1 MONTH OF
FREE
READING

at

www.ForgottenBooks.com

By purchasing this book you are eligible for one month membership to ForgottenBooks.com, giving you unlimited access to our entire collection of over 1,000,000 titles via our web site and mobile apps.

To claim your free month visit:

www.forgottenbooks.com/free948673

ISBN 978-0-260-44649-7
PIBN 10948673

This book is a reproduction of an important historical work. Forgotten Books uses state-of-the-art technology to digitally reconstruct the work, preserving the original format whilst repairing imperfections present in the aged copy. In rare cases, an imperfection in the original, such as a blemish or missing page, may be replicated in our edition. We do, however, repair the vast majority of imperfections successfully; any imperfections that remain are intentionally left to preserve the state of such historical works.

Seventy-Fourth Edition

tatistical Abstract
f the United States
1953

ared under the Direction

Morris B. Ullman in the Office of the

istant Director for Statistical Standards

. DEPARTMENT OF COMMERCE

lair Weeks, Secretary

EAU OF THE CENSUS, Robert W. Burgess, Director

ale by the Superintendent of Documents, U. S. Government Printing Office
lington 25, D. C.   Price $3.50 (Buckram)

BUREAU OF THE CENSUS

ROBERT W. BURGESS, *Director*

A. Ross Eckler, *Deputy Director.*
Howard C. Grieves, *Assistant Director.*
Conrad F. Taeuber, *Assistant Director.*
Morris H. Hansen, *Assistant Director for Statistical Standards.*
Lowell T. Galt, *Assistant Director for Operations.*
Walter L. Kehres, *Assistant Director for Administration.*
Calvert L. Dedrick, *Coordinator, International Statistics.*
Frank R. Wilson, *Information Assistant to the Director.*

ACKNOWLEDGMENTS

The *Statistical Abstract of the United States* has been published annually for the past 74 years, and its present content and form are the result of the work of many persons during that period. Revisions are made each year to adapt it to meet current needs and uses, and to bring the various statistical series up to date.

The *Statistical Abstract* is prepared in the office of Morris H. Hansen, Assistant Director for Statistical Standards. This issue was compiled by William Lerner under the direction of Morris B. Ullman, Chief, Statistical Reports Section. Elma D. Beynon is editorial supervisor and Robert L. Rowland assisted in planning.

The cooperation of many persons acting in either their official positions or as individuals, who contributed to the preparation of this volume, is gratefully acknowledged. The list of tables by source (pp. XII–XV), as well as the source note following each table, indicates the various government and private agencies cooperating in furnishing information, assisting in the selection and preparation of the material, or otherwise contributing to the preparation of the *Statistical Abstract*.

SEPTEMBER 1953.

SUGGESTED BRIEF CITATION

U. S. Bureau of the Census, *Statistical Abstract of the United States: 1953.* (Seventy-fourth edition.) Washington, D. C., 1953.

II

For sale by the Superintendent of Documents, U. S. Government Printing Office, Washington 25, D. C. Price $3.50 (Buckram)

PREFACE

The *Statistical Abstract of the United States*, published annually since 1878, is the standard summary of statistics on the industrial, social, political, and economic organization of the United States. It includes a representative selection of data from most of the important statistical publications, both governmental and private. It is limited, of necessity, primarily to national data, and, to a much lesser extent, to data for regions and individual States. Data for cities or other small geographic units are shown only in a small number of instances.

This book is designed to fulfill two functions: First, to serve as a convenient volume for statistical reference; and second, to serve as a guide to other statistical publications and sources. The source of each table presented is given at the foot of the table. The publications cited usually contain additional statistical detail relating to the subject matter shown, and a more complete discussion of relevant definitions and concepts than can be presented here. Also, they may supply data for smaller geographic units. Where contributing agencies are cited as sources, without mention of publications, more detailed information frequently is available from their unpublished tabulations and records.

1953 edition.—This edition is the seventy-fourth annual issue. The statistics shown are the latest which were available in the early part of the 1953 calendar year. The year, 1953, used to designate this edition, represents both the year during which compilation was made and the year of publication.

Each year several sections are subjected to intensive review. This review introduces new subject material of current interest and eliminates data that are less timely or appear in greater detail than seems warranted.

Worthy of special mention in this edition is the presentation of new data from the 1950 Censuses of Population, Housing, and Agriculture. Availability of these data afforded an opportunity for important additions to several sections. Particularly involved were section 1, Area and Population; section 4, Education; section 8, Labor Force, Employment, and Earnings; section 24, Agriculture—General Statistics; section 25, Agriculture—Production and Related Subjects; and section 29, Construction and Housing. As a result, the presentation in these sections is not only more current but also more complete both in terms of subject coverage and area coverage.

A section which has undergone a significant change in this edition is section 33, Territories, Possessions, and Other Areas Under the Jurisdiction of the United States. This section, which previously included only data on commerce of the Territories and possessions, has been considerably expanded by shifting to it material which was scattered in a number of sections and adding new material from the 1950 Censuses, particularly on population and housing.

Other changes in this edition involve particularly the recent study, *Share Ownership in the United States*, made by the Brookings Institution, from which five tables have been excerpted and added to the Banking and Finance section. The Business Enterprise section provides three new tables dealing with the survival experience of business firms, and two new tables on industrial research and development expenditures. Several new tables on individual and family income have been added to the Income and Expenditures section. New material in other sections includes: Tables showing first marriage and remarriage by age of bride and groom, and divorces and annulments by duration of marriage; Federal prisoners with previous commitments; estimated State distribution of selected Federal expenditures for veterans; number of civilian employees with veteran preference in the executive branch of the Federal Government;

III

value in constant dollars for raw materials production, imports, exports, and appare consumption; votes cast for Governor by States; expenditures by organizations attemp ing to influence national legislation; indexes of production, employment, prices, ret trade, and income for selected foreign countries; and a number of other subjects.

With respect to content other than tabular, efforts to expand and improve the ge eral notes preceding each section were continued, notably in section 18, Commu cations, and section 23, Irrigation, Drainage, and Soil Conservation. On the first pa of text in each section, a note has been added giving the date on which the mater for the section as a whole was organized and sent to the printer. This date ser as a reference point both for those statistics which are subject to revision by t issuing agencies and also to indicate the approximate date on which the section w organized from the latest material available. There are a total of 45 maps and char presented in this edition, as compared to 31 in the last issue. In addition, 1 "Bibliography of Sources" has been expanded and revised.

Historical appendix.—As a result of integrating the annual *Statistical Abstract* wi *Historical Statistics of the United States, 1789–1945*, most of the historical series whi have previously been shown in the historical appendix are now presented in other tab in the *Abstract*. In order to facilitate the location of these tables, the present versi of the historical appendix relates each historical series for which comparable curr data are available to the number of the *Abstract* table in which the series appears.

Present plans are to issue a separate publication which will bring to date, und a single cover, all current series in *Historical Statistics*, together with all known visions in figures published earlier, thus consolidating and supplementing all data whi have been included in the historical appendix of the 1949–1952 editions of the Stat tical Abstract.

Supplements to the *Abstract*.—The *Statistical Abstract*, as an annual one-volu publication, is of necessity limited in amount of detail shown. Businessmen, teache librarians, public officials, professional workers, and others often require data individual cities, counties, metropolitan areas, and other small areas as well as States. Economists, teachers, students, and others frequently need more histori information. To meet such requests for more detail, a series of supplements to t Abstract has been issued.

The most recent supplement, the *County and City Data Book, 1952*, issued in M 1953, brings together 128 items of information for each county, standard metropolit area, and State; and 133 items for each of 484 cities with 25,000 or more inhabitant 1950. Most of the statistics in this volume were obtained from the results of t 1950 Censuses of Agriculture, Population, and Housing. Other subjects covered clude 1950 data for births, deaths, and marriages; bank deposits and E Bond sales; c government finances and employment; city school systems; farm-operator family lev of-living index; and other items of social and economic importance. Final figu for a number of items from the 1948 Census of Business and the 1947 Census of Mar factures are also shown. This volume is on sale by the Superintendent of Documer Government Printing Office, Washington 25, D. C., for $4.25.

Historical Statistics of the United States, 1789–1945, a historical supplement, v published in July 1949. This volume brings together 3,000 statistical series wh extend back through time. Data are shown for each year back to 1789 or to t earliest data available for the series. In the preparation of this supplement t Bureau had the cooperation of a special committee of the Social Science Resea Council set up to advise the Director of the Census on a source book of histori statistics and of the Committee on Research in Economic History under the auspi of the Social Science Research Council. This volume is on sale by the Superintend of Documents, Washington 25, D. C., for $2.75.

asibility.—As implied in the title, the contents of this volume are taken
arge number of sources, as indicated in the list of agencies furnishing material.
ges XII–XV.)   The Bureau of the Census cannot accept the responsibility
accuracy or limitations of the data presented here, other than for those which
ts.   However, the responsibility for selection of the material for the general
l for proper presentation rests with the Bureau, even though carried out with
peration of many technicians who have given unselfishly of their time and
lge in order to assist the Bureau's staff in making the presentation as meaningful
ful as possible.
sooperation of the users must also be acknowledged.   Many persons have
offering suggestions for improving the presentation of the material.   These
have been most helpful and users are urged to continue to make their needs
All suggestions will be carefully considered in planning future editions.

FOR ADDITIONAL INFORMATION ON DATA PRESENTED

e to the agency indicated in the source note to the table which covers the
ed subject.

SUGGESTIONS AND COMMENTS

should be sent to

The Director

Bureau of the Census

Washington 25, D. C.

STATISTICAL ABSTRACT SUPPLEMENTS

County and City Data Book, 1952. A compact presentation of 128 items of statistical data for each county and standard metropolitan area in the United States, and 133 items of statistical data for each of 484 cities having 25,000 or more inhabitants in 1950. Items included based largely on results of 1950 Censuses of Agriculture, Population and Housing. Includes 51 maps, explanatory and definitive text, and source notes. 608 pages. Issued 1953. Price $4.25 (Buckram).

Historical Statistics of the United States, 1789–1945. A supplement to the *Statistical Abstract*, prepared with the cooperation of the Social Science Research Council. A compilation of about 3,000 statistical time series, largely annual, extending back through time to the earliest year for which figures are available. Includes definitions of terms and descriptive text. Specific source notes provide a basic guide to original published sources for further reference and additional data. Detailed alphabetical subject index. 363 pages. Issued 1949. Fourth printing. Price $2.75 (Buckram).

Purchase orders should be addressed to the Superintendent of Documents, U. S. Government Printing Office, Washington 25, D. C.

CONTENTS

CONTENTS   XI

TABLES BY SOURCE

Table numbers followed by "co-op." indicate that the statistics were comp
cooperation with another agency; those followed by "part" indicate that sta
from another source appear in the same table.

Federal Government Agencies

Labor:

Bureau of Employees' Compensation: 415

Bureau of Employment Security: 278–286

Bureau of Labor Statistics:
209–211, 213, 229–231, 233, 235–243, 321, 334–336, 339, 341, 343–346, 349, 404, 424, 498, 499, 560 (co-op.), 570, 662 (co-op.), 854 (part), 862, 902–904, 911, 1025

Mutual Security Agency. *See* Foreign Operations Administration.

National Forest Reservation Commission: 814

Panama Canal: 673–675

Post Office Department: 469, 581–587

President's Materials Policy Commission: 1056

Railroad Retirement Board: 287–289

Reconstruction Finance Corporation: 468

Securities and Exchange Commission: 471, 502, 507, 510, 512, 515, 537, 547 (co-op.)

Selective Service System: 252, 253

State (Bureau of United Nations Affairs): 1108

Tariff Commission: 972

Treasury:

Bureau of Comptroller of Currency: 453–455, 462, 464–467

Bureau of Customs: 685–689, 1078, 1080

Bureau of Internal Revenue: 374–392, 536, 538, 539, 546, 952–954, 956, 957

Bureau of the Mint: 451, 452, 888, 890

Fiscal Service: 366, 367, 393, 395–402, 446, 447

Veterans' Administration: 254–263

Other Government Agencies

New York State, Department of Public Works: 678

United Nations (Statistical Office): 1100–1107, 1109

Nongovernment Agencies

American Bureau of Shipping: 684

American Gas Association: 601–604

American Iron and Steel Institute: 981, 982, 983 (part), 984, 985, (part), 990 (part)

American Medical Association: 84, 85

American Telephone and Telegraph Co.: 561, 562

American Transit Association: 650

Association of American Railroads: 641

Automobile Manufacturers' Association: 615 (part)

Brookings Institution: 516–520

Bureau of Advertising of American Newspaper Publishers Association: 1038

Bus Transportation: 655, 656

Commercial and Financial Chronicle: 449 (part), 508, 514

Congressional Quarterly News Feature: 365

Council of State Governments: 360

F. W. Dodge Corporation: 906, 907

Dun & Bradstreet, Inc.: 551–555

Edison Electric Institute: 594, 598

Electrical Merchandising: 997

Engineering and Mining Journal: 854 (part)

FIG. I.—MAP OF THE UNITED STATES, SHOWING CENSUS DIVISIONS

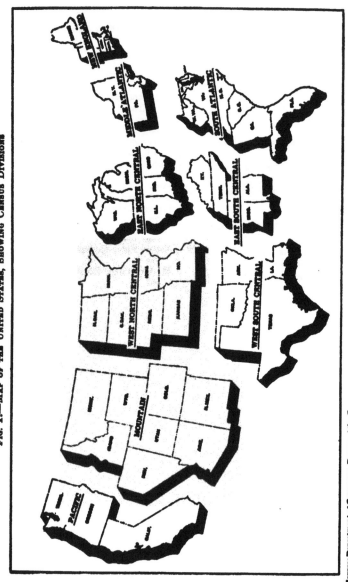

Source: Department of Commerce, Bureau of the Census.

1. Area and Population

This section relates to the population of the United States, its distribution, and its characteristics. The principal source of these data is the Decennial Census of Population, a house-to-house enumeration made once every ten years by the Bureau of the Census. In accordance with a Constitutional provision for a decennial canvass of the population, the first census enumeration was made in 1790. The primary reason for the Census of Population, as set forth in the Constitution, was to provide a basis for the apportionment of members of the House of Representatives among the several States. From 1800 to 1900, the census was conducted by a temporary organization built up by the Superintendent of the Census appointed for each decennial census. In 1902, the Bureau of the Census was established as a permanent agency of the Government, known as the Census Office; it was charged with responsibility for the decennial census and for compiling statistics on other subjects as needed. Currently, figures are supplied by a number of intercensal surveys and estimates in addition to the comprehensive census enumeration.

The data shown here were selected chiefly from the Sixteenth and Seventeenth Censuses (1940 and 1950), and from special Census releases and reports, with the object of giving as complete a description of the population of the United States as space permits. Whenever practicable, a historical series is given in order to show changes that have occurred over periods of time. Most of the data presented apply to continental United States, but some figures for Territories and possessions are included.

Related materials are presented in other sections of this volume. Thus, statistics of marriage and divorce are presented in section 2, Vital Statistics, Health, and Nutrition; statistics on family income are given in section 11, Income and Expenditures; and Census data on employment and occupations are given in section 8, Labor Force, Employment, and Earnings. Data on the population in institutions as enumerated in 1950 are given in this section, but additional data on persons in mental institutions are given in section 2 and on prisoners in section 5, Law Enforcement and Federal Courts. Tables on nativity and citizenship are included in this section, but related data are included in section 3, Immigration, Emigration, and Naturalization.

Decennial censuses.—There are many difficulties involved in the process of obtaining a complete and unduplicated count of the population. Although great efforts are made to obtain such a count, the results fall short of this objective to some degree. These difficulties and their resultant shortcomings are present in all censuses. The magnitude of error, however, may vary from census to census.

In accordance with Census practice dating back to 1790, each person enumerated in the 1950 Census was counted as an inhabitant of his usual place of residence or usual place of abode, that is, the place where he lives and sleeps most of the time. This place is not necessarily the same as his legal residence, voting residence, or domicile, although, in the vast majority of cases, the use of these different bases of classification would produce identical results.

Certain of the data which are presented are indicated as being based on information obtained from a representative sample of the population. For example, tables 28, 29, 31, 33, 37, 38, and 50 include 1950 data based on a representative 20-percent sample of the 1950 Census of Population. A separate line was provided on the population schedules for each person enumerated, with every fifth line designated as a sample line. The sample data in the above tables are based on the persons enumerated on these special lines. Estimates of the number of persons with specified characteristics based on sample data have been obtained by multiplying the number of persons in the sample having these characteristics by five.

Note.—This section presents data for the most recent year or period available on February 18, 1953, when the material was organized and sent to the printer. In a few instances, more recent data were added after that date.

A number of tables also include 1940 data obtained on a sample basis. Sample B is a sample of all individuals from the 1940 Population Schedule; Sample C and Sample W are samples of individual women 15 years old and over from the 1940 and 1910 Population Schedules, respectively. For Sample B, the sample size is 5 percent. Sample C is 5 percent in most areas, but includes a 2½ percent sample in the most populous areas. Sample W is an 8-percent sample for the North and the South, and about 12 percent for the West.

Exact agreement is not to be expected among the various samples, nor between them and the complete count, but the sample data may be used with confidence when large numbers are involved, and may be assumed to indicate patterns and relationships where small numbers are involved. Detailed statements regarding the sampling errors are given in the original sources.

Current Population Survey.—Several tables present statistics based on the Current Population Survey, conducted monthly by the Bureau of the Census. This survey covers a representative sample of about 25,000 households taken in selected areas throughout the United States. A statement indicating the sampling reliability of estimates based on this sample is given in the Sampling Note, p. 181.

Population estimates.—Population estimates for dates after April 1940, which are not the result of sample surveys, are based on data from the 1940 Census and, in some cases, the 1950 Census; statistics of births and deaths provided by the National Office of Vital Statistics, United States Public Health Service; statistics of immigration and emigration reported by the Immigration and Naturalization Service, Department of Justice; and statistics on the armed forces provided by the Department of Defense. Intercensal estimates of State population are based on the same types of data and also make use of school statistics, war ration book registrations, and State censuses.

Urban and rural areas.—In the course of its history, the Bureau of the Census has employed several definitions of urban area.

According to the new urban definition adopted for the 1950 Census, the urban-rural population comprises all persons living in (a) places of 2,500 inhabitants or more incorporated as cities, boroughs, and villages, (b) incorporated towns of 2,500 inhabitants or more except in New England, New York, and Wisconsin, where "towns" are simply minor civil divisions of counties, (c) the densely settled urban fringe, including both incorporated and unincorporated areas, around cities of 50,000 or more, and (d) unincorporated places of 2,500 inhabitants or more outside any urban fringe. The remaining population is classified as rural.

According to the 1940 definition, the urban area was made up for the most part of cities and other incorporated places having 2,500 inhabitants or more. In addition, it included townships and other political subdivisions (not incorporated as municipalities nor containing any areas so incorporated) with a population of 10,000 or more and a population density of 1,000 or more per square mile; and in Massachusetts, Rhode Island, and New Hampshire, those towns (townships) which contain a village of 2,500 or more, comprising either by itself or when combined with other villages within the same town, more than 50 percent of the total population of the town. The remaining area of the country was classified as rural. The definition of urban area used in the 1940 Census was adopted substantially as stated above for the 1910 Census.

In both the new definition of 1950 and the old definition of 1940, incorporated places of 2,500 or more inhabitants constitute the major component of urban territory. The new definition differs from the old definition in substituting specially delineated urban fringes and unincorporated places of 2,500 inhabitants or more for those political subdivisions which were specified as urban under the special rules given above.

In this edition, figures by urban and rural residence for all dates prior to the 1950 Census are in accordance with the old definition. Figures for 1950 and subsequent years are in accordance with the new definition unless otherwise stated.

Farm and nonfarm residence.—The rural population is subdivided into the rural-farm population, which comprises all rural residents living on farms, and the rural-nonfarm population, which comprises the remaining rural population. The method of determining farm and nonfarm residents used in the 1950 Census differs somewhat from that used in earlier surveys and censuses. Persons on "farms" who were paying cash rent for their house and yard only were classified as nonfarm; furthermore, persons in institutions, summer camps, motels, and tourist camps were classified as nonfarm.

Household.—A "household," according to present usage of the Census Bureau, comprises all persons who occupy a dwelling unit, that is, a house, an apartment or other group of rooms, or a room that constitutes "separate living quarters." A household includes the "related persons" (the head of the household and others in the dwelling unit who are related to the head) and also the lodgers and employees, if any, who regularly live in the house. The number of households, thus defined, is the same as the number of "private households" or "families" as used in 1940 census reports. A person living alone or a group of unrelated persons sharing the same dwelling unit as partners is counted as a household.

The term "household" excludes the small number (about 80,000 in 1940) of institutions, hotels, large lodging houses, and other quasi households which are included as households in the Census reports (and in figures shown in this edition) for 1920, 1910, 1890, and earlier years. The figures for 1900 and for 1930 and subsequent years, shown in this edition, are in conformance with the present usage of the term "household" as defined above.

Family.—The term "family," as used here, refers to a group of two or more persons related by blood, marriage, or adoption and residing together, and differs from the meaning of the term as used in the 1930 and 1940 censuses. A primary family consists of the head of a household and all (one or more) other persons in the household related to the head. A secondary family comprises two or more persons such as guests, lodgers or resident employees and their relatives, living in a household or quasi household (other than the negligible number of such groups among inmates of institutions) and related to each other. In a household, a secondary family is not related to the household head, but in a quasi household, a secondary family may include the head of the quasi household.

Subfamily.—A subfamily is a married couple with or without children, or one parent with one or more children under 18 years old, living in a household and related to, but not including, the head of the household or his wife. Members of a subfamily are also members of the primary family with which they live. The number of subfamilies, therefore, is not included in the number of families.

Married couple.—A married couple is defined as a husband and his wife living together.

Unrelated individuals.—The term "unrelated individuals" as used here refers to persons (other than inmates of institutions) who are not living with any relatives. A primary individual is a household head living alone or with persons all of whom are unrelated to him. A secondary individual is a person in a household or a quasi household such as a guest, lodger or a resident employee (excluding inmates of institutions) who is not related to the head or to any other person in the household or quasi household.

Historical statistics.—See preface and historical appendix. Tabular headnotes (as "See also *Historical Statistics*, series B 24–25") provide cross-references, where applicable, to *Historical Statistics of the United States, 1789–1945*.

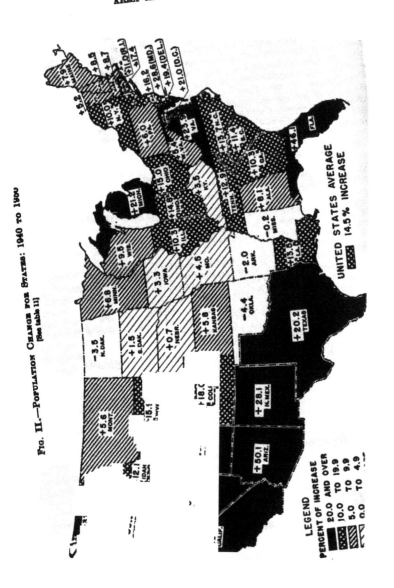

FIG. II.—POPULATION CHANGE FOR STATES: 1940 TO 1950
[See table 11]

LEGEND
PERCENT OF INCREASE

20.0 AND OVER
10.0 TO 19.9
5.0 TO 9.9
0.0 TO 4.9

UNITED STATES AVERAGE
14.5 % INCREASE

FIG. VI.—MARITALA SITUS OF PERSONS 14 YEARS OLD AND OVER, BY
SEX: 1890 TO 1950

[See table 42]

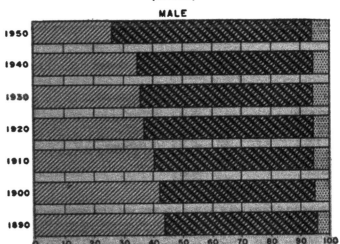

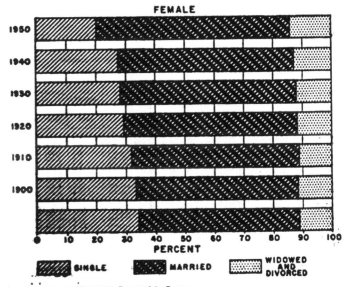

No. 1.—Territorial Expansion of Continental United States and Acquisitions of Principal Territories, Possessions, Etc.

[Boundaries of all territories listed under "Continental United States" were indefinite, at least in part, at time of acquisition. Area figures shown here represent precise determinations of specific territories which have been marked upon maps, based upon interpretations of the several treaties of cession which are necessarily debatable. These determinations were made by a committee consisting of representatives of various governmental agencies in 1912. Adjustments have been made in the areas as remeasured in 1940. See also *Historical Statistics*, series B 24-25]

ACCESSION	Date	Gross area (land and water)	ACCESSION	Date	Gross area (land and water)
		sq. mi.	Other:		*sq. mi.*
Total		3,626,130	The Philippines [2]	1898	116,600
Continental United States		3,022,387	Puerto Rico	1899	3,435
Territory in 1790 [1]		888,811	Guam	1899	206
Louisiana Purchase	1803	827,192	American Samoa	1900	76
By treaty with Spain:			Canal Zone [3]	1904	553
Florida	1819	58,560	Corn Islands [4]	1914	4
Other areas	1819	13,443	Virgin Islands of the U. S.	1917	133
Texas	1845	390,144	The Philippines [2]	1946	116,600
Oregon	1846	285,580	Trust Territory of the Pacific		
Mexican Cession	1848	529,017	Islands [5]	1947	8,475
Gadsden Purchase	1853	29,640	All other [6]		38
Territories		592,825			
Alaska	1867	586,400			
Hawaii	1898	6,423			

[1] Includes that part of drainage basin of Red River of the North, south of 49th parallel, sometimes considered part of Louisiana Purchase.
[2] Ceded by Spain in 1898, the Philippines constituted a territorial possession of the United States from 1898 to 1946. Granted independence as of July 4, 1946, they then became the Republic of the Philippines.
[3] Under jurisdiction of United States in accordance with treaty of Nov. 18, 1903, with Republic of Panama.
[4] Leased (1914) from Republic of Nicaragua for 99 years. [5] Under trusteeship. See table 3, footnote 17.
[6] Includes following islands with gross areas as indicated: Midway (2), Wake (3), Canton and Enderbury (combined area, 27), Swan (1), Navassa (2), Baker, Howland, and Jarvis (combined area, 3), Johnston and Sand (combined area, less than 0.5), Kingman Reef, Quita Sueno Bank, Roncador Cay, and Serrano Bank (each less than 0.5) and other islands specified in table 3, footnote 10, for which area figures are not available.

Source: Department of Commerce, Bureau of the Census; reports and records.

No. 2.—Area and Population of Continental United States: 1790 to 1950

[See also *Historical Statistics*, series B 26-30]

CENSUS DATE	AREA (SQUARE MILES) [1]			POPULATION			
	Gross	Land	Water	Number	Per square mile of land area	Increase over preceding census	
						Number	Percent
1790 (Aug. 2)	892,135	867,980	24,155	3,929,214	4.5		
1800 (Aug. 4)	892,135	867,980	24,155	5,308,483	6.1	1,379,269	35.1
1810 (Aug. 6)	1,720,122	1,685,865	34,257	7,239,881	4.3	1,931,398	36.4
1820 (Aug. 7)	1,792,223	1,753,588	38,635	9,638,453	5.5	2,398,572	33.1
1830 (June 1)	1,792,223	1,753,588	38,635	12,866,020	7.3	3,227,567	33.5
1840 (June 1)	1,792,223	1,755,588	38,635	17,069,453	9.7	4,203,433	32.7
1850 (June 1)	2,997,119	2,944,337	52,782	23,191,876	7.9	6,122,423	35.9
1860 (June 1)	3,026,789	2,973,965	52,824	31,443,321	10.6	8,251,445	35.6
1870 (June 1)	3,026,789	2,973,965	52,824	39,818,449	13.4	8,375,128	26.6
1880 (June 1)	3,026,789	2,973,965	52,824	50,155,783	16.9	10,337,334	26.0
1890 (June 1)	3,026,789	2,973,965	52,824	62,947,714	21.2	12,791,931	25.5
1900 (June 1)	3,026,789	2,974,159	52,630	75,994,575	25.6	13,046,861	20.7
1910 (Apr. 15)	3,026,789	2,973,890	52,899	91,972,266	30.9	15,977,691	21.0
1920 (Jan. 1)	3,026,789	2,973,776	53,013	105,710,620	35.5	13,738,354	14.9
1930 (Apr. 1)	3,022,387	2,977,128	45,259	122,775,046	41.2	17,064,426	16.1
1940 (Apr. 1)	3,022,387	2,977,128	45,259	131,669,275	44.2	8,894,229	7.2
1950 (Apr. 1)	3,022,387	2,974,726	47,661	150,697,361	50.7	19,028,086	14.5

[1] Area figures for each census year represent all continental area under jurisdiction of United States on indicated date, including in some cases considerable areas not then organized or settled, and not covered by the census.
[2] Revised to include adjustments for under enumeration in Southern States; unrevised number is 38,558,371.

Source: Department of Commerce, Bureau of the Census; Reports of Fourteenth, Fifteenth, and Sixteenth Censuses, *Population*, Vol. I; 1950 Population Census releases; and other reports and records. See also Sixteenth Census Reports, *Areas of the United States, 1940*.

—Area and Population of the United States, Territories, Possessions, Etc.: 1930 to 1950

[thin each group are listed in rank order of population in 1950. See also *Historical Statistics*, series B 1–12 and B 25]

AREA	Gross area (land and water) in square miles, 1950	POPULATION		
		1950	1940	1930
d States (aggregate)	3, 628, 120	154, 233, 234	[1]150, 622, 754	[1] 123, 428, 860
tal U. S.	3, 022, 387	150, 697, 361	131, 669, 275	122, 775, 046
s	592, 823	628, 437	495, 294	427, 578
	6, 423	499, 794	[2] 422, 770	[2] 368, 300
	586, 400	128, 643	[4] 72, 524	[4] 59, 278
ne	3, 888	2, 316, 922	1, 920, 902	1, 564, 535
Rico	3, 435	2, 210, 703	1, 869, 255	1, 543, 913
	206	59, 498	22, 290	18, 509
Islands of the U. S.	133	26, 665	24, 889	22, 012
an Samoa	76	18, 937	12, 908	10, 055
y Islands	2	416	437	36
sland	3	349	----------	(5)
Island and Enderbury Island	27	[6] 272	44	(5)
n Island and Sand Island	(7)	[8] 46	[8] 69	(5)
slands	1	[9] 36	(7)	(5)
	[11] 5	(13)	[12] 10	(12)
ne [14]	553	52, 822	51, 827	29, 467
nds [15]	4	[16] 1, 304	[16] 1, 528	(7)
rritory of the Pacific Islands [17]	[18] 8, 475	[19] 54, 843	(20)	(20)
n abroad [21]	----------	[22] 481, 545	118, 933	89, 453
rs of the armed forces	----------	301, 595	}	}
citizens employed by the United States Govern-	----------	26, 910	118, 933	89, 453
s of armed forces personnel or of civilian citizen	----------	107, 350	(23)	(23)
yees	----------	45, 690	(23)	(23)
f merchant vessels				

[es estimated population of the Philippine Islands (1940: 16,356,000; 1930: 13,513,000), not shown sepa-
eded by Spain in 1898, the Philippine Islands constituted a territorial possession of the United States
to 1946. Granted independence as of July 4, 1946, they then became the Republic of the Philippines.
ies inhabitants (560) of Baker, Canton and Enderbury, Howland, Jarvis, Johnston and Sand, and
islands which were enumerated with Hawaii in 1940.
ies inhabitants (36) of Midway Islands which were enumerated with Hawaii in 1930.
s taken as of Oct. 1 of preceding year.
numerated.
bury Island uninhabited at time of enumeration.
han 0.5 square miles.
sland uninhabited at time of enumeration.
Swan Island uninhabited at time of enumeration.
ies Caroline, Christmas, Danger (Pukapuka), Flint, Funafuti, Kingman Reef, Malden, Manahiki,
Nukufetau, Nukulaelai, Nurakita, Penrhyn, Quita Sueno Bank, Rakahanga, Roncador Cay, Serrana
arbuck, Vostok, Phoenix Group (except Canton and Enderbury), and Union (Tokelau) Group, not
ed in decennial censuses; and Baker, Howland, and Jarvis Islands.
figure is for Navassa (area, 2 square miles), and Baker, Howland, and Jarvis (combined area 3 square
cludes Kingman Reef, Quita Sueno Bank, Roncador Cay, and Serrana Bank (each less than 0.5 square
rea of other islands (listed in footnote 10) not available.
numerated or uninhabited at time of enumeration.
lation of Baker, Howland, and Jarvis Islands. Other islands not enumerated or uninhabited at time of
ion.
r jurisdiction of United States in accordance with treaty of Nov. 18, 1903, with Republic of Panama.
d (1914) from the Republic of Nicaragua for 99 years.
es are those of the 1950 and 1940 Censuses of the Republic of Nicaragua, May 1950 and 1940. Little Corn
inhabited at time of both enumerations.
r trusteeship with the United States as administering authority. See *Trusteeship Agreement for the
spaese Mandated Islands (Documentary Supplement No. 1)* of the Security Council of the United
rhich became effective on July 18, 1947.
Department of the Navy. *Handbook on the Trust Territory of the Pacific Islands.* Washington, D. C.,
ernment Printing Office, 1948.
Department of the Navy. *Report on the Administration of the Trust Territory of the Pacific Islands for
July 1, 1949 to June 30, 1950.* Washington, D. C., U. S. Government Printing Office, 1950.
lation 1940, 131,258; 1930, 69,626 (Censuses of Japan).
des United States citizens abroad on private business, travel, etc. Many of these were enumerated in
d States at their usual place of residence as absent members of households.
on 20-percent sample of reports received and consequently subject to sampling variability. Chances
2 out of 3 that the figure that would have been obtained from a complete count would have differed by
1,200 from figure shown here.
vailable.
Department of Commerce, Bureau of Census; *U. S. Census of Population: 1950*, Vol. I.

No. 4.—AREA FOR STATES, TERRITORIES, ETC.: 1950

DIVISION AND STATE	AREA (SQUARE MILES)			DIVISION AND STATE	AREA (SQUARE MILES)		
	Gross	Land [1]	Inland water [2]		Gross	Land [1]	Inland water [2]
Continental United States	3,022,387	2,974,726	47,661	**South Atlantic—Con.**			
				Georgia	58,876	58,483	393
				Florida	58,560	54,262	4,298
New England	66,608	63,159	3,449	**East South Central**	181,964	179,987	1,977
Maine	33,215	31,040	2,175	Kentucky	40,395	39,864	531
New Hampshire	9,304	9,017	287	Tennessee	42,244	41,797	447
Vermont	9,609	9,278	331	Alabama	51,609	51,078	531
Massachusetts	8,257	7,867	390	Mississippi	47,716	47,248	468
Rhode Island	1,214	1,058	156	**West South Central**	429,885	436,381	8,594
Connecticut	5,009	4,899	110	Arkansas	53,104	52,675	439
Middle Atlantic	102,745	100,511	2,234	Louisiana	48,523	45,162	3,361
New York	49,576	47,944	1,632	Oklahoma	69,919	69,031	888
New Jersey	7,836	7,522	314	Texas	267,339	263,513	3,826
Pennsylvania	45,333	45,045	288	**Mountain**	863,887	857,296	6,591
East North Central	248,283	244,867	3,416	Montana	147,138	145,878	1,260
Ohio	41,222	41,000	222	Idaho	83,557	82,769	788
Indiana	36,291	36,205	86	Wyoming	97,914	97,506	408
Illinois	56,400	55,935	465	Colorado	104,247	103,922	325
Michigan	58,216	57,022	1,194	New Mexico	121,666	121,511	155
Wisconsin	56,154	54,705	1,449	Arizona	113,909	113,575	334
West North Central	517,247	510,644	6,603	Utah	84,916	82,346	2,570
Minnesota	84,068	80,009	4,059	Nevada	110,540	109,789	751
Iowa	56,290	56,045	245	**Pacific**	322,866	319,841	4,025
Missouri	69,674	69,226	448	Washington	68,192	66,786	1,406
North Dakota	70,665	70,057	608	Oregon	96,981	96,315	666
South Dakota	77,047	76,536	511	California	158,693	156,740	1,953
Nebraska	77,227	76,663	564				
Kansas	82,276	82,108	168	**Other areas:**			
South Atlantic	278,902	268,040	10,862	Hawaii	6,423	6,407	16
Delaware	2,057	1,978	79	Alaska	586,400	571,065	15,335
Maryland	10,577	9,881	696	Puerto Rico	3,435	3,423	12
Dist. of Columbia	69	61	8	Guam	206	203	3
Virginia	40,815	39,893	922	Virgin Isl. of U. S.	133	132	1
West Virginia	24,181	24,080	101	American Samoa	76	76	
North Carolina	52,712	49,097	3,615	Canal Zone [4]	553	362	191
South Carolina	31,055	30,305	750	Trust Terr. of Pac. [4]	8,475		

[1] Dry land and land temporarily or partially covered by water, such as marshland, swamps, and river flood plains; streams, sloughs, estuaries, and canals less than one-eighth of a statute mile in width; and lakes, reservoirs, and ponds less than 40 acres of area.

[2] Permanent inland water surface, such as lakes, reservoirs, and ponds having 40 acres or more of area; streams, sloughs, estuaries, and canals one-eighth of a statute mile or more in width; deeply indented embayments and sounds, and other coastal waters behind or sheltered by headlands or islands separated by less than 1 nautical mile of water; and islands having less than 40 acres of area. Does not include water surface of the oceans, bays, the Gulf of Mexico, the Great Lakes, Long Island Sound, Puget Sound, and the Straits of Juan de Fuca and Georgia, lying within the jurisdiction of the United States but not defined as inland water.

[3] See table 3, note 14.

[4] See table 3, note 17.

Source: Department of Commerce, Bureau of the Census; *U. S. Census of Population: 1950*, Vol. I, reports and records.

No. 5.—Population per Square Mile, by States: 1800 to 1950

[For United States, population of continental U. S. has been divided by total land area. For each State or Territory, population at given census has been divided by land area as then constituted. However, 1930 figures are based on revised land areas used for 1940. Areas of Indian reservations, outside Indian Territory, are included in areas of States and Territories for all years; however, populations of reservations were not ascertained and therefore were not taken into account in computing densities prior to 1890]

DIVISION AND STATE	1860	1870	1880	1890	1900	1910	1920	1930 [1]	1940	1950
United States	6.1	†13.4	16.9	21.2	25.6	30.9	35.5	41.2	44.2	50.7
New England	12.9	55.3	64.7	75.5	90.2	106.7	119.4	129.2	133.5	147.5
Maine	8.1	21.0	21.7	22.1	23.2	24.8	25.7	25.7	27.3	29.4
New Hampshire	30.4	35.2	38.4	41.7	45.6	47.7	49.1	51.6	54.5	59.1
Vermont	16.9	36.2	36.4	36.4	37.7	39.0	38.6	38.8	35.7	40.7
Massachusetts	52.6	181.3	221.8	278.5	349.0	418.8	479.2	537.4	545.9	596.2
Rhode Island	64.8	203.7	250.2	323.8	401.6	508.5	566.4	649.8	674.2	748.5
Connecticut	52.1	111.5	129.2	154.8	188.5	231.3	286.4	328.0	348.9	400.7
Middle Atlantic	14.0	55.1	105.0	127.1	154.5	193.2	222.6	251.3	274.0	286.1
New York	12.4	92.0	106.7	126.0	152.5	191.2	217.9	262.6	281.2	309.2
New Jersey	25.1	120.6	150.5	192.3	250.7	337.7	420.0	537.3	553.1	642.8
Pennsylvania	13.4	78.6	95.5	117.3	140.6	171.0	194.5	213.8	219.8	233.1
East North Central	.2	27.2	45.7	54.9	65.2	74.3	87.5	103.2	106.7	124.1
Ohio	1.1	65.4	78.5	90.1	102.1	117.0	141.4	161.6	168.0	193.8
Indiana	(3)	46.8	55.1	61.1	70.1	74.9	81.3	89.4	94.7	106.7
Illinois		45.4	55.0	68.3	86.1	100.6	115.7	136.4	141.2	155.8
Michigan		20.6	28.5	36.4	42.1	48.9	63.8	84.9	92.2	111.7
Wisconsin		19.1	23.8	30.6	37.4	42.2	47.6	53.7	57.3	62.8
West North Central		7.6	12.1	17.5	20.3	22.8	24.6	26.0	26.5	27.5
Minnesota		5.4	9.7	16.2	21.7	25.7	29.5	32.0	34.9	37.3
Iowa		21.5	29.2	34.4	40.2	40.0	43.2	44.1	45.3	46.8
Missouri		25.0	31.6	39.0	45.2	47.9	49.5	52.4	54.6	57.1
North Dakota	(4)	(4)		2.7	4.5	8.2	9.2	9.7	9.2	8.8
South Dakota	(4)	(4)		4.5	5.2	7.6	8.3	9.1	8.4	8.5
Nebraska		1.6	5.9	13.8	13.9	15.5	16.9	18.0	17.2	17.3
Kansas		4.5	12.2	17.5	18.0	20.7	21.6	22.9	21.9	23.2
South Atlantic	8.6	21.8	28.2	32.9	38.6	45.3	52.0	58.8	64.4	79.0
Delaware	32.7	63.6	74.6	85.7	94.0	103.0	113.5	120.5	134.7	160.8
Maryland	34.4	78.6	94.0	104.9	119.5	130.3	148.8	165.0	184.2	237.1
Dist. of Columbia	156.6	2,270.7	3,062.5	3,972.3	4,645.3	5,517.8	7,292.9	7,981.5	10,870.3	13,150.5
Virginia	13.7	18.4	25.7	31.8	39.9	50.8	60.9	71.8	79.0	83.2
West Virginia		22.0	28.7	33.2	38.9	45.3	52.5	64.5	72.7	82.7
North Carolina	9.8	23.1	32.6	37.7	44.0	49.7	55.2	56.8	62.1	69.9
South Carolina	11.3	20.2	26.3	31.3	37.7	44.4	49.3	49.7	53.4	58.9
Georgia	1.5	30.2	26.3	31.3	37.7	44.7	49.3	49.7	53.0	58.1
Florida		3.4	4.9	7.1	9.6	13.7	17.7	27.1	35.0	51.1
East South Central	2.9	24.5	31.1	35.8	42.0	46.8	49.5	54.8	56.7	63.8
Kentucky	8.5	32.9	41.0	46.3	53.4	57.0	60.1	55.2	70.9	73.9
Tennessee	2.5	30.2	37.0	42.4	48.5	52.4	56.1	62.4	69.5	78.8
Alabama		19.4	24.6	29.5	35.7	41.7	45.8	51.8	54.5	59.9
Mississippi	.3	17.9	24.4	27.8	33.5	38.8	38.6	42.4	46.1	46.1
West South Central	.6	5.6	9.2	11.0	15.2	20.4	23.8	28.3	30.3	33.8
Arkansas		9.2	15.3	21.5	25.0	30.0	33.4	35.2	37.0	36.3
Louisiana		16.0	20.7	24.6	30.4	36.5	39.6	46.5	52.3	59.4
Oklahoma				[5] 3.7	[5] 11.4	23.9	29.2	34.6	33.7	32.4
Texas	3.1	6.1	8.5	11.6	14.8	17.8	22.1	24.3	29.3	29.3
Mountain		.4	.8	1.4	1.9	3.1	3.9	4.3	4.8	5.9
Montana		.1	.3	1.0	1.7	2.6	3.8	3.7	3.8	4.1
Idaho		.2	.4	1.1	1.9	3.9	5.2	5.4	6.3	7.1
Wyoming		.1	.2	.6	.9	1.5	2.0	2.3	2.6	3.0
Colorado		.4	1.9	4.0	5.2	7.7	9.1	10.0	10.8	12.8
New Mexico		.7	1.0	1.3	1.6	2.7	2.9	3.5	4.4	5.6
Arizona			.4	.8	1.1	1.8	2.9	3.8	4.4	6.6
Utah		1.1	1.8	2.6	3.4	4.5	5.5	6.2	6.7	8.4
Nevada		.4	.6	.4	.4	.7	.7	.8	1.0	1.5
Pacific	2.1	2.5	4.5	5.9	7.6	12.2	17.5	25.6	36.4	45.3
Washington		.4	1.1	5.3	7.8	17.1	20.3	23.3	25.9	35.6
Oregon		1.0	1.8	3.3	4.3	7.0	8.2	9.9	11.3	13.8
California		3.6	5.5	7.8	9.5	15.3	22.0	36.2	44.1	67.5

[1] Based on 1940 land-area measurement.
[2] Revised. Census of Southern States considered incomplete, but there has been no revision of State figures.
[3] Less than one-tenth of 1 person per square mile.
[4] Dakota Territory: Less than one-tenth of 1 person per square mile in 1860, 0.1 in 1870, and 0.9 in 1880.
[5] Oklahoma and Indian Territory combined. Separate data are as follows: Indian Territory 5.9 in 1890 and 12.7 in 1900; Oklahoma, 2.0 in 1890 and 10.3 in 1900.

Source: Department of Commerce, Bureau of the Census; Reports of Fourteenth and Sixteenth Censuses, Population, Vol. I, and U. S. Census of Population: 1950, Vol. I.

No. 6.—Center of Population: 1790 to 1950

["Center of population" is that point which may bee onsidered as center of population gravity of the U. S. or that point upon which the U. S. would balance, if it were a rigid plane without weight and the population distributed thereon with each individual being assumed to have equal weight and to exert an influence on a central point proportional to his distance from the point]

YEAR	North latitude			West longitude			Approximate location
	°	'	''	°	'	''	
1790	39	16	30	76	11	12	23 miles east of Baltimore, Md.
1800	39	16	6	76	56	30	18 miles west of Baltimore, Md.
1810	39	11	30	77	37	12	40 miles northwest by west of Washington, D. C. (in Virginia).
1820	39	5	42	78	33	0	16 miles east of Moorefield, W. Va.[1]
1830	38	57	54	79	16	54	19 miles west-southwest of Moorefield, W. Va.[1]
1840	39	2	0	80	18	0	16 miles south of Clarksburg, W. Va.[1]
1850	38	59	0	81	19	0	23 miles southeast of Parkersburg, W. Va.[1]
1860	39	0	24	82	48	48	20 miles south by east of Chillicothe, Ohio.
1870	39	12	0	83	35	42	48 miles east by north of Cincinnati, Ohio.
1880	39	4	8	84	39	40	8 miles west by south of Cincinnati, Ohio (in Kentucky).
1890	39	11	56	85	32	53	20 miles east of Columbus, Ind.
1900	39	9	36	85	48	54	6 miles southeast of Columbus, Ind.
1910	39	10	12	86	32	20	In the city of Bloomington, Ind.
1920	39	10	21	86	43	15	8 miles south-southeast of Spencer, Owen County, Ind.
1930	39	3	45	87	8	6	3 miles northeast of Linton, Greene County, Ind.
1940	38	56	54	87	22	35	2 miles southeast by east of Carlisle, Haddon Township, Sullivan County, Ind.
1950	38	50	21	88	9	33	8 miles north-northwest of Olney, Richland County, Ill.

[1] West Virginia was set off from Virginia Dec. 31, 1862, and admitted as a State June 19, 1863.

Source: Department of Commerce, Bureau of the Census; *U. S. Census of Population: 1950*, Vol. I.

Fig. VII.—Center of Population: 1790 to 1950

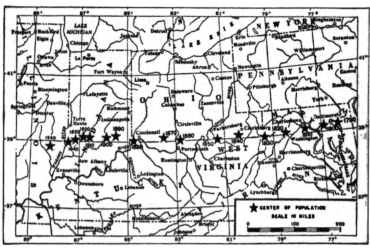

Source: Department of Commerce, Bureau of the Census.

.—ESTIMATED POPULATION OF CONTINENTAL UNITED STATES: JULY 1, 1900 TO 1952

annuals. Estimates for 1900 to 1909 are sums of State estimates based on local data indicative of population pa. Estimates for 1910 to 1952 are based on decennial censuses and statistics of births, deaths, immigration, ration and armed forces. Figures for 1940 to 1952 are provisional]

YEAR	Total population residing in United States	YEAR	Total population residing in United States	YEAR	Total population including armed forces overseas	Total population residing in United States	Civilian population
....	76,094	1918.........	103,203	1936.........	....	125,053	....
....	77,585	1919.........	104,512	1937.........	....	125,825	....
....	79,160	1920.........	106,466	1938.........	....	129,825	....
....	80,632	1921.........	108,541	1939.........	....	130,880	....
....	82,165	1922.........	110,055	1940.........	132,122	131,954	131,658
....	83,820	1923.........	111,950	1941.........	133,402	133,121	131,595
....	85,437	1924.........	114,113	1942.........	134,860	133,920	130,942
....	87,000	1925.........	115,832	1943.........	136,739	134,245	127,409
....	88,709	1926.........	117,399	1944.........	138,397	132,885	126,708
....	90,492	1927.........	119,038	1945.........	139,928	132,481	127,573
....	92,407	1928.........	120,501	1946.........	141,389	140,054	138,385
....	93,868	1929.........	121,770	1947.........	144,126	143,446	142,566
....	95,331	1930.........	123,077	1948.........	146,631	146,093	145,166
....	97,227	1931.........	124,040	1949.........	149,188	148,665	147,578
....	99,118	1932.........	124,840	1950.........	151,677	151,228	150,196
....	100,549	1933.........	125,579	1951.........	154,360	153,353	151,082
....	101,966	1934.........	126,374	1952.........	156,981	155,767	153,234
....	103,266	1935.........	127,250				

ᴇ: Department of Commerce, Bureau of the Census; *Current Population Reports*, Series P-25, Nos. 65, 71; and reports and records on population estimates.

No. 8.—ESTIMATES OF THE FARM POPULATION: APRIL 1910 TO 1951

annuals. Figures represent revised estimates to accord with new definition of farm population adopted in 1950 Census of Population and for current surveys of the Bureau of the Census and the Bureau of Agricultural Economics. New definition excludes from farm population certain groups formerly included. Most important of these groups is population living in houses located on farms, occupants of which pay cash rent for house and yard only without any farm land. Majority of such families have no connection with agriculture and receive no income from agriculture. See also *Historical Statistics*, series B 231]

YEAR	Farm population	YEAR	Farm population	YEAR	Farm population
....	32,077	1924.........	30,493	1938.........	29,573
....	32,110	1925.........	30,440	1939.........	29,388
....	32,210	1926.........	30,162	1940.........	29,047
....	32,270	1927.........	29,647	1941.........	28,786
....	32,320	1928.........	29,509	1942.........	27,805
....	32,440	1929.........	29,564	1943.........	25,757
....	32,530	1930.........	29,447	1944.........	24,647
....	32,326	1931.........	29,723	1945.........	24,342
....	31,741	1932.........	30,229	1946.........	25,543
....	30,886	1933.........	31,198	1947.........	26,147
....	31,556	1934.........	31,071	1948.........	25,093
....	31,638	1935.........	30,887	1949.........	26,134
....	31,558	1936.........	30,420	1950.........	24,235
....	30,873	1937.........	29,903	1951.........	23,276

ᴇ: Department of Commerce, Bureau of the Census and Department of Agriculture, Bureau of Agricultural Economics: cooperative report, Census-BAE, Series No. 17, and records.

No. 9.—PROVISIONAL ESTIMATES OF POPULATION BY STATES: JULY 1, 1943 TO 1

[In thousands. Includes members of armed services stationed in continental United States, but excludes overseas. Based on data from 1940 and 1950 Federal censuses, State censuses, school statistics, vital statistics registrations for war ration books, immigration statistics, and data on armed forces. 1943-49 data in process of revision; see table 7 for revised U. S. totals. For enumerated population, 1790 to 1950, see table 10]

DIVISION AND STATE	1943	1944	1945	1946	1947	1948	1949	1950	1951	1
United States	133,971	132,622	132,127	139,893	143,375	146,045	148,558	151,228	153,383	15
New England	8,364	8,283	8,226	8,768	9,017	9,226	9,364	9,521	9,361	
Maine	802	797	792	843	852	880	904	909	891	
New Hampshire	465	454	450	491	497	508	523	532	532	
Vermont	326	316	322	341	354	358	367	377	372	
Massachusetts	4,244	4,165	4,168	4,449	4,604	4,719	4,772	4,704	4,729	4
Rhode Island	745	772	739	749	767	784	791	789	795	
Connecticut	1,782	1,779	1,755	1,895	1,943	1,979	2,006	2,011	2,031	2
Middle Atlantic	26,322	26,028	25,610	27,776	28,555	29,284	29,944	30,269	30,474	30
New York	12,718	12,637	12,512	13,562	14,041	14,391	14,746	14,882	14,977	15
New Jersey	4,203	4,166	4,050	4,423	4,499	4,657	4,788	4,854	4,973	5
Pennsylvania	9,403	9,225	9,048	9,771	10,014	10,217	10,410	10,533	10,535	10
East North Central	26,530	26,421	26,391	28,293	29,052	29,683	30,114	30,553	30,866	31
Ohio	6,867	6,834	6,880	7,484	7,754	7,949	7,995	7,967	8,034	8
Indiana	3,477	3,434	3,432	3,657	3,729	3,820	3,896	3,961	4,036	4
Illinois	7,748	7,711	7,650	8,147	8,286	8,488	8,626	8,767	8,800	8
Michigan	5,425	5,465	5,483	5,867	6,064	6,175	6,270	6,416	6,524	6
Wisconsin	3,013	2,978	2,946	3,137	3,219	3,261	3,326	3,442	3,472	3
West North Central	12,775	12,298	12,181	12,882	13,136	13,360	13,722	14,117	14,184	14
Minnesota	2,556	2,521	2,534	2,713	2,789	2,850	2,916	2,974	2,984	3
Iowa	2,323	2,246	2,225	2,384	2,429	2,487	2,551	2,637	2,615	2
Missouri	3,711	3,535	3,481	3,713	3,807	3,832	3,907	3,990	4,042	4
North Dakota	550	523	522	541	553	562	583	619	603	
South Dakota	583	549	547	553	571	591	618	655	646	
Nebraska	1,239	1,197	1,192	1,227	1,236	1,243	1,284	1,332	1,343	1
Kansas	1,813	1,727	1,679	1,751	1,749	1,795	1,863	1,910	1,950	2
South Atlantic	19,343	19,217	19,034	19,741	20,187	20,340	20,719	21,236	21,760	22
Delaware	279	284	287	299	310	317	319	321	330	
Maryland	2,093	2,111	2,103	2,288	2,317	2,295	2,339	2,359	2,459	2
District of Columbia	891	881	862	919	920	880	839	806	811	
Virginia	3,100	3,170	3,068	3,171	3,197	3,257	3,297	3,306	3,426	3
West Virginia	1,759	1,711	1,712	1,831	1,899	1,909	1,938	2,014	1,987	1
North Carolina	3,623	3,551	3,515	3,650	3,748	3,836	3,944	4,067	4,146	4
South Carolina	1,942	1,929	1,907	1,894	1,962	1,968	2,004	2,090	2,146	2
Georgia	3,238	3,211	3,161	3,250	3,294	3,272	3,360	3,451	3,494	3
Florida	2,418	2,369	2,420	2,431	2,540	2,606	2,679	2,820	2,968	3
East South Central	10,815	10,497	10,327	10,718	11,023	11,101	11,210	11,479	11,490	11
Kentucky	2,705	2,633	2,580	2,721	2,798	2,822	2,862	2,945	2,940	2
Tennessee	2,962	2,885	2,878	3,064	3,182	3,236	3,267	3,313	3,310	3
Alabama	2,876	2,829	2,811	2,917	2,967	2,986	3,004	3,049	3,049	3
Mississippi	2,273	2,151	2,057	2,016	2,075	2,056	2,076	2,172	2,191	2
West South Central	13,579	13,130	13,071	13,612	13,896	14,191	14,266	14,612	14,962	15
Arkansas	1,836	1,771	1,746	1,762	1,815	1,811	1,835	1,922	1,910	1
Louisiana	2,561	2,513	2,438	2,564	2,590	2,599	2,633	2,716	2,757	2
Oklahoma	2,228	-1,966	2,059	2,137	2,151	2,114	2,125	2,235	2,268	2
Texas	6,953	6,879	6,828	7,148	7,343	7,578	7,673	7,739	8,017	8
Mountain	4,443	4,393	4,237	4,446	4,561	4,684	4,854	5,091	5,245	5
Montana	487	462	463	495	515	535	562	592	588	
Idaho	506	539	509	509	521	553	572	580	580	
Wyoming	257	251	244	259	256	260	276	290	298	
Colorado	1,171	1,148	1,118	1,186	1,201	1,201	1,249	1,329	1,383	1,
New Mexico	541	532	539	556	574	592	632	684	706	
Arizona	701	618	602	646	686	712	726	755	806	
Utah	635	602	612	650	652	663	677	693	706	
Nevada	144	151	148	145	153	159	159	161	171	
Pacific	11,799	12,444	13,060	13,657	13,847	14,275	14,365	14,549	15,060	15,
Washington	2,058	2,162	2,274	2,334	2,279	2,326	2,373	2,381	2,427	2,
Oregon	1,233	1,282	1,294	1,398	1,473	1,482	1,493	1,530	1,554	1,
California	8,508	9,001	9,491	9,925	10,194	10,467	10,499	10,638	11,080	11,

Source: Department of Commerce, Bureau of the Census; *Current Population Reports*, Series P-25, Nos. and 70.

No. 10.—POPULATION, BY STATES AND OTHER AREAS: 1790 TO 1950

[Insofar as possible, population shown is that of present area of State. For regional totals, see also *Historical Statistics*, series B 48-71]

STATE OR OTHER AREA	1790	1800	1810	1820	1830	1840
United States	3,929,214	5,308,483	7,239,881	9,638,453	[1]12,866,020	[1]17,069,453
Regions:						
Northeast	1,968,040	2,635,576	3,486,675	4,359,916	5,542,381	6,761,082
North Central		51,006	292,107	859,305	1,610,473	3,351,542
South	1,961,174	2,621,901	3,461,099	4,419,232	5,707,848	6,950,729
West						
New England	1,009,408	1,233,011	1,471,973	1,660,071	1,954,717	2,234,822
Maine	96,540	151,719	228,705	298,335	399,455	501,793
New Hampshire	141,885	183,858	214,460	244,161	269,328	284,574
Vermont	85,425	154,465	217,895	235,981	280,652	291,948
Massachusetts	378,787	422,845	472,040	523,287	610,408	737,699
Rhode Island	68,825	69,122	76,931	83,059	97,199	108,830
Connecticut	237,946	251,002	261,942	275,248	297,675	309,978
Middle Atlantic	958,632	1,402,565	2,014,702	2,699,845	3,587,664	4,526,260
New York	340,120	589,051	959,049	1,372,812	1,918,608	2,428,921
New Jersey	184,139	211,149	245,562	277,575	320,823	373,306
Pennsylvania	434,373	602,365	810,091	1,049,458	1,348,233	1,724,033
East North Central		51,006	272,324	792,719	1,470,018	2,924,728
Ohio		[2]45,365	230,760	581,434	937,903	1,519,467
Indiana		[3]5,641	[3]24,520	147,178	343,031	685,866
Illinois			[4]12,282	55,211	157,445	476,183
Michigan			[5]4,762	[5]8,896	[5]31,639	212,267
Wisconsin						[6]30,945
West North Central			19,783	66,586	140,455	426,814
Minnesota						
Iowa						[7]43,112
Missouri			19,783	66,586	140,455	383,702
North Dakota						
South Dakota						
Nebraska						
Kansas						
South Atlantic	1,851,806	2,286,494	2,674,891	3,061,063	3,645,752	3,925,299
Delaware	59,096	64,273	72,674	72,749	76,748	78,085
Maryland	319,728	341,548	380,546	407,350	447,040	470,019
Dist. of Columbia		8,144	15,471	23,336	30,261	33,745
Virginia	691,737	807,557	877,683	938,261	1,044,054	1,025,227
West Virginia	55,873	78,592	105,469	136,808	176,924	224,537
North Carolina	393,751	478,103	555,500	638,829	737,987	753,419
South Carolina	249,073	345,591	415,115	502,741	581,185	594,398
Georgia	82,548	162,686	252,433	340,989	516,823	691,392
Florida					34,730	54,477
East South Central	109,368	335,407	708,590	1,190,489	1,815,969	2,575,445
Kentucky	73,677	220,955	406,511	564,317	687,917	779,828
Tennessee	35,691	105,602	261,727	422,823	681,904	829,210
Alabama		[8]1,250	[9]9,046	127,901	309,527	590,756
Mississippi		[8]7,600	[9]31,306	75,448	136,621	375,651
West South Central			77,618	167,680	246,127	449,985
Arkansas			1,062	14,273	30,388	97,574
Louisiana			76,556	153,407	215,739	352,411
Oklahoma						
Texas						
Mountain						
Montana						
Idaho						
Wyoming						
Colorado						
New Mexico						
Arizona						
Utah						
Nevada						
Pacific						
Washington						
Oregon						
California						
Alaska						
Hawaii						
Puerto Rico		[10]155,426				

[1] Includes persons (5,318 in 1830 and 6,100 in 1840) on public ships in service of the United States, not credited to any region, division, or State.
[2] Population of Territory Northwest of River Ohio.
[3] 1800 includes population (3,124) of those portions of Indiana Territory which were taken to form Michigan and Illinois Territories in 1805 and 1809, respectively, and that portion which was separated in 1816; 1810 includes population of area separated in 1816.
[4] Population of Illinois Territory.
[5] Population of Michigan Territory as then constituted; boundaries changed in 1816, 1818, 1834, and 1836.
[6] Includes population of that part of Minnesota northeast of Mississippi River.
[7] Includes population of area constituting that part of Minnesota lying west of Mississippi River and a line drawn from its source northwards to Canadian boundary.

No. 10.—Population, by States and Other Areas: 1790 to 1950—Continued

STATE OR OTHER AREA	1850	1860	1870	1880	1890	1900
United States	23, 191, 876	31, 443, 321	[11]39, 818, 449	50, 155, 783	[12]62, 947, 714	75, 994, 575
Regions:						
Northeast	8, 626, 851	10, 504, 268	12, 298, 730	14, 507, 407	17, 406, 969	21, 046, 695
North Central	5, 403, 595	9, 096, 716	12, 981, 111	17, 364, 111	22, 410, 417	26, 333, 004
South	8, 982, 612	11, 133, 361	12, 288, 020	16, 516, 568	20, 028, 059	24, 523, 527
West	178, 818	618, 976	990, 510	1, 767, 697	3, 102, 269	4, 091, 349
New England	2, 728, 116	3, 135, 283	3, 487, 924	4, 010, 529	4, 700, 749	5, 592, 017
Maine	583, 169	628, 279	626, 915	648, 936	661, 086	694, 466
New Hampshire	317, 976	326, 073	318, 300	346, 991	376, 530	411, 588
Vermont	314, 120	315, 098	330, 551	332, 286	332, 422	343, 641
Massachusetts	994, 514	1, 231, 066	1, 457, 351	1, 783, 085	2, 238, 947	2, 805, 346
Rhode Island	147, 545	174, 620	217, 353	276, 531	345, 506	428, 556
Connecticut	370, 792	460, 147	537, 454	622, 700	746, 258	908, 420
Middle Atlantic	5, 898, 735	7, 458, 985	8, 810, 806	10, 496, 878	12, 706, 220	15, 454, 678
New York	3, 097, 394	3, 880, 735	4, 382, 759	5, 082, 871	6, 003, 174	7, 268, 894
New Jersey	489, 555	672, 035	906, 096	1, 131, 116	1, 444, 933	1, 883, 669
Pennsylvania	2, 311, 786	2, 906, 215	3, 521, 951	4, 282, 891	5, 258, 113	6, 302, 115
East North Central	4, 523, 260	6, 926, 884	9, 124, 517	11, 206, 668	13, 478, 305	15, 985, 581
Ohio	1, 980, 329	2, 339, 511	2, 665, 260	3, 198, 062	3, 672, 329	4, 157, 545
Indiana	988, 416	1, 350, 428	1, 680, 637	1, 978, 301	2, 192, 404	2, 516, 462
Illinois	851, 470	1, 711, 951	2, 539, 891	3, 077, 871	3, 826, 352	4, 821, 550
Michigan	397, 654	749, 113	1, 184, 059	1, 636, 937	2, 093, 890	2, 420, 982
Wisconsin	305, 391	775, 881	1, 054, 670	1, 315, 497	1, 693, 330	2, 069, 042
West North Central	880, 335	2, 169, 832	3, 856, 594	6, 157, 443	8, 932, 112	10, 347, 423
Minnesota	6, 077	172, 023	439, 706	780, 773	1, 310, 283	1, 751, 394
Iowa	192, 214	674, 913	1, 194, 020	1, 624, 615	1, 912, 297	2, 231, 853
Missouri	682, 044	1, 182, 012	1, 721, 295	2, 168, 380	2, 679, 185	3, 106, 665
North Dakota		} [13]4, 837 {	2, 405	36, 909	190, 983	319, 146
South Dakota			11, 776	98, 268	348, 600	401, 570
Nebraska		28, 841	122, 993	452, 402	1, 062, 656	1, 066, 300
Kansas		107, 206	364, 399	996, 096	1, 428, 108	1, 470, 495
South Atlantic	4, 679, 890	5, 364, 703	5, 853, 610	7, 597, 197	8, 857, 922	10, 443, 480
Delaware	91, 532	112, 216	125, 015	146, 608	168, 493	184, 735
Maryland	583, 034	687, 049	780, 894	934, 943	1, 042, 390	1, 188, 044
Dist. of Columbia	51, 687	75, 080	131, 700	177, 624	230, 392	278, 718
Virginia	1, 119, 348	1, 219, 630	1, 225, 163	1, 512, 565	1, 655, 980	1, 854, 184
West Virginia	302, 313	376, 688	442, 014	618, 457	762, 794	958, 800
North Carolina	869, 039	992, 622	1, 071, 361	1, 399, 750	1, 617, 949	1, 893, 810
South Carolina	668, 507	703, 708	705, 606	995, 577	1, 151, 149	1, 340, 316
Georgia	905, 185	1, 057, 286	1, 184, 109	1, 542, 180	1, 837, 353	2, 216, 331
Florida	87, 445	140, 424	187, 748	269, 493	391, 422	528, 542
East South Central	3, 363, 271	4, 020, 991	4, 404, 445	5, 585, 151	6, 429, 154	7, 547, 757
Kentucky	982, 405	1, 155, 684	1, 321, 011	1, 648, 690	1, 858, 635	2, 147, 174
Tennessee	1, 002, 717	1, 109, 801	1, 258, 520	1, 542, 359	1, 767, 518	2, 020, 616
Alabama	771, 623	964, 201	996, 992	1, 262, 505	1, 513, 401	1, 828, 697
Mississippi	606, 526	791, 305	827, 922	1, 131, 597	1, 289, 600	1, 551, 270
West South Central	940, 251	1, 747, 667	2, 029, 965	3, 334, 220	4, 740, 983	6, 532, 290
Arkansas	209, 897	435, 450	484, 471	802, 525	1, 128, 211	1, 311, 564
Louisiana	517, 762	708, 002	726, 915	939, 946	1, 118, 588	1, 381, 625
Oklahoma					258, 657	790, 391
Texas	212, 592	604, 215	818, 579	1, 591, 749	2, 235, 527	3, 048, 710
Mountain	72, 927	174, 923	315, 385	653, 119	1, 213, 935	1, 674, 657
Montana			20, 595	39, 159	142, 924	243, 329
Idaho			14, 999	32, 610	88, 548	161, 772
Wyoming			9, 118	20, 789	62, 555	92, 531
Colorado		34, 277	39, 864	194, 327	413, 249	539, 700
New Mexico	61, 547	[14]93, 516	91, 874	119, 565	160, 282	195, 310
Arizona			9, 658	40, 440	88, 243	122, 931
Utah	11, 380	[15]40, 273	86, 786	143, 963	210, 779	276, 749
Nevada		[16]6, 857	42, 491	62, 266	47, 355	42, 335
Pacific	105, 891	444, 053	675, 125	1, 114, 578	1, 888, 334	2, 416, 692
Washington	[17]1, 201	11, 594	23, 955	75, 116	357, 232	518, 103
Oregon	12, 093	52, 465	90, 923	174, 768	317, 704	413, 536
California	92, 597	379, 994	560, 247	864, 694	1, 213, 398	1, 485, 053
Alaska					32, 052	63, 592
Hawaii	[18]84, 165	[18]69, 800		33, 426	[18]89, 990	154, 001
Puerto Rico		[19]583, 308				[19]953, 243

[a] Population of those parts of Mississippi Territory now in present State.
[b] Population of those parts of present State included in Mississippi Territory as then constituted.
[10] Censuses taken under direction of Spanish Government.
[11] Revised; unrevised figure is 38,558,371. Census of Southern States considered incomplete but there has been no revision of State figures, hence State and region figures do not add to total shown here.
[12] Includes population (325,464) of Indian Territory and Indian reservations, specially enumerated.
[13] Population of Dakota Territory.
[14] Includes population of area taken to form part of Arizona Territory in 1863.
[15] Population of Utah Territory exclusive of that part of present State of Colorado taken to form Colorado Territory in 1861.
[16] Population of Nevada Territory as organized in 1861.

10.—Population, by States and Other Areas: 1790 to 1950—Continued

STATE OR OTHER AREA	1910	1920	1930	1940	1950
nited States	91,972,266	105,710,620	122,775,046	131,669,275	150,697,361
:					
east	25,868,573	29,662,053	34,427,091	35,976,777	39,477,986
Central	29,888,542	34,019,792	38,594,100	40,143,332	44,460,762
	29,380,330	33,125,803	37,857,633	41,665,901	47,197,088
	6,825,821	8,902,972	11,896,222	13,883,265	19,561,535
gland	6,552,681	7,400,909	8,166,341	8,437,290	9,314,453
	742,371	768,014	797,423	847,226	913,774
ampshire	430,572	443,083	465,293	491,524	533,242
nt	355,956	352,428	359,611	359,231	377,747
chusetts	3,366,416	3,852,356	4,249,614	4,316,721	4,690,514
Island	542,610	604,397	687,497	713,346	791,896
cticut	1,114,756	1,380,631	1,606,903	1,709,242	2,007,280
Atlantic	19,315,892	22,261,144	26,260,750	27,539,487	30,163,533
York	9,113,614	10,385,227	12,588,066	13,479,142	14,830,192
ersey	2,537,167	3,155,900	4,041,334	4,160,165	4,835,329
sylvania	7,665,111	8,720,017	9,631,350	9,900,180	10,498,012
rth Central	18,250,621	21,475,543	25,297,185	26,626,342	30,399,368
	4,767,121	5,759,394	6,646,697	6,907,612	7,946,627
a	2,700,876	2,930,390	3,238,503	3,427,796	3,934,224
s	5,638,591	6,485,280	7,630,654	7,897,241	8,712,176
an	2,810,173	3,668,412	4,842,325	5,256,106	6,371,766
sin	2,333,860	2,632,067	2,939,006	3,137,587	3,434,575
rth Central	11,637,921	12,544,249	13,296,915	13,516,990	14,061,394
sota	2,075,708	2,387,125	2,563,953	2,792,300	2,982,483
	2,224,771	2,404,021	2,470,939	2,538,268	2,621,073
uri	3,293,335	3,404,055	3,629,367	3,784,664	3,954,653
Dakota	577,056	646,872	680,845	641,935	619,636
Dakota	583,888	636,547	692,849	642,961	652,740
ska	1,192,214	1,296,372	1,377,963	1,315,834	1,325,510
s	1,690,949	1,769,257	1,880,999	1,801,028	1,905,299
lantic	12,194,895	13,990,272	15,793,589	17,823,151	21,182,335
are	202,322	223,003	238,380	266,505	318,085
and	1,295,346	1,449,661	1,631,526	1,821,244	2,343,001
f Columbia	331,069	437,571	486,869	663,091	802,178
ia	2,061,612	2,309,187	2,421,851	2,677,773	3,318,680
Virginia	1,221,119	1,463,701	1,729,205	1,901,974	2,005,552
Carolina	2,206,287	2,559,123	3,170,276	3,571,623	4,061,929
Carolina	1,515,400	1,683,724	1,738,765	1,899,804	2,117,027
a	2,609,121	2,895,832	2,908,506	3,123,723	3,444,578
a	752,619	968,470	1,468,211	1,897,414	2,771,305
th Central	8,409,901	8,893,307	9,887,214	10,778,225	11,477,181
cky	2,289,905	2,416,630	2,614,589	2,845,627	2,944,806
see	2,184,789	2,337,885	2,616,556	2,915,841	3,291,718
ma	2,138,093	2,348,174	2,646,248	2,832,961	3,061,743
sippi	1,797,114	1,790,618	2,009,821	2,183,796	2,178,914
uth Central	8,784,534	10,242,224	12,176,830	13,064,525	14,537,572
sas	1,574,449	1,752,204	1,854,482	1,949,387	1,909,511
ana	1,656,388	1,798,509	2,101,593	2,363,880	2,683,516
ma	1,657,155	2,028,283	2,396,040	2,336,434	2,233,351
	3,896,542	4,663,228	5,824,715	6,414,824	7,711,194
in	2,633,517	3,336,101	3,701,789	4,150,003	5,074,998
na	376,053	548,889	537,606	559,456	591,024
ing	325,594	431,866	445,032	524,873	588,637
do	145,965	194,402	225,565	250,742	290,529
exico	799,024	939,629	1,035,791	1,123,296	1,325,089
a	327,301	360,350	423,317	531,818	681,187
	204,354	334,162	435,573	499,261	749,587
a	373,351	449,396	507,847	550,310	688,862
a	81,875	77,407	91,058	110,247	160,083
	4,192,304	5,566,871	8,194,433	9,733,262	14,486,527
ngton	1,141,990	1,356,621	1,563,396	1,736,191	2,378,963
n	672,765	783,389	953,786	1,089,684	1,521,341
nia	2,377,549	3,426,861	5,677,251	6,907,387	10,586,223
	64,356	55,036	[20] 59,278	[20] 72,524	128,643
	191,909	255,912	368,336	423,330	499,794
ico	1,118,012	1,299,809	1,543,913	1,869,255	2,210,703

ides population of Idaho and parts of Montana and Wyoming.
uses taken under direction of Hawaiian Government.
us taken as of Nov. 10, 1899.
Census taken as of Oct. 1, 1920; 1940, as of Oct. 1, 1939.
: Department of Commerce, Bureau of the Census; U. S. Census of Population: 1950, Vol. I.

145254°—53——3

No. 11.—POPULATION RANK AND DECENNIAL PERCENT INCREASE FOR STATES: 1890 TO 1950

[Based on population shown in table 10. Minus sign (−) denotes decrease]

DIVISION AND STATE	RANK						PERCENT INCREASE					
	1900	1910	1920	1930	1940	1950	1890 to 1900	1900 to 1910	1910 to 1920	1920 to 1930	1930 to 1940	1940 to 1950
United States							20.7	21.0	14.9	16.1	7.2	
New England							19.0	17.2	12.9	10.3	3.3	
Maine	31	34	35	35	35	35	5.0	6.9	3.5	3.8	6.2	
New Hampshire	37	39	41	42	45	45	9.3	4.6	2.9	5.0	5.6	
Vermont	39	42	45	46	46	46	3.4	3.6	−1.0	2.0	−.1	
Massachusetts	7	6	6	8	8	9	25.3	20.0	14.4	10.3	1.6	
Rhode Island	35	38	38	37	36	37	24.0	26.6	11.4	13.7	3.8	
Connecticut	29	31	29	29	31	28	21.7	22.7	23.9	16.4	6.4	
Middle Atlantic							21.6	25.0	15.2	16.0	4.9	
New York	1	1	1	1	1	1	21.1	25.4	14.0	21.2	7.1	
New Jersey	16	11	10	9	9	8	30.4	34.7	24.4	28.1	2.9	
Pennsylvania	2	2	2	2	2	3	19.9	21.6	13.8	10.5	2.8	
East North Central							18.6	14.2	17.7	17.8	5.3	
Ohio	4	4	4	4	4	5	13.2	14.7	20.8	15.4	3.9	
Indiana	8	9	11	11	12	12	14.8	7.3	8.5	10.5	5.8	
Illinois	3	3	3	3	3	4	26.0	16.9	15.0	17.7	3.5	
Michigan	9	8	7	7	7	7	15.6	16.1	30.5	32.0	8.5	
Wisconsin	13	13	13	13	13	14	22.2	12.8	12.8	11.7	6.8	
West North Central							15.8	12.5	7.8	4.0	1.7	
Minnesota	19	19	17	18	18	18	33.7	18.5	15.0	7.4	8.9	
Iowa	10	15	16	19	20	22	16.7	−.3	8.1	2.8	2.7	
Missouri	5	7	9	10	10	11	16.0	6.0	3.4	6.6	4.3	
North Dakota	40	37	36	38	39	42	67.1	80.8	12.1	5.3	−5.7	
South Dakota	38	36	37	36	38	41	15.2	45.4	9.0	8.8	−7.2	
Nebraska	27	29	31	32	32	33	.3	11.8	8.7	6.3	−4.5	
Kansas	22	22	24	24	29	31	3.0	15.0	4.6	6.3	−4.3	
South Atlantic							17.9	16.8	14.7	12.9	12.9	
Delaware	45	47	47	47	47	47	9.6	9.5	10.2	6.9	11.8	
Maryland	26	27	28	28	24	24	14.0	9.0	11.9	12.5	11.6	
Dist. of Columbia	41	43	42	41	37	36	21.0	18.8	32.2	11.3	36.2	
Virginia	17	20	20	20	19	15	12.0	11.2	12.0	4.9	10.6	
West Virginia	28	28	27	27	25	29	25.7	27.4	19.9	18.1	10.0	
North Carolina	15	16	14	12	11	10	17.1	16.5	16.0	23.9	12.7	
South Carolina	24	26	26	26	26	27	16.4	13.1	11.1	3.3	9.3	
Georgia	11	10	12	14	14	13	20.6	17.7	11.0	.4	7.4	
Florida	33	33	32	31	27	20	35.0	42.4	28.7	51.6	29.2	
East South Central							17.4	11.4	5.7	11.2	9.0	
Kentucky	12	14	15	17	16	19	15.5	6.6	5.5	8.2	8.8	
Tennessee	14	17	19	16	15	16	14.3	8.1	7.0	11.9	11.4	
Alabama	18	18	18	15	17	17	20.8	16.9	9.8	12.7	7.1	
Mississippi	20	21	23	23	23	26	20.3	15.8	−.4	12.2	8.7	
West South Central							37.8	34.5	16.6	18.9	7.3	
Arkansas	25	25	25	25	24	30	16.3	20.0	11.3	5.8	5.1	
Louisiana	23	24	22	22	21	21	23.5	19.9	8.6	16.9	12.5	
Oklahoma	30	23	21	21	22	25	205.6	109.7	22.4	18.1	−2.5	
Texas	6	5	5	5	6	6	36.4	27.8	19.7	24.9	10.1	
Mountain							35.0	57.3	25.7	11.6	12.1	
Montana	43	40	39	39	40	43	70.3	54.5	46.0	−2.1	4.1	
Idaho	46	45	43	43	43	44	82.7	101.3	32.6	3.0	17.9	
Wyoming	48	48	48	48	48	48	47.9	57.7	33.2	16.0	11.2	
Colorado	32	32	33	33	33	34	30.6	48.0	17.6	10.2	8.4	
New Mexico	44	44	44	45	42	40	21.9	67.6	10.1	17.5	25.6	
Arizona	47	46	46	44	44	38	39.3	66.2	63.5	30.3	14.6	
Utah	42	41	40	40	41	39	31.3	34.9	20.4	13.0	8.4	
Nevada	49	49	49	49	49	49	−10.6	93.4	−5.5	17.6	21.1	
Pacific							28.0	73.5	32.8	47.2	18.8	
Washington	34	30	30	30	30	23	45.0	120.4	18.8	15.2	11.1	
Oregon	36	35	34	34	34	32	30.2	62.7	16.4	21.8	14.2	
California	21	12	8	6	5	2	22.4	60.1	44.1	65.7	21.7	

No. **12.**—PROVISIONAL ESTIMATES OF THE COMPONENTS OF CHANGE IN THE CIVILIAN POPULATION BY STATES 940 TO 1950

DIVISION AND STATE	CIVILIAN POPULATION		POPULATION CHANGE, 1940 TO 1950				
	1940, Apr. 1	1950, Apr. 1	Net change	Births	Deaths	Net migration [1]	Net loss to armed forces [2]
United States	131,391,000	149,634,000	+18,242,000	32,294,000	14,195,000	+1,611,000	1,468,000
New England............	8,424,000	9,261,000	+837,000	1,781,000	993,000	+154,000	109,000
Maine..................	845,000	912,000	+67,000	196,000	102,000	−16,000	11,000
New Hampshire.....	491,000	531,000	+40,000	103,000	60,000	+5,000	8,000
Vermont..............	358,000	378,000	+20,000	82,000	43,000	−15,000	4,000
Massachusetts......	4,312,000	4,665,000	+353,000	873,000	517,000	+55,000	56,000
Rhode Island........	710,000	774,000	+65,000	151,000	81,000	+1,000	6,000
Connecticut..........	1,708,000	2,001,000	+293,000	377,000	190,000	+128,000	22,000
Middle Atlantic......	27,505,000	30,083,000	+2,578,000	5,535,000	3,111,000	+448,000	294,000
New York............	13,454,000	14,801,000	+1,346,000	2,625,000	1,539,000	+376,000	116,000
New Jersey..........	4,155,000	4,802,000	+647,000	853,000	473,000	+314,000	46,000
Pennsylvania........	9,895,000	10,480,000	+585,000	2,057,000	1,099,000	−242,000	131,000
East North Central....	26,604,000	30,337,000	+3,733,000	6,088,000	2,966,000	+900,000	290,000
Ohio.................	6,904,000	7,938,000	+1,034,000	1,607,000	799,000	+306,000	81,000
Indiana..............	3,425,000	3,932,000	+508,000	813,000	398,000	+133,000	40,000
Illinois..............	7,886,000	8,672,000	+787,000	1,635,000	898,000	+120,000	71,000
Michigan.............	5,253,000	6,361,000	+1,108,000	1,329,000	550,000	+392,000	63,000
Wisconsin............	3,137,000	3,433,000	+296,000	704,000	321,000	−51,000	36,000
West North Central....	13,506,000	14,032,000	+526,000	2,932,000	1,378,000	−891,000	137,000
Minnesota...........	2,790,000	2,981,000	+191,000	630,000	269,000	−143,000	27,000
Iowa.................	2,537,000	2,621,000	+84,000	544,000	259,000	−176,000	26,000
Missouri.............	3,784,000	3,952,000	+169,000	810,000	432,000	−168,000	41,000
North Dakota.......	642,000	620,000	−22,000	150,000	52,000	−115,000	6,000
South Dakota.......	643,000	650,000	+7,000	145,000	56,000	−76,000	6,000
Nebraska............	1,314,000	1,322,000	+8,000	272,000	126,000	−126,000	13,000
Kansas..............	1,797,000	1,887,000	+90,000	381,000	184,000	−87,000	19,000
South Atlantic........	17,747,000	20,860,000	+3,113,000	5,252,000	1,815,000	−134,000	190,000
Delaware............	266,000	318,000	+52,000	64,000	33,000	+24,000	2,000
Maryland............	1,812,000	2,306,000	+495,000	474,000	222,000	+261,000	18,000
District of Columbia.	657,000	769,000	+112,000	183,000	82,000	+16,000	5,000
Virginia.............	2,650,000	3,220,000	+570,000	768,000	288,000	+106,000	16,000
West Virginia.......	1,902,000	2,005,000	+103,000	522,000	173,000	−217,000	20,000
North Carolina......	3,566,000	4,014,000	+448,000	1,046,000	303,000	−296,000	39,000
South Carolina......	1,894,000	2,096,000	+201,000	664,000	186,000	−261,000	16,000
Georgia..............	3,109,000	3,402,000	+293,000	944,000	297,000	−326,000	27,000
Florida..............	1,892,000	2,729,000	+837,000	547,000	230,000	+559,000	39,000
East South Central....	10,767,000	11,412,000	+645,000	3,133,000	1,049,000	−1,325,000	113,000
Kentucky............	2,838,000	2,913,000	+75,000	759,000	286,000	−372,000	26,000
Tennessee...........	2,916,000	3,281,000	+366,000	848,000	287,000	−160,000	36,000
Alabama.............	2,830,000	3,053,000	+223,000	806,000	268,000	−343,000	31,000
Mississippi..........	2,184,000	2,164,000	−19,000	660,000	208,000	−451,000	21,000
West South Central...	13,029,000	14,380,000	+1,351,000	3,694,000	1,203,000	−988,000	152,000
Arkansas............	1,948,000	1,908,000	−40,000	552,000	157,000	−413,000	22,000
Louisiana...........	2,361,000	2,670,000	+309,000	710,000	233,000	−141,000	27,000
Oklahoma............	2,331,000	2,218,000	−113,000	540,000	196,000	−431,000	26,000
Texas...............	6,389,000	7,584,000	+1,196,000	1,893,000	617,000	−3,000	76,000
Mountain	4,140,000	5,021,000	+881,000	1,196,000	431,000	+172,000	56,000
Montana.............	559,000	589,000	+30,000	129,000	57,000	−35,000	7,000
Idaho................	525,000	588,000	+64,000	138,000	47,000	−21,000	7,000
Wyoming............	246,000	282,000	+36,000	64,000	22,000	−7,000	(²)
Colorado............	1,120,000	1,307,000	+187,000	285,000	124,000	+40,000	14,000
New Mexico.........	532,000	668,000	+136,000	195,000	56,000	+7,000	9,000
Arizona.............	498,000	742,000	+244,000	173,000	60,000	+142,000	10,000
Utah................	550,000	687,000	+137,000	180,000	49,000	+13,000	8,000
Nevada..............	110,000	157,000	+47,000	32,000	16,000	+33,000	2,000
Pacific	9,669,000	14,248,000	+4,579,000	2,683,000	1,250,000	+3,272,000	126,000
Washington.........	1,722,000	2,317,000	+594,000	470,000	213,000	+353,000	16,000
Oregon.............	1,089,000	1,519,000	+430,000	279,000	132,000	+303,000	21,000
California..........	6,858,000	10,413,000	+3,555,000	1,934,000	905,000	+2,615,000	90,000

[1] Comprises both net immigration from abroad and net interdivisional or interstate migration.
[2] Estimated net loss to armed forces less than 500.

Source: Department of Commerce, Bureau of the Census; *Current Population Reports*, Series P-25, No. 47.

No. 13.—POPULATION OF STANDARD METROPOLITAN AREAS: 1940 AND 195

[Minus sign (−) denotes decrease. A standard metropolitan area is a county or group of contiguous co (except in New England) which contains at least one central city of 50,000 inhabitants or more. In addit the county, or counties, containing such a city, or cities, contiguous counties are included in a standard politan area if according to certain criteria they are essentially metropolitan in character and sufficiently grated with the central city. In New England, standard metropolitan areas have been defined on a town than on a county basis. This list of areas is based on "Standard Metropolitan Area Definitions" issued Executive Office of the President, Bureau of the Budget, on October 17, 1950, and "Addendum to list issued October 8, 1952. For detailed explanation of standard metropolitan area concept and data for geog components of each area, see source and *County and City Data Book, 1952*, a supplement to the *Statistical A*

STANDARD METROPOLITAN AREA	1940, Apr. 1	1950, Apr. 1	Percent increase 1940 to 1950	STANDARD METROPOLITAN AREA	1940, Apr. 1	1950, Apr. 1
CONTINENTAL UNITED STATES				**CONTINENTAL UNITED STATES—continued**		
Total, 170 areas	69,424,745	84,715,244	22.0	Grand Rapids (Mich.) area	246,338	288,292
				Green Bay (Wis.) area	83,109	98,314
Akron (Ohio) area	339,405	410,032	20.8	Greensboro-High Point (N. C.) area	153,916	191,057
Albany-Schenectady-Troy (N. Y.) area	465,643	514,490	10.5	Greenville (S. C.) area	136,580	168,152
Albuquerque (N. Mex.) area	69,391	145,673	109.9	Hamilton-Middleton (Ohio) area	120,249	147,203
Allentown-Bethlehem-Easton (Pa.) area	396,673	437,824	10.4	Hampton-Newport News-Warwick (Va.) area	84,499	142,227
Altoona (Pa.) area	140,358	139,514	−.6	Harrisburg (Pa.) area	252,216	292,241
Amarillo (Tex.) area	61,450	87,140	41.8	Hartford (Conn.) area	295,613	358,081
Asheville (N. C.) area	108,755	124,403	14.4	Houston (Tex.) area	528,961	806,701
Atlanta (Ga.) area	518,100	671,797	29.7	Huntington (W. Va.)-Ashland (Ky.) area	225,668	245,795
Atlantic City (N. J.) area	124,066	132,399	6.7			
Augusta (Ga.) area	131,779	162,013	22.9	Indianapolis (Ind.) area	460,926	551,777
				Jackson (Mich.) area	93,108	107,925
Austin (Tex.) area	111,053	160,980	45.0	Jackson (Miss.) area	107,273	142,164
Baltimore (Md.) area	1,083,300	1,337,373	23.5	Jacksonville (Fla.) area	210,143	304,029
Baton Rouge (La.) area	88,415	158,236	79.0	Johnstown (Pa.) area	298,416	291,354
Bay City (Mich.) area	74,981	88,461	18.0	Kalamazoo (Mich.) area	100,085	126,707
Beaumont-Port Arthur (Tex.) area	145,329	195,083	34.2	Kansas City (Mo.) area	688,643	814,357
Binghamton (N. Y.) area	165,749	184,698	11.4	Kenosha (Wis.) area	63,505	75,238
Birmingham (Ala.) area	459,930	558,928	21.5	Knoxville (Tenn.) area	246,088	337,105
Boston (Mass.) area	2,177,621	2,369,986	8.8	Lancaster (Pa.) area	212,504	234,717
Bridgeport (Conn.) area	212,569	258,137	21.4			
Brockton (Mass.) area	119,310	129,428	8.5	Lansing (Mich.) area	130,616	172,941
				Laredo (Tex.) area	45,916	56,141
Buffalo (N. Y.) area	958,487	1,089,230	13.6	Lawrence (Mass.) area	124,849	125,935
Canton (Ohio) area	234,887	283,194	20.6	Lexington (Ky.) area	78,899	100,746
Cedar Rapids (Iowa) area	89,142	104,274	17.0	Lima (Ohio) area	73,303	88,183
Charleston (S. C.) area	121,105	164,856	36.1	Lincoln (Nebr.) area	100,585	119,742
Charleston (W. Va.) area	276,247	322,072	16.6	Little Rock-North Little Rock (Ark.) area	158,085	196,685
Charlotte (N. C.) area	151,826	197,052	29.8	Lorain-Elyria (Ohio) area	112,390	148,162
Chattanooga (Tenn.) area	211,502	246,453	16.5	Los Angeles (Calif.) area	2,916,403	4,367,911
Chicago (Ill.) area	4,825,527	5,495,364	13.9	Louisville (Ky.) area	451,473	576,900
Cincinnati (Ohio) area	787,044	904,402	14.9			
Cleveland (Ohio) area	1,267,270	1,465,511	15.6	Lowell (Mass.) area	130,999	133,928
				Lubbock (Tex.) area	51,782	101,048
Columbia (S. C.) area	104,843	142,565	36.0	Macon (Ga.) area	95,086	135,043
Columbus (Ga.) area	126,407	170,541	34.9	Madison (Wis.) area	130,660	169,357
Columbus (Ohio) area	388,712	503,410	29.5	Manchester (N. H.) area	81,932	88,370
Corpus Christi (Tex.) area	92,661	165,471	78.6	Memphis (Tenn.) area	358,250	482,393
Dallas (Tex.) area	398,564	614,799	54.3	Miami (Fla.) area	267,739	495,084
Davenport (Iowa)-Rock Island-Moline (Ill.) area	196,071	234,256	18.3	Milwaukee (Wis.) area	766,885	871,047
Dayton (Ohio) area	331,343	457,333	38.0	Minneapolis-St. Paul (Minn.) area	940,937	1,116,509
Decatur (Ill.) area	84,693	98,853	16.7	Mobile (Ala.) area	141,974	231,105
Denver (Colo.) area	407,768	563,832	38.3			
Des Moines (Iowa) area	195,835	226,010	15.4	Montgomery (Ala.) area	114,420	138,965
				Muncie (Ind.) area	74,906	90,252
Detroit (Mich.) area	2,377,329	3,016,197	26.9	Nashville (Tenn.) area	257,267	321,758
Dubuque (Iowa) area	63,768	71,337	11.9	New Bedford (Mass.) area	134,435	137,469
Duluth (Minn.)-Superior (Wis.) area	254,036	252,777	−.5	New Britain-Bristol (Conn.) area	126,709	146,983
Durham (N. C.) area	80,244	101,639	26.7	New Haven (Conn.) area	240,750	264,622
El Paso (Tex.) area	131,067	194,968	48.8	New Orleans (La.) area	552,244	685,405
Erie (Pa.) area	180,889	219,388	21.3	New York-Northeastern New Jersey area	11,660,639	12,911,994
Evansville (Ind.) area	130,783	160,422	22.7			
Fall River (Mass.) area	135,137	137,298	1.6	Norfolk-Portsmouth (Va.) area	258,927	446,200
Flint (Mich.) area	227,944	270,963	18.9	Ogden (Utah) area	56,714	83,319
Fort Wayne (Ind.) area	155,084	183,722	18.5	Oklahoma City (Okla.) area	244,159	325,352
Fort Worth (Tex.) area	225,521	361,253	60.2	Omaha (Nebr.) area	325,153	366,395
Fresno (Calif.) area	178,565	276,515	54.9			
Gadsden (Ala.) area	72,580	93,892	29.4			
Galveston (Tex.) area	81,173	113,066	39.3			

—POPULATION OF STANDARD METROPOLITAN AREAS: 1940 AND 1950—Continued

[Minus sign (−) denotes decrease]

D METROPOLITAN AREA	1940, Apr. 1	1950, Apr. 1	Percent increase 1940 to 1950	STANDARD METROPOLITAN AREA	1940, Apr. 1	1950, Apr. 1	Percent increase 1940 to 1950
ENTAL UNITED s—continued				CONTINENTAL UNITED STATES—continued			
ia.) area	70,074	114,950	64.0	Springfield-Holyoke (Mass.) area	364,680	407,255	11.7
) area	211,736	250,512	18.3	Stamford-Norwalk (Conn.)			
ia (Pa.) area	3,199,637	3,671,048	14.7	area	160,274	196,023	22.3
riz.) area	186,193	331,770	78.2	Stockton (Calif.) area	134,207	200,750	49.6
(Pa.) area	2,082,556	2,213,236	6.3	Syracuse (N. Y.) area	295,108	341,719	15.8
Mass.) area	60,996	66,567	9.1	Tacoma (Wash.) area	182,081	275,876	51.5
Maine) area	106,506	119,942	12.6	Tampa-St. Petersburg (Fla.)			
Oreg.) area	501,275	704,829	40.6	area	272,600	409,143	50.4
(R. I.) area	676,766	737,203	8.9	Terre Haute (Ind.) area	99,709	105,160	5.5
hio.) area	66,870	90,188	31.0	Toledo (Ohio) area	344,333	395,551	14.9
				Topeka (Kans.) area	91,247	105,418	15.5
ia.) area	94,047	108,385	16.5	Trenton (N. J.) area	197,318	229,781	16.5
. C.) area	109,544	136,450	24.6				
a.) area	241,884	255,740	5.7	Tulsa (Okla.) area	193,363	251,686	30.2
(Va.) area	262,991	326,050	24.7	Utica-Rome (N. Y.) area	263,163	284,262	8.0
Va.) area	112,184	133,407	18.9	Waco (Tex.) area	101,898	130,194	27.8
(N. Y.) area	438,230	487,632	11.3	Washington (D. C.) area	967,985	1,464,089	51.3
Ill.) area	121,178	152,385	25.8	Waterbury (Conn.) area	138,779	154,656	11.4
s (Calif.) area	170,333	277,140	62.7				
ich.) area	130,468	153,515	17.7	Waterloo (Iowa) area	79,946	100,448	25.6
(Mo.) area	94,067	96,826	2.9	Wheeling (W. Va.)-Steubenville (Ohio) area	364,132	354,092	−2.8
Mo.) area	1,432,088	1,681,281	17.4	Wichita (Kans.) area	143,311	222,290	55.1
Utah) area	211,623	274,895	29.9	Wichita Falls (Tex.) area	73,604	98,493	33.8
(Tex.) area	39,302	58,929	49.9	Wilkes-Barre—Hazleton (Pa)			
io (Tex.) area	338,176	500,460	48.0	area	441,518	392,241	−11.2
dino (Calif.) area	161,108	281,642	74.8	Wilmington (Del.) area	221,836	268,387	21.0
(Calif.) area	280,348	556,808	92.4	Winston-Salem (N. C.) area	126,475	146,135	15.5
ncisco-Oakland area	1,461,804	2,240,767	53.3	Worcester (Mass.) area	252,752	276,336	9.3
Calif.) area	174,949	290,547	66.1	York (Pa.) area	178,022	202,737	13.9
(Ga.) area	117,970	151,481	28.4	Youngstown (Ohio) area	473,605	528,498	11.6
Pa.) area	301,243	257,396	−14.6				
ash.) area	504,980	732,992	45.2	HAWAII			
(La.) area	150,203	176,547	17.5	Honolulu	258,256	353,020	36.7
(Iowa) area	103,627	103,917	.3				
(S. Dak.) area	57,697	70,910	22.9	PUERTO RICO			
d (Ind.) area	161,823	205,058	26.7				
Wash.) area	164,652	221,561	34.6	Mayaguez	76,487	87,307	14.1
(Ill.) area	117,912	131,484	11.5	Ponce	105,116	126,810	20.6
(Mo.) area	90,541	104,823	15.8	San Juan—Rio Piedras	302,765	465,741	53.8
(Ohio) area	96,647	111,661	16.7				

Department of Commerce, Bureau of Census; U. S. Census of Population: 1950, Vol. I, and records.

No. 14.—POPULATION OF CITIES HAVING 50,000 INHABITANTS OR MORE IN 1
1890 TO 1950

[Increase from census to census includes that due to annexation of territory as well as to direct growth

CITY	1890	1900	1910	1920	1930	1940	19
Akron, Ohio	27,601	42,728	69,067	208,435	255,040	244,791	2
Alameda, Calif	11,165	16,464	23,383	28,806	35,033	36,256	6
Albany, N. Y	94,923	94,151	100,253	113,344	127,412	130,577	12
Albuquerque, N. Mex	3,785	6,238	11,020	15,157	26,570	35,449	
Alexandria, Va	14,339	14,528	15,329	18,060	24,149	33,523	
Alhambra, Calif			5,021	9,096	29,472	38,935	
Allentown, Pa	25,228	35,416	51,913	73,502	92,563	96,904	10
Altoona, Pa	30,337	38,973	52,127	60,331	82,054	80,214	7
Amarillo, Tex	482	1,442	9,957	15,494	43,132	51,686	7
Asheville, N. C	10,235	14,694	18,762	28,504	50,193	51,310	5
Atlanta, Ga	65,533	89,872	154,839	200,616	270,366	302,288	3
Atlantic City, N. J	13,055	27,838	46,150	50,707	66,198	64,094	
Augusta, Ga	33,300	39,441	41,040	52,548	60,342	65,919	
Aurora, Ill	19,688	24,147	29,807	36,397	46,589	47,170	
Austin, Tex	14,575	22,258	29,860	34,876	53,120	87,930	12
Baltimore, Md	434,439	508,957	558,485	733,826	804,874	859,100	94
Baton Rouge, La	10,478	11,269	14,897	21,782	30,729	34,719	12
Bay City, Mich	27,839	27,628	45,106	47,554	47,355	47,956	
Bayonne, N. J	19,033	32,722	55,545	76,754	88,979	79,198	
Beaumont, Tex	3,296	9,427	20,640	40,422	57,732	59,061	
Berkeley, Calif	5,101	13,214	40,434	56,036	82,109	85,547	11
Berwyn, Ill			5,841	14,150	47,027	48,451	
Bethlehem, Pa.	6,762	7,293	12,837	50,358	57,892	58,490	
Binghamton, N. Y	35,005	39,647	48,443	66,800	76,662	78,309	
Birmingham, Ala	26,178	38,415	132,685	178,806	259,678	267,583	3
Boston, Mass	448,477	560,892	670,585	748,060	781,188	770,816	8
Bridgeport, Conn	48,866	70,996	102,054	143,555	146,716	147,121	1
Brockton, Mass	27,294	40,063	56,878	66,254	63,797	62,343	
Buffalo, N. Y	255,664	352,387	423,715	506,775	573,076	575,901	5
Burbank, Calif				2,913	16,662	34,337	7
Cambridge, Mass	70,028	91,886	104,839	109,694	113,643	110,879	12
Camden, N. J	58,313	75,935	94,538	116,309	118,700	117,536	12
Canton, Ohio	26,189	30,667	50,217	87,091	104,906	108,401	11
Cedar Rapids, Iowa	18,020	25,656	32,811	45,566	56,097	62,120	
Charleston, S. C	54,955	55,807	58,833	67,957	62,265	71,275	
Charleston, W. Va	6,742	11,099	22,996	39,608	60,408	67,914	
Charlotte, N. C	11,557	18,091	34,014	46,338	82,675	100,899	1
Chattanooga, Tenn	29,100	30,154	44,604	57,895	119,798	128,163	1
Chester, Pa	20,226	33,988	38,537	58,030	59,164	59,285	
Chicago, Ill	1,099,850	1,698,575	2,185,283	2,701,705	3,376,438	3,396,808	3,6
Cicero, Ill	10,204	16,310	14,557	44,995	66,602	64,712	6
Cincinnati, Ohio	296,908	325,902	363,591	401,247	451,160	455,610	5
Cleveland, Ohio	261,353	381,768	560,663	796,841	900,429	878,336	9
Cleveland Heights, Ohio			2,955	15,236	50,945	54,992	
Clifton, N. J				26,470	46,875	48,827	
Columbia, S. C	15,353	21,108	26,319	37,524	51,581	62,396	
Columbus, Ga	17,303	17,614	20,554	31,125	43,131	53,280	
Columbus, Ohio	88,150	125,560	181,511	237,031	290,564	306,087	3
Corpus Christi, Tex	4,387	4,703	8,222	10,522	27,741	57,301	10
Covington, Ky	37,371	42,938	53,270	57,121	65,252	62,018	
Cranston, R. I	8,099	13,343	21,107	29,407	42,911	47,085	
Dallas, Tex	38,067	42,638	92,104	158,976	260,475	294,734	4
Davenport, Iowa	26,872	35,254	43,028	56,727	60,751	66,039	
Dayton, Ohio	61,220	85,333	116,577	152,559	200,982	210,718	2
Dearborn, Mich		844	911	2,470	50,358	63,584	
Decatur, Ill	16,841	20,754	31,140	43,818	57,510	59,305	
Denver, Colo	106,713	133,859	213,381	256,491	287,861	322,412	4
Des Moines, Iowa	50,093	62,139	86,368	126,468	142,559	159,819	17
Detroit, Mich	205,876	285,704	465,766	993,678	1,568,662	1,623,452	1,84
Duluth, Minn	33,115	52,969	78,466	98,917	101,463	101,065	10
Durham, N. C	5,485	6,679	18,241	21,719	52,037	60,195	7
East Chicago, Ind	1,255	3,411	19,098	35,967	54,784	54,637	
East Orange, N. J	13,282	21,506	34,371	50,710	68,020	68,945	7
East St. Louis, Ill	15,169	29,655	58,547	66,767	74,347	75,609	
Elizabeth, N. J	37,764	52,130	73,409	95,783	114,589	109,912	11
El Paso, Tex	10,338	15,906	39,279	77,560	102,421	96,810	11
Erie, Pa	40,634	52,733	66,525	93,372	115,967	116,955	12
Evanston, Ill	9,000	19,259	24,978	37,234	63,338	65,389	7
Evansville, Ind	50,756	59,007	69,647	85,264	102,249	97,062	12
Fall River, Mass	74,398	104,863	119,295	120,485	115,274	115,428	11

For footnotes, see p. 25.

.—POPULATION OF CITIES HAVING 50,000 INHABITANTS OR MORE IN 1950: 1890 TO 1950—Continued

CITY	1890	1900	1910	1920	1930	1940	1950
h.	9,802	13,103	26,550	91,599	136,492	151,543	163,143
ne, Ind	35,393	45,115	63,933	86,549	114,946	118,410	133,607
h, Tex	29,076	26,688	73,312	106,482	163,447	177,662	278,778
llf	10,818	12,470	24,802	45,086	52,513	60,685	91,669
Ala	2,901	4,282	10,587	14,737	24,042	38,975	55,726
, Tex	29,084	37,789	38,981	44,255	52,938	60,862	66,568
			16,802	55,378	100,426	111,719	132,911
			2,746	13,536	62,736	82,582	95,702
Calif							
pids, Mich	60,278	87,565	112,571	137,634	168,592	164,292	176,515
r, Wis	9,069	18,684	25,236	31,017	37,415	46,283	52,735
o, N.C	3,317	10,035	15,895	19,861	53,569	59,319	74,389
, S.C	6,607	11,860	15,741	23,127	29,154	34,734	58,161
Ohio	17,565	22,914	35,279	39,675	52,176	50,892	57,951
l, Ind	6,428	12,376	20,925	36,004	64,560	70,184	87,594
t, Pa	26,385	50,167	64,186	75,917	80,339	83,893	89,544
Conn	53,230	79,850	98,915	138,036	164,072	166,267	177,397
N.J	43,648	59,364	70,324	66,166	59,261	50,118	50,676
Mass	36,537	45,712	57,730	60,203	56,537	53,750	54,661
Tex	27,557	44,633	78,800	138,276	292,352	384,514	596,163
n, W.Va	10,108	11,923	31,161	50,177	75,572	78,836	86,353
lis, Ind	105,436	169,164	233,650	314,194	364,161	386,972	427,173
N.J		5,255	11,877	25,480	56,733	55,329	59,201
Mich	20,798	25,180	31,433	48,374	55,187	49,656	51,088
iss	5,920	7,816	21,262	22,817	48,282	62,107	98,271
le, Fla	17,201	28,429	57,699	91,558	129,549	173,065	204,517
y, N.J	163,003	206,433	267,779	298,103	316,715	301,173	299,017
, Pa	21,805	35,936	55,482	67,327	66,993	66,668	63,232
	23,264	29,353	34,670	38,442	42,993	42,365	51,601
o, Mich	17,853	24,404	39,437	48,487	54,786	54,097	57,704
ty, Kans	38,316	51,418	82,331	101,177	121,857	121,458	129,553
ty, Mo	132,716	163,752	248,381	324,410	399,746	399,178	456,622
Wis	6,532	11,606	21,371	40,472	50,262	48,765	54,368
, Tenn	22,535	32,637	36,346	77,818	106,802	111,580	124,769
, Ohio		3,355	15,181	41,732	70,509	69,160	65,071
Pa	32,011	41,459	47,227	53,150	59,949	61,345	63,774
Mich	13,102	16,485	31,229	57,327	78,397	78,753	92,129
ex	11,319	13,429	14,855	22,710	32,618	39,274	51,910
Mass	44,654	62,559	85,892	94,270	85,068	84,323	80,586
, Ky	21,567	26,369	35,099	41,534	45,736	49,304	55,534
io	18,981	21,723	30,508	41,326	42,357	44,711	50,246
ebr	55,154	40,169	43,973	54,948	75,933	81,984	98,884
k, Ark	25,874	38,307	45,941	65,142	81,679	88,039	102,213
h, Calif	564	2,252	17,809	55,593	142,032	164,271	250,767
hio	4,863	16,028	28,883	37,295	44,512	44,125	51,202
es, Calif	50,395	102,479	319,198	576,673	1,238,048	1,504,277	1,970,358
Ky	161,129	204,731	223,928	234,891	307,745	319,077	369,129
ass	77,696	94,969	106,294	112,759	100,234	101,389	97,249
Tex			1,938	4,051	20,520	31,853	71,747
ss	55,727	68,513	89,336	99,148	102,320	98,123	99,738
n	22,746	23,272	40,665	52,995	53,829	57,865	70,252
Wis	13,426	19,164	25,531	38,378	57,899	67,447	96,056
Mass	23,031	33,664	44,404	49,103	58,036	58,010	59,804
er, N.H	44,126	56,987	70,063	78,384	76,834	77,685	82,732
rt, Pa	20,741	34,227	42,694	46,781	54,632	55,355	51,502
Mass	11,079	18,244	23,150	39,038	59,714	59,063	66,113
Tenn	64,495	102,320	131,105	162,351	253,143	292,942	396,000
la		1,681	5,471	29,571	110,637	172,172	249,276
, Wis	204,468	285,315	373,857	457,147	578,249	587,472	637,392
lis, Minn	164,738	202,718	301,408	380,582	464,356	492,370	521,718
la	31,076	38,469	51,521	60,777	68,202	78,720	129,009
ery, Ala	21,883	30,346	38,136	43,464	66,079	78,084	106,525
rnon, N.Y	10,830	21,228	30,919	42,726	61,499	67,362	71,899
nd	11,345	20,942	24,005	36,524	46,548	49,720	58,479
Tenn	76,168	80,865	110,364	118,342	153,866	167,402	174,307
N.J	181,830	246,070	347,469	414,524	442,337	429,760	438,776
ord, Mass	40,733	62,442	96,652	121,217	112,597	110,341	109,189
ain, Conn	16,519	25,998	43,916	59,316	68,128	68,685	73,726
en, Conn	86,045	108,027	133,605	162,537	162,655	160,605	164,443
ans, La	242,039	287,104	339,075	387,219	458,762	494,537	570,445
heila, N.Y	8,217	14,720	28,867	36,213	54,000	58,408	59,725
Mass	24,379	33,587	39,806	46,054	65,276	69,873	81,904

No. 14.—POPULATION OF CITIES HAVING 50,000 INHABITANTS OR MORE IN 19
1890 TO 950—Continued

CITY	1890	1900	1910	1920	1930	1940	1950
New York, N. Y.[4]	2,507,414	3,437,202	4,766,883	5,620,048	6,930,446	7,454,995	7,891
Niagara Falls, N. Y.	5,502	19,457	30,445	50,760	75,460	78,029	9...
Norfolk, Va.	34,871	46,624	67,452	115,777	129,710	144,332	213
Oakland, Calif.	48,682	66,960	150,174	216,261	284,063	302,163	384
Oak Park, Ill.			19,444	39,858	63,982	66,015	6...
Ogden, Utah	14,889	16,313	25,580	32,804	40,272	43,688	57
Oklahoma City, Okla.	4,151	10,037	64,205	91,295	185,389	204,424	243
Omaha, Nebr.[1]	140,452	102,555	124,096	191,601	214,006	223,844	251
Orlando, Fla.	2,856	2,481	3,894	9,282	27,330	36,736	5...
Pasadena, Calif.	4,882	9,117	30,291	45,354	76,086	81,864	104
Passaic, N. J.	13,028	27,777	54,773	63,841	62,959	61,394	57
Paterson, N. J.	78,347	105,171	125,600	135,875	138,513	139,656	139
Pawtucket, R. I.	27,633	39,231	51,622	64,248	77,149	75,797	81
Peoria, Ill.	41,024	56,100	66,950	76,121	104,969	105,087	111
Philadelphia, Pa.	1,046,964	1,293,697	1,549,008	1,823,779	1,950,961	1,931,334	2,071
Phoenix, Ariz.	3,152	5,544	11,134	29,053	48,118	65,414	106
Pittsburgh, Pa.	6 238,617	6 321,616	533,905	588,343	669,817	671,659	677
Pittsfield, Mass.	17,281	21,766	32,121	41,763	49,677	49,684	5...
Pontiac, Mich.	6,200	9,769	14,532	34,273	64,928	66,626	73
Port Arthur, Tex.		900	7,663	22,251	50,902	46,140	57
Portland, Maine	36,425	50,145	58,571	69,272	70,810	73,643	77
Portland, Oreg.	46,385	90,426	207,214	258,288	301,815	305,394	373
Portsmouth, Va.	13,268	17,427	33,190	54,387	45,704	50,745	8...
Providence, R. I.	132,146	175,597	224,326	237,595	252,981	253,504	248
Pueblo, Colo.	24,558	28,157	7 41,747	43,050	50,096	52,162	6...
Quincy, Mass.	16,723	23,899	32,642	47,876	71,983	75,810	8...
Racine, Wis.	21,014	29,102	38,002	58,593	67,542	67,195	71
Raleigh, N. C.	12,678	13,643	19,218	24,418	37,379	46,897	6...
Reading, Pa.	58,661	78,961	96,071	107,784	111,171	110,568	109
Richmond, Calif.			6,802	16,843	20,093	23,642	9...
Richmond, Va.	81,388	85,050	127,628	171,667	182,929	193,042	230
Roanoke, Va.	16,159	21,495	34,874	50,842	69,206	69,287	9...
Rochester, N. Y.	133,896	162,608	218,149	295,750	328,132	324,975	332
Rockford, Ill.	23,584	31,051	45,401	65,651	85,864	84,637	9...
Sacramento, Calif.	26,386	29,282	44,696	65,908	93,750	105,958	137
Saginaw, Mich.	46,322	42,345	50,510	61,903	80,715	82,794	92
St. Joseph, Mo.	52,324	102,979	77,403	77,939	80,935	75,711	78
St. Louis, Mo.	451,770	575,238	687,029	772,897	821,960	816,048	856
St. Paul, Minn.	133,156	163,065	214,744	234,698	271,606	287,736	311
St. Petersburg, Fla.	273	1,575	4,127	14,237	40,425	60,812	9...
Salt Lake City, Utah	44,843	53,531	92,777	118,110	140,267	149,934	182
San Angelo, Tex.			10,321	10,050	25,308	25,802	52
San Antonio, Tex.	37,673	53,321	96,614	161,379	231,542	253,854	408
San Bernardino, Calif.	4,012	6,150	12,779	18,721	37,481	43,646	6...
San Diego, Calif.	16,159	17,700	39,578	74,361	147,995	203,341	334
San Francisco, Calif.	298,997	342,782	416,912	506,676	634,394	634,536	775
San Jose, Calif.	18,060	21,500	28,946	39,642	57,651	68,457	9...
Santa Monica, Calif.	1,580	3,057	7,847	15,252	37,146	53,500	71
Savannah, Ga.	43,189	54,244	65,064	83,252	85,024	95,996	119
Schenectady, N. Y.	19,902	31,682	72,826	88,723	95,692	87,549	91
Scranton, Pa.	5,215	102,026	129,867	137,783	143,433	140,404	125
Seattle, Wash.	42,837	80,671	237,194	315,312	365,583	368,302	467
Shreveport, La.	11,979	16,013	28,015	43,874	76,655	98,167	127
Sioux City, Iowa	37,806	33,111	47,828	71,227	79,183	82,364	83
Sioux Falls, S. Dak.			14,094	25,202	33,362	40,832	5...
Somerville, Mass.	40,152	61,643	77,236	93,091	103,908	102,177	102
South Bend, Ind.	21,819	35,999	53,684	70,983	104,193	101,268	115
South Gate, Calif.					19,632	26,945	51
Spokane, Wash.	19,922	36,848	104,402	104,437	115,514	122,001	162
Springfield, Ill.	24,963	34,159	51,678	59,183	71,864	75,503	8...
Springfield, Mass.	44,179	62,059	88,926	129,614	149,900	149,554	162
Springfield, Mo.	21,850	23,267	35,201	39,631	57,527	61,238	6...
Springfield, Ohio	31,895	38,253	46,921	60,840	68,743	70,662	78
Stamford, Conn.	10,396	15,997	25,138	35,096	46,346	47,938	74
Stockton, Calif.	14,424	17,506	23,253	40,296	47,963	54,714	78
Syracuse, N. Y.	88,143	108,374	137,249	171,717	209,326	205,967	220
Tacoma, Wash.	36,006	37,714	83,743	96,965	106,817	109,408	143
Tampa, Fla.	5,532	15,839	37,782	51,608	101,161	108,391	124
Terre Haute, Ind.	30,217	36,673	58,157	66,083	62,810	62,693	64
Toledo, Ohio	81,434	131,822	168,497	243,164	290,718	282,349	303
Topeka, Kans.	31,007	33,608	43,684	50,022	64,120	67,833	78

For footnotes, see p. 25.

—POPULATION OF CITIES HAVING 50,000 INHABITANTS OR MORE IN 1950: 1890 TO 1950—Continued

ITY	1890	1900	1910	1920	1930	1940	1950
. J_____	57,458	73,307	96,815	119,289	123,356	124,697	128,009
_____	60,956	60,651	76,813	71,996	72,763	70,304	72,311
_____		1,390	18,182	72,075	141,258	142,187	182,740
, N. J.__	10,643	15,187	21,023	20,651	58,659	55,173	55,837
_____	44,007	56,383	74,419	94,156	101,740	100,518	101,531
_____	14,445	20,666	26,425	38,500	52,848	55,982	84,706
, D. C.*__	188,932	278,718	331,069	437,571	486,869	663,091	802,178
, Conn__	28,646	45,850	73,141	91,715	99,902	96,314	104,477
own____	6,674	12,580	26,693	36,230	44,191	51,743	55,198
W. Va.__	34,522	38,878	41,641	56,208	61,659	61,099	56,591
ans____	23,853	24,671	52,450	72,217	111,110	114,966	168,279
lls, Tex__	1,987	2,480	8,200	40,079	43,690	45,112	68,042
re, Pa__	37,718	51,721	67,105	73,833	86,626	86,236	76,826
, Del.__	61,431	76,508	87,411	110,168	106,597	112,504	110,356
lem, N. C.	10,729	13,650	22,700	48,395	75,274	79,815	87,811
t, R. I.__	20,830	28,204	38,125	43,496	49,376	49,303	50,211
Mass____	84,655	118,421	145,986	179,754	195,311	193,694	203,486
. Y.____	32,033	47,931	79,803	100,176	134,646	142,598	152,798
_____	20,793	33,708	44,750	47,512	55,254	56,712	56,953
n, Ohio__	33,220	44,885	79,066	132,358	170,002	167,720	168,330

em and South Bethlehem boroughs consolidated as Bethlehem city between 1910 and 1920. Combined 1890, 19,823; 1900, 23,999; 1910, 32,810.
ion prior to incorporation.
ed.
ion shown is for New York city as now constituted.
and South Omaha cities consolidated between 1910 and 1920. Combined population, 1890, 148,514; k; 1910, 150,355.
ny city annexed to Pittsburgh in 1907. Combined population, 1890, 343,904; 1900, 451,512.
d figure; exclusive of population (2,648) of certain territory outside city limits.
and West Hoboken towns consolidated as Union City in 1925. Combined population, 1900, 38,281; ; 1920, 60,725.
ion shown for 1900 through 1950 is for District of Columbia, with which the city has been considered since 1895.

Department of Commerce, Bureau of Census; *U. S. Census of Population: 1950*, Vol. I.

No. 15.—POPULATION, SUMMARY OF CHARACTERISTICS: 1790 TO 1950

[See also *Historical Statistics*, series B 13–23, and B 72–80]

	SEX		RACE			RESIDENCE		MEDIAN AGE	
	Male	Female	White	Negro	Other	Urban	Rural	All classes	White
__	--------	--------	3,172,006	757,208	--------	201,655	3,727,559	-----	-----
__	--------	--------	4,306,446	1,002,037	--------	322,371	4,986,112	-----	16.0
__	--------	--------	5,862,073	1,377,808	--------	525,459	6,714,422	-----	16.0
__	4,896,605	4,741,848	7,866,797	1,771,656	--------	693,255	8,945,198	16.7	16.5
__	6,532,489	6,333,531	10,537,378	2,328,642	--------	1,127,247	11,738,773	17.2	17.2
__	8,668,532	8,380,921	14,195,805	2,873,648	--------	1,845,055	15,224,398	17.8	17.9
__	11,837,660	11,354,216	19,553,068	3,638,808	--------	3,543,716	19,648,160	18.9	19.2
__	16,085,204	15,358,117	26,922,537	4,441,830	78,954	6,216,518	25,226,803	19.4	19.7
__	19,492,555	19,064,806	33,589,377	4,880,009	88,985	9,902,361	28,656,010	20.2	20.4
__	25,518,820	24,636,963	43,402,970	6,580,793	172,020	14,129,735	36,026,048	20.9	21.4
__	32,237,101	30,710,613	55,101,258	7,488,676	357,780	22,106,265	40,841,449	22.0	22.5
__	38,816,448	37,178,127	66,809,196	8,833,994	351,385	30,159,921	45,834,654	22.9	23.4
__	47,332,277	44,639,989	81,731,957	9,827,763	412,546	41,998,932	49,973,334	24.1	24.5
__	53,900,431	51,810,189	94,820,915	10,463,131	426,574	54,157,973	51,552,647	25.3	25.6
__	62,137,080	60,637,966	110,286,740	11,891,143	597,163	68,954,823	53,820,223	26.5	26.9
__	66,061,592	65,607,683	118,214,870	12,865,518	588,887	74,423,702	57,245,573	29.0	29.5
__	74,833,239	75,864,122	134,942,028	15,042,286	713,047	1 96,467,686	1 54,229,675	30.2	30.8

definition; old definition: urban, 88,927,464 and rural, 61,769,897. For explanation of old and new urban , see p. 2.

Department of Commerce, Bureau of the Census; Fifteenth Census Reports, *Population*, Vol. II; Census Reports, *Population*, Vol. II, Part 1, and Vol. IV, Part 1, and *U. S. Census of Population: 1950*, art 1.

No. 16.—Population in Urban and Rural Territory, by Size of Place: 1790 to 1950

[See headnote, table 17. For description of old and new definitions, see p. 2. See also *Historical Statistics, series* B 145-159]

CLASS AND SIZE	1790	1800	1820	1840	1860	1880	1900
POPULATION							
United States	3,929,214	5,308,483	9,638,453	17,069,453	31,443,321	50,155,783	75,994,575
Urban territory	201,655	322,371	693,255	1,845,055	6,216,518	14,129,735	30,159,921
Places of 1,000,000 or more	--------	--------	--------	--------	--------	--------	1,208,299
Places of 500,000 to 1,000,000	--------	--------	--------	--------	1,379,198	1,917,018	6,429,474
Places of 250,000 to 500,000	--------	--------	--------	312,710	266,661	1,300,809	1,645,061
Places of 100,000 to 250,000	--------	--------	123,706	204,506	992,922	1,795,783	2,861,291
Places of 50,000 to 100,000	--------	60,515	126,540	187,048	452,060	947,918	3,272,496
Places of 25,000 to 50,000	61,653	67,734	70,474	235,424	670,293	1,446,306	2,709,338
Places of 10,000 to 25,000	48,182	54,479	121,613	404,822	884,433	2,180,447	2,800,628
Places of 5,000 to 10,000	47,569	94,394	155,035	328,741	976,436	1,717,146	4,338,281
Places of 2,500 to 5,000	44,251	45,249	95,887	171,801	594,515	1,617,949	3,204,132
Rural territory	3,727,559	4,986,112	8,945,198	15,224,398	25,226,803	36,026,048	45,834,654
Places of 1,000 to 2,500	(¹)	(¹)	(¹)	(¹)	(¹)	(¹)	3,295,059
PERCENT OF TOTAL POPULATION							
United States	100.0	100.0	100.0	100.0	100.0	100.0	100.0
Urban territory	5.1	6.1	7.2	10.8	19.8	28.2	39.7
Places of 1,000,000 or more	--------	--------	--------	--------	--------	--------	2.4	1.6
Places of 500,000 to 1,000,000	--------	--------	--------	--------	4.4	3.8	2.3
Places of 250,000 to 500,000	--------	--------	--------	1.8	.8	2.6	2.2
Places of 100,000 to 250,000	--------	--------	1.3	1.2	3.2	3.6	4.3
Places of 50,000 to 100,000	--------	1.1	1.3	1.1	1.4	1.9	2.6
Places of 25,000 to 50,000	1.6	1.3	.7	1.4	2.1	2.9	2.7
Places of 10,000 to 25,000	1.2	1.0	1.3	2.4	2.8	4.4	3.7
Places of 5,000 to 10,000	1.2	1.8	1.6	1.9	3.1	3.4	4.2
Places of 2,500 to 5,000	1.1	.9	1.0	1.0	1.9	3.2	3.5
Rural territory	94.9	93.9	92.8	89.2	80.2	71.8	60.3
Places of 1,000 to 2,500	--------	--------	--------	--------	--------	--------	4.3

					1950	
CLASS AND SIZE	1910	1920	1930	1940	Old urban definition	New urban definition
POPULATION						
United States	91,972,266	105,710,620	122,775,046	131,669,275	150,697,361	150,697,361
Urban territory	41,998,932	54,157,973	68,954,823	74,423,702	88,927,464	² 96,467,686
Places of 1,000,000 or more	8,501,174	10,145,532	15,064,555	15,910,866	17,404,450	17,404,450
Places of 500,000 to 1,000,000	3,010,667	6,223,769	5,763,987	6,456,959	9,186,945	9,186,945
Places of 250,000 to 500,000	3,949,839	4,540,838	7,956,228	7,827,514	8,241,560	8,241,560
Places of 100,000 to 250,000	4,840,458	6,519,187	7,540,966	7,792,650	9,614,111	9,478,600
Places of 50,000 to 100,000	4,178,915	5,265,406	6,491,448	7,343,917	9,072,363	8,930,520
Places of 25,000 to 50,000	4,023,397	5,075,041	6,425,663	² 7,417,093	9,495,862	8,977,720
Places of 10,000 to 25,000	5,548,868	7,034,668	9,097,200	9,966,898	12,497,229	11,866,630
Places of 5,000 to 10,000	4,217,420	4,967,625	5,897,156	6,681,894	7,878,675	8,132,260
Places of 2,500 to 5,000	3,728,194	4,385,905	4,717,690	5,025,911	5,565,269	6,490,400
Rural territory	49,973,334	51,552,647	53,820,223	57,245,573	61,769,897	54,229,673
Places of 1,000 to 2,500	4,234,406	4,712,007	4,820,707	5,036,884	5,352,637	6,473,311
PERCENT OF TOTAL POPULATION						
United States	100.0	100.0	100.0	100.0	100.0	100.0
Urban territory	45.7	51.2	56.2	56.5	59.0	² 64.0
Places of 1,000,000 or more	9.2	9.6	12.3	12.1	11.5	11.6
Places of 500,000 to 1,000,000	3.3	5.9	4.7	4.9	6.1	6.1
Places of 250,000 to 500,000	4.3	4.3	6.5	5.9	5.5	5.5
Places of 100,000 to 250,000	5.3	6.2	6.1	5.9	6.4	6.3
Places of 50,000 to 100,000	4.5	5.0	5.3	5.6	6.0	5.9
Places of 25,000 to 50,000	4.4	4.8	5.2	5.6	6.3	6.0
Places of 10,000 to 25,000	6.0	6.7	7.4	7.6	8.3	7.9
Places of 5,000 to 10,000	4.6	4.7	4.8	5.1	5.2	5.4
Places of 2,500 to 5,000	4.1	4.1	3.8	3.8	3.7	4.3
Rural territory	54.3	48.8	43.8	43.5	41.0	36.0
Places of 1,000 to 2,500	4.6	4.5	3.9	3.8	3.6	4.3

¹ Not returned separately.
² Includes population of places under 2,500 (577,992) and unincorporated parts of urbanized areas (7,344,026).

Source: Department of Commerce, Bureau of the Census; *U. S. Census of Population: 1950*, Vol. I.

No. 17.—NUMBER OF PLACES IN URBAN AND RURAL TERRITORY, BY SIZE OF PLACE: 1860 TO 1950

[In 1940 and 1950, the following were counted as separate incorporated places, whereas in 1930 and earlier years each pair was counted as a single place: Bluefield, Va., and Bluefield, W. Va.; Bristol, Tenn., and Bristol, Va.; Delmar, Del., and Delmar, Md.; Harrison, Ohio, and West Harrison, Ind.; Junction City, Ark., and Junction City, La.; Texarkana, Ark., and Texarkana, Texas; Texhoma, Okla., and Texhoma, Texas; and Union City, Ind., and Union City, Ohio. For description of old and new definitions, see p. 2. See also *Historical Statistics*, series B 145-159]

CLASS AND SIZE	1860	1880	1900	1910	1920	1930	1940	1950 Old urban definition	1950 New urban definition
Urban territory	392	939	1,737	2,262	2,722	3,165	3,464	4,023	4,741
Places of 1,000,000 or more		1	3	3	3	5	5	5	5
Places of 500,000 to 1,000,000	2	3	3	5	9	8	9	13	13
Places of 250,000 to 500,000	1	4	9	11	13	24	23	22	23
Places of 100,000 to 250,000	6	12	23	31	43	56	55	66	65
Places of 50,000 to 100,000	7	15	40	59	76	98	107	128	126
Places of 25,000 to 50,000	19	42	82	119	143	185	213	271	252
Places of 10,000 to 25,000	58	146	280	369	465	606	668	814	778
Places of 5,000 to 10,000	136	240	465	605	715	851	965	1,133	1,176
Places of 2,500 to 5,000	163	457	832	1,060	1,255	1,332	1,422	1,570	1,846
Places under 2,500									457
Rural territory			8,931	11,830	12,855	13,433	13,286	13,235	12,907
Places of 1,000 to 2,500			2,128	2,717	3,030	3,087	3,205	3,408	4,158
Places under 1,000			6,803	9,113	9,825	10,346	10,083	9,827	9,649

Source: Department of Commerce, Bureau of the Census; *U. S. Census of Population: 1950*, Vol. I.

No. 18.—MEDIAN AGE OF URBAN AND RURAL POPULATION, BY COLOR AND SEX: 1940 AND 1950

[Definition of median.—The median is the value which divides the distribution into two equal parts—one-half of the cases falling below this value and one-half of the cases exceeding this value. For explanation of old and new urban definitions, see p. 2. See also *Historical Statistics*, series B 72-80]

RESIDENCE AND YEAR	ALL CLASSES			WHITE			NONWHITE		
	Total	Male	Female	Total	Male	Female	Total	Male	Female
1940, OLD URBAN DEFINITION									
Total	29.0	29.1	29.0	29.5	29.5	29.5	25.2	25.4	25.1
Urban	31.0	31.0	31.1	31.3	31.2	31.4	28.9	29.4	28.6
Rural nonfarm	27.7	28.1	27.3	28.0	28.3	27.6	24.9	27.4	24.3
Rural farm	24.4	24.7	23.9	25.4	25.8	25.0	20.0	20.1	19.6
1950, OLD URBAN DEFINITION									
Total	30.2	29.9	30.5	30.8	30.4	31.1	26.1	25.9	26.2
Urban	32.0	31.5	32.4	32.4	31.5	32.8	28.8	28.8	28.8
Rural nonfarm	28.0	27.9	28.1	28.4	28.3	28.5	23.8	23.8	23.7
Rural farm	26.3	26.5	26.1	27.9	28.1	27.7	18.6	18.6	18.7
1950, NEW URBAN DEFINITION									
Total	30.2	29.9	30.5	30.8	30.4	31.1	26.1	25.9	26.2
Urban	31.6	31.2	32.0	32.0	31.5	32.4	28.7	28.7	28.7
Rural nonfarm	27.9	28.2	28.1	28.4	28.2	28.5	23.6	23.6	23.5
Rural farm	26.3	26.4	26.1	27.9	28.0	27.7	18.5	18.4	18.5

Source: Department of Commerce, Bureau of the Census; *U. S. Census of Population: 1950*, Vol II, Part 1, and unpublished data.

No. 19.—POPULATION, URBAN A

[For explanation of old and new urban definitions, see

DIVISION AND STATE	OLD URBAN DEFINITION							
	1920		1930		1940		1950	
	Urban	Rural	Urban	Rural	Urban	Rural	Urban	Rur
United States	54,157,973	51,552,647	68,954,823	53,820,223	74,423,702	57,245,573	88,927,464	61,700
New England	5,620,384	1,780,525	6,311,976	1,854,365	6,420,542	2,016,748	6,922,733	2,301
Maine	299,569	468,445	321,506	475,917	343,057	504,169	374,507	530
New Hampshire	250,438	192,645	273,079	192,214	283,225	208,299	301,249	231
Vermont	109,976	242,452	118,766	240,845	123,239	235,992	137,612	240
Massachusetts	3,468,916	383,440	3,831,426	418,188	3,850,476	457,245	4,122,138	508
Rhode Island	555,146	49,251	635,429	52,068	653,383	59,963	700,410	91
Connecticut	936,339	444,292	1,131,770	475,133	1,188,162	551,080	1,296,817	729
Middle Atlantic	16,783,474	5,477,670	20,394,707	5,866,043	21,147,543	6,391,944	22,643,772	7,519
New York	8,588,586	1,796,641	10,521,952	2,066,114	11,165,893	2,313,249	11,889,008	2,941
New Jersey	2,522,435	633,465	3,339,244	702,090	3,394,773	765,392	3,847,771	987
Pennsylvania	5,672,453	3,047,564	6,533,511	3,097,839	6,586,877	3,313,303	6,906,993	3,591
East North Central	13,050,086	8,425,457	16,794,908	8,502,277	17,444,359	9,181,983	19,982,717	10,416
Ohio	3,677,136	2,082,258	4,507,371	2,139,326	4,612,086	2,294,526	5,273,206	2,675
Indiana	1,482,855	1,447,535	1,795,892	1,442,611	1,887,712	1,540,084	2,217,468	1,716
Illinois	4,403,677	2,081,603	5,635,727	1,994,927	5,809,650	2,087,561	6,486,673	2,208
Michigan	2,241,560	1,426,852	3,302,075	1,540,250	3,454,867	1,801,239	4,099,007	2,272
Wisconsin	1,244,858	1,387,209	1,553,843	1,385,163	1,679,144	1,458,443	1,906,365	1,539
West North Central	4,725,880	7,818,364	5,556,181	7,740,734	5,993,124	7,533,866	7,015,000	7,642
Minnesota	1,051,593	1,335,532	1,257,616	1,306,337	1,390,098	1,402,202	1,607,446	1,375
Iowa	875,495	1,528,526	979,292	1,491,647	1,084,231	1,454,037	1,229,433	1,301
Missouri	1,586,903	1,817,152	1,859,119	1,770,248	1,960,696	1,823,968	2,290,149	1,684
North Dakota	88,239	558,633	113,306	567,539	131,923	510,012	164,817	454
South Dakota	101,872	534,675	120,907	581,942	158,087	484,874	216,157	436
Nebraska	405,293	891,079	486,107	891,856	514,148	801,686	606,530	718
Kansas	616,485	1,152,772	729,834	1,151,165	753,941	1,047,087	903,468	1,001
South Atlantic	4,336,482	9,653,790	5,698,122	10,095,467	6,921,726	10,901,425	8,997,310	12,196
Delaware	120,767	102,236	123,146	115,234	139,432	127,073	147,890	170
Maryland	869,422	580,239	974,869	656,657	1,080,351	740,893	1,274,618	1,068
Dist. of Columbia	437,571		486,869		663,091		802,178	
Virginia	673,984	1,635,203	785,537	1,636,314	944,675	1,733,098	1,335,944	1,982
West Virginia	369,007	1,094,694	491,504	1,237,701	534,292	1,367,682	640,606	1,364
North Carolina	490,370	2,068,753	809,847	2,360,429	974,175	2,597,448	1,238,193	2,659
South Carolina	293,987	1,389,737	371,080	1,367,685	466,111	1,433,693	609,225	1,807
Georgia	727,859	2,167,973	895,492	2,013,014	1,073,808	2,049,915	1,381,868	2,069
Florida	353,515	614,955	759,778	708,433	1,045,791	851,623	1,566,788	1,204
East South Central	1,994,207	6,899,100	2,775,687	7,168,527	3,145,356	7,512,869	4,079,879	7,367
Kentucky	633,543	1,783,087	799,026	1,815,563	849,327	1,996,300	985,739	1,899
Tennessee	611,226	1,726,659	896,538	1,720,018	1,027,206	1,888,635	1,264,159	2,027
Alabama	509,317	1,838,857	744,273	1,901,975	855,941	1,977,020	1,228,209	1,952
Mississippi	240,121	1,550,497	338,850	1,670,971	432,882	1,750,914	601,772	1,577
West South Central	2,969,366	7,272,858	4,427,439	7,749,391	5,203,401	7,841,124	7,706,640	6,636
Arkansas	290,497	1,461,707	382,878	1,471,604	431,910	1,517,477	617,153	1,382
Louisiana	628,163	1,170,346	833,532	1,258,061	980,439	1,383,441	1,363,789	1,319
Oklahoma	538,017	1,490,266	821,681	1,574,389	879,663	1,456,707	1,107,232	1,129
Texas	1,512,689	3,150,539	2,389,348	3,435,367	2,911,389	3,503,435	4,612,666	3,005
Mountain	1,217,968	2,118,113	1,457,922	2,243,867	1,771,742	2,373,261	2,474,628	2,509
Montana	172,011	376,878	181,036	356,570	211,535	347,921	252,906	333
Idaho	119,037	312,829	129,507	315,525	176,708	348,165	234,138	364
Wyoming	57,095	137,307	70,097	155,468	93,577	157,165	144,618	145
Colorado	453,259	486,370	519,882	515,909	590,756	532,540	759,939	563
New Mexico	64,960	295,390	106,816	316,501	176,401	355,417	314,636	366
Arizona	120,788	213,374	149,886	285,717	173,981	325,280	273,794	475
Utah	215,584	233,812	266,264	241,583	305,493	344,817	412,518	276
Nevada	15,254	62,153	34,464	56,594	43,291	66,956	84,079	75
Pacific	3,460,106	2,106,765	5,534,881	2,659,552	6,355,909	3,377,353	9,105,565	5,320
Washington	742,801	613,820	884,539	678,857	921,969	814,222	1,274,152	1,104
Oregon	390,346	393,043	489,746	464,040	531,675	558,009	732,247	786
California	2,326,959	1,099,902	4,160,596	1,516,655	4,902,265	2,005,122	7,099,166	3,457

RURAL, BY STATES: 1920 TO 1950

[For U. S. totals, see also *Historical Statistics*, series B 16–17]

| 1950, NEW URBAN DEFINITION | | | | PERCENT URBAN | | | | | DIVISION AND STATE |
| Urban | Rural | | | 1920 | 1930 | 1940 | 1950 | | |
	Total	Nonfarm	Farm				Old urban definition	New urban definition	
96,467,686	54,229,675	31,181,225	23,048,350	51.2	56.2	56.5	59.0	64.0	United States
7,101,511	2,212,942	1,899,842	403,100	75.9	77.3	76.1	74.3	76.2	New England.
472,600	441,774	319,946	121,828	30.0	40.3	40.5	41.0	51.7	Maine.
308,906	226,436	179,266	47,170	56.5	58.7	57.6	56.5	57.5	New Hampshire.
127,612	240,135	150,003	81,132	31.2	33.0	34.3	36.4	36.4	Vermont.
3,950,229	731,275	651,299	79,976	90.0	90.2	90.4	87.9	84.4	Massachusetts.
687,212	124,664	114,346	10,338	91.9	92.4	91.6	92.4	84.3	Rhode Island.
1,508,642	448,636	385,962	62,656	67.8	70.4	67.8	64.1	77.6	Connecticut.
24,271,680	5,891,844	4,586,683	1,305,161	75.4	77.7	76.8	75.1	80.5	Middle Atlantic.
12,682,448	2,147,746	1,570,092	577,654	82.7	83.6	82.8	80.2	85.5	New York.
4,126,207	649,122	543,822	105,300	79.9	82.6	81.6	79.6	86.6	New Jersey.
7,463,035	3,094,976	2,386,769	705,207	65.1	67.8	66.5	65.8	70.5	Pennsylvania.
21,355,732	9,213,655	5,510,241	3,702,414	64.8	66.4	65.5	65.7	69.7	East North Central.
5,578,274	2,308,353	1,515,255	853,086	63.8	67.5	66.8	66.4	70.2	Ohio.
2,397,190	1,577,028	909,874	667,154	50.6	55.5	55.1	56.4	59.9	Indiana.
6,759,271	1,932,905	1,189,709	703,196	67.9	73.9	73.6	74.5	77.6	Illinois.
4,553,094	1,306,682	1,172,940	694,742	61.1	68.2	65.7	64.3	70.7	Michigan.
1,957,690	1,446,687	721,453	725,234	47.3	52.9	53.5	55.5	57.9	Wisconsin.
7,385,329	6,754,175	3,027,024	3,729,151	37.7	41.8	44.3	48.9	52.0	West North Central.
1,634,914	1,357,569	617,770	730,799	44.1	49.0	49.8	53.9	54.5	Minnesota.
1,250,988	1,370,135	587,485	782,650	36.4	39.6	42.7	46.9	47.7	Iowa.
2,432,715	1,521,988	658,442	863,496	46.6	51.2	51.8	57.9	61.5	Missouri.
164,517	454,819	200,332	254,487	13.6	16.6	20.6	26.6	26.6	North Dakota.
216,730	436,030	182,485	253,545	16.0	18.9	24.6	32.1	33.2	South Dakota.
621,906	703,605	312,170	391,435	31.3	35.3	39.1	45.8	46.9	Nebraska.
963,220	912,079	468,340	443,739	34.8	38.8	41.9	47.4	52.1	Kansas.
10,391,163	10,791,172	6,158,176	4,632,996	31.0	36.1	35.8	42.5	49.1	South Atlantic.
199,122	118,963	84,738	34,225	54.2	51.7	52.3	46.5	62.6	Delaware.
1,615,902	727,099	543,623	183,476	60.0	59.8	59.3	54.4	69.0	Maryland.
802,178				100.0	100.0	100.0	100.0	100.0	Dist. of Columbia.
1,360,115	1,786,855	1,026,804	731,951	29.2	32.4	35.3	40.3	47.0	Virginia.
694,487	1,311,055	900,143	410,922	25.2	28.4	28.1	31.9	34.6	West Virginia.
1,368,101	2,693,628	1,317,268	1,376,560	19.2	25.5	27.3	30.5	33.7	North Carolina.
777,021	1,339,106	638,495	700,611	17.5	21.3	24.5	28.8	36.7	South Carolina.
1,559,447	1,895,131	922,696	962,435	25.1	30.8	34.4	40.1	45.3	Georgia.
1,813,699	957,415	724,609	232,806	36.5	51.7	55.1	56.5	65.5	Florida.
4,694,771	6,982,410	2,944,336	4,048,074	22.4	28.1	29.4	35.5	39.1	East South Central.
1,084,070	1,860,736	886,566	974,170	26.2	30.6	29.8	33.5	36.8	Kentucky.
1,462,692	1,839,116	822,912	1,016,204	26.1	34.3	35.2	38.4	44.1	Tennessee.
1,343,927	1,720,806	760,313	960,493	21.7	28.1	30.2	40.1	43.8	Alabama.
607,182	1,571,752	474,545	1,097,207	13.4	16.9	19.8	27.6	27.9	Mississippi.
6,678,538	6,457,744	3,243,129	3,214,615	28.0	36.4	39.8	53.0	55.6	West South Central.
638,201	1,278,920	477,093	801,827	16.6	20.6	22.2	22.3	33.0	Arkansas.
1,471,696	1,211,320	644,365	567,455	34.9	39.7	41.5	50.8	54.8	Louisiana.
1,139,461	1,093,570	540,804	553,066	26.5	34.3	37.6	49.6	51.0	Oklahoma.
4,628,680	2,873,134	1,580,867	1,292,267	32.4	41.0	45.4	59.8	62.7	Texas.
	2,280,110	1,430,508	856,602	36.5	39.4	42.7	46.8	54.9	Mountain.
	232,990	197,051	135,939	31.3	33.7	37.8	42.8	43.7	Montana.
	296,086	171,126	164,960	27.6	29.1	33.7	30.8	42.9	Idaho.
	145,911	89,207	56,704	29.1	31.1	37.3	49.8	49.5	Wyoming.
	493,771	295,890	196,181	45.2	50.2	52.6	57.4	62.7	Colorado.
	230,296	207,475	131,232	18.0	25.2	33.2	46.2	50.2	New Mexico.
	333,367	266,673	76,914	31.0	34.4	34.8	36.5	55.5	Arizona.
	230,007	188,357	60,520	48.0	52.4	55.5	59.9	65.3	Utah.
91,025	66,455	54,997	12,461	19.7	37.8	39.3	52.5	57.2	Nevada.
	2,634,628	2,554,386	1,679,237	52.2	67.5	65.3	62.9	75.0	Pacific.
1,395,166	875,797	602,026	273,771	54.8	56.6	53.1	53.6	63.2	Washington.
695,316	702,023	473,788	228,235	49.8	51.3	48.8	48.1	63.9	Oregon.
8,585,430	2,046,803	1,478,572	566,231	67.9	73.3	71.0	67.1	80.7	California.

No. 20.—POPULATION, BY SEX, BY STATES: 1930, 1940, AND 1950

[For U. S. totals, see also *Historical Statistics*, series B 13–15]

DIVISION AND STATE	1930			1940			1950		
	Male	Female	Males per 100 females	Male	Female	Males per 100 females	Male	Female	Males per 100 females
United States	62,137,080	60,637,966	102.5	66,061,592	65,607,683	100.7	74,833,239	75,864,122	98.6
New England	4,024,657	4,141,684	97.2	4,154,760	4,282,530	97.0	4,553,770	4,760,683	95.7
Maine	401,285	396,138	101.3	425,821	421,405	101.0	454,145	459,629	98.8
New Hampshire	231,759	233,534	99.2	244,909	246,615	99.3	262,424	270,818	96.9
Vermont	183,260	176,345	103.9	182,224	177,007	102.9	187,754	189,993	98.8
Massachusetts	2,071,672	2,177,942	95.1	2,102,479	2,214,242	95.0	2,270,367	2,420,147	93.8
Rhode Island	235,372	352,125	95.2	349,404	363,942	96.0	390,583	401,313	97.3
Connecticut	801,303	805,600	99.5	849,923	859,319	98.9	988,497	1,018,783	97.0
Middle Atlantic	13,188,681	13,072,069	100.9	13,710,692	13,528,795	99.1	14,793,099	15,379,434	96.2
New York	6,312,520	6,275,546	100.6	6,690,326	6,788,816	98.5	7,239,944	7,590,248	95.4
New Jersey	2,030,644	2,010,690	101.0	2,068,159	2,091,006	99.0	2,382,744	2,452,555	97.2
Pennsylvania	4,845,517	4,785,833	101.2	4,951,207	4,948,973	100.0	5,170,411	5,327,601	97.0
E. North Central	12,904,783	12,392,402	104.1	13,438,325	13,188,017	101.9	15,145,262	15,254,166	99.3
Ohio	3,361,141	3,285,556	102.3	3,461,072	3,446,540	100.4	3,926,534	4,018,093	97.8
Indiana	1,640,051	1,598,442	102.6	1,725,201	1,702,595	101.3	1,956,516	1,975,708	99.1
Illinois	3,873,457	3,757,197	103.1	3,957,149	3,940,092	100.4	4,319,251	4,392,925	98.3
Michigan	2,519,309	2,323,016	108.4	2,694,727	2,561,379	105.2	3,212,119	3,159,647	101.7
Wisconsin	1,510,815	1,428,191	105.8	1,600,176	1,537,411	104.1	1,726,842	1,707,733	101.1
W. North Central	6,785,442	6,511,473	104.2	6,829,335	6,687,855	102.1	7,035,415	7,027,879	100.1
Minnesota	1,316,571	1,247,382	105.5	1,427,545	1,364,755	104.6	1,501,208	1,481,275	101.3
Iowa	1,255,101	1,215,838	103.2	1,280,494	1,257,774	101.8	1,310,283	1,310,790	100.0
Missouri	1,822,866	1,806,501	100.9	1,831,252	1,902,412	96.8	1,940,853	2,013,790	96.4
North Dakota	359,615	321,230	111.9	335,402	345,569	109.4	322,944	295,692	108.3
South Dakota	363,650	329,199	110.5	332,514	310,447	107.1	337,251	315,489	106.9
Nebraska	706,346	671,615	105.2	665,758	650,046	102.4	667,332	655,178	101.4
Kansas	961,291	919,708	104.5	906,340	894,688	101.3	955,534	951,765	100.3
South Atlantic	7,889,634	7,912,955	99.6	8,870,589	8,952,562	99.1	10,496,597	10,685,736	98.2
Delaware	121,257	117,123	103.5	134,333	132,172	101.6	157,344	160,741	97.9
Maryland	821,009	810,517	101.3	915,038	906,206	101.0	1,166,603	1,176,398	99.2
Dist. of Col.	231,883	254,986	90.9	317,522	345,569	91.9	377,918	424,260	89.1
Virginia	1,216,046	1,205,805	100.8	1,349,004	1,328,769	101.5	1,675,216	1,643,404	101.9
West Virginia	889,571	839,334	106.0	905,582	933,392	103.8	1,006,287	999,265	100.7
North Carolina	1,575,208	1,595,066	98.8	1,772,990	1,796,633	98.6	2,017,105	2,044,824	98.6
South Carolina	853,158	885,607	96.3	905,239	964,571	97.0	1,040,540	1,076,487	96.7
Georgia	1,434,527	1,473,979	97.3	1,534,758	1,568,965	96.6	1,688,667	1,755,911	96.2
Florida	737,675	730,536	101.0	943,123	954,291	98.8	1,356,917	1,404,388	97.3
E. South Central	4,947,562	4,939,712	100.2	5,366,024	5,412,201	99.1	5,677,535	5,799,686	97.9
Kentucky	1,322,793	1,291,796	102.4	1,435,812	1,409,815	101.8	1,474,967	1,469,219	100.4
Tennessee	1,304,559	1,311,997	99.4	1,445,829	1,470,012	98.4	1,623,107	1,665,611	97.3
Alabama	1,315,009	1,331,239	98.8	1,399,901	1,433,060	97.7	1,502,640	1,559,105	96.4
Mississippi	1,005,141	1,004,680	100.0	1,084,482	1,099,314	98.7	1,076,791	1,102,122	97.7
W. South Central	6,186,324	5,969,906	103.3	6,588,293	6,596,232	100.8	7,249,397	7,288,175	99.5
Arkansas	939,843	914,639	102.8	962,916	966,471	101.7	951,584	987,977	96.3
Louisiana	1,047,823	1,083,770	99.4	1,172,382	1,191,498	96.4	1,319,166	1,364,340	96.7
Oklahoma	1,233,264	1,162,776	106.1	1,181,892	1,144,542	102.4	1,115,555	1,117,796	99.8
Texas	2,965,994	2,858,721	103.8	3,221,103	3,193,721	100.9	3,863,142	3,848,062	100.4
Mountain	1,949,738	1,751,991	111.3	2,149,398	2,000,605	107.4	2,591,918	2,482,688	104.4
Montana	293,228	244,378	120.0	299,009	261,040	114.8	309,423	281,601	109.9
Idaho	237,347	207,685	114.3	276,579	248,294	111.4	303,397	285,400	106.3
Wyoming	124,785	100,780	123.8	135,055	115,055	117.4	154,853	135,676	114.1
Colorado	530,762	505,039	105.1	568,775	554,518	102.6	665,149	659,940	100.8
New Mexico	219,222	204,095	107.4	271,846	259,972	104.6	347,544	333,646	104.2
Arizona	231,304	204,269	113.2	256,170	241,091	107.1	379,059	370,626	102.3
Utah	259,999	247,848	104.9	278,620	271,669	102.6	347,636	341,226	101.9
Nevada	53,161	37,897	140.3	61,341	48,906	125.4	85,017	75,065	113.3
Pacific	4,268,659	3,925,774	108.7	4,984,176	4,749,086	105.0	7,292,256	7,194,271	101.4
Washington	826,392	737,004	112.1	905,757	830,434	109.1	1,223,851	1,155,112	105.9
Oregon	499,672	454,114	110.0	562,689	526,995	106.8	772,776	748,665	103.2
California	2,942,595	2,734,656	107.6	3,515,730	3,391,657	103.7	5,295,629	5,290,694	100.1

Source: Department of Commerce, Bureau of Census; Sixteenth Census Report, *Population*, Vol. II, and *U. S. Census of Population: 1950*, Vol. II, Part 1.

No. 21.—POPULATION, BY AGE AND SEX, 1920 TO 1950, AND BY COLOR AND RURAL FARM, 1950

[See also *Historical Statistics*, series B 72-144]

E AND SEX	1920	1930	1940	1950 Total	1950 White	1950 Nonwhite	Rural-farm population [1]
tal	105,710,620	122,775,046	131,669,275	150,697,361	134,942,028	15,755,333	23,048,350
years	11,573,230	11,444,390	10,541,524	16,163,571	14,184,504	1,979,067	2,619,670
ars	11,398,075	12,507,609	10,664,622	13,199,685	11,596,572	1,603,113	2,561,239
rears	10,641,137	12,004,877	11,745,935	11,119,268	9,694,529	1,424,739	2,474,958
rears	9,430,556	11,552,115	12,333,523	10,616,598	9,330,520	1,286,078	2,112,974
rears	9,277,021	10,870,378	11,587,835	11,481,828	10,179,187	1,302,641	1,412,315
rears	9,086,491	9,533,608	11,096,638	12,242,260	10,924,804	1,317,456	1,355,382
rears	8,071,193	9,120,421	10,242,388	11,517,007	10,356,331	1,160,676	1,386,713
rears	7,775,281	9,206,645	9,545,377	11,246,386	10,058,473	1,187,913	1,409,971
rears	6,345,557	7,990,195	8,787,843	10,203,973	9,190,290	1,013,683	1,407,246
rears	5,763,620	7,042,279	8,255,225	9,070,465	8,169,354	901,111	1,291,540
rears	4,734,873	5,975,804	7,256,846	8,272,188	7,535,439	736,749	1,196,347
rears	3,549,124	4,645,677	5,842,865	7,235,120	6,695,732	539,388	1,051,816
rears	2,982,548	3,751,221	4,728,340	6,059,475	5,652,606	406,869	898,063
rears	2,068,475	2,770,605	3,806,657	5,002,936	4,585,586	417,350	742,850
rears	1,395,036	1,950,004	2,599,532	3,411,949	3,181,575	230,374	483,169
and over	1,469,704	1,913,196	2,643,125	3,854,652	3,606,526	248,126	534,497
rted	148,699	94,022					
age	26.3	26.5	29.0	30.2	30.8	26.1	26.3
ale	53,900,431	62,137,080	66,061,592	74,833,239	67,129,192	7,704,047	12,078,610
years	5,857,461	5,806,174	5,354,808	8,226,164	7,244,211	991,963	1,337,371
ars	5,753,001	6,381,108	5,418,823	6,714,555	5,915,130	799,425	1,314,554
rears	5,369,306	6,068,777	5,952,329	5,660,399	4,944,535	715,864	1,294,683
rears	4,673,792	5,757,825	6,180,153	5,311,342	4,685,825	625,517	1,144,640
rears	4,527,045	5,336,815	5,692,392	5,606,293	5,002,782	603,511	761,646
rears	4,538,233	4,860,180	5,450,662	5,972,078	5,349,707	622,371	661,587
rears	4,130,783	4,561,786	5,070,312	5,624,723	5,080,610	544,113	688,176
rears	4,074,361	4,679,860	4,745,659	5,517,544	4,955,941	561,603	761,066
rears	3,285,543	4,136,459	4,419,135	5,070,269	4,573,529	496,740	729,737
rears	3,117,580	3,671,924	4,209,299	4,526,366	4,080,174	446,192	674,343
rears	2,535,545	3,131,645	3,752,750	4,128,648	3,756,125	372,523	628,575
rears	1,880,065	2,425,992	3,011,364	3,630,046	3,350,888	279,158	585,688
rears	1,581,800	1,941,508	2,397,816	3,037,838	2,829,399	208,439	501,982
rears	1,079,817	1,417,812	1,896,088	2,421,561	2,223,014	201,547	420,618
rears	708,301	991,647	1,270,967	1,628,829	1,513,308	115,521	277,213
and over	696,963	915,752	1,239,065	1,743,584	1,624,014	119,570	286,731
rted	92,875	51,816					
age	25.8	26.7	29.1	29.9	25.9	26.4	
male	51,810,189	60,637,966	65,607,683	75,864,122	67,812,836	8,051,286	10,969,740
years	5,715,769	5,638,216	5,186,716	7,927,407	6,940,293	987,114	1,282,299
ars	5,645,074	6,226,501	5,265,799	6,485,130	5,681,442	803,688	1,246,685
rears	5,271,831	5,936,100	5,793,606	5,458,869	4,749,994	708,875	1,190,275
rears	4,756,764	5,794,290	6,153,370	5,305,256	4,644,695	660,561	968,334
rears	4,749,976	5,533,563	5,895,443	5,875,535	5,176,405	699,130	650,669
rears	4,548,258	4,973,428	5,645,976	6,270,182	5,575,097	695,085	673,795
rears	3,940,410	4,558,635	5,172,076	5,275,721	5,002,532	616,563	698,537
rears	3,700,920	4,528,785	4,799,718	5,728,842	5,102,532	626,310	738,905
rears	3,060,014	3,853,736	4,366,708	5,133,704	4,616,761	516,943	677,509
rears	2,646,070	3,370,355	4,045,956	4,544,099	4,089,180	454,919	617,197
rears	2,199,328	2,844,159	3,504,096	4,143,540	3,779,314	364,226	566,772
rears	1,669,050	2,219,685	2,832,501	3,605,074	3,344,844	260,230	496,128
rears	1,400,748	1,809,713	2,330,524	3,021,637	2,823,207	198,430	396,681
rears	988,668	1,352,793	1,910,569	2,578,375	2,362,572	215,803	322,232
rears	688,735	958,357	1,298,565	1,783,120	1,668,267	114,853	205,956
and over	772,751	997,444	1,404,060	2,111,068	1,982,512	128,556	237,766
rted	55,824	42,206					
age	24.7	26.2	29.0	30.5	31.1	26.2	26.1

d on new urban definition (see text, p. 2, for explanation).

1: Department of Commerce, Bureau of the Census; *U. S. Census of Population; 1950*, Vol. II, Part 1.

No. 22.—Population by A

[See also Hist

DIVISION AND STATE	Under 5 years	5 to 9 years	10 to 14 years	15 to 19 years	20 to 24 years	25 to 29 years	30 to 34 years	35 to yea
United States	16,163,571	13,199,685	11,119,265	10,616,598	11,481,825	12,242,260	11,517,007	11,246
New England	916,346	746,441	604,122	620,680	694,829	741,414	715,004	682
Maine	99,678	82,366	71,410	70,423	66,659	66,240	61,966	60
New Hampshire	54,519	43,800	37,264	37,464	37,961	38,645	37,611	36
Vermont	41,941	34,434	29,514	28,694	27,484	26,787	25,481	24
Massachusetts	448,816	364,753	295,507	308,506	351,612	373,757	357,956	342
Rhode Island	76,812	60,408	48,821	53,935	66,755	68,360	62,332	58
Connecticut	194,580	160,680	121,606	121,658	144,358	167,625	172,658	161
Middle Atlantic	2,850,072	2,324,909	1,927,478	1,922,554	2,243,213	2,486,192	2,417,377	2,383
New York	1,364,721	1,095,025	892,184	904,034	1,084,812	1,206,923	1,173,267	1,189
New Jersey	458,906	371,826	290,544	295,859	350,403	409,890	409,434	393
Pennsylvania	1,026,445	858,058	744,750	722,661	807,998	869,379	834,676	799
East North Central	3,187,518	2,551,212	2,131,888	1,986,674	2,271,202	2,496,536	2,357,857	2,261
Ohio	846,749	657,864	548,981	506,103	594,909	663,603	620,853	585
Indiana	422,058	342,965	288,473	268,034	300,961	319,721	292,969	280
Illinois	842,842	684,347	565,347	542,280	639,444	712,531	691,503	678
Michigan	703,861	568,686	471,971	431,106	491,167	538,093	504,726	473
Wisconsin	372,008	297,449	257,116	239,151	244,721	256,588	247,806	244
West North Central	1,489,292	1,211,357	1,045,215	1,000,110	1,021,899	1,049,915	983,234	967
Minnesota	332,460	267,652	225,787	207,460	213,712	220,780	212,765	206
Iowa	280,269	226,374	199,225	184,168	189,768	192,843	180,966	174
Missouri	384,391	322,288	279,534	272,330	280,534	296,251	276,758	284
North Dakota	75,408	62,489	54,279	51,213	47,818	44,500	42,407	41
South Dakota	76,713	60,572	53,090	51,179	49,961	48,937	45,014	42
Nebraska	140,169	110,805	97,710	97,265	98,877	99,135	90,629	89
Kansas	199,882	161,677	137,590	136,495	141,009	147,470	134,685	130
South Atlantic	2,478,893	2,070,091	1,784,122	1,688,853	1,755,346	1,794,472	1,631,502	1,572
Delaware	33,237	26,845	21,875	20,877	23,173	26,824	26,727	24
Maryland	258,252	205,897	161,703	155,620	187,272	213,885	199,309	184
Dist. of Columbia	71,353	49,469	40,039	45,411	71,721	84,549	74,377	71
Virginia	381,478	316,410	267,612	266,370	291,406	294,692	266,516	248
West Virginia	240,107	205,390	190,979	166,440	159,550	158,798	142,373	137
North Carolina	501,632	428,599	381,492	365,718	356,326	342,115	301,769	286
South Carolina	279,603	244,044	212,300	194,275	177,014	172,433	149,327	146
Georgia	422,486	355,208	311,293	291,806	276,193	276,270	255,385	254
Florida	290,745	238,229	196,829	182,336	212,691	224,906	215,719	215
East South Central	1,389,281	1,184,284	1,064,540	978,520	902,822	877,099	790,479	796
Kentucky	346,006	295,383	267,054	247,783	226,231	223,963	200,040	196
Tennessee	379,802	321,029	286,603	270,409	265,345	266,935	239,787	227
Alabama	380,124	326,803	293,440	265,240	243,006	234,242	213,437	217
Mississippi	283,349	239,069	217,443	195,088	168,240	151,959	137,215	144
West South Central	1,704,476	1,422,115	1,214,323	1,149,846	1,147,406	1,158,035	1,043,545	1,054
Arkansas	228,279	202,063	179,485	159,765	134,802	131,082	124,709	129
Louisiana	334,466	275,105	235,359	209,922	212,884	213,003	192,202	192
Oklahoma	240,458	211,222	187,701	178,872	166,422	168,673	152,762	155
Texas	901,273	733,725	611,778	601,287	633,298	645,277	573,872	577
Mountain	621,340	505,504	426,874	385,185	391,452	406,893	382,396	364
Montana	68,201	55,357	46,534	40,640	41,716	44,181	45,290	43
Idaho	72,633	61,579	52,457	44,825	41,382	44,103	44,046	42
Wyoming	34,297	27,542	22,703	22,488	24,135	24,350	22,605	21
Colorado	148,275	116,442	99,364	96,320	102,873	109,354	99,891	94
New Mexico	94,944	76,996	65,211	57,130	57,626	57,426	50,133	47
Arizona	92,725	78,957	67,395	57,247	56,918	59,073	56,400	55
Utah	98,307	75,406	62,266	57,091	55,787	55,047	50,074	48
Nevada	16,958	13,523	10,944	9,444	11,015	13,359	13,869	14
Pacific	1,526,353	1,182,972	929,706	884,176	1,053,859	1,237,703	1,192,621	1,166
Washington	263,326	203,786	159,695	157,695	175,619	195,087	188,636	180
Oregon	163,915	131,596	108,140	96,738	105,070	117,706	116,800	117
California	1,099,112	847,590	682,871	629,742	773,170	934,910	887,185	862

Source: Department of Commerce, Bureau of the Census; U. S. Census of Population: 1950, Vol. II, Part

BY STATES: 1950

Statistics, series B31-64]

40 to 44 years	45 to 49 years	50 to 54 years	55 to 59 years	60 to 64 years	65 to 69 years	70 to 74 years	75 to 84 years	85 years and over	Median age	DIVISION AND STATE
10,302,973	9,070,465	8,272,188	7,235,120	6,059,475	5,602,936	3,411,949	3,277,751	576,901	30.2	U. S.
628,079	569,654	552,621	504,874	425,878	345,760	252,807	257,706	47,294	32.3	N. E.
57,186	51,593	49,748	44,344	38,393	33,952	26,019	26,290	5,301	30.0	Maine.
34,963	32,225	31,564	28,429	24,216	20,485	16,341	17,482	3,485	32.3	N. H.
25,506	21,336	19,942	18,306	15,933	13,838	11,234	12,131	2,331	30.0	Vt.
317,850	291,766	286,920	261,480	220,898	181,156	130,527	132,729	24,024	32.8	Mass.
55,296	48,480	46,471	41,968	34,913	28,087	19,704	19,253	3,374	31.7	R. I.
141,188	124,245	118,976	110,347	91,525	71,242	48,982	47,821	8,779	32.7	Conn.
2,216,863	1,990,537	1,887,127	1,628,154	1,352,503	1,057,548	710,256	665,610	112,857	32.7	M. A.
1,131,944	1,033,920	981,891	828,417	684,685	530,103	352,439	320,376	55,539	33.7	N. Y.
357,760	318,504	305,235	263,516	215,546	164,921	109,441	101,632	17,995	32.9	N. J.
721,158	638,113	600,001	536,221	452,272	362,524	248,376	236,602	39,323	31.3	Pa.
2,460,045	1,872,225	1,738,010	1,573,546	1,321,219	1,048,326	719,093	763,540	124,610	31.2	E. N. C.
532,902	477,812	448,936	408,842	344,630	261,805	197,945	195,201	34,024	31.2	Ohio.
264,906	230,512	212,753	192,925	166,976	141,464	99,560	102,055	17,947	30.4	Ind.
622,686	569,734	528,615	479,109	401,148	311,223	207,718	200,356	35,004	32.7	Ill.
424,608	386,068	350,056	312,685	253,776	191,973	127,680	120,310	21,687	29.8	Mich.
225,043	208,099	197,620	179,985	154,489	121,861	86,190	85,918	15,948	31.0	Wis.
911,666	835,639	795,620	733,557	635,162	528,427	380,836	393,344	74,998	31.1	W. N. C.
189,729	176,212	170,905	157,690	134,854	105,188	73,705	75,332	14,905	30.6	Minn.
162,146	151,624	147,203	139,047	120,343	100,809	75,640	80,921	15,628	31.0	Iowa.
275,074	252,646	232,304	210,056	180,800	157,654	112,868	115,894	20,972	32.6	Mo.
37,958	32,870	29,647	27,117	23,854	19,815	13,342	12,777	2,262	27.1	N. Dak.
42,685	36,033	34,864	32,112	28,332	22,239	15,333	14,799	2,925	28.6	S. Dak.
69,161	77,507	75,847	70,790	61,575	49,987	35,673	37,183	7,536	31.0	Nebr.
125,393	111,747	104,950	96,745	85,504	72,735	54,275	56,438	10,770	31.1	Kans.
1,363,532	1,157,345	1,000,527	821,010	664,978	589,256	391,143	357,876	58,733	27.3	S. A.
22,143	19,384	17,961	15,302	12,680	10,404	7,301	7,249	1,306	31.2	Del.
182,980	140,050	125,206	102,064	82,570	66,539	45,359	44,022	7,594	29.7	Md.
63,200	54,792	49,678	39,324	29,825	23,338	15,751	15,017	2,581	32.6	D. C.
211,251	177,199	154,449	126,100	102,656	77,527	60,556	56,857	9,584	27.3	Va.
121,976	106,102	92,963	78,814	65,948	56,835	38,699	37,010	5,982	26.3	W. Va.
245,600	203,510	173,099	137,936	110,141	97,440	63,245	55,700	8,912	25.0	N. C.
130,927	99,968	83,431	67,652	54,555	52,127	32,061	26,624	4,193	23.6	S. C.
219,640	182,855	153,118	126,309	100,096	99,556	60,606	54,540	8,953	26.9	Ga.
196,505	173,485	150,722	127,509	108,507	99,490	67,565	60,851	9,568	30.9	Fla.
715,668	615,910	530,448	444,487	364,016	343,304	226,941	215,508	35,986	26.2	E. S. C.
177,177	159,085	142,306	123,922	104,155	93,069	65,512	65,765	10,897	27.0	Ky.
212,881	180,958	156,013	130,798	106,369	97,134	65,570	62,325	9,855	27.3	Tenn.
191,974	161,656	135,506	110,774	80,233	86,977	54,599	48,705	8,367	25.5	Ala.
133,636	115,211	96,623	78,975	64,259	66,124	41,260	38,713	6,867	24.6	Miss.
844,362	846,902	711,413	600,524	486,665	429,835	284,540	272,535	46,276	27.7	W. S. C.
120,580	108,015	91,813	83,144	67,407	62,715	41,299	38,956	6,035	26.9	Ark.
175,051	153,961	126,887	103,532	81,383	78,961	46,687	43,553	7,648	26.7	La.
147,428	131,715	113,988	100,476	84,703	75,260	53,991	55,499	9,172	28.9	Okla.
521,603	453,221	378,725	313,372	253,172	212,899	142,573	134,527	23,421	27.9	Tex.
321,620	292,268	268,903	214,150	184,272	145,095	99,537	94,189	17,646	27.5	Mt.
37,582	32,160	28,714	26,812	27,940	21,940	13,947	12,602	2,285	29.9	Mont.
27,934	30,706	27,221	24,781	22,170	18,019	12,346	11,233	1,939	27.4	Idaho.
18,734	15,808	14,588	12,949	10,550	7,847	5,033	4,518	767	27.9	Wyo.
65,476	61,698	67,698	61,577	53,526	44,836	32,182	32,565	6,009	29.5	Colo.
38,572	33,282	27,308	23,058	18,167	14,038	8,685	8,698	1,643	24.0	N. Mex.
49,783	41,586	35,173	29,722	23,959	19,163	12,284	10,802	1,992	26.8	Ariz.
40,463	33,904	30,084	25,706	21,745	17,505	11,900	11,039	1,974	25.1	Utah.
12,602	10,694	9,117	7,545	6,215	4,747	3,160	2,642	437	31.7	Nev.
1,023,638	965,985	915,519	714,838	632,782	509,385	346,796	324,149	59,101	31.8	Pac.
159,090	138,714	125,939	115,306	103,916	86,551	59,653	55,144	10,055	30.9	Wash.
105,575	93,228	86,113	77,843	65,230	54,455	37,095	34,979	6,492	31.6	Oreg.
753,973	674,043	603,462	521,689	480,636	368,379	250,046	234,026	42,554	32.1	Calif.

No. 23.—POPULATION 21 YEARS OLD AND OVER, BY STATES: 1940 AND 1950

[Minus sign (−) denotes decrease. See also *Historical Statistics*, series B 244, 258, 273]

DIVISION AND STATE	TOTAL			MALE			FEMALE		
	1940	1950	Percent increase, 1940 to 1950	1940	1950	Percent increase, 1940 to 1950	1940	1950	Per t crea 194 19
United States....	83,996,629	97,403,307	16.0	42,004,816	47,853,694	13.9	41,991,813	49,549,613	
New England:									
Maine............	583,230	576,840	8.2	266,681	283,509	6.3	286,549	293,331	
New Hampshire...	325,206	352,780	8.5	160,697	171,020	6.4	164,509	181,760	
Vermont..........	236,037	237,552	4.2	115,233	116,509	1.2	112,804	120,953	
Massachusetts....	2,916,202	3,206,104	9.9	1,395,179	1,520,510	9.0	1,521,023	1,685,594	
Rhode Island.....	474,195	538,124	13.5	227,801	259,666	14.0	246,394	278,458	
Connecticut......	1,159,601	1,382,373	19.2	571,712	670,521	17.3	587,889	711,852	
Middle Atlantic:									
New York........	9,350,026	10,374,446	11.0	4,603,673	4,994,060	8.5	4,746,353	5,380,386	
New Jersey.......	2,834,600	3,354,160	18.3	1,399,512	1,628,358	16.4	1,435,088	1,725,802	
Pennsylvania.....	6,351,408	6,997,219	10.2	3,161,065	3,408,977	7.8	3,190,343	3,588,242	
East North Central:									
Ohio.............	4,583,907	5,279,761	15.2	2,287,736	2,586,095	13.0	2,296,171	2,693,666	
Indiana..........	2,235,350	2,556,467	14.4	1,121,475	1,261,119	12.5	1,113,875	1,295,348	
Illinois..........	5,381,944	5,956,601	10.7	2,685,444	2,925,046	8.9	2,696,500	3,033,555	
Michigan.........	3,374,373	4,105,606	21.7	1,740,712	2,064,908	18.7	1,633,661	2,040,698	
Wisconsin........	2,018,581	2,222,423	10.1	1,031,000	1,112,677	7.9	987,581	1,109,746	
West North Central:									
Minnesota........	1,796,857	1,910,153	6.3	921,443	958,369	4.0	875,414	951,784	
Iowa.............	1,639,266	1,694,619	3.4	824,442	840,331	1.9	814,824	854,288	
Missouri.........	2,501,472	2,643,129	5.7	1,233,772	1,281,239	3.8	1,267,700	1,361,890	
North Dakota.....	373,216	366,590	−1.8	199,413	194,439	−2.5	173,803	172,151	
South Dakota.....	386,165	401,146	3.3	203,283	209,349	3.0	184,882	191,797	
Nebraska.........	836,581	860,391	2.8	422,251	431,142	2.1	414,330	429,249	
Kansas...........	1,161,868	1,242,541	6.9	581,889	616,047	5.9	579,979	626,494	
South Atlantic:									
Delaware.........	177,635	210,918	18.7	89,250	103,149	15.6	88,385	107,769	
Maryland.........	1,185,654	1,527,089	28.8	593,401	752,882	26.9	592,253	774,207	
Dist. of Col......	484,738	583,338	20.3	229,341	268,844	17.2	255,397	314,494	
Virginia..........	1,575,481	2,025,339	28.6	790,060	1,011,519	28.0	785,421	1,013,820	
West Virginia.....	1,066,732	1,171,878	9.9	547,120	587,373	7.4	519,612	584,505	
North Carolina...	1,929,051	2,311,071	19.8	948,954	1,130,024	19.1	980,097	1,181,047	
South Carolina...	991,536	1,150,867	16.1	481,576	554,085	15.1	509,960	596,782	
Georgia..........	1,772,936	2,008,822	13.3	860,838	964,109	12.0	912,098	1,044,719	
Florida..........	1,218,660	1,822,513	49.6	604,796	887,957	46.8	613,864	935,556	
East South Central:									
Kentucky.........	1,635,781	1,742,978	6.6	823,129	864,430	5.0	812,652	878,548	
Tennessee........	1,707,760	1,978,548	15.9	838,935	961,147	14.6	868,825	1,017,401	
Alabama.........	1,559,680	1,747,759	12.1	763,045	843,927	10.6	796,635	903,832	
Mississippi.......	1,197,617	1,208,023	.9	592,557	587,284	−.9	605,060	620,739	
West South Central:									
Arkansas.........	1,101,800	1,112,866	1.0	557,023	550,158	−1.2	544,837	562,708	
Louisiana........	1,374,947	1,587,145	15.4	678,502	770,580	13.6	696,445	816,565	
Oklahoma........	1,369,196	1,382,108	.9	692,236	682,993	−1.3	676,960	699,115	
Texas............	3,861,721	4,737,225	22.7	1,938,380	2,351,820	21.3	1,923,341	2,385,405	
Mountain:									
Montana..........	356,096	372,345	4.6	195,376	198,368	1.5	160,720	173,977	
Idaho............	312,965	349,016	11.5	168,848	181,675	7.6	144,117	167,341	
Wyoming.........	155,433	178,581	14.9	85,979	96,131	11.8	69,454	82,450	
Colorado.........	713,968	844,748	18.3	362,595	420,846	16.1	351,373	423,902	
New Mexico......	284,295	375,387	32.0	147,842	192,582	30.3	136,454	182,805	
Arizona..........	288,265	441,589	53.3	151,807	225,303	47.0	136,368	215,586	
Utah.............	308,439	389,843	26.4	155,907	196,181	25.8	152,532	193,662	
Nevada..........	75,362	107,173	42.2	43,652	57,810	32.4	31,710	49,363	
Pacific:									
Washington.......	1,192,982	1,559,266	30.7	629,463	799,604	27.0	563,519	759,662	
Oregon...........	748,212	1,001,716	33.9	389,674	509,726	30.8	358,538	491,990	
California........	4,885,541	7,211,825	47.6	2,490,027	3,569,206	43.3	2,395,514	3,642,619	

Source: Department of Commerce, Bureau of the Census; *U. S. Census of Population: 1950*, Vol. II.

.—POPULATION, BY RACE AND SEX, 1930 AND 1940, AND BY RACE AND SEX, URBAN AND RURAL, 1950

[mation of new urban definition, see p. 2. See also *Historical Statistics*, series B 13-23, B 40-47, B 167, B 170]

CE AND SEX	1930	1940	1950, NEW URBAN DEFINITION			
			Total	Urban	Rural nonfarm	Rural farm
al	122,775,046	131,669,275	150,697,361	96,467,686	31,181,325	23,048,350
	110,286,740	118,214,870	134,942,028	86,756,435	28,470,339	19,715,254
	96,303,335	106,795,732	124,780,860	78,267,570	27,350,570	19,162,720
-born	13,983,405	11,419,138	10,161,168	8,488,865	1,119,769	552,534
	11,891,143	12,865,518	15,042,286	9,392,606	2,491,377	3,158,301
a	597,163	588,887	713,047	318,643	219,609	174,795
	332,397	338,969	343,410	56,108	178,678	108,624
b	138,834	126,947	141,768	100,735	14,260	26,773
	74,954	77,504	117,629	109,434	5,844	2,351
r	50,978	50,467	110,240	52,366	20,827	37,047
	62,137,080	66,061,592	74,833,239	46,591,732	15,862,847	12,678,610
	55,922,528	59,448,548	67,129,192	42,249,894	14,489,275	10,390,023
	48,430,037	53,437,533	61,952,802	37,994,340	13,887,315	10,071,147
-born	7,502,491	6,011,015	5,176,390	4,355,554	601,960	318,876
	5,855,669	6,269,038	7,298,722	4,449,766	1,256,115	1,592,841
m	358,883	344,006	405,325	192,122	117,457	95,746
	170,350	171,427	178,824	30,256	91,993	56,575
b	81,771	71,967	76,649	53,458	8,139	15,052
	59,802	57,389	77,008	71,656	3,874	1,478
r	46,960	43,223	72,844	36,752	13,451	22,641
e	60,637,966	65,607,683	75,864,122	49,875,904	15,318,478	10,369,740
	54,364,212	58,766,322	67,812,836	44,506,541	13,981,064	9,325,231
	47,883,298	53,358,199	62,828,058	40,273,230	13,463,255	9,091,573
-born	6,480,914	5,408,123	4,984,778	4,233,311	517,809	233,658
	6,035,474	6,596,480	7,743,564	4,942,842	1,235,262	1,565,460
m	238,280	244,881	307,722	126,521	102,152	79,049
	162,047	162,542	164,586	25,852	86,685	52,049
b	57,063	54,980	65,119	47,277	6,121	11,721
	15,152	20,115	40,621	37,778	1,970	873
r	4,018	7,244	37,396	15,614	7,376	14,406

Department of Commerce, Bureau of the Census: *U. S. Census of Population: 1950*, Vol. II, Part 1.

No. 25.—POPULATION, BY RACE, BY STATES: 1930, 1940, AND 1950

[For U S, totals, see also *Historical Statistics* series B 18–23]

DIVISION AND STATE	1930 White	1930 Negro	1930 Other races	1940 White	1940 Negro	1940 Other races	1950 White	1950 Negro	1950 Other races
U. S.	110,286,740	11,891,143	597,163	118,214,870	12,865,518	588,887	134,942,028	15,042,286	713,047
New England	8,065,220	94,086	7,035	8,329,146	101,509	6,635	9,161,156	142,941	10,356
Maine	795,185	1,096	1,142	844,543	1,304	1,379	910,846	1,221	1,707
New Hampshire	464,351	790	152	490,989	414	121	532,275	731	236
Vermont	358,966	568	77	358,806	384	41	377,188	443	116
Massachusetts	4,192,992	52,365	4,257	4,257,596	55,391	3,734	4,611,503	73,171	5,840
Rhode Island	677,026	9,913	558	701,805	11,024	517	777,015	13,903	978
Connecticut	1,576,700	29,354	849	1,675,407	32,992	843	1,952,329	53,472	1,479
Mid. Atlantic	25,178,861	1,052,899	28,990	26,237,622	1,268,366	33,499	28,237,528	1,875,241	50,764
New York	12,153,191	412,814	22,061	12,879,846	571,221	28,375	13,872,095	918,191	39,906
New Jersey	3,829,663	208,828	2,843	3,931,087	226,973	2,105	4,511,585	318,565	5,179
Pennsylvania	9,196,007	431,257	4,086	9,426,989	470,172	3,019	9,853,848	638,485	5,679
E. N. Central	24,335,980	930,450	30,755	25,528,451	1,069,326	28,565	28,543,307	1,863,698	52,363
Ohio	6,335,173	309,304	2,220	6,566,531	339,461	1,620	7,428,222	513,072	5,333
Indiana	3,125,778	111,982	743	3,305,323	121,916	557	3,758,512	174,168	1,544
Illinois	7,295,267	328,972	6,415	7,504,202	387,446	5,593	8,046,058	645,980	20,138
Michigan	4,663,507	169,453	9,365	5,039,643	208,345	8,118	5,917,825	442,296	11,645
Wisconsin	2,916,255	10,739	12,012	3,112,752	12,158	12,677	3,392,690	28,182	13,703
W. N. Central	12,913,292	331,784	51,539	13,111,519	350,992	54,479	13,576,077	424,178	61,139
Minnesota	2,542,599	9,445	11,909	2,768,982	9,928	13,390	2,953,697	14,022	14,764
Iowa	2,452,677	17,380	882	2,520,691	16,694	883	2,599,546	19,692	1,825
Missouri	3,403,876	223,840	1,651	3,539,187	244,386	1,091	3,655,593	297,088	1,972
North Dakota	671,851	377	8,617	631,464	201	10,270	608,448	257	10,931
South Dakota	670,269	646	21,934	619,075	474	23,412	628,504	727	23,509
Nebraska	1,360,023	13,752	4,185	1,297,624	14,171	4,039	1,301,328	19,234	4,948
Kansas	1,811,997	66,344	2,658	1,734,496	65,138	1,394	1,828,961	73,158	3,180
S. Atlantic	11,349,975	4,421,388	22,226	13,095,227	4,698,863	29,061	16,041,709	5,094,744	45,882
Delaware	205,718	32,602	60	230,528	35,876	101	273,878	43,598	609
Maryland	1,354,226	276,379	921	1,518,481	301,931	832	1,954,975	385,072	2,054
Dist. of Col	353,981	132,068	820	474,326	187,266	1,499	517,865	280,803	5,310
Virginia	1,770,441	650,165	1,245	2,015,583	661,449	741	2,581,555	734,211	2,914
West Virginia	1,614,191	114,893	121	1,784,102	117,754	118	1,890,282	114,867	403
North Carolina	2,234,958	918,647	16,671	2,567,635	981,298	22,690	2,983,121	1,047,353	31,435
South Carolina	944,049	793,681	1,035	1,084,308	814,164	1,332	1,293,405	822,077	1,545
Georgia	1,837,021	1,071,125	360	2,038,278	1,084,927	518	2,380,577	1,062,762	1,209
Florida	1,035,390	431,828	993	1,381,986	514,198	1,230	2,166,051	603,101	9,153
E. S. Central	7,226,017	2,658,238	2,959	7,993,755	2,780,635	3,835	8,770,570	2,698,635	7,976
Kentucky	2,388,452	226,040	97	2,631,425	214,031	171	2,742,090	201,921	795
Tennessee	2,138,644	477,646	266	2,406,906	508,736	199	2,760,257	530,603	858
Alabama	1,700,844	944,834	570	1,849,097	983,290	574	2,079,591	979,617	2,535
Mississippi	998,077	1,009,718	2,026	1,106,327	1,074,578	2,891	1,188,632	986,494	3,788
W. S. Central	9,795,977	2,281,951	98,902	10,569,596	2,425,121	69,808	12,037,250	2,432,028	68,294
Arkansas	1,375,315	478,463	704	1,466,084	482,578	725	1,481,507	426,639	1,365
Louisiana	1,322,712	776,326	2,355	1,511,739	849,303	2,538	1,796,683	882,428	4,405
Oklahoma	2,130,778	172,198	93,064	2,104,228	168,849	63,357	2,032,526	145,503	55,322
Texas	4,967,172	854,964	2,579	5,487,545	924,391	2,888	6,726,534	977,458	7,202
Mountain	3,552,900	30,225	118,664	3,978,913	36,411	134,679	4,845,634	66,429	162,935
Montana	519,898	1,256	16,452	540,468	1,120	17,868	572,038	1,232	17,754
Idaho	438,840	668	5,524	519,292	595	4,986	581,395	1,050	6,192
Wyoming	221,241	1,250	3,074	246,597	956	3,189	284,009	2,557	3,965
Colorado	1,018,793	11,828	5,170	1,106,502	12,176	4,618	1,296,653	20,177	5,259
New Mexico	391,095	2,850	29,372	492,312	4,672	34,834	630,211	8,408	42,568
Arizona	378,551	10,749	46,273	426,792	14,993	57,476	654,311	25,974	66,302
Utah	499,967	1,108	6,772	542,920	1,235	6,155	676,909	2,729	9,224
Nevada	84,515	516	6,027	104,030	664	5,553	149,908	4,302	9,673
Pacific	7,868,518	90,122	235,793	9,370,641	134,295	228,326	13,725,797	504,382	253,338
Washington	1,521,661	6,840	34,895	1,696,147	7,424	30,620	2,316,496	30,691	31,778
Oregon	938,597	2,234	12,955	1,075,731	2,565	11,388	1,497,128	11,529	12,664
California	5,408,260	81,048	187,943	6,596,763	124,306	186,318	9,915,173	462,172	208,878

Source: Department of Commerce, Bureau of the Census; Sixteenth Census Reports, *Population*, Vol. II, and *U. S. Census of Population: 1950*, Vol. II, Part 1.

No. 27.—POPULATION, BY RACE AND NATIVITY, WITH INDIVIDUAL MINOR RACES: 1890 TO 1950

[See also *Historical Statistics*, series B 18–23, B 41–47]

CLASS	1890	1900	1910	1920	1930	1940	1950
All classes	62,947,714	75,994,575	91,972,266	105,710,620	122,775,046	131,669,275	150,697,361
White	55,101,258	66,809,196	81,731,957	94,820,915	110,286,740	118,214,870	134,942,028
Negro	7,488,676	8,833,994	9,827,763	10,463,131	11,891,143	12,865,518	15,042,286
Indian	248,253	237,196	265,683	244,437	332,397	333,969	343,410
Chinese	107,488	89,863	71,531	61,639	74,954	77,504	117,629
Japanese	2,039	24,326	72,157	111,010	138,834	126,947	141,768
All other [1]			3,175	9,488	50,978	50,467	110,240
Native (all races)	53,698,154	65,653,299	78,456,380	91,789,928	106,870,897	120,074,379	139,868,715 [2]
Foreign-born (all races)	9,249,560	10,341,276	13,515,886	13,920,692	14,204,149	11,594,896	10,347,396 [3]
Native white	45,979,391	56,595,379	68,386,412	81,108,161	96,303,335	106,795,732	124,780,860
Foreign-born white	9,121,867	10,213,817	13,345,545	13,712,754	13,983,405	11,419,138	10,161,168
Percent of total	100.0	100.0	100.0	100.0	100.0	100.0	100.0
White	87.5	87.9	88.9	89.7	89.8	89.8	89.5
Negro	11.9	11.6	10.7	9.9	9.7	9.8	10.0
Indian	.4	.3	.3	.2	.3	.3	.2
Chinese	.2	.1	.1	.1	.1	.1	.1
Japanese	(3)	(3)	.1	.1	.1	.1	.1
All other [1]			(3)	(3)	(3)	(3)	(3)
Native (all races)	85.3	86.4	85.3	86.8	88.4	91.2	92.1 [3]
Foreign-born (all races)	14.7	13.6	14.7	13.2	11.6	8.8	6.9 [3]
Native white	73.0	74.5	74.4	76.7	78.4	81.1	82.8
Foreign-born white	14.5	13.4	14.5	13.0	11.4	8.7	6.7

[1] Comprises Asiatic Indians, Koreans, Polynesians, and other nonwhite races.
[2] Based on 20-percent sample.
[3] Less than one-tenth of 1 percent.

Source: Department of Commerce, Bureau of the Census; *U. S. Census of Population: 1950*, Vol. II, Part 1.

No. 28.—WHITE POPULATION, BY NATIVITY AND PARENTAGE: 1890 TO 1950

[Data for native white based on 5-percent sample for 1940; for foreign or mixed parentage based on 5-percent sample for 1940, on 20-percent sample for 1950. Native of native parentage for 1940 and 1950 obtained by subtraction]

CLASS	1890	1900	1910	1920	1930	1940	1950
Total white	55,101,258	66,809,196	81,731,957	94,820,915	110,286,740	118,761,858	134,942,028
Native white	45,979,391	56,595,379	68,386,412	81,108,161	96,303,335	107,282,420	124,780,860
Native parentage	34,475,716	40,949,362	49,488,575	55,421,957	70,400,982	94,124,840	101,191,275
Foreign or mixed parentage	11,503,675	15,646,017	18,897,837	22,686,204	25,902,383	23,157,580	23,589,485
Foreign	8,085,019	10,632,280	12,916,311	15,694,539	17,407,527	15,183,740	14,824,005
Mixed	3,418,656	5,013,737	5,981,526	6,991,665	8,494,856	7,973,840	8,765,480
Foreign-born white	9,121,867	10,213,817	13,345,545	13,712,754	13,983,405	11,419,138	10,161,168
PERCENT OF TOTAL							
Total white	87.9	87.9	88.9	89.7	89.8	89.8	89.5
Native white	73.0	74.5	74.4	76.7	78.4	81.2	82.8
Native parentage	54.8	53.9	53.8	55.3	57.3	63.7	67.1
Foreign or mixed parentage	18.3	20.6	20.5	21.5	21.1	17.5	15.7
Foreign	12.8	14.0	14.0	14.8	14.2	11.5	9.8
Mixed	5.4	6.6	6.5	6.6	6.9	6.0	5.8
Foreign-born white	14.5	13.4	14.5	13.0	11.4	8.6	6.7

Source: Department of Commerce, Bureau of the Census; 15th Census Reports, *Population*, Vol. II; special report of 16th Census, *Nativity and Parentage of the White Population—General Characteristics*; 1950 Census of Population, advance tabulations of special report, *Nativity and Parentage*.

No. 29.—NATIVITY AND PARENTAGE OF THE FOREIGN WHITE STOCK, BY STATES: 1940 TO 1950

[Data for foreign-born white based on complete count; for native white of foreign or mixed parentage, based on 5-percent sample for 1940, based on 20-percent sample for 1950]

DIVISION AND STATE	1940				1950			
	Total foreign white stock		Foreign-born white	Native white of foreign or mixed parentage	Total foreign white stock		Foreign-born white	Native white of foreign or mixed parentage
	Number	Percent			Number	Percent		
United States	34,576,718	100.0	11,419,138	23,157,580	33,756,653	100.0	10,161,168	23,589,485
New England:								
Maine	257,921	.7	83,641	174,280	245,477	.7	74,342	171,135
New Hampshire	207,336	.6	68,296	139,040	191,664	.6	58,134	133,530
Vermont	102,907	.3	31,727	71,180	96,423	.3	28,753	67,670
Massachusetts	2,408,072	7.0	848,852	1,559,220	2,272,919	6.7	713,699	1,559,220
Rhode Island	416,124	1.2	137,784	278,340	387,429	1.1	113,264	274,165
Connecticut	954,381	2.8	327,941	626,440	964,354	2.9	297,859	666,495
Middle Atlantic:								
New York	7,133,650	20.6	2,853,530	4,280,120	6,803,774	20.2	2,500,429	4,303,345
New Jersey	1,971,350	5.7	695,810	1,275,540	2,013,656	6.0	630,761	1,382,895
Pennsylvania	3,128,960	9.0	973,260	2,155,700	2,830,289	8.4	776,609	2,053,680
East North Central:								
Ohio	1,650,306	4.8	519,266	1,131,040	1,578,548	4.7	443,158	1,135,390
Indiana	394,291	1.1	110,631	283,660	400,980	1.2	100,630	300,350
Illinois	2,953,233	8.5	989,373	1,963,860	2,684,567	8.0	783,277	1,901,290
Michigan	2,010,380	5.8	683,030	1,327,320	1,967,465	5.8	603,735	1,363,720
Wisconsin	1,196,194	3.5	286,774	910,420	1,059,349	3.1	218,234	841,115
West North Central:								
Minnesota	1,203,724	3.5	294,904	908,820	1,022,641	3.0	210,231	812,410
Iowa	580,585	1.7	117,245	463,340	482,637	1.4	84,582	398,065
Missouri	479,285	1.4	114,125	365,160	403,865	1.2	92,050	311,815
North Dakota	323,632	.9	74,272	249,360	241,442	.7	49,232	192,210
South Dakota	221,392	.6	44,052	177,340	173,752	.5	30,767	142,985
Nebraska	372,793	1.1	81,853	290,940	299,168	.9	57,273	241,895
Kansas	263,672	.8	51,412	212,260	217,997	.6	38,577	179,420
South Atlantic:								
Delaware	45,973	.1	14,833	31,140	48,304	.1	13,844	34,460
Maryland	265,495	.8	81,715	183,780	313,005	.9	84,440	228,565
Dist. of Columbia	100,314	.3	34,014	66,300	120,332	.4	39,497	80,835
Virginia	73,987	.2	22,987	51,000	128,920	.4	35,070	93,850
West Virginia	131,202	.4	41,782	89,420	110,821	.3	34,586	76,235
North Carolina	25,226	.1	9,046	16,280	46,334	.1	16,134	30,200
South Carolina	15,895		4,915	10,980	24,148	.1	7,503	16,645
Georgia	37,576	.1	11,916	25,660	51,405	.2	16,730	34,675
Florida	180,921	.5	69,861	111,060	336,991	1.0	122,731	214,260
East South Central:								
Kentucky	76,331	.2	15,631	60,700	75,973	.2	16,068	59,905
Tennessee	41,080	.1	11,320	29,760	51,210	.2	15,065	36,145
Alabama	38,057	.1	11,957	26,100	46,378	.1	13,813	32,565
Mississippi	22,988	.1	5,988	17,000	25,269	.1	8,314	16,955
West South Central:								
Arkansas	33,292	.1	7,692	25,600	33,479	.1	9,289	24,190
Louisiana	110,952	.3	27,272	83,680	116,124	.3	28,884	87,240
Oklahoma	98,319	.3	20,359	77,960	84,461	.3	18,906	65,555
Texas	811,808	2.3	234,388	577,420	932,280	2.8	276,645	655,635
Mountain:								
Montana	200,662	.6	55,642	145,020	168,184	.5	43,119	125,065
Idaho	103,716	.3	24,116	79,600	88,427	.3	19,407	69,020
Wyoming	61,259	.2	16,779	44,480	53,490	.2	13,290	40,200
Colorado	260,011	.7	70,471	189,540	244,897	.7	58,987	185,910
New Mexico	54,047	.2	15,247	38,800	60,621	.2	17,336	43,285
Arizona	122,817	.4	36,837	85,980	156,399	.5	45,594	110,805
Utah	138,738	.4	32,298	106,440	135,159	.4	29,844	105,315
Nevada	32,719	.1	10,599	22,120	34,795	.1	10,530	24,265
Pacific:								
Washington	591,803	1.7	203,163	388,640	633,421	1.9	191,001	442,420
Oregon	281,279	.8	87,639	193,640	309,042	.9	83,612	225,430
California	2,406,993	6.9	870,893	1,536,100	2,962,388	8.8	965,333	1,997,055

Source: Department of Commerce, Bureau of the Census; special report of Sixteenth Census, *Nativity and Parentage of the White Population—General Characteristics;* 1950 Census of Population, advance tabulations of special report, *Nativity and Parentage.*

No. 30.—Foreign-Born White Population, by Country of Birth: 1910 to 1950

[Percent not shown where less than 0.1. See also *Historical Statistics*, series B 279-303]

COUNTRY OF BIRTH	1910	1920	1930	1940	1950 Total	1950 Urban	PCT 1910	1920	1930	1940	1950
All countries	13,345,545	13,712,754	13,983,405	11,419,138	10,161,168	8,488,865	100.0	100.0	100.0	100.0	100.0
England and Wales	958,934	879,894	868,889	657,335	584,615	480,012	7.2	6.4	6.2	5.8	5.8
Scotland	261,034	254,567	354,323	279,321	244,200	211,019	2.0	1.9	2.5	2.4	2.4
Northern Ireland	} 1,352,155	1,037,233	178,832	.106,416	15,398	13,769	}10.1	7.6	1.3	.9	.2
Ireland (Eire)			744,810	572,031	504,961	464,043			5.3	5.0	5.0
Norway	403,858	363,862	347,852	262,088	202,294	136,495	3.0	2.7	2.5	2.3	2.0
Sweden	665,183	625,580	595,250	445,070	324,044	242,920	5.0	4.6	4.3	3.9	3.2
Denmark [1]	181,621	189,154	179,474	138,175	107,897	74,088	1.4	1.4	1.3	1.2	1.1
Netherlands	120,053	131,766	133,133	111,064	102,133	69,270	.9	1.0	1.0	1.0	1.0
Belgium	49,397	62,686	64,194	53,958	52,891	41,232	.4	.5	.5	.5	.5
Switzerland	124,834	118,659	113,010	88,293	71,515	49,008	.9	.9	.8	.8	.7
France	117,236	152,890	135,265	102,930	107,924	86,893	.9	1.1	1.0	.9	1.1
Germany	[2] 2,311,085	1,686,102	1,608,814	1,237,772	984,331	776,525	[2] 17.3	12.3	11.5	10.8	9.7
Poland	[2] 937,884	1,139,978	1,268,583	993,479	861,184	762,289	[2] 7.0	8.3	9.1	8.7	8.5
Czechoslovakia	....	362,436	491,638	319,971	278,268	217,315	....	2.6	3.5	2.8	2.7
Austria	[2] 845,506	575,625	370,914	479,906	408,785	346,102	} 3.3	4.2	2.7	4.2	4.0
Hungary	495,600	397,282	274,450	290,228	268,022	228,984	} 3.7	2.9	2.0	2.5	2.6
Yugoslavia [4]	....	169,437	211,416	161,093	143,956	115,181	....	1.2	1.5	1.4	1.4
U.S.S.R. [3]	}1,184,382	1,400,489	1,153,624	1,040,884	894,844	820,512	}18.9	}10.2	8.2	9.1	8.8
Lithuania		135,068	193,606	165,771	147,765	130,245		1.0	1.4	1.5	1.5
Finland	129,609	149,824	142,478	117,210	95,506	57,468	1.0	1.1	1.0	1.0	.9
Rumania	65,920	102,823	146,393	115,940	84,952	78,555	.5	.7	1.0	1.0	.8
Greece	101,264	175,972	174,526	163,252	169,083	157,786	.8	1.3	1.2	1.4	1.7
Italy	1,343,070	1,610,109	1,790,424	1,623,580	1,427,145	1,301,875	10.1	11.7	12.8	14.2	14.0
Spain	21,977	49,247	59,033	47,707	45,565	38,712	.2	.4	.4	.4	.4
Portugal	57,623	67,453	69,993	62,347	54,337	44,933	.4	.5	.5	.5	.5
Other Europe [5]	[4] 27,372	34,571	70,499	60,511	86,375	66,502	[4] .2	.3	.5	.5	.5
Asia [5]	96,535	115,734	159,837	154,321	180,024	162,570	.7	.8	1.1	1.4	1.8
Canada-French	385,083	307,786	370,852	273,366	238,409	191,818	2.9	2.2	2.7	2.4	2.3
Canada-other	[6] 816,063	[6] 823,334	[6] 931,631	[6] 792,114	756,153	599,390	[6] 6.1	[6] 6.0	[6] 6.7	[6] 6.9	7.4
Mexico	219,802	478,383	639,017	377,433	450,562	309,630	1.6	3.5	4.6	3.3	4.4
Other America	32,238	47,298	69,724	66,942	120,297	109,335	.2	.3	.5	.6	1.2
All other	} 40,167	67,512	70,921	58,630	69,658	51,462	} .3	.5	.5	.5	.7
Not reported					77,175	50,927					.8

[1] Iceland included with Denmark prior to 1930; included with "Other Europe" 1930 to 1950.
[2] Persons reported in 1910 as of Polish mother tongue born in Austria, Germany, and U.S.S.R. have been deducted from their respective countries and combined as Poland.
[3] Latvia and Estonia included with U.S.S.R. for 1910 and 1920 and with "Other Europe" from 1930 to 1950.
[4] Includes 4,635 persons born in Serbia and 5,363 persons born in Montenegro, which became parts of Yugoslavia in 1918.
[5] Includes Turkey in Europe.
[6] Includes Newfoundland which in 1950 was a Canadian province.

Source: Department of Commerce, Bureau of the Census; U.S. Census of Population: 1950, Vol. II, Part 1.

.—NATIVITY AND PARENTAGE OF THE FOREIGN WHITE STOCK BY COUNTRY OF ORIGIN: 1940 AND 1950

[foreign-born white based on complete count; for native white of foreign or mixed parentage, based on 5-percent sample for 1940, based on 20-percent sample for 1950]

BY OF BIRTH	1940					1950				
	Total foreign white stock		Foreign-born white	Native white of foreign or mixed parentage		Total foreign white stock		Foreign-born white	Native white of foreign or mixed parentage	
	Number	Percent				Number	Percent			
countries	34,576,718	100.0	11,419,138	23,157,580		33,750,653	100.0	10,161,168	23,589,485	
and Wales	2,124,235	6.1	657,335	1,466,900		2,027,845	6.0	584,615	1,443,230	
	725,861	2.1	279,321	446,540		707,525	2.1	244,200	463,325	
Ireland	377,236	1.1	106,416	270,820		45,288	.1	15,396	29,890	
(ire)	2,410,951	7.0	872,031	1,538,920		2,396,456	7.1	504,961	1,891,495	
	924,688	2.7	262,088	662,600		854,674	2.5	202,294	652,380	
	1,301,390	3.8	445,070	856,320		1,189,689	3.5	324,944	864,605	
	443,815	1.3	138,175	305,640		426,607	1.3	107,897	318,710	
ads	372,384	1.1	111,064	261,320		374,668	1.1	102,133	272,535	
	130,358	.4	53,958	76,400		138,391	.4	52,891	85,500	
nd	293,973	.9	88,293	205,680		287,175	.9	71,515	215,660	
	349,050	1.0	102,930	246,120		361,589	1.1	107,924	253,685	
	5,236,612	15.1	1,237,772	3,998,840		4,726,946	14.0	984,331	3,742,615	
	2,905,859	8.4	993,479	1,912,380		2,786,199	8.3	861,184	1,925,015	
vakia	984,591	2.8	479,906	664,620		984,158	2.9	278,268	705,890	
	1,261,246	3.6	479,906	781,340		1,225,250	3.6	408,785	816,465	
	662,068	1.9	290,228	371,840		705,102	2.1	268,022	437,080	
a	383,393	1.1	161,093	222,300		383,876	1.1	143,956	239,920	
a	2,610,244	7.5	1,040,884	1,569,360		2,542,284	7.5	894,844	1,647,430	
	394,811	1.1	165,771	229,040		397,590	1.2	147,768	249,825	
	284,290	.8	117,210	167,080		267,876	.8	95,506	172,370	
	247,700	.7	115,940	131,760		215,052	.6	84,962	130,180	
	326,672	.9	163,252	163,420		364,318	1.1	169,083	195,235	
	4,594,780	13.3	1,623,580	2,971,200		4,570,550	13.5	1,427,145	3,143,405	
	109,407	.3	47,707	61,700		115,055	.3	45,565	69,490	
	176,407	.5	62,347	114,060		172,012	.5	54,337	117,675	
rope	132,211	.4	60,511	71,700		214,405	.6	86,375	128,030	
	341,541	1.0	154,321	187,220		419,549	1.2	180,024	239,525	
French	908,386	2.6	273,366	635,020		757,904	2.2	238,409	519,495	
ther	2,048,774	5.9	792,114	1,256,660		2,224,478	6.6	758,153	1,466,325	
	1,076,653	3.1	377,433	699,220		1,342,542	4.0	450,562	891,980	
erica and not re-	133,282	.6	66,942	66,340		221,537	.7	120,297	101,240	
	303,850	.9	58,630	245,220		304,133	.9	146,833	157,300	

Department of Commerce, Bureau of the Census; special report of the Sixteenth Census, *Nativity uings of White Population—Country of Origin*; 1950 Census of Population, advance tabulations of special *tivity and Parentage*.

No. 32.—CITIZENSHIP AND NATIVITY OF THE POPULATION 21 YEARS OLD AN:
BY STATES: 1950

[See also *Historical Statistics*, series B 244-250]

DIVISION AND STATE	POPULATION 21 YEARS OLD AND OVER						FOREIGN YEARS AN	
	Total	Citizen			Alien	Citizen-ship not reported	Total	N u i
		All citizens	Native	Natural-ized				
United States	97,403,307	94,862,919	87,330,121	7,471,898	1,870,005	731,283	10,073,186	
New England:								
Maine	576,840	552,096	504,964	47,132	19,319	5,425	71,876	
New Hampshire	352,780	337,585	295,955	41,630	11,053	4,142	56,825	
Vermont	237,552	229,500	210,298	19,202	6,400	1,652	27,254	
Massachusetts	3,206,104	3,038,491	2,498,008	540,483	124,845	42,768	708,096	
Rhode Island	538,124	514,009	425,657	88,352	17,810	6,305	112,467	
Connecticut	1,382,373	1,297,483	1,089,300	208,183	62,739	22,151	293,073	
Middle Atlantic:								
New York	10,374,440	9,796,076	7,869,379	1,926,700	436,252	142,115	2,505,067	
New Jersey	3,354,160	3,217,130	2,733,221	483,909	100,099	36,931	620,039	
Pennsylvania	6,997,219	6,829,625	6,231,007	598,618	101,426	66,168	766,212	
East North Central:								
Ohio	5,279,761	5,181,253	4,844,999	336,254	68,327	30,181	434,762	
Indiana	2,556,467	2,531,960	2,459,062	72,928	15,876	8,602	97,405	
Illinois	5,958,601	5,801,882	5,183,837	618,045	94,264	62,455	774,764	
Michigan	4,106,606	3,968,014	3,515,081	447,933	100,148	43,449	591,525	
Wisconsin	2,222,423	2,184,093	2,007,432	176,661	20,420	17,910	214,991	
West North Central:								
Minnesota	1,910,153	1,873,326	1,703,035	170,291	19,217	17,610	207,118	
Iowa	1,694,619	1,676,476	1,612,069	64,407	9,073	9,070	82,550	
Missouri	2,643,129	2,619,739	2,553,444	66,295	11,836	11,554	89,685	
North Dakota	366,590	358,862	318,208	40,354	3,137	4,891	48,382	
South Dakota	401,146	396,611	371,156	25,355	2,189	2,446	29,990	
Nebraska	860,391	846,047	804,295	41,782	5,697	8,647	56,096	
Kansas	1,242,541	1,231,331	1,205,249	26,082	5,970	5,240	37,292	
South Atlantic:								
Delaware	210,918	207,410	197,406	10,004	2,259	1,249	13,512	
Maryland	1,527,089	1,500,329	1,445,339	54,990	19,129	7,631	81,780	
Dist. of Col	583,338	570,695	543,441	26,652	9,842	3,403	39,897	
Virginia	2,025,339	2,013,357	1,992,413	20,944	8,216	3,766	32,926	
West Virginia	1,171,878	1,160,622	1,138,367	22,255	8,466	2,790	33,511	
North Carolina	2,311,071	2,304,999	2,296,783	8,216	3,920	2,152	14,288	
South Carolina	1,150,567	1,148,289	1,143,909	4,380	1,501	977	6,958	
Georgia	2,005,828	2,003,177	1,993,283	9,858	3,483	2,174	15,545	
Florida	1,823,513	1,790,517	1,696,356	94,161	23,905	9,091	127,157	
East South Central:								
Kentucky	1,742,978	1,737,664	1,728,100	9,564	3,125	2,189	14,878	
Tennessee	1,978,548	1,973,444	1,964,702	8,742	3,277	1,827	13,846	
Alabama	1,747,759	1,743,611	1,734,473	9,138	2,517	1,631	13,286	
Mississippi	1,208,023	1,204,791	1,200,131	4,660	2,172	1,060	7,892	
West South Central:								
Arkansas	1,112,866	1,109,935	1,104,029	5,906	1,818	1,113	8,837	
Louisiana	1,587,149	1,577,244	1,559,048	18,196	6,820	3,081	28,097	
Oklahoma	1,382,108	1,376,350	1,364,263	12,087	3,377	2,381	17,845	
Texas	4,737,225	4,587,285	4,491,044	96,241	128,038	21,902	246,181	
Mountain:								
Montana	372,343	364,203	329,984	34,219	4,420	3,722	42,361	
Idaho	349,016	343,811	329,614	14,197	3,365	1,840	19,402	
Wyoming	178,581	175,136	165,414	9,722	2,294	1,151	13,167	
Colorado	844,748	826,964	785,632	41,332	13,189	4,595	59,116	
New Mexico	375,387	367,433	359,683	7,750	6,348	1,606	15,704	
Arizona	441,589	421,146	397,585	23,561	17,257	3,486	44,304	
Utah	389,843	380,051	360,352	19,699	6,235	3,557	29,491	
Nevada	107,173	103,662	96,592	7,070	2,630	881	10,581	
Pacific:								
Washington	1,559,266	1,507,786	1,367,785	140,001	36,316	15,164	191,481	
Oregon	1,001,716	980,192	918,268	61,924	15,192	6,332	83,448	
California	7,211,825	6,846,302	6,190,469	655,833	294,703	70,820	1,021,356	

Source: Department of Commerce, Bureau of Census; *U. S. Census of Population, 1950,* Vol. II, Pa

-Native Population, by State of Birth and by State of Residence:
1950

[-percent sample; see original source for sampling variability. Excludes small number of native
rn outside continental United States and persons for whom State of birth was not reported. For
torical data, see *Historical Statistics*, series B 182-230]

	BORN IN SPECIFIED STATE			Born in and living in speci- fied State	LIVING IN SPECIFIED STATE		
STATE	Total	Living in other States			Total	Born in other States	
		Number	Percent			Number	Percent
States............	138,072,605	35,284,220	25.6	102,788,385	138,072,605	35,284,220	25.6
d:							
	957,500	231,770	24.2	725,730	827,820	102,090	12.9
pshire......	499,000	172,055	34.5	326,945	469,185	142,240	30.3
	433,295	163,320	37.7	269,975	343,945	73,970	21.5
setts......	4,125,735	818,195	19.8	3,307,540	3,911,175	603,635	15.4
ind............	669,170	160,970	24.1	508,200	668,355	160,155	24.0
it............	1,534,210	325,490	21.2	1,208,720	1,681,565	472,845	28.1
atic:							
	11,760,830	1,904,180	17.0	9,756,700	11,716,430	1,959,730	16.7
y...........	3,493,420	679,400	19.4	2,814,020	4,132,985	1,318,965	31.9
nia.........	10,773,650	2,334,785	21.7	8,438,865	9,588,995	1,150,130	12.0
Central:							
	6,962,625	1,340,835	19.3	5,621,790	7,392,725	1,770,935	24.0
	3,810,930	957,790	25.1	2,853,140	3,793,695	940,555	24.8
	7,835,480	1,966,250	25.1	5,869,230	7,794,005	1,924,775	24.7
	4,903,590	802,330	16.4	4,101,260	5,674,665	1,573,405	27.7
	3,495,725	790,835	22.6	2,704,890	3,183,480	478,590	15.0
Central:							
....	2,998,685	829,100	27.6	2,169,585	2,737,730	568,145	20.8
	3,230,275	1,191,140	36.9	2,039,135	2,509,015	469,880	18.7
	4,463,465	1,609,015	36.0	2,854,450	3,808,260	953,810	25.0
tota............	794,430	361,140	45.5	433,290	564,645	131,355	23.3
tota............	782,255	347,255	44.4	435,000	615,545	180,545	29.3
	1,656,605	719,555	43.4	937,050	1,243,215	306,165	24.6
	2,241,870	998,300	44.5	1,243,570	1,839,495	595,925	32.4
tic:							
	273,230	79,045	28.9	194,185	299,795	105,610	35.2
	1,864,370	398,530	21.4	1,465,840	2,227,335	761,495	34.2
olumbia.........	512,990	249,440	48.6	263,550	740,855	477,305	64.4
	3,391,015	954,190	28.1	2,436,825	3,246,690	809,865	24.9
inia............	2,253,340	631,785	28.0	1,621,555	1,955,920	334,365	17.1
olina.........	4,430,510	900,435	20.3	3,530,075	4,005,315	475,240	11.9
olina.........	2,570,065	717,835	27.9	1,852,230	2,088,220	235,990	11.3
	4,109,885	1,189,185	28.9	2,920,700	3,395,195	474,495	14.0
	1,528,260	326,160	21.3	1,202,100	2,509,995	1,397,895	55.8
Central:							
	3,762,315	1,210,885	32.2	2,551,430	2,902,510	351,080	12.1
	3,669,060	1,050,145	28.6	2,618,915	3,255,640	636,725	19.6
	3,717,000	1,032,250	27.8	2,684,750	3,028,035	343,285	11.3
d............	2,874,955	947,275	32.9	1,927,680	2,153,580	225,900	10.5
Central:							
	2,563,570	1,100,335	42.9	1,463,235	1,883,905	420,670	22.3
	2,859,025	616,040	21.5	2,242,985	2,630,235	387,250	14.7
	2,428,900	1,083,870	44.6	1,345,030	2,190,980	845,950	38.6
	7,125,520	1,315,705	18.5	5,809,815	7,333,375	1,523,560	20.8
	522,670	218,165	41.7	304,505	538,505	234,000	43.5
	499,990	212,210	42.4	287,780	562,745	274,965	48.9
	214,015	104,055	48.6	109,960	273,380	163,420	13.2
	1,039,055	422,135	40.6	616,920	1,240,770	623,850	50.3
ico............	572,420	203,870	35.6	368,560	653,730	285,170	43.6
	455,760	164,070	36.0	291,690	691,650	399,960	57.8
	732,460	219,285	30.0	513,175	651,475	138,300	21.2
	92,925	45,895	49.4	47,030	146,215	99,185	67.8
n............	1,340,680	349,585	26.1	991,095	2,140,620	1,149,525	53.7
	853,720	244,615	28.7	609,105	1,414,490	805,385	56.9
	4,402,145	503,565	11.4	3,898,580	9,324,515	5,425,935	58.2

:partment of Commerce, Bureau of the Census; 1950 Census of Population, advance tabulations of
t, *State of Birth*.

No. 84.—Mobility Status of the Population, by Sex: April 1952

[Figures based on Current Population Survey, see Sampling Note, p. 181]

MOBILITY STATUS AND YEAR OF LAST MOVE	NUMBER			PERCENT		
	Total	Male	Female	Total	Male	Female
Total population, 1 year old and over, April 1952	150,494,000	73,468,000	77,086,000	100.0	100.0	100.0
Same house in 1951	120,016,000	58,356,000	61,660,000	79.8	79.5	80.0
Year of last move:						
Jan. 1950—Mar. 1951	23,198,000	11,492,000	11,706,000	15.4	15.7	15.2
Jan. 1941—Dec. 1949	58,484,000	28,388,000	30,096,000	38.9	38.7	39.0
Before 1941	24,930,000	11,494,000	13,436,000	16.6	15.7	17.4
Never moved	13,404,000	6,982,000	6,420,000	8.9	9.5	8.3
Different house (movers) in 1951	29,840,000	14,660,000	15,180,000	19.8	20.0	19.7
Same county	19,874,000	9,690,000	10,184,000	13.2	13.2	13.2
Different county (migrants)	9,966,000	4,970,000	4,996,000	6.6	6.8	6.5
Within a State	4,854,000	2,416,000	2,438,000	3.2	3.3	3.2
Between States	5,112,000	2,554,000	2,558,000	3.4	3.5	3.3
Abroad in 1951	638,000	392,000	246,000	.4	.5	.3

Source: Department of Commerce, Bureau of Census; *Current Population Reports*, Series P-20, No. 39.

No. 85.—Mobility Status of the Civilian Population, by Sex: April 1949, March 1950, and April 1951

[Figures based on Current Population Survey, see Sampling Note, p. 181]

MOBILITY STATUS AND PERIOD	NUMBER			PERCENT		
	Total	Male	Female	Total	Male	Female
APRIL 1948 TO APRIL 1949						
Civilian population 1 year old and over, April 1949	144,101,000	71,118,000	72,983,000	100.0	100.0	100.0
Same house (nonmovers)	116,496,000	57,321,000	59,177,000	80.8	80.6	81.1
Different house in United States (movers)	27,127,000	13,505,000	13,622,000	18.8	19.0	18.7
Same county	18,792,000	9,204,000	9,588,000	13.0	12.9	13.1
Different county (migrants)	8,335,000	4,301,000	4,034,000	5.8	6.0	5.5
Within a State	3,992,000	2,008,000	1,984,000	2.8	2.8	2.7
Between States	4,344,000	2,293,000	2,050,000	3.0	3.2	2.8
Abroad on April 1, 1948	476,000	292,000	184,000	.3	.4	.3
MARCH 1949 TO MARCH 1950						
Civilian population 1 year old and over, March 1950	146,864,000	72,618,000	74,246,000	100.0	100.0	100.0
Same house (nonmovers)	118,849,000	58,518,000	60,331,000	80.9	80.6	81.3
Different house in United States (movers)	27,526,000	13,769,000	13,757,000	18.7	19.0	18.5
Same county	19,276,000	9,519,000	9,757,000	13.1	13.1	13.1
Different county (migrants)	8,250,000	4,250,000	4,000,000	5.6	5.9	5.4
Within a State	4,360,000	2,278,000	2,082,000	3.0	3.1	2.8
Between States	3,889,000	1,972,000	1,917,000	2.6	2.7	2.6
Abroad on March 1, 1949	491,000	331,000	160,000	.3	.5	.2
APRIL 1950 TO APRIL 1951						
Civilian population 1 year old and over, April 1951	148,400,000	72,618,000	75,782,000	100.0	100.0	100.0
Same house (nonmovers)	116,936,000	56,968,000	59,968,000	78.8	78.4	79.1
Different house in United States (movers)	31,158,000	15,470,000	15,688,000	21.0	21.3	20.7
Same county	20,694,000	10,270,000	10,424,000	13.9	14.1	13.8
Different county (migrants)	10,464,000	5,200,000	5,264,000	7.1	7.2	6.9
Within a State	5,276,000	2,620,000	2,656,000	3.6	3.6	3.5
Between States	5,188,000	2,580,000	2,608,000	3.5	3.6	3.4
Abroad on April 1, 1950	305,000	180,000	125,000	.2	.2	.2

Source: Department of Commerce, Bureau of Census; *Current Population Reports*, Series P-20, No. 39.

LECTED SOCIAL AND ECONOMIC CHARACTERISTICS OF THE POPULATION,
1 YEAR OLD AND OVER, BY MOBILITY STATUS: APRIL 1951

sands. Figures based on Current Population Survey, see Sampling Note, p. 181]

ACTERISTIC	Total civilian population	Same house (non-movers)	DIFFERENT HOUSE IN THE UNITED STATES (MOVERS)					Abroad on April 1, 1950
			Total	Same county	Different county (migrants)			
					Total	Within a State	Between States	
old and over	148, 400	116, 296	31, 155	20, 694	10, 464	5, 276	5, 186	396
AGE								
	37, 626	28, 906	8, 654	5, 662	2, 992	1, 528	1, 464	66
	8, 462	6, 986	1, 490	1, 068	422	340	182	6
	3, 840	2, 686	1, 146	700	446	222	224	8
	10, 730	6, 622	4, 046	2, 588	1, 458	742	716	62
	11, 916	7, 854	4, 002	2, 508	1, 494	698	796	54
	11, 408	8, 478	2, 906	1, 874	1, 032	480	552	24
	21, 062	17, 166	3, 858	2, 718	1, 140	540	600	36
	31, 452	27, 806	3, 908	2, 708	1, 200	652	548	36
	11, 884	10, 732	1, 148	866	280	174	106	4
	30. 7	33. 2	25. 3	25. 7	24. 7	24. 4	25. 1	25. 9
(PERCENT)								
	100. 0	78. 9	20. 9	13. 7	7. 2	3. 6	3. 7	0. 2
	100. 0	78. 1	21. 7	16. 1	5. 6	3. 6	3. 0	. 3
RAL RESIDENCE								
	93, 400	75, 350	19, 856	13, 762	6, 094	2, 490	3, 604	234
	32, 248	34, 528	7, 636	4, 788	2, 868	1, 578	1, 292	64
	22, 752	19, 088	3, 646	2, 144	1, 802	1, 210	392	18
.Y STATUS								
	137, 630	109, 402	27, 980	18, 872	9, 108	4, 486	4, 622	248
	10, 770	7, 534	3, 176	1, 822	1, 356	790	566	56
GENT STATUS								
ars old and over	52, 810	41, 090	10, 710	7, 266	3, 552	1, 534	1, 666	110
	43, 178	33, 996	9, 082	6, 180	2, 902	1, 580	1, 342	96
	42, 134	33, 232	8, 814	6, 014	2, 800	1, 508	1, 292	58
	1, 044	766	268	166	102	42	60	10
	9, 632	7, 992	1, 628	1, 028	600	284	316	12
ears old and over	57, 354	45, 848	11, 404	7, 670	3, 734	1, 882	1, 852	102
	18, 602	14, 570	2, 982	2, 806	1, 176	600	576	50
	17, 888	14, 086	3, 732	2, 636	1, 096	576	520	50
	714	484	230	150	80	24	56	-------
	38, 752	31, 278	7, 422	4, 864	2, 558	1, 282	1, 276	52
N GROUP OF MALES IN CED LABOR FORCE								
	43, 134	33, 964	9, 672	6, 170	2, 962	1, 580	1, 382	96
hnical and kindred	2, 992	2, 312	674	378	296	148	148	6
managers	3, 930	3, 468	462	280	182	130	52	-------
ls, and proprietors,								
d kindred workers	5, 218	4, 296	922	696	226	120	106	-------
men, and kindred	5, 030	3, 964	1, 064	726	338	180	148	12
indred workers	8, 482	6, 618	1, 840	1, 232	608	260	348	24
	9, 040	6, 872	2, 148	1, 506	642	362	280	20
d foremen	2, 554	2, 062	476	362	114	40	74	16
farm and mine	1, 756	1, 288	462	218	244	188	56	8
	4, 018	3, 014	992	742	250	120	130	12

erienced labor force for whom occupation was not reported, not shown separately but included

ment of Commerce, Bureau of the Census; *Current Population Reports*, Series P-20, No. 39.

No. 37.—MOBILITY STATUS OF THE POPULATION, BY STATES: 1950

[Based on 20-percent sample of 1950 census returns; see original source for sampling variability]

DIVISION AND STATE	Total population, 1 year old and over	RESIDENCE IN 1949				PERCENT DISTRIBUTION				R de not pe
		Same house as in 1950	Different house, same county	Different county or abroad	Residence not reported	Total	Same house as in 1950	Different house same county	Different county or abroad	
United States	147,162,995	119,190,100	16,475,275	9,674,960	2,421,660	100.0	81.0	11.2	6.2	
New England:										
Maine	889,455	763,680	81,565	36,000	8,210	100.0	85.9	9.2	4.0	
New Hampshire	519,155	444,465	44,300	25,720	4,670	100.0	85.6	8.5	5.0	
Vermont	367,385	307,165	36,815	20,130	3,275	100.0	83.6	10.0	5.5	
Massachusetts	4,589,565	4,029,310	329,220	165,100	65,935	100.0	87.8	7.2	3.6	
Rhode Island	773,650	659,960	56,610	32,320	24,760	100.0	85.3	7.3	4.2	
Connecticut	1,960,580	1,711,410	153,200	67,100	28,870	100.0	87.3	7.8	3.4	
Middle Atlantic:										
New York	14,531,290	12,701,260	899,655	579,415	350,930	100.0	87.4	6.2	4.0	
New Jersey	4,732,425	4,117,780	325,215	225,340	64,090	100.0	87.0	6.9	4.8	
Pennsylvania	10,272,065	9,008,420	795,065	312,460	156,120	100.0	87.7	7.7	3.0	
East North Central:										
Ohio	7,741,200	6,441,860	846,625	342,830	107,685	100.0	83.2	11.0	4.4	
Indiana	3,833,780	3,142,520	431,585	220,560	39,115	100.0	82.0	11.3	5.8	
Illinois	8,513,800	7,130,945	858,710	384,065	140,080	100.0	83.8	10.1	4.5	
Michigan	6,204,125	5,139,680	671,500	302,525	90,420	100.0	82.8	10.8	4.9	
Wisconsin	3,346,430	2,833,525	327,885	156,120	28,900	100.0	84.7	9.8	4.7	
West North Central:										
Minnesota	2,904,505	2,432,510	271,345	165,425	35,225	100.0	83.7	9.3	5.7	
Iowa	2,572,965	2,111,610	257,750	156,760	46,845	100.0	82.1	10.0	6.1	
Missouri	3,867,885	3,123,310	420,395	252,635	71,545	100.0	80.7	10.9	6.6	
North Dakota	602,920	509,040	49,665	38,850	5,365	100.0	84.4	8.2	6.4	
South Dakota	633,975	521,280	56,200	46,305	6,190	100.0	82.2	9.2	7.0	
Nebraska	1,291,920	1,048,090	132,285	91,760	19,785	100.0	81.1	10.2	7.1	
Kansas	1,860,005	1,467,450	204,620	157,255	30,670	100.0	78.9	11.0	8.5	
South Atlantic:										
Delaware	309,560	261,865	29,750	12,845	5,100	100.0	84.6	9.6	4.1	
Maryland	2,284,780	1,861,375	210,020	162,415	50,970	100.0	81.5	9.2	7.1	
Dist. of Columbia	786,145	603,055	101,670	56,900	24,520	100.0	76.7	12.9	7.2	
Virginia	3,261,850	2,588,050	313,960	259,355	100,485	100.0	79.3	9.6	8.0	
West Virginia	1,955,185	1,621,915	213,980	98,290	21,000	100.0	83.0	10.9	5.0	
North Carolina	3,968,510	3,151,175	527,825	232,810	47,000	100.0	79.6	13.3	5.9	
South Carolina	2,061,565	1,646,200	281,145	108,160	26,060	100.0	79.9	13.6	5.2	
Georgia	3,354,110	2,519,630	512,160	272,195	49,125	100.0	75.1	15.3	8.1	
Florida	2,706,570	1,927,355	426,275	299,695	54,245	100.0	71.2	15.7	11.1	
East South Central:										
Kentucky	2,871,795	2,311,945	362,015	162,505	34,330	100.0	80.5	12.6	5.7	
Tennessee	3,212,420	2,478,885	481,230	207,120	45,185	100.0	77.2	15.0	6.4	
Alabama	3,002,480	2,317,565	460,750	169,570	54,595	100.0	77.2	15.3	5.6	
Mississippi	2,122,435	1,650,580	296,015	148,280	27,560	100.0	77.8	13.9	7.0	
West South Central:										
Arkansas	1,863,360	1,398,175	292,195	154,720	18,270	100.0	75.0	15.7	8.3	
Louisiana	2,625,085	2,114,060	308,100	148,865	54,040	100.0	80.5	11.7	5.7	
Oklahoma	2,183,055	1,603,690	332,490	219,815	27,060	100.0	73.5	15.2	10.1	
Texas	7,512,820	5,531,660	1,117,105	763,065	100,990	100.0	73.6	14.9	10.2	
Mountain:										
Montana	574,280	441,300	68,025	56,130	8,825	100.0	76.8	11.8	9.8	
Idaho	573,045	425,975	77,270	63,410	6,390	100.0	74.3	13.5	11.1	
Wyoming	282,315	201,100	39,690	37,645	3,850	100.0	71.2	14.1	13.3	
Colorado	1,290,475	951,325	170,280	149,720	19,150	100.0	73.7	13.2	11.6	
New Mexico	660,340	479,130	87,385	82,865	10,960	100.0	72.6	13.2	12.5	
Arizona	728,455	507,435	125,500	85,075	10,515	100.0	69.7	17.2	11.7	
Utah	668,005	532,410	80,150	50,415	5,090	100.0	79.7	12.0	7.5	
Nevada	156,055	107,735	22,610	22,885	2,825	100.0	69.0	14.5	14.7	
Pacific:										
Washington	2,320,935	1,713,855	348,965	211,890	46,225	100.0	73.8	15.0	9.1	
Oregon	1,484,225	1,076,775	221,795	164,135	21,520	100.0	72.5	14.9	11.1	
California	10,344,020	7,520,580	1,712,810	893,510	217,120	100.0	72.7	16.6	8.6	

Source: Department of Commerce, Bureau of the Census; *U. S. Census of Population; 1950*, Vol. II, Part 1

TVE POPULATION, BORN IN STATE OF RESIDENCE AND BORN ELSE-
WHERE: 1850 TO 1950

[See also *Historical Statistics*, series B 183-194]

Total	Born in State of residence	BORN IN OTHER STATES		State of birth not reported	Born in outlying possessions	American citizens born abroad or at sea
		Number	Percent			
17,742,961	13,457,049	4,251,250	24.0	34,662		
23,353,386	17,527,069	5,774,434	24.7	49,265		2,618
32,991,142	25,321,340	7,657,320	23.2	12,262	51	169
43,475,840	33,882,734	9,592,764	22.1		51	291
53,372,703	41,871,611	11,094,108	20.8	396,652	322	10,010
65,653,299	51,901,722	13,501,045	20.6	180,488	2,923	67,151
78,456,380	61,185,305	16,910,114	21.6	285,685	7,365	67,911
91,789,928	71,071,013	20,274,450	22.1	313,582	38,020	92,863
108,570,897	82,677,619	25,388,100	23.4	238,469	136,032	130,677
120,074,379	92,609,754	26,905,986	22.4	279,514	156,956	122,160
139,868,715	102,788,385	35,284,220	25.6	1,369,785	329,970	96,355

olored population only.
ulation of Indian Territory and Indian reservations, specially enumerated in 1890, with a
325,451 not distributed by State of birth. These areas were not enumerated prior to 1890.
of 1950 census returns; see original sources for sampling variability.

nt of Commerce, Bureau of the Census; 1950 Census of Population, advance tabulations of
of Birth, and records.

EN, 15 TO 49 YEARS OLD, AND NUMBER OF OWN CHILDREN UNDER
5 YEARS OLD: APRIL 1940 TO 1952

ased on Sample C (see p. 2); statistics for 1947, 1949, and 1952 based on Current Population
Survey (see Sampling Note, p. 181)]

AGE OF WOMAN	1952		CHILDREN UNDER 5 PER 1,000 WOMEN			
	Number of women, married, husband present	Number of children under 5 years old	1940	1947	1949	1952
ED STATES						
) years	26,658,000	15,626,000	452	526	555	586
	4,238,000	4,006,000	720	741	815	945
	4,904,000	5,030,000	796	908	920	1,026
	9,662,000	5,572,000	457	557	568	571
	7,854,000	1,018,000	117	120	127	130
URBAN						
) years	17,772,000	9,522,000	369	477	503	536
	2,848,000	2,442,000	614	662	748	857
	3,310,000	3,192,000	629	834	887	961
	6,424,000	3,362,000	380	522	515	523
	5,190,000	536,000	80	94	102	103
L NONFARM						
) years	5,294,000	3,508,000	516	568	632	663
	896,000	976,000	796	808	885	1,089
	1,008,000	1,166,000	803	970	993	1,157
	1,904,000	1,164,000	486	545	642	611
	1,486,000	202,000	124	139	130	136
AL FARM						
) years	3,592,000	2,596,000	618	641	631	723
	494,000	588,000	864	904	938	1,190
	586,000	692,000	980	1,096	1,049	1,164
	1,334,000	1,046,000	665	699	664	784
	1,178,000	280,000	212	183	202	238

nt of Commerce, Bureau of the Census; *Current Population Reports*, Series P-20, No. 46.

No. 40.—Gross and Net Reproduction Rates, by Color, Urban and Rural Residence, and Regions: 1905 to 1910, 1930 to 1935, 1935 to 1940, 1942 to 1947, and 1944 to 1949

[Statistics for 1905 to 1910 based on Sample W, and those for 1930 to 1935 and 1935 to 1940 based on Sample C (see p. 2): statistics for 1942 to 1947 and for 1944 to 1949 based on Current Population Survey made in April 1947 and April 1949, see Sampling Note, p. 181. Urban-rural classification is in accordance with 1940 definitions; see p. 2. A net reproduction rate of 1,000 means that each generation would just replace itself, if birth and death rates of a specified period were to continue indefinitely, in the absence of net immigration. A rate above 1,000 implies a potentially gaining population, and a rate below 1,000, a potentially declining population. A gross reproduction rate of 1,000 means that if all women born at the beginning of a generation were to live through their reproductive period and continue birth rates existing at the time of their birth, they would barely reproduce themselves, assuming no migration from outside the area. Where gross reproduction rate is less than 1,000, no improvement in mortality alone would prevent a potential decline in population]

COLOR AND AREA	NET REPRODUCTION RATE					GROSS REPRODUCTION RATE			
	1905–10	1930–35	1935–40	1942–47	1944–49	1905–10	1930–35	1935–40	1942–47
COLOR									
All classes	1,336	964	978	1,292	1,385	1,793	1,106	1,101	1,682
White	1,339	972	967	1,269	(¹)	1,740	1,060	1,062	1,396
Nonwhite	1,329	1,074	1,137	1,489	(¹)	2,340	1,336	1,413	1,712
AREA									
United States	1,336	964	978	1,292	1,385	1,793	1,106	1,101	1,682
Urban	937	747	726	1,085	1,186	1,298	839	815	1,177
Rural-nonfarm	1,409	1,150	1,150	1,465	1,628	1,956	1,206	1,294	1,596
Rural-farm	2,022	1,632	1,661	1,859	1,806	2,663	1,844	1,878	2,029
The Northeastern States[2]	1,120	826	794	1,123	(¹)	1,476	919	881	1,202
The North Central States[3]	1,308	943	944	1,267	(¹)	1,626	1,044	1,045	1,356
The South[4]	1,614	1,197	1,182	1,447	(¹)	2,393	1,382	1,363	1,610
The West[5]	1,166	892	941	1,232	(¹)	1,479	1,003	1,067	1,449

[1] Not available.
[2] New England and Middle Atlantic.
[3] East and West North Central.
[4] South Atlantic and East and West South Central.
[5] Mountain and Pacific.

Source: Department of Commerce, Bureau of the Census; special report of Sixteenth Census, *Differential Fertility, 1940 and 1910—Standardized Fertility Rates and Reproduction Rates*; and *Current Population Reports*, Series P-20, Nos. 18 and 27.

No. 41.—Annual Gross and Net Reproduction Rates, by Color: 1940 to 1949

[Statistics based on births reported by National Office of Vital Statistics, adjusted for under registration, and on annual life tables and population estimates by age. For meaning of gross and net reproduction rates, see headnote, table 40. For earlier annual gross reproduction rates, see *Historical Statistics*, series C 37]

YEAR	NET REPRODUCTION RATE			GROSS REPRODUCTION RATE		
	All classes	White	Nonwhite	All classes	White	Nonwhite
1940	1,023	1,000	1,205	1,116	1,079	1,414
1941	1,076	1,054	1,252	1,169	1,133	1,468
1942	1,190	1,173	1,316	1,282	1,253	1,511
1943	1,233	1,214	1,385	1,329	1,297	1,584
1944	1,171	1,141	1,385	1,266	1,216	1,577
1945	1,144	1,111	1,382	1,234	1,180	1,564
1946	1,359	1,340	1,515	1,443	1,411	1,683
1947	1,534	1,502	1,698	1,613	1,575	1,875
1948	1,462	1,415	1,798	1,543	1,484	1,975
1949	1,474	1,419	1,878	1,551	1,485	2,033

Source: Department of Health, Education, and Welfare, Public Health Service, National Office of Vital Statistics; annual report, *Vital Statistics of the United States*.

MARITAL STATUS OF PERSONS 14 YEARS OLD AND OVER, BY SEX—TOTAL POPULATION, 1890 TO 1940, AND CIVILIAN POUPLATION, 1947 TO 1952

[thousands. 1947-1952 based on Current Population Survey; see Sampling Note, p. 181. Civilian (April 1947 to April 1952) includes members of the armed forces living off post or with their families; excludes all other members of the armed forces. Armed forces included are as follows: 1947, 254,000; 1949, 393,000; 1950, 547,000; 1951, 610,000; 1952, 974,000]

Population 14 years old and over	Single	Married	Widowed	Divorced	PERCENT OF TOTAL							
					Crude Rates				Standardized for age [1]			
					Single	Married	Widowed	Divorced	Single	Married	Widowed	Divorced
21,501	9,379	11,205	815	49	43.6	52.1	3.8	0.2	36.7	57.9	5.0	0.2
25,414	11,090	13,956	1,178	84	42.0	52.8	4.5	.3	37.0	56.8	5.7	.4
33,362	13,485	18,093	1,471	156	40.4	54.2	4.4	.5	36.3	57.3	5.5	.5
37,954	13,998	21,882	1,758	235	36.9	57.6	4.6	.6	35.5	58.3	5.4	.6
45,088	16,150	26,328	2,025	489	35.8	58.4	4.5	1.1	34.7	59.1	4.9	1.1
50,554	17,593	30,192	2,144	624	34.8	59.7	4.2	1.2	34.8	59.7	4.2	1.2
52,350	14,760	34,638	2,181	818	28.2	66.2	4.1	1.6	30.9	63.9	3.7	1.5
53,227	14,734	35,411	2,055	1,027	27.7	66.5	3.9	1.9	30.5	64.2	3.5	1.8
53,448	13,952	36,474	2,181	842	26.1	68.2	4.1	1.6	29.3	65.5	3.6	1.5
54,287	14,212	37,022	2,176	878	26.2	68.2	4.0	1.6	29.4	65.5	3.6	1.5
53,420	12,984	37,354	2,216	866	24.3	69.9	4.1	1.6	28.2	66.7	3.5	1.5
53,564	12,868	37,830	2,102	764	24.0	70.6	3.9	1.4	28.1	67.3	3.3	1.3
20,298	8,928	11,126	2,155	72	34.1	54.8	10.6	.4	27.8	57.7	14.0	.4
25,024	8,337	13,814	2,718	115	33.3	55.2	10.9	.5	28.4	57.1	13.9	.5
30,959	9,342	17,688	3,176	185	31.8	57.1	10.3	.6	27.8	58.5	12.9	.6
36,190	10,624	21,324	3,918	273	29.4	58.9	10.8	.8	27.4	58.9	12.8	.8
44,013	12,478	26,175	4,734	573	28.4	59.5	10.8	1.3	26.9	59.7	12.0	1.3
50,549	13,936	30,090	5,700	823	27.6	59.5	11.3	1.6	27.6	59.5	11.3	1.6
54,803	12,078	35,212	6,376	1,140	22.0	64.2	11.6	2.1	24.1	63.1	10.7	2.0
55,364	11,623	35,783	6,725	1,233	21.0	64.6	12.1	2.2	23.3	63.4	11.1	2.2
56,001	11,174	37,012	6,582	1,233	20.0	66.1	11.8	2.2	22.6	64.7	10.5	2.1
56,635	11,126	37,451	6,838	1,220	19.6	66.1	12.1	2.2	22.5	64.8	10.6	2.1
57,354	10,946	38,124	7,064	1,200	19.1	66.5	12.4	2.1	22.2	65.1	10.7	2.0
58,034	11,068	38,670	6,972	1,324	19.1	66.6	12.0	2.3	22.3	65.3	10.2	2.2

[1] ...istribution used as standard. Figures show percent distributions with effects of changes in age
removed.
...arital status not reported, not shown separately.
...artment of Commerce, Bureau of the Census; *Current Population Reports*, Series P-20, No. 41.

No. 48.—MARITAL STATUS OF THE POPULATION 14 YEARS OLD AND OVER, BY BY STATES 1950

DIVISION AND STATE	MALE				FEMALE			
	Population 14 years old and over	Single	Married	Widowed or divorced	Population 14 years old and over	Single	Married	Widowed or divorced
United States	55,311,617	14,518,079	37,399,617	3,393,921	57,042,417	11,454,266	37,503,836	8,0
New England	3,455,230	991,754	2,242,187	221,289	3,709,869	933,848	2,253,679	
Maine	331,780	89,695	217,317	24,768	342,686	74,262	217,857	
New Hampshire	197,099	53,019	129,426	14,654	207,945	46,848	130,117	
Vermont	136,311	39,015	87,803	9,493	141,356	32,358	87,968	
Massachusetts	1,733,192	512,784	1,109,859	110,549	1,905,814	514,744	1,117,604	
Rhode Island	300,768	90,590	192,099	18,079	314,531	79,889	191,832	
Connecticut	756,080	206,651	505,683	43,746	797,537	185,747	508,301	
Middle Atlantic	11,360,821	3,113,110	7,588,008	658,703	12,073,287	2,765,883	7,657,978	
New York	5,616,963	1,549,627	3,751,890	315,446	6,033,574	1,396,777	3,794,988	
New Jersey	1,838,965	484,286	1,251,995	102,684	1,931,114	412,255	1,258,965	
Pennsylvania	3,904,893	1,079,197	2,584,123	241,573	4,108,599	956,851	2,604,025	
East North Central	11,340,558	2,824,558	7,784,716	752,684	11,595,126	2,237,984	7,740,352	
Ohio	2,935,808	690,429	2,038,936	206,443	3,060,868	583,658	2,034,945	
Indiana	1,448,831	334,960	1,014,612	99,259	1,486,515	260,592	1,012,389	
Illinois	3,309,125	846,005	2,241,186	221,934	3,418,775	674,982	2,241,529	
Michigan	2,368,024	595,093	1,620,012	152,919	2,349,955	440,298	1,610,981	
Wisconsin	1,278,770	357,671	841,970	79,129	1,279,013	278,454	840,508	
West North Central	5,224,331	1,386,590	3,512,419	325,322	5,293,994	1,054,374	3,511,187	
Minnesota	1,101,812	325,692	713,846	62,274	1,099,128	249,809	712,817	
Iowa	968,920	247,531	660,592	60,797	985,169	192,515	659,523	
Missouri	1,466,440	348,128	1,015,421	102,891	1,556,891	290,227	1,021,911	
North Dakota	230,502	79,986	139,467	11,049	207,649	47,972	138,449	
South Dakota	245,727	76,817	155,583	13,327	227,366	47,432	154,290	
Nebraska	496,732	134,383	334,216	30,133	497,059	96,769	333,277	
Kansas	712,198	174,053	493,294	44,851	720,732	127,650	490,911	
South Atlantic	7,455,623	2,048,627	5,027,932	382,064	7,734,562	1,581,510	5,071,176	
Delaware	117,542	29,920	80,540	7,082	122,763	25,122	80,971	
Maryland	863,852	227,271	587,425	49,156	884,036	177,646	586,999	
Dist. of Columbia	301,111	89,087	192,729	19,295	347,872	90,420	197,282	
Virginia	1,210,799	360,621	780,730	60,448	1,193,627	252,810	781,345	
West Virginia	700,823	191,384	470,057	39,482	704,919	147,899	469,136	
North Carolina	1,390,072	409,107	926,216	54,749	1,435,312	323,484	938,634	
South Carolina	688,217	203,243	458,853	26,121	733,249	165,525	470,145	
Georgia	1,168,086	307,088	804,327	56,671	1,247,615	235,013	823,792	
Florida	1,018,121	231,006	718,055	69,060	1,065,169	163,691	722,872	
East South Central	3,937,390	1,033,109	2,693,580	210,701	4,109,463	797,984	2,728,773	
Kentucky	1,039,654	282,429	695,990	61,235	1,048,459	209,319	695,284	
Tennessee	1,149,299	292,486	793,477	63,336	1,209,638	233,525	799,722	
Alabama	1,024,915	266,786	708,188	49,941	1,093,798	213,412	724,165	
Mississippi	723,522	191,408	495,925	36,189	757,568	141,728	509,602	
West South Central	5,163,744	1,277,456	3,581,076	305,212	5,268,309	902,033	3,592,059	
Arkansas	659,656	158,910	460,166	40,580	675,397	113,687	464,118	
Louisiana	914,015	236,374	630,055	47,586	968,553	185,330	643,519	
Oklahoma	808,400	193,018	561,938	53,504	822,794	132,665	562,431	
Texas	2,781,613	689,154	1,928,917	163,542	2,801,565	470,351	1,921,991	
Mountain	1,840,271	489,896	1,230,981	119,394	1,761,165	315,513	1,218,239	
Montana	227,271	65,864	144,198	17,209	202,470	34,687	141,691	
Idaho	213,170	53,510	145,650	13,670	198,781	31,992	144,491	
Wyoming	113,645	32,940	73,125	7,580	96,526	14,978	70,764	
Colorado	489,263	126,051	330,744	32,468	490,550	89,480	328,752	
New Mexico	233,244	66,052	154,157	13,035	223,050	44,974	182,913	
Arizona	263,546	68,104	177,562	17,880	259,511	47,636	176,600	
Utah	235,325	60,719	163,130	11,476	234,486	44,850	162,497	
Nevada	64,807	16,316	42,415	6,076	55,791	7,216	40,531	
Pacific	5,530,649	1,353,379	3,766,718	410,552	5,496,642	864,737	3,730,393	
Washington	919,661	238,492	612,237	68,932	862,214	133,118	603,809	
Oregon	576,808	131,916	401,369	43,523	561,087	84,938	397,351	
California	4,034,180	982,971	2,753,112	298,097	4,073,341	646,681	2,729,233	

Source: Department of Commerce, Bureau of the Census; *U. S. Census of Population: 1950,* Vol. II, I

No. 46.—FAMILIES, BY CHARACTERISTICS: APRIL 1952

[Statistics based on Current Population Survey, see Sampling Note, p. 181. For definition of families, see p. 3]

CHARACTERISTIC	ALL FAMILIES		MALE HEAD				FEMALE HEAD	
			Married, wife present		Other marital status			
	Number	Percent	Number	Percent	Number	Percent	Number	Percent
RESIDENCE								
All families	40,442,000	100.0	35,196,000	100.0	1,216,000	100.0	4,030,000	100.0
Urban	26,918,000	66.6	23,090,000	65.6	718,000	59.0	3,110,000	77.2
Rural nonfarm	7,844,000	19.4	6,998,000	19.9	220,000	18.1	626,000	15.5
Rural farm	5,680,000	14.0	5,108,000	14.5	278,000	22.9	294,000	7.3
SIZE OF FAMILY								
All families	40,442,000	100.0	35,196,000	100.0	1,216,000	100.0	4,030,000	100.0
2 persons	13,712,000	33.9	11,162,000	31.7	612,000	50.3	1,938,000	48.1
3 persons	9,974,000	24.7	8,660,000	24.6	306,000	25.2	1,008,000	25.0
4 persons	8,126,000	20.1	7,422,000	21.1	122,000	10.0	584,000	14.5
5 persons	4,402,000	10.9	4,064,000	11.5	100,000	8.2	238,000	5.9
6 persons	2,142,000	5.3	1,980,000	5.6	36,000	3.0	126,000	3.1
7 or more	2,084,000	5.2	1,908,000	5.4	40,000	3.3	136,000	3.4
RELATED CHILDREN UNDER 18 YEARS OLD								
All families	40,442,000	100.0	35,196,000	100.0	1,216,000	100.0	4,030,000	100.0
No related children under 18	17,524,000	43.3	14,746,000	41.9	808,000	66.4	1,970,000	48.9
1 related child under 18	8,902,000	22.0	7,708,000	21.9	182,000	15.0	1,012,000	25.1
2 related children under 18	7,340,000	18.1	6,600,000	18.8	130,000	10.7	610,000	15.1
3 related children under 18	3,668,000	9.1	3,362,000	9.6	60,000	4.9	246,000	6.1
4 or more	3,008,000	7.4	2,780,000	7.9	36,000	3.0	192,000	4.8
OWN CHILDREN UNDER 18 YEARS OLD								
All families	40,442,000	100.0	35,196,000	100.0	1,216,000	100.0	4,030,000	100.0
No own children under 18	19,176,000	47.4	15,670,000	44.5	984,000	80.9	2,522,000	62.6
1 own child under 18	8,164,000	20.2	7,326,000	20.8	114,000	9.4	724,000	18.0
2 own children under 18	6,874,000	17.0	6,348,000	18.0	72,000	5.9	454,000	11.3
3 own children under 18	3,444,000	8.5	3,228,000	9.2	30,000	2.5	186,000	4.6
4 or more	2,784,000	6.9	2,624,000	7.5	16,000	1.3	144,000	3.6
OWN CHILDREN UNDER 6 YEARS OLD								
All families	40,442,000	100.0	35,196,000	100.0	1,216,000	100.0	4,030,000	100.0
No children under 6	28,226,000	69.8	23,530,000	66.9	1,178,000	96.9	3,518,000	87.3
1 child under 6	7,162,000	17.7	6,830,000	19.4	16,000	1.3	316,000	7.8
2 or more	5,054,000	12.5	4,836,000	13.7	22,000	1.8	196,000	4.9
MARITAL STATUS OF HEAD								
All families	40,442,000	100.0	35,196,000	100.0	1,216,000	100.0	4,030,000	100.0
Married, spouse present	35,196,000	87.0	35,196,000	100.0				
Separated	476,000	1.2			92,000	7.6	384,000	9.5
Other married, spouse absent	464,000	1.1			56,000	4.6	406,000	10.1
Widowed	2,862,000	7.1			534,000	43.9	2,328,000	57.8
Divorced	560,000	1.4			60,000	4.9	500,000	12.4
Single	884,000	2.2			474,000	39.0	410,000	10.2
AGE OF HEAD								
All families	40,442,000	100.0	35,196,000	100.0	1,216,000	100.0	4,030,000	100.0
Under 25	1,914,000	4.7	1,738,000	4.9	54,000	4.4	122,000	3.0
25 to 29	4,224,000	10.4	3,954,000	11.2	40,000	3.3	230,000	5.7
30 to 34	4,902,000	12.1	4,556,000	12.9	66,000	5.4	280,000	6.9
35 to 44	9,646,000	23.9	8,676,000	24.7	200,000	16.4	770,000	19.1
45 to 54	8,088,000	20.0	6,954,000	19.8	242,000	19.9	892,000	22.1
55 to 64	6,490,000	16.0	5,442,000	15.5	266,000	21.9	782,000	19.4
65 to 74	3,722,000	9.2	2,902,000	8.2	200,000	16.4	620,000	15.4
75 and over	1,456,000	3.6	974,000	2.8	148,000	12.2	334,000	8.3
Median age (years)	44.5		43.5		55.2		51.9	

Source: Department of Commerce, Bureau of the Census; *Current Population Reports*, Series P-20, No. 44.

ꞮUSEHOLDS, URBAN AND RURAL, 1950, AND NUMBER OF HOUSEHOLDS, 1930 AND 1940, BY STATES

x definition of households, see p. 3. See also *Historical Statistics, series* B 171–175]

AND STATE	House-holds, 1930	House-holds, 1940	HOUSEHOLDS, 1950			
			Total	Urban	Rural non-farm	Rural farm
ates	29,904,663	34,948,666	42,857,335	28,509,435	8,580,048	5,767,852
	1,961,499	2,208,351	2,616,797	2,012,071	500,021	104,705
	197,826	220,272	254,668	134,077	89,760	30,831
Ɪre	119,337	133,714	155,174	89,191	52,852	13,131
	89,188	92,937	103,538	39,087	44,900	19,551
s	1,021,160	1,123,448	1,307,450	1,110,637	175,486	21,327
	165,343	188,028	225,558	192,537	30,228	2,793
	388,645	449,952	570,409	446,542	106,795	17,072
r	6,374,280	7,294,488	8,572,808	7,049,051	1,219,212	304,545
	3,153,124	3,670,802	4,329,699	3,745,342	432,915	151,442
	985,636	1,103,916	1,374,477	1,199,352	145,980	29,145
	2,235,620	2,519,770	2,918,632	2,104,357	640,317	173,958
ꞮƦral	6,362,822	7,290,676	8,829,542	6,254,465	1,576,535	998,542
	1,607,918	1,901,632	2,314,629	1,656,801	429,416	228,412
	843,066	963,470	1,169,305	716,173	264,987	188,146
	1,925,396	2,196,908	2,585,772	2,025,332	346,942	213,508
	1,180,554	1,399,660	1,791,651	1,275,694	328,732	187,225
	711,889	829,006	968,184	580,465	206,558	181,161
ƦꞮral	3,317,881	3,698,161	4,153,167	2,221,222	933,007	998,938
	606,496	730,135	845,733	477,751	183,045	184,937
	635,704	703,440	780,909	383,255	188,304	209,350
	939,476	1,070,909	1,198,977	748,108	207,368	243,501
Ꞵ	145,005	152,774	162,184	45,150	56,357	60,677
Ꞵ	161,013	166,140	182,981	63,893	55,797	65,291
	342,999	361,944	394,615	188,435	98,886	107,294
	487,188	512,819	587,678	314,630	145,160	127,888
	3,511,840	4,291,395	5,540,342	2,950,484	1,555,261	1,034,597
	59,092	70,806	90,361	56,588	24,544	9,229
	385,179	467,476	640,526	457,590	138,845	44,091
lumbia	125,554	174,020	224,099	224,099		
	529,089	630,184	845,716	429,375	248,889	167,452
Ꞵ	373,941	445,576	518,736	201,844	222,020	94,872
ꞮƦ	644,033	790,736	994,441	370,189	330,034	294,218
Ꞵ	365,680	435,211	514,672	211,824	160,340	142,508
	652,793	754,273	889,809	438,416	237,551	213,742
	376,499	523,113	821,982	560,559	202,938	58,485
ꞮꞮral	2,273,359	2,636,791	2,991,927	1,283,131	766,013	942,783
	609,405	699,527	779,669	320,419	224,134	235,116
	600,625	716,635	871,277	415,482	211,559	244,236
	591,625	675,091	786,205	373,196	198,881	214,128
	471,704	535,538	554,776	174,032	131,439	249,305
ꞮƦral	2,868,262	3,355,552	4,103,354	2,383,524	900,209	819,621
	438,639	496,398	524,706	192,192	134,660	197,856
	485,363	563,574	724,534	421,022	172,568	130,944
	554,164	612,461	663,292	360,656	156,981	145,645
	1,380,096	1,684,119	2,190,820	1,409,644	436,000	345,176
	914,406	1,126,190	1,446,725	837,019	390,969	218,737
	136,210	160,769	175,614	81,198	57,849	36,557
	106,044	142,611	169,264	77,102	49,228	42,934
	56,887	69,982	84,288	45,053	23,916	15,319
	257,324	317,225	391,577	255,304	84,258	52,015
	98,546	130,090	177,216	96,911	50,094	30,211
	105,992	131,897	210,403	123,945	67,434	19,024
	115,936	140,025	188,075	127,504	41,492	19,079
	25,469	33,591	50,288	30,002	16,698	3,588
	2,300,191	3,025,062	4,552,673	3,518,468	728,521	305,384
	423,833	540,171	736,988	485,305	174,270	77,413
	266,328	339,082	479,294	269,765	142,933	66,596
	1,610,030	2,146,809	3,336,391	2,763,398	411,618	161,375

rtment of Commerce, Bureau of the Census; Fifteenth Census Reports, *Population*, Vol. VI, Six-Ꞵeports, *Population*, Vol. IV, Part 1, and *U. S. Census of Population: 1950*, Vol. II, Part 1.

No. 48.—HOUSEHOLDS, FAMILIES, SUBFAMILIES, MARRIED COUPLES, AND UNRELATED INDIVIDUALS, URBAN AND RURAL: APRIL 1952

[Average not shown where base is less than 100,000. For definitions, see pp. 2, 3. See Sampling Note, p. 181]

SUBJECT	NUMBER				PERCENT			
	United States	Urban	Rural nonfarm	Rural farm	United States	Urban	Rural nonfarm	Rural farm
All households	45,464,000	30,550,000	8,838,000	6,076,000	100.0	100.0	100.0	100.0
FAMILIES								
All families	40,442,000	26,918,000	7,844,000	5,680,000	100.0	100.0	100.0	100.0
Primary families	40,076,000	26,614,000	7,808,000	5,654,000	99.1	98.9	99.5	99.5
Secondary families	366,000	304,000	36,000	26,000	.9	1.1	.5	.5
SUBFAMILIES								
All subfamilies	2,034,000	1,348,000	322,000	364,000	100.0	100.0	100.0	100.0
Husband-wife subfamilies	1,314,000	884,000	180,000	250,000	64.6	65.6	55.9	68.7
Other subfamilies	720,000	464,000	142,000	114,000	35.4	34.4	44.1	31.3
MARRIED COUPLES								
All married couples	36,510,000	23,974,000	7,178,000	5,358,000	100.0	100.0	100.0	100.0
With own household	34,968,000	22,906,000	6,974,000	5,088,000	95.8	95.5	97.2	95.0
Without own household	1,542,000	1,068,000	204,000	270,000	4.2	4.5	2.8	5.0
UNRELATED INDIVIDUALS								
All individuals	9,178,000	7,017,000	1,447,000	714,000	100.0	100.0	100.0	100.0
Primary individuals	5,388,000	3,936,000	1,030,000	422,000	58.7	56.1	71.2	59.1
Secondary individuals	3,790,000	3,081,000	417,000	292,000	41.3	43.9	28.8	40.9
AVERAGE SIZE OF UNIT [1]								
Households	3.32	3.18	3.37	3.95				
Families	3.54	3.40	3.63	4.10				
Primary families	3.55	3.42	3.63	4.10				
Secondary families	2.52	2.43						
Subfamilies	2.80	2.74	2.88	2.97				

[1] Average population per unit.

Source: Department of Commerce, Bureau of the Census; *Current Population Reports*, Series P-20, No. 44.

No. 49.—HOUSEHOLDS BY REGIONS AND DIVISIONS: APRIL 1940 AND 1950

[For definition of households, see p. 3. See also *Historical Statistics*, series B 17]

REGION AND DIVISION	1940	1950	Percent increase, 1940 to 1950
United States	34,948,666	42,857,335	22.6
Northeast	9,502,839	11,239,605	18.3
New England	2,208,351	2,616,797	18.5
Middle Atlantic	7,294,488	8,622,808	18.2
North Central	10,965,537	12,962,709	18.1
East North Central	7,290,676	8,829,542	21.1
West North Central	3,698,161	4,153,167	12.3
South	10,304,738	12,635,632	22.6
South Atlantic	4,291,395	5,540,342	29.1
East South Central	2,626,791	2,991,927	13.9
West South Central	3,386,552	4,103,354	21.2
West	4,152,252	5,999,396	44.5
Mountain	1,126,190	1,446,725	28.5
Pacific	3,026,062	4,552,673	50.4

Source: Department of Commerce, Bureau of the Census; Sixteenth Census Reports, *Population*, Vol. IV, Part 1, and *U. S. Census of Population: 1950*, Vol. II, Part 1.

No. 51.—Institutional Population, by Sex and by Type of Institution
States: 1950

DIVISION AND STATE	ALL CLASSES			Correctional institutions [1]	Specialized medical institutions	Institutions for aged and dependent [2]	Homes and schools for handicapped	Institutions for juveniles
	Total	Male	Female					
United States	1,566,846	949,628	617,218	264,557	710,003	296,783	155,183	1
New England	125,822	67,332	58,490	10,998	61,734	30,414	14,067	
Maine	9,861	5,583	4,278	1,097	4,379	2,235	1,396	
New Hampshire	7,416	3,852	3,564	536	2,717	2,466	732	
Vermont	4,298	2,214	2,084	449	2,062	820	494	
Massachusetts	69,422	37,266	32,156	5,752	36,664	15,674	7,900	
Rhode Island	8,051	4,109	3,942	551	4,727	1,761	28	
Connecticut	26,774	14,308	12,466	2,613	11,185	7,458	3,507	
Middle Atlantic	375,811	211,294	164,517	43,604	180,353	73,071	41,522	
New York	209,786	117,413	92,373	23,855	108,967	38,403	22,255	
New Jersey	50,479	27,737	22,742	6,193	25,920	8,314	7,222	
Pennsylvania	115,546	66,144	49,402	13,556	45,366	26,354	12,346	
East North Central	331,054	202,790	128,264	50,203	145,309	69,968	38,472	
Ohio	87,724	54,466	33,258	14,582	32,937	22,025	8,915	
Indiana	38,409	23,990	14,419	7,895	13,199	8,963	5,059	
Illinois	99,790	59,081	40,709	13,074	46,028	20,235	11,294	
Michigan	67,596	43,088	24,508	11,968	32,281	10,552	9,318	
Wisconsin	37,535	22,165	15,370	2,684	20,764	7,593	3,886	
West North Central	142,261	83,344	58,917	19,274	56,644	37,756	17,290	
Minnesota	30,887	17,985	12,902	2,976	13,858	7,683	4,970	
Iowa	27,493	16,043	11,450	2,595	9,967	8,952	4,210	
Missouri	38,009	21,277	16,732	6,809	15,893	9,726	2,524	
North Dakota	5,887	3,460	2,427	418	2,548	1,315	1,276	
South Dakota	6,654	4,420	2,234	561	2,710	1,996	876	
Nebraska	14,361	8,069	6,292	1,443	4,981	3,706	1,934	
Kansas	18,970	12,090	6,880	4,472	6,687	4,376	2,200	
South Atlantic	199,042	129,571	69,471	55,698	88,175	24,036	12,282	
Delaware	4,040	2,305	1,735	502	2,250	462	434	
Maryland	27,748	16,689	11,059	5,582	14,253	3,664	2,243	
Dist. of Columbia	13,088	7,964	5,124	1,085	7,721	2,780	305	
Virginia	36,482	25,395	11,087	11,673	14,605	4,723	2,800	
West Virginia	15,265	9,784	5,481	4,718	6,108	2,406	567	
North Carolina	32,692	21,440	11,252	10,252	13,187	2,965	1,866	
South Carolina	12,154	9,424	5,730	4,017	6,394	952	1,651	
Georgia	31,703	20,830	10,873	9,764	15,807	2,191	1,230	
Florida	22,870	15,740	7,130	8,105	7,880	3,873	1,176	
East South Central	85,241	57,384	27,857	19,437	39,143	10,819	5,729	
Kentucky	24,548	16,091	8,457	5,547	11,272	2,658	1,334	
Tennessee	26,612	17,549	9,063	4,686	10,865	5,535	1,585	
Alabama	21,430	15,028	6,402	6,143	10,370	1,062	2,143	
Mississippi	12,651	8,716	3,935	3,061	6,636	1,564	667	
West South Central	104,632	66,804	37,828	23,686	51,445	9,459	8,496	
Arkansas	13,060	8,648	4,412	2,183	8,054	726	542	
Louisiana	18,972	11,646	7,326	4,364	9,835	1,483	1,201	
Oklahoma	19,152	11,895	7,257	3,852	9,640	1,541	1,373	
Texas	53,448	34,615	18,833	13,287	23,416	5,709	5,379	
Mountain	42,447	28,095	14,352	8,729	18,870	6,171	4,351	
Montana	5,283	3,405	1,878	943	2,127	879	618	
Idaho	4,081	2,601	1,480	687	1,223	874	895	
Wyoming	2,754	2,070	684	476	1,436	212	415	
Colorado	15,246	9,380	5,866	2,323	7,609	2,225	1,053	
New Mexico	3,869	2,780	1,089	1,065	1,902	192	219	
Arizona	5,993	4,351	1,642	1,226	2,667	951	125	
Utah	3,906	2,467	1,439	805	1,369	615	919	
Nevada	1,315	1,041	274	504	457	223	7	
Pacific	160,536	103,014	57,522	32,928	68,530	35,689	12,069	
Washington	27,638	17,336	10,302	5,365	11,212	6,678	2,815	
Oregon	14,895	9,144	5,751	2,375	5,964	3,871	1,641	
California	118,003	76,534	41,469	25,188	51,354	25,140	7,633	

[1] Schools for juvenile delinquents included with institutions for juveniles.
[2] Homes exclusively for dependent children included with institutions for juveniles.

Source: Department of Commerce, Bureau of the Census; 1950 Census of Population, advance tabulatio special report, *Institutional Population.*

STATISTICS OF RELIGION—CHURCH MEMBERSHIP AND NUMBER OF CLERGY

[atest information available from religious bodies; excludes a few groups giving no data, such as Church Scientist, and Jehovah's Witnesses. Totals include, substantially, those religious bodies reporting to Census for Census of Religious Bodies in 1936. Not all groups follow same calendar year nor count up in same way; some groups give only approximate figures. Roman Catholics count all baptised including infants; Jews regard as members all Jews in communities having congregations; Eastern Churches include all persons in their nationality or cultural groups; most Protestant bodies count only ho have attained full membership, and previous estimates have indicated that all but a small minority are over 13 years of age; however, many Lutheran bodies and Protestant Episcopal Church now report ed persons, and not only those confirmed]

RELIGIOUS BODY	Year	Number of churches reported	Church member-ship	Number of clergy with charges
1.		264,592	88,673,005	181,123
h membership of 50,000 or over:				
Day Adventists	1951	2,728	245,974	
c Overcoming Holy Church of God	1951	300	75,000	850
ies of God	1951	5,950	318,478	
bodies:				
can Baptist Convention	1951	6,706	1,554,304	5,500
rn Baptist Convention	1951	28,289	7,373,498	20,058
ial Baptist Convention, U.S.A., Inc.	1951	25,350	4,467,779	26,350
ial Baptist Convention of America	1950	10,851	2,645,789	
can Baptist Association	1951	2,105	286,691	
Fill Baptists	1951	2,700	400,000	2,800
al Baptists	1951	654	50,487	400
ial Baptist Evangelical Life and Soul Saving Assembly of				
A	1951	1 264	1 57,674	128
ial Primitive Baptist Convention of the U.S.A.	1950	1,009	79,000	
tive Baptists	1950	1,000	72,000	
i American Free Will Baptist Church	1951	618	78,350	467
a (German Baptist): Church of the Brethren	1951	1,030	186,358	818
st Churches of America	1950	47	73,000	
inity Science Church	1951	3,851	682,172	4,321
n and Missionary Alliance	1950	882	53,935	544
ss of God:				
h of God (Cleveland, Tenn.)	1951	2,418	121,706	2,418
h of God (Anderson, Ind.)	1951	1,904	100,814	1,602
hurch of God	1951	1,508	54,560	1,222
of God in Christ	1951	3,505	323,305	2,864
of the Nazarene	1951	3,616	235,670	3,438
s of Christ	1951	14,500	1,000,000	1 6,500
tional Christian Church	1951	5,620	1,241,477	3,260
s of Christ	1951	7,835	1,792,985	3,692
Churches:				
ian Apostolic Orthodox Church of America	1951	57	130,000	45
Orthodox Church (Hellenic)	1952	320	1,000,000	340
nian Orthodox Church	1952	47	50,000	
nssian Orthodox Greek Catholic Church of North America	1950	399	400,000	
nssian Orthodox Church Outside of Russia	1951	91	55,000	150
n Eastern Orthodox Church	1947	46	75,000	
i Antiochian Orthodox Church	1951	77	75,000	77
tical and Reformed Church	1951	2,746	735,941	1,780
tical United Brethren Church	1951	4,457	720,544	3,126
ed Churches	1936	508	88,411	
: Religious Society of Friends (5 Years Meeting)	1951	490	68,612	279
dent Fundamental Churches of America	1946	650	65,000	
tional Church of the Four Square Gospel	1951	559	64,109	868
Congregations	1951	3,876	5,000,000	2,577
Day Saints:				
h of Jesus Christ of Latter Day Saints	1950	2,117	1,111,314	
anized Church of Jesus Christ of Latter Day Saints	1951	620	126,453	620
un:				
ican Lutheran Conference:				
erican Lutheran Church	1950	1,883	715,640	1,380
gustana Evangelical Lutheran Church	1951	1,121	465,062	783
angelical Lutheran Church	1950	2,501	895,455	1,150
heran Free Church	1949	356	59,860	162
ran Synodical Conference of North America:				
heran Church, Missouri Synod	1950	4,430	1,674,901	3,602
angelical Lutheran Joint Synod of Wisconsin and other States	1951	830	311,477	633
d Lutheran Church in America	1951	3,860	1,925,506	2,915
nite Church	1951	557	58,330	557

ata.

No. 52.—Statistics of Religion—Church Membership and Number of Clergy—Continued

RELIGIOUS BODY	Year	Number of churches reported	Church membership	Number of clergy with charges
Bodies with membership of 50,000 or over—Con.				
Methodist bodies:				
African Methodist Episcopal Church	1951	5,878	1,166,301	5,878
African Methodist Episcopal Zion Church	1951	3,090	728,150	3,440
Colored Methodist Episcopal Church	1951	2,469	392,167	1,820
The Methodist Church	1951	39,961	9,065,727	[1] 21,979
Pentecostal Assemblies:				
Pentecostal Assemblies of the World, Inc	1950	600	50,000	500
United Pentecostal Church	1950	1,200	100,000	1,200
Polish National Catholic Church of America	1951	156	265,879	147
Presbyterian bodies:				
Cumberland Presbyterian Church	1952	1,026	81,086	550
Presbyterian Church in the U. S.	1951	3,665	702,266	1,872
Presbyterian Church in the U. S. A.	1950	8,317	2,364,112	5,343
United Presbyterian Church of N. A.	1951	830	219,027	594
Protestant Episcopal Church	1950	7,116	2,417,464	----------
Reformed bodies:				
Christian Reformed Church	1951	368	155,310	271
Reformed Church in America	1951	767	187,256	278
Roman Catholic Church	1951	20,443	29,241,580	15,653
Salvation Army	1951	1,382	227,821	----------
Scandinavian Evangelical: Evangelical Mission Covenant Church of America	1951	489	51,850	430
Spiritualists: International General Assembly of Spiritualists	1947	175	150,000	----------
Unitarian Churches	1951	357	79,901	399
Universalist Church of America	1951	401	63,975	230
Other bodies		18,066	1,591,501	12,919

[1] 1950 data.

Source: National Council of the Churches of Christ in the United States of America; *Yearbook of American Churches, 1952*, as corrected in Sept. 6, 1952, issue of *Information Service*.

No. 53.—Statistics of Religion—Church Contributions From Living Donors

[Represents data for 47 religious bodies reporting annual contributions]

RELIGIOUS BODY	Reports for year ending—	TOTAL CONTRIBUTIONS		Benevolences [1]	Congregational expenses [2]
		Amount	Per member		
Total, 47 bodies [3]	------------	$1,286,633,160	$34.32	$249,801,078	$1,036,832,082
Bodies with membership of 50,000 or over: [4]					
Baptist: American Convention	Apr. 30, 1952	54,065,373	34.87	8,744,618	45,320,755
National Convention U. S. A., Inc.	June 30, 1952	310,000	.07	310,000	----------
Southern Convention	Jan. 1, 1952	222,838,109	31.53	37,268,172	185,569,937
Brethren, Church of	Sept. 30, 1952	7,367,138	44.01	2,485,442	4,881,696
Congregational Christian	Dec. 31, 1951	53,941,501	43.45	6,225,415	47,716,086
Disciples of Christ	June 30, 1952	60,118,020	33.52	8,263,638	51,854,382
Evangelical and Reformed	Dec. 31, 1951	29,123,386	39.19	4,135,981	24,987,405
Evangelical United Brethren	Oct. 31, 1951	29,451,876	41.09	5,413,872	24,038,004
International Foursquare Gospel	Dec. 31, 1951	3,527,546	46.21	509,930	3,017,616
Lutheran: American	---do------	25,821,698	49.26	4,828,809	20,992,889
Augustana Evangelical	Jan. 31, 1952	16,819,608	50.37	3,047,442	13,772,166
Evangelical	---do------	30,154,098	49.83	7,146,436	23,007,662
Missouri Synod	Dec. 31, 1951	66,431,204	55.51	11,910,393	54,520,811
United	---do------	57,942,546	40.70	13,252,272	44,690,274
Wisconsin and Other States	Dec. 31, 1950	7,487,925	34.92	1,475,795	6,012,130
Mennonite Church	Dec. 31, 1951	3,196,761	48.07	1,866,821	1,329,940
Methodist Church	---do------	268,623,814	29.63	40,120,363	228,503,451
Nazarene, Church of	---do------	27,099,068	111.76	4,480,990	22,618,078
Presbyterian: Cumberland	---do------	1,852,000	23.74	257,280	1,594,720
United	---do------	12,010,256	55.19	2,878,604	9,131,652
U. S.	Mar. 31, 1952	47,766,431	66.19	11,705,414	36,061,017
U. S. A.	Dec. 31, 1951	112,841,865	45.46	18,436,236	94,405,629
Protestant Episcopal	---do------	65,328,485	39.34	10,533,129	54,795,356
Reformed in America	---do------	11,972,727	62.90	2,522,777	9,449,950
Seventh-Day Adventists	---do------	41,056,175	157.80	34,122,264	6,933,911

[1] Includes contributions for home and foreign missions, charitable purposes, and foreign relief.
[2] Represents contributions to expenses of local parish or church (including building funds, repairs, fuel, minister's salary).
[3] Includes data for religious bodies not shown separately. [4] Based on membership 13 years old and over.

Source: National Council of the Churches of Christ in the United States of America; published in *Statistics of Giving*, November 15, 1952.

2. Vital Statistics, Health, and Nutrition

Vital statistics.—Vital statistics, including statistics of births, deaths, marriages, divorces, and communicable diseases, are compiled and published by the National Office of Vital Statistics, Public Health Service. Reports in this field are also issued by the individual State bureaus of vital statistics.

Births and deaths.—The national collection of mortality statistics on an annual basis was begun in 1900. For that year, the death-registration States consisted of 10 States and the District of Columbia. In 1915, the national collection of birth statistics was begun with 10 States and the District of Columbia. Beginning with 1933, the birth and death registration areas have comprised the entire United States.

Births and deaths are classified by place of occurrence and by place of residence [1] of the mother or of the decedent. In most of the following tables, the data are shown by place of residence.

Birth statistics include only live births. Most of the natality data refer to *registered births.* However, a number of tables also present birth statistics corrected for under-registration and corrected for incompleteness of the birth-registration area for years prior to 1933.

Death statistics include only deaths occurring in the continental United States and exclude deaths among armed forces overseas. Fetal deaths (stillbirths) are excluded from death statistics.

Marriages and divorces.—National collections of statistics on marriages and divorces in the United States were made for the years 1867–1906, 1916, 1922–32, 1937–40 and 1944–51. Estimates have been made for the intervening years as well as for years in which collections were not complete. At the present time, records of marriage are filed centrally in three-fourths of the States, and records of divorce in more than one-half of the States. Marriage and divorce data in the following tables are shown by place of occurrence.

Vital statistics rates.—Vital statistics rates are based upon population figures provided by the Bureau of the Census. The special situation created by the changes in size and disposition of the armed forces necessitated the use of different types of population bases during the war and postwar period.[2] Briefly, birth and divorce rates for 1941–46 for the United States are based on the total population including members of the armed forces overseas; those for States on the civilian population in the States. Birth and divorce rates for 1947–49, 1951 and death and marriage rates for 1941–49, 1951 for the United States and States are based on total population present in the area, excluding armed forces overseas. For 1940 and 1950, rates are based on the enumerated population as of April 1; for other years, rates are based on estimated midyear populations.

Cause-of-death classification.—Causes of death are classified according to the *International List of Causes of Death.* The sixth and latest decennial revision was put into effect beginning with data for 1949.[3]

Morbidity.—Statistics on morbidity are compiled and published by the Public Health Service. Each State health officer reports cases of selected diseases weekly and annually. The number of diseases reported to the State health officers depends on

---

Note.—This section presents data for the most recent year or period available on February 13, 1953, when the material was organized and sent to the printer. In a few instances, more recent data were added after that date.

[1] For a discussion of methods of residence allocation and of significance of residence figures, see *Vital Statistics of the United States,* 1949, Part II, pp. V–IX.

[2] For a discussion of the interpretation of crude rates during wartime, see *Summary of Natality and Mortality Statistics, United States,* 1943, Vital Statistics—Special Reports, Vol. 21, No. 1, 1945; and *Marriage and Divorce in the United States, 1867 to 1946,* Vital Statistics—Special Reports, Vol. 23, No. 9, 1946.

[3] For details on comparability of causes of death due to revision, see *The Effect of the Sixth Revision of the International Lists of Diseases and Causes of Death Upon Comparability of Mortality Trends,* Vital Statistics—Special Reports, Vol. 36, No. 10, 1951.

59

laws or regulations within the various States. However, most of the common communicable diseases are reportable in all States. Tables 93 and 94 show selected data on diseases reported to the Public Health Service.

In addition, data on illnesses are obtained by special surveys. The most comprehensive survey in this field is the National Health Survey made in 1935–36. Public Health Bibliography Series No. 5 gives extensive annotated citations to publications based on the National Health Survey. Morbidity studies of specific conditions, such as rheumatism and cancer, are in process. These data are supplemented by more intensive studies in specific localities such as Hagerstown and Baltimore, Md.

Medical care.—Annual statistics of medical care on a Nation-wide basis are obtained from the annual census of hospitals and institutions conducted by the American Medical Association. Such censuses include only hospitals, sanatoriums, and related institutions registered by that organization. Therefore, a relatively large number of institutions are not included in the survey. However, practically all of the large institutions in the country are canvassed with the result that most of the hospital bed facilities are usually included.

An index to one aspect of medical care is also provided by the numbers of births and deaths occurring in hospitals and institutions. These data may be found in the Public Health Service publications on vital statistics. Another aspect of medical care is provided by statistics on patients in hospitals for mental disease, and in institutions for mental defectives and epileptics. Beginning with the 1947 report, the annual reports are issued by the National Institute of Mental Health, Public Health Service; from 1926–46, the data were collected annually by the Bureau of the Census.

Nutrition.—Statistics on the apparent consumption of food per capita by civilians are estimated by the Bureau of Agricultural Economics of the Department of Agriculture. On the basis of these estimates, statistics on the nutritive value of the per capita food supply are computed by the Bureau of Human Nutrition and Home Economics. These statistics are published quarterly by the Bureau of Agricultural Economics in the *National Food Situation*. Methodologies and detailed information back to 1909 are available in Misc. Pub. No. 691, *Consumption of Food in the United States 1909–48*, and its supplements.

Statistics on Federal food distribution programs, and data on the quantity and costs of the food commodities distributed and the number of persons participating in the programs are published annually in *Agricultural Statistics*.

Under the provisions of Federal laws, food commodities are distributed for school lunches and to institutions and welfare cases. Statistics on direct distribution, without charge to recipients, of food commodities acquired by the Government and distributed under provisions of Section 32, Public Law 320 approved in 1935, Section 6 of the National School Lunch Act of 1946, Public Law 471, Eighty-first Congress, and commodities distributed under Section 416 of the Agricultural Act of 1949 on which the recipient paid the freight from point of storage, are presented in tables 98–100. Distribution to ultimate recipients is accomplished through cooperating distributing agencies in States. Cost represents cost to the Federal government of the commodity as delivered to the State distributing agency and includes cost of purchase, handling, warehousing, and transportation charges, but excludes cost of administrative expenses, except that $8.9 million expended for Section 416 commodities excludes transportation charges which were paid by recipients. Statistics on the indemnity plan, which is a subsidy program to expand markets for agricultural products, maintain outlets for government-owned commodities, and support school-lunch programs, are shown in tables 98 and 100. Sponsors of school-lunch programs are reimbursed by the government for local purchases of food on a basis of quality and quantity of meals served. This program was started in 1943.

Historical statistics.—See preface and historical appendix. Tabular headnotes (as "See also *Historical Statistics*, series C 24, C 45, C 77–78) provide cross-references, where applicable, to *Historical Statistics of the United States, 1789–1945*.

No. 54.—Births, Deaths, Marriages and Divorces and Rates Per 1,000 Population: 1900 to 1951

[Births and deaths are for registration States and represent registered births and deaths only; for births adjusted for underregistration, see table 56. For coverage of these areas, see table 55. Marriage and divorce data are for the United States. For additional rates, see Historical Statistics, series C 24, C 45, C 77–78]

YEAR	NUMBER				RATES PER 1,000 POPULATION [1]			
	Births	Deaths	Marriages [2]	Divorces [3]	Births	Deaths	Marriages [2]	Divorces [3]
1900		343,217	709,000	55,751		17.2	9.3	0.7
1905		345,863	842,000	67,976		15.9	10.0	.8
1910		696,856	948,166	83,045		14.7	10.3	.9
1915	776,304	815,500	1,007,595	104,298	25.0	13.2	10.0	1.0
1920	1,508,874	1,118,070	1,274,476	170,505	23.7	13.0	12.0	1.6
1925	1,878,880	1,191,809	1,188,334	175,449	21.3	11.7	10.3	1.5
1930	2,203,958	1,327,240	1,126,856	195,961	18.9	11.3	9.2	1.6
1935	2,155,105	1,392,752	1,327,000	218,000	16.9	10.9	10.4	1.7
1939	2,265,588	1,387,897	1,403,633	251,000	17.3	10.6	10.7	1.9
1940	2,360,399	1,417,269	1,595,879	264,000	17.9	10.8	12.1	2.0
1941	2,513,427	1,397,642	1,695,999	293,000	18.8	10.5	12.7	2.2
1942	2,808,996	1,385,187	1,772,132	321,000	20.8	10.3	13.2	2.4
1943	2,934,860	1,459,544	1,577,050	359,000	21.5	10.9	11.7	2.6
1944	2,794,800	1,411,338	1,452,394	400,000	20.2	10.6	10.9	2.9
1945	2,735,456	1,401,719	1,612,992	485,000	19.5	10.6	12.2	3.5
1946	3,288,672	1,395,617	2,291,045	610,000	23.3	10.0	16.4	4.3
1947	3,699,940	1,445,370	1,991,878	483,000	25.8	10.1	13.9	3.4
1948	3,535,068	1,444,337	1,811,155	408,000	24.2	9.9	12.4	2.8
1949	3,559,529	1,443,607	1,579,798	397,000	23.9	9.7	10.6	2.7
1950	3,554,149	1,452,454	1,667,231	385,144	23.6	9.6	11.1	2.6
1951	[4] 3,758,000	[4] 1,486,000	[4] 1,594,904	[4] 371,000	[4] 24.5	[4] 9.7	[4] 10.4	[4] 2.4

[1] Birth and divorce rates for 1941–46 based on population including armed forces overseas; for 1940 and 1947–51 based on population excluding armed forces overseas. Death and marriage rates for 1940–51 based on population excluding armed forces overseas.
[2] Estimated, except 1925, 1930, and 1944–51.   [3] Estimated, except for 1900, 1905, 1925, 1930 and 1950.
[4] Estimated.   [5] Preliminary.

Source: Department of Health, Education, and Welfare, Public Health Service, National Office of Vital Statistics; annual report, Vital Statistics of the United States, and News Release, FSA–E–33, July 9, 1952.

No. 55.—Birth- and Death-Registration States—Population and Number of States Included: 1900 to 1933

[Beginning with 1933 both birth- and death-registration areas comprise all States. For midyear estimates of population for 1934 and subsequent years, see table 7, p. 13. See also Historical Statistics, series O 1–5]

YEAR	BIRTH-REGISTRATION STATES			DEATH-REGISTRATION STATES		
	Population (midyear estimates)	Percent of U. S. total population	Number of States (incl. D. C.)	Population (midyear estimates)	Percent of U. S. total population	Number of States (incl. D. C.)
1900				19,965,446	26.2	11
1905				21,767,980	26.0	11
1910				47,470,437	51.4	21
1915	31,096,697	30.9	11	61,894,847	61.6	26
1916	32,944,013	32.3	12	66,971,177	65.7	27
1917	55,197,932	53.5	21	70,234,775	68.0	28
1918	55,153,782	53.4	21	79,008,412	76.6	31
1919	61,212,076	58.6	23	83,157,982	79.6	34
1920	63,597,307	59.7	24	86,079,263	80.9	35
1921	70,807,090	65.2	28	87,814,447	80.9	35
1922	79,560,746	72.3	31	92,702,901	84.2	38
1923	81,072,123	72.4	31	96,788,197	86.5	39
1924	87,000,295	76.2	34	99,318,098	87.0	40
1925	88,294,564	76.2	34	102,031,555	88.1	41
1926	90,400,590	77.0	36	103,822,683	88.4	42
1927	104,320,830	87.6	41	107,084,532	90.0	43
1928	113,636,160	94.3	45	113,636,160	94.3	45
1929	115,317,450	94.7	47	115,317,450	94.7	47
1930	116,544,946	94.7	47	117,238,278	95.3	48
1931	117,455,229	94.7	47	118,148,987	95.3	48
1932	118,903,899	95.2	48	118,903,899	95.2	48
1933	125,578,763	100.0	49	125,578,763	100.0	49

Source: Department of Health, Education, and Welfare, Public Health Service, National Office of Vital Statistics; annual report, Vital Statistics of the United States.

FIG. VIII.—VITAL STATISTICS RATES: 1915 TO 1951

[See tables 54 and 56]

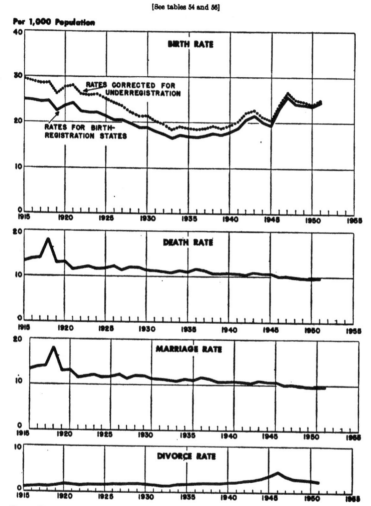

Source: Department of Health, Education, and Welfare, Public Health Service, National Office of Vital Statistics.

No. 56.—Registered Births, Estimated Births Adjusted for Underregistration, and Rates per 1,000 Population, by Race, for the United States: 1935 to 1950

[For total registered births, see table 34, p. 61. See also *Historical Statistics,* series C 25 and C 26]

YEAR	REGISTERED BIRTHS				BIRTHS ADJUSTED FOR UNDERREGISTRATION					
	Number		Rate [1]		Number			Rate [1]		
	White	Non-white	White	Non-white	All races	White	Non-white	All races	White	Non-white
.....	1,___,012	227,098	16.5	20.6	2,377,000	2,043,000	334,000	18.7	17.9	26.5
.....	1,___,___	252,927	16.4	20.1	2,355,000	2,027,000	328,000	18.4	17.6	26.1
.....	1,___,457	274,300	16.7	20.9	2,413,000	2,071,000	342,000	18.7	17.9	26.9
.....	2,___,366	261,017	17.2	21.2	2,496,000	2,148,000	348,000	19.2	18.4	26.3
.....	2,___,671	232,017	16.9	21.2	2,466,000	2,117,000	349,000	18.5	18.0	26.1
.....	2,___,___	284,446	17.5	21.7	2,556,000	2,199,000	360,000	19.4	18.6	26.7
.....	2,___,___	___,24	18.5	22.6	2,703,000	2,330,000	374,000	20.3	19.5	27.3
.....	2,___,694	322,062	20.6	22.3	2,989,000	2,605,000	384,000	22.2	21.6	27.7
.....	2,___,788	340,097	21.2	24.1	3,104,000	2,704,000	400,000	22.7	22.1	28.4
.....	2,___,___	348,100	19.5	28.7	2,939,000	2,545,000	394,000	21.2	20.6	27.5
.....	2,___,___	250,888	18.2	23.3	2,858,000	2,471,000	388,000	20.4	19.8	28.6
.....	2,___,945	373,027	22.0	24.3	3,411,000	2,990,000	420,000	24.1	23.7	28.4
.....	2,___,310	430,230	24.5	28.2	3,817,000	3,347,000	469,000	26.6	26.1	31.1
.....	2,___,318	464,782	22.9	30.5	3,637,000	3,141,000	495,000	24.9	24.9	32.1
.....	2,___,723	475,309	22.3	30.3	3,649,000	3,136,000	512,000	24.6	23.6	32.6
.....	2,___,037	463,313	22.7	31.1	3,632,000	3,108,000	534,000	24.1	23.0	32.8

[1] For 1941–46, rates based on population including armed forces overseas; for 1940 and 1947–50, rates based on population excluding armed forces overseas.

Source: Department of Health, Education, and Welfare, Public Health Service, National Office of Vital Statistics, based on data published in annual report, *Vital Statistics of the United States.*

No. 57.—Percent Completeness of Birth Registration, by Race and by States: 1940 and 1950

By place of occurrence. Percentages for 1940 show results of registration completeness test covering Dec. 1939 and Jan.–Mar. 1940 live births; percentages for 1950 give results of similar test covering live births in Jan.–Mar. 1950. For further details see "Methodology and Summary Results of the 1950 Birth Registration Test in the United States," published in "Estadistica," *Journal of the Inter-American Statistical Institute,* Vol. X, No. 37, Dec. 1952, pp. 601–630]

STATE	ALL RACES		WHITE		NONWHITE		STATE	ALL RACES		WHITE		NONWHITE	
	1940	1950	1940	1950	1940	1950		1940	1950	1940	1950	1940	1950
	92.5	97.9	94.0	98.6	82.0	93.5	Montana	97.6	99.8	98.0	99.8	91.1	96.9
							Nebraska	96.9	99.6	97.0	99.6	83.1	96.7
Alabama	85.2	95.9	86.4	97.1	82.4	94.0	Nevada	96.3	97.8	97.5	98.8	[1] 80.9	[1] 88.6
Arizona	84.4	92.1	93.8	97.5	68.4	86.6	New Hampshire	98.7	99.7	98.6	99.7	(2)	(2)
Arkansas	75.9	83.1	79.6	92.3	68.2	77.9	New Jersey	99.0	99.6	99.0	99.7	98.7	98.7
California	98.0	99.2	98.1	99.2	98.5	98.4	New Mexico	86.4	94.4	91.2	96.9	40.3	84.7
Colorado	92.8	96.8	92.8	96.7	[1] 80.4	97.7	New York	98.7	99.5	98.8	99.6	98.3	98.5
Connecticut	99.4	100.0	99.4	100.0	97.9	100.0	North Carolina	80.1	96.2	88.4	97.6	81.0	95.4
Delaware	97.4	92.3	97.2	99.5	98.6	98.8	North Dakota	94.7	99.3	94.6	99.4	95.2	96.7
Dist. of Col.	97.9	99.1	98.5	99.8	96.6	97.4	Ohio	96.3	99.0	96.3	99.0	98.7	98.0
							Oklahoma	84.8	96.0	87.0	97.3	66.9	86.3
Florida	82.9	97.5	91.3	98.8	86.4	94.1	Oregon	97.1	99.1	97.3	99.1	[1] 84.1	99.4
Georgia	81.3	94.5	83.6	96.7	77.6	91.0	Pennsylvania	97.0	99.4	97.2	99.5	92.9	98.4
Idaho	93.0	93.6	93.1	95.6	[1] 78.3	[1] 98.0	Rhode Island	98.8	99.9	98.8	99.9	[1] 100.0	[1] 100.0
Illinois	96.9	99.0	96.6	99.0	94.0	98.6	South Carolina	77.6	89.5	82.7	95.5	71.8	85.1
Indiana	94.6	92.3	94.7	99.3	[1] 80.1	98.1	South Dakota	93.4	98.4	94.6	99.2	79.6	83.7
Iowa	93.5	99.2	95.6	99.4	92.9	98.7	Tennessee	90.4	98.7	91.4	97.2	75.1	94.4
Kansas	95.8	99.2	95.9	99.3	87.6	94.0	Texas	86.3	96.0	86.3	97.2	66.7	88.9
Kentucky	59.2	94.8	59.2	94.7			Utah	96.6	98.8	97.1	99.1	[1] 59.6	[1] 52.3
							Vermont	97.3	99.4	97.3	99.4	(2)	(2)
Louisiana	86.1	95.5	87.7	97.0	83.7	98.5	Virginia	91.9	97.1	92.5	97.8	90.2	95.0
Maine	96.1	99.0	96.3	99.0	(2)	[1] 100.0	Washington	97.8	99.3	98.0	99.4	88.2	99.0
Maryland	97.1	99.1	97.5	99.3	94.1	98.7	West Virginia	93.8	94.2	95.7	94.5	81.3	90.9
Massachusetts	98.9	99.7	98.9	99.8	94.9	98.1	Wisconsin	96.9	99.6	96.9	99.2	98.2	98.7
Michigan	97.8	98.9	97.9	99.2	94.2	98.8	Wyoming	93.6	98.9	94.9	98.8	[1] 88.4	[1] 100.0
Minnesota	99.3	99.9	99.3	99.9	87.2	98.6							
Mississippi	82.8	97.8	93.8	94.6	84.3	97.2							
Missouri	90.2	98.0	90.7	98.1	82.7	96.5							

[1] Based on 25 to 99 records. Sizable variations in percentages based on these frequencies may arise from random factors.

[2] Not computed. Number of test records less than 25. Percentages based on so few records subject to considerable error.

Source: Department of Health, Education, and Welfare, Public Health Service, National Office of Vital Statistics, annual report, *Vital Statistics of the United States.*

No. 58.—Registered Births and Estimated Births Adjusted for Underregistration by Sex: 1935 to 1950

[For total registered births, see table 54, p. 61; for total estimated births, see table 56, p. 63].

YEAR	REGISTERED BIRTHS		BIRTHS ADJUSTED FOR UNDER-REGISTRATION		
	Male	Female	Male	Female	Male births per 1,000 female births
1935	1,105,489	1,049,618	1,219,000	1,158,000	1,053
1936	1,099,465	1,045,325	1,207,000	1,148,000	1,051
1937	1,130,641	1,072,696	1,238,000	1,175,000	1,053
1938	1,172,541	1,114,421	1,280,000	1,217,000	1,052
1939	1,162,600	1,102,988	1,255,000	1,201,000	1,054
1940	1,211,684	1,148,715	1,313,000	1,246,000	1,054
1941	1,289,734	1,223,693	1,387,000	1,316,000	1,053
1942	1,444,365	1,364,631	1,537,000	1,452,000	1,058
1943	1,506,959	1,427,901	1,593,000	1,510,000	1,055
1944	1,435,301	1,359,499	1,509,000	1,430,000	1,055
1945	1,404,587	1,330,869	1,467,000	1,391,000	1,055
1946	1,691,220	1,597,452	1,754,000	1,657,000	1,058
1947	1,899,876	1,800,064	1,960,000	1,857,000	1,055
1948	1,813,852	1,721,216	1,866,000	1,771,000	1,054
1949	1,826,352	1,733,177	1,872,000	1,777,000	1,054
1950	1,823,555	1,730,594	1,863,000	1,768,000	1,054

Source: Department of Health, Education, and Welfare, Public Health Service, National Office of Vital Statistics; Vital Statistics—Special Reports, Vol. 37, No. 7.

No. 59.—Registered Births by Attendant: 1935 to 1950

YEAR	NUMBER ATTENDED BY—			PERCENT ATTENDED BY—		
	Physician in hospital[1]	Physician not in hospital	Midwife, other, and not specified	Physician in hospital[1]	Physician not in hospital	Midwife, other, and not specified
1935	795,629	1,089,832	269,644	36.9	50.6	12.5
1940	1,316,768	825,271	218,360	55.8	35.0	9.3
1943	2,115,582	615,754	203,524	72.1	21.0	6.9
1944	2,112,963	493,463	188,374	75.6	17.7	6.7
1945	2,155,	402,890	176,	78.8	14.7	6.5
1946	2,708,	402,759	177,	82.4	12.2	5.4
1947	3,136,	375,407	187,	84.8	10.1	5.1
1948	3,025,804	323,434	186,	85.6	9.1	5.3
1949	3,087,228	289,981	182,972	86.7	8.1	5.1
1950	3,128,688	251,539	176,688	88.0	7.1	5.0

[1] It is assumed that all births in hospitals or institutions are attended by physicians.

Source: Department of Health, Education, and Welfare, Public Health Service; annual report, Vital Statistics of the United States.

No. 60.—Birth Rates per 1,000 Female Population, by Age of Mother, for Birth-Registration States: 1920 to 1950

[Rates based on registered births. For 1920, 1925, and 1930, excludes Maine as well as States not in registration areas; for 1935–50, includes entire continental U. S. For coverage of registration areas, see table 55. See also Historical Statistics, series C 28-35]

AGE OF MOTHER	1920	1925	1930	1935	1940	1945	1947	1948	1949	1950
15-44 years[1]	101.0	90.3	79.3	70.0	73.7	82.2	110.1	104.8	105.2	103.9
White	100.6	89.6	78.8	68.9	72.5	81.0	109.6	102.8	102.6	100.3
Nonwhite	107.2	98.9	83.2	78.7	83.3	92.4	114.2	121.5	126.4	126.6
10 to 14	.3	.4	.5	.5	.6	.7	.8	.9	.9	.9
15 to 19	48.5	50.1	49.1	44.7	48.9	48.8	76.7	79.7	81.5	79.1
20 to 24	151.8	134.7	124.9	114.7	125.3	130.1	200.1	192.8	194.8	192.5
25 to 29	150.5	131.1	117.3	107.0	114.4	126.4	160.3	160.3	162.9	165.0
30 to 34	115.5	103.9	87.7	73.5	77.4	94.7	107.5	100.3	99.5	101.5
35 to 39	78.4	69.3	56.1	45.4	41.9	54.6	57.3	53.3	52.6	51.2
40 to 44	31.1	27.2	21.8	17.6	13.9	15.5	15.9	15.1	14.8	14.6
45 to 49	3.8	3.0	3.0	2.4	1.3	1.3	1.2	1.1	1.1	1.0

[1] Rates for age group 15 to 44 years computed by relating total births, regardless of age of mother (including age "Not stated" and ages 50 and over), to female population 15 to 44 years. Figures for age "Not stated" have not been distributed among the specified age groups.

Source: Department of Health, Education, and Welfare, Public Health Service, National Office of Vital Statistics; records and Vital Statistics of the United States.

No. 61.—REGISTERED BIRTHS AND BIRTH RATES PER 1,000 POPULATION, BY STATES: 1940 TO 1950

[By place of residence. See also *Historical Statistics*, series C 24]

STATE	NUMBER OF BIRTHS					RATE PER 1,000 POPULATION [1]				
	1940	1943	1945	1947	1950	1940	1943	1945	1947	1950
United States	2,360,399	2,934,860	2,735,456	3,699,940	3,554,149	17.9	21.5	19.5	25.8	23.6
Alabama	62,938	77,535	70,321	86,116	82,616	22.2	28.2	26.2	30.0	27.0
Arizona	11,503	14,297	13,348	19,153	20,823	23.0	26.1	24.2	29.3	27.8
Arkansas	38,473	42,889	39,628	48,963	45,592	19.7	24.1	23.3	26.7	23.9
California	112,287	174,420	184,380	245,889	244,871	16.3	23.0	21.6	25.0	23.1
Colorado	21,034	24,367	23,511	32,874	33,885	18.7	23.2	22.3	26.6	25.6
Connecticut	25,548	39,005	33,765	45,581	40,620	14.9	22.2	19.3	23.2	20.2
Delaware	4,551	6,229	5,984	7,717	7,643	17.1	22.9	21.6	25.3	24.0
District of Columbia	11,228	16,080	16,141	21,686	19,826	16.9	19.2	19.7	24.4	24.7
Florida	33,799	46,744	47,791	59,807	64,644	17.8	22.9	22.6	23.7	23.3
Georgia	64,757	78,387	74,852	94,944	91,412	20.7	26.2	25.6	29.0	26.5
Idaho	11,789	12,391	11,501	16,255	16,035	22.5	26.5	24.6	31.3	27.2
Illinois	124,615	155,735	138,705	196,007	189,913	15.8	20.5	18.7	23.5	21.8
Indiana	61,660	74,672	68,444	96,359	93,479	18.0	22.1	20.3	25.5	23.8
Iowa	44,854	47,617	44,934	63,858	62,660	17.7	20.6	19.7	25.5	23.9
Kansas	38,885	36,021	33,624	44,535	43,928	16.0	21.2	20.4	24.0	23.1
Kentucky	63,768	65,566	60,892	79,987	75,026	22.4	25.7	24.0	28.5	26.5
Louisiana	50,848	62,005	57,538	74,630	76,362	21.5	26.7	25.0	28.9	28.5
Maine	15,222	18,944	16,687	20,322	21,061	18.0	24.2	21.3	28.0	23.0
Maryland	32,365	47,371	42,791	56,687	54,205	17.8	24.0	21.5	25.2	23.1
Massachusetts	65,551	85,917	77,064	107,791	96,214	15.2	20.9	18.9	23.5	20.5
Michigan	99,021	125,778	112,655	161,085	160,955	18.8	23.6	20.7	26.5	25.3
Minnesota	53,915	58,508	54,556	75,877	75,317	19.0	22.9	21.7	27.0	25.3
Mississippi	52,732	59,846	54,263	66,450	64,904	24.1	29.5	27.2	31.5	29.8
Missouri	61,479	72,458	65,559	90,060	85,924	16.2	20.3	19.1	23.4	21.7
Montana	11,556	11,407	10,601	15,086	15,611	20.7	24.0	22.5	26.4	26.4
Nebraska	22,029	25,048	24,128	32,132	31,799	16.7	20.9	20.7	25.4	24.0
Nevada	2,109	3,026	2,851	4,041	3,667	19.1	22.4	22.8	27.1	22.9
New Hampshire	8,329	9,367	8,338	13,267	11,517	16.9	20.6	18.4	26.2	21.6
New Jersey	59,814	83,032	77,338	106,242	97,802	14.4	20.3	19.3	23.0	20.2
New Mexico	14,792	15,211	15,306	20,322	22,092	27.8	31.1	31.1	34.9	32.4
New York	196,088	248,627	234,754	323,250	301,043	14.5	19.8	19.2	23.1	20.3
North Carolina	80,455	94,566	87,401	112,877	106,486	22.5	26.0	26.0	29.9	26.2
North Dakota	13,135	13,422	13,147	17,064	17,030	20.5	24.7	24.2	29.5	27.5
Ohio	114,663	144,067	132,496	197,311	185,850	16.6	21.1	19.3	25.6	23.4
Oklahoma	44,887	48,639	43,165	53,684	50,120	19.2	23.5	22.3	25.2	22.4
Oregon	17,623	25,450	24,140	36,294	36,079	16.2	22.2	19.5	26.7	23.7
Pennsylvania	165,486	199,366	173,799	248,513	221,635	16.7	21.4	19.1	24.4	21.1
Rhode Island	10,830	14,667	13,635	18,536	16,210	15.2	21.2	19.8	23.9	20.5
South Carolina	44,612	54,144	49,431	59,470	57,450	23.5	30.0	27.3	29.9	27.1
South Dakota	12,064	12,816	12,460	16,539	17,806	18.7	22.9	22.7	27.5	27.3
Tennessee	55,242	70,203	64,966	86,619	81,376	18.9	24.8	22.9	27.4	24.7
Texas	127,072	164,513	157,915	198,662	203,841	19.8	26.2	24.8	26.9	26.4
Utah	13,347	17,161	15,680	21,724	21,192	24.3	29.8	27.7	34.2	30.8
Vermont	6,942	7,303	6,873	9,708	9,003	19.3	22.9	21.8	27.4	23.8
Virginia	57,014	72,187	67,068	85,740	82,021	21.3	26.1	23.9	26.8	24.7
Washington	28,159	44,520	44,573	58,481	55,817	16.2	24.1	21.6	26.5	23.5
West Virginia	42,269	43,372	39,039	55,085	50,307	22.2	25.0	23.0	29.3	25.2
Wisconsin	54,891	64,480	61,437	84,059	82,674	17.5	21.8	20.9	25.9	24.1
Wyoming	5,189	5,822	5,481	7,320	7,806	20.7	26.0	24.1	28.4	26.2

For 1940, 1947, and 1950, rates based on total population in each specified area (excluding armed forces overseas). For 1943 and 1945, rates for the United States based on population including armed forces overseas; rates for States based on civilian population. United States rates on civilian population base were: 23.0 (1943) and 21.4 (1945).

Source: Department of Health, Education, and Welfare, Public Health Service, National Office of Vital Statistics; *Vital Statistics—Special Reports*, Vol. 37, No. 7.

No. 62.—Registered Births by Race, for Urban and Rural Areas, by States: 1950

[By place of residence. For total births by States, see table 61]

STATE	TOTAL		URBAN [1]			RURAL [1]		
	White	Non-white	All races	White	Non-white	All races	White	Non-white
United States	3,063,627	490,522	2,155,061	1,870,858	284,223	1,399,068	1,192,769	206,299
Alabama	49,778	32,838	33,429	20,522	12,907	49,187	29,256	19,931
Arizona	17,635	3,188	10,793	10,087	706	10,030	7,548	2,482
Arkansas	33,216	12,376	15,814	12,101	3,713	29,778	21,115	8,663
California	224,318	20,553	170,070	153,518	16,552	74,801	70,800	4,001
Colorado	33,039	846	21,306	20,581	725	12,579	12,458	121
Connecticut	39,192	1,428	26,661	25,331	1,330	13,959	13,861	98
Delaware	6,256	1,385	3,788	3,055	703	3,885	3,203	682
Dist. of Columbia	11,102	8,724	19,826	11,102	8,724			
Florida	45,877	18,767	40,144	28,449	11,695	24,500	17,428	7,072
Georgia	56,670	34,742	42,887	27,674	15,213	48,525	28,996	19,529
Idaho	15,768	267	7,454	7,379	75	8,581	8,389	192
Illinois	170,014	19,899	145,153	125,793	19,360	44,760	44,221	539
Indiana	88,325	5,154	58,821	53,808	5,013	34,658	34,517	141
Iowa	62,034	626	30,767	30,171	596	31,893	31,863	30
Kansas	41,912	2,016	24,725	22,886	1,839	19,203	19,026	177
Kentucky	69,645	5,381	27,278	23,789	3,489	47,748	45,856	1,892
Louisiana	45,207	31,155	41,372	25,801	15,571	34,990	19,406	15,584
Maine	21,002	59	8,086	8,056	30	12,975	12,946	29
Maryland	42,256	11,949	29,440	21,355	8,085	24,765	20,901	3,864
Massachusetts	93,971	2,243	84,579	82,501	2,078	11,635	11,470	165
Michigan	146,918	14,037	109,583	96,321	13,262	51,372	50,597	775
Minnesota	74,296	1,021	40,822	40,292	530	34,495	34,004	491
Mississippi	27,447	37,457	17,988	9,673	8,315	46,916	17,774	29,142
Missouri	77,577	8,347	52,727	45,529	7,198	33,197	32,048	1,149
Montana	14,772	839	7,997	7,878	119	7,614	6,894	720
Nebraska	31,015	784	16,204	15,534	670	15,595	15,481	114
Nevada	3,376	291	2,091	1,960	131	1,576	1,416	160
New Hampshire	11,503	14	6,537	6,525	12	4,980	4,978	2
New Jersey	88,296	9,506	78,051	69,918	8,133	19,751	18,378	1,373
New Mexico	20,438	1,654	11,251	10,933	318	10,841	9,505	1,336
New York	273,804	27,239	235,806	209,624	26,182	65,237	64,180	1,057
North Carolina	70,205	36,281	35,465	24,749	10,716	71,021	45,456	25,565
North Dakota	16,600	430	5,075	5,042	33	11,955	11,558	397
Ohio	171,021	14,829	130,334	116,433	13,901	55,516	54,588	928
Oklahoma	44,277	5,843	28,064	25,083	2,981	22,056	19,194	2,862
Oregon	35,372	707	21,393	20,895	498	14,686	14,477	209
Pennsylvania	204,177	17,458	149,502	133,069	16,433	72,133	71,108	1,025
Rhode Island	15,796	412	14,263	13,884	379	1,947	1,914	33
South Carolina	30,755	26,695	18,341	12,015	6,326	39,109	18,740	20,369
South Dakota	16,937	869	6,740	6,645	95	11,066	10,292	774
Tennessee	65,230	16,146	32,864	23,289	9,575	48,512	41,941	6,571
Texas	176,345	27,496	139,128	121,398	17,730	64,713	54,947	9,766
Utah	20,846	346	13,181	13,021	160	8,011	7,825	186
Vermont	8,998	5	3,499	3,494	5	5,504	5,504	
Virginia	60,659	21,362	32,804	24,325	8,479	49,217	36,334	12,883
Washington	53,537	1,980	36,128	34,667	1,461	19,689	19,170	519
West Virginia	47,366	3,141	16,663	15,622	1,041	33,844	31,744	2,100
Wisconsin	81,162	1,512	45,740	44,674	1,066	36,934	36,488	446
Wyoming	7,381	225	4,477	4,407	70	3,129	2,974	155

[1] Urban places include every incorporated place having population of 2,500 or more in 1950, as well as certain unincorporated places defined as "urban" according to special rules. "Rural" includes all other areas.

Source: Department of Health, Education, and Welfare, Public Health Service, National Office of Vital Statistics; annual report, Vital Statistics of the United States.

No. 68.—REGISTERED BIRTHS BY ATTENDANT, BY STATES: 1950

[By place of residence. For total births by States, see table 61]

STATE	NUMBER ATTENDED BY—				PERCENT ATTENDED BY—			
	Physician in hospital [1]	Physician not in hospital	Midwife	Other and not specified	Physician in hospital [1]	Physician not in hospital	Midwife	Other and not specified
United States	3,125,975	251,539	161,089	15,536	88.0	7.1	4.5	0.4
a	49,401	14,204	18,024	987	59.8	17.2	21.8	1.2
.	18,887	720	763	453	90.7	3.5	3.7	2.2
as	29,448	8,513	7,275	356	64.6	18.7	16.0	.8
nia	240,463	3,361	266	781	98.2	1.4	.1	.3
lo	31,891	1,618	175	201	94.1	4.8	.5	.6
ticut	40,412	195	5	8	99.5	.5	(²)	(²)
re	6,958	262	401	22	91.0	3.4	5.2	.3
t of Columbia	19,453	360	7	6	98.1	1.8	(²)	(²)
	50,809	4,512	8,961	362	78.6	7.0	13.9	.6
L	63,522	8,227	18,069	1,594	69.5	9.0	19.8	1.7
	15,761	232	14	28	98.3	1.4	.1	.2
	180,862	8,688	181	182	95.2	4.6	.1	.1
.	87,152	5,711	90	526	93.2	6.1	.1	.6
	60,408	2,205	25	22	96.4	3.5	(²)	(²)
	42,092	1,801	17	18	95.8	4.1	(²)	(²)
ky	48,761	21,034	4,600	631	65.0	28.0	6.1	.8
na	63,679	3,852	8,215	616	83.4	5.0	10.8	.8
	19,411	1,633	7	10	92.2	7.8	(²)	(²)
nd	48,197	4,021	1,745	242	88.9	7.4	3.2	.4
husetts	95,092	1,106	5	11	98.8	1.1	(²)	(²)
an	155,916	4,801	111	127	96.9	3.0	.1	.1
ota	73,854	1,216	134	113	98.1	1.6	.2	.2
ippi	29,802	11,320	23,096	686	45.9	17.4	35.6	1.1
ri	73,875	10,681	1,004	364	86.0	12.4	1.2	.4
a	15,230	296	48	37	97.6	1.9	.3	.2
ka	30,785	991	5	18	96.8	3.1	(²)	.1
.	3,588	53	1	25	97.8	1.4	(²)	.7
ampshire	11,362	151	--------	4	98.7	1.3	--------	(²)
rsey	95,446	1,949	333	74	97.6	2.0	.3	.1
exico	16,336	2,771	2,372	613	73.9	12.5	10.7	2.8
ork	296,061	4,442	161	379	98.3	1.5	.1	.1
arolina	74,955	17,563	13,658	310	70.4	16.5	12.8	.3
Dakota	16,257	630	86	57	95.5	3.7	.5	.3
	177,223	8,387	75	165	95.4	4.5	(²)	.1
ma	43,366	5,284	1,037	433	86.5	10.5	2.1	.9
	35,435	540	23	81	98.2	1.5	.1	.2
lvania	208,455	12,940	118	122	94.1	5.8	.1	.1
Island	16,031	165	1	13	98.9	1.0	(²)	.1
arolina	32,827	8,939	15,566	118	57.1	15.6	27.1	.2
Dakota	17,197	409	88	112	96.6	2.3	.5	.6
see	60,402	14,225	4,653	2,096	74.2	17.5	5.7	2.6
	163,008	20,852	18,363	1,618	80.0	10.2	9.0	.8
	20,827	272	56	37	98.3	1.3	.3	.2
t	8,445	553	3	2	93.8	6.1	(²)	(²)
a	60,268	11,381	9,918	454	73.5	13.9	12.1	.6
gton	55,225	504	21	67	98.9	.9	(²)	.1
irginia	33,193	15,806	1,237	271	65.7	31.3	2.4	.5
sin	80,604	1,945	68	57	97.5	2.4	.1	.1
ng	7,343	218	18	27	96.5	2.9	.2	.4

assumed that all births in hospitals or institutions are attended by physicians.
[1] than 0 05 percent.

e: Department of Health, Education, and Welfare, Public Health Service, National Office of Vital cs. Basic figures are published in annual report, *Vital Statistics of the United States.*

No. 64.—Births and Deaths, by Place of Occurrence and by Place of Residence, for Each City Having in 1940, a Population of 100,000 or More: 1949

[Differences between births (or deaths) by place of occurrence and by place of residence may be illustrated as follows: Total number of births occurring in Akron (including births to mothers whose usual residence was elsewhere) was 9,353, whereas total number of births to mothers whose usual residence was in Akron (including births occurring elsewhere) was 7,307]

CITY	BIRTHS Place of occurrence	BIRTHS Place of residence	DEATHS Place of occurrence	DEATHS Place of residence	CITY	BIRTHS Place of occurrence	BIRTHS Place of residence	DEATHS Place of occurrence	DEATHS Place of residence
Akron	9,353	7,307	2,405	2,313	Minneapolis	17,777	13,587	5,625	5,301
Albany	4,543	2,948	2,039	1,928	Nashville	7,226	6,368	2,558	2,226
Atlanta	14,657	8,504	4,230	4,015	Newark, N. J	13,535	9,389	5,005	4,964
Baltimore	26,689	21,831	11,329	10,852	New Bedford	2,040	2,146	1,216	1,325
Birmingham	11,012	8,150	3,439	3,167	New Haven	5,686	3,304	2,201	1,848
Boston	19,035	15,707	11,099	9,621	New Orleans	21,508	14,879	7,550	6,156
Bridgeport	4,946	3,408	1,681	1,602	New York [1]	156,900	152,268	78,586	81,527
Buffalo	17,469	12,463	7,193	6,667	Norfolk	5,760	5,051	2,031	2,016
Cambridge	3,791	2,747	1,525	1,311	Oakland	14,116	8,862	4,704	4,286
Camden	5,734	2,831	1,687	1,395	Oklahoma City	7,927	5,643	2,403	1,939
Canton	5,035	3,443	1,316	1,295	Omaha	7,605	6,049	2,942	2,536
Charlotte	5,689	3,649	1,326	1,096	Paterson	5,476	2,708	1,764	1,606
Chattanooga	5,703	4,060	1,816	1,518	Peoria	5,164	2,437	1,424	1,234
Chicago	78,565	79,136	37,782	41,418	Philadelphia	46,893	42,344	24,576	23,889
Cincinnati	16,825	11,972	7,230	6,373	Pittsburgh	23,600	18,421	8,569	8,115
Cleveland	26,918	22,525	10,509	10,084	Portland	12,386	9,891	4,613	4,547
Columbus	13,716	9,283	4,807	3,880	Providence	10,161	5,188	3,057	2,828
Dallas	14,731	10,815	3,975	3,374	Reading	1,777	2,061	1,138	1,387
Dayton	11,836	9,109	2,929	2,765	Richmond	8,761	5,280	3,296	2,701
Denver	13,892	10,143	4,684	4,297	Rochester	11,091	7,445	4,261	3,865
Des Moines	6,199	4,648	2,231	1,812	Sacramento	6,986	3,195	2,240	1,889
Detroit	50,366	44,063	14,962	16,635	St. Louis	26,172	19,666	11,377	10,534
Duluth	3,231	2,384	1,299	1,155	St. Paul	10,343	8,231	3,574	3,268
Elizabeth	3,733	2,383	1,275	1,143	Salt Lake City	8,041	5,484	1,927	1,542
Erie	4,767	3,502	1,424	1,386	San Antonio	14,843	13,743	3,988	3,851
Fall River	3,110	2,321	1,511	1,360	San Diego	10,425	8,669	3,152	2,981
Flint	7,066	4,280	1,616	1,416	San Francisco	19,226	16,221	9,742	9,559
Fort Wayne	5,064	3,563	1,534	1,356	Scranton	3,990	2,536	1,780	1,639
Fort Worth	8,438	6,988	2,571	2,422	Seattle	14,843	13,608	5,660	5,721
Gary	5,226	4,207	1,223	1,186	Somerville	1,405	2,209	846	1,094
Grand Rapids	6,311	4,903	1,875	1,958	South Bend	4,235	3,140	1,156	1,048
Hartford	8,061	3,934	2,147	1,768	Spokane	5,974	4,066	2,168	1,941
Houston	18,511	17,327	5,152	4,871	Springfield, Mass.	5,213	4,040	1,922	1,836
Indianapolis	12,643	11,382	5,642	5,179	Syracuse	7,929	4,731	2,632	2,566
Jacksonville	7,009	6,056	2,407	2,324	Tacoma	4,625	3,720	1,846	1,597
Jersey City	10,450	6,578	3,618	3,385	Tampa	3,979	3,912	1,607	1,659
Kansas City, Kans	4,180	3,526	1,679	1,388	Toledo	10,753	8,196	4,039	3,605
Kansas City, Mo.	13,275	9,972	5,592	5,346	Trenton	4,882	2,516	1,952	1,449
Knoxville	5,473	3,104	1,623	1,229	Tulsa	5,939	4,385	1,778	1,574
Long Beach	7,256	5,581	2,195	2,551	Utica	3,432	2,109	1,579	1,231
Los Angeles	38,351	41,377	21,273	21,070	Washington, D. C.	27,672	19,814	8,682	8,448
Louisville	13,190	10,687	4,563	4,355	Wichita	5,666	5,071	1,658	1,558
Lowell	3,019	2,237	1,356	1,273	Wilmington	5,213	2,940	1,563	1,396
Memphis	12,533	9,355	4,303	3,590	Worcester	5,703	4,142	2,616	2,344
Miami	5,871	5,306	2,464	2,450	Yonkers	3,054	2,868	1,366	1,457
Milwaukee	19,613	14,814	5,647	6,356	Youngstown	6,295	4,468	2,118	1,802

[1] Represents 5 boroughs.

Source: Department of Health, Education, and Welfare, Public Health Service, National Office of Vital Statistics; annual report, *Vital Statistics of the United States.*

No. 65.—EXPECTATION OF LIFE AND MORTALITY RATES AT SINGLE YEARS OF AGE, BY RACE AND SEX: 1949

[Interpolated from abridged life table prepared by National Office of Vital Statistics, Public Health Service, Department of Health, Education, and Welfare]

AGE (years)	EXPECTATION OF LIFE IN YEARS					MORTALITY RATE PER 1,000				
	Total	White Males	White Females	Nonwhite Males	Nonwhite Females	Total	White Males	White Females	Nonwhite Males	Nonwhite Females
0	67.65	65.88	71.51	58.57	62.93	31.40	32.50	25.00	53.10	42.50
1	68.84	67.09	72.33	60.85	64.71	2.41	2.30	2.04	4.67	3.52
2	68.01	66.25	71.48	60.14	63.96	1.54	1.61	1.27	2.67	2.30
3	67.11	65.35	70.57	59.30	63.10	1.12	1.11	.93	2.02	1.77
4	66.19	64.43	69.64	58.41	62.21	.94	1.00	.77	1.48	1.24
5	65.25	63.49	68.69	57.50	61.29	.78	.93	.57	1.17	1.07
6	64.30	62.54	67.73	56.57	60.36	.69	.80	.54	.99	.83
7	63.34	61.59	66.77	55.62	59.41	.62	.72	.50	.86	.65
8	62.38	60.63	65.80	54.67	58.45	.57	.65	.46	.76	.55
9	61.42	59.67	64.83	53.71	57.48	.54	.62	.44	.73	.50
10	60.45	58.71	63.86	52.75	56.51	.54	.62	.43	.74	.50
11	59.48	57.75	62.89	51.79	55.53	.56	.65	.43	.82	.56
12	58.51	56.78	61.91	50.83	54.56	.62	.71	.44	.96	.67
13	57.55	55.82	60.94	49.88	53.60	.69	.81	.48	1.17	.84
14	56.59	54.87	59.97	48.94	52.65	.79	.93	.52	1.43	1.04
15	55.63	53.92	59.00	48.01	51.70	.91	1.06	.57	1.72	1.26
16	54.68	52.98	58.04	47.10	50.77	1.04	1.22	.62	2.03	1.52
17	53.74	52.04	57.07	46.19	49.85	1.14	1.34	.67	2.33	1.78
18	52.80	51.11	56.11	45.30	48.93	1.23	1.45	.71	2.58	2.02
19	51.86	50.18	55.15	44.42	48.03	1.30	1.53	.74	2.79	2.25
20	50.93	49.26	54.19	43.54	47.14	1.37	1.61	.76	3.02	2.50
21	50.00	48.34	53.23	42.66	46.25	1.45	1.69	.79	3.26	2.74
22	49.07	47.42	52.27	41.80	45.38	1.51	1.75	.82	3.48	2.96
23	48.14	46.50	51.31	40.95	44.51	1.54	1.75	.85	3.59	3.13
24	47.22	45.58	50.36	40.10	43.65	1.55	1.73	.89	3.87	3.26
25	46.29	44.66	49.40	39.25	42.79	1.57	1.71	.93	4.07	3.41
26	45.36	43.74	48.45	38.41	41.93	1.59	1.69	.97	4.28	3.57
27	44.43	42.81	47.49	37.58	41.06	1.64	1.71	1.01	4.46	3.69
28	43.50	41.89	46.54	36.74	40.23	1.68	1.73	1.07	4.62	3.76
29	42.56	40.96	45.59	35.91	39.38	1.75	1.79	1.13	4.76	3.81
30	41.65	40.03	44.64	35.08	38.53	1.83	1.86	1.21	4.91	3.84
31	40.73	39.10	43.69	34.25	37.69	1.91	1.93	1.28	5.10	3.92
32	39.81	38.18	42.75	33.43	36.83	2.04	2.05	1.38	5.39	4.14
33	38.89	37.25	41.81	32.60	35.98	2.19	2.20	1.47	5.79	4.52
34	37.97	36.33	40.87	31.79	35.14	2.38	2.40	1.56	6.32	5.06
35	37.06	35.42	39.93	30.99	34.32	2.58	2.62	1.71	6.92	5.55
36	36.15	34.51	39.00	30.20	33.51	2.81	2.87	1.85	7.52	6.25
37	35.25	33.61	38.07	29.43	32.72	3.05	3.14	2.00	8.12	6.82
38	34.36	32.71	37.15	28.67	31.94	3.30	3.43	2.16	8.71	7.33
39	33.47	31.82	36.23	27.91	31.17	3.56	3.73	2.32	9.30	7.80
40	32.59	30.94	35.31	27.17	30.41	3.83	4.06	2.51	9.92	8.27
41	31.71	30.07	34.40	26.44	29.67	4.16	4.46	2.71	10.61	8.81
42	30.84	29.20	33.49	25.72	28.93	4.52	4.89	2.94	11.38	9.43
43	29.98	28.34	32.59	25.01	28.20	4.93	5.35	3.18	12.25	10.14
44	29.13	27.49	31.69	24.31	27.48	5.37	5.87	3.45	13.23	10.95
45	28.28	26.65	30.80	23.63	26.78	5.86	6.41	3.75	14.24	11.82
46	27.45	25.82	29.91	22.97	26.09	6.38	7.02	4.08	15.30	12.68
47	26.62	25.00	29.03	22.32	25.42	6.96	7.70	4.42	16.48	13.53
48	25.80	24.19	28.16	21.69	24.76	7.56	8.50	4.81	17.72	14.34
49	25.00	23.39	27.29	21.07	24.12	8.22	9.37	5.24	19.06	15.12
50	24.20	22.61	26.43	20.47	23.48	8.94	10.33	5.71	20.48	15.98
51	23.41	21.84	25.58	19.89	22.85	9.70	11.33	6.22	21.92	16.82
52	22.64	21.08	24.73	19.33	22.24	10.48	12.37	6.75	23.42	17.72
53	21.87	20.34	23.90	18.78	21.63	11.31	13.44	7.30	24.94	18.63
54	21.12	19.61	23.07	18.25	21.03	12.16	14.54	7.88	26.50	19.59
55	20.37	18.89	22.25	17.73	20.44	13.10	15.71	8.52	28.21	20.60
56	19.63	18.19	21.43	17.23	19.87	14.11	16.99	9.25	29.97	21.72
57	18.90	17.49	20.63	16.75	19.30	15.21	18.38	10.04	31.53	23.03
58	18.19	16.81	19.83	16.28	18.74	16.43	19.93	10.92	32.80	24.60
59	17.48	16.14	19.05	15.81	18.20	17.75	21.65	11.87	33.86	26.43
60	16.79	15.49	18.27	15.35	17.68	19.15	23.45	12.91	34.64	28.25
61	16.11	14.85	17.50	14.89	17.20	20.67	25.39	14.07	35.61	30.18
62	15.44	14.23	16.75	14.42	16.72	22.48	27.58	15.53	37.40	32.68
63	14.79	13.62	16.00	13.96	16.27	24.67	30.07	17.36	40.52	35.93
64	14.15	13.02	15.28	13.53	15.85	27.22	32.85	19.51	44.71	39.79
65	13.53	12.45	14.57	13.14	15.49	29.98	35.88	21.87	49.74	43.73
66	12.93	11.89	13.88	12.80	15.18	32.88	39.06	24.35	54.76	48.73
67	12.35	11.36	13.22	12.51	14.93	35.85	42.36	27.01	58.96	52.32
68	11.80	10.84	12.57	12.26	14.73	38.79	45.69	29.82	61.43	54.27
69	11.25	10.33	11.94	12.03	14.55	41.76	49.11	32.80	(¹)	(¹)

¹ Not computed because of deficiencies in basic data.

Source: Metropolitan Life Insurance Co., New York, N. Y.; Statistical Bulletin, Nov. 1951.

No. 66.—Selected Life Table Values: 1909-11 to 1949

[See also *Historical Statistics*, series C 6-21]

RACE AND PERIOD	AT BIRTH		AGE 20		AGE 45		AGE 65	
	Male	Female	Male	Female	Male	Female	Male	Female
	ANNUAL RATE OF MORTALITY PER 1,000 LIVING AT AGE INDICATED							
White:								
1909–1911 [1]	123.26	102.26	4.89	4.20	12.64	9.91	43.79	37.86
1919–1921 [2]	80.25	63.92	4.27	4.33	9.26	8.14	34.99	31.68
1929–1931	62.32	49.63	3.18	2.77	9.29	7.02	38.65	31.25
1939–1941	48.12	37.89	2.12	1.45	7.66	5.23	36.85	26.43
1947	34.5	26.5	1.8	.9	6.8	4.1	36.7	23.3
1948	33.4	25.7	1.7	.9	6.5	3.9	36.3	22.4
1949	32.5	25.0	1.6	.8	6.4	3.8	35.9	21.9
Negro: [3]								
1929–1931	87.32	72.04	8.58	8.82	22.40	20.18	50.72	49.35
1939–1941	82.28	65.84	5.44	5.32	18.59	16.02	46.85	40.90
1947 [4]	54.5	44.9	3.6	3.3	14.4	12.1	46.0	42.4
1948 [4]	52.1	42.0	3.3	2.8	14.5	11.7	48.7	43.8
1949 [4]	53.1	42.5	3.0	2.5	14.2	11.8	49.7	44.3
	AVERAGE FUTURE LIFETIME IN YEARS AT AGE INDICATED							
White:								
1909–1911 [1]	50.23	53.62	42.71	44.88	23.86	25.45	11.25	11.97
1919–1921 [2]	56.34	58.53	45.60	46.46	26.00	26.98	12.21	12.75
1929–1931	59.12	62.67	46.02	48.52	25.28	27.39	11.77	12.81
1939–1941	62.81	67.29	47.76	51.38	25.87	28.90	12.07	13.56
1947	65.2	70.5	48.7	53.4	26.3	30.2	12.3	14.2
1948	65.5	71.0	49.0	53.8	26.5	30.5	12.4	14.4
1949	65.9	71.5	49.3	54.2	26.7	30.8	12.4	14.6
Negro: [3]								
1929–1931	47.55	49.51	35.95	37.22	20.59	21.39	10.87	12.24
1939–1941	52.26	55.56	39.52	42.04	21.88	23.89	12.21	13.93
1947 [4]	57.9	61.9	43.1	46.4	23.6	26.6	13.3	15.9
1948 [4]	58.1	62.5	42.9	46.8	23.3	26.7	13.1	15.7
1949 [4]	58.6	62.9	43.5	47.1	23.2	26.8	13.1	15.5

[1] For original registration States.   [2] For death-registration States of 1920.
[3] Values prior to 1929 excluded because of doubt as to reliability of mortality statistics for Negroes.
[4] Values relate to nonwhite population of which only small proportion are of races other than Negro.

Source: Department of Health, Education, and Welfare, Public Health Service, National Office of Vital Statistics; *United States Life Tables and Actuarial Tables, 1939-41*, and *Vital Statistics of the United States*, 1947 to 1949, except for annual rates of mortality at ages 20, 45, and 65 for 1947-49, which were computed by the Metropolitan Life Insurance Company.

No. 67.—Death Rates Per 1,000 Population, by Race and Sex: Death-Registration States, 1900 to 1950

[For coverage of registration areas, see table 55, p. 61. See also *Historical Statistics*, series C 45-51]

YEAR	TOTAL			WHITE			NONWHITE		
	Both sexes	Male	Female	Both sexes	Male	Female	Both sexes	Male	Female
1900	17.2	17.9	16.5	17.0	17.7	16.3	25.0	25.7	24.4
1905	15.9	16.7	15.0	15.7	16.5	14.8	25.5	26.8	24.3
1910	14.7	15.6	13.7	14.5	15.4	13.6	21.7	22.3	21.0
1915	13.2	14.0	12.3	12.9	13.7	12.0	20.2	20.8	19.5
1920	13.0	13.4	12.6	12.6	13.0	12.1	17.7	17.8	17.5
1925	11.7	12.4	10.9	11.1	11.8	10.4	17.4	18.2	16.6
1930	11.3	12.3	10.4	10.8	11.7	9.8	16.3	17.4	15.3
1935	10.9	12.0	9.9	10.6	11.6	9.5	14.3	15.6	13.0
1940 [1]	10.8	12.0	9.5	10.4	11.6	9.2	13.8	15.1	12.6
1945 [1]	10.6	12.7	8.8	10.4	12.5	8.6	12.0	13.9	10.4
1946 [1]	10.0	11.4	8.6	9.8	11.3	8.5	11.1	12.3	9.9
1947 [1]	10.1	11.5	8.7	9.9	11.4	8.5	11.3	12.5	10.2
1948 [1]	9.9	11.3	8.5	9.7	11.2	8.3	11.3	12.6	10.0
1949 [1]	9.7	11.1	8.3	9.5	11.0	8.1	11.1	12.4	9.9
1950 [1]	9.6	11.1	8.2	9.5	10.9	8.1	11.2	12.5	9.9

[1] Based on population excluding armed forces overseas.

Source: Department of Health, Education, and Welfare, Public Health Service, National Office of Vital Statistics. 1900-49, annual report, *Vital Statistics of the United States*.

No. 68.—DEATH RATES PER 1,000 POPULATION, BY AGE: DEATH-REGISTRATION STATES, 1900 TO 1950

[For coverage of registration areas, see table 55, p. 61. See also *Historical Statistics*, series C 52 and C 65–76]

AGE	1900 [1]	1910 [1]	1920 [1]	1930 [1]	1940 [1]	1945 [1]	1947 [1]	1948 [1]	1949 [1]	1950 [1]
Total [2] (unadjusted)_	17.2	14.7	13.0	11.3	10.8	10.6	10.1	9.9	9.7	9.6
Adjusted for age [3]___	17.8	15.8	14.2	12.5	10.7	9.6	9.1	9.0	8.8	8.4
Under 1 year_____	162.4	131.8	92.3	69.0	54.9	41.7	33.8	35.0	34.1	33.0
1–4 years_____	19.8	14.0	9.9	5.6	2.9	2.0	1.6	1.6	1.5	1.4
5–14 years_____	3.9	2.9	2.6	1.7	1.0	.9	.7	.7	.6	.6
15–24 years_____	5.9	4.5	4.9	3.3	2.0	1.9	1.5	1.4	1.3	1.3
25–34 years_____	8.2	6.5	6.8	4.7	3.1	2.7	2.1	2.0	1.9	1.8
35–44 years_____	10.2	9.0	8.1	6.8	5.2	4.6	4.1	4.0	3.8	3.6
45–54 years_____	15.0	13.7	12.2	12.2	10.6	9.7	9.3	9.0	8.7	8.5
55–64 years_____	27.2	26.2	23.6	24.0	22.3	20.3	19.8	19.4	18.9	19.1
65–74 years_____	56.4	55.6	52.5	51.4	48.0	44.5	44.6	44.0	43.5	40.7
75–84 years_____	123.3	122.2	118.9	112.7	112.6	99.5	98.1	96.3	94.5	93.3
85 years and over_____	260.9	250.3	248.3	228.0	228.9	222.5	243.1	247.1	242.0	202.0

[1] Based on population excluding armed forces overseas.
[2] Includes deaths for which age was not stated.
[3] Adjusted for age by the direct method using as the standard population the age distribution of the population of the United States as enumerated in 1940.

Source: Department of Health, Education, and Welfare, Public Health Service, National Office of Vital Statistics; annual report, *Vital Statistics of the United States*.

No. 69.—MATERNAL DEATHS, INFANT DEATHS (UNDER 1 YEAR OF AGE) AND FETAL DEATHS, FOR BIRTH-REGISTRATION STATES: 1915 TO 1950

[For coverage of registration area, see table 55, p. 61. See also *Historical Statistics*, series C 38–39 and C 42]

YEAR	MATERNAL DEATHS [1]		DEATHS UNDER 1 YEAR		FETAL DEATHS [2]	
	Number	Rate per 10,000 live births	Number	Rate per 1,000 live births	Number	Ratio per 1,000 live births
1915_____	4,719	60.8	77,572	99.9	_____	_____
1920_____	12,058	79.9	129,531	85.8	_____	_____
1925_____	12,158	64.7	134,652	71.7	_____	_____
1930_____	14,836	67.3	142,413	64.6	_____	_____
1935_____	12,544	58.2	120,138	55.7	_____	_____
1940_____	8,876	37.6	110,984	47.0	_____	_____
1945_____	5,668	20.7	104,684	38.3	65,513	23.9
1946_____	5,153	15.7	111,063	33.8	74,849	22.8
1947_____	4,978	13.5	119,173	32.2	77,917	21.1
1948_____	4,122	11.7	113,169	32.0	72,788	20.6
1949_____	3,216	9.0	111,531	31.3	70,584	19.8
1950_____	2,960	8.3	103,825	29.2	72,502	20.4

[1] Deaths from deliveries and complications of pregnancy, childbirth, and the puerperium. Beginning with 1949, deaths are classified according to sixth revision of *International Lists of Diseases and Causes of Death*. For deaths in United States as a whole, it is estimated that 9 percent fewer deaths were assigned to maternal causes under sixth revision than under fifth revision of *International List* (1939–48).
[2] Includes only fetal deaths (stillbirths) for which period of gestation was 20 weeks (or 5 months) or more, or was not stated.

Source: Department of Health, Education, and Welfare, Public Health Service, National Office of Vital Statistics; annual report, *Vital Statistics of the United States*.

No. 70.—Deaths and Death Rates Per 1,000 Population, By Age, Race, and Sex: 1949 and 1950

[See also *Historical Statistics*, series C 45–51]

AGE	TOTAL			WHITE			NONWHITE		
	Both sexes	Male	Female	Both sexes	Male	Female	Both sexes	Male	Female
NUMBER OF DEATHS	1949								
Total [1]	1,443,607	821,291	622,316	1,268,848	726,169	542,679	174,759	95,122	79,637
Under 1 year	111,531	64,161	47,370	89,007	51,530	37,477	22,524	12,631	9,893
1–4 years	18,687	10,362	8,325	15,004	8,355	6,649	3,683	2,007	1,676
5–14 years	15,717	9,543	6,174	13,903	7,985	5,018	1,558	1,558	1,156
15–24 years	29,483	18,803	10,680	22,459	15,028	7,431	7,024	3,775	3,249
25–34 years	43,303	25,187	18,116	32,206	19,366	12,842	11,095	5,821	5,274
35–44 years	78,401	46,297	32,104	60,268	36,951	23,317	18,133	9,346	8,787
45–54 years	150,210	93,373	56,837	121,752	77,836	43,916	28,458	15,537	12,921
55–64 years	253,394	159,569	93,825	222,568	142,327	80,241	30,826	17,242	13,584
65–74 years	334,192	192,063	142,129	305,837	176,402	129,435	28,355	15,661	12,694
75–84 years	295,621	152,189	143,432	280,133	143,730	136,403	15,488	8,459	7,029
85 years and over	111,580	48,802	62,778	105,603	46,000	59,603	5,977	2,802	3,175
RATE PER 1,000 POPULATION [2]									
Total [1]	9.7	11.1	8.3	9.5	11.0	8.1	11.1	12.4	9.9
Under 1 year	34.1	38.4	29.6	30.7	34.7	26.5	60.5	67.9	53.5
1–4 years	1.5	1.6	1.4	1.4	1.5	1.2	2.4	2.6	2.2
5–14 years	.6	.8	.5	.6	.7	.5	.8	1.0	.7
15–24 years	1.3	1.7	.9	1.1	1.5	.8	2.6	2.9	2.4
25–34 years	1.9	2.2	1.5	1.5	1.9	1.2	4.5	5.0	4.0
35–44 years	3.8	4.6	3.0	3.2	4.0	2.5	8.8	9.7	8.1
45–54 years	8.7	10.9	6.5	7.8	10.0	5.6	17.7	20.1	15.5
55–64 years	18.9	23.9	14.0	17.9	23.0	12.9	31.6	35.0	28.1
65–74 years	43.5	51.7	35.8	42.6	51.0	34.7	56.8	60.7	52.7
75–84 years	94.5	106.3	84.6	96.0	107.9	86.0	74.5	84.6	65.1
85 years and over	242.0	246.5	238.7	263.3	264.4	262.6	99.6	116.8	88.2
NUMBER OF DEATHS	1950								
Total [1]	1,452,454	827,749	624,705	1,276,085	731,366	544,719	176,369	96,383	79,986
Under 1 year	103,825	59,727	44,098	82,018	47,595	34,423	21,807	12,132	9,675
1–4 years	18,148	10,062	8,086	14,203	7,921	6,282	3,945	2,141	1,804
5–14 years	14,607	8,769	5,838	12,002	7,298	4,704	2,605	1,471	1,134
15–24 years	28,298	18,332	9,966	21,793	14,769	7,024	6,505	3,563	2,942
25–34 years	42,467	25,111	17,356	31,558	19,323	12,235	10,909	5,788	5,121
35–44 years	76,937	45,402	31,535	59,208	36,293	22,915	17,729	9,109	8,620
45–54 years	148,087	92,356	55,731	120,144	77,150	42,994	27,943	15,206	12,737
55–64 years	254,150	160,422	93,728	222,222	142,419	79,803	31,928	18,003	13,925
65–74 years	342,296	198,428	143,868	312,482	181,770	130,712	29,814	16,658	13,156
75–84 years	305,851	157,095	148,756	289,503	147,984	141,519	16,348	9,111	7,237
85 years and over	116,516	51,240	65,276	110,034	48,249	61,785	6,482	2,991	3,491
RATE PER 1,000 POPULATION [2]									
Total [1]	9.6	11.1	8.2	9.5	10.9	8.0	11.2	12.5	9.9
Under 1 year	33.0	37.3	28.5	29.9	34.0	25.7	53.7	59.9	47.5
1–4 years	1.4	1.5	1.3	1.2	1.4	1.1	2.5	2.7	2.3
5–14 years	.6	.7	.5	.6	.7	.5	.9	1.0	.7
15–24 years	1.3	1.7	.9	1.1	1.5	.7	2.5	2.9	2.2
25–34 years	1.8	2.2	1.4	1.5	1.9	1.1	4.4	5.0	3.9
35–44 years	3.6	4.3	2.9	3.1	3.8	2.4	8.1	8.6	7.5
45–54 years	8.5	10.7	6.4	7.7	9.8	5.5	17.1	18.6	15.5
55–64 years	19.1	24.1	14.1	18.0	23.0	12.9	33.7	36.9	30.4
65–74 years	40.7	49.0	33.0	40.2	48.6	32.4	46.0	52.5	39.8
75–84 years	93.3	104.3	84.0	94.2	105.3	84.8	80.4	90.3	70.5
85 years and over	202.0	216.4	191.9	206.8	221.2	196.8	144.7	160.2	133.7

[1] Includes deaths for which age was not stated.
[2] Based on population excluding armed forces overseas.

Source: Department of Health, Education, and Welfare, Public Health Service, National Office of Vital Statistics; annual report, *Vital Statistics of the United States*.

No. 71.—Deaths and Death Rates Per 1,000 Population, by States: 1940 to 1950

[By place of residence. See also *Historical Statistics*, series C 45]

STATE	NUMBER OF DEATHS					RATE PER 1,000 POPULATION [1]				
	1940	1947	1948	1949	1950	1940	1947	1948	1949	1950
United States	1,417,269	1,445,370	1,444,337	1,443,607	1,452,454	10.8	10.1	9.9	9.7	9.6
Alabama	29,554	26,347	26,620	26,750	26,836	10.4	9.0	9.0	8.9	8.8
Arizona	5,556	6,032	6,586	6,397	6,422	11.1	9.2	9.5	9.0	8.6
Arkansas	17,247	15,095	15,224	15,680	15,411	8.8	8.2	8.3	8.5	8.1
California	79,742	96,697	98,905	100,354	98,760	11.5	9.8	9.8	9.7	9.3
Colorado	12,291	12,613	12,582	12,415	12,280	10.9	10.2	10.0	9.6	9.3
Connecticut	18,070	19,153	19,569	18,569	19,123	10.6	9.7	9.7	9.3	9.5
Delaware	3,285	3,345	3,407	3,330	3,501	12.3	11.0	10.9	10.5	11.0
District of Columbia	8,081	8,254	8,197	8,448	8,560	12.2	9.3	9.8	10.5	10.7
Florida	21,614	24,283	24,767	25,376	26,569	11.4	9.6	9.6	9.5	9.6
Georgia	32,485	28,946	29,526	29,608	30,325	10.4	8.8	9.1	8.9	8.8
Idaho	4,924	4,780	4,906	4,701	4,837	9.4	9.2	8.9	8.2	8.2
Illinois	89,099	93,686	91,328	92,568	92,490	11.3	11.2	10.7	10.7	10.6
Indiana	40,555	40,567	39,544	40,026	40,630	11.8	10.7	10.2	10.1	10.3
Iowa	26,297	26,484	26,064	26,106	26,979	10.4	10.6	10.2	10.1	10.3
Kansas	18,589	18,700	18,553	18,814	19,058	10.3	10.1	9.8	9.8	10.0
Kentucky	29,967	28,371	28,050	28,046	27,885	10.5	10.1	10.0	9.8	9.8
Louisiana	25,542	23,395	23,561	23,400	23,738	10.8	9.1	9.1	8.9	8.8
Maine	10,581	9,959	9,988	10,099	9,886	12.5	11.7	11.3	11.2	10.8
Maryland	22,026	22,480	22,440	22,110	22,417	12.1	10.0	9.9	9.5	9.3
Massachusetts	51,122	51,754	52,611	50,767	49,386	11.8	11.3	11.3	10.7	10.5
Michigan	52,183	57,137	56,786	57,422	57,743	9.9	9.4	9.1	9.1	9.1
Minnesota	26,384	27,781	27,400	27,719	28,020	9.4	9.9	9.6	9.4	9.4
Mississippi	23,295	20,212	20,296	20,661	20,784	10.7	9.6	9.6	9.9	9.5
Missouri	43,777	44,872	42,752	43,825	43,710	11.6	11.6	11.1	11.3	11.1
Montana	5,765	5,760	5,884	5,878	5,822	10.3	10.8	10.9	10.3	9.9
Nebraska	12,670	12,871	12,615	12,644	12,617	9.6	10.2	10.0	9.7	9.5
Nevada	1,402	1,623	1,624	1,610	1,588	12.7	10.9	10.4	10.3	9.9
New Hampshire	6,236	6,194	6,172	6,109	6,076	12.7	12.2	11.9	11.5	11.4
New Jersey	45,772	48,181	48,076	47,880	49,100	11.0	10.4	10.1	9.8	10.2
New Mexico	5,484	5,471	5,609	5,576	5,471	10.3	9.4	9.3	8.7	8.0
New York	149,816	157,734	158,242	155,020	156,074	11.1	11.3	10.9	10.4	10.5
North Carolina	31,904	30,187	30,161	31,009	31,130	8.9	8.0	7.9	7.9	7.7
North Dakota	5,257	5,252	·5,146	5,222	5,191	8.2	9.1	8.9	8.7	8.4
Ohio	78,949	82,254	80,891	80,368	80,633	11.4	10.7	10.5	10.1	10.1
Oklahoma	20,885	19,327	19,079	19,394	19,473	8.9	9.1	9.1	9.2	8.7
Oregon	12,180	13,501	14,080	13,891	13,935	11.2	9.9	10.0	9.7	9.2
Pennsylvania	111,977	110,459	109,202	108,363	110,212	11.3	10.8	10.6	10.4	10.5
Rhode Island	8,019	8,368	8,188	·8,071	8,306	11.2	10.8	10.4	10.1	10.5
South Carolina	20,280	17,230	17,957	17,494	17,973	10.7	8.6	9.0	8.6	8.5
South Dakota	5,700	5,730	5,806	5,667	5,880	8.9	9.5	9.5	9.0	9.0
Tennessee	29,383	28,591	28,826	28,993	29,425	10.1	9.0	9.0	9.0	8.9
Texas	62,635	62,662	64,245	63,337	63,349	9.8	8.5	8.4	8.3	8.2
Utah	4,845	4,996	5,070	4,929	4,974	8.8	7.9	7.8	7.3	7.2
Vermont	4,664	4,378	4,096	4,162	4,167	13.0	12.4	11.4	11.3	11.0
Virginia	29,741	29,193	28,976	29,345	29,708	11.1	9.1	9.0	8.9	9.0
Washington	20,080	21,979	22,211	22,491	22,486	11.6	9.9	9.8	9.8	9.5
West Virginia	17,669	17,218	17,600	17,305	17,428	9.3	9.1	9.3	9.0	8.7
Wisconsin	31,563	33,219	32,564	32,993	33,778	10.1	10.2	9.8	9.7	9.8
Wyoming	2,157	2,349	2,385	2,385	2,336	8.6	9.1	8.9	8.6	8.0

[1] Based on total population in each specified area (excluding armed forces overseas).

Source: Department of Health, Education, and Welfare, Public Health Service, National Office of Vital Statistics; *Vital Statistics—Special Reports*, Vol. 37, No. 8.

No. 72.—DEATHS BY RACE, FOR URBAN AND RURAL AREAS, BY STATES: 1949

[By place of residence]

STATE	TOTAL			URBAN [1]			RURAL [1]		
	All races	White	Non-white	All races	White	Non-white	All races	White	Non-white
United States..	1,443,607	1,268,848	174,759	914,658	806,862	107,796	528,949	461,986	66,963
Alabama	26,750	15,395	11,355	10,988	6,112	4,876	15,762	9,283	6,479
Arizona	6,397	5,384	1,013	2,883	2,682	201	3,514	2,702	812
Arkansas	15,680	11,372	4,308	5,942	4,311	1,631	9,738	7,061	2,677
California	100,354	95,098	5,256	73,774	69,684	4,090	26,580	25,414	1,166
Colorado	12,415	12,124	291	8,149	7,909	240	4,266	4,215	51
Connecticut	18,829	18,267	562	12,793	12,295	498	6,036	5,972	64
Delaware	3,330	2,733	597	1,789	1,439	350	1,541	1,294	247
Dist. of Columbia	8,448	5,335	3,113	8,448	5,335	3,113	......	......	
Florida	25,376	18,307	7,069	16,032	11,619	4,413	9,344	6,688	2,656
Georgia	29,608	17,414	12,194	14,281	7,951	6,330	15,327	9,463	5,864
Idaho	4,701	4,604	97	2,183	2,165	18	2,518	2,439	79
Illinois	92,568	84,865	7,703	71,710	64,432	7,278	20,856	20,433	425
Indiana	40,026	37,887	2,139	23,594	21,568	2,026	16,432	16,319	113
Iowa	26,106	25,837	269	13,239	12,996	243	12,867	12,841	26
Kansas	18,814	17,800	1,014	9,741	8,868	873	9,073	8,932	141
Kentucky	28,046	24,700	3,346	11,473	9,213	2,260	16,573	15,487	1,086
Louisiana	23,400	13,489	9,911	13,046	7,878	5,168	10,354	5,611	4,743
Maine	10,099	10,057	42	3,964	3,944	20	6,135	6,113	22
Maryland	22,110	17,453	4,657	13,719	10,501	3,218	8,391	6,952	1,439
Massachusetts	50,767	49,884	883	45,122	44,281	841	5,645	5,603	42
Michigan	57,422	53,365	4,057	37,375	33,656	3,719	20,047	19,709	338
Minnesota	27,719	27,385	334	15,616	15,413	203	12,103	11,972	131
Mississippi	20,661	9,381	11,280	6,170	3,034	3,136	14,491	6,347	8,144
Missouri	43,825	39,536	4,289	25,840	22,238	3,602	17,985	17,298	687
Montana	5,878	5,618	260	3,080	3,034	46	2,798	2,584	214
Nebraska	12,644	12,322	322	6,085	5,829	256	6,559	6,493	66
Nevada	1,610	1,490	120	765	729	36	845	761	84
New Hampshire	6,109	6,099	10	3,464	3,459	5	2,645	2,640	5
New Jersey	47,880	44,228	3,652	38,217	35,132	3,085	9,663	9,096	567
New Mexico	5,576	5,069	507	2,617	2,522	95	2,959	2,547	412
New York	155,020	145,809	9,211	126,655	117,831	8,824	28,365	27,978	387
North Carolina	31,009	20,201	10,808	10,653	6,458	4,195	20,356	13,743	6,613
North Dakota	5,222	5,090	132	1,442	1,429	13	3,780	3,661	119
Ohio	80,368	74,395	5,973	55,815	50,347	5,468	24,553	24,048	505
Oklahoma	19,394	17,118	2,276	9,983	8,835	1,148	9,411	8,283	1,128
Oregon	13,891	13,631	260	8,123	7,976	147	5,768	5,655	113
Pennsylvania	108,363	101,082	7,281	76,704	69,919	6,785	31,659	31,163	496
Rhode Island	8,071	7,868	203	7,296	7,105	191	775	763	12
South Carolina	17,494	8,982	8,512	5,962	3,355	2,607	11,532	5,627	5,905
South Dakota	5,687	5,400	287	1,877	1,845	32	3,810	3,555	255
Tennessee	28,993	22,257	6,736	12,761	8,364	4,397	16,232	13,893	2,339
Texas	63,337	52,743	10,594	37,966	31,388	6,580	25,360	21,355	4,014
Utah	4,929	4,797	132	3,078	3,001	77	1,851	1,796	55
Vermont	4,162	4,159	3	1,569	1,567	2	2,593	2,592	1
Virginia	29,345	20,164	9,181	12,274	8,124	4,150	17,071	12,040	5,031
Washington	22,491	21,850	641	14,082	13,676	406	8,409	8,174	235
West Virginia	17,305	15,940	1,365	6,399	5,806	593	10,906	10,134	772
Wisconsin	32,993	32,549	444	18,777	18,497	280	14,216	14,052	164
Wyoming	2,385	2,315	70	1,141	1,110	31	1,244	1,205	39

[1] "Urban" includes urban places having populations of 2,500 or more, according to the 1940 population census; "rural" includes all other areas.

Source: Department of Health, Education, and Welfare, Public Health Service, National Office of Vital Statistics; annual report, *Vital Statistics of the United States*.

CAUSE OF DEATH	SIXTH REVISION, 1948			FIFTH REVISION, 1938						
	Category numbers	Number 1960 [1]	Rate 1960 [1]	Category numbers	1900	1910	1920	1930	1940 [1]	1960 [1]
All causes		1,452,454	963.8		1,719.1	1,468.0	1,298.9	1,132.1	1,076.4	963.8
Tuberculosis, all forms	001-019	33,939	22.5	13-22	194.4	153.8	113.1	71.1	45.9	22.5
Syphilis and its sequelae	020-029	7,568	5.0	30	12.0	13.5	16.5	16.7	14.4	5.0
Typhoid fever	040	96	.1	1	31.3	6.0	7.6	4.7	1.0	(°)
Dysentery, all forms	045-048	923	.5	27	12.0	6.0	4.0	2.8	1.9	.5
Diphtheria	055	410	.2	10	40.3	21.1	15.3	4.9	1.1	.2
Whooping cough	056	1,118	.7	9	12.2	11.6	12.5	4.8	2.2	.7
Meningococcal infections	057	974	.6	36	(°)	.3	.9	3.6	.8	.6
Acute poliomyelitis	080	1,904	1.3	35		2.9	12.4	1.2	.8	1.3
Measles	085	408	.3	35	13.3	12.4	8.9	(°)	.8	.3
All other infective and parasitic diseases	030-039, 041-044, 049-054, 058-074, 081-084, 086-138	4,230	2.8	2-6, 7, 8, 11, 12, 23-29, 28, 29, 31, 32, 34, 37-44, 115b, 177	345.2	371.9	364.9	414.4	485.7	2.8
Malignant neoplasms, etc.	140-205	210,733	139.8	43-55	64.0	76.2	83.4	97.4	120.3	137.8
Diabetes mellitus	260	24,419	16.2	61	11.0	13.5	16.1	19.1	26.6	26.5
Meningitis, except meningococcal and tuberculous	340	1,839	1.2	81		13.5	4.4	2.6	1.7	1.0
Major cardiovascular-renal diseases	330-334, 400-468, 592-594	709,751	510.8	132	345.2	371.9	364.9	414.4	485.7	489.0
Diseases of cardiovascular system	330-334, 400-468	745,074	494.4	58, 83, 90-103	264.3	287.2	282.5	327.8	405.6	442.7
Vascular lesions affecting central nervous system	330-334	156,751	104.0	83	106.9	96.8	93.0	89.0	90.9	91.7
Rheumatic fever	400-402	1,924	1.3	58	6.3	6.2	3.8	2.5	1.3	1.5
Diseases of heart	410-443	535,705	355.5	90-95	137.4	158.9	159.6	214.2	292.5	326.9
Hypertension without mention of heart and general arteriosclerosis	444-450	43,297	28.7	97, 102	14.7	28.4	26.2	19.0	18.5	19.1
Other diseases of circulatory system	451-468	7,397	4.9	96, 98-101, 103				3.1	3.5	4.5
Chronic and unspecified nephritis and other renal sclerosis	592-594	24,677	16.4	131, 132	81.0	84.6	82.4	86.7	79.0	44.3
Influenza and pneumonia, except pneumonia of newborn	480-493	47,120	31.3	33, 107-109	202.2	155.9	207.5	102.5	70.3	35.2
Ulcer of stomach and duodenum	540, 541	8,214	5.5	117	2.7	4.0	2.6	6.2	6.8	6.4
Gastritis, duodenitis, enteritis, and colitis, except diarrhea of the newborn	543, 571, 572	7,622	5.1	119, 120	142.7	115.4	53.7	28.0	10.3	5.0
Cirrhosis of liver	590, 591	13,855	9.2	124	12.5	13.3	7.1	7.2	8.6	11.2
Acute nephritis, etc.	590-689	3,470	2.8	130	7.7	10.2	6.3	4.3	2.5	1.3
Deliveries and complications of pregnancy, etc.	640-689	2,980	2.0	140-150	13.4	15.3	19.0	12.7	6.7	2.2
Congenital malformations	750-759	18,425	12.2	157	12.0	15.2	16.2	11.2	10.0	12.5
Symptoms, senility, and ill-defined conditions	780-795	22,517	14.9	162, 199, 200	117.5	47.5	31.8	30.4	23.7	11.0
Motor-vehicle accidents	E810-E835	34,763	23.1	170	(°)	1.8	10.3	26.7	26.2	21.3
All other accidents	E800-E802, E840-E962	58,498	37.5	169, 171-176, 178-195	72.3	82.4	69.7	53.1	47.0	40.5
Suicide	E963, E970-E979	17,145	11.4	163, 164	10.2	15.3	10.2	15.6	14.4	11.4
Homicide	E964, E980-E985	7,943	4.3	165-168, 196	1.2	4.6	8.5	8.9	6.3	4.3
All other causes	Residual	103,543	101.9	Residual	388.3	265.6	218.5	181.7	132.2	100.7

[1] Rates based on population excluding armed forces overseas. [2] Excludes aneurysm of the aorta. [3] Includes aneurysm (except of heart). [4] Includes paratyphoid fever, which was not separately classified. [5] Includes all embolism and thrombosis, except puerperal. [6] Excludes disease of the coronary arteries. [7] Excludes automobile collisions with trains and streetcars, and motorcycle accidents. [8] Includes legal executions. [9] Excludes legal executions. (°) Not available.

Source: Department of Health, Education, and Welfare, Public Health Service, National Office of Vital Statistics; annual report, *Vital Statistics of the United States.*

No. 74.—Deaths and Death Rates for Accidents by External Cause of Injury: 1949 and 1950

EXTERNAL CAUSE OF INJURY	NUMBER		RATE [1]	
	1949	1950	1949	1950
All accidents	90, 106	91, 249	60. 7	60. 6
Railway accidents	2, 119	2, 126	1. 4	1. 4
Motor-vehicle accidents	31, 701	34, 763	21. 3	23. 1
Motor-vehicle traffic accidents	30, 863	33, 863	20. 8	22. 5
Motor-vehicle nontraffic accidents	838	900	. 6	. 6
Other road-vehicle accidents	599	533	. 4	. 4
Water-transport accidents	1, 484	1, 502	1. 0	1. 0
Aircraft accidents	1, 549	1, 436	1. 0	1. 0
Accidental poisoning by solid and liquid substances	1, 634	1, 564	1. 1	1. 1
Accidental poisoning by gases and vapors	1, 617	1, 769	1. 1	1. 2
Accidental falls	22, 308	20, 783	15. 0	13. 8
Fall from one level to another	7, 456	7, 117	5. 0	4. 7
Fall on same level	4. 300	4, 569	2. 9	3. 0
Unspecified falls	10, 552	9, 097	7. 1	6. 0
Blow from falling object	1, 604	1, 613	1. 1	1. 1
Accidents caused by machinery	1, 669	1, 771	1. 1	1. 2
Accidents caused by electric current	1, 046	955	. 7	. 6
Accidents caused by fire and explosion of combustible material	5, 982	6, 405	4. 0	4. 3
Accidents caused by hot substance, corrosive liquid, steam, and radiation	950	842	. 6	. 6
Accidents caused by firearm	2, 326	2, 174	1. 6	1. 4
Inhalation and ingestion of food or other object causing obstruction or suffocation	1, 341	1, 350	. 9	. 9
Accidental drowning	5, 330	4, 785	3. 6	3. 2
Excessive heat and insolation	488	137	. 3	. 1
Excessive cold	185	250	. 1	. 2
Hunger, thirst, and exposure	182	176	. 1	. 1
Cataclysm	314	251	. 2	. 2
Lightning	249	219	. 2	. 1
Complications due to nontherapeutic medical and surgical procedures, therapeutic misadventure, and late complications of therapeutic procedures	232	569	. 2	. 4
All other accidents	5, 197	5, 236	3. 5	3. 5

[1] Based on population excluding armed forces overseas.

Source: Department of Health, Education, and Welfare, Public Health Service, National Office of Vital Statistics; basic figures from annual report, *Vital Statistics of the United States*.

No. 75.—DEATH RATES PER 100,000 POPULATION, FOR THE 10 LEADING CAUSES OF DEATH, BY STATES: 1949

[By place of residence. Based on total population present in area, excluding armed forces overseas. For method of selecting the leading causes of death, see The Leading Causes of Death: United States, 1949, Vital Statistics—Special Reports, Vol. 36, No. 20]

STATE	Diseases of heart	Malignant neoplasms, etc.	Vascular lesions affecting central nervous system	Accidents	Certain diseases of early infancy	Pneumonia (exc. of newborn) and influenza	Tuberculosis, all forms	General arteriosclerosis	Chronic and unspecified nephritis, etc.	Diabetes mellitus
United States	349.1	138.9	100.9	60.7	43.2	39.0	26.3	26.5	17.5	16.9
Alabama	253.4	96.3	99.2	59.2	59.8	40.1	30.8	9.7	24.8	11.0
Arizona	196.6	96.9	56.9	77.8	68.6	37.6	72.2	14.2	10.7	8.8
Arkansas	248.7	99.1	87.0	64.7	40.4	44.1	35.3	12.6	26.1	10.6
California	359.3	142.0	94.9	63.1	39.2	27.2	26.7	25.6	11.8	8.9
Colorado	335.1	130.8	88.8	69.5	54.0	53.2	19.3	21.6	17.4	12.7
Connecticut	376.1	170.9	92.4	43.4	30.4	19.0	20.8	18.1	11.4	19.3
Delaware	415.0	141.4	86.5	55.9	41.4	28.8	35.4	24.5	25.4	26.0
District of Columbia	371.6	154.0	85.2	55.8	48.0	26.6	52.2	18.2	14.7	14.2
Florida	306.3	121.6	104.3	62.9	46.6	28.6	25.6	16.6	21.8	13.3
Georgia	256.9	96.4	116.0	57.2	52.1	36.0	26.1	12.1	27.6	11.0
Idaho	279.9	105.1	83.7	82.2	45.1	22.9	9.8	12.8	17.7	11.7
Illinois	423.6	166.2	94.7	61.9	37.4	24.3	26.8	20.2	24.3	26.4
Indiana	368.3	145.1	124.6	69.5	40.2	28.2	20.6	30.8	19.2	18.2
Iowa	373.0	150.4	136.7	64.6	39.4	28.4	9.6	28.1	18.6	16.3
Kansas	350.1	141.7	130.3	72.8	38.9	25.7	11.2	27.1	22.0	19.1
Kentucky	306.6	110.3	106.3	69.1	53.5	46.3	43.9	22.6	21.0	12.2
Louisiana	296.7	117.0	82.2	57.9	60.2	38.5	29.8	10.8	18.1	13.3
Maine	403.7	166.7	135.6	64.8	46.2	34.1	20.9	31.7	20.5	19.1
Maryland	373.6	137.0	82.5	54.0	38.5	23.9	39.4	17.6	15.2	18.3
Massachusetts	435.8	176.1	115.3	51.6	31.0	26.2	23.6	26.0	13.8	20.2
Michigan	318.6	137.5	93.5	62.3	42.9	26.6	22.8	19.0	15.5	25.7
Minnesota	333.8	148.8	120.6	61.7	39.3	27.0	12.9	28.1	9.5	17.0
Mississippi	260.9	100.0	102.9	60.1	56.3	41.4	29.1	10.9	31.9	11.3
Missouri	408.4	158.9	123.5	69.1	38.4	39.8	27.1	22.4	28.6	17.7
Montana	356.2	129.7	106.9	98.2	45.4	27.9	19.4	27.4	18.5	18.1
Nebraska	333.2	153.6	121.0	69.9	36.1	28.8	12.0	24.0	18.0	18.2
Nevada	327.7	120.8	79.2	105.0	48.4	23.3	36.5	11.3	13.8	14.5
New Hampshire	446.8	182.2	126.8	55.3	38.8	29.6	13.2	55.6	21.0	28.3
New Jersey	402.9	173.9	97.1	43.3	34.1	22.3	26.7	20.6	15.0	20.9
New Mexico	165.7	84.0	45.1	79.7	90.3	49.8	44.6	10.1	14.1	6.8
New York	441.5	175.4	91.3	51.1	34.0	28.3	29.6	21.0	13.1	19.8
North Carolina	242.6	82.7	96.6	56.7	55.2	32.9	24.6	11.2	19.5	10.2
North Dakota	281.6	130.8	101.4	73.2	55.2	27.4	11.5	20.9	14.9	18.4
Ohio	354.8	147.5	116.9	61.2	39.9	26.5	24.8	26.3	14.7	22.5
Oklahoma	273.7	121.3	107.0	70.5	43.0	30.5	24.9	16.1	21.5	14.2
Oregon	341.1	134.6	98.7	73.9	36.8	25.7	15.1	24.1	12.7	12.5
Pennsylvania	418.6	152.7	102.0	54.1	39.1	28.9	25.8	25.6	15.6	20.2
Rhode Island	412.3	177.6	92.4	49.2	33.2	14.9	21.2	21.4	18.8	38.7
South Carolina	264.0	84.5	106.0	63.9	56.4	38.0	25.1	16.0	20.7	12.4
South Dakota	287.5	129.3	118.0	74.3	44.0	26.9	18.0	23.1	12.5	20.6
Tennessee	252.8	100.5	104.0	53.0	52.2	41.5	38.0	9.7	20.9	9.0
Texas	231.3	100.4	73.8	67.2	55.7	31.3	31.8	10.5	16.9	10.6
Utah	248.0	84.2	61.2	70.9	52.1	16.5	8.9	11.8	11.1	10.3
Vermont	420.2	166.9	128.9	58.6	51.5	33.0	26.7	45.5	16.6	22.3
Virginia	293.4	100.9	103.0	60.1	55.6	33.2	29.6	16.8	20.7	11.8
Washington	343.6	137.6	104.6	71.3	39.8	30.2	18.4	19.7	12.1	14.3
West Virginia	267.7	104.6	89.8	72.4	56.4	36.9	27.3	15.1	18.4	15.5
Wisconsin	372.5	154.8	117.6	61.8	40.8	23.1	13.6	23.6	14.2	18.9
Wyoming	269.9	101.8	77.2	107.2	61.2	24.6	10.5	11.2	16.3	11.2

Source: Department of Health, Education, and Welfare, Public Health Service, National Office of Vital Statistics, annual report, Vital Statistics of the United States.

No. 76.—Infant Deaths (Under 1 Year of Age) per 1,000 Live Births, by Age Groups, for Birth-Registration States: 1915 to 1950

[For total under 1 year, see also *Historical Statistics*, series C 39]

AGE	1915	1920	1925	1930	1935	1940	1945	1946	1947	1948	1949	1950
Total under 1 year	99.9	85.8	71.7	64.6	55.7	47.0	38.3	33.8	32.2	32.0	31.3	29.2
Under 28 days	44.4	41.5	37.8	35.7	32.4	26.8	24.3	24.0	22.8	22.2	21.4	20.5
Under 1 day	15.0	14.8	15.0	15.0	15.0	13.9	11.2	11.4	10.7	10.7	10.5	10.2
1 day	4.9	4.6	4.2	4.2	3.7	3.5	3.3	3.5	3.4	3.4	3.1	3.1
2 days	3.5	3.4	3.2	2.9	2.4	2.2	2.1	2.2	2.1	2.1	2.1	2.0
3 days											1.1	1.1
4 days	6.7	6.4	5.8	5.1	4.4	3.6	3.1	3.0	3.0	2.8	.7	.6
5 days											.5	.5
6 days											.4	.4
7-13 days	6.0	5.4	4.4	3.9	3.1	2.4	2.1	1.9	1.7	1.6	1.5	1.3
14-20 days	4.6	3.8	2.9	2.5	2.0	1.6	1.3	1.1	1.0	.9	.9	.7
21-27 days	3.7	3.1	2.3	2.1	1.8	1.4	1.2	.9	.9	.8	.7	.6
28-59 days	9.0	7.3	5.8	5.3	4.4	3.5	2.8	2.2	2.0	2.0	2.1	1.8
2 months	7.6	5.7	4.6	4.2	3.5	2.9	2.2	1.6	1.6	1.6	1.6	1.4
3 months			4.0	3.5	2.9	2.4	1.8	1.3	1.3	1.3	1.3	1.2
4 months	16.9	13.1	3.4	2.8	2.3	1.9	1.4	1.0	1.0	1.1	1.1	.9
5 months			2.9	2.4	2.0	1.6	1.2	.8	.8	.9	.9	.7
6 months			2.7	2.3	1.8	1.4	1.1	.7	.7	.7	.7	.6
7 months	12.5	10.0	2.5	2.0	1.6	1.2	.9	.6	.5	.6	.6	.6
8 months			2.3	1.8	1.4	1.0	.8	.5	.5	.5	.5	.5
9 months			2.1	1.7	1.3	.9	.6	.4	.4	.4	.4	.4
10 months	9.5	8.3	1.9	1.5	1.1	.8	.5	.4	.3	.4	.4	.3
11 months			1.8	1.4	1.1	.7	.5	.3	.3	.3	.3	.3

Source: Department of Health, Education, and Welfare, Public Health Service, National Office of Vital Statistics; annual report, *Vital Statistics of the United States*.

No. 77.—Infant Deaths (Under 1 Year of Age), per 1,000 Live Births, by Age, Race, and Sex: 1950

AGE	TOTAL			WHITE			NONWHITE		
	Both sexes	Male	Female	Both sexes	Male	Female	Both sexes	Male	Female
Total under 1 year	29.2	32.8	25.5	26.8	30.2	23.1	44.5	48.9	39.9
Under 28 days	20.5	23.3	17.5	19.4	22.2	16.4	27.5	30.8	24.2
Under 1 day	10.2	11.5	8.8	9.7	11.0	8.3	13.0	14.7	11.2
1 day	3.1	3.6	2.6	3.0	3.5	2.5	3.7	4.2	3.2
2 days	2.0	2.4	1.6	2.0	2.4	1.6	2.3	2.7	1.9
3 days	1.1	1.3	.9	1.0	1.2	.8	1.4	1.5	1.3
4 days	.6	.7	.5	.6	.7	.5	.9	.9	.8
5 days	.5	.5	.4	.4	.5	.4	.8	.9	.8
6 days	.4	.4	.3	.3	.4	.3	.7	.7	.6
7-13 days	1.3	1.5	1.2	1.2	1.3	1.0	2.4	2.6	2.2
14-20 days	.7	.8	.7	.6	.7	.6	1.4	1.5	1.2
21-27 days	.6	.6	.5	.5	.6	.4	1.0	1.1	.9
28-59 days	1.8	2.1	1.6	1.6	1.7	1.3	3.6	4.0	3.1
2 months	1.4	1.5	1.2	1.2	1.3	1.0	2.7	2.8	2.6
3 months	1.2	1.3	1.0	1.0	1.1	.9	2.2	2.4	2.0
4 months	.9	1.0	.9	.8	.8	.7	1.8	1.8	1.7
5 months	.7	.8	.7	.6	.7	.6	1.5	1.6	1.4
6 months	.6	.7	.6	.5	.6	.5	1.3	1.4	1.3
7 months	.6	.6	.5	.5	.5	.4	1.1	1.2	1.0
8 months	.5	.5	.4	.4	.4	.4	.9	.9	.9
9 months	.4	.4	.4	.3	.4	.3	.8	.8	.7
10 months	.3	.3	.3	.3	.3	.3	.6	.6	.6
11 months	.3	.3	.3	.3	.3	.2	.6	.6	.5

Source: Department of Health, Education, and Welfare, Public Health Service, National Office of Vital Statistics; annual report, *Vital Statistics of the United States*.

No. 78.—INFANT DEATHS (UNDER 1 YEAR OF AGE) AND RATES PER 1,000 LIVE BIRTHS, BY STATES: 1940 TO 1950

[By place of residence. See also *Historical Statistics*, series C 39]

STATE	NUMBER OF INFANT DEATHS					RATE PER 1,000 LIVE BIRTHS				
	1940	1947	1948	1949	1950	1940	1947	1948	1949	1950
United States	110,984	119,173	113,169	111,531	103,825	47.0	32.2	32.0	31.3	29.2
Alabama	3,870	3,301	3,228	3,345	3,044	61.5	37.5	37.8	39.6	36.8
Arizona	983	973	1,083	1,034	953	85.5	50.8	56.4	51.0	45.8
Arkansas	1,810	1,445	1,363	1,539	1,209	47.0	29.5	28.4	33.7	26.5
California	4,403	7,233	6,885	6,574	6,115	39.2	29.4	28.6	26.8	25.0
Colorado	1,270	1,234	1,267	1,153	1,167	60.4	37.5	38.4	35.1	34.4
Connecticut	868	1,150	1,026	943	886	34.0	25.2	24.3	23.1	21.8
Delaware	217	239	214	224	235	47.7	31.0	29.5	30.4	30.7
District of Columbia	554	691	531	576	603	49.3	31.9	25.5	29.1	30.4
Florida	1,818	2,285	2,103	2,088	2,078	53.8	38.2	35.3	33.8	32.1
Georgia	3,744	3,251	3,169	3,101	3,064	57.8	34.2	34.2	33.3	33.5
Idaho	506	478	481	431	434	42.9	29.4	29.8	27.0	27.1
Illinois	4,398	5,672	5,123	5,195	4,868	35.3	28.9	27.7	27.4	25.6
Indiana	2,595	2,949	2,760	2,746	2,520	42.1	30.6	29.8	29.1	27.0
Iowa	1,636	1,817	1,610	1,591	1,555	36.5	28.5	26.6	25.7	24.8
Kansas	1,106	1,251	1,151	1,136	1,130	38.3	28.1	26.9	25.9	26.7
Kentucky	3,387	2,971	3,073	3,139	2,616	53.1	37.1	39.8	41.2	34.9
Louisiana	3,268	2,773	2,779	2,810	2,639	64.3	37.2	37.9	37.2	34.6
Maine	810	853	706	713	650	53.2	35.7	32.0	32.5	30.9
Maryland	1,590	1,794	1,537	1,636	1,465	49.1	31.6	28.8	30.5	27.0
Massachusetts	2,458	3,027	2,613	2,347	2,240	37.5	28.1	26.8	24.5	23.3
Michigan	4,032	5,080	4,639	4,545	4,230	40.7	31.5	30.0	28.9	26.3
Minnesota	1,758	2,165	1,959	1,893	1,889	33.2	28.6	26.9	25.6	25.1
Mississippi	2,869	2,448	2,474	2,631	2,385	54.4	36.8	37.9	39.6	36.7
Missouri	2,885	2,929	2,585	2,563	2,510	46.9	32.5	30.3	30.0	29.2
Montana	537	484	461	457	441	46.5	32.1	30.7	29.7	28.2
Nebraska	792	804	835	761	796	36.0	27.8	26.8	24.1	25.0
Nevada	109	134	147	118	139	51.7	33.2	39.8	32.1	37.9
New Hampshire	341	399	361	333	282	40.9	30.1	29.1	27.9	24.5
New Jersey	2,121	2,965	2,585	2,534	2,467	35.5	27.9	26.5	26.0	25.2
New Mexico	1,488	1,379	1,438	1,406	1,211	100.6	67.9	70.1	65.1	54.8
New York	7,297	9,123	8,258	7,878	7,429	37.2	28.2	27.3	26.1	24.7
North Carolina	4,631	3,938	3,858	4,113	3,674	57.6	34.9	35.3	38.1	34.5
North Dakota	593	523	487	517	453	45.1	30.6	29.4	30.7	26.6
Ohio	4,714	5,817	5,693	5,693	4,990	41.4	29.5	30.5	28.1	25.8
Oklahoma	2,238	1,733	1,731	1,531	1,514	49.9	32.3	34.4	30.8	30.2
Oregon	585	895	897	869	812	33.2	24.7	25.5	24.6	22.5
Pennsylvania	7,404	7,741	6,442	6,567	6,126	44.7	31.1	28.4	29.2	27.6
Rhode Island	410	522	444	395	450	37.9	26.3	24.0	24.0	27.8
South Carolina	3,042	2,352	2,331	2,283	2,220	68.2	39.5	40.4	39.0	38.6
South Dakota	466	511	525	448	473	38.7	30.9	32.0	26.0	26.6
Tennessee	2,954	3,144	3,096	3,331	2,961	53.5	36.3	37.7	40.2	36.4
Texas	8,675	8,161	9,131	8,628	7,630	68.3	41.1	46.2	42.7	37.4
Utah	539	545	568	535	503	40.4	25.1	27.4	26.3	23.7
Vermont	309	303	271	301	221	44.5	31.2	28.9	32.4	24.5
Virginia	3,335	3,142	3,163	3,162	2,836	58.5	36.6	38.5	38.1	34.6
Washington	992	1,643	1,537	1,530	1,522	35.2	28.1	27.5	27.1	27.3
West Virginia	2,269	2,091	2,108	2,082	1,822	53.7	38.0	40.2	39.6	36.1
Wisconsin	2,046	2,476	2,148	2,202	2,121	37.3	29.5	26.3	26.5	25.7
Wyoming	232	249	293	280	247	44.7	34.0	39.5	37.4	32.5

Source: Department of Health, Education, and Welfare, Public Health Service, National Office of Vital Statistics; annual report, *Vital Statistics of the United States*.

No. 79.—INFANT DEATHS (UNDER 1 YEAR OF AGE) AND RATES PER 1,000 LIVE BIRTHS, BY RACE, FOR URBAN AND RURAL AREAS, BY STATES: 1949

[By place of residence. For rates by color for U. S., see also *Historical Statistics*, series C 39–41]

STATE	NUMBER OF DEATHS				RATE PER 1,000 LIVE BIRTHS					
	Urban[1]		Rural[1]		Total		Urban[1]		Rural[1]	
	White	Non-white	White	Non-white	White	Non-white	White	Non-white	White	Non-white
United States	50,744	12,253	38,363	10,271	28.9	47.3	27.8	46.0	30.4	49.0
Alabama	604	671	1,100	970	32.6	51.0	30.7	55.6	33.8	48.2
Arizona	328	26	395	283	41.3	112.9	29.7	39.4	61.1	138.4
Arkansas	367	174	718	280	31.7	39.8	31.9	53.7	31.6	34.3
California	3,685	539	2,194	156	26.2	34.0	24.5	32.7	29.5	39.6
Colorado	588	22	533	10	34.9	42.3	30.1	35.0	42.2	78.1
Connecticut	575	54	309	5	22.3	45.7	22.2	45.5	22.6	47.2
Delaware	80	32	83	29	26.7	48.2	24.3	47.5	29.5	48.9
District of Columbia	327	249	---	---	28.1	30.4	28.1	30.4	---	---
Florida	654	513	573	348	27.6	49.9	25.5	50.3	30.5	49.4
Georgia	755	639	921	786	28.6	41.0	31.1	47.5	26.9	36.9
Idaho	210	1	204	16	26.3	73.3	30.2	14.1	23.2	99.4
Illinois	3,262	733	1,166	34	26.0	40.5	26.3	40.2	25.0	49.2
Indiana	1,529	227	985	5	28.2	46.6	29.5	46.9	26.3	33.8
Iowa	854	24	708	5	25.5	51.5	29.0	44.7	22.2	192.3
Kansas	612	58	450	15	25.4	38.3	27.5	33.9	23.0	76.5
Kentucky	859	187	1,986	107	39.9	59.0	38.3	59.2	40.7	58.8
Louisiana	686	695	545	884	27.2	52.3	28.0	48.7	26.2	55.5
Maine	237	1	472	2	33.4	114.3	28.1	50.0	35.1	200.0
Maryland	571	347	536	182	26.5	45.0	27.1	43.5	25.8	47.7
Massachusetts	1,972	73	297	5	24.3	38.0	24.0	37.2	26.1	57.5
Michigan	2,465	487	1,543	50	27.8	40.9	26.9	39.2	29.5	71.4
Minnesota	1,079	26	758	28	25.1	69.1	26.1	81.9	23.9	59.8
Mississippi	341	445	582	1,263	31.7	45.8	36.9	59.6	29.3	42.3
Missouri	1,195	242	1,033	93	28.8	41.8	27.8	36.3	30.1	69.4
Montana	230	13	169	45	27.4	71.6	30.5	146.1	24.1	62.4
Nebraska	390	17	340	14	23.6	46.0	27.0	30.9	20.7	112.9
Nevada	48	2	57	11	31.0	45.0	27.2	16.4	35.2	65.9
New Hampshire	214	1	118	---	27.9	50.0	31.5	83.3	23.0	---
New Jersey	1,605	383	476	70	23.5	49.2	23.4	49.0	23.9	50.0
New Mexico	535	34	693	146	61.0	119.8	54.8	129.3	67.0	117.8
New York	5,277	982	1,587	32	25.0	38.3	24.8	38.5	25.7	33.0
North Carolina	646	620	1,539	1,308	30.2	54.2	26.7	62.3	31.9	51.1
North Dakota	157	2	325	33	29.3	94.3	32.6	66.7	27.9	96.8
Ohio	3,092	550	1,634	39	27.0	41.0	26.4	41.1	28.1	39.4
Oklahoma	689	151	558	133	28.3	50.8	30.7	55.3	25.7	44.5
Oregon	461	15	370	23	24.0	53.1	24.5	30.5	23.4	102.7
Pennsylvania	3,665	748	2,106	48	27.8	47.2	27.2	47.3	28.9	46.1
Rhode Island	322	16	54	3	23.4	45.0	22.7	41.6	28.7	51.1
South Carolina	367	320	566	1,028	28.6	50.2	27.8	53.4	30.8	49.2
South Dakota	166	10	231	41	24.1	70.3	29.5	126.6	21.3	63.5
Tennessee	920	468	1,637	306	37.8	50.7	37.1	52.9	38.2	47.5
Texas	4,354	848	2,923	503	41.4	50.8	39.5	52.7	44.6	48.0
Utah	307	7	209	12	24.7	68.8	25.1	52.2	24.1	- 94.5
Vermont	105	1	194	---	32.3	250.0	30.4	500.0	33.4	---
Virginia	668	456	1,337	701	32.7	53.5	28.6	55.3	34.2	52.5
Washington	855	57	564	54	26.0	58.1	26.0	43.6	26.0	86.6
West Virginia	541	40	1,399	102	39.0	48.9	35.5	46.4	40.6	50.0
Wisconsin	1,158	39	958	47	26.0	59.9	26.5	39.7	25.3	103.8
Wyoming	135	4	126	15	35.7	105.6	38.1	98.0	23.5	109.5

[1] "Urban" includes urban places having populations of 2,500 or more, according to 1940 population census; "rural" includes all other areas.

Source: Department of Health, Education, and Welfare, Public Health Service, National Office of Vital Statistics. Basic figures are published in annual report, *Vital Statistics of the United States.*

No. 80.—MARRIAGE LICENSES ISSUED—UNITED STATES AND MAJOR CITIES (OR COUNTIES), BY MONTH: 1949 TO 1952

[Figures for United States represent marriage licenses and marriages reported. Figures for major-city areas represent licenses issued in 34 cities with populations of 100,000 or more according to the 1950 census, and in 69 counties containing the remaining 72 cities in that population-size group. These areas contain nearly two-fifths of the total population of the United States]

MONTH	UNITED STATES				106 MAJOR CITIES (OR COUNTIES)			
	1949	1950	1951	1952 [1]	1949	1950	1951	1952 [1]
Total	1,595,150	1,591,673	1,621,159	1,563,975	580,468	575,414	543,295	515,590
January	113,001	100,015	126,396	102,083	39,840	35,919	45,804	34,938
February	107,949	101,559	104,208	106,513	37,584	33,501	32,364	35,215
March	104,696	99,083	125,299	100,062	32,854	33,356	44,859	31,839
April	129,367	125,729	119,982	117,786	46,758	45,121	41,973	41,591
May	140,453	138,105	134,140	137,556	53,031	52,169	48,307	49,069
June	185,130	184,564	182,506	172,505	67,594	65,849	63,784	60,190
July	136,326	155,655	134,165	135,825	41,997	48,192	41,695	41,557
August	156,293	180,779	152,455	150,444	57,220	65,453	53,273	50,403
September	147,373	172,737	144,073	138,251	50,421	57,081	45,880	45,015
October	132,175	148,662	133,132	133,061	44,095	49,395	42,919	43,196
November	124,306	134,338	124,771	128,015	40,500	44,231	40,636	40,222
December	131,111	150,347	140,042	141,854	38,574	45,057	41,801	42,494

[1] Preliminary.

Source: Department of Health, Education, and Welfare, Public Health Service, National Office of Vital Statistics; annual report, *Vital Statistics of the United States*; *Vital Statistics—Special Reports*, Vol. 36, No. 22; *Monthly Vital Statistics Report*, Vol. 1, Nos. 1-13.

No. 81.—FIRST MARRIAGE AND REMARRIAGE BY AGE OF BRIDE AND OF GROOM, 8 REPORTING STATES COMBINED: 1948 TO 1950

[By place of occurrence. Data are for Connecticut, Iowa, Kansas, New Hampshire, New York (excluding New York City), South Dakota, Tennessee, and Virginia]

AGE	1948				1949				1950			
	First marriage		Remarriage		First marriage		Remarriage		First marriage		Remarriage	
	Bride	Groom	Bride	Groom	Bride	Groom	Bride	Groom	Bride	Groom	Bride	Groom
Total	165,635	167,270	36,564	35,014	144,051	145,001	33,852	33,015	160,127	161,852	36,387	34,771
Under 15 years	174		1		214				254		1	
15-19 years	55,306	12,338	712	53	49,921	11,067	676	26	57,555	13,350	982	41
20-24 years	74,293	86,043	5,678	2,482	62,950	74,577	4,769	2,151	70,473	86,744	5,189	2,191
25-29 years	21,463	42,081	7,471	5,619	18,221	35,780	6,471	5,007	18,623	37,797	6,821	5,221
30-34 years	7,655	14,667	6,051	5,747	6,491	12,667	5,530	5,043	6,686	12,816	5,839	5,286
35-39 years	3,397	5,980	4,909	4,883	3,177	5,383	4,656	4,709	3,215	5,443	4,890	4,781
40-44 years	1,559	2,782	3,561	3,971	1,455	2,571	3,582	3,686	1,565	2,643	3,794	3,990
45-49 years	795	1,444	2,898	3,203	780	1,367	2,791	3,187	840	1,411	3,025	3,383
50-54 years	386	862	1,972	2,762	367	733	2,600	2,709	370	770	2,178	2,915
55 years and over	337	854	2,985	6,964	310	703	3,068	6,203	383	736	3,384	6,709
Not stated	256	239	366	340	165	153	319	294	163	142	289	254
Median age [1]	21.8	24.1	33.5	36.5	21.7	24.1	34.4	39.4	21.6	23.9	34.3	39.7

[1] In computing median age, marriages for which age was "Not stated" have been distributed.

Source: Department of Health, Education, and Welfare, Public Health Service, National Office of Vital Statistics; *Vital Statistics—Special Reports*, Vol. 35, No. 9; Vol. 36, No. 6; and Vol. 37, No. 5.

No. 82.—MARRIAGES AND DIVORCES—NUMBER AND RATE PER 1,000 POPULATION, BY STATES: 1940, 950, AND 1951

[By place of occurrence. For U. S. rates, see also *Historical Statistics*, series C 77 and C 78]

STATE	MARRIAGES						DIVORCES [1]					
	Number			Rate per 1,000 [2]			Number			Rate per 1,000 [2]		
	1940	1950	1951 [3]	1940	1950	1951 [2]	1940	1950	1951 [3]	1940	1950	1951 [3]
United States..	1,595,879	1,667,231	1,594,904	12.1	11.1	10.4	264,000	385,144	371,000	2.0	2.6	2.4
Alabama	34,010	22,823	21,581	12.0	7.5	7.1	4,444	8,743	8,766	1.6	2.9	2.9
Arizona	23,643	20,031	20,198	47.4	26.7	25.1	1,913	4,062	4,240	3.8	5.4	5.3
Arkansas	43,600	51,584	53,247	22.4	27.0	27.9	5,331	8,800		2.7	4.6	
California	45,069	79,360	74,958	6.5	7.5	6.8	22,904	38,833	38,452	3.3	3.7	3.5
Colorado	7,407	13,735	12,751	6.6	10.4	9.3	2,800	4,400	4,400	2.5	3.3	3.2
Connecticut	17,374	19,474	18,759	10.2	9.7	9.2	1,743	2,712	2,635	1.0	1.4	1.3
Delaware	4,825	2,635	2,525	18.1	8.3	7.7	207	637	600	.8	2.0	1.8
District of Columbia	7,727	10,198	10,029	11.7	12.7	12.4	1,347	1,697	1,383	2.0	2.1	1.7
Florida	32,709	27,588	27,175	17.2	10.0	9.2	11,186	18,033	18,675	5.9	6.5	6.3
Georgia	39,200	44,122	47,795	12.5	12.8	13.7	4,500	9,514		1.4	2.8	
Idaho	8,892	8,345	7,848	16.9	14.2	13.3	1,664	2,606	2,538	3.2	4.6	4.3
Illinois	63,445	93,288	87,876	8.0	10.7	10.0	12,700	23,002	23,716	1.6	2.6	2.7
Indiana	39,900	61,659	62,210	11.6	15.7	15.4	8,400	11,600		2.5	2.9	
Iowa	48,350	27,603	24,300	19.0	10.5	9.3	4,793	5,404	5,105	1.9	2.1	1.9
Kansas	21,333	18,486	16,694	11.8	9.7	8.6	3,777	5,000	4,722	2.1	2.6	2.4
Kentucky	76,300	33,019	27,734	26.8	11.2	9.5	6,000	8,100		2.1	2.8	
Louisiana	27,487	26,900	25,360	11.6	10.0	9.2	3,200	5,400		1.4	2.0	
Maine	10,202	8,617	8,206	12.0	9.4	9.2	1,549	2,175	2,010	1.8	2.4	2.3
Maryland	39,305	50,661	48,593	21.6	21.6	19.9	3,227	5,039	4,978	1.8	2.2	2.0
Massachusetts	44,836	41,711	40,800	10.4	8.9	8.6	4,616	6,515		1.1	1.4	
Michigan	46,342	58,180	53,409	8.8	9.1	8.2	12,054	15,979		2.3	2.5	
Minnesota	27,500	30,991	25,138	9.8	10.4	8.4	2,964	4,049	3,804	1.1	1.3	1.3
Mississippi	34,088	56,738	56,973	15.6	26.0	26.0	3,263	6,065	4,918	1.5	2.8	2.2
Missouri	71,860	34,300	30,571	19.0	8.7	7.6	12,000	12,177	11,632	3.2	3.1	2.9
Montana	8,700	7,235	6,311	15.6	12.2	10.7	1,700	1,951	1,840	3.0	3.3	3.1
Nebraska	15,977	13,828	12,309	12.1	10.4	9.2	2,085	2,554	2,356	1.6	1.9	1.7
Nevada	39,030	49,872	49,209	354.0	311.5	287.8	5,189	8,909		47.1	55.7	
New Hampshire	6,036	7,631	7,507	12.3	14.3	14.1	726	1,040	1,084	1.5	2.0	2.0
New Jersey	41,059	46,291	44,435	9.9	9.6	8.9	3,200	5,434	4,896	.8	1.1	1.0
New Mexico	12,170	22,717	22,013	22.9	33.3	31.3	1,200	2,655	2,942	2.3	3.9	4.2
New York	132,501	141,075	137,483	9.8	9.5	9.1	11,300	11,700		.8	.8	
North Carolina	15,100	29,751	28,608	4.2	7.3	6.9	3,900	6,361		1.1	1.6	
North Dakota	4,174	5,108	4,266	6.5	8.2	7.1	500	589	592	.8	1.0	1.0
Ohio	83,781	75,136	66,376	12.1	9.5	8.2	17,100	21,853	20,922	2.5	2.7	2.6
Oklahoma	33,319	22,400	20,636	14.3	10.0	9.1	9,800	13,900		4.2	6.2	
Oregon	5,998	11,300	10,446	5.5	7.4	6.7	3,419	5,943		3.1	3.9	
Pennsylvania	85,354	89,669	84,936	8.6	8.5	8.0	9,800	12,140	10,688	1.0	1.1	1.0
Rhode Island	6,172	7,501	7,025	8.7	9.5	8.9	653	907		.9	1.1	
South Carolina	43,200	46,175	46,466	22.7	21.8	21.9		2,300			1.1	
South Dakota	4,138	6,969	6,217	6.4	10.7	9.6	793	929	865	1.2	1.4	1.3
Tennessee	30,700	21,692	20,776	10.5	6.6	6.3	5,600	7,828	7,262	1.9	2.4	2.2
Texas	86,500	89,155	88,685	13.5	11.6	11.1	27,500	37,400		4.3	4.9	
Utah	8,245	7,110	6,843	15.0	10.3	9.7	1,500	2,107	2,259	2.7	3.1	3.2
Vermont	4,906	3,569	3,380	13.7	9.4	9.1	428	678	585	1.2	1.8	1.6
Virginia	52,680	36,732	36,992	19.7	11.1	10.9	5,299	5,941	6,003	2.0	1.8	1.8
Washington	26,300	34,438	32,300	15.1	14.5	13.3	6,400	11,197	8,600	3.7	4.7	3.5
West Virginia	8,181	17,199	16,329	4.3	8.6	8.2	2,964	4,200		1.6	2.1	
Wisconsin	23,379	29,081	27,376	7.5	8.5	7.9	3,599	4,845	4,273	1.1	1.4	1.2
Wyoming	2,935	3,549	3,160	11.7	12.2	10.7	1,000	1,151	1,159	4.0	4.0	3.9

[1] Includes reported annulments.
[2] Based on total population in each specified area (excluding armed forces overseas).
[3] Preliminary.
[4] Estimated.
[5] Marriage licenses.

Source: Department of Health, Education, and Welfare, Public Health Service, National Office of Vital Statistics; basic figures from *Vital Statistics—Special Reports*, Vol. 36, No. 2, and News Release, FSA E-33, July 9, 1952.

No. 83.—DIVORCES AND ANNULMENTS BY DURATION OF MARRIAGE, NINE REPORTING STATES: 1948 TO 1950

[By place of occurrence]

YEAR AND DURATION	Total	Connecticut [1]	Florida	Iowa	Mississippi	New Hampshire	Oregon	South Dakota	Tennessee	Virginia
1948										
Total	57,236	2,847	18,015	5,609	[1]6,697	1,260	6,405	1,030	8,292	7,061
Under 1 year	4,608	10	1,561	671	636	53	481	48	1,052	96
1 year	5,745	87	2,095	748	431	110	856	131	1,176	111
2 years	6,290	155	1,731	649	901	121	884	159	996	694
3 years	4,489	152	1,308	448	618	96	560	91	654	560
4 years	3,743	176	1,156	307	459	80	437	64	493	571
5 years	3,665	177	1,223	286	431	66	360	67	439	616
6 years	3,224	219	1,025	280	401	61	333	52	347	505
7 years	2,713	191	832	213	325	64	264	42	346	436
8 years	2,240	162	674	191	254	57	213	44	284	361
9 years	1,843	109	601	159	187	58	198	15	213	303
10-14 years	7,347	589	2,256	609	839	190	665	113	884	1,202
15-19 years	4,276	338	1,305	361	460	108	436	74	538	656
20 years and over	6,618	482	2,131	606	673	190	650	127	791	968
Not stated	435	....	117	81	82	4	68	3	79	1
Median duration [2]	5.0	8.9	4.9	3.8	4.6	6.6	3.9	4.3	3.5	6.9
1949										
Total	54,289	2,811	17,810	5,482	6,285	1,062	6,274	921	7,477	[1]6,167
Under 1 year	4,416	12	1,446	687	565	39	620	76	884	87
1 year	5,395	83	1,841	703	711	98	755	134	967	103
2 years	5,726	143	1,810	651	714	112	791	97	884	534
3 years	5,093	182	1,516	554	605	101	702	81	763	589
4 years	3,530	203	1,100	368	380	71	421	67	474	446
5 years	2,945	154	1,046	217	341	58	315	44	387	383
6 years	2,797	155	953	234	341	54	258	37	337	428
7 years	2,707	223	929	208	282	64	274	32	301	394
8 years	2,252	185	735	164	234	54	235	28	284	333
9 years	1,959	149	647	164	211	46	176	33	230	303
10-14 years	6,858	522	2,172	600	742	144	700	95	784	1,099
15-19 years	3,934	306	1,349	332	400	78	396	63	418	592
20 years and over	6,337	493	2,168	593	678	142	584	131	666	882
Not stated	340	1	98	7	81	1	47	3	98	4
Median duration [2]	5.0	8.4	5.1	3.4	4.4	6.0	3.6	4.1	3.4	7.4
1950										
Total	53,895	2,712	18,033	5,404	6,065	1,040	5,943	929	7,828	5,941
Under 1 year	4,059	3	1,305	673	506	33	605	106	761	67
1 year	5,082	73	1,765	691	715	85	626	101	943	83
2 years	5,332	154	1,705	549	642	96	713	109	872	492
3 years	5,260	171	1,742	560	558	94	647	95	826	567
4 years	4,680	251	1,421	445	570	94	559	66	716	558
5 years	3,095	183	1,029	270	346	52	332	56	415	412
6 years	2,484	148	835	219	259	59	232	38	332	362
7 years	2,459	161	843	217	275	46	237	28	305	347
8 years	2,376	146	817	193	258	61	234	35	295	337
9 years	1,919	121	662	167	207	40	206	34	223	259
10-14 years	6,696	484	2,296	541	692	148	616	99	834	984
15-19 years	3,953	328	1,347	338	365	94	392	56	440	593
20 years and over	6,112	489	2,168	540	592	138	528	104	682	871
Not stated	388	....	96	1	80	....	16	2	184	9
Median duration [2]	4.8	8.5	5.0	3.5	4.0	6.2	3.7	3.8	3.6	7.2

[1] Duration computed by subtracting year of marriage from year of divorce.
[2] In computing median duration in years, divorces and annulments for which years of duration was "Not stated" have been distributed.
Source: Department of Health, Education, and Welfare, Public Health Service, National Office of Vital Statistics; *Vital Statistics—Special Reports*, Vol. 35, No. 12; Vol. 36, No. 7; and Vol. 37, No. 4.

No. 84.—HOSPITALS—TYPE OF CONTROL AND SERVICE: 1909 TO 1951

[Covers hospitals and related institutions registered by the American Medical Association. Registration is a basic recognition extended to hospitals and related institutions in accordance with requirements outlined in *Essentials of a Registered Hospital*, officially adopted by the House of Delegates of the A. M. A. See also *Historical Statistics*, series C 92–117]

YEAR	TYPE OF CONTROL								
	Total			Governmental				All other	
	Hospitals	Beds		Federal		State and local		Hospitals	Beds
		Number	Rate [1]	Hospitals	Beds	Hospitals	Beds		
1909	4,359	421,065	4.7	71	8,827	[2]282	[2]189,049	[2]4,056	[2]223,189
1914	5,037	532,481	5.4	93	12,602	[2]294	[2]232,534	[2]4,650	[2]287,045
1918	5,323	612,251	5.9	110	18,815	[2]303	[2]262,254	[2]4,910	[2]331,182
1920	6,152	817,020	7.7	----	----	----	----	----	----
1923	6,896	802,065	6.9	299	57,091	[2]351	[2]317,264	----	----
1930	6,719	955,869	7.8	288	63,581	1,534	556,145	4,907	336,143
1935	6,246	1,075,139	8.4	316	83,353	1,408	658,359	4,522	333,427
1936	6,189	1,096,721	8.6	323	84,234	1,401	679,606	4,465	332,881
1937	6,128	1,124,548	8.7	329	97,951	1,393	690,798	4,406	335,799
1938	6,166	1,161,380	8.9	330	92,248	1,398	722,888	4,438	346,244
1939	6,236	1,195,026	9.1	329	96,338	1,411	748,808	4,496	349,880
1940	6,291	1,226,245	9.3	336	108,928	1,431	764,761	4,524	352,556
1941	6,358	1,324,381	9.9	428	179,202	1,436	786,309	4,494	358,870
1942	6,345	1,383,827	10.3	474	220,938	1,450	794,843	4,421	368,046
1943	6,655	1,649,254	12.1	827	476,673	1,457	799,466	4,371	373,115
1944	6,611	1,729,945	12.5	798	551,135	1,464	801,143	4,349	377,667
1945	6,511	1,738,944	12.4	705	546,384	1,478	810,334	4,328	382,226
1946	6,280	1,468,714	10.4	464	264,486	1,498	818,248	4,318	385,980
1947	6,276	1,425,222	9.9	401	213,204	1,516	817,001	4,359	396,017
1948	6,335	1,423,520	9.7	372	185,098	1,528	834,669	4,435	403,753
1949	6,572	1,439,030	9.7	361	182,254	1,576	842,901	4,635	413,875
1950	6,430	1,456,912	9.6	355	186,793	1,557	850,248	4,518	419,871
1951	6,637	1,529,968	10.0	388	216,939	1,644	880,781	4,605	432,268

YEAR	TYPE OF SERVICE								
	General			Mental		Tuberculosis		All other	
	Hospitals	Beds		Hospitals	Beds	Hospitals	Beds	Hospitals	Beds
		Number	Rate [1]						
1909	----	----	----	----	----	----	----	----	----
1914	----	----	----	----	----	----	----	----	----
1918	----	----	----	----	----	----	----	----	----
1920	4,013	311,159	2.9	521	295,382	52	10,150	1,566	200,329
1923	4,041	293,301	2.5	589	341,480	466	49,131	1,800	118,153
1930	4,302	371,609	3.0	561	437,919	515	65,940	1,341	80,401
1935	4,257	406,174	3.2	592	529,311	496	70,373	901	69,281
1936	4,207	402,505	3.1	584	548,952	506	73,692	892	71,472
1937	4,245	412,091	3.2	579	570,616	508	76,751	796	65,090
1938	4,286	425,324	3.3	592	591,822	493	76,022	795	68,212
1939	4,356	444,947	3.4	600	605,284	480	75,972	790	67,823
1940	4,432	462,380	3.5	602	621,284	479	78,246	778	64,335
1941	4,518	533,496	4.0	596	638,144	477	82,365	767	70,374
1942	4,557	594,260	4.4	586	646,118	468	82,372	734	61,077
1943	4,885	850,576	6.2	575	650,993	455	79,860	740	67,825
1944	4,833	925,818	6.7	566	648,745	453	79,848	759	75,534
1945	4,744	922,549	6.6	563	657,393	449	78,774	755	80,228
1946	4,523	641,331	4.5	575	674,930	450	83,187	732	69,266
1947	4,539	592,453	4.1	585	680,913	441	81,328	711	70,528
1948	4,589	576,459	3.9	586	691,499	438	81,993	722	73,569
1949	4,761	574,683	3.9	606	705,423	444	82,470	761	75,454
1950	4,713	587,917	3.9	579	711,921	431	85,746	707	71,328
1951	4,890	640,207	4.2	596	728,187	430	88,379	721	73,315

[1] Beds per 1,000 population. [2] Local hospitals included in "all other." State hospitals only.

Source: American Medical Association, Council on Medical Education and Hospitals, Chicago, Ill.; annual report, *Hospital Service in the United States*.

No. 85.—Hospital Facilities, 1930 to 1951, and by States, 1951

[See headnote, table 84]

YEAR AND STATE	Hospitals		Beds		Bassinets		Patients admitted		Average census¹	
	Total	Government	Total	Government	Total	Government	Total	Government	Total	Government
TOTAL										
1930	6,719	1,812	955,869	619,726	49,584	6,303	7,717,154	2,293,052	763,382	550,737
1935	6,246	1,724	1,075,130	741,712	53,310	8,417	10,087,548	2,869,004	875,510	674,921
1940	6,291	1,767	1,226,245	873,689	61,939	10,559	10,257,402	6,399,113	1,026,171	784,672
1945	6,511	2,183	1,738,944	1,356,718	83,131	16,586	16,257,402	6,399,113	1,405,247	1,114,414
1948	6,572	1,937	1,439,030	1,025,155	89,386	16,385	16,659,973	4,258,785	1,234,951	915,843
1950	6,430	1,912	1,456,912	1,037,041	89,200	16,613	17,023,513	4,317,370	1,242,777	931,461
1951	6,637	2,032	1,529,988	1,097,730	92,036	18,422	18,237,118	4,366,415	1,293,653	973,072
1951										
Alabama	111	35	20,450	15,435	1,352	431	274,918	110,987	16,969	13,087
Arizona	69	32	7,182	4,861	591	206	112,930	39,581	5,503	4,004
Arkansas	73	25	15,041	12,106	824	260	173,986	67,075	11,977	10,168
California	385	113	113,044	90,546	5,293	1,390	1,336,314	487,407	94,998	76,806
Colorado	108	29	19,745	13,660	1,027	201	222,687	55,482	15,810	11,446
Connecticut	71	20	23,756	15,024	1,281	21	257,073	16,996	20,195	13,614
Delaware	16	7	4,384	3,090	242	7	41,978	3,643	3,852	2,995
Dist. of Col	26	11	16,497	13,217	861	240	326,346	152,343	16,957	12,797
Florida	141	49	22,600	16,766	1,779	654	326,346	202,925	16,957	13,388
Georgia	129	46	26,915	22,135	1,509	732	376,974	202,925	21,585	18,329
Idaho	82	18	4,451	2,791	542	117	76,334	16,808	3,286	2,305
Illinois	341	80	102,644	71,691	5,456	586	1,115,604	219,923	87,858	68,999
Indiana	137	68	30,454	22,612	2,166	689	434,576	133,624	27,100	20,996
Iowa	131	34	22,590	14,874	1,672	223	302,416	53,040	19,049	13,223
Kansas	134	50	19,177	13,371	1,502	405	257,541	77,604	15,663	11,512
Kentucky	116	37	23,579	17,611	1,328	313	298,227	96,436	19,404	15,283
Louisiana	118	23	22,594	16,902	1,493	504	360,729	142,976	17,728	14,063
Maine	53	11	8,718	5,984	581	41	92,050	8,933	7,440	5,498
Maryland	82	29	26,517	19,116	1,288	418	261,090	91,231	22,825	17,142
Massachusetts	220	71	66,228	49,701	3,620	660	597,027	147,664	57,581	45,395
Michigan	256	96	64,650	48,092	3,946	835	783,263	221,799	56,513	43,448
Minnesota	212	72	31,316	20,318	2,360	532	439,884	85,142	26,024	17,674
Mississippi	94	33	13,550	10,619	853	296	202,391	80,215	10,434	8,542
Missouri	163	47	37,948	25,862	2,510	483	433,975	99,713	32,709	23,153
Montana	57	13	5,914	2,975	643	54	100,193	7,946	4,686	2,498
Nebraska	112	24	13,844	8,835	1,150	118	182,837	32,739	11,043	7,764
Nevada	16	11	1,408	1,153	154	99	25,651	16,284	1,039	886
New Hampshire	40	11	6,322	4,180	495	61	74,292	11,247	5,177	3,777
New Jersey	156	47	51,922	36,853	3,018	520	506,923	96,152	44,901	33,620
New Mexico	47	23	4,482	3,140	436	169	68,273	26,387	3,388	2,582
New York	511	150	220,831	166,797	8,836	1,319	1,868,844	515,266	193,618	151,702
North Carolina	176	52	29,879	20,339	2,387	495	475,839	113,449	23,194	16,596
North Dakota	47	11	6,718	4,142	557	37	92,966	8,507	5,505	3,849
Ohio	243	79	69,685	48,279	4,311	662	883,321	149,818	60,824	43,516
Oklahoma	119	47	18,591	14,319	1,303	441	234,703	76,837	15,118	12,219
Oregon	76	17	11,759	6,963	998	115	188,955	25,448	9,907	6,371
Pennsylvania	343	62	107,104	66,925	6,791	340	1,181,545	119,233	91,922	60,745
Rhode Island	34	8	9,709	7,289	502	70	81,008	16,922	8,142	6,280
South Carolina	65	27	15,445	12,190	1,019	446	217,095	107,490	12,741	10,630
South Dakota	59	18	7,343	4,379	642	88	102,654	11,325	5,718	3,786
Tennessee	135	40	24,474	18,228	1,493	465	334,655	117,462	20,612	16,069
Texas	527	122	56,348	40,192	4,744	1,276	1,020,969	330,038	47,692	36,130
Utah	34	12	4,601	2,783	615	101	79,979	13,291	3,661	2,478
Vermont	29	6	4,161	1,917	327		51,696	4,012	3,796	2,043
Virginia	120	34	32,088	24,743	1,844	443	396,460	140,471	26,703	21,503
Washington	123	46	26,794	19,339	1,860	283	370,725	92,335	21,468	16,280
West Virginia	80	22	14,305	8,786	977	108	241,257	33,318	12,114	7,735
Wisconsin	219	82	36,653	24,372	2,574	317	473,825	92,391	31,021	21,809
Wyoming	22	15	2,687	2,216	282	159	54,761	41,100	2,850	2,663

¹ Average number of patients receiving hospital treatment each day.

Source: American Medical Association, Council on Medical Education and Hospitals, Chicago, Ill.; annual report, Hospital Service in the United States.

No. 86.—PATIENTS IN HOSPITALS FOR MENTAL DISEASE AND IN INSTITUTIONS FOR MENTAL DEFECTIVES AND EPILEPTICS, UNDER PUBLIC AND PRIVATE CONTROL: 1923 TO 1950

[Coverage of hospitals and institutions varies from year to year. In general no adjustments are made for these variations. For details, see source]

YEAR	PATIENTS IN HOSPITALS FOR MENTAL DISEASE AT BEGINNING OF YEAR					MENTAL DEFECTIVES AND EPILEPTICS IN INSTITUTIONS AT BEGINNING OF YEAR				
	Total		Public hospitals		Private hospitals	Total		Public institutions		Private institutions
	Number of patients	Rate [1]	State	Other [2]		Number of patients	Rate [1]	State	City	
1923	267,617	241.7	229,837	28,549	9,231	51,731	46.7	46,580	1,363	3,788
1931	337,573	273.0	292,284	36,731	8,558	72,565	58.7	72,565	(²)	(²)
1935	403,895	318.4	342,167	51,789	9,939	96,101	75.0	89,760	1,103	4,238
1936	419,832	326.7	353,604	55,725	10,503	96,995	75.9	91,754	818	4,423
1937	431,990	336.2	364,563	56,111	11,316	98,765	76.9	93,772	538	4,455
1938	444,989	344.0	374,169	59,774	11,046	102,328	79.1	97,209	538	4,581
1939	459,258	352.2	389,979	58,158	11,121	100,903	77.4	95,996	(²)	4,907
1940	461,358	351.0	393,804	56,849	10,705	102,292	77.8	98,228	521	3,543
1941	480,741	362.4	409,055	61,096	10,588	103,298	77.9	98,853	523	3,902
1942	490,448	364.2	426,291	52,143	12,014	113,597	84.4	107,781	504	5,312
1943	498,828	365.4	432,254	54,643	11,931	112,449	82.4	106,112	500	5,837
1944	501,751	363.4	432,375	57,182	12,194	118,153	85.6	111,650	472	6,031
1945	510,661	365.8	433,763	63,875	13,023	117,783	84.4	111,550	452	5,781
1946	518,672	374.8	439,967	66,704	12,001	118,467	85.6	112,071	417	5,979
1947	530,255	371.9	446,156	71,694	12,405	122,605	86.0	115,870	408	6,327
1948	540,038	372.0	455,972	70,885	13,181	124,673	85.9	118,298	(⁴)	6,375
1949	554,372	375.8	468,799	72,058	13,515	129,402	87.7	122,492	(⁴)	6,910
1950	566,510	377.2	479,056	73,548	13,906	131,040	87.2	124,304	(⁴)	6,736

[1] Per 100,000 estimated population as of Jan. 1, 1923 to 1941; July 1, 1942 to 1945. Per 100,000 estimated civilian population as of July 1, 1946 to 1950.
[2] Covers veterans', county, and city hospitals.   [3] Data not available.
[4] The last city institution was transferred to State auspices in 1948.

No. 87.—MOVEMENT OF PATIENT POPULATION IN HOSPITALS FOR MENTAL DISEASE AND IN INSTITUTIONS FOR MENTAL DEFECTIVES AND EPILEPTICS: 1948, 1949, AND 1950

ITEM	HOSPITALS FOR MENTAL DISEASE				INSTITUTIONS FOR MENTAL DEFECTIVES AND EPILEPTICS			
	1948	1949	1950		1948	1949	1950	
			Total	State			Total	State
Patients on books at beginning of year	620,838	641,630	656,061	553,676	143,721	148,229	149,038	142,247
In hospitals and institutions	540,038	554,372	566,510	479,056	124,673	129,402	131,040	124,304
Absent	80,800	87,258	89,551	80,620	19,048	18,827	17,998	17,943
In family care	2,237	2,917	3,565	3,564	916	1,065	1,071	1,071
On parole or otherwise absent	78,563	84,341	85,986	77,056	18,132	17,762	16,927	16,872
Admissions during the year	[1] 259,080	[1] 259,025	[1] 263,337	180,101	15,174	15,282	15,213	13,659
First admissions	142,526	147,752	151,074	105,588	12,366	12,336	12,326	10,960
Readmissions	50,817	54,881	57,630	35,905	1,282	1,509	1,396	1,273
Transfers from other hospitals for mental disease or institutions for mental defectives and epileptics	12,069	10,618	11,027	8,608	1,526	1,437	1,491	1,426
Separations during the year	241,773	244,270	247,930	134,896	12,337	12,685	11,970	10,604
Discharges	180,747	184,366	187,522	85,615	7,104	7,736	7,328	6,362
Transfers to other hospitals for mental disease or institutions for mental defectives and epileptics	13,605	12,538	13,056	9,098	2,203	1,809	1,681	1,481
Deaths in hospitals or institutions	46,365	45,859	46,127	39,103	2,957	3,037	2,873	2,678
Deaths while on parole	1,056	1,207	1,225	1,080	73	103	88	83
Patients on books at end of year	638,145	656,385	671,468	574,881	146,558	150,826	152,281	145,302
In hospitals or institutions	554,454	564,160	577,246	489,930	127,797	132,861	135,082	128,145
Absent	83,691	92,225	94,222	84,951	18,761	17,965	17,199	17,157
In family care	2,635	3,458	4,910	4,910	1,025	1,126	1,254	1,254
On parole or otherwise absent	81,056	88,767	89,312	80,041	17,736	16,839	15,945	15,903

[1] Includes 53,666 admissions to Veterans' Adm. hospitals not classified by type of admission for 1948, 45,774 for 1949, and 43,608 for 1950.

Source of tables 86 and 87: Department of Health, Education, and Welfare, Public Health Service; annual report, *Patients in Mental Institutions.*

No. 88.—PATIENTS IN HOSPITALS FOR MENTAL DISEASE AND IN INSTITUTIONS FOR MENTAL DEFECTIVES AND EPILEPTICS, BY STATES: 1950

STATE	PATIENTS IN HOSPITALS FOR MENTAL DISEASE [1]				MENTAL DEFECTIVES AND EPILEPTICS IN INSTITUTIONS					
	Resident patients at end of year	First admissions during year			Resident patients at end of year	First admissions during year				
		All hospitals	Public hospitals			All institutions			Public institutions	
			Number	Rate [2]		Total [3]	Defectives	Epileptics	Number	Rate [2]
United States	525,683	151,074	109,781	73.1	135,062	12,326	10,569	1,561	10,969	7.3
Alabama	6,535	1,950	1,459	47.9	1,250	130	117	13	130	4.3
Arizona	1,554	691	691	92.5						
Arkansas	4,957	1,624	1,604	83.5						
California	35,493	17,111	10,089	96.9	7,351	951	871	42	682	6.5
Colorado	5,497	2,231	723	55.2	898	88	64	24	88	6.7
Connecticut	8,933	2,630	1,941	96.8	2,785	173	151	22	153	7.6
Delaware	1,327	388	388	120.9	475	43	43		43	13.4
District of Columbia	6,699	1,267	1,267	162.7	671	42	42		42	5.4
Florida	6,682	2,518	954	34.3	540	93	68	25	68	2.4
Georgia	10,141	2,767	2,065	60.5	707	135	134		135	4.0
Idaho	1,127	389	389	66.0	709	71	64	7	71	12.1
Illinois	36,896	10,243	8,253	94.6	10,097	825	750	68	702	8.0
Indiana	9,645	2,524	1,643	41.5	4,306	366	318	48	366	9.2
Iowa	8,045	2,551	1,280	48.5	3,436	330	268	62	317	12.0
Kansas	4,956	629	511	27.0	2,114	105	64	41	105	5.5
Kentucky	7,115	2,268	1,513	52.0	841	66	66		53	1.8
Louisiana	7,541	2,744	2,016	74.5	978	121	107	14	120	4.4
Maine	2,782	515	507	55.8	1,240	162	162		162	17.8
Maryland	8,617	2,321	1,247	53.7	1,551	173	158	15	156	6.7
Massachusetts	24,100	6,518	5,365	114.6	7,471	660	572	87	586	12.5
Michigan	20,851	6,416	3,663	57.2	8,274	913	814	92	847	13.2
Minnesota	10,815	4,133	2,198	73.9	4,448	241	207	32	204	6.9
Mississippi	5,066	2,263	1,885	87.3	593	91	91		91	4.2
Missouri	12,754	3,042	1,585	39.7	2,561	170	124	45	142	3.6
Montana	1,909	430	430	72.9	534	56	44	4	56	9.5
Nebraska	4,792	1,970	1,756	132.2	1,864	88	65	17	70	5.3
Nevada	363	135	135	85.4						
New Hampshire	2,608	790	742	140.0	660	44	44		44	8.3
New Jersey	19,292	5,260	4,561	94.7	6,607	438	307	102	339	7.0
New Mexico	1,060	468	245	36.5	112	21	21		21	3.1
New York	87,305	18,892	15,797	106.4	22,295	2,055	1,888	154	1,862	12.5
North Carolina	9,269	2,869	2,026	50.4	928	165	165		165	4.1
North Dakota	2,107	388	388	62.7	1,110	50	32	17	48	7.8
Ohio	24,532	6,550	4,520	56.8	6,926	503	361	142	503	6.3
Oklahoma	7,662	2,081	1,391	62.6	1,691	187	129	58	187	8.4
Oregon	4,422	1,705	1,445	94.6	1,252	136	136		136	8.9
Pennsylvania	37,494	6,667	5,286	50.2	9,885	805	609	155	525	5.0
Rhode Island	3,383	1,048	905	116.5	806	63	59	3	62	8.0
South Carolina	5,419	2,120	1,623	78.0	1,307	442	349	63	442	21.2
South Dakota	1,630	383	383	58.8	761	48	38	10	48	7.4
Tennessee	7,642	3,137	1,449	43.9	796	36	36		36	1.1
Texas	15,985	4,831	3,740	49.1	3,890	298	195	103	298	3.9
Utah	1,272	337	337	48.9	750	53	42	11	53	7.7
Vermont	1,952	587	410	108.8	442	68	64	4	68	18.0
Virginia	10,254	3,146	2,309	71.6	2,270	249	214	35	230	7.1
Washington	7,237	2,157	1,935	83.3	2,479	128	121	7	128	5.5
West Virginia	4,697	1,315	1,293	64.2	466	30	30		30	1.5
Wisconsin	14,245	3,945	3,309	96.2	3,520	370	326	35	302	8.8
Wyoming	634	130	130	45.8	435	44	39	4	44	15.5

[1] Excludes patients in Veterans' Administration hospitals.
[2] Rate per 100,000 estimated civilian population, July 1, 1950.
[3] Includes 196 persons neither mentally defective nor epileptic.

Source: Department of Health, Education, and Welfare, Public Health Service; annual report, *Patients in Mental Institutions*.

No. 89.—First Admissions to Hospitals for Mental Disease, by Mental
Disorder and Sex: 1949 and 1950

[Excludes first admissions for whom diagnosis was not reported and data from Veterans' Administration hospitals]

| DIAGNOSIS | NUMBER | | | | PERCENT DISTRIBUTION | | | | Admitted to State hospitals, 1950 |
| | 1949 | 1950 | | | 1949 | 1950 | | | |
		Total	Male	Female		Total	Male	Female	
All patients	139,238	141,001	72,343	68,658	100.0	100.0	100.0	100.0	100,223
Total with psychoses	108,812	109,628	52,016	57,612	78.1	77.3	71.9	83.0	79,926
General paresis	3,875	3,205	2,278	927	2.8	2.3	3.1	1.4	3,000
With other forms of syphilis of the C. N. S.	717	546	360	186	.5	.4	.5	.3	454
With epidemic encephalitis	155	141	80	61	.1	.1	.1	.1	114
With other infectious diseases	232	256	140	116	.2	.2	.2	.2	196
Alcoholic	6,613	5,771	4,614	1,157	4.7	4.1	6.4	1.7	4,485
Due to drugs and other exogenous poisons	774	747	328	419	.6	.5	.5	.6	406
Traumatic	581	754	515	239	.4	.5	.7	.3	544
With cerebral arteriosclerosis	17,581	17,766	9,784	7,982	12.6	12.6	13.5	11.6	15,187
With other disturbances of circulation	757	867	503	364	.5	.6	.7	.5	594
With convulsive disorders	1,608	1,537	860	677	1.2	1.1	1.2	1.0	1,351
Senile	14,866	14,691	6,634	8,057	10.7	10.4	9.2	11.7	10,882
Involutional psychoses	8,486	8,971	2,454	6,517	6.1	6.4	3.4	9.5	4,863
Due to other metabolic, etc., diseases	804	945	455	490	.6	.7	.6	.7	785
Due to new growth	290	294	156	138	.2	.2	.2	.2	221
With organic changes of the nervous system	1,353	1,436	805	631	1.0	1.0	1.1	.9	1,147
Manic-depressive	10,487	10,115	3,495	6,620	7.5	7.2	4.8	9.6	5,240
Schizophrenia (dementia praecox)	29,729	31,548	13,736	17,812	21.4	22.4	19.0	25.9	23,637
Paranoia and paranoid conditions	1,984	2,424	1,078	1,346	1.4	1.7	1.5	2.0	1,009
With psychopathic personality	1,212	1,163	661	502	.9	.8	.9	.7	779
With mental deficiency	2,595	2,593	1,402	1,191	1.9	1.8	1.9	1.7	2,377
Other and undiagnosed psychoses	4,113	3,258	1,678	1,580	3.0	2.3	2.3	2.3	2,555
Psychoneuroses	9,222	9,859	3,659	6,200	6.6	7.0	5.1	9.0	4,653
Total without psychoses	21,204	22,114	16,668	5,446	15.2	15.7	23.0	7.9	15,644
Epilepsy	527	638	372	266	.4	.5	.5	.4	510
Mental deficiency	1,453	1,474	911	563	1.0	1.0	1.3	.8	1,334
Alcoholism	12,171	13,019	10,856	2,163	8.7	9.2	15.0	3.2	7,783
Drug addiction	1,075	1,159	688	471	.8	.8	1.0	.7	508
Personality disorders due to epidemic encephalitis	113	76	44	32	.1	.1	.1	.0	64
Psychopathic personality	1,682	1,920	1,445	475	1.2	1.4	2.0	.7	1,551
Primary behavior disorders	696	976	569	407	.5	.7	.8	.6	723
Other, unclassified, unknown [1]	3,487	2,852	1,783	1,069	2.5	2.0	2.5	1.6	3,171

[1] Includes patients with undiagnosed disorders and with no mental disorder found.

No. 90.—First Admissions to State Hospitals for Mental Disease—Patients
With Psychosis Only, by Sex and Age: 1949 and 1950

| AGE | 1949 | | | 1950 | | |
	Total	Male	Female	Total	Male	Female
Total	79,960	41,691	38,289	79,926	41,300	38,626
Under 15 years	326	176	150	372	187	185
15 to 19	2,541	1,444	1,097	2,815	1,576	1,239
20 to 24	4,955	2,676	2,279	5,074	2,860	2,214
25 to 29	5,944	2,782	3,162	6,376	3,033	3,343
30 to 34	6,458	2,947	3,511	6,046	2,767	3,279
35 to 39	6,659	3,295	3,364	7,045	3,327	3,718
40 to 44	6,534	3,388	3,146	6,045	3,059	2,986
45 to 49	6,102	3,114	2,988	6,098	3,173	2,925
50 to 54	5,376	2,756	2,620	5,191	2,609	2,582
55 to 59	5,133	2,849	2,284	5,123	2,746	2,377
60 to 64	5,395	3,083	2,312	5,129	2,871	2,258
65 to 69	5,774	3,294	2,480	5,800	3,275	2,525
70 and over	18,382	9,628	8,754	18,351	9,596	8,755
Age unknown	401	259	142	551	311	240

Source of tables 89 and 90: Department of Health, Education, and Welfare, Public Health Service; annual report, *Patients in Mental Institutions*.

No. 91.—Patients With Psychosis in State Hospitals for Mental Disease—Discharges, by Psychosis: 1949 and 1950

[Excludes patients who were treated for psychoneuroses and other non-psychotic conditions and discharged patients for whom mental disorder and condition on discharge were not reported]

PSYCHOSIS	1949				1950			
	Total	Recovered	Improved	Unimproved and unclassified	Total	Recovered	Improved	Unimproved and unclassified
Total	56,296	14,836	32,105	9,265	56,386	14,882	35,206	6,298
General paresis	2,323	338	1,567	418	2,091	282	1,620	189
Other forms of syphilis of the C. N. S.	453	84	274	95	370	69	261	40
With epidemic encephalitis	94	13	59	22	90	15	62	13
With other infectious diseases	110	45	51	14	117	56	51	10
Alcoholic	5,077	2,593	1,868	616	5,042	2,555	2,214	273
Due to drugs and other exogenous poisons	458	227	197	34	439	226	199	14
Traumatic	366	69	228	69	392	81	267	44
With cerebral arteriosclerosis	3,608	496	2,235	877	3,623	517	2,493	613
With other disturbances of circulation	212	38	117	57	205	54	125	26
With convulsive disorders	1,201	181	784	236	1,222	161	862	199
Senile	1,646	142	946	558	1,473	119	970	384
Involutional psychoses	4,316	1,410	2,457	449	4,483	1,584	2,628	271
Due to other metabolic, etc., diseases	365	104	201	60	331	95	186	50
Due to new growth	41	8	22	11	48	12	18	18
With organic changes of the nervous system	432	50	228	154	453	60	279	114
Manic-depressive	9,875	4,151	4,980	744	9,503	3,915	5,104	484
Schizophrenia (dementia praecox)	20,150	3,547	12,967	3,636	21,099	3,832	14,630	2,637
Paranoia and paranoid conditions	958	179	573	206	941	185	599	157
With psychopathic personality	1,178	546	495	137	1,117	490	528	99
With mental deficiency	1,768	352	1,034	382	1,681	320	1,043	318
Other, undiagnosed, and unknown	1,575	263	822	490	1,666	254	1,067	345

Source: Department of Health, Education, and Welfare, Public Health Service; annual report, *Patients in Mental Institutions.*

No. 92.—First Admissions to Institutions for Mental Defectives and Epileptics, by Sex, Mental Status, and Type of Epilepsy: 1950

[Based on number of hospitals reporting first admissions by mental status and type of epilepsy]

STATUS AND TYPE	Total	STATE INSTITUTIONS			OTHER INSTITUTIONS		
		Total	Male	Female	Total	Male	Female
Total	11,490	10,211	5,784	4,427,	1,279	685	594
Defective, total	9,899	8,792	4,972	3,820	1,107	590	517
Idiot	2,158	1,915	1,054	861	243	132	111
Imbecile	3,450	3,142	1,785	1,357	308	147	161
Moron	3,588	3,193	1,825	1,368	395	222	173
Unclassified	703	542	308	234	161	89	72
Epileptic, total	1,395	1,295	751	544	100	49	51
Symptomatic	506	469	276	193	37	19	18
Idiopathic	719	676	374	302	43	21	22
Unclassified	170	150	101	49	20	9	11
Neither defective nor epileptic	196	124	61	63	72	46	26

Source: Department of Health, Education, and Welfare, Public Health Service, annual report, *Patients in Mental Institutions.*

No. 98.—Reportable Diseases—Number of Cases Reported for Selected Causes, by Months: 1951

[Includes cases reported in military establishments in the United States. Figures on number of reported cases of communicable disease in this and following table should be interpreted with caution. Reporting of most of these diseases is known to be seriously incomplete, with degree of completeness varying from State to State. However, these figures have proved valuable to health authorities by indicating significant changes in disease incidence. They should not be interpreted as measure of total amount of illness caused by the diseases concerned. Names of diseases are in conformity with the Sixth Revision of the International List, 1948]

Disease	Total	January	February	March	April	May	June	July	August	September	October	November	December
Typhoid fever	2,128	152	83	134	99	156	180	238	296	272	222	180	135
Brucellosis (undulant fever)	3,139	190	178	227	214	281	315	283	274	241	242	200	197
Scarlet fever and streptococcal sore throat	84,151	10,972	11,172	12,094	10,223	9,019	5,273	3,049	2,902	2,886	4,141	5,395	6,975
Diphtheria	3,983	406	381	370	251	241	218	160	233	365	480	474	388
Whooping cough	68,687	7,780	6,271	6,083	5,827	6,796	6,627	4,138	4,906	4,415	4,367	4,900	4,920
Meningococcal infections	4,164	469	457	473	424	322	291	300	236	217	300	292	398
Tularemia	702	60	51	65	48	71	52	60	60	42	42	38	94
Acute poliomyelitis	28,386	650	348	232	256	351	972	3,088	7,420	6,802	4,405	2,371	1,490
Acute infectious encephalitis	1,123	61	66	89	76	107	89	96	133	135	110	80	91
Smallpox	11	1	2	1			2	2	2		1		
Measles	530,118	40,137	57,821	82,553	96,672	105,182	58,963	27,066	8,938	4,111	7,666	12,406	28,492
Endemic typhus fever (murine)	378	26	25	19	20	31	43	14	43	37	31	14	35
Rocky Mountain spotted fever	247	2		3	5	61	81	72	65	24	15	11	7
Malaria	5,600	72	32	105	50	83	200	449	763	800	664	439	176
Venereal diseases:[2]													
Gonococcal infection	254,057			62,628			62,415			68,916			60,096
Syphilis and its sequelae	174,924			47,258			47,416			40,075			40,175

[1] Includes cases not allocated to month of onset or month of report.
[2] Data from Division of Venereal Disease, Public Health Service. Reports received by quarters only.

Source: Department of Health, Education, and Welfare, Public Health Service, National Office of Vital Statistics; Weekly Morbidity Report, Vol. 2, No. 53.

No. 94.—REPORTABLE DISEASES—NUMBER OF CASES REPORTED: 1944 TO 1951

[For qualifications of data, see headnote, table 93. Names of diseases are in conformity with the *Sixth Revision of the International Lists, 1948.* For rates for selected diseases, see *Historical Statistics*, series C 85–91]

DISEASE	1944	1945	1946	1947	1948	1949	1950	1951
Typhoid fever	4,599	4,211	3,268	3,075	2,840	2,795	2,484	2,128
Brucellosis (undulant fever)	4,436	5,049	5,887	6,321	4,991	4,235	3,510	3,139
Scarlet fever and streptococcal sore throat	200,539	185,570	125,511	93,595	91,295	87,220	64,494	84,151
Diphtheria	14,150	18,675	16,354	12,262	9,493	7,969	5,796	3,983
Whooping cough	109,873	133,792	109,860	156,517	74,715	69,479	120,718	68,687
Meningococcal infections	16,312	8,206	5,693	3,420	3,376	3,519	3,788	4,164
Tularemia	781	900	1,355	1,401	1,086	1,179	927	702
Acute poliomyelitis	19,029	13,624	25,698	10,827	27,726	42,033	33,300	28,386
Acute infectious encephalitis	788	785	728	785	730	903	1,135	1,123
Smallpox	397	346	337	176	57	49	39	11
Measles	630,291	146,013	695,843	222,375	615,104	625,281	319,214	530,118
Endemic typhus fever (murine)	5,401	5,193	3,365	2,050	1,171	985	685	378
Rocky Mountain spotted fever	470	472	587	596	547	570	464	347
Malaria	57,626	62,763	48,610	15,116	9,606	4,151	2,184	5,600
Venereal diseases: [1]								
Gonococcal infection	288,020	313,363	415,855	380,666	345,501	317,950	286,746	254,057
Syphilis and its sequelae	402,251	351,767	385,524	355,592	314,313	256,463	217,558	174,924

[1] Data from Division of Venereal Diseases, Public Health Service.

Source: Department of Health, Education, and Welfare, Public Health Service, National Office of Vital Statistics; *Weekly Morbidity Report*, Vol. 2, No. 53.

No. 95.—PHYSICIANS AND DENTISTS, AND MEDICAL AND DENTAL SCHOOLS: 1920 TO 1952

[See also *Historical Statistics*, series C 79–84]

ITEM	1920	1930	1940	1945	1947	1948	1949	1950	1951	1952
Physicians, number	144,977	153,803	175,382	(1)	(1)	199,745	201,277	204,359	206,635	(1)
Medical schools:										
Number	85	76	77	77	78	79	79	79	79	79
Graduates	3,047	4,565	5,097	5,136	6,389	5,543	5,094	5,553	6,135	6,080
Dentists, number	56,152	71,055	70,601	(1)	(1)	75,645	(1)	86,876	(1)	91,066
Dental schools:										
Number	46	38	39	39	40	41	41	42	42	42
Graduates	906	1,561	1,757	3,212	2,225	1,759	1,574	2,565	2,830	2,922

[1] Not available.

Source: Department of Health, Education, and Welfare, Public Health Service. (Compiled from various sources.)

No. 96.—NUTRITION—APPARENT CIVILIAN PER CAPITA CONSUMPTION OF MAJOR FOOD COMMODITIES: 1935 TO 1952

[In pounds. Data on calendar year basis except as follows: Dried fruit, pack year; fresh citrus fruits and rice, crop year beginning previous year; peanuts, crop year beginning September of year indicated. See also *Historical Statistics*, series C 128-155]

COMMODITY	1935-39, average	1946	1947	1948	1949	1950	1951	1952[1]
Meats (carcass weight), total	126.2	153.2	154.3	144.6	143.7	143.5	137.6	142.0
Beef	55.2	61.3	69.1	62.7	63.5	63.0	56.1	60.4
Veal	8.1	9.9	10.8	9.5	8.8	8.0	6.6	7.0
Lamb and mutton	6.8	6.6	5.3	5.0	4.1	3.9	3.4	3.9
Pork (excluding lard)	56.1	75.4	69.1	67.4	67.3	68.6	71.5	70.7
Fish (edible weight), total	11.1	11.0	10.6	11.0	11.4	11.5	11.5	11.4
Fresh and frozen	5.3	6.2	6.2	6.3	6.4	6.3	6.4	(²)
Canned [³]	4.8	3.8	3.6	3.8	4.1	4.3	4.2	(²)
Cured	1.0	1.0	.8	.9	.9	.9	.9	(²)
Poultry products:								
Eggs	37.3	47.1	47.6	48.3	47.7	48.2	51.6	52.7
Eggs (number)	*398*	*377*	*381*	*387*	*381*	*386*	*397*	*406*
Chicken (dressed weight)	17.9	25.7	23.5	23.1	25.1	26.4	26.8	29.5
Turkey (dressed weight)	2.6	4.5	4.4	3.7	4.1	4.9	5.2	5.6
Dairy products:								
Total milk (whole milk equivalent) [⁴]	801	813	787	751	761	776	757	(²)
Cheese	5.5	6.7	6.9	6.9	7.2	7.7	7.2	7.5
Condensed and evaporated milk	16.7	18.5	20.3	20.1	19.6	20.0	18.2	17.9
Fluid milk and cream [⁴]	340	423	396	387	384	385	395	400
Fats and oils, total, fat content	44.7	39.7	41.8	42.4	42.2	45.4	41.8	43.7
Butter, farm and factory (actual weight)	16.7	10.5	11.1	9.9	10.4	10.7	9.6	8.7
Lard	11.0	11.8	12.5	12.7	11.7	12.1	12.2	12.2
Margarine (actual weight)	2.9	3.8	5.0	6.1	5.7	6.1	6.5	7.7
Shortening	11.7	10.1	9.3	9.7	9.7	11.0	9.0	10.0
Other edible fats and oils	6.3	6.2	6.9	7.2	7.8	8.8	7.6	8.3
Fruits:								
Fresh, total [⁴]	138.5	138.3	143.5	130.6	125.0	110.1	117.7	113.0
Citrus [⁴]	48.9	58.7	61.8	53.9	47.4	40.9	44.8	44.3
Apples (commercial)	30.4	23.2	26.3	25.8	24.8	23.1	25.6	22.7
Other (excluding melons)	59.2	56.4	56.4	50.9	52.8	46.1	47.3	46.0
Processed:								
Canned fruit	14.9	21.8	18.2	18.0	18.2	20.9	18.7	19.7
Canned juices	3.9	17.7	15.5	17.3	15.4	13.8	14.8	13.9
Frozen	.8	3.1	3.2	3.0	3.5	4.3	4.7	5.5
Dried	5.8	4.6	4.0	4.2	4.6	4.4	4.4	4.5
Vegetables:								
Fresh [⁴]	235	272	252	261	249	252	254	241
Canned	29.9	46.5	40.2	37.6	38.6	41.8	41.4	41.2
Frozen	4.4	2.0	2.6	3.0	3.0	3.3	4.1	4.2
Potatoes [⁴]	131	127	124	113	108	104	104	102
Sweetpotatoes [⁴]	21.4	18.2	15.9	13.0	14.3	12.8	6.5	7.5
Dry edible beans [⁴]	8.8	8.7	6.4	6.8	7.0	8.6	8.4	8.5
Sugar (refined)	97.0	74.4	91.1	95.7	95.1	95.5	96.3	92-96
Grains:								
Corn products:								
Corn meal	22.9	15.9	14.0	13.8	13.5	13.2	12.7	12.5
Corn sirup	7.6	11.8	12.8	8.2	8.5	9.1	9.0	9.0
Corn starch	1.3	1.8	1.9	1.7	1.8	1.9	1.9	1.9
Corn sugar	2.7	3.8	4.5	4.0	4.1	4.5	4.1	4.0
Breakfast cereals	1.6	1.9	1.4	1.5	1.5	1.5	1.5	1.5
Hominy	1.4	2.7	3.1	2.9	2.7	2.7	2.7	2.7
Oatmeal	3.9	3.1	2.8	2.9	2.9	3.0	3.0	3.0
Barley food products [⁵]	1.4	2.0	1.9	1.5	1.5	1.4	1.4	1.4
Wheat:								
Flour [⁷]	159	156	138	137	135	133	133	133
Breakfast cereals	3.7	3.3	3.3	3.3	3.3	3.3	3.3	3.3
Rye flour	2.2	1.8	1.3	1.4	1.5	1.5	1.5	1.5
Rice, milled	5.6	4.0	4.7	5.0	5.0	5.0	5.8	5.5
Beverages:								
Coffee [⁶]	14.0	19.9	17.3	18.3	18.6	16.1	16.4	16.4
Tea	.67	.57	.58	.57	.59	.60	.65	.64
Cocoa beans	4.4	4.2	4.1	3.8	4.0	4.3	4.0	4.0
Peanuts (shelled)	4.3	5.0	4.6	4.3	4.2	4.3	4.4	4.4

[1] Preliminary.
[2] Data not available.
[3] Excludes canned food products containing small quantities of fish such as clam chowder, etc.
[4] Series in process of revision as result of 1950 Census of Agriculture for all years for total milk, fluid milk and cream, fresh vegetables; 1946 through 1950 for total fresh fruit, fresh citrus fruit; and 1946 through 1949 for potatoes, sweetpotatoes, dry beans.
[5] Average for 1937-39.
[6] In terms of malt equivalent.
[7] Comprises white, whole wheat, and semolina flour.
[8] Green bean basis.

Source: Department of Agriculture, Bureau of Agricultural Economics; published quarterly in *National Food Situation*.

No. 97.—NUTRITION—NUTRIENTS AVAILABLE FOR CIVILIAN CONSUMPTION PER CAPITA PER DAY: 1935 TO 1952

[Computed on basis of estimates of apparent civilian consumption (retail basis) including consumption from urban gardens. No deductions have been made in nutrient estimates for loss or waste in home or for destruction or loss of nutrients during preparation of food. Deductions have been made for inedible refuse. Data for iron, thiamine, riboflavin, and niacin include amounts of these nutrients added to prepared cereals, bread, and white flour under enrichment program. See also *Historical Statistics*, series C 122–127]

NUTRIENTS	Units	1935–39, average	1946	1947	1948	1949	1950	1951	1952 (prel.)
Food energy	Cal	3,280	3,390	3,330	3,260	3,230	3,270	3,240	3,250
Protein	Grams	89	104	97	94	94	94	95	96
Fat	do	132	147	142	142	141	146	141	146
Carbohydrate	do	431	417	411	402	401	399	402	394
Calcium	do	.94	1.15	1.06	1.05	1.05	1.06	1.07	1.08
Iron	Mg	13.6	18.6	17.3	16.5	16.5	16.3	16.5	16.5
Vitamin A value	I.U.	8,100	9,500	8,800	8,600	8,600	8,500	8,000	8,100
Thiamine	Mg	1.43	2.18	1.96	1.93	1.90	1.90	1.96	1.93
Riboflavin	do	1.86	2.58	2.42	2.35	2.34	2.35	2.36	2.38
Niacin	do	15.2	21.3	19.8	19.0	19.0	19.0	19.0	18
Ascorbic acid	do	115	137	129	125	121	117	122	118

Source: Department of Agriculture, Bureau of Human Nutrition and Home Economics; published quarterly in *National Food Situation*.

No. 98.—FEDERAL FOOD PROGRAMS—DIRECT DISTRIBUTION AND INDEMNITY PLAN: 1936 TO 1952

[For years ending June 30. Participation data for peak month. See text p. 60]

YEAR	DIRECT DISTRIBUTION						INDEMNITY PLAN [1] (SCHOOL-LUNCH PROGRAM)	
	Institutions and welfare cases			School-lunch programs				
	Persons participating	Quantity	Cost	Children participating	Quantity	Cost	Children participating	Cost
	1,000	1,000 pounds	$1,000	1,000	1,000 pounds	$1,000	1,000	$1,000
1936	10,431	634,665	31,792	(2)	6,174	244		
1940	11,910	1,694,890	57,674	2,496	92,904	3,962	7	1
1941	10,252	2,169,059	66,684	4,715	340,780	13,119	325	592
1942	6,230	822,251	26,146	6,165	454,503	21,859	731	1,474
1943	3,069	296,983	15,447	5,277	278,659	17,563	2,095	[3] 5,801
1944	1,161	189,616	11,753	2,926	92,776	7,814	3,762	26,585
1945	945	105,600	7,043	3,938	94,390	5,796	4,630	41,613
1946	828	74,130	1,852	3,688	76,622	5,834	5,177	51,290
1947	927	139,750	2,873	4,834	151,350	8,048	6,016	[4] 59,872
1948	1,179	180,191	13,742	7,209	283,313	32,779	6,015	53,975
1949	1,106	173,913	14,002	6,542	286,355	36,025	6,960	58,772
1950	1,113	255,112	24,452	10,129	466,718	55,189	7,840	64,539
1951	1,041	237,780	25,304	9,901	405,340	49,925	8,638	68,275
1952	1,112	40,616	7,326	10,126	196,787	32,173	9,320	66,120

[1] For 1940–43, represents School Milk Program, which was merged with indemnity plan in July 1943. [2] Not available. [3] Includes $975,000 expenditures for indemnity plan started in 1943. [4] Excludes $9,697,000 for nonfood expenditures.

No. 99.—FEDERAL FOOD PROGRAMS—DIRECT DISTRIBUTION, BY FOOD GROUPS: 1952

[For year ending June 30. See text p. 60]

COMMODITY	TOTAL		SCHOOL-LUNCH PROGRAMS		INSTITUTIONS AND WELFARE CASES	
	Quantity	Cost	Quantity	Cost	Quantity	Cost
	1,000 pounds	$1,000	1,000 pounds	$1,000	1,000 pounds	$1,000
Total	237,403	39,499	196,787	32,173	40,616	7,326
Dairy products	30,941	8,447	23,199	6,851	7,742	1,596
Poultry products	6,223	6,285	3,554	3,590	2,669	2,695
Canned vegetables	34,763	4,038	34,763	4,038		
Fresh fruits	67,703	3,724	49,231	2,708	18,472	1,016
Dried fruits	10,076	1,369	10,076	1,369		
Canned fruits	28,110	3,961	28,110	3,961		
Citrus juice	23,368	4,423	17,280	3,271	6,088	1,152
Miscellaneous products	36,219	7,262	30,574	6,395	5,645	867

Source of tables 98 and 99: Department of Agriculture, Production and Marketing Administration; *Agricultural Statistics*.

No. 100.—SCHOOL LUNCH PROGRAM (INDEMNITY PLAN)—SCHOOLS AND CHILDREN
PARTICIPATING: FISCAL YEAR 1952

[See text p. 60]

STATE OR OTHER AREA	ELEMENTARY AND SECONDARY SCHOOLS			CHILDREN IN ELEMENTARY AND SECONDARY SCHOOLS		
	Total number [1]	Number participating (peak month) [2]	Percent participation	Total enrollment [1]	Number participating (peak month) [2]	Percent participation
Total	168,965	55,652	32.9	29,059,023	9,329,441	32.1
Continental U. S.	166,473	53,412	32.1	28,491,566	9,029,217	31.7
Alabama	4,101	1,366	33.3	697,256	259,199	37.2
Arizona	580	258	44.5	146,357	52,777	36.1
Arkansas	2,645	927	35.0	415,157	156,826	37.8
California	4,848	2,820	58.2	1,916,055	599,826	31.3
Colorado	1,871	476	25.4	250,580	57,322	22.9
Connecticut	1,103	338	30.6	338,498	61,415	18.1
Delaware	233	76	32.6	55,074	11,908	21.6
District of Columbia	225	178	79.1	114,513	39,893	34.8
Florida	2,013	846	42.0	470,928	186,917	39.7
Georgia	4,013	1,389	34.6	728,363	281,421	38.6
Idaho	853	389	45.6	126,023	45,783	36.3
Illinois	5,466	3,047	55.7	1,465,081	536,645	36.6
Indiana	3,455	1,297	37.5	759,469	228,751	30.1
Iowa	7,819	1,105	14.1	535,504	165,648	30.9
Kansas	4,728	809	17.1	377,704	79,207	21.0
Kentucky	5,551	1,227	22.1	617,054	203,956	33.1
Louisiana	2,431	1,673	68.8	566,649	380,942	67.0
Maine	1,784	549	30.8	193,968	47,960	24.7
Maryland	1,302	656	50.4	404,826	128,022	31.6
Massachusetts	2,837	1,850	65.2	844,311	303,979	36.0
Michigan	5,293	2,152	40.7	1,259,487	363,599	28.9
Minnesota	6,107	1,300	21.3	567,683	224,129	39.5
Mississippi	4,877	1,106	22.7	539,781	172,592	32.0
Missouri	7,545	1,689	22.4	741,234	214,316	28.9
Montana	1,490	227	15.2	117,846	26,625	22.6
Nebraska	5,677	427	7.5	257,382	52,987	20.6
Nevada	210	66	31.4	26,310	7,465	28.4
New Hampshire	648	276	42.6	96,345	22,119	22.5
New Jersey	2,326	1,131	48.6	844,148	200,362	23.7
New Mexico	903	264	29.2	165,450	37,086	22.4
New York	8,345	3,208	38.4	2,497,904	849,272	34.0
North Carolina	3,895	1,435	36.8	892,062	375,538	42.1
North Dakota	3,349	617	18.4	126,391	39,041	30.9
Ohio	5,030	1,692	33.6	1,400,999	339,950	24.3
Oklahoma	2,963	1,669	56.3	452,366	145,578	32.2
Oregon	1,454	583	40.1	272,140	82,211	30.2
Pennsylvania	8,810	2,753	31.2	1,907,294	402,570	21.1
Rhode Island	483	236	48.9	138,754	27,189	19.6
South Carolina	3,732	1,361	36.5	499,015	205,748	41.2
South Dakota	3,758	217	5.8	128,955	20,496	15.9
Tennessee	4,954	1,911	38.6	675,584	253,723	37.6
Texas	7,829	1,749	22.3	1,430,407	384,178	26.9
Utah	521	335	64.3	155,667	61,812	39.7
Vermont	940	312	33.2	76,444	22,949	30.0
Virginia	3,467	1,214	35.0	617,149	225,080	36.5
Washington	1,689	820	48.5	429,253	116,948	27.2
West Virginia	4,463	1,407	31.5	449,025	125,589	28.0
Wisconsin	7,148	1,861	26.0	638,027	184,923	29.0
Wyoming	709	118	16.6	61,094	16,723	27.4
Alaska	104	9	8.7	14,871	1,166	7.8
Hawaii	213	163	76.5	112,913	68,995	61.1
Puerto Rico	2,161	2,034	94.1	432,157	216,651	50.1
Virgin Islands	34	34	100.0	[2] 7,516	4,412	58.7

[1] Source: U. S. Office of Education. Data for 1949–50.
[2] November 1951. Number of schools and children may have been higher in some States during other months, but November was the peak month in terms of children participating nationally.
[3] Includes private school data for 1951.

3. Immigration, Emigration, and Naturalization

Aliens or citizens arriving or departing by vessel or airplane at ports other than land border ports of the United States are recorded on passenger and crew lists or manifests by officials of the transportation companies, these lists or manifests being delivered to the Immigration and Naturalization Service of the Department of Justice. Persons going by land or air between Mexico or Canada and the United States are required to enter or depart at land border stations where they are registered by officers of the Immigration and Naturalization Service. Statistics of immigration and emigration are prepared from these and other records by the Immigration and Naturalization Service.

Immigration.—Although the reporting of alien arrivals was required at an early date in certain of the colonies and original States, the continuous record of immigration to the United States begins with the fiscal year ending September 30, 1820. Under the Act of March 2, 1819, passenger lists for all vessels arriving from foreign places were to be delivered to the local collector of customs, copies transmitted to the Secretary of State, and the information reported to Congress. Immigration statistics were compiled by the Department of State from 1820 to 1874 and by the Bureau of Statistics of the Treasury Department from 1867 to 1895. Since 1892 there has been a separate office or bureau of immigration, now a part of the Immigration and Naturalization Service. Annual reports were issued by this bureau from 1892 to 1932. From 1933 to 1940, a summary of the work of the Immigration and Naturalization Service was given in the Annual Reports of the Secretary of Labor. For 1941, the *Annual Report of the Attorney General* contained a report on immigration and naturalization. No report was published for 1942. For subsequent fiscal years, Annual Reports of the Immigration and Naturalization Service (submitted by the Commissioner to the Attorney General) were published in mimeographed form.

Since 1820 the official immigration statistics (see table 101) have changed considerably in completeness and in the basis of reporting. The early figures were for arrivals at Atlantic and Gulf coast seaports of the United States. Pacific coast arrivals were first reported in 1850. Aliens arriving at Canadian seaports en route to the United States were included after 1893. The reporting of arrivals over the land borders began in 1904 and was gradually extended up to 1908. Hawaii, Puerto Rico, and Alaska were treated as integral parts of the United States for purposes of immigration and emigration statistics beginning in 1901, 1902, and 1904 respectively. Travel between the Philippine Islands and the United States was not treated as immigration or emigration between July 1, 1898 and May 1, 1934.

Prior to 1868 arriving alien passengers were recorded, thereafter immigrant arrivals (i. e., omitting aliens coming for temporary stay). Subsequent to the passage of the Act of 1891 which increased the number of excludable classes, the basis of reporting was changed from arrivals to admissions (i. e., omitting aliens not permitted to enter the United States), except for the period 1895 to 1897, inclusive, when the reporting of arrivals was resumed.

Two classes of alien admissions are now reported, immigrant and nonimmigrant (see table 102). Included in the nonimmigrant class are aliens admitted under section 3 of the Immigration Act of 1924 (see table 108), returning resident aliens, students, and

Note.—This section presents data for the most recent year or period available on February 13, 1953, when the material was organised and sent to the printer.

others. An immigrant alien is defined as an alien, other than a returning resident, admitted for permanent residence, under either quota or nonquota status. Nonquota immigrants admitted comprise immigrants born in Canada, Newfoundland, Mexico, Cuba, Haiti, the Dominican Republic, the Canal Zone, and independent countries of Central and South America, and their wives and unmarried children under age 18 if accompanying or following to join such immigrants; relatives of citizens of the United States (wives, husbands, unmarried children under age 21); ministers and professors who enter solely for the purpose of carrying on their vocations, and their wives and unmarried children under age 18, if accompanying or following to join such ministers and professors; and others. Certain temporary admissions such as of persons in possession of border-crossing identification cards are not included either in the immigrant or nonimmigrant totals.

Emigration.—No official record of emigration was kept prior to July 1, 1907. Alien departures are classified as emigrant and nonemigrant (see table 102). For statistical purposes an alien emigrant is an alien resident of the United States departing with the declared intention of residing permanently in a foreign country. The nonemigrant category includes both alien residents of the United States departing for a temporary sojourn abroad, and aliens leaving the United States after a temporary stay.

Naturalization.—Naturalization statistics for the United States began with the fiscal year 1907. Prior to this time each court kept records of naturalizations but no national data were compiled. The Act of June 29, 1906, effective September 27, 1906, provided for periodic returns by all courts conducting naturalization proceedings, and for the filing with a central Federal agency of a duplicate copy of each declaration of intention and petition for naturalization filed, and of each certificate of naturalization issued. Naturalization statistics were originally compiled by the Bureau of Immigration and Naturalization of the Department of Commerce and Labor, now the Immigration and Naturalization Service of the Department of Justice.

Alien registration.—The Act of June 28, 1940, required the registration of all aliens remaining in the United States (including Alaska, Hawaii, Puerto Rico, and the Virgin Islands) for a period of thirty days or longer. Aliens resident in the United States on August 27, 1940, were required to register on or before December 26, 1940. Aliens arriving subsequent to August 27, 1940, and not registered by the consul granting visas were required to register within thirty days of arrival.

Historical statistics.—See preface and historical appendix. Tabular headnotes (as "See also *Historical Statistics*, series B 304") provide cross-references, where applicable, to *Historical Statistics of the United States, 1789-1945.*

No. 101.—IMMIGRATION: 1820 TO 1952

[Data are for fiscal years ending June 30, except as noted; for periods they are totals, not annual averages. From 1819 to 1867 figures represent alien passengers arriving; for 1868 to 1891 inclusive and 1895 to 1897 inclusive, immigrant alien arrivals; for 1892 to 1894 and from 1898 to the present time, immigrant aliens admitted. See also *Historical Statistics*, series B 304]

PERIOD	Number	PERIOD	Number	YEAR	Number
1820-1830 [1]	151,824	1911-1915	4,459,831	1949	188,317
1831-1840 [3]	509,125	1916-1920	1,275,980	1950	249,187
1841-1850 [3]	1,713,251	1921-1925	2,638,913	1951	205,717
1851-1860 [3]	2,598,214	1926-1930	1,468,296	1952	265,520
1861-1870 [4]	2,314,824	1931-1935	220,209	Calendar years:	
1871-1880	2,812,191	1936-1940	308,222	1946	148,954
1881-1890	5,246,613	1941-1945	170,952	1947	168,571
1891-1900	3,687,564	1946-1950	864,067	1948	170,420
		1946	108,721	1949	248,987
1901-1905	3,833,076	1947	147,292	1950	203,407
1906-1910	4,962,310	1948	170,570	1951	238,287

[1] Oct. 1, 1819, to Sept. 30, 1830. Calendar years.
[3] Oct 1, 1830, to Dec. 31, 1840.
[4] Jan. 1, 1861, to June 30, 1870.

No. 102.—ALIENS ADMITTED AND DEPARTING: 1911 TO 1952

[See also *Historical Statistics*, series B 304, B 350-352]

PERIOD OR YEAR ENDING—	ADMITTED			DEPARTING			EXCESS OF ADMISSIONS OVER DEPARTURES [1]	
	Total	Immigrant	Nonimmigrant	Total	Emigrant	Nonemigrant	Total	Immigrant over emigrant
June 30:								
1911-1915, total	5,312,007	4,459,831	852,176	2,763,410	1,444,530	1,318,880	2,548,597	3,015,301
1916-1920, total	1,800,075	1,275,980	524,095	1,224,747	702,464	522,283	575,328	573,516
1921-1925, total	3,421,811	2,638,913	782,898	1,414,236	697,397	716,839	2,007,575	1,941,516
1926-1930, total	2,460,279	1,468,296	991,983	1,280,542	347,679	932,863	1,179,737	1,120,617
1931-1935, total	949,903	220,209	729,694	1,188,597	323,863	864,734	-238,694	-103,654
1936-1940, total	1,152,599	308,222	844,377	1,008,053	135,875	872,178	144,546	172,347
1941-1945, total	712,422	170,952	541,470	399,522	42,696	356,826	312,900	128,256
1946-1950, total	2,783,976	864,067	1,919,889	1,862,771	113,703	1,749,068	921,205	750,384
1946	312,190	108,721	203,469	204,353	18,143	186,210	107,837	90,578
1947	513,597	147,292	366,305	323,422	22,501	300,921	190,175	124,791
1948	646,576	170,570	476,006	448,218	20,875	427,343	205,400	163,731
1949	635,589	188,317	447,272	430,069	24,586	405,503	205,500	221,589
1950	676,024	249,187	426,837	456,689	27,596	429,091	219,335	179,543
1951	670,823	205,717	465,106	472,901	26,174	446,727	197,922	243,640
1952	781,602	265,520	516,082	509,497	21,880	487,617	272,105	243,640
Dec. 31:								
1948	641,307	170,420	470,887	438,518	21,776	416,742	202,789	148,644
1949	679,928	248,987	430,941	431,849	26,577	405,272	248,079	222,410
1950	655,614	203,407	452,207	475,646	27,881	447,765	179,968	175,526
1951	703,716	238,287	465,429	477,328	23,422	453,906	226,388	214,865

[1] Excess of departures indicated by a minus (−) sign.

No. 103.—ALIENS EXCLUDED AND DEPORTED: 1901 TO 1952

PERIOD ENDING JUNE 30	Excluded	Deported	YEAR ENDING JUNE 30	Excluded	Deported	Deportable aliens required to depart	Indigent aliens returned at their request
1901-1905, total	37,132	2,999	1943	1,495	4,207	11,947	5
1906-1910, total	71,079	8,559	1944	1,642	7,179	32,270	4
1911-1915, total	115,496	15,879	1945	2,341	11,270	69,490	12
1916-1920, total	62,613	12,033	1946	2,942	14,375	101,945	21
1921-1925, total	103,803	28,427	1947	4,771	18,663	195,880	88
1926-1930, total	85,504	63,730	1948	4,905	20,371	197,	
1931-1935, total	33,277	74,631	1949	3,834	20,040		
1936-1940, total	34,940	42,455	1950	3,571	6,628		
1941-1945, total	10,240	30,772	1951	3,784	13,544		
1946-1950, total	20,023		1952	2,944	20,181		

Source of tables 101, 102, and 1 ... stice, Immigration and Natural...
Report, releases, and records.

FIG. IX.—QUOTA IMMIGRANTS ADMITTED: 1925 TO 1952

[See table 104]

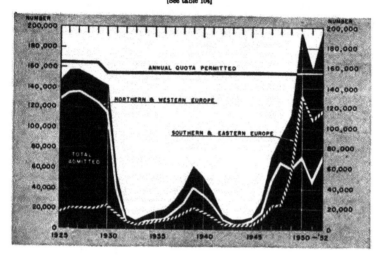

FIG. X.—NATURALIZATION: 1907 TO 1952

[See table 114]

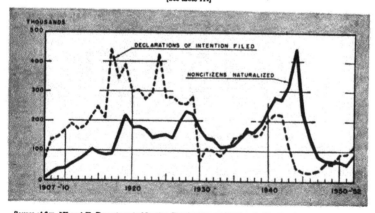

Source of figs. IX and X: Department of Justice, Immigration and Naturalization Service.

No. 104.—ANNUAL QUOTAS ALLOTTED AND QUOTA IMMIGRANTS ADMITTED, BY QUOTA COUNTRY OR REGION: YEARS ENDING JUNE 30, 1936 TO 1952

Number of aliens admitted annually of any nationality subject to the quota law was limited by Immigration Act of 1921 to 3 percent of number of foreign-born of such nationality resident in continental United States as determined by 1910 census; and by population plan of act of 1924, to 2 percent according to 1890 census. National origins clause of 1924 act, effective July 1, 1929, provided that quota of any nationality be computed by applying to 150,000 the ratio between calculated number of inhabitants in continental United States in 1920 owing their origin to nationality concerned and the total inhabitants in the United States of all nationalities subject to quota law. For estimates of white population by countries of origin, calculated as a basis for immigration quotas, see table 97, *Statistical Abstract, 1932*.) Under 1924 act, minimum quota is 100; for nonquota classes, see general note (p. 98)

Quota country or region [1]	Annual quota 1936-1952 [2]	Quota immigrants admitted						
		1936-1940	1941-1945	1946-1950	1949	1950	1951	1952
All countries	154,277	203,330	80,979	602,828	113,046	197,460	156,547	194,247
Europe	150,572	199,792	78,392	494,713	111,443	195,671	154,759	162,754
Northern and western Europe	125,853	127,474	49,386	259,862	59,578	69,368	47,026	73,362
Belgium	1,304	1,432	2,001	5,252	1,270	970	991	1,103
Denmark	1,181	1,188	761	4,738	1,109	1,101	1,082	1,183
France	3,069	3,438	3,850	13,937	2,907	3,187	2,900	2,935
Germany	25,957	90,910	21,723	78,855	12,819	22,811	14,637	35,458
Great Britain and Northern Ireland	65,721	14,551	14,885	96,430	23,543	17,194	15,360	20,368
Iceland	100	23	96	376	68	58	96	96
Ireland	17,853	4,298	1,043	24,930	6,505	6,444	3,810	3,819
Luxembourg	100	81	218	235	94	74	59	109
Netherlands	3,153	2,514	2,048	12,458	2,991	3,067	3,102	3,032
Norway	2,377	1,966	926	9,170	2,308	2,179	2,245	2,353
Sweden	3,314	1,556	627	7,692	2,376	1,876	1,360	1,454
Switzerland	1,707	2,150	1,213	5,909	1,503	1,666	1,372	1,394
Southern and eastern Europe	24,719	72,378	28,814	234,811	51,865	126,306	107,733	119,482
Austria	1,413	978	...	11,460	1,327	6,153	1,361	2,236
Bulgaria	100	422	155	439	66	177	281	330
Czechoslovakia	2,874	9,833	3,316	13,771	3,365	4,058	3,570	4,306
Estonia	116	300	151	7,444	1,716	8,387	2,250	1,366
Finland	569	1,526	628	2,248	497	518	506	494
Greece	310	1,768	1,227	1,348	426	285	3,638	4,621
Hungary	869	4,735	1,300	7,818	1,445	4,054	5,079	7,331
Italy	5,677	16,943	1,344	25,003	5,207	5,861	4,326	5,901
Latvia	236	735	443	21,714	3,634	17,490	11,220	4,999
Lithuania	386	1,426	646	19,326	6,452	11,774	4,568	3,330
Poland	6,524	18,189	10,602	88,957	21,462	50,692	45,766	42,665
Portugal	440	1,656	1,528	2,080	462	426	384	388
Rumania	291	-2,026	1,293	3,844	669	2,019	2,042	5,184
Spain	252	1,296	1,118	881	194	197	286	256
Yugoslavia	236	1,030	728	1,370	177	697	401	374
U. S. S. R. (Russia)	2,798	5,362	3,831	19,545	3,710	10,954	14,019	15,369
Turkey	968	2,171	779	8,486	976	5,359	7,411	17,365
Other southern and eastern Europe	700	1,001	127	1,177	261	385	346	1,045
Asia	1,905	2,349	1,582	5,132	1,003	1,173	1,341	1,065
...	1,300	255	440	1,516	326	328	372	353
...	600	934	655	1,406	272	286	178	135

Persons born in colonies, dependencies, or protectorates, or portions thereof within barred zone, of European countries, who are admissible under immigration laws of United States as quota immigrants, are charged to quota of country to which such colony or dependency belongs or by which it is administered as a protectorate. Aliens who obtain visas during later part of fiscal year may be admitted in following year since visas are valid for period of 4 months. Nationality for quota purposes does not always coincide with actual nationality (Sec. 12, Immigration Act of 1924).

Quota was 119,774 from 1934 to February 5, 1944, when quota of 105 Chinese, authorized by act of December 17, 1943 increased the maximum quota to 153,879. On July 4, 1946, quota for Philippine Islands was increased from 50 to 100, thereby raising total quota to 153,929. Quota was increased to 154,206 on July 27, 1949, by establishment of separate quotas of 100 each for Israel, Syria, and Lebanon, and abolition of combined quota of 123 established for Syria and Lebanon. Quota was increased to 154,277 on Oct. 31, 1950, when quota for Italy was increased to 5,677, quota for Yugoslavia was increased to 938, and a separate quota of 100 was established for Trieste.

Number of quota immigrants exceeds quota because 50 percent of quota for future years may be mortgaged when necessary under Displaced Persons Act of 1948.

Prior to 1946, Austrian quota included with German.

Philippines included in Asia in 1952; previously included in Pacific.

Source: Department of Justice, Immigration and Naturalization Service; *Annual Report*, releases.

No. 105.—IMMIGRATION, BY COUNTRY OF ORIGIN: 1820 TO 1952

[Data are totals, not annual averages, and are for periods ending June 30. Data prior to 1906 refer to country whence aliens came; thereafter, country of last permanent residence. Because of boundary changes and changes in list of countries separately reported, data for certain countries not comparable throughout. See also *Historical Statistics*, series B 304-330]

COUNTRY	Total 133 yrs. 1820-1952	1901-1910	1911-1920	1921-1930	1931-1940	1941-1950	1950	1951	1952
All countries, total	39,796,719	8,795,386	5,735,811	4,107,209	528,431	1,035,039	249,187	205,717	265,520
Europe, total	33,589,510	8,136,016	4,376,564	2,477,853	348,289	621,704	199,115	149,545	193,626
Belgium	175,142	41,635	33,746	15,846	4,817	12,189	1,429	1,802	2,946
Bulgaria [1]	66,241	39,280	22,533	2,945	938	375	13	1	9
Czechoslovakia	128,499	....	3,426	102,194	14,393	8,347	946	88	51
Denmark	342,646	65,285	41,983	32,430	2,559	5,393	1,094	1,076	1,152
Finland	23,128	....	756	16,691	2,146	2,503	506	532	500
France	643,258	73,379	61,897	49,610	12,623	38,809	4,430	4,573	4,878
Germany	6,440,520	341,498	143,945	412,202	}117,621{	226,578	128,592	87,755	104,236
Austria [2]	}4,205,078{	}2,145,266{	453,649	32,868	}117,621{	24,860	16,467	9,761	23,088
Hungary			442,693	30,680	7,861	3,469	190	62	63
Great Britain:									
England	2,784,375	388,017	249,944	157,420	21,756	112,252	10,191	12,393	18,539
Scotland	755,604	120,469	78,357	159,781	6,887	16,131	2,299	2,309	3,390
Wales	90,047	17,464	13,107	13,012	735	3,209	265	196	248
Greece	451,036	167,519	184,201	51,084	9,119	8,973	1,179	4,459	6,996
Ireland	4,625,745	339,065	146,181	220,591	13,167	26,967	5,842	3,144	3,526
Italy	4,797,184	2,045,877	1,109,524	455,315	68,028	57,661	12,454	8,958	11,342
Netherlands	274,741	48,262	43,718	26,948	7,150	14,860	3,060	3,062	3,060
Norway	819,598	190,505	66,395	68,531	4,740	10,100	2,262	2,289	2,354
Poland [3]	422,659	....	4,813	227,734	17,026	7,571	696	98	235
Portugal	265,498	69,149	89,732	29,994	3,329	7,423	1,106	1,078	953
Rumania	158,159	53,008	13,311	67,646	3,871	1,076	155	104	34
Spain	173,944	27,935	68,611	28,958	3,258	2,898	385	442	481
Sweden	1,231,913	249,534	95,074	97,249	3,960	10,665	2,183	2,022	1,778
Switzerland	309,214	34,922	23,091	29,676	5,512	10,547	1,854	1,485	1,502
Turkey in Europe	156,665	79,976	54,677	14,659	737	580	109	118	94
U. S. S. R. (Russia)	3,343,916	1,597,306	921,201	61,742	1,356	548	6	10	11
Yugoslavia	59,144	....	1,888	49,064	5,835	1,576	189	454	327
Other Europe	845,556	565	8,111	22,983	8,865	6,144	1,195	1,274	1,833
Asia, total [4]	963,568	243,567	192,559	97,400	15,344	31,780	3,779	3,921	9,328
China	399,480	20,605	21,278	29,907	4,928	16,709	1,280	335	263
Japan	283,231	129,797	83,837	33,462	1,948	1,555	100	271	3,814
Turkey in Asia	205,596	77,393	79,389	19,165	328	218	13	3	12
Other Asia [4]	75,261	15,772	8,055	14,866	8,140	13,298	2,386	3,312	5,239
America, total	4,864,950	361,888	1,143,671	1,516,716	160,037	354,804	44,191	47,631	61,049
Canada and Newfoundland	3,236,680	179,226	742,185	924,515	108,527	171,718	21,885	25,880	33,354
Mexico	854,076	49,642	219,004	459,287	22,319	60,589	6,744	6,153	9,079
Central America	75,467	8,192	17,159	15,769	5,861	21,665	2,169	2,011	2,637
South America	151,320	17,280	41,899	42,215	7,803	21,831	3,284	3,596	4,591
West Indies	509,270	107,548	123,424	74,899	15,502	49,725	6,208	5,902	6,672
Other America	38,137	....	....	31	25	29,276	3,903	4,089	4,716
Africa	35,203	7,368	8,443	6,286	1,750	7,367	849	845	931
Australia and New Zealand	69,372	11,975	12,348	8,299	2,231	13,805	460	490	545
Pacific Islands (not specified)	19,880	1,049	1,079	427	780	5,437	786	3,265	33
All other countries [4]	254,236	33,523	1,147	228	....	142	7	20	8

[1] Includes Serbia and Montenegro prior to 1920.
[2] Austria included with Germany 1938-45.
[3] From 1899 to 1919 Poland is included with Austria-Hungary, Germany, and Russia.
[4] Philippines included in "Other Asia" in 1952 (1,179); previously included in "All other countries."
[5] Includes 32,897 persons returning to their homes in the United States. After 1906 such aliens have been included in immigration statistics as nonimmigrants; prior to that year, aliens were recorded by countries whence they came (see headnote).

Source: Department of Justice, Immigration and Naturalization Service; releases.

No. 106.—EMIGRANT ALIENS DEPARTING, BY COUNTRY OF FUTURE PERMANENT RESIDENCE: YEARS ENDING JUNE 30, 1948 TO 1952

COUNTRY	1948	1949	1950	1951	1952	COUNTRY	1948	1949	1950	1951	1952
All countries, total	20,875	24,586	27,598	26,174	21,880	Europe—Con. Switzerland	318	300	342	311	341
						U. S. S. R. (Russia)	345	627	157	140	143
Europe, total	10,253	11,893	12,642	11,477	9,691	Yugoslavia	192	82	74	64	77
						Other Europe	273	236	332	281	230
Belgium	244	225	237	155	192						
Bulgaria	18	18	15	2	5	Asia, total	3,220	1,642	2,130	1,902	1,930
Czechoslovakia	145	113	97	36	28						
Denmark	285	324	350	336	350	China	2,267	365	428	376	223
						Japan	143	230	315	282	306
Finland	119	123	160	138	114	Palestine	182	177	101	28	53
France	963	1,274	1,125	1,019	1,172	Syria	161	52	29	26	25
Germany	134	622	1,309	1,101	1,028	Other Asia	447	818	1,257	1,190	1,113
Austria	53	79	98	87	112						
						America, total	5,289	9,330	10,542	11,046	8,796
Great Britain: England	2,262	2,968	2,919	2,882	1,884						
Scotland	320	443	444	465	258	Canada	1,055	1,217	2,267	3,202	2,760
Wales	51	103	72	78	35	Central America	380	775	851	816	576
						Mexico	849	1,096	1,257	1,149	988
Greece	349	380	588	374	435	Newfoundland	110	16			
Hungary	32	29	27	30	14	South America	1,862	2,538	2,873	2,817	1,984
Ireland (Eire)	285	302	372	539	229	West Indies	1,024	3,603	3,190	2,897	2,227
Italy	1,498	1,494	1,636	1,440	1,281	Other America		85	104	165	171
Netherlands	354	368	379	304	327						
Northern Ireland	87	97	189	173	71	Africa	363	345	433	393	317
						Australia	485	177	340	309	267
Norway	577	596	677	576	553	New Zealand	101	67	119	98	89
Poland	127	133	106	72	68	Philippine Islands	615	926	1,181	627	521
Portugal	394	230	228	188	183	Pacific islands, not specified	13	43	51	41	56
Rumania	10	11	8	5	2	Unknown or not reported	531	163	160	191	213
Spain	323	262	218	227	225						
Sweden	510	425	483	451	334						

Source: Department of Justice, Immigration and Naturalization Service; *Annual Report*, releases, and records.

No. 107.—IMMIGRANT ALIENS ADMITTED AND EMIGRANT ALIENS DEPARTING, BY SEX, AGE, AND MAJOR OCCUPATION GROUP: YEARS ENDING JUNE 30, 1936 TO 1952

[See also *Historical Statistics*, series B 331-336]

SEX, AGE, OCCUPATION	1936–40, total	1941–45, total	1946–50, total	1949	1950	1951	1952
Admissions, total	308,222	170,952	864,067	188,317	249,187	205,717	265,520
Males	139,282	70,151	347,836	80,340	119,130	99,327	123,609
Females	168,940	100,801	516,251	107,977	130,057	106,390	141,911
Males per 1,000 females	824	696	674	744	916	934	871
Under 16 years	47,238	24,608	137,214	32,728	50,466	44,023	64,513
16 to 44 years [1]	203,627	107,551	575,407	123,340	152,358	121,823	159,788
45 years and over [2]	57,357	38,793	151,466	32,249	46,361	39,871	41,219
Illiterates, number [3]	5,322	1,403	8,114	1,963	1,677	1,860	2,026
Percent	1.7	.8	.9	1.1	.7	.9	.8
REPORTING OCCUPATIONS							
Professional, technical, and kindred workers	26,113	17,913	64,094	13,884	20,502	15,269	16,496
Farmers and farm managers	4,928	1,691	35,872	8,937	17,642	10,214	10,566
Proprietors, managers, and officials, except farm	26,956	11,284	28,119	6,014	6,396	5,493	5,968
Clerical, sales, and kindred workers	15,849	12,398	69,230	14,797	16,796	14,098	16,724
Craftsmen, foremen, and kindred workers	}21,425	16,205	{59,427	13,693	21,832	16,183	21,223
Operatives and kindred workers			61,935	14,271	19,618	17,858	21,092
Private household workers	19,387	5,765	29,665	6,990	8,900	7,243	9,653
Service workers, except private household	7,204	4,134	19,292	3,937	4,970	5,292	6,418
Farm laborers and foremen	1,978	813	6,486	933	3,976	4,972	6,289
Laborers, except farm and mine	9,700	3,822	21,015	6,192	5,698	5,481	5,960

For footnotes, see p. 102.

No. 107.—Immigrant Aliens Admitted and Emigrant Aliens Departing, by Sex, Age, and Major Occupation Group: Years Ending June 30, 1936 to 1952—Continued

SEX, AGE, OCCUPATION	1936-40, total	1941-45, total	1946-50, total	1949	1950	1951	1952
Departures, total	135,875	42,696	113,703	24,586	27,598	26,174	21,880
Males	84,006	25,006	63,424	12,950	14,331	12,843	10,921
Females	51,869	17,690	50,279	11,636	13,267	13,331	10,959
Males per 1,000 females	1,620	1,414	1,261	1,113	1,080	963	997
Under 16 years	8,561	4,628	9,656	2,032	2,333	2,417	1,918
16 to 44 years [1]	83,215	26,715	59,100	13,895	15,576	15,422	12,318
45 years and over [2]	44,099	11,353	44,947	8,659	9,689	8,335	7,644
REPORTING OCCUPATIONS							
Professional, technical, and kindred workers	7,180	3,723	11,629	2,150	2,631	2,772	2,328
Farmers and farm managers	3,318	627	1,701	306	335	350	263
Proprietors, managers, and officials, except farm	6,095	2,394	9,166	1,819	1,943	1,954	1,693
Clerical, sales, and kindred workers	4,973	2,033	5,555	1,280	1,540	1,799	1,179
Craftsmen, foremen, and kindred workers	} 12,814	3,089	3,629	879	929	950	437
Operatives and kindred workers		{	6,219	1,265	1,222	1,363	902
Private household workers	8,879	1,104	2,547	643	663	757	470
Service workers, except private household	3,680	1,091	3,706	690	730	839	908
Farm laborers and foremen	4,246	1,103	4,565	976	642	253	158
Laborers, except farm and mine	32,111	7,377	8,223	1,702	993	924	4,099

[1] 1940-1944, 16 to 45 years.
[2] 1940-1944, 45 years and over. Includes age unknown.
[3] Immigrants 16 years of age or over unable to read or write in any language.

Source: Department of Justice, Immigration and Naturalization Service, *Annual Report*, releases, and records.

No. 108.—Aliens Admitted, by Classes, Under the Immigration Act of 1924 as Amended: Years Ending June 30, 1946 to 1952

CLASSES	1946	1947	1948	1949	1950	1951	1952
Number admitted, all classes	312,190	513,597	646,576	535,589	676,024	670,823	781,602
Under Section 3	184,017	332,354	431,355	399,775	376,185	413,489	462,445
Government officials, their families, attendants, servants and employees	17,031	16,517	16,822	13,722	13,975	20,881	22,267
Temporary visitors for business	74,913	79,634	78,876	73,338	67,984	83,995	86,745
Temporary visitors for pleasure	59,913	134,924	206,107	225,745	219,810	230,210	269,606
In continuous transit through United States	31,124	96,825	124,780	81,615	68,540	72,027	77,899
To carry on trade under treaty	378	651	711	632	766	850	791
Members of international organizations	658	3,803	4,059	4,723	5,010	5,526	5,137
Under Section 4	99,078	116,542	122,695	122,768	102,379	100,787	124,910
Husbands of United States citizens	269	579	647	3,239	1,459	822	793
Wives of United States citizens	47,679	31,698	30,086	27,967	12,291	8,685	16,058
Unmarried children of United States citizens	1,319	6,462	6,097	4,648	2,525	1,955	2,464
Returning residents	13,306	22,818	32,464	36,984	40,908	44,212	44,980
Natives of nonquota countries	29,396	35,309	37,506	35,969	32,790	34,704	47,744
Their wives and children	106	331	462	425	448	570	664
Ministers and their wives and children	432	1,336	1,592	1,233	833	733	580
Professors and their wives and children	102	834	997	869	603	457	297
Students	5,855	11,008	11,914	10,481	9,744	7,355	8,613
Women who had been United States citizens	63	91	136	110	86	39	32
Miscellaneous classes	551	381	794	843	697	1,255	2,685
Under Section 5 (quota immigrants)	29,095	70,701	92,526	113,046	197,460	156,547	194,247

Source: Department of Justice, Immigration and Naturalization Service; *Annual Report*, releases.

No. 109.—IMMIGRANT ALIENS ADMITTED AND EMIGRANT ALIENS DEPARTING, BY RACE OR NATIONALITY: YEARS ENDING JUNE 30, 1948 TO 1952

RACE OR PEOPLE	1948 Admitted	1948 Departing	1949 Admitted	1949 Departing	1950 Admitted	1950 Departing	1951 Admitted	1951 Departing	1952 Admitted	1952 Departing
Total	170,570	20,875	188,317	24,586	249,187	27,596	205,717	26,174	265,520	21,880
Armenian	390	33	387	172	1,592	44	663	30	546	22
Bohemian and Moravian (Czech)	3,138	64	3,507	105	3,677	64	2,839	61	2,464	52
Bulgarian, Serbian, Montenegrin	347	51	165	33	656	32	1,340	22	898	31
Chinese	3,574	2,238	2,490	547	1,2a9	674	1,083	560	1,152	397
Croatian and Slovenian	573	93	784	63	4,940	52	5,996	62	4,962	67
Cuban	2,827	280	1,956	1,188	1,915	759	1,617	752	2,157	1,049
Dalmatian, Bosnian, Herzegovinian	29	34	35	9	79	19	156	10	100	7
Dutch and Flemish	5,515	501	5,041	616	4,508	514	4,702	435	4,829	514
East Indian	42	184	55	317	70	517	74	383	74	282
English	26,200	3,118	20,620	3,997	15,295	3,583	14,952	3,579	20,633	3,134
Filipino	1,055	545	1,000	903	531	1,170	677	562	957	496
Finnish	747	93	726	110	303	115	177	93	227	86
French	9,702	1,061	7,888	1,209	6,425	1,132	6,749	1,223	8,113	1,455
German	25,038	429	24,030	1,082	28,926	1,234	20,677	1,293	77,877	1,479
Greek	3,060	354	2,537	444	1,497	511	5,051	358	7,725	451
Irish	13,511	513	15,181	573	10,955	751	8,160	909	9,816	582
Italian	16,677	1,485	12,267	1,522	10,215	1,136	8,144	1,279	11,735	1,325
Japanese	316	101	492	225	45	305	-206	259	4,734	475
Korean	36	9	39	18	6	31	24	24	83	33
Latin American	4,169	1,275	4,122	2,651	4,035	2,082	4,042	1,889	5,637	1,905
Lithuanian	826	10	7,594	11	13,755	6	4,880	20	2,006	19
Magyar	1,205	46	2,002	67	5,250	50	6,684	70	5,974	51
Negro	2,231	120	1,954	1,324	1,468	981	1,145	529	1,411	367
Polish	9,000	206	26,787	268	55,146	237	37,380	268	33,854	203
Portuguese	1,230	437	1,509	335	1,156	229	1,200	199	1,227	253
Rumanian	758	22	1,057	40	2,100	25	1,507	26	1,101	31
Russian	3,184	368	5,023	604	17,125	197	22,083	236	14,244	247
Ruthenian (Russniak)	57	1	26	6	901	2	1,454		1,145	5
Scandinavian (Norwegians, Danes, and Swedes)	6,886	1,314	7,098	1,475	6,128	1,521	5,661	1,327	6,157	1,326
Scotch	9,040	477	7,977	664	5,707	722	6,132	793	7,982	599
Slovak	938	149	800	50	600	48	376	14	277	14
Spanish	998	403	1,501	636	787	517	936	463	1,153	559
Syrian	314	70	482	112	537	99	699	100	652	151
Turkish	126	118	146	148	147	123	125	111	219	153
Welsh	939	68	738	97	519	93	469	114	620	58
West Indian (other than Cuban)	1,448	206	1,679	327	2,003	257	1,936	225	2,223	241
All other	14,444	4,399	18,622	2,638	38,899	7,796	25,721	7,891	20,556	3,752

Source: Department of Justice, Immigration and Naturalization Service; *Annual Report.*

No. 110.—DISPLACED PERSONS AND WAR BRIDES ADMITTED: 1946 TO 1952

[Figures included in total immigrants in other tables in this section]

YEAR ENDING JUNE 30	DISPLACED PERSONS [1] Total	Quota	Non-quota	Non-immigrant	WAR BRIDES [2] Total	Husbands	Wives	Alien children
Total	381,473	375,026	5,392	1,055	119,693	333	114,691	4,669
1946	2,551	2,534	17	....	45,557	61	44,775	721
1947	17,414	16,076	942	396	27,212	101	25,736	1,375
1948	21,414	19,446	1,309	659	23,016	94	21,954	968
1949	40,048	39,734	314	....	22,214	71	20,670	1,473
1950	124,353	124,120	233	....	1,694	6	1,556	132
1951	96,515	95,920	595	....	(2)	(2)	(2)	(2)
1952	79,178	77,196	1,982	....	(2)	(2)	(2)	(2)

[1] Legislation authorizing admission was approved June 25, 1948. Admissions prior thereto were under President's Directive of Dec. 22, 1945.
[2] Act of Dec. 28, 1945, which facilitated entry of alien wives, husbands, and children of citizen members of armed forces, expired on Dec. 28, 1948. Public Law 51 of Apr. 21, 1949, authorized admission of certain alien fiances and fiancees and adjustment of their status to that of permanent residence.

Source: Department of Justice, Immigration and Naturalization Service; *Annual Report.*

No. 111.—ALIENS AND CITIZENS—TOTAL ARRIVALS AND DEPARTURES AND
ARRIVALS AT PRINCIPAL PORTS: YEARS ENDING JUNE 30, 1931 TO 1952

[Excludes travelers between continental U S. and outlying possessions, persons habitually crossing and recrossing
international land boundaries, and agricultural and railway track workers admitted from Mexico. Figures for
alien arrivals cover admissions only, excluding aliens among arrivals found inadmissible and debarred from
entering]

PORT AND CLASS	1931–35, average	1936–40, average	1941–45, average	1946–50, average	1949	1950	1951	1952
Arrivals, total	517,967	575,620	279,310	1,064,616	1,255,960	1,339,591	1,431,309	1,588,827
United States citizens	327,986	345,100	136,826	507,821	620,371	663,567	760,486	807,225
Immigrants	44,042	61,644	34,190	172,817	188,317	249,187	205,717	265,520
Nonimmigrants	145,939	168,875	108,294	383,978	447,272	426,837	465,106	516,082
Departures, total	577,771	533,146	182,129	846,412	982,450	1,112,207	1,140,027	1,323,786
United States citizens	340,052	331,535	102,225	473,858	552,361	655,518	667,126	814,289
Emigrants	64,773	27,175	8,539	22,741	24,586	27,508	26,174	21,880
Nonemigrants	172,947	174,436	71,365	349,813	405,503	429,001	446,727	487,617
Excess of arrivals over departures	−59,804	42,474	97,181	218,204	273,510	227,384	291,282	265,041
Citizens permanently departing:								
Naturalized	1,067	1,103	538	3,148	1,042	5,694	11,595	(¹)
Native born	19,673	9,850	5,820	15,062	5,290	17,813	46,325	(¹)
ARRIVALS AT PRINCIPAL PORTS								
New York	367,031	375,260	76,485	470,902	584,388	642,128	693,852	760,016
United States citizens	240,068	228,369	39,340	221,108	302,441	311,856	370,598	375,282
Immigrants	27,717	42,073	7,719	104,100	113,050	166,849	142,903	183,222
Nonimmigrants	99,246	104,818	29,426	145,694	168,897	163,423	180,351	201,512
Boston	12,351	11,709	3,097	28,100	43,094	54,229	32,397	32,471
United States citizens	7,341	6,942	1,675	16,465	24,153	26,175	24,926	25,128
Immigrants	1,040	885	310	8,327	14,318	24,222	3,787	2,968
Nonimmigrants	3,970	3,882	1,113	3,308	4,623	3,832	3,684	4,375
Philadelphia	932	1,318	1,350	3,870	2,671	2,136	1,345	1,710
United States citizens	734	954	601	1,642	655	842	703	670
Immigrants	27	25	381	588	263	370	134	337
Nonimmigrants	170	339	368	1,640	1,153	924	508	703
Baltimore	1,425	1,311	10,792	17,772	11,142	6,535	4,672	2,746
United States citizens	1,195	1,058	8,827	12,185	7,840	5,231	3,692	1,036
Immigrants	56	30	192	771	559	260	148	620
Nonimmigrants	175	224	1,773	4,816	2,743	1,044	832	1,090
Miami	20,796	72,183	82,168	223,295	233,927	246,941	283,056	308,920
United States citizens	17,144	55,362	50,282	140,418	140,884	158,281	184,045	199,835
Immigrants	94	1,445	3,229	6,432	5,711	5,451	5,199	6,209
Nonimmigrants	3,558	15,376	28,656	76,445	87,332	83,209	93,812	102,876
New Orleans	8,520	8,645	10,466	34,325	40,074	47,837	42,237	44,501
United States citizens	6,758	6,997	6,279	22,147	27,084	27,180	23,265	21,289
Immigrants	314	231	469	3,852	3,805	11,320	9,177	12,301
Nonimmigrants	1,448	1,417	3,718	8,326	9,185	9,337	9,796	10,911
San Francisco	12,821	14,433	11,619	34,826	36,064	35,449	37,372	33,006
United States citizens	7,322	8,311	7,472	20,050	23,199	25,970	27,125	20,884
Immigrants	937	712	817	5,756	4,167	2,174	3,841	3,178
Nonimmigrants	4,563	5,410	3,330	9,020	8,698	7,305	6,406	8,944
Seattle	3,810	3,711	1,185	7,732	11,069	10,588	15,180	25,275
United States citizens	2,112	2,211	452	6,768	9,878	9,525	13,706	19,904
Immigrants	196	92	245	294	552	77	382	3,497
Nonimmigrants	1,501	1,407	487	670	639	986	1,092	1,874

Not available.

Source: Department of Justice, Immigration and Naturalization Service; Annual Report, releases.

No. 112.—Passengers Arriving and Departing, by Countries, Flag of Carrier, Mode of Travel: Years Ending June 30, 1945 to 1952

COUNTRY, FLAG, ETC.	1945	1946	1947	1948	1949	1950	1951	1952
Passengers arriving, total	310,112	485,007	829,540	1,023,742	1,104,473	1,182,152	1,282,165	1,433,010
Europe	73,469	159,418	325,001	440,852	479,768	588,204	581,708	653,341
Asia	9,675	17,534	32,775	51,185	49,103	50,077	66,213	83,295
Africa	27,884	14,846	8,081	8,424	6,798	5,192	4,443	7,836
Australia and Pacific	20,323	23,658	23,234	20,048	16,366	18,640	26,296	8,626
Canada and Newfoundland	28,972	33,686	50,926	77,501	96,850	34,585	36,287	45,107
Greenland	1,635	327	96	123	105	108	180	5,304
Mexico	3,295	6,981	2,659	4,422	3,790	4,325	15,452	25,252
West Indies	121,046	196,152	322,547	313,117	337,015	362,829	430,404	460,252
Central America	18,972	23,094	36,183	45,501	47,429	50,766	44,673	53,194
South America	4,842	9,361	28,048	62,569	67,259	67,426	76,519	90,804
Flag: U.S.	252,263	377,236	585,909	648,444	697,039	749,754	763,035	841,885
Foreign	57,850	107,771	243,631	375,298	407,434	432,398	519,130	591,125
By sea	107,143	200,041	356,426	491,427	502,593	601,543	547,866	622,705
By air	202,970	284,966	473,114	532,315	601,880	580,609	734,299	810,305
Aliens	141,387	221,685	401,531	490,211	497,481	530,209	532,463	635,902
Citizens	168,725	263,322	428,009	533,531	606,992	651,943	749,702	797,108
Passengers departing, total	185,301	389,584	695,441	786,319	863,951	981,124	999,574	1,198,593
Europe	45,761	95,851	228,454	292,497	363,678	432,800	400,111	486,086
Asia	2,267	9,020	49,290	54,919	39,512	46,202	28,873	65,173
Africa	15,315	11,654	7,342	7,473	6,442	6,011	6,928	12,009
Australia and Pacific	3,049	11,286	25,117	24,716	17,185	19,462	18,360	9,714
Canada and Newfoundland	15,835	23,095	12,065	5,383	7,145	12,807	7,271	24,854
Greenland	896	201	84	194	138	176	85	5,706
Mexico	10,983	17,372	7,749	4,082	3,717	4,530	14,475	21,255
West Indies	61,368	170,446	280,919	288,401	315,533	382,195	405,972	440,623
Central America	13,953	22,905	38,944	41,102	41,689	38,466	37,993	44,328
South America	16,874	27,774	45,477	67,552	66,612	68,475	79,806	88,755
Flag: U.S.	137,036	295,617	507,528	503,036	527,692	577,358	568,217	690,107
Foreign	49,265	93,967	187,913	283,283	336,259	403,766	431,357	508,396
By sea	47,377	137,045	295,263	375,215	408,081	467,105	398,629	479,467
By air	138,924	252,539	400,178	411,104	455,870	514,019	600,945	719,036
Aliens	85,811	163,276	249,121	312,271	315,599	329,529	335,801	385,859
Citizens	100,490	226,308	446,320	474,048	548,352	651,595	663,773	812,644

Source: Department of Justice, Immigration and Naturalization Service; Annual Report, releases.

No. 113.—Estimated Resident Aliens in Continental United States, for Selected Dates: 1941 to 1945

DATE	Number of aliens [1]	CHANGE IN PRECEDING PERIOD					
		Net decrease	Decrease through naturalization	Decrease through mortality	Decrease through emigration	Decrease through other causes [2]	Increase through immigration
Jan. 1, 1941	4,889,770						
July 1, 1941	4,693,623	196,147	156,794	50,341	7,464	7,215	25,667
July 1, 1942	4,349,269	344,354	269,419	84,864	7,212	11,422	28,563
July 1, 1943	3,949,399	399,870	317,675	83,139	5,088	17,615	23,647
July 1, 1944	3,410,175	539,224	440,174	80,041	5,652	41,796	28,439
July 1, 1945	3,050,803	359,372	237,221	75,800	7,417	76,819	37,855

[1] Estimates do not take into account the considerable temporary movement of aliens into and out of the United States.
[2] Deportations, voluntary departures, expatriations, denaturalizations, etc.

Source: Department of Justice, Immigration and Naturalization Service; records.

No. 114.—NATURALIZATION: 1907 TO 1952

[See also *Historical Statistics*, series B 337–339]

PERIOD OR YEAR ENDING JUNE 30—	Declarations filed[1]	PETITIONS FILED[2]			ALIENS NATURALIZED[3]		
		Total	Civilian	Military	Total	Civilian	Military
1907[4]–1910, total	526,322	164,036	164,036	--------	111,738	111,738	--------
1911–1915, total	1,004,539	496,655	496,655	--------	406,547	406,547	--------
1916–1920, total	1,682,370	884,729	640,429	244,300	722,425	478,125	244,300
1921–1925, total	1,575,809	862,715	818,332	44,383	799,790	755,407	44,383
1926–1930, total	1,133,205	1,021,562	1,008,741	12,821	973,395	961,572	11,823
1931–1935, total	535,266	637,668	629,798	7,870	626,072	619,049	7,023
1936–1940, total	834,213	999,445	982,613	16,832	892,392	879,524	12,868
1941–1945, total	635,146	[5]1,520,053	1,407,062	[5]112,991	[5]1,539,972	1,427,441	[5]112,531
1946–1950, total	285,138	418,013	(6)	(6)	[5]447,056	409,788	[5]37,268
1940	203,536	278,028	276,840	1,188	235,260	232,500	2,760
1941	224,123	277,807	277,807	--------	277,294	275,747	1,547
1942	221,790	343,487	341,979	1,508	270,364	268,762	1,602
1943	115,664	[5]377,125	338,885	[5]38,240	[5]318,933	281,459	[5]37,474
1944	42,368	[5]325,717	275,486	[5]50,231	[5]441,979	392,766	[5]49,213
1945	31,195	[5]195,917	172,905	[5]23,012	[5]231,402	208,707	[5]22,695
1946	26,787	[5]123,864	110,071	[5]13,793	[5]150,062	134,849	[5]15,213
1947	37,771	[5]88,802	70,767	[5]18,035	[5]93,904	77,442	[5]16,462
1948	60,187	68,265	(6)	(6)	70,150	69,080	1,070
1949	64,866	71,044	(6)	(6)	66,594	64,138	2,456
1950	93,527	66,038	(6)	(6)	66,346	64,279	2,067
1951	91,497	61,634	(6)	(6)	54,716	53,741	975
1952	111,461	94,086	(6)	(6)	88,655	87,070	1,585

[1] Declaration of intention to become citizen.
[2] Petition for naturalization.
[3] Certificates of naturalization issued.
[4] From Sept. 27, 1906, to June 30, 1907.
[5] Includes 1,425 in 1943, 6,496 in 1944, 5,666 in 1945, 2,054 in 1946, and 5,370 in 1947 in various theaters of war or areas occupied by American forces. No provision for naturalization in these areas subsequently.
[6] Not available.

Source: Department of Justice, Immigration and Naturalization Service; *Annual Report*, releases.

No. 115.—ALIENS NATURALIZED, BY AGE AND SEX: YEARS ENDING JUNE 30, 1945 TO 1952

[See also *Historical Statistics*, series B 339–341]

AGE AND SEX	1945[1]	1946[1]	1947	1948	1949	1950	1951	1952
Both sexes	225,736	148,008	93,904	70,150	66,594	66,346	54,716	88,655
Under 21 years	1,669	1,244	544	476	987	1,003	726	1,052
21 to 25 years	8,246	7,269	5,495	2,970	6,297	7,742	6,238	9,785
26 to 35 years	26,442	16,641	13,848	7,914	10,960	13,925	13,046	23,529
36 to 45 years	54,375	35,630	25,296	18,980	16,271	14,679	11,606	17,491
46 to 55 years	64,987	40,925	24,668	20,651	17,020	15,176	12,253	18,880
56 to 65 years	50,273	31,784	16,948	13,655	10,914	10,071	7,745	12,655
Over 65 years	19,744	12,515	7,105	5,504	4,145	3,750	3,102	5,163
Male	111,059	74,250	52,998	33,147	27,865	25,745	18,711	28,597
Under 21 years	1,579	1,115	406	257	433	371	282	405
21 to 25 years	4,115	3,297	3,032	711	1,239	1,732	1,019	1,890
26 to 35 years	11,859	8,835	8,214	2,663	3,630	4,401	3,345	6,199
36 to 45 years	24,549	17,053	14,610	9,297	7,511	6,399	4,390	6,424
46 to 55 years	30,558	19,576	13,627	10,214	7,759	6,485	5,060	6,852
56 to 65 years	27,613	17,461	9,246	7,079	5,157	4,523	3,135	4,636
Over 65 years	10,786	6,913	3,863	2,926	2,136	1,834	1,480	2,191
Female	114,677	73,758	40,906	37,003	38,729	40,601	36,005	60,058
Under 21 years	90	129	138	219	554	632	444	647
21 to 25 years	4,131	3,972	2,463	2,259	5,058	6,010	5,219	7,895
26 to 35 years	14,583	9,806	5,634	5,251	7,330	9,524	9,701	17,430
36 to 45 years	29,826	18,577	10,686	9,683	8,760	8,280	7,216	11,067
46 to 55 years	34,429	21,349	11,041	10,437	9,261	8,691	7,193	12,028
56 to 65 years	22,660	14,323	7,702	6,576	5,757	5,548	4,610	8,019
Over 65 years	8,958	5,602	3,242	2,578	2,009	1,916	1,622	2,972

[1] Excludes 5,666 members of the armed forces naturalized overseas in 1945, and 2,054 in 1946.

Source: Department of Justice, Immigration and Naturalization Service; *Annual Report*, releases.

No. 116.—ALIENS NATURALIZED, BY STATES AND TERRITORIES OF RESIDENCE: YEARS ENDING JUNE 30, 1950, 1951, AND 1952

STATE OF RESIDENCE	1950	1951	1952	STATE OF RESIDENCE	1950	1951	1952
Total	66,346	54,716	88,655	New Hampshire	318	252	431
				New Jersey	3,742	2,700	4,131
Alabama	140	126	231	New Mexico	125	134	164
Arizona	341	283	387	New York	20,499	17,990	7,120
Arkansas	44	52	108	North Carolina	188	210	359
California	9,488	7,879	12,258				
Colorado	358	381	533	North Dakota	93	138	108
				Ohio	2,254	1,386	2,855
Connecticut	1,753	1,093	2,864	Oklahoma	160	234	305
Delaware	90	59	178	Oregon	451	278	601
District of Columbia	466	371	615	Pennsylvania	2,443	2,312	4,028
Florida	957	1,276	1,524				
Georgia	200	126	553	Rhode Island	521	419	707
				South Carolina	93	74	134
Idaho	85	93	156	South Dakota	89	73	91
Illinois	3,367	2,201	2,942	Tennessee	106	105	222
Indiana	577	403	1,048	Texas	1,353	1,192	1,989
Iowa	329	257	445	Utah	125	81	162
Kansas	198	265	340				
				Vermont	232	224	258
Kentucky	198	107	290	Virginia	413	456	712
Louisiana	245	270	411	Washington	1,176	1,032	1,755
Maine	475	591	737	West Virginia	175	112	244
Maryland	489	558	949	Wisconsin	623	515	796
Massachusetts	4,861	3,436	6,593	Wyoming	69	56	80
Michigan	3,475	2,763	5,288				
				Territories, etc.:			
Minnesota	567	545	722	Alaska	95	78	104
Mississippi	60	86	111	Hawaii	1,087	512	526
Missouri	502	451	726	Puerto Rico	55	57	78
Montana	166	136	236	Virgin Islands	62	36	35
Nebraska	155	170	253	All other	144	25	56
Nevada	68	55	106				

No. 117.—ALIENS NATURALIZED, BY COUNTRY OF FORMER ALLEGIANCE: YEARS ENDING JUNE 30, 1949 TO 1952

NATIONALITY	1949	1950	1951	1952	NATIONALITY	1949	1950	1951	1952
All countries	66,594	66,346	54,716	88,655	Norway	912	879	660	855
					Poland	4,371	3,793	3,100	5,858
Albania	86	65	42	98	Portugal	971	1,066	703	1,186
Belgium	612	654	563	694	Rumania	632	523	453	575
British Empire	13,284	12,829	10,867	14,993					
Bulgaria	65	59	46	80	Spain	676	614	428	579
					Sweden	1,044	879	627	882
Czechoslovakia	1,294	1,276	953	2,091	Switzerland	464	373	299	415
Denmark	539	515	355	544	U. S. S. R. (Russia)	2,752	2,122	1,830	2,851
Estonia	104	139	101	162	Yugoslavia	809	770	515	944
Finland	489	437	334	522					
France	1,658	1,867	1,641	2,043	Persia (Iran)	55	53	69	96
					Syria	241	192	119	160
Germany	5,777	6,065	5,439	13,538	Turkey	436	352	274	348
Austria	1,194	1,192	1,154	2,183	Philippine Islands	3,478	3,257	1,595	1,813
Greece	1,638	1,667	1,313	1,707					
Hungary	1,036	850	703	1,319	West Indies	614	838	886	942
Italy	8,301	8,743	5,975	9,720	Mexico	2,227	2,323	1,989	2,496
					Central America	375	502	552	602
Latvia	165	186	127	263	South America	391	470	420	508
Lithuania	601	482	320	591	Other countries [1]	8,477	9,442	9,604	16,010
Netherlands	836	872	680	987					

[1] Includes 297 persons in 1949, 586 in 1950, 916 in 1951, and 1,499 in 1952 who were stateless.

Source of tables 116 and 117: Department of Justice, Immigration and Naturalization Service; *Annual Report*, releases.

4. Education

Data on school attendance and on educational attainment were obtained for individuals in the United States as part of the 1940 and 1950 Censuses of Population. Annually, beginning in 1945, the Bureau of the Census has reported on school enrollment (and in 1947 and 1952 on educational attainment and illiteracy) of the population, based on sample data obtained in the Current Population Survey. The Biennial Survey of Education, conducted by the U. S. Office of Education, covers enrollment and attendance, teaching staff, finances, and other information on public education facilities at all levels, with less complete information for private schools. Public library statistics are also collected and published by this office. Other statistical studies of the U. S. Office of Education, publications of the National Education Association, Annual or Biennial Reports of the State Departments of Education, and educational journals are the other chief regular sources of statistical materials in the field of education. Many special studies are made by research divisions of city school systems, by schools of education in colleges and universities, and by educational foundations.

Educational statistics for individuals.—The school attendance statistics are based on the replies to the enumerator's inquiry as to whether the person had attended, or had been enrolled in, any regular school or college within a given period. Regular school enrollment does not include enrollment in kindergarten or nursery school or, generally, enrollment in vocational, trade, business, or correspondence schools.

The 1940 and 1950 Censuses included questions on the formal educational attainment of each person, that is, the last full grade that the person had completed in the regular school system—public, private, or parochial school, college, or university. This question replaced the inquiry on illiteracy included in previous censuses.

The *median* year of school completed may be defined as the year which divides the population group into equal parts—one-half having completed more schooling and one-half having completed less schooling than the median. In the presentation of median year of school completed, the completion of the first year of high school is uniformly indicated by 9 and of the first year of college by 13, although there are some areas with only 7 years of elementary school.

Statistics for schools.—Working through national committees since 1910, the U. S. Office of Education, in cooperation with the State departments of education, has brought about a considerable degree of uniformity in recording and reporting educational statistics. Since about 1930, a similar movement has been in progress with institutions of higher education, the U. S. Office of Education serving as a clearing house for uniform procedures in records and reports.

The statistics presented in the *Abstract* from the Biennial Survey of Education include current national totals and summaries for a period of years. The national totals are reasonably complete for the types of education covered but data are not included for private schools of art, music, drama, etc., for private commercial, trade and vocational schools, or private correspondence schools. The introduction of the junior high school, which includes the 7th and 8th grades from the traditional elementary school and the 9th grade from the regular high school, has made it impossible to compare elementary school or high school data over a period of years except on the basis of grade enrollment, 8 grades as elementary and 4 grades as secondary. Detailed statistics on the major fields of education are published in the reports of the Biennial Survey of Education. Information on vocational education is compiled by the U. S. Office of Education.

Data in this section relate to continental United States except as noted.

Note.—This section presents data for the most recent year or period available on February 18, 1953, when the material was organized and sent to the printer. In a few instances, more recent data were added after that date.

No. 118.—Persons Attending School by Single Years of Age From 5 to 20, by Sex: 1920 to 1950

[Statistics for 1940 and 1950 are based on attendance at or enrollment in any regular school or college, including night schools, extension schools, or vocational schools, if part of regular school system. Excludes correspondence schools. In the 2 prior censuses, school attendance question not restricted as to type of school or college. In 1950, question referred to period between Feb. 1 and Apr. 1, 1950; in 1940, to period between Mar. 1, and Apr. 1, 1940; in 1930, to period between Sept. 1, 1929, and Apr. 1, 1930; and in 1920, to period between preceding Sept. 1 and Jan. 1. Estimates for 1950 based on sample of 1950 census returns]

AGE AND SEX	1920 Number	Percent of population	1930 Number	Percent of population	1940 Number	Percent of population	1950 Number	Percent of population
TOTAL								
5 to 20 years old	21,373,976	64.2	26,849,639	69.9	26,293,224	70.8	27,088,065	72.7
5 years old	441,411	18.8	500,734	20.0	385,160	18.0	¹ 284,625	10.5
6 years old	1,480,714	63.3	1,667,486	66.3	1,420,051	69.1	¹¹1,874,620	67.6
7 years old	1,905,404	83.3	2,207,331	89.4	1,935,819	92.4	2,670,295	94.4
8 years old	2,010,894	88.5	2,451,048	94.1	2,089,528	94.8	2,448,490	95.6
9 years old	1,944,314	90.4	2,401,356	95.6	2,093,679	95.6	2,257,985	96.1
10 years old	2,077,965	93.0	2,427,254	97.1	2,209,240	95.7	2,228,955	96.0
11 years old	1,970,255	93.9	2,260,735	97.5	2,125,664	95.9	2,145,630	96.3
12 years old	2,082,749	93.2	2,408,623	97.1	2,315,270	95.5	2,204,840	95.9
13 years old	1,877,429	92.5	2,242,053	96.5	2,263,495	94.8	2,099,085	96.9
14 years old	1,766,784	86.3	2,212,825	92.9	2,224,670	92.5	2,025,730	94.8
15 years old	1,357,345	72.9	1,943,553	84.7	2,122,996	87.6	1,945,790	91.4
16 years old	1,001,701	50.8	1,569,839	66.3	1,897,179	76.2	1,682,200	80.9
17 years old	642,360	34.6	1,100,018	47.9	1,464,027	60.9	1,426,930	68.2
18 years old	413,619	21.7	728,524	30.7	940,105	36.4	867,695	39.8
19 years old	252,680	13.8	441,814	19.8	509,380	20.9	533,025	24.7
20 years old	148,352	8.3	291,446	13.1	294,962	12.5	392,160	17.9
MALE								
5 to 20 years old	10,663,547	64.1	13,521,768	70.2	13,313,771	71.2	13,793,135	72.4
5 years old	217,446	18.3	247,739	19.5	190,842	17.5	¹140,735	10.2
6 years old	739,300	62.8	832,088	65.5	710,525	68.2	¹944,440	66.9
7 years old	959,128	83.1	1,111,729	89.0	975,904	92.2	1,354,195	94.2
8 years old	1,011,506	88.3	1,234,410	94.0	1,057,382	94.7	1,243,500	95.6
9 years old	982,227	90.3	1,217,161	95.4	1,062,888	95.5	1,146,275	96.0
10 years old	1,048,389	92.9	1,226,457	96.9	1,121,202	95.6	1,131,075	95.9
11 years old	989,744	93.8	1,136,412	97.4	1,071,248	95.8	1,090,870	96.1
12 years old	1,052,563	93.0	1,222,203	96.9	1,176,278	95.3	1,119,490	94.6
13 years old	941,325	92.4	1,126,382	96.4	1,142,178	94.6	1,064,170	95.7
14 years old	890,571	86.2	1,120,553	92.9	1,122,703	92.2	1,031,890	94.7
15 years old	665,948	71.9	979,070	84.8	1,067,177	87.3	986,610	91.5
16 years old	470,433	48.2	777,585	65.8	948,009	75.7	849,510	80.6
17 years old	297,100	32.1	544,739	47.1	734,581	60.5	716,155	67.9
18 years old	192,481	20.5	359,527	31.1	488,650	38.1	458,380	42.4
19 years old	127,011	14.0	239,899	20.8	281,123	23.2	292,600	27.8
20 years old	78,355	9.3	155,714	14.6	166,081	14.4	223,150	21.2
FEMALE								
5 to 20 years old	10,710,429	64.5	13,327,871	69.7	12,979,453	70.4	13,294,920	72.0
5 years old	223,965	19.3	252,995	20.5	194,318	18.4	¹143,890	10.8
6 years old	741,414	63.9	835,398	67.1	709,526	70.1	¹930,180	68.2
7 years old	946,276	83.5	1,095,602	89.7	959,915	92.7	1,316,100	94.5
8 years old	999,388	88.6	1,216,638	94.3	1,032,146	95.0	1,204,900	95.7
9 years old	962,087	90.5	1,184,195	95.7	1,030,791	95.7	1,111,710	96.2
10 years old	1,029,576	93.2	1,200,797	97.2	1,088,038	95.8	1,097,880	96.2
11 years old	980,511	94.1	1,124,323	97.6	1,054,416	96.0	1,054,760	96.4
12 years old	1,030,166	93.4	1,186,420	97.3	1,138,992	95.7	1,085,350	96.3
13 years old	936,104	92.7	1,115,671	96.7	1,123,317	95.1	1,034,915	96.0
14 years old	876,213	86.5	1,092,172	92.9	1,101,967	92.8	993,840	94.9
15 years old	691,397	73.9	964,483	84.5	1,055,818	88.0	959,180	91.2
16 years old	531,268	53.3	792,254	66.8	952,170	76.8	832,690	81.1
17 years old	345,260	37.2	555,279	48.8	729,446	61.3	710,775	68.4
18 years old	221,138	22.8	363,997	30.3	451,455	34.7	409,315	37.2
19 years old	125,669	13.6	211,915	18.8	228,257	18.7	240,425	21.8
20 years old	69,997	7.5	135,732	11.7	128,881	10.6	169,010	14.9

¹ Excludes kindergarten enrollment, largely included in earlier enrollment figures.

Source: Dept. of Commerce, Bureau of Census; U. S. Census of Population: 1950, Vol. II.

FIG. XI.—AVERAGE CURRENT EXPENDITURE PER PUPIL IN AVERAGE DAILY ATTENDANCE FOR PUBLIC ELEMENTARY AND SECONDARY DAY SCHOOLS: 1950

[See table 134]

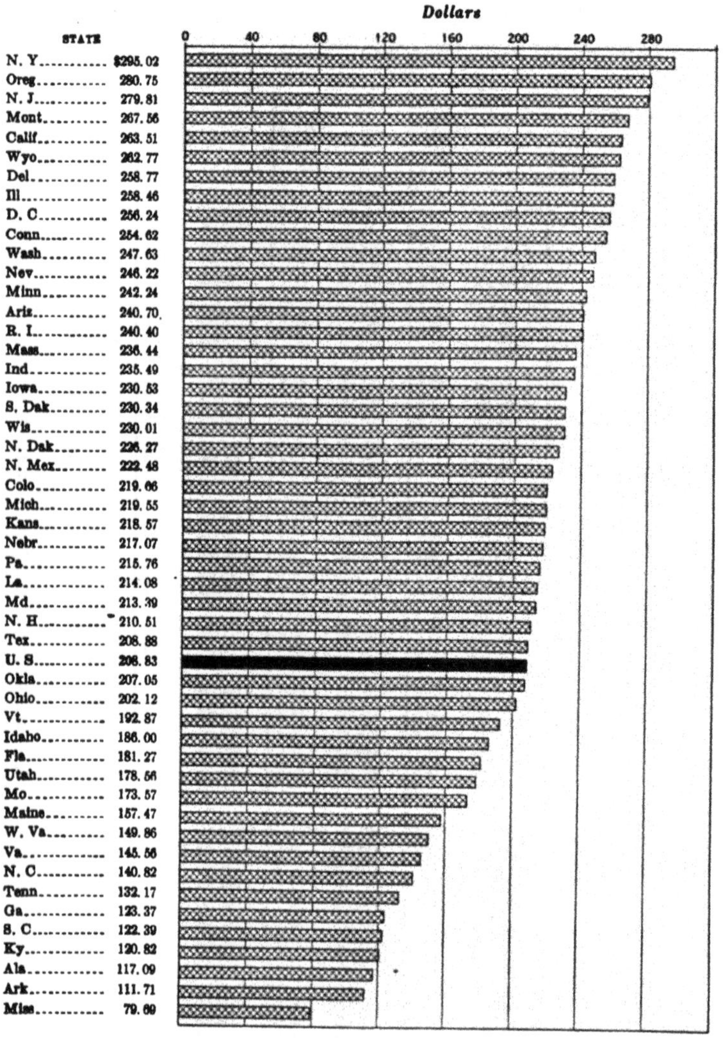
Dollars
0
40
80
120
160
200
240
280
STATE
N. Y. $295.02
Oreg. 280.75
N. J. 279.81
Mont. 267.56
Calif. 263.51
Wyo. 262.77
Del. 258.77
Ill. 258.46
D. C. 256.24
Conn. 254.62
Wash. 247.63
Nev. 246.22
Minn. 242.24
Ariz. 240.70
R. I. 240.40
Mass. 236.44
Ind. 235.49
Iowa 230.53
S. Dak. 230.34
Wis. 230.01
N. Dak. 226.27
N. Mex. 222.48
Colo. 219.66
Mich. 219.55
Kans. 218.57
Nebr. 217.07
Pa. 215.76
La. 214.08
Md. 213.39
N. H. 210.51
Tex. 208.88
U. S. 208.83
Okla. 207.05
Ohio 202.12
Vt. 192.87
Idaho 186.00
Fla. 181.27
Utah 178.56
Mo. 173.57
Maine 157.47
W. Va. 149.86
Va. 145.56
N. C. 140.82
Tenn. 132.17
Ga. 123.37
S. C. 122.39
Ky. 120.82
Ala. 117.09
Ark. 111.71
Miss. 79.69

Source: Department of Commerce, Bureau of the Census. Data are from Department of Health, Education, and Welfare, Office of Education.

No. 119.—SCHOOL ATTENDANCE BY AGE AND SEX: 1940, 1947, AND 1951

[1940 statistics cover total population 5 to 24 years old from 1940 census; 1947 and 1951 figures relate to civilian population 5 to 29 years old, based on Current Population Survey; see Sampling Note, p. 181]

YEAR AND AGE	TOTAL			MALE			FEMALE		
	Popu-lation	Attending school		Popu-lation	Attending school		Popu-lation	Attending school	
		Number	Per-cent		Number	Per-cent		Number	Per-cent
APRIL 1940									
Total, 5 to 24........	46,351,915	26,759,699	57.7	23,243,697	13,614,585	58.6	23,108,218	13,144,514	56.9
5 years...............	2,142,407	[1]385,160	18.0	1,087,811	[1]190,842	17.5	1,054,596	[1]194,318	18.4
6 years...............	2,054,385	[1]1,420,051	69.1	1,041,757	[1]710,525	68.2	1,012,628	[1]709,526	70.1
7 to 9 years.........	6,487,830	6,119,026	94.3	3,289,255	3,096,174	94.1	3,198,575	3,022,852	94.5
10 to 13 years.......	9,340,205	8,915,660	95.5	4,734,213	4,510,906	95.3	4,605,992	4,404,763	95.6
14 to 17 years.......	9,720,419	7,708,871	79.3	4,902,896	3,869,470	78.9	4,817,523	3,839,401	79.7
18 and 19 years.....	5,018,534	1,449,485	28.9	2,495,373	760,773	30.8	2,523,461	679,712	26.9
20 to 24 years.......	11,587,835	760,837	6.6	5,692,392	466,895	8.2	5,895,443	293,942	5.0
APRIL 1947									
Total, 5 to 29...	56,683,000	26,679,000	47.1	27,864,000	13,985,000	50.2	28,819,000	12,694,000	44.0
5 to 24 years........	45,129,000	26,244,000	58.2	22,324,000	13,601,000	60.9	22,805,000	12,643,000	55.4
5 years...............	2,628,000	136,000	5.2	1,342,000	54,000	4.0	1,286,000	82,000	6.4
6 years...............	2,446,000	1,644,000	67.2	1,247,000	834,000	66.9	1,199,000	810,000	67.6
7 to 9 years.........	6,915,000	6,643,000	96.1	3,521,000	3,372,000	95.8	3,394,000	3,271,000	96.4
10 to 13 years.......	8,562,000	8,354,000	97.6	4,347,000	4,245,000	97.7	4,215,000	4,109,000	97.5
14 to 17 years.......	8,689,000	7,057,000	81.2	4,377,000	3,538,000	80.8	4,312,000	3,519,000	81.6
18 and 19 years.....	4,141,000	1,148,000	27.7	1,837,000	565,000	30.8	2,304,000	583,000	25.3
20 to 24 years.......	11,748,000	1,262,000	10.7	5,653,000	993,000	17.6	6,095,000	269,000	4.4
25 to 29 years........	11,554,000	435,000	3.8	5,540,000	384,000	6.9	6,014,000	51,000	.8
OCTOBER 1951									
Total, 5 to 29...	57,650,000	30,466,000	52.8	27,752,000	15,774,000	56.8	29,898,000	14,692,000	49.1
5 to 24 years........	46,038,000	30,178,000	65.6	22,312,000	15,546,000	69.7	23,726,000	14,632,000	61.7
5 years...............	3,044,000	574,000	18.9	1,554,000	304,000	19.6	1,490,000	270,000	18.1
6 years...............	2,816,000	2,622,000	93.1	1,438,000	1,344,000	93.5	1,378,000	1,278,000	92.7
7 to 9 years	8,644,000	8,556,000	99.0	4,414,000	4,374,000	99.1	4,230,000	4,182,000	98.9
10 to 13 years.......	9,464,000	9,390,000	99.2	4,816,000	4,774,000	99.1	4,648,000	4,616,000	99.3
14 and 15 years.....	4,374,000	4,148,000	94.8	2,216,000	2,108,000	95.1	2,158,000	2,040,000	94.5
16 and 17 years.....	4,098,000	3,068,000	74.9	2,026,000	1,506,000	74.3	2,072,000	1,562,000	75.4
18 and 19 years.....	3,714,000	974,000	26.2	1,648,000	534,000	32.4	2,066,000	440,000	21.3
20 to 24 years.......	9,884,000	846,000	8.6	4,200,000	602,000	14.3	5,684,000	244,000	4.3
25 to 29 years........	11,612,000	288,000	2.5	5,440,000	228,000	4.2	6,172,000	60,000	1.0

[1] Includes those attending kindergarten, excluded in 1947 and 1951.

Source: Dept. of Commerce, Bureau of Census; *Current Population Reports*, Series P-20, Nos. 12 and 40.

No. 120.—PERCENT OF POPULATION 5 TO 29 YEARS OLD ENROLLED IN SCHOOL, BY AGE, COLOR, AND SEX: OCTOBER 1951

[Figures relate to civilian population 5 to 29 years old, based on Current Population Survey; see Sampling Note, p. 181]

AGE	TOTAL		MALE		FEMALE	
	White	Nonwhite	White	Nonwhite	White	Nonwhite
Total, 5 to 29 years..................	52.8	53.4	56.8	56.9	49.0	50.3
5 and 6 years.....................	54.5	54.9	55.4	52.8	53.6	57.1
7 to 13 years.....................	99.3	97.3	99.3	98.0	99.4	96.5
14 to 17 years.....................	86.3	77.1	86.6	74.9	86.0	79.2
18 and 19 years.....................	26.9	20.8	33.8	23.6	21.7	17.9
20 to 24 years.....................	8.8	6.2	14.9	9.0	4.3	4.3
25 to 29 years.....................	2.5	2.7	4.2	4.3	.9	1.5

Source: Dept. of Commerce, Bureau of Census; *Current Population Reports*, Series P-20, No. 40.

No. 121.—School and Kindergarten Enrollment by Age, Urban and Rural: 1950

[Number in thousands. Based on 20-percent sample of 1950 census returns; see original source for sampling variability]

AGE	UNITED STATES			URBAN			RURAL NONFARM			RURAL FARM		
	Popu-lation	Enrolled		Popu-lation	Enrolled		Popu-lation	Enrolled		Popu-lation	Enrolled	
		Num-ber	Per-cent		Num-ber	Per-cent		Num-ber	Per-cent		Num-ber	Per-cent
SCHOOL ENROLLMENT												
Total, 5 to 29...	58,709	28,985	49.4	35,929	17,179	47.8	12,854	6,297	49.0	9,926	5,509	55.5
5 and 6 years.......	5,490	2,160	39.3	3,156	1,298	41.1	1,302	480	36.9	1,032	382	37.1
7 to 13 years.........	16,802	16,077	95.7	9,363	9,002	96.1	3,922	3,745	95.5	3,517	3,330	94.7
14 and 15 years.....	4,268	3,964	92.9	2,333	2,211	94.8	964	887	92.1	971	865	89.1
16 and 17 years.....	4,175	3,104	74.4	2,334	1,839	78.8	924	649	70.2	916	616	67.2
18 and 19 years.....	4,344	1,401	32.2	2,686	980	36.5	933	238	25.6	725	182	25.1
20 to 24 years.......	11,440	1,481	12.9	7,680	1,216	15.8	2,353	188	8.0	1,407	77	5.5
25 to 29 years.......	12,189	798	6.5	8,375	632	7.6	2,457	109	4.4	1,357	57	4.2
KINDERGARTEN ENROLLMENT												
Total, 5 and 6 years.	5,490	899	16.4	3,156	743	23.5	1,302	112	8.6	1,032	44	4.3

Source: Dept. of Commerce, Bureau of Census; *U. S. Census of Population: 1950*, Vol. II, Part 1.

No. 122.—Median Income in 1949, for Males 14 Years Old and Over with Income, by Age and Years of School Completed: April 1950

[Based on 20-percent sample of 1950 census returns; see original source for sampling variability. Median not shown where base is less than 3,000]

AGE	Total[1]	YEARS OF SCHOOL COMPLETED								
		None	Elementary			High school		College	
			1 to 4 years	5 to 7 years	8 years	1 to 3 years	4 years	1 to 3 years	4 years or more
Total, 25 years and over......	$2,699	$1,106	$1,365	$2,035	$2,533	$2,917	$3,285	$3,522	$4,407
14 to 17 years....................	494	345	327	305	305	308	411	341	....
18 and 19 years.................	721	485	543	703	881	727	767	451	.....
20 and 21 years.................	1,316	679	826	1,055	1,364	1,471	1,617	796	854
22 to 24 years.................	1,917	848	1,027	1,409	1,840	2,145	2,309	1,413	1,526
25 to 29 years.................	2,538	1,016	1,281	1,763	2,255	2,573	2,892	2,764	2,928
30 to 34 years.................	2,968	1,133	1,453	2,038	2,557	3,053	3,156	3,296	4,113
35 to 44 years.................	3,085	1,267	1,562	2,252	2,803	3,178	3,523	3,962	5,142
45 to 54 years.................	2,980	1,465	1,741	2,371	2,912	3,209	3,687	4,099	5,549
55 to 64 years.................	2,553	1,736	1,727	2,172	2,601	2,927	3,436	3,601	5,142
65 to 74 years.................	1,379	827	846	1,164	1,505	1,771	2,262	2,362	3,597
75 years and over.............	757	491	569	690	800	947	1,217	1,328	1,892

[1] Includes a small number for whom years of school completed was not reported.

Source: Dept. of Commerce, Bureau of Census; 1950 Census of Population, advance tabulations of special report, *Education*.

No. 123.—Type of School Attended by the Enrolled Population, by Age and Sex: April 1940 and October 1951

[1940 statistics cover total population 5 to 24 years old from 1940 census; 1951 figures relate to civilian population 5 to 29 years old, based on Current Population Survey. See Sampling Note, p. 181. Percent not shown where base is less than 100,000]

		TYPE OF SCHOOL					
YEAR, AGE, AND SEX	Total enrolled	Elementary		High school		College or professional school	
		Number	Percent of total enrolled	Number	Percent of total enrolled	Number	Percent of total enrolled
APRIL 1940							
Total, 5 to 24 [1]	26,516,896	18,142,242	68.4	6,839,398	25.8	1,537,340	5.8
5 to 13 years	16,649,812	16,152,553	97.0	497,259	3.0		
14 to 17 years	7,670,146	1,925,461	25.1	5,513,473	71.9	231,212	3.0
18 and 19 years	1,442,481	48,836	3.4	730,209	50.6	663,436	46.0
20 to 24 years	756,451	15,392	2.0	98,458	13.0	642,601	84.9
Male, 5 to 24	13,489,536	9,323,765	69.1	3,352,749	24.9	813,016	6.0
5 to 13 years	8,410,009	8,191,012	97.4	218,997	2.6		
14 to 17 years	3,849,366	1,096,473	28.5	2,654,287	69.0	98,606	2.6
18 and 19 years	765,918	27,428	3.6	418,547	54.6	319,943	41.8
20 to 24 years	464,237	8,852	1.9	60,918	13.1	394,467	85.0
Female, 5 to 24	13,029,360	8,818,477	67.7	3,486,650	26.8	724,233	5.6
5 to 13 years	8,239,803	7,961,541	96.6	278,262	3.4		
14 to 17 years	3,820,780	828,988	21.7	2,859,186	74.8	132,606	3.5
18 and 19 years	676,563	21,408	3.2	311,662	46.1	343,493	50.8
20 to 24 years	292,214	6,540	2.2	37,540	12.8	248,134	84.9
OCTOBER 1951							
Total, 5 to 29	30,466,000	21,842,000	71.7	6,780,000	22.3	1,844,000	6.1
5 to 24 years	30,178,000	21,840,000	72.4	6,748,000	22.4	1,590,000	5.3
5 to 13 years	21,142,000	20,760,000	98.2	382,000	1.8		
14 to 17 years	7,216,000	1,064,000	14.7	5,986,000	83.0	166,000	2.3
18 and 19 years	974,000	8,000	.8	328,000	33.7	638,000	65.5
20 to 24 years	846,000	8,000	.9	52,000	6.1	786,000	92.9
25 to 29 years	288,000	2,000	.7	32,000	11.1	254,000	88.2
Male, 5 to 29	15,774,000	11,278,000	71.5	3,304,000	20.9	1,192,000	7.6
5 to 24 years	15,546,000	11,276,000	72.5	3,286,000	21.1	984,000	6.3
5 to 13 years	10,796,000	10,620,000	98.4	176,000	1.6		
14 to 17 years	3,614,000	648,000	17.9	2,888,000	79.9	78,000	2.2
18 and 19 years	534,000	2,000	.4	196,000	36.7	336,000	62.9
20 to 24 years	602,000	6,000	1.0	26,000	4.3	570,000	94.7
25 to 29 years	228,000	2,000	.9	18,000	7.9	208,000	91.2
Female, 5 to 29	14,692,000	10,564,000	71.9	3,476,000	23.7	652,000	4.4
5 to 24 years	14,632,000	10,564,000	72.2	3,462,000	23.7	606,000	4.1
5 to 13 years	10,346,000	10,140,000	98.0	206,000	2.0		
14 to 17 years	3,602,000	416,000	11.5	3,098,000	86.0	88,000	2.4
18 and 19 years	440,000	6,000	1.4	132,000	30.0	302,000	68.6
20 to 24 years	244,000	2,000	.8	26,000	10.7	216,000	88.5
25 to 29 years	60,000			14,000		46,000	

[1] Excludes persons for whom type of school was not reported.

Source: Department of Commerce, Bureau of the Census; *Current Population Reports*, Series P-20, No. 40, and records.

No. 124.—Kindergarten and School Enrollment, in Public and Private Schools, of Persons 5 to 29 Years Old: October 1951

[Figures relate to civilian population based on Current Population Survey; see Sampling Note, p. 181. Kindergarten enrollment tabulated only for persons 5 and 6 years old]

	NUMBER ENROLLED				PERCENT ENROLLED			
TYPE	Kindergarten	Elementary school	High school	College or professional school	Kindergarten	Elementary school	High school	College or professional school
Total	1,122,000	21,842,000	6,780,000	1,844,000	100.0	100.0	100.0	100.0
Public	890,000	19,296,000	6,168,000	1,062,000	79.3	88.3	91.0	57.6
Private	232,000	2,546,000	612,000	782,000	20.7	11.7	9.0	42.4

Source: Department of Commerce, Bureau of the Census; *Current Population Reports*, Series P-20, No. 40.

No. 125.—Percent Distribution, by Type of School, of Persons 5 to 29 Years
Old, Enrolled in School, by Age, Color, and Sex: October, 1951

[Figures relate to civilian population based on Current Population Survey; see Sampling Note, p. 181.   Percent
not shown where base is less than 100,000]

AGE AND SEX	WHITE				NONWHITE			
	Total enrolled	Elementary school	High school	College or professional school	Total enrolled	Elementary school	High school	College or professional school
Total, 5 to 29 years	100.0	70.8	22.7	6.5	100.0	78.6	18.9	2.4
5 to 13 years	100.0	98.1	1.9	....	100.0	98.8	1.2	....
14 to 17 years	100.0	12.3	85.2	2.5	100.0	34.1	65.2	.7
18 to 24 years	100.0	.4	17.8	81.8	100.0	6.7	54.7	38.7
25 to 29 years	100.0	....	8.6	91.4	....	....	....	....
Male, 5 to 29 years	100.0	70.3	21.5	8.2	100.0	80.6	16.7	2.7
5 to 13 years	100.0	98.3	1.7	....	100.0	98.6	1.4	....
14 to 17 years	100.0	15.0	82.6	2.4	100.0	42.3	57.2	.5
18 to 24 years	100.0	.2	16.4	83.4	....	....	....	....
25 to 29 years	100.0	....	5.8	94.2	....	....	....	....
Female, 5 to 29 years	100.0	71.3	24.0	4.7	100.0	76.6	21.3	2.1
5 to 13 years	100.0	97.9	2.1	....	100.0	99.0	1.0	....
14 to 17 years	100.0	9.5	87.9	2.7	100.0	26.7	72.4	.9
18 to 24 years	100.0	.6	20.3	79.1	....	....	....	....
25 to 29 years	....	....	....	....	....	....	....	....

Source: Department of Commerce, Bureau of the Census; *Current Population Reports*, Series P-20, No. 40.

No. 126.—Persons 5 to 24 Years Old, by Age and Years of School Completed:
1950

[Estimates based on preliminary sample of 1950 census returns; see original sources for sampling variability]

AGE AND YEARS OF SCHOOL COMPLETED	Number	Percent	AGE AND YEARS OF SCHOOL COMPLETED	Number	Percent
5 and 6 years old	5,459,000	100.0	16 and 17 years old	4,203,000	100.0
No school years completed	4,938,000	90.4	Under 1 year of high school [1]	1,095,080	26.1
Grade school: 1 year or more	271,000	5.0	High school: 1 to 3 years	2,873,000	68.3
School years not reported	251,000	4.6	Additional years completed	194,000	4.6
			School years not reported	42,000	1.0
7 to 9 years old	7,824,000	100.0			
No school years completed	1,229,000	15.7	18 to 20 years old	6,472,000	100.0
Grade school: 1 and 2 years	4,855,000	62.0	Under 1 year of high school [1]	1,342,000	20.7
3 years or more	1,580,000	20.2	High school: 1 to 3 years	1,919,000	29.6
School years not reported	163,000	2.1	4 years	2,343,000	36.2
			College: 1 year or more	791,000	12.2
10 to 13 years old	9,246,000	100.0	School years not reported	77,000	1.2
Grade school: Under 5 years [1]	3,841,000	41.5			
5 to 6 years	3,969,000	42.9	21 to 24 years old	9,153,000	100.0
7 years	1,056,000	11.4	Under 1 year of high school [1]	2,128,000	23.2
Additional years completed	234,000	2.5	High school: 1 to 3 years	2,131,000	23.3
School years not reported	149,000	1.6	4 years	3,056,000	33.4
			College: 1 year or more	1,703,000	18.6
14 and 15 years old	4,368,000	100.0	School years not reported	133,000	1.5
Grade school: Under 8 years [1]	1,764,000	40.4			
8 years	1,356,000	31.0			
High school: 1 year or more	1,214,000	27.8			
School years not reported	34,000	.8			

[1] Includes no school years completed.
[2] Includes no school years completed and 1 to 8 years of grade school.

Source: Department of Commerce, Bureau of the Census; *Current Population Reports*, Series P-20, No. 32,
and records.

No. 127.—Persons 25 Years Old and Over, by Years of School Completed, by Age, Color, and Sex: 1940 and 1950

[1940 statistics are final figures from 1940 census. 1950 statistics are estimates based on preliminary sample of 1950 census returns; see original sources for sampling variability]

YEAR, AGE, AND SEX	Population [1]	Median years of school completed	Grade school			High school		College	
			Less than 5 years [2]	5 and 6 years	7 and 8 years	1 to 3 years	4 years	1 to 3 years	4 years or more
APRIL 1940									
Total, 25 and over	74,775,836	8.4	10,104,612	8,515,111	25,897,953	11,181,905	10,551,680	4,075,184	3,497,331
Male	37,463,087	8.3	5,550,390	4,399,910	13,239,380	5,332,803	4,507,244	1,823,981	2,021,228
Female	37,312,749	8.5	4,554,222	4,115,201	12,658,573	5,849,192	6,044,436	2,251,203	1,386,103
White, 25 and over	67,999,523	8.7	7,322,114	7,082,235	24,546,893	10,603,592	10,255,333	3,948,681	3,319,785
Male	34,113,972	8.7	4,034,706	3,725,114	12,619,179	5,089,656	4,381,386	1,769,814	1,975,295
Female	33,885,551	8.8	3,287,408	3,357,121	11,927,714	5,513,936	5,873,947	2,178,867	1,344,490
Nonwhite, 25 and over	6,776,313	5.7	2,782,498	1,432,876	1,351,060	578,403	296,347	126,503	87,546
Male	3,349,115	5.4	1,515,684	674,796	620,201	243,147	125,858	54,167	45,932
Female	3,427,198	6.1	1,266,814	758,080	730,859	335,256	170,489	72,336	41,613
APRIL 1950									
Total, 25 and over	87,675,000	9.3	9,630,000	8,088,000	23,736,000	15,017,000	17,751,000	6,315,000	5,226,000
25 to 29 years	12,060,000	12.1	532,000	583,000	1,855,000	2,613,000	4,136,000	1,245,000	915,000
30 to 34 years	11,619,000	11.5	606,000	660,000	2,284,000	2,524,000	3,519,000	1,041,000	794,000
35 to 44 years	21,158,000	10.2	1,472,000	1,656,000	5,355,000	4,393,000	4,671,000	1,700,000	1,500,000
45 to 54 years	17,351,000	8.8	2,006,000	1,802,000	5,546,000	2,716,000	2,703,000	1,184,000	1,015,000
55 to 64 years	13,176,000	8.4	2,268,000	1,653,000	4,498,000	1,596,000	1,545,000	678,000	591,000
65 years and over	12,311,000	8.2	2,747,000	1,734,000	4,198,000	1,175,000	1,177,000	467,000	411,000
Male, 25 and over	43,039,000	9.0	5,199,000	4,169,000	11,915,000	7,142,000	7,645,000	2,953,000	2,948,000
25 to 29 years	5,905,000	12.0	297,000	310,000	969,000	1,283,000	1,733,000	639,000	567,000
30 to 34 years	5,713,000	11.3	343,000	357,000	1,161,000	1,227,000	1,511,000	528,000	478,000
35 to 44 years	10,458,000	10.0	806,000	832,000	2,655,000	2,122,000	2,104,000	790,000	823,000
45 to 54 years	8,635,000	8.7	1,061,000	914,000	2,906,000	1,299,000	1,163,000	528,000	551,000
55 to 64 years	6,660,000	8.3	1,226,000	895,000	2,328,000	763,000	667,000	275,000	310,000
65 years and over	5,668,000	8.1	1,374,000	861,000	1,896,000	448,000	467,000	190,000	239,000
Female, 25 and over	44,636,000	9.6	4,431,000	3,919,000	11,821,000	7,875,000	10,106,000	3,362,000	2,258,000
25 to 29 years	6,155,000	12.1	235,000	273,000	886,000	1,330,000	2,403,000	606,000	348,000
30 to 34 years	5,906,000	11.8	262,000	303,000	1,123,000	1,297,000	2,008,000	513,000	316,000
35 to 44 years	10,700,000	10.4	574,000	824,000	2,700,000	2,271,000	2,567,000	910,000	677,000
45 to 54 years	8,716,000	8.9	945,000	888,000	2,640,000	1,417,000	1,540,000	656,000	464,000
55 to 64 years	6,516,000	8.5	1,042,000	758,000	2,170,000	833,000	878,000	400,000	281,000
65 years and over	6,643,000	8.3	1,373,000	873,000	2,302,000	727,000	710,000	277,000	172,000
White, 25 and over	79,766,000	9.7	7,312,000	6,635,000	22,069,000	13,979,000	17,158,000	6,046,000	5,062,000
Male	39,132,000	9.3	3,882,000	3,456,000	11,183,000	6,679,000	7,385,000	2,852,000	2,886,000
Female	40,634,000	10.0	3,430,000	3,179,000	10,886,000	7,300,000	9,773,000	3,194,000	2,176,000
Nonwhite, 25 and over	7,909,000	7.0	2,318,000	1,453,000	1,667,000	1,038,000	593,000	269,000	164,000
Male	3,907,000	6.5	1,317,000	713,000	732,000	463,000	260,000	101,000	82,000
Female	4,002,000	7.4	1,001,000	740,000	935,000	575,000	333,000	168,000	82,000

[1] Includes 1,041,976 persons for 1940 and 1,912,000 persons for 1950, not reported by years of school completed and not shown separately in this table.
[2] Includes persons reporting no school years completed.

Source: Department of Commerce, Bureau of the Census; 1950 Census of Population preliminary report, PC-7, No. 6.

No. 128.—Years of School Completed by Persons 25 Years Old and Over, by States: 1950

[Based on 20-percent sample of 1950 census returns; see original source for sampling variability]

DIVISION AND STATE	¹Total, 25 years old and over ¹	YEARS OF SCHOOL COMPLETED						
		Elementary school			High school		College	
		Under 5 years ²	5 to 7 years	8 years	1 to 3 years	4 years	1 to 3 years	4 years or more
United States	87,570,575	9,453,925	13,961,715	17,731,375	14,856,860	17,690,945	6,261,635	5,284,445
New England	5,674,890	451,385	750,200	1,061,725	1,060,535	1,416,015	390,329	379,680
Maine	516,830	34,445	64,825	114,435	102,725	131,440	34,655	24,980
New Hampshire	316,380	19,995	40,385	78,180	55,160	72,435	23,325	18,890
Vermont	212,165	11,610	23,975	56,500	39,690	47,500	17,615	12,485
Massachusetts	2,901,005	228,685	369,680	465,415	560,170	788,420	207,725	208,470
Rhode Island	479,495	46,495	84,910	90,370	96,860	93,060	26,360	27,690
Connecticut	1,249,015	110,155	166,425	276,825	205,930	283,160	80,640	87,165
Middle Atlantic	18,773,800	1,766,750	2,749,250	4,219,850	3,174,395	3,997,530	1,026,090	1,240,630
New York	9,436,500	894,275	1,220,925	2,096,940	1,587,595	2,025,130	551,365	694,545
New Jersey	3,044,080	251,190	461,280	682,640	512,830	653,345	169,655	205,715
Pennsylvania	6,293,220	591,285	1,067,065	1,440,270	1,073,970	1,319,355	305,070	340,370
East North Central	18,102,385	1,320,185	2,424,000	4,490,630	3,187,255	3,960,815	1,250,340	1,010,680
Ohio	4,745,470	329,080	652,925	1,080,855	887,520	1,097,685	321,480	271,140
Indiana	2,289,225	151,125	311,785	553,475	395,005	537,560	146,010	119,505
Illinois	5,393,355	421,260	674,340	1,494,920	880,455	1,134,915	385,325	318,480
Michigan	3,667,840	275,640	491,885	802,015	754,150	801,750	251,560	193,885
Wisconsin	2,006,495	143,130	293,085	599,365	270,125	406,905	145,845	107,670
West North Central	8,743,460	508,515	1,074,275	2,412,210	1,184,450	1,740,640	673,545	432,505
Minnesota	1,725,015	100,140	222,790	535,015	229,880	350,610	150,180	97,235
Iowa	1,539,185	60,455	182,945	439,305	239,995	372,870	126,980	77,575
Missouri	2,404,205	203,885	370,365	700,460	338,800	437,055	159,400	119,435
North Dakota	325,945	28,895	51,995	105,525	34,290	53,315	30,595	14,575
South Dakota	356,675	21,020	43,310	118,590	46,300	67,990	35,595	17,555
Nebraska	773,035	37,915	82,165	212,325	121,895	190,875	66,880	39,435
Kansas	1,119,400	56,205	120,705	299,990	173,290	267,925	103,915	66,695
South Atlantic	11,358,735	2,016,675	2,751,740	1,379,340	1,891,970	1,601,695	753,975	673,015
Delaware	189,215	18,445	31,060	31,790	38,560	38,815	11,290	13,810
Maryland	1,362,490	148,965	318,260	205,605	221,530	242,735	82,465	95,315
Dist. of Columbia	524,880	25,575	71,295	61,435	80,410	125,580	57,255	68,155
Virginia	1,800,165	315,370	488,785	152,770	281,225	261,855	132,855	113,070
West Virginia	1,039,555	142,500	231,805	258,260	135,940	152,295	57,050	44,710
North Carolina	2,020,140	425,335	598,985	182,175	366,795	191,020	120,450	101,670
South Carolina	1,005,575	275,815	200,955	85,735	179,750	78,130	54,685	54,220
Georgia	1,778,475	430,420	476,490	167,165	303,460	176,390	106,365	79,275
Florida	1,637,240	224,280	274,105	234,405	284,300	334,875	131,550	102,790
East South Central	5,942,010	1,204,315	1,387,335	1,037,570	864,405	778,355	318,945	226,815
Kentucky	1,552,505	260,120	329,575	407,220	187,165	198,720	82,495	59,010
Tennessee	1,756,800	321,670	402,640	263,640	251,480	253,510	101,055	71,560
Alabama	1,559,445	352,090	416,485	162,840	260,615	193,995	77,600	56,840
Mississippi	1,073,260	270,435	238,635	145,875	165,145	132,130	57,795	41,305
West South Central	7,871,345	1,463,759	1,611,945	1,043,605	1,433,230	1,175,945	580,136	429,200
Arkansas	1,000,830	197,800	233,060	182,520	165,550	125,935	51,090	31,210
Louisiana	1,415,145	405,720	325,255	134,650	204,960	160,630	75,425	66,555
Oklahoma	1,242,615	136,515	217,960	247,345	227,775	227,775	105,005	77,070
Texas	4,212,755	663,715	835,670	479,090	874,240	661,605	344,715	254,365
Mountain	2,728,595	232,885	311,320	513,630	464,120	639,345	294,785	195,195
Montana	335,745	20,895	40,125	81,855	50,830	77,180	35,875	20,470
Idaho	314,085	13,975	31,960	66,380	58,565	83,085	35,570	17,130
Wyoming	157,505	9,990	16,260	33,240	27,875	39,455	17,355	11,240
Colorado	757,395	53,440	83,640	154,940	123,140	179,215	81,185	61,645
New Mexico	325,900	55,515	49,800	44,040	50,435	56,935	29,855	22,355
Arizona	392,655	55,520	52,055	61,960	63,540	80,885	38,065	29,035
Utah	343,775	11,990	28,480	53,985	71,670	95,050	46,025	26,235
Nevada	96,555	6,570	9,090	16,260	18,065	26,520	10,855	7,085
Pacific	8,880,355	549,465	901,630	1,552,765	1,591,500	2,357,305	973,500	694,725
Washington	1,412,020	65,590	141,090	294,265	252,210	369,685	145,520	101,525
Oregon	910,315	39,355	90,995	206,670	167,720	235,890	93,465	60,515
California	6,558,020	444,520	669,545	1,051,830	1,171,565	1,755,730	734,515	532,685

¹ Includes persons for whom years of school completed was not reported, not shown separately.
² Includes persons reporting no school years completed.

Source: Dept. of Commerce, Bureau of the Census; *U. S. Census of Population: 1950*, Vol. II, Part 1.

No. 129.—SCHOOL AND KINDERGARTEN ENROLLMENT FOR PERSONS 5 TO 29 YEARS OLD AND MEDIAN SCHOOL YEARS COMPLETED BY PERSONS 25 YEARS OLD AND OVER, BY STATES: 1950

[Based on 20-percent sample of 1950 census returns; see original source for sampling variability. For definition of median, see p. 108]

DIVISION AND STATE	PERSONS 5 TO 29 YEARS OLD ENROLLED IN SCHOOL		CHILDREN 5 AND 6 YEARS OLD ENROLLED IN KINDERGARTEN		MEDIAN SCHOOL YEARS COMPLETED BY PERSONS 25 YEARS OLD AND OVER				
					All classes			White	Non-white
	Number	Percent 1	Number	Percent 2	Total	Male	Female		
United States	28,964,965	49.4	896,970	16.4	9.3	9.0	9.6	9.7	6.2
New England	1,697,215	49.7	72,620	23.3	10.4	10.1	10.6	10.4	8.7
Maine	180,085	50.8	8,920	25.8	10.2	9.5	10.8	10.2	8.5
New Hampshire	102,440	52.2	2,200	12.3	9.8	9.4	10.3	9.9	8.8
Vermont	78,170	52.8	1,555	10.8	10.0	9.1	10.7	10.0	
Massachusetts	849,935	50.1	32,505	21.5	10.9	10.6	11.1	10.9	9.1
Rhode Island	135,115	45.2	4,815	18.6	9.3	9.3	9.4	9.4	8.5
Connecticut	350,570	48.8	22,625	33.1	9.8	9.5	10.0	9.8	8.4
Middle Atlantic	5,288,750	48.5	213,135	22.2	9.3	9.2	9.4	9.5	8.4
New York	2,517,060	48.6	121,890	26.6	9.6	9.6	9.6	9.7	8.6
New Jersey	809,865	47.1	51,455	33.1	9.3	9.3	9.3	9.5	8.1
Pennsylvania	1,961,825	49.0	39,790	11.5	9.0	8.9	9.1	9.0	8.2
East North Central	5,663,715	49.5	248,715	23.8	9.6	9.2	9.9	9.7	8.4
Ohio	1,455,800	49.0	47,605	17.9	9.9	9.6	10.2	10.0	8.4
Indiana	755,360	49.6	19,710	13.9	9.6	9.2	9.9	9.7	8.3
Illinois	1,528,575	48.6	62,905	22.3	9.3	9.1	9.5	9.5	8.5
Michigan	1,253,595	50.1	86,275	37.1	9.9	9.5	10.2	10.0	8.5
Wisconsin	670,385	51.7	32,220	25.9	8.9	8.8	9.1	8.9	8.4
West North Central	2,721,120	50.9	106,775	21.2	9.0	8.9	9.8	9.1	8.2
Minnesota	595,985	52.6	23,900	21.8	9.0	8.8	9.8	9.0	8.5
Iowa	516,430	51.6	28,295	30.2	9.8	9.0	10.7	9.9	8.6
Missouri	716,705	49.4	21,890	16.6	8.8	8.8	8.9	8.9	8.0
North Dakota	134,740	51.7	580	2.2	8.7	8.6	8.9	8.8	7.0
South Dakota	132,975	50.2	2,590	10.0	8.9	8.8	9.9	8.9	8.1
Nebraska	256,170	50.6	14,415	30.4	10.1	9.3	10.8	10.1	8.8
Kansas	368,115	50.7	15,105	22.2	10.2	9.4	10.8	10.2	8.7
South Atlantic	4,373,485	48.1	46,435	5.4	8.6	8.3	8.8	9.2	5.9
Delaware	56,695	46.9	875	7.7	9.8	9.4	10.2	10.4	7.2
Maryland	430,670	46.5	10,370	12.0	8.9	8.8	9.0	9.5	6.9
Dist. of Columbia	125,440	43.2	5,815	26.7	12.0	11.7	12.1	12.4	8.8
Virginia	651,675	45.1	5,600	4.2	8.5	8.0	8.8	9.3	6.1
West Virginia	443,990	50.3	1,250	1.5	8.5	8.4	8.6	8.6	7.6
North Carolina	911,295	48.7	4,215	2.4	7.9	7.6	8.2	8.6	5.9
South Carolina	497,785	49.8	2,460	2.4	7.6	7.3	7.9	9.0	4.8
Georgia	742,410	49.2	7,115	4.8	7.8	7.5	8.1	8.8	4.9
Florida	513,525	48.6	8,735	8.5	9.6	9.2	10.0	10.9	5.8
East South Central	2,524,315	50.3	16,525	3.4	8.3	8.1	8.5	8.7	5.7
Kentucky	599,095	47.5	5,170	4.3	8.4	8.3	8.5	8.5	7.2
Tennessee	695,240	49.2	4,265	3.2	8.4	8.3	8.6	8.6	6.5
Alabama	716,645	52.2	3,170	2.3	7.9	7.7	8.2	8.8	5.4
Mississippi	513,335	52.7	3,920	4.0	8.1	7.7	8.4	9.0	5.1
West South Central	3,001,960	49.2	31,950	5.3	8.8	8.6	9.0	9.3	6.0
Arkansas	429,965	53.1	1,870	2.2	8.3	8.2	8.5	8.7	5.6
Louisiana	584,135	50.6	6,670	5.7	7.6	7.4	7.9	8.8	4.6
Oklahoma	490,510	53.8	7,650	8.7	9.1	8.9	9.6	9.4	7.8
Texas	1,497,350	46.4	15,760	5.7	8.9	8.9	9.6	9.7	7.0
Mountain	1,093,315	51.6	26,465	12.4	10.7	10.1	11.3	10.9	7.3
Montana	118,055	52.1	1,635	7.1	10.2	9.1	11.4	10.3	8.0
Idaho	131,885	53.9	890	3.5	11.0	10.4	11.6	11.0	8.6
Wyoming	58,590	48.1	1,755	14.8	11.1	10.2	12.0	11.1	8.5
Colorado	267,210	51.0	8,450	16.9	10.9	10.2	11.5	10.9	9.8
New Mexico	156,810	49.7	2,565	7.7	9.3	9.0	9.7	9.5	5.8
Arizona	162,430	50.7	3,905	11.8	10.0	9.5	10.5	10.6	5.5
Utah	169,945	55.7	5,580	17.5	12.0	11.8	12.0	12.0	8.9
Nevada	28,390	48.3	1,685	28.5	11.5	10.8	12.0	11.7	7.4
Pacific	2,621,110	49.8	126,350	27.6	11.5	11.0	11.9	11.6	8.9
Washington	440,550	49.4	21,950	26.0	11.2	10.5	11.8	11.3	8.8
Oregon	292,490	52.2	5,845	10.7	10.9	10.2	11.6	10.0	8.9
California	1,888,070	49.3	108,555	29.8	11.6	11.2	11.9	11.8	8.9

1 Percent of population 5 to 29 years.
2 Percent of population 5 and 6 years old.
Source: Dept. of Commerce, Bureau of the Census; U. S. Census of Population: 1950, Vol. II, Part 1.

No. 130.—Public Elementary and Secondary Schools—Summary: 1870 to 1950

ITEM	1870	1880	1890	1900	1910
Total population	1 38,558,371	1 50,155,783	1 2 62,622,250	1 2 75,602,515	1 91,972,266
Population 5-17 years, inclusive	1 12,055,443	1 15,065,767	1 2 18,543,201	1 2 21,404,322	1 24,239,948
Percent of total population	31.3	30.1	29.6	28.3	26.4
Pupils enrolled in public schools	6,871,522	9,867,395	12,722,631	15,503,110	17,813,852
Percent of total population	17.8	19.7	20.3	20.5	19.4
Percent of population 5-17, inclusive	57.0	65.5	68.6	72.4	73.5
Average daily attendance	4,077,347	6,144,143	8,153,635	10,632,772	12,827,307
Percent of pupils enrolled	59.3	62.3	64.1	68.6	72.1
Average number of days schools in session	132.2	130.3	134.7	144.3	157.5
Average number of days attended per enrolled pupil	78.4	81.1	86.3	99.0	113.0
Number of teachers	200,515	286,593	363,922	423,062	523,210
Male	77,529	122,795	125,525	126,588	110,481
Female	122,986	163,798	238,397	296,474	412,729
Percent male teachers	38.7	42.8	34.5	29.9	21.1
Salaries: Teachers, supervisors, and principals (thousands of dollars)	37,833	55,943	91,836	137,688	253,915
Average annual salary per teacher	$189	$195	$252	$325	$485
Total expenditure for education (thousands of dollars) 3	63,397	78,095	140,507	214,965	426,250
Per capita of total population	$1.64	$1.56	$2.24	$2.84	$4.64
Per capita of population 5-17, inclusive	$5.26	$5.18	$7.58	$10.04	$17.58
Per pupil enrolled	$9.23	$7.91	$11.04	$13.87	$23.93
Per pupil in average attendance	$15.55	$12.71	$17.23	$20.21	$33.23

ITEM	1920	1930	1940	1946	1948	1950
Total population	1 105,710,620	1 122,775,046	1 131,669,275	4 139,893,406	4 146,113,000	4 151,240,000
Population 5-17 years, inclusive	1 27,728,788	1 31,571,322	1 29,745,246	28,944,000	30,171,000	30,788,000
Percent of total population	26.2	25.7	22.6	20.7	20.6	20.4
Pupils enrolled in public schools	21,578,316	25,678,015	25,433,542	23,299,941	23,944,532	25,111,427
Percent of total population	20.4	20.9	19.3	16.7	16.4	16.6
Percent of population 5-17, inclusive	77.8	81.3	85.5	80.5	79.4	81.6
Average daily attendance	16,150,035	21,264,886	22,042,151	19,848,507	20,909,739	22,283,845
Percent of pupils enrolled	74.8	82.8	86.7	85.2	87.3	88.7
Average number of days schools in session	161.9	172.7	175.0	176.8	177.6	177.9
Average number of days attended per enrolled pupil	121.2	143.0	151.7	150.6	155.1	157.9
Number of teachers	679,533	854,263	875,477	831,026	860,678	913,671
Male	95,686	141,771	194,725	138,209	161,913	194,968
Female	583,867	712,492	680,752	692,817	698,765	718,703
Percent male teachers	14.1	16.6	22.2	16.6	18.8	21.3
Salaries: Teachers, supervisors, and principals (thousands of dollars)	590,120	1,250,427	1,314,342	1,730,563	2,393,630	2,896,480
Average annual salary per teacher 5	$871	$1,420	$1,441	$1,995	$2,639	$3,010
Total expenditure for education (thousands of dollars) 3	1,036,151	2,316,790	2,344,049	2,906,856	4,311,176	5,837,643
Per capita of total population	$9.80	$18.87	$17.77	$20.78	$29.51	$38.60
Per capita of population 5-17, inclusive	$37.37	$73.38	$78.65	$100.43	$142.89	$189.61
Per pupil enrolled 6	$48.02	$89.84	$91.64	$124.27	$178.89	$231.05
Per pupil in average attendance 6	$64.16	$108.49	$105.74	$145.88	$202.81	$258.85

1 Census enumeration as of June 1, 1870 to 1900; Apr. 15, 1910; Jan. 1, 1920; Apr. 1, 1930 and 1940.
2 Excluding population of Indian Territory which is not covered by public-school statistics, and also, for 1890, population of Indian reservations. These were not enumerated at censuses prior to 1890.
3 Current expense, capital outlays, and interest.
4 Census estimate, excludes armed forces overseas.
5 Beginning 1920, based on total number of teachers, supervisors, and principals.
6 Beginning 1920, excludes data for night, summer, part-time, and continuation schools separately reported.

Source (except for population statistics and estimates): Department of Health, Education, and Welfare, Office of Education; *Biennial Survey of Education*, chapter on Statistical Summary of Education and chapter on Statistics of State School Systems.

No. 131.—Number of Schools of Specified Types, by States and Other Areas: 1950

DIVISION, STATE, OR OTHER AREA	PUBLIC SCHOOLS (EXCLUDING KINDERGARTENS)		NONPUBLIC SCHOOLS (EXCLUDING KINDERGARTENS)[1]		INSTITUTIONS OF HIGHER EDUCATION[2]		RESIDENTIAL SCHOOLS FOR EXCEPTIONAL CHILDREN, 1946		Schools of nursing not affiliated with colleges and universities[3]
	Elementary	Secondary	Elementary	Secondary	Publicly controlled[4]	Privately controlled	Public	Private	
Continental U. S.	128,225	24,542	10,375	3,331	641	1,210	307	137	1,065
New England	5,399	1,063	894	439	38	115	28	16	111
Maine	1,432	202	89	61	6	10	4	....	11
New Hampshire	434	107	66	41	3	6	2	....	12
Vermont	801	84	30	25	4	9	2	1	8
Massachusetts	1,731	478	424	204	18	59	11	11	58
Rhode Island	304	64	86	29	2	11	4	1	5
Connecticut	697	128	199	79	5	23	5	3	16
Middle Atlantic	12,965	2,402	2,404	710	56	223	28	60	248
New York	5,927	1,009	1,074	335	30	102	11	31	93
New Jersey	1,528	268	403	127	11	26	9	6	42
Pennsylvania	6,510	1,125	927	248	15	95	8	23	113
East North Central	18,784	4,171	2,792	645	87	234	38	17	211
Ohio	3,074	1,199	601	156	9	60	11	1	57
Indiana	2,271	831	312	41	6	34	7	1	24
Illinois	3,470	942	864	190	19	81	5	5	85
Michigan	3,969	697	455	172	18	28	9	6	23
Wisconsin	6,000	502	560	86	35	31	6	4	22
West North Central	22,697	4,222	1,641	423	104	144	46	8	121
Minnesota	5,122	866	345	74	16	26	11	3	22
Iowa	6,973	977	337	132	21	30	6	2	23
Missouri	6,302	751	399	93	18	37	11	3	24
North Dakota	2,571	407	49	22	11	2	4	....	10
South Dakota	3,391	289	55	23	7	9	4	....	7
Nebraska	4,060	552	217	48	10	14	5	....	10
Kansas	2,778	680	239	31	21	24	5	....	25
South Atlantic	18,580	3,595	568	300	85	202	61	13	168
Delaware	142	52	28	11	2	3	4	....	7
Maryland	858	212	172	60	12	22	6	9	21
District of Columbia	122	37	43	23	2	22	5	2	6
Virginia	2,812	533	66	56	12	32	10	1	31
West Virginia	4,022	374	51	16	11	11	9	....	22
North Carolina	2,852	952	59	32	14	40	9	....	39
South Carolina	3,238	445	30	19	7	25	6	....	16
Georgia	3,133	808	44	28	19	35	7	1	13
Florida	1,401	482	75	55	6	12	5	....	13
East South Central	16,346	2,448	457	232	44	103	24	3	59
Kentucky	4,678	539	235	99	9	31	5	1	12
Tennessee	4,349	488	75	42	7	39	7	1	12
Alabama	3,221	740	96	44	9	17	8	1	15
Mississippi	4,098	681	51	47	19	16	4	....	20
West South Central	11,111	3,783	733	241	93	78	30	6	60
Arkansas	1,983	583	59	20	12	11	4	....	8
Louisiana	1,561	841	238	91	7	11	7	2	14
Oklahoma	1,846	998	82	37	26	9	8	2	11
Texas	5,721	1,561	354	93	48	47	11	2	27
Mountain	5,602	1,174	262	99	48	19	31	1	27
Montana	1,221	206	46	17	8	3	5	....	4
Idaho	653	167	26	7	6	3	4	....	8
Wyoming	600	101	7	1	2	....	3	....	....
Colorado	1,471	287	83	30	13	7	6	1	4
New Mexico	675	147	60	21	7	2	5	....	1
Arizona	449	85	29	17	5	1	3	....	5
Utah	367	140	9	5	6	3	4	....	5
Nevada	166	41	2	1	1	....	1	....	....
Pacific	5,741	1,384	624	242	82	89	21	13	60
Washington	1,167	367	106	49	14	13	8	....	17
Oregon	1,083	271	75	25	7	15	5	1	7
California	3,491	746	443	168	61	61	8	12	36
Alaska	56	31	17	2	1	....	....	....	....
American Samoa	45	4	....	....	....	....	....	....	....
Canal Zone	16	11	....	....	1	....	....	....	....
Hawaii	134	25	49	17	1	....	4	....	3
Puerto Rico	1,739	327	83	55	1	1	3	1	10
Virgin Islands	23	2	9	....	....	....	....	....	....

[1] Estimated.
[2] Includes universities, colleges, professional schools, teachers colleges, normal schools and junior colleges.
[3] January 1, 1950.   [4] Includes 4 U. S. Service Academies.   [5] 1947–48.   [6] 1946–47.   [7] September 1, 1950.

Source: Department of Health, Education, and Welfare, Office of Education; *Biennial Survey of Education*, chapter on Statistical Summary of Education.

No. 132.—Public Elementary and Secondary Schools—Enrollment and Attendance by States and Other Areas 950

[Includes data for kindergartens. Excludes data for residential schools for exceptional children, observation and practice schools, and preparatory departments of colleges and universities]

DIVISION, STATE, OR OTHER AREA	PUPILS ENROLLED			Average daily attendance (1,000)	Average number of days school in session	Average number of days attended per pupil enrolled	High school graduates
	Total	Elementary	Secondary				
Continental U. S.	25,111,427	19,404,693	5,706,734	22,284	177.9	157.9	1,063,444
New England	1,292,728	961,515	331,213	1,156	178.7	159.8	63,691
Maine	158,247	124,058	34,189	145	180.0	164.9	6,763
New Hampshire	71,733	53,316	18,417	66	176.5	161.5	3,841
Vermont	61,143	49,224	11,919	56	170.1	156.6	1 2,423
Massachusetts	632,285	453,852	178,433	560	178.4	158.1	33,032
Rhode Island	96,305	71,308	24,997	84	180.0	156.6	4,202
Connecticut	273,015	209,757	63,258	245	180.7	162.3	13,430
Middle Atlantic	4,223,330	3,095,322	1,128,008	3,692	182.5	159.5	215,334
New York	1,998,129	1,457,855	540,274	1,700	182.6	155.4	97,857
New Jersey	674,915	495,140	179,775	583	182.2	157.4	33,074
Pennsylvania	1,550,286	1,142,327	407,959	1,408	182.6	165.8	84,403
East North Central	4,609,842	3,477,637	1,132,205	4,167	180.4	163.1	224,026
Ohio	1,202,967	916,706	286,261	1,110	178.0	164.2	56,084
Indiana	689,808	524,208	165,600	589	173.7	148.3	31,941
Illinois	1,153,683	871,072	282,611	1,032	186.6	166.9	57,679
Michigan	1,069,435	809,887	259,548	987	180.0	166.1	46,096
Wisconsin	493,949	355,764	138,185	450	181.9	165.6	30,226
West North Central	2,411,630	1,828,121	583,509	2,124	174.9	154.1	118,492
Minnesota	481,612	358,736	122,876	434	171.5	154.6	26,488
Iowa	477,720	364,942	112,778	418	179.3	156.8	23,959
Missouri	644,457	499,126	145,331	558	179.1	155.1	24,925
North Dakota	114,661	87,809	26,852	103	172.7	155.5	5,464
South Dakota	117,675	88,577	29,098	106	175.0	158.2	6,203
Nebraska	227,879	168,063	59,816	204	177.4	158.5	13,365
Kansas	347,626	200,968	86,758	301	1 165.1	142.9	1 18,088
South Atlantic	4,060,552	3,269,350	791,202	3,605	179.1	159.0	128,980
Delaware	46,055	35,325	10,730	41	181.9	161.5	2,024
Maryland	335,018	269,911	65,107	209	184.1	164.1	8,372
District of Columbia	96,323	74,576	21,747	84	176.0	153.0	3,730
Virginia	597,867	497,563	100,304	537	180.0	161.6	20,116
West Virginia	438,498	348,561	89,937	309	175.0	159.2	15,952
North Carolina	884,733	703,698	181,035	798	179.9	162.2	30,485
South Carolina	494,185	415,146	79,039	414	177.4	148.5	12,056
Georgia	718,037	571,329	146,708	620	178.0	153.7	19,760
Florida	449,836	353,241	96,595	415	180.0	166.2	16,485
East South Central	2,430,174	2,009,179	420,995	2,134	176.0	149.3	70,742
Kentucky	562,883	467,159	95,724	484	171.2	147.3	16,850
Tennessee	659,785	539,445	120,340	583	176.7	156.2	19,784
Alabama	680,066	555,892	124,174	595	176.3	154.2	19,700
Mississippi	527,440	446,683	80,757	472	172.5	136.5	14,399
West South Central	2,655,877	2,146,688	539,189	2,326	176.9	153.2	97,836
Arkansas	407,084	328,804	78,280	355	173.9	151.7	14,066
Louisiana	483,363	399,634	83,729	421	179.0	155.8	12,548
Oklahoma	441,263	339,797	101,466	394	184.2	164.5	20,190
Texas	1,354,167	1,078,453	275,714	1,157	174.6	149.1	51,023
Mountain	983,971	761,292	222,679	870	176.5	156.1	41,016
Montana	105,917	79,864	26,053	94	183.5	163.5	4,975
Idaho	122,259	91,232	31,027	111	175.8	159.6	6,126
Wyoming	59,585	46,004	13,581	49	175.0	143.7	2,631
Colorado	229,196	176,097	52,499	201	176.1	154.7	10,317
New Mexico	148,978	121,496	27,482	121	180.0	146.1	4,313
Arizona	139,244	111,557	27,687	127	170.9	155.2	4,837
Utah	153,648	114,917	38,731	142	175.3	162.3	6,678
Nevada	25,144	19,525	5,619	25	176.6	176.4	1,139
Pacific	2,413,323	1,855,589	557,734	2,209	175.2	160.4	103,327
Washington	400,867	308,870	91,997	357	173.8	154.7	18,453
Oregon	255,032	188,786	66,246	229	179.2	160.6	12,257
California	1,757,424	1,357,933	399,491	1,624	175.0	161.7	72,617
Alaska	13,910	11,592	2,318	11	175.0	135.1	374
American Samoa	4,001	3,485	516	(2)	(2)	(2)	16
Canal Zone	9,523	7,594	1,929	8	187.3	164.4	406
Hawaii	89,820	65,074	24,746	85	171.7	163.3	5,385
Puerto Rico	409,639	361,900	47,739	369	191.0	172.1	7,624
Virgin Islands	4,896	4,229	667	5	180.9	169.8	1 94

1 1948 data. Estimated. 2 Not available.

Source: Department of Health, Education, and Welfare, Office of Education, *Biennial Survey of Education*, chapter on Statistics of State School Systems.

No. 168.—PUBLIC ELEMENTARY AND SECONDARY SCHOOLS—NUMBERS AND SALARIES OF TEACHERS, BY STATES AND OTHER AREAS: 1940 TO 1950

DIVISION, STATE, OR OTHER AREA	NUMBER OF TEACHERS [1]			Percent of teachers, male, 1950	NUMBER OF PUPILS PER TEACHER [2]			SALARIES OF TEACHERS, SUPERVISORS AND PRINCIPALS			
	1940	1945	1950		1940	1945	1950	Total, 1950 (1,000 dollars)	Average salary (dollars)		
									1940	1945	1950
Continental U.S.	875,477	860,678	913,671	21.3	25.2	24.3	24.4	2,894,489	1,441	2,639	3,010
New England	43,239	47,168	50,773	22.0	25.2	22.1	22.8	168,888	1,748	2,867	3,153
Maine	6,156	6,117	6,323	20.7	24.1	22.9	22.9	13,374	904	1,767	2,115
New Hampshire	2,945	2,788	2,816	21.8	22.9	22.3	23.3	8,270	1,258	2,355	2,712
Vermont	2,653	2,354	2,405	16.2	21.3	22.7	23.4	6,111	981	2,066	2,345
Massachusetts	24,769	22,287	24,596	24.1	25.4	23.4	22.8	87,992	2,037	3,103	3,535
Rhode Island	3,783	3,620	3,984	21.6	25.4	22.4	21.0	13,134	1,809	3,105	3,394
Connecticut	9,619	9,994	10,649	19.2	20.6	22.2	23.0	40,017	1,861	3,249	3,558
Middle Atlantic	163,500	157,358	162,389	21.5	25.1	22.5	22.7	596,296	2,187	3,191	3,433
New York	60,553	75,025	79,670	24.5	23.8	21.7	21.3	310,097	2,604	3,476	3,706
New Jersey	26,964	23,901	27,109	21.4	25.1	21.4	21.5	99,699	2,093	3,102	3,511
Pennsylvania	60,983	58,432	55,610	26.0	27.4	24.1	23.3	176,502	1,640	2,897	3,006
East North Central	164,354	160,640	172,284	24.2	25.3	24.5	24.2	590,237	1,879	3,127	3,368
Ohio	43,671	41,303	43,650	20.7	25.7	25.3	25.4	139,525	1,587	2,947	3,068
Indiana	21,450	22,125	23,428	29.5	27.5	25.0	25.1	86,077	1,433	3,078	3,401
Illinois	45,955	43,307	47,224	23.8	23.8	22.9	21.8	170,405	1,700	3,016	3,408
Michigan	32,716	33,811	37,157	17.9	24.3	26.5	26.6	131,720	1,876	3,020	3,420
Wisconsin	20,653	20,034	20,805	24.9	23.7	22.2	21.6	62,560	1,379	2,560	3,007
West North Central	115,716	102,509	104,003	19.5	19.8	19.5	20.4	278,035	1,442	2,129	2,589
Minnesota	21,080	19,056	19,574	20.6	21.5	21.7	22.2	60,804	1,276	2,422	3,013
Iowa	22,450	20,902	21,319	16.6	16.5	19.2	19.6	55,447	1,017	2,088	2,490
Missouri	26,423	22,972	22,494	19.3	22.7	23.2	24.8	80,601	1,150	2,088	2,561
North Dakota	7,262	6,388	6,537	20.5	17.3	16.8	16.5	15,195	745	1,666	2,334
South Dakota	7,837	6,729	7,127	21.8	15.3	15.0	14.9	15,575	807	1,853	2,044
Nebraska	13,760	11,855	11,949	16.0	17.6	16.8	17.0	28,316	829	1,919	2,392
Kansas	16,904	14,660	15,003	23.1	19.6	18.9	20.0	43,097	1,014	2,191	2,678
South Atlantic	120,914	124,950	135,013	16.6	27.9	26.5	26.7	343,383	1,014	2,232	2,581
Delaware	1,620	1,761	1,846	29.7	24.1	21.5	22.1	6,437	1,604	2,642	3,273
Maryland	8,638	9,740	11,059	20.5	29.6	27.3	27.0	42,106	1,642	3,321	3,694
District of Columbia	3,057	3,329	3,326	17.5	27.1	25.4	25.2	13,841	2,350	3,411	3,920
Virginia	17,734	17,532	19,055	12.7	27.9	28.3	26.2	49,764	899	2,062	2,328
West Virginia	14,252	13,081	14,145	20.9	28.9	27.7	28.2	38,879	1,170	2,364	2,436
North Carolina	24,530	25,216	27,491	15.1	32.2	29.8	29.0	76,304	946	2,116	2,699
South Carolina	15,042	15,725	16,753	13.9	26.6	28.9	24.7	32,074	743	1,748	1,962
Georgia	22,646	22,700	24,380	17.7	25.6	26.6	25.4	48,972	770	1,724	1,982
Florida	13,189	15,266	16,957	17.0	24.8	24.2	24.5	52,976	1,012	2,541	2,932
East South Central	73,127	74,683	77,538	18.6	25.2	26.9	27.5	188,040	783	1,739	1,982
Kentucky	18,802	17,879	18,097	20.3	26.2	25.4	26.7	37,299	876	1,884	1,996
Tennessee	21,147	20,738	22,302	20.4	24.6	26.4	26.3	51,105	962	1,901	2,292
Alabama	19,405	20,053	21,612	15.8	29.2	28.7	27.5	47,176	744	1,057	2,111
Mississippi	14,773	15,413	15,627	18.2	33.1	29.6	30.2	22,520	559	1,204	1,424
West South Central	93,091	87,791	94,796	19.7	26.5	25.3	24.5	286,973	987	2,226	2,603
Arkansas	12,852	12,508	12,845	21.0	29.1	27.3	27.6	24,109	584	1,545	1,801
Louisiana	14,530	14,125	15,652	14.7	26.8	26.9	26.9	50,229	1,006	2,296	2,933
Oklahoma	20,204	16,050	15,931	19.2	24.0	24.9	24.7	49,711	1,014	2,277	2,786
Texas	45,205	45,008	50,368	21.1	24.7	23.9	22.0	162,914	1,079	2,695	3,122
Mountain	33,663	34,435	36,937	25.4	22.4	22.3	22.2	118,717	1,290	2,643	2,988
Montana	5,195	4,742	4,584	20.0	18.9	18.3	20.6	14,626	1,184	2,582	2,942
Idaho	4,513	3,979	4,449	25.2	23.5	23.8	25.9	11,443	1,087	2,209	2,461
Wyoming	2,551	2,314	2,549	20.6	18.5	19.1	19.2	7,530	1,169	2,187	2,795
Colorado	8,918	8,671	9,223	21.4	22.3	21.3	21.8	27,302	1,393	2,540	2,831
New Mexico	3,798	4,218	4,905	21.2	28.0	25.7	24.6	17,585	1,144	2,741	3,214
Arizona	3,384	4,600	5,140	28.2	26.1	25.0	24.6	19,387	1,544	3,134	3,456
Utah	4,417	4,729	4,911	34.2	28.0	28.0	29.0	16,777	1,394	2,958	3,108
Nevada	...	1,053	1,118	23.2	20.1	21.3	21.7	3,918	1,557	2,988	3,308
Pacific	66,183	71,146	79,959	21.5	26.7	27.7	27.6	345,949	2,101	3,398	4,044
Washington	10,653	13,195	14,624	26.9	26.9	24.6	24.6	54,234	1,705	3,325	3,457
Oregon	7,290	8,344	10,226	23.2	22.8	24.1	22.4	36,789	1,333	2,941	3,322
California	135,304	49,607	55,109	19.7	27.6	29.2	29.8	264,926	2,351	3,690	4,258
Alaska [4]	302	449	529	20.0	(6)	18.7	20.3	2,305	(5)	3,588	4,299
American Samoa	63	105	163	84.0	(6)	(6)	(7)	(5)	(5)	(5)	(5)
Canal Zone	200	250	309	32.7	(6)	24.7	27.0	1,200	1,634	2,550	3,519
Guam	139	212	269	(5)	(6)	(6)	(6)	309	(5)	(5)	(5)
Hawaii	2,091	2,968	3,214	18.0	(6)	24.6	26.6	11,903	1,830	3,639	3,908
Puerto Rico	6,065	8,574	8,955	19.8	(6)	39.4	41.3	14,365	824	1,499	1,509
Virgin Islands	117	170	143	17.6	(6)	(7)	31.0	(5)	680	(7)	(5)

[1] Excludes supervisors and principals except when not reported separately.
[2] Number in average daily attendance in full-time day schools.   [3] For 1938.
[4] Data do not include Federal schools for natives.   [5] Not available.

Source: Department of Health, Education, and Welfare, Office of Education; Biennial Survey of Education.

No. 184.—Public Elementary and Secondary Schools—Value of Property and Expenditures, by States and Other Areas: 1950

[In thousands of dollars, except averages per pupil]

DIVISION, STATE, OR OTHER AREA	VALUE OF SCHOOL PROPERTY		EXPENDITURES						
				Current expenditure for full-time day schools					Adult, summer, and evening schools
	Total	Per pupil [1]	Total	Chargeable to pupils		Not chargeable to pupils	Capital outlay	Interest	
				Amount	Per pupil [1]				
Continental U. S.	11,396,804	$511	5,837,643	4,653,464	$208,83	33,811	1,014,176	100,878	35,614
New England	710,597	615	304,476	262,535	227.10	538	38,422	1,652	1,328
Maine	51,144	353	26,143	22,901	157.47		2,210	89	43
New Hampshire	31,000	472	16,939	13,818	210.51		2,881	92	148
Vermont	22,449	399	11,548	10,855	192.87	24	613	56	
Massachusetts	385,483	688	145,559	132,486	236.44		12,225	3 123	725
Rhode Island	62,543	747	21,538	20,137	240.40	136	879	334	52
Connecticut	157,978	644	83,748	62,438	254.62	377	19,614	959	360
Middle Atlantic	2,842,606	770	1,165,915	968,675	262.38	5,864	153,760	28,515	9,101
New York	1,578,924	929	617,811	501,648	296.02	3,900	87,423	17,690	7,150
New Jersey	401,512	689	199,986	165,146	279.81	1,232	28,739	4,919	1,951
Pennsylvania	862,170	612	348,118	303,882	215.76	732	37,598	5,906	
E. North Central	2,580,437	619	1,306,760	949,687	227.93	15,596	217,641	30,512	3,264
Ohio	612,409	552	291,920	224,314	302.12	1,078	60,408	5,269	3 855
Indiana	4 240,000	4 408	158,180	138,673	235.49		16,111	3,395	
Illinois	792,355	768	358,198	266,682	256.46	13,391	71,214	6,911	
Michigan	631,626	640	274,584	216,618	219.55	1,089	52,260	4,617	
Wisconsin	304,047	676	123,868	103,400	230.01	88	17,682	319	2,409
W. North Central	1,127,028	531	516,359	456,214	214.76		52,395	7,750	
Minnesota	240,145	553	118,163	105,199	242.34		12,135	830	
Iowa	204,635	490	114,174	96,324	230.53		17,018	833	
Missouri	255,464	458	112,463	96,884	173.57		11,413	4,167	
North Dakota	56,527	548	24,905	23,361	226.27		1,172	371	
South Dakota	3 51,748	3 486	27,071	24,804	230.34		2,282	285	
Nebraska	112,613	553	47,193	44,191	217.07		2,503	496	
Kansas	205,896	684	72,391	65,751	218.57		5,872	767	
South Atlantic	1,215,914	337	712,436	548,266	152.09	9,481	131,561	8,283	15,822
Delaware	25,000	612	13,118	10,577	258.77	13	2,369	100	59
Maryland	147,206	493	94,545	63,704	213.39	58	27,389	2,006	1,388
Dist. of Columbia	69,313	828	37,671	21,448	256.24		5,982		441
Virginia	204,720	381	100,502	75,143	145.56		21,347	899	713
West Virginia	144,669	363	69,666	56,761	149.86	244	9,611	3 30	
North Carolina	231,008	290	151,323	112,333	140.82	8,968	28,001	2,021	(4)
South Carolina	90,721	219	63,465	50,615	122.39		7,777	567	4,506
Georgia	157,879	255	95,225	76,468	123.37		11,449	938	6,370
Florida	145,398	350	97,319	75,219	181.27	197	17,636	1,922	2,345
E. South Central	399,868	187	292,528	242,810	113.78	961	43,433	1,512	4,091
Kentucky	131,369	271	68,092	56,485	120.82	428	5,110	514	3,555
Tennessee	4 100,000	4 171	104,576	77,071	132.17		26,855	474	175
Alabama	4 96,500	4 162	79,374	69,627	117.09	363	8,542	480	361
Mississippi	4 72,000	4 152	40,786	37,627	79.69	190	2,926	44	
W. South Central	921,296	396	557,732	452,919	194.58	123	89,764	14,925	
Arkansas	98,526	278	54,354	39,661	111.71		13,615	1,078	
Louisiana	139,861	332	112,753	90,070	214.06	123	20,877	1,682	
Oklahoma	191,041	485	87,611	81,584	207.05		4,627	1,400	
Texas	491,867	425	303,013	241,603	208.88		50,644	10,765	
Mountain	439,781	505	248,669	191,909	220.48	615	52,836	3,350	958
Montana	4 50,500	4 535	31,607	25,259	267.56	29	5,381	144	794
Idaho	46,605	418	26,267	20,653	186.00		5,372	341	
Wyoming	28,417	581	14,737	12,855	262.77		1,647	235	
Colorado	113,524	564	59,458	44,204	219.66	242	13,797	1,215	
New Mexico	57,630	478	33,509	26,898	222.48	166	6,138	308	
Arizona	61,897	489	41,535	30,451	240.70		10,504	580	
Utah	64,633	456	33,800	25,404	178.56	179	7,674	379	164
Nevada	16,177	644	8,757	6,184	246.22		2,423	149	
Pacific	1,159,277	535	830,536	586,436	262.73	612	234,363	14,078	1,650
Washington	257,224	721	113,845	88,343	247.63	612	22,927	913	4 1,050
Oregon	152,053	665	93,325	64,172	280.75		27,286	1,867	
California	750,000	462	623,359	437,911	263.51		184,149	11,298	
Alaska	6,961	629	4,101	3,405	317.19		696		
Canal Zone	(7)	(7)	1,706	1,642	196.40		49		14
Hawaii	(7)	(7)	19,412	18,350	214.82		881		182
Puerto Rico	26,445	716	26,771	25,921	70.21		754		97

[1] Average per pupil in average daily attendance.   [3] 1948 data.   [4] Excludes veterans' program.
[4] Estimated.   [5] Incomplete.   [6] Small amount included in expense for day schools.   [7] Not available.

Source: Department of Health, Education, and Welfare, Office of Education; *Biennial Survey of Education*, chapter on Statistics of State School Systems.

No. 135.—PUBLIC ELEMENTARY AND SECONDARY SCHOOLS—ENROLLMENT, WHITE AND NEGRO, FOR 18 STATES: 1946, 1948, AND 1950

| STATE | ENROLLMENT IN— | | | | | | AVERAGE DAYS ATTENDANCE PER PUPIL ENROLLED, 1950 | |
| | White schools | | | Negro schools | | | White | Negro |
	1946	1948	1950	1946	1948	1950		
Total, 18 States	6,885,762	7,081,552	7,424,114	2,264,229	2,306,662	2,396,946	157.0	147.9
Alabama	412,771	416,172	437,779	225,604	230,702	242,287	156.1	150.6
Arkansas	297,370	304,760	305,287	96,700	98,948	101,797	155.2	141.0
Delaware	34,400	35,830	37,835	7,283	7,693	8,220	161.9	139.5
District of Columbia	54,030	53,751	50,573	40,747	43,763	45,750	152.2	154.0
Florida	271,360	299,320	333,454	101,817	106,285	116,382	167.3	163.0
Georgia	435,271	451,104	467,370	259,111	248,360	250,667	158.4	144.9
Kentucky	490,256	509,458	525,759	36,205	36,619	37,124	147.3	147.3
Louisiana	270,567	273,380	299,766	165,706	169,031	183,597	157.8	152.6
Maryland	225,231	234,797	261,417	63,160	67,619	73,601	165.0	160.9
Mississippi	258,224	259,418	263,643	258,800	259,988	263,797	152.2	120.9
Missouri	574,348	570,575	588,141	50,887	53,182	56,316	154.4	162.0
North Carolina	562,192	589,531	617,638	251,307	258,740	267,095	164.5	157.0
Oklahoma	424,570	421,065	403,570	36,696	35,009	37,693	165.9	149.1
South Carolina	247,224	251,353	272,305	201,020	207,457	221,380	155.6	139.7
Tennessee	492,951	524,473	552,858	102,068	103,966	106,927	156.2	156.1
Texas	1,048,899	1,078,242	1,152,914	197,554	200,796	201,253	149.6	146.7
Virginia	400,282	410,339	440,807	147,699	150,636	157,060	163.0	157.9
West Virginia	385,816	397,984	412,998	24,857	25,266	26,800	158.9	165.1

Source: Department of Health, Education, and Welfare, Office of Education; *Biennial Survey of Education*, chapter on Statistics of State School Systems.

No. 136.—PRIVATE ELEMENTARY AND SECONDARY SCHOOLS—TEACHERS AND ENROLLMENT, BY STATES: 1950

[Includes data for kindergartens. Excludes data for private residential schools for exceptional children and private vocational and trade schools. Partly estimated on basis of earlier surveys]

| STATE | Number of teachers | NUMBER OF PUPILS | | | STATE | Number of teachers | NUMBER OF PUPILS | | |
		Total	Elementary	Secondary			Total	Elementary	Secondary
Cont. U.S.	118,271	3,380,139	2,707,777	672,362	Montana	397	11,929	9,290	2,639
					Nebraska	1,284	29,503	22,633	6,870
Alabama	1,017	17,190	12,109	5,081	Nevada	31	1,166	1,013	153
Arizona	358	7,113	5,195	1,918	N.H.	1,119	26,612	19,989	6,623
Arkansas	306	8,073	6,056	2,017	New Jersey	5,314	169,233	141,334	27,900
California	5,216	158,631	127,164	31,447					
Colorado	848	21,384	16,151	5,233	New Mexico	484	16,472	14,320	2,152
					New York	16,160	499,775	415,824	83,951
Connecticut	2,806	65,483	50,860	14,623	North Carolina	524	7,329	5,108	2,221
Delaware	276	9,019	7,255	1,764	North Dakota	736	11,730	9,385	2,345
Dist. of Col	831	18,190	14,149	4,041	Ohio	6,270	198,032	162,367	35,665
Florida	803	21,092	15,513	5,579					
Georgia	551	10,326	6,357	3,969	Oklahoma	724	11,103	8,606	2,497
					Oregon	715	17,108	13,071	4,037
Idaho	196	3,764	3,175	589	Pennsylvania	11,176	357,008	292,148	64,860
Illinois	10,991	311,398	258,255	53,143	Rhode Island	1,405	42,449	30,947	11,502
Indiana	2,488	69,661	57,840	11,821	South Carolina	279	4,830	3,389	1,441
Iowa	2,419	57,784	45,698	12,086					
Kansas	1,424	30,078	24,576	5,502	South Dakota	512	11,280	9,595	1,685
					Tennessee	829	15,799	9,177	6,622
Kentucky	1,981	54,171	41,694	12,477	Texas	2,681	76,340	63,722	12,518
Louisiana	2,739	85,286	72,542	12,744	Utah	110	2,019	1,395	624
Maine	1,375	35,721	24,661	11,060	Vermont	605	15,301	9,207	6,094
Maryland	2,597	69,808	57,564	12,244					
Massachusetts	7,181	212,036	149,397	62,639	Virginia	1,119	19,282	12,401	6,881
					Washington	1,409	28,386	21,614	6,772
Michigan	8,580	190,062	145,328	44,732	West Virginia	466	10,527	7,567	2,960
Minnesota	2,855	86,071	71,731	14,340	Wisconsin	4,677	144,078	123,321	20,757
Mississippi	511	12,341	9,747	2,594	Wyoming	71	1,509	1,277	232
Missouri	3,572	96,777	76,139	20,638					

Source: Department of Health, Education, and Welfare, Office of Education; *Biennial Survey of Education*, chapter on Statistics of State School Systems.

No. 187.—Public Elementary and Secondary Schools—Enrollment, by Grade: 1940 to 1950

SCHOOL AND GRADE	1940	1942	1944	1946	1948	1950
Pupils enrolled, total	25,433,542	24,562,473	23,266,616	23,299,941	23,944,532	25,111,427
Elementary schools, total	18,832,098	18,174,668	17,713,096	17,677,744	18,291,227	19,404,693
Kindergarten	594,647	625,783	697,468	772,957	988,680	1,034,203
First	3,018,463	2,930,762	2,878,843	2,894,588	2,951,300	3,170,343
Second	2,333,076	2,215,100	2,220,739	2,318,502	2,363,477	2,644,707
Third	2,331,559	2,175,245	2,162,878	2,190,617	2,258,858	2,395,904
Fourth	2,321,567	2,196,732	2,079,788	2,094,352	2,183,171	2,254,028
Fifth	2,347,692	2,166,018	2,016,635	2,008,120	2,055,115	2,150,678
Sixth	2,175,133	2,134,494	1,997,306	1,910,028	1,939,500	2,055,741
Seventh	2,107,667	2,060,752	1,964,997	1,836,897	1,897,740	1,947,227
Eighth	1,700,994	1,679,782	1,693,942	1,653,683	1,653,386	1,751,802
High schools, total	6,601,444	6,387,805	5,553,520	5,622,197	5,653,305	5,706,734
First year	2,011,341	1,927,040	1,774,593	1,728,499	1,672,920	1,756,303
Second year	1,767,312	1,705,746	1,519,638	1,585,302	1,502,743	1,511,906
Third year	1,485,603	1,450,788	1,230,168	1,255,907	1,271,645	1,273,826
Fourth year	1,281,735	1,273,141	1,009,611	1,032,420	1,130,805	1,122,872
Postgraduate	55,453	31,090	19,510	50,069	75,192	41,827

No. 188.—Public Elementary and Secondary Schools—Current Expenditure Per Pupil, by Purpose: 1930 to 1950

PURPOSE	CURRENT EXPENDITURE (EXCLUDING INTEREST)							
	1930		1940		1948		1950 [2]	
	Per pupil [1]	Percent	Per pupil [1]	Percent	Per pupil [1]	Percent	Per pupil [1]	Percent
Total	$86.70	100.0	$88.09	100.0	$181.48	100.0	$208.83	100.0
Administration (general control)	3.70	4.3	4.15	4.7	8.13	4.5	9.88	4.7
Instruction	61.97	71.5	63.66	72.3	122.98	67.8	139.67	66.9
Salaries	58.80	67.9	59.63	67.7	115.63	63.7	131.35	62.9
Textbooks and supplies	3.17	3.6	4.03	4.6	7.35	4.1	8.32	4.0
Operation	10.16	11.7	8.82	10.0	17.06	9.4	19.19	9.2
Maintenance	3.71	4.3	3.33	3.8	8.11	4.5	9.61	4.6
Auxiliary services	4.80	5.5	5.86	6.6	16.10	8.9	18.78	9.0
Fixed charges	2.36	2.7	2.27	2.6	9.10	5.0	11.70	5.6
Capital outlay	17.44		11.70		19.73		45.51	
Interest	4.35		5.94		3.65		4.51	

[1] Average per pupil in average daily attendance. [2] Expenditures for community services, etc., not included.

Source of tables 137 and 138: Department of Health, Education, and Welfare, Office of Education; *Biennial Survey of Education*, chapter on Statistics of State School Systems.

No. 189.—High-School and College Graduates—Number, by Sex: 1890 to 1950

[Data cover graduates of both public and private institutions]

YEAR OF GRADUATION	HIGH SCHOOL			COLLEGE		
	Total	Men	Women	Total	Men	Women
1890	43,731	18,549	25,182	[1] 15,539	12,857	2,682
1900	94,883	38,075	56,808	[1] 27,410	22,173	5,237
1910	156,429	63,676	92,753	[1] 37,199	28,762	8,437
1920	311,266	123,684	187,582	48,622	31,980	16,642
1930	666,904	300,376	366,528	122,484	73,615	48,869
1940	1,221,475	578,718	642,757	186,500	109,546	76,954
1942	1,080,033	466,926	613,107	136,174	58,664	77,510
1948	1,180,909	552,863	627,046	271,019	175,456	95,563
1950	1,199,700	570,700	629,000	432,058	328,841	103,217

[1] Revised. Distribution by sex estimated.

Source: Department of Health, Education, and Welfare, Office of Education; *Biennial Survey of Education*, chapter on Statistical Summary of Education.

No. 140.—SCHOOL AND COLLEGE ENROLLMENT AND EXPENDITURES: 1900 TO 1950

ITEM	1900	1910	1920	1930	1940	1948	1950
ENROLLMENT							
Elementary schools, total.	16,261,846	18,528,535	20,963,722	23,717,796	21,106,655	20,828,958	22,201,505
Kindergartens:							
Public	131,657	[1] 293,970	481,266	723,443	594,647	983,680	1,034,203
Nonpublic	93,737	[1] 52,219	29,683	54,456	57,341	[3] 182,000	[3] 183,000
Residential schools for exceptional children	[2]	[2]	[2]	[4] 5,164	5,777	[4] 4,459	[4] 4,459
Elementary schools:							
Public	14,852,202	16,604,821	18,897,661	20,555,150	18,237,451	17,302,547	18,370,490
Nonpublic	1,147,188	1,506,218	1,455,878	2,255,430	2,095,938	2,269,430	2,574,777
Elementary grades in college and teacher-training elementary schools	[2]	[2]	[2]	[2]	59,547	32,948	35,682
Residential schools for exceptional children	37,062	71,307	[4] 99,234	[4] 124,153	55,954	[4] 48,894	[4] 48,894
Secondary schools, total	699,403	1,115,398	2,500,176	4,804,255	7,123,009	6,365,168	6,437,042
Public high schools [7]	519,251	915,061	2,200,389	4,399,422	6,601,444	5,653,305	5,706,734
Nonpublic high schools	110,797	117,400	213,920	[4] 341,156	457,768	602,484	672,362
Secondary grades in college and teacher-training secondary schools	65,855	78,932	81,367	59,287	54,070	39,595	38,162
Residential schools for exceptional children	3,500	4,005	[4] 4,500	[4] 4,388	9,727	[4] 9,784	[4] 9,784
Higher education, total	237,592	355,215	597,880	1,100,737	1,494,203	2,616,262	2,659,021
Publicly controlled	[5] 90,689	[5] 166,560	[5] 315,382	[5] 532,647	796,531	1,326,147	1,354,902
Privately controlled	[5] 146,903	[5] 188,655	[5] 282,498	[5] 568,090	697,672	1,290,115	1,304,119
EXPENDITURES (thousands of dollars) [10]							
Public elementary and secondary schools [11]	214,965	426,250	1,036,151	2,316,790	2,344,049	4,311,176	5,837,643
Private elementary and secondary schools [11]	[2]	53,542	[2]	233,277	227,000	[9] 530,021	782,967
Public institutions of higher education [13]	45,786	91,896	{ 115,597	288,909	[13] 332,592	[13] 896,184	[13] 1,174,125
Private institutions of higher education [13]			{ 100,769	343,310	[13] 273,163	[13] 801,781	[13] 949,150

[1] 1912 data.   [2] Census estimates.   [3] Not available.   [4] 1927 data.   [5] 1946 data.   [6] 1918 data.
[7] Data from high school reports through 1920; later data from Statistics of State School Systems.   [8] 1938 data.
[9] Estimated.   [10] Includes capital outlay.   [11] Excludes pupils in residential schools for exceptional children.
[12] Expenditures for all departments, including preparatory.
[13] Excludes expenditures for auxiliary enterprises and activities and other noneducational purposes included in prior years, amounting to $59,034,000 for public institutions and $93,665,000 for private institutions for 1940; $235,805,000 and $252,870,000 for 1948; and $255,474,000 and $283,743,000 for 1950.

Source: Department of Health, Education, and Welfare, Office of Education; *Biennial Survey of Education*, chapter on Statistical Summary of Education.

No. 141.—JUNIOR COLLEGES—NUMBER AND ENROLLMENT: 1918 TO 1950

YEAR	ALL SCHOOLS REPORTING		PUBLICLY CONTROLLED		PRIVATELY CONTROLLED	
	Number	Enrollment	Number	Enrollment	Number	Enrollment
1918	46	4,504	14	1,367	32	3,137
1920	52	8,102	10	2,940	42	5,162
1922	80	12,124	17	4,771	63	7,353
1924	132	20,559	39	9,240	93	11,319
1926	153	27,095	47	13,859	106	13,236
1928	248	44,855	114	28,437	134	16,418
1930	277	55,616	129	36,501	148	19,115
1932	342	85,063	159	58,887	183	26,176
1934	322	78,480	152	55,869	170	22,611
1936	415	102,453	187	70,557	228	31,896
1938	453	121,510	209	82,041	244	39,469
1940	456	149,854	217	107,553	239	42,301
1942	461	141,272	231	100,783	230	40,489
1944	413	89,208	210	60,884	203	28,324
1946	464	156,486	242	109,640	222	46,816
1948	472	240,173	242	178,196	230	61,977
1950	483	242,740	256	187,695	227	55,045

Source: Department of Health, Education, and Welfare, Office of Education; *Biennial Survey of Education*, chapter on Statistics of Higher Education, Section 1.

No. 142.—INSTITUTIONS OF HIGHER EDUCATION—STAFF, ENROLLMENT, AND RECIPIENTS OF DEGREES, BY SEX, AND INCOME AND EXPENDITURES: 1940 TO 1950

[All money figures in thousands of dollars. Data cover universities, colleges, professional schools, junior colleges, teachers' colleges, and normal schools, both publicly and privately controlled, regular session. For student enrollment and total expenditures for earlier years, see table 140]

ITEM	1940	1942	1944	1946 [1]	1948 [1]	1950 [1]
Number of institutions reporting staff, enrollment, and degrees conferred	1,708	1,720	1,650	1,768	1,788	1,851
Staff (reduced to full-time basis), total	131,552	134,127	134,451	136,832	196,300	210,349
Men	94,536	96,251	93,794	93,876	143,243	157,691
Women	37,016	37,886	40,657	42,156	53,057	52,658
Resident college enrollment, total	1,494,203	1,463,990	[2]1,155,272	1,676,851	2,616,262	2,659,021
Men	893,250	818,559	578,948	927,662	1,836,339	1,853,068
Women	600,953	585,431	576,324	749,189	779,923	805,953
Degrees conferred:						
Baccalaureate and first professional, total	186,500	185,346	125,863	136,174	271,019	432,058
Men	109,546	103,889	55,865	58,664	175,456	328,841
Women	76,954	81,457	69,998	77,510	95,563	103,217
Masters, including advanced engineering (men and women)	26,731	24,648	13,414	19,209	42,400	58,183
Doctors (men and women)	3,290	3,497	2,305	1,966	4,188	6,633
Number of institutions reporting income and expenditures	1,609	1,628	1,563	1,768	1,788	1,851
Current income	715,211	783,720	1,047,296	1,169,294	2,027,052	2,374,645
Educational and general income	571,288	626,296	863,654	924,958	1,538,076	1,833,845
Student fees	208,897	201,385	154,485	214,344	304,601	394,610
Endowment earnings	71,304	74,075	75,196	89,763	86,680	96,341
Federal Government	33,860	58,232	306,163	197,250	526,476	524,319
State governments	151,222	166,532	175,169	225,161	352,281	491,636
Local governments	24,392	27,057	26,449	31,005	47,521	61,700
Private gifts and grants	40,453	45,916	50,449	77,572	91,466	118,627
Sales and services	32,777	40,308	53,576	67,084	92,725	111,987
Miscellaneous	11,383	12,811	20,167	22,779	36,324	34,625
Auxiliary enterprises and activities	143,923	157,424	183,644	244,436	465,155	511,265
Other noneducational income [3]					23,821	29,535
Receipts for plant expansion	66,209	30,096	22,587	121,837	364,901	528,747
Receipts for increase of permanent funds	44,518	38,510	69,668	[4]	[5]75,881	116,932
Current expenditures	674,689	738,169	974,117	1,068,422	1,883,269	2,245,661
Educational and general	521,990	542,466	753,845	820,326	1,391,594	1,706,444
Administration and general expense	62,827	66,968	69,668	104,808	171,829	213,070
Resident instruction	280,248	298,558	334,188	375,122	657,945	780,994
Organized research	27,266	34,287	58,456	86,812	150,090	225,341
Libraries	19,487	19,763	20,452	26,580	44,208	56,147
Plant operation and maintenance	69,612	72,594	81,201	110,947	201,996	225,110
Organized activities related to instruction	27,225	37,771	48,415	60,604	85,346	119,108
Extension	35,325	42,595	44,421	55,473	71,180	86,674
Other			[6]97,044			
Auxiliary enterprises and activities	124,184	137,328	199,344	242,028	438,988	476,401
Other noneducational expenditures	28,514	28,375	20,928	26,066	52,687	62,816
Expenditures for plant expansion	83,765	50,202	27,427	71,403	306,371	416,831

[1] Includes estimates for institutions not reporting.
[2] Includes 277,755 full time regular session military students.
[3] Not reported separately prior to 1948.   [4] Not available.
[5] Represents receipts from private gifts and grants only; other sources of permanent funds comparatively minor.
[6] Consists of "Federal contract courses" only.

Source: Department of Health, Education, and Welfare, Office of Education; *Biennial Survey of Education*, chapter on Statistics of Higher Education.

No. 143.—INSTITUTIONS OF HIGHER EDUCATION—FALL ENROLLMENT, BY TYPE OF INSTITUTION: 1950, 1951, AND 1952

[Includes estimates. 1950 data based on returns from 1,852 of a total 1,888 institutions covered; 1951 data based on returns from 1,806 of a total 1,859 institutions covered; and 1952 data based on returns from 1,845 of a total 1,907 institutions covered. Includes data for Territories and possessions]

TYPE	1950			1951			1952		
	Total enrollment	First-time students	Veterans	Total enrollment	First-time students	Veterans	Total enrollment	First-time students	Veterans
All institutions	2,296,592	516,836	572,307	2,116,440	472,025	383,747	2,148,284	536,879	232,880
Universities, colleges, and professional schools	1,888,275	357,930	507,201	1,746,319	332,412	344,164	1,735,232	374,950	205,217
Teachers' colleges	190,745	52,395	32,118	170,034	44,081	19,005	173,540	50,987	10,398
Junior colleges	217,572	106,511	32,988	200,087	95,532	26,578	239,512	110,942	17,265

Source: Department of Health, Education, and Welfare, Office of Education: *Fall Enrollment in Higher Educational Institutions*.

No. 144.—Institutions of Higher Education—Enrollment, Faculty, and Earned Degrees Conferred in Negro Institutions: 1940 to 1950

ITEM	1940	1948	1950					
			Total	Universities, colleges, and professional schools		Teachers colleges and normal schools [1]	Junior colleges	
				Publicly controlled	Privately controlled		Publicly controlled	Privately controlled
Number of institutions....	104	108	105	23	54	12	3	13
Faculty (full-time equivalent).................	3,922	5,851	6,600	3,020	2,803	491	65	221
Men	2,311	3,379	3,936	1,851	1,705	234	36	110
Women.................	1,611	2,472	2,664	1,169	1,098	257	29	111
RESIDENT COLLEGE ENROLLMENTS								
Regular session:								
Total.................	42,504	79,391	[2] 76,561	31,599	35,529	6,740	1,116	1,577
Men.................	17,921	42,469	40,677	17,096	19,575	2,369	751	886
Women.................	24,583	36,922	35,884	14,503	15,954	4,371	365	691
Undergraduate........	41,843	77,407	72,922	30,261	33,395	6,651	1,058	1,557
Men.................	17,627	41,606	38,934	16,430	18,535	2,347	743	879
Women.................	24,216	35,801	33,988	13,831	14,860	4,304	315	678
Graduate.................	661	1,984	2,304	882	1,342	[3] 80		
Men.................	294	863	1,161	462	679	[3] 20		
Women.................	367	1,121	1,143	420	663	[3] 60		
First time in any college.	14,612	24,129	21,368	8,480	9,809	2,266	436	665
Men.................	6,254	13,260	10,613	4,436	4,820	809	251	297
Women.................	8,358	10,869	10,755	4,053	4,689	1,457	185	371
Veterans, third week [4]..		26,308	19,320	7,907	9,253	1,193	304	663
Men.................		26,049	19,152	7,825	9,173	1,190	304	660
Women.................		259	168	82	80	3		3
Summer session, 1939, 1947, and 1949............	24,380	39,507	38,976	19,914	15,132	3,514	83	333
Men.................	4,760	16,340	15,258	7,832	6,433	835	69	89
Women.................	19,620	23,167	23,718	12,082	8,699	2,679	14	244
EARNED DEGREES CONFERRED [5]								
Bachelor's and first professional.................	5,302	8,504	13,106	4,866	6,497	1,745		
Men.................	2,078	3,062	6,467	2,508	3,464	495		
Women.................	3,224	5,442	6,641	2,358	3,033	1,250		
Master's and second professional.................	145	433	768	306	400	62		
Men.................	56	184	335	143	172	20		
Women.................	89	249	433	163	228	42		

[1] All publicly controlled.
[2] Includes special students (less than 2 percent of total) omitted from breakdown by level.
[3] Graduate enrollment in teachers colleges estimated.
[4] Veterans of World War II in attendance, third week of fall term.
[5] Doctorate not conferred at any institution in this group.

Source: Department of Health, Education, and Welfare, Office of Education; *Biennial Survey of Education*, chapter on Statistics of Higher Education, Section 1.

No. 145.—Number Surviving Through College Per 1,000 Pupils

GRADE OR YEAR	1930-31	1931-32	1932-33	1933-34	1934-35	1935-36	1936-37	1937-38	1938-39	1939-40	1940-41	1941-42	1942-43
Elementary: Fifth [1].....	1,000	1,000	1,000	1,000	1,000	1,000	1,000	1,000	1,000	1,000	1,000	1,000	1,000
Sixth............	943	929	935	944	963	946	954	954	955	963	968	952	954
Seventh............	872	884	889	895	892	890	895	901	908	916	910	905	909
Eighth............	824	818	831	836	842	830	849	850	853	846	836	834	847
High School: I............	770	780	786	792	806	814	839	811	796	781	781	789	807
II............	652	651	664	688	711	725	704	679	655	673	697	698	713
III............	529	546	570	594	610	587	554	519	532	552	566	581	604
IV............	463	481	510	480	512	466	425	428	444	476	507	514	533
Graduates............	417	432	455	462	467	439	393	398	419	450	481	488	505
Year of graduation........	1938	1939	1940	1941	1942	1943	1944	1945	1946	1947	1948	1949	1950
College: I............	148	154	160	142	129	119	121	(2)	(2)	(2)	(2)	(2)	225
Graduates............	69	69	47	49	51	(2)	(2)	(2)	(2)				
Year of graduation........	1942	1943	1944	1945	1946	1947	1948	1949	1950				

[1] Fourth grade in 11-grade system; fifth grade in 12-grade system.
[2] Because of veteran students, it is not possible to calculate retention rates.

Source: Department of Health, Education, and Welfare, Office of Education; *Biennial Survey of Education*, chapter on Statistical Summary of Education.

No. 146.—Institutions of Higher Education—1952 Fall Enrollment of Total, First-Time Students, and Veterans, by Sex, by States and Other Areas

[See headnote, table 143]

DIVISION, STATE, OR OTHER AREA	TOTAL ENROLLMENT			FIRST-TIME STUDENTS			VETERANS		
	Total	Men	Women	Total	Men	Women	Total	Men	Women
Continental U. S	2,134,242	1,380,357	753,885	532,310	321,310	211,000	231,720	224,884	6,836
New England	156,330	106,231	50,099	38,990	25,096	13,894	15,890	15,427	463
Maine	7,303	4,519	2,784	2,327	1,362	965	393	389	4
New Hampshire	7,898	5,639	2,259	2,478	1,578	900	340	329	11
Vermont	6,873	4,110	2,763	2,117	1,192	925	246	243	3
Massachusetts	93,993	62,953	31,040	21,810	13,948	7,862	10,654	10,304	350
Rhode Island	9,728	6,633	3,095	2,947	1,948	999	679	665	14
Connecticut	30,535	22,377	8,158	7,311	5,068	2,243	3,578	3,497	81
Middle Atlantic	449,276	297,504	151,772	82,380	52,317	30,063	55,279	53,666	1,613
New York	288,640	185,019	103,621	49,240	30,319	18,921	34,145	33,015	1,130
New Jersey	39,478	28,544	10,934	9,286	5,947	3,339	6,519	6,358	161
Pennsylvania	121,158	83,941	37,217	23,854	16,051	7,803	14,615	14,293	322
East North Central	422,098	277,113	144,985	100,476	60,865	39,611	43,991	42,945	1,046
Ohio	110,630	74,169	36,461	25,516	15,677	9,839	12,363	12,065	298
Indiana	56,729	38,431	18,298	15,478	10,033	5,445	7,465	7,249	216
Illinois	125,715	81,122	44,593	28,350	16,457	11,893	13,582	13,234	348
Michigan	87,992	57,783	30,209	19,627	11,945	7,682	7,513	7,403	110
Wisconsin	41,032	25,608	15,424	11,505	6,753	4,752	3,068	2,994	74
West North Central	185,988	117,887	68,101	54,394	31,146	23,248	16,022	15,710	312
Minnesota	40,333	25,221	15,112	11,166	6,152	5,014	2,849	2,766	83
Iowa	33,794	20,909	12,885	10,349	5,948	4,401	2,395	2,348	47
Missouri	50,515	32,583	17,932	13,022	7,097	5,925	6,427	6,320	107
North Dakota	6,944	4,580	2,364	2,624	1,586	1,038	496	495	1
South Dakota	6,495	4,379	2,116	2,726	1,663	1,063	522	512	10
Nebraska	18,918	11,833	7,085	5,344	3,161	2,183	1,327	1,303	24
Kansas	28,989	18,382	10,607	9,163	5,530	3,624	2,006	1,966	40
South Atlantic	250,544	158,151	92,393	65,905	38,030	27,875	28,677	27,729	948
Delaware	3,035	1,990	1,045	812	489	323	210	203	7
Maryland	37,093	26,714	10,379	7,724	5,181	2,543	4,224	4,114	110
Dist. of Columbia	31,790	21,845	9,945	5,665	3,355	2,310	7,086	6,764	322
Virginia	31,452	18,266	13,186	9,621	4,826	4,795	1,949	1,907	42
West Virginia	17,519	10,432	7,087	5,176	3,203	1,973	1,832	1,785	47
North Carolina	41,765	24,128	17,637	13,198	7,305	5,893	2,920	2,849	71
South Carolina	20,472	12,311	8,161	6,168	3,480	2,688	1,480	1,463	17
Georgia	31,849	19,576	12,273	8,068	4,590	3,478	3,224	3,132	92
Florida	35,569	22,889	12,680	9,473	5,601	3,872	5,752	5,512	240
East South Central	107,778	64,945	42,833	30,453	16,922	13,531	10,207	9,991	216
Kentucky	26,800	16,217	10,583	6,998	3,716	3,282	2,793	2,703	90
Tennessee	35,647	21,731	13,916	10,057	5,630	4,427	2,892	2,822	70
Alabama	27,321	16,337	10,984	7,311	4,146	3,165	2,756	2,717	39
Mississippi	18,010	10,660	7,350	6,087	3,430	2,657	1,766	1,749	17
West South Central	206,706	133,046	73,660	54,525	33,493	21,032	23,279	22,678	601
Arkansas	17,067	10,461	6,606	4,844	2,969	1,875	1,846	1,810	36
Louisiana	33,506	20,732	12,774	8,833	5,127	3,706	2,970	2,899	71
Oklahoma	36,650	25,531	11,119	11,023	7,511	3,512	4,850	4,750	100
Texas	119,483	76,322	43,161	29,825	17,886	11,939	13,613	13,219	394
Mountain	87,206	56,378	30,828	26,082	15,866	10,216	10,317	9,932	385
Montana	6,652	4,114	2,538	2,159	1,288	871	543	524	19
Idaho	6,892	4,580	2,312	2,698	1,708	990	563	549	14
Wyoming	3,499	2,182	1,317	857	547	310	254	247	7
Colorado	27,391	17,340	10,051	7,212	4,149	3,063	3,288	3,116	172
New Mexico	8,428	5,867	2,561	2,392	1,649	743	1,157	1,111	46
Arizona	11,609	7,469	4,140	3,961	2,497	1,464	1,313	1,234	79
Utah	21,484	14,019	7,465	6,457	3,844	2,613	3,036	2,991	45
Nevada	1,251	807	444	346	184	162	163	160	3
Pacific	268,316	169,102	99,214	79,105	47,575	31,530	28,058	26,806	1,252
Washington	34,696	22,753	11,945	11,009	6,630	4,379	5,258	5,094	164
Oregon	22,462	14,632	7,830	6,152	3,656	2,496	2,481	2,374	107
California	211,156	131,717	79,439	61,944	37,289	24,655	20,319	19,338	981
Alaska	266	192	74	68	48	20	26	26	
Canal Zone	196	99	97	151	81	70	1	1	
Hawaii	4,648	2,469	2,179	1,339	746	593	344	328	16
Puerto Rico	8,932	3,977	4,955	3,011	1,488	1,523	789	779	10

Source: Department of Health, Education, and Welfare, Office of Education; *Fall Enrollment in Higher Educational Institutions*.

No. 147.—INSTITUTIONS OF HIGHER EDUCATION—NUMBER, STAFF, AND ENROLLMENT, BY STATES AND OTHER AREAS: 1950

[See headnote, table 142]

DIVISION, STATE, OR OTHER AREA	Number of institutions	STAFF (REDUCED TO FULL-TIME BASIS)[1]		Regular session		Undergraduate		Graduate		Freshman, both sexes
		Men	Women	Men	Women	Men	Women	Men	Women	
Continental U. S.	1,851	157,691	52,653	1,853,068	805,953	1,860,641	687,615	172,161	65,047	594,126
New England	156	14,212	3,820	126,806	47,721	107,615	30,655	11,411	2,951	39,640
	16	636	247	6,617	2,697	6,449	2,837	122	24	2,580
	9	762	202	7,332	2,211	6,790	2,044	204	32	2,642
	13	478	198	5,030	2,665	4,872	2,603	111	21	2,301
	77	8,826	1,992	73,561	20,008	58,215	22,907	6,844	2,379	21,068
	13	955	300	10,354	3,471	9,765	2,270	465	156	3,912
	28	2,558	881	23,872	6,509	21,621	5,904	1,633	369	6,877
Middle Atlantic	279	32,580	9,165	334,587	167,117	235,451	116,684	53,465	20,892	102,737
	132	18,705	5,587	236,702	116,203	161,857	60,936	37,283	16,571	60,188
	37	2,197	685	34,344	11,141	29,715	9,390	2,964	200	11,362
	110	10,588	2,593	113,541	39,713	93,879	31,458	12,218	3,615	91,180
East North Central	321	29,029	9,383	397,491	167,640	330,364	134,814	34,537	13,548	117,166
	69	7,541	2,438	102,410	43,514	84,002	34,034	6,090	1,900	31,081
	40	4,510	1,196	58,383	23,889	52,697	21,114	4,602	1,383	17,820
	100	8,518	2,821	117,664	50,446	93,573	40,125	12,442	4,657	33,771
	46	4,297	1,575	80,907	33,368	65,412	24,287	8,364	4,753	21,329
	66	4,100	1,353	38,067	16,423	33,880	15,263	3,090	765	13,465
West North Central	218	15,419	6,500	173,418	77,946	157,224	70,668	14,723	3,917	61,870
	44	3,254	1,471	37,495	17,582	33,397	16,666	3,691	729	12,660
	51	3,215	1,269	32,012	14,950	28,368	13,265	3,313	849	11,182
	65	3,851	1,606	49,307	21,233	43,397	18,770	4,536	1,517	17,070
	13	574	205	6,791	2,686	6,821	2,514	267	43	3,073
	16	694	259	6,454	2,402	6,183	2,268	165	32	2,632
	24	1,653	652	16,133	7,236	14,582	6,613	990	206	6,280
Kansas	45	2,248	1,138	27,226	11,848	24,970	10,828	1,503	477	9,736
South Atlantic	257	18,683	7,657	203,944	96,903	179,054	83,436	18,329	6,191	72,088
Delaware	5	355	102	2,681	1,011	2,095	849	452	122	764
Maryland	31	2,758	765	26,559	9,972	20,772	7,717	2,731	688	7,221
District of Columbia	21	2,107	668	32,823	13,357	21,655	8,484	4,366	1,924	7,316
Virginia	44	2,679	1,270	24,041	14,033	22,904	13,418	892	283	16,232
West Virginia	22	1,271	536	16,472	7,834	15,383	7,128	664	403	8,673
North Carolina	64	3,310	1,437	30,740	16,193	28,359	14,784	2,056	560	18,043
South Carolina	32	1,698	601	16,135	8,123	15,152	7,531	534	411	6,360
Georgia	54	2,311	1,009	20,566	14,737	28,690	13,376	1,555	846	10,322
Florida	18	2,294	873	26,027	11,605	23,951	10,339	1,727	828	9,086
East South Central	147	8,435	4,110	92,157	46,576	84,491	41,728	5,738	2,516	34,714
Kentucky	40	1,718	991	21,611	10,967	19,676	9,929	1,664	613	8,031
Tennessee	46	3,267	1,282	20,944	16,659	27,647	14,115	2,431	1,136	11,648
Alabama	26	1,961	1,017	25,297	11,020	24,000	10,409	874	373	8,438
Mississippi	35	1,489	820	14,275	7,930	13,275	7,275	769	394	6,601
West South Central	171	13,508	5,218	176,116	78,112	157,725	68,141	11,809	6,650	57,388
Arkansas	23	1,540	623	14,036	7,119	13,134	6,871	361	102	6,138
Louisiana	18	2,553	997	20,850	11,425	22,371	9,987	1,737	450	8,908
Oklahoma	35	2,273	914	35,800	13,680	32,811	11,983	2,336	1,130	11,667
Texas	95	7,412	2,683	92,370	45,988	89,409	39,630	7,372	4,902	34,200
Mountain	67	6,529	1,814	79,534	32,153	70,525	27,977	6,466	1,943	27,977
Montana	11	600	208	6,855	3,240	6,403	3,112	329	84	2,370
Wyoming	9	550	179	6,757	2,580	6,463	2,283	142	51	3,221
Idaho	2	341	105	2,817	945	2,524	814	266	68	989
Colorado	20	2,200	570	20,391	10,691	22,529	8,896	2,964	862	8,345
New Mexico	9	800	211	8,349	3,128	7,108	2,412	723	273	2,782
Arizona	6	675	186	9,918	4,103	8,911	3,600	480	212	3,743
Utah	9	1,268	310	17,078	6,916	15,470	6,366	1,442	325	4,307
Nevada	1	175	45	1,401	494	1,298	494	61	39	859
Pacific	171	18,153	4,939	207,450	91,783	150,147	96,490	19,660	6,639	79,644
Washington	27	2,253	881	33,016	13,056	29,987	12,193	2,399	897	11,613
Oregon	22	1,724	555	23,074	11,058	21,292	10,666	1,304	264	4,760
California	122	14,146	3,553	151,330	64,409	128,868	57,611	15,900	5,508	61,371
U. S. Service Academies	4	1,073	2	7,645	....	7,645	....	....	....	1,852
Alaska	1	60	28	258	109	195	100	....	....	308
Canal Zone	1	14	6	153	73	153	73	....	....	128
Hawaii	1	319	137	3,599	2,309	2,636	1,669	149	215	1,355
Puerto Rico	2	681	606	8,271	2,963	6,235	2,944	12	14	1,784

[1] Includes administrative officers, extension service, and organized research, in addition to regular staff.

Source: Department of Health, Education, and Welfare, Office of Education; Biennial Survey of Education, chapter on Statistics of Higher Education, Section 1.

No. 148.—Institutions of Higher Education—Value of Property, Endowments, and Other Permanent Funds, Income and Expenditures, by States and Other Areas: 1950

[In thousands of dollars]

DIVISION, STATE, OR OTHER AREA	Value of plant and plant funds [1]	NONEXPENDABLE FUNDS		INCOME—			EXPENDITURES	
		Endowment and annuity funds [2]	Student loan funds	For current operations	For nonexpendable funds	For plant expansion	Current operations	Plant expansion
Continental U. S.	5,272,590	2,601,222	43,100	2,374,645	116,932	528,747	2,245,661	416,531
New England	390,096	600,096	7,097	197,451	34,583	27,623	188,264	29,779
Maine	24,911	20,084	114	9,664	1,763	576	9,411	2,038
New Hampshire	25,100	29,174	777	11,268	449	465	10,536	1,924
Vermont	13,988	10,405	222	8,520	133	401	8,356	430
Massachusetts	163,025	376,515	4,337	120,477	29,801	10,469	113,671	15,396
Rhode Island	28,929	16,132	150	12,751	369	1,504	12,225	1,098
Connecticut	134,145	147,788	1,497	34,771	2,068	14,208	34,065	8,893
Middle Atlantic	906,435	606,392	7,076	432,722	27,060	87,642	416,712	46,513
New York	485,888	369,113	3,996	255,745	17,237	28,877	245,216	21,320
New Jersey	79,820	75,689	1,274	44,306	3,602	3,522	43,169	2,909
Pennsylvania	340,727	161,590	1,806	132,672	6,151	25,243	128,327	22,284
East North Central	1,054,794	393,685	6,485	496,792	14,065	107,599	473,675	84,304
Ohio	221,283	104,312	1,623	98,348	2,271	18,415	94,770	23,375
Indiana	149,280	39,889	917	73,951	1,898	8,772	69,379	10,474
Illinois	314,591	191,455	1,994	170,978	7,874	45,066	163,109	25,765
Michigan	246,874	36,394	1,476	102,047	1,500	20,403	96,369	17,341
Wisconsin	122,766	21,633	475	51,468	842	14,943	48,048	7,349
West North Central	527,172	162,510	4,750	243,230	4,760	45,479	225,122	41,490
Minnesota	133,699	54,640	1,009	57,508	929	15,354	53,048	12,999
Iowa	99,571	24,335	645	53,239	740	5,501	49,999	8,268
Missouri	141,787	54,386	1,998	55,260	2,567	8,266	51,362	9,693
North Dakota	24,696	6,837	102	9,750	44	4,791	8,301	1,705
South Dakota	21,573	4,522	157	8,886	22	2,142	8,613	1,608
Nebraska	39,597	8,648	355	21,407	335	2,396	20,639	2,765
Kansas	66,249	9,142	484	37,180	123	6,938	32,260	4,452
South Atlantic	723,959	276,051	6,660	286,200	11,829	65,959	265,929	54,032
Delaware	9,212	4,759	16	3,503	....	516	3,309	380
Maryland	93,894	46,821	187	40,349	1,210	11,964	39,589	7,617
District of Columbia	52,529	12,609	228	31,060	565	8,012	28,891	2,301
Virginia	115,267	52,036	1,229	41,584	1,632	7,517	40,394	8,370
West Virginia	46,078	4,225	100	19,612	22	6,873	18,070	3,954
North Carolina	175,642	84,768	1,802	53,253	3,110	21,380	51,433	15,552
South Carolina	61,004	11,882	305	23,126	435	2,210	21,426	1,935
Georgia	86,784	51,949	2,373	34,783	4,670	3,045	33,262	4,284
Florida	83,549	6,921	420	38,929	185	3,533	32,535	9,660
East South Central	266,139	121,965	3,696	125,944	4,116	20,276	118,131	21,061
Kentucky	51,558	30,572	685	26,088	2,340	3,825	37,257	3,114
Tennessee	101,397	62,777	2,168	42,253	1,206	6,586	39,712	8,518
Alabama	66,476	23,060	757	33,877	373	4,121	29,737	5,916
Mississippi	46,708	5,576	86	21,726	197	5,944	21,425	3,513
West South Central	532,142	231,663	3,879	196,381	11,709	76,869	182,615	58,865
Arkansas	38,912	7,549	512	19,812	138	4,143	17,712	3,946
Louisiana	92,917	24,752	452	35,568	256	2,517	35,149	6,140
Oklahoma	109,997	15,765	671	35,805	596	14,999	33,844	12,890
Texas	290,316	183,597	1,944	187,196	10,719	55,210	95,910	35,889
Mountain	195,588	29,695	842	96,910	968	20,400	89,879	23,330
Montana	18,967	5,048	102	8,655	56	1,771	7,991	1,411
Idaho	30,528	7,029	58	9,271	320	2,364	8,315	3,092
Wyoming	15,303	3,505	55	5,402	119	1,882	5,095	2,502
Colorado	61,823	8,286	323	33,060	285	6,853	31,109	6,629
New Mexico	21,319	3,695	18	11,605	73	858	10,923	4,990
Arizona	19,305	213	26	9,795	11	4,859	9,379	3,000
Utah	24,983	949	150	15,877	18	1,745	14,808	1,625
Nevada	3,360	970	100	2,225	86	98	2,259	81
Pacific	578,145	179,146	2,915	280,000	7,802	106,909	264,320	57,370
Washington	104,895	18,377	410	42,142	187	9,610	40,103	10,772
Oregon	60,999	7,274	478	21,052	157	7,669	20,350	5,921
California	412,251	153,496	2,027	216,806	7,458	89,630	203,867	40,677
U. S. Service Academies	96,118			18,014			18,014	86
Alaska	1,988			1,244	....	174	1,042	316
Canal Zone	750			89			91	
Hawaii	6,663			4,571	....	177	4,266	185
Puerto Rico	14,039			9,530	....	1,337	8,879	1,196

[1] Grounds, buildings, equipment, and unexpended plant funds.
[2] Includes other nonexpendable funds except student loans.

Source: Department of Health, Education, and Welfare, Office of Education; Biennial Survey of Education, chapter on Statistics of Higher Education, Section 2.

No. 149.—EARNED DEGREES CONFERRED, BY MAJOR FIELD OF STUDY: 1952

MAJOR FIELD OF STUDY	NUMBER OF DEGREES CONFERRED								
	Bachelor's and first professional [1]			Master's and second professional [2]			Doctor's [3]		
	Total	Men	Women	Total	Men	Women	Total	Men	Women
Total	331,924	227,029	104,895	63,471	43,537	19,934	7,683	6,969	714
Agriculture	9,595	9,451	144	1,608	1,578	30	412	402	10
Animal husbandry	1,022	1,007	15	136	133	3	42	42	
Forestry	1,219	1,218	1	225	225		17	17	
All other	7,354	7,226	128	1,247	1,220	27	353	343	10
Biological sciences [4]	11,196	8,275	2,921	2,307	1,908	399	764	680	84
Biology	6,960	5,148	1,812	570	456	114	132	109	23
Zoology	2,034	1,574	460	569	480	89	154	137	17
All other	2,202	1,553	649	1,168	972	196	478	434	44
Education	62,951	24,599	38,352	26,382	15,194	11,188	1,146	954	192
Education	52,060	16,157	35,903	24,538	13,683	10,855	1,061	884	177
Industrial arts	2,812	2,736	76	420	416	4	10	9	1
Physical education	8,079	5,706	2,373	1,424	1,095	329	75	61	14
Engineering	30,549	30,489	60	4,091	4,073	18	529	526	3
Aeronautical	911	900	11	231	231		25	25	
Chemical	2,857	2,849	8	587	582	5	168	168	
Civil	5,329	5,322	7	583	582	1	45	45	
Electrical	6,453	6,446	7	1,008	1,005	3	120	117	3
Mechanical	7,685	7,677	8	660	656	4	72	72	
All other	7,314	7,295	19	1,022	1,017	5	99	99	
English	14,087	5,805	8,282	1,922	1,043	879	284	237	47
Fine arts	18,191	9,031	9,160	3,597	2,402	1,195	197	164	33
Architecture	2,210	2,098	112	240	230	10			
Music	7,015	3,056	3,959	1,738	1,145	593	55	51	4
Speech and dramatic arts	3,949	1,845	2,004	885	545	340	118	95	23
All other	5,117	2,032	3,085	734	482	252	24	18	6
Foreign languages	4,418	1,706	2,712	916	520	396	235	184	51
Classical	683	476	207	116	72	44	32	23	9
French	1,385	440	945	267	141	126	50	38	12
Spanish	1,605	429	1,176	290	145	145	43	31	12
All other modern	745	361	384	243	162	81	110	92	18
Geography	669	552	117	194	159	35	37	36	1
Healing arts and medical sciences [4]	23,663	17,714	5,949	1,847	1,120	727	152	132	20
Dentistry, D. D. S. only	2,918	2,895	23						
Medicine, M. D. only	6,201	5,871	330						
Nursing	4,137	46	4,091	478	5	473	1		1
Optometry	844	820	24	95	95				
Pharmacy	4,321	3,934	387	151	138	13	51	43	8
Veterinary medicine	1,005	997	8	14	13	1	7	6	1
All other	4,237	3,151	1,086	1,109	869	240	93	83	10
Home economics	7,716	64	7,652	649	32	617	23	6	17
Journalism	2,772	1,959	813	322	268	54	4	4	
Law	12,558	12,158	400	456	440	16	46	46	
Library science	629	85	544	1,088	360	728	4	3	1
Mathematics	4,721	3,389	1,332	802	663	139	206	195	11
Military or naval science	201	199	2						
Physical sciences [6]	12,145	10,813	1,332	3,054	2,830	224	1,720	1,663	57
Chemistry	6,819	5,717	1,102	1,409	1,242	167	1,031	986	45
Geology	2,102	2,026	76	486	469	17	116	116	
Physics	2,247	2,141	106	886	851	35	485	476	9
All other	977	929	48	273	268	5	88	85	3
Philosophy	2,421	2,124	297	287	258	29	102	92	10
Psychology	6,622	3,783	2,839	1,406	1,066	340	540	467	73
Religion	7,139	6,017	1,122	1,262	861	401	191	181	10
Religious education and Bible	2,931	1,974	957	617	262	355	59	49	10
Theology	4,208	4,043	165	645	599	46	132	132	
Social sciences [6]	84,950	67,703	17,247	10,121	7,789	2,332	1,049	957	92
Economics	8,595	7,520	1,075	695	612	83	239	223	16
History	10,216	7,285	2,931	1,445	1,075	370	317	291	26
Political science	4,925	4,016	909	525	449	76	147	135	12
Sociology	6,697	2,986	3,711	517	386	131	141	121	20
Business and commerce	46,683	41,060	5,623	3,826	3,519	307	92	88	4
Social work	1,075	360	715	1,923	827	1,096	27	24	3
All other	6,759	4,476	2,283	1,190	921	269	86	75	11
All other fields	14,731	11,113	3,618	1,160	973	187	42	40	2

[1] Based on curricula of 4 years or more. Includes B. A. and B. S. degrees and first professional degrees such as M. D., D. D. S., D. V. M., LL. B., and B. D.
[2] M. A., M. S. degrees, and professional degrees such as M. Chem. E., LL. M., M. B. A., and Th. M.
[3] Ph. D., Ed. D., S. T. D., and Sc. D. Excludes honorary degrees.
[4] Excludes psychology. [5] Excludes geography. [6] Excludes geography, philosophy, and psychology.

Source: Department of Health, Education, and Welfare, Office of Education; circular No. 360a, *Earned Degrees Conferred by Higher Educational Institutions.*

No. 150.—Institutions of Higher Education—Enrollment in Summer Session and in Extension and Correspondence Work: 1920 to 1950

YEAR	ENROLLMENT		YEAR	ENROLLMENT	
	Summer session [1]	Extension and correspondence [2]		Summer session [1]	Extension and correspondence [2]
1920	132, 489	101, 662	1936	370, 026	297, 921
1922	220, 311	155, 163	1938	429, 864	371, 173
1924	278, 125	194, 147	1940	456, 679	362, 381
1926	340, 461	324, 819	1942	426, 849	362, 387
1928	382, 776	360, 246	1944	479, 326	342, 338
1930	388, 755	354, 133	1946	515, 602	535, 957
1932	414, 260	440, 186	1948	955, 429	759, 909
1934	303, 754	253, 991	1950	943, 021	848, 695

[1] For odd years, 1919, 1921, etc.
[2] Includes both collegiate and noncollegiate students; data on number of noncollegiate students included are available, as follows: 1932, 174,921; 1934, 45,484; 1936, 46,452; 1938, 75,822; 1940, 70,145; 1942, 83,833; 1944, 98,496. Not requested separately for 1946, 1948, and 1950.

Source: Department of Health, Education, and Welfare, Office of Education; *Biennial Survey of Education*, chapter on Statistical Summary of Education.

No. 151.—Public and Private Residential Schools for the Blind, the Deaf, the Mentally Deficient, and Delinquents: 1922 to 1947

TYPE AND YEAR	States reported [1]	Schools reported	Pupils	TYPE AND YEAR	States reported [1]	Schools reported	Pupils
Blind:				Deaf—Continued			
1922	39	48	4, 634	1940	45	79	14, 673
1927	41	51	5, 245	1947	45	79	12, 971
1931	41	55	5, 530				
1936	41	55	5, 851	Mentally deficient:			
1940	40	50	5, 870	1936	47	130	[2] 21, 889
1947	41	54	5, 150	1940	46	104	[2] 21, 806
Deaf:				1947	46	139	[2] 21, 460
1922	43	75	11, 417	Delinquent:			
1927	44	76	13, 928	1936	49	154	31, 174
1931	45	83	14, 854	1940	49	142	29, 109
1936	45	79	15, 366	1947	49	163	[2] 22, 460

[1] Includes District of Columbia.
[2] Includes only children reported for school work.

Source: Department of Health, Education, and Welfare, Office of Education; *Biennial Survey of Education*, chapter on Statistics of Special Schools and Classes for Exceptional Children.

No. 152.—Special Schools and Classes for Exceptional Children—Enrollment for City School Systems, by Type: 1936 to 1948

[Data include home and hospital instruction]

TYPE	1936			1940			1948		
	States reporting [1]	Cities reporting	Pupils enrolled	States reporting [1]	Cities reporting	Pupils enrolled	States reporting [1]	Cities reporting	Pupils enrolled
Blind and partially seeing	27	161	7, 251	28	181	8, 875	33	264	8, 216
Deaf and hard-of-hearing	31	168	9, 318	30	168	13, 476	39	287	13, 977
Mentally deficient	43	643	99, 621	42	565	96, 416	46	729	87, 067
Crippled	30	301	24, 865	31	356	25, 784	47	959	30, 498
Delicate	30	150	23, 517	27	166	26, 792	42	549	19, 071
Socially maladjusted	20	45	12, 653	25	50	10, 477	25	90	15, 340
Speech-defective	22	123	116, 770	29	144	126, 146	40	455	182, 344
Mentally gifted	9	14	3, 009	9	12	3, 255	11	15	20, 712
Epileptic	(?)	(?)	(?)	13	33	499	21	65	390

[1] Includes District of Columbia.
[2] Not available.

Source: Department of Health, Education, and Welfare, Office of Education; *Biennial Survey of Education*, chapter on Statistics of Special Schools and Classes for Exceptional Children.

No. 153.—Public Libraries—Summary, By States and Other Areas: 1945

STATE OR OTHER AREA	NUMBER OF PUBLIC LIBRARIES		Number of volumes at end of year	Number of registered borrowers	Income [1] ($1,000)	OPERATING EXPENDITURES		Number of employees
	Total	Submitting report				Total ($1,000)	Per capita	
Continental U. S.	7,408	6,026	124,675,253	22,890,963	64,917	61,790	$0.70	[2] 37,382
Alabama	64	61	770,157	255,548	339	292	.20	222
Arizona	15	9	137,652	117,428	48	43	.19	19
Arkansas	85	50	432,150	168,090	192	181	.18	155
California	206	165	11,689,004	1,978,012	6,765	6,551	.98	3,925
Colorado	109	66	1,260,027	241,111	512	496	.62	339
Connecticut	197	187	3,820,177	465,216	1,658	1,553	.99	986
Delaware	20	13	295,960	46,791	133	129	.49	75
Dist. of Columbia	1	1	720,972	151,626	823	762	1.15	346
Florida	94	22	535,381	143,718	426	246	.45	151
Georgia	187	146	1,326,931	387,018	670	644	.30	465
Idaho	56	32	341,433	95,307	141	131	.75	97
Illinois	375	326	6,944,783	1,429,273	4,430	4,175	.71	2,391
Indiana	237	216	5,988,806	855,685	2,118	2,107	.84	1,262
Iowa	315	307	3,231,397	530,218	1,182	1,127	.87	877
Kansas	204	189	1,753,832	331,277	553	523	.62	489
Kentucky	74	68	957,236	210,333	502	423	.39	311
Louisiana	34	32	794,898	227,747	525	514	.36	433
Maine	205	122	1,579,563	160,507	381	303	.65	302
Maryland	40	35	1,128,474	247,374	899	859	.63	407
Massachusetts	397	337	11,434,836	1,177,673	4,966	4,828	1.14	2,935
Michigan	306	295	5,348,848	1,045,380	4,131	3,873	.86	1,808
Minnesota	153	151	2,783,434	562,112	1,494	1,466	.95	806
Mississippi	59	43	431,350	130,039	126	118	.14	100
Missouri	196	145	2,745,290	576,248	1,295	1,248	.60	772
Montana	43	39	597,468	110,805	229	209	.70	141
Nebraska	276	241	1,625,358	301,434	473	443	.69	467
Nevada	14	5	108,768	24,109	54	52	1.03	37
New Hampshire	254	206	1,923,030	198,932	406	347	.76	364
New Jersey	291	183	5,799,949	925,217	2,898	2,893	.83	1,439
New Mexico	28	25	212,123	53,121	60	57	.23	47
New York	598	484	11,375,675	2,590,068	7,781	7,498	.66	4,303
North Carolina	130	98	2,559,397	467,438	710	671	.22	430
North Dakota	100	64	279,243	57,311	85	78	.56	62
Ohio	274	236	10,301,324	1,649,169	6,706	6,503	1.07	3,631
Oklahoma	80	61	998,456	266,863	325	307	.46	240
Oregon	96	92	1,484,918	318,397	702	680	.81	464
Pennsylvania	346	216	6,145,891	1,180,068	3,175	3,034	.52	1,741
Rhode Island	72	52	1,165,561	131,174	402	374	.79	296
South Carolina	53	39	526,726	163,503	224	208	.28	166
South Dakota	95	91	601,555	109,662	191	166	.71	183
Tennessee	66	47	1,006,570	257,641	397	386	.24	342
Texas	107	84	2,047,783	730,707	910	890	.34	548
Utah	48	31	622,492	157,856	221	265	.68	191
Vermont	239	186	1,324,648	70,322	209	183	.61	268
Virginia	86	70	998,888	291,925	465	429	.32	299
Washington	144	129	2,041,143	411,370	1,501	1,287	.95	788
West Virginia	51	39	406,727	126,174	176	163	.20	94
Wisconsin	293	269	3,972,990	690,162	2,174	1,944	1.01	1,092
Wyoming	23	19	395,919	73,809	130	118	.59	86
Alaska	[3]	1	6,500		13	13	.98	4
Canal Zone	[3]	1	81,339	9,732	44	44	.85	19
Hawaii	[3]	4	355,210	89,435	444	433	1.03	125
Virgin Islands	[3]	1	20,799	1,300	9	9	.78	8

[1] Excludes balance from previous year.
[2] Includes 15,009 part-time employees.
[3] Not available.

Source: Department of Health, Education, and Welfare, Office of Education; Bulletin 1947, No. 12, Public Library Statistics.

No. 154.—Vocational Schools and Vocational Teacher-Training Courses, Federally Aided—Number of Teachers and Students, by Class of School or Course and by Sex: Years Ending June 30, 1920 to 1951

[Institutions Federally aided are reimbursed from Federal funds provided under act known as "The Smith-Hughes Act," or the "National Vocational Education Act of 1917," and subsequent acts extending benefits of vocational education to Alaska, Hawaii, Puerto Rico, and Virgin Islands, and providing for further development of vocational education. These acts, administered by Office of Education, provide appropriations for reimbursement in part from Federal funds for expenditures by States and local communities for vocational education. Includes data for Hawaii beginning 1930, for Puerto Rico beginning 1940, for Virgin Islands beginning 1951]

CLASS OF SCHOOL OR COURSE	TEACHERS					PUPILS				
	1920	1930	1940	1950	1951	1920	1930	1940	1950	1951
VOCATIONAL SCHOOLS										
Total, all classes [1]				62,959	66,510	265,058	981,882	2,290,741	3,364,613	3,363,420
Male						163,228	603,514	1,279,109	1,715,699	1,682,290
Female						101,830	378,368	1,011,632	1,648,914	1,681,130
Evening	2,565	9,842	17,744	20,902	24,162	73,122	323,154	728,937	1,520,971	1,475,104
Part-time	1,773	5,468	14,600	12,324	11,634	122,974	407,285	525,358	596,295	561,895
All-day	3,331	9,245	24,917	29,733	30,714	68,962	241,486	1,022,284	1,243,419	1,322,433
Day-unit course		319	658				9,957	14,162	3,928	3,988
Agriculture [1]				13,852	17,348	31,301	188,311	584,133	764,975	771,028
Male						29,351	180,490	583,034	764,975	771,028
Female						1,950	7,821	1,099		
Evening		1,878	4,976	3,149	5,330		60,462	192,346	345,007	319,096
Part-time		306	3,727	1,240	1,991		4,164	62,489	43,071	42,625
All-day	1,570	4,346	8,450	9,463	10,027	31,301	113,728	318,223	373,113	405,371
Day-unit course		319	568				9,957	11,175	3,784	3,936
Trade and industrial [1]				25,511	23,005	184,819	618,604	758,499	804,602	792,347
Male						133,872	422,575	602,182	687,847	676,127
Female						50,947	196,029	156,227	116,755	116,220
Evening	1,779	5,030	5,769	8,312	7,773	48,354	165,317	167,908	269,734	268,284
Part-time, total	1,636	4,981	9,449	8,671	7,155	115,241	381,898	383,579	312,129	308,675
Trade extension	350	1,747	7,150			17,159	45,601	(²)	213,346	207,228
Trade preparatory	(²)	(²)	(²)			(²)	(²)	(²)	21,393	21,299
General continuation	1,286	3,234	2,299			98,082	336,297	142,481	77,390	80,148
All-day	1,047	3,054	6,940	8,528	8,077	21,224	71,389	206,922	222,739	215,388
Home economics [1]				19,657	22,164	48,938	174,967	818,766	1,430,366	1,458,605
Male						5	449	24,746	70,336	65,318
Female						48,933	174,518	794,020	1,360,030	1,393,287
Evening	786	2,934	4,857	6,978	8,748	24,768	97,375	245,850	666,676	659,551
Part-time	137	181	1,192	937	806	7,733	21,223	72,790	115,979	97,328
All-day	714	1,845	9,527	11,742	12,610	16,437	56,369	497,139	647,567	701,674
Day-unit course			90					2,987	144	52
Distributive occupations [1]				3,939	3,993			129,433	364,670	341,440
Male								69,147	192,541	169,817
Female								60,286	172,129	171,623
Evening			2,142	2,463	2,311			122,933	239,554	228,173
Part-time			282	1,476	1,682			6,500	125,116	113,267
VOCATIONAL TEACHER-TRAINING COURSES										
Total, all classes	1,082	³843	1,588	(²)	(²)	12,456	20,736	40,491	(²)	(²)
Male	657	³518	957	(²)	(²)	6,985	12,531	22,406	(²)	(²)
Female	425	³325	631	(²)	(²)	5,471	8,205	18,085	(²)	(²)
In agriculture	293	195	392	(²)	(²)	2,310	3,325	6,426	(²)	(²)
Trade and industry	359	334	525	(²)	(²)	6,150	11,205	15,606	(²)	(²)
Home economics	414	316	556	(²)	(²)	3,652	6,206	12,768	(²)	(²)
Distributive occupations			115	(²)	(²)			5,680	(²)	(²)
Other and not specified	16			(²)	(²)	344			(²)	(²)

[1] Totals for teachers omitted for 1920, 1930, and 1940 because of duplications in State reports by types of schools.
² Not available.
³ Excluding duplication.

Source: Department of Health, Education, and Welfare, Office of Education: *Digest of Annual Reports of State Boards for Vocational Education.*

No. 155.—VOCATIONAL EDUCATION AND TEACHER TRAINING, FEDERALLY AIDED—
EXPENDITURES OF FEDERAL, STATE, AND LOCAL FUNDS, 1920 TO 1951, AND BY
STATES AND OTHER AREAS, 1951

[In thousands of dollars. For years ending June 30. See headnote, table 154]

YEAR, STATE OR OTHER AREA	ALL VOCATIONAL EDUCATION [1]				AGRICULTURAL EDUCATION [2]		TRADE AND INDUSTRIAL EDUCATION [2]		HOME ECONOMICS EDUCATION [2]	
	Total funds	Federal	State	Local	Total funds	Federal	Total funds	Federal	Total funds	Federal
TOTAL										
1920	8,535	2,477	2,670	3,388	2,437	890	3,397	700	1,054	156
1924	15,945	4,833	5,175	5,938	5,254	1,898	8,555	1,589	2,745	332
1928	25,716	6,821	7,029	11,865	7,609	2,844	12,021	2,454	3,731	492
1932	33,402	8,415	9,036	15,951	10,213	3,699	15,426	2,547	5,129	1,130
1936	33,428	9,749	8,606	15,073	10,327	3,863	15,006	2,430	5,807	1,429
1940	55,081	20,004	11,737	23,340	16,986	6,709	21,100	6,435	11,718	4,290
1944	64,299	19,958	15,016	29,325	18,448	6,628	24,058	6,093	15,752	4,409
1948	103,339	26,200	25,834	51,305	30,545	9,877	40,872	8,537	28,130	6,260
1950	128,717	26,622	40,534	61,561	38,523	10,087	47,869	8,612	36,916	6,341
1951	137,355	26,685	44,206	66,462	41,492	10,129	50,728	8,646	39,239	6,347
1951										
Alabama	2,753	724	1,987	43	1,164	389	697	118	801	183
Arizona	726	172	130	424	159	60	278	51	255	45
Arkansas	2,584	543	752	1,289	1,233	316	291	60	977	143
California	8,514	1,077	676	6,761	1,545	259	3,539	500	3,049	224
Colorado	1,046	221	184	640	287	83	280	66	304	56
Connecticut	1,933	266	1,467	198	117	58	1,577	128	189	60
Delaware	537	163	206	168	123	51	232	55	145	43
District of Columbia	314	99	214		14	7	194	40	81	40
Florida	3,285	345	94	2,846	775	112	1,445	120	921	89
Georgia	3,679	767	818	2,094	1,602	399	550	132	1,404	199
Idaho	588	162	153	273	253	63	190	54	140	43
Illinois	5,810	1,244	1,820	2,746	2,096	329	1,645	565	1,550	254
Indiana	3,279	664	358	2,257	939	258	1,025	209	1,208	156
Iowa	1,876	573	103	1,200	832	275	336	122	646	146
Kansas	1,326	401	236	691	646	185	279	89	349	104
Kentucky	1,932	709	260	963	918	372	315	119	631	186
Louisiana	3,553	536	451	2,566	1,439	255	739	121	1,273	130
Maine	506	165	122	219	178	70	113	41	209	51
Maryland	1,644	316	741	587	325	93	869	132	404	70
Massachusetts	5,325	560	2,353	2,412	504	71	3,716	353	995	84
Michigan	4,480	903	1,127	2,450	1,074	287	1,987	352	1,142	200
Minnesota	2,863	595	965	1,303	914	269	1,064	148	766	143
Mississippi	2,609	638	925	1,046	1,275	388	365	61	883	162
Missouri	2,792	773	512	1,507	1,020	341	846	207	841	186
Montana	572	173	73	326	226	62	129	50	183	46
Nebraska	1,056	305	155	597	504	149	154	61	337	79
Nevada	194	97	20	77	53	27	61	31	80	40
New Hampshire	410	158	97	155	103	52	133	49	147	45
New Jersey	3,880	565	681	2,643	282	88	3,084	358	426	78
New Mexico	569	172	54	343	229	62	126	51	185	45
New York	12,705	1,849	3,101	7,754	1,318	292	9,270	1,154	1,405	239
North Carolina	4,416	918	2,131	1,367	2,176	491	566	145	1,546	238
North Dakota	664	213	218	233	217	96	193	52	226	51
Ohio	3,741	1,171	494	2,076	1,116	362	1,546	467	904	258
Oklahoma	3,165	552	657	1,956	1,650	274	545	114	852	136
Oregon	1,186	221	473	491	342	86	525	64	273	56
Pennsylvania	6,722	1,545	3,480	1,697	1,338	383	3,686	725	1,456	353
Rhode Island	276	115	39	122	30	15	191	73	55	27
South Carolina	2,467	499	821	1,147	1,061	269	451	74	872	133
South Dakota	585	203	25	357	233	92	106	53	234	47
Tennessee	3,202	713	987	1,501	1,248	370	730	130	1,121	177
Texas	11,209	1,404	9,248	558	4,924	645	1,210	329	4,341	352
Utah	1,152	169	104	879	344	56	444	53	275	46
Vermont	443	154	57	232	133	49	135	53	144	41
Virginia	3,917	626	1,820	1,471	1,249	301	1,014	132	1,447	161
Washington	2,676	329	749	1,599	659	115	1,062	112	831	80
West Virginia	1,553	433	268	852	464	184	587	97	441	128
Wisconsin	4,000	634	327	3,040	1,251	265	1,482	179	1,166	152
Wyoming	475	165	46	264	181	52	121	54	136	44
Hawaii	732	165	568		176	53	277	51	236	46
Puerto Rico	1,347	486	861		548	238	312	75	440	151
Virgin Islands	66	33		33	5	2	36	19	26	11

[1] Includes data for distributive (and, prior to 1948, teacher-training) courses not shown separately.
[2] Beginning 1948, includes expenditures for teacher training previously reported separately.

Source: Department of Health, Education, and Welfare, Office of Education; *Digest of Annual Reports of State Boards for Vocational Education.*

No. 156.—Vocational Courses, Federally Aided—Students Enrolled, by Course, by States and Other Areas: 1950 and 1951

[For years ending June 30. Excludes vocational teacher-training courses. See also headnote, table 154]

STATE OR OTHER AREA	1950					1951				
	Total	Agricultural	Trade and industrial	Home economics	Distributive	Total	Agricultural	Trade and industrial	Home economics	Distributive
Total	**3,364,613**	**764,975**	**804,602**	**1,430,366**	**364,670**	**3,363,420**	**771,028**	**792,347**	**1,458,605**	**341,440**
Alabama	67,477	24,138	20,768	19,420	3,151	69,455	23,455	19,295	22,898	3,591
Arizona	16,244	2,131	4,142	8,089	1,882	15,451	2,278	4,403	7,443	1,327
Arkansas	80,655	28,928	12,404	36,403	2,920	78,732	30,581	10,283	35,191	2,677
California	446,174	32,232	95,390	258,105	60,447	415,388	17,729	104,853	222,509	70,297
Colorado	37,549	2,280	10,540	17,449	7,280	37,961	2,816	11,376	17,731	6,038
Connecticut	28,676	710	17,066	6,783	4,117	25,464	729	15,441	6,922	2,372
Delaware	6,813	969	3,093	2,097	654	7,165	889	3,504	2,103	669
Dist. of Col.	9,831	72	3,907	3,780	2,072	9,509	236	3,543	3,672	2,058
Florida	82,129	11,556	27,760	36,466	6,347	83,144	10,979	33,292	27,283	11,590
Georgia	149,318	56,240	24,426	58,034	10,618	158,166	63,055	26,876	58,281	9,954
Idaho	9,637	2,915	2,397	3,665	660	10,317	3,135	2,782	3,400	1,000
Illinois	95,521	25,021	26,208	38,803	5,489	98,951	26,406	25,480	41,181	5,884
Indiana	72,063	11,342	23,709	27,319	9,693	66,992	11,934	18,229	29,191	7,638
Iowa	59,236	23,202	12,085	23,225	724	52,745	20,010	11,550	19,826	1,359
Kansas	31,608	5,522	7,511	16,355	2,220	28,066	6,257	7,852	12,669	1,288
Kentucky	58,375	15,740	5,090	29,661	7,884	56,672	16,553	7,546	26,266	6,307
Louisiana	63,280	25,333	13,051	20,660	4,236	74,909	25,523	13,397	31,947	4,042
Maine	7,674	1,483	1,452	4,684	55	8,242	1,529	1,708	4,980	25
Maryland	27,304	3,781	8,604	9,248	5,671	26,643	4,444	10,813	8,589	2,797
Massachusetts	66,453	2,123	29,478	31,438	3,414	64,095	1,701	28,281	30,950	3,163
Michigan	113,865	16,265	37,842	47,471	12,287	110,244	18,845	34,220	45,370	11,809
Minnesota	54,438	12,696	11,104	26,582	4,056	55,804	15,242	9,776	27,385	3,401
Mississippi	91,412	41,392	11,472	34,057	4,491	95,436	44,142	11,782	34,305	5,207
Missouri	69,703	18,366	13,295	32,199	5,843	64,614	19,112	15,367	25,470	4,665
Montana	8,389	2,185	2,091	3,657	456	8,436	2,336	2,320	3,438	342
Nebraska	25,706	4,764	5,257	12,838	2,847	25,279	5,294	4,667	12,885	2,433
Nevada	3,469	521	1,138	1,810	......	3,196	578	1,059	1,559	......
New Hampshire	6,235	686	2,077	2,830	642	6,455	745	1,969	3,493	248
New Jersey	28,002	2,100	17,341	6,974	1,587	26,372	2,038	16,082	6,359	1,893
New Mexico	8,321	1,757	1,927	4,181	456	7,878	1,777	1,832	3,870	399
New York	190,030	10,776	98,735	43,048	37,471	162,192	11,018	83,681	34,405	33,088
North Carolina	90,429	30,095	9,036	45,249	6,059	106,866	36,519	8,787	56,409	5,151
North Dakota	10,161	2,792	1,672	4,933	764	10,644	2,667	1,536	5,230	1,211
Ohio	77,378	13,049	29,231	24,433	10,665	72,912	13,485	25,616	25,617	8,194
Oklahoma	53,828	21,703	5,287	22,389	4,449	64,922	24,738	6,588	30,326	3,270
Oregon	28,829	6,768	8,844	11,256	1,961	24,126	3,794	9,232	10,477	623
Pennsylvania	99,931	13,138	44,171	38,070	4,552	102,881	13,326	45,540	37,746	6,269
Rhode Island	3,435	367	1,932	1,136	......	3,741	435	1,665	1,608	33
South Carolina	131,311	68,604	8,715	47,637	6,355	126,820	63,117	8,740	48,897	6,066
South Dakota	8,570	2,563	1,589	4,153	265	9,662	2,587	2,478	4,084	513
Tennessee	72,959	24,376	13,332	30,579	4,672	80,834	27,568	14,130	35,158	3,978
Texas	298,899	94,437	33,049	126,525	44,888	366,766	98,775	35,158	188,021	44,812
Utah	40,713	6,935	5,889	19,877	8,012	30,844	6,569	4,695	13,052	6,528
Vermont	5,222	886	1,800	2,032	504	5,640	1,006	1,679	2,239	716
Virginia	113,383	18,013	17,704	67,171	10,435	106,762	17,154	8,573	71,964	9,071
Washington	112,967	9,769	27,771	37,979	37,448	102,033	10,236	31,386	36,081	24,330
West Virginia	52,208	31,010	10,461	9,469	1,268	45,278	23,507	9,077	11,156	1,538
Wisconsin	99,309	21,547	25,961	44,862	6,939	92,794	22,807	21,864	43,712	4,411
Wyoming	6,113	1,420	997	2,720	976	6,434	1,291	1,239	2,722	1,182
Hawaii	12,368	2,481	3,181	4,867	1,839	13,110	2,181	4,152	5,053	1,724
Puerto Rico	31,013	7,796	2,570	17,698	2,949	35,826	7,849	6,653	17,065	4,259
Virgin Islands	......	......	......	......	......	768	51	300	417	......

Source: Department of Health, Education, and Welfare, Office of Education; *Digest of Annual Reports of State Boards for Vocational Education.*

No. 157.—FEDERAL FUNDS ALLOTTED FOR EDUCATION, BY STATES AND OTHER AREAS: 1951

[In thousands of dollars. For school year ending 1951]

STATE OR OTHER AREA	Total [1]	FUNDS ADMINISTERED BY FEDERAL SECURITY AGENCY		FUNDS ADMINISTERED BY DEPARTMENT OF AGRICULTURE		FUNDS FOR THE EDUCATION OF VETERANS		
		Total [3]	Assistance to federally affected areas [3]	Total [4]	School lunch program	Total [4]	Education and training, Public Law 346	
							Tuition, equipment, supplies, and materials	Subsistence allowances
Total	2,598,646	171,720	66,694	161,668	116,201	2,128,216	896,262	1,366,679
Alabama	81,209	2,904	800	5,682	4,147	72,510	14,356	38,249
Arizona	12,904	2,351	1,446	1,075	752	9,469	2,645	5,840
Arkansas	54,136	2,312	1,140	4,473	2,196	47,342	9,170	33,146
California	149,436	18,532	9,914	7,173	6,186	114,726	35,953	68,603
Colorado	29,946	1,582	796	1,810	990	26,794	7,576	16,188
Connecticut	17,316	1,716	424	1,162	830	14,438	4,360	8,467
Delaware	5,027	609	(5)	370	147	2,047	581	1,320
District of Columbia	25,795	836		288	258	25,632	9,498	15,540
Florida	55,891	2,932	1,116	2,842	2,007	50,127	15,601	32,826
Georgia	82,581	5,873	3,342	5,521	3,899	71,175	12,368	82,348
Hawaii	11,996	812	461	1,029	810	10,155	2,809	6,199
Idaho	101,508	7,456	2,039	5,271	4,010	88,777	32,496	51,304
Illinois	44,350	2,968	689	3,387	2,337	38,005	11,340	28,728
Indiana	33,153	2,374	879	2,767	1,626	27,992	7,761	17,684
Iowa	20,106	2,404	1,452	2,334	1,471	15,367	3,582	10,710
Kansas	45,666	2,916	1,601	4,968	3,502	39,794	7,513	29,446
Kentucky	91,582	1,612	141	5,784	4,737	84,156	21,076	59,408
Louisiana	7,903	807	126	999	612	6,698	1,444	3,901
Maine	31,946	3,660	1,940	1,898	1,106	26,999	5,668	15,627
Maryland	55,079	2,537	627	3,142	2,787	47,400	16,709	24,987
Massachusetts	85,760	6,027	2,780	5,446	4,305	47,288	15,859	26,038
Michigan	36,537	1,466	22	3,988	2,183	33,759	8,929	21,085
Minnesota	71,504	2,112	412	4,719	3,166	64,672	11,755	47,367
Mississippi	78,296	5,352	979	3,887	2,506	70,085	15,985	44,386
Missouri	10,002	984	148	722	393	8,394	2,317	5,267
Montana	22,646	1,336	460	1,466	752	19,778	4,290	13,651
Nebraska	1,388		489	219	87	979	306	606
Nevada	6,658	387	165	656	400	4,309	1,312	2,534
New Hampshire	40,908	2,104	225	2,319	1,923	44,570	16,073	25,667
New Jersey	14,817	1,687	1,392	1,346	929	11,583	2,087	7,716
New Mexico	162,428	6,377	250	7,677	6,382	108,375	64,610	91,674
New York	81,518	5,780	757	6,932	5,081	70,805	13,179	54,206
North Carolina	11,921	484	12	1,083	480	10,404	2,189	6,666
North Dakota	83,816	5,777	1,859	6,616	5,253	71,423	21,140	42,253
Ohio	40,768	5,166	2,833	3,900	2,704	40,721	9,204	25,980
Oklahoma	21,342	2,741	291	1,619	1,123	16,963	5,903	5,901
Oregon	176,663	7,120	660	5,655	4,274	166,878	50,111	105,317
Pennsylvania	10,567	968	279	575	391	9,115	2,961	5,286
Rhode Island	56,397	3,500	1,829	4,522	3,414	47,275	8,775	35,296
South Carolina	16,668	853	366	886	311	8,283	1,812	6,092
South Dakota	91,453	2,861	377	5,879	4,426	82,698	19,106	56,768
Tennessee	164,857	9,655	5,236	8,835	6,358	146,365	36,541	94,530
Texas	16,575	1,920	787	1,257	911	13,608	4,193	8,641
Utah	4,690	407	16	588	283	3,609	977	2,365
Vermont	35,630	5,990	2,990	4,041	2,839	27,089	6,456	18,594
Virginia	55,667	6,667	4,515	2,346	1,668	23,365	7,179	14,025
Washington	32,611	2,385	18	2,571	2,062	16,616	3,490	11,001
West Virginia	34,656	2,105	68	2,368	2,275	29,355	8,220	17,704
Wisconsin	6,660	660	106	546	236	4,264	1,049	2,861
National [7]	73,362	5,331		372				
Canal Zone	1,645							
U. S. Territories and possessions	37,694	4,128	3,177	6,999	5,600	22,041	3,978	18,365
Foreign countries	35,196					15,768	2,692	12,979

[1] Includes $27,049,000 of other Federal funds for education.
[2] Includes, in addition to Federally affected areas, funds for support of land-grant colleges, vocational education below college level, vocational rehabilitation, American Printing House for the Blind, school facilities survey, and surplus property transferred to educational institutions.
[3] Includes those areas affected by Federal activity and employment.
[4] Includes, in addition to school lunch program, funds for Agricultural Experiment Stations, and Cooperative Agricultural Extension Service. [5] Includes also vocational rehabilitation under Public Law 16.
[6] Less than $500. [7] Federal funds allotted to national programs which cannot be reported by States; includes $772,000 of unallotted funds administered by Department of Agriculture.

Source: Department of Health, Education, and Welfare, Office of Education; *Federal Funds for Education.*

5. Law Enforcement and Federal Courts

Criminal justice is administered in the United States for the most part by State and local officers and agencies. The United States Constitution reserves to the States the general police powers, and only offenses against the United States Government or those which involve the crossing of State lines or an interference with interstate commerce can be made Federal offenses by act of Congress. Consequently, unless they occur in Federal territories or reservations, or on the high seas, or are committed by members of the armed forces, the usual criminal offenses such as murder, robbery, burglary, theft, assault, and rape are violations of State laws. There are fifty separate and distinct criminal law jurisdictions in the United States, one in each of the forty-eight States, one in the District of Columbia set up by act of Congress, and the Federal jurisdiction. Each of these has its own criminal law and procedure and its own law enforcement agencies. Yet the general system of law enforcement is quite similar from State to State. Of course, there are among the States differences in detail and often substantial differences in the penalties provided for like offenses.

The administration of criminal justice can be divided into three parts. The first covers the activities of the police agencies, namely the investigation of crimes and the apprehension of persons suspected of committing them. This function involves agencies such as municipal police, county police, State police, sheriffs, constables, marshals, Federal agents, and many kinds of special officers. The second phase of the administration of criminal justice is the prosecution of those charged with criminal offenses to determine whether they are in fact guilty. The agencies concerned include the courts, justices of the peace, municipal, State and Federal grand juries, and prosecuting court officers. The third division of criminal administration is concerned with the punishment or treatment of those convicted of crime. While the courts usually determine the sentence after conviction, the administration of the penalty is carried out by prison, reformatory, jail, probation and parole officials.

Nearly all statistical data on crime and criminals are derived from the records and reports of the various agencies engaged in the administration of criminal law. Police statistics present the number of offenses reported, the number of persons arrested, and the offenses cleared by arrest. Arrest records provide data concerning sex, age, race, and other characteristics of the persons arrested and charged with crime. As the police agencies are largely local, a real problem is involved in collecting statistical data from the large number of such agencies. The Federal Bureau of Investigation obtains reports from police agencies and publishes information for the country as a whole in its semi-annual bulletin, *Uniform Crime Reports*. The great majority of urban communities are now reporting to the Federal Bureau and the reports received cover about three quarters of the population of the United States. Information concerning offenses known to the police and the sex and age of persons arrested are shown by offense. No centralized information is available on the police activities of the Federal agencies. Some information concerning the work of each Federal agency will be found in its respective annual report.

Court statistics for the country as a whole showing the number of persons prosecuted for criminal offenses and the outcome of the prosecutions are quite incomplete. In many States, an annual or biennial publication presents data on the criminal cases disposed of in the trial courts. This information may be published by the State Judicial

Note.—This section presents data for the most recent year or period available on February 18, 1953, when the material was organized and sent to the printer.

138

Council or the Attorney General or some other State agency. The only national compilation of such information was that made by the Bureau of the Census which annually published statistical data on criminal cases disposed of in the general trial courts of from sixteen to thirty States including the District of Columbia. The latest data collected by the Census Bureau were those for 1945.   No national collection is now made.

Comprehensive information is collected on the business of the Federal courts by the Administrative Office of the United States Courts, and is published annually in the *Report of the Director*. The bulk of civil litigation in the country is commenced and determined in the various State courts, and only when the United States Constitution and acts of Congress specifically confer jurisdiction upon the Federal courts may civil litigation be heard and decided by these courts. The question whether a State court or a Federal court has jurisdiction over a particular civil action is often difficult to determine, but generally speaking the Federal courts have jurisdiction over the following types of cases: .

(1) Suits or proceedings by the United States; (2) Suits or proceedings against the United States; (3) Civil actions between private parties arising under the Constitution, laws, or treaties of the United States; (4) Civil actions between private litigants who are citizens of different States; (5) Civil cases involving admiralty, maritime, or prize jurisdiction; (6) All matters and proceedings in bankruptcy.

The Federal courts of original jurisdiction are known as the United States District Courts, and one or more of these courts is established in every State, Territory, or possession. Appeals from the district courts are taken to intermediate appellate courts of which there are eleven. They are known as United States Courts of Appeals. The Supreme Court of the United States is the final and highest appellate court in the Federal system of courts.

Statistics of prisoners committed to penal institutions have been collected and published for a longer period of time than have other criminal statistics. A national compilation of data on prisoners in Federal and State prisons and reformatories was made annually by the Bureau of the Census until after the 1947 data were compiled when this work was transferred to the Bureau of Prisons. Summary statistics covering persons received and discharged from State prisons and reformatories and from Federal prisons and persons executed in the United States under civilian authority, are now published periodically in *National Prisoner Statistics* bulletins of the Bureau of Prisons. The Federal Bureau of Prisons, in its annual report, *Federal Prisons*, also provides as complete statistical information on Federal prisoners as has been issued in this country. In addition, nearly every State publishes annual data either for its whole prison system or for each separate State institution.

Information concerning juvenile delinquents and juvenile delinquency and the operation of many juvenile courts is collected and published by the Children's Bureau, Social Security Administration, Department of Health, Education, and Welfare.

Information on the prosecution and disposition of persons charged with misdemeanors and other minor offenses in the justice of the peace and municipal courts of the country is not compiled at the present time. Statistical data on such prosecutions may be found for some of the larger cities in the annual reports of the municipal court or of the municipal government. Likewise, there is no general compilation of statistical data on persons confined to county jails and local workhouses. The Bureau of the Census made a survey of jail prisoners for the calendar year 1933 and some information on incarcerated prisoners was published in connection with the 1940 and 1950 decennial censuses but there is at present no regular compilation covering this field.

Fig. XII.—Federal Prisoners Received from the Courts, by Major Offense Groups: Years Ending June 30, 1944 to 1952

[See table 170]

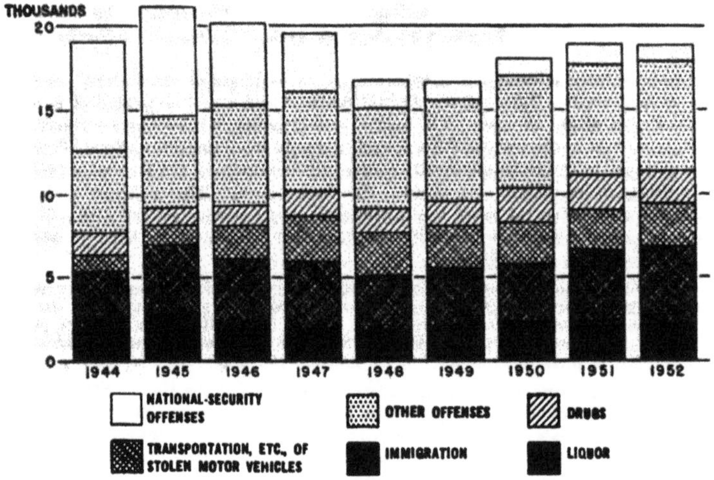

Fig. XIII.—Federal Prisoners with Previous Commitments, by Offense: Year Ending June 30, 1952

[See table 171]

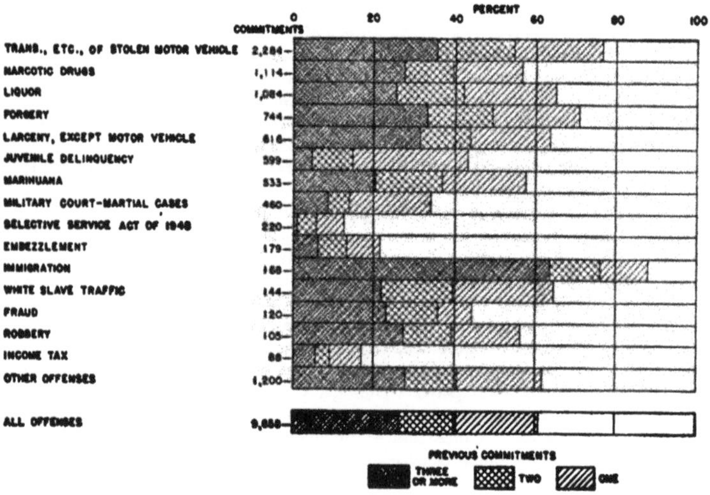

Source of figs. XII and XIII: Department of Justice, Bureau of Prisons.

No. 158.—OFFENSES KNOWN TO THE POLICE—ANNUAL TRENDS, BY POPULATION GROUPS: 1950 AND 1951

[Population figures based on 1950 decennial census]

| POPULATION GROUP | Total | CRIMINAL HOMICIDE | | Rape | Robbery | Aggravated assault | Burglary—breaking or entering | Larceny—theft (except auto theft) | Auto theft |
		Murder, nonnegligent manslaughter	Manslaughter by negligence						
Total, 2,134 cities; total population, 66,117,563:									
1950	1,036,335	3,474	2,273	7,391	34,315	49,314	240,744	595,221	164,193
1951	1,091,039	3,344	2,181	7,635	34,175	48,648	238,193	636,663	120,200
Percent change	+5.2	−3.7	−4.0	+3.3	−.4	−1.4	−1.1	+7.0	+15.4
39 cities over 250,000; population, 26,641,961:									
1950	467,630	1,779	1,103	4,433	23,132	26,223	108,732	248,430	51,798
1951	497,523	1,765	1,066	4,676	22,886	27,303	109,623	267,419	62,785
Percent change	+6.4	−.8	−3.4	+5.5	−1.1	−3.3	+.8	+7.6	+21.2
54 cities, 100,000 to 250,000; population, 9,353,981:									
1950	160,276	567	428	798	4,044	6,321	38,894	92,294	16,990
1951	171,367	532	418	841	4,236	6,212	38,732	101,006	19,390
Percent change	+6.9	−6.2	−2.3	+5.4	+4.7	−1.7	−.4	+9.5	+14.1
121 cities, 50,000 to 100,000; population, 8,592,462:									
1950	132,220	365	273	614	2,574	6,060	30,521	79,455	12,358
1951	136,049	350	236	653	2,704	6,296	29,431	83,105	13,274
Percent change	+2.9	−4.1	−13.6	+6.4	+5.1	+3.9	−3.6	+4.6	+7.4
229 cities, 25,000 to 50,000; population, 7,990,724:									
1950	111,202	276	230	474	1,829	3,554	24,460	70,784	9,605
1951	118,693	269	227	509	1,917	3,929	24,066	76,927	10,849
Percent change	+6.7	−2.5	+3.2	+7.4	+4.8	+10.6	−1.6	+8.7	+13.0
802 cities, 10,000 to 25,000; population, 9,365,264:									
1950	108,966	314	164	614	1,716	3,263	23,926	70,276	8,693
1951	111,186	277	131	581	1,532	3,164	23,390	73,009	9,102
Percent change	+2.0	−11.8	−20.1	−5.4	−10.7	−3.0	−2.2	+3.9	+4.7
1,069 cities under 10,000; population, 6,173,131:									
1950	56,641	173	85	458	1,020	1,893	14,211	34,052	4,749
1951	56,221	151	103	375	900	1,744	12,951	35,197	4,800
Percent change	−.7	−12.7	+21.2	−18.1	−11.8	−7.9	−8.9	+3.4	+1.1

Source: Department of Justice, Federal Bureau of Investigation; annual bulletin, *Uniform Crime Reports for the United States and Its Possessions.*

No. 159.—CRIME RATES—OFFENSES KNOWN TO THE POLICE IN URBAN COMMUNITIES, BY CLASS, BY STATES: 1951

[Rate per 100,000 inhabitants. Population figures based on 1950 decennial census. Offenses reported by 2,421 cities representing an urban population of 69,980,551, except for burglary and larceny-theft which are based on reports of 2,420 cities with a total population of 67,908,946]

DIVISION AND STATE	Murder, nonnegligent manslaughter	Robbery	Aggravated assault	Burglary—breaking or entering	Larceny—theft (except auto theft)	Auto theft
United States	4.88	49.3	70.5	347.2	940.1	173.8
New England	1.24	15.3	12.1	229.8	630.4	122.8
Maine	2.00	7.7	6.6	185.9	667.1	81.8
New Hampshire	.41	4.5	4.1	163.3	557.7	39.4
Vermont		5.9	12.8	181.8	569.1	74.1
Massachusetts	1.14	16.0	9.1	217.4	595.7	139.8
Rhode Island	.90	14.9	14.3	336.2	740.1	127.4
Connecticut	1.77	19.5	23.9	246.0	691.8	106.9
Middle Atlantic	2.56	29.0	34.9	[1] 218.3	[1] 479.5	115.9
New York	1.27	11.4	20.4	191.5	532.0	92.6
New Jersey	2.59	32.1	50.5	293.5	565.8	127.9
Pennsylvania	3.41	39.1	36.6	[2] 186.1	[2] 356.1	125.2
East North Central	4.33	66.2	66.4	312.2	943.8	154.7
Ohio	4.34	42.1	41.9	286.2	951.0	125.5
Indiana	4.78	36.3	42.9	341.8	929.6	176.6
Illinois	4.98	104.3	78.1	317.8	661.9	160.4
Michigan	4.47	80.0	117.3	402.3	1,422.6	194.1
Wisconsin	1.33	10.1	12.3	136.9	852.3	106.1
West North Central	3.05	36.3	52.3	311.5	834.0	144.2
Minnesota	.80	24.5	4.8	222.1	759.6	127.2
Iowa	1.53	14.6	6.4	243.0	734.8	129.8
Missouri	6.71	73.0	138.2	414.1	834.0	173.3
North Dakota		14.0	2.5	250.9	911.4	90.4
South Dakota		14.7	3.5	199.9	800.0	53.0
Nebraska	1.29	21.4	26.2	274.2	958.5	166.5
Kansas	2.83	32.6	31.9	377.9	1,008.7	140.4
South Atlantic [3]	10.30	47.3	214.9	416.5	961.5	226.2
Delaware	4.93	41.1	19.7	531.4	1,369.9	267.7
Maryland	7.53	47.1	100.8	265.6	581.8	390.2
Virginia	10.30	64.8	233.4	426.0	1,306.0	256.2
West Virginia	2.84	28.6	53.6	274.0	554.3	120.2
North Carolina	10.40	31.3	400.1	429.3	849.4	165.6
South Carolina	12.51	17.1	106.8	354.0	940.6	182.0
Georgia	18.23	30.4	161.3	346.1	839.8	216.5
Florida	8.85	54.5	88.1	622.1	1,185.7	201.0
East South Central	12.45	47.9	102.6	413.2	711.5	191.3
Kentucky	10.51	85.9	115.5	502.1	927.3	269.4
Tennessee	12.95	45.9	64.0	411.1	700.5	191.9
Alabama	15.27	32.7	136.9	413.4	613.9	175.7
Mississippi	8.12	22.7	103.4	267.0	595.4	91.8
West South Central	9.11	36.9	75.9	430.1	1,030.1	214.1
Arkansas	8.00	29.2	105.5	297.0	610.3	108.9
Louisiana	7.86	42.3	67.1	249.9	578.4	197.2
Oklahoma	5.73	42.3	44.5	443.5	1,114.5	207.5
Texas	10.53	37.8	84.2	499.2	1,198.6	232.1
Mountain	2.76	53.4	36.3	463.4	1,402.9	215.6
Montana	2.21	36.7	30.5	296.0	1,352.1	285.5
Idaho	3.05	29.5	16.8	432.2	1,613.9	148.7
Wyoming	1.78	37.4	19.6	307.0	1,276.1	194.0
Colorado	2.85	69.7	39.3	577.3	1,251.6	221.1
New Mexico	4.50	26.6	43.4	272.0	823.8	159.9
Arizona	2.63	101.2	75.8	715.1	2,243.0	345.7
Utah	1.86	35.3	19.9	373.5	1,424.7	161.9
Nevada	3.73	89.6	42.9	672.2	1,902.8	218.5
Pacific	3.21	79.1	49.7	510.4	1,652.7	263.9
Washington	2.23	62.9	22.1	450.6	1,638.3	259.9
Oregon	1.93	40.5	22.8	466.5	1,500.3	179.3
California	3.50	85.6	57.1	523.5	1,669.4	272.4

[1] Burglary and larceny based on reports of 532 cities with a total population of 10,291,946.
[2] Burglary and larceny based on reports of 222 cities with a total population of 3,625,770.
[3] Includes District of Columbia.

Source: Department of Justice, Federal Bureau of Investigation; annual bulletin, Uniform Crime Reports for the United States and Its Possessions.

160.—OFFENSES KNOWN, OFFENSES CLEARED BY ARREST, AND PERSONS FOUND GUILTY IN 226 CITIES OF 25,000 AND OVER: 1951

[Population of cities covered was 25,228,419, based on 1950 decennial census. Information presented here ...ming persons found guilty pertains to final dispositions and not the dispositions at any preliminary judi-... according to the questionnaires returned by the cities]

OFFENSE	NUMBER OF OFFENSES—		Number of persons charged (held for prosecution)	PERSONS FOUND GUILTY—			
				Total		Of offense charged	Of lesser offense
	Known to police	Cleared by arrest		Number	Percent of persons charged		
...tal (part I classes)	464,664	122,119	87,809	61,353	69.9	52,406	8,947
l homicide:							
...r and nonnegligent manslaughter.	1,258	1,212	1,133	729	64.3	534	195
...aughter by negligence..........	806	668	539	259	48.1	196	63
----------------------------------	3,929	3,018	2,279	1,362	59.8	902	460
...r..................................	18,120	7,219	5,954	4,326	72.7	3,351	975
...ted assault......................	25,246	18,992	13,507	7,000	51.8	4,816	2,184
...p—breaking or entering..........	96,277	28,185	17,068	12,770	74.9	10,716	2,054
...—theft (except auto theft)........	270,968	52,218	37,728	28,743	76.2	26,669	2,074
...ft................................	48,060	11,607	9,611	6,164	64.1	5,222	942
...tal (part II classes) 1.............	(7)	(7)	8,585,514	6,150,754	71.6	6,086,246	52,588
...saults..........................	(7)	(7)	40,235	24,626	61.2	23,913	713
...and counterfeiting..............	(7)	(7)	3,091	2,461	79.6	2,182	279
...lement and fraud...............	(7)	(7)	6,818	4,680	68.6	4,331	349
...roperty; buying, receiving, etc....	(7)	(7)	1,920	962	50.1	894	68
...is; carrying, possessing, etc........	(7)	(7)	7,387	5,836	79.0	5,631	205
...nses (including prostitution and ...ercialized vice)...............	(7)	(7)	23,219	16,691	71.9	16,070	621
...s against the family and children..	(7)	(7)	13,714	9,049	66.0	8,659	390
...e drug laws....................	(7)	(7)	4,235	2,935	69.3	2,879	56
...laws.............................	(7)	(7)	16,050	13,437	83.7	13,205	232
...nness; disorderly conduct; va- ...y............................	(7)	(7)	689,635	514,707	74.6	512,404	2,303
...ng..............................	(7)	(7)	33,308	22,604	68.1	22,523	171
...while intoxicated...............	(7)	(7)	47,131	36,291	77.0	33,082	3,209
...and motor-vehicle laws 3..........	(7)	(7)	7,580,949	5,426,293	71.6	5,386,178	42,115
...r offenses........................	(7)	(7)	117,822	68,092	57.8	66,295	1,797

...ect to coverage indicated in footnote 3.
...available.
...d on reports of 214 cities, total population, 22,824,023.

...e: Department of Justice, Federal Bureau of Investigation; semiannual bulletin, *Uniform Crime Reports ...nited States and Its Possessions.*

No. 161.—Arrests, by Age Groups: 1951

[Data from arrest records, evidenced by fingerprint cards received at F. B. I. during year, are limited to instances of arrests for violations of State laws and municipal ordinances. Excludes fingerprint cards representing arrests for violations of Federal laws or commitments to any type of penal institution. Data do not represent all persons arrested, as fingerprint cards are not forwarded to Washington for every individual taken into custody. Arrest records in lower age groups probably incomplete because of practice of some jurisdictions not to fingerprint youthful offenders]

OFFENSE CHARGED	Total, all ages	Under 15	15	16	17	18	19	20	21	22	23	24	25–29	30–34	35–39	40–44	45–49	50 and over	Not known
Total	831,288	3,432	4,276	10,931	18,660	28,775	27,369	26,273	29,833	29,996	30,625	29,817	140,184	114,256	100,694	63,968	62,530	89,063	696
Criminal homicide	6,522	16	20	50	110	147	153	191	237	338	367	245	1,258	904	810	632	446	732	4
Robbery	17,997	70	128	414	786	1,346	1,178	1,241	1,217	1,120	1,109	1,015	3,709	2,055	1,207	667	412	321	11
Assault	61,639	44	86	372	773	1,404	1,617	1,745	2,107	2,271	2,407	2,603	13,019	10,274	8,346	5,963	3,773	4,888	47
Burglary—breaking or entering	42,415	1,134	1,069	2,467	3,197	3,705	3,017	2,510	2,371	2,172	2,110	1,828	6,801	3,860	1,674	960	960	1,025	57
Larceny—theft	69,089	622	650	1,930	3,283	4,685	3,674	3,845	3,374	3,006	2,060	2,781	11,706	8,120	6,122	4,762	3,372	4,060	28
Auto theft	20,222	538	873	1,610	1,882	2,094	1,631	1,274	1,202	1,066	980	750	3,014	1,611	846	491	225	184	9
Embezzlement and fraud	19,855	8	6	77	140	271	342	365	564	699	960	780	4,012	3,639	2,841	2,106	1,436	1,966	14
Stolen property; buying, receiving, etc.	3,479	13	12	51	87	123	146	110	143	122	188	126	688	505	438	316	216	348	1
Arson	1,003	13	9	24	33	40	35	26	35	31	33	22	182	115	105	108	70	120	1
Forgery and counterfeiting	10,484	19	32	107	190	327	360	355	397	453	433	453	2,290	1,709	1,215	869	553	900	3
Rape	8,971	13	40	163	388	637	708	609	562	512	477	445	1,615	976	647	411	280	445	6
Prostitution and commercialized vice	9,215	35	4	11	67	168	220	235	397	448	524	513	2,069	1,460	1,136	777	511	647	3
Other sex offenses	20,173	14	48	138	255	498	496	865	726	705	771	773	2,947	3,072	2,446	1,835	1,334	2,500	12
Narcotic drug laws	13,030	10	28	134	306	559	692	738	838	926	894	817	2,933	1,656	926	951	422	666	7
Weapons; carrying, possessing, etc.	9,723	6	19	118	229	429	411	410	490	466	461	460	2,004	1,380	982	776	470	649	5
Offenses against family and children	16,677	2	1	16	52	112	188	313	466	590	736	749	3,970	3,270	2,698	1,774	906	846	9
Liquor laws	12,902	10	18	74	155	541	530	443	296	303	325	318	3,706	3,541	2,724	1,594	1,244	1,921	8
Driving while intoxicated	59,910	3	5	39	159	446	634	866	1,234	1,382	1,626	1,746	10,100	9,941	9,796	8,393	6,061	7,449	83
Road and driving laws	17,960	6	12	123	344	1,037	1,077	978	1,069	1,036	1,010	1,001	3,798	2,396	1,571	3,038	680	778	7
Parking violations	603					10	10	22	8	16	24	19	128	80	176	41	29	41	1
Other traffic and motor vehicle laws	16,980	13	30	110	299	738	827	786	841	834	857	817	3,262	2,157	1,584	1,139	683	886	17
Disorderly conduct	46,687	41	81	314	810	1,779	1,764	1,718	1,979	1,977	1,954	1,863	8,686	6,545	5,405	4,971	4,509	4,509	43
Drunkenness	191,455	34	57	187	631	1,631	2,038	2,263	3,512	3,772	3,988	4,061	24,116	26,533	29,458	29,127	24,153	35,717	197
Vagrancy	40,810	4	83	460	1,004	1,862	1,648	2,494	1,756	1,843	1,783	1,645	7,204	5,879	5,285	4,671	3,834	6,263	57
Gambling	18,644		8	30	66	148	153	166	254	288	355	448	2,458	3,792	3,063	2,678	2,191	3,505	13
Suspicion	43,094	233	292	723	1,790	2,292	1,903	1,780	2,028	1,998	1,829	1,875	7,879	6,008	4,466	3,271	2,174	2,946	34
Not stated	8,690	11	20	63	87	247	201	204	277	294	203	294	208	1,187	1,137	1,033	859	1,102	5
All other offenses	38,259	559	676	1,146	1,440	1,814	1,618	1,468	1,592	1,509	1,060	1,433	6,438	1,740	3,873	2,943	2,235	3,210	27

Source: Department of Justice, Federal Bureau of Investigation; annual bulletin, *Uniform Crime Reports for the United States and Its Possessions.*

No. 162.—U. S. Supreme Court—Cases Filed and Disposition During October Terms: 1940 to 1951

[Statutory term of Court begins first Monday in October, but for statistical purposes new term begins upon adjournment of preceding term, usually in June]

ACTION	1940	1945	1946	1947	1948	1949	1950	1951
Total cases:								
Filed	977	1,316	1,510	1,295	1,465	1,270	1,181	1,234
Disposed of	985	1,292	1,520	1,322	1,425	1,301	1,202	1,207
Remaining on docket	124	168	188	131	171	140	119	146
Original cases filed	4	1			2			1
Appeals filed	84	64	97	69	86	85	77	104
Petitions for certiorari (not in forma pauperis):								
Filed	769	727	731	647	687	633	582	612
Granted	174	155	148	97	144	85	89	94
Denied or dismissed	592	565	586	555	523	556	495	518
Petitions for certiorari in forma pauperis:								
Filed	120	393	528	426	447	441	404	413
Granted	19	15	8	17	18	7	17	19
Denied or dismissed	101	378	520	400	425	436	386	386
Motions for leave to file various writs:								
Filed		131	154	153	243	111	118	104
Granted					2			1
Denied or dismissed		131	154	150	241	108	121	102
Method of disposition:								
By written opinions (number of cases)	195	170	190	143	147	108	114	96
Number of written opinions	165	134	142	110	114	87	91	83
By per curiam opinions	86	45	66	65	91	94	77	101
By final decree—original cases	1				1		5	
By denial or dismissal of certiorari	693	943	1,106	955	948	991	881	904
By denial or withdrawal of motions to file various writs		131	154	150	235	107	121	101
By motion to dismiss or per stipulation	10	3	4	9	3	1	4	5

Source: Administrative Office of the U. S. Courts, *Annual Report of the Director.*

No. 163.—U. S. Courts of Appeals—Cases Filed, Years Ending June 30: 1940 to 1952

CASES	1940	1945	1946	1947	1948	1949	1950	1951	1952
Total cases [1]	3,505	2,730	2,627	2,615	2,758	2,989	2,830	2,962	3,079
Appeals from courts	2,561	2,168	2,188	2,195	2,314	2,455	2,290	2,337	2,410
Administrative appeals, total	800	511	418	400	381	491	485	566	610
Federal Trade Commission	23	26	4	8	9	6	8	38	20
National Labor Relations Board	306	108	107	124	63	172	167	236	244
The Tax Court of the United States	414	331	267	216	244	233	239	238	257
Other administrative appeals	57	46	40	52	65	80	71	54	89

[1] Includes some miscellaneous original proceedings which are neither appeals from courts nor administrative appeals.

Source: Administrative Office of the U. S. Courts, *Annual Report of the Director.*

No. 164.—U. S. District Courts—Trials Begun During Years Ending June 30: 1945 to 1952

[For purposes of this table, a trial was defined as a contested proceeding (other than a hearing on a motion) before either court or jury in which evidence was introduced and final judgment sought]

TYPE OF TRIAL	1945	1946	1947	1948	1949	1950	1951	1952
Total	9,779	9,030	8,818	8,905	9,282	9,572	9,878	10,065
Civil trials, total	5,265	5,220	5,850	6,156	6,426	6,539	6,962	6,661
Court	3,561	3,633	3,989	4,204	4,149	4,276	4,492	4,174
Jury	1,704	1,587	1,861	1,952	2,277	2,263	2,470	2,487
Criminal trials, total	4,514	3,810	2,968	2,749	2,856	3,033	2,916	3,404
Court	1,503	1,250	1,112	892	997	961	1,035	1,168
Jury	3,011	2,560	1,856	1,857	1,859	2,072	1,881	2,236

Source: Administrative Office of the U. S. Courts, *Annual Report of the Director.*

No. 165.—CIVIL CASES FILED IN 86 U. S. DISTRICT COURTS, YEARS ENDING JUNE 30: 1941 TO 1952

[Excludes district courts in D. C., Alaska, Canal Zone, Guam, and Virgin Islands]

TYPE OF CASE	1941 [1]	1945 [1]	1946 [1]	1947 [1]	1948	1949	1950	1951	1952
Total	28,909	52,144	57,512	48,909	36,530	43,351	44,454	41,252	47,734
U. S. cases, total	14,544	42,067	44,931	29,159	15,845	21,396	21,854	18,802	22,243
U. S. plaintiff:									
Land condemnation	1,783	1,263	804	509	544	746	759	874	991
Rationing, price and rent control (OPA-OHE)		26,283	31,094	15,169	3,566	6,624	5,252	3,765	3,283
Defense Production Act 1950								[1] 23	[2] 2,116
Forfeiture: Food and drug	2,265	3,415	3,210	2,382	1,281	2,077	1,582	1,474	1,816
Negotiable instruments	3,206	1,639	1,909	2,235	2,031	2,562	4,156	3,384	3,654
Other	5,402	3,806	3,253	3,416	3,594	4,918	5,977	5,396	5,725
U. S. defendant:									
Habeas corpus (not including deportations)	318	475	379	393	508	481	409	399	406
Admiralty	36	2,016	2,980	2,939	1,301	730	468	349	502
Tax suits	779	462	421	444	503	632	896	1,023	1,068
Federal Tort Claims Act				654	1,475	1,212	1,013	686	822
Other	755	738	1,181	1,018	1,042	1,424	1,342	1,429	1,870
Private cases, total	14,365	10,057	12,581	19,650	20,985	21,955	22,600	22,450	25,491
Federal question	5,427	3,563	5,085	9,298	6,958	6,543	6,743	6,441	7,622
Antitrust laws	110	26	61	62	76	159	155	202	255
Copyright	560	133	146	174	246	126	164	146	194
Patent	953	226	299	370	476	560	689	584	519
Trade-mark	173	91	107	154	157	157	204	164	178
Employers' Liability Act	100	412	661	799	1,038	942	1,084	1,132	1,231
Fair Labor Standards Act	816	597	1,075	[3] 3,482	796	277	245	250	224
Habeas corpus	127	536	492	485	543	584	560	482	541
Jones Act	949	384	451	1,607	1,574	1,620	1,716	1,734	2,227
Rationing, price and rent control (OPA-OHE-Def. Prod. Act 1950)		384	948	1,094	958	1,042	631	526	521
Other	1,639	774	845	1,071	1,094	1,074	1,295	1,221	1,732
Diversity of citizenship	7,286	5,268	6,242	8,586	10,818	12,347	13,124	13,474	15,125
Contract	2,685	2,141	2,462	3,257	4,149	4,531	4,862	4,604	4,869
Tort	3,631	2,763	3,414	4,854	6,114	7,051	7,572	8,309	9,696
Other	970	364	366	475	555	765	690	561	560
Admiralty	1,652	1,226	1,254	1,766	3,209	3,065	2,733	2,535	2,744

[1] Represents 84 districts; data for Hawaii and Puerto Rico excluded prior to 1948.
[2] Excludes rent control cases which are included with rationing, price, and rent control.
[3] Includes 2,236 "portal to portal" cases.

Source: Administrative Office of the U. S. Courts, *Annual Report of the Director*

No. 166.—CIVIL CASES TERMINATED IN 86 U. S. DISTRICT COURTS, BY BASIS OF JURISDICTION AND MAJOR NATURE OF SUIT GROUPS: YEAR ENDING JUNE 30, 1952

[Excludes district courts in D. C., Alaska, Canal Zone, Guam, and Virgin Islands. Excludes data for land condemnation cases]

BASIS OF JURISDICTION AND NATURE OF SUIT	Total	JUDGMENT WITHOUT CONTEST OR BY CONSENT					CONTESTED JUDGMENT			
		Dismissed for want of prosecution	Default judgment	Consent judgment	Consent dismissal	Other disposition	Judgment by decision of court before trial	Judgment after court trial	Judgment by court during jury trial	Judgment on jury verdict
Total cases	42,219	1,295	6,085	7,309	18,646	1,367	3,157	2,880	188	1,391
United States cases	19,259	259	5,599	4,653	5,035	271	1,737	1,631	15	59
Private cases	22,960	1,036	486	2,647	13,611	1,096	1,420	1,249	173	1,342
United States plaintiff	15,127	115	5,591	4,281	3,264	121	856	871	6	22
Enforcement of Federal statutes:										
Rent control—OHE	1,816	3	197	809	380	4	164	254	1	4
Fair Labor Standards Act	467	2	10	328	82	1	8	26		
Other enforcement suits	3,273	51	474	1,784	535	15	218	193	1	2
Forfeitures:										
Food and drug	1,782	2	1,052	498	81	25	116	8		
Liquor	628	2	186	136	72	9	59	157	2	5
Other forfeitures	656	2	358	116	112	4	21	43		
Contract actions:										
Negotiable instruments	3,493	17	2,227	220	917	4	50	57		1
Other contracts	1,388	20	629	62	500	4	117	52		4
Other U. S. plaintiff	1,634	16	458	328	585	55	108	81	2	6
United States defendant	4,132	144	8	372	1,771	150	881	760	9	37
Habeas corpus	753	24		5	170	5	432	117		
Tort Claims Act	676	24	2	132	246	50	44	177		1
Tax suits	939	13	1	12	616	42	72	160	6	17
Other U. S. defendant	1,764	83	5	223	739	53	333	306	3	19
Federal question	6,798	450	212	532	3,964	222	744	417	24	233
Copyright	171	20	13	25	88	4	8	12		1
Employers' Liability Act	1,053	20		35	781	55	8	9	12	133
Fair Labor Standards Act	487	80	3	61	268	12	15	43	2	3
Habeas corpus	510	2		1	69	4	409	25		
Jones Act	1,682	160	4	93	1,268	25	47	24	6	55
Miller Act	158	11	6	12	103		9	15		2
Patent	606	28	2	166	269	18	34	87		4
Other Federal question	2,129	129	184	139	1,118	104	214	202	4	35
Diversity of citizenship	13,385	475	182	1,929	7,548	809	595	690	149	1,008
Contracts:										
Insurance	2,231	22	9	1,084	669	109	68	126	20	124
Other contracts	2,389	138	106	159	1,343	111	173	258	20	81
Real property	664	24	12	43	350	62	66	78	1	28
Torts:										
Personal injury, motor vehicle	4,745	142	26	417	3,075	336	105	97	52	495
Personal injury, other negligence	2,367	104	3	162	1,561	121	102	72	41	201
Other diversity	989	45	26	64	550	70	81	59	15	79
Admiralty	2,777	111	92	186	2,099	65	81	142		1

Source: Administrative Office of the U. S. Courts, *Annual Report of the Director.*

No. 167.—CRIMINAL PROCEEDINGS COMMENCED IN U. S. DISTRICT COURTS, BY MAJOR OFFENSE GROUPS: YEARS ENDING JUNE 30, 1950, 1951, AND 1952

[Figures for defendants are smaller in some instances than corresponding figures for cases, because defendants appearing in more than one case have been counted only once]

NATURE OF PROCEEDING AND OFFENSE	1950		1951		1952	
	Cases	Defendants	Cases	Defendants	Cases	Defendants
Total	36,383	42,582	38,679	44,587	37,959	43,590
Proceeding commenced by:						
Indictment	15,850	20,641	13,939	18,385	15,260	19,384
Information—Indictment waived	6,270	6,850	6,314	6,913	6,378	6,964
Information—other	14,143	14,954	18,337	19,158	16,256	17,165
All other proceedings	120	137	80	111	57	57
Offense:						
Transportation, etc., of stolen motor vehicles	2,794	3,392	2,572	3,064	3,123	3,748
Larceny, fraud, and other theft [1]	9,056	10,271	7,233	8,501	7,407	8,401
White slave traffic	233	270	232	255	240	257
Narcotics	2,366	2,669	2,073	2,464	2,021	2,460

See footnotes at end of table.

No. 167.—CRIMINAL PROCEEDINGS COMMENCED IN U. S. DISTRICT COURTS, BY MAJOR OFFENSE GROUPS: YEARS ENDING JUNE 30, 1950, 1951, AND 1952—Con.

NATURE OF PROCEEDING AND OFFENSE	1950		1951		1952	
	Cases	Defendants	Cases	Defendants	Cases	Defendants
Offense—Continued						
Liquor, Internal Revenue	3,742	5,809	4,004	6,142	3,766	5,628
Other liquor	271	294	248	264	238	256
Antitrust violations	34	488	16	184	12	84
Food and Drug Act	366	579	366	612	271	447
Immigration laws	10,482	10,609	14,965	15,107	13,147	13,279
Impersonation of Federal officer	223	224	211	216	197	193
Juvenile delinquency	968	1,160	1,006	1,226	1,116	1,347
Migratory bird laws	525	699	498	638	483	632
Motor Carrier Act	553	611	454	508	332	382
National defense laws:						
Selective Service Act, 1940	164	164	22	24	11	11
Selective Service Act, 1948	44	43	314	314	664	648
OPA-OHE—Price and rent control	7	17			2	2
Illegal use of uniform	112	109	162	161	176	175
Other [2]	31	42	81	124	219	405
All other U. S. offenses	1,927	2,519	1,813	2,270	2,196	2,742
Offenses: local,[3] on U. S. reservations and high seas:						
Robbery	311	372	240	309	229	296
Assault	385	400	343	348	320	330
Burglary	462	423	420	426	368	366
Larceny	391	384	390	402	455	496
Rape and other sex offenses	203	204	218	217	204	193
All other local, etc., offenses	824	830	789	789	789	796

[1] Includes burglary, embezzlement, forgery, theft, etc., interstate commerce and transportation, etc., of stolen property.
[2] Includes treason, espionage, sabotage, sedition, and other offenses directly associated with national defense.
[3] District of Columbia, Alaska, Canal Zone, Guam, and Virgin Islands.

No. 168.—CRIMINAL DEFENDANTS DISPOSED OF IN 86 U. S. DISTRICT COURTS, BY MAJOR OFFENSE GROUPS: YEAR ENDING JUNE 30, 1952

[Excludes district courts in D. C., Alaska, Canal Zone, Guam, and Virgin Islands]

NATURE OF OFFENSE	Total	NOT CONVICTED			CONVICTED AND SENTENCED			TYPE OF SENTENCE		
		Total	Dismissed	Acquitted	Total	Pleas of guilty or nolo	Convicted	Imprisonment	Probation and suspended sentence	Fine only
Total (excluding juvenile delinquency) [1]	38,622	3,834	2,891	943	34,788	32,734	2,054	15,379	17,018	2,391
Transportation, etc., of stolen motor vehicles	3,519	326	278	48	3,193	3,046	147	2,375	813	5
Larceny, fraud, and other theft [1]	7,819	1,006	801	205	6,813	6,406	407	3,147	3,378	288
White slave traffic	237	35	23	12	202	158	44	159	42	1
Narcotics	2,121	252	184	68	1,869	1,523	346	1,551	312	6
Liquor, Internal Revenue	5,600	810	524	286	4,790	4,233	557	1,949	2,545	296
Other liquor	256	36	27	9	220	208	12	95	96	29
Antitrust violations	103	63	41	22	40	29	11	3	10	27
Food and Drug Act	513	87	69	18	426	406	20	10	71	345
Immigration laws	13,224	205	191	14	13,019	12,980	39	4,311	8,650	58
Impersonating federal officer	196	31	23	8	167	152	15	103	57	7
Migratory bird laws	601	92	34	58	509	490	19	3	17	489
Motor Carrier Act	368	33	25	8	335	332	3		29	306
National defense laws:										
Selective Service Act, 1940	39	27	27		12	12		8	4	
Selective Service Act, 1948	522	221	195	26	301	148	153	264	35	2
OPA-OHE—Price and rent control	20	16	15	1	4	1	3	3		1
Illegal use of uniform	165	11	10	1	154	154		86	59	9
Other [3]	218	73	65	8	145	126	19	34	50	61
Counterfeiting	244	47	29	18	197	155	42	126	66	5
All other U. S. offenses	2,347	401	292	109	1,946	1,783	163	927	593	426
Offenses committed on U. S. reservations and high seas	808	62	38	24	446	392	54	225	191	30
Juvenile delinquency	1,325	70	56	14	1,255		1,255	584	668	2

[1] Juvenile delinquency cases excluded from totals because proceedings differ in nature from ordinary court trial and because Attorney General has power to designate any public or private agency for custody of juvenile during period for which he is committed.
[2] See footnote 1, table 167.   [3] See footnote 2, table 167.

Source of tables 167 and 168: Administrative Office of the U. S. Courts, *Annual Report of the Director.*

No. 169.—Sentenced Prisoners Present at End of Year and Prisoners Received from Courts, by Type of Institution: 1939 to 1951

[Rate per 100,000 of estimated civilian population. Includes estimates for certain State institutions]

YEAR	PRESENT AT END OF YEAR						RECEIVED FROM COURTS					
	All institutions		Federal institutions		State institutions		All institutions		Federal institutions		State institutions	
	Number	Rate	Number	Rate	Number	Rate	Number	Rate	Number	Rate	Number	Rate
1939	179,559	137.5	19,730	15.1	159,829	122.4	(1)	(1)	(1)	(1)	(1)	(1)
1940	172,996	131.4	19,260	14.6	153,736	116.8	73,290	55.7	15,109	11.5	58,181	44.2
1941	164,669	125.2	18,465	14.0	146,204	111.1	69,478	52.8	15,350	11.7	54,128	41.1
1942	149,791	144.5	16,623	12.7	133,168	101.8	59,421	45.4	13,725	10.6	45,696	34.9
1943	136,367	107.0	16,113	12.6	120,254	94.4	50,061	39.3	12,203	9.6	37,858	29.7
1944	131,974	104.2	18,139	14.3	113,835	89.9	50,148	39.6	14,047	11.1	36,101	28.5
1945	123,219	104.4	18,638	14.6	114,581	89.8	52,875	41.4	14,171	11.1	38,704	30.3
1946	139,435	100.8	17,622	12.7	121,813	88.0	60,530	43.7	14,950	10.8	45,580	32.9
1947	150,865	105.8	17,146	12.0	133,719	93.8	63,977	44.8	12,948	9.1	51,029	35.8
1948	155,092	106.8	16,328	11.2	138,764	95.6	62,650	43.2	12,430	8.6	50,220	34.6
1949	163,342	110.7	16,868	11.4	146,474	99.3	68,377	46.4	13,130	8.9	55,247	37.5
1950	165,796	110.4	17,134	11.4	148,662	99.0	68,855	45.8	14,237	9.5	54,618	36.4
1951	164,896	109.2	17,395	11.5	147,501	97.6	66,380	43.9	14,120	9.3	52,360	34.6

1 Comparable data not available.
Source: Department of Justice, Bureau of Prisons; *National Prisoner Statistics* bulletin No. 7, November 1952.

No. 170.—Sentenced Federal Prisoners Received From the Courts, by Offense: Years Ending June 30, 1937 to 1952

OFFENSE	1937	1940	1945	1948	1949	1950	1951	1952
Total	24,282	23,003	21,200	16,787	16,723	18,063	18,950	18,896
Counterfeiting and forgery	1,486	1,589	673	1,018	1,204	1,534	1,438	1,253
Embezzlement and fraud	510	750	340	531	592	609	535	558
Immigration	2,802	2,270	3,995	3,200	3,526	3,463	4,334	4,548
Juvenile Delinquency Act		216	911	677	607	658	684	605
Kidnaping	44	37	20	36	23	41	26	42
Liquor laws	12,238	10,735	2,988	1,838	2,035	2,304	2,323	2,347
National Bank and Federal Reserve Act	120	157	51	141	90	165	142	164
Narcotic-drug laws	1,866	2,250	1,134	1,443	1,503	2,029	2,063	1,932
National Motor Vehicle Theft Act	1,312	1,512	1,072	2,612	2,471	2,486	2,392	2,605
Theft from interstate commerce	308	313	475	430	378	270	327	307
White Slave Traffic Act	370	378	209	221	160	185	182	173
Government reservation, D. C., high seas, and territorial cases	1,033	1,021	986	1,069	1,054	1,145	1,272	1,369
Other	2,083	1,719	1,757	1,898	2,012	2,195	2,160	2,101
National-security offenses	30	56	6,588	1,673	1,068	979	1,072	902
Selective Service Act of 1940			2,613	236	152	97	9	8
Selective Service Act of 1948					74	39	115	273
Other national-defense and security laws [1]		11	2,150	319	182	130	155	157
Military court-martial cases:								
Army	30	45	1,793	851	592	606	775	416
Navy			32	267	88	107	18	48

1 Commitments under national defense and security laws in effect prior to 1940 not classified separately.
Source: Department of Justice, Bureau of Prisons; annual report, *Federal Prisons, 1952*.

No. 171.—FEDERAL PRISONERS WITH PREVIOUS COMMITMENTS, BY OFFENSE: YEAR ENDING JUNE 30, 1952

[Known previous commitments under sentence, of prisoners committed to Federal institutions under sentence of more than 1 year]

OFFENSE	Total committed	WITH KNOWN PREVIOUS COMMITMENTS					Without known previous commitments [1]
		Total		With one	With two	With three or more	
		Number	Percent of total committed				
Total offenses	9,658	5,903	61.1	1,970	1,370	2,563	3,755
Counterfeiting	136	83	61.0	30	17	36	53
Drug laws	1,647	937	56.9	298	222	417	710
Embezzlement	179	39	21.8	15	13	11	140
Forgery	744	527	70.8	159	119	249	217
Fraud	120	53	44.2	10	15	28	67
Immigration	168	148	88.1	20	21	107	20
Impersonating Federal officer	54	37	68.5	11	5	21	17
Income tax	88	15	17.0	7	3	5	73
Juvenile delinquency (except D. C.)	599	260	43.4	171	61	28	339
Kidnapping	42	27	64.3	4	9	14	15
Larceny-theft	2,900	2,140	73.8	629	509	1,002	760
Transportation, etc., of stolen motor vehicle	2,284	1,748	76.5	506	433	809	536
Liquor laws	1,084	704	64.9	247	180	277	380
Robbery	105	59	56.2	18	12	29	46
Securities, transporting false or forged	114	88	77.2	20	12	56	26
Selective Service Act	223	28	12.6	15	11	2	195
Wearing military uniform illegally	31	25	80.6	7	2	16	6
White slave traffic	144	93	64.6	36	25	32	51
Other and unclassifiable	295	177	60.0	54	44	79	118
Military court-martial cases	460	157	34.1	92	25	40	303
Government reservation, D. C., high seas and territorial cases	525	306	58.3	127	65	114	219

[1] Includes 10 with no report as to previous commitments.

Source: Department of Justice, Bureau of Prisons; annual report, *Federal Prisons, 1952*.

No. 172.—MOVEMENT OF SENTENCED PRISONERS IN STATE AND FEDERAL PRISONS AND REFORMATORIES, BY SEX: 1950 AND 1951

[Includes estimates for State institutions in Georgia]

MOVEMENT OF SENTENCED PRISONERS	1950			1951		
	Total	Male	Female	Total	Male	Female
Prisoners present January 1	163,342	157,255	6,087	165,796	159,988	5,808
Admissions, total	108,069	103,438	4,631	107,507	102,632	4,875
Admitted, except transfers	83,437	79,272	4,165	81,666	77,289	4,377
Received from court	68,855	65,556	3,299	66,380	62,857	3,523
Returned as a conditional-release violator	8,692	8,164	528	9,124	8,640	484
Returned from escape	1,993	1,880	113	2,562	2,467	95
Other admissions [1]	3,897	3,672	225	3,600	3,325	275
Transferred from other institutions	24,632	24,166	466	25,841	25,343	498
Discharges, total	105,615	100,705	4,910	108,407	103,794	4,613
Discharged, except transfers	81,021	76,608	4,413	83,133	79,008	4,125
Unconditional and conditional releases	72,179	68,179	4,000	73,937	70,271	3,666
Unconditional	29,943	28,438	1,505	31,991	30,594	1,397
Expiration of sentence	27,857	26,452	1,405	29,486	28,196	1,290
Pardon	54	52	2	178	176	2
Commutation	2,032	1,934	98	2,327	2,222	105
Conditional	42,236	39,741	2,495	41,946	39,677	2,269
Parole	33,572	31,473	2,099	35,303	33,332	1,971
Conditional pardon	1,342	1,290	52	1,855	1,782	73
Other conditional release	7,322	6,978	344	4,788	4,563	225
Death, except execution	782	769	13	713	695	18
Execution [2]	82	82		105	104	1
Escape	2,317	2,207	110	2,896	2,794	102
Other discharges [1]	5,661	5,371	290	5,482	5,144	338
Transferred to other institutions	24,594	24,097	497	25,274	24,786	488
Prisoners present December 31	165,796	159,988	5,808	164,896	158,826	6,070

[1] Include prisoner movement incident to authorized temporary absences for appearances in court and other purposes, and also discharges by court order.
[2] Includes executions carried out under county jurisdiction.

Source: Department of Justice, Bureau of Prisons; *National Prisoner Statistics*, bulletin Nos. 4 and 7.

No. 173.—STATE AND FEDERAL PRISONS AND REFORMATORIES—FELONY PRISONERS RECEIVED FROM COURTS, BY SELECTED OFFENSES: 1942 TO 1950

[Excludes statistics for State institutions as follows: Georgia, all years; Mississippi, 1942 to 1949; Michigan, 1942 to 1945 and 1948 to 1950]

OFFENSE	1942	1943	1944	1945	1946	1947	1948	1949	1950
Number of institutions reporting	146	150	147	150	151	147	147	149	150
NUMBER									
Total	47,761	46,273	41,658	42,251	54,432	54,048	52,363	54,862	57,896
Criminal homicide	3,008	2,648	2,362	2,519	3,732	3,692	3,195	3,764	3,203
Robbery	3,848	3,392	3,658	3,550	5,267	5,714	4,983	5,449	5,722
Aggravated assault	2,519	2,333	2,120	2,528	3,528	3,239	2,631	2,975	2,542
Burglary	7,434	6,356	6,362	7,293	10,150	10,440	9,744	11,282	11,527
Larceny, except auto theft	8,193	6,579	5,466	7,542	9,408	9,292	9,148	8,462	8,796
Auto theft	3,179	2,375	2,744	3,172	5,225	5,058	4,869	4,554	4,957
Rape	1,719	1,597	1,593	1,648	2,227	2,597	1,790	1,755	1,796
All other offenses	17,562	14,361	15,732	14,836	16,564	16,759	17,653	18,619	19,445
PERCENT DISTRIBUTION									
Total	100.0	100.0	100.0	100.0	100.0	100.0	100.0	100.0	100.0
Criminal homicide	6.3	6.8	5.8	5.8	6.6	6.2	6.1	6.7	5.3
Robbery	8.1	8.4	7.4	8.2	9.2	10.2	9.4	9.9	9.9
Aggravated assault	5.9	4.8	4.4	6.0	6.3	5.8	5.1	5.1	4.5
Burglary	15.4	13.8	15.4	14.6	18.7	18.7	18.6	18.9	21.4
Larceny, except auto theft	17.2	14.3	17.5	17.6	17.2	16.5	15.7	14.4	15.1
Auto theft	4.7	4.9	6.7	7.3	9.3	9.1	9.2	8.4	9.7
Rape	3.6	4.2	3.9	4.3	4.1	2.7	3.3	3.1	3.1
All other offenses	26.8	27.8	38.3	34.3	28.4	28.4	32.4	22.1	20.4

Source: Department of Justice, Bureau of Prisons.

No. 174.—STATE AND FEDERAL PRISONS AND REFORMATORIES—PRISONERS PRESENT
JANUARY 1 AND RECEIVED FROM COURTS DURING YEAR: 1947 TO 1951

[Includes estimates for certain State institutions.   Corrects certain Federal and State data previously published]

DIVISION AND STATE	PRISONERS PRESENT JAN. 1					PRISONERS RECEIVED FROM COURTS				
	1947	1948	1949 [1]	1950	1951	1947	1948	1949	1950	1951
United States..........	139,435	150,865	155,397	163,342	165,796	63,977	62,650	68,377	68,855	66,380
Federal institutions [2]...	17,622	17,146	16,328	16,868	17,134	12,948	12,430	13,130	14,237	14,120
State institutions......	121,813	133,719	139,069	146,474	148,662	51,029	50,220	55,247	54,618	52,260
New England:										
Maine...................	570	627	632	650	736	325	303	372	471	371
New Hampshire.........	237	269	268	250	235	105	90	84	72	73
Vermont...............	255	229	218	284	259	201	199	256	210	149
Massachusetts.........	2,374	2,664	2,620	2,537	2,375	997	906	834	851	766
Rhode Island..........	365	403	361	350	284	304	277	270	250	198
Connecticut...........	1,045	1,078	1,084	1,087	1,020	531	472	481	440	467
Middle Atlantic:										
New York.............	12,995	14,090	15,054	15,246	15,313	3,772	3,500	3,703	3,456	3,855
New Jersey............	3,541	3,958	4,190	4,301	3,991	1,694	1,450	1,513	1,555	1,614
Pennsylvania..........	6,586	6,938	7,375	7,616	7,432	1,978	2,085	2,104	1,867	1,682
East North Central:										
Ohio..................	7,264	8,134	8,261	8,835	9,128	2,588	2,357	2,978	2,727	2,418
Indiana...............	3,439	3,942	4,296	4,707	4,738	1,257	1,250	1,320	1,134	1,039
Illinois...............	7,478	7,820	7,784	7,922	7,886	1,934	1,640	1,863	1,868	1,510
Michigan..............	7,829	8,241	8,161	8,589	8,591	2,677	2,600	3,161	3,076	3,199
Wisconsin.............	1,588	1,705	1,915	1,991	2,017	873	1,084	1,107	1,051	1,056
West North Central:										
Minnesota.............	1,586	1,616	1,699	1,777	1,879	560	529	498	679	591
Iowa..................	1,695	1,824	1,990	2,104	2,084	581	651	678	632	644
Missouri..............	2,922	3,161	3,155	3,209	3,400	1,257	1,149	1,326	1,550	1,381
North Dakota.........	240	243	244	242	235	130	120	130	124	115
South Dakota.........	300	363	422	418	451	245	280	240	302	231
Nebraska.............	836	914	1,020	1,193	1,147	535	620	661	623	570
Kansas...............	1,267	1,345	1,458	1,765	1,959	506	553	783	833	716
South Atlantic:										
Delaware.............	169	189	178	157	158	140	149	122	123	85
Maryland.............	3,481	3,597	3,771	4,148	3,892	2,817	2,835	3,431	3,060	3,235
Dist. of Columbia.....	1,115	1,102	1,258	1,372	1,478	450	585	577	580	616
Virginia..............	3,937	3,992	3,984	4,242	4,439	1,572	1,665	1,793	1,751	1,652
West Virginia.........	2,178	2,309	2,484	2,776	2,904	644	595	741	702	706
North Carolina........	3,789	4,046	4,125	4,437	4,335	1,222	1,226	1,375	1,259	1,352
South Carolina........	1,048	1,256	1,387	1,413	1,513	543	549	628	607	617
Georgia...............	3,693	4,597	4,269	4,749	4,845	1,529	1,423	1,583	1,615	1,467
Florida...............	2,952	3,460	3,761	3,851	3,973	1,511	1,504	1,491	1,516	1,374
East South Central:										
Kentucky.............	2,234	2,303	2,906	3,198	3,250	1,204	1,341	1,439	1,365	1,141
Tennessee............	2,380	2,637	2,665	2,715	2,780	924	900	1,022	1,026	940
Alabama..............	3,948	4,432	4,679	5,036	4,454	2,508	2,627	2,998	2,514	2,440
Mississippi...........	1,851	1,915	1,892	1,970	2,158	643	546	728	753	666
West South Central:										
Arkansas.............	1,252	1,446	1,442	1,595	1,541	664	598	691	695	626
Louisiana.............	2,220	2,304	2,288	2,514	2,674	923	902	1,071	1,164	983
Oklahoma.............	2,122	2,224	2,229	2,297	2,401	1,048	1,087	1,112	1,183	1,134
Texas................	4,246	5,675	5,792	5,958	6,424	2,588	2,439	2,635	2,996	3,056
Mountain:										
Montana..............	361	428	464	584	595	287	340	417	410	380
Idaho................	257	326	381	479	514	195	244	318	290	207
Wyoming.............	323	366	356	411	410	191	209	257	237	228
Colorado.............	1,331	1,389	1,456	1,362	1,490	756	795	693	957	802
New Mexico...........	607	630	580	637	705	333	312	397	437	412
Arizona..............	784	941	964	894	878	524	517	478	452	438
Utah.................	409	487	485	476	562	203	183	225	239	180
Nevada...............	278	263	251	300	240	228	193	239	172	138
Pacific:										
Washington...........	1,957	2,044	1,944	2,053	2,290	918	829	870	933	850
Oregon...............	1,106	1,200	1,308	1,400	1,534	578	577	673	689	638
California............	7,373	8,547	9,563	10,377	11,056	2,834	2,985	2,881	3,122	3,252

[1] Due to reclassification effective Jan. 1, 1949, data include 305 prisoners of a State receiving station in New York, previously excluded.
[2] Not included in State figures.

Source: Department of Justice, Bureau of Prisons; State and Federal Prisons and Reformatories release No. 1, and *National Prisoner Statistics*, bulletin Nos. 4 and 7.

No. 175.—State and Federal Prisons and Reformatories—Felony Prisoners Received From Courts, by Color, Nativity, Age, and Sex: 1945 to 1949

COLOR, NATIVITY, AND AGE	1945 [1]	1946 [1]	1947 [2]	1948 [1]			1949 [1]		
				Total	Male	Female	Total	Male	Female
Total	43,281	56,432	56,088	52,303	49,833	2,470	56,802	54,370	2,432
Color and nativity:									
White	29,539	37,146	38,541	36,092	34,658	1,434	39,585	38,155	1,430
Native [3]	27,825	35,333	36,653	34,438	33,035	1,403	37,782	36,395	1,387
Foreign-born	1,714	1,813	1,888	1,654	1,623	31	1,803	1,760	43
Negro	13,207	18,655	16,885	15,561	14,548	1,013	16,614	15,640	974
All other	535	631	662	650	627	23	603	575	28
Age:									
Under 15 years	39	36	29	19	16	3	40	38	2
15 to 17	2,787	3,016	2,419	1,772	1,699	73	2,361	2,271	90
18	2,544	3,040	2,645	2,339	2,243	96	1,962	1,877	85
19	2,352	3,133	3,258	2,917	2,775	142	2,892	2,774	118
20	2,395	3,156	3,269	3,086	2,954	132	3,249	3,140	109
21 to 24	8,722	12,459	12,455	11,820	11,261	559	12,844	12,318	526
25 to 29	7,506	10,364	10,662	10,018	9,495	523	11,548	11,044	504
30 to 34	5,389	7,113	7,014	6,558	6,257	301	7,204	6,868	336
35 to 39	4,067	5,272	5,227	5,113	4,854	259	5,407	5,124	283
40 to 44	2,990	3,524	3,535	3,512	3,317	195	3,748	3,592	156
45 to 49	1,966	2,403	2,553	2,267	2,178	79	2,598	2,488	110
50 to 54	1,245	1,358	1,438	1,361	1,305	56	1,370	1,299	71
55 to 59	666	776	841	800	774	26	826	798	28
60 to 64	338	399	413	427	412	15	436	430	6
65 and over	305	383	330	304	293	11	317	309	8

[1] Excludes statistics for State institutions in Michigan, Georgia, and Mississippi.
[2] Includes statistics covering year ending May 31 for Pennsylvania, and for Georgia, statistics for year ending March 31, 1947, adjusted to a calendar year basis; excludes statistics for Mississippi.
[3] Includes white, unknown nativity.
Source: Department of Justice, Bureau of Prisons.

No. 176.—Prisoners Executed Under Civil Authority, by Race and Offense: 1930 to 1951

[Excludes executions by military authorities. The Army (including the Air Force) carried out 148, all from 1942 to 1950 of which 95 were for murder (including 18 involving rape), 52 for rape, and 1 for desertion. There were no executions in the Navy]

YEAR	ALL OFFENSES				MURDER [1]			RAPE			OTHER OFFENSES [2]		
	Total	White	Negro	Other	Total	White	Negro	Total	White	Negro	Total	White	Negro
All years	3,136	1,413	1,685	38	2,732	1,351	1,345	354	35	317	50	27	23
1930	155	89	65	1	147	89	57	6	.....	6	2	.....	2
1931	153	77	72	4	137	76	57	15	1	14	1	.....	1
1932	140	62	75	3	128	62	63	10	.....	10	2	.....	2
1933	160	77	81	2	151	75	74	7	1	6	2	1	1
1934	168	65	102	1	154	64	89	14	1	13	.....	.....	.....
1935	199	119	77	3	184	115	66	13	2	11	2	2	.....
1936	195	92	101	2	180	85	93	10	2	8	5	5	.....
1937	147	69	74	4	133	67	62	13	2	11	1	.....	1
1938	190	96	92	2	155	90	63	25	1	24	10	5	5
1939	159	80	77	2	144	79	63	12	.....	12	3	1	2
1940	124	49	75	.....	105	44	61	15	2	13	4	3	1
1941	123	59	63	1	102	55	46	20	4	16	1	.....	1
1942	147	67	80	.....	116	57	59	24	4	20	7	6	1
1943	131	54	74	3	118	54	63	13	.....	11	.....	.....	.....
1944	120	47	70	3	96	45	48	24	2	22	.....	.....	.....
1945	117	41	75	1	90	37	52	26	4	22	1	.....	1
1946	131	46	84	1	107	45	61	22	.....	22	2	1	1
1947	152	42	110	.....	128	40	88	23	2	21	1	.....	1
1948	119	35	82	2	95	32	61	22	1	21	2	2	.....
1949	119	50	67	2	107	49	56	10	.....	10	2	1	.....
1950	82	40	42	.....	68	32	32	13	4	9	1	.....	1
1951	105	57	47	1	87	55	31	17	2	15	1	.....	1

[1] Includes 24 females; 14 white, 10 nonwhite.
[2] 18 armed robbery, 13 kidnaping, 10 burglary, 6 espionage (all in 1942), 3 aggravated assault.
Source: Department of Justice, Bureau of Prisons; National Prisoner Statistics, bulletin No. 6.

6. Climate

Climatological data are gathered by the United States Weather Bureau at about 10,000 stations. Of this number nearly 3,000 stations have autographic precipitation records, about 600 take automatic or hourly readings of a series of weather elements, and the remainder record one observation a day. There are few records in existence for stations before 1871, although some earlier and less detailed records began in the 18th century. Data shown in these tables include long-time averages and extremes of the several elements for the vicinities indicated. Where the station has moved, but not out of the general vicinity, the data represent combined values for both the previous and the new locations.

The following tables contain data from a list of cities selected to give a general representation of the climate over the United States. The averages represent the arithmetic means of the period of record at the station. The number of degree days as used in table 189 is the average monthly sum of the differences between 65° and the daily mean temperatures below 65°, i. e. (65°-T°). Experience has shown that, in order to heat buildings to a temperature of approximately 70°, the amount of fuel or heat used per day is proportional to the number of degrees the average outside temperature falls below 65°. The degree-day value is based on this assumption.

Note.—This section presents data for the most recent year or period available on February 18, 1953, when the material was organized and sent to the printer.

No. 177.—Ground Elevation of Stations in Selected Cities

STATION		Ground elevation (feet)	STATION		Ground elevation (feet)
Alabama	Mobile	10	New Jersey	Atlantic City	8
	Montgomery	201	New Mexico	Albuquerque	5,310
Arizona	Phoenix	1,083	New York	Albany	277
Arkansas	Little Rock	257		New York	10
California	Fresno	331		Rochester	543
	Los Angeles	312	North Carolina	Asheville	2,203
	San Francisco	52		Raleigh	400
Colorado	Denver	5,292	North Dakota	Bismarck	1,650
District of Columbia	Washington	72	Ohio	Cleveland	787
Florida	Jacksonville	18	Oklahoma	Oklahoma City	1,254
	Miami	8	Oregon	Portland	30
Georgia	Atlanta	977	Pennsylvania	Harrisburg	335
Idaho	Boise	2,842		Pittsburgh	1,348
Illinois	Chicago	611	South Carolina	Charleston	9
Indiana	Indianapolis	718	South Dakota	Huron	1,282
Iowa	Des Moines	800	Tennessee	Nashville	577
Kansas	Wichita	1,372	Texas	Amarillo	3,590
Kentucky	Louisville	467		El Paso	3,920
Louisiana	New Orleans	9		Fort Worth	688
Maine	Eastport	33		Houston	41
Massachusetts	Boston	12	Utah	Salt Lake City	4,260
Michigan	Detroit	619	Vermont	Burlington	340
	Sault Ste. Marie	721	Virginia	Norfolk	11
Minnesota	Minneapolis	830		Richmond	162
Mississippi	Vicksburg	247	Washington	Seattle	14
Missouri	Kansas City	741		Spokane	2,357
	St. Louis	465	West Virginia	Parkersburg	615
Montana	Helena	3,893	Wisconsin	Madison	938
	Miles City	2,629	Wyoming	Cheyenne	6,139
Nebraska	North Platte	2,783	Alaska	Juneau	15
	Omaha	978	Hawaii	Honolulu	12
Nevada	Winnemucca	4,299	Puerto Rico	San Juan	50

Source: Department of Commerce, Weather Bureau; records.

No. 178.—Mean Temperatures

[Average of daily maximum and minimum temperatures; for period of record through 1951]

Station	Length of record (yrs.)	Jan.	Feb.	Mar.	Apr.	May	June	July	Aug.	Sept.	Oct.	Nov.	Dec.	Annual
Ala.__ Mobile__	80	52.2	54.6	59.6	66.9	74.2	80.3	81.8	81.7	78.2	69.0	59.1	53.4	67.6
Montgomery__	79	49.3	51.7	58.1	65.4	73.4	80.0	81.7	81.0	76.9	66.8	56.1	49.8	65.8
Ariz.__ Phoenix__	56	51.9	55.9	60.8	68.0	75.0	85.1	90.5	88.8	83.5	71.6	60.1	52.8	70.4
Ark.__ Little Rock__	72	42.1	44.9	53.3	62.5	70.0	78.0	81.2	80.4	74.5	64.0	52.0	44.1	62.3
Calif.__ Fresno__	64	46.1	51.3	56.4	61.2	67.7	75.4	81.9	80.2	73.8	64.8	54.7	46.7	63.3
Los Angeles__	74	55.4	56.3	58.1	60.3	62.5	66.5	70.7	71.5	69.9	65.9	62.0	57.2	63.1
San Francisco__	81	50.1	52.7	54.3	55.7	57.0	58.8	58.9	59.3	61.5	60.8	56.8	51.5	56.5
Colo.__ Denver__	80	30.5	33.0	39.2	47.8	56.7	66.7	72.8	71.4	62.9	51.7	40.2	32.7	50.5
D.C.__ Washington__	83	34.8	35.8	43.9	53.9	64.6	73.0	77.3	75.3	68.9	57.7	46.3	37.1	55.7
Fla.__ Jacksonville__	80	56.2	57.9	63.1	68.7	75.1	80.1	81.9	81.6	78.6	70.9	62.4	56.6	69.5
Miami__	41	68.3	68.2	70.5	73.8	77.1	80.1	81.6	82.0	80.9	77.7	72.1	69.3	75.2
Ga.__ Atlanta__	73	43.7	45.7	52.8	61.1	69.4	76.6	78.5	77.7	73.2	63.3	52.0	44.7	61.6
Idaho__ Boise__	12	26.9	35.4	41.4	50.2	57.6	63.5	75.7	72.3	62.7	52.5	39.4	32.0	50.7
Ill.__ Chicago__	81	25.0	26.8	36.1	47.1	57.6	67.6	73.3	72.0	65.3	54.1	40.0	28.1	49.6
Ind.__ Indianapolis__	81	29.2	31.0	40.6	52.2	63.0	72.2	76.1	74.2	67.4	56.0	42.4	32.4	53.1
Iowa__ Des Moines__	73	21.3	24.7	35.7	50.5	61.6	70.9	76.1	73.7	65.6	54.1	38.6	26.3	50.0
Kans.__ Wichita__	63	31.0	36.1	45.0	56.6	66.1	74.9	80.8	78.3	71.1	59.6	45.2	34.6	56.6
Ky.__ Louisville__	79	34.9	36.8	45.8	56.2	66.2	74.9	81.3	80.4	73.6	70.5	60.2	48.4	57.0
La.__ New Orleans__	78	55.1	57.5	53.1	69.5	73.1	81.5	82.4	82.2	79.0	69.0	57.8	46.1	56.7
Maine__ Eastport__	79	21.2	21.6	29.8	39.0	47.5	55.2	60.4	60.7	56.0	47.8	37.4	25.8	41.9
Mass.__ Boston__	80	28.7	28.7	36.6	46.6	57.6	66.7	72.3	70.3	63.8	54.0	42.9	32.4	50.1
Mich.__ Detroit__	81	25.2	25.4	34.2	46.1	57.9	67.8	72.7	70.8	63.9	52.6	39.4	28.1	48.5
Sault Ste. Marie__	63	14.5	19.3	25.1	37.5	49.2	58.7	65.9	62.8	56.0	45.2	32.8	20.8	39.3
Minn.__ Minneapolis__	61	13.7	16.5	30.0	45.9	58.0	67.7	73.5	70.6	62.0	50.0	32.8	19.5	45.0
Miss.__ Vicksburg__	78	48.7	51.5	58.5	65.8	72.8	79.4	81.4	81.1	76.6	67.0	56.7	50.2	65.8
Mo.__ Kansas City__	63	29.9	32.8	43.3	55.2	64.9	74.3	79.7	77.6	69.9	58.9	44.5	32.6	55.4
St. Louis__	79	32.8	35.0	44.8	56.1	65.3	73.3	79.7	77.0	70.7	59.5	45.6	35.5	56.6
Mont.__ Helena__	72	20.0	26.6	32.3	43.7	52.0	59.6	67.7	66.2	55.8	45.6	32.8	24.6	43.7
Miles City__	60	16.9	19.5	31.4	46.7	57.0	66.0	74.4	71.8	60.4	48.4	33.4	22.0	45.7
Nebr.__ North Platte__	77	25.3	27.7	36.8	49.0	58.9	68.6	74.9	73.1	63.9	51.6	37.4	27.7	49.5
Omaha__	79	22.2	26.2	37.6	51.6	62.5	72.0	77.4	75.2	66.6	54.9	39.1	27.3	51.1
Nev.__ Winnemucca__	73	27.8	33.2	39.7	47.4	55.1	63.5	73.9	69.4	59.1	48.4	38.1	30.1	48.6
N.J.__ Atlantic City__	80	34.1	33.8	39.9	48.3	58.4	67.5	72.9	72.6	67.5	57.3	46.4	37.0	53.0
N.Mex.__ Albuquerque__	21	34.1	30.0	46.2	55.2	64.4	73.2	76.2	69.3	57.9	43.7	34.7	34.3	48.3
N.Y.__ Albany__	136	23.7	24.4	33.8	46.7	60.1	68.2	72.4	70.6	62.7	50.9	39.3	27.9	48.3
New York__	80	31.7	31.6	39.0	49.3	60.4	69.1	74.5	73.0	66.0	56.5	45.1	34.9	52.7
Rochester__	80	25.1	24.4	32.7	44.7	56.8	66.5	71.3	69.3	62.8	51.4	39.4	28.9	47.8
N.C.__ Asheville__	49	39.1	39.9	47.0	56.9	65.2	70.4	73.1	72.2	67.2	56.8	46.2	39.4	56.1
Raleigh__	69	42.5	43.8	51.1	60.6	68.5	75.6	78.0	77.4	72.2	61.5	51.8	43.1	60.4
N.Dak.__ Bismarck__	77	8.3	11.5	25.0	43.1	54.7	64.9	70.9	68.3	58.1	45.4	28.4	14.9	41.8
Ohio__ Cleveland__	46	28.7	28.3	34.3	45.2	56.8	66.5	71.0	70.1	64.9	54.2	42.1	31.0	49.7
Okla.__ Oklahoma City__	61	37.4	40.6	50.1	60.4	68.0	77.0	81.3	81.6	73.0	62.4	48.5	39.9	60.2
Oreg.__ Portland__	63	38.5	42.7	47.2	52.5	57.9	62.7	67.6	67.3	62.6	55.1	44.7	41.8	52.7
Pa.__ Harrisburg__	78	30.6	30.7	40.3	51.0	62.3	70.9	75.9	73.9	66.4	55.1	43.5	33.4	52.6
Pittsburgh__	78	31.2	31.5	40.0	50.7	61.3	70.1	74.3	72.4	66.5	55.1	43.0	33.8	52.6
S.C.__ Charleston__	80	49.5	51.3	57.6	64.9	72.8	79.1	81.5	80.9	77.0	67.9	56.4	49.7	65.7
Huron__	76	13.1	16.0	30.0	46.0	57.0	66.9	73.0	70.9	61.4	48.6	31.7	19.3	44.5
Tenn.__ Nashville__	81	39.4	41.7	49.5	59.3	68.2	76.4	79.4	78.3	72.2	61.2	49.0	41.3	59.6
Tex.__ Amarillo__	60	36.7	39.5	47.7	57.0	65.8	74.4	79.0	77.9	70.3	59.8	46.4	38.4	57.9
El Paso__	72	44.7	49.6	55.7	63.6	72.0	80.5	81.4	80.0	74.6	64.6	52.5	45.4	63.7
Fort Worth__	80	45.0	48.8	57.1	65.0	72.6	80.5	84.1	84.5	77.8	67.9	56.3	47.7	65.7
Houston__	72	54.1	56.4	62.7	69.0	76.4	81.3	83.3	83.4	79.1	71.2	61.6	55.0	69.3
Utah__ Salt Lake City__	78	28.2	34.1	41.8	50.9	58.6	67.6	76.9	75.1	65.9	53.2	40.9	29.2	52.1
Vt.__ Burlington__	69	18.7	18.7	29.4	42.9	56.0	66.0	70.0	67.9	60.1	48.7	36.7	24.1	44.7
Va.__ Norfolk__	81	42.0	42.5	48.9	57.2	66.5	74.2	78.5	77.2	72.4	62.3	52.0	43.3	59.3
Richmond__	54	39.2	39.6	48.1	58.0	66.5	74.2	78.0	76.4	70.9	60.1	49.1	40.2	58.3
Wash.__ Seattle__	61	40.2	42.4	45.7	50.3	55.7	60.3	64.2	64.0	60.0	52.9	46.3	42.3	52.1
Spokane__	73	26.9	31.6	40.0	48.4	56.2	62.3	70.3	68.9	60.7	49.2	37.4	30.7	48.5
W.Va.__ Parkersburg__	63	33.7	34.6	43.8	53.3	63.5	71.9	75.2	73.9	67.9	56.3	44.5	35.5	54.5
Wis.__ Madison__	49	17.6	20.1	31.3	45.6	57.0	67.3	72.5	70.1	61.5	50.2	35.2	22.9	46.1
Wyo.__ Cheyenne__	81	24.8	27.3	33.6	41.2	50.6	60.0	67.6	66.0	57.3	46.0	35.4	26.4	44.9
Alaska__ Juneau__	9	26.4	25.8	72.5	38.2	17.3	56.5	55.2	58.9	49.6	41.6	32.1	27.3	40.2
H.__ Honolulu__	47	71.6	71.6	71.8	73.1	74.9	76.4	77.5	78.3	77.2	76.9	74.8	72.4	75.0
P.R.__ San Juan__	53	74.9	74.9	75.4	76.7	78.7	80.0	80.0	80.3	80.3	80.0	78.4	76.4	78.1

Source. Department of Commerce, Weather Bureau; records.

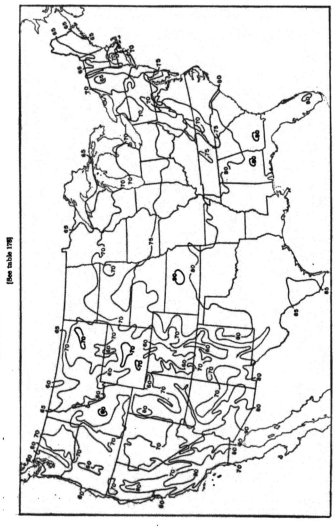

FIG. XIV.—AVERAGE JULY TEMPERATURE

[See table 175]

No. 172.—Average Daily Maximum Temperatures

[For period of record through 1951]

STATION	Length of record (yrs.)	Jan.	Feb.	Mar.	Apr.	May	June	July	Aug.	Sept.	Oct.	Nov.	Dec.	Annual
Ala. Mobile	80	60.6	63.9	67.2	75.2	82.6	88.3	89.6	89.6	86.2	78.0	68.1	62.1	75.9
Ariz. Montgomery	79	58.0	60.9	66.0	75.6	82.5	89.5	90.9	90.0	86.3	77.0	66.2	58.6	73.4
Phoenix	68	64.9	69.1	74.5	82.7	91.3	101.0	103.6	101.5	97.5	86.5	74.6	65.6	84.4
Calif. Little Rock	72	50.3	53.6	62.6	72.0	79.2	87.2	90.4	89.7	84.0	74.1	61.2	52.2	71.4
Fresno	64	54.4	61.3	65.5	74.8	82.1	91.2	99.0	97.3	89.5	76.7	64.6	55.1	75.3
Los Angeles	74	64.5	65.5	67.3	68.6	71.9	76.2	81.2	82.0	80.6	76.3	72.7	66.5	72.9
San Francisco	77	55.1	58.5	60.6	62.1	63.3	64.4	64.3	64.2	68.4	67.8	63.0	56.3	62.5
Colo. Denver	80	42.6	44.8	51.2	60.8	68.6	79.9	83.6	84.4	76.8	64.8	52.0	44.6	63.0
D. C. Washington	80	42.5	44.0	52.9	63.9	74.5	82.7	86.7	84.4	78.3	67.4	54.9	44.6	64.8
Fla. Jacksonville	78	68.0	68.3	72.2	77.5	83.6	88.3	89.9	89.5	85.7	78.5	70.9	65.5	77.8
Miami	41	74.3	74.6	76.6	79.4	82.4	85.3	86.9	87.3	86.0	82.7	77.6	75.3	80.7
Ga. Atlanta	73	51.7	54.4	62.2	70.8	79.3	85.9	87.4	86.3	82.0	72.1	60.7	52.6	70.5
Savannah	13	34.7	43.7	51.8	62.7	70.7	76.9	90.0	90.0	77.0	64.5	39.0	40.3	61.5
Boise	79	31.9	38.2	34.7	55.7	78.5	80.9	79.0	73.7	61.6	50.0	35.6	31.1	51.7
Chicago	73	36.5	38.7	49.0	61.3	72.4	81.5	85.9	85.7	77.0	65.1	49.9	34.2	55.8
Wichita	73	30.1	36.6	46.9	60.6	71.5	80.7	85.6	84.0	75.0	64.6	42.5	34.2	58.6
Louisville	63	41.3	44.2	55.9	67.0	75.1	85.2	90.6	90.1	82.0	70.3	55.2	44.3	66.6
New Orleans	70	43.6	45.1	54.5	66.7	76.0	84.4	88.1	85.4	80.5	69.2	54.9	44.9	66.1
Key West	79	62.8	65.2	71.1	76.9	83.2	90.8	89.6	89.8	86.3	78.5	66.7	63.6	77.1
Newport	79	30.9	33.9	36.1	45.4	55.2	68.4	73.9	68.9	62.8	54.0	43.2	32.6	52.6
Boston	80	36.4	36.6	44.4	54.7	66.1	75.4	80.6	78.4	71.9	61.9	50.3	39.5	58.0
Mich. Detroit	79	31.6	32.3	41.5	56.0	67.4	77.0	82.1	79.7	72.8	60.7	46.0	35.0	56.8
Sault Ste. Marie	68	23.2	23.1	31.7	45.0	59.2	66.7	74.5	72.4	64.6	52.8	37.1	27.1	48.9
Minneapolis	72	22.1	26.0	36.2	56.3	67.9	77.2	83.0	80.4	71.7	60.0	40.2	26.9	53.9
Vicksburg	76	57.1	60.2	67.7	74.9	82.1	88.4	90.1	90.0	85.9	76.6	65.2	58.5	74.2
Kansas City	80	38.3	41.4	53.0	64.7	74.2	83.6	88.7	87.3	79.0	66.6	50.9	41.4	64.5
St. Louis	79	40.2	43.2	53.6	65.1	75.1	84.0	88.4	88.7	79.6	68.4	53.9	43.1	64.2
Helena	72	28.4	33.5	41.5	54.5	65.1	71.1	81.2	79.7	67.8	56.0	41.5	32.6	54.2
North Platte	77	37.3	30.3	43.2	58.6	68.9	77.9	86.0	85.8	73.6	60.3	42.7	31.7	57.4
Omaha	79	36.0	39.9	49.5	61.7	71.0	80.7	87.4	85.0	76.8	65.2	49.7	35.5	62.2
	79	31.0	33.2	47.0	61.7	72.4	81.7	87.4	85.0	76.8	65.2	50.7	35.5	60.6
N. C. Asheville	78	38.5	44.2	52.5	61.7	70.2	79.5	86.9	86.4	77.3	65.0	52.4	41.4	63.4
Charlotte	21	40.5	45.5	55.1	65.1	64.8	72.5	78.5	76.3	73.5	64.1	53.3	43.9	56.5
Raleigh	61	44.1	52.6	60.5	70.0	79.1	86.6	91.9	89.6	82.6	71.0	57.5	46.5	70.0
	61	31.6	32.0	41.7	55.5	66.0	77.9	82.7	80.3	72.8	60.8	44.9	34.5	57.2
	80	31.9	31.6	40.1	55.2	66.3	76.2	80.8	78.4	72.0	59.8	44.9	34.0	60.9
N. C.	45	48.4	48.9	57.4	66.1	74.4	81.1	83.2	82.3	77.7	62.8	48.7	44.2	64.2
	77	18.6	21.9	35.2	54.6	66.7	75.5	83.2	81.4	71.0	57.5	38.8	25.1	53.4
	44	33.0	34.3	43.0	56.3	69.3	78.9	83.5	81.3	74.7	62.6	44.5	33.6	58.2
Oklahoma City	61	47.2	51.1	61.5	71.0	77.9	87.0	91.8	91.9	84.5	73.7	60.0	49.4	70.6
Ohio Cleveland	77	44.2	45.6	54.6	61.4	67.3	72.3	78.4	78.0	72.2	62.8	52.3	46.4	61.6
Columbus	88	37.3	37.7	48.3	61.4	71.9	80.2	84.5	82.0	75.5	63.9	50.8	39.7	61.0
Portland	78	36.7	39.6	48.8	60.5	72.1	80.2	84.0	82.1	76.2	64.5	50.5	40.6	61.5
Philadelphia	78	32.2	38.5	40.4	57.9	69.1	78.6	85.5	83.7	74.5	61.3	42.5	29.3	56.0
Pittsburgh	61	47.4	49.7	59.2	69.2	78.2	86.0	89.9	87.9	82.5	71.9	58.3	49.4	69.1
Columbia	48	44.9	52.6	61.9	70.8	78.4	87.9	91.1	90.2	83.7	72.7	60.4	50.3	70.8
	63	37.0	38.3	49.0	62.1	73.5	85.6	90.9	94.4	91.6	86.5	77.6	65.9	57.2	76.4
Fort Worth	62	50.1	56.3	63.0	71.7	75.6	82.4	90.7	94.2	84.9	88.0	78.6	66.7	57.5	76.0
	63	35.1	46.0	71.7	77.9	84.2	90.2	92.2	92.5	88.1	81.1	70.5	63.7	78.3

Source: Department of Commerce, Weather Bureau; records.

No. 180.—AVERAGE DAILY MINIMUM TEMPERATURES

[For period of record through 1951]

STATION		Length of record (yrs.)	Jan.	Feb.	Mar.	Apr.	May	June	July	Aug.	Sept.	Oct.	Nov.	Dec.	Annual
Ala	Mobile	80	43.8	46.2	52.0	58.5	65.8	72.3	74.0	73.7	70.2	59.9	50.0	44.7	59.3
	Montgomery	79	40.3	42.4	48.2	55.2	63.2	70.2	72.4	71.9	67.5	56.5	46.0	40.9	56.2
Ariz	Phoenix	56	38.8	42.7	47.0	53.3	60.5	69.2	77.4	76.1	69.5	56.7	45.4	39.7	56.4
Ark	Little Rock	72	33.8	36.1	43.9	52.9	60.7	68.8	72.0	71.0	65.0	53.8	42.7	35.9	53.1
Calif	Fresno	64	37.7	41.3	44.3	48.1	53.2	59.5	64.8	63.2	58.0	50.8	42.8	38.2	50.2
	Los Angeles	74	46.1	47.1	48.8	51.0	53.7	56.8	60.1	60.9	59.1	55.4	51.3	47.9	53.2
	San Francisco	77	44.8	47.0	48.3	49.4	50.8	52.3	53.0	53.5	54.7	52.8	50.7	46.6	50.4
Colo	Denver	80	18.4	21.1	27.1	35.7	44.6	53.4	59.5	58.3	49.3	38.5	27.7	20.7	37.9
D. C	Washington	80	27.1	27.6	34.8	43.9	54.4	63.3	67.9	66.1	59.5	47.9	37.7	29.5	46.6
Fla	Jacksonville	78	47.6	49.0	54.1	59.9	66.5	72.0	73.8	73.8	71.5	63.5	54.0	48.1	61.2
	Miami	41	62.3	61.7	64.4	68.2	71.7	74.9	76.2	76.8	75.7	72.7	66.6	63.4	69.6
Ga	Atlanta	78	36.6	37.0	43.3	51.4	59.9	67.2	69.6	69.0	64.4	54.5	43.2	36.7	52.7
Idaho	Boise	12	19.0	27.0	31.0	37.6	44.4	50.0	58.3	56.6	48.4	40.2	30.8	25.0	39.0
Ill	Chicago	79	17.9	19.9	29.2	39.5	49.5	59.6	65.8	65.1	58.0	46.9	33.5	23.2	42.3
Ind	Indianapolis	81	21.8	23.3	32.2	43.1	53.5	62.8	66.7	64.7	57.8	46.8	34.8	25.6	44.4
Iowa	Des Moines	73	12.4	15.7	27.5	40.4	51.3	61.1	65.6	63.4	55.1	43.6	29.6	18.1	40.3
Kans	Wichita	63	22.7	25.0	34.1	45.7	55.1	64.6	69.3	68.4	60.3	48.9	35.3	26.1	46.3
Ky	Louisville	79	27.2	28.6	35.8	46.6	56.3	65.3	68.9	67.2	60.6	49.1	38.1	29.5	47.9
La	New Orleans	78	47.4	49.6	55.1	61.4	68.0	74.0	75.6	75.7	72.9	64.4	54.4	48.6	62.3
Maine	Eastport	76	13.3	14.2	23.4	32.6	40.4	47.0	52.1	53.1	49.2	41.7	31.6	18.7	34.8
Mass	Boston	80	21.0	20.8	28.9	38.6	48.9	57.9	63.9	62.4	55.8	45.8	35.6	25.1	42.1
Mich	Detroit	78	18.8	18.6	26.7	37.3	48.4	58.5	63.5	61.8	55.3	44.6	33.3	23.4	40.8
	Sault Ste. Marie	63	6.7	4.4	14.5	28.9	39.1	47.7	53.2	53.2	47.4	37.9	26.7	14.4	31.2
Minn	Minneapolis	61	5.3	7.9	21.7	36.4	48.0	58.1	63.2	60.8	52.3	40.9	25.4	12.1	36.0
Miss	Vicksburg	78	40.3	42.8	49.3	56.3	63.5	70.3	72.6	72.2	67.2	57.1	47.2	41.8	56.7
Mo	Kansas City	63	21.6	23.7	33.7	45.7	55.6	65.1	69.8	68.2	60.2	49.1	35.7	25.7	46.2
	St. Louis	79	24.5	26.8	36.0	47.1	57.3	66.5	71.0	66.1	61.8	50.5	37.6	28.5	48.1
Mont	Helena	72	11.5	14.7	22.8	32.9	40.9	48.0	54.1	52.7	43.7	35.1	24.0	16.5	33.1
	Miles City	60	6.5	8.8	20.5	34.8	45.0	54.0	60.7	57.8	47.2	35.9	23.0	12.2	33.9
Nebr	North Platte	77	11.7	15.5	24.0	36.3	46.9	56.5	62.3	60.3	50.2	37.2	24.1	15.8	36.7
	Omaha	79	13.4	17.1	28.1	41.5	52.6	62.3	67.4	65.3	56.3	44.6	30.0	19.1	41.5
Nev	Winnemucca	78	16.9	22.2	27.0	33.1	40.0	47.4	53.9	50.3	40.8	31.7	23.8	18.7	33.8
N. J	Atlantic City	78	26.8	26.9	33.2	41.6	51.9	61.3	66.9	66.9	61.5	50.5	39.6	30.1	46.4
N. Mex	Albuquerque	21	22.0	26.4	31.8	40.3	49.7	58.1	64.0	62.7	56.0	43.9	29.9	24.6	42.5
N. Y	Albany	78	15.6	15.4	25.4	37.1	48.7	57.8	62.7	60.6	53.4	42.4	32.4	20.8	39.4
	New York	80	24.8	24.3	31.5	41.2	52.1	61.3	66.8	65.8	59.7	49.2	38.4	28.3	45.3
	Rochester	80	18.3	17.1	25.2	36.1	47.2	56.7	61.8	60.1	53.6	42.9	32.9	22.9	39.6
N. C	Asheville	49	29.7	29.9	36.5	43.7	51.9	59.7	63.0	62.3	56.7	45.3	35.6	30.0	45.4
	Raleigh	65	33.6	34.1	40.7	48.6	58.0	65.9	69.2	68.2	62.8	51.5	41.5	34.6	50.7
N. Dak	Bismarck	77	-2.3	1.1	14.8	31.6	42.6	52.5	57.9	55.2	45.1	33.8	18.2	5.5	29.6
Ohio	Cleveland	46	17.4	18.3	26.0	36.1	46.9	56.5	60.3	59.2	52.9	42.8	31.3	22.6	39.2
Okla	Oklahoma City	61	27.7	30.1	38.7	49.3	58.1	67.0	70.8	70.3	63.1	51.8	39.0	30.5	49.7
Oreg	Portland	77	34.3	36.8	40.1	43.6	48.4	53.1	56.8	56.6	52.8	47.4	41.0	37.2	45.7
Pa	Harrisburg	63	23.9	23.6	32.0	41.7	52.4	61.0	65.6	63.7	57.2	46.2	36.2	27.1	44.2
	Pittsburgh	78	23.6	23.4	31.1	40.9	51.7	60.5	64.5	62.7	56.8	45.7	35.4	26.9	43.6
S. C	Charleston	78	43.2	44.4	50.2	57.3	65.8	72.5	75.0	74.6	70.8	60.9	50.7	44.1	59.1
S. Dak	Huron	70	2.0	5.5	19.7	34.1	44.9	55.3	60.4	58.1	48.3	35.8	21.0	9.2	32.9
Tenn	Nashville	81	31.1	32.4	40.3	49.4	58.2	66.7	69.9	68.6	61.9	50.4	39.6	33.1	50.1
Tex	Amarillo	60	24.4	26.1	33.5	43.2	52.7	61.1	66.6	65.6	56.8	46.5	33.2	26.5	45.0
	El Paso	72	32.3	36.8	42.3	49.9	58.4	67.0	69.8	68.4	62.7	51.7	39.4	33.5	51.0
	Fort Worth	53	35.8	38.2	46.2	54.4	62.7	70.7	73.9	74.1	67.6	57.1	45.9	37.8	55.4
	Houston	61	44.7	47.0	53.5	60.1	66.5	72.4	74.3	74.3	70.3	61.5	52.1	46.3	60.3
Utah	Salt Lake City	78	21.8	26.5	32.8	40.2	47.7	55.8	64.4	62.9	53.0	42.7	32.3	25.2	42.1
Vt	Burlington	60	10.2	9.9	21.4	34.0	45.8	55.3	60.4	58.1	50.9	40.6	30.0	16.3	36.1
Va	Norfolk	77	34.2	34.3	40.2	48.1	57.8	66.3	70.6	70.1	65.5	55.0	44.5	36.3	51.9
	Richmond	54	30.3	30.1	37.7	45.7	55.7	64.2	68.4	67.1	61.2	49.6	39.0	31.4	48.4
Wash	Seattle	61	35.8	37.1	39.3	42.8	47.6	51.9	55.1	55.2	51.9	47.0	41.5	38.1	45.3
	Spokane	71	20.9	24.2	31.1	37.5	44.6	50.8	56.2	54.5	46.6	38.4	30.9	25.5	38.4
W. Va	Parkersburg	63	25.5	25.5	33.6	42.6	52.4	61.4	64.9	63.4	57.0	45.3	35.4	27.7	44.6
Wis	Madison	53	10.2	12.5	23.8	37.2	48.8	58.9	63.9	61.8	54.0	42.6	28.5	16.6	38.2
Wyo	Cheyenne	79	14.7	16.0	21.3	29.4	38.3	47.2	53.4	52.2	43.1	33.1	23.6	17.5	32.5
Alaska	Juneau	9	20.0	19.5	26.7	31.5	38.4	44.5	47.4	45.5	43.0	36.3	27.3	22.6	33.6
T. H	Honolulu	47	66.7	66.8	67.1	68.5	70.3	72.1	73.1	73.8	73.5	72.6	70.4	68.6	70.3
P. R	San Juan	53	69.9	69.8	70.2	71.6	73.6	74.9	75.4	75.7	75.2	74.5	73.2	71.5	73.0

Source: Department of Commerce, Weather Bureau; records.

No. 181.—Highest Temperature of Record

[For period of record through 1951]

STATION		Length of record (yrs.)	Jan.	Feb.	Mar.	Apr.	May	June	July	Aug.	Sept.	Oct.	Nov.	Dec.	Annual
Ala	Mobile	80	83	82	91	90	99	102	103	101	103	95	86	80	103
	Montgomery	79	83	84	90	92	99	106	107	108	105	96	88	83	107
Ariz	Phoenix	36	84	92	95	103	114	118	118	115	116	105	95	87	118
Ark	Little Rock	72	83	87	90	94	97	105	110	108	106	93	84	78	110
Calif	Fresno	64	73	84	87	101	110	112	115	113	111	100	89	76	115
	Los Angeles	74	90	92	99	100	103	105	109	106	108	104	96	92	109
	San Francisco	81	78	80	86	89	97	100	99	92	101	96	83	74	101
Colo	Denver	80	76	77	82	86	95	99	102	105	97	90	79	79	105
D. C	Washington	81	80	84	93	95	97	102	106	105	104	98	87	74	106
Fla	Jacksonville	80	84	86	91	92	99	102	104	101	99	95	86	83	104
	Miami	41	83	85	88	91	92	94	95	93	93	91	88	85	95
Ga	Atlanta	73	79	78	87	93	97	102	103	101	102	94	82	75	103
Idaho	Boise	12	58	66	76	92	95	109	104	106	102	88	78	60	109
Ill	Chicago	81	67	68	82	91	98	102	105	103	100	90	82	69	105
Ind	Indianapolis	81	71	73	84	90	95	101	106	103	100	92	82	80	106
Iowa	Des Moines	73	65	78	88	92	105	103	110	110	102	95	83	75	110
Kans	Wichita	63	74	82	92	98	100	109	112	114	108	95	83	75	114
Ky	Louisville	79	79	78	88	91	98	102	107	105	102	91	83	74	107
La	New Orleans	78	83	85	90	91	97	102	102	100	99	94	80	84	102
Maine	Eastport	79	58	54	76	81	90	92	93	93	92	83	67	60	93
Mass	Boston	80	72	68	86	89	97	100	104	101	102	90	83	69	104
Mich	Detroit	81	67	68	82	88	95	104	105	104	100	89	81	65	105
	Sault Ste. Marie	63	48	50	75	83	91	98	98	98	92	83	74	54	98
Minn	Minneapolis	61	58	64	83	91	106	104	108	103	104	90	77	63	108
Miss	Vicksburg	78	82	84	92	92	97	101	102	101	104	94	86	82	104
Mo	Kansas City	63	75	81	91	95	103	108	110	113	109	98	83	74	113
	St. Louis	81	75	84	92	93	96	104	110	108	103	93	83	75	110
Mont	Helena	72	63	69	73	86	95	102	103	103	96	84	71	64	103
	Miles City	60	66	71	88	91	101	108	111	110	106	91	76	71	111
Nebr	North Platte	77	71	74	88	95	99	104	109	108	105	96	83	76	109
	Omaha	79	69	78	91	94	103	107	114	111	104	96	80	72	114
Nev	Winnemucca	73	61	69	82	88	98	104	108	106	103	90	75	70	108
N. J	Atlantic City	78	68	77	84	90	95	97	102	104	94	91	80	65	104
N. Mex	Albuquerque	21	67	70	81	88	98	101	102	101	98	87	76	66	104
N. Y	Albany	78	71	66	85	93	97	100	104	102	98	91	82	67	104
	New York	81	71	73	84	91	95	97	102	102	100	90	81	70	102
	Rochester	80	74	70	86	90	93	98	99	98	96	92	81	70	102
N. C	Asheville	49	77	80	87	89	93	96	98	98	104	103	101	97	99
	Raleigh	65	79	82	94	95	99	102	104	103	105	97	87	79	114
N. Dak	Bismarck	77	60	65	81	90	102	107	114	109	105	91	74	66	114
Ohio	Cleveland	81	73	73	83	88	92	101	103	102	98	97	86	80	113
Okla	Oklahoma City	61	83	90	97	97	98	99	107	109	113	106	97	86	113
Oreg	Portland	77	65	68	83	93	99	102	107	102	102	88	73	65	107
Pa	Harrisburg	63	73	74	86	93	97	100	103	104	99	97	84	71	104
	Pittsburgh	77	75	77	84	90	95	98	103	103	102	91	80	73	104
S. C	Charleston	81	82	82	94	93	99	104	104	102	100	95	84	81	104
S. Dak	Huron	70	64	70	89	94	106	109	111	110	106	97	79	71	111
Tenn	Nashville	81	78	79	89	90	96	101	106	105	104	93	85	76	106
Tex	Amarillo	60	83	84	96	96	100	107	106	106	102	95	86	83	107
	El Paso	65	77	86	93	95	104	106	107	103	103	94	85	77	107
	Fort Worth	53	93	96	100	100	107	107	109	112	108	106	88	90	112
	Houston	62	84	90	96	93	98	103	104	104	106	99	89	84	106
Utah	Salt Lake City	78	62	69	78	85	93	103	105	102	97	88	74	66	105
Vt	Burlington	66	64	59	84	86	92	96	100	101	95	85	75	67	101
Va	Norfolk	81	80	82	92	95	98	102	104	105	100	94	87	78	105
	Richmond	54	80	82	94	96	98	104	105	107	101	99	88	77	107
Wash	Seattle	61	67	70	81	87	92	98	100	96	92	82	70	65	100
	Spokane	71	62	60	74	90	97	100	108	104	98	87	70	60	108
W. Va	Parkersburg	63	78	77	89	93	96	99	104	106	99	91	83	75	106
Wis	Madison	83	58	63	82	89	101	100	107	101	97	86	77	62	107
Wyo	Cheyenne	79	64	70	77	82	88	97	100	96	92	85	75	69	100
Alaska	Juneau	9	48	46	49	56	82	83	83	78	72	61	56	54	83
T. H	Honolulu	47	83	84	84	83	85	86	87	88	88	87	85	85	88
P. R	San Juan	53	88	91	91	93	94	93	92	93	94	94	93	90	94

Source: Department of Commerce, Weather Bureau; records.

No. 182.—Lowest Temperature of Record

[For period of record through 1951]

STATION		Length of record (yrs.)	Jan.	Feb.	Mar.	Apr.	May	June	July	Aug.	Sept.	Oct.	Nov.	Dec.	Annual
Ala.	Mobile	80	11	-1	24	32	44	50	62	57	48	34	22	14	-1
	Montgomery	79	5	-5	20	30	43	48	61	58	45	31	13	8	-5
Ariz.	Phoenix	56	16	24	30	35	39	49	63	58	49	36	27	22	16
Ark.	Little Rock	72	-8	-12	11	28	39	51	56	52	37	27	10	5	-12
Calif.	Fresno	64	17	24	27	34	38	42	50	51	37	30	27	18	17
	Los Angeles	74	28	28	31	36	40	46	49	49	44	40	34	30	28
	San Francisco	81	29	33	33	40	42	46	47	46	47	43	38	27	27
Colo.	Denver	80	-29	-25	-11	4	19	30	42	40	21	-2	-18	-25	-29
D. C.	Washington	81	-14	-15	4	15	33	43	52	49	36	26	11	-13	-15
Fla.	Jacksonville	80	15	10	25	34	46	54	65	64	49	37	23	14	10
	Miami	41	31	27	34	44	50	65	66	66	67	52	36	30	27
Ga.	Atlanta	73	-2	-9	8	25	38	39	58	55	43	28	3	1	-9
Idaho	Boise	12	-17	-10	12	22	27	34	44	41	32	20	15	-1	-17
Ill.	Chicago	81	-20	-21	-12	17	27	35	49	46	29	14	-2	-23	-23
Ind.	Indianapolis	81	-25	-18	-1	19	31	39	48	44	30	22	-5	-15	-25
Iowa	Des Moines	73	-30	-26	-12	11	26	37	48	40	26	7	-10	-21	-30
Kans.	Wichita	63	-15	-22	-3	15	27	44	53	45	32	14	4	-10	-22
Ky.	Louisville	79	-20	-19	3	21	33	43	49	45	33	23	-1	-7	-20
La.	New Orleans	78	15	7	26	38	52	58	66	63	64	40	29	19	7
Maine	Eastport	79	-20	-23	-10	2	24	30	45	44	30	22	-13	-23	-23
Mass.	Boston	80	-13	-18	-8	11	31	41	50	46	34	25	-2	-17	-18
Mich.	Detroit	81	-16	-20	-7	8	28	38	48	43	30	22	0	-24	-24
	Sault Ste. Marie	63	-32	-37	-27	-13	21	31	36	32	27	15	-12	-24	-37
Minn.	Minneapolis	61	-34	-33	-27	6	22	34	44	40	26	10	-13	-27	-34
Miss.	Vicksburg	78	3	-1	17	31	43	52	59	54	41	31	20	10	-1
Mo.	Kansas City	63	-20	-22	-3	16	27	44	53	46	34	17	4	-13	-22
	St. Louis	81	-22	-18	3	20	32	44	55	52	36	21	3	-15	-22
Mont.	Helena	72	-42	-41	-26	-10	22	31	37	29	6	-8	-22	-40	-42
	Miles City	60	-46	-49	-30	-7	18	32	41	34	17	-8	-26	-43	-49
Nebr.	North Platte	77	-35	-35	-21	-3	19	33	40	36	21	4	-25	-30	-35
	Omaha	79	-32	-26	-16	6	25	39	50	44	30	8	-14	-20	-32
Nev.	Winnemucca	73	-36	-26	-3	12	17	29	33	26	16	10	-9	-27	-36
N. J.	Atlantic City	78	-4	-9	8	15	33	45	52	48	37	29	10	-7	-9
N. Mex.	Albuquerque	21	-1	-6	8	18	30	43	54	53	35	22	5	7	-6
N. Y.	Albany	78	-26	-22	-21	9	29	35	44	35	24	19	-11	-21	-26
	New York	81	-6	-14	3	12	34	44	54	51	39	27	7	-13	-14
	Rochester	80	-14	-23	-7	7	27	35	44	43	28	19	1	-16	-22
N. C.	Asheville	49	-6	-6	7	20	31	40	46	45	35	20	1	-4	-6
	Raleigh	65	2	-2	13	23	34	46	53	51	39	30	14	0	-2
N. Dak.	Bismarck	77	-45	-45	-36	-3	13	31	32	32	10	-10	-28	-42	-45
Ohio	Cleveland	81	-17	-16	-5	11	26	38	46	45	32	24	0	-12	-17
Okla.	Oklahoma City	61	-11	-17	1	20	33	46	55	49	35	16	9	-2	-17
Oreg.	Portland	77	-2	7	20	28	32	39	43	43	35	20	11	3	-2
Pa.	Harrisburg	63	-14	-13	5	11	32	43	49	46	32	25	10	-3	-14
	Pittsburgh	77	-16	-20	-1	11	27	38	46	45	34	20	1	-9	-20
S. C.	Charleston	81	10	7	24	32	45	49	61	62	49	37	17	12	7
S. Dak.	Huron	70	-43	-37	-25	-5	20	31	40	33	18	-6	-28	-34	-43
Tenn.	Nashville	81	-10	-13	3	25	36	42	51	47	36	26	-1	-2	-13
Tex.	Amarillo	60	-11	-16	-3	13	26	38	51	48	32	15	4	-6	-16
	El Paso	72	-6	5	14	26	36	46	56	52	41	26	11	-5	-6
	Fort Worth	53	-2	-8	10	30	34	48	56	55	40	24	19	7	-8
	Houston	63	5	6	21	34	45	55	55	54	45	33	23	15	5
Utah	Salt Lake City	78	-20	-13	0	18	25	32	43	42	29	22	-2	-10	-20
Vt.	Burlington	68	-27	-28	-24	5	25	33	43	38	25	17	-3	-29	-29
Va.	Norfolk	81	5	2	14	23	38	49	57	56	40	31	17	5	2
	Richmond	54	-1	-3	12	19	35	43	52	49	40	28	14	-1	-3
Wash.	Seattle	61	3	4	20	30	36	40	46	46	36	29	15	12	3
	Spokane	71	-30	-23	-10	14	29	34	41	37	22	9	-13	-19	-30
W. Va.	Parkersburg	63	-16	-27	-3	15	29	38	47	45	32	20	4	-10	-27
Wis.	Madison	83	-29	-28	-13	8	27	38	48	43	29	12	-14	-26	-29
Wyo.	Cheyenne	79	-38	-34	-21	-6	8	25	33	25	16	-5	-21	-28	-38
Alaska	Juneau	9	-19	-12	-2	7	26	33	36	27	27	16	-3	-21	-21
T. H.	Honolulu	47	57	56	57	59	63	64	67	66	63	63	61	59	56
P. R.	San Juan	53	63	62	63	65	66	66	70	68	69	68	66	62	62

Source: Department of Commerce, Weather Bureau; records.

No. 183.—Average Precipitation, Inches

[For period of record through 1931]

	STATION	Length of record (yrs.)	Jan.	Feb.	Mar.	Apr.	May	June	July	Aug.	Sept.	Oct.	Nov.	Dec.	Annual
Ala.	Mobile	81	4.74	4.91	6.60	4.05	4.42	5.64	7.28	6.30	5.24	3.32	3.66	4.93	62.40
	Montgomery	59	4.57	5.01	6.26	4.71	3.45	4.19	5.34	4.07	3.17	2.28	2.63	4.73	51.39
Ariz.	Phoenix	50	.80	.60	.65	.41	.13	.06	1.02	1.04	.87	.49	.64	.88	7.75
Ark.	Little Rock	72	4.66	3.89	4.68	4.60	4.81	3.60	3.37	3.46	3.06	2.89	4.10	4.14	47.95
Calif.	Fresno	74	1.89	1.65	1.61	.90	.37	.11	.01	.01	.16	.55	.87	1.55	9.41
	Los Angeles	74	2.90	3.23	2.68	1.01	.35	.07	.01	.00	.20	.61	1.14	2.87	15.10
	San Francisco	103	4.65	3.73	3.11	1.51	.67	.15	.01	.01	.37	1.03	2.45	4.41	21.93
Colo.	Denver	60	.46	.64	1.08	2.03	2.81	1.40	1.46	1.40	1.00	1.02	.68	.46	14.06
D. C.	Washington	61	3.36	3.01	3.56	3.25	3.70	3.99	4.31	4.51	3.60	2.94	2.56	3.09	42.06
Fla.	Jacksonville	60	2.74	2.93	3.25	2.73	3.88	6.02	6.68	6.13	7.20	4.75	1.97	2.56	51.16
	Miami	41	2.11	1.94	2.34	3.43	6.80	6.68	5.48	5.92	8.37	7.88	1.99	1.76	55.20
Ga.	Atlanta	78	4.72	4.70	5.31	3.92	3.40	3.92	4.89	4.13	3.16	2.39	3.12	4.60	46.41
Idaho	Boise	42	1.15	1.47	1.09	1.09	1.20	1.04	.10	.15	.48	1.09	1.42	1.48	11.08
Ill.	Chicago	61	1.96	1.88	2.20	2.87	3.40	3.60	3.20	3.13	3.17	2.46	2.07	2.02	33.08
Ind.	Indianapolis	63	3.09	2.88	3.88	3.67	3.85	4.12	3.65	3.02	2.89	2.25	3.02	2.85	40.00
Iowa	Des Moines	73	1.16	1.15	1.87	2.78	4.61	4.86	3.86	3.90	3.45	2.40	1.37	1.28	32.09
Kans.	Wichita	60	.88	1.24	1.76	3.13	4.41	4.66	3.23	3.18	3.21	2.25	1.04	1.07	30.64
Ky.	Louisville	79	4.15	3.40	4.66	3.90	3.77	3.95	4.26	3.27	2.64	2.55	3.64	4.60	44.35
La.	New Orleans	81	4.61	4.40	5.14	4.87	4.80	5.70	6.66	6.00	5.46	3.44	4.06	4.90	56.05
Maine	Eastport	70	3.61	3.21	3.66	2.87	2.95	3.04	3.12	2.98	3.00	3.80	4.05	3.35	38.95
Mass.	Boston	81	3.97	3.28	3.72	3.48	3.17	3.15	3.27	3.58	3.11	3.31	3.71	3.35	42.09
Mich.	Detroit	61	2.11	2.12	2.45	2.62	3.41	3.36	3.30	2.72	2.60	2.40	2.42	2.20	31.72
	Sault Ste. Marie	61	2.01	1.45	1.77	2.11	2.46	2.01	2.84	3.12	3.09	3.04	2.55	2.24	29.14
Minn.	Minneapolis	61	.85	.87	1.47	2.11	3.47	4.22	3.40	3.12	2.72	1.90	1.15	.92	25.71
Miss.	Vicksburg	60	5.39	4.67	6.65	5.36	4.25	4.75	4.55	4.04	3.35	2.76	4.55	5.56	55.71
Mo.	Kansas City	115	1.37	1.61	2.50	3.80	5.76	4.40	4.44	3.86	4.24	2.87	1.86	2.46	39.25
	St. Louis	113	2.33	2.24	3.50	3.76	4.40	4.44	3.47	3.06	3.24	2.77	2.49	2.72	38.44
Mont.	Helena	72	.77	.67	.75	1.00	1.90	2.26	1.10	.80	1.02	.80	.67	.72	12.44
	Miles City	76	.56	.60	.80	1.05	1.94	2.73	1.40	1.16	1.02	.88	.60	.50	13.01
Nebr.	North Platte	77	.41	.43	.97	2.13	3.11	3.18	3.06	2.31	1.55	1.07	.60	.50	18.50
	Omaha	81	.73	.90	1.35	2.80	5.04	4.07	3.70	3.23	3.05	2.19	1.13	.89	29.50
Nev.	Winnemucca	62	1.06	.93	.91	.81	.84	.67	.23	.17	.35	.70	.90	1.01	8.44
N. J.	Atlantic City	78	3.80	3.02	3.02	3.20	3.02	3.07	4.25	4.18	3.16	3.16	3.16	3.80	40.90
N. Mex.	Albuquerque	71	.37	.44	.58	.60	.70	.55	1.28	1.40	1.14	.81	.44	.57	8.89
N. Y.	Albany	100	2.31	2.38	2.89	2.70	3.33	3.34	3.50	3.34	3.34	2.80	2.90	2.57	34.80
	New York	103	3.36	3.26	3.55	3.32	3.33	3.44	4.25	4.26	3.48	3.45	3.33	3.32	42.50
	Rochester	105	2.38	2.05	2.70	2.53	2.97	3.04	3.25	2.74	2.73	2.48	2.40	2.40	30.04
N. C.	Asheville	45	3.36	3.86	5.14	3.74	4.14	4.97	5.29	5.41	3.92	2.46	3.07	3.05	49.44
	Raleigh	65	3.34	3.70	3.74	3.46	3.95	4.47	5.39	5.41	3.44	2.80	2.83	3.30	44.44
N. Dak.	Bismarck	77	.49	.46	.91	1.31	2.22	3.36	2.48	1.86	1.31	.87	.60	.46	16.22
Ohio	Cleveland	80	2.51	2.33	2.71	2.44	3.12	3.32	3.45	2.77	2.83	2.44	3.04	2.45	34.62
Okla.	Oklahoma City	61	1.36	1.21	2.11	3.38	5.07	3.97	2.65	2.73	3.00	2.72	2.05	1.32	31.55
Oreg.	Portland	51	6.90	5.25	4.87	2.80	2.15	1.65	.56	.61	1.84	3.40	6.18	7.00	43.89
Pa.	Harrisburg	60	2.91	2.44	3.10	2.89	3.55	3.89	3.70	3.80	3.07	2.68	2.63	2.88	36.81
	Pittsburgh	83	2.97	2.60	3.18	3.01	3.22	3.85	4.06	3.36	2.55	2.49	2.33	2.77	36.21
S. C.	Charleston	82	2.66	3.19	3.40	2.75	3.34	5.47	7.38	6.68	5.17	3.36	1.91	3.92	47.30
Tenn.	Memphis	70	.96	.63	1.00	2.16	2.72	3.76	5.97	4.62	3.42	3.30	1.31	.96	30.50
Tex.	Nashville	61	4.46	4.15	5.11	4.14	3.76	3.12	3.97	3.03	2.28	1.74	4.07	.77	49.80
	Amarillo	60	.57	.74	.93	1.66	3.12	2.97	.82	1.72	1.39	1.29	.69	.82	20.06
	El Paso	48	.46	.41	.38	.27	.35	.75	2.16	2.52	1.22	.80	.43	2.03	32.06
	Fort Worth	61	1.97	2.06	2.39	3.74	4.75	3.15	2.65	2.82	2.45	2.78	2.24	2.02	32.06
	Houston	66	3.71	2.96	3.12	3.43	4.74	4.37	4.27	3.73	4.02	3.39	3.11	4.71	45.96
Utah	Salt Lake City	78	1.36	1.44	1.94	1.98	1.87	.86	.95	.87	.67	1.04	1.44	1.36	16.10
Vt.	Burlington	62	1.61	1.62	2.16	2.37	2.97	3.44	3.78	3.25	2.41	2.20	2.20	1.94	33.17
Va.	Norfolk	60	3.16	3.09	3.74	3.38	3.78	4.21	4.70	4.66	3.00	2.70	2.37	3.19	45.80
	Richmond	80	3.35	3.00	3.64	3.38	3.78	3.84	4.73	4.86	3.25	2.80	2.67	3.01	41.72
Wash.	Seattle	74	4.79	3.60	3.18	2.24	1.90	1.45	.62	.70	1.71	2.90	4.67	5.54	33.02
	Spokane	71	2.08	1.64	1.07	1.32	1.20	.54	.36	.99	1.16	2.16	16.10		
W. Va.	Parkersburg	67	3.46	2.85	3.68	3.15	4.16	4.24	3.74	2.76	2.26	2.60	2.80	3.74	39.14
Wis.	Madison	60	1.45	1.41	2.06	2.69	3.55	3.91	3.18	3.02	2.61	1.91	1.56	1.30	31.24
Wyo.	Cheyenne	61	.45	.59	1.04	1.94	2.42	1.71	2.01	1.55	1.18	.96	.54	.49	14.68
Alaska	Juneau	9	4.77	3.56	3.86	3.69	3.82	3.53	5.11	4.79	7.65	6.25	6.13	3.86	52.48
T. H.	Honolulu	47	3.96	2.67	3.05	1.88	1.03	.72	.85	1.06	1.32	2.04	2.35	3.83	24.96
P. R.	San Juan	44	3.97	2.63	2.82	3.96	6.06	5.34	5.98	6.12	6.12	4.44	6.60	5.30	60.95

Source: Department of Commerce, Weather Bureau; records.

No. 184.—AVERAGE NUMBER OF DAYS WITH 0.01 INCH OR MORE OF PRECIPITATION

[For period of record through 1951]

STATION		Length of record (yrs.)	Jan.	Feb.	Mar.	Apr.	May	June	July	Aug.	Sept.	Oct.	Nov.	Dec.	Annual
Ala.	Mobile	81	10	10	10	8	8	12	15	14	9	6	7	10	119
	Montgomery	79	11	10	10	9	9	11	12	11	8	6	7	10	114
Ariz.	Phoenix	56	4	4	4	2	1	1	5	5	3	2	2	4	37
Ark.	Little Rock	72	10	9	10	10	10	10	9	9	7	6	8	9	107
Calif.	Fresno	64	8	7	7	4	2	1	(¹)	(¹)	1	3	4	8	45
	Los Angeles	74	6	6	6	4	2	1	(¹)	(¹)	1	2	3	6	37
	San Francisco	81	11	11	10	6	4	2	1	(¹)	2	4	7	10	68
Colo.	Denver	80	5	6	8	9	10	8	9	9	6	6	5	5	85
D. C.	Washington	81	11	10	12	11	12	11	11	11	9	8	9	10	125
Fla.	Jacksonville	80	8	8	8	7	9	13	16	15	13	9	7	8	121
	Miami	41	8	6	7	7	11	13	16	15	18	15	9	8	133
Ga.	Atlanta	78	12	11	12	10	10	11	12	12	8	7	8	11	124
Idaho	Boise	12	11	11	9	8	8	7	2	2	3	8	11	12	92
Ill.	Chicago	81	11	10	12	11	12	11	9	9	9	9	10	11	124
Ind.	Indianapolis	81	12	10	12	12	13	11	10	9	9	8	11	12	131
Iowa	Des Moines	78	8	7	9	10	12	11	9	9	9	8	7	8	107
Kans.	Wichita	65	5	6	7	8	11	9	8	8	8	7	5	5	87
Ky.	Louisville	79	12	10	12	12	11	11	10	9	8	8	10	11	124
La.	New Orleans	81	10	9	9	7	8	13	15	14	11	7	7	10	120
Maine	Eastport	79	15	13	14	12	12	12	12	11	11	11	12	14	149
Mass.	Boston	81	12	10	12	11	11	10	10	10	9	9	10	11	125
Mich.	Detroit	81	13	12	13	11	12	11	9	9	10	10	12	13	135
	Sault Ste. Marie	63	18	14	12	11	11	11	10	10	13	14	17	18	160
Minn.	Minneapolis	61	8	7	9	10	12	12	9	9	9	8	8	8	110
Miss.	Vicksburg	79	11	10	10	9	8	10	11	9	7	6	8	10	109
Mo.	Kansas City	63	7	7	9	11	12	11	9	9	9	7	6	7	104
	St. Louis	81	9	9	11	11	12	11	8	8	8	8	8	9	112
Mont.	Helena	72	9	8	9	8	11	12	8	6	7	7	7	8	100
	Miles City	60	8	6	8	7	10	11	8	6	6	6	6	7	89
Nebr.	North Platte	77	5	5	6	8	11	10	9	9	6	5	4	5	83
	Omaha	81	6	6	7	10	12	11	9	9	8	7	5	6	96
Nev.	Winnemucca	78	9	9	8	7	7	5	2	2	3	5	6	8	71
N. J.	Atlantic City	78	12	10	12	11	11	11	10	10	10	8	9	10	122
N. Mex.	Albuquerque	21	4	4	4	4	4	4	9	9	7	5	3	4	61
N. Y.	Albany	78	13	11	12	12	12	12	12	12	11	10	10	11	137
	New York	81	12	10	12	11	11	11	11	10	9	8	9	11	126
	Rochester	81	19	17	17	14	13	11	11	11	10	11	12	15	166
N. C.	Asheville	49	11	11	12	11	12	14	15	13	9	7	8	10	133
	Raleigh	65	10	10	11	10	11	11	13	12	8	7	7	10	120
N. Dak.	Bismarck	77	7	7	7	8	10	12	9	8	7	6	6	7	94
Ohio	Cleveland	75	17	15	15	13	13	11	10	9	10	11	14	16	154
Okla.	Oklahoma City	61	6	6	7	8	10	9	6	7	7	6	5	6	83
Oreg.	Portland	80	19	17	17	14	12	10	3	4	8	13	17	19	153
Pa.	Harrisburg	68	11	10	12	11	12	12	11	11	10	9	9	10	126
	Pittsburgh	81	16	14	15	13	13	12	12	10	9	10	12	15	151
S. C.	Charleston	81	9	9	9	8	8	11	13	13	10	6	7	9	112
S. Dak.	Huron	70	7	6	8	9	10	11	9	9	7	6	4	6	93
Tenn.	Nashville	81	12	11	12	11	10	10	11	9	8	7	9	11	121
Tex.	Amarillo	60	4	4	4	6	9	8	9	8	7	6	4	4	73
	El Paso	73	3	3	3	2	2	4	8	8	5	4	3	4	49
	Fort Worth	53	7	7	7	8	9	6	5	5	6	6	6	7	77
	Houston	62	10	8	8	7	7	8	10	9	9	6	8		101
Utah	Salt Lake City	78	10	10	10	9	8	5	4	5	5	7	7	10	90
Vt.	Burlington	46	13	12	13	12	13	12	12	11	11	11	13	13	147
Va.	Norfolk	81	11	11	11	10	11	11	13	12	8	8	8	10	124
	Richmond	54	11	10	11	10	10	11	11	11	8	7	7	10	121
Wash.	Seattle	81	18	16	16	13	12	9	5	5	8	13	17	19	151
	Spokane	71	14	12	11	9	9	8	4	4	6	9	12	15	113
W. Va.	Parkersburg	63	15	13	14	13	13	12	13	12	10	9	11	13	144
Wis.	Madison	78	9	8	10	11	12	11	9	9	10	9	9	9	115
Wyo.	Cheyenne	81	6	6	9	10	12	10	11	10	6	6	5	5	96
Alaska	Juneau	9	20	16	19	16	16	16	19	17	21	23	20	21	226
T. H.	Honolulu	47	13	11	13	12	11	11	13	13	12	15	14	15	162
P. R.	San Juan	53	20	15	15	14	16	17	19	20	18	18	19	21	212

¹ Less than ½ day.

Source: Department of Commerce, Weather Bureau; records.

No. 185.—Average Total Snow, Sleet, and Hail, Inches

[For period of record, through 1951.   T denotes trace]

STATION		Length of record (yrs.)	Jan.	Feb.	Mar.	Apr.	May	June	July	Aug.	Sept.	Oct.	Nov.	Dec.	Annual
Ala.	Mobile	71	0.1	0.1	T	T	T	T	T	T	T	T	T	T	0.2
	Montgomery	70	.2	.2	T	T	T	T	T	T	T	T	T	.3	.7
Ariz.	Phoenix	56	T	T	T	T	T	0	0	0	0	0	T	T	T
Ark.	Little Rock	67	2.0	1.2	.4	T	T	0	0	0	0	0	.1	.9	4.6
Calif.	Fresno	64	.1	T	T	T	0	0	0	0	0	0	T	T	.1
	Los Angeles	74	T	T	T	0	0	0	0	0	0	0	T	T	.2
	San Francisco	81	T	.1	T	T	0	0	0	0	0	0	T	.1	.2
Colo.	Denver	70	6.2	7.7	10.8	9.5	1.9	T	0	T	.7	4.1	6.8	8.2	55.9
D. C.	Washington	64	6.1	6.8	3.7	.4	T	0	0	0	0	.1	.7	3.3	20.1
Fla.	Jacksonville	80	T	T	T	T	T	T	T	0	0	0	T	T	T
	Miami	41	0	T	0	T	T	T	T	0	T	0	T	T	T
Ga.	Atlanta	67	.9	.8	.2	T	T	T	0	T	0	T	T	.3	2.2
Idaho	Boise	12	6.9	5.6	2.1	.7	T	T	0	0	T	.1	2.1	5.6	23.9
Ill.	Chicago	67	8.8	8.5	5.9	1.0	.1	T	0	T	T	.1	2.1	7.4	33.0
Ind.	Indianapolis	68	6.6	4.7	3.5	.7	.1	0	0	0	T	.1	1.3	4.6	20.5
Iowa	Des Moines	67	8.8	7.1	5.9	1.1	.2	T	0	T	T	.3	2.1	7.0	32.3
Kans.	Wichita	63	2.8	3.6	2.8	.4	T	T	0	0	0	.1	1.0	2.9	14.1
Ky.	Louisville	67	4.6	3.7	2.1	.2	T	0	0	0	0	.1	.5	3.1	12.7
La.	New Orleans	81	.1	.1	T	T	0	0	0	0	0	0	0	T	.2
Maine	Eastport	67	16.5	18.3	12.9	6.7	.2	0	0	0	T	.2	4.0	12.3	71.1
Mass.	Boston	81	11.9	12.4	7.1	1.8	T	0	0	0	T	T	1.8	7.6	42.6
Mich.	Detroit	61	10.1	9.6	6.8	1.5	.1	0	0	0	0	.1	3.1	8.6	39.9
	Sault Ste. Marie	63	19.2	14.2	10.4	3.7	.7	T	0	0	T	2.5	13.0	19.6	83.1
Minn.	Minneapolis	61	9.0	7.9	8.6	3.4	.2	T	0	T	T	.5	4.8	7.8	42.2
Miss.	Vicksburg	67	1.0	.4	T	T	T	T	T	T	T	0	T	.3	1.7
Mo.	Kansas City	62	4.7	5.5	3.9	.9	T	T	0	0	T	.2	1.2	4.2	20.6
	St. Louis	68	4.3	4.9	3.6	.3	.1	0	0	0	0	T	1.0	3.3	17.6
Mont.	Helena	72	9.9	8.1	8.2	5.2	1.9	.1	0	T	1.0	3.7	6.7	8.9	54.7
	Miles City	60	6.0	4.5	6.6	2.4	1.4	T	T	T	.2	1.7	3.6	5.6	32.0
Nebr.	North Platte	68	3.5	4.7	6.6	1.9	.4	T	0	T	T	1.0	2.8	4.0	25.2
	Omaha	67	6.7	8.8	6.1	.8	.1	T	0	T	T	.4	2.2	5.4	28.5
Nev.	Winnemucca	72	7.8	5.1	4.1	1.5	.5	.6	T	0	T	.5	2.1	6.2	28.4
N. J.	Atlantic City	68	4.0	4.9	2.1	.2	0	0	0	0	T	.5	2.8	14.5	
N. Mex.	Albuquerque	21	2.1	1.6	1.4	.6	.1	T	0	0	T	T	1.4	1.4	8.6
N. Y.	Albany	67	12.7	15.2	9.3	2.0	.1	0	0	0	T	T	3.4	9.5	50.2
	New York	67	7.6	9.7	5.6	1.0	0	0	0	0	0	T	.6	5.6	31.1
	Rochester	67	17.9	15.4	13.3	3.6	.2	0	0	0	T	.3	6.3	13.2	75.2
N. C.	Asheville	49	2.8	2.6	2.3	.3	T	0	0	0	0	.1	.4	2.1	10.8
	Raleigh	65	1.9	2.5	1.2	.2	T	0	0	0	0	T	.4	1.3	7.3
N. Dak.	Bismarck	66	5.5	5.6	7.7	3.2	.8	T	0	T	.1	1.3	4.9	6.0	35.4
Ohio	Cleveland	56	10.6	10.0	5.6	1.8	.1	T	0	0	T	.2	4.0	9.2	41.4
Okla.	Oklahoma City	61	2.7	2.0	1.3	.1	T	T	0	0	0	T	.3	1.6	9.7
Oreg.	Portland	81	5.7	3.0	.7	.1	T	0	0	0	0	T	.4	2.7	12.6
Pa.	Harrisburg	63	8.7	9.2	6.0	.7	T	0	0	0	0	.1	1.1	5.7	31.5
	Pittsburgh	67	8.6	7.9	6.0	2.9	T	T	0	0	T	T	2.3	6.9	34.7
S. C.	Charleston	61	T	.1	T	0	T	0	0	0	0	0	0	.1	.2
S. Dak.	Huron	70	6.1	5.4	6.3	2.2	.2	T	0	T	T	.6	3.4	5.1	29.3
Tenn.	Nashville	67	2.7	2.6	1.4	.5	T	T	0	0	0	T	.4	1.4	9.0
Tex.	Amarillo	60	3.5	4.4	3.0	1.2	.2	T	T	T	T	.4	2.1	4.4	19.2
	El Paso	73	1.0	.4	.2	T	T	T	T	T	T	T	.3	.7	2.6
	Fort Worth	53	1.1	.5	.4	T	T	T	0	0	0	T	.2	.4	2.6
	Houston	54	.1	T	T	T	T	T	0	0	0	0	T	.1	.1
Utah	Salt Lake City	67	12.3	10.5	10.2	3.3	.3	T	T	T	T	.8	5.8	11.4	54.6
Vt.	Burlington	68	15.1	14.4	12.8	3.8	.1	0	T	T	T	.3	6.7	12.1	65.3
Va.	Norfolk	61	2.5	2.8	1.7	T	T	T	0	0	0	T	.4	1.9	9.0
	Richmond	54	3.5	3.3	2.2	.3	T	T	T	0	T	T	.4	2.7	12.4
Wash.	Seattle	59	5.0	3.4	.9	.1	T	T	0	0	0	T	.8	3.7	11.7
	Spokane	67	12.0	8.3	3.0	.3	T	T	T	0	0	T	.1	4.5	8.7	37.9
W. Va.	Parkersburg	63	6.7	6.4	4.2	.8	T	0	0	0	0	.1	1.8	4.7	24.7
Wis.	Madison	68	9.7	8.0	7.9	1.7	.1	0	0	0	T	.6	3.1	7.5	38.3
Wyo.	Cheyenne	68	6.4	7.6	11.2	11.4	3.7	.5	.2	.5	.6	4.1	5.8	6.1	57.1
Alaska	Juneau	9	17.1	16.1	14.3	4.4	.1	0	0	0	T	.3	11.8	19.4	85.5
T. H.	Honolulu	47	0	T	0	0	0	0	0	0	0	0	0	0	T
P. R.	San Juan	53	0	0	0	0	0	0	0	0	0	0	0	0	0

Source: Department of Commerce, Weather Bureau; records.

No. 186.—AVERAGE PERCENTAGE OF POSSIBLE SUNSHINE

[For period of record through 1951]

STATION	Length of record (yrs.)	Jan.	Feb.	Mar.	Apr.	May	June	July	Aug.	Sept.	Oct.	Nov.	Dec.	Annual
Ala. Mobile	46	51	54	60	67	71	67	59	63	64	70	62	46	61
Montgomery	41	51	54	61	69	73	72	65	69	68	70	54	48	64
Ariz. Phoenix	56	75	77	82	87	93	94	83	83	88	88	84	75	85
Ark. Little Rock	58	47	52	58	62	67	72	71	73	70	69	57	47	62
Calif. Fresno	54	46	62	72	83	88	94	97	97	93	86	73	47	78
Los Angeles	55	70	68	69	68	64	69	78	80	77	76	79	72	73
San Francisco	61	53	57	64	70	70	75	68	63	71	70	62	53	65
Colo. Denver	61	67	67	65	63	61	69	68	67	70	70	67	65	67
D.C. Washington	57	46	54	56	58	61	63	64	62	61	61	53	46	58
Fla. Jacksonville	54	57	59	67	71	71	53	62	63	60	59	62	53	62
Miami	41	66	72	73	73	68	61	65	67	62	62	64	64	66
Ga. Atlanta	56	48	53	58	65	69	69	62	62	65	67	60	47	60
Idaho Boise	12	43	47	58	66	67	73	87	85	77	60	39	34	61
Ill. Chicago	58	44	49	53	57	63	68	73	70	65	61	46	41	59
Ind. Indianapolis	48	42	46	49	56	62	68	73	68	68	62	49	39	57
Iowa Des Moines	58	56	57	56	59	62	66	74	69	65	63	53	49	61
Kans. Wichita	38	61	63	64	64	66	72	80	77	72	68	63	58	68
Ky. Louisville	51	41	47	52	57	64	68	73	69	68	64	51	39	58
La. New Orleans	61	49	49	57	63	66	64	58	58	64	69	60	46	59
Maine Eastport	58	45	50	52	51	52	53	56	57	55	50	38	40	51
Mass. Boston	59	48	56	58	57	59	62	63	63	61	58	50	48	56
Mich. Detroit	61	34	42	49	52	58	64	64	66	60	54	35	29	53
Sault Ste. Marie	52	28	44	50	54	54	59	63	58	45	36	21	22	47
Minn. Minneapolis	37	50	53	55	57	60	64	73	69	60	53	39	40	56
Miss. Vicksburg	58	45	49	57	64	69	72	69	72	73	71	60	44	63
Mo. Kansas City	61	55	57	59	60	64	69	76	73	69	67	59	52	63
St. Louis	60	48	50	55	59	64	67	71	68	67	64	54	44	60
Mont. Helena	58	46	55	58	59	59	62	76	74	63	56	47	43	60
Miles City	[1]20	52	61	58	60	67	69	80	73	65	60	52	51	62
Nebr. North Platte	45	63	64	64	62	64	71	78	75	71	70	63	58	66
Omaha	52	56	58	58	59	63	68	77	70	66	65	54	50	63
Nev. Winnemucca	45	54	59	64	70	75	81	90	85	75	62	53		72
N.J. Atlantic City	55	52	57	58	60	63	64	66	66	64	63	58	52	60
N. Mex. Albuquerque	21	71	71	73	76	80	84	78	76	78	80	78	71	77
N.Y. Albany	55	41	51	53	54	58	61	63	61	58	53	39	38	53
New York	58	51	59	59	60	61	63	65	63	63	61	55	52	59
Rochester	58	31	41	49	53	61	67	70	66	60	50	31	26	50
N.C. Asheville	49	48	52	56	61	63	62	58	58	61	64	59	48	58
Raleigh	55	49	54	59	64	67	64	61	61	63	64	61	51	60
N. Dak. Bismarck	57	52	58	55	57	58	61	73	69	62	58	49	48	59
Ohio Cleveland	52	29	36	46	53	61	67	71	67	62	52	32	24	51
Okla. Oklahoma City	54	57	60	62	64	65	73	78	78	73	68	64	57	67
Oreg. Portland	61	28	32	40	49	52	56	71	66	55	42	28	24	48
Pa. Harrisburg	53	43	52	55	58	62	64	67	63	62	58	47	44	57
Pittsburgh	55	32	38	45	50	58	62	64	61	61	54	39	30	51
S.C. Charleston	55	58	59	65	72	73	69	65	66	67	68	68	58	66
S. Dak. Huron	54	55	62	60	62	64	68	76	72	65	60	51	49	63
Tenn. Nashville	55	42	47	54	60	66	69	68	68	68	65	54	42	59
Tex. Amarillo	46	74	75	77	77	78	84	80	82	78	74	72	72	77
El Paso	45	73	76	81	85	87	87	77	77	79	81	79	72	80
Fort Worth	29	56	57	65	66	67	75	78	78	74	70	63	56	68
Houston	42	49	48	53	57	64	70	69	70	67	67	56	43	59
Utah Salt Lake City	14	50	54	63	70	73	77	81	83	84	69	52	42	68
Vt. Burlington	46	34	43	48	47	53	59	62	59	51	42	26	24	46
Va. Norfolk	52	50	57	60	63	66	65	65	66	63	64	60	51	61
Richmond	49	49	55	60	63	67	65	66	62	63	63	58	49	61
Wash. Seattle	56	26	35	43	51	53	53	64	59	50	34	23	22	43
Spokane	54	27	41	53	63	64	68	82	79	68	52	28	22	58
W. Va. Parkersburg	54	30	36	42	49	55	60	63	59	59	52	36	29	48
Wis. Madison	47	43	48	51	53	57	62	70	68	58	53	39	37	53
Wyo. Cheyenne	55	65	66	65	61	59	68	70	68	69	68	66	63	65
Alaska Juneau	9	26	34	34	35	36	35	24	32	22	17	20	17	28
T.H. Honolulu	46	62	64	60	62	64	66	67	70	70	68	63	60	65
P.R. San Juan	53	64	68	70	65	59	61	64	66	60	63	61	64	64

[1] Through 1942.

Source: Department of Commerce, Weather Bureau; records.

No. 187.—Average Hourly Wind Velocity

[For period of record through 1951. True velocities in miles per hour]

STATION		Length of record (yrs.)	Jan.	Feb.	Mar.	Apr.	May	June	July	Aug.	Sept.	Oct.	Nov.	Dec.	Annual
Ala	Mobile	38	10.1	10.1	10.6	10.0	9.3	8.4	8.0	7.5	8.4	8.8	9.5	9.8	9.2
	Montgomery	7	7.6	7.8	8.6	7.2	6.4	5.8	5.6	5.1	5.9	5.4	6.5	6.7	6.6
Ariz	Phoenix	6	4.6	4.8	5.8	5.6	5.6	5.5	5.8	5.2	4.8	4.5	4.2	4.0	5.0
Ark	Little Rock	72	8.2	8.8	8.8	8.9	7.6	6.7	6.2	5.9	6.1	6.5	7.6	7.9	7.4
Calif	Fresno	64	5.3	5.8	6.4	7.4	8.4	8.6	7.9	7.4	6.6	5.6	4.9	5.1	6.6
	Los Angeles	74	6.3	6.5	6.5	6.4	6.2	6.0	5.8	5.7	5.6	5.7	6.0	6.4	6.1
	San Francisco	62	7.4	7.7	8.6	9.7	10.5	11.2	11.5	10.9	9.3	7.8	6.9	7.1	9.1
Colo	Denver	78	7.6	7.6	8.2	8.4	7.7	7.4	7.0	6.7	6.7	7.0	7.3	7.3	7.4
D. C.	Washington	20	7.6	8.5	8.7	8.3	6.9	6.3	5.8	5.6	5.8	6.2	7.4	7.3	7.0
Fla	Jacksonville	80	8.9	9.3	9.6	9.5	8.9	8.5	8.3	8.0	8.4	9.0	8.7	8.7	8.8
	Miami	9	14.0	13.7	14.9	14.3	12.5	11.4	10.7	10.8	12.7	13.4	13.0	13.3	12.9
Ga	Atlanta	71	11.6	12.0	11.9	10.8	9.1	8.2	7.7	7.4	8.3	9.5	10.6	11.1	9.9
Idaho	Boise	12	9.0	10.0	11.1	10.9	10.1	9.7	9.2	9.1	9.1	9.5	9.2	9.0	9.7
Ill	Chicago	36	11.8	11.8	12.5	12.1	10.5	9.7	8.8	8.5	9.6	10.2	11.8	11.3	10.7
Ind	Indianapolis	71	11.4	11.5	11.9	11.5	10.4	9.4	8.7	8.3	9.1	9.8	11.0	11.0	10.3
Iowa	Des Moines	20	10.3	10.7	11.5	11.1	10.0	9.4	8.1	8.1	10.5	10.5	10.1	9.8	9.8
Kans	Wichita	40	12.4	13.1	14.6	14.6	13.1	12.7	11.4	11.2	12.4	12.3	12.7	12.0	12.7
Ky	Louisville	79	9.9	10.3	10.8	10.0	8.5	7.8	7.0	6.6	7.1	7.8	9.4	8.9	8.7
La	New Orleans	81	8.4	8.7	8.8	8.5	7.6	6.9	6.5	6.5	7.4	7.7	8.0	8.3	7.8
Maine	Eastport	66	13.5	13.3	12.6	11.4	9.7	8.4	7.5	7.4	8.7	10.7	12.3	12.9	10.7
Mass	Boston	81	11.5	11.9	12.1	11.5	10.2	9.6	8.9	11.5	9.2	10.8	11.2	11.5	10.8
Mich	Detroit	70	11.8	11.8	11.7	11.4	10.2	9.4	9.0	8.8	9.5	10.2	11.7	11.7	10.6
	Sault Ste. Marie	63	9.0	9.1	9.9	9.7	9.0	7.6	7.2	7.1	7.9	8.9	9.9	9.5	8.7
Minn	Minneapolis	60	11.2	11.4	12.2	12.6	11.8	10.6	9.7	9.7	10.9	11.4	11.5	11.1	11.2
Miss	Vicksburg	72	8.4	8.6	8.9	8.3	7.3	6.7	6.4	6.2	6.7	6.9	7.6	8.1	7.5
Mo	Kansas City	20	10.3	10.8	12.1	11.6	9.9	9.7	8.6	8.4	8.8	9.0	10.6	9.9	10.0
	St. Louis	79	11.9	12.0	12.6	12.1	11.0	10.1	9.2	9.0	9.8	10.6	11.8	11.6	11.0
Mont	Helena	72	7.3	7.6	8.4	8.8	8.7	8.5	8.1	7.8	7.8	7.6	7.3	7.2	7.9
	Miles City	¹ 51	5.6	5.6	6.5	7.6	7.5	6.5	5.8	5.4	5.6	5.6	5.6	5.4	6.1
Nebr	North Platte	77	7.9	8.4	9.8	10.7	9.9	9.0	8.0	7.6	8.1	8.4	8.1	7.7	8.6
	Omaha	79	9.7	10.2	10.9	10.9	9.8	8.9	8.0	7.9	8.6	9.0	9.7	9.4	9.4
Nev	Winnemucca	72	8.0	8.5	8.6	8.7	7.9	7.7	7.3	6.9	7.0	7.1	7.6	7.7	7.8
N. J.	Atlantic City	30	16.2	16.4	17.0	16.6	15.0	14.0	13.3	13.2	13.9	14.9	15.7	15.4	15.1
N. M.	Albuquerque	21	8.0	8.7	10.3	10.5	10.1	9.5	8.6	7.8	7.8	7.8	7.7	7.3	8.7
N. Y.	Albany	13	10.1	11.3	11.0	10.8	9.2	8.2	7.4	6.6	7.3	8.2	9.3	9.3	9.1
	New York	40	16.6	17.1	17.4	16.0	13.7	13.0	12.2	11.8	12.6	14.1	16.1	16.4	14.8
	Rochester	80	10.9	11.0	10.7	9.9	8.7	7.9	7.4	6.9	7.6	8.3	9.9	10.3	9.1
N. C.	Asheville	49	9.6	10.0	10.2	9.5	7.7	6.6	6.2	6.1	6.6	7.4	8.9	9.2	8.2
	Raleigh	65	7.7	8.3	8.8	8.4	7.1	6.6	6.2	5.9	6.2	6.9	7.3	7.4	7.2
N. Dak	Bismarck	12	10.4	10.3	11.5	12.9	12.7	11.7	9.7	9.9	10.5	10.0	10.5	9.5	10.8
Ohio	Cleveland	44	14.5	14.6	14.5	13.6	12.0	10.9	10.6	10.9	11.9	13.4	14.9	14.6	13.1
Okla	Oklahoma City	19	9.8	10.2	11.1	10.8	9.5	9.5	8.3	8.1	8.4	8.7	9.6	9.4	9.5
Oreg	Portland	80	7.4	7.3	7.2	6.9	6.8	6.6	6.8	6.3	6.2	6.0	6.9	7.3	6.8
Pa	Harrisburg	63	7.8	8.5	8.8	8.5	6.9	6.2	5.8	5.4	5.7	6.3	7.4	7.5	7.1
	Pittsburgh	48	11.7	11.8	12.1	11.5	10.0	9.3	8.7	8.4	8.9	9.7	11.3	11.4	10.4
S. C.	Charleston	20	9.9	10.6	11.1	11.0	10.3	9.8	9.3	9.4	10.1	10.3	10.1	9.9	10.2
S. Dak	Huron	70	10.8	11.1	12.0	13.1	12.1	10.9	9.9	9.5	11.0	11.0	10.9	10.3	11.1
Tenn	Nashville	43	9.7	10.0	10.6	10.3	8.7	7.8	7.1	6.9	7.3	7.8	9.2	9.3	8.7
Tex	Amarillo	60	12.1	12.9	14.1	14.5	13.4	13.1	11.3	10.7	12.0	12.2	11.7	11.4	12.5
	El Paso	73	8.7	10.0	11.2	11.4	10.8	9.6	8.5	7.9	7.9	8.0	8.3	8.5	9.2
	Fort Worth	52	10.7	11.3	12.4	12.3	11.1	10.8	9.5	9.2	9.2	9.5	10.2	10.2	10.5
	Houston	42	10.5	10.9	11.6	11.6	10.6	9.5	8.5	8.4	8.8	9.5	10.3	10.3	10.0
Utah	Salt Lake City	22	7.4	8.0	9.0	9.3	9.4	9.2	9.5	9.5	9.0	8.6	7.6	7.3	8.7
Vt	Burlington	46	11.8	10.9	11.1	10.7	9.6	8.7	8.2	8.2	9.1	10.4	11.6	11.4	10.1
Va	Norfolk	39	12.0	12.2	12.9	12.3	11.0	10.3	9.8	9.6	10.1	10.8	11.4	11.4	11.2
	Richmond	54	8.2	8.5	9.2	8.7	7.3	6.7	6.4	6.2	6.3	6.9	7.5	7.6	7.5
Wash	Seattle	² 18	9.7	9.8	10.0	9.4	8.8	8.4	7.9	7.3	7.4	8.5	9.4	10.4	8.9
	Spokane	71	6.3	6.5	7.4	7.5	7.4	7.2	6.8	6.3	6.3	6.0	6.2	6.3	6.7
W. Va	Parkersburg	63	7.3	7.7	7.9	7.4	6.0	5.5	5.2	4.9	5.1	5.6	6.8	7.0	6.2
Wis	Madison	5	12.5	11.9	13.8	12.9	11.4	10.2	8.8	8.1	10.2	10.5	12.5	11.5	11.2
Wyo	Cheyenne	80	13.9	13.3	13.4	12.4	11.1	10.1	8.9	8.6	9.5	10.6	12.1	12.9	11.4
Alaska	Juneau	9	8.4	7.4	9.2	8.5	7.2	7.1	7.1	7.0	8.0	9.1	8.1	8.5	8.0
T. H.	Honolulu	22	9.4	8.4	9.3	10.3	6.9	9.8	10.0	9.9	9.1	8.7	8.0	9.3	9.5
P. R.	San Juan	52	12.7	11.9	12.6	12.2	11.2	12.0	13.3	12.1	9.5	8.2	9.6	11.5	11.4

¹ Through 1942.
² Through 1950.
Source: Department of Commerce, Weather Bureau; records.

No. 188.—AVERAGE

[For period of record through 1951. Eastern standard time. Hours selected to give, for

STATION		Length of record (yrs.)[1]	JAN.		FEB.		MAR.		APR.		MAY		JUNE	
			7:30 a.m.	1:30 p.m.	7:30 a.m.	1:30 p.m.	7:30 a.m.	1:30 p.m.	7:30 a.m.	1:30 p.m.	7:30 a.m.	1:30 p.m.	7:30 a.m.	1:30 p.m.
Ala	Mobile	12	88	63	86	60	87	60	88	57	87	54	89	61
	Montgomery	64	83	61	81	58	80	54	79	52	79	51	81	53
Ariz	Phoenix	86	69	39	66	39	60	30	50	24	42	18	37	17
Ark	Little Rock	64	80	65	79	61	77	55	77	53	81	56	82	56
Calif	Fresno	64	90	73	87	64	85	55	79	44	71	36	60	31
	Los Angeles	62	65	45	72	50	76	48	80	52	85	56	87	56
	San Francisco	52	85	68	84	66	83	61	83	62	85	64	88	65
Colo	Denver	21	59	43	62	44	63	41	67	39	69	39	67	34
D. C	Washington	64	73	56	71	53	72	48	68	45	73	48	75	52
Fla	Jacksonville	15	89	55	86	52	86	50	84	47	82	47	84	55
	Miami	12	88	60	87	55	84	55	82	55	80	57	82	62
Ga	Atlanta	64	80	64	78	61	77	55	74	51	74	51	77	53
Idaho	Boise	12	83	75	83	72	78	58	73	48	72	46	72	44
Ill	Chicago	33	81	71	79	69	78	63	75	56	75	58	77	59
Ind	Indianapolis	52	83	68	80	64	78	59	72	53	72	50	73	51
Iowa	Des Moines	11	81	70	83	69	84	66	79	56	82	58	85	63
Kans	Wichita	63	78	65	77	63	76	57	75	51	79	52	80	55
Ky	Louisville	64	77	68	77	63	74	58	71	54	73	53	75	54
La	New Orleans	63	85	67	84	64	84	61	83	60	82	59	82	60
Maine	Eastport	2 33	74	69	74	67	76	67	77	69	79	69	82	72
Mass	Boston	61	72	59	69	57	69	54	67	53	69	56	71	57
Mich	Detroit	63	80	71	79	68	79	63	75	53	73	54	74	55
	Sault Ste. Marie	63	78	75	77	71	79	69	78	61	77	58	81	62
Minn	Minneapolis	18	76	67	75	65	78	60	75	52	74	49	78	55
Miss	Vicksburg	63	82	65	80	63	79	57	82	57	84	59	85	59
Mo	Kansas City	63	78	64	78	60	76	55	74	53	76	54	78	55
	St. Louis	64	77	65	76	62	75	56	73	54	74	54	75	54
Mont	Helena	64	68	64	70	62	69	55	60	48	70	45	70	45
	Miles City	3 51	84	73	84	69	83	57	78	47	75	40	76	42
Nebr	North Platte	12	83	61	86	62	85	54	81	51	85	51	86	55
	Omaha	63	79	65	76	63	77	57	74	52	76	53	78	55
Nev	Winnemucca	63	83	66	82	59	77	46	70	37	68	31	60	28
N. J	Atlantic City	64	79	68	77	68	77	66	76	65	78	69	80	71
N. Mex	Albuquerque	21	71	49	66	42	58	33	55	28	53	26	48	24
N. Y	Albany	14	74	62	72	60	76	56	73	50	73	51	76	53
	New York	63	72	61	70	59	69	55	66	53	71	56	74	58
	Rochester	11	81	72	78	70	80	63	77	55	77	54	78	53
N. C	Asheville	45	82	59	80	55	79	52	77	47	80	48	85	52
	Raleigh	11	83	59	78	52	78	49	77	45	80	48	82	52
N. Dak	Bismarck	51	73	66	76	66	77	63	79	51	76	47	80	51
Ohio	Cleveland	62	77	71	77	69	77	61	74	52	73	55	74	55
Okla	Oklahoma City	61	79	62	78	58	76	50	76	50	82	57	82	55
Oreg	Portland	11	87	81	89	81	88	68	88	66	88	66	87	65
Pa	Harrisburg	63	74	61	71	57	71	52	67	49	70	51	73	54
	Pittsburgh	63	77	67	76	65	74	57	72	49	72	51	75	54
S. C	Charleston	11	88	57	84	50	84	52	84	49	84	52	86	59
S. Dak	Huron	63	76	71	77	72	85	70	80	55	78	53	82	58
Tenn	Nashville	64	84	66	80	62	77	56	75	51	78	52	79	52
Tex	Amarillo	60	72	51	73	47	70	41	70	40	76	47	76	42
	El Paso	63	61	41	55	34	45	26	40	22	39	21	43	23
	Fort Worth	53	78	62	77	60	73	52	78	53	82	56	80	53
	Houston	42	85	66	85	63	85	59	87	59	89	59	88	59
Utah	Salt Lake City	2 44	81	71	80	65	75	52	70	42	67	36	64	32
Vt	Burlington	64	81	79	81	76	77	72	72	66	70	66	74	67
Va	Norfolk		79	62	77	57	77	55	74	52	76	55	79	59
	Richmond	54	84	61	78	57	77	54	74	51	76	52	78	55
Wash	Seattle	12	86	80	88	79	86	71	86	64	87	62	87	63
	Spokane	62	85	79	85	76	81	64	76	53	74	50	72	49
W. Va	Parkersburg	60	82	66	81	63	79	56	74	49	74	51	78	56
Wis	Madison	21	80	71	79	69	81	65	77	55	78	55	80	57
Wyo	Cheyenne	63	58	50	62	50	66	49	72	49	75	44	71	43
Alaska	Juneau	9	81	82	80	78	82	76	85	73	88	71	87	72
T. H	Honolulu[4]	5	82	81	80	80	77	76	76	72	76	70	75	69
P. R	San Juan	52	81	74	80	71	77	71	76	74	77	77	77	78

[1] Length of record is for morning observation.
[2] Through 1950.
[3] Through 1942.
[4] Hours 8 a. m. and 2 p. m., 150th meridian time.

RELATIVE HUMIDITY

[most of country, approximation of average highest and average lowest humidity values]

JULY		AUG.		SEPT.		OCT.		NOV.		DEC.		ANNUAL		STATION
7:30 a.m.	1:30 p.m.	7:30 a.m.	1:30 p.m.	7:30 a.m.	1:30 p.m.	7:30 a.m.	1:30 p.m.	7:30 a.m.	1:30 p.m.	7:30 a.m.	1:30 p.m.	7:30 a.m.	1:30 p.m.	
91			81	80	62	80	55	86	56	88	64	86	60	Ala.... Mobile.
		87		85	54	84	50	82	54	84	61	83	55	Montgomery.
		34		35	30	37	29	63	33	69	41	57	30	Ariz.... Phoenix.
		34		45	54	53	52	90	58	81	64	81	57	Ark.... Little Rock.
					34	73	42	81	54	90	73	74	47	Calif... Fresno.
	77			81	51	74	47	60	38	61	44	76	49	Los Angeles.
	71		71			84	59	83	60	83	69	86	65	San Francisco.
				64	34	61	35	59	38	58	40	65	37	Colo.... Denver.
70				81	51	81	51	77	51	74	55	75	52	D. C... Washington.
				83	61	90	57	89	55	90	49	87	54	Fla.... Jacksonville.
84				88	66	88	63	87	61	86	62	86	60	Miami.
82		84		80	55	79	52	77	56	80	64	79	57	Ga.... Atlanta.
	24		23	60	40	60	50	83	69	85	77	72	54	Idaho.. Boise.
78				82	57	80	57	78	64	81	71	79	62	Ill.... Chicago.
72		77		79		79	53	79	62	81	69	77	57	Ind.... Indianapolis.
		46		70	48	82	48	83	65	83	72	83	62	Iowa.. Des Moines.
76				79	48	77	50	76	51	79	65	78	55	Kans.. Wichita.
77			54	81	44	80	53	77	60	78	63	77	57	Ky.... Louisville.
88				84	52	82	59	83	60	85	67	84	62	La.... New Orleans.
			74	84	73	82	70	80	72	77	71	80	71	Maine.. Eastport.
72		72		76	67	75	54	72	58	72	57	71	56	Mass.. Boston.
73				81	56	82	56	82	65	82	71	78	60	Mich.. Detroit.
		64		85	67	87	68	85	76	80	77	82	67	Sault Ste. Marie.
				67	37	80	55	80	66	78	70	78	58	Minn.. Minneapolis.
				67	47	64	56	63	55	82	64	84	59	Miss.. Vicksburg.
				70	43	78	51	75	57	78	64	77	56	Mo.... Kansas City.
			77	46	44	76	53	75	59	77	64	76	57	St. Louis.
				47	70	70	54	70	62	70	66	69	52	Mont.. Helena.
				71	48	80	48	82	59	83	67	78	51	Miles City.
				80	48	85	48	85	54	85	63	85	55	North Platte.
		54		63	53	77	51	77	60	78	66	77	57	Omaha.
				36	26	67	36	75	47	82	65	66	40	Nev.... Winnemucca.
	71			76	64	78	65	78	79	67	70	68	N.J.... Atlantic City.
		37		45	27	63	36	71	49	62	56	62	36	N. Mex Albuquerque.
				86	54	80	62	77	64	78	66	66	N.Y.... Albany.
			41	75	46	73	63	72	61	73	58	New York.
				85	56	85	66	81	70	81	60	Rochester.
				87	60	83	51	82	59	84	54	N. C... Asheville.
				81	53	84	60	83	57	83	53	Raleigh.
				61	53	79	67	78	68	78	56	N. Dak Bismarck.
	77			77	45	77	64	77	70	76	59	Ohio... Cleveland.
			51	79	50	78	55	80	60	79	55	Okla... Oklahoma City.
				66	53	90	83	86	84	88	72	Oreg... Portland.
				79	54	75	55	74	59	74	54	Pa..... Harrisburg.
				81	53	77	62	77	66	76	57	Pittsburgh.
				90	56	88	52	87	56	87	56	S. C... Charleston.
				63	54	80	67	78	74	80	61	S. Dak. Huron.
				84	51	81	48	82	65	81	56	Tenn.. Nashville.
		77		76	46	74	48	73	50	74	45	Tex.... Amarillo.
	77			37	60	60	59	25	63	43	64	32	El Paso.
				78	52	76	52	76	55	77	59	78	54	Fort Worth.
				87	55	84	57	84	57	85	65	87	60	Houston.
				21	70	43	79	59	82	70	70	46	Utah... Salt Lake City.
			74	70	74	76	81	79	77	73	Vt..... Burlington.
				61	56	80	56	79	59	79	68	Va..... Norfolk.
				84	51	81	54	83	60	80	56	Richmond.
				78	43	90	55	83	76	83	72	Wash.. Seattle.
				53	35	80	80	87	82	77	61	Spokane.
				66	33	81	57	81	64	80	56	W. Va.. Parkersburg.
				68	48	82	67	81	72	81	60	Wis.... Madison.
				20	46	60	44	59	47	66	44	Wyo... Cheyenne.
				85	72	86	65	82	82	85	79	Alaska. Juneau.
			77	74	71	79	76	76	77	74	T. H... Honolulu.[4]
			77	63	76	81	75	81	74	80	78	P. R... San Juan.

Source: Department of Commerce, Weather Bureau; records.

No. 189.—AVERAGE MONTHLY AND ANNUAL DEGREE DAYS, 65° BASE

[For period of record, through June 1951. (*) denotes less than ½]

STATION	Length of record (yrs.)	Jan.	Feb.	Mar.	Apr.	May	June	July	Aug.	Sept.	Oct.	Nov.	Dec.	Annual
Ala.... Mobile	52	388	305	178	51	3	0	0	0	1	43	202	366	1,537
Montgomery	62	491	394	246	83	10	(*)	0	0	3	68	281	476	2,052
Ariz.... Phoenix	52	405	257	153	45	6	0	0	0	0	18	165	375	1,424
Ark.... Little Rock	53	702	578	376	144	29	(*)	0	0	11	116	390	675	3,021
Calif.... Fresno	52	582	383	290	148	50	4	0	(*)	5	77	309	563	2,411
Los Angeles	74	302	253	229	160	96	24	1	(*)	8	50	130	247	1,500
San Francisco	53	463	344	319	274	255	197	200	183	125	143	245	430	3,178
Colo.... Denver	53	1,034	888	794	515	275	66	8	5	125	405	716	993	5,827
D.C... Washington	55	913	826	620	338	99	12	0	2	43	243	543	865	4,504
Fla.... Jacksonville	80	292	224	132	36	2	(*)	0	0	(*)	23	139	277	1,125
Miami	41	51	45	28	4	(*)	0	0	0	0	(*)	16	37	181
Ga.... Atlanta	73	662	545	392	164	33	1	(*)	(*)	12	128	396	631	2,964
Idaho... Boise	12	1,181	837	733	445	254	110	4	14	138	393	768	1,021	5,898
Ill.... Chicago	54	1,221	1,081	866	533	258	64	6	7	89	330	723	1,121	6,299
Ind.... Indianapolis	60	1,104	982	751	414	155	22	2	4	65	299	663	1,026	5,487
Iowa... Des Moines	63	1,332	1,135	871	445	175	29	2	3	103	356	787	1,187	6,430
Kans... Wichita	63	1,022	844	623	285	99	9	(*)	1	42	218	592	925	4,660
Ky.... Louisville	79	982	793	600	294	90	6	(*)	1	37	220	556	853	4,382
La.... New Orleans	81	336	246	134	30	1	0	0	0	1	22	132	299	1,221
Maine... Eastport	53	1,347	1,233	1,078	774	528	299	154	143	270	521	819	1,213	8,379
Mass... Boston	48	1,108	1,025	841	538	245	66	7	15	98	338	647	1,008	5,936
Mich... Detroit	80	1,235	1,120	957	570	256	54	7	17	120	397	769	1,114	6,616
Sault Ste. Marie	52	1,575	1,460	1,288	821	490	218	91	110	286	604	967	1,377	9,287
Minn... Minneapolis	61	1,589	1,370	1,087	577	258	60	8	23	163	473	966	1,411	7,985
Miss... Vicksburg	52	501	400	244	82	9	(*)	0	0	0	69	267	475	2,053
Mo.... Kansas City	63	1,088	916	675	319	106	26	0	(*)	53	239	617	972	5,011
St. Louis	52	904	849	613	303	90	7	(*)	1	38	208	567	914	4,584
Mont... Helena	48	1,347	1,157	990	639	413	192	43	66	291	596	944	1,252	7,930
Miles City	[1] 48	1,461	1,267	997	545	275	81	7	20	188	510	918	1,322	7,501
Nebr... North Platte	52	1,297	1,030	853	485	226	51	5	10	132	413	816	1,181	6,439
Omaha	78	1,325	1,099	853	412	157	23	1	5	91	333	776	1,165	6,240
Nev... Winnemucca	73	1,148	890	773	534	322	119	11	22	187	503	809	1,077	6,395
N.J... Atlantic City	49	946	887	750	485	208	37	1	2	39	247	546	867	5,015
N.Mex... Albuquerque	21	958	716	584	300	85	4	0	(*)	23	229	662	876	4,437
N.Y... Albany	45	1,271	1,167	946	560	230	50	4	17	129	415	792	1,146	6,687
New York	53	1,014	944	770	461	173	29	1	4	51	263	586	929	5,225
Rochester	53	1,220	1,152	971	604	282	70	10	26	134	415	751	1,099	6,734
N.C... Asheville	22	766	691	571	293	89	9	2	4	44	241	556	778	4,044
Raleigh	65	701	609	444	209	47	4	0	1	20	160	418	672	3,285
N.Dak... Bismarck	52	1,721	1,490	1,193	647	339	110	21	44	245	590	1,075	1,529	9,014
Ohio... Cleveland	15	1,203	1,086	909	556	247	50	7	14	105	407	761	1,092	6,413
Okla... Okla. City	52	850	676	463	197	57	3	(*)	(*)	22	146	457	779	3,650
Oreg... Portland	53	786	615	534	366	233	105	27	28	103	298	535	720	4,350
Pa.... Harrisburg	52	1,062	970	761	427	143	23	1	6	71	308	639	986	5,397
Pittsburgh	53	1,021	950	748	436	161	27	2	6	69	306	642	965	5,333
S.C... Charleston	52	437	380	240	82	6	1	0	0	1	44	225	422	1,838
S.Dak... Huron	52	1,585	1,352	1,047	577	271	71	9	22	178	496	972	1,416	7,996
Tenn... Nashville	53	783	675	474	220	54	3	0	(*)	20	163	475	743	3,610
Tex... Amarillo	60	867	740	557	283	105	12	1	2	42	224	535	847	4,215
El Paso	50	615	432	291	104	14	1	0	0	6	88	366	615	2,532
Fort Worth	53	594	464	277	97	16	1	0	0	5	70	286	540	2,350
Houston	52	368	266	145	35	2	0	0	0	1	25	159	327	1,328
Utah... Salt Lake City	52	1,095	860	711	437	198	61	3	4	93	357	705	1,017	5,541
Vt... Burlington	31	1,441	1,307	1,095	682	327	93	19	45	196	516	859	1,295	7,875
Va.... Norfolk	48	712	650	483	254	62	5	0	0	6	129	392	668	3,364
Richmond	54	800	717	531	276	70	7	(*)	1	27	180	483	771	3,572
Wash... Seattle	24	759	617	562	396	282	129	45	47	139	340	545	668	4,499
Spokane	53	1,165	934	765	495	287	116	22	37	184	490	832	1,070	6,387
W.Va... Parkersburg	63	971	874	675	367	131	17	1	4	61	292	619	914	4,926
Wis... Madison	52	1,447	1,264	1,012	589	267	64	8	20	148	431	839	1,300	7,409
Wyo... Cheyenne	79	1,215	1,066	1,003	714	448	163	36	48	247	588	894	1,135	7,557
Alaska Juneau	9	1,228	1,120	1,007	805	551	343	302	343	466	726	984	1,170	9,045
T.H... Honolulu	47	(*)	0	0	0	0	0	0	0	0	0	0	0	(*)
P.R... San Juan	53	0	0	0	0	0	0	0	0	0	0	0	0	0

[1] Through 1942.

Source: Department of Commerce, Weather Bureau; records.

7. Public Lands and National Park System

Acquisition of original public domain.—Recognition of its sovereignty over its present continental land area was acquired by the United States Government through a series of international agreements and treaties. The United States, however, did not gain title to all of these lands by such agreements. At the time of acquisition of sovereignty over the areas involved, title to about 463 million acres rested in individual States and their political subdivisions or in private owners, which title was not relinquished to the Federal Government. Title to the remaining 1,442 million acres of land area passed to the United States and, with the exception of lands in the District of Columbia, is known as the *original public domain.* Any of such lands which the Government has not disposed of under the public-land laws, are generally referred to as *public-domain lands* or *public lands.*

In addition to the public domain, the United States Government has from time to time acquired, by purchase, condemnation, and gift, tracts of land needed for various public purposes. Such lands are often referred to as *acquired lands,* to distinguish them from public-domain lands. Complete statistics are not available as to the extent of such acquisitions.

Public-domain lands.—*Public-domain lands* or *public lands,* as used here, refers to those Federally owned lands to which the general body of public land laws apply. (See title 43, Code of Federal Regulations.) In general, it includes that portion of the original public domain not disposed of under the public land laws, and certain other lands declared by the Congress specifically to be *public lands.* As a general rule, it excludes *acquired lands,* as defined above. The term *Indian lands,* as used in tables 193–195, refers to that portion of the public domain lands that was ceded to the United States by Indian tribes on condition that part or all of the proceeds from their sale or other disposition would be covered into the Treasury in trust for the Indians.

Entries, selections, patents, and certifications.—The data on entries, selections, patents, and certifications refer to transactions which involve the disposal, under the public-land laws (including the homestead laws), of Federal public lands to non-Federal owners. In general, *original entries* and *selections* are applications to secure title to public lands which have been accepted as properly filed. Some types of applications, however, are not reported until the final certificate is issued.

Applications become *final entries* (perfected entries) upon issuance of a *final certificate* which is given to the applicant after he has complied fully with the requirements of the laws relating to his application. These requirements may include, in particular settlement upon and improvement of the lands entered, or payment of statutory fees or purchase money. A *final certificate* passes equitable title to the land to the applicant. *Patents* are instruments which pass legal title to the lands to the applicant. *Certifications* are issued in lieu of patents in connection with certain State selections.

Historical statistics.—See preface and historical appendix. Tabular headnotes (as "See also *Historical Statistics,* series F 1–7") provide cross-references, where applicable, to *Historical Statistics of the United States, 1789–1945.*

Note.—This section presents data for the most recent year or period available on February 15, 1952, when the material was organized and sent to the printer.

FIG. XV.—ACQUISITION OF THE TERRITORY OF CONTINENTAL UNITED STATES AND ORIGIN OF THE PUBLIC DOMAIN
[See table 191]

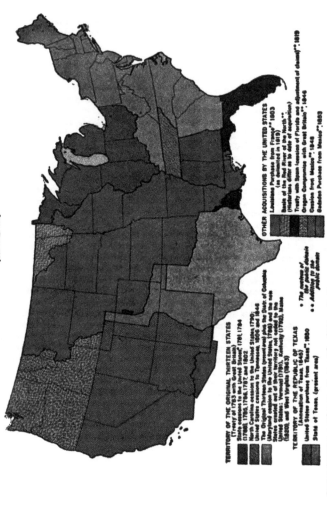

TERRITORY OF THE ORIGINAL THIRTEEN STATES
[Treaty of 1783 with Great Britain]
State cessions to the United States, 1781-1784
(1781, 1782, 1784, 1787, and 1802
War Department cessions to Tennessee 1806 and 1846
United States cessions to Tennessee 1806 and 1846
The Original Thirteen States (present area) plus the State of Columbia
(Maryland cession to the United States, 1790) and the area
States created out of their territory not ceded to the
United States: Vermont (1791), Kentucky (1792), Maine
(1820), and West Virginia (1863)

TERRITORY OF THE REPUBLIC OF TEXAS
United States purchase from Texas", 1850
State of Texas (present area)

OTHER ACQUISITIONS BY THE UNITED STATES
Louisiana Purchase from France", 1803
(as delimited in 1819)
Basin of the Red River of the North"
(Historians differ as to date of acquisition)
Treaty with Spain "cession of Florida and adjustment of classes)", 1819
Oregon Compromise with Great Britain", 1846
Cession from Mexico", 1848
Gadsden Purchase from Mexico", 1853

* The numbers of the public domain
** Adding to the public domain

Source: Department of Interior, Bureau of Land Management.

No. 190.—LANDS IN FEDERAL OWNERSHIP—ACREAGE, BY STATES: 1949

[Submitted by Committee on Public Lands as of September 1950. Compiled from data transmitted by administering agencies during preceding year]

STATE	LAND AREA (ACRES)						
	Total	Under Federal ownership					
		Total	Percent of total area	Administering Agency			
				Dept. of Interior	Dept. of Agriculture	Dept. of Defense	Other
Total	1, 905, 361, 920	455, 146, 726	23.89	262, 155, 710	167, 656, 496	23, 104, 726	2, 229, 792
Alabama	32, 689, 920	1, 099, 722	3. 36	29, 402	632, 389	192, 273	245, 658
Arizona	72, 691, 200	50, 471, 920	69. 43	36, 818, 879	11, 463, 789	2, 160, 923	6, 330
Arkansas	33, 744, 000	3, 031, 431	8. 98	252, 074	2, 425, 437	330, 645	23, 275
California	100, 253, 920	45, 900, 157	45. 74	28, 608, 479	19, 838, 388	2, 413, 936	44, 354
Colorado	66, 538, 560	24, 851, 005	37. 35	10, 097, 183	14, 315, 620	312, 617	125, 585
Connecticut	3, 113, 260	15, 714	. 50	1	11, 832	1, 088	2, 793
Delaware	1, 265, 920	40, 608	3. 21	14, 022	5, 073	20, 298	1, 210
District of Columbia	39, 040	13, 043	33. 41	(1)	(1)	(1)	13, 043
Florida	34, 727, 680	2, 851, 207	8. 21	714, 427	1, 374, 683	730, 702	31, 395
Georgia	37, 451, 570	1, 831, 193	4. 89	396, 635	819, 700	607, 285	17, 673
Idaho	52, 997, 120	34, 285, 000	64. 69	12, 756, 884	20, 432, 505	1, 091, 456	4, 155
Illinois	35, 806, 080	448, 992	1. 25	51, 490	214, 919	159, 113	23, 470
Indiana	23, 171, 200	336, 952	1. 45	185	119, 111	208, 897	8, 779
Iowa	35, 831, 040	105, 310	. 29	27, 552	6, 697	69, 608	1, 453
Kansas	52, 542, 320	322, 118	. 61	50, 928	102, 737	162, 986	6, 467
Kentucky	25, 669, 760	946, 131	3. 69	115, 376	459, 905	296, 435	75, 417
Louisiana	28, 913, 280	1, 053, 161	3. 64	231, 724	580, 719	232, 859	7, 859
Maine	19, 865, 600	143, 131	. 72	50, 823	67, 124	21, 226	3, 858
Maryland	6, 327, 680	229, 392	3. 63	30, 192	56, 534	121, 804	20, 951
Massachusetts	5, 060, 480	52, 671	1. 04	9, 727	1, 708	38, 521	2, 715
Michigan	36, 494, 080	2, 709, 428	7. 42	269, 773	2, 399, 844	25, 717	14, 094
Minnesota	51, 205, 760	3, 819, 665	7. 46	1, 156, 090	2, 628, 994	28, 233	6, 348
Mississippi	30, 348, 800	1, 484, 718	4. 89	87, 041	1, 145, 789	204, 689	47, 194
Missouri	44, 352, 800	1, 641, 502	3. 70	40, 932	1, 350, 659	213, 154	36, 757
Montana	93, 642, 240	34, 212, 875	36. 54	15, 153, 859	18, 465, 197	592, 723	2, 096
Nebraska	49, 057, 920	735, 224	1. 50	258, 214	364, 741	111, 364	905
Nevada	70, 273, 280	59, 526, 969	84. 71	50, 871, 672	5, 071, 643	3, 562, 485	21, 159
New Hampshire	5, 775, 360	682, 600	11. 82	40	669, 365	12, 969	226
New Jersey	4, 814, 080	96, 462	2. 00	13, 999	78	77, 126	5, 364
New Mexico	77, 767, 040	35, 479, 713	45. 62	22, 845, 822	9, 672, 056	2, 815, 598	146, 237
New York	30, 674, 560	358, 214	1. 17	141, 478	32, 917	155, 434	28, 385
North Carolina	31, 450, 880	1, 927, 562	6. 13	442, 360	1, 118, 478	256, 287	110, 437
North Dakota	44, 534, 560	2, 651, 896	5. 91	1, 443, 205	1, 081, 085	127, 430	178
Ohio	26, 316, 080	259, 156	. 98	370	130, 436	104, 838	23, 512
Oklahoma	44, 341, 120	3, 891, 209	8. 78	3, 087, 162	291, 608	487, 681	24, 758
Oregon	61, 664, 000	32, 510, 870	52. 72	17, 494, 598	14, 856, 128	145, 861	14, 268
Pennsylvania	28, 828, 800	590, 522	2. 05	4, 458	509, 663	55, 586	20, 785
Rhode Island	677, 120	18, 917	2. 79	28	10, 722	7, 320	847
South Carolina	19, 380, 160	912, 702	4. 66	130, 830	642, 951	94, 157	44, 764
South Dakota	48, 983, 040	8, 610, 766	17. 23	6, 304, 435	1, 997, 712	293, 234	15, 387
Tennessee	26, 855, 040	1, 646, 281	6. 13	242, 637	647, 346	193, 895	562, 403
Texas	168, 732, 160	2, 246, 872	1. 33	772, 004	790, 304	528, 205	156, 058
Utah	52, 701, 440	37, 592, 044	71. 33	27, 351, 320	7, 886, 244	2, 345, 236	9, 244
Vermont	5, 937, 920	604, 184	11. 69	409, 977	210, 400	13, 531	216
Virginia	25, 533, 360	2, 078, 615	8. 14	263, 040	1, 480, 108	226, 192	9, 275
Washington	42, 865, 280	14, 998, 067	34. 99	4, 900, 998	9, 670, 614	187, 624	238, 874
West Virginia	15, 417, 600	1, 289, 062	8. 36	182	918, 971	367, 767	2, 142
Wisconsin	35, 017, 600	2, 243, 003	6. 41	624, 421	1, 510, 890	97, 367	10, 625
Wyoming	62, 403, 840	32, 207, 086	51. 61	22, 843, 791	9, 152, 902	201, 229	9, 164

1 Included under "other."

Source: 81st Cong., 2d sess.; House of Representatives. Report No. 3116. (Printed 1950.)

No. 191.—ACQUISITION AND EXTENT OF PUBLIC DOMAIN, CONTINENTAL UNITED STATES: 1781 TO 1952

[See also *Historical Statistics*, series F 1-7]

ITEM	ACQUISITION OF THE ORIGINAL PUBLIC DOMAIN			Estimated area of the public domain (selected years) [1]
	Total area	Land area	Water area	
	Acres	*Acres*	*Acres*	*Acres*
Aggregate, 1952	1,462,466,560	1,442,200,320	20,266,240	412,000,000
1912, estimate of public domain				600,000,000
1880, estimate of public domain				900,000,000
1853, Gadsden Purchase	18,988,800	18,961,920	26,880	
1850, estimate of public domain				1,200,000,000
1850, Purchase from Texas	78,926,720	78,842,880	83,840	
1848, Mexican Cession [2]	338,680,960	334,479,360	4,201,600	
1846, Oregon Compromise	183,386,240	180,644,480	2,741,760	
1819, Cession from Spain	46,144,640	43,342,720	[2] 2,801,920	
Red River Basin [4]	29,601,920	29,066,880	535,040	
1803, Louisiana Purchase [2]	529,911,680	523,446,400	6,465,280	
1802, estimate of public domain				200,000,000
1781-1802 (State Cessions)	236,825,600	233,415,680	3,409,920	

[1] Estimated from imperfect data available for indicated years.

[2] Data for Louisiana Purchase exclude area eliminated by Treaty of 1819 with Spain. Such areas are included in figures for Mexican Cession.

[3] Includes 33,920 acres subsequently recognized as part of State of Texas which is not a public domain State.

[4] Represents drainage basin of Red River of the North, south of 49th parallel. Authorities differ as to method and exact date of its acquisition. Some hold it as part of Louisiana Purchase, others maintain it was acquired from Great Britain.

Source: Department of Interior. Estimated area, Bureau of Land Management; all other data, Office of the Secretary, *Areas of Acquisitions to the Territory of the U. S., 1922.*

No. 192.—DISPOSAL OF PUBLIC LANDS: 1861 TO 1952

[For years ending June 30. Data include Alaska except where noted. Period figures are totals, not averages. See also *Historical Statistics*, series F 8-16]

PERIOD OR YEAR	Cash receipts of Bureau of Land Management [1]	Land granted to States [2]	ALL ENTRIES, SELECTIONS, PATENTS, ETC.[3]			HOMESTEAD ENTRIES, EXCEPT ON CEDED INDIAN LANDS		
			All original entries and selections [4]	All final entries	Patents and certifications	Original entries		Final entries [3]
						Number	Acreage	
	1,000 dollars	*1,000 acres*	*1,000 acres*	*1,000 acres*	*1,000 acres*	*Number*	*1,000 acres*	*1,000 acres*
1861-1870	13,324	17,657	[4] 13,341			142,210	15,931	1,379
1871-1880	17,508	3,842	62,202			327,512	39,735	17,887
1881-1890	99,269	23,367	190,697			497,083	69,773	28,961
1891-1900	33,492	14,201	106,299			456,943	62,767	31,878
1901-1910	94,095	20,300	196,841			831,841	130,737	38,819
1911-1920	67,025	8	156,402	[7] 9,778	[7] 13,327	554,026	123,826	74,316
1921-1930	104,453	409	61,231	45,513	66,358	172,503	53,460	40,391
1931-1935	21,659	275	18,232	6,847	8,977	41,610	15,266	6,234
1936-1940	38,597	203	1,037	7,396	9,373	2,944	659	6,783
1941-1945	58,428		404	1,087	3,350	1,233	159	764
1946-1950	141,464		496	436	1,726	2,456	306	155
1949	37,149		134	116	390	681	82	37
1950	36,177		142	150	492	523	73	46
1951	49,082		121	198	386	363	49	63
1952	64,518		113	165	374	458	59	38

[1] Includes receipts from such sources as following: Sales of public and ceded Indian lands; fees and commissions; mineral rentals, royalties, and bonuses; sales of timber; grazing fees and rentals; and land rentals. For period prior to 1861, receipts were $177,230,000.

[2] As of June 30, 1952, process of legal adjudication had not yet been completed for all grants and small changes in data for certain years may occur. For period 1802-60, total land granted to States was 96,977,000 acres. Includes grants for such public purposes as following: Educational, penal, and other public institutions and buildings; bridges, reservoirs, and other internal improvements; reclamation of swamp and arid lands; experiment stations; recreation areas; wildlife and forestry areas; military camps; and payments of bonds issued by local governments. Excludes grants to aid in construction of railroads, wagon roads, canals, and river improvements, or acreage of swamplands lost to States, for which States received indemnity in cash. Excludes data for Alaska and also 10,000 acres which is due to breakage and "less than" items.

[3] Includes homesteads. [4] Includes some classes of final entries and patents prior to 1911.

[5] Excludes commuted homesteads. [6] 1868-1870 only. [7] 1920 only.

Source: Department of Interior, Bureau of Land Management; annual report of the Director, and records.

No. 193.—Public and Indian Land, Entries Under All Acts—Acreage, by States and for Alaska: 1936 to 1952

[For years ending June 30. See general note p. 169. For grand totals for earlier years, see *Historical Statistics*, series F 11–13]

CLASS AND STATE	ORIGINAL ENTRIES							Final entries, 1952	Patented, 1952
	1936–40, total	1941–45, total	1946–50, total	1949	1950	1951	1952		
Total	1,036,849	404,409	496,287	133,773	142,273	120,774	113,153	164,918	373,625
Public land	987,684	400,239	480,487	133,402	135,043	113,078	112,831	162,551	....
Indian land	49,165	4,169	15,800	371	7,230	7,696	322	2,367	....
All homesteads	708,410	162,736	321,638	82,712	79,840	56,209	59,070	41,965	44,725
Stock-raising homesteads	472,920	25,488	3,192	640	....	1,233	640	818	603
Other entries	328,439	241,673	174,649	51,061	62,433	64,565	54,083	122,953	328,900
Alaska	59,034	66,695	171,810	42,269	29,859	18,144	43,681	15,336	16,806
Arizona	80,874	25,157	43,832	13,542	7,724	4,723	3,074	6,076	34,012
California	1 209,426	89,631	59,572	22,150	15,093	23,574	6,889	26,061	41,026
Colorado	107,578	10,209	45,484	21,537	10,424	9,820	8,546	31,349	19,928
Idaho	57,488	21,573	32,543	8,897	10,905	23,988	14,729	15,109	12,721
Montana	84,619	20,929	1,802	504	200	640	257	3,287	9,375
Nevada	2,831	7,851	6,900	2,280	3,675	6,985	9,757	5,736	21,477
New Mexico	176,942	33,435	4,733	1,231	162	1,156	11,194	3,568	113,026
North Dakota	1,860	876						61	550
Oregon	53,878	5,136	2,068	120	913	160	240	5,779	6,288
South Dakota	7,735	550	151					1,234	1,748
Utah	27,091	99,699	71,966	18,046	39,721	19,707	10,733	12,690	39,120
Washington	3,333	760	5,104	641	1,435	730	20	3,561	5,413
Wyoming	138,074	9,830	47,175	1,824	21,186	9,017	2,510	24,637	31,212
Other States	26,086	12,083	3,146	732	976	2,130	1,523	10,434	20,928

1 Includes 150,749 acres acquired by the State of California for State park purposes under act of June 29, 1936.

Source: Department of the Interior, Bureau of Land Management; annual report of the Director.

No. 194.—Public and Indian Land, Entries and Patents—Acreage: 1951 and 1952

[For years ending June 30. Data include Alaska. For grand totals for earlier years, see *Historical Statistics*, series F 11–13]

CLASS	1951			1952		
	Original entries	Final entries	Patented entries	Original entries	Final entries	Patented entries
Total	120,774	197,947	388,428	113,153	164,918	373,625
Homesteads	56,209	70,830	63,424	59,070	41,965	44,725
Stockraising	1,233	923	869	640	818	603
Enlarged	16,202	1,916	2,076	8,919	3,261	1,767
Reclamation	12,226	41,340	31,250	595	21,108	23,490
Forest	293	249	415	103	150	190
Commuted		2,874	2,482		2,092	2,509
Sec. 2289, original act, et al	26,255	23,528	26,332	48,813	14,536	16,166
Deserts	44,686	10,593	11,769	29,255	6,579	6,990
Public auction		101,086	99,009		88,482	74,540
State selection	7,387		1 28,658	12,388		1 8,588
Mineral	7,377	12,800	22,367	10,200	22,217	5,162
Exchange			152,647			215,286
Miscellaneous	5,115	2,638	10,554	2,240	5,675	18,334

1 Includes certifications: 1951, 26,711 acres; 1952, 7,136 acres.

Source: Department of the Interior, Bureau of Land Management; annual report of the Director.

No. 195.—Public Land, Homestead Entries—Acreage, by States and for Alaska: 1931 to 1952

[For years ending June 30. See general note, p. 169. See also *Historical Statistics*, series F 15 and 16]

ITEM AND STATE	ALL HOMESTEADS							
	1931–1935, total	1936–1940, total	1941–1945, total	1946–1950, total	1949	1950	1951	1952
Original entries, total__	15,266,771	659,350	153,567	305,539	82,341	72,610	48,513	88,748
Alaska_____	38,659	58,718	59,559	171,759	42,209	29,859	18,144	43,681
Arizona_____	1,124,034	39,910	8,199	8,134	5,827	162	1,808	103
Arkansas_____	[1] 43,298	(?)						
California_____	909,636	29,127	2,391	25,064	10,870	922	200	157
Colorado_____	1,028,298	58,501	7,533	10,508	972	4,710	3,387	1,200
Florida_____	[1] 9,554	(?)						
Idaho_____	694,481	56,757	16,020	15,626	6,603	1,877	3,465	594
Minnesota_____	[1] 4,947	(?)						
Montana_____	[3]1,384,188	84,102	17,871	644	204	160	640	20
Nebraska_____	[1] 17,468	(?)						
Nevada_____	97,670	1,832	1,812	2,314	1,080	914	507	1,084
New Mexico_____	4,387,629	94,337	13,817	1,378	754	162	978	640
North Dakota_____	79,152	1,860	875					
Oregon_____	561,227	50,963	3,373	1,898	120	913		80
South Dakota_____	220,963	7,695						
Utah_____	609,755	26,811	12,650	32,981	11,787	18,278	16,568	9,699
Washington_____	67,354	2,733	320	2,435	201	61	332	
Wyoming_____	3,894,074	125,425	2,694	30,077	1,262	13,656	403	
Bureau of Land Management [2]____	94,395	20,579	11,453	3,026	732	936	2,084	1,490
Final entries [4]_____	6,233,399	6,783,129	764,204	156,904	36,969	46,127	63,059	37,506

[1] 1931 to 1933.
[2] Entries, if any, included with Bureau of Land Management, for States no longer having local offices.
[3] Includes entries of abandoned military reservations.
[4] Excludes commuted homesteads and ceded Indian lands.

Source: Department of the Interior, Bureau of Land Management; annual report of the Director.

No. 196.—Grazing Districts—Acreage as of June 30, 1952; Permitted Operators and Use, for Fiscal Year 1952

STATE	Area [1] (acres)	Operators (number)	ANIMAL-UNITS-MONTHS OF USE	
			Livestock	Wildlife
Total_____	160,075,550	19,692	15,403,366	1,168,678
Arizona_____	12,960,901	939	925,460	18,320
California_____	4,293,922	458	536,617	61,361
Colorado_____	8,065,525	1,982	943,016	232,772
Idaho_____	13,138,769	2,830	1,485,329	147,186
Montana_____	5,995,791	2,807	973,654	64,211
Nevada_____	47,661,491	1,049	2,507,642	142,040
New Mexico_____	14,383,772	3,618	2,292,411	39,754
Oregon_____	13,433,965	1,288	1,125,877	128,966
Utah_____	25,805,060	3,356	2,563,800	200,980
Wyoming_____	14,333,424	1,365	2,049,412	113,088

[1] Includes vacant public lands within grazing districts, and other federally reserved lands and private lands administered by Bureau of Land Management, by agreement or lease, pursuant to Pierce Act.

Source: Department of the Interior, Bureau of Land Management; annual report of the Director.

No. 197.—RECEIPTS UNDER MINERAL LEASING ACT OF FEB. 25, 1920, THROUGH 1952, AND MINERAL LEASES IN FORCE AS OF JUNE 30, 1952, BY STATES, AND FOR ALASKA

[All money figures in thousands of dollars. Excludes leasing activities of agencies other than Bureau of Land Management. Receipts under all mineral-leasing acts administered by Bureau of Land Management amounted to $51,615,536 in 1952, including those shown here]

STATE	RECEIPTS (YEARS ENDING JUNE 30)							LEASES IN FORCE JUNE 30, 1952[1]	
	Total	1920–47. total	1948	1949	1950	1951	1952	Number	Acres
Total	344,486	157,239	24,351	28,971	28,971	34,951	41,864	63,601	46,736,360
Alabama	217	209	(²)	1	(²)	1	5	22	2,011
Alaska	35	1	1		4	7	23	146	190,663
Arizona	375	42	13	52	30	85	153	1,072	496,217
Arkansas	6	3	1	1	1	(²)	1	19	4,131
California	97,982	61,064	6,631	7,545	7,416	7,969	7,327	5,641	3,211,309
Colorado	28,556	5,542	3,233	4,266	4,180	5,068	6,265	4,730	4,395,707
Florida	3		(²)	(²)			3	47	7,394
Idaho	630	98	11	201	98	118	107	412	446,857
Illinois	(²)	(²)						1	80
Kansas	448	127	26	33	45	141	75	133	46,135
Louisiana	881	719	27	32	23	24	55	130	32,797
Michigan	34	9	2	5	3	5	2	15	7,079
Mississippi	11	1	(²)	1	2	1	3	96	8,098
Montana	12,631	5,966	857	1,145	1,257	1,314	2,092	5,036	4,448,391
Nebraska	76	1	(²)	(²)	7	6	62	277	146,100
Nevada	2,178	82	20	17	480	656	924	6,003	4,022,542
New Mexico	38,118	15,185	3,783	3,833	3,616	4,763	6,939	9,437	8,740,511
North Dakota	978	651	32	4	33	126	131	385	172,668
Oklahoma	240	36	10	17	65	70	41	535	113,246
Oregon	59	8	(²)	9	2	9	31	105	50,094
South Dakota	388	75	10	3	56	59	186	639	636,377
Utah	10,702	3,795	661	974	852	1,548	2,872	6,645	7,488,741
Washington	100	87	3	1	3	3	2	27	5,908
Wyoming	149,858	93,637	9,030	10,827	8,801	12,978	14,585	22,078	15,088,795

[1] Data for all leases except those on acquired lands. See note 1, table 198.
[2] Less than $500.

Source: Department of the Interior, Bureau of Land Management; annual report of the Director.

No. 198.—PUBLIC LANDS—LEASES, PERMITS, AND LICENSES OUTSTANDING, BY CLASS: JUNE 30, 1952

[Data include Alaska]

CLASS	Number	Acres	CLASS	Number	Acres
MINERAL			OTHER		
Grand total	63,957	49,317,000	Grand total	37,757	17,897,360
Leases, total [1]	63,601	48,786,209	Leases, total	37,229	17,295,449
Oil and gas [1]	63,164	48,562,880	Grazing, Taylor Act	11,496	16,254,092
Coal	358	124,478	Grazing, Alaska	27	596,575
Potash	33	69,629	Grazing, Oregon and California	231	264,093
Phosphate	37	23,303	Fur farm, Alaska	5	20,400
Sodium	6	5,438	Aviation	41	20,451
Silica sands	3	481	Mineral or medicinal spring	6	897
			Recreational	12	17,595
Permits, total [1]	310	529,134	Boy Scout camp	1	80
Sulphur	3	1,736	Water well	13	410
Coal	83	115,883	Bathing beach	1	22
Potash	174	319,326	Small tract	26,307	114,332
Sodium	50	92,185	Other	1	480
Vanadium					
			Permits, total [1]	337	1,051
Licenses, total	46	1,657	Special land use		2,230
Coal	46	1,657			

[1] Does not include oil and gas leases within naval reserves and the following on acquired land: 1,192 leases (1,116,261 acres); and various minerals, 132 permits (62,008 acres).
[2] Excludes grazing licenses and permits within grazing district, 19,692 (160,000,000 acres).

Source: Department of the Interior, Bureau of Land Management; annual report of the Director.

No. 199.—LAND GRANTS TO STATES—ACREAGE, BY STATES AND FOR ALASKA, TO JUNE 30, 1952

[In thousands of acres. Includes grants of scrip]

STATE	Total	Support of common schools	Support of other schools	Support of other institutions	Construction of railroads	Construction of wagon roads	Construction of canals and improvement of rivers	Construction of miscellaneous internal improvements	Reclamation of swamplands	Other purposes
Total	245,275	96,532	17,034	¹3,993	37,129	3,359	¹6,104	7,807	64,894	6,426
Alabama	5,006	912	384	(³)	2,747		400	97	441	25
Alaska	21,447	21,009	438	(³)						
Arizona	10,544	8,093	849							1,101
Arkansas	11,937	934	196	500				500	7,687	57
California	8,822	5,534	196		2,564			500	2,193	401
Colorado	4,472	3,686	138	32				500		116
Connecticut	180		180							
Delaware	90		90							
Florida	24,206	975	182		2,219			500	20,325	5
Georgia	270		270							
Idaho	4,251	2,964	387	¹250						650
Illinois	6,235	996	526		2,595		324	209	1,460	124
Indiana	4,040	669	436			171	1,480		1,259	26
Iowa	8,061	1,001	286		4,707		321	500	1,196	50
Kansas	7,795	2,908	151	(³)	4,176			500		59
Kentucky	355		330	25						
Louisiana	11,429	807	256		373			500	9,492	
Maine	210		210							
Maryland	210		210							
Massachusetts	360		360							
Michigan	12,144	1,022	286		3,134	221	1,251	500	5,680	49
Minnesota	16,422	2,875	212		8,047			500	4,707	81
Mississippi	6,097	824	348		1,075			500	3,348	1
Missouri	7,417	1,222	376		1,838			500	3,432	49
Montana	5,963	5,198	389	100						276
Nebraska	3,459	2,731	136	32					500	60
Nevada	2,725	2,062	136	13					500	14
New Hampshire	150		150							
New Jersey	210		210							
New Mexico	12,795	8,711	1,347	750			100			1,887
New York	990		990							
North Carolina	270		270							
North Dakota	3,164	2,495	336	¹250						82
Ohio	2,759	724	699			81	1,204		26	24
Oklahoma	3,096	1,375	1,050	¹671						
Oregon	7,033	3,399	136		2,584			500	286	127
Pennsylvania	780		780							
Rhode Island	120		120							
South Carolina	180		180							
South Dakota	3,435	2,723	366	¹251						86
Tennessee	300		300							
Texas	180		180							
Utah	7,502	5,844	556	500						601
Vermont	150		150							
Virginia	300		300							
Washington	3,044	2,376	236	¹200						132
West Virginia	150		150							
Wisconsin	10,179	982	332		3,652	303	1,022	500	3,361	26
Wyoming	4,343	3,470	136	¹420						316

¹ Includes acreage of grants for "educational and charitable" purposes as follows: Idaho, 150,000; North Dakota, 170,000; South Dakota, 170,000; Washington, 200,000. Includes also 669,000 acres granted to Oklahoma for "charitable, penal, and public building" purposes, and 290,000 acres granted to Wyoming for "charitable, educational, penal, etc." purposes.

² River-improvement grants, 1,505,000 acres (Alabama, 400,000; Iowa, 321,000; New Mexico, 100,000; Wisconsin, 684,000). Canal grants 4,599,000 acres.

³ Less than 500 acres.

Source: Department of the Interior, Bureau of Land Management; annual report of the Director.

No. 200.—Vacant Public Lands—Acreage, by States: June 30, 1900 to 1952

[Vacant public lands are those which are unappropriated and unreserved. The former represent lands not covered by an entry, the latter, lands not reserved for some public purpose, i. e., available for entry or selection under appropriate laws. Data cover vacant public lands outside Alaska withdrawn for classification in furtherance of Taylor Grazing Act and for conservation and development of natural resources. Figures exclude vacant public lands in Alaska estimated at 270,000,000 acres on June 30, 1952. For U. S. totals, see *Historical Statistics*, series F 5]

STATE	1900	1910	1920	1930	1940	1950	1952
Total	627,642,129	343,971,674	300,228,128	178,979,445	178,825,925	176,408,160	171,869,683
Alabama	289,280	166,219	37,200	(²)	15,940	20,926	24,562
Arizona	50,326,988	41,491,369	18,308,909	15,180,589	13,869,348	12,544,779	13,158,451
Arkansas	3,406,444	513,796	276,595	190,989	129,962	133,796	17,637
California	42,487,512	34,864,884	19,865,801	16,623,489	16,988,775	16,305,673	16,382,103
Colorado	38,689,347	21,726,192	8,941,185	8,027,488	7,987,490	8,069,927	8,055,029
Florida	1,392,411	453,000	130,077	13,897	13,775	22,582	20,230
Idaho	43,394,694	34,748,904	8,805,112	10,617,970	11,879,452	10,858,329	12,491,973
Indiana						11	11
Kansas	1,194,900	127,180	4,346	(²)	2,800	2,535	2,432
Louisiana	462,234	88,911	14,390	(²)	5,716	7,290	7,046
Michigan	420,452	107,880	73,523	(²)	15,810	15,604	16,163
Minnesota	4,696,208	1,568,302	256,297	189,845	286,188	93,102	92,002
Mississippi	258,804	47,056	32,300	(²)	12,587	16,713	16,251
Missouri	337,946	2,510	18	(²)	439	924	643
Montana	57,993,687	38,014,942	5,973,741	6,601,677	6,450,800	6,772,660	6,779,452
Nebraska	5,756,688	1,679,486	86,844	22,628	28,600	24,857	18,688
Nevada	61,277,606	56,474,695	54,267,175	51,454,493	51,143,840	47,188,360	46,517,244
New Mexico	56,041,170	36,454,692	18,448,878	15,664,121	15,696,408	14,382,660	13,358,282
North Dakota	15,731,330	1,448,235	81,044	146,506	107,583	96,470	91,308
Oklahoma	5,732,872	5,007	7,404	(²)	23,157	24,601	24,678
Oregon	34,377,907	17,560,573	14,005,757	13,069,196	12,774,194	13,298,154	13,171,571
South Dakota	11,996,989	4,562,804	268,472	436,580	279,087	290,445	308,296
Utah	42,987,451	35,955,554	20,991,715	23,881,445	25,733,585	23,032,410	24,587,943
Washington	11,125,883	2,198,089	1,086,696	920,584	577,419	487,151	476,737
Wisconsin	313,865	14,460	5,184	(²)	6,160	6,043	5,486
Wyoming	46,398,160	34,575,159	19,679,596	16,929,460	15,906,529	16,615,142	16,097,960

[1] Exclusive of Cherokee Strip, containing 8,094,644 acres, and all other lands owned or claimed by Indians in Indian Territory west of ninety-sixth degree of longitude.
[2] Includes acreage of public lands within grazing districts, as follows: 1940, 131,026,135; 1950, 134,874,876; 1952, 148,000,000 (estimated). [3] Data not tabulated.

Source: Department of the Interior, Bureau of Land Management; annual report of the Director and records.

No. 201.—Areas Administered by the National Park Service—Acreage and Number of Visitors: 1952

[For figures for continental U. S. only, see *Historical Statistics*, series F 17–18]

TYPE OF AREA	Number of areas, June 30	Net acreage, June 30	Visitors, year ending Sept. 30, 1952
Areas administered by National Park Service, total	178	23,846,224.34	41,514,644
National Park System:			
Continental United States, total	167	14,766,800.97	37,961,191
National parks	26	10,478,465.37	16,280,562
National monuments	81	4,014,922.99	6,646,316
National military parks	11	34,536.07	[1] 2,169,582
National historical parks	5	10,406.33	2,810,235
National memorial parks	1	62,160.95	127,236
National battlefield parks	2	3,776.55	
National battlefield sites	6	188.33	406,020
National historical sites	10	217.01	
National capital parks	11	2,922.00	810,646
National parkways	9	1,564.02	[2] 1,396,784
	1	[3] 30,145.15	[4] 3,900,595
	1	75,817.12	[5] 3,374,962
National seashore, total	6	7,111,196.97	789,694
	2	2,115,775.64	694,582
	4	4,995,414.43	4,582
Areas administered by National Park Service, total	5	2,020,165.80	2,626,150
	4	2,020,063.80	2,762,441
National historic site (in San Juan, Puerto Rico) [6]	1	40.00	56,718

[1] ... including military parks.
[2] ... administered by National Capital Parks.
[3] ... national demonstration area.
[4] ... administered by National Capital Parks.
[5] ... No record for other 3 parkways.
[6] Areas ... by cooperative agreement with Department of the Army.

Source: Department of the Interior, National Park Service; *Annual Report of the Secretary*.

No. 202.—VISITORS TO NATIONAL PARK SERVICE AREAS: 1916 TO 1952

[Includes data for Alaska and Hawaii. Visitors to these areas were 700,404 in 1952. Record of visitors to National Monuments not available for years prior to 1919. For figures for continental U. S. only, see *Historical Statistics*, series F 13]

YEAR ENDING SEPT. 30	Number	YEAR ENDING SEPT. 30	Number	YEAR ENDING SEPT. 30	Number
1916	356,097	1929	3,248,264	1942	10,766,661
1917	488,268	1930	3,246,656	1943	6,906,749
1918	451,691	1931	3,544,938	1944	8,146,464
1919	811,516	1932	3,754,596	1945	10,521,375
1920	1,058,455	1933	3,481,590	1946	21,682,782
1921	1,171,797	1934	6,337,205	1947	25,265,229
1922	1,216,497	1935	7,676,490	1948	29,608,318
1923	1,493,712	1936	11,989,793	1949	31,864,180
1924	1,670,908	1937	15,133,432	1950	32,782,288
1925	2,054,562	1938	16,331,467	1951	36,706,494
1926	2,314,955	1939	15,530,636	1952	41,516,664
1927	2,797,840	1940	16,755,251		
1928	3,024,544	1941	21,050,425		

Source: Department of the Interior, National Park Service; *Annual Report of the Secretary* and records.

No. 203.—LANDS UNDER JURISDICTION OF BUREAU OF INDIAN AFFAIRS—ACREAGE, BY STATES: 1881 TO 1949

[Taxable lands included in years prior to 1949. Figures for 1949 are for nontaxable lands only]

STATE	1881	1900	1911	1932	JUNE 30, 1949 [1]			
					Total	Trust allotted	Tribal	Government owned
Acres, total	155,632,312	78,372,185	71,646,796	52,651,333	56,004,678	16,534,060	38,607,964	862,626
Arizona	3,092,720	15,150,757	17,358,746	18,657,984	19,457,374	263,996	19,152,712	40,666
Arkansas				80	95	95		
California	415,841	406,398	437,629	625,354	548,408	75,302	456,211	16,895
Colorado	12,467,200	483,780	556,561	443,751	730,513	25,830	704,109	574
Florida		23,062	23,542	125,880	80,028		80,028	
Idaho	2,748,981	1,364,500	770,706	803,239	864,610	446,400	378,171	40,039
Iowa	692	2,965	3,251	3,361	5,040	1,059	3,903	78
Kansas	137,747	28,279	273,408	34,821	36,423	33,710	1,697	1,016
Michigan	66,332	8,317	153,910	20,233	26,397	15,349	7,026	4,022
Minnesota	5,026,447	1,566,707	1,480,647	549,320	863,026	170,509	659,961	32,556
Mississippi				3,863	15,488		15,280	208
Montana	29,356,800	9,500,700	6,263,151	6,055,009	6,502,211	5,163,777	1,217,967	120,467
Nebraska	436,252	74,592	344,375	69,280	28,073	14,214	13,706	153
Nevada	885,015	954,135	696,749	866,176	1,141,362	85,865	1,051,382	4,115
New Mexico	7,228,731	1,667,485	4,520,652	6,188,964	6,717,033	738,504	5,655,863	322,666
New York	86,366	87,677	87,677		86,008		85,978	
North Carolina	65,211	96,211	63,211	57,705	55,784	30	55,399	385
North Dakota	(²)	3,701,724	2,786,162	1,034,123	1,093,882	1,006,678	77,504	9,700
Oklahoma	41,100,915	26,397,237	22,736,473	2,919,896	2,466,770	2,341,356	73,378	54,036
Oregon	3,853,800	1,300,225	1,719,561	1,718,510	1,733,080	396,430	1,331,834	7,816
Pennsylvania					640		640	
South Dakota	³ 36,616,448	8,991,791	7,221,939	5,544,424	5,779,684	4,420,621	1,213,559	145,504
Texas					4,081	1,010		3,071
Utah	2,039,040	2,039,040	291,101	1,871,020	2,509,769	90,895	2,409,289	9,585
Washington	7,079,348	2,333,574	2,943,708	2,712,915	2,723,593	959,050	1,757,754	6,789
Wisconsin	586,026	381,061	590,094	395,919	452,678	147,071	264,318	41,289
Wyoming	2,342,400	1,810,000	³ 318,543	2,249,576	2,080,518	139,209	1,940,315	994

[1] Excludes an estimated 46,500 acres of trust land in Nebraska subject to taxation under the Brown Act of Dec. 30, 1916 (39 Stat. 865), and an estimated 450,000 acres of restricted taxable land in Oklahoma.
[2] Dakota Territory.
[3] Excludes ceded lands amounting to 1,472,000 acres. All other years include ceded land.

Source: Department of the Interior, Bureau of Indian Affairs; *Statistical Supplement to Annual Report of Commissioner of Indian Affairs* and records.

8. Labor Force, Employment, and Earnings

The various series of labor statistics covered in this section may be classified as of one of two types and these types differ somewhat in concept and purpose. One type of labor statistics is obtained by the "population approach," and includes data from the Census of Population and the Current Population Survey of the Bureau of the Census. These surveys involve an enumeration of individual persons and obtain information on employment activity from workers or members of their households. Each employed worker is counted only once, even though he may have held two or more jobs during a given period. The population approach permits a direct enumeration not only of employed persons but also of unemployed workers, the self-employed, unpaid family workers, domestic servants, and others who may not be found on the payrolls of any establishment.

The second type of labor statistics is obtained by the "establishment approach," and includes data from the monthly series of the Bureau of Agricultural Economics of the Department of Agriculture, and the Bureau of Labor Statistics of the Department of Labor. These data are similar to those provided by the Census of Manufactures and other industrial censuses in that they are based on reports from employers; i. e., farms, businesses, or industrial establishments. In adding together data from the reports of different employers the establishment approach counts twice or more any worker who works for two or more employers during a given payroll period, but permits a better analysis of such data as wages, hours, labor turnover, and industry affiliation which can be more accurately obtained from employers' records than by inquiries directed to a worker or a member of his household. The sampling methods usually used in the collection of statistics from establishments yield estimates of employment that may be subject to some error as well as to a small downward bias arising from inadequate representation of new firms entering business. Accurate estimates are maintained, however, by periodic adjustment to "benchmark" data from tabulations of employer reports obtained in connection with government social insurance programs and other sources, and by correcting current figures for selected industries for bias on the basis of past experience.

Labor force.—The labor force as now commonly defined in surveys using the population approach includes persons 14 years old and over who were employed, unemployed, or in the armed forces during a specified week. Employed persons are those who did any work for pay or profit during the week, or who worked without pay for 15 hours or more in a family enterprise (farm or business); also included are persons who did not work or look for work but who had a job or business from which they were temporarily absent during the week. Unemployed persons comprise those who did not work at all during the week but were looking for work. The "experienced civilian labor force" consists of all employed workers and unemployed workers with previous work experience. Population censuses earlier than 1940 used instead a concept of "gainful workers." This differed from the labor force concept in that it included all persons 10 years old and over who reported a gainful occupation, regardless of whether or not they were working or seeking work at the time of the census, and excluded in general new job seekers without previous experience in a gainful occupation.

The Decennial Census of Population provides detailed data for the United States as a whole and for each State, city, and other area, including personal character-

Note.—This section presents data for the most recent year or period available on March 17, 1951, when the material was organized and sent to the printer. In some instances, more recent data were added after that date.

istics (sex, age, color, etc.) of the labor force, the numbers employed and unemployed, the number reported in each occupation and in each industry, and other items. In the 1950 Census, the labor force data relate to the calendar week preceding the enumeration visit (i. e., during the first half of April, for the majority of the population).

The Census Bureau's Current Population Survey, a monthly enumeration of approximately 25,000 households throughout the Nation, provides current data published in *Current Population Reports—Monthly Report on the Labor Force*. Data presented include national totals, by sex and age, of the number of persons in the civilian labor force, during the calendar week containing the 8th of the month, the number employed in nonagricultural industries, the number employed in agriculture, the number unemployed, and the number of nonworkers. Also provided are data on hours of work and major occupation group of those employed and duration of unemployment of those unemployed.

Agricultural employment.—The establishment-type series are available for both agricultural and nonagricultural employment. Agricultural employment estimates, obtained by means of monthly mail returns from crop reporters, have been issued since 1909 by the Department of Agriculture.

Nonagricultural employment.—The monthly estimates of employment in nonagricultural establishments prepared by the Bureau of Labor Statistics are based on voluntary reports from about 42,000 establishments in manufacturing industries and from about 108,000 establishments in selected nonmanufacturing industries, supplemented by data from other government agencies and adjusted at intervals to data from tabulations of reports under government social insurance programs. These estimates exclude proprietors of unincorporated businesses, self-employed persons, domestic servants, and unpaid family workers, most of whom cannot be covered easily by the establishment approach. Persons in the Armed Forces are also excluded.

Estimates are available for total employment for 8 major industry divisions, and for selected nonmanufacturing industries. Both total employment and production-worker estimates are published for 21 major manufacturing groups, 131 manufacturing subgroups, and for mining industries. Average weekly hours and average weekly and hourly earnings are available for production and related workers for over 300 series in manufacturing; in mining, laundries, and cleaning and dyeing industries; and for nonsupervisory employees and working supervisors in other selected nonmanufacturing industries.

The employment data are for all full and part-time employees who worked or received pay for any part of the period reported.

The earnings data are gross, before payroll deductions and include overtime premiums; they exclude irregular bonuses and value of payments in kind. Hours are those actually worked or paid for.

For government and certain other segments of employment, the employment reports of the Bureau of Labor Statistics are supplemented by data from the Interstate Commerce Commission, the Civil Service Commission, the Bureau of the Census and other agencies.

Because of a major revision, continuous data for many currently published series begin with January 1947. Continuity with data prior to 1947 has been maintained for total employment in nonagricultural establishments and the 8 major industry divisions; for total and production-worker employment in all manufacturing, durable and nondurable goods, the 21 major manufacturing industry groups, and the mining industries; for hours and earnings in all manufacturing, durable and nondurable goods, and the mining industries.

Output per man-hour.—The Bureau of Labor Statistics currently prepares annual measures of output per man-hour (or the reciprocal—unit man-hour requirements) by two methods. One involves the construction of industry-wide measures from secondary source material; the other, from establishment reports for specified products selected to represent industry trends. Data under the first program are published for 24 manufacturing industries, 5 mining industries, 4 public utilities and agriculture. Indexes compiled from direct reports cover 18 manufacturing industries. Output per man-hour refers to production, in physical units, per man-hour of work. The indexes measure the relationships between the volume of goods produced and one factor of input—labor time. The data do not measure the specific contribution of labor or capital nor do they reflect increased efficiency resulting from more economical use of fuel and materials, or more efficient integration of industries.

Labor turn-over.—Labor turn-over rates are published monthly in the *Employment and Payrolls Report* of the Bureau of Labor Statistics for approximately 100 industries in 20 major groups in manufacturing and for selected nonmanufacturing industries, on the basis of about 7,000 reports from cooperating establishments. Labor turn-over data are available on a continuous monthly basis from January 1930 for manufacturing as a whole. Because of the adoption of the Standard Industrial Classification beginning with final data for December 1949, labor turn-over rates for many individual industries and industry groups are available on a continuous basis only from December 1949.

Work stoppages.—Statistical data on work stoppages due to labor-management disputes cannot be collected in the same fashion as other labor information since such stoppages are sporadic and cannot be covered by a routine periodic reporting service. The basic measures of strike statistics as now compiled by the Bureau of Labor Statistics are the number of stoppages, the number of workers involved, and the number of unions involved. Basic statistical data are obtained from the employers and unions involved. Leads to where strikes have occurred are obtained from a variety of sources, including newspapers, State employment services, or State and Federal mediation services. From the data given on the schedules, the Bureau prepares annual reports (published in the May *Monthly Labor Review* and later in bulletin form) which give not only the complete and verified total figures for each month of the year but also analyses of strikes by industry, State, city, and by causes, labor organizations involved, and other pertinent classification. Preliminary monthly, semi-annual, and annual figures are issued in press releases.

Historical statistics.—See preface and historical appendix. Tabular headnotes (as "See also *Historical Statistics*, series D 1–10") provide cross-references, where applicable, to *Historical Statistics of the United States, 1789–1945*.

Sampling Note—Current Population Survey

The sample used for the Current Population Survey (Monthly Report on the Labor Force) consists of approximately 25,000 households living in 125 counties and independent cities grouped in 68 areas. The chances are about 19 in 20 that the relative sampling variability of the estimated totals presented from the labor force survey are less than the following:

SEX	CIVILIAN LABOR FORCE			Not in the labor force
	Total	Employed	Unemployed	
	Percent	Percent	Percent	Percent
Both sexes	2	2	18	4
Male	2	2	18	4
Female	2	2	20	2

The percentages shown in this table represent the maximum differences to be expected between totals estimated from the sample and those that would have been obtained by a complete census following the same procedures. These percentages are themselves subject to variation in different time periods, particularly as the magnitudes being estimated change in level. Estimates of change from one month to the next are subject to somewhat smaller sampling variability for some of the items.

The sampling variability indicated above is illustrative of the variability to be expected for other subjects, such as urban-rural distributions, migration, occupation, education, marital status, race, family relationships, income, etc. For specific evaluation of the sampling variability relating to these subjects, see the original releases of the Bureau of the Census.

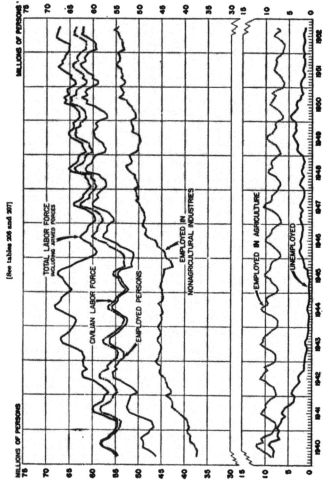

Fig. XVI.—Trends in the Labor Force: 1940 to September 1952

[See tables 206 and 207]

Source: Department of Commerce, Bureau of the Census.

FIG. XVII.—PERCENT CHANGE, 1940 TO 1950, IN NUMBER OF
EMPLOYED PERSONS, BY MAJOR OCCUPATION GROUP

[See table 222]

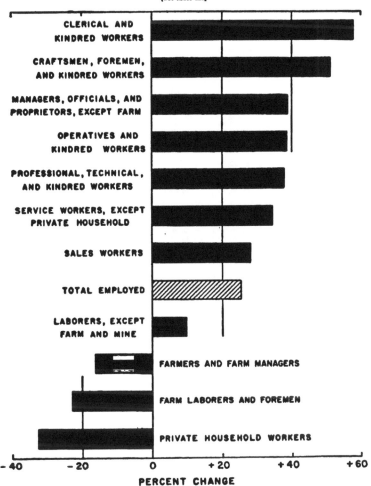

PERCENT CHANGE

Source: Department of Commerce, Bureau of the Census.

No. 204.—LABOR FORCE—GAINFUL WORKERS, 1820 TO 1930, AND EXPERIENCED CIVILIAN LABOR FORCE, 1940 AND 1950, IN FARM AND NONFARM OCCUPATIONS

[For explanation of differences in concept between gainful workers and labor force, see text, p. 179. See also *Historical Statistics*, series D 1-10]

YEAR	Population	GAINFUL WORKERS OR EXPERIENCED CIVILIAN LABOR FORCE				
		Total	Farm occupations [1]		Nonfarm occupations [1]	
				Number	Percent	Number	Percent
			PERSONS 10 YEARS OLD AND OVER				
1820	6,497,815	[2] 2,881,000	2,068,958	71.8	812,042	28.2
1830	8,639,412	[2] 3,931,537	2,772,453	70.5	1,159,084	29.5
1840	11,629,006	[2] 5,420,000	3,719,951	68.6	1,700,049	31.4
1850	16,452,835	[2] 7,697,196	4,901,882	63.7	2,795,314	36.3
1860	22,429,625	[2] 10,532,750	6,207,634	58.9	4,325,116	41.1
1870 [4]	29,123,683	12,924,951	6,849,772	53.0	6,075,179	47.0
1880	36,761,607	17,392,099	8,584,810	49.4	8,807,289	50.6
1890	47,413,559	[5] 23,318,183	9,938,373	42.6	13,379,810	57.4
1900	57,949,824	29,073,233	10,911,998	37.5	18,161,235	62.5
1910	71,580,270	[6] 37,370,794	11,591,767	31.0	25,779,027	69.0
1920	82,739,315	[7] 42,433,535	11,448,770	27.0	30,984,765	73.0
1930	98,723,047	48,829,920	10,471,998	21.4	38,357,922	78.6
			PERSONS 14 YEARS OLD AND OVER				
1930	89,100,555	48,594,592	10,161,212	20.9	38,433,380	79.1
1940	101,102,924	51,742,022	8,833,324	17.1	[8] 42,908,699	82.9
1950	112,354,084	[9] 59,015,464	6,837,652	11.6	[8] 52,177,812	88.4

[1] Data not adjusted for relatively minor differences in farm-nonfarm occupational classification between (a) 1820-1930 series, (b) figures for 1930 and 1940, and (c) figures for 1950.

[2] Figures estimated on basis of returns covering greater part of population.

[3] Figures based on interpolation between 1820 and 1840.

[4] Includes additions due to estimated under-enumeration in 13 Southern States.

[5] Corrected figure; for explanation, see analysis of occupation returns for 1890 in Twelfth Census (1900) Special Reports, *Occupation*, pp. lxvi-lxxiii. Excludes persons in Indian Territory and on Indian reservations, areas specially enumerated at that census, but for which areas no occupation statistics are available.

[6] Figures revised to deduct estimated over-reporting of farm workers.

[7] Figures revised to add estimated under-reporting of gainful workers, partly due to change in census date to January 1.

[8] Includes persons in experienced civilian labor force who did not report occupation.

[9] Figure differs from corresponding item in table 224 due to separate tabulations.

Source: Department of Commerce, Bureau of the Census; 1940 Census Reports on Population, *Comparative Occupation Statistics for the United States, 1870 to 1940* and *U. S. Census of Population: 1950*, Vol. II, Part I.

No. 205.—GAINFUL WORKERS 14 YEARS OLD AND OVER, 1910 TO 1930, AND TOTAL LABOR FORCE, 1940 AND 1950, BY AGE AND SEX

[See also *Historical Statistics*, series D 32-45]

YEAR AND AGE (YEARS)	POPULATION			GAINFUL WORKERS OR LABOR FORCE [1]					
	Total	Male	Female	Total	Male	Female	Percent of population		
							Total	Male	Female
1910									
Total, 14 and over	84, 221, 252	22, 361, 779	20, 959, 473	37, 271, 360	29, 482, 534	7, 788, 826	57.9	86.4	25.2
14 and 15	3, 540, 347	1, 769, 449	1, 770, 808	1, 094, 349	744, 109	350, 140	30.7	41.4	19.8
16 to 19	9, 197, 000	4, 564, 179	4, 632, 821	5, 453, 223	3, 615, 623	1, 847, 800	59.4	79.2	39.9
20 to 44	34, 181, 392	17, 849, 842	16, 331, 449	21, 565, 178	17, 262, 209	4, 302, 969	63.1	96.7	34.3
45 and over	17, 373, 618	9, 149, 305	8, 224, 305	9, 146, 710	7, 880, 593	1, 263, 117	52.7	85.9	15.7
1920									
Total, 14 and over	94, 144, 443	47, 953, 960	46, 190, 483	41, 226, 185	32, 896, 478	8, 629, 707	55.6	86.4	28.3
14 and 15	3, 907, 710	1, 955, 976	1, 943, 734	682, 795	455, 989	225, 806	17.5	23.3	11.6
16 and 17	3, 838, 151	1, 902, 887	1, 935, 264	1, 712, 648	1, 103, 456	609, 192	44.7	58.0	31.6
18 and 19	3, 740, 980	1, 845, 346	1, 895, 734	2, 346, 308	1, 443, 968	902, 235	60.0	78.3	42.3
20 to 24	9, 277, 021	4, 527, 046	4, 749, 979	5, 930, 467	4, 121, 392	1, 809, 075	61.0	91.0	38.1
25 to 44	31, 375, 422	16, 025, 820	15, 249, 602	18, 996, 950	15, 579, 586	3, 417, 373	60.7	97.2	22.4
45 and over	27, 009, 165	9, 114, 869	7, 915, 206	9, 904, 654	8, 562, 175	1, 382, 479	38.3	93.6	17.1
Age unknown	4, 996, 215	2, 485, 071	2, 480, 144	1, 660, 737	1, 492, 887	196, 900	34.3	60.1	8.0
	148, 699	92, 875	55, 824	72, 722	57, 075	15, 647	48.9	61.5	28.0
1930									
Total, 14 and over	89, 100, 555	45, 087, 597	44, 012, 048	48, 594, 592	37, 915, 844	10, 679, 048	54.5	84.1	24.3
14 and 15	4, 678, 084	2, 361, 124	2, 316, 960	431, 790	298, 482	133, 308	9.2	12.6	6.8
16 and 17	4, 653, 157	2, 329, 070	2, 324, 087	1, 478, 841	964, 494	514, 347	31.7	41.2	22.1
18 and 19	4, 364, 107	2, 320, 172	2, 342, 213	2, 346, 308	1, 599, 788	942, 445	55.3	70.7	40.5
20 to 24	10, 570, 378	5, 236, 815	5, 533, 563	7, 147, 053	4, 799, 505	2, 347, 548	65.7	89.9	42.4
25 to 44	39, 944, 030	19, 032, 020	19, 532, 068	11, 823, 004	9, 168, 666	2, 654, 338	62.4	97.2	27.8
45 to 64	27, 108, 840	9, 816, 319	9, 282, 521	10, 500, 540	8, 608, 202	1, 892, 338	61.1	97.8	22.6
65 and over	13, 044, 899	6, 803, 380	6, 214, 514	7, 831, 161	6, 566, 135	1, 265, 026	60.2	96.5	20.4
Age unknown	5, 386, 099	4, 367, 800	4, 029, 298	4, 590, 592	3, 941, 514	649, 078	54.7	90.2	14.1
	6, 681, 808	3, 326, 311	3, 306, 594	2, 304, 967	1, 988, 749	386, 218	33.2	58.3	8.0
	94, 022	51, 816	42, 206	44, 431	31, 029	13, 402	47.3	59.9	31.8
1940									
Total, 14 and over	101, 103, 924	50, 553, 748	50, 546, 176	52, 789, 499	39, 944, 240	12, 845, 259	52.2	79.0	25.4
14 and 15	4, 850, 949	2, 440, 453	2, 387, 796	249, 521	195, 919	53, 602	5.2	8.0	2.2
16 and 17	4, 882, 170	2, 452, 443	2, 429, 727	1, 029, 291	715, 027	314, 264	21.0	29.0	12.9
18 and 19	5, 068, 834	2, 466, 373	2, 523, 461	2, 645, 289	1, 635, 798	1, 009, 491	52.7	65.6	40.0
20 to 24	11, 487, 835	5, 592, 392	5, 895, 443	7, 670, 549	5, 011, 457	2, 659, 092	66.2	88.0	45.1
25 to 44	21, 370, 026	10, 530, 974	10, 818, 082	13, 576, 571	10, 015, 331	3, 561, 240	63.6	95.2	32.9
45 to 64	18, 303, 220	9, 164, 794	9, 168, 426	11, 163, 700	8, 678, 280	2, 465, 420	60.8	94.7	26.9
65 and over	8, 512, 071	7, 862, 019	7, 550, 062	8, 995, 585	7, 329, 310	1, 666, 275	58.0	92.1	22.1
65 and over	20, 572, 206	5, 405, 180	5, 163, 026	5, 378, 609	4, 533, 909	844, 700	50.9	83.8	16.4
	8, 018, 814	4, 405, 120	4, 613, 194	2, 100, 384	1, 829, 209	271, 175	23.3	41.5	5.9
1950 [a]									
Total, 14 and over	111, 703, 400	54, 601, 105	57, 102, 296	59, 642, 990	43, 091, 000	16, 551, 990	53.4	78.9	29.0
14 and 15	4, 297, 396	2, 105, 530	2, 094, 866	444, 530	336, 870	107, 940	10.4	15.5	5.1
16 and 17	4, 153, 735	2, 109, 000	2, 064, 735	1, 123, 450	756, 788	366, 665	26.9	35.9	17.8
18 and 19	4, 441, 492	2, 134, 980	2, 306, 528	2, 392, 195	1, 426, 475	965, 720	55.1	66.8	48.8
20 to 24	11, 437, 945	5, 559, 205	5, 878, 040	7, 089, 440	4, 553, 045	2, 536, 395	62.0	81.9	43.2
25 to 44	11, 487, 390	12, 174, 106	14, 422, 606	10, 555, 926	8, 946, 090	61.0	92.1	31.6	
45 to 64	16, 402, 198	10, 737, 680	13, 820, 410	9, 928, 298	3, 792, 115	64.1	94.5	38.0	
65 and over	8, 444, 615	6, 697, 686	10, 068, 870	7, 801, 908	3, 856, 965	62.1	92.0	32.9	
	6, 540, 160	6, 028, 170	7, 094, 880	5, 482, 138	1, 582, 745	53.2	93.4	23.4	
	3, 208, 360	2, 636, 690	2, 886, 980	2, 379, 345	507, 345	23.6	41.5	7.8	

[1] Figures for 1910 to 1930 represent gainful workers; those for 1940 and 1950 represent the total labor force. For ... p. 179.

... of 1950 Census returns. See source for explanation of sampling variability.

... Bureau of the Census; *Sixteenth Census Reports, Population*, Vol. III, and ... Vol. II, Part 1.

No. 206.—EMPLOYMENT STATUS OF THE NONINSTITUTIONAL POPULATION, BY SEX: 1929 TO 1952

[Thousands of persons 14 years old and over. Data in tables 206-208, and 221, based on Current Population Survey (see Sampling Note, p. 181), are not entirely comparable with those presented in tables 204, 205, 217-220, 222-228, which are based on decennial census reports. See also *Historical Statistics*, series D 11-31]

ANNUAL AVERAGE OR MONTHLY ESTIMATE	Total, noninstitutional population [1]	IN LABOR FORCE						NOT IN LABOR FORCE			
		Total, including armed forces	Civilian labor force					Total	Keeping house	In school	Other
			Total	Employed	Unemployed						
					Number	Percent					
BOTH SEXES											
1929		49,440	49,180	47,630	1,550	3.2					
1930		50,080	49,820	45,480	4,340	8.7					
1931		50,680	50,420	42,400	8,020	15.9					
1932		51,250	51,000	38,940	12,060	23.6					
1933		51,840	51,590	38,760	12,830	24.9					
1934		52,490	52,230	40,890	11,340	21.7					
1935		53,140	52,870	42,260	10,610	20.1					
1936		53,740	53,440	44,410	9,030	16.9					
1937		54,320	54,000	46,300	7,700	14.3					
1938		54,950	54,610	44,220	10,390	19.0					
1939		55,600	55,230	45,750	9,480	17.2					
1940	100,230	56,030	55,640	47,520	8,120	14.6		44,200			
1941	101,370	57,380	55,910	50,350	5,560	9.9		43,990			
1942	102,460	60,230	56,410	53,750	2,660	4.7		42,230	28,690	6,370	7,170
1943	103,510	64,410	55,540	54,470	1,070	1.9		39,100	27,320	5,100	6,680
1944	104,480	65,890	54,630	53,960	670	1.2		38,590	27,350	4,540	6,700
1945	105,370	65,140	53,860	52,820	1,040	1.9		40,230	27,760	4,830	7,640
1946	106,370	60,820	57,520	55,250	2,270	3.9		45,550	31,020	6,360	8,170
1947	107,458	61,608	60,168	58,027	2,142	3.6		45,850	32,441	6,446	6,962
1948	108,482	62,748	61,442	59,378	2,064	3.4		45,733	32,850	6,178	6,706
1949	109,628	63,571	62,105	58,710	3,395	5.5		46,061	33,067	6,093	6,891
1950	110,779	64,599	63,099	59,957	3,142	5.0		46,181	33,058	6,197	6,926
1951	111,994	65,832	62,884	61,005	1,879	3.0		46,092	33,105	5,829	7,159
1952	113,136	66,426	62,966	61,293	1,673	2.7		46,710	33,334	6,040	7,335
MALE											
1940	49,930	41,870	41,480	35,550	5,930	14.3		8,060			
1941	50,420	42,740	41,270	37,350	3,920	9.5		7,680			
1942	50,910	44,110	40,300	38,580	1,720	4.3		6,800	50	2,980	3,770
1943	51,390	45,600	36,940	36,270	670	1.5		5,790	80	2,230	3,480
1944	51,830	46,520	35,460	35,110	350	1.0		5,310	60	1,830	3,420
1945	52,120	45,870	34,530	34,210	620	1.8		6,250	40	2,070	4,140
1946	52,540	43,980	46,740	38,940	1,800	4.4		8,560	70	3,210	5,280
1947	52,935	44,694	43,272	41,677	1,595	3.7		8,242	60	3,437	4,744
1948	53,363	45,150	43,858	42,428	1,430	3.3		8,213	51	3,367	4,795
1949	53,877	45,524	44,075	41,660	2,415	5.5		8,354	62	3,306	4,986
1950	54,376	45,919	44,442	42,287	2,155	4.9		8,457	81	3,244	5,132
1951	54,846	46,524	43,612	42,490	1,123	2.6		8,322	98	2,940	5,284
1952	55,370	46,868	43,454	42,391	1,062	2.4		8,502	69	3,002	5,431
March	55,200	46,252	42,810	41,586	1,224	2.9		8,948	66	3,880	5,002
June	55,321	47,913	44,464	43,326	1,138	2.6		7,408	60	1,384	5,964
September	55,462	46,890	43,468	42,604	864	2.0		8,572	42	3,470	5,060
December			43,240	42,275	965	2.2		9,025	100	3,829	5,096
FEMALE											
1940	50,300	14,160	14,160	11,970	2,190	15.5		36,140			
1941	50,950	14,640	14,640	13,000	1,640	11.2		36,310			
1942	51,550	16,120	16,110	15,170	940	5.8		35,430	28,640	3,390	3,400
1943	52,120	18,810	18,700	18,200	500	2.7		33,310	27,240	2,870	3,200
1944	52,650	19,370	19,170	18,850	320	1.7		33,280	27,290	2,710	3,280
1945	53,250	19,270	19,030	18,610	420	2.2		33,980	27,720	2,760	3,500
1946	53,830	16,840	16,780	16,310	470	2.8		36,990	30,950	3,150	2,890
1947	54,523	16,915	16,896	16,349	547	3.2		37,608	32,380	3,009	2,318
1948	55,118	17,599	17,583	16,950	633	3.6		37,520	32,799	2,810	1,910
1949	55,745	18,048	18,030	17,049	981	5.4		37,697	33,005	2,785	1,906
1950	56,404	18,680	18,657	17,670	987	5.3		37,724	32,977	2,954	1,794
1951	57,078	19,309	19,272	18,515	756	3.9		37,770	33,007	2,888	1,875
1952	57,767	19,550	19,513	18,902	611	3.1		38,208	33,266	3,038	1,904
March	57,562	18,754	18,708	18,128	580	3.1		38,808	33,444	3,984	1,380
June	57,729	19,971	19,926	19,246	680	3.4		37,758	33,686	1,336	2,736
September	57,912	20,276	20,230	19,656	574	2.8		37,636	32,646	3,464	1,526
December			19,681	19,234	447	2.3		38,369	33,221	3,781	1,367

[1] Excludes inmates of penal and mental institutions and homes for the aged, infirm, and needy.

Source: 1929-39, Department of Labor, Bureau of Labor Statistics; *Handbook of Labor Statistics*, 1947 edition. Later data, Department of Commerce, Bureau of the Census; *Current Population Reports*, Series P-50, Nos. 2, 13, 19, 31, and 40, and Series P-57.

No. 207.—CIVILIAN LABOR FORCE, BY AGE AND SEX: 1945 TO 1952

[Thousands of persons 14 years old and over. See headnote, table 206]

ANNUAL AV-ERAGE OR MONTHLY ESTIMATE	MALE						FEMALE					
	Total all ages	14-19 years	20-24 years	25-44 years	45-64 years	65 and over	Total all ages	14-19 years	20-24 years	25-44 years	45-64 years	65 and over
1945	34, 530	2, 950	1, 650	14, 510	13, 260	2, 460	19, 030	2, 720	3, 180	8, 230	4, 410	490
1946	40, 740	2, 680	3, 720	18, 650	13, 350	2, 340	16, 780	2, 160	2, 780	7, 370	4, 020	450
1947	43, 272	3, 073	4, 629	19, 699	13, 495	2, 376	16, 896	2, 067	2, 716	7, 416	4, 283	445
1948	43, 858	3, 173	4, 674	19, 923	13, 706	2, 384	17, 583	2, 083	2, 719	7, 732	4, 537	514
1949	44, 075	3, 054	4, 681	20, 131	13, 756	2, 454	18, 030	2, 053	2, 659	7, 986	4, 777	536
1950	44, 442	3, 127	4, 632	20, 320	13, 911	2, 454	18, 657	1, 980	2, 675	8, 253	5, 166	584
1951	43, 612	2, 987	3, 935	20, 173	14, 078	2, 469	19, 272	2, 013	2, 659	8, 593	5, 457	551
1952	43, 454	2, 896	3, 338	20, 530	14, 276	2, 415	19, 513	1, 996	2, 502	8, 758	5, 668	590
January	42, 864	2, 516	3, 494	20, 322	14, 110	2, 422	18, 916	1, 736	2, 532	8, 610	5, 492	546
February	42, 888	2, 512	3, 488	20, 402	14, 086	2, 370	18, 980	1, 776	2, 474	8, 688	5, 528	514
March	42, 810	2, 518	3, 378	20, 400	14, 218	2, 296	18, 708	1, 686	2, 446	8, 566	5, 518	492
April	42, 946	2, 570	3, 358	20, 456	14, 208	2, 354	18, 798	1, 768	2, 442	8, 586	5, 478	594
May	43, 262	2, 730	3, 322	20, 518	14, 294	2, 398	19, 516	1, 902	2, 462	8, 888	5, 666	598
June	44, 464	3, 678	3, 456	20, 570	14, 308	2, 452	19, 926	2, 514	2, 518	8, 512	5, 496	586
July	44, 720	3, 858	3, 526	20, 602	14, 284	2, 450	19, 456	2, 488	2, 454	8, 508	5, 442	564
August	44, 396	3, 664	3, 424	20, 560	14, 332	2, 416	19, 562	2, 326	2, 502	8, 612	5, 548	574
September	43, 468	2, 834	3, 162	20, 556	14, 406	2, 510	20, 230	2, 010	2, 622	9, 002	5, 980	636
October	43, 196	2, 664	3, 084	20, 600	14, 394	2, 454	19, 950	1, 898	2, 528	8, 914	5, 946	664
November	43, 218	2, 670	3, 078	20, 648	14, 350	2, 472	20, 428	1, 932	2, 608	9, 080	6, 106	702
December	43, 240	2, 532	3, 284	20, 721	14, 312	2, 391	19, 681	1, 917	2, 433	8, 528	5, 828	675

Source: Department of Commerce, Bureau of the Census; *Current Population Reports*, Series P-50, Nos. 2, 13, 19, 31, and 40, and Series P-57.

No. 208.—PERSONS EMPLOYED IN AGRICULTURE AND IN NONAGRICULTURAL INDUSTRIES, BY HOURS WORKED DURING THE SURVEY WEEK: 1943 TO 1952

[Thousands of persons 14 years old and over. See headnote, table 206]

ANNUAL AVERAGE OR MONTHLY ESTIMATE	PERSONS EMPLOYED IN AGRICULTURE				PERSONS EMPLOYED IN NONAGRICULTURAL INDUSTRIES				
	Total	Worked 35 hours or more	Worked 15 to 34 hours	Worked 1 to 14 hours	With a job but not at work [1]	Total	Worked 35 hours or more	Worked 15 to 34 hours	Worked 1 to 14 hours	With a job but not at work [1]
1943	9, 080	7, 740	1, 140	110	90	45, 390	39, 690	3, 510	1, 060	1, 130
1944	8, 950	6, 970	1, 610	160	210	45, 010	38, 060	4, 230	1, 170	1, 550
1945	8, 580	6, 330	1, 800	230	220	44, 240	36, 540	4, 540	1, 370	1, 790
1946	8, 320	6, 250	1, 660	210	200	46, 930	39, 460	4, 200	1, 210	2, 060
1947	8, 266	6, 097	1, 643	241	285	49, 761	41, 538	4, 627	1, 407	2, 188
1948 [2]	7, 973	5, 808	1, 637	242	287	51, 405	40, 411	6, 688	1, 841	2, 465
1949 [2]	8, 026	5, 906	1, 621	291	209	50, 684	38, 479	6, 069	1, 816	2, 321
1950 [2]	7, 507	5, 394	1, 589	294	231	52, 450	39, 856	8, 179	1, 997	2, 417
1951 [2]	7, 054	5, 108	1, 486	263	197	53, 951	42, 554	6, 898	2, 016	2, 483
1952	6, 805	4, 992	1, 418	201	194	54, 488	44, 559	5, 478	1, 831	2, 620
January	6, 186	4, 116	1, 378	316	376	53, 540	44, 046	5, 686	2, 002	1, 806
February	6, 064	4, 390	1, 194	194	286	53, 688	44, 134	5, 652	2, 078	1, 824
March	6, 012	4, 152	1, 378	202	280	53, 702	43, 954	5, 810	2, 012	1, 926
April	6, 412	4, 684	1, 416	150	162	53, 720	43, 002	6, 826	1, 918	1, 974
May	6, 960	5, 416	1, 308	120	116	54, 216	45, 284	4, 946	1, 934	2, 052
June	8, 170	6, 482	1, 408	184	96	54, 402	44, 144	5, 180	1, 642	3, 436
July	7, 598	5, 654	1, 610	174	160	54, 636	42, 112	5, 016	1, 512	5, 996
August	5, 984	5, 030	1, 560	194	180	55, 390	43, 824	4, 924	1, 480	5, 162
September	7, 548	5, 774	1, 380	212	182	54, 712	45, 538	5, 214	1, 576	2, 384
October	7, 274	5, 080	1, 868	218	108	54, 588	45, 688	5, 220	1, 844	1, 836
November	6, 774	5, 254	1, 196	194	128	55, 454	45, 950	5, 934	2, 002	1, 568
December	5, 697	3, 877	1, 323	248	249	55, 812	47, 037	5, 331	1, 968	1, 476

[1] Persons who had a job or business, but who did not work at all during entire survey week because of illness, bad weather, vacation, labor dispute, or because of temporary layoff with definite instructions to return to work within 30 days of layoff. Also persons scheduled to report within 30 days to new job.

[2] Nonagricultural data affected by occurrence of legal holidays in survey weeks and not, therefore, directly comparable with other years shown.

Source: Department of Commerce, Bureau of Census; *Current Population Reports*, Series P-50, Nos. 2, 13, 19, 31, and 40, and Series P-57.

No. 209.—EMPLOYEES IN NONAGRICULTURAL ESTABLISHMENTS, BY INDUSTRY
DIVISION: 1919 TO 1952

[In thousands. Includes all full- and part-time employees who worked during, or received pay for, any part of the pay period ending nearest 15th of month. Excludes proprietors, self-employed persons, domestic servants, and personnel of Armed Forces. Data have been adjusted to 1st quarter 1951 benchmark levels indicated by data from government social insurance programs]

YEAR	Total	Mining	Contract construction	Manufacturing	Transportation and public utilities	Trade [1]	Finance	Service [1]	Government
1919	26,829	1,124	1,021	10,534	3,711	4,664	1,050	2,054	2,671
1920	27,088	1,230	848	10,534	3,998	4,623	1,110	2,142	2,603
1925	28,505	1,080	1,446	9,786	3,824	5,810	1,166	2,591	2,802
1929	31,041	1,078	1,497	10,534	3,907	6,401	1,431	3,127	3,066
1930	29,143	1,000	1,372	9,401	3,675	6,064	1,398	3,084	3,149
1935	26,792	888	912	8,907	2,771	5,602	1,262	2,883	3,477
1940	32,031	16	1,294	10,780	3,013	6,940	1,419	3,477	4,192
1942	39,697	983	2,170	15,051	3,433	7,333	1,440	3,857	5,431
1943	42,042	917	1,567	17,381	3,619	7,189	1,401	3,919	6,049
1944	41,480	883	1,094	17,111	3,798	7,260	1,374	3,934	6,026
1945	40,069	826	1,132	15,302	3,872	7,522	1,394	4,055	5,967
1946	41,412	852	1,661	14,461	4,023	8,602	1,586	4,621	5,607
1947	43,438	943	1,982	15,290	4,122	9,196	1,641	4,807	5,456
1948	44,382	982	2,169	15,321	4,141	9,519	1,711	4,925	5,614
1949	43,295	918	2,165	14,178	3,949	9,513	1,736	5,000	5,837
1950	44,696	889	2,333	14,967	3,977	9,645	1,796	5,098	5,992
1951	47,202	913	2,588	16,082	4,166	10,013	1,861	5,207	6,373
1952	47,993	872	2,572	16,209	4,220	10,251	1,957	5,280	6,633

[1] Beginning 1940, automotive repair service included under "Service"; previously included under "Trade."

Source: Department of Labor, Bureau of Labor Statistics. Monthly figures published currently in *Monthly Labor Review* and mimeographed releases.

No. 210.—ALL EMPLOYEES AND PRODUCTION WORKERS IN MANUFACTURING IN-
DUSTRY GROUPS: 1950 TO 1952

[In thousands. Includes all full- and part-time employees who worked during, or received pay for, any part of the pay period ending nearest 15th of month. Data have been adjusted to 1st quarter 1951 benchmark levels in- dicated by data from government social insurance programs]

INDUSTRY GROUP	ALL EMPLOYEES			PRODUCTION WORKERS		
	1950	1951	1952	1950	1951	1952
Manufacturing	14,967	16,082	16,209	12,317	13,135	13,044
Durable goods	8,085	9,071	9,262	6,690	7,459	7,481
Ordnance and accessories	29.6	77.0	166.4	23.7	61.5	125.7
Lumber and wood products (except furniture)	805	834.4	782.0	743	766.8	713.3
Furniture and fixtures	369	361.3	361.0	321	310.6	309.1
Stone, clay, and glass products	513	551.2	527.9	442	475.1	448.4
Primary metal industries	1,200	1,313.0	1,227.4	1,036	1,132.1	1,039.7
Fabricated metal products (except ordnance machinery, and transportation equipment)	973	1,059.7	1,045.6	810	874.3	850.1
Machinery (except electrical)	1,354	1,601.3	1,642.4	1,043	1,245.1	1,262.5
Electrical machinery	877	1,005.4	1,068.4	670	768.6	806.9
Transportation equipment	1,264	1,510.3	1,674.9	1,036	1,219.8	1,320.5
Instruments and related products	248	292.2	310.2	184	216.7	227.6
Miscellaneous manufacturing industries	453	465.4	456.0	381	388.3	376.7
Nondurable goods	6,882	7,011	6,946	5,627	5,676	5,564
Food and kindred products	1,523	1,544.1	1,538.5	1,143	1,142.4	1,127.1
Tobacco manufactures	103	104.4	107.0	94	95.7	97.9
Textile-mill products	1,292	1,272.7	1,201.7	1,200	1,175.8	1,105.8
Apparel and other finished textile products	1,184	1,187.1	1,190.8	1,065	1,065.9	1,066.9
Paper and allied products	485	511.5	505.6	415	434.3	422.5
Printing, publishing, and allied industries	738	755.5	762.9	485	493.9	494.2
Chemicals and allied products	682	742.8	741.7	494	529.5	515.5
Products of petroleum and coal	238	252.7	258.9	180	188.2	182.6
Rubber products	246	263.3	262.3	198	212.0	208.2
Leather and leather products	392	376.9	381.9	353	338.7	343.1

Source: Department of Labor, Bureau of Labor Statistics. Monthly figures published currently in the *Monthly Labor Review* and mimeographed releases.

No. 211.—Employees (Annual Average) in Nonagricultural Establishments, by State: 1949 to 1952

[In thousands. Prepared in cooperation with State agencies]

DIVISION AND STATE	NONAGRICULTURAL				MANUFACTURING			
	1949	1950	1951	1952	1949	1950	1951	1952
New England:								
Maine	251.3	253.1	272.3	278.4	105.0	108.4	115.6	116.4
New Hampshire	162.3	166.3	172.1	170.2	74.3	78.3	82.2	80.9
Vermont	94.8	96.5	99.4	99.5	34.2	35.7	38.7	38.3
Massachusetts	1,682.7	1,732.0	1,793.2	1,781.2	677.2	707.3	740.5	717.7
Rhode Island	279.6	297.3	308.4	304.7	124.0	146.7	150.5	144.4
Connecticut	729.1	764.7	827.3	846.0	351.0	376.7	423.3	431.1
Middle Atlantic:								
New York	5,508.1	5,618.6	5,795.1	5,864.5	1,764.9	1,829.6	1,918.2	1,942.0
New Jersey	1,586.8	1,646.0	1,755.2	1,789.9	713.6	747.2	810.5	824.4
Pennsylvania	3,475.9	3,540.6	3,716.4	3,666.6	1,356.4	1,403.3	1,494.1	1,444.5
East North Central:								
Ohio	2,622.8	2,732.5	2,929.0	2,954.1	1,120.6	1,199.2	1,315.2	1,317.3
Indiana	1,181.4	1,264.9	1,351.2	1,345.5	513.1	572.3	615.8	609.7
Illinois	3,050.5	3,127.1	3,276.9	3,313.0	1,115.3	1,178.4	1,248.0	1,244.0
Michigan	1,963.5	2,106.9	2,211.9	2,207.9	981.2	1,063.2	1,111.1	1,080.5
Wisconsin	983.8	1,019.2	1,070.6	1,080.4	405.2	428.1	463.9	466.9
West North Central:								
Minnesota	773.4	795.3	826.3	828.8	186.4	194.9	206.6	211.5
Iowa	586.9	603.2	628.0	630.2	147.7	151.6	168.4	169.6
Missouri	1,121.5	1,162.8	1,232.7	1,263.9	334.4	348.3	372.9	391.8
North Dakota	108.5	111.7	112.4	114.2	5.9	5.9	6.1	6.5
South Dakota	118.5	122.0	122.7	122.0	11.3	11.3	11.6	11.3
Nebraska	308.2	316.5	332.0	341.4	48.6	49.8	54.8	59.8
Kansas	445.0	460.5	508.4	541.3	86.8	92.4	116.9	136.0
South Atlantic:								
Delaware	112.1	119.8	128.3	133.7	47.9	51.2	56.0	59.2
Maryland	676.2	693.3	741.4	756.3	219.0	225.2	254.4	259.2
District of Columbia	481.2	484.0	519.5	522.8	16.4	16.7	17.1	17.4
Virginia	766.1	795.6	861.7	878.6	219.1	227.0	242.2	246.4
West Virginia	516.1	517.0	532.3	521.1	127.1	129.7	138.1	134.6
North Carolina	852.1	911.4	970.8	987.3	387.1	418.3	432.9	432.1
South Carolina	432.9	451.2	493.0	524.0	199.5	209.2	218.4	218.1
Georgia	749.7	786.6	849.7	873.5	263.6	284.4	304.4	305.9
Florida	645.8	693.1	746.2	792.4	90.8	97.7	108.7	115.9
East South Central:								
Kentucky	528.2	547.8	589.1	604.5	131.2	139.0	151.6	146.7
Tennessee	703.6	739.8	786.0	806.7	235.8	247.2	264.6	274.3
Alabama	593.0	607.9	650.3	671.5	206.4	216.1	225.3	226.9
Mississippi	281.7	295.1	315.2	318.1	77.4	86.4	94.3	95.2
West South Central:								
Arkansas	264.6	295.1	315.7	314.1	70.0	75.7	82.5	80.8
Louisiana	609.6	621.3	654.5	673.1	138.9	140.2	146.5	150.3
Oklahoma	462.3	473.3	501.8	520.1	64.1	65.6	73.2	90.1
Texas	1,836.1	1,914.4	2,105.5	2,215.2	335.9	353.2	401.9	425.9
Mountain:								
Montana	145.0	147.0	149.0	154.1	17.8	18.0	18.1	18.4
Idaho	125.0	130.5	137.7	137.3	20.0	21.8	24.0	23.5
Wyoming	79.1	80.5	82.7	85.8	6.0	6.0	6.1	6.2
Colorado	334.2	354.4	390.1	412.5	53.9	58.7	65.4	66.8
New Mexico	139.9	150.6	159.9	168.0	10.7	12.2	14.2	15.5
Arizona	152.7	159.2	179.0	195.9	14.5	15.5	22.7	28.1
Utah	183.2	187.8	206.5	213.4	27.7	28.5	31.3	30.9
Nevada	51.3	53.6	58.2	64.6	3.0	3.3	3.6	3.8
Pacific:								
Washington	658.7	672.3	722.2	731.3	169.4	173.9	191.8	192.1
Oregon	416.6	435.3	459.2	457.7	125.3	135.5	147.7	142.6
California	3,088.1	3,209.4	3,515.4	3,662.2	701.5	759.7	892.3	971.2

Source: Department of Labor, Bureau of Labor Statistics. Published quarterly in *Monthly Labor Review* and monthly in *Employment and Payrolls*.

No. 212.—Revised Indexes of Production-Worker Employment in Manufacturing Industries, by Months (Adjusted for Seasonal Variations): 1939 to 1952

[1947–49=100. Based on monthly indexes, adjusted to 1st quarter 1951 benchmark data, published currently in Bureau of Labor Statistics *Monthly Labor Review*]

YEAR	Jan.	Feb.	Mar.	Apr.	May	June	July	Aug.	Sept.	Oct.	Nov.	Dec.	Average
1939	63.2	63.8	64.3	64.6	64.6	64.8	65.2	66.0	67.5	69.8	70.2	70.4	66.2
1940	70.0	69.7	69.0	68.5	68.6	68.8	69.4	71.0	72.6	74.2	75.5	77.2	71.2
1941	78.7	80.1	81.9	84.1	86.3	88.6	90.7	91.8	92.4	92.9	93.4	93.8	87.9
1942	94.9	96.2	97.8	99.5	101.2	102.3	104.2	106.2	108.1	109.9	112.0	114.5	103.9
1943	116.4	117.9	119.4	120.3	120.7	122.0	122.9	122.9	122.8	123.6	124.3	123.3	121.4
1944	122.6	122.2	120.9	119.3	118.8	118.1	117.4	117.0	115.8	115.1	114.6	115.1	118.1
1945	115.5	115.8	115.0	113.7	112.2	109.9	106.6	103.4	88.5	88.6	89.1	89.6	104.0
1946	91.4	85.3	91.2	96.2	97.0	98.4	99.7	101.6	102.6	102.7	104.0	104.1	97.9
1947	104.0	104.1	104.2	104.1	103.0	102.8	102.1	102.3	102.8	103.3	103.8	104.4	103.4
1948	104.6	103.6	103.8	102.0	102.0	102.7	103.4	102.9	102.9	102.6	102.2	100.8	102.8
1949	99.0	97.7	96.4	95.0	93.2	92.7	92.1	92.3	93.5	90.3	96.4	92.4	93.8
1950	93.1	93.0	93.8	95.1	97.7	99.0	100.4	103.1	103.9	105.2	105.2	105.5	99.6
1951	106.6	107.6	107.5	107.8	107.5	107.5	106.8	105.6	104.8	104.4	104.4	104.7	106.2
1952	104.7	104.9	104.9	105.2	104.6	102.6	100.6	104.7	106.8	107.8	109.2	110.0	105.5

Source: Board of Governors of the Federal Reserve System. Published currently in *Federal Reserve Bulletin*.

No. 213.—Employees in Selected Nonmanufacturing Industries: 1950 to 1952

[In thousands. Includes all full- and part-time employees who worked during, or received pay for, any part of the pay period ending nearest 15th of month. Data have been adjusted to 1st quarter 1951 benchmark levels indicated by data from government social insurance programs]

INDUSTRY	1950	1951	1952	1952					
				Feb.	Apr.	June	Aug.	Oct.	Dec
Mining	889	913	872	894	890	816	893	871	870
Metal mining	96.9	100.2	96.4	102.4	102.7	72.1	102.5	98.8	101.9
Iron mining	35.5	37.7	33.3	37.0	38.1	8.0	40.0	39.0	38.8
Copper mining	25.8	25.7	25.9	26.0	26.2	26.3	26.4	24.6	27.0
Lead and zinc mining	19.2	20.4	20.8	22.2	22.0	21.3	19.8	19.3	19.6
Anthracite	75.1	69.1	63.4	62.2	60.5	65.3	63.1	62.5	62.0
Bituminous coal	367.9	372.0	333.8	360.3	350.9	294.2	339.6	330.4	331.2
Crude petroleum and natural gas production	254.2	269.3	276.0	271.9	274.4	281.0	281.2	273.6	273.4
Nonmetallic mining and quarrying	95.1	102.0	102.3	97.5	101.6	102.9	106.2	105.6	101.6
Transportation and public utilities	3,977	4,166	4,220	4,153	4,149	4,225	4,258	4,296	4,293
Transportation	2,765	2,921	2,941	2,889	2,926	2,935	2,946	2,999	2,995
Interstate railroads	1,391	1,449.3	1,399.8	1,391.8	1,404.3	1,396.0	1,394.1	1,423.2	1,406.0
Local railways and bus lines	145	139.0	134.8	137.1	134.8	133.6	133.9	132.3	132.4
Trucking and warehousing	619	675.6	714.	690.8	697.9	704.1	713.5	745.9	761.9
Other transportation and services	610	656.9	692	669.7	688.9	701.4	704.3	697.1	694.9
Telephone	614.8	638.9	672.7	660.3	648.0	673.7	688.1	682.4	686.5
Telegraph	48.7	50.1	48.6	49.3	(1)	47.4	47.6	49.1	48.6
Other public utilities	549	555	563	554	557	558	576	565	562
Trade	9,645	10,013	10,251	9,917	10,152	10,144	10,110	10,442	11,218
Wholesale trade	2,571	2,655	2,721	2,704	2,685	2,700	2,722	2,752	2,787
Retail trade	7,074	7,359	7,530	7,213	7,440	7,444	7,388	7,690	8,431
General merchandise stores	1,409	1,429.3	1,453.2	1,323.8	1,426.9	1,369.6	1,324.6	1,504.8	2,013.2
Food and liquor stores	1,231	1,307.6	1,353.	1,331.8	1,345.2	1,346.9	1,344.8	1,375.8	1,407.2
Automotive and accessories dealers	734	763.7	779	765	761.4	781.	781.6	785.2	815.2
Apparel and accessories stores	555	575.4	584	539	617.6	580	529.7	601.9	705.6
Other retail trade	3,144	3,282.4	3,359	3,251	3,289.0	3,366	3,406.8	3,422.2	3,489.5
Finance, insurance, and real estate [2]	1,796	1,861	1,957	1,906	941	1,972	2,000	1,973	1,978
Banks and trust companies [2]	406	431.0	480.2	469.	473.0	481.2	490.9	484.6	489.6
Security dealers and exchanges	59.6	63.7	64.8	64.	64.5	64.8	65.7	64.4	64.2
Insurance carriers and agents	644	671.4	707.	689.	701.5	709.	721.4	715.2	719.6
Other finance agencies and real estate	686	694.7	704.	683.	702.3	716.	722.1	709.0	704.2
Service [3]	5,098	5,207	5,280	5,154	5,266	5,360	5,378	5,303	5,237
Hotels and lodging places	471	476.5	476.9	450.3	462.8	501.1	545.6	456.3	446.8
Laundries	342.1	342.7	342	336.2	338.9	349.0	348.8	343.7	342.0
Cleaning and dyeing plants	156.7	166.8	172	166.0	174.4	178.9	169.4	176.9	172.5
Motion pictures	248	244.4	236.	233.0	239.1	239.2	238.9	237.2	228.5

[1] Not available.
[2] Beginning January 1952, data include Federal Reserve Banks and mixed ownership of Farm Credit Administration.
[3] Includes industries not shown separately.

Source: Department of Labor, Bureau of Labor Statistics. Monthly figures published currently in *Monthly Labor Review* and in mimeographed releases.

No. 214.—FARM EMPLOYMENT AND WAGE RATES: 1909 TO 1952

[See also *Historical Statistics*, series D 172-176 and E 61-68 for unrevised data]

YEAR	NUMBER OF WORKERS [1] (THOUSANDS)			FARM WAGE RATES [2]				Index of farm wage rates (1910-14=100)
				Per month		Per day		
	Total	Family [3]	Hired [4]	With board	Without board	With board	Without board	
1909	12,209	9,341	2,868	$22.00	$28.00	$1.00	$1.25	96
1910	12,146	9,269	2,877	21.00	28.00	1.05	1.35	96
1915	11,981	9,047	2,934	22.50	30.00	1.10	1.40	102
1917	11,789	8,856	2,933	31.00	40.50	1.55	1.90	141
1918	11,348	8,507	2,841	37.50	48.50	2.05	2.45	177
1920	11,362	8,479	2,883	51.00	65.00	2.80	3.30	241
1925	11,466	8,579	2,887	38.50	49.00	2.00	2.35	183
1926	11,282	8,302	2,980	40.00	51.00	2.00	2.30	187
1930	11,161	8,329	2,832	37.50	48.00	1.80	2.15	175
1935	11,654	9,130	2,524	22.00	30.50	1.10	1.35	110
1940	11,671	8,866	2,805	27.50	37.50	1.30	1.60	131
1944	11,055	8,643	2,412	71.00	91.00	3.50	3.95	328
1945	10,813	8,548	2,265	79.00	101.00	3.85	4.35	366
1946	11,092	8,766	2,326	86.00	108.00	4.20	4.80	399
1947	11,166	8,759	2,407	92.00	117.00	4.50	5.10	434
1948	11,080	8,595	2,485	99.00	124.00	4.80	5.40	445
1948 [5]				101.00	122.00	4.50	4.45	445
1949	10,756	8,326	2,430	99.00	121.00	4.45	4.45	430
1950	10,351	8,043	2,308	99.00	121.00	4.45	4.50	432
1951	10,022	7,799	2,223	113.00	137.00	5.00	5.00	481
1952	9,758	7,595	2,163	119.00	146.00	5.30	5.30	508

[1] Data are arithmetic means of monthly estimates of persons employed during last complete calendar week in each month ending at least one day before last of month.
[2] Weighted averages of wage rates as reported quarterly by crop reporters. U. S. estimates affected by importance of rates in particular regions; see table 216.
[3] Includes farm operators doing one or more hours of farm work and members of their families doing 15 hours or more of unpaid farm work during survey week.
[4] Includes all persons doing one or more hours of farm work for pay during survey week. Members of operators' families doing any farm work for cash wages are counted as hired workers.
[5] New series of wage rates begun in 1948; for description of series, see *Farm Labor, Dec. 1949*.

Source: Department of Agriculture, Bureau of Agricultural Economics; monthly report, *Farm Labor*.

No. 215.—FARM EMPLOYMENT, BY GEOGRAPHIC DIVISIONS: 1950, 1951, AND 1952

[In thousands. For last week in each month ending at least one day before last of month]

GEOGRAPHIC DIVISIONS	1950	1951				1952			
	Dec. 24-30	Mar. 18-24	June 17-23	Sept. 23-29	Dec. 23-29	Mar. 23-29	June 22-28	Sept. 21-27	Dec. 21-27
TOTAL WORKERS									
United States	6,782	8,996	11,334	13,352	6,524	8,790	11,020	13,252	6,485
New England	163	199	260	279	165	205	258	262	159
Middle Atlantic	453	545	695	718	460	536	713	716	472
East North Central	1,184	1,375	1,695	1,608	1,120	1,361	1,688	1,577	1,140
West North Central	1,347	1,511	1,931	1,955	1,282	1,474	1,954	1,932	1,255
South Atlantic	1,159	1,832	2,454	2,664	1,094	1,746	2,372	2,732	1,093
East South Central	980	1,409	1,706	2,880	899	1,396	1,570	2,802	920
West South Central	878	1,396	1,502	2,044	875	1,361	1,404	2,015	818
Mountain	260	300	459	513	258	290	447	498	256
Pacific	378	429	632	691	371	421	614	718	372
HIRED WORKERS [1]									
United States	885	1,672	3,060	3,621	836	1,657	3,025	3,709	848
New England	35	53	80	112	33	56	79	100	33
Middle Atlantic	82	104	193	219	86	104	197	219	90
East North Central	118	171	320	377	104	171	321	369	114
West North Central	103	141	355	328	94	135	397	322	90
South Atlantic	189	446	844	521	173	443	783	577	172
East South Central	99	298	389	824	87	298	379	533	99
West South Central	84	234	370	658	81	229	384	555	69
Mountain	61	63	181	202	62	62	176	193	59
Pacific	114	162	328	380	116	159	309	411	122

[1] Includes all persons doing one or more hours of farm work for pay during survey week. Members of operator's families doing any farm work for cash wages are counted as hired workers.

Source: Department of Agriculture, Bureau of Agricultural Economics; monthly report, *Farm Labor*.

No. 216.—Farm Wage Rates, by Geographic Division: 1951 and 1952

[Some wage rates in certain geographic divisions not obtained because seldom used; U. S. rates include estimates for these divisions]

GEOGRAPHIC DIVISIONS	1951					1952				
	Jan. 1	Apr. 1	July 1	Oct. 1	Annual average	Jan. 1	Apr. 1	July 1	Oct. 1	Annual average
Per month with board and room:										
United States	$105.00	$107.00	$115.00	$116.00	$113.00	$116.00	$114.00	$121.00	$122.00	$119.00
New England	102.00	106.00	112.00	112.00	109.00	112.00	120.00	110.00	120.00	117.00
Middle Atlantic	97.00	102.00	109.00	109.00	106.00	107.00	111.00	112.00	117.00	114.00
East North Central	99.00	107.00	111.00	111.00	109.00	110.00	117.00	119.00	118.00	117.00
West North Central	101.00	113.00	120.00	117.00	115.00	114.00	122.00	127.00	122.00	122.00
Mountain	126.00	142.00	146.00	144.00	142.00	137.00	144.00	153.00	151.00	148.00
Pacific	156.00	160.00	164.00	162.00	161.00	164.00	167.00	178.00	178.00	172.00
Per month with house:										
United States	127.00	128.00	146.00	138.00	137.00	141.00	128.00	155.00	146.00	146.00
New England	140.00	144.00	148.00	142.00	144.00	146.00	151.00	146.00	156.00	151.00
Middle Atlantic	133.00	138.00	143.00	150.00	144.00	148.00	151.00	155.00	159.00	155.00
East North Central	126.00	135.00	140.00	140.00	137.00	142.00	150.00	150.00	150.00	149.00
West North Central	125.00	141.00	144.00	140.00	140.00	140.00	152.00	155.00	148.00	150.00
Mountain	163.00	176.00	176.00	176.00	175.00	178.00	185.00	189.00	195.00	190.00
Pacific	202.00	202.00	209.00	210.00	208.00	217.00	218.00	225.00	226.00	223.00
Per week with board and room:										
United States	24.25	26.00	28.00	28.50	27.25	27.25	28.00	30.00	29.25	28.75
New England	26.00	28.00	31.00	30.50	29.75	30.50	32.00	31.25	33.25	32.00
Middle Atlantic	26.00	27.75	28.25	29.75	28.25	28.00	29.75	30.25	30.50	30.00
Per week without board or room:										
United States	31.75	33.50	35.25	35.25	34.50	35.00	34.75	40.00	35.75	36.50
New England	38.00	40.00	41.00	41.50	40.75	42.00	43.00	44.50	43.75	43.50
Middle Atlantic	36.00	37.75	38.25	40.25	38.50	38.50	39.75	42.25	42.50	41.25
Per day with board and room:										
United States	4.50	4.35	5.40	5.00	5.00	5.00	4.55	5.80	5.10	5.30
East North Central	4.85	5.20	5.50	5.50	5.40	5.40	5.50	6.00	5.80	5.80
West North Central	5.20	5.60	6.30	6.20	6.10	5.70	6.00	6.80	6.30	6.50
Per day with house:										
United States	3.75	3.75	3.90	4.10	3.90	4.20	4.00	4.15	4.25	4.15
South Atlantic	3.55	3.75	3.70	3.85	3.80	3.95	4.00	3.90	4.00	4.00
East South Central	3.00	3.05	3.20	3.30	3.20	3.25	3.25	3.35	3.40	3.35
West South Central	4.15	4.25	4.65	4.70	4.50	4.55	4.45	4.80	5.10	4.70
Per day without board or room:										
United States	4.65	4.70	4.95	5.50	5.00	5.20	5.00	5.20	5.60	5.30
New England	6.80	7.10	7.30	7.40	7.30	7.30	7.50	7.60	7.80	7.60
Middle Atlantic	6.40	6.60	7.10	7.10	7.00	6.90	7.00	7.30	7.40	7.30
East North Central	6.10	6.50	6.90	6.90	6.80	6.90	7.10	7.50	7.30	7.30
West North Central	6.50	7.00	7.80	7.60	7.50	7.20	7.60	8.30	7.80	8.00
South Atlantic	4.25	4.40	4.40	4.65	4.45	4.80	4.60	4.60	4.70	4.65
East South Central	3.60	3.65	3.85	3.95	3.80	3.90	3.95	4.00	4.15	4.00
West South Central	4.70	4.75	5.20	5.40	5.10	5.20	5.10	5.40	5.60	5.40
Mountain	6.20	6.90	7.30	7.50	7.30	7.10	7.40	7.70	7.90	7.70
Per hour with house:										
United States	.59	.57	.75	.81	.69	.65	.61	.80	.87	.74
South Atlantic	.46	.49			.50	.54	.54			.54
East South Central	.41	.42			.43	.44	.44			.46
West South Central	.51	.51			.54	.57	.54			.57
Pacific	.92	.91	.94	.94	.93	.96	.97	.99	1.02	1.00
Per hour without board or room:										
United States	.79	.78	.82	.73	.77	.86	.83	.87	.76	.81
New England	.90	.92	.94	.96	.95	.96	.97	.97	1.01	.99
Middle Atlantic	.84	.87	.90	.93	.91	.89	.92	.94	.96	.94
East North Central	.84	.88	.92	.93	.92	.92	.95	.97	.97	.97
West North Central	.87	.88	.95	.94	.94	.95	.96	1.02	.98	1.00
South Atlantic	.55	.57	.54	.58	.56	.62	.62	.58	.59	.59
East South Central	.49	.50	.51	.52	.52	.54	.54	.54	.54	.54
West South Central	.60	.59	.61	.64	.63	.66	.64	.64	.70	.68
Mountain	.79	.88	.90	.90	.89	.83	.91	.96	.96	.96
Pacific	.97	.98	1.01	1.02	1.01	1.03	1.04	1.05	1.08	1.06

Source: Department of Agriculture, Bureau of Agricultural Economics; monthly report, Farm Labor.

No. 917.—Employment Status of the Population, by Sex and Color, by Region: 1950

EMPLOYMENT STATUS AND SEX	UNITED STATES		NORTHEAST		NORTH CENTRAL		SOUTH		WEST	
	Total	Nonwhite	Total	Nonwhite	Total	Nonwhite	Total	Nonwhite	Total	Nonwhite
Total, 14 years and over	112,354,034	11,038,999	30,389,307	1,877,280	33,454,090	1,744,169	33,677,091	6,961,528	14,638,727	717,062
Total labor force	60,088,998	6,145,243	16,526,074	910,179	17,984,224	964,920	17,083,099	3,961,905	7,890,001	418,181
Civilian labor force	59,071,655	6,078,138	16,395,547	901,742	17,899,874	949,741	17,170,615	3,826,281	7,599,719	400,374
Employed	56,228,449	5,602,283	15,449,372	804,271	17,225,904	844,561	16,498,650	3,605,994	7,066,523	347,437
Unemployed	2,832,206	476,876	947,175	97,471	673,970	100,180	671,965	220,287	534,196	52,937
Not in labor force	52,300,066	4,875,664	14,073,183	957,101	15,469,785	789,789	16,009,022	3,119,863	6,748,126	298,911
Male, 14 years and over	55,311,617	5,332,997	14,816,061	747,973	16,564,889	868,177	16,629,767	3,333,707	7,370,920	367,749
Total labor force	43,553,386	4,066,418	11,592,040	553,001	13,219,642	643,655	12,971,344	2,565,244	5,770,360	294,505
Civilian labor force	42,598,767	3,991,809	11,467,345	544,930	13,139,203	638,742	12,497,205	2,531,018	5,495,014	277,119
Employed	40,519,462	3,681,574	10,752,211	478,425	12,638,904	567,900	12,018,147	2,396,086	5,110,200	340,163
Unemployed	2,079,305	310,235	715,134	66,505	500,299	70,842	479,058	135,932	384,814	36,956
Not in labor force	11,758,231	1,276,189	3,224,011	194,972	3,345,247	214,512	3,658,413	773,463	1,600,560	63,242
Female, 14 years and over	57,042,417	5,688,302	15,783,186	839,307	16,889,139	884,623	17,112,334	3,443,131	7,357,897	349,343
Total labor force	16,500,582	2,088,827	4,934,034	357,178	4,764,582	311,255	4,991,725	1,200,721	2,110,241	123,672
Civilian labor force	16,472,888	2,086,329	4,927,202	356,813	4,760,671	310,999	4,676,310	1,295,263	2,104,705	123,365
Employed	15,712,887	1,993,699	4,697,161	355,848	4,587,000	276,681	4,480,503	1,210,908	1,955,333	107,274
Unemployed	232,001	185,640	232,041	30,966	173,671	34,338	197,807	84,355	149,382	15,981
Not in labor force	40,541,835	3,699,475	10,849,122	472,129	12,124,538	575,277	12,420,609	2,348,400	5,147,566	205,699

1 Figure differs from corresponding item in table 224 due to separate tabulations.

Source: Department of Commerce, Bureau of the Census; U. S. Census of Population: 1950, Vol. II.

No. 218.—EMPLOYMENT STATUS OF THE POPULATION 14 YEARS OLD AND OVER, BY SEX, BY STATES: 1950

[In thousands]

DIVISION AND STATE	TOTAL							MALE LABOR FORCE		FEMALE LABOR FORCE	
	Labor force		Civilian labor force								
					Unemployed		Not in labor force				
	Number	Percent of population 14 years old and over	Total	Employed	Number	Percent of civilian labor force		Number	Percent of population 14 years old and over	Number	Percent of population 14 years old and over
United States	60,054	53.5	59,072	¹ 56,239	2,832	4.8	52,300	43,553	78.7	16,501	28.9
New England	3,896	54.4	3,846	3,611	235	6.1	3,269	2,675	77.4	1,221	32.9
Maine	345	51.2	342	312	30	8.8	330	250	75.5	95	27.7
New Hampshire	218	53.7	217	203	14	6.6	187	150	75.9	68	32.6
Vermont	146	52.4	145	137	8	5.5	132	106	77.5	40	28.3
Massachusetts	1,962	53.9	1,939	1,827	112	5.8	1,677	1,331	76.8	631	33.1
Rhode Island	345	56.0	328	305	24	7.2	271	234	77.9	110	35.0
Connecticut	881	56.7	875	828	47	5.4	672	604	79.9	277	34.8
Middle Atlantic	12,530	53.9	12,551	11,838	713	5.7	10,804	8,918	78.5	2,713	30.8
New York	6,353	54.4	6,325	5,944	381	6.0	5,298	4,406	78.4	1,947	32.3
New Jersey	2,102	55.8	2,068	1,963	105	5.1	1,668	1,485	80.7	618	32.0
Pennsylvania	4,175	52.1	4,158	3,931	226	5.4	3,838	3,027	77.5	1,148	27.9
East North Central	12,447	54.3	12,389	11,873	516	4.2	10,489	9,090	80.2	3,357	29.0
Ohio	3,209	53.5	3,201	3,060	142	4.4	2,787	2,345	79.9	864	28.2
Indiana	1,570	53.5	1,567	1,518	49	3.1	1,366	1,159	80.0	411	27.6
Illinois	3,729	54.4	3,694	3,546	148	4.0	2,999	2,658	80.3	1,071	31.3
Michigan	2,541	53.8	2,530	2,394	136	5.4	2,177	1,808	80.1	643	27.3
Wisconsin	1,399	54.7	1,396	1,355	41	2.9	1,159	1,029	80.5	369	28.9
West North Central	5,537	52.6	5,511	5,353	158	2.9	4,981	4,130	79.0	1,407	26.6
Minnesota	1,188	54.0	1,186	1,144	42	3.5	1,013	874	79.3	314	28.5
Iowa	1,022	52.3	1,021	1,002	19	1.8	932	772	79.7	250	25.3
Missouri	1,577	52.2	1,574	1,522	52	3.3	1,446	1,141	77.8	436	28.0
North Dakota	233	53.1	232	224	9	3.8	206	186	80.5	47	22.6
South Dakota	252	53.3	249	242	7	2.8	221	198	80.7	54	23.7
Nebraska	527	52.9	523	512	12	2.2	469	398	79.7	129	26.0
Kansas	739	51.6	726	708	18	2.5	694	561	78.8	178	24.7
South Atlantic	8,263	54.4	7,965	7,657	309	3.9	6,930	5,899	79.1	2,364	30.5
Delaware	131	54.6	131	127	4	3.1	109	94	79.8	37	30.4
Maryland	973	55.7	938	895	44	4.6	775	699	80.9	275	31.1
Dist. of Columbia	404	62.2	388	373	15	3.9	245	236	78.5	168	48.2
Virginia	1,306	54.3	1,197	1,150	47	3.9	1,099	974	80.5	331	27.8
West Virginia	660	47.0	660	628	31	4.8	746	522	74.5	138	19.6
North Carolina	1,555	55.0	1,513	1,463	50	3.3	1,270	1,114	80.1	441	30.7
South Carolina	798	56.2	782	755	27	3.4	623	553	80.3	246	33.5
Georgia	1,337	55.3	1,299	1,255	44	3.4	1,079	941	80.6	396	31.7
Florida	1,099	52.7	1,057	1,010	48	4.5	985	766	75.2	333	31.2
East South Central	4,055	50.4	3,992	3,839	154	3.8	3,992	3,054	77.6	1,001	24.4
Kentucky	1,013	48.5	991	955	36	3.6	1,075	799	76.9	214	20.4
Tennessee	1,200	50.9	1,182	1,136	46	3.9	1,150	889	77.3	311	25.7
Alabama	1,085	51.2	1,076	1,031	45	4.2	1,033	797	77.7	289	26.4
Mississippi	757	51.1	743	717	26	3.5	724	569	78.7	188	24.8
West South Central	5,345	51.2	5,218	5,003	214	4.1	5,087	4,019	77.8	1,327	25.2
Arkansas	648	48.5	646	616	30	4.7	687	505	76.6	142	21.1
Louisiana	929	49.3	918	876	42	4.6	954	690	75.5	239	24.6
Oklahoma	797	48.8	783	754	30	3.8	835	601	74.4	195	23.8
Texas	2,972	53.2	2,871	2,758	112	3.9	2,611	2,222	79.9	750	26.8
Mountain	1,892	52.5	1,845	1,747	98	5.6	1,709	1,438	78.1	454	25.8
Montana	232	54.0	230	218	12	5.1	198	181	79.7	51	25.1
Idaho	218	53.0	218	206	12	5.5	194	171	80.1	47	23.9
Wyoming	113	56.9	113	108	5	4.3	91	94	82.9	25	26.2
Colorado	513	52.4	498	477	21	4.2	467	376	76.9	137	27.8
New Mexico	230	50.9	218	207	12	5.4	226	179	76.7	51	22.9
Arizona	265	50.8	258	239	20	7.6	258	197	74.9	68	26.2
Utah	243	51.7	241	229	13	5.2	227	186	78.9	57	24.4
Nevada	71	58.8	68	64	5	6.7	50	53	82.0	18	31.9
Pacific	5,988	54.3	5,755	5,319	436	7.6	5,039	4,332	78.3	1,656	30.1
Washington	958	53.7	901	840	61	6.7	824	719	78.1	239	27.7
Oregon	620	54.5	617	577	40	6.5	518	457	79.3	162	28.9
California	4,411	54.4	4,238	3,902	335	7.9	3,697	3,156	78.2	1,255	30.8

¹ Figure differs from corresponding item in table 224 due to separate tabulations.

Source: Dept. of Commerce, Bureau of Census; U. S. Census of Population: 1950, Vol. II, Part I.

No. 219.—LABOR FORCE STATUS OF THE POPULATION 14 YEARS OLD AND OVER, FOR CITIES OF 100,000 OR MORE: 1950

CITY	Population 14 years old and over	LABOR FORCE Number	LABOR FORCE Percent of population 14 years old and over	CITY	Population 14 years old and over	LABOR FORCE Number	LABOR FORCE Percent of population 14 years old and over
Akron, Ohio	210,219	118,606	56.4	Nashville, Tenn.	138,113	76,835	55.6
Albany, N.Y.	108,283	61,526	56.8	Newark, N.J.	346,237	200,842	58.0
Allentown, Pa.	85,400	48,623	56.9	New Bedford, Mass.	86,374	50,932	59.0
Atlanta, Ga.	256,998	152,519	58.9	New Haven, Conn.	131,063	71,463	54.5
Austin, Tex.	102,247	51,466	50.3	New Orleans, La.	435,906	233,979	53.7
Baton Rouge, La.	91,966	49,152	53.5	New York, N.Y.	6,332,984	3,533,813	55.8
Baltimore, Md.	736,014	417,755	56.8	Bronx Borough	1,153,586	628,670	54.5
Berkeley, Calif.	94,396	50,962	54.0	Brooklyn Borough	2,155,211	1,175,806	54.6
Birmingham, Ala.	244,088	134,461	55.1	Manhattan Borough	1,650,125	969,183	58.7
Boston, Mass.	633,234	344,017	54.3	Queens Borough	1,226,284	680,260	55.5
Bridgeport, Conn.	124,824	73,045	58.5	Richmond Borough	147,778	79,894	54.1
Buffalo, N.Y.	457,745	249,804	54.6				
Cambridge, Mass.	97,268	50,522	51.9	Norfolk, Va.	170,112	110,909	65.2
Camden, N.J.	95,436	54,132	56.7	Oakland, Calif.	308,217	174,818	56.7
Canton, Ohio	90,892	51,412	56.6	Oklahoma City, Okla.	186,204	105,169	56.1
				Omaha, Nebr.	194,948	108,759	55.8
Charlotte, N.C.	100,728	64,840	64.4				
Chattanooga, Tenn.	99,507	56,382	56.7	Pasadena, Calif.	86,963	44,779	51.5
Chicago, Ill.	2,871,982	1,698,995	59.2	Paterson, N.J.	111,637	65,919	59.0
Cincinnati, Ohio	396,529	214,460	54.1	Peoria, Ill.	88,154	50,711	57.5
Cleveland, Ohio	716,572	413,916	57.8	Philadelphia, Pa.	1,630,508	891,282	54.7
				Phoenix, Ariz.	82,610	42,497	51.4
Columbus, Ohio	296,967	163,515	55.1				
Corpus Christi, Tex.	74,901	43,086	57.5	Pittsburgh, Pa.	530,001	280,209	52.9
Dallas, Tex.	336,827	205,359	61.3	Portland, Oreg.	297,330	169,546	57.0
Dayton, Ohio	189,837	110,385	58.1	Providence, R.I.	197,055	109,183	55.4
Denver, Colo.	324,473	180,410	55.6	Reading, Pa.	89,008	53,275	59.9
				Richmond, Va.	184,453	108,304	58.7
Des Moines, Iowa	138,074	79,482	57.6				
Detroit, Mich.	1,433,071	819,054	57.2	Rochester, N.Y.	266,491	151,167	56.7
Duluth, Minn.	80,010	44,053	55.1	Sacramento, Calif.	110,096	64,687	58.8
El Paso, Tex.	92,990	51,063	54.9	St. Louis, Mo.	685,042	384,668	56.2
Elizabeth, N.J.	86,855	52,671	59.3	St. Paul, Minn.	239,441	132,935	55.5
				Salt Lake City, Utah	133,175	73,813	55.4
Erie, Pa.	100,057	56,043	56.0				
Evansville, Ind.	97,990	54,615	55.9	San Antonio, Tex.	290,894	153,853	52.9
Fall River, Mass.	86,125	51,053	59.3	San Diego, Calif.	259,842	145,818	56.1
Flint, Mich.	123,624	72,353	58.5	San Francisco, Calif.	642,966	379,897	59.1
Fort Wayne, Ind.	103,209	59,036	57.2	Savannah, Ga.	87,799	49,252	56.1
				Scranton, Pa.	98,704	49,744	50.4
Fort Worth, Tex.	214,022	125,742	58.8				
Gary, Ind.	100,508	57,689	57.4	Seattle, Wash.	375,488	214,746	57.2
Grand Rapids, Mich.	135,576	76,554	56.5	Shreveport, La.	95,293	54,396	57.1
Hartford, Conn.	141,348	87,534	61.9	Somerville, Mass.	79,006	43,815	55.5
Houston, Tex.	450,854	262,414	58.2	South Bend, Ind.	90,035	53,457	59.4
				Spokane, Wash.	124,083	66,684	53.7
Indianapolis, Ind.	331,653	194,096	58.5				
Jacksonville, Fla.	157,134	91,377	58.2	Springfield, Mass.	127,858	72,048	56.4
Jersey City, N.J.	234,506	134,243	57.2	Syracuse, N.Y.	176,620	98,324	55.7
Kansas City, Kan.	96,129	53,974	55.0	Tacoma, Wash.	109,322	58,262	53.3
Kansas City, Mo.	366,665	211,217	57.6	Tampa, Fla.	98,134	54,867	55.9
				Toledo, Ohio	237,686	133,683	56.2
Knoxville, Tenn.	95,191	50,656	53.2				
Little Rock, Ark.	80,182	45,472	56.7	Trenton, N.J.	103,038	59,303	57.6
Long Beach, Calif.	200,752	105,296	52.9	Tulsa, Okla.	140,785	80,479	57.2
Los Angeles, Calif.	1,583,039	876,861	55.4	Utica, N.Y.	80,270	44,121	55.0
Louisville, Ky.	283,290	158,562	56.0	Washington, D.C.	648,963	403,891	62.2
				Waterbury, Conn.	81,006	48,444	59.8
Memphis, Tenn.	301,204	175,419	58.2				
Miami, Fla.	204,179	116,646	57.1	Wichita, Kans.	127,595	72,619	56.9
Milwaukee, Wis.	502,012	293,001	58.4	Wilmington, Del.	87,638	50,448	57.6
Minneapolis, Minn.	415,441	242,054	58.3	Worcester, Mass.	160,518	83,731	52.2
Mobile, Ala.	93,912	53,401	56.9	Yonkers, N.Y.	120,101	67,621	56.3
Montgomery, Ala.	79,224	46,166	58.3	Youngstown, Ohio	131,365	72,147	54.9

Source: Department of Commerce, Bureau of Census; U. S. Census of Population: 1950, Vol. II, Part 1.

No. 220.—LABOR FORCE STATUS OF THE FEMALE POPULATION, BY MARITAL STATUS, AGE, AND COLOR: 1950

[In thousands. Based on 20-percent sample]

COLOR AND AGE	TOTAL FEMALE			SINGLE			MARRIED, SPOUSE PRESENT		
	Popula-tion	Labor force		Popula-tion	Labor force		Popula-tion	Labor force	
		Number	Per-cent of popu-lation		Number	Per-cent of popu-lation		Number	Per-cent of popu-lation
Female, 14 years old and over....	57,102	16,552	29.0	11,418	5,294	46.4	35,569	7,678	21.6
14 to 19 years.........	6,369	1,440	22.6	5,452	1,244	22.8	805	155	19.3
20 to 24 years.........	5,878	2,536	43.2	1,899	1,395	73.4	3,621	948	26.2
25 to 29 years.........	6,277	2,045	32.6	833	661	79.3	4,962	1,098	22.1
30 to 34 years.........	5,897	1,821	30.9	546	422	77.3	4,848	1,082	22.3
35 to 39 years.........	5,713	1,937	33.9	477	361	75.7	4,646	1,187	25.6
40 to 44 years.........	5,125	1,855	36.2	423	318	75.1	4,046	1,107	27.4
45 to 49 years.........	4,553	1,583	34.8	360	258	71.7	3,447	872	25.3
50 years and over.....	17,290	3,334	19.3	1,427	636	44.5	9,195	1,229	13.4
White, 14 years old and over....	51,404	14,441	28.1	10,241	4,870	47.6	32,671	6,757	20.7
14 to 19 years.........	5,571	1,295	23.3	4,796	1,127	23.5	696	138	19.8
20 to 24 years.........	5,178	2,259	43.6	1,680	1,270	75.6	3,253	852	26.2
25 to 29 years.........	5,579	1,745	31.3	734	595	81.1	4,511	951	21.1
30 to 34 years.........	5,282	1,536	29.1	492	386	78.4	4,430	926	20.9
35 to 39 years.........	5,086	1,633	32.1	434	332	76.6	4,226	1,022	24.2
40 to 44 years.........	4,607	1,606	34.9	394	299	75.8	3,715	981	26.4
45 to 49 years.........	4,098	1,376	33.6	338	245	72.6	3,174	777	24.5
50 years and over.....	16,003	2,990	18.7	1,373	615	44.8	8,667	1,111	12.8
Nonwhite, 14 years old and over...........	5,698	2,111	37.0	1,178	424	36.0	2,898	920	31.8
14 to 19 years.........	798	145	18.2	657	116	17.7	109	18	16.2
20 to 24 years.........	700	277	39.6	219	125	57.0	368	96	26.0
25 to 29 years.........	698	300	42.9	99	66	66.5	452	147	32.6
30 to 34 years.........	614	284	46.3	54	37	67.2	418	157	37.5
35 to 39 years.........	626	304	48.6	43	29	66.2	419	165	39.3
40 to 44 years.........	518	249	48.1	29	19	64.9	331	126	38.1
45 to 49 years.........	457	207	45.3	23	13	58.5	273	95	34.7
50 years and over.....	1,287	344	26.7	54	20	37.1	527	118	22.3

Source: Department of Commerce, Bureau of the Census; U. S. Census of Population: 1950, Vol. II, Part 1.

No. 221.—Major Occupation Group of Employed Persons, by Sex: 1952

[Thousands of persons 14 years old and over. See headnote, table 206]

MAJOR OCCUPATION GROUP	MALE				FEMALE			
	Jan.	Apr.	July	Oct.	Jan.	Apr.	July	Oct.
Total employed	41,480	41,896	42,476	42,482	18,246	18,234	18,758	19,380
Professional, technical, and kindred workers	3,218	3,162	3,018	3,350	2,140	2,026	1,580	1,872
Farmers and farm managers	3,662	3,866	3,818	3,738	190	166	204	208
Managers, officials, and proprietors, except farm	5,114	5,022	5,238	5,336	998	978	986	1,054
Clerical and kindred workers	2,806	2,830	2,928	2,668	5,288	5,284	5,444	5,240
Sales workers	2,322	2,272	2,206	2,282	1,368	1,416	1,354	1,476
Craftsmen, foremen, and kindred workers	7,872	8,514	8,802	8,732	258	244	280	270
Operatives and kindred workers	8,798	8,702	8,812	8,612	3,526	3,496	3,592	3,868
Private household workers	34	38	116	36	1,724	1,748	1,814	1,708
Service workers, except private household	2,558	2,500	2,504	2,448	2,034	2,134	2,162	2,390
Farm laborers and foremen	1,580	1,522	2,048	1,886	636	614	1,202	1,186
Laborers, except farm and mine	3,516	3,470	3,986	3,394	84	126	140	108

Source: Department of Commerce, Bureau of the Census; *Current Population Reports*, Series P-57, Nos. 115, 118, 121, and 124.

No. 222.—Major Occupation Group of Employed Persons, by Sex: 1940 and 1950

[In thousands. 1950 figures may differ from corresponding items in table 224 due to separate tabulations]

MAJOR OCCUPATION GROUP	TOTAL		MALE		FEMALE	
	1940	1950	1940	1950	1940	1950
Total	44,888	56,229	33,750	40,519	11,138	15,720
Professional, technical, and kindred workers	3,566	4,910	2,075	2,971	1,491	1,940
Farmers and farm managers	5,144	4,309	4,992	4,192	152	116
Managers, officials, and proprietors, excluding farm	3,620	5,018	3,231	4,341	389	677
Clerical and kindred workers	4,371	6,895	2,013	2,603	2,358	4,293
Sales workers	3,072	3,927	2,261	2,597	811	1,330
Craftsmen, foremen, and kindred workers	5,152	7,783	5,030	7,547	122	236
Operatives and kindred workers	8,052	11,140	6,032	8,120	2,020	3,020
Private household workers	2,083	1,408	114	73	1,969	1,335
Service workers, except private household	3,188	4,287	1,962	2,372	1,226	1,914
Farm laborers, except unpaid, and foremen	1,934	1,490	1,836	1,358	96	132
Farm laborers, unpaid family workers	1,165	910	942	593	223	317
Laborers, except farm and mine	3,123	3,431	3,017	3,303	106	127
Occupation not reported	418	732	245	449	173	283

Source: Department of Commerce, Bureau of the Census; *U. S. Census of Population: 1950*, Vol. II, Part 1.

No. 223.—Class of Worker of Employed Persons, by Sex: 1940 and 1950

CLASS OF WORKER	TOTAL		MALE		FEMALE	
	1940	1950	1940	1950	1940	1950
Total	44,888,063	¹ 56,229,449	33,749,905	¹ 40,519,462	11,138,178	¹ 15,719,987
Private wage and salary workers	30,120,692	40,037,668	21,656,899	27,793,416	8,463,793	12,244,282
Government workers	3,566,567	5,495,690	2,255,554	3,466,249	1,311,013	2,029,441
Self-employed workers	9,757,736	9,591,482	8,818,829	8,624,154	938,907	967,328
Unpaid family workers	1,443,068	1,114,609	1,018,623	635,643	424,465	478,966

¹ Figure differs from corresponding item in table 224 due to separate tabulations.

Source: Department of Commerce, Bureau of the Census; *U. S. Census of Population: 1950*, Vol. II, Part 1.

No. 224.—Detailed Occupation of the Experienced Civilian Labor Force and of Employed Persons, by Sex: 1950

["N. e. c." means not elsewhere classified. For definition of "Employed," and "Experienced Civilian Labor Force," see text, page 179]

OCCUPATION	EXPERIENCED CIVILIAN LABOR FORCE			EMPLOYED		
	Total	Male	Female	Total	Male	Female
Total, 14 years old and over	58,996,943	42,553,838	16,445,105	56,225,340	40,510,176	15,715,164
Professional, technical, and kindred workers	4,988,012	3,024,430	1,963,582	4,909,241	2,970,256	1,938,985
Accountants and auditors	383,496	327,119	56,377	376,285	320,767	55,518
Actors and actresses	18,453	11,967	6,486	14,886	9,809	5,077
Airplane pilots and navigators	14,191	13,993	198	13,720	13,535	185
Architects	25,000	24,046	954	24,756	23,823	933
Artists and art teachers	80,535	49,779	30,756	77,473	47,907	29,566
Athletes	12,389	11,628	761	11,572	10,867	705
Authors	16,184	9,949	6,235	15,651	9,592	6,059
Chemists	75,747	68,118	7,629	74,433	66,982	7,451
Chiropractors	13,064	11,169	1,915	12,903	11,061	1,842
Clergymen	168,419	161,572	6,847	167,471	160,694	6,777
College presidents, professors, and instructors (n. e. c.)	125,640	96,432	29,208	124,743	95,811	28,932
Dancers and dancing teachers	17,239	5,031	12,208	16,097	4,659	11,438
Dentists	75,025	72,949	2,076	74,855	72,810	2,045
Designers	40,108	29,376	10,732	36,720	26,517	10,203
Dietitians and nutritionists	22,826	1,386	21,440	22,400	1,341	21,059
Draftsmen	124,749	116,128	8,621	121,668	113,298	8,370
Editors and reporters	91,472	62,183	29,289	89,325	60,730	28,595
Engineers, technical	534,424	527,772	6,652	525,256	518,781	6,475
Aeronautical	17,925	17,589	336	17,635	17,304	331
Chemical	33,072	32,414	658	32,522	31,893	629
Civil	125,568	123,601	1,967	123,318	121,386	1,932
Electrical	108,137	106,867	1,270	106,515	105,278	1,237
Industrial	40,985	40,524	461	40,200	39,750	450
Mechanical	112,664	112,067	597	110,164	109,588	576
Metallurgical, and metallurgists	11,490	11,240	250	11,340	11,099	241
Mining	10,991	10,864	127	10,765	10,656	109
Not elsewhere classified	73,592	72,606	986	72,797	71,827	970
Entertainers (n. e. c.)	16,311	11,642	4,669	14,936	10,643	4,293
Farm and home management advisors	12,316	6,231	6,085	12,242	6,210	6,032
Foresters and conservationists	27,052	26,193	859	26,127	25,297	830
Funeral directors and embalmers	39,914	37,236	2,678	39,400	36,757	2,643
Lawyers and judges	181,226	174,893	6,333	180,461	174,205	6,256
Librarians	55,749	6,394	49,355	55,329	6,303	49,026
Musicians and music teachers	161,266	81,681	79,585	153,415	75,612	77,803
Natural scientists (n. e. c.)	40,695	34,735	5,960	40,065	34,226	5,839
Nurses, professional	403,793	9,863	393,930	398,534	9,613	388,921
Nurses, student professional	76,671	1,607	75,064	76,146	1,572	74,574
Optometrists	14,711	13,865	846	14,596	13,758	838
Osteopaths	5,167	4,377	790	5,149	4,366	783
Personnel and labor relations workers	52,858	37,592	15,266	52,086	37,070	15,016
Pharmacists	88,997	81,640	7,357	88,115	80,854	7,261
Photographers	54,734	45,253	9,481	52,489	43,401	9,088
Physicians and surgeons	192,317	180,532	11,785	191,947	180,233	11,714
Radio operators	16,421	14,914	1,507	15,911	14,429	1,482
Recreation and group workers	16,799	9,737	7,062	16,046	9,353	6,693
Religious workers	41,698	12,725	28,973	41,431	12,593	28,838
Social and welfare workers, except group	76,393	23,545	52,848	75,414	23,193	52,221
Social scientists	35,895	24,255	11,640	35,203	23,827	11,376
Sports instructors and officials	45,823	34,559	11,264	44,987	33,854	11,133
Surveyors	28,394	27,398	996	27,466	26,520	946
Teachers (n. e. c.)	1,125,688	285,847	839,836	1,118,453	283,467	834,996
Technicians, medical and dental	78,038	34,057	43,981	76,328	33,053	43,275
Technicians, testing	76,962	59,780	17,182	75,507	58,707	16,800
Technicians (n. e. c.)	27,471	23,158	4,313	26,882	22,639	4,243
Therapists and healers (n. e. c.)	24,905	12,578	12,327	24,465	12,347	12,118
Veterinarians	13,489	12,634	855	13,379	12,547	832
Professional, technical, and kindred workers (n. e. c.)	117,283	94,912	22,371	114,506	92,628	21,885
Farmers and farm managers	4,320,576	4,202,683	117,893	4,306,253	4,189,882	116,371
Farmers (owners and tenants)	4,285,462	4,170,291	115,171	4,271,413	4,157,234	114,179
Farm managers	35,114	32,892	2,222	34,840	32,648	2,192

No. 224.—DETAILED OCCUPATION OF THE EXPERIENCED CIVILIAN LABOR FORCE
AND OF EMPLOYED PERSONS, BY SEX: 1950—Continued

OCCUPATION	EXPERIENCED CIVILIAN LABOR FORCE			EMPLOYED		
	Total	Male	Female	Total	Male	Female
Managers, officials, and proprietors, excluding farm	5,076,436	4,391,611	684,825	5,017,465	4,340,687	676,778
Buyers and department heads, store	144,656	107,381	27,275	142,247	106,120	36,127
Buyers and shippers, farm products	26,809	26,056	753	26,196	27,876	360
Conductors, railroad	55,036	54,674	362	55,711	54,359	352
Credit men	33,326	26,069	7,267	22,699	25,748	7,151
Floormen and floor managers, store	11,061	5,990	5,071	10,520	5,515	5,095
Inspectors, public administration	56,807	54,420	2,387	55,905	53,639	2,266
Federal public administration and postal service	27,338	26,422	906	26,850	26,018	832
State public administration	9,362	9,280	362	9,463	9,125	358
Local public administration	16,887	15,768	1,119	16,979	16,466	1,076
Managers and superintendents, building	66,620	43,945	22,675	65,716	43,331	22,385
Officials, administration and engineers, ship	41,387	40,228	1,159	38,104	36,975	1,129
Officials and administrators (n. e. c.), public administration	155,236	128,683	26,553	153,792	127,470	26,322
Federal public administration and postal service	50,042	44,670	5,372	49,520	44,208	5,315
State public administration	23,308	20,400	2,808	23,134	20,338	2,796
Local public administration	51,906	33,523	18,373	51,138	63,929	18,209
Officials, lodge, society, union, etc.	27,060	24,111	2,949	26,045	23,760	2,285
Postmasters	33,031	22,114	16,717	36,700	22,032	14,696
Purchasing agents and buyers (n. e. c.)	64,147	58,291	5,860	62,034	57,316	4,718
Managers, officials, and proprietors (n. e. c.)—salaried	1,811,419	1,593,632	217,787	1,787,334	1,573,585	213,749
...	58,164	56,147	2,017	85,563	53,602	1,961
...	416,443	389,731	26,712	412,462	386,146	26,315
...	96,663	93,214	3,469	96,845	93,419	3,436
Transportation, communication, and utilities and ...	61,584	55,560	6,014	61,366	55,390	4,978
Wholesale trade	158,719	149,583	9,136	157,062	148,067	6,995
...	521,373	441,530	79,853	513,837	435,360	78,475
Food and dairy products stores, and ...	103,030	90,533	12,506	101,706	89,384	12,321
General merchandise and five and ...	60,165	46,735	13,430	56,439	44,191	12,248
... ten cent stores	42,530	28,766	13,762	42,002	28,483	13,519
Apparel, home furnishings, and ...	27,820	25,246	2,574	27,578	25,048	2,530
... stores	57,015	56,085	1,930	56,422	54,510	1,912
Gasoline service stations retailing	36,058	34,425	633	35,414	34,791	623
Eating and drinking places	70,991	51,116	19,875	68,740	49,337	19,403
Hardware, farm implement, and ... material retail	43,901	42,330	1,581	43,669	42,098	1,571
Other retail trade	79,854	66,292	13,562	75,876	65,827	13,351
... dairy homes	119,364	104,521	12,423	118,715	106,354	12,361
... real estate	70,429	58,777	11,652	70,142	58,568	11,574
... hotel	28,162	22,984	5,178	27,666	22,608	5,058
Automobile services and garages	24,045	23,638	407	23,729	23,329	400
... repair services	4,374	4,142	232	4,330	4,103	227
All other industries (including not reported)	66,689	44,360	22,328	65,007	43,270	21,737
...	155,511	117,155	38,356	151,589	114,380	37,200
Managers, officials, and proprietors (n. e. c.)—self-employed	2,541,051	2,203,027	338,094	2,518,402	2,181,961	336,441
Construction	203,088	200,419	2,669	199,482	196,838	2,844
Manufacturing	239,128	224,558	14,570	237,458	222,987	14,491
Transportation	51,926	49,510	2,416	51,279	48,877	2,402
Telecommunications, and utilities and sanitary services	5,782	5,526	266	5,723	5,467	256
Wholesale trade	179,405	171,999	7,406	177,929	170,570	7,369
Retail trade	1,426,326	1,183,570	342,756	1,414,556	1,172,895	241,661
Food and dairy products stores, and milk retailing	401,120	329,816	71,304	397,995	326,917	71,078
General merchandise and five and ten cent stores	65,881	51,466	14,085	65,196	51,169	14,029
Apparel and accessories stores	85,909	59,345	25,984	84,676	58,798	25,878
Furniture, home furnishings, and equipment stores	65,538	62,831	5,707	65,251	62,845	4,896
Motor vehicles and accessories retailing	60,116	55,581	1,535	59,688	59,277	1,381
Gasoline service stations	147,769	142,334	5,435	146,504	141,088	5,416
Eating and drinking places	398,649	216,592	76,357	208,602	252,771	76,531
Hardware, farm implement, and building material retail	98,500	52,050	4,191	84,930	80,738	4,182
Other retail trade	230,306	182,008	38,168	218,602	180,572	38,090

No. 224.—DETAILED OCCUPATION OF THE EXPERIENCED CIVILIAN LABOR FORCE
AND OF EMPLOYED PERSONS, BY SEX: 1950—Continued

OCCUPATION	EXPERIENCED CIVILIAN LABOR FORCE			EMPLOYED		
	Total	Male	Female	Total	Male	Female
Managers, etc.—Con.						
Managers, officials, and proprietors (n. e. c.)—self-employed—Con.						
Banking and other finance	21,995	20,965	1,030	21,912	20,883	1,029
Insurance and real estate	45,019	39,061	5,958	44,901	38,962	5,939
Business services	34,101	29,294	4,807	33,831	29,065	4,766
Automobile repair services and garages	60,458	59,384	1,074	60,099	59,030	1,069
Miscellaneous repair services	29,806	28,489	1,317	29,586	28,276	1,310
Personal services	145,380	105,909	39,471	144,273	104,980	39,293
All other industries (including not reported)	98,637	84,343	14,294	97,373	83,151	14,222
Clerical and kindred workers	7,070,023	2,678,679	4,391,344	6,894,374	2,602,610	4,291,764
Agents (n. e. c.)	126,085	106,450	19,635	124,257	104,961	19,296
Attendants and assistants, library	12,760	3,251	9,509	12,329	3,160	9,169
Attendants, physician's and dentist's office	41,794	2,093	39,701	40,727	2,028	38,699
Baggagemen, transportation	8,101	7,945	156	7,915	7,762	153
Bank tellers	64,497	35,646	28,851	63,980	35,332	28,648
Bookkeepers	736,091	169,312	566,779	720,972	164,743	556,229
Cashiers	234,335	44,192	190,143	226,428	42,842	183,586
Collectors, bill and account	23,953	20,422	3,531	23,368	19,918	3,450
Dispatchers and starters, vehicle	31,508	27,800	3,708	30,761	27,217	3,544
Express messengers and railway mail clerks	18,881	18,594	287	18,688	18,409	279
Mail carriers	167,880	164,268	3,612	165,162	161,702	3,460
Messengers and office boys	58,813	48,307	10,506	55,387	45,289	10,098
Office machine operators	145,943	25,804	120,139	142,066	25,149	116,917
Shipping and receiving clerks	297,125	276,466	20,659	284,491	264,608	19,883
Stenographers, typists, and secretaries	1,621,862	90,750	1,531,112	1,589,479	88,390	1,501,089
Telegraph messengers	8,038	7,233	805	7,178	6,427	751
Telegraph operators	34,915	27,304	7,611	34,331	26,891	7,440
Telephone operators	365,709	16,495	349,214	357,862	16,155	341,707
Ticket, station, and express agents	59,895	52,110	7,785	59,290	51,634	7,656
Clerical and kindred workers (n. e. c.)	3,011,838	1,534,237	1,477,601	2,489,903	1,439,710	1,439,710
Sales workers	4,044,143	2,665,824	1,378,319	3,926,510	2,596,786	1,329,724
Advertising agents and salesmen	33,729	28,814	4,915	32,381	27,809	4,572
Auctioneers	5,453	4,955	498	5,280	4,826	454
Demonstrators	13,946	2,544	11,402	13,308	2,415	10,893
Hucksters and peddlers	23,197	19,913	3,284	21,950	18,871	3,079
Insurance agents and brokers	307,497	281,160	26,337	304,088	278,120	25,968
Newsboys	99,222	95,265	3,957	96,168	92,301	3,867
Real estate agents and brokers	142,564	121,974	20,590	140,602	120,325	20,277
Stock and bond salesmen	11,257	10,108	1,149	10,972	9,886	1,086
Salesmen and sales clerks (n. e. c.)	3,407,278	2,101,091	1,306,187	3,301,761	2,042,233	1,259,528
Manufacturing	326,846	303,694	23,152	320,723	298,271	22,452
Wholesale trade	414,588	399,106	15,482	406,819	391,757	15,062
Retail trade	2,530,550	1,294,927	1,235,623	2,445,436	1,253,113	1,192,323
Other industries (including not reported)	135,294	103,364	31,930	128,783	99,092	29,691
Craftsmen, foremen, and kindred workers	8,152,743	7,907,504	245,239	7,772,560	7,537,016	235,544
Bakers	124,214	109,587	14,627	119,202	105,195	14,007
Blacksmiths	44,313	44,104	209	42,697	42,497	200
Boilermakers	38,930	38,569	361	35,529	35,211	318
Bookbinders	32,426	14,245	18,181	31,200	13,684	17,516
Brickmasons, stonemasons, and tile setters	175,828	174,816	1,012	165,323	164,399	924
Cabinetmakers	76,421	75,300	1,121	73,298	72,224	1,064
Carpenters	985,443	980,272	5,171	912,537	907,728	4,809
Cement and concrete finishers	32,653	32,441	212	29,478	29,293	185
Compositors and typesetters	178,696	167,406	11,290	175,443	164,366	11,077
Cranemen, derrickmen, and hoistmen	106,864	106,036	828	102,965	102,188	777
Decorators and window dressers	45,029	31,582	13,447	43,342	30,339	13,003
Electricians	324,046	321,677	2,369	309,230	307,013	2,217
Electrotypers and stereotypers	11,941	11,474	467	11,752	11,317	435
Engravers, except photoengravers	10,039	8,732	1,287	9,732	8,499	1,233
Excavating, grading, and road machinery operators	111,026	110,505	521	105,351	104,855	496
Foremen (n. e. c.)	853,525	784,193	69,332	843,150	775,224	67,926
Construction	66,439	66,163	276	66,563	66,316	267

No. 224.—DETAILED OCCUPATION OF THE EXPERIENCED CIVILIAN LABOR FORCE AND OF EMPLOYED PERSONS, BY SEX: 1950—Continued

OCCUPATION	EXPERIENCED CIVILIAN LABOR FORCE					
	Total	Male	Female	Total	Male	Female
Craftsmen, etc.—Con.						
Foremen (n. e. c.)—Con.						
Manufacturing				510,754	460,412	50,342
Metal industries				83,307	81,581	1,726
Machinery, including electrical				80,189	75,469	4,720
Transportation equipment				46,936	46,085	851
Other durable goods				75,618	70,007	5,611
Textiles, textile products, and apparel				68,968	47,922	21,036
Other nondurable goods (including not specified manufacturing)				152,746	136,348	16,396
Railroads and railway express service				53,932	53,685	247
Transportation, except railroad				19,820	19,585	235
Telecommunications, and utilities and sanitary services				40,212	39,227	965
Other industries (including not reported)				159,849	143,989	15,880
Forgemen and hammermen		13,		13,124	12,864	260
Furriers		11,		11,014	9,430	1,585
Glaziers		10,		10,263	9,969	294
Heat treaters, annealers, and temperers				17,780	17,495	285
Inspectors, scalers, and graders, log and lumber				17,199	16,461	738
Inspectors (n. e. c.)				95,790	89,062	6,728
Construction				5,083	7,949	54
Railroads and railway express service				36,753	36,624	129
Transport, exc. r. r., communication, and other public utilities				12,463	11,976	488
Other industries (including not reported)				38,511	32,514	5,997
Jewelers, watchmakers, goldsmiths, and silversmiths		45,109		45,687	43,226	2,461
Job setters, metal		24,702		24,447	24,147	300
Linemen and servicemen, telegraph, telephone, and power		211,		212,897	207,962	4,938
Locomotive engineers		72,		72,842	72,412	430
Locomotive firemen		55,		54,140	53,944	196
Loom fixers		30,610		30,298	29,958	340
Machinists		525,156		513,225	506,095	8,130
Mechanics and repairmen	642			1,706,499	1,685,538	20,961
Airplane	720			70,714	69,567	1,147
Automobile	693			650,631	646,549	4,082
Office machine	289			15,896	15,687	238
Radio and television	250			74,821	72,794	2,027
Railroad and car shop	339			47,473	47,252	221
Not elsewhere classified	442			846,965	833,719	13,246
Millers, grain, flour, feed, etc.				9,601	9,534	67
Millwrights				57,947	57,706	241
Molders, metal				60,546	59,879	667
Motion picture projectionists				26,107	25,625	482
Opticians, and lens grinders and polishers		102		19,161	16,643	2,518
Painters, construction and maintenance		488		390,085	381,994	8,091
Paperhangers		498		20,935	17,994	2,941
Pattern and model makers, except paper		000	1,248	35,867	34,663	1,204
Photoengravers and lithographers		893	1,098	28,511	27,449	1,062
Piano and organ tuners and repairmen		716		7,744	7,478	266
				60,312	59,820	492
				277,864	275,892	1,972
				49,124	46,988	2,136
Rollers and roll hands, metal				20,359	29,700	659
Roofers and slaters				44,363	44,126	237
Shoemakers and repairers, except factory		414		57,118	54,969	2,149
Stationary engineers		1,480		213,938	212,504	1,434
Stone cutters and stone carvers		239		8,703	8,477	226
Structural metal workers				49,230	48,963	267
Tailors and tailoresses				83,483	66,435	16,048
Tinsmiths, coppersmiths, and sheet metal workers		1,261		122,828	121,660	1,163
Toolmakers, and die makers and setters		1,111		182,647	181,568	1,080
Upholsterers		5,470		81,181	80,942	4,279
Craftsmen and kindred workers (n. e. c.)		1,254		79,822	78,388	1,134
Members of the armed forces		470				

No. 224.—DETAILED OCCUPATION OF THE EXPERIENCED CIVILIAN LABOR FORCE AND OF EMPLOYED PERSONS, BY SEX: 1950—Continued

OCCUPATION	EXPERIENCED CIVILIAN LABOR FORCE			EMPLOYED		
	Total	Male	Female	Total	Male	Female
Operatives and kindred workers	11,715,606	8,536,065	3,179,541	11,146,220	8,127,433	3,018,787
Apprentices	119,801	116,442	3,359	115,176	112,008	3,168
Auto mechanics	3,879	3,723	156	3,693	3,546	147
Bricklayers and masons	6,471	6,447	24	6,144	6,122	22
Carpenters	10,753	10,664	89	9,972	9,890	82
Electricians	9,194	9,106	86	8,854	8,776	78
Machinists and toolmakers	15,704	15,531	173	15,285	15,126	159
Mechanics, except auto	5,539	5,027	512	6,282	5,822	460
Plumbers and pipe fitters	12,373	11,824	549	11,920	11,387	533
Building trades (n. e. c.)	4,254	4,220	34	3,997	3,967	30
Metalworking trades (n. e. c.)	6,848	6,773	75	5,622	5,551	71
Printing trades	15,569	15,158	411	15,210	14,817	393
Other specified trades	13,124	12,628	496	12,602	12,130	472
Trade not specified	15,093	14,339	754	14,595	13,874	721
Asbestos and insulation workers	16,425	15,987	438	15,196	14,791	405
Attendants, auto service and parking	247,421	240,627	6,794	236,015	229,382	6,633
Blasters and powdermen	11,485	11,388	97	10,909	10,818	91
Boatmen, canalmen, and lock keepers	8,450	8,246	204	8,104	7,901	203
Brakemen, railroad	80,530	80,210	320	78,435	78,131	304
Bus drivers	157,144	152,141	5,003	154,935	149,984	4,951
Chainmen, rodmen, and axmen, surveying	7,397	7,228	169	6,952	6,789	163
Conductors, bus and street railway	11,439	11,223	216	11,281	11,073	208
Deliverymen and routemen	247,403	242,947	4,456	238,551	234,281	4,270
Dressmakers and seamstresses, except factory	142,679	3,999	138,680	138,127	3,809	134,318
Dyers	25,389	24,296	1,093	24,210	23,167	1,043
Filers, grinders, and polishers, metal	155,701	148,563	7,138	147,724	141,021	6,703
Fruit, nut, and vegetable graders and packers, excluding factory	34,369	13,254	21,115	28,745	11,451	17,294
Furnacemen, smeltermen, and pourers	57,547	56,266	1,281	55,392	54,153	1,239
Heaters, metal	9,679	9,241	438	9,270	8,854	416
Laundry and dry cleaning operatives	448,637	148,277	300,360	428,336	140,802	287,534
Meat cutters, except slaughter and packing house	176,315	172,741	3,574	170,624	167,153	3,471
Milliners	12,855	1,358	11,497	12,327	1,305	11,022
Mine operatives and laborers (n. e. c.)	604,627	599,665	4,962	573,437	568,724	4,713
Coal mining	381,209	379,791	1,418	362,102	360,789	1,313
Crude petroleum and natural gas extraction	108,317	107,833	484	102,611	102,159	452
Mining and quarrying, except fuel	115,101	112,041	3,060	108,724	105,776	2,948
Motormen, mine, factory, logging camp, etc	24,322	24,094	228	23,851	23,637	214
Motormen, street, subway, and elevated railway	26,795	26,425	370	26,540	26,190	350
Oilers and greasers, except auto	61,558	60,579	979	58,870	57,936	934
Painters, except construction and maintenance	122,747	108,669	14,078	116,595	103,241	13,354
Photographic process workers	29,289	16,211	13,078	28,019	15,556	12,463
Power station operators	21,613	20,774	839	21,471	20,642	829
Sailors and deck hands	51,109	50,254	855	40,287	39,533	754
Sawyers	97,614	95,621	1,993	93,722	91,835	1,887
Spinners, textile	84,946	21,708	63,238	80,828	20,239	60,589
Stationary firemen	126,806	125,647	1,159	121,847	120,742	1,105
Switchmen, railroad	62,146	61,660	486	61,313	60,837	476
Taxicab drivers and chauffeurs	212,422	208,823	3,599	202,090	198,681	3,409
Truck and tractor drivers	1,396,609	1,388,053	8,556	1,329,197	1,321,146	8,051
Weavers, textile	102,627	62,475	40,152	97,912	59,316	38,596
Welders and flame-cutters	275,545	265,578	9,967	266,305	256,890	9,415
Operatives and kindred workers (n. e. c.)	6,444,165	3,935,395	2,508,770	6,119,627	3,741,415	2,378,212
Manufacturing	5,686,349	3,352,069	2,334,280	5,405,551	3,190,562	2,214,989
Durable goods	2,525,783	1,859,756	666,027	2,407,514	1,773,164	634,360
Sawmills, planing mills, and miscellaneous wood products	192,955	176,457	16,498	184,868	169,245	15,623
Sawmills, planing mills, and mill work	148,278	143,040	5,238	142,621	137,650	4,971
Miscellaneous wood products	44,677	33,417	11,260	42,247	31,595	10,652
Furniture and fixtures	129,124	101,661	27,463	123,815	97,560	26,255
Stone, clay, and glass products	185,399	140,026	45,373	182,292	135,477	46,815
Glass and glass products	74,603	52,058	22,545	72,299	50,563	21,796
Cement, and concrete, gypsum, and plaster products	29,419	28,495	924	28,401	27,511	890
Structural clay products	22,067	17,936	4,131	21,182	17,198	3,984
Pottery and related products	34,352	19,784	14,568	33,343	19,157	14,186
Miscellaneous nonmetallic mineral and stone products	27,958	21,753	6,205	27,067	21,048	6,019

c. 224.—Detailed Occupation of the Experienced Civilian Labor Force and of Employed Persons, by Sex: 1950—Continued

	EXPERIENCED CIVILIAN LABOR FORCE			EMPLOYED		
	Total	Male	Female	Total	Male	Female
Operatives, etc.—Con. peratives, etc. (n. e. c.)—Con.						
Manufacturing—Durable goods—Con.						
Metal industries...		448, 690	96, 026	522, 201	421, 272	91, 929
Primary metal industries...		265, 402	19, 422	256, 068	239, 505	18, 562
Blast furnaces, steel works, and rolling mills...		124, 222	6, 086	126, 651	120, 728	5, 826
Other primary iron and steel industries...	73, 427	69, 065	4, 362	68, 562	64, 450	4, 142
Primary nonferrous industries...	64, 089	56, 115	5, 974	61, 925	52, 333	8, 592
Fabricated metal industries		201, 288	76, 804	265, 123	191, 766	73, 367
Cutlery, hand tools, and other hardware (incl. not spec. metal)		179, 472	62, 913	221, 517	171, 338	60, 279
Fabricated nonferrous metal products...		19, 015	12, 788	30, 105	17, 871	12, 234
Not specified metal industries...		2, 796	908	3, 811	2, 587	864
Machinery, except electrical...		292, 731	63, 907	343, 387	282, 065	61, 272
Agricultural machinery and tractors...		47, 618	3, 385	50, 096	46, 746	3, 392
Office and store machines and devices...		25, 534	12, 145	37, 063	24, 607	12, 476
Misc. machinery...		219, 879	47, 877	256, 236	210, 722	45, 804
Electrical machinery, equipment, and supplies...		161, 108	196, 080	394, 361	154, 619	179, 946
Transportation equipment...		387, 079	71, 108	437, 344	362, 347	66, 097
Motor vehicles and motor vehicle equipment...		299, 511	60, 186	326, 568	280, 218	56, 330
Aircraft and parts...		56, 966	8, 741	62, 239	54, 664	7, 775
Ship and boat building and repairing...		14, 151	621	12, 797	12, 360	537
Railroad and misc. transportation equipment...		16, 551	1, 556	15, 740	14, 306	1, 435
Professional and photographic equipment, and watches...		41, 239	37, 092	74, 532	39, 371	35, 161
Professional equipment and supplies...		22, 847	18, 824	40, 099	21, 962	18, 137
Photographic equipment and supplies...		10, 122	6, 386	15, 740	9, 787	5, 953
Watches, clocks, and clockwork-operated devices...	20, 242	8, 900	11, 882	16, 698	7, 622	11, 071
Misc. manufacturing industries...		109, 665	119, 482	218, 544	102, 282	111, 362
Manufacturing—Nondurable goods...		1, 470, 680	1, 545, 518	2, 980, 579	1, 397, 664	1, 566, 915
Food and kindred products...		332, 704	208, 262	489, 921	303, 409	186, 452
Dairy products...		91, 609	37, 277	129, 728	88, 174	35, 549
Canning and preserving fruits, vegetables, and sea foods...		80, 460	9, 918	54, 468	48, 100	9, 384
Grain-mill products...		31, 852	56, 145	66, 837	25, 717	43, 120
Bakery products...		27, 646	5, 086	31, 506	26, 768	4, 742
Confectionery and related products...		31, 480	34, 930	63, 187	29, 785	32, 402
Beverage industries...		17, 027	32, 202	44, 001	15, 637	28, 464
Misc. food preparations and kindred products...		46, 299	9, 588	52, 857	43, 639	9, 015
Not specified food industries...		21, 348	16, 101	35, 029	18, 789	15, 219
Tobacco manufactures...		5, 053	7, 065	11, 310	4, 758	6, 554
Textile mill products...		20, 330	47, 127	61, 585	18, 485	43, 110
Knitting mills...		234, 748	385, 562	680, 088	310, 395	369, 798
Dyeing and finishing textiles...		42, 127	123, 521	160, 466	40, 585	119, 681
Carpets, rugs, and other floor coverings...		19, 622	5, 640	24, 340	18, 791	5, 449
Yarn, thread, and fabric mills...		14, 224	10, 933	24, 464	13, 861	10, 603
Misc. textile mill products...		232, 331	231, 060	441, 409	221, 355	230, 064
Apparel and other fabricated textile products...		16, 444	14, 408	29, 489	15, 662	13, 905
Apparel and accessories...	170, 527	668, 371	796, 642	186, 496	640, 344
Misc. fabricated textile products...		154, 441	628, 851	743, 256	141, 347	601, 969
		16, 086	40, 490	55, 596	15, 151	38, 435
Paper and allied products...		151, 668	72, 796	215, 374	147, 545	70, 839
Pulp, paper, and paperboard mills...	104, 010	87, 780	16, 230	101, 679	85, 964	15, 715
Paperboard containers and boxes...	61, 938	32, 714	26, 224	59, 140	32, 290	26, 850
Misc. paper and pulp products...	59, 626	30, 184	29, 332	57, 555	29, 291	28, 264
Printing, publishing, and allied industries...	78, 276	43, 482	34, 794	74, 935	41, 799	33, 136
Chemicals and allied products...	189, 906	145, 257	43, 649	183, 268	141, 851	41, 408
Synthetic fibers...	25, 427	17, 755	5, 672	25, 596	17, 306	5, 360
Drugs and medicines...	14, 752	5, 838	8, 896	14, 336	5, 714	8, 615
Paints, varnishes, and related products...	15, 046	15, 888	2, 748	17, 434	14, 796	3, 628
Misc. chemicals and allied products.	130, 681	107, 341	23, 340	125, 908	104, 084	21, 699

No. 224.—DETAILED OCCUPATION OF THE EXPERIENCED CIVILIAN LABOR FORCE AND OF EMPLOYED PERSONS, BY SEX: 1950—Continued

OCCUPATION	EXPERIENCED CIVILIAN LABOR FORCE			EMPLOYED		
	Total	Male	Female	Total	Male	Female
Operatives, etc.—Con.						
Operatives, etc. (n. e. c.)—Con.						
Manufacturing—Nondurable goods—Con.						
Petroleum and coal products	53, 739	52, 248	1, 491	52, 622	51, 206	1, 416
Petroleum refining	47, 086	45, 856	1, 230	46, 188	45, 022	1, 166
Miscellaneous petroleum and coal products	6, 653	6, 392	261	6, 434	6, 184	250
Rubber products	123, 587	85, 821	37, 766	119, 095	82, 836	36, 259
Leather and leather products	299, 395	152, 685	146, 710	283, 884	143, 710	140, 174
Leather: tanned, curried, and finished	30, 820	25, 935	4, 885	29, 394	24, 751	4, 643
Footwear, except rubber	219, 935	104, 773	115, 162	209, 629	98, 911	110, 718
Leather products, except footwear	48, 640	21, 977	26, 663	44, 861	20, 048	24, 813
Not specified manufacturing industries	41, 468	21, 753	19, 715	37, 458	19, 744	17, 714
Nonmanufacturing industries (including not reported)	787, 816	563, 306	174, 510	714, 076	550, 853	163, 223
Construction	69, 233	67, 761	1, 472	64, 020	62, 633	1, 387
Railroads and railway express service	93, 977	92, 769	1, 208	90, 849	89, 695	1, 154
Transportation, except railroad	36, 211	31, 233	4, 978	34, 334	29, 744	4, 590
Telecommunications, and utilities and sanitary services	51, 212	47, 791	3, 421	49, 800	46, 516	3, 284
Wholesale and retail trade	301, 861	186, 922	114, 939	284, 489	176, 655	107, 834
Business and repair services	52, 411	45, 472	6, 939	49, 627	42, 996	6, 631
Personal services	21, 051	9, 380	11, 671	19, 867	8, 699	11, 168
Public administration	52, 492	45, 853	6, 639	50, 284	44, 077	6, 207
All other industries (incl. not reported)	79, 368	56, 125	23, 243	70, 806	49, 838	20, 968
Private household workers	1, 487, 574	77, 636	1, 409, 938	1, 407, 466	73, 156	1, 334, 310
Housekeepers, private household	145, 453	5, 882	139, 571	139, 711	5, 258	134, 453
Living in	52, 755	567	52, 188	52, 755	567	52, 188
Living out	92, 698	5, 315	87, 383	86, 956	4, 691	82, 265
Laundresses, private household	73, 485	2, 310	71, 175	71, 181	2, 203	68, 978
Living in	643	5	638	643	5	638
Living out	72, 842	2, 305	70, 537	70, 538	2, 198	68, 340
Private household workers (n. e. c.)	1, 268, 636	69, 444	1, 199, 192	1, 196, 574	65, 695	1, 130, 879
Living in	162, 141	11, 952	150, 189	162, 141	11, 952	150, 189
Living out	1, 106, 495	57, 492	1, 049, 003	1, 034, 433	53, 743	980, 690
Service workers, except private household	4, 511, 996	2, 503, 975	2, 008, 621	4, 287, 763	2, 373, 410	1, 914, 283
Attendants, hospital and other institution	210, 713	86, 023	124, 690	204, 337	83, 117	121, 220
Attendants, professional and personal service (n. e. c.)	50, 081	16, 734	33, 347	47, 601	16, 014	31, 587
Attendants, recreation and amusement	64, 206	59, 170	5, 036	58, 826	54, 070	4, 756
Barbers, beauticians, and manicurists	388, 804	195, 368	193, 436	382, 464	192, 594	189, 870
Bartenders	207, 836	193, 938	13, 898	193, 467	180, 036	13, 431
Boarding and lodging house keepers	29, 190	7, 921	21, 269	28, 845	7, 793	21, 052
Bootblacks	14, 794	14, 297	497	13, 841	13, 376	465
Charwomen and cleaners	124, 336	49, 920	74, 416	119, 312	47, 196	72, 116
Cooks, except private household	463, 210	211, 672	251, 538	434, 739	192, 341	242, 398
Counter and fountain workers	92, 939	45, 870	47, 069	86, 543	42, 120	44, 423
Elevator operators	94, 167	65, 758	28, 409	89, 089	62, 160	26, 929
Firemen, fire protection	110, 773	110, 319	454	109, 960	109, 416	444
Guards, watchmen, and doorkeepers	248, 979	243, 626	5, 353	237, 203	231, 987	5, 216
Housekeepers and stewards, except private household	108, 971	24, 169	84, 802	105, 828	22, 924	82, 904
Janitors and sextons	471, 750	417, 022	54, 728	454, 522	401, 327	53, 195
Marshals and constables	6, 561	6, 398	153	6, 494	6, 312	182
Midwives	1, 815	314	1, 501	1, 698	307	1, 391
Policemen and detectives	194, 313	190, 718	3, 595	192, 164	188, 663	3, 501
Government	173, 672	171, 271	2, 401	172, 337	169, 969	2, 368
Private	20, 641	19, 447	1, 194	19, 827	18, 694	1, 133
Porters	173, 784	169, 888	3, 896	161, 891	158, 261	3, 630
Practical nurses	144, 240	5, 948	138, 292	135, 902	5, 598	130, 304
Sheriffs and bailiffs	18, 710	17, 947	763	18, 465	17, 710	755
Ushers, recreation and amusement	25, 185	16, 754	8, 431	23, 266	15, 430	7, 836
Waiters and waitresses	713, 112	128, 262	584, 850	664, 828	[119, 263	545, 565
Watchmen (crossing) and bridge tenders	11, 717	11, 248	469	11, 501	11, 044	457
Service workers, except private household (n. e. c.)	541, 790	214, 691	327, 099	505, 017	194, 351	310, 666

No. 224.—DETAILED OCCUPATION OF THE EXPERIENCED CIVILIAN LABOR FORCE AND OF EMPLOYED PERSONS, BY SEX: 1950—Continued

OCCUPATION	EXPERIENCED CIVILIAN LABOR FORCE			EMPLOYED		
	Total	Male	Female	Total	Male	Female
Farm laborers and foremen	2,514,780	2,047,538	467,242	2,399,794	1,950,458	449,336
Farm foremen	17,143	16,576	567	16,741	16,295	446
Farm laborers, wage workers	1,569,112	1,423,316	145,796	1,463,601	1,333,274	130,327
Farm laborers, unpaid family workers	918,598	599,238	319,660	910,352	592,774	317,578
Farm service laborers, self-employed	9,627	8,408	1,219	9,100	8,115	985
Laborers, except farm and mine	3,780,990	3,611,846	139,144	3,417,222	3,290,252	126,979
Fishermen and oystermen	72,186	71,162	1,026	67,308	66,340	968
Garage laborers, car washers and greasers	70,154	67,764	2,390	66,082	63,859	2,223
Gardeners, except farm, and groundskeepers	155,002	151,387	3,615	145,518	142,226	3,292
Longshoremen and stevedores	69,822	69,074	748	63,699	63,033	666
Lumbermen, raftsmen, and wood choppers	188,972	187,261	1,691	172,075	170,495	1,580
Teamsters	22,254	21,915	339	21,165	20,851	314
Laborers (n. e. c.)	3,172,898	3,043,263	129,335	2,863,414	2,745,479	117,935
Manufacturing	1,172,222	1,098,335	73,587	1,091,673	1,024,219	67,454
Durable goods	734,594	702,967	31,627	686,472	656,561	29,921
Sawmills, planing mills, and miscellaneous wood products	165,503	161,341	4,162	156,181	152,276	3,905
Sawmills, planing mills, and mill work	147,947	145,472	2,475	139,898	137,582	2,316
Miscellaneous wood products	17,360	15,869	1,687	16,263	14,694	1,569
Furniture and fixtures	20,163	19,686	1,477	19,973	18,569	1,405
Stone, clay, and glass products	82,052	78,846	3,206	77,709	74,662	3,047
Glass and glass products	15,235	13,904	1,331	14,271	13,019	1,252
Cement, and concrete, gypsum, and plaster products	32,966	32,778	186	21,794	21,611	183
Structural clay products	27,934	27,242	692	26,633	25,977	656
Pottery and related products	6,715	5,990	725	6,327	5,621	706
Miscellaneous nonmetallic mineral and stone products	9,202	8,932	270	8,684	8,404	280
Metal industries	281,631	273,116	8,515	263,561	255,544	8,017
Primary metal industries	221,064	217,990	3,074	207,096	204,262	2,834
Blast furnaces, steel works, and rolling mills	140,718	139,104	1,614	132,524	131,043	1,481
Other primary iron and steel industries	82,802	51,974	828	48,621	47,849	782
Primary nonferrous industries	27,544	26,912	632	25,961	25,360	591
Fabricated metal industries (including not specified metal)	60,567	55,126	5,441	56,465	51,282	5,183
Fabricated steel products	54,655	49,775	4,880	50,904	66,346	4,648
Fabricated nonferrous metal products	4,997	4,495	502	4,610	4,131	479
Not specified metal industries	915	356	59	551	505	56
Machinery, except electrical	56,392	54,337	2,055	53,395	51,416	1,979
Agricultural machinery and tractors	13,255	12,858	397	12,819	12,432	387
Office and store machines and devices	1,730	1,587	143	1,618	1,482	136
Miscellaneous machinery	41,407	39,892	1,515	38,958	37,502	1,456
Electrical machinery, equipment, and supplies	31,655	26,409	5,246	29,541	24,640	4,901
Transportation equipment	74,702	71,739	2,968	66,140	63,481	2,659
Motor vehicles and motor vehicle equipment	49,775	47,400	2,375	45,817	43,629	2,188
Aircraft and parts	3,842	3,636	206	3,551	3,359	192
Ship and boat building and repairing	15,205	14,981	224	12,014	11,873	141
Railroad and miscellaneous transportation equipment	5,880	5,722	158	4,758	4,630	128
Professional and photographic equipment and watches	4,594	3,803	791	4,377	3,622	755
Professional equipment and supplies	2,602	2,144	458	2,500	2,057	443
Photographic equipment and supplies	1,103	962	141	1,050	925	125
Watches, clocks, and clockwork-operated devices	889	697	192	827	640	187
Misc. manufacturing industries	14,902	12,690	3,212	15,806	12,643	2,963

No. 224.—DETAILED OCCUPATION OF THE EXPERIENCED CIVILIAN LABOR FORCE AND OF EMPLOYED PERSONS, BY SEX: 1950—Continued

OCCUPATION	EXPERIENCED CIVILIAN LABOR FORCE			EMPLOYED		
	Total	Male	Female	Total	Male	Female
Laborers, etc.—Con.						
Laborers (n. e. c.)—Con.						
Manufacturing—Con.						
Nondurable goods	427, 918	386, 882	41, 036	396, 149	359, 337	36, 812
Food and kindred products	155, 733	143, 472	12, 261	141, 452	130, 616	10, 836
Meat products	36, 199	32, 927	3, 272	34, 158	31, 033	3, 125
Dairy products	14, 818	14, 105	713	14, 205	13, 523	682
Canning and preserving fruits, vegetables, and sea foods	24, 910	20, 855	4, 055	19, 288	16, 211	3, 077
Grain-mill products	19, 348	19, 053	295	18, 208	17, 940	268
Bakery products	9, 285	8, 089	1, 196	8, 732	7, 582	1, 150
Confectionery and related products	4, 064	3, 412	652	3, 665	3, 073	592
Beverage industries	24, 444	23, 711	733	22, 656	21, 976	680
Misc. food preparations and kindred products	19, 533	18, 668	865	17, 687	16, 876	811
Not specified food industries	3, 132	2, 652	480	2, 853	2, 402	451
Tobacco manufactures	9, 191	6, 421	2, 770	7, 104	5, 417	1, 687
Textile mill products	63, 919	55, 168	8, 751	60, 176	51, 813	8, 363
Knitting mills	2, 967	2, 091	876	2, 804	1, 956	848
Dyeing and finishing textiles, excluding knit goods	3, 144	3, 020	124	2, 987	2, 870	117
Carpets, rugs, and other floor coverings	5, 938	5, 467	471	5, 747	5, 292	455
Yarn, thread, and fabric mills	48, 145	41, 361	6, 784	45, 151	38, 682	6, 469
Miscellaneous textile mill products	3, 725	3, 229	496	3, 487	3, 013	474
Apparel and other fabricated textile products	11, 255	7, 162	4, 093	10, 377	6, 510	3, 867
Apparel and accessories	8, 541	5, 048	3, 493	7, 869	4, 562	3, 307
Miscellaneous fabricated textile products	2, 714	2, 114	600	2, 508	1, 948	560
Paper and allied products	46, 273	43, 008	3, 265	44, 053	40, 946	3, 107
Pulp, paper, and paperboard mills	28, 401	27, 586	815	27, 201	26, 412	789
Paperboard containers and boxes	9, 513	8, 101	1, 412	8, 933	7, 599	1, 334
Miscellaneous paper and pulp products	8, 359	7, 321	1, 038	7, 919	6, 935	984
Printing, publishing, and allied industries	11, 738	10, 505	1, 233	11, 141	9, 963	1, 178
Chemicals and allied products	67, 213	64, 187	3, 026	63, 183	60, 526	2, 657
Synthetic fibers	3, 239	3, 022	217	3, 056	2, 848	208
Drugs and medicines	1, 954	1, 627	327	1, 881	1, 568	313
Paints, varnishes, and related products	4, 777	4, 511	266	4, 505	4, 259	246
Miscellaneous chemicals and allied products	57, 243	55, 027	2, 216	53, 741	51, 851	1, 890
Petroleum and coal products	30, 682	30, 346	336	25, 984	25, 677	307
Petroleum refining	24, 728	24, 480	248	23, 398	23, 174	224
Miscellaneous petroleum and coal products	5, 954	5, 866	88	5, 586	5, 503	83
Rubber products	16, 962	14, 713	2, 249	16, 003	13, 893	2, 110
Leather and leather products	14, 952	11, 900	3, 052	13, 676	10, 976	2, 700
Leather: tanned, curried, and finished	7, 236	6, 409	827	6, 572	5, 959	613
Footwear, except rubber	5, 706	4, 009	1, 697	5, 264	3, 655	1, 609
Leather products, except footwear	2, 010	1, 482	528	1, 840	1, 362	478
Not specified manufacturing industries	10, 710	9, 486	1, 224	9, 052	8, 031	1, 021
Nonmanufacturing industries (including not reported)	1, 999, 376	1, 943, 928	55, 448	1, 791, 741	1, 741, 260	50, 481
Construction	752, 847	746, 997	5, 850	654, 386	649, 341	5, 045
Railroads and railway express service	283, 317	276, 957	6, 360	262, 873	256, 389	6, 484
Transportation, except railroad	114, 477	112, 134	2, 343	104, 312	102, 188	2, 124
Telecommunications, and utilities and sanitary services	131, 994	130, 315	1, 679	125, 660	124, 132	1, 528
Wholesale and retail trade	334, 652	316, 608	18, 044	312, 317	295, 363	16, 954
Business and repair services	14, 532	13, 923	609	13, 451	12, 864	587
Personal services	79, 599	73, 046	6, 553	71, 711	65, 528	6, 183
Public administration	104, 554	101, 691	2, 863	98, 195	95, 693	2, 502
All other industries (including not reported)	182, 904	172, 257	10, 647	148, 836	139, 762	9, 074
Occupation not reported	1, 366, 064	905, 547	460, 517	746, 522	483, 229	263, 293

Source: Department of Commerce, Bureau of the Census; U. S. Census of Population: 1950, Vol. II, Part 1.

No. 225.—MAJOR OCCUPATION GROUP OF EMPLOYED PERSONS, BY SEX, BY STATES: 1950

[Figures may differ from corresponding items in table 224 due to separate tabulations]

DIVISION AND STATE	Total employed	Professional, technical, and kindred workers	Farmers and farm managers	Managers, officials, and proprietors, etc. farm	Clerical and kindred workers	Sales workers	Craftsmen, foremen, and kindred workers	Operatives and	Private household workers
U. S.	40,519,462	2,970,665	4,152,100	4,340,579	2,682,662	2,596,980	7,545,804	8,130,313	72,344
N. E.	2,450,203	199,738	62,502	280,226	171,689	174,615	529,134	608,875	4,962
Maine	224,024	11,924	16,372	26,632	11,563	12,817	29,815	52,438	516
N. H.	133,333	8,569	6,916	14,749	7,206	5,712	26,182	38,646	279
Vt.	99,282	5,779	13,152	10,076	5,203	5,219	17,029	18,966	283
Mass.	1,224,105	110,172	13,655	142,371	98,373	94,182	266,621	302,489	3,088
R. I.	200,376	12,984	1,847	22,314	13,721	14,079	44,985	57,236	315
Conn.	564,081	49,310	10,560	85,584	40,021	38,806	138,802	139,310	1,551
M. A.	8,302,003	737,000	206,606	1,818,288	688,906	583,342	1,687,286	1,856,343	14,144
N. Y.	4,099,158	399,934	94,240	871,961	385,076	318,783	782,742	807,868	8,160
N. J.	1,373,479	134,621	20,520	178,361	112,213	92,065	300,679	304,555	2,819
Pa.	2,829,371	202,445	91,846	268,087	202,619	172,394	608,782	743,986	4,456
E. N. C.	8,654,994	633,002	636,290	865,656	680,851	536,362	1,786,261	2,045,489	14,787
Ohio	2,232,905	167,858	141,854	221,643	186,011	141,177	469,597	644,701	3,196
Ind.	1,121,441	72,109	124,023	106,173	65,942	65,721	225,897	297,291	1,810
Ill.	2,518,808	202,663	170,699	272,953	206,168	164,640	508,815	594,296	5,446
Mich.	1,786,025	126,641	110,375	186,046	115,311	106,905	381,852	510,252	1,901
Wis.	905,815	63,531	150,034	93,813	54,615	56,509	180,580	208,949	1,004
W. N. C.	3,983,910	239,438	911,573	404,436	223,194	344,577	649,564	580,318	4,165
Minn.	833,978	54,616	169,050	85,179	80,680	82,871	137,887	121,513	811
Iowa	737,435	40,301	196,565	73,479	54,597	48,871	110,088	103,269	577
Mo.	1,100,006	71,151	185,941	113,810	76,085	74,801	176,100	185,755	1,815
N. Dak.	178,054	8,042	67,088	16,008	6,633	8,016	18,622	11,504	66
S. Dak.	189,763	9,000	66,938	17,879	6,586	9,081	21,563	15,974	95
Nebr.	385,287	21,883	106,618	38,404	19,930	33,013	54,234	30,914	277
Kans.	534,320	34,415	118,364	60,676	28,772	31,809	91,640	72,279	517
S. A.	5,405,788	330,730	631,826	511,622	292,896	318,279	905,730	1,092,344	14,538
Del.	90,414	8,752	5,778	9,473	5,518	4,877	19,346	17,372	340
Md.	634,067	58,667	26,956	66,733	90,074	41,229	138,347	116,026	1,672
D. C.	212,957	31,300	113	27,174	35,031	13,962	34,551	27,082	831
Va.	837,202	55,212	99,979	77,474	47,949	47,008	146,515	165,213	2,275
W. Va.	493,781	24,990	36,866	39,625	22,112	21,896	89,015	175,356	480
N. C.	1,045,251	42,285	220,718	82,354	36,799	56,902	142,838	220,697	2,367
S. C.	519,764	20,972	100,646	38,955	16,221	26,431	73,162	106,628	1,346
Ga.	877,207	41,622	153,257	77,310	41,258	51,697	134,620	164,187	2,331
Fla.	603,093	45,863	58,003	84,311	36,736	53,270	139,586	98,703	2,804
E. S. C.	2,831,721	138,636	691,643	222,266	115,940	141,360	397,926	515,596	6,789
Ky.	748,658	24,405	169,729	57,432	35,228	36,141	107,392	152,260	1,584
Tenn.	839,122	45,080	172,205	70,366	38,782	47,744	139,385	151,580	2,287
Ala.	765,249	33,787	155,190	58,264	25,532	37,233	105,791	151,199	1,768
Miss.	538,022	22,414	193,519	36,344	14,467	21,182	82,458	63,837	1,120
W. S. C.	3,730,630	243,833	579,451	390,119	191,730	226,223	614,940	595,544	4,752
Ark.	481,338	21,051	139,627	29,619	15,772	26,345	64,581	65,800	666
La.	646,496	40,709	86,818	60,458	35,723	33,866	99,091	111,284	1,420
Okla.	564,458	42,685	107,733	62,668	29,046	35,111	95,249	83,077	705
Tex.	2,037,753	139,143	245,368	233,374	111,180	131,979	363,080	337,363	3,961
Mt.	1,315,413	100,827	175,376	149,670	69,324	77,537	239,621	204,215	1,456
Mont.	169,835	10,814	33,554	17,501	8,145	8,439	26,013	23,087	144
Idaho	161,004	9,153	35,535	14,564	6,254	8,692	34,979	22,332	150
Wyo.	83,823	6,178	11,908	8,897	3,725	3,415	14,914	14,667	63
Colo.	345,896	30,112	41,475	41,531	21,368	25,991	61,237	51,530	368
N. Mex.	187,680	12,964	20,342	17,822	6,948	7,728	27,347	23,686	207
Ariz.	175,090	13,470	11,765	21,909	8,706	11,897	31,619	29,334	301
Utah	174,848	14,341	17,946	19,497	11,580	11,434	35,719	31,076	140
Nev.	47,172	3,795	2,851	6,169	2,880	2,361	8,773	7,760	74
Pac.	3,794,782	349,591	136,133	494,666	328,899	368,215	784,396	627,586	7,766
Wash.	616,635	50,110	43,702	71,642	52,421	52,140	120,609	105,342	789
Oreg.	424,204	29,070	37,986	62,782	21,898	32,466	76,476	74,592	484
Calif.	2,753,943	270,411	104,445	360,716	181,040	238,661	578,130	447,645	6,485

No. 225.—MAJOR OCCUPATION GROUP OF EMPLOYED PERSONS, BY SEX, BY STATES: 1950—Continued

DIVISION AND STATE	MALE—continued					FEMALE			
	Service workers, except private household	Farm laborers, unpaid family workers	Farm laborers, except unpaid, and farm foremen	Laborers, except farm and mine	Occupation not reported	Total employed	Professional, technical, and kindred workers	Farmers and farm managers	Managers, officials, and proprietors, exc. farm
U. S.	2,372,457	592,905	1,358,160	3,303,206	449,287	15,719,987	1,939,543	116,435	677,357
N. E.	165,122	5,349	43,256	182,024	22,602	1,161,107	145,497	2,802	38,339
Maine	10,174	1,357	9,196	30,526	2,504	88,302	11,760	485	3,545
N. H.	7,436	553	4,094	11,820	1,171	64,346	7,868	364	2,473
Vt.	4,509	1,854	8,304	7,929	1,029	37,995	5,970	396	1,710
Mass.	93,458	797	11,865	83,993	10,161	602,602	77,103	788	18,715
R. I.	14,412	121	1,578	13,242	1,952	104,136	10,180	94	3,065
Conn.	35,143	666	8,219	34,414	5,695	263,726	32,616	695	8,831
M. A.	624,062	21,696	106,910	680,418	84,199	3,536,054	420,732	7,146	134,377
N. Y.	368,725	8,357	48,202	282,370	43,706	1,845,103	229,416	3,321	76,126
N. J.	92,147	1,487	17,465	103,589	12,358	589,153	64,266	1,314	22,524
Pa.	163,210	11,852	41,243	294,459	28,133	1,101,798	127,050	2,511	35,727
E. N. C.	494,963	75,770	174,416	634,799	92,314	3,217,961	375,122	16,025	126,578
Ohio	118,979	13,149	35,113	176,247	23,150	826,700	96,051	3,326	31,611
Ind.	57,353	9,689	27,421	89,877	13,730	397,001	43,502	2,645	16,586
Ill.	171,734	14,441	49,517	190,448	26,067	1,027,243	115,483	2,619	41,506
Mich.	98,976	11,376	32,935	112,746	19,787	607,549	76,082	3,035	23,430
Wis.	47,941	27,115	38,430	64,481	9,580	359,468	44,013	4,400	13,445
W. N. C.	179,314	121,760	174,483	270,550	50,146	1,369,039	189,535	14,246	61,237
Minn.	39,567	30,857	32,884	52,986	7,856	304,897	44,153	2,911	11,907
Iowa	30,101	22,702	42,763	47,965	9,608	244,745	36,357	2,373	10,192
Mo.	55,849	20,514	34,824	83,342	16,019	421,811	46,632	4,202	18,937
N. Dak.	6,156	12,204	13,117	8,365	2,143	45,488	8,485	694	2,257
S. Dak.	6,254	10,656	13,558	9,934	2,153	52,505	9,500	849	2,840
Nebr.	16,108	12,766	19,485	26,938	5,715	126,362	19,132	1,212	5,725
Kans.	22,279	12,061	17,852	41,020	6,652	173,231	25,376	2,005	9,379
S. A.	281,467	140,790	251,256	517,035	68,059	2,250,707	253,568	20,888	85,005
Del.	4,618	372	5,904	8,904	1,285	36,223	4,475	181	1,336
Md.	38,588	2,719	19,052	63,676	7,728	260,708	30,440	784	10,093
D. C.	26,914	19	193	19,474	2,980	160,533	19,660	37	5,240
Va.	40,549	13,525	43,511	85,392	10,563	312,902	39,478	2,078	11,756
W. Va.	17,439	8,316	13,602	38,993	6,601	132,376	20,771	859	6,791
N. C.	42,267	50,269	47,239	81,397	12,879	418,101	44,142	5,813	11,576
S. C.	19,909	28,074	31,089	48,786	5,923	235,614	23,684	4,845	6,060
Ga.	41,953	33,023	43,597	91,333	10,957	377,728	36,467	4,051	12,228
Fla.	49,130	4,473	49,191	79,080	9,173	316,522	34,511	2,240	19,925
E. S. C.	115,349	122,184	135,154	239,400	36,347	957,068	110,630	24,125	38,657
Ky.	30,522	29,165	38,358	49,848	9,675	206,328	25,410	2,264	9,706
Tenn.	39,706	25,257	35,506	66,887	12,374	296,524	35,276	2,917	11,195
Ala.	29,070	32,506	31,894	76,683	8,332	276,057	31,035	5,623	10,577
Miss.	15,951	36,256	29,304	45,982	5,966	178,159	18,900	13,321	7,179
W. S. C.	187,667	69,233	215,777	355,930	45,571	1,272,728	160,380	16,137	69,806
Ark.	15,505	18,554	36,364	44,985	6,279	133,908	16,404	4,101	7,495
La.	36,666	13,299	31,621	82,401	8,106	229,112	29,170	2,963	10,652
Okla.	25,680	12,870	21,048	39,870	7,741	189,023	26,820	2,218	11,738
Tex.	109,816	24,510	126,744	187,774	23,443	720,685	87,986	6,855	39,921
Mt.	74,786	22,084	86,628	107,621	15,303	431,255	67,395	4,639	27,753
Mont.	8,982	3,448	13,531	12,531	2,075	48,625	8,312	781	3,232
Idaho	7,321	4,122	11,502	12,983	1,616	44,989	7,181	583	2,619
Wyo.	4,097	1,361	7,006	6,567	995	23,943	3,871	331	1,752
Colo.	20,159	4,940	18,204	27,058	3,653	130,748	19,973	988	7,834
N. Mex.	8,247	3,388	11,414	15,172	2,803	48,864	7,965	617	3,575
Ariz.	10,750	2,270	15,990	15,486	1,794	63,805	9,822	914	4,633
Utah	9,149	2,299	6,433	13,267	1,708	54,018	8,043	277	2,673
Nev.	6,061	265	2,727	3,557	569	16,463	2,228	148	1,435
Pac.	249,797	13,040	176,299	336,329	34,716	1,524,068	216,574	10,427	95,605
Wash.	36,057	3,646	20,414	67,223	7,361	223,427	33,200	2,017	13,025
Oreg.	21,641	3,356	17,865	56,078	3,991	152,306	21,239	1,986	10,380
Calif.	192,099	6,038	132,001	213,028	23,364	1,148,335	162,135	6,424	72,200

No. 225.—Major Occupation Group of Employed Persons, by Sex, by States: 1950—Continued

DIVISIONS AND STATES	Clerical and kindred workers	Sales workers	Craftsmen, foremen, and kindred workers	Operatives and kindred workers	Private household workers	Service workers, except private household	Farm laborers, unpaid family workers	Farm laborers, except unpaid, and farm foremen	Laborers, except farm and mine	Occupation not reported
U. S.	4,292,671	1,329,636	238,096	3,019,901	1,334,573	2,914,071	317,453	191,747	127,375	252,579
N. E.			21,454	356,433		165,266	2,691	2,469	9,830	15,697
	17,811		1,051	20,776		9,572	331	334	1,142	1,574
N. H.	13,106		1,009	23,220		6,308	241	226	640	796
Vt.	8,697		509	7,116		4,862	651	239	286	664
	175,633	45,055	11,413	175,858		57,960	351	919	4,192	6,230
R. I.	24,790	6,830	2,453	43,060		7,164	71	73	908	1,667
Conn.	70,846		5,019			19,583	436	662	2,732	4,056
M. A.	445		62,702			347,229	12,667	7,412	26,460	50,396
N. Y.	450		33,317			179,719	5,845	3,538	9,865	20,279
N. J.	841		10,354			47,157	2,041	1,532	4,719	7,678
			19,031			120,353	5,981	2,803	11,873	16,899
E. N. C.		675	53,350			414,850	53,339	9,433	22,274	55,697
		326	15,307			111,974	9,616	2,372	7,404	14,643
		895	7,247			82,064	6,844	1,345	5,005	9,907
	343,046	263	19,592			120,901	5,566	1,758	11,010	17,423
Wis.	179,033	086	10,212			153,322	1,863	5,470	10,649	
	91,040	105	5,722			46,589	26,641	2,280	3,385	6,815
W. N. C.			19,401			196,277	74,466	7,548	11,632	27,178
			4,318			45,833	16,761	1,611	1,996	5,490
			3,223			35,486	14,595	1,743	2,286	7,900
			7,102			53,031	13,229	1,863	3,718	11,982
			354			7,906	4,957	395	212	1,364
			488			5,769	4,730	439	402	1,336
			1,611			19,603	8,700	748	1,651	4,459
			2,295		11,187	26,757	9,484	724	1,357	4,617
S. A.			23,784			249,846	71,464	51,866	18,440	41,555
Del.			422			4,313	130	363	543	703
		265	4,263			20,196	1,536	1,335	2,085	3,862
		867	1,605			21,636	8	54	926	2,128
		088	3,779			35,097	2,541	3,009	2,733	6,593
		129	1,491			19,246	941	326	1,283	3,097
		377	3,678			35,072	24,242	8,739	3,217	8,991
		880	1,563			17,744	20,810	9,579	1,928	4,222
			3,500			37,481	16,919	10,560	3,215	7,163
			3,073			49,056	4,287	17,821	2,587	4,896
E. S. C.	705		19,635			114,864	41,434	16,296	7,248	22,519
	530		3,096			28,000	3,260	788	1,643	4,900
	378		4,272			37,619	5,262	2,214	3,194	6,575
	789		2,112			31,072	16,668	6,230	2,106	7,200
	018		1,155			20,113	16,213	7,066	1,175	3,854
W. S. C.	423		13,913		121	192,127	36,995	19,561	8,610	25,464
	980		1,261		053	19,412	7,700	3,907	1,184	4,220
	277		1,831		204	32,519	6,917	5,681	1,890	3,896
Okla.	000		2,196		053	30,901	6,674	1,215	1,210	4,380
Tex.	171		8,625			108,305	14,804	8,758	4,376	13,180
	119,223		4,711	22,751	29,663	75,486	11,344	3,535	2,464	9,966
	12,485		424	2,482	2,575	9,575	1,886	628	304	1,071
	11,274		452	3,029	3,028	8,029	2,096	492	327	1,029
	6,250	414	183	1,278	1,391	4,675	766	201	121	697
	30,308	154	1,738	11,287	7,966	21,661	3,690	865	896	2,374
	12,181	627	474	3,380	4,652	8,012	1,657	264	823	1,847
	15,208	807	520	6,168	5,894	10,871	1,105	399	244	1,502
	17,812	854	787	5,307	2,671	8,522	505	387	324	966
	4,520		129	875	1,022	4,135	148	70	65	322
Pac	481,203		21,116	184,334	99,390	212,368	12,128	13,649	10,326	21,783
Wash.	69,446		2,856	19,680	13,047	37,036	3,452	1,980	1,596	3,754
Oreg.	43,568		1,829	14,261	9,492	24,310	3,863	2,404	1,530	2,754
Calif.	368,189		16,431	150,893	76,721	152,610	5,848	9,265	6,964	15,275

Source: Department of Commerce, Bureau of the Census; *U. S. Census of Population: 1950*, Vol. II, Part 1.

No. 226.—Industry Group of Employed Persons, by Sex: 1940 and 1950

INDUSTRY GROUP	TOTAL		MALE		FEMALE	
	1940	1950	1940	1950	1940	1950
Total	44,888,083	¹ 56,239,449	33,749,905	¹ 40,519,462	11,138,178	¹ 15,719,987
Agriculture, forestry and fisheries	8,496,147	7,005,403	8,007,578	6,412,172	488,569	593,231
Agriculture	8,391,022	6,884,970	7,904,629	6,297,221	486,393	587,749
Forestry and fisheries	105,125	120,433	102,949	114,951	2,176	5,482
Mining	913,600	929,152	902,661	906,066	10,939	23,086
Construction	2,075,274	3,439,924	2,038,907	3,341,544	36,367	98,380
Manufacturing	10,557,842	14,575,692	8,243,300	10,933,379	2,334,542	3,642,312
Durable goods	5,116,483	7,756,923	4,558,915	6,518,208	557,568	1,238,714
Furniture, and lumber and wood products	903,202	1,189,025	857,811	1,098,430	45,391	90,595
Primary metal industries	1,495,350	2,003,433	1,379,716	1,780,071	115,634	223,362
Fabricated metal industries, incl. not specified metal	724,166	1,294,922	659,406	1,121,815	64,760	173,107
Machinery, except electrical	370,184	789,300	269,783	513,849	100,401	275,451
Electrical machinery, equipment, and supplies	571,431	868,683	522,110	759,353	49,321	109,330
Motor vehicles and motor vehicle equipment	304,872	478,542	294,866	429,886	10,006	48,656
Transportation equipment, except motor vehicle	747,278	1,133,017	575,223	814,804	172,055	318,213
Other durable goods	5,267,788	6,696,510	3,548,579	4,330,123	1,719,209	2,366,377
Nondurable goods	1,091,728	1,399,070	893,834	1,081,153	197,894	317,917
Food and kindred products	1,168,974	1,240,238	691,273	712,642	477,701	527,596
Textile mill products	785,564	1,063,442	268,654	310,912	516,910	752,530
Apparel and other fabricated textile products	636,277	853,239	503,823	640,259	132,454	212,980
Printing, publishing and allied industries	426,145	658,931	351,211	530,039	74,934	128,892
Chemicals and allied products	1,159,100	1,481,590	839,784	1,055,128	319,316	426,462
Other nondurable goods	183,571	122,260	135,806	85,038	47,765	37,222
Not specified manufacturing industries						
Transportation, communication, and other public utilities	3,107,568	4,368,302	2,767,224	3,687,592	340,344	680,710
Transportation	2,185,671	2,940,663	2,108,015	2,746,128	77,656	194,535
Railroads and railway express service	1,135,019	1,385,684	1,099,361	1,313,022	35,658	72,662
Trucking service and warehousing	493,763	700,682	472,811	653,250	20,952	47,432
Other transportation	556,889	854,297	535,843	779,856	21,046	74,441
Telecommunications	368,915	645,732	163,470	254,919	205,445	390,813
Utilities and sanitary service	552,982	781,907	495,739	686,545	57,243	95,362
Wholesale and retail trade	7,545,918	10,547,569	5,517,878	6,998,784	2,028,040	3,548,785
Wholesale trade	1,204,761	1,975,817	1,022,914	1,596,506	181,847	379,311
Retail trade	6,341,157	8,571,752	4,494,964	5,402,278	1,846,193	3,169,474
Food and dairy products stores, and milk retailing	1,489,303	1,717,495	1,206,548	1,238,033	282,755	479,462
Eating and drinking places	1,114,002	1,685,499	636,362	822,691	477,640	862,808
Other retail trade	3,737,852	5,168,758	2,652,054	3,341,554	1,085,798	1,827,204
Finance, insurance, and real estate	1,472,397	1,916,220	1,016,347	1,135,806	456,050	780,414
Business and repair services	890,904	1,411,357	812,227	1,228,490	78,677	182,867
Business services	245,827	458,268	186,246	317,897	59,581	140,371
Repair services	645,077	953,089	625,981	910,593	19,096	42,496
Personal services	3,974,717	3,488,551	1,134,505	1,159,439	2,538,212	2,329,112
Private households	2,326,879	1,634,695	266,943	206,179	2,059,936	1,428,516
Hotels and lodging places	518,355	523,191	269,705	269,181	248,650	254,010
Other personal services	1,129,483	1,330,665	599,857	684,079	529,626	646,586
Entertainment and recreation services	419,527	554,029	335,256	413,019	84,271	141,010
Professional and related services	3,289,881	4,674,548	1,423,578	1,956,967	1,866,303	2,717,581
Medical and other health services	1,022,815	1,629,320	423,471	580,531	599,344	1,039,789
Educational services	1,559,588	2,067,698	527,572	747,116	1,032,016	1,320,582
Educational services, government	1,221,037	1,537,095	402,577	540,173	818,460	996,922
Educational services, private	338,551	530,603	124,995	206,943	213,556	323,660
Other professional and related services	707,478	977,530	472,535	620,320	234,943	357,210
Public administration	1,406,472	2,488,778	1,097,874	1,836,835	308,598	651,943
Industry not reported	727,836	838,924	450,570	509,369	277,266	329,555

¹ Figure differs from corresponding item in table 224 due to separate tabulations.

Source: Department of Commerce, Bureau of the Census; *U. S. Census of Population: 1950*, Vol. II, Part I.

No. 227.—MAJOR INDUSTRY GROUP OF EMPLOYED PERSONS, BY STATES: 1950

DIVISION AND STATE	Total employed	Agriculture, forestry, and fisheries	Mining	Construction	MANUFACTURING			Transportation, communication, and other public utilities
					Total [1]	Durable goods	Non-durable goods	
United States	56,209,440	7,005,403	926,152	3,430,924	14,575,082	7,755,922	6,806,510	4,368,302
New England	4,511,339	142,505	4,632	288,289	1,391,846	655,490	736,411	321,810
Maine	312,238	94,700	617	16,771	106,929	32,617	73,932	22,625
New Hampshire	202,691	18,625	188	13,290	81,884	25,596	56,124	11,636
Vermont	137,277	26,506	1,853	7,154	33,705	19,815	13,788	9,419
Massachusetts	1,836,797	23,914	1,458	100,783	692,640	286,096	380,704	127,011
Rhode Island	304,513	5,346	175	16,510	122,975	53,357	79,741	12,162
Connecticut	832,807	24,000	587	45,572	332,513	236,000	113,122	43,956
Middle Atlantic	11,230,046	382,731	205,779	646,124	3,916,047	1,896,317	1,962,966	1,016,476
New York	5,944,361	176,148	9,456	310,365	1,773,567	770,434	963,573	522,237
New Jersey	1,962,682	51,779	4,062	121,897	739,860	344,587	388,708	162,232
Pennsylvania	3,021,166	154,804	192,263	215,672	1,304,320	775,306	610,715	330,906
East North Central	11,972,562	1,665,276	105,137	596,989	4,177,741	2,913,554	1,237,378	921,266
Ohio	3,059,926	213,386	30,629	185,767	1,121,006	781,390	331,529	239,979
Indiana	1,516,449	176,102	14,279	77,426	527,596	390,224	141,434	115,914
Illinois	3,456,061	282,873	42,562	175,890	1,125,944	699,992	424,855	232,981
Michigan	2,205,574	162,081	15,543	118,418	978,312	802,608	168,167	181,085
Wisconsin	1,925,268	204,153	3,036	46,546	414,543	249,342	161,385	85,296
West North Central	5,203,348	1,294,063	47,872	312,154	824,911	368,973	443,665	443,675
Minnesota	1,140,673	290,531	15,808	68,292	186,905	87,742	96,406	96,353
Iowa	1,069,180	305,626	3,231	54,954	151,984	76,500	72,968	68,412
Missouri	1,621,617	257,860	9,582	84,447	331,885	147,675	179,722	136,663
North Dakota	223,543	66,949	765	11,286	6,519	1,505	4,943	18,677
South Dakota	242,398	90,229	2,731	15,111	11,781	3,076	8,600	12,995
Nebraska	511,649	151,648	1,073	39,888	46,915	14,620	31,582	46,810
Kansas	709,621	162,879	14,756	40,345	88,922	37,855	40,864	67,776
South Atlantic	7,600,008	1,390,346	186,929	597,634	1,661,847	589,811	1,063,234	611,304
Delaware	129,637	11,438	84	10,494	41,076	9,490	31,166	9,671
Maryland	804,776	40,386	3,792	68,270	228,201	115,172	105,366	82,231
District of Columbia	372,490	747	121	23,576	27,361	7,848	19,363	26,474
Virginia	1,193,164	174,159	29,006	83,577	236,434	90,274	143,684	90,625
West Virginia	628,157	61,770	134,315	32,160	118,511	70,569	47,327	52,311
North Carolina	1,466,242	362,666	3,134	86,388	406,932	107,621	299,634	64,375
South Carolina	718,278	198,268	1,126	41,966	210,779	44,163	165,843	29,645
Georgia	1,304,465	277,394	5,047	71,865	288,198	99,205	187,429	75,955
Florida	1,008,816	134,074	5,302	90,528	106,325	45,258	62,410	78,707
East South Central	3,528,719	1,063,422	115,160	226,227	706,282	331,691	365,646	286,486
Kentucky	904,668	344,006	60,708	54,017	130,688	74,380	74,425	72,938
Tennessee	1,135,648	343,806	14,447	70,984	226,437	89,151	146,738	76,751
Alabama	1,031,308	252,477	27,401	54,771	294,721	119,896	104,219	56,043
Mississippi	716,851	304,032	3,617	36,455	90,336	48,274	41,283	20,764
West South Central	5,042,688	979,526	160,506	304,846	664,627	287,725	373,443	391,490
Arkansas	615,768	217,695	6,775	38,281	84,123	50,601	33,976	35,435
Louisiana	874,608	160,396	24,209	64,929	132,476	49,010	82,734	76,780
Oklahoma	782,511	156,106	36,611	66,360	74,119	31,281	42,348	52,114
Texas	3,769,448	445,899	96,911	296,276	372,909	156,843	213,485	227,170
Mountain	1,742,678	345,885	78,190	142,786	166,582	83,741	81,178	167,446
Montana	312,490	54,960	9,342	14,771	18,515	11,845	6,611	22,500
Idaho	292,996	66,108	5,374	15,501	18,989	11,893	6,943	18,577
Wyoming	107,436	22,378	8,726	9,116	5,490	1,705	4,724	13,913
Colorado	478,044	73,467	10,254	32,085	56,279	25,678	31,600	44,002
New Mexico	302,341	38,377	16,532	22,280	12,146	5,820	6,229	16,963
Arizona	326,232	85,209	10,490	20,444	20,986	11,051	9,785	21,132
Utah	292,709	78,768	12,077	17,005	27,062	14,172	13,605	21,920
Nevada	58,770	8,715	5,464	3,255	1,568	1,671	7,406	
Pacific	5,388,488	401,271	35,847	410,529	1,072,719	636,610	431,155	445,404
Washington	808,159	65,954	3,589	66,948	178,430	117,607	60,079	76,886
Oregon	497,559	73,395	1,689	42,987	130,609	96,255	33,565	49,605
California	3,966,673	264,119	30,303	204,675	763,680	421,748	337,511	318,913

[1] Includes persons classified in not specified manufacturing industries.
[2] Figure differs from corresponding item in table 224 due to separate tabulations.

No. 227.—MAJOR INDUSTRY GROUP OF EMPLOYED PERSONS, BY STATES: 1950—Con.

DIVISION AND STATE	Wholesale and retail trade	Finance, insurance, and real estate	Business and repair services	Personal services	Entertainment and recreation services	Professional and related services	Public administration	Industry not reported
United States	10,547,569	1,916,220	1,411,267	3,488,551	554,029	4,674,548	2,486,778	839,924
New England	652,037	140,470	96,582	191,464	28,704	337,807	156,586	43,893
Maine	52,626	6,727	8,170	18,575	2,121	25,400	12,097	4,959
New Hampshire	31,971	5,064	5,071	11,792	1,584	18,343	7,029	2,244
Vermont	21,469	3,446	3,769	9,371	977	13,359	5,358	1,892
Massachusetts	352,720	77,553	43,587	95,604	15,155	183,091	87,969	20,007
Rhode Island	54,479	9,314	6,420	14,150	2,817	23,831	15,988	4,164
Connecticut	188,772	38,376	19,565	41,972	6,050	73,783	28,145	10,627
Middle Atlantic	2,281,734	551,848	319,523	693,615	122,439	1,028,013	496,522	171,221
New York	1,240,961	336,789	179,631	387,106	76,315	566,650	270,532	94,215
New Jersey	350,971	98,659	51,056	109,426	16,178	149,865	80,887	24,660
Pennsylvania	689,802	116,400	88,836	197,083	29,946	311,498	145,103	52,346
East North Central	2,170,840	361,019	287,299	574,860	105,571	926,964	418,066	165,155
Ohio	558,092	85,710	72,540	151,351	27,667	236,686	122,254	41,439
Indiana	296,487	39,277	32,806	71,983	11,843	115,029	47,923	23,542
Illinois	691,225	138,715	95,052	182,522	33,360	281,657	133,149	50,361
Michigan	421,247	64,436	55,377	112,580	21,589	187,502	73,802	31,674
Wisconsin	203,789	32,881	32,115	56,424	11,112	106,090	40,938	18,139
West North Central	1,035,560	162,134	142,441	255,055	45,541	460,156	197,615	100,673
Minnesota	228,208	37,326	32,695	51,322	9,955	107,156	39,689	15,496
Iowa	192,366	27,639	26,465	44,392	8,275	87,573	30,238	20,024
Missouri	296,261	50,489	37,741	83,344	12,538	118,499	60,330	31,939
North Dakota	39,580	4,027	6,399	7,823	1,575	18,812	8,336	3,933
South Dakota	42,977	4,595	6,856	9,512	2,041	21,317	9,543	4,240
Nebraska	97,365	17,388	14,128	23,461	4,494	43,514	20,276	11,739
Kansas	137,103	20,330	18,157	35,201	6,363	63,285	29,203	13,302
South Atlantic	1,294,180	199,615	151,821	643,356	64,442	574,575	468,212	117,361
Delaware	20,376	3,984	2,822	9,044	1,045	10,170	8,892	2,541
Maryland	166,668	32,174	20,397	61,804	8,479	78,592	76,383	12,704
District of Columbia	65,582	17,284	7,514	39,822	3,568	41,256	114,687	5,477
Virginia	188,590	30,065	21,759	86,051	8,182	87,034	99,166	18,134
West Virginia	97,495	9,994	11,603	30,198	4,723	47,524	16,584	9,969
North Carolina	208,439	24,414	25,896	106,693	10,202	97,847	38,469	22,545
South Carolina	101,965	13,361	11,109	65,158	3,962	48,916	18,623	10,591
Georgia	201,754	30,192	23,135	122,764	9,255	82,125	48,450	18,991
Florida	240,311	38,157	27,586	122,121	15,026	81,110	51,959	16,409
East South Central	589,553	76,553	73,327	263,577	26,575	265,554	122,721	64,254
Kentucky	147,580	20,494	21,894	53,212	7,589	65,100	29,142	16,553
Tennessee	193,228	25,678	23,630	83,107	7,964	85,215	37,423	20,987
Alabama	153,153	21,254	16,869	90,183	6,372	69,991	38,152	15,919
Mississippi	95,592	9,127	11,134	57,075	3,650	45,248	18,004	10,795
West South Central	1,007,686	143,710	125,296	397,680	47,471	399,503	209,575	81,664
Arkansas	97,546	10,566	11,720	40,437	4,334	42,591	16,527	11,856
Louisiana	169,845	21,969	20,158	77,839	9,071	72,028	33,446	13,253
Oklahoma	150,071	22,361	20,920	49,087	7,990	67,920	40,724	14,088
Texas	590,224	88,814	72,498	230,317	26,076	216,964	118,878	42,467
Mountain	350,713	49,819	52,084	107,012	22,344	169,613	102,926	28,853
Montana	41,628	5,018	6,266	10,488	1,960	19,232	10,107	3,635
Idaho	39,493	4,816	6,202	10,757	2,134	17,033	7,913	3,096
Wyoming	18,307	2,325	3,147	5,816	1,025	9,237	5,571	1,880
Colorado	100,431	16,947	15,146	29,675	5,715	50,975	26,582	7,086
New Mexico	39,145	4,550	5,871	13,610	1,966	21,220	13,585	5,189
Arizona	52,376	7,276	7,425	19,615	2,740	24,023	12,727	3,862
Utah	46,699	7,319	6,099	10,815	2,837	22,905	21,458	3,012
Nevada	12,634	1,568	1,928	6,236	3,967	4,988	4,983	1,093
Pacific	1,164,966	231,062	172,293	341,932	91,942	512,363	316,554	66,850
Washington	173,970	32,062	24,024	46,715	8,884	81,805	46,629	12,766
Oregon	118,388	19,573	18,009	32,174	6,263	52,546	23,695	7,866
California	872,608	179,417	130,260	263,043	76,795	378,012	246,230	46,218

Source: Department of Commerce, Bureau of the Census; U. S. Census of Population: 1950, Vol. II, Part I.

No. 228.—CLASS OF WORKER OF EMPLOYED PERSONS, BY SEX, BY STATES: 1950

DIVISION AND STATE	MALE					FEMALE				
	Total	Private wage and salary workers	Government workers	Self-employed workers	Unpaid family workers	Total	Private wage and salary workers	Government workers	Self-employed workers	Unpaid family workers
U. S.	[1] 40,519,462	27,793,416	3,666,349	8,634,154	635,643	[1] 15,719,987	12,244,252	2,829,441	967,328	473,966
N. E.	2,450,203	1,872,130	221,068	346,736	7,299	1,161,107	999,640	114,816	47,787	7,865
Maine	224,024	158,548	18,747	46,050	1,681	88,302	70,570	10,645	5,548	1,439
N. H.	133,331	101,023	12,892	23,652	717	64,346	53,980	6,831	3,964	571
Vt.	93,282	65,089	7,477	24,693	2,023	37,968	28,940	4,930	3,049	1,057
Mass.	1,224,105	947,175	126,312	148,106	1,512	602,602	519,147	60,184	20,572	2,399
R. I.	200,379	155,392	18,695	26,155	320	104,136	91,337	8,858	3,492	449
Conn.	564,031	449,045	36,964	77,036	1,036	263,726	227,585	23,669	10,832	1,640
M. A.	8,302,005	6,346,805	762,782	1,222,679	28,672	3,536,064	2,968,999	362,137	158,800	26,318
N. Y.	4,099,155	3,099,839	394,738	632,085	11,476	1,845,108	1,502,887	184,088	81,720	16,402
N. J.	1,373,479	1,070,285	106,033	195,515	2,646	589,153	499,684	56,687	26,610	6,172
Pa.	2,829,371	2,396,761	202,961	375,079	14,550	1,101,796	926,428	111,412	50,214	13,744
E. N. C.	8,654,994	6,460,680	602,891	1,528,432	63,121	3,217,961	2,579,374	364,814	179,766	84,867
Ohio	2,232,905	1,680,256	161,478	387,413	14,759	826,700	668,940	97,201	44,311	16,248
Ind.	1,121,441	808,394	71,912	232,610	10,583	397,001	315,373	44,422	25,478	10,827
Ill.	2,518,808	1,915,755	186,814	432,730	16,599	1,027,243	858,960	101,041	52,923	14,319
Mich.	1,780,022	1,367,630	122,102	263,228	9,861	607,549	483,140	78,924	35,068	10,417
Wis.	995,813	660,364	63,585	252,437	26,409	369,468	263,051	41,725	21,926	32,736
W. N. C.	3,833,910	2,217,544	291,962	1,347,666	126,734	1,369,630	987,540	192,192	92,898	96,741
Minn.	838,977	484,635	61,192	260,038	31,910	304,897	223,607	40,437	17,729	22,727
Iowa	757,435	401,437	36,084	282,487	23,427	244,745	172,937	35,968	17,019	18,937
Mo.	1,100,006	894,959	77,019	306,198	21,839	421,811	338,360	47,809	27,368	16,874
N. Dak.	178,054	69,713	12,574	83,223	12,544	45,489	27,364	9,187	3,201	5,946
S. Dak.	189,763	75,381	14,628	87,722	11,004	52,805	31,366	10,628	3,554	6,125
Nebr.	385,257	191,906	30,413	149,540	12,396	128,362	84,469	19,874	9,196	10,838
Kans.	534,390	299,216	48,094	178,382	12,704	173,231	117,484	28,299	14,743	12,716
S. A.	5,405,796	4,538,574	544,962	1,180,528	144,716	2,299,767	1,665,516	345,718	127,780	91,654
Del.	90,414	66,421	6,166	14,304	423	36,238	29,844	3,982	2,011	386
Md.	634,067	486,129	85,200	80,455	3,283	260,706	201,006	44,078	12,023	3,602
D. C.	212,957	117,328	77,214	16,418	107	160,633	82,630	73,412	4,010	446
Va.	837,902	536,684	112,307	172,039	14,232	312,902	231,713	61,218	15,162	4,769
W. Va.	425,781	283,767	30,580	73,476	8,978	132,376	98,166	22,170	3,047	8,993
N. C.	1,015,251	621,361	64,278	308,103	51,509	418,101	320,025	48,348	22,010	27,718
S. C.	519,764	317,704	34,457	138,885	28,718	235,614	172,159	27,437	13,328	22,690
Ga.	877,207	649,987	65,042	227,577	34,061	377,726	290,604	45,980	21,714	20,340
Fla.	693,093	560,372	69,109	138,303	5,408	316,532	240,437	38,880	28,191	9,034
E. S. C.	2,831,721	1,622,060	226,239	927,896	138,576	967,068	694,542	122,526	74,791	52,649
Ky.	748,658	437,752	45,354	235,407	30,145	206,328	156,377	26,787	15,104	4,060
Tenn.	879,122	603,809	67,002	247,397	26,124	295,524	220,725	40,297	17,423	8,089
Ala.	735,249	451,604	56,172	212,052	33,380	276,057	197,675	39,482	19,050	19,850
Miss.	538,692	294,264	34,619	232,842	34,947	178,159	112,066	24,289	23,204	18,600
W. S. C.	3,720,630	2,345,149	315,896	996,329	74,966	1,272,729	913,842	188,191	112,294	58,379
Ark.	431,588	248,340	31,355	185,745	19,448	132,908	87,492	21,015	14,538	10,573
La.	646,490	436,700	58,416	151,155	14,110	229,112	167,625	34,678	16,907	9,902
Okla.	564,485	316,344	58,416	175,982	12,884	186,023	125,551	33,908	18,669	10,805
Tex.	2,037,758	1,346,886	171,293	482,436	27,173	730,685	533,194	98,600	61,892	27,099
Mt.	1,315,415	897,687	151,404	332,699	24,438	431,355	287,749	61,963	42,824	18,719
Mont.	162,535	96,239	15,681	82,227	3,704	48,625	31,197	6,089	5,000	2,725
Idaho	161,004	89,031	12,746	54,730	4,497	44,989	29,152	5,161	4,454	3,212
Wyo.	83,892	62,400	9,016	20,969	1,488	23,943	14,365	5,679	2,895	1,304
Colo.	345,806	216,567	35,659	85,173	8,447	130,748	92,012	22,127	11,031	4,578
N. Mex.	157,530	94,061	21,335	38,509	3,725	48,864	30,548	10,778	5,025	2,913
Ariz.	175,050	115,357	19,771	34,244	2,718	63,805	41,945	10,970	8,316	2,374
Utah	174,848	108,540	23,723	36,761	2,594	54,018	37,571	11,516	3,808	1,125
Nev.	47,172	30,948	4,453	9,406	325	16,468	10,939	3,118	1,708	653
Pac.	3,794,782	2,586,657	426,376	769,771	17,546	1,534,049	1,123,722	327,235	130,017	33,064
Wash.	616,035	402,576	76,549	122,637	4,373	233,427	189,118	35,170	19,821	6,618
Oreg.	424,204	284,372	37,736	97,957	4,139	152,306	106,844	22,833	16,255	6,354
Calif.	2,753,943	1,849,839	314,091	666,977	9,036	1,148,335	857,770	176,212	94,241	20,113

[1] Figure differs from corresponding item in table 224 due to separate tabulations.

Source: Department of Commerce, Bureau of the Census; U. S. Census of Population: 1950, Vol. II, Part I.

No. 229.—INDEXES OF PRODUCTIVITY FOR SELECTED INDUSTRIES: 1929 TO 1951

[1939=100. Productivity refers to output in physical units per man-hour of work (or per worker in agriculture and telegraph). Indexes of output per man-hour obtained by dividing indexes of production by indexes of man-hours. For explanation of various indexes used, see *Handbook of Labor Statistics*, 1950, p. 166. See also *Historical Statistics*, series D 213-217]

INDUSTRY	1929	1933	1935	1937	1940	1945	1947	1948	1949	1950	1951
All manufacturing:											
Output per man-hour	78.1	81.9	90.8	90.0							
Mining: [1]											
Output per man-hour	69.9	78.8	84.9	88.0	102.1	106.1	111.1	110.9	108.6	117.4	
Agriculture:											
Output per worker	91.6	89.2	87.5	105.3	102.5	120.1	115.9	130.1	133.9	131.0	
Steam railroad transportation: [2]											
Revenue traffic per man-hour	75.1	83.0	87.6	95.2	105.2	139.5	135.0	133.2	131.5	149.9	158.5
Electric light and power: [3]											
Output per man-hour	64.1	68.1	82.5	89.6	108.6	182.5	167.0	171.0			
Telephone: [4]											
Output per man-hour			88.2	88.8	103.0	98.8	94.0	93.3	99.1	104.5	
Telegraph: [5]											
Output per employee			86.4	93.0	92.5	116.4	121.0	117.0	122.0	134.8	
SELECTED MANUFACTURING INDUSTRIES											
(Output per man-hour)											
Beet-sugar refining	68.4	97.9	82.6	86.9	104.2	79.6	93.1	91.8	104.5	115.0	105.0
Canning and preserving group			100.4	88.7	110.2	113.9	111.1	116.4	127.6	131.6	142.2
Cement	71.7	84.4	80.9	99.1	100.4	90.1	111.5	117.8	120.4	129.4	137.0
Clay construction products	88.0	87.8	84.3	88.2	105.2	88.0	106.1	114.9	117.3	125.9	127.0
Coke group	92.8	74.3	85.0	94.0	104.4	100.5	106.7	102.9	98.5	106.5	108.1
Glass containers					99.2	118.4	129.6	122.3	123.9	130.1	129.3
Hosiery group					109.0	131.4	114.9	118.3	127.3	138.1	146.5
Malt liquors					102.2	118.0	117.0	115.8	125.3	126.9	125.9
Paper and pulp	74.0	86.9	87.5	92.6	105.3	87.6	91.6	94.6	99.1	109.7	114.2
Primary smelting and refining of copper, lead, and zinc	89.5	88.5	76.2	87.6	103.7	89.5	95.1	93.9	96.9	106.7	99.7
Rayon and other synthetic fibers	30.4	60.7	67.8	79.4	113.4	170.2	206.9	235.5	239.9	296.1	302.5
Tobacco products group	63.7	73.7	86.7	90.5	100.6	115.7	115.8	123.3	131.2	137.1	140.7

[1] For 1929 and 1933, covers almost all industries; for 1935 to 1950, represents 6 principal industries (bituminous coal; anthracite; crude petroleum, natural gas and natural gasoline; iron; copper; and lead and zinc). [2] Refers to Class I steam line-haul railroads. [3] Refers to privately owned utilities. [4] Refers to Class A telephone carriers. [5] For principal wire-telegraph and ocean-cable carriers. As satisfactory data on average weekly hours are not available before 1943, an index of output per man-hour is not presented.

Source: Department of Labor, Bureau of Labor Statistics. Published in *Handbook of Labor Statistics*.

No. 230.—GROSS AND NET SPENDABLE AVERAGE WEEKLY EARNINGS OF PRODUCTION WORKERS IN MANUFACTURING INDUSTRIES, IN CURRENT AND 1947–49 DOLLARS: 1939 TO 1952

[Net spendable average weekly earnings represent average gross earnings of production workers in manufacturing industries less social security and income taxes for which specified worker is liable. These net spendable average weekly earnings are then divided by the Bureau's consumers' price index adjusted to an average 1947–49 base, to obtain net spendable weekly earnings in 1947–49 dollars]

PERIOD	GROSS AVERAGE WEEKLY EARNINGS		NET SPENDABLE AVERAGE WEEKLY EARNINGS			
			Worker with no dependents		Worker with three dependents	
	Amount	Index (1947–49 =100)	Current dollars	1947–49 dollars	Current dollars	1947–49 dollars
1939	$23.86	45.1	$23.58	$39.70	$23.62	$39.76
1940	25.20	47.6	24.69	41.22	24.95	41.65
1941	29.58	55.9	28.05	44.59	29.28	46.55
1942	36.65	69.2	31.77	45.58	36.28	52.05
1943	43.14	81.5	36.01	48.65	41.39	55.93
1944	46.08	87.0	38.29	50.92	44.06	58.59
1945	44.39	83.8	36.97	48.08	42.74	55.58
1946	43.82	82.8	37.72	45.23	43.20	51.80
1947	49.97	94.4	42.76	44.77	48.24	50.51
1948	54.14	102.2	47.43	46.14	53.17	51.72
1949	54.92	103.7	48.09	47.34	53.83	52.88
1950	59.33	112.0	51.09	49.70	57.21	55.65
1951	64.71	122.2	54.04	48.68	61.28	55.21
1952	67.97	128.4	55.66	49.04	63.62	56.05

Source: Department of Labor, Bureau of Labor Statistics; *Monthly Labor Review*, *Handbook of Labor Statistics*, 1950 edition, and mimeographed releases.

No. 231.—Hours and Earnings, Gross and Excluding Overtime, of Production Workers in Manufacturing Industries: 1941 to 1952

[Overtime is defined as work in excess of 40 hours per week and paid for at time and one-half. Computation of averages hourly earnings exclusive of overtime makes no allowance for special rates of pay for work done on holidays. See also *Historical Statistics*, series D 117-119]

	Average weekly earnings	Average weekly hours	AVERAGE HOURLY EARNINGS			PERIOD	Average weekly earnings	Average weekly hours	AVERAGE HOURLY EARNINGS		
PERIOD			Gross amount	Excluding overtime					Gross amount	Excluding overtime	
				Amount	Index 1947-49 =100					Amount	Index 1947-49=100
1941		40.6	$0.729	$0.702	54.5	1952					
1942		42.9	.853	.806	62.5	January	$66.50	40.8	$1.63	$1.57	121.9
1943		44.9	.961	.894	69.4	February	66.75	40.7	1.64	1.58	122.7
1944		45.2	1.019	.947	73.5	March	66.99	40.6	1.65	1.59	123.4
1945		43.4	1.023	.963	74.8	April	65.67	39.8	1.65	1.60	124.2
						May	66.33	40.2	1.65	1.60	124.2
1946		40.4	1.086	1.051	81.6	June	66.83	40.5	1.65	1.60	124.2
1947		40.4	1.237	1.198	93.0	July	65.44	39.9	1.64	1.60	124.2
1948		40.1	1.350	1.310	101.7	August	67.23	40.5	1.66	1.61	125.0
1949		39.2	1.401	1.367	106.1	September	69.63	41.2	1.69	1.63	126.6
1950		40.5	1.465	1.415	109.9	October	70.38	41.4	1.70	1.63	126.6
1951		40.7	1.59	1.52	118.8	November	70.28	41.1	1.71	1.65	128.1
1952		40.7	1.67	1.61	125.0	December	72.14	41.7	1.73	1.65	128.1

1 Eleven-month average; August 1945 excluded because of VJ holiday period.

Source: Department of Labor, Bureau of Labor Statistics; published in *Monthly Labor Review* and in mimeographed releases.

No. 232.—Hourly and Weekly Earnings in Constant and Current Prices for Selected Industries: 1940 to 1952

[Figures are monthly averages for production and related workers]

YEAR AND TYPE OF EARNINGS	ALL MANUFACTURING		DURABLE GOODS MANUFACTURING		NONDURABLE GOODS MANUFACTURING		BUILDING CONSTRUCTION		RETAIL TRADE	
	Current prices	1952 prices [1]	Current prices	1952 prices [1]	Current prices	1952 prices [1]	Current prices	1952 prices [1]	Current prices	1952 prices [1]
1940: Hourly	$0.661	$1.252	$0.724	$1.271	$0.602	$1.140	$0.966	$1.814	(2)	(2)
Weekly	25.20	47.73	28.44	53.95	22.27	42.18	31.70	60.04	(2)	(2)
1941: Hourly	.729	1.316	.806	1.458	.640	1.155	1.010	1.823	(2)	(2)
Weekly	29.58	53.39	34.04	61.44	24.92	44.98	35.14	63.43	(2)	(2)
1942: Hourly	.853	1.389	.947	1.542	.723	1.178	1.148	1.870	(2)	(2)
Weekly	36.65	59.69	42.73	69.59	29.13	47.44	41.80	68.06	(2)	(2)
1943: Hourly	.961	1.474	1.069	1.624	.803	1.232	1.252	1.920	(2)	(2)
Weekly	43.14	66.17	49.30	75.61	34.12	52.33	48.13	73.82	(2)	(2)
1944: Hourly	1.019	1.537	1.117	1.685	.861	1.299	1.319	1.989	(2)	(2)
Weekly	46.08	69.50	52.07	78.54	37.12	55.99	52.18	78.70	(2)	(2)
1945: Hourly	1.023	1.509	1.111	1.639	.904	1.333	1.379	2.034	(2)	(2)
Weekly	44.39	65.47	49.05	72.35	38.29	56.47	53.73	79.26	(2)	(2)
1946: Hourly	1.086	1.478	1.156	1.573	1.015	1.381	1.478	2.011	(2)	(2)
Weekly	43.82	59.62	46.49	63.25	41.14	55.97	56.24	76.52	(2)	(2)
1947: Hourly	1.237	1.471	1.292	1.536	1.171	1.392	1.661	1.999	$1.009	$1.200
Weekly	49.97	59.42	52.46	62.38	46.96	55.84	63.30	75.27	40.66	48.35
1948: Hourly	1.350	1.490	1.410	1.556	1.278	1.411	[3]1.848	[3]2.040	1.088	1.201
Weekly	54.14	59.76	57.11	63.04	50.61	55.86	[3]69.85	[3]74.99	43.55	48.40
1949: Hourly	1.401	1.502	1.469	1.638	1.325	1.477	1.935	2.157	1.137	1.246
Weekly	54.92	61.23	58.03	64.69	51.41	57.31	70.96	79.10	45.93	51.20
1950: Hourly	1.465	1.617	1.537	1.695	1.378	1.521	2.031	2.242	1.176	1.296
Weekly	59.33	65.49	63.32	69.89	54.71	60.39	73.73	81.38	47.63	52.57
1951: Hourly	1.59	1.63	1.67	1.71	1.48	1.51	2.19	2.24	1.36	1.39
Weekly	64.71	66.17	69.47	71.03	56.46	58.73	81.47	83.30	50.65	51.79
1952: Hourly	1.67	1.67	1.76	1.76	1.54	1.54	2.31	2.31	1.39	1.39
Weekly	67.97	67.97	73.04	73.04	60.98	60.98	86.01	86.01	52.67	52.67

[1] Current prices divided by consumer price index on base 1952=100.
[2] Not available.
[3] Beginning 1948, not strictly comparable with previous data.

Source: Office of the Economic Adviser to the President, *Economic Indicators*. Based on Department of Labor.

No. 233.—HOURS AND GROSS EARNINGS OF PRODUCTION WORKERS OR NONSUPERVISORY EMPLOYEES: 1950 TO 1952

[Data are based upon reports from cooperating establishments covering both full- and part-time production and related workers or nonsupervisory employees who worked during, or received pay for, any part of the pay period ending nearest the 15th of the month]

INDUSTRY GROUP AND INDUSTRY	AVERAGE WEEKLY EARNINGS			AVERAGE WEEKLY HOURS			AVERAGE HOURLY EARNINGS		
	1950	1951	1952	1950	1951	1952	1950	1951	1952
Mining:									
Metal mining	$65.58	$74.56	$81.65	42.2	43.6	43.9	$1.554	$1.71	$1.86
Anthracite	63.24	66.66	71.19	32.1	30.3	31.5	1.970	2.20	2.26
Bituminous-coal	70.35	77.79	78.32	35.0	35.2	34.2	2.010	2.21	2.29
Petroleum and natural-gas production (except contract services)	73.69	79.76	85.90	40.6	40.9	41.1	1.815	1.95	2.09
Nonmetallic mining and quarrying	59.88	67.05	71.10	44.0	45.0	45.0	1.361	1.49	1.58
Contract construction	73.73	81.49	87.85	37.2	37.9	38.7	1.982	2.15	2.27
Nonbuilding construction	73.46	80.78	86.72	40.9	40.8	41.1	1.796	1.98	2.11
Building construction	73.73	81.47	88.01	36.3	37.2	38.1	2.031	2.19	2.31
Manufacturing	59.33	64.71	67.97	40.5	40.7	40.7	1.465	1.59	1.67
Durable goods	63.32	69.47	73.04	41.2	41.6	41.5	1.537	1.67	1.76
Nondurable goods	54.71	58.46	60.98	39.7	39.5	39.6	1.378	1.48	1.54
Ordnance and accessories	64.79	74.12	77.22	41.8	43.6	42.9	1.550	1.70	1.80
Food and kindred products	55.29	59.92	63.23	41.6	41.9	41.1	1.329	1.43	1.52
Meat products	60.07	65.78	70.30	41.6	41.9	41.6	1.444	1.57	1.69
Dairy products	56.11	60.83	63.80	44.5	44.4	44.0	1.261	1.37	1.45
Canning and preserving	46.81	50.80	51.88	39.3	40.0	39.3	1.191	1.27	1.32
Grain-mill products	58.03	65.85	69.15	43.5	45.1	44.9	1.334	1.46	1.54
Bakery products[1]	53.54	58.24	61.57	41.5	41.6	41.6	1.290	1.40	1.48
Sugar	58.81	60.15	64.41	43.4	41.2	42.1	1.355	1.46	1.53
Confectionery and related products	46.72	49.97	52.27	39.9	40.3	39.9	1.171	1.24	1.31
Beverages	62.91	68.39	71.14	41.5	41.7	41.6	1.516	1.64	1.71
Miscellaneous food products[1]	54.99	57.11	59.78	42.2	42.3	42.1	1.303	1.35	1.42
Tobacco manufactures	40.77	43.51	44.93	38.1	38.5	38.4	1.070	1.13	1.17
Cigarettes	50.19	54.37	56.45	39.0	39.4	39.2	1.287	1.38	1.44
Cigars	35.76	39.10	40.13	36.9	37.6	37.5	.969	1.04	1.07
Tobacco and snuff	42.79	45.99	47.87	37.7	37.7	37.4	1.135	1.22	1.28
Tobacco stemming and redrying	37.59	38.02	38.91	39.4	39.2	39.3	.954	.97	.99
Textile-mill products	48.95	51.60	53.18	39.6	38.8	39.1	1.236	1.33	1.36
Scouring and combing plants		57.82	62.80		39.6	40.0		1.46	1.57
Yarn and thread mills	45.01	47.86	49.15	38.9	38.6	38.7	1.157	1.24	1.27
Broad-woven fabric mills	49.28	51.74	51.99	40.1	39.2	38.8	1.229	1.32	1.34
Narrow fabrics and smallwares		51.48	54.14		39.6	40.1		1.30	1.35
Knitting mills	44.13	47.10	49.02	37.4	36.8	38.3	1.180	1.28	1.28
Dyeing and finishing textiles	53.87	56.77	62.58	40.9	39.7	42.0	1.317	1.43	1.49
Carpets, rugs, other floor coverings	62.33	63.44	68.23	41.5	39.9	41.1	1.502	1.59	1.66
Hats (except cloth and millinery)		49.87	53.20		36.4	37.2		1.37	1.43
Miscellaneous textile goods		57.11	60.06		40.5	40.6		1.41	1.48
Apparel and other finished textile products[1]	43.68	46.31	47.45	36.4	35.9	36.5	1.200	1.29	1.30
Men's and boys' suits and coats	50.22	52.63	52.15	36.9	35.8	35.0	1.361	1.47	1.49
Men's and boys' furnishings and work clothing	36.43	38.16	40.50	36.8	36.0	37.5	.990	1.06	1.08
Women's outerwear	49.41	51.16	52.39	34.7	34.8	35.4	1.424	1.47	1.48
Women's, children's under garments	38.38	41.22	43.62	36.9	36.8	37.6	1.040	1.12	1.16
Millinery	54.21	57.60	58.60	35.2	36.0	36.4	1.540	1.60	1.61
Children's outerwear	38.98	41.38	43.52	36.5	36.3	37.2	1.068	1.14	1.17
Miscellaneous apparel and accessories		42.44	43.15		36.9	37.2		1.15	1.16
Other fabricated textile products	42.06	44.49	46.46	38.2	37.7	38.4	1.101	1.18	1.21
Lumber and wood products (exc. furniture)	55.31	59.98	63.45	41.0	40.8	41.2	1.349	1.47	1.54
Logging camps and contractors	66.23	71.53	77.68	38.9	39.3	41.1	1.703	1.82	1.89
Sawmills and planing mills	54.95	59.13	63.24	40.7	40.5	40.8	1.350	1.46	1.55
Millwork, plywood, and prefabricated structural wood products	60.52	64.02	66.94	43.2	42.4	42.1	1.401	1.51	1.59
Wooden containers	46.03	48.85	50.39	40.7	41.3	41.3	1.311	1.18	1.22
Miscellaneous wood products	47.07	51.24	53.63	41.4	42.0	41.9	1.137	1.22	1.28
Furniture and fixtures	53.67	57.27	60.59	41.2	41.5	41.5	1.281	1.39	1.46
Household furniture	51.91	55.08	58.93	41.9	40.8	41.5	1.239	1.35	1.42
Office, public-building, and professional furniture		66.53	68.36		43.2	42.2		1.54	1.62
Partitions, shelving, lockers, and fixtures		69.66	71.17		41.6	40.9		1.66	1.74
Screens, blinds, and miscellaneous furniture and fixtures		53.43	57.69		41.1	41.5		1.30	1.39
Paper and allied products	61.14	65.51	68.91	43.3	43.1	42.8	1.412	1.52	1.61
Pulp, paper, and paperboard mills	65.06	71.04	73.68	43.9	43.6	43.6	1.482	1.60	1.69
Paperboard containers and boxes[1]	57.96	60.19	64.45	43.0	41.8	42.4	1.348	1.44	1.52
Other paper and allied products	55.48	59.77	62.40	42.0	41.8	41.6	1.321	1.43	1.50
Printing, publishing, and allied industries	73.99	77.21	80.48	38.8	38.8	38.8	1.907	1.99	2.10
Newspapers	80.00	83.45	87.12	36.9	36.6	36.3	2.168	2.28	2.40
Periodicals	74.18	79.20	83.60	39.5	39.8	40.0	1.878	1.99	2.09
Books	64.08	67.32	71.24	39.1	39.6	39.8	1.639	1.70	1.79
Commercial printing	72.34	75.20	80.00	39.9	40.0	40.2	1.813	1.88	1.99

[1] 1950 data not strictly comparable with those shown for later years.

No. 233.—HOURS AND GROSS EARNINGS OF PRODUCTION WORKERS OR NONSUPER-VISORY EMPLOYEES: 1950 TO 1952—Continued

INDUSTRY GROUP AND INDUSTRY	AVERAGE WEEKLY EARNINGS			AVERAGE WEEKLY HOURS			AVERAGE HOURLY EARNINGS		
	1950	1951	1952	1950	1951	1952	1950	1951	1952
Manufacturing—Con.									
Printing, publishing, etc.—Con.									
Lithographing	$73.04	$75.79	$81.61	40.0	40.1	40.2	$1.826	$1.89	$2.03
Greeting cards		43.47	45.84		37.5	38.2		1.15	1.20
Bookbinding and related industries		62.24	62.33		39.9	39.2		1.56	1.59
Miscellaneous publishing and printing services		91.42	98.25		38.9	39.3		2.35	2.50
Chemicals and allied products	62.67	67.81	70.45	41.5	41.6	41.2	1.510	1.63	1.71
Industrial inorganic chemicals	67.59	74.98	77.06	40.9	41.6	41.6	1.660	1.80	1.85
Industrial organic chemicals	65.69	71.08	75.11	40.8	40.9	40.6	1.615	1.74	1.85
Drugs and medicines	59.59	62.47	63.44	40.9	41.1	39.9	1.457	1.52	1.59
Soap, cleaning and polishing preparations		70.89	73.93		41.7	41.3		1.70	1.79
Paints, pigments, and fillers	64.80	58.55	71.28	43.3	41.5	41.5	1.532	1.64	1.72
Gum and wood chemicals		56.55	59.36		42.7	42.1		1.34	1.41
Vegetable and animal oils	47.00	52.33	56.22	41.3	43.2	42.6	1.138	1.34	1.34
Miscellaneous chemicals	53.46	59.34	61.51	44.5	46.6	45.0	1.175	1.29	1.34
		62.50	65.35		41.5	43.1		1.53	1.59
Products of petroleum and coal	76.01	80.98	84.85	40.9	40.9	40.6	1.854	1.98	2.09
Petroleum refining	77.98	84.66	88.44	40.4	40.7	40.2	1.929	2.08	2.20
Coke and other petroleum and coal products		69.39	73.74		41.8	41.9		1.65	1.76
Rubber products	64.42	66.61	74.45	40.9	40.6	40.7	1.575	1.69	1.83
Tires and inner tubes	72.45	78.01	85.65	39.5	39.6	40.4	1.831	1.97	2.12
Other rubber products	52.21	57.81	62.22	40.1	41.0	40.4	1.302	1.41	1.54
Leather and leather products	58.76	63.19	66.58	42.2	41.3	41.1	1.416	1.53	1.62
Leather tanned, curried, and finished	44.56	46.86	50.66	37.6	36.9	38.4	1.185	1.27	1.32
Leather belting and packing	57.21	60.61	64.45	39.7	39.1	39.8	1.441	1.55	1.62
Boot and shoe cut stock and findings		64.50	64.12		43.0	41.1		1.50	1.56
		46.25	49.40		37.6	38.9		1.23	1.27
Footwear (except rubber)	41.99	44.38	48.20	36.9	36.0	38.0	1.138	1.23	1.27
		53.72	56.84		39.5	40.6		1.15	1.18
Handbags and small leather goods		43.59	45.08		37.9	38.2		1.15	1.18
Gloves and miscellaneous leather goods		42.67	44.18		41.3	41.1		1.15	1.19
Stone, clay, and glass products	59.20	63.91	66.17	41.2	41.5	41.1	1.497	1.64	1.61
Glass and glassware, pressed or blown		53.85	55.06		40.9	40.6		2.08	2.13
Glass products made of purchased glass		50.20	62.06		40.0	39.8		1.48	1.56
		53.19	56.20		40.6	40.5		1.31	1.38
Cement, hydraulic	60.13	65.21	67.72	41.7	41.8	41.8	1.442	1.56	1.62
Structural and related products	54.19	60.03	60.09	40.5	41.4	40.6	1.338	1.45	1.48
Pottery and related products	52.16	57.91	61.18	37.5	38.1	38.7	1.391	1.52	1.58
Concrete, gypsum, and plaster products	62.64	66.25	70.65	45.0	45.2	45.0	1.393	1.51	1.57
Cut-stone and stone products		56.93	60.01		41.5	41.1		1.42	1.46
Miscellaneous nonmetallic mineral products		58.46	66.83		42.0	40.6		1.63	1.73
Primary metal industries	67.24	75.12	77.33	40.8	41.5	40.7	1.646	1.81	1.90
Blast furnaces, steel works, and rolling mills	67.47	77.30	79.60	39.9	40.9	40.0	1.691	1.89	1.99
Iron and steel foundries	65.32	71.66	72.22	41.9	42.4	40.8	1.599	1.69	1.77
Primary smelting and refining of nonferrous metals	63.71	69.97	75.46	41.0	41.4	41.7	1.554	1.69	1.81
Secondary smelting and refining of nonferrous metals		64.94	68.15		41.1	41.3		1.58	1.65
Rolling, drawing, and alloying of nonferrous metals	66.75	66.78	74.86	41.9	40.7	41.6	1.593	1.66	1.80
	67.56	73.74	77.79	41.5	41.9	41.6	1.625	1.76	1.87
Miscellaneous primary metal industries		80.65	82.15		42.9	41.7		1.88	1.97
Fabricated metal products (except ordnance, machinery, and transportation equipment)	63.42	68.81	72.36	41.4	41.7	41.6	1.532	1.65	1.74
Tin cans and other tinware	66.90	68.49	69.72	41.6	41.3	41.5	1.654	1.63	1.67
Cutlery, hand tools, and hardware	61.01	66.30	69.06	41.5	41.7	41.1	1.470	1.59	1.68
Heating apparatus (except electric) and plumber's supplies	63.91	66.71	70.99	41.1	40.9	40.8	1.538	1.68	1.74
Fabricated structural metal products	63.26	71.49	74.87	41.1	42.3	42.3	1.540	1.69	1.77
Metal stamping, coating, and engraving	64.22	68.38	74.29	41.3	40.7	41.5	1.555	1.68	1.79
Lighting fixtures		64.64	66.00		40.4	40.0		1.60	1.70
Fabricated wire products		66.08	68.30		40.9	40.9		1.59	1.67
Miscellaneous fabricated metal products		72.11	73.02		43.7	42.7		1.65	1.71
Machinery (except electrical)	67.21	76.38	79.61	41.5	43.4	42.8	1.608	1.76	1.86
Engines and turbines	69.43	79.12	82.36	40.7	43.0	42.4	1.706	1.84	1.94
Agricultural machinery and tractors	64.00	73.26	75.41	40.1	40.7	39.9	1.611	1.80	1.89
Construction and mining machinery	65.97	75.82	77.61	42.4	44.6	43.6	1.556	1.70	1.78
Metalworking machinery	71.54	85.74	91.57	43.2	46.6	46.4	1.656	1.84	1.98
Special-industry machinery (except metalworking machinery)	65.74	74.73	77.40	41.9	43.7	43.0	1.569	1.71	1.80
General industrial machinery	65.33	77.08	79.24	41.9	44.3	43.3	1.583	1.74	1.83
Office and store machines and devices	66.95	73.33	75.28	41.1	41.9	40.9	1.630	1.75	1.84
Service-industry and household machines	67.28	70.44	75.81	41.7	40.6	41.2	1.613	1.74	1.84
Miscellaneous machinery parts	66.15	74.30	75.36	42.0	43.2	42.1	1.575	1.72	1.79

1950 data not strictly comparable with those shown for later years.

No. 233.—Hours and Gross Earnings of Production Workers or Nonsupervisory Employees: 1950 to 1952—Continued

INDUSTRY GROUP AND INDUSTRY	AVERAGE WEEKLY EARNINGS			AVERAGE WEEKLY HOURS			AVERAGE HOURLY EARNINGS		
	1950	1951	1952	1950	1951	1952	1950	1951	1952
Manufacturing—Con.									
Electrical machinery	$60.21	$64.84	$68.64	41.1	41.3	41.1	$1.465	$1.57	$1.67
Electrical generating, transmission, distribution, and industrial apparatus	63.75	70.31	73.99	41.1	42.1	41.8	1.551	1.67	1.77
Electrical appliances		67.32	72.32		39.6	40.4		1.70	1.79
Insulated wire and cable		64.87	72.11		42.4	43.7		1.53	1.65
Electrical equipment for vehicles	66.22	69.08	72.98	41.7	40.4	40.1	1.588	1.71	1.82
Electric lamps		58.20	58.89		40.7	39.0		1.43	1.51
Communication equipment	55.49	60.27	64.21	41.1	41.0	40.9	1.350	1.47	1.57
Miscellaneous electrical products		60.60	65.93		40.4	40.7		1.50	1.62
Transportation equipment	71.18	75.67	81.56	41.0	40.9	41.4	1.736	1.85	1.97
Automobiles	73.25	75.45	83.03	41.2	39.5	40.5	1.778	1.91	2.05
Aircraft and parts	68.39	78.40	81.70	41.6	43.8	43.0	1.644	1.79	1.90
Ship and boat building and repairing	63.28	69.83	75.17	38.4	39.9	40.2	1.648	1.75	1.87
Railroad equipment	66.33	76.48	77.74	39.6	40.9	40.7	1.675	1.87	1.91
Other transportation equipment	64.44	68.53	73.02	41.9	42.3	42.7	1.538	1.62	1.71
Instruments and related products	60.81	68.20	72.07	41.2	42.1	41.9	1.476	1.62	1.72
Laboratory, scientific, and engineering instruments		86.85	93.11		45.0	45.2		1.93	2.06
Mechanical measuring and controlling instruments		68.69	71.66		42.4	42.4		1.62	1.69
Optical instruments and lenses		72.07	76.50		42.9	42.5		1.68	1.80
Surgical, medical, and dental instruments		60.86	64.68		41.4	41.2		1.47	1.57
Ophthalmic goods	50.88	55.49	56.63	40.7	40.8	39.6	1.250	1.36	1.43
Photographic apparatus	65.59	73.08	76.73	41.2	42.0	41.7	1.592	1.74	1.84
Watches and clocks	53.25	59.57	60.55	39.8	40.8	40.1	1.338	1.46	1.51
Miscellaneous manufacturing industries	54.04	57.67	61.50	41.0	40.9	41.0	1.318	1.41	1.50
Jewelry, silverware, and plated ware	58.42	61.30	65.99	42.8	41.7	42.3	1.365	1.47	1.56
Musical instruments and parts		63.65	68.64		40.8	41.1		1.56	1.67
Toys and sporting goods	50.98	53.60	58.73	40.4	39.7	40.5	1.262	1.35	1.45
Pens, pencils, and other office supplies		54.91	57.26		41.6	40.9		1.32	1.40
Costume jewelry, buttons, notions	49.52	53.73	55.74	40.0	40.1	40.1	1.238	1.34	1.39
Fabricated plastic products		60.59	64.79		41.5	41.8		1.46	1.55
Other manufacturing industries		59.18	62.02		41.1	40.8		1.44	1.52
Transportation and public utilities:									
Local railway and bus lines	67.69	72.23	76.56	45.4	46.3	46.4	1.491	1.56	1.65
Telephone	54.38	58.26	61.22	38.9	39.1	38.5	1.398	1.49	1.59
Telegraph	64.19	68.24	72.48	44.7	44.6	43.4	1.436	1.53	1.67
Gas and electric utilities	66.60	71.65	75.12	41.6	41.9	41.5	1.601	1.71	1.81
Trade:									
Wholesale trade	60.36	64.31	67.80	40.7	40.7	40.6	1.483	1.58	1.67
Retail trade (except eating and drinking places)	47.63	50.65	52.67	40.5	40.2	39.9	1.176	1.26	1.32
General merchandise stores	35.95	37.75	38.41	36.8	36.3	35.9	.977	1.04	1.07
Food and liquor stores	51.79	54.54	56.52	40.4	40.1	39.8	1.282	1.36	1.42
Automotive and accessories dealers	61.65	66.28	69.61	45.7	45.4	45.2	1.349	1.46	1.54
Apparel and accessories stores	40.70	42.24	43.68	36.5	36.1	35.8	1.115	1.17	1.22
Finance, insurance and real estate:									
Banks and trust companies	46.44	50.32	52.50						
Security dealers and exchanges	81.48	83.66	81.07						
Insurance carriers	58.49	61.31	63.38						
Service:									
Hotels, year-round	33.85	35.42	37.06	43.9	43.2	42.6	.771	.82	.87
Laundries	35.47	37.81	38.63	41.2	41.1	41.1	.861	.92	.94
Cleaning and dyeing plants	41.69	43.99	45.10	41.2	41.5	41.0	1.012	1.06	1.10
Motion picture production and distribution [1]	92.79	93.95	90.49						

[1] 1950 data not strictly comparable with those shown for later years.

Source: Department of Labor, Bureau of Labor Statistics. Monthly figures published currently in the *Monthly Labor Review* and in mimeographed releases.

No. 234.—Average Rates Per Hour for Unskilled Labor Employed in Road Building on Federal-Aid Projects, by Geographic Divisions: 1931 to 1952

YEAR	United States [1]	New England	Middle Atlantic	South Atlantic	East South Central	West South Central	East North Central	West North Central	Mountain	Pacific
1931	$0.36	$0.45	$0.38	$0.21	$0.20	$0.23	$0.37	$0.36	$0.45	$0.51
1932	.32	.35	.36	.19	.19	.26	.36	.32	.44	.48
1933	.38	.37	.37	.26	.24	.31	.42	.37	.51	.52
1934	.42	.43	.41	.31	.30	.35	.50	.44	.55	.58
1935	.41	.45	.43	.31	.30	.36	.53	.47	.56	.57
1936	.40	.45	.47	.28	.29	.32	.52	.43	.53	.57
1937	.40	.47	.48	.26	.28	.30	.58	.46	.53	.62
1938	.40	.45	.50	.27	.28	.37	.60	.46	.55	.66
1939	.42	.48	.52	.29	.29	.37	.60	.45	.56	.65
1940	.46	.51	.54	.30	.34	.38	.62	.47	.55	.69
1941	.48	.55	.57	.36	.36	.40	.65	.50	.59	.75
1942	.58	.66	.67	.47	.42	.44	.76	.61	.72	.96
1943	.71	.89	.93	.58	.56	.54	.93	.78	.86	1.06
1944	.74	.91	.93	.66	.62	.61	.97	.81	.92	1.11
1945	.78	.95	.98	.69	.70	.68	.99	.84	.84	1.19
1946	.83	1.04	1.00	.71	.67	.70	1.00	.84	1.00	1.21
1947	.91	1.11	1.13	.74	.69	.76	1.13	.93	1.11	1.32
1948	1.02	1.24	1.26	.83	.73	.81	1.25	1.07	1.23	1.51
1949	1.13	1.18	1.48	.95	.78	.84	1.39	1.12	1.37	1.66
1950	1.19	1.43	1.54	.93	.88	.89	1.52	1.14	1.38	1.73
1951	1.27	1.44	1.57	.95	.93	.95	1.61	1.26	1.48	1.78
1952	1.41	1.47	1.84	1.00	.98	1.03	1.76	1.37	1.68	1.97

[1] Changes in United States wage rates are affected by relative number of men employed in areas with higher or lower wage rates.

Source: Department of Commerce, Bureau of Public Roads; records.

No. 235.—Indexes of Union Wage Rates and Weekly Hours in Selected Trades: 1943 to 1952

[Data for recent years cover 77 cities. From 1943 to 1946 study made as of July 1. Since 1947 data collected as of July 1 for all trades except streetcar and bus operators for whom data are shown as of Oct. 1, and printing data for 1948 as of Jan. 2. Relative rates are percentages which indicate changes in minimum hourly wage scales. Relative hours are percentages showing changes in straight-time weekly hours, account not being taken of loss of time from slack work or other causes, nor of overtime work. Year to year changes in union scales are based on comparable quotations for each trade weighted by membership for current year. For indexes based on 1939=100, see also *Historical Statistics*, series D 152-163]

[1947-49 average=100, except for printing where 1945-49 average=100]

TRADE	1943	1944	1945	1946	1947	1948	1949	1950	1951	1952
Building trades, total:										
Rate	70.2	70.8	72.2	80.5	92.1	101.8	106.1	110.7	117.8	125.1
Hours	100.9	101.1	101.1	100.1	100.0	100.0	100.1	100.2	100.1	100.1
Journeyman:										
Rate	71.2	71.7	73.0	80.9	92.3	101.7	106.0	110.5	117.4	124.6
Hours	101.0	101.2	101.2	100.1	99.9	100.0	100.1	100.2	100.1	100.1
Helpers and laborers:										
Rate	63.3	64.0	67.0	77.9	91.1	102.6	106.4	112.2	119.9	127.7
Hours	100.8	100.8	100.8	100.1	100.1	100.0	100.0	100.0	99.9	100.1
Printing trades, total:										
Rate	61.1	62.6	63.5	74.3	(1)	94.3	105.7	107.9	112.4	118.8
Hours	104.6	104.6	104.6	102.0	(1)	100.1	99.9	99.8	99.7	99.5
Book and job:										
Rate	60.7	62.3	63.1	74.2	(1)	94.3	105.7	108.2	112.1	119.3
Hours	106.1	106.1	106.1	102.4	(1)	100.1	99.9	99.8	99.5	99.2
Newspaper:										
Rate	61.9	63.3	64.1	74.5	(1)	94.3	105.7	107.4	112.7	117.6
Hours	101.7	101.7	101.7	101.3	(1)	100.3	99.7	99.5	99.4	99.3
Motortruck drivers and helpers:										
Rate	68.4	70.0	71.5	79.6	91.9	100.0	108.1	111.9	118.2	124.7
Hours	105.6	105.5	105.3	103.1	100.7	99.8	99.5	98.8	96.7	98.3
Streetcar and bus operators, rate	68.6	69.1	69.9	81.9	92.4	101.7	105.9	110.9	118.2	127.0
Bakery workers:										
Rate	70.1	70.6	71.5	81.9	92.9	100.3	106.8	111.3	117.7	123.9
Hours	100.6	100.6	100.6	100.2	100.1	100.1	99.7	99.7	99.6	99.6

[1] No study made in 1947.

Source: Department of Labor, Bureau of Labor Statistics; published annually in *Monthly Labor Review* and special pamphlets.

No. 236.—Estimated Number of Disabling Work Injuries, by Major Industry Group: 1948 to 1952

[In thousands. Includes employees and self-employed. For additional data on accidents, consult index]

INDUSTRY GROUP	1948	1949	1950	1951	1952 [1]	1948	1949	1950	1951	1952 [1]
	Total					Fatalities				
All industries [1]	2,019.9	1,870.0	1,952.0	2,121.0	2,031.0	16.0	15.0	15.5	16.0	15.6
Agriculture [3]	340.0	340.0	340.0	330.0	320.0	4.4	4.3	4.3	4.0	3.8
Mining and quarrying [4]	87.2	70.0	72.0	75.0	75.0	1.4	1.0	1.0	1.2	1.0
Construction [5]	193.0	183.0	205.0	230.0	220.0	2.1	2.1	2.3	2.5	2.4
Manufacturing [6]	469.2	381.0	426.0	510.0	450.0	2.6	2.3	2.6	2.7	2.4
Public utilities [6]	27.4	27.0	24.0	21.0	21.0	.4	.4	.3	.3	.3
Trade, wholesale and retail [6]	347.3	329.0	335.0	381.0	375.0	1.5	1.5	1.5	1.6	1.5
Transportation [7]	195.5	172.0	177.0	186.0	190.0	1.5	1.3	1.3	1.4	1.4
Finance, service, government, and miscellaneous industries [6]	360.3	368.0	373.0	388.0	380.0	2.2	2.1	2.2	2.3	2.2
	Permanent disabilities					Temporary-total disabilities				
All industries [1]	88.5	81.0	84.9	91.0	84.0	1,915.4	1,774.0	1,851.6	2,014.0	1,932.0
Agriculture [3]	[8]	[8]	[8]	[8]	[8]	[8]	[8]	[8]	[8]	[8]
Mining and quarrying [4]	[8]	[8]	[8]	[8]	[8]	[8]	[8]	[8]	[8]	[8]
Construction [5]	8.1	7.6	8.5	8.9	7.9	182.8	173.3	194.2	218.6	209.7
Manufacturing [6]	23.9	19.4	21.7	25.2	22.4	442.7	359.8	401.7	482.1	425.2
Public utilities [6]	.6	.6	.6	.6	.6	26.4	26.0	23.1	20.1	20.1
Trade, wholesale and retail [6]	8.5	8.0	8.1	8.8	8.0	337.3	319.5	325.4	370.6	365.5
Transportation [7]	[8]	[8]	[8]	[8]	[8]	[8]	[8]	[8]	[8]	[8]
Finance, service, government, and miscellaneous industries [6]	[8]	[8]	[8]	[8]	[8]	[8]	[8]	[8]	[8]	[8]

[1] Preliminary. [2] Does not include domestic service.
[3] Based on fragmentary data. [4] Based largely on Bureau of Mines data. [5] Based on small sample studies.
[6] Based on comprehensive survey. [7] Includes data for railroads, based on reports of Interstate Commerce Commission.
[8] Data not shown separately, but included in totals for all industries.

Source: Department of Labor, Bureau of Labor Statistics; *Monthly Labor Review* and *Handbook of Labor Statistics*.

No. 237.—Selected Injury-Frequency and Severity Rates: 1946 to 1951

[Frequency rate is average number of disabling injuries for each million employee-hours worked. Severity rate is average number of days lost for each thousand employee-hours worked. Standard time-loss ratings for fatalities and permanent disabilities are given in *Method of Compiling Industrial Injury Rates*, approved by American Standards Association, 1945]

INDUSTRY	INJURY-FREQUENCY RATES						SEVERITY RATES					
	1946	1947	1948	1949	1950	1951	1946	1947	1948	1949	1950	1951
Manufacturing	19.9	18.8	17.2	14.5	14.7	15.5	1.6	1.4	1.5	1.4	1.2	1.3
Construction	40.2	40.9	36.7	39.9	41.0	39.3	3.8	3.6	5.0	3.9	3.8	4.2
Heat, light and power	17.3	18.1	17.1	16.0	13.8	13.2	1.9	2.3	2.1	2.3	1.9	2.0
Waterworks	18.0	21.0	25.1	27.5	21.9	23.5	2.6	.9	1.5	1.1	1.6	1.4
Personal services	9.7	10.0	10.2	8.9	10.0	9.9	.6	.7	.5	.5	.5	.4
Business services	5.6	4.5	4.4	3.9	3.9	4.4	.3	.3	.3	.3	.3	.2
Educational services	7.8	8.0	8.3	7.6	7.9	8.2	.4	.5	.4	.4	.3	.6
Fire departments	23.5	24.8	30.9	32.1	35.5	30.4	1.9	2.4	1.6	2.5	1.9	2.1
Police departments	29.3	29.1	28.2	27.5	32.4	36.5	3.1	3.1	2.2	2.4	1.5	1.6
Trade	14.2	16.4	15.1	12.7	12.3	12.9	.8	.8	.9	.6	.6	.6

Source: Department of Labor, Bureau of Labor Statistics; published periodically in *Monthly Labor Review*.

No. 238.—Monthly Labor Turn-Over Rates (Per 100 Employees) in Manufacturing Industries: 1939 to 1952

[Month-to-month employment changes as indicated by labor turn-over rates are not precisely comparable to those in table 212, as the former are based on data for entire month while the latter refer to a one-week period ending nearest middle of month. Labor turn-over data, beginning in Jan. 1943, refer to wage and salary workers. The turn-over sample is not so extensive as that of the employment survey—proportionately fewer small plants are included; printing and publishing (since April 1943), canning and preserving, and several other industries are not covered]

CLASS OF TURN-OVER AND YEAR	Jan.	Feb.	Mar.	Apr.	May	June	July	Aug.	Sept.	Oct.	Nov.	Dec.
Accession:												
1939	4.1	3.1	3.3	2.9	3.3	3.9	4.2	5.1	6.2	5.9	4.1	2.8
1943	8.3	7.9	8.3	7.4	7.2	8.4	7.8	7.6	7.7	7.2	5.6	5.2
1951	5.2	4.5	4.6	4.5	4.5	4.9	4.2	4.5	4.3	4.4	3.9	3.0
1952	4.4	3.9	3.9	3.7	3.9	4.9	4.4	5.9	5.6	5.2	4.0	3.3
Total separation:												
1939	3.2	2.6	3.1	3.5	3.5	3.3	3.3	3.0	2.8	2.9	3.0	3.5
1943	7.1	7.1	7.7	7.5	6.7	7.1	7.6	8.3	8.1	7.0	6.4	6.6
1951	4.1	3.8	4.1	4.6	4.8	4.3	4.4	5.3	5.1	4.7	4.3	3.5
1952	4.0	3.9	3.7	4.1	3.9	3.9	5.0	4.6	4.9	4.2	3.5	3.5
Quit:												
1939 [1]	.9	.6	.8	.8	.7	.7	.7	.8	1.1	.9	.8	.7
1943	4.5	4.7	5.4	5.4	4.8	5.2	5.6	6.3	6.3	5.2	4.5	4.4
1951	2.1	2.1	2.5	2.7	2.8	2.5	2.4	3.1	3.1	2.5	1.9	1.4
1952	1.9	1.9	2.0	2.2	2.2	2.2	2.2	3.0	3.5	2.8	2.1	1.7
Discharge:												
1939	.1	.1	.1	.1	.1	.1	.1	.1	.1	.2	.2	.1
1943	.5	.5	.6	.5	.6	.6	.7	.7	.6	.6	.6	.6
1951	.3	.3	.3	.4	.4	.4	.3	.4	.3	.4	.3	.3
1952	.3	.3	.3	.3	.3	.3	.3	.3	.4	.4	.4	.3
Lay-off:												
1939	2.2	1.9	2.2	2.6	2.7	2.5	2.5	2.1	1.6	1.8	2.0	2.7
1943	.7	.5	.5	.6	.5	.5	.5	.5	.5	.6	.7	1.0
1951	1.0	.8	.8	1.0	1.2	1.0	1.3	1.4	1.3	1.4	1.7	1.5
1952	1.4	1.3	1.1	1.3	1.1	1.1	2.2	1.0	.7	.7	.7	1.1
Misc. (including military):												
1943	1.4	1.4	1.2	1.0	.8	.8	.8	.8	.7	.7	.6	.6
1951	.7	.6	.5	.5	.4	.4	.4	.4	.4	.4	.4	.3
1952	.4	.4	.3	.3	.3	.3	.3	.3	.3	.3	.3	.3

[1] Includes miscellaneous (including military) separations.

Source: Department of Labor, Bureau of Labor Statistics; *Monthly Labor Review*, and mimeographed releases.

No. 239.—Labor Union Membership: 1933 to 1951

[Membership data are estimates, not to be construed as data verified by Government. See also *Historical Statistics*, series D 218–223]

YEAR	All unions, total membership (1,000)	AMERICAN FEDERATION OF LABOR Number of affiliated unions	AMERICAN FEDERATION OF LABOR Total membership (1,000)[1]	CONGRESS OF INDUSTRIAL ORGANIZATIONS Number of affiliated unions	CONGRESS OF INDUSTRIAL ORGANIZATIONS Total membership (1,000)	Independent or unaffiliated unions, total membership (1,000)
1933	2,857	108	2,127			730
1934	3,249	109	2,608			641
1935	3,728	109	3,045			683
1936	4,164	111	3,422			742
1937	7,218	100	2,861	32	3,718	639
1938	8,265	102	3,623	42	4,038	604
1939	8,980	104	4,006	45	4,000	974
1940	8,944	105	4,247	42	3,625	1,072
1941	10,489	106	4,569	41	5,000	920
1942	10,762	102	5,483	39	4,195	1,084
1943	13,642	99	6,564	40	5,285	1,793
1944	14,621	100	6,807	41	5,935	1,879
1945	14,796	102	6,931	40	6,000	1,865
1946	14,974	102	7,152	40	6,000	1,822
1947	15,414	105	7,578	40	6,000	1,836
1948	[2] 14,000-16,000	105	7,221	40	(3)	2,200-2,500
1949	[2] 14,000-16,000	107	7,341	39	(3)	2,200-2,300
1950	[2] 14,000-16,000	107	7,143	30	(3)	2,400-2,800
1951	[2] 16,500-17,000	109	7,846	33	5,000	2,000-2,500

[1] Based upon per capita payments paid to AFL by affiliated unions which tend to understate total membership; average AFL membership in 1951 would appear to be about 9,500,000.
[2] Includes Canadian members of labor unions with headquarters in U. S. (796,000 in 1951).
[3] Not available.

Source: Department of Labor, Bureau of Labor Statistics; *Handbook of Labor Statistics*.

No. 240.—Work Stoppages: 1932 to 1952

[Excludes work stoppages involving fewer than 6 workers or lasting less than 1 day. Information obtained directly from companies and unions involved as well as from various Government labor boards, conciliation services, and other neutral parties. See also *Historical Statistics*, series D 224-229, 234]

YEAR	WORK STOPPAGES BEGINNING IN YEAR		WORKERS INVOLVED		MAN-DAYS IDLE			INDEXES (1935-39=100)		
	Number	Average duration (calendar days)	Number (thousands)[1]	Percent of total employed[2]	Number (thousands)	Percent of estimated working time[3]	Per worker involved	Work stoppages	Workers involved	Man-days idle
1932	841	19.6	324	1.8	10,500	0.23	32.4	29	29	62
1933	1,695	16.9	1,170	6.3	16,900	.36	14.4	59	104	100
1934	1,856	19.5	1,470	7.2	19,600	.38	13.4	65	130	116
1935	2,014	23.8	1,120	5.2	15,500	.29	13.8	70	99	91
1936	2,172	23.3	789	3.1	13,900	.21	17.6	76	70	82
1937	4,740	20.3	1,860	7.2	28,400	.43	15.3	166	165	168
1938	2,772	23.6	688	2.8	9,150	.15	13.3	97	61	54
1939	2,613	23.4	1,170	4.7	17,800	.28	15.2	91	104	105
1940	2,508	20.9	577	2.3	6,700	.10	11.6	88	51	40
1941	4,288	18.3	2,360	8.4	23,000	.32	9.8	150	210	136
1942	2,968	11.7	840	2.8	4,180	.05	5.0	104	75	25
1943	3,752	5.0	1,980	6.9	13,500	.15	6.8	131	176	80
1944	4,956	5.6	2,120	7.0	8,720	.09	4.1	173	188	51
1945	4,750	9.9	3,470	12.2	38,000	.47	11.0	166	308	224
1946	4,985	24.2	4,600	14.5	116,000	1.43	25.2	174	408	684
1947	3,693	25.6	2,170	6.5	34,600	.41	15.9	129	193	204
1948	3,419	21.8	1,960	5.5	34,100	.37	17.4	119	174	201
1949	3,606	22.5	3,030	9.0	50,500	.59	16.7	126	269	298
1950	4,843	19.2	2,410	6.9	38,800	.44	16.1	169	214	229
1951	4,737	17.4	2,220	5.5	22,900	.23	10.3	166	197	135
1952	5,117	19.6	3,540	8.8	59,100	.57	16.7	179	315	349

[1] Includes duplication where same workers were involved in more than 1 stoppage during year.

[2] "Total employed workers" includes all workers except those in occupations and professions where strikes rarely if ever occur. In general, "total employed workers" includes all employees except following groups: Government workers, agricultural wage earners on farms employing less than 6 workers, managerial and supervisory employees, and certain groups which because of nature of work cannot or do not strike (such as college professors, clergymen, and domestic servants). Self-employed and unemployed persons are excluded.

[3] Obtained by multiplying average number of employed workers each year by number of days worked by most employees during year.

Source: Department of Labor, Bureau of Labor Statistics; *Handbook of Labor Statistics* and other records. Basic data are currently published in May issues of *Monthly Labor Review*.

No. 241.—Work Stoppages—Major Issues Involved and Duration: 1950, 1951, and 1952

[See headnote, table 240. Data by issues based on stoppages beginning in year; duration data based on stoppages ending in year. See also *Historical Statistics*, series D 230-238]

MAJOR ISSUES AND DURATION	NUMBER OF WORK STOPPAGES			NUMBER OF WORKERS INVOLVED [1] (thousands)			NUMBER OF MAN-DAYS IDLE (thousands)		
	1950	1951	1952	1950	1951	1952	1950	1951	1952
MAJOR ISSUES									
All issues	4,843	4,737	5,117	2,410	2,220	3,540	38,800	22,900	59,100
Wages and hours	2,559	2,102	2,447	1,460	1,180	1,450	32,500	14,300	23,100
Union organization, wages and hours	270	206	240	54	53	725	789	1,840	28,100
Union organization	649	682	599	76	83	116	1,560	1,620	1,220
Other working conditions	1,065	1,342	1,378	746	761	974	3,450	4,180	5,320
Interunion or intraunion matters	255	326	334	66	132	256	419	894	1,240
Not reported	45	79	119	7	11	14	66	63	69
DURATION									
All stoppages	4,812	4,758	5,096	2,810	2,200	3,540	52,100	21,800	59,400
1 day	584	602	639	242	247	256	243	247	256
2-3 days	835	919	916	362	422	415	700	842	828
4 days and less than 1 week	739	723	784	361	358	471	1,250	1,130	1,510
1 week and less than ½ month	1,045	1,009	1,059	684	848	458	3,720	3,270	2,760
½ and less than 1 month	727	680	722	306	303	726	4,040	4,050	7,320
1 and less than 2 months	545	426	556	193	140	424	4,280	4,110	8,980
2 and less than 3 months	170	161	217	104	119	182	4,150	4,570	6,800
3 months or more	164	148	203	560	65	645	33,700	3,690	30,900

[1] See note 1, table 240.

Source: Department of Labor, Bureau of Labor Statistics; May issues of *Monthly Labor Review*; *Handbook of Labor Statistics*, and annual bulletin, *Analysis of Work Stoppages*.

No. 243.—Work Stoppages, by Industry Groups: 1947 to 1951

[See headnote, table 242]

GROUP	NUMBER OF WORK STOPPAGES BEGINNING [1]					NUMBER OF WORKERS INVOLVED [2]					NUMBER OF MAN-DAYS IDLE DURING YEAR				
	1947	1948	1949	1950	1951	1947	1948	1949	1950	1951	1947	1948	1949	1950	1951
All industries [1]	3,693	3,419	3,606	4,843	4,737	2,170,000	1,960,000	3,030,000	2,410,000	2,220,000	34,600,000	34,100,000	50,500,000	38,800,000	22,900,000
MANUFACTURING															
Food and kindred products	183	162	199	183	197	84,200	188,000	94,600	87,000	77,000	649,000	4,720,000	1,490,000	601,000	819,000
Tobacco manufactures	9	3	4	8	3	9,000	9,000	4,900	4,800	1,000	105,000	4,300	19,900	33,000	16,100
Textile-mill products	82	82	83	147	121	33,500	21,300	11,300	17,900	188,000	976,000	719,000	413,800	668,000	3,463,000
Apparel and other finished products, etc	131	131	102	187	210	10,500	24,800	92,000	27,800	14,000	199,000	207,000	173,000	223,000	264,000
Lumber and wood products (except furniture)	109	100	71	119	99	22,500	13,700	11,600	22,000	22,000	850,000	166,000	703,000	315,000	281,000
Furniture and fixtures	37	63	59	70	51	7,000	13,700	11,800	22,000	22,000	227,000	158,000	160,000	310,000	464,000
Paper and allied products	66	43	63	80	77	9,500	10,400	9,700	10,400	1,200	157,000	142,000	458,000	360,000	30,300
Printing, publishing, and allied industries											171,000	537,000	212,000	240,000	
Chemicals and allied products	94	73	72	98	67	30,800	21,400	30,000	30,300	20,000	432,000	538,000	353,000	793,000	301,000
Products of petroleum and coal	14	19	18	26	19	9,000	21,300	4,390	16,400	4,300	310,000	752,000	81,500	792,000	44,500
Rubber products	41	48	64	126	156	47,000	72,300	84,700	124,600	187,000	382,000	624,000	714,000	383,000	700,000
Leather and leather products	81	43	84	84	75	24,000	9,800	18,100	24,300	20,000	223,000	211,000	499,000	157,000	221,000
Stone, clay, and glass products	94	90	68	132	82	23,300	22,200	13,300	44,400	10,000	563,000	365,000	114,000	652,000	281,000
Primary metal industries	185	163	147	309	305	102,000	68,700	467,000	142,000	214,000	1,130,000	1,450,000	12,200,000	1,180,000	1,660,000
Fabricated metal products (except ordnance machinery, and transportation equipment)	215	131	131	278	212	114,300	37,000	94,000	93,300	94,300	883,000	403,000	1,020,000	902,000	1,240,000
Machinery (except electrical)	252	189	176	317	235	114,100	162,000	114,300	224,000	188,000	2,810,000	2,020,000	725,000	4,410,000	2,170,000
Electrical machinery	80	64	67	163	132	35,100	31,000	27,100	251,000	104,000	611,000	402,000	232,000	1,420,000	1,040,000
Transportation equipment	106	107	89	171	194	171,000	271,000	281,000	283,000	380,000	4,200,000	3,170,000	2,190,000	8,540,000	2,900,000
Professional, photographic, and controlling instruments; watches and clocks															
NON-MANUFACTURING															
Agriculture, forestry, and fishing	22	22	21	12	21	12,200	23,100	18,300	22,700	17,200	287,000	531,000	259,000	152,000	245,000
Mining	478	614	476	508	622	517,000	641,000	1,280,000	198,000	264,000	2,440,000	10,400,000	19,200,000	9,700,000	1,280,000
Construction	382	350	615	611	631	175,000	103,000	197,000	287,000	232,000	2,770,000	1,430,000	2,700,000	2,460,000	1,180,000
Trade	335	241	329	381	277	60,000	38,200	44,300	70,100	40,000	1,010,000	537,000	1,440,000	927,000	288,000
Finance, insurance, and real estate	33	18	22	31	21	2,600	1,900	1,900	11,000	14,300	46,300	46,900	23,300	52,500	23,000
Transportation, communication, etc	252	203	347	338	387	465,000	160,000	184,000	405,000	281,000	11,520,000	3,220,000	2,220,000	2,380,000	1,700,000
Services—personal, business, and other	147	150	130	152	179	20,200	30,700	14,000	13,800	31,300	723,000	300,000	219,000	101,000	235,000

[1] Strikes affecting more than 1 industry have been counted as separate strikes in each industry affected, with proper allocation of workers and man-days idle.

[2] Indicate duplication where same workers were involved in more than 1 stoppage during year.

[3] Includes industries not shown separately.

Source: Department of Labor, Bureau of Labor Statistics; published in May issues of *Monthly Labor Review*.

9. Military Services and Veterans' Affairs

This section includes data on the Army, the Navy, the Air Force, Selective Service, and on the various aspects of government programs for veterans.

Military services.—Data on the activities and status of the military services are compiled from information supplied by the various branches of the Armed Forces, the Bureau of the Budget, the Bureau of Labor Statistics, and the Selective Service System. For additional figures showing Federal Government expenditures on military services by branch of service, see Section 14, Federal Government Finances and Employment.

Veterans' Administration.—The Veterans' Administration administers laws authorizing benefits for former members of the armed forces and for the dependents and other beneficiaries of deceased former members of such forces. The Veterans' Administration benefits available under various acts of Congress include: Compensation for service-connected disability or death; pension for non-service-connected disability or death; emergency officers' retirement pay; vocational rehabilitation for service-connected disability; education and training; guaranty or insurance of home, farm, and business loans and, under certain conditions, direct home loans; readjustment allowances for unemployment or self-employment; U. S. Government and National Service Life Insurance; hospitalization; domiciliary care; outpatient medical and dental care for service-connected disability; prosthetic and other appliances; special housing for certain seriously disabled veterans; automobiles or other conveyances for certain disabled veterans; World War I adjusted service certificates; a guardianship program for the protection of estates derived from Veterans' Administration benefits paid to incompetent or minor beneficiaries; burial allowances; and burial flags.

Note.—This section presents data for the most recent year or period available on March 17, 1953, when the material was organized and sent to the printer.

No. 243.—Military Personnel and Pay: 1936 to 1950

[In thousands]

YEAR	PERSONNEL (AVERAGE FOR YEAR)					PAY (TOTAL FOR YEAR)[1]					
		Branch		Sex			Branch		Type of pay		
	Total	Army and Air Force[2]	Navy[3]	Men	Women	Total	Army and Air Force	Navy[4]	Pay roll[5]	Muster-ing-out pay	Family allow-ances[6]
1936	298	167	131	....	....	$272,473	$121,572	$150,901	$272,473	....	....
1937	318	178	140	....	....	290,592	132,089	158,503	290,592	....	....
1938	331	185	146	....	....	304,895	138,267	166,629	304,895	....	....
1939	345	192	154	....	....	331,523	155,482	176,041	331,523	....	....
1940	532	324	208	....	....	431,030	211,925	219,105	431,030	....	....
1941	1,644	1,291	353	1,639	5	1,262,927	855,900	407,027	1,262,927	....	....
1942	3,968	3,071	897	3,952	16	4,696,264	3,410,056	1,286,208	4,553,362	....	$142,902
1943	8,944	6,733	2,211	8,833	111	11,181,079	8,143,833	3,037,246	10,148,745	....	1,032,334
1944	11,372	7,889	3,483	11,161	211	16,840,205	11,130,018	5,710,187	14,067,813	$229,214	2,543,179
1945	11,608	7,734	3,874	11,350	258	20,392,101	13,478,703	6,913,398	16,097,640	1,367,520	2,926,941
1946	3,751	2,291	1,460	3,675	76	[7]10,093,750	6,285,071	3,808,679	6,463,180	2,177,308	736,949
1947	1,671	1,059	612	1,650	21	[7]5,350,396	3,461,632	1,888,764	3,336,934	177,015	308,220
1948	1,492	964	528	1,477	15	[7]3,442,961	2,136,384	1,305,577	2,993,124	95,452	317,258
1949	1,641	1,089	552	1,623	18	[7]3,647,147	2,343,312	1,303,834	3,268,443	49,680	328,385
1950[8]	1,513	1,020	493	1,492	22	[7]1,908,422	1,228,269	680,153	[9]1,889,843	18,439	(9)

[1] Excludes pay of retired and inactive reserve personnel.
[2] Prior to March 1944, includes persons on induction furlough; prior to June 1942 and after April 1945, includes Philippine Scouts.
[3] Covers Navy, Marine Corps, and Coast Guard. Includes missing personnel and personnel in hands of enemy.
[4] Covers Navy, Marine Corps, and Coast Guard. For Navy proper and Coast Guard, includes cash payments for clothing allowance balances.
[5] Includes men's share of family allowances but excludes Government's contribution. Represents actual expenditures for Army through April 1947 and for Coast Guard for all periods. Other data represent estimated obligations based on monthly personnel count.
[6] Represents Government's contribution. Excludes men's share.
[7] Includes leave payments of $716,313,000 in 1946, $1,528,227,000 in 1947, $37,127,000 in 1948, $639,000 in 1949, and $140,000 in 1950 (representing face value of bonds and cash payments) to enlisted personnel discharged prior to Sept. 1, 1946, for accrued and unused leave, and to officers and enlisted personnel then on active duty for leave accrued in excess of 60 days.
[8] Data for January-June only. Starting July 1950, data restricted. [9] Family allowances included under payroll.

Source: Department of Labor, Bureau of Labor Statistics. Current data restricted.

No. 244.—FEDERAL GOVERNMENT EXPENDITURES FOR MILITARY SERVICES AND VETERANS' SERVICES AND BENEFITS, IN RELATION TO TOTAL FEDERAL BUDGET EXPENDITURES: 1915 TO 1953

[Amounts in millions of dollars. For fiscal years ending June 30. Categories are from the functional classification of Budget expenditures (see table 300). Figures include expenditures of agencies, other than military and veterans' Administration, for activities primarily related to military and veterans' programs. For example, figures for military services include General Services Administration expenditures for stockpiling of strategic and critical materials, and expenditures of the National Advisory Committee for Aeronautics. Similarly, figures for veterans' services and benefits include General Services Administration expenditures for veterans' educational facilities and expenditures of the Department of Labor, Bureau of Veterans' Reemployment Rights. Figures exclude expenditures for programs which, though closely related to military or veterans' services, have a primary relationship to other categories of the functional classification. Examples of expenditures excluded are those by Corps of Engineers for rivers and harbors (included in Transportation and Communication and in Natural Resources), and those by Veterans' Administration for direct loans to veterans to aid in purchase of homes (included in Housing and Community Development). For further detail as to classification of particular figures in 1952 and 1953, see Special Analysis B of the Budget of the United States, 1954, pp. 1079-90]

FISCAL YEAR	Total budget expenditures	MILITARY SERVICES		VETERANS' SERVICES AND BENEFITS		FISCAL YEAR	Total budget expenditures	MILITARY SERVICES		VETERANS' SERVICES AND BENEFITS	
		Amount	Percent of total	Amount	Percent of total			Amount	Percent of total	Amount	Percent of total
1915	746	297	39.8	176	23.6	1935	6,521	711	10.9	607	9.3
1916	713	305	42.8	171	24.0	1936	8,494	914	10.8	2,350	27.7
1917	1,954	602	30.8	171	8.7	1937	7,756	937	12.1	1,137	14.6
1918	12,710	9,960	78.1	225	1.8	1938	6,979	1,030	14.7	581	8.3
1919	18,523	14,556	78.4	324	1.7	1939	8,966	1,077	12.0	560	6.2
1920	6,357	3,997	62.9	332	5.2	1940	9,183	1,500	16.3	552	6.0
1921	5,059	2,551	61.0	646	12.8	1941	13,387	6,387	47.7	566	4.2
1922	3,289	929	28.2	666	20.0	1942	34,187	26,600	78.6	550	1.6
1923	3,137	917	29.7	767	23.5	1943	79,622	70,267	88.2	606	.7
1924	2,908	887	22.4	676	23.4	1944	95,315	83,766	87.9	745	.8
1925	2,881	591	20.5	741	25.7	1945	98,703	84,570	85.7	2,090	2.1
1926	2,888	598	20.4	772	26.7	1946	60,703	45,134	74.3	4,416	7.3
1927	2,857	586	20.4	795	27.7	1947	39,289	14,316	36.4	7,381	18.8
1928	2,961	615	20.8	800	27.5	1948	33,791	10,963	32.4	6,554	19.7
1929	3,127	681	24.7	812	26.0	1949	40,057	11,915	29.7	6,726	16.8
1930	3,320	734	22.1	821	24.7	1950	40,156	12,381	30.6	6,647	16.5
1931	3,577	733	20.5	1,045	29.1	1951	44,633	20,462	45.8	5,342	12.0
1932	4,659	703	15.1	985	21.1	1952	66,145	39,727	60.1	4,863	7.4
1933	4,623	648	14.0	863	18.7	1953	74,503	44,390	59.5	4,546	6.1
1934	6,694	540	8.1	557	8.3						

¹ Estimated.

Source: Bureau of the Budget. 1948-1953, Special Analysis L, Budget of the United States Government, 1954.

No. 245.—FEDERAL GOVERNMENT EXPENDITURES FOR MILITARY SERVICES: 1951, 1952, AND 1953

[In billions of dollars. For fiscal years ending June 30]

CATEGORY, PROGRAM, OR AGENCY	1951 actual	1952 actual	1953 estimated
Total	20.5	39.7	44.4
Department of Defense, military functions:			
Military personnel	7.0	11.0	11.4
Operation and maintenance	5.4	12.2	9.8
Major procurement and production:			
Aircraft	2.4	5.4	7.4
Ships	.4	.6	.9
Other	2.1	5.0	6.2
Military construction	.4	1.8	2.3
Civilian components	.5	.6	.7
Research and development	.7	1.1	1.4
Industrial mobilization	.3	.2	.1
Department-wide activities	.6	1.0	1.0
Activities supporting military services:			
Stockpiling of strategic and critical materials	.7	.8	1.1
Other	.1	(¹)	.1

¹ Less than one million.

Source: Bureau of the Budget; Budget of the United States Government, 1954.

265554°—54——16

FIG. XVIII.—FEDERAL GOVERNMENT EXPENDITURES FOR MILITARY SERVICES AND VETERANS' SERVICES AND BENEFITS, IN RELATION TO TOTAL FEDERAL BUDGET EXPENDITURES: 1939 TO 1953

[See table 244]

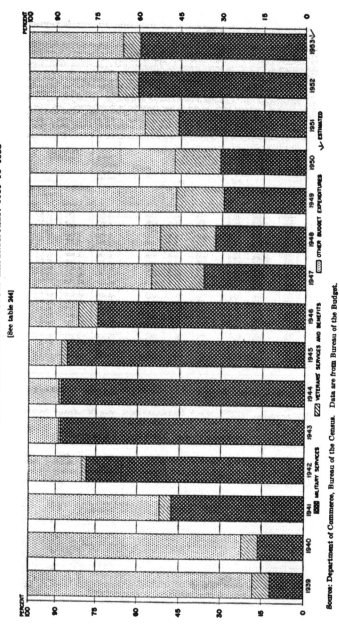

Source: Department of Commerce, Bureau of the Census. Data are from Bureau of the Budget.

No. 246.—MILITARY PERSONNEL ON ACTIVE DUTY: 1925 TO 1952

[Including National Guard, Reserve, and retired Regular personnel on extended or continuous active duty. Warrant officers and flight officers are included under officers. Enlisted data include West Point cadets, Annapolis midshipmen and other officer candidates. Excludes Coast Guard]

YEAR OR	Grand total	ARMY [1]			NAVY [2]			MARINE CORPS		
		Total	Officers	Enlisted	Total	Officers	Enlisted	Total	Officers	Enlisted
MALE AND FEMALE:										
1925		137,048	14,504	122,464	95,288	8,918	86,370	19,476	1,166	18,310
		134,088	14,142	120,706	93,416	9,091	84,325	19,154	1,170	17,976
		134,620	14,080	120,500	95,036	9,440	85,585	19,198	1,168	17,932
		134,684	14,019	122,066	96,013	9,401	86,612	19,020	1,168	17,852
		138,118	14,047	125,071	97,319	9,434	87,885	18,796	1,181	17,615
		138,376	14,151	125,227	97,044	9,548	87,534	18,380	1,208	18,172
1931		140,516	14,159	125,357	98,407	9,849	89,558	18,782	1,198	17,886
		134,957	14,111	120,846	93,435	9,967	83,468	16,561	1,196	15,365
		136,971	13,896	122,651	91,356	9,947	81,409	16,068	1,196	14,876
		138,464	13,761	124,703	92,489	9,972	82,496	16,341	1,187	15,174
		139,486	13,471	126,015	96,480	10,118	86,964	17,203	1,169	16,097
		167,816	13,512	154,304	106,198	10,347	95,946	17,248	1,209	16,040
		179,988	13,740	166,238	113,369	10,397	103,022	18,223	1,216	16,918
		185,488	13,975	171,513	118,436	10,738	107,911	18,356	1,309	16,997
		194,466	14,466	175,369	125,202	12,023	113,179	19,432	1,349	18,082
		269,023	18,326	250,697	160,997	13,644	147,353	28,277	1,738	26,545
1940	1,049,101	462,214	99,536	1,362,779	284,427	20,062	264,234	54,153	3,339	51,020
		675,060	204,432	2,860,186	640,570	69,844	571,008	143,413	7,153	135,475
		804,472	576,576	414,896	1,741,750	179,676	1,562,074	309,320	21,354	287,120
		760,780	775,080	7,217,770	981,348	278,132	2,705,212	475,604	32,798	442,816
		885,080	6637,376	2,053	250,517	331,370	3,045,035	87,087	427,443	
	7,621,978	591,011	287,144	1,633,867	985,288	141,239	844,049	155,679	14,208	141,471
		624,255	132,504	566,781	468,661	52,434	444,227	95,053	7,906	86,547
		680,473	66,178	485,549	419,162	45,416	373,746	84,007	6,007	78,081
		77,272	583,201	449,575	47,975	401,600	85,965	7,390	78,775	
		308,167	72,566	530,601	381,538	44,641	336,897	74,279	7,254	67,026
1950	3,249,074	591,774	130,540	1,401,254	736,680	70,513	666,167	192,620	15,150	177,470
	3,685,975	1,596,419	148,427	1,447,992	824,265	82,247	742,018	261,977	16,413	245,554
Regulars:										
1925	4,304	5,432	5,432	....	671	671	....			
	14,323	12,475	12,475	....	1,776	1,776	....			
	128,165	91,548	34,222	56,326	30,973	9,266	21,717	5,643	344	5,399
	119,623	47,736	71,267	73,991	16,610	57,381	17,477	797	16,680	
	132,350	16,860	16,609	22,413	8,391	14,022	2,230	163	2,067	
	19,794	14,744	7,660	7,084	4,775	2,681	2,094	248	215	
	14,452	8,086	4,239	3,206	4,054	2,436	1,618	167	8	159
	15,082	9,277	5,021	4,256	5,131	2,511	2,620	352	30	322
	22,092	10,982	4,431	6,551	5,193	2,447	2,746	580	45	535
1951	28,925	17,852	4,970	10,882	9,458	4,190	5,268	2,055	63	2,992
	42,686	17,484	7,206	10,228	11,366	4,026	7,342	3,462	115	3,347

YEAR	AIR FORCE [6]						Army personnel assigned to Air Force command [7]	Air Force personnel assigned to Army command [8]
	Male and female			Female				
	Total	Officers	Enlisted	Total	Officers	Enlisted		
1948	387,730	48,957	338,773	2,166	733	1,433	27,902	8,419
1949	419,347	57,851	361,496	3,320	973	2,347	25,496	139
1950	411,277	57,005	354,271	5,314	1,532	3,782	13,725	....
1951	788,381	107,099	681,282	10,349	2,735	7,514	13,978	....
1952	983,251	128,742	854,509	14,770	3,827	10,943	86,930	....

[1] Includes Philippine Scouts; excludes contract surgeons. Data for 1925–47 include personnel in Army Air Forces and its predecessors (Air Service and Air Corps). For 1948 and 1949 includes Air Force personnel assigned to Army command; excludes Army personnel assigned to Air Force command. Beginning 1950, figures consist entirely of Army Department personnel, since Air Force Department personnel no longer assigned to U. S. Army organizations. [2] Nurse Corps included with officers. [3] Includes field clerks.
[3] Includes 178 Navy medical officers on duty with Army.
[4] Number of women in services 1925 to 1940 relatively small.
[6] 1948 and 1949 include Army personnel assigned to Air Force command; exclude Air Force personnel assigned to Army command. No Air Force personnel assigned to Army command beginning 1950.
[7] Included in Air Force. [8] Included in Army.
[9] Includes 9,787 Army personnel in training for subsequent assignment to Air Force commands.

Source: Department of Defense, Office of Secretary of Defense; annual reports of the Departments, and De-

No. 247.—PRINCIPAL WARS IN WHICH THE ARMY OF THE UNITED STATES HAS ENGAGED—NUMBER OF TROOPS AND CASUALTIES

ACTION	Total troops engaged	CASUALTIES							
		Deaths					Wounded (not mortally)	Taken prisoner	Missing
		Total	Killed in action	Died of wounds	Died of disease	Other			
War of the Revolution.	(¹)	² 4,044					6,004	6,642	2,124
War of 1812	³ 528,274	³ 1,950					4,000		
Mexican War	116,597	12,946	1,044	505	(⁴)	(⁴)	3,393		
Civil War ⁵	2,128,948	359,528	67,058	43,012	224,586	24,872	(⁶)	211,411	
Spanish American War	280,564	6,472	496	202	5,423	349	2,974		
Philippine Insurrection	126,468	4,165	777	227	2,572	589	2,911		
China Relief Expedition	5,000	102	33	18	47	4			
World War I	4,057,101	119,956	37,568	12,942	62,670	6,776	⁷ 193,663	4,416	
World War II	⁸ 10,400,000	⁹ 306,005	175,407	26,706	15,120	¹⁰ 88,772	¹¹ 571,822	¹² 114,558	¹³ 1,204

¹ Estimates on total troops run from 250,000 to 395,000. Greatest strength of Continental Army was about 35,000 in November 1778.
² Number of battle deaths accounted for on available records. Total number undoubtedly much larger. No figures available on deaths by disease or other causes.
³ Believed to represent enlistments and not individual soldiers, hence is considerably in excess of actual number of troops employed.
⁴ Number who died of disease cannot be definitely determined. Records show 10,986 "ordinary deaths" and 411 accidental and other deaths. It is believed that many who died of wounds are reported as cases of ordinary deaths.
⁵ Union only. Number of deaths believed to be somewhat larger as records, especially those of southern prisoners, are far from complete.
⁶ Not available.
⁷ Number incurred among 182,674 individuals.
⁸ Represents Army and Air Force personnel, Dec. 1, 1941 through Aug. 31, 1945.
⁹ Represents Army and Air Force personnel for period, Dec. 1, 1941 through Dec. 31, 1945. Battle casualties audited as of July 1, 1946, subject to change. Nonbattle casualties based on records through Jan. 31, 1948.
¹⁰ Includes 23,042 declared dead, 11,332 died of other causes as a result of battle, and 562 reported dead from missing in action. Includes deaths from accidents, homicide, and suicide.
¹¹ Excludes 26,706 who subsequently died of wounds.
¹² Excludes 11,332 who died of other causes (see footnote 10).
¹³ Excludes 23,042 declared dead, 562 reported dead from missing in action (see footnote 10), and 23,941 who were returned to duty. An audit, as of Sept. 30, 1947, shows a new balance of 12 remaining in a missing status.

Source: Department of the Army; *The Army Almanac, 1950.*

No. 248.—NAVY AND MARINE CORPS CASUALTIES IN PRINCIPAL WARS IN WHICH THE UNITED STATES HAS ENGAGED

ACTION	Total	NAVY		MARINE CORPS	
		Killed	Wounded	Killed	Wounded
War of the Revolution	575	342	114	49	70
War of 1812	815	265	439	45	66
Mexican War	62	1	3	11	47
Civil War, 1861–65	4,101	2,112	1,710	148	131
Spanish American War	84	10	47	6	21
Philippine Insurrection	9	9			
China Relief Expedition, 1900	56	4	26	9	17
Occupation of Vera Cruz, 1914	92	17	57	5	13
World War I, 6 April 1917–11 November 1918	¹ 13,236	² 436	³ 819	2,461	9,520
Nicaragua Pacification, 1927–33	116	1	2	47	66
World War II, 7 December 1941–31 December 1946	161,541	⁴ 36,950	⁵ 37,778	19,606	67,207

¹ Excludes 856 missing in action.
² Excludes 457 lost at sea.
³ Excludes 65 who subsequently died but counted as killed.
⁴ Includes 111 killed in October 1941.
⁵ Includes 29 wounded in October 1941; excludes 1,838 who subsequently died but counted as killed.

Source: Department of Navy and Marine Corps. Data published in *The Army Almanac, 1950.*

No. 249.—Ships of the U. S. Navy as of June 30: 1950 to 1952

[Includes vessels in active fleet, reserve fleet, under conversion for change of status in shipyards, in custody of or use by district commandants, naval reserve training, and on loan. Excludes service craft and floating dry docks]

CLASS	1950	1951	1952
Total	2,844	3,065	3,137
Total, excluding Military Sea Transportation Service vessels [1]	2,659	2,621	2,622
Warships	729	720	727
Amphibious	761	746	709
Mine warfare vessels	212	213	240
Patrol vessels	398	424	411
Auxiliary vessels	559	518	535
Military Sea Transportation Service vessels [2]	185	444	515

[1] Excludes ships under construction, small boats, and small landing craft.
[2] Includes all Military Sea Transportation Service ships and miscellaneous craft.

Source: Department of the Navy, Office of the Comptroller.

No. 250.—Aircraft of the U. S. Navy, as of January 1: 1943 to 1952

TYPE	1943	1944	1945	1946	1947	1948	1949	1950	1951	1952
Number, total	11,813	25,892	36,721	30,535	[1] 15,983	14,664	14,947	14,015	13,412	13,213
Combat	5,434	15,164	25,780	19,402	8,104	8,505	8,416	7,450	(3)	(3)
Transport and utility	624	1,367	2,437	2,876	1,268	1,225	1,300	1,374		
Training [2]	5,714	9,057	7,883	7,280	6,593	4,910	5,148	5,133		
Miscellaneous	41	304	621	977	18	24	83	58		

[1] Partly estimated.
[2] Includes combat-type airplanes used for training.
[3] Not available.

Source: Navy Department, Bureau of Aeronautics.

No. 251.—Airplanes on Hand in the U. S. Air Force, as of January 1: 1942 to 1952

TYPE	1942	1943	1944	1945	1946	1947	1948	1949	1950	1951	1952
Total	12,297	33,304	64,232	72,726	44,782	30,035	23,814	20,068	17,222	17,337	19,904
Combat	4,477	11,607	27,448	41,961	26,077	17,186	13,118	9,031	8,004	8,159	(1)
Transport	254	1,857	6,466	10,456	7,500	4,538	3,536	3,712	2,839	2,859	
Trainer	7,340	17,044	26,051	17,060	7,617	6,297	5,714	6,177	5,811	5,961	
Communications	226	2,796	4,267	3,249	3,588	2,014	1,446	1,148	568	358	

[1] Not available.

Source: Department of the Air Force, United States Air Force Statistical Digest.

No. 252.—Summary of Selective Service Data, by States and Other Areas,
as of June 30, 1952

[State allocations of registrants forwarded by Selective Service local boards for examination and induction are affected by number of voluntary enlistments and number ordered to active duty as Armed Forces reserves in addition to number deferred and eligible. Each State is credited with its inductions as well as its enlistments and reserves called to active duty. Because of time lag in reporting to local boards, credits given for each State are not necessarily in complete accord with present strength of Armed Forces contributed by that State]

STATE OR OTHER AREA	NUMBER OF LIVING REGISTRANTS				Registrants forwarded to Armed Forces [2][3]	REJECTIONS [3]		Inductions [3]	Net credits [4]
	All ages	18-18½	18½-26	26 and over [1]		Pre-induction examination	Induction inspection		
Total	13,225,218	426,453	8,805,846	3,992,919	2,695,819	1,078,013	52,487	998,531	3,189,477
Continental U. S.	12,925,825	416,601	8,586,197	3,923,627	2,596,485	1,013,811	51,172	967,386	3,138,577
Alabama	289,311	10,491	202,357	76,463	61,303	34,484	1,534	18,175	68,222
Arizona	63,122	2,120	43,108	17,895	11,763	4,824	221	3,841	16,273
Arkansas	171,679	6,485	120,671	44,523	35,947	21,457	1,187	9,718	38,257
California	809,502	19,826	512,445	277,231	136,906	41,253	3,081	51,468	197,134
Colorado	110,323	3,695	72,816	33,812	18,288	5,658	320	6,750	28,098
Connecticut	165,369	4,929	109,940	50,500	28,257	9,223	447	11,335	46,835
Delaware	26,295	797	16,945	8,553	5,798	2,352	62	1,999	5,893
Dist. of Col.	62,710	1,291	38,915	22,504	11,279	4,607	170	4,799	15,355
Florida	207,133	6,759	139,928	60,446	34,219	15,133	460	12,123	54,682
Georgia	312,149	13,581	218,133	80,435	63,586	33,361	1,082	19,754	75,748
Idaho	52,395	1,727	35,481	15,187	7,017	2,145	109	3,422	13,683
Illinois	721,883	20,013	465,308	236,562	180,770	61,176	5,703	65,555	171,518
Indiana	344,099	10,501	224,823	108,775	65,112	20,671	1,184	29,866	81,811
Iowa	220,750	7,250	148,120	65,389	41,382	9,926	550	20,196	59,894
Kansas	162,212	5,870	106,907	49,435	27,120	6,643	850	11,924	41,451
Kentucky	274,950	10,350	190,401	74,199	76,076	36,742	1,389	24,066	66,643
Louisiana	241,304	7,811	165,482	68,011	69,998	41,114	1,515	16,362	51,578
Maine	81,324	2,485	55,287	23,552	11,653	4,806	176	4,771	24,346
Maryland	191,839	5,766	124,889	61,184	36,660	13,597	949	14,927	48,456
Massachusetts	382,407	10,618	248,044	123,745	58,376	18,194	879	22,603	109,490
Michigan	568,157	17,632	368,889	181,636	136,862	51,448	2,164	51,264	131,452
Minnesota	250,616	8,141	166,430	76,045	43,888	10,487	824	18,933	64,048
Mississippi	201,013	7,004	144,282	49,727	42,426	24,128	705	13,669	43,230
Missouri	329,466	10,897	219,227	99,342	73,720	26,410	1,393	29,233	83,550
Montana	49,548	1,869	32,516	15,163	9,353	2,462	125	3,471	13,435
Nebraska	117,288	3,843	78,001	35,444	22,371	6,326	331	10,770	31,470
Nevada	11,537	382	7,424	3,731	1,471	441	43	783	3,473
New Hampshire	44,311	1,627	29,255	13,429	6,631	1,961	91	2,507	13,788
New Jersey	393,755	10,325	258,067	125,363	83,380	27,348	809	34,573	96,873
New Mexico	60,970	2,711	41,263	16,996	11,584	4,892	338	4,533	13,647
New York City	658,759	15,765	433,379	209,615	200,661	79,024	3,226	65,485	150,406
New York (excluding New York City)	555,526	24,219	374,213	157,094	93,096	29,187	1,468	39,535	134,848
North Carolina	398,483	14,345	274,380	109,758	77,180	36,335	1,726	27,324	85,580
North Dakota	59,710	2,081	41,794	15,835	12,318	2,826	123	5,671	16,958
Ohio	680,764	22,033	437,031	221,700	144,801	48,959	2,009	56,561	164,315
Oklahoma	198,231	7,619	133,997	56,615	25,453	9,358	802	9,957	47,702
Oregon	121,376	3,707	78,738	38,931	14,450	5,269	329	7,021	31,431
Pennsylvania	930,473	27,931	608,094	294,448	128,539	51,807	2,972	60,228	210,333
Rhode Island	65,638	2,060	41,599	21,950	14,884	5,561	102	4,648	19,160
South Carolina	202,025	7,309	142,212	52,504	54,498	35,121	1,102	14,979	45,972
South Dakota	59,617	2,204	40,511	16,902	12,354	3,205	146	6,089	15,984
Tennessee	301,874	10,749	208,167	82,958	67,743	34,154	1,272	21,209	73,100
Texas	691,221	22,992	464,164	204,065	102,462	39,230	3,124	41,995	150,750
Utah	65,438	2,463	43,887	19,088	13,233	3,374	140	4,865	15,406
Vermont	32,338	1,178	22,072	9,088	4,470	1,711	73	1,590	9,355
Virginia	293,759	10,239	196,279	87,241	70,932	35,945	1,258	23,024	72,615
Washington	175,318	5,301	114,701	58,316	28,837	8,982	581	10,493	46,036
West Virginia	194,974	6,777	132,591	55,606	42,009	17,564	700	14,925	54,647
Wisconsin	295,230	9,441	196,708	89,081	72,011	21,949	1,264	26,827	77,728
Wyoming	24,635	763	16,326	7,546	3,388	981	64	1,570	5,927
Alaska	8,170	246	5,271	2,653	1,436	537	49	781	1,404
Canal Zone	544	40	480	24	131	15	1	35	98
Guam	6,148	139	5,779	230	244	97	2	81	798
Hawaii	50,930	1,698	34,360	14,872	13,346	5,751	40	6,060	14,120
Puerto Rico	231,269	8,245	171,971	51,053	82,910	57,087	1,169	23,679	33,836
Virgin Islands	2,332	84	1,788	460	1,267	715	4	509	644

[1] Legally exempted registrants; no longer liable for service because of age.

[2] Cumulative since the inception of the Universal Military Training and Service Act, as amended, September 1948.

[3] Includes voluntary enlistments and deferments between time of preinduction examination and notice of induction.

[4] Cumulative net credits resulting from inductions plus home address reports minus separation reports, as reported by the armed forces September 1948 through June 1952.

Source: Selective Service System, National Headquarters.

No. **253.**—CLASSIFICATION STATUS OF SELECTIVE SERVICE REGISTRANTS, AGED 18½–26: DECEMBER 31, 1951 AND 1952

[In thousands]

CLASSIFICATION STATUS	1951 [1]		1952 [1]	
	Number	Percent	Number	Percent
Total	8,638	100.0	8,993	100.0
Unclassified	[2] 468	5.4	[2] 164	1.8
Classified	8,170	94.6	8,829	98.2
Available for military service (I–A & I–A–O)	1,155	13.4	1,117	12.4
Inducted or enlisted, including discharges and reserves (I–C)	2,083	24.1	3,031	33.7
Member of reserve component or National Guard (I–D)	292	3.4	333	3.7
Occupational deferments (II–A, II–A (App.), II–C, II–S, and I–S) [3]	364	4.2	405	4.5
Dependency (III–A)	923	10.7	1,077	12.0
Veteran of World War II (IV–A)	1,996	23.1	1,253	13.9
Physically, mentally, or morally unfit (IV–F)	1,282	14.8	1,532	17.1
Miscellaneous deferments (IV–B, IV–C, IV–D, I–O)	75	.9	81	.9

[1] Under Universal Military Training and Service Act, as amended, approved June 19, 1951 (1) age of military liability was extended to 35 years for certain specified kinds of registrants, and (2) registrants under 19 years of age were made eligible for classification.
[2] Derived.
[3] Class II–S, college students, and Class I–S, high school and college students, did not come into existence until Sept. 27, 1951.

Source: Selective Service System, National Headquarters.

No. **254.**—ESTIMATED NUMBER OF VETERANS IN CIVIL LIFE, BY PERIOD OF SERVICE: 1945 TO 1952

[Thousands]

PERIOD OF SERVICE	ESTIMATED NUMBER AS OF JUNE 30							
	1945	1946	1947	1948	1949	1950	1951	1952
All veterans [1]	6,498	16,655	18,262	18,745	18,943	19,076	18,869	19,288
World War II [2]	2,469	12,687	14,361	14,914	15,182	15,386	15,200	15,369
No service since June 27, 1950	2,469	12,687	14,361	14,914	15,182	15,386	15,050	14,827
And service since June 27, 1950							150	542
Service since June 27, 1950 [3]							226	921
No service in World War II							76	379
And service in World War II							150	542
World War I [4]	3,821	3,766	3,711	3,651	3,587	3,518	3,446	3,381
Other wars and Regular Establishment [5]	208	200	190	180	174	172	167	150

[1] Excludes persons who served in the Armed Forces only in peacetime (Regular Establishment) unless they are receiving Veterans' Administration compensation for service-connected disability. A small but unknown number of persons with service in two or more periods prior to June 27, 1950 are included more than once. Veterans with service both in World War II and since June 27, 1950 are counted only once.
[2] Estimated cumulative returns to civil life since September 16, 1940 of all persons who served in the Armed Forces of the United States at any time through July 25, 1947 (including persons who served both in that period and since June 27, 1950), less estimated deaths out of service and less estimated returns to active duty from civil life.
[3] Estimated cumulative returns to civil life since June 27, 1950 of all persons who served in the Armed Forces of the United States since that date (including persons who had also served in World War II), less estimated deaths out of service and less estimated returns to active duty from civil life.
[4] Estimated by application of appropriate survival rates to the 1918 age distribution of World War I participants
[5] Includes veterans of Civil War, Indian Wars, Spanish-American War. Only former members of Regular Establishment (peacetime service only) who are receiving Veterans' Administration compensation for service-connected disability are included. Spanish-American War totals estimated by application of appropriate survival rates to the 1902 age distribution of living Spanish-American War participants.

Source: Veterans' Administration, records.

No. 255.—EXPENDITURES OF VETERANS' ADMINISTRATION AND PREDECESSOR ORGANIZATIONS

[In thousands of dollars]

| YEAR ENDING JUNE 30— | Total[1] | COMPENSATION AND PENSIONS | | | | | | Military and naval insurance | U. S. Government life insurance fund |
		Civil War	Spanish-American War	World War I	World War II	Other wars[2]	Regular Establishment		
Total.....	77,784,943	8,174,639	3,245,699	9,081,945	8,074,631	323,782	576,564	2,282,597	1,378,966
To 1937.......	22,380,882	7,934,171	1,168,695	3,365,763	....	267,056	147,507	2,006,484	311,411
1938.......	629,630	39,233	118,183	230,203	....	3,650	11,515	82,522	31,636
1939.......	600,222	33,179	125,298	242,866	....	3,536	11,840	38,304	35,331
1940.......	639,127	27,790	127,427	254,846	....	3,278	15,812	19,602	69,813
1941.......	614,357	23,174	127,357	261,940	....	2,989	17,669	15,391	55,827
1942.......	647,334	19,525	128,674	263,871	201	2,734	19,294	15,491	44,481
1943.......	656,652	16,553	122,989	270,957	6,591	2,471	22,812	14,489	39,815
1944.......	828,392	13,896	125,056	268,269	61,668	2,279	23,207	10,298	44,719
1945.......	2,271,318	11,874	142,797	312,244	238,128	2,301	24,900	19,756	32,273
1946.......	4,772,072	10,417	139,342	345,510	694,342	2,125	24,061	15,385	48,594
1947.......	7,805,355	9,035	145,130	436,665	1,110,033	1,960	29,156	11,105	56,095
1948.......	7,184,961	9,019	165,098	471,952	1,143,095	1,922	29,605	8,316	[8] 295,699
1949.......	7,076,749	7,888	162,583	513,888	1,165,292	1,876	39,782	7,386	56,363
1950.......	9,782,983	6,823	156,158	572,594	1,223,182	1,874	49,037	6,765	113,603
1951.......	5,937,501	6,930	149,624	619,167	1,202,734	1,798	55,740	5,960	59,353
1952.......	5,987,208	5,133	144,288	651,210	1,228,565	22,133	54,647	5,178	83,953

| YEAR ENDING JUNE 30— | NATIONAL SERVICE LIFE INSURANCE | | Adjusted service certificates[6] | READJUSTMENT BENEFITS (PUBLIC LAW 346) | | | Hospital and domiciliary facilities (construction and related costs)[7] | Administration and other benefits[8] | All other[9] |
	Appropriation[4]	Trust fund[5]		Education and training	Readjustment allowances for unemployment and self-employment	Loan guaranty			
Total....	4,412,226	5,990,088	3,816,509	13,548,765	3,805,830	412,247	860,216	7,584,525	4,216,404
To 1937....	....	....	3,718,626	....	....	....	96,697	923,257	2,441,215
1938........	....	....	13,838	....	....	....	9,347	85,881	3,822
1939........	....	....	7,414	....	....	....	10,958	87,913	3,493
1940........	....	....	9,235	....	....	....	13,638	94,456	3,230
1941........	....	7	2,657	....	....	....	4,541	99,545	3,260
1942........	....	960	43,227	....	....	....	4,045	104,696	3,135
1943........	31,542	6,549	997	....	....	....	2,720	114,662	3,505
1944........	102,429	33,898	1,648	....	....	....	4,851	130,980	5,200
1945........	1,117,548	136,847	11,223	8,693	23,512	....	15,801	159,559	13,562
1946........	1,380,001	285,910	3,820	350,561	1,000,909	5,229	34,313	384,350	47,303
1947........	828,473	255,816	1,075	2,122,292	1,447,916	75,493	153,880	882,129	229,102
1948........	142,507	[10] 374,868	906	2,498,884	677,256	64,354	16,990	911,089	373,409
1949........	87,405	339,453	614	2,703,863	509,592	40,037	124,024	941,186	375,537
1950........	473,581	2,080,657	576	2,595,728	138,191	40,672	151,532	901,988	313,223
1951........	44,310	542,045	356	1,943,341	8,378	90,108	103,878	864,570	239,219
1952........	204,430	1,014,078	295	1,325,403	76	79,355	113,011	898,264	158,189

[1] $65,865,513,056 was paid from appropriations and $11,919,430,753 from trust and working funds.

[2] War of the Revolution, $70,000,000; War of 1812, $46,218,391; Indian Wars, $107,863,642; Mexican Wars, $61,763,723; unclassified, $16,513,426; Korean Conflict, $21,154,282; $268,114 for participants in yellow fever experiments, 1932–51.

[3] Includes a cumulative adjustment for prior years of $225,715,729.

[4] Amount transferred by voucher to NSLI trust fund for payment of claims traceable to extra hazards of military or naval service and certain direct payments.

[5] Includes special dividend as follows: 1950, $2,634,537,050; 1951, $221,619,914; and 1952, $556,362,479.

[6] Includes amounts reimbursed to U. S. Government Life Insurance fund on account loans made from that fund.

[7] Includes expenditures from funds allotted under National Recovery Act of 1933, Public Works Administration Act of 1938 and Grants to Republic of Philippines for construction and equipping of hospitals for fiscal year 1952, $200,000. Also includes $415,323,692 transferred to the Department of the Army, Corps of Engineers, for the construction of hospitals as follows: 1946, $7,500,000; 1947, $135,250,000; 1949, $90,000,000; 1950, $100,000,000; 1951, $42,573,692; and 1952, $40,000,000.

[8] Includes salaries and other administrative costs. Also includes fees for counseling of veterans; partial benefit payments made under Public Laws 16 and 346 for fiscal years 1944–47; reimbursement to States for administrative expenses, and expenditures under Federal Tort Claims Act. Medical, hospital and domiciliary services costs included beginning fiscal year 1932; expenditures for State and Territorial Homes included beginning fiscal year 1934.

[9] Includes expenditures for medical, hospital and domiciliary services prior to fiscal 1932; National Home for Disabled Volunteer Soldiers and State and Territorial Homes prior to fiscal year 1934; payments for subsistence, tuition, supplies, and equipment under Public Law 16; burial allowances; homes for paraplegics; automobiles and other conveyances for disabled veterans; vocational training (World War I); allotments and allowances; marine and seamen's insurance; operation of Civil Service and Canal Zone retirements and disability systems to August 31, 1934; Servicemen's Indemnities; Veterans' Special Term Insurance; Service Disabled Veterans' Insurance; and other miscellaneous expenditures.

[10] Includes a cumulative adjustment for prior years of $69,935,268.

Source: Veterans' Administration, Annual Report of Administrator of Veterans' Affairs.

No. 256.—Estimated Distribution of Selected Federal Expenditures for Veterans, by States: Year Ending June 30, 1952

[In thousands of dollars]

STATE	Total expenditures [1]	Compensations and pensions [2]	National Service Life Insurance (death benefits)	Vocational rehabilitation (Public Law 16)	READJUSTMENT BENEFITS (Public Law 346)		Administration and other benefits	Hospital and domiciliary facilities (construction and related costs)
					Education and training	Loan guaranty		
Total	5,019,513	2,105,973	427,854	97,902	1,326,466	75,355	916,264	73,011
Continental U. S.	4,925,373	2,027,841	402,904	97,347	1,297,912	75,207	905,500	72,800
Alabama	122,308	46,204	7,465	3,204	47,071	2,327	16,667	631
Alaska	20,091	14,494	2,140	539	5,062	173	7,437	112
Arizona	54,715	30,691	4,857	2,868	31,474	368	13,907	206
Arkansas	362,021	162,660	29,972	5,730	73,784	15,207	71,910	2,647
California	54,567	21,779	4,108	1,664	16,374	534	12,990	946
Colorado	47,362	25,206	5,435	790	7,794	1,148	6,188	672
Connecticut	8,351	3,661	711	57	1,050	301	2,401	29
Delaware	116,337	17,872	1,960	725	17,182	1,480	73,361	3,964
Dist. of Columbia	115,792	50,480	7,067	1,927	39,126	1,816	14,901	215
Florida	127,757	42,885	6,053	3,745	47,733	1,601	21,364	1,027
Georgia	20,985	7,645	1,823	903	7,160	146	2,940	305
Idaho	225,068	98,578	23,900	2,479	52,239	2,312	46,910	13,108
Illinois	92,679	45,749	10,050	1,849	23,748	1,146	15,380	1,460
Indiana	75,641	29,069	7,464	1,856	22,185	616	12,352	381
Iowa	56,068	24,461	5,613	842	10,805	434	15,562	207
Kansas	102,494	49,262	8,222	3,487	22,367	236	14,856	2,720
Kentucky	116,973	34,886	5,636	2,221	61,496	1,457	12,674	230
Louisiana	34,679	12,371	2,736	228	3,122	462	5,145	50
Maine	46,995	27,426	5,514	283	12,608	1,471	11,183	150
Maryland	165,922	54,857	13,939	2,797	25,015	2,765	80,951	8,198
Massachusetts	147,851	75,105	15,515	3,040	26,244	2,917	22,237	3,155
Michigan	100,704	43,268	8,596	2,276	21,539	1,534	20,468	3,805
Minnesota	92,632	29,148	4,667	3,025	44,462	522	11,829	49
Mississippi	126,965	53,969	10,222	4,494	43,441	1,212	18,396	3,578
Missouri	20,944	8,348	1,902	539	6,550	153	3,311	83
Montana	42,730	14,625	3,751	1,412	14,921	193	7,596	195
Nebraska	4,766	2,072	384	45	787	31	1,447	2
Nevada	14,490	7,298	1,566	277	2,513	410	2,325	39
New Hampshire	117,278	80,638	13,031	1,214	22,383	5,471	15,003	239
New Mexico	28,260	11,125	2,516	400	7,835	287	5,403	714
New York	435,390	159,970	38,093	6,432	104,945	9,448	80,739	4,842
North Carolina	126,189	63,795	9,353	1,340	49,279	559	14,227	6,353
North Dakota	22,052	6,611	1,296	1,280	9,435	138	3,619	75
Ohio	212,778	111,504	20,482	4,139	35,579	2,440	34,977	3,126
Oklahoma	81,795	34,966	6,559	3,175	23,704	1,545	8,066	3,340
Oregon	46,647	21,025	4,163	619	9,312	363	9,665	215
Pennsylvania	321,628	149,901	30,701	5,529	83,710	4,687	52,472	3,380
Rhode Island	24,862	12,135	2,210	452	4,848	609	4,610	26
South Carolina	64,372	22,289	4,860	1,877	30,232	695	6,462	....
South Dakota	34,760	7,165	1,583	315	8,346	107	6,741	150
Tennessee	132,229	46,501	8,806	3,642	45,251	985	26,601	92
Texas	206,902	119,665	21,254	7,555	90,966	3,876	42,756	1,179
Utah	22,788	5,286	2,085	369	8,550	160	2,799	53
Vermont	11,694	5,241	1,068	218	2,283	394	2,474	8
Virginia	86,716	37,210	8,205	1,299	18,310	789	20,565	120
Washington	75,166	31,826	4,509	1,178	15,385	1,528	17,531	365
West Virginia	58,854	26,701	6,128	1,155	8,657	345	11,344	331
Wisconsin	87,369	38,847	5,957	1,962	18,179	753	18,379	436
Wyoming	12,377	3,448	907	241	3,434	66	4,026	135
U. S. Territories and possessions	40,390	13,222	1,917	513	14,856	148	9,460	11
Foreign countries	53,904	54,910	23,033	42	12,636	....	3,003	200

[1] Includes $12,750,000 for expenditures not shown separately. Excludes $957,695,800 not allocable by States.
[2] Compensation on pension benefits paid to living veterans and dependents of deceased veterans, including certain retirement pay.

Source: Veterans' Administration, *Annual Report of Administrator of Veterans' Affairs.*

No. 257.—COMPENSATION, PENSIONS, AND EMERGENCY AND RESERVE OFFICERS' RETIREMENT PAY—NUMBER ON ROLLS, AND EXPENDITURES FOR BENEFITS: 1866 TO 1952

JUNE 30 OR YEAR ENDING JUNE 30—	NUMBER ON ROLLS			Expenditures ($1,000)	JUNE 30 OR YEAR ENDING JUNE 30—	NUMBER ON ROLLS			Expenditures ($1,000)
	Total	Living	Deceased			Total	Living	Deceased	
1866	126,722	55,652	71,070	15,450	1929	831,964	525,961	306,003	418,821
1870	198,686	87,521	111,165	29,351	1930	840,833	542,610	298,223	418,433
1875	234,821	122,989	111,832	29,270	1931	1,079,987	790,782	289,205	488,389
1880	250,802	145,410	105,392	56,689	1932	1,278,046	994,351	283,695	545,777
1885	345,125	247,146	97,979	65,172	1933	1,270,667	997,918	272,749	550,559
1890	537,944	415,654	122,290	106,094	1934	838,855	581,225	257,630	321,377
1895	970,524	751,456	219,068	139,812	1935	838,937	585,955	252,982	374,407
1900	993,529	752,510	241,019	138,462	1936	852,032	600,562	251,470	398,992
1905	998,441	717,761	280,680	141,143	1937	841,937	598,510	243,427	396,030
1910	921,083	602,622	318,461	159,974	1938	836,953	600,848	236,105	402,769
1915	748,147	437,723	310,424	165,518	1939	842,431	602,757	239,674	416,704
1916	709,572	403,372	306,200	159,155	1940	849,298	610,122	239,176	429,138
1917	673,111	370,147	302,964	160,895	1941	856,441	618,926	237,515	433,114
1918	649,497	341,632	307,865	180,177	1942	859,594	623,659	236,035	431,284
1919	673,832	338,216	335,616	233,461	1943	860,080	621,572	238,508	442,360
1920	769,543	419,627	349,916	316,418	1944	1,066,920	813,469	253,451	[1]494,364
1921	768,572	422,691	345,881	380,026	1945	1,513,586	1,144,088	369,498	[1]732,538
1922	772,379	430,942	341,437	377,158	1946	2,631,981	2,130,353	501,628	[1]1,215,688
1923	778,180	436,776	341,404	388,607	1947	2,920,765	2,354,297	566,468	[1]1,731,973
1924	762,547	427,153	335,394	345,490	1948	2,918,325	2,315,039	603,286	[1]1,820,685
1925	790,139	456,530	333,609	346,748	1949	2,949,133	2,313,545	635,588	[1]1,891,283
1926	807,088	472,623	334,465	372,281	1950	3,026,361	2,368,238	658,123	[1]2,009,462
1927	816,380	489,805	326,575	403,630	1951	3,056,178	2,373,577	682,601	[1]2,035,988
1928	834,364	516,566	317,798	410,765	1952	3,124,828	2,417,998	706,830	[1]2,105,973

DESCRIPTION	NUMBER ON ROLLS, JUNE 30 [3]						AVERAGE PAYMENT RATE, JUNE 30 (ANNUAL BASIS)[3]					
	1930	1940	1945	1950	1951	1952	1930	1940	1945	1950	1951	1952
All wars	840,833	849,298	1,513,586	3,026,361	3,056,178	3,124,828	$475	$498	$548	$669	$658	$664
Living	542,610	610,122	1,144,088	2,368,238	2,373,577	2,417,998	514	510	546	646	634	643
Deceased	298,223	239,176	369,498	658,123	682,601	706,830	404	467	553	750	742	735
War of 1812: Deceased	10	1	1				540	240	240			
War with Mexico: Deceased	630	130	55	24	22	19	586	580	576	536	541	532
Indian Wars	9,645	6,271	3,788	2,329	2,012	1,869	446	492	570	682	662	653
Living	5,454	2,216	1,115	530	376	316	513	736	843	1,136	1,130	1,132
Deceased	4,191	4,055	2,673	1,799	1,636	1,553	359	358	456	548	552	556
Civil War	216,692	52,522	24,750	11,147	10,266	8,901	852	1,162	1,188	1,392	1,440	1,440
Living	49,018	2,381	229	15	6	3	852	1,162	1,188	1,392	1,440	1,440
Deceased	167,674	50,141	24,821	11,132	10,260	8,898	452	457	452	538	548	553
Spanish-American War	217,730	216,950	200,059	171,608	165,694	160,546	389	582	707	868	858	851
Living	186,811	159,230	128,104	91,984	85,246	79,110	389	660	861	1,106	1,109	1,117
Deceased	30,919	57,720	71,955	79,624	80,448	81,436	389	367	433	593	592	593
Regular Establishment	19,491	46,177	56,591	71,235	81,370	79,196	232	362	437	673	692	673
Living	15,661	36,051	42,925	53,765	58,748	60,308	235	378	430	631	625	622
Deceased	3,830	10,126	13,666	17,470	22,622	18,888	219	304	457	802	866	835
World War I	376,635	527,247	587,589	805,035	858,986	899,929	499	477	545	719	717	726
Living	285,666	410,244	425,589	520,925	562,288	593,765	553	459	545	777	778	793
Deceased	90,969	117,003	162,000	284,110	296,698	305,164	331	538	546	613	603	595
World War II			640,753	1,964,983	1,936,840	1,945,640			514	631	614	615
Living			546,126	1,701,019	1,666,694	1,669,069			482	581	561	565
Deceased			94,627	263,964	270,146	276,571			698	953	938	917
Public Law 28, 82d Congress [4]					988	28,728					1,102	941
Living					219	15,427					1,177	845
Deceased					769	13,301					1,080	1,052

[1] Excludes any increased compensation for vocational rehabilitation subsistence allowance under Public Law 16.
[2] For expenditures by wars, see table 255.
[3] Averages calculated by dividing total annual value of benefits, as of June 30, by number on rolls.
[4] Veterans with service on or after June 27, 1950.

Source: Veterans' Administration, *Annual Report of Administrator of Veterans' Affairs.*

No. 258.—U. S. GOVERNMENT LIFE INSURANCE AND NATIONAL SERVICE LIFE INSURANCE IN FORCE, BY PLAN, AS OF JUNE 30, 1952

[Amounts in thousands of dollars. Veterans' Administration operates two insurance programs: (1) United States Government Life Insurance for veterans of World War I; and (2) National Service Life Insurance for veterans of World War II and later. These two programs are segregated and administered separately in all particulars]

PLAN	UNITED STATES GOVERNMENT LIFE INSURANCE		NATIONAL SERVICE LIFE INSURANCE							
			Fund [1]		Appropriation [2]		Service-disabled veterans fund [3]		Veterans special term fund [4]	
	Number	Amount	Number	Amount	Number	Amount	Number	Amount	Number	Amount
Total	448,827	1,952,637	7,078,204	48,810,729	8,350	46,395	109	876	3,239	27,272
5-year term	25,654	165,792	4,973,339	38,995,866	4,833	30,567	67	546	3,239	27,272
Ordinary life	142,196	721,796	396,956	2,250,862	1,102	5,695	13	110		
20-payment life	178,620	662,596	985,668	4,179,057	1,162	4,651	24	187		
30-payment life	25,978	134,668	370,512	1,915,272	465	2,154	5	33		
20-year endowment	22,450	56,356	160,350	563,264	374	1,325				
20-year endowment	16,796	74,601								
Endowment at age 60			84,121	446,140	190	898				
Endowment at age 62	22,877	108,206								
Endowment at age 65			45,536	259,777	95	521				
Extended insurance	10,846	21,798	58,182	199,238	128	585				
Paid-up insurance	3,411	6,822	1,440	1,254	1	1				

[1] Fund is administered as a trust fund for benefit of policyholders and their beneficiaries. All premiums collected on insurance issued and all interest earned thereon are paid into the fund; disbursements are made from the fund for death claims, dividends, and other benefits. Government, however, bears cost of administration of this fund in addition to expenses for certain types of losses.

[2] Nonparticipating insurance for disabled veterans for whom good health provisions are waived because of disabilities resulting from active service between October 8, 1940 and September 2, 1945.

[3] For veterans discharged on or after April 25, 1951 with service-connected disability which would be compensable, if ten percent or more in degree.

[4] For veterans who were entitled to indemnity protection under the Servicemen's Indemnity Act of 1951 and who were ordered to active service for a period in excess of 30 days; no medical examination required. Issued only on the 5-year renewable nonconvertible term plan.

Source: Veterans' Administration, *Annual Report of Administrator of Veterans' Affairs* and records.

No. 259.— U. S. GOVERNMENT LIFE INSURANCE IN FORCE: 1921 TO 1952

[Amounts in thousands of dollars. U. S. Government life insurance is granted to veterans of World War I (including those now serving with land, air, and naval forces) upon application, payment of premiums, and satisfactory proof of good health. No person may carry a combined amount of insurance with the government in excess of $10,000 at any one time]

JUNE 30—	INSURANCE POLICIES		JUNE 30—	INSURANCE POLICIES		JUNE 30—	INSURANCE POLICIES	
	Number	Amount		Number	Amount		Number	Amount
1921	651,054	3,849,376	1943	586,631	2,499,656	1948	513,263	2,237,325
1925	582,340	2,865,029	1944	578,641	2,494,900	1949	500,784	2,182,181
1930	648,248	3,042,743	1945	567,941	2,454,864	1950	484,793	2,116,060
1935	590,865	2,605,400	1946	551,823	2,390,154	1951	470,257	2,055,684
1940	609,094	2,565,327	1947	531,053	2,310,344	1952	448,827	1,952,637

Source: Veterans' Administration, *Annual Report of Administrator of Veterans' Affairs* and records.

No. 260.—Veterans Receiving Vocational Training and Education: June 1950 to September 1952

STATUS	1950		1951		1952		
	June 30	Dec. 31	June 30	Dec. 31	Mar. 31	June 30	Sept. 30
Vocational rehabilitation program: [1]							
Applications received [2]	741,892	1,151,229	1,169,545	1,183,930	1,191,757	1,199,403	1,206,993
In training	122,867	106,189	65,188	58,142	50,239	36,426	31,146
School	44,331	45,811	20,739	23,517	21,289	11,214	9,312
Institutional on-farm	42,949	36,193	28,375	22,824	18,884	16,529	14,278
Job	35,587	24,185	16,074	11,801	10,066	8,683	7,556
Rehabilitated [2]	204,031	238,041	272,283	238,042	305,742	321,172	328,494
Education and training program: [2]							
Applications received [2]	9,233,327	9,787,305	10,065,439	10,230,438	10,235,387	10,238,529	10,241,449
In training	1,492,868	1,716,064	1,152,891	1,433,741	1,182,328	741,901	587,924
School	975,608	1,286,785	776,615	1,099,649	907,173	508,036	390,642
Institutional on-farm	318,503	281,532	263,256	237,519	195,796	169,808	145,501
Job	196,757	147,747	113,020	96,573	79,359	64,057	51,781

[1] Authorised under Public Law 16, 78th Congress and Public Law 894, 81st Congress.
[2] Cumulative from inception of program.   [3] Authorized under Public Law 346, 78th Congress.

Source: Veterans' Administration. *Annual Report of Administrator of Veterans' Affairs* and records.

No. 261.—Veterans' Readjustment Allowances—Number of Claimants and Amount of Payments: September 1944 to December 1952

[Payments in thousands of dollars. Allowances provided veterans of World War II under Servicemen's Readjustment Act of 1944]

MONTH	Total payments	UNEMPLOYMENT ALLOWANCES		SELF-EMPLOYMENT ALLOWANCES	
		Amount of payments	Number of continued claims (last wk. in period)	Amount of payments	Total claims (filed during period)
1944: September–December	4,215	4,113	24,000	102	1,751
1945: January–June	19,940	16,606	36,900	3,334	36,958
July–December	106,690	98,349	632,000	8,341	108,077
1946: January–June	917,398	809,782	1,744,105	107,616	1,302,708
July–December	826,316	681,511	934,704	144,805	1,449,595
1947: January–June	609,319	485,356	721,213	123,963	1,392,715
July–December	361,224	287,012	443,290	74,212	783,307
1948: January–June	315,596	265,333	385,282	50,263	588,898
July–December	194,472	161,137	354,711	33,335	353,723
1949: January–June	320,016	288,556	585,780	31,460	341,831
July–December	110,179	98,080	61,039	12,009	122,918
1950: January–June	27,212	26,084	27,148	1,128	12,383
July–December	7,440	6,903	5,756	537	5,562
1951: January–June	1,789	1,699	1,233	90	1,029
July–December	444	424	[1] 727	20	308
1952: January–June	313	304	[1] 320	9	109
July–December	64	61	[1] 70	3	25
Total (cumulative)	[2] 3,822,630	3,231,309	----------	[2] 591,321	----------

[1] Weekly average for last month in period.
[2] Adjusted total; not equal to sum of semiannual figures.

Source: Veterans' Administration, *Annual Report of Administrator of Veterans' Affairs* and records.

No. 262.—Veterans Receiving Hospital or Domiciliary Care Authorized by Veterans' Administration: 1932 to 1952

[During fiscal year 1952, 2,492,361 visits were made by veterans to staff or fee physicians for out-patient medical care. On June 30, 1952, 7,560 veterans were domiciled in State and Territorial homes. For each person, Federal Government reimbursed these States at rate of $120 per year through August 1939, $240 per year through December 17, 1943, $300 per year through May 31, 1948, and $500 per year thereafter]

	Total receiving hospital or domiciliary care at end of year	VETERANS RECEIVING HOSPITAL TREATMENT, ALL FACILITIES AND HOSPITALS [1]				Veterans receiving domiciliary care at end of year	VETERANS' ADMINISTRATION FACILITIES				
		Average daily patients	Patients remaining at end of year				Hospital [2]			Domiciliary	
YEAR ENDING JUNE 30—			Total	Tuberculosis	Neuropsychiatric	General		Average daily patients	Operating expenses (1,000 dollars)	Per diem cost (dollars) [3]	Average daily domiciliary care	Operating expenses (1,000 dollars)
1932	42,216	42,445	42,557	6,409	20,160	16,908	13,688	25,046	31,066	2.44		
1933	51,022	41,172	42,599	5,134	23,358	14,107	9,323	39,030	39,556	2.78	10,406	4,024
1934	53,135	42,616	41,542	4,539	24,447	12,556	9,596	40,972	42,886	2.82	12,066	4,474
1935	57,190	44,942	44,142	4,789	26,394	14,959	11,623	41,999	43,262	2.81	10,364	4,299
1936	76,934	48,004	50,670	4,857	29,387	16,544	14,254	44,639	44,304	2.65	13,514	4,872
1937	78,367	52,805	52,561	4,912	31,190	17,758	15,426	46,147	47,688	2.68	15,706	5,218
1940	79,114	56,304	56,596	4,644	33,015	18,996	16,518	52,409	49,921	2.60	16,706	5,546
1941	73,288	55,478	56,160	4,637	34,506	19,015	13,976	54,582	55,444	2.78	16,998	5,670
1942	67,046	57,680	56,073	4,900	34,659	16,514	11,573	54,636	50,065	2.96	14,871	5,836
1943	65,688	56,072	54,641	4,974	36,369	15,298	6,997	53,470	64,664	3.37	10,430	5,580
1944	72,578	61,305	66,500	6,180	40,382	17,228	8,576	58,388	72,111	3.38	9,447	5,427
1945	84,986	66,376	71,290	6,752	44,636	19,861	8,779	64,317	80,294	3.42	9,002	5,174
1946	98,868	78,236	84,637	6,102	49,399	28,334	11,052	71,498	136,248	5.22	10,347	7,655
1947	117,936	96,146	104,443	12,490	53,962	38,001	13,436	85,623	234,844	8.67	13,064	12,736
1948	117,851	105,861	108,576	13,045	54,790	35,741	14,275	92,534	322,389	9.05	14,387	14,144
1949	115,540	105,698	107,673	14,610	55,160	37,112	14,367	94,639	399,275	18.24	15,208	17,363
1950	118,107	102,638	102,208	14,361	54,419	33,522	16,694	96,040	403,699	10.90	16,831	19,134
1951	114,763	104,991	100,517	15,067	52,132	32,317	16,279	96,305	426,148	11.66	16,775	19,987
1952	120,464	105,110	108,774	15,645	53,818	34,311	16,710	96,024	491,560	13.24	16,876	22,922

	VETERANS UNDER HOSPITAL OR DOMICILIARY CARE, BY CLASS OF BENEFICIARY								
TYPE OF CARE AND YEAR (JUNE 30)	All wars and regular establishment			World War II		World War I		Public Law 28 [4]	Other [5]
	Total	Service connected	Non-service	Service connected	Non-service	Service connected	Non-service		
Hospital treatment:									
	42,599	12,046	30,553			10,746	27,287		4,566
	55,596	12,328	44,268			10,552	40,360		5,984
	71,329	23,337	47,992	11,655	9,119	9,696	35,092		5,667
	85,537	27,790	58,047	16,087	21,273	9,639	33,343		5,495
	104,443	35,525	68,918	22,981	26,049	10,451	34,896		6,046
	105,576	34,872	68,704	22,472	26,232	10,249	36,631		5,692
	107,072	35,919	71,154	22,399	29,768	10,078	37,452		6,376
	102,208	34,596	67,707	22,364	27,794	9,714	36,344		6,087
	100,517	35,597	64,920	23,407	26,137	9,145	35,817	537	6,474
	108,774	36,182	67,592	23,253	26,358	8,831	35,970	3,001	6,361
Domiciliary care:									
	9,323	919	8,404			727	6,739		1,857
	16,518	1,146	15,372			949	14,298		1,276
	6,779	560	6,219	57	298	414	7,174		831
	11,052	684	10,368	107	826	506	8,951		982
	13,456	994	12,464	143	563	709	10,667		1,336
	14,275	1,299	12,986	164	613	963	11,190		1,235
	16,397	1,814	14,483	296	818	1,301	12,407		1,443
	16,694	1,896	14,799	337	957	1,380	12,674		1,376
	16,279	1,922	14,357	342	973	1,376	12,254		1,342
	16,710	2,064	14,646	436	1,091	1,376	12,479		1,340

[1] Veterans' Administration beneficiaries cared for in Army, Navy, other Federal, and State and civil institutions.
[2] Includes hospitals operated in connection with Veterans' Administration domiciliaries.
[3] Includes hospitals operated for only part of year under unusual conditions.
[4] Veterans of service on or after June 27, 1950.
[5] Veterans of all other wars, and of regular establishment.

Source: Veterans' Administration, Annual Report of Administrator of Veterans' Affairs and records.

No. 263.—VETERANS' GUARANTEED AND INSURED LOANS—NUMBER AND AMOUNT OF LOANS CLOSED, BY TYPE OF LOAN, NOVEMBER 1944 TO DECEMBER 1952

[Amounts in thousands of dollars. Cumulative totals may not equal sum of monthly figures because of adjustments]

PERIOD OR MONTH ENDING	TOTAL			HOME		FARM		BUSINESS	
	Number	Amount of loans	Amount of guaranty and insurance	Number	Amount of loans	Number	Amount of loans	Number	Amount of loans
Cumulative:									
To Dec. 29, 1945..	49, 219	[1] 212, 512	80, 557	44, 731	[1] 198, 913	1, 064	[1] 3, 585	3, 424	[1] 10, 014
To Dec. 25, 1946..	517, 980	2, 697, 440	1, 250, 028	455, 293	2, 494, 547	18, 202	66, 844	44, 485	136, 049
To Dec. 25, 1947..	1, 117, 879	6, 183, 772	2, 891, 490	996, 510	5, 777, 068	37, 995	144, 609	83, 374	262, 095
To Dec. 25, 1948..	1, 495, 669	8, 161, 134	3, 857, 795	1, 346, 075	7, 653, 976	48, 403	186, 614	101, 191	320, 544
To Dec. 25, 1949..	1, 789, 402	9, 634, 546	4, 600, 870	1, 622, 867	9, 077, 565	53, 349	204, 147	113, 186	352, 834
To Dec. 25, 1950..	2, 303, 975	12, 759, 732	6, 281, 187	2, 120, 463	12, 150, 993	58, 507	223, 554	125, 005	385, 185
To Dec. 25, 1951..	2, 797, 469	16, 472, 960	8, 426, 331	2, 567, 536	15, 765, 472	62, 137	239, 574	167, 496	467, 914
1952: Jan. 25	40, 182	313, 030	178, 906	34, 283	301, 276	183	689	5, 766	11, 065
Feb. 25	32, 454	252, 689	143, 905	27, 357	242, 103	218	887	4, 879	9, 699
Mar. 25	31, 355	245, 443	139, 654	26, 692	238, 651	273	1, 137	4, 390	8, 655
Apr. 25	31, 361	252, 096	142, 469	27, 568	244, 042	253	1, 056	3, 540	6, 998
May 25	25, 918	208, 985	119, 698	23, 162	202, 758	219	945	2, 537	5, 282
June 25	24, 863	201, 536	115, 194	22, 518	195, 986	172	721	2, 173	4, 829
July 25	22, 892	192, 683	111, 271	21, 462	189, 189	102	384	1, 328	3, 060
Aug. 25	24, 601	207, 230	119, 448	22, 933	202, 746	123	517	1, 545	3, 967
Sept. 25	25, 641	220, 944	127, 802	24, 219	217, 292	130	458	1, 292	3, 194
Oct. 25	25, 949	223, 004	129, 001	24, 869	220, 008	96	439	984	2, 557
Nov. 25	28, 132	246, 253	142, 314	26, 898	243, 087	91	331	1, 143	2, 835
Dec. 25	26, 061	230, 131	133, 443	24, 872	226, 936	101	410	1, 088	2, 785
Cumulative to Dec. 25, 1952	3, 136, 518	19, 263, 696	10, 029, 030	2, 874, 302	18, 483, 391	64, 082	247, 466	198, 134	532, 769

[1] Estimated.

Source: Veterans' Administration records.

No. 264.—AMERICAN NATIONAL RED CROSS—EXPENDITURES AND ADULT MEMBERSHIP: YEARS ENDING JUNE 30, 1944 TO 1952

ITEM	1944	1945	1946	1947	1948	1949	1950	1951	1952
Adult membership (thousands):									
Total, including insular and foreign	36, 544	36, 645	21, 986	18, 110	18, 098	18, 138	18, 090	18, 635	[1] 20, 000
Continental U. S. and Alaska	36, 371	36, 502	21, 874	18, 044	17, 989	17, 896	17, 839	18, 500	[1] 19, 850
Percent of total population [2]	26. 3	27. 7	16. 6	13. 7	13 7	13. 6	12. 6	12. 0	13. 0
Expenditures, total ($1,000) [3]	108, 904	130, 671	133, 274	65, 808	50, 929	43, 698	39, 561	45, 917	56, 948
Services to the armed forces and to veterans	89, 997	112, 345	107, 335	33, 047	16, 429	14, 891	12, 428	16, 613	18, 257
Disaster preparedness and relief.	3, 150	3, 463	2, 214	8, 887	12, 533	6, 804	5, 589	3, 765	19, 039
Blood program			29	1, 192	1, 778	5, 100	5, 847	9, 847	6, 437
Health services	2, 831	2, 610	3, 011	2, 251	1, 987	2, 112	1, 774	1, 962	1, 798
School and college activities	713	988	1, 550	1, 476	1, 417	1, 374	1, 124	925	780
Volunteer services	413	374	342	192	276	304	(4)	(4)	(4)
Services and assistance to chapters	7, 206	2, 097	2, 558	2, 700	2, 330	2, 372	[4] 2, 356	[4] 3, 077	[4] 3, 515
Public relations	693	684	784	669	715	640	540	456	581
Fund raising	1, 295	1, 569	1, 172	804	707	608	597	652	519
International program	5, 319	4, 034	10, 949	3, 568	1, 935	884	375	401	353
General executive offices	2, 287	2, 478	3, 090	1, 935	1, 864	1, 616	1, 948	1, 793	1, 451
Purchase and improvement of land and buildings				1, 159	137	451		2, 418	81
Operating facilities				7, 928	9, 425	6, 452	6, 983	4, 008	4, 137

[1] Estimated.

[2] Based on population estimates of Bureau of Census.

[3] Data for chapter budgets not included; additional expenditures by chapters estimated at approximately $46,567,600 for year ending June 30, 1952. Activities common to all services, such as stenographic section, files, etc., previously prorated to the various services, are included with "Operating facilities" beginning 1947. In fiscal year 1951 and 1952, applicable proportion of cost of telecommunications, duplicating service, insurance and retirement charged directly to program services.

[4] Beginning 1950 volunteer services combined with services and assistance to chapters.

Source: The American National Red Cross, annual report.

10. Social Security and Related Programs

Broadly considered, "social security" includes (1) all public provisions for payments to individuals on an insurance or similar basis to compensate for part of the wage loss resulting from old age, sickness, disability, unemployment, or death (social insurance and related programs); (2) assistance, or payments on a needs basis, to persons with inadequate income (public aid); and (3) medical and hospital care and services to individuals to improve their health, earning power, and welfare (health and medical services and other welfare services).

The *Social Security Bulletin* carries current data on many of these programs, and summarizes annual data for them in an annual Statistical Supplement. Summary data have also appeared in the *Annual Report of the Federal Security Agency*.

Social insurance for industrial and commercial workers.—The two social insurance programs established by the Social Security Act provide protection against wage loss resulting from old age or death (Federal old-age and survivors insurance) or unemployment (Federal-State unemployment insurance). In addition, three States—Rhode Island, California, and New Jersey—administer cash benefits for workers covered by the State unemployment insurance law who suffer a wage loss because of temporary disability; temporary disability benefits are also paid in New York under a law patterned on workmen's compensation and administered by the State workmen's compensation board. In general, these programs cover employment in industry and commerce. The major groups presently excluded under old-age and survivors insurance are the self-employed in certain professions, self-employed farmers, farm and domestic workers not "regularly" employed, and most Federal Government employees.

Old-age and survivors insurance provides monthly retirement benefits to fully insured workers (see table 277) at age 65 or over and supplementary monthly benefits to their wives, if they are aged 65 or have a child of the wage earner in their care, to dependent husbands, and to dependent children under age 18. Monthly survivor benefits are payable to certain dependents of fully or currently insured workers. A lump-sum death payment is made in the case of all insured deaths.

Covered workers and their employers each pay contributions of 1.5 percent on the worker's wages, not counting amounts above the first $3,600 in a year. The rate is scheduled to rise by steps until it reaches 3.25 percent each in 1970. Self-employed persons pay 1.5 times the employee rate. An amount equal to the contributions collected is appropriated for deposit in the old-age and survivors insurance trust fund, from which benefits and administrative costs are paid.

State unemployment insurance laws pay benefits to unemployed covered workers who meet the qualifying conditions specified in the State law. In most States, a waiting period of 1 week must be served before payments begin. Benefits are payable for a maximum number of weeks, ranging from 16 to 26 weeks among the States; maximum weekly benefits range from $20 to $30 under the several State laws. In 10 States maximum allowances for dependents ranging from $5 to $18 raise the range of maximum augmented benefits to $26 to $48.

The standard rate of contributions payable by employers for unemployment insurance (Federal and State) is 3.0 percent of the first $3,000 a year paid to an employee. All States adjust employer contribution rates according to their experience with the risk of unemployment, so that total Federal and State contributions may be considerably less than 3.0 percent; in 10 States with penalty rates, combined contributions may be more than 3.0 percent. In 2 States, employees also contribute. Contributions collected by States are deposited to State accounts in the Federal unemployment trust fund, from which States withdraw amounts needed for benefit payments. The Federal Government makes grants to States to cover administrative costs of State systems that meet statutory Federal requirements.

Note.—This section presents data for the most recent year or period available on March 17, 1953, when the material was organized and sent to the printer.

Social insurance for railroad workers.—The social insurance programs under the Railroad Retirement Act and Railroad Unemployment Insurance Act cover employees of railroads (including the Railway Express Agency and the Pullman Company) subject to part I of the Interstate Commerce Act, affiliated companies such as refrigerator-car loan companies performing services connected with railroad transportation, organizations such as railroad and traffic associations maintained by two or more covered employers, and standard railway-labor organizations, national in scope. These programs are administered by the Railroad Retirement Board, which publishes operations data in its *Monthly Review* and *Annual Report*.

The Railroad Retirement Act provides retirement annuities for aged and disabled workers and for wives of retired employees, and monthly and lump-sum benefits to survivors of deceased workers. The credits of employees who die or retire with less than 10 years of railroad service are transferred to old-age and survivors insurance under the Social Security Act, and any benefits which may be due (except a residual payment) are paid under that program.

Funds for the retirement and survivor system come from a tax on earnings up to $300 a month under the Railroad Retirement Tax Act. The tax, divided equally between the employer and employee, is now at the maximum rate of 12½ percent.

The Railroad Unemployment Insurance Act provides benefits for unemployment and sickness (including maternity). Benefits ranging from $3.00 to $7.50 per day are payable for each day over 7 in the first 14-day registration period, and over 4 in subsequent registration periods, up to a maximum of 130 days in a benefit year for each type of benefit. The most recent changes in the Railroad Unemployment Insurance Act became effective on July 1, 1952; consequently, the data in the tables do not reflect the higher benefit rates described here.

The unemployment insurance program is financed entirely by contributions from covered employers, paid directly to the Board. The contribution rate for any year depends upon the balance in the unemployment insurance account and may vary from ½ to 3 percent of payrolls (exclusive of individual earnings in excess of $300 a month). Since January 1, 1948, the minimum rate has been in effect.

Retirement systems for Federal Government employees.—One contributory retirement system for Federal civilian employees and two noncontributory systems (for special classes of employees) are administered by the Civil Service Commission. In addition, there are separate retirement systems, some contributory and others noncontributory, in operation for the armed forces and special classes of Federal employees.

The Civil Service Retirement Act provides for age, optional, disability and discontinued service annuities for employees in the executive, judicial, and legislative branches of the United States Government and in the municipal government of the District of Columbia not subject to another retirement system, except those employees excluded by executive order because the tenure of employment is intermittent or of uncertain duration. It also provides annuities for the widows and minor children of deceased employees, and, under certain conditions, to the survivors of deceased annuitants. Approximately 1,700,000 employees were subject to this Act as of June 30, 1952. The employee contribution rate, computed on base pay, has been 6 percent since July 1948.

The Act does not require specific payments from the Government as employer, but implies that the Government will furnish the amounts necessary to finance the fund and to continue the Act in full force and effect. Appropriations have been made annually by the Congress to the fund since the fiscal year 1929.

Workmen's compensation.—All States now have programs providing protection against work-connected injuries and deaths. In addition to the State laws, there are Federal workmen's compensation laws covering employees of the Federal Government, private employees in the District of Columbia, and longshoremen and harbor workers. Most of the State workmen's compensation laws exempt such employments as agriculture, domestic service and casual labor; the majority exempt employers who have fewer than a specified number of employees. Occupational diseases, or at least specified diseases, are compensable under most laws.

In most States, total payments to injured workers or to survivor families are limited as to time, amount, or both. All compensation acts require that medical aid be furnished to injured employees; in about one-third of the laws, there are either duration or cost limitations—or both—on the amount of medical benefits provided.

Public assistance.—Public assistance is provided through five major programs, all administered by the States and localities. Payments to four groups of needy persons—the aged, the blind, the permanently and totally disabled, and children whose need arises from certain causes—are financed in part from Federal funds granted to States under the Social Security Act. Aid to other needy persons is furnished for the most part through general assistance, toward which the Federal Government makes no contribution.

To receive a Federal grant for assistance payments and administrative expenses under any of the four programs established by the Social Security Act, a State must have a plan approved as meeting the requirements of the Federal Act. Each State establishes the conditions under which needy people may receive assistance and determines how much they shall get.

Health and welfare service.—Programs providing health and welfare services are aided through Federal grants to States for maternal and child-health services, services for crippled children, child-welfare services, vocational rehabilitation, and public health services (including water-pollution control, hospital survey and construction, and control of specific diseases). The Children's Bureau, a part of the Social Security Administration, administers the first three of these programs; the others are administered by the Office of Vocational Rehabilitation and the Public Health Service, both units of the Department of Health, Education, and Welfare.

Fig. XIX.—Social Security Operations: 1942 to 1952

[Old-age and survivors insurance: Average monthly number and amount of monthly benefits (current payment status). Unemployment insurance: Average weekly number of beneficiaries and average monthly amount of benefits paid under all State laws. Public assistance: Average monthly number of recipients and average monthly amount of payments under all State programs]

INDIVIDUALS RECEIVING PAYMENTS

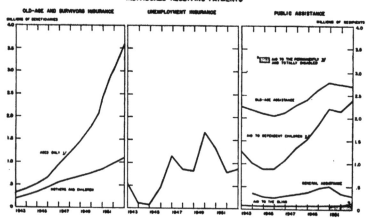

SOCIAL SECURITY PAYMENTS

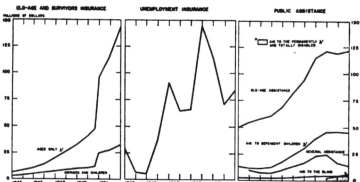

[1] Receiving old-age, wife's or husband's, widow's or widower's, or parent's benefit. Beginning September 1950, includes a small proportion of wife beneficiaries under age 65 with child beneficiaries in their care.
[2] Children plus one adult per family when adults are included in assistance group; before October 1950, partly estimated.
[3] Program initiated October 1950.

Source: Department of Commerce, Bureau of the Census. Data are from Department of Health, Education, and Welfare, Social Security Administration.

No. 285.—EXPENDITURES FOR CIVILIAN SOCIAL SECURITY AND RELATED PUBLIC PROGRAMS, BY SOURCE OF FUNDS AND BY PROGRAM: FISCAL YEARS 1950 AND 1951

[In millions of dollars. Preliminary data corrected to July 1952. Includes administrative expenditures unless otherwise indicated. Fiscal years for Federal Government, most States, and some localities ending June 30; fiscal years for other States and localities cover various 12-month periods ending within year]

PROGRAM	1950			1951		
	Total	Federal	State and local	Total	Federal	State and local
Total	12,394.0	6,791.2	6,904.8	12,687.5	7,432.9	6,294.8
Social insurance and related programs	6,973.3	4,161.5	2,811.8	6,786.5	4,561.4	1,225.1
Old-age and survivors insurance	784.1	784.1		1,568.5	1,568.5	
Railroad retirement	304.4	304.4		321.0	321.0	
Public employee retirement systems	723.2	433.7	289.5	891.2	555.2	336.0
Employment security [1]	2,081.5	213.6	1,868.2	1,060.4	184.4	876.0
Railroad unemployment insurance	119.6	119.6		26.3	26.3	
Railroad temporary disability insurance	31.1	31.1		26.9	26.9	
State temporary disability insurance	69.1		69.1	80.7		80.7
Veterans' program [2]	2,249.8	2,249.8		2,144.0	2,144.0	
Workmen's compensation [3]	600.2	25.2	875.0	604.5	32.1	632.4
Public aid	2,468.7	1,095.8	1,362.9	2,582.2	1,187.7	1,395.5
Special types of public assistance [4]	2,126.6	1,095.5	1,028.8	2,250.5	1,187.7	1,071.8
General assistance	363.1		348.1	228.7		228.7
Health and medical services [5]	2,945.0	1,615.8	1,329.2	3,342.8	1,646.9	2,197.0
Hospital and medical care	1,657.6	644.0	1,013.6	1,763.3	642.7	1,120.6
New hospital construction	521.7	219.7	302.0	571.0	254.0	317.0
Community and related health services	661.7	65.8	595.9	801.4	61.2	740.2
Maternal and child health care [7]	28.6	19.1	9.7	34.4	23.1	11.3
Medical rehabilitation	6.4	3.2	3.2	6.5	3.3	3.3
Medical and public health research	60.6	58.6	2.0	58.7	54.7	2.0
Health manpower training	5.2	5.4	2.5	7.6	5.0	2.6
Other welfare services	1,150.0	438.1	708.9	1,044.0	326.9	717.2
Vocational rehabilitation	23.6	17.8	5.8	34.4	18.4	6.0
Veterans' program [8]	787.1	316.0	471.1	547.6	212.9	334.7
Institutional and other care	261.6	6.6	245.0	336.9	6.9	330.0
School lunch program	122.4	88.4	38.0	128.3	82.8	45.5
Child welfare	4.3	4.3	(9)	5.9	5.9	(9)

[1] State unemployment insurance and employment service programs.
[2] Excludes expenditures from Government life insurance fund.
[3] Includes expenditures for medical services, approximately $185 million in 1950 and $210 million in 1951. Includes payments by employers and private insurance carriers of benefits payable under public law.
[4] Excludes administrative expenditures.
[5] Old-age assistance, aid to blind, aid to dependent children, and beginning October 1950, aid to permanently and totally disabled.
[6] Excludes all medical expenditures of Military Establishment and Atomic Energy Commission; health services provided in connection with public education; medical services included under public aid programs above; medical care included under workmen's compensation above; international health activities; professional training of nurses, physicians, etc.; and expenditures for medical services and research subordinate to performance of other functions.
[7] Federal includes programs for maternal and child health services and for crippled children. State and local expenditures represent required matching of Federal grants.
[8] Federal represents Veterans' Administration programs for vocational rehabilitation, automobiles and other conveyances for disabled veterans, housing for paraplegic veterans and domiciliary care for veterans; State and local are for bonus and other payments and services to veterans.
[9] Not available.

Source: Department of Health, Education, and Welfare, Social Security Administration; Social Security Bulletin.

No. 266.—SELECTED SOCIAL INSURANCE AND RELATED PROGRAMS—ESTIMATED PAYROLLS IN COVERED EMPLOYMENT IN RELATION TO CIVILIAN WAGES AND SALARIES: 1946 TO 1951

[Amounts in millions of dollars. Data for calendar years; corrected to Nov. 5, 1952]

PROGRAM	1946	1947	1948	1949	1950	1951
AMOUNT						
Total earnings [1]	148,156	158,669	174,484	168,168	182,957	211,836
All wages and salaries [1]	111,236	122,042	134,327	133,418	145,582	169,874
Civilian	103,294	117.974	130,357	129,169	140,583	161,234
Payrolls covered by retirement programs	93,604	107,444	118,442	118,155	128,719	155,056
Old-age and survivors insurance [2]	79,003	92,088	101,892	99,989	109,421	133,800
Railroad retirement [2]	4,866	5,107	5,531	5,119	5,320	6,101
Federal civil-service retirement [2]	5,195	4,809	4,469	5,707	6,068	6,396
State and local government [2]	4,540	5,440	6,530	7,340	7,910	8,760
Payrolls covered by unemployment insurance programs	78,011	91,341	101,262	96,639	108,155	124,344
State unemployment insurance [2]	73,145	86,234	95,731	92,520	102,835	118,243
Railroad unemployment insurance [2]	4,866	5,107	5,531	5,119	5,320	6,101
Payrolls covered by workmen's compensation programs [4]	79,500	91,500	101,500	100,000	109,500	127,200
PERCENT						
Civilian wages and salaries [1]	100.0	100.0	100.0	100.0	100.0	100.0
Payrolls covered by retirement programs	90.6	91.1	90.9	91.5	91.6	96.2
Old-age and survivors insurance [2]	76.5	78.1	78.2	77.4	77.8	83.0
Railroad retirement [2]	4.7	4.3	4.2	4.0	3.8	3.8
Federal civil-service retirement [2]	5.0	4.1	3.4	4.4	4.3	4.0
State and local government [2]	4.4	4.6	5.0	5.7	5.6	5.4
Payrolls covered by unemployment insurance programs	75.5	77.4	77.4	76.4	76.9	77.1
State unemployment insurance [2]	70.8	73.1	73.4	72.4	73.1	73.3
Railroad unemployment insurance [2]	4.7	4.3	4.2	4.0	3.8	3.8
Payrolls covered by workmen's compensation programs [4]	77.0	77.6	77.9	77.4	77.9	78.9

[1] Data from Dept. of Commerce, Off. Bus. Econ. Total earnings include earnings of self-employed; all wages and salaries represent civilian wages and salaries in cash and in kind in continental U. S., and pay of Federal civilian and military personnel in all areas. Includes employee contributions under contributory systems.
[2] Continental United States only.   [3] Includes Alaska and Hawaii.
[4] Payrolls of employers insuring with private carriers, State funds, or self-insured, and Federal programs; excludes railroads.

Source: Department of Health, Education, and Welfare, Social Security Administration, Division of Research and Statistics. Data appear periodically in *Social Security Bulletin*.

No. 267.—FEDERAL GRANTS TO STATE AND LOCAL GOVERNMENTS, BY PURPOSE: FISCAL YEARS 1935 TO 1951

[In thousands except per capita. On basis of checks issued. For original sources of data, see source publication]

YEAR ENDING JUNE 30—	TOTAL		SOCIAL SECURITY AND RELATED PURPOSES						
	Amount	Per capita [1]	Total	Assistance payments and administration [2]	Employment security administration	Health services [3]	Other welfare services [4]	Education [5]	All other
1935	$2,196,577	$17.09	$2,773		$1,257		$1,516	$12,722	$2,181,082
1939	1,029,557	7.79	328,403	$246,898	62,858	$14,754	3,893	25,411	675,743
1940	965,239	7.24	359,105	271,135	61,539	21,873	4,588	25,137	581,001
1941	858,591	6.39	426,988	330,408	65,632	25,870	5,078	25,620	405,984
1942	827,478	6.10	483,200	374,568	74,034	29,057	5,541	25,811	318,467
1943	850,995	6.24	468,323	395,623	36,480	30,396	5,824	26,158	356,514
1944	896,926	6.56	509,010	404,942	35,229	60,223	8,616	25,644	362,272
1945	864,905	6.38	532,319	410,364	33,730	78,555	9,670	25,131	307,454
1946	840,098	6.22	578,209	439,132	54,547	71,169	13,361	25,341	236,549
1947	1,187,478	8.32	874,974	613,831	99,252	63,134	98,757	31,145	281,359
1948	1,452,644	9.94	999,236	718,359	133,610	55,309	91,958	35,813	417,594
1949	1,814,751	12.19	1,233,700	927,897	140,314	66,646	98,843	36,951	544,100
1950	2,195,473	14.50	1,563,356	1,123,418	207,617	119,158	113,163	38,501	562,617
1951	2,242,921	14.55	1,631,092	1,185,764	173,838	168,938	102,553	49,123	562,705

[1] Based on Census Bureau estimates of total population, excluding armed forces overseas, as of July 1; data for 1950 and 1951 for Territories and possessions based on 1950 Census.
[2] Old-age assistance, aid to dependent children, aid to blind, and, beginning October 1950, aid to permanently and totally disabled.
[3] Maternal and child health services, services for crippled children, and other public health programs.
[4] Vocational rehabilitation and State and Territorial homes for disabled soldiers and sailors; child welfare services, beginning 1936; community war service day care in 1943; and national school lunch program, beginning 1947.
[5] Colleges of agricultural and mechanic arts, vocational education, education of the blind, and State and municipal marine schools; emergency Office of Education grants from 1936 to 1941; maintenance and operation of schools in certain areas, beginning 1947; and school survey and construction in certain areas, 1951.

Source: Department of Health, Education, and Welfare, Social Security Administration; *Social Security Bulletin*.

268.—FEDERAL GRANTS TO STATE AND LOCAL GOVERNMENTS, BY PURPOSE, BY STATES AND OTHER AREAS: FISCAL YEAR 1951

[In thousands of dollars, except per capita. See headnote and footnotes, table 267]

AND OTHER AREA	TOTAL		SOCIAL SECURITY AND RELATED PURPOSES					
	Amount	Per capita	Total	Assistance payments and administration	Employment security administration	Health services	Other welfare services	Education	All other
total	2,242,903	14.35	1,602,482	1,365,764	173,534	261,286	182,283	48,132	592,786
[state]	62,685	15.46	57,901	33,708	2,341	6,361	1,388	1,118	5,411
[state]	25,996	21.86	24,442	7,457	1,396	1,117	384	434	7,211
[state]	62,129	24.76	31,350	28,871	1,636	4,362	2,385	1,332	24,765
[state]	196,583	14.78	162,461	126,671	14,460	4,786	4,773	4,605	26,562
[state]	34,703	21.86	34,360	30,406	1,402	1,817	738	346	3,863
[state]	21,762	16.75	21,134	4,777	2,713	1,488	1,357	476	3,904
[state]	4,758	14.82	3,039	573		489	346	394	3,190
of Columbia	1,543	7.12	4,547	2,387	608	1,034	446	86	3,366
[state]	57,756	14.14	42,196	32,534	2,462	4,353	3,362	898	9,351
[state]	96,533	17.36	61,364	28,544	3,824	6,651	1,655	2,236	15,343
[state]	14,594	22.44	7,446	5,249		807	488	346	3,323
[state]	91,928	14.46	43,362	44,679	8	3,734	4,288	2,175	24,368
[state]	35,514	4.77	34,468	31,632	3	2,816	2,340	1,432	4,734
[state]	34,643	15.14	35,066	19,399	1	2,446	1,438	766	14,463
[state]	22,659	17.24	22,463	17,075	1,865	1,677	1,388	1,681	20,368
ky	41,566	14.78	34,174	22,346	2,106	5,362	2,995	888	11,662
na	57,929	30.46	66,406	56,734	2,517	3,920	3,326	657	14,245
nd	16,529	17.97	11,362	7,602	1,687	2,157	533	451	4,686
husetts	19,732	6.46	11,454	7,665	2,557	2,103	1,052	888	3,392
	66,161	14.74	61,675	51,202	7,424	4,174	1,671	888	38,343
[state]	51,524	12.74	53,452	45,715	7,441	4,423	3,673	1,633	14,436
ota	45,556	15.15	36,963	22,482	2,641	2,573	1,786	766	15,647
ippi	34,696	16.06	36,584	15,343	1,767	6,341	2,013	914	7,680
ri	77,682	19.57	62,632	52,159	3,151	3,963	2,438	1,606	14,963
ha	16,706	27.94	8,243	6,016	965	836	405	354	4,306
ka	21,354	15.99	12,691	9,541	866	1,243	741	356	4,137
[state]	6,937	42.36	1,987	1,040	394	256	168	316	4,688
ampshire	5,741	16.51	5,655	3,453	865	950	367	339	3,767
rsey	33,696	6.97	23,675	11,904	6,654	3,239	1,781	798	9,644
exico	17,576	25.44	8,640	6,144	887	1,053	556	824	4,411
ork	156,965	10.45	130,137	78,361	27,696	8,696	4,573	3,247	33,460
arolina	50,157	12.29	35,141	20,633	3,065	6,894	4,632	1,163	14,833
Dakota	13,424	21.48	7,992	4,146	563	834	439	304	7,141
[state]	67,029	10.93	62,901	45,596	7,731	3,918	3,654	2,043	22,673
ma	66,567	50.73	52,505	43,664	2,009	4,533	2,397	1,906	14,276
[state]	24,965	16.37	16,019	10,637	2,274	1,853	1,055	404	8,541
lvania	106,346	10.06	77,354	52,154	12,913	8,038	4,346	1,971	37,021
Island	11,542	15.63	7,654	4,704	1,530	988	431	340	3,646
arolina	30,577	14.42	20,584	11,754	1,937	4,302	2,604	688	8,368
Dakota	14,721	22.31	6,606	5,065	460	743	318	340	7,776
see	51,335	15.57	38,537	27,741	2,669	4,716	3,418	941	11,857
[state]	117,361	15.20	92,274	69,811	6,192	10,549	5,721	2,939	22,136
[state]	14,952	21.51	8,420	5,604	1,145	1,089	602	429	6,102
t	6,635	15.86	3,957	2,307	657	738	354	243	1,835
a	21,543	9.52	18,262	8,915	1,717	5,150	2,480	1,713	11,508
gton	53,233	22.35	41,281	34,464	3,570	1,650	1,597	1,330	10,621
irginia	27,710	13.78	20,550	15,339	1,385	1,833	1,993	540	6,631
sin	42,342	12.27	28,601	21,787	2,649	2,496	1,868	782	12,759
ng	8,506	29.23	3,322	2,109	549	410	254	363	4,902
[area]	3,428	25.21	2,492	902	373	1,173	43	146	799
[area]	8,689	17.89	4,739	2,960	603	826	330	347	3,903
Rico	14,691	6.63	8,397	1,964	313	2,891	3,229	829	5,765
Islands	550	20.67	395	54	10	239	93	34	121

d on Census Bureau estimates of total population, excluding armed forces overseas, as of July 1; for Terri-
ad possessions, based on 1950 Census.

e: Department of Health, Education, and Welfare, Social Security Administration; *Social Security Bulletin.*

No. 269.—SOCIAL INSURANCE AND RELATED PROGRAMS—BENEFICIARIES AND BENEFITS BY RISK AND PROGRAM: 1940 TO 1951

[Corrected to July 25, 1952. Partly estimated. Data for State and local government, Federal civil-service, and other contributory retirement systems, exclude refunds of employee contributions]

RISK AND PROGRAM	BENEFICIARIES (thousands) [1]				AMOUNT OF BENEFITS (millions of dollars)			
	1940	1945	1950	1951	1940	1945	1950	1951
Total					1,545.4	2,621.0	6,462.6	6,792.8
Old-age retirement					330.3	602.3	1,466.4	2,167.7
Old-age and survivors insurance	77.2	591.8	1,918.1	2,756.8	21.1	187.4	718.5	1,361.0
Railroad retirement	102.0	129.1	174.8	182.0	83.3	105.2	176.9	187.1
Federal retirement					103.1	141.0	293.4	319.5
Civil-service	47.4	62.5	111.0	120.4	46.1	64.8	135.3	152.4
Other contributory [3]	.6	1.0	1.7	1.7	.7	1.3	2.1	1.8
Noncontributory [7]	82.2	37.6	67.3	60.0	53.3	74.9	156.0	165.2
State and local government retirement [4]	113.0	155.0	213.0	230.0	103.0	143.0	230.0	246.0
Veterans' program [3]	26.2	59.1	53.5	50.2	19.8	54.7	57.6	54.1
Survivorship:								
Monthly benefits					162.9	422.4	924.5	1,194.4
Old-age and survivors insurance	35.7	533.5	1,093.9	1,396.5	7.8	104.2	299.7	523.5
Railroad retirement	3.0	4.4	136.3	146.8	1.4	1.8	43.9	49.5
Federal civil-service		.3	18.3	30.2		.1	8.4	14.0
State and local government retirement [4]	25.0	32.0	40.0	42.0	16.0	20.0	26.0	28.0
Veterans' program [3]	323.2	542.1	991.7	1,011.2	105.7	254.2	491.6	519.4
Workmen's compensation	(8)	(8)	(8)	(8)	[7] 32.0	[7] 42.0	[7] 55.0	[7] 60.0
Lump-sum payments					36.7	65.3	86.7	116.1
Old-age and survivors insurance	(8)	(8)	(8)	(8)	11.7	26.1	32.7	57.3
Railroad retirement	(8)	(8)	(8)	(8)	2.5	8.1	12.7	12.7
Federal retirement	(8)	(8)	(8)	(8)	6.0	10.5	8.4	8.1
Civil-service	(8)	(8)	(8)	(8)	5.8	10.2	8.1	7.8
Other contributory	(8)	(8)	(8)	(8)	.2	.2	.3	.4
State and local government retirement	(8)	(8)	(8)	(8)	[4] 12.5	[4] 15.5	[4] 20.0	[4] 25.0
Veterans' program [4]	(8)	(8)	(8)	(8)	4.0	5.0	12.7	12.9
Workmen's compensation	(8)	(8)	(8)	(8)	(7)	(7)	(7)	(7)
Disability					480.9	956.1	2,457.1	2,451.7
Workmen's compensation	(8)	(8)	(8)	(8)	[7] 129.0	[7] 244.0	[7] 363.0	[7] 415.0
Veterans' program [5]	590.9	1,148.1	2,301.8	2,326.2	298.1	643.1	1,674.6	1,593.9
Railroad retirement	39.3	39.0	76.0	79.1	30.8	30.9	77.3	81.6
Federal civil-service	15.5	23.7	43.0	45.8	13.0	18.9	40.5	44.1
Federal noncontributory [5]			73.1	75.4			178.7	183.0
State and local government retirement [4]	14.3	21.0	32.0	35.0	10.0	14.5	24.0	26.0
State temporary disability insurance [8]		5.4	30.4	26.9		4.7	70.9	81.8
Railroad temporary disability insurance [9]			31.2	26.9			28.1	26.3
Unemployment					534.7	563.2	1,466.2	862.8
State unemployment insurance [10]	982.4	465.0	1,305.0	796.0	518.7	445.9	1,373.4	840.4
Railroad unemployment insurance [9]	41.5	3.3	76.8	29.0	16.0	2.4	59.8	20.2
Veterans' unemployment allowances [11]		88.9	32.1	2.8		115.0	33.0	2.1
Self-employment allowances to veterans [11]		12.1	1.5	1.0		11.7	1.7	.1

[1] Average monthly number, except as otherwise noted.
[2] Includes a small but unknown number and amount of disability and survivor beneficiaries and benefits.
[3] Old-age retirement data include small amount of survivor payments and, for years prior to 1950, significant amount of disability payments now shown separately.
[4] Fiscal year (usually ending June 30); beneficiaries for last month of fiscal year. Data for 1950 and 1951 preliminary.
[5] Under Veterans' Administration. Retirement data only for veterans of Spanish-American War, Boxer Rebellion, and Philippine Insurrection. Disability data include pensions and compensation, and subsistence payments to disabled veterans undergoing training. Lump-sum payments are for burial of deceased veterans.
[6] Comparable data not available.
[7] A small but unknown amount of lump-sum death payments included with monthly survivor payments. Disability benefits exclude payments for medical care. Data for 1950 and 1951, preliminary.
[8] Benefits payable in Rhode Island beginning April 1943, in California beginning December 1946, and in New Jersey beginning January 1949. Excludes New York; data not available. Includes private-plan benefits in California and New Jersey and private-plan beneficiaries in California. Maternity data included for Rhode Island; hospitalization benefits excluded for California. Number represents average weekly number of beneficiaries.
[9] Number represents average number of beneficiaries during 14-day registration period. Temporary disability benefits first payable July 1947; includes maternity data.
[10] Average weekly number.
[11] Average monthly number.

Source: Department of Health, Education, and Welfare, Social Security Administration; *Social Security Bulletin*.

No. 270.—Old-Age and Survivors Insurance—Employee Accounts Established, Workers and Amount of Taxable Wages; Workers in Covered Employment and Amount of Total Payrolls: 1940 to 1952

[Data exclude joint coverage under the railroad retirement and old-age and survivors insurance programs. Corrected to January 14, 1953]

CALENDAR YEAR OR QUARTER	Employee accounts established (thousands) [1]	Workers with taxable wages during period (thousands) [2]	TAXABLE WAGES [3]		Workers in covered employment during period (thousands) [4]	TOTAL PAYROLLS IN COVERED EMPLOYMENT [4]	
			Total (millions)	Average per worker		Total (millions)	Average per worker
1940	5,227	35,393	$32,974	$932	35,393	$35,668	$1,008
1941	6,675	40,976	41,848	1,021	40,976	45,463	1,110
1942	7,636	46,363	52,939	1,142	46,363	56,219	1,256
1943	7,426	47,656	62,423	1,310	47,656	69,553	1,462
1944	4,537	46,296	64,426	1,392	46,296	73,349	1,584
1945	3,321	46,392	62,945	1,357	46,392	71,560	1,543
1946	3,022	48,845	69,088	1,414	48,845	79,290	1,623
1947	2,728	48,908	78,372	1,602	48,908	92,449	1,890
1948	2,720	49,018	84,122	1,716	49,018	102,255	2,086
1949	2,340	46,796	81,806	1,748	46,796	99,989	2,137
1950 [6]	2,891	48,100	87,498	1,819	48,100	109,804	2,283
1951 [6][7]	4,927	54,500	111,075	2,038	54,500	133,800	2,455
1951 [6][7]							
January–March	1,302	44,000	30,175	686	44,000	30,900	702
April–June	1,399	45,500	30,600	673	45,800	32,900	718
July–September	1,333	45,500	27,700	609	47,000	34,000	722
October–December	894	42,000	22,600	538	47,000	36,000	766
1952 [6][7]							
January–March	1,300	45,000	33,000	733	45,000	34,000	756

[1] Excludes number under railroad-retirement program.
[2] Partly estimated. Quarterly data unadjusted for workers employed during quarter but not reported after quarter in which they received their first $3,000 in year prior to 1951, and $3,600 in year after 1950.
[3] Unadjusted for nontaxable wages erroneously reported and wages excluded in benefit computations. Wages in excess of $3,000 a year prior to 1951 and $3,600 a year after 1950 paid to worker by any 1 employer are not taxable.
[4] Partly estimated. Quarterly data adjusted for workers employed during quarter but not reported after quarter in which they received their first $3,000 in year prior to 1951 and their first $3,600 in year after 1950.
[5] Includes all wages of workers earning over $3,000 a year prior to 1951 and $3,600 a year after 1950.
[6] Preliminary, except employee accounts established.
[7] Except for employee accounts established, excludes newly-covered self-employed persons. Although quarterly data on employment and earnings including self-employed persons are not available, annual estimates are obtainable for all covered persons. Annual totals for 1951, including the self-employed, are: 58 million workers; $119.5 billion in taxable earnings; $2,050 average taxable earnings per worker.

Source: Department of Health, Education, and Welfare, Social Security Administration, Bureau of Old-Age and Survivors Insurance. Data appear periodically in *Social Security Bulletin*.

No. 271.—Old-Age and Survivors Insurance—Amount of Payments Certified: 1944 to 1952

[In thousands of dollars. Data corrected to February 6, 1953]

TYPE	1944	1945	1946	1947	1948	1949	1950	1951	1952
Total payments	218,097	287,757	387,691	482,457	575,938	689,010	1,050,885	1,941,868	2,292,267
Payments under 1939, 1946, 1950, and 1952 amendments:									
Monthly benefits, total [1]	195,951	261,622	360,424	452,939	543,623	655,852	1,018,144	1,884,531	2,228,969
Old-age	101,285	133,768	196,078	255,202	312,534	387,765	614,757	1,168,767	(²)
Wife's or husband's	16,454	21,935	32,011	41,523	50,595	62,331	96,801	180,540	(²)
Child's	41,928	56,077	69,419	81,591	91,938	101,868	154,898	281,196	(²)
Widow's or widower's	14,517	20,883	28,642	37,677	48,907	61,446	95,186	159,462	(²)
Mother's	21,017	28,005	33,119	35,315	37,697	40,223	52,639	85,713	(²)
Parent's	751	954	1,155	1,632	1,952	2,220	3,864	8,853	(²)
Lump-sum	22,124	26,115	27,251	29,511	32,315	33,158	32,740	57,337	63,298
Lump-sum payments under 1935 act [3]	22	19	16	6	(⁴)	(⁴)	(⁴)		

[1] Distribution by type estimated.
[2] Data not yet available.   [3] Payable with respect to workers who died prior to January 1940.   [4] Less than $500.

Source: Department of Health, Education, and Welfare, Social Security Administration, Bureau of Old-Age and Survivors Insurance.

No. 272.—OLD-AGE AND SURVIVORS INSURANCE—NUMBER AND AMOUNT OF MONTHLY BENEFITS, BY TYPE: 1945 TO 1952

[Amounts in thousands. Data corrected to February 2, 1953]

YEAR	Total	Old-age	Wife's or husband's	Child's	Widow's or widower's	Mother's	Parent's
BENEFITS IN CURRENT-PAYMENT STATUS, END OF YEAR							
Number:							
1945	1,288,107	518,234	159,168	390,134	93,781	120,581	6,209
1946	1,642,209	701,708	215,984	461,756	127,046	128,410	7,398
1947	1,978,245	874,724	269,174	524,783	164,309	135,229	10,026
1948	2,314,557	1,047,085	320,928	581,265	210,253	142,223	11,903
1949	2,742,808	1,285,893	390,583	639,437	261,336	152,121	13,438
1950	3,477,243	1,770,984	508,380	699,703	314,189	160,438	14,579
1951	4,378,085	2,278,470	646,890	846,247	384,265	203,782	19,331
1952	5,025,549	2,643,932	738,859	938,751	454,563	227,984	21,460
Total monthly amount:							
1945	$23,801	$12,538	$2,040	$4,858	$1,893	$2,391	$81
1946	31,081	17,230	2,805	5,804	2,568	2,577	97
1947	38,277	21,779	3,545	6,702	3,352	2,764	135
1948	45,572	26,564	4,307	7,549	4,331	2,959	162
1949	56,074	33,437	5,376	8,427	5,442	3,207	185
1950	126,857	77,675	11,995	19,366	11,481	5,801	535
1951	154,791	96,008	14,710	22,739	13,849	6,776	709
1952	205,179	130,217	19,178	28,141	18,482	8,273	887
Average monthly amount:							
1945		$24.19	$12.82	$12.45	$20.19	$19.83	$13.05
1946		24.55	12.99	12.57	20.21	20.07	13.11
1947		24.90	13.17	12.77	20.40	20.44	13.46
1948		25.35	13.42	12.99	20.60	20.81	13.61
1949		26.00	13.76	13.18	20.82	21.06	13.77
1950		43.86	23.60	27.68	36.54	34.24	36.70
1951		42.14	22.74	26.87	36.04	33.25	36.68
1952		49.25	25.96	29.98	40.66	36.29	41.33
BENEFITS AWARDED DURING YEAR							
Number:							
1945	462,463	185,174	63,066	127,514	29,844	55,108	1,755
1946	547,150	258,980	88,515	114,875	38,823	44,190	1,767
1947	572,909	271,488	94,189	115,754	45,249	42,807	3,422
1948	596,201	275,902	96,554	118,955	55,667	44,276	2,846
1949	682,241	337,273	117,356	118,922	62,928	43,087	2,675
1950 (under 1939 amendments)	384,334	153,223	66,665	67,730	40,681	24,595	1,420
1950 (under 1950 amendments)	578,294	383,908	96,083	54,911	26,054	16,506	832
1951	1,336,431	762,990	228,876	230,502	89,582	78,332	6,149
1952 (under 1950 amendments)	472,977	203,197	73,751	103,168	53,204	37,342	2,405
1952 (under 1952 amendments)	580,326	326,099	103,958	80,176	39,096	27,535	1,462
Total monthly amount:							
1945	$8,805	$4,650	$622	$1,614	$602	$1,094	$23
1946	10,972	6,584	1,172	1,493	785	914	24
1947	11,881	7,114	1,282	1,570	939	928	48
1948	12,748	7,489	1,392	1,667	1,171	989	41
1949	15,343	9,575	1,728	1,688	1,346	969	39
1950 (under 1939 amendments)	8,749	5,315	1,002	970	841	557	21
1950 (under 1950 amendments)	17,485	12,761	1,894	1,253	961	585	31
1951	42,282	26,388	4,701	5,322	3,125	2,524	221
1952 (under 1950 amendments)	15,315	8,054	1,591	2,486	1,866	1,232	86
1952 (under 1952 amendments)	27,434	19,065	3,102	2,449	1,593	1,162	64
Average monthly amount:							
1945		$25.11	$13.03	$12.66	$20.17	$19.85	$13.11
1946		25.42	13.24	13.00	20.22	20.68	13.58
1947		26.20	13.61	13.56	20.75	21.68	14.03
1948		27.14	14.12	14.01	21.04	22.34	14.41
1949		28.39	14.71	14.19	21.39	22.49	14.58
1950 (under 1939 amendments)		29.02	15.03	14.32	21.66	22.65	14.79
1950 (under 1950 amendments)		33.24	19.71	22.82	36.88	35.44	37.26
1951		37.54	20.54	23.09	34.88	32.22	35.94
1952 (under 1950 amendments)		39.65	21.57	24.10	35.07	33.00	35.89
1952 (under 1952 amendments)		58.11	29.83	30.55	40.75	42.20	43.56

Source: Department of Health, Education, and Welfare, Social Security Administration, Bureau of Old-Age and Survivors Insurance. Data appear periodically in *Social Security Bulletin*.

No. 273.—OLD-AGE AND SURVIVORS INSURANCE—ESTIMATED NUMBER OF EMPLOYERS REPORTING TAXABLE WAGES, THEIR PAY-PERIOD EMPLOYMENT AND AMOUNT OF TAXABLE WAGES, BY SIZE OF FIRM: JANUARY-MARCH 1945 TO 1949

[Data corrected to Nov. 6, 1951]

PERIOD JAN.-MAR.	Total	SIZE OF FIRM (NUMBER OF EMPLOYEES) [1]									
		0	1-3	4-7	8-19	20-49	50-99	100-499	500-999	1,000-9,999	10,000 or more
EMPLOYERS (THOUSANDS) [2]											
1945	2,001.0	23.3	1,174.3	404.0	233.4	100.5	34.0	25.6	3.2	2.6	0.2
1946	2,280.0	29.2	1,268.0	482.1	293.3	115.9	38.1	27.7	3.1	2.6	.2
1947	2,456.7	40.4	1,415.7	519.6	314.8	121.6	39.6	28.9	3.3	2.8	.2
1948	2,580.0	42.4	1,488.5	537.2	325.0	122.3	39.3	29.0	3.3	2.7	.2
1949	2,639.3	50.0	1,544.8	535.4	317.1	120.0	38.4	27.7	3.1	2.6	.2
PAY PERIOD EMPLOYMENT (THOUSANDS) [3]											
1945	32,802	0	1,949	2,078	2,759	3,018	2,322	5,299	2,333	6,554	6,682
1946	32,493	0	2,194	2,507	3,496	3,483	2,611	5,681	2,157	6,163	4,270
1947	35,067	0	2,382	2,650	3,704	3,599	2,676	5,782	2,299	6,794	5,201
1948	35,805	0	2,497	2,739	3,832	3,663	2,690	5,779	2,381	6,512	5,513
1949	34,689	0	2,607	2,758	3,705	3,577	2,611	5,437	2,098	6,485	5,411
TAXABLE WAGES (MILLIONS) [4]											
1945	$17,928	$23	$682	$793	$1,148	$1,408	$1,165	$2,740	$1,242	$4,043	$4,715
1946	16,840	18	779	1,010	1,614	1,800	1,386	2,992	1,190	3,570	2,483
1947	20,805	26	960	1,193	1,917	2,086	1,505	3,542	1,437	4,534	3,533
1948	22,080	35	1,059	1,310	2,112	2,289	1,728	3,847	1,587	4,975	4,138
1949	22,376	42	1,121	1,366	2,204	2,360	1,769	3,754	1,523	4,940	4,397

[1] Measured by employer's pay period employment.
[2] An employer is a legal entity, such as corporation, partnership, or single ownership, for which a single tax return is filed.
[3] Total number of workers employed during pay period ending nearest to Mar. 15.
[4] Wages paid by employers for covered employment during period, excluding wages over $3,000 paid by any one employer to any worker in a calendar year.

Source: Department of Health, Education, and Welfare, Social Security Administration, Bureau of Old-Age and Survivors Insurance.

No. 274.—Old-Age and Survivors Insurance—Percentage Distribution of Workers, by Age and Sex: 1947 to 1950

[Data are estimated; corrected to February 3, 1953]

SEX	1947	1948	1949	1950 [1]	AGE	1947	1948	1949	1950 [1]
All workers [2]...	100.0	100.0	100.0	100.0	Total [2]............	100.0	100.0	100.0	100.0
Male...............	66.9	67.3	67.5	67.8	Under 20............	10.8	10.5	9.2	9.2
Female.............	33.1	32.7	32.5	32.2	20–24...............	15.7	15.4	14.8	14.6
					25–29...............	13.9	13.7	14.0	13.9
1 to 3 quarters [3]...	36.0	34.1	33.4	34.7	30–34...............	12.2	12.4	12.4	12.4
Male...............	21.0	19.7	19.7	20.0	35–39...............	11.1	11.1	11.6	11.6
Female.............	15.1	14.3	13.8	14.8	40–44...............	9.7	9.9	10.3	10.4
					45–49...............	8.1	8.1	8.5	8.5
4 quarters [4].......	64.0	65.9	66.6	65.3	50–54...............	6.6	6.7	6.7	7.0
Male...............	46.0	47.6	47.9	47.8	55–59...............	5.3	5.2	5.4	5.4
Female.............	18.0	18.3	18.7	17.5	60–64...............	3.7	3.8	3.9	3.9
					65 and over.........	3.1	3.1	3.2	3.1

[1] Preliminary.
[2] Workers with $1 or more in wages during calendar year.
[3] Workers with $1 or more in wages in 1, 2 or 3 calendar quarters of year.
[4] Workers with $1 or more in wages in each calendar quarter of year.
[5] Age at birthday in specified year.

Source: Department of Health, Education, and Welfare, Social Security Administration, Bureau of Old-Age and Survivors Insurance.

No. 275.—Old-Age and Survivors Insurance—Percentage Distribution of Workers, by Amount of Wage Credits and Median Wages: 1947 to 1950

[Data corrected to February 3, 1953]

ITEM	1947	1948	1949	1950 [1]		
				All workers	1 to 3 quarters	4 quarters
Estimated number of workers with wage credits (thousands)[1].........	48,900	49,100	47,200	48,100	16,700	31,400
PERCENTAGE DISTRIBUTION [2]						
All workers................	100.0	100.0	100.0	100.0	100.0	100.0
$1–$199..................	13.6	12.4	12.3	11.9	33.5	.3
$200–$399................	7.8	7.2	7.0	6.3	16.2	1.1
$400–$599................	6.1	5.6	5.3	4.9	11.7	1.3
$600–$799................	5.1	4.7	4.5	4.2	8.7	1.8
$800–$999................	4.5	4.2	4.1	4.0	6.6	2.5
$1,000–$1,199............	4.4	4.0	3.9	3.6	4.5	3.2
$1,200–$1,399............	4.6	4.1	4.1	3.7	3.6	3.8
$1,400–$1,599............	4.7	4.2	4.1	3.8	3.0	4.3
$1,600–$1,799............	4.7	4.2	4.2	3.8	2.4	4.6
$1,800–$1,999............	4.7	4.4	4.5	4.3	2.1	5.4
$2,000–$2,199............	4.6	4.4	4.5	4.4	2.1	5.6
$2,200–$2,399............	4.3	4.2	4.3	4.4	1.5	5.9
$2,400–$2,599............	4.0	4.1	4.2	4.4	1.2	6.1
$2,600–$2,799............	3.9	4.0	4.1	4.2	1.2	5.7
$2,800–$2,999............	3.5	3.7	3.8	3.7	1.2	5.1
$3,000..................	19.7	24.6	25.1	28.5	.6	43.3
MEDIAN WAGES						
All workers................	$1,570	$1,772	$1,821	$2,000	$400	$2,750
Male...............	2,084	2,337	2,361	2,550	450	3,150
Female.............	907	1,013	1,075	1,200	300	1,900

[1] Preliminary estimate. [2] Percentage distribution of workers by wage credits.

Source: Department of Health, Education, and Welfare, Social Security Administration, Bureau of Old-Age and Survivors Insurance.

No. 276.—OLD-AGE AND SURVIVORS INSURANCE—INDIVIDUAL BENEFICIARIES AND BENEFITS, BY STATES AND OTHER AREAS: JUNE 30, 1952

[In thousands. Estimates; corrected to December 22, 1952]

STATE OR OTHER AREA	BENEFITS IN CURRENT-PAYMENT STATUS, JUNE 30, 1952		AMOUNT OF PAYMENTS CERTIFIED IN FISCAL YEAR 1952					Number of lump-sum payments certified in fiscal year 1952 [3]
			Total	Monthly benefits [1]			Lump-sum payments [2]	
	Number	Monthly amount		Old-age	Supplementary	Survivor		
Total	4,593.8	$161,739	$2,634,573	$1,221,996	$198,863	$555,564	$58,270	444.7
Alabama	68.7	1,932	24,164	12,113	2,009	9,279	763	6.6
Arizona	19.1	627	7,778	4,296	674	2,567	241	1.9
Arkansas	36.9	907	12,320	6,990	1,108	3,850	372	3.4
California	371.6	13,589	169,870	111,369	16,084	37,901	4,536	34.3
Colorado	37.0	1,242	15,419	9,406	1,542	4,096	375	3.1
Connecticut	82.8	3,333	42,698	26,794	4,414	10,236	1,154	7.8
Delaware	10.8	396	4,966	3,038	483	1,299	146	1.1
District of Columbia	17.2	605	7,674	4,517	591	2,275	291	2.4
Florida	102.6	3,532	43,260	28,331	4,706	9,263	961	8.0
Georgia	68.6	1,899	23,584	11,765	1,845	9,181	793	7.4
Idaho	14.0	427	5,356	3,204	481	1,520	151	1.3
Illinois	283.5	10,608	134,994	82,039	13,175	35,466	4,314	31.8
Indiana	132.7	4,582	57,656	34,294	6,013	15,681	1,866	13.2
Iowa	62.0	1,973	24,608	14,936	2,606	6,343	723	6.1
Kansas	45.1	1,408	17,703	10,687	1,887	4,641	488	4.0
Kentucky	72.9	2,165	26,992	14,032	2,432	9,770	768	6.2
Louisiana	54.7	1,632	20,180	10,749	1,614	7,186	631	5.4
Maine	40.6	1,366	17,317	11,084	1,751	4,062	430	3.3
Maryland	64.6	2,285	28,711	16,231	2,580	8,996	934	6.9
Massachusetts	210.9	8,099	102,924	65,465	10,579	24,262	2,618	19.2
Michigan	200.3	7,513	94,480	53,924	9,474	28,199	2,883	20.7
Minnesota	75.5	2,591	32,202	19,950	3,310	8,121	821	6.4
Mississippi	30.8	786	9,555	4,808	780	3,684	263	2.7
Missouri	113.3	3,842	48,334	30,006	4,824	12,111	1,393	11.1
Montana	15.3	508	6,341	3,804	541	1,787	209	1.7
Nebraska	26.5	820	10,177	6,244	1,059	2,582	292	2.4
Nevada	4.5	159	2,019	1,300	123	525	71	.5
New Hampshire	24.8	870	10,958	7,152	1,092	2,456	258	2.0
New Jersey	182.6	7,146	90,497	55,125	9,313	23,293	2,766	19.4
New Mexico	11.0	305	3,705	1,712	276	1,597	120	1.0
New York	529.1	20,024	252,850	158,976	24,560	61,952	7,342	53.0
North Carolina	78.3	2,191	27,283	13,254	2,229	10,864	936	8.3
North Dakota	7.2	207	2,533	1,480	229	752	72	.7
Ohio	284.2	10,521	133,593	79,356	14,133	36,222	3,882	28.3
Oklahoma	47.3	1,420	17,571	9,901	1,610	5,568	492	4.2
Oregon	58.4	2,050	25,814	17,000	2,552	5,632	630	4.7
Pennsylvania	401.0	15,108	191,629	113,856	19,515	53,026	5,232	37.6
Rhode Island	36.1	1,375	17,520	11,216	1,822	4,013	469	3.4
South Carolina	40.1	1,070	13,362	6,019	987	5,838	518	4.7
South Dakota	9.5	284	3,520	2,035	339	1,028	118	1.0
Tennessee	68.4	1,951	24,250	12,665	2,037	8,787	771	6.8
Texas	144.6	4,352	53,979	28,173	4,570	19,406	1,830	15.6
Utah	16.7	546	6,821	3,514	690	2,429	188	1.5
Vermont	13.6	456	5,739	3,542	589	1,487	121	1.0
Virginia	74.5	2,293	28,660	14,879	2,438	10,415	928	7.7
Washington	88.4	3,214	40,485	27,002	3,961	8,543	959	7.3
West Virginia	69.0	2,260	28,309	14,449	2,580	10,616	664	4.9
Wisconsin	105.7	3,743	47,144	28,501	5,049	12,244	1,350	10.1
Wyoming	5.9	196	2,457	1,527	204	651	75	.6
Alaska	2.3	75	942	638	32	249	23	.2
Hawaii	10.9	337	4,243	2,501	308	1,357	77	.7
Puerto Rico	.8	22	216	38	1	158	13	.1
Virgin Islands	(4)	1	12	7	1	4	(4)	(4)
Foreign	20.7	805	9,299	6,112	1,016	2,034	137	1.0

[1] Distribution by type estimated. Supplementary benefits paid to wives, dependent aged husbands and children of retired (old-age) beneficiaries. Survivor benefits paid to following survivors of deceased insured workers: Aged widows, dependent aged widowers, children, younger widows with child beneficiaries in their care, or dependent aged parents.

[2] Payable with respect to workers who died after December 1939, and before September 1950, if no survivor could be entitled to monthly benefits for month in which worker died, or with respect to all workers who died after August 1950.

[3] Exceeds number of deceased workers with respect to whose wage records payments were certified.

[4] Less than 50.

[5] Less than $500.

Source: Department of Health, Education, and Welfare, Social Security Administration; *Social Security Bulletin*.

No. 277.—Old-Age and Survivors Insurance—Sample (1 Percent) of Workers With Wage Credits at Some Time in 1937-50, by Cumulative Wage Credits in 1937-50, Insurance Status January 1, 1951, and Age Group

[1-percent sample of all workers with wage credits identified for posting by July 1951, only partly adjusted for duplication of workers with more than 1 account. Includes workers who became entitled to benefits before Jan. 1, 1951, and all but 2,229 of the workers dying during the period 1937-50. Age represents age at birthday in 1960. Since data are derived from a sample, they are subject to a sampling variation which may be relatively large where figures shown are small. Because of mechanical processes and extent of adjustments for delayed wage records, data may differ slightly from corresponding data in other published tables. Data corrected to Jan. 6, 1953]

CUMULATIVE WAGE CREDITS AND INSURANCE STATUS	Total [1]	AGE GROUP						
		Under 20	20-24	25-34	35-44	55-59	60-64	65 and over
Total, 1-percent sample [2]	**885,648**	**52,826**	**109,399**	**240,558**	**189,475**	**50,784**	**40,664**	**62,018**
$1-$1,999	319,961	44,591	47,581	80,900	53,971	14,719	12,093	22,772
$2,000-$2,999	58,028	4,005	11,187	17,483	10,392	2,454	2,067	3,903
$3,000-$4,199	54,930	2,344	10,810	16,918	10,240	2,379	1,988	3,722
$4,200-$5,399	125,537	1,807	24,601	41,329	25,032	5,985	4,975	8,685
$5,400-$12,599	86,818	70	11,564	31,745	18,029	4,291	3,475	5,737
$12,600-$16,799	64,685	5	3,273	25,531	15,405	3,555	2,770	4,329
$16,800-$20,999	45,691	(³)	365	13,895	13,806	3,007	2,581	3,980
$21,000-$25,199	35,896	(³)	17	7,042	12,639	2,959	2,353	2,791
$25,200-$29,399	29,093	2	1	3,684	11,044	2,815	2,287	2,170
$29,400-$33,599	27,456	1	(³)	1,634	10,182	3,124	2,349	1,915
$33,600-$41,999	30,609	1	(³)	395	8,469	4,630	3,114	2,144
$42,000 and over	3,744	(³)	(³)	2	266	866	617	459
Fully insured [4]	**631,142**	**13,296**	**74,167**	**180,024**	**147,151** 1	**38,255**	**30,228**	**43,219**
$1-$1,999	72,009	6,185	13,018	21,520	12,936	2,908	2,383	5,108
$2,000-$2,999	55,895	3,630	10,616	16,588	9,641	2,143	1,795	3,435
$3,000-$4,199	53,189	2,297	10,716	16,722	9,923	2,185	1,782	3,420
$4,200-$5,399	127,547	1,805	24,597	41,279	24,859	5,818	4,782	8,376
$5,400-$12,599	86,576	70	11,564	31,734	17,985	4,257	3,419	5,692
$12,600-$16,799	64,645	5	3,273	25,530	15,401	3,546	2,766	4,321
$16,800-$20,999	45,685	(³)	365	13,894	13,805	3,006	2,581	3,980
$21,000-$25,199	35,893	(³)	17	7,042	12,639	2,958	2,353	2,789
$25,200-$29,399	29,093	2	1	3,684	11,044	2,815	2,287	2,170
$29,400-$33,599	27,454	1	(³)	1,634	10,182	3,123	2,349	1,914
$33,600-$41,999	30,609	1	(³)	395	8,469	4,630	3,114	2,146
$42,000 and over	3,744	(³)	(³)	2	266	866	617	459
Uninsured [4]	**253,277**	**38,530**	**35,231**	**60,420**	**41,944**	**12,202**	**10,039**	**18,296**
$1-$1,999	247,521	38,406	34,562	59,347	40,957	11,761	9,654	17,541
$2,000-$2,999	3,928	375	571	876	671	255	202	377
$3,000-$4,199	1,307	47	94	172	239	130	112	212
$4,200-$5,399	462	2	4	23	69	50	57	145
$5,400-$12,599	48	(³)	(³)	1	6	5	14	16
$12,600-$16,799	7	(³)	(³)	(³)	2	(³)	(³)	3
$16,800 and over	4	(³)	(³)	1	(³)	1	(³)	2

[1] Includes 6,726 workers of unknown age, of whom 946 were fully insured and 5,780 were uninsured.
[2] Includes 2,229 workers who were currently insured at death prior to September 1950 on whose wage records benefits were awarded.
[3] No workers in sample cell.
[4] If a worker is fully insured as of a given date, certain of his survivors, in event of his death on or before that date, are eligible for survivors benefits. In addition, all fully insured workers who have attained age 65 are eligible for old-age benefits. An uninsured worker is one on basis of whose wage record no benefits would be payable. Changes in insurance status resulting from wage credits for military service and coordination with Railroad Retirement programs are only partially reflected.

Source: Department of Health, Education, and Welfare, Social Security Administration, Bureau of Old-Age and Survivors Insurance.

No. 278.—Unemployment Insurance—Workers With Wage Credits, Average Employment, and Total Wages, by States and Territories: 1950 and 1951

[In thousands. Corrected to July 1, 1952]

STATE AND TERRITORY	1951 minimum coverage provisions for size of firm [1]	WORKERS WITH WAGE CREDITS [2]		AVERAGE EMPLOYMENT [3]		WAGES [4]	
		1950	1951	1950	1951	1950	1951
Total	8 in 20 weeks	45,600	45,800	32,887	34,968	$103,129,637	$115,717,346
Alabama	8 in 20 weeks	680	744	410	431	1,054,480	1,184,112
Arizona	3 in 20 weeks	200	237	106	121	323,915	402,086
Arkansas	1 in 10 days	435	462	223	240	483,927	565,407
California	1 at any time [5]	4,050	4,334	2,525	2,764	8,610,333	10,183,978
Colorado	8 in 20 weeks	350	375	205	222	512,278	734,334
Connecticut	4 in 13 weeks	834	877	616	675	1,999,469	2,422,664
Delaware	1 in 20 weeks	144	152	100	106	336,357	379,873
District of Columbia	1 at any time	429	436	222	225	670,826	736,086
Florida	8 in 20 weeks	799	826	407	443	1,062,141	1,236,209
Georgia	do	932	924	533	571	1,312,912	1,507,744
Idaho	1 at any time [6]	196	194	94	96	208,598	203,817
Illinois	6 in 20 weeks	3,334	3,442	2,325	2,434	8,054,590	9,151,576
Indiana	8 in 20 weeks	1,371	1,402	915	953	3,021,887	3,554,145
Iowa	8 in 18 weeks	574	600	348	348	1,617,531	1,172,632
Kansas	8 in 20 weeks [7]	448	520	255	252	751,682	978,011
Kentucky	4 in 3 quarters [8]	580	617	391	418	1,063,570	1,235,144
Louisiana	4 in 20 weeks	742	768	459	480	1,208,397	1,501,964
Maine	8 in 20 weeks	266	271	166	176	440,941	527,078
Maryland	1 at any time	833	902	562	607	1,573,920	1,526,007
Massachusetts	1 in 13 weeks	1,989	2,150	1,431	1,486	4,146,408	4,640,286
Michigan	8 in 20 weeks	2,300	2,266	1,626	1,715	6,077,686	6,951,641
Minnesota	1 in 20 weeks [9]	810	866	553	578	1,637,634	1,808,565
Mississippi	8 in 20 weeks	356	380	179	195	338,768	454,131
Missouri	do	1,213	1,239	782	836	2,362,343	2,672,368
Montana	1 in 20 weeks [10]	181	183	101	104	291,785	322,910
Nebraska	8 in 20 weeks [11]	280	291	166	176	466,822	526,984
Nevada	1 at any time [12]	68	74	37	41	122,467	142,130
New Hampshire	4 in 20 weeks	184	195	126	131	326,774	360,906
New Jersey	do	1,906	1,986	1,294	1,394	4,324,118	5,081,008
New Mexico	2 in 13 weeks [13]	209	219	101	107	280,009	339,274
New York	4 in 15 days	6,300	6,338	4,200	4,433	14,948,591	16,479,982
North Carolina	8 in 20 weeks	975	991	658	695	1,601,135	1,795,011
North Dakota	do	92	89	47	47	132,685	142,224
Ohio	3 in 1 day	3,040	3,156	2,175	2,346	7,196,471	8,655,826
Oklahoma	8 in 20 weeks	533	548	281	296	838,381	961,648
Oregon	4 in 6 weeks [14]	517	556	314	333	1,049,566	1,230,154
Pennsylvania	1 at any time	3,915	3,845	3,027	3,160	8,975,126	10,230,923
Rhode Island	4 in 20 weeks	230	330	234	241	673,545	743,046
South Carolina	8 in 20 weeks	482	543	319	346	747,296	870,597
South Dakota	do	96	96	53	53	146,027	156,622
Tennessee	do	823	843	496	526	1,296,986	1,463,500
Texas	do	2,286	2,364	1,229	1,344	3,604,200	4,276,363
Utah	1 at any time [15]	315	290	127	135	367,362	426,922
Vermont	8 in 20 weeks	92	95	60	63	161,172	189,516
Virginia	do	792	824	505	537	1,315,004	1,525,513
Washington	1 at any time	784	855	509	542	1,675,721	1,946,666
West Virginia	8 in 20 weeks	530	560	375	381	1,145,083	1,317,012
Wisconsin	6 in 13 weeks [16]	1,090	1,124	742	786	2,352,171	2,770,925
Wyoming	1 at any time [17]	103	112	54	55	159,391	175,989
Alaska	1 at any time	60	78	25	34	120,994	202,290
Hawaii	do	138	152	91	96	244,140	272,305

[1] Employer becomes subject to State unemployment insurance law when he has employed specified minimum number of workers on at least 1 day in each of specified number of weeks within current or preceding calendar year. Coverage provisions shown are in effect for 1950 and 1951.
[2] Estimated number of different workers in each State who have earned wages in covered employment sometime during calendar year. Totals adjusted to eliminate duplication due to shifting of workers between States during year.
[3] Average of 12 monthly figures, each of which is total of number of workers in covered employment in pay period of each type (weekly, semimonthly, etc.) ending nearest 15th of month.
[4] Total wages in covered employment for all pay periods ending in year.
[5] And wages of $100 in any calendar quarter.
[6] And wages of $75 in a calendar quarter. [7] Or 25 in 1 week.
[8] Wages of at least $50 to each of at least 4 workers during each of 3 calendar quarters.
[9] But 1 in 20 weeks for employers located outside the corporate limits of a city, village, or borough of 10,000 or more population. [10] Or wages of $500 in a calendar year. [11] Or wages of $10,000 in any calendar quarter.
[12] And wages of $225 in any calendar quarter. [13] Or wages of $450 in a calendar quarter.
[14] And wages of $250 in same calendar quarter. [15] And wages of $140 in any calendar quarter.
[16] Or wages of $6,000 in preceding calendar year. Includes employers with wages of $10,000 in a calendar quarter toward which not more than $1,000 per employee need be counted. [17] And wages of $500 in a calendar year.

Source: Department of Labor, Bureau of Employment Security.

No. 279.—Unemployment Insurance—Average Employment and Total Wages, by Major Industry Group: 1950

[In thousands. Data corrected to July 1, 1951]

INDUSTRY DIVISION AND MAJOR INDUSTRY GROUP [1]	AVERAGE EMPLOYMENT		WAGES	
	Number of workers [2]	Percent of total, all industries	Amount [3]	Percent of total, all industries
Total, all industries	32,887	100.0	$103,129,637	100.0
Agriculture, forestry, and fishing	67	.2	185,633	.2
Farms	10	(4)	27,403	(4)
Agriculture and similar service establishments	40	.1	93,848	.1
Forestry	1	(4)	2,807	(4)
Fishing	16	(4)	61,575	.1
Mining	894	2.7	3,102,159	3.0
Metal mining	98	.3	349,258	.3
Anthracite mining	75	.2	233,069	.2
Bituminous and other soft-coal mining	389	1.2	1,277,147	1.2
Crude-petroleum and natural-gas production	238	.7	932,984	.9
Nonmetallic mining and quarrying	94	.3	309,701	.3
Contract construction	2,065	6.3	7,217,614	7.0
Building construction—general contractors	769	2.3	2,541,672	2.5
General contractors, other than building	430	1.3	1,567,558	1.5
Construction—special-trade contractors	866	2.6	3,108,384	3.0
Manufacturing	14,781	44.9	48,972,535	47.5
Ordnance and accessories	26	.1	93,805	.1
Food and kindred products	1,507	4.6	4,650,642	4.5
Tobacco manufactures	96	.3	218,246	.2
Textile-mill products	1,290	3.9	3,559,673	3.5
Apparel and other finished products of fabrics	1,172	3.6	2,906,412	2.8
Lumber and wood products (except furniture)	740	2.2	1,896,122	1.8
Furniture and fixtures	365	1.1	1,104,011	1.1
Paper and allied products	483	1.5	1,680,695	1.6
Printing, publishing, and allied industries	709	2.2	2,735,920	2.7
Chemicals and allied products	671	2.0	2,535,031	2.5
Products of petroleum and coal	238	.7	1,025,932	1.0
Rubber products	245	.7	867,088	.8
Leather and leather products	391	1.2	995,984	1.0
Stone, clay, and glass products	507	1.5	1,656,898	1.6
Primary metal industries	1,190	3.6	4,436,487	4.3
Fabricated metal products (except ordnance, machinery, and transportation equipment)	987	3.0	3,488,708	3.4
Machinery (except electrical)	1,350	4.1	5,073,962	4.9
Electrical machinery, equipment, and supplies	872	2.7	2,937,785	2.8
Transportation equipment	1,255	3.8	4,911,570	4.8
Professional, scientific, and controlling instruments; photographic and optical goods; watches and clocks	245	.7	866,596	.8
Miscellaneous manufacturing industries	444	1.4	1,331,168	1.3
Transportation, communication, and other public utilities [3]	2,498	7.6	8,177,670	7.9
Local railways and bus lines	143	.4	484,912	.5
Trucking and warehousing for hire	865	1.7	1,861,086	1.8
Other transportation, except water transportation	289	.9	877,488	.9
Water transportation	132	.4	554,201	.5
Services allied to transportation, n. e. c	158	.5	439,446	.4
Communication: Telephone, telegraph, and related services	662	2.0	2,020,625	2.0
Utilities: Electric and gas	527	1.6	1,882,793	1.8
Local utilities and local public services, n. e. c	21	.1	57,059	.1

See footnotes at end of table.

No. 279.—UNEMPLOYMENT INSURANCE—AVERAGE EMPLOYMENT AND TOTAL WAGES, BY MAJOR INDUSTRY GROUP: 1950—Continued

[In thousands]

INDUSTRY DIVISION AND MAJOR INDUSTRY GROUP [1]	AVERAGE EMPLOYMENT		WAGES	
	Number of workers [2]	Percent of total, all industries	Amount [3]	Percent of total, all industries
Wholesale and retail trade	8,176	34.9	$32,441,767	22.7
Full-service and limited-function wholesalers	1,279	3.9	4,648,140	4.5
Wholesale distributors, other than full-service and limited-function wholesalers	988	3.0	3,927,977	3.8
Wholesale and retail trade combined, not elsewhere classified	330	1.0	1,089,599	1.1
Retail general merchandise	1,315	4.0	2,799,448	2.7
Retail food and liquor stores	959	2.9	2,520,012	2.4
Retail automotive	648	2.0	2,402,718	2.3
Retail apparel and accessories	488	1.5	1,179,543	1.1
Retail trade, not elsewhere classified	1,015	3.1	2,755,662	2.7
Eating and drinking places	1,015	3.1	1,794,147	1.7
Retail filling stations	140	.4	334,521	.3
Finance, insurance, and real estate	1,530	4.7	4,895,798	4.7
Banks and trust companies	380	1.2	1,224,809	1.2
Security dealers and investment banking	56	.2	285,937	.3
Finance agencies, not elsewhere classified	112	.3	362,321	.4
Insurance carriers	498	1.5	1,633,180	1.6
Insurance agents, brokers, and services	100	.3	334,863	.3
Real estate	334	1.0	861,303	.8
Real estate, insurance, loans, law offices: Any combination	41	.1	139,523	.1
Holding companies (except real estate)	9	[4]	53,862	.1
Service	2,813	8.6	6,986,155	6.8
Hotels, rooming houses, camps, and other lodging places	425	1.3	766,435	.7
Personal services	670	2.0	1,389,806	1.3
Business services, not elsewhere classified	417	1.3	1,448,820	1.4
Employment agencies and commercial and trade schools	41	.1	120,784	.1
Automobile repair services and garages	136	.4	372,111	.4
Miscellaneous repair services and hand trades	87	.3	271,272	.3
Motion pictures	235	.7	635,721	.6
Amusement and recreation and related services, not elsewhere classified	248	.8	496,914	.5
Medical and other health services	177	.5	386,447	.4
Law offices and related services	53	.2	162,440	.2
Educational institutions and agencies	21	.1	48,418	[4]
Other professional and social-service agencies and institutions	91	.3	386,484	.4
Nonprofit membership organizations	188	.6	452,222	.4
Private households	14	[4]	29,170	[4]
Regular governmental establishments	8	[4]	19,111	[4]
Establishments not elsewhere classified [6]	63	.2	150,306	.1

[1] Industry titles from 1942 edition of *Social Security Board Industrial Classification Code* for nonmanufacturing industries and 1945 edition of *Standard Industrial Classification Manual* for manufacturing industries.
[2] Average of 12 monthly figures, each of which is total of numbers of workers in covered employment in pay period of each type (weekly, semimonthly, etc.) ending nearest fifteenth of month.
[3] Total wages in covered employment for all pay periods ending in year.
[4] Less than 0.05 percent of total.
[5] Excludes railroad and allied groups subject, as of July 1, 1939, to Railroad Unemployment Insurance Act.
[6] Includes data for firms whose activities are not classifiable in any of above industries and data for firms not yet classified due to lack of sufficient information regarding nature of business.

Source: Department of Labor, Bureau of Employment Security.

No. 280.—Unemployment Insurance—Claims Received, Weeks Compensated, Benefit Payments, and Federal Grants, by States and Territories: 1952

[In thousands. Corrected to Jan. 30, 1953]

STATE AND TERRITORY	CLAIMS RECEIVED IN LOCAL OFFICES		WEEKS COMPENSATED		AMOUNT OF BENEFIT PAYMENTS [4]		FEDERAL GRANTS FOR ADMINISTRATION [5]	
	Initial [1]	Continued [2]	All unemployment [3]	Total unemployment	All unemployment [3]	Total unemployment [4]	July 1950–June 1951	July 1951–June 1952
Total	11,523	54,311	45,777	41,920	$1,005,022	$955,340	[6]$172,725	[6]$187,511
Alabama	139	858	641	606	11,229	10,847	2,616	2,700
Arizona	31	121	69	65	1,403	1,349	1,295	1,449
Arkansas	90	481	337	310	5,737	5,429	1,614	1,827
California	968	5,179	4,583	4,244	102,170	97,490	17,927	18,867
Colorado	22	92	64	58	1,314	1,234	1,325	1,403
Connecticut	183	686	545	510	11,088	10,701	2,799	2,869
Delaware	15	65	55	51	1,042	996	408	441
District of Columbia	22	112	96	95	1,738	1,716	1,168	1,210
Florida	124	628	448	427	7,533	7,283	2,744	2,854
Georgia	121	717	573	534	9,505	9,061	2,674	2,878
Idaho	25	162	127	123	2,880	2,803	855	917
Illinois	628	3,340	2,590	2,139	57,628	53,027	8,442	9,294
Indiana	302	1,108	916	832	20,943	19,803	3,047	3,154
Iowa	61	301	240	213	4,949	4,615	1,433	1,463
Kansas	44	198	179	163	3,937	3,720	1,298	1,450
Kentucky	155	989	802	747	15,216	14,529	2,003	2,194
Louisiana	138	810	645	593	13,256	12,593	2,517	2,687
Maine	82	424	342	306	5,353	4,972	1,027	1,096
Maryland	142	560	552	491	11,104	10,377	2,906	3,077
Massachusetts	565	2,906	2,550	2,345	59,435	57,151	7,427	8,364
Michigan	700	2,981	2,398	2,295	63,827	62,429	7,786	8,651
Minnesota	112	750	642	600	11,631	11,138	2,598	2,953
Mississippi	87	481	373	343	6,086	5,758	1,775	1,973
Missouri	209	969	739	634	13,655	12,588	3,012	3,344
Montana	22	135	117	117	2,168	2,167	903	936
Nebraska	26	115	104	99	2,177	2,115	849	881
Nevada	13	56	52	49	1,244	1,191	568	581
New Hampshire	70	359	302	265	5,798	5,424	822	949
New Jersey	567	2,401	2,207	2,016	51,400	48,868	6,562	7,369
New Mexico	17	88	74	71	1,546	1,503	858	933
New York	2,468	9,138	7,927	7,117	186,738	176,614	25,138	29,673
North Carolina	278	1,293	1,257	1,171	20,206	19,367	3,000	3,381
North Dakota	10	72	68	62	1,621	1,519	548	587
Ohio	408	1,940	1,543	1,415	36,196	34,520	7,803	8,396
Oklahoma	83	437	332	312	6,191	5,955	1,995	2,079
Oregon	158	783	686	648	15,054	14,581	2,179	2,332
Pennsylvania	1,216	5,434	4,597	4,258	110,348	104,819	12,403	14,325
Rhode Island	181	826	762	731	16,497	16,092	1,589	1,741
South Carolina	92	500	408	384	7,307	7,058	1,906	2,309
South Dakota	8	41	34	31	673	636	454	488
Tennessee	153	1,316	1,078	1,026	17,918	17,265	2,702	2,920
Texas	114	637	477	454	7,959	7,729	6,050	6,744
Utah	27	154	128	116	3,089	2,893	1,087	1,344
Vermont	21	131	114	104	2,369	2,248	539	607
Virginia	97	486	411	390	7,052	6,832	1,722	1,839
Washington	224	1,210	993	949	23,377	22,576	3,561	3,671
West Virginia	130	835	729	629	14,007	12,600	1,432	1,419
Wisconsin	132	697	575	525	14,167	13,244	2,589	2,835
Wyoming	7	32	30	27	727	671	527	555
Alaska	18	116	137	138	4,192	4,098	509	554
Hawaii	22	156	129	103	2,342	2,080	561	609

[1] Includes transitional initial claims.
[2] Represents weeks claimed by continued claims.
[3] Benefits for other than total unemployment are not provided by State law in Montana.
[4] Unadjusted for voided benefit checks.
[5] Advances for unemployment insurance administration certified to State agencies during fiscal year. Totals include, but State figures exclude, expenses for postage.
[6] Includes $334,000 and $5,000 granted to Puerto Rico and Virgin Islands, respectively, in fiscal 1951 for employment service administration and $420,000 and $20,000, respectively, in fiscal 1952.

Source: Department of Labor, Bureau of Employment Security.

No. 281.—UNEMPLOYMENT INSURANCE—CONTRIBUTIONS COLLECTED AND BENEFITS PAID UNDER STATE LAWS, BY STATES AND TERRITORIES: 1951 AND 1952

[In thousands of dollars (except rates). Corrected to January 30, 1953]

STATE AND TERRITORY	Month and year bene-fits first payable	Funds available for bene-fits as of Dec. 31, 1950 [1]	CONTRIBUTIONS COLLECTED [2]		BENEFITS PAID [3]		RATIO (PER-CENT) OF BENEFITS TO CONTRI-BUTIONS		FUNDS AVAILABLE FOR BENEFITS [1]	
			1951	1952	1951	1952	1951	1952	Dec. 31, 1951	Dec. 31, 1952
Total		6,972,296	1,492,509	1,367,679	840,411	998,267	56.3	73.0	7,782,048	8,327,530
Alabama	Jan. 1938	66,580	15,749	15,802	8,218	11,267	52.2	71.6	65,705	71,672
Arizona	do	30,265	5,334	5,943	1,281	1,390	24.0	23.4	35,018	40,400
Arkansas	Jan. 1937	36,550	7,460	8,198	4,494	5,797	60.1	69.6	40,326	43,704
California	Jan. 1938	673,564	182,457	176,987	95,082	101,678	52.1	57.4	674,488	765,519
Colorado	Jan. 1936	59,137	5,388	6,204	1,236	1,311	22.9	21.0	61,550	67,927
Connecticut	Jan. 1938	156,130	32,608	35,723	10,419	11,044	32.0	30.9	181,915	210,922
Delaware	Jan. 1937	14,900	1,819	1,880	964	1,023	53.0	54.2	15,789	16,966
Dist. of Columbia	Jan. 1938	46,775	4,417	4,019	1,587	1,700	35.3	42.3	50,078	54,162
Florida	Jan. 1937	73,589	6,196	9,710	6,860	7,483	71.8	77.1	77,757	81,710
Georgia	do	108,989	15,225	16,269	8,455	9,491	55.5	58.3	116,170	127,045
Idaho	Sept. 1938	27,747	4,960	4,613	1,903	3,802	38.4	62.0	31,413	31,857
Illinois	July 1939	450,344	76,316	75,758	56,877	57,646	80.9	76.7	478,873	503,954
Indiana	Apr. 1938	166,004	27,788	21,291	13,967	20,642	50.2	97.0	217,405	222,729
Iowa	July 1938	100,710	5,572	4,814	3,094	4,987	55.5	103.6	106,405	107,624
Kansas	Jan. 1938	61,531	7,752	8,849	3,849	3,912	52.1	44.2	68,680	76,142
Kentucky	do	123,670	19,090	19,472	14,512	14,188	39.7	73.0	133,061	140,869
Louisiana	Jan. 1938	97,540	19,671	21,320	13,354	13,181	67.4	61.8	106,189	116,761
Maine	do	33,744	7,219	7,316	3,608	5,326	77.0	72.5	39,219	42,106
Maryland	do	112,170	15,123	15,177	6,758	10,930	68.0	72.0	121,001	127,975
Massachusetts	do	92,665	94,434	97,995	48,625	56,193	51.4	60.3	140,935	153,300
Michigan	July 1938	347,847	76,335	76,505	47,120	61,987	59.3	81.9	386,804	378,441
Minnesota	do	113,225	14,525	11,096	9,105	11,012	64.6	99.3	127,274	130,146
Mississippi	Apr. 1938	41,983	5,679	5,203	5,641	6,005	93.1	115.5	40,294	45,377
Missouri	Jan. 1938	194,574	27,142	15,192	12,907	15,944	44.6	90.9	214,143	230,907
Montana	Jan. 1937	23,032	6,083	5,329	2,765	3,155	45.0	60.5	33,535	34,526
Nebraska	Jan. 1938	35,035	4,174	2,601	1,518	2,172	36.4	83.7	38,079	40,467
Nevada	do	13,587	1,920	2,601	1,275	1,245	66.4	47.8	13,444	15,108
New Hampshire	do	23,744	5,094	6,094	2,720	2,790	53.4	86.0	31,184	21,908
New Jersey	Jan. 1938	451,227	65,737	66,109	43,344	51,393	66.8	78.1	450,485	477,060
New Mexico	Dec. 1938	37,309	5,094	5,309	1,927	1,661	39.2	27.7	26,094	32,256
New York	Jan. 1938	904,616	325,598	291,173	180,065	185,211	55.4	63.6	1,050,518	1,191,005
North Carolina	do	162,036	24,976	20,796	17,464	20,162	73.6	97.0	172,257	176,777
North Dakota	Jan. 1939	9,622	1,902	1,892	1,183	1,616	62.2	85.4	10,349	11,096
Ohio	Dec. 1935	544,888	79,027	75,354	55,125	35,976	35.3	47.0	571,600	624,457
Oklahoma	Jan. 1938	37,897	7,607	8,946	5,948	6,173	72.5	68.9	40,431	38,356
Oregon	Jan. 1938	74,791	15,272	11,794	10,446	15,000	78.7	122.2	79,192	77,996
Pennsylvania	Jan. 1938	537,498	127,398	47,302	66,386	109,982	52.2	229.6	610,440	561,026
Rhode Island	do	23,290	16,588	16,225	17,408	16,404	104.9	101.1	22,660	22,629
South Carolina	July 1938	50,530	11,753	14,075	6,171	7,292	52.5	51.8	57,574	65,715
South Dakota	Jan. 1939	10,405	1,604	1,357	712	673	44.6	49.6	11,622	12,574
Tennessee	Jan. 1938	96,177	19,488	19,017	14,039	17,909	72.0	94.1	103,784	107,186
Texas	do	229,327	19,962	22,258	5,986	7,843	30.0	35.7	248,274	265,108
Utah	do	31,321	3,506	3,790	2,338	3,054	66.7	80.6	33,188	34,068
Vermont	do	14,290	2,470	2,407	1,374	3,365	55.4	98.3	15,718	16,108
Virginia	do	81,049	12,700	8,964	15,004	23,279	44.5	85.7	170,577	187,502
Washington	Jan. 1938	126,291	33,972	12,017	8,192	13,366	46.9	106.7	90,351	91,529
West Virginia	Jan. 1936	53,172	17,646	16,928	7,354	14,122	41.0	74.6	237,400	247,583
Wisconsin	July 1936	222,140	17,646	16,928	7,354	723	42.7	34.4	13,985	15,686
Wyoming	Jan. 1939	12,041	1,857	2,196	798	723	42.7	34.4	13,985	15,686
Alaska	do	9,141	2,428	3,778	1,785	4,171	73.7	110.5	9,968	9,785
Hawaii	do	21,778	2,641	2,349	1,813	2,336	68.7	108.7	23,690	23,430

[1] Sum of balances in State clearing account and benefit-payment account, and in State unemployment trust fund account in U. S. Treasury. State unemployment trust fund accounts include interest credited.

[2] Contributions, penalties, and interest from employers and contributions from employees. Adjusted for refunds of contributions and for dishonored contribution checks.

[3] Adjusted for voided benefit checks.

Source: Department of Labor, Bureau of Employment Security.

No. 282.—Unemployment Insurance—Summary of Selected Operations Under State Unemployment Insurance Laws: 1942 to 1952

[Data corrected to January 30, 1953]

YEAR AND MONTH	COVERED EMPLOYMENT [1]		Beneficiaries [4]	Weeks compensated	Continued claims [5]	Benefit payments [6] (thousands)
	Workers [2] (thousands)	Wages [3] (thousands)				
1942	29,349	$54,796,162	2,815,127	26,157,730	33,761,947	$344,084
1943	30,828	66,116,563	664,015	6,003,608	7,664,664	79,643
1944	30,044	62,139,035	533,406	4,123,924	5,480,621	62,385
1945	28,407	66,642,128	2,861,190	34,179,769	30,633,727	445,866
1946	30,234	73,402,152	4,461,032	50,813,263	67,333,494	1,094,850
1947	32,278	86,595,237	3,953,603	44,324,983	51,859,949	[7] 776,165
1948	33,088	96,004,825	4,008,393	42,604,939	50,961,844	[7] 793,265
1949	31,605	93,863,033	7,363,886	86,638,269	102,612,247	[7] 1,737,279
1950	32,657	103,129,637	5,211,883	67,859,529	78,654,227	[7] 1,373,426
1951	34,858	115,717,346	4,127,133	41,596,339	50,392,621	840,411
1952						
January	34,461	(7)	4,383,151	45,777,240	54,311,286	998,267
February	34,565	} 30,035,667	1,185,164	5,451,753	6,530,099	116,469
March	34,713		1,146,445	4,513,067	5,483,269	105,023
April	35,045		1,112,772	4,673,550	5,145,386	101,564
May	35,201	} 30,907,910	992,634	4,367,591	5,149,793	94,385
June	35,421		918,424	4,041,065	4,706,011	86,958
			918,139	3,856,182	4,505,664	83,511
July	(7)	(7)	870,894	4,006,114	5,306,110	88,612
August	(7)	(7)	979,887	4,115,526	4,679,644	95,389
September	(7)	(7)	630,800	2,775,521	3,155,685	62,094
October	(7)	(7)	529,958	2,437,809	2,882,991	54,227
November	(7)	(7)	535,869	2,143,476	2,705,947	47,730
December	(7)	(7)	672,497	3,093,486	4,053,687	69,061

[1] Excludes railroads and allied groups subject as of July 1, 1939, to Railroad Unemployment Insurance Act.
[2] Until January 1945, represents covered employment on last payroll of each type (weekly, semimonthly, etc.) ending in month; thereafter, employment on payroll of each type ending nearest fifteenth of month. Annual figures represent averages of 12 monthly figures.
[3] Total wages in covered employment for all pay periods ending within period.
[4] Annual figures represent first payments made to beneficiaries; monthly figures represent average weekly number of weeks of unemployment compensated during month.
[5] Beginning with January 1949, represents weeks claimed by continued claims.
[6] Annual amounts adjusted, but monthly figures not adjusted, for voided benefit checks.
[7] Includes $1,019,000 for 1947, $3,331,000 for 1948, $1,287,000 for 1949, and $312,000 for 1950 paid to seamen under the Reconversion Unemployment Benefits for seamen program. Program expired June 30, 1950.
[8] Not available.

Source: Department of Labor, Bureau of Employment Security.

No. 283.—Placements Made by Public Employment Offices: 1940 to 1952

[Beginning 1950, includes Alaska, Hawaii and Puerto Rico. Full responsibility of Employment Service for Farm Placement Program terminated June 1943, resumed January 1, 1948]

YEAR AND MONTH	PLACEMENTS		MONTH	PLACEMENTS	
	Total	Nonagricultural		Total	Nonagricultural
1940	5,226,712	3,661,040	July	2,097,008	585,575
1941	7,427,969	5,404,291	August	1,824,864	627,849
1942	10,220,967	6,919,892	September	2,106,355	620,890
1943	12,253,224	9,393,196	October	2,136,966	609,794
1944	12,219,112	11,446,007	November	1,008,281	498,395
1945	10,811,100	9,808,476	December	639,694	426,441
1946	7,139,778	5,518,631			
1947	6,328,100	5,279,979	**1952**		
1948	11,909,995	5,385,533			
1949	13,508,400	4,442,554	January	596,807	472,999
1950	13,409,326	5,624,701	February	504,506	427,200
1951	15,326,383	6,532,034	March	535,602	464,566
1952	15,554,965	6,800,813	April	690,425	565,672
			May	1,315,319	571,862
1951			June	2,068,042	581,251
January	573,666	485,788	July	1,461,814	555,569
February	487,891	437,542	August	1,669,197	588,165
March	579,497	512,671	September	2,527,846	657,903
April	659,845	551,631	October	2,369,854	641,000
May	1,343,230	610,200	November	1,116,704	507,041
June	1,869,086	585,258	December	698,849	467,484

Source: Department of Labor, Bureau of Employment Security.

.—Nonagricultural Placements Made by Public Employment Offices, r Sex, and Veteran Status, by States and Other Areas: 1952

l AND STATE HER AREA	Total	SEX		VETERAN STATUS		PERCENT OF TOTAL	
		Male	Female	Veteran	Non-veteran	Male	Veteran
----------------	6,500,813	3,919,745	2,581,068	1,482,711	5,018,102	60,3	22,8
JARTER							
arch...........	1,364,865	786,059	578,806	310,179	1,054,686	57.6	22.7
....	1,718,785	1,078,002	640,783	387,673	1,331,112	62.7	22.6
aber...........	1,801,638	1,090,184	711,454	401,125	1,400,513	60.5	22.3
cember........	1,615,525	965,500	650,025	383,734	1,231,791	59.8	23.8
OTHER AREA							
----------------	133,768	82,311	51,457	23,078	110,690	61.5	17.3
----------------	61,415	44,410	17,005	15,715	45,700	72.3	25.6
----------------	131,052	89,208	41,844	27,112	103,940	68.1	20.7
----------------	433,482	276,945	156,537	135,663	297,819	63.9	31.3
----------------	81,099	60,383	20,716	24,361	56,738	74.5	30.0
:...............	104,581	54,286	50,295	19,987	84,594	51.9	19.1
----------------	14,821	7,655	7,166	2,064	12,757	51.6	13.9
umbia........	48,733	27,011	21,722	10,494	38,239	55.4	21.5
----------------	184,476	104,540	79,936	40,482	143,994	56.7	21.9
----------------	144,056	89,035	55,021	23,349	120,707	61.8	16.2
----------------	39,833	30,054	9,779	16,706	23,125	75.5	41.9
----------------	212,478	144,147	68,331	59,464	153,014	67.8	28.0
----------------	121,596	71,747	49,851	29,501	92,097	59.0	24.3
----------------	101,912	75,017	26,895	28,295	73,617	73.6	27.8
----------------	104,433	78,780	25,653	28,098	76,335	75.4	26.9
----------------	35,542	21,472	14,070	7,091	28,451	60.4	20.0
----------------	98,437	62,657	35,780	22,507	75,930	63.7	22.9
----------------	34,552	20,321	14,231	6,666	27,886	58.8	19.3
----------------	77,410	47,674	29,736	18,595	58,815	61.6	24.0
tts...........	219,574	107,099	112,475	46,399	173,175	48.8	21.1
----------------	172,788	123,917	48,871	45,879	126,909	71.7	26.6
----------------	127,601	95,005	32,596	47,771	79,830	74.5	37.4
----------------	91,334	53,544	37,790	15,173	76,161	58.6	16.6
----------------	171,470	98,403	73,067	31,203	140,267	57.4	18.2
----------------	37,288	30,626	6,662	12,773	24,515	82.1	34.3
----------------	72,960	60,997	11,963	26,117	46,843	83.6	35.8
----------------	28,724	20,783	7,941	10,520	18,204	72.4	36.6
shire.........	22,825	14,298	8,527	5,056	17,769	62.6	22.2
----------------	146,028	61,917	84,111	19,542	126,486	42.4	13.4
)...............	57,423	46,409	11,014	15,389	42,034	80.8	26.8
----------------	861,395	339,027	522,368	124,365	737,030	39.4	14.4
ina...........	175,034	101,302	73,732	29,380	145,654	57.9	16.8
ts...........	25,636	18,828	6,808	6,751	18,885	73.4	26.3
----------------	328,799	233,019	95,780	93,482	235,317	70.9	28.4
----------------	152,863	111,318	41,545	45,813	107,050	72.8	30.0
----------------	82,302	62,452	19,850	30,014	52,288	75.9	36.5
ia...........	234,921	114,034	120,887	46,222	188,699	48.5	19.7
d.............	27,940	10,030	17,910	3,487	24,453	35.9	12.5
ina...........	91,121	58,246	32,875	15,285	75,836	63.9	16.8
ta...........	20,234	15,629	4,605	6,669	13,565	77.2	33.0
----------------	143,943	84,666	59,277	38,740	105,203	58.8	26.9
----------------	583,357	372,520	210,837	121,260	462,097	63.9	20.8
----------------	55,286	41,266	14,020	17,923	37,363	74.6	32.4
----------------	11,710	7,730	3,980	3,195	8,515	66.0	27.3
.. ------------	96,707	52,292	44,415	14,455	82,252	54.1	14.9
----------------	91,341	69,668	21,673	26,902	64,439	76.3	29.5
ia.............	24,797	13,123	11,674	5,506	19,291	52.9	22.2
----------------	125,751	75,386	50,365	24,995	100,756	59.9	19.9
----------------	14,715	11,609	3,106	4,729	9,986	78.9	32.1
----------------	10,033	6,805	3,228	3,037	6,996	67.8	30.3
----------------	11,375	9,103	2,272	2,701	8,674	80.0	23.7
----------------	18,476	10,139	8,337	2,697	15,779	54.9	14.6
ids...........	1,384	902	482	51	1,333	65.2	3.7

epartment of Labor, Bureau of Employment Security.

No. 285.—Nonagricultural Placements Made by Public Employment Offices, by Sex, Veteran Status, and Industry Division: 1952

INDUSTRY DIVISION	Total	SEX		VETERAN STATUS	
		Male	Female	Veteran	Non-veteran
All industries	6,500,813	3,919,745	2,581,068	1,482,711	5,018,102
Forestry and fishing	9,635	7,269	2,366	2,127	7,508
Mining	47,696	44,564	3,132	18,532	29,164
Construction	661,471	650,036	11,435	223,788	437,683
Manufacturing	2,016,521	1,239,517	777,004	471,217	1,545,304
Transportation, communication, and other public utilities	332,118	308,294	23,824	135,652	196,466
Wholesale and retail trade	1,299,824	830,915	468,909	317,278	982,546
Finance, insurance, and real estate	94,091	42,745	51,346	15,613	78,478
Service	1,841,759	652,464	1,189,295	224,007	1,617,752
Domestic	1,213,608	292,839	920,769	95,799	1,117,809
Government	190,147	137,061	53,086	72,399	117,748
Establishments, n. e. c.	7,551	6,880	671	2,098	5,453
PERCENTAGE DISTRIBUTION BY INDUSTRY DIVISION					
Total	100.0	100.0	100.0	100.0	100.0
Forestry and fishing	.1	.2	.1	.1	.1
Mining	.7	1.1	.1	1.2	.6
Construction	10.2	16.6	.4	15.1	8.7
Manufacturing	31.1	31.6	30.1	31.9	30.8
Transportation, communication, and other public utilities	5.1	7.9	.9	9.1	3.9
Wholesale and retail trade	20.0	21.2	18.2	21.4	19.6
Finance, insurance, and real estate	1.4	1.1	2.0	1.1	1.6
Service	28.4	16.6	46.1	15.1	32.3
Domestic	18.7	7.5	35.7	6.5	22.3
Government	2.9	3.5	2.1	4.9	2.3
Establishments, n. e. c.	.1	.2	(¹)	.1	.1
PERCENTAGE DISTRIBUTION BY SEX AND VETERAN STATUS					
Total	100.0	60.3	39.7	22.8	77.2
Forestry and fishing	100.0	75.4	24.6	22.1	77.9
Mining	100.0	93.4	6.6	38.9	61.1
Construction	100.0	98.3	1.7	33.8	66.2
Manufacturing	100.0	61.5	38.5	23.4	76.6
Transportation, communication, and other public utilities	100.0	92.8	7.2	40.8	59.2
Wholesale and retail trade	100.0	63.9	36.1	24.4	75.6
Finance, insurance, and real estate	100.0	45.4	54.6	16.6	83.4
Service	100.0	35.4	64.6	12.2	87.8
Domestic	100.0	24.1	75.9	7.9	92.1
Government	100.0	72.1	27.9	38.1	61.9
Establishments, n. e. c.	100.0	91.1	8.9	27.8	72.2

¹ Less than 0.05 percent.

Source: Department of Labor, Bureau of Employment Security.

No. 286.—Nonagricultural Placements Made by Public Employment Offices, by Major Occupational Group: 1948 to 1952

[See headnote, table 283]

OCCUPATIONAL GROUP	1948	1949	1950	1951	1952
All occupations	5,385,533	4,442,554	5,624,701	6,552,034	6,500,813
Professional and managerial	61,052	52,461	66,972	87,454	83,137
Clerical and sales	607,783	542,254	694,915	763,479	749,481
Service	1,354,281	1,338,240	1,513,037	1,753,047	1,820,276
Skilled	365,544	269,643	400,073	426,807	370,071
Semiskilled	697,933	567,388	741,596	836,956	857,688
Unskilled and other	2,298,940	1,652,568	2,208,106	2,684,291	2,620,160

Source: Department of Labor, Bureau of Employment Security.

No. 287.—Railroad Employees and Railroad Retirement and Survivor Benefits, By Class: 1940 to 1952

ITEM	1940	1945	1947	1948	1949	1950	1951	1952
Number of employees (1,000)	1,703	2,010	2,471	2,316	2,090	2,034	2,070	(¹)
NUMBER OF BENEFITS								
Monthly benefits awarded, total	23,817	24,213	124,019	81,050	63,154	62,474	56,709	146,402
Retirement annuities and pensions	22,180	23,242	43,874	32,930	36,020	35,815	²33,531	²126,271
Survivor benefits	1,637	971	80,145	48,120	27,134	26,659	23,178	20,131
Monthly benefits terminated, total	13,343	14,770	27,219	28,232	31,340	34,316	34,973	45,359
Retirement annuities and pensions	12,212	13,915	23,581	18,344	20,164	21,293	²21,560	²31,264
Survivor benefits	1,131	855	3,638	9,888	11,176	13,023	13,413	14,095
Monthly benefits in current-payment status, total	149,241	177,289	290,160	345,408	370,071	396,797	416,786	514,392
Retirement annuities and pensions	145,978	172,875	211,566	226,053	241,627	255,065	²267,092	²357,952
Survivor benefits	3,263	4,414	78,594	119,355	128,444	141,732	149,694	156,440
Lump-sum death benefits awarded, total	13,378	20,381	16,253	28,051	33,205	34,938	29,716	25,705
AMOUNT OF BENEFITS ($1,000)								
Total	118,111	147,050	202,449	253,566	291,630	310,845	²330,976	²449,690
Retirement annuities and pensions	114,166	137,140	177,053	208,642	240,894	254,240	²268,733	²361,200
Survivor benefits:								
Monthly	1,448	1,772	19,283	36,011	39,257	43,884	49,527	74,085
Lump-sum	2,497	8,138	6,114	8,914	11,480	12,722	12,716	13,745

¹ Not available.
² Includes annuities to spouses of retired employees which became payable Nov. 1, 1951.

Source: Railroad Retirement Board. Data are published on a fiscal-year basis in *Annual Report* and currently in *The Monthly Review.*

No. 288.—Railroad Unemployment and Sickness Benefits—Summary of Operations Through June 1952

FISCAL YEAR	Applications received ¹	Claims received	BENEFIT PAYMENTS		Amount of benefits (in thousands) ²	Number of beneficiaries	Accounts exhausted
			Number	Average amount			
UNEMPLOYMENT BENEFITS							
1939–40	210,823	1,441,213	(³)	(³)	$14,810	161,000	29,398
1940–41	181,157	1,257,822	(³)	(³)	17,609	164,000	26,682
1941–42	90,151	517,394	450,698	$19.86	8,890	80,000	11,366
1942–43	21,816	100,826	80,584	22.22	1,753	18,000	2,512
1943–44	6,539	27,495	21,587	26.44	547	5,000	434
1944–45	8,989	34,874	27,547	26.47	726	6,000	626
1945–46	201,112	847,009	731,435	28.01	20,517	157,000	15,388
1946–47	256,900	1,763,264	1,585,998	29.41	46,617	225,000	47,639
1947–48	266,671	1,346,574	1,145,940	28.57	32,427	210,000	22,460
1948–49	346,795	1,706,112	1,531,124	30.70	46,745	286,000	20,331
1949–50	562,294	3,730,733	3,475,121	32.72	113,769	506,000	53,131
1950–51	233,403	1,027,727	911,677	27.53	24,780	181,000	16,733
1951–52	219,527	906,331	823,374	28.06	22,741	162,000	10,700
SICKNESS BENEFITS (INCLUDING MATERNITY BENEFITS)							
1947–48	234,926	799,903	734,276	⁴39.02	25,604	150,000	15,957
1948–49	213,570	921,918	873,464	⁴39.57	29,823	179,000	20,627
1949–50	197,023	896,024	851,780	⁴40.36	29,487	160,000	22,107
1950–51	185,671	825,905	782,883	⁴40.08	27,003	143,000	21,866
1951–52	191,620	800,562	757,850	40.48	25,898	143,000	19,847

¹ Application submitted for unemployment when worker applies for unemployment benefits for first time with respect to benefit year, for sickness at the beginning of each spell of sickness. Beginning with 1947–48, data include some applications submitted in June with respect to following year.
² Adjusted for settlement of underpayments and recovery of overpayments.
³ Not reported on comparable basis.   ⁴ Excluding maternity benefits.

Source: Railroad Retirement Board, *Annual Report.* Data published currently in *The Monthly Review.*

No. 289.—RAILROAD RETIREMENT, SURVIVOR, UNEMPLOYMENT, AND SICKNESS BENEFITS, BY STATE OF RESIDENCE OF BENEFICIARY: 1952

[In thousands. Retirement and survivor payment distributions based on preliminary estimates]

STATE	Total	Retire-ment [1]	Survivor [1]	Unem-ployment	Sickness (including maternity)
Total	$535,512	$361,200	$97,830	$41,793	$34,689
Alabama	7,449	4,571	1,289	1,045	545
Arizona	3,117	2,054	385	396	283
Arkansas	5,419	3,903	814	373	329
California	34,372	25,321	5,172	1,502	2,377
Colorado	6,469	4,707	962	410	390
Connecticut	3,100	2,074	736	41	249
Delaware	1,854	1,349	319	101	85
District of Columbia	1,569	897	409	73	190
Florida	12,244	9,672	1,389	730	453
Georgia	8,620	5,558	1,592	742	728
Idaho	1,919	1,211	376	171	162
Illinois	38,901	26,227	7,052	2,430	3,191
Indiana	18,952	13,633	2,942	1,282	1,094
Iowa	11,276	8,483	1,921	356	516
Kansas	10,454	7,560	1,766	445	683
Kentucky	11,932	8,126	1,852	1,131	822
Louisiana	5,416	3,503	1,101	464	348
Maine	2,975	2,129	523	144	178
Maryland	8,767	5,822	1,657	797	492
Massachusetts	8,907	5,828	2,087	391	601
Michigan	13,790	9,500	2,244	1,290	755
Minnesota	14,893	10,054	2,387	1,600	851
Mississippi	4,566	3,096	709	506	255
Missouri	17,716	12,288	2,772	1,451	1,206
Montana	3,322	2,320	513	231	259
Nebraska	6,041	4,266	978	318	479
Nevada	978	688	177	39	74
New Hampshire	1,751	1,281	306	58	106
New Jersey	15,289	11,137	2,895	315	942
New Mexico	2,605	1,335	493	533	243
New York	38,380	25,745	7,162	2,614	2,859
North Carolina	6,029	3,872	1,150	613	393
North Dakota	1,720	1,065	300	221	135
Ohio	34,983	24,591	5,620	2,508	2,264
Oklahoma	4,528	3,211	703	307	307
Oregon	5,338	4,023	717	290	309
Pennsylvania	63,061	41,000	9,432	8,825	3,804
Rhode Island	1,056	686	210	92	68
South Carolina	3,207	2,024	632	367	184
South Dakota	1,420	941	263	129	88
Tennessee	10,845	7,408	1,755	973	709
Texas	18,949	13,005	3,298	1,054	1,593
Utah	2,775	1,848	569	178	181
Vermont	1,498	1,106	232	73	87
Virginia	13,120	8,663	2,451	1,086	920
Washington	8,546	6,419	1,250	455	422
West Virginia	9,267	5,698	1,473	1,329	767
Wisconsin	10,841	7,573	1,805	971	493
Wyoming	1,705	1,192	312	83	119
Outside continental United States	3,580	2,580	632	266	102

[1] State distribution based on projection of 11 months figures.

Source: Railroad Retirement Board. Data published on fiscal-year basis in *Annual Report*.

No. 290.—CIVIL SERVICE RETIREMENT ACT—ANNUITIES AND LUMP-SUM PAYMENTS: 1939 TO 1952

[Dollar amounts in thousands. See general note, p. 340]

JUNE 30 OR YEAR ENDING JUNE 30—	ANNUITIES [1]					LUMP-SUM PAYMENTS					
	Number certified	Number terminated	Number in force		Annual value	Separated employees [2]		Deceased employees [3]		Deceased annuitants [4]	
			Total [5]	Disability		Number	Amount	Number	Amount	Number	Amount
1939	5,796	3,541	68,385	14,315	$57,074	14,800	$2,727	2,871	$3,155	2,242	$1,405
1940	7,367	5,635	62,027	15,394	59,879	15,153	2,857	3,612	3,723	3,145	1,482
1941	6,233	4,122	66,115	16,768	63,488	21,100	3,518	3,736	4,290	2,778	1,735
1942	7,594	4,442	68,179	18,022	66,456	45,562	5,506	3,780	2,904	2,611	1,686
1943	9,679	4,984	72,972	19,802	71,450	111,363	7,178	6,312	4,987	2,666	2,003
1944	10,043	5,650	78,354	21,158	75,653	360,264	21,536	9,061	5,155	2,915	2,343
1945	13,290	5,511	85,228	22,369	82,346	900,858	62,377	16,374	7,441	3,082	2,476
1946	18,034	5,113	98,146	26,537	91,587	1,450,434	185,086	17,924	8,546	2,990	2,562
1947	20,159	6,666	111,416	31,502	108,321	943,026	175,853	17,304	10,372	3,971	2,718
1948	22,879	7,442	126,597	35,353	124,244	432,000	112,846	10,968	9,361	3,563	2,890
1949	21,371	8,998	148,296	39,076	154,252	226,554	61,407	6,336	3,925	4,572	4,685
1950	32,308	9,451	172,208	42,859	181,878	239,151	36,194	4,850	3,712	6,827	4,194
1951	26,484	10,771	197,148	45,601	205,641	166,962	64,914	4,387	3,998	7,384	3,946
1952	30,960	11,985	216,232	47,964	227,448	146,714	71,036	4,308	4,347	7,575	3,982

[1] Through June 30, 1940, data relate entirely to employees retired voluntarily or involuntarily under various age and length of service requirements and to employees with at least 5 years of service who became totally disabled for the position occupied prior to eligibility for retirement. Beginning Jan. 1, 1940, employees may elect a joint and survivor annuity, and beginning Feb. 29, 1948, widows and minor children of deceased employees and annuitants are eligible for survivor annuities under certain conditions; number of survivor annuities in force as of June 30 increased from 26 in 1941 to 39,902 in 1952. Beginning Jan. 24, 1942, employees with at least 5 years service who separate voluntarily or involuntarily prior to eligibility for retirement may obtain deferred annuity at age 62; such annuitants increased from 5 as of June 30, 1942, to 32,182 as of June 30, 1952. Prior to 1952, excludes annuities purchased by voluntary contributions.
[2] Data relate to refunds of amounts to employees' credit in fund paid to employees not eligible for an annuity or who, if eligible, elected to take a refund.
[3] Data relate to refunds of amounts to employees' credit paid to designated or other beneficiaries of employees who died while in service or after separation.
[4] Data relate to refunds of balance of amount to annuitants' credit at time of death paid to designated or other beneficiaries of annuitants. Includes refunds to disability annuitants, whose entitlement to an annuity was suspended, and unexpended balances paid upon termination of survivor annuities.
[5] Due to adjustments, number in force at end of fiscal year does not in all cases equal number certified less number terminated in that year, plus number in force at end of preceding fiscal year.

Source: Civil Service Commission, annual retirement report.

No. 291.—CIVIL SERVICE RETIREMENT ACT—NUMBER OF EMPLOYEE ANNUITANTS AND SURVIVOR ANNUITANTS ON THE ROLL, BY RATES OF ANNUITY: JUNE 30, 1952

RATES OF ANNUITY [1]	NUMBER ON ROLL		RATES OF ANNUITY [1]	NUMBER ON ROLL	
	Employee annuitants	Survivor annuitants		Employee annuitants	Survivor annuitants
Annuitants, total	176,239	39,962	$1,560–$1,679	8,173	102
			$1,680–$1,799	5,885	77
Under $300	312	3,842	$1,800–$1,919	5,265	57
	6,736	8,226	$1,920–$2,039	4,055	46
	15,742	6,260	$2,040–$2,159	3,398	38
	11,755	4,982	$2,160–$3,279	2,746	35
	9,404	4,019	$2,280–$2,399	2,342	24
	8,924	6,883	$2,400–$2,999	6,045	35
	9,271	1,433	$3,000–$3,599	1,805	7
	8,653	1,200	$3,600–$4,199	717	1
	5,630	885	$4,200–$4,799	307	
	5,699	731	$4,800–$5,399	177	
	6,454	504	$5,400–$5,999	69	
	6,666	320	$6,000 and over	55	
	25,301	204			

[1] Includes increases under sec. 8 as amended by acts of Feb. 28, 1948 (Public Law 426, 80th Cong.), and July 6, 1950 (Public Law 555, 81st Cong.); includes annuities purchased by voluntary contributions; does not include increases under act of July 16, 1952 (Public Law 555, 82d Cong.).

Source: Civil Service Commission, annual retirement report.

No. 292.—WORKMEN'S COMPENSATION PAYMENTS, BY STATES: 1942 TO 1951

[Estimated by Social Security Administration. Payments represent cash and medical benefits and include insurance losses paid by private insurance carriers (compiled from the *Spectator*), net disbursements of State funds (from *Spectator, Argus Casualty and Surety Chart*, and State reports; estimated for some States), and self-insurance payments (estimated from available State data). Calendar year data, except fiscal year data for Federal employees, for a few States with State funds, and for 1949 figures for Montana and 1949-1951 for West Virginia. Includes benefit payments under Longshoremen's and Harbor Workers' Compensation Act and Defense Bases Compensation Act for States in which such payments are made]

[In thousands of dollars]

STATE	1942	1943	1944	1945	1946	1947	1948	1949	1950	1951
Total......	330,492	355,862	386,628	410,828	435,213	487,490	537,202	569,838	616,789	707,075
Alabama........	2,083	3,120	2,644	2,648	2,278	2,377	2,587	2,659	2,137	3,264
Arizona........	2,639	3,297	3,478	3,865	4,133	5,328	7,450	8,218	5,800	5,900
Arkansas........	1,917	2,267	2,394	2,379	2,618	3,100	3,149	3,501	3,705	4,430
California......	26,081	32,024	37,881	40,268	40,991	45,067	50,536	52,672	57,070	66,570
Colorado........	2,632	2,475	2,254	2,285	2,289	2,640	2,956	3,154	3,568	3,200
Connecticut....	5,515	6,106	6,760	7,202	7,764	8,814	9,244	9,438	9,500	11,182
Delaware........	442	473	417	438	494	549	627	670	720	840
Dist. of Col.....	1,496	1,379	1,286	1,193	1,382	1,572	1,972	2,279	2,360	2,635
Florida........	2,719	3,407	3,727	4,193	4,571	5,356	6,402	6,815	7,418	9,340
Georgia........	2,060	2,531	2,896	2,921	2,831	3,227	3,601	3,806	4,287	5,180
Idaho..........	1,340	1,435	1,249	1,193	1,317	1,490	1,822	1,920	1,950	2,008
Illinois........	18,379	20,694	22,710	23,457	23,507	26,999	30,219	29,941	31,370	35,090
Indiana........	5,486	6,498	6,482	6,625	7,013	7,972	8,563	8,694	8,920	11,270
Iowa..........	2,464	2,464	2,356	2,666	3,154	3,584	3,561	4,192	4,985	5,510
Kansas........	2,013	3,135	2,987	2,977	2,961	3,113	3,682	3,682	4,260	4,917
Kentucky......	4,716	5,211	5,508	5,716	5,297	6,171	5,242	6,508	6,767	7,400
Louisiana......	4,868	5,513	6,382	6,982	6,969	8,122	9,139	9,915	11,400	13,070
Maine..........	1,628	1,847	2,206	2,224	2,055	2,046	1,996	1,854	1,600	2,040
Maryland......	4,031	5,088	5,421	5,853	5,893	5,921	6,379	6,506	6,920	8,410
Massachusetts..	9,555	10,126	11,406	11,771	15,149	17,759	19,516	20,916	24,100	27,600
Michigan......	11,211	12,423	13,701	14,790	16,698	18,797	20,079	20,007	23,243	24,100
Minnesota......	4,546	5,258	5,469	5,853	6,561	7,663	8,680	9,302	9,662	11,200
Mississippi....	23	34	23	34	76	75	95	1,383	2,420	3,310
Missouri........	6,051	5,711	7,724	8,365	8,908	8,848	9,777	10,170	10,520	12,146
Montana........	2,127	1,994	1,943	2,003	1,851	1,972	2,353	2,422	2,544	2,990
Nebraska......	1,151	1,440	1,220	1,334	1,601	1,726	1,987	2,178	2,360	2,758
Nevada........	1,024	1,190	1,197	1,046	1,052	1,176	1,340	1,571	1,500	2,295
New Hampshire.	933	950	960	1,002	1,250	1,339	1,550	1,546	1,670	1,855
New Jersey....	17,689	19,612	21,835	21,961	20,339	26,208	27,200	27,681	29,010	36,390
New Mexico.....	944	601	675	652	803	1,115	1,303	1,760	2,330	2,640
New York......	62,876	61,061	67,866	75,092	84,232	89,122	100,139	112,051	119,188	134,590
North Carolina.	3,010	3,258	3,476	3,542	4,291	5,027	5,791	5,812	6,430	7,500
North Dakota...	747	685	731	743	771	854	891	1,080	1,100	1,255
Ohio..........	23,471	22,617	23,064	25,603	27,369	32,938	35,464	38,065	40,000	40,600
Oklahoma........	3,797	4,565	5,098	5,456	5,842	6,243	6,998	7,525	8,044	9,890
Oregon..........	4,822	5,146	5,679	5,666	5,557	5,911	6,875	7,923	8,983	11,248
Pennsylvania...	25,197	25,029	24,248	24,552	26,318	27,600	28,907	29,138	30,830	34,370
Rhode Island...	2,402	3,210	4,330	5,449	5,381	4,208	3,730	3,516	3,800	4,520
South Carolina.	2,427	2,702	2,779	2,813	3,024	3,753	3,933	3,968	4,000	3,920
South Dakota...	339	309	315	355	434	518	686	802	950	963
Tennessee......	2,931	3,480	3,896	4,027	3,750	4,084	4,406	4,721	5,429	6,352
Texas..........	12,996	14,669	17,192	18,218	20,445	23,497	28,133	30,437	33,380	38,979
Utah..........	1,575	1,673	1,475	1,312	1,475	1,579	1,657	1,781	1,880	2,090
Vermont........	489	462	544	522	627	750	750	842	900	1,115
Virginia........	3,598	3,587	3,343	3,361	3,794	4,481	5,057	5,256	5,640	6,250
Washington....	7,062	8,245	8,966	9,588	10,810	11,862	14,147	14,656	14,770	17,300
West Virginia...	6,820	7,466	7,598	7,735	7,926	8,296	8,800	9,423	9,632	10,096
Wisconsin......	7,223	7,888	8,673	9,162	9,903	10,665	11,881	12,362	13,356	15,049
Wyoming........	411	442	521	503	579	720	878	930	1,011	1,080
Federal employ-ees............	10,562	11,065	11,623	13,163	10,881	14,566	13,672	14,210	23,370	30,427

Source: Department of Health, Education, and Welfare, Social Security Administration, Division of Research and Statistics. Preliminary estimates appear periodically in *Social Security Bulletin*.

93.—PUBLIC ASSISTANCE—FEDERAL GRANTS TO STATES FOR PUBLIC ASSISTANCE, 1950, 1951, AND 1952, AND BY STATES AND OTHER AREAS, 1952

[In thousands. Advances certified from appropriations in specified fiscal year]

FISCAL YEAR AND STATE OR OTHER AREA	Total	Old-age assistance	Aid to dependent children	Aid to the blind	Aid to the permanently and totally disabled
)49-50	$1,123,418	$843,161	$256,067	$24,169	....
)50-51	1,185,764	826,075	316,477	26,195	$17,017
)51-52	1,177,688	799,845	303,286	29,397	45,165
ia	23,293	15,186	6,113	333	1,662
).	7,907	5,166	2,464	277	....
as	15,966	11,335	4,197	407	28
nia	123,005	89,785	29,328	3,891	....
lo	20,660	16,008	3,097	116	1,438
ticut	10,097	6,767	3,211	119	....
ire	1,084	472	495	80	37
t of Columbia	2,819	927	1,360	89	443
	29,639	20,215	8,408	1,015	....
	33,748	23,767	9,030	841	110
	4,671	3,067	1,257	68	278
	53,211	36,711	14,120	1,509	871
	19,035	13,578	4,849	607	....
	19,066	15,531	3,078	457	....
	16,112	12,588	2,512	204	807
ky	25,012	15,855	8,511	647	....
na	53,536	37,964	10,621	569	4,382
	7,390	4,633	2,555	201	....
nd	7,656	3,374	3,181	161	941
husetts	43,133	34,137	6,966	574	1,456
an	45,163	30,306	14,015	646	196
iota	22,668	17,532	4,678	458	....
ippi	13,888	10,739	2,388	604	157
ri	62,290	46,683	10,960	668	3,979
na	5,574	3,729	1,344	195	305
ka	9,257	7,415	1,575	267	....
.	1,023	1,023	(¹)	(¹)	....
ampshire	3,084	2,150	834	100	....
rsey..	10,842	7,238	2,886	309	410
[exico	6,976	3,424	2,715	152	685
ork	88,901	41,192	34,466	1,698	11,545
Carolina	20,706	11,309	7,251	1,288	858
Dakota	4,075	2,863	963	42	206
	47,874	36,370	8,377	1,293	1,835
ma	45,476	32,246	11,741	899	590
	10,582	7,744	2,109	145	864
lvania	53,302	23,421	21,603	3,641	4,638
Island	5,292	3,134	2,009	68	80
Carolina	13,767	9,679	2,710	393	985
Dakota	5,439	3,819	1,489	67	64
see	25,235	15,371	9,039	825	....
	67,118	57,884	7,429	1,806	....
	5,692	3,266	1,802	80	544
nt	2,851	2,221	515	62	53
a	8,474	3,835	3,611	393	636
gton	29,982	22,288	4,799	268	2,627
irginia..	14,899	6,013	8,101	288	497
sin	20,998	15,581	4,666	465	286
ing	1,907	1,376	322	29	180
	929	556	373	(²)	....
	2,759	591	1,732	35	400
Rico	3,526	1,721	1,394	43	367
Islands	97	59	31	4	3

approved plan in operation.
gram approved September 29, 1952, retroactive to October 1, 1951. Federal grant not made until succeeding ear.

ce: Department of Health, Education, and Welfare, Social Securiy Administration, Bureau of Public nce.

No. 294.—Public Assistance—Recipients of Assistance, by States and Other Areas: June 1952

State or other area	Old-age assistance	Aid to Dependent Children			Aid to the blind	Aid to the permanently and totally disabled	General assistance
		Families	Recipients				
			Total number [1]	Children			
Total	², 659, 661	589, 968	2, 041, 549	1, 527, 353	² 97, 690	145, 345	² 294, 600
Alabama	7?, 445	16, 099	65, 141	50, 746	1, 505	8, 547	180
Arizona	1?, 979	3, 617	13, 663	10, 265	707	....	1, 310
Arkansas	57, 946	13, 099	48, 348	36, 950	1, 881	223	⁴ 2, 211
California	273, 245	54, 719	171, 596	129, 427	³ 11, 582	....	27, 782
Colorado	51, 667	5, 006	18, 424	13, 942	343	3, 725	1, 810
Connecticut	17, 279	4, 580	15, 081	10, 995	309	....	3, 504
Delaware	1, 738	739	2, 856	2, 195	224	140	734
District of Columbia	2, 742	1, 996	8, 192	6, 386	258	1, 277	714
Florida	67, 173	17, 566	57, 850	43, 211	3, 141	....	⁴ 5, 000
Georgia	95, 271	16, 460	61, 670	47, 131	2, 973	....	3, 396
Idaho	9, 247	2, 107	7, 307	5, 381	199	807	⁴ 145
Illinois	109, 847	22, 485	80, 862	60, 053	3, 961	3, 010	25, 245
Indiana	42, 925	8, 319	27, 964	20, 716	1, 713	....	⁷ 10, 518
Iowa	47, 805	5, 399	18, 988	14, 129	1, 281	....	3, 294
Kansas	37, 012	4, 113	14, 593	11, 062	602	2, 713	1, 582
Kentucky	61, 709	19, 327	70, 216	51, 883	2, 525	....	2, 754
Louisiana	120, 604	22, 544	82, 872	61, 788	1, 916	14, 942	7, 066
Maine	14, 086	4, 416	15, 346	11, 113	588	....	3, 949
Maryland	11, 276	4, 980	19, 252	14, 722	461	2, 692	3, 064
Massachusetts	98, 076	13, 078	43, 082	31, 756	1, 662	5, 304	13, 900
Michigan	91, 164	25, 370	82, 218	58, 561	1, 854	1, 090	20, 787
Minnesota	54, 430	7, 680	26, 100	19, 911	1, 138	....	5, 380
Mississippi	57, 586	10, 644	40, 274	30, 995	2, 846	920	905
Missouri	131, 377	21, 679	73, 584	54, 258	³ 3, 290	11, 562	9, 221
Montana	11, 030	2, 274	7, 937	5, 900	519	1, 107	567
Nebraska	20, 595	2, 699	9, 214	6, 800	723	....	1, 366
Nevada	2, 716	⁵ 28	⁵ 102	⁵ 74	⁵ 39	....	⁵ 300
New Hampshire	6, 990	1, 398	4, 848	3, 548	301	17	1, 079
New Jersey	21, 892	5, 164	17, 192	13, 021	818	1, 610	⁷ 6, 160
New Mexico	10, 784	5, 369	18, 451	14, 323	461	2, 346	363
New York	113, 375	51, 931	175, 669	125, 595	4, 109	30, 408	⁷ 41, 457
North Carolina	51, 412	17, 156	62, 406	47, 944	4, 436	5, 200	2, 101
North Dakota	8, 805	1, 567	5, 528	4, 180	112	653	317
Ohio	114, 917	13, 170	48, 833	36, 845	3, 752	5, 153	19, 967
Oklahoma	95, 114	19, 518	65, 780	49, 578	2, 512	2, 691	6, 300
Oregon	22, 460	3, 376	11, 398	8, 560	381	1, 898	4, 454
Pennsylvania	71, 928	30, 077	110, 631	82, 971	³ 15, 615	9, 782	18, 523
Rhode Island	9, 356	3, 311	11, 047	7, 963	186	279	4, 076
South Carolina	42, 497	6, 697	24, 573	19, 307	1, 591	4, 655	2, 080
South Dakota	11, 796	2, 609	8, 469	6, 346	204	228	593
Tennessee	59, 535	20, 058	72, 552	54, 462	2, 807	....	2, 284
Texas	218, 636	15, 775	61, 528	45, 997	6, 026	....	⁴ 6, 600
Utah	9, 717	2, 840	9, 832	7, 256	221	1, 536	1, 181
Vermont	6, 992	1, 018	3, 573	2, 765	172	206	⁴ 1, 100
Virginia	18, 604	7, 519	28, 166	21, 441	1, 448	3, 190	2, 242
Washington	66, 894	9, 609	30, 058	21, 868	⁴ 830	5, 302	8, 564
West Virginia	26, 232	16, 874	61, 994	47, 985	1, 124	3, 127	3, 383
Wisconsin	51, 115	8, 319	28, 201	20, 765	1, 331	989	4, 523
Wyoming	4, 187	498	1, 824	1, 371	95	463	126
Alaska	1, 649	768	2, 496	1, 813	29	....	126
Hawaii	2, 185	3, 173	11, 718	9, 148	104	1, 114	1, 691
Puerto Rico	36, 940	27, 020	81, 036	61, 308	740	6, 538	1, 723
Virgin Islands	679	222	714	633	45	21	247

[1] Includes children and 1 parent or other adult in families in which adult was considered in determining amount of assistance.

² Includes 534 recipients of payments made without Federal participation in California, 12 in Washington, 941 in Missouri, and 6,291 in Pennsylvania.

³ Partly estimated; total not as large as sum of State figures because of adjustment. See footnote 7.

⁴ Excludes some cases for program not administered by State agency.   ⁵ Estimated.

⁶ Excludes cases receiving assistance in kind only and, for a few counties, cases receiving cash payments.

⁷ Includes unknown number of cases receiving medical care, hospitalization, or burial only.

⁸ Represents program administered without Federal participation.

Source: Department of Health, Education , and Welfare, Social Security Administration, Bureau of Public Assistance. Data appear periodically in *Social Security Bulletin*.

,—PUBLIC ASSISTANCE—PAYMENTS, BY STATES AND OTHER AREAS: FISCAL YEAR 1952

[In thousands of dollars. Includes vendor payments for medical care]

OR OTHER AREA	Total	Old-age assistance	Aid to dependent children	Aid to the blind	Aid to the permanently and totally disabled	General assistance
	2,322,560	1,487,605	547,268	1 58,209	75,067	224,411
	30,113	19,648	7,715	434	2,282	33
	12,674	8,352	3,261	485	----------	576
	22,615	15,376	6,051	607	13	1 569
	321,958	218,711	74,915	1 11,175	----------	17,157
	56,649	45,356	5,955	262	2,068	3,012
	27,472	15,851	7,345	284	----------	1 3,992
	1,887	621	701	120	62	283
olumbia	5,480	1,633	2,419	164	772	492
	44,326	31,370	10,450	1,601	----------	1 905
	47,520	33,640	11,985	1,194	----------	701
	9,812	5,562	2,821	131	464	1 834
	126,870	66,672	30,549	2,707	1,680	25,281
	34,479	22,586	7,623	927	----------	3,343
	39,683	29,416	6,335	947	----------	2,985
	33,264	23,035	4,571	399	1,465	3,814
	35,360	22,983	10,616	951	----------	810
	94,841	68,436	15,908	1,022	6,735	2,740
	14,817	7,470	3,880	333	----------	3,134
	14,193	5,504	5,282	261	1,399	1,747
ts	118,670	83,304	18,406	1,462	2,802	12,696
	101,883	53,569	28,044	1,177	731	18,362
	53,259	38,278	9,668	917	----------	4,396
	17,473	13,525	2,823	825	167	134
	94,250	69,073	14,118	1 1,809	5,712	3,538
	12,219	7,001	2,431	360	686	1,740
	18,536	13,947	3,239	572	----------	779
	2,614	1,819	4 14	25	----------	1 756
shire	7,453	4,408	2,008	205	2	830
	26,491	13,819	6,178	567	614	5,314
	10,268	5,154	3,611	220	913	370
	238,084	90,464	75,223	3,696	24,467	44,232
ina	29,767	15,379	9,453	1,820	1,357	1,759
ta	8,459	5,707	1,827	75	424	426
	100,611	69,499	11,566	2,207	2,227	15,112
	77,735	56,816	17,581	1,594	633	1,111
	25,837	15,366	4,128	310	1,379	4,655
ia	101,579	37,612	36,946	1 8,544	5,832	12,644
d	13,044	5,440	3,746	128	135	3,596
ina	19,213	13,364	3,341	535	1,392	582
ta	9,350	5,924	2,177	99	62	1,067
	36,260	22,514	12,118	1,262	----------	366
	101,489	87,261	9,918	2,694	----------	1,616
	12,141	6,312	3,805	154	1,047	824
	4,604	3,279	655	92	94	1 444
	12,541	5,205	4,864	551	1,085	836
	71,811	51,074	11,190	1 759	3,850	4,938
ia	23,315	8,389	11,813	417	658	2,037
	50,406	32,634	11,622	949	721	4,479
	4,303	2,854	657	62	303	427
	1,890	1,119	618	7	----------	146
	6,031	898	3,190	54	569	1,320
'	4,771	2,285	1,864	48	288	266
ds	170	90	42	6	3	29

payments to 534 recipients of aid to partially self-supporting blind in California and 12 in Washington; nts are made without Federal participation. For Pennsylvania and Missouri, includes payments ut Federal participation.
i local funds not administered by State agency.   1 Estimated.
its program administered without Federal participation.
epartment of Health, Education, and Welfare. Social Security Administration, Bureau of Public Data appear periodically in Social Security Bulletin.

No. 296.—Public Assistance—Recipients and Payments: 1946 to 1952

[Partly estimated; subject to revision. Data through Sept. 1950 cover continental U. S., Alaska and Hawaii; thereafter, include Puerto Rico and Virgin Islands. Recipients for December; payments for calendar years]

PROGRAM	1946	1947	1948	1949	1950	1951	1952
NUMBER OF RECIPIENTS (1,000)							
Old-age assistance	2,196	2,332	2,498	2,736	2,786	2,701	2,635
Aid to dependent children:							
Families	346	416	475	599	651	592	569
Recipients [1]					2,233	2,041	1,991
Children	885	1,060	1,214	1,521	1,661	1,523	1,495
Aid to the blind	77	81	86	93	97	97	98
Aid to the permanently and totally disabled					69	124	161
Cases receiving general assistance	315	356	396	562	413	328	280
PAYMENTS ($1,000)							
Total assistance	1,182,594	1,485,759	1,736,985	2,186,543	2,369,324	2,291,277	2,323,517
Old-age assistance	822,061	989,716	1,132,604	1,380,398	1,461,624	1,433,990	1,468,060
Aid to dependent children	208,857	294,961	364,160	475,361	551,653	552,890	542,214
Aid to the blind	30,748	26,253	41,382	48,532	52,606	54,535	59,689
Aid to the permanently and totally disabled					7,967	54,608	81,790
General assistance	120,928	164,830	198,838	282,252	295,383	195,254	171,764

[1] Includes children and 1 parent or other adult in families in which adult was considered in determining amount of assistance.

Source: Department of Health, Education, and Welfare, Social Security Administration, Bureau of Public Assistance.

No. 297.—Maternal and Child Health and Welfare Services—Grants to States and Other Areas: Fiscal Year 1952

[In thousands of dollars. Based on checks issued less refunds]

STATE OR OTHER AREA	Maternal and child health services	Services for crippled children	Child welfare services	STATE OR OTHER AREA	Maternal and child health services	Services for crippled children	Child welfare services
Total	12,676.8	11,109.5	7,245.4	Nevada	61.1	55.6	25.7
				New Hampshire	90.4	70.3	50.0
Alabama	479.6	414.2	298.7	New Jersey	187.6	217.3	69.1
Arizona	165.8	[1] -1.7	64.5	New Mexico	125.5	86.1	98.0
Arkansas	252.0	294.0	121.6	New York	449.7	365.8	99.3
California	437.4	299.1	291.9	North Carolina	599.2	461.8	283.1
Colorado	213.3	130.2	79.3	North Dakota	91.0	83.2	39.9
Connecticut	119.1	177.2	113.8	Ohio	417.8	325.2	152.9
Delaware	88.5	71.4	51.6	Oklahoma	197.4	312.0	178.9
Dist. of Columbia	145.0	149.5	42.3	Oregon	110.4	97.3	80.8
Florida	261.3	183.1	129.9	Pennsylvania	491.0	350.3	315.3
Georgia	499.6	351.2	230.4	Rhode Island	82.0	116.9	40.6
Idaho	89.7	97.2	39.2	South Carolina	271.1	316.6	95.0
Illinois	316.8	312.7	196.8	South Dakota	69.5	91.1	92.3
Indiana	256.9	138.4	75.9	Tennessee	452.6	350.8	311.7
Iowa	164.9	240.1	206.7	Texas	552.3	484.6	413.8
Kansas	134.4	131.1	118.4	Utah	138.9	103.4	62.7
Kentucky	383.2	395.8	263.8	Vermont	76.6	72.9	57.5
Louisiana	333.9	257.6	212.3	Virginia	333.8	324.7	201.3
Maine	110.1	107.0	73.8	Washington	184.2	159.3	130.6
Maryland	274.2	243.1	110.8	West Virginia	260.4	216.6	204.6
Massachusetts	275.4	184.8	72.4	Wisconsin	236.8	276.1	186.3
Michigan	414.2	312.4	196.2	Wyoming	88.8	38.9	42.8
Minnesota	217.5	229.5	151.9				
Mississippi	347.2	315.1	264.1	Alaska	124.6	118.1	49.4
Missouri	254.1	215.0	186.6	Hawaii	129.1	164.6	43.1
Montana	71.5	96.4	43.2	Puerto Rico	372.1	315.3	228.0
Nebraska	106.6	127.2	23.5	Virgin Islands	70.7	63.2	31.1

[1] Negative quantity represents refund to Federal government.

Source: Department of Health, Education, and Welfare, Social Security Administration, Children's Bureau.

No. 298.—MATERNAL AND CHILD-HEALTH SERVICES: 1947 TO 1951

[Services administered or supervised by State health agencies under Social Security Act. Includes data for Alaska, Hawaii, Puerto Rico, and the Virgin Islands. Subject to revision]

TYPE OF SERVICE	NUMBER REPORTED				
	1947	1948	1949	1950	1951
MEDICAL SERVICES					
Maternity service:					
Cases admitted to antepartum medical service	151,000	153,000	168,000	175,000	189,000
Visits by antepartum cases to medical conferences	466,000	456,000	511,000	525,000	555,000
Cases given postpartum medical examination	40,000	45,000	55,000	59,000	53,000
Infant hygiene:					
Individuals admitted to medical service	246,000	264,000	295,000	303,000	395,000
Visits to medical conferences	742,000	762,000	865,000	827,000	1,090,000
Preschool hygiene:					
Individuals admitted to medical service	320,000	379,000	399,000	420,000	565,000
Visits to medical conferences	690,000	745,000	839,000	832,000	1,022,000
School hygiene:					
Examinations by physicians	1,878,000	2,072,000	2,299,000	2,223,000	2,394,000
PUBLIC-HEALTH NURSING SERVICES					
Maternity service:					
Cases admitted to antepartum nursing service	227,000	229,000	242,000	258,000	268,000
Field and office visits to and by antepartum cases	646,000	627,000	640,000	649,000	671,000
Cases given nursing service at delivery	6,000	7,000	6,000	5,000	4,000
Cases admitted to postpartum nursing service	215,000	223,000	243,000	246,000	279,000
Nursing visits to postpartum cases	449,000	458,000	506,000	509,000	572,000
Infant hygiene:					
Individuals admitted to nursing service	516,000	530,000	552,000	537,000	677,000
Field and office nursing visits	1,483,000	1,472,000	1,539,000	1,546,000	1,668,000
Preschool hygiene:					
Individuals admitted to nursing service	495,000	542,000	577,000	560,000	697,000
Field and office nursing visits	1,188,000	1,273,000	1,369,000	1,407,000	1,631,000
School hygiene:					
Field and office nursing visits	2,199,000	2,427,000	2,672,000	2,894,000	2,160,000
IMMUNIZATIONS					
Smallpox	2,072,000	1,403,000	1,562,000	1,617,000	1,521,000
Diphtheria	1,597,000	1,551,000	1,556,000	1,554,000	1,531,000
OTHER SERVICES					
Inspections by dentists or dental hygienists:					
Preschool children	56,000	53,000	76,000	72,000	80,000
School children	1,575,000	1,984,000	2,315,000	2,559,000	2,466,000
Visits for midwife supervision	28,000	27,000	28,000	32,000	32,000

Source: Department of Health, Education, and Welfare, Social Security Administration, Children's Bureau.

No. 299.—SERVICES FOR CRIPPLED CHILDREN: 1948 TO 1951

[Services provided or purchased by official State crippled children's agencies under the Social Security Act. Includes data for Alaska, Hawaii, Puerto Rico, and the Virgin Islands. Subject to revision]

TYPE OF SERVICE	NUMBER REPORTED			
	1948	1949	1950 [1]	1951 [1]
Crippled children on State registers at end of year	522,000	585,000	649,000	689,000
Total number of children who received physician's services	155,000	181,000	214,000	229,000
Clinic service:				
Number of children	131,000	151,000	172,000	156,000
Number of visits	284,000	320,000	364,000	386,000
Average number of visits per child	2.2	2.1	2.1	2.1
Physician's office and home services:				
Number of children	12,000	21,000	25,000	24,000
Number of visits	39,000	61,000	91,000	88,000
Average number of visits per child	3.1	3.0	3.7	3.7
Hospital in-patient care:				
Number of children	32,000	38,000	43,000	43,000
Number of days' care	1,335,000	1,454,000	1,425,000	1,322,000
Average number of days per child	41.5	37.8	32.8	30.5
Convalescent-home care:				
Number of children	5,000	5,600	5,500	5,600
Number of days' care	484,000	556,000	529,000	528,000
Average number of days per child	97.1	98.9	96.9	94.2

[1] Excludes data for Arizona which did not participate in crippled children's program under Social Security Act during this period.

Source: Department of Health, Education, and Welfare, Social Security Administration, Children's Bureau.

No. 300.—Children Receiving Service from Public Welfare Agencies on Mar. 31, 1952 and Percent Change from Mar. 31, 1946, by State or Other Area

[Includes only States with complete reporting coverage, Mar. 31, 1946–52]

STATE OR OTHER AREA	NUMBER OF CHILDREN SERVED, MARCH 31, 1952			PERCENT CHANGE FROM 1946 TO 1952		
	Total [1]	In homes of parents or relatives	In foster family homes	Total [1]	In homes of parents or relatives	In foster family homes
Total	220,096	87,266	93,266	+11	+4	+27
Alabama	8,298	6,199	1,227	+26	+24	+60
Arizona	1,841	933	779	+1	−13	+29
Arkansas	1,601	884	611	+47	+26	+90
Colorado	2,360	1,355	735	+53	+60	+56
Delaware	859	248	525	+29	+2	+35
District of Columbia	2,550	801	877	+4	−26	−18
Florida	1,951	777	978	+28	+32	+23
Idaho	342	273	38	+24	+41	(2)
Illinois	5,864	1,890	3,483	[3]+121	+190	+104
Indiana	13,106	5,841	4,916	−14	−18	+2
Louisiana	3,102	566	2,278	+29	−21	+50
Maine	3,329	986	2,089	+5	−2	+16
Maryland	4,318	803	2,909	[3]+149	+102	+155
Massachusetts	7,969	818	6,394	−17	+11	+21
Minnesota	8,705	5,293	2,667	[3]−55	−60	−26
Mississippi	3,323	2,831	292	+171	+223	(2)
Missouri	4,113	2,119	1,712	+17	+17	+18
Montana	1,100	547	434	+2	−34	+113
Nebraska	1,962	875	515	−16	−34	+40
New Hampshire	2,360	1,006	966	+1	−4	+16
New Jersey	7,243	1,312	4,797	−35	−56	−10
New Mexico	1,848	738	595	+54	+69	+60
New York	40,421	4,625	21,806	(4)	−37	+13
North Carolina	11,660	6,637	2,873	[3]+84	+94	+50
North Dakota	3,1b9	2,934	122	[3]+159	+183	−18
Ohio	16,859	4,198	8,232	+39	+59	+58
Oklahoma	1,822	313	636	−9	−25	+9
Rhode Island	1,979	641	1,050	+16	+69	+5
South Carolina	3,731	2,611	470	+23	+10	+64
South Dakota	739	405	245	+9	+1	+21
Tennessee	2,493	1,308	955	+129	+84	+408
Texas	2,750	1,945	583	−22	−31	+37
Utah	1,006	431	525	+31	+84	−1
Vermont	1,717	687	751	−11	−14	−14
Virginia	8,284	2,707	4,715	+44	+43	+50
Washington	5,571	2,205	2,839	+36	+16	+31
West Virginia	7,823	5,387	1,875	+24	+28	+20
Wisconsin	8,054	3,384	3,847	+28	(2)	+80
Alaska	696	222	165	+65	+50	+42
Hawaii	2,759	1,463	1,000	+79	+109	+117
Puerto Rico	10,760	8,073	502	+53	+32	+39

[1] Includes some 39,625 children living in institutions or elsewhere, not shown separately.
[2] Not computed; 1946 figure less than 100.
[3] Large percent change reflect refinements in State reporting procedures or changes in policy and organization, as well as fluctuations in volume.
[4] Less than 1 percent.

Source: Department of Health, Education, and Welfare, Social Security Administration, Children's Bureau.

No. 801.—VOCATIONAL REHABILITATION OF DISABLED PERSONS—NUMBER, BY TYPE OF DISABILITY AND OCCUPATION: 1947 TO 1952

[For fiscal years ending June 30]

TYPE	1947	1948	1949	1950	1951	1952 [1]
DISABILITY						
Total	43,880	53,131	58,630	59,597	66,198	63,632
Amputated or missing members	5,949	7,276	7,396	7,582	7,986	7,821
Impairment of extremities	12,022	13,510	14,296	13,720	14,852	13,645
Impairment of other parts of body [2]	3,040	3,532	3,584	4,501	4,980	4,990
Visual:						
Blind	2,157	2,569	3,166	3,210	3,614	3,731
Other visual	3,026	3,631	3,895	3,890	4,551	4,010
Aural:						
Deaf	965	1,064	1,152	1,267	1,488	1,178
Hard of hearing	2,428	3,436	3,935	4,024	4,206	3,773
Speech defect	392	538	648	675	874	873
Tuberculosis, pulmonary	3,519	4,433	4,738	4,913	5,807	5,633
Cardiac	1,734	2,125	2,284	2,308	2,592	2,506
Other diseases	6,091	7,745	8,780	9,657	10,626	10,914
Mental disorders	2,546	3,237	3,838	3,845	4,608	4,302
Not reported	17	35	6	15	7	86
JOB OR OCCUPATION						
Total	43,880	53,131	58,630	59,597	66,198	63,632
Professional	2,273	2,749	3,025	3,117	3,094	3,161
Semiprofessional	1,160	1,320	1,299	1,193	1,329	1,384
Managerial and official	888	969	997	1,691	1,606	1,665
Clerical and kindred	6,790	7,955	8,667	7,852	10,267	10,134
Sales and kindred	2,373	3,176	3,496	3,361	3,094	2,865
Service occupations	6,076	7,533	8,652	9,142	9,756	9,865
Agriculture, fishing, etc	3,446	4,221	5,039	5,731	5,416	5,576
Skilled	7,516	8,654	8,808	9,305	10,329	9,077
Semiskilled	6,539	7,796	7,765	7,962	10,350	9,407
Unskilled	3,901	4,923	5,113	4,096	5,295	4,436
Family workers and housewives	2,847	3,807	4,843	6,131	5,679	6,034
Not reported	81	28	24	17	29	47

[1] Subject to revision.

[2] Includes spine, neck, head, facial disfigurement, dwarf.

Source: Department of Health, Education, and Welfare, Office of Vocational Rehabilitation.

No. 302.—VOCATIONAL REHABILITATION OF DISABLED PERSONS—NUMBER AND EXPENDITURES, BY STATE OR OTHER AREA: 1952

[Expenditures in thousands of dollars. For year ending June 30]

STATE OR OTHER AREA	Number rehabili- tated	Number in process of reha- bilita- tion on June 30	EXPENDITURES				
			Total	By State boards of vocational educa- tion		By State agencies for the blind	
				Total	Federal	Total	Federal
Total	63,632	127,451	32,689	29,486	19,737	3,203	2,385
Alabama	1,721	4,637	967	967	598	....	....
Arizona	213	336	120	94	65	26	20
Arkansas	1,066	2,516	459	459	314	....	....
California	3,922	7,960	2,138	2,138	1,601	....	....
Colorado	561	920	226	178	132	48	34
Connecticut	1,190	2,844	411	379	256	32	27
Delaware	475	766	245	195	128	50	35
District of Columbia	347	884	265	265	180	....	....
Florida	1,931	4,636	1,044	811	523	233	177
Georgia	3,194	7,783	2,052	2,052	1,354	....	....
Idaho	164	283	85	69	46	16	14
Illinois	4,049	5,923	1,772	1,772	1,200	....	....
Indiana	1,187	3,191	552	491	325	61	48
Iowa	860	1,695	411	388	272	23	17
Kansas	752	1,145	321	258	176	63	48
Kentucky	722	1,518	223	223	145	....	....
Louisiana	1,390	3,661	737	661	465	96	78
Maine	254	603	144	108	73	36	22
Maryland	1,028	2,696	488	488	349	....	....
Massachusetts	705	1,449	363	358	215	5	5
Michigan	3,500	7,740	1,477	1,348	920	129	89
Minnesota	874	2,595	466	377	257	89	67
Mississippi	1,088	2,339	625	511	345	114	89
Missouri	1,243	2,911	654	548	380	106	84
Montana	401	745	208	175	127	33	25
Nebraska	593	985	284	236	158	48	35
Nevada	56	121	32	32	24	....	....
New Hampshire	112	284	72	61	42	11	11
New Jersey	1,076	2,262	604	492	348	112	92
New Mexico	227	470	150	128	85	22	17
New York	4,487	8,776	2,067	1,747	1,152	320	226
North Carolina	2,998	5,603	1,216	899	560	317	222
North Dakota	204	404	142	142	92	....	....
Ohio	1,327	2,578	680	494	322	186	131
Oklahoma	1,282	3,778	718	718	484	....	....
Oregon	617	1,807	419	365	235	54	37
Pennsylvania	3,574	6,859	2,449	2,161	1,432	288	222
Rhode Island	329	851	156	121	84	35	27
South Carolina	1,816	3,210	693	656	453	37	29
South Dakota	160	519	115	91	59	24	18
Tennessee	1,869	2,942	945	766	514	179	132
Texas	2,435	7,126	1,417	1,219	813	198	153
Utah	369	711	143	143	109	....	....
Vermont	181	379	134	112	73	22	17
Virginia	1,703	3,365	727	684	435	43	29
Washington	1,060	2,506	863	810	488	53	31
West Virginia	1,780	4,512	730	730	503	....	....
Wisconsin	1,429	3,696	741	679	467	62	52
Wyoming	175	329	112	112	80	....	....
Alaska	2	16	7	7	7	....	....
Hawaii	243	585	208	176	119	32	24
Puerto Rico	691	1,507	392	392	253	....	....

Source: Department of Health, Education, and Welfare, Office of Vocational Rehabilitation.

11. Income and Expenditures

The income statistics in this section are of two fundamental types: First, those which provide data on aggregate amounts (national income and national product data) and second, those which provide data on the distribution of families or persons by size of their income (size distribution data). Statistics representing the former type are compiled primarily by the Office of Business Economics of the Department of Commerce and are based on a wide variety of data from government and private sources. Statistics representing the latter type of income data are derived from sample surveys of income conducted by several different agencies. Since these surveys were taken at different times and for different purposes, they differ somewhat in the definitions of income and the income-receiving unit. In addition to the income data, expenditures and savings of families and single persons have been included in this section.

Nation's economic accounts.—The Nation's economic accounts are designed to give a synoptic picture of the economy. (See table 303.) They show the magnitudes of income and expenditure of major economic groups, net additions and absorption of saving by these groups, and the gross national product or income. Statistics are based on the "National income and product" accounts of the Department of Commerce.

Business receipts retained include corporate retained earnings plus inventory valuation adjustment and capital consumption allowances of all business. Government receipts and expenditures are shown on an income and product account basis, rather than on either a cash or a conventional budget basis, so as to be consistent with the receipt and expenditure accounts of the other sectors and with the gross national product total. Government transfer payments, such as social security and veterans' benefits and interest charges represent income to the recipients, but are not included in the gross national product. Therefore, these payments are subtracted from both receipts and expenditures.

A fuller explanation of the Nation's economic accounts may be found in the Annual Review of the Council of Economic Advisers, included in the *Economic Report of the President to Congress.*

Aggregate income.—The aggregate income statistics presented here are of three general types: Gross national product or expenditure, national income (by distributive shares and by industrial origin), and income payments to individuals by States.

Gross national product is the market value of the output of goods and services produced by the Nation's economy, before deduction of depreciation charges and other allowances for business and institutional consumption of durable capital goods.

Note.—This section presents data for the most recent year or period available on March 17, 1953, when the material was organized and sent to the printer. In a few instances, more recent data were added after that date.

273

Other business products used up by business in the accounting period are excluded. The Nation's economy in this context refers to the labor and property supplied by residents of the Nation. Gross national product comprises the purchases of goods and services by consumers and government, gross private domestic investment, and net foreign investment. Gross national product differs from national income mainly in that no allowance is made for depreciation or for indirect business taxes, both of which items constitute expenses in the computation of business net incomes.

National income is the aggregate earnings of labor and property which arise from the current production of goods and services by the Nation's economy. Thus, it measures the total factor costs of the goods and services produced by the economy. Earnings are recorded in the forms in which they accrue to residents of the Nation, inclusive of taxes on those earnings.

National income originating by industry is the sum of factor costs incurred by the industry in production. Hence, it is the net value added to production by the industry, measured at factor costs.

Personal income is the current income received by persons from all sources, inclusive of transfers from government and business but exclusive of transfers among persons.

Income payments to individuals is a measure of income received from all sources during the calendar year by residents of each State. It comprises income received by individuals in form of (1) wages and salaries, after deduction of employees' contributions to social security, railroad retirement, railroad unemployment insurance, and government retirement programs; (2) proprietors' incomes, representing net income of unincorporated establishments, including farms, before owners' withdrawals; (3) property income, consisting of dividends, interest, and net rents and royalties; and (4) "other" income, which includes public assistance and other direct relief; labor income items such as work relief, government retirement payments, veterans' pensions and benefits, workmen's compensation, and social insurance benefits; mustering-out payments to discharged servicemen; family-allowance payments and voluntary allotments of pay to dependents of military personnel; enlisted men's cash terminal leave payments; and State government bonuses to veterans of World War II. For discussion of distribution by State, see headnote, table 312.

Size distribution of income.—The statistics on the size distribution of income are based on data collected in various field surveys of income which have been conducted since 1936. The primary purpose of these field surveys was to show the distribution of families or persons by income levels rather than the aggregate amounts of income received by these families. Whereas the aggregate income data provide an indication of the level of total purchasing power, the field survey size distribution data, by showing the numbers and kinds of families and persons in each income bracket, provide an indication of the distribution of purchasing power in the population. In each of these field surveys trained enumerators interviewed representative samples of the civilian noninstitutional population with respect to the income received by the respondents or their families during the previous year.

The income represented in these tables is consumer money income, defined as the sum of civilian money wages and salaries; net farm entrepreneurial income; net nonfarm entrepreneurial income from business or profession; interest, dividends, and periodic income from estates and trusts; rents and royalties; armed forces pay of persons living in private households at the time of the survey; dependency allotments and contributions from members of the armed forces; veterans payments; social security payments, unemployment and workmen's compensation, pensions and assistance; and miscellaneous items such as periodic contributions for support from persons not in the household, periodic payments from insurance policies or annuities, and alimony. The income is for the calendar year and is before deduction of income taxes or social security taxes. Nonmoney items of income are not covered. None of the aggregate income concepts (gross national product, national income, or personal income) is comparable with consumer money income. The nearest approximation is personal income.

Expenditures and savings.—The Bureau of Labor Statistics most recent survey of family income, expenditures, and savings on a Nation-wide basis for which tabulations are available is for the year 1944. The Survey of Prices Paid by Consumers in 1944 was based on a sample of 1,700 families and single persons in 28 metropolitan districts and 20 cities with populations under 50,000 outside of metropolitan districts. These places were selected to represent (with respect to region, State and city size) all cities in the United States with a population of 2,500 or more.

For this study a family is defined as a group of persons dependent on a common or pooled income for the major items of expense and usually living in the same household. A single person is one who lives alone or with unrelated people in a private home, lodging house, or hotel. From 1945 through 1949, the Bureau has made similar surveys of family expenditure in selected cities each year to obtain data necessary to check the prices and weighting patterns used in the consumers' price index; 1945 expenditure data were obtained for Birmingham, Ala.; Indianapolis, Ind.; and Portland, Oreg. (see *Monthly Labor Review*, June 1948); 1946 data for Milwaukee, Wis.; Scranton, Pa., and Savannah, Ga. (available upon request to the Bureau of Labor Statistics); 1947 data for Washington, D. C.; Manchester, N. H.; and Richmond, Va. (see *Monthly Labor Review*, April, June-August, and October 1949); 1948 data for Denver, Colo.; Detroit, Mich.; and Houston, Tex. (see *Monthly Labor Review*, December 1949); and 1949 data for Memphis, Tenn. (see *Monthly Labor Review*, June 1951). These data from 1948-49, both inclusive, are now also available in Bulletin No. 1065, *Family Income, Expenditures, and Savings in 10 Cities.*

A Nation-wide Consumer Expenditure Survey was made for 1950 by the Bureau of Labor Statistics in 91 cities yielding 12,500 usable schedules from families and single consumers. Data from this survey were not available for inclusion here at the time this section was sent to the printer. For field methods and purposes, see *Monthly Labor Review*, January 1951. For selection of cities for the survey, see *Monthly Labor Review*, April 1951.

National Surveys of Consumer Finances have been conducted annually since 1946 for the Board of Governors of the Federal Reserve System by the Survey Research Center of the University of Michigan. These samples of about 2,500 to 3,000 family units or 2,800 to 3,500 spending units are taken at 60 to 66 sampling points. Information is obtained on many aspects of consumer finances—income, assets, debts, saving, etc.—which provide data on size distributions, aggregates, and distributions of aggregates, and on the interrelationships of economic and social variables. Reports of survey findings are published in the *Federal Reserve Bulletin*.

1950 Census data.—As a part of the 1950 Census of Population, the Bureau of the Census collected data on the distribution of income from a sample of the population. Figures in this section from the 1950 Census (see table 322) are final figures based on a representative 20-percent sample of the population.

Historical statistics.—See preface and historical appendix. Tabular headnotes (as "See also *Historical Statistics*, series A 101-116") provide cross-references, where applicable, to *Historical Statistics of the United States, 1789-1945.*

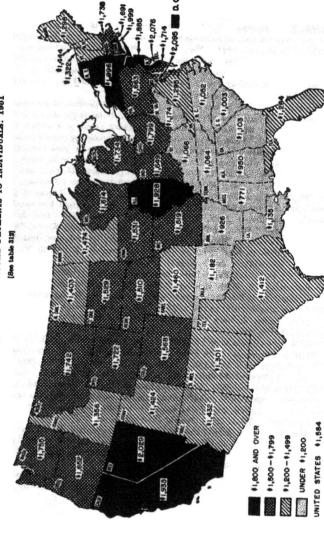

FIG. XX.—PER CAPITA INCOME PAYMENTS TO INDIVIDUALS: 1951
[See table 315]

$1,800 AND OVER
$1,500—$1,799
$1,200—$1,499
UNDER $1,200

UNITED STATES $1,584

Source: Department of Commerce, Office of Business Economics.

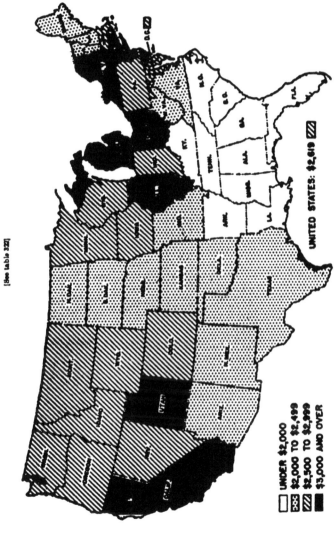

Fig. XXI.—Median Income in 1949 of Families and Unrelated Individuals: 1950

[See table XXI]

UNITED STATES: $2,619

UNDER $2,000
$2,000 TO $2,499
$2,500 TO $2,999
$3,000 AND OVER

Source: Department of Commerce, Bureau of the Census.

No. 308.—THE NATION'S ECONOMIC ACCOUNTS: 1951 AND 1952

[Billions of dollars. Based on national income and product statistics of Dept. of Commerce. For explanation of Nation's economic accounts, see text, p. 273]

ECONOMIC GROUP	1951			1952, FIRST HALF			1952, SECOND HALF [1]		
	Receipts	Expenditures	Excess of receipts (+) or expenditures (−)	Receipts	Expenditures	Excess of receipts (+) or expenditures (−)	Receipts	Expenditures	Excess of receipts (+) or expenditures (−)
Gross national product	329.2	329.2	....	341.2	341.2	....	349.1	349.1	....
Consumers:									
Disposable personal income	225.0	....	....	231.0	....	....	238.6	....	....
Personal consumption expenditures	....	208.0	....	....	214.0	....	....	218.0	....
Personal net saving (+)	....	....	+17.0	....	....	+16.9	....	....	+20.6
Business:									
Gross retained earnings	33.0	....	....	36.2	....	....	36.4	....	....
Gross private domestic investment	....	58.5	....	....	49.6	....	....	53.1	....
Excess of investment (−)	....	....	−25.5	....	....	−13.4	....	....	−16.7
International:									
Net foreign investment	....	.2	....	....	1.3	....	....	−.7	....
Excess of receipts (+) or investment (−)	....	....	−.2	....	....	−1.3	....	....	+.7
Government (Federal, State, and local):									
Tax and nontax receipts or accruals	86.8	....	....	91.5	....	....	94.2	....	....
Less: Transfers, interest, and subsidies (net)	16.9	....	....	17.0	....	....	16.9	....	....
Equals: Net receipts	69.9	....	....	74.5	....	....	77.3	....	....
Total government expenditures	....	79.5	....	....	93.2	....	....	95.6	....
Less: Transfers, interest, and subsidies (net)	....	16.9	....	....	17.0	....	....	16.9	....
Equals: Purchases of goods and services	....	62.6	....	....	76.2	....	....	78.7	....
Surplus (+) or deficit (−) on income and product account	....	....	+7.3	....	....	−1.6	....	....	−1.4
Statistical discrepancy	1.4	....	+1.4	−.5	....	−.5	−3.2	....	−3.2

[1] Estimates based on incomplete data.

Source: Council of Economic Advisers; published in *Economic Report of the President*, January 1953.

No. 304.—RELATION OF GROSS NATIONAL PRODUCT, NATIONAL INCOME, AND PERSONAL INCOME IN CURRENT DOLLARS: 1929 TO 1952

[In millions of dollars. For definitions of gross national product, national income, and personal income, see text, p. 273]

ITEM	1929	1933	1940	1945	1947	1948	1949	1950	1951	1952
Gross national product	103,828	55,760	101,443	215,210	233,264	259,045	258,229	284,187	329,232	345,390
Less:										
Capital consumption allowances	8,816	7,245	8,440	12,410	14,845	17,612	19,371	21,538	24,636	26,100
Depreciation charges	7,553	6,608	7,228	10,885	12,086	14,368	16,409	18,001	20,062	23,400
Accidental damage to fixed capital	413	275	246	381	567	574	518	614	987	700
Capital outlays charged to current expense	850	362	966	1,144	2,192	2,670	2,444	2,923	3,597	3,900
Equals: Net national product	95,012	48,515	93,003	202,800	218,419	241,433	238,858	262,649	304,686	318,300
Plus: Subsidies minus current surplus of Government enterprises	−147	18	420	835	−75	−21	−12	419	541	100
Less:										
Indirect business tax and nontax liability	7,003	7,055	10,021	15,522	18,658	20,390	21,644	23,751	25,329	27,200
Business transfer payments	587	659	431	532	674	739	781	840	860	900
Statistical discrepancy	−80	1,235	1,624	4,890	324	−3,186	162	−693	1,404	−100
Equals: National income	87,365	39,584	81,347	182,691	198,688	223,449	216,259	239,170	277,554	290,400
Less:										
Undistributed corporate profits	2,597	−2,428	2,398	3,803	11,968	13,484	8,821	12,270	9,625	8,000
Corporate profits tax liability	1,398	524	2,878	11,215	11,940	13,028	10,817	18,383	24,213	22,600
Corporate inventory valuation adjustment	472	−2,143	−148	−564	−5,757	−2,051	2,062	−4,815	−1,205	800
Contributions for social insurance	243	265	2,262	6,138	5,683	5,220	5,737	6,851	8,164	8,200
Excess of wage accruals over disbursements	0	0	0	14	15	30	−45	36	29	−100
Plus:										
Net interest paid by Government	983	1,170	1,291	3,663	4,378	4,451	4,614	4,735	4,893	5,000
Government transfer payments	912	1,454	2,688	5,647	11,129	10,546	11,625	14,292	11,504	11,900
Business transfer payments	587	659	431	532	674	739	781	849	860	900
Equals: Personal income	85,127	46,629	78,347	171,927	191,669	209,494	205,867	226,513	254,075	265,300

Source: Department of Commerce, Office of Business Economics; *Survey of Current Business*, July 1952 and February 1953.

No. 305.—GROSS NATIONAL PRODUCT OR EXPENDITURE IN CURRENT DOLLARS: 1929 TO 1952

[In millions of dollars. For definition of gross national product, see text, p. 273. See also *Historical Statistics*, series A 101-116]

ITEM	1929	1933	1940	1945	1947	1948	1949	1950	1951	1952
Gross national product	103,828	55,760	101,443	215,210	233,264	259,045	258,229	284,187	329,232	345,390
Personal consumption expenditures	78,761	46,346	72,052	122,079	165,570	177,890	180,588	194,277	207,972	216,300
Durable goods	9,362	3,503	7,854	8,472	21,369	22,883	23,840	29,152	27,130	25,800
Nondurable goods	37,742	22,254	37,594	74,896	95,142	100,889	99,223	102,760	113,505	119,000
Services	31,657	20,589	26,604	39,721	49,059	54,118	57,525	66,365	67,347	71,500
Gross private domestic investment	15,824	1,306	13,949	10,733	30,187	42,693	33,465	50,349	58,515	52,100
New construction	7,894	1,142	5,566	3,934	13,904	17,716	17,250	22,889	23,252	23,500
Producers' durable equipment	6,438	1,783	6,108	7,545	17,080	19,948	18,697	21,989	24,927	25,500
Change in business inventories	1,562	−1,619	2,275	−746	−797	5,029	−2,482	5,471	10,336	3,100
Net foreign investment	771	158	1,509	−1,438	8,895	1,864	528	−2,304	198	200
Government purchases of goods and services	8,472	7,958	13,933	82,536	26,612	36,596	43,648	41,965	63,542	77,800
Federal	1,311	2,018	6,170	74,796	15,784	21,022	25,449	22,165	40,861	54,400
National security	} 1,344	} 2,022	{ 2,223	75,923	13,328	16,062	19,274	18,497	37,065	49,200
Other			{ 3,956	1,031	3,751	5,570	6,570	3,909	4,202	5,600
Less: Government sales	33	4	9	2,158	1,295	631	395	241	406	400
State and local	7,161	5,940	7,763	8,040	12,828	15,576	18,199	19,700	21,671	23,400

Source: Department of Commerce, Office of Business Economics; *Survey of Current Business*, July 1952 and February 1953.

FIG. XXII.—GROSS NATIONAL PRODUCT IN CURRENT AND CONSTANT DOLLARS: 1929 TO 1952

[See tables 305 and 306]

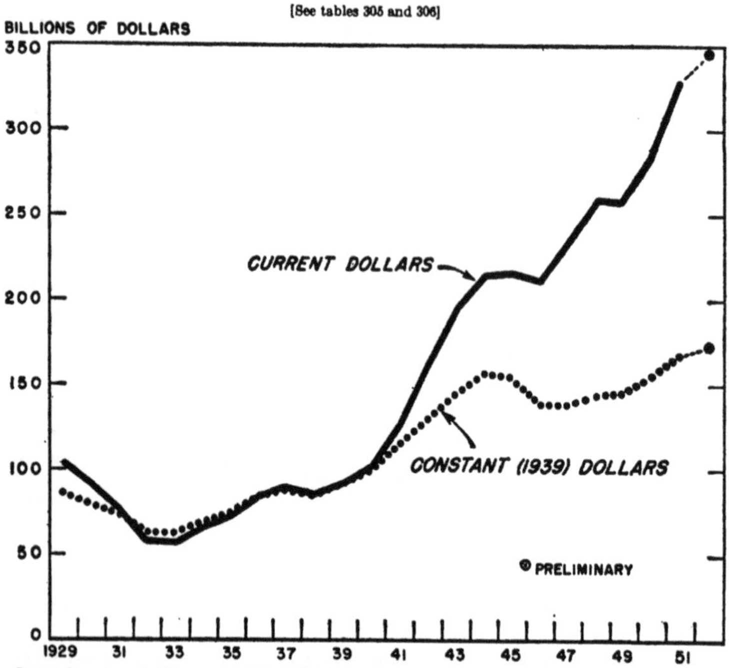

Source: Department of Commerce, Office of Business Economics.

No. 306.—GROSS NATIONAL PRODUCT OR EXPENDITURE IN CONSTANT (1939) DOLLARS: 1929 TO 1952

[In billions of 1939 dollars. Constant-dollar figures obtained by dividing current-dollar estimates shown in table 305 in as fine a product detail as possible, by appropriate price indexes based on 1939 as 100, in order to eliminate from the current-dollar estimates all price change as compared with 1939. For definition of gross national product, see text, p. 273]

ITEM	1929	1933	1940	1945	1947	1948	1949	1950	1951	1952
Gross national product	**85.9**	**61.5**	**100.0**	**153.4**	**138.6**	**143.5**	**144.0**	**154.8**	**167.3**	**171.2**
Personal consumption expenditures	62.2	51.1	71.3	86.3	98.3	100.3	103.2	108.5	108.4	110 4
Durable goods	8.0	3.8	7.7	5.3	12.3	12.6	12.9	15.4	13.3	12.5
Nondurable goods	29.1	24.9	37.1	47.9	49.5	49.7	50.7	51.6	52.4	54.6
Services	25.1	22.4	26.5	33.2	36.4	38.0	39.6	41.5	42.6	43.3
Gross private domestic investment	14.9	1.6	13.7	8.3	19.3	22.7	18.0	25.8	28.0	24.0
New construction	7.4	1.5	5.4	2.6	6.9	8.0	7.9	9.8	9.2	9.0
Producers' durable equipment	6.1	2.0	6.0	6.7	11.8	12.6	11.4	13.1	13.6	13.6
Change in business inventories	1.5	−1.8	2.3	−1.0	.6	2.1	−1.3	2.8	5.1	1.4
Net foreign investment	.8	.1	1.2	−1.8	4.8	1.4	.6	......	2.0	1.6
Government purchases of goods and services	7.9	8.7	13.8	60.6	16.1	19.2	22.2	20.6	28.9	35.1
Federal	1.3	2.3	6.1	54.6	8.5	10.9	12.9	10.9	18.9	24.6
State and local	6.6	6.4	7.7	6.0	7.6	8.2	9.3	9.7	10.1	10.5
Gross private product [1]	81.5	56.5	92.1	129.7	128.8	133.7	133.7	144.3	154.0	156.9
Gross Government product [2]	4.4	5.0	7.8	23.7	9.8	9 7	10.3	10.5	13.3	41.3

[1] Gross national product less compensation of general government employees.
[2] Compensation of general government employees.

Source: Department of Commerce, Office of Business Economics; *Survey of Current Business*, July 1952 and February 1953.

No. 307.—NATIONAL INCOME BY DISTRIBUTIVE SHARES: 1929 TO 1952

[In millions of dollars. For definition of national income, see text, p. 274. See also *Historical Statistics*, series A 117-133]

TYPE OF SHARE	1929	1933	1940	1945	1947	1948	1949	1950	1951	1952 (prel.)
National income	87,355	39,584	81,347	182,691	198,688	223,466	216,259	239,179	277,554	296,600
Compensation of employees	50,786	29,230	51,795	123,026	127,986	140,166	139,915	153,375	178,880	190,400
Wages and salaries [1]	50,145	28,825	49,587	117,672	122,050	134,257	133,356	145,603	169,906	181,100
Private	45,209	23,660	41,130	82,101	104,803	115,550	112,978	123,442	141,159	148,700
Military	312	270	591	22,596	4,066	3,970	4,348	4,999	8,640	(?)
Government civilian [3]	4,647	4,896	7,866	12,974	13,195	14,728	16,130	17,162	20,107	(?)
Supplements to wages and salaries	521	505	2,199	5,353	6,929	5,809	6,559	7,772	8,974	9,200
Employer contributions for social insurance	101	123	1,624	3,805	3,565	3,042	3,503	3,962	4,748	4,800
Other labor income	520	372	575	1,548	2,364	2,767	3,056	3,810	4,226	4,800
Income of unincorporated enterprises and inventory valuation adjustment	13,927	5,207	12,680	31,347	36,365	39,731	34,406	37,915	41,778	42,800
Business and professional	8,262	2,935	7,720	18,719	19,776	22,085	21,690	22,967	26,210	27,800
Income of unincorporated enterprise	8,120	3,450	7,772	18,832	21,223	22,480	20,906	24,907	26,691	(?)
Inventory valuation adjustment	142	-525	-52	-113	-1,547	-395	621	-1,240	-381	(?)
Farm [4]	5,065	2,282	4,940	12,528	16,589	17,666	12,776	13,348	15,568	15,300
Rental income of persons	5,811	2,018	3,630	6,256	7,069	7,506	7,720	8,175	8,871	9,800
Corporate profits and inventory valuation adjustment	10,290	-1,961	9,177	19,153	24,732	31,711	26,189	34,796	41,579	40,500
Corporate profits before tax	9,818	162	9,325	19,717	30,480	33,762	27,107	39,610	42,874	39,700
Corporate profits tax liability	1,398	594	2,878	11,215	11,940	13,028	10,817	18,363	24,218	22,600
Corporate profits after tax	8,420	-362	6,447	8,502	18,549	20,734	16,290	21,227	18,661	17,100
Dividends	5,823	2,066	4,049	4,699	6,561	7,250	7,469	8,957	9,035	9,100
Undistributed profits	2,597	-2,428	2,398	3,803	11,988	13,484	8,844	10,545	11,330	8,000
Inventory valuation adjustment	472	-2,143	-148	-564	-5,757	-2,051	2,082	-4,815	-1,295	800
Net interest	6,541	5,010	4,104	3,009	3,544	4,335	5,030	5,810	6,446	7,000

[1] Includes employee contributions to social insurance funds.

[2] Not available.

[3] Includes pay of employees of government enterprises and of permanent U. S. residents employed in U. S. by foreign governments and international organizations.

[4] Inventory valuation adjustment data for farms are not available separately.

Source: Department of Commerce, Office of Business Economics; *Survey of Current Business*, July 1952 and February 1953.

No. 308.—PERSONAL INCOME AND DISPOSITION OF INCOME: 1929 TO 1952

[Millions of dollars. For definition of personal income, see text, p. 274. See also *Historical Statistics*, series A 134-144]

ITEM	1929	1933	1940	1945	1947	1948	1949	1950	1951	1952 (prel.)
Personal income	85,127	46,639	78,347	171,927	191,600	209,494	205,867	226,312	254,975	268,300
Wage and salary disbursements	50,165	25,825	49,587	117,659	122,044	134,327	133,401	145,567	169,877	181,400
Wage and salary receipts, total	50,023	25,673	48,929	115,326	119,926	132,149	131,167	142,678	166,461	177,900
Other labor income [1]	520	372	575	1,548	2,364	2,767	3,056	3,810	4,226	4,800
Proprietors' and rental income [2]	19,738	7,225	16,280	37,503	42,434	47,257	42,125	46,190	50,649	52,600
Personal interest income	5,832	2,066	4,049	4,699	6,561	7,240	7,469	8,957	9,035	9,100
Transfer payments [3]	7,594	4,180	4,395	6,672	7,922	8,786	9,844	10,545	11,330	12,000
Less: personal contributions for social insurance [4]	1,499	2,113	3,119	6,179	11,803	11,285	12,406	15,132	12,364	12,700
...	142	152	666	2,333	2,118	2,175	2,234	2,889	3,416	3,800
Personal tax and nontax payments	2,643	1,464	2,604	20,867	21,506	21,142	18,625	20,908	29,100	34,000
Federal	1,263	474	1,364	19,379	19,650	18,997	16,159	18,129	26,100	30,700
State and local	1,380	990	1,240	1,488	1,856	2,145	2,467	2,688	3,000	3,300
Disposable personal income	82,484	45,165	75,743	151,060	169,494	188,352	187,241	205,804	234,975	234,300
Personal consumption expenditures	78,761	46,346	72,052	123,079	165,570	177,890	180,589	194,277	207,973	214,300
Personal saving	3,723	-1,181	3,691	27,981	3,924	10,462	6,653	11,227	17,008	18,600

[1] Includes compensation for injuries, employer contributions to private pension and welfare funds, and other payments.

[2] Includes business and professional income, farm income, and rental income of unincorporated enterprise; also the corresponding inventory valuation adjustment.

[3] Includes government social insurance benefits, direct relief, mustering-out pay, veterans' readjustment allowances and other payments, as well as consumer bad debts and other business transfers.

[4] Includes government employee contributions only; thereafter, personal contributions of self-employed persons are also included.

Source: Department of Commerce, Office of Business Economics; *Survey of Current Business*, July 1952 and February 1953.

No. 309.—Personal Consumption Expenditures: 1929 to 1951

[Millions of dollars. Represents market value of purchases of goods and services by individuals and nonprofit institutions, and value of food, clothing, housing, and financial services received by them as income in kind. Includes rental value of owner-occupied houses, but not purchases of dwellings, which are classified as capital goods]

TYPE OF PRODUCT	1929	1933	1940	1945	1946	1947	1948	1949	1950	1951
Total	78,761	46,346	72,052	123,079	146,907	165,570	177,890	180,588	194,277	207,972
Durable commodities	9,362	3,503	7,854	8,472	16,573	21,369	22,883	23,840	29,152	27,120
Nondurable commodities	37,742	22,254	37,594	74,886	85,849	95,142	100,889	99,223	102,780	113,505
Services	31,657	20,589	26,604	39,721	44,485	49,059	54,118	57,525	62,365	67,347
Food and tobacco	21,374	12,777	22,600	45,924	53,738	60,483	63,884	63,145	65,748	73,861
Clothing, accessories, and jewelry	11,018	5,365	8,791	20,347	22,419	23,144	24,213	23,007	23,025	24,630
Personal care	1,116	660	1,107	2,077	2,186	2,261	2,245	2,216	2,303	2,415
Housing	11,421	7,849	9,217	12,205	13,047	14,603	16,466	18,080	19,877	21,765
Household operation	10,509	6,396	10,292	14,865	19,012	22,717	24,450	23,540	26,451	27,383
Medical care and death expenses	3,620	2,307	3,591	5,902	7,015	7,812	8,496	8,885	9,463	10,145
Personal business	5,221	3,063	3,845	4,787	5,536	6,232	7,024	7,576	8,741	9,502
Transportation	7,496	3,920	7,007	6,694	11,648	14,876	16,867	19,274	22,526	21,788
Recreation	4,327	2,199	3,740	6,314	8,934	9,733	10,031	10,276	11,330	11,308
Private education and research	664	481	639	871	1,033	1,316	1,515	1,663	1,793	1,847
Religious and welfare activities	1,196	872	1,000	1,572	1,605	1,589	1,745	1,762	1,857	1,955
Foreign travel and remittances, net.	799	367	223	1,621	734	804	954	1,164	1,163	1,373

Source: Department of Commerce, Office of Business Economics; *Survey of Current Business*, July 1952, and *National Income Supplement*, 1951.

No. 310.—Disposable Personal Income in Current and 1952 Prices: 1929 to 1952

PERIOD	TOTAL DISPOSABLE PERSONAL INCOME (BILLIONS OF DOLLARS)		PER CAPITA DISPOSABLE PERSONAL INCOME (DOLLARS)		Population [2] (thousands)
	Current prices	1952 prices [1]	Current prices	1952 prices [1]	
1929	82.5	127.3	677	1,045	121,881
1930	73.7	118.9	598	965	123,188
1931	63.0	113.5	507	914	124,149
1932	47.8	97.6	383	782	124,949
1933	45.2	97.0	360	773	125,690
1934	51.6	104.7	408	828	126,485
1935	58.0	115.5	455	906	127,362
1936	66.1	130.6	516	1,020	128,181
1937	71.1	135.2	551	1,048	128,961
1938	65.5	127.4	504	981	129,969
1939	70.2	138.2	536	1,055	131,028
1940	75.7	147.6	573	1,117	132,114
1941	92.0	169.4	690	1,271	133,377
1942	116.7	191.0	866	1,417	134,631
1943	132.4	198.5	968	1,451	136,719
1944	147.0	210.0	1,062	1,517	138,390
1945	151.1	208.7	1,080	1,492	139,934
1946	158.9	204.2	1,124	1,445	141,396
1947	169.5	198.2	1,176	1,375	144,129
1948	188.4	208.6	1,285	1,423	146,621
1949	187.2	209.9	1,255	1,407	149,149
1950	205.5	225.1	1,355	1,484	151,677
1951	225.0	229.4	1,458	1,486	154,360
1952 [3]	234.8	234.8	1,496	1,496	156,981

[1] Dollar estimates in current prices divided by an over-all implicit price index for personal consumption expenditures. This price index is based on Department of Commerce data shifted from a 1939 base.
[2] Provisional intercensal estimates of the population of continental United States including armed forces oversees, taking into account the final 1950 census total population count as of July 1.
[3] Estimates based on incomplete data.

Source: Department of Commerce and Council of Economic Advisers; *The Economic Report of the President*, January 1953.

No. 311.—NATIONAL INCOME BY INDUSTRIAL ORIGIN: 1929 TO 1951

[In millions of dollars. National income (for definition, see text, p. 274) originating in each industry is the sum of factor costs incurred by the industry in production. Hence, it is net value added to production by industry, measured at factor costs]

INDUSTRIAL DIVISION	1929	1933	1940	1945	1947	1948	1949	1950	1951
All industries, total	87,355	39,584	81,347	182,691	198,688	223,469	216,259	239,170	277,554
Agriculture, forestry, and fisheries	8,002	3,521	6,599	15,642	19,424	21,829	16,789	17,378	19,967
Farms	7,791	3,402	6,419	15,276	18,949	21,310	16,274	16,825	19,384
Mining, total	2,097	662	1,903	2,789	4,350	5,445	4,576	4,986	5,831
Metal	478	41	445	349	557	686	568	652	851
Anthracite	285	130	138	219	302	343	261	276	284
Bituminous and other soft-coal	652	255	628	1,204	1,827	2,112	1,479	1,696	1,854
Crude petroleum and natural gas	486	195	543	795	1,293	1,870	1,820	1,883	2,282
Nonmetallic mining and quarrying	196	41	149	222	371	434	448	479	560
Contract construction	3,691	735	2,593	4,571	8,550	10,551	10,441	12,404	14,520
Manufacturing, total	22,012	7,563	22,368	51,919	59,459	67,215	63,286	74,496	86,863
Food and kindred products	2,157	1,335	2,483	5,009	5,822	6,637	6,522	6,680	6,861
Tobacco manufactures	258	142	291	243	370	429	517	555	580
Textile-mill products	1,797	697	1,511	2,973	4,687	5,229	4,125	4,578	5,243
Apparel and other finished fabric products	1,240	532	1,109	2,726	3,342	3,441	3,253	3,237	3,655
Lumber and timber basic products	850	122	595	1,067	1,914	2,204	1,804	2,356	2,716
Furniture and finished lumber products	678	183	551	1,052	1,535	1,762	1,657	1,974	2,249
Paper and allied products	563	290	660	1,336	2,234	2,377	2,202	2,682	3,252
Printing, publishing, etc	1,580	790	1,247	2,250	3,073	3,277	3,412	3,613	4,000
Chemicals and allied products	1,136	600	1,489	3,250	3,846	4,383	4,627	5,341	6,601
Products of petroleum and coal	993	17	686	1,326	2,488	3,632	2,838	3,347	4,122
Rubber products	356	103	319	919	1,125	1,063	978	975	1,500
Leather and leather products	601	270	456	898	1,115	1,313	1,100	1,151	1,342
Stone, clay, and glass products	799	208	757	1,147	1,851	2,154	2,089	2,688	3,117
Iron and steel and their products	2,973	682	3,057	7,376	7,647	8,712	7,629	10,100	12,385
Nonferrous metals and their products	767	155	793	1,659	1,934	2,079	2,138	2,483	3,172
Machinery (except electrical)	1,903	426	2,181	5,191	6,324	7,115	6,314	7,409	10,033
Electrical machinery	1,048	276	1,136	3,047	3,432	3,661	3,414	4,665	5,530
Transportation equipment (except automobiles)	317	69	813	7,732	1,548	1,874	1,908	1,998	3,441
Automobiles and auto. equipment	1,394	384	1,602	1,120	3,557	4,132	4,931	6,632	6,275
Wholesale and retail trade, total	13,090	5,375	13,748	27,999	37,324	42,192	40,940	42,783	47,882
Wholesale trade	3,955	1,631	4,108	7,598	10,850	12,611	11,659	11,624	14,266
Retail trade and auto. services	9,135	3,744	9,640	20,401	26,474	29,581	29,281	31,159	33,616
Finance, insurance, and real estate, total	13,098	5,661	8,489	13,278	15,666	17,780	18,929	20,532	22,380
Banking	1,980	493	973	1,854	2,180	2,444	2,614	2,861	3,223
Insurance carriers	788	514	821	1,008	1,281	1,753	2,123	2,095	2,189
Insurance agents and combination offices	533	367	507	754	1,094	1,219	1,227	1,373	1,491
Real estate	8,978	4,060	5,903	9,076	10,524	11,583	12,034	13,119	14,278
Transportation, total	6,562	2,958	4,915	10,495	11,481	12,641	11,853	13,204	14,536
Railroads	4,600	1,849	2,934	6,034	6,311	7,161	6,366	7,122	7,799
Highway freight, etc	482	356	702	1,383	1,946	2,240	2,321	2,794	3,161
Communications and public utilities, total	2,878	2,000	3,039	4,283	5,157	5,939	6,572	7,165	8,068
Telephone, telegraph, etc	1,130	692	1,022	1,772	2,085	2,471	2,661	2,959	3,301
Utilities: electric and gas	1,640	1,237	1,860	2,240	2,748	3,109	3,537	3,789	4,262
Services, total	10,168	5,447	8,637	14,135	18,345	19,821	20,618	22,311	24,382
Hotels and lodging places	577	193	471	1,005	1,177	1,215	1,241	1,296	1,396
Personal services	1,229	667	1,129	2,065	2,555	2,573	2,696	2,822	3,023
Private households	3,117	1,177	1,933	2,445	3,070	3,369	3,626	4,275	4,726
Medical and health services	1,522	937	1,444	2,450	3,363	3,746	3,987	4,307	4,678
Legal services	689	561	719	974	1,280	1,457	1,500	1,623	1,692
Government and government enterprises, total	5,114	5,349	8,795	37,423	18,529	19,609	21,797	23,366	30,121
Federal—general government	900	1,187	3,537	30,614	9,356	8,922	9,972	10,712	16,242
Federal—govt. enterprises	581	485	741	1,153	1,426	1,618	1,790	1,878	2,082
State and local—general govt	3,456	3,531	4,280	5,296	7,262	8,517	9,445	10,159	11,120
State and local—govt. enterprises	177	146	238	360	485	552	590	617	676
Rest of the world [1]	643	293	260	158	403	447	458	545	684

[1] Profits received by domestic corporations from foreign branches excluded here and included in industry of recipient corporation.

Source: Department of Commerce, Office of Business Economics; *Survey of Current Business*, July 1952 and *National Income Supplement*, 1951.

No. 312.—Income Payments to Individuals, by States: 1929 to 1951

["Income payments to individuals" is a measure of income received from all sources during the calendar year by the residents of each State. For six States and the District of Columbia, however, totals shown below are not strictly measures of income received by residents. Totals for District of Columbia, New York, and Maine are too high—and those for Maryland, Virginia, New Jersey, and New Hampshire too low—in terms of measures of total income received by residents. Estimates shown here for D. C. include income paid out to residents of Maryland and Virginia employed in D. C., but exclude income of D. C. residents employed in these 2 States. Estimates for New York include income paid to residents of New Jersey employed in New York, but do not include income of New York residents employed in New Jersey. Similarly, estimates for Maine include income paid to residents of New Hampshire employed in Maine. In computation of per capita income for these 7 States, income totals shown here were first adjusted to a residence basis before division by population. Following are amounts (in millions) of adjustments for 1951: District of Columbia, −592; Maryland, +308; Virginia, +284; New York, −567; New Jersey, +563; Maine, −24; New Hampshire, +24. For definition of income payments to individuals, see text, p. 274]

STATE	AMOUNT (MILLIONS OF DOLLARS)							PER CAPITA (DOLLARS)						
	1929	1933	1940	1945	1949	1950	1951	1929	1933	1940	1945	1949	1950	1951
United States	82,617	46,273	75,852	157,190	196,772	217,672	242,947	680	368	575	1,191	1,325	1,439	1,584
Alabama	802	419	763	2,056	2,306	2,562	2,890	305	154	269	732	768	840	950
Arizona	245	120	237	604	836	936	1,151	573	263	466	1,007	1,152	1,240	1,432
Arkansas	562	288	493	1,245	1,457	1,582	1,769	305	152	254	716	794	873	996
California	5,217	3,113	5,606	13,882	16,824	18,609	21,306	946	511	803	1,466	1,602	1,758	1,933
Colorado	633	358	589	1,274	1,698	1,855	2,158	616	336	570	1,143	1,359	1,396	1,568
Connecticut	1,459	888	1,417	2,604	3,209	3,572	4,071	918	540	827	1,483	1,600	1,776	1,999
Delaware	218	127	239	399	536	609	683	919	513	892	1,390	1,680	1,897	2,076
District of Columbia	638	495	905	1,617	1,891	2,072	2,291	1,191	806	1,087	1,405	1,728	1,955	2,095
Florida	695	425	900	2,521	2,960	3,402	3,801	484	272	468	1,045	1,105	1,704	1,284
Georgia	956	596	986	2,484	2,935	3,309	3,844	329	200	316	794	874	958	1,103
Idaho	230	115	232	540	705	739	800	518	242	443	1,100	1,233	1,255	1,356
Illinois	7,036	3,335	5,740	10,849	14,059	15,397	17,001	932	431	727	1,416	1,630	1,756	1,928
Indiana	1,877	978	1,858	4,113	5,127	5,768	6,655	583	296	542	1,199	1,316	1,455	1,649
Iowa	1,348	644	1,233	2,451	3,303	3,716	4,019	546	258	488	1,105	1,295	1,409	1,531
Kansas	997	474	737	1,929	2,272	2,570	2,847	532	258	423	1,157	1,220	1,346	1,460
Kentucky	964	534	880	1,967	2,480	2,700	3,115	371	199	309	760	867	917	1,066
Louisiana	862	487	847	2,018	2,653	2,834	3,128	415	222	358	832	1,008	1,042	1,135
Maine	449	297	431	867	1,030	1,083	1,182	566	364	499	1,049	1,119	1,174	1,298
Maryland	1,106	720	1,222	2,539	3,070	3,417	3,875	703	441	708	1,272	1,408	1,555	1,714
Massachusetts	3,787	2,386	3,309	5,606	6,903	7,545	8,223	897	553	764	1,339	1,447	1,604	1,738
Michigan	3,543	1,641	3,425	6,902	8,956	10,158	11,352	745	348	648	1,260	1,428	1,583	1,734
Minnesota	1,443	812	1,424	2,699	3,634	3,992	4,414	566	307	511	1,066	1,246	1,341	1,474
Mississippi	544	256	444	1,224	1,331	1,527	1,689	273	123	204	598	641	702	771
Missouri	2,210	1,244	1,914	3,831	5,045	5,580	6,141	612	337	506	1,101	1,291	1,397	1,519
Montana	325	158	321	579	764	942	1,026	602	290	577	1,251	1,359	1,591	1,742
Nebraska	764	374	569	1,370	1,660	1,969	2,035	587	275	434	1,150	1,293	1,478	1,510
Nevada	74	43	92	215	266	300	347	817	447	821	1,483	1,673	1,863	2,029
New Hampshire	302	200	269	467	620	673	747	652	420	561	1,117	1,201	1,293	1,444
New Jersey	3,268	1,985	3,138	5,797	7,030	7,786	8,813	947	535	803	1,474	1,569	1,710	1,885
New Mexico	161	90	190	456	679	775	916	383	196	356	857	1,074	1,133	1,301
New York	14,479	8,509	11,830	20,647	26,151	28,415	30,555	1,125	644	863	1,641	1,741	1,875	1,996
North Carolina	966	677	1,131	2,651	3,361	3,887	4,350	309	205	316	757	852	956	1,052
North Dakota	264	126	237	579	692	790	849	389	190	372	1,111	1,187	1,276	1,403
Ohio	4,920	2,601	4,448	9,122	11,360	12,618	14,509	748	386	642	1,326	1,421	1,584	1,799
Oklahoma	1,079	537	829	1,839	2,285	2,394	2,677	455	226	359	894	1,075	1,071	1,182
Oregon	603	337	633	1,671	2,076	2,318	2,572	640	337	575	1,281	1,390	1,515	1,652
Pennsylvania	7,338	4,027	6,225	11,469	14,363	16,141	17,552	767	414	626	1,264	1,350	1,532	1,663
Rhode Island	579	366	511	952	1,113	1,237	1,341	851	533	716	1,317	1,407	1,564	1,691
South Carolina	438	209	545	1,319	1,586	1,756	2,131	252	167	287	697	791	838	1,003
South Dakota	288	118	242	624	726	839	989	417	172	379	1,153	1,175	1,281	1,529
Tennessee	905	516	927	2,495	2,841	3,182	3,530	349	190	316	868	870	960	1,064
Texas	2,668	1,552	2,652	6,676	9,211	9,874	11,285	465	257	413	978	1,200	1,276	1,412
Utah	272	143	265	658	812	876	1,008	537	275	478	1,066	1,199	1,206	1,424
Vermont	216	127	187	332	408	449	493	601	351	521	1,031	1,112	1,191	1,322
Virginia	987	639	1,127	2,679	3,230	3,566	4,099	422	266	446	940	1,046	1,146	1,295
Washington	1,104	598	1,100	3,095	3,496	3,866	4,257	713	369	632	1,357	1,473	1,622	1,755
West Virginia	793	474	760	1,497	1,943	2,117	2,343	464	265	398	875	1,003	1,051	1,174
Wisconsin	1,849	938	1,622	3,488	4,471	4,936	5,610	634	312	516	1,184	1,344	1,434	1,614
Wyoming	154	87	151	289	408	442	508	687	369	604	1,180	1,478	1,519	1,722

Source: Department of Commerce, Office of Business Economics; *Survey of Current Business*, August 1952.

No. 313.—Income Payments to Individuals—Percent Distribution of Total Income in Each State and Region, by Major Sources: 1951

[See headnote, table 312]

STATE AND REGION	Agricultural income[1]	Government income payments[2]	Manufacturing payrolls	Trade and service income[3]	All other income	STATE AND REGION	Agricultural income[1]	Government income payments[2]	Manufacturing payrolls	Trade and service income[3]	All other income
United States	7.6	15.3	22.9	25.9	27.3	Southwest	13.9	17.9	18.8	25.4	22.0
						Arizona	21.6	18.3	5.8	24.7	29.6
New England	1.7	14.8	32.6	24.4	26.5	New Mexico	15.8	22.2	5.4	22.6	34.0
Connecticut	1.6	10.0	39.2	22.3	26.9	Oklahoma	12.0	21.2	9.4	25.6	31.8
Maine	3.7	17.1	28.0	23.7	27.5	Texas	13.4	16.7	12.2	25.7	32.0
Massachusetts	1.0	16.3	30.2	25.7	26.8						
New Hampshire	3.0	15.9	32.5	24.8	23.8	Central	8.2	12.0	30.9	24.4	24.5
Rhode Island	.6	17.1	34.7	23.3	24.3	Illinois	5.9	11.7	28.6	26.0	27.8
Vermont	9.2	14.1	25.2	24.0	27.5	Indiana	9.6	11.4	34.8	22.8	21.4
						Iowa	29.0	12.3	14.9	22.3	21.5
Middle East	1.7	14.7	26.1	27.7	29.8	Michigan	3.4	11.4	41.6	23.0	20.6
Delaware	4.7	9.8	34.4	19.4	31.7	Minnesota	16.5	13.5	16.5	25.5	28.0
Dist. of Col	...	48.6	3.0	27.2	21.2	Missouri	11.3	14.2	20.1	27.7	26.7
Maryland	3.1	19.2	21.9	26.3	29.5	Ohio	3.5	11.7	36.5	23.5	24.8
New Jersey	1.9	12.7	34.5	24.4	26.5	Wisconsin	11.0	11.2	31.3	23.8	22.7
New York	1.2	13.4	23.3	31.4	30.7						
Pennsylvania	2.0	12.8	31.2	24.3	29.7	Northwest	21.5	16.5	9.7	24.5	27.8
West Virginia	4.1	13.3	20.2	21.0	41.4	Colorado	11.7	20.4	10.5	27.0	30.4
						Idaho	30.7	15.3	11.0	23.7	20.3
Southeast	13.1	13.9	17.5	24.8	24.7	Kansas	14.6	14.9	15.4	23.9	31.2
Alabama	11.7	20.6	20.8	24.3	22.6	Montana	26.1	13.8	6.3	22.7	29.1
Arkansas	24.8	17.8	10.9	24.4	22.1	Nebraska	26.3	14.8	9.0	25.4	24.5
Florida	9.0	19.6	7.6	31.8	32.0	North Dakota	36.4	14.7	2.0	25.0	19.9
Georgia	12.4	19.5	19.6	26.0	22.5	South Dakota	43.3	14.7	3.7	21.8	16.5
Kentucky	12.8	18.8	15.2	23.7	29.5	Utah	9.2	22.2	10.5	34.6	33.5
Louisiana	9.8	19.7	14.0	25.4	31.1	Wyoming	24.0	17.2	5.2	21.9	31.7
Mississippi	24.3	21.8	11.8	24.0	18.1						
North Carolina	17.4	16.3	24.8	21.9	19.6	Far West	7.0	18.2	17.6	28.3	28.9
South Carolina	14.8	20.0	25.8	21.1	18.3	California	6.9	18.2	17.1	28.7	29.1
Tennessee	10.5	18.1	21.4	25.3	24.7	Nevada	10.9	17.5	4.1	32.5	35.0
Virginia	8.7	26.3	16.7	23.2	25.1	Oregon	8.0	14.1	22.5	27.4	28.0
						Washington	6.6	20.8	18.5	26.5	27.6

[1] Consists of net income of farm proprietors (including value of change in inventories of crops and livestock), arm wages, and net rents to landlords living on farms.

[2] Consists of pay of State and local and of Federal civilian employees, net pay of armed forces, family-allowance payments to dependents of enlisted military personnel, voluntary allotments of military pay to individuals, mustering-out payments to discharged servicemen, veterans' benefit payments, interest payments to individuals, public assistance and other direct relief, and benefit payments from social insurance funds.

[3] Consists of wages and salaries and proprietors' income.

Source: Department of Commerce, Office of Business Economics; *Survey of Current Business*, August 1952.

No. 314.—Percent Distribution of Family Units, Income Before Taxes and Liquid Assets, by Income Groups: 1951

[National estimate based on sample interview survey of 2,501 families, defined as all (one or more) persons living in same household and related by blood, marriage, or adoption. Universe covered is population of U. S. residing in private households during interview period, which was January through March 1952. Following groups are excluded: (1) Members of armed forces living at military reservations; (2) residents of hospitals and in religious, educational, and penal institutions; and (3) floating population, that is, people living in hotels, large boarding houses, and tourist camps. For liquid asset holdings of individuals and businesses, see table 472, p. 438]

ANNUAL 1951 MONEY INCOME BEFORE TAXES	Family units	Total money income	Liquid assets [1]
All income groups	100	100	100
Under $1,000	11	1	6
$1,000–$1,999	13	4	7
$2,000–$2,999	16	9	8
$3,000–$3,999	17	14	12
$4,000–$4,999	15	16	10
$5,000–$7,499	17	24	18
$7,500 and over	11	32	39

[1] Liquid assets include all U. S. Government securities, checking accounts, savings accounts in banks, postal savings, and shares in savings and loan associations and credit unions held at time of survey in early 1951. Currency is excluded.

Source: Board of Governors of the Federal Reserve System. Based on unpublished data from 1951 Survey of Consumer Finances conducted by Survey Research Center of University of Michigan for Board of Governors.

No. 315.—Share of Total Money Income Received by Each Tenth of the Nation's Spending Units, by Size of Income: 1947 to 1951

[Data for each year based on interviews in January–March of following year]

SPENDING UNITS RANKED FROM LOWEST TO HIGHEST INCOME [1]	PERCENT OF TOTAL MONEY INCOME BEFORE FEDERAL INCOME TAX					PERCENT OF TOTAL MONEY INCOME AFTER FEDERAL INCOME TAX [2]				
	1947	1948	1949	1950	1951	1947	1948	1949	1950	1951
Lowest tenth	1	1	1	1	1	1	1	1	1	1
Second tenth	3	3	3	3	3	3	4	3	3	3
Third tenth	4	5	5	5	5	5	5	5	5	5
Fourth tenth	6	6	6	6	6	6	7	7	7	7
Fifth tenth	7	8	8	8	8	8	8	8	8	8
Sixth tenth	9	9	9	9	9	9	9	9	10	9
Seventh tenth	10	10	11	11	10	10	10	11	11	11
Eighth tenth	12	12	12	13	12	12	12	13	13	13
Ninth tenth	15	15	15	15	15	15	15	15	15	15
Highest tenth	33	31	30	29	31	31	29	28	27	28

[1] Ranking based on size of money income before or after tax.
[2] Estimated liability on Federal income tax, excluding tax on capital gains. Tax liability was not obtained directly from interviews or from tax returns, but from comprehensive data on family composition and income obtained in connection with Consumer Finances Surveys. For method of estimating, see Federal Reserve Bulletin, Aug. 1950, pp. 961–962.

Source: Board of Governors of the Federal Reserve System. Based on data from 1949, 1950, and 1951 Surveys of Consumer Finances, conducted by Survey Research Center of University of Michigan for Board of Governors.

No. 316.—Average Income of Each Tenth of Nation's Spending Units When Ranked by Size of Income, 1946–51 With Percentage Increase Since 1946

[See headnote, table 317]

SPENDING UNITS RANKED BY SIZE OF INCOME	AVERAGE MONEY INCOME BEFORE TAXES [1]						PERCENT INCREASE SINCE 1946				
	1946	1947	1948	1949	1950	1951	1947	1948	1949	1950	1951
All spending units	$2,570	$3,290	$3,450	$3,270	$3,520	$3,520	15	20	14	23	23
Lowest tenth [2]	410 (?)	390 (?)	480 540	260 410	340 490	310 460	−5 (?)	17 (?)	−37 (?)	−17 (?)	−24 (?)
Second tenth	900	1,020	1,140	1,010	1,130	1,120	13	27	12	26	24
Third tenth	1,340	1,450	1,730	1,540	1,700	1,790	8	29	15	27	34
Fourth tenth	1,740	1,910	2,180	2,030	2,230	2,410	10	25	17	28	39
Fifth tenth	2,130	2,340	2,590	2,520	2,780	2,940	10	22	18	31	38
Sixth tenth	2,500	2,800	3,040	2,970	3,270	3,460	12	22	19	31	38
Seventh tenth	2,920	3,260	3,490	3,460	3,820	4,030	12	20	18	31	38
Eighth tenth	3,420	3,850	4,110	4,090	4,470	4,720	13	20	20	31	38
Ninth tenth	4,240	4,870	5,080	5,070	5,430	5,750	15	20	20	28	36
Highest tenth	9,100	11,020	10,660	9,740	10,090	11,710	21	17	7	11	29

[1] Average (mean) income has been computed for each income tenth (decile) as well as for whole population. Sampling error, which was approximately $180 for whole population, is not yet available for individual tenths. It will be much larger than $180 for the highest tenth and much smaller for the middle tenths.
[2] Negative incomes caused by farm or business losses included in upper line and excluded in lower line.
[3] Not available.

Source: Board of Governors of the Federal Reserve System; *Federal Reserve Bulletin*, September 1952. Based on data from 1949-1952 Surveys of Consumer Finances, conducted by Survey Research Center of University of Michigan for Board of Governors.

No. 317.—Mean and Median Incomes Within Occupational Groups: 1946 to 1951

[Data based on approximately 2,800 to 3,500 interviews taken in 60 sampling areas throughout country. Interview unit defined as all persons living in the same dwelling and belonging to the same family who pool their incomes to meet their major expenses. Mean income is the average obtained by dividing aggregate money income before taxes by number of spending units. Median income is that of middle spending unit when units are ranked by size of money income before taxes]

OCCUPATION OF HEAD OF SPENDING UNIT	MEAN INCOME						MEDIAN INCOME					
	1946	1947	1948	1949	1950	1951	1946	1947	1948	1949	1950	1951
All spending units	$2,570	$3,290	$3,450	$3,270	$3,520	$3,820	$2,300	$2,530	$2,840	$2,700	$3,606	$3,300
Professional and semiprofessional	4,940	5,450	5,140	5,350	5,630	6,020	4,000	4,000	4,000	4,000	4,500	4,500
Managerial and self-employed	5,920	6,730	6,300	5,630	5,790	7,100	3,700	4,500	4,500	4,500	4,500	4,780
Managerial	(1)	(1)	(1)	5,960	6,580	8,960	(1)	(1)	(1)	(1)	4,950	5,350
Self-employed	(1)	(1)	(1)	5,400	5,330	5,820	(1)	(1)	(1)	(1)	4,100	4,180
Clerical and sales	2,900	3,220	3,350	3,260	3,910	3,920	2,600	2,900	3,000	2,800	3,200	3,410
Skilled and semiskilled	2,820	3,120	3,470	3,350	3,530	3,970	2,700	3,000	3,300	3,200	3,600	3,800
Unskilled and service	1,730	1,900	2,280	2,200	2,350	2,320	1,600	1,750	2,100	2,100	2,100	2,100
Farm operator	1,890	2,080	2,690	2,570	2,480	2,660	1,300	1,500	1,800	1,500	1,900	1,880
Other [2]	(1)	2,010	2,030	2,040	2,020	2,330	(1)	(1)	(1)	(1)	(1)	(1)

[1] Not available.
[2] Includes spending units headed by housewives, protective service workers, unemployed persons, and students.

Source: Board of Governors of the Federal Reserve System; *Federal Reserve Bulletin*, September 1952. Based on data from 1949-1952 Surveys of Consumer Finances, conducted by Survey Research Center of University of Michigan for Board of Governors.

No. 318.—Percent Distribution of Spending Units Having Specified Characteristics, by Amount of Net Worth, Early 1950

[Net worth is defined as difference between total selected assets and total debt reported in interviews during January–March 1950. Selected assets include liquid assets (U. S. Government securities, checking accounts, savings accounts in banks, postal savings, and shares in savings and loan associations and credit unions), owner-occupied homes and farms, other real estate, farm machinery, crops and livestock, automobiles, interests in unincorporated nonfarm businesses and privately held corporations, and common and preferred stock in corporations open to investment by the general public. Liabilities include all forms of debt other than charge accounts. For method of computing net worth, see *Federal Reserve Bulletin*, December 1950, pp. 1610–1611. Net worth figures should be considered as minimum estimates because of omission of assets such as currency, corporate bonds, reserve value of life insurance policies, consumer durable goods other than automobiles, jewelry, etc., and because of under-reporting of assets covered]

CHARACTERISTIC OF SPENDING UNIT	ALL CASES Number	ALL CASES Percent	AMOUNT OF NET WORTH Negative	$1–$999	$1,000–$4,999	$5,000–$24,999	$25,000 and over	Not ascertained
All units	1 3,512	100	8	27	23	32	8	2
1949 money income before taxes:								
Under $1,000	479	100	8	43	20	24		2
$1,000–$1,999	604	100	12	42	18	23	2	3
$2,000–$2,999	672	100	10	30	28	26	2	2
$3,000–$3,999	615	100	8	31	29	36	4	1
$4,000–$4,999	397	100	6	16	28	43	5	2
$5,000–$7,499	437	100	3	5	23	51	14	4
$7,500 and over	269	100	(²)	1	6	35	55	3
Occupation of head of unit:								
Professional and semi-professional	287	100	7	17	31	34	10	1
Managerial and self-employed	466	100	2	5	15	48	22	8
Clerical and sales	486	100	6	33	28	28	4	1
Skilled and semi-skilled	895	100	10	31	28	29	1	1
Unskilled and service	344	100	17	37	26	19		1
Farm operators	410	100	3	12	19	40	22	4
Unemployed	187	100	11	43	20	23	1	2
Retired	180	100	1	27	9	44	19	(²)
Place of residence of unit:								
Metropolitan area	1,157	100	9	27	23	32	7	2
City, 50,000 to 600,000	494	100	10	32	23	28	5	2
Town, 2,500 to 50,000	759	100	7	28	22	33	7	3
Town, under 2,500	493	100	8	27	26	31	6	2
Open country	302	100	6	18	23	36	14	3
Age of head of unit:								
18–24	342	100	14	59	19	5	1	2
25–34	779	100	13	31	33	19	2	2
35–44	777	100	8	23	25	34	7	3
45–54	670	100	5	16	23	43	11	2
55–64	495	100	5	17	16	46	13	3
65 and over	419	100	1	26	15	42	14	3
Years married:								
Not married ³	996	100	7	42	24	20	5	2
Less than 3	205	100	17	36	25	16	4	2
3–4	250	100	13	29	30	22	4	2
5–9	377	100	10	21	31	30	5	3
10–19	693	100	9	20	22	38	8	3
20 and over	972	100	4	14	18	48	13	3

¹ Includes spending units headed by students, housewives, etc., not included in occupational classification.
² Less than one-half of 1 percent.
³ Includes those divorced, separated, or widowed.

Source: Board of Governors of the Federal Reserve System. Based on 1950 Survey of Consumer Finances conducted by Survey Research Center of University of Michigan for Board of Governors.

No. 319.—Percent of Money Income Received by Each Fifth of the Nation's Families and Single Persons

[Data for "families and single persons" not on comparable basis with data for "spending units" in table 318]

FAMILIES AND SINGLE PERSONS RANKED FROM LOWEST TO HIGHEST INCOME	PERCENTAGE OF MONEY INCOME				AVERAGE MONEY INCOME IN DOLLARS OF 1948 PURCHASING POWER [1]			PERCENT INCREASE IN AVERAGE INCOME	
	1935-36	1941	1944	1948	1935-36	1941	1948	1935-36 to 1948	1941 to 1948
All groups	100.0	100.0	100.0	100.0	$2,564	$3,396	$4,231	59	25
Lowest fifth	4.0	3.5	3.6	4.2	534	592	893	67	51
Second fifth	8.7	9.1	10.1	10.5	1,159	1,846	2,232	93	44
Third fifth	13.6	15.3	16.3	16.1	1,810	2,597	3,410	88	31
Fourth fifth	20.5	22.5	23.0	22.3	2,734	3,816	4,711	72	23
Highest fifth	53.2	49.6	47.0	46.9	7,083	8,418	9,911	40	18

[1] Current dollars divided by consumers' price index on base 1948=100 to give a rough measure of changes in purchasing power of income.

Sources: 1935-36, National Resources Planning Board; 1941, Department of Labor; 1944, National Bureau of Economic Research; and 1948, Council of Economic Advisers. Published in *Economic Report of the President*, January 1950 and July 1951.

No. 320.—Income Shares of Upper and Lower Groups of Total Population: 1919 to 1948

[Data are based on comparisons between Federal tax data and countrywide totals of income receipts by individuals. Individuals' incomes underlying the basic and economic income variants are defined as receipts for the participation of individuals or of their property in the production process; include employee compensation and other payments to labor, entrepreneurial income, rent, interest, dividends; exclude capital gains and other transfers and do not allow deductions except of business expenses. The basic variant is a first approximation to shares in income thus defined. The economic income variant represents an adjustment of the basic variant to take account of some items omitted from the tax data (compensation of nonfederal government employees and imputed rent on owner-occupied houses), to allow for a finer division of tax returns by distinguishing between head of family and nonhead returns, and to allow for the effect of classifying returns by net income, as defined for tax purposes, instead of by economic income. The disposable income variant measures shares in individuals' incomes after deducting Federal income taxes and including gains and losses from sales of assets. See also *Historical Statistics*, series A 195-197]

YEAR	Top 1 percent	2d to 5th percentage band	Lower 95 percent	Top 1 percent			Top 5 percent		
				Basic variant	Economic income variant	Disposable income variant	Basic variant	Economic income variant	Disposable income variant
		Basic variant							
1919	12.8			12.8	14.0	12.2	22.9	26.1	24.3
1920	12.3			12.3	13.6	11.8	22.1	25.5	24.0
1921		11.4		13.5	16.2	14.2	25.5	31.7	29.3
1922				13.4	15.6	14.4	24.8	30.4	29.0
1923				12.3	14.0	13.1	22.0	26.1	27.0
1924		11.4		12.9	14.7	14.3	24.3	29.1	28.7
1925				13.7	15.7	16.6	25.2	30.2	31.1
1926				13.9	15.8	16.3	25.2	30.2	30.8
1927		11.6		14.4	16.5	17.2	26.0	31.2	31.9
1928		11.8		14.9	17.2	19.1	26.8	32.1	34.1
1929				14.5	17.2	18.9	26.1	31.9	33.5
1930				13.8	15.6	15.1	25.7	30.7	30.3
1931		9	0	12.3	15.6	14.6	24.2	32.0	31.2
1932		9	4	13.9	18.3	12.3	26.0	32.1	29.6
1933		9	0	12.1	14.4	12.6	24.6	30.5	29.3
1934		9	2	13.0	15.6	13.4	24.0	30.1	27.8
1935		11.7	2	12.1	13.6	12.8	23.8	28.8	27.9
1936		11.4	2	13.4	14.7	13.7	24.8	29.3	28.3
1937		11.1	75.9	13.0	14.1	13.0	24.1	28.6	27.4
1938		11.4	77.0	11.5	12.5	12.1	23.0	27.8	27.0
1939	11.9		76.3	11.9	13.3	13.3	23.7	28.1	27.1
1940	12.0		77.0	12.0	12.8	11.5	23.0	27.1	25.7
1941	11.5	10.6		11.5	12.5	10.0	22.2	26.0	23.2
1942	10.2	9.0		10.2	10.8	7.9	19.2	22.7	19.2
1943	9.5	8.5		9.5	10.1	6.8	18.0	21.1	14.5
1944	8.7	8.1	83.2	8.7	9.1	6.7	16.8	19.9	14.9
1945	8.9	8.7	82.4	8.9	9.5	7.4	17.6	19.5	14.8
1946	9.1	9.3	81.6	9.1	9.7	7.6	18.4	20.2	17.9
1947	8.6	82.4		8.6	(1)	(1)	17.6	(1)	(1)
1948	8.5	9.4	82.2	8.5	(1)	(1)	17.6	(1)	(1)

[1] Not available.

Source: National Bureau of Economic Research; *Shares of Upper Income Groups in Income and Savings* and *Income*.

No. 321.—AVERAGE MONEY INCOME, EXPENDITURES AND SAVINGS OF FAMILIES AND SINGLE PERSONS IN CITIES, BY INCOME CLASS: 1944

[Estimates based on sample survey of 1,700 consumer units in cities of 2,500 inhabitants or more. Data relate to all civilians except inmates of institutions. Families are defined as economic units of two or more persons contributing to or mainly dependent on a common or pooled income. Single persons are those who live alone or as lodgers or servants in private homes, rooming houses or hotels]

ITEM	ANNUAL MONEY INCOME AFTER PERSONAL TAXES								
	Under $500	$500-1,000	$1,000-1,500	$1,500-2,000	$2,000-2,500	$2,500-3,000	$3,000-4,000	$4,000-5,000	$5,000 and over
ALL FAMILIES AND SINGLE PERSONS									
Percent of families in each class	4.2	7.7	7.1	11.9	13.9	13.2	19.9	9.6	12.5
Average number of persons	1.42	1.82	2.11	2.55	2.77	3.00	3.61	3.97	4.02
Average number of earners	.28	.68	1.07	1.16	1.22	1.28	1.56	1.96	2.08
Money income after personal taxes	$291	$764	$1,243	$1,769	$2,251	$2,747	$3,481	$4,406	$7,534
Expenditures, current	594	939	1,317	1,690	1,946	2,375	2,816	3,428	4,324
Food	235	368	506	646	747	908	1,084	1,147	1,383
Clothing	41	82	157	231	268	353	456	621	836
Housing, fuel, light, and refrigeration	178	231	285	328	379	424	484	546	635
Household operation	33	50	64	81	89	109	140	166	306
Furnishings and equipment	5	24	33	43	52	84	92	131	159
Automobile	6	13	36	42	61	104	122	175	171
Other transportation	6	21	28	47	53	52	63	83	114
Medical care	48	67	78	93	95	119	147	191	260
Personal care	12	20	34	42	45	55	64	84	109
Recreation	5	15	25	45	52	62	82	104	137
Tobacco	7	16	25	40	40	47	58	70	75
Reading	8	11	15	18	21	27	32	38	43
Formal education	1	2	1	8	8	14	13	29	41
Other	9	19	30	26	35	17	29	43	55
Personal taxes	1	33	70	124	198	283	407	584	2,357
Gifts and contributions	17	31	52	82	92	136	127	211	454
Net savings or deficit	-320	-206	-126	-2	213	236	538	767	2,856
War bonds	16	62	40	117	163	230	323	414	1,193
Life and annuity insurance premiums	10	20	43	50	64	80	106	141	269
Other	-346	-288	-209	-170	-14	-74	107	212	1,394
FAMILIES OF 2 OR MORE PERSONS									
Percent of families in each class	1.5	5.2	5.3	10.7	14.0	14.7	23.0	11.2	14.4
Average number of persons	2.45	2.45	2.78	3.03	3.10	3.13	3.69	4.01	4.13
Average number of earners	.35	.72	1.15	1.22	1.27	1.31	1.57	1.97	2.12
Money income after personal taxes	$313	$776	$1,243	$1,779	$2,259	$2,757	$3,480	$4,408	$7,595
Expenditures, current	887	1,053	1,407	1,788	2,051	2,410	2,838	3,439	4,305
Food	374	434	555	701	797	913	1,043	1,150	1,386
Clothing	42	80	163	234	283	364	462	623	848
Housing, fuel, light and refrigeration	257	251	298	341	394	430	488	547	616
Household operation	56	47	66	83	93	110	140	166	296
Furnishings and equipment	5	25	39	49	60	88	95	132	157
Automobile	16	19	29	42	69	105	119	177	171
Other transportation	7	20	26	44	50	51	63	84	109
Medical care	62	88	94	105	104	123	149	190	265
Personal care	21	19	33	41	48	56	65	84	110
Recreation	3	15	28	46	55	63	82	105	137
Tobacco	16	15	21	41	41	48	59	71	76
Reading	14	13	14	18	22	27	31	37	43
Formal education	1	2	2	11	9	15	13	29	42
Other	13	25	39	32	26	17	29	44	50
Personal taxes	2	13	33	86	180	270	408	559	2,385
Gifts and contributions	26	30	47	66	86	119	119	203	454
Net savings or deficit	-600	-307	-211	-75	122	228	523	766	2,836
War bonds	15	81	28	82	147	283	316	410	1,206
Life and annuity insurance premiums	14	25	40	59	70	83	109	140	263
Other	-629	-413	-279	-216	-95	-91	98	216	1,367

[1] Family size based on equivalent persons, with 52 weeks of family membership considered equivalent to 1 person; 26 weeks equivalent to 0.5 person, etc.
[2] Earner defined as a family member that worked for pay (as wage or salary worker or on his own account) at any time during year.
[3] Personal taxes (income, poll and personal property) have been deducted from money income. Total money income may be obtained by combining amounts shown for both items. Inheritances and large gifts are not considered current income; inheritances and gift taxes excluded from personal taxes.
[4] Includes expenditures for alcoholic beverages.
[5] Includes rents for tenant-occupied dwellings and for lodging away from home and current operation expenses of home owners. Excludes principal payments on mortgages on owned homes.
[6] Value of bonds purchased less those cashed.
[7] Represents differences between income and expenditures plus net war bond purchases and insurance premium payments. Includes amounts deducted for social security, retirement plans, etc., not available separately.

Source: Department of Labor, Bureau of Labor Statistics; Monthly Labor Review, January 1946.

No. 322.—NUMBER OF FAMILIES AND UNRELATED INDIVIDUALS BY INCOME LEVEL IN 1949, AND MEDIAN INCOME, BY STATES: 1950

[Based on 20-percent sample of 1950 Census returns. "Family" refers to a group of two or more related persons residing in same household. "Unrelated individual" refers to a person living alone or with persons not related to him. See source for explanation of sampling variability. Medians computed from $500 intervals]

DIVISION AND STATE	Total [1]	Less than $1,000	$1,000 to $1,999	$2,000 to $2,999	$3,000 to $3,999	$4,000 to $5,999	$6,000 to $9,999	$10,000 and over	MEDIAN INCOME [2] Total	Urban and rural non-farm
United States	49,362,630	10,379,755	7,685,690	8,468,880	7,636,390	7,646,535	3,467,625	1,210,315	$2,619	$2,782
N. E.	3,061,810	549,290	469,710	583,290	525,185	498,370	280,730	76,040	2,801	2,836
Maine	290,770	69,380	55,040	63,065	42,315	32,560	11,180	4,090	2,213	2,277
N. H.	178,610	39,630	28,400	37,555	27,680	23,520	8,305	2,505	2,405	2,431
Vt.	122,655	32,825	23,495	25,640	16,845	13,355	4,440	1,630	2,101	2,229
Mass.	1,545,190	262,755	194,670	289,900	278,595	262,225	112,765	39,995	2,909	2,917
R. I.	251,990	48,600	39,305	51,150	41,985	41,360	15,435	5,060	2,630	2,609
Conn.	651,595	96,110	68,800	115,980	117,765	125,420	57,585	22,760	3,155	3,167
M. A.	9,367,815	1,643,460	1,190,330	1,786,715	1,743,340	1,773,295	867,085	317,575	3,020	3,052
N. Y.	5,089,035	537,930	604,560	870,080	863,975	913,085	437,850	186,650	3,055	3,085
N. J.	1,570,085	219,610	162,305	255,505	296,285	317,355	166,310	57,795	3,285	3,302
Pa.	3,298,695	885,920	423,465	661,120	593,080	542,255	242,925	71,130	2,834	2,874
E. N. C.	10,654,195	1,795,265	1,195,345	1,762,630	1,966,275	1,871,975	864,039	271,375	3,063	3,146
Ohio	2,602,070	436,150	310,675	458,995	488,830	472,660	208,295	64,465	3,024	3,091
Ind.	1,298,600	246,070	172,230	236,485	232,465	225,985	88,665	25,730	2,827	2,914
Ill.	2,997,610	481,295	339,900	482,525	523,680	577,050	293,895	102,620	3,163	3,214
Mich.	2,053,535	234,015	217,035	326,035	415,325	403,245	193,660	54,155	3,195	3,278
Wis.	1,102,380	205,735	155,285	198,580	205,975	192,835	79,515	24,405	2,860	3,069
W. N. C.	4,728,975	1,069,275	755,370	862,710	734,630	687,275	273,549	100,998	2,432	2,677
Minn.	962,560	193,405	150,625	181,690	169,975	157,625	64,830	22,015	2,663	2,838
Iowa	883,435	177,225	141,340	166,315	147,825	137,960	56,650	19,643	2,612	2,656
Mo.	1,364,470	347,970	234,340	230,955	188,085	170,330	69,050	25,955	2,200	2,435
N. Dak.	189,260	39,990	33,320	34,650	27,730	27,320	12,995	5,065	2,446	2,517
S. Dak.	207,860	47,570	37,415	39,695	31,135	27,540	11,745	4,535	2,337	2,394
Nebr.	446,410	92,685	78,035	87,465	67,485	59,085	23,860	9,360	2,389	2,452
Kans.	655,980	150,930	110,295	121,750	102,385	88,125	34,410	14,420	2,377	2,486
S. A.	6,541,345	1,697,595	1,267,970	1,141,770	816,365	751,615	340,905	122,025	2,081	2,380
Del.	102,935	20,305	14,505	17,140	14,950	15,460	7,800	3,295	2,680	2,815
Md.	755,075	134,860	107,910	128,000	118,835	119,955	63,900	20,600	2,811	2,891
Dist. of Col.	340,375	50,185	43,620	63,350	51,840	53,240	34,970	13,970	2,975	------
Va.	1,046,290	249,050	205,320	179,860	133,560	125,380	64,975	19,625	2,172	2,374
W. Va.	574,530	136,515	91,870	129,170	86,295	71,340	26,595	7,960	2,344	2,514
N. C.	1,146,565	323,360	254,740	206,805	129,690	115,680	42,810	15,870	1,864	2,126
S. C.	578,075	195,295	130,660	91,770	61,490	56,925	19,935	6,480	1,647	1,979
Ga.	1,011,725	330,415	219,800	159,175	102,815	91,365	36,475	13,965	1,644	1,934
Fla.	985,470	258,010	209,545	165,500	116,630	102,270	43,445	20,260	1,950	2,009
E. S. C.	3,225,430	1,161,390	722,230	527,415	336,375	279,185	109,165	46,620	1,555	1,943
Ky.	864,730	265,330	185,345	153,240	96,540	80,540	30,815	11,575	1,774	2,094
Tenn.	975,485	298,210	217,655	162,570	108,120	91,250	35,470	13,910	1,749	2,032
Ala.	865,395	305,330	181,380	140,570	90,040	74,540	29,040	9,780	1,580	1,956
Miss.	619,820	292,520	137,650	71,035	41,675	32,855	12,840	5,355	1,028	1,456
W. S. C.	4,634,470	1,285,755	904,645	743,110	581,510	551,755	233,450	96,720	2,021	2,330
Ark.	568,605	227,515	131,990	82,140	48,355	37,160	13,720	6,115	1,315	1,642
La.	802,690	236,460	173,950	124,080	68,695	85,330	38,060	14,965	1,810	2,015
Okla.	737,950	202,340	141,735	125,650	99,615	85,680	33,920	13,290	2,050	2,220
Tex.	2,515,135	602,540	456,370	411,240	344,845	343,585	147,720	64,350	2,273	2,407
Mt.	1,664,000	335,545	264,070	291,410	261,145	254,415	104,815	39,585	2,620	2,711
Mont.	204,045	40,560	31,135	34,510	36,570	31,725	13,535	5,520	2,718	2,887
Idaho	186,800	32,630	30,085	36,450	33,350	29,120	11,725	4,110	2,685	2,787
Wyo.	102,150	17,210	15,295	15,890	18,145	18,945	7,440	2,765	2,964	3,109
Colo.	462,105	97,785	76,150	83,475	72,610	66,780	28,320	11,555	2,514	2,569
N. Mex.	201,880	47,205	35,680	32,495	27,855	27,065	12,725	4,855	2,301	2,447
Ariz.	240,345	55,860	41,025	40,370	38,080	33,040	12,370	5,210	2,375	2,446
Utah	204,805	33,670	26,040	28,385	44,100	36,825	13,450	3,805	3,001	3,043
Nev.	61,850	10,325	8,680	9,465	10,775	10,925	5,250	1,765	2,982	3,080
Pac.	5,402,990	967,880	746,530	930,240	961,435	992,640	464,905	143,380	3,004	3,042
Wash.	878,405	162,345	125,285	130,665	160,310	160,350	66,175	19,565	2,955	3,016
Oreg.	543,920	102,195	74,380	89,755	100,825	99,780	40,510	13,150	2,933	3,021
Calif.	3,980,655	703,440	546,865	609,820	660,500	732,510	358,220	110,665	3,021	3,081

[1] Includes 2,873,940 with income not reported. [2] For definition of median, see headnote, table 18, p. 27.

Source: Department of Commerce, Bureau of the Census, U. S. Census of Population: 1950, Vol. II, Parts.

No. 323.—Percent Distribution of Families and Unrelated Individuals by Total Money Income, Urban and Rural: 1951

[Data based on sample. See source for evaluation of sampling reliability. Includes data for families and individuals in quasi households, hotels, large rooming houses, etc., as well as households. See also headnote, table 325]

TOTAL MONEY INCOME	FAMILIES AND INDIVIDUALS				FAMILIES				UNRELATED INDIVIDUALS			
	Total	Urban	Rural non-farm	Rural farm	Total	Urban	Rural non-farm	Rural farm	Total	Urban	Rural non-farm	Rural farm
Number (1,000)	49,457	33,795	9,288	6,374	40,442	26,918	7,844	5,680	9,015	6,877	1,444	694
Percent	100.0	100.0	100.0	100.0	100.0	100.0	100.0	100.0	100.0	100.0	100.0	100.0
Under $500	8.0	6.2	9.8	14.1	4.4	2.8	5.0	11.3	25.6	21.3	38.0	38.3
$500 to $999	7.4	6.0	8.4	13.4	4.7	2.9	5.6	12.0	21.0	19.6	25.0	25.0
$1,000 to $1,499	5.9	4.3	6.7	12.5	3.5	3.5	6.5	12.2	8.7	8.2	7.4	15.6
$1,500 to $1,999	6.6	5.6	7.1	11.0	6.1	4.6	7.3	11.5	9.1	10.1	5.9	7.2
$2,000 to $2,499	7.9	7.4	8.0	10.7	7.6	6.6	8.3	11.5	9.4	10.8	6.1	3.9
$2,500 to $2,999	7.6	7.6	8.0	6.8	7.8	7.5	8.6	7.5	6.8	8.1	4.6	.6
$3,000 to $3,499	9.5	9.7	10.9	6.5	9.9	10.0	11.9	7.0	7.3	8.4	5.1	2.2
$3,500 to $3,999	8.9	9.7	8.4	5.9	9.8	10.6	9.5	6.3	4.7	5.6	1.8	2.2
$4,000 to $4,499	8.1	8.8	8.0	4.8	9.2	10.1	8.9	5.3	2.7	3.0	2.6	
$4,500 to $4,999	5.6	6.3	4.9	2.8	6.4	7.4	5.7	3.0	1.4	1.7	.5	1.1
$5,000 to $5,999	9.2	10.4	8.9	3.6	10.8	12.4	10.1	3.9	1.7	1.6	2.0	1.7
$6,000 to $6,999	5.8	6.9	4.4	2.5	6.8	8.2	5.0	2.8	.9	1.0	.5	
$7,000 to $9,999	6.4	7.4	4.8	3.5	7.5	8.9	5.5	3.9	.5	.5	.3	.6
$10,000 to $14,999	2.0	2.5	1.2	.8	2.4	3.0	1.4	.7	.2	.1	.3	1.1
$15,000 and over	1.0	1.1	.6	1.1	1.2	1.4	.7	1.2	.1	.1		.6
Median income [1]	$3,348	$3,661	$3,093	$1,953	$3,709	$4,071	$3,365	$2,131	$1,195	$1,540	$740	$733

[1] For definition of median, see headnote, table 18, p. 27.

No. 324.—Percent Distribution of Families and Unrelated Individuals by Total Money Income, by Color, Urban and Rural: 1951

[Data based on sample. See source for evaluation of sampling reliability]

TOTAL MONEY INCOME	FAMILIES AND INDIVIDUALS			FAMILIES			UNRELATED INDIVIDUALS		
	Total	White	Non-white	Total	White	Non-white	Total	White	Non-white
UNITED STATES									
Percent	100.0	100.0	100.0	100.0	100.0	100.0	100.0	100.0	100.0
Under $500	8.0	7.0	16.7	4.4	3.7	11.7	25.6	24.5	32.2
$500 to $999	7.4	6.7	14.6	4.7	4.0	12.6	21.0	21.0	20.7
$1,000 to $1,499	5.9	5.2	11.7	5.3	4.6	12.5	8.7	8.6	9.0
$1,500 to $1,999	6.6	5.9	13.3	6.1	5.5	12.3	9.1	7.9	16.1
$2,000 to $2,499	7.9	7.5	11.5	7.6	7.2	11.7	9.4	9.2	10.8
$2,500 to $2,999	7.6	7.4	9.1	7.8	7.5	10.1	6.8	7.0	5.9
$3,000 to $3,499	9.5	9.8	6.7	9.9	10.1	8.0	7.3	8.1	2.8
$3,500 to $3,999	8.9	9.4	4.5	9.8	10.2	5.6	4.7	5.3	.9
$4,000 to $4,499	8.1	8.6	3.7	9.2	9.6	4.8	2.7	3.1	.3
$4,500 to $4,999	5.6	5.9	2.4	6.4	6.7	3.2	1.4	1.7	
$5,000 to $5,999	9.2	9.9	3.1	10.8	11.4	3.9	1.7	1.8	.6
$6,000 to $6,999	5.8	6.3	1.5	6.8	7.3	2.0	.9	1.0	......
$7,000 to $9,999	6.4	7.0	.9	7.5	8.2	1.0	.5	.5	.6
$10,000 to $14,999	2.0	2.2	......	2.4	2.6	......	.2	.2	......
$15,000 and over	1.0	1.1	.2	1.2	1.3	.3	.1	.1	......
MEDIAN INCOME [1]									
Total	$3,348	$3,524	$1,763	$3,709	$3,859	$2,032	$1,195	$1,258	$929
Urban	3,661	3,851	2,078	4,071	4,229	2,457	1,540	1,650	1,040
Rural nonfarm	3,093	3,168	1,206	3,365	3,427	(²)	740	766	(²)
Rural farm	1,953	2,178	941	2,131	2,351	966	733	750	(²)

[1] For definition of median, see headnote, table 18, p. 27.
[²] Fewer than 100 cases in sample reporting on income.

Source of tables 323 and 324: Department of Commerce, Bureau of the Census; *Income of Families in the United States: 1951*, Series P-60, No. 12.

No. 325.—PERCENT DISTRIBUTION OF PRIMARY FAMILIES AND UNRELATED INDIVIDUALS WITH WAGE OR SALARY INCOME, BY WAGE OR SALARY INCOME AND RECEIPT OF NONWAGE INCOME, URBAN AND RURAL: 1939 TO 1951

[Based on samples of population residing in households only; see source for evaluation of sampling variability. Excludes small number of families and individuals residing in quasi households (hotels, large rooming houses, etc.). "Primary family" refers to head of household and all persons related to him. A "primary individual" refers to household head who has no relatives living with him. These terms were not used in 1940 Census. Wage or salary income includes all money received in compensation for work or services performed as employees, including commissions, tips, piece-rate payments, bonuses, Armed Forces pay, etc., as well as receipts commonly referred to as wages or salaries. It excludes value of income in kind, such as living quarters, meals, clothing, etc. A primary family was considered to have other income if any person 14 years of age and over in family had $30 or more of income from sources other than money wages or salaries. For explanation of urban and rural areas, see p. 2]

WAGE OR SALARY INCOME AND RECEIPT OF NONWAGE INCOME	PRIMARY FAMILIES AND INDIVIDUALS						PRIMARY FAMILIES						PRIMARY UNRELATED INDIVIDUALS					
	1939	1945	1947	1949	1950	1951	1939	1945	1947	1949	1950	1951	1939	1945	1947	1949	1950	1951
UNITED STATES																		
Total	100.0	100.0	100.0	100.0	100.0	100.0	100.0	100.0	100.0	100.0	100.0	100.0	100.0	100.0	100.0	100.0	100.0	100.0
$1 to $499	20.2	10.2	6.1	7.7	7.9	6.9	18.9	9.3	5.3	6.5	7.1	6.0	28.1	22.9	19.1	13.2	13.4	14.2
$500 to $999	21.0	8.6	6.4	5.7	5.7	4.7	20.6	7.5	5.7	5.2	5.1	4.1	27.6	10.7	17.0	12.8	13.5	11.4
$1,000 to $1,499	19.0	9.6	8.1	7.2	6.0	4.5	19.2	9.3	7.5	6.8	5.7	4.1	16.2	14.3	16.3	12.5	12.3	8.8
$1,500 to $1,999	16.3	11.8	9.5	8.6	7.2	6.1	16.7	11.4	9.3	8.8	6.7	4.8	11.7	14.3	16.3	15.8	12.1	10.2
$2,000 to $2,499	9.8	13.2	12.1	11.3	9.9	8.8	10.2	13.1	12.0	10.9	9.8	8.7	4.6	14.5	13.1	16.4	12.1	10.2
$2,500 to $2,999	5.2	10.2	11.9	11.3	9.4	8.8	5.4	12.3	11.2	11.0	9.8	8.7	4.7	7.0	7.6	14.7	10.9	10.5
$3,000 to $4,999	7.2	26.3	31.9	32.3	34.8	35.1	7.6	27.7	33.3	33.7	36.1	37.2	2.3	6.5	10.8	14.7	19.9	28.8
$5,000 and over	2.3	8.8	16.8	16.8	18.9	25.1	2.4	9.3	15.7	17.9	20.3	27.0	.9	1.3	3.4	2.8	2.4	3.3
Median wage or salary income [1]	$1,231	$2,390	$2,884	$2,969	$3,216	$3,515	$1,272	$2,476	$2,955	$3,095	$3,353	$3,560	$714	$1,361	$1,424	$1,890	$1,725	$2,100
Without nonwage income																		
$1 to $499	16.4	4.0	2.5	2.4	3.3	2.1	14.8	2.4	1.4	1.6	2.2	1.2	38.1	20.9	16.3	10.1	13.5	11.2
$500 to $999	20.8	6.4	5.2	4.0	4.4	2.7	20.1	5.2	4.2	3.1	3.3	1.9	27.6	18.3	17.8	12.8	13.8	10.6
$1,000 to $1,499	20.5	8.6	6.9	6.0	6.5	3.5	20.7	7.9	6.7	6.8	4.6	2.8	17.4	15.4	17.6	13.3	13.5	10.0
$1,500 to $1,999	17.0	12.0	9.0	7.6	7.3	5.4	17.6	11.6	8.1	8.8	6.6	4.9	10.6	16.2	13.2	13.0	13.5	10.7
$2,000 to $2,499	10.8	16.3	12.6	11.7	10.6	9.0	11.3	16.4	12.6	11.1	10.2	8.1	4.1	7.6	13.0	17.7	9.8	11.1
$2,500 to $2,999	6.8	15.0	12.4	12.4	9.8	8.8	5.9	16.7	12.6	12.3	9.9	8.6	1.6	4.0	8.0	11.9	9.0	11.2
$3,000 to $4,999	6.3	23.3	31.9	32.1	38.7	40.8	7.7	31.6	37.6	38.1	40.8	40.4	8.6	7.6	11.1	9.3	20.2	26.2
$5,000 and over	1.7	9.6	16.6	18.9	20.3	27.7	1.8	10.4	16.5	20.5	22.5	30.3	.5	1.3	2.8	2.3	1.7	3.2
Median wage or salary income [1]	$1,312	$2,627	$3,094	$3,323	$3,466	$3,792	$1,363	$2,741	$3,232	$3,493	$3,650	$3,962	$729	$1,351	$1,454	$1,999	$1,838	$2,215
URBAN AND RURAL NONFARM																		
Median wage or salary income:[1]																		
Total	$1,345	[2]	$3,042	$3,162	$3,408	$3,664	$1,389	[2]	$3,184	$3,317	$3,547	$3,817	$764	[2]	$1,478	$1,902	$1,799	$2,127
Without nonwage income	$1,380	[2]	$3,191	$3,408	$3,545	$3,848	$1,431	[2]	$3,340	$3,577	$3,728	$4,021	$781	[2]	$1,491	$2,000	$1,890	$2,299
RURAL FARM																		
Median wage or salary income:[1]																		
Total	$453	[2]	$1,510	$1,202	$1,313	$1,741	$461	[2]	$1,646	$1,209	$1,335	$1,703	$336	[2]	$750	[2]	[2]	[2]
Without nonwage income	$455	[2]	$2,008	$1,933	$1,899	$2,575	$459	[2]	$2,073	$2,000	$2,030	$2,673	$331	[2]	$850	[2]	[2]	[2]

[1] For definition of median, see headnote, table 18, p. 27.   [2] Median not shown, where there were fewer than 100 cases in the sample reporting "with income."   [3] Comparable figures not available.

Source: Department of Commerce, Bureau of the Census: *Income of Families in the United States: 1951*, Series P-60, No. 12.

No. 326.—Percent Distribution of Persons 14 Years of Age and Over by Total Money Income in 1951 and Major Occupation Group in April 1952, by Sex

[Data based on sample. See source for evaluation of sampling reliability]

TOTAL MONEY INCOME AND SEX	Total	Total employed civilians	Professional, technical, and kindred workers			Farmers and farm managers	Managers, officials, and proprietors, except farm		
			Total	Self-employed	Salaried		Total	Self-employed	Salaried
MALE									
Number of persons......thousands..	52,736	41,896	3,162	526	2,636	3,866	5,022	2,784	2,238
Number of persons with income thousands..	47,497	40,687	3,120	517	2,603	3,795	4,958	2,726	2,232
Percent of those with income...	100.0	100.0	100.0	100.0	100.0	100.0	100.0	100.0	100.0
Loss................................	.4	.5	.6	4.0	......	2.6	1.0	1.8	.2
$1 to $499.........................	8.7	5.1	2.9	4.0	2.7	16.5	2.5	4.2	.5
$500 to $999.......................	8.4	5.3	2.0	1.6	2.1	15.7	2.3	4.1	.3
$1,000 to $1,499...................	7.0	6.0	2.9	3.2	2.8	14.9	3.2	4.5	1.8
$1,500 to $1,999...................	6.9	6.6	2.3	1.6	2.4	11.1	3.1	4.1	2.0
$2,000 to $2,499...................	9.6	10.4	3.6	4.0	3.5	10.4	7.5	10.3	4.5
$2,500 to $2,999...................	9.8	10.8	6.8	2.4	7.6	6.7	8.7	10.0	7.3
$3,000 to $3,499...................	12.3	13.9	11.9	9.6	12.3	5.3	10.1	10.5	9.6
$3,500 to $3,999...................	10.3	11.7	10.6	5.6	11.5	2.9	9.7	7.9	11.8
$4,000 to $4,499...................	8.0	9.1	13.0	3.2	14.7	2.9	9.3	7.4	11.3
$4,500 to $4,999...................	4.7	5.4	7.4	4.8	7.8	1.3	6.5	5.2	8.0
$5,000 to $5,999...................	6.4	7.1	12.2	4.8	13.4	3.0	11.9	9.8	14.1
$6,000 to $6,999...................	2.8	3.2	8.9	7.2	9.2	1.6	5.7	4.2	7.3
$7,000 to $9,999...................	2.6	2.8	8.7	14.4	7.7	2.2	8.6	4.7	12.8
$10,000 to $14,999.................	1.0	1.2	4.1	20.8	1.1	1.2	4.8	4.8	4.6
$15,000 and over...................	.9	1.0	2.3	8.8	1.1	1.9	5.2	6.4	4.0
Median income [1]..................	$2,952	$3,193	$4,250	$6,167	$4,176	$1,518	$4,100	$3,529	$4,547
FEMALE									
Number of persons......thousands..	57,580	18,234	2,026	90	1,936	166	978	588	390
Number of persons with income thousands..	25,179	15,529	1,798	74	1,724	148	841	481	360
Percent of those with income...	100.0	100.0	100.0	100.0	100.0	100.0	100.0	100.0	100.0
Loss................................	.2	.3		(²)	......	(²)	4.3	7.0	(²)
$1 to $499.........................	29.2	16.3	5.6	(²)	4.2	(²)	12.9	19.7	(²)
$500 to $999.......................	19.6	14.4	8.9	(²)	8.3	(²)	14.2	16.2	(²)
$1,000 to $1,499...................	10.9	11.9	4.6	(²)	4.6	(²)	7.7	11.3	(²)
$1,500 to $1,999...................	12.3	16.3	12.4	(²)	12.5	(²)	9.4	8.5	(²)
$2,000 to $2,499...................	11.0	15.9	18.0	(²)	18.7	(²)	10.7	12.7	(²)
$2,500 to $2,999...................	7.2	10.8	13.9	(²)	14.3	(²)	9.9	9.2	(²)
$3,000 to $3,499...................	4.9	7.5	18.0	(²)	18.7	(²)	8.6	.7	(²)
$3,500 to $3,999...................	2.2	3.3	8.7	(²)	8.9	(²)	6.9	2.8	(²)
$4,000 to $4,499...................	1.0	1.4	3.7	(²)	3.6	(²)	4.7	3.5	(²)
$4,500 to $4,999...................	.5	.8	2.5	(²)	2.6	(²)	3.4	1.4	(²)
$5,000 to $5,999...................	.5	.7	2.1	(²)	2.0	(²)	3.4	2.8	(²)
$6,000 to $6,999...................	.2	.3	.8	(²)	.8	(²)	2.1	2.1	(²)
$7,000 to $9,999...................	.2	.1	.4	(²)	.4	(²)	.9	.7	(²)
$10,000 to $14,999.................	.1	.1	.4	(²)	.2	(²)	.9	1.4	(²)
$15,000 and over...................	.1		......	(²)	......	(²)	......	......	(²)
Median income [1]..................	$1,045	$1,718	$2,517	(²)	$2,556	(²)	$2,070	$1,313	(²)

For footnotes, see p. 295.

No. 326.—Percent Distribution of Persons 14 Years of Age and Over by Total Money Income in 1951 and Major Occupation Group in April 1952, by Sex—Continued

TOTAL MONEY INCOME AND SEX	Employed as civilians in April 1952—continued								In armed forces or not employed in April 1952
	Clerical and kindred workers	Sales workers	Craftsmen, foremen, and kindred workers	Operatives and kindred workers	Private household workers	Service workers, except private household	Farm laborers and foremen	Laborers, except farm and mine	
MALE									
Number of persons...thousands	2,830	2,272	8,514	8,702	38	2,500	1,522	3,470	10,838
Number of persons with income thousands	2,763	2,174	8,419	8,543	38	2,426	1,088	3,363	6,810
Percent of these with income	100.0	100.0	100.0	100.0	100.0	100.0	100.0	100.0	100.0
Loss		.4	.1		(2)	.3		.2	.2
$1 to $499	2.6	6.5	1.1	2.5	(2)	7.8	22.0	9.1	29.2
$500 to $999	3.9	4.0	2.1	3.8	(2)	7.1	25.7	7.3	25.2
$1,000 to $1,499	2.9	3.3	3.0	5.0	(2)	7.7	20.6	11.3	12.9
$1,500 to $1,999	4.6	3.9	5.0	6.3	(2)	12.0	14.2	12.4	8.6
$2,000 to $2,499	8.5	7.7	8.7	13.4	(2)	16.0	6.4	17.2	5.3
$2,500 to $2,999	13.0	7.4	10.4	14.8	(2)	12.4	3.0	13.8	4.5
$3,000 to $3,499	17.2	13.2	14.7	19.1	(2)	14.7	2.7	18.5	3.3
$3,500 to $3,999	18.2	13.7	15.6	13.8	(2)	10.3	2.4	6.6	2.5
$4,000 to $4,499	12.7	9.3	13.0	9.5	(2)	6.0	.3	3.0	1.7
$4,500 to $4,999	6.5	6.7	7.9	5.0	(2)	3.2	.7	2.3	.7
$5,000 to $5,999	5.7	9.2	11.4	5.1	(2)	1.4	1.4	.8	2.0
$6,000 to $6,999	2.6	4.8	4.6	1.4	(2)	.3		.2	.9
$7,000 to $9,999	1.2	6.9	1.9	.4	(2)	.6		.3	1.8
$10,000 to $14,999	.4	2.1	.4		(2)				.3
$15,000 and over		.9	.1		(2)	.2	.7		.1
Median income [1]	$3,424	$3,628	$3,656	$3,108	(2)	$2,474	$1,087	$2,281	$893
FEMALE									
Number of persons...thousands	5,264	1,416	244	3,496	1,748	2,134	614	128	39,346
Number of persons with income thousands	4,743	1,118	233	3,161	1,472	1,821	84	111	9,651
Percent of these with income	100.0	100.0	100.0	100.0	100.0	100.0	100.0	100.0	100.0
Loss			(2)		.2	.4	(2)	(2)	.1
$1 to $499	6.8	28.0	(2)	10.3	50.7	22.3	(2)	(2)	49.0
$500 to $999	8.5	13.5	(2)	10.2	32.3	23.3	(2)	(2)	27.5
$1,000 to $1,499	8.9	15.1	(2)	17.3	10.5	18.7	(2)	(2)	9.5
$1,500 to $1,999	18.7	16.0	(2)	23.5	4.8	16.3	(2)	(2)	6.2
$2,000 to $2,499	21.6	15.7	(2)	19.1	1.1	11.7	(2)	(2)	3.3
$2,500 to $2,999	17.0	5.0	(2)	12.7	.2	3.0	(2)	(2)	1.8
$3,000 to $3,499	10.4	2.5	(2)	5.3		2.7	(2)	(2)	.9
$3,500 to $3,999	4.8	1.9	(2)	1.3	.2	.6	(2)	(2)	.5
$4,000 to $4,499	1.9	1.3	(2)	.1			(2)	(2)	.3
$4,500 to $4,999	.7	.6	(2)	.1		.2	(2)	(2)	.1
$5,000 to $5,999	.5		(2)			.6	(2)	(2)	.1
$6,000 to $6,999	.3		(2)				(2)	(2)	
$7,000 to $9,999			(2)				(2)	(2)	.4
$10,000 to $14,999			(2)				(2)	(2)	
$15,000 and over		.3	(2)			.2	(2)	(2)	.1
Median income [1]	$2,165	$1,281	(2)	$1,758	$492	$1,106	(2)	(2)	$516

[1] Based on number of persons with income. For definition of median, see headnote, table 18, p. 27.
[2] Fewer than 100 cases in sample reporting with income.

Source: Department of Commerce, Bureau of the Census; Income of Persons in the United States: 1951, Series P-60, No. 11.

No. 327.—Percent of Aggregate Wage or Salary Income (Before Taxes) Received by Each Fifth of Wage or Salary Recipients Ranked by Income: 1939 to 1951

[Data based on sample. See source for evaluation of sampling reliability and for explanation of method of estimating aggregate income]

WAGE OR SALARY RECIPIENTS	1939	1945	1947	1948	1949	1950	1951
Total	100.0	100.0	100.0	100.0	100.0	100.0	100.0
Lowest fifth	3.4	2.9	2.9	2.9	2.6	2.3	3.0
Second fifth	8.4	10.1	10.3	10.2	10.1	9.7	10.6
Middle fifth	15.0	17.4	17.8	18.6	18.7	18.3	18.9
Fourth fifth	23.9	25.7	24.7	25.5	26.2	25.7	25.9
Highest fifth	49.3	43.9	44.3	42.8	42.4	44.0	41.6

Source: Department of Commerce, Bureau of the Census; *Income of Persons in the United States: 1951*, Series P-60, No. 11.

No. 328.—Percent Distribution of Persons 14 Years of Age and Over by Total Money Income, by Sex, Urban and Rural: 1944 to 1951

[Data based on sample. See source for evaluation of sampling reliability]

TOTAL MONEY INCOME	MALE					FEMALE				
	1944	1948	1949	1950	1951	1944	1948	1949	1950	1951
UNITED STATES										
Total persons	100.0	100.0	100.0	100.0	100.0	100.0	100.0	100.0	100.0	100.0
Percent with income	88.9	89.9	89.9	89.9	89.8	47.9	40.9	41.8	43.2	43.7
Percent without income	11.1	10.1	10.1	10.1	10.2	52.1	59.1	58.2	56.8	56.3
Percent of those with income	100.0	100.0	100.0	100.0	100.0	100.0	100.0	100.0	100.0	100.0
Loss	.5	.5	.8	.7	.4	.1	.3	.3	.3	.2
$1 to $499	13.0	9.6	11.6	10.6	8.7	30.5	28.9	31.3	31.7	29.2
$500 to $999	12.2	10.4	10.7	9.4	8.4	23.7	20.6	20.0	19.8	19.6
$1,000 to $1,499	11.1	9.8	9.4	8.0	7.0	19.3	14.5	13.5	11.4	10.9
$1,500 to $1,999	11.9	9.3	9.3	8.4	6.9	12.9	13.9	12.7	12.2	12.3
$2,000 to $2,499	14.1	13.2	11.7	11.4	9.6	7.3	11.6	11.2	11.6	11.0
$2,500 to $2,999	11.6	11.5	11.6	10.2	9.8	2.9	5.2	5.2	6.5	7.2
$3,000 to $3,499	9.5	12.2	11.5	12.5	12.3	1.2	2.4	3.1	3.3	4.9
$3,500 to $3,999	5.6	7.3	7.7	8.4	10.3	.6	1.0	1.0	1.2	2.2
$4,000 to $4,499	3.0	5.1	4.8	6.2	8.0	.4	.5	.9	.8	1.0
$4,500 to $4,999	2.0	2.9	2.9	3.4	4.7	.3	.2	.3	.4	.5
$5,000 to $5,999	2.2	3.6	3.4	4.6	6.4	.3	.3	.2	.3	.5
$6,000 to $9,999	2.0	3.1	3.0	4.0	5.5	.3	.3	.3	.3	.4
$10,000 and over	1.2	1.6	1.4	2.0	1.9	.3	.2	.1	.2	.1
Median income for persons with income [1]	$2,046	$2,396	$2,346	$2,570	$2,952	$909	$1,009	$960	$953	$1,045
URBAN AND RURAL NONFARM										
Total persons	100.0	100.0	100.0	100.0	100.0	100.0	100.0	100.0	100.0	100.0
Percent with income	90.0	90.7	90.5	90.8	90.5	51.5	43.1	44.1	45.2	46.1
Percent without income	10.0	9.3	9.5	9.2	9.5	48.5	56.9	55.9	54.8	53.9
Median income for persons with income [1]	$2,265	$2,585	$2,563	$2,784	$3,130	$969	$1,222	$1,049	$1,043	$1,147
RURAL FARM										
Total persons	100.0	100.0	100.0	100.0	100.0	100.0	100.0	100.0	100.0	100.0
Percent with income	84.7	85.5	87.0	86.7	85.8	29.4	29.7	28.0	31.0	27.7
Percent without income	15.3	14.5	13.0	13.3	14.2	70.6	70.3	72.0	69.0	72.3
Median income for persons with income [1]	$951	$1,385	$1,054	$1,328	$1,486	$439	$467	$392	$417	$440

[1] For definition of median, see headnote, table 18, p. 27.

Source: Department of Commerce, Bureau of the Census; *Income of Persons in the United States: 1951*, Series P-60, No. 11.

No. 329.—Percent Distribution of Persons 14 Years of Age and Over With Wage or Salary Income, by Wage or Salary Income, by Sex: 1939 and 1951

[Data based on sample. See source for evaluation of sampling reliability]

WAGE OR SALARY INCOME	BOTH SEXES		MALE		FEMALE	
	1939	1951	1939	1951	1939	1951
Percent of those with wage or salary income	100.0	100.0	100.0	100.0	100.0	100.0
$1 to $999	60.0	23.6	52.8	14.1	79.0	41.9
$1,000 to $1,999	29.2	16.8	33.4	12.5	18.1	25.3
$2,000 to $2,499	5.3	11.3	6.8	10.2	1.6	13.5
$2,500 to $2,999	2.0	10.2	2.6	10.8	.5	9.1
$3,000 to $4,999	2.4	29.7	3.1	39.9	.6	9.7
$5,000 and over	1.0	8.4	1.4	12.4	.1	.5
Median wage or salary income [1]	$789	$2,422	$939	$3,063	$555	$1,361

[1] For definition of median, see headnote, table 18, p. 27.

No. 330.—Median Wage or Salary Income of Persons 14 Years of Age and Over With Wage or Salary Income, by Color, Major Industry Group, and Major Occupation Group, by Sex: 1939 and 1951

[Data based on sample. See source for evaluation of sampling reliability. Wage or salary income includes all money received in compensation for work or services performed as employees including commissions, tips, piece rate payments, bonuses, armed forces pay, etc., as well as receipts commonly referred to as wages or salaries. Excludes value or income in kind, such as living quarters, meals, clothing, etc. Median wage or salary income based on number of persons reporting $1 or more of wage or salary income, except where otherwise specified. For definition of median, see headnote, table 18, p. 27]

COLOR AND MAJOR INDUSTRY OR OCCUPATION GROUP	BOTH SEXES		MALE		FEMALE	
	1939 [1]	1951	1939 [1]	1951	1939 [1]	1951
COLOR [2]						
White	$956	$2,875	$1,112	$3,345	$676	$1,855
Nonwhite	364	1,572	460	2,060	246	781
MAJOR INDUSTRY GROUP [3]						
Agriculture, forestry, and fisheries	292	1,187	301	1,206	154	(?)
Mining	957	3,667	956	3,683	1,077	(?)
Construction	777	2,752	777	2,766	804	(?)
Manufacturing	988	3,003	1,141	3,393	646	1,923
Transportation, communication, and other public utilities	1,365	3,302	1,425	3,348	1,066	2,221
Wholesale trade	1,215	3,278	1,326	3,000	828	(?)
Retail trade	793	2,062	969	2,705	599	1,470
Finance, insurance, and real estate	1,257	2,633	1,487	3,462	977	2,012
Business and repair services	971	2,727	995	2,903	838	(?)
Personal services	360	782	738	1,875	292	653
Entertainment and recreation services	814	1,625	888	(?)	639	(?)
Professional and related services	995	2,359	1,235	3,004	806	2,061
Public administration	1,492	3,338	1,625	3,565	1,233	2,631
MAJOR OCCUPATION GROUP [4]						
Professional, technical, and kindred workers	1,373	3,342	1,809	4,071	1,028	2,495
Farmers and farm managers	372	472	373	482	348	(?)
Managers, officials, and proprietors, except farm	2,030	3,926	2,136	4,143	1,107	2,879
Clerical and kindred workers	1,152	2,494	1,421	3,366	966	2,147
Sales workers	1,032	2,516	1,277	3,539	636	1,176
Craftsmen, foremen, and kindred workers	1,298	3,568	1,309	3,601	827	(?)
Operatives and kindred workers	850	2,646	1,007	3,064	582	1,739
Private household workers	304	455	429	(?)	296	447
Service workers, except private household	693	1,679	833	2,426	493	996
Farm laborers and foremen	305	934	309	982	176	(?)
Laborers, except farm and mines	667	2,142	673	2,170	538	(?)

[1] Data for 1939 exclude public emergency workers.
[2] Data refer to persons who were employed as wage and salary workers during survey week.
[3] Median not shown where there were fewer than 100 cases in the sample reporting with wage or salary income.
[4] Data refer to persons who were in the experienced civilian labor force during survey week. 1939 data include members of armed forces, but exclude persons with less than $100 of wage or salary income.

Source of tables 329 and 330: Department of Commerce, Bureau of the Census; *Income of Persons in the United States: 1951*, Series P-60, No. 11.

No. 331.—Percent Distribution of the Experienced Civilian Labor Force With Wage or Salary Income, and of Their Aggregate Wage or Salary Income (Before Taxes), by Sex and Major Occupation Group: 1939 and 1951

[Data based on sample. See source for evaluation of sampling reliability and for explanation of method of estimating aggregate income]

MAJOR OCCUPATION GROUP	MALE				FEMALE			
	1939		1951		1939		1951	
	Income recipients	Wage or salary income	Income recipients	Wage or salary income	Income recipients	Wage or salary income	Income recipients	Wage or salary income
Total in experienced civilian labor force [1]	100.0	100.0	100.0	100.0	100.0	100.0	100.0	100.0
Professional, technical, and kindred workers	(?)	(?)	(?)	(?)	13.6	21.7	11.9	17.3
Clerical and kindred workers	8.7	10.5	8.1	8.2	25.5	33.7	31.5	38.1
Sales workers	7.3	9.1	5.5	6.5	6.9	6.0	7.5	5.6
Craftsmen, foremen, and kindred workers	18.2	19.3	24.7	27.4	1.1	1.3	1.2	1.3
Operatives and kindred workers	24.3	20.0	24.9	22.8	21.9	17.2	21.8	21.8
Private household workers	(?)	(?)	(?)	(?)	16.7	7.7	10.4	3.5
Service workers, excluding private household	8.0	6.0	5.4	4.7	10.6	7.6	11.7	7.7
Laborers, except farm and mine	12.7	7.3	10.2	6.7	1.1	.8	.6	.4
Other occupations [2]	20.8	27.8	20.2	23.7	2.6	3.9	3.3	4.2

[1] Base of distribution of income recipients is 34.4 million males and 14.4 million females for 1951 and 27.0 million males and 9.2 million females for 1939. 1951 data relate to persons having $1 or more of wage or salary income; 1939 data relate to persons having $100 or more of wage or salary income. 1939 excludes public emergency workers, but includes members of armed forces.
[2] Included in other occupations.
[3] Includes a relatively large proportion of workers not primarily dependent upon wage or salary income. See also note 2.

Source: Department of Commerce, Bureau of the Census; *Income of Persons in the United States: 1951*, Series P-60, No. 11.

No. 332.—Percent of Aggregate Wage or Salary Income (Before Taxes) Received by Each Fifth of Wage or Salary Recipients in the Experienced Civilian Labor Force, for Selected Major Occupation Groups Ranked by Income, by Sex: 1939 and 1951

[Data based on sample. See source for evaluation of sampling reliability and for explanation of method of estimating aggregate income]

SEX AND MAJOR OCCUPATION GROUP	1939					1951				
	Lowest fifth	Second fifth	Middle fifth	Fourth fifth	Highest fifth	Lowest fifth	Second fifth	Middle fifth	Fourth fifth	Highest fifth
MALE										
Clerical and kindred workers	6.7	13.6	17.7	24.0	38.0	8.4	16.5	20.2	23.6	31.3
Sales workers	5.0	10.6	15.5	22.1	46.8	5.7	13.9	17.8	22.4	40.2
Craftsmen, foremen, and kindred workers	6.6	13.3	18.8	24.2	37.1	8.8	15.7	19.6	23.6	32.3
Operatives and kindred workers	6.5	13.0	18.4	24.7	37.4	7.8	16.1	20.2	23.6	32.3
Service workers, except private household	5.5	11.5	16.5	24.1	42.4	4.7	14.0	20.2	25.9	35.2
Laborers, except farm and mine	6.3	11.6	17.4	25.8	38.9	4.8	9.1	24.5	26.3	35.3
FEMALE										
Professional, technical, and kindred workers	5.9	12.2	16.5	23.8	41.6	6.0	15.5	19.8	24.8	33.9
Clerical and kindred workers	7.3	14.9	19.1	23.8	34.9	6.5	15.3	20.7	24.7	32.8
Sales workers	6.6	13.1	19.4	23.6	37.3	3.9	7.6	17.7	28.9	41.9
Operatives and kindred workers	8.2	14.1	19.3	23.8	34.6	5.8	14.6	20.2	25.2	34.2
Private household workers	8.5	12.2	17.1	22.7	39.5	8.5	8.5	12.0	25.4	45.6
Service workers, except private household	7.6	11.3	18.2	24.5	38.4	4.4	10.9	17.5	26.5	40.7

Source: Department of Commerce, Bureau of the Census; *Income of Persons in the United States: 1951*, Series P-60, No. 11.

No. 388.—INCOME OF NONSALARIED PHYSICIANS, LAWYERS, AND DENTISTS: 1929 TO 1951

[Data are based on mail questionnaire surveys of the three professions, usually in cooperation with the professional associations. At intervals, large-scale surveys have been conducted to establish benchmark data, most recently in 1948 (lawyers), 1949 (dentists), and 1950 (physicians). For later years, smaller, interim surveys are conducted to obtain indexes for extending the benchmark data forward]

	PHYSICIANS		DENTISTS		LAWYERS	
YEAR	Average gross income [1]	Average net income [2]	Average gross income [1]	Average net income [2]	Average gross income [1]	Average net income [2]
1929	$8,567	$5,224	$7,112	$4,267	$7,997	$5,534
1930	8,173	4,870	6,814	4,020	7,504	5,194
1931	7,191	4,178	6,004	3,422	7,463	5,090
1932	5,775	3,178	4,591	2,479	6,397	4,156
1933	5,368	2,948	4,052	2,188	5,923	3,866
1934	5,871	3,382	4,347	2,391	6,362	4,218
1935	6,295	3,695	4,438	2,485	6,434	4,272
1936	7,020	4,204	4,868	2,726	6,581	4,394
1937	7,276	4,285	5,148	2,883	6,726	4,483
1938	7,083	4,093	5,263	2,870	6,470	4,273
1939	7,261	4,229	5,705	3,096	6,615	4,391
1940	7,632	4,441	6,592	3,314	6,747	4,507
1941	8,524	5,047	7,020	3,782	7,172	4,794
1942	10,969	6,735	8,320	4,625	8,197	5,527
1943	13,414	8,370	10,126	5,715	8,802	5,945
1944	15,387	9,802	11,591	6,649	9,741	6,504
1945	17,380	10,975	12,115	6,922	10,398	6,861
1946	16,536	10,202	11,429	6,381	10,645	6,951
1947	17,742	10,726	12,032	6,610	11,498	7,437
1948	18,921	11,327	12,703	7,039	12,660	8,121
1949	19,710	11,744	12,981	7,146	13,079	8,093
1950	20,713	12,324	13,202	7,436	13,634	8,540
1951	22,298	13,432	14,085	7,820	14,171	8,730

[1] Gross business receipts from independent professional practice only.
[2] Income from independent professional practice after deduction of business expenses but before payment of income taxes.

Source: Department of Commerce, Office of Business Economics; *Survey of Current Business*, August 1949, January 1950, July 1951, and July 1952.

12. Prices

The indexes issued by the Bureau of Labor Statistics have been, since the beginning of the century, the major source of price statistics in summarized form. This agency prepares weekly and monthly indexes of wholesale prices, a daily index based on spot market prices of 22 commodities; indexes of food prices at retail in 56 large cities; and indexes of consumers' prices for moderate-income families in 34 large cities.

Wholesale price index.—Since 1902, the official monthly wholesale price index has been prepared as an indicator of general price trends and average changes in commodity prices at primary market levels. The official series on the base, 1926=100, has been carried back to 1890; separate monthly indexes are available for major groups of commodities from January 1890, and for subgroups of commodities beginning with 1913. This index, based on 1926=100, is the official index for December 1951 and all earlier dates.

A newly-revised index, based on 1947–49=100, is now the official index for January 1952 and all subsequent months. Weights used represent all sales at the primary market level during the calendar year 1947. Moreover, the new index has expanded the number of commodities covered to 2,000 instead of the 900 measured by the earlier index. For a detailed description of the new index, see the *Monthly Labor Review*, February 1952.

The index measures average changes in commodity prices of commodities at the primary market level—usually the level at which the commodity is first sold commercially in substantial volume. The prices are ordinarily those charged by representative manufacturers or producers to the types of distributors or industrial consumers who are characteristic buyers of the product. Wherever feasible the prices are f. o. b. point of production or sale. In the case of some commodities, prices quoted in organized commodity markets are used.

The index measures completely the price changes of only the commodities which are specifically defined for pricing both physically and in terms of market structure. It is not an over-all measure of the "general price level" or of "the purchasing power of the dollar"—it does not include all classses of commodities (real estate, securities, services, etc.) which are factors in the "general price level."

Consumers' price index.—This index measures average changes in retail prices of goods, rents and services, purchased by wage-earners and lower-salaried clerical workers in large cities. The weights used in calculating the index are based on studies of actual expenditures by families of wage-earners and lower-salaried workers. A study conducted in 1917–19 provided the weights used from 1913 to 1935. From 1935 to January 1950, time-to-time changes in retail prices were weighted by 1934–36 average expenditures of urban families whose annual incomes averaged $1,524 in 1934–36. Weights used beginning January 1950 have been adjusted to 1949–50 spending patterns.

The index does not measure changes in the total amount families spend for living or relative differences in prices or living costs between cities. The list of items priced for the index includes approximately 225 goods and services. For many goods a number of different articles or qualities of articles are included in the index. Sales taxes are reflected wherever applicable, but income taxes, social security deductions, and bond deductions are not included. Since March 1943, food indexes have been based upon changes in food prices in 56 cities. From September 1940 through June 1947, consumers' price indexes were computed monthly for 21 cities, and in March,

Note.—This section presents data for the most recent year or period available on March 17, 1953, when the material was organized and sent to the printer. In a few instances, more recent data were added after that date.

300

June, September, and December for 13 additional cities; beginning July 1947, indexes have been computed monthly for 10 cities, and once every 3 months for 24 additional cities according to a staggered schedule. Since July 1947, the following schedule has been in effect:

Food prices and indexes for 56 cities each month;

Fuel prices and indexes for 34 cities each month;

Commodities (other than food and fuel) and services indexes for 10 cities monthly and for 24 additional cities quarterly on a rotating cycle;

Rents quarterly for 34 cities, on a rotating cycle;

All items and group indexes for 10 cities monthly, and for 24 additional cities quarterly on a rotating cycle;

National indexes (average of large cities) for all items and groups, monthly, based upon prices in the cities surveyed and estimated changes in the unpriced cities.

The **retail food price indexes** presented in this section are one component of the consumers' price index. For periods from January 1935 to March 1943 they are based on the distribution of expenditures as shown by the 1934–36 study of expenditures of wage-earners' and lower-salaried clerical workers' families. In March 1943, the weights for this index were revised to take account of changes in food purchases due to wartime shortages and rationing. In January 1946, these wartime weight adjustments were eliminated and certain other revisions made in the calculating procedures. In January 1950, the weights were adjusted to estimated 1949–50 spending patterns. The indexes are computed from prices of 54 foods for the period from January 1935 to March 1943, 61 foods for the period March 1943 to June 1947, 50 foods from June 1947 to January 1950, and 60 foods thereafter. Aggregate costs of these foods in each of 56 cities (51 cities prior to March 1943), weighted to represent total purchases, have been combined for the United States with the use of population weights. Indexes for all periods prior to January 1935 are converted from indexes computed for corresponding periods on the 1923–25 base.

Other indexes.—The Bureau of Agricultural Economics prepares currently indexes of prices received for farm products and of prices paid by farmers. (See text, p. 605.)

In comparing the movement of the indexes of consumers' prices and of the prices paid by farmers for commodities bought for family living (table 726), it should be noted that the consumers' price index includes rents and other services and the farm index does not, and that the list of commodities included in the two indexes and their geographic coverage differs because farm family buying differs considerably from that of city families, and farm and city workers are located in different parts of the country.

Historical statistics.—See preface and historical appendix. Tabular headnotes (as "See also *Historical Statistics*, series L 41–47") provide cross-references, where applicable, to *Historical Statistics of the United States, 1789–1945*.

FIG. XXIII.—WHOLESALE PRICE INDEXES: 1926 TO 1952

[1947-49=100. Prices in primary markets. See table 334]

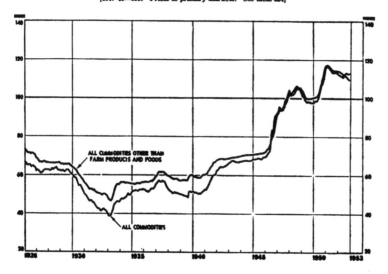

FIG. XXIV.—CONSUMERS' PRICE INDEX: 1913 TO 1952

[1935-39=100. See table 339]

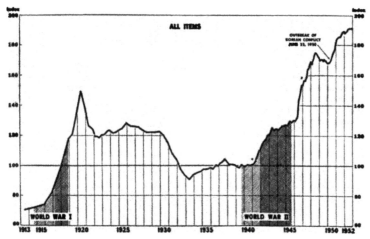

*Estimates of World War II and Postwar understatement by the index were not included. See *Monthly Labor Review* for March 1947.

Source of figs. XXIII and XXIV: Department of Labor, Bureau of Labor Statistics.

No. 334.—WHOLESALE PRICE INDEXES FOR ALL COMMODITIES, AND FOR ALL COMMODITIES OTHER THAN FARM PRODUCTS AND FOODS: 1926 TO 1952

[1947-49=100. This index is the official price index, beginning with January 1952. Although the new index has been computed back to 1926, for comparison, the official index for December 1951 and all earlier dates is that based on 1926=100, shown in tables 325 and 326 of the 1952 Abstract]

YEAR	Yearly average	Jan.	Feb.	Mar.	Apr.	May	June	July	Aug.	Sept.	Oct.	Nov.	Dec.
ALL COMMODITIES													
1926	65.0	67.0	66.3	65.4	65.2	65.3	65.3	64.6	64.4	64.8	64.6	64.0	63.6
1927	62.0	62.0	62.7	62.3	61.6	61.1	61.2	61.3	61.9	62.6	62.5	62.6	62.6
1928	62.9	62.6	62.3	62.1	62.5	63.4	62.9	63.3	63.4	64.1	62.9	62.5	62.3
1929	61.9	62.3	62.0	62.5	62.1	61.5	61.9	62.7	62.6	62.5	61.5	60.7	60.6
1930	56.1	60.1	59.4	58.6	58.5	57.7	56.4	54.8	54.8	54.9	53.9	52.8	51.7
1931	47.4	50.8	49.9	49.4	48.8	47.6	46.9	46.8	46.9	46.3	45.7	45.5	44.6
1932	42.1	43.5	43.1	42.9	42.6	41.9	41.6	41.9	42.3	42.5	41.9	41.5	40.7
1933	42.8	39.6	38.8	38.1	39.2	40.8	42.2	44.8	44.2	44.0	44.3	44.2	44.0
1934	48.7	46.9	47.5	47.9	47.7	47.9	48.5	48.6	49.7	50.4	49.7	48.8	50.0
1935	52.0	51.2	51.7	51.6	52.0	52.1	51.9	51.6	52.3	52.4	52.3	52.4	52.6
1936	52.5	52.4	52.4	51.7	51.8	51.1	51.5	52.3	52.0	53.0	53.0	54.5	54.7
1937	56.1	55.8	56.1	57.0	57.2	56.8	56.6	57.1	56.9	56.5	55.5	54.1	53.1
1938	51.1	52.6	51.9	51.5	51.1	50.8	50.9	51.2	50.7	50.9	50.5	50.3	50.1
1939	50.1	50.0	50.0	49.9	49.5	49.5	49.2	49.0	48.7	51.4	51.6	51.4	51.5
1940	51.1	51.6	51.2	50.9	51.1	50.9	50.4	50.5	50.3	50.7	51.2	51.7	52.0
1941	56.8	52.1	52.4	53.0	54.1	55.2	56.6	57.7	58.7	59.7	60.1	60.1	60.9
1942	64.2	62.4	62.8	63.4	64.1	64.2	64.1	64.1	64.4	64.5	65.0	65.2	65.6
1943	67.0	66.2	66.6	67.2	67.4	67.6	67.4	67.1	67.0	67.0	67.0	66.9	67.1
1944	67.6	67.1	67.2	67.5	67.4	67.6	67.7	67.7	67.5	67.6	67.7	67.7	67.8
1945	68.5	68.2	68.3	68.4	68.7	68.9	69.0	68.9	68.7	68.4	68.8	69.4	69.6
1946	78.7	68.6	70.0	70.8	71.8	72.1	73.3	81.1	83.9	80.6	87.2	90.8	91.6
1947	96.4	92.3	96.1	96.4	94.8	94.3	94.3	96.3	96.5	98.4	99.6	100.7	102.6
1948	104.4	104.5	102.5	102.5	103.3	103.8	104.6	105.5	106.2	106.1	105.0	104.7	104.0
1949	99.2	102.8	101.2	100.9	99.9	99.0	98.2	98.0	98.2	98.3	97.9	97.8	97.7
1950	103.1	97.7	96.3	96.5	96.5	99.6	99.6	100.2	103.0	105.2	107.1	107.7	109.2	112.1
1951	114.8	115.0	116.5	116.5	116.3	115.9	115.1	114.3	113.7	113.4	113.7	113.6	113.5
1952	111.6	113.0	112.5	112.3	111.8	111.6	111.2	111.8	112.1	111.8	111.1	110.7	109.6
ALL COMMODITIES OTHER THAN FARM PRODUCTS AND FOODS													
1926	71.5	73.3	72.7	72.0	71.5	71.6	71.6	71.1	71.2	71.2	71.1	70.9	70.1
1927	67.2	69.0	68.5	67.6	66.9	66.8	66.5	66.5	67.0	67.1	66.9	66.5	66.7
1928	66.4	66.4	66.4	66.2	66.3	66.4	66.2	66.2	66.4	66.5	66.4	66.5	66.5
1929	65.5	66.0	65.7	65.9	65.6	65.4	65.7	65.8	65.3	65.5	65.5	65.4	64.7
1930	60.9	64.0	63.6	63.1	62.8	62.4	61.3	60.4	59.8	59.5	58.7	58.0	57.4
1931	53.6	56.5	56.0	55.2	54.2	53.7	53.0	52.9	53.0	52.5	52.2	52.1	51.7
1932	50.2	51.3	51.0	50.7	50.7	50.3	50.1	49.8	50.1	50.3	50.2	49.9	49.3
1933	50.9	48.1	47.2	47.0	48.7	47.5	49.2	51.7	52.0	54.4	54.2	55.2	55.4
1934	56.0	56.3	56.3	56.1	56.2	56.4	56.5	56.0	56.0	56.0	56.0	56.3	56.7
1935	55.7	55.6	55.4	55.3	55.2	55.5	55.8	55.8	55.7	55.6	56.0	56.3	56.3
1936	56.9	56.3	56.5	56.4	56.4	56.3	56.4	56.8	57.0	56.9	57.2	57.0	56.8
1937	61.0	59.6	60.1	61.2	61.8	61.7	61.6	61.4	60.9	60.3	59.3	58.8	58.8
1938	58.4	59.7	59.4	59.1	58.6	58.4	58.1	58.2	58.2	58.2	58.0	57.6	57.4
1939	58.1	57.3	57.4	57.5	57.6	57.6	57.7	57.7	57.3	58.7	59.9	60.1	60.0
1940	59.4	60.9	60.5	60.3	59.6	59.0	58.8	58.8	58.7	58.8	59.7	60.2	60.2
1941	63.7	60.3	60.3	60.7	61.4	62.5	63.4	64.1	64.9	65.5	66.8	66.9	67.0
1942	68.3	67.9	67.5	68.1	68.3	68.4	68.4	68.4	68.3	68.3	68.3	68.5	68.6
1943	69.3	68.7	68.8	69.0	69.1	69.2	69.2	69.3	69.4	69.5	69.5	70.6	69.2
1944	70.4	69.9	70.1	70.1	70.3	70.4	70.4	70.5	70.5	70.5	70.5	70.6	70.7
1945	71.3	70.8	70.9	71.0	71.0	71.1	71.2	71.2	71.4	71.4	71.5	71.7	71.9
1946	78.8	72.1	72.4	73.1	73.8	74.3	75.5	78.3	79.8	80.2	82.5	86.3	89.2
1947	95.3	91.8	92.2	93.6	94.0	93.8	93.9	94.6	95.8	96.9	97.9	98.6	100.4
1948	103.4	102.0	101.6	101.6	102.0	102.0	102.5	103.5	104.7	105.1	105.2	105.5	105.4
1949	101.3	104.9	104.0	103.3	102.0	100.8	100.1	99.8	100.0	100.0	100.0	100.0	100.2
1950	106.0	100.4	100.6	100.7	100.8	101.5	102.2	103.8	105.9	108.2	110.1	111.6	114.1
1951	115.9	116.6	117.2	117.3	117.1	116.5	116.2	115.7	114.9	114.8	114.5	114.5	114.6
1952	113.2	114.3	114.2	113.3	113.3	113.0	112.6	112.5	112.9	113.2	113.0	112.8	112.9

Source: Department of Labor, Bureau of Labor Statistics; annual report, Wholesale Prices; and Monthly Labor Review.

No. 335.—Wholesale Price Indexes, by Groups and Subgroups of Commodities: 1947 to 1952

[Base 1947–49=100. See headnote, table 334]

COMMODITY GROUP	1947	1948	1949	1950	1951	1952 Average	1952 June	1952 December
All commodities	96.4	104.4	99.2	103.1	114.8	111.6	111.2	109.6
All commodities other than farm products and foods	95.3	103.4	101.3	105.0	115.9	113.2	112.6	112.9
Special groups:								
All foods	98.1	105.7	96.2	98.5	110.3	108.8	108.1	104.5
Special metals and metal products [1]	91.2	103.2	105.6	109.7	120.7	122.2	120.8	123.0
Building materials	94.0	104.0	102.0	109.5	119.6	118.2	117.8	118.3
Farm products	100.0	107.3	92.8	97.5	113.4	107.0	107.2	99.2
Fresh and dried fruits and vegetables	98.4	102.4	99.2	91.4	97.2	120.3	124.2	112.3
Grains	110.9	104.9	84.3	89.7	99.3	98.2	95.4	96.1
Livestock and live poultry	97.6	110.3	92.2	99.0	116.9	102.4	107.2	84.8
Plant and animal fibers	97.4	103.3	99.3	116.2	143.9	115.1	118.7	101.9
Fluid milk	98.1	111.6	90.3	88.7	104.8	109.6	103.5	108.9
Eggs	96.0	103.9	100.1	84.9	106.0	95.9	81.0	99.6
Hay, hayseeds and oilseeds	107.0	109.7	83.3	89.8	102.7	98.3	98.5	98.3
Other farm products	96.1	100.0	103.9	127.8	138.5	136.7	136.7	134.7
Processed foods	98.2	106.1	95.7	99.8	111.4	108.8	108.5	104.3
Cereal and bakery products	100.6	102.3	97.1	99.0	106.9	106.9	106.7	106.8
Meats, poultry and fish	94.4	109.8	95.8	101.5	116.7	108.3	110.1	93.9
Dairy products and ice cream	96.1	107.3	96.6	94.8	107.7	113.6	110.1	113.0
Canned, frozen, fruits and vegetables	100.4	100.1	99.5	99.8	105.5	105.0	103.5	105.0
Sugar and confectionery	101.2	102.9	95.9	98.4	106.4	109.2	110.9	108.2
Packaged beverage materials	89.5	101.0	109.5	148.3	161.3	162.2	161.9	161.9
Other processed foods	93.8	98.4	107.9	118.1	123.0	119.0	118.4	116.9
Textile products and apparel	100.1	104.4	95.5	99.2	110.6	99.8	99.0	98.2
Cotton products	103.1	105.1	91.8	99.5	111.5	98.5	95.4	97.7
Wool products	90.6	104.4	105.0	112.9	144.6	113.0	112.8	112.6
Synthetic textiles	96.6	106.3	96.2	95.3	97.0	88.9	88.5	87.8
Silk products	117.2	92.8	89.9	99.7	128.8	133.7	129.8	139.7
Apparel	101.2	103.2	95.6	96.3	103.8	100.0	100.3	98.3
Other textile products	103.6	100.7	95.8	110.5	141.6	101.0	98.7	84.4
Hides, skins and leather products	101.0	102.1	96.9	104.6	120.3	97.2	95.9	99.6
Hides and skins	109.1	102.1	88.9	103.0	119.0	63.0	59.5	70.6
Leather	105.8	100.8	93.4	107.0	124.7	89.4	88.9	92.9
Footwear	96.1	102.7	101.3	106.5	121.6	112.4	111.0	112.0
Other leather products	99.9	102.5	97.6	98.2	112.3	100.8	100.6	100.3
Fuel, power, and lighting materials	90.9	107.1	101.9	103.0	106.7	106.6	105.9	107.2
Coal	88.0	106.2	105.8	106.2	108.4	108.7	105.3	116.1
Coke	84.2	104.3	111.6	116.1	124.0	124.7	124.3	129.0
Gas	96.1	102.4	101.5	98.2	100.7	103.7	102.0	104.9
Electricity	98.0	99.2	102.8	100.1	98.9	98.6	98.5	98.5
Petroleum and products	88.2	111.7	100.1	103.7	110.5	109.3	109.6	107.9
Chemicals and allied products	101.4	103.8	94.8	96.3	110.0	104.5	104.3	103.3
Industrial chemicals	98.8	104.9	96.2	101.1	120.7	115.2	114.9	112.3
Paint and paint materials	99.1	101.0	99.9	96.8	108.9	107.3	107.0	106.1
Drugs, pharmaceuticals, and cosmetics	105.3	101.0	93.6	92.5	95.6	92.5	92.2	91.3
Fats and oils, inedible	127.6	115.9	56.6	68.7	88.8	50.0	52.0	52.8
Mixed fertilizer	94.0	101.5	104.5	101.3	107.3	109.3	108.7	111.1
Fertilizer materials	95.0	100.6	104.6	101.7	106.3	110.6	109.9	113.0
Other chemicals and products	100.7	104.2	95.1	94.6	108.4	103.3	103.0	103.1
Rubber and products	96.0	102.1	98.9	130.5	148.0	134.0	133.4	127.7
Crude rubber	103.0	103.4	93.6	157.3	215.1	157.8	152.7	137.3
Tires and tubes	99.4	101.8	98.8	113.6	133.9	129.8	130.5	126.3
Other rubber products	96.3	101.8	101.9	109.9	130.9	126.7	127.1	124.3
Lumber and wood products	92.7	107.2	99.2	113.9	123.9	120.3	119.9	119.7
Lumber	94.5	107.3	98.2	114.5	123.6	120.5	120.1	119.8
Millwork	87.3	105.1	107.6	114.6	130.1	127.0	126.4	128.3
Plywood	95.9	109.0	95.2	106.5	115.1	105.0	105.7	102.3
Pulp, paper and allied products	96.6	102.9	96.5	100.9	119.6	116.5	116.7	115.9
Woodpulp	95.6	107.3	97.0	95.6	114.4	111.5	113.3	108.8
Wastepaper	148.3	90.4	61.3	119.5	188.3	70.1	55.1	89.3
Paper	93.4	102.8	103.8	106.5	119.1	124.0	124.2	124.9
Paperboard	99.2	102.0	98.8	105.0	131.8	127.4	129.3	124.4
Converted paper and paperboard	100.5	102.4	97.1	97.7	117.0	113.8	113.7	112.3
Building paper and board	93.0	102.8	104.2	107.6	113.4	115.5	115.8	118.2
Metals and metal products	91.8	103.9	104.8	110.3	123.0	121.0	121.1	124.0
Iron and steel	89.7	104.3	106.0	113.1	123.2	124.7	122.4	127.0
Nonferrous metals	95.6	105.7	98.7	104.1	124.2	123.5	120.0	122.3
Metal containers	90.6	100.6	108.8	109.2	121.1	122.0	120.5	125.4
Hardware	92.9	101.1	106.0	114.2	125.8	125.4	123.9	125.9
Plumbing equipment	94.7	102.7	102.7	108.2	122.5	117.4	118.0	118.1

[1] Includes items to make this group comparable to former index (1926=100) for metals and metal products.

No. 335.—Wholesale Price Indexes, by Groups and Subgroups of Commodities: 1947 to 1952—Continued

[Base 1947–49=100]

COMMODITY GROUP	1947	1948	1949	1950	1951	1952 Average	1952 June	1952 December
Metals and metal products—Continued								
Heating equipment	95.3	101.2	103.6	105.1	114.6	113.8	113.5	113.6
Fabricated structural metal products	96.8	102.4	100.9	104.2	117.5	115.1	115.4	113.9
Fabricated nonstructural metal products	84.3	104.0	111.7	115.6	125.4	124.9	124.4	126.5
Machinery and motive products	92.5	100.9	106.5	108.6	119.0	121.5	121.3	121.4
Agricultural machinery and equipment	90.3	101.4	108.3	110.7	120.1	121.6	121.5	121.7
Construction machinery and equipment	90.0	101.8	108.3	111.5	123.6	125.4	125.4	126.3
Metal working machinery and equipment	93.6	100.8	105.6	112.0	125.8	128.5	127.9	129.0
General purpose machinery and equipment	92.6	100.9	106.5	110.3	123.5	122.6	122.4	121.9
Miscellaneous machinery	93.8	101.1	105.1	107.4	119.4	119.4	119.0	119.6
Electrical machinery and equipment	96.1	100.7	103.2	106.4	121.9	120.3	120.0	119.6
Motor vehicles	91.3	100.8	107.9	107.2	112.9	119.6	119.7	119.7
Furniture and other household durables	95.6	101.4	103.1	105.3	114.1	112.0	111.6	112.3
Household furniture	95.6	102.8	101.5	105.2	116.4	113.0	112.7	113.0
Commercial furniture	94.6	101.1	104.3	109.7	124.5	123.0	123.2	123.2
Floor covering	95.7	101.8	102.5	115.0	137.8	122.8	119.1	122.7
Household appliances	97.1	101.8	101.1	101.9	107.9	107.3	106.8	107.5
Radio, television and phonographs	96.3	100.1	103.6	96.8	92.8	(1)	93.8	93.8
Other household durable goods	93.4	99.7	107.0	108.7	117.3	118.8	119.3	119.6
Nonmetallic minerals, structural	93.9	101.7	104.4	106.9	113.6	113.6	113.8	114.6
Flat glass	95.0	100.1	105.0	107.4	114.0	114.3	114.4	114.4
Concrete ingredients	93.0	101.8	105.2	106.8	113.0	113.0	112.9	113.1
Concrete products	96.1	100.8	103.1	105.5	112.3	112.5	112.4	112.7
Structural clay products	93.3	101.4	103.3	112.6	121.4	122.0	121.4	124.0
Gypsum products	94.5	103.2	102.3	104.6	117.4	117.7	117.7	117.7
Prepared asphalt roofing	94.1	103.1	102.8	101.3	104.8	102.9	106.0	106.0
Other nonmetallic minerals	93.7	102.6	103.8	106.8	111.0	112.3	111.9	115.3
Tobacco manufacturing and bottled beverages	96.0	100.4	101.6	102.4	105.1	110.6	110.8	110.8
Cigarettes	97.5	99.7	102.8	104.0	105.8	105.5	107.3	105.7
Cigars	99.5	99.8	100.6	100.8	100.6	100.1	98.0	102.4
Other tobacco products	97.6	100.3	102.2	104.1	108.4	116.6	114.8	118.4
Alcoholic beverages	97.5	101.0	101.5	102.3	106.5	110.7	111.2	111.2
Nonalcoholic beverages	99.6	100.1	100.3	101.0	119.7	119.7	119.7	119.7
Miscellaneous	100.8	103.1	96.1	96.6	104.9	108.3	108.1	105.1
Toys, sporting goods	97.1	101.4	101.5	106.9	116.2	113.5	113.5	113.1
Manufactured animal feeds	103.4	104.9	91.7	91.4	100.5	108.0	107.9	102.1
Notions and accessories	103.2	103.7	93.3	92.0	101.3	93.8	91.5	92.9
Jewelry and photographic equipment	99.9	100.6	99.5	97.4	101.1	101.0	101.0	101.0
Other miscellaneous	94.1	101.9	104.1	108.6	120.6	120.8	120.5	120.8

¹ Not available.

Source: Department of Labor, Bureau of Labor Statistics; annual report, *Wholesale Prices;* and *Monthly Labor Review.*

No. 336.—Indexes of Spot Primary Market Prices of 22 Commodities: 1939 to 1952

[1947–49=100. Figures in column heads represent number of commodities. Index is computed daily; represents unweighted geometric average of daily price quotations of 22 commodities, traded on organized exchanges. The index is much more sensitive to changes in market conditions than is monthly or weekly wholesale price index]

DATE	All commodities (22)	Foodstuffs (9)	Raw industrials (13)	Livestock and products (5)	Metals (5)	Textiles and fibers (4)	Fats and oils (4)
1939—Aug. 15	33.6	26.9	39.2	31.9	43.1	31.2	28.6
1941—Dec. 6	53.0	46.1	58.3	53.0	54.6	56.3	55.6
1945—Aug. 17	61.7	57.5	64.6	62.6	55.8	62.6	62.4
1946—June 28	67.1	63.5	69.6	64.0	60.7	71.8	67.7
1947—June 17	98.7	100.7	97.2	96.3	92.5	108.2	91.9
1948—June 15	113.6	120.6	108.8	118.1	109.8	102.8	132.9
1949—June 14	77.4	76.2	78.1	72.3	76.0	85.8	56.6
1950—June 20	88.4	85.1	90.7	71.4	98.8	96.3	59.4
1951—June 19	123.3	102.3	140.0	107.8	129.4	140.4	92.8
1952—Mar. 18	100.9	93.6	106.1	68.6	128.3	96.8	64.7
June 17	96.9	93.5	99.3	71.3	113.2	95.4	65.0
Sept. 16	95.1	90.8	98.1	67.2	114.5	98.2	62.8
Dec. 16	89.7	84.6	93.2	60.7	107.8	91.6	56.4

Source: Department of Labor, Bureau of Labor Statistics; annual report, *Wholesale Prices;* also published daily and weekly in mimeographed reports.

No. 337.—Purchasing Power of the Dollar: 1935 to 1952

[Base 1935-1939=100. Computed from indexes compiled by the U. S. Department of Labor, Bureau of Labor Statistics]

YEAR	MONTHLY AVERAGE AS MEASURED BY—			YEAR	MONTHLY AVERAGE AS MEASURED BY—		
	Whole-sale prices	Con-sumers' prices	Retail food prices		Whole-sale prices	Con-sumers' prices	Retail food prices
1935	100.5	101.9	99.5	1944	77.3	79.6	73.4
1936	99.6	100.9	98.6	1945	76.0	77.8	71.8
1937	93.2	97.4	94.9	1946	66.4	71.7	62.6
1938	102.3	99.2	102.1	1947	54.2	62.7	51.5
1939	104.3	100.6	104.9	1948	50.1	58.2	47.6
1940	102.3	99.8	103.4	1949	52.7	58.8	49.5
1941	92.1	95.1	94.7	1950	50.7	58.2	48.9
1942	81.4	85.8	80.6	1951	45.5	53.9	44.0
1943	78.0	80.8	72.4	1952	46.8	52.7	43.1

Source: Department of Commerce, Office of Business Economics; *Survey of Current Business.*

No. 338.—Wholesale Price Indexes, All Commodities and by Economic Classes: 1930 to 1952

[1929=100. Indexes are computed from price series collected by Bureau of Labor Statistics reclassified according to use and durability of product priced]

YEAR	All commodities	Pro-ducers' goods	Con-sumers' goods	Duarble goods	Non-durable goods [1]	YEAR	All commodities	Pro-ducers' goods	Con-sumers' goods	Durable goods	Non-durable goods [1]
1930	90.5	88.4	93.2	93.0	89.1	1944	110.4	112.5	108.0	112.2	110.2
1931	76.5	73.1	80.7	84.7	72.7	1945	112.6	115.4	109.1	113.8	112.6
1932	67.4	64.9	70.6	78.5	61.5	1946	129.1	131.2	126.5	124.6	131.8
1933	69.4	68.3	70.9	80.2	64.1	1947	161.7	167.2	155.2	159.2	163.7
1935	83.4	83.1	83.9	86.5	81.2	1948	175.2	182.0	166.6	175.9	175.5
1937	90.8	93.1	88.0	98.7	87.2	1949	166.4	172.8	158.2	179.6	160.4
1939	80.6	82.1	78.6	95.4	74.0	1950	173.0	181.9	161.0	186.7	166.7
1941	92.1	94.3	89.6	104.2	87.2	1951	192.6	204.3	176.5	204.9	187.0
1942	104.5	105.8	103.2	110.3	102.9	1952 [2]	187.2	196.8	174.4	205.7	178.7
1943	109.4	110.3	108.4	110.6	109.5						

[1] Perishable and semidurable.
[2] Preliminary.

Source: National Bureau of Economic Research.

No. 339.—Consumers' Price Index for Moderate-Income Families in Large Cities: 1913 to 1952

[1935-39=100. For detailed explanation, see general note, p. 300. The Consumers' Price Index has been adjusted to incorporate a correction of new unit bias in rent index beginning with indexes for 1940 and adjusted population and commodity weights beginning with indexes for January 1950. These adjustments make a continuous comparable series. See also *Historical Statistics*, series L 41-47]

YEAR AND MONTH	All items	Food	Apparel	Rent	FUEL, ELECTRICITY, AND REFRIGERATION				House-furnishings	Miscellaneous[1]
					Total	Gas and electricity	Other fuels	Ice		
1913	70.7	79.9	69.3	92.2	61.9				59.1	50.9
1914	71.8	81.8	69.8	92.2	62.3				60.7	51.9
1915	72.5	80.9	71.4	92.9	62.5				63.6	55.6
1916	77.9	90.8	78.3	94.0	65.0				70.9	56.3
1917	91.6	116.9	94.1	93.2	72.4				82.8	65.1
1918	107.5	134.4	127.5	94.9	84.2				106.4	77.8
1919	123.8	149.8	168.7	102.7	91.1				134.1	87.6
1920	143.3	168.8	201.0	120.7	106.9				164.6	100.5
1921	127.7	128.3	154.8	138.6	114.0				138.5	104.3
1922	119.7	119.9	125.6	142.7	113.1				117.5	101.2
1923	121.9	124.0	125.9	146.4	115.2				126.1	100.8
1924	122.2	122.8	124.9	151.6	113.7				124.0	101.4
1925	125.4	132.9	122.4	152.2	115.4				121.5	102.2
1926	126.4	137.4	120.6	150.7	117.2				118.8	102.6
1927	124.0	132.3	118.3	148.3	115.4				115.9	103.2
1928	122.6	130.8	116.5	144.8	113.4				113.1	103.8
1929	122.5	132.5	115.3	141.4	112.5				111.7	104.6
1930	119.4	126.0	112.7	137.5	111.4				108.9	105.1
1931	108.7	103.9	102.6	130.3	108.9				98.0	104.1
1932	97.6	86.5	90.8	116.9	103.4				85.4	101.7
1933	92.4	84.1	87.9	100.7	100.0				84.2	98.4
1934	95.7	93.7	96.1	94.4	101.4				92.8	97.9
1935	98.1	100.4	96.8	94.2	100.7	102.8	98.4	100.0	94.8	98.1
1936	99.1	101.3	97.6	98.4	100.2	100.8	99.8	100.0	96.3	98.7
1937	102.7	105.3	102.8	100.9	100.2	99.1	101.7	100.0	104.3	101.0
1938	100.8	97.8	102.2	104.1	99.9	99.0	101.0	100.0	103.3	101.5
1939	99.4	95.2	100.5	104.3	99.0	98.9	99.1	100.2	101.3	100.7
1940	100.2	96.6	101.7	104.6	99.7	98.0	101.9	100.4	100.5	101.1
1941	105.2	105.5	106.3	106.4	102.2	97.1	108.3	104.1	107.3	104.0
1942	116.6	123.9	124.2	108.8	105.4	96.7	115.1	110.0	122.2	110.9
1943	123.7	138.0	129.7	108.7	107.7	96.1	120.7	114.2	125.6	115.8
1944	125.7	136.1	138.8	109.1	109.8	95.8	126.0	115.8	136.4	121.3
1945	128.6	139.1	145.9	109.5	110.3	96.0	128.3	115.9	145.8	124.1
1946	139.5	159.6	160.2	110.1	112.4	92.3	136.9	115.9	159.2	128.8
1947	159.6	193.8	185.8	113.6	121.1	92.0	156.1	125.9	184.4	139.9
1948	171.9	210.2	198.0	121.2	133.9	94.3	183.4	135.2	195.8	149.9
1949	170.2	201.9	190.1	126.4	137.5	96.7	187.7	141.7	189.0	154.6
1950	171.2	204.1	188.0	124.1	141.1	97.0	194.8	147.8	190.8	157.1
1951	185.9	227.2	206.2	128.8	146.0	97.3	204.5	155.6	212.6	165.8
Mar. 15	184.5	225.4	204.6	127.3	146.3	97.2	205.7	154.4	212.7	165.6
June 15	185.5	227.0	205.5	128.3	145.1	97.2	202.3	156.0	214.6	166.3
Sept. 15	186.5	226.3	210.7	130.0	146.3	97.3	204.8	157.8	212.8	167.5
Dec. 15	190.0	233.9	209.1	131.8	147.1	97.5	207.0	166.3	211.8	170.5
1952:										
Mar. 15	188.4	229.2	205.6	132.9	147.4	97.8	207.1	156.5	209.2	172.0
June 15	191.1	236.0	204.0	134.0	145.9	98.7	202.1	156.8	205.7	173.9
Sept. 15	191.4	234.7	203.6	134.7	149.5	99.2	207.9	165.8	206.6	175.5
Dec. 15	191.0	230.9	202.5	137.8	153.4	99.8	217.0	166.5	206.7	176.8
ADJUSTED BASIS[2]										
1950	171.9	204.5	187.7	131.0	140.6	96.8	194.1	147.8	190.2	156.5
1951	185.6	227.4	204.5	136.2	144.1	97.2	204.5	155.6	210.9	165.4
Mar. 15	184.5	226.2	203.1	134.7	144.2	97.2	205.0	154.4	210.7	164.3
June 15	185.2	226.9	204.0	135.7	143.6	97.1	202.8	156.0	212.5	164.8
Sept. 15	186.6	227.3	209.0	137.1	144.4	97.3	204.9	157.8	211.1	166.0
Dec. 15	189.1	232.2	206.8	139.2	144.9	97.5	206.6	156.3	210.2	169.1
1952:										
Mar. 15	188.0	227.6	203.5	140.5	145.3	97.9	206.8	156.5	207.6	170.7
June 15	189.6	231.5	202.0	141.6	144.8	98.4	203.4	156.8	204.4	172.5
Sept. 15	190.8	233.2	202.3	142.4	147.6	99.0	210.1	165.8	205.0	173.8
Dec. 15	190.7	229.9	201.1	145.3	149.9	99.6	216.5	166.5	205.3	175.0

[1] Includes transportation, medical care, recreation, household operation, personal care, etc.
[2] Weights adjusted to current spending patterns.

Source: Department of Labor, Bureau of Labor Statistics; *Handbook of Labor Statistics* and *Monthly Labor Review*.

No. 340.—Cost of Living Index: 1820 to 1913

[1913=100. See also *Historical Statistics*, series L 36, for complete presentation of series and for detailed references to basic sources]

YEAR	Index	YEAR	Index	YEAR	Index	YEAR	Index	YEAR	Index
1820	65	1860	61	1892	77	1900	80	1908	91
1825	58	1865	102	1893	75	1901	82	1909	91
1830	54	1870	91	1894	73	1902	84	1910	96
1835	60	1875	86	1895	73	1903	88	1911	96
1840	60	1880	80	1896	74	1904	87	1912	102
1845	54	1885	75	1897	75	1905	87	1913	100
1850	54	1890	78	1898	75	1906	90		
1855	67	1891	76	1899	77	1907	95		

Source: Federal Reserve Bank of New York, *Index of Estimated Cost of Living in the U. S.* (1938 revision).

No. 341.—Consumers' Price Index for Moderate-Income Families in 34 Large Cities: 1929 to 1952

[1935–39 average= 100. For detailed explanation, see general note, p. 300]

CITY	DECEMBER 15, INDEX OF CONSUMERS' PRICES—ALL ITEMS						DECEMBER 15, 1952, INDEX [1] FOR—						
	1929	1932	1939	1941	1950 [1]	1951 [1]	All items	Food	Apparel	Rent	Fuel, electricity, refrigeration	House-furnish-ings	Miscellaneous
U. S. (34 cities) [2]	122.8	93.5	99.6	110.5	178.8	189.1	190.7	229.9	201.1	145.3	149.9	205.3	175.0
Atlanta	124.6	91.8	98.7	110.6	[3] 180.7	[3] 196.1	[3] 198.6	228.4	[3] 215.4	[3] 157.0	163.4	[3] 215.7	[3] 185.8
Baltimore	118.2	93.3	98.9	112.5	183.1	193.3	196.7	241.3	195.8	146.2	154.7	202.6	179.5
Birmingham	128.1	90.1	99.5	114.0	183.9	196.0	196.1	221.0	211.1	[3] 209.0	140.3	194.2	171.5
Boston	124.0	95.8	97.9	108.2	171.2	180.9	181.0	215.7	187.5	[4] 133.4	168.8	192.5	167.5
Buffalo	121.8	92.9	99.7	113.4	[3] 174.1	[3] 186.9	[3] 190.3	224.0	[3] 195.6	[4] 142.3	159.1	[3] 209.9	[3] 180.3
Chicago	129.3	93.8	99.8	110.6	183.4	194.2	195.1	232.1	206.0	163.0	139.8	192.7	177.3
Cincinnati	122.2	92.0	98.2	110.3	178.4	187.9	189.5	232.6	196.2	133.5	157.1	191.8	173.0
Cleveland	118.1	90.4	100.0	113.3	[3] 179.6	[3] 192.0	[3] 193.6	234.3	[3] 200.5	[3] 156.6	154.9	[3] 184.6	[3] 170.7
Denver	117.0	91.3	99.7	109.4	[3] 178.1	[3] 191.2	[3] 194.5	232.5	[3] 206.0	[3] 166.7	116.1	[3] 229.0	[3] 172.7
Detroit	124.7	86.2	99.8	112.7	181.3	191.9	195.8	230.7	193.5	[3] 151.2	161.5	219.0	190.6
Houston	120.7	89.3	101.3	111.5	186.1	196.0	197.5	241.2	215.2	[3] 174.6	103.1	199.4	177.9
Indianapolis	122.4	91.3	99.6	113.3	[3] 178.9	[3] 189.9	[3] 193.1	225.0	[3] 193.2	[3] 151.1	162.1	[3] 193.5	[3] 182.3
Jacksonville	128.7	92.8	99.3	114.3	185.6	195.9	198.6	236.1	193.6	168.5	143.8	199.5	186.8
Kansas City, Mo.	117.9	94.6	99.3	108.7	[3] 169.0	[3] 180.4	[3] 185.5	214.7	[3] 192.5	[3] 151.9	135.3	[3] 190.6	[3] 179.2
Los Angeles	124.4	95.0	100.4	112.4	178.5	190.4	192.7	235.4	195.9	[3] 171.0	101.8	202.4	172.0
Manchester	[5]	[5]	99.0	110.7	[3] 176.6	[3] 187.0	[3] 189.3	220.3	[3] 191.5	[3] 139.6	176.1	[3] 213.8	[3] 163.1
Memphis	121.5	90.7	98.9	111.2	182.7	191.4	191.3	233.1	215.2	163.3	142.4	182.8	161.5
Milwaukee	[5]	[5]	98.1	109.4	[3] 180.3	[3] 195.3	[3] 198.4	220.1	[3] 199.9	[3] 181.4	164.0	[3] 217.0	[3] 173.3
Minneapolis	117.2	92.8	101.1	110.7	177.7	187.7	189.7	221.6	209.1	[3] 152.2	148.2	196.5	179.2
Mobile	124.7	93.0	99.7	116.5	177.1	187.3	188.0	227.1	202.8	159.9	131.1	173.5	164.4
New Orleans	119.6	92.4	100.4	113.5	[3] 180.1	[3] 190.0	[3] 191.7	240.2	[3] 206.9	[3] 153.3	112.0	[3] 205.4	[3] 154.6
New York	123.0	97.3	100.1	108.8	175.4	184.0	185.4	228.6	204.8	[3] 120.2	152.0	196.8	174.2
Norfolk	122.4	93.6	98.5	115.6	[3] 179.3	[3] 191.7	[3] 194.5	234.6	[3] 190.5	[3] 164.4	164.4	[3] 199.2	[3] 170.9
Philadelphia	123.4	93.4	98.6	108.8	178.1	189.2	190.8	230.7	197.1	[3] 133.2	153.9	212.2	175.2
Pittsburgh	124.9	93.8	98.8	110.8	180.2	191.7	192.8	235.0	228.3	[4] 133.6	153.3	206.5	171.9
Portland, Maine	119.0	95.8	97.6	108.7	171.3	179.9	182.0	213.3	203.3	133.4	165.0	200.7	167.9
Portland, Oreg.	117.8	91.8	100.9	113.7	[3] 184.3	[3] 195.8	[3] 199.2	242.6	[3] 200.1	[3] 161.2	149.3	[3] 197.6	[3] 179.7
Richmond	118.3	92.9	98.8	110.1	[3] 173.8	[3] 183.8	[3] 186.4	216.1	[3] 203.3	[3] 158.4	151.6	[3] 216.9	[3] 163.6
St. Louis	123.6	92.3	99.1	110.6	178.8	190.2	191.8	240.4	200.0	137.2	148.0	184.7	170.1
San Francisco	118.1	95.2	100.2	111.3	181.5	193.1	197.6	240.6	195.0	141.5	107.3	173.6	191.3
Savannah	124.4	94.1	99.7	114.1	[3] 183.6	[3] 198.8	[3] 201.8	242.9	[3] 206.4	[3] 174.8	172.9	[3] 212.2	[3] 178.9
Scranton	126.9	96.1	97.4	108.3	[3] 173.1	[3] 185.4	[3] 187.9	228.9	[3] 209.7	[3] 126.6	174.5	[3] 182.4	[3] 161.3
Seattle	119.7	92.8	100.9	114.7	[3] 183.1	[3] 194.6	[3] 197.6	236.5	[3] 199.5	[3] 168.2	129.6	[3] 205.2	[3] 183.1
Washington, D. C.	114.5	94.1	98.9	109.8	[3] 173.5	[3] 184.7	[3] 186.9	225.2	[3] 218.0	[3] 128.4	158.9	[3] 216.4	[3] 177.8

[1] Adjusted basis. Weights adjusted to current spending patterns. See headnote, table 339.
[2] Indexes for food based on prices in 51 cities through 1942, 56 cities thereafter. Data for Milwaukee, except for food, not included prior to December 1940.
[3] November.   [4] September.   [5] October.   [6] Not available.

Source: Department of Labor, Bureau of Labor Statistics; *Handbook of Labor Statistics*, Bulletin 699, and *Monthly Labor Review*.

No. 342.—Consumers' Price Indexes in Selected Cities: 1939 to 1951

[January 1935=100. Annual averages of 12 monthly indices unless otherwise noted. Data cover prices of important commodities and services entering into family living expense, i. e., food, housing, clothing, fuel, light, housefurnishings, medical fees, automobile purchase and operation, carfare, etc.]

CITY	1939	1941	1944	1946	1946 [1]	1947 [2]	1948	1949	1950 [1]	1951 [3]
Akron	99.9	109.2	127.9	129.2	138.4	156.7	165.6	164.1	165.2	175.3
Atlanta	99.3	104.0	124.1	126.1	134.1	153.1	159.8	155.5	157.9	172.6
Baltimore	99.9	105.5	128.5	130.2	127.7	156.4	165.6	163.6	164.6	176.9
Birmingham	99.5	105.5	127.1	128.8	136.6	153.4	161.1	158.4	160.3	174.0
Boston	98.6	104.8	122.6	134.5	135.1	151.7	151.8	150.1	161.6	172.6
Bridgeport	100.0	106.7	128.8	127.1	138.2	154.4	166.3	162.3	162.8	174.2
Buffalo	100.7	109.0	128.3	129.4	137.4	156.5	167.4	166.6	160.4	182.4
Chattanooga	99.0	103.4	126.6	128.1	137.2	154.8	161.1	154.4	157.5	171.0
Chicago	99.5	105.6	123.5	125.6	134.5	154.5	166.4	163.5	167.9	180.1
Cincinnati	99.3	105.2	124.0	128.9	134.9	155.0	165.6	164.1	166.1	178.8
Cleveland	99.5	105.4	125.4	127.8	138.9	154.6	165.2	162.2	164.0	175.6
Dallas	99.4	102.9	134.2	127.3	133.8	149.1	159.0	160.4	167.0	180.0
Dayton	98.6	106.9	134.2	128.6	128.8	151.8	160.7	158.0	160.4	178.9
Denver	100.0	103.7	123.3	126.0	133.7	151.0	160.6	158.7	160.2	172.7
Des Moines	100.4	106.0	122.8	124.8	132.6	151.0	161.1	158.4	161.1	174.6
Detroit	99.5	107.0	128.8	131.2	139.3	156.9	166.6	164.0	164.8	180.2
Duluth	100.1	104.8	122.6	125.9	135.5	154.2	166.0	162.2	163.8	182.0
Erie, Pa.	100.6	106.4	131.6	132.8	143.4	164.5	174.0	172.0	175.6	186.8
Fall River	99.9	104.9	124.8	126.7	134.6	150.5	160.9	159.3	158.8	174.6
Grand Rapids	98.7	106.1	128.5	131.6	138.6	157.4	167.1	162.6	165.9	184.4
Green Bay, Wis.	[4]	[4]	122.0	125.1	132.4	151.2	160.8	163.5	165.1	178.2
Houston	98.4	104.4	122.5	124.4	132.0	149.0	150.0	156.3	160.2	172.8
Huntington, W. Va.	[4]	[4]	128.3	131.4	139.8	155.0	163.6	157.7	159.9	172.0
Indianapolis	99.8	107.1	127.2	130.1	140.5	156.5	165.6	165.6	162.8	180.0
Kansas City, Mo.	99.9	103.7	123.5	125.7	133.1	149.1	156.0	154.0	154.6	167.5
London	[4]	107.2	130.7	132.4	141.3	156.8	166.6	162.0	164.3	183.7
Los Angeles	99.5	104.8	125.6	128.0	135.3	150.0	158.7	156.1	156.5	172.5
Louisville	98.9	105.4	124.1	127.8	138.6	161.4	171.5	167.3	167.8	180.6
Miami	98.8	105.5	131.1	132.1	138.8	156.6	163.5	159.8	[4]	[4]
Memphis	100.0	106.1	126.5	127.9	136.5	153.1	150.5	156.9	157.1	167.7
Milwaukee	99.5	105.6	124.4	126.6	134.6	151.5	163.9	165.2	172.8	190.2
Minneapolis	100.6	106.0	125.8	127.9	137.1	157.0	169.0	165.6	[5]166.2	[5]179.1
Muskegon	[4]	110.4	130.8	133.8	144.8	164.5	172.2	169.2	169.9	187.3
Newark	98.6	104.6	123.1	124.6	133.1	149.4	160.5	158.5	156.6	166.5
New Haven	98.9	105.2	119.7	120.9	129.5	146.0	155.8	152.4	152.2	165.0
New Orleans	100.4	107.6	128.2	130.6	139.6	150.7	166.3	162.7	164.9	175.1
New York	100.0	105.7	124.6	126.1	134.6	151.5	161.2	158.9	159.5	170.6
Omaha	100.6	106.6	125.3	128.2	136.6	156.5	167.3	163.4	163.4	180.3
Peoria	98.5	105.3	125.3	127.3	136.1	153.1	163.0	158.2	159.4	178.4
Pittsburgh	98.7	105.8	124.0	125.8	134.7	153.4	163.6	160.7	161.9	177.9
Portland, Oreg.	100.2	106.7	127.3	128.4	137.2	153.8	164.0	163.1	165.2	179.2
Providence	100.1	104.6	124.4	127.9	136.5	153.1	163.0	160.2	161.0	171.0
Seattle, Va.	98.7	106.0	126.7	130.3	138.1	156.6	166.9	163.6	164.5	177.5
Richmond	[4]	[4]	129.9	131.1	140.0	150.6	166.7	167.1	167.6	182.3
Rockford	100.0	106.1	127.4	129.5	138.5	157.1	164.9	165.7	168.3	183.2
Rockford [2]	[4]	[4]	131.9	134.0	142.1	168.6	174.6	172.4	[4]	[4]
Sacramento	100.4	104.3	126.6	128.4	136.6	158.5	163.2	161.4	163.4	183.6
St. Louis	99.5	104.3	125.0	128.6	134.3	152.1	161.8	158.0	160.0	176.8
San Antonio	100.5	104.7	122.6	128.9	132.9	154.3	165.7	161.7	[4]	[4]
San Francisco-Oakland	98.4	103.7	124.8	128.1	138.2	155.5	165.9	165.0	164.2	178.9
Seattle	100.4	106.6	127.2	128.9	137.9	154.5	164.1	161.0	161.5	174.9
Spokane	100.0	106.7	125.2	127.5	136.7	151.9	160.9	159.2	161.9	174.4
Tacoma	[4]	104.7	126.5	127.9	135.7	156.6	161.4	158.5	160.9	172.7
Toledo	98.9	104.7	127.3	130.9	140.2	156.0	166.7	163.2	166.6	180.3
Wichita, Wis.	100.1	107.2	125.9	128.4	137.7	157.0	166.0	165.7	[4]	[4]
Wilmington, Del.	100.0	106.2	124.1	125.1	134.3	150.1	159.2	156.8	156.9	180.4
Youngstown	98.7	107.4	127.3	130.5	138.3	154.5	163.5	150.6	[4]	[4]

[1] Average of four quarterly indexes.
[2] Weighted average of two quarterly indexes and six monthly indexes.
[3] 12-month average. Beginning March 1950: Price movements in 10 key cities measured monthly; for other cities (surveyed quarterly on a staggered schedule), preceding surveyed index used for each nonsurveyed month.
[4] Not available.
[5] Discontinued.
[6] St. Paul combined with Minneapolis.

Source: National Industrial Conference Board, New York, N. Y.; The Economic Almanac.

No. 348.—Indexes of Retail Prices of Foods, by Group: 1929 to 1952

[1935-39 average=100. See general note, p. 300]

YEAR AND MONTH	All foods	Cereals and bakery products	Meats, poultry, and fish	Dairy products	Eggs	Fruits and Vegetables					Beverages	Fats and oils	Sugar and sweets
						Total	Frozen [1]	Fresh	Canned	Dried			
1929	132.5	107.6	127.1	131.0	143.8	169.0		173.5	124.3	171.0	164.8	127.2	114.3
1930	126.0	104.3	119.1	121.0	121.4	177.5		185.7	118.6	158.7	143.4	119.2	107.4
1931	103.9	91.4	101.1	102.8	95.6	125.7		125.7	103.3	118.7	124.6	96.0	99.1
1932	86.5	82.6	79.3	84.9	82.3	103.5		106.9	91.1	91.2	112.6	71.1	89.6
1933	84.1	84.7	68.9	82.8	77.9	113.8		118.9	87.9	88.4	102.4	66.4	94.3
1934	93.7	98.3	78.9	90.9	88.6	119.1		122.3	103.9	101.1	107.6	76.4	97.9
1935	100.4	101.8	99.9	97.5	104.2	99.7		98.8	106.2	100.8	104.0	110.3	100.7
1936	101.3	100.7	98.9	101.6	103.3	104.8		106.2	100.9	96.6	99.4	102.8	99.6
1937	105.3	103.3	105.8	105.4	101.2	107.9		106.6	103.2	116.0	103.6	105.8	101.2
1938	97.8	99.8	98.9	99.6	100.3	93.2		92.1	97.4	93.3	97.7	93.5	97.9
1939	95.2	94.5	96.6	95.9	91.0	94.5		95.1	92.3	93.3	95.5	87.7	100.6
1940	96.6	96.8	95.8	101.4	93.8	96.5		97.3	92.4	100.6	92.5	82.2	96.8
1941	105.5	97.9	107.5	112.0	112.2	103.2		104.2	97.9	106.7	101.5	94.0	106.4
1942	123.9	105.1	126.0	125.4	136.5	130.8		132.8	121.6	136.3	122.1	119.6	126.5
1943	138.0	107.6	133.8	134.6	161.9	169.8		178.0	130.6	158.9	124.8	126.1	127.1
1944	136.1	108.4	129.9	133.6	153.9	168.2		177.2	129.5	164.5	124.3	123.3	126.5
1945	139.1	109.0	131.2	133.9	164.4	177.1		188.2	130.2	168.2	124.7	124.0	126.5
1946	159.6	125.0	161.3	165.1	168.8	182.4		190.7	140.8	190.4	139.6	152.1	143.9
1947	193.8	155.4	217.1	186.2	200.8	199.4		201.5	166.2	263.5	186.8	197.5	180.0
1948	210.2	170.9	246.5	204.8	208.7	205.2		212.4	158.0	246.8	205.0	195.3	174.0
1949	201.9	169.7	233.4	186.7	201.2	208.1		218.8	152.9	227.4	220.7	148.4	176.4
ADJUSTED BASIS [2]													
1950	204.5	172.7	243.6	184.7	173.6	199.2		206.1	146.0	228.5	312.5	144.3	179.9
Jan. 15	196.0	169.0	219.4	184.2	152.3	204.8		217.2	143.3	223.9	299.5	135.2	178.9
Feb. 15	194.9	169.1	222.0	183.6	140.8	199.3		208.7	142.7	222.1	303.3	133.6	178.0
Mar. 15	196.6	169.1	229.3	182.4	149.5	195.1		202.0	142.6	221.5	308.5	134.3	177.0
Apr. 15	197.3	169.3	231.1	179.6	149.8	198.9		208.1	142.3	221.6	305.5	135.6	175.1
May 15	199.8	169.8	240.2	178.3	143.7	202.2		213.6	142.0	222.9	299.1	137.7	174.4
June 15	203.1	169.8	246.5	177.8	148.4	209.3		224.3	142.7	222.9	296.5	140.1	174.3
July 15	208.2	171.5	255.7	180.7	163.3	211.5		227.7	142.7	222.9	303.0	141.8	175.7
Aug. 15	209.9	175.5	260.7	184.3	182.2	193.4		196.9	145.7	227.6	321.3	153.9	185.6
Sept. 15	210.0	176.9	261.0	186.9	192.1	186.9		183.9	147.6	229.8	327.3	154.8	185.4
Oct. 15	210.6	177.2	253.3	191.9	206.2	189.8		187.7	151.6	236.1	333.4	152.9	184.8
Nov. 15	210.6	177.1	250.3	192.8	205.4	195.7		195.9	153.2	242.2	325.5	152.9	184.6
Dec. 15	216.3	177.7	253.4	194.0	249.4	203.9	100.0	207.3	155.3	248.8	327.5	158.5	184.9
1951	227.4	188.5	272.2	206.0	211.3	217.9	98.6	223.3	165.9	249.9	344.5	168.8	186.6
Jan. 15	221.9	185.4	263.6	202.6	191.5	214.1	100.2	220.0	160.6	253.4	340.6	171.5	185.6
Feb. 15	226.0	187.1	270.1	204.4	179.8	224.3	100.8	233.4	165.1	256.7	342.7	176.5	186.0
Mar. 15	226.2	187.5	272.2	204.6	195.2	217.1	101.2	220.7	167.0	257.4	342.6	177.3	186.0
Apr. 15	225.7	188.3	272.6	204.1	191.2	214.8	100.2	215.9	168.9	257.8	343.5	178.3	185.9
May 15	227.4	188.2	272.7	203.5	198.4	221.6	99.6	229.5	169.6	256.7	345.3	176.7	185.4
June 15	226.9	188.4	271.6	203.9	201.2	219.9	98.8	223.5	170.4	254.4	345.2	175.2	186.1
July 15	227.7	189.0	273.2	205.1	211.5	218.5	98.8	221.8	170.0	250.7	344.8	168.8	188.0
Aug. 15	227.0	188.7	275.0	205.9	225.8	208.9	98.0	209.1	165.8	248.5	345.2	162.7	188.3
Sept. 15	227.3	189.4	275.6	206.4	239.2	205.1	97.5	204.3	164.2	245.6	345.0	161.5	188.2
Oct. 15	229.2	189.4	276.6	207.9	243.4	210.8	97.5	214.4	162.8	240.6	345.8	160.6	187.0
Nov. 15	231.4	190.2	273.5	210.4	241.8	223.5	95.9	235.0	162.7	239.1	346.6	158.5	186.7
Dec. 15	232.2	190.4	270.1	213.2	216.7	236.5	95.0	255.4	163.3	238.9	346.8	137.8	186.4
1952:													
Jan. 15	232.4	190.6	272.1	215.8	184.3	241.4	95.0	263.2	163.8	238.6	346.7	155.3	185.9
Feb. 15	227.5	190.9	271.1	217.0	166.5	223.5	94.2	234.6	163.6	238.4	347.1	150.9	185.1
Mar. 15	227.6	191.2	267.7	215.7	161.3	232.1	92.5	248.4	163.9	238.3	347.1	145.6	184.3
Apr. 15	230.0	191.1	266.7	212.6	165.9	247.2	91.5	272.8	163.5	236.9	347.3	143.1	186.2
May 15	230.8	193.8	266.0	210.6	164.0	253.8	88.7	283.4	163.7	236.8	346.6	139.9	187.3
June 15	231.5	193.9	265.0	209.8	169.1	250.0	90.0	278.1	162.3	237.1	346.5	140.1	187.7
July 15	234.9	194.4	270.4	212.3	206.7	253.2	90.1	283.0	162.4	238.9	346.4	140.6	188.9
Aug. 15	235.5	194.2	273.3	213.8	217.2	242.3	90.8	265.3	162.6	241.4	346.6	141.4	189.9
Sept. 15	233.2	194.1	277.0	216.7	221.4	227.6	90.3	241.0	164.2	243.5	346.6	141.1	190.4
Oct. 15	232.4	194.3	271.5	218.1	230.6	227.3	89.0	240.3	164.8	244.7	346.8	140.7	190.7
Nov. 15	232.3	194.3	265.5	218.2	226.0	236.7	89.0	254.3	166.0	248.1	346.1	140.3	190.6
Dec. 15	229.9	194.5	262.4	217.1	201.8	236.4	88.3	254.0	165.9	248.8	347.0	139.8	190.5

[1] December 1950=100.
[2] Weights adjusted to current spending patterns.

Source: Department of Labor, Bureau of Labor Statistics; *Handbook of Labor Statistics*, Serial No. R1172, and *Monthly Labor Review*.

No. 844.—INDEXES OF RETAIL PRICES OF FOODS, BY CITY: 1929 TO 1952

[1935-39 average=100. Sales taxes included wherever applicable. See general note, p. 309]

REGION AND CITY	1929	1933	1939	1941	1945	1949	1950 [1]	1951 [1] Avg.	1951 [1] June	1951 [1] Dec.	1952 [1] June	1952 [1] Dec.
United States [2]	132.5	84.5	95.2	105.5	139.1	201.9	204.5	227.4	226.9	222.2	231.5	229.9
New England:												
Boston	137.1	80.2	95.3	102.7	133.6	192.9	195.6	215.0	214.9	219.3	219.9	215.7
Bridgeport	137.2	86.1	94.8	104.9	135.9	200.0	203.8	225.7	226.9	228.9	230.2	230.0
Fall River	130.5	84.6	96.0	104.9	132.9	198.8	200.9	220.9	221.3	223.8	225.2	219.5
Manchester	177.0	82.9	96.1	104.5	136.2	199.4	200.9	219.9	221.0	220.9	223.9	220.3
New Haven	128.4	85.2	94.7	105.9	136.0	198.0	190.1	230.0	230.5	222.2	225.3	222.0
Portland, Maine	137.3	90.9	93.6	103.5	133.6	191.9	194.1	213.1	213.9	216.1	219.0	213.3
Providence	132.9	86.6	94.9	104.6	136.1	207.1	207.8	230.2	230.6	234.1	238.5	229.0
Middle Atlantic:												
Buffalo	132.6	85.7	96.9	105.5	136.8	196.2	196.7	231.8	234.3	236.7	237.0	234.0
Newark	137.2	89.3	96.7	106.7	141.4	198.6	202.2	225.3	225.5	227.2	226.4	220.2
New York	133.4	92.5	96.5	106.0	140.1	202.7	204.7	226.3	224.4	230.5	226.9	226.8
Philadelphia	130.3	86.5	94.4	102.4	137.1	197.4	201.3	223.8	222.2	226.8	226.5	220.7
Pittsburgh	135.4	83.9	93.6	106.2	136.6	205.8	208.1	230.4	230.3	234.6	232.9	224.6
Rochester	131.8	84.6	94.9	106.9	135.6	198.5	197.7	230.4	232.9	227.4	236.7	226.7
Scranton	140.6	88.7	94.8	104.9	139.4	201.4	202.6	236.0	236.7	230.9	230.8	226.9
East North Central:												
Chicago	133.2	87.5	94.9	106.2	137.8	207.4	209.4	233.3	233.4	238.1	239.3	222.1
Cincinnati	135.6	82.9	92.3	105.0	137.6	201.5	206.2	227.9	226.9	230.4	236.9	226.8
Cleveland	131.1	82.4	96.3	107.7	143.2	209.0	211.4	235.0	235.1	238.5	242.5	234.3
Columbus	131.5	83.6	92.8	102.2	131.8	194.3	186.5	207.6	208.5	211.3	214.3	214.1
Detroit	133.9	78.5	92.7	104.9	135.6	196.6	205.5	230.2	229.4	234.5	234.3	230.7
Indianapolis	138.3	85.5	93.5	105.3	135.4	197.9	201.5	228.6	222.4	227.0	226.9	225.0
Milwaukee	131.6	87.1	93.7	104.0	137.4	202.2	208.8	228.7	229.9	232.6	237.9	230.1
Peoria	136.6	81.6	96.0	106.2	143.3	212.4	216.9	238.0	241.2	242.5	243.3	232.6
Springfield	131.7	81.7	95.5	106.6	144.2	208.0	213.3	238.4	236.5	242.6	245.9	240.6
West North Central:												
Cedar Rapids [4]	(4)	(4)	(4)	104.1	142.5	206.1	211.1	235.9	237.2	239.8	240.6	235.3
Kansas City, Mo.	129.5	84.2	94.3	101.2	133.0	188.9	191.2	213.0	212.8	218.0	216.8	214.7
Minneapolis	125.0	80.3	97.2	106.6	132.6	192.0	195.2	215.4	219.4	224.0	226.8	221.6
Omaha	128.8	81.4	94.7	103.7	131.9	196.4	197.8	219.7	219.6	227.0	225.9	221.5
St. Louis	128.1	80.4	95.7	107.5	141.4	206.9	213.7	235.9	236.2	233.7	235.3	230.4
St. Paul	128.3	82.5	96.1	104.1	130.9	189.7	192.7	216.4	216.2	223.7	225.1	220.4
Wichita	(4)	(4)	(4)	105.9	140.6	213.1	213.3	238.4	234.9	245.8	344.9	247.5
South Atlantic:												
Atlanta	141.8	86.1	94.3	103.8	140.0	199.3	201.8	228.5	228.1	230.7	236.8	228.4
Baltimore	124.1	83.0	96.7	107.0	147.4	212.8	215.3	238.3	238.9	242.5	242.4	241.3
Charleston, S.C.	128.0	84.9	96.4	104.7	136.9	192.4	191.8	218.5	211.6	221.5	222.8	222.1
Jacksonville	121.8	84.8	96.7	106.6	148.2	206.3	209.5	233.0	231.9	235.0	236.2	226.1
Norfolk	136.0	88.6	94.2	107.4	143.5	204.2	204.4	230.0	229.2	233.6	226.0	234.6
Richmond	133.9	85.4	92.9	103.4	136.4	196.8	196.8	217.2	216.4	218.3	214.6	216.1
Savannah	133.4	84.1	96.7	109.8	153.7	211.4	216.8	237.9	239.6	241.7	242.9	242.9
Washington	134.6	80.2	96.0	104.4	139.9	200.5	202.6	234.3	234.2	226.9	227.2	226.2
Winston-Salem [3]	(4)	(4)	(4)	102.0	140.5	198.8	200.0	220.7	220.6	222.8	219.0	222.5
East South Central:												
Birmingham	143.5	86.3	91.9	103.3	142.4	198.2	196.6	219.7	216.4	222.7	217.4	221.0
Jackson	(4)	(4)	(4)	111.4	149.7	205.6	206.0	235.3	231.9	239.2	235.2	227.6
Knoxville	(4)	(4)	(4)	104.9	159.3	223.5	227.9	262.7	349.8	256.6	251.5	255.4
Louisville	132.9	80.5	93.9	104.2	132.8	191.1	192.3	215.1	215.6	219.1	215.6	214.6
Memphis	138.0	86.8	92.7	103.8	145.1	213.2	212.1	234.3	233.0	238.9	235.6	232.3
Mobile	136.5	85.5	96.3	108.9	147.1	206.2	203.9	226.8	226.7	231.4	230.4	227.1
West South Central:												
Austin	137.2	85.1	92.5	101.0	135.9	204.4	206.4	230.6	227.9	235.4	232.0	231.2
Dallas	130.1	80.3	97.5	108.9	138.7	211.6	214.5	247.4	245.2	241.3	247.3	241.2
Houston	135.5	79.9	94.8	104.3	136.6	199.7	203.8	234.9	226.2	239.9	226.7	228.0
New Orleans	134.3	84.0	95.1	110.7	153.3	212.6	216.9	240.3	238.2	244.3	241.4	240.2
Mountain:												
Butte	132.2	84.6	96.0	105.9	134.6	201.7	203.7	226.7	225.5	233.7	231.7	226.6
Denver	130.6	81.6	94.6	102.2	138.6	203.4	207.6	222.3	222.6	229.9	225.1	232.5
Salt Lake City	128.9	81.7	96.8	105.1	142.9	204.8	204.7	228.2	230.0	223.4	224.8	233.6
Pacific:												
Los Angeles	136.2	85.5	96.2	107.7	145.6	205.8	205.5	232.0	230.9	240.7	235.4	235.4
Portland, Oreg.	128.1	84.7	98.3	111.5	149.5	215.6	221.4	240.9	241.3	243.9	240.0	242.6
San Francisco	127.5	80.5	96.0	107.0	148.2	215.3	213.2	226.6	227.4	246.4	247.4	245.0
Seattle	128.6	87.4	97.2	116.2	144.4	208.9	211.1	234.5	233.6	239.9	237.5	236.5

[1] Adjusted basis. Weights adjusted to current spending patterns.
[2] Based on costs in 51 cities prior to March 1943, 56 cities thereafter.
[3] Based on June 1940=100. [4] Not available.

Source: Department of Labor, Bureau of Labor Statistics; Handbook of Labor Statistics and Monthly Labor Review.

No. 345.—Average Retail Prices of Selected Foods: 1913 to 1952

[Prices in cents per pound except for milk (cents per quart), eggs and oranges (cents per dozen), and tomatoes (cents per No. 2 can). Data are averages of prices as reported by retail dealers in 51 large cities prior to 1943 and in 56 cities thereafter. Prices for individual cities combined with use of population weights]

YEAR AND MONTH	Wheat flour	Corn meal	Bread, white	Round steak	Chuck roast	Pork chops	Bacon, sliced	Ham, whole	Lamb, leg	Chickens, roasting	Butter	Cheese
1913	3.3	3.0	5.6	22.3	16.0	21.0	27.0	......	18.9	21.3	38.3	22.1
1920	8.1	6.5	11.5	39.5	26.2	42.3	52.3	......	39.3	44.7	70.1	41.6
1922	5.1	3.9	8.7	32.3	19.7	33.0	39.8	......	36.6	36.0	47.9	32.9
1929	5.1	5.3	8.8	46.0	31.4	37.5	43.9	......	40.2	41.2	55.5	39.5
1932	3.2	3.6	7.0	29.7	18.5	21.5	24.2	......	23.8	25.6	27.8	24.4
1939	3.8	4.0	7.9	36.0	23.4	30.4	31.9	27.5	28.2	30.6	32.5	25.3
1941	4.5	4.3	8.1	1	5	34.3	34.3	30.4	29.7	32.6	41.1	30.0
1945	6.4	6.4	8.8	6	1	37.1	41.1	34.7	40.0	46.6	50.7	35.6
1946	7.1	7.5	10.4	.1	.6	48.5	53.3	47.8	48.7	52.6	71.0	50.1
1947	9.6	9.8	12.5	6	.5	72.1	77.7	67.5	64.2	55.3	80.5	59.0
1948	9.8	10.8	13.9	39.5	25.4	77.2	76.9	68.0	71.1	61.3	86.7	65.6
1949	9.6	9.1	14.0	88.3	84.5	74.3	66.5	63.4	72.5	(1)	72.5	(1)
1950	9.8	9.0	14.3	93.6	.6	4	7	62.0	74.4	(2)	72.9	51.8
Mar. 15	9.7	8.4	14.0	85.4	8	4	0	58.2	71.0	(2)	73.0	52.0
June 15	9.8	8.7	14.0	97.5	0	7	.7	63.5	77.3	(2)	71.1	51.1
Sept. 15	9.9	9.7	14.6	97.2	61.6	75.4	63.2	68.7	76.3	(2)	72.3	51.8
Dec. 15	9.9	9.4	14.7	100.8	63.5	66.5	69.5	62.5	77.5	(2)	76.3	52.6
1951	10.4	9.6	15.7	109.3	74.1	79.4	2	66.5	83.1	(2)	81.9	59.1
Mar. 15	10.4	9.6	15.6	107.5	73.2	77.9	0	67.6	80.7	(2)	81.6	60.2
June 15	10.4	9.4	15.7	108.9	73.9	77.7	8	67.0	84.2	(2)	81.5	59.2
Sept. 15	10.4	9.6	15.7	109.2	74.0	85.2	67.9	67.4	84.1	(2)	80.0	58.7
Dec. 15	10.5	9.8	15.8	112.7	76.4	74.6	66.0	63.8	86.3	(2)	87.9	59.6
1952:												
Mar. 15	10.5	10.2	15.8	111.6	75.3	74.3	61.3	62.2	79.6	(2)	80.5	60.1
June 15	10.5	10.2	16.1	111.5	73.9	85.0	63.8	66.4	83.9	(2)	81.4	60.0
Sept. 15	10.4	10.6	16.2	109.7	73.0	87.8	70.8	69.3	83.0	(2)	85.9	61.0
Dec. 15	10.4	10.5	16.2	108.1	70.4	72.3	64.6	65.0	75.3	(2)	81.7	61.8

YEAR AND MONTH	Milk, fresh (delivered)	Eggs	Bananas	Oranges	Cabbage	Onions	Potatoes	Tomatoes		Coffee	Lard	Sugar
1913	8.9	34.5					1.7			29.8	15.8	5.5
1920	16.7	68.1	12.6	63.2	6.4	7.1	6.3	14.8	28.1	47.0	29.5	19.4
1922	13.1	44.4	10.3	57.4	4.6	7.9	2.8	13.4	20.1	36.1	17.0	7.3
1929	14.4	52.7	9.7	44.7	5.3	6.7	3.2	12.8	15.3	47.9	18.1	6.4
1932	10.7	30.2	6.5	30.2	4.1	5.0	1.7	9.3	9.2	29.4	8.7	5.0
1939	12.2	32.1	6.3	28.9	3.6	3.8	2.5	8.6	8.9	22.4	11.0	5.4
1941	13.6	39.7	7.2	31.0	4.2	5.0	2.3	9.1	9.8	23.6	12.7	5.7
1945	15.6	58.1	10.4	48.5	6.1	6.9	4.9	12.2	17.5	30.5	18.8	6.7
1946	17.6	56.6	11.6	49.9	5.9	6.9	4.7	15.0	19.1	34.4	26.3	7.7
1947	19.6	69.6	15.1	43.4	7.3	7.4	5.0	19.3	24.7	46.9	31.5	9.7
1948	21.8	72.3	15.9	44.7	6.6	10.6	5.6	16.5	21.4	51.4	29.6	9.4
1949	21.1	69.6	16.6	51.8	6.7	7.4	5.5	15.2	23.1	55.4	19.2	9.5
1950	20.6	60.4	16.3	49.3	5.9	6.8	4.6	14.7	24.6	79.4	19.1	9.7
Mar. 15	20.3	52.0	16.8	50.2	6.8	6.4	4.7	14.3	23.7	78.1	16.5	9.8
June 15	19.6	51.6	16.4	48.9	6.6	7.7	5.3	14.5	24.2	74.2	17.3	9.4
Sept. 15	20.9	66.8	14.9	49.3	5.0	6.2	4.3	14.8	24.7	84.5	23.3	10.1
Dec. 15	21.9	86.8	16.4	47.3	5.9	5.5	4.0	15.8	27.0	83.3	22.3	10.0
1951	23.1	73.7	16.3	48.7	8.6	7.9	5.1	18.8	27.4	86.8	24.6	10.1
Mar. 15	22.8	68.1	16.6	47.3	14.5	7.3	4.4	19.4	27.6	86.3	25.9	10.1
June 15	22.7	70.2	16.4	47.7	6.5	10.2	5.6	20.6	27.6	87.2	24.7	10.0
Sept. 15	23.3	83.5	16.0	55.3	5.8	7.0	4.7	18.0	27.8	86.9	24.2	10.1
Dec. 15	23.9	75.6	16.1	46.8	10.0	8.6	6.5	17.5	26.5	86.9	23.1	10.1
1952:												
Mar. 15	24.1	56.2	17.0	45.7	7.4	12.9	6.9	29.3	25.9	87.0	19.3	10.0
June 15	23.7	50.0	16.8	48.4	8.6	11.4	8.6	33.0	26.9	86.8	18.2	10.2
Sept. 15	24.5	77.2	16.2	57.8	7.5	9.0	7.6	17.3	27.1	86.7	17.5	10.5
Dec. 15	24.8	70.4	16.1	47.2	7.7	10.9	7.3	28.1	28.0	86.6	16.1	10.1

[1] Not available.
[2] Pricing discontinued. Fryers substituted April 1949.

Source: Department of Labor, Bureau of Labor Statistics, *Handbook of Labor Statistics*, Serial No. R1172, and *Monthly Labor Review*.

No. 846.—COAL—AVERAGE RETAIL PRICES AND INDEXES FOR LARGE CITIES COMBINED: 1935 TO 1952

[Unweighted average for bituminous; weighted average for anthracite. Prices not directly comparable because of change in number of dealers reporting number of quotations received or number of cities from which prices are collected over period covered. See also *Historical Statistics*, series L 50-51]

YEAR AND MONTH	AVERAGE PRICE PER TON OF 2,000 POUNDS			INDEX (1935-39=100)		
	Bitumi-nous	Pennsylvania anthracite		Bitumi-nous	Pennsylvania anthracite	
		Stove	Chestnut		All sizes	Chestnut
1935	$8.29	$11.38	$11.14	97.2	101.1	100.9
1939	8.52	10.79	10.84	101.1	98.4	98.1
1941	9.10	11.92	11.97	108.2	108.5	107.8
1946	10.95	15.96	15.97	132.4	145.0	143.8
1947	12.99	17.23	17.11	156.5	157.3	155.7
1948	15.40	19.24	19.10	186.2	176.6	174.1
1949	15.83	20.34	20.13	193.1	186.7	182.2
1950	16.48	21.38	21.07	200.2	195.9	190.9
1951	16.87	23.70	23.16	204.6	214.9	210.8
1951: September	16.84	23.90	23.32	204.7	216.6	212.3
December	17.08	24.22	23.67	207.3	219.0	215.2
1952: March	¹ 16.16	(²)	23.31	207.3	219.3	215.2
June	¹ 16.02	(²)	21.77	205.5	208.8	201.0
September	¹ 16.28	(²)	22.92	208.7	216.8	211.6
December	¹ 16.72	(²)	24.69	214.4	235.7	227.9

¹ Weighted average price; not comparable with previous data.
² Not available.

Source: Department of Labor, Bureau of Labor Statistics; data through 1941 from Bulletin No. 707. Later data published currently in monthly releases and in *Monthly Labor Review*.

No. 347.—AVERAGE TYPICAL BILLS FOR SPECIFIED QUANTITIES OF ELECTRIC ENERGY IN CITIES OF 50,000 POPULATION OR MORE: 1933 TO 1952

[25,100, and 250 kilowatt-hour consumptions were chosen to represent the typical usage, respectively, of residential consumers who use electricity for lighting and the operation of small appliances only; for lighting, small appliances, and refrigeration; and for lighting, small appliances, refrigeration, and cooking]

DATE	AVERAGE BILL IN DOLLARS FOR—			AVERAGE BILL IN CENTS PER KILOWATT-HOUR FOR—			INDEX OF AVERAGE BILL (JAN. 1, 1935=100) FOR—		
	25 kw.-hrs.	100 kw.-hrs.	250 kw.-hrs.	25 kw.-hrs.	100 kw.-hrs.	250 kw.-hrs.	25 kw.-hrs.	100 kw.-hrs.	250 kw.-hrs.
Oct. 1, 1933	1.63	4.58	9.26	6.5	4.6	3.7	103.8	102.9	103.3
Oct. 1, 1934	1.58	4.47	8.98	6.3	4.5	3.6	100.6	100.4	100.2
Jan. 1, 1935 ¹	1.57	4.45	8.96	6.3	4.5	3.6	100.0	100.0	100.0
Jan. 1, 1935 ²	1.60	4.47	8.90	6.3	4.5	3.6	100.0	100.0	100.0
Jan. 1, 1936	1.53	4.21	7.85	6.1	4.2	3.1	95.6	94.2	88.2
Jan. 1, 1937	1.45	4.10	7.51	5.8	4.1	3.0	90.6	91.7	84.4
Jan. 1, 1938	1.43	4.03	7.34	5.7	4.0	2.9	89.4	90.2	82.5
Jan. 1, 1939	1.40	3.96	7.21	5.6	4.0	2.9	87.5	88.6	81.0
Jan. 1, 1940	1.36	3.88	7.05	5.4	3.9	2.8	85.0	86.6	79.2
Jan. 1, 1941	1.34	3.83	6.96	5.4	3.8	2.8	83.8	85.7	78.4
Jan. 1, 1942	1.34	3.80	6.95	5.4	3.8	2.8	83.8	85.0	78.1
Jan. 1, 1943	1.33	3.80	6.94	5.3	3.8	2.8	83.1	85.0	78.0
Jan. 1, 1944	1.33	3.78	6.92	5.3	3.8	2.8	83.1	84.6	77.8
Jan. 1, 1945	1.32	3.76	6.89	5.3	3.8	2.8	82.5	84.1	77.4
Jan. 1, 1946	1.28	3.73	6.86	5.1	3.7	2.7	80.0	83.4	77.1
Jan. 1, 1947	1.23	3.64	6.78	4.9	3.6	2.7	76.9	81.4	76.2
Jan. 1, 1948	1.24	3.64	6.79	5.0	3.6	2.7	77.5	81.4	76.3
Jan. 1, 1949	1.25	3.68	6.87	5.0	3.7	2.7	78.1	82.3	77.2
Jan. 1, 1950	1.24	3.64	6.81	5.0	3.6	2.7	77.5	81.4	76.5
Jan. 1, 1951	1.24	3.62	6.77	5.0	3.6	2.7	77.5	81.0	76.1
Jan. 1, 1952	1.24	3.63	6.79	5.0	3.6	2.7	77.5	81.2	76.3

¹ Average bills for 1935 and prior years are for 150 cities of 50,000 population or more. The index numbers are adjusted to be comparable with subsequent years.
² Average bills for 1935 and subsequent years are for all cities of 50,000 population or more.

Source: Federal Power Commission; annual report, *Typical Electric Bills, Including Residential, Commercial and Industrial Service: Cities of 50,000 Population and More*.

No. 348.—Lowest and Highest Net Monthly Residential Electric Bills for 100 Kilowatt-Hours Use, Based on Rates as of Jan. 1, 1952, for Communities of 2,500 Population and More, by States

DIVISION AND STATE	SERVED BY PRIVATELY OWNED UTILITIES		SERVED BY PUBLICLY OWNED UTILITIES		COMMUNITIES OF 50,000 POPULATION AND MORE		COMMUNITIES OF 10,000 TO 50,000 POPULATION		COMMUNITIES OF 2,500 TO 10,000 POPULATION	
	Utilities	Communities	Utilities	Communities	Lowest bills	Highest bills	Lowest bills	Highest bills	Lowest bills	Highest bills
New England:										
Maine	6	45	3	3	¹ $4.70	¹ $4.70	$4.40	$4.70	*$4.00	$5.92
New Hampshire	6	20	1	1	¹ 4.72	¹ 4.72	4.01	4.94	4.05	*5.00
Vermont	4	16	1	1	(²)	(²)	*4.07	5.00	4.00	5.00
Massachusetts	28	119	22	23	3.15	4.74	*2.93	5.77	*2.41	6.80
Rhode Island	3	23			4.60	4.61	4.58	4.61	4.58	4.61
Connecticut	8	58	7	8	3.60	4.16	*3.26	4.31	3.60	4.60
Middle Atlantic:										
New York	16	236	24	25	2.78	5.10	*2.41	5.17	*2.53	5.53
New Jersey	6	215	6	7	3.67	4.62	3.67	*5.75	3.67	*5.90
Pennsylvania	22	381	24	24	3.65	5.00	3.55	5.00	3.55	6.05
East North Central:										
Ohio	10	178	46	48	3.35	3.82	3.35	*4.60	3.35	*5.30
Indiana	6	88	34	34	*2.75	3.95	*3.20	*4.75	*3.05	*5.15
Illinois	12	219	34	34	2.78	3.85	2.78	4.55	2.78	*6.50
Michigan	11	123	30	31	3.45	3.73	*2.96	4.15	*3.00	*5.05
Wisconsin	11	71	34	35	2.60	4.51	*2.60	4.51	*2.50	4.84
West North Central:										
Minnesota	7	43	47	47	3.56	3.96	*2.30	4.61	3.15	*6.25
Iowa	11	68	27	27	3.00	4.80	2.85	*5.00	3.00	*6.08
Missouri	11	77	38	38	2.85	3.65	2.85	*4.74	2.85	*6.00
North Dakota	3	11	2	2	(²)	(²)	3.75	4.00	*3.38	4.48
South Dakota	6	19	7	7	¹ 3.75	¹ 3.75	*4.25	5.01	3.75	*6.00
Nebraska			29	40	*2.79	*3.20	*2.64	*3.95	*3.20	*4.70
Kansas	8	37	32	32	*2.80	3.80	*2.60	*5.20	*3.25	*7.50
South Atlantic:										
Delaware	1	4	6	6	¹ 4.50	¹ 4.50	(²)	(²)	4.55	*6.30
Maryland	6	36	3	3	¹ 3.77	¹ 3.77	2.88	4.92	2.88	5.96
Virginia	6	72	13	14	2.88	3.82	*2.50	4.25	3.40	5.50
West Virginia	7	56	2	2	3.82	3.82	3.82	4.25	3.75	4.41
North Carolina	5	67	36	37	3.20	3.40	3.20	*4.70	3.20	*6.20
South Carolina	5	60	18	19	3.20	3.92	3.20	*4.00	*2.56	*4.32
Georgia	6	65	39	39	3.35	4.40	*3.10	*4.60	*2.50	*4.90
Florida	5	77	25	25	3.75	*5.33	4.00	*6.00	4.00	*6.94
District of Columbia	1	1			¹ 2.88	¹ 2.88				
East South Central:										
Kentucky	6	56	16	16	2.50	3.78	*2.25	*4.85	*2.25	5.80
Tennessee	3	3	58	68	*2.50	*2.50	*2.00	3.35	*2.00	*4.65
Alabama	5	56	30	32	2.75	3.10	*2.00	*4.55	*2.00	*4.75
Mississippi	2	32	21	21	¹ 3.94	¹ 3.94	*2.00	*5.00	*2.00	*6.45
West South Central:										
Arkansas	6	50	14	14	¹ 3.75	¹ 3.75	3.69	4.12	*3.22	*5.50
Louisiana	6	56	23	23	3.68	4.05	3.68	*5.50	3.68	*6.50
Oklahoma	4	58	29	29	3.57	3.69	3.57	*5.50	3.57	*6.61
Texas	12	227	52	56	2.83	4.48	2.83	5.23	*2.15	*7.25
Mountain:										
Montana	3	24	2	2	(²)	(²)	3.83	3.83	3.14	*5.00
Idaho	7	28	4	4	(²)	(²)	3.11	*3.40	*2.79	4.36
Wyoming	9	17	3	3	(²)	(²)	3.35	4.18	3.60	5.55
Colorado	7	23	12	13	3.30	4.07	*3.35	*4.37	*3.11	*5.50
New Mexico	5	16	8	8	¹ 3.56	¹ 3.56	3.75	4.62	3.56	*5.90
Arizona	7	26	3	3	¹ 3.45	¹ 3.45	*3.00	3.17	3.29	5.30
Utah	3	19	14	14	3.10	3.10	*2.79	*2.79	*2.70	4.52
Nevada	5	8	2	2	(²)	(²)	2.16	3.51	2.16	5.70
Pacific:										
Washington	3	35	21	32	*1.70	2.76	2.72	*3.25	*1.75	*3.50
Oregon	6	45	9	9	¹ 3.05	¹ 3.05	*1.80	3.38	*2.25	*3.65
California	9	264	23	29	*2.77	3.54	2.38	*4.90	*2.82	5.35

*Publicly owned utility.
¹ Only 1 community in this population group.
² No community in this population group.

Source: Federal Power Commission; annual report on typical residential electric bills, Jan. 1, 1952.

No. 349.—Gas Prices—Net Monthly Bills for Specified Quantities, by Cities

[Based on rates as of Dec. 15, 1950 and 1951. One therm=100,000 British thermal units]

City and kind of gas	Heating value per cubic foot in British thermal units (Dec. 15, 1951)	Net Monthly Bills							
		10.6 therms		19.6 therms		30.6 therms		40.6 therms	
		1950	1951	1950	1951	1950	1951	1950	1951
Atlanta [1] _natural_	1,029	$1.47	$1.52	$2.03	$2.09	$2.02	$2.09	$3.15	$3.25
Baltimore [2] _do_	1,051	[2]2.57	2.56	[3]3.60	3.58	[4]4.87	4.83	[5]6.01	5.96
Birmingham _manufactured_	520	1.62	1.62	2.66	2.66	3.75	3.75	4.52	4.52
Boston: Co. No. 1 _do_	530	2.72	2.74	5.81	5.95	8.17	8.24	10.31	10.40
Co. No. 2 _do_	536	3.04	3.18	5.26	5.53	7.06	7.46	8.88	9.41
Buffalo [6] _mixed_	900	1.19	1.19	1.94	1.94	2.85	2.85	3.68	3.68
_do_	800	1.65	1.65	2.63	2.63	3.47	3.47	4.17	4.17
Chicago _do_	1,050	[1]1.00	1.00	1.59	1.59	2.26	2.26	2.88	2.87
Cincinnati _natural_	1,075	.88	.88	1.33	1.33	1.90	1.90	2.41	2.41
Cleveland _do_	830	1.58	1.58	2.25	2.25	2.93	2.93	3.42	3.42
Denver [6] _do_	830	1.58	1.58	2.25	2.25	2.93	2.93	3.42	3.42
Detroit [7] _do_	990	1.25	1.24	2.04	2.02	2.96	2.95	3.83	3.79
Houston: Co. No. 1 _do_	1,077	.93	.93	1.43	1.43	2.04	2.04	2.60	2.60
Co. No. 2 _do_	1,081	.93	.93	1.43	1.43	2.04	2.04	2.60	2.60
Co. No. 3 _do_	1,081	.87	.87	1.33	1.33	1.99	1.99	2.40	2.40
Indianapolis _manufactured_	570	1.58	1.49	2.92	2.61	4.57	3.92	6.05	4.97
Jacksonville [6] _do_	510	4.50	4.01	7.70	6.82	11.54	10.18	14.88	13.12
Kansas City, Mo. [3] _natural_	994	.68	.70	1.09	1.11	1.59	1.62	2.04	2.08
Los Angeles _do_	1,100	1.36	1.36	1.85	1.85	2.45	2.45	2.95	2.95
Manchester _manufactured_	570	3.91	4.02	5.94	6.13	8.02	8.33	9.89	10.29
Memphis _natural_	980	1.39	1.39	2.26	2.26	3.27	3.28	3.68	3.83
Milwaukee _do_	980	[2]2.13	2.13	[3]3.26	3.26	[4]4.56	4.56	[5]5.74	5.74
Minneapolis _do_	1,000	1.48	1.47	2.05	2.03	2.74	2.71	3.37	3.33
Mobile _do_	1,053	1.60	1.60	2.51	2.33	3.19	3.22	3.70	3.72
New Orleans _do_	1,071	1.07	1.07	1.58	1.58	2.20	2.20	2.75	2.75
New York:									
3 boroughs [10] _manufactured_	540	2.88	2.91	4.72	4.77	6.80	6.87	8.54	8.62
Brooklyn: Co. No. 4 _do_	538	2.86	2.89	4.80	4.84	6.84	6.89	8.53	8.60
Co. No. 5 _natural_	1,030	[3]3.24	3.18	[5]5.44	5.46	[7]7.64	7.66	[10]9.56	9.60
Co. No. 6 _do_	1,058	[3]3.23	3.26	[5]5.48	5.53	[7]7.87	7.95	[9]9.75	9.35
Richmond _do_	1,027	3.31	3.34	5.52	5.58	7.69	7.76	9.27	9.36
Norfolk [11] _do_	1,175	[2]2.96	2.51	[5]5.25	4.08	[8]8.03	5.54	[10]10.38	6.66
Philadelphia _mixed_	650	[2]2.01	2.01	[3]3.54	3.54	[5]5.33	5.33	[6]6.84	6.84
Pittsburgh: Co. No. 1 _natural_	1,115	[1]1.00	1.00	1.06	1.06	1.64	1.64	2.18	2.18
Co. No. 2 _do_	1,033	1.22	1.23	1.79	1.80	2.48	2.48	3.11	3.11
Co. No. 3 _do_	1,100	1.18	1.18	1.72	1.72	2.37	2.37	2.96	2.96
Portland, Maine [2] _manufactured_	581	3.69	4.47	6.00	7.13	7.60	8.82	9.39	10.41
Portland, Oreg. _do_	570	2.73	2.73	4.61	4.61	6.05	6.05	7.54	7.54
Richmond [12] _natural_	1,100	[3]3.56	3.04	[5]5.70	4.38	[7]7.85	5.95	[9]9.47	6.95
St. Louis [1] _do_	1,026	1.74	1.74	2.93	2.93	4.38	4.38	5.44	5.44
San Francisco _do_	1,100	.95	1.17	1.27	1.58	1.66	2.06	2.01	2.49
Savannah [1] _manufactured_	500	3.32	4.37	5.75	7.48	8.33	10.44	10.33	13.01
Scranton _do_	521	2.87	3.33	4.56	4.29	5.76	6.68	7.58	8.60
Seattle [13] _do_	527	4.84	4.93	8.14	8.33	7.63	7.91	9.62	9.99
Washington, D. C. [3] _natural_	1,100	1.78	1.55	2.96	2.72	4.30	4.06	5.42	5.21

[1] 1951 bills include 3% State sales tax.
[2] Bills include 2% sales tax.
[3] Manufactured gas.
[4] Bills include 1% county sales tax.
[5] Minimum bill.
[6] Bills include 2% State sales tax and 1% city tax.
[7] Bills include 3% State sales tax.
[8] In 1950 bills include 10% city utility tax.
[9] Bills include 2% city tax in 1950, 3% in 1951.
[10] Manhattan, Bronx, and Queens.
[11] Bills include 8% city utility tax in 1950, 10% in 1951.
[12] Bills include 5% city utility tax.
[13] Bills include 3% city tax in 1950; bills for 1951 include 2% State sales tax and 1% city tax.

Source: Department of Labor, Bureau of Labor Statistics; published annually in special bulletin, _Gas and Electricity, Price Changes and Residential Bills._

No. 350.—ANNUAL AVERAGE UNIT VALUES OF IMPORTANT ARTICLES IMPORTED: 1925 TO 1951

[Values required by law to represent values *in foreign markets* whence exported to United States. "Ton" signifies long ton of 2,240 pounds except where otherwise specified. Averages obtained by dividing total value of imports of specified article by total quantity. Where, as in some commodities considerable price variations may exist between different grades, methods of packing, etc., and proportions of grades, etc., may vary from year to year, such averages may show actual price movements only roughly]

YEAR	Cheese, per pound	FISH, CURED, PER BARREL (200 POUNDS)		HIDES AND SKINS, PER POUND		Wheat, per bushel	Bananas, per bunch	Cocoa, per pound	Coffee, per pound	Tea, per pound
		Herring	Mackerel	Cattle	Goat					
	Cents	Dollars	Dollars	Cents	Cents	Dollars	Cents	Cents	Cents	Cents
1925	27.8	13.30	15.60	16.0	40.7	1.39	53.52	10.0	22.3	31.2
1926	26.9	12.09	12.05	14.7	44.6	1.39	56.33	10.0	21.6	32.7
1927	30.7	12.69	13.10	17.4	43.6	1.31	56.17	13.4	18.4	31.6
1928	30.3	13.15	13.96	23.1	46.0	1.17	55.02	12.4	21.3	30.3
1929	29.2	12.54	15.45	16.0	47.4	1.11	55.34	9.8	20.4	28.9
1930	26.7	14.13	12.40	13.0	40.7	.98	55.46	8.4	13.1	26.6
1931	23.6	12.39	9.30	8.4	31.6	.64	52.69	5.6	10.0	21.6
1932	22.5	9.32	6.66	5.6	20.0	.53	49.94	4.1	9.1	13.1
1933	21.9	8.94	8.11	7.8	21.0	.56	51.00	4.0	7.8	14.2
1934	22.4	10.02	9.82	7.9	26.4	.78	50.55	4.4	8.7	21.3
1935	22.9	10.66	10.56	8.6	24.3	.78	50.95	4.4	7.8	19.9
1936	21.2	9.64	10.52	9.9	28.7	.91	49.18	5.2	7.7	21.7
1937	21.1	8.38	12.67	12.6	33.0	1.12	47.22	8.5	8.9	22.5
1938	21.2	8.74	10.35	8.7	22.6	.67	48.61	4.4	6.9	22.5
1939	21.7	9.30	9.45	9.0	23.3	.56	50.91	4.2	6.9	21.6
1940	23.0	9.63	10.17	8.8	23.1	.68	55.57	4.4	6.2	22.9
1941	19.5	9.63	15.70	10.4	23.0	.72	57.54	5.6	7.9	27.2
1942	18.9	12.87	18.95	12.7	29.7	.72	59.49	7.7	12.0	37.0
1943	17.4	14.43	27.21	13.3	30.2	1.12	62.26	6.8	12.4	32.4
1944	21.6	18.59	28.45	13.9	33.3	1.34	66.45	6.8	12.5	33.5
1945	25.1	18.80	27.43	13.1	40.2	1.34	69.32	7.4	12.7	34.9
1946	39.0	18.76	30.06	20.6	54.7	1.44	78.78	9.5	17.2	36.3
1947 (prel.)	53.9	20.85	31.60	25.4	67.7	1.45	82.50	25.5	24.1	40.7
1948 (prel.)	54.0	21.75	32.18	24.7	72.7	1.12	84.20	35.4	25.1	49.3
1949 (prel.)	52.6	20.78	27.79	19.0	66.9	2.11	96.38	19.7	27.2	48.5
1950 (prel.)	42.7	19.73	29.09	21.7	62.7	1.90	108.36	25.0	44.8	47.1
1951 (prel.)	43.0	19.53	32.78	34.4	75.2	1.67	110.59	32.1	50.6	47.0

YEAR	Cane sugar, per pound	Whiskey, per proof gallon	Wines, per gallon	Rubber, crude, per pound	Shellac, per pound	Copra, per pound	TOBACCO, LEAF, PER POUND		Cotton, unmanufactured, per pound
							Cigar wrappers	Other leaf	
	Cents	Dollars	Dollars	Cents	Cents	Cents	Dollars	Cents	Cents
1925	2.76	3.47	1.93	48.4	51.0	5.0	2.34	80.27	33.7
1926	2.47	(1)	2.76	54.6	33.6	5.1	2.25	75.88	25.5
1927	3.06	(1)	2.32	35.6	41.4	4.6	2.15	64.90	22.2
1928	2.68	(1)	2.44	25.0	42.4	4.5	2.06	62.02	24.9
1929	2.14	(1)	2.40	19.1	38.4	4.2	1.84	65.37	23.9
1930	1.85	(1)	2.62	12.9	27.3	3.7	1.60	52.99	19.7
1931	1.77	(1)	2.56	6.6	16.3	2.4	1.47	45.92	9.9
1932	1.63	(1)	2.23	3.5	13.3	1.8	1.33	39.22	9.9
1933	1.87	(1)	3.75	4.9	9.9	1.4	1.82	34.11	10.6
1934	1.96	4.95	3.42	9.8	17.7	1.2	2.00	39.32	13.4
1935	2.26	4.53	3.17	11.4	13.6	2.1	2.18	36.65	14.0
1936	2.66	4.18	3.15	14.5	11.7	2.1	2.19	38.65	13.2
1937	2.60	3.76	2.73	18.5	10.8	3.3	1.97	46.08	12.4
1938	2.19	4.15	2.48	14.1	8.9	1.8	2.03	52.70	9.0
1939	2.15	4.22	2.30	16.0	8.0	1.6	1.67	51.54	8.0
1940	1.94	3.98	2.24	17.4	11.9	1.3	1.56	49.88	8.1
1941	2.05	4.03	2.46	18.2	13.6	1.7	1.51	50.69	7.3
1942	2.70	4.43	2.49	18.9	25.1	3.3	1.72	49.26	12.2
1943	2.76	4.34	2.25	27.1	26.9	3.6	1.76	56.15	15.6
1944	2.75	4.26	2.35	31.2	29.0	3.4	2.03	82.24	15.8
1945	3.07	4.00	3.02	31.4	29.6	3.0	2.38	98.69	11.2
1946	3.70	4.16	3.95	27.4	42.1	3.8	3.21	104.73	19.0
1947 (prel.)	4.92	4.68	4.05	20.1	48.7	7.9	3.12	100.84	25.8
1948 (prel.)	4.88	5.09	4.09	18.8	49.3	12.3	3.83	90.35	27.2
1949 (prel.)	4.99	5.30	3.80	16.3	47.3	8.1	4.77	83.35	16.5
1950 (prel.)	5.17	5.72	3.52	25.5	35.6	8.8	4.94	81.81	21.7
1951 (prel.)	5.17	5.37	3.40	49.1	44.4	9.2	4.75	77.75	42.2

1 No importations.

No. 350.—ANNUAL AVERAGE UNIT VALUES OF IMPORTANT ARTICLES IMPORTED: 1925 TO 1951—Continued

YEAR	Jute and jute butts, per ton	Jute burlaps, per pound	Flax, per ton	Sisal, per ton	Manila, per ton	WOOL, PER POUND			Silk, raw, per pound
						Carpet	Clothing	Combing	
	Dollars	Cents	Dollars	Dollars	Dollars	Cents	Cents	Cents	Dollars
1925	190.69	13.6	680.59	170.79	290.51	30	46	53	6.21
1926	215.06	13.7	478.07	182.86	263.92	26	35	39	5.91
1927	131.52	11.8	479.06	153.32	255.49	26	34	37	5.27
1928	129.45	12.9	698.47	145.10	202.65	25	44	44	4.87
1929	128.35	12.0	579.24	156.58	186.95	27	38	38	4.91
1930	107.76	9.1	429.26	138.50	138.08	20	26	25	3.57
1931	69.71	6.7	222.45	83.44	95.60	12	24	20	2.28
1932	64.19	5.0	216.50	50.10	62.91	9	14	15	1.54
1933	56.27	6.1	276.17	56.89	56.99	10	19	18	1.52
1934	62.95	7.4	374.08	70.91	66.31	13	24	23	1.27
1935	72.82	7.0	490.07	71.03	80.52	14	23	21	1.43
1936	82.09	6.4	442.68	104.45	144.99	18	26	27	1.70
1937	83.69	6.3	412.63	115.06	177.95	27	33	33	1.84
1938	84.35	5.6	613.35	88.43	115.58	19	32	30	1.61
1939	100.90	6.3	454.34	72.90	90.83	18	25	24	2.34
1940	126.55	9.0	504.55	84.25	94.99	23	22	24	2.79
1941	104.78	9.7	496.57	77.62	133.10	21	25	27	2.67
1942	157.21	12.2	558.96	117.09	167.22	21	31	29	2.53
1943	146.01	12.0	825.38	142.82	213.00	24	31	31	1.75
1944	160.53	13.4	639.65	148.79	224.83	19	31	31	--------
1945	167.82	14.2	315.20	151.17	225.18	21	32	32	10.41
1946	160.16	13.8	526.24	172.64	201.14	21	29	30	7.86
1947 (prel.)	261.83	20.1	596.03	269.33	377.35	23	30	38	6.39
1948 (prel.)	348.99	25.9	786.31	303.00	547.12	27	39	54	2.72
1949 (prel.)	384.05	23.1	521.84	288.26	519.53	33	49	65	2.53
1950 (prel.)	281.26	21.6	462.74	251.00	485.17	46	66	70	2.66
1951 (prel.)	281.75	33.5	731.19	415.94	597.90	97	144	136	4.07

YEAR	Boards, planks, deals, per M board feet [1]	Pulpwood, per cord	Wood pulp, per ton	Newsprint paper, per pound	Petroleum, crude, per gallon	Manganese ore, per pound	Copper, pigs, ingots, bars, per pound [2]	Nickel, pigs, ingots, bars, per pound	Tin, bars, blocks, pigs, per pound	Sodium nitrate, per ton
	Dollars	Dollars	Dollars	Cents	Cents	Cents	Cents	Cents	Cents	Dollars
1925	30.33	10.20	55.09	3.6	2.9	1.17	12.9	20.49	55.40	47.23
1926	28.79	10.25	59.01	3.3	3.1	1.41	12.6	26.75	60.63	46.79
1927	27.82	10.32	57.37	3.3	3.2	1.36	11.8	26.42	63.30	40.34
1928	26.96	10.45	53.27	3.2	2.7	1.13	12.4	25.20	49.80	35.81
1929	27.52	10.81	52.75	3.0	2.4	1.15	16.1	25.53	47.06	37.52
1930	23.84	10.76	49.63	2.9	2.5	1.08	13.2	25.05	33.31	37.71
1931	20.86	10.97	42.72	2.7	2.0	.99	8.5	25.33	24.82	38.34
1932	19.29	8.61	35.45	2.4	1.6	.96	5.7	25.06	21.12	26.19
1933	22.03	7.41	33.09	1.9	1.3	.95	6.2	24.83	36.36	19.07
1934	25.39	7.54	38.34	1.7	1.7	.95	7.0	25.36	50.02	19.32
1935	24.54	7.48	⁴ 36.59	1.7	1.7	.99	6.9	25.28	48.50	20.32
1936	24.01	7.84	⁴ 36.37	1.8	1.7	.95	8.3	25.16	44.30	19.30
1937	27.45	8.14	⁴ 41.04	1.8	1.8	1.03	11.7	24.83	52.84	18.53
1938	24.65	8.53	⁴ 42.55	2.2	1.7	1.30	9.2	25.07	40.30	18.59
1939	26.86	8.34	⁴ 37.45	2.2	1.6	1.19	9.6	25.09	44.95	18.55
1940	31.45	8.49	⁴ 49.15	2.3	1.8	1.31	10.0	25.00	45.89	18.74
1941	33.37	8.85	⁴ 57.03	2.2	2.0	1.52	9.9	25.04	47.40	⁵ 17.80
1942	36.11	9.98	⁴ 58.72	2.2	2.3	1.50	9.9	25.18	48.91	⁵ 19.11
1943	45.30	11.33	⁴ 59.05	2.5	2.5	1.60	10.4	25.18	49.00	⁵ 19.96
1944	50.28	12.29	⁴ 67.47	2.7	2.6	1.95	10.7	25.87	50.37	⁵ 21.52
1945	52.15	13.47	⁴ 66.00	2.8	2.5	2.00	10.8	27.30	48.43	⁵ 21.84
1946	61.41	14.59	⁴ 75.21	3.5	2.8	2.01	11.7	27.16	53.24	⁵ 21.60
1947 (prel.)	74.20	16.67	⁴ 110.42	4.4	3.9	1.70	18.8	30.13	76.53	⁵ 27.23
1948 (prel.)	78.92	17.64	⁴ 125.18	4.7	5.2	1.66	20.2	33.13	93.75	⁵ 32.47
1949 (prel.)	69.93	17.72	⁴ 103.47	4.7	5.2	1.98	18.1	37.15	99.11	⁵ 36.50
1950 (prel.)	75.83	17.22	⁴ 100.70	4.6	5.1	1.56	18.2	42.22	82.42	⁵ 36.28
1951 (prel.)	88.92	19.66	⁴ 149.28	5.2	5.0	2.50	24.5	56.63	118.0	⁵ 37.23

¹ Excludes cabinet woods; includes clapboard beginning 1939.
² Unrefined copper.
⁴ Tons of 2,000 pounds, air-dry weight.
⁵ Short tons.

Source: Department of Commerce, Bureau of Census; basic data through 1946 published in annual report, Foreign Commerce and Navigation of the United States.

No. 351.—ANNUAL AVERAGE UNIT VALUES OF IMPORTANT DOMESTIC ARTICLES EXPORTED: 1929 TO 1951

[Values of goods required by law to represent market value at port of exportation. See headnote, table 350]

YEAR	Lard, per lb.	Milk, condensed and evaporated, per lb.	Cheese, per lb.	Eggs, per doz.	Corn, per bu.	Rice, per lb.	Wheat, per bu.	Wheat flour, per bbl.	Sugar, per lb.	Tobacco leaf, per lb.	Cotton, per lb. [1]	BOARDS, PLANKS, AND SCANTLINGS, PER M BOARD FEET	
												Softwoods	Hardwoods
	Cts.	Cts.	Cts.	Cts.	Dols.	Cts.	Dols.	Dols.	Cts.	Cts.	Cts.	Dols.	Dols.
1929	12.7	12.1	27.8	33.8	1.01	3.7	1.34	5.91	3.0	26.2	19.7	32.27	66.45
1930	11.4	11.5	25.7	27.2	.94	3.8	1.00	5.31	2.4	25.8	14.4	29.45	62.50
1931	9.0	10.5	22.4	22.7	.69	2.7	.62	3.57	2.1	21.8	9.0	22.91	50.96
1932	5.8	8.5	18.3	21.7	.36	1.9	.60	3.19	1.6	16.8	7.3	20.35	41.09
1933	5.9	6.8	18.5	20.6	.49	2.4	.54	3.49	1.6	19.5	9.0	22.16	43.98
1934	6.1	7.4	19.5	24.1	.76	3.2	.60	4.04	1.5	29.7	11.8	27.93	54.54
1935	12.3	7.4	22.0	29.7	1.50	3.0	.91	4.53	2.3	35.1	12.4	28.41	50.46
1936	12.1	7.8	23.5	26.0	1.05	3.1	.99	4.78	2.2	33.6	12.5	32.30	50.08
1937	11.8	8.5	24.2	27.4	.67	3.1	1.11	5.67	2.2	32.1	11.9	35.50	54.38
1938	8.9	7.8	20.9	29.7	.64	2.6	.90	4.44	2.1	32.8	9.8	33.78	51.45
1939	7.3	7.0	21.2	25.8	.62	3.0	.58	3.17	2.8	23.5	9.9	33.50	51.87
1940	6.3	7.4	22.2	23.3	.67	2.9	.78	3.70	3.1	20.1	10.9	35.01	57.73
1941	9.8	8.0	20.7	27.2	.87	3.9	.85	4.13	3.1	24.8	13.5	41.21	69.30
1942	13.3	9.5	25.1	38.4	.92	6.1	1.08	4.75	4.6	28.5	18.4	53.88	94.41
1943	16.4	9.9	26.9	48.1	1.20	6.4	1.37	5.87	4.4	43.3	22.4	80.79	109.82
1944	16.8	12.1	30.3	39.9	1.42	6.9	1.63	6.92	5.7	52.5	22.4	66.93	105.16
1945	16.1	13.1	31.9	46.4	1.42	6.8	1.87	7.15	[3]6.1	50.7	21.9	61.53	96.30
1946	19.1	12.4	32.7	44.6	1.80	7.8	2.09	8.63	[3]5.4	54.6	26.0	64.55	116.55
1947	25.8	14.6	38.1	50.2	1.89	9.5	2.56	11.93	[3]7.4	54.7	30.8	81.91	131.19
1948	25.9	16.4	45.5	52.4	1.82	9.7	2.78	12.64	[3]7.7	51.5	35.6	88.66	150.12
1949	14.6	15.0	36.0	50.3	1.56	7.7	2.46	10.03	6.8	51.0	33.7	82.52	155.42
1950	13.3	14.3	15.5	43.2	1.58	7.7	1.96	8.29	5.0	53.1	35.6	85.15	165.59
1951	19.2	15.3	31.8	51.7	1.90	8.7	2.10	9.34	6.9	62.8	44.4	86.80	164.77

YEAR	COAL, PER SHORT TON		Petroleum, crude, per gal.	Motor fuel, gasoline, and naphtha, per gal.[2]	Kerosene, per gal.	Lubricating oils, per gal.	Iron and steel scrap, per ton	Tin plate, terneplate, taggers' tin, per lb.	Copper, refined, per lb.	Motor-trucks, busses, and chassis, per unit (new)	Passenger cars, per unit (new)
	Anthracite	Bituminous									
	Dols.	Dols.	Cts.	Cts.	Cts.	Cts.	Dols.	Cts.	Cts.	Dols.	Dols.
1929	9.56	3.77	3.4	10.6	10.1	23.2	13.91	4.9	18.0	567	690
1930	9.61	3.73	3.2	9.4	9.0	21.9	15.51	5.0	13.4	663	692
1931	9.59	3.58	1.9	5.9	6.6	18.9	14.38	4.1	9.4	525	611
1932	9.26	3.37	2.4	5.6	5.2	17.1	8.17	3.7	6.1	469	573
1933	8.74	3.16	2.1	5.3	5.2	16.3	8.89	3.6	6.8	453	499
1934	8.54	3.72	2.9	5.6	5.2	18.5	10.46	4.1	7.6	478	540
1935	8.20	3.62	2.8	5.7	5.6	17.7	10.15	4.3	7.7	512	548
1936	8.21	3.62	2.1	6.1	5.3	18.1	11.00	4.4	9.2	519	572
1937	7.73	3.71	3.4	6.7	5.7	19.0	18.91	4.9	13.0	605	587
1938	7.67	3.63	3.4	6.0	5.3	17.6	15.10	5.3	10.0	624	620
1939	7.69	3.69	3.1	6.2	4.7	18.3	15.40	4.7	11.0	601	614
1940	7.95	3.69	3.1	7.7	6.1	21.8	16.87	5.2	11.5	831	645
1941	8.19	4.15	3.4	[4]8.5	5.5	21.4	18.74	5.4	11.3	1,007	743
1942	8.63	4.63	3.5	[4]9.9	5.5	26.8	23.39	5.3	11.3	1,649	946
1943	9.14	4.85	3.7	[4]11.8	6.5	28.4	18.66	5.2	10.5	2,576	1,159
1944	9.69	5.06	4.0	[4]15.2	6.3	28.0	18.12	5.3	10.0	2,284	1,689
1945	9.87	5.29	3.9	[4]13.5	4.6	30.3	17.38	5.3	10.7	2,448	1,200
1946	9.83	5.78	4.1	[4]6.6	5.9	25.1	19.17	5.5	13.5	1,351	1,047
1947	10.60	7.70	5.1	[4]8.7	7.6	33.0	29.18	7.0	20.4	1,617	1,256
1948	12.91	8.55	6.7	[4]11.7	9.5	36.9	36.24	7.9	22.2	1,697	1,352
1949	13.11	8.35	7.1	[4]12.0	9.2	32.6	26.30	8.4	20.8	(5)	1,464
1950	16.06	8.11	7.0	[4]12.5	9.8	30.4	28.25	8.0	20.1	(5)	1,489
1951	14.95	8.74	7.9	[4]13.2	10.0	38.1	32.89	10.2	27.0	(5)	1,567

[1] Excludes linters. [2] Refined sugar only. [3] Including natural gasoline.
[4] Includes mineral spirits not reported separately since 1940. [5] Not available.

Source: Department of Commerce, Bureau of Census; basic data through 1946 published in annual report, *Foreign Commerce and Navigation of the United States.*

13. Elections

The conduct of elections in the United States for Federal, State, and local offices and on State and local issues, is regulated by State laws or, in some cities and a few counties, by local charters. An important exception is that the United States Constitution prescribes the basis of representation in Congress and the manner of electing the President of the United States and grants to Congress the right to regulate the times, places, and manner of electing Federal officers. Almost all of the more than 120 thousand governmental units in the United States conduct elections at various intervals—annual, biennial, quadrennial, or longer—for different types of offices and other purposes. No regular and complete system exists for reporting either the number of elections held or the numbers of votes cast for the multitude of candidates, except for Federal offices, and in most States, for State offices. Few States require central reporting on local elections. The numbers of governments holding elections and the numbers of voters participating vary between Presidential and the intervening Congressional election years, and between even-numbered and odd-numbered years.

The election of the President of the United States is provided for in the Constitution, article II, section 1, through the establishment of an electoral college in each State, for each Presidential election. The method of casting the electoral vote was modified in 1804 by the adoption of the 12th Amendment to the Constitution. The number of electors, and therefore of electoral votes, is "equal to the whole number of Senators and Representatives to which the State may be entitled in Congress." The electors are elected by popular vote in all States.

The number of members in the House of Representatives is fixed by the Congress at the time of each apportionment; since 1912 it has remained constant. The 14th Amendment to the Constitution, in effect at the present time, provides that "Representatives shall be apportioned among the several States according to their respective numbers, counting the whole number of persons in each State . . ." The Constitution also requires that each State have at least one Representative.

Historical statistics.—See preface and historical appendix. Tabular headnotes (as "See also *Historical Statistics*, series P 27–31") provide cross-references, where applicable, to *Historical Statistics of the United States, 1789–1945.*

Note.—This section presents data for the most recent year or period available on March 31, 1953, when the material was organized and sent to the printer.

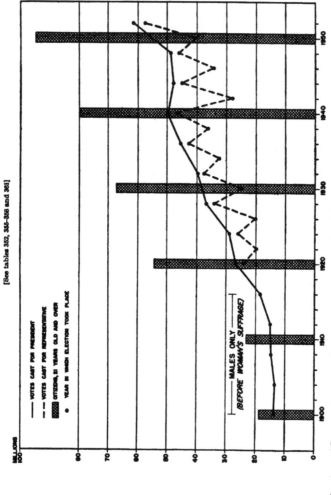

FIG. XXV.—PARTICIPATION IN NATIONAL ELECTIONS: 1900 TO 1952

[See tables 352, 355-358 and 361]

VOTES CAST FOR PRESIDENT
VOTES CAST FOR REPRESENTATIVE
CITIZENS, 21 YEARS OLD AND OVER
YEAR IN WHICH ELECTION TOOK PLACE

MALES ONLY (BEFORE WOMAN'S SUFFRAGE)

MILLIONS

Source: Department of Commerce, Bureau of the Census. For source of election data, see headnote.

No. 852.—Vote for Presidential Electors, by Major Political Parties: 1888 to 1952

YEAR	Total [1]	Republican	Democratic	Socialist and Socialist-Labor	Miscellaneous independent [2]	Prohibition	Communist	PERCENT OF TOTAL — Rep.	Dem.
1888	11,381,408	5,444,337	5,540,050		146,897	250,124		47.8	48.7
1892	12,043,603	5,190,802	5,554,414		1,027,329	271,058		43.1	46.1
1896	13,813,243	7,035,638	[5]6,467,946	[4]36,454	131,329	141,676		50.9	[3]46.5
1900	13,904,518	7,219,530	6,358,071	127,519	50,232	209,166		51.7	45.5
1904	13,523,519	7,628,834	5,084,491	436,184	114,753	259,257		56.4	37.6
1908	14,887,133	7,679,006	6,409,106	434,645	111,693	252,683		51.6	43.1
1912	15,031,169	3,483,922	6,286,214	926,090	4,126,020	208,923		23.2	41.8
1916	18,527,863	8,533,507	9,127,695	600,014	45,590	221,057		46.1	49.3
1920	26,813,268	16,147,249	9,140,864	927,004	410,054	188,097	[6]36,386	60.2	34.1
1924	[5]29,091,417	15,725,016	8,386,503	[4]36,428	4,848,355	57,520	[6]46,770	54.1	28.8
1928	36,811,717	21,391,381	15,016,443	289,023	64,823	81,869	102,991	39.7	57.4
1932	39,751,438	15,761,841	22,821,857	918,057	196,832	37,082	80,159	36.5	60.2
1936	45,647,117	16,679,583	27,476,673	110,426	[7]472,431	57,732	48,579	44.8	53.8
1940	49,820,312	[7]22,304,400	[8]26,826,742	106,442	[8]1,011,918	74,754		45.9	51.6
1944	47,975,263	22,006,285	[9]24,776,864	168,070	[10]2,487,829	103,216		45.0	49.4
1948	48,833,680	21,969,170	[10]24,105,695	47,655	[11]292,217	72,768		55.0	44.4
1952	61,551,978	33,824,351	[11]27,314,987						

[1] Totals for years prior to 1928 exclude votes cast for names not appearing on electoral tickets for parties specified. Totals for 1928–44 exclude void and blank ballots.

[2] For 1888, Union Labor Party; 1892, 1900, and 1904, Populist; 1896, National Democrat; 1908, Populist and Independent; 1912, Progressive; 1916 to 1952, miscellaneous.

[3] Democrat-Populist.

[4] Socialist-Labor only. In 1924 practically all Socialist votes cast for La Follette and Wheeler, official candidates of both Socialist and Independent Progressive parties, included in miscellaneous.

[5] Includes scattering votes; 445 in Iowa; 633 in New Jersey; and 131 in Pennsylvania.

[6] Workers.

[7] Included with miscellaneous are 798 Union votes cast in endorsement of Republican candidate.

[8] Included with miscellaneous are 417,418 American Labor votes cast in endorsement of Democratic candidate.

[9] Included with miscellaneous are 496,405 American Labor and 329,235 Liberal votes cast in endorsement of Democratic candidate.

[10] Included with miscellaneous are 1,169,021 votes for Thurmond (States' Rights Democrats) and 1,156,103 votes cast for Wallace (Progressives, etc.); included with Democratic are 222,562 Liberal votes cast for Democratic nominees.

[11] Included with Democratic are 416,711 Liberal Party votes.

Source: 1888–1912, reports of State officials on file in Department of State. 1916, *The Presidential Vote 1896–1932*, E. E. Robinson. 1920, 1924, 1948, and 1952, U. S. Congress, Clerk of the House; *Statistics of Presidential and Congressional Election*. 1928–44, Dept. of Commerce, Bureau of Census; Elections, 1944: No. 5, *Vote Cast in Presidential and Congressional Elections, 1928–44*.

No. 358.—Apportionment of Congressional Representation, by States, From Adoption of Constitution to 1950

[Until 1940, population for apportionment purposes excluded Indians not taxed and, until 1870, two-fifths of slaves. In 1940, all Indians were held subject to Federal taxation. Until 1850, apportionment ratios chosen arbitrarily; 1850 to 1900, ratios were apportionment population of U. S. divided by number of Representatives; from 1910 on, apportionments computed from priority lists, not from ratios. No apportionment in 1920. For discussion of apportionment methods, see S. Doc. No. 304, 76th Cong., 3d sess., *A Survey of Methods of Apportionment in Congress*, by Edward V. Huntington. See also *Historical Statistics*, series P 57–61, which shows apportionment totals under Apportionment Act, *excluding* Representatives assigned after apportionment (footnote 6 below)]

STATE	Constitution [1]	1790	1800	1810	1820	1830	1840	1850	1860	1870	1880	1890	1900	1910	1930	1940	1950
							RATIOS UNDER CONSTITUTION AND APPORTIONMENT ACTS										
	30,000 [1]	33,000	33,000	35,000	40,000	47,700	70,680	93,423	127,381	131,425	151,911	173,901	194,182	(7)	(7)	(7)	(7)
							NUMBER OF REPRESENTATIVES										
Total	65	106	142	186	213	242	232	[3]237	[4]243	[5]293	332	357	391	435	435	435	435
Alabama				[6]1	3	5	7	7	6	8	8	9	9	10	9	9	9
Arizona														[7]1	1	2	2
Arkansas					[6]1	2	3	4	3	4	5	6	7	7	7	7	6
California						[6]2	2	3	4	6	7	8	11	20	23	30
Colorado									[6]1	1	2	3	4	4	4	4
Connecticut	5	7	7	7	6	6	4	4	4	4	4	5	5	6	6	6
Delaware	1	1	1	2	1	1	1	1	1	1	1	1	1	1	1	1
Florida						[6]1	1	1	2	2	2	3	4	5	6	8
Georgia	3	2	4	6	7	9	8	8	7	9	10	11	11	12	10	10	10
Idaho										[6]1	1	1	2	2	2	2
Illinois				[6]1	1	3	7	9	14	19	20	22	25	27	27	26	25
Indiana			[6]1	3	7	10	11	11	13	13	13	13	13	13	12	11	11
Iowa						[6]2	2	6	9	11	11	11	11	9	8	8
Kansas								1	3	7	8	8	8	7	6	6
Kentucky		2	[6]6	10	12	13	10	10	9	11	11	11	11	9	9	8
Louisiana			[6]1	3	3	4	4	5	6	6	6	7	8	8	8	8
Maine			[6]7	7	8	7	6	5	5	4	4	4	4	3	3	3
Maryland	6	8	9	9	8	6	6	5	6	6	6	6	6	6	6	7
Massachusetts	8	14	17	13	13	12	10	11	10	11	12	13	14	16	15	14	14
Michigan					[6]1	3	4	6	9	11	12	12	13	17	17	18
Minnesota							[6]2	2	3	5	7	9	10	9	9	9
Mississippi				[6]1	1	2	4	5	6	7	7	8	8	7	7	6
Missouri				1	2	5	7	9	13	14	15	16	16	13	13	11
Montana										[6]1	1	1	2	2	2	2
Nebraska								[6]1	1	3	6	6	6	5	4	4
Nevada								[6]1	1	1	1	1	1	1	1	1
N. Hampshire	3	4	5	6	6	5	4	3	3	2	2	2	2	2	2	2
New Jersey	4	5	6	6	6	6	5	5	5	7	7	8	10	14	14	14
New Mexico													[7]1	1	2	2
New York	6	10	17	27	34	40	34	33	31	33	34	34	37	43	45	45	43
N. Carolina	5	10	12	13	13	13	9	8	7	8	9	9	10	10	11	12	12
N. Dakota										[6]1	1	2	3	2	2	2
Ohio			[6]1	6	14	19	21	21	19	20	21	21	21	22	24	23	23
Oklahoma												[6]5	8	9	8	6
Oregon							[6]1	1	1	1	2	2	3	3	4	4
Pennsylvania	8	13	18	23	26	28	24	25	24	27	28	30	32	36	34	33	30
Rhode Island	1	2	2	2	2	2	2	2	2	2	2	2	3	2	2	2
S. Carolina	5	6	8	9	9	9	7	6	4	5	7	7	7	6	6	6
S. Dakota										[6]2	2	2	3	2	2	2
Tennessee		[6]1	3	6	9	13	11	10	8	10	10	10	10	9	10	9
Texas						[6]2	2	4	6	11	13	16	18	21	21	22
Utah											[6]1	1	2	2	2	2
Vermont		2	4	6	5	5	4	3	3	3	2	2	2	1	1	1
Virginia	10	19	22	23	22	21	15	13	11	10	10	10	10	9	9	10
Washington										[6]1	2	3	5	6	6	7
West Virginia								3	3	4	4	5	6	6	6	6
Wisconsin						[6]2	3	6	8	9	10	11	11	10	10	10
Wyoming										[6]1	1	1	1	1	1	1

[1] Number of Representatives not to exceed 1 for each 30,000 inhabitants.
[2] See headnote.
[3] Membership increased from 233 to 234 by act of July 30, 1852 (10 Stat. L. 25). See note 6.
[4] Membership increased from 233 to 241 by act of Mar. 4, 1862 (12 Stat. L. 353). See note 6.
[5] Membership originally fixed at 283 but increased to 292 by act of May 30, 1872 (17 Stat. L. 192). One Member assigned to Colorado after apportionment.
[6] Assigned after apportionment.
[7] Included in apportionment act in anticipation of Statehood.
[8] Included in the 20 Members originally assigned to Massachusetts but credited to Maine after its admission as a State, Mar. 15, 1820 (3 Stat. L. 555).

Source: Department of Commerce, Bureau of the Census, records.

No. 354.—ELECTORAL VOTE FOR PRESIDENT, BY MAJOR POLITICAL PARTIES, BY STATES: 1924 TO 1952

[See also *Historical Statistics*, series P 27–31]

STATE	1924 Rep.	1924 Dem.	1928 Rep.	1928 Dem.	1932 Rep.	1932 Dem.	1936 Rep.	1936 Dem.	1940 Rep.	1940 Dem.	1944 Rep.	1944 Dem.	1948[1] Rep.	1948[1] Dem.	1952 Rep.	1952 Dem.
Total	382	136	444	87	59	472	8	523	82	449	99	432	189	303	442	89
Plurality	246		357			413		515		367		333		114	353	
Ala		12		12		11		11		11		11				11
Ariz	3		3			3		3		3		4		4	4	
Ark		9		9		9		9		9		9		9		8
Calif	13		13			22		22		22		25		25	32	
Colo	6		6			6		6	6		6			6	6	
Conn	7		7		8			8		8		8	8		8	
Del	3		3		3			3		3		3	3		3	
Fla		6	6			7		7		7		8		8	10	
Ga		14		14		12		12		12		12		12		12
Idaho	4		4			4		4		4		4		4	4	
Ill	29		29			29		29		29	28			28	27	
Ind	15		15			14		14	14		13		13		13	
Iowa	13		13			11		11	11		10		10		10	
Kans	10		10			9		9	9		8		8		8	
Ky	13		13			11		11		11		11		11		10
La		10		10		10		10		10		10				10
Maine	6		6		5		5		5		5		5		5	
Md	8		8			8		8		8		8	8		9	
Mass	18			18		17		17		17		16		16	16	
Mich	15		15			19		19	19			19	19		20	
Minn	12		12			11		11		11		11		11	11	
Miss		10		10		9		9		9		9				8
Mo	18		18			15		15		15		15		15	13	
Mont	4		4			4		4		4		4		4	4	
Nebr	8		8			7		7	7		6		6		6	
Nev	3		3			3		3		3		3		3	3	
N. H	4		4		4			4		4		4	4		4	
N. J	14		14		16			16		16		16	16		16	
N. M	3		3			3		3		3		4		4	4	
N. Y	45		45			47		47		47		47	47		45	
N. C		12	12			13		13		13		14		14		14
N. Dak	5		5			4		4	4		4		4		4	
Ohio	24		24			26		26		26	25			25	25	
Okla		10	10			11		11		11		10		10	8	
Oreg	5		5			5		5		5	6		6		6	
Pa	38		38		36			36		36	35		35		32	
R. I	5			5		4		4		4		4		4	4	
S. C		9		9		8		8		8		8				8
S. Dak	5		5			4		4	4		4		4		4	
Tenn		12	12			11		11		11		12		11	11	
Tex		20	20			23		23		23		23		23	24	
Utah	4		4			4		4		4		4		4	4	
Vt	4		4		3		3		3		3		3		3	
Va		12	12			11		11		11		11		11	12	
Wash	7		7			8		8		8		8		8	9	
W. Va	8		8			8		8		8		8		8		8
Wis	(²)	(²)	13			12		12	12		12			12	12	
Wyo	3		3			3		3		3	3			3	3	

[1] Total of 531 electors also includes 39 for States' Rights Democrat candidates, as follows: Alabama, 11; Louisiana, 10; Mississippi, 9; South Carolina, 8; and Tennessee, 1.

[2] Electoral votes of Wisconsin cast for LaFollette and Wheeler, Independent Progressive candidates.

Source: U. S. Congress, Clerk of the House; *Statistics of Presidential and Congressional Election*.

No. 355.—Vote for Presidential Electors, by States: 1916 to 1944

[For current figures, see table 356]

STATE	1916	1920	1924	1928	1932	1936	1940	1944
Total........	18,537,843	26,813,268	29,091,417	36,811,717	39,751,438	45,647,117	49,928,322	47,976,263
Alabama..........	130,728	237,636	166,593	248,982	245,034	275,744	294,219	244,743
Arizona	58,019	66,570	73,961	91,254	118,251	124,163	150,039	137,634
Arkansas..........	168,374	183,637	138,532	197,693	220,562	179,423	201,838	212,956
California.........	999,781	943,344	1,281,778	1,796,656	2,266,972	2,638,882	3,268,791	3,520,975
Colorado..........	294,364	292,053	342,260	392,242	457,696	488,676	549,004	505,039
Connecticut.......	213,874	365,518	400,295	553,031	594,207	690,723	781,502	831,990
Delaware	51,810	94,875	90,865	105,891	112,901	127,603	136,374	125,361
Florida...........	80,734	193,206	109,154	253,674	276,252	327,365	485,492	482,592
Georgia...........	158,710	148,251	166,577	229,159	255,590	293,178	312,553	328,100
Idaho.............	134,615	135,592	148,295	154,230	186,520	198,632	235,168	208,321
Illinois	2,190,217	2,094,714	2,470,067	3,107,489	3,407,926	3,956,522	4,217,985	4,036,061
Indiana	718,986	1,262,964	1,272,390	1,421,314	1,576,927	1,650,897	1,782,747	1,672,091
Iowa	514,703	895,076	976,960	1,009,362	1,036,687	1,142,733	1,215,430	1,052,599
Kansas	628,298	570,243	662,451	713,200	791,978	865,013	861,297	733,776
Kentucky	520,069	918,708	815,332	940,604	983,063	926,206	970,063	867,921
Louisiana	92,962	126,057	121,951	215,833	268,804	329,778	372,305	349,383
Maine	138,314	197,840	192,192	262,171	298,444	304,240	320,840	296,400
Maryland	262,039	438,442	358,630	528,348	511,054	624,896	660,104	608,439
Massachusetts....	531,764	993,720	1,129,909	1,577,827	1,580,114	1,840,357	2,026,993	1,960,665
Michigan	646,873	1,047,819	1,160,298	1,372,082	1,664,628	1,805,093	2,085,929	2,205,223
Minnesota	365,395	735,838	822,146	970,976	1,002,843	1,129,975	1,251,198	1,125,529
Mississippi	86,130	82,492	112,515	151,692	146,034	162,090	175,824	180,080
Missouri	798,793	1,332,800	1,307,985	1,500,721	1,609,894	1,828,635	1,833,729	1,571,677
Montana	177,679	178,998	174,423	194,108	216,479	230,512	247,873	207,355
Nebraska	287,313	382,653	464,169	547,138	570,135	608,032	615,878	563,126
Nevada	33,316	27,194	26,921	32,417	41,430	43,848	53,174	54,234
New Hampshire ...	89,127	159,092	164,769	196,747	205,520	218,114	235,419	229,625
New Jersey	494,438	910,251	1,088,054	1,549,381	1,630,063	1,820,437	1,974,920	1,963,761
New Mexico	66,805	103,401	112,830	118,014	151,606	168,920	183,014	152,225
New York	1,706,305	2,898,513	3,256,319	4,405,626	4,688,614	5,596,398	6,301,596	6,316,790
North Carolina ..	289,835	538,741	482,687	636,070	711,501	839,462	822,648	790,554
North Dakota	113,390	205,776	199,081	239,847	256,290	273,716	280,775	220,171
Ohio	1,164,091	2,021,653	2,016,237	2,508,346	2,610,088	3,012,425	3,319,912	3,153,056
Oklahoma	292,327	484,610	528,415	618,427	704,633	749,740	826,212	722,636
Oregon	261,650	238,522	279,488	319,942	368,751	414,021	481,240	480,147
Pennsylvania	1,297,382	1,551,230	2,144,852	3,150,615	2,859,002	4,138,105	4,078,714	3,794,793
Rhode Island	87,816	167,981	210,115	237,194	266,170	311,149	321,148	299,276
South Carolina ..	63,852	66,808	50,751	68,605	104,407	115,437	99,830	103,375
South Dakota	128,942	182,237	203,868	261,865	288,438	296,452	308,427	232,076
Tennessee	272,190	435,636	300,273	363,473	390,638	475,531	522,823	510,692
Texas	373,114	486,326	657,309	708,999	863,426	843,482	1,041,168	1,150,326
Utah	143,145	145,526	156,990	176,604	206,579	216,677	247,819	248,319
Vermont	64,475	89,961	102,912	135,191	136,980	143,689	143,062	125,361
Virginia	153,994	231,033	223,726	305,358	297,942	334,590	346,607	388,485
Washington	392,904	398,705	421,549	500,840	614,814	692,338	793,833	856,328
West Virginia ...	289,671	509,942	583,082	642,752	743,774	830,072	868,076	715,596
Wisconsin	447,555	701,280	840,779	1,016,872	1,114,815	1,258,712	1,405,540	1,339,152
Wyoming	51,546	52,530	78,900	82,835	96,962	103,382	112,240	101,340

Source: 1916, The Presidential Vote, 1896-1932, E. E. Robinson; 1920 and 1924, U. S. Congress, Clerk of the House, Statistics of Congressional and Presidential Elections; 1928-44, Department of Commerce, Bureau of Census, Elections. See No. 5. Vote Cast in Presidential and Congressional Elections, 1928-44.

No. 856.—VOTE FOR PRESIDENTIAL ELECTORS, BY MAJOR POLITICAL PARTIES BY STATES: 1948 AND 1952

[In thousands]

STATE	1948						1952					
	Total	Democratic	Republican	Other parties	Percent of total		Total	Democratic	Republican	Other parties	Percent of total	
					Democratic	Republican					Democratic	Republican
Total	48,834	24,106	21,969	2,759	49.4	45.0	61,552	27,315	33,824	413	44.4	55.0
Alabama	215	....	41	174	....	19.0	426	275	149	2	64.6	35.0
Arizona	177	95	78	4	53.8	43.8	261	109	152	....	41.7	58.3
Arkansas	242	150	51	42	61.7	21.0	405	226	177	1	55.9	43.8
California	4,022	1,913	1,895	213	47.6	47.1	5,142	2,198	2,897	47	42.7	56.3
Colorado	515	267	240	8	51.9	46.5	630	245	380	5	39.0	60.3
Connecticut	884	423	438	22	47.9	49.5	1,097	482	611	4	43.9	55.7
Delaware	139	68	70	2	48.8	50.0	174	83	90	1	47.9	51.8
Florida	578	282	194	101	48.8	33.6	989	445	544	(1)	45.0	55.0
Georgia	419	255	77	87	60.8	18.3	656	457	199	(1)	69.7	30.3
Idaho	215	107	102	6	50.0	47.3	276	95	181	(1)	34.4	65.4
Illinois	3,984	1,995	1,961	28	50.1	49.2	4,481	2,014	2,457	10	44.9	54.8
Indiana	1,656	808	821	27	48.8	49.6	1,955	802	1,136	18	41.0	58.1
Iowa	1,038	522	494	22	50.3	47.6	1,269	452	809	8	35.6	63.8
Kansas	789	352	423	14	44.6	53.6	896	273	616	7	30.5	68.8
Kentucky	823	467	341	15	56.7	41.5	993	496	495	2	49.9	49.8
Louisiana	416	136	73	207	32.7	17.5	652	345	307	....	52.9	47.1
Maine	265	112	150	3	42.3	56.7	352	119	232	....	33.8	66.0
Maryland	597	287	295	15	48.0	49.4	902	395	499	7	43.8	55.3
Massachusetts	2,155	1,152	909	4 94	53.4	42.2	2,383	1,084	1,292	8	45.5	54.2
Michigan	2,110	1,003	1,039	68	47.6	49.2	2,799	1,231	1,552	16	44.0	55.4
Minnesota	1,212	693	484	36	57.2	39.9	1,379	608	763	8	44.1	55.3
Mississippi	192	19	5	168	10.1	2.6	286	173	....	5 112	60.4	....
Missouri	1,579	917	655	6	58.1	41.5	1,892	930	959	3	49.1	50.7
Montana	224	119	97	8	53.1	43.1	265	106	157	1	40.1	59.4
Nebraska	489	224	265	......	45.8	54.2	610	188	422	......	30.8	69.2
Nevada	62	31	29	1	50.4	47.3	82	32	51	......	38.6	61.4
New Hampshire	231	108	121	2	46.7	52.4	273	107	166	......	39.1	60.9
New Jersey	1,950	895	981	73	45.9	50.3	2,420	1,016	1,375	29	42.0	56.8
New Mexico	186	105	80	......	56.8	43.2	239	106	132	1	44.3	55.4
New York	6,275	4 2,780	2,841	4 653	44.3	45.3	6 3,105	3,105	3,953	71	43.6	55.5
North Carolina	791	459	259	74	58.0	32.7	1,211	653	558	......	53.9	46.1
North Dakota	221	96	115	10	43.4	52.2	270	77	192	2	28.4	71.0
Ohio	2,936	1,453	1,446	38	49.5	49.2	3,701	1,600	2,100	......	43.2	56.8
Oklahoma	722	453	269	......	62.7	37.3	949	431	518	......	45.4	54.6
Oregon	524	243	261	20	46.4	49.8	695	271	421	4	38.9	60.5
Pennsylvania	3,735	1,752	1,902	81	46.9	50.9	4,581	2,146	2,416	19	46.9	52.7
Rhode Island	326	189	135	3	57.8	41.4	414	203	211	(1)	49.0	50.9
South Carolina	143	34	5	103	24.1	3.8	341	173	7 168		50.7	49.3
South Dakota	250	118	130	3	47.0	51.8	294	90	204	......	30.7	69.3
Tennessee	550	270	203	77	49.1	36.9	893	444	446	3	49.7	50.0
Texas	1,147	751	282	114	65.4	24.6	2,076	969	1,103	4	46.7	53.1
Utah	276	149	124	3	54.0	45.0	330	135	194	......	41.1	58.9
Vermont	123	46	76	2	36.9	61.5	154	43	110	(1)	28.2	71.5
Virginia	419	201	172	46	47.9	41.0	620	269	349	2	43.4	56.3
Washington	905	476	386	43	52.6	42.7	1,103	493	599	11	44.7	54.3
West Virginia	749	429	316	3	57.3	42.2	874	454	420	......	51.9	48.1
Wisconsin	1,277	647	591	39	50.7	46.3	1,607	622	980	5	38.7	61.0
Wyoming	101	52	48	1	51.6	47.3	129	48	81	(1)	37.1	62.7

1 Less than 500.   3 Includes 48,201 blanks and 633 scattering.
2 Independent votes (pledged to Republican candidate).
4 Includes 222,562 Liberal Party votes.
5 Includes 97,119 blanks, 128 scattering, and 71 void.   6 Includes 416,711 Liberal Party votes.
7 Includes 158,289 votes by separate set of electors, by petition, for Republican candidates.

Source: U. S. Congress, Clerk of the House; *Statistics of the Presidential and Congressional Election.*

No. 357.—Vote for United States Representatives, by States: 1934 to 1948

[For explanation and current figures, see table 358]

STATE	1934	1936	1938	1940	1942	1944	1946	1948
Total	32,532,700	42,885,505	36,295,629	46,950,848	28,074,365	45,103,042	34,396,450	46,142,485
Alabama	164,885	255,052	123,877	269,645	69,131	222,338	179,488	197,084
Arizona	96,044	108,750	104,088	139,784	79,747	128,036	112,812	158,975
Arkansas	137,375	160,305	143,956	208,890	98,361	217,207	151,333	229,403
California	2,074,563	2,242,308	2,391,138	2,771,954	1,901,538	3,007,499	2,335,262	3,561,390
Colorado	395,698	457,759	449,537	525,026	342,396	493,862	332,072	497,411
Connecticut	548,038	682,933	623,397	780,646	560,248	825,116	674,499	920,610
Delaware	96,857	126,663	105,571	134,778	84,726	126,440	112,621	140,535
Florida	131,817	284,937	153,061	380,237	107,111	416,372	186,763	353,013
Georgia	52,833	277,073	66,087	271,523	61,875	274,374	161,578	365,356
Idaho	163,039	194,972	178,684	231,636	139,287	205,579	178,758	211,869
Illinois	2,747,438	3,731,539	3,104,444	4,006,860	2,862,842	3,874,845	3,446,920	3,848,640
Indiana	1,456,307	1,617,839	1,572,649	1,761,417	1,286,729	1,651,216	1,332,648	1,633,401
Iowa	846,253	1,054,364	902,636	1,114,963	664,747	972,759	593,076	939,743
Kansas	757,234	799,860	737,025	788,652	493,692	664,192	554,860	703,910
Kentucky	460,479	917,647	533,959	890,898	342,605	843,843	583,302	740,538
Louisiana	186,112	291,963	152,410	321,044	84,987	282,569	106,009	321,576
Maine	270,295	301,048	281,619	246,673	160,841	183,771	174,248	213,694
Maryland	455,630	543,381	486,472	585,418	337,436	544,324	444,955	534,186
Massachusetts	1,373,555	1,783,326	1,719,677	1,964,738	1,327,242	1,889,753	1,617,314	2,155,346
Michigan	1,212,525	1,696,280	1,547,215	1,987,352	1,170,694	2,163,487	1,604,732	2,064,536
Minnesota	995,605	1,091,195	1,070,927	1,205,753	761,276	1,109,109	875,005	1,181,726
Mississippi	57,327	148,441	35,439	146,219	51,602	152,712	50,037	152,537
Missouri	1,320,336	1,810,975	1,245,032	1,816,729	925,319	1,520,412	1,084,741	1,565,102
Montana	199,739	208,474	208,710	237,975	169,508	197,217	190,088	214,549
Nebraska	542,316	569,336	477,715	575,316	357,009	514,926	372,040	460,451
Nevada	41,683	43,764	45,441	50,746	39,389	51,744	49,046	58,705
New Hampshire	170,213	204,272	181,003	218,206	156,215	215,857	161,092	220,363
New Jersey	1,326,407	1,688,941	1,531,121	1,862,386	1,203,455	1,859,425	1,381,993	1,852,441
New Mexico	148,268	166,373	155,157	182,057	105,947	151,888	126,939	185,224
New York	3,657,908	5,311,612	4,487,956	6,083,201	3,875,271	6,024,597	4,705,410	5,997,987
North Carolina	493,694	800,884	479,267	797,655	314,827	754,658	452,222	763,513
North Dakota	277,979	235,576	216,340	235,286	182,380	197,594	144,394	190,803
Ohio	2,085,897	2,863,364	2,313,460	3,078,196	1,735,181	2,964,334	2,216,750	2,808,530
Oklahoma	553,487	694,180	468,257	766,041	351,968	684,560	492,141	685,065
Oregon	293,400	389,944	365,943	461,902	276,423	442,476	334,670	491,142
Pennsylvania	2,925,819	4,070,414	3,783,638	4,005,607	2,508,778	3,712,570	3,111,987	3,657,029
Rhode Island	244,562	304,920	300,220	314,023	236,604	293,481	272,394	318,577
South Carolina	22,156	115,285	46,196	99,672	23,356	100,862	26,358	140,654
South Dakota	277,555	286,449	274,416	296,551	178,111	225,738	157,805	240,720
Tennessee	275,242	392,553	264,404	417,157	156,212	398,622	193,448	448,973
Texas	439,690	819,690	365,208	1,019,418	278,418	1,058,419	347,395	1,061,853
Utah	179,976	215,786	182,532	246,881	150,493	247,681	196,672	274,333
Vermont	129,725	140,395	112,552	140,477	58,070	123,036	73,066	122,598
Virginia	148,171	322,276	126,043	316,576	90,067	342,980	253,864	383,160
Washington	479,365	646,858	586,493	744,286	428,186	803,093	644,930	817,578
West Virginia	619,946	825,738	622,821	870,115	460,287	718,509	537,357	788,631
Wisconsin	885,874	890,207	912,365	1,269,393	748,873	1,162,858	963,918	1,211,341
Wyoming	91,383	98,313	94,500	106,888	74,855	96,102	79,438	97,464

Source: 1934–44, Department of Commerce, Bureau of Census; Elections, 1944: No. 5, *Vote Cast in Presidential and Congressional Elections, 1928–44.* U. S. Congress, Clerk of the House; *Statistics of the Congressional Election of Nov. 5, 1946,* and *Statistics of the Presidential and Congressional Election of Nov. 2, 1948.*

No. 358.—VOTE FOR UNITED STATES REPRESENTATIVES, BY MAJOR POLITICAL PARTIES, BY STATES: 1950 AND 1952

[In thousands. In each State, totals represent the sum of votes cast in each Congressional District, except as follows: In New Mexico and North Dakota, no representatives were elected from districts, but more than one was elected from the State at large; in these States, each party total represents votes cast for that candidate of the party receiving highest vote. In Delaware, Nevada, Vermont, and Wyoming only one representative is elected at large. In Connecticut, Ohio (1950), Texas (1952), and Washington (1952), representatives are elected by district except one, who is elected at large; the at-large vote is not reflected in this tabulation. In numerous States, one or other of the major parties had no candidate in some districts. In those cases where votes of a party, as such, are cast in endorsement of a candidate of another party, the votes are here counted as for the endorsing party. See also notes below]

STATE	1950						1952					
	Total	Demo-cratic	Re-pub-lican	Other parties	Percent of total		Total	Demo-cratic	Re-pub-lican	Other parties	Percent of total	
					Dem-ocrat-ic	Re-pub-lican					Dem-ocrat-ic	Re-pub-lican
Total	40,490	19,785	19,750	894	48.9	48.9	57,560	28,179	28,543	838	49.0	49.6
Alabama	152	151	1		99.4	.6	343	324	19		94.6	5.4
Arizona	178	116	62		65.0	35.0	248	128	121		51.5	48.5
Arkansas	296	296			100.0		362	309	52	1	85.3	14.3
California ¹	3,359	1,481	1,754	124	44.1	52.2	4,564	1,874	2,539	150	41.1	55.6
Colorado	443	214	226	3	48.4	51.0	607	270	335	1	44.5	55.3
Connecticut	861	436	425		50.6	49.4	1,098	504	587	2	46.1	53.7
Delaware	129	56	73		43.3	56.7	170	82	88		48.1	51.9
Florida	253	229	24		90.4	9.6	739	547	192	(²)	74.1	25.9
Georgia	253	253			100.0		547	547		(²)	100.0	
Idaho	200	91	109		45.6	54.4	265	107	157		40.6	59.4
Illinois	3,510	1,617	1,891	2	46.1	53.9	4,352	2,004	2,349	(²)	46.0	54.0
Indiana	1,587	727	850	9	45.8	53.6	1,936	831	1,094	11	42.9	56.5
Iowa	820	317	500	2	38.7	61.0	1,143	379	762	2	33.1	66.7
Kansas	607	249	358		41.0	59.0	824	334	490		40.6	59.4
Kentucky	489	308	181		63.0	37.0	951	495	455	1	52.1	47.8
Louisiana	227	227			100.0		416	380	36		91.3	8.7
Maine	238	101	137		42.4	57.6	234	77	157	1	32.8	66.9
Maryland	573	284	286	3	49.5	49.9	841	405	436		48.2	51.8
Massachusetts	1,947	921	930	⁵ 96	47.3	47.8	2,289	1,064	1,210	15	46.5	52.9
Michigan	1,805	839	956	9	46.5	53.0	2,772	1,311	1,453	8	47.3	52.4
Minnesota	1,018	⁴ 474	539	6	⁴ 46.6	52.9	1,388	639	749		46.0	54.0
Mississippi	88	83	3		94.2	3.3	241	235	6		97.5	2.5
Missouri	1,250	698	552	1	55.8	44.2	1,861	971	890		52.2	47.8
Montana	211	108	100	2	51.4	47.5	256	111	144	1	43.3	56.4
Nebraska	436	164	272		37.7	62.3	566	180	386	(²)	31.8	68.2
Nevada	60	32	28		52.8	47.2	81	40	41		49.5	50.5
New Hampshire	185	73	112		39.3	60.7	258	95	163		36.9	63.1
New Jersey	1,571	690	859	22	43.9	54.7	2,316	978	1,317	20	42.2	55.9
New Mexico	173	98	75		56.4	43.6	⁵ 234	121	112		52.0	48.0
New York	5,052	⁶ 2,163	⁶ 2,384	⁶ 505	42.8	47.2	6,910	2,780	3,619	512	40.2	52.4
North Carolina	522	366	157		70.0	30.0	1,122	763	356	2	68.0	31.8
North Dakota	181	62	119		34.4	65.6	⁵ 231	50	181	(²)	21.6	78.4
Ohio	2,767	1,257	1,451	58	45.5	52.4	3,382	1,471	1,836	75	43.5	54.3
Oklahoma	608	364	243		60.0	40.0	933	546	384	4	58.5	41.1
Oregon	499	201	288	10	40.3	57.7	666	258	408		38.7	61.3
Pennsylvania	3,512	1,673	1,834	5	47.6	52.2	4,506	2,151	2,353	3	47.7	52.2
Rhode Island	293	182	112		61.9	38.1	407	220	187		54.1	45.9
South Carolina	50	50			100.0		284	278	6		98.0	2.0
South Dakota	248	98	151		39.3	60.7	287	90	197		31.4	68.6
Tennessee	263	165	72	25	63.0	27.4	700	480	204	17	68.5	29.1
Texas	360	326	34		90.5	9.5	1,719	1,697	22		98.7	1.3
Utah	264	138	125		52.5	47.5	327	145	182		44.4	55.6
Vermont	89	23	65	1	25.6	73.4	153	43	110	(²)	28.2	71.8
Virginia	212	155	51	5	73.4	24.3	447	298	139	10	66.7	31.0
Washington	724	342	378	3	47.3	52.3	1,016	441	574	1	43.4	56.5
West Virginia	663	375	288		56.6	43.4	875	471	403		53.9	46.1
Wisconsin	1,110	470	639	1	42.4	57.6	1,568	603	955	(²)	38.4	61.6
Wyoming	93	42	51		45.5	54.5	127	51	76		39.9	60.1

¹ In California a person may be candidate of one or more parties for same office, so that party votes for candidates are not segregable. Party vote shown is computed by assigning to a party total votes for candidates who are members of that party.
² Less than 500.   ³ Includes 87,673 blanks.
⁴ Democratic-Farmer-Labor party.
⁵ Voters entitled to vote for 2 candidates; total ascertained by adding the vote of the highest candidate in each party.
⁶ Included in Republican are 40,575 endorsing votes cast for Democrats; included in "Other" are 164,695 endorsing votes cast for Democrats and 25,355 for Republicans.

Source: U. S. Congress, Clerk of the House; Statistics of the Congressional Election of Nov. 7, 1950, and Statistics of the Presidential and Congressional Election of Nov. 4, 1952.

No. 359.—VOTE FOR UNITED STATES SENATORS, BY MAJOR POLITICAL PARTIES, BY STATES: 1950 AND 1952

[In thousands. Years in which no regular elections occur indicated by leaders. Elections to fill vacancies for unexpired terms excluded]

STATE	1950						1952					
	Total	Democratic	Republican	Other parties	Percent of total Democratic	Percent of total Republican	Total	Democratic	Republican	Other parties	Percent of total Democratic	Percent of total Republican
Total	32,409	15,298	16,166	945	47.2	49.9	44,802	20,029	23,242	1,532	44.7	51.9
Alabama	164	126	....	38	76.5	....						
Arizona	185	116	69	....	62.8	37.2	257	125	132	....	48.7	51.3
Arkansas	303	303	....	....	100.0	....						
California	3,686	1,503	2,183	(1)	40.8	59.2	4,542	....	3,982	560	....	87.7
Colorado	450	210	240	....	46.7	53.3						
Connecticut	863	454	409	....	52.6	47.4	1,093	485	574	35	44.4	52.5
Delaware							171	78	93	....	45.5	54.5
Florida	313	239	74	....	76.3	23.7	618	617	....	1	99.8	....
Georgia	261	261	....	....	100.0	....						
Idaho	201	77	124	....	38.3	61.7						
Illinois	3,623	1,658	1,952	13	45.8	53.9						
Indiana	1,599	741	844	13	46.4	52.8	1,946	911	1,021	14	46.8	52.4
Iowa	859	384	471	4	44.7	54.8						
Kansas	619	271	336	12	43.8	54.3						
Kentucky	617	334	278	4	54.2	45.1						
Louisiana	252	221	31	....	87.7	12.3						
Maine							237	83	139	15	34.9	58.7
Maryland	616	283	326	6	46.0	53.0	856	406	450	....	47.5	52.5
Massachusetts							2,360	1,212	1,141	7	51.3	48.3
Michigan							2,821	1,383	1,428	9	49.0	50.6
Minnesota							1,387	590	786	12	42.5	56.6
Mississippi							234	234	....	....	100.0	....
Missouri	1,279	686	593	1	53.6	4.1	1,868	1,009	858	1	54.0	45.9
Montana							262	133	127	2	50.7	48.6
Nebraska							592	165	409	18	27.8	69.1
Nevada	62	36	26	....	58.0	42.0	81	39	42	....	48.3	51.7
New Hampshire	190	72	106	11	38.2	56.0						
New Jersey							2,318	1,011	1,287	20	43.6	55.5
New Mexico							240	123	117	....	51.1	48.9
New York	5,473	²2,320	2,367	¹³786	42.4	43.3	6,980	2,522	3,854	605	36.1	55.2
North Carolina	548	376	172	....	68.7	31.3						
North Dakota	187	61	126	....	32.4	67.6	238	55	158	25	23.3	66.3
Ohio	2,860	1,214	1,646	....	42.5	57.5	3,442	1,563	1,879	....	45.4	54.6
Oklahoma	631	346	285	....	54.8	45.2						
Oregon	503	117	377	10	23.2	74.8						
Pennsylvania	3,549	1,694	1,820	34	47.7	51.3	4,519	2,169	2,331	20	48.0	51.6
Rhode Island							411	225	186	....	54.8	45.2
South Carolina	50	50	....	....	100.0	....						
South Dakota	251	91	161	....	36.1	63.9						
Tennessee							735	545	153	36	74.2	20.9
Texas							1,895	1,895	....	....	100.0	....
Utah	264	121	142	1	45.8	53.9	327	150	177	....	45.7	54.3
Vermont	89	20	70	(1)	22.0	78.0	184	43	111	....	27.7	72.3
Virginia							544	399	(1)	145	73.4	....
Washington	745	398	342	5	53.4	46.0	1,059	595	461	3	56.2	43.5
West Virginia							877	470	407	....	53.6	46.4
Wisconsin	1,118	516	595	5	46.2	53.3	1,605	731	870	....	45.6	54.2
Wyoming							130	63	67	....	48.4	51.6

¹ Less than 500.
² Included in "Other" are 312,594 Liberal votes cast in endorsement of Democratic candidate.
³ Includes 244,654 blanks, void, and scattering.

Source: U. S. Congress, Clerk of the House; *Statistics of the Congressional Election of Nov. 7, 1950*, and *Statistics of the Presidential and Congressional Election of Nov. 4, 1952.*

No. 360.—REGISTERED VOTERS AND VOTES CAST FOR GOVERNOR, BY STATES

STATE	REGISTERED VOTERS		VOTES CAST		
	Year	Number	Year	General election	Primary election [1]
Alabama		(2)	1950	170,541	402,177
Arizona	1950	279,533	1950	195,227	163,220
Arkansas	1951	522,783	1950	317,067	327,559
California	1950	5,244,837	1950	3,796,090	2,997,264
Colorado	1951	655,626	1950	450,994	146,850
Connecticut	1950	1,069,321	1950	878,735	(2)
Delaware		(4)	1948	(4)	(5)
Florida	1950	1,067,155	1948	457,612	681,766
Georgia	1950	1,229,164	1950	234,975	563,037
Idaho	1950	⁵ 300,000	1950	204,792	127,567
Illinois		(2)	1948	3,940,257	1,322,750
Indiana	1950	2,273,985	1948	1,652,312	(2)
Iowa		(3)	1950	857,213	332,190
Kansas		(3)	1950	619,310	337,865
Kentucky		(2)	1947	677,479	419,845
Louisiana	1950	818,031	1948	76,566	643,915
Maine		(2)	1950	241,177	214,404
Maryland	1950	917,937	1950	645,631	380,375
Massachusetts	1950	2,475,396	1950	1,910,180	649,467
Michigan		(2)	1950	1,879,382	866,636
Minnesota		(2)	1950	1,046,632	870,295
Mississippi		(2)	1947	166,095	365,226
Missouri		(2)	1948	1,567,338	712,849
Montana	1950	272,103	1948	222,964	136,402
Nebraska		(2)	1950	459,319	323,125
Nevada	1950	83,950	1950	61,773	56,838
New Hampshire	1950	311,294	1950	191,165	74,422
New Jersey	1950	2,066,897	1949	1,414,527	450,063
New Mexico		(2)	1950	180,205	117,691
New York	1950	6,432,770	1950	5,473,048	(2)
North Carolina		(2)	1948	780,525	432,125
North Dakota		(2)	1950	153,772	168,558
Ohio	1950	2,673,626	1950	2,902,819	986,343
Oklahoma		(2)	1950	644,276	563,347
Oregon	1950	751,270	1950	519,125	344,802
Pennsylvania	1950	4,761,660	1950	3,510,059	2,003,385
Rhode Island	1951	373,375	1950	296,808	(2)
South Carolina	1950	567,467	1950	50,642	236,329
South Dakota	1951	⁵ 300,000	1950	253,316	100,751
Tennessee		(2)	1950	236,194	481,271
Texas		(2)	1950	394,747	1,086,564
Utah		(2)	1948	275,067	122,928
Vermont	1950	189,665	1950	87,061	74,817
Virginia	1949	⁵ 671,800	1949	262,332	325,500
Washington	1950	1,217,942	1948	883,141	540,266
West Virginia	1950	1,080,113	1948	768,061	453,349
Wisconsin		(2)	1950	1,138,148	898,442
Wyoming		(2)	1950	96,959	65,911

1 Includes figures only for initial primary elections—not run-off primaries.
2 Registration not required or no central records maintained.
3 Candidates for Governor nominated at party conventions.
4 Not available.
5 Estimate.

Source: The Council of State Governments, Chicago, Ill.; *The Book of the States, 1952-53.*

No. 361.—MALE CITIZENS OF VOTING AGE, 1900 AND 1910, AND ALL CITIZENS OF VOTING AGE, 1920 TO 1950, BY STATES

[For *total* population, 21 years old and over, for 1950, see table 23. For U. S. totals, see also *Historical Statistics*, series B 244 and B 258]

DIVISION AND STATE	MALE CITIZENS 21 YEARS OLD AND OVER		CITIZENS 21 YEARS OLD AND OVER			
	1900	1910	1920	1930	1940	1950
United States	[1] 18,973,994	[2] 23,257,240	[2] 54,418,928	67,288,952	72,863,451	[3] 94,974,460
New England	1,373,696	1,542,217	3,637,179	4,251,856	5,015,624	5,969,164
Maine	192,202	201,861	420,711	439,062	493,506	552,096
New Hampshire	110,127	111,052	235,490	257,350	295,859	337,585
Vermont	97,029	100,540	198,609	203,406	214,248	229,500
Massachusetts	647,019	754,547	1,861,269	2,197,605	2,575,477	3,038,491
Rhode Island	100,705	119,620	289,645	357,669	424,876	514,009
Connecticut	226,014	254,597	631,455	796,764	1,011,658	1,297,483
Middle Atlantic	3,860,713	4,516,538	10,984,026	14,179,853	16,951,733	19,842,834
New York	1,828,887	2,110,318	5,129,209	6,783,504	8,327,563	9,796,079
New Jersey	467,018	592,234	1,526,693	2,179,216	2,592,978	3,217,130
Pennsylvania	1,564,808	1,814,086	4,328,124	5,217,043	6,031,192	6,829,625
East North Central	4,129,263	4,835,329	11,609,924	14,486,613	16,796,537	19,662,232
Ohio	1,143,426	1,317,652	3,228,349	3,882,029	4,404,423	5,181,253
Indiana	691,286	775,688	1,702,578	1,944,828	2,198,935	2,531,990
Illinois	1,250,283	1,453,840	3,462,573	4,428,680	5,119,854	5,801,882
Michigan	611,015	733,615	1,879,272	2,575,816	3,131,722	3,963,014
Wisconsin	434,273	554,534	1,337,152	1,655,260	1,941,603	2,184,093
West North Central	2,646,505	3,122,829	6,839,372	7,760,810	8,501,797	9,001,992
Minnesota	412,186	521,198	1,232,866	1,461,311	1,730,547	1,873,326
Iowa	594,797	607,050	1,366,919	1,472,456	1,608,926	1,676,476
Missouri	822,548	916,609	1,969,089	2,271,259	2,463,726	2,619,739
North Dakota	70,893	139,167	289,868	340,664	358,090	358,562
South Dakota	93,799	151,030	313,279	374,337	378,405	396,511
Nebraska	264,228	315,065	684,973	784,745	817,280	846,047
Kansas	388,054	472,710	982,878	1,106,038	1,144,823	1,231,331
South Atlantic	2,453,531	2,978,380	7,048,935	8,282,868	10,285,903	[3] 12,871,228
Delaware	51,318	56,785	126,254	142,052	171,856	207,410
Maryland	307,821	343,807	818,143	958,671	1,153,510	1,500,329
District of Columbia	80,504	98,122	292,964	330,866	474,793	570,093
Virginia	443,237	514,781	1,192,560	1,293,254	1,567,517	2,013,357
West Virginia	241,473	310,831	710,927	874,116	1,046,107	1,160,622
North Carolina	416,514	502,506	1,202,558	1,538,977	1,925,483	2,304,999
South Carolina	282,054	333,171	776,847	817,584	989,841	1,148,259
Georgia	497,748	615,893	1,414,819	1,494,096	1,768,969	[3] 2,175,612
Florida	133,162	202,484	513,863	833,252	1,187,827	1,790,517
East South Central	1,778,419	2,074,883	4,493,821	5,201,377	6,084,611	6,659,510
Kentucky	537,526	596,140	1,278,411	1,416,323	1,630,772	1,737,664
Tennessee	483,505	547,905	1,208,226	1,413,523	1,703,391	1,973,444
Alabama	410,533	507,186	1,135,559	1,343,283	1,555,369	1,743,611
Mississippi	346,855	423,652	871,623	1,028,248	1,195,079	1,204,791
West South Central	1,416,912	2,143,281	4,973,325	6,366,907	7,536,731	8,650,814
Arkansas	310,218	391,232	861,540	964,956	1,098,986	1,109,935
Louisiana	312,751	397,717	897,236	1,118,843	1,364,933	1,577,244
Oklahoma	105,767	420,741	980,448	1,277,419	1,362,438	1,376,350
Texas	688,176	933,591	2,234,101	3,005,689	3,710,374	4,587,285
Mountain	486,597	736,526	1,656,604	1,953,152	2,393,992	2,982,406
Montana	84,572	117,906	264,244	298,982	343,180	364,203
Idaho	47,314	94,770	218,411	237,144	305,311	343,811
Wyoming	32,823	49,597	102,698	124,224	150,031	175,136
Colorado	163,665	233,617	519,205	586,255	688,410	826,964
New Mexico	51,067	81,142	159,914	202,566	275,227	367,433
Arizona	35,107	46,091	125,923	202,369	263,346	421,146
Utah	57,767	83,703	206,671	248,410	296,160	380,051
Nevada	14,282	29,700	40,538	53,202	70,327	103,662
Pacific	722,893	1,253,604	3,102,227	4,805,516	6,296,523	9,334,280
Washington	165,752	347,470	741,213	916,864	1,123,725	1,507,786
Oregon	123,779	211,875	447,823	579,547	717,121	980,192
California	433,362	694,259	1,913,191	3,309,105	4,455,677	6,846,302

[1] Includes 95,745 males in Indian Territory.
[2] 1910 and 1920 State figures include foreign-born Negroes (not naturalized) excluded from U. S. totals, but exclude native born of all other nonwhite races included in U. S. totals.
[3] Figures for Georgia, where minimum voting age is 18, includes all persons (172,441), citizens and noncitizens, 18 to 20 years of age.

Source: Department of Commerce, Bureau of the Census. 12th Census Reports, *Population*, Vol. I, Pt. 1; 13th Census Reports, *Abstract of the Census;* 14th Census Reports, *Population*, Vol. III; 15th Census Reports, *Population*, Vol. II; 16th Census Reports, *Population*, Vol. II, Pt. 1; and *U. S. Census of Population: 1950*, Vol. II, Pt. 1.

No. 362.—COMPOSITION OF CONGRESS BY POLITICAL PARTY AFFILIATIONS:[*] 1915 TO 1953

[D=Democratic, R=Republican. See also *Historical Statistics*, series P 50-56]

YEAR	President	Congress	HOUSE			SENATE		
			Major party	Principal minority party	Other (except vacancies)	Major party	Principal minority party	Other (except vacancies)
1915–1917	D (Wilson)	64th	D—230	R—196	9	D—56	R—40	
1917–1919	D (Wilson)	65th	D—216	R—210	6	D—53	R—42	
1919–1921	D (Wilson)	66th	R—240	D—190	3	R—49	D—47	
1921–1923	R (Harding)	67th	R—301	D—131	1	R—59	D—37	
1923–1925	R (Coolidge)	68th	R—225	D—205	3	R—51	D—43	2
1925–1927	R (Coolidge)	69th	R—247	D—183	4	R—56	D—39	1
1927–1929	R (Coolidge)	70th	R—237	D—195	3	R—49	D—46	1
1929–1931	R (Hoover)	71st	R—267	D—167	1	R—56	D—39	1
1931–1933	R (Hoover)	72d	D—220	R—214	1	R—48	D—47	1
1933–1934	D (F. Roosevelt)	73d	D—310	R—117	5	D—60	R—35	1
1935–1936	D (F. Roosevelt)	74th	D—319	R—103	10	D—69	R—25	2
1937–1938	D (F. Roosevelt)	75th	D—331	R—89	13	D—76	R—16	4
1939–1941	D (F. Roosevelt)	76th	D—261	R—164	4	D—69	R—23	4
1941–1942	D (F. Roosevelt)	77th	D—268	R—162	5	D—66	R—28	2
1943–1944	D (F. Roosevelt)	78th	D—218	R—208	4	D—58	R—37	1
1945–1946	D (F. Roosevelt) / D (Truman)	79th	D—242	R—190	2	D—56	R—38	1
1947–1948	D (Truman)	80th	R—245	D—188	1	R—51	D—45	
1949–1950	D (Truman)	81st	D—263	R—171	1	D—54	R—42	
1951–1952	D (Truman)	82d	D—234	R—199	2	D—49	R—47	
1953	R (Eisenhower)	83d	R—221	D—211	1	R—48	D—47	1

[*] Source: Party affiliation of The President: U. S. Congress, Clerk of the House; *Platforms of Two Great Political Parties, 1899 to 1944*. Other data: Tabulations of Library of Congress, Legislative Reference Service, *Political Trends—Both Houses of Congress—1789-1944*; and *Congressional Directory*.

FIG. XXVI.—COMPOSITION OF CONGRESS BY POLITICAL PARTY AFFILIATIONS: 1927 TO 1953

[See table 362]

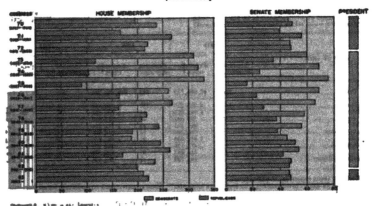

Source: Department of Commerce, Bureau of the Census. For source of data, see table 362.

No. 363.—Congressional Bills, Acts, and Resolutions: 1937 to 1952

[Excludes simple and concurrent resolutions. See also *Historical Statistics*, series P 40-44 and P 47]

ITEM	75th Cong.	76th Cong.	77th Cong.	78th Cong.	79th Cong.	80th Cong.	81st Cong.	82d Cong.
Period of session	1937-1938	1939-1941	1941-1942	1943-1944	1945-1946	1947-1948	1949-1950	1951-1952
Measures introduced, total	16,156	16,105	11,334	8,334	10,330	10,797	14,988	12,730
Bills	15,120	15,174	10,793	7,845	9,748	10,108	14,219	12,062
Joint resolutions	1,036	931	541	489	582	689	769	668
Measures enacted, total	1,759	1,662	1,485	1,157	1,625	1,363	2,024	1,617
Public	919	1,005	850	568	733	906	921	594
Private	840	657	635	589	892	457	1,103	1,023

Source: U. S. Congress, *Calendars of the U. S. House of Representatives* and *History of Legislation*, and tabulations of Library of Congress Legislative Reference Service.

No. 364.—Congressional Bills Vetoed: 1913 to 1952

[See also *Historical Statistics*, series P 32-37]

PERIOD	President	VETOED BILLS			Vetoes sustained	Bills passed over veto
		Total	Regular	Pocket		
1913-1921	Wilson	44	33	11	38	6
1921-1923	Harding	6	5	1	6	
1923-1929	Coolidge	50	20	30	46	4
1929-1933	Hoover	37	21	16	34	3
1933-1945	F. Roosevelt	631	371	260	622	9
1945-1952	Truman	250	180	70	238	12

Source: U. S. Congress, Senate Library, *Veto Messages . . . 1889-1948*; U. S. Congress, *Calendars of the U. S. House of Representatives* and *History of Legislation*.

No. 365.—Expenditures by Organizations Attempting to Influence National Legislation (Lobbies): 1949, 1950, and 1951

[Represents tabulation of reports made under Federal Regulation of Lobbying Act. Excludes personal reports of individuals representing organizations for which no separate report was filed. Classification of an organization is based on what appears to be the basic nature of the group's membership, determined largely by the organization name rather than on legislative interest]

TYPE OF ORGANIZATION	1949		1950		1951	
	Number of groups [1]	Expenditures [2]	Number of groups [1]	Expenditures [2]	Number of groups [1]	Expenditures [2]
Total	256	$7,969,710	312	$10,303,204	269	$8,771,096
Business	140	3,280,278	141	3,410,054	117	3,089,742
Citizens	30	1,015,073	45	1,799,803	36	1,498,309
Employee	17	257,301	30	518,413	30	541,488
Farm	11	391,595	13	1,212,214	10	1,281,785
Foreign policy	14	718,556	13	744,904	11	581,005
Professional	15	1,672,043	21	1,596,835	18	673,442
Reclamation	11	374,174	11	389,374	11	412,004
Tax	13	154,967	31	443,186	31	524,896
Veterans, military	5	105,723	7	188,421	5	128,425

[1] Excludes those reporting no expenditure.
[2] Reported as spent "in connection with legislative interests." Some groups report expenditures for all purposes; others report an allocation of spending for legislative purposes.

Source: Congressional Quarterly News Features, Washington, D. C.; *Congressional Quarterly Almanac.* (Material copyrighted; written permission required for reproduction rights.)

14. Federal Government Finances and Employment

The Government's proposed budget for the ensuing fiscal year is transmitted to the Congress by the President in January, and contains the President's recommendations for budget appropriations and other authorizations for the maintenance of the various departments and establishments. It includes estimates to carry out both existing laws and proposed legislation. Data from *The Budget of the United States Government* for the fiscal year ending June 30, 1954, are presented in tables 368–373. The Treasury Department publishes a *Digest of Appropriations* each year, which summarizes appropriation legislation enacted by the Congress, and also publishes yearly the *Combined Statement of Receipts, Expenditures and Balances*, an abstract of the Treasury books relating to all of the receipt accounts and appropriation accounts which report disbursements under the appropriations made by the Congress.

The day-to-day financial operations of the Federal Government are reported in the *Daily Statement of the United States Treasury*, which covers all of the receipts and expenditures of the Government, including those arising under public debt operations. The *Daily Treasury Statement* for the first working day of each month contains a statement of the public debt as of the last day of the month just ended. The *Daily Treasury Statement* of the fifteenth of the month contains certain special tables. The *Treasury Bulletin*, a monthly publication, contains analytical material on fiscal operations and related Treasury activities. The *Annual Report of the Secretary of the Treasury* is a convenient summary of yearly data relating to somewhat broader fields, and, in addition, contains reports on the finances of the Federal Government and developments in Treasury operations. The *Annual Report of the Commissioner of Internal Revenue* gives a detailed account of tax collections by kind of tax and by geographic area.

Two other special aspects of Federal finances are presented in the Treasury Department's *Circulation Statement of United States Money* (monthly) and *Prices and Yields of Public Marketable Securities* . . . (monthly).

Data from income tax returns are compiled by the Bureau of Internal Revenue of the Treasury Department. This Bureau's annual report, *Statistics of Income*, Part 1, is compiled from data reported on individual income tax returns, taxable fiduciary income tax returns, Federal estate tax returns, and gift tax returns. *Statistics of Income*, Part 2, also published annually, presents data from corporation income and declared value excess-profits tax returns, corporation excess-profits tax returns, and personal holding company returns. See tables 379–392, 536, 538, 539, and 546.

Data from a special study on debt by the Office of Business Economics of the Department of Commerce are presented in table 394. These data are published annually in the *Survey of Current Business*. Gross debt, as defined in this study, consists of all classes of legal indebtedness except the following: (1) Deposit liability of banks and the amount of bank notes in circulation; (2) value of outstanding policies and annuities of life insurance carriers; (3) short-term debts among individuals and unincorporated nonfinancial business firms; and (4) nominal debt of corporations, such as bonds which are authorized but unissued or outstanding but reacquired.

Note.—This section presents data for the most recent year or period available on March 31, 1953, when the material was organized and sent to the printer. In a few instances, more recent data were added after that date.

Net public and private debt outstanding is a comprehensive aggregate of indebtedness of borrowers after elimination of certain duplicating governmental and corporate debt. This measure of indebtedness provides a more significant indication of trends in debt structure than does gross debt, since effects of nominal changes in financial practices and organization are largely removed. To obtain net figures, gross or total debt is adjusted for specific types of duplications pertaining to the following sectors of the economy: (1) Federal Government and its corporations and agencies generally; (2) State and local governments treated as a single entity; and (3) within the corporate area, those affiliated but legally distinct corporations which operate under a single management, treated here as a unit. In the noncorporate private area, data are gross throughout with no adjustments for duplications.

Federal employment figures are compiled primarily by the Civil Service Commission. The figures are issued by that agency in its regular *Annual Report* and in its *Monthly Report on Employment*. The Commission also publishes an annual report on the pay of Federal employees entitled *Pay Structure of the Federal Civil Service*. Data on Federal employment are also issued by the Bureau of Labor Statistics in its *Monthly Labor Review*.

TREASURY FUND STRUCTURE

All receipts of the Government, with a few exceptions, are deposited to the credit of the general fund of the Treasury irrespective of their ultimate disposition or availability for expenditure. However, these receipts are recorded by the Treasury in accounts classified generally according to the source, and according to whether or not the receipts are earmarked in some degree for expenditure.

Under the Constitution, no money may be withdrawn from the Treasury unless appropriated by the Congress. All disbursements of the Government, with a few exceptions, are made from the general fund irrespective of the source of funds or authority for such disbursements. These disbursements are further classified by accounts reflecting various types of authorizations or conditions under which they may be expended. A brief description of these various classes of accounts follows:

Budget accounts.—General receipt accounts are a record of receipts which are available to finance the general operations of the Government to the extent appropriations are made by the Congress. If expenditures out of these appropriations exceed budget receipts, the Secretary of the Treasury is authorized to borrow on the credit of the United States. The principal sources of general receipts are income taxes, excise taxes, employment taxes, customs duties, and miscellaneous receipts.

Special receipt accounts (earmarked moneys) are funds received generally under Federal projects pursuant to special authorizations of law, which may be expended only for the particular purpose specified and not for general purposes. The Congress appropriates these receipts for the special purpose involved. Examples of some of the special fund receipts relate to the Reclamation Fund, Alaska Railroad Fund, the Mineral Leasing Act, and the National Forest Funds.

Expenditure (appropriation) accounts record the amounts authorized by the Congress, and expenditures therefrom, for the general support of the Government. They are classified according to the period of availability (i. e., 1-year, multiple year, no-year), as to amount (definite or indefinite), or whether or not requiring annual appropriation action by the Congress.

Revolving and management fund accounts are funds authorized by specific provisions of law to: (a) Finance a continuing cycle of operations with receipts derived from such operations available without further action by Congress; or, (b) facilitate accounting for and administration of intragovernmental operations. Examples of such accounts are the General Supply Fund of the General Services Administration;

the Working Capital Fund of the Public Buildings Administration; and corporate operations such as those under the Reconstruction Finance Corporation and the Commodity Credit Corporation.

Nonbudget accounts.—Trust accounts are receipts and expenditures (appropriation) accounts maintained to record the receipt and expenditure of moneys held in trust by the Government for the benefit of individuals, or classes of individuals, which may be expended only in accordance with the terms of a trust agreement or statute. Examples are the Civil Service Retirement Fund, Federal Old-Age and Survivors Insurance Trust Fund, Unemployment Trust Fund, and National Service Life Insurance Fund. These moneys are not available for general purposes and do not enter into the budget surplus or deficit.

Deposit fund accounts are receipts that are either: (a) Held in suspense temporarily and later refunded or transferred into some other account of the Government; or, (b) held by the Government as banker or agent for others and paid out at the direction of the owners. These funds have no effect on the budget surplus or deficit. In Treasury reports these accounts are reported on a net basis (excess of expenditures or excess of receipts for the period). Examples are employees' payroll allotment accounts for the purchase of U. S. savings bonds, and accounts for the accumulation of taxes withheld from employees' salaries.

BASIS OF TABLES

Many tables dealing with Federal fiscal affairs *are based upon, or reconciled with*, financial data as reported in the *Daily Treasury Statement*. This *Statement* is compiled from the latest available reports received from Government depositaries and disbursing offices.

Expenditures (disbursement basis).—Expenditures of the Government are stated by the Treasury Department in its published reports on two bases:

1. In the *Daily Treasury Statement*, expenditures are reported to quite an extent upon the basis of checks issued as furnished daily by teletype from Government disbursing offices; the main exception is the Department of Defense, the figures of which are currently on a checks-paid basis. Also included as expenditures are transfers from general appropriation accounts to trust funds.

2. In the annual *Combined Statement of Receipts, Expenditures and Balances* expenditures are stated on the basis of checks-issued during the fiscal year, as reported by Government disbursing offices; the Treasury holds its books open for this purpose until all such reports have been received.

Receipts.—Similarly, the Treasury Department utilizes three bases for the reporting of receipts:

1. In order to state receipts of the Government as promptly as possible, revenues and miscellaneous receipts are reported in the *Daily Treasury Statement* on the basis of the latest available reports of deposits in Government depositaries.

2. However, certificates of deposit covering actual deposits in Treasury offices and depositaries cannot reach the Treasury immediately and for that reason all receipts for a fiscal year cannot be covered by warrants (formally documented) immediately upon the close of each fiscal year. In the *Combined Statement of Receipts, Expenditures and Balances* receipts are compiled on a warrants-issued basis and include in-transit items in such a manner as to take into account all certificates of deposit applying to a particular fiscal year.

3. Collection basis—Statements showing receipts on this basis are compiled from reports of collectors in the field and from depositaries for withheld taxes. These reports do not coincide with others because collecting officers make collections during the last few days of the fiscal year which are not deposited until after the close of the fiscal year and because many employers deposit withheld taxes directly in depositary

banks. The depositary receipts are later submitted to collectors who report them in addition to the cash payments they have received. The moneys represented by the depositary receipts have been reported in the *Daily Treasury Statement* sometimes several months before it is possible to report them as collections. This reporting basis has the advantage of providing statistical details which are not available elsewhere.

Public debt accounts.—Tables on this basis indicate the status of the public debt after taking into consideration items in transit at the end of the period. The basis differs from that used in the *Daily Treasury Statement* since the Treasury believes that it is not practical to delay publication of that report in order to include all transactions for a particular day.

Historical statistics.—See preface and historical appendix. Tabular headnotes (as "See also *Historical Statistics*, series P 89-98") provide cross-references, where applicable, to *Historical Statistics of the United States, 1789-1945*.

Fig. **XXVII.**—Net Public and Private Debt, by Major Components: 1916 to 1951

[See table 394]

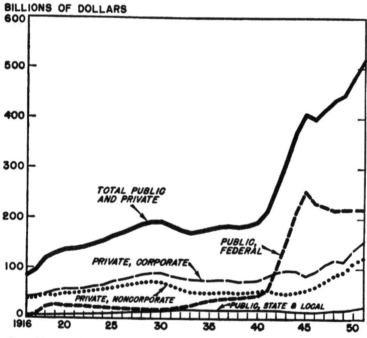

BILLIONS OF DOLLARS

Source: Department of Commerce, Office of Business Economics.

No. 366.—RECEIPTS AND SURPLUS OR DEFICIT OF THE FEDERAL GOVERNMENT: 1789 TO 1952

[In thousands of dollars. On basis of warrants issued through 1915, thereafter on basis of daily Treasury statements except as noted. General, special, emergency, and trust accounts combined through 1930; thereafter, trust accounts excluded. For explanation of bases and accounts, see general note, p. 333. See also *Historical Statistics*, series P 89-98]

YEARLY AVERAGE OR YEAR ENDING JUNE 30—	Net [1]	Total [2]	Customs [3]	Internal revenue		Sales of public lands [4]	Other receipts	Surplus (+) or deficit (−), receipts compared with expenditures
				Income and profits taxes	Other			
1789-1800 [5]	5,717	5,717	5,020		[6] 375	[6] 9	313	−59
1801-1810 [7]	13,056	13,056	12,046		201	457	352	+3,970
1811-1820 [7]	21,032	21,032	16,383		1,845	1,624	1,481	−2,911
1821-1830 [7]	21,923	21,923	19,852		32	1,380	660	+5,761
1831-1840 [7]	30,461	30,461	20,470		5	7,452	2,533	+5,996
1841-1850 [7]	26,545	26,545	25,649		[6] 1		909	−5,553
1851-1860	60,237	60,237	54,498			4,583	1,157	+74
1861-1865	160,907	160,907	68,980	[9] 28,005	[9] 54,566	555	19,994	−522,578
1866-1870	447,301	447,301	178,902	50,604	171,316	2,110	44,368	+66,650
1871-1875	236,530	236,530	186,200	7,760	112,217	2,223	26,429	+49,370
1876-1880	285,124	285,124	146,594	(9)	116,697	1,025	23,808	+32,526
1881-1885	366,961	366,961	201,953	[10] 29	132,102	6,086	26,790	+109,270
1886-1890	375,448	375,448	216,557		126,663	8,097	24,111	+96,314
1891-1895	362,901	362,901	176,951	[11] 77	150,228	2,650	23,136	−10,708
1896-1900	434,877	434,877	185,089		206,622	1,526	41,859	−22,574
1901-1905	580,481	580,481	260,117		255,374	5,670	38,521	+23,922
1906-1910	628,506	628,506	310,599	[12] 26,962	257,145	7,310	49,265	−10,670
1911-1915	710,227	710,227	289,363	49,738	307,116	3,755	60,256	−10,026
1916-1920	3,482,653	3,482,663	225,301	1,962,471	962,212	1,812	410,855	−4,551,680
1921-1925	4,306,673	4,306,673	464,027	2,111,093	1,062,604	846	678,104	+727,684
1926-1930	4,069,138	4,069,138	566,636	2,234,637	671,331	494	584,140	+896,331
1931-1935	2,770,683	2,838,216	322,729	1,116,203	1,186,406	138	212,645	−2,443,900
1936-1940	5,025,444	5,442,480	378,997	2,108,871	2,740,962	121	212,660	−3,231,753
1941-1945	26,156,670	27,653,194	378,227	19,470,535	6,146,915	136	1,657,680	−35,095,851
1946-1950	39,514,193	43,735,853	431,982	29,521,286	10,435,566	(12)	3,094,346	−3,297,291
1946	4,088,097	4,115,957	386,512	1,426,375	2,086,276	74	216,219	−4,424,549
1947	4,975,603	5,293,390	446,367	2,163,414	2,423,726	71	210,022	−3,777,421
1948	5,761,694	6,341,661	350,187	2,640,286	3,084,084	96	266,060	−1,176,617
1949	5,103,597	5,697,594	316,597	2,186,757	2,972,464	248	187,517	−3,962,156
1950	5,264,685	5,893,346	346,591	2,125,325	3,177,809	117	241,826	−3,915,016
1941	7,227,361	7,995,612	391,570	3,469,638	3,392,037	178	341,895	−6,159,272
1942	12,695,326	13,676,680	386,948	7,960,445	3,672,653	90	284,325	−21,490,243
1943	22,301,622	23,402,322	334,291	16,068,660	6,050,300	129	921,863	−57,420,430
1944	43,891,673	45,441,049	431,382	34,654,852	7,090,186	96	3,334,711	−51,423,398
1945	44,762,650	47,780,308	354,776	35,173,051	6,736,951	184	3,466,346	−53,940,916
1946	40,026,892	44,238,125	435,478	30,864,796	9,425,537	127	3,493,200	−20,676,171
1947	40,042,996	44,508,189	494,879	30,305,556	10,073,840	148	4,634,560	+753,795
1948	42,210,770	46,098,807	421,735	31,170,968	10,692,517	214	3,923,383	+8,419,470
1949	38,245,666	42,772,506	384,468	30,482,294	10,825,002	(13)	[13] 2,081,726	−1,811,440
1950	37,044,734	41,310,628	432,659	28,392,671	11,185,936	(13)	[13] 1,490,270	−3,122,102
1951	48,142,606	53,368,672	624,008	37,752,554	13,353,541	(13)	[13] 1,639,569	+3,509,783
1952	62,728,607	67,999,870	550,696	51,346,525	14,286,369	(13)	[13] 1,813,779	−4,016,640

[1] Net receipts equal total receipts less (a) appropriations to Federal old-age and survivors insurance trust fund beginning 1937 and (b) refunds of receipts beginning 1931.

[2] ... beginning 1931 on account of refunds of receipts and capital transfers.

[3] ... tonnage tax prior to 1882. Beginning 1882, tonnage tax is included in other receipts.

[4] On basis of warrants issued 1789 through 1893; thereafter, on basis of checks issued.

[5] Average for period Mar. 4, 1789, through Dec. 31, 1800.

[6] ... included though there were no accounts under these items for certain years.

[7] ... to 1843; revenue for 1844-50 is for period Jan. 1, 1841, through June 30, 1850.

[8] ...

[9] Average for June and 1894.

[10] One year only, 1886.

[11] One year only, 1895.

[12] Sales of public lands included in other receipts.

Source: Treasury Department, *Annual Report o the Secretary*; annual and current data published in *Daily Statement of the U. S. Treasury*.

Fig. **XXVIII.**—Total Receipts of the Federal Government, by Major Sources: Years Ending June 30, 1945 to 1952

[See table 366]

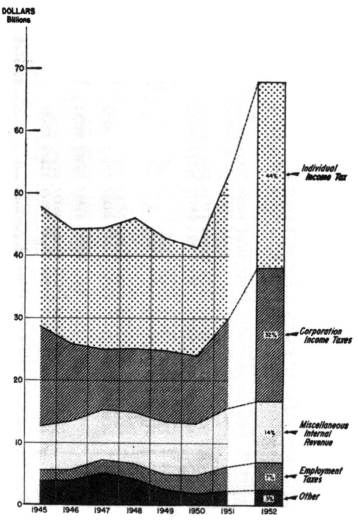

Source: Treasury Department.

FIG. XXIX.—EXPENDITURES OF THE FEDERAL GOVERNMENT, BY MAJOR CLASSIFICATIONS: YEARS ENDING JUNE 30, 1945 TO 1952

[See table 367]

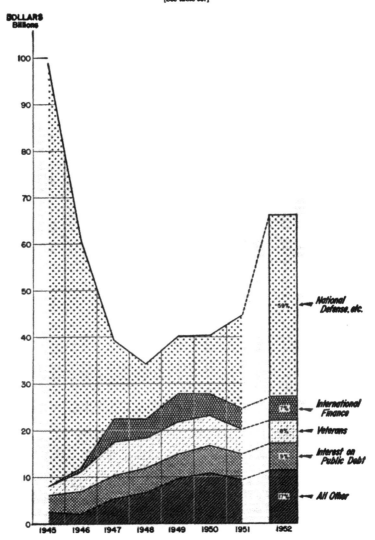

Source: Treasury Department.

No. 367.—EXPENDITURES AND GROSS DEBT OF THE FEDERAL GOVERNMENT: 1789 TO 1952

[See headnote, table 366. See also *Historical Statistics*, series P 99–107 and P 132–133]

YEARLY AVER-AGE OR YEAR ENDING JUNE 30—	EXPENDITURES (thousands of dollars)							GROSS DEBT [5]	
	Total [1]	Depart-ments of Army and Air Force [2]	Depart-ment of Navy [2]	In-dians [3]	Veterans' pensions [3]	Interest on the public debt	All other [4]	Amount (millions of dol-lars)	Per capita (dol-lars)
1789–1800 [6]	5,776	1,464	745	27	82	2,629	829	83	15.87
1801–1810 [6]	9,086	1,632	1,637	164	79	3,704	1,871	53	7.46
1811–1820 [6]	23,943	10,742	4,676	317	741	4,877	2,589	91	9.58
1821–1830 [6]	16,162	3,919	3,295	599	1,248	3,956	3,145	49	3.83
1831–1840 [6]	24,495	8,321	5,042	2,612	2,572	331	5,616	4	.21
1841–1850 [6]	34,097	13,491	7,619	1,458	1,790	1,701	8,039	63	2.77
1851–1860	60,163	15,784	11,997	3,267	1,531	2,776	24,807	65	2.06
1861–1865	683,785	547,753	65,330	3,203	4,858	34,601	28,040	2,678	75.01
1866–1870	377,642	127,816	28,383	4,488	23,428	135,441	58,087	2,436	61.06
1871–1875	287,460	40,186	23,327	7,504	30,166	111,580	74,696	2,156	47.84
1876–1880	255,596	37,170	15,990	5,405	35,051	100,191	61,791	2,091	41.60
1881–1885	257,691	43,010	15,863	7,328	57,790	63,742	69,958	1,579	27.86
1886–1890	279,134	44,085	17,872	6,429	82,657	44,027	88,064	1,122	17.80
1891–1895	363,599	50,326	29,185	10,651	140,186	29,402	103,849	1,097	15.76
1896–1900	457,451	111,278	48,086	11,832	141,642	38,164	106,450	1,263	16.60
1901–1905	535,559	133,362	86,287	11,711	140,114	27,849	136,236	1,132	13.51
1906–1910	639,178	169,050	112,872	15,338	151,329	22,673	167,916	1,147	12.41
1911–1915	720,268	198,792	134,062	20,744	164,897	22,519	179,239	1,191	11.85
1916–1920	8,065,333	3,212,420	882,132	30,833	187,143	375,371	3,377,434	24,299	228.23
1921–1925	3,578,989	540,176	427,748	42,125	244,784	973,696	1,350,460	20,516	177.12
1926–1930	3,182,807	404,999	340,343	37,676	223,507	737,680	1,438,602	16,185	131.51
1931–1935	5,214,874	458,730	358,770	25,384	279,008	695,549	3,397,430	28,701	225.55
1936–1940	8,267,197	696,674	649,179	36,795	408,758	904,707	5,569,085	42,968	325.23
1941–1945	64,242,521	32,143,689	17,673,156	30,207	514,797	2,080,921	11,799,780	258,682	1,848.60
1946–1950	42,801,425	12,744,084	6,722,097	(7)	(7)	5,196,058	18,139,185	257,357	1,696.61
1936	8,493,486	618,587	528,882	28,876	399,066	749,397	6,168,678	33,779	263.79
1937	7,756,021	628,104	556,674	36,933	396,047	866,384	5,271,879	36,425	282.75
1938	6,938,240	644,264	596,130	33,378	402,779	926,281	4,335,409	37,165	286.27
1939	8,965,555	695,256	672,722	46,964	416,721	940,540	6,193,351	40,440	308.98
1940	9,182,682	907,160	891,485	37,821	429,178	1,040,936	5,876,103	42,968	325.23
1941	13,386,554	3,938,943	2,313,058	33,588	433,148	1,110,693	5,557,124	48,961	367.09
1942	34,186,529	14,325,506	8,579,589	31,839	431,294	1,260,085	9,558,213	72,422	537.13
1943	79,621,982	42,525,563	20,888,349	24,665	442,394	1,806,160	13,932,801	136,696	999.83
1944	95,315,065	49,438,330	26,537,634	31,266	494,959	2,608,980	16,203,896	201,003	1,452.44
1945	98,702,525	50,490,102	30,047,152	29,680	772,190	3,616,686	13,746,715	258,682	1,848.60
1946	60,703,060	27,986,769	15,164,412	35,495	1,261,415	4,721,958	11,533,010	269,422	1,905.42
1947	39,298,819	9,172,139	5,597,203	37,369	1,929,226	4,957,922	17,594,959	258,286	1,792.05
1948 [8]	33,791,301	7,698,556	4,284,619	41,147	2,080,130	5,211,102	14,475,746	252,292	1,720.71
1949 [8]	40,057,108	9,552,858	4,434,706	(7)	(7)	5,339,396	20,730,148	252,770	1,694.75
1950	40,166,836	9,310,100	4,129,546	(7)	(7)	5,749,913	20,977,277	257,357	1,696.61
1951 [8]	44,632,822	14,994,543	5,862,549	(7)	(7)	5,612,655	18,163,076	255,222	1,653.50
1952	66,145,247	30,419,425	10,231,265	(7)	(7)	5,859,263	[10] 19,635,294	259,105	1,650.19

[1] Excludes debt retirements and beginning 1931, refunds of receipts and capital transfers.
[2] Excludes civil expenditures under War and Navy Depts. in Washington through 1915. Subsequent to 1915 includes all expenditures made by Depts. of Army (including rivers and harbors and Panama Canal), Navy, and, beginning 1949, Air Force, irrespective of original sources of funds. Expenditures of Dept. of Air Force for 1949 were $1,590,461,000, for 1950, $3,520,653,000, for 1951, $6,358,604,000, and for 1952, $12,851,619,000.
[3] On basis of warrants issued through 1930; thereafter, on basis of checks issued. Expenditures for Indians exclude interest accounts, which are included in trust fund expenditures beginning 1940. Veterans' pensions represent expenditures under appropriation "Army and Navy pensions," administered by Veterans' Administration.
[4] Includes civil expenditures under War and Navy Depts. in Washington through 1915, expenditures of Office of Secy. of Defense, unavailable funds charged off under Act of June 3, 1922, expenditures for "Govt. corporations (wholly owned)," etc. (net)" beginning 1932, and expenditures for Indians and veterans' pensions beginning 1949.
[5] Represents gross debt as of end of each period; e. g., 1800, 1810, etc.
[6] Years ending Dec. 31 through 1842; average for 1789–1800 begins Mar. 4, 1789; average for 1841–50 is for Jan. 1, 1841–June 30, 1850. See note 5 concerning gross debt.   [7] Included in all other.
[8] For comparability with earlier years, all transactions relating to Foreign Economic Cooperation Trust Fund (amounting to $3,000,000,000) have been consolidated with budget expenditures.
[9] Beginning 1951, investments of wholly owned Government corporations in public debt securities are excluded from budget expenditures.
[10] Includes $21,365,000 for Department of Defense, not segregated as to respective departments.

Source: Treasury Department, *Annual Report of the Secretary;* annual and current data published in *Daily Statement of the U. S. Treasury.*

No. 368.—FEDERAL GOVERNMENT EXPENDITURES BY ORGANIZATION UNIT: 1945 TO 1952

[In millions of dollars. For years ending June 30. Expenditures reported on a checks-issued basis, adjusted in total to daily Treasury statement basis (which is partly checks issued and partly checks paid). "Budget" receipts, expenditures, and authorizations, as used in this and following tables, are mainly those of general and special accounts. Two important exceptions are appropriations from general fund to Federal old-age and survivors trust fund and refunds of receipts, both of which are excluded from expenditures and deducted from receipts. Budget expenditures also include net transactions (expenditures minus receipts) of wholly owned Government corporations and enterprises; omitted from both expenditures and receipts are transfers of capital between wholly owned Government corporations and the United States Treasury, and debt transactions of Government enterprises (expenditures from public debt authorizations are included; see also table 371). Figures in early years have not been revised to reflect recent changes in organizational structure]

DESCRIPTION OR ORGANIZATION UNIT	1945	1946	1947	1948	1949	1950	1951	1952
Total budget expenditures	95,706	60,700	39,289	¹ 33,791	40,057	² 40,156	44,632	66,145
Legislative branch	31	22	40	43	47	57	61	62
The Judiciary	12	15	17	20	21	24	25	27
Executive Office of the President	408	196	29	8	8	8	9	9
Funds appropriated to the President		¹ 5	¹ 47	¹ 164	¹ 4,044	3,627	4,188	4,953
Independent offices:								
Atomic Energy Commission			170	466	621	550	897	1,670
Civil Service Commission	315	265	237	361	344	328	324	392
Export-Import Bank of Washington	(³)	557	957	460	⁴ 87	40	76	30
General Accounting Office	32	39	40	34	35	35	32	32
National Advisory Committee for Aeronautics	33	32	35	38	49	54	62	67
Philippine War Damage Commission			3	36	170	136	87	(⁴)
Railroad Retirement Board	324	306	316	778	594	569	614	778
Reconstruction Finance Corporation	184	287	282	155	355	587	⁴ 90	⁴ 940
Tennessee Valley Authority	26	⁴ 7	7	34	27	19	72	188
United States Maritime Commission	5,540	1,785	614	292	153	(⁴)	(⁴)	(⁴)
Veterans Administration	2,094	4,411	7,325	6,474	6,587	6,626	5,380	4,933
War Assets Administration	12	98	421	287				
Other independent offices	305	247	185	78	228	87	97	330
Federal Security Agency	780	743	928	1,028	1,313	1,443	1,571	1,671
Federal Works Agency	280	214	347	486				
General Services Administration					809	576	840	1,070
Housing and Home Finance Agency	⁴ 900	⁴ 168	228	⁴ 71	⁴ 77	⁴ 919	461	655
Department of Agriculture	2,285	1,387	1,527	1,225	2,750	2,968	834	1,342
Department of Commerce	152	126	164	173	662	963	903	970
Department of Defense:								
Office of the Secretary of Defense				(⁴)	7	199	362	362
Department of the Air Force	11,030	4,276	800	1,124	1,800	3,600	6,349	12,708
Department of the Army:								
Military functions	36,558	22,818	7,222	5,671	5,615	3,985	7,477	15,766
Civil functions	150	221	794	1,486	2,121	1,353	994	719
Department of the Navy	26,662	14,508	5,769	4,297	4,442	4,102	5,562	10,161
Department of the Interior	201	210	273	349	485	568	587	665
Department of Justice	104	104	113	118	129	131	151	195
Department of Labor	14	82	112	86	15	257	233	263
Post Office Department (general fund)	16	169	246	207	534	568	626	740
Department of State	77	168	318	676	317	361	361	258
Treasury Department:								
Interest on public debt	3,622	4,747	4,958	5,168	5,352	5,720	5,615	5,853
Other	2,440	1,830	4,476	2,396	734	676	748	774
District of Columbia (United States share)	6	6	8	12	12	12	11	11
Adjustment to daily Treasury statement basis	+255	+1,077	+305	−385	+272	+330	−705	−855
Total trust account expenditures	1,992	4,564	3,564	3,756	3,896	6,946	3,654	⁷ 5,317
Unemployment trust fund: Withdrawals by States and other expenditures	71	1,146	869	856	1,327	2,013	898	1,067
Federal old-age and survivors insurance trust fund: Benefit payments and administrative expenses	267	358	466	559	660	783	1,565	2,067
Railroad retirement account: Benefit payments and other expenditures	141	152	173	222	278	204	221	301
Veterans' life insurance funds: Insurance losses and refunds	153	330	349	377	393	3,101	691	1,088
Federal employees' retirement funds: Annuities and refunds	151	266	323	244	221	268	270	300
Other trust accounts: Misc. trust expenditures	446	1,706	685	509	348	348	257	492
Deposit funds	⁴ 1,609	647	372	175	433	62	⁴ 541	186
Sales and redemptions of obligations of Government corporations and credit agencies in the market (net)	1,552	96	359	⁴ 107	74	(⁴)	(⁴)	(⁴)
Adjustment to daily Treasury statement basis	−71	−136	+388	+915	+165	+66	+190	−244

¹ Excludes transfer of $3 billion of 1948 surplus to foreign economic cooperation trust fund for expenditure in 1949.
² Excludes $11,036,000 representing net purchases of United States securities which is included in Treasury totals (see table 367).
³ Other expenditures are shown under various agencies to which funds are allocated.
⁴ Less than $500,000.   ⁵ Deduct.   ⁶ Included with Department of Commerce.
⁷ Includes transactions of mixed-ownership corporations of $365,696,000 (net) which are shown separately in the Daily Treasury Statement.
⁸ Since 1950, sales and redemptions of obligations of wholly-owned Government corporations have been excluded from this table.

Source: Bureau of the Budget; Budget of the United States Government.

No. 369.—Receipts From and Payments to the Public by the Federal Government: 1929 to 1952

In billions. For years ending June 30. Receipts from and payments to public exclude intragovernmental financial transactions but include operations of trust accounts as well as budget accounts of Federal Government. This table therefore shows flow of money on cash basis between Federal Government as a whole and the public. Net borrowing or repayment of borrowing from the public excludes borrowing by Treasury from Federal trust accounts and Government corporations, and also excludes certain types of public debt transactions like issuance and redemption of armed forces leave bonds. The public is defined to include individuals; banks (including Federal Reserve and Postal Savings System); businesses; private corporations; State, local and foreign governments; and international organizations. For additional explanation, see 1954 Budget, pp. 1076–77, headnote to table 366, and general note, p. 333]

YEAR	Receipts from the public [1] (1)	Payments to the public [1] (2)	Excess of receipts from (+) or payments to (−) the public (3)=(1)−(2)	Receipts from exercise of monetary authority [2] (4)	Excess of Treasury cash income (+) or outgo (−) [3] (5)=(3)+(4)	Decrease (+) or increase (−) in Treasury cash balance (6)	Decrease (+) or increase (−) in Exchange Stabilization Fund balance (7)	Net borrowing (−) or repayment of borrowing (+) from the public (8)=(5)+(6)+(7)
1929	$3.8	$2.9	+$0.9	(4)	+$0.9	−$0.1	----------	+$0.8
1930	4.0	3.1	+.9	(4)	+.9	(4)	----------	+.9
1931	3.2	4.1	−1.0	(4)	−1.0	−.2	----------	−1.1
1932	2.0	4.8	−2.7	(4)	−2.7	+.1	----------	−2.7
1933	2.1	4.7	−2.6	(4)	−2.6	−.4	----------	−3.0
1934	3.1	6.5	−3.3	$2.8	−.5	−1.7	−$2.0	−4.2
1935	3.8	6.3	−2.4	.2	−2.2	+.7	----------	−1.5
1936	4.2	7.6	−3.5	.2	−3.2	−.8	----------	−4.1
1937	5.6	8.4	−2.8	.1	−2.7	+.1	----------	−2.6
1938	7.0	7.2	−.1	.1	(4)	+.3	----------	+.3
1939	6.6	9.4	−2.9	.1	−2.7	−.6	----------	−3.4
1940	6.9	9.6	−2.7	.1	−2.6	+.9	----------	−1.7
1941	9.2	14.0	−4.8	.1	−4.7	−.7	----------	−5.4
1942	15.1	34.5	−19.4	.1	−19.3	−.4	----------	−19.7
1943	25.1	78.9	−53.8	.1	−53.7	−6.5	----------	−60.2
1944	47.8	94.0	−46.1	(4)	−46.1	−10.7	----------	−56.8
1945	50.2	95.2	−45.0	.1	−44.9	−4.5	----------	−49.5
1946	43.5	61.7	−18.2	.3	−17.9	+10.5	----------	−7.4
1947	43.5	36.9	+6.6	.1	+6.7	+10.9	+1.8	+19.4
1948	45.4	36.5	+8.9	(4)	+8.9	−1.6	----------	+7.3
1949	41.6	40.6	+1.0	(4)	+1.0	+1.5	----------	+2.5
1950	40.9	43.2	−2.2	(4)	−2.2	−2.0	----------	−4.2
1951	53.4	45.8	+7.6	(4)	+7.6	−1.8	----------	+5.8
1952	68.0	68.0	(4)	.1	+.1	+.4	----------	+.5

[1] Net of refunds of receipts.
[2] Consists of the increment resulting from reduction in weight of the gold dollar and the seigniorage on silver.
[3] Comparable to "net cash operating income or outgo" currently published in monthly Treasury Bulletin.
[4] Less than $50 million.

Source: Bureau of the Budget; Budget of the United States Government.

No. 370.—BUDGET RECEIPTS AND EXPENDITURES OF THE FEDERAL GOVERNMENT, BY FUNCTION: 1945 TO 1952

[In millions of dollars. For years ending June 30. For explanation of terms, see general note, p. 333, and headnote to table 368]

SOURCE AND FUNCTION	1945	1946	1947	1948	1949	1950	1951	1952
Excess of budget expenditures	53,941	20,676			1,811	3,111		4,017
Excess of budget receipts			754	8,419			3,510	
Total budget receipts	44,762	46,027	40,043	42,211	38,246	37,045	48,143	62,128
Total budget expenditures [1]	96,703	60,703	39,289	33,791	40,057	40,156	44,633	66,145
Budget receipts, total	44,762	46,027	40,043	42,211	38,246	37,045	48,143	62,128
Direct taxes on individuals	19,789	19,008	20,408	21,896	18,725	18,115	24,095	30,713
Direct taxes on corporations	16,399	12,906	9,676	10,174	11,554	10,854	14,388	21,467
Excise taxes	5,934	6,696	7,270	7,402	7,551	7,597	8,698	8,893
Employment taxes	1,793	1,714	2,039	2,396	2,487	2,892	3,940	4,573
Customs	355	435	494	422	384	423	624	550
Miscellaneous receipts	3,480	3,479	4,621	3,809	2,072	1,430	1,629	1,803
Deduct:								
Appropriation to Federal old-age and survivors insurance trust fund	1,310	1,238	1,459	1,516	1,690	2,106	3,120	3,569
Refunds of receipts (excluding interest)	1,679	2,973	3,006	2,272	2,838	2,160	2,107	2,302
Budget expenditures, total [1]	96,703	60,703	39,289	33,791	40,057	40,156	44,633	66,145
Military services, total	84,570	45,134	14,316	10,963	11,915	12,281	20,462	39,727
Direction and coordination of defense				1	9	12	37	60
Air Force defense	49,958	25,362	6,295	{1,117; 5,248}	{1,754; 5,239}	{3,600; 3,982}	{6,349; 7,468}	{12,709; 15,635}
Army defense	30,088	16,764	5,557	4,196	4,377	4,083	5,567	10,142
Naval defense	4,523	3,009	2,464	399	535	604	1,040	1,181
Activities supporting defense								
Veterans' services and benefits, total	2,095	4,416	7,381	6,654	6,726	6,647	5,342	4,863
Veterans' education and training		351	2,122	2,506	2,703	2,596	1,943	1,326
Other veterans' readjustment benefits	9	1,000	1,519	807	631	278	163	122
Veterans' compensation and pensions	772	1,261	1,929	2,080	2,154	2,223	2,171	2,178
Veterans' insurance and servicemen's indemnities	1,137	1,395	840	151	96	480	50	216
Veterans' hospitals and medical care	118	216	461	592	737	764	745	784
Other veterans' services and administration	58	192	510	518	405	306	270	238
International security and foreign relations, total	677	1,463	6,541	4,781	6,459	4,805	4,727	5,268
Conduct of foreign affairs	114	97	118	164	173	233	230	242
Military and economic assistance	564	1,367	6,423	4,617	6,286	4,572	4,497	5,026
Social security, welfare, and health, total	988	994	1,263	1,806	1,843	2,142	2,296	2,491
Retirement and dependents' insurance	328	315	304	764	582	587	612	772
Public assistance	409	430	653	737	923	1,125	1,187	1,180
Aid to special groups	25	31	115	119	118	139	137	152
Work relief and direct relief	4	5	3	8	9			
Accident compensation	15	18	17	15	15	24	27	36
Promotion of public health	186	173	146	139	171	242	304	328
Prisons and probation	18	21	25	23	26	24	28	23
Defense community facilities and services	1	1						
Housing and community development, total	[1]193	[1]199	346	82	282	262	602	735
Public housing programs	112	77	413	98	42	[1]37	124	136
Aids to private housing	[1]416	[1]331	[1]117	[1]58	312	300	452	500
Research and other general housing aids	5	3	13	7	1	2	7	10
Provision of community facilities	106	51	39	35	[1]72	[1]8	6	9
Urban development and redevelopment							2	6
Civil defense								33
Defense housing, community facilities and services								12
Disaster insurance, loans, and relief								28
Education and general research, total	158	85	66	65	75	123	115	171
Promotion of education	25	27	34	38	39	41	51	126
Educational aid to special groups	2	2	3	3	3	5	6	6
Library and museum services	5	6	8	8	9	10	10	11
General-purpose research	126	51	22	16	24	68	48	29
Agriculture and agricultural resources, total	1,602	743	1,243	574	2,512	2,733	650	1,045
Stabilization of farm prices and farm income	1,470	452	650	[1]92	1,725	1,844	[1]461	46
Financing farm ownership and operation	[1]340	[1]252	[1]119	[1]3	65	146	339	272
Financing rural electrification and rural telephones	16	68	185	239	305	298	276	243
Conservation and development of agricultural land and water resources	325	380	388	285	341	337	346	341
Research, and other agricultural services	131	126	160	146	177	163	149	143

See footnotes at end of table.

No. 370.—BUDGET RECEIPTS AND EXPENDITURES OF THE FEDERAL GOVERNMENT, BY FUNCTION: 1945 TO 1952—Continued

[In millions of dollars. For years ending June 30]

SOURCE AND FUNCTION	1945	1946	1947	1948	1949	1950	1951	1952
Natural resources, total	247	254	626	1,113	1,536	1,624	2,051	2,948
Conservation and development of land and water resources	169	171	343	505	756	884	948	1,038
Conservation and development of forest resources	39	44	53	61	66	78	81	95
Conservation and development of mineral resources	23	21	24	33	42	50	50	56
Conservation and development of fish and wildlife	8	8	11	12	18	23	26	30
Recreational use of natural resources	5	6	12	17	19	24	30	33
Development and control of atomic energy			174	475	622	550	897	1,670
Defense production activities							2	5
General resource surveys	3	4	10	10	13	16	18	21
Transportation and communication, total	3,364	786	546	1,213	1,600	1,703	1,685	1,923
Promotion of the merchant marine	3,183	375	³ 881	183	124	100	101	230
Provision of navigation aids and facilities	63	90	244	222	289	299	301	292
Provision of highways	103	87	235	351	453	498	455	470
Promotion of aviation including provision of airways and airports	100	67	86	99	143	159	160	169
Regulation of transportation	30	22	23	15	15	15	15	18
Other services to transportation	³ 145	³ 86	³ 8	34	40	33	20	³ 4
Postal service (from general fund)	1	161	242	304	530	593	626	740
Regulation of communication	31	11	6	6	7	7	7	7
Finance, commerce, and industry, total	236	9	112	132	127	213	176	241
Promotion or regulation of financial institutions	³ 61	³ 67	³ 61	³ 16	³ 8	³ 6	³ 9	³ 24
Promotion or regulation of trade and industry	13	20	23	23	24	26	26	26
Business loans and guarantees	34	³ 128	21	80	83	166	³ 19	³ 57
War damage insurance	³ 3	³ 2	1	20				
Promotion of defense production and economic stabilization	252	186	127	24	28	26	178	277
Labor, total	204	174	194	183	193	262	228	243
Mediation and regulation of labor relations	20	17	11	8	12	13	12	13
Unemployment compensation and placement activities	120	144	161	156	163	227	189	202
Labor standards and training	58	6	12	11	13	15	17	18
Labor information, statistics, and general administration	6	7	10	7	5	8	9	8
Defense production activities							1	2
General government, total	840	951	1,334	1,368	1,070	1,164	1,290	1,411
Legislative functions	19	23	26	32	34	39	40	42
Judicial functions	12	13	16	18	19	25	28	28
Executive direction and management	21	8	7	7	7	7	9	9
Federal financial management	322	397	415	416	378	390	413	438
Other central services	94	97	505	495	197	155	183	235
Retirement for Federal civilian employees	198	248	224	247	228	308	308	313
Protective services and alien control	121	102	77	87	93	98	115	164
Territories and possessions, and the District of Columbia	17	13	12	20	21	22	22	50
Other general government	36	49	50	43	94	121	173	131
Interest, total	3,663	4,816	5,012	5,248	5,445	5,817	5,714	5,934
Interest on the public debt	3,622	4,747	4,958	5,188	5,352	5,720	5,615	5,853
Interest on refunds of receipts	36	66	50	57	87	93	93	76
Interest on uninvested trust funds	3	2	5	4	6	4	6	5
Adjustment to daily Treasury statement basis	+252	+1,077	+306	−366	+272	+330	−705	−855
MEMORANDUM								
Capital transfers from expenditures to receipt accounts	16	36	210	263	802	276	208	266
Refunds of receipts (excluding interest)	1,679	2,973	3,036	2,272	2,838	2,160	2,107	2,302
Investments of Government-owned corporations and enterprises in United States securities [1]						11	104	101

[1] Expenditures for 1949 and prior years include investments in United States securities.
[2] Expenditures for Army defense include some expenditures for support of the Air Force financed from 1949 and prior year appropriations.   [3] Deduct, excess of repayments and collections over expenditures.

Source: Bureau of the Budget; *Budget of the U. S. Government, 1954.*

No. 371.—BUDGET APPROPRIATIONS AND OTHER AUTHORIZATIONS FOR FEDERAL AGENCIES, BY ORGANIZATION UNIT: 1952

[In millions of dollars. For year ending June 30. The Budget total of "new obligational authority" represents total of new authorizations enacted for any fiscal year for Federal agencies to incur obligations. This total includes "net new appropriations," "reappropriations," "contract authorizations," and "authorizations to expend from public debt receipts." "Net new appropriations" represent total of all appropriations less appropriations enacted to liquidate prior year contract authorizations. "Reappropriations" continue available in the succeeding fiscal year the unused balance of an appropriation which would otherwise expire for obligation purposes. "Contract authorizations" permit placement of specific obligations or contracts but require subsequent appropriations to "liquidate" them (i. e., to authorize withdrawal of funds from Treasury in payment of obligations). "Authorizations to expend from public debt receipts" authorize use of proceeds of Treasury borrowing to finance certain types of Government programs. See also general note, p. 333, and headnote to table 368]

ORGANIZATION UNIT	Appropriations	Deduct: Appropriations to liquidate contract authorizations	Net appropriations	New contract authorizations	Authorizations to expend from public debt receipts	Reappropriations	Total new obligational authority
Total	¹ ² 91,096	2,858	88,238	³ 716	⁴ 2,696	1,145	⁵ 92,878
Legislative branch	78	3	75				75
The Judiciary	27		27				27
Executive Office of the President	10		10				10
Funds appropriated to the President:							
Disaster relief	56		56				56
Emergency fund for the President, national defense	1		1			5	6
Expansion of defense production					500		500
India emergency food aid					27		27
Mutual security	7,328	44	7,284			728	8,012
Independent offices:							
Atomic Energy Commission	1,606	340	1,266	1		40	1,307
Civil Service Commission	337		337				337
Economic Stabilization Agency	101		101				101
Export-Import Bank of Washington					1,000		1,000
Federal Civil Defense Administration	75		75				75
Railroad Retirement Board	778		778				778
Reconstruction Finance Corporation					100		100
Tennessee Valley Authority	238		238				238
Veterans' Administration	4,410	27	4,383			71	4,454
Other	213	12	201				201
Federal Security Agency	1,751	144	1,607	2			1,609
General Services Administration	¹ 988	200	788				788
Housing and Home Finance Agency	98		98	100	265		⁴ 479
Department of Agriculture	1,086		1,086		732	1	⁴ 1,887
Department of Commerce	949	623	326	611		4	941
Department of Defense:							
Military functions	61,635	1,425	60,210			364	60,574
Civil functions	655		655				655
Department of the Interior	590	37	553	2		(⁶)	555
Department of Justice	203	(⁶)	203				203
Department of Labor	253		253				253
Post Office Department (general fund)	740		740				740
Department of State	262	3	259			3	262
Treasury Department:							
Interest on the public debt	5,853		5,853				5,853
Other	² 764		764				764
District of Columbia (Federal contribution)	11		11				11

¹ Refunds of receipts under Renegotiation Act (excluding interest) amounting to $8 million are deducted.
² Refunds of receipts (excluding interest) amounting to $2,278 million are deducted.
³ Includes $43 million of reauthorizations of contract authority.
⁴ Includes $43 million of reauthorizations to expend from public debt receipts.
⁵ Includes $84 million of authorizations to expend from corporate debt receipts ($16 million in Housing and Home Finance Agency and $68 million in Department of Agriculture).
⁶ Less than $500,000.

Source: Bureau of the Budget; *Budget of the U. S. Government, 1954.*

No. 372.—FEDERAL EXPENDITURES—INVESTMENT, OPERATING AND OTHER BUDGET EXPENDITURES: 1952 AND 1953

[In millions of dollars. For years ending June 30. Based on existing and proposed legislation]

DESCRIPTION AND CATEGORY	1952 actual	1953 esti- mate	DESCRIPTION AND CATEGORY	1952 actual	1953 esti- mate
Total budget expenditures...	66,145	74,593	Current expenses for aids and special services, total.........	12,246	13,205
			Agriculture.....................	463	547
Additions to Federal assets, total.........................	17,964	25,499	Direct Federal programs.....	414	486
Loans¹............................	1,699	1,850	Grants-in-aid..................	49	61
International security and foreign relations............	441	196	Business........................	1,041	1,018
Housing and community de- velopment.................	796	728	Labor...........................	200	206
			Direct Federal programs.....	14	12
To private borrowers......	623	661	Grants-in-aid..................	186	194
To State and local govern- ments....................	173	67	Home owners and tenants......	² 129	² 123
Agriculture and agricultural resources.................	512	726	Direct Federal programs.....	² 141	² 158
Finance, commerce, and in- dustry...................	² 20	203	Grants-in-aid..................	12	35
Other............................	² 30	² 3	Veterans........................	4,710	4,411
Physical assets.................	16,265	22,648	Direct Federal programs.....	4,465	4,288
Public works—sites and di- rect construction.........	4,214	4,953	Payments to trust funds.....	241	118
Civil........................	2,383	2,603	Grants-in-aid..................	4	5
Military....................	1,831	2,350	International aids..............	4,596	5,616
Major commodity inven- tories—net change.......	489	1,350	Civil........................	4,596	5,586
Civil........................	² 317	288	Military....................		30
Military....................	806	1,062	Other aids......................	1,364	1,530
Major equipment..............	11,140	16,742	Direct Federal programs.....	87	93
Civil........................	140	242	Grants-in-aid..................	1,278	1,437
Military....................	11,000	16,500			
Other physical assets........	422	603	Other services and current op- erating expenses, total......	33,171	31,767
Civil........................	421	600	Repair, maintenance, and op- eration of physical assets (excluding special services).	12,398	10,024
Military....................	1	3	Civil........................	333	324
			Military....................	12,065	9,700
Expenditures for other develop- mental purposes, total.......	2,874	3,436	Regulation and control.......	545	488
Physical assets (non-Federal)..	1,023	1,227	Operation and administration of other civil activities....	1,427	1,458
State and local assets........	570	782	International activities.......	210	221
Direct Federal programs....	1	2	Federal financial activities....	409	412
Grants-in-aid..............	569	779	Other direct Federal pro- grams.....................	416	401
Private physical assets......	453	445	Payments to Federal em- ployees' retirement funds..	329	343
Direct Federal programs....	390	382	Shared revenues and other grants-in-aid..............	65	81
Grants-in-aid..............	63	62	Other military operation and administration..............	12,867	13,277
Education, training, and health...................	283	294	Interest........................	5,934	6,520
Direct Federal programs.....	93	86	On the public debt..........	5,853	6,450
Grants-in-aid...............	190	208	Other interest...............	81	70
Research and development....	1,495	1,838			
Civil........................	337	381	Noncost payments...............	744	661
Direct Federal programs....	323	367	Reserve for contingencies.......		25
Grants-in-aid..............	14	14	Adjustment to daily Treasury statement basis..............	−855	
Military......................	1,158	1,457			
Engineering and natural re- source surveys.............	73	77			
Direct Federal programs.....	72	77			
Grants-in-aid................	2	1			

¹ Excludes collections going directly to miscellaneous receipts.
² Deduct, excess of repayments and collections over expenditures.

Source: Bureau of the Budget; *Budget of the U. S. Government, 1954*, Special Analysis D.

No. 373.—COMMITMENTS AND EXPENDITURES FOR MAJOR FEDERAL CREDIT PROGRAMS: 1952 AND 1953

[In millions of dollars. For years ending June 30. Based on existing and proposed legislation. Commitments are defined as approvals by Federal agencies of direct loans or of insurance or guarantees of private loans. They are on a gross basis without deductions for commitments not subsequently utilized. Net expenditures reflect new loans less collections on old loans]

AGENCY OR PROGRAM	NEW COMMITMENTS		NET EXPENDITURES	
	1952 actual	1953 estimate	1952 actual	1953 estimate
Total, budget expenditures for loans			1,468	1,604
Adjustment for repayments going directly into miscellaneous receipts			231	246
Total (including repayments to miscellaneous receipts)	14,950	17,578	1,699	1,850
Expansion of defense production	1,445	1,325	105	147
Mutual Security Agency	381	39	378	70
Veterans' Administration	3,367	3,161	73	85
Export-Import Bank	551	697	74	129
Reconstruction Finance Corporation	114	201	−164	55
Housing and Home Finance Agency	5,694	7,280	684	595
Federal National Mortgage Association	836	1,253	489	498
Slum clearance and urban redevelopment	12	76	7	9
College housing	19	75	1	22
Federal Housing Administration	3,844	4,894	28	31
Public Housing Administration	983	982	159	35
Department of Agriculture	3,398	4,875	373	549
Rural Electrification Administration	206	200	186	171
Farmers' Home Administration	166	175	45	30
Commodity Credit Corporation	949	2,177	33	276
Federal Intermediate Credit Banks	2,077	2,323	109	72
Treasury Department: Loan to United Kingdom			−44	−45
Other agencies or programs			−11	19

Source: Bureau of the Budget; *Budget of the U. S. Government, 1954*, Special Analysis E.

No. 374.—INTERNAL REVENUE COLLECTIONS, BY PRINCIPAL SOURCES: 1936 TO 1952

[In millions of dollars. For years ending June 30. Data differ from those in table 366 which represent deposits of these collections in Treasury or depositaries during fiscal years concerned; see text, p. 335. See also *Historical Statistics*, series P 109–129]

TAX SOURCE	1936–40, average	1941–45, average	1946–50, average	1948	1949	1950	1951	1952
Internal revenue collections, total	4,871	25,342	40,212	41,865	40,463	38,957	50,446	65,010
Income and profits taxes:								
Individual income	1,013	9,721	18,650	20,998	18,052	17,153	[1] 22,997	[1] 29,274
Corporation income and profits [2]	1,098	9,452	10,962	10,174	11,554	10,854	14,388	21,467
Employment taxes	516	1,425	2,245	2,381	2,476	2,645	[1] 2,627	[1] 4,464
Alcohol taxes	576	1,444	2,337	2,255	2,211	2,219	2,547	2,549
Tobacco taxes	562	865	1,271	1,300	1,322	1,328	1,380	1,565
Estate and gift taxes	364	488	772	899	797	706	730	833
Manufacturers' excise taxes [3]	419	636	1,521	1,649	1,772	1,836	2,384	2,349
All other	323	1,310	2,254	2,207	2,281	2,215	2,393	2,508

[1] Estimated. Income tax withheld and employment tax (old-age insurance) withheld not reported separately after 1950.
[2] Includes excess profits on Army and Navy contracts, and unjust enrichment for 1937–1947.
[3] Excludes taxes on soft drinks and taxes on adulterated, process or renovated butter, mixed flour, and filled cheese.

Source: Treasury Department, Bureau of Internal Revenue; *Annual Report of the Commissioner*.

No. 375.—INTERNAL REVENUE COLLECTIONS, BY TAX SOURCES IN DETAIL:
1951 AND 1952

[In thousands of dollars. For years ending June 30. Data differ from those in table 366, which represent deposits of these collections in Treasury or depositaries, during fiscal years concerned; see text, p. 325. See also *Historical Statistics*, series P 109–129]

TYPE OF TAX	1951	1952	TYPE OF TAX	1951	1952
Grand total, all collections	50,445,686	65,009,586	Miscellaneous internal revenue—Continued		
Income and profits taxes, total	37,384,879	50,741,017	Manufacturers' excise taxes—Continued.		
Individual income taxes, total	22,997,309	29,274,107	Parts and accessories for automobiles	119,475	164,135
Withheld by employers [1]	13,089,770	17,929,047	Electrical energy	93,184	53,094
Other	9,907,539	11,345,060	Electric, gas, and oil appliances	121,996	89,544
Corporation income and profits taxes	14,387,569	21,466,910	Electric light bulbs and tubes	30,284	30,736
			Radio and telev. sets, phonographs, components, etc.	128,187	118,244
Employment taxes [1]	3,627,479	4,464,264	Phonograph records	7,007	6,880
Miscellaneous internal revenue, total	9,433,329	9,804,305	Musical instruments	10,756	9,412
			Mechanical pencils, etc.		4,880
Estate tax	638,523	750,591	Mech. refrigerators, freezers, air-conditioners, etc.	96,319	57,970
Gift tax	91,207	82,556	Matches	10,169	8,032
			Business and store machines	44,491	48,515
Alcohol taxes, total	2,546,808	2,549,120	Photographic apparatus	46,020	33,766
Distilled spirits (imported, excise)	172,362	187,479	Sporting goods	17,862	16,501
Distilled spirits (domestic, excise)	1,574,473	1,402,252	Firearms, shells, and cartridges	17,846	10,679
Distilled spirits rectification tax	38,053	31,812	Pistols and revolvers	762	1,172
Wines, cordials, etc. (imported, excise)	3,738	3,753	Retailers' excise taxes, total	457,013	475,466
Wines, cordials, etc. (domestic, excise)	63,516	68,621	Furs	57,604	51,436
Rectifiers; liquor dealers; manufactures of stills (special taxes)	9,161	15,249	Jewelry	210,239	220,338
Stamps for distilled spirits intended for export	12	28	Luggage	82,831	90,799
Case stamps for distilled spirits bottled in bond	1,090	1,285	Toilet preparations	106,339	112,892
Container stamps	14,921	12,080	Miscellaneous taxes, total	1,842,598	1,947,472
Floor taxes	12	93,808	Wagering, excise		4,372
Fermented malt liquors	665,009	727,604	Wagering, special		973
Brewers; dealers in malt liquors (special taxes)	4,462	5,148	Sugar	80,192	78,473
			Telephone, telegraph, etc.	354,660	395,434
Tobacco taxes, total	1,380,396	1,565,162	Local telephone service	290,320	310,337
Cigars (large and small)	44,275	44,810	Transportation of oil by pipe line	24,946	26,881
Cigarettes (large and small)	1,293,973	1,474,072	Transportation of persons, seats, berths	237,617	275,174
Snuff	7,235	4,796	Transportation of property	381,342	388,589
Tobacco (chewing and smoking)	33,870	22,817	Leases of safe deposit boxes	9,569	10,211
Floor taxes and other	1,043	18,667	Admissions to theaters, concerts, etc.	346,492	330,816
Stamp taxes	93,107	84,995	Admissions to cabarets, roof gardens, etc.	42,646	45,489
Manufacturers' excise taxes, total	2,383,677	2,348,943	Club dues and initiation fees	30,120	33,592
Lubricating oils	97,238	95,286	Bowling alleys, pool tables, etc.	3,610	3,597
Gasoline, incl. floor tax	569,048	713,174	Coin-operated devices	20,731	18,823
Tires and tubes	196,383	161,328	Adulterated and processed or renovated butter, and filled cheese	11	4
Automobile trucks and busses	121,285	147,445	Narcotics, including marihuana and special taxes	866	915
Other automobiles and motorcycles	653,363	578,149	Coconut and other vegetable oils processed	19,088	15,365
			Firearms transfer and occupational taxes	9	29
			Diesel oil		7,138
			All other, including repealed taxes not listed above	381	1,261

[1] Estimated. Income tax withheld and employment tax (old-age insurance) withheld not reported separately

Source: Treasury Department, Bureau of Internal Revenue; *Annual Report of the Commissioner.*

No. 376.—INTERNAL REVENUE COLLECTIONS, BY STATES AND OTHER AREAS; 1951 AND 1952

[In thousands of dollars. For years ending June 30. See headnote, table 375. Tax receipts are credited to States in which collections made. Receipts in the various States do not indicate the tax burden of the respective States, since burden may eventually be borne by persons in other States]

DIVISION, STATE OR OTHER AREA	TOTAL [1]		INDIVIDUAL INCOME AND EMPLOYMENT TAXES [2]		CORPORATION INCOME TAXES [3]	
	1951	1952	1951	1952	1951	1952
Total	50,445,686	65,009,586	26,624,788	33,738,370	14,267,569	21,466,910
New England	2,807,541	3,573,669	1,729,973	2,126,244	751,588	1,119,169
Maine	127,370	163,357	81,137	100,658	37,278	52,906
New Hampshire	87,177	111,753	61,758	78,630	18,792	26,947
Vermont	48,675	67,181	34,783	42,281	9,552	20,351
Massachusetts	1,486,571	1,838,263	900,211	1,083,225	418,602	575,126
Rhode Island	239,708	293,139	150,112	174,627	66,309	93,441
Connecticut	818,039	1,099,976	501,972	646,823	199,054	350,296
Middle Atlantic	14,590,708	19,360,296	7,632,113	9,535,343	4,698,609	7,464,199
New York	9,243,924	12,327,411	4,720,431	5,634,496	3,243,066	5,115,907
New Jersey	1,460,314	1,900,154	843,492	1,077,968	353,519	526,709
Pennsylvania	3,886,470	5,132,731	2,068,190	2,622,879	1,101,995	1,821,498
East North Central	13,944,736	17,653,569	6,506,585	8,092,489	4,661,044	6,797,185
Ohio	3,292,928	4,537,755	1,674,500	2,252,561	1,065,565	1,765,050
Indiana	1,702,617	1,358,804	506,521	629,499	249,422	339,960
Illinois	4,329,997	5,350,912	2,281,609	2,733,659	1,322,809	1,917,371
Michigan	4,156,022	5,090,018	1,541,525	1,845,918	1,658,005	2,325,758
Wisconsin	963,172	1,286,080	496,431	630,822	265,183	448,902
West North Central	3,458,615	4,503,444	2,067,617	2,798,648	922,015	1,266,560
Minnesota	786,759	972,842	458,461	556,937	222,838	305,570
Iowa	438,240	522,707	302,484	349,615	100,206	135,446
Missouri	1,392,272	2,004,932	751,902	1,207,512	414,960	557,255
North Dakota	57,680	69,364	46,889	57,066	7,295	8,550
South Dakota	64,282	76,069	49,089	60,108	9,057	11,157
Nebraska	334,021	392,654	217,248	209,395	61,636	63,097
Kansas	385,362	464,876	241,553	298,015	106,032	128,764
South Atlantic	5,503,105	6,900,814	2,611,145	3,297,070	1,245,566	1,805,992
Delaware	566,957	768,958	192,975	209,513	354,874	546,003
Maryland [4]	1,413,474	1,745,229	901,046	1,173,165	217,129	283,682
Dist. of Columbia	(4)	(4)	(4)	(4)	(4)	(4)
Virginia	863,146	1,051,424	325,965	423,080	148,917	222,035
West Virginia	245,969	316,761	154,027	189,568	69,914	102,840
North Carolina	1,257,160	1,522,193	315,730	383,049	187,543	270,668
South Carolina	191,327	263,641	119,752	154,041	60,262	94,174
Georgia	497,148	637,359	282,049	367,268	125,174	169,434
Florida	467,624	595,249	319,601	397,385	81,066	117,206
East South Central	1,867,552	2,212,225	756,496	943,245	314,566	434,542
Kentucky	1,056,515	1,191,985	221,018	280,275	113,575	157,506
Tennessee	398,606	494,019	264,102	315,606	102,788	135,409
Alabama	298,452	386,402	199,745	247,157	77,718	113,669
Mississippi	113,977	139,819	81,632	100,207	20,877	27,868
West South Central	2,719,259	3,425,432	1,661,292	2,020,720	709,665	999,168
Arkansas	130,984	157,253	89,263	106,052	30,623	40,281
Louisiana	410,122	494,047	237,581	285,796	102,686	133,177
Oklahoma	494,893	639,575	241,491	309,563	155,446	219,765
Texas	1,683,259	2,134,557	1,092,956	1,319,309	411,300	605,915
Mountain	929,962	1,326,669	627,706	928,326	193,290	274,097
Montana	91,691	116,004	66,495	86,119	18,121	21,979
Idaho	91,354	117,674	64,049	80,433	21,571	29,243
Wyoming	48,984	63,644	35,799	48,874	8,497	9,900
Colorado	353,849	575,122	209,909	384,264	84,372	125,947
New Mexico	80,607	102,222	64,521	81,198	10,595	13,471
Arizona	104,438	142,526	82,899	107,211	15,912	25,103
Utah	109,532	146,668	69,295	94,751	27,443	38,624
Nevada	47,506	62,809	34,741	45,456	6,849	9,770
Pacific	4,483,610	5,864,620	2,935,062	3,862,363	966,634	1,328,864
Washington	563,872	755,069	382,860	516,900	129,759	176,847
Oregon	361,511	464,266	259,549	324,150	77,558	114,264
California	3,558,227	4,645,285	2,292,653	3,021,223	727,717	1,032,753
Alaska	38,762	44,349	34,940	37,716	1,985	3,391
Hawaii	98,023	134,996	66,361	88,992	23,525	35,614
Puerto Rico	3,812	9,503	1,502	7,196		

[1] Includes miscellaneous taxes in the following amounts: 1951, $9,433,329,000; 1952, $9,804,305,000.
[2] Includes taxes withheld on salaries and wages.
[3] Includes excess profits taxes.
[4] Collections for the District of Columbia included with Maryland; separate data not available.

Source: Treasury Department, Bureau of Internal Revenue; Annual Report of the Commissioner.

No. 377.—Effective Rates of Individual Income Tax Under Revenue Acts of 1913–1951, for Selected Income Groups

[In percent. Maximum earned net income assumed]

REVENUE ACT	INCOME YEAR	SINGLE PERSON, NO DEPENDENT, WITH NET INCOME—									
		$600	$1,000	$2,000	$3,000	$5,000	$8,000	$10,000	$25,000	$100,000	$500,000
1913	3/1/13–12/31/15					0.4	0.6	0.7	1.1	2.5	5.0
1916	1916					.8	1.3	1.4	2.0	3.9	8.6
1917	1917			1.0	1.3	2.4	3.4	4.0	7.3	16.2	38.5
1918	1918			3.0	4.0	4.8	8.1	9.5	15.4	35.2	64.6
	1919–1920			2.0	2.7	3.2	5.6	6.7	11.8	31.3	60.7
1921	1921			2.0	2.7	3.2	5.6	6.7	11.8	31.3	60.7
	1922			2.0	2.7	3.2	5.3	6.0	10.6	30.2	52.1
	1923			1.5	2.0	2.4	3.9	4.5	7.9	22.7	39.1
1924	1924			.8	1.0	1.2	1.9	2.3	6.5	22.7	39.9
1926	1925–1927			.3	.6	.8	1.3	1.5	4.9	16.1	23.2
1928	1928, 1930–1931			.3	.6	.8	1.3	1.5	4.4	15.8	23.2
	1929			.1	.2	.3	.7	.9	3.7	14.9	22.2
1932	1932–1933			2.0	2.7	3.2	5.3	6.0	10.6	30.2	52.7
1934	1934–1935			1.6	2.3	2.8	4.7	5.6	11.2	31.4	53.0
1936, 1938	1936–1939			1.6	2.3	2.8	4.7	5.6	11.2	33.4	61.0
1940	1940 [1]		0.4	2.2	2.8	3.4	5.6	6.9	17.0	44.3	66.2
1941	1941		2.1	2.9	7.4	9.7	12.9	14.9	28.9	53.2	69.1
1942	1942 [1]	2.5	8.9	13.7	15.7	18.4	21.8	23.9	38.5	64.6	82.9
	1943 [1][3]	2.6	10.7	16.7	19.1	22.1	25.7	27.8	42.6	69.7	88.4
1944 [4]	1944–1945	3.8	11.5	17.3	19.5	22.1	25.4	27.6	42.4	69.9	88.9
1945	1946–1947	3.2	9.5	14.3	16.2	18.4	21.5	23.5	37.5	63.5	81.6
1948	1948–1949		6.6	11.6	13.6	16.2	19.3	21.2	34.4	58.8	77.0
1950	1950		7.0	12.2	14.3	16.9	20.0	22.0	35.6	60.8	79.2
1951	1951		8.2	14.3	16.6	19.3	22.7	24.9	39.9	67.3	86.0
	1952		8.9	15.5	18.1	21.0	24.9	27.2	43.8	69.7	87.2

REVENUE ACT	INCOME YEAR	MARRIED PERSON, NO DEPENDENT, WITH NET INCOME—									
		$600	$1,000	$2,000	$3,000	$5,000	$8,000	$10,000	$25,000	$100,000	$500,000
1913	3/1/13–12/31/15					0.2	0.5	0.6	1.0	2.5	5.0
1916	1916					.4	1.0	1.2	1.9	3.9	8.6
1917	1917				0.7	1.6	2.9	3.6	7.1	16.2	38.5
1918	1918				2.0	3.6	6.6	8.3	14.9	35.0	64.6
	1919–1920				1.3	2.4	4.6	5.9	11.5	31.2	60.6
1921	1921				.7	2.0	4.6	5.9	11.5	31.2	60.6
	1922				.7	2.0	4.3	5.2	10.2	30.1	52.1
	1923				.5	1.5	3.2	3.9	7.7	22.6	39.1
1924	1924				.3	.8	1.3	1.7	6.3	22.6	39.9
1926	1925–1927					.3	.7	1.0	4.6	16.1	23.2
1928	1928, 1930–1931					.3	.7	1.0	4.1	15.8	23.2
	1929					.1	.3	.5	3.5	14.9	22.2
1932	1932–1933				.7	2.0	3.8	4.8	10.1	30.1	52.7
1934	1934–1935				.3	1.6	3.1	4.2	10.0	30.6	52.8
1936, 1938	1936–1939				.3	1.6	3.1	4.2	10.0	32.5	60.8
1940	1940 [1]				1.0	2.2	4.0	5.3	15.4	43.5	66.0
1941	1941			2.1	4.6	7.5	10.9	13.1	27.5	52.7	69.0
1942	1942 [1]	0.2		7.0	10.8	14.9	19.2	21.5	36.9	64.1	82.8
	1943 [1][3]	.2	1.5	9.4	13.5	17.9	22.3	24.7	40.1	68.6	88.1
1944 [4]	1944–1945	.5	1.5	12.3	15.8	19.5	23.6	25.9	41.2	69.4	88.8
1945	1946–1947			9.5	12.7	16.0	19.7	21.9	36.3	63.1	81.5
1948	1948–1949			6.6	10.0	12.6	15.1	16.2	23.5	46.4	71.9
1950	1950 [6]			7.0	10.4	13.2	15.7	16.9	24.3	48.0	74.1
1951	1951 [6]			8.2	12.2	15.5	18.0	19.3	27.5	53.5	80.9
	1952 [6]			8.9	13.3	16.9	19.7	21.0	30.0	56.9	82.5

See footnotes at end of table.

No. 377.—Effective Rates of Individual Income Tax Under Revenue Acts of 1913–1951, for Selected Income Groups—Continued

[In percent. Maximum earned net income assumed]

REVENUE ACT	INCOME YEAR	MARRIED PERSON, 2 DEPENDENTS, WITH NET INCOME—									
		$500	$1,000	$2,000	$3,000	$5,000	$8,000	$10,000	$25,000	$100,000	$500,000
1913	3/1/13–12/31/15					0.2	0.5	0.6	1.0	2.5	5.0
1916	1916					.4	1.0	1.2	1.9	3.9	8.6
1917	1917				0.4	1.3	2.7	3.	7.1	16.2	38.5
1918	1918				1.2	3.1	6.0	7.8	14.7	35.0	64.6
	1919–1920				.8	2.1	4.2	5.6	11.4	31.2	60.6
1921	1921					1.4	3.8	5.3	11.3	31.1	60.6
	1922					1.4	3.5	4.6	10.0	30.1	52.1
	1923					1.0	2.6	3.4	7.5	22.6	39.1
1924	1924					.5	1.0	1.4	6.1	22.5	39.9
1926	1925–1927					.2	.5	.8	4.5	16.0	28.1
1928	1928, 1930–1931					.2	.5	.8	4.0	15.7	28.1
	1929					.1	.2	.4	3.4	14.8	22.2
1932	1932–1933					1.4	3.0	4.2	9.8	30.0	52.7
1934	1934–1935					1.0	2.3	3.4	9.3	30.2	52.7
1936, 1938	1936–1939					1.0	2.3	3.4	9.3	32.0	60.7
1940	1940[1]					1.5	3.1	4.4	14.3	42.9	65.9
1941	1941				1.9	5.4	9.0	11.2	25.9	52.2	86.9
1942	1942[2]			0.7	6.4	11.8	16.5	19.1	35.3	63.5	82.7
	1943[2][3]	0.2	1.4	2.9	8.9	14.6	19.4	21.1	38.3	67.8	88.0
1944[4]	1944–1945	.5	1.5	2.3	9.2	15.1	19.8	22.5	38.8	66.6	88.6
1945	1946–1947				6.3	11.8	16.2	18.6	34.1	62.3	81.3
1948	1948–1949				3.3	8.6	12.2	13.6	21.9	45.6	71.7
1950	1950[5]				3.5	9.0	12.7	14.2	22.7	47.2	73.9
1951	1951[6]				4.1	10.6	14.7	16.2	25.6	52.6	80.7
	1952[6]				4.4	11.5	16.0	17.7	28.0	56.0	82.2

[1] Includes defense tax.
[2] Tax liabilities for 1942 and 1943 unadjusted for transition to current payment basis.
[3] Includes net Victory tax. Computed by assuming that deductions are 10 percent of Victory tax net income; i. e., that Victory tax net income is ten-ninths of selected net income.
[4] Individual Income Tax Act of 1944.
[5] Taking into account maximum effective rate limitation of 77 percent.   [6] Split income basis.

Source: Treasury Department, Bureau of Internal Revenue.

No. 378.—Individual Income Tax Liability Under Revenue Acts of 1913–1951, for Selected Income Groups

[Maximum earned net income assumed]

REVENUE ACT	INCOME YEAR	SINGLE PERSON, NO DEPENDENT, WITH NET INCOME—									
		$500	$1,000	$2,000	$3,000	$5,000	$8,000	$10,000	$25,000	$100,000	$500,000
1913	3/1/13–12/31/15					$20	$50	$70	$270	$2,520	$25,020
1916	1916					40	100	140	490	3,940	42,940
1917	1917			$20	$40	120	275	395	1,820	16,220	192,720
1918	1918			60	120	240	650	950	3,540	35,150	323,150
	1919–1920			40	80	160	450	670	2,960	31,270	303,270
1921	1921			40	80	160	450	670	2,640	31,270	300,720
	1922			40	80	160	420	600	2,640	30,220	260,720
	1923			30	60	120	315	450	1,980	22,665	195,540
1924	1924			15	30	60	150	225	1,635	22,645	199,645
1926	1925–1927			6	17	40	101	154	1,234	16,134	116,134
1928	1928, 1930–1931			6	17	40	101	154	1,099	15,844	115,844
	1929			2	6	13	52	90	922	14,930	110,930
1932	1932–1933			40	80	160	420	600	2,640	30,220	263,720
1934	1934–1935			32	68	140	378	560	2,804	31,404	264,844
1936, 1938	1936–1939			32	68	140	378	560	2,804	33,354	305,224
1940	1940[1]		$4	44	84	172	449	686	4,253	44,268	330,933
1941	1941		21	117	221	483	1,031	1,498	7,224	53,214	345,654
1942	1942[2]	$15	89	273	472	920	1,742	2,390	9,626	64,641	414,616
	1943[2][3]	17	107	333	574	1,105	2,052	2,783	10,644	69,065	441,863
1944[4]	1944–1945	23	115	345	585	1,105	2,035	2,755	10,590	69,870	444,350
1945	1946–1947	19	95	285	485	922	1,720	2,347	9,362	63,541	407,897
1948	1948–1949		66	232	409	811	1,546	2,124	8,600	58,762	385,000
1950	1950		70	244	428	843	1,604	2,201	8,898	60,770	396,221
1951	1951		82	286	498	964	1,816	2,486	9,976	67,274	429,750
	1952		89	311	542	1,052	1,992	2,728	10,940	69,688	436,164

See footnotes at end of table.

No. 378.—INDIVIDUAL INCOME TAX LIABILITY UNDER REVENUE ACTS OF 1913-1951, FOR SELECTED INCOME GROUPS—Continued

[Maximum earned net income assumed]

REVENUE ACT	INCOME YEAR	MARRIED PERSON, NO DEPENDENT, WITH NET INCOME—									
		$600	$1,000	$2,000	$3,000	$5,000	$8,000	$10,000	$25,000	$100,000	$500,000
1913	3/1/13-12/31/15					$10	$40	$60	$260	$2,510	$25,010
1916	1916					20	80	120	470	3,920	42,920
1917	1917				$20	80	235	355	1,780	16,180	192,680
1918	1918				60	180	530	830	3,720	35,030	323,030
	1919-1920				40	120	370	590	2,880	31,190	303,190
1921	1921				20	100	370	590	2,880	31,190	303,190
	1922				20	100	340	520	2,560	30,140	260,640
	1923				15	75	255	390	1,920	22,605	195,480
1924	1924				8	38	105	165	1,565	22,575	199,575
1926	1925-1927					17	56	101	1,159	16,059	116,059
1928	1928, 1930-1931					17	56	101	1,024	15,769	115,769
	1929					6	22	52	862	14,870	110,870
1932	1932-1933				20	100	300	480	2,520	30,100	263,600
1934	1934-1935				8	80	248	415	2,489	30,594	263,944
1936, 1938	1936-1939				8	80	248	415	2,489	32,469	304,144
1940	1940[1]				31	110	317	528	3,843	43,476	330,156
1941	1941			$42	138	375	873	1,305	6,864	52,704	345,084
1942	1942[1]			140	324	746	1,532	2,152	9,220	64,060	414,000
	1943[1][3]	$1	$15	188	405	894	1,780	2,467	10,035	68,584	440,747
1944[4]	1944-1945	3	15	245	475	975	1,885	2,585	10,295	69,435	443,895
1945	1946-1947			190	380	798	1,577	2,185	9,082	63,128	407,465
1948	1948-1949			133	299	631	1,206	1,621	5,877	46,403	359,662
1950	1950[6]			139	313	661	1,257	1,686	6,087	47,994	370,657
1951	1951[6]			163	367	775	1,443	1,928	6,874	53,516	404,500
	1952[6]			178	400	844	1,577	2,104	7,508	56,932	412,328

REVENUE ACT	INCOME YEAR	MARRIED PERSON, TWO DEPENDENTS, WITH NET INCOME—									
		$600	$1,000	$2,000	$3,000	$5,000	$8,000	$10,000	$25,000	$100,000	$500,000
1913	3/1/13-12/31/15					$10	$40	$60	$260	$2,510	$25,010
1916	1916					20	80	120	470	3,920	42,920
1917	1917				$12	64	219	339	1,764	16,164	192,664
1918	1918				36	156	482	782	3,672	34,982	322,982
	1919-1920				24	104	338	558	2,848	31,158	303,158
1921	1921					68	266	526	2,816	31,126	303,126
	1922					68	276	456	2,496	30,076	260,576
	1923					51	207	342	1,872	22,557	195,432
1924	1924					26	81	141	1,525	22,535	199,535
1926	1925-1927					8	42	83	1,129	16,029	116,029
1928	1928, 1930-1931					8	42	83	994	15,739	115,739
	1929					3	14	40	838	14,846	110,846
1932	1932-1933					68	236	416	2,456	30,036	263,536
1934	1934-1935					48	184	343	2,327	30,162	263,464
1936, 1938	1936-1939					48	184	343	2,327	31,997	303,568
1940	1940[1]					75	246	440	3,571	42,948	329,637
1941	1941				88	271	717	1,117	6,480	52,160	344,476
1942	1942[1]			$13	191	592	1,322	1,914	8,814	63,479	413,384
	1943[1][3]	$1	$14	58	267	730	1,553	2,208	9,574	67,803	439,931
1944[4]	1944-1945	3	15	45	275	755	1,585	2,245	9,705	68,565	442,985
1945	1946-1947				190	589	1,292	1,862	8,522	62,301	406,600
1948	1948-1949[6]				100	432	974	1,361	5,476	45,643	358,677
1950	1950[6]				104	452	1,016	1,417	5,672	47,208	369,645
1951	1951[6]				122	530	1,174	1,622	6,406	52,640	403,408
	1952[6]				133	577	1,282	1,774	7,004	56,032	411,224

[1] Includes defense tax.
[2] Tax liabilities for 1942 and 1943 unadjusted for transition to current payment basis.
[3] Includes net Victory tax. Computed by assuming that deductions are 10 percent of Victory tax net income; i. e., that Victory tax net income is ten-ninths of selected net income.
[4] Individual Income Tax Act of 1944.
[5] Taking into account maximum effective rate limitation of 77 percent.
[6] Split income basis.

Source: Treasury Department, Bureau of Internal Revenue.

No. 379.—Individual and Taxable Fiduciary Income Tax Returns—Summary: 1925 to 1950

Includes data for Alaska, District of Columbia, and Hawaii; based on returns as filed, unaudited except to insure proper execution. Under revenue laws, the filing requirements applicable to individuals (citizens or residents of the United States), for the years shown, are as follows: (1) Single, or married and not living with husband or wife: for 1925 and 1930, net income of $1,500 or over; 1935, $1,000 or over; 1940, gross income of $800 or over; (2) Married and living with husband or wife: for 1925 and 1930, combined net income of $3,500 or over; 1935, $2,500 or over; for 1940, combined gross income of $2,000 or over; (3) For 1945, every individual with gross income of $500 or over; and for 1948-50, $600 or over; for refund purposes, returns are also required with respect to gross incomes under $500 for 1945, or under $600 for 1948-50, from which taxes have been withheld. (For 1925-35, returns are required to be filed by individuals having gross income of $5,000 or over if single, or married and not living with husband or wife; or having combined gross income of $5,000 or over if married and living with husband or wife; regardless of net income.) *Data for returns showing no net income or no adjusted gross income, filed in accordance with these provisions, are not included in statistics given here.* Fiduciaries are required to file returns on same basis as single individuals except that a return is required for every estate or trust of which any beneficiary is a nonresident alien and, beginning 1938, for every trust having net income of $100 or over. Partnership net profit or net loss is reported on individual returns of copartners according to their shares. See also *Historical Statistics*, series P 144-147]

ITEM	1925	1930	1935	1940	1945	1948	1949	1950 (prel.)
Number of individual returns, total ¹..........thousands..	4,171	3,706	4,575	14,665	49,751	51,746	51,302	52,656
Taxable...............do....	2,501	2,038	2,111	7,505	42,651	36,411	35,628	38,187
Nontaxable...............do....	1,670	1,670	2,464	7,161	7,100	15,334	15,674	14,469
Net income or adjusted gross income ²......millions of dollars..	21,895	18,119	14,910	36,589	120,301	164,174	161,373	179,874
Total tax ³...............do....	735	477	657	⁴ 1,496	17,050	15,442	14,538	18,375
Average per return: ⁵ Income...................	$5,249	$4,887	$3,259	$2,495	$2,418	$3,173	$3,146	$3,416
Tax.......................	$176	$129	$144	$102	$343	$298	$283	$349
Tax per capita of total population ³..	$6.35	$3.87	$5.14	$11.32	$128	$105	$98	$121
Percent of population filing returns ⁵.............................	3.60	3.01	3.58	11.10	37.43	35.27	34.37	34.67
Taxable fiduciary returns: ¹ Number............thousands..	(¹)	(¹)	(¹)	(¹)	114	101	100	115
Total income..millions of dollars..					857	967	927	1,284
Total tax...............do....					176	176	144	209

¹ Taxable fiduciary returns included with individual returns through 1940, shown separately thereafter.
² *Net income* (shown for 1940 and prior years) is total income less statutory deductions, but before deduction of exemption or credits allowable in computing amount subject to tax. *Adjusted gross income* (shown for 1945-50) is defined as gross income minus allowable trade and business deductions, expenses of travel and lodging in connection with employment, reimbursed expenses in connection with employment, deductions attributable to rents and royalties, certain deductions of life tenants and income beneficiaries of property held in trust, and allowable losses from sales of property.
³ Tax tabulated for 1940 and prior years is before deduction of credits for tax paid at source and tax paid to a foreign country or possession of United States, while tax for 1945-50 is after deduction of such credits.
⁴ Includes defense tax.
⁵ For individual returns only, 1945 and later years.

Source: Treasury Department, Bureau of Internal Revenue; *Statistics of Income*, Part 1.

No. 880.—INDIVIDUAL AND TAXABLE FIDUCIARY INCOME TAX RETURNS—ANALYSIS: 1946 TO 1950

[Money figures in millions of dollars. See headnote, table 379. See also *Historical Statistics*, series P 144, 146, and 147]

DISTRIBUTION	1946	1947	1948	1949	1950 (prel.) Total	1950 (prel.) Individual	1950 (prel.) Fiduciary
Adjusted gross income [1]	135,396	151,269	165,161	162,300	181,108	179,874	1,234
Salaries, wages, commissions, etc.[2]	99,144	114,737	125,815	124,799	138,956	138,956	....
Dividends, domestic and foreign [3]	4,137	4,776	5,458	5,748	6,824	6,131	693
Interest [4]	1,172	1,210	1,364	1,596	1,679	1,583	96
Rents and royalties: [5]							
Net profit	1,993	2,304	2,690	3,127	3,290	3,184	106
Net loss	194	229	238	268	283	281	2
Business and profession: [6]							
Net profit	16,055	16,422	18,075	15,647	16,890	16,847	43
Net loss	444	521	648	637	843	840	3
Partnership: [7]							
Net profit	8,151	8,288	8,093	7,936	8,601	8,554	47
Net loss	109	153	167	250	225	224	2
Sales or exchanges of capital assets: [8]							
Net gain	3,551	2,557	2,600	1,995	3,394	3,181	213
Net loss	235	263	290	335	316	314	2
Sales or exchanges of property other than capital assets: [9]							
Net gain	123	99	108	102	105	101	3
Net loss	68	68	83	102	133	132	1
Annuities and pensions [10]	231	226	293	442	430	430	....
Income from estates and trusts [11]	1,120	1,239	1,322	1,452	1,710	1,690	21
Miscellaneous income [12]	768	665	768	1,048	1,030	1,009	22
Total tax	16,281	18,249	15,618	14,682	18,584	18,375	209
Number of returns (thousands)	52,722	54,910	51,847	51,402	52,771	52,656	115

[1] See note 2, table 379.

[2] Salaries, wages, commissions, etc., include annuities, pensions, and retirement pay not reported in schedule for annuities and pensions, but exclude wages of not more than $100 per return from which no tax is withheld, reported on Form W-2 for 1946-47, and on Form 1040A for 1948-50. (See note 12.)

[3] Dividends received exclude amounts received through partnerships and fiduciaries; exclude amounts not exceeding $100 per return reported on Form W-2 for 1946-47 and on Form 1040A for 1948-50. (See note 12.)

[4] Interest received includes interest on notes, mortgages, bank deposits, corporation bonds before amortization of bond premium, and taxable and partially tax-exempt interest on Government obligations before amortization of bond premium; also includes, when received through partnerships and fiduciaries, partially tax-exempt interest on Government obligations and partially tax-exempt dividends on share accounts in Federal savings and loan associations. Excludes amounts not exceeding $100 per return reported on Form W-2 for 1946-47 and on Form 1040A for 1948-50. (See note 12.)

[5] Net profit from rents and royalties is excess of gross rents over depreciation, repairs, interest, taxes, and other rent expenses and excess of gross royalties over depletion and other royalty expenses. Conversely, net loss from these sources is excess of expenses over gross receipts.

[6] Net profit from business is excess of gross receipts over business expenses and net operating loss deduction due to net operating loss from business, partnership, and common trust funds for two preceding years. Conversely, net loss from business is excess of business expenses and net operating loss deduction over gross receipts from business.

[7] Partnership profit or loss excludes partially tax-exempt interest on Government obligations, dividends on Federal savings and loan association shares issued prior to Mar. 28, 1942, and net gain or loss from sales of capital assets. In computing partnership profit or loss, charitable contributions are not deductible nor is the net operating loss deduction allowed.

[8] Capital assets consist of all property held by taxpayer *other than* (1) stock in trade or other property held primarily for sale to customers, or (2) kinds of property specified in note 9. Net gain or loss reported is a combination of current year capital gains and losses to be taken into account (including those from partnerships or common trust funds in which taxpayer participates) and net capital loss carry-over from five preceding years but not prior to 1942. Allowable net loss is limited to amount of such loss, or to net income (adjusted gross income if taxed under Supplement T) computed without regard to gains and losses from sales of capital assets, or to $1,000, whichever is smallest. For details as to portion of gains and losses taken into account, description of capital loss carry-over, and special treatment of certain gains and losses, see *Statistics of Income*, Part 1.

[9] Sales of (1) property used in trade or business of a character which is subject to allowance for depreciation, (2) Government obligations issued on or after Mar. 1, 1941, on a discount basis and payable, without interest, within 1 year from issue, and (3) real property used in trade or business.

[10] Income shown from annuities and pensions is only the taxable portion of amounts received. Amounts received to extent of 3 percent of cost are reported annually, until aggregate of amounts received and excluded from income equals cost. Thereafter, entire amounts received are taxable and must be included in income. Annuities, pensions, and retirement pay from which tax is withheld may be reported as salaries and wages.

[11] Income from estates and trusts excludes partially tax-exempt interest on Government obligations and dividends on Federal savings and loan association shares issued prior to Mar. 28, 1942. Such income is reported in partially tax-exempt interest.

[12] Miscellaneous income includes all taxable income not accounted for elsewhere in this table; also includes wages not subject to withholding, dividends, and interest, not exceeding in total $100 per return reported on Form W-2 for 1946-47 and on Form 1040A for 1948-50.

Source: Treasury Department, Bureau of Internal Revenue; *Statistics of Income*, Part 1.

No. 381.—Individual Income Tax Returns, by Adjusted Gross Income Classes: 1949 and 1950

[Money figures in thousands of dollars. See headnote, table 379]

ADJUSTED GROSS INCOME CLASS (thousands of dollars)	NUMBER OF RETURNS		ADJUSTED GROSS INCOME [1]		TOTAL TAX		EFFECTIVE TAX RATE ON ADJUSTED GROSS INCOME	
	1949	1950 [2]	1949	1950 [2]	1949	1950 [2]	1949	1950 [2]
Total	51,301,910	52,655,564	161,373,205	179,874,478	14,538,141	18,374,322	9.01	10.22
Under 0.5	3,926,316	3,780,013	1,326,810	1,265,066	-----	-----	-----	-----
0.5 under 1	3,759,620	3,581,769	3,048,085	2,880,443	38,437	40,337	1.26	1.40
1 under 1.5	5,530,342	5,076,702	6,910,656	6,351,090	191,102	197,079	2.77	3.10
1.5 under 2	4,792,180	5,472,877	10,161,002	9,578,992	394,473	413,125	3.88	4.31
2 under 2.5	6,107,906	5,643,345	13,735,888	12,704,101	650,080	647,870	4.73	5.10
2.5 under 3	6,029,740	5,785,796	16,542,737	15,902,166	875,700	890,984	5.29	5.60
3 under 4	9,203,154	9,836,800	31,832,646	34,107,192	1,919,402	2,177,241	6.03	6.38
4 under 5	4,935,227	5,965,385	22,007,436	26,707,551	1,609,178	2,043,783	7.31	7.65
5 under 10	4,837,794	6,114,699	30,970,696	39,046,068	3,039,306	3,983,698	9.81	10.20
10 under 15	581,572	679,114	6,971,530	8,146,940	951,897	1,157,379	13.65	14.20
15 under 20	220,420	256,019	3,783,153	4,395,990	625,709	757,996	16.54	17.24
20 under 25	116,446	139,527	2,588,897	3,110,483	491,165	615,381	18.97	19.78
25 under 50	171,261	220,107	5,763,891	7,425,461	1,401,017	1,887,944	24.31	25.43
50 under 100	46,130	62,689	3,074,224	4,192,517	1,062,365	1,517,006	34.56	36.18
100 under 150	8,025	11,564	961,006	1,385,519	407,379	613,196	42.39	44.23
150 under 200	4,520	5,716	895,192	1,335,847	430,870	668,220	48.13	50.02
300 under 500	775	1,290	289,204	482,179	155,141	263,252	53.64	54.60
500 under 1,000	379	623	254,332	419,462	148,465	239,881	56.37	57.19
1,000 and over	120	219	255,500	433,407	146,459	260,550	57.32	60.12

[1] See note 2, table 379.   [2] Preliminary.

Source: Treasury Department, Bureau of Internal Revenue; *Statistics of Income*, Part 1.

No. 382.—Individual Income Tax Returns, by Family Relationship: 1945 to 1950

[Money figures in thousands of dollars. See headnote, table 379]

FAMILY RELATIONSHIP	1945	1946	1947	1948	1949	1950 [1]
Number of returns	49,750,991	52,600,470	54,799,936	51,745,697	51,301,910	52,655,564
Joint returns of husbands and wives	24,586,056	26,332,777	26,010,512	29,484,845	30,050,190	31,231,923
Separate returns of husbands and wives:						
Men [2]	1,932,840	2,062,824	2,542,268	1,146,292	1,131,888	1,160,151
Women [2]	1,903,196	2,041,965	2,690,948	1,247,711	1,226,710	1,114,417
Separate community property returns:						
Men [3]	1,029,782	1,065,873	1,594,446	228,359	(3)	(3)
Women [3]	996,066	989,978	1,643,794	228,067	(3)	(3)
Returns of single persons:						
Men	8,790,401	10,581,162	10,767,013	10,405,679	10,337,361	10,442,269
Women	10,423,650	9,535,891	9,550,935	9,004,724	8,553,761	8,606,804
Adjusted gross income [4]	120,301,131	134,330,096	150,295,275	164,173,861	161,373,205	179,874,478
Joint returns of husbands and wives	68,726,636	77,003,356	82,321,452	118,549,475	118,377,474	134,679,222
Separate returns of husbands and wives:						
Men	9,405,380	10,672,264	12,202,471	3,390,452	3,414,483	3,653,702
Women	4,541,274	5,121,373	6,190,806	2,435,848	2,685,901	2,524,186
Separate community property returns:						
Men	4,050,276	4,574,918	7,117,655	942,193	(3)	(3)
Women	3,735,452	4,246,183	5,979,593	934,978	(3)	(3)
Returns of single persons:						
Men	14,526,588	17,759,551	20,266,550	21,066,176	20,221,921	21,491,996
Women	15,315,523	14,952,367	16,216,945	16,854,765	16,673,427	17,525,370

[1] Preliminary.
[2] An unequal number of returns of husbands and wives results from use of sampling in certain income areas, from the fact that some returns lack sufficient information to identify the family relationship, and from deferment of filing returns by members of the armed forces for 1945 and 1946.
[3] Included in "Separate returns of husbands and wives."
[4] See note 2, table 379.

Source: Treasury Department, Bureau of Internal Revenue; *Statistics of Income*, Part 1.

No. 388.—INDIVIDUAL INCOME TAX RETURNS—INCOME DISTRIBUTED BY SOURCE, BY ADJUSTED GROSS INCOME CLASSES: 1950

[Amounts in thousands of dollars. Data are preliminary. See headnote, table 379]

ADJUSTED GROSS INCOME CLASS [1] (thousands of dollars)	Salaries, wages, etc.[2]	Dividends[3]	Interest[4]	RENTS AND ROYALTIES[5]		BUSINESS AND PROFESSION[6]		PARTNERSHIP[7]	
				Net profit	Net loss	Net profit	Net loss	Net profit	Net loss
AMOUNT									
Total	138,956,127	6,130,906	1,582,898	3,183,655	280,980	16,846,649	849,420	8,554,469	223,547
Under 0.6	1,093,015	13,255	19,571	50,527	11,600	114,280	47,672	21,497	6,835
0.6 under 1	2,247,748	44,003	44,154	123,492	7,260	324,004	39,257	60,550	8,190
1 under 1.5	5,003,951	83,102	74,529	193,824	13,043	760,470	64,971	141,159	13,267
1.5 under 2	7,856,925	88,256	77,866	191,576	14,485	1,028,688	51,545	194,078	19,079
2 under 2.5	10,880,068	93,956	68,066	192,682	19,569	1,112,835	51,063	258,331	9,209
2.5 under 3	13,096,835	101,619	66,922	168,665	20,199	1,148,598	62,001	296,255	12,493
3 under 4	30,717,185	207,767	119,396	298,103	39,168	1,987,815	85,685	590,004	16,965
4 under 5	23,861,823	227,541	126,364	274,183	37,628	1,512,663	68,706	533,728	18,105
5 under 10	31,515,233	780,146	318,921	634,310	56,455	3,433,953	117,613	1,671,464	38,639
10 under 15	4,175,514	525,708	145,219	206,130	15,574	1,672,108	55,590	979,046	15,778
15 under 20	1,855,309	398,190	92,049	157,472	9,165	980,517	29,375	655,394	9,770
20 under 25	1,205,394	335,540	68,683	106,199	7,014	657,762	22,685	531,980	7,036
25 under 50	2,616,134	1,026,017	180,436	272,269	14,895	1,382,215	57,243	1,342,406	18,808
50 under 100	1,256,008	866,875	98,683	143,211	7,413	518,650	35,151	790,584	12,928
100 under 150	330,615	386,392	31,302	46,968	3,012	108,929	16,664	232,532	4,863
150 under 300	240,312	430,328	25,261	38,394	2,586	72,389	17,765	183,826	5,104
300 under 500	57,638	184,186	9,293	13,532	1,296	15,114	6,424	40,947	2,065
500 under 1,000	27,827	158,822	7,035	8,065	519	10,005	6,157	20,875	2,843
1,000 and over	7,693	179,203	6,148	5,026	182	5,684	4,658	9,513	1,590

PERCENT	ITEMS OF INCOME AND LOSS FROM EACH SOURCE AS A PERCENTAGE OF AGGREGATE POSITIVE INCOME								
Total	76.49	3.37	0.87	1.75	0.15	9.27	0.46	4.71	0.12
Under 0.6	80.80	.98	1.45	3.74	.86	8.45	3.52	1.59	.51
0.6 under 1	76.20	1.49	1.50	4.19	.25	10.98	1.33	2.05	.28
1 under 1.5	77.31	1.28	1.15	2.99	.20	11.75	1.00	2.18	.20
1.5 under 2	81.17	.91	.80	1.98	.15	10.61	.53	2.00	.20
2 under 2.5	84.90	.73	.53	1.50	.15	8.68	.40	2.02	.07
2.5 under 3	87.36	.63	.42	1.05	.13	7.17	.39	1.85	.08
3 under 4	89.56	.61	.35	.87	.11	5.80	.25	1.72	.05
4 under 5	88.77	.85	.47	1.02	.14	5.63	.26	1.99	.07
5 under 10	80.09	1.98	.81	1.61	.14	8.73	.30	4.25	.10
10 under 15	50.80	6.36	1.76	3.22	.19	20.22	.67	11.84	.19
15 under 20	41.55	8.92	2.06	3.53	.21	21.96	.66	14.68	.22
20 under 25	38.15	10.62	2.17	3.36	.22	20.82	.72	16.84	.22
25 under 50	34.68	13.60	2.39	3.61	.20	18.32	.76	17.80	.25
50 under 100	29.51	20.35	2.32	3.36	.17	12.18	.83	18.56	.30
100 under 150	23.39	27.33	2.21	3.26	.21	7.71	1.18	16.47	.34
150 under 300	17.63	31.56	2.07	2.81	.19	5.31	1.30	13.48	.37
300 under 500	11.69	37.37	1.89	2.75	.25	3.07	1.30	8.31	.42
500 under 1,000	6.47	36.92	1.64	1.87	.12	2.33	1.43	4.85	.66
1,000 and over	1.75	40.71	1.40	1.14	.04	1.29	1.06	2.16	.36

See footnotes at end of table.

No. 383.—INDIVIDUAL INCOME TAX RETURNS—INCOME DISTRIBUTED BY SOURCE, BY ADJUSTED GROSS INCOME CLASSES: 1950—Continued

[Amounts in thousands of dollars]

ADJUSTED GROSS INCOME CLASS [1] (thousands of dollars)	SALES OR EX-CHANGES OF CAPITAL ASSETS [8]		SALES OR EX-CHANGES OF PROPERTY OTHER THAN CAPITAL ASSETS [9]		Annuities and pensions [10]	Income from estates and trusts [11]	Miscellaneous income [12]	AGGREGATE		Adjusted gross income
	Net gain	Net loss	Net gain	Net loss				Positive income	Negative income	
AMOUNT										
Total....	3,181,051	313,886	101,494	122,306	429,767	1,689,754	1,008,812	181,665,582	1,791,139	179,874,478
Under 0.6.......	16,430	14,405	1,167	7,204	4,206	5,084	13,776	1,352,778	87,716	1,265,068
0.6 under 1......	25,107	9,336	3,222	5,307	25,592	11,820	40,100	2,949,792	60,350	2,880,443
1 under 1.5......	52,092	18,784	4,318	11,421	61,683	17,428	80,014	6,472,570	121,486	6,351,090
1.5 under 2......	61,613	16,147	8,478	11,368	67,900	26,407	79,830	9,691,617	112,624	9,578,992
2 under 2.5......	60,680	19,241	6,168	11,739	38,220	20,176	83,741	12,814,923	110,821	12,704,101
2.5 under 3......	82,557	19,412	4,193	5,327	36,791	24,362	94,800	16,021,597	119,432	15,902,168
3 under 4.......	150,798	34,281	10,234	13,864	38,239	42,447	135,158	34,297,146	180,953	34,107,192
4 under 5.......	169,433	33,559	11,983	14,248	40,279	38,657	83,126	26,879,780	172,246	26,707,551
5 under 10......	548,260	69,552	24,346	20,408	58,675	172,947	190,480	39,348,735	302,667	39,046,068
10 under 15.....	271,947	25,486	9,628	7,049	16,993	143,653	62,480	8,268,426	119,477	8,148,940
15 under 20.....	178,163	15,040	4,368	4,462	5,740	99,243	35,555	4,465,000	68,012	4,396,900
20 under 25.....	134,689	9,397	3,571	3,226	5,460	88,526	22,025	3,159,829	49,348	3,110,483
25 under 50.....	376,266	19,041	5,954	7,664	13,223	275,548	82,651	7,543,119	117,652	7,425,461
50 under 100....	304,552	7,506	2,720	4,427	7,290	243,147	27,315	4,259,935	67,425	4,192,517
100 under 150...	156,603	1,496	416	1,159	2,577	114,135	3,822	1,413,716	27,194	1,386,519
150 under 300...	214,551	904	581	1,224	2,514	149,632	2,717	1,363,405	27,565	1,335,847
300 under 500...	113,649	170	81	810	713	57,123	599	492,875	10,699	482,179
500 under 1,000..	132,375	91	48	1,305	351	64,476	294	430,176	10,715	419,462
1,000 and over...	131,283	38	18	294	321	94,943	329	440,163	6,757	433,407

	ITEMS OF INCOME AND LOSS FROM EACH SOURCE AS A PERCENTAGE OF AGGREGATE POSITIVE INCOME									
PERCENT										
Total......	1.75	0.17	0.06	0.07	0.24	0.93	0.56			
Under 0.6.......	1.21	1.06	.09	.53	.31	.38	1.02			
0.6 under 1......	.85	.32	.11	.18	.87	.40	1.36			
1 under 1.5......	.80	.29	.07	.18	.95	.27	1.24			
1.5 under 2......	.64	.17	.09	.12	.70	.27	.82			
2 under 2.5......	.47	.15	.05	.09	.30	.16	.65			
2.5 under 3......	.52	.12	.03	.03	.23	.15	.59			
3 under 4.......	.44	.10	.03	.04	.11	.12	.39			
4 under 5.......	.63	.12	.04	.05	.15	.14	.31			
5 under 10......	1.39	.18	.06	.05	.15	.44	.48			
10 under 15.....	3.29	.31	.12	.09	.21	1.74	.76			
15 under 20.....	3.99	.34	.10	.10	.20	2.22	.80			
20 under 25.....	4.26	.30	.11	.10	.17	2.80	.70			
25 under 50.....	4.99	.25	.08	.10	.18	3.65	.70			
50 under 100....	7.15	.18	.06	.10	.17	5.71	.64			
100 under 150...	11.08	.11	.03	.08	.18	8.07	.27			
150 under 300...	15.74	.07	.04	.09	.18	10.97	.20			
300 under 500...	23.06	.03	.02	.16	.14	11.59	.12			
500 under 1,000..	30.77	.02	.01	.26	.08	14.99	.07			
1,000 and over...	29.83	.01	(13)	.07	.07	21.57	.07			

[1] See note 2, table 379.
[8-12] See footnotes 2 through 12, table 380.
[13] Less than 0.005 percent

Source: Treasury Department, Bureau of Internal Revenue; *Statistics of Income,* Part 1.

No. 384.—INDIVIDUAL INCOME TAX RETURNS, BY

[Money figures, except average per return

DIVISION, STATE, OR TERRITORY	1948			1949			1950 [1]	
	Number of returns	Adjusted gross income [2]	Tax	Number of returns	Adjusted gross income [2]	Tax	Number of returns	Adjusted gross income [2]
Total [3]	51,785,057	164,311,497	15,460,095	51,499,609	162,209,696	14,580,806	52,470,856	180,064,994
New England	3,830,083	11,596,817	1,079,771	3,706,617	11,069,996	981,473	3,785,596	12,361,652
Maine	336,902	825,415	59,554	322,300	781,219	56,381	320,488	847,446
N. Hampshire	211,073	565,176	42,075	201,461	515,591	38,463	210,103	578,200
Vermont	131,103	331,730	23,562	127,061	307,216	21,774	126,495	352,663
Massachusetts	1,947,809	5,949,883	543,751	1,902,361	5,912,113	518,417	1,931,414	6,309,165
Rhode Island	331,699	1,025,377	101,231	321,008	902,320	78,973	327,753	1,055,155
Connecticut	871,497	2,901,236	309,598	826,436	2,651,537	267,465	870,345	3,219,023
Middle Atlantic	12,270,392	40,731,522	4,626,423	12,022,086	39,759,776	3,800,445	12,192,839	43,704,835
New York	6,203,398	21,437,148	2,265,751	6,106,261	21,202,910	2,137,040	6,123,930	22,977,615
New Jersey	1,993,768	6,628,354	615,496	1,941,010	6,453,503	590,326	2,008,440	7,307,069
Pennsylvania	4,073,136	12,656,320	1,145,176	3,974,815	12,094,363	1,073,079	4,060,469	13,420,151
E. N. Central	11,913,367	39,396,216	3,739,954	11,606,854	38,646,107	3,487,275	11,683,192	42,319,385
Ohio	3,090,508	10,096,564	949,747	2,977,078	9,636,409	879,644	3,066,256	10,711,935
Indiana	1,441,605	4,364,014	374,381	1,409,222	4,374,124	371,821	1,464,200	4,816,972
Illinois	3,690,962	12,959,004	1,344,871	3,619,255	12,510,306	1,226,823	3,399,658	13,469,090
Michigan	2,410,194	8,175,360	752,115	2,333,556	7,760,425	700,399	2,477,041	9,204,619
Wisconsin	1,285,103	3,802,274	318,840	1,267,742	3,764,843	308,588	1,285,947	4,116,769
W. N. Central	4,899,392	14,150,634	1,228,794	4,939,604	14,231,909	1,137,528	4,922,878	15,229,692
Minnesota	1,066,112	3,071,655	267,983	1,064,193	2,993,559	238,292	1,076,359	3,429,054
Iowa	925,204	2,736,718	216,959	954,663	2,735,521	207,742	938,132	2,887,396
Missouri	1,287,540	3,784,449	347,794	1,358,024	4,152,012	351,445	1,345,968	4,346,393
North Dakota	198,521	610,211	47,331	217,305	565,172	37,986	198,629	549,467
South Dakota	212,645	595,537	45,329	214,937	540,617	36,833	215,239	557,868
Nebraska	466,436	1,402,937	121,768	475,954	1,356,295	109,937	478,657	1,474,351
Kansas	645,843	1,948,127	173,592	654,528	1,888,733	144,593	669,904	2,075,564
South Atlantic	2,380,951	16,611,243	1,414,589	5,967,149	17,211,365	1,413,300	6,224,395	19,405,018
Delaware	122,255	485,791	72,369	120,793	448,332	77,209	128,079	545,893
Maryland	958,698	3,036,471	279,068	1,104,645	3,381,243	290,284	1,162,059	3,817,212
Dist. of Col	339,450	1,128,555	124,884	396,604	1,376,868	141,467	373,782	1,418,048
Virginia	905,559	2,568,408	205,210	917,380	2,606,750	203,112	956,580	2,927,108
West Virginia	618,189	1,730,289	128,794	596,898	1,620,262	109,570	599,684	1,727,911
N. Carolina	901,457	2,359,574	177,614	906,710	2,335,044	165,890	958,858	2,759,007
S. Carolina	424,012	1,058,583	72,500	426,338	1,114,879	75,146	452,555	1,306,858
Georgia	741,220	2,060,766	161,964	725,497	2,064,459	161,959	770,782	2,308,074
Florida	749,657	2,184,806	192,187	770,284	2,263,498	188,663	822,036	2,594,907
E. S. Central	2,380,951	6,399,489	390,878	2,344,033	6,363,608	461,127	2,446,814	7,149,781
Kentucky	713,550	1,934,941	146,904	679,542	1,829,511	132,687	715,431	2,116,609
Tennessee	769,354	2,041,261	166,520	771,088	2,155,940	158,539	804,601	2,376,817
Alabama	616,539	1,679,746	121,400	610,931	1,634,742	116,224	634,960	1,836,199
Mississippi	281,508	743,541	56,054	282,472	743,415	53,677	291,822	820,156
W. S. Central	3,538,098	10,851,772	1,071,842	3,674,591	11,332,309	1,034,783	3,826,411	12,827,340
Arkansas	304,152	808,796	63,875	326,192	859,742	57,636	344,316	948,913
Louisiana	619,475	1,841,078	170,322	623,020	1,895,155	167,711	637,844	2,079,747
Oklahoma	577,105	1,719,212	153,119	600,921	1,713,487	136,048	606,613	1,925,065
Texas	2,037,366	6,482,687	684,526	2,124,368	6,863,925	673,388	2,237,638	7,874,215
Mountain	1,587,297	4,880,412	414,815	1,615,418	4,952,753	406,719	1,656,179	5,574,680
Montana	210,143	664,243	56,269	210,026	629,115	51,468	208,597	694,052
Idaho	190,204	519,785	38,408	187,650	529,031	39,354	191,116	580,309
Wyoming	99,279	320,222	29,868	101,625	327,108	28,461	101,191	353,090
Colorado	440,969	1,333,092	124,155	459,267	1,454,809	123,524	471,209	1,609,065
New Mexico	155,758	472,944	40,598	175,767	531,172	45,204	179,164	630,901
Arizona	206,126	660,433	55,947	203,174	642,640	50,452	214,002	747,769
Utah	221,326	653,441	43,289	216,304	630,231	42,750	225,356	712,171
Nevada	63,492	256,252	26,081	61,605	207,747	22,506	65,544	287,323
Pacific	5,519,542	19,114,147	1,953,449	5,446,542	18,710,015	1,806,708	5,541,769	20,517,994
Washington [4]	902,167	2,970,439	290,582	906,292	2,949,863	271,847	910,934	3,254,719
Oregon	557,588	1,835,879	179,862	541,639	1,781,983	162,938	552,769	2,004,899
California	4,060,087	14,307,829	1,483,005	3,998,611	13,978,169	1,373,923	4,078,066	15,558,376
Hawaii	182,227	586,944	57,618	182,803	540,156	47,120	179,871	583,616

[1] Preliminary.   [2] See note 2, table 379.

[3] Aggregates shown in this table differ somewhat from corresponding United States totals in other tables prepared from income tax returns of individuals, due to the use of rounded ratios in extending data from samples.

STATES AND TERRITORIES: 1948, 1949, AND 1950

and tax per capita, in thousands of dollars]

					1950 ¹—Continued					
	Average per return		Tax per capita of total population	Percentage, returns to total population	Percent of U. S. total				DIVISION, STATE, OR TERRITORY
Tax	Adjusted gross income	Tax			Population	Returns	Adjusted gross income	Tax	
18,389,534	$3,422	$350	$121	34.55	100.00	100.00	100.00	100.00	Total ²
1,240,653	3,265	338	137	40.61	6.14	7.22	6.87	6.96	New England.
65,225	2,644	204	72	35.23	.60	.61	.47	.35	Maine.
49,158	2,782	234	92	39.49	.35	.40	.32	.27	New Hampshire.
26,871	2,788	212	71	33.55	.25	.24	.20	.15	Vermont.
650,438	3,267	337	138	41.06	3.10	3.66	3.50	3.54	Massachusetts.
109,031	3,219	333	138	41.44	.52	.62	.59	.50	Rhode Island.
379,930	3,699	437	189	43.28	1.32	1.66	1.79	2.07	Connecticut.
4,713,605	3,584	397	156	40.28	19.93	23.34	24.27	25.63	Middle Atlantic.
2,626,329	3,752	429	176	41.15	9.80	11.67	12.76	14.28	New York.
742,887	3,638	370	153	41.38	3.20	3.83	4.06	4.04	New Jersey.
1,344,389	3,305	331	128	38.54	6.94	7.74	7.45	7.31	Pennsylvania.
4,401,940	3,619	376	144	38.27	20.12	22.28	23.50	23.94	East North Central.
1,087,976	3,493	355	137	38.49	5.25	5.84	5.95	5.92	Ohio.
449,731	3,290	307	113	36.95	2.61	2.79	2.66	2.45	Indiana.
1,511,346	3,962	445	172	38.77	5.77	6.48	7.48	8.22	Illinois.
968,137	3,716	391	151	38.60	4.23	4.72	5.11	5.26	Michigan.
384,750	3,201	299	112	37.36	2.27	2.45	2.29	2.09	Wisconsin.
1,393,159	3,112	283	99	34.85	9.30	9.38	8.51	7.58	West North Central.
299,539	3,186	278	101	36.17	1.96	2.05	1.90	1.63	Minnesota.
247,277	3,078	264	94	35.56	1.74	1.79	1.60	1.34	Iowa.
438,202	3,229	326	110	33.70	2.63	2.57	2.41	2.38	Missouri.
41,173	2,766	207	67	32.09	.41	.38	.31	.23	North Dakota.
40,509	2,592	188	62	32.86	.43	.41	.31	.22	South Dakota.
135,422	3,080	263	102	35.94	.86	.91	.82	.74	Nebraska.
191,037	3,098	285	100	35.07	1.26	1.28	1.15	1.04	Kansas.
1,869,947	3,118	289	85	29.28	14.00	11.86	10.78	9.79	South Atlantic.
110,067	4,262	859	343	39.90	.21	.24	.30	.60	Delaware.
367,626	3,285	316	156	49.24	1.55	2.21	2.12	2.00	Maryland.
170,054	3,794	455	211	46.31	.53	.71	.79	.92	District of Col.
253,349	3,060	255	76	26.86	2.18	1.82	1.63	1.38	Virginia.
132,030	2,881	220	66	29.78	1.33	1.14	.96	.72	West Virginia.
218,691	2,877	228	54	23.57	2.68	1.83	1.53	1.19	North Carolina.
101,903	2,888	225	49	21.59	1.38	.86	.73	.55	South Carolina.
192,170	2,904	249	56	22.32	2.27	1.47	1.28	1.04	Georgia.
254,167	3,157	309	90	29.09	1.86	1.57	1.44	1.38	Florida.
604,629	2,922	247	53	21.31	7.54	4.66	3.97	3.26	East South Central.
178,429	2,950	249	61	24.29	1.94	1.36	1.18	.97	Kentucky.
210,346	2,954	261	63	24.28	2.18	1.53	1.32	L.14	Tennessee.
148,496	2,892	234	49	20.81	2.01	1.21	1.02	.81	Alabama.
66,758	2,810	229	31	13.42	1.43	.56	.46	.36	Mississippi.
1,338,897	3,352	350	92	26.17	9.63	7.29	7.12	7.28	West South Central.
74,320	2,756	216	39	17.91	1.27	.66	.53	.40	Arkansas.
201,705	3,261	316	74	23.45	1.79	1.22	1.15	1.10	Louisiana.
180,553	3,173	296	81	27.13	1.47	1.16	1.07	.98	Oklahoma.
882,519	3,519	394	114	28.91	5.10	4.26	4.37	4.80	Texas.
521,665	3,366	315	102	32.52	3.35	3.16	3.10	2.83	Mountain.
63,194	3,327	306	108	35.24	.39	.40	.39	.35	Montana.
44,927	3,036	235	76	32.45	.39	.36	.32	.24	Idaho.
34,327	3,489	339	118	34.77	.19	.19	.20	.19	Wyoming.
160,012	3,415	340	120	35.46	.88	.90	.89	.87	Colorado.
57,740	3,466	322	84	26.19	.45	.34	.34	.31	New Mexico.
74,810	3,494	350	99	28.34	.50	.41	.42	.41	Arizona.
53,033	3,160	235	77	32.57	.46	.43	.40	.29	Utah.
32,262	3,926	492	200	40.71	.11	.12	.14	.18	Nevada.
2,281,635	3,757	412	156	37.87	9.64	10.56	11.56	12.40	Pacific.
335,349	3,573	368	133	36.16	1.66	1.74	1.81	1.82	Washington. ⁴
205,952	3,627	373	135	36.13	1.01	1.05	1.11	1.12	Oregon.
1,739,734	3,815	427	164	38.53	6.97	7.77	8.64	9.46	California.
54,964	3,245	306	111	36.19	.33	.34	.32	.30	Hawaii.

⁴ Includes Alaska.

Source: Treasury Department, Bureau of Internal Revenue; *Statistics of Income*, Part 1.

No. 385.—INDIVIDUAL INCOME TAX RETURNS—ANALYSIS, BY ADJUSTED GROSS INCOME CLASSES: 1950

[Money figures, except average tax per return, in thousands of dollars. Data are preliminary. See headnote, table 379]

ADJUSTED GROSS INCOME CLASS [1]	Number of returns	Adjusted gross income [1]	Exemptions [2]	Total tax	DISTRIBUTION OF TAX	
					Normal tax and surtax	Alternative tax
Total	52,655,564	179,874,478	82,589,707	18,374,922	16,244,356	2,130,566
Under $600 nontaxable	3,780,012	1,265,068	3,159,403			
$600 under $1,000 taxable	1,570,113	1,310,810	942,068	40,337	40,337	
$600 under $1,000 nontaxable	2,011,656	1,560,653	2,785,208			
$1,000 under $1,500 taxable	2,663,366	3,381,544	1,870,039	197,079	197,079	
$1,000 under $1,500 nontaxable	2,413,336	2,969,546	4,222,864			
$1,500 under $2,000 taxable	3,333,412	5,818,935	2,768,516	413,125	413,125	
$1,500 under $2,000 nontaxable	2,139,465	3,760,057	4,690,191			
$2,000 under $2,500 taxable	4,132,168	9,290,893	4,474,606	647,870	647,870	
$2,000 under $2,500 nontaxable	1,511,177	3,413,208	3,997,673			
$2,500 under $3,000 taxable	4,585,740	12,652,390	6,042,221	890,984	890,984	
$2,500 under $3,000 nontaxable	1,200,056	3,249,778	3,511,387			
$3,000 under $4,000 taxable	8,668,606	30,154,986	14,021,751	2,177,241	2,177,241	
$3,000 under $4,000 nontaxable	1,168,194	3,952,206	4,010,732			
$4,000 under $5,000 taxable	5,740,400	25,557,601	10,692,688	2,043,783	2,043,783	
$4,000 and over nontaxable	244,985	1,149,860	1,002,281			
$5,000 under $10,000 taxable	6,114,699	39,046,068	11,670,321	3,983,698	3,983,698	
$10,000 under $15,000	679,114	8,148,940	1,328,820	1,157,379	1,157,379	
$15,000 under $20,000	256,019	4,396,990	510,469	757,996	757,996	
$20,000 under $25,000	139,837	3,110,483	282,271	615,381	613,307	2,074
$25,000 under $50,000	220,107	7,425,461	445,054	1,887,944	1,743,779	144,165
$50,000 under $100,000	62,689	4,192,517	123,404	1,517,006	882,277	634,729
$100,000 under $150,000	11,564	1,396,519	21,937	613,196	246,088	367,108
$150,000 under $300,000	6,716	1,335,847	12,422	668,220	222,004	446,216
$300,000 under $500,000	1,290	482,179	2,268	263,252	69,232	194,020
$500,000 under $1,000,000	623	419,462	1,009	239,881	66,944	172,937
$1,000,000 and over	219	433,407	344	260,550	91,233	169,317

ADJUSTED GROSS INCOME CLASS [1]	PERCENT DISTRIBUTION			Average total tax per return	Effective tax rate on adjusted gross income
	Returns	Adjusted gross income	Total tax		
Total	100.00	100.00	100.00	$349	10.22
Under $600 nontaxable	7.18	.70			
$600 under $1,000 taxable	2.98	.73	.22	26	3.08
$600 under $1,000 nontaxable	3.82	.87			
$1,000 under $1,500 taxable	5.06	1.88	1.07	74	5.83
$1,000 under $1,500 nontaxable	4.58	1.65			
$1,500 under $2,000 taxable	6.33	3.23	2.25	124	7.10
$1,500 under $2,000 nontaxable	4.06	2.09			
$2,000 under $2,500 taxable	7.85	5.17	3.53	157	6.97
$2,000 under $2,500 nontaxable	2.87	1.90			
$2,500 under $3,000 taxable	8.71	7.03	4.85	194	7.04
$2,500 under $3,000 nontaxable	2.28	1.81			
$3,000 under $4,000 taxable	16.46	16.76	11.85	251	7.22
$3,000 under $4,000 nontaxable	2.22	2.20			
$4,000 under $5,000 taxable	10.90	14.21	11.12	356	8.00
$4,000 and over nontaxable	.47	.64			
$5,000 under $10,000 taxable	11.61	21.71	21.68	651	10.20
$10,000 under $15,000	1.29	4.53	6.30	1,704	14.20
$15,000 under $20,000	.49	2.44	4.13	2,961	17.24
$20,000 under $25,000	.27	1.73	3.35	4,401	19.78
$25,000 under $50,000	.42	4.13	10.27	8,577	25.43
$50,000 under $100,000	.12	2.33	8.26	24,199	36.18
$100,000 under $150,000	.02	.77	3.34	53,026	44.23
$150,000 under $300,000	.01	.74	3.64	99,497	50.02
$300,000 under $500,000	(3)	.27	1.43	204,071	54.60
$500,000 under $1,000,000	(3)	.23	1.31	385,042	57.19
$1,000,000 and over	(3)	.24	1.42	1,189,726	60.12

[1] See note 2, table 279.

[2] Exemptions include $600 per capita exemption for the taxpayer, his spouse, and each closely related dependent (specified by law) who had less than $500 income and who received more than one-half his support from the taxpayer, together with additional exemptions for the taxpayer and/or his spouse, of $600 if blind and $600 if age 65 or over.

[3] Less than 0.005 percent.

Source: Treasury Department, Bureau of Internal Revenue; Statistics of Income, Part 1.

No. 386.—CORPORATION INCOME TAX RETURNS—SUMMARY: 1925 TO 1950

[Includes data for Alaska, District of Columbia, and Hawaii; based on returns as filed, prior to audit adjustments or other changes made after the returns were filed, as the result of carry-backs, relief granted under section 722 of the Internal Revenue Code, recomputation of amortization of emergency facilities, or renegotiation of war contracts. All corporations are required to file returns except those specifically exempt, such as mutual, fraternal, civic, and charitable organizations not operating for profit. Returns of inactive corporations are excluded from these tabulations, except as noted. In comparing data over a period of years, changes in law must be taken into consideration, especially discontinuance for 1934-41 of privilege of filing consolidated returns (except by railroad corporations and their related holding or leasing companies and, in 1940-41, by Pan American trade corporations) and the restoration of this privilege in 1942. See source publications for effect of changes on statistical items. For other corporation data based on income tax returns, see pp. 480-483 and 486. See also Historical Statistics, series P 159-164]

[Money figures in millions of dollars]

ITEM	1925	1930	1935	1940	1945	1948	1949	1950 [1]
ALL INCOME AND DECLARED VALUE EXCESS PROFITS TAX RETURNS								
Number of returns (excluding inactive corporations)	430,072	463,096	477,113	473,042	421,125	594,243	614,842	629,370
Total compiled receipts [3]	134,780	136,588	114,660	145,287	255,443	410,966	393,450	455,718
Net income less deficit [4]	7,621	1,551	1,696	6,919	21,139	34,425	28,196	42,561
Total tax liability	1,170	712	735	2,549	10,795	11,920	9,817	17,396
Income tax	1,170	712	710	2,144	4,183	11,920	9,817	15,911
Declared value excess profits tax			25	31	55			
Excess profits tax				374	6,557			1,385
Dividends paid in cash and assets other than own stock	5,189	5,184	5,941	6,089	6,081	9,386	9,869	11,759
RETURNS WITH NET INCOME								
Number of returns	252,334	221,420	164,231	220,977	303,019	395,860	384,772	423,677
Total compiled receipts [3]	114,087	89,911	77,639	125,180	229,046	379,309	350,169	428,394
Net income [4]	9,584	6,429	5,168	11,203	22,146	36,273	30,577	44,087
Total tax liability	1,170	712	735	2,549	10,795	11,920	9,817	17,396
Income tax	1,170	712	710	2,144	4,183	11,920	9,837	15,911
Declared value excess profits tax			25	31	55			
Excess profits tax				374	6,557			1,385
Dividends paid in cash and assets other than own stock	4,817	4,823	4,651	5,898	5,918	9,279	9,409	11,641
RETURNS WITH NO NET INCOME								
Number of returns [5]	177,738	241,616	312,882	262,065	118,106	198,383	230,070	199,393
Total compiled receipts [3]	20,693	46,677	37,011	23,056	16,402	31,656	43,281	27,324
Deficit [4]	1,963	4,878	3,469	2,284	1,026	1,848	2,382	1,506
Dividends paid in cash and assets other than own stock	372	1,361	1,290	200	163	108	160	118
Inactive corporations, number of returns	([7])	55,700	56,518	43,741	33,335	26,427	35,315	34,095
RETURNS WITH EXCESS PROFITS TAX [6]								
Number of returns				13,440	52,097			50,200
Excess profits net income				2,996	14,185			26,681
Adjusted excess profits net income				912	8,368			8,976

[1] Preliminary.

[3] Total compiled receipts consist of gross sales (less returns and allowances), gross receipts from operations (where inventories are not an income-determining factor), all interest received on Government obligations (less amortizable bond premium), other interest, rents, royalties, excess of net short-term capital gain over net long-term capital loss, excess of net long-term capital gain over net short-term capital loss, net gain from sale or exchange of property other than capital assets, dividends, and other taxable income. Total compiled receipts exclude nontaxable income other than tax-exempt interest received on certain Government obligations.

[4] Net income (or deficit), in general, represents taxable income less allowable deductions, except that for 1925 and 1930, and for 1925-30, amount shown is before deduction due to net operating loss of prior years. (For amounts of such deductions, see table 538, p. 481). Beginning 1936, dividends received on stock of domestic corporations are included in taxable income. For 1936 and later years, contributions or gifts are deductible in arriving at net income and are limited to 5 percent of net income before deduction.

[5] Includes returns tax.

[6] Number of returns with no net income, for 1925, includes returns of inactive corporations, not available separately.

[7] For data reported, see above.

Source: Treasury Department, Bureau of Internal Revenue; Statistics of Income, Part 2.

No. 387.—CORPORATION INCOME TAX RETURNS, BY STATES AND TERRITORIES: 1949

[Money figures in thousands of dollars. See headnote and footnotes, table 386]

DIVISION, STATE, OR TERRITORY	Total number of returns [1]	RETURNS WITH NET INCOME				RETURNS WITH NO NET INCOME		
		Number of returns	Net income	Income tax	Dividends paid in cash and assets other than own stock	Number of returns	Deficit	Dividends paid in cash and assets other than own stock
Total	649,957	384,772	30,576,517	9,817,308	9,409,065	230,670	2,381,680	160,027
New England	57,709	33,545	1,887,365	513,729	547,480	22,289	192,797	13,890
Maine	4,101	2,369	83,872	27,045	22,429	1,545	13,404	525
New Hampshire	2,249	1,320	43,885	14,288	11,028	885	6,763	594
Vermont	1,516	849	31,429	6,384	4,971	644	5,272	258
Massachusetts	32,318	18,849	1,021,148	274,110	323,217	12,631	96,189	5,644
Rhode Island	5,121	2,975	133,448	44,643	37,527	1,838	23,593	3,431
Connecticut	12,404	7,183	573,583	147,269	148,308	4,746	47,576	3,348
Middle Atlantic	226,300	128,599	10,911,456	3,315,753	3,588,253	86,918	834,865	71,568
New York	160,375	90,093	7,754,846	2,334,992	2,802,455	63,848	585,126	48,785
New Jersey	36,533	20,449	1,021,493	261,190	193,320	14,380	99,066	10,989
Pennsylvania	29,392	18,057	2,135,119	719,571	592,478	9,790	150,673	11,794
East North Central	122,773	75,552	8,582,037	2,995,076	2,355,645	39,688	520,788	28,158
Ohio	31,147	20,025	1,976,956	663,649	596,680	10,073	153,453	8,317
Indiana	14,456	9,243	512,735	170,469	116,692	4,063	40,752	1,495
Illinois	40,764	24,538	2,531,483	875,089	756,746	13,619	162,004	11,190
Michigan	19,839	11,604	2,906,028	1,055,347	756,809	6,855	130,583	5,436
Wisconsin	16,567	10,052	654,835	210,522	128,718	5,078	33,895	1,720
West North Central	49,305	33,196	1,926,699	636,539	505,948	13,305	113,892	9,545
Minnesota	11,388	7,461	486,025	159,174	138,174	3,161	31,492	3,167
Iowa	7,881	5,500	249,396	75,164	44,890	1,842	13,260	1,644
Missouri	16,421	10,703	803,206	275,498	223,592	4,893	45,574	3,269
North Dakota	1,806	1,345	28,564	6,636	4,709	422	1,401	122
South Dakota	2,141	1,508	25,435	7,665	4,709	513	1,453	60
Nebraska	4,354	3,074	137,511	43,444	37,071	1,081	7,707	.518
Kansas	5,344	3,605	199,360	68,958	53,203	1,393	13,005	765
South Atlantic	65,563	42,445	2,709,369	840,242	933,553	22,789	223,330	12,886
Delaware	3,055	1,930	805,887	223,106	446,002	935	16,850	4,394
Maryland	8,691	5,100	322,954	99,144	96,239	2,958	39,079	1,526
District of Columbia	3,994	2,380	142,907	43,928	38,465	1,428	12,672	848
Virginia	8,820	5,930	292,330	96,207	60,484	2,635	37,422	1,243
West Virginia	6,441	3,902	139,656	46,486	41,744	2,154	16,570	1,865
North Carolina	10,560	7,053	415,406	139,619	102,484	3,117	26,901	1,150
South Carolina	5,035	3,227	140,183	45,370	25,646	1,467	9,812	165
Georgia	7,737	5,161	282,539	86,667	78,871	2,423	22,513	847
Florida	14,170	7,762	197,507	59,713	34,618	5,672	41,401	798
East South Central	19,878	13,296	661,929	219,701	149,923	6,071	65,354	3,254
Kentucky	5,444	3,713	230,416	79,066	61,241	1,567	19,215	1,212
Tennessee	6,539	4,447	232,758	75,634	50,257	1,907	22,980	1,277
Alabama	4,739	3,029	150,267	50,212	29,204	1,589	15,929	331
Mississippi	3,156	2,047	48,488	14,789	9,221	1,008	7,230	434
West South Central	34,712	21,911	1,495,405	502,131	537,194	10,769	122,199	6,192
Arkansas	3,191	2,211	66,952	21,879	15,649	859	5,553	181
Louisiana	6,641	4,337	233,993	77,975	75,738	1,992	17,576	880
Oklahoma	5,171	3,420	334,439	119,240	129,863	1,524	16,637	1,530
Texas	19,709	11,943	860,021	283,037	315,944	6,394	82,433	3,602
Mountain	15,752	10,648	410,363	136,297	111,006	6,438	45,737	1,817
Montana	3,296	1,921	43,038	13,456	10,986	1,158	3,598	246
Idaho	2,143	1,095	46,959	14,987	11,838	600	4,267	370
Wyoming	1,212	797	16,612	5,002	4,146	366	4,247	305
Colorado	5,359	3,039	170,929	57,340	51,745	1,866	12,364	211
New Mexico	1,185	793	24,705	8,099	6,488	349	3,358	36
Arizona	1,865	1,000	33,044	10,884	6,828	761	6,649	253
Utah	2,875	1,574	58,613	18,731	15,900	967	8,113	325
Nevada	815	429	15,862	7,798	3,075	371	3,141	43
Pacific	56,436	34,804	1,932,076	639,569	659,566	20,034	253,521	12,173
Washington	10,963	4,936	259,522	81,554	63,521	3,955	37,382	1,695
Oregon	5,501	2,929	134,838	44,457	31,961	1,983	16,698	698
California	33,974	16,939	1,537,716	513,558	564,083	14,096	199,441	9,780
Alaska	354	165	4,734	1,558	652	113	1,046	20
Hawaii	1,243	671	53,092	16,703	19,846	556	8,161	543

[1] Includes returns with net income, returns with no net income, and returns of inactive corporations.

Source: Treasury Department, Bureau of Internal Revenue; *Statistics of Income*, Part 2.

). 388.—Corporation Income Tax Returns—Total Compiled Receipts, Net Income or Deficit, and Total Tax, by Industrial Divisions: 1925 to 1949

[Money figures in millions of dollars. See headnote and footnotes, table 386]

All industrial divisions [1] / Agriculture, forestry, and fishery [2]

AR	Total compiled receipts, all returns	Returns with net income — Number	Net income	Total tax	Returns with no net income — Number	Deficit	Total compiled receipts, all returns	Returns with net income — Number	Net income	Total tax	Returns with no net income — Number	Deficit
5...	134,780	252,334	9,564	1,170	177,738	1,962	794	4,662	77	9	5,242	89
)...	136,588	221,420	6,429	712	241,616	4,878	672	3,475	40	4	6,431	86
5...	114,650	164,231	5,165	735	312,882	3,469	591	2,321	44	6	6,784	40
)...	148,237	220,977	11,203	2,549	252,065	2,284	643	3,213	49	10	5,187	32
5...	255,448	303,019	22,165	10,795	118,106	1,026	998	3,865	150	64	2,287	16
7...	367,746	382,531	33,381	10,981	169,276	1,939	1,671	4,444	239	77	2,885	24
8...	410,966	395,860	36,273	11,920	198,383	1,848	1,862	4,553	246	79	3,141	26
)...	393,430	384,772	30,577	9,817	230,070	2,382	1,902	4,312	210	67	3,604	32

Mining and quarrying [3] / Construction [3]

AR	Total compiled receipts, all returns	Returns with net income — Number	Net income	Total tax	Returns with no net income — Number	Deficit	Total compiled receipts, all returns	Returns with net income — Number	Net income	Total tax	Returns with no net income — Number	Deficit
5...	4,936	5,488	454	55	13,675	210	2,309	9,701	156	18	5,637	43
)...	3,010	4,700	194	21	7,533	238	3,046	8,871	151	15	9,674	82
5...	2,633	4,527	165	22	9,188	174	1,496	4,242	49	7	11,806	86
)...	3,264	3,956	315	68	6,427	109	2,525	6,716	102	23	9,033	94
5...	3,954	3,694	300	118	3,602	57	2,948	7,811	146	62	5,934	53
7...	6,037	4,954	860	292	3,340	73	7,048	14,353	430	140	5,934	39
8...	7,907	5,503	1,222	414	3,582	69	9,389	16,155	625	210	7,325	46
)...	6,825	4,766	805	268	4,385	109	9,918	16,290	591	200	9,456	74

Manufacturing / Public utilities [3]

AR	Total compiled receipts, all returns	Returns with net income — Number	Net income	Total tax	Returns with no net income — Number	Deficit	Total compiled receipts, all returns	Returns with net income — Number	Net income	Total tax	Returns with no net income — Number	Deficit
5...	60,921	54,137	4,383	547	34,537	682	11,911	14,862	1,469	186	8,751	135
0...	58,726	40,641	2,758	317	50,363	1,640	16,027	12,109	1,334	157	9,522	334
5...	47,947	37,976	2,483	357	55,700	666	11,604	10,600	927	129	14,833	572
0...	66,991	47,168	5,682	1,553	38,420	325	13,710	11,479	1,592	362	10,574	279
5...	141,284	61,680	10,577	6,112	17,432	326	22,663	12,966	3,134	1,548	6,770	197
7...	180,325	74,612	17,516	6,319	37,572	864	26,797	14,857	3,614	1,013	8,872	208
8...	200,011	73,639	18,928	6,822	43,108	814	29,676	15,304	3,594	1,205	9,921	146
9...	187,347	66,317	15,342	5,497	48,953	1,095	28,724	14,810	3,024	1,056	11,008	180

Trade [3] / Finance, insurance, real estate, and lessors of real property [3]

AR	Total compiled receipts, all returns	Returns with net income — Number	Net income	Total tax	Returns with no net income — Number	Deficit	Total compiled receipts, all returns	Returns with net income — Number	Net income	Total tax	Returns with no net income — Number	Deficit
5...	39,860	71,910	1,264	145	37,678	288	10,884	73,246	1,524	180	42,701	456
0...	37,217	59,741	651	64	71,746	739	13,691	72,102	1,065	109	64,477	1,567
5...	37,540	57,813	767	109	87,066	301	9,124	33,231	603	86	91,702	1,382
0...	47,216	71,766	1,270	296	66,083	188	9,913	58,988	2,031	198	83,614	1,162
5...	66,640	97,550	3,439	1,902	22,398	76	10,827	90,568	3,786	687	45,005	262
7...	122,332	133,192	6,368	2,221	44,105	287	13,835	105,918	4,114	648	45,125	272
8...	137,505	136,304	6,129	2,128	56,444	370	15,474	112,038	4,762	814	48,605	236
9...	132,291	126,320	4,387	1,493	74,705	547	17,048	116,587	5,526	1,010	49,690	242

Services [3] / Nature of business not allocable

AR	Total compiled receipts, all returns	Returns with net income — Number	Net income	Total tax	Returns with no net income — Number	Deficit	Total compiled receipts, all returns	Returns with net income — Number	Net income	Total tax	Returns with no net income — Number	Deficit
5...	2,941	16,571	246	28	12,410	72	323	1,757	20	2	17,107	17
0...	4,167	18,741	234	24	19,472	179	33	1,040	2	(³)	1,898	12
5...	3,710	13,358	127	18	36,289	269	6	163	1	(³)	1,560	9
0...	3,846	16,091	203	39	26,294	96	124	1,600	9	2	5,433	38
5...	5,972	22,977	649	317	12,130	47	166	1,908	15	5	3,480	11
7...	8,496	28,154	815	264	17,821	92	206	2,047	25	7	3,632	10
8...	9,018	29,412	755	246	21,044	125	122	953	12	4	3,213	12
9...	9,286	29,466	682	224	24,510	125	109	902	9	3	3,579	8

A corporation is classified industrially according to the business reported on the return. When diversified activities are reported, the classification is determined by the industry which accounts for the largest percentage of al receipts.

For changes in classification affecting comparability of data, see "Statistics of Income for 1938, Part 2."

Less than $500,000.

Source: Treasury Department, Bureau of Internal Revenue; Statistics of Income, Part 2.

No. 889.—CORPORATION INCOME TAX RETURNS—NUMBER OF RETURNS, TOTAL
PAID, BY INDUSTRIAL

[Money figures in thousands of dollars.

Line number	MAJOR INDUSTRIAL GROUP [1]	Total number of returns [2]	RETURNS WITH NET INCOME	
			Number of returns	Total compiled receipts [2]
1	All industrial groups	649,957	384,772	350,168,722
2	Agriculture, forestry, and fishery	8,362	4,312	1,616,695
3	Farms and agricultural services	7,642	4,010	1,568,878
4	Forestry	288	139	23,094
5	Fishery	432	163	24,033
6	Mining and quarrying	11,029	4,766	5,863,422
7	Metal mining	1,696	175	854,624
8	Anthracite mining	218	93	316,177
9	Bituminous coal and lignite mining	2,210	1,033	1,578,787
10	Crude petroleum and natural gas production	4,385	2,276	2,395,858
11	Nonmetallic mining and quarrying	2,520	1,189	717,976
12	Construction	27,041	16,290	8,676,131
13	General building contractors	7,108	4,041	2,712,628
14	General contractors other than building	3,601	2,418	2,456,781
15	General contractors not allocable	1,207	718	595,265
16	Special trade contractors	14,033	8,679	2,779,736
17	Other construction	1,092	434	131,721
18	Manufacturing	120,502	68,317	167,534,041
19	Beverages	3,555	1,786	4,957,037
20	Food and kindred products	11,665	7,056	23,644,861
21	Tobacco manufactures	206	114	3,200,423
22	Textile-mill products	6,143	3,692	9,459,263
23	Apparel and products made from fabrics	14,759	7,613	6,123,972
24	Lumber and wood products, except furniture	5,939	3,365	3,362,450
25	Furniture and fixtures	4,372	2,581	1,935,233
26	Paper and allied products	2,627	1,698	5,002,330
27	Printing, publishing, and allied industries	13,125	8,547	5,838,843
28	Chemicals and allied products	7,790	4,273	12,491,858
29	Petroleum and coal products	704	428	17,523,579
30	Rubber products	663	427	2,873,770
31	Leather and products	2,959	1,620	2,420,065
32	Stone, clay, and glass products	4,326	2,750	3,758,426
33	Primary metal industries	3,085	1,773	13,740,551
34	Fabricated metal products, except ordnance, machinery, and transportation equipment.	9,792	5,798	7,635,478
35	Machinery, except transportation equipment and electrical	10,095	5,607	12,516,574
36	Electrical machinery and equipment	3,146	1,656	7,689,844
37	Transportation equipment, except motor vehicles	1,132	525	3,368,648
38	Motor vehicles and equipment, except electrical	1,388	693	14,406,603
39	Ordnance and accessories	64	23	180,401
40	Scientific instruments; photographic equipment; watches, clocks..	1,850	1,008	1,727,660
41	Other manufacturing	11,117	5,283	3,676,172
42	Public utilities	27,450	14,810	26,199,477
43	Transportation	19,592	10,274	15,714,956
44	Railroads, railway express	713	397	9,183,543
45	Urban, suburban, and interurban railways (with or without buses)	85	41	187,573
46	Trucking and warehousing	9,738	5,828	2,338,223
47	Other motor vehicle transportation, including taxicabs and buses.	3,965	1,610	881,404
48	Pipeline transportation	157	108	315,309
49	Water transportation	1,748	968	1,736,122
50	Air transportation and allied services	1,059	229	612,785
51	Services incidental to transportation	1,943	1,039	432,542
52	Other transportation	184	54	24,455
53	Communication	4,466	2,413	3,424,906
54	Telephone (wire or radio)	2,811	1,540	3,058,166
55	Telegraph (wire and radio)	24	6	15,121
56	Radio broadcasting and television	1,606	860	351,192
57	Other communication	25	7	427
58	Electric and gas utilities	1,307	968	6,897,649
59	Electric light and power	686	523	5,389,588
60	Gas production and distribution, except natural gas production..	621	445	1,508,061
61	Other public utilities	2,085	1,155	161,966
62	Water supply	1,624	931	127,955
63	Public utilities not elsewhere classified	461	224	34,011

For footnotes, see p. 366.

COMPILED RECEIPTS, NET INCOME OR DEFICIT, INCOME TAX, AND DIVIDENDS GROUPS: 1949

[See headnote and footnotes, table 336]

RETURNS WITH NET INCOME—Continued			RETURNS WITH NO NET INCOME				Line number
Net income [4]	Income tax	Dividends paid in cash and assets other than own stock	Number of returns	Total compiled receipts [5]	Deficit [4]	Dividends paid in cash and assets other than own stock	
30,576,517	9,817,308	9,408,065	230,070	43,280,970	2,331,630	160,027	1
202,591	65,637	58,722	3,894	286,266	12,249	1,245	2
202,055	64,629	56,293	2,326	209,754	20,538	980	3
5,481	1,457	2,174	128	3,723	1,042	225	4
2,054	561	255	240	12,728	1,669	40	5
854,561	267,682	405,045	4,385	962,051	108,784	12,587	6
151,989	48,334	109,474	655	111,499	10,416	2,412	7
21,677	5,283	18,544	113	116,243	4,448	2,332	8
122,803	43,038	55,532	1,037	348,511	25,480	2,095	9
397,936	131,825	195,010	1,830	335,132	60,404	4,437	10
110,156	39,202	34,485	750	50,664	7,946	310	11
591,250	200,106	68,385	9,456	1,241,459	73,737	2,637	12
146,765	49,417	16,692	2,509	405,403	22,199	1,533	13
235,856	83,338	27,943	1,071	227,688	15,164	400	14
34,239	11,751	3,240	896	50,791	5,817	21	15
165,340	52,654	19,839	5,009	515,949	30,169	608	16
9,050	2,846	871	381	21,628	2,388	6	17
15,342,817	5,497,255	4,785,674	48,953	19,812,782	1,095,151	68,608	18
471,046	171,910	107,185	1,581	497,423	27,912	1,102	19
1,181,586	428,965	346,790	4,263	6,296,608	107,800	7,960	20
290,209	97,599	90,055	53	34,795	1,320	64	21
736,863	273,375	219,483	2,341	1,355,451	87,338	8,746	22
289,316	81,822	42,714	6,985	1,672,347	88,142	8,185	23
339,599	105,711	78,964	2,434	999,875	82,150	1,967	24
153,113	54,365	31,624	1,727	357,853	20,713	860	25
583,745	214,666	154,247	888	465,229	26,307	1,156	26
557,700	194,640	145,024	4,239	393,156	41,056	1,978	27
1,715,658	606,108	587,784	3,240	843,313	61,134	9,395	28
1,169,223	344,484	843,316	238	663,874	30,929	1,920	29
164,387	58,396	56,613	221	193,506	11,871	991	30
114,010	40,658	36,961	1,207	592,253	20,297	2,296	31
520,457	190,574	148,527	1,474	232,166	18,419	459	32
1,844,828	497,810	351,690	1,224	897,834	49,721	4,462	33
793,548	279,287	199,509	3,806	925,406	87,063	3,728	34
1,434,195	531,505	364,476	4,252	1,118,427	96,685	5,981	35
714,080	270,351	222,771	1,411	515,055	47,518	1,844	36
331,742	53,873	90,741	554	463,946	37,018	3,426	37
2,112,098	790,077	529,047	651	540,449	73,500	653	38
14,962	6,420	6,280	31	1,713	504		39
180,778	66,303	54,322	783	129,853	17,653	475	40
301,965	107,853	67,854	5,290	837,095	67,030	1,800	41
3,624,043	1,056,198	1,317,550	11,098	2,524,271	150,282	12,187	42
1,296,100	447,853	861,849	8,305	2,092,880	125,981	11,424	43
723,180	255,481	223,274	222	507,011	38,049	5,550	44
7,798	2,093	6,309	36	255,246	11,367	2,092	45
167,001	56,170	22,066	3,555	383,157	17,724	480	46
79,334	25,370	13,810	2,222	307,874	17,094	424	47
62,908	23,351	17,376	33	26,117	771	221	48
108,482	58,409	42,640	643	165,451	18,270	760	49
37,078	9,001	2,512	722	238,862	17,271	1,906	50
49,898	17,275	12,533	820	103,044	7,089	273	51
2,031	701	829	53	3,508	346		52
372,006	136,452	237,124	1,768	327,078	17,334	383	53
329,742	121,969	220,731	1,130	23,614	3,172	222	54
948	295	12	12	207,462	3,180		55
41,265	14,177	7,372	620	95,747	10,954	181	56
56	13	0	6	255	36		57
1,524,234	461,774	203,748	270	73,302	4,070	226	58
1,085,948	376,934	557,500	126	26,822	1,687	82	59
238,296	84,840	148,178	154	44,380	2,383	144	60
31,703	10,119	12,825	748	31,111	2,897	154	61
27,337	8,760	12,006	567	7,000	787	144	62
4,346	1,359	624	181	24,111	2,110	10	63

No. 389.—CORPORATION INCOME TAX RETURNS—NUMBER OF RETURNS, TOTAL COMPILED INDUSTRIAL GROUPS:

[Money figures in thousands of dollars.

Line number	MAJOR INDUSTRIAL GROUP [1]	Total number of returns [2]	RETURNS WITH NET INCOME	
			Number of returns	Total compiled receipts [3]
64	Trade	297,953	129,320	116,457,145
65	Wholesale	69,371	42,346	55,759,352
66	Commission merchants	9,983	5,441	2,988,920
67	Other wholesalers	59,388	36,905	52,770,432
68	Food	8,982	5,577	10,993,396
69	Alcoholic beverages	2,314	1,399	4,430,290
70	Apparel and dry goods	5,827	3,152	2,956,216
71	Chemicals, paints, and drugs	2,745	1,561	2,396,098
72	Hardware, electrical goods, plumbing and heating equipment	5,749	4,066	5,763,541
73	Lumber, millwork, and construction materials	3,347	2,358	2,305,391
74	Machinery and equipment	5,153	3,101	2,847,221
75	Farm products (raw materials)	3,234	2,416	5,164,104
76	Wholesalers not elsewhere classified	18,541	11,370	13,423,919
77	Wholesalers not allocable	3,496	1,905	2,490,256
78	Retail	120,617	75,632	54,105,286
79	Food	9,293	5,257	11,820,096
80	General merchandise	7,570	5,093	14,111,411
81	Department stores	2,626	2,095	11,028,508
82	Mail-order houses	590	936	337,194
83	Variety stores	686	412	2,067,075
84	Other general merchandise	3,669	2,350	678,634
85	Apparel and accessories	16,165	9,743	4,371,404
86	Furniture and house furnishings	10,405	6,497	2,017,865
87	Automotive dealers and filling stations	23,241	16,756	12,704,437
88	Automobiles and trucks	18,506	14,056	11,662,809
89	Parts, accessories, tires, batteries	2,319	1,259	456,323
90	Filling stations	2,416	1,441	585,305
91	Drug stores	5,240	3,536	1,208,115
92	Eating and drinking places	15,223	6,612	1,359,135
93	Building materials and hardware	11,969	8,960	2,766,608
94	Lumber and building materials	7,117	5,396	2,062,063
95	Hardware and farm equipment	4,852	3,564	704,545
96	Other retail trade	21,510	13,178	3,746,215
97	Liquor stores	2,656	1,608	231,583
98	Jewelry stores	2,763	1,521	377,489
99	Other retail stores	11,872	7,153	2,099,801
100	Retail trade not allocable	4,219	2,896	1,037,342
101	Trade not allocable	17,965	11,342	6,592,507
102	Finance, insurance, real estate, and lessors of real property	174,057	116,587	16,182,500
103	Finance	38,933	29,489	6,303,245
104	Banks and trust companies	14,992	14,235	3,766,917
105	Credit agencies other than banks	14,531	9,128	964,830
106	Holding and other investment companies	7,764	5,283	1,423,149
107	Security and commodity-exchange brokers and dealers	1,646	843	148,349
108	Insurance carriers and agents	10,166	7,499	6,709,986
109	Insurance carriers	2,556	2,158	6,330,697
110	Insurance agents and brokers	7,610	5,341	379,289
111	Real estate, except lessors of real property other than buildings	118,706	76,010	2,896,964
112	Lessors of real property, except buildings	6,252	3,589	272,285
113	Services	57,533	29,468	7,556,431
114	Hotels and other lodging places	6,287	3,584	1,267,249
115	Personal services	11,950	6,689	1,191,893
116	Business services	11,448	6,067	1,827,037
117	Automotive repair services and garages	4,389	2,488	295,286
118	Miscellaneous repair services, hand trades	2,411	1,190	203,061
119	Motion pictures	5,811	3,558	1,731,826
120	Amusement, except motion pictures	7,555	2,822	508,034
121	Other services, including schools	7,682	3,070	535,025
122	Nature of business not allocable	16,630	902	83,570

[1] See note 1, table 388.
[2] Includes returns with net income, returns with no net income, and returns of inactive corporations.
[3] See note 2, table 388.

LED RECEIPTS, NET INCOME OR DEFICIT, INCOME TAX, AND DIVIDENDS PAID, BY IN-
149—Continued

e headnots and footnotes, table 386]

	RETURNS WITH NET INCOME—continued		RETURNS WITH NO NET INCOME				
Net income [4]	Income tax	Dividends paid in cash and assets other than own stock	Number of returns	Total compiled receipts [2]	Deficit [4]	Dividends paid in cash and assets other than own stock	Line number
4,367,406	1,432,595	946,733	74,796	15,834,124	547,048	29,534	64
1,694,835	575,979	372,263	25,581	8,125,009	257,442	11,083	65
140,744	44,112	34,996	4,262	615,305	24,741	1,360	66
1,554,081	531,867	337,287	21,319	7,509,704	232,701	9,723	67
192,844	63,586	42,721	3,247	1,945,647	29,466	1,313	68
126,150	45,305	19,810	848	317,140	8,237	527	69
97,909	32,670	19,275	2,595	754,173	32,535	1,315	70
85,763	29,063	30,361	1,124	189,883	9,306	150	71
214,488	75,528	46,001	1,594	461,487	19,526	723	72
81,035	26,578	12,756	938	268,151	9,026	432	73
142,718	50,245	21,620	1,979	351,541	17,573	1,309	74
100,408	32,899	20,752	765	462,989	8,448	341	75
453,245	154,875	111,308	6,837	2,261,515	85,564	2,679	76
59,512	19,518	12,598	1,392	497,078	12,930	922	77
2,449,197	836,772	531,041	43,160	6,553,322	247,296	14,511	78
312,969	113,290	56,435	3,808	666,244	16,555	258	79
880,480	325,096	278,367	2,369	632,940	21,356	7,907	80
676,651	250,607	201,626	504	401,334	11,004	7,675	81
9,685	3,462	3,002	330	46,816	2,681	5	82
166,941	63,624	66,353	267	50,184	1,367	36	83
25,223	7,403	5,386	1,268	134,606	6,304	191	84
172,951	54,253	38,960	6,213	904,260	41,459	1,046	85
97,065	29,462	11,822	3,766	515,099	24,015	1,322	86
586,696	196,549	69,662	6,103	1,552,820	50,791	1,254	87
532,806	180,862	57,342	4,195	1,370,004	42,789	1,140	88
17,343	5,412	3,279	1,001	113,028	6,127	77	89
36,547	12,275	9,041	907	69,706	1,875	47	90
45,739	13,835	12,427	1,624	301,118	6,412	362	91
57,148	17,102	11,432	8,335	699,799	31,917	529	92
148,628	44,635	28,588	2,913	366,557	15,811	717	93
114,350	35,375	24,274	1,648	250,786	10,603	490	94
34,269	9,260	4,314	1,255	117,771	5,206	227	95
147,521	42,551	23,348	8,029	912,476	38,970	1,106	96
5,556	1,220	582	1,027	98,767	2,768	83	97
18,811	5,551	3,271	1,216	143,205	9,307	240	98
82,369	24,094	12,644	4,550	485,179	19,446	591	99
40,905	11,686	6,851	1,236	185,825	7,449	193	100
243,384	77,843	43,409	5,964	1,155,792	42,310	3,930	101
5,525,919	1,910,279	1,645,456	49,696	865,559	241,932	30,266	102
2,282,920	404,973	1,217,892	8,368	136,617	91,087	15,890	103
1,031,341	310,677	359,111	611	42,235	13,297	3,439	104
293,141	96,199	90,392	4,910	38,944	25,107	4,126	105
929,234	78,732	761,731	2,228	19,736	47,104	8,142	106
29,234	7,365	6,658	619	35,702	5,579	183	107
2,353,770	261,418	197,330	2,415	175,299	17,761	1,002	108
2,293,155	244,030	178,778	337	119,457	12,272	865	109
60,615	17,388	18,552	2,078	55,842	5,489	137	110
741,256	201,923	138,132	36,603	523,118	123,143	12,517	111
147,963	52,055	92,104	2,304	30,525	9,941	857	112
682,310	223,745	176,740	24,510	1,729,144	124,911	3,823	113
115,486	37,904	22,875	2,547	264,255	18,944	170	114
78,044	22,765	14,388	4,922	316,611	16,048	272	115
153,279	51,076	37,082	4,737	332,179	23,030	849	116
27,911	7,911	3,318	1,776	86,292	5,445	148	117
14,145	4,542	1,274	1,174	65,845	4,840	65	118
182,736	60,023	75,263	1,967	313,303	22,770	764	119
62,262	23,955	15,055	4,008	178,909	19,188	1,171	120
48,447	14,908	7,485	3,379	171,660	14,528	384	121
9,430	2,711	1,758	2,579	26,375	7,586	1,150	122

¹ See note 2, table 386.

Source: Treasury Department, Bureau of Internal Revenue; *Statistics of Income*, Part 2.

No. 390.—FEDERAL GIFT TAX RETURNS—SUMMARY: 1945 TO 1948

[Money figures and net gift classes in thousands of dollars]

ITEM	TOTAL				1948: TAXABLE RETURNS—NET GIFT CLASSES					1948 non-taxable returns, no net gifts
	1945	1946	1947	1948	Under 50	50–200	200–600	600–1,000	1,000 and over	
Number of returns [1]	20,095	24,826	24,857	26,200	5,721	693	121	10	14	19,641
Total gifts	535,559	755,604	777,613	740,923	181,453	112,519	45,066	9,967	41,527	350,392
Real estate	77,397	111,675	119,273	110,989	27,727	6,141	4,505	841	53	71,722
Stocks and bonds	261,116	407,537	394,306	399,622	89,215	75,528	28,450	7,104	31,309	168,016
Cash	117,054	151,193	152,860	138,313	39,679	18,628	9,032	1,999	5,357	63,616
Insurance	8,604	9,913	9,314	8,672	3,954	1,502	13	22	4	3,176
Miscellaneous	71,387	75,286	102,070	83,329	20,877	10,721	3,065		4,804	43,862
Gifts of taxpayer reported by spouse [2]				95,213	28,759	15,142	10,673	457	3,109	37,073
Gifts of spouse reported by taxpayer [2]				95,213	19,888	14,328	8,174		3,109	49,715
Exclusions [3]	94,347	119,946	121,761	130,497	34,297	6,043	1,188	126	360	88,484
Total gifts after exclusions	441,212	635,658	655,852	610,427	138,284	105,662	41,379	9,383	41,167	274,550
Deductions	271,586	370,412	399,318	401,279	72,750	40,543	4,467	1,606	7,363	274,550
Charitable gifts after exclusions	61,996	102,216	129,723	131,753	14,590	29,551	2,768	1,200	7,303	76,281
Marital deduction [4]				31,275	6,882	3,523	843	195		19,830
Specific exemption [5]	209,590	268,196	269,596	238,252	51,278	7,469	855	150	60	178,439
Net gifts	169,625	265,246	256,534	209,148	65,533	65,120	36,913	7,779	33,803	
Tax	36,633	62,336	64,402	45,338	7,743	12,906	9,375	1,992	13,322	

[1] A return is required of every citizen or resident alien who transferred by gift during calendar year to any one donee property exceeding $3,000 in value or who, regardless of value, made a gift of future interest in property. A nonresident alien is similarly required to file a return if gift consists of property situated in the United States.
[2] The Revenue Act of 1948 provides that gifts of husband or wife to third party after Apr. 2, 1948, may be considered made one-half by each.
[3] An exclusion is allowed of the first $3,000 of gifts, except gifts of future interest in property, made to any one donee during calendar year.
[4] Deduction allowed citizens or residents for gifts made after Apr. 2, 1948, to the donor's spouse.
[5] The specific exemption of $30,000 less the sum of amounts allowed in prior years may be taken in one year or spread over a period of years, at option of donor. A nonresident alien donor is not entitled to this exemption.

No. 391.—FEDERAL ESTATE TAX RETURNS—SUMMARY: 1935 TO 1949

[All money figures in thousands of dollars. An estate tax return is required to be filed (1) for estate of every citizen and resident alien who died (a) in period Sept. 9, 1916, through 10:24 a. m., Feb. 26, 1926, or in period 5 p. m., June 6, 1932, through Aug. 30, 1935, the value of whose gross estate exceeds $50,000; (b) in period 10:25 a. m., Feb. 26, 1926, through 4:59 p. m., June 6, 1932, the value of whose gross estate exceeds $100,000; (c) in period Aug. 31, 1935 through Oct. 21, 1942, the value of whose gross estate exceeds $40,000; and (d) on or after Oct. 22, 1942, the value of whose gross estate exceeds $60,000; and (2) for estate of every nonresident alien who died (a) prior to Oct. 22, 1942, any part of whose estate is situated in U. S., at date of death; and (b) on or after Oct. 22, 1942, only if gross estate situated in U. S., at date of death exceeds $2,000. The estate of an individual who died after 5 p. m., June 6, 1932, is subject to 2 Federal estate taxes—basic tax and additional tax. Basic tax is computed at rates provided by Revenue Act of 1926, which rates are embodied in Internal Revenue Code as basic estate tax. Additional tax is excess of tentative tax computed at rates provided by act in force at date of death, over basic tax]

FILING PERIOD	RETURNS FILED		GROSS ESTATE		NET TAXABLE ESTATE [1]		TAX [1]	
	Citizens [2] and resident aliens	Nonresident aliens [3]	Citizens [2] and resident aliens	Nonresident aliens [3]	Citizens [2] and resident aliens	Nonresident aliens [3]	Citizens [2] and resident aliens	Nonresident aliens [3]
1935	11,110	1,614	2,435,282	24,609	1,316,838	22,888	153,763	1,703
1936	11,605	1,716	2,296,257	16,163	1,245,395	14,627	195,301	1,069
1937	15,037	1,995	2,767,739	26,019	1,622,618	23,995	305,784	2,665
1938	15,932	1,710	3,046,977	22,648	1,724,589	20,670	314,620	2,182
1939	15,221	1,705	2,746,143	21,745	1,537,975	20,347	276,707	2,231
1940	15,435	1,441	2,632,659	15,540	1,479,268	13,916	250,360	1,196
1941	15,977	1,145	2,777,657	15,733	1,561,215	14,553	291,758	1,641
1942	16,215	1,181	2,724,513	12,620	1,524,881	11,455	308,342	1,349
1943	15,187	846	2,627,367	10,471	1,396,607	8,703	362,164	1,212
1944	14,303	554	2,907,620	8,712	1,508,963	7,272	404,635	1,146
1945	15,898	652	3,436,901	13,524	1,900,159	10,997	531,052	1,876
1947 [4]	20,899	1,108	4,224,210	27,198	2,319,310	21,872	621,966	4,389
1948	23,356	1,025	4,774,783	16,266	2,584,595	12,602	714,707	1,825
1949	24,552	1,352	4,933,215	24,511	2,106,827	19,356	567,421	3,409

[1] Net taxable estate is net estate for additional tax plus regular net estate for returns filed under the 1926 and prior acts. Tax shown is total net estate tax liability—the sum of net basic tax and net additional tax— and includes defense tax (10 percent of net tax) effective only for estates of individuals who died in period June 26, 1940 through Sept. 20, 1941.
[2] Excludes returns for estates of nonresident citizens who died prior to May 11, 1934.
[3] Includes returns for estates of nonresident citizens who died prior to May 11, 1934.
[4] No data compiled for 1946.

Source of tables 390 and 391: Treasury Department, Bureau of Internal Revenue; *Statistics of Income*, Part 1.

	1946	1947	1948	Total, 1949	Nontaxable, 1949	TAXABLE, 1949							Taxable under 1941 and prior acts
						Total under 1942 and 1940 acts, by net estate before specific exemption (classes)[1]							
						60–100	100–200	200–300	300–600	600–1,000	1,000–5,000	5,000 and over	
Number of returns													
Gross estate, total													
Real estate													
Federal Government bonds													
State and municipal bonds													
Other bonds													
Capital stock of corporations													
Mortgages, notes, and cash													
Insurance													
Deductions, total													
Funeral and administration expenses													
Debts, mortgages, and liens													
Losses during administration													
Support of dependents													
Charitable, public, and similar bequests													
Marital deduction													
Property previously taxed, net deduction													
Specific exemption													
Disallowed deductions[3]													
Allowable deductions													
Net estate before exemption[4]													
Net estate for basic tax[5]													
Net estate for additional tax[6]													
Tax before tax credits													
Total tax before tax credits													
Tax credits[7]													
Net tax													
Estate tax													
Total tax liability													

[1] Net estate classes are based on amount of net estate for additional tax plus specific exemption. (See note 2.)

[2] The specific exemption tabulated (a) for estates subject to additional tax is $60,000 under 1942 and 1940 acts; $40,000 under 1941, 1940, and 1935 acts; $50,000 under 1934 and 1932 acts; and (b) for estates subject to earlier acts is $100,000 under 1926 act; and $50,000 under 1924 and prior acts.

[3] Represents excess of (total amount of) funeral and administration expenses, debts of decedent, mortgages and liens, and support of dependents, over value of property includible in gross estate subject to claims.

[4] Excess of gross estate over allowable deductions, exclusive of specific exemption.

[5] Net estate after deducting specific exemption of $100,000, except for returns filed under 1924 or prior acts for which specific exemption is $50,000.

[6] Applies only to estates of individuals who died subsequent to June 6, 1932.

[7] Credits for (a) estate, inheritance, legacy, or succession taxes paid to States, etc., (b) gift taxes paid to the Federal Government, and (c) death duties paid to foreign countries with which conventions are in effect.

Source: Treasury Department, Bureau of Internal Revenue; Statistics of Income, Part 1.

No. 393.—PUBLIC DEBT OF THE UNITED STATES: 1800 TO 1952

[All figures except per capita in millions of dollars. On basis of public debt accounts prior to 1920 and on basis of daily Treasury statements for 1920 and thereafter. See also *Historical Statistics*, series P 132-143]

JUNE 30 [1]	GROSS DEBT Amount	GROSS DEBT Per capita [2]	Interest bearing [3]	Matured [3]	Non-interest bearing [4]	JUNE 30 [1]	GROSS DEBT Amount	GROSS DEBT Per capita [2]	Interest bearing [3]	Matured	Non-interest bearing [4]
1800	83	$15.87				1919	25,482	$242.54	25,234	11	236
1810	53	7.46				1920	24,299	228.23	24,063	7	230
1820	91	9.58				1921	23,977	220.91	23,739	11	228
1830	49	3.83				1922	22,963	208.65	22,710	25	228
1840	4	.21				1923	22,350	199.64	22,007	99	244
1850	63	2.77				1924	21,251	186.23	20,981	30	239
1855	36	1.30	35	(5)		1925	20,516	177.12	20,211	30	275
1860	65	2.06	65	(5)		1926	19,643	167.32	19,384	13	246
1865	2,678	75.01	2,218	2	458	1927	18,512	155.51	18,253	15	245
1870	2,436	61.06	2,036	4	397	1928	17,604	146.09	17,318	45	241
1875	2,156	47.84	1,709	11	436	1929	16,931	139.04	16,639	51	241
1880	2,091	41.60	1,710	8	373	1930	16,185	131.51	15,922	32	232
1885	1,579	27.86	1,182	4	392	1931	16,801	135.45	16,520	52	230
1890	1,122	17.80	711	2	409	1932	19,487	156.10	19,161	60	266
1895	1,097	15.76	716	2	379	1933	22,539	179.48	22,158	66	315
1900	1,263	16.60	1,023	1	239	1934	27,053	214.07	26,480	54	518
1901	1,222	15.74	967	1	233	1935	28,701	225.55	27,645	231	825
1902	1,178	14.88	931	1	246	1936	33,779	263.79	32,989	169	620
1903	1,159	14.38	915	1	244	1937	36,425	282.75	35,800	119	506
1904	1,136	13.83	895	2	239	1938	37,165	286.27	36,576	141	447
1905	1,132	13.51	895	1	236	1939	40,440	308.98	39,886	142	411
1906	1,143	13.37	895	1	246	1940	42,968	325.23	42,376	205	386
1907	1,147	13.19	895	1	251	1941	48,961	367.09	48,387	205	369
1908	1,178	13.28	898	4	276	1942	72,422	537.13	71,968	98	356
1909	1,148	12.69	913	3	232	1943	136,696	999.83	135,380	141	1,175
1910	1,147	12.41	913	2	231	1944	201,003	1,452.44	199,543	201	1,259
1911	1,154	12.29	915	2	237	1945	258,682	1,848.60	256,357	269	2,057
1912	1,194	12.52	964	2	228	1946	269,422	1,905.42	268,111	376	935
1913	1,193	12.27	966	2	226	1947	258,286	1,792.05	255,113	231	2,942
1914	1,188	11.99	968	2	219	1948	252,292	1,720.71	250,063	280	1,949
1915	1,191	11.85	970	2	220	1949	252,770	1,694.75	250,762	245	1,764
1916	1,225	12.02	972	1	252	1950	257,357	1,696.61	255,209	265	1,883
1917	2,976	28.77	2,713	14	249	1951	255,222	1,653.50	252,852	512	1,858
1918	12,244	117.11	11,986	20	238	1952	259,105	1,650.19	256,863	419	1,834

INTEREST-BEARING DEBT

JUNE 30	Total	Public issues Marketable Bills	Public issues Marketable Certificates	Public issues Marketable Notes	Public issues Marketable Treasury bonds [6]	Public issues Marketable Other bonds [7]	Public issues Nonmarketable U.S. savings bonds	Public issues Nonmarketable Treasury savings notes	Public issues Nonmarketable Treasury bonds, investment series	Public issues Nonmarketable Other bonds [8]	Special issues
1940	42,376	1,302	....	6,383	26,555	196	2,905	....	....	261	4,775
1941	48,387	1,603	....	5,698	30,215	196	4,314	....	....	241	6,120
1942	71,968	2,508	3,096	6,689	38,084	196	10,188	3,015	....	307	7,885
1943	135,380	11,864	16,561	9,168	57,520	196	21,256	7,495	....	448	10,871
1944	199,543	14,734	28,822	17,405	79,244	196	34,606	9,557	....	692	14,287
1945	256,357	17,041	34,136	23,497	106,449	196	45,586	10,136	....	505	18,812
1946	268,111	17,039	34,804	18,261	119,323	180	49,035	6,711	....	427	22,332
1947	255,113	15,775	25,296	8,142	119,322	166	51,367	5,560	....	2,118	27,366
1948	250,063	13,757	22,588	11,375	112,462	164	53,274	4,394	959	879	30,211
1949	250,762	11,536	29,427	3,596	110,425	162	56,260	4,860	954	765	32,776
1950	255,209	13,533	18,418	20,404	102,795	160	57,536	8,472	954	582	32,356
1951	252,852	13,614	9,509	35,806	78,833	156	57,572	7,818	14,526	366	34,653
1952	256,863	17,219	28,423	18,963	75,660	142	57,685	6,612	14,046	373	37,739

[1] Figures for 1800-1840 as of Jan. 1.
[2] Based on Bureau of Census estimated population for continental U. S. as of July 1 of each year beginning 1850.
[3] Excludes bonds issued to Pacific railways and Navy pension fund.
[4] Includes old demand notes; U. S. notes (gold reserve deducted since 1900); postal currency and fractional currency less amounts officially estimated to have been destroyed; and also deposits held by Treasury for various purposes. Excludes gold, silver and currency certificates, and Treasury notes of 1890 for redemption of which an exact equivalent of the respective kinds of money or bullion was held in the Treasury.
[5] Less than $500,000.
[6] Bank eligible bonds and beginning 1942 also includes bank restricted bonds.
[7] Consists of postal savings and Panama Canal bonds, and also conversion bonds prior to 1947.
[8] Consists of depositary bonds, and adjusted service bonds until they matured on June 15, 1945. Also includes armed forces leave bonds for 1947-51.

Source: Treasury Department; *Annual Report of the Secretary*, Statement of the Public Debt published in *Daily Statement of the U. S. Treasury*, and *Treasury Bulletin*.

No. 394.—PUBLIC AND PRIVATE DEBT: 1929 to 1951

[In billions of dollars. Data as of end of calendar year except for State and local government debt as of June 30. See general note, p.333]

YEAR	Public and private, total	PUBLIC			PRIVATE						
		Total	Federal	State and local	Total	Corporate		Individual and noncorporate			
						Long-term	Short-term	Mortgage		Nonmortgage	
								Farm [2]	Non-farm [1]	Farm [1]	Non-farm [1]
GROSS DEBT											
1929	214.4	34.8	17.5	17.2	179.6	85.6	50.4	9.6	31.7	2.6	28.7
1930	214.5	35.5	17.5	18.5	179.0	61.1	48.3	8.4	32.7	2.4	27.1
1931	204.0	38.6	19.1	19.5	165.4	60.1	40.3	9.1	31.7	2.0	22.3
1932	186.3	42.4	22.8	19.6	153.8	58.8	37.3	8.5	30.1	1.6	17.5
1933	191.7	47.5	27.7	19.8	144.2	57.2	35.2	7.7	27.6	1.4	15.2
1934	198.4	57.0	37.9	19.2	141.4	53.2	37.4	7.6	26.8	1.3	15.1
1935	201.4	61.0	41.7	19.3	140.4	52.6	37.8	7.4	26.1	1.5	15.6
1936	207.0	64.7	45.1	19.6	142.3	50.5	40.4	7.2	25.7	1.4	17.1
1937	208.5	67.4	47.8	19.6	142.2	51.8	38.7	7.0	25.7	1.6	17.8
1938	204.5	67.0	47.4	19.6	137.8	52.8	33.9	6.6	25.9	2.2	16.2
1939	208.9	70.1	50.1	20.0	138.8	52.1	34.7	6.6	26.3	2.2	16.8
1940	216.8	73.8	53.6	20.2	142.9	51.2	37.7	6.5	27.2	2.6	17.7
1941	242.3	89.2	69.0	20.2	154.1	51.2	46.3	6.4	28.4	2.9	18.8
1942	300.8	142.9	123.2	19.7	157.9	50.2	56.2	6.0	27.9	3.0	14.7
1943	386.1	205.4	186.7	18.7	159.3	48.4	62.0	5.4	27.2	2.8	14.1
1944	431.7	271.2	253.7	17.5	160.5	47.0	62.0	4.9	27.0	2.8	16.8
1945	464.2	309.2	292.6	16.6	155.0	46.3	54.3	4.7	27.9	2.5	20.5
1946	459.4	288.1	272.1	15.9	171.3	48.4	60.9	4.8	33.6	2.8	20.9
1947	487.7	296.6	280.8	15.8	201.1	55.0	73.2	4.9	40.1	3.5	24.4
1948	500.3	276.7	258.0	18.7	223.5	62.5	75.9	5.1	46.5	5.5	27.7
1949	515.0	287.0	266.1	20.9	231.0	67.7	69.1	5.4	51.9	6.4	30.5
1950	541.1	290.6	266.4	24.2	270.5	71.7	88.8	5.8	61.1	6.1	34.9
1951	601.6	297.4	270.5	27.0	304.2	77.8	106.0	6.3	69.5	7.0	38.7
NET DEBT											
1929	191.1	29.7	16.5	13.2	161.5	47.3	41.6	9.6	31.7	2.6	28.7
1930	191.4	30.6	16.5	14.1	160.8	51.1	38.2	9.4	32.7	2.4	27.1
1931	182.6	34.0	18.5	15.5	148.6	50.3	33.2	9.1	31.7	2.0	22.3
1932	175.7	37.9	21.3	16.6	137.8	49.2	30.8	8.5	30.1	1.6	17.5
1933	169.7	41.0	24.3	16.7	128.8	47.9	29.1	7.7	27.6	1.4	15.2
1934	172.6	46.3	30.4	15.9	126.3	44.6	30.9	7.6	26.8	1.3	15.1
1935	175.9	50.5	34.4	16.0	125.4	43.6	31.2	7.4	26.1	1.5	15.6
1936	181.4	53.9	37.7	16.2	127.5	42.5	33.5	7.2	25.7	1.4	17.1
1937	182.3	55.3	39.2	16.1	127.9	43.5	32.3	7.0	25.7	1.6	17.8
1938	180.5	54.5	38.5	16.0	124.3	44.5	26.4	5.8	25.9	2.2	16.2
1939	184.5	58.9	42.6	16.3	125.5	44.4	29.2	6.6	26.3	2.2	16.8
1940	198.5	61.3	44.8	16.5	129.6	43.7	31.9	6.5	27.2	2.6	17.7
1941	212.0	72.6	56.3	16.3	140.0	43.6	39.8	6.4	28.4	2.9	18.8
1942	260.7	117.5	101.7	15.8	143.2	42.7	49.0	6.0	27.9	3.0	14.7
1943	314.3	169.3	154.4	14.9	145.0	41.0	54.5	5.4	27.2	2.8	14.1
1944	371.6	226.0	211.9	14.1	145.7	39.8	54.3	4.9	27.0	2.8	16.8
1945	407.3	265.5	252.7	13.7	140.8	38.3	47.0	4.7	27.9	2.5	20.5
1946	394.5	243.3	229.7	13.6	155.5	41.3	52.2	4.8	33.6	2.8	20.9
1947	426.5	257.7	242.3	14.4	181.8	46.1	62.8	4.9	40.1	3.6	24.4
1948	458.3	252.7	236.5	16.2	202.6	52.5	65.3	5.1	46.6	5.5	27.7
1949	446.7	236.7	218.6	18.1	210.0	56.5	58.3	5.4	51.9	6.4	30.5
1950	466.8	238.4	218.7	20.7	246.4	59.8	76.6	5.8	61.1	6.1	34.9
1951	519.2	242.0	218.7	23.3	277.2	64.8	91.0	6.3	69.5	7.0	38.7

[1] Data are for noncorporate borrowers only.
[2] Comprises real-estate farm debt contracted for productive purposes and owed to institutional lenders.
[3] Comprises debt incurred for commercial (nonfarm), financial and consumer purposes, including debt owed by agriculture for financial and consumer purposes.

Source: Department of Commerce, Office of Business Economics (based upon data from various governmental sources). Survey of Current Business, October 1950 and September 1952.

No. 895.—Computed Interest Charge and Computed Interest Rate on Federal Securities: 1930 to 1952

[Dollar amounts in millions. Based on *Daily Treasury Statement*. See also *Historical Statistics*, series P 137 and P 138 for charge and rate on interest bearing debt]

END OF FISCAL YEAR	TOTAL INTEREST-BEARING SECURITIES				COMPUTED ANNUAL INTEREST RATE					
	Amount outstanding		Computed annual interest charge		Total interest-bearing securities [1]	Public debt				Guaranteed securities [1]
	Public debt and guaranteed securities [1]	Public debt	Public debt and guaranteed securities [1]	Public debt		Total public debt	Total marketable issues [2]	Non-marketable issues [2]	Special issues	
1930.........	15,922	15,922	606	606	3,807	3,807	(4)	(4)	(4)	......
1935.........	31,768	27,645	863	751	2,716	2,716	(4)	(4)	3,289	2,730
1940.........	47,874	42,376	1,203	1,095	2,514	2,583	2,492	2,908	3,027	1,978
1945.........	256,766	256,357	4,969	4,964	1,935	1,936	1,718	2,473	2,436	1,321
1946.........	268,578	268,111	5,357	5,351	1,995	1,996	1,773	2,567	2,448	1,410
1947.........	255,197	255,113	5,376	5,374	2,107	2,107	1,871	2,593	2,510	1,758
1948.........	250,132	250,063	5,457	5,455	2,182	2,182	1,942	2,623	2,588	1,924
1949.........	250,785	250,762	5,606	5,606	2,236	2,236	2,001	2,629	2,596	2,210
1950.........	255,226	255,209	5,613	5,613	2,200	2,200	1,958	2,569	2,589	2,684
1951.........	252,879	252,852	5,740	5,740	2,270	2,270	1,981	2,623	2,606	2,655
1952.........	256,907	256,863	5,962	5,961	2,329	2,329	2,051	2,659	2,675	2,578

[1] Excludes guaranteed securities held by Treasury.
[2] Includes bills, certificates, notes, treasury bonds, postal savings bonds, Panama Canal bonds and, prior to 1947, conversion bonds.
[3] Annual interest charge and annual interest rate on U. S. savings bonds are computed on basis of rate to maturity applied against amount outstanding.
[4] Not available.

Source: Treasury Department; *Treasury Bulletin*.

No. 896.—Ownership of U. S. Government Securities, Direct and Fully Guaranteed, as of June 30: 1925 to 1952

[Par value.[1] In millions of dollars. Holdings of Federal Reserve Banks and U. S. Government agencies and trust funds are reported figures; holdings of other investor groups for 1940-1952 are estimates by Treasury Department]

ITEM	1925	1930	1935	1940	1945	1950	1951	1952
Gross debt, total [2]	20,516	16,185	32,824	48,496	259,115	257,377	255,251	259,151
U. S. Government agencies and trust funds: [3]								
Special issues	95	764	633	4,775	18,812	32,356	34,653	37,739
Public issues	434	237	1,389	2,305	6,128	5,474	6,305	6,596
Held by the public	19,987	15,184	30,802	41,416	234,175	219,547	214,293	214,816
Federal Reserve Banks	353	591	2,433	2,466	21,792	18,331	22,982	22,906
Commercial banks [4]	4,632	4,977	12,716	16,100	84,200	65,600	58,400	61,100
Mutual savings banks	1,128	519	1,542	3,100	9,600	11,600	10,200	9,600
Insurance companies	(5)	(5)	2,600	6,500	22,700	19,800	17,100	15,700
Other corporations	(5)	(5)	(5)	2,100	22,900	19,000	21,100	20,000
State and local governments [6]	(5)	(5)	(5)	400	5,300	8,700	9,400	10,400
Individuals: [7]								
Savings bonds	......	......	(5)	2,600	40,700	49,900	49,100	49,100
Other securities	(5)	(5)	(5)	7,500	18,300	17,000	15,300	14,400
Miscellaneous investors [8]	(5)	(5)	(5)	700	8,900	9,700	10,800	11,700

[1] Holdings of commercial banks and mutual savings banks for 1925 to 1935 are reported book values, and holdings of residual investors therefore deviate from par values in these years. U. S. savings bonds, Series A-F and J, included at current redemption value.
[2] Includes all securities issued or guaranteed by U. S. Government, but excludes guaranteed securities held by the Treasury.
[3] Includes Postal Savings System.
[4] Consists of commercial banks, trust companies, and stock savings banks in United States and in Territories and insular possessions. Figures exclude securities held in trust departments.
[5] Not available separately. Combined totals of these items as follows: 1925, $13,874,000,000; 1930, $9,097,000,000; and 1935, $11,511,000,000.
[6] Comprises trust, sinking, and investment funds of State and local governments and their agencies, and Territories and insular possessions.
[7] Includes partnerships and personal trust accounts.
[8] Includes savings and loan associations, dealers and brokers, foreign accounts, corporate pension funds, and nonprofit institutions.

Source: Treasury Department, monthly data published currently in *Treasury Bulletin* and *Federal Reserve Bulletin*.

No. 397.—Interest-Bearing Governmental Securities—Estimated Ownership Outstanding, by Issuer: 1943 to 1952

[Par value. In billions of dollars. Figures represent par values except in the case of data which include U. S. savings bonds, Series A–F and J, which are included on basis of current redemption values]

JUNE 30—	Total amount outstanding	HELD BY BANKS		Held by U.S. Government investment accounts	HELD BY PRIVATE NONBANK INVESTORS						
		Commercial banks	Federal Reserve Banks		Total	Individuals[1]	Insurance companies	Mutual savings banks	Corporations[3]	State and local governments[3]	Miscellaneous investors[4]
Securities of U. S. Government and Federal instrumentalities guaranteed by U. S.[5]											
1943	139.5	52.2	7.2	14.3	65.7	29.6	13.1	5.3	12.9	1.5	3.4
1944	201.1	68.4	14.9	19.1	98.6	44.9	17.3	7.3	19.9	2.2	6.1
1945	256.8	84.2	21.8	24.9	125.9	58.2	22.7	9.6	21.9	5.3	8.3
1946	268.6	84.4	23.8	29.1	131.2	62.2	24.9	11.5	17.6	6.5	8.6
1947	255.2	70.0	21.9	32.8	130.5	65.4	24.6	12.1	13.9	7.1	7.4
1948	250.1	64.6	21.4	35.8	128.4	64.8	22.8	12.0	13.6	7.8	7.5
1949	250.8	63.0	19.3	38.3	130.1	65.8	20.5	11.6	15.7	8.0	8.5
1950	255.2	65.6	18.3	37.8	133.5	65.9	19.8	11.6	19.0	8.7	8.4
1951	252.9	58.4	23.0	41.0	130.6	63.3	17.1	10.2	21.1	9.4	9.5
1952	256.9	61.1	22.9	44.3	128.5	62.5	15.7	9.6	20.0	10.4	10.5
Securities of Federal instrumentalities not guaranteed by United States[6]											
1943	1.9	.6		.6	.7	.6	(7)	(7)	.1		(7)
1944	1.5	.6		.2	.7	.6	(7)	(7)	.1		(7)
1945	1.0	.5		(7)	.5	.4	(7)	(7)	.1		(7)
1946	1.1	1.0			.1	.1	(7)	(7)	(7)		(7)
1947	.5	.4			.1	.1	(7)	(7)	(7)		(7)
1948	.8	.6			.2	.1	(7)	(7)	.1		(7)
1949	.9	.7			.2	.1	(7)	(7)	.1		(7)
1950	.7	.6			.1	.1	(7)	(7)			(7)
1951	1.3	.8		(7)	.5	.4	(7)	(7)	.1		(7)
1952	1.2	.7		(7)	.5	.4	(7)	(7)	(7)		(7)
Securities of State and local governments, Territories, and possessions[8]											
1943	18.5	3.5		.6	14.4	7.5	1.8	.2	.5	3.8	.5
1944	17.2	3.5		.6	13.3	7.3	1.6	.2	.4	3.4	.4
1945	16.4	3.8		.5	12.1	7.2	1.1	.1	.4	2.9	.4
1946	15.7	4.1		.5	11.2	7.0	.9	.1	.4	2.4	.4
1947	16.6	5.0		.5	11.1	6.9	.9	.1	.4	2.4	.4
1948	18.4	5.6		.5	12.3	7.7	1.1	.1	.4	2.5	.5
1949	20.5	6.0		.4	14.2	8.8	1.6	.1	.5	2.7	.5
1950	23.8	7.4		.4	16.0	9.2	2.2	.1	.5	3.5	.5
1951	26.7	8.6		.6	17.6	10.1	2.5	.1	.6	3.7	.6
1952	29.2	9.9		.7	18.6	10.6	2.7	.2	.6	3.9	.6

[1] Includes partnerships, personal trust accounts.　[2] Exclusive of banks and insurance companies.
[3] Comprises trust, sinking, and investment funds of State and local governments, Territories, and possessions.
[4] Includes savings and loan associations, nonprofit associations, corporate pension trust funds, dealers and brokers, and investments of foreign balances and international accounts in this country.
[5] Data on *Daily Treasury Statement* basis. Since data exclude noninterest-bearing debt, they differ slightly from those in table 396. Includes special issues to Federal agencies and trust funds, and excludes guaranteed securities held by Treasury.
[6] Includes Federal land bank bonds only through June 30, 1946; on June 27, 1947, the U. S. proprietary interest in these banks ended. Excludes stocks and interagency loans.
[7] Less than $50 million.　[8] Excludes obligations of the Philippine Islands after June 30, 1946.

Source: Treasury Department, *Annual Report of the Secretary.*

No. 398.—Interest-Bearing Securities Issued by All Governmental Units in the United States—Estimated Amounts Outstanding, by Tax Status and Issuer: 1913 to 1952

[U. S. Govt. data on basis of public debt accounts prior to 1920; beginning 1920, on basis of *Daily Treasury Statement*. "Total amount outstanding" of securities of the several issuers differs from gross indebtedness of these issuers in that former excludes noninterest-bearing debt. "Total privately held securities" differs from net indebtedness of borrowers in several additional respects. Former derived by deducting from total amount of interest-bearing securities outstanding the amount of such securities held by Federal agencies, Federal Reserve Banks, and by public sinking, trust, and investment funds. Net indebtedness derived by deducting from gross indebtedness an amount equivalent to total volume of sinking fund assets of respective borrowers, with no allowance for any other public assets. For exception to par value, see table 397]

[Par value. In millions of dollars]

JUNE 30—	Total	TAX STATUS					ISSUER			
		Tax-exempt			Tax-able[3]	U. S. Govt. special issues	U. S. Govt.	Federal instrumentalities		State local, and territorial governments[6]
		Total	Wholly[1]	Partially[2]				Guaranteed[4]	Nonguaranteed[5]	
TOTAL AMOUNT OUTSTANDING										
1913	5,523	5,523	5,523	--------	--------	--------	966	--------	--------	4,557
1915	6,420	6,420	6,420				970			5,450
1920	32,253	32,253	11,303	20,950			24,063		401	7,790
1925	34,681	34,586	16,645	17,941		95	20,211		1,506	12,965
1930	35,943	35,179	23,606	11,573		764	15,922		1,871	18,180
1935	53,283	52,650	34,446	18,204		633	27,545	4,123	2,399	19,116
1938	63,001	60,320	32,278	28,042	6	2,676	36,576	4,853	2,262	19,310
1939	67,362	63,583	30,873	32,710	9	3,770	39,886	5,450	2,265	19,761
1940	70,117	65,327	30,240	35,087	15	4,775	42,376	5,498	2,199	20,044
1941	76,954	62,855	26,823	36,032	7,979	6,120	48,387	6,360	2,200	20,007
1942	98,244	58,594	25,498	33,096	31,766	7,885	71,968	4,549	2,210	19,517
1943	159,858	55,222	23,052	32,270	93,665	10,871	135,380	4,092	1,852	18,534
1944	219,826	47,326	19,837	27,489	158,213	14,287	199,543	1,516	1,453	17,314
1945	274,191	42,847	17,191	25,656	212,532	18,812	256,357	409	1,008	16,417
1946	285,407	37,250	15,916	21,335	225,824	22,332	268,111	467	1,093	15,736
1947	272,274	37,685	16,746	20,939	207,222	27,366	255,197	(7)	497	16,580
1948	269,358	36,389	18,563	17,826	202,758	30,211	250,132	(7)	827	18,399
1949	272,199	36,887	20,700	16,187	202,536	32,776	250,785	(7)	876	20,538
1950	279,776	36,841	23,964	12,877	210,579	32,356	255,226	(7)	746	23,804
1951	280,887	36,120	26,844	9,276	210,114	34,653	252,879	(7)	1,320	26,688
1952	287,344	36,761	29,359	7,402	212,843	37,739	256,907	(7)	1,220	29,217
PRIVATELY HELD SECURITIES										
a. 1913–35: Includes holdings by trust and investment funds of States, localities, Territories, and possessions.										
1913	4,902	4,902	4,902	--------	--------	--------	966	--------	--------	3,936
1915	5,675	5,675	5,675				961			4,714
1920	30,420	30,420	10,024	20,396			23,476			6,709
1925	31,914	31,914	14,748	17,167			19,328		1,384	11,202
1930	31,786	31,786	20,714	11,072			14,303		1,765	15,718
1935	45,782	45,782	29,172	16,610			23,502	3,757	1,471	17,052
b. 1938–52: Excludes holdings by trust and investment funds of States, localities, Territories, and possessions.										
1938	50,340	50,335	25,351	24,984	6	--------	29,249	4,528	1,415	15,148
1939	53,553	53,545	24,166	29,379	9		31,344	5,164	1,421	15,624
1940	55,005	54,989	23,884	31,105	15		32,691	5,212	1,355	15,746
1941	60,229	52,614	20,568	32,046	7,615		37,364	6,086	1,385	15,394
1942	78,671	48,800	19,398	29,402	29,873		58,113	4,261	1,386	14,911
1943	131,846	46,588	17,688	28,900	85,258		112,682	3,806	1,292	14,068
1944	178,440	40,342	15,555	24,788	138,098		162,535	1,335	1,267	13,302
1945	218,815	37,080	13,770	23,310	181,735		204,374	403	1,007	13,030
1946	223,191	32,710	13,035	19,675	190,481		208,748	458	1,098	12,892
1947	207,577	(7)	13,804	(7)	(7)		193,406	(7)	497	13,674
1948	201,456	(7)	15,537	(7)	(7)		185,219	(7)	827	15,410
1949	203,428	(7)	17,523	(7)	(7)	--------	185,154	(7)	876	17,398
1950	210,974	(7)	20,029	(7)	(7)		190,322	(7)	746	19,906
1951	203,276	(7)	22,548	(7)	(7)		179,532	(7)	1,316	22,428
1952	205,139	(7)	24,726	(7)	(7)		179,309	(7)	1,216	24,614

[1] Securities the income from which is exempt from both normal and surtax rates of Federal income tax.
[2] Securities the income from which is exempt only from normal rates of Federal income tax.
[3] Securities the income from which is subject to both normal and surtax rates of Federal income tax.
[4] Excludes securities held by Treasury.
[5] Includes Federal land bank bonds only through June 30, 1946; on June 27, 1947, United States proprietary interest in these banks ended. Excludes stocks and intergency loans.
[6] Wholly tax-exempt. Excludes obligations of Philippine Islands after June 30, 1946.
[7] Included with U. S. Govt.   [8] Not available.

Source: Treasury Department, *Annual Report of the Secretary.*

No. 399.—Securities Other Than World War I and World War II Obligations of Foreign Governments Owned by the U. S. Government: June 30, 1952

[All figures in thousands of dollars. On basis of face value of securities received by United States, with due allowances for repayments. To extent that securities are not held in the custody of Treasury, statement is made from reports received from other Government departments and establishments]

SECURITY	Amount	SECURITY	Amount
Total this amount	19,566,346	Other securities—Continued	
Capital stock	1,681,429	Federal Housing Administration:	
Banks for cooperatives	176,500	Mortgage notes and contracts on sales	
Commodity Credit Corporation	100,000	of acquired real estate	32,524
Defense Homes Corporation	10,000	Stock in rental and war housing cor-	
Export-Import Bank of Washington	1,000,000	porations	439
Federal Crop Insurance Corporation	27,000	Title I defaulted notes	48,556
Federal Farm Mortgage Corporation	10	Federal Security Agency: Student war	
Federal intermediate credit banks	60,000	loans	971
Federal National Mortgage Associa-		General Services Admin. (Public Works	
tion	20,000	Admin.): Loans to States, munici-	
Federal Savings and Loan Insurance		palities, railroads, and others	84,840
Corporation	93,284	Housing and Home Finance Admin.:	
Inland Waterways Corporation	15,000	Alaska housing program loans	8,212
Production credit corporations	34,235	Community facilities service loans	1,299
Public Housing Administration	1,000	Interior Department: Indian loans	12,828
Reconstruction Finance Corporation	100,000	Maritime Admin.: Ship construction,	
Smaller War Plants Corporation	39,400	and reconditioning loans, ship sales	
War Damage Corporation	1,000	notes, etc	(7)
Paid-in surplus	6,835	Mutual Security Agency: Loans to	
Federal intermediate credit banks	5,835	foreign governments	308,728
Federal National Mortgage Association	1,000	Public Housing Administration:	
Bonds and notes	9,864,423	Farm Security Admin. program	78
Commodity Credit Corporation	1,970,000	Public war housing program	14,146
Export-Import Bank of Washington	1,086,100	Puerto Rico Reconstruction Admin.:	
Housing and Home Finance Adminis-		Certificates of Cafeteros de Puerto	
trator:		Rico	5
Federal National Mortgage Associa-		Loans	5,913
tion	2,037,893	Reconstruction Finance Corporation	
Housing loans for educational institu-		affiliate, assets held for U. S. Trea-	
tions	2,000	sury:	
Prefabricated housing loans program	32,170	Loans	812
Slum clearance program	10,000	Other securities	3,097
Mutual Security Agency:		Rural Electrification Admin.: Loans	
Guaranty program	2,510	for rural electrification and rural tele-	
Loan program	1,147,453	phone service	99,850
Public Housing Administration	685,000	Treasury Department:	
Reconstruction Finance Corporation	197,173	Advances to Federal Reserve Banks	27,546
Rural Electrification Administration	1,731,326	Credit to United Kingdom	3,705,664
Secretary of Agriculture: Farmers'		Loan	7,000
Home Administration program	78,369	Railroads	5,950
Tennessee Valley Authority	39,000	Subscriptions to International Bank	
Veterans' Administration (direct loan		for Reconstruction and Develop-	
program)	177,978	ment and to International Mone-	
Defense Production Act of 1950:		tary Fund	3,365,000
Defense Materials Procurement		Veterans' Administration: Guaranteed	
Agency	333,700	loans to veterans	26,291
Export-Import Bank of Washington	61	Virgin Islands Corporation, The: Loans	
Reconstruction Finance Corporation	57,200	to aid agriculture and industry	78
Secretary of the Interior (Defense		Defense Production Act of 1950:	
Minerals Exploration Administra-		Department of the Army: Guaranteed	
tion)	4,500	loans	7,188
Other securities	8,335,689	Dept. of the Navy: Guaranteed loans	4,597
Department of the Army: Guaranteed			
loans (World War II)	5,217	Less:	
Department of the Navy: Guaranteed		Face amount of above securities ac-	
loans (World War II)	439	quired by Government corporations	
Disaster loans, etc., revolving fund		or agencies from funds or by ex-	
(Farmers' Home Administration)	41,165	change for obligations	22,000
Farm Credit Administration: Loans		Capital stock:	
from Agricultural Marketing Act		Housing and Home Finance	
revolving fund	4,987	Administrator	20,000
Farmers Home Administration: Loans		Reconstruction Finance Corpora-	
to aid agriculture	476,015	tion	1,000
		Paid-in surplus: Housing and Home	
		Finance Administrator	1,000

Amount due United States from central branch Union Pacific R. R. on account of bonds issued (Pacific Railway Aid Acts, approved July 1, 1862, July 2, 1864, and May 7, 1878):

Principal	1,600
Interest	1,464
Total	3,064

[1] Includes loan amounting to $7,500,000 held by U. S. Treasury as of June 30, 1952.
[2] Funds of Housing and Home Finance Administrator.
[3] Reconstruction Finance Corporation funds.
[4] Excludes net payments from Treasury, or transfer of assets authorized by law, for which no formal receipts or other evidence of payments are held by Secretary of the Treasury in stock and nonstock corporations amounting to $1,469,152,000. [5] Reserves amounting to $146,138,000 established against these securities.
[6] Crop, livestock, and commodity loans. [7] Not available.

Source: Treasury Department, Annual Report of the Secretary.

No. **400.**—U. S. SAVINGS BONDS—SALES AND REDEMPTIONS BY SERIES, CUMULATIVE THROUGH DECEMBER 31, 1952

[In millions of dollars. On basis of *Daily Treasury Statement*. Series A-F and J sales at issue price and total redemptions and amounts outstanding at current redemption values. Series G, H, and K shown at face value. Matured bonds redeemed included in redemptions. Series A-D sold from March 1935 through April 1941 and Series E, F, and G sold since May 1941. Beginning May 1, 1952, rate of interest accrual on Series E increased and Series F and G replaced by two new issues, Series J and K, also at higher interest rates. A new current-income bond, Series H, similar in interest return to Series E, sold since June 1, 1952]

SERIES	Sales	Accrued discount	Sales plus accrued discount	Redemptions	AMOUNT OUTSTANDING		Percent of redemptions to sales plus accrued discount
					Matured debt (Series A-D)	Interest-bearing debt	
Total, Series A-K	99,799	7,991	107,790	49,744	106	57,940	
Series A-D (matured), total	3,949	1,054	5,003	4,897	106		43.63
Interest-bearing, total	95,850	6,937	102,787	44,847		57,940	43.63
Series E and H	67,095	6,372	73,467	¹ 38,143		35,324	51.92
Series F, G, J, and K	¹ 28,755	565	29,320	6,704		22,616	22.86

¹ Includes exchanges of matured Series E bonds for Series G bonds beginning May 1951 and for Series K bonds beginning May 1952.

Source: Treasury Department; *Treasury Bulletin*, February 1953.

No. **401.**—U. S. SAVINGS BONDS—AMOUNTS OUTSTANDING, SALES, ACCRUED DISCOUNT, AND REDEMPTIONS AND MATURITIES, FOR FISCAL YEARS 1935 TO 1952, AND BY QUARTERS 1950 TO 1952

[In millions of dollars. Includes data for Series A-D not shown separately: these series have not been issued since April 1941. See also headnote, table 400]

PERIOD	Amount outstanding at end of period (all series)¹	FUNDS RECEIVED FROM SALES DURING PERIOD				Accrued discounts during period (all series)	Redemptions and maturities during period (all series)
		All series	Series E and H	Series F and J	Series G and K		
Year ending June:							
1935–40	2,905	3,120		67	395	96	311
1941	4,314	1,492	203	67	395	65	148
1942	10,188	5,994	3,526	435	2,032	88	207
1943	21,256	11,789	8,271	758	2,759	128	848
1944	34,606	15,498	11,820	802	2,876	223	2,371
1945	45,586	14,891	11,553	679	2,658	387	4,298
1946	49,035	9,612	6,739	407	2,465	573	6,717
1947	51,367	7,208	4,287	360	2,561	691	5,545
1948	53,274	6,235	4,026	301	1,907	804	5,113
1949	56,260	7,141	4,278	473	2,390	927	5,067
1950	57,536	5,673	3,993	231	1,449	1,045	5,422
1951	57,572	5,143	3,272	347	¹ 1,523	1,149	6,137
1952	57,685	3,925	3,296	121	¹ 508	1,207	5,109
Quarter:							
1950—March	57,331	1,812	1,127	96	590	270	1,546
June	57,536	1,236	909	46	281	269	1,323
September	57,396	1,077	831	32	214	283	1,517
December	58,019	1,949	801	243	905	280	1,454
1951—March	57,764	1,221	895	48	279	292	1,741
June	57,572	895	745	25	126	294	1,426
September	57,488	897	755	23	119	290	1,309
December	57,587	947	796	28	123	306	1,176
1952—March	57,680	1,113	936	35	141	296	1,332
June	57,685	970	810	35	126	316	1,292
September	57,758	1,053	915	29	110	294	1,284
December	57,940	1,027	915	30	82	315	1,166

¹ Interest-bearing debt.
² Includes exchanges of matured Series E bonds for Series G bonds beginning May 1951 and for Series K bonds beginning May 1952.

Source: Treasury Department; monthly data published currently in *Treasury Bulletin* and *Federal Reserve Bulletin*.

402.—U. S. Savings Bonds—Sales of Series E Through K, by States, From Inception of Program Through December 31, 1952

[Thousands of dollars. Data are for calendar years and represent issue price on basis of *Daily Treasury Statement*. See also headnote, table 400]

	SERIES E AND H SAVINGS BONDS				SERIES F, G, J AND K SAVINGS BONDS			
	1941–52, total	1950	1951	1952	1941–52, total	1950	1951	1952
	67,095,053	3,668,087	3,190,490	3,574,839	28,735,213	2,604,844	770,130	885,982
	709,741	27,779	24,669	888	146	15,826	7,106	6,868
	292,131	12,157	9,578	907	520	4,835	3,090	1,847
	412,187	20,472	17,146	18,310	124,825	7,413	4,182	3,909
	4,966,420	222,805	178,399	188,071	1,715,492	102,523	36,381	34,782
	338,368	30,426	22,928	013	005	15,858	7,709	3,741
	1,122,107	48,019	46,554	431	099	34,408	11,146	4,640
	182,806	8,032	6,463	943	501	6,940	2,487	1,264
ct of Columbia....	806,025	41,868	38,242	394	929	22,239	7,688	4,844
a	790,204	41,976	34,053	007	532	32,342	11,488	6,087
la	784,553	35,428	33,915	410	123	15,497	5,273	3,528
	192,500	6,968	4,902	222	803	5,448	1,989	2,084
s	5,194,924	329,891	261,841	710	129	189,143	80,065	61,030
nn	1,782,469	98,071	88,411	823	259	35,096	26,965	22,286
	1,738,329	108,970	76,711	001	450	84,476	36,255	24,444
	1,017,240	61,463	43,994	172	379	22,702	15,380	12,401
cky	711,848	38,012	31,808	323	907	24,309	12,342	9,986
ana	701,104	32,091	26,041	508	414	17,300	5,463	6,261
and	277,600	12,913	11,071	307	208	10,074	3,079	2,141
and	839,702	39,082	37,082	507	143	25,290	8,992	5,538
chusetts	2,161,121	102,369	90,442	502	144	108,411	23,730	15,888
	3,516,486	195,844	193,313	031	300	64,410	26,782	26,646
	1,401,994	78,746	54,197	264	310	46,067	18,545	15,514
	430,743	18,324	15,355	145	844	7,687	4,080	3,573
	1,786,877	107,584	86,746	037	037	53,656	27,927	19,884
	331,179	17,329	12,878	920	305	7,731	3,360	4,600
ska	890,433	66,844	45,272	378	432	39,104	15,497	15,008
a	75,730	3,666	3,178	255	442	2,448	1,098	1,137
Iampshire	173,949	7,046	7,085	240	032	6,827	1,810	906
ersey	2,405,301	148,009	130,461	524	973	53,719	25,256	15,087
Mexico	182,665	8,556	7,066	316	859	3,607	2,085	1,629
York	8,062,361	464,479	380,848	060	4,542,046	382,380	98,327	64,084
Carolina	820,834	35,431	32,290	11?	207,701	15,213	7,604	5,718
Dakota	345,142	18,230	13,506	143	119,973	8,009	3,944	5,181
	4,046,729	220,192	214,457	288	1,542,094	90,303	44,582	36,827
oma	805,234	47,086	36,325	671	224,308	16,177	9,323	7,315
	746,933	28,966	22,627	722	006	16,301	7,019	4,985
	5,207,771	317,514	300,783	471	2,158,479	129,084	65,161	42,764
	349,365	17,249	14,372	418	198,032	12,614	2,849	1,895
	433,570	17,622	16,196	623	143,312	8,718	3,321	5,696
	381,848	24,086	18,463	198	121,626	7,885	5,801	5,776
	766,399	32,613	28,330	37?	630	20,755	5,828	7,896
	2,487,348	131,277	96,581	010	916	49,974	25,342	20,139
	270,744	11,080	9,968	282	355	4,393	1,729	1,549
	99,095	3,766	3,703	784	575	3,632	1,508	1,100
	1,113,277	51,883	49,651	552	213	16,112	7,975	6,350
	1,223,801	52,691	44,743	517	455	36,728	10,844	7,174
	616,066	36,766	37,555	711	192	10,608	5,869	3,913
	1,480,417	82,874	66,739	271	819	58,185	26,380	20,963
	138,107	8,151	6,345	415	980	2,787	1,678	1,636
	¹ 30,075				349			
	42,909	3,158	1,990	1,795		146	51	187
	812,990	9,045	11,725	12,604		3,626	1,299	1,171
	42,464	1,105	1,284	1,507	14,258	206	53	43
	2,094	58	59	63	³ 944	1	100	
	⁵ 4,906	739				14		
					1,767,101	445,326		
	+1,686,675	+152,621	+197,362	+237,344		+1,856	−10,010	+3,600

mulative through Mar. 31, 1947.
mulative through July 1951.
mulative through Sept. 1950.
mulative through Aug. 1950.
mmercial banks were eligible to purchase Series F and G for limited amounts during certain months. Sales tributed by States.

rce: Treasury Department; *Annual Report of the Secretary* and *Treasury Bulletin.*

No. 403.—Government Corporations and Credit Agencies—Principal Assets and Liabilities as of September 30, 1952

[In millions of dollars. Includes figures for certain business-type activities of U. S. Government]

Corporation or agency	Total	Assets, other than interagency items [1]							Liabilities, other than interagency items				
		Cash	Loans receivable	Commodities, supplies, and materials	Investments		Land, structures, and equipment	Other assets	Bonds, notes, and debenture payable		Other liabilities	U. S. Government interest	Privately owned interest
					U. S. Govt. securities	Other securities [2]			Fully guaranteed by U. S.	Other			
Total [2]	26,922	932	16,890	1,377	2,371	3,436	3,212	704	39	1,301	1,434	25,730	367
Department of Agriculture:													
Farm Credit Administration:													
Banks for cooperatives	437	22	366		43		(²)	5		120	1	290	
Federal intermediate credit banks	936	41	322		61			11		804	12	80	25
Production credit corporations	62	(³)			43	8	(³)	(³)			(³)	82	
Agricultural Marketing Act	1	(³)	1					1				1	
Federal Farm Mortgage Corporation	30	2	27						1		1	29	
Rural Electrification Administration	1,987	46	1,871		1		102	69			1	1,985	
Commodity Credit Corporation	2,223	11	856	1,064			(²)	220	(³)		490	1,733	
Farmers Home Administration [3]	615	75	510					29			7	608	
Federal Crop Insurance Corporation	41	32			1			9			2	30	
Housing and Home Finance Agency:													
Home Loan Bank Board:													
Federal home loan banks	1,042	25	715		298		(²)	4		317	383	(²)	342
Federal Savings and Loan Insurance Corporation	206	1			203			4			5	203	
Public Housing Administration	2,092	106	751			(²)	1,216	21			16	2,076	
Federal Housing Administration	478	55	33		299	(³)	1	90	38		225	215	
Office of the Administrator:													
Federal National Mortgage Association	2,108	(²)	2,097				(²)	10			4	2,104	
Other	110	31	47				29	4			3	107	
Reconstruction Finance Corporation:													
Assets held for U. S. Treasury [4]	399	6	1	153		2	201	37			50	399	
Other [7]	819	14	695	41		40	1	29			33	773	
Export-Import Bank	2,563	1	2,546				(³)	17			34	2,528	
Federal Deposit Insurance Corporation	1,438	(²)			1,423		(³)	14			43	1,344	
Tennessee Valley Authority	1,540	304	19				1,209	8			43	1,497	
All other [8]	9,802	162	5,551	130	(²)	3,385	453	122			61	9,741	

[1] Assets are shown on a net basis, i. e., after reserve for losses.
[2] Includes U. S. investment of $635 million in stock of International Bank for Reconstruction and Development and its subscription of $2,750 million to International Monetary Fund.
[3] Excludes U. S. Maritime Commission. Latest available figure for this agency are as of Mar. 31, 1947.
[4] Includes "Disaster Loans, etc., Revolving Fund."
[5] Assets representing unrecovered costs to Corporation in its national defense, war, and reconversion activities, which are held for Treasury for liquidation purposes.
[6] Includes figures for Smaller War Plants Corporation being liquidated by RFC.
[7] Figures for one small agency are as of Aug. 31, 1952.
[8] Less than $500,000.

Source: Board of Governors of the Federal Reserve System; Federal Reserve Bulletin, January 1953.

No. 404.—Employment and Payrolls of the Federal Government by Branch: 1929 to 1952

[Includes data for employees outside continental United States, force-account (temporary) construction workers, and fourth-class postmasters. See also *Historical Statistics* series P 71-72, P 82-83]

YEAR OR MONTH	EMPLOYMENT (THOUSANDS)				PAYROLLS (THOUSANDS OF DOLLARS)			
	Average for year or as of first of month				Total for year or for month			
	Total	Execu-tive [1]	Legis-lative	Judicial	Total	Executive [1]	Legis-lative	Judicial
1929	596	591	4	2	1,079,794	1,063,056	11,303	5,435
1930	611	605	4	2	1,117,830	1,100,273	11,686	5,871
1931	624	618	4	2	1,128,630	1,110,677	11,904	6,049
1932	622	615	4	2	1,059,138	1,041,792	11,552	5,794
1933	630	624	4	2	972,126	956,562	10,555	5,009
1934	719	712	5	2	1,169,370	1,151,547	12,521	5,302
1935	820	813	5	2	1,417,991	1,398,383	13,906	5,702
1936	894	886	5	2	1,604,860	1,584,485	14,429	5,946
1937	902	895	5	2	1,613,699	1,593,227	14,455	6,017
1938	900	893	5	2	1,626,622	1,605,741	14,511	6,370
1939	969	961	5	2	1,757,292	1,735,834	14,787	6,691
1940	1,078	1,069	6	2	1,978,152	1,955,068	15,640	7,444
1941	1,433	1,424	6	3	2,524,903	2,501,105	16,032	7,766
1942	2,233	2,224	6	3	4,431,091	4,406,373	16,625	8,093
1943	3,165	3,157	6	3	7,856,131	7,831,305	17,785	9,041
1944	3,337	3,328	6	3	8,301,111	8,273,709	18,127	9,275
1945	3,569	3,560	6	3	8,153,686	8,122,973	20,537	10,176
1946	2,704	2,694	7	3	6,754,625	6,717,837	23,929	12,880
1947	2,153	2,143	7	3	5,966,107	5,922,339	29,074	14,694
1948	2,067	2,056	7	3	6,223,486	6,176,414	30,891	16,181
1949	2,101	2,089	8	4	6,705,700	6,654,101	34,436	17,163
1950	2,081	2,069	8	4	7,026,908	6,969,497	38,577	18,834
1951	2,466	2,454	8	4	8,994,754	8,934,726	39,834	20,194
1952	2,612	2,599	9	4				
January	2,524	2,512	8	4	846,065	840,578	3,661	1,826
February	2,538	2,525	8	4	801,375	796,100	3,546	1,729
March	2,551	2,539	8	4	807,727	802,514	3,604	1,609
April	2,559	2,547	9	4	826,843	821,276	3,721	1,846
May	2,571	2,559	9	4	826,104	820,611	3,725	1,768
June	2,583	2,570	9	4	827,347	821,860	3,687	1,800
July	2,619	2,606	9	4	[2] 880,590	[2] 874,892	[2] 3,819	[2] 1,879
August	2,622	2,609	9	4				
September	2,610	2,598	9	4				
October	2,592	2,580	9	4				
November	2,588	2,575	9	4				
December	2,986	2,973	9	4				

[1] Includes Government corporations. Based, for the most part, on reports of respective agencies to Civil Service Commission adjusted to improve comparability throughout period. Differs from data in tables compiled by Civil Service Commission in following respects: (1) Excludes seamen and trainees on ships contracted by U. S. Maritime Commission and substitute rural mail carriers; (2) includes temporary employees of Post Office Department hired to handle Christmas mail each year, Federal Reserve banks, and mixed-ownership banks of Farm Credit Administration.
[2] Comparable data not available subsequently.

Source: Department of Labor, Bureau of Labor Statistics. Data for executive branch based mainly on reports of Civil Service Commission. Current data published in *Monthly Labor Review* and in mimeographed releases.

No. 405.—Paid Civilian Employment in the Executive Branch of the Federal Government, by Area and Sex: June 1945 to 1952

[Represents number in active-duty status as of last day of month. Prior to 1947, excludes seamen and trainees of U. S. Maritime Commission, and beginning 1948, excludes Central Intelligence Agency. See also *Historical Statistics*, series P 63 for earlier data on Washington, D. C., metropolitan area total]

AREA AND SEX	1945	1946	1947	1948	1949	1950	1951	1952
Continental U. S., total..	2,915,476	9,299,007	1,849,781	1,859,807	1,928,524	1,819,489	2,312,982	2,419,185
Men	1,822,939	1,652,703	1,409,184	1,436,110	1,494,465	1,413,051	1,739,832	1,822,368
Women	1,092,537	646,304	440,597	423,697	434,059	406,438	573,150	596,817
Percent women	38	28	24	23	23	22	25	25
Washington, D. C., metropolitan area, total [1]	257,808	235,109	205,237	206,110	217,237	213,776	256,096	251,341
Men	103,964	119,199	111,847	113,640	119,530	119,970	138,722	138,552
Women	153,844	115,910	93,390	92,470	97,707	93,806	117,374	112,789
Percent women	60	49	46	45	45	44	46	45

[1] For definition of Washington metropolitan area, see table 410, footnote 4.

No. 406.—Accessions to and Separations From Paid Civilian Full-Time Employment in the Executive Branch of the Federal Government: Fiscal Years 1949 to 1952

ITEM	CONTINENTAL UNITED STATES				WASHINGTON, D. C., METROPOLITAN AREA			
	1949	1950	1951	1952	1949	1950	1951	1952
Accessions:								
Total number	562,457	330,307	1,070,774	687,112	59,047	41,783	103,440	62,606
Average monthly rate [1]	2.8	1.7	4.8	2.7	2.4	1.7	3.8	2.1
Separations:								
Total number	511,244	431,037	593,002	615,595	49,044	47,755	63,540	66,450
Average monthly rate [1]	2.5	2.2	2.6	2.4	2.0	1.9	2.3	2.3
Type of separation:								
Quit [2]	242,138	160,331	355,146	417,059	29,400	23,468	42,354	47,033
Reduction in force	53,748	103,281	17,039	29,323	2,666	6,142	971	2,403
Discharge [3]	12,515	9,229	17,288	25,494	853	780	1,112	1,376
Other [4]	202,843	158,196	203,529	143,719	16,125	17,365	19,103	15,638

[1] Per 100 full-time employees.
[2] Represents resignation, transfer to other Federal agency, and abandonment of position.
[3] Represents separation required by an agency for disqualification or inefficiency, and removal for misconduct, delinquency, or other serious cause.
[4] Represents termination of appointment, and separation for extended leave without pay, military leave, retirement, death, legal incompetency, and disability not entitled to retirement.

No. 407.—Paid Civilian Employment in the Executive Branch of the Federal Government, by Type of Position, and Persons Examined, Passed, and Appointed Under Civil Service Regulations: June 1947 to 1952

[Includes data for employees outside continental United States. See headnote, table 405. See also *Historical Statistics*, series P 62 and P 65–68]

TYPE OF POSITION	1947	1948	1949	1950	1951	1952 [1]
Total	2,128,648	2,090,732	2,109,642	1,966,448	2,486,491	2,603,267
Subject to competitive requirements of Civil Service Act:						
Number	1,733,019	1,750,823	1,802,708	1,687,594	2,175,668	2,278,446
Percent of total reported	81	84	85	86	87	88
Persons examined [2]	1,388,345	1,434,033	1,947,147	1,682,830	1,905,024	2,132,469
Persons passed [2]	(3)	(3)	1,122,023	935,813	1,069,442	1,223,068
Persons appointed [2]	[4] 329,002	[4] 514,808	[4] 504,660	[4] 336,500	[4] 578,539	[4] 503,865
Excepted from competitive requirements of Civil Service Act	395,629	339,909	306,934	278,854	310,823	324,821

[1] In continental United States, 2,241,941, or 93 percent, of 2,419,185 employees were in positions subject to competitive requirements of Civil Service Act.
[2] During fiscal year ending June 30.
[3] Not available.
[4] Excludes temporary appointments pending establishment of registers.

Source of tables 405–407: Civil Service Commission, *Annual Report* and records.

No. 408.—PAID CIVILIAN EMPLOYMENT IN FULL-TIME POSITIONS IN THE EXECUTIVE BRANCH OF THE FEDERAL GOVERNMENT AND AVERAGE PAY BY COMPENSATION AUTHORITY: 1950, 1951, AND 1952

[Covers all full-time civil employees in continental United States except relatively small number of employees on fee, piece work, or other basis, employees for whom pay rates were not specified, and employees of Board of Governors of Federal Reserve System. Some agencies reported as of dates other than specified]

COMPENSATION AUTHORITY	JUNE 30, 1950		JUNE 30, 1951		JUNE 30, 1952	
	Number of employees	Average pay [1]	Number of employees	Average pay [1]	Number of employees	Average pay [1]
Total	1,627,812	$3,504	2,130,968	$3,481	2,201,746	$3,553
Classification Act of 1949 (per annum)	800,748	3,667	1,004,624	3,596	1,032,492	4,039
General schedule	701,824	2,788	885,925	3,700	917,173	4,149
Crafts, protective, and custodial schedule	98,924	2,807	118,699	2,814	115,319	3,166
Postal Pay Act	362,133	3,488	348,123	3,522	360,910	4,003
Wage boards	429,739	3,133	718,896	3,945	766,274	3,471
Other acts and administrative orders	35,192	4,502	49,326	4,302	52,072	4,780

[1] Based on annual rates and other rates converted to annual equivalent for 52 40-hour weeks.

Source: Civil Service Commission: annual report, *Pay Structure of the Federal Civil Service*.

No. 409.—PAID CIVILIAN EMPLOYMENT IN FULL-TIME POSITIONS IN THE EXECUTIVE BRANCH OF THE FEDERAL GOVERNMENT BY ANNUAL EQUIVALENT PAY GROUP AND COMPENSATION AUTHORITY: JUNE 30, 1952

[Covers civil employees in continental United States. 1952 survey covered 2,201,746, or 99.5 percent of 2,212,909 full-time employees reported as of June 30, 1952, on Civil Service Commission's monthly employment report. The survey excludes 3 employees on fee, piecework, or other basis, 10,155 employees for whom pay rates were not specified, and 678 employees in Board of Governors, Federal Reserve System. One agency reported as of June 21, 1952]

ANNUAL EQUIVALENT PAY GROUP	TOTAL		COMPENSATION AUTHORITY							
			Classification Act of 1949		Wage boards		Postal Pay Act		Other acts and administrative orders	
	Number	Percent	Number	Percent	Number	Percent	Number	Percent	Number	Percent
All groups	2,201,746	100.0	1,032,492	100.0	766,274	100.0	360,910	100.0	52,072	100.0
Less than $2,000	22,202	1.0	41	(¹)	8,072	1.1	12,355	3.5	1,734	3.3
	66,054	3.1	11,069	1.1	51,671	6.7	4,717	1.3	1,607	3.1
	392,512	17.8	231,153	21.4	150,633	20.8	4,778	1.4	7,048	13.5
	539,909	25.4	308,510	29.9	206,408	26.9	38,678	11.0	6,314	12.1
	388,531	17.6	130,971	12.7	167,455	21.9	78,095	22.3	10,010	19.2
	392,066	17.9	98,473	9.5	116,827	15.2	171,882	48.9	6,074	11.7
	109,462	5.0	57,779	5.6	31,262	4.1	16,478	4.7	3,944	7.6
	90,609	4.1	57,559	5.6	13,958	1.8	16,127	4.6	2,965	5.7
	65,607	3.0	52,020	5.0	7,294	1.0	4,746	1.4	1,587	3.0
	21,934	1.0	17,775	1.7	1,499	.2	1,497	.4	1,153	2.2
	12,961	.6	10,895	1.1	569	.1	835	.2	662	1.3
	27,391	1.2	24,564	2.4	635	.1	423	.1	1,469	2.8
	4,492	.2	3,643	.6	344	.1	167	.1	296	.5
	14,496	.7	12,617	1.2	200	(¹)	186	.1	1,463	2.9
	9,327	.4	7,531	.7	105	(¹)	69	(¹)	1,522	2.9
	3,296	.2	2,913	.3	107	(¹)	15	(¹)	191	.4
	7,368	.3	5,612	.5	60	(¹)	28	(¹)	1,669	3.2
	9,064	.4	7,184	.7	80	(¹)	36	(¹)	2,382	4.5

¹ Less than 0.05 percent.

Source: Civil Service Commission: annual report, *Pay Structure of the Federal Civil Service*.

No. 410.—Paid Civilian Employment in the Executive Branch of the Federal Government, 1938 to 1952, and for Selected Agencies, 1952, by State

[Partially estimated   See headnote, table 405]

STATE OR OTHER AREA	TOTAL EMPLOYMENT				EMPLOYMENT BY AGENCY, JUNE 1952			
	December 1938 [1]	June 1945 [2]	June 1951	June 1952	Department of Defense	Post Office Department	Veterans' Administration	Other departments and agencies
Total	865,407	3,769,646	2,486,491	2,603,267	1,337,095	523,779	174,597	567,796
Outside cont. U. S	33,574	854,170	173,509	184,082	120,763	2,178	1,281	59,860
Territories and possessions	28,697	(3)	84,376	83,311	46,607	2,178	859	33,667
Foreign countries	4,877	(3)	89,133	100,771	74,156		422	26,193
Continental U. S	831,833	2,915,476	2,312,982	2,419,185	1,216,332	521,601	173,316	507,936
Wash., D. C., metro. area [4]	[5]119,874	257,806	256,096	251,341	94,318	8,149	11,840	137,034
48 States [4]	711,959	2,657,668	2,056,886	2,167,844	1,122,014	513,452	161,476	370,902
Alabama	15,213	53,663	48,296	52,786	34,253	6,731	3,302	8,500
Arizona	7,477	17,900	14,594	15,389	5,671	2,072	1,464	6,182
Arkansas	9,388	25,907	15,534	16,826	6,038	4,999	2,734	3,055
California	48,334	317,236	249,039	265,008	183,462	36,842	13,209	31,495
Colorado	8,692	28,839	30,104	37,646	19,070	4,653	3,626	10,297
Connecticut	5,784	12,394	11,100	11,476	1,881	6,472	955	2,168
Delaware	1,240	3,335	2,272	2,542	544	980	514	504
Florida	9,426	76,747	37,464	40,451	23,638	7,888	2,682	6,243
Georgia	12,595	70,231	57,179	61,058	37,384	9,975	4,498	9,201
Idaho	3,780	9,877	5,795	6,535	1,567	1,647	508	2,813
Illinois	44,316	133,085	108,256	114,923	46,691	39,610	9,107	19,515
Indiana	12,330	42,903	39,605	41,052	21,814	11,588	3,092	4,558
Iowa	10,560	19,078	15,743	15,965	337	9,654	2,638	3,336
Kansas	8,964	32,455	21,242	22,501	7,474	7,508	3,500	4,019
Kentucky	10,117	27,330	30,404	34,191	16,779	7,862	2,884	6,666
Louisiana	11,002	41,858	25,044	27,564	10,143	6,887	2,529	8,005
Maine	6,997	25,707	15,567	17,795	11,798	3,587	973	1,437
Maryland [4]	18,326	50,651	47,594	51,143	31,186	5,165	2,246	12,546
Massachusetts	28,137	103,516	66,060	71,678	39,573	17,934	5,856	8,315
Michigan	17,722	49,828	44,243	47,320	17,687	18,016	4,141	7,476
Minnesota	13,048	21,841	24,131	25,489	1,554	13,518	4,747	5,670
Mississippi	11,661	24,529	16,247	16,250	5,926	4,699	2,436	3,189
Missouri	21,590	54,206	55,191	53,384	17,419	19,556	3,158	13,251
Montana	8,157	9,150	8,801	8,253	865	2,156	597	4,635
Nebraska	8,979	27,850	21,121	20,889	8,192	6,960	1,525	4,211
Nevada	1,891	6,753	5,485	5,513	2,905	535	282	1,791
New Hampshire	2,199	4,360	3,218	3,364	300	2,023	424	617
New Jersey	15,743	81,968	53,156	55,404	34,493	13,178	2,769	4,964
New Mexico	7,201	16,206	15,365	16,368	7,005	1,806	1,127	6,430
New York	87,483	293,021	192,682	209,133	76,999	75,567	15,418	41,149
North Carolina	10,623	40,156	26,807	27,228	11,415	8,629	2,705	4,479
North Dakota	3,820	6,047	7,105	6,718	695	3,175	691	2,157
Ohio	28,722	111,269	105,536	107,187	58,164	28,999	6,588	13,436
Oklahoma	10,631	47,878	47,292	48,549	33,989	7,039	1,411	6,110
Oregon	9,113	18,827	17,836	18,399	4,397	4,745	1,849	7,408
Pennsylvania	50,619	196,540	145,957	152,629	91,807	34,949	11,586	14,287
Rhode Island	6,702	23,191	12,495	13,751	9,972	2,157	850	772
South Carolina	8,826	47,302	23,748	24,718	16,600	4,358	1,145	2,615
South Dakota	4,691	10,438	9,285	9,177	1,863	2,981	1,520	2,813
Tennessee	17,149	44,382	44,522	44,147	10,406	8,473	5,418	19,850
Texas	27,777	140,899	115,411	122,279	72,388	22,446	8,884	18,561
Utah	3,886	37,665	30,798	33,840	27,911	1,959	620	3,350
Vermont	2,052	3,172	3,117	3,351	196	1,796	504	855
Virginia [4]	21,005	107,601	77,660	80,942	58,743	8,019	4,356	9,834
Washington	15,520	100,359	67,956	66,501	44,234	6,506	3,131	12,630
West Virginia	5,891	11,110	11,352	11,491	1,724	5,219	2,340	2,208
Wisconsin	13,485	22,314	21,303	22,144	2,764	10,885	4,060	4,435
Wyoming	3,095	5,067	6,575	6,070	1,699	1,049	876	2,446
Undistributed		1,027	1,599	827	399			428

[1] From geographic study which excluded temporary postal substitutes; distribution for June 1938 not available.
[2] Represents peak of total employment.   [3] Not available.
[4] Beginning 1950, Washington, D. C., metropolitan area includes Dist. of Columbia; Alexandria and Falls Church Cities, Arlington and Fairfax Counties, Virginia; and Montgomery and Prince Georges Counties, Maryland. In 1945, only parts of these counties were included. These areas excluded from data for 48 States.
[5] Relates to District of Columbia only.

No. 411.—PAID CIVILIAN EMPLOYMENT IN THE EXECUTIVE BRANCH OF THE FEDERAL GOVERNMENT BY AGENCY AND AREA: JUNE 1952

[For coverage, see headnote, table 405. For definition of areas, see table 410, footnote 4]

AGENCY	Total all areas	CONTINENTAL UNITED STATES			OUTSIDE CONTINENTAL UNITED STATES		
		Total	Washington, D. C. metropolitan area	48 States	Total	Territories and possessions	Foreign countries
All agencies	2,603,257	2,419,185	251,341	2,167,844	184,002	83,311	100,771
Percent distribution	100	93	10	83	7	3	4
Executive Office of the President:							
White House Office	245	245	245				
Bureau of the Budget	498	496	476	22			
Executive Mansion and Grounds	121	121	121				
National Security Resources Board	178	178	178				
Office of Defense Mobilization	161	161	161				
Other	208	208	193	15			
Executive Departments:							
State	31,302	11,068	8,143	2,925	20,234	15	20,219
Treasury	89,460	88,417	16,939	71,478	1,043	923	120
Department of Defense:							
Office of the Secretary of Defense	2,253	2,199	2,183	16	54		54
Department of the Army	543,853	492,403	39,457	452,946	51,450	16,844	34,606
Department of the Navy	481,326	447,084	43,731	403,353	34,242	22,111	12,131
Department of the Air Force	309,653	274,046	8,947	265,699	35,017	7,652	27,365
Justice	32,194	31,026	9,827	22,099	868	440	138
Post Office	523,779	521,001	8,149	513,482	2,178	2,178	
Interior	60,677	52,633	5,955	46,678	8,044	7,927	117
Agriculture	76,349	74,431	10,014	66,417	1,818	1,069	749
Commerce	65,172	61,447	21,955	39,492	3,725	3,369	356
Labor	7,815	7,616	3,548	4,068	199	66	133
Independent agencies:							
American Battle Monuments Comm	457	16	16		441		441
Atomic Energy Commission	6,734	6,729	1,072	5,657	5		5
Board of Governors, Fed. Res. System	580	580	547	13			
Canal Zone Government	2,529				2,529	2,529	
Civil Aeronautics Board	582	572	516	56	10	10	
Civil Service Commission	4,694	4,686	2,288	2,398	8	7	1
Defense Materials Procurement Agency	158	154	154		4		4
Defense Production Administration	464	464	464				
Defense Transport Administration	216	216	216				
Displaced Persons Commission	107	54	52	2	53		53
Economic Stabilization Agency	17,297	17,051	3,926	13,125	246	246	
Export-Import Bank	136	136	136				
Federal Civil Defense Administration	1,106	1,106	791	317			
Federal Communications Commission	1,138	1,113	742	371	25	25	
Federal Deposit Insurance Corp	1,013	1,013	306	707			
Federal Mediation & Conciliation Serv	370	370	61	309			
Federal Power Commission	699	699	568	131			
Federal Security Agency	35,458	35,095	10,321	24,874	363	268	95
Federal Trade Commission	680	680	587	113			
General Accounting Office	6,114	6,114	4,632	1,482			
General Services Administration	29,142	29,047	13,001	16,046	95	43	52
Government Printing Office	7,676	7,676	7,409	267			
Housing and Home Finance Agency	12,626	12,488	3,479	9,009	138	131	7
Interstate Commerce Commission	2,093	2,093	1,391	702			
Mutual Security Agency	4,916	1,236	1,213	23	3,680		3,680
Natl. Adv. Committee for Aeronautics	7,654	7,654	167	7,487			
Natl. Capital Housing Authority	353	353	353				
National Labor Relations Board	1,173	1,152	437	715	21	21	
National Mediation Board	114	114	39	75			
National Science Foundation	117	117	117				
Panama Canal Company	16,809	555	31	294	16,314	16,314	
Railroad Retirement Board	2,199	2,199	38	2,161			
Reconstruction Finance Corporation	2,545	2,537	982	1,555	8	6	2
Selective Service System	559	559	257	302			
Securities and Exchange Commission	567	567	372	205			
Veterans' Administration	8,160	7,922	262	7,670	258	258	
War Claims Commission	324	324	201	123			
Virgin Islands Corporation	946	939	779	160	7		7
[illegible]	734	734	734				
[illegible]	193	193	186	7			
[illegible]	123	123	123				
Court of the United States	21,300	21,300	6	21,294			
Tennessee Valley Authority	174,597	173,316	11,840	161,476	1,281	859	422
[illegible]	185	161	162		24		24
[illegible]	94	94	84	10			

Source: Civil Service Commission, *Annual Report* and *Monthly Report of Employment*.

No. 412.—Paid Civilian Employment in the Executive Branch of the Federal Government, by Selected Agency: 1943 to 1952

[Includes data for employees outside continental United States. See headnote, table 405]

JUNE	ALL AGENCIES		DEPARTMENT OF DEFENSE [1]		POST OFFICE DEPARTMENT		VETERANS' ADMINISTRATION		OTHER AGENCIES	
	Number	Percent	Number	Percent	Number	Percent	Number	Percent	Number	Percent
1943	3,157,	100	2,088,892	66	316,357	10	53,349	2	698,515	22
1944	3,312,	100	2,256,846	68	352,773	10	50,510	2	652,127	20
1945	3,769,	100	2,634,075	70	378,849	10	65,143	2	691,579	18
1946	2,722,	100	1,416,225	52	488,623	18	169,643	6	647,340	24
1947	2,128,	100	859,142	41	471,787	22	216,753	10	580,966	27
1948	2,090,	100	870,962	42	503,607	24	195,545	9	520,615	25
1949	2,109,	100	579,875	42	517,743	25	195,488	9	516,536	24
1950	1,966,	100	753,149	38	500,679	25	188,392	10	524,228	27
1951	2,486,113	100	1,235,498	50	498,281	20	182,812	7	569,900	23
1952	2,603,###	100	1,337,095	51	533,779	20	174,597	7	557,796	22

[1] Through June 1947, represents War Department and Navy Department combined.

Source: Civil Service Commission, *Annual Report* and *Monthly Report of Employment*.

No. 413.—Federal Employees Subject to the Civil Service Retirement Act: September 30, 1947

[Includes employees outside continental United States. Covers employees in the executive, legislative, and judicial branches and in the District of Columbia government. Partly estimated]

CHARACTERISTICS	NUMBER OF EMPLOYEES				PERCENT DISTRIBUTION			AVERAGE SALARY		
	Total	Men	Women	Percent men	Total	Men	Women	Total	Men	Women
By age group: [1]										
Under 20 years	7,189	3,562	3,627	49.5	0.5	0.3	0.9	2,065	2,024	2,106
20 to 24 years	119,239	58,931	60,308	49.4	7.9	5.2	15.8	2,272	2,271	2,272
25 to 29 years	203,771	143,087	60,684	70.2	13.5	12.7	15.9	2,587	2,655	2,427
30 to 34 years	219,068	170,485	48,583	77.8	14.5	15.1	12.7	2,916	3,026	2,526
35 to 39 years	203,156	156,596	46,560	77.1	13.4	13.9	12.2	3,064	3,223	2,528
40 to 44 years	176,841	132,640	44,201	75.0	11.7	11.8	11.6	3,121	3,319	2,528
45 to 49 years	171,073	128,118	42,955	74.9	11.3	11.4	11.2	3,119	3,308	2,552
50 to 54 years	185,753	150,599	35,154	81.1	12.3	13.3	9.2	3,100	3,227	2,556
55 to 59 years	130,010	106,399	23,611	81.8	8.6	9.4	6.2	3,133	3,264	2,539
60 to 64 years	62,797	51,974	10,823	82.8	4.2	4.6	2.8	3,168	3,312	2,475
65 to 69 years	26,202	21,717	4,485	82.9	1.7	1.9	1.2	3,126	3,266	2,445
70 to 74 years	4,618	3,842	776	83.2	.3	.3	.2	2,795	2,923	2,160
75 years and over	953	878	75	92.1	.1	.1	(3)	2,780	2,830	2,194
By salary group: [2]										
Under $1,000	11,472	5,747	5,725	50.1	.8	.5	1.5	656	645	668
$1,000 to $1,999	133,645	86,961	46,684	65.1	8.8	7.7	12.2	1,770	1,772	1,768
$2,000 to $2,999	783,657	506,768	276,889	64.7	51.9	44.9	72.5	2,462	2,494	2,404
$3,000 to $3,999	405,331	364,344	40,987	89.9	26.8	32.3	10.7	3,301	3,298	3,327
$4,000 to $4,999	103,193	94,939	8,254	92.0	6.8	8.4	2.2	4,423	4,427	4,380
$5,000 to $5,999	37,042	34,698	2,344	93.7	2.5	3.1	.6	5,530	5,561	5,072
$6,000 to $6,999	15,352	14,822	530	96.5	1.0	1.3	.1	6,393	6,394	6,388
$7,000 to $7,999	11,969	11,668	301	97.5	.8	1.0	.1	7,296	7,296	7,325
$8,000 to $8,999	5,643	5,562	81	98.6	.4	.5	(3)	8,330	8,328	8,443
$9,000 to $9,999	1,919	1,889	30	98.4	.1	.2	(3)	9,678	9,680	9,518
$10,000 and over	1,447	1,430	17	98.8	.1	.1	(3)	10,399	10,401	10,294
By length of service group: [4]										
Under 5 years	350,436	193,692	156,744	55.3	23.2	17.2	41.0	2,410	2,538	2,252
5 to 9 years	642,632	492,563	150,069	76.6	42.5	43.6	39.3	2,800	2,969	2,504
10 to 14 years	192,943	157,512	35,431	81.6	12.8	14.0	9.3	3,359	3,500	2,731
15 to 19 years	90,367	78,600	11,767	87.0	6.0	7.0	3.1	3,392	3,481	2,793
20 to 24 years	83,129	74,571	8,558	89.7	5.5	6.6	2.2	3,286	3,335	2,860
25 to 29 years	87,671	74,253	13,418	84.7	5.8	6.6	3.5	3,381	3,429	3,116
30 to 34 years	37,766	33,065	4,701	87.6	2.5	2.9	1.2	3,614	3,680	3,152
35 to 39 years	15,939	15,288	651	95.9	1.1	1.3	.2	3,646	3,667	3,151
40 to 44 years	8,256	7,862	394	95.2	.5	.7	.1	3,705	3,809	3,166
45 to 49 years	1,391	1,285	106	92.4	.1	.1	(3)	4,088	4,148	3,358
50 years and over	140	137	3	97.9	(3)	(3)	(3)	4,312	4,356	2,303

[1] Average age is 40.6 years for all employees, 41.6 years for men, and 37.7 years for women. Age is determined by subtracting birth year from year 1947.
[2] Less than 0.1 percent.
[3] Pay rates represent base pay before any deductions for retirement, taxes, or bonds, but exclude overtime, bonuses, night differentials, etc. Pay rates other than annual rates are converted to annual full-time equivalent.
[4] Average length is 10.2 years for all employees, 11.3 years for men, and 7.2 years for women. Service represents all Federal employment, whether or not retirement deductions were taken from pay, and military service.

Source: Civil Service Commission, records.

No. 414.—Paid Civilian Employees With Veteran Preference in the Executive Branch of the Federal Government, by Selected Characteristics: June 1949 to 1952

[For coverage, see headnote, table 405. For definition of areas, see table 410, footnote 4]

ITEM	CONTINENTAL UNITED STATES				WASHINGTON, D. C., METROPOLITAN AREA			
	1949	1950	1951	1952	1949	1950	1951	1952
Total [1]	896,325	895,536	1,070,503	1,119,656	76,377	78,775	88,503	89,534
Veterans	880,607	878,703	1,050,878	1,098,627	73,480	75,628	85,358	86,394
Sex:								
Men	856,555	855,087	1,023,539	1,070,538	69,291	71,807	81,192	82,305
Women	24,052	23,616	27,339	28,089	4,189	3,821	4,166	4,089
Type of preference:								
Disabled (10-point)	124,410	138,940	164,027	172,497	7,776	9,444	10,683	10,659
Other (5-point)	756,197	739,763	886,851	926,130	65,704	66,184	74,675	75,735
Wives, widows, and mothers of veterans (10-point)	17,718	16,833	19,625	21,029	2,897	3,147	3,145	3,140

[1] Excludes certain employees for whom distribution is not available.
Source: Civil Service Commission, Annual Report.

No. 415.—Accidental Injuries to Civilian Employees of the Federal Government: 1938 to 1952

[For years ending June 30. Includes all employees covered under provisions of Federal Employees' Compensation Act. Excludes emergency relief acts except where specifically indicated]

ITEM	1938–1940, average	1949	1950	1951	1952
Injury cases reported, total	41,571	84,012	81,163	89,909	100,458
Index	100	202	195	216	242
Nonfatal	41,265	83,214	79,907	85,455	94,996
Fatal	306	798	1,256	4,454	5,462
Employment coverage	920,000	2,100,000	2,067,498	2,234,868	2,459,173
Casualty rates:					
Frequency per million man-hours	12.68	8.12	8.35	8.37	8.43
Severity per thousand man-hours	1.23	.55	.66	.62	.66
Cost per $100 payroll	$0.31	$0.15	$0.31	$0.30	$0.30
Cost per employee	$5.59	$4.36	$10.00	$10.14	$10.83
Final disposition of injury cases, total	41,496	84,083	88,481	95,366	106,323
Index	100	203	214	230	262
Minor injury cases	18,746	43,187	42,599	45,096	51,852
Disability 1-3 days	5,301	10,547	11,339	12,183	13,097
Covered by leave	8,858	16,932	20,758	18,291	20,948
Compensated, nonfatal	5,012	7,881	8,036	11,143	12,502
Compensated, fatal	98	557	472	549	244
Disapproved	2,974	2,520	2,268	4,015	4,232
All other	417	2,459	3,009	4,089	5,358
Average evaluation per fatal case	$9,800	$12,926	$31,166	$34,301	$33,662
Average evaluation per nonfatal disabling injury	$149	$162	$370	$377	$406
Average days lost per nonfatal disabling injury	38	25	41	41	41
Disbursements, total	$11,311,156	$14,209,790	$23,370,109	$30,427,296	$36,077,534
Medical treatment and supplies	612,433	2,941,729	4,985,351	4,367,405	5,352,698
Disability compensation	1,905,357	5,887,400	9,362,234	13,944,370	15,496,766
Death compensation	1,733,374	3,892,102	6,317,405	7,653,287	9,558,780
Emergency Relief Acts	6,986,865	545,740	809,872	960,284	896,508
Other	73,127	942,819	1,895,247	3,501,950	4,775,702

Source: Department of Labor, Bureau of Employees' Compensation; Annual Report.

15. State and Local Government Finances and Employment

The governmental structure of the United States includes, in addition to the National Government and the 48 States, a total of nearly 117,000 distinct units of local government, created or authorized by the States. A majority of these—some 67,000—are local school districts, but there are large numbers also of county and township governments, municipalities, and numerous kinds of "special districts."

This section provides figures relating to State and local governments as such—their numbers, finances, and employment. Statistics regarding particular functions in which State and local governments have an important role are presented in other sections (for example, the sections on Education, Roads and Motor Vehicles, and Social Security and Related Programs).

The primary official source of most of these tabulations is the current Census Bureau series on *State Finances, City Finances, Governmental Finances in the United States,* and *Public Employment.* (A descriptive leaflet, *Census Bureau Publications on Governments,* is issued annually by the Bureau.) Basic information for these series is obtained mainly by mail canvass from State and local officials; however, financial data for each of the 48 State governments and the 41 cities of over 250,000 are compiled from their official records and reports by Census personnel, and classified into uniform categories for statistical reporting.

Number of governments.—The figures for governmental units shown in table 416 include all agencies or bodies having an organized existence, governmental character, and substantial autonomy. While most of these governments can impose taxes, many of the special districts—such as independent public housing authorities, the New York Port Authority, and numerous local irrigation, power, and other types of districts—lack this power but are financed from rentals, charges for services, benefit assessments, grants from other governments, and other nontax sources. The figures exclude semi-autonomous agencies through which States, cities, and counties sometimes provide for certain functions—for example "dependent" school systems, State institutions of higher education, and certain other "authorities" and special agencies which are under the administrative or fiscal control of an established governmental unit.

Financial data.—Unless otherwise stated, financial data in this section relate to the fiscal years of the respective governments. Federal and State government amounts are for fiscal years ending on June 30 of the year specified, except for 6 States with earlier closing dates—3 in the same calendar year and 3 in the latter part of the preceding calendar year. Local government figures are for fiscal years ending in the calendar year specified, except for a few units which close their fiscal years in the succeeding January. Practically all school districts have fiscal years ending on June 30, but a majority of other local governments operate on a calendar fiscal year.

Nation-wide government finance statistics must be classified and presented in terms of uniform concepts and categories, rather than according to the highly diverse terminology, organization, and fund structure of individual governments. Accordingly, financial statistics which appear here for individual States and large cities, although based upon the official records and reports of these governments, will not agree directly with amounts appearing in such original sources except where particular segments of the official accounts conform explicitly to standard Census reporting categories.

Note.—This section presents data for the most recent year or period available on March 31, 1953, when the material was organized and sent to the printer. In some instances, more recent data were added after that date.

The framework for Census statistics on governmental finances makes a basic distinction between general government, utilities and liquor stores, and insurance trust activities. These are distinguished as to revenue according to the nature of the source involved, as to expenditure according to the purpose of the spending, and as to debt and related borrowing and debt redemption according to the purpose (general government or utility) for which the debt was incurred.

The utility sector involves only water supply, electric, gas, and transit systems operated by local governments and liquor stores operated by 16 States and by a few local governments. The scattering of other kinds of semi-commercial activities carried on by some governments are included in the general government category.

Insurance trust amounts relate to employee retirement, unemployment compensation, and other social insurance systems administered by State and local governments. The general government sector comprises all activities and amounts other than those classified as utility or insurance trust in nature.

Revenue and expenditure reported for each of these sectors and in total, in the basic framework of Census statistics, represent only external transactions, and exclude transfers among agencies and funds of the government concerned. Such internal transactions are shown separately, however, in related tables.

Some of these features of Census financial data represent a change from the framework which applied to reporting for 1950 and earlier years. Pending a recasting of prior data to the new structure, financial data appearing in this section cannot in all respects be directly related to government finance series included in the volume *Historical Statistics of the United States, 1789–1945*, or to the more detailed financial data for years up to 1946 which appear in the Census publication, *Historical Review of State and Local Government Finances*.

Employment statistics.—Figures in this section regarding public employment and payrolls are primarily based upon the Census Bureau's regular mail canvass survey covering all State governments and a scientific sample of local governments. Payroll amounts include all salaries, wages, and individual fee payments for the month specified, and employment numbers relate to all persons on governmental payrolls during the pay period ending nearest the close of the month covered—including paid officials, temporary help, and (except where otherwise specified) part-time as well as full-time personnel. As in the case of financial data, amounts shown for individual governments, such as States, cover major dependent agencies such as institutions of higher education, as well as the ordinary central departments and agencies of the government.

Historical statistics.—See preface and historical appendix. Tabular headnotes (as "See also *Historical Statistics*, series P 189–190") provide cross-references, where applicable, to *Historical Statistics of the United States, 1789–1945*.

FIG. **XXX.**—TAX REVENUE OF STATE AND LOCAL GOVERNMENTS:
1945 TO 1951

[See table 419]

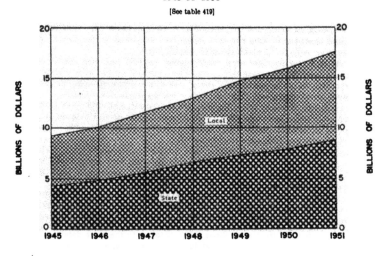

FIG. **XXXI.**—EMPLOYEES AND MONTHLY PAYROLLS OF STATE AND LOCAL
GOVERNMENTS AS OF OCTOBER: 1940 TO 1952

[See table 423]

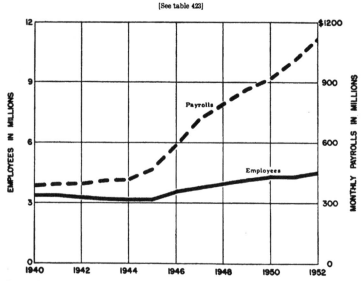

Source of figs. XXX and XXXI: Department of Commerce, Bureau of the Census.

No. 416.—GOVERNMENTAL UNITS, BY STATES AND BY TYPE OF GOVERNMENT: 1952

[Limited to governments actually in existence in 1952. Excludes, therefore, a few counties and numerous townships and "incorporated places" which exist as areas for which statistics can be presented as to population and other subjects, but which lack any separate organized county, township, or municipal government]

| STATE | All governmental units[1] | LOCAL GOVERNMENTS EXCEPT SCHOOL DISTRICTS | | | | | School districts[5] |
		Total	Counties[2]	Municipalities	Townships[3]	Special districts[4]	
Total	116,743	49,348	3,049	16,778	17,202	12,319	67,346
Alabama	548	439	67	302	....	70	108
Arizona	367	96	14	48	....	34	270
Arkansas	1,089	666	75	360	....	231	422
California	3,764	1,753	57	305	....	1,390	2,010
Colorado	1,963	600	62	241	....	297	1,362
Connecticut	363	359	8	33	152	166	3
Delaware	106	92	3	49	....	40	15
District of Columbia	2	2	....	1	....	1	....
Florida	617	549	67	294	....	188	67
Georgia	976	788	159	475	....	154	187
Idaho	938	632	44	193	....	395	305
Illinois	7,723	4,238	102	1,157	1,433	1,546	3,484
Indiana	3,050	1,934	92	540	1,009	293	1,115
Iowa	5,857	1,203	99	934	....	170	4,653
Kansas	6,933	2,948	105	605	1,514	734	3,984
Kentucky	796	563	120	313	....	130	232
Louisiana	489	421	62	215	....	144	67
Maine	664	659	16	42	473	128	4
Maryland	328	327	23	146	....	158	....
Massachusetts	584	563	12	39	312	230	....
Michigan	6,766	1,920	83	489	1,264	84	4,845
Minnesota	9,026	2,798	87	796	1,844	71	6,227
Mississippi	693	599	82	263	....	254	93
Missouri	7,002	2,110	114	781	329	886	4,891
Montana	1,598	310	56	121	....	133	1,287
Nebraska	7,981	1,588	93	533	477	485	6,392
Nevada	243	76	17	15	....	44	166
New Hampshire	551	322	10	12	222	78	228
New Jersey	1,151	669	21	334	233	81	481
New Mexico	289	182	32	72	....	78	106
New York	5,483	2,567	57	610	932	968	2,915
North Carolina	608	607	100	401	....	106	....
North Dakota	3,968	1,888	53	348	1,393	94	2,079
Ohio	3,936	2,470	88	904	1,338	140	1,465
Oklahoma	2,771	670	77	499	....	94	2,100
Oregon	1,723	651	36	208	....	407	1,071
Pennsylvania	5,156	2,649	66	990	1,564	29	2,506
Rhode Island	89	88	....	7	32	49	....
South Carolina	413	363	46	237	2	78	49
South Dakota	4,917	1,517	64	307	1,090	56	3,399
Tennessee	435	421	95	241	....	85	13
Texas	3,963	1,483	254	738	....	491	2,479
Utah	385	344	29	209	....	106	40
Vermont	414	393	14	71	238	70	20
Virginia	366	365	100	223	....	42	....
Washington	1,539	993	39	240	70	644	545
West Virginia	350	294	55	216	....	23	55
Wisconsin	7,256	1,959	71	534	1,281	73	5,296
Wyoming	519	200	23	86	....	91	318

[1] Includes Federal Government and the 48 States.
[2] Number of county governments; excludes areas corresponding to counties but having no organized county government.
[3] Includes towns in the 6 New England States, New York, and Wisconsin.
[4] Includes 15 special districts operating in more than one State. Each such district is counted only once in the tabulation—in the State in which its principal office is located.
[5] Excludes local school systems operated as part of State, county, municipal, or township governments.

Source: Department of Commerce, Bureau of the Census; *Governments in the United States, 1952.*

No. 417.—FEDERAL EXPENDITURES—AID TO STATE AND LOCAL GOVERNMENTS: 1952 AND 1953

[In millions of dollars. For years ending June 30. Based on existing and proposed legislation]

TYPE OF AID, FUNCTION, AND MAJOR PROGRAM	1952 actual	1953 estimate	TYPE OF AID, FUNCTION, AND MAJOR PROGRAM	1952 actual	1953 estimate
Federal aid to State and local governments, total	2,604	2,945	Grants-in-aid—Continued Agriculture and agricultural resources—Continued Commodity Credit Corporation:		
Grants-in-aid, total	2,393	2,828	Donation of commodities	5	1
Veterans' services and benefits	7	10	Other	14	13
Supervision of on-the-job training	2	5	Natural resources	20	25
Other	5	5	Forestry cooperation	10	10
Social security, welfare, and health	1,475	1,637	Other	10	15
Public assistance	1,178	1,341	Transportation and communication	448	538
National school lunch program	84	84	Federal-aid postwar highway construction	406	499
Vocational rehabilitation	22	22	Federal-aid airport program	33	33
Hospital construction	124	121	Other	9	6
Maternal and child welfare	31	33	Labor: Unemployment compensation and employment service administration	187	194
Defense community facilities and services		2	General government	16	18
Disease control and other public health	36	34	District of Columbia—Federal contribution	11	11
Housing and community development	34	89	Grants to American Samoa, Guam, and Trust Territories	5	7
Defense community facilities and services		8	**Shared revenues**	38	48
Disaster relief	16	12	Agriculture and agricultural resources	1	(¹)
Civil defense	1	24	Natural resources	37	48
Low-rent housing—annual contributions	13	27	Mineral Leasing Act	15	18
Slum clearance and urban redevelopment		8	National forests fund	14	17
Other community facilities	4	10	Tennessee Valley Authority: Payments in lieu of taxes	3	3
Education and general research	122	221	Other	5	10
Vocational education	26	25	**Loans and repayable advances: Housing and community development**	173	69
Education of children on Federal property and in areas especially affected by Federal activities	91	191	United States Housing Act	159	35
Other	5	5	Other	14	34
Agriculture and agricultural resources	84	96			
Cooperative extension work	32	32			
Removal of surplus commodities	33	50			

¹ Less than $500,000.

Source: Bureau of the Budget; *Budget of the United States Government*, 1954, Special Analysis G.

No. 418.—FEDERAL, STATE, AND LOCAL GENERAL REVENUE BEFORE AND AFTER INTERGOVERNMENTAL TRANSACTIONS: 1950 AND 1951

[In millions of dollars. Differences between totals of intergovernmental revenue and intergovernmental expenditure primarily reflect variance in fiscal years among governments]

ITEM	TOTAL		FEDERAL		STATE AND LOCAL					
					Total		State		Local	
	1950	1951	1950	1951	1950	1951	1950	1951	1950	1951
General revenue from own sources	58,454	72,643	40,027	52,254	18,427	20,390	8,841	9,896	9,586	10,492
Plus intergovernmental revenue	6,847	7,297			6,847	7,297	2,423	2,508	4,424	4,789
Equals gross general revenue	65,301	79,940	40,027	52,254	25,274	27,687	11,264	12,406	14,010	15,281
Minus intergovernmental expenditure	6,895	7,609	¹2,341	¹2,393	4,554	5,216	4,223	4,702	331	514
Equals general revenue for own purposes	58,406	72,331	37,686	49,861	20,720	22,471	7,041	7,704	13,679	14,767

¹ Includes grants, advances, and loans (except United States Housing Act loans) and reimbursements for contract research, tuition of veterans in State and local schools, etc.; excludes distribution of commodities and other payments in kind and United States Housing Act loans.

Source: Department of Commerce, Bureau of the Census; annual report, *Governmental Revenue in 1951*.

No. 419.—FEDERAL, STATE, AND LOCAL TAX REVENUE, BY TYPE: 1942 TO 1951

[See also *Historical Statistics*, series P 189-190]

ITEM	Total [1]	Individual income	Corporation income [2]	Sales, gross receipts, and customs	Property	Death and gift	Licenses, permits, and other
	AMOUNTS IN MILLIONS						
Total:							
1942	$20,797	$3,527	$4,998	$5,687	$4,544	$532	$1,509
1945	50,075	18,726	15,547	8,454	4,802	770	1,776
1946	46,128	16,399	12,225	9,828	4,990	810	1,878
1947	46,642	18,257	9,059	11,314	5,507	936	1,560
1948	51,122	19,762	10,273	12,106	6,128	1,074	1,779
1949	50,358	16,105	11,844	12,596	6,842	969	2,012
1950	50,957	16,472	11,043	12,986	7,349	870	2,247
1951	63,586	22,569	14,795	14,938	7,926	906	2,450
Federal:							
1942	12,270	3,251	4,726	3,334		419	540
1945	40,882	18,344	15,089	6,020		636	793
1946	36,037	15,977	11,778	6,838		667	777
1947	35,088	17,802	8,602	7,593		770	321
1948	37,792	19,219	9,681	7,661		890	341
1949	35,568	15,461	11,196	7,780		780	351
1950	35,053	15,684	10,450	7,832		698	389
1951	46,031	21,696	14,101	9,117		708	409
State and local:							
1942	8,527	276	272	2,353	4,544	113	969
1945	9,193	383	458	2,434	4,802	134	983
1946	10,091	422	447	2,990	4,990	143	1,101
1947	11,554	455	457	3,721	5,507	167	1,248
1948	13,331	543	591	4,445	6,128	184	1,438
1949	14,790	644	648	4,816	6,842	179	1,661
1950	15,914	788	593	5,154	7,349	172	1,858
1951	17,555	873	694	5,821	7,926	199	2,041
State:							
1942	3,903	249	269	2,220	271	112	781
1945	4,307	357	453	2,278	276	132	811
1946	4,934	389	442	2,806	253	142	902
1947	5,721	418	451	3,415	261	165	1,011
1948	6,732	499	585	4,045	279	180	1,143
1949	7,376	593	641	4,365	276	176	1,325
1950	7,930	724	586	4,670	307	168	1,475
1951	8,934	805	687	5,270	346	196	1,631
Local:							
1942	4,624	27	3	133	4,273	1	188
1945	4,886	26	5	156	4,526	1	172
1946	5,157	33	5	183	4,737	1	198
1947	5,833	37	6	306	5,246	1	237
1948	6,599	44	7	400	5,850	3	295
1949	7,414	51	7	451	6,566	3	336
1950	7,984	64	7	484	7,042	4	383
1951	8,621	68	7	551	7,580	3	410
	PER CAPITA, 1951 [3]						
Total	$411.95	$146.22	$95.85	$96.78	$51.35	$5.87	$15.87
Federal	298.22	140.56	91.36	59.07		4.59	2.65
State and local	113.73	5.66	4.50	37.71	51.35	1.29	13.22
State	57.88	5.22	4.45	34.14	2.24	1.27	10.57
Local	55.85	.44	.05	3.57	49.11	.02	2.66
	PERCENT DISTRIBUTION, BY LEVEL OF GOVERNMENT, 1951						
Total	100.0	100.0	100.0	100.0	100.0	100.0	100.0
Federal	72.4	96.1	95.3	61.0		78.1	16.7
State and local	27.6	3.9	4.7	39.0	100.0	22.0	83.3
State	14.1	3.6	4.6	35.3	4.4	21.6	66.6
Local	13.6	.3	(4)	3.7	95.6	.3	16.7

[1] Excludes employer and employee contributions for social insurance except Federal unemployment compensation tax act receipts which have been included in Federal "licenses, permits, and other taxes."
[2] Federal amounts include excess profits tax, as well as normal tax and surtax, and for years prior to 1948 include unjust enrichment tax.
[3] Based on estimated July 1, 1951, population of continental United States, including armed forces overseas.
[4] Less than 1⁄10 of 1 percent.

Source: Department of Commerce, Bureau of Census; annual report, *Governmental Revenue in 1951*.

No. 420.—GROSS DEBT OF FEDERAL, STATE, AND LOCAL GOVERNMENTS: 1902 TO 1952

[In millions of dollars. Beginning 1940, data are as of June 30; earlier data as of end of fiscal years]

YEAR	Total	Federal[1]	STATE AND LOCAL[2]								
			Total	State	Local						
					Total	County	City	Town-ship	School district	Special district	
1902	3,378	1,178	2,195	270	1,925	205	1,612	57	46	5	
1912	5,692	1,194	4,498	423	4,075	393	3,447	80	119	36	
1922	33,219	22,963	10,256	1,163	9,093	1,387	5,810	130	1,127	639	
1932	39,063	19,487	19,576	2,896	16,680	2,775	9,909	433	2,170	1,393	
1942	92,112	72,422	19,690	3,211	16,479	1,846	9,806	273	1,701	2,853	
1945	275,271	258,682	16,589	2,425	14,164	1,545	8,411	(³)	1,363	2,667	
1947	275,111	258,286	16,825	2,978	13,847	1,481	8,097	(³)	1,355	2,734	
1948	270,994	252,292	18,702	3,722	14,980	1,408	8,859	276	1,560	2,877	
1949	273,645	252,770	20,875	4,024	16,851	1,603	9,496	310	2,147	3,295	
1950	281,548	257,357	24,191	5,361	18,830	1,707	10,908	339	2,710	3,166	
1951	282,262	255,222	27,040	6,373	20,667	1,875	11,721	411	3,257	3,403	
1952	288,728	259,105	29,623	7,040	22,583	2,066	12,437	420	3,801	3,860	

[1] Public debt of the United States Government; includes general treasury obligations incurred on behalf of Federal agencies and excludes Federal agency debt incurred outside of general treasury.
[2] Comprises debt both for general purposes and for government enterprises.
[3] Estimates included in total; not shown separately.

No. 421.—ANNUAL INTEREST PAYMENTS ON DEBT OF FEDERAL, STATE, AND LOCAL GOVERNMENTS: 1932 TO 1951

[Data are for fiscal years of various governments ending within specified calendar year, except that State data and all 1942 amounts are for fiscal years ending June 30 of year specified or within 12 preceding months]

YEAR	PAYMENTS (in millions of dollars)						PER CAPITA[1]				
	Total	Fed-eral[2]	State and local				Total	Fed-eral	State and local		
			Total	State	Local				Total	State	Local
					Total	Cities only					
1932	1,439	599	840	114	726	419	$12	$5	$7	$1	$6
1942	1,967	1,260	707	123	584	345	15	9	5	1	4
1945	4,226	3,622	604	95	509	303	30	26	4	1	4
1947	5,474	4,958	516	78	438	272	38	34	4	1	3
1948	5,732	5,188	544	87	457	282	39	35	4	1	3
1949	5,930	5,352	578	98	480	288	40	36	4	1	3
1950	6,111	5,496	615	111	504	313	41	36	4	1	3
1951	6,264	5,615	649	130	519	317	41	36	4	1	3

[1] Based on estimated population, including armed forces overseas, as of July 1 except for 1950 data, which are based on April 1 enumeration for continental United States.
[2] On basis of Public Debt accounts.

No. 422.—OUTSTANDING DEBT OF STATE AND LOCAL GOVERNMENTS, BY TYPE OF DEBT: JUNE 30, 1952

[In millions of dollars]

TYPE OF DEBT	Total	State	LOCAL					
			Total	County	City	Town-ship	School district	Special district
Gross debt	29,623	7,040	22,583	2,066	12,437	420	3,801	3,860
Long-term debt	27,720	6,756	20,964	1,986	11,840	358	3,669	3,110
Full faith and credit	22,718	4,930	17,788	1,797	9,382	356	3,669	2,583
Nonguaranteed	5,002	1,826	3,176	189	2,458	2	....	527
Offsets to long-term debt	3,229	1,131	2,098	109	1,606	6	205	171
Net long-term debt	24,491	5,625	18,866	1,877	10,234	353	3,464	2,939

Source of tables 420-422: Department of Commerce, Bureau of the Census; annual report, *Governmental Debt in 1952.*

No. 423.—EMPLOYEES AND PAYROLLS OF FEDERAL, STATE, AND LOCAL
GOVERNMENTS: 1942 TO 1952

[Data for 1942 through 1951 are for October. See also *Historical Statistics*, series P 69–88, for average annual monthly
employment and payrolls]

TYPE OF GOVERN-MENT	1942	1946	1947	1948	1949	1950	1951	1952			
								Jan.	Apr.	July	Oct.
	NUMBER OF EMPLOYEES (THOUSANDS)										
Total	6,515	6,586	5,791	6,042	6,303	6,402	6,502	6,798	6,936	6,364	7,106
Federal (civilian)[1]	2,664	3,275	2,002	3,076	2,047	2,117	2,515	2,834	2,539	2,619	2,583
State and local	3,261	3,181	3,789	3,966	4,156	4,285	4,287	4,274	4,366	3,645	4,522
School[2]	1,320	1,267	1,529	1,581	1,658	1,723	1,759	1,779	1,801	981	1,873
Nonschool	1,931	1,914	2,260	2,385	2,497	2,562	2,528	2,495	2,565	2,664	2,649
State	868	473	688	677	731	745	754	752	759	784	768
Local	1,426	1,441	1,622	1,707	1,767	1,817	1,774	1,743	1,806	1,880	1,851
City	872	879	986	1,039	1,082	1,106	1,102	1,084	1,111	1,163	1,154
County	333	316	375	408	410	429	435	429	445	459	454
Other	223	246	251	262	275	282	237	230	250	258	273
	AMOUNT OF MONTHLY PAYROLL (MILLIONS OF DOLLARS)										
Total	896.2	1,109.9	1,182.7	1,329.0	1,466.0	1,527.9	1,865.4	1,876.1	1,879.3	1,729.1	1,973.5
Federal (civilian)[1]	498.1	642.3	481.4	532.9	539.2	613.4	857.4	846.1	826.5	865.2	855.9
State and local	394.1	467.6	702.3	795.1	866.7	914.6	1,008.0	1,030.0	1,052.5	872.9	1,123.7
School[2]	175.4	200.0	318.5	353.0	384.5	409.4	452.5	462.3	465.5	268.6	502.9
Nonschool	218.7	267.6	383.7	442.0	481.9	505.2	555.5	567.7	584.0	615.3	620.8
State	69.5	72.9	115.0	134.0	151.3	157.4	177.7	183.2	185.6	195.0	195.3
Local	159.2	194.7	267.7	308.0	330.6	347.8	377.8	384.5	398.2	420.3	425.6
City	109.7	133.2	181.2	206.2	219.7	230.2	253.9	250.1	280.0	281.7	282.7
County	34.5	43.6	55.1	66.6	72.6	75.7	86.1	98.3	92.9	95.9	97.0
Other	15.0	18.9	26.4	35.2	37.3	38.9	37.8	37.1	39.3	42.7	45.8

[1] October 1952 data from Civil Service Commission; data prior to October 1952 from Bureau of Labor Statistics. Includes data for Federal civilian employees working outside continental United States.
[2] Excludes all school board members. Data for 1946–52 based on returns to quarterly mail canvass of Bureau of Census; those for prior years based on information furnished by U.S. Office of Education.

Source: Department of Commerce, Bureau of Census; annual report, *Public Employment in October 1952*.

No. 424.—ESTIMATED AVERAGE MONTHLY EMPLOYMENT OF STATE AND LOCAL
GOVERNMENTS: 1929 TO 1952

[In thousands. Includes school districts and other special-purpose agencies. Excludes military and work-relief
employment. See also *Historical Statistics*, series P 73–80]

YEAR	Total	Educa-tion	Other	YEAR	Total	Educa-tion	Other
1929	2,532	1,121	1,411	1941	3,320	1,362	1,957
1930	2,622	1,150	1,472	1942	3,270	1,383	1,887
1931	2,704	1,160	1,544	1943	3,174	1,361	1,813
1932	2,666	1,148	1,518	1944	3,116	1,352	1,764
1933	2,601	1,122	1,479	1945	3,137	1,353	1,784
1934	2,647	1,122	1,525	1946	3,341	1,395	1,946
1935	2,728	1,151	1,577	1947	3,582	1,468	2,114
1936	2,842	1,174	1,668	1948	3,787	1,516	2,271
1937	2,923	1,206	1,717	1949	3,948	1,585	2,363
1938	3,054	1,239	1,815	1950	4,098	1,644	2,454
1939	3,080	1,257	1,823	1951	4,113	1,681	2,431
1940	3,206	1,299	1,907	1952	4,230	1,749	2,481

Source: Department of Labor, Bureau of Labor Statistics. Based on data from the State, County, and Municipal Survey, the U.S. Office of Education, and the Bureau of the Census.

No. 425.—NUMBER OF PUBLIC EMPLOYEES, BY STATES: OCTOBER 1952

[In thousands]

State	Total employees	Federal civilian[1]	STATE[2] AND LOCAL		State[3]	LOCAL					
			Total	Full-time employees only		Total	Cities	Counties	Townships	School districts	Special districts
United States	6,322.5	2,400.8	4,521.7	3,844.3	1,103.4	3,418.3	1,341.7	529.8	189.1	1,234.4	123.3
Alabama	125.8	82.6	73.2	66.0	19.0	54.2	12.0	9.6	......	32.0	.6
Arizona	40.0	15.3	24.7	21.9	7.0	17.7	3.9	3.6	......	9.1	1.0
Arkansas	59.5	16.6	43.0	36.2	12.4	30.6	6.6	3.2	......	19.2	1.5
California	655.9	260.8	395.1	347.5	78.3	316.8	92.8	72.7	......	133.7	17.6
Colorado	84.3	37.4	47.0	39.0	12.1	34.9	10.9	6.4	......	17.0	.5
Connecticut	72.3	11.5	60.8	51.2	19.3	41.5	21.7	.4	17.3	.5	1.6
Delaware	12.8	2.5	10.3	9.4	5.6	4.7	2.6	.6	......	1.3	.1
District of Columbia	279.6	[1,4]258.8	20.8	20.1	......	20.8	20.4	......	......	......	.4
Florida	140.2	40.2	100.0	92.6	26.2	73.8	29.3	10.7	......	32.7	1.1
Georgia	147.3	60.4	86.9	79.4	20.0	66.9	20.2	10.1	......	35.0	1.6
Idaho	26.8	6.4	20.5	14.5	6.5	14.0	3.1	3.0	......	6.6	1.3
Illinois	352.5	113.8	238.7	205.7	43.9	194.9	55.1	20.0	7.6	79.3	32.8
Indiana	153.6	42.5	111.1	91.6	26.1	85.0	24.2	16.0	1.9	40.7	2.3
Iowa	105.6	16.0	89.7	70.4	23.0	66.6	19.2	12.7	......	34.8	.2
Kansas	86.7	22.2	64.5	51.6	16.7	47.9	11.8	8.9	2.1	24.1	1.0
Kentucky	95.9	33.6	62.3	54.6	18.0	44.3	12.7	5.3	......	26.2	.1
Louisiana	105.3	26.7	78.6	71.0	28.3	50.3	16.0	5.9	......	26.8	1.6
Maine	47.4	17.7	29.7	22.1	9.6	20.1	6.2	.8	12.2	.1	.8
Maryland	114.2	[1]50.7	63.5	58.3	17.4	46.1	22.9	20.6	......	......	2.5
Massachusetts	235.8	71.5	164.3	140.9	32.3	132.0	74.5	5.0	42.7	......	9.7
Michigan	244.5	43.1	201.5	168.4	38.7	162.7	59.9	19.7	7.9	74.5	.7
Minnesota	132.7	25.4	107.4	77.1	26.0	81.3	28.7	13.1	7.8	31.5	.3
Mississippi	70.8	16.8	54.1	44.2	16.3	37.8	8.0	22.0	......	7.5	.3
Missouri	155.7	52.0	103.7	87.2	22.8	80.9	29.2	7.1	1.7	39.9	3.0
Montana	28.7	8.0	20.7	16.9	6.8	13.9	2.6	3.5	......	7.5	.4
Nebraska	69.5	20.9	48.5	39.7	11.0	37.5	8.2	6.1	.9	16.8	5.5
Nevada	12.5	5.4	7.1	6.1	1.9	5.2	1.1	2.0	......	1.9	.2
New Hampshire	23.3	3.4	20.0	12.7	6.2	13.8	5.0	.8	4.3	3.2	.5
New Jersey	190.5	55.4	135.2	118.0	25.7	109.5	60.6	15.5	7.5	24.5	1.4
New Mexico	38.5	16.4	22.2	18.9	8.6	13.6	3.2	1.1	......	8.9	.4
New York	723.6	206.2	517.4	470.7	89.7	427.7	290.8	33.0	27.2	70.3	6.4
North Carolina	129.8	27.1	102.7	90.0	76.0	26.7	17.4	7.4	......	......	2.0
North Dakota	31.7	6.6	25.1	16.0	5.2	19.9	4.1	3.4	4.0	8.2	.2
Ohio	337.6	106.6	230.9	184.0	41.6	189.3	70.9	25.2	11.4	78.4	3.4
Oklahoma	117.2	48.2	68.9	57.9	20.2	48.7	12.9	8.2	......	27.4	.2
Oregon	71.5	18.1	53.4	43.3	17.7	35.7	9.0	6.0	......	18.8	2.0
Pennsylvania	391.7	151.7	240.0	193.5	65.9	174.0	55.8	13.9	11.3	90.8	2.3
Rhode Island	34.6	13.7	20.9	19.1	7.6	13.3	10.1	......	3.2	......	(¹)
South Carolina	79.4	24.0	55.3	50.0	14.6	40.8	8.7	5.2	......	26.2	.6
South Dakota	33.7	9.0	24.7	17.3	5.4	19.3	4.2	3.2	2.8	8.9	.1
Tennessee	124.5	44.0	80.6	70.1	18.7	61.9	30.4	30.6	......	.5	.4
Texas	330.4	121.7	208.7	186.4	44.5	164.2	54.3	22.3	......	83.2	4.4
Utah	58.9	33.3	25.6	19.2	8.4	17.3	5.6	2.6	......	8.9	.2
Vermont	16.4	3.3	13.1	8.9	4.6	8.5	2.5	(⁴)	5.2	.4	.3
Virginia	166.2	[1]79.4	86.8	77.4	30.9	55.9	25.7	28.8	......	......	1.4
Washington	151.3	64.8	86.5	69.7	22.1	64.4	17.9	11.3	.2	27.8	7.2
West Virginia	61.9	11.5	50.4	44.3	19.8	30.6	6.1	2.6	......	21.9	......
Wisconsin	136.8	21.8	115.0	84.5	21.9	93.0	41.1	17.9	9.9	23.1	.9
Wyoming	17.0	6.0	11.1	8.9	3.2	7.8	1.6	1.6	......	4.4	.3

[1] Data from Civil Service Commission, as of Sept. 30, 1952. Excludes employees working outside continental United States.

[2] See footnotes, table 428.

[3] District of Columbia consists of employees in Washington, D. C., metropolitan area and includes substantial numbers of employees working in suburban locations in Maryland and Virginia.

[4] Includes a small number of judicial employees and employees in executive agencies not allocable by State.

[5] Less than 50 employees.

Source: Department of Commerce, Bureau of the Census; annual report, *State Distribution of Public Employment in 1952*.

No. 426.—STATE AND LOCAL GOVERNMENT PAYROLLS, BY TYPE OF GOVERNMENT AND BY STATES: OCTOBER 1952

[In thousands of dollars]

STATE	STATE AND LOCAL		State [1]	LOCAL					
	Total	For full-time employees only		Total	Cities	Counties	Townships	School districts	Special districts
United States	1,122,745	1,075,455	270,856	852,898	345,837	112,655	24,513	338,551	31,143
Alabama	14,733	14,220	3,756	10,975	2,290	1,674		6,930	142
Arizona	6,811	6,635	1,695	5,116	951	966		2,997	273
Arkansas	7,056	6,792	2,120	4,987	804	561		3,392	279
California	121,962	117,171	26,801	95,151	29,787	16,625		44,497	4,242
Colorado	10,608	10,144	2,835	7,773	2,472	1,200		4,054	46
Connecticut	15,939	15,298	4,791	11,148	6,398	85	4,280	129	255
Delaware	2,702	2,650	1,349	1,353	760	119		440	25
District of Columbia	6,467	6,344		6,467	6,347				120
Florida	22,155	21,720	5,479	16,674	6,363	1,817		8,251	243
Georgia	17,941	16,922	4,096	13,146	3,573	1,847		7,477	247
Idaho	3,945	3,554	1,319	2,639	524	441		1,469	165
Illinois	66,918	66,121	11,308	55,610	14,915	4,997	632	25,183	9,853
Indiana	30,943	25,781	6,058	20,885	4,492	2,736	88	12,979	580
Iowa	18,447	17,443	4,873	13,574	2,695	2,578		8,292	9
Kansas	12,535	12,921	2,564	9,981	1,973	1,799	141	5,830	218
Kentucky	12,660	12,259	3,545	9,115	2,281	819		6,001	14
Louisiana	17,558	17,069	5,957	11,601	3,269	815		7,264	263
Maine	4,803	4,524	1,849	2,954	1,204	126	1,470	19	136
Maryland	16,945	16,546	4,278	12,668	6,352	5,525			791
Massachusetts	40,539	39,259	8,819	31,721	19,498	1,213	7,826		3,184
Michigan	59,546	57,554	11,917	47,629	17,095	5,364	524	24,402	155
Minnesota	24,412	22,317	6,732	17,681	5,693	3,052	255	8,643	28
Mississippi	8,890	8,309	2,936	5,954	1,083	3,416		1,434	22
Missouri	22,545	21,425	4,558	17,987	6,195	1,356	104	9,941	291
Montana	5,137	4,846	1,689	3,449	541	705		2,134	69
Nebraska	10,052	9,631	2,261	7,791	1,270	1,110	42	3,909	1,461
Nevada	1,826	1,770	607	1,219	257	418		492	37
New Hampshire	3,413	3,146	1,347	2,066	1,028	94	221	674	49
New Jersey	36,980	35,631	7,230	29,750	17,716	3,689	1,363	6,557	425
New Mexico	4,229	4,022	1,787	3,442	640	227		2,507	68
New York	154,262	150,736	27,537	126,726	93,163	8,112	3,631	19,832	1,966
North Carolina	28,147	21,931	15,048	5,099	3,256	1,418			425
North Dakota	4,506	4,270	1,366	3,140	388	661	61	2,009	21
Ohio	53,351	50,940	9,789	43,472	15,591	5,347	680	21,222	752
Oklahoma	14,143	13,479	4,116	10,026	2,045	1,481		6,464	17
Oregon	14,086	13,371	4,530	9,565	2,126	1,505		5,514	410
Pennsylvania	60,431	54,705	16,060	44,370	13,389	3,262	1,217	26,016	486
Rhode Island	5,066	4,996	1,698	3,373	2,715		558		(7)
South Carolina	10,405	10,130	3,041	7,362	1,468	783		5,018	102
South Dakota	4,316	3,966	1,199	3,117	527	846	17	1,967	14
Tennessee	16,045	15,306	3,496	12,549	6,390	5,972		99	89
Texas	48,289	47,009	9,847	38,422	11,525	4,750		21,257	899
Utah	5,453	5,022	1,913	3,540	859	475		2,179	27
Vermont	2,208	2,028	938	1,270	420	2	748	92	7
Virginia	18,327	17,799	6,013	12,314	6,027	6,146			141
Washington	23,857	21,858	6,655	17,202	5,476	2,619	1	7,562	1,544
West Virginia	11,449	11,140	3,747	7,702	451			6,212	7
Wisconsin	27,057	25,646	5,508	21,549	9,895	4,653	575	6,085	341
Wyoming	2,474	2,345	799	1,675	292	248		1,081	54

[1] See footnote, table 425.
[2] Less than $500.

Source: Department of Commerce, Bureau of the Census; annual report, *State Distribution of Public Employment in 1952*.

No. 427.—EMPLOYMENT AND PAYROLLS OF STATE AND LOCAL GOVERNMENTS, BY TYPE OF GOVERNMENT AND BY FUNCTION: OCTOBER 1952

FUNCTION	NUMBER OF EMPLOYEES (in thousands)								OCTOBER PAYROLLS (in millions of dollars)							
	Total	State	Local Total	City	County	School district	Township	Special district	Total	State	Local Total	City	County	School district	Township	Special district
Education, total	1,873	336	1,537	188	76	1,224	39	--	602.9	75.6	427.3	62.3	16.6	339.6	9.8	--
Elementary and secondary schools	1,561	46	1,515	177	76	1,224	39	--	434.2	11.7	422.5	59.9	16.6	338.2	9.8	--
Institutions of higher education	281	269	22	11	--	11	--	--	61.3	56.5	4.8	2.4	--	2.3	--	--
Other	30	30	--	--	--	--	--	--	7.3	7.3	--	--	--	--	--	--
Highways	456	187	269	109	108	--	45	7	107.0	46.9	60.1	26.2	25.3	--	6.2	2.5
Public welfare	92	37	56	21	32	--	3	--	21.5	9.1	12.5	5.0	7.2	--	.3	--
Health	73	27	46	28	15	--	2	1	18.4	6.8	11.6	7.9	3.4	--	.2	.1
Hospitals	389	183	176	84	85	--		2	75.0	40.9	34.1	17.3	16.4	--	.4	--
Police	238	21	217	175	31	--	11	--	67.1	6.1	61.0	51.4	7.5	--	2.0	.3
Local fire protection	174	--	174	150	--	--	14	10	37.5	--	37.5	35.5	--	--	.9	1.0
Natural resources	121	83	37	--	11	--	--	26	26.0	19.5	6.6	--	2.4	--	--	4.2
Sanitation	106	--	106	97	--	--	2	7	26.8	--	26.8	24.4	--	--	.4	2.0
Local parks and recreation	61	--	61	54	--	--	1	6	14.0	--	14.0	12.1	--	--	.2	1.7
Housing and community redevelopment	22	--	22	7	--	--	(1)	16	6.0	--	6.0	2.0	--	--	(1)	4.0
Employment security administration	44	44	--	--	--	--	--	--	12.8	12.8	--	--	--	--	--	--
State liquor stores	14	14	--	--	--	--	--	--	3.5	3.5	--	--	--	--	--	--
Local utilities, total	227	--	227	184	2	--	--	41	68.6	--	68.6	54.1	--	--	--	
Water supply	92	--	92	81	2	--	--	9	23.8	--	23.8	21.2	--	--	--	
Electric light and power	46	--	46	40	--	--	--	6	14.3	--	14.3	12.4	--	--	--	
Transit	85	--	85	60	--	--	--	25	29.4	--	29.4	20.0	--	--	--	
Gas supply	4	--	4	3	--	--	--	1	1.1	--	1.1	.6	--	--	--	
All other	661	172	489	241	172	--	67	8	135.6	49.6	86.9	46.9	34.8	--	3.8	1.5

1 Less than 500 employees or $50,000 October payroll.

Source: Department of Commerce, Bureau of the Census; annual report, *State Distribution of Public Employment in 1952.*

No. 428.—State Government Employees, by Function and byStates: October 1952

STATE	Total [1]	Education	High-ways	Health and hospitals	Police	Public welfare	Natural re-sources	State liquor stores	All other [1]
Total [1]	1,102,441	336,551	186,781	216,071	21,007	26,744	83,361	14,235	215,601
Alabama	18,963	5,960	3,002	3,586	800	947	2,412	721	2,855
Arizona [4]	6,985	2,133	1,738	639	118	321	466	....	1,595
Arkansas	12,377	4,470	2,687	3,868	160	548	1,002	....	917
California	78,272	24,802	9,161	11,802	2,430	489	6,980	....	22,549
Colorado	12,118	5,192	1,286	2,221	263	174	1,070	....	1,912
Connecticut [4]	19,206	5,298	2,767	4,775	492	786	920	....	4,273
Delaware	5,550	1,630	1,014	1,088	186	261	415	....	536
Florida [4]	26,219	6,506	5,568	2,700	600	700	2,186	....	7,900
Georgia	19,951	5,847	4,897	3,376	487	210	2,422	....	2,772
Idaho	6,580	2,441	1,124	679	146	176	920	226	788
Illinois [4]	43,868	10,942	6,102	10,154	913	3,379	1,637	....	10,741
Indiana [4]	20,113	11,534	(7)	(7)	(7)	(7)	(7)	....	(7)
Iowa	22,096	5,910	2,326	4,987	276	1,847	1,649	842	2,604
Kansas	16,686	7,326	2,745	2,535	124	359	1,004	....	2,466
Kentucky [4]	17,974	4,208	5,768	2,719	348	681	1,679	....	2,571
Louisiana	28,316	7,110	4,735	7,626	334	1,836	2,578	....	4,097
Maine [4]	9,560	1,306	2,406	1,304	185	315	1,121	201	1,453
Maryland	17,432	4,666	2,817	4,684	376	44	1,018	....	3,527
Massachusetts	32,281	2,538	4,180	11,513	446	1,222	1,002	....	11,356
Michigan	38,717	15,939	2,768	7,360	806	1,878	2,334	875	6,665
Minnesota	26,013	9,715	3,983	5,631	230	401	1,786	....	4,308
Mississippi	16,296	4,138	2,536	2,981	302	700	4,092	....	1,555
Missouri	22,782	5,639	4,208	4,179	461	1,746	1,515	....	5,003
Montana	6,794	1,906	1,446	617	111	312	1,043	385	863
Nebraska	11,036	3,584	1,800	2,076	190	38	1,114	....	2,586
Nevada [4]	1,946	341	656	133	32	53	223	....	408
New Hampshire	6,176	1,538	1,494	1,189	74	196	461	231	990
New Jersey	25,674	4,441	3,690	6,255	663	1,011	1,762	....	7,822
New Mexico	8,548	2,306	1,566	774	93	672	739	....	1,310
New York	86,728	8,800	11,760	33,218	919	1,584	5,468	....	24,304
North Carolina	75,968	52,151	11,319	4,103	567	96	2,536	....	5,184
North Dakota	5,214	1,697	926	889	46	102	487	....	1,087
Ohio	41,640	12,546	7,002	(7)	766	(7)	1,618	1,817	(7)
Oklahoma	20,187	7,555	2,374	3,960	458	1,121	1,975	....	2,745
Oregon	17,665	4,459	2,638	2,134	374	829	2,414	512	4,104
Pennsylvania	64,996	8,176	15,480	(7)	1,900	(7)	3,182	4,914	(7)
Rhode Island [4]	7,612	1,375	941	1,907	182	561	417	....	2,220
South Carolina [4]	14,575	5,664	3,624	2,089	354	612	1,822	....	2,410
South Dakota	5,366	1,910	1,129	650	86	342	235	....	1,072
Tennessee	18,669	5,147	4,143	2,487	763	1,078	2,748	....	2,398
Texas	44,499	17,049	9,780	6,314	671	1,861	2,992	....	5,832
Utah	8,362	3,668	1,180	686	103	213	745	193	1,567
Vermont	4,627	1,277	990	510	152	106	420	98	1,063
Virginia	30,883	7,396	10,117	5,907	590	(7)	2,391	1,314	(7)
Washington	22,089	7,975	3,037	2,152	512	1,281	2,456	935	3,652
West Virginia	19,818	5,680	6,291	2,101	259	712	1,812	941	2,022
Wisconsin	21,946	10,628	778	2,493	(7)	1,711	2,180	....	4,056
Wyoming	3,206	1,102	620	337	86	169	462	21	430

[1] Includes estimates for missing items.
[2] Includes data for legislative, executive, judicial, fiscal management and general administrative activities. Also includes employment security administration.
[3] November 1952 data, except education.
[4] April 1952 data. Includes nonschool part-time employees.
[5] Includes nonschool part-time employees.
[6] April 1952 data, except education.
[7] Not available; estimates included in totals.
[8] August 1952 data, except education. Includes nonschool part-time employees.
[9] Except for education, data for employment and payrolls (see table 426) from separate sources, therefore, not strictly comparable.

Source: Department of Commerce, Bureau of the Census; annual report, *State Distribution of Public Employment in 1952*.

No. 429.—STATE GOVERNMENT PAYROLLS, BY FUNCTION AND BY STATES:
OCTOBER 1952

[In thousands of dollars]

STATE	Total [1]	Education	Highways	Health and hospitals	Police	Public welfare	Natural resources	State liquor stores	All other [2]
Total [1]	270,849.7	75,591.0	46,879.3	47,753.8	6,149.1	9,054.6	19,468.9	3,511.5	62,451.5
Alabama	3,757.8	1,022.0	594.2	406.4	132.2	215.9	446.4	171.6	769.1
Arizona [3]	1,694.5	371.6	563.5	137.7	41.9	57.4	124.4		398.0
Arkansas	2,119.6	723.2	481.6	348.9	35.6	98.9	173.1		258.3
California	26,801.4	7,235.0	(4)	(4)	(4)	(4)	(4)		(4)
Colorado	2,834.8	1,039.4	406.6	502.4	79.2	45.9	255.9		504.4
Connecticut [5]	4,791.2	1,131.1	847.4	1,082.0	137.6	168.3	232.7		1,192.1
Delaware	1,349.3	558.9	240.3	190.9	47.7	51.1	55.6		194.8
Florida [6]	5,479.1	1,436.4	988.5	475.0	123.0	152.0	463.2		1,841.0
Georgia	4,094.9	1,172.5	938.6	658.4	94.9	56.1	436.4		738.0
Idaho	1,319.1	358.6	332.0	124.5	38.0	44.4	198.4	33.1	190.1
Illinois [6]	11,308.0	2,754.0	1,685.2	2,357.1	290.1	856.6	428.2		2,936.8
Indiana [7]	6,057.5	2,499.9	(4)	(4)	(4)	(4)	(4)		(4)
Iowa	4,872.7	1,839.3	624.8	899.7	76.6	253.9	358.8	176.9	642.7
Kansas	3,563.5	1,466.6	693.5	481.5	30.7	79.4	213.4		506.1
Kentucky [8]	3,544.6	785.6	1,197.1	433.0	80.9	157.1	283.9		607.0
Louisiana	5,967.3	1,488.4	961.0	1,237.9	90.1	501.8	555.2		1,102.9
Maine [6]	1,849.4	265.4	497.2	269.8	49.8	73.8	258.1	70.3	365.0
Maryland	4,277.6	1,000.9	768.6	1,074.2	92.1	15.7	277.4		1,048.7
Massachusetts	8,818.7	618.9	1,158.7	2,732.3	153.9	329.4	279.6		3,545.9
Michigan	11,917.3	4,415.3	1,035.1	2,215.5	321.4	598.5	717.0	271.9	2,342.6
Minnesota	6,731.7	2,469.3	1,016.5	1,425.9	75.2	96.8	478.3		1,169.7
Mississippi	2,935.8	733.1	475.5	426.0	76.9	162.6	611.1		450.6
Missouri	4,558.0	933.7	1,009.6	648.9	128.2	328.2	359.5		1,149.9
Montana	1,688.5	404.6	511.0	144.1	31.1	71.5	239.9	78.0	208.3
Nebraska	2,261.0	516.4	454.0	382.1	53.1	11.6	269.4		574.4
Nevada [7]	606.6	103.6	231.4	29.8	8.9	14.6	100.4		117.9
New Hampshire	1,347.4	274.0	327.0	263.7	23.6	47.4	99.1	60.6	252.0
New Jersey	7,230.0	1,144.2	1,143.0	1,537.8	227.2	333.6	412.7		2,431.5
New Mexico	1,786.5	593.0	359.4	138.4	31.7	152.0	162.1		349.9
New York	27,536.5	2,633.4	3,287.8	9,146.4	296.2	500.3	1,320.6		10,351.8
North Carolina	18,048.3	12,953.5	2,401.8	683.6	151.6	25.9	580.8		1,251.1
North Dakota	1,366.4	489.5	279.6	152.3	13.4	22.6	131.7		277.3
Ohio	9,789.0	2,423.9	1,943.1	(4)	236.5	(4)	416.3	419.8	(4)
Oklahoma	4,116.1	1,544.4	503.7	654.3	109.3	258.2	405.3		640.9
Oregon	4,530.4	885.3	956.5	502.9	120.8	217.2	604.0	141.8	1,101.9
Pennsylvania	16,060.2	1,938.3	3,931.5	(4)	579.9	(4)	669.3	1,197.3	(4)
Rhode Island [6]	1,693.2	301.3	189.7	281.6	28.3	154.2	82.2		655.9
South Carolina	3,041.2	790.8	678.7	402.7	85.2	142.2	335.8		605.8
South Dakota	1,196.9	420.7	290.1	93.1	22.0	62.0	60.6		250.4
Tennessee	3,495.5	945.5	778.7	404.6	171.6	246.9	412.4		535.8
Texas	9,847.0	3,247.6	2,778.1	1,103.5	184.0	394.8	608.0		1,531.0
Utah	1,913.1	796.4	345.5	153.2	30.0	55.2	139.6	33.7	358.5
Vermont	938.2	218.2	237.8	107.3	40.1	26.7	100.4	22.4	185.3
Virginia	6,012.9	1,494.2	1,622.3	1,138.8	166.5	(4)	489.9	336.7	(4)
Washington	5,654.9	1,757.2	1,006.4	510.4	154.7	367.0	736.3	253.6	869.3
West Virginia	3,746.9	760.6	1,443.2	336.7	66.1	137.9	296.4	238.0	466.0
Wisconsin	5,508.2	2,382.2	283.7	608.0	(4)	458.6	561.0		1,192.0
Wyoming	799.0	252.8	186.0	63.0	17.7	39.0	118.9	5.8	115.8

[1] Includes estimates for missing items.
[2] Includes data for legislative, executive, judicial, fiscal management and general administrative activities. Also includes employment security administration.
[3] November 1952 data, except education.
[4] Not available; estimates included in totals.
[5] April 1952 data. Includes nonschool part-time payrolls.
[6] Includes nonschool part-time payrolls.
[7] April 1952 data, except education.
[8] August 1952 data, except education. Includes nonschool part-time payrolls.
[9] Except for education, data for employment (see table 428) and payrolls from separate sources, therefore, not strictly comparable.

Source: Department of Commerce, Bureau of the Census: annual report, *State Distribution of Public Employment in 1952.*

No. 430.—RETIREMENT COVERAGE OF STATE AND LOCAL GOVERNMENT EMPLOYEES, BY TYPE OF GOVERNMENT: OCTOBER 1952

ITEM	Total	COVERED BY STATE OR LOCAL RETIRE-MENT PLAN [1]		COVERED BY FED-ERAL OLD-AGE AND SURVIVORS INSUR-ANCE		WITHOUT RETIRE-MENT OR PENSION COVERAGE	
		Number	Percent of total	Number	Percent of total	Number	Percent of total
State and local	4,510,040	3,021,254	67.0	436,071	9.7	1,050,715	23.3
State	1,101,519	745,722	67.7	135,881	12.3	219,916	20.0
Education	315,872	166,008	52.6	26,402	8.4	123,462	39.1
Nonschool	785,647	579,714	73.8	109,479	13.9	96,454	12.3
Local	3,408,521	2,275,532	66.8	302,190	8.9	830,799	24.4
Education	1,537,148	1,208,425	78.6	64,036	4.2	264,687	17.2
Nonschool, total	1,871,373	1,067,107	57.0	288,154	12.7	566,112	30.3
City	1,157,922	759,751	65.6	112,294	9.7	285,877	24.7
County	441,541	211,221	47.8	99,433	22.5	130,887	29.6
Township	145,921	36,087	24.7	7,791	5.3	102,043	69.9
Special district	125,989	60,048	47.7	18,636	14.8	47,305	37.5

[1] Employees covered by Federal OASI and also by supplemental State or local plans counted only once, in latter category.

Source: Department of Commerce, Bureau of the Census; special study, *Retirement Coverage of State and Local Government Employees.*

No. 431.—SUMMARY OF FINANCES OF STATE-ADMINISTERED PUBLIC-EMPLOYEE RETIREMENT SYSTEMS: 1944 TO 1951

[In thousands of dollars]

ITEM	RECEIPTS					PAYMENTS				Assets, end of fiscal year
	Total	Em-ployee contri-butions	Government contributions		Earn-ings on invest-ments	Total	Bene-fits [1]	With-draw-als [1]	Other	
			State	Local						
1944	195,234	76,357	50,243	26,354	42,280	[2] 70,175	48,062	18,857	1,752	1,241,772
1945	220,095	89,370	63,656	21,945	45,122	75,352	52,464	20,962	1,856	1,390,349
1946	265,715	110,131	71,533	36,460	47,285	90,596	60,034	27,976	2,585	1,607,224
1947	317,051	144,805	96,105	33,282	47,900	105,320	70,560	31,579	3,181	1,789,848
1948	428,514	182,315	127,099	60,918	58,279	121,380	83,492	33,836	4,032	2,092,571
1949	580,975	221,943	142,802	74,335	62,095	141,501	95,017	39,614	6,870	2,436,980
1950	608,857	260,494	180,308	97,948	70,242	165,908	109,731	46,307	9,955	2,870,683
1951	723,863	319,591	211,363	118,329	83,581	398,519	130,003	61,135	8,381	3,441,064
General (State and local)	239,704	152,443	78,282	67,293	31,686	79,076	41,439	34,242	3,395	1,306,993
Educational:										
Teachers	315,820	127,372	100,722	43,108	44,617	108,449	83,948	21,139	4,362	1,842,709
School-nonteachers	5,716	1,961	803	2,465	487	2,082	1,421	545	116	21,716
School employees [3]	16,431	7,997	7,459		965	5,780	3,822	1,876	82	50,458
University and col-lege	7,574	2,730	3,722		1,132	2,099	1,563	424	112	31,477
General and teachers	30,046	11,281	15,020	745	3,000	5,277	3,048	2,034	145	122,629
Police	3,464	1,069	1,553	434	368	1,409	1,167	186	56	15,623
Firemen	514	108	273	91	47	210	195	6	9	2,019
Judicial	722	370	298		45	418	400	16	2	2,191
Other	13,903	5,296	3,239	4,193	1,244	2,719	1,950	667	102	45,319

[1] Amounts for withdrawals shown separately when available; otherwise included with benefit payments.
[2] Includes $867,500 not distributed according to object of payment.
[3] Teachers and nonteachers not reported separately.

Source: Department of Commerce, Bureau of the Census; annual reports, *Compendium of State Government Finances.*

No. 432.—Financial Transactions of State-Administered Public-Employee Retirement Systems, by States: 1951

[In thousands of dollars. Investment transactions are excluded]

STATE	RECEIPTS					PAYMENTS			
	Total	Employee contributions	Government contributions		Earnings on investments	Total	Benefits [1]	Withdrawals [1]	Other
			State	Local					
Total	722,863	310,591	211,362	118,329	83,581	206,519	139,003	61,135	8,381
Alabama	7,172	2,563	3,770	187	652	856	250	497	109
Arizona	2,913	1,843	233	677	160	584	213	345	26
Arkansas	3,953	1,541	2,076	....	336	971	651	280	40
California	105,646	47,395	35,691	13,127	9,433	31,986	22,490	7,401	2,095
Colorado	3,933	1,866	1,191	672	204	940	306	592	42
Connecticut	10,638	4,772	3,944	643	1,279	4,318	3,367	914	37
Delaware	18	9	9	....	....	61	61	....	....
Florida	11,967	7,816	2,891	619	641	3,611	2,157	1,388	66
Georgia	8,318	3,630	3,518	613	557	1,875	1,022	751	102
Idaho	2,819	1,099	1,087	525	108	620	223	379	18
Illinois	26,289	13,028	8,309	4,963	1,989	10,502	8,020	2,079	403
Indiana	12,997	4,894	4,913	1,331	1,859	6,364	5,589	696	79
Iowa	11,409	5,625	1,349	4,257	178	1,508	1,417	21	70
Kansas	2,332	1,381	801	....	150	705	251	422	32
Kentucky	3,281	1,261	1,630	....	400	839	515	272	52
Louisiana	16,945	5,819	4,268	5,457	1,401	2,212	1,168	956	88
Maine	2,764	1,691	1,516	273	284	1,603	1,221	336	46
Maryland	8,672	3,063	4,470	429	710	1,527	1,012	447	68
Massachusetts	17,904	9,176	6,218	14	2,496	9,799	8,044	1,507	248
Michigan	24,312	10,816	10,417	1,288	1,791	8,179	5,053	2,978	148
Minnesota	8,515	5,824	1,770	126	795	3,226	1,420	1,664	142
Mississippi	1,495	1,044	319	....	132	571	328	219	24
Missouri	3,910	1,856	61	1,795	198	603	265	288	50
Montana	3,682	2,095	493	880	214	1,494	881	510	103
Nebraska	1,319	1,133	19	71	96	488	151	305	32
Nevada	1,722	841	539	276	66	539	246	244	49
New Hampshire	3,404	1,359	1,017	818	210	679	447	208	24
New Jersey	37,634	13,458	12,676	4,628	6,872	11,369	8,631	2,599	139
New Mexico	746	345	274	64	63	757	570	158	29
New York	122,239	50,353	17,145	36,783	17,958	32,003	20,322	10,370	1,311
North Carolina	20,674	7,583	9,695	947	2,449	2,657	1,203	1,425	29
North Dakota	1,597	834	156	520	87	438	312	92	34
Ohio	48,172	18,638	3,414	18,879	7,241	16,676	11,248	5,060	368
Oklahoma	3,922	2,530	1,063	....	309	1,063	409	612	62
Oregon	11,335	5,040	2,240	3,284	771	3,037	983	1,936	118
Pennsylvania	54,634	22,539	13,889	7,381	10,825	17,542	12,025	5,214	303
Rhode Island	2,887	1,364	914	419	190	746	564	171	11
South Carolina	8,589	2,900	4,346	840	503	1,799	1,160	519	120
South Dakota	248	217	....	....	31	91	17	67	7
Tennessee	7,512	3,450	3,403	98	561	1,797	1,074	618	105
Texas	28,269	12,523	13,391	....	2,355	5,376	2,647	1,769	960
Utah	3,427	2,056	883	208	280	1,169	671	478	20
Vermont	1,566	665	764	....	137	352	224	115	13
Virginia	12,853	5,252	6,538	22	1,041	2,719	1,477	1,120	122
Washington	16,548	6,147	7,599	2,006	796	5,623	4,267	1,167	189
West Virginia	7,210	2,746	3,790	....	674	1,592	1,159	381	52
Wisconsin	21,649	8,097	6,420	3,045	4,087	4,855	3,146	1,534	175
Wyoming	823	424	223	164	12	178	126	31	21

[1] Amounts for withdrawals shown separately when available; otherwise included with benefit payments.

Source: Department of Commerce, Bureau of the Census; annual report, *Compendium of State Government Finances in 1951*.

No. 433.—SUMMARY OF STATE GOVERNMENT FINANCES: 1951

[Amounts, except per capita, in millions of dollars. N. e. c. signifies "not elsewhere classified." See also *Historical Statistics*, series P 188-211, and P 294-349]

ITEM	Amount	Per capita[1]	ITEM	Amount	Per capita[1]
Revenue and borrowing	16,868	$112.96	Expenditure—Continued		
			General expenditure—Con.		
Borrowing	1,284	8.54	Education—Con.		
			Intergovernmental expenditure	2,299	$15.06
Revenue	15,574	103.52	Other	287	1.91
General revenue	12,408	82.46	Highways	2,989	19.87
Taxes	9,964	56.38	Regular State highway facilities	2,134	14.18
Sales and gross receipts	5,270	35.03	State toll highway facilities	179	1.19
General	2,001	13.30	Intergovernmental expenditure	676	4.49
Motor fuels	1,710	11.37	Health and hospitals	1,139	7.57
Alcoholic beverages	469	3.12	State hospitals and institutions for the handicapped	864	5.74
Tobacco products	430	2.86	Other	276	1.53
Other	660	4.38	Nonhighway transportation	58	.39
Licenses	1,369	9.04	Housing and community redevelopment	13	.09
Motor vehicle	793	5.27	Natural resources	518	3.44
Corporations in general	211	1.40	Employment security administration	166	1.10
Alcoholic beverages	77	.51	General control	346	2.30
Other	279	1.86	Miscellaneous and unallocable	1,327	8.82
Individual income	805	5.35	Veterans' services	336	2.22
Corporation net income	687	4.57	Intergovernmental expenditure, n. e. c.	607	4.04
Property	346	2.30	State aid for unspecified purposes only	513	3.41
Death and gift	196	1.30	Interest	130	.86
Severance	222	1.47	Other	255	1.69
Other	50	.33	Liquor stores expenditure	782	5.20
Intergovernmental revenue	2,508	16.67	Insurance trust expenditure	1,293	8.59
From Federal Government	2,350	15.68	Employee retirement	200	1.33
Public welfare	1,185	7.88	Unemployment compensation	916	6.09
Education	329	2.18	Workmen's compensation	140	.93
Highways	430	2.86	Other	37	.24
Health and hospitals	103	.68			
Employment security administration	175	1.17	Expenditure by character and object:		
Other	127	.91	Direct expenditure	10,397	69.10
From local governments	149	.99	Current operation	4,863	32.32
Charges and miscellaneous	964	6.40	Capital outlay	2,506	16.65
Current charges	674	4.48	Construction	2,217	14.73
Education	372	2.47	Contract construction only	1,998	13.28
Commercial activities of institutions of higher education only	237	1.57	Purchase of land and existing structures	142	.94
Highways	53	.35	Equipment	148	.98
Toll facilities only	45	.30	Assistance and subsidies	1,604	10.06
Health and hospitals	93	.62	Interest on debt	130	.86
Other	156	1.04	Insurance benefits and repayments	1,292	8.59
Earnings on property and investments	196	1.30	Intergovernmental expenditure	4,702	31.25
Other	94	.62	Total personal services[2]	2,656	17.65
Liquor stores revenue	914	6.08			
Insurance trust revenue	2,254	14.98	Debt outstanding at end of fiscal year:		
Employee retirement	513	3.41	Total	6,228	41.36
Unemployment compensation	1,483	9.86			
Workmen's compensation	191	1.27	Long-term	5,974	39.70
Other	66	.44	Full faith and credit	4,688	31.16
			Nonguaranteed	1,286	8.55
Expenditure and debt redemption	15,445	102.66	Short-term	249	1.66
			Net long-term	4,944	32.86
Debt redemption	346	2.30	Full faith and credit only	3,761	25.00
			Cash and security holdings end of fiscal year	19,591	130.22
Expenditure	15,086	100.35			
General expenditure	13,022	86.56	Unemployment fund balance in U. S. Treasury	7,140	47.46
Current operation only	354	2.35	Cash and other deposits	3,319	22.06
Capital outlay only	215	1.43	Securities	9,132	60.70
Public welfare	2,390	15.90	Total by purpose:		
Aid to dependent children	1,397	9.28	Insurance trust	11,840	78.71
[Other]	520	3.46	Debt offsets	1,030	6.84
[ ]	51	.34	Other	7,021	46.67
[ ]	17	.11			
Other, including all public welfare administration, n. e. c.	240	1.60			
[Education]	165	1.10			
[ ]	3,722	24.74			
[Operation of commercial activities of higher education]	1,186	7.73			
Operation of commercial activities only	220	1.46			

[1] Computed on the basis of amounts rounded to the nearest thousand. Based on estimated population on July 1, 1950. [2] Included in items shown above.

Source: Department of Commerce, Bureau of the Census; annual report, *Compendium of State Government*

No. 434.—General Revenue and General Expenditure

[In thousands of dollars. See also

| STATE | GENERAL REVENUE | | | | | GENERAL EXPENDITURE | | |
| | Total | Taxes [1] | Intergovernmental revenue | | Charges and miscellaneous | Total | Public safety | Public welfare |
			From Federal government	From local governments				
1 Total	12,406,193	8,934,449	2,358,888	149,252	963,604	13,022,934	353,772	2,396,311
2 Alabama	188,354	116,921	51,239	3,240	16,954	200,406	3,945	29,998
3 Arizona	92,487	66,534	19,271	504	6,188	87,196	1,665	15,383
4 Arkansas	147,722	92,485	47,262	658	7,317	147,808	1,703	31,617
5 California	1,292,915	958,093	247,346	9,744	77,732	1,261,376	47,505	289,554
6 Colorado	158,825	100,357	41,752	848	15,868	149,676	3,854	53,046
7 Connecticut	163,585	123,931	22,065	2,749	14,840	169,203	7,764	33,226
8 Delaware	36,819	28,485	4,673	352	3,309	53,724	1,326	2,475
9 Florida	274,654	205,193	54,116	2,065	13,280	280,356	4,721	53,063
10 Georgia	239,343	152,579	67,901	2,423	16,440	216,970	3,773	43,678
11 Idaho	58,587	34,121	16,034	696	7,736	60,781	1,290	10,225
12 Illinois	530,388	419,249	91,613	980	18,546	587,622	24,442	132,284
13 Indiana	316,964	238,803	44,856	3,549	29,756	272,694	8,386	32,701
14 Iowa	232,011	162,409	43,402	9,454	16,746	247,109	5,212	38,607
15 Kansas	175,819	122,856	34,984	1,218	16,761	170,824	5,073	30,351
16 Kentucky	182,421	122,911	48,314	152	11,044	183,477	5,650	30,042
17 Louisiana	384,850	262,069	79,933	1,732	41,116	361,732	4,539	98,840
18 Maine	66,919	43,160	14,734	3,270	5,755	69,360	2,324	15,513
19 Maryland	185,994	144,417	20,823	2,308	18,446	222,736	8,333	14,735
20 Massachusetts	409,988	294,340	84,890	12,061	18,697	447,775	12,539	100,847
21 Michigan	604,320	452,749	86,488	7,138	57,945	632,018	17,029	94,953
22 Minnesota	309,318	215,581	49,927	2,961	40,849	289,311	9,411	38,203
23 Mississippi	156,496	101,105	41,498	2,704	11,189	147,257	2,836	20,150
24 Missouri	272,120	180,511	80,428	225	10,956	262,876	5,742	97,985
25 Montana	65,206	34,771	20,004	1,566	8,863	67,516	1,440	13,104
26 Nebraska	91,066	52,556	24,005	4,038	10,465	89,664	2,871	19,693
27 Nevada	26,121	13,040	7,617	572	4,892	24,641	639	2,234
28 New Hampshire	36,877	22,528	8,234	1,634	4,481	40,835	1,360	7,562
29 New Jersey	227,660	167,768	33,126	11,939	14,832	263,912	11,341	26,577
30 New Mexico	101,791	59,648	22,817	298	19,028	87,704	1,653	10,808
31 New York	1,118,450	915,144	145,181	3,628	54,497	1,158,067	37,065	217,128
32 North Carolina	342,063	255,667	54,632	2,579	29,185	407,770	7,696	26,270
33 North Dakota	79,113	42,352	13,794	1,632	21,335	72,759	1,425	8,695
34 Ohio	537,692	418,745	84,434	6,843	27,670	543,062	12,844	104,407
35 Oklahoma	269,230	176,136	69,114	591	23,389	284,778	5,790	77,805
36 Oregon	157,094	109,718	27,372	5,671	14,333	167,763	4,449	30,420
37 Pennsylvania	660,733	496,106	103,146	10,306	49,175	1,024,039	24,760	137,510
38 Rhode Island	59,184	42,998	11,614	1,132	3,440	64,201	1,708	14,645
39 South Carolina	151,846	103,790	32,815	858	14,383	150,987	3,096	18,575
40 South Dakota	68,761	41,954	15,463	1,661	9,683	55,229	1,251	9,104
41 Tennessee	236,566	165,458	56,232	4,361	10,515	232,660	4,649	43,373
42 Texas	559,129	352,224	138,404	5,785	62,716	553,126	9,789	109,189
43 Utah	74,765	49,948	17,324	277	7,216	72,856	3,004	11,746
44 Vermont	30,021	22,151	5,429	606	1,835	28,648	1,387	4,693
45 Virginia	225,854	162,049	29,093	1,741	32,971	230,222	9,817	12,892
46 Washington	311,582	226,213	59,269	2,955	23,145	404,721	4,855	107,293
47 West Virginia	142,812	107,053	26,842	474	8,443	160,437	3,864	25,940
48 Wisconsin	311,069	233,460	46,275	6,915	24,439	292,247	6,585	39,460
49 Wyoming	40,589	22,126	13,103	157	5,203	42,903	1,342	3,692

[1] See also table 433.

OF STATE GOVERNMENTS, BY STATES: 1951

Historical Statistics, series P 192–211]

	GENERAL EXPENDITURE—continued											
Education				Health and hospitals							Total inter-govern-mental expend-iture	
Total[9]	State institu-tions of higher educa-tion	Inter-govern-mental	High-ways	State hospitals and institu-tions for the handi-capped	Other	Natural re-sources	General control	Veter-ans' services	Interest	All other		
3,728,122	1,105,997	2,304,552	2,905,731	862,665	275,534	517,552	346,217	234,732	129,986	1,100,054	4,701,654	1
81,286	21,990	99,025	42,404	7,000	5,059	7,544	4,767	326	2,144	11,831	116,265	2
32,091	11,476	13,452	20,660	2,906	1,094	2,955	2,749	11	122	14,647	27,639	3
48,364	15,071	30,276	34,798	6,131	3,953	5,701	3,213	23	4,243	6,232	43,780	4
304,622	87,934	204,111	205,657	51,067	27,064	108,262	42,153	6,314	7,644	113,454	702,789	5
31,655	19,958	11,346	35,721	10,037	2,014	5,336	3,428	98	405	4,089	77,575	6
34,634	14,874	13,562	32,566	20,982	3,292	4,519	5,005	166	2,190	12,867	22,456	7
24,746	3,596	6,929	28,329	3,239	1,228	1,005	1,490	206	2,159	1,426	10,379	8
95,416	26,892	83,955	79,175	12,067	7,229	17,696	7,538	225	622	12,350	76,330	9
63,824	21,440	55,262	47,270	10,877	9,880	5,160	4,479	606	247	5,047	71,044	10
16,499	8,448	5,876	18,637	3,252	1,456	5,155	1,306	29	55	2,986	9,646	11
164,729	62,623	75,208	112,380	53,646	14,873	16,476	15,555	4,905	8,807	26,516	154,471	12
165,361	46,641	87,639	66,978	20,540	4,296	5,750	7,233	516	538	10,075	123,920	13
38,208	26,514	24,204	77,172	13,344	2,399	11,972	4,351	6,450	448	31,632	51,921	14
56,792	27,370	38,098	44,480	12,807	2,342	5,415	4,321	280	202	12,146	71,612	15
27,602	12,535	31,375	62,098	7,645	3,864	9,229	7,184	53	293	5,755	37,481	16
59,692	32,504	67,160	55,930	25,764	2,919	12,960	7,126	1,589	8,085	34,327	100,896	17
15,608	4,390	6,062	33,099	4,092	1,525	5,031	1,986	1	819	3,102	9,084	18
62,131	16,477	31,388	51,610	21,721	6,995	5,373	7,320	55	2,551	21,449	84,507	19
19,435	10,435	36,047	90,943	45,775	5,551	6,847	14,538	616	4,482	117,397	201,390	20
8,725	77,891	155,565	111,449	20,355	21,424	15,552	11,163	1,379	3,765	76,215	299,723	21
68,774	42,605	48,725	61,368	36,125	3,230	12,720	4,632	18,458	2,568	17,742	107,953	22
58,551	14,557	31,613	31,545	5,660	9,063	7,473	3,116	132	2,272	12,329	58,251	23
71,296	34,187	64,046	39,375	12,536	3,350	7,316	7,344	276	1,215	5,580	59,651	24
17,028	7,055	9,701	19,550	4,753	930	5,635	1,795	149	406	2,287	16,998	25
17,338	11,891	4,631	31,758	7,657	1,165	4,276	1,440	46	44	3,399	34,989	26
1,988	1,958	2,588	9,231	322	280	4,664	759	8	23	1,606	3,734	27
4,679	1,694	947	11,399	4,177	864	3,063	1,623	31	308	3,830	2,841	28
45,490	17,053	27,051	112,954	17,921	6,395	6,187	11,228	314	2,540	19,384	65,781	29
35,943	12,121	26,191	21,308	2,154	1,470	3,395	3,234	60	762	3,922	27,712	30
391,737	35,745	248,427	155,091	140,434	32,076	35,422	45,753	7,063	23,545	161,878	605,579	31
171,177	96,541	92,561	130,161	17,463	5,545	10,306	5,602	262	5,818	15,340	68,562	32
14,669	6,929	6,765	18,536	3,070	761	3,226	1,655	2,630	1,162	15,366	11,266	33
148,516	47,670	98,851	145,945	37,353	5,565	9,937	13,761	1,307	3,570	56,004	348,066	34
27,488	14,495	42,737	62,498	17,969	4,092	9,257	5,134	185	2,116	5,783	72,827	35
29,317	16,417	24,294	45,580	7,705	1,584	15,252	6,967	344	872	7,989	29,696	36
179,684	31,680	122,308	264,403	76,684	19,242	32,012	20,416	222,063	18,213	46,942	163,463	37
56,229	6,509	3,589	9,115	6,137	1,418	982	3,152	15	1,322	15,326	11,908	38
16,366	16,396	34,947	36,907	4,922	3,362	5,334	3,069	254	2,225	12,092	55,616	39
3,565	3,548	17,636	676	2,796	1,058	2,901	754	5,972	6,189		40	
41,591	25,862	57,666	60,306	7,252	7,091	7,039	4,160	167	1,806	15,024	52,542	41
49,562	170,148	122,307	21,049	6,573	13,794	10,037	269	1,444	11,322	187,906	42	
14,055	15,055	14,817	14,189	2,152	1,176	3,346	2,109	23	17	3,074	21,056	43
1,419	2,987	9,278	1,951	998	1,692	1,474	31	80	1,380	5,903	44	
23,062	44,356	65,506	23,067	5,435	5,963	7,380	214	1,091	15,959	72,697	45	
110,900	102,657	72,568	64,611	9,310	5,969	15,490	6,673	28,716	2,951	18,919	119,373	46
24,739	41,307	41,987	7,634	2,250	4,699	5,398	1	1,664	6,638	43,797	47	
48,705	29,338	64,906	11,343	6,261	14,890	6,521	154	120	76,223	174,718	48	
52,255	5,149	7,973	12,631	1,229	584	2,252	970		61	3,401	14,785	49

[9] Includes amounts for items not shown separately.

Source: Department of Commerce, Bureau of the Census; annual report, *Compendium of State Government Finances in 1951*.

No. 485.—STATE TAX COLLECTIONS, BY TYPE OF TAX, BY STATES: 1952

[In thousands of dollars. Includes local shares of State-imposed taxes. Preliminary data]

STATE	Total [1]	SALES AND GROSS RECEIPTS					Motor vehicle and opera- tors li- censes	Indi- vidual income	Corpo- ration net in- come [3]	Prop- erty
		Total [1]	General sales or gross receipts	Motor vehicle fuels	Alco- holic bev- erages	To- bacco prod- ucts				
Number of States using tax	48	48	31	48	48	41	48	31	33	45
Total	9,537,556	5,729,517	2,229,295	1,670,856	441,559	448,966	923,558	[3] 905,472	[5] 830,235	369,502
Alabama	131,670	88,989	37,165	36,929	1,511	7,746	7,887	[3] 16,258	[3] 1,093	8,237
Arizona	68,997	42,972	22,246	13,454	2,291	2,040	4,265	[3] 11,172	(3)	8,770
Arkansas	99,569	69,908	27,569	26,559	6,059	6,625	9,803	4,149	8,661	259
California	1,063,915	657,349	416,494	160,301	19,156		70,051	91,176	119,396	71,612
Colorado	106,302	63,173	30,986	24,350	3,802		7,529	14,053	6,121	7,441
Connecticut	132,118	85,919	35,164	21,466	5,595	8,443	12,084		22,189	468
Delaware	24,071	9,150	[4] 2	5,032	971	1,085	1,467	4,607		985
Florida	226,784	174,212	54,115	63,938	26,006	4,075	27,546			5,068
Georgia	226,124	170,007	93,654	51,639	10,267	8,890	6,242	15,856	23,524	8,064
Idaho	38,268	16,636		11,292	817	1,651	4,265	6,752	4,064	2,439
Illinois	455,172	382,756	191,934	82,435	22,098	26,919	48,984			442
Indiana	258,051	205,882	126,746	46,840	12,788	13,319	26,005			12,843
Iowa	168,244	104,489	59,289	31,620	3,094	5,022	33,842	19,703	2,884	127
Kansas	132,956	88,368	44,664	29,250	5,227	5,317	16,750	10,941	3,790	7,319
Kentucky	129,010	71,460		41,453	9,523	5,533	9,358	18,112	10,853	10,650
Louisiana	283,158	161,847	54,288	50,215	16,578	18,780	8,817	[3] 22,766	(3)	12,951
Maine	56,238	37,483	11,212	14,114	2,071	5,325	7,024			6,248
Maryland	153,347	87,109	29,246	28,135	6,754		16,849	22,240	14,627	2,979
Massachusetts	300,038	106,035		37,231	21,204	26,743	17,937	59,371	[3] 29,114	169
Michigan	502,554	372,457	245,660	78,951	6,861	24,148	51,338		21,696	28,105
Minnesota	232,648	86,551		38,556	12,897	11,383	26,610	45,761	12,403	
Mississippi	109,826	79,123	30,864	32,450	4,272	6,993	3,794	5,226	10,042	1,339
Missouri	184,957	119,244	83,287	22,872	5,395		20,563	[3] 25,436	(3)	6,738
Montana	37,332	17,821		10,999	1,653	2,761	2,812	5,325	2,284	3,915
Nebraska	56,178	30,556		22,723	2,805	3,987	3,322			19,308
Nevada	14,480	8,161		4,861	612	863	2,148			2,330
New Hampshire	25,373	14,081		6,768	1,022	3,069	4,678	1,228		1,371
New Jersey	178,203	99,979	22,618	39,584	15,894	19,099	45,635			3,004
New Mexico	64,699	43,924		15,358	1,438	2,555	6,323	[3] 3,504	(3)	3,660
New York	1,023,582	322,162		102,494	46,252	59,769	86,087	296,989	218,129	2,027
North Carolina	278,482	151,111	51,821	69,648	10,911		21,650	36,468	42,564	5,356
North Dakota	44,961	27,046	12,290	7,454	2,923	3,110	7,127	4,091	1,391	3,687
Ohio	451,026	345,211	165,246	87,024	31,982	19,816	58,353			18,710
Oklahoma	187,756	111,182	40,990	42,514	5,932	10,767	23,689	9,695	8,850	
Oregon	128,340	34,943		29,373	1,308		18,776	42,825	22,071	19
Pennsylvania	537,509	238,352		116,308	43,220	44,265	60,790		127,854	1,582
Rhode Island	53,225	36,543	12,526	6,889	1,836	3,344	5,120		[4] 7,983	
South Carolina	147,046	104,664	37,581	36,178	13,419	5,761	5,818	12,088	17,520	1,659
South Dakota	38,912	32,672	16,137	9,516	2,410	1,717	2,634		161	845
Tennessee	179,468	127,777	50,022	49,600	8,047	13,221	13,882	3,608	16,791	[4] 49
Texas	413,669	188,330		95,684	15,800	33,292	35,220			33,843
Utah	54,380	31,309	16,890	10,859	787	916	3,227	7,303	3,227	5,886
Vermont	28,497	11,318		5,101	2,743	1,894	4,940	7,042	2,912	349
Virginia	166,559	74,805		49,101	8,018		15,467	24,595	22,425	9,512
Washington	249,085	208,191	135,230	43,954	1,407	10,343	13,389			15,231
West Virginia	122,829	104,522	65,535	19,006	4,138	5,748	11,593			220
Wisconsin	243,753	69,214		35,323	11,139	10,418	28,998	57,132	58,029	16,261
Wyoming	24,155	14,554	7,804	5,455	526	214	2,861			4,982

[1] Includes amounts for types of tax not shown separately.
[3] Includes unincorporated businesses.
[3] Combined corporation and individual income taxes as reported by 5 States (Alabama, Arizona, Louisiana, Missouri, and New Mexico) tabulated with individual income taxes. Amount shown as corporation tax for Alabama represents only taxes on financial institutions.
[4] Back taxes only; not counted with "number of States using tax."
[5] Excludes amounts for corporation excise taxes and surtaxes measured in part by net income and in part by corporate excess.
[6] Includes corporate excess tax.

Source: Department of Commerce, Bureau of the Census; annual report, *State Tax Collections in 1952.*

No. 436.—Debt of State Governments Outstanding at End of Fiscal Year, by States: 1952

STATE	Total debt	LONG-TERM DEBT			Short-term debt	Offsets to long-term debt	Net long-term debt	PER CAPITA DEBT [1]	
		Total	Full faith and credit	Non-guaranteed				Total	Net long-term
Total	7,049,206	6,764,394	4,939,329	1,825,965	284,914	1,131,397	5,624,997	$46.14	$36.87
Alabama	72,806	72,806	61,855	10,841		19,929	52,778	23.90	17.35
Arizona	3,281	3,281	663	2,568		402	2,829	4.01	3.51
Arkansas	130,382	130,382	122,001	8,381		8,020	122,362	66.36	64.06
California	522,304	522,304	492,474	29,830		237,531	284,773	47.38	25.82
Colorado	16,492	16,492		16,492		909	15,583	11.99	11.32
Connecticut	252,735	92,450	92,450		150,265	3,535	78,624	114.19	38.53
Delaware	92,962	90,863	40,637	50,626	2,100		90,863	282.56	276.18
Florida	71,093	71,093		71,093		6,574	64,519	24.01	21.79
Georgia	20,699	20,699		20,699		615	20,084	5.94	5.76
Idaho	1,646	1,646		1,646		31	1,615	2.79	2.74
Illinois	382,154	382,154	363,348	18,806		17,124	365,030	43.23	41.30
Indiana	18,133	18,133		18,133	80	4,383	13,750	4.51	3.41
Iowa	32,873	32,878	29,750	3,128			32,878	12.82	12.82
Kansas	6,600	6,600	3,250	2,350		1,165	4,435	3.67	2.77
Kentucky	11,061	11,061		11,061		787	10,274	3.79	3.52
Louisiana	215,699	215,699	174,816	40,722		14,647	200,892	78.18	72.87
Maine	26,609	26,609	5,902	20,707		367	26,242	29.83	29.42
Maryland	205,458	205,458	91,531	113,927		42,482	162,976	54.17	65.77
Massachusetts	402,007	396,692	365,882	30,800	5,315	7,924	388,768	54.95	52.16
Michigan	351,049	351,049	234,507	116,542		7,181	343,868	53.64	52.54
Minnesota	120,525	120,525	118,905	1,620		9,206	111,319	40.26	37.18
Mississippi	74,361	74,361	4,761	69,590		6,771	67,590	32.92	30.96
Missouri	26,092	26,092	22,000	4,092		7,852	18,240	6.45	4.51
Montana	44,964	44,964	5,611	39,123		5,772	39,192	76.29	68.40
Nebraska	826	826		826			826	.61	.61
Nevada	885	885	885			66	819	5.18	4.79
New Hampshire	26,277	20,177	19,075	1,102	6,100	2,209	17,968	49.21	33.85
New Jersey	339,798	339,798	94,576	245,217		3,000	336,798	68.31	67.71
New Mexico	29,543	29,543	19,175	10,368		3,035	26,508	14.96	37.66
New York	1,012,784	952,784	922,685	30,719	60,000	477,128	475,616	67.40	31.65
North Carolina	274,357	274,357	273,444	913		57,693	216,664	66.35	52.40
North Dakota	34,634	34,634	33,305	1,330		22,394	12,240	57.25	20.23
Ohio	165,186	165,186	162,570	2,616		3,328	161,858	20.49	20.07
Oklahoma	135,735	135,735	43,327	92,408		15,167	120,568	59.90	53.21
Oregon	116,564	116,564	116,427	137		33,085	82,479	74.82	53.56
Pennsylvania	895,055	895,055	483,641	411,414		28,928	866,127	84.77	82.03
Rhode Island	51,837	51,837	50,242	1,596		5,636	46,201	65.37	58.26
South Carolina	125,960	125,960	78,495	47,464		9,515	116,444	59.27	54.80
South Dakota	21,123	21,122	20,815	308		15,646	5,477	22.66	8.47
Tennessee	100,262	100,262	97,364	2,898		9,955	90,307	30.22	27.22
Texas	94,005	94,005	55,957	38,048		7,566	86,439	11.76	10.82
Utah	1,424	1,424	470	954		517	907	2.01	1.28
Vermont	4,999	4,999	4,999				4,999	13.40	13.40
Virginia	37,519	37,519	12,009	25,510		10,017	27,502	11.08	8.12
Washington	235,865	175,682	142,649	33,033	60,183	11,331	164,551	97.26	67.77
West Virginia	345,551	345,551	77,927	167,624		11,524	234,027	123.08	117.31
Wisconsin	5,027	5,027		5,027			5,027	1.45	1.45
Wyoming	4,457	4,457	270	4,187		46	4,411	15.11	14.96

[1] Based on estimated total population of 48 States on July 1, 1951, excluding armed forces overseas (152,572,000).

Source: Department of Commerce, Bureau of the Census; annual report, *Governmental Debt in 1952*.

No. 437.—STATE UNEMPLOYMENT-COMPENSATION FUND FINANCES: 1945 TO 1951

[In thousands of dollars]

ITEM	1945	1946	1947	1948	1949	1950	1951
Total receipts	1,364,172	1,161,817	1,098,787	1,202,947	1,129,567	1,176,412	1,483,395
Contributions from general funds (unemployment compensation tax)	1,253,781	1,033,591	969,227	1,059,413	972,929	1,028,033	1,336,678
Interest	110,391	128,226	129,560	143,534	156,638	148,379	146,717
Benefit payments	70,372	964,661	880,360	755,646	1,114,739	1,844,663	916,139
Assets, end of fiscal year	6,457,321	6,664,593	6,885,449	7,292,921	7,166,900	6,595,621	7,160,797

Source: Department of Commerce, Bureau of the Census; annual reports, *Compendium of State Government Finances.*

No. 438.—INCOME AND EXPENSE STATEMENT OF THE 16 STATE-OPERATED ALCOHOLIC-BEVERAGE MONOPOLY SYSTEMS, BY STATES: 1952

[In thousands of dollars]

STATE	Net sales of goods	Cost of goods sold	Gross profit on sales	Operating expense	Net operating revenue	Other income	Other expense	Net income
Total	921,591	690,567	231,024	52,425	178,599	653	63	179,189
Alabama	40,608	27,391	13,217	1,962	11,255	70		11,325
Idaho	11,888	8,180	3,708	632	3,076			3,076
Iowa	39,074	28,293	10,781	2,781	8,000	45		8,045
Maine	19,449	13,928	5,521	1,179	4,342			4,342
Michigan	139,640	106,801	32,839	3,780	29,059	106		29,165
Montana	16,159	12,032	4,127	1,253	2,874	16		2,890
New Hampshire	16,984	12,532	4,452	865	3,587			3,587
Ohio	160,546	134,973	25,573	6,299	19,274	75		19,349
Oregon	41,533	28,701	12,832	2,292	10,540		49	10,491
Pennsylvania	203,980	147,559	56,421	18,053	38,368	210		38,578
Utah	13,235	8,465	4,770	851	3,919			3,919
Vermont	6,587	5,856	731	345	386	2		388
Virginia	100,978	78,686	22,292	5,075	17,217			17,217
Washington	63,320	42,534	20,786	3,218	17,568	66	14	17,620
West Virginia	41,268	29,083	12,185	3,653	8,532	63		8,595
Wyoming	6,342	5,553	789	187	602			602

Source: Department of Commerce, Bureau of the Census; annual report, *Compendium of State Government Finances in 1951.*

No. 439.—NATIONAL SUMMARY OF CITY FINANCES: 1951

[Amounts in millions. The 481 cities having more than 25,000 inhabitants in 1950]

ITEM	Amount	Per capita	ITEM	Amount	Per capita
Revenue and borrowing, total	$7,116	$114.85	Expenditures—Continued By purpose: General expenditure	$4,797	$77.43
Borrowing, total	1,065	17.20	Police	495	7.99
General	792	12.79	Fire	378	6.10
Utility	273	4.41	Highways	542	8.74
Revenue, total	6,050	97.66	Sanitation	517	8.34
General revenue, total	4,513	77.06	Public assistance	336	5.42
Taxes, total	3,187	51.43	Other public welfare	85	1.38
Property	2,416	39.00	Education	800	12.92
Sales and gross receipts	466	7.52	Libraries	66	1.07
Licenses and other	304	4.91	Health and hospitals	395	6.37
Intergovernmental revenue, total	971	15.67	Own hospitals	272	4.38
From State governments only	872	14.07	Other	123	1.99
Charges and miscellaneous	656	10.58	Recreation	231	3.73
Current charges	376	6.07	General control	246	3.97
Special assessments	69	1.11	General public buildings	60	.97
Other and unallocable	211	3.40	Interest on general debt	167	2.70
Utility revenue, total	1,054	17.01	Other and unallocable	478	7.72
Water system	443	7.15	Utility expenditure	1,222	19.73
Electric power system	250	4.03	Water system	509	8.21
Gas supply system	38	.61	Electric system	297	4.80
Transit system	319	5.15	Gas supply system	28	.45
Liquor stores	5	.07	Transit system	385	6.21
Insurance trust revenue	184	2.97	Liquor stores	3	.05
Employee-retirement	179	2.88	Insurance trust expenditure	208	3.36
Unemployment compensation	5	.08	Employee retirement	206	3.32
			Unemployment compensation	2	.04
Expenditure and debt redemption, total	6,767	109.23	Debt outstanding at end of fiscal year, total	9,975	161.01
Debt redemption, total	540	8.71	Long-term: Total	9,628	155.41
General	441	7.12	Full faith and credit	8,123	131.12
Utility	99	1.59	Nonguaranteed	1,506	24.29
Expenditure, total	6,227	100.51	Net long-term	8,149	131.64
By character and object:			Short-term	347	5.60
Current operation	3,928	63.40			
Capital outlay, total	1,412	22.80	Long-term debt issued, total	1,076	17.37
Construction	1,167	18.84			
Contract construction only	1,053	17.00	Original issues	1,020	16.46
Land and existing structures	119	1.92	Refunding issues	57	.91
Equipment	126	2.03	Long-term retired, total	527	8.50
Intergovernmental expenditure	44	.71	Redeemed	454	7.33
Assistance and subsidies	357	5.76	Refunded	73	1.18
Interest on debt	278	4.48			
Insurance trust benefits and withdrawals	208	3.36			
Total personal services [1]	2,967	47.83			

[1] Included in items shown above.

Source: Department of Commerce, Bureau of the Census; annual report, *Compendium of City Government Finances in 1951*.

No. 440.—FINANCES OF CITY OPERATED UTILITIES, BY TYPE OF UTILITY: 1951

[Dollar amounts in thousands]

ITEM	All utilities [1]	Water supply systems	Electric systems	Gas supply systems	Transit systems
Number	502			24	17
Utility revenue [2]	$1,053,650			$37,664	$319,000
Utility expenditure, total [3]	1,222,065	508,533	137,166	27,946	364,928
Current operation [3]	677,989	217,212	180,184	20,221	300,010
Capital outlay	433,355			7,321	40,061
Interest paid on utility debt	110,722			404	44,867
Debt outstanding	3,614,703	1,853,412		15,840	1,326,061
Utility services charged to parent city	18,187			441	

[1] Includes 1 liquor store system with amounts as follows (in thousands): revenue, $4,608; expenditure (all current operation), $3,270.

[2] Net of receipts from utility services charged to parent city.

[3] Gross current operation expenditure minus any utility services charged to parent city.

Source: Department of Commerce, Bureau of the Census; annual report, *Compendium of City Government Finances in 1951*.

No. 441.—GENERAL REVENUE AND GENERAL EXPENDITURE

[In thousands

		GENERAL REVENUE						GENERAL EXPENDITURES	
POPULATION GROUP AND CITY	Total	Taxes			Inter-govern-mental revenue	Charges and miscel-laneous	Total	Total, less capital outlay
		Total taxes	Prop-erty	Other city taxes				
1	Total	4,812,541	3,186,514	2,416,346	770,168	970,635	655,692	4,796,964	3,813,024
2	Over 1,000,000, total	1,858,131	1,231,099	846,426	384,673	408,400	218,632	1,830,901	1,431,684
3	New York	1,280,964	843,099	580,285	262,814	314,885	131,980	1,251,725	986,178
4	Chicago	164,642	122,551	79,101	43,450	33,116	8,975	170,087	136,067
5	Philadelphia	145,472	106,918	56,884	50,034	6,292	32,262	167,671	121,646
6	Los Angeles	111,490	69,119	44,091	25,028	20,254	22,117	111,269	82,056
7	Detroit	146,563	89,412	86,065	3,347	33,853	23,298	129,549	105,137
8	500,000 to 1,000,000, total	846,962	561,365	439,244	122,121	191,779	93,838	830,139	674,268
9	Baltimore	105,668	59,883	51,502	8,381	37,260	9,525	119,847	89,804
10	Cleveland	57,046	33,636	31,846	1,790	14,677	8,733	55,704	45,357
11	St. Louis	49,909	40,959	23,509	17,450	2,656	6,294	44,935	40,639
12	Washington, D. C.	126,227	103,171	46,602	56,569	16,299	6,757	109,223	95,102
13	Boston	149,150	100,514	97,152	3,362	39,384	9,261	146,361	132,367
14	San Francisco	97,916	57,984	50,125	7,859	31,795	8,137	91,370	68,124
15	Pittsburgh	30,169	26,276	21,521	4,755	2,171	1,722	34,815	27,746
16	Milwaukee	44,434	24,250	20,726	3,524	14,572	5,612	45,455	34,178
17	Houston	25,586	20,554	18,332	2,222	873	4,159	30,088	18,731
18	Buffalo	54,804	31,792	29,948	1,844	16,585	6,427	51,009	44,594
19	New Orleans	35,612	20,583	10,228	10,355	6,083	8,946	37,789	27,534
20	Minneapolis	31,735	24,085	22,165	1,920	2,015	5,635	26,084	21,374
21	Cincinnati	37,717	17,678	15,588	2,090	7,409	12,630	36,669	28,708
22	250,000 to 500,000, total	537,528	332,762	249,468	83,294	86,373	118,693	523,078	406,369
23	Seattle	26,366	14,867	9,019	5,848	5,367	6,132	23,508	16,913
24	Kansas City, Mo	20,378	16,662	9,488	7,174	1,288	2,428	23,837	15,819
25	Newark	55,984	48,911	41,190	7,721	4,509	2,564	49,607	46,326
26	Dallas	21,230	15,548	12,556	2,992	1,191	4,491	26,688	16,139
27	Indianapolis	17,227	12,678	12,302	376	2,464	2,085	17,733	14,548
28	Denver	43,137	19,964	13,045	6,919	17,482	5,691	44,195	36,764
29	San Antonio	12,095	9,048	8,093	955	526	2,521	15,477	9,492
30	Memphis	22,958	11,807	9,005	2,802	7,077	4,074	27,982	20,295
31	Oakland	21,490	14,139	9,958	4,181	3,126	4,225	20,698	16,402
32	Columbus	14,054	8,244	3,929	4,315	3,392	2,418	14,660	10,792
33	Portland, Oreg	19,454	13,064	9,176	3,888	1,798	4,592	20,856	13,675
34	Louisville	23,034	14,487	7,837	6,650	650	7,897	22,247	18,720
35	San Diego	17,414	9,847	6,112	3,735	3,906	3,661	16,403	11,325
36	Rochester	34,215	19,130	18,024	1,106	10,268	4,817	33,409	29,453
37	Atlanta	17,899	12,978	9,168	3,810	944	3,977	20,285	16,460
38	Birmingham	11,468	6,923	3,336	3,587	2,523	2,012	11,395	7,785
39	St. Paul	24,896	17,225	15,348	1,877	4,438	3,233	23,125	20,769
40	Toledo	18,380	10,776	2,611	8,165	3,635	3,969	17,713	13,486
41	Jersey City	35,501	30,947	28,292	2,655	1,520	3,034	34,721	32,766
42	Fort Worth	16,193	7,533	6,575	958	2,254	6,405	16,390	9,493
43	Akron	15,052	6,396	5,933	463	4,620	4,036	13,002	10,931
44	Omaha	8,868	6,736	4,822	1,914	929	1,203	9,386	5,794
45	Long Beach	40,545	4,852	3,649	1,203	2,466	33,227	19,761	12,222
46	100,000 to 250,000, total	596,025	403,690	336,468	67,222	116,024	76,311	613,086	491,783
47	50,000 to 100,000, total	516,904	351,498	292,235	59,263	87,878	77,528	522,899	427,109
48	25,000 to 50,000, total	456,971	306,100	252,505	53,595	80,181	70,690	476,861	387,421

OF CITIES HAVING MORE THAN 25,000 INHABITANTS: 1951

of dollars]

Police	Fire	High- ways	Sani- tation	Public wel- fare	Edu- cation	Li- braries	Health and hos- pitals	Recrea- tion	General control	General public build- ings	Interest on general debt	Other	
625,204	377,923	541,585	514,942	421,108	600,366	66,305	394,941	221,027	246,243	60,282	166,905	677,905	1
198,580	201,961	164,375	171,680	232,543	287,459	17,745	168,686	70,517	84,229	20,162	84,628	229,604	2
63,047	32,080	89,229	93,421	199,749	285,104	8,647	124,083	30,551	51,244	11,908	60,282	147,183	3
22,158	14,529	20,218	10,243	18,089	....	4,090	11,627	1,247	9,357	2,222	2,994	23,806	4
22,383	24,371	18,866	5,274	88	2,355	1,908	12,154	9,571	12,785	2,068	14,487	37,480	5
27,383	13,925	32,215	16,054	....	8,468	2,677	4,511	9,688	6,238	1,655	2,864	14,730	6
25,385	12,704	33,785	20,676	8,468	....	483	13,718	10,360	6,604	2,200	6,231	16,298	7
93,673	66,076	89,340	97,123	78,435	125,894	12,812	87,899	44,823	45,123	11,317	21,254	89,684	8
8,637	13,494	9,386	11,587	36,907	....	1,896	6,709	3,666	4,788	3,307	4,308	8,339	9
8,483	6,637	6,616	10,343	3,360	....	....	7,180	4,048	2,672	464	2,637	4,447	10
5,653	4,159	8,393	3,646	515	71	901	10,977	3,754	2,734	373	746	4,806	11
32,640	4,300	7,280	7,902	7,393	27,732	1,371	20,606	4,280	5,706	1,220	11	11,097	12
13,559	10,604	9,917	6,630	29,691	25,254	2,931	16,780	4,630	6,894	1,093	4,397	12,451	13
3,436	2,735	8,789	11,612	21,924	....	1,048	7,815	7,611	6,514	1,250	1,804	7,711	14
5,531	4,365	6,336	5,506	82	....	1,372	2,547	3,039	2,380	515	1,024	2,150	15
6,521	4,378	6,306	9,366	5	2,250	1,366	1,680	2,437	2,383	537	178	2,854	16
5,673	3,160	6,322	6,468	337	....	285	2,506	1,422	1,221	150	1,707	1,808	17
5,204	3,763	6,078	4,627	15	20,289	8	174	2,965	1,849	1,028	1,225	4,146	18
3,511	3,395	6,386	6,340	356	505	311	778	1,798	3,386	667	1,872	6,222	19
3,813	3,085	6,703	2,221	1,308	1,645	1,323	3,636	3,014	1,468	412	1,023	1,782	20
2,907	3,160	3,886	....	....	7,201	....	5,802	2,160	1,867	287	1,825	1,681	21
57,403	30,191	69,284	63,079	34,351	78,039	16,387	40,606	34,896	25,743	8,533	18,382	44,119	22
8,223	4,615	6,615	2,392	....	14	1,008	1,486	2,368	1,805	1,436	820	1,100	23
5,015	3,660	6,003	1,903	42	....	....	3,353	3,061	1,608	228	848	2,632	24
5,130	4,130	1,583	8,635	2,702	17,504	1,841	4,723	1,232	1,787	1,732	1,752	963	25
3,384	3,666	6,064	7,733	172	....	262	2,265	1,554	1,071	184	382	1,996	26
3,083	2,392	3,229	2,421	....	....	....	2,753	1,141	445	87	342	1,290	27
2,336	3,402	5,364	2,478	16,906	....	613	3,297	3,717	3,314	235	360	2,178	28
3,463	3,670	3,314	3,614	....	....	276	1,405	795	636	20	729	1,879	29
3,783	3,283	3,321	3,782	124	8,706	334	3,009	1,147	677	14	712	1,643	30
3,453	3,615	3,715	1,931	6	8	1,207	678	1,917	1,103	250	333	3,401	41
3,542	3,130	3,620	2,694	30	....	385	494	968	937	129	867	961	32
3,642	3,843	3,843	5,675	....	....	771	1,692	982	203	377	1,710	33
3,270	3,400	3,353	4,044	784	4,192	552	1,817	1,156	886	111	2,078	1,625	34
3,612	4,612	3,691	2,019	24	3	564	420	2,520	1,046	197	153	2,682	35
3,640	3,460	3,480	3,072	33	11,070	622	1,717	1,778	1,369	355	629	4,531	36
3,683	3,687	3,687	2,587	29	6,645	658	767	840	889	111	446	1,374	37
1,871	1,466	1,236	908	287	1,326	262	315	725	749	1,173	532	824	38
1,845	2,979	2,643	1,101	668	9,133	566	991	1,208	755	277	646	1,244	39
3,455	3,183	3,846	2,682	904	2,381	....	528	1,067	869	646	229	1,161	40
3,416	746	2,980	886	11,945	491	7,602	979	322	958	888	41
2,438	3,452	2,122	105	....	206	1,511	928	471	156	714	4,840	42
2,563	2,640	2,201	567	3,080	362	403	892	305	343	543	43
3,376	757	....	....	183	265	1,710	630	180	157	679	44
3,641	3,622	1,763	....	1,005	468	601	1,850	1,721	358	232	4,330	45
66,363	34,340	74,636	25,153	126,046	16,494	35,477	31,387	31,067	5,955	18,007	44,205	46
44,303	42,633	66,733	61,591	31,223	89,188	7,816	36,085	24,743	28,730	7,279	13,662	42,136	47
45,463	47,633	50,733	50,857	22,537	89,765	7,061	23,864	22,741	23,332	6,741	12,290	37,391	48

Source: Department of Commerce, Bureau of the Census; annual report, Compendium of City Government Finances for 1951.

No. 442.—OUTSTANDING DEBT OF CITIES HAVING MORE THAN 25,000 INHABITANTS: 1951

[In thousands of dollars]

CITY	ALL CITY DEBT (GENERAL AND UTILITY) AT END OF FISCAL YEAR							LONG-TERM UTILITY DEBT AT END OF FISCAL YEAR	
	Total	Long term			Short term	Net long term	All offsets to long-term debt	Total	Full faith and credit
		Total	Full faith and credit	Non-guaranteed					
Total	9,974,908	9,628,059	8,123,113	1,504,946	346,849	8,149,055	1,479,004	3,614,703	2,822,679
Over 1,000,000, total	5,463,340	5,199,087	4,527,630	671,457	264,253	4,131,633	1,067,454	2,387,421	2,101,586
New York	4,099,892	3,913,998	3,476,040	437,958	185,894	2,972,934	941,064	1,919,860	1,919,860
Chicago	248,358	194,596	127,794	66,802	53,762	170,292	24,304	50,098	5
Philadelphia	505,312	505,117	503,767	1,350	195	440,719	64,398	39,610	39,610
Los Angeles	294,744	294,744	136,691	158,053	....	289,637	5,107	204,992	49,250
Detroit	315,034	290,632	283,338	7,294	24,402	258,051	32,581	92,861	92,861
500,000 to 1,000,000, total	1,174,538	1,162,292	1,067,560	94,732	12,246	987,199	175,093	278,888	265,755
Baltimore	219,519	219,519	219,519	....	....	182,920	36,599	61,546	61,546
Cleveland	125,168	125,168	88,091	37,077	....	113,812	11,356	42,237	5,160
St. Louis	27,719	27,719	27,469	250	....	26,608	1,111	....	....
Washington, D. C.									
Boston	150,119	140,119	140,119	....	10,000	71,387	68,732	120	120
San Francisco	182,165	182,165	182,078	87	....	180,099	2,066	101,691	101,691
Pittsburgh	53,066	53,066	53,066	....	....	52,472	594	1,062	1,062
Milwaukee	17,538	17,538	14,388	3,150	....	15,941	1,597	400	....
Houston	114,245	114,245	78,339	35,906	....	108,757	5,488	4,530	4,530
Buffalo	65,478	63,232	46,967	16,265	2,246	52,328	10,904	13,468	13,468
New Orleans	65,365	65,365	63,368	1,997	....	56,873	8,492	....	....
Minneapolis	60,757	60,757	60,757	....	....	56,252	4,505	8,286	8,286
Cincinnati	93,399	93,399	93,399	....	....	69,750	23,649	9,892	9,892
250,000 to 500,000, total	868,647	847,980	660,370	187,610	20,667	769,007	78,973	304,373	152,280
Seattle	121,756	120,088	25,097	94,991	1,668	114,402	5,686	93,597	....
Kansas City, Mo.	48,938	48,938	46,155	2,783	....	48,248	690	10,081	7,799
Newark	53,631	51,255	51,255	....	2,376	47,299	3,956	9,653	9,653
Dallas	79,321	79,321	71,357	7,964	....	76,582	2,739	22,484	21,903
Indianapolis	16,579	16,579	15,732	847	....	15,816	763	....	....
Denver	60,498	60,498	58,575	1,923	....	60,303	195	40,453	40,453
San Antonio	50,762	50,762	21,120	29,642	....	45,508	5,254	29,403	....
Memphis	36,477	36,477	36,477	....	....	33,659	2,818	4,359	4,359
Oakland	17,422	17,422	17,422	....	....	17,133	289	....	....
Columbus	28,924	27,478	27,478	....	1,446	25,197	2,281	6,696	6,696
Portland, Oreg.	21,372	20,874	20,874	....	498	15,965	4,909	4,758	4,758
Louisville	62,270	62,148	44,254	17,894	122	47,336	14,812	....	....
San Diego	25,151	25,151	25,151	....	....	25,088	63	17,434	17,434
Rochester	27,779	17,954	13,623	4,331	9,825	17,805	149	1,266	1,266
Atlanta	27,329	27,329	20,245	7,084	....	26,452	877	5,795	87
Birmingham	23,170	22,512	22,512	....	658	20,435	2,077	3,110	....
St. Paul	26,209	25,088	25,088	....	1,121	18,606	6,482	5,242	5,242
Toledo	14,668	11,905	6,884	5,021	2,763	5,400	6,505	2,932	331
Jersey City	38,893	38,703	38,703	....	190	29,503	9,200	11,913	11,913
Fort Worth	42,875	42,875	32,245	10,630	....	42,753	122	19,497	8,867
Akron	17,300	17,300	12,800	4,500	....	16,227	1,073	6,748	2,627
Omaha	11,681	11,681	11,681	....	....	10,479	1,202	....	....
Long Beach	15,642	15,642	15,642	....	....	8,811	6,831	8,892	8,892
100,000 to 250,000, total	1,038,768	1,025,414	805,721	219,693	13,354	942,859	82,555	329,548	178,327
50,000 to 100,000, total	721,422	701,527	560,140	141,387	19,895	669,616	31,911	174,085	85,641
25,000 to 50,000, total	708,193	691,759	501,692	190,067	16,434	648,741	43,018	220,388	99,090

Source: Department of Commerce, Bureau of the Census; annual report, *Compendium of City Government Finances in 1951.*

No. 443.—EMPLOYMENT AND PAYROLLS OF CITY GOVERNMENTS: OCTOBER 1952

| | NUMBER OF EMPLOYEES | | | | | PAYROLL ($1,000) | |
| | | Nonschool | | | | | |
CITY	Total	All	General government	Utility	School	Total	Non-school
All cities	1,341,744	1,154,093	970,445	183,645	187,651	345,635.6	282,735.4
Over 1,000,000	342,229	283,227	213,816	70,111	58,296	115,362.1	94,240.2
New York	232,314	174,018	126,250	47,768	58,296	77,121.6	55,978.7
Chicago	30,152	30,152	26,694	3,488		10,985.2	10,985.2
Philadelphia	22,706	22,706	21,549	1,157		6,612.7	6,612.7
Los Angeles	29,281	29,281	18,767	10,514		10,907.1	10,907.1
Detroit	27,770	27,770	20,456	7,314		9,755.5	9,795.5
500,000 to 1,000,000, total	187,760	138,878	117,053	16,836	22,892	46,078.7	39,639.4
Baltimore	20,127	12,966	12,130	836	7,161	5,475.6	3,877.5
Cleveland	15,771	15,771	10,285	5,486		4,975.1	4,975.1
St. Louis	12,291	12,291	11,319	972		3,361.1	3,361.1
Washington, D. C.	20,395	14,718	14,171	547	5,677	6,347.5	4,337.0
Boston	23,054	17,683	17,187	496	5,371	6,251.6	4,286.8
San Francisco	14,849	14,849	10,575	4,274		5,256.9	5,256.9
Pittsburgh	6,513	6,513	6,330	483		2,158.4	2,158.4
Milwaukee	8,267	8,267	7,817	450		2,752.1	2,752.1
Houston	5,842	5,842	5,231	611		1,510.7	1,510.7
Buffalo	9,577	6,105	4,755	350	3,472	3,377.3	1,914.3
New Orleans	6,742	6,675	5,585	1,090	67	1,665.1	1,642.5
Minneapolis	5,727	5,727	5,192	535		1,665.8	1,666.8
Cincinnati	8,306	6,171	5,476	695	2,134	2,200.3	1,820.2
250,000 to 500,000, total	111,973	94,736	79,579	15,157	17,237	31,649.0	26,635.3
Seattle	7,607	7,607	3,640	3,967		2,570.9	2,570.9
Kansas City, Mo.	4,955	4,955	4,483	472		1,170.9	1,170.9
Newark	11,153	6,892	6,560	332	4,261	3,835.9	1,981.5
Dallas	5,137	5,137	4,472	665		1,361.9	1,361.9
Indianapolis	4,077	4,077	4,077			972.1	972.1
Denver	6,047	6,047	5,425	622		1,594.4	1,594.4
San Antonio	4,721	4,721	3,007	1,714		1,141.7	1,141.7
Memphis	10,680	7,372	4,619	2,753	3,248	2,274.4	1,626.2
Oakland	3,596	3,596	3,596			1,254.6	1,254.6
Columbus	3,122	3,122	2,568	554		871.3	871.3
Portland, Oreg.	3,809	3,809	3,387	422		1,104.2	1,104.2
Louisville	5,451	4,682	4,053	629	769	1,219.1	985.8
San Diego	3,170	3,170	2,751	419		1,021.4	1,021.4
Rochester	7,069	4,045	3,885	160	3,024	2,071.1	1,077.0
Atlanta	4,048	4,048	3,614	434		1,068.7	1,068.7
Birmingham	1,738	1,738	1,724	14		454.6	454.6
St. Paul	4,885	2,573	2,240	333	2,312	1,602.5	791.3
Toledo	3,218	2,704	2,405	299	514	1,015.9	898.3
Jersey City	(1)	(1)	(1)	(1)	2,639	(1)	(1)
Fort Worth	2,899	2,899	2,601	298		770.8	770.8
Akron	2,259	1,789	1,551	238	470	615.8	519.4
Omaha	1,360	1,360	1,360			366.6	366.6
Long Beach	3,260	3,260	2,720	540		1,078.3	1,078.3
Under 250,000, total	729,786	641,552	559,997	81,555	88,234	149,994.6	122,840.6

1 Not available; estimates included in group total.

Source: Department of Commerce, Bureau of the Census; annual report, *City Employment in 1952*.

16. Banking and Finance

Banking and monetary system.—Banks in this country are organized under the laws of both the States and the Federal government. "National" banks organized under Federal law, passed in 1863, are supervised by the Comptroller of the Currency, and State-chartered banks are supervised by officials of the respective States. The Federal Reserve System was established in 1914 to exercise central banking functions, some of which are shared with the United States Treasury. The Reserve System includes national banks and such State banks as voluntarily join the System. The Federal Deposit Insurance Corporation, established on January 1, 1934, insures each deposit account up to $10,000 in banks which are members of the Federal Reserve System and in such nonmember banks as join the insurance fund.

Condition of banks.—The Comptroller of the Currency, who has charge of the supervision of national banks, has collected condition reports since 1863 from these banks and has tabulated and published summaries of these reports in detail in the *Abstract of Reports of National Banks* (now usually four times a year). The call report data are also summarized in the annual reports of the Comptroller.

After the Federal Reserve System was established in 1914, State bank members of the Federal Reserve System began to submit their statements of condition at the same time and in substantially the same form as national banks. These have been consolidated by the Board of Governors of the Federal Reserve System with data for national banks collected by the Comptroller of the Currency into totals for all member banks of the Federal Reserve System, and are published in the *Member Bank Call Report* (usually four times a year) and in summary form in the *Federal Reserve Bulletin*. *Banking and Monetary Statistics*, which was published in 1943 by the Board of Governors of the Federal Reserve System, makes available in one volume and on a uniform basis statistics of banking, monetary, and other financial developments. The statistics generally cover the period beginning with 1914.

Since the establishment of the Federal Deposit Insurance Corporation in 1934, insured banks not members of the Federal Reserve System have been reporting their condition for the end of June and December in the same manner as member banks, and consolidation of all these reports gives totals for all insured banks, which include nearly all commercial banks in the country. Beginning with June 30, 1947, a revised all-bank series has been tabulated twice a year by the Federal Deposit Insurance Corporation, replacing the three series previously compiled by the three Federal banking supervisory agencies. Data for noninsured banks are obtained largely through the cooperation of State banking officials. A monthly series, based in part on the new all-bank series, is prepared and published by the Board of Governors of the Federal Reserve System.

Statistics of the Postal Savings System, which is under the management of the Post Office Department and which performs certain banking functions, are available monthly in the *Federal Reserve Bulletin* and annually in the *Report of Operations of the Postal Savings System*.

Currency.—Currency, including coin and paper money, represents a relatively small part of the total media of exchange in the United States, as most money payments are made by check. All currency is now issued by the Federal Reserve Banks and the Treasury.

Note.—This section presents data for the most recent year or period available on March 31, 1953, when the material was organized and sent to the printer. In a few instances, more recent data were added after that date.

"Currency in circulation" or "money in circulation" (official *Treasury Circulation Statement*) refers to all coin and paper money outside the Treasury and Federal Reserve Banks, with the exception of gold and silver coin known to have been exported and, beginning with January 31, 1934, all gold coin. It includes all coin and paper money held by the public in the United States whether in current active use or held idle—also some currency which, strictly speaking, is not a part of the money supply in the hands of the public, that is, cash in vaults of commercial and savings banks, currency lost or destroyed, and currency carried abroad by travelers and not appearing in the official gold and silver export figures. The Board of Governors of the Federal Reserve System derives a monthly figure for "currency outside banks" by subtracting from the Treasury "circulation" figure an amount representing vault cash held by commercial and mutual savings banks, and this figure more nearly approximates true circulation. Historical data on the stock of money and money in circulation may be found in the *Annual Report of the Secretary of the Treasury.*

Government credit agencies.—Government corporations and credit agencies make available credit of specified types or to specified groups of private borrowers, either by lending directly or by insuring or guaranteeing loans made by private lending institutions. The purposes and activities of the more than 20 credit agencies reflect mandates and powers given them by Congress. Some of these agencies were created to meet financial problems precipitated by the depression, others are geared to meeting certain broad social problems, particularly in the form of foreign aid and aid to housing.

Foreign loans of Government credit agencies include those of the Export-Import Bank and the Mutual Security Agency, as well as the Treasury loan to the United Kingdom, which was made in 1946–48. Credit for agricultural purposes is provided by the Rural Electrification Administration; the Commodity Credit Corporation, which makes price support loans on certain farm products; the Farmers Home Administration; and several credit agencies operating under the supervision of the Farm Credit Administration. (See table 403.) Loans for housing purposes represent largely purchases of insured and guaranteed home mortgages by the Federal National Mortgage Association from private lenders, but also include loans of the Federal Home Loan Banks to member institutions and the loans of the Public Housing Administration to local housing authorities to aid in the construction of low-cost housing. Credits extended by the Reconstruction Finance Corporation are largely to businesses.

Since the war, Congress has provided for financing a number of special programs by increasing the authority of Federal credit agencies to insure or guarantee certain types of loans made by private institutions. Most Federal guaranteeing and insurance operations are reflected in activities of the Veterans' Administration and the Federal Housing Administration.

Statistics on the assets and liabilities of Government credit agencies are published quarterly in the *Daily Statement of the United States Treasury* and in the *Treasury Bulletin.* Statistics relating to the operations of Government credit agencies are also available in reports of the individual agencies.

Private credit agencies other than banks.—In addition to commercial banks, savings banks, and Government credit agencies, there are a considerable number of other types of credit agencies in the United States. The most important of these are savings and loan associations, insurance companies, finance companies dealing primarily in installment sales financing, credit unions, and personal loan companies. Statistics of savings and loan associations are collected by the Home Loan Bank Board. Statistics on loans, investments, cash, etc., of life insurance companies are collected and published principally by the Spectator Company, which also publishes statistics on other types of insurance. Federal credit unions are under the supervision of the Bureau of Federal Credit Unions of the Department of Health, Education, and Welfare and statistics on them are compiled and published by that organization. These data are combined with information on credit unions other than Federal by the Bureau of Labor Statistics and published in the *Monthly Labor Review*. (See tables 498 and 499.) Consumer credit statistics are published currently in the *Federal Reserve Bulletin*.

SAVINGS AND LIQUID ASSETS

Individuals' saving.—The Securities and Exchange Commission releases quarterly detailed estimates of individuals' saving showing the increase in liquid assets held by individuals less the increase in their debt, exclusive of gains or losses from revaluation of assets. In addition to total saving, these figures show the components contributing to it, such as changes in securities, cash, insurance, consumers' indebtedness, etc. A continuous series starting with 1940 is published quarterly in a special release and in the Commission's *Statistical Bulletin*. (See table 471.) Annual estimates prior to 1940 were published in the *National Income Supplement to the Survey of Current Business*, July 1951, and in the issue of September 1949. The Home Loan Bank Board compiles statistics on changes in selected types of individual long-term savings. (See table 470.) The Board of Governors of the Federal Reserve System releases annual data covering the distribution of liquid assets and occasional data covering positive, negative, and net savings of families, by income groups. These estimates are based on the Board's Survey of Consumer Finances, a nation-wide interview survey of private households. (See table 314, p. 286.)

Liquid asset holdings of individuals and businesses.—The Board of Governors of the Federal Reserve System prepares annual estimates of the amount of currency, demand deposits, time deposits, shares in savings and loan associations, and U. S. Government securities held by individuals and businesses. Separate estimates are shown for five categories of holders, and the series, which begins in December 1939, is published annually in the *Federal Reserve Bulletin*. (See table 472.)

SECURITIES MARKETS

New issues and retirement of securities.—Statistical information on new security issues has been provided for many years by the *Journal of Commerce* (since 1906), the *Commercial and Financial Chronicle* (since 1919) (see table 514), and the Standard and Poor's Corporation (since 1924). The statistics of the *Commercial and Financial Chronicle*, include, in addition to domestic and foreign corporate issues and State and local government securities, the issues of independent agencies of the United States Government, and of foreign governments and their subdivisions.

A more comprehensive series of new issues with detailed information on the intended uses of net proceeds has been compiled by the Securities and Exchange Commission on a monthly basis beginning with January 1934. The data cover substantially all new issues offered for cash sale in the United States in amounts over $100,000 and with terms to maturity of more than one year. Included are issues privately placed as well as issues publicly offered, and unregistered issues as well as issues registered under the Securities Act of 1933. (See tables 512 and 515.) This series is published monthly in the *Statistical Bulletin* of the Securities and Exchange Commission, the *Federal Reserve Bulletin*, and the *Survey of Current Business*.

In addition, the Commission has been compiling statistics since 1933 on changes in security holdings of institutional groups and individuals, and net change in outstanding corporate securities through cash transactions. The latter data are published in the *Federal Reserve Bulletin*. The Commission also publishes data from time to time on cost of flotation of securities registered under the Securities Act of 1933 and privately placed issues.

Trading in securities.—(See tables 504, 507, 508, 510.) Monthly figures on the total value and volume of securities sold on each of the national securities exchanges have been published since October 1934 by the Securities and Exchange Commission. These figures, reported in connection with the fees paid under Section 31 of the Securities Exchange Act of 1934, include all sales effected on exchanges except, since March 1944, United States Government issues. They cover odd lots as well as round lots. The Commission also publishes figures on the total daily round-lot volume of trading in stocks on the New York Stock Exchange and the American Stock Exchange, showing short sales and several categories of member and nonmember purchases and sales. Daily odd-lot purchases and sales are reported separately.

Prior to 1934, the only available statistical data on the volume of trading in securities were the daily figures on the number of shares and the principal amount of bonds reported sold on the New York Stock Exchange and on most of the other securities exchanges. "Reported" volume of stock sales on the New York Stock Exchange represents sales in round lots reported on the ticker and does not include certain types of round-lot transactions such as stopped sales, private sales, split openings, cross transactions, and errors of omission, which ordinarily amount to from five to ten percent of total round-lot sales on the Exchange.

Security price averages.—Among the most widely known indices of security prices are the Dow-Jones averages, which provide a continuous series of common stock prices on a daily basis since 1897. This series is now based on 65 common stocks divided into 30 industrial, 20 railroad, and 15 public utility stocks. Indices of the Standard and Poor's Corporation, available since 1918, are now based on the Wednesday closing prices of nearly 500 stocks. (See table 503.) The Securities and Exchange Commission compiles an index of weekly closing prices of 265 stocks listed on the New York Stock Exchange, comprising 37 industry groups, conforming with the Standard Industrial Classification. These indices are published in the Commission's *Statistical Bulletin.* (See table 502.)

INSURANCE

Insurance statistics.—There are no complete statistics of insurance for the United States as a whole. Individual States collect statistics on insurers operating within their respective jurisdictions; organizations representing certain classes of insurers, or of insurance, collect statistics for those classes; insurance publishers gather the only statistics approaching comprehensiveness. This situation arises primarily from the fact that the regulation of insurance and the collection of primary information on insurance are in the hands of the various States, Territories, and the District of Columbia. While insurance is now largely subject to Federal regulation, the Federal Government has not exercised its power nor has it taken any steps to collect comprehensive statistics of insurance on a national basis. Basic theory and practice are parallel throughout insurance, but application of theory and details of practice, including vocabulary, differ enormously by class of insurance and by class of insurer. Sound combination or comparison of figures is often difficult or impossible.

Types of insurance.—Insurance is traditionally classified as life, fire and marine, and casualty. With some overlapping between classes, an insurer is authorized to write insurance falling in one of these three classes, though there is now a tendency in the direction of permitting insurers, other than life, to write all kinds of insurance except life. *Life insurance* and *marine insurance* are each fairly homogeneous, the one having to do with life contingencies, and the other with losses connected with transportation. *Fire insurance,* as such, offers protection against loss by fire, but insurers in that business write several allied classes of insurance, principally against loss by windstorm, by damage to motor vehicles, by damage to aircraft, by sprinkler leakage, by earthquake, and by riot. *Casualty insurance* is a miscellaneous class, the principal subclasses of which are liability insurance (protecting against loss due to claims for damages) and workmen's compensation insurance (protecting an employer against loss due to his obligations under a workmen's compensation law). (See section 10, Social Security.) Casualty insurers also write several unrelated kinds of insurance, including fidelity and surety bonds.

Types of insurer.—The principal classes of insurer are stock companies and mutual companies or associations. Of less importance are fraternal insurers, reciprocal exchanges, Lloyds, State funds, and savings banks. *Stock companies* are corporations owned and controlled by stockholders, usually for the purpose of making profits. *Mutuals* are owned and controlled by insured members for the purpose of meeting their insurance needs at cost. *Fraternal insurers* emphasize social purposes as well as insurance; *reciprocal exchanges* are organizations of individual insureds operating through an attorney-in-fact; *Lloyds* are groups of individuals writing insurance in syndicates; *State funds* are insurers operated by individual States and are almost entirely devoted to writing workmen's compensation insurance either as exclusive insurers or in competition with private insurers; *savings banks* write life insurance in three States.

Historical statistics.—See preface and historical appendix. Tabular headnotes (as "See also *Historical Statistics*, series N 172–178") provide cross-references, where applicable, to *Historical Statistics of the United States, 1789–1945.*

Fig. **XXXII.**—Stock Prices: 1946 to 1952

[1935–39 = 100. Indexes based on Wednesday figures. See table 503]

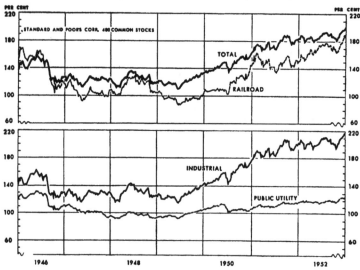

Source: Board of Governors of the Federal Reserve System.

No. 444.—Consolidated Condition Statement for Banks and the Monetary System: 1929 to 1952

[In millions of dollars. Figures partly estimated. Comprises all commercial and savings banks, Federal Reserve Banks, Postal Savings System, and Treasury currency funds. Treasury funds included are the gold account, Treasury currency account, and Exchange Stabilization Fund]

ITEM	1929 (June 29)	1933 (June 30)	1939 (Dec. 30)	1945 (Dec. 31)	1950 (Dec. 30)	1951 (Dec. 31)	1952 (Dec. 2)
Total assets or liabilities, net	64,698	48,465	78,171	191,786	198,009	208,724	220,865
ASSETS							
Gold	4,037	4,031	17,644	20,065	22,706	22,695	23,187
Treasury currency	2,019	2,296	2,963	4,339	4,636	4,706	4,812
Bank credit, total	58,642	42,148	54,564	167,381	171,667	181,323	192,866
Loans, net	41,082	21,987	22,157	30,387	60,366	67,597	75,484
U. S. Government obligations, total	5,741	10,328	23,105	128,417	96,360	97,808	100,005
Commercial and savings banks	5,499	8,199	19,417	101,288	72,894	71,343	72,740
Federal Reserve Banks	216	1,998	2,484	24,262	20,778	23,601	24,697
Other	26	131	1,204	2,867	2,888	2,664	2,571
Other securities	11,819	9,863	9,302	8,577	14,741	15,918	17,874
LIABILITIES							
Capital and miscellaneous accounts, net	8,922	6,436	6,812	10,979	14,624	15,320	16,647
Deposits and currency, total	55,776	42,029	66,350	180,806	184,385	193,404	204,220
Foreign bank deposits, net	365	50	1,217	2,141	2,518	2,279	2,301
U. S. Government balances:							
Treasury cash	204	264	2,409	2,287	1,293	1,279	1,270
At commercial and savings banks	381	852	845	24,608	2,989	3,615	5,250
At Federal Reserve Banks	36	35	634	977	668	347	389
Deposits adjusted and currency outside banks	54,790	40,828	61,253	150,798	176,917	185,984	194,801
Demand deposits adjusted [1]	22,540	14,411	29,793	75,851	92,272	96,234	101,508
Time deposits adjusted [2]	28,611	21,656	27,059	48,452	59,347	61,447	65,799
Commercial banks	19,557	10,849	15,258	30,135	36,314	37,889	40,666
Mutual savings banks [3]	8,905	9,621	10,522	15,385	20,009	20,887	22,586
Postal Savings System	149	1,186	1,278	2,932	2,922	2,701	2,547
Currency outside banks	3,639	4,761	6,401	26,490	25,398	26,303	27,494

[1] Demand deposits, other than interbank and U. S. Government, less cash items reported as in process of collection.
[2] Excludes interbank time deposits; United States Treasurer's time deposits, open account; and deposits of Postal Savings System in banks.
[3] Prior to June 30, 1947, includes a relatively small amount of demand deposits.

Source: Board of Governors of the Federal Reserve System. Figures published currently in *Federal Reserve Bulletin*.

No. 445.—Deposits and Currency—Adjusted Deposits of all Banks and Currency Outside Banks: 1892 to 1952

[In millions of dollars. Figures partly estimated. See also *Historical Statistics*, series N 172-176]

JUNE 30—	Total deposits (adj.) and currency	Currency outside banks	DEPOSITS				Total demand deposits (adj.) and currency
			Total	Demand (adj.) [1]	U. S. Govt. [2]	Time [3]	
1892	5,538	1,015	4,523	2,580	14	1,929	3,595
1900	8,865	1,331	7,534	4,520	99	3,015	5,751
1910	16,977	1,725	15,252	8,254	54	6,944	9,979
1915	20,682	1,575	19,107	9,828	48	9,231	11,403
1920	39,859	4,105	35,754	19,616	304	15,834	20,721
1925	48,323	3,573	44,750	21,376	180	23,194	24,949
1930	54,389	3,369	51,021	21,706	322	28,992	25,075
1933	40,391	4,763	45,099	20,433	811	21,962	25,216
1935	46,952	5,699	60,029	31,962	828	27,462	38,661
1940	102,784	25,097	137,687	69,053	24,542	44,253	94,150
1945	155,507	26,299	129,208	52,160	1,367	55,455	108,485
1950	167,875	25,638	142,237	62,697	2,185	57,380	108,335
1951	167,990	25,296	142,694	61,877	2,304	56,682	107,143
1952	173,765	26,185	148,580	65,040	1,801	56,730	110,225
	181,015	25,776	155,240	63,948	6,332	59,948	114,738
	191,025	26,474	164,551	94,754	6,121	65,676	121,228

[1] Demand deposits other than interbank and U. S. Govt., less cash items reported as in process of collection.
[2] Beginning with December 1938, includes U. S. Treasurer's *time* deposits, open account.
[3] Includes amounts held by commercial banks, mutual savings banks and Postal Savings System. Excludes interbank time deposits; U. S. Treasurer's *time* deposits, open account; and deposits of Postal Savings System in banks. Prior to June 30, 1947, includes a relatively small amount of demand deposits at mutual savings banks.

Source: Board of Governors of the Federal Reserve System; *Banking and Monetary Statistics*, and *Federal Reserve Bulletin*. Figures published currently in *Federal Reserve Bulletin*.

Fig. **XXXIII.**—Deposits of All Banks and Currency Outside Banks: 1930 to 1952

Years ending June 30. See table 445]

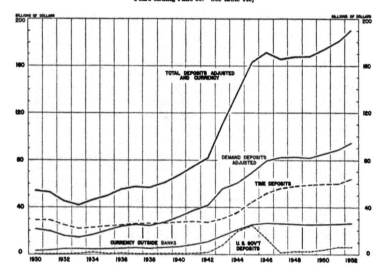

Fig. **XXXIV.**—Principal Assets of All Banks: 1935 to 1952

[As of end of December 1935 to 1944; end of June and December thereafter. See table 456]

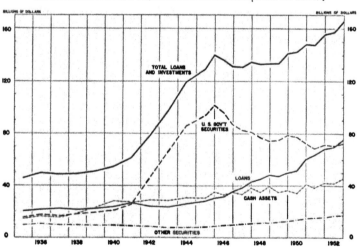

Source of figs. **XXXIII** and **XXXIV**: Board of Governors of the Federal Reserve System.

No. 446.—MONEY STOCK AND MONEY IN CIRCULATION: 1800 TO 1952

figures except per capita in thousands of dollars. For sake of comparability figures in this table for earlier years have been revised in conformity with revisions in circulation statement in 1922 and 1927. For explanations of these revisions, see annual reports of Secretary of Treasury 1922, p. 433, and 1928, pp. 70–71. Per capita figures for 1800–40 based on Bureau of Census population figures for continental United States on census dates; beginning 1860, based on estimated population as of July 1 and Dec. 31. See also *Historical Statistics*, series N 148–151]

| Stock of money in United | MONEY HELD IN TREASURY | | | | | MONEY OUTSIDE TREASURY [1] | | |
| | Total | In trust against gold and silver certificates [2] | Gold reserve against United States notes [3] | Held for Federal Reserve Banks and agents [3] | All other money | Held by Federal Reserve Banks and agents | In circulation | |
							Amount	Per capita (dollars)
						1, 800	26, 800	4. 99
						2, 000	67, 100	6. 96
						3, 664	196, 306	10. 91
						6, 695	435, 407	13. 82
	186, 994	82, 085				124, 910	774, 966	19. 42
	225, 922	13, 758	100, 000			112, 168	972, 382	19. 37
1, 123	664, 250	426, 387	100, 000			155, 872	1, 439, 261	22. 67
1, 360	701, 539	483, 947	100, 000			117, 391	1, 601, 968	23. 02
2, 220	969, 492	654, 503	150, 000			134, 990	2, 081, 281	27. 38
2,	1, 245, 501	948, 347	150, 000			146, 152	2, 622, 340	31. 30
3,	1, 603, 198	1, 285, 014	150, 000			165, 172	3, 148, 584	34. 07
4,	1, 967, 665	1, 619, 429	152, 977			195, 259	3, 319, 582	33. 01
8, 158, 496	2, 375, 664	704, 638	152, 979	1, 184, 276		337, 771	5, 467, 589	51. 36
8, 299, 382	4, 176, 281	2, 059, 799	153, 821	1, 782, 744		210, 217	4, 815, 208	41. 87
8, 306, 564	4, 021, 987	1, 978, 448	156, 039	1, 796, 229		91, 211	4, 521, 988	36. 74
15, 113, 035	9, 997, 362	7, 131, 431	156, 039	5, 539, 590		2, 709, 891	5, 567, 093	43. 75
28, 457, 900	21, 896, 996	19, 651, 067	156, 039	14, 958, 896		2, 029, 829	7, 847, 801	59. 40
44, 803, 301	23, 173, 608	20, 878, 641	156, 039	16, 194, 111	2, 139, 012	3, 811, 797	22, 804, 342	162. 61
43, 009, 400	22, 202, 115	19, 923, 738	156, 039	15, 859, 079	2, 122, 328	3, 745, 512	26, 746, 438	191. 61
49, 648, 011	23, 649, 365	20, 397, 855	156, 039	15, 927, 596	2, 085, 441	3, 863, 941	26, 344, 997	199. 76
50, 599, 352	23, 632, 353	22, 318, 880	156, 039	17, 623, 458	1, 158, 433	3, 763, 994	26, 297, 227	196, 32
52, 601, 129	26, 890, 134	24, 563, 122	156, 039	19, 443, 973	1, 170, 982	3, 926, 896	27, 902, 559	190. 31
53, 103, 980	28, 982, 365	26, 554, 811	156, 039	20, 459, 710	1, 180, 808	3, 874, 816	27, 402, 910	184. 33
52, 440, 153	26, 646, 409	26, 348, 625	156, 039	20, 168, 654	1, 141, 744	3, 819, 755	27, 156, 290	179. 02
50, 983, 939	24, 175, 565	22, 894, 641	156, 039	17, 696, 728	1, 124, 884	4, 197, 063	27, 809, 230	180. 17
53, 853, 745	25, 810, 840	24, 528, 270	156, 039	19, 397, 733	1, 126, 530	4, 217, 518	29, 025, 925	184. 86
1951	53, 535, 281	25, 130, 266	23, 859, 773	156, 039	18, 662, 510	1, 114, 444	4, 406, 308	29, 205, 979	187. 47
1952	53, 420, 084	25, 664, 834	24, 386, 290	156, 039	19, 170, 160	1, 113, 496	4, 847, 436	30, 432, 973	192. 08

[1] eginning 1870, excludes gold and silver certificates and Treasury notes of 1890 outside Treasury. Beginning excludes amount (gold certificates) held for Federal Reserve Banks and agents. These items are excluded gold and silver held as security against them are included.

[2] both items include also reserve against Treasury notes of 1890.

[3] 1914 to date, gold certificates. Amount excluded from total since gold held as security against gold certificates is included in column "In trust against gold and silver certificates."

ncludes total stock of silver dollars and subsidiary silver.

Source: Treasury Department; *Annual Report of the Secretary; Circulation Statement of United States Money*, published monthly.

No. 447.—MONEY STOCK AND MONEY IN CIRCULATION, BY KIND, JUNE 30: 1930 TO 1952

[In thousands of dollars. See also *Historical Statistics*, series N 148, 151–165]

	1930	1935	1940	1945	1950	1951	1952
Money stock, total [1]	8, 306, 564	15, 113, 035	28, 457, 900	48, 009, 400	52, 440, 353	52, 935, 929	53, 353, 745
Gold coin and bullion [2]	4, 534, 966	9, 115, 643	19, 963, 091	20,	24, 230, 720	21, 755, 888	23, 346, 498
Silver bullion		312, 309	1, 353, 162	1, 520, 296	2, 022, 835	2, 057, 227	2, 092, 041
Silver dollars	539, 980	546, 642	547, 078	493, 943	492, 563	492, 349	491, 897
Subsidiary silver	310, 978	312, 416	402, 251	525, 796	1, 001, 574	1, 041, 946	1, 117, 899
United States notes	346, 681	346, 681	346, 681	346, 681	378, 463	346, 681	346, 681
Minor coin	126, 001	133, 040	909	303, 539	378, 463	386, 646	402, 702
Federal Reserve notes	1, 746, 601	3, 492, 654	778	21, 680, 975	602, 680	24, 874, 934	25, 756, 570
Federal Reserve Bank notes ..	2, 360	94, 354	808	533, 979	277, 202	345, 987	223, 100
National bank notes	693, 317	768, 086	190	121, 215	57, 618	82, 382	78, 367
Percentage of gold to total money	54. 59	60. 32	70. 15	42. 10	46. 21	42. 67	43. 34

See footnotes at end of table.

No. 447.—Money Stock and Money in Circulation, by Kind, June 30: 1930 to 1952—Continued

[In thousands of dollars]

KIND	1930	1935	1940	1945	1950	1951	1952
Money in circulation, total__	4,521,968	5,567,093	7,847,501	26,746,438	27,156,290	27,809,230	29,625,325
Gold coin [1]_____	357,236						
Gold certificates_____	994,841	117,167	66,793	52,084	40,772	39,070	37,855
Silver dollars_____	38,629	32,308	46,020	125,178	170,185	180,013	191,306
Silver certificates_____	386,915	701,474	1,581,662	1,650,689	2,177,251	2,092,174	2,067,611
Treasury notes of 1890_____	1,260	1,182	1,163	1,150	1,145	1,145	1,145
Subsidiary silver_____	281,231	295,773	354,187	788,283	964,709	1,019,824	1,092,891
Minor coin_____	117,436	125,126	168,977	291,996	360,886	378,350	393,482
United States notes_____	288,389	285,417	247,887	322,587	320,781	318,173	318,330
Federal Reserve notes_____	1,402,066	3,222,913	5,163,284	22,867,459	22,760,285	23,456,016	24,605,158
Federal Reserve Bank notes__	3,206	81,470	22,373	527,001	273,788	243,261	220,584
National bank notes_____	650,779	704,263	165,155	120,012	86,488	81,202	77,384

[1] Totals involve duplication to extent that United States notes and Federal Reserve notes, included in full, are in part secured by gold, also included in full. Gold certificates, silver certificates, and Treasury notes of 1890 excluded, since they are complete duplications of equal amounts of gold or silver held as security therefor and included in totals.

[2] By proclamation of the president dated Jan. 31, 1934, weight of gold dollar reduced from 25.8 to 15 5/21 grains of gold, 0.9 fine. Hence, value of gold based on $35 per fine ounce beginning June 1934; theretofore, based on $20.67 per fine ounce.

[3] Gold Reserve Act of 1934, which was culmination of gold actions of 1933, vested in United States title to all gold coin and gold bullion. Gold coin was withdrawn from circulation and formed into bars. Gold coin ($287,000,000) shown on Treasury records as being then outstanding was dropped from monthly circulation statement as of Jan. 31, 1934.

Source: Treasury Department; *Annual Report of the Secretary; Circulation Statement of United States Money,* published monthly.

No. 448.—Bank Debits and Deposit Turnover: 1920 to 1952

[All figures in millions of dollars. Figures represent debits or charges on books of reporting member and non-member banks of Federal Reserve System to deposit accounts of individuals, firms, and corporations, and of United States, State, county, and municipal governments, including debits to savings accounts, payments from trust accounts, and certificates of deposit paid. Excludes debits to accounts of other banks or in settlement of clearinghouse balances, payment of cashier's checks, charges to expense and miscellaneous accounts, corrections, and similar charges. See also *Historical Statistics,* series N 76–79]

YEAR	DEBITS TO TOTAL DEPOSIT ACCOUNTS [1]				ANNUAL RATE OF TURNOVER OF TOTAL DEPOSITS [1]		DEBITS TO DEMAND DEPOSIT ACCOUNTS [1]		ANNUAL RATE OF TURNOVER OF DEMAND DEPOSITS [1]	
	Total, all reporting centers	New York City [2]	140 other centers [3]	Other reporting centers [4]	New York City	Other reporting centers	New York City	Other leading cities	New York City	Other leading cities
1920_____	490,468	241,431	241,595	7,442						
1925_____	605,843	313,373	256,689	35,781						
1930_____	702,959	384,639	277,317	41,003						
1935_____	402,718	184,006	190,167	28,545			178,498	175,902	31.5	22.7
1940_____	445,863	171,582	236,952	37,329			167,373	217,744	17.1	18.6
1942 (old series)_____	607,071	210,961	342,430	53,679			200,337	308,913	18.0	18.4
1942 (new series) [5]__	641,778	226,865	347,837	67,074	16.1	13.1				
1944_____	891,910	345,585	462,354	83,970	17.1	10.8	298,902	403,400	22.4	17.3
1945_____	974,102	404,543	479,760	89,799	18.2	9.7	351,602	412,800	24.2	16.1
1946 (old series)_____	}1,050,021	417,475	527,336	105,210	18.9	10.0	{374,365	449,414	25.5	16.9
1946 (new series) [6]__							407,946	522,944	25.2	16.5
1947_____	1,125,074	405,929	599,639	119,506	21.0	11.9	400,468	596,445	24.1	18.0
1948_____	1,249,630	449,002	667,934	132,695	23.6	12.9	445,221	600,155	27.2	19.2
1949_____	1,231,053	452,897	648,976	129,179	24.1	12.4	447,150	639,772	28.2	18.7
1950_____	1,403,752	513,970	742,458	147,324	26.6	13.4	508,166	731,511	31.4	20.3
1951_____	1,577,857	551,889	854,050	171,917	26.9	14.5	540,990	837,491	32.2	21.7
1952_____	1,692,136	615,670	895,906	180,560	28.7	14.4	598,855	871,030	34.8	21.5

[1] Except interbank.
[2] Weekly reporting member bank series; excludes interbank and Government.
[3] National series for which bank debits figures available beginning with 1919.
[4] Annual figures for 1930 and 1935 include from 121 to 131 centers and for 1940 and 1942 (old series) include 133 centers. Figures for 1942 (new series) to November 1947 include 193 centers; from December 1947 through December 1950, 192 centers; and thereafter 201.
[5] Partly estimated for first 4 months.
[6] Estimated for first 6 months.

Source: Board of Governors of the Federal Reserve System, annual and current reports on bank debits and *Federal Reserve Bulletin.*

No. 449.—BANK CLEARINGS AT PRINCIPAL CITIES: 1920 TO 1952

[Millions of dollars. Comparability of figures for different years is affected by tendency toward consolidation of banks, eliminating former clearings between 2 or more banks. Debits to individual account (table 448) are a better measure of volume of payment. Cities listed in order of importance according to clearings in 1952. See also *Historical Statistics*, series N 86-89]

YEAR	Total, 143 cities	New York City	142 cities outside New York City	YEAR	Total, 143 cities	New York City	142 cities outside New York City
	438,847	243,135	195,712	1938	295,644	165,156	130,488
	444,919	249,868	195,051	1939	307,311	165,914	141,397
	499,515	283,619	215,896	1940	315,228	160,878	154,350
	511,689	290,355	221,334	1941	378,244	183,263	194,981
	543,614	321,234	222,380	1942	419,971	192,939	227,032
	622,538	391,727	230,811	1943	514,051	248,560	265,491
	714,889	477,242	237,647	1944	569,877	286,349	283,528
	543,854	347,110	196,744	1945	631,635	334,433	297,202
	411,161	263,270	147,891	1946	709,961	366,065	343,896
	258,145	160,138	98,007	1947	751,796	361,238	390,558
	243,556	157,414	86,142	1948	803,597	371,554	432,043
	263,816	161,507	102,309	1949	770,297	358,845	411,452
	300,402	181,551	118,851	1950	806,107	399,309	406,798
	330,993	193,549	137,444	1951	(?)	431,775	(?)
	335,899	186,740	149,159	1952	(?)	461,724	(?)

CITY	1920	1925	1930	1935	1940	1945	1949	1950	1951	1952
Total, 35 cities	424,173	481,922	528,962	291,351	304,211	611,908	738,134	829,719	918,585	965,001
York	243,135	283,619	347,110	181,561	160,878	334,433	358,845	399,309	431,775	461,724
delphia	26,095	29,079	26,360	16,900	21,485	34,710	45,243	51,102	55,433	56,635
go	32,060	35,392	28,706	13,195	16,695	27,280	36,807	40,675	44,780	45,097
ngeles	3,904	7,945	8,807	5,852	7,544	17,144	25,178	26,506	31,189	32,853
n	18,617	22,482	23,080	10,646	11,944	19,890	22,953	26,348	28,335	28,995
t	6,104	8,431	9,440	4,525	6,312	16,473	19,485	22,855	26,622	28,372
rancisco	8,122	9,479	9,589	6,409	7,774	15,743	19,513	21,983	27,350	26,769
land	6,907	5,997	6,638	3,417	5,734	11,529	15,177	17,684	21,581	22,094
urgh	6,983	8,857	9,247	5,246	7,075	12,979	14,755	16,782	18,484	19,189
s City, Mo	11,615	7,036	6,302	4,348	4,908	10,856	15,147	16,707	18,042	18,447
ts	1,869	2,557	2,122	1,969	2,087	6,638	12,259	14,451	16,445	17,532
nis	3,257	3,604	2,258	2,205	3,431	8,264	11,603	12,910	15,192	16,235
apolis	8,294	7,627	6,146	3,941	4,822	9,734	13,604	14,896	15,994	16,019
on	4,613	4,463	4,016	3,045	3,787	8,196	12,697	14,114	15,843	15,941
on	1,504	1,766	1,676	1,420	2,569	5,082	10,488	11,922	14,088	14,687
ore	4,806	5,832	4,820	2,911	4,302	8,318	10,797	12,155	13,646	14,280
nati	3,597	3,710	3,203	2,466	3,245	6,305	8,517	9,929	11,055	11,327
and	3,048	2,839	2,257	1,697	2,237	4,518	6,430	7,199	8,195	8,676
nd, Oreg	1,907	2,015	1,770	1,279	1,800	3,830	7,214	7,991	8,180	8,354
	2,073	2,205	1,908	1,460	2,113	4,768	5,795	6,909	8,195	8,466
s	2,094	2,188	2,182	1,503	1,614	3,968	5,911	6,838	7,994	7,980
ville	1,290	1,744	1,850	1,395	1,933	4,028	6,088	6,934	7,578	7,928
rleans	3,815	3,170	2,315	1,434	2,190	4,665	6,330	6,871	7,436	7,899
ngham	991	1,372	1,010	816	1,290	3,125	4,842	5,583	6,594	7,365
r	1,981	1,668	1,694	1,204	1,627	3,209	5,175	5,972	6,986	7,117
nville	626	1,446	675	625	1,106	2,801	4,247	5,128	6,085	6,777
his	1,191	1,233	954	828	1,286	2,620	4,929	5,371	5,776	5,954
d	1,670	1,681	1,200	1,171	1,459	2,628	4,541	5,185	5,627	5,796
	2,255	2,782	2,604	1,478	1,583	3,312	4,059	4,671	5,409	5,690
ngton, D. C	897	1,353	1,318	985	1,414	2,499	3,890	4,608	5,241	5,246
	1,796	2,062	1,497	829	1,142	1,945	3,087	3,734	4,306	4,954
	1,180	1,122	1,079	697	1,066	2,140	3,518	3,987	4,544	4,706
	892	806	918	648	843	1,562	2,804	3,095	3,517	3,687
	943	904	1,002	724	1,063	1,679	2,738	3,064	3,285	3,516
	(?)	1,129	1,701	918	985	1,580	2,123	2,417	2,710	2,707
tion, Ohio	781	805	793	596	577	967	1,707	1,900	2,030	2,128
rd	551	703	768	535	629	870	1,314	1,385	1,527	1,685
ort	697	715	684	400	603	982	1,295	1,499	1,576	1,612

data available.

Source: Commercial and Financial Chronicle, New York, N. Y., except for data for Los Angeles, which were supplied by Los Angeles Clearing House Association.

No. 450.—ANALYSIS OF CHANGES IN GOLD STOCK: 1915 TO 1952

[In millions of dollars. Gold valued at $20.67 per fine ounce through January 1934; at $35 thereafter. See also *Historical Statistics*, series N 166-171]

YEAR	GOLD STOCK (end of period)		Increase in total gold stock	Domestic gold production [2]	Net gold import (+) or export (−)	Earmarked gold: Decrease (+) or increase (−)	Gold under earmark (end of period) [3]
	Total [1]	Treasury					
1915	2,025	2,025	499.1	99.7	+420.5		
1920	2,639	2,639	−68.4	49.9	+95.0	[4] −145.0	22.0
1925	4,112	4,112	−100.1	48.0	−134.4	+32.2	13.0
1930	4,306	4,306	309.6	43.4	+290.1	−2.4	137.7
1935	10,126	10,125	1,868.0	110.7	+1,739.0	+.2	8.8
1940	22,042	21,995	4,342.5	170.2	+4,744.5	−644.7	1,807.7
1945	20,063	20,065	−547.8	32.0	−106.3	−356.7	4,293.8
1949	24,563	24,427	164.6	67.3	+686.5	−495.7	4,273.3
1950	22,820	22,706	−1,743.3	80.1	−371.3	−1,352.4	5,625.7
1951	22,873	22,695	52.7	66.3	−549.0	+617.6	5,008.2
1952	23,252	23,186	378.9	67.8	+684.8	−304.8	5,313.0

[1] Includes gold in Exchange Stabilization Fund beginning 1935; gold in active portion of this fund not included in Treasury gold stock.
[2] Estimate of the United States mint through 1951; figure for 1952 is estimate of American Bureau of Metal Statistics.
[3] Held at Federal Reserve Banks for foreign and international accounts.
[4] Adjusted for changes in gold held under earmark abroad by the Federal Reserve banks.

Source: Board of Governors of the Federal Reserve System; *Banking and Monetary Statistics* and *Federal Reserve Bulletin*.

No. 451.—COINAGE OF GOLD, SILVER, AND MINOR COIN: 1840 TO 1952

[In thousands of dollars. Coinage figures represent face amount of coin. See also *Historical Statistics*, series N 179-182]

YEAR	Total	Gold coin [1]	Silver coin	Minor coin	YEAR	Total	Gold coin [1]	Silver coin	Minor coin
1840	3,427	1,675	1,727	25	1925	216,457	192,380	19,874	4,203
1850	33,892	31,982	1,866	44	1930	8,731	2,440	2,658	3,632
1860	25,939	23,474	2,259	206	1935	38,581		31,237	7,344
1870	24,927	23,190	1,378	350	1940	50,158		29,360	20,798
1880	90,111	62,308	27,412	391	1945	101,132		75,871	25,261
1890	61,055	20,467	39,203	1,385	1947	48,044		35,323	12,720
1900	137,649	99,273	36,345	2,031	1948	49,848		36,860	12,989
1905	58,269	49,638	6,332	2,299	1949	28,346		18,651	9,695
1910	111,505	104,724	3,744	3,037	1950	41,891		34,006	7,885
1915	30,145	23,968	4,114	2,063	1951	74,736		61,434	13,302
1920	50,214	16,990	25,057	8,167	1952	95,736		79,264	16,472

[1] Coinage of domestic gold coin discontinued in 1933.

No. 452.—SILVER—PRICES, BULLION VALUE, AND RATIO TO GOLD: 1840 TO 1951

[London price converted to basis of ounce 1.000 fine and converted to American money at par of exchange through 1930; from 1931 through 1944, at current rate of exchange; beginning 1945, (London price) reported on basis of ounce 0.999 fine and converted to American money at current rate of exchange. Commercial ratio computed on basis of London quotations through 1914; thereafter, on basis of New York average price. Beginning 1934, monetary value of gold is $35.00 per fine ounce, as against $20.67+ in previous years. Value of fine silver (371½ grains) in dollar computed on basis of London quotations through 1917; thereafter, on basis of New York average price. See also *Historical Statistics*, series N 183-184, for data on commercial ratio to gold and value of silver in dollar]

[All figures, except "Commercial ratio to gold," expressed in dollars]

CALENDAR YEAR	London, per fine ounce	NEW YORK, PER FINE OUNCE			Commercial ratio to gold	Bullion value of silver dollar	CALENDAR YEAR	London, per fine ounce	NEW YORK, PER FINE OUNCE			Commercial ratio to gold	Bullion value of silver dollar
		Average	High	Low					Average	High	Low		
1840	1.323				15.62	1.023	1918	1.042	.984	1.019	.889	21.00	0.761
1850	1.316				15.70	1.018	1920	1.346	1.019	1.379	.604	20.28	.788
1860	1.352				15.29	1.045	1925	.703	.694	.732	.668	29.78	.537
1870	1.328				15.57	1.027	1930	.387	.385	.472	.311	53.74	.298
1880	1.145	1.139	1.150	1.113	18.05	.886	1935	.639	.646	.813	.501	54.19	.500
1890	1.046	1.053	1.205	.958	19.75	.809	1940	.384	.351	.359	.351	99.76	.271
1900	.620	.621	.658	.598	33.33	.480	1945	.513	.519	.708	.448	67.40	.402
1905	.610	.610	.665	.556	33.87	.472	1948	.756	.744	.775	.700	47.07	.575
1910	.541	.542	.576	.508	38.22	.418	1949	.756	.719	.733	.700	48.61	.587
1915	.519	.511	.580	.478	40.48	.401	1950	.756	.742	.800	.718	47.14	.574
1917	.895	.840	1.165	.731	24.61	.692	1951	.908	.894	.902	.800	39.12	.692

Source of tables 451 and 452: Treasury Dept., Bureau of the Mint; *Annual Report of the Director*.

No. 453.—ALL ACTIVE BANKS—PRINCIPAL ASSETS AND LIABILITIES, BY CLASS OF BANKS: 1834 TO 1951

[Includes banks in Alaska, Hawaii, Puerto Rico, Philippine Islands (through 1941), and beginning with 1935, those in Virgin Islands and with 1936, those in Canal Zone, Guam (except 1943–44), and American Samoa. Data for banks other than national for earlier years are not as of June 30 and are incomplete, especially through 1888. Figures for mutual savings banks include some stock savings banks for years prior to 1910 and also a few in several more recent years. Private banks are not included prior to 1887; statistics for private banks, except for 1935, cover only banks under State supervision and those voluntarily reporting; for 1935 they include also private banks which submitted reports to the Comptroller of the Currency under provisions of the Banking Act of 1933. See also *Historical Statistics*, series N 19–34, and N 43–48]

[Money figures in millions of dollars]

ON OR ABOUT JUNE 30—	Number of banks	Total assets or liabilities [1]	SELECTED ASSETS			SELECTED LIABILITIES			
			Loans and discounts including overdrafts [3]	U. S. Govt. and other securities [5]	Cash and balances with other banks [1][6]	Capital stock [4]	Surplus, undivided profits, and reserve [8]	Circulation [7]	Total deposits [1]
All banks:									
1834	506	418.9	324.1	6.1	76.1	200.0		94.5	102.3
1840	901	657.5	462.9	42.4	98.7	358.4		107.0	119.9
1850	1,562	909.9	691.9	70.3	195.7	421.9		207.1	209.7
1860	3,355	2,398.9	1,662.3	904.2	665.6	565.2	260.3	318.4	2,222.1
1870	10,382	10,755.5	5,687.7	2,496.4	2,256.0	1,024.7	882.3	285.5	5,513.0
1910	22,095	22,480.3	12,521.6	4,667.6	4,437.3	1,879.9	1,955.6	675.6	17,554.2
1915	27,062	27,304.1	15,758.7	5,840.1	5,008.5	2,162.8	2,372.7	722.7	22,031.7
1920	30,139	52,826.2	30,650.1	11,252.0	8,367.4	2,702.6	3,251.3	688.2	41,725.2
1925	28,841	61,698.1	33,596.5	15,374.9	9,908.5	3,169.7	4,180.8	648.5	51,995.1
1930	24,079	73,463.4	40,510.1	17,944.7	11,178.0	3,859.4	6,392.1	652.3	59,547.2
1935	16,053	60,386.9	20,419.3	24,217.2	12,397.5	3,899.6	4,230.3	222.1	51,586.1
1940	15,017	80,212.6	22,557.7	29,074.9	25,683.9	3,091.5	5,233.3		71,153.5
1944 (Dec. 30)	14,579	152,947.2	26,101.6	94,011.0	30,977.2	3,053.0	6,640.2		142,310.8
1945 (Dec. 31)	14,566	175,361.1	30,466.9	110,518.7	35,614.6	3,187.4	7,434.3		166,530.1
1946 (Dec. 31)	14,633	169,406.4	34,522.9	95,636.7	35,217.5	3,299.5	8,128.5		156,801.4
1947 (Dec. 31)	14,755	176,024.1	43,231.1	92,397.3	36,360.1	3,342.6	8,654.6		162,726.7
1948 (Dec. 31)	14,735	176,075.4	45,452.7	85,963.4	36,683.5	3,428.2	9,130.6		162,041.4
1949 (Dec. 31)	14,705	180,043.1	49,825.3	91,436.2	36,675.9	3,546.7	9,616.9		165,344.0
1950 (Dec. 31)	14,666	192,240.7	60,711.1	88,004.6	41,235.5	3,670.2	10,245.6		176,130.2
1951 (Dec. 31)	14,636	203,862.6	68,001.0	87,586.3	45,716.6	3,840.0	10,960.3		184,603.7
National banks:									
1865	1,294	1,126.5	362.4	394.0	343.9	325.8	54.5	131.5	614.2
1870	2,076	2,035.5	994.7	451.5	517.5	455.9	166.5	318.1	1,085.1
1880	2,732	4,944.2	2,644.2	774.6	1,400.3	621.5	391.5	266.3	3,621.5
1910	7,145	9,896.6	5,455.9	1,576.2	2,549.9	969.6	861.4	675.6	7,257.0
1915	7,605	11,795.7	6,665.1	2,026.5	2,697.0	1,056.5	1,056.8	722.7	8,821.2
1920	8,030	23,276.3	12,502.1	4,050.9	4,495.4	1,224.2	1,397.9	686.2	17,166.6
1925	8,072	24,263.7	12,596.2	5,706.2	4,791.9	1,369.4	1,600.6	648.5	19,921.8
1930	7,252	28,872.4	14,897.2	6,888.2	5,415.3	1,744.0	2,232.2	652.3	23,268.9
1935	5,431	26,066.5	7,366.7	10,716.4	6,868.2	1,809.5	1,276.9	221.1	22,518.2
1940	5,170	36,885.1	9,179.2	12,905.3	13,577.1	1,534.6	1,941.8		33,074.4
1944 (Dec. 30)	5,031	76,949.9	11,497.5	47,022.3	17,637.2	1,566.9	2,708.0		72,128.9
1945 (Dec. 31)	5,029	90,535.8	13,946.0	55,611.6	20,178.8	1,658.8	2,996.9		85,342.9
1946 (Dec. 31)	5,013	84,550.3	17,309.8	46,642.8	20,067.2	1,756.6	3,395.2		79,049.8
1947 (Dec. 31)	5,011	88,447.0	21,480.5	44,010.0	23,075.6	1,779.8	3,641.6		82,275.4
1948 (Dec. 31)	4,997	88,135.1	23,818.5	40,228.4	23,024.3	1,828.5	3,842.1		81,648.0
1949 (Dec. 31)	4,983	90,230.3	23,928.3	44,207.8	21,043.0	1,916.3	4,018.0		83,344.3
1950 (Dec. 31)	4,965	97,240.1	29,277.5	43,022.5	23,813.4	2,001.7	4,327.3		90,529.6
1951 (Dec. 31)	4,946	102,724.6	32,423.8	43,043.6	26,012.2	2,105.3	4,564.8		94,431.6
State (commercial banks): [2]									
1840	901	657.7	462.9	42.4	98.7	358.4		107.0	119.9
1850	1,562	909.9	691.9	70.3	195.7	421.9		207.1	209.7
1860	650	451.5	292.1	61.9	109.9	109.3	35.5	.5	317.9
1870	5,009	3,376.4	1,963.5	589.9	707.0	388.8	260.6		2,659.0
1910	14,378	8,741.2	5,230.3	1,424.9	1,695.2	871.5	795.0		6,840.2
1915	17,794	11,511.4	6,808.5	1,928.4	2,133.2	1,073.6	962.4		9,123.7
1920	20,068	28,720.3	14,427.5	4,452.6	3,606.0	1,465.1	1,414.4		19,199.7
1925	19,635	29,506.3	16,736.7	6,263.4	4,544.3	1,789.5	1,820.0		24,794.0
1930	15,853	34,180.0	19,661.4	7,162.4	5,460.9	2,136.9	2,052.6		27,281.4
1935	9,583	22,441.0	7,586.9	8,890.0	4,915.1	1,701.3			18,696.5
1940	8,230	31,192.9	8,403.5	10,531.6	10,731.9	1,540.2	1,967.6		27,202.1
1944 (Dec. 30)	8,971	61,001.4	10,187.8	37,231.3	12,707.3	1,475.3	2,546.5		58,625.5
1945 (Dec. 31)	9,009	70,545.2	12,184.7	42,354.6	14,772.7	1,617.7	2,829.7		66,604.5
1946 (Dec. 31)	9,082	65,521.1	13,504.5	34,657.1	14,263.3	1,521.7	2,990.5		60,640.0

See footnotes at end of table.

No. 453.—ALL ACTIVE BANKS—PRINCIPAL ASSETS AND LIABILITIES, BY CLASS OF BANKS: 1834 TO 1951—Continued

[Money figures in millions of dollars]

ON OR ABOUT JUNE 30—	Number of banks	Total assets or liabilities [1]	SELECTED ASSETS			SELECTED LIABILITIES			
			Loans and discounts including overdrafts [2]	U. S. Govt. and other securities [3]	Cash and balances with other banks [1][4]	Capital stock [5]	Surplus, undivided profits, and reserve [6]	Circulation [7]	Total deposits [1]
State (commercial banks): [11]—Continued									
1947 (Dec. 31)_____	9,092	67,396.3	16,684.9	34,482.1	15,488.4	1,550.4	3,104.6	_____	62,283.1
1948 (Dec. 31)_____	9,090	67,025.3	18,832.2	31,812.5	15,621.9	1,581.8	3,268.1	_____	61,610.4
1949 (Dec. 31)_____	9,101	67,915.9	19,227.4	33,211.9	14,672.6	1,622.1	3,455.2	_____	62,267.5
1950 (Dec. 31)_____	9,081	72,215.6	23,178.5	31,611.2	16,526.0	1,658.0	3,651.7	_____	66,221.8
1951 (Dec. 31)_____	9,075	77,305.6	25,616.1	31,981.5	18,723.8	1,729.6	3,869.4	_____	70,932.2
Mutual savings banks:									
1875_____	674	896.2	532.5	295.7	41.2	_____	45.6	_____	849.6
1880_____	629	881.7	385.4	390.8	39.1	_____	56.0	_____	819.1
1900_____	652	2,336.5	1,001.6	1,128.1	114.0	_____	195.5	_____	2,134.7
1910_____	638	3,652.4	1,727.2	1,676.1	160.7	_____	289.3	_____	3,360.6
1915_____	630	4,319.4	2,170.0	1,869.9	206.3	_____	360.0	_____	3,951.1
1920_____	620	5,619.0	2,591.5	2,716.3	226.7	_____	422.5	_____	5,187.1
1925_____	611	7,913.0	4,183.1	3,351.2	243.3	_____	749.7	_____	7,151.8
1930_____	606	10,295.3	5,896.0	3,872.4	296.8	_____	1,068.7	_____	9,215.9
1935_____	571	11,172.5	5,342.5	4,511.4	522.8	[13] 25.6	1,199.1	_____	9,919.8
1940_____	551	11,952.2	4,926.5	5,261.5	979.4	8.0	1,288.1	_____	10,631.4
1944 (Dec. 30)_____	535	14,761.3	4,362.3	9,543.6	582.5	4.9	1,370.3	_____	13,350.6
1945 (Dec. 31)_____	534	16,987.1	4,271.8	11,905.4	607.8	4.9	1,584.9	_____	15,354.5
1946 (Dec. 31)_____	533	18,665.0	4,515.3	13,157.5	816.4	4.9	1,778.5	_____	16,835.2
1947 (Dec. 31)_____	533	19,713.9	4,944.4	13,696.2	886.3	5.0	1,884.1	_____	17,762.8
1948 (Dec. 31)_____	532	20,473.5	5,686.2	13,708.7	877.9	4.7	1,994.5	_____	18,404.9
1949 (Dec. 31)_____	531	21,492.9	6,578.1	13,822.2	872.6	5.3	2,116.5	_____	19,293.4
1950 (Dec. 31)_____	529	22,384.9	8,136.8	13,209.4	796.9	5.4	2,241.8	_____	20,031.3
1951 (Dec. 31)_____	529	23,438.8	9,861.7	12,397.6	886.2	[13]	[12] 2,406.9	_____	20,915.3
Private banks:									
1890_____	1,358	165.2	108.4	8.0	36.2	41.4	14.4	_____	105.4
1900_____	989	126.8	78.4	5.8	34.7	19.4	5.6	_____	97.7
1910_____	934	160.0	108.4	10.4	31.5	18.9	9.7	_____	126.4
1915_____	1,036	177.7	115.0	15.3	32.0	20.5	12.5	_____	135.7
1920_____	799	212.6	128.9	32.2	37.4	13.3	16.5	_____	171.8
1925_____	523	155.2	80.5	35.2	27.3	10.8	10.4	_____	127.5
1930_____	361	114.6	65.5	21.7	15.0	8.6	8.7	_____	81.0
1935_____	243	716.8	121.2	399.4	91.5	69.1	89.1	_____	511.5
1940_____	57	182.4	48.4	76.5	45.4	8.9	15.8	_____	145.5
1944 (Dec. 30)_____	42	234.6	53.7	123.7	50.3	5.9	15.4	_____	205.4
1945 (Dec. 31)_____	38	273.0	62.4	144.1	55.5	5.9	16.7	_____	238.1
1946 (Dec. 31)_____	35	310.0	73.3	149.4	70.7	6.3	16.0	_____	267.4
1947 (Dec. 31)_____	119	466.9	121.4	209.1	109.9	7.5	24.5	_____	407.4
1948 (Dec. 31)_____	116	441.5	115.9	183.9	111.5	7.9	25.9	_____	378.2
1949 (Dec. 31)_____	92	395.1	94.4	194.4	85.6	5.0	27.1	_____	338.9
1950 (Dec. 31)_____	91	400.1	118.4	161.6	99.4	5.1	24.8	_____	337.4
1951 (Dec. 31)_____	86	379.6	99.4	163.5	94.5	5.0	25.1	_____	324.6

[1] Reciprocal interbank demand balances with banks in U. S. are reported net, beginning 1942.
[2] Acceptances of other banks and bills of exchange or drafts sold with endorsements are excluded for national and State banks beginning with 1920 and for other banks beginning with 1929.
[3] Securities borrowed excluded for national banks beginning with 1903 and for other banks beginning with 1929. Not reported separately for prior years.
[4] Includes lawful reserve and exchanges for clearing house. Beginning 1936, excludes cash items not in process of collection.
[5] Beginning 1934, includes capital notes and debentures for banks other than national.
[6] Interest, taxes, and other expenses accrued and unpaid are excluded for national banks beginning with 1920 and for other banks beginning with 1929.
[7] Figures for national banks represent national bank circulation only; comparatively small amounts of State bank notes outstanding for 1870 to 1910, for which national banks converted from State banks or merged with State banks assumed liability, are not included in the figures for national banks or for all banks.
[8] Capital only.
[9] U. S. Government securities only.
[10] Includes State bank circulation outstanding.
[11] Includes loan and trust companies, and with some exceptions (see headnote), stock savings banks.
[12] Figures given under capital for 1935 include capital stock of one stock savings bank (see headnote).
[13] Not available.
[14] Includes book value of capital notes and debentures.

Source: Treasury Department, Comptroller of the Currency; *Annual Report*.

No. 454.—ALL ACTIVE BANKS—ASSETS AND LIABILITIES: 1948 TO 1951

[Money figures in millions of dollars. Includes data for U. S. possessions]

ITEM	1948 (Dec. 31)	1949 (Dec. 31)	1950 (Dec. 31)	1951 (Dec. 31)
Number of banks	14, 735	14, 705	14, 666	14, 636
Assets, total	176, 075	180, 043	192, 241	203, 863
Loans, total	48, 453	49, 828	60, 711	66, 001
Loans on real estate	16, 704	18, 350	21, 925	24, 648
Commercial and industrial loans (including open-market paper)	19, 055	17, 195	22, 068	26, 040
Other loans, including overdrafts	13, 332	15, 070	17, 645	18, 310
Less valuation reserves	638	787	927	997
Securities, total	85, 933	91, 436	88, 005	87, 566
U. S. Government obligations, direct and guaranteed	74, 462	78, 754	73, 188	71, 595
Obligations of States and political subdivisions	5, 754	6, 657	8, 249	9, 393
Other bonds, notes, and debentures	5, 200	5, 505	6, 011	5, 969
Corporate stocks, including stocks of Federal Reserve banks	517	520	557	609
Currency and coin	2, 145	2, 185	2, 343	2, 591
Balances with other banks, including reserve balances and cash items in process of collection	37, 490	34, 491	38, 893	42, 826
Bank premises owned, furniture and fixtures	1, 123	1, 173	1, 241	1, 331
Real estate owned other than bank premises	32	32	33	37
Investments and other assets indirectly representing bank premises or other real estate	78	96	103	105
Customers' liability on acceptances outstanding	205	191	235	349
Interest, commissions, rent, and other income earned or accrued but not collected	616	621	677	737
Other assets				
Liabilities, total	163, 521	166, 878	178, 325	189, 157
Deposits, total	162, 041	165, 244	176, 120	186, 604
Deposits of individuals, partnerships, and corporations:				
Demand	83, 166	83, 454	91, 314	97, 006
Time	53, 355	54, 416	55, 203	57, 472
U. S. Government and postal savings deposits	2, 521	3, 325	3, 069	3, 728
Deposits of States and political subdivisions	8, 562	8, 957	9, 546	10, 102
Deposits of banks	12, 285	12, 721	14, 050	15, 104
Other deposits (certified and cashiers' checks, etc.)	2, 152	2, 371	2, 938	3, 192
Bills payable, rediscounts, and other liabilities for borrowed money	64	27	95	44
Acceptances executed by or for account of reporting banks and outstanding	228	222	270	378
Interest, discount, rent, and other income collected but not earned				
Interest, taxes, and other expenses accrued and unpaid	1, 188	1, 385	1, 840	2, 131
Other liabilities				
Capital accounts, total	12, 554	13, 165	13, 916	14, 706
Capital notes and debentures	48	48	47	40
Preferred stock	79	69	62	51
Common stock	3, 296	3, 431	3, 561	3, 749
Surplus	6, 008	6, 385	6, 854	7, 262
Undivided profits	2, 506	2, 626	2, 809	3, 027
Reserves and retirement account for preferred stock and capital notes and debentures	617	606	583	577

Source: Treasury Department, Comptroller of the Currency; *Annual Report.*

No. 455. — ALL ACTIVE BANKS—SUMMARY, BY STATES AND OTHER AREAS: DEC. 31, 1951

[Money figures in millions of dollars]

REGION, STATE, OR OTHER AREA	Number of banks	Total assets or liabilities	SELECTED ASSETS			SELECTED LIABILITIES			
			Loans and discounts including overdrafts	U.S. Govt. and other securities	Cash and balances with other banks [1]	Capital, surplus, undivided profits and reserve [2]	Deposits		
							Total	Demand	Time (incl. postal savings)
Total	14,636	263,862.6	68,001.6	87,586.3	45,716.6	14,706.3	186,603.7	126,680.0	59,923.7
Continental U. S.	14,594	263,903.4	67,608.1	87,260.9	45,530.9	14,623.1	185,755.6	126,179.6	59,576.1
New England States	854	15,634.7	5,457.5	7,619.6	2,360.6	1,468.7	14,015.6	6,386.7	7,628.8
Maine	95	817.6	260.2	426.8	122.6	84.6	729.5	288.3	441.2
New Hampshire	109	660.7	248.8	320.8	85.8	75.7	583.0	182.7	400.3
Vermont	76	404.6	202.8	137.9	59.5	39.4	363.4	115.6	247.8
Massachusetts	368	8,961.6	3,262.3	4,235.6	1,349.2	859.6	7,994.5	3,856.5	4,138.1
Rhode Island	22	1,189.3	423.6	575.3	172.6	95.0	1,080.2	501.4	578.8
Connecticut	184	3,600.9	1,059.7	1,923.2	570.3	314.5	3,265.0	1,442.2	1,822.7
Eastern States	2,283	76,712.8	27,594.1	32,294.4	15,551.8	6,463.5	68,757.3	43,786.4	24,976.9
New York	749	52,227.7	20,270.6	20,322.5	10,782.7	4,432.9	46,462.9	29,780.7	16,682.2
New Jersey	341	6,220.7	1,853.2	3,223.3	1,064.0	427.7	5,757.0	3,030.9	2,726.1
Pennsylvania	967	13,806.5	4,262.2	6,540.2	2,830.4	1,267.9	12,442.5	8,138.6	4,304.0
Delaware	38	699.1	216.7	334.9	140.6	70.5	623.9	439.9	183.9
Maryland	169	2,411.3	618.8	1,272.2	481.6	184.8	2,212.5	1,373.5	839.0
District of Columbia	19	1,347.5	372.6	601.2	352.5	79.8	1,258.4	1,016.8	241.7
Southern States	3,878	29,598.3	8,864.6	11,582.5	8,786.6	1,841.6	27,532.9	22,679.8	4,453.1
Virginia	315	2,396.0	812.0	950.6	603.9	168.2	2,209.8	1,537.3	672.5
West Virginia	181	1,118.0	300.8	519.6	265.7	90.4	1,020.1	757.4	262.7
North Carolina	225	2,291.5	707.8	947.7	610.4	144.9	2,113.4	1,680.3	433.1
South Carolina	149	849.8	210.3	376.4	256.8	48.4	796.8	702.3	94.5
Georgia	386	2,152.7	741.2	744.5	639.8	140.5	1,990.5	1,664.6	325.9
Florida	208	2,366.9	561.0	1,148.6	624.1	143.1	2,211.0	1,808.3	402.7
Alabama	226	1,487.8	424.9	623.3	422.8	98.9	1,378.0	1,108.0	269.9
Mississippi	202	940.3	236.1	433.2	262.4	57.2	879.4	744.0	135.5
Louisiana	166	2,150.5	505.3	925.2	693.7	109.6	2,022.8	1,727.3	295.5
Texas	909	8,589.5	2,713.9	2,877.1	2,864.9	494.3	8,028.9	7,291.2	737.7
Arkansas	230	946.9	220.7	422.7	297.6	64.6	880.0	776.0	104.0
Kentucky	383	1,938.9	586.3	767.9	571.8	131.4	1,797.8	1,558.8	238.9
Tennessee	296	2,369.5	844.6	845.5	652.5	150.1	2,204.4	1,724.2	480.2
Middle Western States	4,972	48,938.8	14,331.0	22,619.3	11,593.3	2,975.4	45,654.7	32,377.2	13,277.5
Ohio	659	9,234.4	2,770.6	4,331.4	2,040.6	567.6	8,609.1	5,618.5	2,990.6
Indiana	485	3,781.3	941.7	1,895.2	914.9	222.3	3,542.0	2,563.1	978.9
Illinois	895	14,749.6	3,944.1	7,033.2	3,673.0	888.0	13,753.8	10,364.3	3,389.5
Michigan	435	6,425.2	1,845.7	3,189.2	1,330.7	355.9	6,016.8	3,708.7	2,308.1
Wisconsin	557	3,513.0	986.6	1,723.5	774.4	216.5	3,286.3	2,007.8	1,278.5
Minnesota	681	3,452.5	1,170.4	1,442.4	811.7	229.1	3,197.4	2,160.6	1,036.8
Iowa	661	2,574.2	901.0	1,077.0	580.1	175.6	2,394.1	1,844.2	550.0
Missouri	599	5,208.5	1,770.9	1,927.4	1,467.8	320.4	4,855.2	4,110.1	745.1
Western States	2,097	9,556.0	2,688.4	4,153.7	2,647.6	573.3	8,939.1	7,700.4	1,238.7
North Dakota	150	640.3	152.7	368.3	115.6	36.9	601.1	440.7	160.3
South Dakota	169	566.6	175.5	263.2	123.6	33.7	530.4	435.4	95.0
Nebraska	416	1,551.7	459.9	668.1	414.3	94.1	1,446.8	1,296.5	150.3
Kansas	607	1,966.0	565.2	827.5	562.8	120.3	1,840.6	1,652.0	188.6
Montana	110	647.2	163.1	315.4	163.8	28.7	615.3	513.6	101.8
Wyoming	52	324.5	82.8	143.8	95.5	17.5	305.9	253.4	52.4
Colorado	157	1,405.4	436.9	578.9	380.5	84.1	1,313.5	1,050.8	262.7
New Mexico	51	427.2	116.7	166.8	139.6	22.9	403.3	347.0	56.4
Oklahoma	385	2,027.2	536.1	821.6	650.9	135.1	1,882.3	1,711.1	171.2
Pacific States	510	22,462.6	8,671.9	8,991.4	4,491.6	1,300.7	20,856.2	12,855.1	8,001.1
Washington	121	2,466.2	859.3	996.5	583.9	150.0	2,304.6	1,557.2	747.4
Oregon	71	1,623.2	587.2	668.2	344.8	95.7	1,514.0	1,077.8	436.2
California	201	16,379.7	6,523.0	6,504.6	3,120.1	943.8	15,173.3	8,840.8	6,332.5
Idaho	42	504.2	174.7	218.6	106.7	25.9	467.5	359.0	116.7
Utah	54	698.8	240.9	280.3	171.7	40.5	653.6	460.3	193.3
Nevada	8	215.7	62.6	112.1	38.0	11.7	202.0	135.2	66.9
Arizona	13	572.8	224.1	211.1	126.3	33.1	532.9	424.9	108.1
Other areas	42	959.2	392.8	325.4	185.8	83.1	848.0	500.4	347.6
Alaska	20	123.2	28.8	55.5	37.5	6.6	116.4	82.4	34.0
Canal Zone (Panama)	(3)	24.6	1.1	3.8	4.2	....	24.6	22.3	2.3
Guam	(4)	19.2	2.4		.9		19.0	12.3	6.7
Hawaii	9	421.0	191.3	140.0	82.1	33.7	384.3	202.2	182.1
Puerto Rico	11	364.7	167.7	122.3	60.0	42.3	297.8	178.0	119.8
American Samoa	1	1.3	.1	1.1	.2	.1	1.2	.7	.5
Virgin Islands	1	5.2	1.6	2.7	.9	.4	4.8	2.5	2.3

[1] Includes reserve balances and cash items in process of collection.
[2] Includes capital notes and debentures and retirement account for preferred stock and capital notes, etc.
[3] 4 branches of 2 American national banks.
[4] 2 branches of an American national bank.

Source: Treasury Department, Comptroller of the Currency; *Annual Report.*

No. 456.—All Banks in Continental United States—Principal Assets and Liabilities, and Number of Banks: 1930 to 1952

[Money figures in millions of dollars. In general, data cover national banks, State commercial banks, trust companies, mutual and stocks savings banks, and such private, Morris Plan, and industrial banks for which data are available. For member bank data, see table 458; for figures on all active banks including those in territories and possessions, see table 455]

ITEM	1930, Dec. 31	1935, Dec. 31	1940, Dec. 31	1945, Dec. 31	1949, Dec. 31	1950, Dec. 30	1951 June 30	1951 Dec. 31	1952 June 30	1952 Dec. 31
Loans and investments, total	58,602	45,779	54,177	140,227	140,508	148,021	147,742	154,869	157,528	155,636
Loans	38,062	20,355	23,736	30,362	49,544	60,386	63,840	67,608	69,742	75,512
Investments, total	18,550	25,424	30,422	109,865	91,064	87,635	83,901	87,261	87,786	90,114
U. S. Government obligations	(1)	15,527	20,972	101,288	78,433	72,894	68,726	71,343	70,783	72,740
Other securities	(1)	9,896	9,449	8,577	12,621	14,741	15,176	15,918	17,002	17,374
Cash assets [1]	(1)	14,849	28,090	35,415	36,522	41,086	38,235	45,531	41,667	45,584
Deposits, total [2]	52,093	55,389	75,996	165,612	164,467	175,296	171,860	185,756	184,120	195,552
Interbank [2]	5,155	6,570	10,934	14,065	12,710	14,039	11,947	15,067	13,513	15,221
Other:										
Demand	(1)	25,427	38,558	105,935	96,156	104,744	102,527	111,644	109,247	116,632
Time	(1)	23,392	26,503	45,513	55,601	56,513	57,386	59,025	61,399	63,596
Capital accounts, total	(1)	7,787	8,302	10,542	13,088	13,937	14,236	14,623	15,039	15,367
Number of banks	22,773	15,900	14,896	14,553	14,687	14,650	14,636	14,618	14,599	14,575

[1] Not available.
[2] Beginning June 30, 1942, excludes reciprocal interbank balances, which on Dec. 31, 1942, aggregated $512 million at all member banks and $525 million at all insured commercial banks.

No. 457.—Federal Reserve System, All Member Banks—Earnings, Expenses, and Dividends: 1930 to 1951

[Money figures in millions of dollars; ratios in percentages. See also Historical Statistics, series N 66–75]

ITEM	1930	1935	1940	1945	1950	1951 Total	1951 National	1951 State
Number of banks	8,062	6,387	6,496	6,884	6,873	6,840	4,939	1,901
Current earnings, total	2,157.9	1,206.6	1,323.0	2,102.2	3,364.7	3,606.7	2,446.1	1,222.6
Interest earned	1,887.5	967.1	1,025.6	1,707.9	2,663.2	3,017.0	2,051.2	965.8
Expenses, total	1,604.3	832.5	921.0	1,267.6	2,019.7	2,231.9	1,474.1	757.9
Interest paid	771.0	209.7	147.6	185.2	274.9	314.6	223.2	91.5
Salaries and wages	461.8	334.5	400.2	572.6	909.9	1,125.3	739.8	386.5
Net current earnings [1]	553.6	374.1	402.0	834.5	1,344.9	1,436.8	972.1	464.7
Recoveries, profits on securities, etc.	118.2	376.0	302.8	452.8	218.6	148.6	96.2	52.5
Losses and charge-offs [1]	368.3	538.2	355.7	226.9	313.7	335.9	230.4	105.4
Profits before income taxes	}(1)	(1)	(1)	}1,058.5	1,149.9	1,246.5	856.8	460.5
Taxes on net income				270.1	369.1	490.9	331.8	159.1
Net profits	205.5	211.9	349.1	788.4	780.8	755.6	505.0	250.7
Cash dividends declared [2]	357.0	186.8	210.5	245.9	345.5	370.5	247.3	123.2
Loans [3]	25,018.0	11,985.0	14,286.0	19,815.0	39,098.0	47,016.0	(4)	(4)
Securities [3]	10,377.0	16,912.0	20,623.0	77,361.0	64,314.0	60,668.0	(4)	(4)
Capital accounts [3]	6,722.9	5,113.0	5,897.0	7,343.0	9,455.0	9,947.0	(4)	(4)
Ratios to capital accounts:								
Net current earnings [1]	8.2	7.3	7.2	11.5	13.2	14.4	(4)	(4)
Net profits	4.6	4.1	6.2	10.9	9.3	7.6	(4)	(4)
Cash dividends declared	5.5	2.7	3.5	3.4	3.7	3.7	(4)	(4)
Ratios to total assets:								
Total current earnings [1]	4.6	2.9	2.3	1.7	2.4	2.6	(4)	(4)
Net current earnings [1]	1.3	.9	.7	.7	.9	1.0	(4)	(4)

[1] Beginning with 1942, taxes on net income, previously included in expenses, are reported separately, and re- depreciation on banking-house furniture and fixtures, previously included in losses and charge-offs, is included in expenses.

[2] Includes interest on capital notes and debentures beginning 1932, when first issued.

[3] Figures are a simple average of amounts reported for every call date in year and final call date in preceding year. Prior to 1941, averages of amounts reported for call dates at beginning, middle, and end of year were used, plus the 13 mid-month figures for the 10 intervening months.

[4] Figures are on the 13-month basis used for all member banks.

Source: Tables 456 and 457: Board of Governors of the Federal Reserve System; figures through 1941, Banking and Monetary Statistics; published currently in Federal Reserve Bulletin.

No. 458.—FEDERAL RESERVE SYSTEM, ALL MEMBER BANKS—PRINCIPAL ASSETS AND LIABILITIES: 1925 TO 1952

[Money figures in millions of dollars. Data as of Dec. 31. See also *Historical Statistics*, series N 49-55, for data as of June 30 on all member banks]

ITEM	ALL MEMBER BANKS							
	1925	1930	1935	1940	1945	1950	1951	1952
Number of banks	9,489	8,052	6,387	6,486	6,884	6,873	6,840	6,798
ASSETS								
Loans and investments, total	30,884	34,860	29,985	37,126	107,183	107,424	112,247	119,547
Loans	21,996	23,870	12,175	15,321	22,775	44,705	49,561	55,034
Investments, total	8,888	10,989	17,810	21,805	84,408	62,719	62,687	64,514
U. S. Govt. obligations [1]	3,728	4,125	12,268	15,823	78,338	52,365	51,621	32,763
Other securities	5,160	6,864	5,541	5,982	6,070	10,355	11,065	11,751
Reserve with Federal Reserve Banks	2,238	2,475	5,573	13,992	15,811	17,459	19,912	19,810
Cash in vault	575	593	665	991	1,438	1,643	2,062	2,081
Balances with domestic banks [2]	2,155	2,456	3,776	6,185	7,117	6,868	7,463	7,378
LIABILITIES								
Deposits, total	34,250	37,029	38,454	56,430	129,670	133,089	141,015	147,527
Interbank:								
Domestic banks [2]	} 4,169	3,980	5,847	9,716	12,380	11,693	12,656	12,626
Foreign banks		784	449	706	1,260	1,755	1,768	1,991
U. S. Government [3]	304	267	844	651	22,275	2,698	3,344	4,870
Postal savings	96	189	218	22	3	7	14	18
All other:								
Demand	19,124	18,796	21,056	33,213	69,640	87,783	92,867	95,453
Time	10,557	13,012	10,041	12,122	24,111	29,153	30,366	32,570
Demand deposits adjusted [4]	15,943	15,860	18,801	30,429	64,184	78,370	83,100	85,543
Net demand deposits subject to reserve	19,360	18,969	22,169	35,262	70,918	87,160	92,770	96,786
Borrowings	740	513	14	3	208	79	26	165
Capital accounts	4,678	6,593	5,145	5,698	7,589	9,695	10,218	10,761

ITEM	NEW YORK [5]			CHICAGO [5]			RESERVE CITY BANKS			COUNTRY BANKS		
	1950	1951	1952	1950	1951	1952	1950	1951	1952	1950	1951	1952
Number of banks	23	22	22	13	13	13	336	321	319	6,501	6,484	6,444
ASSETS												
Loans and investments, total	20,612	21,379	22,130	5,569	5,731	6,240	40,685	42,694	45,583	40,558	42,444	45,594
Loans	9,729	11,146	12,376	2,083	2,468	2,748	17,906	19,651	21,697	14,988	16,296	18,213
Investments, total	10,883	10,233	9,754	3,487	3,264	3,493	22,779	23,043	23,886	25,570	26,148	27,381
U. S. Govt. obligations [1]	8,993	8,129	7,678	2,911	2,711	2,912	19,084	19,194	19,624	21,377	21,587	22,549
Other securities	1,890	2,104	2,076	576	552	581	3,695	3,849	4,262	4,193	4,561	4,832
Reserve with Federal Reserve Banks	4,693	5,246	5,059	1,216	1,407	1,144	6,806	7,582	7,788	4,745	5,676	5,870
Cash in vault	118	159	148	30	32	32	519	639	651	976	1,231	1,250
Balances with domestic banks [2]	78	79	84	133	165	169	2,206	2,356	2,419	4,450	4,862	4,706
LIABILITIES												
Deposits, total	25,646	26,859	27,309	7,109	7,462	7,686	51,437	54,466	57,357	48,897	52,288	55,175
Interbank:												
Domestic banks [2]	3,208	3,386	3,354	1,177	1,269	1,311	6,184	6,704	6,670	1,124	1,298	1,291
Foreign banks	1,430	1,447	1,611	51	38	39	264	273	330	10	11	11
U. S. Government [3]	488	901	1,202	177	247	347	1,034	1,206	1,917	999	990	1,404
Postal savings							2	3	3	5	11	15
All other:												
Demand	18,836	19,490	19,361	4,604	4,710	4,789	32,366	34,094	35,281	31,977	34,572	36,022
Time	1,684	1,636	1,780	1,099	1,138	1,201	11,587	12,187	13,156	14,782	15,406	16,433
Demand deposits adjusted [4]	15,898	16,439	16,288	3,954	4,121	4,126	27,938	29,489	30,609	30,581	33,051	34,519
Net demand deposits subject to reserve	20,642	21,734	21,850	5,220	5,506	5,645	33,114	35,160	36,912	28,184	30,371	32,379
Borrowings	70	5	132				4	8	9	16	16	25
Capital accounts	2,351	2,425	2,505	490	513	541	3,322	3,521	3,745	3,532	3,760	3,970

[1] Both direct and guaranteed obligations.
[2] Prior to Dec. 31, 1935, excludes balances with private banks to extent that such balances were reported in "Other assets." Prior to Dec. 31, 1933, excludes time balances with domestic banks which then amounted to $62,000,000 and which, prior to that time, were reported in "Other assets." Beginning June 30, 1942, excludes reciprocal bank balances which on Dec. 31, 1942, aggregated $513,000,000.
[3] Beginning with 1940, includes U. S. Treasurer's time deposits, open account.
[4] Demand deposits other than interbank and U. S. Government, less cash items reported as in process of collection and, prior to Dec. 31, 1935, less cash items reported on hand but not in process of collection.
[5] Central reserve city banks only.

Source: Board of Governors of the Federal Reserve System. Figures published currently in *Federal Reserve Bulletin*.

No. 459.—FEDERAL RESERVE BANKS—PRINCIPAL ASSETS: 1920 TO 1952

[In thousands of dollars. See also *Historical Statistics*, series N 114–119, for data on all Federal Reserve Banks]

DEC. 22—	Total assets	Reserves	RESERVE BANK CREDIT OUTSTANDING				
				Loans and securities			
			Total [1]	Total [2]	Discounts and advances	Acceptances purchased	U. S. Govt. securities
All F. R. banks:							
1920 (Dec. 29)	8, 254, 105	2, 250, 400	3, 384, 682	3, 254, 828	2, 687, 393	260, 405	287, 029
1925	5, 109, 494	2, 834, 371	1, 439, 172	1, 396, 122	642, 998	374, 356	374, 566
1930	4, 200, 648	3, 061, 517	1, 373, 332	1, 351, 652	251, 396	363, 844	729, 467
1935	11, 025, 800	7, 835, 351	2, 485, 631	2, 472, 733	4, 672	4, 686	2, 430, 731
1940	23, 251, 805	20, 085, 582	2, 274, 219	2, 194, 553	2, 915		2, 184, 100
1945	46, 082, 896	17, 902, 934	25, 091, 365	24, 513, 094	248, 905		24, 262, 348
1948	45, 643, 097	23, 176, 223	19, 498, 711	18, 964, 512	77, 848		18, 884, 897
1950	47, 172, 314	21, 497, 632	22, 215, 951	20, 847, 518	67, 396		20, 777, 857
1951	49, 899, 836	21, 408, 087	25, 009, 207	23, 825, 342	19, 347		23, 801, 258
1952	51, 852, 494	21, 985, 705	25, 834, 594	24, 857, 283	156, 379		24, 697, 012
Boston:							
1949	2, 492, 749	916, 600	1, 329, 097	1, 306, 430	5, 619		1, 308, 811
1950	2, 643, 116	846, 109	1, 514, 612	1, 425, 870	125		1, 433, 745
1951	2, 811, 226	717, 416	1, 749, 510	1, 643, 246	2, 510		1, 640, 736
1952	2, 890, 696	753, 330	1, 790, 147	1, 695, 226	2, 214		1, 693, 012
New York:							
1949	12, 442, 428	7, 399, 964	4, 598, 699	4, 496, 536	23, 377		4, 473, 461
1950	12, 442, 611	6, 355, 896	5, 284, 219	4, 945, 795	61, 960		4, 883, 908
1951	13, 276, 342	6, 895, 931	5, 819, 335	5, 511, 102	2, 895		5, 598, 485
1952	13, 456, 392	6, 112, 901	6, 574, 746	6, 328, 276	114, 924		6, 213, 352
Philadelphia:							
1949	2, 789, 740	1, 257, 428	1, 334, 080	1, 296, 521	7, 255		1, 294, 381
1950	2, 874, 305	1, 180, 843	1, 448, 477	1, 384, 042	3, 640		1, 378, 198
1951	3, 001, 310	1, 201, 383	1, 564, 412	1, 492, 408	3, 440		1, 485, 205
1952	3, 147, 504	1, 328, 296	1, 565, 962	1, 519, 487	5, 476		1, 510, 542
Cleveland:							
1949	3, 660, 491	1, 508, 288	1, 814, 394	1, 748, 596	6, 849		1, 741, 745
1950	3, 973, 060	1, 544, 108	2, 100, 031	1, 921, 226	149		1, 921, 075
1951	4, 232, 249	1, 566, 177	2, 265, 367	2, 205, 581	670		2, 204, 911
1952	4, 372, 845	1, 532, 109	2, 487, 218	2, 403, 285	4, 184		2, 399, 101
Richmond:							
1949	2, 699, 007	1, 139, 428	1, 285, 834	1, 218, 247	5, 806		1, 212, 335
1950	2, 749, 618	1, 002, 926	1, 454, 354	1, 339, 632	575		1, 338, 925
1951	2, 940, 288	994, 835	1, 624, 616	1, 571, 979	2, 340		1, 569, 546
1952	3, 131, 707	1, 068, 080	1, 688, 753	1, 630, 134	5, 704		1, 624, 364
Atlanta:							
1949	2, 309, 532	1, 035, 661	1, 044, 273	1, 015, 339	2, 879		1, 012, 460
1950	2, 364, 712	930, 341	1, 198, 180	1, 110, 117	25		1, 110, 085
1951	2, 539, 983	973, 336	1, 339, 755	1, 274, 598	300		1, 273, 684
1952	2, 684, 046	936, 261	1, 435, 952	1, 393, 840	2, 584		1, 391, 034
Chicago:							
1949	7, 788, 614	4, 457, 964	2, 892, 994	2, 827, 655	9, 732		2, 817, 903
1950	8, 194, 781	4, 260, 426	3, 376, 992	3, 142, 930	106		3, 142, 824
1951	8, 620, 623	4, 343, 917	3, 782, 904	3, 522, 316	341		3, 521, 975
1952	8, 909, 398	4, 590, 307	3, 635, 991	3, 444, 388	7, 360		3, 437, 028
St. Louis:							
1949	1, 980, 708	729, 760	1, 056, 226	1, 023, 063	2, 502		1, 020, 561
1950	2, 016, 164	631, 080	1, 208, 107	1, 138, 113	500		1, 137, 613
1951	2, 087, 591	604, 034	1, 335, 362	1, 286, 957	55		1, 286, 902
1952	2, 210, 564	668, 510	1, 335, 677	1, 303, 827	1, 246		1, 302, 581
Minneapolis:							
1949	1, 154, 445	446, 505	636, 681	613, 216	1, 787		611, 351
1950	1, 159, 603	387, 261	671, 840	641, 379			641, 194
1951	1, 316, 450	350, 279	777, 130	749, 487			749, 353
1952	1, 344, 300	353, 185	794, 177	765, 802	1, 267		764, 400
Kansas City:							
1949	1, 909, 007	863, 346	938, 506	916, 812	3, 402		913, 410
1950	2, 072, 822	865, 464	1, 005, 870	961, 993	315		961, 678
1951	2, 126, 606	775, 121	1, 183, 327	1, 118, 498	7, 096		1, 111, 402
1952	2, 220, 227	936, 080	1, 102, 637	1, 064, 607	2, 526		1, 062, 083
Dallas:							
1949	1, 605, 637	712, 225	842, 310	819, 265	2, 432		816, 853
1950	1, 607, 252	648, 078	968, 659	940, 787			940, 787
1951	1, 915, 791	561, 917	1, 153, 080	1, 129, 869			1, 129, 530
1952	2, 058, 183	744, 678	1, 126, 469	1, 102, 742	1, 151		1, 101, 591
San Francisco:							
1949	4, 709, 899	2, 719, 304	1, 749, 737	1, 679, 511	6, 185		1, 673, 326
1950	4, 874, 270	2, 573, 061	1, 998, 582	1, 892, 635			1, 892, 635
1951	4, 148, 088	2, 468, 709	2, 494, 280	2, 319, 630			2, 319, 630
1952	4, 633, 478	2, 985, 048	2, 398, 528	2, 215, 679	7, 744		2, 207, 985

[1] ... to total loans and securities, amounts due from foreign banks and Reserve bank float.
... investments, industrial loans, etc., not listed separately.

Source: ... of the Federal Reserve System: *Banking and Monetary Statistics, Annual Report*. ... Figures published currently in *Federal Reserve Bulletin*.

No. 460.—FEDERAL RESERVE BANKS—PRINCIPAL LIABILITIES: 1920 TO 1952

[Money figures in thousands of dollars. See also *Historical Statistics*, series N 120–123, for data on all Federal Reserve Banks]

DEC. 31—	Capital	Surplus [1]	DEPOSIT LIABILITY		Federal Reserve notes	Reserve percentage [2]
			Total	Member bank reserves		
All F. R. banks:						
1920 (Dec. 29)	99, 821	202, 096	1, 861, 496	1, 780, 679	3, 336, 281	43. 3
1925	117, 237	220, 310	2, 257, 388	2, 212, 096	1, 838, 164	69. 0
1930	169, 640	274, 636	2, 517, 133	2, 470, 583	1, 663, 538	73. 7
1935	130, 512	169, 736	6, 385, 809	5, 587, 206	3, 709, 074	77. 6
1940	138, 579	183, 849	16, 126, 567	14, 025, 633	5, 930, 997	90. 8
1945	177, 095	385, 783	18, 199, 5⁴0	15, 914, 980	24, 649, 132	41. 7
1949	210, 891	515, 716	18, 906, 292	16, 568, 088	23, 482, 646	54. 7
1950	225, 102	537, 565	19, 809, 583	17, 680, 744	23, 587, 018	49. 4
1951	236, 613	565, 885	21, 191, 576	20, 055, 716	25, 064, 109	46. 4
1952	252, 634	612, 219	21, 344, 064	19, 950, 372	26, 250, 299	46. 2
Boston:						
1949	12, 001	33, 790	837, 096	711, 482	1, 397, 144	41. 0
1950	12, 223	35, 257	925, 056	783, 608	1, 423, 788	36. 0
1951	12, 986	37, 203	918, 961	873, 756	1, 525, 817	29. 3
1952	13, 612	39, 473	922, 277	835, 721	1, 603, 208	29. 8
New York:						
1949	72, 426	155, 468	6, 313, 547	5, 347, 438	5, 430, 262	62. 2
1950	73, 383	160, 609	6, 323, 274	5, 665, 077	5, 342, 941	56. 4
1951	75, 472	167, 062	6, 956, 979	6, 368, 672	5, 588, 434	54. 7
1952	80, 139	174, 822	6, 748, 339	6, 184, 727	5, 796, 489	48. 7
Philadelphia:						
1949	15, 084	42, 604	918, 064	788, 335	1, 632, 189	49. 3
1950	15, 675	44, 199	956, 671	822, 286	1, 665, 849	45. 0
1951	16, 765	45, 982	964, 916	912, 100	1, 769, 888	43. 9
1952	17, 186	48, 067	1, 010, 335	929, 318	1, 857, 370	46. 3
Cleveland:						
1949	19, 432	46, 963	1, 331, 846	1, 185, 987	2, 050, 079	47. 3
1950	22, 001	49, 020	1, 500, 498	1, 323, 910	2, 112, 367	42. 7
1951	22, 498	51, 654	1, 536, 281	1, 471, 670	2, 286, 836	41. 7
1952	24, 215	55, 070	1, 572, 447	1, 497, 699	2, 410, 657	38. 5
Richmond:						
1949	9, 223	27, 128	851, 278	708, 359	1, 580, 160	44. 9
1950	9, 845	28, 516	861, 045	750, 834	1, 616, 465	40. 5
1951	10, 383	30, 374	881, 188	848, 054	1, 785, 153	37. 3
1952	11, 013	32, 597	912, 174	849, 025	1, 887, 063	38. 0
Atlanta:						
1949	8, 240	21, 956	798, 992	685, 366	1, 290, 999	49. 5
1950	8, 954	23, 131	859, 026	740, 422	1, 276, 091	43. 6
1951	9, 711	24, 633	947, 769	915, 858	1, 382, 155	41. 8
1952	10, 408	26, 565	957, 876	895, 538	1, 445, 086	39. 0
Chicago:						
1949	26, 885	73, 458	2, 800, 823	2, 627, 072	4, 501, 280	61. 1
1950	28, 698	76, 774	3, 031, 776	2, 797, 828	4, 559, 980	56. 1
1951	30, 375	81, 030	3, 337, 186	3, 227, 710	4, 764, 081	53. 6
1952	32, 342	86, 057	3, 180, 912	3, 066, 258	4, 971, 415	55. 8
St. Louis:						
1949	6, 894	19, 639	700, 997	611, 854	1, 090, 460	40. 7
1950	7, 398	20, 816	740, 075	651, 163	1, 097, 441	34. 3
1951	8, 366	22, 309	775, 637	740, 738	1, 167, 160	31. 1
1952	8, 800	24, 149	796, 990	731, 518	1, 230, 998	34. 0
Minneapolis:						
1949	4, 709	13, 567	455, 665	394, 920	612, 217	41. 8
1950	5, 073	14, 241	441, 571	391, 855	610, 643	36. 8
1951	5, 363	15, 136	490, 145	464, 389	632, 029	31. 2
1952	5, 719	16, 204	482, 080	437, 867	650, 889	31. 2
Kansas City:						
1949	7, 379	19, 182	876, 890	768, 824	918, 194	48. 1
1950	8, 306	20, 184	946, 577	837, 399	919, 844	46. 5
1951	8, 886	21, 504	978, 474	952, 309	972, 743	39. 7
1952	9, 477	23, 062	1, 010, 279	957, 907	1, 022, 199	46. 2
Dallas:						
1949	8, 456	17, 180	913, 455	814, 892	640, 274	45. 8
1950	9, 610	18, 159	990, 138	891, 215	639, 322	39. 8
1951	10, 712	19, 517	1, 035, 411	1, 011, 045	702, 162	33. 5
1952	12, 238	26, 688	1, 096, 205	1, 051, 212	759, 282	40. 1
San Francisco:						
1949	20, 163	44, 692	2, 107, 579	1, 923, 559	2, 339, 368	61. 1
1950	23, 936	46, 659	2, 233, 846	2, 025, 147	2, 322, 307	56. 5
1951	25, 096	49, 481	2, 368, 629	2, 269, 415	2, 487, 651	50. 7
1952	27, 485	59, 465	2, 652, 140	2, 513, 582	2, 615, 673	56. 7

[1] Includes surplus sec. 13b beginning December 1935.

[2] Ratio of reserves (shown in table 459) to aggregate of total deposit and Federal Reserve note liabilities.

Source: Board of Governors of the Federal Reserve System; *Banking and Monetary Statistics*, *Annual Report* and *Federal Reserve Bulletin*. Figures published currently in *Federal Reserve Bulletin*.

No. 461.—Federal Reserve Banks—Discount Rates[1] in Effect Jan. 1, 1935, and Changes to Dec. 31, 1952

[Percent per annum]

Month established	Boston	New York	Philadelphia	Cleveland	Richmond	Atlanta	Chicago	St. Louis	Minneapolis	Kansas City	Dallas	San Francisco
	DISCOUNTS FOR AND ADVANCES TO MEMBER BANKS UNDER SECS. 13 AND 13(a) OF FEDERAL RESERVE ACT[2]											
In effect Jan. 1, 1935	2	1½	2½	2	3	2½	2½	2½	3	2½	3	2
1935—Jan.			2		2½	2	2	2	2½		2½	
May				1½	2				2	2	2	
1937—Aug.		1			1½	1½	1½		1½		1½	
Sept.	1½		1½					1½		1½		1½
1939—Sept.	1					(3)	(3)	(3)		(3)	(3)	
1942—Feb.							1					
Mar.			1		1	1		1	1		1	
Apr.				1						1		1
Oct.	(4)	(4)	(4)	(4)	(4)	(4)	(4)	(4)	(4)	(4)	(4)	(4)
1948—Jan.	1¼	1¼	1¼	1¼	1¼	1¼	1¼	1¼	1¼	1¼	1¼	1¼
Aug.	1½	1½	1½	1½	1½	1½	1½	1½	1½	1½	1½	1½
1950—Aug.	1¾	1¾	1¾	1¾	1¾	1¾	1¾	1¾	1¾	1¾	1¾	1¾
In effect Dec. 31, 1952	1¾	1¾	1¾	1¾	1¾	1¾	1¾	1¾	1¾	1¾	1¾	1¾
	ADVANCES TO MEMBER BANKS UNDER SEC. 10(b) OF FEDERAL RESERVE ACT[3]											
In effect Jan. 1, 1935	4	4	4	4	4½	4½	4	4½	5	4	4	4
1935—Jan.		2½				4						
Aug.										2½		
Sept.	2½				2½	2½	2½					2½
Oct.		2		2				2½	2½		2½	
Nov.			2½									
1937—Aug.						2	2		2		2	
Sept.	2		2		2			2		2		2
1942—Mar.								1½				
Aug.							1½					
Sept.				1½								
Oct.	1½	1½	1½		1½	1½			1½	1½	1½	1½
1948—Jan.	1¾	1¾	1¾	1¾	1¾	1¾	1¾	1¾	1¾	1¾	1¾	1¾
Aug.	2	2	2	2	2	2	2	2	2	2	2	2
1950—Aug.	2¼	2¼	2¼	2¼	2¼	2¼	2¼	2¼	2¼	2¼	2¼	2¼
In effect Dec. 31, 1952	2¼	2¼	2¼	2¼	2¼	2¼	2¼	2¼	2¼	2¼	2¼	2¼
	ADVANCES TO INDIVIDUALS, PARTNERSHIPS, AND CORPORATIONS (EXCEPT MEMBER BANKS), SECURED BY DIRECT OBLIGATIONS OF U. S. (last par. sec. 13 of Federal Reserve Act)											
In effect Jan. 1, 1935	4	3½	4	4	4	4	4	4½	4½	4	4	4
1935—Feb.								4				
May				3½						3½		
1936—Apr.	2½					2½				2½	2½	
Oct.									3			
1939: To banks—												
Aug.		1										
Sept.	1		1½	[8] 1½	1½	1	1	1	1½	1	1	1½
To others—												
Sept.			2½									
1942: To banks—												
Mar.			1		1				1			
Apr.				1								1
To others—												
Mar.								3				
Oct.	2	2½	2	2	2½	2	2	2	2½	2	3	2½
1946—Mar.	(7)		(7)	(7)	(7)	(7)	(7)	(7)	[7] 2		(7)	
Apr.		(7)								(7)		(7)
1948—Jan.	2½					2½	2½	2½	2½	2½		
Feb.											2¾	
Aug.			2½	2¼			2¾		2¾			
1950—Aug.				2¾		2¾						
In effect Dec. 31, 1952	2½	2½	2½	2¾	2½	2¾	2¾	2½	2¾	2½	2¾	2½

1 For rates for 1914 to 1921, see Statistical Abstract 1928, table 249; for 1922 to 1932, Statistical Abstract 1933, table [illegible]; for 1933 and 1934, Statistical Abstract 1942, table 268. For rates on industrial advances authorized by sec. 13b of Federal Reserve Act, which are not shown in this table, see source.

2 Rediscounts of notes, drafts, and bills eligible for discount under Federal Reserve Act, and advances secured by such paper, by direct obligations of U. S., by certain obligations guaranteed as to principal and interest by U. S., and by obligations of Federal intermediate credit banks maturing within 6 months.

3 1 percent on advances secured by Government obligations.

4 ½ percent on advances secured by Government obligations maturing or callable in 1 year or less. This preferential rate eliminated in April and May 1946.

5 Advances secured to satisfaction of Federal Reserve Bank.

6 [illegible] percent to other lenders (than banks) in effect until Apr. 11, 1942.

7 Preferential rate to banks eliminated.

Source: Board of Governors of the Federal Reserve System; *Banking and Monetary Statistics*, *Annual Report*, and *Federal Reserve Bulletin*. Figures published currently in *Federal Reserve Bulletin*.

No. 462.—NATIONAL BANKS—ASSETS AND LIABILITIES: 1950 AND 1951

[Money figures in thousands of dollars. Includes banks in Alaska, Hawaii, and Virgin Islands]

ASSETS AND LIABILITIES	1950 (Dec. 30)	1951 (Dec. 31)				
		All banks	Central reserve cities	Other reserve cities	Country banks	Non-member banks [1]
Number of banks	4,965	4,946	15	211	4,713	7
Assets, total	97,240,093	102,738,560	18,699,887	43,886,307	39,875,532	276,834
Loans and securities, total	72,300,103	75,467,394	13,510,663	31,900,654	29,844,006	212,068
Loans and discounts, including overdrafts	29,277,480	32,423,777	6,349,531	14,831,796	11,135,775	106,675
U. S. Government securities, direct obligations	35,687,933	35,146,687	5,409,602	14,188,958	15,455,276	92,851
Obligations guaranteed by U S. Gov't [2]	3,627	9,656		7,468	2,188	
Obligations of States and political subdivisions	4,667,048	5,333,230	1,097,115	1,875,695	2,350,665	9,755
Other bonds, notes, and debentures	2,468,442	2,373,149	606,159	924,794	839,409	2,787
Corporate stocks, including stock of Federal Reserve Banks	175,573	180,895	48,256	71,943	60,695	1
Cash in vault	1,147,089	1,418,564	78,198	448,832	873,618	20,916
Reserve with Federal Reserve Banks	11,420,505	12,821,432	3,057,212	5,666,571	4,049,034	[3] 28,615
Balances with other banks and cash items	11,245,961	11,772,162	1,791,435	5,280,811	4,688,593	11,323
Other assets	1,126,555	1,259,008	262,379	572,439	420,279	3,911
Liabilities and capital accounts, total	97,240,093	102,738,560	18,699,887	43,886,307	39,875,532	276,834
Deposits, total	89,529,632	94,431,561	16,432,039	40,719,774	37,021,109	258,639
Demand deposits of individuals, partnerships, and corporations	52,051,784	54,855,841	10,318,828	22,760,651	21,677,545	98,817
Time deposits of individuals, partnerships, and corporations	19,010,542	19,825,659	1,448,090	8,173,287	10,106,911	97,371
Deposits of U. S. Government and postal savings	1,910,944	2,243,626	574,198	928,013	703,156	38,259
Deposits of States and polit. subdivisions	5,707,194	5,924,592	324,732	2,638,815	2,941,690	19,355
Deposits of banks	9,135,365	9,789,974	3,159,513	5,569,264	1,058,740	2,457
Other deposits (certified and cashiers' checks, etc.)	1,713,803	1,791,869	606,678	649,744	533,067	2,380
Other liabilities	1,381,472	1,636,881	908,376	530,749	196,452	1,304
Capital stock	2,001,650	2,105,345	449,684	822,203	828,183	5,275
Surplus	2,925,104	3,083,495	662,491	1,249,295	1,164,394	7,315
Undivided profits	1,124,223	1,212,538	211,869	472,726	526,373	1,570
Reserves	278,012	268,740	35,428	91,560	139,021	2,731

[1] National banks in Alaska, Hawaii, and Virgin Islands.
[2] Federal Housing Administration debentures.   [3] Reserve with approved national banking associations.

Source: Treasury Department, Comptroller of the Currency; *Abstract of Reports of Condition of National Banks.*

No. 463.—FEDERAL RESERVE SYSTEM, MEMBER BANK RESERVE REQUIREMENTS: 1917 TO 1952

[Percent of deposits. See also *Historical Statistics,* series N 131-134]

EFFECTIVE DATE OF CHANGE	NET DEMAND DEPOSITS [1]			Time deposits (all member banks)	EFFECTIVE DATE OF CHANGE	NET DEMAND DEPOSITS [1]			Time deposits (all member banks)
	Central reserve city banks	Reserve city banks	Country banks			Central reserve city banks	Reserve city banks	Country banks	
June 21, 1917	13	10	7	3	May 5, 1949	24	21		[3] 7
Aug. 16, 1936	19½	15	10½	4½	June 30, 1949		20		[3] 6
Mar. 1, 1937	22¾	17½	12¼	5¼	July 1, 1949			14	[3] 6
May 1, 1937	26	20	14	6	Aug. 1, 1949			13	
Apr. 16, 1938	22¾	17½	12	5	Aug. 11, 1949	23½	19½		[3] 5
Nov. 1, 1941	26	20	14	6	Aug. 16, 1949			12	[3] 5
Aug. 20, 1942	24				Aug. 18, 1949	23	19		
Sept. 14, 1942	22				Aug. 25, 1949	22½	18½		
Oct. 3, 1942	20				Sept. 1, 1949	22	18		
Feb. 27, 1948	22				Jan. 11, 1951	23	19		[3] 6
June 11, 1948	24				Jan. 16, 1951			13	[3] 6
Sept. 16, 1948			16	[3] 7½	Jan. 25, 1951	24	20		
Sept. 24, 1948	26	22		[3] 7½	Feb. 1, 1951			14	
May 1, 1949			15	[3] 7	In effect Dec. 31, 1952	24	20	14	6

[1] Demand deposits subject to reserve requirements, i. e., total demand deposits minus cash items in process of collection and demand balances due from domestic banks (also minus war loan and series E bond accounts during period Apr. 13, 1943-June 30, 1947, and all U. S. Government demand accounts Apr. 24, 1917-Aug. 22, 1935).
[2] Requirement became effective at country banks.
[3] Requirement became effective at central reserve and reserve city banks.

Source: Board of Governors of the Federal Reserve System, *Federal Reserve Bulletin.*

4.—NATIONAL BANKS—SUMMARY, BY STATES AND OTHER AREAS: DEC. 31, 1951

[Money figures in thousands of dollars]

	Number of banks	Total assets or liabilities	SELECTED ASSETS			Capital, surplus, undivided profits, and reserve	Total	Demand	Time (incl. postal savings)
			Loans and discounts, including overdrafts	U.S. Government and other securities	Cash and balances with other banks[1]				
	4,946	102,738,560	32,423,777	43,643,617	26,012,158	6,670,118	94,431,561	73,156,255	21,275,273
and	230	5,396,961	1,737,447	2,187,272	1,378,534	426,430	4,893,560	4,140	882,430
impshire	32	255,609	64,000	111,963	56,588	24,586	229,693	774	76,819
t	51	230,443	75,309	58,109	64,964	21,961	207,875	877	42,996
t	38	152,215	54,292	61,974	34,101	14,470	136,600	614	96,076
usetts	115	3,563,544	1,201,243	1,372,505	918,935	287,905	3,210,331	2,107	672,224
Island	6	213,994	75,101	93,737	42,568	14,821	199,153	071	92,082
tient	48	979,151	246,602	458,984	261,378	62,687	909,818	097	179,121
	1,272	27,631,665	8,889,435	11,741,024	6,544,805	2,179,682	24,541,572	19,305,477	5,236,075
ork	372	15,255,621	5,331,549	5,923,447	3,736,083	1,155,672	13,215,611	11,336,880	1,678,731
rsey	202	2,849,478	800,255	1,460,804	854,306	182,748	2,652,185	1,573,718	1,078,467
lvania	619	7,598,898	2,448,314	2,559,115	1,802,021	738,660	7,105,234	5,105,712	1,999,822
re	11	35,758	11,585	16,386	7,231	4,501	30,922	19,351	11,572
nd	59	825,528	198,601	392,903	225,628	55,139	767,744	507,134	180,610
Columbia	9	816,379	199,131	388,279	219,536	42,256	769,875	662,702	107,173
	1,184	18,672,809	5,501,709	7,133,958	5,733,108	1,099,535	17,437,008	14,908,156	2,533,853
	123	1,377,924	444,455	564,955	352,006	96,094	1,273,639	912,892	340,747
rginia	74	596,119	149,062	278,582	162,871	44,203	548,465	732	121,723
arolina	46	800,987	177,732	232,579	173,948	36,445	550,319	313	96,006
arolina	25	831,779	136,445	234,177	156,881	25,866	802,216	169	86,947
	61	1,206,083	396,991	426,773	367,820	66,306	1,130,957	622	144,345
	63	1,582,220	325,854	753,755	450,605	96,089	1,476,875	187	305,888
	70	1,127,307	316,219	477,179	321,342	71,174	1,046,310	009	301,301
pi	24	251,719	61,766	112,665	74,886	14,208	236,002	161	44,441
	36	1,409,896	333,877	646,928	467,147	71,109	1,382,833	658	160,175
	443	6,951,836	2,204,177	2,292,219	2,341,957	394,061	6,501,307	140	900,167
y	52	602,145	118,334	226,039	153,500	33,236	467,179	247	56,932
e	93	774,156	332,142	332,403	233,118	49,269	721,385	004	312,381
	74	1,710,038	604,655	609,811	476,577	101,363	1,598,921	021	806,800
atern	1,277	27,406,659	7,676,688	12,494,776	7,020,268	1,609,269	25,627,416	933	6,861,423
	239	4,342,333	1,215,787	2,031,037	1,052,786	201,810	4,056,077	112	1,068,965
	125	2,080,990	491,840	1,021,345	855,657	118,439	1,959,209	313	887,966
	386	10,700,057	2,995,638	4,878,524	2,758,141	652,370	9,983,447	567	2,396,880
n	78	3,333,556	896,092	1,663,981	745,905	163,178	3,139,749	504	912,245
in	95	1,676,992	400,618	837,452	423,633	97,495	1,573,242	709	467,533
ta	178	2,317,450	757,425	904,630	634,928	146,058	2,148,012	1,602,123	486,889
	97	859,461	251,767	371,100	229,306	62,147	801,849	652,992	751,827
	79	2,059,820	607,021	785,777	619,852	117,500	1,962,771	1,714,673	348,098
akota	736	6,386,265	1,717,874	2,725,014	1,893,906	366,091	5,987,014	836	770,179
akota	40	284,790	76,349	143,880	202,412	14,763	208,291	800	60,491
	35	234,105	91,601	120,233	70,034	15,168	276,655	879	81,976
	123	1,105,825	327,667	454,789	315,393	62,699	1,032,377	657	110,720
	174	1,106,963	281,040	477,526	341,843	60,880	1,042,633	946	93,847
	39	823,417	73,867	104,431	56,510	13,781	312,407	209	41,198
c	24	225,038	56,667	103,548	64,023	11,295	213,704	351	35,363
o	77	1,033,697	300,478	435,412	292,632	60,966	908,150	001	145,249
xico	26	305,179	81,046	121,306	102,981	16,624	290,817	504	40,313
na	198	1,698,579	429,161	601,852	558,048	102,895	1,580,980	749	134,281
	180	16,917,367	6,693,949	6,601,179	3,380,633	972,220	15,686,352	870	5,994,482
	35	1,945,237	665,206	747,774	508,370	112,503	1,821,814	252	386,588
	20	1,403,723	511,622	568,258	203,295	83,739	1,307,540	570	385,970
	63	12,256,574	5,043,925	4,748,656	2,281,168	706,820	11,326,412	198	96,075
	13	573,065	126,896	168,936	73,916	18,723	352,317	244	96,075
	11	356,375	111,774	143,968	90,909	17,854	335,473	763	76,706
	5	170,875	49,563	91,331	27,594	9,775	159,269	488	44,063
	3	411,518	178,937	132,200	92,431	22,500	353,227	303	54,873
	6	77,475	15,142	37,436	24,250	3,409	73,900	845	28,435
	1	104,134	89,951	65,275	35,698	13,064	179,917	781	35,156
ands	1	5,225	1,582	2,683	900	418	4,762	490	3,272

[1] deral Reserve banks and cash items in process of collection.

nent, Comptroller of the Currency; Annual Report and Abstract of Reports of

No. 465.—National Banks—Number, Capital Stock, Capital Funds, Earnings and Expenses: 1929 to 1951

[Money figures in thousands of dollars. Figures for previous years published in Comptroller of Currency annual report for 1935, p. 115. See also Historical Statistics, series N 60-97]

Year ending Dec. 31	Number of banks	Capital stock (par value) [1]			Capital funds [1]	Gross earnings	Expenses [2]	Net current earnings	Net losses including depreciation (−) or net recoveries (+) [3]	Net profits before dividends	Dividends			Net profits before dividends	
		Total	Preferred	Common							On preferred stock	On common stock		Ratio to capital stock	Ratio to capital funds
												Cash	Stock	Percent	Percent
1929	7,408	1,650,574	....	1,650,574	3,754,898	1,405,544	985,408	418,141	−129,197	291,944	....	225,082	21,235	17.69	7.78
1930	7,038	1,724,028	....	1,724,028	3,919,930	1,325,404	989,842	335,562	−177,151	158,411	....	211,272	5,016	9.19	4.04
1931	6,373	1,680,780	....	1,680,780	3,758,412	1,153,145	580,942	303,103	−347,683	*44,560	....	192,196	827	*2.65	*1.18
1932	6,016	1,597,037	....	1,597,037	3,322,596	1,000,226	760,210	360,016	−514,753	*154,737	....	188,381	....	*10.53	*4.96
1933	*5,159	1,600,303	92,469	1,507,834	2,961,678	801,626	556,123	326,802	−552,808	*226,116	565	71,106	859	*17.68	*12.60
1934	*5,457	1,709,043	349,470	1,359,573	2,982,006	908,778	657,667	251,109	−604,560	*163,451	10,108	80,915	1,207	*9.92	*5.16
1935	5,392	1,791,324	510,511	1,280,813	3,094,092	794,156	449,146	345,008	−89,517	155,491	18,982	94,377	4,409	8.55	5.14
1936	5,331	1,705,028	447,001	1,258,027	3,143,029	824,593	505,613	308,920	+53,996	312,526	18,166	101,560	16,019	18.39	9.98
1937	5,299	1,691,788	365,842	1,285,946	3,200,194	839,094	565,221	273,873	−44,853	228,021	11,552	110,231	26,672	14.33	7.11
1938	5,230	1,577,793	267,495	1,310,243	3,281,819	837,857	677,272	290,585	−91,599	198,549	9,978	113,347	19,780	12.59	6.06
1939	5,193	1,511,521	241,075	1,220,446	3,380,740	848,419	581,264	267,155	−18,579	261,576	8,911	122,847	9,300	18.11	7.44
1940	5,150	1,532,315	204,244	1,328,071	3,483,563	864,749	599,444	265,305	−23,840	241,465	8,176	124,174	12,009	15.76	6.97
1941	5,123	1,523,454	182,055	1,341,398	3,590,865	926,693	641,648	284,015	−14,720	299,295	7,816	124,506	14,945	17.68	7.49
1942	5,067	1,511,123	156,739	1,354,384	3,684,882	962,837	695,034	267,803	−24,460	243,343	6,683	121,177	8,844	16.10	6.60
1943	5,046	1,508,170	135,713	1,372,457	3,860,443	982,837	748,434	315,329	+36,128	350,457	6,158	126,357	41,378	23.24	9.08
1944	5,031	1,551,116	110,597	1,440,519	4,114,972	1,061,763	846,094	360,170	+81,665	411,844	5,298	126,012	33,900	26.55	10.01
1945	5,023	1,616,884	80,672	1,636,212	4,467,718	1,349,523	987,224	361,998	+128,168	494,133	4,131	161,825	77,305	30.31	10.97
1946	5,013	1,960,583	63,302	1,963,038	4,963,036	1,573,814	1,137,664	435,950	+58,948	494,988	2,437	167,702	28,155	29.11	10.11
1947	5,011	1,749,405	33,359	1,738,676	5,293,067	1,724,834	1,263,497	461,337	−9,354	452,948	1,373	182,147	23,450	23.48	8.56
1948	4,997	1,894,490	20,128	1,778,962	5,545,968	1,900,671	1,360,780	539,871	−115,764	424,727	1,284	192,653	35,691	23.20	7.84
1949	4,981	1,894,352	20,979	1,983,373	5,811,044	2,004,906	1,443,906	562,300	−87,619	474,681	1,100	203,644	86,964	25.20	8.17
1950	4,965	1,965,977	16,070	1,949,898	6,152,799	2,192,713	1,592,558	600,155	−62,545	537,610	712	228,792	47,049	27.35	8.74
1951	4,946	2,058,050	12,032	2,046,018	6,505,378	2,454,358	1,812,299	642,059	−133,364	508,695	615	247,220	56,807	24.02	7.79

[1] Averages of amounts from reports of condition made in each year.
[2] Including income tax.
[3] Difference between "recoveries and profits" and "losses and charge-offs."
[4] Deficit.
[5] Licensed banks, i. e., those operating on an unrestricted basis.

Source: Treasury Department, Comptroller of the Currency; Annual Report.

No. 466.—NATIONAL BANKS—LOANS AND SECURITIES, BY CLASS, AS OF DEC. 31, 1930 TO 1951

[In millions of dollars]

CLASS	1930	1935	1940	1945	1950 (Dec. 30)	1951
Loans and discounts, total [1]	14,360.4	7,508.4	10,027.8	13,948.0	23,277.8	32,423.8
Commercial and industrial loans, including open-market paper	(4)	(4)	4,318.4	5,681.8	13,401.9	15,089.3
Agricultural loans	(4)	(4)	729.0	707.2	1,423.5	1,000.2
Loans to brokers and dealers in securities	932.7	426.2	274.1	1,424.4	728.5	704.7
Other loans for the purpose of purchasing or carrying stocks, bonds, and other securities	(4)	(4)	369.4	1,904.1	532.9	591.5
Real estate loans:						
On farm land (including improvements)	301.7	209.0	254.1	193.2	270.9	284.8
On residential property (other than farm)	1,274.5	1,111.2	1,371.6	1,622.6	5,461.1	5,008.2
On other properties	415.7	63.6	491.5	389.7	1,146.2	1,348.1
Loans to banks	11,356.8	5,006.8	22.7	20.6	39.5	65.3
All other loans, including overdrafts	11,356.8	5,006.8	2,217.1	4,907.4	6,570.8	6,702.2
Loss valuation reserves					358.1	479.5
Securities, total	7,092.1	11,477.5	13,568.0	55,611.6	43,022.4	43,043.5
U. S. Government direct obligations	2,654.8	6,634.3	7,568.5	51,460.0	35,557.9	35,146.7
Obligations guaranteed by U. S.		1,267.3	2,094.1	7.9	3.6	9.7
Obligations of States and political subdivisions	1,107.9	1,452.9	2,008.5	2,341.7	4,067.9	5,233.2
Other bonds, notes, and debentures	3,076.2	1,996.2	1,694.1	1,636.9	2,465.4	2,373.1
Corporate stocks	212.5	216.3	212.0	145.3	175.6	180.9
Claims, judgments, etc.	40.7					

[1] Includes overdrafts.
[2] Net loans. Figures for various loan items are reported gross, i. e., before deduction of valuation reserves, and are not entirely comparable with prior years. [4] Not available.
Source: Treasury Department, Comptroller of the Currency; Annual Report and Abstract of Reports of Condition of National Banks.

No. 467.—NATIONAL BANKS—FIDUCIARY ACTIVITIES: 1930 TO 1951

[Money figures, except averages, in millions of dollars]

ITEM	1930 (June 30)	1935 (June 30)	1940 (June 30)	1945 (Dec. 31)	1950 (Dec. 30)	1951 (Dec. 31)
Banks authorized to exercise fiduciary powers:						
Number, total	2,472	1,992	1,877	1,788	1,776	1,773
Number exercising powers	1,829	1,578	1,540	1,504	1,516	1,512
Number having authority but not exercising powers	643	384	337	284	260	461
Assets, total	23,520.1	22,543.5	32,307.3	76,015.8	81,960.8	86,081.9
Trusts, individual, total number	79,912	120,711	157,829	153,833	191,874	240,760
Living trusts	(2)	60,162	71,062	81,727	107,130	94,440
Court trusts	(2)	60,549	66,367	72,106	64,735	67,149
Agency, custodian, escrow, safekeeping etc., trusts						78,171
Trusts assets, individual, total value	4,478.0	9,264.3	9,345.4	15,764.5	34,507.2	38,136.6
Investments, total	3,705.9	8,342.0	7,492.5	12,051.5	18,390.0	19,967.9
Bonds	(2)	4,006.3	3,700.9	5,052.4	11,984.4	12,006.8
Stocks	(2)	2,442.4	2,310.1	2,522.1	4,314.9	4,606.9
Real-estate mortgages	(2)	602.9	516.4	520.9	763.9	520.1
Real estate	(2)	571.8	582.1	465.1	608.9	425.4
Miscellaneous				224.7		387.7
Deposits in savings banks	8.7	20.3				
Deposits in own banks	163.5	354.3	526.7	749.2	1,045.0	1,317.1
Deposits in other banks	18.5	8.5				
Other assets	580.4	525.6	1,326.2	2,063.5	15,150.2	14,601.0
Estates, corporate, number	11,511	16,201	16,278	15,507	25,300	17,597
Bond issues outstanding, bank acting as trustee	11,822.7	11,605.1	9,317.7	8,193.1	10,049.2	14,590.6
Gross earnings of trust departments reporting fees			31.7		(5)	(5)
Average per trust	$848	$504	$308	$388	$322	$350
Average per trust department	$14,850	$15,725	$22,742	$28,504	$45,256	$51,356

[2] Agency, etc., trusts included with living trusts prior to 1951.
[5] No data available. [6] Based on earnings of banks reporting trust earnings.
Source: Treasury Department, Comptroller of the Currency; Annual Report.

No. 468.—Reconstruction Finance Corporation—Disbursements, Repayments and Other Reductions, and Outstanding Balances for Period Ending December 31, 1952

[In thousands]

CHARACTER OF LOAN	1952 (Jan. 1–Dec. 31)		Outstanding balances, Dec. 31, 1952
	Disbursements	Repayments and other reductions	
Total	$186,771	$236,448	$798,197
Industrial and commercial enterprises	173,025	148,324	471,703
Business loans:			
Approved—Under Sections 4 (a) and 5 (d) 2 RFC Act	99,974	140,611	378,696
Direct loans	55,849	115,796	303,473
Immediate participations	42,676	18,734	64,740
Deferred participations	1,449	6,079	10,485
Approved—Under Section 714 DPA	4,807	644	4,163
Direct loans	4,060	416	3,644
Deferred participations	747	228	519
Approved—Under Section 302 DPA	68,244	7,069	88,842
Direct loans	64,160	6,147	85,680
Deferred participations	4,084	922	3,162
Railroads—loans and securities purchased		18,786	70,855
Financial institutions		37,568	46,801
Purchase of preferred stock, capital notes and debentures of banks and trust companies		29,509	46,535
Loans on preferred stock of banks and trust companies		86	32
Loans on preferred stock of insurance companies		7,972	210
Loans to mortgage loan companies		1	24
Political subdivisions of States and Territories	8,167	4,479	22,198
Public agency loans	8,167	2,047	13,044
Drainage, levee and irrigation		459	5,398
Municipal securities purchased from FWA		1,973	3,756
Mortgages partially guaranteed by Veterans' Administration		6,437	71,725
Mortgages insured by Federal Housing Administration		90	195
Mortgage loans acquired from Defense Homes Corporation (less equity of U. S. Treasury of $13,702,106)		1,226	29,500
Catastrophe	7,579	3,560	17,130
Direct loans	7,448	3,462	16,852
Immediate participations	131	98	278
Loans to foreign governments: Republic of the Philippines		6,000	54,000

Source: Reconstruction Finance Corporation, records.

No. 469.—Postal Savings Business—Summary, as of June 30: 1930 to 1952

[Data include Alaska, Hawaii, Puerto Rico, and Virgin Islands. See also *Historical Statistics*, series N 109–113]

ITEM	1930	1935	1940	1945	1950	1951	1952
Depositories in operation, total	6,795	8,111	7,980	8,050	8,235	8,247	8,261
Offices	5,998	7,301	7,172	7,162	7,215	7,208	7,200
Branches and stations	797	810	808	888	1,020	1,039	1,061
Deposits ($1,000)	159,959	944,969	923,266	1,739,341	1,827,913	1,603,327	1,460,415
Withdrawals ($1,000)	138,332	938,017	892,149	1,113,902	2,007,999	1,912,444	1,631,050
Balance to credit of depositors, June 30 ($1,000)[1]	175,272	1,204,863	1,293,409	2,659,575	3,097,316	2,788,199	2,617,564
Increase or decrease:							
Amount ($1,000)	21,627	6,943	31,117	625,438	−180,095	−309,117	−170,635
Percent	14.1	.6	2.5	30.7	−5.5	−10.0	−6.1
Number of depositors, June 30[1]	466,401	2,508,291	2,816,408	3,921,937	3,779,784	3,529,527	3,339,373
Average principal per depositor	$376	$464	$459	$678	$819	$790	$784
Balance on deposit in banks, June 30 ($1,000)	148,255	384,510	43,132	7,904	9,507	22,509	22,379

[1] Includes account shown on balance sheet as unclaimed.

Source: Post Office Department, Office of the Postmaster General; *Operations of the Postal Savings System*.

No. 470.—ESTIMATED SAVINGS OF INDIVIDUALS IN SELECTED MEDIA: 1920 TO 1951

[In millions of dollars]

Dec. 31—	Total	Savings and loan assns.[1]	Life insurance companies[2]	Mutual savings banks[3]	Commercial banks[4]	Postal savings[5]	U. S. savings bonds[6]	Net increase during year
1920	22,608	1,741	5,485	5,906	10,546	166	761	
1925	36,670	3,811	9,508	7,340	16,314	138	375	3,217
1930	47,169	6,237	13,362	8,797	19,164	160	....	1,345
1935	46,697	5,204	13,860	8,364	18,947	280	....	1,098
1936	41,677	4,780	14,613	8,506	10,979	1,239	....	−1,474
1940	45,547	4,254	17,203	9,829	12,899	1,229	153	2,528
1941	52,768	4,118	22,064	10,431	14,365	1,318	1,990	3,794
1942	58,746	4,322	24,668	15,615	15,402	1,342	2,910	3,445
1943	64,679	4,632	26,502	16,490	15,823	1,392	4,458	4,951
1944	114,236	6,306	34,212	13,332	23,371	2,466	34,200	23,922
1945	134,648	7,365	37,560	15,332	29,929	3,012	42,908	19,722
1946	147,100	8,548	40,713	16,812	33,447	3,379	44,200	11,032
1947	154,784	9,753	43,820	17,744	34,694	3,523	44,288	8,984
1948	162,700	10,964	47,139	18,385	34,970	3,442	47,808	8,966
1949	169,718	12,471	50,251	19,209	35,145	3,202	49,500	7,018
1950	174,446	13,975	53,890	20,002	35,290	3,035	48,689	5,727
1951 (prel.)		16,079	57,000	20,909	(7)		48,698	(7)

[1] Estimated private investment in savings and loan associations, including deposits and investment securities. Excludes shares pledged against shortage loans. Source: Home Loan Bank Board.
[2] Estimated accumulations in U. S. life insurance companies include reserves plus dividends left to accumulate, minus premium notes and policy loans. Source: Institute of Life Insurance.
[3] Deposits. Prior to 1936 data based on savings deposits in mutual savings banks as reported by Comptroller of Currency. All figures include a small percentage of Christmas savings and other special accounts in addition to ordinary deposits. Source: National Association of Mutual Savings Banks and Federal Deposit Insurance Corporation.
[4] Time deposits of individuals, partnerships and corporations. From 1920 to 1935, based on Comptroller of Currency figures as of June 30 for all national, state commercial and stock savings banks and trust companies. Thereafter as of December 31, prepared by Home Loan Bank Board. From 1936 to 1945, December 31 figures as reported by Comptroller of Currency and Federal Deposit Insurance Corporation. Source: Comptroller of the Currency, Federal Deposit Insurance Corporation and Home Loan Bank Board.
[5] Due depositors. Outstanding principal and accrued interest on certificates of deposit, outstanding savings stamps and unclaimed deposits. Source: Post Office Department.
[6] Current redemption value of savings held by individuals at year-end—from 1920 to 1928, War Savings Securities; 1935 to date includes U. S. Savings Bonds, Series A–O. Source: U. S. Treasury Department.
[7] Not available.

Source: Housing and Home Finance Agency, Home Loan Bank Board.

No. 471.—SAVING BY INDIVIDUALS IN THE UNITED STATES: 1944 TO 1952

[In billions of dollars. Includes unincorporated business savings of types specified but excludes corporate or governmental saving. Current data are necessarily estimates and therefore subject to revision]

Type	1944	1945	1946	1947	1948	1949	1950	1951	1952
Gross saving, total	+49.6	+36.7	+32.4	+33.8	+34.1	+35.0	+43.8	+39.2	+52.0
Liquid saving, total	+41.6	+37.9	+12.6	+6.6	+2.8	−1.0	+1.5	+11.8	+14.6
Currency and deposits	+17.9	+17.6	+1.1	+2.0	−1.5	−1.4	+4.2	+6.7	+5.7
Savings and loan assns.	+1.5	+1.5	+1.2	+1.1	+1.2	+1.5	+1.6	+2.1	+3.1
Insurance and pension reserves	+4.6	+4.6	+7.0	+7.1	+6.1	+6.0	+4.9	+4.6	+9.5
(Life insurance)	+6.0	+6.1	+5.4	+3.3	+3.7	+3.7	+3.9	+4.3	+4.6
Securities	+5.5	+4.1	+4.5	+1.5	+1.8	+1.1	+1.1	+4.3	+4.6
U. S. savings bonds	+11.8	+6.9	+1.8	+.8	+2.1	+1.5	+.6	−.4	+.3
Other U. S. Government	+.6	+3.6	−.7	−.5	−.5	−1.2	−.3	−.3	+.3
State and local	(3)	−.1	−.1	+.4	−1.1	−.1	+.5	+.3	+1.0
Other	+.3	−.2	+.7	−.6	+1.1	+1.1	+.7	+3.1	+1.9
Less: Debt	+.3	−.4	−.7	−.4	−4.4	−2.9	−7.9	−6.4	
Net saving, durable goods	−.2	−.9	−2.8	−4.6	−2.5	−2.9	−3.2	−.4	−8.1
Other	+1.9	+2.9	+44.3	+42.2	+25.0	+20.5	+40.3	+36.2	+35.8

[a] Includes bank loans made for purpose of purchasing or carrying securities.
[b] Institutions on one- to four-family nonfarm dwellings.
[c] Applicable to purchases of automobiles and other durable consumer goods, although including loans for purchases of consumption goods. Other segments of individuals' debt have been allocated to other categories, such as savings bank loans on life insurance, and securities.
[d] Purchase of one- to four-family nonfarm dwellings less net acquisition of properties by nonindividuals and small amount of construction by nonprofit institutions.
[e] Expenditures on durable goods as estimated by Department of Commerce.

Source: Securities and Exchange Commission; data are published quarterly in a special release and in the...

No. 472.—Liquid Asset Holdings of Individuals and Businesses: 1942 to 1951

[In billions of dollars. Data estimated as of December]

TYPE OF HOLDER	1942	1943	1944	1945	1946	1947	1948	1949	1950	1951 (prel.)
Total [1]	116.2	156.4	195.9	227.5	231.5	237.2	238.8	243.0	250.2	260.5
Currency	13.1	18.0	22.6	25.5	25.7	26.4	25.0	24.3	24.3	25.2
Demand deposits [2]	36.8	47.1	52.1	60.2	64.6	66.2	64.5	63.8	65.8	70.7
Time deposits [3]	27.7	32.0	39.0	47.7	53.0	55.2	56.1	57.0	57.5	59.6
Savings and loan shares [3]	4.8	5.4	6.2	7.2	8.4	9.6	10.8	12.2	13.8	15.8
U. S. Government Securities [4]	33.8	53.9	75.0	86.9	79.8	80.8	82.4	85.7	88.8	89.2
Business holdings, total	39.4	55.9	67.5	73.0	66.3	64.6	64.5	66.7	70.5	74.5
Currency	2.8	3.6	4.3	4.7	4.9	4.8	4.7	4.6	4.6	4.8
Demand deposits	21.7	28.9	31.3	33.7	33.5	33.9	33.7	34.2	34.6	38.0
Time deposits	2.1	2.3	2.7	3.1	3.4	3.5	3.5	3.5	3.6	3.7
Savings and loan shares	.1	.2	.2	.2	.3	.3	.3	.3	.4	.4
U. S. Government securities	12.7	20.9	29.0	31.3	24.2	22.1	22.3	24.1	27.3	27.6
Corporations, total	27.1	38.6	44.7	45.1	38.9	38.1	39.3	41.9	46.3	49.2
Currency	.8	.9	.9	.9	1.0	1.0	1.0	1.0	1.0	1.0
Demand deposits	16.0	20.9	23.1	22.1	21.8	22.2	22.7	23.1	23.7	26.0
Time deposits	.7	.7	.7	.7	.7	.7	.7	.7	.7	.7
Savings and loan shares		.1	.1	.1	.1	.1	.1	.1	.1	.1
U. S. Government securities	9.6	16.0	20.9	21.3	15.3	14.1	14.8	17.0	20.8	21.4
Financial corporations, total [5]	2.5	3.1	3.5	4.8	4.4	4.3	4.5	5.2	5.4	5.7
Demand deposits	1.2	1.3	1.5	2.0	2.1	2.2	2.2	2.3	2.5	2.6
Time deposits	.1	.1	.1	.1	.1	.1	.1	.1	.1	.1
U. S. Government securities	1.2	1.7	2.3	2.7	2.2	2.0	2.2	2.8	2.8	3.0
Nonfinancial corporations, total	24.6	35.5	40.9	40.3	34.5	33.8	34.8	36.7	40.9	43.5
Currency	.8	.9	.9	.9	1.0	1.0	1.0	1.0	1.0	1.0
Demand deposits	14.8	19.6	20.6	20.1	19.7	20.0	20.5	20.8	21.2	23.4
Time deposits	.6	.6	.6	.6	.6	.6	.6	.6	.6	.6
Savings and loan shares			.1	.1	.1	.1	.1	.1	.1	.1
U. S. Government securities	8.4	14.3	18.7	18.6	13.1	12.1	12.6	14.2	18.0	18.4
Unincorporated business, total	12.3	17.3	22.8	27.9	27.4	26.5	25.2	24.8	24.2	25.3
Currency	2.0	2.7	3.4	3.8	3.9	3.8	3.7	3.6	3.6	3.8
Demand deposits	5.7	8.0	9.2	11.6	11.7	11.7	11.0	11.1	10.9	12.0
Time deposits	1.4	1.6	2.0	2.4	2.7	2.8	2.8	2.8	2.9	3.0
Savings and loan shares	.1	.1	.1	.1	.2	.2	.2	.2	.3	.3
U. S. Government securities	3.1	4.9	8.1	10.0	8.9	8.0	7.5	7.1	6.5	6.2
Personal holdings, total	76.8	100.5	128.4	154.5	165.2	172.6	174.3	176.3	179.7	186.0
Currency	10.3	14.4	18.3	20.8	20.8	20.6	20.3	19.7	19.7	20.4
Demand deposits	15.1	18.2	21.8	26.5	31.1	32.3	30.8	29.6	31.2	32.7
Time deposits	25.6	29.7	36.3	44.6	49.6	51.7	52.6	53.5	53.9	55.9
Savings and loan shares	4.7	5.2	6.0	7.0	8.1	9.3	10.5	11.9	13.4	15.4
U. S. Government securities	21.1	33.0	46.0	55.6	55.6	58.7	60.1	61.6	61.5	61.6
Trust funds total [6]	6.9	10.0	12.4	15.9	19.4	21.6	22.9	24.0	26.5	29.2
Demand deposits	1.2	1.3	1.4	1.6	1.7	1.6	1.6	1.5	1.6	1.6
Time deposits	.2	.2	.2	.2	.3	.3	.5	.5	.8	1.0
Savings and loan shares	.1	.1	.1	.1	.2	.2	.2	.3	.5	
U. S. Government securities	5.4	8.4	11.7	14.0	17.2	19.5	20.6	21.7	23.8	26.1
Other personal, total [7]	69.9	90.5	115.9	138.6	145.8	151.0	151.4	152.3	153.2	156.8
Currency	10.3	14.4	18.3	20.8	20.8	20.6	20.3	19.7	19.7	20.4
Demand deposits	13.9	16.9	20.4	24.9	29.4	30.7	29.2	28.1	29.6	31.1
Time deposits	25.4	29.5	36.1	44.4	49.3	51.4	52.1	53.0	53.1	54.9
Savings and loan shares	4.6	5.1	5.9	6.9	7.9	9.1	10.3	11.6	13.1	14.9
U. S. Government securities	15.7	24.6	34.3	41.6	38.4	39.2	39.5	39.9	37.7	35.5

[1] Excludes figures for banks, insurance companies, savings and loan associations, nonprofit associations, foreigners, and governmental bodies and agencies.

[2] Estimates of demand deposit balances as they would appear on the records of depositors. They differ from figures based on bank records such as given in regular banking statistics. Depositor-record estimates are lower than bank-record estimates; for example, total demand deposits as of Dec. 31, 1951 on a holder-record basis (see table) amounted to 70.7 billion dollars while on a bank-record basis these deposits amount to 90.9 billion.

[3] Private share capital in all operating savings and loan associations including private repurchasable shares, deposits, and investment certificates.

[4] Includes outstanding amounts of excess profits tax refund bonds beginning December 1945, and armed forces leave bonds beginning December 1947.

[5] Includes real estate companies, finance and credit companies, insurance agencies (not carriers), investment trusts, security brokers and dealers, holding companies not otherwise classified, etc.

[6] Includes only amounts administered by corporate trustees.

[7] Includes holdings of farmers and professional persons.

Source: Board of Governors of the Federal Reserve System. Published in Federal Reserve Bulletin, July 1952.

No. 473.—BANK SUSPENSIONS—NUMBER OF BANKS AND AMOUNT OF DEPOSITS: 1864 TO 1952

[Banks closed either permanently or temporarily, on account of financial difficulties, by order of supervisory authorities or by directors of bank. "Member" refers to membership in Federal Reserve System. All National banks in continental U. S. are Federal Reserve System members; all Federal Reserve System members are insured. See also, *Historical Statistics*, series N 135-147]

PERIOD	NUMBER OF BANKS				PERIOD	NUMBER OF BANKS			
	Total	National	State	Private		Total	National	State	Private
1864-1870	44	15	29		1892-1900	1,174	226	521	427
1871-1880	365	61	304		1901-1910	808	119	397	292
1881-1891	346	67	279		1911-1920	944	83	675	186

YEAR OR PERIOD	NUMBER OF BANKS					DEPOSITS (THOUSANDS OF DOLLARS)				
	Total	National	State member	State and private nonmember		Total	National	State member	State and private nonmember	
				Noninsured	Insured [1]				Noninsured	Insured [1]
1921-1929	5,714	706	229	4,779		1,626,665	363,324	128,677	1,133,467	
1930	1,352	161	27	1,164		853,363	202,599	480,518	937,541	
1931	2,294	409	107	1,778		1,690,669	436,171	263,957	957,541	
1932	1,456	276	55	1,125		715,626	214,190	55,153	446,325	
1933	4,004	1,101	174	2,729		3,598,975	1,610,549	783,399	1,205,027	
1930-1933	9,106	1,947	363	6,796		6,858,633	2,494,316	1,334,908	3,089,400	
1934-1940	313	16	6	54	207	131,934	14,872	26,548	40,325	49,880
1941-1945	22	6		4	12	12,056	8,126		409	3,524
1946	1			1		167			167	
1947	0					0				
1948	5			4		2,448			2,448	
1949	3			1		42			42	
1950	1					113			113	
1951	2									
1952	3			1	2	1,403			135	1,268

[1] Deposit insurance by Federal Deposit Insurance Corporation; became operative Jan. 1, 1934.

Source: 1864-1891, U. S. Treasury, Comptroller of Currency; 1951 Annual Report. Later data, Board of Governors of the Federal Reserve System; figures published currently in *Federal Reserve Bulletin*.

No. 474.—DEPOSIT INSURANCE—NUMBER OF OPERATING BANKS AND BRANCHES BY INSURANCE STATUS AND CLASS OF BANK: DECEMBER 31, 1952

TYPE OF BANK OR OFFICE	All banks	COMMERCIAL AND STOCK SAVINGS BANKS AND NONDEPOSIT TRUST COMPANIES						MUTUAL SAVINGS BANKS	
		Total	Insured			Noninsured		Insured	Noninsured
			Members F. R. system		Not members F. R. system	Banks of deposit	Nondeposit trust companies		
			National	State					
Total	20,460	19,673	7,445	3,436	8,024	952	65	384	392
All banks	14,917	14,088	4,009	1,886	6,644	264	65	209	123
Unit banks	12,046	11,641	3,461	1,645	5,929	262		128	277
Banks operating branches	1,971	1,447		448	1,180	99	2	75	49
Branches	5,533	5,337	2,336	1,550	1,350	99		177	69
Continental United States	20,338	19,512	7,445	3,436	7,942	408	65	383	392
All banks	14,873	14,046	4,009	1,886	6,627	264	65	206	123
Unit banks	13,000	12,545	4,461	1,643	5,914	267		128	277
Banks operating branches	1,865	1,443	448	241	713	27		75	46
Branches	5,713	5,467	4,556	1,550	1,320	39		177	69
Other areas	152	152			77	30			
All banks	42	42			17	10			
Unit banks	26	26			6	10			
Banks operating branches	16	16			11				
Branches	120	120			60	60			

Source: Federal Deposit Insurance Corporation; *Annual Report*.

No. 475.—Changes in Number and Classification of Operating Banking Offices in the United States and Possessions by Insurance Status: 1946 to 1952

TYPE OF CHANGE	1946	1947	1948	1949	1950	1951	1952
Banking offices, total	18,979	19,175	19,366	19,600	19,851	20,155	20,450
Number of banks	14,751	14,767	14,753	14,736	14,693	14,661	14,617
Number of branches	4,219	4,408	4,613	4,864	5,158	5,494	5,833
Net change during year	+86	+205	+191	+234	+251	+304	+295
Offices opened	374	333	305	344	381	425	433
Banks	148	113	80	80	69	65	71
Branches	226	220	225	264	312	360	362
Offices closed	288	128	114	110	130	121	138
Banks	114	97	94	97	106	97	115
Branches	174	31	20	13	24	24	23
INSURED							
Banking offices, total	17,593	17,817	18,027	18,299	18,624	18,979	19,308
Number of banks	13,550	13,597	13,612	13,628	13,640	13,657	13,645
Number of branches	4,043	4,220	4,415	4,671	4,984	5,322	5,663
Net change during year	+102	+224	+210	+272	+325	+355	+329
Offices opened	346	307	273	308	359	398	411
Banks	132	99	62	61	59	53	62
Branches	214	208	211	247	300	345	349
Offices closed	271	114	100	92	118	99	122
Banks	102	83	80	83	95	76	102
Branches	169	31	20	9	23	23	20
Changes in classification [1]	+27	+31	+37	+56	+84	+56	+40
NONINSURED							
Banking offices, total	1,377	1,358	1,339	1,301	1,227	1,176	1,142
Number of banks	1,201	1,170	1,141	1,108	1,053	1,004	972
Number of branches	176	188	198	193	174	172	170
Net change during year	−16	−19	−19	−38	−74	−51	−34
Offices opened	28	26	32	36	22	27	22
Banks	16	14	18	19	10	12	9
Branches	12	12	14	17	12	15	13
Offices closed	17	14	14	18	12	22	16
Banks	12	14	14	14	11	21	13
Branches	5			4	1	1	3
Changes in classification [1]	−27	−31	−37	−56	−84	−56	−40

[1] Net change in number of insured and noninsured banking offices, respectively, resulting from admissions of noninsured banks to insurance and from absorptions or successions of noninsured banks by insured banks and of insured banks by noninsured banks.

No. 476.—Insured Commercial Banks—Assets and Liabilities as of Dec. 31: 1946 to 1952

[Money figures in millions of dollars]

ITEM	1946	1947	1948	1949	1950 [1]	1951	1952
Number of banks	13,359	13,403	13,419	13,436	13,446	13,455	13,439
Assets, total	147,365	152,773	152,163	155,319	166,792	177,449	186,682
Cash, balances with other banks, and cash items in process of collection	33,704	36,936	38,097	35,222	39,865	44,242	44,299
Securities, total	81,469	76,712	70,339	75,824	73,198	73,673	76,280
U. S. Government obligations, direct and guaranteed	73,575	67,960	61,407	65,847	61,047	60,599	62,408
Obligations of States and political subdivisions	4,301	5,131	5,511	6,403	7,959	9,016	10,006
Other securities	3,593	3,621	3,421	3,574	4,192	4,058	3,866
Loans, discounts, and overdrafts	30,740	37,592	41,979	42,499	51,809	57,371	63,824
Miscellaneous assets	1,452	1,533	1,748	1,774	1,921	2,164	2,279
Liabilities and capital accounts, total	147,365	152,773	152,163	155,319	166,792	177,449	186,682
Deposits, total	137,030	141,889	140,683	143,194	153,498	163,172	171,357
Demand deposits of individuals, partnerships, and corporations	79,903	83,738	81,699	82,129	89,993	95,701	98,898
Time deposits of individuals, partnerships and corporations	32,761	33,963	34,262	34,462	34,582	36,057	38,795
U. S. Government	3,047	1,433	2,436	3,232	2,979	3,615	5,296
Other deposits	21,319	22,755	22,286	23,371	25,943	27,799	28,368
Miscellaneous liabilities	1,047	1,148	1,320	1,476	2,013	2,354	2,740
Capital, surplus, undivided profits, etc.	9,288	9,736	10,160	10,649	11,281	11,923	12,585

[1] Dec. 30.

Source of tables 475 and 476: Federal Deposit Insurance Corporation, Annual Report.

No. 477.—DEPOSIT INSURANCE—NUMBER AND DEPOSITS OF ALL OPERATING BANKS, BY INSURANCE STATUS AND BY STATES AS OF DEC. 31, 1951 AND 1952

[Deposits in millions of dollars. Includes commercial and stock savings banks, nondeposit trust companies, and mutual savings banks]

STATE	1951				1952			
	Number		Deposits		Number		Deposits	
	In-sured	Nonin-sured	In-sured	Nonin-sured	In-sured	Nonin-sured	In-sured	Nonin-sured
Total	13,657	1,004	178,540	8,064	13,645	972	186,142	8,289
Alabama	226	------	1,378	------	229	------	1,451	------
Arizona	12	1	530	3	13	1	609	3
Arkansas	224	6	877	3	224	6	928	3
California	190	11	15,115	56	189	10	16,341	57
Colorado	147	10	1,308	6	148	12	1,405	6
Connecticut	98	86	1,873	1,392	99	85	1,964	1,483
Delaware	35	3	531	93	35	2	520	79
Dist. of Columbia	19	------	1,266	------	19	------	1,271	------
Florida	204	4	2,203	8	209	4	2,464	8
Georgia	337	66	1,974	17	341	62	2,063	16
Idaho	41	1	467	9	39	1	504	9
Illinois	882	18	13,710	44	883	11	14,444	30
Indiana	474	11	3,509	34	474	11	3,740	34
Iowa	606	57	2,305	89	609	56	2,398	92
Kansas	468	139	1,681	160	474	135	1,785	167
Kentucky	361	22	1,778	20	362	18	1,840	18
Louisiana	165	1	2,022	1	166	1	2,104	1
Maine	61	34	479	251	63	33	518	260
Maryland	164	5	2,064	128	160	5	2,197	130
Massachusetts	173	195	4,480	3,514	173	195	4,510	3,713
Michigan	414	21	5,862	155	412	17	6,455	160
Minnesota	664	17	3,182	15	665	15	3,403	12
Mississippi	198	4	871	8	199	3	903	9
Missouri	575	24	4,831	24	576	22	5,021	19
Montana	110	------	615	------	109	------	654	------
Nebraska	367	49	1,407	40	369	46	1,485	41
Nevada	8	------	202	------	8	------	235	------
New Hampshire	58	51	241	342	58	51	247	366
New Jersey	337	4	5,751	6	331	4	6,026	6
New Mexico	51	------	403	------	51	------	444	------
New York	740	9	45,981	482	725	9	47,914	508
North Carolina	224	1	2,088	26	225	1	2,183	26
North Dakota	145	5	488	113	146	7	496	117
Ohio	652	7	8,600	9	647	7	9,069	9
Oklahoma	374	11	1,876	6	376	9	1,996	5
Oregon	69	2	1,506	8	67	2	1,624	8
Pennsylvania	951	16	12,376	67	930	17	12,788	66
Rhode Island	14	8	869	211	15	6	927	186
South Carolina	134	15	788	9	134	15	832	9
South Dakota	169	------	530	------	170	------	553	------
Tennessee	291	7	2,199	5	290	7	2,293	6
Texas	870	44	7,945	84	877	42	8,485	91
Utah	54	------	654	------	55	------	696	------
Vermont	75	1 1	363	------	73	1 1	376	------
Virginia	315	------	2,210	------	315	------	2,371	------
Washington	118	3	2,286	18	118	3	2,414	21
West Virginia	177	4	1,007	13	178	4	1,023	13
Wisconsin	548	9	3,277	9	548	9	3,490	9
Wyoming	52	------	306	------	52	------	314	------
Other areas	16	27	264	584	17	25	386	493

1 Nondeposit trust company.

Source: Federal Deposit Insurance Corporation, *Annual Report.*

No. 478.—FEDERAL DEPOSIT INSURANCE CORPORATION—DISBURSEMENTS TO PROTECT DEPOSITORS, AND NUMBER AND DEPOSITS OF INSURED BANKS PLACED IN RECEIVERSHIP OR ABSORBED WITH THE CORPORATION'S AID: 1934 TO 1952

CLASSIFICATION	DISBURSEMENT BY FDIC (THOUSANDS OF DOLLARS)[1]			NUMBER OF BANKS			DEPOSITS (THOUSANDS OF DOLLARS)		
	Total	Receiverships	Absorptions[2]	Total	Receiverships	Absorptions	Total	Receiverships	Absorptions
All banks, cumulative total	276,044	87,044	189,000	420	245	175	540,653	109,590	**431,063**
By class of bank:									
National banks	52,883	14,808	38,075	73	21	52	112,530	19,474	93,056
State banks, members F. R. system	101,205	20,934	80,271	22	6	16	187,656	26,537	161,119
Banks not members F. R. system	121,956	51,302	70,654	325	218	107	240,467	63,579	176,988
Calendar year:									
1934	941	941		9	9		1,968	1,968	
1935	8,890	6,025	2,865	25	24	1	13,320	9,091	4,229
1936	14,781	8,056	6,725	69	42	27	27,508	11,241	16,267
1937	19,160	12,044	7,116	75	50	25	33,349	14,960	18,389
1938	30,479	9,092	21,387	74	50	24	59,684	10,296	49,388
1939	67,771	26,197	41,574	60	32	28	157,772	32,738	125,034
1940	74,134	4,895	69,239	43	19	24	142,430	5,657	136,773
1941	23,880	12,278	11,602	15	8	7	29,717	14,730	14,987
1942	10,825	1,612	9,213	20	6	14	19,185	1,816	17,369
1943	7,172	5,500	1,672	5	4	1	12,525	6,637	5,888
1944	1,503	404	1,099	2	1	1	1,915	456	1,459
1945	1,768		1,768	1		1	5,695		5,695
1946	265		265	1		1	347		347
1947	1,724		1,724	5		5	7,040		7,040
1948	2,990		2,990	3		3	10,657		10,687
1949	2,551		2,551	4		4	5,475		5,475
1950	3,986		3,986	4		4	5,501		5,501
1951	1,885		1,885	2		2	3,408		3,408
1952	1,339		1,339	3		3	3,157		3,157
Banks with deposits of—									
$100,000 or less	4,946	4,308	638	106	83	23	6,358	4,947	1,411
$100,000 to $250,000	12,906	11,554	1,352	109	86	23	17,759	13,920	3,839
$250,000 to $500,000	14,588	10,223	4,365	59	36	23	20,976	12,462	8,514
$500,000 to $1,000,000	27,868	13,901	13,967	58	24	34	43,427	17,590	25,837
$1,000,000 to $2,000,000	30,960	8,961	21,999	41	9	32	59,248	11,748	47,500
$2,000,000 to $5,000,000	46,813	12,421	34,392	29	5	24	88,315	16,279	72,036
$5,000,000 to $10,000,000	23,400		23,400	10		10	65,397		65,397
$10,000,000 to $25,000,000	40,910	25,676	15,234	4	2	2	79,755	32,644	47,111
$25,000,000 to $50,000,000	73,653		73,653	4		4	159,418		159,418

[1] Includes only principal disbursement; excludes expenses incident to transactions, greater part of which has been recovered.

[2] Excludes excess collections turned over to banks as additional purchase price at time of termination of liquidations.

Source: Federal Deposit Insurance Corporation, *Annual Report.*

No. 479.—Federal Home Loan Banks—Principal Assets and Liabilities as of December 31, 1932 to 1952

[In thousands of dollars]

YEAR AND FEDERAL HOME LOAN BANK DISTRICT	Total assets [1]	PRINCIPAL ASSETS			PRINCIPAL LIABILITIES AND CAPITAL				
		Advances outstanding	Investments in Government securities (face amount)	Cash [1]	Member deposits	Consolidated obligations	Paid-in on capital stock		Surplus reserves and undivided profits
							Members	U.S. Government	
All banks:									
1932	94,668	84,446	2,311	7,215	389		14,747	75,746	
1933	109,888	96,508	14,345	5,460	1,926		21,952	81,846	
1934	125,316	102,856	15,864	6,984	4,063		24,471	94,196	3,279
1935	174,468	145,287	9,476	19,153	10,745		26,316	117,809	3,495
1936	261,273	200,088	22,407	27,640	12,588	77,700	34,634	124,741	3,554
1937	294,271	198,943	44,635	35,529	21,906	65,500	37,971	124,741	4,793
1938	282,586	181,313	49,479	30,305	29,617	45,500	40,978	124,741	6,629
1939	301,544	201,492	49,815	45,345	26,921	90,500	44,541	124,741	11,256
1940	316,300	218,446	62,775	35,336	29,836	90,500	44,815	124,741	12,976
1941	287,510	129,213	121,421	35,504	34,438	40,800	51,703	124,741	14,851
1942	394,436	110,088	151,275	31,785	20,834	44,300	57,377	124,741	16,664
1943	308,013	130,368	143,813	30,322	35,744	66,500	61,805	124,741	17,782
1944	342,710	194,573	117,177	25,572	41,002	65,500	72,658	124,810	22,086
1945	478,864	293,455	143,151	39,714	70,245	160,000	84,525	122,051	22,026
1946	694,189	435,573	135,445	45,504	87,566	281,700	105,678	122,472	24,134
1947	828,945	515,016	271,845	34,386	133,545	416,500	131,257	115,708	25,117
1948	785,303	433,429	272,793	53,079	267,112	206,500	136,339	93,519	25,897
1949	1,065,470	815,957	197,486	41,479	294,096	361,000	182,647	85,022	29,968
1950	1,101,532	805,937	248,088	37,795	361,396	529,900	270,052		31,997
1951	1,235,227	844,199	318,686	42,882	419,661	448,556	315,488		34,413
Boston	106,020	82,267	40,880	2,860	15,896	61,800	25,547		2,418
New York	145,228	92,783	46,229	581	64,402	24,700	28,431		5,111
Pittsburgh	97,982	73,793	19,550	2,703	33,241	40,400	21,256		2,470
Greensboro	134,652	90,846	32,160	3,308	75,134	11,600	40,052		3,722
Cincinnati	110,104	86,256	47,834	3,579	41,234	26,000	38,288		3,340
Indianapolis	93,230	50,950	35,505	3,492	45,006	22,400	22,240		3,203
Chicago	163,196	122,566	35,250	5,170	43,130	79,000	34,330		3,417
Des Moines	87,413	62,712	22,780	1,818	27,043	17,800	14,336		3,185
Little Rock	47,676	33,176	11,540	2,752	7,347	22,000	15,057		1,650
Topeka	43,726	25,450	15,915	2,365	6,309	21,150	12,271		1,707
San Francisco	196,068	175,450	16,201	8,369	55,327	89,000	44,258		2,707

[1] Includes interbank deposits.

Source: Housing and Home Finance Agency, Home Loan Bank Board; records.

No. 480.—Federal Home Loan Bank System—Member Institutions: 1948 to 1952

[Money figures in thousands of dollars]

ITEM	1948	1949	1950	1951	1952
Member institutions as of Dec. 31:					
Number	3,769	3,900	3,980	3,981	4,066
Federal savings and loan associations	1,485	1,508	1,526	1,549	1,551
State-chartered savings and loan associations	2,245	2,314	2,368	2,401	2,447
Mutual savings banks	26	20	29	25	23
Life insurance companies	10	8	7	4	5
Assets	12,900,808	14,202,823	16,197,414	18,391,438	21,571,000 [1]
Federal savings and loan associations	6,164,489	7,103,902	8,452,940	9,789,930	11,762,000
State-chartered savings and loan associations	5,568,868	6,174,413	7,015,005	8,067,040	9,394,000
Mutual savings banks	702,578	798,327	629,505	443,549	431,000
Life insurance companies	364,969	126,191	80,268	90,018	94,000
Federal Home Loan Bank loans to members:					
Loans made during year	258,612	264,693	674,767	422,977	388,653
Loans repaid during year	290,390	337,250	282,229	432,967	427,382
Loans outstanding Dec. 31	515,976	433,429	815,937	805,937	844,199

[1] Preliminary.

Source: Housing and Home Finance Agency, Home Loan Bank Board; records.

No. 481.—All Savings and Loan Associations—Total Number and Selected Financial Items: 1920 to 1952

[Amounts in millions of dollars. Data cover continental United States, Alaska, Hawaii, and Puerto Rico. See also *Historical Statistics*, series H 114 and H 129-132]

END OF YEAR	Number of associations	Total assets	Mortgage loans	U. S. government and other securities	Savings capital-private	Mortgage pledged shares	FHLB advances and other borrowed money	General reserves and undivided profits	Mortgage loans made during year
1920	8,633	2,520	(¹)	(¹)	1,741	(¹)	(¹)	(¹)	(¹)
1922	10,009	3,343	2,009	(¹)	2,210	541	(¹)	(¹)	862
1925	12,403	5,509	5,085	(¹)	3,811	881	(¹)	(¹)	1,620
1930	11,777	8,829	7,760	(¹)	6,296	1,358	(¹)	(¹)	1,282
1935	10,266	5,875	3,947	(¹)	4,254	655	(¹)	(¹)	564
1940	7,521	5,733	4,415	108	4,322	290	233	464	1,200
1941	7,211	6,049	4,823	139	4,682	245	256	475	1,379
1944	6,279	7,438	4,963	1,703	6,308	183	199	572	1,454
1945	6,149	8,747	5,531	2,456	7,365	145	336	645	1,913
1946	6,098	10,203	7,276	2,047	8,548	135	402	751	2,584
1947	6,045	11,687	8,971	1,787	9,753	115	541	855	3,811
1948	6,011	13,028	10,469	1,525	10,964	104	590	969	3,607
1949	5,983	14,622	11,714	1,527	12,471	98	499	1,105	3,636
1950	5,992	16,846	13,714	1,535	13,978	92	880	1,279	5,237
1951	5,995	19,164	15,610	1,671	16,073	90	884	1,453	5,250
1952 (prel.)	6,000	22,700	18,533	1,879	19,211	89	960	1,665	6,617

¹ Not available.

Source: Housing and Home Finance Agency, Home Loan Bank Board; annual study, *Trends in the Savings and Loan Field*.

No. 482.—Federal Savings and Loan Insurance Corporation—Summary of Insured Institutions as of December: 1946 to 1952

[Money figures in thousands of dollars]

ITEM	1946	1947	1948	1949	1950	1951	1952 ¹
Number of associations	2,496	2,536	2,616	2,756	2,860	3,020	3,172
Total assets	7,293,662	8,537,578	9,714,561	11,278,155	13,644,166	16,145,828	19,656,000
Mortgage loans	5,216,897	6,572,195	7,777,308	9,022,016	11,152,747	13,191,167	16,092,500
Savings capital—private	6,184,005	7,176,684	8,254,709	9,699,525	11,359,433	13,619,359	16,732,000
Savings capital—U. S. Gov't	14,819	7,061	5,031	1,317	414		
Federal Home Loan Bank advances	267,531	391,442	447,243	368,427	743,383	744,056	816,600
Number of investors	4,860,400	5,415,000	6,122,000	7,076,000	8,111,000	9,354,000	10,805,600
Operations:							
New savings capital	2,565,992	2,787,082	3,217,139	3,687,942	4,543,291	5,666,877	7,102,680
Withdrawals	1,612,645	1,816,299	2,241,612	2,424,639	3,210,867	3,769,836	4,266,963
Mortgage loans made	2,796,878	2,864,846	2,754,577	2,886,670	4,351,928	4,500,600	5,847,555

¹ Preliminary.

Source: Housing and Home Finance Agency, Home Loan Bank Board.

No. 462.—ALL SAVINGS AND LOAN ASSOCIATIONS—TOTAL NUMBER AND SELECTED FINANCIAL ITEMS BY STATE OR OTHER Area: DEC. 31, 1951

[Amounts in thousands of dollars]

DISTRICT AND STATE	Number of associations	Total assets	Mortgage loans	U. S. Government and other securities	Savings capital—total	PHLB advances and other borrowed money	General reserves and undivided profits
United States	5,995	19,144,441	15,665,530	1,671,697	14,672,045	533,573	1,453,150
No. 1 Boston	335	1,513,641	1,266,145	136,691	1,361,502	60,734	127,561
Connecticut	32	230,755	207,904	21,124	212,135	13,342	15,508
Maine	35	47,608	41,526	2,645	34,691	4,323	6,448
Massachusetts	308	1,016,973	838,772	93,668	845,532	37,754	88,189
New Hampshire	26	60,486	52,949	4,848	50,374	3,591	5,137
Rhode Island	5	115,574	101,409	6,944	101,507	1,040	10,450
Vermont	10	19,573	14,689	1,552	16,496	944	1,539
No. 2 New York	722	2,460,030	1,990,803	245,840	2,112,574	171,551	161,312
New Jersey	466	811,111	646,432	87,764	708,140	39,767	47,945
New York	255	1,643,732	1,346,302	156,076	1,405,579	81,173	144,652
Puerto Rico	1	5,187	4,069		3,853	669	186
No. 3 Pittsburgh	972	2,029,730	1,544,832	95,689	1,197,177	71,295	104,713
Delaware	41	27,397	24,464	823	21,137	2,063	1,136
Pennsylvania	894	1,243,110	1,082,074	60,536	1,036,982	67,933	97,169
West Virginia	37	60,482	56,207	4,886	57,086	4,263	6,417
No. 4 Greensboro	668	2,476,050	2,162,134	143,749	2,086,050	166,364	166,136
Alabama	26	81,824	67,372	4,716	74,437	473	5,933
District of Columbia	28	435,387	398,685	15,400	362,189	13,598	39,794
Florida	90	474,005	377,899	40,823	405,906	19,065	32,720
Georgia	73	286,800	264,201	14,938	251,890	8,104	20,007
Maryland	378	474,043	368,873	26,350	378,483	27,046	42,168
North Carolina	177	377,553	327,796	21,584	322,622	15,578	27,178
South Carolina	74	102,386	138,815	9,499	141,214	6,196	11,326
Virginia	70	180,971	154,454	8,439	152,409	6,342	15,997
No. 5 Cincinnati	765	2,824,440	2,135,713	385,552	2,451,680	63,447	245,296
Kentucky	118	230,804	257,741	34,214	236,124	9,922	23,481
Ohio	607	2,448,086	1,794,412	316,228	2,050,622	47,425	210,445
Tennessee	39	135,800	163,560	15,080	164,934	6,120	10,969
No. 6 Indianapolis	303	1,977,950	620,162	114,125	913,343	57,136	57,932
Indiana	231	620,110	475,562	78,145	525,480	31,846	53,190
Michigan	70	437,799	363,600	36,090	396,754	25,340	34,153
No. 7 Chicago	726	2,120,545	1,723,856	181,800	1,704,474	154,553	153,610
Illinois	573	1,666,373	1,347,606	149,269	1,346,420	131,075	118,119
Wisconsin	153	442,172	376,160	32,531	358,064	23,478	35,491
No. 8 Des Moines	343	1,185,285	918,216	59,684	963,899	55,292	64,295
Iowa	99	234,586	186,564	17,298	192,517	12,050	13,389
Minnesota	73	497,686	352,601	19,484	387,372	17,386	21,804
Missouri	154	376,521	320,572	18,480	315,190	23,635	27,170
North Dakota	15	60,761	38,322	6,476	44,314	1,401	3,363
South Dakota	12	16,309	13,391	983	14,116	522	669
No. 9 Little Rock	334	916,900	771,992	61,306	776,852	47,606	66,722
Arkansas	62	77,197	66,552	4,650	66,619	2,978	5,301
Louisiana	76	376,814	228,189	19,212	228,258	16,939	24,476
Mississippi	35	60,802	51,637	3,514	53,157	2,511	4,121
New Mexico	19	40,279	34,008	1,818	34,747	1,501	3,060
Texas	142	451,437	381,006	32,783	394,121	23,151	29,315
No. 10 Topeka	272	768,795	626,471	74,888	645,376	26,344	63,723
Colorado	53	166,712	134,745	18,323	141,078	5,719	14,118
Kansas	105	227,207	186,602	16,861	184,328	12,776	16,967
Nebraska	66	141,167	106,196	25,950	117,546	2,040	14,167
Oklahoma	60	231,619	196,928	14,997	202,512	5,709	15,541
11 San Francisco	347	2,405,230	2,067,197	195,846	2,409,151	114,738	156,531
Alaska	1	1,901	1,187	360	1,342	199	100
Arizona	6	61,397	36,045	2,684	53,456	4,196	2,466
California	189	1,708,685	1,461,672	96,819	1,945,686	98,779	130,015
Hawaii	7	31,600	27,397	1,661	36,400	1,043	2,716
Idaho	10	42,460	32,653	2,793	37,130	1,559	2,664
Montana	19	37,064	28,810	4,542	33,816	635	3,644
Nevada	2	4,901	4,479	517	5,074	29	744
Oregon	36	143,313	111,184	16,796	119,388	9,189	7,742
Utah	19	97,566	76,972	7,647	77,369	1,214	7,646
Washington	45	254,280	222,601	56,366	310,918	7,527	26,947
Wyoming	13	26,716	18,470	2,685	20,471	369	1,606

Source: Housing and Home Finance Agency, Home Loan Bank Board; annual study, Trends in the Savings and Loan Field.

No. 484.—Savings and Loan Associations—Failures: 1920 to 1951

[Liabilities and estimated loss in thousands of dollars. Liabilities not available prior to 1930. See also *Historical Statistics*, series H 123–135]

YEAR	Number failed	Liabilities	Estimated loss	YEAR	Number failed	Liabilities	Estimated loss
1920	2		1	1939	153	84,901	27,040
1925	26		500	1940	129	69,560	6,744
1929	159		2,313	1941	44	8,575	1,052
1930	190	80,438	24,676	1942	18	8,919	1,789
1931	122	52,518	26,337	1943	11	1,484	361
				1944	5	2,508	155
1933	88	215,517	43,955				
1934	68	34,728	10,174	1945–46	0	0	0
1935	239	31,946	15,782	1947	1	92	0
1936	144	20,316	9,052	1948–49	0	0	0
1937	269	44,739	15,775	1950	1	50	0
1938	277	36,025	11,281	1951	0	0	0

Source: United States Savings and Loan League, Chicago, Ill., *Annual Statistical Report*.

No. 485.—Nonfarm Mortgages Recorded—Number and Amount, by Type of Mortgagee, for Continental United States: 1942 to 1952

[Amounts in thousands of dollars. Estimates based on mortgage recordings of $20,000 or less in more than 500 counties and similar political subdivisions, which contain about three-fifths of total nonfarm population]

PERIOD	Total	Savings and loan associations	Insurance companies	Commercial banks	Mutual savings banks	Individuals	Other mortgagees
NUMBER							
1942	1,351,290	424,709	75,726	268,158	43,734	356,511	182,452
1943	1,273,993	423,335	66,524	230,121	38,554	376,049	159,390
1944	1,445,616	496,357	51,130	249,206	42,031	445,952	100,940
1945	1,638,557	574,816	47,477	299,035	51,647	498,698	166,884
1946	2,497,122	827,129	96,065	589,292	101,153	625,260	268,223
1947	2,566,632	799,207	135,105	616,672	105,771	592,194	317,683
1948	2,534,702	765,505	156,290	552,938	123,031	613,361	323,577
1949	2,487,521	761,870	159,815	506,719	126,848	574,430	357,839
1950	3,032,442	935,499	227,236	628,247	165,212	610,291	465,967
1951	2,877,860	901,503	207,123	583,010	145,163	630,921	410,140
1952	3,028,157	1,026,964	170,813	599,619	153,205	670,523	407,033
AMOUNT							
1942	3,942,613	1,170,546	361,743	885,803	165,581	732,697	626,243
1943	3,861,401	1,237,505	379,866	752,643	152,054	857,681	581,752
1944	4,605,931	1,559,850	257,070	878,272	165,065	1,130,718	614,956
1945	5,649,819	2,017,066	249,849	1,097,039	216,981	1,402,487	666,397
1946	10,589,168	3,483,173	502,746	2,711,888	547,870	2,043,791	1,298,700
1947	11,726,677	3,650,249	847,129	3,003,794	596,481	2,006,208	1,622,816
1948	11,882,114	3,628,818	1,015,211	2,663,560	744,769	2,149,477	1,679,279
1949	11,828,001	3,646,196	1,046,068	2,445,722	749,697	2,038,593	1,901,725
1950	16,179,196	5,059,612	1,618,020	3,364,889	1,064,141	2,298,962	2,773,572
1951	16,405,367	5,294,689	1,615,173	3,370,407	1,013,366	2,539,452	2,572,280
1952	18,017,677	6,452,357	1,420,246	3,599,856	1,136,621	2,757,931	2,650,666

No. 486.—Index of Estimated Number of Nonfarm Real Estate Foreclosures for Continental United States: 1942 to 1952

[1935–1939=100. Adjusted for seasonal variation]

YEAR	Jan.	Feb.	Mar.	Apr.	May	June	July	Aug.	Sept.	Oct.	Nov.	Dec.	Average
1942	31.9	30.7	28.8	29.1	27.5	27.7	27.7	24.5	24.9	24.5	22.5	21.7	26.8
1943	20.6	18.4	17.2	18.2	16.9	15.9	15.8	15.0	15.3	13.4	13.6	13.4	16.1
1944	11.5	13.4	12.4	9.9	10.9	11.1	10.2	9.8	10.9	9.9	10.7	10.5	10.9
1945	8.1	9.6	9.5	8.0	8.0	9.0	7.4	7.6	7.4	7.5	8.0	7.1	8.1
1946	7.7	7.0	7.4	6.9	6.5	5.9	5.8	6.1	5.9	6.2	7.7	6.8	6.7
1947	6.8	7.0	7.4	6.5	6.6	7.0	6.9	6.6	6.6	5.8	6.7	6.7	6.7
1948	7.5	7.6	8.1	7.8	7.4	8.3	8.8	8.4	8.9	8.9	8.6	9.2	8.3
1949	9.4	9.7	10.3	9.7	9.7	10.9	11.8	12.8	11.9	11.9	11.8	13.8	11.2
1950	14.1	14.5	15.3	14.1	13.7	14.6	12.9	14.1	13.7	13.1	11.9	12.8	13.7
1951	12.9	12.6	12.1	11.2	11.3	11.2	11.0	12.0	11.6	10.8	11.0	11.1	11.6
1952	11.5	11.6	11.7	11.3	11.1	12.1	11.7	12.4	11.1	11.6	10.6	11.8	11.6

Source of tables 485 and 486: Housing and Home Finance Agency, Home Loan Bank Board.

No. 457.—Mortgage Loans on One- to Four-Family Nonfarm Homes, Estimated Balance Outstanding: 1941 to 1952

[In millions of dollars. Represents estimates on basis of recent surveys and more detailed analyses of mortgage holdings. See also *Historical Statistics*, series H 120-126]

TYPE OF MORTGAGES	1941	1942	1943	1944	1945	1946	1947	1948	1949	1950	1951	1952 (prel.)
Total	18,368	18,236	17,835	17,947	18,543	21,669	26,161	33,361	37,406	45,072	51,872	54,155
Savings and loan associations	4,349	4,349	4,365	4,617	5,156	6,340	6,475	9,641	11,117	13,104	14,801	17,590
Life insurance companies	1,976	2,255	2,410	2,436	3,258	2,570	3,450	4,925	5,970	8,392	10,514	11,800
Mutual savings banks	2,189	2,136	2,083	1,957	1,894	3,063	2,363	2,538	6,364	7,317	5,331	6,160
Commercial banks	2,672	2,752	2,706	2,703	2,875	4,876	6,302	7,396	7,966	9,481	10,275	11,260
Home Owners' Loan Corporation	1,777	1,567	1,333	1,091	852	636	486	360	231	10		
Federal National Mortgage Association	205	205	60	60	7	6	4	199	806	1,228	1,618	2,310
Individuals and others	5,192	4,969	4,933	5,081	5,501	6,368	7,151	7,697	8,062	8,445	8,830	8,125

Source: Housing and Home Finance Agency, Home Loan Bank Board; *Annual Report.*

No. 458.—Farm Credit—Loans and Discounts Not Secured by Farm Mortgages, by Type of Lender: 1930 to 1952

[In thousands of dollars. Continental United States only. Farmers Home Administration succeeded Farm Security Administration on Nov. 1, 1946; it took over from Farm Credit Administration for liquidation the emergency crop and feed loans, including those for drought-relief and orchard rehabilitation, on that date and loans of the regional agricultural credit corporations, on April 16, 1949. See also *Historical Statistics*, series R 289, R 281-286]

ITEM	1930	1935	1940	1945	1950	1951	1952
Commercial banks: Agricultural loans outstanding, Jan. 1 [1]	3,490,742	840,857	1,134,578	1,377,405	3,023,280	3,506,115	3,496,878
Federal intermediate credit banks: [3] Loans to and discounts for—							
Single-purpose institutions:							
Made during year [3]	162,906	118,137	67,316	72,089	160,456	226,396	258,100
Outstanding, Jan. 1	47,303	55,063	32,316	26,965	50,825	68,075	77,841
Production credit associations:							
Made during year [3]	109,927	44,011	4,503	4,082	9,844	14,129	8,900
Outstanding, Jan. 1	26,073	33,969	1,835	700	2,400	2,389	6,000
Banks for cooperatives:							
Made during year		6,508	31,069	58,462	145,415	128,077	116,566
Outstanding, Jan. 1			17,560	65,008	46,982	45,125	65,906
Banks for cooperatives: [4]							
Loans made during year		66,296	100,455	329,980	396,209	665,180	826,013
Loans outstanding, Jan. 1		27,831	75,843	212,472	300,885	342,969	421,518
Production credit associations:							
Loans made during year [3]		194,959	347,145	609,579	1,085,745	1,310,034	1,298,920
Loans outstanding, Jan. 1 [4]		60,450	153,425	186,906	387,454	450,673	561,371
Farmers Home Administration: [7]							
Loans made during year	5,940	187,087	110,192	97,665	126,443	124,906	176,200
Loans outstanding, Jan. 1	5,940	198,325	424,973	479,865	360,490	342,585	212,464
Farm Security Administration:							
Loans made during year [10]		10	66,297	57,006	271,811	237,123	208,264
Loans outstanding, Jan. 1 [9]			152,349	360,424	1,206,896	1,529,969	1,735,157
Commodity Credit Corporation:							
Loans outstanding, Jan. 1 [12]		27,162	234,606	146,232	699,615	342,451	401,649

[1] All active banks. Includes loans guaranteed by Commodity Credit Corporation.
[2] Excludes loans to production credit associations. Includes renewals.
[3] Includes loans guaranteed by Commodity Credit Corporation.
[4] Includes all loans made by Banks for Cooperatives whether or not discounted with F. I. C. B.
[5] Includes loans of associations in liquidation. Excludes loans subject to repurchase agreement with Commodity Credit Corporation.
[6] Includes loans to cooperative and defense relocation corporations; also includes loans made by Emergency Crop and Feed Loan offices and by regional agricultural credit corporations.
[7] Includes only emergency crop, feed, and drought-relief loans made by Farm Credit Administration and its predecessors.
[8] July 1.   [9] Net advances after deducting amounts repaid.
[10] Cumulative net advances minus principal repayments.
[11] Includes loans made in first instance by Commodity Credit Corporation and guaranteed loans purchased from

No. 489.—Farm Credit—Farm Mortgage Loans Held by Principal Lender Groups, Loans Closed, and Interest Payable: 1930 to 1952

[In thousands of dollars except where noted. Continental United States only. Loans held by Federal Farm Mortgage Corporation were made by Land Bank Commissioner: authority to make new loans expired July 1, 1947. Farmers Home Administration succeeded Farm Security Administration on Nov. 1, 1946. Joint-stock land banks have been in liquidation since May 12, 1933; includes banks in receivership. See also *Historical Statistics*, series E 244-255]

ITEM	1930	1935	1940	1945	1949	1950	1951	1952
Total debt outstanding, Jan. 1..	9,630,763	7,584,459	6,586,399	4,932,942	5,106,183	5,407,310	5,827,585	6,299,576
Federal land banks and Federal Farm Mortgage Corporation [1]...	1,201,732	2,564,179	2,723,110	1,556,963	946,076	964,727	991,439	1,026,906
Life insurance companies [1].........	2,118,439	1,301,562	984,290	933,723	1,035,719	1,172,157	1,340,705	1,525,411
Commercial banks [2].............	997,468	496,842	534,170	449,582	847,841	879,416	943,387	980,436
Farmers Home Administration.....	....	....	31,927	193,377	188,893	188,855	214,047	233,374
Joint-stock land banks [1].............	637,789	277,020	91,726	5,455	462	270	....	....
Individuals and others.............	4,675,340	2,942,856	2,221,176	1,793,822	2,089,192	2,201,885	2,338,008	2,533,449
LOANS CLOSED BY								
Federal land banks and Federal Farm Mortgage Corporation.....	47,146	443,479	100,317	120,581	180,643	203,154	211,435	(7)
Joint-stock land banks.............	5,236	275	123	14	....	....	....	....
INTEREST PAYABLE								
Interest rates on mortgage loans recorded (percent)................	6.4	5.4	(3)	[4] 4.7	[4] 4.7	(3)	[4] 4.7	(3)
Interest rates on mortgage loans outstanding, Jan. 1 (percent) [5]...	6.0	5.5	4.6	4.5	4.6	4.6	4.7	4.7
Interest charges [6].................	569,756	396,092	293,091	220,113	242,392	261,885	284,213	[7] 308,037
Index of interest charges per acre (1910-14=100).................	206	135	98	69	76	82	89	[7] 96

[1] Includes purchase-money mortgages and sales contracts in addition to regular mortgages.
[2] Begining 1935, includes insured commercial banks; prior to 1935, open State and national banks.
[3] Not available.
[4] Average of rates on mortgages recorded during month of March only.
[5] Average contract rates, except for temporarily reduced rates on outstanding loans of Federal land banks, 1935 and 1940, and Federal Farm Mortgage Corporation, 1940 and 1945.
[6] Payable during calendar year on outstanding loans. Excludes amounts paid by Secretary of Treasury to Federal land banks, 1935 and 1940, and Federal Farm Mortgage Corporation, 1940 and 1945, as reimbursement for interest reductions granted borrowers.
[7] Preliminary.

Source: Department of Agriculture, Bureau of Agricultural Economics; *Agricultural Finance Review*.

No. 490.—Federal Land Banks—Principal Assets and Liabilities as of Dec. 31: 1942 to 1952

[In thousands of dollars]

DECEMBER 31—	ASSETS				LIABILITIES					
	Total assets	Mortgage loans [1]	U.S. Govt. obligations, direct and fully guaranteed	Cash on hand and in banks	Unmatured farm loan bonds outstanding [2]	Capital stock		Paid-in surplus, U.S. Govt.	Reserve and undivided profits [4]
						U.S. Govt.	National farm loan associations [3]		
1942........	2,086,397	1,599,275	258,123	51,238	1,532,618	117,176	100,330	146,086	127,581
1943........	1,901,061	1,355,757	398,416	34,348	1,361,802	120,260	87,999	142,022	128,919
1944........	1,441,484	1,135,150	220,149	30,834	845,167	118,941	75,696	123,874	141,579
1945........	1,231,881	1,026,980	144,725	33,935	630,975	117,790	68,106	50,252	162,061
1946........	1,114,105	943,133	135,848	28,216	705,127	39,879	61,917	36,924	178,582
1947........	990,409	866,290	104,249	22,638	661,573	....	56,955	....	196,501
1948........	970,443	855,347	101,313	20,568	646,924	....	55,918	....	201,256
1949........	1,011,355	897,704	106,308	19,932	715,702	....	57,886	....	205,928
1950........	1,042,079	944,718	87,813	19,851	714,537	....	60,197	....	216,568
1951........	1,108,184	993,987	83,194	18,255	784,149	....	62,902	....	226,342
1952........	1,180,913	1,076,691	82,105	15,063	815,323	....	67,204	....	247,578

[1] Less payments on principal and principal of delinquent and extended installments; before deductions for reserves. [2] Excludes bonds owned by banks.
[3] For 1951 and prior years, includes capital stock owned by individual borrowers.
[4] Not including special reserves set up against particular assets. Includes earned surplus.

Source: Department of Agriculture, Farm Credit Administration; *Annual Report*, and records.

No. 491.—FARM CREDIT ADMINISTRATION—LOANS AND DISCOUNTS MADE AND OUTSTANDING: 1932 TO 1952

[In thousands of dollars]

YEAR	FARM MORTGAGE LOANS BY—		LOANS TO COOPERATIVES BY—			FEDERAL INTERMEDIATE CREDIT BANKS, LOANS TO AND DISCOUNTS FOR—		Production credit associations [14]
	Federal land banks	Land Bank Commissioner	Federal intermediate credit banks (direct) [1]	Banks for cooperatives, including central bank [2]	Agricultural Marketing Act revolving fund [1]	Prod. credit associations, banks for co-ops [2]	Other financing institutions	
Made during year—								
Cumulative to Dec. 31, 1932	1,725,240		815,425		369,479		819,230	
1933	151,634	70,812	27,910	27,144	60,687	27	250,756	27
1934	730,367	853,136	57,369	40,371	9,555	110,162	228,283	107,216
1935	248,071	190,395	44,509	66,348	7,402	220,204	145,442	195,306
1936	109,170	77,258	3,755	81,294	20,449	271,700	105,206	228,060
1937	63,092	40,020	5,129	97,584	5,935	342,979	101,438	265,520
1938	51,418	29,395	2,958	94,946	7,911	370,858	90,466	300,153
1939	81,082	27,417	4,138	83,390	1,214	381,222	96,558	320,463
1940	64,273	36,964	4,590	101,221	3,094	419,072	92,593	348,383
1941	68,068	27,533	5,651	181,509	3,900	539,297	102,261	418,196
1942	53,974	28,534	9,397	252,379	5,017	696,522	110,078	477,715
1943	61,900	30,497	5,000	398,581	1,417	827,474	94,962	501,212
1944	70,275	35,017	3,402	363,637	509	782,402	81,744	490,477
1945	92,985	29,462	4,032	533,702	660	759,297	74,491	491,166
1946	130,162	15,055	11,575	390,709	975	922,816	95,022	614,668
1947	130,764	16,696	14,128	531,246	1,400	1,126,163	111,967	737,611
1948	130,514	[4] 17	15,839	494,418	1,000	1,266,714	165,710	924,314
1949	182,357	[4] 19	5,900	382,617	700	1,416,948	162,593	968,990
1950	206,953	[4] 25	9,044	402,170	700	1,443,367	174,051	1,075,710
1951	214,220	[4] 38	15,176	368,981	200	1,545,205	236,504	1,320,397
1952	254,581	[4] 41	8,000	328,113	378	1,789,137	225,109	1,341,709
Outstanding Dec. 31—								
1932	1,128,564		9,865		156,885		82,518	
1933	1,232,707	70,738	15,211	18,607	157,732	27	134,233	37
1934	1,915,762	616,825	33,900	27,331	54,863	61,024	94,322	30,852
1935	2,071,925	794,725	2,731	50,013	44,433	104,706	47,162	59,910
1936	2,064,158	836,779	1,641	69,647	32,754	129,872	41,017	105,680
1937	2,038,307	812,749	1,813	97,633	30,982	165,194	46,454	124,749
1938	1,982,224	752,881	929	97,496	28,722	168,392	35,545	145,678
1939	1,904,655	690,580	1,324	76,252	20,547	165,256	33,354	158,674
1940	1,851,218	648,296	1,400	74,741	16,463	186,923	34,103	171,866
1941	1,784,398	596,802	2,187	113,444	16,914	226,017	39,222	187,497
1942	1,602,846	512,197	2,000	144,644	12,551	272,564	39,050	164,962
1943	1,357,902	406,180	2,000	235,174	5,351	285,671	14,778	108,734
1944	1,136,928	329,700	700	212,835	3,067	267,185	31,197	101,664
1945	1,027,087	228,397	2,042	187,545	2,665	241,879	27,870	138,899
1946	944,421	140,197	4,161	191,550	2,202	276,461	43,344	235,308
1947	892,322	103,195	4,000	274,777	2,007	334,901	42,908	300,620
1948	856,571	75,227	3,700	301,987	1,914	425,696	61,091	391,280
1949	869,472	56,720	2,400	344,378	1,366	485,823	57,941	455,472
1950	949,482	42,415	4,000	425,012	1,453	611,677	52,441	562,419
1951	997,622	31,864	4,000	320,562	608	627,108	91,223	635,116
1952	1,074,462	23,374	2,000	418,304				

[1] Includes renewals.
[2] Excludes advances in connection with Commodity Credit Corporation programs.
[3] Duplicates amount of credit extended and outstanding for the 2 agencies concerned.
[4] For loans made, excludes associations in liquidation subsequent to beginning of liquidation; for loans outstanding, excludes for each date associations which had been placed in liquidation.
[5] Represents refinancing of existing commissioner loans; lending authority of Land Bank Commissioner expired July 1, 1947.

Source: Department of Agriculture, Farm Credit Administration; Annual Report, Semiannual Report on Loans and Discounts, and records.

No. 492.—Farm Credit Administration—Loans and Discounts Made During Year Ending Dec. 31, 1952

[In thousands of dollars]

DISTRICT AND STATE	FARM MORTGAGE LOANS BY—		LOANS TO COOPERATIVES BY—			FEDERAL INTERMEDIATE CREDIT BANKS, LOANS TO AND DISCOUNTS FOR [3]		Production credit associations [2]
	Federal land banks	Land Bank Commissioner [1]	Federal intermediate credit banks (direct) [2]	Banks for cooperatives including central bank	Agricultural Marketing Act revolving fund [1]	Prod. credit assoc'ns and banks for co-ops [2]	Other financing institutions	
Total	254,581	41	8,000	528,118	375	[4] 1,789,137	223,109	1,341,709
District No. 1	9,837		8,000	85,930		77,967	706	64,964
Maine	373			16,687		7,503	244	5,040
New Hampshire	280			165		1,172		1,016
Vermont	1,348			222		7,856		7,447
Massachusetts	927			58,537		4,331	249	3,220
Rhode Island	26					759		645
Connecticut	653			1,099		5,476		4,315
New York	4,769		8,000	8,994		43,038	85	37,287
New Jersey	1,451			226		7,822	128	5,914
District No. 2	10,275			11,663		68,976	11,960	64,799
Pennsylvania	3,042			3,850		20,973		19,265
Delaware	244					2,493		2,450
Maryland	1,362			1,141		14,367		13,526
Virginia	1,956			3,538		16,038	98	14,889
West Virginia	682			29		3,676		3,179
Puerto Rico	2,989			3,105		12,429	10,962	11,389
District No. 3	15,947			61,463		130,192	1,399	107,981
North Carolina	4,418			2,297		38,081	755	31,386
South Carolina	3,409			268		22,679	56	19,494
Georgia	5,081			17,952		41,230	6	32,726
Florida	3,039			40,946		28,202	782	23,175
District No. 4	19,045			27,941		185,806	9,691	136,798
Ohio	6,286			8,557		55,745	3,948	46,731
Indiana	6,620			7,278		64,838	1,351	50,712
Kentucky	3,053			1,337		38,026	2,085	21,588
Tennessee	3,086			10,769		27,197	2,307	17,767
District No. 5	13,997			15,439		100,449	24,409	99,849
Alabama	5,847			1,220		17,232	1,511	17,421
Mississippi	5,388			8,029		50,195	19,998	49,698
Louisiana	2,762			6,190		33,022	2,900	32,730
District No. 6	23,587			49,161		197,411	9,937	146,507
Illinois	13,940			10,679		73,184	2,838	67,681
Missouri	6,321			15,316		74,275	2,635	47,630
Arkansas	3,296			23,166		49,952	4,464	31,196
District No. 7	38,163			55,970		126,100	9,567	87,999
Michigan	9,160			9,477		19,056	35	14,952
Wisconsin	10,047			18,778		31,628	4,805	27,491
Minnesota	15,206			27,061		56,178	3,302	35,439
North Dakota	3,750			654		19,238	1,825	10,117
District No. 8	40,066		13	27,340		148,169	12,686	120,419
Iowa	19,087		9	21,206		60,482	3,617	51,105
South Dakota	8,698			902		25,326	2,668	22,039
Nebraska	10,522		2	5,192		46,807	1,548	33,793
Wyoming	1,759		2	40		15,554	4,853	12,482
District No. 9	19,820			49,616	125	127,813	22,836	110,414
Kansas	8,676			23,925		35,483	1,749	31,700
Oklahoma	5,624			21,978	125	35,118	8,011	29,430
Colorado	3,874			2,314		40,516	7,762	35,137
New Mexico	1,646			1,399		16,696	5,314	14,147
District No. 10	27,068			56,103	250	223,697	56,564	151,288
Texas	27,068			56,103	250	223,697	56,564	151,288
District No. 11	19,322		1	71,294		178,974	55,679	120,269
Arizona	627			248		18,904	18,522	13,406
Utah	1,628			6,300		19,585	8,547	15,284
Nevada	436			82		7,711	2,787	4,019
California	16,631		1	64,664		132,774	25,823	86,560
District No. 12	17,474		27	16,196		192,875	9,075	130,492
Montana	3,805		10	93		64,500	1,282	43,977
Idaho	5,681		6	1,319		50,409	404	37,344
Washington	4,029		3	5,785		31,388	1,686	14,511
Oregon	3,959		8	9,001		46,078	1,703	34,660

[1] Represents refinancing of existing commissioner loans; lending authority of Land Bank Commissioner expired July 1, 1947.

[2] Includes renewals.

[3] Duplicates credit extended by the 2 agencies concerned.

[4] Includes $30,018,000 of direct loans made to the Central Bank for Cooperatives which cannot be allocated by States.

Source: Department of Agriculture, Farm Credit Administration; *Annual Report, Semiannual Report on Loans and Discounts*, and records.

No. 493.—FARM CREDIT ADMINISTRATION—LOANS AND DISCOUNTS OUTSTANDING, DEC. 31, 1952

[In thousands of dollars]

DISTRICT AND STATE	FARM MORTGAGE LOANS BY—		LOANS TO COOPERATIVES BY—			FEDERAL INTERMEDIATE CREDIT BANKS LOANS TO AND DISCOUNTS FOR—		Production credit associations
	Federal land banks	Land Bank Commissioner	Federal intermediate credit banks (direct)	Banks for cooperatives (including central bank)	Agricultural Marketing Act revolving fund	Prod. credit assoc'ns and banks for co-ops [1]	Other financing institutions	
Total	1,078,493	23,374	2,000	418,504	905	627,106	91,225	606,116
District No. 1		2,114	2,000					
Maine		156						
New Hampshire		55						
Vermont		106						
Massachusetts		287						
Rhode Island	756	47						
Connecticut		255						
New York		513	2,000					
New Jersey		418						
District No. 2		1,387						
Pennsylvania		225						
Delaware		16						
Maryland		94						
Virginia		155						
West Virginia		95						
Puerto Rico		997						
District No. 3		2,062				250		
North Carolina		405						
South Carolina		461						
Georgia		572				250		
Florida		474						
District No. 4		772				150		
Ohio		167						
Indiana		257						
Kentucky		163						
Tennessee		205				150		
District No. 5		629						
Alabama		121						
Mississippi		239						
Louisiana		269						
District No. 6		1,588				5		
Illinois		496				5		
Missouri		744						
Arkansas		345						
District No. 7		4,939						
Michigan		618						
Wisconsin		1,081						
Minnesota		1,335						
North Dakota		1,305						
District No. 8		2,697						
Iowa		631						
South Dakota		538						
Nebraska		776						
Wyoming		152						
District No. 9		1,226				250		
Kansas		432						
Oklahoma		424				250		
Colorado		214						
New Mexico		156						
District No. 10		1,992				250		
Texas		1,992				250		
District No. 11		4,265						
Arizona		160						
Utah		254						
Nevada		32						
California		1,919						
District No. 12		1,767						
Montana		635						
Idaho		434						
Washington		189						
Oregon		409						

[1] Duplicates loans outstanding for the 2 agencies concerned.

[2] Includes $26,196,000 of direct loans made to the Central Bank for Cooperatives which cannot be allocated by States.

Source: Department of Agriculture, Farm Credit Administration; Annual Report and Report on Loans and Discounts, and reports.

No. 494.—Farmers Home Administration—Real-Estate and Non-Real-Estate Loans to Individuals, by States and Other Areas

[In thousands of dollars. Includes loans made from corporation trust funds]

DIVISION, STATE, OR OTHER AREA	REAL-ESTATE LOANS[1]				NON-REAL-ESTATE LOANS				Emergency crop and feed loans outstanding Jan. 1, 1953
	Direct farm ownership		Farm housing		Production and subsistence[3]		Disaster[7]		
	Amount of loans in 1952[2]	Amount of loans outstanding Jan. 1, 1953[3]	Amount of loans in 1952[4]	Amount of loans outstanding Jan. 1, 1953	Amount of loans in 1952	Amount of loans outstanding Jan. 1, 1953[4]	Amount of loans in 1952	Amount of loans outstanding Jan. 1, 1953[5]	
Total	22,521	193,123	26,332	69,680	141,171	294,483	33,194	23,771	27,965
New England	280	2,386	366	1,009	3,121	5,880	189	358	112
Maine	96	850	243	738	1,678	2,808	45	96	86
New Hampshire	35	157	18	25	476	1,029	8	15	6
Vermont	118	708	37	54	564	1,185	1	117	9
Massachusetts	21	420	27	85	166	332	86	53	3
Rhode Island	0	28	5	6	17	72	18	26	1
Connecticut	10	223	36	101	220	324	3	21	8
Middle Atlantic	617	6,927	907	2,415	6,277	13,196	338	516	168
New York	142	2,336	215	610	2,731	6,997	281	261	62
New Jersey	207	1,467	310	571	996	2,236	41	227	40
Pennsylvania	268	3,124	382	1,234	2,550	5,963	13	28	66
East North Central	2,090	17,627	1,597	5,180	15,663	33,327	507	1,016	653
Ohio	457	3,570	240	681	3,239	5,907	45	37	80
Indiana	357	3,685	378	1,126	2,549	4,636	43	28	86
Illinois	260	2,651	281	946	3,227	6,349	54	66	59
Michigan	253	3,034	406	1,510	3,351	7,942	175	335	141
Wisconsin	763	4,207	292	917	3,327	7,663	190	550	247
West North Central	5,106	36,347	3,116	8,591	24,924	52,649	10,128	5,121	14,163
Minnesota	724	6,512	397	934	5,313	10,306	335	96	900
Iowa	882	4,945	539	1,218	2,777	5,190	218	70	11
Missouri	1,340	9,631	982	2,451	3,963	8,443	8,730	4,103	2,334
North Dakota	579	3,084	394	844	3,441	4,613	9	53	7,468
South Dakota	604	2,683	191	795	4,028	8,606	324	136	3,907
Nebraska	484	3,845	286	1,299	3,097	6,243	80	68	461
Kansas	493	5,447	327	1,050	2,305	6,448	432	595	1,110
South Atlantic	4,455	31,238	5,932	14,969	19,483	36,183	3,972	2,699	2,104
Delaware	7	204	13	17	97	265	0	1	20
Maryland	128	1,284	243	544	799	2,487	1	23	186
Virginia	393	2,764	673	1,662	1,458	3,007	475	440	392
West Virginia	474	1,822	366	1,152	1,387	3,520	0	26	36
North Carolina	1,411	7,342	1,406	3,095	5,004	9,499	363	339	171
South Carolina	417	5,394	1,002	2,668	3,727	7,909	1,540	619	452
Georgia	1,117	10,417	1,466	4,287	4,926	10,763	1,294	556	484
Florida	508	2,181	671	1,894	2,085	9,173	299	305	363
East South Central	3,125	30,865	4,968	11,543	14,647	29,695	5,281	3,750	668
Kentucky	391	2,493	829	1,658	3,061	5,261	222	216	41
Tennessee	510	5,388	704	2,200	2,252	4,002	724	594	133
Alabama	1,273	9,612	1,855	4,213	3,810	7,907	547	552	173
Mississippi	951	16,407	1,580	3,472	5,504	12,235	3,788	2,488	318
West South Central	3,300	39,268	5,275	13,495	26,477	61,197	15,557	10,568	3,774
Arkansas	700	9,448	1,204	2,287	5,170	12,364	4,974	2,149	849
Louisiana	618	5,931	1,027	2,480	4,652	7,227	1,051	350	593
Oklahoma	609	8,690	1,196	3,739	6,107	16,192	2,073	1,807	275
Texas	1,373	15,199	1,846	4,980	12,548	25,454	7,759	6,172	2,057
Mountain	2,133	15,639	2,213	6,695	16,357	36,962	1,532	2,638	4,997
Montana	117	2,416	264	738	3,711	8,123	155	394	2,147
Idaho	544	4,192	357	1,568	3,062	6,008	82	287	120
Wyoming	272	1,802	147	633	2,276	5,460	112	318	327
Colorado	452	2,095	435	1,008	3,827	8,353	495	1,036	700
New Mexico	364	1,504	470	845	2,767	5,175	43	72	447
Arizona	88	624	243	498	962	1,676	7	23	78
Utah	253	2,725	256	1,271	1,412	3,351	137	318	78
Nevada	43	371	41	134	350	852	2	190	10
Pacific	1,845	6,664	1,291	4,136	5,151	18,656	822	1,873	2,352
Washington	819	2,872	248	1,072	3,031	7,329	308	620	1,497
Oregon	530	2,223	319	1,099	1,969	4,042	152	355	384
California	216	1,569	724	1,965	3,151	6,685	372	906	471
Hawaii	12	726	202	552	130	440	0	31	(9)
Puerto Rico	34	2,395	345	952	1,949	2,494	0	(9)	14
Alaska	4	86	0	1	48	133	0	1	21
Virgin Islands	0	13	30	42	4	41	0	0	1

[1] Excludes insured mortgage farm ownership loans.
[2] Amount obligated for tenant purchase, farm enlargement and farm development loans.
[3] Includes project liquidation loans. [4] Amount obligated. [4] Includes water facilities loans.
[4] Includes rural rehabilitation, construction and wartime adjustment loans.
[5] Includes fur and orchard loans.
[6] Includes flood damage, flood and windstorm restoration loans, and Regional Agricultural Credit Corporation loans made by Farm Credit Administration prior to transfer of funds to Farmers Home Administration on April 16, 1949.
[9] Less than $500.

Source: Department of Agriculture, Farmers Home Administration.

No. 495.—Consumer Credit, by Major Parts: 1933 to 1952

[In millions of dollars. Estimated amounts outstanding. For revised series, see *Federal Reserve Bulletin*, April 1953]

END OF YEAR	Total consumer credit	INSTALLMENT CREDIT					NONINSTALLMENT CREDIT			
		Total installment credit	Sale credit			Loans [1]	Total	Single-payment loans [2]	Charge accounts	Service credit
			Total	Automobile	Other					
....	3,439	1,586	1,122	450	688	466	1,851	303	1,081	467
....	3,846	1,860	1,317	576	741	543	1,986	332	1,203	451
....	4,772	2,622	1,805	940	865	817	2,151	287	1,292	472
....	5,933	3,518	2,436	1,289	1,147	1,082	2,415	476	1,419	520
....	6,513	3,960	2,752	1,384	1,368	1,208	2,553	537	1,459	557
....	6,128	3,596	2,313	970	1,343	1,282	2,533	523	1,487	523
....	7,031	4,424	2,792	1,267	1,525	1,632	2,607	530	1,544	533
....	8,163	5,417	3,450	1,729	1,721	1,967	2,746	536	1,650	560
....	8,826	5,867	3,744	1,942	1,802	2,143	2,939	565	1,764	610
....	5,092	3,048	1,617	482	1,135	1,431	2,644	483	1,513	648
....	4,600	2,001	882	175	707	1,119	2,599	414	1,498	687
....	4,976	2,061	891	200	691	1,170	2,915	428	1,758	729
....	5,627	2,364	942	227	715	1,422	3,263	510	1,981	772
....	8,677	4,000	1,648	544	1,104	2,352	4,677	749	3,054	874
....	11,862	6,434	3,086	1,151	1,935	3,348	5,428	896	3,612	920
....	14,366	8,400	4,528	1,961	2,567	4,072	5,766	949	3,854	963
....	16,809	10,890	6,240	3,144	3,096	4,650	5,919	1,018	3,909	992
....	20,097	13,450	7,904	4,126	3,778	5,555	6,638	1,322	4,239	1,087
....	20,644	13,510	7,846	4,039	3,507	5,964	7,134	1,436	4,567	1,111
....	23,975	16,506	9,388	5,190	4,198	7,118	7,469	1,552	4,768	1,149

[1]...des repair and modernization loans insured by Federal Housing Administration.
[2]...installment loans (single-payment loans of commercial banks and pawnbrokers).

No. 496.—Consumer Installment Loans: 1933 to 1952

[In millions of dollars. Estimated amounts outstanding. For revised series, see *Federal Reserve Bulletin*, April 1953]

END OF YEAR	Total	Commercial banks [1]	Small loan companies	Industrial banks [1]	Industrial loan companies [1]	Credit unions	Miscellaneous lenders	Insured repair and modernization loans [2]
....	466	29	246	121		20	50	....
....	543	44	264	125		25	60	25
....	817	88	287	156		37	79	170
....	1,062	161	325	191		56	102	244
....	1,208	268	374	221		63	125	147
....	1,282	312	380	129	98	103	117	146
....	1,632	323	448	131	99	135	96	200
....	1,967	692	496	132	104	174	99	268
....	2,143	784	531	134	107	200	102	285
....	1,431	426	417	89	72	130	91	206
....	1,119	316	364	67	59	104	86	123
....	1,170	357	364	68	60	100	88	113
....	1,422	477	439	76	79	103	93	164
....	2,352	956	597	117	98	153	109	322
....	3,348	1,435	701	166	134	225	119	568
....	4,072	1,709	817	204	160	312	131	739
....	4,650	1,951	929	250	175	462	142	801
....	5,555	2,431	1,084	291	208	525	157	854
....	5,964	2,510	1,268	301	229	542	176	938
....	7,118	3,092	1,440	365	273	698	193	1,057

[1]...des only personal installment cash loans, retail automobile direct loans, and other retail direct loans.
[2]...des only loans insured by Federal Housing Administration adjusted by Federal Reserve to exclude ...umer loans.

...of tables 495 and 496: Board of Governors of the Federal Reserve System. Figures published cur-...Federal Reserve Bulletin.

No. 497.—CONSUMER INSTALLMENT SALE CREDIT, EXCLUDING AUTOMOBILE CREDIT: 1933 TO 1952

[In millions of dollars. Estimated amounts outstanding. For revised series, see *Federal Reserve Bulletin*, April 1953]

END OF YEAR	Total, excluding automobile	Department stores and mail order houses	Furniture stores	Household appliance stores	Jewelry stores	All other retail stores
1933	663	119	299	119	29	97
1934	741	146	314	131	35	115
1935	865	186	336	171	40	132
1936	1,147	256	405	255	56	174
1937	1,368	314	469	307	68	210
1938	1,343	302	485	206	70	220
1939	1,525	377	536	273	93	246
1940	1,721	439	599	302	110	271
1941	1,802	466	619	313	120	284
1942	1,135	252	440	188	76	179
1943	707	172	289	78	57	111
1944	691	183	263	50	56	109
1945	715	198	296	51	57	113
1946	1,104	337	386	118	89	174
1947	1,935	650	587	249	144	305
1948	2,567	874	750	387	152	404
1949	3,096	1,010	935	500	163	488
1950	3,778	1,245	1,029	710	(1)	794
1951	3,807	1,186	971	613	(1)	737
1952	4,198	1,461	1,146	709	(1)	882

1 Included in all other.

Source: Board of Governors of the Federal Reserve System. Figures published currently in *Federal Reserve Bulletin*.

No. 498.—STATE AND FEDERAL CREDIT UNIONS—RELATIVE DEVELOPMENT: 1937 TO 1951

[See headnote, table 499]

YEAR	TOTAL NUMBER OF CREDIT UNIONS		CREDIT UNIONS REPORTING		MEMBERS		AMOUNTS OF LOANS OUTSTANDING, END OF YEAR ($1,000) [2]		ASSETS ($1,000)	
	Total [1]	State	Total [1]	State	Total [1]	State	Total [1]	State	Total [1]	State
1937	6,219	3,792	5,424	3,128	1,538,177	1,055,736	77,217	62,317	116,338	97,068
1938	7,158	4,299	6,730	3,977	1,868,262	1,236,826	107,861	84,143	147,294	117,672
1939	8,077	4,782	7,849	4,677	2,309,183	1,459,377	148,773	111,306	193,600	145,803
1940	9,152	5,267	8,914	5,175	2,826,612	1,700,390	190,251	134,741	253,150	180,649
1941	10,042	5,663	9,650	5,506	3,304,390	1,907,694	219,856	150,605	322,215	216,558
1942	10,099	5,622	9,470	5,400	3,144,603	1,797,084	148,772	105,885	340,348	221,115
1943	9,549	5,285	8,983	5,124	3,023,603	1,721,240	122,468	87,240	355,263	228,315
1944	9,041	4,993	8,702	4,907	2,933,507	1,629,706	120,955	86,552	397,930	253,664
1945	8,882	4,923	8,615	4,858	2,842,989	1,626,364	126,278	91,122	434,627	281,524
1946	8,968	5,003	8,715	4,954	3,019,748	1,717,616	187,464	130,663	495,249	322,083
1947	9,168	5,155	8,942	5,097	3,339,859	1,893,944	279,923	188,551	591,127	380,751
1948	9,497	5,273	9,329	5,271	3,749,047	2,120,708	398,387	260,745	701,461	443,060
1949	10,073	5,427	9,897	5,402	4,090,721	2,271,115	504,133	329,425	827,089	510,726
1950	10,586	5,602	10,571	5,587	4,610,278	2,487,455	679,596	415,861	1,005,476	599,641
1951	11,279	5,881	11,284	5,886	5,196,393	2,732,495	747,476	447,720	1,198,328	693,613

1 Covers data for State and Federal credit unions.
2 Some State unions report on fiscal-year basis (seven in 1951); other data apply to calendar year.

Source: Department of Labor, Bureau of Labor Statistics; *Monthly Labor Review*.

No. 499.—CREDIT UNIONS—OPERATIONS, 1950 AND 1951, AND BY STATES, 1951

[Data for State-chartered associations furnished by State officials—usually Superintendent of Banks—charged with supervision of credit unions. All data for Federal credit unions furnished by Bureau of Federal Credit Unions, Department of Health, Education, and Welfare. 1950 figures based on later data than that shown in table 498]

YEAR AND STATE	NUMBER OF ASSOCIATIONS		Number of members	Amount of loans outstanding at end of year ($1,000)	Paid-in share capital ($1,000)	Total assets ($1,000)	Net earnings ($1,000)
	Total active	Reporting[1]					
Total: 1950	10,586	10,571	4,610,278	679,865	850,483	1,005,475	35,060
1951	11,279	11,264	5,196,393	747,476	1,040,442	1,196,328	39,762
State associations:							
1950	5,002	5,587	2,483,455	416,129	488,564	599,641	20,301
1951	5,881	5,896	2,732,495	447,720	583,040	603,615	21,430
Federal associations:							
1950	4,954	4,954	2,126,823	263,736	361,925	405,835	15,760
1951	5,398	5,398	2,463,898	299,756	457,402	504,713	18,336
1951							
Alabama	111	111	38,277	8,946	10,494	12,250	574
Arizona	36	36	10,877	1,780	2,096	2,268	92
Arkansas	42	42	8,346	789	1,063	1,206	50
California	684	682	432,291	75,723	93,212	106,363	4,044
Colorado	135	135	55,561	9,434	11,977	13,783	452
Connecticut	314	314	140,594	16,726	34,326	37,466	1,073
Delaware	7	7	4,552	636	841	909	39
District of Columbia	125	125	129,239	14,468	20,947	23,001	852
Florida	245	254	83,811	13,791	17,143	19,142	807
Georgia	180	180	72,871	10,002	4,814	14,002	463
Idaho	36	37	7,929	1,000	1,201	1,312	48
Illinois	1,018	1,018	510,300	67,974	115,030	124,971	4,605
Indiana	340	340	155,328	20,165	32,923	36,175	1,145
Iowa	216	216	60,528	9,148	12,689	14,523	377
Kansas	154	153	50,557	7,122	10,013	11,043	428
Kentucky	128	126	39,902	7,350	9,106	10,285	372
Louisiana	212	212	73,533	8,879	11,066	12,454	500
Maine	53	53	22,200	2,354	3,058	3,468	122
Maryland	96	96	54,397	6,245	6,779	7,083	300
Massachusetts	558	559	359,907	51,441	75,251	88,483	1,407
Michigan	451	451	274,459	50,266	65,860	76,008	2,454
Minnesota	239	239	111,820	24,121	28,555	32,736	865
Mississippi	36	36	11,067	1,367	1,675	1,806	85
Missouri	424	424	145,305	21,792	31,141	34,289	821
Montana	50	50	11,732	1,612	1,935	2,155	85
Nebraska	104	104	34,482	5,999	6,710	7,266	269
Nevada	16	16	4,560	385	451	490	20
New Hampshire	17	17	9,663	2,437	3,214	3,359	98
New Jersey	325	325	165,683	14,875	29,985	32,844	920
New Mexico	30	30	7,636	773	889	1,016	44
New York	788	788	395,238	40,997	69,215	77,800	2,304
North Carolina	222	222	57,554	6,727	8,883	11,369	721
North Dakota	90	94	16,709	3,061	4,008	5,249	110
Ohio	699	699	335,607	44,667	68,075	74,157	2,436
Oklahoma	91	91	37,148	6,322	8,542	9,178	352
Oregon	76	76	29,804	5,058	6,395	7,035	270
Pennsylvania	600	600	356,601	36,730	58,144	65,822	2,006
Rhode Island	54	54	61,534	17,252	13,779	28,481	650
South Carolina	34	34	13,846	1,224	1,590	1,842	70
South Dakota	63	63	8,053	881	1,402	1,650	68
Tennessee	167	167	51,238	13,103	16,515	19,582	765
Texas	540	540	214,454	38,399	48,275	54,275	2,315
Utah	80	80	26,266	5,675	6,667	6,754	400
Vermont	32	31	5,648	320	452	497	16
Virginia	129	129	61,175	6,572	8,829	7,331	284
Washington	194	195	72,976	11,140	14,060	15,473	662
West Virginia	73	73	30,926	2,446	2,814	3,051	147
Wisconsin	556	556	213,014	32,820	40,562	54,710	1,858
Wyoming	22	22	4,349	473	599	668	27
Alaska	12	12	2,679	397	426	450	14
Canal Zone	5	5	2,075	105	143	152	3
Hawaii	110	110	50,575	11,008	18,455	21,250	702
Puerto Rico	70	70	13,464	1,620	1,108	1,565	27

[1] In some States number reporting is greater than total at end of year because former includes associations which, although transacting some business during year, had ceased operation by end of year.
[2] Estimated.
[3] Fiscal year ending June 30.
[4] Federal credit unions only; no State-chartered associations in this State or area.
[5] Fiscal year ending September 30.
[6] Excludes loans on real estate, which can be made only from surplus funds.

Source: Department of Labor, Bureau of Labor Statistics, Monthly Labor Review, February 1952.

No. 500.—MONEY RATES—OPEN-MARKET RATES IN NEW YORK CITY: 1890 TO 1952

[Percent per annum. See also *Historical Statistics*, series N 185-187, for data on prime commercial paper, stock exchange time loans, and call loan renewals]

YEARLY AVERAGE	Prime commercial paper, 4 to 6 months	Prime bankers' acceptances, 90 days	Stock exchange time loans, 90 days	Stock exchange call loan renewals	YIELDS ON U. S. GOVERNMENT SECURITIES		
					3-month bills [1]	9- to 12-month taxable issues	3- to 5-year taxable issues
1890	6.91		5.31	5.84			
1900	5.71		3.94	2.94			
1910	5.72		4.03	2.98			
1920	7.50	6.06	8.06	7.74			
1930	3.59	2.48	3.26	2.94			
1940	.56	.44	1.25	1.00	.014		
1945	.75	.44	1.25	1.00	.375	.81	1.18
1947	1.03	.87	1.50	1.38	.594	.88	1.32
1948	1.44	1.11	1.55	1.55	1.040	1.14	1.62
1949	1.48	1.12	1.63	1.63	1.102	1.14	1.43
1950	1.45	1.15	1.63	1.63	1.218	1.26	1.50
1951	2.17	1.60	2.30	2.17	1.552	1.73	1.93
1952	2.33	1.75	2.59	2.49	1.766	1.81	2.13

[1] Rate on new issues within period. Tax-exempt bills prior to March 1941; taxable bills thereafter.

Source: Board of Governors of the Federal Reserve System, *Banking and Monetary Statistics*. Monthly and weekly figures published currently in *Federal Reserve Bulletin*.

No. 501.—BUSINESS LOAN RATES—AVERAGES OF INTEREST RATES CHARGED ON SHORT-TERM LOANS TO BUSINESSES, BY BANKS IN SELECTED CITIES AND BY SIZE OF LOAN: 1940 TO 1952

[Percent per annum. Estimates based on statistics reported by 91 large banks in 19 leading cities. Short term loans include loans maturing in one year or less. "Interest rate," as used here, includes discount rates. See also *Historical Statistics*, series N 188-191]

YEAR	Total 19 cities	New York City	7 other Northern and Eastern cities	11 Southern and Western cities	SIZE OF LOAN			
					$1,000 to $10,000	$10,000 to $100,000	$100,000 to $200,000	$200,000 and over
1940	2.1	1.8	2.0	2.5	4.3	3.0	2.0	1.8
1945	2.2	2.0	2.5	2.5	4.3	3.2	2.3	2.0
1947	2.1	1.8	2.2	2.6	4.2	3.1	2.5	1.8
1948	2.5	2.2	2.6	2.9	4.4	3.5	2.8	2.2
1949	2.7	2.4	2.7	3.1	4.6	3.7	3.0	2.4
1950	2.7	2.4	2.7	3.2	4.5	3.6	3.0	2.4
1951	3.1	2.8	3.1	3.5	4.7	4.0	3.4	2.9
1952	3.5	3.3	3.5	3.8	4.9	4.2	3.7	3.3

Source: Board of Governors of the Federal Reserve System. Annual totals published currently in *Federal Reserve Bulletin*.

No. 502.—STOCK PRICES—AVERAGES OF WEEKLY INDEXES, BY TYPE OF INDUSTRY: 1940 TO 1952

[Base: 1939=100. Figures are annual averages of indexes of weekly closing prices of 265 common stocks, distributed as follows: 96 for durable goods manufacturing, 72 for nondurable goods manufacturing, 21 for transportation, 28 for utilities, 32 for trade, finance, and service, and 14 for mining]

TYPE OF INDUSTRY	1940	1945	1947	1948	1949	1950	1951	1952
Composite index	90.6	131.2	131.0	132.3	127.6	154.1	184.7	195.0
Manufacturing, total	93.4	129.0	132.7	136.2	132.1	165.7	206.6	220.2
Durable goods	92.5	129.0	120.1	124.4	116.0	150.4	178.2	188.8
Nondurable goods	94.2	129.3	145.1	147.0	147.2	180.2	233.1	249.3
Transportation	99.1	190.0	149.1	158.1	138.8	159.9	198.0	230.6
Utilities	97.7	112.9	105.5	99.4	96.1	107.2	112.6	117.9
Trade, finance, and service	86.7	149.1	162.8	156.9	160.5	183.2	207.9	204.8
Mining	75.9	114.3	117.2	133.2	129.2	143.5	204.0	275.7

Source: Securities and Exchange Commission. Annual and current data are published by the Council of Economic Advisers in their monthly publication, *Economic Indicators*.

[See also *Historical Statistics*, series N 213–214]

CLASS	1929	1930	1935	1940	1945	1949	1950	1951	1952
BOND PRICES	DOLLARS PER $100 BOND								
U. S. Government[1]					102.0	102.7	102.5	98.9	97.3
Standard and Poor's Corp.:									
Municipal (15 issues)[2]	98.5	99.0	108.6	123.6	139.6	136.9	133.4	133.0	128.3
Corporate, high grade (17 bonds, A1+ issues)[3]	99.09	90.85	106.5	116.3	121.6	121.0	121.9	117.7	115.8
STOCK PRICES	DOLLARS PER SHARE (EXCEPT INDEXES)								
Standard and Poor's Corp.:									
Preferred (15 issues)[4]	136.7	141.5	151.4	169.2	189.1	176.4	181.5	170.4	169.7
Common (index, 1935–39 = 100):[5]									
Total (420 issues)	300.9	189.2	82.9	85.1	121.5	123.4	146.4	176.5	187.7
Industrial (353 issues)	171.1	127.0	82.2	87.9	123.3	127.6	186.4	192.3	221.0
Railroad (20 issues)	300.7	331.3	99.2	71.1	135.9	96.6	116.7	149.9	161.5
Public utility (50 issues)	374.1	280.7	83.9	95.8	106.1	97.5	107.2	112.4	113.2
Dow-Jones and Co. Inc.:[6]									
Total (65 issues)	125.43	95.64	41.97	45.28	63.72	64.37	77.69	93.98	103.71
Industrial (30 issues)	311.24	236.34	120.00	134.74	169.52	179.48	216.31	257.64	270.76
Railroad (20 issues)	180.66	132.13	23.83	28.50	56.56	47.77	60.73	81.58	97.06
Public utility (15 issues)[7]	104.43	84.80	22.15	22.61	32.15	36.44	41.29	44.03	48.95
Moody's per share, monthly average:[8]									
Total (200 issues)	96.00	64.90	32.44	33.84	46.02	46.66	56.23	66.98	71.73
Industrial (125 issues)	81.45	48.38	34.09	31.76	43.94	48.82	57.23	70.72	76.63
Railroad (25 issues)	108.82	90.77	26.15	26.16	34.94	24.35	28.60	45.72	46.35
Public utility (24 issues)	133.20	107.67	27.20	23.64	36.29	26.37	31.29	32.50	35.48

[1] Straight average of market prices of all taxable marketable bonds due or callable in 15 years and over; beginning April 1952, in 12 years and over.

[2] Prices derived from average yields on basis of a 4 percent 20-year bond based on Wednesday closing prices.

[3] Based on composite of data (including industrial, utility, and railroad) and are a conversion of yield indexes, based on yield to maturity of each bond and assuming a 4 percent coupon with 20 years to maturity. From April 1937 to date, prices are averages of weekly data for 17 A1+ bonds; from January 1928 to March 1937, data based on a varying group of A1+ bonds, one price monthly (first of month) being used.

[4] Prices derived from average of median yields on noncallable high-grade stocks on basis of a $7 annual dividend. Data from Board of Governors, Federal Reserve System.

[5] Based on Wednesday closing prices, or last preceding sale price; indexes weighted by number of shares of each stock outstanding in base period. Number of stocks represents number currently used; continuity of series not affected by changes in number.

[6] Averages of daily closing figures. Changes have been made in stocks used at various times. However, the stock prices have remained constant except for public utilities (see note 7).

[7] For 20 stocks prior to June 2, 1938.

[8] Based on prices end of month. 200 stocks used represent for the most part, an identical list, except in public utility group, which is a different composite of 24 electric utilities (representing combined holding and operating electric companies prior to 1942 and operating electric companies thereafter). Data for A. T. & T. Co., included in figures for 200 stocks; excluded from utilities in order to show more clearly the trend for electric operating stocks.

[9] Includes also 15 banks and 10 insurance stocks and 1 additional public utility stock (see note 8).

Source: Department of Commerce, Office of Business Economics; *Survey of Current Business*, except as noted. (For original sources see table stub.)

[Value except average price, in millions of dollars]

	BONDS			STOCKS			JAN. 1—	BONDS[1]			STOCKS		
	Face value	Market value	Average price	Shares (millions)	Market value	Average price		Face value	Market value	Average price	Shares (millions)	Market value	Average price
		37,088	91.37	1,404	47,491	34.24	1947	137,165	140,758	$102.64	1,771	68,604	38.73
				1,455	46,466	32.09	1948	134,727	136,207	99.62	1,807	66,313	36.69
				1,455	41,501	28.69	1949	137,308	131,306	100.18	2,015	67,048	33.22
				1,495	55,785	26.43	1950	126,410	128,404	102.43	2,166	76,302	35.22
				671	39,012	31.17	1951	114,509	115,602	100.96	2,350	93,807	39.87
				868	46,619	27.01	1952	102,808	100,381	97.63	2,610	105,434	41.53
	141,108	118,...	103.51	1,802	72,765	46.23	1953			97.61			
	148,111	106.64											

[1] These figures include bonds of International Bank for Reconstruction and Development. These are excluded in computing average price of all listed bonds.

Source: New York Stock Exchange, New York, N. Y.; *Year Book*.

No. 505.—Bond and Stock Yields—Percent: 1929 to 1952

[See also *Historical Statistics*, series N 197-200, 203-205]

CLASS	1929	1930	1935	1940	1945	1949	1950	1951	1952
BONDS									
U. S. Government [1]					2.37	2.31	2.32	2.57	2.68
Municipal (Standard & Poor's Corp., 15 issues)	4.27	4.07	3.40	2.50	1.67	2.21	1.98	2.00	2.19
Municipal (Bond Buyer, 20 issues)	4.31	4.12	3.38	2.52	1.49	2.15	1.90	1.97	2.20
Corporate (Moody's Investors' Service), by type: [2]									
Total (105 issues)	5.21	5.09	4.46	3.55	2.87	2.96	2.86	3.06	3.19
Industrial (35 issues)	5.31	5.25	4.02	3.10	2.68	2.74	2.67	2.89	3.00
Railroad (30 issues)	5.18	4.96	4.95	4.30	3.06	3.24	3.10	3.26	3.26
Public utility (40 issues)	5.14	5.05	4.43	3.25	2.89	2.90	2.82	3.09	3.20
Corporate, by years to maturity: [3]									
5 years	4.72	4.40	2.37	1.28	1.53	1.92	[4]1.90	[4]2.22	[5]
10 years	4.57	4.40	3.00	1.95	2.14	2.32	2.30	2.39	2.73
20 years	4.45	4.40	3.37	2.55	2.55	2.62	2.48	2.59	2.88
50 years [6]	4.40	4.40	3.50	[4]2.70	[4]2.55	2.80	[4]2.63	2.72	3.09
STOCKS									
Preferred (Standard & Poor's Corp., 11 issues) [7]	5.12	4.95	4.63	4.14	3.70	3.97	3.85	4.11	4.13
Common (Moody's Investors' Service): [8]									
Total (200 issues) [9]	3.4	4.5	4.1	5.3	4.2	6.6	6.3	6.1	5.5
Industrial (125 issues)	3.8	4.9	3.5	5.3	4.0	6.8	6.5	6.3	5.6
Railroad (25 issues)	4.4	5.6	4.0	5.4	5.5	8.5	6.5	6.3	5.9
Public utility (24 issues)	2.1	3.5	5.1	6.0	5.0	5.9	5.7	5.8	5.4

[1] Average yields on taxable bonds due or callable in 15 years and over; beginning April 1952, in 12 years and over.
[2] Number of issues as of Dec. 1, 1952; number varies for earlier years.
[3] Estimated yields prevailing on highest grade issues in first quarter of each year prior to 1951 and in February only beginning 1951. Data from National Bureau of Economic Research
[4] More than usually liable to error.
[5] Not available.
[6] Represents bonds of 40 years to maturity beginning 1945.
[7] Based on 11 stocks (15 stocks, 1929-45). Yield determined from average of 9 median yields. Issues converted to a price equivalent to $100 par and a 7 percent annual dividend before averaging.
[8] Average of monthly figures computed by dividing the aggregate annual dividends being paid as of the end of each month by the market value of all outstanding shares of the companies as of the same date.
[9] Includes also 15 bank and 10 insurance stocks, and 1 additional public utility (see note 8, table 503).

Source: Department of Commerce, Office of Business Economics; *Survey of Current Business*, except as noted.

No. 506.—Dividends Per Share (Annual Rates) for 200 Common Stocks: 1930 to 1952

YEAR	Total, 200 stocks [1]	Industrial, 125 stocks	Public utility, 24 stocks	Railroad, 25 stocks	Bank, 15 stocks	Insurance, 10 stocks
1930	$2.93	$2.38	$3.55	$4.95	$4.69	$2.32
1935	1.30	1.05	1.32	1.03	2.24	1.34
1940	1.78	1.67	1.54	1.08	2.08	1.62
1941	1.90	1.81	1.44	1.28	2.07	1.64
1942	1.75	1.64	1.26	1.46	1.95	1.71
1943	1.73	1.55	1.28	1.77	1.94	1.69
1944	1.84	1.67	1.31	1.99	1.93	1.63
1945	1.92	1.75	1.30	2.19	2.00	1.62
1946	2.02	1.85	1.43	2.19	2.20	1.83
1947	2.38	2.33	1.56	1.92	2.32	1.88
1948	2.74	2.78	1.60	2.06	2.33	1.88
1949	3.09	3.19	1.66	2.41	2.36	2.06
1950	3.53	3.77	1.76	2.18	2.50	2.46
1951	4.09	4.44	1.88	2.55	2.64	2.73
1952	3.94	4.20	1.91	2.72	2.65	2.86

[1] Includes American Telephone and Telegraph Co. stock; excluded from "public utility."

Source: Moody's Investors' Service, New York, N. Y.

507.—SALES OF STOCKS AND BONDS ON ALL REGISTERED EXCHANGES: 1943 TO 1952

[Money figures in millions of dollars; number of shares of stock in millions. Stock sales include rights and units and cover actual volume of sales as distinguished from ticker or "reported" volume in table 508]

| | ALL REGISTERED EXCHANGES | | | | | NEW YORK STOCK EXCHANGE | | | | |
| | | Stocks | | Bonds | | | | Stocks | | Bonds | |
YEAR	Market value of all sales	Shares	Market value	Par value	Market value	Market value of all sales	Shares	Market value	Par value	Market value
	10,056	455	9,024	3,530	1,902	9,457	362	7,672	3,300	1,750
	11,780	454	9,799	3,122	1,981	10,080	342	8,264	2,900	1,710
	15,112	767	16,270	3,091	1,842	15,190	597	13,474	2,600	1,710
	20,001	802	18,814	1,872	1,187	16,675	531	15,562	1,400	1,000
	12,541	512	11,557	1,274	956	10,617	398	9,747	1,170	
	12,749	570	12,904	1,172	944	11,781	435	10,892	1,110	
	11,443	516	10,740	938	208	9,074	380	9,012		
	22,340	807	21,802	1,278	1,088	19,735	682	18,735	1,225	
	22,127	863	20,302	935	652	18,013	643	18,215	911	
	16,179	733	17,398	900	791	16,531	522	14,781	850	

Source: Securities and Exchange Commission; *Statistical Bulletin*, published monthly.

508.—SALES ON NEW YORK STOCK EXCHANGE—VOLUME: 1940 TO 1952

[See also *Historical Statistics*, series N 228–232]

| YEAR | Stocks, millions of shares[1] | BONDS, PAR VALUE (MILLIONS OF DOLLARS)[2] | | | | | Stocks, millions of shares[1] | BONDS, PAR VALUE (MILLIONS OF DOLLARS)[2] | | | |
		Total	Corporate	U. S. Govern-ment	State, municipal, foreign	YEAR		Total	Corporate	U. S. Govern-ment	State, municipal, foreign
	164	638	592	(3)	43	1940	208	1,660	1,414	30	216
	173	961	907	3	51	1941	171	2,112	1,929	20	163
	227	3,977	827	2,861	289	1942	126	2,311	2,181		124
	454	3,384	2,332	391	661	1943	270	2,234	3,130	2	125
	1,125	2,982	3,182	142	658	1944	263	3,695	3,585		104
	810	2,764	1,027	116	721	1945	369	2,262	2,145		106
	425	2,967	1,643	370	755	1946	364	1,706	1,576	19	111
	552	2,368	1,069	501	769	1947	254	1,678	970		162
	523	2,170	2,293	683	672	1948	290	1,678	910		85
	496	3,576	1,869	519	559	1949	277	816	712	(3)	101
	400	2,760	2,007	349	347	1951	444	1,112	1,008	2	92
	397	1,828	1,464	127	249	1952	525	824	730	2	80
	302	2,046	1,480	311	255			773	666	(3)	

Source: *Commercial and Financial Chronicle*, New York, N. Y.

[Footnotes indicating ticker or "reported" volume which excludes odd-lots, stopped sales, private sales, split openings, ... transactions, and errors of omission. Totals are therefore less than the actual volume shown in table 507.] Exclusive of stopped sales. Less than ...

509.—PRINCIPAL COMMODITY FUTURES—VOLUME OF TRADING ON ALL CONTRACT MARKETS: 1940–41 TO 1951–52

[Compiled from daily reports of all clearing members of each contract market]

YEAR BEGINNING JULY	Wheat (million bush-els)	Corn (million bush-els)	Oats (million bush-els)	Rye (million bush-els)	Soybeans (million bushels)	Cotton (thousand bales)	Eggs (carlots)
	4,783.9	798.6	246.5	856.3	611.4	34,306	36,466
	3,831.0	1,255.6	524.6	790.0	681.6	64,069	41,978
	2,703.7	851.5	610.6	1,499.7	16.9	42,755	9,006
	2,641.7	(3)	790.4	691.1		39,190	6,065
	2,425.0	491.2	1,000.2	4,074.6		37,613	40,220
	1,424.0	117.3	1,095.9	1,662.5		110,345	79,357
	2,122.4	2,006.9	946.9			110,345	135,325
	3,700.5	5,506.3	1,956.9	21.1		110,583	128,020
	4,514.9	5,672.5	1,176.5	355.4	557.7	40,385	91,191
	4,202.0	2,013.4	1,045.7	561.0	1,513.9	35,007	85,969
	4,675.7	2,206.6	1,017.0	476.9	2,412.0	78,007	142,511
	4,341.7	2,636.6	2,209.2	426.6	2,963.2	94,687	90,699

Trading suspended.

Source: Department of Agriculture, Commodity Exchange Authority, annual report, *Commodity Futures Statistics*.

No. 510.—Securities—Sales Effected on Securities Exchanges: 1952

[In thousands. Value and volume of sales effected on registered securities exchanges are reported in connection with fees paid under sec. 31 of the Securities Exchange Act of 1934. For most exchanges, figures represent transactions cleared during year. Figures may differ from those in table 507 due to revision of data by exchanges]

EXCHANGE	Total market value	STOCKS [1]		BONDS [2]		RIGHTS AND WARRANTS	
		Market value	Number of shares	Market value	Principal amount	Market value	Number of units
All registered exchanges	18,179,060	17,328,422	626,922	791,437	899,125	59,221	104,691
Boston	193,795	191,935	4,288	17	15	1,842	1,034
Chicago Board of Trade	(3)	(3)	(4)				
Cincinnati	21,443	21,395	589	7	12	41	42
Detroit	75,025	74,957	3,795			68	207
Los Angeles	181,097	180,735	9,429	0	0	362	480
Midwest	464,225	462,094	14,585	413	372	1,718	3,197
New Orleans	1,827	1,780	54	47	45		
New York Curb	1,305,301	1,273,902	111,515	19,934	28,647	11,465	6,289
New York Stock	15,581,422	14,720,397	431,821	769,491	866,447	41,534	89,761
Philadelphia-Baltimore	166,730	165,323	4,655	420	598	988	1,325
Pittsburgh	25,825	25,825	1,148	0	0		
Salt Lake	2,782	2,782	21,885				
San Francisco Mining	452	452	5,119				
San Francisco Stock	202,753	200,627	16,617	994	810	1,293	2,305
Spokane	964	964	1,777				
Washington	5,459	5,275	244	184	179		
All exempted exchanges	7,626	7,472	878	154	170		
Colorado Springs	73	73	131				
Honolulu	6,505	6,351	720	154	170		
Richmond	559	559	11				
Wheeling	489	489	16				

[1] Includes voting trust certificates, American depositary receipts, and certificates of deposit for stocks.
[2] Includes mortgage certificates and certificates of deposit for bonds. Since Mar. 18, 1944, United States Government bonds have not been included in these data.
[3] $500 or less.   [4] 500 shares or less.

Source: Securities and Exchange Commission.

No. 511.—Customers' Debit Balances, Money Borrowed, and Related Items—Stock Exchange Firms Carrying Margin Accounts: 1939 to 1952

[All figures in millions of dollars. Data relate to member firms of New York Stock Exchange carrying margin accounts. Figures derived from money balances as shown by ledger and exclude value of securities carried for customers or owned by firms. For detailed discussion, see Federal Reserve Bulletin, September 1936]

END OF MONTH	DEBIT BALANCES				CREDIT BALANCES				
	Customers' debit balances (net) [1]	Debit balances in investment and trading accounts of—		Cash on hand and in banks	Money borrowed [2]	Customers' credit balances [1]	Credit balances in investment and trading accounts of—		Credit balances in capital accounts (net)
		Partners	Firm				Partners	Firm	
1939—December	906	16	78	207	637	335	23	7	277
1940—December	677	12	99	204	427	335	22	5	247
1941—December	600	8	86	211	368	352	17	5	213
1942—December	543	7	154	160	378	324	15	4	182
1943—December	789	11	188	181	557	419	14	5	198
1944—December	1,041	7	260	209	726	568	18	8	227
1945—December	1,138	12	413	313	795	766	29	13	299
1946—December	540	5	312	456	218	814	30	10	290
1947—December	578	7	315	393	240	788	23	15	273
1948—December	550	10	312	349	257	698	28	5	278
1949—December	881	5	400	306	523	792	26	15	271
1950—December	1,356	9	399	397	745	1,120	36	12	317
1951—June	1,275	10	375	364	680	1,059	26	13	319
December	1,292	12	392	378	695	1,075	42	11	314
1952—June	1,327	9	427	365	912	927	23	16	334
December	1,362	8	406	343	920	924	35	9	315

[1] Excludes balances with reporting firms (1) of member firms of New York Stock Exchange and other national securities exchanges and (2) of firms' own partners.
[2] Includes money borrowed from banks and also from other lenders (not including member firms of national securities exchanges).

Source: Board of Governors of the Federal Reserve System; Banking and Monetary Statistics; monthly figures published currently in Federal Reserve Bulletin.

No. 512.—SECURITIES—NEW SECURITIES OFFERED FOR CASH SALE, BY TYPE AND
ISSUER: 1934 TO 1952

[Estimated gross proceeds in millions of dollars. Gross proceeds are derived by multiplying principal amounts
or number of units by offering price, except for municipal issues where principal amount is used. Covers
substantially all new issues of securities offered for cash sale in United States in amounts over $100,000 and
with terms of maturity of more than 1 year. Figures represent offerings, not actual sales. Includes issues
privately placed, publicly offered, unregistered issues and those registered under Securities Act of 1933]

SECURITY AND ISSUER	1934	1935	1940	1945	1948	1949	1950	1951	1952 (prel.)
TYPE OF SECURITY									
All types, total	4,910	6,062	6,554	54,712	20,250	21,110	19,598	21,256	27,096
Bonds	397	2,332	2,677	6,011	7,078	6,062	6,361	7,741	8,721
...	4,512	4,342	3,857	48,701	13,172	15,059	13,589	13,623	17,375
Bonds, debentures, and notes, total	4,894	6,576	5,273	53,526	19,145	19,949	18,453	19,214	25,100
Corporate	371	2,235	2,286	4,355	5,973	4,800	4,920	5,691	7,725
Noncorporate	4,512	4,342	3,857	48,701	13,172	15,059	13,532	13,523	17,375
Preferred stock	6	84	183	758	492	425	631	838	572
Common stock	19	32	108	397	614	736	811	1,212	1,425
ISSUER									
Corporate, total	397	2,322	2,677	6,011	7,078	6,062	6,361	7,741	8,721
Manufacturing	(²)	(²)	(²)	(²)	2,236	1,414	1,300	3,122	4,106
Electric, gas, and water	(²)	(²)	(²)	(²)	2,187	2,320	2,649	2,456	2,757
Railroad	(²)	(²)	(²)	(²)	902	571	399	612	894
Other transportation	176	136	394	1,024	632	460	564	385	517
Real estate and financial	(²)	(²)	(²)	(²)	132	340	259	169	450
Commercial and miscellaneous	71	125	159	(²)11	594	549	747	525	456
Noncorporate, total	4,512	4,342	3,857	48,701	13,172	15,059	13,532	13,523	17,375
U. S. Government (including agency issues guaranteed)	3,535	2,936	2,517	47,353	10,327	11,304	9,887	9,778	12,577
Federal agency (issues not guaranteed)	12	116	109	506	0	216	36	110	459
State and municipal	959	1,299	1,238	799	2,689	2,987	3,532	3,189	4,105
Foreign government	5	59	0	45	150	116	1,263	1,419	1,223
Eleemosynary and other nonprofit	1	8	24	2	6	15	20	26	10

¹ Not available.
² Includes ... million International Bank.
³ Includes ... million International Bank.
⁴ Includes ... million International Bank.

Source: Securities and Exchange Commission; monthly data published in *Statistical Bulletin*.

No. 513.—U. S. PURCHASES OF FOREIGN CAPITAL ISSUES (GOVERNMENTAL AND
CORPORATE) PUBLICLY OFFERED IN THE U. S.: 1925 TO 1952

[Amounts in thousands of dollars. Excludes privately taken issues and small issues for which data are not
available. Excludes issues of U. S. possessions after 1945]

YEAR	Number of issues	Total nominal capital	Estimated refunding to Americans ¹	Estimated new nominal capital	YEAR	Number of issues	Total nominal capital	Estimated refunding to Americans ¹	Estimated new nominal capital
1925	184	1,316,186	239,700	1,076,486	1945	8	76,800	60,800	16,000
1926	149	705,768	34,537	671,231	1946	8	135,400	127,800	7,600
1927	121	1,087,580	182,227	905,353	1947	13	406,300	130,800	275,500
1928	11	73,988	9,958	64,030	1948 ³				
1929	3	2,125		2,125	1949	1	97,500	50,832	46,699
1930	4	5,072	4,000	1,072	1950	9	217,611	184,751	32,860
1931					1951	18	483,720	19,500	464,220
1932	4	92,300	90,000	2,300	1952 ³	17	325,761		325,761
1933	5	31,409	14,700	16,700					

¹ As a result of previous repatriations and purchases by investors of other countries these figures include, especially through 1930, substantial amounts of bonds not held in United States at time of their redemption.
² No issues. ³ Preliminary.

Source: Department of Commerce. Office of Business Economics; Balance of Payments Division records.

462 BANKING AND FINANCE

No. 514.—Capital Issues—Summary, by Classes: 1920 to 1952

[In millions of dollars. Data cover domestic and foreign issues in United States. Preferred stocks of no par value and all common stocks are taken at offering price, other issues at par. Privileged stock subscriptions included in figures and issues of less than $100,000. See also *Historical Statistics*, series N 221–237]

YEAR	Total issues	New capital	Refund-ing	TOTAL ISSUES, BY KINDS						
				Corporate				Farm-loan and Gov't agencies	State and munic-ipal [2]	Foreign govern-ment
				Rail-roads	Public utilities	Indus-trials [1]	Miscel-laneous			
1920	4,010.0	3,634.8	375.2	377.9	496.8	1,627.6	464.0	....	609.5	344.3
1925	7,126.0	6,220.2	905.9	514.7	1,710.0	1,270.2	1,243.2	188.2	1,408.4	791.3
1929	11,592.2	10,182.8	1,409.4	817.2	2,442.8	2,459.8	4,306.6		1,435.7	130.1
1930	7,677.0	7,023.4	653.7	1,026.5	2,566.2	1,151.9	728.6	86.5	1,497.6	619.6
1935	4,782.3	1,412.1	3,340.2	195.7	1,283.5	706.5	80.4	1,137.1	1,231.8	116.0
1940	4,805.9	1,950.5	2,855.4	372.3	1,274.1	764.2	352.0	804.3	1,239.0	
1941	5,545.9	2,853.9	2,692.0	365.3	1,383.0	675.5	195.0	1,969.0	954.1	4.0
1942	2,114.5	1,075.1	1,039.4	48.6	467.2	490.1	36.6	548.2	523.7	
1943	2,228.2	643.5	1,584.7	152.4	399.1	503.2	26.1	622.1	435.2	90.0
1944	4,295.9	936.4	3,359.5	622.8	1,384.3	1,005.7	168.3	433.2	660.6	21.1
1945	8,046.2	1,774.7	6,271.5	1,507.7	2,397.4	1,906.0	447.5	937.9	799.7	30.0
1946	8,728.0	4,643.9	4,084.0	729.9	2,114.6	3,146.0	661.6	861.2	1,161.3	83.5
1947	9,752.8	7,688.4	2,064.5	269.7	3,122.8	2,377.5	548.0	661.2	2,327.9	445.8
1948	10,453.0	9,318.0	1,135.0	627.0	3,016.9	2,084.4	820.2	1,062.2	2,692.4	180.0
1949	9,832.8	8,240.0	1,592.8	475.5	2,886.6	1,644.6	594.7	1,176.2	2,939.2	116.0
1950	11,067.3	8,346.7	2,720.6	492.4	3,090.7	1,463.6	840.3	1,385.7	3,542.4	242.2
1951	12,577.0	10,317.5	2,259.5	331.4	3,017.3	2,968.9	547.5	2,066.2	3,193.8	451.9
1952	15,384.7	12,647.4	2,737.3	530.9	3,260.9	4,160.0	635.1	2,146.4	4,328.4	323.0

CORPORATE ISSUES BY CLASS OF SECURITY (NEW CAPITAL AND REFUNDING)

YEAR	Total	Long-term bonds and notes	Short-term bonds and notes	Stocks	YEAR	Total	Long-term bonds and notes	Short-term bonds and notes	Stocks
1920	2,966.3	1,234.4	660.8	1,071.1	1944	3,181.1	2,655.7	13.6	511.9
1925	4,738.1	3,040.2	386.9	1,311.0	1945	6,258.6	4,891.4	46.4	1,320.7
1929	10,026.4	2,842.3	262.6	6,921.4	1946	6,652.1	4,532.1	38.3	2,081.7
1930	5,473.3	3,248.0	657.0	1,868.3	1947	6,317.9	4,731.1	70.7	1,516.1
1935	2,267.4	2,066.1	50.5	150.8	1948	6,548.4	5,600.9	7.4	940.1
1940	2,762.6	2,396.1	38.6	327.9	1949	5,601.4	4,567.8	7.9	1,025.6
1941	2,618.8	2,276.5	43.1	299.1	1950	5,886.9	4,417.9	177.4	1,291.6
1942	1,042.5	908.4	4.7	129.4	1951	6,865.1	5,058.0	6.2	1,800.9
1943	1,080.9	869.1	38.0	173.8	1952	8,587.0	6,749.1	38.5	1,799.4

[1] Comprises the following classifications given in original detailed statements: Iron, steel, coal, copper, etc., equipment manufacturers, motors and accessories, oil, rubber, and miscellaneous industrials.
[2] Includes bonds issued by States, Territories and possessions, counties and municipalities, and by school and road districts and other independent governmental bodies. Beginning 1935, excludes funds obtained by States and municipalities from any agency of Federal Government.

Source: *Commercial and Financial Chronicle*, New York, N. Y.

imated gross proceeds	2,640	2,456	2,787
imated net proceeds	2,563	2,418	2,716
ew money	1,765	1,198	2,502
Plant and equipment	1,711	2,149	2,492
Working capital	17	27	11
Retirements	686	173	202
Funded debt	516	80	91
Other debt	102	87	108
Preferred stock	67	6	2
Other purposes	77	58	5
RAILROAD			
imated gross proceeds	554	235	517
imated net proceeds	549	232	513
ew money	301	207	287
Plant and equipment	282	202	285
Working capital	20	5	(¹)
Retirements	234	25	226
Funded debt	185	24	216
Other debt	30	1	11
Preferred stock	0	0	0
Other purposes	15	0	0

New money	480	348	411
Plant and equipment	34	16	6
Working capital	435	253	404
Retirements	192	102	51
Funded debt	99	61	43
Other debt	91	36	3
Preferred stock	2	5	5
Other purposes	87	45	20
COMMERCIAL AND MISCELLANEOUS			
Estimated gross proceeds	653	533	599
Estimated net proceeds	636	516	583
New money	262	337	435
Plant and equipment	94	113	208
Working capital	168	224	188
Retirements	155	114	42
Funded debt	30	65	16
Other debt	92	48	24
Preferred stock	33	11	2
Other purposes	171	66	55

¹ Less than $500,000.

Source: Securities and Exchange Commission; monthly data published in *Statistical Bulletin*.

No. 516.—SHAREHOLDINGS OF RECORD IN REPORTING CORPORATIONS, CLASSIFIED BY TYPE OF BUSINESS: 1951

[Covers 3,954 common and preferred stocks representing close to 25 percent of all publicly owned issues, including one or more issues of virtually all larger companies. Relates to share ownership held in the United States (including shares of companies incorporated in other countries) rather than to ownership of United States corporations. Canvass covered all publicly owned corporations with stocks listed on the several exchanges, together with a large number whose stock are not listed on any exchange. Only publicly owned corporations are included; family and closely held companies of all types are excluded, as are those whose shares are restricted by agreements or options affecting their resale. Cooperative associations are also excluded. A number of companies for which data are included are not corporations in a strict sense, but their shares are comparable to those of corporations in practically all respects. For most corporations, figures apply within period between Nov. 1, 1951, and Feb. 1, 1952; for a number of companies with fiscal years ending prior to Nov. 1, figures are for an earlier date in 1951]

TYPE OF BUSINESS	Number of corporations	Number of issues	Shares outstanding	SHAREHOLDINGS OF RECORD			
				Number	Average number of shares	Market value, Dec. 1951	Average value per shareholding [1]
			1,000	*1,000*		*Million*	
Total	2,991	3,954	3,695,279	20,320.6	181.8	$132,087.8	$6,500
Manufacturing	1,425	1,895	1,521,525	8,157.3	186.5	57,608.5	7,062
Steel and iron	138	165	138,295	874.4	158.2	5,335.7	6,094
Other metals and their products	39	54	46,050	164.7	279.6	2,196.5	13,337
Machinery except electrical	215	283	155,032	826.6	187.5	4,424.3	5,352
Electrical machinery	97	116	112,334	752.0	148.2	3,932.2	5,189
Railroad equipment	20	27	23,959	200.8	119.3	624.3	3,100
Automobiles and equipment	79	101	184,582	1,114.2	165.6	6,842.1	6,141
Aircraft	32	37	34,045	205.4	165.7	697.1	3,393
Shipbuilding	8	11	3,416	27.4	134.9	110.9	4,054
Building materials and equipment	82	107	55,319	289.0	231.4	1,897.5	6,558
Glass	18	25	27,967	94.0	297.6	1,268.1	13,496
Office equipment	20	26	21,748	132.8	163.6	1,143.0	8,607
Furniture and furnishings	16	19	6,317	33.6	187.8	123.7	3,679
Rubber and rubber products	29	43	25,315	184.9	150.5	1,302.2	7,763
Chemicals and drugs	105	150	226,265	946.2	238.6	14,156.5	14,929
Paper and paper products	76	117	76,906	291.0	243.7	2,439.2	8,383
Printing and publishing	25	33	15,934	76.9	207.2	267.5	3,479
Textiles	107	146	85,949	324.5	264.9	2,430.6	7,492
Leather and leather products	18	22	10,236	47.0	217.7	270.3	5,748
Food and food products	166	225	143,337	974.7	147.1	4,424.5	4,539
Beverages	49	58	46,746	174.4	268.0	1,392.5	7,983
Tobacco	26	41	29,622	211.1	140.3	1,130.5	5,354
Miscellaneous	60	79	60,178	283.7	212.1	1,635.2	5,763
Petroleum, including refining	123	138	459,306	1,718.3	267.3	23,545.9	13,703
Mining	154	168	251,772	711.4	353.9	4,893.9	6,879
Transportation	155	226	184,669	1,190.4	155.1	6,529.8	5,485
Railroads	99	153	123,203	930.0	132.5	5,462.2	5,873
Airlines	19	22	28,933	142.7	202.7	536.5	3,759
Automotive	17	23	17,534	79.7	223.6	223.6	2,805
Ship operating	13	19	11,857	28.0	423.5	272.9	9,747
Miscellaneous	7	9	2,842	10.0	265.3	34.6	3,473
Public utilities	260	472	531,010	4,734.8	112.1	19,946.7	4,213
Electric and gas	150	298	350,362	2,807.9	124.8	10,078.9	3,589
Gas	61	96	102,230	550.8	185.5	2,819.0	5,118
Communications	31	49	69,807	1,324.0	52.7	6,909.2	5,219
Miscellaneous	18	32	8,611	52.1	165.3	139.6	2,680
Real estate	37	48	16,068	71.8	223.9	528.2	7,359
Retail trade and service	181	258	171,771	780.0	220.2	5,624.3	7,211
Amusements	20	25	34,213	193.1	177.2	468.6	2,401
Finance and investment	590	664	505,117	2,660.5	189.9	12,536.7	4,712
Banks and trust companies	319	325	139,207	1,112.8	125.1	6,242.7	5,610
Finance companies	34	64	26,302	191.2	137.6	820.3	4,290
Insurance companies	68	76	45,236	261.1	173.3	2,278.2	8,727
Investment companies—closed end	44	67	46,780	305.9	152.9	1,074.8	3,514
Investment companies—open end	112	113	234,379	728.0	321.9	1,970.0	2,706
Miscellaneous	13	19	13,213	61.5	214.9	150.7	2,451
Unclassified	46	54	19,828	103.0	192.5	410.2	3,983

[1] Because of numerous large nonindividual shareholdings (see table 517), average value per shareholding should be used with caution.

Source: The Brookings Institution, Washington, D. C.; *Share Ownership in the United States.*

No. 517.—SHAREHOLDINGS OF RECORD IN REPORTING CORPORATIONS CLASSIFIED BY TYPE OF HOLDER: 1951

[See headnote, table 516]

TYPE OF HOLDER	Number of holders of record [1]	Number of shares	Average number of shares	Market value, Dec. 1951	Average value per share-holding
UNADJUSTED	1,000	1,000		Million	
Total	20,220.6	3,006,279.0	151.6	$122,067.8	94,500
Men	7,564.7	1,050,236.7	138.8	$1,747.6	4,197
Women	8,432.4	823,223.9	97.6	28,152.6	3,461
Joint accounts	2,584.5	234,096.4	90.5	5,249.1	2,253
Fiduciaries	976.3	250,573.0	261.3	11,538.0	11,530
Institutions and foundations	144.5	70,276.9	485.2	3,303.0	22,527
Brokers and dealers [2]	239.7	281,685.5	1,592.2	70,179.2	42,489
Nominees [3]	140.2	375,114.9	2,675.7	18,020.2	128,530
Others	237.7	506,181.6	2,126.6	22,342.9	93,887
ADJUSTED FOR BENEFICIAL HOLDINGS [4]					
Total	26,156.0	3,006,279.0	146.9	122,067.8	5,351
Men	9,001.4	1,264,361.7	140.5	38,126.9	4,236
Women	9,379.7	946,739.9	100.9	33,366.1	3,557
Joint accounts	2,983.8	267,464.3	91.2	6,803.7	2,218
Fiduciaries	3,105.5	461,423.5	148.5	21,067.4	6,790
Institutions and foundations	226.3	105,970.1	462.9	4,939.4	21,562
Brokers and dealers [5]	42.1	25,157.3	853.7	708.7	16,143
Others	464.3	634,212.2	1,344.7	27,051.6	53,307

[1] Represents number of listings in stock transfer books (or other records). "Shareholder" thus differs from "share owner" (or stockholder) who may own shares in more than one corporation, or in more than one issue of the same corporation. See tables 518–520 for number of share owners.
[2] Includes holdings for buyers on margin, since they are not fully paid; and holdings of fully paid shares held mainly for convenience of the beneficial (or actual) owners who may be abroad or who for other reasons find it advantageous to have brokers retain their securities.
[3] Nominees include all partnerships, individuals, and organizations created as a business convenience to appear as holders of record on behalf of the beneficial (or actual) owners. A very large portion of all nominee holdings is accounted for by fiduciaries or trust accounts.
[4] Estimated to show how shareholdings would appear if all shareholdings were registered in the names of the actual owners rather than in the names of nominees or brokers (see notes 2 and 3). Each person with an interest in a common trust fund is counted as a separate beneficial holder.
[5] Relates only to holdings for other brokers and dealers.

Source: The Brookings Institution, Washington, D. C.; Share Ownership in the United States.

No. 518.—INDIVIDUAL SHARE OWNERS OF PUBLICLY OWNED STOCKS DISTRIBUTED BY EDUCATIONAL LEVEL: 1952

[If an individual owns shares in five stocks he is counted as one share owner, but in tables 516 and 517 he is represented by five shareholdings. Fiduciaries, institutions and foundations, and other nonindividual holders are excluded. Analysis is based on data obtained through a nation-wide field survey conducted during Jan.-Feb. 1952. This survey embraces interviews pertaining to 13,553 persons represented in a cross section of 5,000 family spending units. For an explanation of sample design and probable variability, see source publication]

LAST YEAR OF SCHOOL COMPLETED	POPULATION 21 YEARS AND OVER		INDIVIDUAL SHARE OWNERS [1]		
	Percent	Number	Percent of group population	Estimated number	Percent of total
Total	100.0	99,230,000	6.4	6,350,000	100.0
8th grade or less	39.6	39,300,000	3.1	1,220,000	19.4
1 to 3 years high school	19.6	19,440,000	3.2	630,000	9.9
4 years high school	23.9	23,790,000	7.7	1,840,000	29.0
1 to 3 years college	8.9	8,830,000	15.1	1,330,000	20.9
4 or more years college	7.3	7,210,000	18.0	1,300,000	20.5
Current students	.7	720,800	2.8	20,000	.3

[1] Excludes 140,000 share owners under 21 years of age.

Source: The Brookings Institution, Washington, D. C.; Share Ownership in the United States.

No. 519.—INDIVIDUAL SHARE OWNERS OF PUBLICLY OWNED STOCKS DISTRIBUTED BY OCCUPATIONAL GROUPS: 1952

[See headnote, table 518]

OCCUPATION	Population	INDIVIDUAL SHARE OWNERS		
		Percent of group population	Estimated number	Percent of total
Total	155,520,000	4.2	6,490,000	100.0
Administrative executives	670,000	44.8	300,000	4.6
Operating supervisory officials	3,190,000	19.4	620,000	9.6
Professional persons, personal service	2,980,000	12.4	370,000	5.7
Professional persons, technical fields	2,270,000	13.2	300,000	4.6
Sales personnel [1]	1,780,000	11.2	200,000	3.1
Merchants [2]	2,360,000	10.6	250,000	3.9
Clerical and kindred workers	7,790,000	7.6	590,000	9.1
Farmers	4,700,000	6.8	320,000	4.9
Skilled workers, foremen	9,310,000	4.4	410,000	6.3
Public service workers	1,180,000	3.4	40,000	.6
Semiskilled workers	15,090,000	1.4	210,000	3.2
Unskilled workers	5,640,000	.2	10,000	.2
Members of armed forces [3]	1,820,000	1.1	20,000	.3
Employed, occupation unidentified	390,000	(⁴)	(⁴)	(⁴)
Nonemployed adults	2,250,000	1.3	30,000	.5
Nonemployed—retired, dependent	6,180,000	9.1	560,000	8.6
Housewives—nonemployed	35,600,000	6.0	2,130,000	32.8
Students and preschool age	52,320,000	.2	130,000	2.0

[1] Representatives of wholesalers and manufacturers.
[2] Includes wholesale.
[3] Includes only those members of armed forces who are members of family groups.
[4] Less than 10,000 share owners in the group.

Source: The Brookings Institution, Washington, D. C.; *Share Ownership in the United States.*

No. 520.—INDIVIDUAL SHARE OWNERS OF PUBLICLY OWNED STOCKS DISTRIBUTED BY INCOMES REPORTED FOR THEIR FAMILIES AS UNITS: 1952

[Based on anticipated 1952 income before taxes, as reported by a representative family member, usually the head. See also headnote, table 518]

REPORTED COMBINED FAMILY INCOME	TOTAL POPULATION		INDIVIDUAL SHARE OWNERS		
	Percent	Number	Percent of group population	Estimated number	Percent of total
Total individuals	100.0	155,520,000	4.2	6,490,000	100.0
Less than $2,000	16.5	25,660,000	1.1	280,000	4.3
$2,000 to $3,000	15.7	24,460,000	1.4	350,000	5.4
$3,000 to $4,000	23.1	35,900,000	1.6	590,000	9.1
$4,000 to $5,000	17.6	27,370,000	3.0	830,000	12.8
$5,000 to $10,000	23.0	35,820,000	8.0	2,880,000	44.4
$10,000 and over	4.1	6,310,000	24.7	1,560,000	24.0

Source: The Brookings Institution, Washington, D. C.; *Share Ownership in the United States.*

No. 521.—Life Insurance Companies—Summary of Financial Condition and Policy Account: 1880 to 1951

[All figures in millions of dollars. Includes domestic and foreign business of U. S. companies but excludes operations of Veterans' Admn. (see p. 235), and U. S. business of foreign companies]

YEAR	Assets (admitted) Dec. 31	Liabilities,[1] Dec. 31	Total income[2]	Premium income[3]	Payment to policy holders[2]	INSURANCE WRITTEN AND PAID FOR DURING YEAR			INSURANCE IN FORCE DEC. 31			
						Group	Ordinary	Industrial	Total	Group	Ordinary[4]	Industrial
1880	465		81		56				1,602		1,582	21
1890	771	675	197	135	90		742	242	4,060		3,621	429
1900	1,742	1,408	421	325	169		1,280	366	8,561		7,093	1,468
1910	3,876	3,665	731	503	367		1,832	735	16,404		12,227	3,177
1915	5,180	4,933	1,043	784	545	(4)	2,631	974	22,777	(4)	18,349	4,427
1917	5,941	5,634	1,249	929	590	(4)	3,840	1,061	27,159	(4)	21,966	5,223
1920	6,675	6,202	1,325	994	710	(4)	3,985	1,208	29,870	(4)	24,167	5,763
1925	7,850	6,980	1,764	1,385	746	(4)	5,490	1,615	42,381	1,637	33,455	7,190
1930	11,988	10,957	3,018	2,384	1,343	1,254	10,563	3,656	71,660	4,399	54,567	12,834
1935	17,482	16,807	4,397	3,360	1,963	1,572	12,966	4,738	108,146	9,121	76,123	17,902
1936	18,688	17,862	4,584	3,534	2,347	1,556	12,604	4,860	107,945	9,386	79,775	18,287
1938	25,585	19,285	4,632	3,322	2,616	821	8,268	4,673	97,965	8,912	71,919	17,154
1939	31,350	22,220	5,073	3,692	2,535	1,303	8,113	4,722	109,730	10,470	71,963	18,298
1940	30,802	29,406	5,668	3,944	2,651	1,609	7,806	3,718	117,794	15,382	81,069	21,344
1943	37,762	35,443	6,443	4,421	2,407	1,469	8,540	3,586	140,309	22,961	91,777	26,571
1944	41,064	39,249	7,011	4,865	2,528	2,158	9,536	3,734	149,071	24,446	97,577	27,048
1945	44,797	42,342	7,674	5,249	2,779	1,519	10,944	3,970	155,732	22,770	104,458	28,497
1946	48,197	45,576	8,006	5,727	2,848	6,111	16,776	4,842	174,453	32,198	116,110	36,147
1947	51,743	48,307	8,982	6,435	3,290	6,204	16,897	5,193	191,294	33,565	120,206	37,493
1948	55,512	51,808	9,608	7,131	3,602	6,670	17,091	5,043	206,578	38,210	133,669	31,694
1949	59,650	55,138	10,138	7,408	3,806	5,096	17,387	6,016	230,516	43,075	144,458	32,982
1950	64,020	59,361	11,057	8,050	4,240	10,980	19,781	6,433	342,018	52,586	155,071	34,391
1951	68,278	63,428	11,666	8,704	4,734	9,331	20,808	6,079	261,550	60,120	165,965	35,464

[1] Not including unapportioned surplus and capital. Prior to 1906 apportioned surplus is also excluded. For amount of this item in recent years, see table 522.
[2] Beginning 1951 reported on accrual basis; previous years on cash basis.
[3] Amounts of policies in force for 1840, 369,600,000; 1850, $180,000,000; 1870, $2,363,000,000.
[4] Group business included in ordinary.

Source: 1880, Frederick L. Hoffman, insurance statistician, Newark, N. J.; 1890 and subsequent years, The Spectator, Philadelphia, Pa.; Insurance Yearbook, Life Volume.

No. 522.—Life Insurance Companies—Percentage Distribution of Assets: 1920 to 1951

[Percent]

YEAR	U. S. Government securities	Foreign government, State, provincial, and local bonds	Securities of business and industry	Mortgages	Real estate	Policy loans	Miscellaneous assets	Total
1920			[4] 49.0	29.7	2.3	11.7	7.3	100.0
1925	4.0	5.5	35.9	41.5	2.3	12.5	5.3	100.0
1930	2.0	4.9	35.0	41.7	2.7	13.6	6.1	100.0
1935	1.5	6.0	26.3	40.1	2.9	14.9	6.0	100.0
1940	4.3	6.6	26.4	32.0	6.1	18.0	7.7	100.0
1945	12.6	7.6	25.0	22.0	6.6	15.3	5.0	100.0
1950	19.0	8.1	29.6	19.3	6.7	10.0	7.1	100.0
1936	32.0	5.9	26.1	16.3	2.6	6.2	4.7	100.0
1940	44.5	4.6	24.5	14.8	1.9	4.6	2.9	100.0
1945	44.9	4.6	27.3	14.8	1.9	4.6	2.8	100.0
1947	29.7	5.8	31.3	16.8	1.7	4.7	4.1	100.0
1948	29.3	4.9	34.6	19.5	1.7	4.7	2.9	100.0
1949	23.3	4.3	35.9	21.5	1.9	4.8	4.8	100.0
1950	21.0	4.0	34.3	24.6	2.1	4.7	7.5	100.0
1951	16.1	3.9	37.2	28.2	2.4	4.7	7.5	100.0

[4] Total of all classes of bonds.

Source: The Spectator, Philadelphia, Pa.; Insurance Yearbook, Life Volume; and Institute of Life Insurance.

No. 528.—Life Insurance Companies—Financial Condition and Business: 1945 to 1951

[Amounts in thousands of dollars. See headnote, table 521]

ITEM	1945	1949	1950	1951
Number of companies	348	435	440	418
Income, total [1]	7,673,987	10,137,699	11,087,123	11,665,739
Premium income, total	5,243,542	7,406,463	8,050,438	8,703,953
New premiums (except annuities)	470,589	574,139	621,878	619,379
Renewals (except annuities)	4,118,780	5,352,042	5,626,992	[2] 6,165,193
Annuities first year	171,850	124,844	128,503	65,094
Annuities renewal	397,958	642,952	810,867	[3] 895,668
Accident and health premiums		590,108	732,839	958,618
Supplementary contracts involving life contingencies	89,655	124,318	129,359	(4)
Interest, dividends, and real estate income	1,323,460	1,891,073	2,065,109	1,937,686
Other receipts	1,101,685	838,223	941,576	1,024,161
Disbursements, total [1]	4,218,570	6,253,846	6,949,891	11,142,552
Paid to policyholders and beneficiaries, total	2,716,795	3,865,827	4,239,743	4,722,534
Death claims	1,282,156	1,483,706	1,593,337	[5] 1,749,304
Matured endowments	413,736	469,653	493,830	504,000
Annuities	184,790	239,692	257,230	345,687
Lapsed, surrendered, and purchased policies	240,675	588,661	666,307	618,625
Dividends to policyholders	472,441	634,462	679,252	796,892
Disabilities and double indemnities	124,097	128,453	132,679	[6] 101,736
Accident and health benefits		320,900	417,109	607,688
Paid on supplementary contracts	301,496	477,941	530,757	(7)
Dividends to stockholders	30,481	35,871	82,548	[8] 43,859
Profit and loss, etc	46,672	89,820	150,510	[9] 4,486,930
Insurance, taxes (incl. real estate), licenses, and fees	153,043	163,086	198,409	[10] 206,910
Real estate repairs and expenses	50,082	48,018	50,248	(11)
Commissions, new	164,264	217,761	236,488	250,773
Commissions, renewal	273,186	383,093	396,807	[12] 423,738
Commissions, annuities	12,689	11,174	12,465	12,259
Commissions, accident and health		81,638	95,442	121,508
Salaries and expenses of agents	147,328	271,610	289,723	(11)
Salaries of officers and employees	154,538	291,613	313,257	(11)
Rents	31,311	35,596	39,378	(11)
Other expenses	134,484	281,098	314,116	[13] 914,700
Admitted assets, Dec. 31, total	44,797,041	59,629,541	64,019,686	68,278,226
Real estate owned	856,703	1,246,779	1,444,585	1,618,900
Mortgages	6,635,982	12,905,901	16,102,008	19,313,784
U. S. Government bonds	20,582,788	15,290,380	13,459,211	11,009,037
Other bonds owned	12,023,085	23,983,952	25,906,417	28,641,551
Stock owned	998,609	1,712,604	2,103,059	2,221,542
Collateral loans	3,181	12,276	12,527	15,495
Premium notes	67,892	47,389	61,464	23,957
Loans to policyholders	1,893,964	2,192,260	2,351,866	2,565,768
Other assets	1,734,816	2,238,000	2,578,548	2,868,192
Liabilities, Dec. 31, total	[14] 41,555,657	55,471,987	59,380,541	63,428,107
Life insurance and annuity reserve	34,705,862	46,001,252	49,149,586	52,450,475
Disability and double indemnity reserve	1,208,240	1,312,541	1,332,610	1,355,496
Unearned premium reserve on accident and health		173,989	202,588	317,175
Reserve on supplementary contracts	2,752,743	3,955,685	4,198,134	4,404,454
All other liabilities	[14] 2,888,812	4,028,520	4,497,623	4,900,507
Special voluntary contingency, etc., reserves	796,608	1,205,009	1,371,821	1,083,381
Unassigned funds and capital	2,454,776	2,952,545	3,267,323	3,766,737
Surplus apportioned	465,433	620,569	698,923	735,264
New business:				
Total: Number	19,100,513	24,466,240	26,406,059	25,178,955
Amount	16,432,947	28,380,195	37,143,605	36,213,415
Ordinary: Number	5,415,323	7,534,635	8,605,190	8,901,255
Amount	10,943,529	17,266,691	19,780,976	20,802,667
Group: Number	4,805	9,866	11,545	12,793
Amount	1,519,455	5,097,819	10,929,582	9,331,996
Industrial: Number	13,680,385	16,621,739	17,789,324	16,264,907
Amount	3,969,964	6,015,685	6,433,047	6,079,353
Insurance in force, Dec. 31:				
Total: Number	154,306,989	175,625,616	179,711,192	182,385,804
Amount	155,722,778	220,515,545	242,017,831	261,549,686
Ordinary: Number	50,171,542	65,315,835	68,473,364	71,189,099
Amount	104,456,033	144,457,931	155,071,050	165,964,830
Group: Number	37,877	60,586	68,130	76,335
Amount	22,769,796	43,075,182	52,555,781	60,130,479
Industrial: Number	104,097,570	110,249,195	111,169,698	111,120,370
Amount	28,496,958	32,982,432	34,391,000	35,464,378

[1] Beginning 1951 reported on accrual basis; previous years on cash basis. [2] Includes industrial and group premiums, new and renewals. [3] Includes first year group annuities. [4] Included with "other receipts". [5] Includes double indemnity. [6] Disability only. [7] Included with "Profit and loss, etc." [8] Surplus item, not included in disbursements. [9] Includes $3,693,583,000 increase in reserves. [10] Excludes taxes on investments. [11] Not shown separately. [12] Includes industrial and group commissions, new and renewals. [13] General insurance expenses, exclusive of investment expenses. [14] Revised to exclude special voluntary reserves; treated as surplus for later years.

Source: The Spectator, Philadelphia, Pa.; Insurance Yearbook, Life Volume.

No. 524.—LIFE INSURANCE OF FRATERNAL ORDERS: 1935 TO 1951

[Amounts in thousands of dollars. Covers transactions (domestic and foreign) of fraternal orders in U. S. Excludes U. S. business of foreign concerns]

ITEM	1935	1940	1945	1949	1950	1951
Number reporting	206	215	180	176	196	200
Income, total	206, 102	222, 086	268, 448	291, 528	295, 967	306, 664
Net amount received from members	152, 176	187, 786	182, 108	202, 727	202, 265	209, 221
All other receipts	55, 626	65, 270	86, 339	88, 596	93, 702	97, 443
Expenditures, total [1]	155, 542	185, 898	170, 903	202, 178	205, 401	216, 097
Paid for claims	111, 065	117, 575	160, 378	131, 926	131, 725	135, 077
Agents' commissions and examiners' fees	12, 126	9, 917	12, 452	18, 275	19, 033	18, 476
Expenses of management [2]	27, 308	26, 624	34, 826	57, 045	59, 176	66, 146
Assets, invested and other, Dec. 31	994, 314	1, 252, 924	1, 644, 527	1, 977, 726	2, 039, 845	2, 126, 455
Liabilities, Dec. 31	715, 860	1, 090, 625	1, 384, 385	1, 678, 672	1, 729, 607	1, 790, 294
Insurance account:						
Number of certificates in force at end of year	6, 462, 293	7, 096, 148	7, 740, 156	8, 419, 527	8, 364, 071	8, 349, 654
Amount written during year	562, 794	622, 306	648, 775	906, 620	876, 565	752, 188
Amount in force at end of year	6, 162, 535	6, 291, 644	6, 923, 682	8, 117, 089	6, 346, 349	7, 746, 744

[1] Includes expenditures not shown separately.
[2] Includes taxes.

Source: The Spectator, Philadelphia, Pa.; *Insurance Yearbook, Life Volume.*

No. 525.—LIFE INSURANCE OF ASSESSMENT LIFE ASSOCIATIONS: 1935 TO 1951

[Amounts in thousands of dollars. Covers transactions (domestic and foreign) of associations in U. S. Excludes U. S. business of foreign associations]

ITEM	1935	1940	1945	1949	1950	1951
Number reporting	50	55	43	58	51	71
Income, total	15, 950	25, 694	60, 875	110, 558	115, 977	128, 791
Net amount received from members	14, 610	24, 336	64, 443	105, 545	111, 111	115, 948
All other receipts	1, 250	1, 290	4, 132	5, 007	4, 666	6, 843
Expenditures, total [1]	14, 596	21, 372	54, 262	95, 662	105, 152	112, 554
Paid for death claims	2, 590	2, 651	5, 146	9, 020	7, 665	6, 668
Other payments to members	4, 563	7, 066	24, 560	44, 959	56, 191	50, 603
Paid to agents and medical examiners	2, 960	8, 357	14, 451	32, 567	21, 909	94, 636
Expenses of management [1]	2, 707	3, 766	7, 941	18, 458	22, 247	21, 627
Total admitted assets, Dec. 31	25, 462	27, 152	77, 315	136, 712	144, 307	154, 627
Total liabilities, Dec. 31	17, 526	20, 944	51, 282	86, 374	80, 452	92, 544
Insurance account:						
Number of certificates in force at end of year	637, 918	1, 073, 031	2, 192, 228	3, 136, 532	[4] 398, 594	[4] 536, 767
Amount written during year	74, 726	71, 330	47, 527	73, 594	[6] 64, 750	[6] 102, 946
Amount in force at end of year	251, 767	204, 317	264, 545	399, 745	438, 990	444, 176

[1] Includes expenditures not shown separately.
[2] Includes taxes.
[4] 35 companies reporting.
[5] 37 companies reporting.
[6] 22 companies reporting.
[6] 45 companies reporting.

Source: The Spectator, Philadelphia, Pa.; *Insurance Yearbook, Life Volume.*

No. 526.—ACCIDENT AND HEALTH BUSINESS OF CASUALTY AND LIFE INSURANCE COMPANIES: 1950 AND 1951

[In thousands of dollars]

ITEM	1950			1951		
	Aggregate	Casualty	Life	Aggregate	Casualty	Life
Premiums written:	1,316,74			1,574,95		
Accident and health	674, 226	292, 604	381, 622	740, 461	318, 275	422, 186
Group accident and health	642, 448	235, 562	406, 886	854, 024	323, 985	530, 039
Premiums earned:						
Accident and health	668, 503	296, 711	374, 792	722, 319	310, 066	412, 254
Group accident and health	633, 143	231, 452	401, 690	565, 073	234, 605	530, 466
Losses incurred (including adjustment expense):						
Accident and health	332, 147	160, 368	171, 779	361, 542	167, 836	193, 706
Group accident and health	484, 183	182, 370	301, 813	732, 247	275, 926	456, 322
Underwriting expense incurred:						
Accident and health	264, 169	135, 865	168, 265	302, 649	128, 974	394, 635
Group accident and health	96, 398	36, 354	60, 085	152, 272	47, 205	76, 447

Source: The Spectator, Philadelphia, Pa.; *Insurance Yearbook, Casualty and Surety Volume.*

No. 527.—Mutual Accident and Sick Benefit Associations—Financial Condition and Business Transacted: 1901 to 1948

[Money figures in thousands of dollars. Although many small companies have not reported all years, large companies have reported regularly, and figures are fairly comparable from year to year]

YEAR	Number of companies	Admitted assets	Net surplus	Premiums or assessments	Income (including interest)	Paid for claims	Paid to agents, medical examiners, and for management	Total disbursements	Number of certificates written during year	Number of certificates in force at end of year
1901	[1] 102	1,617	1,490	2,957	3,201	1,643	1,753	3,348	286,183	310,092
1905	[1] 165	3,769	3,198	6,134	7,513	3,513	3,330	6,862	657,809	887,804
1910	[1] 197	5,169	3,685	9,291	10,938	5,169	4,258	10,434	946,340	1,382,415
1915	[1] 177	7,103	4,483	10,969	12,555	6,955	4,354	11,769	693,654	1,359,366
1920	67	13,709	9,690	19,538	22,712	10,580	8,771	19,944	713,270	1,853,328
1925	167	46,682	31,558	40,807	44,903	22,395	15,019	36,672	807,722	2,170,582
1930	156	39,551	25,901	47,036	50,542	29,185	18,086	48,338	963,011	2,483,753
1935	109	39,419	21,417	32,707	35,764	20,011	12,274	32,964	716,697	1,914,519
1940	110	56,772	25,680	45,304	48,501	23,588	17,266	42,161	1,136,309	2,543,771
1941	104	65,137	30,877	52,046	55,671	26,696	19,988	48,038	1,101,257	2,589,476
1942	103	72,291	33,904	59,752	62,898	27,133	23,377	51,267	1,263,425	2,987,059
1943	99	85,435	38,552	67,014	71,234	29,029	26,428	56,663	1,230,189	3,063,913
1944	81	97,238	43,109	74,474	80,776	33,578	29,655	64,437	977,753	3,059,509
1945	79	115,450	45,678	86,863	91,710	39,208	29,836	66,076	[2] 800,141	[2] 2,891,108
1946	65	114,524	52,564	93,603	96,027	45,841	33,176	80,543	[3] 354,897	[2] 1,477,852
1947	65	133,250	57,913	111,667	115,864	52,337	42,260	96,707	[2] 1,161,441	[2] 3,765,000
1948	43	136,757	58,732	112,942	116,891	58,113	39,656	99,606	[2] 1,060,911	[2] 3,678,041

[1] Includes all known companies, whether reporting or not.
[2] 49 companies reporting in 1945; 43 companies in 1946; 46 companies in 1947; 34 companies in 1948.
[3] 32 companies reporting in 1948.

Source: The Spectator, Philadelphia, Pa.; *Insurance Yearbook*, Casualty and Surety Volume.

No. 528.—Fire Losses, Total and Per Capita: 1876 to 1951

[Amounts, except per capita, in thousands of dollars. Continental United States only. Prior to 1916 figures are as compiled by the New York Journal of Commerce and include losses of $10,000 or over in the principal cities of the United States, adding 15 percent for small and unreported losses. These figures are not comparable with those shown for later years (the 1916 Journal of Commerce figure being $214,531,000 as against $258,378,000) which cover all fires reported to the Actuarial Bureau Committee, adding 25 percent for unreported and uninsured losses prior to 1935 and 30 percent thereafter. Estimated fire losses are based on paid losses]

YEARLY AVERAGE OR YEAR	Loss Amount	Index [1] 1926=100	YEAR	Loss Amount	Index [1] 1926=100	YEAR	Loss Amount	Index [1] 1926=100	Per capita [2]
1876–1880	69,912	....	1915	172,033	77.3	1933	271,453	62.1	$2.16
1881–1885	95,753	....	1916	[2] 258,378	103.6	1934	271,197	56.5	2.15
1886–1890	113,627	....	1917	289,535	103.1	1935	235,263	47.9	1.85
1891–1895	148,988	....	1918	353,879	110.1	1936	266,659	56.1	2.08
1896–1900	136,043	....	1919	320,540	91.6	1937	284,959	52.1	1.97
1901	165,818	139.1	1920	447,887	99.1	1938	258,478	54.4	1.99
1902	161,078	133.5	1921	495,406	135.4	1939	275,102	57.7	2.10
1903	145,302	114.9	1922	506,541	123.0	1940	285,879	57.3	2.17
1904	229,198	168.9	1923	535,373	110.9	1941	303,895	56.1	2.28
1905	165,222	113.8	1924	549,062	115.6	1942	314,295	49.7	2.35
1906	518,612	342.8	1925	559,418	109.8	1943	373,000	60.4	2.78
1907	215,085	125.7							
1908	217,886	129.7	1926	561,981	100.0	1944	437,273	69.6	3.29
1909	188,705	105.9	1927	472,934	88.3	1945	484,274	(4)	3.66
1910	214,003	112.2	1928	464,607	84.4	1946	554,070	(4)	3.96
1911	217,005	110.9	1929	459,446	79.0	1947	647,860	(4)	4.52
1912	206,439	102.5	1930	501,981	94.0	1948	715,074	(4)	4.89
1913	203,754	98.0	1931	451,644	89.8	1949	651,534	(4)	4.38
1914	221,439	104.1	1932	400,860	88.6	1950	648,909	(4)	4.29
						1951	730,084	(4)	4.76

[1] Adjusted for fluctuations in commodity prices and for variations in amount of property exposed to loss.
[2] Based on population estimates of the Bureau of the Census. Excludes armed forces overseas.
[3] See headnote. [4] Not available.

Source: National Board of Fire Underwriters, New York, N. Y.; *Report of the Committee on Statistics and Origin of Fires*.

No. 529.—BUSINESS OF FIRE, MARINE, AND CASUALTY INSURERS: 1935 TO 1951

[In thousands of dollars except number of companies. Data cover transactions of both United States and foreign stock, mutual, and reciprocal companies in continental U. S., Territories, and possessions]

ITEM	1935	1940	1945	1949	1950	1951
ALL COMPANIES						
Total admitted assets, Dec. 31	3,951,855	5,072,220	7,670,729	11,909,183	13,084,540	14,303,897
Total liabilities except capital, Dec. 31 [1]	1,906,829	2,654,036	4,486,578	7,810,212	8,579,174	9,605,691
Unearned premiums reserve	1,071,343	1,379,654	1,968,186	3,887,976	4,314,733	4,864,705
Reserve for losses [2]	632,489	864,527	1,502,129	2,597,887	2,842,333	3,237,975
Capital paid up, Dec. 31 [3]	487,673	551,120	638,630	706,088	824,817	849,374
Surplus over capital and liabilities [4]	1,468,302	1,797,064	2,545,321	3,329,683	3,680,548	4,048,532
Net premiums written	1,633,836	3,141,178	3,110,134	5,931,652	6,813,660	7,797,065
Premiums earned	1,548,191	2,024,901	2,860,638	5,553,117	6,251,352	7,300,416
Total income	1,811,628	2,341,612	3,361,537	(5)	(5)	(5)
Losses paid	648,455	842,449	1,321,362	2,308,279	2,784,717	3,527,570
Expense paid	641,013	776,484	1,016,048	2,308,334	2,783,426	3,664,865
Losses incurred [6]	754,209	1,024,937	1,627,802	2,827,403	3,320,314	3,907,648
Expenses incurred (includes taxes)	659,948	844,029	1,106,656	3,042,296	2,326,924	3,527,743
STOCK COMPANIES						
Number reporting	513	551	564	613	585	582
Total admitted assets, Dec. 31	3,430,367	4,284,336	6,332,533	9,536,216	10,706,400	11,582,674
Total liabilities except capital, Dec. 31 [1]	1,712,701	2,177,817	3,565,348	6,161,434	6,882,389	7,588,611
Unearned premiums reserve	940,484	1,177,071	1,551,849	3,340,630	3,653,382	3,968,589
Reserve for losses [2]	519,466	668,189	1,216,167	1,900,312	2,130,734	2,360,712
Capital paid up, Dec. 31	481,320	532,854	633,053	729,046	781,275	808,680
Surplus over capital and liabilities [4]	1,236,346	1,523,866	2,144,312	2,647,746	3,041,539	3,316,302
Net premiums written	1,364,355	1,729,639	2,464,405	4,708,709	5,189,868	5,931,978
Premiums earned	1,317,322	1,643,411	2,286,134	4,344,634	4,826,182	5,443,363
Total income	1,508,836	1,902,109	2,675,849	(5)	(5)	(5)
Losses paid	549,477	685,008	1,076,877	1,855,400	2,096,717	2,690,160
Expense paid	570,944	673,070	870,525	1,602,902	2,265,640	3,427,655
Dividends paid to stockholders	81,949	90,846	101,826	125,652	7,139,222	7,161,634
Dividends paid to policyholders	3,674	9,791	15,016	33,790	27,023	22,502
Net remittance to home office	19,985	12,910	13,846	7,948	15,897	8,236
Other disbursements	135,941	343,975	395,043	(5)	(5)	(5)
Losses incurred [6]	654,834	834,296	1,263,811	2,137,162	2,608,345	2,747,390
Expenses incurred (includes taxes)	588,013	730,465	936,352	1,604,963	1,986,526	2,113,347
MUTUAL COMPANIES						
Number reporting	194	271	266	332	286	327
Total admitted assets, Dec. 31	462,535	676,162	1,206,638	2,161,425	2,135,308	2,391,605
Total liabilities except capital, Dec. 31 [1]	257,028	427,824	827,909	1,514,612	1,525,950	1,584,204
Unearned premiums reserve	116,614	180,298	290,563	886,629	508,671	795,808
Reserve for losses [2]	96,539	180,604	354,009	651,957	652,543	756,816
Guaranty fund	6,383	14,977	12,824	30,885	26,208	36,964
Surplus over capital and liabilities [4]	199,154	233,350	355,105	615,966	583,523	730,406
Net premiums written	245,767	360,419	578,111	1,086,304	1,452,288	1,694,941
Premiums earned	230,608	326,864	540,978	1,341,205	1,256,847	1,221,465
Total income	296,430	384,086	612,604	(5)	(5)	(5)
Losses paid	85,583	137,708	228,863	434,316	618,048	728,390
Expense paid	59,712	87,861	127,214	466,366	466,029	568,607
Dividends paid to policyholders	56,023	72,041	101,260	161,063	7,148,178	7,182,197
Other disbursements	21,248	39,671	58,941	(5)	(5)	(5)
Losses incurred [6]	99,375	164,881	300,162	658,909	739,678	915,380
Expenses incurred (includes taxes)	71,835	88,566	147,260	329,373	330,991	404,602
RECIPROCAL ORGANIZATIONS						
Number reporting	29	57	51	44	51	66
Total admitted assets, Dec. 31	58,963	91,722	132,358	208,542	243,042	349,618
Total liabilities except capital, Dec. 31 [1]	26,100	48,588	83,501	134,176	180,920	243,574
Unearned premiums reserve	14,245	22,380	25,744	60,708	67,730	102,738
Reserve for losses [2]	8,460	15,844	31,953	45,638	56,055	98,446
Guaranty fund	(5)	2,360	2,752	9,187	7,382	(5)
Surplus over capital and liabilities [4]	32,863	40,040	46,104	66,179	75,780	99,835
Net premiums written	33,714	51,121	67,608	73,849	170,543	340,116
Premiums earned	(5)	54,927	63,526	67,279	166,324	235,563
Total income	36,182	55,468	72,994	(5)	(5)	(5)
Losses paid	13,396	19,787	28,521	28,663	68,952	116,097
Expense paid	10,258	15,588	30,309	45,076	50,762	98,423
Dividends paid to subscribers	5,559	9,670	7,461	13,083	10,609	14,480
Other disbursements	3,065	8,960	9,960	(5)	(5)	(5)
Losses incurred [6]	(5)	25,820	43,630	31,343	92,391	145,043
Expenses incurred (includes taxes)	(5)	15,979	20,054	17,941	50,407	68,604

[1] Includes voluntary reserve. [2] Includes adjustment expenses. [3] Includes guaranty fund.
[4] Net worth. [5] Not available. [6] Based on incomplete returns.
Includes... Full basis not available.

Source: The Spectator, Philadelphia, Pa.; Insurance Yearbook, Fire and Marine Volume and Casualty and Surety Volume.

No. 530.—LIFE, FIRE, AND CASUALTY INSURANCE BUSINESS, BY STATES: 1951

[In thousands of dollars. Totals in this table differ from figures for corresponding items in preceding tables because data by States are compiled for all companies operating in each State whereas aggregates shown in other tables cover data for companies from which annual reports were obtained]

STATE	LIFE			FIRE AND CASUALTY	
	Premiums received	Insurance in force, Dec. 31	Death claims	Premiums written	Losses paid
Total	7,221,866	279,843,427	20,120,022	9,821,653	4,934,653
Alabama	86,470	3,196,631	460,487	89,426	37,594
Arizona	19,450	762,236	45,745	35,225	15,633
Arkansas	32,757	1,276,812	176,571	67,857	27,735
California	407,496	17,942,304	1,134,524	862,827	417,793
Colorado	53,704	2,092,169	158,665	75,071	32,855
Connecticut	129,017	4,959,870	259,431	171,955	98,298
Delaware	22,040	843,790	63,860	20,828	7,917
District of Columbia	47,824	2,095,519	200,216	42,451	18,258
Florida	119,029	3,821,918	561,677	164,787	75,461
Georgia	125,870	4,481,599	687,975	138,749	58,014
Idaho	15,621	570,808	40,786	29,622	14,947
Illinois	483,377	18,863,338	1,175,461	666,542	334,064
Indiana	169,689	7,238,023	512,227	260,108	128,358
Iowa	93,154	3,682,424	201,732	159,182	79,605
Kansas	67,678	2,750,804	192,689	116,299	67,529
Kentucky	90,349	2,960,478	327,577	111,577	46,356
Louisiana	174,660	2,954,756	318,194	129,814	56,105
Maine	40,749	1,162,489	86,322	46,764	20,976
Maryland	116,272	4,386,215	326,061	128,133	60,754
Massachusetts	250,170	9,053,996	556,945	364,806	198,182
Michigan	265,551	11,832,160	946,868	456,247	251,865
Minnesota	112,342	4,563,914	291,437	175,788	88,223
Mississippi	31,585	1,234,186	145,601	63,579	30,654
Missouri	164,948	6,664,901	522,948	225,434	105,136
Montana	18,680	714,654	44,704	33,657	13,021
Nebraska	49,977	1,992,923	113,415	79,545	37,120
Nevada	5,109	195,777	13,377	11,054	5,082
New Hampshire	24,857	873,605	52,484	39,787	21,221
New Jersey	300,479	11,562,537	544,309	364,459	233,784
New Mexico	14,843	551,060	64,475	36,604	17,220
New York	919,930	35,814,064	1,894,071	1,403,153	758,278
North Carolina	153,385	4,553,567	500,071	147,974	65,704
North Dakota	14,829	583,120	38,373	29,897	11,959
Ohio	426,997	17,664,301	1,094,412	484,809	242,982
Oklahoma	58,602	2,506,148	244,209	126,395	60,889
Oregon	51,621	1,986,160	115,289	105,403	45,237
Pennsylvania	567,005	21,987,935	1,440,448	602,987	316,487
Rhode Island	43,516	1,539,525	115,929	48,409	26,721
South Carolina	70,915	2,425,079	446,907	72,401	32,150
South Dakota	16,690	616,399	37,645	33,565	13,381
Tennessee	94,585	3,762,257	428,953	137,011	62,802
Texas	245,521	10,692,245	1,154,829	471,335	220,796
Utah	25,485	1,056,768	97,110	30,163	12,195
Vermont	15,675	517,663	32,237	20,735	12,088
Virginia	118,373	4,331,641	429,128	140,832	62,456
Washington	82,256	3,310,596	225,369	138,323	62,714
West Virginia	56,281	2,329,988	187,200	77,260	39,050
Wisconsin	160,638	6,260,410	333,707	209,230	101,719
Wyoming	8,900	360,411	22,280	15,079	5,707
Alaska	1,562	56,582	4,991		
Canal Zone	315	12,700	1,725		
Hawaii	22,179	779,602	49,530		
Puerto Rico	5,234	139,769	15,035		
Canada	394,875	17,369,887	649,964	356,425	181,596
Mexico	195	57,967	5,901		
Philippine Islands	6,741	134,212	13,771		
Foreign countries	6,192	163,514	19,927		
Miscellaneous	119,712	3,527,021	294,248		

Source: The Spectator, Philadelphia, Pa.; *Insurance Yearbook*, Life Volume, Fire and Marine Volume, and Casualty and Surety Volume.

17. Business Enterprise

Statistics in this section relate in general to the place and the behavior of the business firm and business initiative in the American economy. More specifically, the data show measures of and changes in business population, corporate assets and liabilities, certain types of business income and expenditure, patents and designs, and research expenditures.

Business population and turnover.—These estimates of the Office of Business Economics (see tables 531–535) are based on data from a number of sources, particularly Bureau of the Census, Bureau of Internal Revenue, and Bureau of Old-Age and Survivors Insurance. A firm is defined here as a business organization under a single management and may include one or more plants or outlets; a firm doing business in more than one industry is counted only in that industry accounting for the highest proportion of its total employment. A self-employed person is considered a firm only if he has either one or more employees or has an established place of business. This count of business population differs from that of the Bureau of the Census which ordinarily represents a count of establishments, i. e., manufacturing plants or retail stores.

The number of new and discontinued businesses is estimated from tabulations prepared by the Bureau of Old-Age and Survivors Insurance, which show the number of employer identification numbers issued and canceled each quarter.

Business transfers represent purchases of going businesses, acquisitions of businesses through inheritance, transfers of businesses to a trustee or executor as well as changes in the form of business organization.

Information on new incorporations is collected by Dun & Bradstreet and is available monthly, by States, beginning in July 1945. The statistics include both completely new businesses which are incorporated, and changes in existing businesses from the noncorporate to the corporate form of organization, the transfer of an existing corporation to a new State, etc.

Corporate assets and liabilities.—These data are from the Bureau of Internal Revenue and the Securities and Exchange Commission. In its annual report, *Statistics of Income*, Part 2, the Bureau of Internal Revenue presents abbreviated balance sheet and income account data for all United States corporations. In a quarterly release entitled *Net Working Capital of U. S. Corporations*, the Securities and Exchange Commission publishes data on the net working capital position of all United States corporations, exclusive of banks and insurance companies, showing the principal components of current assets and liabilities.

Corporation income, profits, dividends, and taxes.—The Bureau of Internal Revenue, the Office of Business Economics of the Department of Commerce, and the Board of Governors of the Federal Reserve System are the principal sources of statistics on these subjects. The statistics of these agencies overlap in many respects but are not comparable because of differing purposes of compilation.

Corporation statistics based on income tax returns are published by the Bureau of Internal Revenue in the annual *Statistics of Income*, Part 2.

Corporate data of the Office of Business Economics are from statistics on national income and product which may be found in its *Survey of Current Business*. In particular, see regular February and July monthly issues, and the 1951 *National Income Supplement*. These data are defined as required for purposes of national income estimation.

The primary sources of data for the Office of Business Economics estimates of profits, taxes, dividends, and undistributed profits are the original corporate tax returns sub-

Note.—This section presents data for the most recent year or period available on April 22, 1953, when the material was organized and sent to the printer.

473

mitted to the Bureau of Internal Revenue and summarized in the annual report on *Statistics of Income*, Part 2. Various adjustments of the *Statistics of Income* data have been required by the national income treatment, particularly with respect to depletion, capital gain or loss, and intercorporate dividends and because the original corporate income statements do not represent the final stage of information. For details of these adjustments, see table 38 of the reports on national income and product in the *National Income Supplement* cited above. That table provides a reconciliation between the national income profit series and those reported in *Statistics of Income*.

Unincorporated enterprises.—These data also are from the national income and product statistics of the Office of Business Economics. Net income of these enterprises is a composite income share. It includes return on proprietors' investment and risk, as well as return from proprietors' own labor and any labor contributed by proprietors' families to the business.

Sources and uses of corporate funds.—These data indicate capital requirements of corporations and manner in which they are financed. Sources of funds should be equal to their uses. Certain discrepancies, however, apart from errors in estimation interfere with this equality. These discrepancies are not particularly significant and are due to omission of such factors as (1) money accruing to corporations from an excess of sales over purchases of used plant and equipment (2) transactions in securities held as permanent investments except public offerings, and (3) the fact that net new issues omit entrepreneurial capital for new corporations where no offering or sales of securities are made to the public or to institutions. Liquidation of such corporations is similarly not reflected.

Business sales and inventories.—These data include all companies, both corporate and noncorporate, major activities of which are in manufacturing or trade. Farm and other nonfarm businesses are not included. The manufacturing figures are the sum of (1) totals for corporations from Bureau of Internal Revenue *Statistics of Income* data for 1939–49 and projections of 1949 figures by means of a representative sample of manufacturing corporations for 1950–52, and (2) estimates for unincorporated enterprises projected, by means of sample data, back to 1939 and forward to 1952 from benchmarks on sole proprietorships and partnerships from Bureau of Internal Revenue for the years 1939, 1945, 1947 and 1949.

Retail and wholesale trade estimates are based on figures in 1939 and 1948 Censuses of Business, interpolated and carried forward by means of sample data, Bureau of Internal Revenue compilations, and other information.

Net change in business inventories.—To ascertain net physical change in nonfarm inventories, book values of beginning and ending inventories of each year are expressed in terms of constant base year prices by means of selected Bureau of Labor Statistics wholesale price indexes appropriate to each industry. Net increment in deflated book value figures is then converted to a current price basis by index ratios of current prices to base year prices. No inventory valuation adjustment is shown for farm inventories because change in farm inventories is estimated (by Bureau of Agricultural Economics) from physical quantity data.

Plant and equipment expenditures of U. S. business.—A joint survey by the Securities and Exchange Commission and the Department of Commerce presents quarterly data on actual expenditures of U. S. business, other than agriculture, and anticipated expenditure for the next two quarters. In addition, a survey is made at the beginning of each year of plans of business as regards expansion during that year. The data are based on reports submitted by corporations registered with the Securities and Exchange Commission and by a large sample of nonregistered manufacturing companies, unincorporated as well as corporate, reporting to the Department of Commerce.

Historical statistics.—See preface and historical appendix. Tabular headnotes (as "See also *Historical Statistics*, series P 176–187") provide cross-references, where applicable, to *Historical Statistics of the United States, 1789–1945.*

No. 531.—AVERAGE NUMBER OF FIRMS IN OPERATION, 1929 TO 1952, AND NEW AND DISCONTINUED BUSINESSES, 1944 TO 1952

[In thousands except new incorporations. Data are for continental United States. Excludes firms in agriculture, forestry, fishing and the professional services. New businesses include only firms which have been newly established; going concerns which have been purchased are considered business transfers. Discontinued businesses include closures of all kinds without reference to reason for discontinuing—e. g., failure, retirement, illness of proprietor, etc.]

TYPE AND STATUS OF FIRMS	All industries	Mining and quarrying	Contract construction	Manufacturing	Transportation, communication, and other public utilities	Wholesale trade	Retail trade	Finance, insurance, and real estate	Service industries
FIRMS IN OPERATION									
(Annual averages)									
1929	3,097.1	38.0	233.0	257.6	117.2	114.9	1,341.1	234.8	670.5
1932	2,947.2	34.2	184.7	167.1	106.5	110.0	1,304.4	299.1	662.1
1935	3,066.3	37.2	179.8	205.7	125.0	122.0	1,403.8	301.8	699.8
1940	3,282.8	37.3	199.2	228.7	148.0	146.8	1,596.0	310.5	718.3
1944	3,062.2	31.0	153.4	245.2	123.8	146.1	1,393.3	312.3	657.1
1945	3,256.4	31.2	176.7	262.8	130.9	159.7	1,456.6	325.4	706.0
1946	3,605.4	32.4	342.6	301.9	163.0	181.1	1,574.0	337.6	772.8
1947	3,879.4	33.8	289.3	329.6	180.8	196.6	1,673.0	344.7	830.6
1948	3,990.7	35.2	321.0	329.6	188.3	202.7	1,709.6	346.8	857.4
1949	3,954.8	34.6	335.0	312.0	189.3	203.0	1,693.2	344.7	853.0
1950	3,980.4	34.2	358.0	303.0	194.2	204.0	1,685.2	347.2	854.5
1951	4,005.9	34.2	375.4	305.9	204.4	207.1	1,672.3	352.1	857.5
1952 (prel.)	4,063.5	34.4	395.3	304.1	214.7	210.9	1,662.9	357.0	862.5
NEW BUSINESSES									
1944	354.9	3.8	29.4	34.0	25.6	18.5	127.3	26.5	87.8
1945	429.8	4.0	56.0	48.3	27.9	22.4	130.1	26.3	94.8
1946	619.8	5.0	94.9	76.7	40.0	31.9	216.4	26.7	128.3
1947	476.4	5.1	74.9	50.2	28.7	22.4	170.5	20.0	103.6
1948	404.6	4.9	66.6	40.6	22.5	18.8	143.3	18.7	86.8
1949	358.6	4.2	58.6	32.1	20.0	16.5	136.7	17.7	73.0
1950	397.5	4.8	71.5	42.9	34.5	17.2	130.6	23.2	73.5
1951	405.7	4.7	68.2	45.2	29.4	17.4	142.5	25.5	72.9
1952: 1st quarter	122.8	1.4	24.2	12.0	9.4	4.3	41.6	6.8	21.2
2d quarter	110.6	1.2	22.2	10.5	7.6	4.6	39.6	5.9	18.6
DISCONTINUED									
1944	198.4	3.9	16.5	31.9	11.2	6.8	76.0	14.7	45.7
1945	202.6	3.7	18.1	26.7	11.1	7.3	75.6	13.8	46.4
1946	235.4	3.2	26.6	28.3	14.8	8.9	79.1	14.1	51.2
1947	281.9	4.0	36.5	41.1	17.1	12.1	102.7	16.3	60.9
1948	371.0	4.9	42.4	47.6	19.7	16.3	141.4	18.6	79.1
1949	380.3	4.6	46.9	55.0	19.2	16.4	150.5	19.4	75.3
1950	336.3	4.8	46.5	43.2	16.4	15.1	150.2	18.3	72.6
1951	377.4	4.7	53.4	44.1	18.0	14.0	155.5	20.1	66.9
1952: 1st quarter	100.8	1.2	12.0	12.1	5.5	3.7	41.6	5.2	17.6
2d quarter	96.6	1.3	12.4	12.8	4.1	3.9	40.3	4.8	16.0

ITEM	1945	1946	1947	1948	1949	1950	1951	1952	
								1st quarter	2d quarter
TRANSFERS AND INCORPORATIONS									
Business transfers (new series)	447.6	619.7	557.2	496.3	489.8	467.0	418.6	120.2	101.0
New incorporations [1]	96,291	123,856	112,889	95,102	85,691	91,235	82,699	23,397	24,018
NEW BUSINESSES BY TYPE OF ORGANIZATION									
All types	429.8	619.8	476.4	404.6	358.6	397.5	405.8	122.8	110.6
Individual	291.3	399.8	308.7	269.9	243.3	269.4	278.3	84.5	72.6
Partnership	117.5	179.4	125.3	96.5	80.3	87.5	90.9	25.0	26.2
Corporate	39.4	40.0	40.8	36.6	33.6	39.0	35.9	11.8	11.5
Other	1.6	1.7	1.6	1.6	1.4	1.6	1.7	.5	.4

[1] Compiled by Dun and Bradstreet, Inc. Available only since July 1945.

[2] Excludes (includes Louisiana).

Source: Department of Commerce, Office of Business Economics; published currently in Survey of Current Business.

FIG. XXXV.—BUSINESS EXPENDITURES FOR NEW PLANT AND
EQUIPMENT: 1945 TO 1953

[Excludes agriculture. See table 547

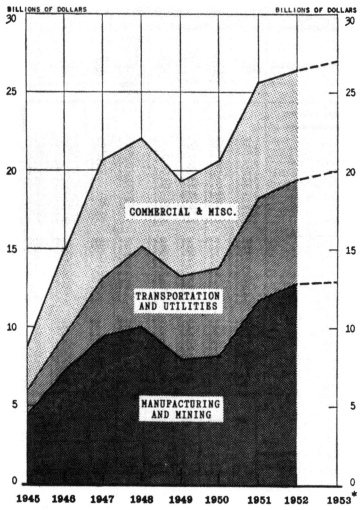

*Anticipated by business.

Source: Securities and Exchange Commission and Department of Commerce, Office of Business Economics.

No. 532.—Number of Firms in Operation by Year of Acquisition: Dec. 31, 1944 to 1951

[In thousands]

YEAR OF ACQUISITION	Total businesses started 1944–51 [1]	FIRMS REMAINING IN OPERATION UNDER THE SAME OWNERSHIP ON DECEMBER 31							
		1944	1945	1946	1947	1948	1949	1950	1951
All years	16,296.0	3,142.2	3,360.3	3,762.7	3,947.4	3,951.1	3,953.3	3,965.6	4,014.0
Prior to 1944	2,985.8	2,857.1	2,259.9	1,963.3	1,796.6	1,648.8	1,525.2	1,415.1	1,326.0
1944	955.4	555.1	400.7	303.7	245.5	206.9	180.5	157.4	141.0
1945	877.4		708.8	500.4	378.6	308.3	260.4	224.7	196.3
1946	1,229.5			975.3	694.2	520.7	414.9	344.5	295.1
1947	1,033.7				532.5	586.9	435.6	345.2	280.7
1948	809.0					708.4	492.1	382.1	289.8
1949	818.4						644.6	465.4	345.2
1950	864.6							680.2	484.7
1951	821.3								642.2

[1] For years 1944–51, all firms newly established, reorganized, purchased or otherwise acquired by transfer; for years prior to 1944, all firms in operation, December 31, 1943. Total in columns is equal to sum of all sole proprietorships and other management entities counted separately for each business operated at any time during 1944–51.

Source: Department of Commerce, Office of Business Economics; *Survey of Current Business*, December 1952.

No. 533.—Business Firm Turnover Rates, 1949–1951, and Rank by Median Age Attained, 1945–1950, by Industry Group

ITEM	1949–51 ANNUAL AVERAGE TURNOVER RATES [1]				RANK	
	Entry rate	Discontinuance rate	Transfer rate	Discontinuance plus transfer rate	By rate sold or liquidated	By 1945–50 average median age attained
All industries	98	95	112	207		
Mining and quarrying	112	145	73	218	6	7
Contract construction	193	141	45	186	8	3
Manufacturing	130	150	71	221	7	6
Food and kindred products	43	175	82	258	9	
Textiles and textile products	96	113	58	171	8	
Leather and leather products	75	113	47	160	5	
Lumber and lumber products	280	283	80	363	10	
Paper and allied products	90	79	45	124	3	
Printing and publishing	51	38	71	110	1	
Chemicals and allied products [3]	84	167	61	228	8	
Stone, clay, and glass products	50	153	84	157	3	
Primary and metal products	50	82	69	151	4	
Other manufacturing [3]	100	141	65	206	7	
Transportation, communication and other public utilities	128	94	56	150	8	4
Wholesale trade	83	75	56	131	2	1
Retail trade	83	90	160	250	8	8
General merchandise	83	54	77	131	1	
Food and liquor	62	90	142	232	5	
Automotive	90	85	91	176	4	
Apparel and accessories	80	80	74	154	3	
Eating and drinking places	114	127	284	411	6	
Filling stations	102	99	319	418	7	
Other retail trade	76	67	83	150	2	
Finance, insurance, and real estate	64	48	64	112	1	2
Service industries	90	84	95	179	4	5
Hotels and other lodging places	89	89	154	243	6	
Personal services	65	73	105	178	5	
Business services	111	75	50	135	2	
Automobile repair	96	101	72	173	4	
Miscellaneous repair	100	75	55	133	1	
Motion pictures	91	63	87	150	3	
Other services	102	106	103	209	7	

[1] Number of new, discontinued or transferred firms during period per 1,000 firms in operation at beginning of period. Turnover rates computed separately for each year; three-year annual averages shown.
[2] Includes products of petroleum and coal.
[3] Includes tobacco, rubber products and miscellaneous manufactures.

Source: Department of Commerce, Office of Business Economics; *Survey of Current Business*, December 1952.

No. 534.—NUMBER OF FIRMS IN OPERATION AND NEW, DISCONTINUED, AND TRANSFERRED BUSINESSES, BY INDUSTRY: 1950 AND 1951

[In thousands. See headnote, table 531]

INDUSTRY	FIRMS IN OPERATION (annual averages)		NEW BUSINESSES		DISCONTINUED BUSINESSES		TRANSFERRED BUSINESSES	
	1950	1951	1950	1951	1950	1951	1950	1951
All industries	3,960.4	4,008.9	397.5	405.7	365.2	377.4	467.0	415.6
Mining and quarrying	34.2	34.2	4.8	4.7	4.8	4.7	2.7	2.3
Contract construction	358.0	375.4	71.5	68.2	45.5	53.4	16.1	13.5
Manufacturing	303.0	305.9	42.9	45.2	42.2	44.1	23.5	19.5
Food and kindred products	27.8	24.1	1.4	1.3	5.2	4.9	2.5	2.0
Textile mill products	11.0	11.2	.7	.5	.3	.5	.4	.3
Apparel and other finished textile products	31.2	30.4	3.7	3.1	4.5	4.2	2.3	1.7
Leather and leather products	5.8	5.6	.5	.4	.8	.4	.3	.2
Lumber and timber basic products	64.4	70.8	22.9	25.6	17.5	21.4	5.9	5.3
Furniture and finished lumber products	10.6	10.5	.7	.6	.7	.7	.7	.5
Paper and allied products	4.1	4.2	.4	.4	.3	.3	.2	.2
Printing and publishing	47.3	47.8	2.5	2.1	1.8	1.8	3.6	2.9
Chemicals and allied products	8.3	7.6	.7	.7	1.4	1.7	.5	.4
Products and petroleum and coal	1.5	1.5	.1	.2	.2	(1)	.1	.1
Stone, clay, and glass products	10.3	9.5	.9	.8	1.5	1.4	1.0	.7
Primary metal industries	5.8	5.9	.3	.3	.3	.2	.3	.3
Fabricated metals	17.9	18.3	1.6	1.4	1.2	1.1	1.5	1.2
Machinery except electrical	19.2	21.3	2.1	3.7	1.1	.9	1.5	1.6
Electrical machinery	5.0	5.4	.7	.8	.4	.4	.3	.2
Transportation equipment	5.5	5.2	.7	.9	.9	1.1	.4	.3
Professional, scientific, and controlling instruments	3.5	3.4	.3	.3	.3	.3	.2	.2
Rubber products	1.5	1.5	.2	.1	.2	.1	.1	.1
Miscellaneous	22.5	21.6	2.5	2.0	3.2	2.8	1.6	1.2
Transportation, communication, and other public utilities	194.2	204.4	24.8	29.4	16.4	18.9	11.2	9.9
Wholesale trade	204.0	207.1	17.2	17.4	15.1	14.0	12.1	9.6
Retail trade	1,685.2	1,672.3	139.6	142.5	150.2	155.5	297.0	267.4
General merchandise	50.3	50.4	3.3	1.3	2.8	1.6	4.4	2.3
General stores with food	29.7	29.1	1.2	1.7	1.9	2.2	2.5	2.5
Grocery, with and without meats	316.9	305.9	16.0	16.7	26.3	28.0	50.6	42.2
Meat and seafood	24.1	21.8	1.6	1.5	3.4	3.9	2.9	2.4
Other food	105.0	104.0	9.5	8.7	10.3	9.5	12.8	11.1
Liquor	21.0	20.6	1.4	1.3	1.8	1.7	3.6	3.4
Motor vehicles	54.8	57.9	6.0	7.3	4.9	3.4	5.8	4.8
Automotive parts and accessories	22.8	23.0	1.8	1.4	1.2	1.5	2.0	1.4
Apparel	83.7	83.2	7.1	6.5	6.7	7.8	6.8	5.4
Shoes	14.7	15.0	1.2	1.1	.8	.8	1.1	1.1
Eating and drinking places	319.5	314.5	36.2	37.4	38.7	43.5	94.5	85.8
Filling stations	227.5	228.3	21.8	27.5	22.9	25.0	73.4	73.9
Home furnishings	44.4	46.0	4.7	4.9	3.3	2.9	3.4	2.8
Appliances and radios	27.6	29.3	3.3	3.2	2.2	2.9	2.8	1.9
Drugs	48.9	48.5	1.4	1.5	2.1	1.7	4.3	3.8
Hardware and farm implements	47.3	47.6	2.4	2.4	2.4	1.9	5.4	4.6
Lumber and building materials	40.2	40.6	4.7	2.7	3.4	2.8	2.8	2.4
Jewelry	20.9	20.5	1.4	1.4	2.0	1.7	2.1	1.4
Miscellaneous retail	185.7	186.3	14.6	14.0	13.3	14.6	16.3	14.2
Finance, insurance, and real estate	347.2	352.1	23.2	25.5	18.3	20.1	20.6	18.9
Service industries	854.5	857.5	73.5	72.9	72.6	66.9	83.9	74.8
Hotels and other lodging places	75.5	76.9	6.2	8.7	7.1	6.7	12.0	12.4
Laundry, cleaning and garment repair	113.5	113.5	8.2	7.9	8.1	8.3	14.2	11.3
Barber and beauty shops	207.3	205.4	12.8	13.7	16.0	14.4	21.2	19.1
Other personal services	100.2	99.6	6.7	5.8	7.1	5.9	10.7	9.8
Business services	86.4	89.6	9.7	9.3	6.5	5.7	5.5	4.3
Automobile repair	92.1	90.8	7.8	7.9	9.1	8.4	6.8	5.8
Miscellaneous repair	107.8	110.9	11.4	10.3	8.2	6.9	6.2	5.4
Motion pictures	14.8	15.0	1.5	1.0	.9	1.2	1.4	1.2
Other amusements	56.9	55.7	9.3	8.2	9.6	9.4	6.0	5.5

[1] Less than 50.

Source: Department of Commerce, Office of Business Economics; *Survey of Current Business*.

No. 535.—NUMBER OF FIRMS IN OPERATION, MARCH 31, 1950 TO 1952, AND NUMBER OF NEW AND DISCONTINUED BUSINESSES, 1950 AND 1951, BY STATES AND REGIONS

[In thousands. Data are for continental U. S. Based on data from Bureau of Old-Age and Survivors Insurance. Firms doing business in more than 1 State counted only once and classified in State of firm's reporting headquarters]

STATE AND REGION	FIRMS IN OPERATION			NEW BUSINESSES		DISCONTINUED BUSINESSES	
	1950	1951	1952 [1]	1950	1951 [1]	1950	1951 [1]
United States	3,965.4	4,007.4	4,036.0	397.5	405.8	365.2	377.4
New England	269.8	269.5	270.4	23.6	22.4	22.3	24.9
Connecticut	59.1	59.3	60.5	5.4	5.1	5.4	4.5
Maine	29.0	30.2	30.8	3.1	3.2	2.2	2.3
Massachusetts	131.7	129.6	128.3	10.7	10.8	10.2	14.2
New Hampshire	17.0	17.0	17.3	1.6	1.6	1.7	1.4
Rhode Island	22.4	22.5	22.9	1.9	1.6	1.9	1.4
Vermont	10.6	10.8	10.5	.9	1.0	.8	1.1
Middle East	1,067.4	1,079.4	1,093.1	108.5	99.3	85.7	85.8
Delaware	9.6	9.9	9.9	.9	1.1	.6	.9
District of Columbia	23.4	23.6	24.3	1.9	2.0	1.6	1.5
Maryland	52.5	53.7	55.9	5.3	5.8	4.2	3.9
New Jersey	149.4	150.7	152.3	13.4	13.4	11.8	12.0
New York	540.3	547.2	555.8	55.0	53.1	45.8	48.3
Pennsylvania	252.8	254.0	254.1	19.9	19.6	17.9	20.5
West Virginia	39.4	40.2	40.8	4.1	4.4	3.7	3.6
Southeast	607.5	622.7	638.5	72.4	79.7	52.1	65.0
Alabama	48.1	49.6	50.9	5.1	6.5	5.0	4.3
Arkansas	34.5	34.3	35.7	3.4	3.7	3.9	4.2
Florida	87.8	91.2	97.3	14.3	14.4	9.1	11.0
Georgia	61.0	62.5	64.8	8.0	9.8	7.3	7.1
Kentucky	52.3	54.7	54.9	5.8	5.8	3.5	5.2
Louisiana	51.9	51.8	53.9	6.0	7.4	6.0	6.1
Mississippi	32.5	33.1	33.1	3.5	3.1	2.8	3.0
North Carolina	72.8	74.7	78.7	8.0	8.8	5.1	5.3
South Carolina	35.8	37.8	38.3	4.2	4.4	2.8	2.8
Tennessee	60.1	60.6	59.2	6.8	8.4	7.1	8.5
Virginia	70.7	72.4	71.7	8.3	7.5	6.4	7.6
Southwest	290.1	295.0	301.9	35.7	36.7	30.9	31.1
Arizona	18.9	18.8	19.1	2.6	2.7	2.8	2.7
New Mexico	15.9	15.8	15.9	2.2	2.3	2.5	2.1
Oklahoma	52.9	53.3	53.8	5.9	5.6	5.5	5.4
Texas	202.4	207.1	213.1	25.0	26.1	20.0	20.8
Central	1,065.0	1,092.2	1,088.7	96.4	94.8	90.5	97.7
Illinois	255.4	266.5	267.3	21.1	23.0	23.6	24.5
Indiana	97.6	96.6	97.2	8.0	8.8	9.3	8.7
Iowa	75.1	74.6	73.5	4.9	6.0	6.3	6.5
Michigan	161.4	165.5	165.8	16.8	15.3	13.8	14.0
Minnesota	79.5	79.6	79.2	5.9	5.7	6.0	5.9
Missouri	106.2	107.8	107.1	9.1	10.3	9.6	10.0
Ohio	203.1	205.1	203.0	18.3	18.9	14.9	20.6
Wisconsin	96.7	96.5	95.7	6.2	6.8	6.9	7.4
Northwest	219.5	222.0	217.7	20.6	21.7	20.0	22.3
Colorado	37.1	37.4	35.9	4.4	4.7	4.3	5.9
Idaho	14.8	14.6	13.8	1.9	1.8	2.2	2.3
Kansas	56.5	58.6	60.3	4.9	5.4	3.3	3.2
Montana	18.3	18.3	17.8	1.7	1.6	1.8	1.9
Nebraska	37.5	37.6	35.6	2.7	3.1	3.2	4.3
North Dakota	14.4	14.2	13.4	1.0	1.0	1.1	1.7
South Dakota	17.8	17.6	17.1	1.4	1.4	1.7	1.9
Utah	14.9	15.3	15.4	1.6	1.6	1.5	1.2
Wyoming	8.3	8.5	8.4	.9	1.1	.9	1.0
Far West	429.1	426.5	425.6	53.4	50.1	58.6	49.6
California	311.9	309.6	307.8	37.6	36.3	40.6	35.1
Nevada	5.4	5.2	5.2	.7	1.0	1.0	.9
Oregon	48.6	49.4	50.5	7.9	6.4	6.8	6.2
Washington	63.2	62.3	62.2	7.1	6.4	8.3	7.5

Preliminary.

Source: U. S. Department of Commerce, Office of Business Economics; *Survey of Current Business*.

No. 536.—Corporation Assets and Liabilities: 1930 to 1949

[Money figures in millions of dollars. See headnote, table 538]

ITEM	1930	1935	1940	1945	1947	1948	1949
Returns of active corporations, number	463,036	477,113	473,042	421,125	551,807	594,243	614,842
Balance sheets, number [1]	403,173	415,205	413,716	374,950	496,821	536,833	554,573
Total assets or liabilities [2]	334,002	303,150	320,478	441,461	494,615	526,136	543,562
ASSETS							
Cash [3]	21,012	23,664	41,423	57,717	64,369	65,737	63,864
Notes and accounts receivable [4]	59,675	38,690	42,864	51,630	75,959	84,597	85,526
Inventories	18,771	14,788	19,463	26,067	44,009	48,293	44,726
Investments, government obligations [5]	10,228	21,863	29,570	129,935	108,774	104,519	110,959
Other investments	83,809	90,163	80,429	74,026	78,363	84,202	91,152
Capital assets [6]	120,994	100,480	100,214	92,057	112,194	125,650	135,617
Other assets	19,511	13,501	6,514	10,029	10,945	11,538	11,709
LIABILITIES							
Notes and accounts payable	26,870	25,332	22,683	24,663	35,826	38,527	36,697
Bonded debt and mortgages	50,282	49,822	49,199	40,987	50,108	57,326	61,851
Other liabilities	95,568	89,066	110,210	221,286	227,114	232,064	238,716
Capital stock: [7]							
Preferred	19,117	19,523	17,138	14,764	15,007	14,957	15,365
Common	87,067	82,733	72,292	64,747	72,463	76,774	78,944
Surplus and undivided profits [8]	61,832	48,828	61,633	83,585	101,404	113,607	122,357
Deficit [9]	6,734	12,163	12,676	8,571	8,307	8,118	8,260
Net surplus	55,098	36,665	48,957	75,014	93,097	105,489	113,988

[1] Excludes returns with fragmentary balance sheet data.
[2] Adjustments are made in tabulating data as follows: (1) Reserves for depreciation, depletion, amortization, and bad debts, when reported under liabilities are used to reduce corresponding asset account, and "Total assets" and "Total liabilities" are decreased by amount of such reserves; and (2) a deficit in surplus, reported under assets, is transferred to liabilities, and "Total assets" and "Total liabilities" are decreased by amount of deficit.
[3] Cash in till and deposits in banks.
[4] Less reserve for bad debts. Includes loans and discounts of banks.
[5] Consists of obligations of United States or any agency or instrumentality thereof; obligations of States, Territories, and political subdivisions thereof, District of Columbia, and United States possessions.
[6] Less depreciation and depletion reserves. Includes land.
[7] For balance sheets in which common and preferred stock are not reported separately, combined amount is tabulated as "Common stock."
[8] Consists of sum of positive amounts of "Paid-in or capital surplus," "Earned surplus and undivided profits," and "Surplus reserves."
[9] Consists of negative amounts for "Earned surplus and undivided profits."

Source: Treasury Department, Bureau of Internal Revenue; Statistics of Income, Part 2.

No. 537.—Current Assets and Liabilities of U. S. Corporations: 1942 to 1952

[In billions of dollars. Covers all U. S. corporations excluding banks and insurance companies. 1942-1949 based on Bureau of Internal Revenue Statistics of Income, covering virtually all corporations in United States; for 1950-52 estimated (subject to revision), based on data compiled from many different sources, including data on corporations registered with Securities and Exchange Commission. Figures as of end of specified years]

ASSETS AND LIABILITIES	1942	1943	1944	1945	1946	1947	1948	1949	1950	1951	1952
Current assets, total	83.6	93.8	97.2	97.4	108.1	123.6	133.0	133.1	156.1	174.4	183.4
Cash on hand and in banks	17.6	21.6	21.6	21.7	22.8	25.0	25.3	26.5	27.4	29.6	31.0
U. S. Government securities	10.1	16.4	30.9	21.1	15.3	14.1	14.8	16.8	20.5	21.3	21.0
Receivables from U. S. Government [1]	4.0	5.0	4.7	2.7	.7	} 36.6	42.4	43.0	53.9	58.8	66.4
Other notes and accounts receivable	23.3	21.9	21.6	23.2	30.0						
Inventories	27.3	27.6	26.8	26.3	37.6	44.6	48.9	45.3	52.6	62.6	62.7
Other current assets [2]	1.3	1.3	1.4	2.4	1.7	1.6	1.6	1.4	1.7	2.1	2.3
Current liabilities, total	47.3	51.6	51.7	45.8	51.9	61.5	64.4	60.7	77.7	91.9	96.9
Advances and prepayments, U. S. Government [1]	2.0	2.2	1.8	.9	.1	} 37.6	39.4	37.5	47.2	55.4	61.4
Other notes and accounts payable	24.0	24.1	25.0	24.8	31.5						
Federal income tax liabilities	12.6	16.6	15.5	10.4	6.5	10.7	11.5	9.3	14.8	19.7	16.8
Other current liabilities [3]	8.7	8.7	9.4	9.7	11.8	13.2	13.5	14.0	15.7	16.7	18.7
Net working capital	36.3	42.1	45.6	51.6	56.2	62.1	68.6	72.4	78.4	82.5	86.5

[1] Receivables from and payables to U. S. Government exclude amounts offset against each other on corporation's books or amounts arising from subcontracting which are not directly due from or to U. S. Government.
[2] Includes marketable securities other than U. S. Government.
[3] Includes provisions for renegotiation other than those combined with income tax liabilities.

Source: Securities and Exchange Commission; Statistical Series, Net Working Capital of U. S. Corporations. Data are published quarterly.

No. 538.—CORPORATION RECEIPTS, DEDUCTIONS, PROFITS, AND TAX: 1925 TO 1949

[Includes data for Alaska, District of Columbia, and Hawaii; based on income tax returns as filed, prior to audit adjustments or other changes made after the returns were filed, as the result of carry-backs, relief granted under section 722 of the Internal Revenue Code, recomputation of amortization of emergency facilities, or renegotiation of war contracts. All corporations are required to file returns except those specifically exempt, such as mutual, fraternal, civic, and charitable organizations not operating for profit. Returns of inactive corporations are excluded from these tabulations, except as noted. In comparing data over a period of years, changes in law must be taken into consideration, especially discontinuance for 1934–41 of privilege of filing consolidated returns (except by railroad corporations and their related holding or leasing companies and, in 1940–41, by Pan American trade corporations) and the restoration of this privilege in 1942. See source publications for effect of changes on statistical items. Data represent combined totals for returns reporting net income and those reporting no net income. For number of returns, see table 386, p. 361]

[In millions of dollars]

ITEM	1925	1930	1935	1940	1945	1947	1948	1949
Compiled receipts, total [1]	134,789	136,355	114,850	148,237	255,449	387,746	419,966	395,480
Gross sales	106,532	97,941	85,332	114,642	203,578	304,296	339,089	320,296
Gross receipts from other operations	(?)	25,267	19,790	24,466	48,455	49,456	56,484	56,529
Other receipts	26,253	10,283	5,801	8,329	10,904	13,506	15,007	15,590
Tax-exempt income:								
Dividends from domestic corporations [3]	1,175	2,571	3,014	(?)	(?)	(?)	(?)	(?)
Interest on Government obligations [4]	526	526	714	763	513	446	369	493
Compiled deductions, total [5]	125,464	131,940	109,227	138,889	234,102	356,180	376,378	365,068
Cost of goods sold	84,716	76,190	66,279	86,739	157,377	294,200	261,404	247,311
Cost of operations	(?)	(?)	9,190	13,297	22,666	28,205	32,820	29,396
Interest paid	3,617	4,861	5,251	2,701	2,308	2,501	2,759	3,046
Taxes paid [6]	(?)	2,297	2,628	4,317	4,585	6,893	7,463	8,361
Depreciation and depletion [8]	3,336	4,449	3,701	4,003	4,620	6,489	8,049	8,897
Other deductions	33,801	44,142	24,167	28,852	39,545	57,742	63,864	65,413
Compiled net profit or loss [9]	9,316	4,649	5,428	9,348	21,345	31,515	34,588	28,387
Net income or deficit [10]	7,621	1,551	1,698	8,919	21,139	31,423	34,435	28,195
Deduction due to net loss for prior year [11]	243	166	-----	128	142	186	206	196
Total tax [12]	1,176	712	735	2,549	10,795	10,921	11,920	9,817
Compiled net profit less total tax	8,146	3,937	4,668	6,800	10,551	20,594	22,668	18,560
Dividends paid:								
Cash	5,198	8,184	3,941	6,089	6,081	8,366	9,396	9,460
Stock	544	414	136	140	334	761	1,025	664

[1] Total compiled receipts consist of gross sales (less returns and allowances), gross receipts from operations (where inventories are not an income-determining factor), all interest received on Government obligations (less amortizable bond premium), other interest, rents, royalties, excess of net short-term capital gain over net long-term capital loss, excess of net long-term capital gain over net short-term capital loss, net gain from sale or exchange of property other than capital assets, dividends, and other taxable income. Total compiled receipts exclude nontaxable income other than tax-exempt interest received on certain Government obligations.

[2] Not available.

[3] Beginning 1936, "Dividends from domestic corporations" are taxable income, tabulated with "Other receipts."

[4] Beginning 1934, includes in addition to the wholly tax-exempt interest, that which is partially tax-exempt. Interest on Treasury notes issued on or after Dec. 1, 1940, and obligations issued on or after Mar. 1, 1941, by the United States or any agency or instrumentality thereof, is wholly taxable and is included in "Other receipts" for 1941-49.

[5] Beginning 1936, includes contributions or gifts (limited to 5 percent of net income before this deduction).

[6] Excludes (1) Federal income tax and Federal excess-profits taxes; (2) estate, inheritance, legacy, succession, and gift taxes; (3) income taxes paid to a foreign country or possession of United States, if any portion is claimed as a tax credit; (4) taxes assessed against local benefits; (5) Federal taxes paid on tax-free covenant bonds; and (6) taxes reported in "Cost of goods sold" and "Cost of operations."

[7] Tabulated with "Other deductions."

[8] Includes amortization of emergency facilities for 1940 and later years.

[9] Compiled receipts less compiled deductions.

[10] Net income (or deficit), in general, represents taxable income less allowable deductions, except that for 1925 and 1930, and for 1948-49, amount shown is before deduction due to net operating loss of prior years.

[11] Estimated by corporations reporting net income.

[12] In addition to income tax, includes declared value excess-profits tax, 1933-45; defense tax, 1940; and excess profits tax under provisions of Second Revenue Act of 1940, 1940-46.

Source: Treasury Department, Bureau of Internal Revenue; Statistics of Income, Part 2.

No. 539.—CORPORATION INCOME TAX RETURNS, BY TOTAL-ASSETS CLASSES, BY INDUSTRIAL DIVISIONS: 1949

[All money figures (except assets classes) in millions of dollars. See headnote, table 538]

TOTAL-ASSETS CLASS (thousands of dollars)	Number of returns [1]	Total assets or liabilities [1]	Total compiled receipts [2]	Net income or deficit [3]	Income tax	Number of returns [1]	Total assets or liabilities [1]	Total compiled receipts [2]	Net income or deficit [3]	Income tax
	All industrial divisions					Agriculture, forestry, and fishery				
Total	554,573	543,561.7	387,635.6	27,941.1	9,688.5	6,820	1,933.9	1,533.3	171.4	63.7
Under 50	242,765	5,159.4	12,935.6	[4] 81.1	64.4	2,537	58.5	109.5	[4] .9	.8
50–100	99,878	7,176.6	15,282.1	287.7	113.6	1,352	98.3	137.5	2.8	1.5
100–250	104,262	16,435.9	32,963.2	938.0	340.2	1,565	248.4	258.4	10.1	4.7
250–500	44,634	15,567.0	29,310.2	1,105.8	433.8	706	247.9	203.1	13.6	5.7
500–1,000	25,651	17,903.3	28,962.6	1,292.5	527.8	392	273.0	207.0	19.6	7.9
1,000–5,000	27,798	59,296.1	61,612.8	3,633.7	1,400.7	239	430.8	292.0	22.0	8.5
5,000–10,000	4,680	32,383.4	24,261.0	1,752.7	661.2	22	143.1	79.0	4.8	1.7
10,000–50,000	3,761	75,811.8	53,772.3	4,448.9	1,588.5	6	95.8	73.3	15.5	5.1
50,000 and over	1,179	313,826.3	128,545.7	14,563.0	4,558.2	1	338.0	473.4	83.9	27.8
	Mining and quarrying					Construction				
Total	8,094	9,261.1	6,730.9	697.5	264.9	23,402	4,637.1	9,690.7	510.4	196.3
Under 50	2,585	53.5	86.3	[4] 4.2	1.0	11,574	233.2	870.1	[4] 1.2	3.8
50–100	1,212	88.2	117.2	[4] 1.8	1.6	4,131	294.3	845.3	20.1	7.0
100–250	1,668	266.7	309.3	9.2	6.1	4,217	660.4	1,700.4	62.8	22.4
250–500	1,004	357.8	396.0	20.4	10.1	1,863	650.1	1,509.6	76.4	28.9
500–1,000	674	470.5	482.4	22.8	13.4	887	607.6	1,280.0	74.7	28.9
1,000–5,000	713	1,481.6	1,278.3	90.5	41.0	649	1,258.6	2,239.7	151.1	57.7
5,000–10,000	114	805.5	526.2	47.7	19.1	52	364.8	493.0	34.2	13.5
10,000–50,000	105	2,246.6	1,566.7	170.6	59.4	29	568.1	752.6	92.3	34.2
50,000 and over	24	3,490.8	1,967.7	342.2	113.3					
	Manufacturing					Public utilities				
Total	110,269	123,755.1	155,285.3	14,154.9	5,446.4	22,496	71,620.0	28,410.1	2,533.1	1,040.7
Under 50	41,603	901.6	2,489.2	[4] 71.0	9.4	10,952	212.8	465.7	[4] 5.6	2.8
50–100	18,171	1,312.9	3,191.6	17.4	20.8	3,610	259.2	425.2	11.2	4.6
100–250	21,701	3,477.1	8,021.3	167.1	85.0	3,525	554.6	809.4	34.1	12.8
250–500	11,400	4,015.8	8,806.2	298.7	139.5	1,580	549.4	756.0	44.4	17.1
500–1,000	7,286	5,111.2	10,488.9	464.6	209.2	1,045	738.3	940.9	59.2	24.1
1,000–5,000	7,595	15,812.5	27,936.3	1,724.5	717.9	1,076	2,252.3	2,105.5	181.2	70.8
5,000–10,000	1,193	8,377.5	12,968.1	995.7	398.0	200	1,413.6	830.3	91.5	35.5
10,000–50,000	1,033	21,092.8	30,694.0	2,886.5	995.1	276	6,092.2	2,658.7	297.3	114.1
50,000 and over	287	63,653.7	80,669.5	7,970.4	2,871.6	232	59,547.5	19,418.4	2,117.7	758.9
	Trade					Finance, insurance, real estate, and lessors of real property				
Total	187,530	42,965.4	129,965.0	3,808.3	1,468.9	146,129	281,962.8	16,767.9	5,230.6	992.5
Under 50	85,053	1,900.3	7,154.4	[4] 97.9	22.4	56,645	1,257.0	434.4	39.5	15.2
50–100	38,392	2,761.6	9,200.5	126.9	46.5	25,375	1,821.3	426.4	77.9	20.2
100–250	38,200	5,966.4	19,660.4	422.3	141.5	27,176	4,300.8	855.9	167.5	45.0
250–500	14,302	4,948.7	16,019.4	436.5	164.6	11,646	4,060.4	697.4	158.7	45.5
500–1,000	6,592	4,505.4	13,955.9	430.5	171.2	7,663	5,448.1	745.8	163.5	49.7
1,000–5,000	4,253	8,111.7	24,166.5	804.7	308.1	12,432	28,295.2	1,965.4	515.7	138.9
5,000–10,000	414	2,845.3	7,747.0	254.4	97.7	2,587	17,856.6	1,042.8	272.3	76.2
10,000–50,000	264	4,965.1	14,615.6	473.4	178.3	2,007	39,977.1	2,771.7	736.8	173.7
50,000 and over	50	5,979.9	17,445.1	897.5	338.6	579	178,966.3	7,828.2	3,098.7	427.9
	Services					Nature of business not allocable				
Total	46,588	7,063.1	8,850.3	533.2	212.4	3,264	323.2	103.1	2.7	2.6
Under 50	29,232	513.9	1,307.7	[4] .5	8.8	2,584	28.7	18.1	[4] 1.4	.2
50–100	7,382	523.3	931.4	33.2	11.4	253	17.5	7.1	.1	.1
100–250	5,964	922.4	1,323.1	64.3	22.4	251	39.0	14.9	.6	.3
250–500	2,058	710.4	911.1	57.4	22.3	75	26.4	11.5	[4] .4	.1
500–1,000	1,023	706.2	850.8	57.2	23.0	59	42.1	10.8	.4	.3
1,000–5,000	801	1,594.6	1,614.6	143.5	57.4	35	60.7	14.5	.4	.4
5,000–10,000	86	564.7	553.5	51.9	19.5	2	12.4	1.2	.1	(5)
10,000–50,000	36	677.5	614.9	73.6	27.6	5	96.5	24.9	2.7	1.1
50,000 and over	6	850.1	743.3	52.5	20.0					

[1] Excludes returns of inactive corporations and returns on which balance sheet data are incomplete. See note 2, table 536.
[2] For items included in "Total compiled receipts," see note 1, table 538.
[3] Compiled receipts (exclusive of wholly tax-exempt interest) less compiled deductions. See table 538.
[4] Deficit.
[5] Less than $500,000.

Source: Treasury Department, Bureau of Internal Revenue; Statistics of Income, Part 2.

No. 540.—Income of Unincorporated Enterprises, by Industry: 1945 to 1951

[In millions of dollars. Income of unincorporated enterprises measures monetary earnings and income in kind of sole proprietorships, partnerships, and producers' cooperatives from their current business operations—other than supplementary income of individuals derived from renting property. Income equals business receipts (exclusive of capital gains and expenses) less business expenses (exclusive of capital losses and depletion allowances)]

INDUSTRY	1945	1946	1947	1948	1949	1950	1951
All industries, total	31,360	37,194	34,912	40,146	33,774	38,255	42,159
Agriculture, forestry, and fisheries	12,667	14,960	15,788	17,881	12,999	13,585	15,826
Farms	12,528	14,790	15,589	17,666	12,776	13,348	15,568
Other [1]	139	170	199	215	222	237	258
Mining	107	138	232	334	208	264	235
Contract construction	1,375	1,885	2,265	2,629	2,578	3,234	3,306
Manufacturing	1,929	1,976	1,400	1,072	928	1,432	1,240
Wholesale and retail trade	9,826	11,723	10,330	10,694	9,304	11,172	12,080
Wholesale trade	1,800	1,944	1,605	1,650	1,178	1,419	1,740
Retail trade and automotive services	8,126	9,789	8,725	9,044	8,126	9,753	10,340
Finance, insurance, and real estate	843	910	949	1,091	1,025	1,260	1,319
Transportation	382	422	471	509	506	558	679
Communications and public utilities	17	18	18	19	20	22	23
Services	4,434	5,152	5,459	5,917	6,204	6,858	7,309
Medical and other health services	1,604	1,902	2,101	2,282	2,379	2,608	2,665
Legal services	799	943	1,023	1,174	1,195	1,335	1,339
Personal services	702	786	735	690	810	890	980
Other services	1,329	1,551	1,601	1,770	1,820	1,970	2,225

[1] Agricultural and similar service establishments; forestry; and fisheries.

Source: Department of Commerce, Office of Business Economics; Survey of Current Business, July 1952 and National Income Supplement, 1951.

No. 541.—Corporate Income Before Federal and State Income and Excess Profits Taxes, by Industry: 1945 to 1951

[In millions of dollars. Corporate income before taxes, as included in national income statistics, represents earnings of corporations organized for profit which accrue to residents of the Nation, measured before Federal and State profit taxes, without deduction of depletion charges and exclusive of capital gains and losses. Profits accruing to residents are measured by eliminating intercorporate dividends from profits of domestic corporations and by adding net receipts of dividends and branch profits from abroad. In other respects, definition of profits is in accordance with Federal income tax regulations. Corporate income before taxes is measured net of capital gains and losses, dividends received, renegotiation refunds, and accelerated emergency amortization charges, but before deduction of depletion charges. Definition with respect to depletion charges has an important effect on data for mining industries]

INDUSTRY	1945	1946	1947	1948	1949	1950	1951
All industries, total	19,717	23,464	30,489	33,762	27,107	39,610	42,874
Agriculture, forestry, and fisheries	119	171	199	204	162	221	266
Farms	115	167	197	201	162	219	264
Forestry and fisheries	4	4	2	3	(1)	2	2
Mining	422	843	1,123	1,647	1,127	1,388	1,609
Contract construction	94	219	389	583	532	981	845
Manufacturing	10,437	12,046	17,355	19,029	14,989	23,762	24,378
Food and kindred products	1,499	2,106	1,905	1,606	1,551	1,824	1,696
Textile-mill products	784	1,462	1,593	1,582	694	1,259	1,115
Chemicals and allied products	1,024	1,474	1,776	1,696	1,665	2,778	3,090
Products of petroleum and coal	550	964	1,708	2,617	1,844	2,096	2,745
Iron and steel and their products, including ordnance	1,245	1,060	1,972	2,434	1,682	2,944	3,645
Machinery (except electrical)	805	736	1,540	1,834	1,405	1,985	2,754
Transportation equipment except automobiles	985	-34	-7	251	202	290	343
Automobiles and automobile equipment	175	102	1,259	1,680	2,100	2,405	2,749
Other	3,319	4,176	5,609	5,360	4,137	7,199	8,331
Wholesale and retail trade	3,536	5,748	6,263	5,935	3,960	5,613	5,491
Wholesale trade	1,347	2,523	2,775	2,449	1,525	2,146	2,430
Retail trade and automotive services	2,189	3,225	3,488	3,486	2,435	3,467	3,061
Finance, insurance, and real estate	1,573	1,738	1,875	2,331	2,711	2,677	2,698
Transportation	1,386	861	1,199	1,703	1,142	1,982	1,910
Communications and public utilities	1,334	1,569	1,602	1,699	1,730	2,170	2,516
Services	800	726	671	804	521	622	556
	17	186	218	207	222	313	374

[1] Less than $500,000.
[2] Profits received by domestic corporations from foreign branches are excluded here and included in industry of domestic corporation.

Source: Department of Commerce, Office of Business Economics; Survey of Current Business, July 1952 and National Income Supplement, 1951.

No. 542.—Corporate Profits, Taxes and Dividends: 1941 to 1952

[In billions of dollars. These series are as presented in official national income statistics. Corporate profits figures represent earnings of corporations organized for profit which accrue to residents of the Nation. (See also headnote, table 541.) They are given both before and after Federal and State taxes on corporate earnings. Disbursement of tax refunds have been deducted from tax liability in year in which tax liability was incurred. Net corporate dividend payments represent amount of cash dividends disbursed to residents of the Nation, and therefore are measured after elimination of intercorporate dividends. Undistributed corporate profits comprise difference between corporate profits after taxes and net dividend payments. Quarterly data are seasonally adjusted at annual rates]

YEAR AND QUARTER	Profits before taxes	Income tax liability	Profits after taxes	Dividends	Undistributed profits
1941	17.2	7.8	9.4	4.5	4.9
1942	21.1	11.7	9.4	4.3	5.1
1943	25.1	14.4	10.6	4.5	6.2
1944	24.3	13.5	10.8	4.7	6.1
1945	19.7	11.2	8.5	4.7	3.8
1946	23.5	9.6	13.9	5.8	8.1
1947	30.5	11.9	18.5	6.6	12.0
1948	33.8	13.0	20.7	7.2	13.5
1949	27.1	10.8	16.3	7.5	8.8
1950	39.6	18.4	21.2	9.0	12.3
1951	42.9	24.2	18.7	9.0	9.6
1st quarter	50.1	28.4	21.7	8.6	13.1
2d quarter	43.3	24.5	18.8	9.0	9.8
3d quarter	38.6	21.8	16.9	9.2	7.7
4th quarter	39.5	22.2	17.3	9.3	8.0
1952 [1]	39.7	22.6	17.1	9.1	8.0
1st quarter	42.7	24.3	18.4	8.9	9.5
2d quarter	38.2	21.8	16.4	9.6	6.8
3d quarter	37.2	21.2	16.0	9.3	6.7
4th quarter	40.3	23.0	17.3	9.0	8.3

[1] Fourth quarter preliminary estimates of profits based upon past relationship of corporate profits and inventory valuation adjustment to private nonfarm gross national product.

Source: Department of Commerce, Office of Business Economics; *Survey of Current Business*, July 1952 and February 1953, and the *National Income Supplement*, 1951.

No. 543.—Profits and Dividends of Public Utility Corporations: 1941 to 1952

[In millions of dollars]

YEAR AND QUARTER	RAILROAD [1]				ELECTRIC POWER [2]				TELEPHONE [3]			
	Operating revenue	Profits before taxes [4]	Profits after taxes [5]	Dividends	Operating revenue	Profits before taxes [4]	Profits after taxes [5]	Dividends	Operating revenue	Profits before taxes [4]	Profits after taxes [5]	Dividends
1941	5,347	674	500	186	3,029	774	527	437	1,334	297	187	162
1942	7,466	1,658	902	202	3,216	847	490	408	1,506	364	168	151
1943	9,055	2,211	873	217	3,464	913	502	410	1,691	420	176	156
1944	9,437	1,972	667	246	3,615	902	507	398	1,815	451	168	155
1945	8,902	756	450	246	3,681	905	534	407	1,979	433	174	162
1946	7,628	271	287	235	3,815	964	638	458	2,148	313	209	168
1947	8,665	777	479	236	4,291	954	643	494	2,283	215	138	131
1948	9,672	1,148	699	289	4,530	983	657	493	2,694	292	196	178
1949	8,580	700	438	252	5,055	1,129	757	553	2,967	333	207	213
1950	9,473	1,384	783	312	5,431	1,303	824	619	3,342	580	331	276
1951	10,391	1,260	693	328	5,867	1,480	818	661	3,729	691	341	318
1st quarter	2,440	229	104	101	1,504	413	229	157	904	175	90	77
2d quarter	2,596	275	146	63	1,419	344	195	161	918	174	92	79
3d quarter	2,583	250	124	53	1,423	320	168	162	931	160	72	81
4th quarter	2,772	505	320	111	1,521	403	226	181	976	182	86	81
1952 [6]	10,580	1,436	816	336	6,224	1,718	922	709	4,136	787	384	355
1st quarter	2,587	295	141	80	1,603	498	257	172	993	194	93	85
2d quarter	2,532	261	149	74	1,491	400	214	173	1,023	205	98	87
3d quarter	2,633	368	208	66	1,513	382	207	177	1,037	182	88	91
4th quarter [6]	2,828	512	318	116	1,618	439	244	186	1,084	206	104	93

[1] Class I line-haul railroads, covering about 95 percent of all railroad operations.
[2] Class A and B electric utilities, covering about 95 percent of all electric power operations.
[3] Revenues and profits for telephone operations of Bell System Consolidated (including the 20 operating subsidiaries and Long Lines and General departments of American Telephone and Telegraph Company) and for 2 affiliated telephone companies, which together represent about 85 percent of all telephone operations. Dividends for the 20 operating subsidiaries and 2 affiliates.
[4] After all charges and before Federal income taxes and dividends.
[5] After all charges and taxes and before dividends. [6] Preliminary.

Source: Board of Governors of the Federal Reserve System; published currently in *Federal Reserve Bulletin*.

No. 544.—Annual Sales, Profits, and Dividends of Large Manufacturing Corporations: 1942 to 1951

[In millions of dollars. Includes data for 200 corporations with assets of $10,000,000 and over. Asset classification is as of end of 1946. Profits before and after taxes are as published by the 200 companies except for certain adjustments, chiefly to exclude special charges and credits and intercorporate dividends where large. Series includes little or no representation of some important nondurable goods groups such as meatpacking, tobacco and rubber]

ASSET GROUP OR INDUSTRY	1942	1943	1944	1945	1946	1947	1948	1949	1950	1951
Assets of $50,000,000 and over (300 corporations):										
Sales	21,841	26,312	30,411	26,802	21,389	30,935	37,028	36,739	44,118	51,087
Profits before taxes	3,405	3,693	3,539	2,429	2,039	4,109	5,319	5,088	7,883	8,557
Profits after taxes	1,234	1,283	1,258	1,132	1,206	2,527	2,814	2,101	4,055	3,411
Dividends	763	779	851	864	946	1,171	1,405	1,680	2,340	1,985
Assets of $20,000,000 and over (81 corporations):										
Sales	18,544	24,160	26,851	22,280	17,415	25,686	31,239	31,578	37,631	43,390
Profits before taxes	2,876	3,111	2,982	1,976	1,573	3,423	4,593	4,506	6,902	7,492
Profits after taxes	1,056	1,007	1,091	984	932	2,106	2,380	2,788	3,566	2,975
Dividends	672	688	755	764	804	1,000	1,210	1,474	2,013	1,784
Assets of $10,000,000 to $50,000,000 (119 corporations):										
Sales	3,297	4,152	4,560	4,322	3,974	5,249	5,790	5,161	6,287	7,677
Profits before taxes	532	582	557	453	466	686	726	582	908	1,065
Profits after taxes	168	167	167	168	274	420	452	333	420	436
Dividends	91	91	96	100	142	170	194	196	226	222
NONDURABLE GOODS INDUSTRIES										
Total (94 corporations):[1]										
Sales	6,470	7,671	8,321	8,440	8,996	11,425	12,441	12,853	14,777	17,371
Profits before taxes	1,079	1,302	1,346	1,139	1,430	1,793	2,212	1,847	2,702	3,184
Profits after taxes	441	509	532	588	911	1,170	1,477	1,213	1,515	1,411
Dividends	308	327	354	364	451	563	656	710	889	848
Foods and kindred products (28 corporations):[2]										
Sales	1,760	2,116	2,399	2,538	2,800	3,239	3,538	3,323	3,492	3,873
Profits before taxes	264	326	358	369	441	428	413	379	469	407
Profits after taxes	122	139	124	149	238	263	259	235	287	190
Dividends	81	85	86	89	107	131	137	135	143	140
Chemicals and allied products (36 corporations):[2]										
Sales	2,035	2,481	2,468	2,424	2,520	3,111	3,549	3,557	4,447	5,433
Profits before taxes	463	526	508	417	461	546	656	675	1,110	1,388
Profits after taxes	157	169	160	177	281	336	409	404	560	482
Dividends	130	132	147	149	180	214	254	312	438	355
Petroleum refining (14 corporations):[2]										
Sales	1,481	1,793	2,132	2,153	2,060	2,906	3,945	3,865	4,234	4,999
Profits before taxes	179	280	286	192	269	456	721	525	550	861
Profits after taxes	112	153	190	166	214	350	548	406	442	516
Dividends	63	76	83	85	92	223	375	234	205	231
DURABLE GOODS INDUSTRIES										
Total (106 corporations):[3]										
Sales	15,371	20,641	22,000	18,162	12,394	19,510	23,587	23,886	29,341	33,696
Profits before taxes	2,330	2,391	2,193	1,290	609	2,316	3,107	3,191	5,192	5,374
Profits after taxes	783	755	726	574	296	1,357	1,837	1,887	2,542	2,000
Dividends	457	452	497	600	496	618	747	950	1,351	1,141
Primary metals and products (30 corporations):										
Sales	6,765	7,673	7,704	6,653	5,429	7,545	9,066	8,187	10,446	12,501
Profits before taxes	982	829	697	442	451	891	1,174	998	1,700	2,092
Profits after taxes	316	309	280	227	270	545	720	578	854	775
Dividends	203	200	194	193	211	247	270	285	377	230
Machinery (37 corporations):										
Sales	2,592	3,571	3,930	3,563	2,082	3,642	4,550	4,353	5,056	6,160
Profits before taxes	519	615	548	377	39	447	569	519	847	1,000
Profits after taxes	134	130	129	129	−8	273	334	330	424	345
Dividends	81	83	86	93	98	116	126	138	208	191
Automobiles and equipment (15 corporations):[3]										
Sales	4,098	6,403	7,341	5,562	3,725	6,692	8,063	9,577	11,806	12,426
Profits before taxes	567	678	697	310	809	809	1,131	1,473	3,205	1,915
Profits after taxes	250	236	240	148	−8	445	639	861	1,037	704
Dividends	120	122	170	171	138	196	282	451	671	420

[1] Includes 26 companies not shown separately, as follows: textile mill products (10); paper and allied products (15); and miscellaneous (1).

[2] For certain items, data for years 1942–44 are partly estimated for 7 companies: foods (3); chemicals (2); petroleum, textiles, and paper (1 each).

[3] Includes 25 companies not shown separately, as follows: building materials (12); transportation equipment other than automobile (6); and miscellaneous (7).

Source: Board of Governors of the Federal Reserve System; published in part in the *Federal Reserve Bulletin.*

No. 545.—Sources and Uses of Corporate Funds: 1947 to 1952

[Billions of dollars. Covers nonfinancial business corporations only, excluding banking and insurance companies which are primarily suppliers of capital funds for business or intermediaries in flow of savings from consumers to business. Based on Securities and Exchange Commission and other financial data]

ITEM	1947	1948	1949	1950	1951	1952
Uses, total	**32.9**	**28.3**	**15.4**	**40.0**	**40.3**	**31.0**
Plant and equipment	17.1	19.1	16.4	16.9	22.2	23.0
Inventories (book values)	7.1	4.2	−3.6	8.0	10.2	1.0
Receivables	7.6	4.0	−.5	9.9	4.6	4.5
From business	6.0	2.4	−2.2	7.9	1.6	(¹)
From consumers	1.8	1.4	1.4	1.5	.4	(¹)
From government	−.2	.2	.3	.5	2.6	(¹)
Cash and deposits	2.2	.3	1.1	.9	2.1	}
U. S. Government securities	−1.0	.7	2.2	4.0	.8	2.0
Other current assets	−.1	(²)	−.2	.3	.4	.5
Sources, total	**32.4**	**29.0**	**14.9**	**41.1**	**40.0**	**31.0**
Retained profits (including depletion)	11.6	12.8	8.0	11.6	9.0	7.0
Depreciation	5.2	6.2	7.2	7.8	8.8	10.5
Payables (trade)	4.6	1.2	−2.0	6.7	4.3	2.5
Federal income-tax liability	2.3	.8	−2.3	7.4	5.6	−1.0
Other current liabilities	1.0	(²)	.3	1.5	.8	1.5
Bank loans (excluding mortgage loans)	2.6	1.1	−1.9	1.5	4.2	1.5
Short-term	1.6	.5	−.8	2.0	3.6	(²)
Long-term	1.0	.6	−1.1	−.5	.6	(²)
Mortgage loans	.8	.7	.7	.9	.9	1.0
Net new issues	4.4	5.9	4.9	3.7	6.4	8.0
Stocks	1.3	1.2	1.6	1.7	2.8	2.5
Bonds	3.1	4.7	3.3	2.0	3.6	5.5
Discrepancy between total uses and total sources	−.5	−.7	+.5	−1.1	+.3	----

¹ Not available　² Less than $50,000,000.

Source: Department of Commerce, Office of Business Economics.

No. 546.—Corporate Dividends Paid, by Industrial Divisions: 1925 to 1949

[In millions of dollars. See headnote, table 538]

DIVISION	1925		1930		1935		1940	
	Cash	Stock	Cash	Stock	Cash	Stock	Cash	Stock
All industrial divisions	5,189.5	544.4	8,184.2	414.2	5,940.6	135.9	6,068.8	140.0
Agriculture, forestry, and fishery ¹	30.9	4.1	25.0	3.2	34.7	3.5	25.9	.1
Mining and quarrying ¹	335.1	3.9	302.6	12.6	257.1	3.1	282.6	3.7
Construction ¹	70.0	11.6	95.5	7.8	29.8	4.2	30.9	2.0
Manufacturing	2,223.8	267.4	3,161.0	121.9	2,193.5	49.7	2,399.6	48.0
Public utilities ¹	1,006.8	77.2	2,223.9	40.2	1,283.8	5.6	1,075.3	11.3
Trade ¹	506.1	90.5	560.8	61.7	510.1	28.6	512.5	19.1
Finance, insurance, real estate, and lessors of real property ¹	896.8	78.6	1,646.8	155.3	1,559.6	38.4	1,655.1	53.1
Services ¹	107.9	9.5	166.1	11.3	71.1	2.3	91.4	2.4
Nature of business not allocable	11.8	1.7	2.5	.1	1.0	.4	15.4	.2

DIVISION	1945		1947		1948		1949	
	Cash	Stock	Cash	Stock	Cash	Stock	Cash	Stock
All industrial divisions	6,080.8	334.4	8,365.0	700.8	9,386.5	1,024.7	9,569.1	684.2
Agriculture, forestry, and fishery ¹	27.6	1.0	59.6	1.2	63.2	4.9	60.0	2.7
Mining and quarrying ¹	159.8	1.9	315.7	9.8	464.1	25.9	420.6	13.5
Construction ¹	29.5	3.2	42.9	11.7	67.5	37.2	71.0	19.2
Manufacturing	2,824.7	146.2	4,159.2	398.8	4,636.8	637.3	4,852.3	360.1
Public utilities ¹	1,243.0	6.7	1,307.7	30.0	1,452.6	38.3	1,329.7	19.1
Trade ¹	557.4	60.7	990.8	182.3	1,077.9	199.0	976.3	161.3
Finance, insurance, real estate, and lessors of real property ¹	1,101.1	106.7	1,297.0	55.7	1,448.9	66.9	1,675.7	97.2
Services ¹	132.3	7.9	186.1	11.0	172.9	13.0	180.6	10.8
Nature of business not allocable	5.5	.2	5.9	.4	2.7	2.3	2.9	.4

¹ For changes in classification affecting comparability of data, see *Statistics of Income,* for 1938, Part 2.

Source: Treasury Department, Bureau of Internal Revenue; *Statistics of Income,* Part 2.

No. 547.—BUSINESS EXPENDITURES FOR NEW PLANT AND EQUIPMENT: 1939 TO 1953

[Millions of dollars. Figures differ from totals in gross national product (table 305) which include agricultural investment and certain equipment and construction outlays charged to current expense]

INDUSTRY GROUP	1939	1945	1947	1948	1949	1950	1951	1952	1953 [1]
Total [2]	5,512	8,682	20,612	22,060	19,295	20,605	25,644	26,455	26,391
Manufacturing	1,943	3,962	8,703	9,124	7,149	7,491	10,862	11,904	12,039
Durable goods industries	756	1,590	3,407	3,452	2,594	3,135	5,168	5,784	5,323
Primary iron and steel	122	198	636	772	596	599	1,196	1,528	1,350
Primary nonferrous metals	30	54	178	198	151	134	310	396	329
Fabricated metal products	91	216	370	343	271	350	433	335	335
Electrical machinery and equipment	49	138	304	280	216	245	272	276	444
Machinery except electrical	100	316	519	527	383	411	663	772	632
Motor vehicles and equipment	138	263	504	474	340	510	551	396	372
Transportation equipment excluding motor vehicles	42	56	95	106	87	82	219	233	211
Stone, clay and glass products	71	100	326	269	181	280	307	315	270
Other durable goods	118	265	473	510	360	534	704	632	697
Nondurable goods industries	1,187	2,366	4,296	5,651	4,555	4,356	5,654	6,210	6,516
Food and kindred products	205	337	869	721	636	523	579	540	506
Beverages	38	97	277	332	249	257	274	245	235
Textile mill products	136	209	510	618	471	480	531	400	314
Paper and allied products	67	116	371	383	368	327	620	394	380
Chemicals and allied products	176	276	1,060	941	670	771	1,247	1,451	1,571
Petroleum and coal products	403	879	1,735	2,100	1,789	1,587	2,102	2,596	2,658
Rubber products	38	119	143	102	81	102	150	130	134
Other nondurable goods	134	261	530	454	371	350	382	454	469
Mining	326	283	691	882	792	707	929	890	910
Railroad	380	648	889	1,319	1,382	1,111	1,474	1,301	1,294
Other transportation	345	574	1,296	1,285	897	1,212	1,490	1,353	1,380
Electric and gas utilities	520	505	1,539	2,543	3,125	3,309	3,664	4,236	4,368
Commercial and miscellaneous	2,078	2,699	7,492	6,806	5,980	6,775	7,235	6,980	7,000

[1] Estimates based on anticipated capital expenditures of business as reported in mid-February and mid-March, 1953.
[2] Excludes agriculture.

Source: Securities and Exchange Commission and Department of Commerce, Office of Business Economics. Data published quarterly in Statistical Series releases of the Securities and Exchange Commission and in Survey of Current Business.

No. 548.—GROSS PRIVATE DOMESTIC INVESTMENT AND ITS COMPONENTS: 1929 TO 1952

[In billions of dollars. Consists of acquisitions of newly produced capital goods by private business and nonprofit institutions and of value of change in volume of inventories held by them; covers all private new dwellings, including those acquired by owner-occupants]

CLASS	1929	1933	1940	1945	1947	1948	1949	1950	1951	1952 [1]
Gross private domestic investment, total [2]	15.8	1.3	13.9	10.7	30.2	42.7	33.5	50.3	58.5	51.4
Nonfarm producers' plant and equipment, total [3]	9.8	2.3	7.4	8.7	20.3	23.4	21.7	25.4	29.6	31.0
Equipment [3]	5.6	1.6	5.3	6.3	14.6	16.7	15.3	18.4	20.8	22.0
Construction [4]	4.2	.7	2.1	2.4	5.7	6.7	6.4	7.0	8.8	9.0
Farm equipment and construction [5]	1.1	.3	1.0	1.4	3.5	4.6	4.7	5.4	5.9	5.5
Residential construction (nonfarm) [6]	2.8	.3	3.0	1.1	6.3	8.6	8.3	12.6	11.0	11.1
Other private construction [7]	.5	.1	.2	.2	.7	1.0	1.3	1.5	1.7	1.7
Net change in business inventories, total	1.6	—1.6	2.3	—.7	—.8	5.0	—2.5	5.5	10.3	2.0
Nonfarm	1.8	—1.3	2.0	—.6	1.4	3.7	—1.6	4.6	9.4	1.4
Farm	—.3	—.3	.2	—.1	—2.2	1.3	—.9	.9	.9	.6

[1] Estimates by Council of Economic Advisers; based on incomplete data.
[2] Items for 1945 and earlier years are not comparable with those for later years. (See notes 4 and 6.)
[3] Total producers' durable equipment less "farm machinery and equipment" and farmers' purchases of tractors and business motor vehicles. These figures assume that farmers purchase 85 and 15 percent, respectively, of all tractors and motor vehicles used for productive purposes.
[4] Industrial buildings, public utilities, gas- and oil-well drilling, warehouses, office and loft buildings, stores, restaurants, and garages. Includes hotel construction prior to 1947 only.
[5] Farm construction (residential and nonresidential) plus "farm machinery and equipment" and farmers' purchases of tractors and business motor vehicles. (See footnote 3.)
[6] Includes construction of hotels, tourist cabins, motor courts, and dormitories beginning 1947.
[7] Religious, educational, social and recreational, hospital and institutional, miscellaneous nonresidential and all other private.

Source: Department of Commerce, Office of Business Economics (except as noted). Published in Economic Report of the President, January 1953.

No. 549.—BUSINESS SALES AND INVENTORIES: 1940 TO 1952

[In billions of dollars. A new series on retail sales and inventories beginning in 1951 has been substituted for the series previously published. These estimates are based on a change in the method of estimation adopted by the Bureau of Census. Retail estimates are shown in this table on the previously published basis 1940–51 and on the new basis 1951 to date. For a description of the retail sales and inventories series on the new basis see *Survey of Current Business*, September and November, 1952]

INDUSTRY	1940	1945	1947	1948	1949	1950	1951	NEW SERIES	
								1951	1952
Business sales, total (unadjusted)...	145.6	286.2	397.9	437.3	416.0	473.1	528.2	533.4	546.5
Manufacturing, total	70.3	154.5	191.0	211.6	197.0	231.7	268.0	268.0	276.5
Durable goods	29.7	75.2	80.3	91.1	84.8	106.4	126.7	126.7	132.8
Nondurable goods	40.6	79.3	110.7	120.4	112.2	125.4	141.4	141.4	143.6
Wholesale trade, total	28.9	53.7	87.3	95.2	88.3	97.7	107.2	107.2	106.1
Durable goods	7.5	10.9	24.4	27.4	24.7	31.1	34.4	34.4	32.9
Nondurable goods	21.4	42.8	62.8	67.7	63.6	66.6	72.8	72.8	73.1
Retail trade, total	46.4	78.0	119.6	130.5	130.7	143.7	153.0	158.2	164.0
Durable goods	13.6	16.0	36.7	41.9	43.9	52.9	53.2	54.5	55.2
Nondurable goods	32.8	62.0	88.0	88.6	86.8	90.8	99.8	103.7	108.8
Business inventories, end of year (seasonally adjusted) book value, total	22.2	30.9	50.6	55.6	52.3	62.4	73.2	74.1	74.9
Manufacturing, total	12.8	18.4	28.9	31.7	29.0	34.1	43.0	43.0	43.6
Durable goods	6.3	8.8	14.3	15.9	14.1	16.8	22.9	22.9	24.1
Nondurable goods	6.5	9.6	14.6	15.9	14.9	17.3	20.2	20.2	19.5
Wholesale trade, total	3.2	4.6	7.6	8.1	8.0	9.7	10.3	10.3	10.2
Durable goods	1.1	1.5	3.2	3.7	3.7	4.5	5.1	5.1	5.1
Nondurable goods	2.1	3.1	4.4	4.4	4.3	5.2	5.2	5.2	5.1
Retail trade, total	6.1	7.9	14.1	15.8	15.3	18.7	19.9	20.8	21.1
Durable goods	2.5	2.4	5.5	6.7	6.4	8.2	9.1	9.7	9.6
Nondurable goods	3.6	5.5	8.6	9.1	8.9	10.5	10.8	11.0	11.5
Ratio of inventories to sales: [1]									
Manufacturing, total	2.06	1.48	1.71	1.72	1.86	1.56	1.76	1.76	1.88
Durable goods	2.29	1.58	2.03	1.96	2.15	1.66	1.88	1.88	2.11
Nondurable goods	1.89	1.39	1.48	1.54	1.64	1.48	1.65	1.65	1.65
Wholesale trade, total	1.30	.91	1.01	.99	1.08	1.04	1.16	1.16	1.13
Durable goods	1.70	1.40	1.48	1.51	1.80	1.49	1.76	1.76	1.82
Nondurable goods	1.16	.78	.83	.77	.80	.84	.88	.88	.82
Retail trade, total	1.49	1.21	1.27	1.40	1.43	1.37	1.54	1.60	1.49
Durable goods	1.97	1.74	1.67	1.80	1.87	1.57	2.07	2.15	2.02
Nondurable goods	1.29	1.07	1.14	1.22	1.21	1.26	1.26	1.31	1.23
Manufacturing inventories, by stages of fabrication, total (unadjusted)	12.9	18.5	29.0	31.8	29.0	34.2	43.1	43.1	43.7
Purchased materials	(²)	(²)	12.6	13.2	11.4	14.7	17.0	17.0	16.6
Goods in process	(²)	(²)	7.2	7.5	6.7	8.3	11.0	11.0	12.2
Finished goods	(²)	(²)	9.2	11.1	10.9	11.1	15.1	15.1	14.8

[1] Ratio of average inventories to monthly sales; average inventories based on centered averages of end of period figures.
[2] Not available.

Source: Department of Commerce, Office of Business Economics; *Survey of Current Business* and records.

No. 550.—Net Change in Business Inventories: 1929 to 1951

[Millions of dollars. Net change in business inventories measures change in physical inventories, valued at average prices current during year. Difference between change in business inventories as thus measured and change in book value of inventories constitutes inventory valuation adjustment]

ITEM	1929	1933	1946	1945	1947	1948	1949	1950	1951
Net change in business inventories, total	1,562	−1,418	2,275	−746	−797	8,029	−2,482	5,471	10,336
Farm	−252	−271	240	−148	−2,205	1,312	−873	911	908
Nonfarm	1,814	−1,348	2,035	−598	1,408	3,717	−1,600	4,560	9,398
Net change in nonfarm inventories	1,814	−1,348	2,035	−598	1,408	3,717	−1,600	4,560	9,398
Corporate	1,558	−871	1,633	−1,027	1,383	2,158	−1,488	3,212	8,885
Noncorporate	256	−477	402	429	25	1,564	−113	1,348	513
Change in book value	1,200	1,329	2,235	79	8,712	6,168	−4,322	10,615	11,074
Corporate	1,086	1,272	1,781	−463	7,140	4,204	−3,578	8,027	10,180
Noncorporate	114	48	454	542	1,572	1,960	−744	2,588	894
Inventory valuation adjustment	614	−2,668	−200	−677	−7,304	−3,446	2,713	−6,055	−1,676
Corporate	472	−2,143	−148	−564	−5,757	−2,051	2,082	−4,515	−1,295
Noncorporate	142	−525	−52	−113	−1,547	−395	631	−1,240	−381
Net change in nonfarm inventories by industrial groups	1,814	−1,348	2,035	−598	1,408	3,717	−1,600	4,560	9,398
Manufacturing	941	−875	1,274	−1,367	965	1,314	−1,476	1,889	5,106
Change in book value	598	528	1,363	−1,132	4,417	2,746	−2,704	5,144	5,896
Inventory valuation adjustment	343	−1,406	−89	−435	−3,452	−1,532	1,228	−3,255	−780
Wholesale trade	31	−89	102	342	−21	783	122	625	426
Change in book value	−74	268	187	646	1,067	726	−418	1,638	606
Inventory valuation adjustment	105	−357	5	−164	−1,088	46	540	−1,095	−270
Retail trade	260	−485	575	258	596	1,750	−37	1,982	437
Change in book value	87	223	656	352	2,305	2,337	−762	3,294	958
Inventory valuation adjustment	173	−708	−81	−94	−1,707	−587	725	−1,312	−521
All other	612	−196	24	129	206	−30	−218	66	429
Change in book value	589	1	59	173	923	355	−43	519	525
Inventory valuation adjustment	29	−197	−35	−44	−657	−385	220	−453	−96

Source: Department of Commerce, Office of Business Economics; *Survey of Current Business*, July 1952, and *National Income Supplement*, 1951.

No. 551.—Industrial and Commercial Failures—Number and Liabilities: 1857 to 1952

[Excludes all railroad failures. Series revised beginning 1933 to exclude real estate and financial companies. These revisions bring failure record more nearly in accordance with type of concerns covered by "Total number of concerns in business," in which no changes were made. Beginning 1939, new series includes voluntary discontinuances with loss to creditors and small concerns forced out of business with insufficient assets to cover all claims, in addition to failures included in former series]

YEAR OR YEARLY AVERAGE	Total number of concerns in business [1]	Number of failures	Current liabilities (1,000 dollars)	Average liability	YEAR OR YEARLY AVERAGE	Total number of concerns in business [1]	Number of failures	Current liabilities (1,000 dollars)	Average liability
1857–1860	324,397	4,185	192,926	$91,762	1930	2,183,008	26,355	668,282	25,357
1861–1865	501,874	3,039	92,873	25,944	1931	2,125,288	28,285	736,340	26,082
1866–1870	591,373	2,648	76,488	28,905	1932	2,076,480	31,822	928,313	29,172
1871–1875	622,340	5,147	158,221	30,740	1933 [1]	1,960,701	19,859	457,520	23,761
1876–1880	677,347	7,967	186,014	16,700	1933 [1]	1,960,701	19,859	457,520	23,320
1881–1884	835,337	6,022	142,228	16,338	1934	1,973,000	12,001	333,959	27,621
1885–1890	1,036,606	10,387	148,905	14,338	1935	1,982,905	12,244	310,580	25,366
1891–1895	1,105,445	12,989	190,376	15,351	1936	2,009,935	9,607	203,173	21,148
1896–1900	1,127,566	12,147	148,094	12,192	1937	2,056,398	9,490	183,253	19,310
1901–1905	1,294,304	11,681	196,578	16,836	1938	2,101,083	12,836	246,505	19,204
1906–1910	1,653,022	12,735	176,000	14,056	1939 [1]	2,116,092	11,408	166,604	14,744
1911–1915	1,807,291	17,072	263,410	15,545	1940	2,116,008	14,768	182,620	12,350
1916–1920	1,785,249	11,932	330,617	16,917	1941	2,166,480	13,619	182,584	12,320
1921–1925	1,813,406	20,775	655,531	28,740	1942	2,170,615	11,848	135,104	11,488
1926–1930	2,104,096	23,005	514,086	21,779	1943	2,181,540	5,640	100,763	10,712
1931–1935	2,023,975	20,860	194,496	30,496	1944	2,023,007	3,221	45,338	14,069
1936–1940	2,032,785	12,064	196,437	16,282	1945	1,909,096	809	30,225	36,321
1941–1945	2,021,660	5,301	90,852	20,256	1946	2,141,897	1,129	67,349	44,654
1946–1950	2,406,660	5,052	212,305	44,783	1947	2,404,883	3,474	204,612	58,869
1951	2,047,302	20,615	441,226	39,381	1948	2,350,015	5,280	234,620	44,609
1852	2,115,312	31,214	441,744	39,018	1949	2,679,300	9,246	308,109	33,315
1853	2,177,589	33,773	400,268	19,705	1950	2,086,296	9,162	248,283	27,099
1854	3,177,568	33,146	520,105	22,471	1951	2,607,527	8,058	259,547	32,210
1855	2,199,040	33,842	463,159	20,670	1952	2,687,604	7,555	282,814	37,224
1856	2,112,770	32,909	458,268	21,094					

[1] Data for 1857–70 based on census of business by Mercantile Agency in 1857 and 1870; thereafter data represent number of concerns listed in July issue of Reference Book. See table 554 for class of industrial covered.

[1] See headnote regarding revisions. Figures in italics are comparable with preceding years.

Source: Dun & Bradstreet, Inc., New York, N. Y. Monthly data published currently in Dun's Statistical Review.

No. 552.—INDUSTRIAL AND COMMERCIAL FAILURES—NUMBER AND LIABILITIES, BY MONTHS: 1947 TO 1952

[Liabilities in thousands of dollars. Current liabilities include all accounts and notes payable and all obligations, whether in secured form or not, known to be held by banks, officers, affiliated companies, supplying companies, or the Government. Deferred liabilities (the difference between current, as defined above, and the total) are therefore long-term obligations held by the public]

YEAR	Jan.	Feb.	Mar.	Apr.	May	June	July	Aug.	Sept.	Oct.	Nov.	Dec.
Number:												
1947	202	238	254	277	378	283	297	287	292	336	313	317
1948	356	417	477	404	426	463	420	439	398	459	460	531
1949	566	685	847	877	775	828	719	810	732	802	835	770
1950	864	811	884	806	874	725	694	787	648	707	683	679
1951	775	599	732	693	755	699	685	678	620	643	587	612
1952	671	619	715	780	638	671	590	594	539	631	590	563
Current liabilities:												
1947	15,193	12,976	15,251	16,080	17,326	18,982	20,701	14,903	10,034	21,322	16,845	25,499
1948	12,965	26,619	17,481	15,296	13,814	12,163	13,876	21,442	20,703	25,114	24,416	31,731
1949	19,159	27,567	37,188	31,930	24,583	28,161	21,804	31,175	20,598	23,894	22,799	19,251
1950	26,436	22,156	27,900	21,250	22,672	18,072	19,538	18,448	15,254	16,649	18,864	21,044
1951	21,685	16,009	17,652	17,064	23,504	22,773	21,068	26,417	26,643	29,742	17,567	19,403
1952	26,208	19,474	29,232	29,530	21,193	21,222	22,789	16,322	20,138	35,049	18,757	23,400
Total liabilities:												
1947	15,193	12,976	15,251	16,080	17,521	19,297	21,512	14,903	10,099	22,229	16,624	25,499
1948	13,010	26,338	17,554	15,378	14,513	12,163	14,026	21,442	20,885	27,229	25,069	32,072
1949	19,159	27,695	38,284	33,899	24,620	29,279	22,494	31,720	20,648	24,129	23,496	19,432
1950	26,556	22,585	28,310	21,500	22,856	23,065	19,538	18,717	15,254	16,706	18,904	21,044
1951	21,912	16,414	17,652	18,054	23,641	23,143	21,532	26,528	26,826	30,122	17,592	19,403
1952	26,300	19,624	29,387	30,285	21,209	21,537	22,973	16,672	20,178	35,299	18,859	23,775

No. 553.—INDUSTRIAL AND COMMERCIAL FAILURES—NUMBER AND LIABILITIES, BY INDUSTRIAL GROUPS AND SIZE OF LIABILITIES: 1951 AND 1952

[Liabilities in thousands of dollars. See headnote, table 552]

INDUSTRIAL GROUP AND SIZE OF LIABILITIES	1951				1952			
	Number	Percent	Current liabilities	Total liabilities	Number	Percent	Current liabilities	Total liabilities
Total	8,058	100.0	259,547	262,821	7,511	100.0	283,314	286,098
Under $5,000	1,832	22.7	5,269	5,269	1,428	18.8	4,272	4,272
$5,000 to $25,000	4,160	51.6	52,227	52,227	3,884	51.0	46,016	46,016
$25,000 to $100,000	1,634	20.3	74,097	74,097	1,769	23.3	81,583	81,583
$100,000 to $1,000,000	412	5.1	89,115	91,249	512	6.7	114,032	116,098
$1,000,000 and over	20	.3	38,839	39,979	18	.2	37,411	38,129
Manufacturing	1,533	100.0	90,979	92,644	1,581	100.0	104,984	107,044
Under $5,000	239	15.6	689	689	171	10.8	504	504
$5,000 to $25,000	668	43.6	8,206	8,206	668	42.3	8,027	8,027
$25,000 to $100,000	442	28.8	21,840	21,840	509	32.2	24,664	24,664
$100,000 to $1,000,000	172	11.2	37,749	38,283	222	14.0	51,967	53,339
$1,000,000 and over	12	.8	22,486	23,626	11	.7	19,792	20,510
Wholesale trade	827	100.0	41,572	42,461	748	100.0	40,896	41,165
Under $5,000	115	13.9	342	342	95	12.7	283	283
$5,000 to $25,000	423	51.2	5,155	5,155	339	45.3	4,250	4,250
$25,000 to $100,000	221	26.7	10,840	10,840	240	32.1	11,233	11,233
$100,000 to $1,000,000	63	7.6	12,691	13,580	70	9.4	13,244	13,513
$1,000,000 and over	5	.6	12,544	12,544	4	.5	11,886	11,886
Retail trade	4,068	100.0	72,936	73,300	3,833	100.0	75,547	75,727
Under $5,000	1,143	28.0	3,280	3,280	925	24.1	2,773	2,773
$5,000 to $25,000	2,244	54.9	28,695	28,695	2,141	55.9	24,504	24,504
$25,000 to $100,000	626	15.3	26,158	26,158	670	17.5	29,371	29,371
$100,000 to $1,000,000	74	1.8	13,653	14,017	97	2.5	18,899	19,079
$1,000,000 and over	1	.0	1,150	1,150				
Construction	957	100.0	37,473	37,731	838	100.0	36,145	36,175
Under $5,000	168	17.6	486	486	114	13.6	342	342
$5,000 to $25,000	480	50.2	6,092	6,092	423	50.5	5,538	5,538
$25,000 to $100,000	233	24.3	10,359	10,359	221	26.4	10,553	10,553
$100,000 to $1,000,000	74	7.7	17,877	18,135	80	9.5	19,712	19,742
$1,000,000 and over	2	.2	2,659	2,659				
Commercial service	653	100.0	16,596	16,685	511	100.0	25,772	25,987
Under $5,000	167	25.6	472	472	123	20.1	370	370
$5,000 to $25,000	345	52.8	4,079	4,079	313	51.2	3,697	3,697
$25,000 to $100,000	112	17.2	4,900	4,900	129	21.1	5,762	5,762
$100,000 to $1,000,000	29	4.4	7,145	7,234	43	7.1	10,210	10,425
$1,000,000 and over					3	.5	5,733	5,733

Source of tables 552 and 553: Dun & Bradstreet, Inc., New York, N. Y. Monthly data published currently in *Dun's Statistical Review*.

No. 554.—INDUSTRIAL AND COMMERCIAL FAILURES—NUMBER AND LIABILITIES, BY INDUSTRIAL GROUPS AND INDUSTRIES: 1950, 1951, AND 1952

INDUSTRIAL GROUP	NUMBER			CURRENT LIABILITIES (THOUSANDS OF DOLLARS)		
	1950	1951	1952	1950	1951	1952
Grand total	9,162	8,058	7,611	248,283	259,547	283,314
Mining and manufacturing	2,074	1,533	1,581	95,094	90,970	104,954
Mining—Coal, oil, miscellaneous	26	38	42	3,335	6,820	3,794
Food and kindred products	261	209	164	16,225	14,474	12,648
Textile-mill products and apparel	420	397	388	14,909	17,313	19,669
Lumber and products	312	220	245	11,295	15,262	11,758
Paper, printing, and publishing	112	89	101	5,395	5,963	7,038
Chemicals and allied products	56	49	43	5,601	6,056	3,937
Leather and products	103	67	82	4,106	2,944	4,553
Stone, clay, and glass products	66	31	40	2,940	591	1,886
Iron, steel, and products	71	40	50	5,839	1,670	4,234
Machinery	209	106	131	10,330	10,360	19,680
Transportation equipment	62	18	44	3,772	937	2,530
Miscellaneous	376	269	251	11,346	8,580	12,028
Wholesale trade	1,016	827	748	33,594	41,572	40,896
Food and farm products	277	253	217	11,214	14,553	10,363
Apparel	39	41	51	1,336	1,265	1,745
Dry goods	26	21	35	600	387	1,475
Lumber, building materials, hardware	104	57	62	4,424	3,137	3,501
Chemicals and drugs	43	32	23	971	900	1,140
Motor vehicles and auto equipment	71	31	32	1,732	2,097	1,150
Miscellaneous	456	392	328	13,317	19,233	21,522
Retail trade	4,429	4,068	3,833	72,691	72,936	75,547
Food and liquor	941	1,063	919	10,297	13,870	13,343
General merchandise	208	139	185	4,664	4,365	3,086
Apparel and accessories	735	600	570	12,927	9,509	10,730
Furniture, home furnishings	462	408	428	9,943	12,075	10,877
Lumber, building materials, hardware	260	233	187	4,936	4,335	6,705
Automotive group	437	310	302	6,639	5,215	6,225
Eating and drinking places	831	864	828	15,020	16,498	16,097
Drug stores	116	108	107	1,714	1,845	1,908
Miscellaneous	439	363	357	6,551	5,134	6,776
Construction	912	957	838	25,651	37,473	34,145
General building contractors	282	346	317	9,235	19,779	20,812
Building subcontractors	588	577	494	14,407	13,653	14,037
Other contractors	42	34	27	2,009	4,041	1,296
Commercial service	731	653	611	21,253	16,596	25,772
Passenger and freight transportation	187	200	178	6,371	8,216	14,909
Miscellaneous public services	38	27	34	2,009	713	1,893
Hotels	29	22	28	1,948	577	1,290
Cleaning, dyeing, repairing	93	95	87	2,247	1,762	1,283
Laundries	47	42	40	1,010	1,066	851
Undertakers	10	5	10	200	100	273
Other personal services	57	57	56	659	677	987
Business and repair services	270	205	178	6,809	3,485	4,286

Source: Dun & Bradstreet, Inc., New York, N. Y. Monthly data published currently in *Dun's Statistical Review*.

No. 555.—INDUSTRIAL AND COMMERCIAL FAILURES—NUMBER AND LIABILITIES, BY STATES: 1950, 1951, AND 1952

| | NUMBER OF CONCERNS IN BUSINESS [1] | | FAILURES | | | | CURRENT LIABILITIES (THOUSANDS OF DOLLARS) | | |
| DIVISION AND STATE | | | Number | | | As percent of concerns in business | | | |
	1951	1952	1950	1951	1952	1952	1950	1951	1952
United States	2,697,977	2,537,004	9,162	8,058	7,611	0.29	248,283	259,547	283,314
New England	178,076	179,245	864	658	720	.40	21,774	22,786	27,550
Maine	16,333	16,326	48	32	32	.20	1,091	325	659
New Hampshire	10,081	9,909	47	29	25	.25	1,094	1,174	1,848
Vermont	7,217	7,187	14	5	13	.18	260	143	648
Massachusetts	88,352	89,573	500	369	368	.41	13,623	14,190	13,930
Rhode Island	16,557	15,840	89	92	87	.55	1,500	1,481	2,984
Connecticut	40,536	40,410	166	131	195	.48	4,106	5,474	7,481
Middle Atlantic	566,528	579,501	2,917	3,021	2,978	.51	78,738	92,316	114,619
New York	287,468	293,934	2,151	2,327	2,335	.79	59,786	69,092	87,729
New Jersey	94,094	96,730	346	307	319	.33	10,926	11,961	18,627
Pennsylvania	184,966	188,837	420	387	324	.17	8,056	11,263	10,263
East North Central	537,229	541,305	1,416	1,066	931	.17	36,304	29,814	35,622
Ohio	132,644	133,569	326	223	205	.15	7,019	6,530	11,254
Indiana	69,990	69,057	62	46	49	.07	2,938	1,219	1,773
Illinois	165,956	166,051	479	417	378	.23	12,925	11,317	13,158
Michigan	96,967	99,217	280	181	170	.17	8,252	6,355	5,944
Wisconsin	71,672	72,781	267	199	129	.18	5,167	4,398	3,493
West North Central	277,656	280,891	331	255	226	.08	10,615	9,138	9,361
Minnesota	56,558	57,940	59	73	69	.12	1,879	3,197	2,010
Iowa	53,043	53,338	46	47	32	.06	1,115	1,256	852
Missouri	74,883	75,788	136	81	75	.10	4,988	2,823	3,846
North Dakota	11,779	11,791	9	6	5	.04	485	109	263
South Dakota	13,815	13,969	10	6	7	.05	246	222	175
Nebraska	29,382	29,557	41	14	13	.04	721	471	557
Kansas	38,196	38,508	30	28	27	.07	611	1,048	1,658
South Atlantic	297,819	302,171	669	546	467	.15	20,107	26,627	22,150
Delaware	6,071	6,333	3	4	7	.11	139	87	174
Maryland	33,740	34,410	152	87	69	.20	5,799	4,909	3,962
District of Columbia	9,367	9,295	18	5	24	.26	639	341	695
Virginia	47,497	47,240	97	58	70	.15	2,063	4,352	1,512
West Virginia	27,863	27,688	51	71	47	.17	1,615	2,079	2,666
North Carolina	53,343	55,136	95	70	46	.08	2,956	2,601	3,384
South Carolina	24,712	24,258	11	7	10	.04	731	583	923
Georgia	45,536	43,824	94	92	51	.12	2,222	5,078	2,237
Florida	49,690	53,987	148	152	143	26	3,943	6,597	6,597
East South Central	148,300	150,804	213	193	194	.13	4,833	5,534	6,626
Kentucky	41,733	42,670	45	33	33	.08	805	684	778
Tennessee	43,936	44,904	64	82	92	.20	1,445	2,964	2,447
Alabama	35,345	35,321	59	37	41	.12	1,685	1,037	1,328
Mississippi	27,286	27,909	45	41	28	.10	898	849	473
West South Central	242,548	242,399	332	223	191	.08	11,753	16,006	10,384
Arkansas	29,590	29,617	38	27	17	.06	1,142	1,006	726
Louisiana	37,103	37,703	66	66	58	.15	2,834	6,321	1,912
Oklahoma	39,340	38,278	47	41	22	.06	834	759	1,895
Texas	136,515	136,801	181	89	94	.07	6,943	7,920	5,851
Mountain	95,145	94,889	213	174	163	.17	5,933	6,128	6,676
Montana	11,676	11,330	6	2	5	.04	285	33	280
Idaho	10,956	10,721	19	16	21	.20	523	369	447
Wyoming	6,321	6,220	4	2	1	.02	36	23	25
Colorado	28,519	28,770	55	35	12	.04	2,549	2,964	1,278
New Mexico	12,588	12,323	8	19	10	.08	223	522	250
Arizona	10,404	10,697	70	59	49	.46	1,509	1,171	1,754
Utah	11,260	11,571	34	31	50	.43	475	507	1,304
Nevada	3,421	3,257	17	10	15	.46	333	539	1,329
Pacific	263,676	265,799	2,207	1,922	1,739	.65	58,826	51,208	49,926
Washington	43,237	43,677	211	137	115	.26	4,452	2,769	3,735
Oregon	31,117	30,899	149	66	73	.24	2,820	3,067	2,677
California	189,322	191,223	1,847	1,719	1,551	.81	51,554	45,372	43,514

Represents number of names listed in July issue of the Reference Book. See table 554 for class of industries covered.

Source: Dun & Bradstreet, Inc., New York, N. Y. Monthly data published currently in *Dun's Statistical Review*.

No. 556.—PATENT APPLICATIONS AND PATENTS AND CERTIFICATES OF REGISTRATION: 1901 TO 1952

[Data include patents issued to citizens of United States and residents of foreign countries. For information on copyrights, see table 580, p. 506. See also *Historical Statistics*, series P 176–187]

CALENDAR YEAR OR PERIOD	Patent applications [1]	PATENTS ISSUED					CERTIFICATES OF REGISTRATION ISSUED				
		Total	Patents	Plant patents	Designs	Reissues	Total	Trade-marks	Trade-mark renewals	Labels	Prints
1901–1905	302,417	148,291	143,791		3,953	547	18,580	12,795		4,579	1,342
1906–1910	307,187	175,618	171,560		3,207	761	34,375	32,060		2,856	1,450
1911–1915	360,937	194,387	186,341		7,295	651	32,381	27,369		3,523	1,460
1916–1920	368,737	207,108	197,644		8,486	978	35,364	30,681		3,411	1,272
1921–1925	426,591	217,525	203,977		12,336	1,222	81,556	68,881	2,278	7,361	3,066
1926–1930	480,904	234,857	219,384		13,796	1,677	97,488	71,469	12,796	8,736	4,457
1931–1935	342,861	256,219	239,092	161	15,079	1,887	72,731	52,432	9,220	8,495	4,008
1936–1940	360,544	229,514	200,903	276	26,463	1,879	71,785	52,709	8,408	8,125	3,549
1941–1945	294,272	184,573	164,436	239	18,853	1,022	52,308	34,447	17,756	(2)	(3)
1946–1950	400,342	163,122	144,160	335	18,018	609	55,654	61,372	24,282	(2)	(3)
1946	91,072	24,775	21,819	56	2,779	121	13,841	8,116	5,725	(2)	(3)
1947	85,313	22,433	20,149	62	2,102	120	15,121	8,981	6,140	(2)	(3)
1948	75,992	25,095	22,973	44	2,945	111	16,530	11,474	5,056	(2)	(3)
1949	74,510	38,809	35,147	92	4,451	118	19,769	15,972	3,797	(2)	(3)
1950	74,396	48,009	43,072	90	4,718	129	20,393	16,839	3,564	(2)	(3)
1951	84,949	48,719	44,368	58	4,164	134	20,730	17,380	3,350	(2)	(3)
1952	68,341	46,890	43,667	101	2,969	166	19,598	16,179	3,419	(2)	(3)

[1] Figures include patents for inventions, designs, and reissues of patents. Includes applications without fees from 1918 to date.
[2] Data are for the year 1925.
[3] Figures for 1940 are for the six-months period ended June 30, 1940. On July 1, 1940, jurisdiction of prints and labels was transferred to the Copyright Office, Library of Congress, and data concerning them are compiled by that organization. (See table 580.)
[4] Excludes 150 trade-mark republications (under Trade-Mark Act of 1946) of trade-marks registered under prior acts for 1947; 19,730 for 1948; 12,963 for 1949; 2,053 for 1950; 1,297 for 1951; and 1,182 for 1952.

Source: Department of Commerce, United States Patent Office; records (not published elsewhere). Fiscal year figures published in *Annual Report of the Secretary*.

No. 557.—PATENTS AND DESIGNS GRANTED TO RESIDENTS OF FOREIGN COUNTRIES: 1948 TO 1952

[See also *Historical Statistics*, series P 180]

COUNTRY	1948	1949	1950	1951	1952	COUNTRY	1948	1949	1950	1951	1952
Total	1,994	3,166	4,406	4,888	5,635	Italy	4	13	38	82	106
						Japan			2	3	8
Argentina	24	24	25	33	57	Mexico	6	13	14	25	24
Australia	37	68	68	69	80	Netherlands	94	266	357	356	435
Austria	1	8	21	44	87	New Zealand	2	7	10	17	19
Belgium	16	31	47	91	90						
Brazil	7	10	7	11	20	Norway	7	26	42	53	64
						Poland	2			3	6
Canada	289	403	492	556	522	Scotland	25	30	59	72	81
Czechoslovakia	5	31	47	96	67	Spain	4	8	18	24	35
Cuba	8	10	20	23	18	Sweden	94	180	294	333	402
Denmark	21	17	60	74	85						
England	842	1,179	1,521	1,612	1,774	Switzerland	197	307	439	427	530
						Union of South Africa	13	13	25	27	21
Finland		4	9	23	20	Union of Soviet Socialist Republics			1	3	2
France	188	374	685	672	746	Wales	6	12	6	6	10
Germany	25	13	25	78	256	All other countries	30	48	74	69	105
Greece	9	2	3	11	6						
	3	6	9	2	5						

[1] Includes Northern Ireland and Eire.

Source: Department of Commerce, United States Patent Office; (records not published elsewhere).

No. 558.—PATENTS AND DESIGNS ISSUED TO CITIZENS OF THE UNITED STATES, BY STATE OR OTHER AREA, AND MILITARY ORGANIZATIONS: 1943 TO 1952

STATE OR OTHER AREA	1943	1944	1945	1946	1947	1948	1949	1950	1951	1952
Total	30,704	28,441	27,124	22,962	20,676	25,991	36,569	43,439	43,659	41,040
Alabama	55	80	116	63	63	80	145	134	189	139
Arizona	40	30	29	30	23	42	53	93	101	93
Arkansas	33	33	25	32	34	38	60	72	78	72
California	2,326	2,108	2,223	2,042	1,719	2,231	3,144	3,990	4,084	3,922
Colorado	134	139	108	85	106	153	216	284	288	330
Connecticut	1,114	987	916	728	738	817	1,242	1,468	1,365	1,270
Delaware	297	279	300	314	213	235	297	332	304	262
Florida	171	181	148	127	134	184	287	323	403	329
Georgia	156	108	89	82	66	107	147	214	199	215
Idaho	35	26	16	27	15	29	41	68	81	70
Illinois	3,393	3,128	2,871	2,325	2,074	2,448	3,572	4,229	4,263	4,105
Indiana	839	742	643	562	513	663	990	1,117	1,087	1,021
Iowa	259	183	183	159	109	197	288	371	377	420
Kansas	132	121	106	92	86	144	210	246	250	259
Kentucky	108	115	103	80	72	78	109	152	162	123
Louisiana	106	131	92	95	99	140	217	231	215	193
Maine	69	50	59	58	50	43	63	76	75	77
Maryland	337	365	340	310	306	353	566	671	678	604
Massachusetts	1,506	1,378	1,259	1,106	1,046	1,336	1,841	1,912	1,925	1,817
Michigan	1,876	1,697	1,607	1,189	1,083	1,346	2,024	2,417	2,642	2,347
Minnesota	468	451	368	265	270	357	512	698	734	731
Mississippi	37	35	27	20	19	27	48	59	78	67
Missouri	640	538	518	356	332	479	601	780	912	815
Montana	24	32	25	19	28	30	59	63	77	51
Nebraska	66	56	44	47	28	49	77	129	130	114
Nevada	14	17	13	11	10	17	27	36	30	39
New Hampshire	81	73	67	45	56	46	78	86	88	159
New Jersey	2,563	2,409	2,427	2,218	2,063	2,399	3,217	3,701	3,612	3,231
New Mexico	25	45	17	45	30	28	50	57	58	61
New York	5,506	5,180	4,882	4,382	3,690	4,664	6,313	7,209	6,893	6,063
North Carolina	109	103	106	77	79	116	172	248	266	234
North Dakota	74	8	16	10	38	17	24	38	41	41
Ohio	2,592	2,440	2,362	1,864	1,623	2,056	2,896	3,412	3,627	3,481
Oklahoma	274	263	330	201	208	177	378	494	529	493
Oregon	132	134	132	120	94	124	225	294	326	329
Pennsylvania	2,313	2,127	2,050	1,701	1,488	1,953	2,590	3,099	3,077	2,957
Rhode Island	258	220	338	249	293	551	382	409	313	329
South Carolina	50	37	44	29	23	49	70	98	83	76
South Dakota	17	24	12	13	12	18	29	43	40	41
Tennessee	138	137	109	97	120	123	241	294	264	287
Texas	602	522	485	414	371	511	740	992	1,060	1,108
Utah	43	37	43	21	31	30	41	70	59	77
Vermont	36	51	32	27	25	31	43	66	55	73
Virginia	190	200	150	159	159	192	296	356	327	322
Washington	239	199	228	180	203	235	382	480	438	490
West Virginia	103	127	109	102	84	85	114	162	156	123
Wisconsin	808	812	665	490	484	640	967	1,114	1,114	1,036
Wyoming	24	17	17	13	12	16	33	32	23	34
Alaska	3	3	2	5	2		3	12	8	11
Canal Zone	3	5	3	2		9	5	2	6	3
District of Columbia	205	206	203	202	157	205	279	348	385	384
Guam						1				
Hawaii	22	13	16	17	12	8	14	31	31	40
Philippine Islands	5	5								
Puerto Rico	3	1	4	2	3	2	4	6	3	6
Virgin Islands						1		2		1
U.S. Army	19	13	22	12	15	19	24	16	9	12
U.S. Navy	30	20	21	59	61	57	99	97	77	47
U.S. Marine Corps	2		4	2	2	1	2	2	2	2
U.S. Coast Guard						4	1		4	3
U.S. Air Force							1	1		1

Source: Department of Commerce, United States Patent Office; records (not published elsewhere).

No. 559.—RESEARCH AND DEVELOPMENT EXPENDITURES: 1941 TO 1952

[Government data derived from actual Federal budget expenditures for research and development plus estimates of procurement expenditures used for research and development. Industry data based on nationwide survey conducted in mid-1952 (see table 560). University data based on sample survey completed early in 1953]

YEAR	Total	SOURCE OF FUNDS			USE OF FUNDS BY—		
		Government	Industry	University	Government	Industry	University
EXPENDITURES (million dollars)							
1941	900	370	510	20	200	660	40
1942	1,070	490	560	20	240	780	50
1943	1,210	780	410	20	300	850	60
1944	1,380	940	420	20	390	910	80
1945	1,520	1,070	430	20	430	990	100
1946	1,780	910	840	30	470	1,190	120
1947	2,280	1,160	1,060	60	520	1,570	170
1948	2,610	1,390	1,150	70	570	1,820	220
1949	2,610	1,560	980	70	550	1,790	270
1950	2,870	1,610	1,180	80	570	1,980	320
1951	3,360	1,980	1,300	80	700	2,300	360
1952	3,750	2,240	1,430	80	800	2,530	410
PERCENT OF TOTAL							
1941	100.0	41.0	57.0	2.0	22.0	73.0	5.0
1942	100.0	46.0	52.0	2.0	22.0	72.0	5.0
1943	100.0	64.0	34.0	2.0	25.0	70.0	5.0
1944	100.0	68.0	30.0	2.0	28.0	66.0	6.0
1945	100.0	70.0	28.0	2.0	28.0	65.0	7.0
1946	100.0	51.0	47.0	2.0	26.0	67.0	7.0
1947	100.0	51.0	47.0	2.0	23.0	69.0	8.0
1948	100.0	52.0	44.0	3.0	22.0	70.0	8.0
1949	100.0	59.0	38.0	3.0	21.0	69.0	10.0
1950	100.0	56.0	41.0	3.0	20.0	69.0	11.0
1951	100.0	59.0	39.0	2.0	21.0	68.0	11.0
1952	100.0	60.0	38.0	2.0	21.0	68.0	11.0

Source: Department of Defense, Research and Development Board.

No. 560.—INDUSTRIAL RESEARCH AND DEVELOPMENT—RESEARCH COST AND PERSONNEL, BY INDUSTRY: 1951

[Figures cover approximately 85 percent of all industrial research and development. Based on nationwide survey of companies engaged in scientific and engineering research and development conducted in mid-1952]

INDUSTRY	Number of companies reporting	COST OF RESEARCH			RESEARCH PERSONNEL		COST RATIOS [1]	
		Total cost ($1,000)	Percent of total sales	Percent financed by Federal government	Total research employees	Number of engineers and scientists [2]	Average cost per research employee	Average cost per engineer or scientist [3]
All industries	1,994	[4] 1,783,042	2.0	47.0	[5] 230,157	[6] 80,851	$8,990	$22,100
Manufacturing	1,597	1,613,493	2.0	46.5	196,517	70,203	9,960	22,700
Food and kindred products	72	22,764	.3	3.7	2,941	1,357	8,700	16,900
Textile mill products and apparel	49	15,817	.9	14.4	1,989	734	8,500	19,200
Chemicals and allied products	275	204,170	2.5	7.1	25,211	13,181	7,900	16,500
Petroleum refining	49	92,942	.6	3.1	12,363	4,953	8,100	20,900
Stone, clay, and glass products	38	20,752	1.3	2.7	3,115	1,210	6,600	18,600
Primary metal industries	49	34,415	.4	9.6	3,705	1,703	10,100	21,600
Fabricated metal products	130	38,404	.9	31.1	6,311	2,491	6,000	16,500
Machinery (except electrical)	182	99,334	1.5	23.9	12,868	5,333	8,100	18,600
Electrical machinery	233	431,944	6.4	57.0	51,172	17,243	9,400	28,100
Transportation equipment	104	516,605	4.5	70.7	89,243	21,557	10,000	27,700
Motor vehicles and equipment	26	94,303	1.2	9.4	8,896	1,445	10,700	48,600
Aircraft and parts	62	410,085	12.7	85.0	49,915	20,166	8,700	24,300
Other transportation equipment	16	6,217	.9	52.5	432	246	15,500	30,800
Professional, scientific, and controlling instruments	182	94,447	5.7	57.6	13,442	5,664	7,500	17,900
Photographic equipment and supplies	24	30,794	4.8	29.1	4,330	1,954	7,500	17,300
Other professional, scientific, and controlling instruments	128	60,653	6.4	72.8	9,112	3,740	7,500	18,200
Other manufacturing	174	49,895	.8	31.4	7,527	3,547	6,400	14,300
Nonmanufacturing	407	170,169	1.7	50.8	33,640	10,548	5,300	16,000
Commercial consulting services	291	43,620	47.2	65.5	7,181	3,391	7,400	16,000
Nonprofit research agencies	37	28,517	84.3	56.0	4,568	2,515	6,900	11,700
Other nonmanufacturing	80	98,032	1.0	42.9	11,871	4,639	9,300	29,300

[1] Based on reports from 1,660 companies reporting both research cost and employment.
[2] Professional research staff.
[3] Operating cost of all research and development divided by average employment of research engineers and scientists.
[4] Based on reports from 1,754 companies; total including estimates for 170 companies not reporting is $1,859,100,000.
[5] Based on reports from 1,901 companies; total including estimates for 133 companies not reporting is 254,000.
[6] Based on reports from 1,795 companies; total including estimates for 170 companies not reporting is 94,000.

Source: Department of Labor, Bureau of Labor Statistics, and Department of Defense, Research and Development Board. Industrial Research and Development, January 1953 (a preliminary report).

18. Communications

This section includes financial and operating data for telephone, wire-telegraph, ocean-cable, and radiotelegraph carriers, data on newspapers, periodicals, and books, and data on the postal service. Also included are financial and statistical data relating to authorized standard (AM), FM and television radio broadcast stations and networks. Additional data on communications (e. g., number of telephones on farms, radios in occupied dwelling units, and the manufacture of communication equipment) appear in other sections of this *Abstract*.

Telephone and telegraph systems.—Since the establishment of the Federal Communications Commission in 1934, statistical coverage of communications has been concentrated in that agency. The Commission issues annually *Statistics of the Communications Industry in the United States*, which contains most of the data shown here. Additional data may be obtained from the annual reports of the American Telephone & Telegraph Co., and the Western Union Telegraph Co. Beginning in 1902, reports on the telephone and telegraph industries covering all systems and lines have been compiled at 5-year intervals by the Bureau of the Census in the Census of Electrical Industries. The last Census was taken for the year 1937.

According to the Communications Act of 1934, as amended, only common carriers engaged in interstate, or foreign, communication service are subject to the full jurisdiction of the Commission, and are required to file annual and monthly reports. The companies controlling these carriers are also required to file annual reports. Practically all the wire-telegraph, ocean-cable, and radiotelegraph carriers are subject to the full jurisdiction of the Commission. A large number of telephone carriers engaged only in intrastate service are not fully subject to the Act. However, it is estimated that the gross operating revenues of the telephone carriers reporting annually cover over 90 percent of the revenues of all telephone carriers in the United States.

The term "system" in general is used for aggregations of lines operated by the larger companies. "Bell System" as referred to in this section, consists of the American Telephone & Telegraph Co., and its principal telphone subsidiaries.

Broadcasting.—Data are from the Federal Communications Commission. The number of broadcast stations refers to the number licensed or holding construction permits. Total broadcast revenues are defined as total time sales of all networks and stations, less commissions to agencies and plus incidental revenues, such as sale of talent, program material, etc. Reports filed with the Federal Communications Commission by radio broadcast stations and networks cover substantially all units in the industry which operate in the United States and its possessions or between the United States and foreign countries.

United States Postal Service.—Data on the postal service are obtained from the *Annual Reports of the Postmaster General*. The postal statistics, unless otherwise noted, include data for outlying Territories, possessions, etc., except the Canal Zone; the Philippine Islands are excluded for all years.

Historical statistics.—See preface and historical appendix. Tabular headnotes (as "See also *Historical Statistics*, series P 170–175") provide cross-references, where applicable, to *Historical Statistics of the United States, 1789–1945*.

Note.—This section presents data for the most recent year or period available on April 22, 1953, when the material was organized and sent to the printer.

No. 561.—American Telephone & Telegraph Co. and Principal Telephone Subsidiaries (Bell Telephone System)—Summary: 1925 to 1952

[Figures are as of December 31]

ITEM	1925	1930	1935	1940	1945	1950	1951	1952
Telephones (thousands)....	11,910	15,187	13,573	17,484	22,446	35,342	37,414	39,414
Central offices (number)...	6,147	6,689	6,896	7,052	7,374	8,470	8,671	8,870
Miles of pole line............	394,529	426,212	407,454	399,838	420,009	502,892	518,987	545,934
Miles of wire (thousands)...	44,943	74,124	78,626	89,306	99,759	141,781	149,381	159,112
In underground cable..	27,769	45,116	47,639	54,339	60,789	86,963	91,007	98,689
In aerial cable...........	12,535	23,777	26,425	30,307	33,966	48,240	51,634	55,509
Open wire...............	4,230	5,231	4,562	4,660	5,084	6,578	6,750	6,914
Percent total wire mileage in cable............	90.3	92.9	94.2	94.8	95.0	96.3	96.5	96.7
Average daily telephone conversations total (thousands).	50,141	64,034	60,290	79,303	90,548	140,782	145,136	149,360
Local........................	48,051	61,150	58,066	76,560	85,877	134,870	139,125	143,231
Toll and long distance..	2,090	2,884	2,224	2,743	4,671	5,912	6,011	6,129
Total plant ($1,000)........	3,166,909	4,626,536	4,187,790	4,747,674	5,702,057	10,101,522	10,949,886	11,971,435
Operating revenue ($1,000).	787,560	1,073,228	919,116	1,174,322	1,930,890	3,261,528	3,636,462	4,036,664
Taxes ($1,000)..............	55,113	84,732	94,507	184,770	399,917	499,451	629,380	706,627
Employees (number)[1].....	306,556	391,746	268,754	323,701	474,527	602,466	648,459	682,396
American Tel. and Tel. Co., stockholders (number)	362,179	567,694	657,465	690,902	663,897	985,583	1,092,433	1,220,509

[1] Includes employees of Western Electric Co. and Bell Telephone Laboratories.

Source: American Telephone & Telegraph Co., New York, N. Y.; Annual Report.

No. 562.—Telephones—Number and Wire Mileage in All Systems, and Number of Telephones in the Bell System: 1880 to 1952

[Number of telephones represents total number of instruments in service]

DEC. 31—	Total telephones [1]	Total miles of wire [1]	Telephones in Bell System [2]	DEC. 31—	Total telephones [1]	Total miles of wire [1]	Telephones in Bell System [2]
1880...........	47,900	30,000	47,900	1933.........	16,711,000	87,000,000	16,635,000
1885...........	155,800	156,000	155,800	1934.........	16,869,000	86,800,000	16,797,000
1890...........	227,900	332,000	227,900	1935.........	17,424,000	87,200,000	17,344,000
1895...........	328,500	732,000	308,802	1936.........	18,423,000	88,100,000	18,342,000
1900...........	1,355,900	2,807,000	855,911	1937.........	[2] 19,453,401	[2] 90,831,421	19,365,000
1905...........	4,126,900	5,470,000	2,530,924	1938.........	19,953,000	92,850,000	19,855,000
1910...........	7,635,400	16,927,000	5,882,719	1939.........	20,831,000	95,150,000	20,784,000
1915...........	10,523,800	24,798,000	9,172,495	1940.........	21,928,000	99,250,000	21,861,000
1920...........	13,329,400	32,000,000	12,601,935	1941.........	23,321,000	105,550,000	23,441,000
1921...........	13,875,200	34,000,000	13,380,219	1942.........	24,919,000	108,300,000	24,852,000
1922...........	[2] 14,347,395	[2] 37,265,955	13,915,279	1943.........	26,381,000	108,000,000	26,315,000
1923...........	15,389,500	41,400,000	15,000,181	1944.........	26,869,000	109,000,000	26,943,000
1924...........	16,672,500	46,800,000	15,822,934	1945.........	27,867,000	110,700,000	27,868,000
1925...........	16,935,500	52,200,000	16,720,224	1946.........	31,611,000	116,600,000	31,597,000
1926...........	17,746,000	57,980,000	17,574,252	1947.........	34,867,000	125,500,000	34,854,000
1927...........	[2] 18,522,767	[2] 63,536,182	18,365,000	1948.........	38,205,000	137,600,000	38,193,000
1928...........	19,341,000	68,130,000	19,197,000	1949.........	40,709,000	147,300,000	40,699,000
1929...........	20,068,800	76,460,000	19,958,000	1950.........	43,004,000	156,700,000	42,904,000
1930...........	20,325,000	83,210,000	20,098,000	1951.........	45,636,000	165,100,000	45,628,000
1931...........	19,650,000	84,100,000	19,696,000	1952.........	48,056,000	176,000,000	48,052,000
1932...........	[2] 17,424,405	[2] 87,677,586	17,341,000				

[1] Partly estimated, except as indicated.
[2] Bell-owned and Bell-connecting (owned by other companies).
[2] From Bureau of the Census.

Source: American Telephone & Telegraph Co., New York, N. Y.; Annual Report and records.

No. 563.—TELEPHONE SYSTEMS—SELECTED DATA OF CLASS A CARRIERS, BY STATES AND OTHER AREAS: 1951

[For year ending Dec. 31. Class A carriers are those having average annual operating revenues exceeding $100,000]

STATE AND OTHER AREA	Miles of wire in cable (thousands)	Miles of aerial wire (thousands)	Central offices	NUMBER OF CALLS ORIGINATING FROM COMPANY AND SERVICE TELEPHONES (thousands) [1]		COMPANY TELEPHONES (thousands)			State taxes (thousands) [2]
				Local	Toll	Total	Business	Residence	
Grand total	149,311	5,499	10,270	66,630,929	2,146,403	39,915	12,346	27,569	$276,296
States, total	148,895	5,471	10,153	66,396,641	2,131,993	39,769	12,290	27,479	[3] 275,196
Alabama	1,503	123	113	1,074,662	16,118	408	108	300	1,620
Arizona	465	64	51	316,478	8,798	170	63	108	1,977
Arkansas	644	102	97	455,480	10,365	213	69	145	1,311
California	14,915	257	724	5,606,034	183,742	3,444	1,171	2,272	30,022
Colorado	1,124	123	186	757,578	13,239	454	143	311	2,197
Connecticut	3,327	48	126	1,186,031	71,196	831	229	602	2,814
Delaware	481	9	34	178,086	9,598	128	39	88	225
Dist. of Col	1,535		32	773,450	12,892	523	248	275	2,471
Florida	2,354	93	100	963,419	19,747	505	209	296	3,766
Georgia	2,167	167	164	1,352,916	22,814	554	167	387	3,555
Idaho	253	75	100	235,271	7,294	137	48	89	870
Illinois	10,350	141	368	3,597,066	165,208	2,632	905	1,727	24,307
Indiana	3,204	172	287	1,699,113	52,382	940	254	686	5,671
Iowa	1,447	160	183	892,900	24,812	507	131	376	2,046
Kansas	1,397	196	234	783,369	17,812	489	127	362	3,119
Kentucky	1,369	131	181	833,391	16,914	391	104	287	1,716
Louisiana	2,110	138	158	1,409,184	20,528	537	156	380	4,288
Maine	655	66	145	314,189	16,238	213	56	157	1,154
Maryland	2,777	73	169	939,411	33,774	703	195	508	4,469
Massachusetts	5,623	63	330	2,451,632	126,895	1,646	481	1,165	9,591
Michigan	7,735	184	475	3,473,056	68,160	2,036	535	1,502	8,866
Minnesota	2,366	142	206	1,383,066	29,999	709	202	508	3,929
Mississippi	777	123	164	545,029	14,451	234	69	165	2,190
Missouri	3,840	171	279	1,896,356	38,019	1,001	314	688	5,632
Montana	203	68	97	232,793	4,762	138	42	95	674
Nebraska	694	75	123	391,111	8,922	215	62	153	1,536
Nevada	163	32	25	46,991	1,665	30	12	18	355
New Hampshire	423	44	112	196,917	13,118	146	38	109	671
New Jersey	6,736	53	246	2,113,372	248,864	1,740	496	1,244	13,384
New Mexico	287	55	58	226,494	5,429	124	50	74	607
New York	21,881	155	815	7,630,887	244,403	5,451	1,963	3,488	60,473
North Carolina	1,693	156	202	998,835	25,612	457	138	319	4,149
North Dakota	158	67	134	180,620	4,746	89	26	63	722
Ohio	8,573	202	513	3,842,441	83,248	2,202	504	1,696	12,123
Oklahoma	1,849	156	205	1,059,316	23,534	519	158	361	3,198
Oregon	1,389	80	170	752,040	25,676	421	130	290	3,397
Pennsylvania	10,660	134	529	3,991,658	180,119	2,591	786	2,104	7,063
Rhode Island	869	10	40	389,023	14,112	247	71	176	1,985
South Carolina	895	93	77	485,382	11,126	214	63	151	1,768
South Dakota	209	57	143	204,036	4,888	116	32	84	645
Tennessee	2,210	160	216	1,670,698	21,906	642	178	464	4,458
Texas	7,869	446	624	4,021,090	77,703	1,828	585	1,242	12,316
Utah	469	50	71	429,178	6,709	203	56	147	954
Vermont	195	47	89	116,789	7,800	85	23	62	429
Virginia	2,726	119	191	1,116,307	33,405	648	201	447	3,228
Washington	2,253	151	249	1,220,262	35,367	714	228	492	6,085
West Virginia	929	60	129	600,583	18,365	343	95	248	1,412
Wisconsin	2,629	112	138	1,134,566	24,385	734	220	514	5,124
Wyoming	215	41	49	135,084	3,150	75	24	51	410
Canada	[4]	4							1
Cuba	1								112
Hawaii	335	16	46	236,388	5,703	109	35	74	539
Puerto Rico	80	8	71	57,900	2,707	36	21	15	448

[1] Party estimated.
[2] Includes county, municipal and other taxing-district taxes. Excludes excise taxes collected by telephone carriers from users of telephone services.
[3] Includes $396,000 not distributed by States.
[4] Less than 500.

Source: Federal Communications Commission; annual report, *Statistics of the Communications Industry in the United States.*

No. 564.—TELEPHONE SYSTEMS—SUMMARY, CLASS A CARRIERS: 1926 TO 1951

[Excludes intercompany duplications. Covers class A telephone carriers filing annual reports with F. C. C. Class A carriers are those whose average annual operating revenues exceeded $100,000. Gross operating revenues of class A carriers (excluding intercompany duplications of Bell System) reporting in 1937 represented approximately 94 percent of revenues of all telephone carriers as reported for Census of Electrical Industries for that year. Figures include data for carriers consolidated and merged for which annual data are available]

[All money figures in thousands]

YEAR	Miles of wire (thousands)	Telephones (thousands)	Employees, number [1]	Total compensation [2]	YEAR	Miles of wire (thousands)	Telephones (thousands)	Employees, number [1]	Total compensation
1926	54,541	14,412	323,217	$432,210	1943	102,064	22,529	348,127	$751,711
1927	73,775	17,026	357,778	550,210	1944	102,747	23,868	364,967	806,890
1928	84,660	17,139	347,106	555,981	1945	104,368	24,514	398,768	936,000
1929	92,349	14,336	267,871	370,073	1946	110,029	28,308	536,175	1,206,431
1930	92,878	15,187	266,699	402,836					
1937 [2]	96,612	17,086	296,777	480,721	1947	117,651	31,277	586,682	1,435,809
1938	98,689	18,396	304,596	387,145	1948	129,206	34,234	585,486	1,686,687
1939	98,761	20,697	344,949	602,981	1949	138,367	36,416	559,718	1,754,108
1940	102,587	22,168	350,465	670,274	1950	147,380	38,295	564,964	1,797,841
					1951	154,810	40,426	586,809	1,975,585

YEAR	Number of carriers	Investment in telephone plant	DEPRECIATION AND AMORTIZATION RESERVES		Operating revenues	Operating ratio [4] (percent)	Taxes	Net operating income after all tax deductions	Net income	Dividends declared
			Amount	Ratio to investment (percent)						
1926	91	$4,471,737	$1,105,264	24.74	$973,043	59.65	$96,176	$196,107	$150,976	$184,963
1927	87	4,546,662	1,191,737	26.20	1,052,215	64.25	121,542	233,594	204,329	185,582
1928 [2]	81	4,657,695	1,266,009	27.05	1,112,644	67.27	142,386	221,821	201,301	189,602
1929	81	4,793,944	1,323,849	27.60	1,115,020	66.00	152,065	204,702	170,730	185,384
1930	78	4,904,826	1,375,177	24.10	1,172,129	66.13	163,895	232,107	205,984	185,026
1937	78	5,071,277	1,437,737	28.34	1,243,292	65.33	193,627	237,391	221,234	185,080
1941	78	5,289,237	1,525,542	28.21	1,274,776	64.40	243,454	245,912	209,916	184,461
1942	78	5,645,345	1,647,905	29.18	1,555,437	63.42	337,151	231,123	175,719	182,915
1943	75	5,745,125	1,814,873	31.56	1,742,474	63.53	398,706	241,937	194,819	182,474
1944	77	5,852,545	1,986,875	33.94	1,869,022	64.17	438,457	231,174	184,232	186,236
1945	76	6,056,982	2,166,601	35.77	2,037,079	65.99	420,628	274,193	190,645	193,206
1946	74	6,681,967	2,349,391	35.16	2,211,519	75.73	273,162	263,634	227,237	199,314
1947	73	7,736,202	2,513,296	32.28	2,355,810	80.38	260,761	201,421	170,664	203,973
1948	71	9,105,035	2,664,206	29.26	2,773,408	78.92	310,634	274,121	228,475	218,755
1949	71	9,962,486	2,795,205	28.00	3,066,485	77.47	366,640	322,099	252,214	234,261
1950	71	10,702,322	2,979,466	27.84	3,444,568	71.52	525,985	454,999	371,820	295,723
1951	66	11,546,513	3,186,344	27.60	3,817,537	70.66	589,279	460,160	377,423	303,375

[1] Number on Dec. 31 prior to 1943; end of October, thereafter.
[2] Data for 1926 through 1930 include estimates.
[3] In comparing figures in this table, consideration should be given to the minor effect of revisions of Uniform System of Accounts, effective Jan. 1, 1932, and Jan. 1, 1937, resulting in certain changes in and rearrangements of the balance sheet and income statement.
[4] Ratio of operating expenses to operating revenues.

Source: Federal Communications Commission; annual report, *Statistics of the Communications Industry in the United States.*

No. **565.**—Domestic and International Telegraph Carriers—Summary: 1930 to 1951

[All money figures in thousands except average compensation. Figures show development of principal carriers filing annual reports with F. C. C. Data for earlier years restated on basis of currently effective systems of accounts: Radiotelegraph effective Jan. 1, 1940; wire-telegraph and ocean-cable effective Jan. 1, 1943]

ITEM	1930	1935	1940	1945	1948	1949	1950	1951
DOMESTIC TELEGRAPH								
Number of carriers	2	2	2	1	1	1	1	1
Investment in plant and equipment	$379,869	$383,216	$375,021	$357,784	$310,295	$306,316	$294,451	$284,293
Depreciation and amortization reserves	$53,095	$42,574	$97,746	$157,243	$136,267	$133,979	$128,227	$123,825
Capital stock [1]	$104,144	$106,282	$109,874	$104,836	$104,836	$104,836	$104,836	$104,836
Funded debt [1] [3]	$157,602	$175,858	$88,861	$90,981	$80,408	$77,261	$55,922	$51,122
Total surplus [4]	$111,332	$115,986	$114,256	$56,233	$48,105	$45,607	$52,084	$54,670
Number of revenue messages transmitted (1,000) [5]	211,971	176,250	191,645	244,629	201,878	185,673	188,947	189,637
Message revenues	$132,041	$92,776	$96,670	$154,585	$153,692	$141,100	$146,054	$154,909
Total operating revenues	$148,522	$106,262	$114,587	$182,048	$183,429	$171,393	$177,994	$192,069
Operating revenue deductions [4]	$139,141	$96,076	$110,856	$174,848	$185,362	$173,505	$167,280	$182,023
Operating ratio (percent)	93.87	90.41	96.74	96.04	101.05	101.23	93.98	94.76
Operating income [4]	$8,596	$10,186	$6,222	$7,200	*$1,932	*$1,112	$8,664	$6,059
Net income transferred to earned surplus	$3,942	$3,213	$372	*$7,854	$1,265	*$3,468	$7,353	$4,711
Dividends declared	$8,188	$2,090	$1,045	$2,433	$1,228		$2,450	$3,381
Miles of wire in cable (1,000)	357	425	449	481	386	373	333	370
Miles of aerial wire (1,000)	1,912	1,820	1,820	1,766	1,246	1,065	929	855
Number of employees	[7] 84,962	62,257	[6] 59,670	[6] 63,446	[6] 48,967	[6] 41,660	[6] 40,482	[6] 40,319
Total compensation	$108,557	$65,030	$74,736	$126,662	$140,901	$125,871	$116,937	$127,818
Average compensation per employee per annum	$1,278	$1,045	$1,252	$1,996	$2,877	$3,021	$2,889	$3,170
INTERNATIONAL TELEGRAPH								
Ocean-cable:								
Number of carriers	5	5	5	5	5	5	4	4
Investment in plant and equipment	$119,966	$116,329	$111,129	$109,317	$98,256	$96,289	$97,283	$88,496
Depreciation and amortization reserves	$53,930	$61,579	$64,492	$69,722	$64,614	$64,689	$63,911	$55,420
Capital stock [1]	$73,723	$60,723	$45,841	$24,941	$23,180	$22,255	$22,255	$18,255
Funded debt [1] [3]	$26,050	$21,768						
Total surplus [4]	$26,876	$9,515	*$10,926	$10,587	$2,737	[6] $737	$1,212	$2,104
Number of revenue messages transmitted (1,000) [5]	15,258	9,050	7,667	10,531	11,022	10,390	9,969	10,059
Message revenues	$27,245	$15,633	$16,733	$25,334	$22,655	$21,453	$23,392	$21,190
Total operating revenues	$27,811	$16,093	$17,840	$26,727	$23,857	$23,154	$24,649	$27,062
Operating revenue deductions [4]	$19,813	$14,948	$16,039	$21,704	$24,303	$23,262	$22,263	$23,829
Operating ratio (percent)	71.24	92.89	89.90	81.21	101.87	100.47	90.32	88.05
Operating income [4]	$7,712	$1,002	$1,434	$4,013	*$464	*$132	$1,937	$2,179
Net income transferred to earned surplus	$9,403	$962	$1,573	$5,524	*$824	$188	$2,165	$1,949
Dividends declared	$15,416	$2,710	$987	$20	$706	$353	$884	$353
Miles of wire in cable (1,000)	104	109	111	107	107	100	98	[6] 89
Miles of aerial wire (1,000)	10	7	8	9	9	7	7	7
Number of employees	[7] 6,880	[6] 5,394	[6] 4,534	[6] 4,962	[6] 5,973	[6] 5,671	[6] 5,495	[6] 5,483
Total compensation	$9,795	$6,926	$6,602	$10,982	$13,265	$13,037	$12,031	$13,037
Average compensation per employee per annum	$1,424	$1,284	$1,456	$2,213	$2,220	$2,301	$2,189	$2,391
Radio-telegraph:								
Number of carriers	7	8	8	6	7	7	7	7
Investment in plant and equipment	$27,270	$31,379	$30,886	$28,306	$37,370	$38,043	$38,885	$38,812
Depreciation and amortization reserves	$11,064	$15,034	$16,748	$16,475	$17,473	$18,208	$18,929	$18,509
Capital stock [1]	$15,922	$7,554	$7,724	$10,456	$13,614	$13,614	$13,614	$13,182
Funded debt [3]	$4,875	$15,812	$1,227	$1,026	$7,236	$7,821	$8,807	$8,419
Total surplus [4]	$1,242	$3,200	$18,600	$14,098	$10,986	$11,411	$13,777	$16,924
Number of revenue messages transmitted (1,000) [5]	5,151	6,619	8,952	10,516	11,114	10,501	12,609	13,984
Message revenues	$6,358	$8,314	$12,537	$18,903	$19,683	$20,367	$22,239	$25,278
Total operating revenues	$7,549	$9,267	$14,247	$23,152	$22,491	$23,441	$25,684	$29,887
Operating revenue deductions [4]	$7,197	$8,745	$10,996	$16,201	$23,132	$22,697	$22,963	$25,258
Operating ratio (percent)	95.34	94.37	77.18	69.98	102.85	96.83	89.41	84.51
Operating income [4]	$272	$479	$2,259	$771	*$1,145	$243	$1,867	$2,178
Net income transferred to earned surplus	$372	*$269	$2,025	$2,383	*$454	$431	$2,373	$2,577
Dividends declared		$1,400	$838	$850	$2	$5	$8	$10
Number of employees	[7] 2,119	[6] 2,740	[6] 3,549	[6] 4,617	[6] 5,671	[6] 5,483	[6] 5,264	[6] 5,628
Total compensation	$3,809	$4,107	$6,207	$14,171	$18,452	$18,232	$18,209	$20,083
Average compensation per employee per annum	$1,798	$1,499	$1,749	$3,069	$3,254	$3,325	$3,459	$3,568

[1] Data for Western Union included in domestic telegraph; not segregable between domestic telegraph and ocean-cable operations. [3] Includes long-term advances from affiliates.
[5] Principally as estimated by reporting carriers on basis of actual counts for test periods.
[4] Includes depreciation and operating taxes.
[5] After recorded provision for Federal income taxes for entire company operations (including non-communications activities). [6] Deficit or other reverse item.
[7] End of June.   [6] End of December.   [6] End of October.

Source: Federal Communications Commission; annual report, *Statistics of the Communications Industry in the United States.*

No. 566.—RADIOTELEPHONE SERVICE, BY CLASS: DECEMBER 31, 1951

[Covers radiotelephone service offered by 35 of the 56 class A telephone carriers; in addition, radiotelephone service with revenue amounting to $1,279,595 is offered by 3 radiotelegraph carriers, 1 cable carrier, and 4 small telephone carriers, details for which were not reported]

CLASS OF SERVICE	Number of chargeable calls	Gross revenues
FIXED STATIONS		
Message service, total	1,151,532	$10,645,796
Overseas, total	876,292	9,831,349
Bermuda and trans-Atlantic	328,772	4,132,195
Central and South American and Caribbean	251,511	2,688,640
Trans-Pacific	296,009	3,604,414
Interstate, intrastate, intraterritory and intrapossession	275,300	817,537
Private line service		342,162
MOBILE STATIONS		
Marine service to mobile stations	500,916	757,531
General service	381,562	692,157
Dispatching service	119,354	65,374
Domestic public land mobile radio services	2,783,883	3,383,152
General service	1,922,263	2,490,607
Direct dispatching service	811,180	834,990
Signalling or paging service	50,421	50,296
Other		8,349
Private mobile radiotelephone systems		1,915,835

[1] Includes monthly charges, installation and move charges.

Source: Federal Communications Commission; annual report, *Statistics of the Communications Industry in the United States.*

No. 567.—WESTERN UNION TELEGRAPH CO.—LINE AND WIRE MILEAGE, OFFICES AND FINANCES: 1867 TO 1952

YEAR ENDING—	Miles of pole line and cable [1]	Miles of wire [1]	Number of offices [2]	Receipts	Expenses	Net income [5]
June 30—				*Dollars*	*Dollars*	*Dollars*
1867	46,270	85,291	2,565	6,568,925	3,944,008	2,624,920
1870	54,109	112,191	3,972	7,138,738	4,910,772	2,227,966
1880	85,645	233,534	9,077	12,782,895	6,948,957	5,833,938
1890	183,917	678,997	19,382	22,387,029	15,074,304	7,312,735
1900	192,705	933,153	22,900	24,758,570	18,593,206	6,165,364
1910	214,360	1,429,049	24,825	33,889,202	26,614,302	7,274,900
Dec. 31—						
1915	238,940	1,610,709	25,142	52,475,721	40,972,541	11,503,180
1920	246,214	1,449,710	24,881	121,473,685	108,134,041	13,339,644
1925	246,307	1,635,236	24,428	129,151,617	112,861,832	16,289,785
1930	256,763	1,948,938	24,296	133,235,751	123,987,519	9,248,232
1935	254,691	1,905,858	20,964	91,389,312	86,131,234	5,258,078
1940	249,343	1,914,615	19,140	101,277,546	97,655,965	3,621,581
1945	276,064	2,291,164	18,687	[4] 194,271,046	[4] 189,836,541	[4] 4,434,505
1946	[6] 215,892	[6] 2,067,687	18,588	185,189,220	196,189,919	[7] [6] 11,000,699
1947	[6] 167,616	[6] 1,786,285	18,232	208,969,995	199,828,649	9,141,346
1948	[6] 158,564	[6] 1,675,558	17,460	197,782,367	197,953,988	[7] [6] 171,621
1949	[6] 146,990	[6] 1,477,925	16,835	181,944,962	185,308,346	[7] [6] 3,363,401
1950	[6] 132,274	[6] 1,337,768	16,202	189,436,704	180,500,859	[6] 8,935,845
1951	[6] 122,566	[6] 1,264,293	15,355	203,792,458	197,824,468	[6] 5,967,990
1952	[6] 120,797	[6] 1,233,473	14,704	196,435,299	195,157,510	[6] 1,277,789

[1] Pole and wire mileages reflect acquisition on Oct. 7, 1943, of facilities of Postal Telegraph Companies.
[2] Excludes agency and commission offices, numbering 10,974 on Dec. 31, 1952.
[3] Figures for 1915 and prior years represent net income before bond interest.
[4] Effective Jan. 1, 1943, the Federal Communications Commission prescribed a new system of accounts for telegraph carriers, and receipts and expenses as stated above for subsequent years are not fully comparable with results for prior years.
[5] Net income from current operations, before extraordinary adjustments of income applicable to prior years.
[6] Excludes controlled pole lines and wires no longer recorded in plant records.
[7] Deficit.   [8] After extraordinary credits and charges.

Source: Western Union Telegraph Co., New York, N. Y.; *Annual Report.*

No. 568.—COMMERCIAL BROADCAST STATIONS ON THE AIR, BY STATES AND OTHER AREAS: 1952 AND 1953

[Stations licensed or holding construction permits]

STATE OR OTHER AREA	1952 (as of Jan. 1)				1953 (as of Jan. 1)			
	Total	AM	FM	TV	Total	AM	FM	TV
Total	3,039	2,287	644	108	3,125	2,367	629	129
Alabama	89	72	15	2	101	79	18	4
Arizona	27	25	1	1	30	27	1	2
Arkansas	47	42	5		50	44	6	
California	184	132	40	11	191	140	40	11
Colorado	36	33	3		38	32	3	3
Connecticut	36	26	9	1	34	25	8	1
Delaware	9	6	2	1	9	6	2	1
District of Columbia	19	7	8	4	20	7	9	4
Florida	98	76	20	2	102	79	21	2
Georgia	102	77	22	3	105	80	22	3
Idaho	27	23	4		26	23	3	
Illinois	122	75	42	5	124	78	41	5
Indiana	66	43	21	2	71	46	22	3
Iowa	66	47	18	1	67	49	16	2
Kansas	38	36	2		39	37	2	
Kentucky	58	45	11	2	57	45	10	2
Louisiana	57	44	12	1	58	45	12	1
Maine	16	14	2		17	15	2	
Maryland	36	22	11	3	36	23	10	3
Massachusetts	74	50	22	2	75	51	22	2
Michigan	92	61	25	6	96	67	23	6
Minnesota	58	49	7	2	57	48	7	2
Mississippi	48	44	4		49	45	4	
Missouri	63	49	12	2	66	53	11	2
Montana	25	25			25	25		
Nebraska	24	21	2	1	26	23	1	2
Nevada	11	10	1		11	10	1	
New Hampshire	15	12	3		15	12	3	
New Jersey	32	19	12	1	32	19	11	2
New Mexico	25	24		1	28	27		1
New York	153	94	46	13	156	98	45	13
North Carolina	139	97	40	2	141	99	40	2
North Dakota	13	13			13	13		
Ohio	127	71	42	14	129	74	41	14
Oklahoma	50	42	6	2	52	45	5	2
Oregon	52	44	8		55	46	8	1
Pennsylvania	174	114	53	7	171	113	49	9
Rhode Island	17	11	5	1	16	11	4	1
South Carolina	58	45	13		59	46	13	
South Dakota	13	12	1		14	13	1	
Tennessee	72	61	9	2	72	61	9	2
Texas	216	184	26	6	221	187	24	10
Utah	22	18	2	2	22	18	2	2
Vermont	9	9			10	10		
Virginia	78	57	19	2	82	59	20	3
Washington	60	52	7	1	62	53	7	2
West Virginia	52	37	14	1	55	39	15	1
Wisconsin	75	57	17	1	77	61	15	1
Wyoming	13	13			14	14		
Alaska	10	10			10	10		
Hawaii	12	12			14	12		2
Puerto Rico	23	23			23	23		
Virgin Islands	1	1			2	2		

Source: Federal Communications Commission, *Annual Report.*

No. 569.—Total Broadcast Revenues of All Networks and Stations, AM and AM-FM, FM and TV: 1937 to 1951

[Total broadcast revenues are defined as total time sales of all networks and stations, less commissions to agencies and plus incidental revenues, such as sale of talent, program material, etc.]

YEAR	TOTAL		AM AND AM-FM [1]		FM (INDEPENDENTS)		TV [2]	
	Number of stations	Revenues (thousands)	Number of stations	Revenues (thousands)	Number of stations	Revenues (thousands)	Number of stations	Revenues (thousands)
1937	629	$114,223	629	$114,223				
1938	660	111,346	660	111,346				
1939	706	123,662	706	123,662				
1940	765	147,147	765	147,147				
1941	826	165,785	817	165,779	2		6	36
1942	902	176,694	851	176,839	5	$13	6	42
1943	892	215,428	841	215,318	5	26	6	84
1944	886	275,580	875	275,299	4	32	6	219
1945	912	299,715	901	299,338	5	30	6	336
1946	1,043	339,236	1,025	322,553	8	17	10	666
1947	1,581	365,032	1,464	363,714	52	422	15	1,906
1948	1,974	416,867	1,834	406,995	103	1,261	37	8,621
1949	2,323	446,544	2,621	413,785	104	1,429	98	34,320
1950	2,336	550,400	2,143	442,100	86	1,400	107	106,900
1951	2,374	686,100	2,200	449,200	66	1,200	108	235,700

[1] Includes revenues of 4 nationwide networks and regional networks.
[2] Includes revenues of 4 TV networks beginning in 1948 when commercial TV network operation started.

Source: Federal Communications Commission.

No. 570.—Employment, Hours, and Earnings in the Radio and Television Broadcasting Industry: October 1950

CLASSIFICATION	TOTAL			NETWORKS AND OWNED AND OPERATED STATIONS			OTHER BROADCASTING STATIONS [1]		
	Number of employees	Average scheduled weekly—		Number of employees	Average scheduled weekly—		Number of employees	Average scheduled weekly—	
		Hours	Earnings		Hours	Earnings		Hours	Earnings
All full-time employees except general officers and assistants	46,793	40.0	$73.00	9,350	38.5	$96.00	37,443	40.0	$68.50
Staff program employees:									
Supervisory	2,301	41.0	97.00	224	39.0	177.00	2,077	41.5	88.50
Nonsupervisory	14,203	38.5	73.00	2,255	36.0	107.00	11,948	39.0	67.00
Technical employees:									
Supervisory	2,429	41.5	98.50	199	39.5	160.00	2,230	42.0	90.50
Nonsupervisory	10,670	40.5	76.00	1,888	39.5	104.50	8,782	41.0	70.00
Commercial employees:									
Supervisory	1,205	41.5	120.00	98	39.0	197.50	1,107	41.5	113.00
Nonsupervisory	3,897	41.0	86.50	281	38.5	138.00	3,616	41.0	82.50
Promotion and publicity employees:									
Supervisory	319	40.0	114.50	94	39.5	150.50	225	40.0	96.00
Nonsupervisory	486	39.5	72.00	224	39.5	92.00	262	39.5	54.50
Clerical employees	9,103	40.0	48.00	3,155	40.5	55.00	5,948	40.0	44.50
Building-service employees	1,716	37.5	47.00	707	37.0	59.50	1,009	38.5	38.00
All other employees except general officers and assistants	464	39.0	78.00	225	40.0	107.00	239	38.0	59.50
Full-time general officers and assistants	2,769	[3]	[4]162.50	164	[3]	[4]391.00	2,605	[3]	[4]146.50
All part-time employees except general officers and assistants	10,503	[3]	[4]69.00	3,323	[3]	[4]162.00	7,180	[3]	[4]32.00
Part-time general officers and assistants	567	[3]	[4]77.50				567	[3]	[4]77.50

[1] Includes all stations not owned and operated by networks.
[3] Not reported.
[4] Average actual weekly earnings.

Source: Department of Labor, Bureau of Labor Statistics.

No. 571.—Radio Stations Authorized and Operators Licensed, by Class, as of June 30: 1950, 1951, and 1952

CLASS OF STATION OR OPERATOR	1950	1951	1952	CLASS OF STATION OR OPERATOR	1950	1951	1952
Safety and special radio authorization	**66,382**	**96,944**	**98,393**	Land transportation—Con.			
				Urban transit	100	111	110
Aeronautical	23,794	34,061	32,603	Intercity bus	30	31	34
Aircraft	20,118	30,832	29,963	Taxicab	2,750	3,152	3,639
Ground	3,676	3,229	2,640	Highway truck	107	270	341
Marine	24,921	29,544	35,500	Automobile emergency	58	85	146
Ship	22,601	26,681	32,229	Experimental	466	404	369
Ship radar	1,125	1,625	1,958	Disaster communications		2	71
Coast	130	116	107				
Alaskan coastal	340	344	379	Broadcast stations [1]	4,510	4,592	4,762
Alaskan fixed public	524	517	568	Standard (AM)	2,303	2,385	2,420
Other	201	261	259	Frequency modulation (FM)	732	659	648
				Television (TV)	109	109	108
Public safety	7,607	9,129	11,143	Television (experimental and auxiliary)	206	213	221
Police	5,618	6,198	7,008	Noncommercial educational (FM)	82	95	104
Fire	276	432	764	Facsimile	(2)	(2)	(2)
Forestry—Conservation	1,307	1,728	2,070	International	40	40	40
Highway maintenance	238	408	555	Remote pickup	1,003	1,043	1,175
Special emergency	168	313	670	Studio transmitter (ST)	29	42	44
State Guard		50	76	Developmental	6	6	2
Industrial	6,009	9,551	13,680	**Radio operators and amateur stations**	**712,895**	**792,019**	**904,597**
Power	3,601	5,016	6,065	Commercial operators	416,881	474,155	561,572
Petroleum	1,380	2,416	3,787	Aircraft radiotelephone operators	120,550	137,988	117,564
Forest products	246	453	685	Amateur operators	86,662	88,729	110,968
Special industrial	724	1,451	2,740	Amateur stations	87,967	90,587	113,092
Low-power industrial	93	150	259	Citizens stations	335	560	1,401
Relay press	26	35	51				
Motion picture	20	21	23				
Other	9	9	50				
Land transportation	3,495	4,253	5,027				
Railroad	450	604	757				

[1] Stations licensed or holding construction permits.
[2] Commercial facsimile broadcasting is now authorized over FM broadcast facilities.

Source: Federal Communications Commission; *Annual Report.*

No. 572.—Comparative Financial Data for All Networks and Standard Broadcast Stations: 1947 to 1951

[In thousands of dollars, except number of networks and stations]

ITEM	1947	1948	1949	1950	1951
Number of networks	7	7	7	7	7
Number of stations	1,464	1,824	2,021	2,143	2,200
Broadcast revenues, total	363,714	406,995	413,785	443,058	419,226
Broadcast expenses of networks and stations	291,918	342,904	357,522	372,314	389,975
Broadcast income before Federal income tax	71,796	64,092	56,263	70,743	59,251
BROADCAST REVENUES					
Revenues from time sales, net	326,117	366,428	375,050	401,089	404,551
Commissions to regularly established agencies, representatives, brokers and others	*47,970*	*50,292*	*50,307*	*52,476*	*51,561*
Revenues from time sales, total	374,087	416,720	425,357	453,565	456,112
Revenues from network time sales, net	134,727	141,052	134,898	131,530	122,034
Payments to foreign stations and elimination of miscellaneous duplications	*3,551*	*3,896*	*1,863*	*1,411*	*431*
Network time sales to:					
Nationwide networks	131,265	137,619	130,766	126,044	113,984
Regional networks	4,975	4,868	3,854	3,962	4,664
Miscellaneous networks and stations	2,038	2,462	2,141	2,935	3,817
Revenues from non-network time sales to:					
National and regional advertisers and sponsors	91,581	104,760	108,315	118,824	119,539
Local advertisers and sponsors	147,779	170,908	182,144	203,211	214,519
Revenues from incidental broadcast activities, total	37,597	40,567	38,735	41,968	44,675
Talent	19,599	22,196	21,998	25,202	26,889
Sundry broadcast revenues	17,998	18,371	16,737	16,766	17,786

Source: Federal Communications Commission. Published annually in multilithed release, *Final AM and FM Financial Data.*

No. 573.—COMPARATIVE FINANCIAL DATA FOR THE 4 NATIONWIDE STANDARD BROADCAST NETWORKS AND THEIR KEY STATIONS: 1947 TO 1951

ITEM	1947	1948	1949	1950	1951
Number of key stations	11	11	11	11	11
Total broadcast revenues	$91,222,718	$95,785,942	$95,409,849	$95,609,651	$89,066,007
Total broadcast expenses	75,091,412	80,506,811	79,995,870	80,435,393	82,251,085
Broadcast income (before Federal income taxes)	16,141,306	15,280,131	15,413,979	15,174,258	6,836,922

No. 574.—COMPARATIVE FINANCIAL DATA FOR 1,830 STANDARD BROADCAST STATIONS BY CLASS OF STATION AND TIME OF OPERATION: 1950 AND 1951

[All broadcast income is before Federal income taxes. Only those stations identical for both years with respect to class, time and network affiliation are included. Excludes 12 stations of networks]

ITEM	1950	1951	Percent increase 1950 to 1951
Averages per station:			
Total (1,830 stations):			
Total broadcast revenues	$178,883	$182,443	2.0
Total broadcast expenses	148,610	154,314	3.8
Broadcast income	30,273	28,129	[1] 7.1
Clear channel 50 kilowatts unlimited (58 stations [2]):			
Total broadcast revenues	1,067,756	1,035,328	[1] 3.0
Total broadcast expenses	795,149	812,863	2.2
Broadcast income	272,607	222,465	[1] 18.4
Clear channel 5 to 25 kilowatts unlimited (42 stations):			
Total broadcast revenues	342,236	347,085	1.4
Total broadcast expenses	286,578	295,948	2.5
Broadcast income	55,656	51,137	[1] 4.7
Clear channel 5 to 25 kilowatts part-time (6 stations):			
Total broadcast revenues	214,316	235,773	10.0
Total broadcast expenses	177,644	185,429	4.4
Broadcast income	36,672	50,344	37.3
Regional unlimited (847 stations):			
Total broadcast revenues	249,567	254,412	1.9
Total broadcast expenses	204,992	212,880	3.8
Broadcast income	44,575	41,532	[1] 6.8
Regional part-time (215 stations):			
Total broadcast revenues	92,988	94,128	5.5
Total broadcast expenses	85,782	89,423	4.2
Broadcast income	7,206	8,700	20.7
Local unlimited (736 stations):			
Total broadcast revenues	93,110	98,029	5.3
Total broadcast expenses	82,199	86,413	5.1
Broadcast income	10,911	11,616	6.5
Local day and part-time (119 stations):			
Total broadcast revenues	64,538	67,210	4.2
Total broadcast expenses	60,567	63,608	5.0
Broadcast income	3,971	4,302	8.3

[1] Decrease.   [2] Includes 5 stations clear channel 50 kilowatts, part-time.

No. 575.—BROADCAST REVENUES AND INCOME OF STANDARD BROADCAST STATIONS AND NETWORKS: 1950 AND 1951

SOURCE	1950				1951			
	Total broadcast revenues		Broadcast income [1]		Total broadcast revenues		Broadcast income [1]	
	Amount	Percent of total	Amount	Percent of total	Amount	Percent of total	Amount	Percent of total
Total	$443,067,945	100.00	$70,742,312	100.00	$443,228,953	100.00	$59,256,749	100.00
Networks, including owned and operated stations	110,475,458	24.94	18,984,342	26.84	104,028,974	23.16	10,094,533	17.04
Networks and their key stations	97,461,908	22.00	15,134,406	21.40	91,792,076	20.43	7,215,392	12.18
Other network owned and operated stations	13,014,550	2.94	3,849,936	5.44	12,236,898	2.73	2,879,441	4.86
Other stations	332,579,387	75.06	51,758,920	73.16	345,197,109	76.84	49,155,916	82.96
Network outlet stations	232,788,768	52.54	42,154,659	61.00	235,538,934	52.43	39,316,136	66.3
Other stations	99,790,619	22.52	9,604,261	12.16	109,658,175	24.41	9,839,780	16.6

[1] Before Federal income taxes.

Source of tables 573–575: Federal Communications Commission. Published annually in multilithed release, Final AM and FM Financial Data.

No. 576.—Financial Data of Television Networks and Broadcast Stations: 1950 and 1951

[In millions of dollars]

ITEM	1950			1951		
	Broadcast revenues	Broadcast expenses	Broadcast income [1]	Broadcast revenues	Boradcast expenses	Broadcast income [1]
Industry total	105.9	115.1	[2] 9.2	235.7	194.1	41.6
4 networks (including owned and operated stations)	55.5	65.5	[2] 10.0	128.4	117.4	11.0
Other stations	50.4	49.6	.8	107.3	76.7	30.6

[1] Before Federal income tax. [2] Represents loss.

Source: Federal Communications Commission; annual report, *Statistics of the Communications Industry in the United States.*

No. 577.—Periodicals—Number, Circulation, and Receipts, by Type: 1947

[Circulation and money figures in thousands]

TYPE	Number published	Aggregate circulation per issue	Receipts	TYPE	Number published	Aggregate circulation per issue	Receipts
Total	4,610	384,628	$1,045,523	Labor	183	3,694	$6,877
				Legal	85	273	3,319
Agriculture and farm, general	95	16,514	38,060	Medical and dental	143	1,894	11,392
				Military and naval	21	622	1,841
Agriculture and farm, specified	144	6,005	10,957	Motion picture	31	8,272	15,032
Art, music, and drama	54	2,730	5,322	Religious	951	47,191	42,752
Business and finance	127	2,013	31,211	Science and technology	106	3,918	13,658
Comics	263	89,478	41,829	Sports, outdoor, hobbies, etc	206	8,977	36,412
Educational	177	14,565	21,845	Trade. merchandising	472	5,310	62,348
Fashions	38	5,746	31,603	Trade: professional, institutional, and service	298	3,099	31,146
Fiction	180	35,332	44,572				
Fraternal and clubs	98	14,388	9,163	Trade: industrial, engineering, and technical	489	6,166	79,421
General interest, news, and current events	203	64,228	343,865	University, college, and school	17	64	418
Geography and travel	20	1,187	6,293	Women's service	21	22,556	100,489
Home and garden	32	11,867	39,874	All other	139	5,699	8,766
Juvenile	17	2,837	7,058				

Source: Department of Commerce, Bureau of the Census; 1947 Census of Manufactures report.

No. 578.—NEWSPAPERS AND PERIODICALS—NUMBER AND CIRCULATION, BY FREQUENCY OF ISSUE, AND RECEIPTS: 1929 TO 1947

[Circulation and money figures in thousands]

FREQUENCY OF ISSUE AND RECEIPTS	1929	1931	1933	1935	1937	1939	1947
NEWSPAPERS							
Total number	10,176	9,299	6,884	8,266	8,826	9,173	10,282
Aggregate circulation per issue [1]	91,778	86,457	76,299	87,696	96,296	96,476	119,587
Daily (except Sunday):							
Morning:							
Number	459	455	432	464	506	473	400
Circulation	15,742	15,480	14,782	15,984	17,311	17,152	21,796
Evening:							
Number	1,627	1,589	1,471	1,573	1,560	1,567	1,484
Circulation	26,274	25,813	22,849	24,887	26,034	25,814	31,490
Sunday:							
Number	578	555	489	523	526	542	416
Circulation	29,012	27,453	25,454	29,196	32,713	33,007	42,736
Weekly:							
Number	7,075	6,313	4,218	5,337	5,839	6,212	7,705
Circulation	18,884	16,173	12,048	15,185	17,287	18,295	21,408
Semiweekly:							
Number	381	339	240	332	348	343	228
Circulation	1,580	1,353	1,028	1,724	1,720	1,990	928
Triweekly:							
Number	56	48	34	37	46	36	21
Circulation	287	184	140	121	231	219	151
Other:							
Number							56
Circulation							1,069
Receipts, total	$1,073,119	$886,523	$667,820	$760,247	$861,689	$845,687	$1,792,328
Subscription and sales	275,781	261,569	239,147	260,224	287,509	306,192	599,925
Advertising	797,338	624,954	428,673	500,023	574,180	539,495	1,192,413
PERIODICALS							
Total number	5,157	4,887	3,459	4,019	4,202	4,985	4,610
Aggregate circulation [1]	202,022	183,527	174,759	178,621	224,275	229,693	354,628
Daily:							
Number	207	204	177	196	163	230	112
Circulation	932	831	794	682	791	1,979	842
Triweekly:							
Number	8	9	6	7	8	12	5
Circulation	25	31	25	22	33	27	5
Semiweekly:							
Number	27	38	30	27	45	50	21
Circulation	1,402	1,284	1,811	2,129	2,556	2,995	182
Weekly:							
Number	1,158	1,066	878	966	954	1,109	892
Circulation	34,495	30,782	39,365	42,648	56,115	55,825	69,393
Semimonthly:							
Number	224	205	145	171	179	198	233
Circulation	9,168	6,375	4,593	5,808	7,548	8,135	13,832
Monthly:							
Number	2,799	2,552	1,664	2,009	2,063	2,328	2,253
Circulation	133,048	122,671	103,193	102,194	124,521	134,766	194,824
Quarterly:							
Number	562	629	462	510	547	698	647
Circulation	20,605	19,576	23,238	23,277	25,806	26,238	45,535
Other:							
Number	172	184	97	133	243	380	447
Circulation	2,346	1,978	1,742	2,161	6,903	9,726	60,015
Receipts, total	$597,445	$497,254	$269,294	$329,564	$407,835	$409,027	$1,045,522
Subscription and sales	184,545	163,698	128,292	143,466	171,961	184,572	419,782
Advertising	322,900	243,556	141,002	186,098	235,874	224,455	625,741

[1] Calculated by totaling returns for average circulation per issue as made for individual publications.

Source: Department of Commerce, Bureau of Census; 1947 Census of Manufactures report.

No. 579.—Book Publishing—Number of Copies Sold and Receipts, by Type: 1947

[In thousands]

TYPE	ALL EDITIONS			
	Number of copies sold			Receipts
	Total	Hard-bound	Paper-bound	
Books, total	487,216	277,450	209,766	$435,134
Textbooks:				
Elementary and high school	74,254	53,285	20,969	55,068
College	23,821	22,547	1,274	52,513
School workbooks (except educational tests)	41,070	843	40,227	13,227
Religious books:				
Bibles and testaments	9,248	4,703	4,545	9,285
Prayer books	2,606	1,372	1,234	1,558
General religious books and hymnals	30,689	15,619	15,070	18,050
Technical and professional books	17,467	11,676	5,791	48,837
Mail-order books, including book clubs	54,429	45,546	8,883	65,423
Subscription books	14,626	13,880	746	63,851
Trade books:				
Adult	140,414	48,673	91,741	69,963
Juvenile	53,752	49,962	3,790	20,289
Other books	24,840	9,344	15,496	20,070
All pamphlets, total, including educational test	402,290	....	402,290	20,656

Source: Department of Commerce, Bureau of the Census; 1947 Census of Manufactures report.

No. 580.—Registration of Copyrights by Subject Matter: Fiscal Years, 1947 to 1952

[For information on patents, see table 556, p. 493. See also *Historical Statistics*, series P 170-175 for data on total registrations and on the registration of books, musical compositions, and commercial prints and labels]

SUBJECT MATTER OF COPYRIGHT	1947	1948	1949	1950	1951	1952
Total	230,215	238,121	201,190	210,564	200,354	203,705
Books	53,925	54,774	51,562	54,894	50,533	49,402
Printed in the United States	49,243	51,546	48,323	50,144	45,879	44,834
Books proper	9,903	9,786	10,254	11,323	11,272	11,623
Pamphlets, leaflets, etc	34,940	35,797	33,929	34,383	31,199	29,991
Contributions to newspapers and periodicals	4,400	5,963	4,140	4,438	3,408	3,320
Printed abroad in a foreign language	3,970	2,545	2,644	3,710	3,536	3,382
English books registered for ad interim copyright	712	683	595	1,040	1,118	1,187
Periodicals (numbers)	58,340	59,699	54,163	55,436	55,129	56,509
Lectures, sermons, addresses	972	1,203	1,036	1,007	698	837
Dramatic or dramatico-musical compositions	6,456	6,128	5,159	4,427	3,992	3,766
Musical compositions	68,709	72,339	48,210	52,309	48,319	51,538
Maps	1,779	1,456	2,314	1,638	1,992	2,422
Works of art, models, or designs	4,044	3,938	3,281	4,013	3,428	3,305
Reproductions of works of art	540	309	239	326	453	520
Drawings or plastic works of a scientific or technical character	2,147	1,619	1,063	1,316	953	980
Photographs	1,838	1,844	1,134	1,143	770	995
Commercial prints and labels	9,674	10,619	13,233	13,320	11,981	11,770
Prints and pictorial illustrations	6,506	6,686	4,358	4,309	3,590	2,891
Motion picture photoplays	666	632	667	782	835	798
Motion pictures not photoplays	1,418	999	1,096	1,113	1,314	1,281
Renewals of commercial prints and labels	21	20	13,675	14,531	16,372	16,690
Renewals of all classes	13,180	15,796				

Source: The Library of Congress, *Annual Report*.

No. 581.—United States Postal Service—Summary: 1800 to 1952

[See text, p. 496. Leaders indicate no data. For financial data, see also *Historical Statistics*, series P 155-167]

YEAR ENDING JUNE 30—	Number of post offices	Mileage of post routes [1]	FINANCES (thousands of dollars)			Revenue per capita, dollars	MONEY ORDERS ISSUED (thousands of dollars)		Number of ordinary postage stamps issued, millions	Number of pieces of mail handled, millions [4]
			Gross revenue	Gross expenditure	Surplus (+) or deficit (—)[2]		Domestic [5]	International [7]		
1800	903	20,817	281	214	+67					
1810	2,300	36,406	552	496	+56					
1820	4,500	72,492	1,112	1,161	—49					
1830	8,450	115,176	1,851	1,933	—82					
1840	13,468	155,739	4,544	4,718	—175	0.27				
1850	18,417	178,672	5,500	5,212	+287	.94			[6] 2	
1860	28,498	340,504	8,518	19,171	—10,658	.37			216	
1865	20,550	142,340	14,556	12,695	+917	.42	[6] 1,360		387	
1870	28,492	231,232	18,880	23,999	—5,096	.49	34,054	[7] 22	466	
1875	35,547	277,873	26,791	33,611	—6,820	.61	77,431	1,965	682	
1880	42,989	343,888	33,315	36,542	—3,222	.66	100,353	3,464	876	
1885	51,252	365,251	42,061	50,046	—7,481	.76	117,559	6,840	1,465	
1890	62,401	427,990	60,882	66,260	—5,384	.97	114,363	13,230	2,220	4,005
1895	70,064	456,026	76,983	87,180	—10,200	1.12	156,709	12,906	2,795	5,134
1900	76,688	500,980	102,355	107,740	—5,410	1.34	228,921	16,749	3,999	7,130
1905	68,131	486,805	152,827	167,399	—14,504	1.83	306,903	47,516	5,751	10,188
1910	59,580	447,998	224,139	229,977	—5,881	2.43	547,994	99,743	9,067	14,850
1915	56,380	432,334	287,248	296,546	—11,332	2.85	666,139	60,772	11,236	
1920	52,641	435,342	437,150	454,322	—17,370	4.11	1,322,709	32,980	13,213	
1925	50,957	464,260	599,591	639,282	—39,745	5.28	1,532,567	32,660	17,387	26,525
1930	49,063	503,915	705,484	803,667	—98,216	5.75	1,714,876	72,708	16,209	27,828
1935	45,685	514,126	630,795	696,503	—65,808	4.94	1,820,957	30,429	13,610	22,362
1940	44,024	541,514	766,949	807,629	—40,764	5.84	2,094,543	21,666	16,381	27,749
1944	42,161	549,093	1,112,877	1,068,987	+43,892	8.06	4,371,873	29,961	19,105	34,931
1945	41,792	550,903	1,314,240	1,145,002	+169,139	9.41	4,810,300	33,137	20,340	37,912
1946	41,751	551,415	1,224,572	1,353,650	—129,062	8.69	4,748,066	32,736	19,180	36,318
1947	41,769	608,900	1,399,141	1,504,805	—305,655	9.02	4,199,610	41,523	19,542	37,428
1948	41,664	640,339	1,410,971	1,687,759	—276,834	9.62	4,554,944	51,264	20,432	40,280
1949	41,607	662,379	1,571,851	2,149,297	—577,471	10.53	4,846,918	41,796	21,047	43,555
1950	41,464	668,266	1,677,487	[8] 2,222,906	—545,462	11.06	4,598,024	56,978	20,647	45,064
1951	41,193	674,488	1,776,816	2,341,382	—564,563	11.51	5,237,970	28,495	21,522	46,906
1952	40,919	(7)	1,947,316	2,666,844	—719,584	12.40	5,933,646	38,604	22,087	49,741

[1] Excluding rural free delivery routes, ocean mail routes, and airmail routes to foreign countries.
[2] Audited postal surplus or deficit which is greater or less than excess of receipts or expenditures by the amount of adjusted losses and contingencies.
[3] Domestic excludes and international includes foreign countries on domestic basis.
[4] Continental United States only. Data for years prior to 1926 are estimates.
[5] Postage stamps first issued under act of Mar. 3, 1847, and placed on sale at New York July 1, 1847.
[6] From Nov. 1, 1864, when money-order system first went into operation, to June 30, 1865.
[7] From Sept. 1, 1869, to June 30, 1870. International money orders first issued under convention of Oct. 12, 1867.
[8] Reduced by $1,747 for repayment of items over 10 years old. [9] Not available.

No. 582.—Postal Service Revenues, by Source: 1920 to 1952

[In thousands of dollars. For years ending June 30. See text, p. 496.]

ITEM	1920	1925	1930	1935	1940	1945	1950	1951	1952
Total	437,150	599,591	705,484	630,795	764,949	1,314,246	1,677,487	1,776,816	1,947,316
Ordinary postal revenue	434,409	585,333	696,429	595,358	732,137	1,246,777	1,606,940	1,696,744	1,860,708
Stamps, postal cards, etc.[1]	379,587	507,572	574,851	473,407	521,753	958,770	882,313	882,357	948,430
Second-class postage paid in money (pound rates)[1]	25,100	29,619	28,594	18,431	23,082	25,296	[2] 40,261	[2] 41,304	[2] 44,230
Other postage paid in money under permit	12,960	29,301	73,545	95,206	176,502	252,318	[2] 678,042	[2] 742,009	[2] 839,163
Box rents	6,143	7,817	8,586	6,595	7,681	11,033	14,407	15,101	15,768
Miscellaneous	414	1,024	996	3,718	2,917	4,371	10,917	13,781	18,120
Money-order revenues	10,314	12,909	17,498	20,434	28,995	46,671	63,416	65,755	70,417
Revenue from postal savings	2,420	1,349	1,562	12,013	10,817	20,792	8,131	14,318	14,191

[1] For volume of this item, see table 586.
[2] Beginning 1945, includes fees; previously included with miscellaneous.
Source of tables 581 and 582: Post Office Department, *Annual Report of the Postmaster General.*

No. 583.—Postal Service Expenditures, by Object: 1920 to 1951

[In thousands of dollars. For years ending June 30. See text, p. 496; for total expenditures, see table 581. Data cover expenditures during specified fiscal year, whether on account of that year or of previous years]

ITEM	1920	1925	1930	1935	1940	1945	1950	1951
Service in post offices (total)	234,102	338,046	429,571	378,407	479,731	721,871	1,404,390	1,395,016
Salaries of postmasters	40,108	47,562	52,850	44,588	49,238	72,544	109,100	111,920
Salaries of clerks, etc	102,319	153,336	201,972	173,510	222,778	368,147	728,860	747,906
City delivery service	63,626	95,161	127,890	113,153	145,355	191,182	406,015	397,455
All other expenditures	28,049	41,987	46,860	47,156	62,360	89,998	160,411	137,733
Railway Mail Service	36,711	52,906	61,888	52,251	60,136	86,288	142,012	146,120
Rural Delivery Service	75,794	93,163	106,347	90,519	91,446	106,847	159,470	172,537
Transportation of domestic mail	99,520	142,141	176,984	134,676	155,883	219,347	413,820	524,960
By railroads	70,714	99,720	117,265	93,328	101,890	134,371	222,965	335,184
By other means	28,805	42,421	59,720	41,348	53,994	84,975	190,855	189,775
Transportation foreign mail	5,912	9,175	24,449	36,806	16,248	4,614	92,380	90,297
Payment account of invalid money orders	264	138	131	232	187	694	630	496
Post Office Department [1]		3,712	4,296	3,612	3,998	5,441	10,247	11,673

[1] Paid out of the General Treasury prior to 1923.

No. 584.—Transportation of Domestic Mails, by Class of Service: 1930 to 1952

[Data as of June 30 or for year ending June 30. See text, p. 496. Railway mail space units of service vary in size and character and may consist of a car, a section of a car, or a closed pouch carried on a car. Some cars are railway post offices, others are for storage only, about 20 classes of units being distinguished]

CLASS OF SERVICE AND ITEM	1930	1935	1940	1945	1950	1951	1952
Steam railway service: [1]							
Length of routes (miles)	220,416	199,016	181,500	173,138	158,878	[3]149,858	[3]140,661
Annual travel (thousand miles)—							
Regular space units	564,801	455,214	455,836	496,391	552,555	[3]502,692	[3]490,573
Prorated to 60-foot car basis	228,478	192,130	208,113	260,140	341,085	299,169	297,317
Annual expenditure (thousand dollars) [2]—							
Regular authorizations	103,970	86,806	92,217	114,658	217,274	[3]299,245	[3]292,471
Annual cost	125,243	99,676	108,485	145,267	287,781	340,539	(4)
Average rate of cost—							
Per mile of length (dollars)	471.70	436.17	508.09	662.24	1,367.55	[3]1,996.85	[3]2,079.26
Per unit mile traveled (cents)	18.41	19.06	20.23	23.09	39.32	[3]59.53	[3]59.62
Per 60-foot car mile (cents)	45.70	45.40	44.31	44.01	63.70	[3]100.03	[3]98.37
Electric railway service:							
Number of routes	224	135	85	66	35	30	24
Length of routes (miles)	7,012	4,459	2,690	1,963	1,040	912	819
Annual travel of space units (thousand miles)	9,829	6,047	3,786	3,140	1,374	1,152	1,024
Annual rate of obligation (thousand dollars)	571	349	236	224	190	171	161
Average cost per unit mile traveled (cents)	5.81	5.77	6.24	7.13	13.81	14.87	15.69
Power boat service:							
Number of routes	265	196	175	146	125	115	115
Length of routes (miles)	40,130	21,043	19,613	8,701	6,541	6,132	(4)
Annual travel (thousand miles)	4,806	2,860	2,451	1,505	1,262	1,145	[5]1,130
Annual rate of obligation (thousand dollars)	1,401	1,085	924	521	818	806	860
Average cost per mile traveled (cents)	29.15	37.95	37.71	34.64	64.84	70.36	[6]76.05
Air mail service:							
Length of routes (miles)	14,907	26,884	37,943	56,849	158,977	163,000	162,167
Miles traveled with mail (thousands)	14,939	31,149	59,236	166,576	339,160	368,702	429,107
Mail carried (million pound-miles)	(7)		6,790	18,671	122,909	84,351	[3]137,429
Cost of service (thousand dollars)	14,618	8,838	19,426	[3]35,259	[3]67,644	[3]67,946	[3]67,844
Average cost per mile (dollars)	0.98	0.28	0.33	0.21	0.20	0.18	0.16

[1] Annual expenditure (regular authorizations) represents estimated cost for transporting normal mail traffic over regular routes only, based on contracts outstanding at end of each fiscal year. Annual cost includes emergency and side and transfer service. Average rates based on regular authorizations.
[2] Subject to revision. [3] For expenditures for Railway Mail Service, see table 583. [4] Not available.
[5] Annual scheduled miles. [6] Rate per annual scheduled miles. [7] Not computed.

Source of tables 583 and 584: Post Office Department, *Annual Report of the Postmaster General.*

No. 585.—DELIVERY SERVICE—CITY AND RURAL FREE DELIVERY AND STAR ROUTE SERVICE: 1870 TO 1952

[See text, p. 496. Free city delivery was instituted in 1863; rural free delivery in 1897. Star routes are mail routes between towns which are let on a contract basis. Star route service in Alaska is not included here; data for 1952 as follows: Number of routes, 19; annual rate of obligation, $80,707]

AS OF JUNE 30	CITY FREE DELIVERY			RURAL FREE DELIVERY				STAR ROUTES	
	Number of offices	Number of carriers	Annual cost [1] (1,000 dollars)	Number of routes	Length of routes (miles)	Annual travel (1,000 miles)	Annual cost (1,000 dollars)	Number of routes (regular service)	Annual cost (1,000 dollars)
1870	51	1,362	1,231					7,295	5,050
1880	104	2,628	2,364					9,863	7,721
1885	456	5,066	7,978					15,887	5,322
1890	604	12,714	12,145					20,733	5,754
1895	796	15,822	14,671	1,259	26,685		420	22,894	5,066
1900	1,144	21,778	20,923	32,110	721,237		20,865	17,199	7,342
1905	1,692	28,715	31,738	41,079	993,068	308,007	36,915	15,425	5,926
1910	1,808	32,902	39,829	43,856	1,076,225	326,305	52,366	11,557	5,713
1915	2,096	36,142	62,841	43,445	1,151,532	348,627	75,795	10,739	11,106
1920	3,401	46,251	98,587	45,189	1,227,654	370,273	95,131	10,906	18,774
1930	3,080	53,762	126,426	43,278	1,334,842	404,738	106,338	11,785	14,281
1933	3,111	49,064	111,648	34,848	1,355,078	411,361	90,425	11,838	11,357
1934	3,124	53,852	126,371	34,118	1,368,063	415,433	92,437	11,963	10,862
1937	3,172	54,644	123,908	33,601	1,377,088	418,248	91,799	11,872	10,800
1938	3,215	55,713	126,205	33,144	1,387,445	420,107	91,196	11,893	11,055
1939	3,226	56,617	126,408	33,539	1,393,647	421,854	91,170	11,463	10,846
1940	3,275	58,531	143,766	33,646	1,401,600	424,704	91,441	11,369	10,928
1941	3,308	61,065	145,759	33,445	1,411,573	427,756	91,502	11,477	11,385
1942	3,247	63,919	155,190	33,292	1,420,971	430,725	91,636	11,400	12,027
1943	3,408	58,602	170,879	32,179	1,425,860	432,281	95,512	11,236	14,287
1944	3,732	58,046	184,113	32,112	1,428,475	433,120	104,691	11,170	16,909
1945	3,894	57,968	190,574	32,108	1,435,059	435,209	105,863	11,201	18,556
1946	4,058	65,770	245,406	32,161	1,441,536	437,248	117,403	11,218	20,063
1947	4,167	67,723	287,029	32,249	1,449,767	439,750	128,582	11,296	21,700
1948	4,270	74,127	308,435	32,412	1,455,196	444,424	131,119	11,394	23,211
1949	4,413	85,330	392,848	32,559	1,480,710	449,361	152,704	11,437	36,522
1950	4,632	90,189	405,816	32,619	1,493,365	453,290	159,387	11,599	37,446
1951	4,653	84,927	397,378	32,513	1,495,775	451,290	168,556	11,665	34,044
1952	4,765	85,345	454,800	32,546	1,499,910	455,345	188,785	11,656	36,394

[1] Represents audited expenditures; in 1880 and 1890, some incidental expense included.

No. 586.—POSTAL SERVICE OPERATION—SUMMARY FOR PRINCIPAL ITEMS: 1930 TO 1952

[For years ending June 30. See text, p. 496. For sales of postage stamps and other stamped paper and postage collected on second-class matter, see table 582]

ITEM	1930	1935	1940	1945	1950	1951	1952
Transactions in stamped paper:							
Ordinary postage stamps issued (millions)	16,369	13,610	16,241	20,240	20,647	21,522	22,067
Stamped envelopes (millions)	3,164	1,618	1,650	2,065	2,052	2,005	2,275
Postal cards issued (millions)	1,642	1,764	2,257	2,282	3,872	4,184	2,984
Pieces of mail carried [1] (millions)	27,886	22,322	27,749	37,912	45,064	46,906	48,741
Second-class matter carried:							
Free in county (1,000 pounds)	75,226	57,360	60,626	59,787	79,287	78,545	76,466
Paid at pound rates (1,000 pounds)	1,654,415	1,068,389	1,283,673	1,319,567	2,146,599	2,205,162	2,367,209
Foreign mails dispatched by sea:							
Letters, post cards (1,000 pounds)	7,108	4,602	4,231	31,426	5,283	4,861	5,361
Other articles (1,000 pounds)	53,377	53,066	62,257	474,160	364,073	316,028	319,134
Mail registered:							
Domestic, paid (1,000 pieces)	76,489	41,315	40,588	[2] 51,094	[2] 67,971	[2] 71,180	[2] 67,538
International, paid (1,000 pieces)	7,860	3,444	2,713	(2)	(2)	(2)	(2)
Official, free (1,000 pieces)	8,863	10,852	12,082	[2] 22,907	[2] 18,084	[2] 18,540	[2] 15,055
Registry fees (1,000 dollars)	12,807	[2] 7,100	6,835	[2] 17,705	[2] 18,477	[2] 19,308	[2] 21,676
Mail insured:							
Domestic, parcel post (1,000 pieces)	126,421	71,960	80,918	131,384	196,509	196,784	201,294
International (1,000 pieces)	649	311	280	(2)	(2)	(2)	(2)
Total fees paid (1,000 dollars)	4,775	5,349	5,702	[2] 12,389	[2] 22,028	[2] 22,394	[2] 22,121
Mail sent C. O. D.:							
Total pieces sent (1,000)	46,249	31,118	34,645	[2] 44,146	[2] 62,104	[2] 60,109	[2] 46,814
Total fees (1,000 dollars)	5,825	4,208	4,748	[2] 10,830	[2] 18,906	[2] 18,241	[2] 20,196

[1] Continental U. S. only.
[2] Includes "insured mail treated as registered mail," formerly included with regular insured mailings.
[2] Not published.
[2] Excludes data for international mail included in prior years.
[2] Total surcharges (effective July 1, 1932) amounting to $3,815,000 in 1935, $2,674,000 in 1940, $7,371,000 in 1945, $5,000,000 in 1950, $4,726,000 in 1951, and $5,942,000 in 1952.

Source of tables 585 and 586: Post Office Department, Annual Report of the Postmaster General and records.

No. 587.—Postal Service Operation—Number of Offices, Mileage of Rural Routes, and Gross Receipts, by States and Other Areas

[Figures for years ending June 30]

DIVISION, STATE, AND OTHER AREA	Number of post offices, 1952	Mileage of rural free-delivery routes, 1952	GROSS POSTAL RECEIPTS (thousands of dollars)[1]					
			1935	1940	1945	1950	1951	1952
Grand total	40,919	1,499,910	595,661	729,780	1,243,674	1,603,628	1,691,189	1,848,754
Continental United States	40,445	1,499,697	591,800	726,172	1,216,094	1,593,127	1,681,558	1,837,249
New England	2,264	46,018	46,111	54,022	77,245	112,173	117,352	125,666
Maine	666	13,000	3,588	3,925	5,834	6,765	6,945	7,424
New Hampshire	332	6,544	2,216	2,718	3,815	5,203	5,524	6,106
Vermont	345	8,170	1,659	1,846	2,406	3,239	3,334	3,632
Massachusetts	568	8,766	26,890	29,796	42,120	63,032	65,626	69,791
Rhode Island	70	1,485	3,018	3,514	5,970	7,961	8,377	8,834
Connecticut	283	8,053	9,740	12,224	17,100	25,972	27,546	29,817
Middle Atlantic	4,911	120,217	164,613	195,685	324,915	437,889	456,757	495,261
New York	1,905	51,426	102,748	120,888	210,835	275,433	286,300	311,476
New Jersey	627	9,287	18,553	23,207	35,122	53,059	56,130	61,013
Pennsylvania	2,379	59,504	43,312	51,590	78,958	109,397	114,327	122,772
East North Central	5,587	317,755	143,663	180,346	259,651	372,850	389,080	419,554
Ohio	1,316	71,905	34,046	41,668	62,071	86,039	90,272	98,787
Indiana	881	60,961	13,388	16,810	26,745	35,755	37,838	40,869
Illinois	1,439	74,742	62,916	79,257	104,734	157,303	162,750	174,569
Michigan	1,008	56,141	20,048	26,870	42,100	58,635	62,635	66,997
Wisconsin	913	54,005	13,265	15,740	23,402	34,318	35,584	38,332
West North Central	6,353	340,325	66,925	76,171	111,234	155,302	162,048	175,982
Minnesota	1,029	55,947	15,089	17,600	24,886	35,556	37,032	40,009
Iowa	1,097	65,660	10,932	12,912	18,531	25,354	26,926	29,226
Missouri	1,433	65,008	22,748	25,806	37,517	55,684	58,826	63,698
North Dakota	506	29,506	2,562	2,747	3,583	4,579	4,836	5,074
South Dakota	537	25,575	2,433	2,614	3,686	4,663	4,809	5,230
Nebraska	658	38,088	6,217	6,925	10,397	13,704	14,364	15,606
Kansas	903	60,541	6,945	7,569	12,633	14,763	15,433	17,036
South Atlantic	6,507	221,725	51,213	65,939	124,543	150,838	163,414	180,256
Delaware	66	3,186	1,251	1,759	2,574	3,727	3,905	4,181
Maryland	539	12,581	7,706	9,435	15,328	19,877	21,135	23,649
Dist. of Columbia	1	138	6,307	8,242	18,637	19,731	21,734	23,879
Virginia	1,631	34,015	7,688	9,617	18,013	21,198	22,985	25,542
West Virginia	1,474	13,509	4,274	5,142	8,725	9,349	10,001	11,803
North Carolina	1,088	50,979	7,475	9,407	19,175	23,247	24,841	27,595
South Carolina	488	29,244	2,037	2,532	4,897	6,656	7,437	8,479
Georgia	870	59,801	8,452	10,630	18,631	23,812	25,824	25,693
Florida	650	18,272	6,023	8,875	18,561	23,242	25,553	29,435
East South Central	4,484	171,804	21,330	26,881	49,905	58,411	62,521	69,221
Kentucky	2,109	32,219	6,161	7,304	12,472	14,804	16,328	17,932
Tennessee	782	51,631	7,676	9,796	17,528	22,629	24,030	26,698
Alabama	890	45,852	4,524	5,961	11,991	13,118	14,059	15,878
Mississippi	703	42,102	2,969	3,820	7,914	7,860	8,404	8,712
West South Central	4,620	186,177	33,206	42,606	81,886	98,003	104,773	117,064
Arkansas	1,067	31,081	3,265	4,115	7,995	8,441	8,887	9,663
Louisiana	729	22,145	5,017	6,684	13,778	14,781	15,804	17,403
Oklahoma	843	45,772	6,217	7,375	13,032	14,720	15,467	17,208
Texas	1,981	87,179	18,707	24,433	47,080	60,061	64,615	72,760
Mountain	2,853	39,891	15,914	19,778	32,171	41,878	45,921	50,174
Montana	529	7,303	2,422	2,813	3,682	4,856	5,075	5,526
Idaho	387	8,058	1,488	1,878	2,815	3,597	3,906	4,072
Wyoming	259	1,405	992	1,189	1,811	2,302	2,456	2,724
Colorado	546	15,163	5,929	7,158	10,701	14,801	15,976	17,588
New Mexico	459	3,419	1,162	1,631	2,997	3,881	4,244	4,859
Arizona	265	2,255	1,456	1,990	4,228	5,460	5,800	6,468
Utah	287	2,077	1,928	2,434	4,591	5,487	6,040	6,632
Nevada	121	211	537	686	1,345	1,495	1,622	1,903
Pacific	2,696	55,785	48,823	64,743	155,143	166,583	180,291	203,333
Washington	669	18,156	8,026	9,964	21,402	23,370	24,895	27,273
Oregon	589	12,568	5,004	6,719	11,152	15,591	16,372	17,902
California	1,438	25,061	35,793	48,060	122,589	127,622	139,023	158,356
Alaska	254	51	98	170	413	982	1,119	1,425
Hawaii	98	73	834	1,480	22,726	3,955	4,086	4,800
Puerto Rico	107	89	568	809	2,489	2,415	2,793	3,336
Virgin Islands	5		17	36	48	75	82	101
Other areas [2]	10		2,340	1,101	1,903	2,892	215	247
Philatelic agency							1,336	1,595

[1] Revenues from money-order business, postal savings, and certain miscellaneous items not included.
[2] Includes Canton Island, Guam, Samoa (Tutuila), Wake, Caroline, Mariana and Marshall Islands.

Source: Post Office Department, *Annual Report of the Postmaster General*.

19. Power

Energy for supplying mechanical power, heat, light and refrigeration for the complex machinery and processes necessary to maintain productivity and comfort in the United States is derived primarily from coal, oil, water, natural gas, wood and waste, wind, certain basic chemical and physical reactions, and the rays of the sun. Of these an increasing percentage of the coal, oil, water, and gas are being converted to electric energy for application to the energy requirements of our economic system. In 1950 approximately 23 percent of the coal, 8 percent of the oil, practically all of the water power, and 11 percent of the natural gas were consumed in the production of electric energy.

Statistics on these various sources of energy are compiled by numerous agencies but only a few of the series are reasonably complete or arranged to avoid duplication in a manner that permits ready computation of total energy requirements. Oil, coal, natural gas, and wood yield many products as well as power and, consequently, enter into many statistical series.

Data on coal, oil, and natural gas production, utilization, and related subjects are compiled annually by the Bureau of Mines and are published in the *Minerals Yearbook* For summaries of statistical material from this source, see section 28, Mining and Mineral Products. Data on natural gas utilization and the production of manufactured gas from coal, oil, and related products, its utilization, and related statistics are published by the American Gas Association in its monthly bulletins and annual statistical numbers. Annual summary data are included in this section.

Data on the production of electric energy by type of prime mover and showing the quantities of basic fuels—coal, oil, natural gas, and others—used in production, and the capacity of all generating plants by type of prime mover and related statistics are compiled and published annually by the Federal Power Commission. These data cover both generation for public use by electric utilities and for use by the producer where generated by non-utility establishments. Data on sales, revenues, and customers by classes of service, on rates and typical bills, and related matters are also published by the Commission. Monthly statistics on production, fuels used in production, sales by classes of service, salaries and wages, taxes, and other costs are also published and distributed by the Federal Power Commission in a loose-leaf current data series known as *Electric Power Statistics*. Statistics on the distribution of electric energy by utilities for public use are presented monthly and annually by the Edison Electric Institute in its *Statistical Bulletins*. Summaries of these statistics appear in the following tables.

Data on the use of power by manufacturing, extracting, and related industries are issued from time to time by the Bureau of the Census in its Censuses of Manufactures and Mineral Industries. Statistics based on these studies appear in the sections on manufacturing and mineral industries in this *Abstract*.

Over-all statistics on water as an actual and potential source of power are compiled by the Federal Power Commission and are shown in table 605.

The Bureau of the Census in the Census of Electrical Industries compiled at five-year intervals beginning in 1902 a report on the Electric Light and Power Industry. The last survey made was for the year 1937. Summary statistics from this report are shown in table 593.

Data in this section relate to continental United States except as indicated.

Historical statistics.—See preface and historical appendix. Tabular headnotes (as "See also *Historical Statistics*, series G 159-170") provide cross-references, where applicable, to *Historical Statistics of the United States, 1789-1945*.

Note.—This section presents data for the most recent year or period available on April 22, 1953, when the material was organized and sent to the printer.

Fig. XXXVI.—Installed Capacity of Electric Utility Generating
Plants: 1920 to 1952

[See table 590]

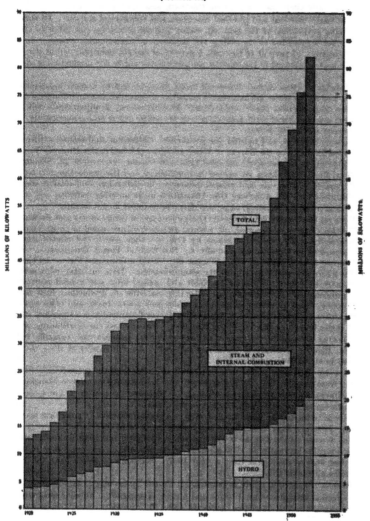

Source: Federal Power Commission.

No. 588.—ENERGY FROM MINERAL FUELS AND WATER POWER—ANNUAL SUPPLY: 1889 TO 1951

In trillions of British thermal units. Unit heat values employed are: Anthracite, 12,700 B. t. u. per pound; bituminous coal and lignite, 13,100 B. t. u. per pound; petroleum, 5,800,000 B. t. u. per barrel; natural gas, 1,075 B. t. u. per cubic foot. Water power includes installations owned by manufacturing plants and mines, as well as Government- and privately-owned public utilities. Fuel equivalent of water power calculated from kilowatt-hours of power produced wherever available, as is true of all public-utility plants since 1919. Otherwise, fuel equivalent calculated from reported horsepower of installed water wheels, assuming capacity factor of 20 percent for factories and mines and of 40 percent for public utilities. See also *Historical Statistics*, series G 150–170]

				MINERAL FUELS					
				Coal			Petroleum and natural gas		
YEAR	Total energy	Water power [1]	Total	Total	Pennsylvania anthracite	Bituminous and lignite	Total	Petroleum (crude)		Natural gas (marketed production)
								Domestic production	Imports	
1889	(²)	(²)	4,126	3,664	1,157	2,507	472	204	......	268
1890	7,409	238	7,171	6,600	1,535	5,065	571	331	......	240
1900	7,869	290	7,648	7,030	1,457	5,563	628	368	......	254
1901–05 avg.	10,075	323	9,753	6,536	1,696	7,140	915	592	1	323
1906–10 avg.	13,798	477	13,317	11,544	2,061	9,783	1,473	1,002	1	470
1911–15 avg.	16,630	611	15,919	12,794	2,367	11,537	2,125	1,437	70	610
1916–20 avg.	20,256	708	19,548	16,327	2,356	13,981	3,211	2,162	287	830
1921–25 avg.	20,568	653	19,915	14,582	1,972	12,610	5,233	3,758	550	1,024
1926–30 avg.	23,675	785	22,890	15,541	1,946	13,595	7,350	5,196	394	1,780
1931–35 avg.	18,494	719	17,775	10,571	1,363	9,207	7,206	5,158	232	1,634
1936–40 avg.	23,671	863	22,315	12,943	1,298	10,945	9,975	7,205	158	2,582
1941–45 avg.	30,528	1,222	29,306	16,617	1,503	15,114	12,779	8,916	227	3,636
1946–50 avg.	34,217	1,485	32,732	15,673	1,329	14,243	17,150	10,935	749	5,478
1947	35,574	1,436	34,366	17,975	1,453	16,522	16,273	10,771	576	4,926
1948	35,686	1,481	35,155	17,188	1,451	15,707	17,967	11,717	746	5,534
1949	31,503	1,529	29,964	12,557	1,095	11,473	17,407	10,683	897	5,527
1950 (prel.)	34,431	1,573	33,858	14,647	1,120	13,527	19,211	11,449	1,009	6,753
1951 (prel.)	38,635	1,559	37,076	15,071	1,054	14,017	22,005	13,021	1,029	7,955

[1] Assuming average central-station practice for each year; declined from about 7.05 pounds of coal per kilowatt-hour in 1889 to 1.14 pounds in 1951.
[2] Not available.

Source: Department of Interior, Bureau of Mines; *Minerals Yearbook*. Preliminary data published in annual report, *Bituminous Coal and Lignite*.

No. 589.—ELECTRIC UTILITIES—NUMBER OF ELECTRIC UTILITY SUPPLY SYSTEMS AND GENERATING PLANTS, BY CLASS OF OWNERSHIP: 1922 TO 1951

Duplications of establishments operating in two or more States have been eliminated. Each type of prime mover in combination generating plants counted separately; nonutility generating plants, approximately 4,890 in 1951, producing primarily for industrial use, are not included]

DEC. 31	Total, all classes	Privately owned	PUBLICLY OWNED				
			Total	Municipal	Federal	Public utility districts and State projects	Cooperatives
1922: Total electric supply systems	6,355	3,774	2,581	2,581	......	......	......
Systems with generating plants	4,380	2,650	1,730	1,730	......	......	......
Number of generating plants	5,444	3,615	1,829	1,829	......	......	......
1927: Total electric supply systems	3,430	1,627	1,802	1,799	3	......	......
Systems with generating plants	1,788	923	865	862	3	......	......
Number of generating plants	4,339	3,244	1,095	1,085	10	......	......
1937: Total electric supply systems	3,501	1,407	2,094	1,877	25	11	181
Systems with generating plants	1,812	818	994	965	17	6	16
Number of generating plants	4,027	2,916	1,111	1,014	27	43	27
1942: Total electric supply systems	4,061	1,080	2,981	2,092	74	26	800
Systems with generating plants	1,594	492	1,102	990	18	11	83
Number of generating plants	3,866	2,400	1,466	1,187	96	101	142
1947: Total electric supply systems	3,950	776	3,174	2,173	75	37	889
Systems with generating plants	1,522	419	1,103	973	19	14	97
Number of generating plants	3,879	2,370	1,503	1,146	98	111	180
1950: Total electric supply systems	3,944	815	3,129	2,074	61	81	913
Systems with generating plants	1,507	408	1,099	945	14	38	92
Number of generating plants	3,886	2,371	1,517	1,146	79	140	152
1951: Total electric supply systems	4,007	821	3,186	2,072	55	91	913
Systems with generating plants	1,495	395	1,103	945	15	43	92
Number of generating plants	3,887	2,394	1,399	1,136	63	145	166
Total electric supply systems	3,955	778	3,157	2,079	57	94	977
Systems with generating plants	1,461	570	1,040	947	13	43	92
Number of generating plants	3,806	2,385	1,521	1,194	91	145	161

Source: Federal Power Commission; annual report, *Production of Electric Energy and Capacity of Generating Plant*, and related data.

No. 590.—PRODUCTION OF ELECTRIC ENERGY AND NUMBER AND CAPACITY OF GENERATING PLANTS, BY CLASS OF OWNERSHIP AND TYPE OF PRIME MOVER: 1925 TO 1951

[Installed capacity as of Dec. 31. Industrial series first available for 1939; detail by type of prime mover for 1943. See also *Historical Statistics*, series G 171-190 and G 200-224]

ITEM	1925	1930	1935	1940	1945	1949	1950	1951
CLASS OF OWNERSHIP								
Production, total (millions of kilowatt-hours)				179,907	271,255	345,066	388,674	433,358
Electric utilities (for public use), total	61,451	91,112	95,287	141,837	222,486	291,100	329,141	370,673
Privately owned	58,685	86,108	89,330	125,411	180,926	233,112	266,860	301,845
Publicly owned	2,766	5,003	5,958	16,426	41,560	57,988	62,281	68,828
Municipal	2,302	3,604	4,229	6,188	9,624	13,410	15,244	17,617
Federal	103	465	555	8,584	28,001	38,102	40,388	44,120
Cooperatives, power districts, State projects	172	518	732	1,175	3,146	5,643	5,793	6,204
Noncentral stations	189	416	442	479	790	832	857	987
Industrial plants [1]				38,070	48,769	53,967	59,533	62,685
Installed capacity, total (thousands of kilowatts)				50,962	62,868	76,570	82,850	90,127
Electric utilities (for public use), total	21,472	32,384	34,436	39,927	50,111	63,100	68,919	75,775
Privately owned	20,045	30,285	31,820	34,399	40,307	50,484	55,176	60,192
Publicly owned	1,427	2,099	2,615	5,528	9,804	12,616	13,743	15,583
Municipal	1,125	1,601	2,002	2,977	3,586	4,727	4,970	5,293
Federal	198	226	300	1,944	5,081	6,210	6,921	8,099
Cooperatives, power districts, State projects	49	154	175	435	891	1,417	1,538	1,875
Noncentral stations	56	118	139	173	245	263	314	316
Industrial plants [1]				11,035	12,757	13,470	13,931	14,353
TYPE OF PRIME MOVER								
Electric utilities (for public use):								
Number of plants, total [2]	3,738	4,043	4,023	3,918	3,886	3,888	3,867	3,806
Hydro	1,250	1,446	1,476	1,474	1,505	1,465	1,458	1,428
Steam	2,004	1,626	1,424	1,153	1,057	1,054	1,051	1,048
Internal combustion	484	971	1,123	1,291	1,324	1,369	1,358	1,330
Production, total (millions of kilowatt-hours)	61,451	91,112	95,287	141,837	222,486	291,100	329,141	370,673
Hydro	21,798	31,190	38,372	47,321	79,970	89,748	95,938	99,751
Steam	39,367	59,293	56,144	93,002	140,435	197,878	229,543	267,252
Internal combustion	286	629	771	1,514	2,081	3,473	3,660	3,671
Hydro as percent of total	35.5	34.2	40.3	33.4	35.9	30.8	29.1	26.9
Installed capacity, total (thousands of kilowatts)	21,472	32,384	34,436	39,927	50,111	63,100	68,919	75,775
Hydro	5,922	8,585	9,399	11,224	14,912	16,654	17,675	18,868
Steam	15,368	23,386	24,471	27,775	34,113	44,640	49,333	54,865
Internal combustion	182	414	566	928	1,087	1,806	1,911	2,041
Hydro as percent of total	27.6	26.5	27.3	28.1	29.8	26.4	25.6	24.9
Production per kilowatt of installed capacity (kilowatt-hours) [3]	2,862	2,813	2,767	3,552	4,440	4,613	4,776	4,892
Industrial plants: [1]								
Production, total (millions of kilowatt-hours)				38,070	48,769	53,967	59,533	62,685
Hydro					4,777	5,025	4,946	4,626
Fuel					43,992	48,942	54,587	58,060
Hydro as percent of total					9.8	9.3	8.3	7.4
Installed capacity, total (thousands of kilowatts)				11,035	12,757	13,470	13,931	14,353
Hydro					980	1,008	1,000	1,002
Steam					11,135	11,831	12,162	12,507
Internal combustion					641	630	770	843
Hydro as percent of total					7.7	7.5	7.2	7.0

[1] Industrial classification comprises production and capacity of approximately 3,338 industrial electric power plants of 100 kilowatts and over in 1951, including amounts for stationary electric power plants of railroads and railways.

[2] Each prime mover type in combination plants counted separately.

[3] Based on capacity in service at end of year.

Source: Federal Power Commission; annual report, *Production of Electric Energy and Capacity of Generating Plants*, and industrial electric power summaries.

No. 591.—GENERATING PLANTS—INSTALLED CAPACITY OF ELECTRIC UTILITIES AND INDUSTRIAL PLANTS, BY TYPE OF PRIME MOVER AND BY CLASS OF OWNERSHIP, BY STATES: 1951

[Thousands of kilowatts]

DIVISION AND STATE	Total	TYPE OF PRIME MOVER				ELECTRIC UTILITIES				Industrial plants
		Electric utilities and industrial		Electric utilities		Total	Privately owned	Publicly owned		
		Fuel	Hydro	Fuel	Hydro			Municipal	Other	
United States....	90,128	70,257	19,870	55,907	13,866	75,775	60,192	5,293	10,290	14,353
New England........	5,589	4,254	1,264	2,268	987	4,255	4,105	125	24	1,264
Maine.............	658	296	392	142	270	412	400	2	1	246
New Hampshire.....	480	175	311	136	262	394	396	3	......	91
Vermont...........	238	44	195	31	180	211	197	14	(¹)	27
Massachusetts.....	2,377	2,140	237	1,804	182	1,796	1,701	86	9	581
Rhode Island.......	436	425	11	366	3	359	352	......	7	77
Connecticut.......	1,310	1,203	107	909	80	1,048	1,090	21	2	222
Middle Atlantic......	17,220	15,543	1,677	12,614	1,586	14,210	13,961	209	28	3,010
New York.........	8,035	6,810	1,225	5,722	1,150	6,873	6,747	105	17	1,162
New Jersey........	2,679	2,670	9	2,177	6	2,183	2,153	28	3	496
Pennsylvania......	6,506	6,063	443	4,714	440	5,154	5,082	64	9	1,352
East North Central.....	20,945	20,016	929	16,390	858	17,226	15,657	1,309	242	3,737
Ohio.............	4,718	4,702	15	4,662	12	4,674	4,320	341	13	1,044
Indiana..........	3,016	2,980	36	2,426	36	2,462	2,171	290	1	554
Illinois.........	5,363	5,310	54	4,614	49	4,662	4,441	177	44	701
Michigan.........	4,571	4,163	408	3,081	394	3,475	3,005	299	171	1,096
Wisconsin........	2,376	1,861	415	1,597	367	1,964	1,750	101	113	312
West North Central.....	6,173	5,543	631	5,001	579	5,590	3,753	1,066	732	589
Minnesota........	1,478	1,296	180	1,107	137	1,244	938	230	67	222
Iowa.............	1,390	1,251	138	1,133	135	1,271	994	199	78	118
Missouri.........	1,284	1,133	151	1,004	151	1,155	949	189	17	129
North Dakota......	203	203	......	199	......	199	151	11	38	4
South Dakota......	218	206	13	191	5	195	152	37	6	23
Nebraska.........	662	519	142	505	142	648	1	147	500	14
Kansas...........	946	940	6	952	6	868	506	274	25	78
South Atlantic.......	12,110	9,326	2,786	7,477	2,317	9,794	8,737	511	546	2,316
Delaware.........	192	191	1	148	1	148	137	12	......	44
Maryland.........	1,404	1,131	272	937	271	1,199	1,162	28	9	205
Dist. of Columbia..	525	522	3	505	3	508	505	......	3	17
Virginia..........	1,763	1,557	206	1,098	183	1,276	1,219	34	23	487
West Virginia.....	1,996	1,788	208	1,354	101	1,455	1,454	1	(¹)	541
North Carolina....	2,340	1,379	961	1,171	662	1,833	1,505	111	217	507
South Carolina....	1,303	615	679	418	658	1,087	804	7	187	226
Georgia..........	1,323	879	444	749	432	1,181	1,058	18	105	142
Florida..........	1,275	1,262	13	1,115	13	1,128	804	301	22	147
East South Central.....	5,386	2,986	2,999	2,390	2,991	5,280	2,160	111	3,019	517
Kentucky.........	1,105	702	406	660	406	1,066	719	42	305	42
Tennessee........	2,175	802	1,373	657	1,373	2,020	132	25	1,873	145
Alabama..........	2,009	849	1,230	610	1,212	1,822	983	1	839	247
Mississippi.......	455	455	......	372	......	372	336	43	3	83
West South Central.....	7,104	6,556	548	4,917	545	5,462	4,323	533	597	1,642
Arkansas.........	763	606	156	436	153	590	462	41	87	173
Louisiana........	1,409	1,409	......	988	......	988	876	83	28	421
Oklahoma.........	857	783	74	734	74	908	611	79	118	49
Texas............	4,075	3,758	318	2,759	318	3,077	2,383	330	365	999
Mountain...........	4,757	2,130	2,627	1,466	2,622	4,069	2,164	159	1,746	688
Montana..........	556	94	462	81	461	542	454	......	88	13
Idaho............	496	42	454	5	453	458	394	14	50	38
Wyoming.........	231	139	92	68	92	160	66	2	92	71
Colorado.........	686	536	145	494	144	638	474	80	84	94
New Mexico.......	379	354	25	298	25	323	255	23	45	56
Arizona..........	1,272	505	767	302	767	1,069	246	2	821	203
Utah.............	470	375	94	208	94	303	262	36	4	167
Nevada...........	622	34	587	9	586	506	14	1	541	36
Pacific............	10,496	4,075	6,421	2,484	3,873	9,887	5,273	1,360	3,254	639
Washington.......	3,363	432	2,932	202	2,906	3,104	571	523	2,019	259
Oregon..........	1,143	343	800	206	783	989	418	52	519	154
California........	5,990	3,300	2,690	2,076	2,685	5,764	4,285	775	704	226

¹ Less than 500.

Source: Federal Power Commission; based on annual report, *Production of Electric Energy and Capacity of Generating Plants*, 1951.

No. 592.—ELECTRIC ENERGY—PRODUCTION BY ELECTRIC UTILITIES AND INDUSTRIAL PLANTS, BY TYPE OF PRIME MOVER AND BY CLASS OF OWNERSHIP, BY STATES: 1951

[Millions of kilowatt-hours]

| DIVISION AND STATE | Total | TYPE OF PRIME MOVER | | | | ELECTRIC UTILITIES | | | | Industrial plants |
| | | Electric utilities and industrial | | Electric utilities | | Total | Privately owned | Publicly owned | | |
		Fuel	Hydro	Fuel	Hydro			Municipal	Other	
United States	433,359	328,982	104,377	270,922	99,751	370,673	301,845	17,617	51,211	62,685
New England	21,174	16,486	5,687	13,042	4,448	17,490	17,073	344	73	3,684
Maine	2,913	712	2,203	278	1,515	1,792	1,779	10	3	1,121
New Hampshire	1,925	703	1,222	583	979	1,562	1,555	7		363
Vermont	969	49	920	32	842	874	829	45	(1)	95
Massachusetts	8,304	7,368	936	6,223	764	6,987	6,735	227	25	1,317
Rhode Island	1,778	1,760	18	1,612	9	1,621	1,592		29	157
Connecticut	5,284	4,896	389	4,315	339	4,654	4,584	55	15	630
Middle Atlantic	81,444	71,065	10,378	60,064	9,963	70,028	69,377	517	133	11,416
New York	36,485	28,140	8,345	24,957	7,958	32,915	32,547	261	107	3,570
New Jersey	11,647	11,599	48	9,899	40	9,939	9,831	95	13	1,708
Pennsylvania	33,312	31,327	1,984	25,209	1,965	27,174	27,000	161	13	6,138
East North Central	100,418	95,622	4,796	79,995	4,396	84,391	79,872	3,555	964	16,027
Ohio	29,366	29,324	42	24,590	27	24,617	23,509	1,077	32	4,749
Indiana	15,099	14,941	158	12,299	158	12,457	11,654	802	1	2,642
Illinois	25,379	25,171	207	22,456	187	22,644	22,039	460	144	2,735
Michigan	21,254	19,300	1,954	14,749	1,887	16,636	15,319	891	425	4,618
Wisconsin	9,320	6,886	2,435	5,900	2,137	8,037	7,351	325	361	1,283
West North Central	23,566	19,877	3,690	17,766	3,405	21,170	15,971	2,774	2,425	2,396
Minnesota	5,629	4,499	1,130	3,925	870	4,795	4,071	581	143	834
Iowa	5,562	4,652	930	4,055	930	4,985	4,376	449	160	597
Missouri	4,581	3,682	899	3,192	899	4,091	3,604	457	1	490
North Dakota	684	684		680		680	543	30	106	4
South Dakota	675	638	37	592	14	606	500	101	6	69
Nebraska	2,298	1,626	672	1,600	670	2,270	1	308	1,961	28
Kansas	4,118	4,096	22	3,722	22	3,744	2,876	820	49	374
South Atlantic	61,232	51,702	9,529	42,225	7,529	49,754	46,241	1,561	1,953	11,478
Delaware	707	707		547		547	528	19		160
Maryland	6,737	5,278	1,461	3,836	1,456	5,291	5,205	62	24	1,446
Dist. of Columbia	1,741	1,737	4	1,703	4	1,707	1,703		4	34
Virginia	9,590	8,885	705	6,816	617	7,433	7,290	109	64	2,157
West Virginia	12,121	11,117	1,003	8,813	455	9,269	9,268	1		2,852
North Carolina	12,016	8,447	3,568	7,529	2,342	9,871	8,498	306	1,067	2,145
South Carolina	4,719	3,169	1,550	2,542	1,479	3,721	3,159	4	558	998
Georgia	7,136	5,929	1,207	5,173	1,145	6,318	6,098	44	176	818
Florida	6,465	6,433	32	5,565	32	5,597	4,521	1,016	60	868
East South Central	30,605	15,678	14,928	13,056	14,903	27,959	12,153	278	15,506	2,646
Kentucky	5,582	3,927	1,655	3,786	1,655	5,441	3,998	132	1,311	141
Tennessee	10,800	3,787	7,013	3,058	7,013	10,071	55	52	9,493	729
Alabama	11,692	5,433	6,259	4,019	6,234	10,253	5,550		4,704	1,439
Mississippi	2,530	2,530		2,193		2,193	2,099	94		337
West South Central	36,650	35,300	1,350	25,655	1,341	26,997	23,559	1,765	1,673	9,653
Arkansas	3,955	3,528	429	2,437	420	2,856	2,465	91	299	1,099
Louisiana	7,703	7,703		5,498		5,498	5,191	247	60	2,205
Oklahoma	3,647	3,246	401	3,014	401	3,415	3,105	160	457	232
Texas	21,345	20,824	521	14,707	521	15,228	13,105	1,266	857	6,117
Mountain	20,526	7,971	12,556	5,084	12,543	17,626	10,445	477	6,705	2,900
Montana	3,326	66	3,259	44	3,250	3,304	2,927		376	22
Idaho	3,035	115	2,921	(1)	2,915	2,915	2,543	67	306	120
Wyoming	811	399	412	226	412	638	232	1	405	173
Colorado	2,648	2,287	362	1,907	355	2,262	1,908	229	125	386
New Mexico	1,451	1,425	27	1,171	27	1,197	1,061	52	84	254
Arizona	4,826	2,222	2,604	1,329	2,604	3,933	1,017	7	2,909	893
Utah	1,781	1,345	435	394	435	830	695	118	17	951
Nevada	2,648	111	2,537	11	2,536	2,547	62	1	2,484	101
Pacific	57,744	16,282	41,462	14,036	41,222	55,258	27,134	6,345	21,779	2,486
Washington	20,909	952	19,958	160	19,755	19,914	3,384	2,372	14,158	995
Oregon	6,501	781	5,720	256	5,663	5,969	1,767	212	3,989	532
California	30,334	14,550	15,785	13,591	15,785	29,375	21,983	3,762	3,631	959

1 Less than 500,000.

Source: Federal Power Commission; based on annual report, *Production of Electric Energy and Capacity of Generating Plants,* 1951.

No. 593.—ELECTRIC LIGHT AND POWER INDUSTRY—SUMMARY: 1902 TO 1937

[Figures cover all establishments engaged either in generation and distribution of electric energy, or distribution or transmission of electric energy, to public or private consumers. Excludes establishments which consume all current generated, such as manufacturing and mining companies, railroads, railways, hotels, and other enterprises not in nature of public utilities, unless a portion of generated output was sold commercially. Plants operated by Federal Government or by States excluded unless energy sold commercially]

ITEM	1902	1912	1917	1922	1927	1932	1937
Number of reporting establishments,[1] total	3,620	5,221	6,542	6,355	4,238	3,429	3,501
Generating all or part of current	(?)	4,646	5,124	4,389	2,331	1,788	1,812
Distributing or transmitting only	(?)	575	1,418	1,966	2,004	1,641	1,689
Number of separate generating stations	(?)	(?)	5,962	5,444	4,803	4,339	[2] 4,027
Prime movers, hp. (thousands)	1,645	7,530	12,937	19,851	35,710	47,967	50,230
Steam engines	} 1,394 {	1,808	1,762	1,371	904	649	712
Steam turbines		3,054	6,747	12,355	34,338	32,804	33,177
Internal-combustion engines	12	111	210	308	546	561	1,101
Hydroturbines and water wheels	436	2,469	4,277	5,822	9,844	13,572	15,230
Generators, rated kilowatt capacity (thousands)	1,212	5,165	8,994	14,313	25,631	34,623	34,481
Output,[4] kilowatt-hours (millions)		14,183	31,044	50,274	96,529	111,716	168,300
Reported as generated	2,507	11,569	25,438	40,292	74,685	79,657	121,097
Reported as purchased or received from other sources	(?)	2,614	5,606	9,983	22,142	32,058	47,202
Number of customers (thousands)		2,838	7,179	12,710	21,790	25,862	27,219
Revenue from elec. service ($1,000)	[3] 94,187	[3] 287,139	[3] 502,080	[3] 1,020,430	1,802,655	1,975,304	2,356,512
Sales, kilowatt-hours (millions)	(?)	(?)	35,752	41,965	79,011	88,265	132,080
Distribution for other purposes (non-revenue), kilowatt-hours (millions)	(?)	(?)	(?)	(?)	17,817	23,451	35,370
Operating expenses, ($1,000) [6]	(?)	(?)	(?)	553,088	[7] 750,484	805,180	1,042,198
Value of electric utility plant ($1,000,000)) [8]	505	2,176	3,080	4,465	[9] 9,297	12,664	12,941
Employees, number	30,326	79,335	163,541	150,762	251,020	244,575	261,225
Salaries and wages ($1,000)	20,647	61,182	95,242	212,433	[7] 367,632	[7] 323,980	470,258

[1] The term "establishment" as here used may represent a single electric station (either generating or distributing or both) or a number of such stations operated under the same ownership. [2] Not available.
[2] Comprises 1,112 stations operated by steam; 1,283 by internal-combustion; 1,426 by water; and 206 composite (stations having more than 1 type of prime mover).
[4] Comprises generated output and energy purchased and received from other sources. Since the energy "Received from other sources" was, in a large part, purchased from other electric light and power companies, a considerable duplication is involved, as such energy would also be included in the "Generated."
[5] Includes "Estimated value of free service."
[6] Includes cost of fuel purchased and interchanged power, maintenance and other operating expenses.
[7] Reported by commercial establishments only. No data for municipal establishments.
[8] Includes value of plant and equipment, $902,000,000, owned by companies engaged in the operation of electric light and power plants and other public utilities, not distributed among the several utilities.
[9] Not comparable with other years; includes only salaries and wages chargeable to electric operating service.

Source: Department of Commerce, Bureau of the Census; Census of Electrical Industries, report on Electric Light and Power Industry. Survey discontinued.

No. 594.—ELECTRIC LIGHT AND POWER INDUSTRY—ENERGY GENERATED, SALES, REVENUE, AND CUSTOMERS: 1930 TO 1952

[Figures for energy generated obtained by Edison Electric Institute from Federal Power Commission. Figures for sales, revenue, and customers for 1930 and 1935 not strictly comparable with those for 1940 and subsequent years due to change in classification of sales. See also Historical Statistics, series G 225-233]

CLASS	1930 [1]	1935 [1]	1940	1945	1950	1952
Energy generated million kilowatt-hours	91,112	96,287	141,837	222,486	329,141	398,924
Sales to ultimate customers do	74,906	77,396	115,643	193,553	266,539	342,534
Residential or domestic [2]	11,018	13,973	23,318	34,184	67,030	90,780
Rural (distinct rural rates) [3]	1,472	1,211	1,991	3,066	7,400	8,536
Commercial and industrial:						
Small light and power	13,944	13,588	22,373	30,428	50,446	62,080
Large light and power	40,148	40,865	58,557	107,490	139,065	167,358
All other	8,323	7,955	11,405	17,777	16,568	17,770
Revenue from ultimate customers $1,000	1,990,355	1,911,989	2,446,218	3,341,578	5,084,445	6,137,272
Residential or domestic [2]	654,441	700,358	805,961	1,167,356	1,931,696	2,400,899
Rural (distinct rural rates) [3]	24,824	21,572	49,472	90,345	157,611	184,479
Commercial and industrial:						
Small light and power	575,598	519,213	689,263	880,213	1,333,755	1,584,219
Large light and power	566,468	531,107	631,428	1,001,957	1,404,980	1,664,073
All other	169,924	139,729	174,112	201,647	256,435	263,612
Ultimate customers, Dec. 31 thousands	24,698	26,213	29,191	34,681	44,584	48,459
Residential or domestic [2]	20,332	21,019	24,942	28,117	37,533	40,748
Rural (distinct rural rates) [3]	190	216	686	1,284	1,596	1,063
Commercial and industrial:						
Small light and power	3,626	3,711	4,240	4,208	5,468	5,684
Large light and power	347	305	178	162	225	256
All other	89	62	115	119	136	158

[1] See footnote. [2] Prior to 1940 covers residential and eastern farms. [3] Prior to 1940 covers western farms.
Source: Edison Electric Institute, New York, N. Y.; annual statistical bulletin.

No. **595.**—Electric Utilities—Balance Sheet and Income Account of Privately Owned Classes A and B Companies: 1937 to 1951

[In thousands of dollars. For years ending Dec. 31. Data cover reports of all companies having annual electric revenues in excess of $250,000. These concerns represent approximately 98 percent of the total privately owned electric utility industry]

ITEM	1937	1940	1945	1949	1950	1951
COMPOSITE BALANCE SHEET						
Assets and other debits, total	15,378,135	15,579,209	14,568,323	19,001,350	20,589,713	22,438,288
Electric utility plant	9,614,616	10,447,232	12,175,986	17,163,780	18,805,882	20,622,128
Other utility plant	1,512,880	1,650,694	1,823,914	2,282,013	2,450,725	2,594,287
Unclassified utility plant	2,724,087	2,309,061	490,882	181,499	184,381	155,160
Total utility plant	13,851,583	14,406,987	14,490,782	19,627,292	21,440,988	23,371,575
Reserve for depreciation and amortization	*1,495,250*	*1,912,974*	*3,064,919*	*4,069,111*	*4,385,860*	*4,734,081*
Total utility plant less reserves	12,356,333	12,494,013	11,425,863	15,558,181	17,055,728	18,637,494
Utility plant adjustments	(¹)	(¹)	(¹)	² 595	² 2,055	² 1,107
Investment and fund accounts	1,462,433	1,380,403	1,089,443	²1,272,434	²1,234,927	² 1,234,542
Current and accrued assets	959,076	1,122,902	1,695,721	1,898,688	2,058,124	2,307,468
Other assets	600,293	581,891	357,296	271,452	238,879	287,677
Liabilities and other credits, total	15,378,135	15,579,209	14,568,323	19,001,350	20,589,713	22,438,288
Common capital stock	4,306,364	4,392,601	3,879,314	4,623,226	5,046,117	5,409,072
Preferred capital stock	2,125,431	2,078,219	2,071,133	2,392,487	2,574,886	2,731,382
Premiums, assessments, etc	96,590	100,032	111,815	239,958	322,908	398,547
Total capital stock	6,528,385	6,570,852	6,062,262	7,255,671	7,943,911	8,539,001
Capital surplus	223,098	256,800	230,439	355,351	323,508	326,131
Earned surplus	802,981	860,351	765,522	1,197,125	1,345,981	1,444,373
Long-term debt	6,850,195	6,895,460	6,141,453	8,572,086	9,188,616	9,994,047
Current and accrued liabilities	692,384	692,038	964,830	1,358,533	1,527,186	1,857,190
Other liabilities	280,892	303,609	394,517	262,584	260,511	277,546
COMPOSITE INCOME ACCOUNT						
Electric utility operating income:						
Operating revenues	2,157,277	2,403,712	3,171,457	4,381,849	4,783,860	5,238,259
Operating expenses	928,629	1,013,189	1,453,615	2,319,926	2,454,994	2,654,623
Depreciation and amortization	212,865	256,306	315,858	385,418	434,434	472,296
Taxes	305,427	397,400	639,096	786,449	938,827	1,139,434
Total operating revenue deductions	1,446,921	1,666,985	2,408,569	3,491,793	3,828,255	4,266,352
Net operating revenues	710,356	736,727	762,888	890,056	955,605	971,907
Income from electric plant leased to others	7,514	7,625	4,750	5,195	5,200	3,953
Electric utility operating income	717,870	744,352	767,638	895,251	960,805	975,860
Other utility operating income	51,095	60,536	65,082	60,766	72,273	83,951
Total utility operating income	768,965	804,888	832,720	956,017	1,033,078	1,059,811
Other income	70,698	68,149	54,338	65,733	68,156	62,475
Gross income	839,663	873,037	887,058	1,021,750	1,101,234	1,122,286
Income deductions:						
Interest on long-term debt	282,905	266,607	210,771	242,687	259,705	280,491
Other income deductions (net)	47,279	58,766	141,833	21,804	19,586	27,572
Total income deductions	330,184	325,373	352,604	264,491	279,291	308,063
Net income	509,479	547,664	534,454	757,259	821,943	814,223

¹ Included with utility plant.   ² Less reserves.

Source: Federal Power Commission; annual report, *Statistics of Electric Utilities in the United States.*

No. **596.**—Electric Utility Depreciation Practices—Relationship of Reserves and Expenses to Electric Plant: 1937 to 1951

[Money figures in millions. See headnote, table 595. Excludes amounts related to other than electric facilities; covers only those utilities segregating *electric* plant and reserve accounts from *all* plant and reserve accounts]

ITEM	1937	1945	1948	1949	1950	1951
Number of utilities	121	253	249	249	249	255
Total electric plant, value	$5,358	$8,880	$10,784	$12,807	$14,490	$16,835
Estimated depreciable electric plant, value	(¹)	$7,928	$9,292	$11,050	$12,667	$14,930
Electric depreciation reserves:						
Amount	$635	$1,900	$2,408	$2,676	$2,971	$3,406
Ratio to total plant (percent)	11.9	21.4	22.3	20.9	20.5	20.2
Ratio to depreciable plant (percent)		24.0	25.9	24.2	23.5	22.8
Electric depreciation expense:						
Amount	$103	$214	$246	$288	$331	$385
Ratio to total plant (percent)	1.92	2.41	2.28	2.25	2.28	2.28
Ratio to depreciable plant (percent)		2.70	2.65	2.61	2.61	2.56

¹ Not available.

Source: Federal Power Commission; *Electric Utility Depreciation Practices.*

No. 597.—Consumption of Fuels by Electric Utilities for Production of Electric Energy: 1920 to 1952

[Use of fuels for stand-by purposes is included. See also *Historical Statistics*, series G 194-199]

| CALENDAR YEAR | CONSUMPTION OF FUELS | | | | | | Consumption of coal and coal equivalent of other fuels (thousand tons [1]) | Output by fuels [4] (million kilowatt-hours) | Consumption per kilowatt-hour (pounds) |
| | Coal (thousand tons [1]) | | | | Fuel oil (thousand barrels [3]) | Gas (million cubic feet) | | | |
	Total	Bituminous [2]	Anthracite	Lignite [3]					
1920	31,540	30,099	1,540	....	12,690	22,136	35,791	23,405	3.0
1925	36,615	33,803	1,812	....	9,794	45,472	40,014	39,442	2.0
1930	40,278	28,130	2,148	....	8,803	110,552	47,545	59,552	1.60
1935	32,715	30,936	1,779	....	11,257	124,118	40,797	56,089	1.44
1940	51,474	47,721	2,348	1,405	16,325	180,096	62,942	93,953	1.34
1943	77,301	73,072	3,265	963	17,986	201,987	93,275	143,786	1.30
1944	80,084	75,720	3,427	936	20,862	368,784	99,251	153,885	1.29
1945	74,736	70,621	3,122	982	20,298	225,212	92,842	142,231	1.30
1946	72,197	67,623	3,453	1,120	26,316	306,942	93,471	144,555	1.29
1947	89,631	85,033	3,522	976	44,309	372,054	115,672	176,923	1.21
1948	99,586	94,470	3,966	1,151	42,645	478,097	130,122	199,796	1.30
1949	83,963	79,397	3,334	1,213	66,301	560,131	124,574	200,965	1.24
1950	91,871	86,855	3,609	1,407	75,420	628,919	138,421	232,313	1.19
1951	105,708	100,378	3,870	1,521	63,945	763,895	154,498	270,531	1.14
1952 (prel.)	107,040	101,823	3,767	1,449	67,120	911,867	161,090	293,928	1.10

[1] Of 2,000 pounds. [3] Lignite included with bituminous coal prior to 1940. [4] Of 42 gallons.
[4] Output by use of wood and waste not included except small amount in 1952.

Source: Federal Power Commission; annual report, *Consumption of Fuels for Production of Electric Energy*; also, related monthly reports.

No. 598.—Farm Electrification: 1930 to 1952

ITEM	1930	1940	1945	1949	1950 [1]	1951	1952
Total number of farms [2]	6,286,648	6,096,799	5,859,169	....	5,382,162	....	....
Total number of farms served, Dec. 31	646,900	2,050,000	2,929,000	4,994,700	4,424,000	4,554,000	4,574,000
By private companies	....	1,448,500	1,707,100	2,407,046	1,998,000	2,059,000	2,117,000
By public authorities, total	....	601,500	1,221,900	2,587,654	2,426,000	2,585,000	2,787,000
By REA cooperatives [5]	....	517,500	1,051,000	2,343,738	2,168,000	2,318,000	2,475,000
Other public [6]	....	84,000	170,900	243,916	258,000	267,000	282,000
EASTERN FARMS [5]							
Number of customers (farms served), average	428,300	1,431,028	2,160,265	3,578,506	3,288,000	3,516,000	3,685,000
Sales, kilowatt-hours (1,000)	315,597	1,535,360	3,394,000	7,761,264	7,677,000	9,280,000	10,847,000
Revenue ($1,000)	22,106	66,535	124,309	252,692	244,138	285,135	317,899
Kilowatt-hours per customer	745	1,073	1,571	2,169	2,335	2,639	2,864
Annual bill, average	$52.37	$46.46	$57.50	$70.71	$74.26	$81.28	$86.31
Revenue per kilowatt-hour (cents)	7.08	4.33	3.66	3.26	3.18	3.08	3.01
WESTERN FARMS [5]							
Number of customers (farms served), average	189,661	413,989	637,600	1,128,460	956,000	1,023,000	1,077,000
Sales, kilowatt-hours (1,000)	1,473,195	1,820,000	2,514,600	6,080,408	4,632,000	6,695,000	6,932,000
Revenue ($1,000)	24,524	35,500	52,595	108,929	86,470	115,030	122,963
Kilowatt-hours per customer	7,768	4,398	3,943	5,388	4,832	6,439	6,439
Annual bill, average	$129.95	$85.72	$82.41	$96.45	$92.31	$112.63	$115.17
Revenue per kilowatt-hour (cents)	1.66	1.95	2.09	1.79	1.91	1.72	1.79

[1] Beginning 1950, data reflect change in Census definition of farm, which tends to decrease number of farms.
[2] Census figures; relate to Apr. 1 for 1930, 1940, and 1950 and Jan. 1 for 1945.
[5] REA cooperatives only and excludes customers of all other agencies (companies and municipals) supplied in whole or in part by REA.
[6] Customers served by municipal systems and various power districts not financed by REA.
[5] "Eastern farms" are those located in the area not affected by heavy irrigation pumping and their statistics give an indication of use of electricity on the average farm. "Western farms" are those where irrigation may be involved. Possibly less than one-fifth of farms in irrigation States do actual pumping, but statistics are not available to make a more accurate separation. Figures for "Western farms," therefore, are more a reflection of fluctuation in the economy than they are of the conventional farm requirements.

Source: Edison Electric Institute, New York, N. Y.; annual statistical bulletin.

No. 599.—RURAL ELECTRIFICATION ADMINISTRATION—SUMMARY OF OPERATIONS: 1935 TO 1952

YEAR	TOTAL LOANS APPROVED AS OF DEC. 31 [1]		DATA FOR SYSTEMS IN OPERATION						
			As of Dec. 31			During year			
	Bor-row-ers [2]	Amount	Sys-tems [3]	Miles ener-gized [4]	Con-sumers connected	Kilowatt hours generated	Kilowatt hours purchased	Kilowatt hours billed	Total reve-nue
	Number	$1,000	Number	Miles	Number	1,000	1,000	1,000	$1,000
1935		6,977	2	0	0				
1940	791	351,455	685	267,846	674,495	(5)	(5)	(5)	(5)
1943	873	473,742	811	390,058	1,087,801	199,228	1,828,132	1,679,381	55,588
1944	904	517,700	826	410,471	1,216,798	213,462	2,106,332	1,925,734	64,043
1945	961	666,954	848	449,579	1,406,918	258,397	2,344,550	2,136,384	73,607
1946	1,009	988,009	869	506,838	1,683,901	319,913	2,730,265	2,477,509	89,943
1947	1,029	1,190,527	911	603,064	2,046,095	433,282	3,720,705	3,396,290	114,998
1948	1,044	1,574,924	952	759,494	2,518,450	718,283	5,018,725	4,757,051	151,674
1949	1,066	1,999,280	995	943,385	3,040,425	903,412	6,541,739	6,227,471	197,029
1950	1,076	2,311,637	1,007	1,088,777	3,413,407	1,076,946	8,164,801	7,778,735	241,373
1951	1,076	2,484,444	1,012	1,177,234	3,657,502	1,384,542	9,961,744	9,655,486	285,074
1952 [6]	1,081	2,668,946	1,019	1,244,665	3,851,227	1,651,106	11,730,511	11,500,197	322,926

[1] For years prior to 1948, includes amounts not yet under loan contract.
[2] Organizations, mainly cooperatives, to which loans for extending central station electric service in rural areas are made.
[3] Rural electric distribution, generation, and transmission systems operated by REA borrowers.
[4] Pole miles of electric distribution and transmission line in service. [5] Not available. [6] Preliminary.

Source: Department of Agriculture, Rural Electrification Administration.

No. 600.—NATURAL-GAS COMPANIES—COMPOSITE INCOME ACCOUNT: 1940 TO 1951

[In thousands of dollars. For years ending Dec. 31. Natural-gas companies deriving 50 percent or more of utility operating income from natural-gas operations]

ITEM	1940	1945	1948	1949	1950	1951
Gas utility operating income:						
Operating revenues	496,522	654,362	958,607	1,066,790	1,336,060	1,654,163
Operating expenses	287,046	387,372	613,600	695,312	861,643	1,058,750
Depreciation and amortization	52,046	62,393	80,323	89,909	101,934	131,906
Taxes:						
Federal taxes on income	} 55,531	} 95,888	63,547	59,235	91,944	129,781
Other taxes			45,893	53,668	62,742	77,834
Total operating revenue deductions	394,923	545,653	803,363	899,124	1,118,263	1,398,271
Net operating revenues	101,599	108,709	155,244	168,666	217,797	257,892
Income from gas plant leased to others	89	394	308	206	874	1,425
Gas utility operating income	101,688	109,103	155,552	168,872	218,671	259,317
Other utility operating income	1,277	1,178	1,181	1,612	1,812	1,336
Total utility operating income	102,965	110,281	156,733	170,484	220,483	260,653
Other income	6,364	5,065	10,655	12,674	15,636	11,739
Gross income	109,329	115,346	167,388	183,158	236,119	272,392
Income deductions:						
Interest on long-term debt	20,818	16,763	27,905	42,637	54,510	65,728
Interest on debt to associated companies	4,861	5,249	4,633	5,811	5,893	7,702
Interest charged to construction-credit	} 3,551	5,267	52	15,125	19,358	14,377
Other income deductions—net				8,317	11,080	11,080
Total income deductions	29,230	27,279	32,486	41,340	52,145	70,138
Net income	80,099	88,067	134,902	141,818	183,974	202,254

Source: Federal Power Commission; annual report, *Statistics of Natural Gas Companies*.

No. 601.—GAS UTILITY INDUSTRY—CUSTOMERS, SALES, AND REVENUES, BY TYPE OF GAS: 1951 AND 1952

[See headnote, table 602]

TYPE OF GAS	CUSTOMERS (1,000) [1]			SALES (1,000,000 THERMS)			REVENUES ($1,000)		
	1951	1952 [2]	Percent change	1951	1952 [2]	Percent change	1951	1952 [2]	Percent change
All types	24,953	26,016	+4.3	48,222	52,457	+8.8	2,228,109	2,459,513	+10.4
Natural gas	16,037	18,535	+15.6	44,718	49,074	+9.7	1,667,154	1,953,540	+17.2
Manufactured gas	5,804	3,897	−32.9	1,763	1,232	−30.1	362,923	254,947	−29.8
Mixed gas	2,803	3,270	+16.7	1,653	2,072	+25.3	177,101	228,781	+29.2
Liquefied petroleum gas	309	314	+1.6	88	79	−10.2	20,931	22,245	+6.3

[1] Yearly averages. [2] Preliminary.

Source: American Gas Association, New York, N. Y.; yearbook, *Gas Facts*.

602.—Gas Utility Industry—Customers and Revenues, by Class of Service: 1932 to 1952

[ers natural, manufactured, mixed, and liquid petroleum gas. Based on questionnaire mailed to all privately ned gas utilities and municipally owned gas departments in the United States, except those with annual enues less than $25,000, which in the aggregate account for only a negligible portion of the industry]

R	CUSTOMERS (1,000)[1]					REVENUES ($1,000)				
	Total	Residential	Commercial	Industrial	Other	Total	Residential	Commercial	Industrial	Other
....	15, 536	456		78	8	728, 302	537, 207	92, 816	90, 678	2, 601
...·	15, 874	776	1, 018	72	8	727, 004	505, 339	90, 556	130, 459	2, 639
....	16, 185	041	1, 058	77	9	770, 349	516, 218	97, 362	151, 996	4, 774
....	16, 620	481	1, 056	74	9	801, 298	526, 359	99, 774	167, 081	6, 084
....	16, 907	727	1, 095	75	10	777, 261	522, 956	101, 150	144, 956	8, 125
....				73	8	814, 232	537, 629	105, 346	165, 197	5, 160
..·.				73	8	871, 735	573, 361	111, 970	182, 527	3, 877
....				78	7	914, 036	574, 842	114, 323	220, 384	4, 487
....				76	8	994, 318	622, 686	127, 686	228, 227	6, 262
....				77	8	1, 064, 044	647, 556	127, 528	280, 283	8, 726
....	18, 320	1, 177		82	6	1, 105, 162	666, 735	123, 120	297, 927	10, 380
..·.				80	12	1, 180, 623	711, 767	142, 041	280, 907	15, 907
....				87	15	1, 211, 262	761, 274	153, 781	284, 517	11, 860
....				91	16	1, 305, 616	869, 400	182, 917	325, 642	17, 657
....	20, 562	1, 571		94	18	1, 579, 462	957, 926	229, 906	377, 408	23, 223
....	21,	1,		97	17	1, 686, 596	1, 061, 393	328, 077	394, 589	53, 666
....	22,	1,		99	17	1, 945, 002	1, 177, 070	365, 571	476, 610	35, 751
....	23,	1,		101	23	2, 226, 109	1, 234, 987	394, 435	557, 066	41, 689
....	24,	1,		106	23	2, 458, 513	1, 446, 761	321, 450	640, 429	50, 873

y averages.   [2] Preliminary.

rce: American Gas Association, New York, N. Y.; yearbook, *Gas Facts*.

603.—Manufactured Gas—Solid Fuels and Oil Used by Utilities, by Type of Use: 1932 to 1951

[Solid fuels in thousands of tons; oil in millions of gallons. See headnote, table 602]

	1932	1936	1940	1945 [1]	1947 [1]	1948 [1]	1949 [1]	1950 [1]	1951 [1]
ANTHRACITE COAL									
otal	115	126	214	252	470	690	382	329	241
r gas generator fuel	33	44	86	94	181	272	135	109	33
fuel	82	82	128	160	344	355	214	199	186
				[3] 38	[3] 45	[3] 53	[3] 33	[3] 21	[3] 20
BITUMINOUS COAL									
otal	8, 193	7, 949	6, 682	8, 098	7, 515	7, 894	6, 529	6, 297	5, 780
r gas generator fuel	477	480	304	432	379	393	366	341	221
r fuel	428	382	340	487	492	461	328	340	170
and retort charge	7, 191	6, 972	6, 220	7, 171	6, 843	6, 452	5, 836	5, 615	5, 377
h and producer fuel	7	15	18	8	1	(7)	(1)	1	1
COKE									
otal	2, 915	2, 639	2, 099	3, 551	3, 651	3, 728	3, 365	3, 213	1, 912
r gas generator fuel	1, 595	1, 314	1, 552	2, 225	2, 591	2, 485	2, 196	2, 258	1, 341
fuel	599	512	364	585	542	547	472	399	306
and producer fuel	781	793	663	741	[4] 748	[4] 702	[4] 536	[4] 586	[4] 865
OIL									
otal	648	510	677	984	1, 289	1, 326	1, 196	1, 185	873
r gas enricher	536	465	592	797	1, 635	1, 075	929	912	578
fuel	9	11	27	[5] 24	57	61	68	75	68
s production	60	34	58	113	147	172	185	192	227

cludes fuel used in production of manufactured gas during periods of peak demand or emergency only, for systems regularly distributing natural gas.
en and retort charge.
ss than 500 tons.
cludes 10,000 tons used as oven and retort charge in 1947, 7,000 tons in 1948, 5,000 tons in 1949, 7,000 tons in and 4,000 tons in 1951.
cludes 500,000 gallons used as bench and producer fuel.

ce: American Gas Association, New York, N. Y.; yearbook, *Gas Facts*.

No. 604.—GAS UTILITY INDUSTRY—CUSTOMERS AND REVENUES, BY TYPE OF GAS, CLASS OF SERVICE, AND STATE: 1951

[See headnote, table 602]

TYPE OF GAS, DIVISION, AND STATE	CUSTOMERS (1,000) [1]					REVENUES ($1,000)				
	Total	Residential	Commercial	Industrial	Other	Total	Residential	Commercial	Industrial	Other
United States, all types	24,953.3	23,042.5	1,787.2	100.7	22.9	2,226,109	1,334,967	294,435	557,068	41,639
Natural gas	16,036.9	14,742.0	1,218.7	88.3	17.9	1,667,154	930,360	203,648	496,086	37,060
Manufactured gas	5,803.8	5,389.4	384.9	24.8	4.7	362,923	258,732	63,052	37,102	4,037
Mixed gas	2,803.3	2,627.8	158.1	17.1	.3	177,101	130,711	22,673	23,259	458
Liquefied petroleum gas	309.3	283.3	25.5	.5	(²)	20,931	15,164	5,062	621	84
New England	1,643.7	1,557.1	78.2	7.6	.8	108,575	81,028	14,796	12,185	544
Connecticut	370.5	350.3	18.3	1.8	.1	26,691	19,263	3,637	3,719	72
Maine	39.7	37.6	2.0	.1	(²)	2,707	2,020	477	209	1
Massachusetts	1,006.3	951.2	49.9	4.6	.6	65,706	49,563	8,636	7,084	423
New Hampshire	38.5	36.0	2.2	.3	(²)	2,516	1,806	510	191	9
Rhode Island	167.5	161.8	4.9	.7	.1	9,912	7,582	1,339	935	56
Vermont	21.2	20.2	.9	.1	(²)	1,043	794	199	47	3
Middle Atlantic	6,811.8	6,310.2	466.9	28.9	5.8	501,099	343,609	68,990	84,638	3,862
New Jersey	1,228.7	1,139.1	84.0	8.6	(²)	71,277	52,630	11,087	7,352	208
New York	3,641.5	3,357.0	265.6	14.7	4.2	235,412	169,478	39,364	23,962	2,608
Pennsylvania	1,941.6	1,814.1	117.3	8.6	1.6	194,410	121,501	18,539	53,324	1,046
East North Central	5,634.0	5,274.2	331.1	22.6	6.1	538,951	346,194	60,767	128,817	3,173
Illinois	1,759.2	1,654.4	92.4	11.4	1.0	136,293	80,546	15,050	40,528	169
Indiana	593.8	556.6	34.6	1.6	1.0	52,548	30,600	6,284	15,173	491
Michigan	1,140.7	1,074.6	62.3	3.8	(²)	115,115	85,324	11,647	18,011	133
Ohio	1,696.3	1,568.6	119.6	4.0	4.1	199,885	124,361	23,812	50,154	1,558
Wisconsin	444.0	420.0	22.2	1.8	(²)	35,110	25,363	3,974	4,951	822
West North Central	1,943.7	1,787.2	147.5	8.5	.5	224,309	131,052	27,852	60,643	4,762
Iowa	305.3	280.4	24.2	.7	(²)	30,878	19,446	4,771	6,590	71
Kansas	401.9	361.5	38.2	1.9	.3	53,396	25,364	5,961	19,476	2,595
Minnesota	357.7	337.8	18.5	1.4	(²)	36,582	23,777	3,242	9,208	355
Missouri	614.5	572.1	39.6	2.8	(²)	67,765	43,262	7,508	16,599	396
Nebraska	198.0	175.5	20.8	1.5	.2	27,256	14,476	4,339	7,475	966
North Dakota	27.4	25.0	2.3	.1	(²)	2,749	1,826	693	130	100
South Dakota	38.9	34.9	3.9	.1	(²)	5,663	2,901	1,388	1,165	279
South Atlantic	1,710.0	1,575.3	125.9	4.4	4.4	155,975	95,662	23,151	34,273	2,889
Delaware	51.8	48.9	2.9	(²)	(²)	3,573	2,760	476	331	6
District of Columbia	177.6	162.4	13.6	.6	1.0	14,638	11,123	2,784	300	431
Florida	179.1	166.8	11.2	.2	.9	15,099	8,954	3,615	1,773	757
Georgia	249.2	225.7	21.4	2.1	(²)	31,420	15,051	3,554	12,469	346
Maryland	405.9	379.0	26.0	.5	.4	29,823	22,428	3,863	3,249	283
North Carolina	68.4	62.0	6.3	.1		5,504	3,627	1,743	122	12
South Carolina	43.9	39.6	4.3	(²)		3,375	2,338	944	93	
Virginia	238.0	221.7	15.3	.3	.7	17,055	12,701	2,628	1,336	390
West Virginia	296.1	269.2	24.9	.6	1.4	35,488	16,680	3,544	14,600	664
East South Central	829.4	744.9	80.1	3.4	1.0	109,229	50,982	13,992	37,805	6,450
Alabama	207.3	190.5	16.3	.5	(²)	32,778	12,702	3,193	16,851	32
Kentucky	280.5	253.0	26.2	.5	.8	27,970	17,723	3,787	5,913	547
Mississippi	161.4	141.8	18.2	1.3	.1	20,271	8,396	2,780	8,581	514
Tennessee	180.2	159.6	19.4	1.1	.1	28,210	12,161	4,232	6,460	5,357
West South Central	2,564.1	2,296.7	249.6	14.3	3.5	244,778	103,180	28,285	107,919	5,394
Arkansas	184.9	159.7	23.8	1.4	(²)	22,182	8,819	3,329	9,829	205
Louisiana	431.4	392.2	35.8	2.6	.8	46,200	15,880	3,114	26,350	856
Oklahoma	462.0	410.9	47.2	2.8	1.1	19,936	5,909	5,909	12,792	905
Texas	1,485.8	1,333.9	142.8	7.5	1.6	136,854	58,545	15,933	58,948	3,428
Mountain	656.9	584.8	68.9	2.4	.8	88,989	42,020	14,510	28,960	3,479
Arizona	139.5	124.1	14.7	.6	.1	17,068	5,745	1,794	9,419	110
Colorado	208.6	183.9	24.4	.3	(²)	29,829	15,083	6,456	6,520	1,770
Idaho	.6		.1			56	30	26		
Montana	79.5	70.5	8.6	.4	(²)	11,597	6,209	2,411	2,578	399
Nevada	5.1	4.5	.6			603	350	233	4	16
New Mexico	95.4	86.3	8.4	.3	.4	12,875	5,762	1,664	4,506	943
Utah	83.0	75.4	7.1	.5		10,105	5,405	668	4,032	
Wyoming	45.2	39.6	5.0	.3	.3	6,856	3,436	1,258	1,921	241
Pacific	3,159.7	2,912.1	239.0	8.6	(²)	256,204	141,240	42,090	61,806	11,046
California	2,963.4	2,755.4	220.2	7.8	(²)	239,143	129,672	37,268	61,137	11,006
Oregon	100.9	91.5	8.9	.5		9,386	6,777	2,251	358	
Washington	75.4	65.2	9.9	.3		7,675	4,791	2,571	313	

[1] Averages for the year.   [²] Less than 50 customers.

Source: American Gas Association, New York, N. Y.; yearbook, Gas Facts.

No. 605.—WATER POWER—DEVELOPED, 1920 TO 1951, AND ESTIMATED UNDEVELOPED

[In thousands of kilowatts]

DIVISION AND STATE	DEVELOPED WATER POWER (CAPACITY OF ACTUAL INSTALLATIONS ONLY)										Estimated undeveloped water power, Jan. 1952
	Electric utilities only		Electric utilities and industrial plants								
			Dec. 1939		Dec. 1950			Dec. 1951			
	Dec. 1920	Dec. 1930	Total	Utilities	Total	Utilities	Industrial	Total	Utilities	Industrial	
United States	3,704	8,528	12,675	11,604	13,675	17,676	1,000	19,570	18,568	1,002	36,174
New England	391	788	1,115	823	1,290	971	268	1,254	987	267	3,329
Maine	40	174	301	186	301	270	121	392	270	122	1,604
New Hampshire	43	212	292	235	312	262	80	311	262	49	687
Vermont	49	166	173	156	192	177	15	196	180	15	532
Massachusetts	114	129	228	161	222	166	56	237	182	55	301
Rhode Island	2	2	14	3	11	3	8	11	3	5	
Connecticut	44	79	107	85	107	89	18	107	89	18	114
Middle Atlantic	662	1,290	1,632	1,542	1,678	1,602	76	1,677	1,596	81	6,598
New York	540	1,074	1,229	1,165	1,225	1,155	70	1,225	1,150	75	3,077
New Jersey	1	1	6	3	9	6	3	9	6	3	225
Pennsylvania	120	215	399	395	444	441	3	443	440	3	3,296
East North Central	372	662	790	763	991	838	73	929	868	71	2,315
Ohio	17	13	16	12	16	12	4	15	12	3	212
Indiana	11	35	36	36	37	37		36	36		323
Illinois	43	50	51	49	54	49	5	54	49	5	1,111
Michigan	167	258	368	344	399	384	15	408	394	14	353
Wisconsin	134	347	318	323	395	395	40	415	367	48	316
West North Central	297	279	537	601	629	577	52	631	579	62	5,982
Minnesota	98	122	156	128	181	138	43	180	137	43	227
Iowa	135	124	127	127	137	137		135	135		414
Missouri	12	13	151	151	151	151		151	151		2,472
North Dakota			(1)								652
South Dakota	5	4	4	4	11	3	8	13	5	8	1,279
Nebraska	7	11	87	86	142	142	(1)	142	142	(1)	466
Kansas	7	6	9	7	6	6		6	6		290
South Atlantic	539	1,693	2,234	1,869	2,767	2,297	470	2,786	2,317	469	8,395
Delaware			(1)		1	1		1	1		
Maryland	1	273	273	271	272	271	1	272	271	1	383
District of Columbia	2	3	3	2	3	3		2	3		
Virginia	45	83	204	182	207	183	24	206	183	23	1,432
West Virginia	9	56	209	101	208	101	107	208	101	107	2,097
North Carolina	144	397	651	400	962	662	300	961	662	299	1,272
South Carolina	281	508	520	495	679	653	26	679	653	26	940
Georgia	155	271	349	337	425	412	13	444	432	12	2,042
Florida	4	14	14	14	13	13		13	13		90
East South Central	170	563	1,270	1,140	2,729	2,721	8	2,999	2,991	8	4,612
Kentucky		105	111	111	271	271		406	406		1,576
Tennessee	97	127	432	310	1,226	1,238		1,372	1,373		846
Alabama	72	632	727	719	1,230	1,212	8	1,230	1,212	8	1,780
Mississippi											410
West South Central	4	19	140	139	466	463	3	548	546	3	2,886
Arkansas	1	11	67	67	148	145	3	196	153	3	1,606
Louisiana			1								50
Oklahoma	1	2	2	2	74	74		74	74		963
Texas	2	6	71	71	245	245	(1)	318	318	(1)	847
Mountain	487	784	1,633	1,581	2,286	2,282	4	2,627	2,623	4	22,989
Montana	212	300	321	321	427	426	1	462	461	1	6,085
Idaho	135	226	367	367	441	440	1	454	453	1	8,849
Wyoming	2	12	47	47	79	79		92	92		785
Colorado	45	52	67	66	92	91	1	145	144	1	1,327
New Mexico	1	1	1	1	25	25		25	25		209
Arizona	23	87	382	208	541	541		767	767		3,476
Utah	58	98	93	93	94	94		94	94		1,397
Nevada	9		504	504	587	586	1	587	586	1	111
Pacific	672	2,391	2,783	2,741	5,979	5,933	46	6,421	6,373	48	29,798
Washington	241	508	812	784	2,591	2,544	27	2,938	2,908	29	15,516
Oregon	65	166	286	278	783	785	17	800	783	17	6,723
California	566	1,640	1,685	1,680	2,606	2,604	2	2,690	2,688	2	7,460

[1] Less than 500.

Source: Federal Power Commission. Developed water power published in annual report, *Production of Electric Energy and Capacity of Generating Plants*.

20. Roads and Motor Vehicles

Public roads.—Federal Government statistics on public roads are compiled and published by the Bureau of Public Roads of the Department of Commerce. Since 1945, such data have been published annually in *Highway Statistics*. For statistics prior to 1945, the same Bureau's publication, *Highway Statistics, Summary to 1945*, shows available public roads data carried back over periods ranging from 20 to 50 years.

The first road mileage survey was made in 1904. Other road mileage surveys were made in 1909, 1914, and 1921. Data for these surveys appear in Department of Agriculture, Bulletin 1279, *Rural Highway Mileage, Income, and Expenditures, 1921–1922*.

The term "rural" as used here may be roughly defined as the area which lies outside of communities having 2,500 inhabitants or more. The data shown here, which are compiled on the basis of individual reports from the different States, are largely consistent with this definition of "rural." "Urban extensions" are continuations of designated State-system roads in or through cities or towns of 2,500 inhabitants or more. "County and other local roads" are rural roads over which the State exercises no direct control.

Motor vehicles and fuel.—Motor-vehicle production data are compiled by the Automobile Manufacturers Association and published in the annual report, *Automobile Facts and Figures*. The Bureau of the Census compiles and publishes statistics on the motor-vehicles and equipment industry which are published in the Census of Manufactures reports and are also included in section 30, Manufactures, in this volume.

Motor-vehicle registration figures are based on reports and records of State motor-vehicle registration departments. The statistics are compiled and published by the Bureau of Public Roads in the annual report, *Highway Statistics*. The same report also includes statistics on motor fuel consumption.

Historical statistics.—See preface and historical appendix. Tabular headnotes (as "See also *Historical Statistics*, series K 177–181") provide cross-references, where applicable, to *Historical Statistics of the United States, 1789–1945*.

Note.—This section presents data for the most recent year or period available on April 22, 1953, when the material was organized and sent to the printer.

No. 606.—Rural Roads in the United States—Approximate Mileage: 1921 to 1951

[In **thousands of miles.** Rural roads include roads outside of incorporated areas and certain of the more populous unincorporated areas. Figures cover continental U. S. and refer to existing mileage at end of calendar year. See also *Historical Statistics*, series K 177–181]

TYPE AND CONTROL	1921	1925	1930	1935	1940	1945	1949	1950	1951
All rural roads, total.........	2,925	3,006	3,009	3,032	2,990	3,012	3,003	2,990	2,987
Primary State highways...........	} 203	} 275	} 324	332	329	339	358	363	367
Secondary State highways........				58	81	84	85	88	92
County roads under State control..	....	....	....	115	114	118	121	122	125
County and local roads [1]..........	2,722	2,731	2,685	2,527	2,466	2,471	2,439	2,417	2,403
Surfaced rural roads, total..	387	521	694	1,063	1,340	1,495	1,617	1,679	1,722
Primary State highways...........	} 84	} 145	} 227	280	302	316	344	351	355
Secondary State highways........				39	65	71	69	73	78
County roads under State control..	....	....	....	38	55	63	77	83	88
County and local roads [1]..........	303	376	467	706	918	1,045	1,127	1,172	1,201
Nonsurfaced rural roads, total [2].............	2,538	2,485	2,315	1,969	1,650	1,517	1,386	1,311	1,264
Primary State highways...........	} 119	} 130	} 97	52	27	23	14	12	11
Secondary State highways........				19	16	13	16	15	14
County roads under State control..	....	....	....	77	59	55	44	39	37
County and local roads [1][2].........	2,419	2,355	2,218	1,821	1,548	1,426	1,312	1,245	1,202

[1] Includes mileage in national and State parks, forests, reservations, etc., not included as part of State highway systems.   [2] Includes mileage not classified by type of surface.

Source: Department of Commerce, Bureau of Public Roads; *Highway Statistics, Summary to 1945*, and subsequent annual reports.

607.—Existing Rural Road Mileage, by Type and by Governmental Control, by States, End of 1951

[Excludes roads outside incorporated areas and certain more populous unincorporated areas. Compiled for latest available year from reports of State authorities and planning survey data]

STATE		Surfaced			Nonsur-faced	GOVERNMENTAL CONTROL		
	Total	Total	Low type [1]	High type [1]		State	Local	Federal [2]
Continental U. S.	2,987,430	1,723,175	1,450,224	272,951	1,264,253	[3] 532,291	2,381,073	74,066
	59,984	41,874	37,222	4,642	18,110		41,670	370
	27,568	10,042	7,784	2,258	17,526		19,401	8,204
	64,621	28,266	23,587	4,679	36,355		64,417	
	97,656	58,864	45,140	13,724	38,822		74,479	10,300
	72,031	19,782	14,023	5,759	52,249	11,	59,407	793
	10,323	10,006	7,187	2,819	317	2,	7,798	
	3,501	3,088	2,179	907	713	[4] 3,		
	41,464	19,596	17,410	2,186	21,868	9,	38,720	1,136
	88,190	25,795	20,258	5,537	62,395	13,781	74,408	
	40,509	20,321	18,371	2,020	19,978	4,552	37,309	8,846
	103,432	87,722	75,535	12,187	15,710		92,990	
	84,337	75,588	63,228	12,300	8,749		74,614	
	101,098	71,572	65,565	6,007	29,530		92,302	
	125,935	53,296	50,627	2,669	72,639		116,695	15
	60,004	37,757	32,548	5,209	22,217		63,621	251
	39,779	24,557	18,755	5,802	15,222		26,775	
	20,727	17,135	16,015	1,120	3,592		9,948	36
	16,542	14,001	11,346	2,655	2,541		12,047	
	17,795	16,745	13,679	3,066	1,050		14,738	
	92,761	68,637	61,049	7,553	24,124		84,663	
nesota	108,456	84,798	79,299	5,499	23,658		94,085	1,151
ssippi	61,785	34,265	31,043	3,222	27,520		53,781	1,029
uri	99,799	74,282	69,284	4,998	25,517		90,642	770
ana	69,679	21,001	18,495	2,506	48,678		64,171	6,962
ka	100,031	33,509	31,993	1,516	66,522		90,804	390
a	25,405	6,558	6,553	5	18,847		19,416	
ampshire	12,519	8,917	8,326	591	3,602		8,742	118
rsey	18,367	14,678	11,904	2,774	3,689		16,436	
Mexico	61,712	9,430	5,299	4,131	52,282		47,672	1,966
ork	79,502	62,220	41,449	27,771	10,292		64,608	
Carolina	65,346	47,252	36,564	10,688	18,094			1,146
Dakota	113,952	29,381	29,271	110	84,571		108,885	682
ma	86,258	76,084	58,495	17,589	10,174		70,210	
ma	92,006	28,378	22,429	5,949	63,628		83,272	87
	52,478	27,742	24,144	3,598	24,736		30,799	14,028
lvania	88,015	54,837	35,231	19,606	33,178		45,777	322
Island	1,658	1,521	1,276	245	137		1,094	
Carolina	47,464	18,946	16,524	2,422	28,518		26,378	
Dakota	93,570	31,859	30,440	1,419	61,711	6,231	84,326	963
co	64,331	52,952	48,686	4,266	11,379	7,743	55,938	658
	196,306	86,571	72,673	13,898	109,825		188,290	
	24,917	11,204	8,319	2,885	13,713	4,	16,197	3,036
t	12,909	10,233	9,207	1,026	2,736	1,	11,111	22
	49,691	45,757	42,796	2,961	3,934	48,	619	969
on	46,874	35,035	30,095	4,941	11,538	6,	36,076	4,773
rginia	33,579	18,650	14,046	4,604	14,929	31,	1,943	814
n	86,287	77,471	70,016	7,455	8,816	10,	75,814	410
	25,937	7,931	4,849	3,082	18,006		19,332	1,943

[1] Low type includes soil surfaced; slag, gravel, or stone; bituminous surfaced treated; and mixed bituminous (bituminous penetration (nonrigid base). High type includes mixed bituminous and bituminous penetration (rigid base); bituminous concrete and sheet asphalt; Portland cement concrete; brick; and block.

[2] Includes only mileage of roads not forming a part of State or local highway systems.

[3] Includes 8,217 miles of State park, forest, institutional, and other roads, rural and urban, that are not part of regular local highway systems.

[4] Includes county roads under State control in Alabama (3 counties), Delaware, North Carolina, Virginia (all counties), and West Virginia. Also in Virginia, includes mileage maintained by State in incorporated places of less than 3,500 population.

Source: Department of Commerce, Bureau of Public Roads, Highway Statistics, 1951.

No. 608.—State Highway Systems—Existing Mileage, Mileage Built, Funds Available and Disbursements: 1930 to 1951

[Figures cover continental U. S. and refer to calendar years for most States. See also *Historical Statistics*, series K 184–188 for data on total mileage built by State highway departments]

ITEM	1930	1935	1940	1945	1949	1950	1951
Total mileage at end of year	[1] 324,498	523,474	551,766	573,234	596,699	606,468	629,316
Mileage under State control	[7]	520,351	548,499	570,239	596,176	[5] 606,468	[5] 629,316
Primary State-highway systems	[1] 324,498	331,867	329,472	338,310	357,650	365,213	366,973
Nonsurfaced roads	[1] 97,726	52,060	26,991	22,873	13,192	12,007	11,071
Surfaced roads	[1] 226,772	279,807	302,481	315,437	344,458	351,206	355,902
Low type [4]	[1] 142,659	168,282	180,091	182,786	206,770	[5] 168,554	[5] 169,285
High type [4]	[1] 84,113	111,525	122,390	132,651	137,688	[5] 182,652	[5] 186,617
Secondary roads	[7]	173,603	195,245	202,356	205,833	209,339	217,101
Urban extensions of State-highway systems	[7]	14,881	23,782	29,573	32,693	[5] 35,916	[5] 37,025
Other State roads							[5] 8,217
Connecting streets not under State control	[3]	3,123	3,267	2,995	2,523	[9]	[9]
Total mileage built during year by State-highway departments [7]	35,277	26,814	32,5°4	15,278	45,176	55,487	51,471
Graded and drained	7,813	3,284	2,207	283	2,329	3,364	2,531
Surfaced	27,464	23,530	30,387	14,995	42,847	52,123	48,940
Mileage built—State controlled	35,277	26,814	29,695	14,827	35,241	44,265	41,864
Earth roads	7,813	3,284	1,423	250	1,517	1,784	1,603
High-type surface	10,787	3,806	5,223	3,971	7,487	13,379	15,122
Low-type surface	16,677	19,724	23,049	10,606	26,237	29,102	25,139
State-highway funds available ($1,000) [8] [9]	1,423,164	1,205,945	2,037,606	2,242,572	4,583,325	5,068,196	5,565,091
Disbursements of State-highway funds ($1,000) [8] [10]	1,330,545	1,267,838	1,678,009	1,299,381	3,201,008	3,561,513	3,980,534

[1] No segregation of secondary State highways from primary systems in 1930; figures shown include an undetermined amount of municipal street mileage on State systems or connecting these systems. Not strictly comparable with subsequent years, since county road mileage had not yet been taken over by State highway departments.
[2] Not available.
[3] Mileage formerly shown as "Connecting streets not under State control," now included with "Urban extensions of State highway systems," with exception of mileage in Kentucky, Maryland, Mississippi, and District of Columbia. These mileages reclassified as local city streets.
[4] Low type includes soil-surfaced; slag, gravel, or stone; bituminous surface-treated; and mixed bituminous surfaces. High type includes bituminous penetration; bituminous concrete and sheet asphalt; Portland cement concrete; brick; and block.
[5] Beginning 1950, mixed bituminous and bituminous penetration on "nonrigid base" shown as low type and surfacing on "rigid base" included as high-type mileage.
[6] Mileage of State park, forest, institutional, toll, and other roads under State control not previously included.
[7] Prior to 1940, represents State-controlled only.
[8] Includes funds transferred to or from local units and proceeds of highway-user imposts allotted by the State treasurer for (1) county and other local roads and streets, and for (2) nonhighway purposes.
[9] Available funds include accumulated reserves.
[10] Includes estimated highway transactions of Port of New York Authority.

Source: Department of Commerce, Bureau of Public Roads; *Highway Statistics, Summary to 1945*, and subsequent annual reports.

No. 609.—Public Roads—State Highway Finances: 1920 to 1951

[In thousands of dollars. See also *Historical Statistics*, series K 193–204]

YEAR	State revenues used for highway purposes	Federal funds received for highways	ALLOCATION OF NET RECEIPTS FROM STATE IMPOSTS ON HIGHWAY USERS				DISBURSEMENTS FOR STATE HIGHWAY PURPOSES						State highway debt outstanding
			Total net funds distributed	State highway	Local roads and streets	Non-highway	Total	State highway		Administrative, highway patrol, etc.	Interest		
								Construction	Maintenance				
1920	154,986	61,966	98,672				320,507	240,340	56,468	21,699			225,406
1925	142,716	93,343	393,738	300,628	85,931	7,179	613,342	403,543	119,304	62,034	28,161		789,347
1930	129,791	94,111	829,822	627,855	181,807	20,160	1,018,530	728,887	193,929	42,534	53,181		1,572,455
1935	53,622	219,381	908,676	523,399	238,134	147,143	750,681	438,306	187,122	49,401	75,822		2,160,299
1940	60,964	196,139	1,274,389	754,479	323,331	196,579	941,332	563,074	218,776	81,460	78,022		2,159,025
1945	102,094	59,954	1,186,220	770,705	315,681	99,834	636,378	210,467	286,678	82,267	56,966		1,637,904
1946	204,420	147,230	1,544,298	1,037,058	412,662	94,578	1,012,778	502,316	326,574	130,612	53,276		1,571,577
1947	127,186	288,336	1,764,567	1,110,272	483,777	170,518	1,484,406	882,351	373,677	178,404	49,974		1,536,930
1948	191,006	364,852	1,997,085	1,236,848	570,867	189,370	1,823,042	1,138,674	465,616	167,223	51,524		1,735,362
1949	209,520	429,198	2,241,512	1,449,285	626,116	166,111	2,092,121	1,361,950	488,037	185,325	56,806		1,928,330
1950	190,604	425,587	2,487,094	1,597,704	672,352	217,038	2,283,513	1,533,859	501,487	187,453	60,714		2,141,038
1951	235,426	415,628	2,750,182	1,739,686	743,725	266,771	2,581,632	1,739,579	562,272	215,154	64,627		2,475,803

Source: Department of Commerce, Bureau of Public Roads.

No. 615.—MOTOR VEHICLES—FACTORY SALES AND REGISTRATIONS: 1900 TO 1951

[For 1924 and subsequent years includes data for motor vehicles assembled in foreign countries from parts made in United States. Excludes motorcycles. See also *Historical Statistics*, series K 225-232]

	FACTORY SALES						REGISTRATIONS (IN THOUSANDS)		
YEAR	Number (in thousands)			Wholesale value [3] (thousands of dollars)			Total (excl. publicly owned)	Passenger cars, and taxis [4]	Motor trucks and busses [3]
	Total	Passenger cars	Motor trucks [1]	Total	Passenger cars	Motor trucks [1]			
1900	4	4		4,899	4,899		8	8	
1905	25	24	1	40,000	38,670	1,330	79	77	1
1910	187	181	6	225,000	215,340	9,660	469	458	10
1915	970	896	74	701,778	575,978	125,800	2,491	2,332	159
1920	2,237	1,906	322	2,238,420	1,809,171	423,249	9,239	8,132	1,108
1924	3,603	3,186	417	2,288,677	1,970,097	318,581	17,613	15,436	2,177
1925	4,266	3,725	531	2,916,770	2,458,370	458,400	19,941	17,440	2,501
1926	4,301	3,784	517	3,092,188	2,640,065	452,123	22,053	19,221	2,832
1927	3,401	2,937	465	2,584,802	2,164,671	420,131	23,140	20,142	2,997
1928	4,359	3,815	543	3,013,622	2,576,690	437,132	24,512	21,308	3,204
1929	5,358	4,587	771	3,413,148	2,847,119	566,030	26,503	23,060	3,442
1930	3,356	2,785	571	2,094,835	1,645,309	384,437	26,532	22,973	3,559
1931	2,390	1,973	417	1,373,691	1,111,274	262,418	25,862	22,330	3,532
1932	1,371	1,135	235	754,685	618,391	136,193	24,133	20,622	3,200
1933	1,920	1,574	347	948,805	762,737	186,069	23,877	20,586	3,290
1934	2,753	2,178	575	1,487,260	1,147,116	330,144	24,964	21,472	3,482
1935	3,947	3,252	695	2,088,834	1,709,426	379,408	26,290	22,496	2,725
1936	4,454	3,670	785	2,478,467	2,015,646	462,820	28,172	24,108	4,064
1937	4,809	3,916	893	2,778,227	2,243,732	534,495	29,705	25,391	4,315
1938	2,489	2,004	485	1,570,950	1,236,802	334,148	29,443	25,167	4,276
1939	3,577	2,867	710	2,260,018	1,765,189	494,829	30,615	26,140	4,476
1940	4,472	3,717	755	2,938,474	2,370,654	567,820	32,085	27,272	4,663
1941	4,841	3,780	1,061	3,637,008	2,567,208	1,069,800	34,472	29,524	4,948
1942	1,042	223	819	1,591,270	163,814	1,427,457	32,579	27,869	4,710
1943	700	(4)	700	1,451,896	102	1,451,794	30,500	25,913	4,587
1944	738	1	738	1,701,376	447	1,700,929	30,096	25,466	4,630
1945	725	70	656	1,269,210	87,255	1,181,955	30,638	25,691	4,947
1946	3,090	2,149	941	3,023,028	1,979,781	1,043,247	33,946	28,100	5,846
1947	4,796	3,556	1,240	5,673,739	3,963,896	1,709,843	37,360	30,719	6,642
1948	5,285	3,909	1,376	6,711,612	4,853,402	1,856,210	40,542	33,201	7,341
1949	6,254	5,119	1,134	8,175,853	6,768,418	1,407,435	44,140	36,312	7,828
1950	8,003	6,666	1,337	10,380,752	8,633,272	1,747,480	48,185	40,185	8,382
1951	6,765	5,337	1,428	9,737,254	7,371,207	2,366,047	51,292	42,526	8,766

[1] Includes busses. A substantial part of the trucks and busses reported comprises chassis without body; hence value of bodies for these chassis not included. Includes military trucks; total sales for the period Sept. 1, 1939, through 1945, amounted to 2,575,000, valued at $5,257,588,000. Production for the period Jan. 1, 1940, through 1945 was 2,601,000. [3] Beginning 1937, represents standard equipment.
[2] Prior to 1926, busses included with passenger cars. [4] Less than 500.

Source: Factory sales—Automobile Manufacturers Association, Detroit, Mich.; *Automobile Facts and Figures*. Registrations—Department of Commerce, Bureau of Public Roads; *Highway Statistics, Summary to 1945*, and subsequent annual reports.

No. 616.—MOTOR FUEL CONSUMPTION: 1943 TO 1951

[In millions of gallons. Excludes exports and Federal purchases for military use. Data obtained chiefly from reports of State authorities. See also *Historical Statistics*, series K 283-235 for data on total highway and non-highway usage]

USE	1943	1944	1945	1946	1947	1948	1949	1950	1951
Total consumption	18,571	19,524	22,304	29,201	32,636	34,797	36,835	40,280	42,961
Total usage	16,642	19,392	22,047	28,877	31,681	34,329	36,440	39,831	42,473
Highway	14,004	16,430	19,140	25,649	28,216	30,451	32,431	35,653	38,128
Nonhighway	2,630	2,962	2,808	3,228	3,465	3,869	4,009	4,178	4,345
Private and commercial use, total	15,196	16,637	21,576	25,382	31,030	33,616	35,690	39,033	41,639
Highway	14,668	16,090	18,798	25,269	27,714	29,909	31,830	35,034	37,479
Nonhighway	2,528	2,748	2,778	3,113	2,315	3,707	3,840	3,999	4,160
Public, total	447	455	471	493	551	713	750	798	834
Federal, highway	42	62	43	44	59	64	67	99	75
State, county, and municipal	405	412	428	450	502	649	682	729	759
Highway	394	298	305	335	443	488	514	561	575
Nonhighway	111	115	120	115	149	182	169	179	184
Losses allowed for evaporation, handling, etc.	229	232	257	325	255	378	396	449	478

Source: Department of Commerce, Bureau of Public Roads; *Highway Statistics, Summary to 1945*; and subsequent annual reports.

No. 617.—Motor-Vehicle Registrations (Combined Figures for Passenger Cars, Busses, and Motor Trucks), by States: 1915 to 1951

[Excludes publicly owned vehicles. For uniformity, figures have been adjusted to a calendar year basis as registration years in States differ. Figures represent net numbers where possible, excluding reregistrations and nonresident registrations]

[In thousands]

DIVISION AND STATE	1915	1920	1925	1930	1935	1940	1945	1950	1951
Continental U. S.	2,491	9,239	19,941	26,532	26,230	32,035	30,638	48,567	51,292
New England	206	573	1,281	1,699	1,682	2,020	1,967	2,784	2,921
Maine	22	63	140	186	181	206	207	272	276
New Hampshire	13	35	81	112	117	135	128	169	176
Vermont	11	32	70	87	82	94	90	119	123
Massachusetts	103	274	637	846	786	904	859	1,266	1,330
Rhode Island	16	50	102	137	149	187	178	249	259
Connecticut	41	119	251	331	367	494	505	709	757
Middle Atlantic	497	1,474	3,537	4,921	4,964	5,976	5,311	8,235	8,714
New York	255	676	1,696	2,306	2,331	2,743	2,330	3,603	3,888
New Jersey	82	228	561	853	888	1,087	1,020	1,564	1,670
Pennsylvania	160	570	1,330	1,760	1,745	2,146	1,961	2,978	3,156
East North Central	687	2,229	4,917	6,383	6,065	7,296	6,884	10,419	10,944
Ohio	181	621	1,346	1,759	1,715	1,919	1,905	2,768	2,912
Indiana	97	333	725	875	851	1,000	984	1,424	1,502
Illinois	181	569	1,263	1,638	1,526	1,926	1,721	2,632	2,769
Michigan	115	413	989	1,328	1,219	1,552	1,454	2,409	2,530
Wisconsin	93	293	594	783	754	901	820	1,186	1,231
West North Central	500	1,782	2,942	3,582	3,494	3,960	3,663	5,437	5,666
Minnesota	98	324	570	733	727	871	730	1,156	1,207
Iowa	145	437	689	778	699	794	693	1,060	1,083
Missouri	76	297	604	762	766	922	854	1,253	1,310
North Dakota	25	91	145	183	164	182	181	273	281
South Dakota	29	120	168	205	179	196	179	287	296
Nebraska	50	219	339	426	406	412	406	563	602
Kansas	73	294	487	595	558	583	600	844	883
South Atlantic	161	806	1,920	2,518	2,657	3,406	3,453	5,822	6,273
Delaware	5	18	40	56	57	72	68	107	115
Maryland	31	103	234	322	346	444	459	679	731
District of Columbia	19	34	103	187	171	162	111	191	187
Virginia	21	115	283	376	386	500	548	906	970
West Virginia	13	81	218	286	246	305	284	475	482
North Carolina	21	141	340	453	463	592	606	1,035	1,110
South Carolina	15	94	168	218	236	337	336	570	638
Georgia	25	146	248	342	394	503	522	888	969
Florida	11	74	286	328	356	495	518	971	1,081
East South Central	68	358	879	1,215	1,129	1,513	1,517	2,768	2,919
Kentucky	20	113	262	331	346	464	435	774	809
Tennessee	26	102	245	366	352	450	460	842	888
Alabama	12	75	195	279	245	340	359	675	719
Mississippi	10	68	177	237	186	259	263	477	503
West South Central	84	773	1,794	2,411	2,360	2,891	2,767	4,918	5,193
Arkansas	8	59	184	220	207	257	275	471	493
Louisiana	11	73	207	275	269	365	404	699	738
Oklahoma	25	213	424	550	502	575	505	819	853
Texas	40	428	979	1,366	1,382	1,694	1,583	2,929	3,119
Mountain	81	371	677	964	959	1,239	1,193	2,039	2,168
Montana	15	61	95	135	150	191	157	249	271
Idaho	7	51	82	119	118	163	151	257	276
Wyoming	4	24	48	62	70	86	82	142	146
Colorado	29	129	240	309	285	352	342	556	590
New Mexico	7	18	49	84	92	125	118	233	254
Arizona	8	35	68	111	103	138	143	284	287
Utah	9	43	74	114	106	140	154	243	260
Nevada	2	10	21	30	35	44	46	75	84
Pacific	227	873	1,994	2,739	2,900	3,730	3,852	6,145	6,493
Washington	39	174	329	446	454	562	614	903	948
Oregon	24	115	217	252	294	394	414	678	679
California	164	584	1,448	2,041	2,152	2,774	2,855	4,564	4,866

Source: Department of Commerce, Bureau of Public Roads; *Highway Statistics, Summary to 1945*; and subsequent annual reports.

No. 618.—Motor-Vehicle Registrations and Revenues, by States: 1951

DIVISION AND STATE	NUMBER OF MOTOR CARS						RECEIPTS FROM MOTOR-VEHICLE ADMINISTRATION (thousands of dollars)	
	Total	Registered vehicles, private and commercial		Publicly owned vehicles, Federal, State, county, etc. [1]	Trailers, registered (including official) [5]	Motor-cycles, registered (including official) [4]	Total receipts [3]	Registration, motor cars [6]
		Passenger cars and taxis	Trucks and busses					
Continental U.S.	51,913,945	42,535,217	8,766,380	622,368	2,581,538	439,690	1,603,790	795,601
New England	2,956,676	2,513,777	406,332	36,487	122,480	15,673	46,736	32,290
Maine	390,141	313,390	62,622	4,129	21,139	2,290	5,722	5,682
New Hampshire	186,162	142,734	33,532	3,896	19,118	1,745	4,026	3,875
Vermont	128,968	107,709	15,162	1,117	9,870	889	4,190	3,646
Massachusetts	1,346,830	1,169,413	170,648	16,489	86,690	5,170	14,592	7,178
Rhode Island	261,024	226,092	32,475	2,467	5,092	1,781	4,903	3,888
Connecticut	764,241	654,430	92,393	7,409	22,483	3,780	11,704	8,054
Middle Atlantic	8,566,661	7,561,716	1,163,174	91,171	340,819	61,537	186,976	149,372
New York	3,931,540	3,435,200	402,896	43,464	193,286	25,575	82,533	73,546
New Jersey	1,685,304	1,430,086	220,272	14,946	27,713	9,922	44,309	29,103
Pennsylvania	3,159,198	2,696,430	470,007	32,761	93,520	26,040	59,134	46,721
East North Central	11,044,262	9,413,397	1,536,274	99,681	667,062	108,316	199,928	167,180
Ohio	2,940,388	2,555,025	357,451	27,912	202,899	24,735	57,880	44,218
Indiana	1,512,026	1,244,495	257,234	11,296	128,184	19,567	25,362	21,518
Illinois	2,789,546	2,400,584	368,485	20,477	64,816	24,778	46,918	41,478
Michigan	2,644,287	2,218,227	312,090	24,940	242,431	19,489	45,089	37,496
Wisconsin	1,946,126	1,000,066	231,014	15,056	17,734	8,747	24,679	22,480
West North Central	5,722,391	4,459,368	1,176,814	84,309	422,707	43,235	187,964	95,788
Minnesota	1,217,480	1,001,112	206,569	10,709	124,797	10,818	26,344	24,717
Iowa	1,100,191	896,948	191,931	12,312	116,448	10,681	31,444	26,525
Missouri	1,320,113	1,035,451	274,700	9,982	79,746	6,981	19,188	16,302
North Dakota	283,809	194,465	86,636	2,708	3,289	934	6,352	5,623
South Dakota	296,412	219,354	75,409	3,649	32,934	1,895	4,763	4,448
Nebraska	608,464	467,321	134,808	6,355	56,964	4,515	7,468	5,143
Kansas	896,932	675,717	207,761	10,454	18,487	7,801	12,528	9,990
South Atlantic	6,342,362	5,004,968	1,174,298	89,097	277,087	60,747	114,245	82,144
Delaware	116,780	92,586	22,590	1,602	4,749	689	2,135	1,540
Maryland	736,827	619,409	111,284	6,134	16,441	5,607	19,272	9,063
District of Columbia	191,316	166,604	20,915	4,787	1,733	813	4,185	1,635
Virginia	984,276	788,436	181,898	13,942	37,871	11,159	14,340	11,193
West Virginia	490,211	370,817	111,546	7,848	10,366	3,313	14,937	10,596
North Carolina	1,129,454	899,374	221,122	18,957	78,731	10,388	22,183	19,129
South Carolina	648,297	522,629	115,000	10,668	9,298	5,409	5,638	4,147
Georgia	969,167	752,616	208,436	10,115	31,866	7,684	8,539	4,351
Florida	1,096,085	854,848	185,508	15,004	86,002	15,593	26,016	20,648
East South Central	2,966,627	2,296,984	667,444	47,637	34,369	23,159	59,145	34,873
Kentucky	830,239	635,024	174,406	10,909	19	6,374	12,646	6,308
Tennessee	905,298	702,426	186,138	17,734	104	7,400	14,775	11,276
Alabama	730,104	547,874	171,043	11,487	12,603	6,951	13,870	10,372
Mississippi	510,286	345,660	156,819	7,507	21,453	2,425	7,854	6,918
West South Central	5,263,178	3,991,194	1,261,126	65,790	224,631	41,246	113,777	79,445
Arkansas	499,642	331,387	161,455	6,830	25,445	2,005	9,586	5,334
Louisiana	735,997	567,202	161,120	7,655	32,792	5,161	8,675	4,373
Oklahoma	855,530	639,485	213,046	12,999	14,478	6,696	22,304	14,961
Texas	3,157,009	2,453,120	665,544	38,306	151,906	27,384	72,360	48,965
Mountain	2,210,794	1,631,690	536,674	43,440	136,573	14,976	38,966	21,843
Montana	277,031	188,126	83,074	5,831	7,985	1,129	5,006	4,110
Idaho	281,372	200,625	75,501	5,234	37,821	2,327	2,144	2,350
Wyoming	149,324	103,482	42,369	3,513	15,636	940	1,600	1,190
Colorado	599,613	456,125	133,400	10,088	26,831	4,282	5,779	3,895
New Mexico	256,238	186,310	67,523	5,005	7,951	2,780	4,411	4,556
Arizona	306,533	221,460	64,412	6,971	23,849	3,411	4,114	2,574
Utah	304,711	210,940	49,432	4,348	2,345	1,353	2,915	2,369
Nevada	86,062	64,642	18,972	2,448	5,255	744	846	590
Pacific	6,887,728	5,801,148	962,522	92,887	446,334	68,729	139,604	122,682
Washington	968,793	783,262	164,836	21,596	49,495	6,026	25,044	19,350
Oregon	691,397	605,151	164,535	11,961	23,208	6,037	11,500	9,951
California	4,926,543	4,202,630	643,533	60,390	398,671	54,666	119,230	103,672

[1] Excludes vehicles owned by military services.
[2] As reported. State registration requirements differ widely.
[3] Includes registration fees, certificates of title, transfer or registration fees, permits, fines, etc.; excludes motor-fuel and motor-carrier taxes; for California, includes $69,844,690 vehicle license fees and for Washington, $10,757,000 motor-vehicle excise taxes.
[4] Excludes fees for registration of automobiles (including taxicabs), busses, and trucks and tractor trucks.
[5] Commercial full trailers included with trucks. [6] Includes fees for registration of trailers.
[6] Trucks under 1,500 pounds capacity included with automobiles.
[7] Excludes automobiles of the diplomatic corps.
[8] Represents publicly owned only. Heavy semitrailers registered with tractors (as a unit). Automobile trailers not required to register.
[9] Trailers with gross weight of 4,500 pounds or less included with automobiles.

Source: Department of Commerce, Bureau of Public Roads; Highway Statistics, 1951.

No. 619.—Number of Deaths From Motor-Vehicle Accidents, by Place of Death and Place of Residence: 1950

[Exclusive of deaths among armed forces overseas]

STATE	By place of death	By place of resi-dence	STATE	By place of death	By place of resi-dence	STATE	By place of death	By place of resi-dence
United States....	34,763	34,763	Kentucky............	753	722	North Dakota........	105	111
			Louisiana...........	585	551	Ohio................	1,850	1,892
Alabama............	859	855	Maine..............	161	155	Oklahoma...........	504	510
Arizona............	333	278	Maryland..........	480	442	Oregon.............	461	465
Arkansas...........	365	383	Massachusetts......	492	544	Pennsylvania.......	1,656	1,744
California..........	3,082	3,171	Michigan..........	1,627	1,692	Rhode Island.......	87	89
Colorado...........	415	406	Minnesota.........	556	587	South Carolina.....	627	633
Connecticut........	287	291	Mississippi........	525	519	South Dakota.......	198	196
Delaware...........	84	80	Missouri..........	902	942	Tennessee..........	801	778
Dist. of Col........	102	134	Montana..........	209	191	Texas..............	2,499	2,498
Florida............	882	842	Nebraska..........	317	305	Utah...............	199	202
Georgia............	928	906	Nevada...........	122	81	Vermont...........	69	82
Idaho.............	243	226	New Hampshire....	103	96	Virginia...........	929	857
Illinois............	1,963	2,042	New Jersey.......	715	646	Washington........	534	548
Indiana............	1,136	1,067	New Mexico.......	340	263	West Virginia......	400	422
Iowa..............	620	634	New York.........	1,961	2,098	Wisconsin..........	857	806
Kansas............	546	529	North Carolina.....	1,153	1,113	Wyoming..........	149	117

No. 620.—Motor-Vehicle Accident Deaths by Age, Race, and Sex: 1950

AGE	ALL RACES			WHITE			NONWHITE		
	Both sexes	Male	Female	Both sexes	Male	Female	Both sexes	Male	Female
All ages...............	34,763	26,516	8,247	30,955	23,574	7,381	3,808	2,942	866
Under 1 year...........	264	146	118	232	128	104	32	18	14
1 to 4 years...........	1,503	865	638	1,337	773	564	166	92	74
5 to 9 years...........	1,266	834	432	1,103	737	366	163	97	66
10 to 14 years.........	886	633	253	788	566	222	98	67	31
15 to 19 years.........	3,145	2,458	687	2,888	2,265	623	257	193	64
20 to 24 years.........	4,455	3,737	718	4,003	3,386	617	452	351	101
25 to 34 years.........	5,855	4,727	1,128	5,059	4,081	978	796	646	150
35 to 44 years.........	4,359	3,439	920	3,731	2,943	788	628	496	132
45 to 54 years.........	3,848	2,905	943	3,331	2,479	852	517	426	91
55 to 64 years.........	3,880	2,884	996	3,515	2,589	926	365	295	70
65 to 74 years.........	3,264	2,377	887	3,051	2,208	843	213	169	44
75 years and over.....	1,987	1,466	521	1,880	1,387	493	107	79	28
Not stated............	51	45	6	37	32	5	14	13	1

Source of tables 619 and 620: Department of Health, Education, and Welfare, Public Health Service, National Office of Vital Statistics; annual report, *Vital Statistics of the United States.*

No. 621.—Number of Traffic Accident Fatalities by Hour of Accident and Place of Accident, Urban and Rural: Reporting Area, 1949

HOUR OF ACCIDENT	Total	Urban	Rural	HOUR OF ACCIDENT	Total	Urban	Rural
Total.................	29,945	7,938	22,007	12 m. to 12:59 p.m.........	901	183	718
				1 p.m. to 1:59 p.m.........	1,119	226	893
12 p.m. to 12:59 a.m.....	1,359	321	1,038	2 p.m. to 2:59 p.m.........	1,412	336	1,076
1 a.m. to 1:59 a.m........	1,099	299	800	3 p.m. to 3:59 p.m.........	1,635	331	1,304
2 a.m. to 2:59 a.m........	667	142	525	4 p.m. to 4:59 p.m.........	1,951	556	1,395
3 a.m. to 3:59 a.m........	441	94	347				
				5 p.m. to 5:59 p.m.........	2,045	535	1,510
4 a.m. to 4:59 a.m........	488	101	387	6 p.m. to 6:59 p.m.........	1,972	567	1,405
5 a.m. to 5:59 a.m........	569	129	440	7 p.m. to 7:59 p.m.........	1,570	450	1,120
6 a.m. to 6:59 a.m........	615	131	484	8 p.m. to 8:59 p.m.........	1,360	363	997
7 a.m. to 7:59 a.m........	640	114	526				
				9 p.m. to 9:59 p.m.........	1,307	334	973
8 a.m. to 8:59 a.m........	729	149	580	10 p.m. to 10:59 p.m......	1,550	376	1,174
9 a.m. to 9:59 a.m........	823	171	652	11 p.m. to 11:59 p.m......	840	205	635
10 a.m. to 10:59 a.m......	904	211	693	Hour not stated............	2,636	1,283	1,353
11 a.m. to 11:59 a.m......	1,313	331	982				

Source: Department of Health, Education, and Welfare, Public Health Service, National Office of Vital Statistics; *Motor-Vehicle Accident Fatalities, 1949.*

21. Transportation, Air and Land

Steam railways.—Because of the long period in which it has been subject to close Federal regulation and the degree of its consolidation, there is an extensive coverage of important statistical items relating to the railway industry. The *Statistics of Railways in the United States*, published annually by the Interstate Commerce Commission since 1888, is the most important source for steam railway statistics. Various other periodical reports are also issued by the Interstate Commerce Commission. The Association of American Railroads supplements official railway statistics with various releases.

The term "steam railways" as used in this section includes electrified divisions operated by such carriers. The total steam railroad mileage of the United States comprises: (a) Regular interstate carriers (and their nonoperating subsidiaries) reporting to the Interstate Commerce Commission; (b) switching and terminal railroads, also reporting to the Commission; and (c) private railroads (defined by the Commission as "circular" because they report on brief circulars and as "unofficial"). Except in certain mileage data the circular and unofficial companies are not included in any of the statistics. The switching and terminal roads were formerly included with operating railways, but are now separated, and data for them do not appear in most of the tables.

Nonoperating subsidiaries include proprietary companies, which are covered by the reports of operating carriers, and lessor companies which have no traffic and whose reports appear only in statistics of capitalization, dividends, and investment.

Operating railways are divided into three classes, according to the amount of their annual operating revenues, class I, having more than $1,000,000 of such revenue; class II, from $100,000 to $1,000,000; and class III, less than $100,000. During recent years more detailed reports are required from class I carriers than from smaller companies. The basis of the figures in each table is indicated by notes. Omission of class II and class III railroads affects very little the comparability of statistics with those of earlier years as regards most items, since the bulk of the business is done by class I.

The Interstate Commerce Commission divides railroads geographically into three districts and eight subsidiary regions. Each railroad is treated as a unit and placed wholly in some one district or region. Broadly speaking, the eastern district includes territory east of Chicago and north of the Ohio and Potomac Rivers; southern district, territory east of the Mississippi River and south of the Ohio and Potomac Rivers; and western district, the remainder of the country.

Electric railways.—The Interstate Commerce Commission issues annually an abstract of the annual reports of electric railways, chiefly interurban, which report to it. The American Transit Association publishes street railway statistics in its annual *Transit Fact Book*. The Bureau of the Census has published a quinquennial report on electric railways from 1902 to 1937. In the more recent years the report also covered affiliated trolley-bus and motor-bus operations. The last Census of Electrical Industries was for the year 1937.

Motor carriers.—Statistics of class I for-hire carriers (those with $100,000 or more of gross annual operating revenues) are compiled by the Interstate Commerce Commission from annual and quarterly reports submitted to it by these carriers. Beginning with reports for the year 1950, the class I minimum became $200,000. This series begins with 1939 data.

The annual review and statistical number of *Bus Transportation*, a McGraw-Hill publication, summarizes operations of common carriers and school busses.

Civil aeronautics.—Federal promotion and regulation of civil aviation are carried out by two bodies—the Civil Aeronautics Administration and the Civil Aeronautics Board. The Civil Aeronautics Board is an independent agency concerned primarily with the issuance of certificates of public necessity, economic regulation, the formula-

Note.—This section presents data for the most recent year or period available on April 22, 1953, when the material was organized and sent to the printer. In a few instances, more recent data were added after that date.

tion of safety regulations and the investigation of accidents to civil aircraft. The Civil Aeronautics Administration is an operating agency of the Department of Commerce. Its principal activities are the building and operation of air navigation aids, the enforcement of safety regulations and promotion of a national airport system.

The *Statistical Handbook of Civil Aviation* is published by the Civil Aeronautics Administration. This *Handbook* brings together all official statistical data on the development of civil aviation in the United States, including summaries of statistics published by the Civil Aeronautics Board. The Civil Aeronautics Administration has also published a detailed historical record of America's aircraft production during the recent war. This publication is entitled *U. S. Military Aircraft Acceptances, 1940–45—Aircraft, Engine, and Propeller Production.*

Historical statistics.—See preface and historical appendix. Tabular headnotes (as "See also *Historical Statistics*, series K 28–33") provide cross-references, where applicable, to *Historical Statistics of the United States, 1789–1945.*

No. 622.—STEAM RAILWAYS—MILEAGE OWNED AND MILEAGE OPERATED: 1925 TO 1951

[As of Dec. 31. See also *Historical Statistics*, series K 28–33]

ITEM	1925	1930	1935	1940	1945	1950	1951
Number of operating companies [1]	947	775	661	574	517	471	462
Road owned, first track (miles) [2]	249,398	249,052	241,822	233,670	226,696	223,779	223,427
Miles operated: [3]							
All railways, road, first track	261,871	262,215	254,347	246,739	240,156	236,999	236,599
Total, reporting railways [4]	417,954	429,883	419,228	405,975	396,054	396,380	395,831
Road, first track	258,631	260,440	252,930	245,740	239,438	236,857	236,476
Other main tracks	40,962	42,742	41,916	41,373	41,106	40,456	40,157
Yard track and sidings	118,361	126,701	124,382	118,862	117,510	119,067	119,198
Class I railways, road, first track	236,848	242,391	237,491	232,524	227,877	226,101	225,974

	1950			1951		
		Miles of road			Miles of road	
CLASS OF COMPANIES	Companies	Owned [3]	Operated [3]	Companies	Owned [3]	Operated [3]
Total	1,038	223,779	236,999	1,031	223,427	236,599
Class I line-haul operating	127	182,051	226,101	127	183,551	225,974
Lessors to Class I	179	26,705	....	175	25,080	....
Class II line-haul operating	171	7,397	8,397	167	7,134	8,202
Lessors to Class II	6	183	....	9	306	....
Class III line-haul operating	166	2,198	2,359	164	2,141	2,300
Lessors to Class III	9	70	....	8	67	....
Switching and terminal	[5] 253	(6)	(6)	[5] 255	(6)	(6)
Proprietary [7]	100	4,783	....	100	4,770	....
Circular	18	281	106	20	297	106
Unofficial	9	111	34	6	81	15

[1] Classes I, II, III, circular, and unofficial.
[2] First track. Covers continental U. S. only, excluding all duplication.
[3] Includes some duplication under trackage rights and some mileage in Canada operated by U. S. companies.
[4] Excludes circular and unofficial, figures for which cover road, first track only.
[5] Includes 215 operating, 13 lessor, 15 proprietary, 9 circular, and 1 unofficial in 1950, and 218 operating, 13 lessor, 14 proprietary, 9 circular, and 1 unofficial in 1951.
[6] Figures omitted as "miles of road" of switching and terminal companies is not comparable with that of line-haul companies.
[7] Excludes proprietary companies in systems which file consolidated reports combining mileage, investment, and other items on a net system basis.

Source: Interstate Commerce Commission; annual lreport, *Statistics of Railways in the United States.*

No. 625.—STEAM RAILWAYS (ALL REPORTING COMPANIES)—EQUIPMENT IN SERVICE: 1925 TO 1951

["All reporting companies" include switching and terminal but not circular and unofficial lines. Data for tractive effort and capacity of cars exclude switching roads, also smaller roads during recent years; they would not be materially different if all carriers were included. Excludes the large number of cars owned by private car lines. See also Historical Statistics, series K 34-36]

	LOCOMOTIVES								FREIGHT-CARRYING CARS [3]			
		Steam			Electric locomotive units	Diesel electric locomotive units				Capacity [1]		Passenger-train cars
YEAR ENDING DEC. 31—	Total number [1]	Number	Tractive effort [1]			Number	Tractive effort [1]		Total number (1,000)	Aggregate (1,000 tons)	Average (tons)	
			Aggregate (1,000 lb.)	Average (lb.)			Aggregate (1,000 lb.)	Average (lb.)				
1925	68,096	67,712	2,586,806	40,666	379	1	(4)	(4)	2,414	105,570	44.3	54,814
1930	60,189	59,406	2,636,940	45,225	648	77	(4)	(4)	2,322	104,180	46.9	53,584
1935	49,541	48,477	2,206,201	45,367	884	130	(4)	(4)	1,867	82,677	48.3	42,428
1940	44,333	43,410	2,638,284	50,906	900	967	43,929	55,130	1,684	82,722	50.0	28,308
1941	44,375	41,911	2,039,428	51,217	896	1,517	69,347	54,733	1,733	85,682	50.3	28,234
1942	44,671	41,755	2,046,064	51,811	892	1,978	91,589	54,942	1,774	88,187	50.5	38,446
1943	44,496	41,963	2,083,618	52,451	907	2,476	117,300	55,200	1,784	88,946	50.7	38,331
1944	44,305	41,921	2,095,046	52,822	902	3,432	171,957	56,398	1,797	89,960	50.8	38,217
1945	44,253	41,018	2,067,639	53,217	885	4,301	213,198	55,868	1,787	89,872	51.1	38,683
1946	45,511	39,592	2,017,807	53,735	867	5,008	248,129	55,872	1,768	90,391	51.2	38,697
1947	44,344	36,942	1,913,503	54,806	864	6,496	328,255	56,524	1,760	89,225	51.5	39,057
1948	44,476	34,581	1,816,890	55,170	867	8,961	455,287	58,255	1,785	91,294	51.9	39,494
1949	43,272	30,344	1,681,633	55,333	856	12,025	617,506	58,714	1,779	91,981	52.4	38,006
1950	42,961	26,680	1,463,413	57,078	827	15,396	807,523	57,487	1,746	90,458	52.6	37,359
1951	42,473	22,590	1,271,671	56,476	817	19,014	1,018,119	58,202	1,778	92,671	52.9	36,326

[1] Includes locomotives other than classes shown.
[2] Excludes caboose cars.
[3] Class I roads.
[4] Not available.

No. 626.—STEAM RAILWAYS—CARS IN SERVICE, BY CLASS: 1935 TO 1951

["All operating companies" include switching and terminal companies but not circular and unofficial lines. Excludes cars owned by private car lines, roughly equaling one-tenth of those owned by railway companies]

	ALL OPERATING COMPANIES					CLASS I, 1951			
CLASS	1935	1940	1945	1950	1951	Total	Eastern district	Southern district	Western district
Freight-train cars	1,892,375	1,704,287	1,812,271	1,768,963	1,882,699	1,775,788	721,878	421,697	632,523
Steel [1]	809,612	956,004	1,152,145	1,335,676	1,401,275	1,401,275	665,105	351,637	394,533
Steel underframe [1]	908,206	640,428	570,318	374,532	341,462	341,462	67,641	62,469	221,352
Freight-carrying cars	1,867,381	1,684,171	1,787,973	1,745,778	1,777,678	1,732,486	713,866	414,632	603,463
Box	812,776	705,683	745,901	718,180	730,563	735,059	276,316	134,228	325,615
Flat	53,496	65,782	71,062	67,712	71,929	66,011	9,337	15,498	41,176
Stock	68,455	54,674	54,484	46,281	43,805	43,762	6,172	5,387	34,203
Gondola and hopper (open and closed tops)	793,779	809,538	874,558	874,801	883,772	867,007	418,381	253,455	195,171
Tank	9,266	8,836	9,030	8,436	8,271	7,576	3	133	7,440
Refrigerator	26,703	21,772	21,001	19,083	18,599	18,591	880	794	16,917
Other	72,080	14,917	11,012	11,215	11,930	10,494	1,909	5,534	2,981
Caboose cars	24,994	22,216	25,198	24,205	24,221	23,358	8,890	5,058	9,420
Passenger-train cars	42,436	38,306	36,833	37,359	34,836	34,130	19,226	5,343	11,561
Steel [1]	28,961	29,897	31,838	33,320	32,627	32,627	17,501	4,730	10,306
Steel underframe [1]	8,394	6,442	5,576	3,651	3,327	3,327	1,579	582	1,166
Coach	(5)	17,470	17,668	16,488	15,850	15,792	9,680	2,057	4,055
Combination coach	(5)	3,207	2,748	2,231	2,188	2,100	1,147	319	634
Parlor and sleeping [2]	(5)	422	731	437	494	494	149	41	384
Dining	1,535	1,582	1,836	1,784	1,784	682	319	783	
Club, lounge, and observation	(5)	370	278	430	436	436	71	60	305
Mail	1,829	1,701	1,770	1,702	1,702	888	255	559	
Baggage, express, and other nonpassenger	(5)	15,087	13,671	13,817	13,687	13,657	6,549	2,264	4,844
Other passenger	(5)	105	26	20	24	24	15	9	—
Other passenger-train	(5)	269	208	230	234	211	45	19	147
Railway type company service equipment	79,394	77,811	90,036	95,547	96,183	93,411	28,546	19,096	45,769
Work cars and trailers	4,446	4,064	3,899	3,697	3,644	3,644	2,982	354	308

[1] Data represent class I roads only; figures exclude caboose cars.
[2] Excludes cars owned or leased by Pullman Co.
[3] No comparable data available.

Source of tables 625 and 626: Interstate Commerce Commission, annual report, Statistics of Railways in the United States.

No. 627.—Steam Railways (Class I)—Equipment Installed and Permanently Withdrawn From Service: 1936 to 1951

[Includes owned and leased equipment]

YEAR	LOCOMOTIVES		FREIGHT-TRAIN CARS		PASSENGER-TRAIN CARS	
	New units installed	Units permanently withdrawn [1]	New units installed	Units permanently withdrawn [1]	New units installed	Units permanently withdrawn [1]
1936	98	1,644	37,554	113,582	159	988
1937	441	973	09,118	81,451	576	842
1938	252	1,129	15,213	60,827	275	1,009
1939	298	1,660	23,236	74,229	209	790
1940	421	1,260	60,455	54,846	154	754
1941	632	718	76,392	26,693	297	587
1942	716	579	58,595	15,257	273	364
1943	891	268	28,000	13,516	8	255
1944	1,245	519	38,970	24,589	104	222
1945	901	1,110	37,132	44,247	111	378
1946	712	1,424	38,823	52,713	481	521
1947	1,398	2,739	55,543	62,594	858	736
1948	2,350	2,377	95,979	69,363	951	802
1949	2,884	4,099	80,815	85,577	939	923
1950	3,215	3,495	40,032	72,669	1,078	1,188
1951	3,514	4,093	86,627	54,496	183	1,109

[1] Permanently withdrawn for sale or demolition.

Source: Interstate Commerce Commission; annual report, *Statistics of Railways in the United States*.

No. 628.—Steam Railways (Class I)—Fuel Consumption and Rail and Tie Replacements: 1925 to 1951

[Excludes rails and ties laid in new construction. Short ton is 2,000 pounds; long ton 2,240 pounds]

CLASS	ALL DISTRICTS						
	1925	1930	1935	1940	1945	1950	1951
Consumption of fuel by steam locomotives:							
Anthracite......1,000 short tons..	2,174	1,140	508	286	139	41	6
Bituminous coal..........do....	117,714	98,400	71,335	79,628	115,154	55,410	48,311
Fuel oil...........1,000 gallons..	2,457,827	2,366,569	1,998,176	2,502,868	4,413,072	2,277,220	2,036,249
Other fuel equivalent, 1,000 short tons..				34	32	39	44
Total, coal equivalent,[1] 1,000 short tons..	[2] 135,420	[3] 114,458	[3] 84,783	96,067	143,806	(3)	(3)
Rails laid in replacement and betterment:							
Total tonnage ..1,000 long tons..	3,485	2,674	1,159	1,912	2,956	2,191	2,059
Total charges [4].....1,000 dollars..	126,487	98,521	36,218	64,516	106,010	124,894	123,962
Ties laid in previously constructed tracks:							
Cross ties...........thousands..	82,717	63,354	44,326	43,621	43,912	30,494	29,062
Switch and bridge ties, 1,000 board feet..	[3] 282,630	235,315	156,536	145,553	130,520	98,400	92,799
Total charges [4].....1,000 dollars..	[3] 120,644	94,207	52,370	59,047	97,908	92,912	94,570

CLASS	1950			1951		
	Eastern district	Southern district	Western district	Eastern district	Southern district	Western district
Consumption of fuel by steam locomotives:						
Anthracite.................1,000 short tons..	41			6		
Bituminous.....................do....	26,315	15,148	13,947	22,157	13,047	13,107
Fuel oil....................1,000 gallons..	12,717	27,253	2,237,250	8,850	22,528	2,004,871
Other fuel equivalent....1,000 short tons..	1		38	1		43
Total, coal equivalent [1]...1,000 short tons..	(3)	(3)	(3)	(3)	(3)	(3)
Rails laid in replacement and betterment:						
Total tonnage.............1,000 long tons..	584	587	1,020	609	547	903
Total charges [4]...........1,000 dollars..	32,862	33,011	59,021	37,023	32,655	54,284
Ties laid in previously constructed tracks:						
Cross ties..................thousands..	8,190	8,123	14,181	7,509	8,148	13,405
Switch and bridge ties......1,000 board feet..	27,994	26,931	43,475	27,329	25,762	39,708
Total charges [4]...................1,000 dollars..	28,066	24,216	40,630	27,620	25,952	40,998

[1] Ratio of fuel oil to coal left to experience of each road.
[2] Includes equivalent of a small amount of miscellaneous fuel.
[3] Not available.
[4] Excludes labor cost of applying rails or ties.
[5] Excludes 1,435 linear feet of steel ties.

Source: Interstate Commerce Commission; annual report, *Statistics of Railways in the United States*.

No. 636.—Steam Railways (Class I)—Railway Tax Accruals, by States: 1930 to 1951

[Excludes switching and terminal companies and includes nonoperating subsidiaries. Total railroad taxes, Federal and State in 1963, by classes, were as follows: Class I and subsidiaries, $1,265,753,611 (including $4,177,-488 Canadian, $1,390,607 Mexican, $323 Cuban, and $11 Great Britain taxes); class II and subsidiaries, $17,550,-827; class III and subsidiaries, $3,942,843; switching and terminal companies, $53,707,919; grand total, $1,276,-853,200]

STATE	AMOUNT (thousands of dollars)						PER MILE OF LINE (dollars)			
	1930	1935	1940	1945	1950	1951	1940	1945	1950	1951
Total	363,297	238,272	307,391	822,940	1,134,655	1,186,072	1,589	3,534	5,885	6,029
U. S. Government taxes	40,966	26,796	183,546	551,004	868,037	856,106	830	2,548		
New England:										
Maine	1,908	1,232	1,161	1,795	1,909	1,930	636	1,001	1,090	1,113
New Hampshire	1,125	718	538	522	627	631	530	365	600	605
Vermont	407	413	298	266	310	309	361	402	430	434
Massachusetts	4,709	2,964	3,832	4,414	5,004	5,441	2,147	2,574	2,938	3,190
Rhode Island	687	664	625	798	770	841	3,567	4,885	4,402	4,852
Connecticut	1,672	711	946	1,416	1,289	1,362	1,071	1,636	1,550	1,640
Middle Atlantic:										
New York	27,378	23,685	24,186	29,878	34,594	36,127	3,276	4,070	4,901	5,034
New Jersey	30,442	17,530	19,793	20,901	16,162	17,051	10,368	16,767	8,990	9,438
Pennsylvania	12,440	9,342	10,734	9,378	12,539	13,451	1,098	986	1,350	1,450
South Atlantic:										
Delaware	166	151	180	154	179	181	309	322	607	615
Dist. of Columbia	144	128	234	253	364	372	6,410	7,430	10,711	10,928
Maryland	2,076	1,748	2,110	3,529	3,678	3,743	1,870	3,179	3,234	3,397
Virginia	7,318	5,192	5,800	7,810	9,383	9,990	1,338	1,990	2,420	2,576
West Virginia	8,109	6,229	8,686	7,870	10,591	12,094	2,806	2,572	2,940	3,445
North Carolina	5,302	3,696	4,110	4,907	5,091	5,337	1,131	1,362	1,361	1,448
South Carolina	3,499	2,306	1,697	2,848	2,471	2,487	639	644	816	826
Georgia	3,908	2,434	2,519	3,146	3,414	3,847	473	592	1,685	931
Florida	4,994	3,039	2,132	3,046	4,470	4,569	446	721	990	1,008
East North Central:										
Ohio	19,928	10,452	11,063	12,722	16,124	17,675	1,320	1,534	1,945	2,131
Indiana	12,882	6,520	6,278	7,488	10,416	10,313	946	1,141	1,573	1,575
Illinois	22,084	13,610	12,900	19,040	24,127	24,697	1,103	1,640	2,094	2,146
Michigan	10,816	5,346	5,035	5,538	5,751	7,164	742	853	891	1,114
Wisconsin	7,201	4,921	4,455	4,361	5,437	5,606	653	728	871	904
West North Central:										
Minnesota	6,778	4,291	6,529	9,871	12,209	13,441	815	1,210	1,498	1,651
Iowa	8,026	3,804	2,986	3,398	5,196	5,775	334	386	606	673
Missouri	4,284	3,336	2,757	2,900	5,262	5,525	399	424	785	829
North Dakota	4,110	2,114	2,559	2,954	4,903	4,962	499	546	945	956
South Dakota	2,696	2,191	1,063	1,115	1,665	1,624	287	282	421	410
Nebraska	4,622	3,060	2,978	3,689	5,519	5,734	493	634	982	980
Kansas	8,871	6,232	5,327	6,322	9,801	10,702	523	750	1,167	1,274
East South Central:										
Kentucky	5,373	3,592	5,048	5,380	7,336	7,535	1,411	1,553	2,060	2,151
Tennessee	3,629	2,588	2,841	5,784	6,600	7,556	844	1,767	2,020	2,347
Alabama	3,681	2,378	2,736	3,502	3,886	3,478	611	819	888	799
Mississippi	5,047	2,937	3,079	3,962	4,639	4,717	840	1,110	1,316	1,338
West South Central:										
Louisiana	5,096	4,087	3,854	4,318	5,093	5,168	1,001	1,169	1,394	1,418
Texas	7,614	5,487	6,260	5,562	7,174	6,987	389	365	501	489
Oklahoma	6,468	3,667	3,723	4,277	5,986	6,163	603	726	1,005	1,032
Arkansas	3,025	2,290	2,038	2,880	3,526	3,020	497	722	1,051	831
Mountain:										
Montana	5,178	4,460	4,066	4,058	6,380	6,621	809	818	1,281	1,329
Wyoming	1,970	1,671	1,715	1,970	2,834	2,785	925	1,110	1,498	1,476
Colorado	4,271	3,363	3,021	4,026	5,977	6,201	748	1,009	1,536	1,585
New Mexico	2,785	1,883	1,788	2,019	2,148	2,168	651	824	887	893
Arizona	3,100	3,055	2,597	3,154	5,228	5,229	1,274	1,454	2,563	2,583
Utah	2,404	2,243	2,309	2,956	3,063	3,561	1,135	1,605	1,733	2,012
Nevada	1,970	1,786	1,813	1,819	2,126	2,194	1,073	1,229	1,442	1,488
Idaho	3,244	2,516	2,524	2,949	4,027	4,515	942	1,111	1,521	1,706
Pacific:										
Washington	7,430	3,892	3,346	4,734	5,459	5,724	664	892	1,088	1,152
Oregon	3,064	2,413	2,207	2,673	5,187	5,242	707	801	1,778	1,793
California	13,210	6,229	7,047	13,496	15,753	19,048	1,018	2,022	2,366	2,771

Source: Interstate Commerce Commission; annual report, *Statistics of Railways in the United States.*

No. 637.—STEAM-RAILWAY FREIGHT SERVICE—SUMMARY STATISTICS: 1936 TO 1951

[Excludes switching and terminal roads except as noted. Tons of 2,000 pounds. See also *Historical Statistics*, series K 43–52]

ITEM	ALL ROADS						
	1936–1940, average	1941–1945, average	1946–1950, average	1948	1949	1950	1951
Freight revenue, rail line ($1,000)	3,313,398	6,221,235	7,236,485	8,090,194	7,151,237	7,933,764	8,757,874
Per train-mile [1]	$6.95	$9.29	$12.72	$13.64	$14.14	$15.18	$16.33
Per loaded car-mile (cents) [1]	23.6	27.9	35.7	38.6	39.5	39.8	41.9
Revenue tons originated (1,000)	986,094	1,481,798	1,466,130	1,580,480	1,284,197	1,420,891	1,547,238
Total revenue tons carried (1,000)	1,778,746	2,925,421	2,751,640	2,997,976	2,425,123	2,710,919	2,940,872
Tons carried 1 mile: Revenue freight (millions)	341,322	654,687	602,917	641,104	529,111	591,550	649,831
Revenue ton-miles per mile of road	1,370,519	2,711,448	2,532,696	2,695,708	2,229,430	2,496,927	2,748,700
Revenue per ton-mile (cents) [2]	.971	.950	1.200	1.262	1.352	1.341	1.346
Freight-train miles (1,000)	478,402	666,694	569,388	593,448	506,407	522,816	536,582
Freight-train car-miles: Loaded (revenue and non-revenue) (1,000)	13,882,934	21,969,322	20,051,850	20,745,520	17,947,564	19,735,505	20,709,222
Empty (1,000)	8,371,016	11,938,016	10,427,275	10,858,378	10,206,987	10,195,410	10,659,317
Average miles per car per day [1][3]		46.2	42.8	44.1	39.3	42.5	43.8
Revenue ton-miles per train-mile	713	977	1,059	1,080	1,045	1,131	1,211
Ton miles per loaded car-mile [4]	24.6	29.7	30.1	30.9	29.5	30.0	31.4
Haul per ton: U. S. as a system (miles)	346.13	439.36	411.23	405.64	412.02	416.32	419.99
Individual railway (miles)	191.89	222.44	216.75	213.85	218.18	218.21	220.97
Revenue per ton: U. S. as a system	$3.36	$4.20	$4.94	$5.12	$5.57	$5.56	$5.66
Individual railway	$1.86	$2.13	$2.60	$2.70	$2.95	$2.93	$2.98

ITEM	CLASS I							
	Total		Eastern district		Southern district		Western district	
	1950	1951	1950	1951	1950	1951	1950	1951
Freight revenue, rail line ($1,000)	7,817,263	8,634,101	2,874,913	3,162,446	1,597,858	1,820,995	3,344,492	3,650,661
Per train-mile	$15.18	$16.33	$17.76	$19.20	$14.12	$15.68	$13.94	$14.74
Per loaded car-mile (cents)	39.8	41.9	45.9	48.9	39.8	42.2	35.7	37.2
Revenue tons originated (1,000)	1,354,196	1,477,402	502,239	538,002	367,067	406,092	484,890	533,308
Total revenue tons carried (1,000)	2,570,153	2,790,817	1,148,872	1,231,147	603,779	663,609	817,502	896,061
Tons carried 1 mile: Revenue freight (millions)	588,578	646,620	198,354	212,736	135,094	153,228	255,130	280,657
Revenue and nonrevenue (millions)	619,945	677,491	206,397	220,417	142,436	160,190	271,112	296,884
Revenue ton-miles per mile of road	2,598,236	2,860,589	3,713,659	3,989,773	2,925,647	3,329,789	2,010,454	2,215,657
Revenue per ton mile (cents) [2]	1.329	1.336	1.451	1.488	1.183	1.188	1.311	1.301
Freight-train miles (1,000)	514,971	528,573	161,888	164,685	113,137	116,157	239,946	247,731
Freight-train car miles: Loaded (revenue and nonrevenue) (1,000)	19,644,438	20,614,551	6,273,036	6,477,496	4,014,968	4,315,824	9,356,434	9,821,231
Empty (1,000)	10,139,511	10,601,562	3,207,412	3,284,914	2,250,717	2,457,583	4,681,382	4,859,065
Average miles per car per day [3]	42.5	43.8	31.6	32.3	45.2	48.1	53.4	54.5
Revenue ton-miles per train-mile	1,157	1,238	1,247	1,314	1,203	1,330	1,074	1,146
Ton miles per loaded car-mile [4]	31.6	32.9	32.9	34.0	35.6	37.1	29.1	30.2
Haul per ton: U. S. as a system (miles)	434.6	437.7	394.9	395.4	368.0	377.3	526.2	526.3
Individual railway (miles)	229.0	231.7	172.7	172.8	223.7	230.9	312.1	313.2
Revenue per ton: U. S. as a system	$5.77	$5.84	$5.72	$5.88	$4.35	$4.48	$6.90	$6.85
Individual railway	$3.04	$3.10	$2.51	$2.57	$2.65	$2.74	$4.09	$4.07

[1] Class I roads only. [2] Based on freight revenue from rail-line operations. [3] Includes switching and terminal companies. [4] Based on revenue ton miles; nonrevenue ton miles not available for all roads. [5] Based on revenue and nonrevenue ton miles.

Source: Interstate Commerce Commission; annual report, *Statistics of Railways in the United States.*

No. 638.—STEAM RAILWAYS—PASSENGERS CARRIED AND PASSENGER REVENUE: 1936 TO 1951

[Passenger service revenue per train-mile includes revenue from mail, express, etc., but average revenue per passenger-mile is computed only from revenue from passengers themselves. See also *Historical Statistics*, series X 39-47]

ITEM	ALL ROADS					
	1936–40, average	1941–45, average	1946–50, average	1948	1949	1950	1951
Passengers carried (thousands)	471,362	772,303	628,334	545,535	556,741	486,019	485,458
Passengers carried 1 mile (millions)	23,068	71,713	43,775	41,224	35,123	31,790	34,640
Average journey per passenger (miles)	48.94	92.55	66.58	61.96	63.11	65.14	71.35
Passenger train-miles (thousands)	403,715	468,217	408,855	406,371	382,213	359,055	346,391
Passenger train car-miles (thousands)	2,992,350	4,167,194	3,791,382	3,790,476	3,572,595	3,450,642	3,477,732
Passenger revenue ($1,000)	419,760	1,342,958	973,796	955,680	862,139	814,741	901,019
Passenger service train revenue per train-mile	1.49	3.86	3.39	3.33	3.13	3.61	3.76
Revenue per passenger per mile (cents)	1.82	1.87	2.23	2.34	2.45	2.56	2.60
Average passengers per train	57	158	100	101	92	89	97

ITEM	CLASS I							
	Total		Eastern district		Southern district		Western district	
	1950	1951	1950	1951	1950	1951	1950	1951
Passengers carried (thousands)	486,194	483,533	348,523	341,783	58,026	59,314	79,645	82,736
Passengers carried 1 mile (millions)	31,760	34,614	15,199	15,935	4,926	5,537	11,686	13,141
Average journey per passenger (miles)	65.32	71.54	43.61	46.62	84.87	93.34	146.10	158.83
Passenger train-miles (thousands)	357,846	356,126	139,898	139,399	61,527	61,796	156,426	153,914
Passenger train car-miles (thousands)	3,446,482	2,474,472	1,310,902	1,305,221	612,519	630,767	1,523,080	1,534,484
Passenger revenue ($1,000)	813,355	900,239	430,117	460,885	121,030	138,987	262,208	300,367
Passenger service train revenue per train-mile	3.61	3.76	4.34	4.51	3.31	3.42	3.09	3.22
Revenue per passenger per mile (cents)	2.56	2.60	2.63	2.90	2.46	2.51	2.26	2.29
Average passengers per train	89	97	109	114	80	90	74	85

[1] Based on data for class I roads only.

Source: Interstate Commerce Commission; annual report, *Statistics of Railways in the United States*.

No. 639.—STEAM RAILWAYS (CLASS I)—OPERATING REVENUES, FREIGHT AND PASSENGER REVENUE, AND FREIGHT TON-MILES, BY MONTHS: 1925 TO 1952

[Except at times of general revisions in freight rates, changes in freight revenue closely parallel those of ton-mileage. Excludes class I switching and terminal companies]

YEAR	Average	Jan.	Feb.	Mar.	Apr.	May	June	July	Aug.	Sept.	Oct.	Nov.	Dec.
	TOTAL OPERATING REVENUES (millions of dollars)												
1925	510.2	479.2	450.1	481.1	469.6	463.5	501.7	517.1	549.9	559.9	585.3	527.4	518.7
1930	440.1	448.2	422.2	447.7	445.9	457.6	439.7	451.2	481.0	462.5	478.0	394.3	373.0
1935	287.5	284.2	254.9	280.6	274.7	278.5	281.3	275.3	294.0	308.8	341.6	301.2	306.1
1940	326.2	344.4	313.6	327.1	321.6	343.5	345.0	366.2	381.5	382.7	418.7	375.5	381.9
1945	741.6	720.9	712.8	812.9	775.6	823.6	819.9	795.7	784.9	675.9	697.0	651.2	673.7
1946	624.6	641.6	578.1	646.2	595.6	651.6	612.0	574.1	710.2	660.4	710.0	658.3	637.7
1947	704.0	722.7	716.8	778.6	739.0	794.4	526.1	342.9	643.2	727.1	794.8	765.9	804.3
1948	714.4	730.7	675.8	739.1	747.3	741.1	728.5	700.7	743.8	695.3	648.2	704.8	730.8
1949	739.4	657.0	584.9	743.3	713.8	745.4	778.2	772.2	889.8	872.0	925.4	862.3	827.9
1950	843.9	843.7	715.8	875.8	851.6	835.6	817.0	910.2	856.7	965.8	903.3	902.2	
1951	851.7	867.0	846.0	875.5	847.5	870.3	814.3	790.7	900.7	942.1	980.2	908.0	935.1
	FREIGHT REVENUE (millions of dollars)												
1925	340.2	332.0	327.0	345.2	345.6	354.1	321.4	347.1	354.5	363.3	385.5	310.9	280.7
1930	253.0	211.5	208.5	239.2	232.0	234.0	225.0	221.1	235.7	260.6	255.4	245.7	224.4
1935	204.5	283.1	257.7	296.7	295.3	284.7	286.7	300.7	310.7	316.1	346.2	315.2	306.4
1940	444.2	396.4	396.5	427.0	430.5	601.8	624.7	648.2	680.7	547.3	463.8	463.7	401.2
1945	681.4	537.3	452.0	630.5	601.8	634.7	642.2	652.7	745.1	725.0	794.5	710.6	673.6
1950	719.6	708.7	600.2	741.0	722.0	724.1	710.7	674.1	755.9	718.5	814.3	743.4	669.4
1951	722.4	715.9	704.8	739.3	762.1	720.1	662.9	644.8	744.6	796.0	826.1	760.6	762.5

No. 639.—STEAM RAILWAYS (CLASS I)—OPERATING REVENUES, FREIGHT AND PASSENGER REVENUE, AND FREIGHT TON-MILES, BY MONTHS—Continued

YEAR	Average	Jan.	Feb.	Mar.	Apr.	May	June	July	Aug.	Sept.	Oct.	Nov.	Dec.
PASSENGER REVENUE (millions of dollars)													
1930	60.8	70.5	61.3	61.8	59.6	60.4	67.2	65.8	67.4	59.1	52.4	48.7	55.4
1935	29.8	30.5	27.3	27.7	27.2	27.1	31.0	31.6	33.9	30.8	28.6	27.8	34.4
1940	34.8	36.1	31.9	33.3	30.0	29.7	35.9	37.7	41.0	36.1	33.5	31.2	40.8
1945	143.0	139.2	125.9	133.6	129.2	138.9	152.2	150.7	153.3	140.1	146.5	145.6	161.1
1950	67.8	69.7	57.8	59.6	60.6	56.8	71.7	76.0	78.2	71.6	66.3	65.9	79.3
1951	75.0	78.2	63.8	70.6	66.8	70.7	80.6	80.6	83.8	74.1	71.1	71.8	88.2
1952	75.5	82.3	73.5	74.1	71.9	76.0	81.7	80.5	80.5	70.6	66.0	66.0	84.1
FREIGHT TON-MILES (millions) [1]													
1930	35,179	36,718	34,347	35,301	34,900	36,573	34,417	35,595	37,423	36,232	39,294	32,310	29,034
1935	26,031	24,967	24,124	27,596	23,340	24,672	25,951	23,174	25,938	27,731	31,218	27,482	26,179
1940	33,820	32,518	29,642	31,118	29,909	33,081	32,900	33,716	36,406	37,060	38,614	35,955	34,903
1945	60,504	60,676	56,924	68,224	65,215	68,631	66,538	64,696	60,487	56,078	53,260	53,453	49,844
1950	51,883	41,793	36,383	50,937	49,687	51,155	51,865	51,982	59,415	57,941	61,980	54,817	54,608
1951	56,573	56,511	48,367	59,057	56,863	58,753	56,649	53,276	60,023	58,118	61,843	56,746	52,668
1952	53,709	54,700	54,089	55,949	52,147	54,557	47,293	44,817	56,949	58,213	58,066	56,975	50,753

[1] Revenue and nonrevenue (freight trains).

Source: Interstate Commerce Commission; monthly reports, *Operating Revenues and Operating Expenses of Class I Steam Railways* and *Operating Statistics of Class I Steam Railways.*

No. 640.—STEAM RAILWAYS (CLASS I)—REVENUE FREIGHT ORIGINATED, BY COMMODITY GROUPS: 1930 TO 1951

[In thousands of tons of 2,000 pounds. Excludes switching and terminal roads. Excludes nonrevenue freight; this is a large item in the case of a few commodities, notably coal. See also *Historical Statistics*, series K 52–59]

ITEM	1930	1935	1940	1945	1948	1949	1950	1951
Total	1,153,197	789,627	1,009,421	1,424,913	1,506,878	1,226,503	1,354,196	1,477,402
Products of agriculture	110,728	76,338	88,821	159,571	145,176	140,383	129,175	140,810
Animals and their products	23,129	15,125	15,456	23,748	16,865	15,284	14,321	14,362
Products of mines:								
Coal and coke	407,937	320,628	372,663	485,109	527,162	376,914	439,365	465,803
Other	234,600	124,508	197,557	247,832	318,478	276,845	307,443	353,570
Products of forests	69,371	42,483	58,221	75,604	86,104	69,257	78,860	86,521
Manufactures and miscellaneous [1]	277,765	196,506	262,010	412,216	394,827	335,228	374,144	405,955
All less than carload	29,667	14,039	14,693	20,833	18,266	12,592	10,888	10,379

ITEM	EASTERN DISTRICT		SOUTHERN DISTRICT		WESTERN DISTRICT	
	1950	1951	1950	1951	1950	1951
Total	502,239	538,002	367,067	406,092	484,890	533,308
Products of agriculture	23,699	24,702	16,105	17,237	89,371	96,872
Animals and their products	3,377	3,266	1,614	1,501	9,330	9,595
Products of mines:						
Coal and coke	213,368	220,457	183,858	203,134	42,139	42,212
Other	64,642	73,874	66,936	76,449	175,865	203,247
Products of forests	3,980	4,695	32,134	35,448	42,746	46,379
Manufactures and miscellaneous [1]	188,024	206,010	63,941	69,997	122,179	129,948
All less than carload	5,149	4,999	2,479	2,325	3,260	1,055

[1] Includes forwarder traffic beginning 1940.

Source: Interstate Commerce Commission; annual report, *Statistics of Railways in the United States.*

No. 641.—STEAM RAILWAYS (CLASS I)—NUMBER OF CARS OF REVENUE FREIGHT LOADED, BY PRINCIPAL COMMODITIES: 1925 TO 1952

[In thousands. Figures are 52-week totals]

YEAR	Total	Grain and grain products	Live-stock	Coal	Coke	Forest products	Ore	Miscel-laneous	Mdse., less than carload
1925	51,224	2,306	1,636	8,905	623	3,737	2,012	18,513	13,193
1930	45,873	2,368	1,285	7,927	486	2,369	1,662	17,661	12,201
1934	30,846	1,646	1,074	6,135	333	1,149	793	11,474	8,241
1935	31,504	1,577	714	6,145	340	1,384	1,036	12,227	6,081
1936	36,109	1,805	759	6,937	480	1,663	1,622	14,546	6,276
1937	37,670	1,789	722	6,977	508	1,838	2,208	15,174	6,466
1938	30,457	1,967	708	5,541	275	1,418	846	12,026	7,062
1939	33,911	1,940	694	6,083	414	1,584	1,615	13,751	7,331
1940	36,358	1,835	686	6,320	549	1,800	2,148	14,842	7,679
1941	42,352	2,028	681	7,806	679	2,190	2,682	15,476	8,040
1942	42,771	2,185	745	8,386	722	2,445	3,016	19,755	5,537
1943	42,440	2,648	838	8,507	752	2,229	2,816	19,571	5,080
1944	42,408	2,521	892	8,890	751	2,271	2,649	20,007	5,426
1945	41,918	2,734	804	8,296	695	2,029	2,474	19,255	5,529
1946	41,341	2,497	925	8,004	587	2,263	1,996	18,744	6,335
1947	44,502	2,724	770	9,088	732	2,415	2,651	20,049	6,071
1948	42,719	2,668	630	8,690	739	2,348	2,701	19,686	5,457
1949	35,911	2,563	551	6,218	588	1,952	2,210	17,220	4,569
1950	38,902	2,466	491	7,340	727	2,226	2,529	18,955	4,269
1951	40,499	2,588	497	7,503	838	2,368	3,004	19,840	3,866
1952	37,963	2,569	492	6,719	673	2,270	2,653	18,912	3,685

Source: Association of American Railroads, Car Service Division, Washington, D. C.; annual summary, *Cars of Revenue Freight Loaded*. Weekly reports are published currently.

No. 642.—STEAM RAILWAYS—NUMBER AND COMPENSATION OF EMPLOYEES: 1920 TO 1951

[Excludes switching and terminal companies. See also *Historical Statistics*, series K 82–83]

YEAR	ALL OPERATING CARRIERS		CLASS I CARRIERS					
	Average number of employees	Total yearly compensation (1,000 dollars)	Average number of employees	Total hours (thousands)	Total yearly compensation (1,000 dollars)	Average hours per employee	Average compensation	
							Per hour [1]	Per year
1920	2,075,896	3,754,261	2,022,832	5,446,741	3,681,901	2,692.6	$0.676	$1,820
1925	1,794,411	2,916,198	1,744,311	4,521,361	2,869,609	2,597.8	.631	1,640
1930	1,517,043	2,688,896	1,467,839	3,739,772	2,580,789	2,527.0	.675	1,714
1934	1,027,426	1,541,313	1,007,702	2,393,809	1,519,352	2,375.6	.635	1,508
1935	1,013,654	1,666,229	994,871	2,397,353	1,643,879	2,410.9	.686	1,653
1936	1,086,405	1,873,819	1,065,894	2,675,545	1,846,636	2,510.6	.691	1,735
1937	1,136,912	2,013,677	1,114,663	2,799,530	1,985,447	2,511.6	.709	1,781
1938	965,290	1,771,063	939,171	2,329,606	1,746,141	2,480.5	.750	1,859
1939	1,006,711	1,889,130	987,873	2,488,635	1,863,334	2,519.7	.749	1,887
1940	1,045,738	1,990,631	1,026,848	2,615,903	1,964,125	2,547.5	.751	1,913
1941	1,159,025	2,360,369	1,139,925	2,989,768	2,331,680	2,622.8	.780	2,045
1942	1,290,818	2,966,062	1,270,667	3,440,967	2,932,070	2,708.0	.852	2,307
1943	1,374,518	3,556,189	1,355,114	3,816,420	3,520,926	2,816.3	.923	2,598
1944	1,434,167	3,807,755	1,414,776	3,996,873	3,857,957	2,825.1	.968	2,727
1945	1,436,545	3,900,928	1,419,505	3,976,637	3,862,001	2,808.5	.970	2,721
1946	1,377,700	4,213,530	1,359,263	3,682,339	4,170,767	2,672.3	1.146	3,068
1947	1,370,510	4,399,296	1,351,865	3,613,290	4,352,047	2,672.1	1.204	3,219
1948	1,345,076	4,820,747	1,326,597	3,545,081	4,766,836	2,672.2	1.345	3,595
1949	1,209,192	4,468,545	1,192,619	3,016,786	4,415,790	2,532.5	1.464	3,707
1950	1,236,879	4,644,900	1,220,401	3,576,864	4,594,432	2,357.1	1.597	3,745
1951	1,292,000	5,328,072	1,275,744	2,976,870	5,273,975	2,335.0	1.770	4,133

[1] Calculated for all classes of employees, including those not paid on an hourly basis.

Source: Interstate Commerce Commission; annual report, *Statistics of Railways in the United States*.

No. 643.—STEAM RAILWAYS (CLASS I)—NUMBER AND COMPENSATION OF EMPLOYEES BY DISTRICTS AND BY CLASS: 1950 AND 1951

[For years ending Dec. 31. Includes class I switching and terminal companies]

DISTRICT OR CLASS	AVERAGE NUMBER OF EMPLOYEES		TOTAL COMPENSATION (1,000 dollars)		AVERAGE PER DAY OR HOUR, STRAIGHT TIME		AVERAGE PER MONTH, TOTAL COMPENSATION	
	1950	1951 [1]	1950	1951 [1]	1950	1951 [1]	1950	1951 [1]
DISTRICT								
All employees, all districts	1,267,815	1,326,655	4,778,876	5,492,972			$422	
Daily basis	96,872		490,894		$17.46			
Hourly basis	1,170,943	1,326,655	4,287,982	5,492,972	1.512	$1.740	305	$345
Eastern district	533,205	547,285	1,999,913	2,282,874			410	
Daily basis	41,685		204,921		17.44			
Hourly basis	481,520	547,285	1,794,992	2,282,874	1.538	1.767	311	348
Southern district	234,971	249,502	866,803	1,009,434			447	
Daily basis	18,025		96,674		17.54			
Hourly basis	216,946	249,502	770,129	1,009,434	1.474	1.705	296	337
Western district	509,639	529,868	1,912,160	2,200,664			424	
Daily basis	37,162		189,299		17.44			
Hourly basis	472,477	529,868	1,722,861	2,200,664	1.503	1.729	304	346
CLASS								
Executives, officials, and staff assistants	15,845	16,194	130,085	144,614	27.89	[2] 3.716	684	[2] 744
Daily basis	15,845	[2] 16,194	130,085	[2] 144,614				
Professional, clerical, and general	212,425	219,165	769,565	872,820			369	
Daily basis	41,447		183,436		16.20			
Hourly basis	170,978	219,165	586,129	872,820	1.566	1.824	286	332
Maintenance of way and structures	243,389	257,025	711,390	849,259			420	
Daily basis	4,845		24,399		16.86			
Hourly basis	238,544	257,025	686,991	849,259	1.353	1.537	240	275
Maintenance of equipment and stores	359,040	381,047	1,252,323	1,450,224			440	
Daily basis	11,415		60,252		17.30			
Hourly basis	347,625	381,047	1,192,071	1,450,224	1.555	1.745	286	317
Transportation (other than train service, engine, and yard)	156,468	158,830	548,247	615,796			278	
Daily basis	16,688		55,606		11.01			
Hourly basis	139,780	158,830	492,641	615,796	1.477	1.638	294	323
Transportation (yardmasters, switch tenders, and hostlers)	16,951	17,496	81,799	95,649			466	
Daily basis	6,632		37,116		16.08			
Hourly basis	10,319	17,496	44,683	95,649	1.415	1.887	361	456
Transportation (train and engine service)	263,697	276,898	1,285,467	1,464,610			406	
Hourly basis	263,697	276,898	1,285,467	1,464,610	1.582	1.758	406	441

[1] Beginning January 1951, all employees reported on hourly basis.
[2] Hourly basis.

Source: Interstate Commerce Commission; annual report, *Wage Statistics of Class I Steam Railways in the United States.*

No. 644.—Steam-Railway Accidents—Number of Persons Killed and Injured, by Status: 1891 to 1951

[For various reasons, including fact that returns were required under different acts, statistics are not strictly comparable. Prior to 1921, train accidents were those causing damage to railway property in excess of $150 or any damage and a resulting casualty. From 1921 to 1947 they were considered as such when damage exceeded $150 with or without a casualty; for 1948, accidents causing damages in excess of $260, with or without a casualty, were classified as train accidents; for 1949 to 1950, train accidents were those causing damage of $375 or more; for 1951, the damage limit was $300. Where damage was less than the amounts specified and there was a reportable casualty it was classified as a train-service accident. Figures for years 1911-15 include industrial and other nontrain accidents to employees only, and for years 1906-10 exclude switching and terminal roads. Otherwise, data cover all reportable accidents, including those due to suicide, mental derangement, and attempting to escape custody. See also Historical Statistics, series K 84-93]

YEARLY AVERAGE OR YEAR ENDING—	TOTAL		PASSENGERS [1]		EMPLOYEES [2]		OTHER PERSONS		TRESPASSERS	
	Killed	Injured	Killed	Injured	Killed	Injured	Killed	Injured	Killed	Injured
June 30:										
1891-1895	6,821	36,313	292	2,987	2,315	27,061	595	1,283	3,618	4,011
1896-1900	6,946	42,346	222	3,297	2,054	32,793	634	1,547	4,036	4,672
1901-1905	8,336	72,943	392	7,894	3,349	57,209	891	2,798	4,796	5,047
1906-1910	10,210	105,617	385	11,635	3,572	83,502	994	4,590	5,256	5,650
1911-1915	10,174	174,941	273	13,362	3,273	148,640	1,362	6,836	5,366	6,053
Dec. 31:										
1916-1920	8,682	176,698	304	7,419	2,855	137,523	2,074	8,460	3,439	3,391
1921-1925	6,618	141,688	173	5,578	1,654	125,790	2,235	9,420	2,566	2,904
1926-1930	6,635	90,643	101	3,687	1,395	73,522	2,686	9,822	2,521	2,532
1931-1935	5,127	29,834	38	1,996	589	18,222	1,811	6,530	2,688	3,087
1936-1940	4,997	37,292	56	2,583	613	19,765	1,866	6,882	2,452	2,111
1941-1945	6,060	53,812	174	4,274	980	41,222	2,040	7,056	1,838	1,278
1946-1950	3,918	41,866	97	3,706	808	30,778	1,777	6,348	1,446	1,141
1943	5,051	60,948	278	8,166	1,072	46,971	1,946	7,076	1,755	1,125
1944	4,906	61,251	367	4,854	1,087	46,812	1,905	6,683	1,860	1,152
1945	4,812	61,515	188	4,840	972	46,632	2,052	6,370	1,632	1,173
1946	4,506	52,026	128	4,714	738	39,472	1,971	6,670	1,671	1,170
1947	4,285	46,819	70	4,346	791	36,880	1,902	6,862	1,512	1,191
1948	3,883	43,107	59	3,607	622	31,361	1,726	6,400	1,476	1,130
1949	3,426	32,123	37	2,545	450	22,993	1,614	5,506	1,325	1,079
1950	3,486	32,367	120	3,419	392	22,566	1,669	6,129	1,245	1,133
1951	3,459	34,454	150	3,184	432	24,266	1,698	5,908	1,194	1,011

[1] Data cover passengers on trains and travelers not on trains. Casualties sustained in nontrain accidents included with "other persons."
[2] Prior to 1921 casualties sustained by employees not on duty in nontrain accidents included with "other persons."
Source: Interstate Commerce Commission; annual report, Accident Bulletin—Steam Railways.

No. 645.—Accidents at Highway Grade Crossings (All Steam Railways)—Automobile and Total Casualties: 1937 to 1951

[Excludes casualties due to suicide, mental derangement, and attempting to escape custody. See also headnote, table 644]

YEAR	Number of accidents	ALL PERSONS		ACCIDENTS WHICH INVOLVED AUTOMOBILES		
		Number killed	Number injured	Persons killed	Persons injured	Total casualties per 10,000 automobiles registered
1937	4,489	1,875	5,196	1,607	4,804	2.19
1938	3,494	1,817	4,018	1,307	3,763	1.73
1939	3,476	1,398	3,900	1,190	3,744	1.61
1940	4,164	1,808	4,682	1,576	4,430	1.77
1941	4,320	1,981	4,885	1,679	4,667	1.85
1942	4,180	1,970	4,616	1,621	4,386	1.84
1943	3,781	1,732	4,217	1,378	3,944	1.74
1944	3,811	1,840	4,214	1,512	3,963	1.83
1945	4,100	1,908	4,446	1,677	4,126	1.88
1946	4,001	1,851	4,397	1,668	4,137	1.68
1947	4,015	1,790	4,251	1,521	4,055	1.49
1948	3,994	1,613	4,255	1,355	4,054	1.28
1949	3,522	1,507	3,774	1,307	3,607	1.11
1950	4,000	1,576	4,206	1,348	4,206	1.15
1951	3,996	1,578	4,335	1,396	4,161	1.08

Source: Interstate Commerce Commission; annual report, Accident Bulletin—Steam Railways.

No. 646.—The Alaska Railroad—Summary of Passenger and Freight Services:
Years Ending June 30, 1951 and 1952

ITEM	1951	1952	ITEM	1951	1952
Road mileage operated—monthly average............	536	537	**FREIGHT TRAFFIC**		
			Freight-train miles.............	532,839	600,821
			Loaded cars, 1 mile, freight and mixed trains............	8,430,000	10,238,000
PASSENGER TRAFFIC			Empty cars, 1 mile, freight and mixed trains............	5,913,000	7,959,000
Passenger-train miles [1]........	234,482	273,902	All cars, 1 mile................	14,343,000	18,197,000
Passenger-car miles, passenger trains [1].................	820,181	1,120,612	Tons of revenue freight carried:		
Total revenue passengers carried..............	112,080	143,040	Coal......................	314,361	451,118
Revenue passengers carried 1 mile...................	14,438,713	19,769,697	Miscellaneous..............	779,365	903,962
Total passenger revenue.......	$638,004	$962,053	Tons of revenue freight carried 1 mile..................	178,983,000	227,012,000
Average revenue per passenger per mile..................	$0.04420	$0.04866	Total freight revenue..........	$12,487,587	$14,995,352
			Average revenue per ton per mile..................	$0.06977	$0.06606

[1] Including motor miles.

Source: Department of the Interior, The Alaska Railroad.

No. 647.—Electric Railways—Summary: 1890 to 1937

[The census of street railways, which was first taken in 1890, and which has been taken at quinquennial intervals through 1937 beginning with the inquiry for 1902, covers (1) all street railways, without regard to kind of motive power, and (2) all interurban railways using other than steam as motive power. The nonelectric railroads included are those operated principally by cable and gasoline engines. Operations of electrified divisions of steam-railway companies are not included. Figures in this table do not include data for motorbus and trolley-bus operations of electric street railways. (For motorbus and trolley-bus statistics from census reports, see source)]

ITEM	1890	1902	1912	1922	1927	1932	[1] 1937
Number of companies..................	789	967	1,260	[2] 1,200	[2] 963	[2] 706	[2] 478
Miles of line operated [3].............	5,783	16,645	30,438	31,264	27,948	20,110	14,214
Miles of all track operated [3]..........	8,123	22,577	41,065	43,932	40,722	31,548	23,770
Value of road and equipment (thousand dollars).................	389,357	2,167,634	4,596,563	5,058,762	[4]	4,143,381	4,399,768
Number of employees [3].............	70,764	140,769	282,461	300,119	264,575	[4] 182,165	152,475
Number of passenger cars............	32,505	60,290	76,162	77,301	70,309	59,692	44,864
Revenue passengers, including pay-transfer (thousands).............	2,023,010	4,774,212	9,545,555	12,666,558	12,174,592	[7] 7,955,981	7,485,290
Operating revenues (thousand dollars) [3].................	90,617	247,554	567,512	1,016,719	927,774	566,290	513,129
Operating expenses (thousand dollars) [3].................	62,011	142,313	332,896	727,795	694,460	442,607	406,119
Operating ratio (percent).............	68.4	57.5	58.7	71.6	74.9	78.2	79.1

[1] Excludes data for 22 companies, operating on a part-year basis. These companies reported 36,810,221 passengers; 9,108,009 car-miles; 1,042,866 car-hours; $2,388,295, operating revenue; and $2,412,010, operating expense.
[2] Includes certain companies in Pennsylvania which maintained separate organizations, though controlled through stock ownership by other companies. For 1912 these companies were treated as merged and not included in the number reported.
[3] Includes small mileage of track lying outside United States.
[4] Data incomplete. Some of the companies engaged in both light-and-power and electric-railway operations were unable to report separately the values of plant and equipment assignable to their railway activities.
[5] Number reported as of June 30, for 1890, 1922, 1927, and 1932; for 1902, average for the year; for 1912, as of Sept. 16. Figures for 1937 represent an average of numbers reported on June 30 and Dec. 31.
[6] Includes 334 trolley-bus operators.
[7] Includes 29,721,000 trolley-bus passengers.
[8] Includes auxiliary operating revenues of $8,905,000 for 1927 and $91,242,000 for 1922; auxiliary expenses, $7,822,000 for 1927, and $49,232,000 for 1922. Data for operating revenues and operating expenses of auxiliary operations excluded so far as possible for earlier years.

Source: Department of Commerce, Bureau of the Census; Census of Electrical Industries, report on Street Railways and Trolley-Bus and Motorbus Operations. Survey discontinued.

No. 648.—EXPRESS COMPANIES—INCOME ACCOUNT: 1921 TO 1951

[In thousands of dollars. Mileage operated by Railway Express Agency, Inc., 1951: Total, 221,237; steam road, 788,083; electric line, 1,208; steamboat line, 13, 282; motor carrier, 14, 679; airplane, 186,086]

CALENDAR YEAR	Receipts for transportation	Paid for express privileges	Total operating revenues [1]	Operating expenses	Net operating revenues	Express taxes	Operating income [2]	Other income	Net income [3]
American Railway Express Co.:									
1921	294,664	113,491	184,897	182,266	2,631	2,095	806	2,074	2,309
1926	290,303	143,582	149,715	146,433	3,282	2,059	1,196	1,086	2,184
1928	41,104	18,554	23,063	22,560	523	227	198	198	281
Railway Express Agency, Inc.:									
1929 [4]	242,216	127,591	117,628	115,535	2,098	1,343	734	667	20
1930	138,751	52,170	86,068	84,899	3,180	1,548	1,608	148	4
1935	167,179	57,803	111,976	104,158	7,818	6,967	831	192	2
1940	176,521	56,053	119,957	111,478	8,479	7,589	907	178	4
1941	195,606	63,117	135,262	125,638	9,624	8,486	1,106	225	188
1942	260,360	107,706	155,306	144,448	10,858	9,785	1,055	320	191
1943	380,215	146,042	207,545	193,590	13,965	13,074	861	432	66
1944	400,685	150,095	254,734	235,017	15,717	15,518	1,172	349	219
1945	437,130	157,075	284,428	266,960	17,468	16,734	712	272	[5] 222
1946	427,341	105,814	296,230	305,462	20,747	19,861	876	411	[5] 57
1947	436,683	220,315	312,981	288,186	24,845	24,187	628	461	[5] 222
1948	419,973	130,254	294,833	276,557	18,270	17,858	379	1,178	55
1949	385,295	90,825	250,667	234,584	16,063	15,654	313	1,185	[5] 165
1950	314,806	77,178	222,661	207,054	15,607	14,137	1,437	1,047	70
1951	319,558	101,030	223,343	209,116	14,227	13,680	537	1,086	99
Southeastern Express Co.:									
1921 [7]	4,374	1,649	2,781	2,719	61	25	37	10	47
1925	5,041	3,912	4,241	4,086	185	86	67	20	87
1930	5,007	3,900	4,244	4,098	146	110	35	28	73
1935	5,620	2,334	3,406	3,250	156	96	57	3	60
1938 [8]	3,122	746	2,436	2,270	166	166	6	1	7

[1] Includes revenues from sources other than transportation.
[2] Deducting, besides taxes, a small amount of uncollectible revenue.
[3] Sum of 2 preceding columns less deductions.
[4] Result of operations for 2 months ended Feb. 28, 1929, when taken over by Railway Express Agency, Inc.
Result of operations for 10 months ended Dec. 31, 1929. [5] Deficit.
Result of operations for 6 months ended Dec. 31, 1921.
Result of operations for 7 months ended July 31, 1938, when taken over by Railway Express Agency, Inc.

No. 649.—PULLMAN COMPANY—SUMMARY OF OPERATIONS: 1910 TO 1950

[All money figures in thousands of dollars]

YEAR ENDING—	Total revenues, car operations	Association and contract revenues, debit [1]	EXPENSES, CAR OPERATIONS		Net revenues, car operation	Operating income	REVENUE PASSENGERS CARRIED	
			Total	Conducting car operations			Thousands	Number per car-day
June 30:								
1910	35,334	969	23,962	[2]	11,372	13,151	20,208	14
1915	38,722	2,421	26,633	11,716	12,660	10,816	24,362	12
Dec. 31:								
1920	72,124	13,155	61,031	30,905	11,098	9,304	39,255	16
1925	80,195	8,873	63,513	32,347	16,685	12,546	35,526	12
1930	76,234	5,534	68,960	35,379	7,274	4,937	29,360	9
1935	45,426	2,683	49,077	19,720	[3] 648	[3] 1,647	15,479	9
1940	57,962	2,131	51,942	21,940	6,020	2,365	14,765	8
1942	96,875	13,570	72,531	36,150	23,344	9,151	26,068	11
1943	120,529	26,888	92,766	50,107	27,763	5,553	32,632	13
1944	141,289	19,080	107,999	60,922	33,290	10,721	35,833	13
1945	142,575	13,647	117,885	60,361	34,690	9,045	31,434	12
1946	131,592	2,380	115,804	62,541	12,908	4,780	25,945	11
1947	110,280	3,680	104,946	51,611	5,314	[3] 1,006	21,012	13
1948	110,272	4,364	99,436	51,649	10,834	3,734	18,660	12
1949	101,951	3,346	92,008	50,573	9,948	4,090	16,022	11
1950	106,721	1,219	93,696	52,896	12,085	6,873	15,806	11

[1] Amounts due other carriers under provisions of definite contracts. [2] Not separated. [3] Deficit.
Source of tables 648 and 649: Interstate Commerce Commission; annual report, *Statistics of Railways in the United States.*

No. 650.—TRANSIT INDUSTRY—SUMMARY: 1930 TO 1951

[Represents entire transit industry comprising all organized local passenger transportation agencies except taxicabs and suburban railroads. Based on financial and statistical reports received by American Transit Association from transit companies representing 85 to 95 percent of the industry]

ITEM	1930	1935	1940	1945	1948	1949	1950	1951
Miles of route operated (Dec. 31):								
Electric railway—miles of single track	35,400	26,700	19,602	17,702	12,964	11,931	10,813	9,457
Surface	34,320	25,470	18,360	16,480	11,740	10,700	9,590	8,240
Subway and elevated	1,080	1,230	1,242	1,222	1,224	1,231	1,223	1,217
Trolley coach—miles of negative overhead wire	146	548	1,925	2,313	2,905	3,318	3,482	3,647
Motorbus—miles of route round trip	60,900	58,100	78,000	90,400	96,500	96,400	98,000	99,700
Passenger vehicles owned (Dec. 31), total	96,263	74,844	75,464	89,758	90,507	88,129	86,310	85,338
Electric railway cars	64,790	50,466	37,662	36,377	26,250	24,728	22,986	20,804
Surface	55,150	40,050	26,630	26,160	16,824	14,859	13,228	10,980
Subway and elevated	9,640	10,416	11,032	10,217	9,456	9,869	9,758	9,644
Trolley coaches	173	578	2,802	3,711	5,687	6,366	6,504	7,074
Motorbusses	21,300	23,800	35,000	49,670	58,540	57,035	56,820	57,660
Investment (Dec. 31), total (millions)	(¹)	(¹)	$4,096	$4,262	$3,900	$3,940	$3,918	$3,899
Electric railway	(¹)	(¹)	3,588	3,620	3,111	3,110	3,060	2,997
Surface	(¹)	(¹)	1,574	1,570	1,060	998	913	811
Subway and elevated	(¹)	(¹)	2,014	2,050	2,051	2,112	2,147	2,186
Trolley coach	(¹)	(¹)	58	76	118	137	144	162
Motorbus	(¹)	(¹)	450	566	671	693	714	740
Operating revenues, total (millions)	$963	$681	$737	$1,380	$1,489	$1,491	$1,452	$1,473
Electric railway	803	520	455	709	666	621	578	534
Surface	649	388	328	560	474	403	362	319
Subway and elevated	154	132	128	149	192	218	216	215
Trolley coach	2	5	25	68	91	112	122	132
Motorbus	158	156	256	603	732	758	752	807
Vehicle miles operated, total (millions)	2,707	2,327	2,596	3,254	3,311	3,183	3,007	2,913
Electric railway	1,995	1,544	1,316	1,398	1,157	1,015	906	811
Surface	1,540	1,097	845	940	699	555	463	387
Subway and elevated	455	447	471	458	458	460	443	424
Trolley coach	6	19	86	133	178	200	206	209
Motorbus	706	764	1,194	1,723	1,976	1,968	1,895	1,893
Passengers carried, total (millions)	15,567	12,226	13,098	23,254	21,368	19,008	17,246	16,125
Electric railway	13,072	9,512	8,325	12,124	9,112	7,185	6,168	5,290
Surface	10,513	7,276	5,943	9,426	6,506	4,839	3,904	3,101
Subway and elevated	2,559	2,236	2,382	2,698	2,606	2,346	2,264	2,189
Trolley coach	16	96	534	1,244	1,528	1,661	1,658	1,633
Motorbus	2,479	2,618	4,239	9,886	10,728	10,162	9,420	9,202
Revenue passengers carried, total (millions)	12,528	9,782	10,504	18,982	17,312	15,251	13,845	12,881
Electric railway	10,346	7,408	6,465	9,636	7,213	5,683	4,903	4,212
Surface	7,782	5,156	4,183	7,081	4,740	3,480	2,790	2,171
Subway and elevated	2,564	2,252	2,282	2,555	2,473	2,203	2,113	2,041
Trolley coach	13	77	419	1,001	1,206	1,268	1,261	1,231
Motorbus	2,169	2,297	3,620	8,345	8,893	8,300	7,681	7,438
Number of employees (average), total	276,444	209,200	202,400	242,000	261,000	253,000	240,000	232,000
Electric railway	247,244	164,400	122,500	129,200	109,000	98,000	90,900	81,000
Trolley coach	400	1,300	6,400	8,500	14,000	15,000	15,400	16,500
Motorbus	28,800	43,500	73,500	104,300	138,000	140,000	133,700	134,500
Payroll, total (millions)	$479	$321	$360	$632	$829	$841	$835	$872

¹ Not available.

Source: American Transit Association, New York, N. Y.; annual report, Transit Fact Book.

No. 651.—CLASS I INTERCITY MOTOR CARRIERS OF PROPERTY—SUMMARY OF FINANCIAL AND OPERATING STATISTICS: 1946 TO 1950

[All money figures, except average revenue and expenses per vehicle-mile, in thousands of dollars. Covers common and contract carriers with average annual operating revenues of $200,000 or more in 1950, and for prior years $100,000 or more, engaged wholly or preponderantly in intercity service subject to general jurisdiction of I. C. C.]

ITEM	1946	1947	1948	1949	1950
Number of carriers reporting	1,516	1,603	1,825	2,012	1,621
Investment in carrier operating property	314,561	396,769	516,383	615,449	747,756
Less reserve for depreciation and amortization	143,703	166,639	215,458	270,706	309,430
Net investment in carrier operating property	170,858	230,130	300,845	344,743	438,326
Income statement:					
Operating revenue, total	883,806	1,232,846	1,662,882	1,804,586	2,376,713
Common carrier	808,457	1,122,814	1,515,283	1,722,744	2,180,779
Contract carrier	59,689	78,164	105,688	126,735	143,771
Other operating revenue	18,860	30,566	38,911	45,109	55,164
Expenses, total	852,292	1,174,211	1,552,772	1,793,814	2,215,008
Operation and maintenance expenses	666,741	1,032,719	1,379,114	1,589,049	1,968,089
Equipment maintenance and garage	132,337	145,638	194,045	206,597	261,903
Transportation	217,618	437,503	764,702	809,078	1,127,354
Terminal	166,851	255,095	171,214	197,762	249,578
Traffic	21,988	26,075	37,368	47,361	56,839
Insurance and safety	51,087	71,116	97,915	108,131	121,552
Administrative and general	74,940	92,392	112,865	131,220	150,843
Depreciation and amortization [1]	31,873	44,761	60,815	74,207	94,497
Operating taxes and licenses [2]	54,489	64,116	73,167	83,317	105,408
Operating rents, net	96,189	32,615	39,676	47,241	50,012
Operating ratio (percent expenses of operating revenue)	96.4	95.3	93.4	94.7	93.1
Net operating revenue	31,514	58,235	110,109	100,774	164,707
Losses of distinct operating unit—Net	333	377	719	430	440
Other income, less income deductions	1,184	3,489	1,965	2,704	4,608
Net income before income taxes	30,046	54,439	107,425	97,640	168,845
Net income after income taxes	21,020	27,012	72,184	63,572	92,582
Dividend appropriations and withdrawals [3]	9,491	12,590	18,047	21,029	23,482
Number and compensation of employees:					
All employees:					
Number [4]	145,942	157,590	141,421	153,902	175,190
Compensation [5]	391,544	474,403	465,119	533,229	668,840
Equipment maintenance and garage:					
Number	12,428	13,626	11,205	11,840	12,843
Compensation	34,728	41,792	37,190	41,298	47,478
Transportation:					
Drivers and helpers: [6]					
Number	53,316	51,120	64,423	70,354	79,866
Compensation	146,104	161,305	220,868	253,817	316,894
Others:					
Number	3,052	3,406	2,741	3,017	3,271
Compensation	10,802	12,690	11,287	13,191	15,067
Terminal:					
Number	53,819	68,914	45,209	48,944	55,241
Compensation	140,413	185,238	127,981	146,242	157,564
Sales, tariff, and advertising:					
Number	3,351	3,825	4,085	5,070	5,585
Compensation	11,698	14,537	16,556	21,125	26,904
Administrative and general:					
General officers:					
Number	2,799	3,063	2,319	2,457	2,279
Compensation	22,334	26,792	23,524	26,006	30,386
Others, including insurance and safety:					
Number	12,171	13,696	11,439	12,118	13,105
Compensation	26,478	31,672	28,023	31,580	35,546
Operating statistics and averages:					
Owned revenue vehicles, total	112,300	127,912	151,027	169,469	191,243
Trucks	30,737	22,223	25,232	28,038	26,900
Truck-tractors	26,308	41,882	48,985	54,202	61,060
Semitrailers	52,274	60,804	72,764	82,732	90,629
Full trailers	2,991	3,293	4,096	4,497	4,654
Intercity vehicle-miles (millions)	3,407	3,069	3,810	4,332	5,382
Tons of intercity revenue freight carried [7] (thousands)	112,266	135,426	165,826	176,452	212,997
Miles per owned vehicle	46,147	47,461	46,863	48,088	53,683
Revenue per vehicle-mile (intercity)	$0.359	$0.393	$0.426	$0.426	$0.434
Expenses per vehicle-mile (intercity) [8]	$0.354	$0.384	$0.406	$0.403	$0.414

[1] Amortization represents a very small part of this total.   [2] Does not include Federal or State income taxes.
[3] Withdrawals of sole proprietors and partners.
[4] Beginning 1948, excludes employees of Common Carriers of other than general freight and contract carriers in 1944, 48,674, compensation $135,759,000; 1949, 48,603, compensation $155,600,000; 1950, 49,025, compensation $168,400,000.
[5] Does not include drivers of equipment engaged by these carriers to perform "purchased transportation."
[6] Includes pickup and delivery employees (subsequently included with drivers, etc.) as follows: 1946, 34,630, compensation $92,920,000; 1947, 35,560, compensation $103,970,000.
[7] Includes tonnage on account of tonnage received from connecting motor carriers.
[8] Includes expenses of operating vehicles in local services not available separately.

Source: Interstate Commerce Commission; annual report, Statistics of Class I Motor Carriers.

No. 652.—CLASS I INTERCITY MOTOR CARRIERS OF PROPERTY—SELECTED OPERATING STATISTICS, BY REGIONS: 1945 TO 1950

[See headnote, table 651. Regions: 1, Conn., Maine, Mass., N. H., R. I., Vt.; 2, Del., D. C., Md., N. J., N. Y., Pa., W. Va.; 3, Ill., Ind., Mich. (Lower Pen.), Ohio; 4, Ala., Fla., Ga., Ky., Miss., N. C., S. C., Tenn., Va.; 5, Mich. (Upper Pen.), Minn., N. Dak., S. Dak., Wis.; 6, Iowa, Kans., Mo., Nebr.; 7, Ark., La., Okla., Tex.; 8, Colo., Idaho, Mont., N. Mex., Utah, Wyo.; 9, Ariz., Calif., Nev., Oreg., Wash.]

| REGION AND YEAR | Number of carriers reporting | Operating revenue ($1,000) | Total expenses ($1,000) | OWNED REVENUE VEHICLES [1] | | | | Vehicle-miles, total intercity service (1,000) | EMPLOYEES [2] | |
				Trucks	Truck-tractors	Semi-trailers	Full trailers		Average number	Compensation ($1,000)
Total:										
1945	1,445	746,394	745,002	19,610	33,534	44,081	2,940	2,164,808	132,904	335,403
1946	1,516	883,806	852,292	20,727	36,308	52,274	2,991	2,406,622	145,942	391,544
1947	1,603	1,232,546	1,174,211	22,233	41,582	60,804	3,293	3,059,474	157,590	474,403
1948	1,825	1,662,882	1,552,772	25,232	48,935	72,764	4,096	3,809,696	182,027	603,878
1949	2,012	1,894,588	1,793,814	28,038	54,202	82,732	4,497	4,338,273	199,405	698,829
1950	1,621	2,379,713	2,215,006	28,990	61,060	96,539	4,654	5,351,624	224,215	854,806
1. New England:										
1945	141	54,504	54,110	2,047	2,588	3,399	7	122,697	9,763	27,539
1946	150	65,270	62,057	2,139	2,921	4,330	28	132,828	11,066	32,201
1947	167	81,243	77,668	2,218	3,494	5,064	33	151,220	12,192	37,996
1948	181	92,684	89,994	2,343	3,762	5,522	36	161,096	13,206	44,150
1949	203	100,791	97,496	2,534	4,127	6,068	62	172,503	13,792	48,339
1950	149	116,224	109,960	2,299	4,173	6,422	27	192,303	14,216	54,753
2. Middle Atlantic:										
1945	357	150,177	149,500	3,611	7,539	9,701	45	377,021	26,935	69,256
1946	393	179,472	174,043	4,073	8,478	11,466	29	419,274	30,711	82,074
1947	397	243,466	231,553	4,303	9,807	13,295	39	513,177	32,740	99,457
1948	446	317,472	297,866	4,623	11,200	15,752	159	636,238	37,468	122,086
1949	487	357,983	339,363	5,073	12,016	17,691	202	711,578	40,910	142,044
1950	365	429,805	404,049	5,039	12,528	19,104	208	832,847	43,932	166,962
3. Central:										
1945	348	222,515	222,408	3,387	10,326	14,787	783	701,878	39,278	101,852
1946	346	272,203	259,846	3,265	10,919	17,348	665	822,264	42,979	118,121
1947	392	410,216	393,751	3,532	12,346	20,288	760	1,142,951	46,052	144,125
1948	456	580,075	540,676	4,073	14,754	24,479	963	1,452,140	53,608	195,266
1949	483	645,573	611,947	4,300	15,795	26,830	1,151	1,610,454	57,103	210,489
1950	419	850,779	792,997	4,540	18,623	32,797	1,260	2,051,481	66,341	267,058
4. Southern:										
1945	152	83,473	84,285	1,973	4,086	4,776	17	277,428	15,810	33,588
1946	167	91,554	88,731	2,052	4,186	5,520	37	279,141	15,903	37,048
1947	173	116,698	110,723	2,203	4,629	6,347	36	329,302	16,145	41,304
1948	191	163,859	151,048	2,583	5,278	7,580	44	421,051	18,583	54,225
1949	216	203,293	190,643	3,038	6,233	9,384	70	514,292	22,103	68,490
1950	192	266,761	247,452	3,422	7,402	11,645		661,807	27,007	89,989
5. Northwestern:										
1945	69	34,893	34,816	955	1,834	2,183	4	104,281	6,990	16,708
1946	67	42,911	41,934	1,080	2,073	2,684	4	118,560	8,008	21,086
1947	68	58,060	56,346	1,166	2,244	2,955	1	133,947	8,917	26,204
1948	73	74,390	70,559	1,244	2,540	3,370	2	156,511	9,793	32,067
1949	85	79,560	76,991	1,341	2,808	3,701	25	176,495	9,926	34,800
1950	71	97,380	92,084	1,380	3,224	4,428	3	203,592	11,104	42,727
6. Midwestern:										
1945	77	37,600	38,043	1,017	1,782	2,078	26	128,284	6,861	16,103
1946	89	49,052	47,057	1,192	2,167	2,804	61	152,630	8,213	20,732
1947	95	70,058	66,977	1,248	2,565	3,322	57	191,731	9,450	26,808
1948	109	93,593	87,808	1,437	3,057	3,979	94	244,041	10,791	33,575
1949	125	126,190	120,777	1,959	3,787	5,430	48	310,171	13,767	46,843
1950	101	155,248	146,765	2,139	4,408	6,471	71	386,832	15,228	56,629
7. Southwestern:										
1945	124	64,988	64,354	2,387	3,106	3,755	82	212,069	13,330	28,240
1946	122	72,814	70,270	2,537	3,184	4,244	80	220,947	13,705	32,237
1947	112	90,643	84,443	2,590	3,337	4,488	78	244,587	13,705	36,079
1948	129	122,913	113,135	3,066	4,271	5,429	102	310,171	16,055	47,364
1949	142	140,419	130,254	3,285	4,758	6,272	67	354,512	17,538	54,934
1950	119	175,573	159,853	3,480	5,554	7,219	121	445,203	19,746	67,761
8. Rocky Mountain:										
1945	31	16,890	16,893	554	316	518	185	49,204	2,864	6,675
1946	36	22,200	21,609	667	438	664	273	62,736	3,280	8,881
1947	44	44,651	40,939	909	929	1,377	221	112,615	5,021	15,677
1948	55	55,620	50,314	1,055	1,022	1,516	249	126,032	5,638	19,440
1949	61	67,888	61,854	1,188	1,284	1,809	269	157,645	6,638	23,876
1950	50	79,577	69,521	1,117	1,353	1,937	274	182,760	6,846	26,301
9. Pacific:										
1945	146	80,264	80,593	3,679	1,957	2,884	1,791	191,946	11,373	35,402
1946	146	88,330	86,745	3,722	1,942	3,174	1,814	198,242	12,077	39,164
1947	155	117,511	111,791	4,064	2,231	3,668	2,068	239,027	13,368	46,751
1948	185	162,275	151,372	4,808	3,051	5,137	2,447	302,416	16,885	63,703
1949	210	172,891	164,489	5,320	3,394	5,547	2,603	330,623	17,628	69,014
1950	155	206,366	192,325	5,574	3,795	6,516	2,690	394,800	19,795	82,626

[1] Excludes equipment used under lease, including operations conducted under "purchased transportation arrangements."
[2] Excludes drivers of equipment engaged by these carriers to perform "purchased transportation" service.

Source: Interstate Commerce Commission; annual report, *Statistics of Class I Motor Carriers.*

No. 653.—Class I Intercity Motor Carriers of Passengers—Summary of Financial and Operating Statistics: 1946 to 1950

[All money figures, except average fare and average revenue and expense per vehicle-mile, in thousands of dollars. Covers carriers with average annual operating revenues of $200,000 or more in 1950, and for prior years $100,000 or more, engaged wholly or preponderantly in intercity service subject to jurisdiction of Interstate Commerce Commission. This table does not include carriers subject to the Commission's jurisdiction engaged wholly or preponderantly in local or suburban service or carriers engaged in transportation of both property and passengers]

ITEM	1946	1947	1948	1949	1950
Number of carriers reporting	264	253	260	272	172
Investment in carrier operating property	174, 455	226, 363	282, 533	295, 628	286, 600
Less reserve for depreciation and amortization	91, 209	99, 643	113, 260	133, 047	144, 489
Net investment in carrier operating property	83, 246	126, 725	170, 864	159, 933	141, 512
Income statement:					
Operating revenue, total	380, 627	367, 424	401, 823	379, 751	380, 751
Passenger revenue [1]	365, 103	348, 707	377, 504	354, 314	354, 629
Special bus revenue	6, 641	8, 404	10, 696	11, 470	11, 604
Other operating revenue	8, 883	10, 313	13, 123	14, 067	14, 528
Expenses, total	299, 217	312, 517	350, 622	345, 365	314, 773
Operation and maintenance expenses	246, 992	267, 756	296, 921	279, 206	264, 906
Depreciation and amortization [2]	17, 720	19, 868	26, 794	30, 906	27, 188
Operating taxes and licenses [3]	28, 574	29, 272	31, 764	30, 801	28, 649
Operating rents, net	5, 931	5, 696	5, 183	4, 873	4, 050
Operating ratio (percent expenses of operating revenue)	78.6	85.1	87.4	91.0	89.7
Net operating revenue	81, 410	54, 907	50, 701	34, 146	35, 978
Loss of carrier property, net	484	275	109	105	100
Other income, less income deductions	1, 678	130	568	997	758
Net income before income taxes	82, 604	54, 768	50, 230	32, 604	33, 121
Net income after income taxes	50, 414	33, 494	31, 172	19, 974	18, 908
Dividend appropriations and withdrawals [4]	31, 796	32, 280	20, 611	15, 942	16, 088
Number of employees and compensation:					
All employees:					
Number	46, 587	45, 820	47, 868	45, 961	40, 148
Compensation	129, 185	126, 123	151, 474	151, 261	139, 280
Equipment maintenance and garage:					
Number	12, 028	11, 639	12, 230	11, 802	9, 856
Compensation	31, 316	31, 665	35, 548	34, 945	31, 376
Transportation:					
Drivers of passenger revenue vehicles: Number	19, 295	19, 494	20, 900	20, 809	19, 081
Compensation	59, 333	65, 065	74, 446	74, 454	69, 855
Others: Number	1, 820	1, 816	1, 859	1, 861	1, 565
Compensation	6, 225	6, 520	6, 680	7, 263	5, 313
Station:					
Number	7, 581	7, 079	6, 903	6, 326	5, 843
Compensation	15, 005	15, 243	16, 065	16, 032	15, 085
Traffic, solicitation, and advertising:					
Number	761	777	822	802	748
Compensation	2, 353	2, 639	2, 850	2, 935	2, 819
Administrative and general:					
General officers: Number	566	574	566	569	434
Compensation	5, 654	5, 332	5, 306	5, 170	4, 345
Others, including insurance and safety: Number	4, 534	4, 441	4, 479	4, 191	3, 620
Compensation	9, 269	9, 669	10, 389	10, 449	9, 449
Operating statistics and averages:					
Passenger vehicles owned [5]	13, 106	14, 149	15, 290	14, 963	13, 200
Vehicle-miles of owned and leased passenger vehicles: [6]					
Regular route intercity service (thousands)	964, 227	978, 364	1,051,056	987, 512	987, 724
Special, charter, and sightseeing service (thousands)	17, 630	22, 274	27, 987	29, 410	25, 570
Local and suburban service [7] (thousands)	60, 798	55, 732	50, 760	48, 760	41, 936
Number of revenue passengers carried:					
Regular route intercity service (thousands)	433, 730	412, 332	420, 758	367, 074	304, 348
Special, charter, and sightseeing service (thousands)	7, 216	8, 667	9, 716	9, 694	7, 996
Local service (thousands)	121, 014	105, 454	106, 293	92, 714	77, 564
Miles per vehicle [8]	77, 677	76, 055	72, 533	69, 088	65, 411
Average fare per passenger, per carrier, intercity service	$0.796	$0.802	$0.852	$0.912	$1.010
Passenger revenue per vehicle-mile:					
Regular route intercity	.359	.338	.341	.339	.346
Special, charter, and sightseeing service	.377	.377	.362	.380	.405
Local service	.315	.322	.376	.398	.405
Expense per vehicle-mile	.267	.296	.310	.334	.332

[1] Regular route intercity and local revenue.
[2] Amortization represents a very small part of this total.
[3] Includes Federal or State income taxes.
[4] Dividends, small in amount, of sole proprietors and partners.
[5] Owned vehicles owned at close of year.
[6] Includes bus-miles of vehicles operated under "purchased transportation arrangements."
[7] Includes only service on local and suburban runs of preponderantly intercity carriers.
[8] Average for owned and leased vehicles.

Source: Interstate Commerce Commission; annual report, Statistics of Class I Motor Carriers.

No. 654.—CLASS I INTERCITY MOTOR CARRIERS OF PASSENGERS—SELECTED OPERATING STATISTICS, BY REGIONS: 1945 TO 1950

[See headnote, table 653; for description of regions, see headnote, table 652]

REGION AND YEAR	Number of carriers reporting	Operating revenue ($1,000)	Total expenses ($1,000)	PASSENGER VEHICLES		REGULAR-ROUTE INTERCITY			EMPLOYEES	
				Intercity[1]	Total[2]	Vehicle-miles (1,000)	Revenue passengers carried (1,000)	Average fare per passenger, per carrier	Average number	Total compensation ($1,000)
Total:										
1945	231	377,933	264,934	12,281	13,393	860,485	434,614	$0.793	42,394	108,394
1946	254	380,627	299,217	12,558	13,636	964,227	433,730	.796	46,587	129,185
1947	253	367,424	312,517	12,915	14,040	978,364	412,332	.802	45,820	136,123
1948	260	401,333	350,632	14,622	15,831	1,051,056	420,758	.852	47,808	151,474
1949	262	379,751	345,585	14,988	16,115	987,512	367,074	.912	45,961	151,261
1950	172	350,751	314,773	13,621	14,566	887,725	304,348	1.010	40,148	139,280
1. New England:										
1945	18	11,412	10,255	559	584	26,097	23,132	.450	1,601	4,493
1946	18	10,274	9,682	495	513	26,801	20,647	.445	1,647	4,545
1947	19	10,542	10,282	512	558	27,779	19,395	.473	1,684	4,973
1948	21	12,295	12,240	647	679	31,290	21,404	.499	1,783	5,553
1949	21	12,257	12,157	638	680	30,743	18,357	.573	1,796	5,748
1950	13	9,199	9,409	470	505	22,391	9,143	.859	1,221	4,208
2. Middle Atlantic:										
1945	34	39,965	32,567	1,556	1,772	87,191	64,620	.546	4,874	12,615
1946	41	45,322	38,638	1,749	2,001	102,498	67,469	.581	5,565	15,696
1947	41	44,506	40,374	1,767	1,964	104,648	65,074	.594	5,479	16,621
1948	42	48,731	44,988	1,999	2,240	107,760	67,732	.605	6,024	19,001
1949	43	39,167	37,962	1,743	1,965	84,593	54,654	.578	4,775	15,921
1950	36	38,013	36,074	1,581	1,798	78,957	49,137	.616	4,456	15,536
3. Central:										
1945	46	59,516	44,467	1,876	2,124	131,498	69,215	.753	7,129	19,115
1946	46	64,643	52,085	2,007	2,268	157,616	70,182	.809	8,019	23,058
1947	47	64,044	55,879	2,122	2,422	157,683	66,499	.823	7,870	24,639
1948	44	66,330	61,391	2,283	2,623	164,690	67,625	.880	7,906	26,394
1949	43	71,898	67,426	2,581	2,920	172,027	64,209	.968	8,683	29,530
1950	29	69,649	62,320	2,378	2,711	159,035	55,929	1.080	7,639	27,450
4. Southern:										
1945	53	113,114	78,789	3,926	4,133	274,011	148,586	.724	12,405	30,113
1946	59	108,029	83,905	3,954	4,122	295,673	147,936	.692	13,296	33,851
1947	60	101,529	85,260	3,916	4,162	296,437	140,139	.678	12,941	35,228
1948	62	106,249	90,435	4,133	4,388	298,502	134,290	.735	12,745	36,640
1949	59	101,001	88,087	4,221	4,412	276,404	114,004	.819	11,969	36,099
1950	34	89,213	77,857	3,722	3,781	244,256	94,293	.879	10,083	32,310
5. Northwestern:										
1945	6	13,355	8,299	367	367	32,029	11,657	1.097	1,169	3,233
1946	9	14,535	10,031	426	430	37,099	12,601	1.105	1,460	4,660
1947	10	14,802	11,729	476	481	41,252	12,935	1.090	1,604	5,050
1948	12	16,872	14,568	635	639	47,364	14,784	1.062	1,770	5,976
1949	14	11,529	12,244	564	564	35,801	10,344	1.027	1,509	5,044
1950	5	13,897	13,045	556	556	38,541	11,001	1.167	1,588	5,614
6. Midwestern:										
1945	12	18,383	11,391	529	529	44,966	12,929	1.374	1,909	5,168
1946	14	18,910	13,097	548	548	49,793	13,133	1.389	2,109	6,093
1947	14	23,631	19,187	764	764	65,723	14,543	1.535	2,693	8,632
1948	16	25,121	20,955	840	840	69,405	15,535	1.510	2,792	9,275
1949	16	22,509	19,575	826	826	60,461	12,800	1.611	2,725	9,292
1950	9	20,120	17,597	719	719	54,340	10,259	1.792	2,427	8,544
7. Southwestern:										
1945	38	61,214	40,506	2,044	2,105	148,409	61,487	.946	6,954	16,662
1946	41	59,176	44,543	1,898	1,912	158,478	60,151	.936	7,201	19,665
1947	34	49,754	41,155	1,821	1,830	143,010	50,571	.941	6,262	17,590
1948	34	63,244	54,141	2,315	2,324	183,811	56,835	1.049	7,374	23,124
1949	36	63,302	56,508	2,553	2,559	187,752	52,399	1.125	7,588	24,739
1950	26	56,674	51,030	2,474	2,475	167,403	42,422	1.322	6,673	22,585
8. Rocky Mountain:										
1945	9	5,291	3,359	178	225	11,938	3,899	1.177	581	1,457
1946	10	4,831	3,496	172	210	12,532	2,882	1.482	574	1,619
1947	11	4,562	3,641	173	195	12,495	2,383	1.678	522	1,652
1948	11	4,868	4,029	200	224	13,185	2,714	1.542	615	1,826
1949	11	4,516	3,983	201	229	13,116	2,586	1.497	528	1,762
1950	6	3,468	2,983	166	167	10,160	1,873	1.583	376	1,372
9. Pacific:										
1945	15	55,663	35,301	1,246	1,554	104,346	39,089	1.178	5,772	15,538
1946	16	54,907	43,740	1,309	1,632	123,737	38,729	1.182	6,716	19,998
1947	17	53,964	45,010	1,364	1,664	129,337	40,793	1.099	6,765	21,738
1948	18	55,623	47,885	1,570	1,874	135,049	39,839	1.142	6,859	23,585
1949	19	53,572	47,643	1,661	1,960	126,615	37,661	1.144	6,398	23,136
1950	14	50,519	44,457	1,555	1,854	112,442	30,290	1.322	5,665	21,667

[1] Includes vehicles owned, leased, and operated under "purchased transportation arrangements," operated in intercity revenue service.

[2] Includes average number operated in intercity service during year and number owned in local operations at close of year.

Source: Interstate Commerce Commission; annual report, Statistics of Class I Motor Carriers.

No. 655.—Motorbus Lines—Summary of Operations of Common Carriers and School Busses: 1949 to 1952

ITEM	1949	1950	1951	1952 (prel.)
COMMON CARRIER BUS OPERATIONS				
Number of operating companies (Dec. 31):				
City and city suburban	1,799	1,626	1,676	1,628
Intercity	2,080	2,888	2,844	2,847
Number of busses (Dec. 31):				
City and city suburban	57,500	57,570	58,364	58,488
Intercity	30,280	28,711	29,386	28,863
Miles of highway covered (Dec. 31): [1]				
City and city suburban	54,000	53,310	50,680	54,239
Intercity	416,500	400,284	438,447	438,438
Total bus miles (1,000):				
City and city suburban	1,795,611	1,861,862	1,781,714	1,749,842
Intercity	1,598,023	1,500,430	1,437,549	1,444,182
Revenue passengers, line service (1,000):				
City and city suburban [2]	8,502,055	7,750,000	7,580,000	7,485,452
Intercity	854,981	815,172	907,912	899,844
Operating revenue ($1,000):				
City and city suburban	786,351	798,982	830,757	859,404
Intercity	537,575	510,815	541,853	555,705
Taxes assignable to operations ($1,000): [3]				
City and city suburban	56,556	62,025	58,914	48,655
Intercity	42,880	42,508	43,578	45,380
Net operating revenue ($1,000):				
City and city suburban	−5,906	8,540	22,829	20,355
Intercity	30,912	37,982	41,409	38,878
Number of employees (Dec. 31): [4]				
City and city suburban	125,696	129,043	126,850	118,617
Intercity	66,749	66,570	62,676	64,709
SCHOOL BUS OPERATIONS				
Number of schools using busses	45,300	43,813	43,649	41,208
Number of busses	97,600	104,179	105,594	119,347
Total bus-miles (1,000)			689,563	1,119,696
Children carried daily (1,000)	5,730	6,264	6,410	7,054
Cost of service annually ($1,000)	177,532	180,183	207,718	288,385

[1] Includes duplication between carriers.   [2] Includes revenue transfer passengers.   [3] Excludes income taxes.   [4] Operating companies only.

No. 656.—Trolley Bus and Street Car Lines—Summary of Operations: 1949 to 1952

ITEM	1949	1950	1951	1952 (prel.)
TROLLEY BUS LINES				
Number of operating companies (Dec. 31)	42	42	43	41
Number of busses owned (Dec. 31)	6,355	6,497	7,089	7,182
Miles of highway covered (Dec. 31)	1,425	1,457	1,496	1,487
Total bus-miles (millions)	176	192	206	210
Revenue passengers (millions) [1]	1,149	1,198	1,226	1,205
Operating revenue ($1,000)	102,724	121,960	131,880	141,739
Taxes assignable to operations ($1,000) [2]	4,581	4,912	5,343	7,080
Net operating revenue ($1,000)	11,372	15,384	15,828	15,407
Number of employees on payroll	15,570	15,650	16,350	16,742
STREETCAR LINES				
Number of operating companies	101	88	81	74
Number of cars owned	15,805	13,226	10,960	10,000
Miles of single track	10,700	9,590	8,240	7,500
Miles of first main track	5,707	5,110	4,407	4,000
Operating revenue ($1,000)	410,500	361,700	318,900	290,000
Number of passengers (millions)	3,480	2,790	2,171	1,790
Revenue-miles operated (millions)	555	463	387	334

[1] Includes revenue transfer passengers.   [2] Does not include income taxes.

Source of tables 655 and 656: *Bus Transportation*, Annual Review of Industry Progress Number; published by McGraw-Hill Publishing Co., Inc., New York, N. Y.

No. 657.—CIVIL AERONAUTICS—SUMMARY OF CIVIL FLYING: 1934 TO 1952

[As of Dec. 31 or for year ending Dec. 31. See also *Historical Statistics*, series K 246–273]

ITEM	1934	1940	1945	1950	1951	1952
Miles of controlled civil airways..............	19,081	32,100	43,285	70,253	74,424	72,328
Total civil aircraft........................	8,322	17,928	37,789	¹ 92,809	¹ 88,545	¹ 89,317
Hours in civil flying (1,000).................	846	3,200	(⁴)	(⁴)	8,613	(²)
Certificated airplane pilots....	13,949	69,829	296,895	(²)	580,574	(²)
Miles flown, other than scheduled air carrier (thousands)...........................	75,602	264,000	(²)	(²)	994,765	(²)
Instructional...........................	17,360	126,264	(²)	(²)	190,195	(²)
Commercial ²...........................	20,980	31,961	(²)	(²)	209,765	(²)
Business...............................	11,697	25,910	(²)	(²)	379,845	(²)
Pleasure..............................	25,565	79,865	(²)	(²)	200,265	(²)
Fuel consumed (1,000 gallons):						
Gasoline..............................	28,556	88,075	(²)	(²)	131,833	(²)
Oil...................................	1,018	1,764	(²)	(²)	2,930	(²)
Radio range stations, total ⁴...............	112	292	360	749	760	760
Low/medium frequency..................	112	290	344	378	375	372
Very high frequency...................	----------	2	16	371	385	388
Nondirectional radio beacons ⁴...........	73	48	88	141	152	166
Airport traffic control towers, federally operated ⁴.....	----------	----------	107	172	157	141
Airway traffic control centers, federally operated ⁴	----------	11	29	31	31	31
Combined tower stations...................	----------	----------	----------	----------	19	34
Interstate airways communications stations...	205	365	438	451	427	415
Airports in operation, as recorded by CAA, total...........................	2,297	2,331	4,026	6,403	6,237	6,042
Municipal ⁵............................	980	1,031	1,220	2,272	2,316	⁶ 2,336
Commercial ⁷..........................	872	860	1,509	2,329	2,042	⁸ 1,731
CAA intermediate ⁸....................	259	289	216	76	57	} ⁹ 1,975
All others ⁹...........................	186	151	1,081	1,726	1,822	
Total accidents in non-air-carrier flying operations........	1,491	3,471	4,652	4,505	3,824	(²)

¹ Includes gliders. ² Not available.
³ Includes noncertificated irregular air carrier and noncertificated cargo-carrier operations (for which no comparable classification existed for 1934 and 1940), as well as contract, charter, and other revenue-producing operations.
⁴ Data include continental United States, and Territories and possessions wherever applicable.
⁵ Public use and public services, public control.
⁶ Not strictly comparable due to changes in airport use types. See table 663 for current definitions.
⁷ Public use and public services, private control.
⁸ No public services, CAA control.
⁹ Includes military (no public services, military control); no public services, private control; no public services, Federal Government control (Forest Service, etc.).

Source: Department of Commerce, Civil Aeronautics Administration, and Civil Aeronautics Board. Published in *CAA Statistical Handbook of Civil Aviation*.

No. 658.—CIVIL AERONAUTICS—SCHEDULED AIR CARRIER OPERATING REVENUES AND EXPENSES: 1940 TO 1951

[In thousands of dollars]

ITEM	DOMESTIC AIR CARRIERS				INTERNATIONAL AIR CARRIERS			
	1940	1945	1950	1951	1940	1945	1950	1951
Net operating income.................	5,967	34,117	63,158	107,001	1,256	7,346	11,808	18,071
Operating revenues, total..........	76,864	214,743	557,803	702,364	26,922	69,111	260,131	287,936
Passenger............................	53,308	166,520	444,506	591,186	8,812	38,859	160,673	184,692
Mail................................	20,090	33,693	63,788	57,422	13,439	12,246	55,689	53,213
Express and freight..................	2,078	10,835	35,122	36,914	893	7,315	21,664	25,245
Excess baggage......................	551	2,298	5,077	6,069	306	1,570	3,244	3,809
Other...............................	836	1,396	9,310	10,773	3,472	9,121	18,861	20,977
Operating expenses, total..........	¹ 70,897	180,626	494,645	595,363	25,666	61,765	248,323	269,865
Aircraft.............................	35,178	69,223	241,060	287,941	(²)	22,918	122,776	129,221
Flying operations.....................	22,093	43,421	141,816	173,023	(²)	15,296	70,980	75,102
Direct maintenance flight equipment...	7,496	16,393	57,841	71,686	(²)	5,199	26,158	29,856
Depreciation flight equipment.......	5,590	9,409	41,403	43,232	(²)	2,422	25,638	24,263
Ground and indirect expense.........	35,028	111,404	253,584	307,422	(²)	38,847	125,547	140,644

¹ Includes total operating expenses for Colonial; distribution by type not available.
² Not available.

Source: Department of Commerce, Civil Aeronautics Administration, and Civil Aeronautics Board. Published in *CAA Statistical Handbook of Civil Aviation*.

No. 669.—CIVIL AERONAUTICS—SUMMARY OF SCHEDULED AIR CARRIER OPERATIONS: 1934 TO 1952

[As of Dec. 31 or for year ending Dec. 31. See also *Historical Statistics*, series K 248–273]

ITEM	1934	1940	1945	1950	1951	1952 (prel.)
Number of operators:						
Domestic	24	19	20	38	36	35
International	3	3	4	12	12	13
Route miles in operation	50,801	95,079	87,401	182,841	187,676	196,442
Domestic [1]	28,609	42,757	48,516	77,440	78,913	77,977
International [2]	22,192	52,322	38,885	106,401	108,763	110,465
Airplanes in service	522	437	518	1,120	1,121	1,227
Domestic	423	369	421	980	981	1,078
International	99	68	97	160	140	149
Average available seats: [3]						
Domestic	8.96	16.54	19.66	27.47	38.96	41.64
International	(⁴)	18.26	18.91	40.96	46.38	46.67
Average speed (miles per hour):						
Domestic	(⁴)	(⁴)	155.4	181.2	194.6	190.8
International	(⁴)	(⁴)	160.7	218.4	223.4	223.8
Fuel consumed (1,000 gal.):						
Gasoline	25,136	74,535	160,911	572,246	657,402	770,455
Domestic	18,925	65,675	134,834	415,442	491,484	585,322
International	6,211	8,860	26,087	156,804	165,919	185,126
Oil	839	1,286	2,025	6,675	7,288	8,658
Domestic	669	1,104	1,710	5,007	5,546	6,987
International	170	184	316	1,668	1,742	1,681
Total personnel employed	6,477	22,051	68,261	82,766	95,752	(⁵)
Domestic	4,201	15,984	50,313	61,903	72,898	(⁵)
International	2,276	6,067	17,966	20,863	22,855	(⁵)
Revenue miles flown (all services) (thousands)	49,065	119,753	241,578	456,087	503,739	542,065
Domestic	41,526	110,101	208,969	364,266	406,105	448,688
International	7,539	9,652	32,609	98,821	97,634	105,599
Revenue passengers carried	[6] 572,265	[6] 2,965,398	7,061,510	19,016,189	24,662,366	27,377,633
Domestic	[6,6] 475,461	[6] 2,802,781	6,576,252	17,342,681	22,552,179	25,016,684
International	[6] 96,804	162,617	475,558	1,675,477	2,041,807	2,366,607
Revenue passenger miles flown, domestic (thousands)	[6] 189,306	1,052,156	3,362,455	6,003,826	10,566,282	12,598,826
Average passenger-mile rate, domestic	$0.059	$0.0607	$0.0496	$0.0555	$0.0560	(⁷)
Express and freight, ton-miles flown	(⁴)	(⁴)	36,914,363	211,912,648	214,585,945	233,491,916
Domestic	[6] 597,293	3,476,234	22,196,852	151,351,080	143,624,785	160,527,232
International	(⁴)	(⁴)	8,717,611	60,569,569	71,295,378	78,464,688
Mail, ton-miles flown, domestic	[6] 2,237,175	10,117,858	[10] 66,092,921	67,006,947	63,848,234	66,341,652
Accidents, domestic: [11]						
Number of accidents	71	30	40	35	45	43
Revenue miles flown per accident	584,869	3,663,790	5,234,222	10,118,294	9,645,980	(⁷)
Total fatalities	29	45	86	109	170	54
Fatalities per 1,000,000 revenue miles flown	0.70	0.41	0.43	0.26	0.40	(⁷)
Accidents, international: [11]						
Number of accidents	2	6	5	6	10	13
Revenue miles flown per accident	3,769,555	1,608,622	6,521,741	15,985,584	10,263,478	(⁷)
Total fatalities	9	------	27	56	40	103
Fatalities per 1,000,000 revenue miles flown	1.19	------	0.83	0.58	0.39	(⁷)

[1] 1934 as of Dec. 31; 1940 and 1945, average for December; and 1950–52, based on fourth quarter.
[2] 1934 and 1940, as of Dec. 31; 1945, average for December; and 1950–52, based on fourth quarter.
[3] Obtained by dividing passenger seat miles by revenue miles flown in passenger service.
[4] Not available.
[5,6] Data for domestic passengers include duplication.
[6] Includes nonrevenue passengers.
[6a] Includes nonrevenue miles.
[8] Excludes Colonial Airlines, Inc., and Hawaiian Airlines, Ltd.
[9] Excludes 294,236 ton-miles flown by U. S. Army.
[10] Includes regular mail carried under special contract.
[11] Revenue operations accidents.

Source: Department of Commerce, Civil Aeronautics Administration, and Civil Aeronautics Board. Published in *Statistical Handbook of Civil Aviation*.

No. 660.—Civil Airplane Output, by Power and Types: 1946 to 1952

ITEM	1946	1947	1948	1949	1950	1951	1952
Airplanes produced, number	35,001	15,617	7,302	3,545	3,520	2,477	3,509
Under 3,000 lbs. airframe weight	34,568	15,339	7,039	3,379	3,391	2,279	3,057
3,000 lbs. airframe weight and over	433	278	263	166	129	198	452
Airplanes produced, by size:							
1- and 2-place	30,766	7,273	3,302	996	1,029	614	544
3- to 5-place	3,802	8,066	3,737	2,383	2,362	1,661	2,512
Over 5-place	433	278	263	166	129	202	453
Airplanes produced, by horsepower: [1]							
1–74	20,659	2,372	} 2,990	930	597	150	85
75–99	9,122	4,690					
100–399	4,736	8,246	} 4,026	2,441	2,789	2,123	2,971
400–3,999	345	129	} 286	174	134	204	453
4,000 and over	139	180					

[1] Total rated horsepower of all engines.

Source: Department of Commerce, Civil Aeronautics Administration and Bureau of Census. Published in CAA Statistical Handbook of Civil Aviation.

No. 661.—Civil Aeronautics—Domestic Scheduled Air Carrier Personnel: 1934 to 1951

TYPE OF PERSONNEL	1934	1940	1945	1948	1949	1950	1951
Total	4,201	15,984	50,313	60,416	59,886	61,963	72,599
Pilots and copilots	667	1,939	4,967	5,307	5,257	5,785	6,668
Other flight personnel		18	108	312	642	776	1,012
Pursers, stewards, stewardesses		914	2,075	3,038	3,199	3,372	4,106
Meteorologists and dispatchers		193	2,613	2,612	2,497	2,450	2,617
Mechanics	1,650	4,054	10,844	16,428	15,674	15,788	18,906
Other hangar and field personnel	923	1,880	7,012	9,222	9,336	9,822	11,475
Office employees	961	5,855	19,241	21,396	21,136	21,894	25,770
All others		1,131	3,453	2,101	2,145	2,016	2,322

Source: 1934 and 1940, Department of Commerce, Civil Aeronautics Administration; 1945–51, Civil Aeronuatics Board. Published in CAA Statistical Handbook of Civil Aviation.

No. 662.—Employment, Hours, and Earnings in Aircraft Industries (Annual Averages): 1947 to 1951

ITEM	1947	1948	1949	1950	1951
EMPLOYMENT [1]					
(Prime contracting plants)					
All plants, number of employees	(²)	194,176	216,791	231,342	377,266
Airframe plants	151,242	151,163	167,595	180,187	300,363
Engine plants	33,830	35,101	40,763	42,584	66,340
Propeller plants	(²)	7,912	8,433	8,571	10,563
HOURS AND EARNINGS					
Average weekly earnings:					
Aircraft industries	$53.99	$60.21	$62.69	$67.15	$75.82
Aircraft engines and parts industries	$56.30	$63.40	$65.24	$71.40	$85.90
Average hourly earnings:					
Aircraft industries	$1.360	$1.465	$1.548	$1.622	$1.751
Aircraft engines and parts industries	$1.411	$1.550	$1.603	$1.696	$1.892
Average weekly hours:					
Aircraft industries	39.7	41.1	40.5	41.4	43.3
Aircraft engines and parts industries	39.9	40.9	40.7	42.1	45.4

[1] Data for week ending nearest middle of month.
[2] Not available.

Source: Department of Labor, Bureau of Labor Statistics, and Department of Commerce, Civil Aeronautics Administration and Bureau of Census. Published in CAA Statistical Handbook of Civil Aviation.

No. 663.—AIRPORTS AND AIRFIELDS, BY CLASS AND BY TYPE, BY STATES: JAN. 1, 1953

[Data cover existing airports and airfields recorded with Civil Aeronautics Administration. See also *Historical Statistics*, series K 257-268 for total and lighted airports]

STATE	Total	CLASS						TYPE [2]				
		I (incl. Sub I) [1]	II	III	IV	V	VI and over	Commercial	Municipal	Limited	Military	Private
Total	6,042	3,685	976	571	437	181	192	1,731	2,396	1,231	363	381
Alabama	76	36	15	14	10	1	2	18	37	5	16	2
Arizona	179	75	43	30	12	14	5	24	50	61	31	4
Arkansas	80	51	10	10	9			22	34	21		3
California	495	273	78	46	38	32	28	126	169	195	50	55
Colorado	107	51	26	22	2		6	30	53	12	2	10
Connecticut	22	13	1	2	5	1		11	8	1		2
Delaware	19	12	2	2	1		2	8	2	3	1	5
Dist. of Columbia	3				1	1	1		1		2	
Florida	175	45	21	39	40	11	19	34	84	4	51	2
Georgia	108	40	16	21	22	2	7	10	50	19	18	10
Idaho	148	122	14	7	2		3	6	69	48	1	24
Illinois	169	101	43	12	8	3	2	109	43	19	3	4
Indiana	124	80	25	9	8	2		74	35	7	4	4
Iowa	156	127	14	6	8		1	33	58	56	2	7
Kansas	184	121	26	13	4	9	9	33	101	27	8	15
Kentucky	47	31	5	6	4		1	14	18	8	2	5
Louisiana	94	54	15	12	7	3	3	12	35	34	6	7
Maine	67	42	5	13	2	2	3	15	24	21	4	3
Maryland	49	25	10	4	6		4	21	7	8	6	7
Massachusetts	71	41	12	8	6		4	33	22	5	5	
Michigan	247	173	41	15	11	2	5	59	109	64	6	9
Minnesota	116	72	32	6	4	1	1	26	87		1	2
Mississippi	85	48	11	16	8	1	1	20	33	20	7	1
Missouri	109	76	15	10	5	2	1	38	51	17	2	1
Montana	123	89	15	7	6	2	4	14	83	19	1	6
Nebraska	128	96	13	4	2	2	11	33	71	21	1	2
Nevada	70	33	7	10	10	9	1	12	28	27	5	3
New Hampshire	31	20	5	3	2		1	13	12	2	1	3
New Jersey	76	50	12	7	5	1	1	59	10	4	2	1
New Mexico	98	51	16	7	7	9	8	5	37	42	4	10
New York	214	147	32	12	14	6	3	90	43	66	9	6
North Carolina	132	79	19	15	12	2	5	62	36	13	13	4
North Dakota	122	101	11	2	8			13	68	41		
Ohio	217	154	40	10	6	2	5	132	36	28	3	14
Oklahoma	145	88	21	13	12	7	4	22	79	30	7	7
Oregon	123	81	10	12	14	4	2	28	52	45	1	2
Pennsylvania	199	147	29	14	7	1	1	131	47	14	4	3
Rhode Island	11	5	1	1	2	2		5	4		2	
South Carolina	64	28	13	2	13	5	3	16	38	4	5	1
South Dakota	69	47	8	6	4	2	2	13	50	4	1	1
Tennessee	58	35	12	3	4	4		20	25	7	3	3
Texas	617	350	127	55	43	24	18	104	163	192	47	111
Utah	60	25	13	13	2	6	1	8	42	5	5	
Vermont	22	18		3			1	9	9	1	1	2
Virginia	113	73	17	8	11	2	2	43	28	25	14	3
Washington	167	106	22	11	16	3	9	38	70	46	11	2
West Virginia	41	26	5	3	3	1		20	16	3		2
Wisconsin	160	107	34	14	3		2	75	68	14	1	2
Wyoming	50	20	9	13	6	1	1	6	34	8	1	1

[1] Sub I facilities are those which do not come up to Class I standards.

[2] Airport type definitions: Municipal—public use, aircraft services generally available, public ownership and/or control. Commercial—public use, aircraft services generally available, nonpublic ownership and/or control. Limited—intended for private use but public not prohibited, aircraft services limited or not available, public or nonpublic ownership and/or control. Military—some civil use, military ownership and/or control. Private—authorized use only, public or nonpublic ownership and/or control.

Source: Department of Commerce, Civil Aeronautics Administration; *Statistical Handbook of Civil Aviation*.

22. Waterways, Water Traffic, and Shipping

Data in this section vary as to area coverage, the variation depending upon the source of compilation. The data from Corps of Engineers, Department of Army, are for continental United States and Territories, possessions, etc.; data from Bureau of Census, and Bureau of Customs are for United States customs area which includes Alaska, Hawaii, and Puerto Rico and from 1935 through 1939, Virgin Islands; data from Maritime Administration and War Shipping Administration are for continental United States.

Units of measurement.—"Cargo tonnage" represents weight of cargo in long tons (2,240 pounds) or short tons (2,000 pounds). All other tonnage figures refer to capacity of vessels. The terms gross and net tonnage refer to space measurement, 100 cubic feet being called 1 ton. Gross tonnage is the capacity of the entire space within the frames and the ceiling of the hull, together with those closed-in spaces above deck available for cargo, stores, passengers or crew, with certain minor exemptions. Net or registered tonnage is what remains after deducting from the gross tonnage the spaces occupied by the propelling machinery, fuel, crew quarters, master's cabin, and navigation spaces. It represents substantially space available for cargo and passengers. The net tonnage capacity of a ship recorded as "entered with cargo" may bear little relation to actual weight of cargo. Dead weight tonnage is the weight in long tons required to depress a vessel from light water line (that is, with only the machinery and equipment on board) to load line. It is therefore the weight of the cargo, fuel, etc., which a vessel is designed to carry with safety. Displacement tonnage (naval vessels) has reference to weight of the vessel itself with its normal equipment, fuel, etc.

Types of vessel shipments.—Shipments by dry cargo vessels include shipments on all types of watercraft except tanker vessels, and shipments by tanker vessels include all types of cargo both liquid and dry carried by tanker vessels.

Vessel entrances and clearances.—The tables on vessel entrances and clearances show the number and net registered tonnage of American and foreign dry cargo and tanker vessels with cargo and in ballast entering and clearing the United States customs area in the foreign trade and indicate the customs districts at which these vessels first entered and from which they last cleared. With minor exceptions, all types of watercraft engaged in the foreign trade which are required to make formal entrance and clearance under United States customs regulations are included in the statistics. Army and Navy vessels entering or clearing without commercial cargo are not included in the figures. The tons shown in tables 679–682 are net tons of 100 cubic feet carrying capacity of the vessels (as defined in Part 16 of Title 46, "Code of Federal Regulations, Measurements of Vessels") and do not represent the actual weight of cargo carried.

A vessel is reported as entered at the first port in the United States at which entry is made, regardless of whether any cargo is unladen at that port. A vessel is reported as cleared from the last port where outward cargo is completed or where the vessel cleared in ballast.

Vessels touching at a United States port in distress, or for other temporary causes without discharging cargo are not included in the figures.

Historical statistics.—See preface and historical appendix. Tabular headnotes (as "See also *Historical Statistics*, series K 132–145") provide cross-references, where applicable, to *Historical Statistics of the United States, 1789–1945*.

Note.—This section presents data for the most recent year or period available on April 22, 1953, when the material was organized and sent to the printer.

No. 664.—Water-Borne Commerce of the United States—Cargo Tonnage, Foreign and Domestic: 1946 to 1951

[In thousands of short tons of 2,000 pounds. See also *Historical Statistics*, series K 132-145]

CLASS	1946	1947 [1]	1948 [1]	1949 [1]	1950 [1]	1951 [1]
Foreign commerce, total	148,877	188,256	162,971	165,366	169,226	232,013
Imports, through seaports	47,948	57,306	66,078	77,153	96,290	101,812
Exports, through seaports	76,589	101,906	64,404	65,740	43,640	97,603
Imports, Great Lakes ports	4,163	4,796	4,219	4,839	5,662	6,682
Exports, Great Lakes ports	20,177	24,098	25,270	17,626	22,608	25,705
Domestic commerce, unadjusted total	729,296	(1)	(1)	(1)	(1)	(1)
Coastwise, between ports	127,609	152,096	174,061	161,431	182,544	186,673
Great Lakes, between ports	138,617	163,180	172,491	145,892	169,681	176,463
Local traffic of seaports and Great Lakes ports	91,225	[4] 112,666	[4] 113,959	[3] 102,637	[3] 106,906	[3] 122,030
Traffic between ports and river points [2]	81,668	149,815	160,698	165,703	190,789	213,405
Traffic between ports of Territories and possessions of the United States [4]					1,239	1,417
Traffic on rivers, canals, and connecting channels [3]	280,807					
Imports and domestic, unadjusted total	878,863	(1)	(1)	(1)	(1)	(1)
Deductions of duplications:						
Traffic between seaports and river points	81,668	(1)	(1)	(1)	(1)	(1)
Other duplications (canals, etc.) [3]	180,103	(1)	(1)	(1)	(1)	(1)
Net total, foreign and domestic	617,092	706,817	793,200	746,721	839,584	884,000
Approximate net total, domestic	[7] 468,155	578,561	630,229	575,363	651,289	681,987

[1] Figures are net for each type of traffic; no adjustments required to arrive at net totals.
[2] Represents traffic local to seaports, Great Lakes ports, and communities on inland waterways.
[3] Represents traffic among ports and communities utilizing inland waterways exclusively.
[4] Included in other types of domestic traffic prior to 1950.
[5] Excluding St. Marys Falls Canal traffic and additional Detroit River traffic, data for which are already included in figures for Great Lakes traffic; also excluding duplications relating to rivers and canals themselves.
[6] Principally coastwise and lake traffic passing through canals and connecting channels other than the St. Marys Falls Canal and Detroit River.
[7] Estimated from figures in this table on assumption that all deductions represent duplications in domestic traffic; includes some minor duplications in figures for foreign traffic.

Source: Department of the Army, Corps of Engineers, *Annual Report of Chief of Engineers*, Part II, except for 1951 data, which are preliminary.

No. 665.—Estimated Employment on American Flag Merchant Vessels: 1929 to 1952

[Represents personnel employed on active steam and motor merchant vessels of 1,000 gross tons and over, engaged in deep-sea trades (overseas foreign, nearby foreign, intercoastal, and coastwise). Includes only freight, combination passenger and freight, and tanker vessels]

YEAR	Average monthly employment [1]	YEAR	Average monthly employment [1]	Date	Number employed [1]
1929	61,825	1938	50,908	Dec. 31, 1947	118,500
1930	63,360	1939	52,445	June 30, 1948	94,900
1931	57,180	1940	50,975	Dec. 31, 1948	78,200
1932	52,800	1941	50,275	June 30, 1949	76,200
1933	54,620	1942	47,550	Dec. 31, 1949	65,650
1934	56,298	1943	76,800	June 30, 1950	61,550
1935	56,575	1944	125,755	Dec. 31, 1950	68,040
1936	55,025	1945	158,755	June 30, 1951	94,300
1937	57,170	1946	127,175	Dec. 31, 1951	97,630
				June 30, 1952	76,650
				Dec. 31, 1952	70,850

[1] Includes masters of vessels; excludes personnel employed on vessels under bareboat charter, or vessels owned by Army or Navy.

Source: Department of Commerce, Maritime Administration; records.

No. **666.**—Water-Borne Imports and Exports—Cargo Tonnage, by Flag of
Carrier Vessel, 1921 to 1952, and by Coastal Districts, 1946 to 1952

[In cargo tons of 2,240 pounds. Excludes cargoes (small in aggregate) carried by ships of less than 100 tons
gross capacity prior to 1946]

YEAR AND DISTRICT	IMPORTS BY FLAGS OF CARRIER VESSELS			EXPORTS BY FLAGS OF CARRIER VESSELS		
	Total	American	Foreign	Total	American	Foreign
Total:						
1921	33,184,790	23,454,831	9,729,959	48,640,044	18,557,464	30,082,580
1925	43,135,154	21,214,626	21,920,528	49,666,499	15,716,692	33,949,807
1930	47,562,416	24,822,560	22,739,856	49,730,870	14,913,598	34,817,272
1932	28,710,280	13,324,302	15,385,978	31,844,566	8,147,086	23,697,480
1933	26,566,967	11,017,462	15,549,505	32,385,550	8,354,909	24,030,641
1934	29,813,903	12,767,083	17,046,820	37,821,061	9,435,147	28,385,914
1935	33,965,678	14,125,363	19,840,315	38,145,865	8,740,017	29,405,848
1936	38,395,748	13,196,753	25,198,996	39,714,046	8,615,976	31,098,070
1937	42,092,521	13,363,122	28,692,399	54,557,728	10,882,780	43,674,945
1938	32,818,162	12,077,522	20,740,640	55,612,107	10,356,772	45,255,334
1939	37,548,452	11,124,084	26,424,368	55,086,843	9,425,982	45,660,861
1940	39,881,161	15,465,891	24,415,270	54,401,306	11,553,134	42,848,152
1941	24,458,000	15,535,000	8,923,000	37,205,000	14,488,000	22,717,000
1943	27,668,000	22,089,000	5,579,000	42,647,000	22,591,000	20,056,000
1944	29,750,000	23,401,000	6,349,000	49,299,000	30,359,000	18,940,000
1945	35,202,000	28,049,000	7,153,000	55,003,000	33,687,000	21,316,000
1946	43,914,094	28,874,571	15,039,523	77,716,542	44,463,070	33,253,472
1947	52,860,000	33,645,000	19,215,000	110,997,000	54,520,000	56,477,000
1948	60,192,997	36,185,590	24,007,407	78,849,620	30,804,647	48,044,973
1949	69,081,139	36,932,206	32,148,933	64,164,776	23,335,624	40,829,152
1950	86,342,305	37,739,650	48,602,655	55,969,164	18,195,757	37,773,407
1951	89,823,763	38,245,983	51,577,780	103,294,219	38,599,961	64,694,258
1952	95,867,770	37,192,161	58,675,609	91,684,583	27,010,116	64,674,467
Dry cargoes:						
1946	22,606,662	12,730,414	9,876,248	64,160,404	39,050,784	25,109,620
1947	28,634,000	15,492,000	13,142,000	97,635,000	49,772,000	47,863,000
1948	32,732,094	15,359,212	17,372,882	67,702,862	27,283,247	40,419,615
1949	35,023,498	12,672,750	22,350,748	55,019,687	19,942,857	35,076,830
1950	41,616,924	13,234,760	28,382,164	47,837,917	14,669,123	33,168,794
1951	44,690,068	15,885,924	28,804,144	90,385,549	34,255,468	56,130,081
1952	44,957,497	16,536,006	28,421,491	78,935,652	23,329,787	55,605,865
Tanker cargoes:						
1946	21,307,432	16,144,157	5,163,275	13,556,138	5,412,286	8,143,852
1947	24,226,000	18,153,000	6,073,000	13,362,000	4,748,000	8,614,000
1948	27,460,903	20,826,378	6,634,525	11,146,758	3,521,399	7,625,359
1949	34,057,641	24,259,456	9,798,185	9,145,089	3,392,767	5,752,322
1950	44,725,381	24,504,890	20,220,491	8,131,247	3,526,634	4,604,613
1951	45,133,695	22,360,059	22,773,636	12,906,670	4,344,493	8,564,177
1952	50,910,273	20,656,155	30,254,118	12,748,931	3,680,330	9,068,601
Atlantic ports:						
1946	34,353,241	23,792,915	10,560,326	33,574,089	22,412,865	11,161,224
1947	40,704,000	(³)	(³)	57,031,000	(³)	(³)
1948	46,743,960	(³)	(³)	32,225,600	(³)	(³)
1949	52,052,017	(³)	(³)	25,373,754	(³)	(³)
1950	67,912,822	(³)	(³)	13,596,490	(³)	(³)
1951	69,796,810	(³)	(³)	48,780,177	(³)	(³)
1952	73,523,220	(³)	(³)	37,732,551	(³)	(³)
Gulf ports:						
1946	3,915,955	2,763,806	1,152,149	20,073,599	12,552,943	7,520,656
1947	6,239,000	(³)	(³)	23,922,000	(³)	(³)
1948	7,319,684	(³)	(³)	18,061,724	(³)	(³)
1949	9,463,434	(³)	(³)	16,996,765	(³)	(³)
1950	9,759,324	(³)	(³)	15,016,177	(³)	(³)
1951	9,743,716	(³)	(³)	20,041,283	(³)	(³)
1952	10,740,596	(³)	(³)	21,144,995	(³)	(³)
Pacific ports:						
1946	2,140,427	1,489,510	650,917	6,460,909	4,223,500	2,237,409
1947	2,189,000	(³)	(³)	9,297,000	(³)	(³)
1948	2,628,806	(³)	(³)	6,222,034	(³)	(³)
1949	3,252,244	(³)	(³)	6,071,153	(³)	(³)
1950	3,656,037	(³)	(³)	6,490,791	(³)	(³)
1951	4,219,999	(³)	(³)	13,365,945	(³)	(³)
1952	5,266,552	(³)	(³)	12,273,533	(³)	(³)
Great Lakes ports:						
1948	3,500,547	(³)	(³)	22,340,262	(³)	(³)
1949	4,313,444	(³)	(³)	15,723,104	(³)	(³)
1950	5,014,122	(³)	(³)	20,865,706	(³)	(³)
1951	6,061,200	(³)	(³)	21,106,815	(³)	(³)
1952	6,337,401	(³)	(³)	20,533,505	(³)	(³)

[1] Excludes U. S. Army, Navy cargo, and Great Lakes.
[2] Excludes U. S. Army and Navy cargo. Includes Alaska, Hawaii, and Puerto Rico. Beginning July 1950,
excludes commodities classified for security reasons as "special category." 1947-52 data subject to revision.
[3] Not available.

Source: Department of Commerce, Bureau of the Census; annual report, *Foreign Commerce and Navigation of
the United States,* and records.

No. 667.—WATER-BORNE IMPORTS—SHIPPING WEIGHT ON DRY CARGO AND TANKER VESSELS, BY TRADE AREA: 1949, 1950, AND 1951

[In millions of pounds. Represents general imports. Totals represent sums of unrounded figures; may vary from sums of rounded amounts. See 1951 Abstract, table 641, for latest data available by countries]

TRADE AREA	1949 [1]			1950 [1]			1951 [1]		
	Total	On American vessels	Percent American	Total	On American vessels	Percent American	Total	On American vessels	Percent American
DRY CARGO									
Trade area, total	78,452.6	26,397.6	34.2	92,221.9	29,645.9	31.5	100,195.5	35,594.5	35.5
Foreign except Canadian	58,947.6	24,471.7	41.5	68,642.5	26,462.7	38.3	75,437.4	31,996.8	42.3
Caribbean	15,271.9	3,990.5	26.1	15,578.7	3,552.5	23.0	17,436.0	7,090.0	40.7
East Coast South America	4,436.7	1,958.4	44.1	5,320.0	1,808.6	34.2	5,841.3	2,438.9	41.6
West Coast South America	9,550.4	7,537.0	78.9	9,259.4	7,844.9	84.7	10,013.3	7,732.5	77.2
West Coast Central America and Mexico	1,611.7	1,228.1	76.2	1,769.4	1,221.0	69.0	1,771.9	1,017.8	57.4
Gulf Coast Mexico	572.6	167.5	29.3	735.7	231.7	29.4	612.5	139.2	22.7
United Kingdom and Eire	575.2	208.6	33.9	1,706.6	627.0	35.4	1,785.2	690.7	38.5
Baltic, Scandinavia, Iceland and Greenland	6,174.8	1,498.2	24.3	7,138.1	1,505.4	21.0	7,672.2	2,118.0	27.5
Bayonne-Hamburg Range	3,016.0	624.6	20.7	6,380.9	1,684.6	26.3	8,535.0	1,876.2	22.0
Portugal and Spanish Atlantic	384.2	118.7	36.9	547.5	190.3	34.7	647.9	127,3	19.6
Azores, Mediterranean, and Black Sea	3,109.1	884.5	28.4	4,109.5	1,028.8	24.9	4,227.0	1,330.7	31.5
West Coast Africa	1,635.7	365.8	22.4	2,115.9	478.5	22.6	2,686.1	582.1	21.7
South and East Africa	2,000.0	1,378.1	68.8	2,830.2	1,354.9	47.8	2,596.3	1,351.4	52.0
Australasia	566.5	215.4	38.0	640.1	224.0	34.9	691.6	243.2	35.9
India, Persian Gulf, and Red Sea	3,863.6	1,004.4	35.1	3,302.4	991.4	30.0	3,344.6	1,146.1	34.3
Straits Settlements and Netherlands East Indies	2,475.7	1,350.3	54.5	2,436.1	1,306.7	53.6	2,292.5	1,382.2	60.3
South China, Formosa, and Philippines	3,672.3	1,676.1	45.6	3,800.4	1,632.5	42.9	4,475.3	1,817.9	40.6
North China including Shanghai and Japan	730.6	179.5	24.6	1,162.2	608.6	52.3	804.6	440.1	54.7
Canadian	19,505.6	5,918.2	30.1	24,379.4	3,242.1	12.2	24,665.4	3,797.7	15.6
Pacific Canada	2,948.6	1,128.5	38.3	4,733.2	1,279.3	27.0	2,777.2	912.4	32.9
Great Lakes Canada	8,925.3	2,091.3	23.4	9,884.1	1,436.0	14.5	12,040.8	1,540.6	12.8
Atlantic Canada and Newfoundland	7,631.5	696.4	9.1	9,762.2	526.6	5.3	9,850.3	2,356.6	13.7
TANKER CARGO									
Trade area, total	76,299.1	54,341.2	71.2	100,184.9	54,891.0	54.7	101,699.5	56,066.5	49.5
Foreign except Canadian	76,126.4	54,222.5	71.2	100,158.3	54,875.7	54.7	101,661.4	56,065.5	49.5
Caribbean	61,013.7	45,836.0	75.1	80,851.4	46,391.5	50.8	79,979.6	42,906.7	53.5
East Coast South America				(?)	(?)	100.0	2.3		
West Coast South America	296.0	241.6	81.6	4.1			40.0	16.6	42.0
West Coast Central America and Mexico	8.4			22.8	15.6	68.6	43.2	30.7	71.1
Gulf Coast Mexico	3,090.8	1,854.9	60.0	5,994.5	3,703.0	61.7	6,132.1	3,728.7	60.8
United Kingdom and Eire	208.2	62.4	30.7	276.2	67.4	34.3	562.4	166.5	29.6
Baltic, Scandinavia, Iceland, and Greenland	34.8			140.3	29.9	21.3	113.9		
Bayonne-Hamburg Range	81.0	7.5	9.3	297.1	129.7	43.6	1,216.3	512.7	42.2
Portugal and Spanish Atlantic	(?)			2.9			2.0		
Azores, Mediterranean, and Black Sea	347.5	197.0	56.7	333.0			4,730.8	380.4	8.1
West Coast Africa	1.6	(?)	2.7						
South and East Africa									
Australasia	(?)						.3		
India, Persian Gulf, and Red Sea	11,045.5	6,020.0	54.5	12,232.6	2,534.6	20.7	7,067.4	2,363.3	32.6
Straits Settlements, Netherlands East Indies	.1	.1	100.0	(?)	(?)	100.0	1,045.9		
South China, Formosa, and Philippines	(?)	(?)	100.0				122.0	42.7	35.0
North China including Shanghai and Japan	(?)			3.5	3.5	99.9			
Canadian	166.7	117.7	73.2	26.6	15.3	57.3	36.1	18.0	49.8
Pacific Canada	13.4	2.0	14.9	5.0	4.9	98.0	2.5	.4	16.0
Great Lakes Canada	139.9	115.7	82.7	8.1	8.1	100.0	17.6	17.6	100.0
Atlantic Canada and Newfoundland	7.4	(?)	(?)	12.5	2.3	16.6	10.0	(?)	.4

[1] Preliminary. [2] Less than 50,000 pounds. [3] Less than 0.05 percent.

Source: Department of Commerce, Bureau of the Census; current summary reports, FT 973, U. S. Water-Borne Trade by Trade Area.

No. 666.—Water-Borne Imports and Exports—Cargo Tonnage, by Flag of Carrier Vessel, 1921 to 1952, and by Coastal Districts, 1946 to 1952

[In cargo tons of 2,240 pounds. Excludes cargoes (small in aggregate) carried by ships of less than 100 tons gross capacity prior to 1946]

YEAR AND DISTRICT	IMPORTS BY FLAGS OF CARRIER VESSELS			EXPORTS BY FLAGS OF CARRIER VESSELS		
	Total	American	Foreign	Total	American	Foreign
Total:						
1921	33, 184, 790	23, 454, 831	9, 729, 959	48, 640, 044	18, 557, 464	30, 082, 580
1925	43, 135, 154	21, 214, 626	21, 920, 528	49, 666, 499	15, 716, 692	33, 949, 807
1930	47, 562, 416	24, 822, 560	22, 739, 856	49, 730, 870	14, 913, 596	34, 817, 272
1932	28, 710, 280	13, 324, 302	15, 385, 978	31, 844, 566	8, 147, 086	23, 697, 480
1933	26, 566, 967	11, 017, 462	15, 549, 505	32, 325, 550	8, 354, 909	24, 630, 641
1934	29, 813, 903	12, 767, 083	17, 046, 820	37, 821, 061	9, 435, 147	28, 385, 914
1935	33, 965, 678	14, 125, 363	19, 840, 315	38, 145, 865	8, 740, 017	29, 405, 848
1936	38, 395, 748	13, 196, 753	25, 198, 995	39, 714, 046	8, 615, 976	31, 098, 070
1937	42, 062, 821	13, 363, 422	28, 699, 399	54, 557, 725	10, 882, 780	43, 674, 945
1938	32, 818, 162	12, 077, 522	20, 740, 640	55, 612, 107	10, 328, 778	45, 283, 334
1939	37, 548, 452	11, 124, 084	26, 424, 368	55, 086, 843	9, 425, 952	45, 660, 891
1940	39, 881, 161	15, 465, 891	24, 415, 270	54, 401, 806	11, 553, 124	42, 848, 182
1942 [1]	24, 458, 000	15, 535, 000	8, 923, 600	37, 205, 000	14, 488, 000	22, 717, 000
1943 [1]	27, 665, 000	22, 086, 000	5, 579, 000	42, 647, 000	22, 591, 000	20, 056, 000
1944 [1]	29, 780, 000	23, 401, 000	6, 349, 000	49, 299, 000	30, 359, 000	18, 940, 000
1945 [1]	35, 202, 000	28, 049, 000	7, 153, 000	55, 003, 000	33, 687, 000	21, 316, 000
1946 [2]	43, 914, 094	28, 874, 571	15, 039, 523	77, 716, 542	44, 463, 070	33, 253, 572
1947 [2]	52, 860, 000	33, 645, 000	19, 215, 000	110, 997, 000	54, 520, 000	56, 477, 000
1948 [2]	60, 192, 997	36, 185, 590	24, 007, 407	78, 849, 820	30, 904, 647	48, 044, 673
1949 [2]	69, 061, 139	36, 932, 206	32, 148, 933	64, 164, 776	23, 335, 624	40, 829, 152
1950 [2]	86, 342, 305	37, 739, 650	48, 602, 655	55, 969, 164	18, 195, 757	37, 773, 407
1951 [2]	89, 823, 763	38, 245, 983	51, 577, 780	103, 294, 219	38, 599, 961	64, 694, 258
1952 [2]	95, 867, 770	37, 192, 161	58, 675, 609	91, 684, 583	27, 010, 116	64, 674, 467
Dry cargoes:						
1946 [2]	22, 606, 662	12, 730, 414	9, 876, 248	64, 160, 404	39, 080, 784	25, 109, 620
1947 [2]	28, 634, 000	15, 492, 000	13, 142, 000	97, 635, 000	49, 772, 000	47, 863, 000
1948 [2]	32, 732, 094	15, 359, 212	17, 372, 882	67, 702, 862	27, 283, 247	40, 419, 615
1949 [2]	35, 023, 498	12, 672, 750	22, 350, 748	55, 019, 687	19, 942, 857	35, 076, 830
1950 [2]	41, 616, 924	13, 234, 760	28, 382, 164	47, 837, 917	14, 669, 123	32, 168, 794
1951 [2]	44, 690, 068	15, 885, 924	28, 804, 144	90, 385, 549	34, 255, 468	56, 130, 081
1952 [2]	44, 957, 497	16, 536, 006	28, 421, 491	78, 935, 652	23, 329, 787	55, 605, 965
Tanker cargoes:						
1946 [2]	21, 307, 432	16, 144, 157	5, 163, 275	13, 556, 138	5, 412, 286	8, 143, 852
1947 [2]	24, 226, 000	18, 153, 000	6, 073, 000	13, 362, 000	4, 748, 000	8, 614, 000
1948 [2]	27, 460, 903	20, 826, 378	6, 634, 525	11, 146, 758	3, 521, 399	7, 625, 359
1949 [2]	34, 057, 641	24, 259, 456	9, 798, 185	9, 145, 089	3, 392, 767	5, 752, 322
1950 [2]	44, 725, 381	24, 504, 890	20, 220, 491	8, 131, 247	3, 526, 634	4, 604, 613
1951 [2]	45, 133, 695	22, 360, 059	22, 773, 636	12, 908, 670	4, 344, 493	8, 564, 177
1952 [2]	50, 910, 273	20, 656, 155	30, 254, 118	12, 748, 931	3, 680, 330	9, 068, 601
Atlantic ports:						
1946 [2]	34, 353, 241	23, 792, 915	10, 560, 326	33, 574, 089	22, 412, 865	11, 161, 224
1947 [2]	40, 704, 000	[3]	[3]	57, 031, 000	[3]	[3]
1948 [2]	46, 743, 980	[3]	[3]	32, 225, 800	[3]	[3]
1949 [2]	52, 052, 017	[3]	[3]	25, 373, 754	[3]	[3]
1950 [2]	67, 912, 822	[3]	[3]	13, 596, 490	[3]	[3]
1951 [2]	69, 796, 810	[3]	[3]	48, 780, 177	[3]	[3]
1952 [2]	73, 523, 220	[3]	[3]	37, 732, 551	[3]	[3]
Gulf ports:						
1946 [2]	3, 915, 955	2, 763, 806	1, 152, 149	20, 073, 599	12, 552, 943	7, 520, 656
1947 [2]	6, 239, 000	[3]	[3]	23, 922, 000	[3]	[3]
1948 [2]	7, 319, 684	[3]	[3]	18, 061, 724	[3]	[3]
1949 [2]	9, 463, 434	[3]	[3]	16, 996, 765	[3]	[3]
1950 [2]	9, 759, 324	[3]	[3]	15, 016, 177	[3]	[3]
1951 [2]	9, 743, 716	[3]	[3]	20, 041, 283	[3]	[3]
1952 [2]	10, 740, 896	[3]	[3]	21, 144, 995	[3]	[3]
Pacific ports:						
1946 [2]	2, 140, 427	1, 489, 510	650, 917	6, 460, 909	4, 223, 500	2, 237, 409
1947 [2]	2, 189, 000	[3]	[3]	9, 297, 000	[3]	[3]
1948 [2]	2, 628, 805	[3]	[3]	6, 222, 034	[3]	[3]
1949 [2]	3, 252, 244	[3]	[3]	6, 071, 153	[3]	[3]
1950 [2]	3, 656, 037	[3]	[3]	6, 490, 791	[3]	[3]
1951 [2]	4, 219, 999	[3]	[3]	13, 365, 945	[3]	[3]
1952 [2]	5, 266, 552	[3]	[3]	12, 273, 533	[3]	[3]
Great Lakes ports:						
1948 [2]	3, 500, 547	[3]	[3]	22, 340, 262	[3]	[3]
1949 [2]	4, 313, 444	[3]	[3]	15, 723, 104	[3]	[3]
1950 [2]	5, 014, 122	[3]	[3]	20, 865, 706	[3]	[3]
1951 [2]	6, 061, 239	[3]	[3]	21, 106, 815	[3]	[3]
1952 [2]	6, 337, 401	[3]	[3]	20, 533, 505	[3]	[3]

[1] Excludes U. S. Army, Navy cargo, and Great Lakes.

[2] Excludes U. S. Army and Navy cargo. Includes Alaska, Hawaii, and Puerto Rico. Beginning July 1950, excludes commodities classified for security reasons as "special category." 1947-52 data subject to revision.

[3] Not available.

Source: Department of Commerce, Bureau of the Census; annual report, *Foreign Commerce and Navigation of the United States,* and records.

No. 667.—Water-Borne Imports—Shipping Weight on Dry Cargo and Tanker Vessels, by Trade Area: 1949, 1950, and 1951

[In millions of pounds. Represents general imports. Totals represent sums of unrounded figures; may vary from sums of rounded amounts. See 1951 Abstract, table 641, for latest data available by countries]

TRADE AREA	1949 [1]			1950 [1]			1951 [1]		
	Total	On American vessels	Percent American	Total	On American vessels	Percent American	Total	On American vessels	Percent American
DRY CARGO									
Trade area, total	78,452.6	28,257.0	36.2	90,231.9	29,645.9	31.8	100,195.8	25,534.5	25.5
Foreign except Canadian	58,947.0	24,471.7	41.5	68,542.5	25,463.7	38.3	75,437.4	23,506.6	42.3
Caribbean	15,271.9	3,990.5	26.1	15,576.7	3,583.5	23.0	17,436.0	7,089.0	40.7
East Coast South America	4,436.7	1,962.4	44.1	5,220.0	1,808.6	34.2	6,341.3	2,432.9	41.6
West Coast South America	9,550.4	7,537.0	78.9	9,350.4	7,844.9	84.7	10,013.3	7,732.6	77.2
West Coast Central America and Mexico	1,611.7	1,228.1	76.2	1,768.4	1,221.9	69.0	1,771.9	1,017.6	57.1
Gulf Coast Mexico	572.6	167.5	29.3	786.7	231.7	29.4	612.5	139.3	22.7
United Kingdom and Eire	876.2	296.6	33.6	1,706.6	627.0	35.4	1,785.2	990.7	22.5
Baltic, Scandinavia, Iceland and Greenland	6,176.6	1,468.0	34.3	7,128.1	1,308.4	21.0	7,672.3	2,113.0	27.5
Bayonne-Hamburg Range	3,016.0	634.6	20.7	6,360.9	1,684.6	26.3	6,535.0	1,576.3	23.0
Portugal and Spanish Atlantic, Azores, Mediterranean, and Black Sea	304.2	112.7	30.9	547.5	190.3	34.7	647.9	127,9	19.6
West Coast Africa	3,109.1	994.5	32.4	4,109.8	1,028.3	34.9	4,237.0	1,330.7	31.5
South and East Africa	1,635.7	365.5	22.4	2,115.9	478.8	22.6	2,688.1	833.1	31.7
Australasia	3,030.0	1,270.1	68.8	2,820.2	1,364.9	47.8	2,395.3	1,451.4	36.3
India, Persian Gulf, and Red Sea	566.5	215.4	38.0	640.1	224.0	34.9	691.6	945.2	35.8
Straits Settlements and Netherlands East Indies	2,863.6	1,004.4	35.1	3,302.4	991.4	30.0	3,344.6	1,146.1	34.3
South China, Formosa, and Philippines	2,471.7	1,360.3	54.5	2,434.1	1,306.7	53.6	2,292.5	1,382.2	60.3
North China including Shanghai and Japan	3,672.3	1,676.1	45.6	3,800.4	1,683.5	42.9	4,475.3	1,617.9	40.6
	730.6	179.5	24.6	1,162.2	608.6	52.3	804.6	440.1	54.7
Canadian	19,505.6	3,915.3	20.1	24,579.4	3,342.1	13.3	24,668.4	3,797.7	15.4
Pacific Canada	2,949.6	1,128.5	38.3	4,733.2	1,279.3	27.0	2,777.2	912.4	32.9
Great Lakes Canada	8,926.3	2,091.3	23.4	9,884.1	1,436.0	14.5	12,040.5	1,540.6	12.8
Atlantic Canada and Newfoundland	7,631.5	695.4	9.1	9,762.2	536.8	5.3	9,850.3	1,254.6	12.7
TANKER CARGO									
Trade area, total	76,200.1	54,341.2	71.2	100,134.9	54,591.6	54.7	161,099.5	80,695.5	49.5
Foreign except Canadian	76,132.4	54,223.5	71.2	100,150.3	54,575.7	54.7	161,069.4	80,965.5	49.5
Caribbean	61,013.7	45,838.0	75.1	80,553.4	46,301.6	50.8	76,970.5	42,906.7	57.5
East Coast South America				(?)	(?)	100.0	2.2		
West Coast South America	396.0	341.8	81.6	4.1			60.0	18.8	62.0
West Coast Central America and Mexico	8.4			22.8	15.6	66.6	43.2	30.7	71.1
Gulf Coast Mexico	3,095.6	1,864.9	60.0	5,994.5	3,703.0	61.7	6,132.1	3,726.7	60.8
United Kingdom and Eire	203.2	62.4	30.7	276.2	67.4	24.3	562.4	166.5	29.6
Baltic, Scandinavia, Iceland, and Greenland	34.5			140.3	29.9	21.3	113.9		
Bayonne-Hamburg Range	81.0	7.5	9.3	307.1	130.7	43.6	1,216.3	512.7	42.2
Portugal and Spanish Atlantic	(?)			2.9			2.0		
Azores, Mediterranean, and Black Sea	347.5	197.0	56.7	232.0			4,730.8	380.4	8.1
West Coast Africa	1.6	(?)	2.7						
South and East Africa									
Australasia	(?)						.3		
India, Persian Gulf, and Red Sea	11,048.5	6,020.0	54.5	12,292.6	2,534.6	20.7	7,087.4	2,352.3	33.6
Straits Settlements, Netherlands East Indies	.1	.1	100.0	(?)	(?)	100.0	1,045.9		
South China, Formosa, and Philippines	(?)	(?)	100.0				122.0	42.7	35.0
North China including Shanghai and Japan	(?)			2.5	2.5	99.9			
Canadian	168.7	117.7	73.2	26.4	15.3	57.3	30.1	15.0	58.8
Pacific Canada	12.4	2.9	14.9	5.9	4.9	98.0	2.5	.4	16.0
Gulf Lakes Canada	139.9	115.7	82.7	8.1	8.1	100.0	17.6	17.6	100.0
Atlantic Canada and Newfoundland	7.4	(?)	(?)	13.5	2.3	16.6	10.0	(?)	.4

[1] Preliminary. [2] Less than 50,000 pounds. [3] Less than 0.05 percent.

Source: Department of Commerce, Bureau of the Census; current summary reports. FT 973, U. S. Water-Borne Trade by Trade Area.

No. 668.—WATER-BORNE EXPORTS—SHIPPING WEIGHT ON DRY CARGO AND TANKER VESSELS, BY TRADE AREA: 1949, 1950, AND 1951

[In millions of pounds. Covers domestic and foreign merchandise. Totals represent sums of unrounded figures: may vary from sums of rounded amounts. See 1951 *Abstract*, table 641, for latest data available by countries]

TRADE AREA	1949 [1]			1950 [1]			1951 [1]		
	Total	On American vessels	Per-cent American	Total	On American vessels	Per-cent American	Total	On American vessels	Per-cent American
DRY CARGO									
Trade area, total	123,244.1	44,672.0	36.2	107,156.9	32,853.8	30.7	202,463.6	76,732.2	37.9
Foreign except Canadian	88,773.3	34,700.4	39.1	61,277.3	22,018.5	35.9	155,882.1	64,856.3	41.6
Caribbean	8,796.7	4,095.7	46.6	8,127.9	3,255.8	40.1	8,818.0	3,424.1	38.8
East Coast South America	3,997.5	1,104.5	27.6	4,971.7	1,101.1	22.1	10,126.3	3,536.1	34.9
West Coast South America	2,192.0	1,049.6	47.9	1,779.8	698.8	39.3	2,729.5	1,121.1	41.1
West Coast Central America and Mexico	235.8	131.0	55.6	246.6	129.2	52.4	300.7	140.1	46.6
Gulf Coast Mexico	539.9	187.7	34.8	929.2	282.4	30.4	965.3	325.7	33.7
United Kingdom and Eire	5,692.3	1,793.9	31.5	5,786.4	2,122.7	36.7	13,630.7	4,542.0	33.3
Baltic, Scandinavia, Iceland, and Greenland	4,430.4	1,189.2	26.8	2,675.8	696.1	26.0	10,399.6	2,829.3	27.2
Bayonne-Hamburg Range	23,880.8	7,952.0	33.3	14,132.6	5,319.5	37.6	53,168.7	24,063.0	45.3
Portugal and Spanish Atlantic	1,240.0	28.8	2.3	877.5	258.1	29.4	1,018.5	110.8	10.9
Azores, Mediterranean, and Black Sea	18,523.6	10,237.5	55.3	8,503.2	2,907.2	34.2	24,889.9	10,386.6	41.7
West Coast Africa	1,307.6	396.5	30.3	783.0	222.8	28.4	1,436.9	387.6	27.0
South and East Africa	2,307.1	907.0	39.3	1,207.4	496.2	41.1	1,625.7	1,038.8	63.9
Australasia	1,824.5	366.4	20.1	1,207.5	253.1	21.0	1,632.8	331.5	20.3
India, Persian Gulf, and Red Sea	4,143.5	1,389.4	33.5	3,059.6	752.5	24.6	8,632.1	5,401.5	62.6
Straits Settlements, and Netherlands East Indies	1,025.0	412.1	40.2	574.2	253.2	44.1	998.4	496.5	49.9
South China, Formosa, and Philippines	3,824.4	2,113.0	55.3	2,742.7	1,400.9	51.1	2,640.9	1,471.8	55.7
North China, incl. Shanghai and Japan	4,812.3	1,346.3	28.0	3,672.1	1,868.9	50.9	12,868.1	5,241.8	40.7
Canadian	34,470.8	9,971.6	28.9	45,879.7	10,840.4	23.6	46,581.5	11,882.0	25.5
Pacific Canada	482.2	187.5	38.9	533.4	195.8	36.7	579.6	264.0	45.5
Great Lakes Canada	31,865.5	9,772.1	30.7	42,429.1	10,643.3	25.1	42,986.6	11,593.1	27.0
Atlantic Canada and Newfoundland	2,123.1	12.0	.6	2,917.2	1.3	(3)	3,015.3	24.9	.8
TANKER CARGO									
Trade area, total	20,485.0	7,599.8	37.1	18,214.0	7,899.7	43.4	28,915.4	9,731.7	33.7
Foreign except Canadian	12,226.8	4,245.5	34.7	9,682.3	4,022.4	41.5	20,291.1	4,752.9	23.4
Caribbean	2,560.4	1,320.8	51.6	2,320.2	1,533.2	66.1	3,118.9	2,085.6	66.9
East Coast South America	454.4	173.8	38.2	310.1	87.4	28.2	484.1	277.0	57.2
West Coast South America	438.9	68.4	15.6	757.3	246.4	32.5	721.6	334.0	46.3
West Coast Central America and Mexico	724.9	255.9	35.3	1,426.3	380.5	26.6	1,720.0	499.2	29.0
Gulf Coast Mexico	59.4	15.7	26.4	34.6	11.9	34.4	24.8	9.9	39.9
United Kingdom and Eire	3,650.6	1,125.6	30.8	2,088.7	433.6	20.8	4,443.7	332.9	7.5
Baltic, Scandinavia, Iceland, and Greenland	1,196.9	241.2	20.2	543.4	267.7	49.3	1,293.1	101.7	7.9
Bayonne-Hamburg Range	1,452.6	673.6	46.4	987.6	564.1	57.1	1,457.0	348.4	23.9
Portugal and Spanish Atlantic	122.1			46.4			43.8	2.3	5.3
Azores, Mediterranean, and Black Sea	561.4	214.7	38.2	739.3	361.1	48.8	715.0	203.0	28.4
West Coast Africa	196.7	20.1	10.2	92.0	71.7	78.0	235.9	42.6	18.1
South and East Africa	(3)	(3)	100.0	100.4	32.0	31.8	419.9	110.2	26.2
Australasia	371.8	135.3	36.4	23.5	2.5	10.6	1,354.7	111.9	8.3
India, Persian Gulf, and Red Sea	30.2	.2	.7	.1	.1	75.2	810.6	64.1	7.9
Straits Settlements, Netherlands East Indies	31.9			(3)			638.9		
South China, Formosa, and Philippines	249.7			46.3			440.5	57.7	13.1
North China, incl. Shanghai and Japan	124.7	.2	.2	164.2	30.1	18.3	2,368.6	172.3	7.3
Canadian	8,258.2	3,354.3	40.6	8,531.7	3,877.3	45.4	8,624.3	4,978.8	57.7
Pacific Canada	3,635.5	1,690.9	46.5	4,221.7	2,111.8	50.0	4,272.9	2,645.0	61.9
Great Lakes Canada	3,733.5	933.8	25.0	3,845.6	1,382.3	35.9	3,921.9	2,067.2	52.7
Atlantic Canada and Newfoundland	889.3	729.6	82.0	464.3	383.2	82.5	429.5	266.5	62.0

[1] Preliminary. [2] Less than 0.05 percent. [3] Less than 50,000 pounds.

Source: Department of Commerce, Bureau of the Census; current summary reports, FT 973, *U. S. Water-Borne Trade by Trade Area*.

No. 669.—Commerce of Principal United States Ocean Ports: 1951

[In thousands of short tons of 2,000 pounds. In addition to commerce here shown, many ports have (1) commerce with ports on internal rivers and canals; (2) purely local port traffic, including, for New York and San Francisco, what is called intraport traffic between parts of a harbor for which separate statistics are maintained. These forms of traffic, although aggregate tonnage is large, are of much less economic importance than foreign and coastwise traffic]

PORT	Imports	Exports	COASTWISE Receipts	COASTWISE Shipments	PORT	Imports	Exports	COASTWISE Receipts	COASTWISE Shipments
Total¹	101,812	97,668	196,806	194,646	GULF PORTS—continued				
ATLANTIC COAST PORTS					Mobile Harbor, Ala.	2,682	627	491	877
Searsport Harbor, Maine	182	81	381	14	Gulfport Harbor, Miss.	495	40	8	1
Portland Harbor, Maine	7,081	182	2,638	414	New Orleans, La.	4,256	6,027	998	7,400
Portsmouth Harbor, N.H.	215		848	3	Baton Rouge, La.	786	714	892	4,...
Salem Harbor, Mass.	17		288		Lake Charles, La.²	36	467	19	...
Boston, Mass.	5,101	382	11,704	980	Terrebonne Bay, La.				1,704
New Bedford and Fairhaven Harbor, Mass.	2		380	41	Orange, Tex.	7	53		163
Fall River Harbor, Mass.	348		1,404	85	Beaumont, Tex.	10	446	3,074	16,308
Providence River and Harbor, R.I.	808	3	6,225	407	Port Arthur, Tex.	7	1,374	3,127	14,440
New London Harbor, Conn.	204		288	198	Galveston, Tex.	233	5,233	44	1,...
New Haven Harbor, Conn.	730		3,749	668	Texas City, Tex.	34	633	527	7,...
Bridgeport Harbor, Conn.	207		1,628	323	Houston, Tex.	1,789	5,406	700	31,...
Norwalk Harbor, Conn.			287		Freeport, Tex.	10	387	6	929
Stamford Harbor, Conn.			650	28	Port Aransas, Tex.	1	388	148	14,...
New York Harbor, N.Y.	22,187	9,803	45,737	9,705	Corpus Christi, Tex.	20	621	7	8,729
Hempstead Harbor, N.Y.			1,283	2,788	Brazos Island Harbor, Tex.	239	536	18	663
Huntington Harbor, N.Y.			184	904	PACIFIC COAST PORTS				
Port Jefferson Harbor, N.Y.			487	297	San Diego Harbor, Calif.	17	1	1,246	
Seawout Harbor, N.Y.			8	40	Los Angeles Harbor, Calif.	1,006	3,225	8,214	4,...
Albany, N.Y.	186	1,073	2,668	13	Long Beach Harbor, Calif.	359	2,825	838	1,646
Northport Bay and Harbor, N.Y.			28	2,190	San Luis Obispo Harbor, Calif.			204	2,...
Delaware River and tributaries	28,244	6,632	22,631	7,034	Ventura Harbor, Calif.		15	35	2,...
Baltimore Harbor and Channels, Md.	14,498	7,980	7,138	1,587	Ellwood, Calif.			40	...
Hampton Roads, Va.	2,922	28,505	4,972	11,333	Estero Bay, Calif.		610	64	1,...
Morehead City, N.C.	130		168		El Segundo, Calif.	14		263	1,404
Wilmington, N.C.	201	42	3,087	9	San Francisco Bay Area, Calif.	1,694	3,069	13,333	9,697
Charleston Harbor, S.C.	1,134	632	2,063	184	Humboldt Harbor and Bay, Calif.		20	145	34
Savannah Harbor, Ga.	1,402	381	1,616	44	Stockton, Calif.	7	264	6	138
Jacksonville Harbor, Fla.	733	214	2,480	60	Coos Bay, Oreg.		341	167	406
Palm Beach Harbor, Fla.	155	336	97		Portland, Oreg.	106	1,781	5,824	652
Port Everglades Harbor, Fla.	288	167	1,236	179	Astoria, Oreg.	8	206	68	15
Miami Harbor, Fla.	230	62	516	8	Vancouver, Wash.		430	90	88
San Juan Harbor, P.R.	632	73	1,239	549	Longview, Wash.	13	613	156	176
Mayaguez Harbor, P.R.	35		146	192	Grays Harbor and Chehalis River, Wash.	4	94	204	194
Ponce Harbor, P.R.	154	203	206	230	Tacoma Harbor, Wash.	364	697	698	270
GULF COAST PORTS					Seattle Harbor, Wash.	349	863	5,148	632
Charlotte Harbor, Fla.		178		849	Bellingham Bay and Harbor, Wash.	281	46	36	34
Tampa Harbor, Fla.	204	1,406	2,222	1,486	Port Angeles Harbor, Wash.	49	17	123	105
Port St. Joe Harbor, Fla.		11	1,778		Whittier, Alaska			266	19
Panama City Harbor, Fla.	67	87	348	86	Seward Harbor, Alaska			604	4
					Honolulu Harbor, T.H.	64	10	1,...	...
					Kahului Harbor, T.H.	8		128	264
					Hilo Harbor, T.H.	29	1	168	264
					Nawiliwili Harbor, T.H.	9		40	187
					Pearl Harbor, T.H.	76	12	191	9

¹ Includes data for ports not shown separately.
² Including Calcasieu River and Pass.

Source: Department of the Army, Corps of Engineers. Data are preliminary and are subject to revision in Annual Report of Chief of Engineers, Part II.

No. 670.—COMMERCE OF PRINCIPAL GREAT LAKES PORTS: 1948 TO 1951

[In thousands of short tons of 2,000 pounds. Foreign imports and exports, lakewise receipts and shipments, and coastwise receipts and shipments only are included]

PORT	RECEIPTS				SHIPMENTS			
	1948	1949	1950	1951	1948	1949	1950	1951
Total	176,741	150,471	175,637	185,444	197,767	163,244	193,511	204,197
Agate Bay (Two Harbors), Minn	217	177	216	194	20,787	16,369	18,948	21,870
Alabaster, Mich					539	535	538	685
Alpena Harbor, Mich	364	400	442	451	2,049	2,082	2,382	2,651
Ashland Harbor, Wis	340	515	685	543	5,871	4,726	5,422	3,049
Ashtabula, Ohio	11,622	8,996	10,447	10,997	4,897	2,437	3,302	2,635
Buffalo, N. Y.	16,994	16,122	16,458	18,594	1,804	2,229	2,417	2,294
Buffington, Ind.	993	1,020	1,019	1,146	108	91	121	126
Calcite, Mich	132	89	150	126	13,099	11,856	14,018	15,457
Chicago, Ill.¹	14,771	12,570	15,813	16,374	3,032	3,427	4,093	5,008
Cleveland, Ohio	17,082	15,323	17,375	19,294	1,611	698	382	317
Conneaut Harbor, Ohio	12,937	10,870	9,562	12,450	3,081	1,909	2,522	2,122
Detour, Mich	501	382	523	524				
Detroit, Mich	18,040	16,067	21,090	21,631	751	1,314	1,296	1,131
Drummond Island, Mich	7	8	8	6	972	1,452	1,515	2,104
Duluth-Superior, Minn. and Wis	11,319	6,694	10,117	7,933	57,866	49,951	58,009	65,180
Erie Harbor, Pa.	4,705	4,393	4,340	5,356	2,047	1,718	2,276	2,095
Escanaba Harbor, Mich	431	205	372	268	5,270	4,233	5,561	7,349
Fairport, Ohio	1,254	975	972	1,435	1,767	1,082	1,297	1,166
Frankfort Harbor, Mich	1,207	896	1,071	1,213	668	587	882	758
Gary Harbor, Ind	8,297	8,406	9,182	9,215	160	97	171	
Grand Haven Harbor and Grand River, Mich	125	186	135	163	911	921	798	969
Great Sodus Bay, N. Y.					2,111	1,383	2,151	2,299
Green Bay, Wis.	3,451	2,517	3,944	3,196	4	4	8	7
Holland, Mich.	205	221	231	213				
Huron Harbor, Ohio	1,925	1,642	1,468	2,397	1,614	1,106	1,810	1,091
Indiana Harbor, Ind.	9,483	8,779	10,355	10,575	4,299	5,168	5,182	5,383
Kewaunee Harbor, Wis.	389	354	455	397	624	549	571	685
Lorain Harbor, Ohio	9,137	7,086	8,153	9,072	3,671	2,518	3,264	3,190
Ludington, Mich.	1,862	1,654	1,681	2,055	1,551	1,206	1,726	1,588
Manistee Harbor, Mich	234	192	209	215	590	682	819	647
Manistique Harbor, Mich	110	72	136	125	277	184	283	222
Manitowoc Harbor, Wis	1,241	1,063	1,498	1,320	953	825	944	1,002
Marblehead, Ohio					1,107	1,020	1,091	1,086
Marquette Harbor, Mich	222	136	214	240	486	513	688	646
Marysville, Mich	793	758	919	804	9	27	16	19
Menominee Harbor and River, Mich, and Wis.	848	491	881	790	88	76	82	85
Milwaukee Harbor, Wis.	7,021	5,538	7,357	6,836	1,564	1,522	1,421	1,453
Muskegon Harbor, Mich	1,623	1,727	2,124	2,221	1,028	985	1,220	1,230
Ogdensburg, N. Y.	263	218	368	434	270	179	249	240
Oswego, N. Y.	1,457	1,379	1,267	1,677	903	346	809	708
Port Huron, Mich.	568	524	554	677	5	4	10	30
Port Inland Harbor, Mich.	1		2		3,993	4,135	4,523	4,740
Port Washington Harbor, Wis.	677	733	968	1,177				
Presque Isle Harbor, Mich.		1		1	4,029	3,818	3,880	4,665
Racine Harbor, Wis.	357	225	145	158		13	9	
Rochester, N. Y.	270	170	29	10	1,473	891	1,218	1,252
Rockport, Mich.	8				1,033			
Saginaw River, Mich., and ports	3,433	2,993	4,019	3,613	37	118	54	54
St. Joseph Harbor, Mich.	348	337	314	292				
Sandusky Harbor, Ohio	2	2	1	2	11,820	6,165	9,822	7,363
Sault Ste. Marie, Mich.	456	487	502	447	9	2	2	6
Sheboygan Harbor, Wis.	658	432	641	508				
Toledo Harbor, Ohio	4,608	4,203	4,640	4,300	25,844	21,115	29,307	25,901
Tonawanda, N. Y.	403	267	402	423	3	4	31	
All other	2,880	2,007	2,883	3,356	1,082	970	1,279	1,918

¹ Includes Chicago Harbor and River, Calumet Harbor and River, Lake Calumet, Calumet-Sag Channel, and Chicago Sanitary and Ship Canal to Sag Junction.

Source: Department of the Army, Corps of Engineers; *Annual Report of Chief of Engineers*, Part II, except for 1951 data which are preliminary.

No. 671.—COMMERCE ON PRINCIPAL RIVERS, CANALS, AND CONNECTING CHANNELS OF THE UNITED STATES: 1946 TO 1951

[In thousands of short tons of 2,000 pounds. Excludes general ferry traffic, non-regulated car ferry traffic, and cargoes in transit]

WATERWAY	1946	1947	1948	1949	1950	1951
RIVERS						
Connecticut River below Hartford, Conn	1,400	1,604	1,584	1,802	1,983	2,001
Hudson River, N. Y. (South of Spuyten Duyvil Creek to Waterford, N. Y.)	9,151	10,949	12,716	13,598	14,574	15,575
Delaware River, Philadelphia, Pa., to Trenton, N. J.	5,008	5,832	7,219	6,901	7,095	7,505
Delaware River, Philadelphia, Pa., to the sea	37,151	41,997	42,375	36,635	66,292	72,111
Potomac River below Washington, D. C.	1,971	2,041	2,450	2,290	2,412	3,101
James River, Va	2,214	2,806	3,101	3,255	3,610	4,576
Wilmington Harbor, N. C.[1]	2,103	2,345	2,951	3,107	4,022	4,496
Mobile River, Ala., tributaries	2,576	3,274	3,179			
Black Warrior, Warrior, and Tombigbee Rivers, Ala	1,372	1,848	2,069	2,160	2,603	2,712
Bayou Teche, La	510	614	709	906	1,241	910
Lake Pontchartrain, La	508	447	597	614	1,390	1,308
Mermentau River, Bayou Nespique, and Bayou Des Cannes, La	512	1,180	1,306	1,549	1,792	1,448
Bayou Lafourche, La	849	879	1,351	1,551	2,152	2,390
Bayou Terrebonne, La	488	750	1,046	1,221	1,507	1,394
Petit Anse, Tigre, and Carlin Bayous, La	1,104	1,382	1,515	1,784	1,916	1,996
San Bernard River, Tex						1,618
San Joaquin River, Calif	1,026	730	1,003	1,227	1,496	1,951
Sacramento River, Calif	1,078	1,380	1,543	1,610	1,591	1,976
Columbia and Lower Willamette Rivers below Vancouver, Wash., and Portland, Oreg	14,282	15,938	15,889	16,369	16,576	19,949
Columbia River from Vancouver, Wash., to The Dalles, Oreg	1,836	2,005	2,684	3,034	2,845	3,085
Columbia River and tributaries above Celilo Falls to Mallory Lock and Dam, Oreg. and Wash	744	830	697	906	852	1,032
Willamette River above Portland and Yamhill River, Oreg	3,979	4,942	4,170	4,149	3,945	4,394
Snohomish River, Wash	1,782	1,852	1,697	1,609	1,657	1,742
Illinois Waterway, Ill	6,914	10,165	12,273	12,905	16,421	17,612
Red River below Fulton, Ark	54	49	81	161	872	1,123
Mississippi River, Minneapolis, Minn., to the Passes	41,305	51,477	57,148	59,332	66,925	72,611
Missouri River:						
Kansas City to the mouth	751	621	797	917	763	816
Kansas City to Sioux City	276	377	811	800	809	1,372
Sioux City to Fort Benton	26	14	15	4		70
Allegheny River, Pa	2,565	2,734	3,270	3,013	3,504	4,268
Monongahela River, Pa. and W. Va	26,430	31,742	30,015	25,346	28,510	32,084
Kanawha River, W. Va	4,534	5,367	5,911	4,956	6,346	7,052
Ohio River, Pittsburgh to mouth	36,551	41,307	42,702	41,300	48,596	56,641
Cumberland River, Tenn., and Ky	1,027	1,206	1,352	1,479	1,647	1,980
Tennessee River, Tenn., Ala., and Ky	2,399	2,792	2,953	2,767	3,061	3,749
FEDERAL CANALS AND CONNECTING CHANNELS						
Cape Cod Canal, Mass	10,656	11,925	12,113	11,619	12,625	13,128
Inland Waterway from Delaware River to Chesapeake Bay, Del. and Md	3,608	3,386	4,397	6,342	7,398	8,666
Lake Charles Deep Water Channel, La	6,854	8,494	10,540	11,342	12,164	13,532
Gulf Intracoastal Waterway, Plaquemine to Morgan City, alternate route	1,532	1,878	2,188	2,191	1,819	2,084
Gulf Intracoastal Waterway, Apalachee Bay, Fla., to the Mexican border	20,457	22,801	27,866	26,291	31,520	35,828
Sabine-Neches Waterway, Tex	43,395	47,644	55,596	64,063	45,386	34,306
Port Aransas (Aransas Pass) Corpus Christi Waterway, Tex	19,885	22,942	22,962	19,290	21,122	24,608
Detroit River, Mich	110,984	137,440	132,734	108,464	127,292	131,318
St. Marys Falls Canal, Mich.[3]	91,587	116,732	115,414	95,532	148,140	119,804
Green Bay Passage, Mich	5,217	6,885	6,353	5,870	6,045	6,182
Multnomah Channel, Oreg	1,466	1,589	1,639	1,536	997	1,695
Canals and locks at Willamette Falls, Oreg	2,079	1,906	1,977	1,806	1,664	1,864
Lake Washington Ship Canal, Wash	2,197	2,015	2,115	2,012	2,056	2,082
STATE AND PRIVATE CANALS						
New York State Barge Canal[4]	3,682	3,760	4,514	3,960	4,916	4,241
Innerharbor Navigation Canal, La	1,576	2,044	2,123	2,832	3,338	3,647

[1] Reported as "Cape Fear River at and below Wilmington, N. C." prior to 1946.
[2] See also table 677.
[3] See also table 676.
[4] See also table 678.

Source: Department of the Army, Corps of Engineers; Annual Report of Chief of Engineers, Part II, except for 1951 data which are preliminary.

No. 672.—Freight Carried on Inland Waterways, by System: 1946 to 1951

[In thousands of ton-miles]

SYSTEM	1946	1947	1948	1949	1950	1951
Total	123,973,219	146,714,238	161,846,212	139,396,230	163,343,977	182,173,704
Atlantic coast rivers	1,541,611	1,721,868	4,510,915	4,414,348	6,497,249	10,396,724
Gulf coast rivers	374,997	494,457	575,992	658,655	1,228,645	1,141,914
Pacific coast rivers	1,467,037	1,388,673	1,459,041	1,624,795	1,686,494	4,376,387
Mississippi River system, including Ohio River and tributaries	18,358,220	23,479,053	27,923,751	27,399,055	33,597,816	36,754,185
Other waterways	8,947	9,656	10,683	8,022	7,720	6,570
Canals and connecting channels [1]	6,200,361	7,455,210	8,658,700	7,788,007	8,638,713	9,556,340
Great Lakes system [2]	96,022,046	112,165,321	118,707,121	97,503,348	111,687,340	119,941,384

[1] Except Great Lakes.
[2] Excludes traffic between foreign ports on the Great Lakes.

Source: Department of the Army, Corps of Engineers; *Annual Report, Chief of Engineers*, Part II, except for 1951 data which are preliminary.

No. 673.—Panama Canal—Revenues, Expenses, and Computed Surplus: 1914 to 1951

[In thousands of dollars]

YEAR ENDING JUNE 30	Tolls [1]	Civil revenues	Business profits [3]	Total revenues	Net appropriation expenses [3]	Net revenues [3]	Capital interest, 3 percent [4]	Computed surplus [3]
Total	642,884	7,829	22,595	674,307	401,343	272,964	473,375	*199,411*
1914 to 1931, total	271,864	4,178	8,748	284,790	138,903	145,886	165,558	*19,672*
1932	20,707	327	557	21,591	10,239	11,352	14,944	*3,592*
1933	19,621	310	1,136	21,067	9,556	11,511	14,908	*3,397*
1934	24,065	97	1,367	25,528	7,931	17,597	15,039	2,558
1935	23,339	82	1,021	24,442	9,481	14,961	15,124	*163*
1936	23,507	120	920	24,547	9,675	14,872	15,160	*288*
1937	23,147	99	917	24,164	10,290	13,874	15,205	*1,331*
1938	23,215	90	825	24,130	9,576	14,555	15,230	*675*
1939	23,699	107	681	24,488	10,145	14,342	15,250	*908*
1940	21,177	118	1,034	22,330	10,042	12,288	15,243	*2,956*
1941	18,190	276	1,009	19,475	9,614	9,861	15,275	*5,414*
1942	9,772	[5] 219	734	10,726	9,407	1,319	15,302	*13,983*
1943	7,369	[6] 55	1,493	8,916	11,269	*2,352*	15,432	*17,785*
1944	5,474	239	1,553	7,267	12,634	*5,368*	15,484	*20,851*
1945	7,223	239	1,469	8,931	13,905	*4,975*	15,476	*20,450*
1946	14,792	268	[7] 208	[7] 15,267	15,214	*53*	15,427	[7] *15,374*
1947	17,642	110	1,726	19,478	18,074	1,404	15,478	*14,073*
1948	20,004	294	[8] 1,582	21,881	[9] 19,527	2,354	15,490	*13,136*
1949	20,612	133	[10] 845	21,590	21,217	373	15,689	*15,316*
1950	24,512	299	667	25,478	22,558	2,920	16,024	*13,104*
1951	23,952	169	[11] 5,898	18,223	22,085	*3,863*	15,636	*19,498*

[1] Adjusted for overcharges and undercollections.
[3] Italics denote deficit.
[3] After deduction of canal earnings repaid to appropriations.
[4] No interest charge against the Canal is actually made by the Treasury. In order to present the net results of operation of the Canal, interest on capital invested is computed at a rate considered reasonable for Government borrowings over an indefinite period. Computed interest prior to July 12, 1920, is included in capital investment account.
[5] Includes adjustment of $15,000 in postal surplus.
[6] Includes adjustment of $44,000 in postal surplus.
[7] Actual business profits of $877,000 adjusted by $669,000 for write-off of reimbursable capital expenditures, public works, Republic of Panama.
[8] Includes $23,000 for prior fiscal years.
[9] Includes $292,000 for judgments rendered by Court of Claims for overtime compensation in prior years.
[10] Adjusted by a net reduction of $162,000 for prior fiscal years.
[11] Actual business profits of $638,000 have been adjusted by a net decrease in the amount of $6,536,000 representing surplus adjustments applicable to prior fiscal years

Source: The Panama Canal, *Annual Report of the Governor*.

No. 674.—COMMERCIAL TRAFFIC THROUGH THE PANAMA CANAL, TOTAL, 1915 TO 1951, AND BY NATIONALITY OF VESSEL, 1951

[See general note, p. 568. Figures cover ocean-going commercial traffic which includes only tolls-paying vessels of 300 net tons and over, Panama Canal measurement, and vessels paying tolls on displacement tons of 800 displacement tons and over. Foreign naval vessels such as colliers, transports, supply ships, etc., with a measurement of 300 net tons or more and foreign naval vessels such as battleships, cruisers, destroyers, submarines, etc., with a displacement of 800 tons or more, classified as ocean-going commercial vessels]

YEAR ENDING JUNE 30	Number of transits	Net tonnage (thousands)	Tolls (thousands of dollars)	Tons of cargo (thousands of long tons)	NATIONALITY OF VESSELS (year ending June 30, 1951)	Number of transits	Net tonnage (thousands)	Tolls (thousands of dollars)	Tons of cargo (thousands of long tons)
Total	151,844	697,045	643,343	725,872	Belgian	1	4	4	6
					British	1,004	5,780	5,150	6,464
Cumulative to June 30, 1920	9,850	30,704	33,692	26,845	Chilean	52	226	202	208
1921	2,791	10,687	11,369	11,596	Chinese	6	31	26	49
1922	2,665	10,568	11,192	10,852	Colombian	75	102	92	77
1923	2,905	17,206	17,504	19,546					
1924	5,180	24,181	24,285	26,968	Costa Rican	3	7	6	10
1925	4,592	21,134	21,304	23,967	Danish	191	738	679	700
					Ecuadorean	247	236	208	98
1926	5,057	22,506	22,930	26,080	Finnish	1	4	3	(*)
1927	5,299	24,345	24,212	27,734	French	108	846	812	884
1928	6,253	27,229	26,922	28,616					
1929	6,289	27,385	27,111	30,648	German	4	11	9	8
1930	6,027	27,716	27,060	30,018	Greek	105	538	478	534
					Honduran	844	916	775	543
1931	5,370	25,590	24,625	25,065	Icelandic	3	2	2	(*)
1932	4,362	21,842	20,695	19,790	Italian	70	391	340	358
1933	4,162	21,004	19,804	18,141					
1934	5,234	26,416	24,047	24,704	Japanese	40	201	191	318
1935	5,180	25,730	23,307	26,310	Liberian	22	64	57	97
					Mexican	9	29	26	34
1936	5,382	25,928	23,479	26,506	Netherland	115	491	441	402
1937	5,397	25,430	23,102	26,108	Nicaraguan	8	5	4	3
1938	5,534	25,960	23,170	27,386					
1939	5,903	27,170	23,661	27,787	Norwegian	513	2,326	2,045	2,004
1940	5,370	24,144	21,145	27,299	Panamanian	220	1,010	962	1,271
					Peruvian	24	53	48	65
1941	4,727	20,643	18,156	24,951	Philippine	25	129	114	142
1942	2,668	11,010	9,782	13,607	Portuguese	9	41	22	30
1943	1,822	8,234	7,357	10,600					
1944	1,562	6,073	5,456	7,008	Spanish	23	88	72	57
1945	1,939	8,381	7,244	8,604	Swedish	148	680	599	655
					United States	2,203	12,449	10,528	14,882
1946	3,747	17,517	14,774	14,978	Venezuelan	17	44	30	36
1947	4,260	20,232	17,597	21,671					
1948	4,678	22,902	19,987	24,118					
1949	4,793	23,472	20,541	25,305					
1950	5,445	23,013	24,430	26,872					
1951	5,593	27,180	23,906	30,073					

1 Panama Canal net tonnages prior to 1936 are estimates, based on revised measurement rules, effective Mar. 1, 1938.
2 Canal opened to traffic Aug. 15, 1914.
3 Less than 500 tons.

No. 675.—COMMERCIAL TRAFFIC THROUGH THE PANAMA CANAL—SUMMARY, YEARS ENDING JUNE 30: 1943 TO 1951

[See general note, p. 568]

ITEM	1943	1944	1945	1946	1947	1948	1949	1950	1951
Number of transits	1,822	1,562	1,939	3,747	4,260	4,678	4,793	5,445	5,593
Measurement tonnage registered:									
Gross (thousands)	10,874	8,046	11,427	23,928	27,530	31,085	31,726	37,391	36,692
Net (thousands)	8,578	6,012	8,934	14,528	16,456	18,563	18,844	22,367	21,466
Panama Canal, net (thousands)	8,234	6,073	8,381	17,517	20,232	22,902	23,472	23,013	27,180
Tons of cargo, total (thousands of long tons)	10,600	7,008	8,604	14,978	21,671	24,115	25,305	26,872	30,073
Atlantic to Pacific	4,945	3,354	4,296	6,118	8,295	9,070	9,899	9,484	11,128
Pacific to Atlantic	5,655	3,649	4,309	8,860	13,376	15,430	15,406	19,388	18,942

Source of tables 674 and 675: The Panama Canal, Annual Report of the Governor.

No. 676.—FREIGHT AND PASSENGER TRAFFIC ON ST. MARYS FALLS CANAL (SAULT STE. MARIE): 1890 TO 1951

[Includes both American and Canadian canals and traffic to and from Canadian as well as American ports. Average distances, ton-miles, freight charges, etc., based on total haul from port of origin to port of destination in process of performance by vessels passing through canals]

SEASON	FREIGHT CARRIED (1,000 SHORT TONS OF 2,000 POUNDS)					Total ton-miles (millions)	FREIGHT CHARGES	
	Total	East-bound	West-bound	By American vessels	By Canadian and other foreign vessels		Amount (1,000 dollars)	Average per ton per mile (mills)
1890	9,041	6,429	2,612	8,679	362	7,207	9,472	1.30
1895	15,063	12,030	3,033	14,497	566	12,503	14,239	1.14
1900	25,643	20,532	5,111	24,896	747	21,179	24,953	1.18
1905	44,271	36,779	7,492	42,061	2,210	36,893	31,421	.85
1910	62,363	47,134	15,229	58,569	3,794	52,406	38,711	.74
1915	71,290	56,369	14,921	66,877	4,413	59,317	41,984	.71
1920	79,282	63,464	15,818	74,866	4,416	64,702	85,742	1.33
1925	81,875	67,305	14,570	75,764	6,111	65,577	71,093	1.08
1930	72,898	57,067	15,831	67,560	5,338	59,058	61,159	1.04
1935	48,293	37,192	11,101	41,532	6,761	39,141	41,783	1.07
1939	69,850	58,483	11,367	60,045	9,805	56,539	66,054	1.17
1940	89,360	76,635	12,782	79,116	10,244	71,807	74,118	1.03
1941	110,768	95,774	14,994	97,387	13,381	88,946	102,792	1.15
1942	120,119	104,139	15,980	105,255	14,864	95,903	111,470	1.16
1943	115,578	97,380	18,198	102,404	13,174	92,069	110,377	1.20
1944	116,985	98,480	18,505	103,579	13,406	93,424	122,786	1.31
1945	112,983	96,729	16,254	96,858	14,125	90,390	(1)	(1)
1946	91,587	72,614	18,973	89,648	1,939	(1)	(1)	(1)
1947	110,732	91,784	18,948	96,971	13,761	(1)	(1)	(1)
1948	115,414	95,346	20,068	100,536	14,878	(1)	(1)	(1)
1949	95,832	83,670	12,162	82,020	13,812	(1)	(1)	(1)
1950	106,140	89,191	16,949	91,038	15,102	(1)	(1)	(1)
1951	119,864	105,559	14,305	100,963	18,901	(1)	(1)	(1)

COMMODITY	1920	1925	1930	1935	1940	1945	1950	1951
Passengers carried ....number..	68,451	56,956	45,303	32,937	53,129	46,044	63,366	43,834
Freight, east-bound..........1,000 tons [2]..	63,464	67,305	57,067	37,192	76,635	96,729	89,191	105,559
Flour..............................do..	748	929	853	684	480	108	63	100
Wheat.............................do..	4,304	8,785	7,318	5,388	6,660	14,436	5,714	9,246
Other grain.......................do..	1,236	3,163	1,204	876	1,087	3,031	2,462	2,818
Lumber...........................do..	358	367	303	72	47	2		1
Pulpwood.........................do..				239	692	619	444	644
Iron ore..........................do..	56,643	53,821	46,990	29,277	65,842	77,719	79,962	89,997
All other.........................do..	175	240	399	656	1,827	814	546	2,753
Freight, west-bound..........1,000 tons [2]..	15,818	14,570	15,831	11,101	12,725	16,254	16,949	14,305
Coal..............................do..	14,156	12,874	14,059	9,162	10,174	13,837	13,464	10,732
All other.........................do..	1,662	1,696	1,772	1,939	2,551	2,417	3,485	3,573

[1] Not available. [2] Short tons of 2,000 pounds.

No. 677.—FREIGHT AND PASSENGER TRAFFIC ON OHIO RIVER: 1941 TO 1951

YEAR	Short tons	Ton-miles	Passengers carried [1]	YEAR	Short tons
	Thousands	Thousands	Number		Thousands
1941	36,557	5,197,440	1,554,319	1950—Total	48,598
1942	38,281	5,299,847	1,034,190	Up [4]	11,279
1943	36,610	5,996,347	1,191,350	Down [4]	11,154
1944	37,801	7,004,099	1,148,294	Inbound	19,946
1945	33,868	6,064,690	1,145,626	Outbound	6,219
1946	35,851	4,999,560	1,053,511		
1947	41,397	5,746,076	1,534,856	1951—Total [3]	56,541
1948	42,792	6,585,854	[2] 61,130	Up [4]	13,021
1949	41,300	6,904,147	78,267	Down [4]	12,818
1950	48,598	8,800,451	95,631	Inbound	22,543
1951 [3]	56,541	9,760,268	110,285	Outbound	8,159

[1] No data included for ferry traffic. [2] Largest excursion boat destroyed by fire in September 1947.
[3] Preliminary. [4] Includes through traffic.

Source of tables 676 and 677: Department of the Army, Corps of Engineers; *Annual Report of Chief of Engineers,* Part II, and records.

No. 678.—Freight Traffic on New York State Canals—Tonnage Moved: 1837 to 1952

[In short tons of 2,000 pounds. Excludes tonnage handled over State terminals but not moved through any portion of canal channel. East-bound tonnage is that moving toward Albany; west-bound is that moving away from Albany. See also *Historical Statistics*, series K 170-171]

YEARLY AVERAGE	All canals	Erie division	YEARLY AVERAGE	All canals	Erie division	YEARLY AVERAGE OR YEAR	All canals	Erie division
1837-1840	1,239,016	771,741	1886-1890	5,261,441	3,569,651	1936-1940	4,523,271	3,794,843
1841-1845	1,613,317	894,522	1891-1895	4,112,061	2,961,828	1941-1945	3,392,596	2,799,941
1846-1850	2,781,410	1,556,896	1896-1900	3,544,963	2,441,065	1946-1950	3,987,962	3,725,510
1851-1855	3,976,501	2,141,476	1901-1905	3,335,230	2,141,492	1946	2,530,541	2,455,516
1856-1860	3,911,407	1,888,785	1906-1910	3,235,120	2,206,606	1947	2,769,050	2,514,643
1861-1865	5,049,341	2,762,069	1911-1915	2,445,237	1,625,461	1948	4,375,617	4,122,411
1866-1870	5,967,724	3,015,330	1916-1920	1,346,365	797,706	1949	3,949,733	3,665,669
1871-1875	5,974,097	3,228,073	1921-1925	1,905,201	648,406	1950	4,415,612	4,230,346
1876-1880	6,219,695	3,542,050	1926-1930	2,904,575	2,357,042	1951	4,316,402	3,956,304
1881-1885	5,210,299	3,465,560	1931-1935	4,014,260	3,515,522	1952	4,657,565	2,412,460

COMMODITY	1935	1940	1945	1950	1951	1952
Freight, east-bound, tons	1,468,315	2,234,684	1,912,584	799,251	1,159,842	1,044,586
Petroleum and its products	33,179	313,654	784,717	179,491	156,914	805,457
Grain	614,865	656,673	664,306	226,061	663,376	485,424
Pulpwood	9,480	32,480	164,306	79,820	115,962	216,599
Other	851,849	921,366	330,027	222,580	196,509	168,622
Freight, west-bound, tons	3,660,387	2,842,326	1,186,128	3,905,662	4,651,137	3,463,550
Petroleum and its products	1,772,627	1,788,346	848,945	3,472,462	3,726,566	3,368,824
Other	1,226,280	1,054,980	337,183	433,200	273,084	290,726

Source: State of New York, Department of Public Works; annual statements on canal tonnage.

No. 679.—Vessels Entered and Cleared in Foreign Trade—Net Registered Tonnage: 1840 to 1952

[In thousands of net tons. Excludes domestic trade. For definition of net registered tonnage and vessel entrances and clearances, see general note, p. 568. Figures cover years ending June 30 to and including 1918, calendar years thereafter. Seaports include all ports except northern border ports; see table 680. See, also *Historical Statistics*, series K 146-157]

YEARLY AVERAGE OR YEAR	ENTERED		CLEARED		YEARLY AVERAGE OR YEAR	ENTERED		CLEARED	
	Seaports	Other ports	Seaports	Other ports		Seaports	Other ports	Seaports	Other ports
1840	1,728	501	1,861	492	1936-1940	55,521	11,595	56,967	11,575
1850	3,169	1,179	3,167	1,194	1941-1945	52,620	15,374	56,304	16,489
1860	5,000	3,275	5,257	3,588	1946-1950	75,094	12,309	74,689	12,201
1870	6,270	3,896	6,302	3,807	1940	45,392	13,181	48,992	13,176
1871-1875	8,462	2,997	9,514	2,984	1941	42,616	16,448	46,143	16,454
1876-1885	12,134	2,792	12,197	2,807	1942	28,258	15,684	31,976	15,780
1886-1895	12,604	2,931	12,781	2,917	1943	44,739	16,345	50,322	16,484
1896-1905	13,479	2,602	13,655	2,593	1944	66,306	15,535	71,717	15,066
1906-1915	16,201	2,816	16,905	2,878	1945	81,182	12,839	91,452	13,107
1916-1925	20,931	3,869	21,077	4,007	1946	68,520	10,738	66,376	10,849
1926-1935	24,551	5,939	24,633	5,918	1947	90,889	12,907	84,508	12,652
1906-1910	29,651	8,072	29,156	8,086	1948	76,910	14,023	75,714	13,715
1911-1915	36,028	11,879	35,954	12,081	1949	74,701	10,999	73,068	11,233
1916-1920	38,071	13,440	40,137	13,511	1950	73,451	13,173	74,789	13,044
1921-1925	52,959	13,334	53,575	13,075					
1926-1930	63,746	15,296	64,441	15,319	1951	93,674	14,412	94,186	13,979
1931-1935	54,926	16,462	55,214	10,361	1952	97,965	15,112	94,397	15,095

[1] Year ending Sept. 30. [2] Average for period July 1, 1918, to Dec. 31, 1920.
[3] Preliminary data, subject to revision.
[4] Vessels under time or voyage charter to Military Sea Transportation Service excluded from clearances after May 1951 and from entrances after March 1952.

Source: Department of Commerce, Bureau of the Census; annual report, *Foreign Commerce and Navigation of the United States*, and records.

No. 680.—Vessels Entered and Cleared in Foreign Trade—Net Registered Tonnage by Regions, 1921 to 1952, and by Customs Districts, 1949 to 1952

[In thousands of net tons. See headnote, table 679]

CUSTOMS DISTRICT	1949 [1]		1950 [1]		1951 [1][2]		1952 [1][2]	
	Entered	Cleared	Entered	Cleared	Entered	Cleared	Entered	Cleared
Grand total	85,700	84,286	86,529	87,829	106,886	105,164	113,677	109,521
Seaports, total	74,701	73,063	73,451	74,785	93,674	94,185	97,965	94,527
North Atlantic coast, total	45,043	44,308	44,702	44,675	58,505	58,922	59,304	57,066
Maine, New Hampshire	1,851	1,518	2,195	1,987	3,124	2,739	3,493	2,961
Massachusetts	3,391	2,195	4,170	2,814	3,940	2,771	3,787	2,571
Rhode Island	301	420	307	425	343	390	357	347
Connecticut	153	374	405	408	434	346	511	392
New York	21,454	23,657	22,489	25,301	24,472	26,111	27,043	27,331
Philadelphia	7,519	5,547	9,117	7,132	9,722	7,587	9,310	7,537
Maryland	5,879	4,738	4,667	4,188	6,877	5,455	6,950	5,431
Virginia	4,495	5,889	1,352	2,420	9,668	13,220	7,853	10,296
South Atlantic coast, total	2,603	2,598	3,259	3,255	3,461	3,894	3,922	4,278
North Carolina	96	84	157	85	129	136	256	116
South Carolina	703	497	765	551	1,046	1,007	1,192	960
Georgia	567	516	610	728	687	647	802	847
Puerto Rico	894	1,120	1,367	1,490	1,244	1,697	1,244	1,821
Virgin Islands [3]	343	381	360	401	354	384	366	504
Gulf coast, total	15,719	14,860	13,385	14,206	15,733	16,006	16,688	17,689
Florida	2,224	2,326	2,851	2,941	3,208	2,863	3,947	3,002
Mobile	2,243	1,019	2,049	924	1,949	990	2,594	1,123
New Orleans	4,709	5,580	4,486	5,411	4,938	5,663	5,868	5,792
Sabine	1,890	1,301	770	962	951	947	1,195	1,031
Galveston	4,653	4,652	3,229	3,968	4,686	5,513	5,534	6,110
Mexican border, Laredo	343	340	368	430	430	419	313	391
Pacific coast, total	10,993	10,957	11,737	12,229	15,545	14,943	14,330	15,713
Washington	2,739	2,453	194	103	3,275	3,228	3,571	2,370
Oregon	1,499	1,237	3,993	3,820	1,994	1,692	2,081	1,466
San Francisco	1,921	2,514	2,242	3,205	3,627	3,480	4,213	4,193
Los Angeles	3,360	3,101	1,153	975	5,259	5,368	4,929	4,312
Alaska	343	400	3,064	2,966	304	306	314	317
Hawaii	928	915	315	348	911	902	1,045	995
San Diego	203	37	776	812	165	67	196	60
Northern border, total	10,999	11,223	13,178	13,044	14,412	13,979	15,112	15,095
St. Lawrence	80	48	159	60	156	44	128	43
Rochester	951	933	1,643	1,557	1,828	1,622	1,305	1,284
Buffalo	666	444	872	453	1,134	580	1,335	710
Ohio	4,367	6,005	2,052	1,108	5,487	6,664	5,792	6,682
Michigan	1,943	1,677	270	218	1,858	1,719	2,167	1,879
Chicago	507	827	1,863	1,869	524	736	604	896
Wisconsin	266	192	454	585	304	286	338	359
Duluth and Superior	2,197	1,097	5,875	7,494	3,119	2,327	3,443	3,242

YEARLY AVERAGE OR YEAR	ATLANTIC COAST		GULF COAST		PACIFIC COAST		Mexican border, total	NORTHERN BORDER	
	Total	With cargo	Total	With cargo	Total	With cargo		Total	With cargo
Entrances:									
1921–1925	30,979	27,133	12,390	8,243	9,562	6,070	28	13,334	6,475
1926–1930	36,884	33,003	11,634	7,415	15,100	8,247	150	15,293	7,700
1931–1935	31,721	28,668	8,058	4,858	14,968	9,239	180	10,462	4,997
1936–1940	30,634	26,925	10,115	5,593	14,108	9,366	663	11,595	5,187
1941–1945	34,914	18,397	6,454	4,463	11,211	6,153	40	15,374	5,060
1946	44,046	25,382	14,684	5,494	10,636	5,317	254	10,738	2,325
1947 [1]	52,904	30,857	16,689	7,269	10,581	5,426	414	12,906	2,579
1948 [1]	49,513	35,199	16,501	8,273	10,493	6,227	388	14,023	2,900
1949 [1]	47,646	36,408	15,719	9,193	10,993	7,495	343	10,999	2,967
1950 [1]	47,961	18,797	13,385	3,937	11,737	3,785	368	13,178	3,021
1951 [1]	61,966	47,997	15,733	9,730	15,545	8,848	430	14,412	3,412
1952 [1][2]	63,226	51,282	16,088	10,500	16,339	10,559	313	15,112	3,997
Clearances:									
1921–1925	30,537	24,284	12,833	9,589	9,890	8,360	28	13,075	9,296
1926–1930	36,351	28,698	12,326	10,641	15,656	13,148	95	15,319	10,504
1931–1935	30,668	23,563	9,018	8,079	15,411	13,220	127	10,351	7,309
1936–1940	30,472	22,450	11,064	9,601	14,752	13,394	677	11,575	9,412
1941–1945	38,545	27,351	7,636	6,494	13,082	11,286	40	15,489	12,657
1946	41,382	27,048	16,080	13,056	9,779	7,629	233	10,849	9,548
1947 [1]	54,214	40,508	18,516	16,149	11,513	10,645	355	12,552	11,284
1948 [1]	48,497	32,395	16,516	14,169	10,380	9,169	312	13,735	12,339
1949 [1]	46,905	30,230	14,860	12,536	10,957	9,846	340	11,223	9,382
1950 [1]	47,930	10,488	14,206	4,702	12,229	6,259	420	13,044	11,540
1951 [1][2]	52,316	41,088	16,006	13,635	14,943	13,742	419	13,979	12,384
1952 [1][2]	61,364	37,662	17,069	14,241	15,713	13,969	391	15,095	12,578

[1] Preliminary data, subject to revision.

[2] Vessels under time or voyage charter to Military Sea Transportation Service excluded from clearances after June 1951 and from entrances after March 1952.

[3] Reported as a foreign country prior to Jan. 1, 1935.

Source: Department of Commerce, Bureau of the Census; annual report, *Foreign Commerce and Navigation of the United States*, and records.

No. 681.—Vessels Entered in Foreign Trade—Net Registered Tonnage, by
Classes: 1881 to 1952

[All figures except number of vessels and percentages in thousands of net tons. See headnote, table 679.
Totals represent sums of unrounded figures; may vary from sum of rounded amounts. See also *Historical
Statistics*, series K 146-151]

YEARLY AVERAGE OR YEAR	Number of vessels, all ports	ALL PORTS				SEAPORTS				
		Total	American vessels	Foreign vessels	Percent American	All vessels	Sailing vessels	Steam vessels	With cargo	In ballast
1881–1890	28,086	16,208	3,295	12,913	20.8	13,442	5,251	8,391	11,809	1,632
1891–1900	31,791	22,289	4,878	17,391	22.4	18,888	3,816	15,080	14,184	4,652
1901–1905	34,040	30,458	4,832	25,888	22.3	24,451	2,495	21,945	19,205	5,245
1906–1910	34,275	37,728	6,372	29,350	22.2	29,451	1,816	27,834	25,021	4,429
1911–1915	38,951	47,914	12,205	35,700	26.4	36,035	1,374	34,461	27,778	4,257
1916–1920 [1]	42,713	51,511	21,000	29,512	42.7	36,071	1,880	34,173	26,139	12,062
1921–1925	41,548	65,293	28,645	36,648	44.7	53,939	1,084	51,955	41,471	11,628
1926–1930	44,046	79,062	30,314	48,748	38.3	65,766	479	65,296	46,710	14,628
1931–1935	31,328	65,390	23,847	41,543	34.5	54,939	527	54,701	42,535	12,628
1936–1940	28,954	67,117	19,343	47,875	28.7	55,621	183	55,419	41,951	13,870
1941–1945 [1]	28,907	67,004	34,488	32,536	51.6	56,690	37	55,853	28,905	32,628
1946–1950 [1]	48,813	87,462	46,205	41,257	52.5	76,694	(2)	(2)	50,208	34,628
1941	37,535	55,061	26,940	28,121	24.5	43,616	49	43,576	32,819	4,797
1942	31,338	48,942	12,611	26,331	31.0	39,267	38	39,228	15,077	16,181
1943	36,640	61,094	29,392	31,702	48.0	44,739	37	44,702	28,792	36,047
1944	30,824	51,869	46,977	32,789	48.7	58,306	30	58,275	32,397	34,688
1945	48,318	94,621	61,875	32,646	64.3	81,123	44	81,128	37,982	43,180
1946	49,082	80,308	53,045	27,213	64.1	68,220	34	68,495	36,345	33,172
1947 [1]	50,449	98,794	53,627	45,170	57.2	80,580	12	80,577	43,572	37,046
1948 [1]	50,228	90,927	47,728	43,199	52.5	70,916	(2)	(2)	51,044	36,628
1949 [1]	48,378	55,700	41,251	44,451	48.1	74,704	(2)	(2)	55,405	18,628
1950 [1]	46,936	96,629	36,376	51,261	48.6	78,451	(2)	(2)	63,771	9,628
1951 [1]	48,466	108,086	44,571	63,515	41.2	93,674	(2)	(2)	66,868	34,628
1952 [1] [4]	49,347	113,077	42,038	71,039	37.2	97,966	(2)	(2)	72,556	34,628

YEARLY AVERAGE OR YEAR	SEAPORTS—continued					NORTHERN BORDER PORTS			
	American vessels		Foreign vessels		Percent American	Total	American vessels	Foreign vessels	With cargo
	Total	With cargo	Total	With cargo					
1881–1890	2,983	2,550	10,800	9,001	21.7	2,766	462	2,304	1,628
1891–1900	3,619	2,956	15,247	11,228	19.2	3,408	1,288	2,044	1,628
1901–1905	3,962	3,246	20,599	15,960	16.1	5,599	2,490	3,098	2,628
1906–1910	4,175	3,471	24,475	20,150	14.1	8,072	4,197	3,875	2,527
1911–1915	5,276	4,200	30,789	22,578	14.6	11,879	6,919	4,960	4,454
1916–1920 [1]	14,506	11,375	23,568	13,753	38.1	12,440	7,490	4,950	5,646
1921–1925	22,536	18,404	30,433	23,066	42.5	13,334	7,119	6,315	6,478
1926–1930	23,182	18,809	40,586	29,901	36.4	15,268	7,123	8,102	7,700
1931–1935	19,554	16,570	35,074	25,965	36.1	10,462	5,066	6,469	4,197
1936–1940	16,090	13,865	39,432	28,086	29.0	11,596	3,154	8,441	5,187
1941–1945 [1]	30,059	16,877	22,580	12,118	57.1	16,374	4,899	10,778	6,628
1946–1950 [1]	42,168	26,318	32,926	23,970	56.2	12,369	4,097	8,382	3,798
1941	16,767	14,688	25,949	17,161	30.3	16,445	4,174	12,271	4,628
1942	10,326	3,004	17,931	10,072	36.5	15,684	3,285	12,400	4,628
1943	24,508	14,135	20,231	9,857	54.6	16,345	4,784	11,561	5,628
1944	42,195	20,509	24,109	11,788	63.6	15,556	4,975	9,080	4,049
1945	56,499	36,080	24,682	11,912	69.6	12,839	4,876	7,963	3,751
1946	49,143	23,437	20,378	12,911	70.7	10,736	3,902	6,835	2,834
1947 [1]	49,044	28,029	31,544	17,543	60.6	12,902	4,582	8,228	3,079
1948 [1]	43,270	26,107	33,640	22,987	54.2	14,025	4,467	9,568	3,300
1949 [1]	37,626	27,470	37,076	26,924	53.4	10,999	3,685	7,375	2,337
1950 [1]	31,757	26,536	41,696	37,235	43.2	13,178	3,619	9,568	2,628
1951 [1]	40,482	26,005	53,192	38,568	43.2	14,412	4,089	10,328	2,412
1952 [1] [4]	37,547	27,114	60,418	45,444	38.3	15,112	4,491	10,621	2,997

[1] Average for period July 1, 1915, to Dec. 31, 1920.
[2] Preliminary data, subject to revision.
[3] Not available.
[4] Vessels under time or voyage charter to Military Sea Transportation Service excluded after March 1952.

Source: Department of Commerce, Bureau of the Census; annual report, *Foreign Commerce and Navigation of the United States*, and records.

No. 682.—VESSELS CLEARED IN FOREIGN TRADE—NET REGISTERED TONNAGE, BY CLASSES: 1881 TO 1952

[All figures except number of vessels and percentages in thousands of net tons. See headnote, table 679. Totals represent sums of unrounded figures; may vary from sum of rounded amounts. See also *Historical Statistics*, series K 152-157]

YEARLY AVERAGE OR YEAR	Number of vessels, all ports	ALL PORTS				SEAPORTS				
		Total	American vessels	Foreign vessels	Percent American	All vessels	Sailing vessels	Steam vessels	With cargo	In ballast
1881-1890	32,159	16,473	3,450	13,023	20.9	13,719	5,363	8,356	12,795	924
1891-1900	31,902	22,463	5,088	17,425	22.4	19,021	3,818	15,203	17,514	1,507
1901-1905	33,863	30,551	6,812	23,739	22.3	24,633	2,621	22,012	22,460	2,173
1906-1910	33,897	37,192	8,282	28,910	22.3	29,156	1,850	27,306	26,768	2,388
1911-1915	38,790	48,015	12,512	35,503	26.1	35,954	1,654	34,301	32,827	3,126
1915-1920 [1]	42,687	53,647	23,005	30,643	42.9	40,137	2,057	38,080	34,851	5,285
1921-1925	40,120	66,653	29,554	37,099	44.3	53,578	984	52,594	42,233	11,345
1926-1930	44,082	79,760	30,709	49,051	38.5	64,441	467	63,973	52,581	11,860
1931-1935	30,520	65,565	23,616	41,949	36.0	55,214	221	54,993	44,990	10,224
1936-1940	32,706	68,541	19,448	49,093	28.4	56,967	102	56,864	46,126	10,841
1941-1945	33,195	71,792	37,283	34,509	51.9	56,304	41	56,262	45,147	11,167
1946-1950 [3]	45,135	87,190	44,942	42,244	51.5	74,889	(²)	(²)	54,584	20,302
1941	38,024	62,596	21,869	40,726	34.9	46,142	44	46,098	32,714	13,428
1942	30,506	47,706	16,354	31,352	34.3	31,975	32	31,943	26,464	5,511
1943	35,915	66,716	33,682	33,034	50.5	50,232	37	50,195	42,470	7,762
1944	40,321	87,385	53,050	34,335	60.7	71,717	52	71,665	60,095	11,622
1945	46,210	94,559	61,460	33,099	65.0	81,452	42	81,410	63,992	17,461
1946	44,464	77,225	49,124	28,101	63.6	66,376	33	66,343	47,828	18,547
1947 [3]	48,374	97,160	54,088	43,072	55.7	84,508	14	84,494	67,483	17,024
1948 [3]	46,067	89,449	45,775	43,667	51.2	75,714	(²)	(²)	56,154	19,582
1949 [3]	43,503	84,286	39,681	44,604	47.1	73,063	(²)	(²)	52,759	20,304
1950 [3]	43,268	87,829	36,043	51,778	41.0	74,785	(²)	(²)	48,695	26,064
1951 [3][4]	45,326	108,164	44,738	63,425	41.4	94,185	(²)	(²)	68,726	25,456
1952 [3][4]	45,382	109,621	38,803	70,818	35.4	94,527	(²)	(²)	66,127	28,399

YEARLY AVERAGE OR YEAR	SEAPORTS—continued					NORTHERN BORDER PORTS			
	American vessels		Foreign vessels		Percent American	Total	American vessels	Foreign vessels	With cargo
	Total	With cargo	Total	With cargo					
1881-1890	2,978	2,541	10,741	10,254	21.7	2,754	472	2,282	1,778
1891-1900	3,644	2,914	15,377	14,600	19.2	3,442	1,394	2,048	2,129
1901-1905	4,000	3,284	20,633	19,176	16.2	5,918	2,812	3,106	3,825
1906-1910	4,084	3,498	25,072	23,270	14.0	8,036	4,198	3,838	5,673
1911-1915	5,361	4,522	30,594	28,305	14.9	12,061	7,151	4,909	8,567
1915-1920 [1]	15,455	11,505	24,681	23,346	38.5	13,511	7,550	5,962	9,637
1921-1925	22,556	14,974	31,022	27,259	42.1	13,075	6,998	6,077	9,236
1926-1930	23,338	17,071	41,102	35,510	36.2	15,319	7,371	7,948	10,504
1931-1935	19,653	15,729	35,561	29,261	35.6	10,351	3,962	6,388	7,309
1936-1940	16,302	13,116	40,665	33,009	28.6	11,575	3,146	8,429	9,412
1941-1945	32,585	26,377	23,718	18,770	57.9	15,489	4,698	10,789	12,657
1946-1950 [3]	40,933	29,510	33,953	25,073	54.7	12,301	4,010	8,291	10,819
1941	17,701	12,251	28,441	20,462	38.4	16,454	4,169	12,285	13,824
1942	13,149	10,827	18,826	15,637	41.1	15,730	3,205	12,525	13,782
1943	28,826	24,140	21,406	18,330	57.0	16,484	4,856	11,628	13,638
1944	46,919	39,960	24,798	20,134	65.4	15,668	6,131	9,538	12,016
1945	56,332	44,705	25,120	19,286	69.2	13,107	5,129	7,979	10,027
1946	45,113	31,963	21,263	15,865	68.0	10,849	4,012	6,837	9,548
1947 [3]	49,558	38,783	34,949	28,700	58.6	12,652	4,530	8,122	11,284
1948 [3]	41,348	29,840	34,358	26,314	54.6	13,735	4,428	9,309	12,339
1949 [3]	36,136	25,446	36,927	27,313	49.5	11,223	3,545	7,677	9,382
1950 [3]	32,510	21,520	42,269	27,175	43.5	13,044	3,533	9,509	11,540
1951 [3][4]	40,999	30,375	53,185	38,353	43.5	13,979	3,739	10,240	12,384
1952 [3][4]	34,350	24,713	60,177	41,413	36.3	15,095	4,453	10,641	12,578

[1] Average for period July 1, 1915, to Dec. 31, 1920.
[2] Preliminary data, subject to revision.   [3] Not available.
[4] Vessels under time or voyage charter to Military Sea Transportation Service excluded after June 1951.

Source: Department of Commerce, Bureau of the Census; annual report, *Foreign Commerce and Navigation of the United States*, and records.

No. 683.—United States Flag Steam and Motor Merchant Vessels: 1946 to 1952

Dead weight tonnage in thousands. Covers seagoing vessels of 1,000 gross tons and over engaged in foreign and domestic trade, and inactive vessels. Excludes special types and vessels employed on Great Lakes]

DATE AND TYPE OF VESSEL	ALL VESSELS		ACTIVE VESSELS													INACTIVE VESSELS		SPECIAL SERVICE	
			Total		Foreign trade		Total		Domestic trade											
									Coastwise		Intercoastal		Noncontiguous							
	Num-ber	Dead weight tons	Num-ber	Dead weight tons	Num-ber	Dead weight tons	Num-ber	Dead weight tons	Num-ber	Dead weight tons	Num-ber	Dead weight tons	Num-ber	Dead weight tons			Num-ber	Dead weight tons	Num-ber	Dead weight tons
1946, Sept. 30	4,422	46,540	2,332	25,400	1,890	20,593	442	4,807	297	3,483	54	843	91	761			2,090	21,140		
Combination	96	555	25	166	15	128	10	38				561	10	38			61	380		
Cargo	3,442	33,380	1,633	18,111	1,607	18,201	226	1,910	101	730	1		72	619			1,609	15,290		
Tankers	894	12,605	474	7,123	268	4,264	206	2,839	196	2,733	2		8	104			420	6,482		
1947, Dec. 31	3,696	38,882	2,114	23,651	1,603	17,238	511	6,413	381	5,104	68	742	62	567			1,582	15,231		
Combination	95	742	38	284	32	259	6	25					6	25			57	458		
Cargo	2,977	29,206	1,628	16,561	1,434	14,779	194	1,782	82	659	65	692	47	431			1,349	12,645		
Tankers	624	8,934	448	6,806	137	2,200	311	4,606	299	4,445	3	50	9	111			176	2,128		
1948, June 30	3,499	34,774	1,722	19,583	1,246	13,767	477	5,783	327	4,329	66	721	84	735			1,787	17,223		
Combination	77	601	48	385	41	357	7	28					7	28			29	216		
Cargo	2,857	25,674	1,221	12,424	1,023	10,592	198	1,832	66	559	63	667	68	606			1,636	13,250		
Tankers	536	7,499	454	6,743	182	2,818	272	3,925	259	3,760	4	54	9	111			72	755		
1949, June 30	3,373	34,225	1,396	18,644	1,094	11,416	383	4,626	262	3,437	63	700	58	491			1,993	20,194		
Combination	73	600	47	336	43	275	4	13					4	13			25	221		
Cargo	2,799	25,442	949	10,063	813	8,025	156	1,437	59	416	20	657	44	264			1,530	19,370		
Tankers	501	7,177	370	3,593	148	2,415	223	3,176	200	3,021	3	43	10	114			131	1,584		
1950, June 30	3,406	34,826	1,145	13,638	711	8,383	434	6,474	279	3,716	87	1,131	68	626			2,282	23,688		
Combination	63	639	51	417	45	389	6	28					6	28			32	223		
Cargo	2,846	28,927	682	7,075	505	5,367	177	1,708	65	150	56	640	53	1,000			2,164	21,581		
Tankers	479	6,959	412	6,335	161	2,397	251	3,737	213	3,157	29	423	9	96			67	634		
1951, June 30	3,386	34,336	1,414	16,761	988	11,426	426	5,333	287	3,924	88	667	81	741			1,732	17,683	240	3,189
Combination	266	2,067	51	428	46	404	5	24					5	24			203	1,530	12	109
Cargo	2,650	27,376	919	9,614	743	7,892	176	1,721	65	464	53	626	68	611			1,506	15,381	225	2,401
Tankers	470	6,893	444	6,718	190	3,129	245	3,587	232	3,440	3	41	10	105			23	163	3	19
1952, June 30	3,359	36,951	1,177	14,242	782	9,043	395	5,199	291	4,023	86	690	49	448			1,903	19,166	278	3,784
Combination	280	2,044	45	397	44	393	1	4					1	4			198	1,491	17	155
Cargo	2,629	27,210	717	7,490	582	5,009	135	1,202	66	517	41	449	28	337			1,682	17,164	230	2,467
Tankers	451	6,627	415	6,355	156	2,461	259	3,984	233	3,516	15	341	11	127			43	461	3	13

1 Includes ships originally constructed as cargo ships but converted to transports, hospital ships, etc., previously included in the cargo classification as follows: 1951, 183 ships of 1,426,000 deadweight tons; 1952, 181 ships of 1,415,300 deadweight tons.

Source: Department of Commerce, Maritime Administration; records.

No. 684.—Merchant Vessels Completed by U. S. Shipyards: 1914 to 1952

[Represents self-propelled steel vessels of 2,000 gross tons and over. For explanation of gross-tons and deadweight tons, see text p. 568]

YEAR	Number	Gross tons	PASSENGER-CARGO/ TRANSPORT			CARGO			TANKER		
			Number	Gross tons	Dead-weight tons	Number	Gross tons	Dead-weight tons	Number	Gross tons	Dead-weight tons
1914	26	135,164	1	2,662	800	17	87,585	130,278	8	44,917	67,222
1915	24	128,337	3	19,967	12,600	17	88,262	131,388	4	20,088	29,862
1916	74	369,955	1	6,063	7,490	49	200,824	299,623	24	163,068	246,953
1917	125	642,120	1	10,206	9,940	92	413,602	627,002	32	218,312	314,226
1918	414	1,769,629	5	29,736	24,297	375	1,508,003	2,282,585	34	231,890	339,368
1919	723	3,369,884	2	1C,285	10,650	679	3,066,207	4,680,321	42	273,392	394,712
1920	467	2,395,545	12	99,911	111,000	375	1,758,086	2,695,753	80	537,548	778,027
1921	183	1,359,426	22	256,436	243,380	57	316,909	485,418	104	786,081	1,156,053
1922	19	168,024	3	41,293	34,384	10	78,442	155,680	6	48,289	70,652
1923	18	117,042	7	33,947	26,110	9	67,582	110,410	2	15,513	23,420
1924	12	84,302	7	43,740	19,788	4	34,016	48,450	1	6,546	10,544
1925	12	83,916	3	18,850	11,470	9	65,066	92,200	---	---	---
1926	8	54,043	5	28,789	15,880	2	16,302	25,625	1	8,952	15,262
1927	19	154,700	7	51,294	27,459	9	72,936	104,300	3	30,470	49,752
1928	7	71,916	3	44,190	37,400	---	---	---	4	27,726	44,086
1929	8	65,313	2	23,614	19,800	5	32,603	49,200	1	9,096	15,190
1930	18	163,500	5	50,311	39,269	2	15,824	24,000	11	97,365	161,219
1931	14	150,949	9	108,968	85,413	---	---	---	5	41,981	69,526
1932	15	145,470	13	129,348	82,572	2	16,122	21,800	---	---	---
1933	4	49,527	4	49,527	32,367	---	---	---	---	---	---
1934	2	9,544	---	---	---	2	9,544	15,180	---	---	---
1935	2	19,022	---	---	---	---	---	---	2	19,022	29,760
1936	8	63,428	---	---	---	---	---	---	8	63,428	104,860
1937	15	121,852	---	---	---	---	---	---	15	121,852	191,929
1938	24	181,366	---	---	---	6	39,196	56,100	18	142,170	227,982
1939	28	241,052	3	30,063	20,436	14	91,560	128,484	11	119,429	193,112
1940	53	444,727	6	68,943	61,222	31	227,275	334,660	16	148,509	238,352
1941	95	749,108	6	58,107	56,515	61	423,022	597,943	28	267,979	434,039
1942	724	5,392,848	11	101,847	81,290	652	4,678,880	6,842,689	61	612,121	982,381
1943	1,661	12,485,629	20	219,760	180,047	1,410	10,103,245	14,921,082	231	2,162,624	3,420,405
1944	1,463	11,403,163	48	461,291	330,311	1,175	8,455,475	11,857,797	240	2,486,397	3,954,967
1945	1,041	7,614,898	46	509,163	311,046	807	5,336,152	7,206,201	188	1,769,593	2,797,397
1946	83	645,706	9	76,719	84,667	66	487,354	728,583	8	81,633	120,900
1947	39	247,327	8	73,664	68,225	28	154,402	223,657	3	19,261	36,166
1948	24	158,915	1	15,359	10,513	17	92,049	158,863	6	51,507	87,693
1949	33	540,559	---	---	---	---	---	---	33	540,559	863,292
1950	26	404,617	---	---	---	3	26,854	43,500	23	377,763	608,593
1951	10	147,569	2	47,438	23,580	4	28,993	42,994	4	71,138	116,438
1952	16	249,857	1	53,329	12,810	7	58,703	83,460	8	137,825	203,266

Source: American Bureau of Shipping, New York, N. Y.; published annually in *The Bulletin*.

No. 685.—UNITED STATES MERCHANT MARINE—SUMMARY: 1789 TO 1952

[For definition of "gross ton" see general note, p. 568. See also *Historical Statistics*, series K 94-104 and K 124-129]

JUNE 30 (EXCEPT AS INDICATED)	NUMBER OF VESSELS			GROSS TONNAGE OF VESSELS (THOUSANDS)								
					Major class			Material of which built		Type of trade in which engaged		
	Total	Steam and motor	All other	Total	Steam and motor	Sailing [1]	Canal boats and barges [1]	Metal [2]	Wood	Foreign trade	Coastwise and internal	Other [3]
1789 (Dec. 31)				202		202				124	69	9
1800 (Dec. 31)				972		972				667	272	33
1810 (Dec. 31)				1,425	1	1,424				981	405	33
1820 (Dec. 31) [4]				1,280	22	1,258				584	588	108
1830 (Dec. 31) [4]				1,192	64	1,127				538	517	137
1840 (Sept. 30)				2,181	202	1,978				763	1,177	241
1850				3,535	526	3,010				1,440	1,798	296
1860				5,354	868	4,486				2,379	2,645	330
1870	26,998	3,524	25,474	4,247	1,075	2,363	808			1,449	2,638	159
1880	24,712	4,717	19,995	4,068	1,212	2,366	490			1,314	2,638	116
1900	23,497	5,965	17,502	4,424	1,859	2,109	456	627	3,798	928	3,409	87
1900	23,333	7,053	16,280	5,165	2,658	1,885	622	1,593	3,572	817	4,287	62
1910	25,740	12,452	13,288	7,508	4,900	1,655	953	4,117	3,391	783	6,669	57
1915	26,701	15,948	10,753	8,389	5,944	1,384	1,061	5,305	3,085	1,863	6,486	40
1920	28,153	18,814	9,369	16,374	13,823	1,272	1,228	12,448	3,876	9,925	6,386	62
1925	26,367	18,637	7,730	17,406	14,976	1,125	1,304	14,499	2,907	8,151	9,216	39
1930	25,214	19,211	7,003	16,068	13,757	757	1,554	13,514	2,554	6,296	9,733	40
1935	24,919	18,495	6,424	14,654	12,535	441	1,677	12,469	2,185	4,560	10,049	44
1939	27,470	19,606	7,864	14,632	11,952	221	2,430	12,159	2,473	3,312	11,298	22
1940	27,212	19,504	7,708	14,018	11,353	300	2,406	(5)	(5)	3,638	10,352	29
1941 (Jan. 1)	27,075	19,382	7,693	13,772	11,047	182	2,493	11,393	2,329	3,047	10,654	21
1942 (Jan. 1)	27,325	19,471	7,854	13,860	11,072	166	2,621	11,641	2,218	4,109	9,744	7
1943 (Jan. 1)	27,612	19,974	7,638	16,762	14,052	142	2,566	14,647	2,115	9,285	7,471	6
1944 (Jan. 1)	28,690	21,511	7,179	25,795	23,217	129	2,449	23,837	1,959	18,685	7,105	5
1945 (Jan. 1)	29,797	22,772	7,025	32,813	30,247	115	2,452	30,898	1,915	26,043	6,766	5
1946 (Jan. 1)	31,386	24,355	7,031	38,501	35,928	98	2,475	36,571	1,929	29,705	8,791	4
1947 (Jan. 1)	32,760	25,532	7,228	37,532	35,149	95	2,888	35,897	1,936	26,535	11,354	3
1948 (Jan. 1)	33,843	26,633	7,210	33,167	30,469	87	2,611	31,211	1,956	22,021	11,143	3
1949 (Jan. 1)	35,264	27,862	7,407	32,182	29,323	87	2,771	30,212	1,969	20,634	11,525	3
1950 (Jan. 1)	36,063	28,793	7,290	31,215	28,327	82	2,806	29,263	1,952	19,154	12,048	14
1951 (Jan. 1)	36,745	29,429	7,316	30,341	27,424	71	2,846	28,417	1,974	18,876	11,464	3
1952 (Jan. 1)	37,389	30,189	7,200	30,416	27,459	66	2,891	28,559	1,857	19,979	11,134	4

CLASSES	NUMBER OF VESSELS					GROSS TONNAGE OF VESSELS (THOUSANDS)				
	1941	1949	1950	1951	1952	1941	1949	1950	1951	1952
Total	27,075	35,264	36,063	36,745	37,389	13,722	32,182	31,215	30,341	30,416
By location:										
Atlantic and Gulf [6]	16,627	21,071	21,623	22,069	22,530	9,812	20,318	20,420	19,968	20,989
Pacific [7]	6,727	9,801	10,086	10,303	10,344	1,954	9,066	8,446	8,072	7,196
Northern lakes	2,023	1,964	2,026	2,043	2,027	1,641	2,076	1,628	1,865	1,846
Western rivers	1,698	2,428	2,368	2,430	2,488	305	721	721	736	736
By rig:										
Steam	3,796	5,020	4,795	4,551	4,432	9,814	27,226	26,272	25,390	25,356
Motor	15,586	22,942	23,998	24,878	25,757	1,233	2,099	2,055	2,052	2,103
Sailing	517	303	290	208	249	182	87	82	71	66
Unrigged	7,176	7,099	7,000	7,048	6,951	2,493	2,771	2,806	2,846	2,891

[1] Canal boats and barges included with sailing prior to 1868.
[2] Includes iron, steel, composite, and concrete.
[3] Includes whale fisheries and cod and mackerel fisheries. Beginning 1939, figures exclude mackerel.
[4] Decrease of tonnage arises principally from registered tonnage having been corrected in 1818, 1829, and 1830 by omitting all vessels with registers granted prior to 1815, which were presumed to have been lost at sea, captured, etc.
[5] Not available.
[6] Including Puerto Rico and Virgin Islands.
[7] Including Hawaii and Alaska.

Source: Treasury Department, Bureau of Customs; annual report, *Merchant Marine Statistics*.

No. 686.—U. S. MERCHANT MARINE—NUMBER AND GROSS TONNAGE OF VESSELS ON JAN. 1, 1952, BY YEAR OF BUILD

YEAR OF BUILD	Number	Gross tons	YEAR OF BUILD	Number	Gross tons	YEAR OF BUILD	Number	Gross tons
Total..	37,389	30,416,339	1888.........	46	6,051	1921.........	299	236,850
			1889.........	28	4,056	1922.........	345	109,843
Unknown...	970	114,121	1890.........	33	5,461	1923.........	482	122,256
1849.........	1	19	1891.........	67	10,427	1924.........	602	147,539
1851.........	1	14	1892.........	54	9,278	1925.........	645	139,540
1852.........	1	14	1893.........	42	3,961	1926.........	703	141,604
1857.........	3	191	1894.........	30	2,960	1927.........	788	212,240
1862.........	1	36	1895.........	36	6,352	1928.........	809	182,817
1863.........	1	1,318	1896.........	68	43,610	1929.........	847	168,560
1864.........	1	225	1897.........	61	27,487	1930.........	770	157,479
1865.........	4	121	1898.........	95	42,555	1931.........	538	123,696
1866.........	4	224	1899.........	98	45,109	1932.........	374	129,761
1867.........	5	138	1900.........	152	79,946	1933.........	315	52,164
1868.........	6	1,647	1901.........	169	61,202	1934.........	412	38,031
1869.........	4	237	1902.........	167	85,646	1935.........	586	61,914
1870.........	2	3,706	1903.........	164	72,803	1936.........	763	134,162
1871.........	8	474	1904.........	163	53,160	1937.........	871	216,283
1872.........	8	461	1905.........	226	195,591	1938.........	750	165,169
1873.........	7	310	1906.........	248	273,298	1939.........	768	194,139
1874.........	7	884	1907.........	253	278,217	1940.........	893	377,974
1875.........	9	778	1908.........	273	201,870	1941.........	955	514,127
1876.........	8	447	1909.........	237	128,977	1942.........	1,536	3,436,741
1877.........	7	3,159	1910.........	266	155,630	1943.........	2,278	7,414,329
1878.........	10	3,505	1911.........	332	101,689	1944.........	2,288	5,930,677
1879.........	9	1,770	1912.........	368	85,771	1945.........	1,891	4,766,318
1880.........	9	2,081	1913.........	394	122,081	1946.........	1,536	600,450
1881.........	30	3,006	1914.........	361	89,873	1947.........	1,433	276,655
1882.........	32	2,016	1915.........	356	57,565	1948.........	1,294	235,170
1883.........	30	1,533	1916.........	362	144,030	1949.........	1,165	237,055
1884.........	31	2,899	1917.........	533	211,096	1950.........	1,030	225,216
1885.........	37	3,062	1918.........	498	134,945	1951.........	992	306,825
1886.........	28	2,017	1919.........	524	229,726			
1887.........	37	2,866	1920.........	476	244,828			

Source: Treasury Department, Bureau of Customs; annual report, *Merchant Marine Statistics.*

No. 687.—U. S. MERCHANT MARINE—NUMBER AND GROSS TONNAGE OF VESSELS ON JAN. 1, 1952, BY TONNAGE GROUPINGS

TONNAGE GROUPINGS	TOTAL		STEAM VESSELS		MOTOR VESSELS		SAILING VESSELS		UNRIGGED VESSELS	
	Number	Gross tons (1,000)	Number	Gross tons (1,000)	Number	Gross tons (1,000)	Number	Gross tons (1,000)	Number	Gross tons (1,000)
Total....................	37,389	30,416	4,432	25,356	25,757	2,103	249	66	6,951	2,891
5 to 49 tons..................	21,962	394	74	2	21,015	369	192	3	681	20
50 to 99 tons..................	2,729	192	174	14	2,204	152	11	1	340	25
100 to 499 tons..................	6,801	1,840	601	140	2,082	411	13	3	4,105	1,286
500 to 999 tons..................	1,758	1,155	141	99	165	109	11	10	1,441	938
1,000 to 2,499 tons..............	617	871	139	223	121	155	17	30	340	463
2,500 to 4,999 tons..............	328	1,248	170	668	112	414	5	20	41	143
5,000 to 9,999 tons..............	2,835	20,717	2,787	20,350	45	351	......	......	3	16
10,000 to 19,999 tons..........	351	3,820	338	3,677	13	144	......	......	......	......
20,000 tons and over..........	8	183	8	183	......	......	......	......	......	......

Source: Treasury Department, Bureau of Customs; annual report, *Merchant Marine Statistics.*

No. 688.—U. S. MERCHANT MARINE—CHANGES IN GROSS TONNAGE OF DOCUMENTED
VESSELS: 1940 TO 1951

[In thousands of gross tons. Documented vessels of 5 net tons or more. For definition of "gross ton" see general note, p. 568. Vessels may be added to merchant marine by way of redocumentation. However, figures are available only for vessels documented. See also *Historical Statistics*, series K 105–118]

YEAR	Gross tonnage of vessels built and documented	GROSS TONNAGE OF VESSELS REMOVED					Net increase (+) or decrease (−) [1]
		Total	Lost and abandoned	Sold to aliens	Sold to United States	All other	
1940	447	1,697	274	1,114	([2])	308	[3] −297
1941	647	1,064	127	333	245	358	+138
1942	4,544	1,876	166	70	323	1,316	+2,802
1943	10,432	1,727	199	102	216	1,210	+8,094
1944	8,032	1,425	417	104	288	616	+7,018
1945	6,314	901	138	75	198	490	+5,687
1946	548	1,745	344	1,193	87	121	−608
1947	267	5,914	257	4,930	383	345	−4,665
1948	200	1,713	245	1,207	136	124	−985
1949	195	1,380	449	330	404	196	−987
1950	194	1,238	163	488	147	440	−574
1951	309	484	123	75	30	226	+75

[1] Difference in total gross tonnage between current and previous year as shown in table 685.
[2] Included in all other.
[3] 6 months' decrease.

Source: Treasury Department, Bureau of Customs; annual report, *Merchant Marine Statistics*.

No. 689.—U. S. MERCHANT MARINE—NUMBER AND GROSS TONNAGE OF VESSELS
BUILT IN UNITED STATES AND DOCUMENTED: 1940 TO 1951

[Documented vessels of 5 net tons or more. See also *Historical Statistics*, series K 119–123]

YEAR	ALL VESSELS		Steam and motor	Sailing	Canal boats and barges
	Number of vessels	Gross tons			
1940	705	446,894	385,661	87	61,126
1941	703	647,097	596,443	---	60,654
1942	1,108	4,543,946	4,504,398	14	39,534
1943	1,901	10,431,734	10,339,670	23	92,041
1944	1,723	8,032,009	8,009,277	129	22,603
1945	1,744	6,313,977	6,258,608	---	55,369
1946	1,275	548,262	509,538	7	38,717
1947	1,259	267,331	186,109	16	81,206
1948	1,118	200,290	108,206	---	92,084
1949	978	195,190	85,288	39	109,863
1950	861	194,370	103,358	7	91,005
1951	992	308,825	165,064	---	143,761

Source: Treasury Department, Bureau of Customs; annual report, *Merchant Marine Statistics*.

No. 690.—MERCHANT VESSELS LAUNCHED IN THE WORLD AND IN THE UNITED STATES: 1910 TO 1952

[Vessels of 100 gross tons and over. For definition of "gross ton" see general note, p. 568. Beginning 1941 sailing ships and nonpropelled craft are included for Great Britain and N. Ireland only. For 1939-1945, figures exclude information from enemy and enemy-occupied countries and Russia; for 1946-1949, figures exclude Germany and Russia. Beginning 1950, figures include Germany, but exclude Russia, Poland, and China]

CALENDAR YEAR	WORLD				UNITED STATES	
	Total		Steam and motor			
	Number	Gross tons	Number	Gross tons	Number	Gross tons
1910-1914, average	1,533	2,739,079	1,180	2,631,779	162	252,864
1915-1920, average [1]	1,488	4,046,860	1,296	3,918,746	518	1,877,322
1921-1925, average	942	2,581,653	830	2,531,592	99	315,114
1926-1930, average	873	2,468,515	808	2,427,929	74	188,788
1931-1935, average	484	1,020,444	461	1,010,567	25	83,485
1936-1940, average	931	2,427,144	841	2,376,050	127	310,706
1941-1945, average	1,442	8,520,091	1,390	8,510,700	963	6,718,446
1946-1950, average	934	2,645,026	858	2,630,349	67	372,579
1941	564	2,498,061	510	2,491,173	187	1,035,229
1942	1,359	7,828,705	1,300	7,815,369	861	5,670,530
1943	2,122	13,893,978	2,078	13,884,776	1,625	11,579,522
1944	1,822	11,182,310	1,738	11,169,503	1,261	9,339,067
1945	1,344	7,197,402	1,326	7,192,679	880	5,967,581
1946	747	2,127,421	690	2,114,702	96	891,294
1947	837	2,111,886	787	2,102,621	70	164,848
1948	997	2,332,604	872	2,309,743	49	126,418
1949	1,012	3,146,145	928	3,131,805	66	633,306
1950	1,075	3,507,073	1,013	3,492,876	52	437,031
1951	1,101	3,658,485	1,022	3,642,564	64	165,863
1952	1,074	4,395,578	1,074	4,395,578	64	467,545

[1] Figures covering war period are for allied and neutral countries.

Source: Lloyd's Register of Shipping, London; *Annual Summary of Mercantile Shipbuilding of the World* and records.

No. 691.—MERCHANT MARINE OF THE WORLD AND OF THE UNITED STATES

[Vessels of 100 tons and over. Prior to 1919 tonnage figures are gross for steamers and net for sailing vessels, thereafter gross for both. Wooden vessels on Great Lakes and vessels on Caspian Sea excluded. Japanese sailing vessels and most sailing vessels belonging to Greece, Turkey, and southern Russia excluded. Figures for Philippine Islands included with United States, 1910-39. See general note, p. 568. Data not compiled during last war period]

YEAR	World total	United States	YEAR	World total	United States	YEAR	World total	United States
	1,000 tons	*1,000 tons*		*1,000 tons*	*1,000 tons*		*1,000 tons*	*1,000 tons*
1895	25,086	2,165	1925	64,641	15,377	1949	83,346	28,224
1900	28,957	2,750	1930	69,608	14,046	1950	85,303	27,896
1905	35,998	3,996	1935	64,886	12,852	1951	87,961	27,702
1910	41,915	5,059	1939	69,440	12,003	1952	90,868	27,601
1915	49,262	5,893	1947	84,356	32,891			
1920	57,314	16,049	1948	81,074	29,602			

ITEM	NUMBER				THOUSANDS OF TONS (SEE HEADNOTE)				
	1930	1939	1950	1951	1952	1920	1930	1939	1950	1951	1952
World total	32,713	31,186	31,732	32,112	32,318	57,314	69,608	69,440	85,303	87,961	90,868
Steam and motor	29,996	29,763	30,852	31,226	31,461	53,905	68,024	68,509	84,583	87,245	90,180
Steel and iron	27,595	27,507	27,922	28,374	28,751	51,661	67,304	68,007	83,996	86,678	89,636
Wood and composite	2,401	2,256	2,930	2,852	2,710	2,244	720	503	587	567	545
Sailing and nonpropelled	2,717	1,423	880	886	857	3,409	1,584	930	720	716	688
Steel and iron	742	743	611	643	628	1,524	654	572	557	578	565
Wood and composite	1,975	680	269	243	229	1,885	930	358	163	138	1:3
United States	4,223	3,375	5,213	5,160	5,114	16,049	14,046	12,003	27,898	27,702	27,601
Steam and motor	3,517	2,958	4,953	4,909	4,876	14,574	13,202	11,490	27,513	27,331	27,245
Steel and iron	3,001	2,560	4,531	4,484	4,458	13,341	12,914	11,342	27,404	27,225	27,139
Wood and composite	516	398	422	425	418	1,234	288	148	109	106	105
Sailing and nonpropelled	706	417	260	251	238	1,475	844	513	385	371	356
Steel and iron	147	187	154	160	157	304	288	272	260	270	268
Wood and composite	559	230	106	91	81	1,171	556	241	125	101	88

Source: Lloyd's Register of Shipping, London; Appendix to *Lloyd's Register Book*.

23. Irrigation, Drainage, and Soil Conservation

Irrigation.—The 17 Western States and Arkansas, Louisiana, and Florida are the States in which most of the irrigated land in the Nation is located. In these States a special census of irrigation was made as part of the 1950 Census of Agriculture conducted by the Bureau of the Census. Information on acres irrigated, irrigation works, capital investment, and a number of other items was obtained from the irrigation companies, districts, and other organizations, and from farms that operate their own irrigation supply works. For the remaining eastern, midwestern, and southern States information on irrigation was limited to that reported in the farm census.

The definition of irrigated land in the 1950 Census was the net acreage of farm land to which irrigation water was actually applied during 1949. It did not include land that could be irrigated or that usually is irrigated, but that was not irrigated during 1949. Land in irrigated farms that was used for purposes such as roads and farmsteads, to which irrigation water was not applied, was excluded. Also excluded was irrigated land used for purposes other than farming, such as that in rural residential areas, cemeteries, parks, and golf courses.

The Bureau of Reclamation has operated since 1902 as the principal Federal agency engaged in the development of irrigation projects. By Congressional directive its activities are confined to the 17 Western States and Alaska. However, Kansas does not appear in any of the Reclamation tables because work on developments in that State has not yet progressed to a point to warrant its inclusion. Actual operation of irrigation works is transferred to water users organizations as soon as the projects are fully developed and these organizations are willing and able to assume the responsibility of operating the works.

Reclamation crop data, compiled since 1906, are obtained from the annual crop census conducted by the Bureau. Information on reclamation project charges and rentals are obtained from the financial records of the Bureau. Data on reclamation hydroelectric plants have been compiled semi-annually by the Bureau since July 1944.

Drainage.—Drainage works for farm lands are constructed primarily for three purposes, namely, (1) the reclamation or improvement of the land, (2) protection of the land against overflow, and (3) to rid the land of seepage from irrigation ditches or for control or prevention of alkali formation. Ninety percent of all drainage enterprises were organized for reclamation and improvement of land.

The farmers in the Eastern United States need drainage to take surplus rainfall off some of their lands. Most of this is gravity drainage, although pumps are sometimes used. In the Western States drainage is mainly for the purpose of taking seepage water off irrigated lands and to carry off alkali salts.

In the 1950 National Census of Drainage, in general, only those organized enterprises with 500 acres or more of drained farm land were included in the enumeration. A few irrigation enterprises of smaller size which had their own drainage works were also included. In previous Censuses (1910-1940) all organized enterprises draining farm lands were included in the enumeration regardless of size. Privately drained lands of less than 500 acres have not been enumerated in any of the four Drainage Censuses. The change in census procedure for 1950 materially reduced the number of enterprises enumerated, but affected very little the amount of drained land enumerated.

In taking the 1950 Census, differences in form of organization and management of drainage enterprises made it necessary for the Bureau of the Census to divide somewhat arbitrarily the 40 States with drainage enterprises into two groups: the 10 "county-drain" States and the 30 "drainage-district" States. The eight States with no drainage enterprises are the six New England States, Pennsylvania, and West Virginia. In the 10 "county-drain" States (Delaware, Indiana, Iowa, Kentucky, Michigan, Minnesota, North Dakota, Ohio, Oklahoma, South Dakota), statistics were gathered for the county as a unit, rather than for each separate enterprise as for the 30 "drainage-district" States. In most of the "county-drain" States, the management of drainage enterprises is under the county government. Generally, the maintenance work on existing ditches has been done by reorganizing the land of an earlier enterprise into a new project. Since the number of enterprises for "county-drain" States would be meaningless, the number was not obtained for these 10 States.

Note.—This section presents data for the most recent year or period available on April 23, 1953, when the material was organized and sent to the printer.

593

In the Western States most of the drained land is located in irrigation enterprises which were chartered to do both irrigation and drainage work under one organization. In the case of irrigation enterprises having their own drainage, the cost of construction and operation and maintenance of the irrigation works is usually far greater than that for drainage. Separate records are seldom kept for expenditures for drainage and irrigation. Data were not included in the 1950 Census of Drainage for cost, collections, and indebtedness of irrigation enterprises having their own drainage. Therefore, the data for 1950 are not fully comparable with those for earlier years.

Soil conservation.—Basic soil conservation district legislation has now been enacted in all of the 48 States and 4 of the Territories and possessions. Each of these laws contains an effective date after which soil conservation districts could be organized by local farmers and operators. A soil conservation district is a political subdivision of a State which is determined by petition and referendum of farmers residing in the area, and approved by the State Soil Conservation Committee. Districts, in most cases, have authority to solicit Federal, State, county, and private assistance in carrying on their soil and water conservation program within the area. On request of the local governing body of each soil conservation district, the Department of Agriculture provides technical and other assistance to districts, through its several agencies. These memorandums of understanding form the basis on which any departmental assistance is provided to a district for use on the farms and ranches within the district. After the basic memorandum with the Department has been signed, the Soil Conservation Service signs a supplemental memorandum with each district governing body requesting assistance, to cover activities which the Soil Conservation Service will help each district to carry out.

Historical statistics.—See preface and historical appendix. Tabular headnotes (as "See also *Historical Statistics*, series F 56–59") provide cross-references, where applicable, to *Historical Statistics of the United States, 1789–1945.*

No. 692.—IRRIGATION ENTERPRISES—SUMMARY: 1910 TO 1950

[Data are for the 17 Western States, Arkansas, Louisiana, and, for 1940 and 1950, Florida. Tables 692, 694 and 696 relate to irrigation enterprises of all types, including those operated by individual farmers. They are based on reports of management of enterprises. An enterprise is defined as "an independent irrigation establishment owning or operating works for supplying water to agricultural land." See also *Historical Statistics*, series F 86-99]

ITEM	CENSUS OF—				
	1910	1920	1930	1940 [4]	1950 [1]
Approximate land area..........1,000 acres..	1,294,063	1,222,980	1,222,980	[1]1,290,784	1,265,972
Farms (irrigated and nonirrigated) [2]....number..	1,776,046	1,916,391	2,062,813	1,960,093	1,689,447
Land in all farms [3]..........1,000 acres..	414,463	505,441	566,694	637,388	734,577
Irrigation enterprises:					
Enterprises..........number..	50,856	66,396	75,517	96,255	123,926
Area irrigated..........1,000 acres..	14,436	19,192	19,548	21,136	26,332
Investment in irrigation enterprises....1,000 dollars..	321,454	697,657	892,736	1,069,105	1,887,738
Increase over preceding census......percent..	....	250.2	117.0	26.0	19.6	76.2
Average per acre irrigated..........dollars..	22.27	36.35	45.67	50.11	71.68
Increase over preceding census......percent..	....	63.2	25.6	9.7	42.6
Average annual cost per acre irrigated for maintenance and operation of irrigation works..........dollars..	[4]1.97	2.43	2.77	2.19	[4]4.89

[1] Includes Florida; see headnote.
[2] Represents redeterminations and therefore differs from figures shown for earlier years.
[3] From Census of Agriculture.
[4] Excludes cost of operation and maintenance for rice-growing districts in Gulf States; consequently figure is not comparable with those for later years.

Source: Department of Commerce, Bureau of Census; *U. S. Census of Agriculture: 1950*, Vol. III.

No. 693.—FARM DRAINAGE—ANNUAL COST AND FUNDS COLLECTED, FOR ALL DRAINAGE STATES: 1940 TO 1949

[See table 697 for States included]

FINANCIAL ITEMS	All drainage States, amount	30 STATES [1]		10 States, amount [2]
		Number of enterprises reporting	Amount	
Cost of construction and operation and maintenance, 1940 to 1949............	$179,832,778	2,436	$116,321,689	$62,892,699
1940............	11,116,467	1,513	6,196,439	4,982,028
1941............	11,858,943	1,519	6,668,374	4,390,468
1942............	11,622,561	1,516	6,722,109	4,900,442
1943............	11,680,225	1,577	7,063,851	4,056,464
1944............	13,754,590	1,582	8,135,637	4,618,213
1945............	15,874,309	1,671	9,077,448	6,796,951
1946............	18,866,027	1,853	11,645,339	7,222,688
1947............	23,635,739	2,022	15,294,054	8,411,685
1948............	29,105,402	2,133	19,222,181	9,881,281
1949............	31,517,308	2,214	20,306,448	11,211,760
Cost of new drainage works, 1940 to 1949............	23,872,422	983	16,288,346	7,584,076
1940............	292,905	28	211,662	81,243
1941............	595,553	36	456,885	138,668
1942............	666,364	38	485,030	183,334
1943............	761,825	55	552,887	208,938
1944............	847,874	58	585,754	262,120
1945............	1,841,360	106	1,209,478	631,882
1946............	2,656,197	175	1,845,545	810,652
1947............	3,982,765	285	2,675,951	1,306,814
1948............	5,480,198	334	3,811,674	1,668,824
1949............	6,745,381	309	4,453,480	2,291,901
Funds collected for drainage, 1940 to 1949............	209,919,661	2,471	144,416,844	65,502,817
1940............	14,826,778	1,544	9,876,982	4,949,796
1941............	16,069,107	1,516	10,964,089	5,095,018
1942............	16,454,645	1,534	11,257,936	5,176,709
1943............	16,604,413	1,549	11,745,320	4,859,093
1944............	17,857,447	1,574	12,352,396	5,505,051
1945............	19,893,508	1,650	13,748,625	6,144,883
1946............	24,077,324	1,792	16,740,225	7,337,099
1947............	25,989,339	1,866	18,062,647	7,606,692
1948............	28,080,532	2,072	19,551,253	8,538,349
1949............	30,406,966	2,107	20,116,051	10,288,917

[1] Largely States with organized drainage districts and other corporate and private enterprises.
[2] Largely county-drain States. See text, p. 589.

Source: Department of Commerce, Bureau of the Census; *U. S. Census of Agriculture: 1950*, Vol. IV.

No. 694.—IRRIGATION ENTERPRISES—AREA IRRIGATED, 1939 AND 1949, AND CAPITAL INVESTED, 1940 AND 1950, BY STATES AND BY PRINCIPAL DRAINAGE BASINS

[Data are for the 17 Western States and Arkansas, Louisiana, and Florida. Minus sign (−) denotes decrease]

STATE OR DRAINAGE BASIN	AREA IRRIGATED				CAPITAL INVESTED			
	1939	1949			1940	1950		
		Total	Proportion of total	Increase 1939–49		Total	Proportion of total	Increase 1940–50
	Acres	Acres	Percent	Percent	Dollars	Dollars	Percent	Percent
20 States, total	21,136,101	26,233,215	100.0	24.1	1,059,105,122	1,887,738,707	100.0	78.2
Arkansas	161,601	419,101	1.6	159.3	5,766,895	14,171,467	.8	145.7
Louisiana	447,095	597,966	2.3	33.7	11,565,513	21,503,040	1.1	85.9
Florida	132,362	362,938	1.4	174.2	7,055,921	19,549,139	1.0	177.1
17 Western States, total	20,395,043	24,853,210	94.7	21.9	1,034,716,793	1,832,515,061	97.1	77.1
Arizona	653,263	979,114	3.7	49.9	83,526,608	137,575,193	7.3	64.7
California	5,009,568	6,596,839	25.2	30.2	318,889,218	646,474,185	33.9	100.8
Colorado	3,220,685	2,943,895	11.2	−8.6	106,846,343	163,295,813	8.7	52.8
Idaho	2,277,857	2,167,879	8.3	−4.8	102,585,798	129,973,554	6.9	26.7
Kansas	99,980	140,902	.5	41.0	2,153,886	5,882,265	.3	173.1
Montana	1,711,409	1,806,576	6.9	5.7	67,352,505	81,256,990	4.3	20.6
Nebraska	610,379	887,239	3.4	45.4	39,056,207	56,463,881	3.0	44.6
Nevada	739,863	722,896	2.8	−2.3	16,906,790	20,181,476	1.1	19.4
New Mexico	554,039	691,476	2.6	24.8	32,735,997	61,137,909	3.2	86.8
North Dakota	21,615	35,759	.1	65.4	1,755,489	2,957,763	.2	68.5
Oklahoma	4,160	44,209	.2	962.7	272,186	13,076,010	.7	4,704.1
Oregon	1,049,176	1,337,517	5.1	27.5	50,961,251	74,360,981	3.9	45.9
South Dakota	60,198	84,356	.3	40.1	5,395,610	6,617,914	.4	22.7
Texas	1,045,224	3,150,527	12.0	201.4	66,441,376	144,445,313	7.7	117.4
Utah	1,176,116	1,166,972	4.4	−.8	41,896,532	56,539,436	3.0	35.0
Washington	615,013	618,129	2.4	.5	56,415,196	178,289,988	9.4	216.0
Wyoming	1,486,498	1,474,835	5.6	−.8	41,522,801	59,986,390	3.2	44.5
PRINCIPAL DRAINAGE BASIN								
17 Western States, total	20,395,043	24,853,210	100.0	21.9	1,034,716,793	1,832,515,061	100.0	77.1
North Pacific Coast	3,914,119	3,974,363	16.0	1.5	212,872,435	386,371,143	21.1	81.5
South Pacific Coast	4,602,833	6,100,040	24.5	32.5	295,405,297	580,233,136	31.7	96.4
Great Basin	2,073,727	2,142,927	8.6	3.3	59,698,865	81,034,792	4.4	35.7
Gulf of California	2,646,618	2,973,557	12.0	12.4	156,027,509	274,209,408	15.0	75.7
Gulf of Mexico, excluding Mississippi River	1,987,475	3,858,135	15.5	94.1	99,664,965	181,375,505	9.9	82.0
Mississippi River	5,165,778	5,796,252	23.3	12.2	210,917,156	329,128,643	18.0	56.0
Hudson Bay (Red River of the North)	4,493	7,936	(1)	76.6	130,566	162,434	(1)	24.4

1 0.05 percent or less.

Source: Department of Commerce, Bureau of the Census; *U. S. Census of Agriculture: 1950*, Vol. III.

No. 695.—IRRIGATION ENTERPRISES—DAMS, RESERVOIRS, CANALS, PIPE LINES, AND WELLS, BY STATES AND BY PRINCIPAL DRAINAGE BASINS: 1950

[Data are for the 17 Western States and Arkansas, Louisiana, and Florida]

STATE OR DRAINAGE BASIN	Diversion dams	Reservoirs	RESERVOIRS WITH CAPACITY REPORTED		Canals and ditches	Pipe lines and siphons	WELLS	
			Reservoirs	Total capacity			Flowing	Pumped
	Number	Number	Number	Acre-feet	Miles	Miles	Number	Number
20 States, total	50,131	7,717	7,002	42,407,489	138,987	15,851	10,634	190,688
Arkansas	108	86	74	40,431	683	19	18	3,662
Louisiana	319	58	57	31,249	3,477	62	849	3,365
Florida	355	180	168	3,343	695	482	4,161	7,298
17 Western States, total	49,349	7,393	6,703	42,332,466	134,112	15,288	5,586	176,063
Arizona	552	269	237	3,625,679	4,800	316	214	4,361
California	4,708	1,684	1,502	8,711,667	21,183	10,068	573	72,147
Colorado	7,709	1,182	1,106	2,028,550	18,729	251	1,371	4,068
Idaho	5,121	364	313	5,124,956	15,159	487	466	896
Kansas	127	48	42	25,505	542	13	11	1,343
Montana	8,139	639	577	1,598,899	15,499	110	70	142
Nebraska	488	114	94	133,934	4,613	88	80	7,157
Nevada	4,065	202	176	687,179	3,388	123	289	254
New Mexico	1,286	476	448	3,186,401	5,763	168	196	3,846
North Dakota	15	11	6	1,101	193	7		4
Oklahoma	20	29	27	148,945	354	19		190
Oregon	6,231	538	471	2,421,138	8,406	572	138	2,770
South Dakota	281	100	94	204,698	964	8	14	27
Texas	438	566	508	1,402,883	10,092	1,168	152	15,070
Utah	3,080	511	476	2,224,361	9,621	300	1,926	560
Washington	1,861	222	205	6,436,522	4,964	1,514	69	2,008
Wyoming	5,228	458	419	4,370,044	9,822	56	96	248
PRINCIPAL DRAINAGE BASIN								
17 Western States, total	49,349	7,393	6,703	42,332,466	¹134,112	15,288	5,586	176,063
North Pacific Coast	14,776	1,108	985	14,375,186	30,572	2,627	879	5,727
South Pacific Coast	4,407	1,605	1,440	8,591,567	19,334	9,511	515	69,828
Great Basin	7,667	784	670	3,312,809	11,504	685	2,380	2,219
Gulf of California	6,619	1,061	966	4,657,623	19,904	745	209	5,488
Gulf of Mexico, excluding Mississippi River	2,105	964	883	4,050,962	16,171	1,321	1,554	14,389
Mississippi River	13,770	1,901	1,757	7,334,599	36,615	393	286	16,412
Hudson Bay (Red River of the North)	5	5	2	720	8	6		

¹ Total does not agree with sum of detail shown due to rounding; data reported in tenths of miles.

Source: Department of Commerce Bureau of the Census; *U. S. Census of Agriculture: 1950* Vol. III.

No. 696.—Irrigated Land in Farms, by States: 1939, 1944 and 1949

[In 1940, the schedule called for land from which irrigated crops were harvested in 1939, and for land irrigated in 1939 and used for grazing or pasture; in 1945 and 1950, for total land in farms irrigated in 1944 and 1949]

DIVISION AND STATE	FARMS REPORTING			ACRES IRRIGATED			BY SPRINKLER, 1949	
	1939	1944	1949	1939	1944	1949	Farms report-ing	Acres irri-gated
United States	299,604	288,195	305,061	17,962,830	20,539,470	25,787,455	25,049	639,987
The North	13,656	12,448	18,348	667,820	861,979	1,256,321	5,372	110,320
The South	32,639	29,008	39,087	1,601,384	2,372,296	4,553,481	3,098	137,894
The West	253,309	246,739	247,626	15,713,626	17,305,195	19,976,653	16,679	391,773
New England	328	322	1,581	2,846	12,153	31,450	922	18,752
Maine	33	3	123	143	100	2,299	111	2,131
New Hampshire	7	10	51	25	63	622	38	536
Vermont		2	22		6	303	14	259
Massachusetts	231	274	1,053	2,049	11,355	18,507	483	6,705
Rhode Island	10	9	52	109	132	1,631	42	1,462
Connecticut	57	24	280	520	496	8,088	245	7,660
Middle Atlantic	1,446	1,415	2,208	17,260	30,792	54,616	1,783	42,630
New York	567	646	838	5,948	10,316	19,248	732	16,361
New Jersey	580	675	1,033	7,956	11,712	28,117	811	19,058
Pennsylvania	299	94	287	3,356	8,764	7,251	240	6,611
East North Central	1,491	1,206	2,110	10,833	12,795	36,237	1,883	31,295
Ohio	658	463	458	4,536	4,178	5,706	431	5,134
Indiana	136	123	164	685	830	5,339	160	5,285
Illinois	72	47	139	307	368	1,510	119	1,400
Michigan	462	347	995	2,960	2,850	13,901	898	11,894
Wisconsin	163	226	354	2,345	4,569	9,781	275	7,492
West North Central	10,391	9,905	12,449	636,881	806,239	1,136,018	673	18,342
Minnesota	216	27	274	2,968	210	4,235	248	4,097
Iowa	88	54	76	2,258	1,197	1,386	54	1,149
Missouri	140	118	142	960	1,113	2,069	121	931
North Dakota	479	206	304	19,975	22,814	35,294	9	318
South Dakota	967	708	807	54,073	52,895	78,069	12	391
Nebraska	6,913	7,156	9,680	473,775	631,762	876,259	153	8,295
Kansas	1,578	636	1,166	82,872	96,248	138,686	76	3,121
South Atlantic	4,119	4,199	6,516	128,037	224,446	361,044	2,410	89,777
Delaware	2	3	10	7	22	404	10	404
Maryland	17	8	30	67	287	697	20	568
District of Columbia		16	2		45	13	2	13
Virginia	53	31	71	687	1,419	2,817	64	2,762
West Virginia	23	11	9	270	42	40	3	14
North Carolina	37	19	96	246	229	2,083	82	1,883
South Carolina	14	5	84	411	62	6,408	53	1,793
Georgia	26	14	139	158	423	3,161	92	2,249
Florida	3,947	4,092	6,075	126,191	221,917	365,421	2,084	80,091
East South Central	111	211	180	891	1,113	6,950	121	1,794
Kentucky	46	34	67	205	230	485	48	346
Tennessee	21	21	35	311	393	1,012	29	971
Alabama	37	153	34	281	487	367	31	300
Mississippi	7	3	44	94	3	5,086	13	177
West South Central	28,409	24,596	32,391	1,472,456	2,146,737	4,164,487	567	46,323
Arkansas	1,529	2,229	3,060	159,412	288,665	422,107	40	1,676
Louisiana	7,037	7,185	7,438	413,969	535,619	576,775	36	1,067
Oklahoma	275	74	466	4,437	2,237	34,071	76	2,072
Texas	19,568	15,110	21,427	894,638	1,320,216	3,131,534	415	41,508
Mountain	135,414	127,963	122,280	9,912,862	10,703,164	11,642,484	976	43,324
Montana	15,057	12,997	13,457	1,587,602	1,555,480	1,716,792	250	15,520
Idaho	29,898	28,571	29,413	1,895,048	2,026,280	2,137,237	344	9,995
Wyoming	8,637	7,793	7,831	1,284,027	1,353,873	1,431,767	14	581
Colorado	29,766	28,054	27,121	2,467,548	2,698,579	2,872,348	183	8,194
New Mexico	15,811	14,299	12,691	436,402	534,640	655,257	53	1,822
Arizona	10,339	9,634	7,822	575,464	736,027	963,560	51	4,011
Utah	22,612	23,543	21,126	911,135	1,124,081	1,137,995	48	1,766
Nevada	3,264	3,072	2,819	755,636	674,204	727,498	33	1,435
Pacific	117,895	118,776	125,346	5,800,764	6,602,031	8,334,169	15,703	348,449
Washington	17,426	15,974	16,928	493,982	520,153	589,035	3,411	67,852
Oregon	16,159	15,597	17,663	1,030,228	1,129,059	1,306,810	4,140	98,769
California	84,310	87,205	90,755	4,276,554	4,952,819	6,438,324	8,152	181,828

Source: Department of Commerce, Bureau of the Census; *U. S. Census of Agriculture: 1950*, Vols. II and III.

No. 697.—NUMBER OF DRAINAGE ENTERPRISES, LAND IN ENTERPRISES, AND FINANCIAL DATA, BY STATES: 1920 TO 1950

STATE	Approximate land area in 1950 (acres)	NUMBER OF DRAINAGE ENTERPRISES [1]		LAND IN DRAINAGE ENTERPRISES, TOTAL ACRES (NET) [1]				FUNDS COLLECTED JAN. 1, 1940 TO DEC. 31, 1949 [1]	
		1940	1950	1920	1930	1940	1950	Number of enterprises reporting	Amount ($1,000)
Total 49 States	1,819,122,640	(2)	(2)	65,405,026	84,468,062	84,947,620	102,608,321	(2)	206,919
Total 30 States [4]	1,451,365,760	9,402	14,006	22,291,273	36,687,719	39,872,238	50,655,190	3,471	144,416
Alabama	32,698,930	1	10	....	30,640	388,681	28,045	76,671	7	73
Arizona	72,688,000	23	23	30,640	388,681	298,632	197,263	3	22
Arkansas	33,713,000	346	844	3,470,501	4,631,155	4,562,736	4,701,095	199	10,313
California	100,312,600	1,067	2,047	1,108,319	2,283,714	2,687,194	3,554,576	152	24,120
Colorado	66,610,680	397	630	171,466	386,719	406,822	622,976	17	1,196
Florida	34,727,680	948	1,380	1,637,078	3,944,694	5,699,622	6,062,676	297	28,300
Georgia	37,426,120	52	56	65,433	94,255	94,374	96,369	23	132
Idaho	52,972,160	280	379	64,642	375,466	650,126	435,171	44	1,096
Illinois	35,795,400	1,095	1,632	3,909,049	5,032,062	5,091,364	5,370,526	572	17,000
Kansas	52,648,120	133	121	98,886	257,166	258,113	356,965	60	1,040
Louisiana	28,908,680	1,130	928	2,206,326	3,664,482	4,219,694	12,161,665	406	18,072
Maryland	6,332,940	126	93	....	....	183,337	325,615	20	139
Mississippi	30,236,720	278	441	1,691,444	2,965,406	3,890,618	3,025,744	367	8,215
Missouri	44,304,640	296	318	2,596,204	3,150,022	3,087,063	3,147,484	223	14,046
Montana	93,361,920	399	404	168,682	167,629	372,661	289,189	25	452
Nebraska	49,004,320	195	472	607,730	879,450	916,181	821,088	77	1,934
Nevada	70,204,960	44	82	15,940	162,980	153,373	251,164	5	194
New Jersey	4,814,080	...	5	....	....	....	11,206	5	30
New Mexico	77,767,040	182	232	140,219	176,392	205,835	344,961	5	356
New York	30,604,160	...	14	....	....	....	66,465	13	460
North Carolina	31,422,080	396	412	542,838	679,236	825,576	1,126,809	261	1,416
Oregon	61,641,600	336	1,087	4,000	211,182	348,826	415,858	30	1,063
South Carolina	19,395,200	24	45	140,081	206,349	204,396	349,011	37	358
Tennessee	26,730,080	155	151	368,671	695,560	601,592	615,536	48	427
Texas	168,646,220	180	545	2,166,128	2,883,356	4,218,580	5,794,786	96	11,686
Utah	52,701,440	240	471	112,623	156,052	202,068	202,155	29	919
Virginia	25,531,520	2	30	....	15,042	15,714	45,460	26	111
Washington	42,743,040	375	533	94,924	367,342	406,709	431,613	120	1,416
Wisconsin	35,011,200	398	206	794,549	902,713	761,208	514,700	53	606
Wyoming	62,403,840	175	150	95,474	245,703	312,662	335,951	19	582
Total 19 States [1]	367,755,680	(2)	(2)	43,213,765	47,780,274	47,064,801	52,053,141	(2)	65,564
Delaware	1,205,920	(3)	(3)	....	....	395,014	382,547	....	120
Indiana	23,171,300	(3)	(3)	10,087,163	10,214,014	10,121,982	11,017,709	(3)	6,729
Iowa	35,808,800	(3)	(3)	5,224,478	6,127,649	6,164,344	6,734,663	(3)	13,704
Kentucky	25,512,920	(3)	(3)	363,480	885,525	465,270	969,802	(3)	602
Michigan	36,494,080	(3)	(3)	9,736,171	9,180,851	8,978,386	10,194,430	(3)	21,326
Minnesota	51,205,760	(3)	(3)	9,232,708	11,474,683	10,960,499	11,399,962	(3)	15,982
North Dakota	44,836,480	(3)	(3)	1,340,326	1,064,142	1,375,041	1,572,230	(3)	964
Ohio	26,240,000	(3)	(3)	8,107,204	8,165,494	7,720,267	8,923,562	(3)	5,117
Oklahoma	44,179,840	(3)	(3)	12,180	170,158	197,646	300,894	(3)	376
South Dakota	48,963,040	(3)	(3)	222,089	697,755	676,472	707,953	(3)	471

See footnotes at end of table.

No. 697.—NUMBER OF DRAINAGE ENTERPRISES, LAND IN ENTERPRISES, AND FINANCIAL DATA, BY STATES: 1920 TO 1950—Continued

STATE	CAPITAL INVESTED PRIOR TO DATE OF CENSUS ($1,000)			COST OF CONSTRUCTION AND OPERATION AND MAINTENANCE, JAN. 1, 1940, TO DEC. 31, 1949 [1]				OUTSTANDING INDEBTEDNESS DEC. 31 OF YEAR PRECEDING CENSUS [1]			
				Total		Cost of new works (for lands not previously drained)		1940		1950	
	1920	1930	1940	Number of enterprises reporting	Amount ($1,000)	Number of enterprises reporting	Amount ($1,000)	Number of enterprises reporting	Amount ($1,000)	Number of enterprises reporting	Amount ($1,000)
Total 48 States	372,274	686,260	691,726	(2)	178,034	(2)	23,872	4,626	137,745	(2)	63,422
Total 38 States[4]	188,850	394,682	411,479	3,436	116,232	983	16,288	1,664	126,542	696	52,893
Alabama			410	8	70	7	59	1	41	1	8
Arizona	414	1,875	1,119					2	94		
Arkansas	14,147	37,533	39,451	127	5,540	28	392	139	13,235	49	3,806
California	47,687	66,452	70,144	159	15,927	16	135	90	17,123	39	3,806
Colorado	1,082	4,359	4,890	47	778	5	22	38	1,853	13	217
Florida	13,847	45,468	43,357	207	18,603	63	2,707	94	32,296	51	12,760
Georgia	795	1,919	2,065	22	133	23	107	62	410	14	332
Idaho	1,669	5,112	7,567	44	906	12	133	33	1,906	19	563
Illinois	43,595	74,566	72,567	892	16,860	103	1,217	158	6,974	80	2,850
Kansas	937	2,701	3,734	60	1,117	10	279	20	1,806	14	235
Louisiana	9,022	20,753	23,362	392	16,652	142	5,316	140	10,798	80	8,685
Maryland			44	28	183	22	130			12	31
Mississippi	7,076	23,601	23,260	345	5,703	156	441	233	6,688	92	3,052
Missouri	20,723	47,340	49,050	225	8,282	9	114	169	8,174	70	2,658
Montana	665	1,879	2,828	25	462	9	166	17	1,503	8	130
Nebraska	4,589	6,847	7,579	75	1,533	27	758	36	1,279	6	204
Nevada	118	1,350	1,338	5	194	2	62	5	649	1	4
New Jersey				5	39	5	34				
New Mexico	1,711	3,279	5,722	5	75			13	3,901	3	77
New York				12	177	7	75			3	78
North Carolina	3,624	4,719	5,468	250	1,439	158	738	32	687	8	151
Oregon	200	4,166	5,482	50	2,176	17	477	30	1,782	19	341
South Carolina	582	1,265	1,241	33	319	27	207	24	636	7	40
Tennessee	2,926	6,367	6,502	26	271	23	256	133	1,898	3	
Texas	5,701	12,003	14,047	89	9,534	32	1,822	64	4,574	24	10,872
Utah	1,005	4,772	4,869	30	837	13	29	18	2,769	4	31
Virginia		242	201	26	111	27	96	2	129		
Washington	1,397	4,638	5,333	131	1,541	24	204	54	490	44	195
Wisconsin	4,163	6,207	4,255	92	611	15	296	39	392	16	85
Wyoming	1,176	5,251	5,595	14	163	2	12	26	4,455	16	1,069
Total 10 States[5]	183,424	285,568	280,245	(2)	68,802	(2)	7,584	2,374	11,203	(2)	16,529
Delaware			455	(2)	173	(2)	3	6	1		
Indiana	31,148	54,111	47,540	(2)	8,206	(2)	786	20	429	(2)	221
Iowa	49,627	77,479	75,374	(2)	13,303	(2)	2,143	277	1,287	(2)	2,499
Kentucky	1,522	5,358	4,648	(2)	711	(2)	45	33	759	(2)	58
Michigan	24,684	37,677	40,412	(2)	20,236	(2)	2,556	673	810	(2)	2,477
Minnesota	42,017	64,140	65,576	(2)	18,311	(2)	1,595	768	6,035	(2)	3,774
North Dakota	2,208	3,149	3,673	(2)	890	(2)	245	5	184	(2)	183
Ohio	30,680	36,836	35,216	(2)	6,189	(2)	148	313	303	(2)	300
Oklahoma	76	2,284	1,971	(2)	299	(2)	62	13	262	(2)	197
South Dakota	1,461	4,535	5,079	(2)	483			20	1,133	(2)	722

[1] Including irrigation enterprises having their own drainage. An interstate enterprise is counted in each State in which a part is located, but is counted only once in the total.
[2] Data for irrigation enterprises not included in 1950.
[3] Not available.
[4] Largely States with organized drainage districts and other corporate and private enterprises.
[5] Largely county-drain States. See text, p. 589.

Source: Department of Commerce, Bureau of the Census; U. S. Census of Agriculture: 1950, Vol. IV.

No. 698.—NUMBER AND AREA OF DRAINAGE ENTERPRISES CLASSIFIED BY SIZE: 1920 TO 1950

SIZE GROUP	Number of enterprises, 1950	AREA OF ENTERPRISES (ACRES) [1]						
		All drainage States			30 States [2]			
		1920	1930	1940	1920	1930	1940	1950
Total	14,066	95,629,291	128,495,678	132,528,451	23,657,216	41,644,155	45,397,327	54,617,706
Under 100 acres	} 8,273	} 1,152,025 {	324,157	525,455	} 12,395	{ 2,727	4,362	} 608,554
100 to 199 acres			1,040,664	1,446,870		12,057	19,496	
200 to 499 acres	5,222,615	5,964,023	7,093,485	99,112	147,705	230,974	} 1,098,279
500 to 999 acres	1,586	9,091,516	11,130,096	11,234,727	308,736	910,371	965,985	
1,000 to 1,999 acres	1,398	} 29,522,536 {	34,074,009	{ 14,558,019	} 3,153,867	4,996,968	{ 1,726,342	} 1,962,013
2,000 to 4,999 acres	1,314			20,511,078			3,960,638	4,162,149
5,000 to 9,999 acres	651	13,357,936	15,865,002	16,387,515	2,820,328	4,484,862	4,542,720	4,826,261
10,000 to 19,999 acres	433	} 23,826,149	35,075,951	{ 16,964,180	} 9,423,712	14,768,991	{ 6,041,949	6,068,763
20,000 to 49,999 acres	268			20,141,844			10,047,929	7,636,801
50,000 to 99,999 acres	87	8,605,536	11,403,982	10,760,472	4,880,449	6,304,255	6,816,045	6,984,562
100,000 to 199,999 acres	25	} 4,850,978	10,218,995	{ 5,925,431	} 2,868,617	} 10,014,219	{ 3,794,141	2,568,363
200,000 to 499,999 acres	19			3,155,492			2,954,853	6,571,335
500,000 acres and over	12		3,378,199	4,123,883			4,123,382	12,172,486

[1] The sum of the areas in the individual enterprises without deduction for area in more than one enterprise (overlapped).

[2] Largely States with organized drainage districts and other corporate and private enterprises. See text, p. 589.

Source: Department of Commerce, Bureau of the Census; *U. S. Census of Agriculture: 1950*, Vol. IV.

No. 699.—FEDERAL RECLAMATION IRRIGATION PROJECTS—ACREAGE AND CROP VALUE: 1939 TO 1951

[Acreage in thousands and value in thousands of dollars. Includes projects constructed by United States and those for which supplemental water is furnished from storage works built by United States. Net area in cultivation and value exclude data for lands on Government projects cropped without irrigation]

YEAR	ENTIRE AREA				WARREN ACT LAND [1]			REGULAR AND SUPPLEMENTAL WATER PROJECTS			
	Irrigable acreage	Irrigated acreage	Net area in cultivation	Crop value	Irrigated acreage	Net area in cultivation	Crop value	Irrigable acreage	Irrigated acreage	Net area in cultivation	Crop value
1939	3,890	3,141	3,078	114,083	1,218	1,175	40,313	2,493	1,923	1,903	73,770
1940	4,180	3,391	3,316	117,789	1,238	1,177	37,600	2,709	2,153	2,139	80,008
1941	4,946	3,389	3,380	159,896	1,140	1,202	49,486	2,850	2,199	2,178	110,400
1942	4,849	3,881	3,822	272,049	1,608	1,562	116,429	3,392	2,278	2,205	155,620
1943	4,854	4,055	4,014	388,671	1,633	1,615	170,607	2,882	2,422	2,399	218,064
1944	4,940	4,164	4,139	411,226	1,695	1,664	186,543	2,916	2,469	2,475	224,683
1945	5,030	4,163	4,196	435,184	1,746	1,731	202,639	2,958	2,417	2,465	232,545
1946	5,151	4,322	4,397	530,624	1,808	1,830	250,913	3,038	2,514	2,567	279,711
1947	5,167	4,462	4,554	555,420	1,832	1,871	254,946	3,092	2,630	2,683	300,475
1948	5,390	4,559	4,700	534,624	1,894	1,939	257,463	3,221	2,665	2,760	277,161
1949	5,679	4,821	4,916	516,329	2,028	2,067	238,981	3,296	2,792	2,849	277,348
1950	6,025	5,077	5,189	578,238	2,220	2,271	290,554	3,396	2,857	2,918	287,694
1951	6,713	5,876	5,942	821,722	2,280	2,318	376,314	4,049	3,596	3,624	445,408

[1] Warren Act contracts are those which provide for sale of excess water to irrigation districts, i. e., water over and above project requirements. Lands served are usually located outside project proper. The act also provides for joint construction and financing of irrigation works by Federal Government and irrigation districts.

Source: Department of the Interior, Bureau of Reclamation: *Annual Report of Secretary* and official records.

No. 700.—FEDERAL RECLAMATION IRRIGATION PROJECTS—CHARGES AND RENTALS, BY PROJECT, TO JUNE 30, 1952

[In thousands of dollars. Cumulative from inception of program; data by project for fiscal year only]

STATE AND PROJECT	CONSTRUCTION WATER-RIGHT CHARGES [1]			OPERATION AND MAINTENANCE CHARGES			RENTALS OF IRRIGATION WATER		
	Amount due	Amount paid	Due and unpaid	Amount due	Amount paid	Due and unpaid	Amount due	Amount paid	Due and unpaid
Total	99,272	98,011	1,261	56,666	56,558	108	24,912	24,784	128
Arizona: Gila							211	198	18
Salt River	212	212							
Arizona-California:									
All-American Canal (Imperial Div.)				40	6	34			
Yuma and Yuma Aux	110	106	4	177	169	8	6	6	
California: Cachuma							3	3	
Central Valley							1,295	1,294	1
Orland	54	44	10	94	93	1	1	1	
Colorado:									
Cole.-Big Thompson							4	4	
Fruitgrowers Dam	6	6							
Grand Valley	66	66					23	23	
Mancos				7	7				
Pine River	22	19	4	5	5		3	3	
Uncompahgre	60	60							
Idaho: Boise	523	514	9	31	31		258	156	95
Minidoka	377	375	2	84	84				
Rathdrum Prairie-Post Falls	5	5		3	3				
Montana: Bitter Root	14	14							
Frenchtown	5	5							
Huntley	38	38							
Milk River	101	63	38	146	110	36	1	1	
Missoula Valley				2	2				
Missouri River Basin:									
Savage Unit				6	6				
Sun River	109	108	1	5	5				
Montana-North Dakota:									
Lower Yellowstone	142	94	48						
Missouri River Basin:									
Missouri-Souris Dist							22	15	7
Nebraska: Mirage Flats	1	1							
Nebraska-Wyoming:									
North Platte	301	286	15	107	93	14			
Nevada: Humboldt	34	34							
Newlands	95	95							
Truckee Storage	25	25							
New Mexico: Carlsbad	64	64		7	7				
Tucumcari							203	203	
New Mexico-Texas:									
Rio Grande	212	212		940	940				
Oklahoma: W. C. Austin	77	77		175	175				
Oregon: Arnold	4	4							
Baker	6	6							
Burnt River	15	15							
Deschutes	37	37					244	244	
Umatilla	35	3	32				18	18	
Vale	88	88		5	5				
Oregon-California:									
Klamath	101	100	1	120	119	1	212	207	5
Oregon-Idaho: Owyhee	216	216		1	1				
South Dakota: Belle Fourche	39	39		2	2				
Rapid Valley	13	13		5	5				
Texas: Balmorhea	3	3							
Utah: Hyrum	18	18							
Moon Lake	40	40							
Newton	9	9							
Ogden River	74	74							
Provo River	718	718					73	73	
Salt River Basin	88	88		7	7				
Sanpete	9	9							
Scofield	5	5							
Strawberry Valley	71	71							
Washington:									
Columbia Basin	3	3					30	30	
Okanogan	9	9							
Yakima	374	374		407	393	14			
Wyoming: Kendrick							19	19	
Riverton	82	41	41				22	21	1
Shoshone	135	135		7	7		66	65	1
Total, prior years	94,426	[2]93,370	1,056	56,283	[2]56,283		22,203	[2]22,203	

[1] Construction water-right charges equal amount for amortization of allocated construction charges.
[2] Includes charges maturing in prior years but paid during fiscal year 1952.

Source: Department of the Interior, Bureau of Reclamation; official records.

No. 701.—FEDERAL RECLAMATION IRRIGATION PROJECTS—ACREAGE AND CROP VALUE, BY PROJECT: 1951

STATE AND PROJECT	PROJECTS ENTIRELY CONSTRUCTED BY BUREAU			PROJECTS FURNISHED SUPPLEMENTAL WATER FROM WORKS CONSTRUCTED BY BUREAU			SPECIAL AND WARREN ACT CONTRACTORS RECEIVING WATER FROM BUREAU WORKS[3]		
	Irrigable acreage[1]	Acreage in cultivation	Crop value (1,000)	Irrigable acreage[1]	Acreage in cultivation	Crop value (1,000)	Irrigable acreage[1]	Acreage in cultivation	Crop value (1,000)
Total[3]	2,782,007	2,345,125	$325,520	1,267,402	1,168,602	$106,063	2,663,606	2,317,714	$375,314
Arizona:									
Gila	27,538	14,401	2,706				1,610	1,610	212
Salt River	238,907	224,257	64,939				95,499	83,788	24,580
Arizona-California: Yuma	71,159	57,177	15,800						
California:									
All-American Canal:									
Coachella Division	60,715	33,489	18,778						
Imperial Division							517,000	440,000	75,250
Central Valley							726,609	546,988	144,730
Orland	19,375	17,130	1,822						
Colorado:									
Colorado-Big Thompson				615,000	615,000	63,300			
Fruitgrowers Dam				2,662	2,099	280			
Grand Valley	40,471	27,205	3,642				8,045	7,685	1,089
Mancos				8,592	7,389	367			
Paonia	11,500	10,063	1,012						
Pine River				35,812	33,899	1,144			
Pine River Indian Irrigation				9,493	9,273	334			
Uncompahgre	71,969	57,349	5,316				17,112	16,858	760
Idaho:									
Lewiston Orchards	3,504	2,681	562						
Minidoka	218,281	197,467	17,432	112,000	103,606	6,865	727,940	704,273	61,368
Preston Bench				6,660	4,744	389			
Rathdrum Prairie	4,196	3,256	280						
Idaho-Oregon: Boise	224,001	194,150	19,682				132,197	128,375	12,997
Montana:									
Bitter Root	16,665	16,309	571						
Buffalo Rapids	22,524	21,695	1,211						
Frenchtown	4,985	3,027	175						
Huntley	32,508	16,991	1,066						
Intake	881	473	25						
Milk River	124,041	63,267	2,937						
Missoula Valley	977	492	13						
Missouri River Basin:									
Yellowstone Division:									
Savage Unit	2,216	1,940	63						
Sun River	97,275	85,665	2,442						
Montana-North Dakota:									
Lower Yellowstone	57,200	49,223	2,776						
Nebraska: Mirage Flats	11,659	11,331	688						
Nebraska-Wyoming:									
North Platte	223,768	201,871	13,287				108,715	105,382	6,688
Nevada:									
Humboldt				40,012	25,438	1,811			
Newlands	72,136	52,317	2,456						
Truckee Storage				28,793	24,298	2,233			
New Mexico:									
Carlsbad	25,055	24,717	4,451						
Fort Sumner	6,500	5,188	486						
Tucumcari	42,214	33,318	1,978						
New Mexico-Texas:									
Rio Grande	[4] 155,000	147,353	43,469				20,000	17,752	4,149
North Dakota:									
Buford-Trenton	8,199	8,003	396						
Oklahoma: W. C. Austin	47,810	46,322	5,160						
Oregon:									
Arnold				4,315	3,267	226			
Baker				7,312	7,305	299			
Burnt River				15,291	15,240	651			
Deschutes	50,000	47,582	7,938	46,713	43,082	5,150	2,520		
Grants Pass				10,350	7,544	884			
Ochoco							8,500	7,940	924
Umatilla	18,134	12,066	624	14,352	10,340	822			
Vale	32,000	30,910	2,627						

See footnotes at end of table.

No. 701.—FEDERAL RECLAMATION IRRIGATION PROJECTS—ACREAGE AND CROP VALUE, BY PROJECT: 1951—Continued

STATE AND PROJECT	PROJECTS ENTIRELY CONSTRUCTED BY BUREAU			PROJECTS FURNISHED SUPPLEMENTAL WATER FROM WORKS CONSTRUCTED BY BUREAU			SPECIAL AND WARREN ACT CONTRACTORS RECEIVING WATER FROM BUREAU WORKS [2]		
	Irrigable acreage [1]	Acreage in cultivation	Crop value (1,000)	Irrigable acreage [1]	Acreage in cultivation	Crop value (1,000)	Irrigable acreage [1]	Acreage in cultivation	Crop value (1,000)
Oregon-California: Klamath	85, 369	74, 992	$12, 842				87, 286	81, 460	$8, 314
Oregon-Idaho: Owyhee	105, 126	97, 525	11, 911				13, 800	13, 110	2, 781
South Dakota:									
Belle Fourche	59, 129	54, 137	2, 328						
Rapid Valley				8, 900	7, 101	$227			
Texas: Balmorhea				10, 191	8, 086	1, 169			
Utah:									
Hyrum				6, 475	5, 674	386			
Mona Lake				75, 233	58, 729	1, 544			
Newton				2, 552	1, 962	143			
Ogden River				22, 861	15, 964	2, 061			
Provo River				46, 609	40, 680	4, 605			
Sanpete				13, 653	12, 911	419			
Scofield				14, 754	14, 154	992			
Strawberry Valley	40, 069	37, 262	2, 729				3, 987	3, 864	327
Weber River				108, 917	90, 817	11, 787			
Washington:									
Columbia Basin	6, 915	5, 335	739						
Okanogan	5, 342	3, 514	1, 127						
Yakima	262, 645	217, 914	41, 663				190, 841	162, 329	32, 174
Wyoming:									
Kendrick	14, 482	9, 341	347						
Riverton	61, 299	52, 026	2, 223				1, 945	1, 871	81
Shoshone	96, 318	74, 394	3, 465						

[1] Area for which Bureau is prepared to supply water.
[2] Includes acreage provided either a full or supplemental irrigation water supply under the Warren Act and other special service contracts.
[3] Excludes 110,572 acres of temporarily suspended, other leased and water rental lands (crop value $11,508,000).
[4] Although there are 178,003 acres that can be irrigated within project limits, area for which there is considered to be a safe and reliable water supply is 155,000 acres.

Source: Department of the Interior, Bureau of Reclamation: *1951 Crop Summary and Related Data, Federal Reclamation Projects.*

No. 702.—Hydroelectric Plants on Reclamation Projects, Operating and Under Construction, as of December 31, 1952

STATE AND PROJECT	Plant	Year of initial operation	Present name-plate capacity (kw.)	Ultimate name-plate capacity (kw.)
Total			4,600,327	[1] 7,796,877
Constructed and operated by Bureau of Reclamation, total			4,421,200	4,609,700
Arizona-Nevada: Boulder Canyon	Hoover [5]	1936	1,346,800	1,322,300
Davis Dam	Davis	1951	225,000	225,000
Arizona-California: Parker	Parker	1942	120,000	120,000
California: Central Valley	Keswick	1949	75,000	75,000
	Shasta	1944	379,000	379,000
Yuma	Siphon Drop	1926	1,600	1,600
Colorado: Colorado-Big Thompson	Estes	1950	45,000	45,000
	Green Mountain	1943	21,600	21,600
	Marys Lake	1951	8,100	8,100
Idaho: Boise	Anderson Ranch	1950	27,000	[4] 40,350
	Black Canyon	1925	8,000	8,000
	Boise Diversion	1912	1,500	1,500
Minidoka	Minidoka	1909	13,400	13,400
Montana: Hungry Horse	Hungry Horse	1952	142,500	285,000
New Mexico: Rio Grande	Elephant Butte	1940	24,300	24,300
South Dakota: Missouri River Basin	Angostura	1951	1,200	1,200
Washington: Columbia Basin	Grand Coulee [4][5]	1941	1,974,000	1,974,000
Yakima	Prosser [6]	1922	2,400	2,400
Wyoming: Kendrick	Seminoe	1939	32,400	32,400
Missouri River Basin	Boysen	1952	15,000	15,000
	Kortes	1950	36,000	36,000
North Platte and Missouri River Basin	Guernsey	1927	4,800	14,800
North Platte	Lingle	1919	1,400	1,400
Riverton	Pilot Butte	1925	1,600	1,600
Shoshone	Heart Mountain	1948	5,000	5,000
	Shoshone	1922	5,000	5,000
Constructed by Bureau of Reclamation but operated by others, total			30,327	30,327
Arizona: Salt River	Arizona Falls [7]	1912	850	850
	Cross Cut [7]	1914	5,100	5,100
	Roosevelt	1909	15,400	15,400
	S. Consolidated [7]	1912	1,600	1,600
Colorado: Grand Valley	Grand Valley (Palisade)	1937	3,000	3,000
Nevada: Newlands	Lahontan	1911	1,640	1,640
Oregon: Deschutes	Cove [8]	1946	1,500	1,500
Utah: Strawberry Valley	Spanish Fork [9]	1916	1,550	1,550
Washington: Yakima	Rocky Ford	1916	187	187
Constructed and operated by water users organizations, total			72,900	82,900
Arizona: Salt River	Chandler [10]	1919	600	600
	Horse Mesa [10]	1927	30,000	30,000
	Mormon Flat [10]	1926	7,080	7,080
	Stewart Mountain [10]	1930	10,400	10,400
California: All-American	Drop Nos. 3 and 4 [11]	1941	24,000	24,000
Oregon: Klamath	"C" Canal Drop [12]	1924	800	800
Constructed and operated by Army Engineers, total			86,000	195,000
Montana: Fort Peck [10]	Fort Peck	1943	85,000	185,000
Under construction by Bureau of Reclamation, total				542,050
Alaska: Eklutna	Eklutna	1954		30,000
California: Central Valley	Folsom	1954		108,000
	Nimbus	1955		13,500
Colorado: Colorado-Big Thompson	Flatiron	1953		69,700
	Polehill	1953		33,200
Idaho: Palisades	Palisades	1956		114,000
Montana: Missouri River Basin	Canyon Ferry	1953		50,000
	Kroll	1952		1,000
	Tiber	1957		2,000
	Little Porcupine	1955		15,000
Washington: Yakima-Kennewick	Chandler	1955		12,000
Wyoming: Kendrick	Alcova	1954		36,000
Under construction by Army Engineers, total [13]				1,345,000
North Dakota: Missouri River Basin	Garrison	1955		400,000
South Dakota: Missouri River Basin	Ft. Randall	1953		320,000
	Gavins Point	1954		100,000
	Oahe	1958		525,000

[1] Includes 1,041,800 kilowatt capacity of 26 additional plants authorized but not under construction.
[2] Power plant units operated by power allottees under agency contract.
[3] 27,000 kilowatts; space provided in plant for third unit.
[4] Power marketed by Bonneville Power Administration.
[5] Main units with a nameplate rating at 105,000 kilowatts have continuous operating capacity of 130,000 kilowatts.
[6] Prosser will be removed when Chandler is constructed.
[7] Power plant constructed by Bureau of Reclamation with Salt River Valley Water Users' Association funds.
[8] Unit No. 3 installed in Pacific Power and Light Company's Cove No. 2 plant.
[9] Three plants: (a) Spanish Fork (upper); (b) Spanish Fork (lower); (c) Payson.
[10] Salt River Valley Water Users' Association's plant. [11] Imperial Irrigation District's plant.
[12] Enterprise Irrigation District's plant. [13] Power to be marketed by Bureau of Reclamation.

Source: Department of the Interior, Bureau of Reclamation; official records.

No. 703.—Growth of Conservation Districts, by Fiscal Years, to June 30, 1952

[See text, p. 590]

YEAR ENDING JUNE 30	DISTRICTS ORGANIZED		TOTAL AREA IN DISTRICTS		DISTRICTS WITH SUPPLEMENTAL MEMORANDUMS	
	Each year	Cumulative total	New districts and additions	Cumulative total	Each year	Cumulative total
	Number	*Number*	*1,000 acres*	*1,000 acres*	*Number*	*Number*
1938	69	69	36, 107	36, 107	34	34
1939	92	161	52, 339	88, 446	79	113
1940	153	314	101, 306	189, 752	120	233
1941 [1]	241	555	145, 091	334, 843	201	434
1942	230	785	122, 727	457, 570	219	653
1943	116	901	60, 102	517, 672	159	812
1944	213	1, 114	102, 819	620, 491	171	983
1945 [2]	232	1, 346	120, 368	740, 859	221	1, 204
1946 [3]	292	1, 638	143, 119	883, 977	223	1, 427
1947	251	1, 889	118, 991	1, 002, 969	315	1, 742
1948	144	2, 033	111, 035	1, 114, 003	174	1, 916
1949	131	2, 164	64, 760	1, 178, 763	158	2, 074
1950	121	2, 285	74, 721	1, 253, 484	133	2, 207
1951	88	2, 373	51, 626	1, 305, 110	122	2, 329
1952	94	2, 467	53, 803	1, 358, 913	89	2, 418

[1] Includes wind-erosion districts and grazing districts for 1941 and subsequent years
[2] Totals at end of each year hereafter are net, including corrections and adjustments made during year.
[3] Includes Imperial irrigation district, California.

Source: Department of Agriculture, Soil Conservation Service; *Report of Chief of Soil Conservation Service.*

No. 704.—Conservation Practices Newly Applied in Conservation Districts, with Soil Conservation Service Assistance, Fiscal Years: 1949 to 1952

[See text, p. 590]

PRACTICES	Unit	1949	1950	1951	1952	Cumulative to June 30, 1952 [1]
Contour farming	Acres	3, 352, 922	3, 491, 511	3, 185, 039	2, 910, 867	28, 601, 869
Cover cropping	do	2, 614, 797	3, 111, 387	2, 809, 720	3, 296, 085	19, 171, 931
Stubble mulching	do	6, 611, 273	7, 140, 297	6, 893, 178	6, 316, 467	47, 957, 022
Strip cropping	do	692, 995	829, 200	880, 383	805, 125	7, 370, 853
Seeding range and pasture	do	1, 358, 856	1, 876, 832	2, 306, 365	2, 920, 412	12, 213, 204
Woodland management	do	3, 077, 106	3, 391, 551	859	2, 844, 943	18, 882, 506
Farm and ranch ponds	Number	31, 206	37, 780	3, 068, 843	61, 578	277, 122
Tree planting [2]	Acres	107, 057	126, 784	187, 435	154, 883	931, 799
Terraces	Miles	96, 621	100, 612	006	66, 853	858, 967
Diversions	do	5, 126	5, 892	78, 420	5, 526	36, 569
Farm drainage	Acres	1, 103, 412	1, 161, 402	1, 173, 582	1, 314, 682	7, 545, 646
Irrigation land preparation	do	264, 905	315, 519	384, 690	407, 851	1, 836, 923
Improved water application	do	562, 667	617, 606	616, 371	538, 373	3, 770, 108
Combined treatment	do	22, 115, 560	26, 071, 342	25, 596, 642	27, 216, 161	162, 726, 125

[1] These data are for first-time application only and do not include duplication of acreage for reapplication or maintenance of those same practices year after year.
[2] Includes acreage of windbreak planting.

Source: Department of Agriculture, Soil Conservation Service; *Report of Chief of Soil Conservation Service.*

No. 705.—SOIL CONSERVATION DISTRICTS—SUMMARY, BY STATES AND OTHER AREAS: CUMULATIVE TO JUNE 30, 1952

[See text, p. 590]

STATE OR OTHER AREA	Date district law became effective	Districts organized [1]	APPROXIMATE AREA AND FARMS WITHIN ORGANIZED DISTRICTS			Districts having memo. of understanding with D. A. [2]	SOIL CONSERVATION DISTRICT COOPERATORS [3]		
			Total area	Farms and ranches	Land in farms		Cooperators	Total area	Treated area
		Number	1,000 acres	Number	1,000 acres	Number	Number	1,000 acres	1,000 acres
Total		2,447	1,566,912	4,956,876	956,140	2,436	1,119,571	444,423	162,728
Cont. U. S.		2,431	1,551,149	4,955,650	955,457	2,396	1,119,250	831,689	152,472
Alabama	Mar. 18, 1939	12	32,688	225,368	19,048	12	47,106	7,840	5,289
Arizona	June 14, 1941	46	1,390	8,048	1,390	46	4,018	914	435
Arkansas	July 1, 1937	66	33,141	188,721	14,880	64	47,970	5,415	4,426
California	June 26, 1938	74	35,960	40,626	12,433	79	16,871	3,914	1,645
Colorado	May 6, 1937	95	34,365	39,524	22,663	95	11,586	10,706	6,159
Connecticut	July 18, 1945	7	2,486	19,371	1,273	7	3,604	204	109
Delaware	Apr. 3, 1943	3	1,266	8,296	923	3	1,261	314	78
Florida	June 30, 1937	53	27,049	54,929	11,710	53	14,347	3,941	2,383
Georgia	Mar. 23, 1937	27	37,226	224,005	22,586	25	74,541	14,321	9,386
Idaho	Mar. 9, 1939	31	20,608	23,009	8,097	31	9,086	3,240	1,344
Illinois	July 9, 1937	95	32,116	194,822	30,225	95	27,414	4,692	2,163
Indiana	Mar. 15, 1937	86	14,812	104,901	12,304	86	13,274	1,481	1,045
Iowa	July 4, 1939	100	34,467	205,934	34,467	90	33,500	6,144	3,699
Kansas	Apr. 10, 1937	105	52,107	187,630	46,572	105	45,988	14,334	8,094
Kentucky	June 11, 1940	119	34,378	226,992	15,946	119	47,689	4,006	2,554
Louisiana	July 27, 1938	26	27,045	129,563	9,992	26	34,412	5,073	2,554
Maine	Mar. 25, 1941	15	15,496	39,745	4,370	15	7,980	1,019	349
Maryland	June 1, 1937	23	6,090	40,210	4,043	23	11,113	1,628	647
Massachusetts	June 28, 1945	15	5,025	36,915	2,478	15	4,487	808	104
Michigan	July 23, 1937	67	24,676	144,999	15,361	67	17,535	2,194	841
Minnesota	Apr. 26, 1937	54	17,514	93,390	15,607	53	15,403	2,852	1,333
Mississippi	Apr. 4, 1938	74	50,349	253,526	19,616	74	48,916	8,198	5,445
Missouri	July 23, 1943	26	8,794	54,353	8,170	27	7,201	1,398	617
Montana [5]	Feb. 28, 1939	79	80,784	34,277	48,185	77	9,811	20,317	9,793
Nebraska	May 18, 1937	87	45,250	311,845	47,753	87	34,604	11,266	4,980
Nevada	Mar. 30, 1937	26	43,028	1,885	3,564	22	1,113	785	312
New Hampshire	May 10, 1945	10	5,775	18,786	2,017	10	3,152	562	225
New Jersey	July 1, 1937	8	4,785	36,143	1,837	8	4,641	885	197
New Mexico	Mar. 17, 1937	60	55,003	26,273	39,311	60	10,571	21,822	12,373
New York	July 20, 1940	38	18,560	106,637	12,884	38	21,675	2,982	1,118
North Carolina	Mar. 22, 1937	28	28,901	268,279	17,484	28	57,870	5,989	3,778
North Dakota	Mar. 16, 1937	79	43,147	67,418	38,812	79	20,632	12,148	7,265
Ohio	June 5, 1941	83	23,858	206,708	20,743	82	20,383	2,881	1,412
Oklahoma	Apr. 15, 1937	85	43,625	162,507	35,210	85	62,436	15,368	8,320
Oregon	Apr. 7, 1939	36	13,563	17,351	7,099	36	4,472	2,231	1,050
Pennsylvania	July 3, 1937	28	12,825	82,086	7,023	28	15,582	1,973	469
Rhode Island	Apr. 26, 1943	3	677	2,603	265	3	851	101	64
South Carolina	Apr. 17, 1937	44	19,580	147,745	11,022	44	32,463	5,479	3,822
South Dakota	July 1, 1937	53	78,280	49,841	29,280	53	21,308	12,383	8,271
Tennessee	Mar. 10, 1939	58	17,046	155,273	12,608	53	21,934	3,029	1,947
Texas [6]	Apr. 24, 1939	163	186,349	364,595	126,745	187	121,272	61,793	24,803
Utah	Mar. 23, 1937	47	44,264	28,187	18,038	45	7,704	4,141	1,969
Vermont	Apr. 18, 1939	13	5,931	26,490	3,931	13	6,575	1,290	247
Virginia	Apr. 1, 1938	28	22,906	182,910	14,808	28	26,145	4,425	2,049
Washington	Mar. 17, 1939	72	35,861	57,945	15,147	60	18,099	6,643	3,906
West Virginia	June 12, 1939	14	15,279	97,380	8,606	14	24,473	2,390	1,452
Wisconsin	July 1, 1937	68	31,357	166,018	22,558	63	34,464	3,896	1,886
Wyoming	May 22, 1941	38	34,219	8,685	14,422	38	4,187	5,329	1,982
Alaska	Mar. 25, 1947	9	4,376	1,265	137	8	218	28	4
Hawaii	May 19, 1947	8	1,417	5,008	581	8	800	237	44
Puerto Rico	July 1, 1946	17	1,896	55,508	1,586	17	7,642	485	155
Virgin Islands	June —, 1946	2	85	1,150	85	2	375	84	21

[1] For specific procedure on organization of soil conservation districts, see respective State soil conservation district law. By provision of most State district laws, State soil conservation committee has responsibility for organization of districts. Local district governing bodies administer affairs of each individual district.

[2] Soil Conservation Service furnishes technical and other assistance to practically all districts that have entered into memorandums of understanding with Department of Agriculture.

[3] Includes all farmer-district cooperative agreements for initial, advanced and basic conservation plans (formerly shown as active conservation plans only, not including initial and advanced agreements). Cancellations caused by death, change in ownership, or mutual consent have been deducted. Data on plans and treated areas included only work done through farmer-district cooperative agreements since Aug. 1937 with assistance of Soil Conservation Service.

[4] Includes Imperial irrigation district.

[5] Includes 29 State cooperative grazing districts.

[6] Includes 5 wind-erosion districts.

Source: Department of Agriculture, Soil Conservation Service; Report of Chief of Soil Conservation Service.

24. Agriculture—General Statistics

Statistics on agriculture are for the most part prepared by the Bureau of the Census, Department of Commerce, which conducts the Federal Census of Agriculture, and by the Department of Agriculture which prepares current annual estimates.

Beginning with 1840 a Census of Agriculture has been taken every 10 years in conjunction with the Decennial Census of Population. In 1925, 1935, and 1945 a mid-decennial Census of Agriculture has also been taken. Information at each census has been obtained by a personal canvass of individual farms by census enumerators. The first Census of Agriculture was limited in scope. It included such items as an inventory of the principal classes of domestic animals, the production of wool, the .value of poultry, the value of products of the dairy, and the production of the principal crops. The number of farms and the acreage and value of farm land were first included in the Census of 1850. In 1880 information was first secured as to the tenure under which the farms were operated. A detailed classification of farm land according to use was first obtained in 1925; in earlier censuses, farm land was classified only as improved land, woodland, and other unimproved land.

A farm as defined by the Bureau of the Census is all the land on which some agricultural operations are performed by a person, either by his own labor alone or with the assistance of members of his household, or hired employees. In 1950, places of 3 or more acres were counted as farms only if agricultural products, exclusive of a home garden, with a value of $150 or more were produced in 1949. Also, in 1950, places of less than 3 acres were counted as farms only if the value of agricultural products sold in 1949 amounted to $150 or more. In each census from 1925 to 1945, places of 3 or more acres were counted as farms if any agricultural products, other than a small home garden, were produced during the preceding year while places of less than 3 acres were counted as farms if the agricultural production was valued at $250 or more. (For definitions used in earlier censuses, see *U. S. Census of Agriculture: 1950*, Vol. II, Introduction.)

Agricultural operations consist of the production of crops or plants, vines or trees (excluding forestry operations), or of the keeping, grazing, or feeding of livestock for animal products, animal increase, or value enhancement. Included as farms are such agricultural enterprises as nurseries, greenhouses, hothouses, fur farms, mushroom houses, apiaries, and cranberry bogs. Excluded are fish farms, fish hatcheries, oyster farms, frog farms, kennels, game preserves, parks, and the like. When a landowner has one or more tenants, renters, croppers, or managers, the land operated by each is considered a farm for census purposes. Thus, for a plantation, each cropper and tenant operation is considered a separate farm even though the entire plantation may be handled essentially as a single farm enterprise.

The land in farms includes considerable areas of land not actually under cultivation or used for pasture or grazing, but all such land must have been under the control of the operator and considered a part of his farm. Land used for grazing or pasture that was neither owned nor leased by the farm operator generally was not included under land in farms. Rent-free lands were included in an operator's farm only if he had sole use of such lands. Thus vast acreages of land used for grazing, such as national forests, Taylor grazing land, State lands, or other public lands, and some railroad and other privately owned lands, are not included as land in farms even though used for agricultural purposes.

Note.—This section presents data for the most recent year or period available on April 22, 1952, when the material was organized and sent to the printer.

Information on prices received by farmers for products they sell and prices paid for articles they buy for production and family living are obtained by the Bureau of Agricultural Economics from about 33,000 voluntary reporters, which include farmers. local merchants, and handlers of agricultural products. Season average prices received by farmers are calculated by weighting midmonth prices by monthly sales during the crop marketing season, beginning with the first month when a particular crop harvest begins.

The index numbers of prices received and of prices paid by farmers (see tables 726 and 727) are based on current midmonth prices for these commodities. For information concerning methods of construction of the indexes, see Supplement No. 1 to the January 1950 issue of *Agricultural Prices*, issued by the Bureau of Agricultural Economics. The ratio of the index of prices received to the index of prices paid by farmers measures the monthly variation in the average per unit exchange value of farm products in terms of commodities and services bought by farmers.

Cash income is the cash receipts from farm marketings and represents the quantities of crops, livestock, and livestock products sold by farmers multiplied by the prices received per unit of production at the local market. Gross farm income includes Government payments, value of farm products consumed on the farm, and rental value of farm homes, as well as cash receipts from farm marketings.

Historical statistics.—See preface and historical appendix. Tabular headnotes (as "See also *Historical Statistics*, series E 1–16") provide cross-references, where applicable, to *Historical Statistics of the United States, 1789–1945*.

Fig. **XXXVIII.**—Gross Farm Income—Net Income and Production
Expenses of Farm Operators: 1929 to 1952

[See table 726]

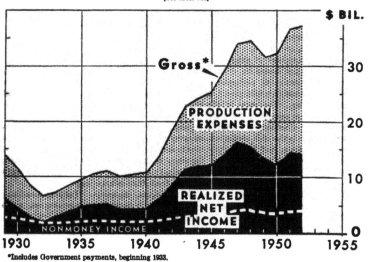

*Includes Government payments, beginning 1933.

Fig. **XXXIX.**—Indexes of Prices Received and Paid by Farmers:
1910 to 1952

[See table 726]

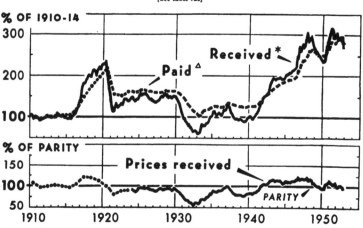

*Monthly data.
△ Includes interest, taxes, and wage rates. Annual average data, 1910–23; by quarters, 1924–36; by months, 1937
to date.

Source of figs. XXXVIII and XXXIX: Department of Agriculture, Bureau of Agricultural Economics.

No. 706.—COMPARATIVE BALANCE SHEET OF AGRICULTURE: JANUARY 1, 1945 TO 1953

[In millions of dollars. Estimated; margin of error varies with item]

ITEM	1945	1946	1947	1948	1949	1950	1951	1952	1953 (prel.)
ASSETS									
Total	97,009	106,019	121,467	133,365	140,063	136,274	155,271	170,446	166,632
Physical assets:									
Real estate	54,939	61,542	69,843	74,976	77,701	75,255	85,895	93,912	92,000
Non-real-estate:									
Livestock	9,011	9,717	11,916	13,257	14,426	12,892	17,127	19,600	
Machinery and motor vehicles	6,289	6,296	6,612	8,396	10,909	13,018	13,660	15,533	
Crops, stored on and off farms [1]	6,396	6,030	6,852	8,789	8,417	7,837	7,657	8,884	50,892
Household furnishings and equipment [2]	4,672	4,803	5,332	6,133	6,949	7,685	8,696	9,259	
Financial assets:									
Deposits and currency	10,800	12,500	14,900	15,300	14,800	14,300	14,400	15,200	
United States savings bonds	3,714	4,496	4,504	4,781	5,025	5,250	5,300	5,300	24,100
Investment in cooperatives	1,188	1,333	1,487	1,731	1,856	2,037	2,226	2,418	
CLAIMS									
Total	97,009	106,019	121,467	133,365	140,063	136,274	155,271	170,446	166,632
Liabilities, total	8,338	7,830	8,296	9,049	11,174	12,364	12,806	14,149	15,900
Real estate debt	4,933	4,682	4,777	4,882	5,108	5,407	5,828	6,300	
Non-real-estate debt:									
To principal institutions:									
Excluding loans held or guaranteed by Commodity Credit Corporation	1,622	1,671	1,954	2,293	2,714	2,838	3,372	4,071	(3)
Loans held or guaranteed by Commodity Credit Corporation	683	277	65	74	1,152	1,719	806	578	
To others [4]	1,100	1,200	1,500	1,800	2,200	2,400	2,800	3,200	
Proprietors' equities	88,671	100,189	113,171	124,316	128,909	125,910	142,465	156,297	150,792

[1] Includes all crops held on farms and crops held in bonded warehouses as security for Commodity Credit Corporation loans; latter on Jan. 1, 1952 totaled $305,000,000.
[2] Estimated valuation for 1940 plus purchases minus depreciation. (Revised series.)
[3] Not yet available.
[4] Tentative. Includes individuals, merchants, dealers, and other miscellaneous lenders.

Source: Department of Agriculture, Bureau of Agricultural Economics; annual report, The Balance Sheet of Agriculture.

FIG. XL.—VALUE OF FARM ASSETS: JANUARY 1, 1940 TO 1952

[See table 706]

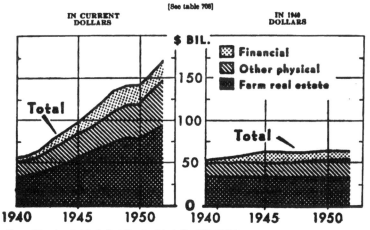

IN CURRENT DOLLARS

IN 1940 DOLLARS

$ BIL.

Financial
Other physical
Farm real estate

Total

Total

1940 1945 1950 1940 1945 1950

Source: Department of Agriculture, Bureau of Agricultural Economics.

No. 707.—NATIONAL FARM PRODUCT IN CURRENT DOLLARS: 1910 TO 1950

[Millions of dollars. Gross national farm product differs in content and movement from measures of the total output of farm products. As a value-added concept, the gross farm product measures only production actually occurring on farms, without duplications. That is, the value of materials used up by farmers in the production process, such as feed, fertilizer, and motor fuel, is deducted from the value of total farm output to arrive at the gross farm product. It is termed "gross" only because depreciation and other capital consumption allowances are not deducted. Value of materials used up in production, technically known as "intermediate products," has risen greatly in recent decades relative to the value of total farm output. Thus, gross farm product has risen significantly less than total farm output over the period 1910–50]

ITEM	1910	1920	1930	1940	1945	1946	1947	1948	1949	1950
Value of farm output	7,503	16,256	11,141	10,486	24,496	28,256	32,124	36,127	31,183	33,232
Cash receipts from farm marketings and CCC loans [1]	5,793	12,608	9,023	8,367	21,516	24,964	30,014	30,544	28,012	26,773
Products consumed on farms where produced	1,177	2,406	1,537	1,254	2,256	2,624	3,095	2,936	2,510	2,344
Net change in all farm inventories [2]	+151	+348	−249	+240	−148	−227	−2,205	+1,313	−720	+752
Gross rental value of farm homes	382	894	830	625	874	998	1,220	1,334	1,351	1,364
Less: Value of intermediate products consumed [3]	1,705	4,397	3,541	3,580	7,730	8,896	10,725	11,642	10,762	11,916
Intermediate products other than rents [3]	1,079	3,058	2,394	2,750	5,998	6,872	8,307	9,088	8,475	9,389
Gross rents paid to nonfarm landlords [4]	626	1,339	1,147	830	1,732	2,024	2,418	2,554	2,287	2,527
Discrepancy			+134	−188	−60	−206	−216	−58	+81	+163
Equals: Gross national farm product	5,798	11,859	7,466	7,094	16,828	19,566	21,615	24,968	20,310	21,154
Less: Capital consumption allowances	610	1,575	1,111	973	1,744	1,897	2,334	2,816	3,214	3,519
Depreciation charges	560	1,453	1,004	876	1,563	1,686	2,115	2,570	2,971	3,269
Capital outlays charged to current expense	50	122	107	97	181	211	219	246	243	250
Equals: Net national farm product	5,188	10,284	6,355	6,121	15,084	17,669	19,281	21,752	17,096	17,635
Less: Indirect business taxes	150	438	519	372	494	533	610	664	715	752
Plus: Government payments to farm landlords				670	686	685	278	222	181	248
Equals: National farm income	5,033	9,846	5,836	6,419	15,276	17,821	18,949	21,310	16,542	17,131

[1] Includes imputed value of food and firewood consumed on farm where produced.
[2] Adjustment necessary to convert sales figures to a commodity output basis.
[3] Includes current expenses for feed and livestock, seed, fertilizer, operation of motor vehicles, irrigation, and other purchased items. Some intermediate products are direct purchases by one farmer from another. Bulk of purchased materials represents production, or value added, by nonfarm industries.
[4] Counted as an expense to farmers, since only the rental value of farm-owned property is considered to originate in farm sector.

Source: Department of Commerce, Office of Business Economics; Survey of Current Business, September 1951.

No. 708.—NATIONAL FARM PRODUCT IN CONSTANT DOLLARS: 1910 TO 1950

[Millions of 1939 dollars. See headnote, table 707]

ITEM	1910	1920	1930	1940	1945	1946	1947	1948	1949	1950
Value of farm output	7,080	7,571	8,409	9,994	11,419	11,809	11,700	12,284	12,154	12,720
Cash receipts from farm marketings and CCC loans [1]	5,250	5,611	6,793	7,889	9,936	10,163	10,300	10,140	10,637	10,734
Products consumed on farms where produced	1,186	1,184	1,113	1,197	1,075	1,154	1,179	1,084	1,056	1,032
Net change in all farm inventories [2]	+87	+136	−138	+282	−219	−151	−442	+377	−240	+240
Gross rental value of farm homes	557	640	641	626	627	643	663	683	701	714
Less: Value of intermediate products consumed [3]	1,747	2,369	2,801	3,561	4,770	5,036	5,271	5,266	5,425	5,755
Intermediate products other than rents [3]	1,172	1,652	1,953	2,675	3,910	4,165	4,381	4,361	4,514	4,831
Gross rents paid to nonfarm landlords [4]	575	717	848	886	860	871	890	905	911	924
Discrepancy			+98	−172	−23	−73	−64	−24	+26	+54
Equals: Gross national farm product	5,333	5,202	5,510	6,605	6,672	6,846	6,493	7,042	6,703	6,911

[1-4] See footnotes 1–4, table 707.

Source: Department of Commerce, Office of Business Economics; Survey of Current Business, September 1951.

No. 709.—FARMS AND FARM PROPERTY—SUMMARY: 1920 TO 1952

[Revised estimates of farm population as of Apr. 1 by Bureau of Agricultural Economics and Bureau of Census; farm values, Bureau of Agricultural Economics as of Mar. 1. See also *Historical Statistics*, series E 1-16]

ITEM	1920	1930	1940	1945	1949	1950	1951	1952
Farm population (1,000)	31,974	30,529	30,547	25,295	25,954	25,058	24,037	24,819
Percent of total population [1]	30.1	24.9	23.2	18.1	17.5	16.6	15.6	15.9
Number of farms (1,000) [2]	6,448	6,289	6,097	5,859	5,890	5,382		
Total value, selected items of farm property ($1,000,000) [3]	78,668	57,963	41,883	80,988	102,454	101,185	116,992	129,345
Farm land and buildings, value ($1,000,000)	66,316	47,880	33,642	54,008	77,119	75,355	85,595	93,912
Average value per farm	$10,284	$7,614	$5,548	$9,320	$13,766	$13,991	$15,959	$17,499
Average value per acre	$69.38	$49.52	$31.71	$47.83	$66.78	$64.96	$74.14	$81.05
Index of estimated value per acre: [4]								
1912-14=100	170	115	84	128	178	169	198	211
1935-39=100	205	138	102	152	211	204	238	255
Farms changing ownership per 1,000 farms (estimated number), total [5]	48.4	61.5	63.0	69.7	56.9	52.3	54.9	52.4
Voluntary sales and trades [6]		23.7	30.2	51.5	40.8	37.1	38.4	37.5
Forced sales and related defaults		20.8	15.9	3.6	1.6	1.8	1.8	2.0
Foreclosures of mortgages, bankruptcies, etc. [7]	4.0	15.7	12.6	1.9	1.2	1.6	1.5	1.5
Delinquent taxes		5.1	3.3	1.1	.4	.4	.3	.5
Other transfers [8]		17.6	16.9	13.2	14.5	13.4	12.5	12.9
Percentage of voluntary sales and trades:								
Purchased by local residents		82	82	82	80	79	78	(9)
Purchased for operation		81	73	76	80	80	78	(9)
Occupation of purchase:								
Active farmer		73	66	66	67	67	65	(9)
Retired farmer		4	4	3	5	5	3	(9)
Other occupation		24	28	34	28	28	32	(9)

[1] Total population includes armed forces serving overseas.
[2] Revised series—intercensal years interpolated on basis of change in farm population.
[3] Includes farm land and buildings, implements and machinery and livestock, including poultry. Turkeys excluded from 1929 to date.
[4] As of March 1. [5] Year ending Mar. 15. [6] Includes contracts to purchase (but not options).
[7] Includes loss of title by default of contract, and surrender of title or transfers to avoid foreclosures.
[8] Includes inheritance and gift transfers; sales in settlement of estates; and miscellaneous and unclassified sales. [9] Not available.

Source: Department of Agriculture, Bureau of Agricultural Economics; annual reports, *The Farm Income Situation* and *The Farm Real Estate Situation*.

No. 710.—LAND UTILIZATION—TREND IN THE UNITED STATES: 1880 TO 1950

[In millions of acres. Total farm and nonfarm land areas are for year indicated. Cropland and pasture acreages usually relate to preceding years. Total, 1880-1940, represents area measurement for 1940 Census; remeasured in 1950 and revised to 1,904,000,000 acres. See also *Historical Statistics*, series F 25-36, where total for 1880-1945 represents area measurement for 1880 Census]

LAND USE ITEM	1880	1890	1900	1910	1920	1930	1940	1950
Total	1,905	1,905	1,905	1,905	1,905	1,905	1,905	1,904
In farms	536	623	839	879	956	987	1,061	1,159
Pasture	122	144	276	364	328	379	461	485
Not plowable					223	270	350	416
Plowable					105	109	111	[1] 69
Crop failure and cropland lying idle or fallow	10	15	24	25	40	54	78	64
Cropland harvested	178	233	296	322	362	369	321	345
Farmsteads, lanes and waste	36	41	56	57	35	45	44	45
Forests and cut-over land	190	190	191	191	168	189	157	220
Pastured					98	77	85	[2] 135
Not pastured					92	91	66	85
Not in farms	1,369	1,283	1,066	1,026	949	918	844	745
Roads, railroads, cities, parks, ungrazed desert, and other waste land	[3] 118	[3] 120	[3] 128	[3] 125	[3] 128	[3] 132	[3] 137	144
Pasture [4]	863	818	625	600	502	437	369	[5] 290
Forest land capable of producing timber of commercial quantity and quality	368	344	318	301	319	349	335	[6] 311

[1] Cropland used for pasture only. Not comparable to previous estimates of plowable pasture.
[2] Includes 34,000,000 acres of arid woodland and brush land.
[3] Estimated. [4] Includes idle grassland in first decades and arid woodland (pinon, juniper, chaparral).
[5] Includes about 80,000,000 to 100,000,000 acres of arid woodland and brush land used for grazing.
[6] Largely commercial forest land. Includes approximately 110,000,000 acres used to some extent for grazing.

Source: Dept. of Commerce, Bureau of Census and Dept. of Agriculture, Bureau of Agricultural Economics; comparative report, *Graphic Summary of Land Utilization in the United States*, and records.

No. 711.—FARMS—NUMBER, ACREAGE, AND VALUE, BY STATES: 1935 TO 1950

[See also *Historical Statistics*, series E 19 and 31]

DIVISION AND STATE	NUMBER OF FARMS				ALL LAND IN FARMS (thousands of acres)			
	1935	1940	1945	1950	1935	1940	1945	1950
United States	6,812,350	6,096,799	5,859,169	5,382,162	1,054,515	1,060,852	1,141,615	1,152,586
New England	155,241	135,190	150,311	103,225	15,463	13,371	14,497	12,547
Maine	41,907	38,980	42,184	30,358	4,722	4,223	4,613	4,182
New Hampshire	17,695	16,554	18,786	13,391	2,116	1,809	2,017	1,714
Vermont	27,061	23,582	26,490	19,043	4,013	3,667	3,931	3,527
Massachusetts	35,094	31,897	37,007	22,220	2,196	1,938	2,078	1,660
Rhode Island	4,327	3,014	3,603	2,598	308	222	265	191
Connecticut	32,157	21,163	22,241	15,615	2,080	1,512	1,593	1,272
Middle Atlantic	397,684	348,100	347,477	294,702	36,455	33,639	34,406	31,855
New York	177,025	153,238	149,490	124,977	18,686	17,170	17,568	16,017
New Jersey	29,375	25,835	26,226	24,838	1,914	1,874	1,818	1,725
Pennsylvania	191,284	169,027	171,761	146,887	15,855	14,594	15,020	14,113
East North Central	1,083,687	1,006,095	963,797	885,404	116,957	113,655	115,564	112,086
Ohio	255,146	233,783	220,575	199,359	22,858	21,908	21,928	20,969
Indiana	200,835	184,545	175,970	166,627	20,519	19,801	20,027	19,650
Illinois	231,312	213,439	204,239	195,268	31,661	31,033	31,602	30,978
Michigan	196,517	187,589	175,268	155,589	18,460	18,038	18,392	17,270
Wisconsin	199,877	186,735	177,745	168,561	23,459	22,876	23,615	23,221
West North Central	1,179,856	1,090,574	1,031,993	962,735	273,077	274,423	283,248	284,329
Minnesota	203,302	197,351	188,952	179,101	32,818	32,607	33,140	32,883
Iowa	221,986	213,318	208,934	203,159	34,359	34,149	34,454	34,265
Missouri	278,454	256,100	242,934	230,045	35,055	34,740	35,278	35,123
North Dakota	84,606	73,962	69,520	65,401	39,118	37,936	41,001	41,194
South Dakota	83,303	72,454	68,705	66,452	37,102	39,474	43,032	44,786
Nebraska	133,616	121,062	111,756	107,183	46,616	47,344	47,783	47,467
Kansas	174,580	156,327	141,192	131,304	48,010	48,174	48,589	48,611
South Atlantic	1,147,133	1,019,451	1,043,475	953,998	95,987	92,555	94,661	102,170
Delaware	10,381	8,994	9,296	7,448	921	896	923	851
Maryland	44,412	42,110	41,275	36,107	4,384	4,198	4,200	4,056
District of Columbia	89	65	40	28	3	2	2	1
Virginia	197,632	174,885	173,051	150,997	17,646	16,445	16,358	15,572
West Virginia	104,747	99,282	97,600	81,434	9,424	8,909	8,720	8,215
North Carolina	300,967	278,276	287,412	288,508	19,936	18,845	18,618	19,318
South Carolina	165,504	137,558	147,745	139,364	12,330	11,239	11,022	11,879
Georgia	250,544	213,033	225,897	198,191	25,297	23,684	23,676	25,751
Florida	72,857	62,248	61,159	56,921	6,048	8,338	13,084	16,528
East South Central	1,137,219	1,023,349	969,829	913,002	79,101	77,086	76,198	79,576
Kentucky	278,298	252,894	238,501	218,476	20,699	20,294	19,725	19,442
Tennessee	273,783	247,617	234,431	231,631	19,086	18,493	17,789	18,534
Alabama	273,455	231,746	223,369	211,512	19,661	19,143	19,068	20,889
Mississippi	311,683	291,092	263,528	251,383	19,655	19,156	19,617	20,711
West South Central	1,137,571	964,370	877,831	780,423	201,118	200,527	204,995	211,469
Arkansas	253,013	216,674	198,769	182,429	17,742	18,045	17,456	18,871
Louisiana	170,216	150,007	129,295	124,181	10,444	9,996	10,040	11,202
Oklahoma	213,325	179,687	164,790	142,246	35,335	34,803	36,162	36,007
Texas	501,017	418,002	384,977	331,567	137,597	137,683	141,338	145,389
Mountain	271,392	233,497	212,527	194,858	173,881	191,901	244,577	250,213
Montana	50,564	41,823	37,747	35,085	47,512	46,452	55,787	59,247
Idaho	45,113	43,663	41,498	40,294	9,952	10,298	12,503	13,224
Wyoming	17,487	15,018	13,076	12,614	28,162	28,026	33,117	34,421
Colorado	63,644	51,436	47,618	45,578	29,978	31,527	36,218	37,953
New Mexico	41,369	34,105	29,695	23,599	34,397	38,860	49,608	47,522
Arizona	18,824	18,468	13,142	10,412	14,019	25,651	37,856	39,916
Utah	30,695	25,411	26,322	24,176	6,239	7,302	10,309	10,865
Nevada	3,696	3,573	3,429	3,110	3,622	3,785	6,178	7,064
Pacific	299,567	276,173	281,929	266,815	62,476	63,694	71,529	74,310
Washington	84,381	81,686	79,887	69,820	14,680	15,182	15,720	17,369
Oregon	64,826	61,829	63,125	59,827	17,358	17,988	19,754	20,328
California	150,360	132,658	138,917	137,168	30,438	30,524	35,054	36,613

No. 711.—FARMS—NUMBER, ACREAGE, AND VALUE, BY STATES: 1935 TO 1950—Con.

DIVISION AND STATE	AVERAGE ACREAGE PER FARM		VALUE OF FARMS (LAND AND BUILDINGS)							
			Total (thousands of dollars)				Average value per farm (dollars)		Average value per acre (dollars)	
	1945	1950	1935	1940	1945	1950[1]	1945	1950[1]	1945	1950[1]
United States...	194.8	215.3	32,858,844	33,641,739	46,288,926	75,266,666	7,917	13,963	40.63	64.96
New England.......	96.4	121.5	391,271	748,588	928,517	1,222,687	6,244	11,529	64.74	97.49
Maine...........	109.4	127.7	142,539	124,083	150,981	226,515	3,755	7,462	34.81	54.17
New Hampshire....	107.4	122.0	66,987	62,206	80,396	124,545	4,260	9,338	30.84	73.85
Vermont........	146.4	155.2	115,996	111,109	134,576	196,405	5,060	10,514	34.34	45.06
Massachusetts...	56.2	74.7	256,677	213,014	255,332	314,710	7,167	14,162	127,62	180.54
Rhode Island.....	73.5	72.5	35,238	26,234	32,610	44,238	9,883	17,062	124.51	283.02
Connecticut......	71.6	81.5	252,584	204,761	263,023	315,251	11,826	20,190	165.09	247.77
Middle Atlantic....	99.0	107.4	2,141,412	2,638,079	3,290,676	3,485,486	6,875	11,747	69.44	149.42
New York........	117.5	126.2	1,045,392	947,074	1,087,562	1,467,452	7,375	11,742	61.90	95.62
New Jersey.......	69.3	69.5	234,313	237,806	292,981	506,278	11,171	20,343	161.15	292.34
Pennsylvania.....	87.4	95.1	861,707	864,200	1,006,574	1,512,755	5,872	10,299	67.15	107.19
East North Central....	121.2	125.6	6,896,844	7,323,632	9,965,796	14,768,512	10,442	14,597	86.19	121.17
Ohio............	99.4	105.2	1,277,456	1,443,917	1,906,351	2,858,060	8,470	14,343	85.20	139.34
Indiana.........	113.5	118.0	1,040,228	1,251,492	1,794,315	2,691,273	10,197	16,151	89.50	136.90
Illinois.........	164.7	158.6	2,205,800	2,537,117	3,693,545	5,394,806	17,633	27,628	115.90	174.15
Michigan........	104.9	111.0	826,251	912,845	1,190,290	1,701,440	6,843	10,935	65.32	98.32
Wisconsin.......	132.9	137.8	1,346,880	1,188,550	1,434,293	2,058,925	8,089	12,203	60.74	85.36
West North Central....	274.5	286.5	9,365,141	8,796,913	12,115,624	19,044,226	11,739	19,279	43.77	46.96
Minnesota.......	175.4	182.4	1,883,072	1,443,021	1,932,763	2,777,312	9,705	15,507	55.33	84.46
Iowa...........	164.9	168.7	2,462,812	2,695,744	3,611,140	5,005,670	17,294	27,105	104.63	140.71
Missouri........	145.2	148.7	1,099,951	1,107,303	1,526,951	2,354,930	6,295	9,720	43.35	63.06
North Dakota....	536.8	659.9	707,130	495,197	708,322	1,188,960	10,189	18,178	17.28	26.36
South Dakota....	628.3	674.0	691,983	506,452	764,300	1,401,787	11,124	21,095	17.76	31.30
Nebraska........	427.3	442.9	1,552,812	1,137,808	1,906,210	2,735,030	15,205	25,517	35.86	57.62
Kansas.........	344.1	370.0	1,478,659	1,421,387	1,971,331	3,196,628	13,962	24,344	40.87	65.80
South Atlantic....	92.6	96.6	2,791,939	3,188,550	4,232,536	7,189,765	4,042	7,466	43.88	76.08
Delaware.......	99.3	114.3	51,476	54,809	72,694	97,141	7,820	13,043	76.72	114.11
Maryland.......	101.8	112.3	242,714	273,080	354,307	507,226	8,596	14,048	84.46	135.07
Dist. of Columbia...	46.4	45.2	7,182	5,943	4,961	4,666	124,034	166,643	2,676.02	3,686.54
Virginia........	94.5	102.1	596,855	674,975	865,808	1,277,684	5,021	8,456	53.11	89.01
West Virginia....	99.3	100.0	237,644	260,827	341,008	487,309	3,494	5,953	39.11	59.31
North Carolina...	64.8	67.0	622,719	736,708	1,002,982	1,906,714	3,490	6,605	68.55	98.55
South Carolina...	74.6	85.2	265,516	338,495	440,632	830,349	2,952	5,896	39.98	69.06
Georgia........	104.2	128.9	426,755	480,345	654,344	1,114,806	2,896	5,623	27.69	43.28
Florida.........	213.9	290.1	321,078	334,378	498,400	945,871	8,149	16,617	38.09	57.28
East South Central....	79.4	87.2	1,915,218	2,324,727	3,094,649	5,166,668	3,224	5,662	40.41	64.96
Kentucky.......	82.7	86.0	620,409	778,694	1,015,796	1,572,250	4,250	7,196	51.80	89.87
Tennessee......	75.9	80.0	556,751	664,474	870,948	1,431,966	3,715	6,182	46.96	77.26
Alabama........	85.4	96.5	368,220	406,782	560,743	1,017,075	2,506	4,809	29.36	46.59
Mississippi.....	74.4	82.4	370,839	474,986	647,862	1,147,791	2,457	4,566	23.01	55.42
West South Central....	233.5	271.0	4,029,762	4,231,841	5,816,259	10,635,466	6,636	12,616	28.37	38.25
Arkansas.......	97.8	103.4	376,086	456,948	662,770	1,135,671	3,394	6,225	37.97	50.18
Louisiana.......	77.6	90.2	205,618	352,874	473,238	920,239	3,653	7,416	47.08	82.21
Oklahoma......	219.4	253.1	784,994	831,141	1,106,154	1,853,460	6,712	12,016	30.59	41.42
Texas..........	367.1	438.5	2,573,705	2,586,979	3,574,998	6,718,426	9,286	20,263	26.39	46.21
Mountain.......	1,150.3	1,254.1	1,772,429	1,779,843	2,786,169	5,512,389	12,969	28,294	11.27	20.86
Montana........	1,557.4	1,665.7	375,841	350,172	517,991	999,063	13,720	28,475	8.81	16.86
Idaho..........	301.3	226.3	307,396	339,194	492,831	922,920	11,882	22,920	38.46	60.52
Wyoming.......	2,392.6	2,727.1	166,774	155,971	232,043	454,603	17,746	36,060	7.01	13.21
Colorado.......	780.6	832.7	418,755	385,344	564,804	1,211,818	11,855	26,568	15.60	31.93
New Mexico.....	1,670.6	2,013.7	170,180	187,826	326,751	713,360	11,004	30,228	15.10	15.01
Arizona........	3,980.6	3,521.7	132,650	152,677	287,876	608,551	21,906	57,996	7.80	15.12
Utah..........	391.7	449.4	158,303	154,358	261,518	471,342	9,047	19,492	25.40	45.37
Nevada........	1,801.7	2,271.2	42,569	47,594	71,986	135,907	20,985	43,700	11.65	19.24
Pacific........	253.7	256.5	3,324,578	3,234,636	5,662,686	9,396,578	16,629	31,245	71.66	112.19
Washington.....	209.3	246.5	550,720	598,366	900,194	1,470,208	11,268	21,057	43.54	84.44
Oregon........	312.9	348.6	448,712	476,817	697,773	1,216,088	11,064	20,227	35.42	50.52
California......	232.3	266.9	2,325,446	2,168,453	3,464,649	6,650,279	25,084	41,192	99.40	154.22

[1] Based on reports for only a sample of farms.
[2] Based on average value per acre for farms in sample for which value of land and buildings was reported.
[3] Average for farms reporting value of land and buildings.

Source: Department of Commerce, Bureau of the Census; U. S. Census of Agriculture: 1950, Vol. II.

No. 712.—FARM LAND, BY USE, BY STATES: 1944 AND 1949

[In thousands of acres. For total land in farms, see table 711]

DIVISION AND STATE	CROPLAND HARVESTED		CROPLAND USED ONLY FOR PASTURE		CROPLAND NOT HARVESTED AND NOT PASTURED		OTHER THAN CROPLAND	
	1944	1949	1944 [1]	1949	1944 [2]	1949	1944	1949
United States	352,866	344,399	47,449	69,332	88,879	64,106	690,921	680,728
New England	3,987	2,805	375	847	232	564	9,903	8,330
Maine	1,316	932	74	221	101	254	3,128	2,775
New Hampshire	436	290	48	101	26	59	1,507	1,263
Vermont	1,160	859	93	219	28	78	2,650	2,371
Massachusetts	581	376	77	151	45	97	1,376	1,036
Rhode Island	62	40	10	26	9	15	184	111
Connecticut	433	308	72	129	25	61	1,064	775
Middle Atlantic	14,441	12,211	1,450	2,851	1,613	2,459	16,902	14,335
New York	6,922	5,792	705	1,579	740	1,114	9,202	7,533
New Jersey	916	782	116	161	104	148	681	635
Pennsylvania	6,604	5,637	626	1,111	769	1,196	7,018	6,166
East North Central	61,117	58,570	9,411	10,862	3,789	4,687	41,246	36,996
Ohio	10,837	10,296	1,867	2,049	598	1,034	8,626	7,501
Indiana	10,912	11,001	1,817	2,051	811	777	6,487	5,830
Illinois	20,302	20,364	2,150	2,591	1,131	987	8,019	7,035
Michigan	8,521	7,797	1,786	1,983	903	1,263	7,182	6,227
Wisconsin	10,545	10,112	1,791	2,187	346	606	10,933	10,315
West North Central	132,778	133,302	10,024	14,480	16,761	20,151	123,686	116,396
Minnesota	18,589	19,709	1,316	1,560	2,418	1,192	10,847	10,422
Iowa	21,562	22,547	2,612	3,144	768	358	9,512	8,215
Missouri	12,902	12,264	2,916	5,104	1,039	1,389	18,421	16,366
North Dakota	20,817	20,353	710	935	3,576	6,340	15,896	13,567
South Dakota	16,536	17,528	641	816	1,337	1,478	24,529	24,964
Nebraska	19,596	19,407	942	1,400	2,890	2,970	24,325	28,691
Kansas	22,817	21,494	887	1,521	4,733	6,425	20,153	19,173
South Atlantic	27,494	25,022	4,047	6,308	5,460	6,530	59,600	64,311
Delaware	416	389	63	72	85	74	359	316
Maryland	1,745	1,531	394	448	226	306	1,836	1,771
District of Columbia	1	(⁷)	(⁷)	(⁷)	(⁷)	(⁷)	(⁷)	(⁷)
Virginia	3,933	3,314	1,169	1,564	690	911	10,566	9,784
West Virginia	1,490	1,218	312	787	172	349	6,747	5,860
North Carolina	6,126	5,782	526	733	950	1,183	11,016	11,619
South Carolina	4,149	3,960	238	494	800	932	5,835	6,493
Georgia	7,824	7,008	784	1,273	2,035	2,116	13,632	15,264
Florida	1,809	1,728	563	937	505	659	10,206	13,204
East South Central	23,802	22,494	8,000	11,323	4,422	5,396	39,974	40,362
Kentucky	5,322	5,054	4,038	5,265	1,039	1,282	9,325	7,840
Tennessee	5,844	5,575	2,260	2,856	1,170	1,489	8,516	8,613
Alabama	6,163	5,729	854	1,596	1,249	1,394	10,801	12,167
Mississippi	6,473	6,136	849	1,604	963	1,231	11,332	11,740
West South Central	51,043	49,083	9,062	13,236	5,627	6,979	139,264	142,171
Arkansas	5,995	5,930	1,651	2,472	1,127	1,252	8,683	9,217
Louisiana	3,490	3,149	1,032	1,804	613	705	4,904	5,545
Oklahoma	14,088	11,896	1,759	2,318	1,117	1,802	19,198	19,991
Texas	27,469	28,108	4,619	6,643	2,772	3,220	106,477	107,419
Mountain	23,103	24,500	1,879	4,212	7,375	10,964	212,222	210,537
Montana	7,439	7,576	400	1,271	3,479	5,081	47,468	48,319
Idaho	3,442	3,648	322	485	825	1,097	7,914	7,995
Wyoming	1,843	1,901	112	405	264	407	30,897	31,709
Colorado	6,035	6,863	513	970	2,007	3,165	27,662	26,925
New Mexico	1,957	1,898	135	446	410	495	47,106	44,683
Arizona	652	884	230	184	77	198	36,898	36,651
Utah	1,248	1,279	128	305	288	468	8,645	8,812
Nevada	487	421	36	145	23	53	5,632	6,444
Pacific	15,102	15,412	3,202	5,214	5,101	6,396	48,124	47,287
Washington	4,290	4,237	439	715	2,403	2,760	9,589	9,649
Oregon	3,276	3,219	566	969	1,067	1,349	14,845	14,790
California	7,536	7,957	2,196	3,531	1,631	2,278	23,691	22,848

For footnotes, see next page.

No. 712.—FARM LAND, BY USE, BY STATES: 1944 AND 1949—Continued

[In thousands of acres]

DIVISION AND STATE	OTHER THAN CROPLAND							
	1944				1949			
	Wood-land pastured	Wood-land not pastured	Other pasture	Other land	Wood-land pastured	Wood-land not pastured	Other pasture	Other land
United States	26,673	71,251	481,577	42,863	134,715	85,699	413,600	45,364
New England	2,494	4,467	2,261	723	1,784	4,354	1,498	704
Maine	611	1,530	430	234	383	1,840	273	270
New Hampshire	446	755	331	79	305	744	149	75
Vermont	857	604	1,022	70	723	788	788	96
Massachusetts	309	640	347	159	195	845	146	151
Rhode Island	18	92	41	33	14	65	13	19
Connecticut	232	447	270	115	164	362	157	92
Middle Atlantic	2,536	4,697	7,254	2,266	2,320	4,375	5,062	2,067
New York	1,529	2,100	4,550	1,022	1,562	2,111	3,126	884
New Jersey	30	259	175	209	44	276	125	190
Pennsylvania	974	2,328	2,638	1,005	633	2,491	1,811	933
East North Central	11,206	5,619	17,171	7,245	11,975	7,346	10,329	7,545
Ohio	1,560	1,107	4,582	1,407	1,606	1,441	3,692	1,467
Indiana	1,710	984	2,675	1,339	1,690	1,215	1,497	1,455
Illinois	1,687	787	3,903	1,645	2,041	1,009	3,286	1,720
Michigan	2,275	1,228	2,287	1,304	2,145	1,276	1,101	1,408
Wisconsin	3,976	1,535	3,954	1,407	4,434	2,002	3,482	1,487
West North Central	11,006	4,014	98,682	15,646	13,334	5,877	52,711	16,464
Minnesota	3,096	1,209	3,525	2,757	3,340	1,743	3,618	1,712
Iowa	1,452	225	5,730	2,076	1,902	415	3,731	2,164
Missouri	5,189	1,973	9,487	1,683	6,305	2,604	6,088	1,681
North Dakota	316	155	12,089	3,355	484	246	10,735	2,102
South Dakota	194	70	22,492	1,704	495	143	23,943	1,470
Nebraska	378	132	22,185	1,620	603	217	21,415	1,456
Kansas	900	237	17,054	1,752	744	417	16,283	1,740
South Atlantic	12,537	29,290	14,590	3,424	17,636	31,876	11,310	4,190
Delaware	9	222	40	57	11	206	26	71
Maryland	127	974	472	363	163	1,006	351	351
District of Columbia	(³)	(³)	(³)	(³)	(³)	(³)	(³)	(³)
Virginia	1,177	4,648	3,169	580	1,386	5,375	2,270	674
West Virginia	1,100	2,127	3,944	276	1,304	1,980	2,234	238
North Carolina	1,088	6,105	1,059	715	1,421	8,272	1,087	886
South Carolina	985	5,828	620	360	1,207	4,358	440	442
Georgia	3,508	7,214	1,611	360	4,371	8,930	1,188	790
Florida	4,527	1,274	4,006	390	7,255	1,762	3,396	788
East South Central	8,994	16,197	11,965	3,918	11,706	17,314	7,540	4,982
Kentucky	1,172	3,353	5,653	1,117	1,609	3,294	1,698	2,341
Tennessee	1,332	3,720	2,447	1,016	1,902	3,966	1,687	2,088
Alabama	2,917	4,639	2,440	783	3,712	6,030	1,706	719
Mississippi	3,571	3,376	3,384	1,001	4,463	4,024	2,290	963
West South Central	22,969	5,877	165,696	4,412	40,657	8,762	87,790	6,012
Arkansas	2,382	3,105	2,329	804	3,345	3,579	1,566	808
Louisiana	1,398	1,494	1,872	651	1,804	1,945	1,182	624
Oklahoma	4,119	399	13,351	1,229	4,619	890	12,748	1,347
Texas	16,051	818	87,654	1,756	30,890	2,278	72,317	2,334
Mountain	14,437	436	179,381	4,099	23,062	2,611	179,406	5,148
Montana	976	99	44,856	827	2,758	405	41,227	982
Idaho	946	114	6,230	624	1,242	309	5,626	817
Wyoming	261	11	30,346	359	275	72	30,946	913
Colorado	1,311	96	26,417	570	617	430	22,603	1,075
New Mexico	4,647	94	41,914	761	114	608	36,261	720
Arizona	6,007	14	30,815	362	986	74	31,113	928
Utah	173	11	6,263	196	1,454	102	6,415	441
Nevada	76	7	4,420	129	96	30	6,217	130
Pacific	7,975	1,655	36,929	2,306	52,341	2,642	29,916	4,669
Washington	1,862	474	6,602	430	2,433	938	5,397	557
Oregon	2,772	690	11,086	497	3,618	892	9,955	557
California	3,341	691	18,211	1,448	6,290	1,082	13,544	1,982

¹ Land used only for pasture that had been plowed within 7 years.
² Crop failure and cropland idle or fallow.
³ 500 acres or less.

Source: Department of Commerce, Bureau of the Census; U. S. Census of Agriculture: 1950, Vol. II.

No. 713.—FARM REAL ESTATE—INDEXES OF ESTIMATED VALUE PER ·ACRE, BY STATES: MARCH 1, 1912 TO 1953

[1935-39 = 100]

DIVISION AND STATE	1912	1915	1920	1925	1930	1933	1935	1940	1945	1950	1951	1952	1953 [1]
United States	117	124	205	153	138	88	95	102	152	204	233	255	253
New England	14	94	133	121	121	100	99	101	123	150	155	161	163
Maine	105	101	149	131	131	99	99	100	125	144	137	138	144
New Hampshire	105	109	139	120	120	100	98	102	127	147	154	160	165
Vermont	101	103	149	125	123	101	100	101	129	175	184	195	195
Massachusetts	88	88	128	118	117	101	99	101	119	136	146	152	153
Rhode Island	84	86	110	108	113	100	99	101	122	155	168	171	171
Connecticut	79	80	110	110	112	100	99	100	121	154	164	169	172
Middle Atlantic	111	113	154	129	120	93	96	102	134	178	195	215	215
New York	115	117	156	130	120	95	98	100	128	177	186	205	205
New Jersey	86	87	114	109	110	97	97	102	132	171	180	202	206
Pennsylvania	113	115	161	132	123	90	95	104	142	181	207	230	229
East North Central	131	140	217	157	130	83	91	106	160	224	262	285	283
Ohio	135	147	219	151	124	81	91	106	167	231	276	308	307
Indiana	141	148	235	149	117	77	89	108	181	254	303	332	336
Illinois	142	150	233	168	133	79	90	110	163	236	278	302	307
Michigan	111	118	175	150	137	91	94	103	164	225	258	276	263
Wisconsin	113	121	198	151	136	93	96	97	128	169	188	200	201
West North Central	140	151	265	181	187	92	98	94	138	203	235	256	255
Minnesota	111	128	250	186	186	92	97	100	134	196	231	249	256
Iowa	133	155	296	189	156	81	92	103	149	219	254	269	261
Missouri	164	172	282	189	166	93	98	100	154	210	245	273	272
North Dakota	150	159	225	169	148	102	103	80	117	177	193	220	225
South Dakota	185	195	349	221	179	106	105	79	119	188	216	243	234
Nebraska	139	143	255	176	161	99	102	83	122	185	218	239	240
Kansas	133	135	198	151	148	92	96	93	146	219	245	269	274
South Atlantic	96	97	196	146	127	79	92	106	163	224	251	280	280
Delaware	116	117	161	130	129	93	95	103	142	184	199	236	231
Maryland	100	107	170	135	126	92	94	103	152	206	227	260	263
Virginia	91	91	177	145	126	83	91	106	161	221	251	281	292
West Virginia	118	122	187	145	127	89	95	104	129	169	189	200	201
North Carolina	76	80	174	146	123	67	87	108	175	269	296	332	347
South Carolina	122	114	278	167	125	69	92	108	196	247	273	295	302
Georgia	128	122	284	151	130	74	93	107	173	237	261	293	307
Florida	74	75	137	132	132	93	97	102	142	162	194	217	228
East South Central	96	98	197	139	126	78	92	110	177	261	295	324	324
Kentucky	100	103	206	145	131	82	90	117	195	282	322	357	342
Tennessee	97	101	202	138	126	79	92	109	179	268	297	321	323
Alabama	84	84	151	131	122	75	94	104	153	223	248	274	288
Mississippi	99	99	222	139	124	74	92	108	168	251	289	318	329
West South Central	100	105	186	151	143	86	95	104	146	201	236	266	250
Arkansas	106	102	239	172	152	86	95	103	179	265	305	334	326
Louisiana	90	87	180	128	120	81	94	110	147	204	218	236	245
Oklahoma	107	104	182	144	139	83	94	102	143	225	264	285	277
Texas	99	107	183	153	144	87	96	103	144	191	226	250	239
Mountain	133	133	204	142	138	93	95	103	163	211	238	254	250
Montana	183	188	236	141	135	89	95	104	168	236	266	286	270
Idaho	119	114	205	147	138	91	96	102	166	188	198	207	200
Wyoming	149	156	271	153	150	95	96	104	177	244	286	304	298
Colorado	169	161	242	159	142	92	92	105	186	256	281	296	285
New Mexico	124	124	178	134	136	93	94	104	163	232	264	282	269
Arizona	101	103	175	129	130	95	97	101	154	182	214	237	249
Utah	114	111	190	148	144	95	95	102	138	161	174	180	175
Nevada	141	149	198	150	146	96	96	102	134	160	171	178	172
Pacific	89	101	146	137	133	90	95	101	161	169	186	200	196
Washington	120	122	171	138	135	90	94	103	164	192	203	216	206
Oregon	122	125	162	138	135	90	93	105	163	177	191	202	195
California	77	92	139	136	133	90	96	100	160	163	182	197	194

[1] Preliminary.

Source: Department of Agriculture, Bureau of Agricultural Economics; periodic report, *Current Developments in the Farm Real Estate Market.*

No. 714.—Farms—Number, by Size, by States: 1950

Division and state	Total number of farms	Under 3 acres	3 to 9 acres	10 to 29 acres	30 to 49 acres	50 to 99 acres	100 to 179 acres	180 to 259 acres	260 to 499 acres	500 to 999 acres	1,000 acres and over
United States	5,382,162	76,609	466,366	863,608	634,342	1,047,801	1,102,543	437,326	478,984	152,364	121,362
New England	162,225	3,447	9,533	15,697	8,947	28,565	32,356	10,226	9,655	2,362	405
Maine	30,366	409	1,234	2,769	2,740	7,709	8,363	3,461	2,726	700	147
New Hampshire	12,391	319	1,100	1,840	1,268	2,839	3,862	1,341	1,245	574	59
Vermont	19,043	240	904	1,576	939	2,603	4,906	5,273	3,432	873	122
Massachusetts	22,220	1,577	2,610	4,980	2,655	4,034	3,070	1,143	665	211	52
Rhode Island	2,398	296	362	527	300	565	367	117	87	32	5
Connecticut	15,615	666	2,152	3,396	1,920	3,123	3,543	908	677	162	23
Middle Atlantic	304,702	8,220	24,812	39,536	27,364	70,363	75,516	38,413	15,191	2,348	609
New York	124,977	2,831	7,945	13,486	9,674	30,754	34,780	16,067	11,307	1,534	281
New Jersey	24,528	1,542	4,747	5,961	2,518	4,026	3,895	1,271	677	152	50
Pennsylvania	146,887	3,835	12,120	20,080	15,162	39,484	37,862	11,075	6,117	964	196
East North Central	865,484	10,906	51,661	82,436	56,712	202,714	260,489	112,490	72,018	9,895	1,219
Ohio	199,359	2,943	15,740	24,690	19,440	51,238	54,284	18,919	10,530	1,421	166
Indiana	166,627	3,486	12,270	20,027	17,125	37,294	43,026	19,468	12,907	1,536	211
Illinois	195,368	2,662	11,947	15,685	12,381	29,088	86,711	35,844	27,625	3,859	409
Michigan	155,589	1,598	7,131	15,223	20,800	42,917	43,296	15,511	5,922	1,186	217
Wisconsin	168,561	1,368	4,573	6,876	11,067	42,177	63,173	34,458	13,086	1,588	195
West North Central	982,725	8,704	36,688	47,333	47,388	128,484	266,828	184,840	191,668	75,376	34,668
Minnesota	179,101	1,444	4,601	4,360	6,634	26,077	62,568	34,782	29,539	4,468	800
Iowa	203,159	1,963	7,998	9,068	7,245	25,525	77,486	42,391	28,110	2,639	264
Missouri	230,045	1,893	11,361	20,340	28,200	44,556	60,039	31,742	27,479	6,283	1,162
North Dakota	65,401	131	461	619	461	919	5,338	5,396	28,316	22,095	8,775
South Dakota	66,452	340	1,064	1,190	981	2,219	10,410	7,998	21,838	11,705	8,767
Nebraska	107,183	1,119	3,611	3,408	2,219	6,815	26,300	19,167	26,909	16,530	7,206
Kansas	131,304	1,814	6,047	6,315	4,603	11,973	23,956	17,605	33,674	17,466	7,689
South Atlantic	988,906	10,584	85,122	227,696	160,781	228,245	142,545	69,197	40,282	14,896	7,196
Delaware	7,448	246	827	1,073	875	1,661	1,506	704	503	127	36
Maryland	36,107	796	3,677	5,544	3,708	7,193	8,022	3,461	2,460	634	123
Dist. of Columbia	26	13		4	4	1			2		
Virginia	180,997	2,043	17,081	31,228	19,635	32,795	25,850	10,131	6,532	2,577	525
West Virginia	81,434	1,064	7,777	13,687	11,049	20,960	18,853	5,836	3,972	1,287	320
North Carolina	288,508	2,582	26,855	84,994	46,913	67,111	33,796	9,455	6,343	1,861	500
South Carolina	139,364	1,689	11,736	45,022	26,794	26,180	15,183	5,061	4,446	2,020	998
Georgia	198,191	1,326	10,880	32,141	34,139	62,474	36,220	13,088	11,147	4,647	2,800
Florida	56,921	1,689	7,378	13,108	6,964	9,909	7,086	2,590	2,774	1,476	1,736
East South Central	912,082	7,760	82,406	226,496	154,407	213,091	135,564	48,226	31,579	10,342	4,443
Kentucky	218,476	2,615	21,659	37,612	28,770	59,229	44,952	14,010	8,601	1,843	405
Tennessee	231,631	2,366	21,546	52,864	36,593	57,782	37,441	11,556	7,850	1,896	445
Alabama	211,612	1,370	15,996	47,432	46,631	50,496	28,135	8,822	7,545	3,208	1,880
Mississippi	251,388	1,214	23,014	87,308	42,413	47,096	26,753	8,840	7,713	3,209	1,733
West South Central	780,423	8,660	96,568	126,130	100,343	146,872	145,919	62,430	78,127	36,722	34,673
Arkansas	182,429	1,240	15,109	39,547	31,863	46,121	20,537	10,778	8,835	3,145	1,254
Louisiana	124,181	1,780	13,403	41,584	26,029	20,206	10,429	3,628	3,653	1,836	1,331
Oklahoma	142,246	1,602	6,199	10,265	11,498	22,525	36,429	15,609	24,676	6,302	4,046
Texas	331,567	4,028	21,797	36,354	27,953	58,020	68,523	32,423	40,963	27,436	18,042
Mountain	194,853	4,040	15,874	15,266	14,668	24,877	28,780	11,643	22,449	20,696	35,344
Montana	35,085	287	969	1,341	984	2,008	3,655	1,925	4,785	6,300	13,064
Idaho	40,284	471	3,272	3,696	4,506	6,982	7,399	2,875	4,162	2,606	2,353
Wyoming	12,614	150	304	298	328	869	2,048	954	1,717	1,556	4,204
Colorado	46,578	985	3,408	4,046	2,260	4,882	6,706	2,849	5,051	6,172	7,940
New Mexico	23,800	307	3,168	3,946	1,668	3,160	2,341	974	2,416	2,270	4,389
Arizona	10,412	446	1,459	1,597	1,112	1,287	1,121	404	778	570	1,319
Utah	24,170	1,411	3,014	2,851	2,685	4,246	3,109	1,431	1,636	1,052	1,431
Nevada	3,110	63	190	360	319	511	413	191	275	344	654
Pacific	265,515	14,311	47,786	66,145	33,196	34,125	34,329	10,416	14,665	16,140	13,127
Washington	89,820	1,502	13,040	17,610	9,085	9,449	6,327	2,687	3,710	3,081	2,005
Oregon	54,527	1,266	9,153	12,777	7,211	9,324	7,653	2,332	3,788	2,299	2,857
California	137,168	11,013	26,453	35,068	16,949	15,369	10,346	4,517	6,617	4,699	6,295

Source: Department of Commerce, Bureau of the Census; U. S. Census of Agriculture: 1950, Vol. II.

No. 715.—FARMS—NUMBER AND ACREAGE, 1920 TO 1950, AND AVERAGE VALUE OF LAND AND BUILDINGS, 1950, BY SIZE OF FARM

[1950 data, except number of farms, based on reports for only a sample of farms. May not agree with other sample data, since size data were not adjusted to agree with total count of farms]

SIZE OF FARM	1920	1925	1930	1935	1940	1945	1920	1925	1930	1935	1940	1945
	Number of farms						Percent distribution of number of farms					
Total	6,448,343	6,371,640	6,288,648	6,812,350	6,096,799	5,859,169	100.0	100.0	100.0	100.0	100.0	100.0
Under 10 acres	288,772	378,535	358,504	570,831	506,402	594,561	4.5	5.9	5.7	8.4	8.3	10.1
Under 3 acres	20,350	15,151	43,007	35,573	35,977	98,966	.3	.2	.7	.5	.6	1.7
3 to 9 acres	268,422	363,384	315,497	535,258	470,425	495,595	4.2	5.7	5.0	7.9	7.7	8.5
10 to 29 acres	(1)	(1)	(1)	1,241,433	1,012,971	945,608	(1)	(1)	(1)	18.2	16.6	16.1
10 to 19 acres	507,763	588,049	559,617	683,452	559,254	(1)	7.9	9.2	8.9	10.0	9.2	(1)
20 to 29 acres	(1)	(1)	(1)	557,979	453,717	(1)	(1)	(1)	(1)	8.2	7.4	(1)
30 to 49 acres	1,505,782	1,450,645	1,440,588	1,440,145	1,221,096	(1)	23.3	22.8	22.9	21.1	20.0	(1)
30 to 49 acres	(1)	(1)	(1)	882,164	767,289	708,796	(1)	(1)	(1)	12.9	12.6	12.1
50 to 99 acres	1,474,745	1,421,078	1,374,965	1,444,007	1,291,048	1,157,320	22.9	22.3	21.9	21.2	21.2	19.8
100 to 174 acres	1,449,620	1,385,777	1,348,937	1,404,897	1,278,617	(1)	22.5	21.7	21.4	20.6	21.0	(1)
100 to 179 acres	(1)	(1)	(1)	1,438,017	1,309,741	1,199,809	(1)	(1)	(1)	21.1	21.5	20.5
175 to 259 acres	559,800	502,417	530,593	540,267	517,400	(1)	8.2	7.9	8.5	7.9	8.5	(1)
180 to 259 acres	(1)	(1)	(1)	506,547	486,336	493,215	(1)	(1)	(1)	7.4	8.0	8.4
260 to 499 acres	475,677	438,961	451,338	473,239	458,787	473,184	7.4	6.9	7.2	6.9	7.5	8.1
500 to 999 acres	149,819	143,852	159,696	167,452	163,694	173,777	2.3	2.3	2.5	2.5	2.7	3.0
1,000 acres and over	67,405	63,328	80,620	88,662	100,531	112,899	1.0	1.0	1.3	1.3	1.6	1.9

SIZE OF FARM	1920	1925	1930	1935	1940	1945	1920	1925	1930	1935	1940	1945
	All land in farms (thousands of acres)						Percent distribution of land in farms					
Total	955,884	924,319	986,771	1,054,515	1,060,852	1,141,615	100.0	100.0	100.0	100.0	100.0	100.0
Under 10 acres	1,600	2,097	1,908	3,057	2,668	2,805	.2	.2	.2	.3	.3	.2
Under 3 acres	34	23	61	51	51	141	(2)	(2)	(2)	(2)	(2)	(2)
3 to 9 acres	1,567	2,074	1,847	3,006	2,617	2,664	.2	.2	.2	.3	.2	.2
10 to 29 acres	(1)	(1)	(1)	22,272	18,111	16,864	(1)	(1)	(1)	2.1	1.7	1.5
10 to 19 acres	7,087	8,060	7,789	9,369	7,607	(1)	.7	.9	.8	.9	.7	(1)
20 to 29 acres	(1)	(1)	(1)	12,903	10,504	(1)	(1)	(1)	(1)	1.2	1.0	(1)
30 to 49 acres	48,406	46,405	46,252	46,594	39,892	(1)	5.1	5.0	4.7	4.4	3.8	(1)
30 to 49 acres	(1)	(1)	(1)	33,691	29,388	27,074	(1)	(1)	(1)	3.2	2.8	2.4
50 to 99 acres	105,631	101,906	98,685	104,016	93,317	83,206	11.1	11.0	10.0	9.9	8.8	7.3
100 to 174 acres	194,681	186,703	180,214	188,859	172,030	(1)	20.4	20.1	18.3	17.9	16.2	(1)
100 to 179 acres	(1)	(1)	(1)	194,805	177,509	162,375	(1)	(1)	(1)	18.5	16.7	14.2
175 to 259 acres	112,563	106,475	110,205	114,408	109,777	(1)	11.8	11.5	11.2	10.8	10.5	(1)
180 to 259 acres	(1)	(1)	(1)	108,462	104,289	105,802	(1)	(1)	(1)	10.3	9.8	9.3
260 to 499 acres	164,244	151,731	156,522	164,268	159,569	164,648	17.2	16.4	15.9	15.6	15.0	14.4
500 to 999 acres	100,976	97,468	108,924	114,244	111,935	118,836	10.6	10.5	11.0	10.8	10.6	10.4
1,000 acres and over	220,636	224,472	276,213	309,701	364,060	460,006	23.1	24.3	28.0	29.4	34.3	40.3

				1950				
SIZE OF FARM	Number of farms	All land in farms (1,000 acres)	Cropland harvested (1,000 acres)	Average value of land and buildings		Percent distribution		
				Per farm	Per acre	Number of farms	All land in farms	Cropland harvested
Total	5,382,162	1,159,789	346,528	$13,911	$66.75	100.0	100.0	100.0
Under 10 acres	484,014	2,430	973	5,522	1,066.55	9.0	.2	.3
10 to 29 acres	853,606	15,391	8,175	4,981	272.10	15.9	1.3	2.4
30 to 49 acres	624,242	23,945	10,694	5,586	144.25	11.6	2.1	3.1
50 to 69 acres	1,047,801	75,638	30,621	7,760	106.67	19.5	6.5	8.9
50 to 69 acres	426,587	24,736	9,960	6,727	114.04	7.9	2.1	2.9
70 to 99 acres	620,214	50,892	20,761	8,460	102.66	11.5	4.4	6.0
100 to 179 acres	1,102,562	149,942	66,989	13,138	96.27	20.5	12.9	19.4
100 to 139 acres	579,111	67,550	27,856	10,977	94.04	10.8	5.8	8.1
140 to 179 acres	523,451	82,392	39,133	15,524	98.04	9.7	7.1	11.3
180 to 259 acres	487,325	105,388	48,704	20,306	94.31	9.1	9.1	14.1
180 to 219 acres	275,009	54,547	24,283	18,442	93.19	5.1	4.7	7.0
220 to 259 acres	212,316	50,841	24,421	22,708	95.52	3.9	4.4	7.1
260 to 499 acres	478,084	166,584	76,561	27,969	80.03	8.9	14.4	22.2
500 to 999 acres	182,264	125,981	48,506	39,422	57.53	3.4	10.9	14.1
1,000 acres and over	121,362	494,501	54,216	92,478	24.23	2.3	42.6	15.7

1 Not available.   2 0.05 percent or less.

Source: Department of Commerce, Bureau of the Census; *U. S. Census of Agriculture: 1950*, Vol. II.

No. 716.—FARMS—NUMBER, BY COLOR AND TENURE OF OPERATOR, WITH ACREAGE AND VALUE BY TENURE OF OPERATOR: 1910 TO 1950

[See also *Historical Statistics*, series E 19-24, 31-60]

YEAR, COLOR, AND REGION	All farms	Full owner	Part owner	Manager	TENANT	
					Cash [1]	Other
NUMBER OF FARMS						
United States, total:						
1910	6, 361, 502	3, 354, 897	593, 235	58, 104	712, 394	1, 642, 382
1920	6, 448, 343	3, 366, 510	548, 580	68, 449	480, 009	1, 974, 796
1930	6, 288, 648	2, 911, 644	656, 730	615, 696	480, 210	2, 175, 155
1940	6, 096, 799	3, 084, 136	615, 099	34, 351	514, 438	1, 808, 553
1945	5, 859, 169	3, 301, 361	649, 622	23, 025	402, 175	1, 466, 346
1950	5, 382, 162	3, 099, 583	824, 683	22, 327	212, 790	1, 221, 320
White:						
1910	5, 440, 619	3, 159, 068	548, 413	56, 980	447, 851	1, 228, 707
1920	5, 498, 454	3, 174, 109	517, 759	60, 223	373, 835	1, 508, 328
1930	5, 372, 578	2, 752, 787	612, 697	62, 767	387, 534	1, 558, 209
1940	5, 377, 728	2, 916, 562	581, 517	33, 634	444, 305	1, 390, 616
1945	5, 169, 984	3, 126, 212	629, 734	39, 363	326, 787	1, 062, 668
1950	4, 801, 243	2, 936, 122	768, 573	22, 056	171, 375	901, 117
Nonwhite:						
1910	920, 883	195, 809	45, 412	1, 544	264, 443	413, 675
1920	949, 889	192, 401	40, 821	3, 226	106, 174	608, 267
1930	916, 070	158, 857	43, 983	3, 132	101, 376	68, 182
1940	719, 071	167, 876	33, 582	717	70, 353	417, 888
1945	649, 215	175, 149	20, 788	622	75, 388	877, 286
1950	580, 919	153, 461	55, 350	471	41, 415	330, 282
The South, total:						
1910	3, 097, 547	1, 329, 390	215, 121	18, 284	433, 080	1, 091, 692
1920	3, 206, 664	1, 405, 762	191, 488	18, 318	219, 199	1, 371, 998
1930	3, 223, 816	1, 190, 983	224, 002	17, 388	288, 032	1, 503, 731
1940	3, 007, 170	1, 327, 690	216, 607	12, 880	254, 351	1, 794, 042
1945	2, 881, 138	1, 508, 066	193, 607	12, 193	232, 234	922, 645
1950	2, 652, 423	1, 431, 121	325, 969	9, 979	119, 853	785, 487
White:						
1910	2, 207, 406	1, 154, 100	171, 944	5, 084	192, 094	671, 184
1920	2, 283, 730	1, 227, 204	152, 482	16, 548	118, 913	768, 648
1930	2, 342, 130	1, 050, 187	183, 489	16, 329	140, 112	942, 882
1940	2, 326, 904	1, 185, 788	185, 246	13, 215	189, 667	712, 988
1945	2, 215, 722	1, 348, 076	165, 853	12, 771	188, 092	550, 448
1950	2, 094, 333	1, 289, 641	274, 135	9, 740	80, 295	430, 894
Nonwhite:						
1910	890, 141	175, 290	43, 177	1, 200	260, 988	420, 508
1920	922, 914	178, 558	39, 031	1, 770	100, 275	603, 350
1930	881, 667	140, 496	41, 523	629	97, 920	530, 619
1940	680, 266	141, 902	31, 361	365	64, 684	441, 954
1945	665, 413	160, 980	28, 232	442	73, 142	477, 797
1950	559, 090	141, 482	51, 864	239	38, 862	335, 945
LAND IN FARMS (1,000 acres)						
United States, total:						
1910	878, 798	464, 923	133, 634	53, 731	67, 847	158, 669
1920	955, 884	461, 350	178, 325	54, 139	65, 095	191, 983
1930	986, 771	372, 450	245, 926	61, 695	71, 370	235, 030
1940	1, 060, 852	382, 008	300, 325	66, 530	74, 388	227, 601
1945	1, 141, 615	412, 258	371, 261	106, 272	61, 121	190, 413
1950	1, 158, 566	418, 970	422, 794	105, 341	42, 203	169, 757
VALUE OF FARMS (LAND AND BUILDINGS) ($1,000)						
United States, total:						
1910	34, 801, 126	17, 340, 639	5, 056, 266	1, 455, 959	10, 977, 233	
1920	66, 316, 002	30, 710, 721	9, 153, 502	2, 665, 216	6, 012, 819	17, 773, 744
1930	47, 879, 838	21, 125, 468	5, 134, 335	2, 336, 678	3, 801, 132	12, 580, 406
1940	33, 641, 730	15, 397, 274	6, 112, 411	1, 443, 687	2, 227, 608	5, 891, 788
1945	46, 345, 926	21, 104, 511	10, 029, 155	2, 354, 583	3, 265, 430	10, 010, 267
1950	75, 200, 608	(4)	(4)	(4)	(4)	

[1] For 1910, standing renters (renters paying a fixed quantity of products) were included with "Cash tenants" for all States; for 1920, those for northern and western States were included with "Cash tenants," and those for the South with "Other tenants."
[2] Of these acreages, operator owned 130,745,000 in 1930, 144,890,000 in 1940, and 192,280,000 in 1945.
[3] Of these values, part owners owned property valued at $2,961,522,000 in 1940 and $5,098,872,000 in 1945.
[4] Based on reports for only a sample of farms.
[5] Averages only available. See table 719.

Source: Department of Commerce, Bureau of the Census; *U. S. Census of Agriculture*, 1950, Vol. II.

No. 717.—FARMS—NUMBER, BY TENURE OF OPERATOR, BY STATES: 1945 AND 1950

[For total number of farms (all tenures combined), see table 711. See also *Historical Statistics*, series E 19-24]

DIVISION AND STATE	NUMBER OF FARMS OPERATED BY—								TENANTS AS PERCENT OF TOTAL NUMBER	
	Full owners		Part owners		Managers		Tenants			
	1945	1950	1945	1950	1945	1950	1945	1950	1945	1950
United States	3,301,361	3,089,583	660,502	824,923	38,885	23,527	1,858,421	1,444,129	31.7	26.8
New England	132,943	86,845	9,370	11,784	2,383	817	5,615	3,779	3.7	3.7
Maine	38,736	27,180	1,900	2,203	211	102	1,337	783	3.2	2.6
New Hampshire	16,606	11,366	1,274	1,490	238	94	668	441	3.6	3.3
Vermont	23,300	15,273	1,567	2,741	321	142	1,302	887	4.9	4.7
Massachusetts	33,269	18,766	1,903	2,440	868	277	967	737	2.6	3.3
Rhode Island	2,745	1,997	433	394	113	31	312	176	8.7	6.8
Connecticut	18,287	12,263	2,293	2,426	632	171	1,029	755	4.6	4.8
Middle Atlantic	270,001	234,472	35,813	36,987	4,511	1,934	37,152	23,309	10.7	7.9
New York	116,070	97,576	19,045	18,934	2,038	833	12,337	7,634	8.3	6.1
New Jersey	19,759	19,557	3,221	3,054	575	312	2,671	1,915	10.2	7.7
Pennsylvania	134,172	117,339	13,547	14,999	1,898	789	22,144	13,760	12.9	9.4
East North Central	588,434	562,255	134,460	144,522	6,346	3,165	224,587	175,462	23.5	19.8
Ohio	146,331	134,909	24,835	28,026	1,399	722	48,010	35,642	21.8	17.9
Indiana	108,199	105,365	26,891	28,615	978	539	39,902	32,108	22.7	19.3
Illinois	87,527	87,234	35,266	39,771	1,680	793	79,766	67,470	39.1	34.6
Michigan	126,589	113,914	27,096	27,231	1,047	492	20,536	13,952	11.7	9.0
Wisconsin	119,788	120,773	20,372	20,879	1,242	619	36,343	26,290	20.4	15.6
West North Central	468,942	482,546	204,906	220,872	4,057	2,520	354,086	276,797	34.3	28.2
Minnesota	103,363	106,487	34,354	34,843	750	375	50,485	37,396	26.7	20.9
Iowa	94,573	94,833	25,195	30,229	921	561	88,245	77,536	42.2	38.2
Missouri	145,426	146,427	31,552	36,674	810	555	65,146	46,389	26.8	20.2
North Dakota	22,160	25,483	27,775	25,403	261	125	19,324	14,300	27.8	21.9
South Dakota	17,329	20,697	24,808	25,334	312	224	26,166	20,197	38.1	30.4
Nebraska	33,622	37,939	24,603	27,164	432	333	53,099	41,747	47.5	38.9
Kansas	52,460	50,680	36,531	41,135	571	347	51,621	39,232	38.6	29.9
South Atlantic	583,525	546,883	57,915	100,491	6,614	3,936	395,421	307,688	37.9	32.1
Delaware	6,527	5,194	629	917	205	72	1,935	1,265	20.8	17.0
Maryland	28,386	25,671	2,564	3,387	532	338	9,493	6,711	23.0	18.6
District of Columbia	17	16	2	2	20	9	1	1	2.5	3.6
Virginia	124,383	108,338	12,219	16,209	1,273	571	35,176	25,879	20.3	17.1
West Virginia	78,398	67,583	4,398	5,280	417	218	14,387	8,353	14.7	10.3
North Carolina	144,450	142,085	19,835	35,422	550	516	122,577	110,485	42.6	38.3
South Carolina	59,757	59,282	7,486	16,495	473	401	80,029	63,186	54.2	45.3
Georgia	96,134	95,908	7,217	16,619	1,008	844	121,538	84,820	53.8	42.8
Florida	45,473	42,806	3,565	6,160	1,836	967	10,285	6,988	16.8	12.3
East South Central	498,413	478,925	52,090	97,736	2,182	2,062	407,144	334,279	42.4	36.6
Kentucky	159,889	143,455	14,332	25,493	435	416	63,845	49,112	26.8	22.5
Tennessee	139,072	134,670	17,615	28,851	390	377	77,354	67,733	33.0	29.2
Alabama	100,072	97,747	13,218	25,716	389	436	109,690	87,613	49.1	41.4
Mississippi	99,380	103,053	6,925	17,676	968	833	156,255	129,821	59.3	51.6
West South Central	427,118	385,315	83,602	127,772	4,397	3,981	362,714	263,355	41.3	33.7
Arkansas	99,694	93,643	9,904	19,640	561	544	88,610	68,602	44.6	37.6
Louisiana	58,761	62,810	6,433	11,584	560	588	63,541	49,199	49.1	39.6
Oklahoma	70,669	63,723	27,552	33,315	698	481	65,771	44,727	39.9	31.4
Texas	197,994	165,139	39,613	63,233	2,578	2,368	144,792	100,827	37.6	30.4
Mountain	119,910	112,155	51,262	49,543	2,536	1,922	38,819	31,238	18.3	16.0
Montana	16,622	16,090	14,530	13,573	317	267	6,278	5,155	16.6	14.7
Idaho	26,109	25,947	6,785	6,890	240	164	8,364	7,283	20.2	18.1
Wyoming	5,772	6,008	4,406	4,249	301	214	2,597	2,143	19.9	17.0
Colorado	22,986	23,582	10,809	11,255	528	366	13,295	10,375	27.9	22.8
New Mexico	18,232	14,535	7,088	5,731	299	278	4,076	3,047	13.7	13.0
Arizona	9,064	6,718	1,867	2,115	525	343	1,686	1,236	12.8	11.9
Utah	18,483	16,854	5,440	5,371	193	196	2,206	1,755	8.4	7.3
Nevada	2,642	2,423	337	359	133	94	317	234	9.2	7.5
Pacific	212,075	200,187	31,082	35,216	5,859	3,190	32,913	28,222	11.7	10.6
Washington	61,280	53,284	9,042	9,456	596	361	8,969	6,719	11.2	9.6
Oregon	47,847	46,069	7,934	8,282	521	273	6,823	5,203	10.8	8.7
California	102,948	100,834	14,106	17,478	4,742	2,556	17,121	16,300	12.3	11.9

Source: Department of Commerce, Bureau of the Census; *U. S. Census of Agriculture: 1950*, Vol. II.

No. 718.—Farm Acreage, by Tenure of Operator, by States:[1] 1945 and 1950

[In thousands of acres. For total farm acreage (all tenures combined), see table 711. See also *Historical Statistics*, series E 31-35]

DIVISION AND STATE	ALL LAND IN FARMS OPERATED BY—									
	Full owners		Part owners				Managers		Tenants	
			Total		Rented					
	1945	1950	1945	1950	1945	1950	1945	1950	1945	1950
United States	412,282	418,970	371,251	422,394	178,902	195,295	104,272	105,341	267,634	211,990
The North	176,048	174,526	143,634	163,197	66,541	69,397	9,583	9,692	134,431	116,975
The South	173,119	172,513	71,402	192,324	34,390	52,915	28,957	29,834	79,316	67,345
The West	64,191	70,332	156,195	106,133	78,391	72,936	67,732	67,316	27,697	26,740
New England:										
Maine	4,066	3,522	270	510	101	121	71	70	108	79
New Hampshire	1,616	1,266	228	342	72	97	97	50	67	57
Vermont	3,280	2,578	308	722	122	213	101	63	202	165
Massachusetts	1,459	1,159	216	348	78	110	147	90	45	55
Rhode Island	169	122	46	46	20	19	20	9	22	14
Connecticut	1,066	770	340	373	126	138	126	55	69	74
Middle Atlantic:										
New York	11,872	10,927	3,446	2,712	1,213	1,348	687	308	1,296	1,070
New Jersey	1,061	1,606	264	463	136	146	171	113	291	201
Pennsylvania	10,494	10,609	1,941	2,285	604	796	463	306	2,122	1,813
East North Central:										
Ohio	11,340	10,886	4,089	4,655	1,843	2,161	440	267	6,079	5,160
Indiana	8,898	8,619	4,962	5,330	2,372	2,746	331	251	5,946	5,409
Illinois	8,929	8,745	7,886	8,982	3,952	4,535	524	364	14,296	12,985
Michigan	10,498	10,440	4,530	4,672	1,855	1,900	418	225	2,870	1,852
Wisconsin	14,218	14,979	3,695	3,889	1,390	1,388	414	285	5,298	4,068
West North Central:										
Minnesota	14,590	16,175	8,967	9,042	3,604	3,736	260	188	9,590	7,478
Iowa	12,505	12,481	8,531	7,080	2,587	2,501	314	218	15,774	16,303
Missouri	18,103	19,044	7,460	8,736	3,317	3,575	463	420	9,234	8,524
North Dakota	5,827	11,862	22,471	21,644	10,947	9,401	444	204	9,250	7,404
South Dakota	4,091	7,551	26,579	27,438	14,390	12,188	1,363	1,763	9,998	9,032
Nebraska	10,044	12,407	18,582	19,775	7,240	7,599	1,500	2,013	16,460	13,272
Kansas	10,973	10,332	21,194	24,062	10,963	12,586	790	714	15,693	12,614
South Atlantic:										
Delaware	511	497	94	158	39	82	86	38	264	198
Maryland	2,368	2,439	376	563	147	218	278	167	1,177	906
Dist. of Columbia	(2)	(2)	(2)	(2)	(2)	(2)	2	1	(2)	(2)
Virginia	11,085	10,505	1,643	2,447	602	985	769	531	2,690	1,949
West Virginia	6,776	6,410	677	892	261	321	176	116	1,092	806
North Carolina	10,483	10,544	1,646	3,148	608	1,263	205	326	6,196	5,340
South Carolina	6,043	6,149	919	2,229	347	954	501	565	3,560	2,806
Georgia	12,350	14,076	1,306	3,788	510	1,546	1,137	1,484	8,793	6,463
Florida	6,402	7,279	3,569	4,965	1,878	2,509	2,381	3,300	1935	996
East South Central:										
Kentucky	12,467	12,692	1,878	2,862	696	1,096	321	228	4,468	9,681
Tennessee	10,886	11,031	1,926	3,162	696	1,117	217	345	4,790	4,097
Alabama	10,044	10,689	2,004	4,418	699	2,004	501	683	6,493	5,149
Mississippi	11,534	11,756	1,230	3,193	502	1,690	1,148	1,072	5,714	4,691
West South Central:										
Arkansas	10,388	10,318	1,777	3,716	760	1,791	614	610	4,388	4,227
Louisiana	5,368	5,326	1,126	2,390	569	1,375	580	1,201	2,804	2,345
Oklahoma	9,841	9,838	12,455	15,980	6,827	7,495	1,475	1,087	11,410	9,115
Texas	50,965	44,435	37,954	54,332	19,440	28,566	18,538	18,062	33,980	26,897
Mountain:										
Montana	9,109	10,909	39,642	39,078	18,325	14,776	5,291	4,000	4,745	5,771
Idaho	4,812	5,316	5,519	5,819	2,470	2,518	668	650	1,504	1,388
Wyoming	2,380	3,806	19,519	20,170	5,052	7,992	7,806	8,382	2,501	2,060
Colorado	7,616	8,248	19,976	20,425	6,741	8,244	3,696	3,767	5,097	4,423
New Mexico	6,705	7,725	24,780	24,073	14,081	12,062	13,123	12,735	3,022	2,969
Arizona	1,584	3,066	11,581	11,892	9,187	8,445	25,548	24,126	1,173	902
Utah	3,694	3,666	4,344	4,682	1,904	1,904	1,880	2,202	421	255
Nevada	1,533	2,392	1,290	1,611	635	669	3,123	2,855	253	208
Pacific:										
Washington	8,062	4,542	7,062	5,685	3,396	4,220	818	1,217	2,906	3,774
Oregon	7,705	8,066	8,760	9,094	3,601	2,764	1,566	1,440	1,778	1,679
California	11,189	11,396	12,863	14,814	7,341	8,219	6,309	5,911	4,674	4,443

[1] Includes land subrented to others.
[2] 500 acres or less.

Source: Department of Commerce, Bureau of the Census; *U. S. Census of Agriculture: 1950*, Vol. II.

No. 719.—AVERAGE VALUE OF FARMS (LAND AND BUILDINGS), BY TENURE OF OPERATOR, BY STATES: 1945 AND 1950

[Based on reports for only a sample of farms. For total value of farms and average value per farm for all tenures combined, see table 711]

DIVISION AND STATE	AVERAGE VALUE PER FARM (DOLLARS)								AVERAGE VALUE PER ACRE (DOLLARS), 1950			
	Full owners		Part owners		Managers		Tenants		Full owners	Part owners	Managers	Tenants
	1945	1950	1945	1950	1945	1950	1945	1950				
United States	6,393	10,716	15,184	25,133	60,552	128,255	6,941	12,943	79.06	49.24	34.60	87.93
The North	7,262	11,947	15,306	25,873	41,760	75,692	13,178	23,997	91.07	67.80	79.38	109.01
The South	4,508	7,588	9,982	16,860	60,530	125,761	3,103	5,818	63.21	50.22	38.91	65.35
The West	11,145	19,352	26,847	53,090	99,304	226,324	15,256	31,969	86.49	29.36	23.71	71.51
New England:												
Maine	3,577	6,991	6,923	13,642	20,324	63,748	2,752	5,416	52.99	58.27	84.45	52.79
N. Hamp	3,810	7,894	6,574	14,465	24,930	44,672	4,217	12,264	73.92	59.18	101.70	88.73
Vermont	4,718	9,490	8,201	14,205	16,728	39,823	4,932	10,414	55.57	56.10	84.50	49.59
Massachusetts	5,999	12,362	11,926	20,552	43,484	68,928	5,395	9,321	200.54	138.63	225.12	150.96
Rhode Island	7,609	14,328	15,714	29,141	49,491	88,147	7,458	10,776	227.34	240.63	196.52	267.18
Connecticut	9,127	16,216	16,088	32,286	79,669	160,940	8,628	26,073	260.05	203.76	448.12	198.34
Middle Atlantic:												
New York	5,924	10,256	11,179	18,915	49,161	59,238	7,043	12,276	90.39	91.97	196.05	84.69
New Jersey	8,913	17,231	16,302	29,879	65,783	77,462	9,934	22,148	340.74	228.85	245.34	192.05
Pennsylvania	4,989	8,907	9,208	16,584	38,784	74,683	6,359	13,583	102.81	107.25	202.55	124.50
E. N. Central:												
Ohio	6,370	10,948	14,120	23,982	42,560	70,724	10,958	20,670	132.27	139.08	189.22	142.70
Indiana	7,172	10,816	16,013	26,969	37,183	74,964	13,818	25,804	126.16	138.42	157.18	154.03
Illinois	11,077	16,123	23,092	35,733	48,999	109,688	22,519	38,701	153.95	158.32	224.61	199.23
Michigan	5,609	9,219	10,375	16,544	38,258	57,991	8,185	14,243	99.32	94.35	124.36	100.53
Wisconsin	7,075	10,817	10,212	16,268	27,991	62,237	9,465	14,941	86.25	86.95	142.67	97.04
W. N. Central:												
Minnesota	7,941	12,735	12,112	19,848	28,033	48,516	11,405	20,112	81.94	75.56	118.62	98.73
Iowa	14,079	20,985	23,196	26,637	36,274	77,612	18,831	31,945	154.61	156.17	189.52	168.77
Missouri	5,078	7,839	10,125	15,219	34,838	71,159	6,766	11,195	50.63	63.14	95.85	74.47
North Dakota	8,538	15,085	12,442	21,666	27,832	52,584	8,605	16,163	32.40	26.24	29.33	31.05
South Dakota	8,986	15,607	13,316	25,667	37,802	80,344	10,137	19,247	43.14	24.36	10.69	47.72
Nebraska	12,144	19,505	21,211	35,796	52,226	134,884	14,058	24,463	57.46	48.77	18.71	77.96
Kansas	9,394	14,798	21,659	36,623	42,278	90,408	12,845	24,014	69.66	63.52	49.21	68.89
South Atlantic:												
Delaware	6,237	10,982	9,508	20,133	57,420	73,613	7,355	12,501	122.24	113.62	141.13	89.61
Maryland	7,370	12,519	12,942	22,009	42,342	71,321	8,131	14,146	129.84	130.44	172.31	99.05
Virginia	4,845	8,086	7,181	12,540	45,498	96,407	3,425	5,552	83.70	81.74	99.94	70.42
West Virginia	3,375	5,534	5,807	9,111	27,333	55,915	2,742	4,673	59.00	56.88	102.92	51.06
North Carolina	3,727	6,530	4,405	8,274	30,179	73,898	2,943	5,558	89.97	95.75	110.13	117.80
South Carolina	4,026	6,733	4,471	8,675	33,732	80,863	1,882	3,298	69.27	64.48	68.07	74.65
Georgia	3,675	6,036	5,438	9,257	29,492	64,419	1,909	3,230	44.28	40.12	41.12	42.18
Florida	6,925	12,768	12,341	20,412	62,959	243,890	2,324	4,907	77.72	28.34	56.75	40.53
E. S. Central:												
Kentucky	4,169	6,589	5,255	9,480	72,339	92,102	3,797	7,094	75.04	83.56	183.79	94.49
Tennessee	3,860	6,054	5,253	8,805	43,313	64,730	2,906	4,749	75.07	80.32	114.09	78.92
Alabama	2,903	4,996	4,749	7,964	38,610	57,341	1,745	3,033	48.07	47.29	39.44	53.07
Mississippi	3,333	5,727	5,800	9,884	61,422	103,075	1,400	2,172	51.75	55.45	81.55	61.29
W. S. Central:												
Arkansas	3,405	5,410	6,424	11,257	58,676	94,878	2,560	4,905	50.76	60.32	87.19	80.57
Louisiana	3,942	6,565	9,079	15,941	77,938	161,587	2,182	3,988	81.87	82.33	76.40	86.56
Oklahoma	4,807	8,435	13,575	22,886	40,182	92,519	5,422	11,257	54.05	47.87	44.91	55.48
Texas	7,552	14,099	20,444	36,560	105,635	203,122	6,890	16,153	53.81	42.46	22.38	56.44
Mountain:												
Montana	8,368	17,831	19,670	39,604	97,533	162,214	9,887	21,947	26.69	14.18	11.09	21.50
Idaho	8,960	16,567	21,227	40,790	46,838	78,212	12,451	25,445	83.37	51.94	25.62	126.53
Wyoming	9,354	18,495	26,814	51,478	105,786	217,089	10,808	24,155	27.21	11.40	6.89	24.86
Colorado	8,227	17,270	18,911	43,251	49,224	196,820	10,905	23,404	43.99	24.34	18.20	57.42
New Mexico	5,536	14,498	19,992	53,802	164,885	203,491	8,541	23,870	27.55	13.55	7.10	25.54
Arizona	11,151	25,120	39,425	84,234	164,623	375,048	15,878	38,587	52.94	14.80	8.67	52.56
Utah	8,029	16,250	14,702	26,764	72,569	100,282	8,812	16,716	74.76	34.48	9.51	76.85
Nevada	13,777	29,259	33,897	53,713	142,922	198,599	16,167	22,208	30.13	16.24	10.87	42.89
Pacific:												
Washington	7,430	13,019	28,496	51,279	52,720	118,225	17,372	38,415	145.07	56.15	41.74	91.21
Oregon	8,233	14,803	24,675	44,149	53,740	135,294	11,737	25,325	86.43	41.85	25.08	81.82
California	17,950	27,070	49,493	86,377	106,602	272,856	25,291	47,749	244.63	110.93	109.31	172.93

Source: Department of Commerce, Bureau of the Census; U. S. Census of Agriculture: 1950, Vol. II.

No. 720.—FARMS—NUMBER, ACREAGE, AND AVERAGE VALUE, BY COLOR OF OPER-
ATOR, BY STATES: 1945 AND 1950

[Acreage in thousands; average value in dollars. See also *Historical Statistics*, series K 43-45]

DIVISION AND STATE	NUMBER OF FARMS				ALL LAND IN FARMS				AVERAGE VALUE (LAND AND BUILDINGS)			
	White		Nonwhite		White		Nonwhite		Per farm		Per acre	
	1945	1950	1945	1950	1945	1950	1945	1950	White, 1950	Non-white, 1950	White, 1950	Non-white, 1950
U. S.	5,100,954	4,301,343	689,215	559,919	1,100,859	1,095,919	46,787	62,867	(¹)	(¹)	(¹)	(¹)
N. E.:												
Maine	42,145	30,330	39	19	4,615	4,180	3	2	(¹)	(¹)	(¹)	(¹)
N. H.	18,788	12,388	6	5	2,017	1,713	(¹)	(¹)	(¹)	(¹)	(¹)	(¹)
Vt.	26,470	19,032	14	11	3,626	3,335	3	2	(¹)	(¹)	(¹)	(¹)
Mass.	26,602	22,121	234	99	2,073	1,637	6	4	(¹)	(¹)	(¹)	(¹)
R. I.	3,507	2,504	76	4	365	191	(¹)	(¹)	(¹)	(¹)	(¹)	(¹)
Conn.	22,177	16,586	64	29	1,591	1,271	2	1	(¹)	(¹)	(¹)	(¹)
M. A.:												
N. Y.	148,528	134,602	662	375	17,524	15,982	46	34	(¹)	(¹)	(¹)	(¹)
N. J.	35,659	24,189	697	480	1,799	1,710	19	10	(¹)	(¹)	(¹)	(¹)
Pa.	171,412	146,600	349	278	14,001	14,097	20	16	(¹)	(¹)	(¹)	(¹)
E. N. C.:												
Ohio	219,470	198,420	1,116	930	21,851	20,928	77	61	(¹)	(¹)	(¹)	(¹)
Ind.	175,304	166,306	378	321	20,008	19,636	24	20	(¹)	(¹)	(¹)	(¹)
Ill.	206,235	194,465	914	830	31,549	30,620	62	52	(¹)	(¹)	(¹)	(¹)
Mich.	174,347	154,792	1,021	797	18,234	17,237	58	43	(¹)	(¹)	(¹)	(¹)
Wis.	177,466	166,339	279	222	23,564	23,304	27	15	(¹)	(¹)	(¹)	(¹)
W. N. C.:												
Minn.	188,745	178,064	207	147	33,119	33,669	21	21	(¹)	(¹)	(¹)	(¹)
Iowa	208,750	203,069	144	90	34,444	34,386	70	9	(¹)	(¹)	(¹)	(¹)
Mo.	238,987	228,813	2,997	3,212	35,101	34,981	178	163	(¹)	(¹)	(¹)	(¹)
N. Dak.	68,789	64,800	731	601	40,783	40,925	218	269	(¹)	(¹)	(¹)	(¹)
S. Dak.	67,156	65,227	1,549	1,215	41,854	42,723	1,145	2,063	(¹)	(¹)	(¹)	(¹)
Nebr.	111,547	107,049	210	134	47,724	47,435	30	32	(¹)	(¹)	(¹)	(¹)
Kans.	160,408	130,920	750	474	48,478	48,568	112	58	(¹)	(¹)	(¹)	(¹)
S. A.:												
Del.	8,905	7,056	691	392	888	831	36	20	12,941	5,689	115.32	106.06
Md.	37,657	33,504	4,218	3,603	3,947	3,865	232	191	15,082	5,419	135.30	113.02
D. C.	57	27	3	1	1	(¹)	(¹)	(¹)				
Va.	138,890	122,800	34,963	28,943	14,807	14,021	1,851	1,651	6,674	3,434	84.36	66.86
W. Va.	96,900	81,062	700	372	8,195	8,195	20	19	5,800	3,080	56.72	64.84
N. C.	313,130	215,956	74,273	72,552	14,308	14,191	3,310	3,127	7,125	4,384	97.33	106.03
S. C.	76,689	70,022	69,136	61,842	8,203	9,316	2,419	2,562	7,837	2,765	70.63	66.15
Ga.	164,469	147,834	78,411	50,357	19,017	22,309	4,688	3,549	6,361	2,523	44.30	36.32
Fla.	50,734	49,415	10,438	7,506	12,572	15,967	811	580	17,443	2,809	56.70	31.83
E. S. C.:												
Ky.	232,542	213,888	8,909	4,893	19,499	19,941	236	201	7,223	3,696	80.08	86.08
Tenn.	262,902	207,570	27,829	24,061	15,608	17,814	1,121	1,021	6,480	3,103	77.44	73.40
Ala.	186,130	164,318	67,220	47,294	15,000	17,974	3,466	2,915	5,625	1,968	80.57	38.56
Miss.	121,213	126,294	142,313	123,089	14,393	16,118	6,323	4,592	6,538	1,960	36.35	54.40
W. S. C.:												
Ark.	147,494	141,588	51,275	40,841	15,728	17,413	1,720	1,488	7,030	2,536	50.34	70.29
La.	88,164	93,825	46,131	40,656	8,335	9,802	1,768	1,600	9,057	2,646	53.26	77.28
Okla.	153,596	133,228	11,304	9,018	35,040	34,086	1,121	951	12,622	3,642	51.83	35.36
Tex.	320,027	297,062	45,950	34,518	138,628	143,224	2,710	2,165	22,071	3,156	46.07	52.17
Mt.:												
Mont.	36,608	34,261	1,220	804	57,820	57,088	967	1,259	(¹)	(¹)	(¹)	(¹)
Idaho	40,951	30,824	537	460	12,481	13,047	52	177	(¹)	(¹)	(¹)	(¹)
Wyo.	12,731	12,391	325	223	32,814	33,332	302	2,008	(¹)	(¹)	(¹)	(¹)
N. Mex.	47,008	45,150	610	428	35,531	37,195	667	828	(¹)	(¹)	(¹)	(¹)
Ariz.	27,806	21,615	1,800	1,784	46,481	40,826	2,157	6,496	(¹)	(¹)	(¹)	(¹)
Utah	12,194	9,317	1,006	1,098	35,060	20,428	1,000	19,496	(¹)	(¹)	(¹)	(¹)
Nev.	25,988	22,951	439	326	10,277	10,130	32	735	(¹)	(¹)	(¹)	(¹)
	2,987	2,753	642	387	5,838	6,122	340	941	(¹)	(¹)	(¹)	(¹)
Pac.:												
Wash.	79,678	62,944	809	876	16,616	16,856	102	511	(¹)	(¹)	(¹)	(¹)
Oreg.	62,657	58,337	638	636	19,068	19,321	85	407	(¹)	(¹)	(¹)	(¹)
Calif.	136,279	132,484	2,638	4,694	34,736	36,345	317	869	(¹)	(¹)	(¹)	(¹)

¹ Based on reports for only a sample of farms. ² Not available. ³ 500 acres or less.

Source: Department of Commerce, Bureau of the Census; *U. S. Census of Agriculture: 1950*, Vol. II.

No. 721.—MORTGAGED FARMS—NUMBER, ACREAGE, VALUE, AND AMOUNT OF INDEBTEDNESS IN COMPARISON WITH ALL FARMS, BY TENURE AND REGION: 1935 TO 1950

[1950 data based on sample of farms and exclude District of Columbia]

REGION AND TENURE	FARMS Total number	Mortgaged farms Number	Mortgaged farms Per cent of total	LAND IN FARMS All farms, acres (1,000)	Mortgaged farms Acres (1,000)	Mortgaged farms Per cent of total	VALUE OF FARMS (LAND AND BUILDINGS) All farms ($1,000)	Mortgaged farms Amount ($1,000)	Mortgaged farms Per cent of total	MORTGAGE DEBT Total ($1,000)	Ratio to value of mortgaged farms (percent)	Debt per acre	Debt per farm	Equity per mortgaged farm
United States, all tenures 1935	6,812,350	2,350,313	34.5	1,054,515	(¹)	(¹)	32,858,844	15,873,779	47.2	7,654,469	41.5	(¹)	3,227	(³)
1940	6,096,799	2,363,777	38.8	1,060,852	457,874	43.1	33,641,789		35.1	6,556,929	39.5	$14.40	2,786	$4,299
1945	5,859,169	1,713,855	29.3	1,141,615	273,125	24.1	46,385,926			4,949,915	24.2	18.24	2,893	9,417
1950	5,382,134	1,480,401	27.5	1,163,545	303,610	26.2	74,704,673	22,046,126	26.3	5,677,378	25.3	18.38	3,710	11,128
Full owners 1935	3,310,224	1,270,107	39.6	390,075	181,505	46.5	14,626,646	7,385,406	49.5	3,652,364	60.2	20.25	2,890	2,870
1940	3,084,138	1,276,312	41.4	382,098	180,452	47.2	15,754,974	7,987,195	51.6	3,353,375	42.5	18.68	2,623	3,547
1945	3,301,361	997,205	30.2	412,355	149,105	36.2	23,106,611	8,106,198	34.7	2,639,787	32.9	18.04	2,697	5,592
1950	3,089,057	894,095	28.9	418,970	135,343	32.3	32,406,373	11,273,373	34.5	3,116,307	27.6	23.03	3,485	9,128
Part owners (owned portion only)² 1935	698,867	336,416	54.7	181,709	93,882	64.9	3,564,202	2,384,405	66.2	1,165,864	46.9	11.78	3,287	3,724
1940	615,039	336,416	54.7	144,639	90,897	64.9	3,864,202	2,862,721	66.2	1,105,864	46.9	11.78	3,287	3,724
1945	640,002	277,929	41.5	162,259	89,897	44.8	5,899,671		44.5	875,038	30.6	9.73	3,194	7,256
1950	924,921	281,475	34.1	229,304	90,079	39.5	11,440,118	4,855,278	40.1	1,178,637	25.7	13.08	4,187	12,108
Tenant- and manager-operated farms (including rented portion of part-owner farms)² 1935	2,913,259	731,148	25.1	531,834	183,040	34.3	14,780,262	6,659,213	38.1	2,127,390	27.8	(¹)	(¹)	(³)
1940	2,397,622	749,049	31.2	534,115	183,119	35.0	19,375,664	5,347,605	38.1	1,376,692	37.8	11.63	4,235	(³)
1945	1,867,346	442,721	23.3	534,968	134,119	26.0	30,574,466	6,163,476		1,284,544	20.7	10.26	3,092	(³)
1950	1,467,646	304,830	20.8	611,291	75,188	10.3	30,636,681			1,789,290	24.0	15.43	3,933	(³)
The North, all tenures 1935	2,919,486	1,125,440	38.5	441,953	191,630	44.0	19,028,131	9,026,390	47.7	4,122,160	45.7	21.61	4,255	4,349
1940	2,463,676	884,975	35.7	433,088		43.0	15,451,414		37.4	3,031,631	31.9	18.41	3,655	7,297
1945	2,449,096	729,097	33.0	447,715		39.2	23,047,895	11,314,573		2,986,114	28.4	24.02	4,113	11,677
1950	3,121,923	988,780	28.8	440,528	194,320		32,782,988		34.3	1,857,183				(³)
The South, all tenures 1935	3,077,170	1,008,319	33.4	370,206	163,471	44.2	9,716,128	4,220,891	43.4	1,502,187	35.6	9.19	1,676	2,710
1940	2,881,135	660,309	22.9	370,186	115,409	30.5	13,148,534	4,073,520	31.0	1,184,935	29.1	10.27	1,795	4,575
1945	2,652,396	549,113	22.1	377,795	102,683	24.5	22,698,745	6,122,049	27.1	1,470,261	24.0	14.32	2,604	7,937
The West, all tenures 1935	970,359	236,063	41.4	355,356	102,273	40.0	6,097,317	2,635,489	52.4	962,663	26.6	9.41	4,621	7,181
1940	509,070	233,763	45.7	285,596	93,004	29.4	7,833,677	2,805,740	35.8	992,663	33.8	7.70	4,528	12,455
1950	461,673	168,191	36.4	316,105	76,007	22.6	14,048,127	4,612,405	32.8	1,123,903	34.8	14.66	6,676	30,717

¹ Not available.
² Acres, value, and debt for part-owner farms are for owned portion only; rented portion included with data for tenants and managers.
³ Average per farm not shown because acres and value include rented portion of part-owner farms.

Source: Department of Commerce, Bureau of the Census and Department of Agriculture, Bureau of Agricultural Economics; cooperative report, *Farm Mortgage Debt* (U.S. Census of Agriculture: 1950, Vol. V, pt. 8).

No. 722.—Mortgaged Farms—Number, Amount of Indebtedness, Acreage, and Value, by States: 1945 and 1950

DIVISION AND STATE	TOTAL NUMBER OF MORTGAGED FARMS		PERCENT OF ALL FARMS		TOTAL AMOUNT OF FARM-MORTGAGE DEBT ($1,000)		ALL MORTGAGED FARMS					
							Acreage (1,000)		Value of land and buildings ($1,000)		Ratio of debt to value (percent)	
	1945	1950	1945	1950	1945	1950	1945	1950	1945	1950	1945	1950
U. S.	1,712,285	1,466,461	28.3	27.5	4,940,915	5,579,278	273,123	269,610	16,375,954	22,049,128	30.2	25.3
New England	53,274	41,027	35.4	39.8	114,866	141,975	5,265	4,843	368,166	506,455	32.1	28.4
Maine	10,670	8,805	25.3	29.2	16,713	20,470	1,322	1,258	50,895	72,715	32.5	28.6
N. H.	6,068	5,349	32.2	40.1	9,705	15,570	660	654	27,649	50,159	34.1	31.0
Vt.	8,597	8,772	36.2	44.1	21,975	21,855	1,643	1,643	54,385	92,452	40.4	24.5
Mass.	17,138	10,429	46.3	46.9	36,778	38,526	934	724	117,631	141,239	31.3	27.5
R. I.	1,300	1,020	36.1	39.3	3,863	4,227	77	70	12,143	16,061	26.3	26.4
Conn.	8,821	6,630	36.3	42.5	26,105	31,028	563	501	95,457	126,245	27.3	24.6
Middle Atlantic	112,727	98,382	32.4	33.5	386,792	373,125	11,801	10,859	831,371	1,249,579	35.8	28.9
N. Y.	55,828	45,765	37.8	37.4	147,200	168,426	6,765	5,950	418,734	569,369	35.2	30.8
N. J.	10,785	9,818	41.1	39.5	36,235	44,914	744	640	123,378	210,842	31.8	21.6
Pa.	46,114	42,776	26.8	29.1	197,358	147,781	4,292	4,280	269,239	470,368	37.1	31.4
E. N. Central	422,707	377,728	33.3	31.4	1,530,538	1,133,491	46,346	33,532	5,472,319	4,145,412	31.7	27.4
Ohio	60,941	56,804	27.0	30.5	187,452	228,681	5,992	5,604	228,539	510,453	31.7	31.2
Ind.	65,790	57,129	37.4	34.3	176,466	200,426	7,785	6,453	604,242	856,345	32.6	33.3
Ill.	50,486	45,970	24.7	22.5	269,946	366,755	8,801	6,521	1,136,846	1,185,777	32.7	22.4
Mich.	65,391	43,996	37.3	31.4	144,946	155,514	6,953	4,931	446,994	496,916	32.4	31.3
Wis.	81,127	66,804	44.6	39.7	382,072	383,036	10,684	8,944	665,263	833,515	30.4	34.0
W. N. Central	304,270	307,126	32.4	31.3	1,642,640	1,327,612	107,454	76,076	4,534,363	5,373,584	33.1	24.9
Minn.	53,256	64,999	44.1	36.3	304,641	276,807	15,127	11,805	864,356	905,872	33.2	32.3
Iowa	58,987	67,809	41.6	32.4	425,039	433,878	15,154	11,537	1,584,856	1,791,603	33.3	24.2
Mo.	81,466	72,419	32.5	31.5	197,529	167,053	12,434	10,017	592,861	654,363	33.1	25.5
N. Dak.	27,646	19,215	30.8	29.4	91,461	69,108	14,046	10,009	260,808	300,968	35.1	23.0
S. Dak.	28,310	19,662	42.7	29.6	106,761	87,596	15,457	10,718	297,560	349,516	35.9	25.1
Nebr.	41,112	29,509	26.6	27.5	204,174	157,954	19,019	12,597	649,611	682,229	31.4	23.1
Kans.	46,608	34,322	31.0	26.1	171,535	145,375	16,216	9,306	614,939	631,677	27.0	23.0
S. Atlantic	309,835	199,369	26.1	20.2	225,712	442,526	34,238	22,441	1,688,363	1,696,875	26.8	26.1
Del.	2,705	2,039	28.1	27.3	6,498	9,630	282	232	20,261	27,744	32.0	30.2
Md.	13,884	11,863	33.6	32.0	40,627	53,640	1,564	1,281	128,688	183,399	31.6	30.2
Va.	30,072	23,918	17.4	15.6	61,765	74,723	8,682	3,764	220,114	272,912	28.3	27.6
W. Va.	13,411	12,747	12.7	15.6	18,658	24,804	1,456	1,420	69,724	90,441	31.5	27.4
N. C.	48,341	49,869	16.8	17.3	73,917	88,010	3,045	3,637	228,242	349,835	33.1	25.4
S. C.	33,892	27,555	22.3	19.6	37,500	41,124	3,048	2,357	118,759	177,949	31.7	23.1
Ga.	57,361	52,107	25.4	26.3	65,344	84,072	7,585	6,696	203,727	313,643	32.0	22.4
Fla.	11,870	13,645	19.4	24.0	30,313	65,795	2,796	4,046	113,823	280,556	26.6	23.4
E. S. Central	222,550	202,203	23.2	22.1	297,230	372,486	20,066	16,663	925,198	1,385,515	32.1	28.9
Ky.	44,712	41,717	18.7	19.1	81,579	102,902	4,496	3,966	276,311	373,250	35.2	27.0
Tenn.	42,942	46,540	18.3	20.1	66,433	86,015	4,083	3,772	210,227	337,605	31.1	26.1
Ala.	60,419	50,213	27.0	23.7	66,564	80,396	5,120	5,439	188,291	304,798	35.4	26.3
Miss.	74,484	63,733	26.3	25.4	83,744	101,234	5,967	5,465	250,369	369,764	32.4	27.4
W. S. Central	226,214	190,110	31.0	24.4	551,969	654,966	70,996	61,899	2,039,944	3,029,964	26.6	21.5
Ark.	47,899	40,189	32.9	22.0	62,696	85,320	5,096	4,872	224,206	334,885	28.1	24.5
La.	26,572	23,021	22.3	18.6	48,070	62,196	3,043	2,486	153,409	221,337	31.3	23.6
Okla.	50,397	40,211	30.5	25.3	116,780	116,917	12,287	9,867	352,726	491,035	33.0	23.6
Tex.	101,446	86,724	26.4	26.3	323,358	400,554	49,600	44,664	1,298,613	1,902,897	24.8	20.1
Mountain	65,466	70,635	32.2	35.9	262,291	494,562	66,257	58,017	959,294	1,779,318	27.4	26.9
Mont.	10,544	10,830	27.9	30.9	41,664	92,449	15,777	13,584	152,659	272,060	32.3	28.0
Idaho	17,134	15,745	41.3	39.1	56,494	79,269	5,144	4,770	216,500	333,590	27.0	23.8
Wyo.	5,945	5,206	44.7	42.0	24,954	54,622	12,965	9,259	97,749	159,555	26.4	33.9
Colo.	16,387	17,529	34.4	35.8	55,054	105,309	12,463	11,560	197,413	424,888	30.1	28.5
N. Mex.	5,391	6,904	17.8	29.4	24,924	47,606	12,764	9,792	102,678	214,545	33.2	22.2
Ariz.	2,741	3,928	28.4	27.7	22,334	38,751	5,096	3,689	78,794	165,348	34.8	24.9
Utah	8,634	8,767	32.8	36.2	25,720	42,312	3,307	2,564	93,875	174,569	27.7	24.2
Nev.	900	1,008	37.2	32.2	6,120	12,981	1,360	1,612	20,603	44,633	28.7	29.0
Pacific	95,168	95,166	35.2	26.8	663,998	695,465	26,617	20,586	1,555,187	1,896,367	36.0	34.7
Wash.	38,966	22,811	38.7	34.1	73,995	121,009	4,089	4,919	282,388	483,712	28.9	25.8
Oreg.	20,809	22,147	33.0	37.0	69,218	114,331	8,418	7,148	265,816	480,132	26.0	23.8
Calif.	55,385	32,208	39.9	26.1	315,845	460,866	12,890	9,434	1,531,177	1,942,435	24.0	25.3

[1] For 1945 includes data for District of Columbia.

Source: Department of Commerce, Bureau of the Census and Department of Agriculture, Bureau of Agricultural Economics; cooperative report, Farm Mortgage Debt (U. S. Census of Agriculture: 1950, Vol. V, pt. 6).

No. 728.—FARM-MORTGAGE DEBT—TOTAL AMOUNT OUTSTANDING, BY STATES, AS OF JANUARY 1: 1945 TO 1952

[Thousands of dollars]

DIVISION AND STATE	1945	1946	1947	1948	1949	1950	1951	1952
United States	4,932,942	4,681,720	4,777,355	4,881,744	5,106,183	5,407,310	5,827,586	6,299,576
New England	114,860	109,247	110,082	113,526	117,405	130,519	125,385	129,100
Maine	16,713	16,431	17,681	18,732	19,364	20,098	21,258	22,216
New Hampshire	9,706	9,584	9,822	10,586	11,409	12,094	12,976	13,086
Vermont	21,975	22,814	25,768	27,006	28,088	28,573	29,401	30,577
Massachusetts	36,778	32,980	30,361	31,277	32,086	32,924	33,662	34,082
Rhode Island	3,583	3,569	3,544	3,567	3,759	3,857	4,129	4,350
Connecticut	26,105	23,899	22,906	22,358	22,699	23,273	23,959	24,780
Middle Atlantic	293,792	304,891	307,979	323,595	335,401	345,385	360,610	371,296
New York	147,200	144,002	151,922	155,466	160,368	162,783	167,581	172,350
New Jersey	39,235	37,955	40,619	43,417	48,275	48,818	56,493	57,232
Pennsylvania	107,358	102,844	115,434	124,622	126,758	133,814	136,536	141,714
East North Central	1,020,226	966,659	961,627	976,692	1,011,676	1,052,619	1,129,613	1,195,838
Ohio	167,463	160,916	162,263	166,965	175,333	178,567	191,081	200,770
Indiana	176,466	168,391	169,400	173,568	183,430	194,406	207,928	223,766
Illinois	269,947	245,260	250,712	217,606	217,159	220,464	237,900	255,537
Michigan	144,363	144,940	155,705	163,424	175,418	186,087	200,196	214,053
Wisconsin	262,072	244,152	243,546	264,477	260,327	272,735	292,468	301,712
West North Central	1,594,067	1,427,603	1,346,752	1,261,197	1,248,475	1,295,396	1,359,539	1,452,062
Minnesota	304,641	273,364	257,608	244,485	237,572	244,853	266,728	265,865
Iowa	525,930	465,567	424,761	361,863	383,949	392,809	419,252	449,923
Missouri	197,520	193,533	198,380	198,921	204,877	212,192	223,614	234,729
North Dakota	91,461	80,778	76,146	70,361	67,387	70,026	75,043	79,457
South Dakota	98,786	87,222	80,626	70,632	67,847	71,730	77,071	84,878
Nebraska	204,174	175,922	160,963	141,935	139,870	147,788	156,642	163,926
Kansas	171,595	151,216	148,150	143,120	146,998	156,499	169,188	188,775
South Atlantic	325,712	344,262	391,547	433,481	471,934	505,006	557,376	619,950
Delaware	6,466	6,174	7,287	8,898	10,351	11,409	12,613	13,269
Maryland [1]	40,627	39,975	43,883	48,781	50,449	53,987	57,848	62,285
Virginia	61,765	64,685	72,256	78,123	87,265	94,532	101,530	111,486
West Virginia	18,656	17,870	20,229	21,601	22,585	23,574	26,996	30,667
North Carolina	73,917	76,810	87,836	96,041	96,252	97,373	101,268	108,206
South Carolina	37,500	37,868	40,542	45,112	49,029	52,564	58,053	62,953
Georgia	66,344	69,538	78,919	87,549	98,078	108,296	121,400	134,559
Florida	20,313	31,363	40,615	48,356	57,925	63,301	77,668	96,525
East South Central	297,320	296,977	322,368	342,155	366,546	397,405	428,044	463,242
Kentucky	81,579	79,125	82,650	86,569	91,922	97,870	108,110	116,859
Tennessee	65,433	65,830	70,121	76,965	82,576	89,678	95,703	105,081
Alabama	66,564	66,306	70,255	74,634	79,651	87,186	90,189	96,164
Mississippi	83,744	88,716	99,342	103,987	112,396	122,701	134,092	145,138
West South Central	551,903	529,092	556,891	586,535	617,473	674,348	730,745	802,661
Arkansas	63,695	66,536	72,477	76,897	86,102	98,525	101,235	111,375
Louisiana	48,070	51,693	55,826	59,796	64,282	71,214	76,347	83,319
Oklahoma	116,780	107,829	111,400	112,963	117,806	124,898	138,151	152,465
Texas	323,358	303,034	317,188	334,879	349,283	384,711	415,012	455,502
Mountain	242,291	259,790	284,530	322,004	361,225	399,757	453,993	507,003
Montana	41,664	39,904	40,912	42,143	45,676	49,357	56,301	64,845
Idaho	58,404	54,768	56,522	61,914	68,074	74,515	84,780	96,030
Wyoming	24,951	24,025	25,414	28,463	32,391	36,167	41,414	46,157
Colorado	58,064	59,444	66,738	75,187	86,755	96,337	112,547	130,036
New Mexico	24,924	27,039	32,499	41,863	49,018	55,950	59,909	63,025
Arizona	22,334	22,541	27,117	30,699	33,128	36,403	43,495	45,880
Utah	25,720	25,592	27,805	32,130	34,596	37,394	39,752	41,487
Nevada	6,120	6,477	7,523	9,605	11,570	13,824	15,795	17,543
Pacific	462,668	460,268	495,543	533,249	575,048	616,675	652,282	726,433
Washington	73,995	73,527	74,093	79,222	86,201	96,153	103,108	109,236
Oregon	69,218	68,779	78,862	85,574	92,497	100,582	110,517	125,671
California	318,845	317,962	342,608	368,453	396,350	419,340	438,657	493,526

[1] Includes District of Columbia.

Source: Department of Agriculture, Bureau of Agricultural Economics; annual report, *Agricultural Finance Review*.

No. 724.—Cash Receipts From Farm Marketings and Government Payments,
BY STATES: 1951

[In millions of dollars]

DIVISION AND STATE	Total	Crops	Live-stock and prod-ucts	Gov-ern-ment pay-ments	DIVISION AND STATE	Total	Crops	Live-stock and prod-ucts	Gov-ern-ment pay-ments
United States	32,907.5	15,652.9	19,069.0	205.6	S. Atlantic—Con.				
					Virginia	611.3	225.4	277.4	5.4
New England	775.1	216.4	555.7	4.8	West Virginia	142.3	24.9	116.1	1.2
Maine	181.1	72.3	107.3	1.0	North Carolina	965.3	731.5	155.5	8.0
New Hampshire	69.0	9.4	59.0	.5	South Carolina	416.4	328.7	84.4	2.7
Vermont	120.0	18.3	100.5	1.2	Georgia	837.6	673.9	423.9	2.6
Massachusetts	211.5	58.0	152.9	.7	Florida	530.3	396.0	130.3	2.4
Rhode Island	26.3	6.5	19.7	.1					
Connecticut	171.2	51.4	119.3	.5	East South Central	2,162.5	1,108.5	454.4	42.0
					Kentucky	680.0	351.1	281.0	7.4
Middle Atlantic	2,106.7	550.6	1,541.7	14.4	Tennessee	682.9	287.0	278.9	7.0
New York	904.0	235.5	655.1	7.1	Alabama	430.5	265.0	173.2	4.3
New Jersey	360.0	119.1	240.0	.9	Mississippi	568.1	355.2	164.7	5.2
Pennsylvania	842.7	192.7	643.6	6.4					
					West South Central	3,609.3	1,912.3	1,646.5	40.5
East North Central	6,134.0	1,754.4	4,396.8	41.7	Arkansas	573.5	362.5	204.4	6.5
Ohio	1,077.3	312.2	756.7	7.4	Louisiana	303.0	245.6	116.4	11.6
Indiana	1,145.5	311.5	830.2	6.9	Oklahoma	631.7	218.9	462.5	.2
Illinois	2,058.6	763.4	1,304.5	10.4	Texas	2,205.5	1,067.5	1,119.2	22.2
Michigan	734.1	243.4	476.9	3.2					
Wisconsin	1,135.5	117.9	1,009.7	3.0	Mountain	2,497.3	953.5	1,454.8	42.1
					Montana	441.3	200.4	234.6	4.8
West North Central	8,354.6	2,112.5	6,051.6	69.6	Idaho	357.6	177.0	174.3	1.9
Minnesota	1,294.5	301.3	993.7	7.5	Wyoming	196.0	20.1	145.5	1.7
Iowa	2,372.7	290.3	2,070.7	11.7	Colorado	561.2	170.1	385.5	4.7
Missouri	1,171.2	264.6	896.0	10.9	New Mexico	235.5	70.6	145.8	3.0
North Dakota	560.4	395.2	405.3	6.6	Arizona	359.1	231.6	124.1	1.5
South Dakota	697.1	196.4	405.2	6.5	Utah	191.2	44.5	142.2	4.2
Nebraska	1,163.0	308.2	844.7	9.1	Nevada	63.1	6.3	55.4	.3
Kansas	1,066.4	356.1	691.3	8.0					
					Pacific	3,716.7	2,236.8	1,459.0	31.0
South Atlantic	3,545.1	2,299.2	1,395.2	23.7	Washington	557.6	346.3	207.2	4.1
Delaware	113.0	22.4	89.1	.5	Oregon	424.4	233.2	207.9	2.4
Maryland	271.3	85.2	184.5	1.7	California	2,734.7	1,657.5	1,073.4	23.5

Source. Department of Agriculture, Bureau of Agricultural Economics; published in *The Farm Income Situation*.

No. 725.—Farm Income—Estimated Cash Receipts From Crops, Livestock
AND Products, BY Kind: 1930 to 1952

[In millions of dollars]

KIND	1930	1935	1940	1945	1948	1949	1950	1951	1952 (prel.)
CROPS									
All crops, total	3,864	3,367	3,436	9,419	13,136	12,526	12,352	13,063	14,627
Cotton and cottonseed	826	712	643	1,206	2,553	2,632	2,404	3,849	3,202
Tobacco	244	242	242	598	945	958	1,061	1,157	1,090
Feed grains	500	421	479	1,552	2,704	2,339	1,977	1,806	2,066
Oilbearing crops	72	69	126	610	1,043	846	982	1,086	1,021
Food grains and hay	557	302	576	1,434	2,103	3,290	2,156	1,916	2,175
Vegetables	722	489	871	1,594	1,773	1,641	1,406	1,670	1,800
Fruits and tree nuts	536	408	417	1,407	1,063	1,013	1,290	1,214	1,350
Sugar crops	90	73	79	186	155	161	205	182	140
Other crops	317	241	302	580	807	751	987	1,081	1,083
LIVESTOCK AND PRODUCTS									
All livestock and products, total	5,184	4,117	4,897	11,944	17,671	15,359	15,976	19,560	18,600
Hogs	1,135	682	836	2,393	3,680	3,125	3,184	3,504	3,446
Cattle and calves	1,184	1,063	1,376	3,318	5,385	4,849	5,673	6,687	6,487
Sheep and lambs	182	152	180	319	409	351	395	457	477
Wool	69	70	105	119	113	106	125	298	151
Dairy products	1,607	1,310	1,580	3,021	4,390	3,745	3,719	4,021	4,801
Poultry and eggs	1,002	799	833	2,921	3,190	3,115	2,821	3,587	3,456
Other	37	41	47	93	76	63	65	79	76

Source: Department of Agriculture, Bureau of Agricultural Economics; prior to 1940, data published in *Net Farm Income and Parity Report, 1948*; thereafter, *The Farm Income Situation*.

No. 726.—Farm Income, Prices Received and Paid by Farmers: 1930 to 1952

[Farm income in millions of dollars. See also *Historical Statistics*, series E 88-104]

ITEM	1930	1935	1940	1945	1949	1950	1951	1952 (prel.)
FARM INCOME								
Gross income	11,420	9,585	10,920	25,323	31,763	32,086	36,731	37,274
Cash receipts, total	9,050	7,647	9,056	22,125	28,129	28,611	32,908	33,417
Crops	3,864	2,987	3,435	9,419	12,585	12,352	13,053	14,627
Livestock and livestock products	5,186	4,117	4,897	11,964	15,359	15,976	19,569	18,498
Government payments		573	724	742	185	283	286	292
Value of home consumption	1,540	1,317	1,239	2,218	2,189	2,007	2,200	2,117
Rental value of dwellings	830	621	625	980	1,445	1,468	1,623	1,740
Total expenses of agricultural production	6,990	5,085	6,622	13,037	18,170	19,742	22,432	22,955
Net income of farm operators from current operations	4,430	4,500	4,298	12,286	13,593	12,344	14,299	14,319
Adjustment for inventory changes	−300	+536	+270	−462	−875	+918	+1,345	+352
Farm wages to laborers living on farms	805	551	731	1,617	2,001	1,909	2,049	2,064
Net cash income to persons on farms from farming	3,055	3,117	2,857	10,785	10,514	9,304	10,909	11,778
INDEX NUMBERS OF PRICES RECEIVED AND PAID (1910-14=100)								
Prices received by farmers:								
All farm products	125	109	100	206	249	256	302	288
Crops	116	104	91	203	223	232	264	267
Livestock and products	134	114	108	210	272	278	335	307
Retail prices paid by farmers:								
Living and production	140	123	122	179	240	246	271	273
Living	144	124	121	182	243	246	268	271
Production	135	122	123	176	238	246	273	274
Payable per acre:								
Interest payable	206	135	98	69	76	82	89	96
Taxes payable	281	178	186	181	275	296	311	327
Prices paid, including interest, taxes, and wage rates	151	124	124	189	250	255	281	286
PARITY RATIO								
Ratio of prices received to prices paid, including interest, taxes, and wage rates	83	88	81	109	100	100	107	101

Source: Department of Agriculture, Bureau of Agricultural Economics: Farm income—*The Farm Income Situation;* indexes—annual report, *Agricultural Statistics,* and published currently in *Agricultural Prices.*

No. 727.—Prices Received by Farmers—Indexes, by Major Groups of Products: 1915 to 1952

[1910-14=100. Indexes cover 45 major farm products. See also *Historical Statistics,* series E 95-97]

PERIOD	All groups	CROPS							LIVESTOCK AND PRODUCTS		
		Food grains	Feed grains and hay	Tobacco	Cotton	Fruits	Truck crops	Oil bearing crops	Meat animals	Dairy products	Poultry and eggs
1915-19	164	193	161	183	175	126		201	162	147	153
1920-24	150	147	125	189	197	157	[1] 152	155	121	159	163
1925-29	148	141	118	169	150	146	145	135	145	161	155
1930-34	88	70	76	117	77	98	104	78	83	105	94
1935-39	107	94	95	172	87	95	95	113	117	119	108
1940-44	154	123	119	241	138	150	164	170	166	169	145
1945-49	250	222	205	378	240	216	206	289	291	264	213
1947	275	270	249	374	272	212	226	363	329	272	219
1948	285	250	250	380	270	174	214	351	361	300	235
1949	249	219	170	398	245	199	201	242	311	251	219
1950	256	224	187	402	280	200	185	276	340	247	181
1951	302	243	220	436	335	193	239	339	411	284	226
1952	288	244	227	432	309	195	254	296	358	302	203
March	288	251	229	435	309	176	265	284	372	305	177
June	292	238	226	· 437	319	220	250	289	380	277	181
September	288	240	234	428	329	200	182	305	349	307	227
December	269	247	218	428	268	206	256	300	291	309	221

[1] 1924 only.

Source: Department of Agriculture, Bureau of Agricultural Economics; annual report, *Crops and Markets.* Also published currently in *Agricultural Prices.*

No. 728.—FARM INCOME AND EXPENDITURES—ESTIMATED NET CASH AVAILABLE
TO FARM OPERATORS AFTER FARM EXPENDITURES: 1929 TO 1952

[In millions of dollars]

YEAR	Cash receipts [1]	CASH EXPENDITURES							Farm operators' net cash income from farming
		Total	Current operating expenses [2]	Farm capital expenditures	Interest on farm mortgage debt	Taxes on farm property	Total cash wages of hired labor	Net rent to nonfarm landlords [3]	
1929	11,299	7,543	3,409	1,414	582	641	955	542	3,756
1930	9,060	6,355	3,087	1,044	570	638	875	391	2,405
1931	6,369	4,927	2,328	600	552	581	570	195	1,442
1932	4,735	3,803	1,874	300	526	504	490	309	922
1933	5,430	3,826	1,875	377	472	454	454	214	1,613
1934	6,760	4,318	2,076	570	430	420	508	319	2,442
1935	7,647	4,922	2,230	872	396	431	577	407	2,725
1936	8,634	5,509	2,544	1,059	364	436	653	453	3,125
1937	9,155	6,163	2,868	1,310	341	448	755	441	2,992
1938	8,149	5,703	2,653	1,196	330	444	767	369	2,446
1939	8,552	6,123	2,916	1,226	305	452	782	442	2,430
1940	9,056	6,754	3,336	1,408	293	446	816	460	2,302
1941	11,619	7,891	3,737	1,600	284	457	1,013	710	3,728
1942	16,136	9,706	4,965	1,682	272	461	1,345	981	6,430
1943	20,003	10,833	5,885	1,455	246	472	1,687	1,088	9,170
1944	21,153	11,777	6,320	1,766	230	495	1,861	1,103	9,376
1945	22,126	12,667	6,929	1,891	220	554	1,962	1,131	9,488
1946	25,336	15,144	7,891	2,968	216	617	2,155	1,307	10,192
1947	30,020	18,323	9,473	4,183	222	708	2,373	1,387	11,697
1948	30,464	20,292	10,398	5,072	229	765	2,540	1,288	10,172
1949	28,129	19,256	9,571	5,124	242	822	2,415	1,082	8,871
1950	28,611	20,874	10,648	5,597	262	865	2,304	1,198	7,737
1951	32,908	23,670	12,515	6,179	284	917	2,467	1,308	9,238
1952	33,417	23,322	12,627	5,607	307	969	2,485	1,327	10,005

[1] From farm marketings and Government payments.
[2] Excludes hired labor.
[3] Includes share rent as well as cash rent paid to nonfarm landlords because their share included in cash receipts.

Source: Department of Agriculture, Bureau of Agricultural Economics; *The Farm Income Situation.*

No. 729.—FARM TAXES AND INSURANCE: 1925 TO 1951

[See also *Historical Statistics* E 76-87]

ITEM	1925	1930	1935	1940	1945	1949	1950	1951
Taxes levied on farm real estate, total (million dollars)	517	567	394	402	471	699	735	775
Amount per acre (dollars)	.56	.57	.37	.38	.41	.64	.64	.68
Amount per $100 of value (dollars)	1.07	1.20	1.15	1.22	.90	1.10	1.01	.98
Taxes levied on farm personal property (millions of dollars)	63	71	37	44	[1] 83	[1] 124	[1] 130	[1] 142
State automotive taxes paid by farmers:								
Motor vehicle licenses and permits (million dollars)	41	55	47	59	90	102	108	116
Motor fuel taxes (million dollars) [2]	22	68	66	79	90	136	143	150
FARMERS' MUTUAL FIRE INSURANCE [3]								
Number of companies [4]	1,839	1,896	1,941	1,896	1,841	1,808	[5] 1,776	
Insurance in force at end of year (million dollars)	9,477	11,382	11,083	12,394	16,170	22,486	[5] 24,310	[6] 28,187
Cost per $100 of insurance, total (cents)	27.8	31.6	22.2	25.3	23.6	22.3	[5] 22.1	[5] 22.8
Losses (cents)	21.1	24.8	14.7	17.1	15.6	14.0	[5] 14.7	[5] 14.3
Expenses (cents)	6.7	6.8	7.8	8.1	8.0	8.3	[5] 8.4	[5] 8.5
Surplus and reserves, end of year (thousand dollars) [6]			33,464	45,474	70,644	108,083	[5] 120,002	[6] 147,300

[1] Preliminary.
[2] Beginning 1945 includes taxes on gasoline used in farm tractors.
[3] For 1925-30 includes companies with more than 65 percent of their insurance on farm property; for later years, 90 percent. About 85 percent of their total insurance is on farm property, for both periods.
[4] Number of companies for which data were obtained; perhaps not entirely complete for any year.
[5] Estimate based on sample of companies.
[6] Excess of assets over liabilities. Most of farmers' mutuals are assessment companies and as such are not required to set up unearned premium reserves. Data not compiled prior to 1934.

Source: Department of Agriculture, Bureau of Agricultural Economics; *Agricultural Finance Review.*

No. 730.—Farm Labor—Farms Reporting, Persons Working on Farms Week Preceding Enumeration 1950; and Wages Paid, 1949

[Based on reports for only a sample of farms. Relates to farm operators and hired workers doing farm work, and also to unpaid family members working 15 hours or more. Excludes housework and contract construction work]

DIVISION AND STATE	FAMILY AND/OR HIRED WORKERS		FAMILY WORKERS, INCLUDING OPERATOR		HIRED WORKERS		CASH WAGES PAID FOR HIRED LABOR IN 1949	
	Farms reporting	Persons working	Farms reporting	Persons working	Farms reporting	Persons working	Farms reporting	Amount ($1,000)
United States	4,547,947	8,538,064	4,470,603	6,982,795	703,134	1,555,269	2,670,043	2,418,461
New England	82,178	160,512	79,338	112,050	21,241	45,762	48,619	95,177
Maine	23,440	39,628	22,871	30,470	4,234	9,158	14,246	23,573
New Hampshire	10,747	19,112	10,424	14,226	2,329	4,886	5,531	7,888
Vermont	16,003	31,426	15,449	23,193	4,966	8,233	10,552	11,042
Massachusetts	17,361	37,398	16,586	23,861	5,102	13,532	9,428	26,357
Rhode Island	2,120	4,583	2,022	2,937	690	1,646	1,146	2,717
Connecticut	12,504	28,670	11,986	17,363	3,920	11,307	7,116	23,594
Middle Atlantic	252,019	511,784	245,754	388,651	63,651	123,133	150,817	200,189
New York	106,316	207,155	103,241	154,409	29,024	52,746	68,561	94,444
New Jersey	21,339	55,807	20,529	32,594	8,789	23,213	13,936	39,096
Pennsylvania	124,364	248,822	121,984	201,648	25,838	47,174	68,320	66,619
East North Central	763,963	1,352,607	754,151	1,177,658	116,225	174,349	465,796	276,589
Ohio	169,331	293,044	167,729	257,499	21,874	35,545	93,772	55,064
Indiana	141,124	237,471	139,561	210,033	17,813	27,438	80,907	41,054
Illinois	171,520	299,979	168,924	250,124	34,586	49,855	112,281	77,667
Michigan	126,384	214,902	126,782	190,717	14,686	24,185	76,578	47,436
Wisconsin	153,044	306,611	151,155	269,285	27,266	37,326	102,258	55,349
West North Central	877,669	1,600,672	869,486	1,437,531	114,621	163,141	589,135	304,425
Minnesota	163,132	307,833	161,729	277,047	22,127	30,786	114,106	57,113
Iowa	187,161	336,324	185,270	296,194	30,845	46,130	131,307	68,269
Missouri	197,360	339,548	195,429	305,595	20,998	33,953	108,246	47,853
North Dakota	56,719	111,471	56,111	99,742	7,906	11,729	44,067	32,131
South Dakota	60,811	113,395	60,239	101,819	8,492	11,576	45,750	25,765
Nebraska	97,429	183,692	96,595	167,056	11,841	16,636	65,854	35,790
Kansas	115,197	208,409	114,113	190,078	12,412	18,331	79,785	39,514
South Atlantic	787,669	1,542,610	771,645	1,229,839	119,928	312,771	432,734	269,111
Delaware	5,925	12,290	5,623	8,357	1,768	3,933	3,840	5,693
Maryland	30,950	67,795	29,770	46,544	10,026	21,251	19,604	26,437
Dist. of Columbia [1]	26	70	26	36	1	34	8	118
Virginia	122,339	220,754	119,324	176,023	20,764	44,731	61,579	42,767
West Virginia	63,492	105,056	62,576	92,482	7,055	12,574	25,865	10,863
North Carolina	239,439	433,658	236,225	379,885	27,459	53,773	148,013	48,182
South Carolina	117,284	243,295	114,916	198,027	16,411	45,268	62,745	27,648
Georgia	165,024	327,608	161,928	263,313	25,269	64,385	86,509	42,629
Florida	43,216	132,064	41,283	65,208	11,176	66,856	24,579	64,893
East South Central	745,739	1,285,717	734,945	1,101,901	80,820	183,816	356,679	137,863
Kentucky	178,520	298,140	175,542	254,003	24,692	44,137	96,982	36,208
Tennessee	187,540	312,964	184,407	266,497	24,088	46,467	94,951	30,727
Alabama	174,637	311,792	172,352	273,888	17,492	37,904	77,605	26,838
Mississippi	205,042	362,821	202,644	307,513	14,548	55,308	81,171	44,212
West South Central	645,820	1,212,666	633,963	969,841	92,525	252,825	371,900	442,621
Arkansas	151,103	263,455	149,531	220,221	13,790	43,234	73,350	62,889
Louisiana	100,314	189,717	98,907	147,452	11,916	42,265	43,356	38,901
Oklahoma	121,286	210,395	119,958	191,585	11,626	18,810	60,145	42,698
Texas	273,117	549,099	265,557	400,583	55,193	148,516	195,049	298,133
Mountain	169,823	351,666	166,147	261,368	38,077	90,296	115,185	304,422
Montana	30,010	58,226	29,444	45,651	6,357	12,575	22,424	29,260
Idaho	35,933	66,549	35,493	54,169	6,534	12,424	26,203	32,197
Wyoming	11,547	25,581	11,175	18,236	3,177	7,345	7,933	16,146
Colorado	40,346	84,145	39,466	64,924	9,610	19,221	29,135	42,691
New Mexico	19,222	41,047	18,672	29,015	4,585	12,032	11,305	23,190
Arizona	8,750	28,472	8,283	12,225	3,435	16,247	5,745	39,106
Utah	21,375	40,480	21,075	33,060	3,457	7,420	13,706	16,069
Nevada	2,640	7,122	2,539	4,088	922	3,034	1,734	5,764
Pacific	222,990	520,130	215,184	313,956	56,046	206,174	142,778	485,974
Washington	59,251	109,262	58,209	85,860	10,236	23,402	33,445	61,246
Oregon	50,148	92,398	49,402	72,601	8,140	19,797	27,464	45,828
California	113,591	318,470	107,573	155,495	37,670	162,975	81,869	378,899

[1] Data not included in totals.

Source: Department of Commerce, Bureau of the Census; U. S. Census of Agriculture: 1950, Vol. II.

No. 731.—Specified Farm Expenditures: 1869 to 1949

[All 1950 data and data for livestock and poultry purchased and for seeds, bulbs, plants, and trees purchased for 1945 are based on reports for only a sample of farms]

ITEM	FARMS REPORTING		AMOUNT EXPENDED		
	Number	Percent of all farms	Total	Average per farm (based on all farms)	Average per farm reporting
			1,000 dollars	*Dollars*	*Dollars*
All farms...................1950..	5, 379, 250	100. 0	....	....	....
Specified farm expenditures [1]...........1949..	4, 792, 184	88. 9	10, 895, 148	2, 026	2, 278
Machine hire and/or hired labor.............1949..	2, 548, 279	88. 0	3, 680, 084	866	654
Machine hire...............1949..	2, 757, 864	51. 3	611, 823	114	222
Hired labor [2]...............1899..	(2)	(2)	248, 229	46	(2)
1899..			557, 369	62	
1909..	2, 922, 279	45. 9	521, 730	60	179
1919..	2, 988, 999	44. 8	1, 608, 713	170	280
1924..	2, 596, 721	39. 5	864, 988	130	341
1929..	2, 631, 601	41. 8	964, 420	132	342
1930..	2, 360, 227	37. 1	781, 792	136	346
1944..	2, 799, 026	47. 8	1, 365, 026	215	488
1949..	2, 670, 043	49. 6	2, 415, 461	450	905
Feed for livestock and poultry...............1909..	2, 398, 906	37. 2	250, 940	47	127
1919..	3, 811, 121	54. 4	1, 697, 226	179	312
1924..	3, 190, 739	50. 1	730, 445	118	225
1929..	3, 359, 400	52. 8	919, 190	146	280
1930..	3, 342, 715	54. 5	732, 117	129	249
1944..	4, 271, 642	72. 9	2, 406, 726	414	568
1949..	3, 875, 704	72. 0	3, 022, 341	562	780
Livestock and poultry purchased............1944..	2, 765, 691	47. 2	1, 317, 441	226	476
1949..	2, 948, 908	54. 5	2, 350, 509	444	810
Seeds, bulbs, plants, and trees purchased....1944..	3, 008, 028	51. 3	296, 263	51	99
1949..	3, 335, 882	62. 0	542, 987	101	143
Gasoline and other petroleum fuel and oil for the farm business...............1939..	2, 896, 614	47. 8	322, 286	58	112
1949..	2, 953, 476	55. 5	1, 183, 708	211	380
Farm machinery repairs [4].................1949..	2, 762, 064	51. 2	774, 819	144	282
Tractor repairs...............1949..	2, 039, 485	37. 7	390, 023	72	192
Other farm machinery repairs.............1949..	2, 333, 378	43. 4	385, 796	72	165

[1] Many expense items excluded such as fertilizer and lime, maintenance of buildings, taxes, mortgage interest, insurance, rents, containers, veterinary fees, and others of varying degrees of importance. Specified expenditures, shown in this table, amounted to approximately 60 percent of all farm production costs for 1949 according to estimates of United States Department of Agriculture.

[2] For 1924 to 1949, cash payments for farm labor; for 1899 to 1949, housework specifically excluded; for 1929, 1944, and 1949, excludes expenditures for contract construction work, machine hire, or labor included in cost of machine hire; for 1889, 1899, 1909 and 1919, value of board included.

[3] Not available.

[4] Amount spent for repairing (both labor and parts) and amount spent for repair parts and other replacement parts; excludes motortruck and automobile repairs.

Source: Department of Commerce, Bureau of the Census; *U. S. Census of Agriculture: 1950*, Vol. II.

No. 732.—FARM FACILITIES, ROADS, MOTOR VEHICLES, TRACTORS, AND RESIDENCE OF FARM OPERATORS, BY STATES: 1950

[Based on reports for only a sample of farms]

DIVISION AND STATE	NUMBER OF FARMS REPORTING—							
	Electricity	Electric water pump	Telephone	Distance to trading center visited most frequently				
				Under 1 mile	1 to 4 miles	5 to 9 miles	10 miles and over	Average distance reported (miles)
United States	4,213,599	2,018,578	2,057,556	391,234	2,074,939	1,640,239	1,114,973	6
New England	93,618	53,643	75,182	8,679	46,291	29,028	14,764	
Maine	26,195	14,793	19,467	2,611	12,821	8,658	5,370	5
New Hampshire	12,696	7,919	10,055	1,013	5,690	4,150	2,118	6
Vermont	17,533	7,595	13,267	1,975	8,899	5,153	2,591	5
Massachusetts	20,358	10,294	17,309	1,892	10,930	5,526	2,366	5
Rhode Island	2,416	1,867	2,003	158	1,011	746	489	4
Connecticut	14,420	11,175	13,081	1,030	6,940	4,795	1,830	6
Middle Atlantic	274,442	185,523	182,693	20,926	125,029	92,144	48,091	6
New York	117,253	79,725	87,683	10,363	55,746	38,471	16,417	6
New Jersey	23,280	19,432	17,829	1,928	10,992	7,567	3,113	5
Pennsylvania	133,909	86,366	77,181	8,635	58,291	46,106	28,561	5
East North Central	811,437	557,792	533,183	49,395	373,367	304,281	135,663	6
Ohio	185,691	117,811	119,736	11,526	85,869	65,452	31,115	6
Indiana	152,834	99,268	102,963	9,741	68,422	57,190	26,767	6
Illinois	169,625	105,229	127,528	11,729	81,116	65,093	31,351	6
Michigan	146,895	114,250	83,135	6,986	66,687	55,520	22,426	6
Wisconsin	156,392	121,234	99,821	9,413	71,273	61,036	24,004	5
West North Central	765,706	387,526	603,699	59,929	345,172	342,871	211,441	7
Minnesota	150,610	101,206	107,279	8,007	65,896	69,101	33,833	6
Iowa	184,760	116,941	166,343	13,174	78,935	73,690	32,858	6
Missouri	159,187	53,456	106,768	18,233	91,862	72,121	41,093	6
North Dakota	44,214	19,811	27,219	2,659	15,894	22,791	22,711	9
South Dakota	45,892	16,646	36,850	3,131	16,690	22,242	23,650	9
Nebraska	83,315	38,130	69,484	6,431	34,285	38,741	24,949	7
Kansas	97,728	41,276	89,756	8,294	41,610	44,185	32,347	7
South Atlantic	714,126	261,396	146,123	66,797	363,799	287,309	210,078	6
Delaware	6,112	4,665	4,900	494	3,263	2,662	491	5
Maryland	30,302	20,765	19,457	2,904	15,749	10,121	6,348	6
District of Columbia	[1] 18	[1] 1		[1] 17	[1] 26	[1] 1		(²)
Virginia	114,241	40,690	35,847	14,007	56,202	37,830	38,524	7
West Virginia	59,137	13,904	21,719	7,735	32,736	19,683	19,003	6
North Carolina	219,422	71,055	23,342	19,676	111,337	85,498	62,154	6
South Carolina	95,060	32,865	11,896	6,635	51,902	47,865	29,191	6
Georgia	149,323	53,232	18,619	11,595	73,390	66,754	40,656	6
Florida	40,529	24,220	10,253	3,751	19,220	16,776	13,711	7
East South Central	595,852	144,999	123,228	89,021	364,959	241,674	190,352	6
Kentucky	145,246	28,945	45,813	26,846	90,410	52,607	41,129	5
Tennessee	165,551	41,689	43,541	25,827	94,713	57,025	45,843	6
Alabama	144,569	38,160	17,438	16,684	80,801	56,360	50,560	7
Mississippi	140,486	36,205	16,436	19,664	99,035	75,682	52,820	6
West South Central	559,173	181,446	158,595	58,781	282,165	228,644	186,334	7
Arkansas	121,832	30,763	19,177	16,132	77,044	50,517	34,356	6
Louisiana	83,189	30,489	14,380	15,697	53,779	29,948	20,187	5
Oklahoma	93,324	30,521	45,901	7,103	45,054	47,291	38,594	7
Texas	260,828	89,673	79,137	19,849	106,288	100,888	93,197	8
Mountain	155,380	81,473	86,000	16,191	57,744	46,194	68,535	11
Montana	26,282	15,123	9,988	1,592	7,353	7,956	17,636	14
Idaho	37,195	25,872	22,242	2,539	14,457	12,433	9,832	8
Wyoming	9,437	4,720	4,739	641	2,958	2,284	6,428	15
Colorado	36,574	18,623	27,060	2,702	13,828	11,349	16,295	10
New Mexico	14,057	5,595	3,493	1,849	6,381	4,500	9,657	13
Arizona	8,054	4,635	4,413	928	3,421	2,308	3,171	11
Utah	21,597	5,448	12,515	5,724	8,397	4,574	4,460	6
Nevada	2,184	1,457	1,550	216	949	700	1,056	17
Pacific	243,865	164,780	148,853	21,515	116,413	68,094	49,715	6
Washington	64,733	42,380	40,198	4,912	29,037	19,397	14,287	6
Oregon	54,564	36,724	30,080	4,498	22,740	16,072	14,970	7
California	124,568	85,676	78,575	12,105	64,636	32,625	20,458	6

[1] Not included in totals.
[2] 0.5 or less.

No. 732.—Farm Facilities, Roads, Motor Vehicles, Tractors, and Residence of Farm Operators, by States: 1950—Continued

DIVISION AND STATE	MOTOR TRUCKS ON FARMS [1]		TRACTORS ON FARMS [1]		AUTOMOBILES ON FARMS [1]		FARM OPERATORS REPORTING RESIDENCE	
	Farms reporting	Number	Farms reporting	Number	Farms reporting	Number	On farm operated	Not on farm operated
United States	1,840,291	2,306,670	2,535,206	3,600,381	3,329,772	4,190,234	4,961,330	368,176
New England	51,023	69,661	46,352	63,868	72,086	96,240	96,601	4,390
Maine	14,854	19,197	12,794	16,665	19,879	23,937	23,245	1,426
New Hampshire	6,708	8,643	5,405	8,946	9,446	12,068	12,682	480
Vermont	8,819	10,600	8,417	10,682	13,107	16,580	17,081	526
Massachusetts	10,625	15,365	10,322	14,697	15,763	21,443	20,601	1,014
Rhode Island	1,521	2,485	1,290	1,944	1,955	2,778	2,390	114
Connecticut	8,495	13,376	8,124	11,954	11,946	18,434	14,689	568
Middle Atlantic	126,570	162,481	188,461	271,192	228,536	308,184	277,280	11,942
New York	56,610	72,440	81,985	119,202	97,294	129,806	116,587	5,680
New Jersey	15,624	23,938	15,374	26,039	18,864	27,756	23,262	999
Pennsylvania	54,336	66,103	91,122	125,851	112,608	151,582	137,441	5,253
East North Central	365,597	342,787	614,276	962,060	731,621	916,426	520,944	35,729
Ohio	56,661	64,780	127,390	182,481	163,216	208,027	190,305	8,358
Indiana	53,583	59,511	106,037	183,980	129,235	168,223	154,411	6,916
Illinois	79,068	86,776	141,986	234,789	189,653	195,587	181,944	9,407
Michigan	49,493	56,966	111,373	149,377	130,187	164,756	145,241	6,007
Wisconsin	66,812	74,454	127,488	171,433	145,330	182,503	161,143	5,051
West North Central	387,391	444,462	705,670	1,031,047	798,946	991,751	997,922	54,691
Minnesota	63,077	70,357	142,911	204,200	155,539	196,663	169,461	6,925
Iowa	58,600	62,375	141,305	240,941	180,974	225,097	191,750	7,026
Missouri	71,804	77,250	100,312	125,536	144,532	162,848	213,880	10,543
North Dakota	44,037	55,732	56,336	96,676	56,285	73,597	55,909	7,488
South Dakota	31,668	37,730	56,267	88,274	58,687	77,508	60,355	4,518
Nebraska	45,796	54,193	87,567	127,154	94,432	128,947	98,047	4,740
Kansas	71,720	88,535	98,970	146,366	108,507	133,006	117,502	10,582
South Atlantic	249,521	281,561	222,363	264,163	409,596	552,613	806,179	39,764
Delaware	3,340	4,059	4,046	6,125	5,418	7,063	6,748	337
Maryland	16,917	21,443	20,532	29,905	26,805	36,476	33,549	1,639
District of Columbia	11	15	1	14	6	29	23	4
Virginia	41,702	49,099	36,515	48,183	77,078	94,010	141,102	5,684
West Virginia	21,621	24,615	11,602	13,984	32,831	37,266	76,157	3,319
North Carolina	55,306	60,410	62,666	73,497	140,009	159,201	308,365	6,431
South Carolina	25,440	29,714	26,432	30,282	69,963	81,449	130,121	6,608
Georgia	55,306	62,865	48,253	60,369	89,237	100,535	165,068	7,706
Florida	20,899	29,356	15,275	22,018	28,199	36,029	46,044	6,151
East South Central	202,642	234,182	171,254	216,065	323,936	360,350	664,529	30,396
Kentucky	49,794	54,957	49,342	56,818	102,938	119,846	203,467	8,474
Tennessee	55,600	60,272	50,798	59,796	99,095	113,072	215,060	8,327
Alabama	47,102	52,743	37,783	45,751	64,417	71,212	199,511	6,281
Mississippi	50,166	66,210	33,332	51,608	67,486	76,220	238,471	7,364
West South Central	269,188	315,667	299,241	422,076	400,715	470,866	799,367	51,367
Arkansas	56,510	62,435	41,360	60,308	57,981	65,077	171,683	6,616
Louisiana	30,918	36,534	23,485	35,735	44,480	56,183	117,358	3,665
Oklahoma	59,903	68,871	71,710	93,706	83,390	94,796	128,668	9,910
Texas	121,827	146,537	162,676	232,326	210,975	254,510	392,396	30,573
Mountain	121,546	165,777	126,149	197,741	141,562	187,113	171,365	19,616
Montana	26,602	36,670	27,151	44,860	26,726	34,937	31,073	3,615
Idaho	22,796	30,662	27,541	39,308	31,825	39,995	36,029	2,774
Wyoming	9,115	12,617	9,230	15,610	9,319	12,812	11,534	931
Colorado	31,005	42,681	32,162	53,117	35,719	46,536	41,100	3,754
New Mexico	11,728	16,072	10,596	15,780	11,627	14,947	20,862	2,158
Arizona	5,590	8,600	4,878	9,746	7,025	11,761	9,022	1,243
Utah	12,824	14,352	12,908	15,987	17,346	20,709	18,023	4,345
Nevada	1,907	3,123	1,783	3,213	2,005	3,056	2,742	296
Pacific	125,713	190,063	151,420	222,069	212,465	302,521	241,628	21,352
Washington	34,854	48,127	40,247	55,061	54,275	69,400	65,943	2,811
Oregon	29,710	30,402	36,537	52,426	47,450	61,516	55,970	3,071
California	71,149	110,563	74,336	124,582	110,731	171,205	119,715	15,470

[1] Not included in totals.
[2] Based on reports for only a sample of farms.

Source: Department of Commerce, Bureau of the Census; U. S. Census of Agriculture: 1950, Vol. II.

No. 733.—FARM MACHINERY AND EQUIPMENT: 1930 TO 1952

[Money figures in millions. See also *Historical Statistics*, series E 105–110]

ITEM	1930	1935	1940	1945	1949	1950	1951	1952 [1]
Value of farm implements and machinery [2]	$3,302	$2,153	$3,060	$6,208	$10,827	$12,944	$13,810	$15,765
Tractors on farms, Jan. 1 (1,000)	920	1,048	1,545	2,422	3,315	3,615	3,940	4,170
Motor trucks on farms, Jan. 1 (1,000)	900	890	1,047	1,490	2,065	2,209	2,310	2,410
Automobiles on farms, Jan. 1 (1,000)	4,135	3,642	4,144	4,148	4,290	4,207	4,280	4,350
Sales of farm equipment, machinery, and parts [3]	$346.7	$372.3	$429.5	$612.6	$1,550.9	$1,562.2	$1,917.7	(4)
Farmers' expenditures:								
Motor vehicles [5]	$289	$297	$429	$446	$1,400	$1,482	$1,727	(5)
Machinery and equipment	$334	$235	$377	$749	$1,655	$1,841	$2,178	(5)

[1] Preliminary.
[2] Data represent inventory valuations at beginning of year. Includes family share of automobiles.
[3] For use in United States from domestic manufacture; from Bureau of Census, Facts for Industry Series M35A.
[4] Not available.
[5] Excludes family share of automobiles.

Source: Department of Agriculture, Bureau of Agricultural Economics (except as noted).

No. 734.—FERTILIZER CONSUMPTION: 1880 TO 1951

[In thousands of tons of 2,000 pounds. Based on tag sales, records of Government officials, or estimates. Beginning 1935, figures include tonnage distributed by Agricultural Adjustment Administration and by Tennessee Valley Authority, data for the latter representing fiscal years ending June 30. Data for phosphate rock used in Illinois and Florida, available only since 1939, have been excluded from annual comparisons. In addition to tonnage for consumption, fertilizers and fertilizer materials produced in continental U. S. are exported to island possessions]

YEAR	Quantity	YEAR	Quantity	YEAR	Quantity	YEAR	Quantity
1880	1,150	1919	6,626	1930	8,222	1941	9,183
1890	1,980	1920	7,177	1931	6,354	1942	9,949
1900	2,200	1921	4,863	1932	4,385	1943	11,463
1910	5,453	1922	5,671	1933	4,908	1944	12,055
1912	5,767	1923	6,445	1934	5,583	1945	13,202
1913	6,337	1924	6,826	1935	6,276	1946	14,892
1914	7,100	1925	7,334	1936	6,931	1947	15,039
1915	5,324	1926	7,329	1937	8,226	1948	15,980
1916	5,128	1927	6,844	1938	7,548	1949	16,449
1917	5,926	1928	7,986	1939	7,707	1950	17,984
1918	6,467	1929	8,012	1940	8,249	1951	18,666

Source: The National Fertilizer Association, Washington, D. C. Published in *The Fertilizer Review*.

No. 735.—FARMERS' MARKETING, PURCHASING, AND SERVICE ASSOCIATIONS— ESTIMATED BUSINESS: 1950–51

COMMODITY	Number of associations	Gross business ($1,000)	Net business ($1,000)[1]	COMMODITY	Number of associations	Gross business ($1,000)	Net business ($1,000)[1]
Total	[2] 9,977	10,473,184	8,103,668	Purchasing	7,335	2,390,716	1,644,206
				Farm machinery and equipment	2,149	104,053	63,152
Marketing	7,276	7,982,609	6,359,601	Feed	4,707	896,882	683,268
Dry beans	175	38,450	31,137	Fertilizer	3,521	255,771	153,538
Cotton and products	550	349,934	320,019	Petroleum products	2,848	574,005	366,013
Dairy products	2,072	2,298,201	1,933,174	Seed	3,930	120,908	89,248
Fruits and vegetables	951	1,024,577	701,777	Other supplies	5,937	439,097	288,989
Grains, soybeans, meal, and oil	2,740	2,051,297	1,355,392	Services	4,144	99,859	[3] 99,859
Livestock and live-stock products	753	1,406,328	1,321,248	Trucking, storage, grinding, misc.	3,448	75,498	75,498
Nuts	81	141,012	113,485	Cotton ginning	480	21,800	21,800
Poultry products	760	303,716	263,380	Livestock trucking	216	2,561	2,561
Rice	32	131,191	90,729				
Tobacco	24	125,842	125,842				
Wool and mohair	258	30,882	29,270				
Miscellaneous	405	81,179	74,168				

[1] Adjusted for duplication. This figure approximately represents value at level at which farmer does business with his cooperative; excludes wholesale business of farm supply cooperatives or terminal market sales performed for local associations.
[2] Excludes duplications caused by associations engaged in handling more than one commodity.
[3] Charges for services in which no duplication occurs.

Source: Department of Agriculture, Farm Credit Administration; annual report, *Statistics of Farmers' Marketing, Purchasing, and Service Cooperatives*.

No. 736.—FARMERS' MARKETING AND PURCHASING ASSOCIATIONS—NUMBER, MEMBERSHIP, AND BUSINESS: 1913 TO 1951

[Comprises independent local associations, federations, large-scale centralized associations]

PERIOD [1]	ASSOCIATIONS LISTED			ESTIMATED MEMBERSHIP [2]			ESTIMATED BUSINESS ($1,000) [3]		
	Total	Marketing	Purchasing	Total	Marketing	Purchasing	Total	Marketing	Purchasing
1913	3,099	2,988	111				310,313	304,385	5,928
1915	4,424	4,149	275	651,186	591,683	59,503	635,839	624,161	11,678
1921	7,374	6,476	898				1,256,214	1,198,493	57,721
1925–26	10,803	9,586	1,217	2,700,000	2,453,000	247,000	2,400,000	2,265,000	135,000
1930–31	11,950	10,362	1,588	3,000,000	2,608,000	392,000	2,400,000	2,185,000	215,000
1935–36	10,500	8,388	2,112	3,660,000	2,710,000	950,000	1,840,000	1,596,000	254,000
1936–37	10,745	8,142	2,601	3,270,000	2,414,000	856,000	2,194,000	1,882,600	312,400
1937–38	10,900	8,300	2,600	3,400,000	2,500,000	900,000	2,400,000	2,060,000	340,000
1938–39	10,700	8,100	2,600	3,200,000	2,410,000	890,000	2,100,000	1,765,000	335,000
1939–40	10,700	8,051	2,649	3,200,000	2,300,000	900,000	2,087,000	1,728,000	359,000
1940–41	10,600	7,943	2,657	3,400,000	2,420,000	980,000	2,230,000	1,911,000	349,800
1941–42	10,550	7,824	2,726	3,600,000	2,430,000	1,170,000	2,840,000	2,360,000	480,000
1942–43	10,450	7,708	2,742	3,860,000	2,590,000	1,270,000	3,780,000	3,180,000	600,000
1943–44	10,300	7,522	2,778	4,280,000	2,760,000	1,520,000	5,160,000	4,430,000	730,000
1944–45	10,150	7,400	2,750	4,505,000	2,895,000	1,610,000	5,645,000	4,825,000	819,000
1945–46	10,150	7,378	2,772	5,010,000	3,150,000	1,860,000	6,070,000	5,147,000	923,000
1946–47	10,125	7,268	2,857	5,436,000	3,378,000	2,058,000	7,116,000	6,005,000	1,111,000
1947–48	10,135	7,159	2,976	5,890,000	3,620,000	2,290,000	8,635,000	7,195,000	1,440,000
1948–49	10,075	6,993	3,082	6,384,000	3,973,000	2,411,000	9,390,000	7,700,000	1,690,000
1949–50	10,035	6,922	3,113	6,584,000	4,075,000	2,509,000	8,725,000	7,082,600	1,642,400
1950–51 [4]	9,977	[5] 6,769	3,208	[4] 7,054,568	[4] 4,211,890	[4] 2,842,878	[6] 10,473,184	[6] 8,022,468	[6] 2,350,716

[1] Marketing season during which farm products are moved into channels of trade. Marketing seasons overlap.
[2] For years since about 1945, comprises members, contract members, and shareholders, but excludes patrons not in these categories.
[3] Includes value of commodities sold or purchased for patrons and charges for rendering other essential services in marketing or purchasing. Most duplication in value from intra-association transactions eliminated.
[4] Covers operations of associations whose fiscal years ended during July 1, 1950, through June 30, 1951, with limited exceptions.
[5] Includes Service Associations.
[6] Data not comparable with figures for previous years. These are gross figures. Net figures obtained after adjusting for duplication resulting from business done between cooperatives are: Total net business, $8,103,695,000; marketing, $6,459,490,000; purchasing, $1,644,205,000.

No. 737.—FARMERS' MARKETING, PURCHASING, AND SERVICE ASSOCIATIONS—NUMBER, MEMBERSHIP, AND BUSINESS, BY STATES: 1950–51

[See headnote, table 736]

DIVISION AND STATE	Associations listed	Estimated membership [1]	Estimated business [2] ($1,000)	DIVISION AND STATE	Associations listed	Estimated membership [1]	Estimated business [2] ($1,000)
United States [3]	9,977	7,054,568	10,473,184	S. Atlantic—Continued			
New England	146	116,592	242,497	Virginia	123	213,005	135,659
Maine	27	22,263	34,114	West Virginia	45	47,564	19,228
New Hampshire	10	10,542	29,600	North Carolina	92	313,030	98,696
Vermont	37	24,961	63,706	South Carolina	34	36,587	19,425
Massachusetts	39	31,317	63,840	Georgia	79	148,948	132,396
Rhode Island	5	4,805	8,671	Florida	107	16,503	148,538
Connecticut	28	16,702	42,476	East South Central	387	728,387	333,114
Middle Atlantic	622	361,556	1,042,166	Kentucky	55	383,450	115,794
New York	383	166,267	580,540	Tennessee	106	163,223	68,500
New Jersey	56	39,208	149,578	Alabama	66	61,577	34,023
Pennsylvania	182	156,081	312,042	Mississippi	130	120,637	120,797
East North Central	2,133	1,918,552	2,492,801	West South Central	911	442,382	699,644
Ohio	303	334,375	464,793	Arkansas	107	55,248	78,745
Indiana	156	383,307	415,919	Louisiana	55	19,904	54,124
Illinois	578	613,099	730,104	Oklahoma	201	162,483	166,516
Michigan	233	183,606	290,429	Texas	548	204,547	400,279
Wisconsin	861	403,565	571,556	Mountain	552	295,646	651,678
West North Central	3,991	2,041,512	2,965,769	Montana	172	52,567	125,375
Minnesota	1,261	561,453	791,055	Idaho	109	55,074	137,277
Iowa	710	377,317	615,125	Wyoming	27	14,195	53,775
Missouri	289	390,971	313,087	Colorado	117	77,789	180,676
North Dakota	560	207,268	372,606	New Mexico	32	11,686	22,475
South Dakota	305	138,453	179,872	Arizona	15	44,870	46,215
Nebraska	415	214,256	310,849	Utah	74	35,612	80,402
Kansas	351	151,773	321,115	Nevada	6	3,553	3,582
South Atlantic	547	862,141	664,611	Pacific	787	292,362	1,490,549
Delaware	14	15,912	22,560	Washington	193	100,181	395,609
Maryland	62	71,592	83,099	Oregon	133	69,420	181,782
District of Columbia	1	(4)	(4)	California	461	122,817	962,449

[1] See note 2, table 736.   [2] See note 3 and 6, table 736.   [3] See note 4, table 736.
[4] Membership and business allocated to States.

Source of tables 736 and 737: Department of Agriculture, Farm Credit Administration; annual report, Statistics of Farmers' Marketing, Purchasing, and Service Cooperatives.

No. 788.—Commodity Credit Corporation—Inventories of Commodities
Owned as of June 30: 1950, 1951, and 1952

[Amounts in thousands]

COMMODITY AND UNIT OF QUANTITY	1950		1951		1952	
	Quantity	Cost	Quantity	Cost	Quantity	Cost
Total		$2,643,153		$1,500,731		$1,130,882
Barley	bu	31,497	46,434	20,388	31,643	9,012	14,291
Beans, dry	cwt	9,687	79,690	6,180	50,478	4,326	34,095
Corn	bu	332,460	505,864	413,424	643,182	313,895	499,995
Cotton	bale	3,414	580,406	83	17,726	2	418
Eggs, dried	lbs	93,919	103,290	40,411	40,180	5,307	5,399
Flour and related grain products	do	15,147	725				
Meat, Mexican	do	68,891	16,485	7,308	1,493		
Milk and milk products	do	583,483	164,877	40,006	5,943	30,449	5,265
Oats	bu	12,109	10,744	9,031	8,691	4,776	4,756
Oilseeds and products:							
Cottonseed linters	lbs					53,593	5,044
Cottonseed oil	do					78,476	14,010
Flaxseed	bu	13,374	69,767	3,163	13,118	152	637
Linseed oil	lbs	471,667	134,846	521,386	116,897	496,627	112,208
Peanuts, Farmer Stock	do	5,668	608	117	13	142,273	17,433
Soybeans	bu	53	163	34	105	38	105
All other			3,231		717		803
Rosin	lbs	384,686	29,120	144,164	10,191	164,783	11,874
Seeds, various	do	13,131	1,206	409,515	23,410	370,013	32,578
Sorghums, grain	cwt	41,274	104,699	15,831	40,744	1,190	3,209
Turpentine	gal	2,587	1,217	500	224	525	251
Wheat	bu	327,654	760,444	196,505	483,559	143,333	364,271
Wool	lbs	455	402	2,607	6,426		
All other			28,935		5,991		4,240

Source: Department of Agriculture, Production and Marketing Administration.

No. 739.—Commodity Credit Corporation—Cost of Acquisition of Agricultural Commodities for All Purposes During Years Ending June 30: 1950,
1951, and 1952

[Thousands of dollars. Includes purchases under price-support, supply and foreign purchase programs as well
as acquisitions in settlement of price-support loans]

COMMODITY	1950	1951	1952	COMMODITY	1950	1951	1952
Total	2,735,451	884,398	469,714	Domestic acquisitions— Continued			
				Potatoes, Irish	81,072	66,284	62
Domestic acquisitions	2,704,659	821,680	430,250	Rice	10,847	10,931	2,941
Barley	26,518	10,468	2,575	Sugar	19,934	694	
Beans, dry	41,055	12,200	14,333	Sorghum, grain	101,639	28,792	555
Corn	545,531	227,459	41,112	Wheat	640,581	156,472	192,242
Cotton [1]	600,366	16,437	18,172	Wool	32,823	21	
Eggs	84,735	24,208		Other	66,943	32,143	45,843
Flour and related grain products	16,234	14,384	4,581				
Fruit, processed	8,299		121	Purchases foreign coun- tries	30,792	62,718	39,464
Meat and meat pro- ducts	22,732	11,361	1,857	Cotton, extra long staple		42,728	29,916
Mexican meat, canned [2]	7,253			Fats and oils	873		
Milk and milk pro- ducts	197,006	68,444	10,809	Kenaf fiber			52
Oats	3,971	826	699	Kenaf seed		48	1,076
Oilseeds and products:				Mexican beef, frozen	1,064	4,132	
Cotton linters			4,934	Rice	[3] 55		
Cottonseed products, other			23,069	Sugar	28,937	2,509	3,989
Flaxseed and lin- seed oil	79,915	36,979	627	Wool		13,301	4,431
Peanuts	82,190	77,702	50,079				
Soybeans	11,743	13,842	6,121				
All other	23,272	12,033	518				

[1] Includes cotton pooled for account of producers.
[2] Not a purchase by CCC; transfer from Bureau of Animal Industry for disposition.
[3] Denotes credit resulting from an accounting adjustment to prior years transactions.

Source: Department of Agriculture, Production and Marketing Administration.

No. 740.—Farms—Number and Percent Distribution, by Type: 1950

[Based on reports for only a sample of farms. Type of farm determined on basis of relationship of value of sales, from a particular source to total value of products sold for each farm. In general, value of sales from a particular source was 50% or more of total sales when a farm was classified as that type. Part-time farms include those with a value of products sold of $250–$1,199 and with operator either reporting 100 days or more of off-farm work or other income exceeding value of farm products sold. Residential farms include those with a value of farm products sold of less than $250. Abnormal farms include public and private institutional farms, experiment stations, community projects, etc.]

TYPE OF FARM	Number of farms	Percent distribution (commercial farms)	TYPE OF FARM	Number of farms	Percent distribution (commercial farms)
All farms	5,379,250		Commercial farms—Continued		
Commercial farms	3,706,412	100.0	General farms:		
Cash-grain farms	430,369	11.6	Primarily crop	84,589	2.3
Cotton farms	609,307	16.4	Primarily livestock	134,066	3.6
Other field-crop farms	409,421	11.0	Crop and livestock	275,060	7.4
Vegetable farms	46,415	1.2	Miscellaneous types	50,368	1.4
Fruit-and-nut farms	82,175	2.2	Other farms	1,672,838	
Dairy farms	602,093	16.2	Part-time farms	639,230	
Poultry farms	175,876	4.7	Residential farms	1,029,392	
Livestock farms other than dairy and poultry	806,080	21.7	Abnormal farms	4,216	

Source: Department of Commerce, Bureau of the Census; U. S. Census of Agriculture: 1950, Vol. II.

No. 741.—Value of All Farm Products Sold, With Farms Reporting, by Source of Income: 1940, 1945, and 1950

[Value of farm products refers to preceding calendar year]

SOURCE OF INCOME	NUMBER OF FARMS REPORTING			VALUE OF FARM PRODUCTS SOLD					
				Total ($1,000)			Average per farm reporting (dollars)		
	1940	1945	1950	1940	1945	1950	1940	1945	1950
All farms	[1] 6,096,799	[1] 5,859,169	5,382,162	(2)	(2)	22,052,264	(2)	(2)	4,097
Farms with no farm products sold	440,189	523,894	360,987						
All farm products sold	5,617,066	5,327,687	5,021,175	6,681,581	16,230,627	22,052,266	1,190	3,046	4,392
All crops sold	4,225,175	3,702,481	(2)	3,094,947	7,507,597	9,802,545	732	2,028	(2)
Field crops, other than vegetables and fruits and nuts sold	3,825,478	3,216,106	(2)	2,470,727	5,621,108	8,012,055	646	1,748	(2)
Vegetables sold	458,011	579,579	346,526	199,526	876,593	607,018	436	906	1,752
Fruits and nuts sold	668,783	581,039	381,124	295,351	1,078,643	791,666	442	2,021	2,077
Horticultural specialties sold	25,774	34,690	(2)	129,343	231,259	392,098	4,495	6,666	(2)
All livestock and livestock products sold	4,456,306	4,336,641	(2)	3,547,482	8,644,671	12,114,902	796	1,993	(2)
Dairy products sold	2,647,851	2,472,709	2,006,831	1,115,198	2,531,408	3,079,132	422	1,024	1,534
Poultry and poultry products sold	3,507,902	3,401,918	2,730,178	555,412	1,586,549	1,828,232	158	466	666
Livestock and livestock products, other than dairy and poultry, sold	(2)	3,476,763	(2)	1,873,575	4,526,714	7,212,438	(2)	1,302	(2)
Forest products sold	276,611	221,901	(2)	36,152	73,359	134,509	142	353	(2)

[1] Includes 29,542 unclassified farms for 1940 and 7,586 for 1945 for which value of farm products sold are not available.

[2] Not available.

Source: Dept. of Commerce, Bureau of the Census; U. S. Census of Agriculture: 1950, Vol. II.

No. 742.—FARMS—NUMBER, BY TYPE OF FARM, BY STATES: 1950

[See headnote, table 740]

DIVISION AND STATE	All farms	COMMERCIAL FARMS										Other farms
		Total [1]	Cash grain	Cotton	Other field crop	Vegetable	Fruit and nut	Dairy	Poultry	Livestock other than dairy and poultry	General	
United States	5,379,250	3,706,412	430,389	609,307	408,421	46,415	82,178	602,093	175,876	806,080	494,285	1,672,838
New England	103,191	59,169	100	.....	6,108	1,642	1,964	27,780	13,131	2,204	2,646	44,022
Maine	30,368	15,790	90	.....	4,192	335	587	4,999	2,786	583	1,085	14,578
New Hampshire	13,382	6,385	5	.....	87	70	219	3,003	2,077	259	365	6,997
Vermont	19,043	13,082			111	30	74	10,823	761	391	458	5,961
Massachusetts	22,205	13,173			816	744	762	4,515	4,202	561	431	9,032
Rhode Island	2,606	1,585			102	95	35	595	532	75	26	1,021
Connecticut	15,587	9,154	5		800	368	287	3,845	2,773	335	281	6,433
Middle Atlantic	296,310	194,341	6,560	.....	4,707	7,546	5,610	102,751	30,798	11,621	18,783	101,969
New York	124,780	87,967	2,974	.....	1,765	3,614	3,445	55,169	9,260	3,406	5,903	36,813
New Jersey	24,779	18,055	327	.....	866	2,888	871	4,041	6,577	553	862	6,724
Pennsylvania	146,751	88,319	3,259	.....	2,076	1,044	1,294	43,541	14,961	7,662	12,018	58,432
E. N. Central	885,171	671,384	120,837	151	7,897	7,147	7,995	226,808	27,215	153,897	112,108	213,787
Ohio	199,220	134,595	21,687	.....	2,827	1,413	1,377	32,556	7,510	34,316	30,993	64,625
Indiana	166,638	123,222	22,458	.....	1,701	654	516	16,057	6,813	46,281	27,757	43,416
Illinois	195,212	160,867	60,172	151	111	1,296	754	15,866	4,800	51,106	25,311	34,345
Michigan	155,519	106,847	14,972	.....	1,977	2,600	4,736	45,800	5,266	10,857	19,021	48,672
Wisconsin	168,582	145,853	1,548	.....	1,281	1,184	612	116,529	2,826	11,337	9,026	22,729
W. N. Central	982,411	847,189	190,859	13,373	3,068	1,718	1,215	103,870	23,269	358,576	148,233	135,222
Minnesota	179,119	157,259	24,842	.....	928	611	220	50,118	6,289	35,492	37,772	21,890
Iowa	203,155	187,702	26,244	.....	82	314	130	7,007	4,017	120,306	28,224	15,453
Missouri	229,958	164,600	12,938	13,373	536	468	645	29,743	6,979	78,099	21,090	65,358
North Dakota	65,302	62,650	39,109	.....	690	5	5	2,558	281	10,170	9,751	2,652
South Dakota	66,331	62,726	13,667	.....	98	40	5	1,931	832	34,583	11,477	3,605
Nebraska	107,174	99,934	33,088	.....	657	75	70	2,912	1,941	43,231	17,691	7,240
Kansas	131,372	112,338	40,973	.....	97	205	140	8,701	2,930	36,695	22,228	19,034
South Atlantic	958,403	560,966	10,255	104,487	247,627	10,819	10,733	31,336	31,654	47,878	53,886	397,437
Delaware	7,452	5,556	611	.....	10	324	19	1,229	2,466	248	625	1,896
Maryland	36,162	23,655	1,398	.....	4,990	1,173	232	6,828	3,598	2,178	2,839	12,507
Dist. of Col.[2]	28	16			2				1			12
Virginia	150,823	78,103	2,396	366	34,794	856	974	8,110	5,915	13,697	9,352	72,720
West Virginia	81,418	23,337	337	.....	1,242	111	401	4,341	3,331	9,957	2,903	58,081
North Carolina	288,473	193,679	3,141	21,441	135,227	1,348	732	5,312	5,391	6,262	12,076	94,794
South Carolina	139,195	84,231	1,148	40,172	27,565	1,174	661	1,590	1,520	3,035	6,241	54,964
Georgia	198,037	122,355	1,070	41,622	38,040	1,708	476	2,936	7,382	8,089	16,907	75,682
Florida	56,843	30,050	154	886	5,759	4,125	7,238	930	2,051	4,412	2,943	26,793
E. S. Central	912,408	547,666	6,956	243,192	109,805	2,614	1,827	33,478	6,870	69,609	66,808	364,742
Kentucky	218,237	134,595	2,128	582	70,025	215	467	9,041	1,414	26,548	23,239	83,642
Tennessee	231,524	138,232	2,457	44,898	27,508	578	565	14,611	1,686	22,685	21,697	93,292
Alabama	211,361	118,143	870	75,245	11,766	767	474	2,554	2,042	9,284	12,910	93,218
Mississippi	251,286	156,696	1,501	122,467	506	1,054	321	7,272	1,728	11,092	8,962	94,590
W. S. Central	779,992	503,163	45,244	238,416	17,185	5,307	6,419	27,883	15,547	91,809	51,942	276,829
Arkansas	182,386	113,189	3,751	73,432	306	718	1,978	6,608	4,689	12,994	7,793	69,197
Louisiana	124,022	70,473	4,474	42,579	5,945	892	2,159	3,157	643	6,223	3,795	53,549
Oklahoma	142,168	92,808	14,982	15,772	3,276	528	410	8,449	2,066	24,087	17,303	49,360
Texas	331,416	226,693	17,057	106,633	7,658	3,169	1,872	9,669	8,149	47,905	23,051	104,723
Mountain	194,766	149,611	33,853	4,015	8,861	2,146	2,966	17,568	5,209	49,501	24,154	45,155
Montana	35,074	29,999	10,370	.....	860	70	185	1,821	314	12,963	3,180	5,075
Idaho	40,311	32,388	7,133	.....	4,468	166	337	6,286	539	5,511	7,591	7,923
Wyoming	12,615	10,527	2,005	.....	286	5	5	822	128	5,696	1,455	2,088
Colorado	45,586	36,426	9,396	.....	1,944	1,039	971	3,135	1,168	12,290	6,076	9,110
New Mexico	23,503	14,056	2,413	2,712	457	162	273	671	241	5,640	1,419	9,447
Arizona	10,412	6,755	834	1,303	40	243	349	838	552	1,907	569	3,657
Utah	24,198	17,140	1,644	.....	786	456	576	3,641	2,162	4,201	3,410	7,058
Nevada	3,117	2,320	58	.....	20	5		354	105	1,293	454	797
Pacific	266,598	172,923	15,725	5,673	4,163	7,476	43,719	30,519	22,183	20,985	15,725	93,675
Washington	69,821	39,355	6,392	.....	1,056	1,400	6,048	10,535	4,420	4,646	3,147	30,466
Oregon	59,747	34,404	3,562	.....	1,636	1,297	4,049	6,618	3,336	6,033	6,057	25,343
California	137,030	99,164	5,771	5,673	1,471	4,779	33,622	13,466	14,427	10,306	6,521	37,866

[1] Includes miscellaneous commercial farms not shown separately.   [2] Data not included in totals.

Source: Department of Commerce, Bureau of the Census, U. S. Census of Agriculture: 1950, Vol. II.

No. 743.—VALUE OF ALL FARM PRODUCTS SOLD, WITH FARMS REPORTING, BY SOURCE OF INCOME, BY STATES: 1950

[Value of farm products refers to calendar year 1949]

DIVISION AND STATE	ALL FARMS REPORTING PRODUCTS SOLD		Field crops other than vegetables and fruits and nuts sold, value ($1,000)	VEGETABLES SOLD		FRUITS AND NUTS SOLD		Horticultural specialties sold, value ($1,000)
	Farms reporting [1]	Value ($1,000)		Farms reporting	Value ($1,000)	Farms reporting	Value ($1,000)	
United States	5,021,175	22,853,256	5,012,665	346,535	607,012	381,134	791,665	302,000
New England	96,692	631,706	111,172	16,517	12,316	16,619	15,997	39,912
Maine	26,069	125,515	87,075	4,354	2,530	3,704	5,604	1,772
New Hampshire	11,355	46,500	1,926	937	769	1,263	1,646	1,795
Vermont	17,572	86,968	2,366	755	264	852	1,335	657
Massachusetts	19,785	135,350	15,802	2,899	4,488	3,195	7,143	14,460
Rhode Island	2,393	16,034	1,302	305	530	344	388	2,471
Connecticut	12,506	121,269	31,600	1,367	2,418	1,410	2,510	6,738
Middle Atlantic	273,750	1,398,647	146,694	36,890	79,275	32,849	51,996	67,116
New York	116,502	630,401	61,509	15,919	37,154	15,302	27,031	34,466
New Jersey	20,487	214,319	17,164	6,350	20,328	3,308	10,760	19,391
Pennsylvania	132,761	544,927	70,631	14,385	15,796	14,230	14,775	12,400
East North Central	846,693	4,042,395	1,196,740	73,000	71,479	66,093	57,197	99,722
Ohio	187,042	711,661	188,114	10,392	12,798	12,981	9,079	20,047
Indiana	159,279	731,694	205,951	8,602	7,941	6,685	4,117	12,465
Illinois	180,808	1,361,578	542,761	6,520	14,170	5,424	7,911	22,646
Michigan	147,025	472,612	120,578	19,290	17,497	12,560	20,680	14,994
Wisconsin	164,089	764,629	48,394	28,187	19,073	9,353	5,460	7,751
West North Central	998,443	5,691,252	1,716,497	15,746	16,056	26,765	7,497	31,879
Minnesota	176,014	950,553	287,177	5,475	10,651	4,558	1,300	8,063
Iowa	200,841	1,635,350	306,391	3,065	2,505	5,695	573	5,451
Missouri	215,377	719,878	185,690	4,384	2,989	9,906	4,077	4,644
North Dakota	65,130	400,622	265,286	164	56	274	34	476
South Dakota	65,900	430,400	121,937	222	152	651	57	637
Nebraska	106,007	779,521	257,663	963	508	2,095	385	2,000
Kansas	128,075	764,728	322,112	1,575	1,096	3,574	1,072	3,448
South Atlantic	859,353	2,124,731	1,005,334	93,465	106,129	57,393	162,004	63,444
Delaware	7,014	76,288	6,636	2,172	3,572	622	1,011	1,273
Maryland	33,103	172,157	36,146	7,711	9,806	2,317	2,900	6,550
Dist. of Columbia	27	570	2	4	4	4	(*)	434
Virginia	133,562	309,644	106,465	9,555	9,455	5,711	11,612	6,030
West Virginia	55,447	82,146	5,178	2,841	619	4,455	4,008	2,013
North Carolina	262,419	556,628	440,661	20,672	7,565	5,422	3,732	3,734
South Carolina	126,674	213,562	155,428	15,081	7,630	4,433	3,636	1,447
Georgia	180,006	375,152	213,290	24,427	9,930	14,730	6,276	4,609
Florida	50,111	338,645	42,467	10,942	56,743	18,619	130,981	17,372
East South Central	842,241	1,371,301	779,657	34,539	16,727	46,536	12,067	13,826
Kentucky	196,162	417,061	201,206	3,318	1,285	8,496	2,367	2,606
Tennessee	215,403	340,542	167,301	9,381	3,286	10,400	3,184	4,600
Alabama	192,128	274,037	167,968	11,046	3,406	16,908	2,751	5,210
Mississippi	235,548	339,661	243,191	10,885	2,748	10,737	3,755	1,321
West South Central	728,396	2,862,635	1,775,658	56,071	41,399	51,165	32,697	15,762
Arkansas	160,254	592,851	282,134	9,566	3,308	11,092	7,042	1,170
Louisiana	109,380	245,730	173,828	7,412	3,234	10,450	6,945	1,660
Oklahoma	132,683	471,002	245,152	5,221	2,916	12,047	2,736	2,000
Texas	306,079	1,753,052	1,073,915	28,272	31,752	17,579	16,975	11,816
Mountain	184,326	1,631,339	640,329	53,199	53,099	12,536	15,996	12,111
Montana	34,098	279,069	112,399	505	418	1,097	535	606
Idaho	36,734	281,025	146,027	1,982	3,346	2,843	3,302	1,392
Wyoming	12,100	121,836	26,376	152	138	206	31	255
Colorado	42,723	426,448	156,348	5,314	11,443	3,350	4,186	4,764
New Mexico	20,172	154,740	64,921	1,334	2,508	1,720	1,391	548
Arizona	9,496	203,937	99,505	642	30,238	1,097	3,799	861
Utah	26,651	130,298	29,771	3,760	4,611	2,796	5,252	1,410
Nevada	2,944	34,007	4,623	131	278	117	36	127
Pacific	341,999	2,406,249	727,393	17,600	212,466	36,455	436,069	64,634
Washington	61,612	365,209	142,741	4,435	14,995	14,627	67,520	5,736
Oregon	53,990	298,079	98,384	3,631	16,738	15,167	27,505	9,111
California	126,397	1,741,961	486,168	9,004	180,932	56,661	330,327	44,757

[1] Number of farms reporting sales and number of farms reporting no sales were based on reports for only a sample of farms and adjusted to equal total number of farms as obtained in complete enumeration.
[2] $500 or less.

No. 748.—VALUE OF ALL FARM PRODUCTS SOLD WITH FARMS REPORTING, BY SOURCE OF INCOME, BY STATES: 1950—Continued

DIVISION AND STATE	DAIRY PRODUCTS SOLD		POULTRY AND POULTRY PRODUCTS SOLD		Livestock and livestock products sold, value [3] ($1,000)	Forest products sold, value ($1,000)	Farms with no farm products sold (number)[1]
	Farms reporting	Value ($1,000)	Farms reporting	Value ($1,000)			
United States	2,006,831	3,078,132	2,730,178	1,823,332	7,212,438	134,509	360,987
New England	38,622	183,023	34,813	128,055	46,211	10,619	12,622
Maine	10,093	22,071	9,218	26,182	7,132	4,538	4,269
New Hampshire	4,583	15,376	4,788	19,905	3,882	1,201	2,036
Vermont	12,443	62,358	5,386	6,065	10,527	3,405	1,471
Massachusetts	5,961	40,125	8,233	39,958	10,720	623	2,435
Rhode Island	785	6,631	1,006	3,489	1,090	23	305
Connecticut	4,788	36,461	6,182	32,456	6,859	227	2,107
Middle Atlantic	140,967	569,886	146,130	268,517	176,617	7,676	22,952
New York	68,394	319,323	48,274	80,425	66,500	3,882	8,475
New Jersey	4,938	50,146	13,023	72,841	18,253	210	1,351
Pennsylvania	67,635	200,416	84,833	115,252	91,864	3,584	13,126
East North Central	537,534	904,117	541,752	302,873	1,496,537	12,710	37,311
Ohio	108,950	142,221	119,231	73,650	253,462	2,511	12,317
Indiana	91,591	93,910	107,908	70,100	334,799	1,599	7,348
Illinois	106,548	127,166	140,798	64,761	580,258	905	5,460
Michigan	89,651	143,115	74,369	41,215	101,581	3,031	8,564
Wisconsin	140,794	397,705	99,346	53,147	228,436	4,664	3,622
West North Central	615,877	511,791	719,227	411,810	2,968,503	5,618	22,292
Minnesota	134,536	188,440	129,356	117,918	375,036	2,158	3,087
Iowa	143,659	116,436	165,735	120,315	1,077,850	440	2,318
Missouri	113,205	79,246	152,067	60,340	378,419	2,573	11,668
North Dakota	43,308	24,145	37,718	8,946	101,844	31	262
South Dakota	40,708	21,396	50,067	24,263	261,868	100	552
Nebraska	69,263	34,048	81,679	40,391	444,469	59	1,086
Kansas	74,198	48,080	93,585	39,637	349,017	257	3,319
South Atlantic	160,709	212,135	363,512	262,769	279,211	50,505	99,615
Delaware	2,018	6,812	4,678	54,401	2,771	153	434
Maryland	11,722	47,218	20,402	45,536	23,932	1,058	3,004
District of Columbia	2	96	5	2	41	(²)	1
Virginia	44,744	46,243	77,681	45,774	77,502	6,550	17,415
West Virginia	24,043	15,436	38,640	18,840	32,898	2,255	15,987
North Carolina	35,635	26,227	104,779	28,908	35,905	9,874	25,089
South Carolina	17,610	11,442	34,133	10,675	18,141	5,030	12,660
Georgia	22,531	23,994	66,765	45,022	50,913	21,839	18,185
Florida	2,404	34,667	16,429	13,611	37,109	3,744	6,810
East South Central	212,755	131,369	407,877	52,053	346,883	24,731	70,761
Kentucky	85,365	41,316	120,842	15,783	149,300	3,199	20,314
Tennessee	68,309	45,280	129,511	13,827	98,501	4,470	16,228
Alabama	28,242	19,439	80,533	11,702	53,605	9,967	18,384
Mississippi	30,839	25,334	76,991	10,741	45,477	7,094	15,835
West South Central	148,620	157,072	364,124	113,914	715,236	8,646	60,027
Arkansas	36,703	17,011	75,299	30,221	48,396	3,481	13,175
Louisiana	6,337	19,703	39,625	3,922	35,257	1,963	14,801
Oklahoma	52,603	36,424	81,099	18,897	160,600	401	9,563
Texas	52,977	83,934	168,101	60,874	470,984	2,802	22,488
Mountain	78,661	101,435	79,568	55,284	750,129	2,872	10,460
Montana	14,338	11,166	15,942	4,150	148,313	643	987
Idaho	24,197	27,818	15,520	6,134	92,369	867	1,530
Wyoming	5,164	4,380	5,870	1,901	86,625	132	454
Colorado	18,539	21,801	22,812	12,622	213,103	290	1,855
New Mexico	3,230	6,552	6,988	2,252	76,384	183	3,427
Arizona	1,763	10,873	3,021	2,914	55,035	712	916
Utah	10,640	16,373	8,335	24,568	51,961	42	1,125
Nevada	800	2,473	1,080	743	26,340	2	166
Pacific	70,085	308,303	82,175	228,056	417,111	11,733	24,946
Washington	26,550	51,507	24,670	31,186	54,774	3,580	8,208
Oregon	22,377	37,492	21,987	28,870	73,609	6,368	5,967
California	21,158	219,304	35,518	168,000	288,728	1,785	10,771

[1] Number of farms reporting sales and number of farms reporting no sales were based on reports for only a sample of farms and adjusted to equal total number of farms as obtained in complete enumeration. [2] $500 or less. [3] Other than dairy and poultry.

Source: Department of Commerce, Bureau of the Census; U. S. Census of Agriculture: 1950, Vol. II.

No. 744.—NUMBER OF FARMS, BY VALUE OF SALES, BY DIVISIONS AND STATES: 1950

[Based on reports for only a sample of farms, adjusted to equal complete enumeration]

DIVISION AND STATE	NUMBER OF FARMS, BY VALUE OF SALES										
	Total	No sales	$1 to $249	$250 to $399	$400 to $599	$600 to $999	$1,000 to $1,499	$1,500 to $2,499	$2,500 to $3,999	$4,000 to $5,999	$6,000 to $9,999	$10,000 and over
U. S.	5,382,162	399,987	672,915	311,439	326,677	519,305	463,368	640,082	606,459	500,000	392,445	483,254
New England	102,225	12,632	17,015	6,017	5,212	6,410	5,062	7,528	8,912	9,066	10,344	14,746
Maine	30,356	4,269	5,646	2,160	1,694	2,136	1,537	2,376	2,336	2,330	2,265	3,607
N. H	13,391	2,036	2,658	948	838	931	649	1,042	1,054	806	1,014	1,235
Vt	19,043	1,471	2,535	897	727	982	870	1,897	2,136	2,668	2,909	2,251
Mass	22,230	2,435	3,345	1,116	1,246	1,471	1,267	1,731	1,939	1,772	2,097	3,511
R. I.	2,598	306	303	128	149	202	92	165	242	166	229	522
Conn.	15,615	2,107	2,436	768	608	708	647	914	1,213	1,202	1,790	3,230
Middle Atlantic	306,762	22,953	37,547	16,616	14,933	29,718	17,361	26,772	22,368	22,336	27,212	37,672
N. Y	124,977	8,475	13,583	5,999	5,419	7,991	6,996	11,153	14,713	15,970	18,566	16,452
N. J	34,838	1,351	2,378	1,050	1,124	1,631	1,336	1,760	1,828	1,986	3,196	7,262
Pa	146,987	13,126	22,616	9,567	8,300	11,196	9,049	13,822	15,727	14,374	15,220	13,790
E. N. Central	865,464	37,311	76,826	35,449	46,796	63,162	63,170	100,596	124,062	130,969	124,417	96,344
Ohio	199,359	13,317	24,269	10,632	11,095	15,789	15,210	22,465	26,311	24,263	22,685	12,082
Ind	166,927	7,348	15,399	8,071	8,604	12,902	13,229	18,899	22,186	20,122	22,219	12,556
Ill	195,208	5,460	13,063	6,946	7,015	10,709	10,017	15,910	20,416	24,623	34,732	44,337
Mich	155,599	5,864	16,134	5,890	9,477	14,695	14,897	22,150	22,846	17,624	13,770	7,163
Wis	165,561	5,622	7,831	3,931	4,605	8,197	10,017	21,164	33,101	34,397	28,011	12,785
W. N. Central	982,726	22,262	49,055	22,855	31,495	53,574	59,319	111,666	147,799	157,548	177,226	144,062
Minn	179,101	2,087	7,626	4,275	4,726	8,727	10,067	19,553	26,351	31,905	37,131	22,151
Iowa	203,159	2,318	5,439	3,074	3,907	6,362	6,923	14,984	34,009	33,412	51,070	51,551
Mo	230,045	11,668	24,682	14,044	14,607	23,580	23,317	34,004	31,587	22,376	17,395	12,394
N. Dak	66,401	262	980	586	855	1,939	2,743	7,450	12,609	14,270	14,136	9,551
S. Dak	66,452	552	1,186	753	996	2,034	2,938	6,906	11,656	14,001	14,868	10,762
Nebr	107,183	1,086	2,394	1,730	2,031	3,614	4,702	10,952	17,625	21,122	22,065	18,843
Kans	131,394	3,319	6,778	3,896	4,211	7,618	8,729	17,160	21,462	20,452	19,919	17,850
S. Atlantic	955,996	99,615	172,271	65,604	59,336	105,145	93,544	133,366	104,562	51,254	31,591	25,460
Del	7,448	434	761	447	418	462	362	614	674	529	770	1,977
Md	36,107	2,004	4,749	2,167	1,948	2,692	2,353	3,383	3,704	3,316	4,173	4,618
D. C	28	1	5	2	2	4	2	4	2	......	3	5
Va	150,997	17,415	34,306	11,920	11,104	15,843	13,569	16,978	12,817	8,554	4,579	5,522
W. Va	81,434	15,987	27,789	7,912	6,536	7,436	4,351	4,230	2,907	1,507	1,396	1,291
N. C	285,508	25,089	41,424	16,218	16,513	26,444	26,653	52,761	47,378	22,277	9,450	3,251
S. C	139,364	12,690	21,952	11,323	12,960	19,998	16,914	20,450	15,620	4,840	2,305	2,130
Ga	198,191	18,185	30,600	14,900	16,221	26,691	22,747	29,160	19,426	9,207	6,357	5,067
Fla	84,921	6,810	10,695	4,313	4,132	5,847	4,861	4,074	2,834	2,558	3,209	
E. S. Central	912,963	70,761	163,126	82,453	89,675	145,323	114,723	119,929	64,981	29,736	16,667	15,055
Ky	218,476	20,314	37,737	14,562	16,606	26,603	24,351	30,238	21,404	12,303	8,327	5,349
Tenn	231,631	16,228	41,794	19,088	21,604	38,540	29,842	31,662	18,082	8,134	4,918	3,631
Ala	211,512	18,384	40,934	21,757	22,962	34,892	25,507	24,230	12,172	4,950	2,916	2,918
Miss	251,382	15,835	41,663	26,925	28,434	47,188	35,033	32,798	13,323	4,449	2,508	3,237
W. S. Central	786,423	60,927	112,166	50,927	53,360	86,212	77,322	97,162	75,509	53,379	40,596	64,112
Ark	182,429	13,175	29,560	14,355	14,455	26,446	22,309	25,807	14,762	8,237	5,987	6,374
La	134,181	14,801	20,006	9,120	10,069	17,384	16,020	17,480	8,676	3,929	2,877	3,809
Okla	142,246	9,563	19,996	9,670	9,362	13,866	12,451	17,018	16,046	12,475	11,455	10,344
Tex	331,567	22,488	42,604	17,782	18,964	28,514	26,562	36,797	36,325	28,738	20,187	43,586
Mountain	194,866	19,400	15,055	7,455	7,176	11,677	11,644	18,751	22,899	23,196	26,734	39,822
Mont	35,085	987	1,898	916	1,017	1,764	1,957	3,640	4,322	4,935	5,972	7,992
Idaho	40,284	1,530	2,615	1,159	1,179	2,379	2,291	4,049	5,653	5,715	6,408	7,206
Wyo	12,614	454	582	377	321	502	687	1,180	1,774	1,587	1,320	3,340
Colo	45,578	1,855	3,125	1,612	1,615	2,357	2,520	4,190	5,285	5,495	6,696	10,837
N. Mex	23,599	3,427	3,426	1,565	1,188	1,660	1,353	1,714	1,562	1,739	2,104	3,841
Ariz	10,412	916	1,198	526	843	716	716	931	740	685	729	2,722
Utah	34,176	1,125	2,313	1,123	1,209	1,985	1,886	2,763	3,187	2,774	2,678	3,162
Nev	3,110	166	203	177	104	323	264	294	345	275	317	732
Pacific	396,915	34,946	38,412	12,142	13,061	13,784	16,783	34,965	34,448	22,543	26,988	51,029
Wash	69,639	8,209	10,664	4,040	4,150	5,543	4,448	6,540	5,596	4,908	5,841	9,666
Oreg	59,927	5,967	9,043	3,759	3,628	4,699	4,283	5,698	5,480	4,415	5,165	7,742
Calif	137,166	10,771	10,706	5,343	5,303	6,543	6,065	13,772	13,432	13,220	15,653	26,361

No. 744.—Number of Farms, by Value of Sales, by Divisions and States: 1950—Continued

DIVISION AND STATE	PERCENT OF ALL FARMS, BY VALUE OF SALES										
	No sales	$1 to $349	$250 to $399	$400 to $599	$600 to $999	$1,000 to $1,499	$1,500 to $2,499	$2,500 to $3,999	$4,000 to $5,999	$6,000 to $9,999	$10,000 and over
U.S.	6.7	12.5	5.8	6.1	9.5	8.5	11.9	11.3	9.3	9.3	9.2
New England	12.2	16.5	5.8	5.1	6.2	4.9	7.6	8.6	8.8	9.9	14.2
Maine	14.1	18.6	7.1	5.6	7.0	5.1	7.8	7.7	7.7	7.5	11.9
N.H.	15.2	19.8	7.1	6.2	7.0	4.8	7.8	7.9	6.7	7.6	10.0
Vt.	7.7	13.3	4.7	3.8	5.1	4.6	8.4	11.2	14.1	15.3	11.8
Mass.	11.0	15.1	5.0	5.6	6.6	5.7	7.8	8.7	8.0	9.4	17.2
R.I.	11.7	15.1	4.9	5.7	7.8	3.5	6.5	9.3	6.5	8.8	20.1
Conn.	13.5	15.6	4.9	4.3	4.5	4.1	5.9	7.8	7.7	11.1	20.6
Middle Atlantic	7.7	12.5	5.6	5.0	7.0	5.9	9.0	10.9	10.9	12.6	12.7
N.Y.	8.8	10.3	4.8	4.3	6.4	5.6	8.9	11.8	12.8	15.1	13.2
N.J.	5.4	9.6	4.2	4.5	6.2	5.4	7.1	7.4	5.0	12.9	29.4
Pa.	8.9	15.4	6.5	5.7	7.6	6.2	9.4	10.7	9.8	10.4	9.4
E.N. Central	4.3	8.7	4.3	4.6	7.0	7.0	11.4	14.1	13.7	14.1	10.9
Ohio	6.2	12.2	5.4	5.6	7.9	7.6	11.3	13.2	12.2	11.4	7.0
Ind.	4.4	9.2	4.8	5.2	7.7	7.4	11.3	13.3	12.1	13.3	11.1
Ill.	2.8	6.7	3.6	3.6	5.5	5.1	8.1	10.5	12.6	18.8	22.7
Mich.	5.5	10.4	5.6	6.1	9.4	9.4	14.2	14.7	11.3	8.9	4.6
Wis.	2.1	4.6	2.3	2.7	4.9	5.9	12.6	19.6	20.3	17.2	7.6
W.N. Central	2.3	5.0	2.9	3.2	5.5	6.0	11.4	15.0	16.0	16.0	14.7
Minn.	1.7	4.3	2.4	2.6	4.9	5.6	10.9	16.1	17.8	20.7	12.9
Iowa	1.1	2.7	1.5	2.0	3.1	3.4	7.4	11.8	16.4	25.1	25.4
Mo.	5.1	10.7	6.1	6.3	10.3	10.1	15.0	13.7	9.7	7.6	5.3
N. Dak.	.4	1.5	.9	1.3	2.9	4.2	11.4	19.3	21.8	21.6	14.6
S. Dak.	.8	1.8	1.2	1.5	3.0	4.4	10.5	17.5	21.1	22.0	16.2
Nebr.	1.0	2.2	1.6	1.9	3.4	4.4	10.2	16.4	19.7	21.5	17.6
Kans.	2.5	5.2	3.0	3.2	5.8	6.6	13.1	16.3	15.6	15.2	13.6
S. Atlantic	10.4	18.0	7.1	7.3	11.0	9.8	13.9	10.9	5.3	3.3	3.1
Del.	5.8	10.2	6.0	5.6	6.2	4.9	8.2	9.0	7.1	10.3	20.5
Md.	8.3	13.2	6.0	5.4	7.5	6.5	9.4	10.3	9.2	11.6	12.8
D.C.	3.6	17.9	7.1	7.1	7.1	14.3	7.1	7.1	----	10.7	17.9
Va.	11.5	22.8	7.9	7.4	10.5	9.0	11.2	8.5	4.3	3.0	3.9
W. Va.	19.6	34.1	9.7	8.0	9.1	5.3	5.2	3.4	2.0	1.7	1.7
N.C.	8.7	14.4	5.3	5.7	9.2	9.9	18.3	16.4	7.7	3.3	1.1
S.C.	9.1	15.8	8.3	9.3	14.3	12.1	14.7	9.8	3.5	1.7	1.5
Ga.	9.2	15.4	7.3	8.2	13.5	11.5	14.7	9.8	4.7	3.2	2.6
Fla.	12.0	18.8	7.6	7.3	9.8	8.5	10.3	7.2	5.0	4.5	9.2
E.S. Central	7.8	17.8	9.0	9.8	15.9	12.6	13.0	7.1	3.3	2.0	1.7
Ky.	9.3	17.3	6.7	7.6	12.2	11.1	13.9	9.8	5.6	3.8	2.7
Tenn.	7.0	18.0	8.2	9.4	15.8	12.9	13.7	7.8	3.5	2.1	1.6
Ala.	8.7	19.4	10.3	10.8	16.5	12.1	11.5	5.8	2.3	1.4	1.4
Miss.	6.3	16.6	10.7	11.3	18.8	13.9	13.0	5.3	1.8	1.0	1.3
W.S. Central	7.7	14.4	6.5	6.9	11.0	9.9	12.4	9.7	6.8	6.3	8.2
Ark.	7.2	16.2	7.9	8.5	14.5	12.2	14.1	8.1	4.5	3.3	3.5
La.	11.9	16.1	7.3	8.1	14.0	12.9	14.1	7.0	3.2	2.3	3.1
Okla.	6.7	14.1	6.8	6.6	9.7	8.8	12.0	11.3	8.8	8.1	7.3
Tex.	6.8	12.8	5.4	5.7	8.6	8.0	11.1	11.0	8.7	8.8	13.1
Mountain	5.4	7.7	3.8	3.7	6.0	6.0	9.6	11.8	11.9	13.7	20.4
Mont.	2.8	4.5	2.6	2.9	5.0	5.6	10.4	12.3	14.1	17.0	22.8
Idaho	3.8	6.5	2.9	2.9	5.9	5.7	10.1	14.0	14.2	15.9	18.1
Wyo.	3.6	4.6	3.0	2.5	4.7	5.4	9.4	14.1	12.6	14.4	25.7
Colo.	4.1	6.9	3.5	3.5	5.2	5.5	9.2	11.6	12.1	14.7	23.8
N. Mex.	14.5	14.5	6.6	5.0	7.0	5.7	7.3	6.7	7.3	8.9	16.3
Ariz.	8.8	11.5	5.1	5.2	6.9	6.9	8.8	7.1	6.6	7.0	26.1
Utah	4.7	9.6	4.6	5.0	8.2	7.7	11.4	13.2	11.5	11.1	13.1
Nev.	5.3	6.5	4.7	3.3	7.5	8.5	9.5	11.1	8.8	10.2	23.6
Pacific	9.3	11.4	4.9	4.9	7.0	6.3	9.4	9.2	8.4	10.0	19.1
Wash.	11.8	15.3	5.8	5.9	7.9	6.4	9.4	7.9	7.0	8.4	14.2
Oreg.	10.0	15.1	5.3	6.1	7.9	7.2	9.4	9.2	7.4	8.6	12.9
Calif.	7.9	7.8	3.9	3.9	6.2	5.9	9.3	9.8	9.6	11.4	24.3

Source: Department of Commerce, Bureau of the Census; U. S. Census of Agriculture: 1950, Vol. II.

25. Agriculture—Production and Related Subjects

The data in this section are, for the most part, from the Bureau of the Census, Department of Commerce, and from various bureaus in the United States Department of Agriculture. In general, statistics for agriculture census years are from the Bureau of the Census. Estimates for intervening years, and adjustments, where necessary, to a January 1 basis are from the Bureau of Agricultural Economics, United States Department of Agriculture.

Annual agricultural statistics of a wide variety have been issued currently by the United States Department of Agriculture for 90 years—the first being as of May 1, 1863. The 41 field offices design the samples and collect data from voluntary reporters. State estimates and other information are sent to the Crop Reporting Board of the Bureau of Agricultural Economics in Washington, where, after review, reports are issued containing State, Regional, and United States data.

Statistics compiled by the Bureau of Agricultural Economics on crops, livestock, and livestock products, agricultural prices, farm employment, and other related subjects are based mainly on data obtained through mail questionnaires. The basic information is obtained from nearly three-quarters of a million reporters, located in every agricultural county in the United States, who report on one or more items during a year. These reporters, mostly farmers, report for their own and nearby farms on some 80 crops and scores of other items pertaining to agricultural production and farm family living.

The most extensive of the current survey data are gathered by the Bureau of Agricultural Economics from questionnaires handled in cooperation with the Post Office Department through its rural mail carriers. These surveys obtain livestock data in June and December and crop acreage data in October. For each survey the rural carrier distributes 10 to 20 cards to farmers on his route. The farmer is asked to complete his questionnaire for his own farm and return the card to his mail box.

In the data prepared by the Bureau of Agricultural Economics, estimates of crop acreage and production for the census years are set up currently on available information. Later, if necessary, these data are revised to a level based largely on the census enumerations. The estimates for intercensal years are based on sample data obtained each year from individual reporters. This information is supplemented by other data, such as State assessors' enumerations of agricultural information, crop meter frontage measurements, reports of carlot shipments, warehouse receipts, local surveys, personal observations by field statisticians as well as reports from other sources having a knowledge of farming, agricultural production, and processing. Cotton acreage and production are also based on sample data and, in large measure, on ginning information gathered by the Bureau of the Census. Usually, all known sources of information pertaining to agriculture in general, from the farm to the consumer's household are tapped for basic facts used in compiling current statistics on agriculture.

For each decade from 1840 through 1900, the Census of Agriculture was taken as of June 1. The five decennial censuses since then have been taken as of April 15, 1910; January 1, 1920; and April 1, 1930, 1940, and 1950. The 1925, 1935, and 1945 quinquennial Censuses of Agriculture were taken as of January 1. Comparison of inventory numbers of livestock from census to census is seriously affected by a change in the date of enumeration. From January to April there are material changes in num-

Note.—This section presents data for the most recent year or period available on May 20, 1953, when the material was organized and sent to the printer.

245354°—53——42   641

bers on hand in most parts of the country due to births, marketings, farm slaughter, etc. In an effort to obtain as much comparability as possible the censuses taken in April either excluded recently born animals from the enumeration or provided for their enumeration in a separate age group. Volume II of the 1950 Census of Agriculture Reports shows a complete history of the enumeration of livestock and presents a discussion of the comparability from census to census.

For most kinds of domestic livestock, there are comparatively short, cyclic fluctuations in numbers, even though the trend over a long period of time may be definitely in one direction. A single census may be taken at a time when such a cycle is at the peak or at the trough of numbers and hence gives no true indication of the long-time trend.

Annual inventory numbers of livestock on farms prepared by the Department of Agriculture together with estimates of livestock, dairy, and poultry production are based on information furnished by individual farmers, supplemented by State assessors' data in a number of States, and by such records as brand inspections, rail and truck shipments, and inspected slaughter. The level for these inventories is based in large part on census enumerations for years when census data are available.

Data on imports and exports are now compiled by the Department of Commerce, Bureau of the Census, and are published in the annual report, *Foreign Commerce and Navigation of the United States.* (See also section 32, Foreign Commerce.) The official trade statistics based on the fiscal year are usually preferable to data presented on a calendar year basis, for use in comparing imports and exports with crop production since, for most crops, they coincide more nearly with the crop year.

For a historical summation of raw materials production, imports, exports, and consumption, which includes figures for agricultural materials, see table 1056.

Historical statistics.—See preface and historical appendix. Tabular headnotes (as "See also *Historical Statistics*, series E 72–75") provide cross-references, where applicable, to *Historical Statistics of the United States, 1789–1945.*

No. 745.—FARM PRODUCTION INDEXES AND ACREAGE OF 52 CROPS: 1929 TO 1952

[For certain series, data prior to 1950 subject to adjustment to 1950 Census results. See also *Historical Statistics*, series E 72-75]

ITEM	1929	1930	1935	1940	1945	1948	1949	1950	1951	1952
INDEXES OF VOLUME OF PRODUCTION 1935-39=100										
Gross farm production [1]	101	96	97	108	123	131	130	125	128	132
Farm output for human use	97	95	96	110	129	141	140	136	139	144
Farm produced, horse and mule power	124	120	106	92	76	59	53	50	46	41
Product added by live-stock: [2]										
Total livestock	101	102	96	107	130	120	126	126	130	132
Livestock, exc. horses and mules	97	99	94	110	139	131	130	139	145	147
Crops and pasture, total [3]	100	96	97	108	120	136	132	126	127	132
Feed grains, hay, and pasture	108	94	103	111	124	135	128	126	122	126
Food grains	106	115	84	107	142	167	147	132	126	156
Truck crops	86	86	94	111	126	137	139	145	145	146
Vegetables exc. truck crops	92	94	107	102	111	121	114	111	88	91
Fruits and tree nuts	86	84	104	108	111	113	123	122	126	115
Sugar crop	73	83	90	102	94	92	94	112	87	91
Cotton and cottonseed	113	106	81	96	69	112	122	76	117	114
Tobacco	103	112	90	99	136	155	135	140	137	162
Oil crops	60	66	98	165	274	343	320	286	342	345
Production for sale and for home consumption, total	99	96	91	110	124	127	126	125	140	145
Livestock and products, total [4]	99	99	93	112	141	128	134	136	141	145
Meat animals	103	100	90	118	147	133	137	138	143	146
Poultry and eggs	100	106	92	112	170	153	160	179	191	200
Dairy products	93	94	98	105	119	111	113	113	112	111
Crops, total [4]	98	96	89	107	122	150	144	134	130	144
Food grains	113	109	81	110	155	186	160	148	145	191
Feed grains and hay	103	83	91	114	144	199	177	171	154	165
Cotton and cotton-seed	113	106	81	96	68	115	125	77	117	116
Tobacco	62	68	96	171	291	371	339	309	261	351
Oil-bearing crops	106	113	89	101	137	136	136	140	160	182
Truck crops	87	91	92	111	142	143	144	147	160	154
Fruits and tree nuts	73	89	95	110	113	115	121	126	127	121
Vegetables	90	90	104	101	110	122	112	113	88	90
Sugar crops	74	85	89	104	94	88	90	112	89	90
AGGREGATE ACREAGE, 52 CROPS										
Planted or grown (1,000 acres)	363,028	369,550	361,889	347,969	356,222	359,280	365,040	353,524	361,842	354,699
Harvested (1,000 acres)	355,295	359,896	336,060	231,649	345,443	347,943	352,114	336,801	335,791	340,985

[1] Measures calendar-year production of all crops and pasture consumed by all livestock, and the product added in conversion of feed and pasture into livestock and livestock products for human use and into farm-produced horse and mule power.

[2] Estimated value, at 1935-39 average prices, of all feed (including commercial feeds) and pasture consumed by each class of livestock subtracted from total value, at 1935-39 average prices, of livestock and livestock products.

[3] Includes miscellaneous crops not included in groups shown.

[4] Volume of sales and home consumption during calendar year.

[5] Total crop production minus quantities retained for feed and seed and quantities not harvested or lost.

Source: Department of Agriculture, Bureau of Agricultural Economics; annual report, *Agricultural Statistics*.

No. 746.—Farm Labor Productivity and Man-Hours Required: 1910 to 1952

[Data for farm output prior to 1950 subject to adjustment to 1950 Census results]

YEAR	Man-hours of labor required on farms [1] (millions)	Index of farm output per man-hour (1935-39=100) [2]	YEAR	Man-hours of labor required on farms [1] (millions)	Index of farm output per man-hour (1935-39=100) [2]
1910	22,343	74	1944	20,768	130
1915	22,938	80	1945	19,765	136
1920	23,770	81	1946	19,465	144
1925	23,643	82	1947	18,988	142
1930	22,753	87	1948	18,808	157
1935	20,903	96	1949	18,667	156
1940	20,520	112	1950	17,384	164
1941	20,149	118	1951	17,890	162
1942	21,057	127	1952	17,175	173
1943	20,910	125			

[1] Expressed in terms of man-equivalent hours, that is, time used by average adult males in performing farm operations.
[2] Index of farm output (production available for human use) divided by index of man-hour requirements.

Source: Department of Agriculture, Bureau of Agricultural Economics. Published in *Agricultural Statistics*.

No. 747.—Agricultural Products Exported—Value, by Major Groups: 1921 to 1952

[In million of dollars. Excludes reexports of foreign products. Includes shipments under foreign aid programs such as UNRRA, Interim Aid, ECA, and MDAP (MSA); Civilian Supply shipments are included in 1948 and subsequent years]

PERIOD	Total agricultural exports	Animals and products, edible	Dairy products and eggs	Grains and preparations	Vegetables, fruits, and nuts	Miscellaneous animal and vegetable products	Cotton	Tobacco
1921-1925, average	2,013.2	283.2	38.8	474.3	102.0	145.3	805.0	164.6
1926-1930, average	1,691.6	189.8	23.6	318.6	144.3	105.1	765.7	144.5
1931-1935, average	731.7	63.9	6.9	55.4	94.4	40.8	366.5	103.7
1936-1940, average	701.2	44.6	8.6	104.6	91.4	59.2	282.9	109.8
1941-1945, average	1,654.4	490.7	376.6	174.0	170.7	153.0	151.7	137.7
1946-1950, average	3,222.5	216.4	269.6	1,205.4	282.0	307.0	674.2	267.9
1946	3,140.0	446.6	450.2	788.8	314.6	250.5	538.2	351.2
1947	3,130.9	234.4	338.7	1,242.5	321.9	299.4	423.3	270.7
1948	3,419.9	136.3	255.9	1,704.7	350.1	247.5	511.0	214.5
1949	3,568.5	151.2	200.5	1,457.4	243.5	389.7	874.2	251.9
1950	2,853.1	113.8	102.8	833.9	179.9	348.0	1,024.5	250.2
1951	4,038.3	203.2	153.0	1,483.8	211.8	514.4	1,146.4	325.5
1952 (prel.)	3,427.0	152.8	93.9	1,481.8	251.2	328.2	873.6	245.5

Source: Department of Commerce, Bureau of the Census; annual report, *Foreign Commerce and Navigation of the U. S.*, and records.

No. 748.—Agricultural Products Exported—Indexes of Quantity: 1941 to 1952

[January 1924-December 1929 = 100]

YEAR ENDING JUNE 30—	Total [1]	Cotton, including linters	Agricultural, except cotton	Tobacco, unmanufactured	Fruits	Wheat and flour	Other grains	Cured pork	Lard, including neutral
1941	25	15	34	35	38	22	46	7	24
1942	49	14	82	61	62	19	51	70	84
1943	55	15	92	62	52	18	36	81	70
1944	67	15	115	74	70	27	39	75	106
1945	64	20	105	97	69	31	49	38	109
1946	96	43	146	110	75	175	70	6	57
1947 [2]	100	46	151	122	99	201	168	8	41
1948	90	24	151	83	89	266	109	2	43
1949	109	56	158	92	66	278	165	4	62
1950	97	68	125	101	63	172	180	6	69
1951	93	50	132	99	63	204	194	11	65
1952	111	66	153	111	81	261	178	15	96

[1] Based on data for 74 agricultural export classifications.
[2] Beginning January 1947, includes exports under various special programs including ECA.

Source: Department of Agriculture, Office of Foreign Agricultural Relations; annual report, *Agricultural Statistics*. Published currently in *Foreign Agricultural Trade*. Compiled from official records of Bureau of Census.

No. 749.—AGRICULTURAL PRODUCTS EXPORTED—VALUE OF CHIEF PRODUCTS: 1931 TO 1952

[In millions of dollars. Excludes reexports of foreign products. Includes shipments under foreign aid programs such as UNRRA, Interim Aid, ECA, and MDAP (MSA); Civilian Supply shipments are included in 1948 and subsequent years].

PRODUCTS	1931–1935, average	1936–1940, average	1941–1945, average	1946–1950, average	1948	1949	1950	1951	1952 (prel.)
Total	731.7	701.2	1,654.4	2,222.5	2,419.9	2,362.5	2,363.1	4,620.3	3,427.6
Live animals	1.5	1.8	3.5	12.2	7.2	7.0	7.2	9.0	10.9
Meats	23.7	21.3	373.2	114.4	47.8	42.0	32.3	85.6	80.2
Eggs and dairy products	6.9	8.0	376.6	209.4	255.9	200.5	102.5	183.0	98.9
Animal fats and oils	37.0	18.2	109.2	105.5	99.0	124.5	112.1	214.3	147.3
Hides and skins	3.2	4.5	1.1	15.7	11.6	21.0	11.6	12.7	19.5
Bread grains [1]	40.4	55.6	112.6	666.4	1,420.9	1,025.1	499.7	1,013.4	907.2
Coarse grains	9.3	35.3	30.5	224.9	188.0	341.3	246.8	375.0	385.8
Rice	4.7	6.9	30.2	82.9	85.9	90.1	45.0	96.0	187.1
Fodders and feeds	9.3	9.5	3.9	19.0	14.1	23.0	16.6	33.4	18.8
Vegetables	8.0	12.2	50.0	73.2	82.0	62.0	62.5	71.2	90.7
Fruits and preparations	52.2	74.0	83.5	127.5	113.4	100.9	111.5	117.3	160.0
Vegetable oils (expressed), oilseeds, and nuts	6.5	11.3	46.1	145.2	166.7	240.1	165.7	202.5	151.9
Coffee and substitutes	1.9	2.2	1.2	7.2	7.6	7.3	5.1	8.0	6.1
Sugar and related products	4.8	8.1	26.8	34.6	16.1	8.5	20.1	22.0	15.7
Seeds, except oilseeds	1.9	2.5	13.0	15.0	13.0	12.0	7.0	8.0	5.5
Tobacco	103.7	100.8	137.7	267.9	214.5	251.9	260.2	325.5	345.5
Cotton	366.5	262.9	151.7	674.2	511.0	674.2	1,034.5	1,145.4	575.5
Wool and hair	1.5	2.1	6.8	9.7	3.6	16.4	10.4	4.9	2.4
All other	17.6	27.1	37.5	122.1	162.9	100.2	91.1	110.9	68.9

[1] Wheat and rye; flour and flour products.

Source: Department of Commerce, Bureau of the Census; annual report, *Foreign Commerce and Navigation of the U. S.*, and records.

No. 750.—AGRICULTURAL PRODUCTS IMPORTED—VALUE, BY MAJOR GROUPS: 1931 TO 1952

[In millions of dollars. General imports through 1932, imports for consumption thereafter. Excludes distilled liquors and candy]

GROUP	1931–35, average	1936–40, average	1941–45, average	1946–50, average	1948	1949	1950	1951	1952
Agricultural imports,[1] total		1,240.1	1,866.7	2,016.6	2,120.3	2,504.3	2,966.5	5,779.0	4,517.6
Commodities listed, total	532.3	1,177.9	1,829.0	2,874.9	2,683.2	2,765.7	2,819.4	4,972.9	4,328.1
Animals and products, edible	16.1	45.7	52.4	116.0	169.4	135.9	189.3	245.7	177.8
Dairy products and eggs	14.2	14.2	5.8	17.2	14.8	21.1	31.0	25.7	40.1
Hides and skins, except reptile	38.6	50.1	68.2	88.9	105.5	69.9	114.1	127.0	56.0
Animal fats, inedible	3.5	1.1	2.7	.4	.2	.5	.5	.8	1.0
Grains and preparations	25.2	44.3	112.3	42.5	26.9	75.3	75.4	131.4	165.7
Fodders and feeds	6.7	11.3	16.4	23.1	18.9	94.1	33.4	42.1	74.2
Vegetables, fruits, nuts	66.3	79.2	93.0	303.9	230.7	199.3	215.4	221.9	218.8
Vegetable oils (expressed) and oilseeds	71.7	112.9	84.4	203.5	254.4	165.0	215.2	211.7	181.6
Cocoa, coffee, tea, spices	188.6	206.1	347.5	946.5	970.6	1,007.6	1,391.6	1,672.2	1,566.5
Sugar and related products	122.0	152.1	207.6	343.0	349.1	396.2	406.1	439.8	466.2
Beverages, excluding spirits	6.1	11.4	14.0	20.5	16.6	18.1	23.6	25.5	27.5
Crude rubber	74.6	206.3	151.8	312.3	309.2	240.3	688.2	809.3	619.1
Tobacco, unmanufactured	27.1	34.3	50.5	80.8	77.6	73.2	76.4	86.4	80.7
Cotton, unmanufactured	7.4	11.4	20.2	41.2	42.0	22.4	43.3	42.4	41.2
Wool and mohair, unmanufactured	18.7	61.3	347.9	291.3	307.6	222.2	427.8	713.5	382.6
Raw silk	115.1	105.7	12.6	33.0	15.4	7.3	20.6	19.5	36.6
Vegetable fibers, except cotton and silk	17.6	39.4	43.6	60.8	93.9	88.0	96.1	158.2	128.1

[1] Value of total agricultural imports not available on calendar year basis prior to 1934.

Source: Department of Commerce, Bureau of the Census; annual report, *Foreign Commerce and Navigation of the U. S.*, and records.

No. 751.—AGRICULTURAL EXPORTS AND IMPORTS—VALUE: 1857 TO 1952

[All figures, except percentages, in millions of dollars. Excludes forest products. Crude rubber and similar gums (now mainly plantation products) are included in agricultural products]

YEARLY AVERAGE OR YEAR ENDING JUNE 30—	AGRICULTURAL EXPORTS [1]			AGRICULTURAL IMPORTS [1] [4]				Excess of domestic agricultural exports over supplementary imports
	Domestic products		Foreign products (re-exports)	Total	Percent of all imports	Supplementary imports [5]	Complementary imports [5]	
	Total [3]	Percent of all exports [3]						
1857–1861	214	80.4	10.2	118	37.1			
1862–1866	147	74.7	9.2	122	43.0			
1867–1871	250	76.6	8.6	181	42.6			
1872–1876	396	78.3	9.0	266	47.0			
1877–1881	589	80.1	8.6	272	51.4			
1882–1886	555	75.9	9.7	322	48.4			
1887–1891	572	74.6	7.2	378	49.8			
1892–1896	636	72.7	9.4	413	53.5			
1897–1901	826	65.8	12.9	401	53.4			
1902–1906	878	59.4	14.5	523	49.7			
1907–1911	974	53.8	16.8	701	49.9			
1912–1916	1,254	45.1	28.0	1,024	55.4			
1917–1921	2,856	42.6	82.7	2,162	61.5			
1922–1926	1,950	45.9	58.6	1,982	54.3			
1927–1931	1,621	35.9	57.8	1,943	51.2	(6)	(6)	(6)
1932–1936	713	36.4	20.3	872	50.9	443	429	270
1937–1941	679	20.3	32.3	1,281	51.0	628	652	51
1942–1946	1,976	18.9	92.0	1,645	45.5	1,024	621	952
1947 (prel.)	3,610	28.4	135.9	2,704	50.2	1,387	1,317	2,223
1948 (prel.)	3,505	25.4	56.0	2,862	45.3	1,444	1,418	2,062
1949 (prel.)	3,830	30.2	51.6	3,001	43.0	1,532	1,469	2,298
1950 (prel.)	2,986	29.6	53.2	3,177	45.2	1,553	1,625	1,433
1951 (prel.)	3,411	27.1	96.4	5,147	47.9	2,289	2,858	1,122
1952 (prel.)	4,047	26.1	70.0	4,698	45.0	1,970	2,728	2,077

[1] Excludes distilled liquor.
[2] Beginning Jan. 1, 1942, includes food exported for relief or charity; beginning Jan. 1, 1947, also includes exports under Army Civilian Supply Program.
[3] Based on total exports of domestic merchandise.
[4] Imports for consumption beginning 1934; general imports prior thereto.
[5] Supplementary agricultural imports consist of all imports similar to agricultural commodities produced commercially in the United States, together with all other agricultural imports interchangeable to any significant extent with such United States commodities. Complementary agricultural imports include all others, about 95 percent of which consist of rubber, coffee, raw silk, cacao beans, wool for carpets, bananas, tea, and spices.
[6] Average not computed; data not available prior to 1929.

Source: Department of Agriculture, Office of Foreign Agricultural Relations, from official records of Bureau of the Census and U. S. Tariff Commission. Published in annual report, *Agricultural Statistics.*

No. 752.—AGRICULTURAL PRODUCTS IMPORTED—INDEXES OF QUANTITY: 1939 TO 1952

[January 1924–December 1929=100]

YEAR ENDING JUNE 30—	Total [1]	Complementary [2]	Supplementary [2]	Wool (excl. free for carpets)	Hides and skins	Dairy products	Sugar	Vegetable oils and oilseeds	Grains, grain products, and feeds	Tobacco, leaf
1939	91	102	77	46	71	50	66	116	79	75
1940	102	113	87	112	76	51	82	103	111	75
1941	128	146	104	328	104	22	89	93	118	79
1942	102	100	104	389	116	32	62	98	119	77
1943	78	44	122	898	103	36	48	43	220	92
1944	89	61	125	488	70	21	82	57	805	80
1945	84	67	106	382	57	5	90	53	445	86
1946	86	79	94	561	47	17	52	42	123	84
1947	102	104	98	457	53	25	72	81	38	100
1948	100	110	87	296	62	16	80	72	15	80
1949	102	114	86	179	42	23	87	62	124	92
1950	104	111	96	255	59	41	79	69	188	91
1951	119	121	115	332	67	55	92	86	211	100
1952	108	115	98	248	49	49	91	54	307	110

[1] Based on data for 122 agricultural import classifications.
[2] Supplementary agricultural imports consist of all imports similar to agricultural commodities produced commercially in the United States, together with all other agricultural imports interchangeable to any significant extent with such United States commodities. Complementary agricultural imports include all others, about 95 percent of which consist of rubber, coffee, raw silk, cacao beans, wool for carpets, bananas, teas, and spices.

Source: Department of Agriculture, Office of Foreign Agricultural Relations; annual report, *Agricultural Statistics.* Published currently in *Foreign Agricultural Trade.* Compiled from official records of Bureau of the Census and Tariff Commission.

No. 753.—ALL CROPS—ACREAGE, VALUE, AND CROPLAND HARVESTED: 1879 TO 1949

[Minus sign (−) denotes decrease]

CROP AND YEAR	ACREAGE (THOUSANDS)			VALUE (THOUSANDS OF DOLLARS)			Average value per acre (dollars)
	Total	Increase		Total	Increase		
		Acres	Percent		Amount	Percent	
Cropland harvested:							
1919 [1]	348,604	−4,054	−1.2				
1924	344,549						
1929	350,243	14,698	4.2				
1934	295,634	−53,618	−17.7				
1939	321,242	25,618	8.7				
1944	352,866	31,623	9.8				
1949	344,399	−8,467	−2.4				
All crops:							
1879	166,187			(2)	(2)	(2)	(2)
1889	219,706	53,519	32.2	(2)	(2)	(2)	(2)
1899	283,218	63,513	28.9	2,866,050	(2)	(2)	10.20
1909	311,293	28,075	9.9	5,387,774	2,309,724	80.1	16.99
1919	348,604	37,310	12.0	14,646,178	9,358,404	177.0	42.01
1924	(2)	(2)	(2)	7,472,535	−7,173,643	−49.0	(2)
1929 [3]	361,945	(2)	(2)	8,223,515	750,980	10.0	22.72
1934	298,642	−63,302	−17.5	4,479,015	−3,744,500	−45.5	15.00
1939	324,238	25,596	8.6	5,705,464	1,226,449	27.4	17.60
1944 [3][4]	353,355	29,116	9.0	14,439,931	8,734,466	153.1	40.87
1949	351,526	−1,829	−.5	16,297,089	1,857,158	12.9	46.36
Field crops: [4]							
1899	282,840			2,725,292			9.64
1909	309,913	27,073	9.6	4,942,686	2,217,874	81.4	15.95
1919 [5]	346,875	36,962	11.9	12,272,568	8,329,982	168.5	35.38
1929	342,660	5,785	1.7	6,900,066	−5,372,502	−46.0	19.57
1934 [7]	286,421	−64,239	−18.3	3,949,725	−2,950,371	−42.8	13.60
1939	315,660	27,239	9.4	4,763,656	813,931	20.6	15.09
1944 [5]	343,798	28,128	8.9	11,891,732	7,128,076	149.6	34.80
1949	342,664	−1,134	−.3	14,322,355	2,430,628	20.4	41.80
Vegetables: [5][8]							
1899	1,009			65,749			
1919	1,424	415	41.1	534,436	(10)	(10)	
1929	2,812	1,387	97.4	522,010	−12,426	−2.3	
1934	3,774	962	34.2	137,029	(10)	(10)	
1939	3,053	−720	−19.1	410,916	(10)	(10)	
1944 [9]	4,370	1,317	43.1	1,032,626	621,710	151.3	
1949	3,718	−652	−14.9	607,018	−425,608	−41.2	
Fruits and nuts and horticultural specialties:							
1889 [12]	379			162,757			
1900 [12]	371	−7	−1.9	279,358	116,601	71.6	
1910 [12]	304	−67	−18.1	539,144	559,786	200.4	
1920 [13]	6,473	(10)	(10)	801,409	−37,735	−4.5	123.83
1924 [7]	6,448	−25	−.4	392,261	−409,148	−51.1	60.84
1930	5,525	−923	−14.3	520,892	128,631	35.3	94.09
1944 [14]	5,187	−338	−6.1	1,515,572	994,680	185.5	292.21
1949 [14]	5,145	−41	−.8	1,367,716	−147,857	−9.8	265.51

[1] For Census of 1920, cropland harvested was obtained by adding the acres of individual crops harvested. See note 6.
[2] Not available.
[3] Total acreage of crops harvested for which figures are available. Includes any acreage of alfalfa seed and clover and grass seeds enumerated, some of which was harvested from land also cut for hay.
[4] Total for specified crops.
[5] Irish and sweet potatoes included with "Field crops," not with "Vegetables."
[6] Excludes corn cut for fodder (acreage, 14,503,000; value, $306,935,000) probably duplicated in acreage of corn harvested for grain.
[7] Only strawberries included in small fruits; other small fruits included in field crops.
[8] Acreage represents vegetables harvested for sale only; acreage in farm gardens not available. Value includes both vegetables for home use and for sale, except as noted.
[9] Vegetables harvested for sale.
[10] Available data not comparable.
[11] Farm garden vegetables for home use only.
[12] Acreage in fruit orchards, vineyards, and planted nut trees not secured prior to 1930 Census.
[13] Acreage of horticultural specialties not included.
[14] Excludes acreage on farms reporting less than one-half acre in orchards, vineyards, and planted nut trees.

Source: Department of Commerce, Bureau of the Census; U. S. Census of Agriculture: 1950, Vol. II.

No. 754.—CROPS—ACREAGE, PRODUCTION, AND VALUE, BY KIND: 1944 AND 1949

[Leaders indicate no data available. See also *Historical Statistics*, series E 181-343]

CROP	ACREAGE (THOUSANDS)		PRODUCTION (1,000 UNITS)			VALUE ($1,000)	
	1944	1949	Unit	1944	1949	1944	1949
All crops harvested		[1] 351,528					16,297,089
Specified crops, harvested [2]	349,303					14,439,931	[1] 16,103,848
All field crops [4]		342,064					14,222,355
Specified field crops [5]	340,246					11,891,732	14,149,357
Corn for all purposes [5]	92,269	83,336				3,291,109	3,823,424
Sorghum for all purposes except sirup	17,224	10,069				306,980	228,783
All wheat threshed	[6] 65,286	[6] 71,161	Bushels	[6] 1,032,660	[6] 1,006,559	[6] 1,458,641	[6] 1,874,371
Oats threshed	35,425	35,331	...do......	1,041,112	1,135,700	721,162	739,724
Oats cut for feeding unthreshed	4,187	1,533				83,710	40,781
Barley threshed	11,694	[6] 9,180	Bushels	261,425	[6] 220,963	262,369	[6] 331,735
Rye threshed	2,029	[6] 1,418	...do......	21,349	[6] 16,563	23,256	[6] 20,237
Mixed grains threshed	[6] 11,146	1,763	...do......	[6] 7 30,812	45,769	[6] 7 31,225	51,910
Flax threshed	2,477	[6] 4,813	...do......	20,765	[6] 40,189	60,324	[6] 144,703
Rice threshed	[6] 1,294	[6] 1,819	...do......	[6] 65,044	[6] 89,432	[6] 114,192	[6] 158,436
Soybeans harvested for beans		10,148	...do......	[6] 187,726	212,440	[6] 389,512	451,129
Soybeans hogged or grazed or cut for silage		583					9,818
Cowpeas harvested for dry peas		382	Bushels	3,603	1,954	13,182	6,885
Cowpeas harvested for green peas [9]		151	Bu. in shell.		2,092		4,005
Cowpeas hogged or grazed or cut for silage		312					5,154
Soybeans and cowpeas cut for hay	3,072	1,394	Tons....	3,350	1,643	78,804	37,296
Peanuts harvested for nuts	[6] 2,966	2,134	Pounds..	[6] 2,008,656	1,721,913	[6] 162,727	177,000
Peanut vines or tops saved for hay		1,335	Tons....	1,041	674	17,307	9,844
All dry field and seed beans	[6] 1,898	1,780	Bushels.	[6] 26,075	32,367	[6] 97,802	131,846
All dry field and seed peas other than cowpeas and Austrian peas	[6] 697	366	...do......	[6] 14,285	5,215	[6] 42,064	11,466
All hay, excluding sorghum for hay and specified annual legumes	[6] 69,215	65,636	Tons....	[6] 94,914	90,051	[6] 1,630,084	1,884,072
Alfalfa cut for hay	14,977	16,412	...do......	32,670	35,254	605,966	793,601
Clover or timothy cut for hay	22,603	18,557	...do......	30,749	23,957	583,028	547,072
Lespedeza cut for hay	[6] 5,941	[6] 6,929	...do......	[6] 5,569	[6] 7,934	[6] 132,475	[6] 162,254
Small grains cut for hay	1,542	3,046	...do......	1,884	3,141	30,950	63,548
Wild hay cut	15,526	[6] 14,297	...do......	14,422	[6] 11,616	128,482	[6] 172,150
Other hay cut	8,625	[6] 6,390	...do......	9,620	[6] 6,655	149,183	[6] 183,141
Silage made from grass or hay crops [10]		297	...do......		1,495		12,305
Alfalfa seed harvested	[6] 827	1,055	Bushels	[6] 946	1,882	[6] 19,527	43,341
Red clover seed harvested	[6] 1,914	1,326	...do......	[6] 603	1,268	[6] 30,294	30,938
Lespedeza seed harvested	[6] 811	1,007	Pounds..	[6] 174,183	231,939	[6] 14,221	17,057
Vetch seed harvested		180	...do......		36,317	2,666	5,499
Cotton harvested (lint)	[6] 18,962	26,599	Bales...	[6] 11,838	15,419	[6] 1,266,373	2,212,902
Cottonseed			Tons....	[6] 4,896	6,410	[6] 260,465	278,395
Tobacco harvested	[6] 1,630	1,532	Pounds..	[6] 1,778,769	1,769,769	[6] 740,747	820,045
Sugarcane cut for sugar	[6] 269	319	Tons....	[6] 5,061	6,301	[6] 25,548	37,820
Sugarcane or sorghum for sirup	[6] 11 88	[6] 64	Gallons.	[6] 11 13,048	[6] 7,160	[6] 11 13,928	[6] 7,560
Sugar beets harvested for sugar	[6] 546	662	Tons....	[6] 6,841	9,944	[6] 73,312	107,593
Hops harvested	26	37	Pounds..	32,493	44,491	21,615	25,328
Chufas harvested for nuts	1	1	Bushels.	17	13	127	90
Irish potatoes harvested	2,537	13 1,514	...do......	356,547	366,528	519,678	468,391
Sweetpotatoes harvested	[6] 673	13 392	...do......	[6] 63,288	39,424	[6] 118,423	83,060
Vegetables, total [4]						1,032,626	[3] 607,018
Vegetables grown for home use						456,033	
Vegetables harvested for sale	4,370	3,718				576,593	607,018

For footnotes, see next page.

No. 754.—Crops—Acreage, Production, and Value, by Kind: 1944 and 1949—Continued

CROP	ACREAGE (THOUSANDS)		PRODUCTION (1,000 UNITS)			VALUE ($1,000)	
	1944	1949	Unit	1944	1949	1944	1949
All fruits and nuts and horticultural specialties		[13] 5,145					2,897,716
Specified fruits and nuts and horticultural specialties [9]	[14] 5,157					1,515,572	1,347,473
Strawberries	73	102	Quarts	96,306	168,708	27,713	50,090
Other berries and small fruits	113	116				19,360	26,210
Tree fruits, nuts and grapes (nurseries excluded)	5,091	[13] 4,716				1,397,900	866,220
Apples			Bushels	[8] 136,665	121,353	[8] 206,379	187,430
Peaches			...do....	65,011	66,457	136,180	80,465
Pears			...do....	37,766	38,890	68,175	36,659
Cherries			Pounds	[8] 346,236	372,065	[8] 36,695	35,459
Plums and prunes			Bushels	16,525	20,226	44,909	36,559
Grapes			Pounds	5,360,034	5,013,655	211,551	95,322
Apricots			Bushels	[8] 12,790	8,989	[8] 26,253	12,292
Oranges, including satsumas, tangerines, and mandarins			Tons	[8] 3,929	3,766	[8] 246,086	234,462
Grapefruit			...do....	[8] 1,547	1,164	[8] 61,457	36,151
Lemons			Field beans	[8] 16,761	16,377	[8] 38,734	52,045
Limes			Pounds	[8] 5,575	16,453	[8] 556	810
Pecans			...do....	[8] 96,180	61,064	21,553	12,521
Walnuts, English or Persian			...do....	[8] 126,511	186,980	[8] 27,476	24,094
Almonds			...do....	[8] 84,184	77,386	[8] 29,807	12,202
Filberts and hazelnuts			...do....	[8] 11,414	17,386	[8] 3,118	1,699
Tung nuts			...do....	[8] 62,683	167,585	[8] 3,120	4,723
Horticultural specialties		211				281,269	392,098

[1] Total acreage of crops harvested for which figures are available. Includes any acreage of alfalfa seed and clover and grass seeds enumerated, some of which was harvested from land also cut for hay.

[2] Excludes crops for which data were not obtained in 1944.

[3] Value of vegetables grown for home use not obtained in 1949.

[4] Irish and sweetpotatoes included with "Field crops," not with "Vegetables."

[5] Includes sweet corn, popcorn, "Egyptian corn," kafir, and milo maize.

[6] Totals are for States for which data are available.

[7] Excludes flax and wheat mixtures.

[8] Totals are for 8 States having separate inquiry on questionnaire.

[9] Includes wild hay and lespedeza in those States where separate inquiries were not on the questionnaire.

[10] Silage crops other than corn and sorghums.

[11] Does not include sorghum for sirup.

[12] Does not include acreage for farms with less than 15 bushels harvested.

[13] Excludes acreage on farms with less than ½ acre of fruit orchards, groves, vineyards, and planted nut trees.

[14] Acreage for horticultural specialties not included.

Source: Department of Commerce, Bureau of the Census; *U. S. Census of Agriculture: 1950*, Vol. II.

No. 755.—Principal Crops—Acreage, Production, and Value: 1866 to 1952

[Tons are of 2,000 pounds. For weights of units of measurement for principal products, see Appendix II. Approximate weights of units of measurement for other products are as follows: Number of pounds to a bushel—sweetpotatoes, 55; sorghums for grain, 56; clover seed, 60. Number of pounds to a barrel of cranberries, 100. Prices and yields for periods are weighted averages except for cotton and cottonseed, which are simple averages of prices and yields for individual years. Acreage, production, and yield of all crops revised to census data. See also *Historical Statistics*, series E 181–230, for acreage harvested, production, and price data for corn, wheat, oats, barley, flaxseed, potatoes, sweetpotatoes, cotton, cottonseed, soybeans, and hay]

YEARLY AVERAGE OR YEAR	CORN					WHEAT				
	Acreage harvested	Production	Farm value [1]	Yield per acre	Price [2]	Acreage harvested	Production	Farm value [1]	Yield per acre	Price [2]
	1,000 acres	1,000 bushels	1,000 dollars	Bushels	Cents per bushel	1,000 acres	1,000 bushels	1,000 dollars	Bushels	Cents per bushel
1866-1875	40,138	1,028,963	561,163	25.6	54.5	21,918	270,595	337,186	12.3	124.6
1876-1885	63,645	1,607,510	523,608	26.2	39.1	34,553	448,337	413,730	13.0	92.3
1886-1895	76,327	1,696,608	725,042	25.4	36.5	38,496	526,076	356,288	13.7	67.7
1896-1900	81,263	2,193,585	711,706	27.7	28.2	47,256	630,354	413,935	13.3	65.7
1901-1905	93,220	2,539,114	1,115,625	26.6	44.0	47,002	674,843	483,123	14.4	71.6
1906-1910	97,894	2,735,480	1,450,885	27.9	53.1	45,105	664,299	579,992	14.7	87.3
1911-1915	100,294	2,609,562	1,720,900	26.0	66.0	53,247	801,080	712,938	15.0	89.0
1916-1920	102,681	2,704,765	3,342,953	26.4	123.4	59,485	790,773	1,526,204	13.3	193.0
1921-1925	101,275	2,706,500	2,035,203	26.7	75.3	57,558	787,082	875,067	13.7	111.2
1926-1930	99,462	2,484,935	1,919,033	25.0	77.2	60,300	866,470	883,173	14.4	101.9
1931-1935	102,306	2,330,431	1,137,535	22.8	48.8	51,926	680,868	407,254	13.1	60.0
1936-1940	90,790	2,347,110	1,432,758	25.9	61.0	57,687	795,913	614,156	13.8	77.2
1941-1945	90,285	2,928,542	2,027,701	32.8	103.4	56,396	984,580	1,252,433	17.5	127.2
1946-1950	84,534	3,094,663	4,699,940	36.6	151.9	70,312	1,184,749	2,398,392	16.8	202.4
1940	86,429	2,457,146	1,518,719	28.4	61.8	53,273	814,646	555,547	15.3	68.2
1941	85,357	2,651,889	1,991,103	31.1	75.1	55,935	941,970	889,561	16.8	94.4
1942	87,367	3,068,562	2,813,772	35.1	91.7	49,773	969,381	1,064,789	19.5	110.0
1943	92,060	2,965,980	3,328,496	32.2	112.0	51,355	843,813	1,148,845	16.4	136.0
1944	94,014	3,087,982	3,353,205	32.8	109.0	59,749	1,060,111	1,498,081	17.7	141.0
1945	87,625	2,868,795	3,651,929	32.7	127.0	65,167	1,107,623	1,660,891	17.0	150.0
1946	7,585	3,217,076	5,028,250	36.7	150.0	67,105	1,152,118	2,201,036	17.2	191.0
1947	82,888	2,354,739	5,082,655	28.4	216.0	74,519	1,358,911	3,109,445	18.2	229.0
1948	84,778	3,605,078	4,675,149	42.5	130.0	72,418	1,294,911	2,577,191	17.9	199.0
1949	85,602	3,238,618	4,034,035	37.8	125.0	75,910	1,098,415	2,061,897	14.5	188.0
1950	81,817	3,057,803	4,679,612	37.4	153.0	61,610	1,019,389	2,042,392	16.5	200.0
1951	80,736	2,899,169	4,813,520	35.9	166.0	61,492	980,810	2,073,645	16.0	211.0
1952 (prel.)	81,359	3,306,735	5,193,570	40.6	157.0	70,585	1,291,447	2,699,275	18.3	209.0

YEARLY AVERAGE OR YEAR	OATS					RYE				
	Acreage harvested	Production	Farm value [1]	Yield per acre	Price [2]	Acreage harvested	Production	Farm value [1]	Yield per acre	Price [2]
1866-1875	10,616	281,394	122,375	26.5	43.5	1,589	17,210	15,864	10.8	92.2
1876-1885	17,954	494,612	158,927	27.5	32.1	1,905	22,185	14,205	11.6	64.1
1886-1895	28,113	753,240	215,561	26.8	28.6	2,160	27,209	14,895	12.6	54.0
1896-1900	29,741	865,863	199,211	29.1	23.0	2,262	29,088	12,888	12.9	44.3
1901-1905	32,122	975,626	315,133	30.4	32.3	2,323	30,640	17,570	13.2	57.1
1906-1910	34,869	954,648	383,118	27.4	40.1	2,166	29,137	20,369	13.5	69.9
1911-1915	37,531	1,155,906	454,401	30.8	39.3	2,905	39,714	29,681	13.4	74.7
1916-1920	41,100	1,312,199	834,158	31.9	63.6	5,455	65,481	96,895	12.0	148.0
1921-1925	42,441	1,248,349	497,621	29.4	39.9	4,857	63,746	47,739	13.1	74.9
1926-1930	40,266	1,189,317	477,416	29.5	40.1	3,394	40,928	30,826	12.1	75.3
1931-1935	37,597	973,920	252,598	25.9	25.9	2,980	33,134	13,888	11.1	41.9
1936-1940	34,826	1,052,573	328,974	30.2	31.3	3,526	41,474	21,149	11.8	51.0
1941-1945	39,350	1,267,222	759,269	32.2	59.9	2,800	34,344	28,118	12.3	81.9
1946-1950	39,983	1,353,850	1,083,373	33.9	80.0	1,789	21,846	36,173	12.2	165.6
1940	35,431	1,246,450	377,319	35.2	30.3	3,204	39,725	16,679	12.4	42.0
1941	38,161	1,182,509	485,659	31.0	41.1	3,573	43,878	23,766	12.3	54.2
1942	38,197	1,342,681	655,738	35.2	48.8	3,792	52,929	31,934	14.0	60.3
1943	38,914	1,139,831	823,297	29.3	72.2	2,652	28,680	28,173	10.8	98.2
1944	39,741	1,149,240	815,376	28.9	70.9	2,132	22,525	24,597	10.6	109.0
1945	41,739	1,523,851	1,016,276	36.5	66.7	1,850	23,708	32,119	12.8	135.0
1946	42,812	1,477,573	1,195,146	34.5	80.9	1,597	18,487	35,456	11.6	192.0
1947	37,855	1,176,142	1,232,230	31.1	105.0	1,991	25,497	57,719	12.8	226.0
1948	39,260	1,450,186	1,048,437	36.9	72.3	2,058	25,886	37,697	12.6	146.0
1949	39,236	1,254,885	825,053	32.0	65.7	1,554	18,102	21,949	11.6	121.0
1950	40,733	1,410,464	1,115,999	34.6	79.1	1,744	21,257	28,046	12.2	132.0
1951	36,525	1,321,288	1,087,396	36.2	82.3	1,710	21,301	32,647	12.5	153.0
1952 (prel.)	38,643	1,268,280	1,064,070	32.8	83.9	1,385	15,910	28,233	11.5	177.0

[1] Values are based on season average or Dec. 1 prices. See notes on "Price" column.

[2] Received by farmers. Beginning 1908, prices are season average prices for the crop-marketing season; prior thereto, Dec. 1 prices. Prices for certain years include an allowance for unredeemed loan and purchase agreement deliveries.

No. 755.—PRINCIPAL CROPS—ACREAGE, PRODUCTION, AND VALUE: 1866 TO 1952—Continued

YEARLY AVERAGE OR YEAR	Acreage harvested	Production	Farm value [1]	Yield per acre	Price [2]	Acreage harvested	Production	Farm value [1]	Yield per acre	Price [2]
		BARLEY					BUCKWHEAT			
	1,000 acres	1,000 bushels	1,000 dollars	Bushels	Cents per bushel	1,000 acres	1,000 bushels	1,000 dollars	Bushels	Cents per bushel
1866–1875...	1,202	26,346	26,830	21.7	98.0	766	10,426	9,085	13.6	87.1
1876–1885...	2,296	50,208	31,000	22.1	61.6	816	10,442	6,640	12.8	65.6
1886–1895...	3,513	82,767	39,376	23.6	47.6	812	11,256	6,165	13.9	54.6
1896–1900...	4,308	102,596	37,485	23.8	36.5	814	12,640	5,927	15.5	46.9
1901–1905...	5,281	151,417	65,080	22.3	43.0	819	14,568	6,854	15.2	59.5
1906–1910...	7,250	163,200	90,976	22.5	55.7	841	14,601	10,125	17.4	69.2
1911–1915...	7,562	177,192	101,286	23.5	57.2	778	12,927	9,838	16.6	76.1
1916–1920...	7,636	173,712	174,922	22.1	100.7	806	12,642	18,985	15.1	150.2
1921–1925...	7,210	160,478	98,800	22.3	58.2	707	12,062	11,287	17.0	92.7
1926–1930...	11,282	263,142	144,123	23.4	54.8	665	9,918	8,747	14.9	88.2
1931–1935...	10,608	211,714	77,607	20.0	36.7	480	8,187	4,191	17.1	51.2
1936–1940...	11,034	243,144	113,228	22.0	46.6	401	6,445	4,143	16.1	64.3
1941–1945...	12,778	331,040	266,085	24.1	80.5	425	7,385	7,805	17.4	101.6
1946–1950...	10,853	280,614	361,286	25.9	128.7	348	5,894	8,024	16.9	135.1
1940.........	13,525	311,278	123,542	23.0	39.7	398	6,476	3,482	16.7	48.6
1941.........	14,276	362,568	191,741	25.4	52.9	327	6,028	4,072	17.9	67.4
1942.........	16,986	429,480	271,331	25.3	63.2	375	6,656	5,612	17.7	84.6
1943.........	14,900	322,913	319,871	21.7	99.1	505	8,530	11,113	17.5	135.0
1944.........	12,301	276,275	280,434	22.5	102.0	508	8,966	9,061	17.6	101.0
1945.........	10,454	266,994	271,662	25.5	102.0	401	6,467	7,685	16.1	118.0
1946.........	10,390	265,089	360,773	25.5	136.0	383	6,812	10,089	17.8	148.0
1947.........	10,955	281,868	478,552	25.7	170.0	506	7,177	13,610	14.2	190.0
1948.........	11,906	315,537	363,286	26.5	115.0	390	6,085	6,825	18.4	112.0
1949.........	9,872	237,071	246,291	24.0	104.0	269	4,955	4,721	18.4	95.3
1950.........	11,153	303,588	357,258	27.2	118.0	253	4,439	4,906	17.5	111.0
1951.........	9,436	254,287	315,270	26.9	124.0	201	3,340	4,673	16.6	140.0
1952 (prel.).	8,284	237,008	319,108	27.5	141.0	161	3,162	4,671	19.6	148.0
		RICE, ROUGH					FLAXSEED			
	1,000 acres	1,000 bags	1,000 dollars	Lbs.	Dollars per bag	1,000 acres	1,000 bushels	1,000 dollars	Bushels	Cents per bushel
1906–1910...	598	9,532	17,436	1,644	1.77	2,384	20,590	26,662	8.6	126
1911–1915...	677	10,814	20,679	1,597	1.91	2,041	17,197	23,444	8.4	148
1916–1920...	1,056	18,793	68,093	1,780	3.62	1,580	10,135	30,872	6.4	305
1921–1925...	922	16,187	41,234	1,758	2.59	2,166	17,749	37,631	8.2	213
1926–1930...	968	19,234	40,513	1,997	2.10	2,968	20,064	40,885	6.7	202
1931–1935...	852	18,214	25,526	2,135	1.40	1,778	10,161	13,201	5.7	130
1936–1940...	1,054	23,782	38,784	2,286	1.63	1,663	14,195	21,715	8.5	163
1941–1945...	1,424	28,617	105,891	2,010	3.74	3,952	35,868	91,690	9.1	256
1946–1950...	1,714	37,083	184,098	2,104	4.98	4,134	40,346	188,915	9.7	460
1940.........	1,099	24,495	44,208	2,291	1.80	3,182	30,924	43,796	9.7	142
1941.........	1,214	23,086	69,800	1,902	3.01	3,265	32,133	57,482	9.8	179
1942.........	1,457	29,082	105,082	1,996	3.61	4,408	40,976	96,880	9.3	226
1943.........	1,473	29,254	116,024	1,988	3.96	5,691	50,009	141,554	8.8	283
1944.........	1,480	30,974	121,614	2,093	3.92	2,610	21,665	62,941	8.3	291
1945.........	1,499	30,668	122,136	2,046	3.98	3,785	34,557	99,912	9.1	289
1946.........	1,562	32,497	162,644	2,054	5.00	2,423	22,886	91,153	9.3	404
1947.........	1,708	35,217	210,287	2,062	5.97	4,129	40,618	249,843	9.8	615
1948.........	1,804	38,275	186,682	2,122	4.88	4,973	54,603	312,975	11.0	571
1949.........	1,857	40,737	167,105	2,194	4.10	5,048	43,976	186,073	8.5	363
1950.........	1,620	28,669	196,773	2,288	6.09	4,090	40,236	134,531	8.8	334
1951.........	1,967	45,797	220,877	2,338	4.82	3,904	34,696	129,841	8.6	371
1952 (prel.).	1,972	48,660	285,855	2,468	5.87	3,309	31,002	117,200	9.4	378

[1] Values are based on season average or Dec. 1 prices. See notes on "Price" column.

[2] Received by farmers. Prices are season average prices as follows: Barley, buckwheat, and flaxseed, beginning 1908; rice, beginning 1909. Prices for prior years are as of Dec. 1. Prices for certain years for barley, rice, and flaxseed include an allowance for unredeemed loans and purchase agreement deliveries.

No. 755.—PRINCIPAL CROPS—ACREAGE, PRODUCTION, AND VALUE: 1866 TO 1952—Continued

YEARLY AVERAGE OR YEAR	Acreage harvested	Production	Farm value [1]	Yield per acre	Price [4]	Acreage harvested	Production	Farm value [1]	Yield per acre	Price [4]
	POTATOES					SWEETPOTATOES				
	1,000 acres	1,000 bushels	1,000 dollars	Bushels	Cents per bushel	1,000 acres	1,000 bushels	1,000 dollars	Bushels	Cents per bushel
1866–1875...	1,488	129,276	81,370	86.9	62.9	376	29,170	25,517	77.6	87.5
1876–1885...	2,074	173,138	87,877	83.5	50.8	464	35,625	20,063	76.8	54.9
1886–1895...	2,635	214,022	102,644	81.2	48.0	526	44,448	22,071	84.5	51.0
1896–1900...	2,918	246,703	101,576	84.5	41.2	542	44,452	20,926	82.0	48.8
1901–1905...	3,115	286,091	162,270	91.8	56.7	565	52,815	30,841	93.5	58.4
1906–1910...	3,465	342,430	205,664	98.8	60.1	615	59,337	41,211	96.5	69.5
1911–1915...	3,473	349,277	234,639	100.6	67.2	597	57,063	48,339	95.6	84.7
1916–1920...	3,455	336,280	472,515	97.3	140.5	736	71,633	99,374	97.4	138.7
1921–1925...	3,359	357,535	350,071	106.5	97.9	702	62,198	77,909	88.6	125.3
1926–1930...	3,132	359,142	354,962	114.7	99.2	664	62,593	71,188	94.3	113.7
1931–1935...	3,510	377,616	201,396	107.6	53.4	945	77,491	49,987	82.0	64.5
1936–1940...	2,906	355,109	241,653	122.2	68.1	741	61,991	49,110	83.7	79.2
1941–1945...	2,809	397,362	495,610	134.7	124.7	729	65,726	107,166	90.2	163.0
1946–1950...	1,993	431,699	466,095	216.6	108.0	521	49,679	103,229	95.4	207.8
1940........	2,832	376,990	203,748	133.1	54.1	648	51,609	44,160	79.8	85.4
1941........	2,693	355,697	285,500	132.1	80.3	731	62,517	57,660	85.5	92.2
1942........	2,671	368,899	428,432	138.1	116	687	65,469	77,548	95.3	118
1943........	3,219	458,887	595,754	141.7	130	857	71,142	146,413	83.1	206
1944........	2,780	383,926	570,442	138.1	149	726	68,261	129,912	94.0	190
1945........	2,664	419,399	597,922	157.4	143	646	61,289	124,305	94.8	203
1946........	2,527	487,315	602,823	192.9	124	637	60,825	131,643	95.5	216
1947........	2,001	388,985	128,172	194.4	161	547	49,642	107,279	90.8	216
1948........	1,981	449,805	690,660	227.1	154	455	43,094	94,923	94.6	220
1949........	1,759	402,353	515,876	228.8	128	472	45,003	96,205	95.3	214
1950........	1,606	429,806	392,963	253.4	91.7	492	49,825	86,097	101.2	173
1951........	1,534	320,519	522,190	240.3	163	314	28,796	87,807	91.7	305
1952 (prel.)..	1,396	347,504	793,732	248.6	228	326	28,292	93,887	86.8	332

YEARLY AVERAGE OR YEAR	Acreage harvested	Production	Farm value [1]	Yield per acre	Price [4]	Production	Farm value [1]			Price [4]
	COTTON (EXCLUDING LINTERS) [11]					COTTONSEED				
	1,000 acres	1,000 bales [12]	1,000 dollars	Lbs.	Cents per pound	1,000 short tons	1,000 dollars			Dols. per ton
1866–1875...	9,046	3,389		162.6		1,382				
1876–1885...	15,147	5,706	253,959	172.2	9.30	2,419				
1886–1895...	20,016	7,691	289,493	181.5	7.70	3,389				
1896–1900...	24,425	10,036	354,063	197.4	7.04	4,486				
1901–1905...	28,041	10,801	485,555	183.8	8.98	4,800				
1906–1910...	31,057	11,847	658,884	182.3	11.29	4,799	120,640			25.07
1911–1915...	33,649	14,167	729,245	200.7	10.44	6,292	125,791			20.59
1916–1920...	33,534	11,918	1,468,022	169.9	24.91	5,295	277,640			53.28
1921–1925...	35,895	11,515	1,277,208	151.2	22.22	5,112	169,432			33.11
1926–1930...	42,212	14,834	1,126,700	167.8	15.38	6,500	184,899			28.83
1931–1935...	31,671	12,684	551,305	190.9	9.16	5,505	95,829			19.16
1936–1940...	27,058	13,534	646,935	239.1	9.67	5,684	132,166			23.49
1941–1945...	20,619	11,247	1,110,463	262.4	19.84	4,602	228,712			49.83
1946–1950...	21,421	12,303	1,974,508	272.9	32.72	4,961	338,783			70.96
1940........	23,861	12,566	621,284	252.5	9.89	5,286	114,817			21.72
1941........	22,236	10,744	914,313	231.9	17.03	4,553	216,961			47.65
1942........	22,602	12,817	1,219,716	272.4	19.04	5,202	237,221			45.60
1943........	21,610	11,427	1,135,605	254.0	19.88	4,688	244,059			52.10
1944........	19,617	12,230	1,267,857	299.4	20.73	4,902	258,163			52.70
1945........	17,029	9,015	1,014,823	254.1	22.52	3,664	187,155			51.10
1946........	17,584	8,640	1,409,668	235.7	32.64	3,514	252,697			71.90
1947........	21,330	11,860	1,892,949	266.6	31.93	4,682	402,058			85.90
1948........	22,911	14,877	2,260,089	311.3	30.38	5,945	399,755			67.20
1949........	27,439	16,128	2,304,640	281.8	28.58	6,559	284,810			43.40
1950........	17,843	10,012	2,005,169	269.0	40.07	4,105	354,593			86.40
1951........	26,687	15,144	2,867,668	271.9	37.88	6,286	435,891			69.30
1952 (prel.)..	24,995	15,038	2,774,230	288.4	36.90	6,108	427,746			70.00

[1] Values are based on season average or Dec. 1 prices. See notes on "Price" column.
[4] Received by farmers. Beginning with 1908 for potatoes and cotton, 1909 for sweetpotatoes, and cottonseed, prices are season average prices. Figures for prior years are Dec. 1 prices. Prices for certain years for cotton and cottonseed include an allowance for unredeemed loans and purchase agreement deliveries.
[5] Average for 8 years. [6] Average for 6 years. [7] Average for 7 years. [8] Average for 4 years.
[9] Includes following quantities of commercial early potatoes not marketed and excluded in computing value (1,000 bushels): 1928, 7,462; 1931, 66; 1932, 2,175; 1939, 1,240; 1943, 440; 1950, 1,235; 1951, 1,093.
[10] Includes 1,504,000 bushels unharvested but purchased by the Government under price-support program.
[11] State production figures, which conform with census annual ginning enumeration, with allowance for cross State ginnings, rounded to thousands and added for United States totals. Cotton grown in Baja, California, ginned in California from 1913 to 1924, has been excluded.
[12] Production is in running bales prior to 1899; 500-pound gross weight bales thereafter.
[13] Data for 1909 and 1910.

No. 755.—PRINCIPAL CROPS—ACREAGE, PRODUCTION, AND VALUE: 1866 TO 1952—Continued

YEARLY AVERAGE OR YEAR	Acreage harvested	Production	Farm value [1]	Yield per acre	Price [14]	Acreage harvested	Production	Farm value [1]	Yield per acre	Price [14]
	SORGHUMS FOR GRAIN					PEANUTS (PICKED AND THRESHED)				
	1,000 acres	1,000 bushels	1,000 dollars	Bush- els	Cents per bu. [14]	1,000 acres [15]	1,000 pounds	1,000 dollars	Lbs.	Cents per lb. [16]
1916–1920....						1,004	798,945	52,095	725.5	6.53
1921–1925....						926	640,834	32,425	684.9	5.08
1926–1930....	[18] 3,800	[18] 43,794	[18] 29,014	[18] 12.5	[18] 66.3	1,059	780,062	35,206	715.1	4.46
1931–1935....	4,038	53,543	23,763	13.5	44.1	1,434	998,782	24,207	695.2	2.40
1936–1940....	4,705	61,306	31,926	13.0	52.1	1,770	1,352,243	45,952	764.0	3.40
1941–1945....	6,921	122,755	111,216	17.7	90.6	3,032	1,998,497	135,650	664.0	6.95
1946–1950....	7,279	142,441	176,591	19.6	126	2,878	2,081,398	213,450	737	10.2
1943........	6,589	109,596	124,896	15.9	114.0	3,698	2,176,430	156,026	617.0	7.12
1944........	9,386	184,975	168,596	19.7	91.3	3,066	2,060,825	167,352	675.0	8.04
1945........	6,234	96,088	114,786	15.2	119.0	3,160	2,042,235	168,878	646.0	8.27
1946........	6,609	108,025	147,402	15.9	139.0	3,141	2,036,005	195,364	648.0	9.10
1947........	5,480	98,217	171,082	17.0	183.0	3,377	2,181,695	220,210	646.0	10.1
1948........	7,317	131,384	168,235	18.0	128.0	3,296	2,335,940	245,190	709.0	10.5
1949........	6,502	148,399	166,760	22.5	112.0	2,303	1,864,780	193,496	805.0	10.4
1950........	10,235	232,278	245,024	22.6	105	2,205	2,036,670	222,052	898	10.9
1951........	5,487	100,195	211,939	18.9	132	2,009	1,675,955	174,875	834	10.4
1952 (prel.)..	5,089	83,316	137,313	16.4	165	1,613	1,365,000	149,762	902	11.0
	BEANS, DRY, EDIBLE					SOYBEANS (FOR BEANS)				
	1,000 acres	1,000 bags [19]	1,000 dollars [19]	Lbs.	Dollars per bag [17]	1,000 acres	1,000 bushels	1,000 dollars	Bush- els	Cents per bu. [17]
1916–1920....	1,239	8,397	59,814	631.8	7.79					
1921–1925....	1,208	8,949	46,022	663.9	5.46	[21] 4,911	[24] 4,911	[23] 11,796	[21] 11.4	[23] 240
1926–1930....	1,802	11,597	61,578	643.7	5.73	679	8,685	14,947	12.8	172
1931–1935....	1,687	12,465	31,127	739.2	2.66	1,391	23,597	17,616	16.4	75
1936–1940....	1,709	15,009	47,639	831.7	3.36	3,430	61,995	53,379	18.1	86
1941–1945....	1,968	17,587	91,725	897.0	5.22	9,432	174,028	221,668	18.4	125
1946–1950....	1,747	18,432	147,267	1,035	7.99	11,384	230,167	580,796	20.4	252
1943........	2,362	21,002	117,492	888.0	6.05	10,397	190,133	345,032	18.3	181
1944........	1,996	16,147	94,418	809.0	6.28	10,245	192,121	393,892	18.8	205
1945........	1,487	12,091	78,317	880.0	6.55	10,740	193,167	402,234	16.0	208
1946........	1,623	15,840	136,289	977.0	10.60	9,932	203,395	522,140	20.5	257
1947........	1,778	17,265	184,019	971.0	11.60	11,411	186,451	621,477	16.3	333
1948........	1,998	20,916	182,443	1,074.0	7.86	10,682	227,217	516,069	21.3	227
1949........	1,885	21,279	130,979	1,134	6.59	10,482	234,194	506,474	22.3	216
1950........	1,512	16,896	112,604	1,117	7.44	13,814	299,279	737,632	21.7	247
1951........	1,498	17,341	125,544	1,282	7.91	13,845	282,477	769,926	20.9	273
1952 (prel.)..	1,272	16,777	132,857	1,319	8.52	14,075	291,682	823,881	20.7	292
	RED CLOVER SEED [25]					HOPS				
	1,000 acres	1,000 bushels	1,000 dollars	Bushels	Dollars per bushel [17]	1,000 acres	1,000 pounds	1,000 dollars	Lbs.	Cents per lb. [26]
1916–1920....	[27] 1,004	[27] 1,287	[27] 22,741	[28] 1.18	[28] 17.67	30	32,665	10,796	1,096	32.0
1921–1925....	945	981	11,891	1.04	12.12	23	26,616	4,456	1,215	14.7
1926–1930....	1,061	1,190	15,959	1.12	13.41	23	30,363	5,366	1,314	16.4
1931–1935....	843	953	6,587	1.13	7.23	30	36,224	6,090	1,212	17.3
1936–1940....	1,205	1,236	11,410	1.02	9.23	22	35,966	7,944	1,151	22.5
1941–1945....	1,711	1,332	21,005	.78	15.77	36	44,760	24,760	1,243	55.4
1946–1950....	1,951	1,711	39,186	.88	22.88	40	52,880	29,980	1,321	55.7
1943........	1,389	1,092	19,676	.79	18.02	32	42,445	26,623	1,318	62.2
1944........	2,412	1,784	33,363	.74	18.70	37	46,146	31,485	1,296	68.3
1945........	2,163	1,559	26,993	.72	18.60	41	57,614	37,401	1,407	64.9
1946........	2,581	1,929	42,399	.75	21.98	41	53,751	33,736	1,312	62.8
1947........	1,433	1,145	32,132	.80	28.07	40	50,786	34,736	1,275	68.4
1948........	1,628	1,696	43,960	.93	25.04	40	60,464	27,984	1,246	46.5
1949........	1,360	1,313	31,575	.97	24.36	38	50,796	22,260	1,353	67.0
1950........	2,556	2,478	45,306	.97	18.29	39	55,351	31,082	1,308	62.1
1951........	1,459	1,439	27,368	.99	19.03	41	63,239	31,853	1,535	65.4
1952 (prel.)..	1,608	1,620	39,873	.96	18.27	38	61,263	25,734	1,609	60.5

[1] Values are based on season average or Dec. 1 prices. See notes on "Price" column.
[14] Received by farmers. Prices for certain years for grain sorghums, peanuts, dry edible beans, soybeans, and red clover seed include an allowance for unredeemed loans and purchase agreement deliveries. See also notes on prices for each crop.
[15] Based on the reported price of grain sorghums.
[16] Equivalent solid acreage.
[17] Prices are season average prices, prices of beans being for cleaned beans.
[18] Average for 1929 and 1930.
[19] Bags of 100 pounds (uncleaned).
[20] Farm value of dry edible beans equals the price of cleaned beans applied to the production of cleaned beans rather than to the total production.
[21] Average for 1924 and 1926.
[22] Average for 1919 and 1920.
[25] Dec. 1 prices, 1916 to 1921; beginning 1922, season average prices.
[26] Excludes 4,496,000 pounds in 1935, 4,365,000 pounds in 1937, 3,160,650 pounds in 1938, 2,612,000 pounds in 1939, not available for marketing because of economic conditions and the marketing agreement allotments. Sales adjustments under marketing agreement were 38,000,050 pounds in 1948, 39,035,000 pounds in 1949, 46,830,000 pounds in 1951, and 30,200,000 pounds in 1952. Prices and values are computed on the marketed crop.

No. 755.—PRINCIPAL CROPS—ACREAGE, PRODUCTION, AND VALUE: 1866 TO 1952—Continued

YEARLY AVERAGE OR YEAR	Acreage harvested	Production	Farm value [1]	Yield per acre	Price [30]	Acreage harvested	Production	Farm value [1]	Yield per acre	Price [30]
	HAY [27]					TOBACCO				
	1,000 acres	1,000 tons	1,000 dollars	Short tons	Dollars per ton [28]	1,000 acres	1,000 pounds	1,000 dollars	Lbs.	Cents per lb. [29]
1866–1875	20,296	23,356	332,744	1.15	14.21	450	330,207	34,829	754	10.3
1876–1885	28,704	36,056	350,467	1.26	9.72	711	518,825	38,817	730	7.5
1886–1895	39,492	48,007	427,727	1.22	8.91	916	669,297	52,244	731	7.8
1896–1900	42,467	54,137	422,324	1.27	7.80	1,064	818,926	53,322	770	6.6
1901–1905	46,147	61,592	557,465	1.33	9.05	1,126	923,378	67,718	820	7.3
1906–1910	50,542	66,001	706,860	1.31	10.71	1,173	977,963	95,680	834	9.8
1911–1915	67,402	80,341	906,605	1.19	11.28	1,286	1,048,825	107,974	816	10.3
1916–1920	72,407	90,020	1,513,078	1.24	16.81	1,742	1,386,048	322,244	795	23.2
1921–1925	73,322	87,935	1,085,952	1.20	12.35	1,633	1,279,550	247,642	774	19.4
1926–1930	69,118	83,980	948,691	1.22	11.30	1,831	1,410,902	249,531	771	17.7
1931–1935	68,190	76,969	651,795	1.13	8.47	1,569	1,268,339	175,681	808	13.9
1936–1940	68,842	85,404	790,145	1.24	9.25	1,641	1,491,701	277,578	909	18.6
1941–1945	75,861	103,385	1,754,218	1.36	16.97	1,542	1,603,694	618,116	1,040	38.5
1946–1950	73,211	98,759	2,159,228	1.35	21.86	1,718	2,080,043	973,970	1,211	46.8
1943	77,004	103,128	1,913,356	1.34	18.60	1,458	1,406,190	569,974	964	40.5
1944	77,639	102,889	2,145,300	1.33	20.90	1,750	1,950,940	819,803	1,115	42.0
1945	76,697	107,438	2,068,523	1.40	19.30	1,821	1,991,108	848,216	1,094	42.6
1946	73,741	99,518	2,084,794	1.35	20.90	1,961	2,314,807	1,044,230	1,181	45.1
1947	74,666	100,576	2,240,809	1.35	22.30	1,852	2,107,160	917,889	1,138	43.6
1948	71,817	96,172	2,266,742	1.34	23.60	1,554	1,979,581	954,698	1,274	48.2
1949	71,464	95,055	2,013,260	1.33	21.20	1,623	1,969,100	904,531	1,213	45.9
1950	74,368	102,476	2,190,536	1.38	21.40	1,599	2,029,567	1,048,503	1,269	51.7
1951	74,442	107,991	2,481,003	1.45	23.00	1,783	2,330,787	1,190,963	1,307	51.1
1952 (prel.)	74,664	104,424	2,630,069	1.40	25.20	1,776	2,207,477	1,103,337	1,243	50.0

YEARLY AVERAGE OR YEAR	Acreage harvested	Production	Farm value [1]	Yield per acre	Price [30]	Production	Farm value [1]	Price [30]
	SORGHUMS FOR FORAGE					ORANGES AND TANGERINES (5 STATES) [30]		
	1,000 acres	1,000 tons	1,000 dollars	Short tons	Dols. per ton [31]	1,000 boxes [32]	1,000 dollars [33]	Dols. per box [33]
1919–1920						29,097	69,625	2.39
1921–1925						31,650	72,772	2.30
1926–1930	[34] 4,849	[34] 6,505	[34] 63,763	[34] 1.34	[34] 9.80	43,096	100,560	2.33
1931–1935	7,103	8,628	55,114	1.21	6.39	52,950	64,016	1.22
1936–1940	8,640	10,934	64,616	1.27	5.91	73,721	76,669	1.06
1941–1945	8,339	12,557	109,794	1.51	8.74	99,745	246,689	2.47
1946–1950	4,644	6,565	97,321	1.41	14.82	113,471	196,698	1.73
1943	8,404	10,982	142,848	1.31	13.00	106,651	279,622	2.64
1944	7,586	11,552	125,789	1.52	10.90	113,210	300,024	2.69
1945	7,357	9,543	115,071	1.30	12.10	104,350	303,939	2.93
1946	5,987	8,181	119,589	1.37	14.60	118,540	179,429	1.55
1947	4,590	5,666	98,496	1.23	17.40	114,510	147,224	1.30
1948	4,680	6,659	106,658	1.42	16.00	104,120	179,820	1.74
1949	3,633	5,729	73,566	1.58	12.80	108,475	238,763	2.22
1950	4,361	6,592	88,295	1.51	13.40	121,710	238,253	1.97
1951	4,660	6,455	129,360	1.39	20.00	122,590	181,361	1.49
1952 (prel.)	5,005	4,441	111,785	.89	25.20	126,350	182,640	1.45

[1] Value based on season average or Dec. 1 prices. See notes on "Price" column.
[30] Received by farmers. Prices as of Dec. 1 except as noted.   [27] Tame hay only, prior to 1911.
[28] Prices are season average prices beginning 1911; Dec. 1 prices theretofore. Beginning 1939, prices are for hay sold baled; prior years, for hay sold loose. Price for hay sold loose in 1948 was $18.90 per ton.
[29] Prices are season average prices beginning 1919; Dec. 1 prices theretofore.
[30] Prior to 1942, data are for 7 States. Production figures include fruit consumed on farms, sold locally, and used for manufacturing, as well as that shipped; they exclude fruit which ripened on trees but was destroyed prior to picking. Figures relate to crop produced from bloom of year shown. In California, picking season usually extends from about Oct. 1 to Dec. 31 of following year. In other States, season begins about Oct. 1 and ends in early summer.
[31] Prior to 1942, price of sweet sorghums for forage and hay.
[32] Net content of boxes varies. In California and Arizona, approximate average is 77 lbs.; in other states, 90 lbs. Production includes following quantities donated to charity, unharvested, and/or eliminated on account of economic conditions (1,000 boxes): 1933, 977; 1934, 1,395; 1935, 614; 1936, 1,023; 1937, 1,204; 1938, 2,949, 1939, 1,236; 1940, 1,322; 1941, 762; 1942, 654; 1943, 830; 1944, 1,771; 1945, 731; 1946, 2,639; 1947, 1,563; 1948, 881; 1949, 894, 1950, 799; 1951, 1063. Price and value are computed on remaining crop.
[33] Season average returns to growers. Price and value apply to entire crop exclusive of that portion donated to charity, unharvested, and/or eliminated on account of market conditions. (See note 32.) Prices are equivalent packing-house-door returns for all methods of sale and are weighted by production to obtain U. S. averages.
[34] Average for 1929 and 1930.

Source: Department of Agriculture, Bureau of Agricultural Economics; annual report, *Agricultural Statistics*, and annual summaries of crop statistics.

No. 756.—WHEAT FLOUR PRODUCTION BY STATES: 1944 TO 1951

[1,000 sacks of 100 lbs. Figures represent total wheat flour production of all commercial mills (excluding custom)]

STATE	1944	1945	1946	1947	1948	1949	1950	1951 [1]
United States	[2] 243,400	[2] 274,400	[2] 278,900	305,499	279,123	284,351	234,899	229,292
California	4,725	4,945	4,403	4,860	4,000	4,356	4,607	4,896
Colorado	3,063	4,266	4,662	5,487	5,540	4,368	3,765	4,065
Georgia	611	701	609	733	532	508	395	(²)
Idaho	1,486	1,867	2,348	2,583	2,269	1,796	1,514	(³)
Illinois	13,270	14,741	12,649	14,322	14,197	12,082	12,434	13,344
Indiana	3,404	3,671	4,306	4,483	4,155	3,720	3,096	2,692
Iowa	4,111	4,407	4,463	4,459	3,720	3,089	3,125	3,070
Kansas	36,988	40,429	43,883	52,124	51,119	36,686	35,007	36,006
Kentucky	3,452	3,545	3,637	4,653	3,993	4,157	3,799	(²)
Maryland	963	1,424	1,431	1,437	1,401	1,049	1,189	(²)
Michigan	3,308	4,065	4,281	4,482	4,629	4,530	4,276	4,105
Minnesota	29,126	26,139	33,910	40,080	31,055	26,113	27,998	25,929
Missouri	18,625	22,850	23,020	27,377	26,491	21,906	20,239	21,932
Montana	2,947	3,426	4,121	4,267	3,615	3,076	3,129	3,049
Nebraska	6,237	7,327	7,379	8,521	7,960	6,777	5,690	6,996
New York	29,691	32,028	33,456	32,476	30,183	26,225	27,011	26,230
North Carolina	1,801	1,700	1,702	2,442	2,246	2,022	1,959	(²)
North Dakota	3,143	4,089	4,198	4,765	3,307	2,784	2,701	2,748
Ohio	9,211	9,701	9,377	9,142	9,500	9,556	9,639	9,357
Oklahoma	10,870	12,037	12,170	14,300	13,149	10,787	10,483	9,776
Oregon	6,638	7,617	7,096	7,411	5,802	5,033	4,631	5,707
Pennsylvania	1,464	2,021	2,338	2,834	2,401	2,006	2,136	(²)
South Carolina	235	310	335	264	319	270	158	(²)
Tennessee	3,990	4,230	4,166	4,780	3,784	3,343	3,154	(²)
Texas	14,897	18,888	19,067	21,609	19,608	14,657	12,446	12,417
Utah	2,901	3,344	3,292	3,668	3,704	3,649	3,811	4,057
Virginia	2,772	3,319	3,338	3,912	3,462	2,055	1,827	(²)
Washington	12,192	13,216	12,854	12,639	11,791	9,531	9,118	9,645
West Virginia	213	282	326	(²)	(²)	(²)	156	(²)
Wisconsin	2,110	2,022	2,101	2,481	2,519	2,299	(²)	(²)
Other States	1,807	2,177	2,340	2,942	2,522	2,495	4,830	21,090

[1] Estimates based on monthly reports of mills with daily capacity over 400 sacks.
[2] Includes 7,031,000 sacks in 1944, 4,596,000 sacks in 1945, and 5,705,000 sacks in 1946 not distributed by State.
[3] Included in "Other States."

Source: Department of Commerce, Bureau of the Census. Monthly data are published in *Facts for Industry*, Series M16A.

No. 757.—WHEAT—SUPPLY AND DISAPPEARANCE: 1936 TO 1951

[In thousands of bushels; pounds per bushel, 60. For years beginning July 1. For continental United States only. See also *Historical Statistics*, series E 190-195]

ITEM	1936–1940 average	1941–1945 average	1946–1950 average	1947	1948	1949	1950	1951 (prel.)
Supply, total	983,030	1,467,688	1,410,282	1,442,876	1,492,354	1,407,890	1,455,929	1,408,549
Stocks, July 1, total	181,389	440,028	222,373	53,537	195,943	307,285	424,714	366,394
On farms	58,311	136,059	61,787	40,501	94,453	66,808	65,861	72,638
Interior mills, elevators, and warehouses	27,340	78,484	51,016	10,116	30,645	76,434	129,522	88,180
Commercial [2]	40,941	125,872	73,753	8,129	34,055	126,158	168,467	157,948
Merchant mills [2] [3]	54,697	81,717	32,001	24,591	34,340	32,401	55,934	73,627
C. C. C. wheat in transit and in steel and wood bins		23,896	3,816	500	2,530	3,797	4,900	3,002
New crop	795,913	984,580	1,184,749	1,256,911	1,294,911	1,098,415	1,019,389	980,810
Imports	7,829	37,081	3,141	130	1,500	2,190	11,826	31,506
Disappearance, total	750,947	1,078,580	1,128,660	1,246,935	1,185,069	983,176	1,059,695	1,122,955
Food	490,604	480,036	483,183	488,385	479,392	483,781	481,014	479,911
Feed	114,725	303,949	133,962	174,008	97,608	111,830	112,777	96,629
Other [4]	145,618	294,605	511,825	584,542	608,069	387,575	465,904	577,415
Stocks, June 30 [5]	230,149	389,099	281,603	195,943	307,285	424,714	396,234	285,594

[2] Prior to 1937 some new wheat included, thereafter only old-crop wheat.
[3] Estimated total based on Bureau of Census item, "In mills and mill elevators attached to mills," 1931-44.
[4] Imports include full duty wheat, wheat imported for feed and dutiable flour in terms of wheat.
[5] Includes exports to foreign countries, shipments to Territories and possessions, military procurement, and other.
[5] For individual items see supply, above.

Source: Department of Agriculture, Bureau of Agricultural Economics, except for imports which are from Bureau of Census. Published in annual report, *Agricultural Statistics*, and in *The Wheat Situation*.

No. 758.—WHEAT—ACREAGE, PRODUCTION, AND VALUE, BY STATES: 1941 TO 1952

[Pounds per bushel, 60. Prices are season average prices received by farmers. See also *Historical Statistics*, series E 186–188, for U. S. totals for acreage harvested, production, and price]

DIVISION AND STATE	ACREAGE HARVESTED			YIELD PER ACRE			PRODUCTION			PRICE FOR CROP OF[1]		FARM VALUE	
	1941-50, avg.	1951	1952[2]	1941-50, avg.	1951	1952[2]	1941-50, avg.	1951	1952[2]	1951	1952[2]	1951	1952[2]
	1,000 acres	1,000 acres	1,000 acres	Bu.	Bu.	Bu.	1,000 bu.	1,000 bu.	1,000 bu.	Cts. per bu.	Cts. per bu.	1,000 dol.	1,000 dol.
U. S.	63,354	61,492	70,585	17.2	16.0	18.3	1,084,664	980,810	1,291,447	211	209	2,073,645	2,699,275
M. A.:													
N. Y.	334	413	444	25.2	25.0	29.0	8,504	10,319	12,856	221	205	22,792	26,350
N. J.	65	81	80	22.6	26.0	25.0	1,481	2,106	2,000	212	205	4,465	4,100
Pa.	885	837	845	20.9	22.5	22.5	18,548	18,832	19,012	209	200	39,359	38,024
E. N. C.:													
Ohio	1,996	1,906	2,249	23.3	18.0	24.5	46,908	34,308	55,100	221	200	75,821	110,200
Ind.	1,434	1,426	1,540	20.4	16.5	24.0	29,828	23,529	36,960	217	200	51,958	73,920
Ill.	1,390	1,757	1,810	19.0	19.0	23.0	27,106	33,383	41,630	218	210	72,775	87,423
Mich.	991	1,232	1,429	24.4	25.0	25.5	24,625	30,800	36,440	221	200	68,068	72,880
Wis.	88	80	75	22.4	23.2	24.5	2,000	1,856	1,838	209	208	3,872	3,817
W. N. C.:													
Minn.	1,182	1,076	1,155	17.3	18.6	14.7	20,346	20,022	16,998	215	220	43,058	37,432
Iowa	208	145	163	19.6	19.3	22.0	4,160	1,489	3,579	212	210	3,163	7,516
Mo.	1,264	1,318	1,199	15.9	17.0	22.0	20,644	22,406	26,378	210	205	47,053	54,075
N. Dak.	9,323	10,485	9,917	15.4	13.9	10.1	140,940	145,732	100,069	210	221	306,323	220,812
S. Dak.	3,323	3,839	3,813	12.7	14.9	8.2	41,914	57,260	31,412	211	214	120,813	67,365
Nebr.	3,540	4,005	4,390	19.5	14.5	22.4	70,067	58,073	98,367	216	210	125,370	206,538
Kans.	12,491	9,701	14,649	15.9	13.0	21.0	197,949	126,113	307,629	213	210	268,621	646,021
S. A.:													
Del.	63	58	58	18.8	20.5	21.0	1,178	1,189	1,218	203	190	2,414	2,314
Md.	329	262	262	19.4	20.5	20.5	6,402	5,371	5,371	206	190	11,064	10,205
Va.	452	357	353	17.0	21.0	21.5	7,661	7,497	7,590	212	200	15,894	15,180
W. Va.	83	60	60	17.7	18.5	21.0	1,452	1,110	1,260	215	205	2,386	2,583
N. C.	435	392	396	15.4	23.0	21.0	6,693	9,016	8,316	210	205	18,934	17,048
S. C.	213	161	184	13.9	20.5	20.0	2,934	3,300	3,680	208	205	6,864	7,544
Ga.	172	97	130	12.6	18.5	19.0	2,162	1,794	2,470	211	205	3,785	5,064
E. S. C.:													
Ky.	330	223	230	15.6	16.0	20.0	5,173	3,568	4,600	218	210	7,778	9,660
Tenn.	316	195	211	13.9	15.5	19.0	4,405	3,022	4,009	218	215	6,588	8,619
Ala.	14	6	11	14.8	21.0	19.0	209	126	209	230	215	277	449
Miss.	11	3	9	21.8	25.0	26.0	244	75	234	209	215	157	503
W. S. C.:													
Ark.	28	18	22	13.2	15.5	18.0	367	279	396	209	210	583	832
Okla.	5,365	4,095	5,790	13.2	9.5	18.5	71,737	38,902	107,115	220	210	85,584	224,942
Tex.	4,744	1,994	3,011	12.4	9.0	11.5	60,347	17,946	34,626	219	210	39,302	72,715
Mt.:													
Mont.	4,210	5,910	5,811	17.5	16.1	14.4	72,532	95,033	83,548	196	198	186,641	165,655
Idaho	1,178	1,480	1,536	27.4	25.7	26.4	32,160	37,968	40,598	197	197	74,872	80,139
Wyo.	283	375	393	19.2	18.0	16.3	5,468	6,750	6,410	200	199	13,487	12,749
Colo.	1,959	2,483	3,117	19.2	14.0	17.6	37,371	34,870	54,932	211	210	73,511	115,271
N. Mex.	354	165	130	11.3	6.6	6.6	4,105	1,094	859	211	212	2,307	1,824
Ariz.	26	22	23	22.0	26.0	26.0	571	572	598	217	220	1,241	1,316
Utah	322	422	433	22.8	21.5	17.7	7,236	9,081	7,678	200	203	18,129	15,588
Nev.	17	18	19	27.8	29.6	25.2	482	532	478	206	206	1,094	985
Pac.:													
Wash.	2,421	2,774	2,889	26.8	27.5	27.9	64,395	76,224	80,541	213	215	162,358	173,163
Oreg.	912	1,048	1,102	25.8	28.2	28.0	23,350	29,522	30,856	217	220	64,062	67,883
Calif.	602	573	647	18.3	17.0	21.0	10,990	9,741	13,587	223	225	21,722	30,571

[1] Includes an allowance for unredeemed loan and purchase agreement deliveries valued at average rate.
[2] Preliminary.

Source: Department of Agriculture, Bureau of Agricultural Economics; annual summaries, *Acreage, Yield, and Production of Principal Crops* and *Season Average Prices and Value of Production*.

No. 759.—CORN—ACREAGE, PRODUCTION, AND VALUE, BY STATES: 1941 TO 1952

[Pounds per bushel, 56. Covers corn for all purposes, including hogged and silged corn and that cut and fed without removing ears, as well as that husked and snapped for grain. Prices are season average prices received by farmers. See also *Historical Statistics*, E 151–153, for U. S. totals for acreage harvested, production, and price]

DIVISION AND STATE	ACREAGE HARVESTED			YIELD PER ACRE			PRODUCTION			PRICE FOR CROP OF		FARM VALUE	
	1941–50, avg.	1951	1952	1941–50, avg.	1951	1952	1941–50, avg.	1951	1952	1951	1952	1951	1952
	1,000 acres	1,000 acres	1,000 acres	Bu.	Bu.	Bu.	1,000 bu.	1,000 bu.	1,000 bu.	Cts. per bu.	Cts. per bu.	1,000 dol.	1,000 dol.
U. S.	96,098	80,736	81,399	34.7	36.9	40.6	3,611,652	2,966,149	3,306,735	168	157	4,813,539	5,192,570
N. E.:													
Maine	13	15	14	33.3	36.0	31.0	430	540	434	216	200	1,166	868
N. H.	13	14	14	43.1	43.0	41.0	551	602	574	211	195	1,270	1,119
Vt.	61	66	64	42.0	41.0	42.0	2,566	2,788	2,668	211	196	5,883	5,342
Mass.	36	36	36	43.2	47.0	46.0	1,680	1,692	1,656	211	194	3,570	4,280
R. I.	8	7	7	40.3	41.0	44.0	314	287	308	211	195	606	601
Conn.	46	38	35	43.5	45.0	40.0	1,968	1,710	1,400	211	195	3,608	2,730
M. A.:													
N. Y.	686	689	645	38.4	44.0	47.0	25,346	26,116	30,315	188	180	52,958	54,567
N. J.	187	185	196	43.0	42.8	52.5	7,984	9,712	10,290	199	188	18,550	19,088
Pa.	1,329	1,321	1,347	42.7	46.0	49.0	56,703	60,766	66,008	187	180	113,632	118,205
E. N. C.:													
Ohio	3,473	3,582	3,567	50.2	46.0	55.0	174,260	169,850	196,051	174	160	294,968	303,482
Ind.	4,380	4,365	4,046	49.1	55.0	50.0	215,425	241,415	202,300	165	153	403,577	360,029
Ill.	8,534	8,736	8,911	51.0	55.0	58.0	450,052	480,680	516,838	170	144	816,816	691,980
Mich.	1,648	1,964	1,984	35.9	41.5	50.0	59,153	80,856	83,280	169	150	116,705	123,920
Wis.	2,545	2,413	2,413	43.7	43.0	56.0	111,416	103,759	139,954	168	150	174,315	206,931
W. N. C.:													
Minn.	5,206	5,444	5,261	41.9	39.5	56.0	232,046	215,038	296,680	140	140	301,053	373,398
Iowa	10,516	10,190	10,908	50.4	43.5	64.0	532,301	443,265	697,702	161	150	713,857	1,046,588
Mo.	4,308	3,823	4,332	34.5	34.0	41.0	145,301	132,022	173,512	177	140	232,679	242,909
N. Dak.	1,183	1,215	1,069	22.0	18.5	19.5	26,010	22,478	20,846	145	140	32,593	29,184
S. Dak.	3,673	3,892	3,597	26.5	22.0	26.0	97,944	85,624	103,516	153	140	105,315	144,922
Nebr.	7,625	7,080	7,080	29.3	26.4	37.0	223,512	187,620	261,960	166	156	390,911	408,658
Kans.	2,535	2,429	2,730	25.5	24.0	22.0	71,594	58,294	59,840	173	160	100,862	95,744
S. A.:													
Del.	136	185	169	31.0	27.0	38.0	4,219	5,735	6,422	182	180	10,438	10,275
Md.	481	464	572	36.5	45.0	46.0	17,636	20,430	21,712	185	166	37,327	35,225
Va.	1,130	968	968	34.0	43.0	33.0	38,113	41,624	31,614	190	180	74,923	56,905
W. Va.	311	314	303	34.8	39.0	41.0	11,306	8,346	8,405	190	180	15,774	15,549
N. C.	2,283	2,181	2,203	26.5	31.0	18.5	59,640	67,611	35,176	170	180	114,939	101,117
S. C.	1,476	1,316	1,253	17.6	20.0	15.0	26,118	26,320	18,945	170	185	44,744	35,048
Ga.	3,343	3,096	2,099	13.4	16.0	12.0	44,673	40,536	37,162	172	190	85,202	82,321
Fla.	656	601	637	11.2	16.0	15.5	7,378	9,616	9,874	161	180	15,482	17,773
E. S. C.:													
Ky.	2,370	2,151	2,086	32.8	37.5	38.0	77,241	80,662	55,408	178	180	144,385	105,134
Tenn.	2,329	2,012	1,992	27.9	30.0	20.0	64,486	60,360	30,840	184	190	111,062	75,966
Ala.	2,527	2,437	2,769	16.6	19.0	11.0	46,470	44,303	29,258	177	185	81,962	51,393
Miss.	2,442	1,774	1,721	18.3	21.5	15.0	44,293	38,141	27,536	175	195	66,767	55,686
W. S. C.:													
Ark.	1,522	688	689	19.2	23.5	15.0	28,821	23,218	13,935	170	180	39,471	25,083
La.	1,070	709	666	16.6	23.0	19.0	17,493	16,307	12,642	185	190	26,907	24,042
Okla.	1,308	984	777	18.4	21.5	13.0	25,052	21,156	10,101	184	180	34,696	18,182
Tex.	3,520	2,278	2,232	16.5	18.5	18.5	56,561	42,143	41,292	167	180	70,379	74,336
Mt.:													
Mont.	195	165	145	16.2	14.5	14.0	3,073	2,392	2,030	182	185	4,353	3,756
Idaho	34	36	46	47.0	54.5	57.0	1,592	1,962	2,622	190	195	3,728	5,113
Wyo.	80	52	51	16.6	15.0	21.0	1,306	780	1,071	179	180	1,396	1,928
Colo.	722	537	501	20.9	26.0	26.5	14,632	14,482	13,276	184	180	26,647	23,897
N. Mex.	142	72	80	14.6	15.5	14.0	2,046	1,116	1,120	206	195	2,388	2,184
Ariz.	32	32	35	12.3	10.0	12.0	398	320	420	239	215	765	903
Utah	26	31	36	31.8	37.0	38.0	831	1,147	1,368	212	210	2,432	2,873
Nev.	2	3	3	31.1	40.0	42.0	74	120	126	220	220	264	277
Pac.:													
Wash.	21	19	21	48.6	58.0	59.0	1,011	1,102	1,209	202	195	2,226	2,382
Oreg.	30	25	28	37.6	42.0	44.0	1,310	1,092	1,232	213	205	2,325	2,526
Calif.	71	69	78	32.7	34.0	35.0	2,321	2,346	2,730	217	205	5,091	5,596

[1] Includes an allowance for unredeemed loan and purchase agreement deliveries valued at average rate.
[2] Preliminary.

Source: Department of Agriculture, Bureau of Agricultural Economics; annual summaries, *Acreage, Yield, and Production of Principal Crops* and *Season Average Prices and Value of Production*.

No. 760.—Oats—Acreage, Production, and Value, by States: 1941 to 1952

[Pounds per bushel, 32. Prices are season average prices received by farmers. See also *Historical Statistics*, series E 196-198, for U. S. totals for acreage harvested, production and price]

DIVISION AND STATE	ACREAGE HARVESTED			YIELD PER ACRE			PRODUCTION			PRICE FOR CROP OF [1]		FARM VALUE	
	1941-50 avg.	1951	1952 [2]	1941-50 avg.	1951	1952 [2]	1941-50 avg.	1951	1952 [2]	1951	1952 [2]	1951	1952 [2]
	1,000 acres	1,000 acres	1,000 acres	Bu.	Bu.	Bu.	1,000 bu.	1,000 bu.	1,000 bu.	Cts. per bu.	Cts. per bu.	1,000 dol.	1,000 dol.
U. S.	39,667	36,525	38,643	33.0	36.2	32.8	1,310,736	1,321,288	1,268,280	82.3	83.9	1,087,396	1,064,070
N. E.:													
Maine	82	114	82	39.4	44.0	30.0	3,243	5,016	2,460	92	93	4,615	2,288
N. H.	6	5	4	36.1	36.0	36.0	233	180	144	108	108	194	156
Vt.	41	36	34	32.2	41.0	36.0	1,334	1,476	1,224	108	108	1,594	1,322
Mass.	6	5	4	30.8	40.0	31.0	181	200	124	108	108	216	134
R. I.	1	1	1	31.3	32.0	31.0	31	32	31	108	108	35	33
Conn.	5	4	4	32.8	31.0	30.0	160	124	120	108	108	134	130
M. A.:													
N. Y.	705	755	770	32.4	48.0	37.0	23,365	36,240	28,490	87	90	31,529	25,641
N. J.	43	42	42	31.3	39.0	33.0	1,336	1,638	1,386	93	94	1,523	1,303
Pa.	785	770	755	31.4	42.0	29.0	24,681	32,340	21,895	89	93	28,783	20,362
E. N. C.:													
Ohio	1,131	1,196	1,268	37.1	41.0	37.0	42,692	49,036	46,916	85	86	41,681	40,348
Ind.	1,339	1,348	1,416	35.1	37.0	35.5	47,212	49,876	50,268	82	82	40,898	41,220
Ill.	3,566	3,359	3,359	39.6	40.0	37.0	141,681	134,360	124,283	82	82	110,175	101,912
Mich.	1,368	1,486	1,516	36.4	40.5	33.5	50,477	60,183	50,786	81	84	48,748	42,660
Wis.	2,735	2,895	2,953	42.8	49.5	45.0	117,913	143,302	132,885	82	84	117,508	111,623
W. N. C.:													
Minn.	4,734	4,948	5,245	36.7	43.0	39.0	174,803	212,764	204,555	77	78	163,828	159,553
Iowa	5,531	5,672	6,182	36.8	33.5	35.0	205,288	190,012	216,370	86	82	163,410	177,423
Mo.	1,762	1,206	1,194	24.6	23.0	22.0	43,602	27,738	26,268	87	88	24,132	23,116
N. Dak.	2,220	1,959	1,704	29.6	29.0	23.0	66,413	56,811	39,192	65	69	36,927	27,042
S. Dak.	2,906	3,145	3,554	30.5	37.0	26.5	89,073	116,365	94,181	73	77	84,946	72,519
Nebr.	2,269	2,172	2,454	27.2	28.0	19.0	61,349	60,816	46,626	84	83	51,085	38,700
Kans.	1,374	797	888	22.7	18.0	20.5	31,817	14,346	18,142	93	95	13,342	17,235
S. A.:													
Del.	6	8	7	30.4	32.0	31.0	165	256	217	87	94	223	204
Md.	40	55	58	31.3	36.0	34.5	1,237	1,980	2,001	89	92	1,762	1,841
Va.	134	146	143	27.7	33.0	33.0	3,717	4,818	4,719	85	89	4,095	4,200
W. Va.	67	52	54	27.0	32.0	29.5	1,780	1,664	1,593	103	100	1,714	1,593
N. C.	341	385	373	27.6	35.5	34.0	9,495	13,668	12,682	89	93	12,165	11,794
S. C.	643	576	582	24.8	28.0	30.0	15,972	16,128	17,460	91	94	14,676	16,412
Ga.	566	396	471	24.1	26.0	30.0	13,509	10,296	14,130	99	105	10,193	14,836
Fla.	25	20	36	17.2	25.0	30.0	454	500	1,080	132	115	660	1,242
E. S. C.:													
Ky.	92	89	104	22.8	24.0	25.0	2,103	2,136	2,600	103	105	2,200	2,730
Tenn.	211	182	200	25.6	26.0	28.0	5,400	4,732	5,600	104	108	4,921	6,048
Ala.	200	76	114	23.6	27.0	28.5	4,650	2,052	3,249	117	115	2,401	3,736
Miss.	311	115	167	29.5	29.0	37.0	9,294	3,335	6,179	103	105	3,435	6,488
W. S. C.:													
Ark.	263	122	123	27.2	25.0	32.5	7,166	3,050	3,998	103	102	3,142	4,078
La.	100	43	48	26.8	28.0	35.0	2,719	1,204	1,680	108	108	1,300	1,814
Okla.	1,067	298	402	19.0	16.0	21.0	20,643	4,768	8,442	92	94	4,387	7,935
Tex.	1,304	543	820	21.1	15.0	25.5	28,263	8,145	20,910	101	93	8,226	19,446
Mt.:													
Mont.	385	300	309	33.4	34.0	33.5	12,999	10,200	10,352	77	88	7,854	9,110
Idaho	184	191	186	41.8	42.0	46.5	7,704	8,022	8,602	89	95	7,140	8,172
Wyo.	143	149	145	30.7	31.5	31.0	4,395	4,694	4,495	93	100	4,365	4,495
Colo.	200	182	191	30.7	28.5	33.0	6,138	5,187	6,303	99	100	5,135	6,303
N. Mex.	40	28	27	22.1	18.5	22.0	893	518	594	107	105	554	624
Ariz.	10	9	11	36.5	41.0	52.0	386	369	572	114	120	421	686
Utah	48	41	44	43.9	46.0	46.0	2,106	1,886	2,024	104	110	1,961	2,226
Nev.	8	8	8	40.8	40.0	44.0	338	320	352	109	115	349	405
Pac.:													
Wash.	161	145	136	46.2	46.0	50.0	7,454	6,670	6,800	93	98	6,203	6,664
Oreg.	336	288	289	29.1	26.1	33.8	9,753	7,515	9,775	104	102	7,816	9,970
Calif.	172	163	170	29.6	26.5	32.5	5,118	4,320	5,525	111	114	4,795	6,298

[1] Includes an allowance for unredeemed loan and purchase agreement deliveries valued at average rate.
[2] Preliminary.

Source: Department of Agriculture, Bureau of Agricultural Economics; annual summaries, *Acreage, Yield, and Production of Principal Crops* and *Season Average Prices and Value of Production*.

No. 761.—BARLEY AND RICE—ACREAGE, PRODUCTION, AND VALUE, BY STATES: 1941 TO 1952

[Pounds per bushel of barley, 48; rice (rough), 45. Prices are season average prices received by farmers. See also Historical Statistics, series E 200-202, for U. S. barley totals for acreage harvested, production, and price]

DIVISION AND STATE	ACREAGE HARVESTED			YIELD PER ACRE			PRODUCTION			PRICE FOR CROP OF [1]		FARM VALUE	
	1941-50 avg.	1951	1952 [2]	1941-50 avg.	1951	1952 [2]	1941-50 avg.	1951	1952 [2]	1951	1952 [2]	1951	1952 [2]
BARLEY	1,000 acres	1,000 acres	1,000 acres	Bu.	Bu.	Bu.	1,000 bu.	1,000 bu.	1,000 bu.	Cents per bu.	Cents per bu.	1,000 dol.	1,000 dol.
U. S.	12,215	9,436	8,264	34.9	26.9	27.5	306,127	254,287	227,008	124	141	315,270	319,188
N. E.:													
Maine	4	6	4	29.8	32.0	28.0	129	192	112	128	130	246	146
Vt.	3	1	1	24.9	33.0	30.0	67	33	30	142	145	47	44
M. A.:													
N. Y.	101	74	70	26.9	34.0	31.0	2,603	2,516	2,170	121	130	3,044	2,821
N. J.	12	18	15	31.3	28.0	36.5	385	684	546	124	130	848	712
Pa.	134	157	148	32.3	34.5	37.0	4,332	5,416	5,476	118	125	6,391	6,845
E. N. C.:													
Ohio	29	19	18	27.4	26.0	30.0	787	494	540	119	135	588	729
Ind.	45	19	24	25.1	21.5	27.0	1,120	408	648	128	130	514	842
Ill.	62	29	22	27.1	28.0	29.5	1,652	812	649	132	135	1,072	878
Mich.	147	114	88	29.7	24.0	29.0	4,386	2,876	2,552	130	120	4,661	3,062
Wis.	255	201	97	34.2	33.0	35.0	8,364	6,633	3,395	127	145	8,484	4,923
W. N. C.:													
Minn.	1,098	1,402	1,136	25.9	27.5	25.0	28,563	38,555	28,400	120	135	46,266	38,340
Iowa	66	33	28	25.9	31.0	30.0	1,712	663	890	114	130	790	823
Mo.	100	60	60	20.5	21.5	25.0	1,999	1,290	1,500	128	135	1,651	2,025
N. Dak.	2,291	2,275	1,820	22.1	22.5	19.0	50,917	51,186	34,580	108	125	55,263	43,225
S. Dak.	1,579	838	628	20.0	23.5	15.5	31,989	19,698	9,734	106	125	20,875	12,165
Nebr.	903	210	172	19.2	22.0	20.0	17,892	4,620	3,440	120	130	5,544	4,472
Kans.	619	119	86	17.5	13.0	15.5	10,580	1,547	1,233	125	130	1,934	1,733
S. A.:													
Del.	10	11	10	26.7	31.0	30.0	268	341	300	114	120	389	360
Md.	74	76	66	30.1	32.5	33.0	2,220	2,470	2,178	114	120	2,816	2,614
Va.	79	82	82	28.6	32.0	34.0	2,260	2,624	2,788	116	125	3,044	3,485
W. Va.	10	12	11	27.9	26.0	32.0	289	312	352	126	140	424	493
N. C.	36	35	43	25.0	36.0	32.5	938	1,260	1,398	123	135	1,676	1,887
S. C.	23	16	18	22.0	25.0	27.0	492	400	486	143	145	572	705
Ga.	7	4	5	20.3	22.5	27.0	147	90	135	149	155	134	209
E. S. C.:													
Ky.	78	53	56	23.9	22.5	26.5	1,842	1,192	1,484	121	140	1,442	2,078
Tenn.	86	53	55	19.4	18.5	20.0	1,672	980	1,100	134	145	1,313	1,596
W. S. C.:													
Ark.	8	4	5	19.2	18.0	21.0	147	72	105	115	130	83	136
Okla.	242	18	26	16.0	11.0	17.5	3,912	198	455	130	135	257	614
Tex.	209	45	60	16.8	11.5	14.5	3,649	518	870	127	130	658	1,131
Mt.:													
Mont.	643	460	460	25.9	27.5	28.0	16,563	12,650	12,880	107	125	13,526	16,100
Idaho	342	328	326	35.3	32.0	37.0	12,066	10,432	12,062	128	140	13,144	16,887
Wyo.	134	139	132	29.7	33.0	32.0	3,962	4,587	4,234	120	135	5,504	5,702
Colo.	662	406	349	24.7	23.5	28.5	16,477	9,541	9,946	129	140	12,308	13,924
N. Mex.	30	21	24	20.4	20.5	22.0	610	430	528	122	150	588	792
Ariz.	92	98	107	41.1	50.0	55.0	4,028	4,900	5,885	144	155	7,056	9,122
Utah	129	138	141	44.6	44.0	44.0	5,757	6,072	6,204	148	150	8,501	9,306
Nev.	22	21	19	35.3	34.0	37.0	762	714	703	153	160	1,092	1,125
Pac.:													
Wash.	181	94	84	35.5	36.0	36.0	6,604	3,384	3,024	125	150	4,568	4,536
Oreg.	286	337	276	33.3	30.0	37.0	9,565	10,110	10,212	130	100	14,053	16,339
Calif.	1,476	1,412	1,497	29.6	30.0	36.0	44,236	42,360	53,892	151	160	63,964	86,227
RICE (ROUGH)	1,000 acres	1,000 acres	1,000 acres	Lb.	Lb.	Lb.	1,000 bags [3]	1,000 bags [3]	1,000 bags [3]	Dollars per bag [3]	Dollars per bag [3]	1,000 dollars	1,000 dollars
U. S.	1,533	1,997	1,972	2,084	2,238	2,468	32,950	45,797	48,660	4.31	5.37	230,877	265,865
Miss.	----	27	48	----	2,480	2,200	662	1,066	4.80	5.70	3,178	6,019	
Ark.	313	445	454	2,195	2,025	2,075	6,871	9,011	9,420	4.50	5.90	44,875	54,696
La.	858	612	588	1,743	1,980	2,150	10,248	11,994	12,642	4.55	5.80	54,200	73,334
Tex.	429	569	552	2,002	2,375	2,475	8,666	13,514	13,662	4.95	5.90	80,906	80,906
Calif.	238	314	330	2,929	3,400	3,609	7,090	10,676	11,880	4.95	6.00	52,846	71,280

[1] Includes an allowance for unredeemed loan and purchase agreement deliveries valued at average rate. [2] Preliminary. [3] Bags of 100 pounds.

Source: Department of Agriculture, Bureau of Agricultural Economics; annual summaries, Acreage, Yield, and Production of Principal Crops and Season Average Prices and Values of Production.

No. 762.—RYE AND SORGHUMS FOR GRAIN—ACREAGE, PRODUCTION, AND VALUE, BY STATES: 1941 TO 1952

[Pounds per bushel of rye, 56; sorghums for grain, 56 and 50. Prices are season average prices received by farmers]

STATE	ACREAGE HARVESTED			YIELD PER ACRE			PRODUCTION			PRICE FOR CROP OF—		FARM VALUE	
	1941-50, avg.	1951	1952	1941-50, avg.	1951	1952	1941-50, avg.	1951	1952	1951	1952	1951	1952
RYE	1,000 acres	1,000 acres	1,000 acres	Bu.	Bu.	Bu.	1,000 bu.	1,000 bu.	1,000 bu.	Cents per bu.	Cents per bu.	1,000 dol.	1,000 dol.
United States...	2,294	1,710	1,385	12.1	12.5	11.5	28,095	21,301	15,910	153	177	32,647	28,233
New York	15	12	9	17.7	18.5	19.5	263	222	176	148	180	329	317
New Jersey	14	11	8	17.2	19.0	18.5	241	209	148	149	145	311	274
Pennsylvania	33	12	12	14.9	15.5	17.0	478	186	204	149	160	277	328
Ohio	44	18	15	16.8	16.0	17.5	727	288	262	165	185	475	485
Indiana	82	43	47	13.4	12.5	14.0	1,099	538	658	165	185	888	1,217
Illinois	52	41	33	12.7	13.0	14.0	661	533	462	165	185	879	855
Michigan	62	62	45	13.8	14.0	14.0	861	868	630	159	180	1,380	1,134
Wisconsin	102	97	58	11.3	11.5	11.5	1,142	1,116	667	153	165	1,707	1,101
Minnesota	171	190	129	13.5	15.0	13.5	2,317	2,850	1,742	156	180	4,446	3,136
Iowa	14	8	7	14.6	14.0	15.5	210	112	108	153	180	171	194
Missouri	40	25	25	11.5	11.0	12.0	453	275	300	171	195	470	585
North Dakota	369	178	180	12.1	15.0	10.5	4,724	2,670	1,575	146	165	3,898	2,599
South Dakota	434	512	287	12.3	13.0	11.0	5,435	6,656	3,157	147	170	9,784	5,367
Nebraska	329	202	170	10.6	8.5	10.0	3,570	1,717	1,700	149	170	2,558	2,890
Kansas	73	30	42	10.6	9.5	11.0	780	285	462	155	175	442	808
Delaware	16	19	14	13.6	14.5	14.0	218	276	196	152	180	420	353
Maryland	17	14	13	14.6	14.5	15.5	248	203	202	157	175	319	354
Virginia	31	19	16	13.4	14.5	15.0	412	276	240	161	195	444	468
West Virginia	4	2	2	12.6	13.0	13.5	45	26	27	172	190	45	51
North Carolina	29	15	15	11.4	14.0	15.0	330	210	225	220	240	462	540
South Carolina	14	6	7	9.5	12.5	11.5	135	75	80	225	250	169	200
Georgia	10	4	7	8.7	11.0	10.5	85	44	74	251	270	110	200
Kentucky	29	17	21	13.3	12.0	13.5	384	204	284	188	215	384	611
Tennessee	31	15	20	10.2	10.0	11.0	317	150	220	200	220	300	484
Oklahoma	70	45	115	8.3	5.0	8.0	603	225	920	159	180	358	1,656
Texas	24	13	27	9.1	6.0	8.0	214	78	216	150	180	117	389
Montana	25	9	6	12.1	10.5	10.0	307	94	60	130	155	122	93
Idaho	5	3	4	14.5	15.0	13.0	70	45	52	149	180	67	94
Wyoming	14	6	5	10.8	11.0	9.0	157	66	45	146	160	96	72
Colorado	69	27	27	9.4	8.0	8.0	684	216	216	152	165	328	356
New Mexico	8	5	4	9.8	5.0	10.0	76	25	40	151	165	38	66
Utah	8	5	6	10.4	9.0	8.5	80	45	51	166	175	75	89
Washington	19	14	10	11.8	11.0	10.0	232	154	100	155	170	239	170
Oregon	30	23	21	13.5	12.0	15.0	416	276	315	147	170	406	536
California	10	8	8	11.5	11.0	12.0	121	88	96	151	170	133	163
SORGHUM GRAIN													
United States...	7,100	8,687	5,089	18.4	18.9	16.4	132,598	160,195	83,316	132	165	211,929	137,313
Indiana	2	1	2	28.5	28.0	33.0	45	28	66	148	157	41	104
Missouri	44	23	30	19.7	17.0	18.0	865	391	540	147	160	575	864
South Dakota	87	18	14	12.3	12.0	14.5	1,025	216	203	135	148	292	300
Nebraska	119	128	97	19.5	13.0	23.0	2,374	1,664	2,231	132	148	2,196	3,302
Kansas	1,327	2,605	1,324	18.0	22.0	14.0	25,109	57,310	18,536	132	157	75,649	29,102
North Carolina	11	33	43	25.8	30.0	27.0	290	990	1,161	143	176	1,416	2,043
South Carolina	5	4	4	17.4	18.5	16.5	81	74	66	163	185	121	122
Alabama	26	19	11	17.0	17.0	16.0	461	323	176	154	165	497	290
Arkansas	12	15	10	15.4	21.0	17.0	186	315	170	146	157	460	267
Louisiana	2	1	2	15.4	16.0	19.0	27	16	38	143	157	23	60
Oklahoma	686	1,048	472	13.4	16.0	9.0	9,420	16,768	4,248	129	168	21,631	7,137
Texas	4,174	3,913	2,682	18.9	18.5	18.0	79,096	72,250	48,236	130	165	93,925	79,589
Colorado	181	229	140	14.4	12.0	8.0	2,694	2,748	1,120	133	160	3,792	1,792
New Mexico	257	359	129	14.8	9.5	7.0	4,311	3,410	903	133	165	4,535	1,490
Arizona	53	26	34	38.1	42.0	48.0	2,076	1,092	1,632	180	193	1,966	3,150
California	124	65	95	38.2	40.0	42.0	4,724	2,600	3,990	185	193	4,810	7,701

[1] Includes an allowance for unredeemed loan and purchase agreement deliveries valued at average rate.
[2] Preliminary.   [3] Short-time average.

Source: Department of Agriculture, Bureau of Agricultural Economics; annual summaries, *Acreage, Yield, and Production of Principal Crops* and *Season Average Prices and Value of Production*.

No. 763.—GRAIN PRICES—AVERAGE MARKET PRICES, BY KIND, BY MARKET: 1909 TO 1951

[Weighted average market price per bushel of reported cash sales]

YEARLY AVERAGE OR CROP YEAR BEGINNING—	Wheat, July-June			Corn, Nov.-Oct.		Oats, Aug.-July		Barley, Aug.-July	Rye, July-June	Flaxseed, Aug.-July [1]	Kafir, Nov.-Oct. [3]
	No. 1, Dark Northern Spring, Minneapolis	No. 2, Hard Winter, Kansas City	No. 2, Red Winter, Chicago	No. 3, Yellow, Chicago	No. 3, Yellow, Kansas City	No. 3, White, Chicago	No. 3, White, Minneapolis	No. 2, Minneapolis [3]	No. 2, Minneapolis	No. 1, Minneapolis	No. 2, White, Kansas City
1909-1913	[4] $0.99	$0.95	$0.99	$0.61	$0.60	$0.40	$0.38	$0.64	$0.70	$1.91	$1.84
1914-1920	[4] 1.90	1.70	1.82	1.15	1.12	.60	.56	1.02	1.43	3.02	2.17
1921-1925	1.44	1.27	1.33	.79	.78	.43	.38	.64	.57	2.47	1.59
1926-1930	1.26	1.16	1.26	.85	.79	.44	.42	.64	.86	2.32	1.81
1931-1935	.93	.73	.78	.67	.67	.31	.32	.60	.37	1.61	1.48
1936-1940	1.06	.92	.98	.60	.66	.35	.33	.72	.64	1.98	1.68
1941-1945	1.45	1.40	1.46	1.19	1.12	.68	.61	1.12	1.06	2.90	1.90
1946-1950	2.48	2.25	2.20	1.61	1.62	.86	.85	1.71	1.96	5.00	2.60
1941	1.10	1.12	1.12	.80	.78	.46	.46	.79	.66	2.11	1.19
1942	1.29	1.26	1.26	.94	.90	.54	.50	.92	.78	2.88	1.85
1943	1.55	1.45	1.67	1.14	1.13	.76	.74	1.28	1.08	3.05	2.37
1944	1.59	1.56	1.58	1.18	1.10	.71	.67	1.30	1.10	3.10	2.01
1945	1.71	1.60	1.68	1.92	1.67	.67	.67	1.31	1.72	3.14	2.42
1946	2.34	2.09	2.09	1.84	1.84	.92	.85	1.78	2.05	4.52	2.91
1947	2.66	2.82	2.48	2.14	2.24	1.06	1.14	2.33	2.65	6.38	3.15
1948	2.37	2.19	2.27	1.35	1.31	.72	.71	1.40	1.57	5.56	2.35
1949	2.37	2.16	1.96	1.31	1.27	.73	.73	1.30	1.42	3.92	2.15
1950	2.46	2.28	2.30	1.74	1.63	.86	.82	1.54	1.62	3.96	2.42
1951	2.50	2.43	2.30	1.80	1.79	.90	.96	1.47	1.79	4.10	2.61

[1] Average closing price through December 1920. [3] Special No. 2, 1920-33; No 2 Malting, thereafter.
[3] Price per 100 pounds. [4] No. 1 Northern Spring.

Source: Department of Agriculture, Bureau of Agricultural Economics; annual report, *Agricultural Statistics*, and records.

No. 764.—WHEAT, CORN, AND OATS—RECEIPTS AT PRIMARY MARKETS, BY CROP YEARS: 1945 TO 1951

[In thousands of bushels. Pounds per bushel: Wheat, 60; corn, 56; oats, 32]

YEAR BEGINNING—	Total 12 markets	Chicago	Milwaukee	Minneapolis	Duluth	St. Louis	Kansas City	Peoria	Omaha	Indianapolis	Sioux City	St. Joseph	Wichita
WHEAT													
July 1:													
1945	575,597	23,383	5,375	119,747	146,874	27,896	135,354	5,045	36,797	12,623	6,886	17,362	36,336
1946	512,020	21,992	3,605	133,868	90,332	18,518	140,361	4,726	40,016	7,363	6,107	16,064	29,067
1947	609,973	42,659	4,983	141,346	104,088	20,609	178,530	3,215	42,346	8,338	4,645	15,008	41,983
1948	629,365	32,486	5,489	153,740	125,373	26,253	156,080	4,130	51,085	9,397	5,388	18,473	34,537
1949	468,636	29,941	5,131	117,428	100,362	18,464	99,337	2,945	30,866	8,604	3,302	14,524	29,657
1950	518,343	21,533	3,549	155,718	99,708	17,754	127,351	4,771	35,337	5,804	3,175	17,132	26,591
1951	538,620	15,698	726	150,499	109,445	22,388	119,260	4,582	32,447	4,906	4,376	15,516	36,833
CORN													
Oct. 1:													
1945	271,655	100,046	8,523	19,742	691	17,476	22,379	26,960	23,145	20,349	15,229	7,290	27
1946	447,212	165,204	11,190	25,367	4,462	35,846	46,620	44,529	52,542	30,594	17,708	13,220	3
1947	231,657	86,265	5,751	15,268	5,109	14,933	18,677	30,448	30,797	16,908	12,908	4,443	
1948	346,396	121,250	7,874	30,462	16,016	26,772	27,870	37,126	28,920	36,108	22,100	7,388	2
1949	355,149	125,411	9,273	32,041	21,503	23,520	32,465	25,962	36,547	34,949	15,713	6,776	4
1950	376,063	121,041	9,470	24,155	9,673	20,868	41,015	22,968	57,071	34,314	26,381	13,396	
1951	397,336	119,038	8,701	18,352	2,639	27,164	28,568	24,050	30,841	26,680	14,080	7,234	55
OATS													
July 1:													
1945	219,135	37,235	4,850	80,397	28,434	9,691	10,061	4,837	13,373	5,151	12,256	6,276	83
1946	198,900	44,579	3,927	60,757	15,504	11,067	10,822	5,890	10,104	4,260	13,144	6,085	
1947	154,329	30,391	4,499	61,730	12,669	5,147	4,552	5,077	2,455	12,149	4,556		
1948	142,217	35,479	1,609	41,667	17,185	6,509	7,148	5,617	8,192	4,140	14,115	5,449	12
1949	190,436	36,526	2,343	51,150	15,306	7,852	5,620	2,894	7,212	4,848	14,667	5,643	12
1950	102,914	31,001	2,347	27,745	4,627	5,752	5,408	2,324	9,735	16,719	4,263		4
1951	121,000	35,021	1,780	33,028	2,747	5,181	4,988	2,204	9,708	16,902	5,350		

Source: Department of Agriculture, Bureau of Agricultural Economics; compiled from *Chicago Journal of Commerce*.

No. 765.—TOBACCO—ACREAGE, PRODUCTION, AND VALUE, BY STATES: 1941 TO 1952

[Prices are season average prices received by farmers]

STATE	ACREAGE HARVESTED			YIELD PER ACRE			PRODUCTION			PRICE FOR CROP OF—	
	1941-50, average	1951	1952¹	1941-50 aver-age	1951	1952¹	1941-50, average	1951	1952¹	1951	1952¹
	Acres	*Acres*	*Acres*	*Lbs.*	*Lbs.*	*Lbs.*	*1,000 pounds*	*1,000 pounds*	*1,000 pounds*	*Cts. per lb.*	*Cts. per lb.*
U.S....	1,630,060	1,782,900	1,775,500	1,124	1,307	1,243	1,841,869	2,330,787	2,207,477	51.1	50.0
Mass........	6,840	6,800	6,000	1,566	1,545	1,574	10,694	10,505	9,444	69.8	91.8
Conn........	17,900	16,900	17,300	1,366	1,378	1,425	24,416	23,281	24,652	92.4	113.0
N.Y........	720	300	200	1,348	1,400	1,400	980	420	280	23.8	......
Pa...........	34,740	34,900	23,500	1,448	1,610	1,550	50,451	56,186	36,428	19.0	......
Ohio.......	20,950	18,900	19,700	1,157	1,387	1,393	24,160	26,222	27,450	42.6	40.8
Ind........	9,790	10,800	11,000	1,210	1,298	1,298	11,929	13,850	14,280	47.8	44.9
Wis........	22,100	15,500	16,100	1,469	1,477	1,478	32,468	22,889	23,799	28.7	......
Minn.......	540	300	300	1,258	1,300	1,300	676	390	390	22.0	......
Mo.........	5,680	5,000	5,000	1,052	800	1,150	5,965	4,000	5,750	51.7	50.0
Kans.......	240	100	100	1,020	920	1,000	245	92	100	50.0	49.0
Md.........	43,770	53,000	51,000	758	785	800	33,702	41,605	40,800	44.9	......
Va.........	122,910	136,500	137,500	1,120	1,295	1,339	138,489	176,788	184,105	52.2	50.0
W.Va.......	2,930	3,100	3,300	1,107	1,380	1,375	3,268	4,278	4,538	52.5	51.0
N.C........	655,030	750,200	750,200	1,118	1,332	1,231	736,834	998,930	923,840	53.5	50.1
S.C........	111,700	132,000	132,000	1,134	1,330	1,280	128,052	175,560	168,960	50.6	52.2
Ga.........	88,770	112,100	112,100	1,033	1,225	1,125	92,991	137,361	126,145	47.0	50.3
Fla.........	20,660	26,600	26,700	957	1,218	1,141	19,990	32,392	30,458	72.3	70.6
Ky.........	356,700	348,800	349,700	1,110	1,324	1,272	397,950	461,930	444,650	49.3	......
Tenn.......	107,400	110,100	112,900	1,182	1,301	1,246	128,139	143,214	140,670	50.5	......
Ala........	360	600	600	847	1,050	930	304	630	558	47.0	47.5
La.........	330	400	300	506	660	600	167	264	180	60.0	......

¹ Preliminary.

Source: Department of Agriculture, Bureau of Agricultural Economics; annual summaries, *Acreage, Yield, and Production of Principal Crops* and *Season Average Prices and Value of Production.*

No. 766.—WHEAT, CORN, RICE, AND TOBACCO—QUANTITY EXPORTED AND IMPORTED: 1932 TO 1952

[Year ending June 30]

PRODUCT	1932-36 avg.	1937-41 avg.	1942-46 avg.	1947-51 avg.	1949	1950	1951	1952
DOMESTIC EXPORTS ¹								
Wheat and flour (in terms of grain) 1,000 bu..	50,295	67,879	99,150	408,142	505,303	314,231	374,014	478,188
Corn and meal (in terms of grain) 1,000 bu..	4,170	45,726	13,954	91,716	90,621	109,670	116,260	80,102
Rice, milled ² ...1,000 lbs..	152,298	281,173	520,703	932,322	914,143	1,013,596	978,957	1,709,905
Tobacco, unmanufactured.......1,000 lbs..	418,195	374,397	375,915	482,355	451,091	480,598	477,398	517,739
IMPORTS FOR CONSUMPTION ³								
Wheat and flour (in terms of grain) 1,000 bu..	21,106	16,512	47,350	7,721	4,571	11,840	20,006	37,412
Corn and meal (in terms of grain) 1,000 bu..	10,507	23,018	2,265	695	637	704	760	856
Rice.........1,000 lbs..	41,448	86,060	7,221	12,656	4,533	5,136	43,942	50,006
Tobacco, unmanufactured.......1,000 lbs..	62,974	74,398	75,343	87,330	88,455	86,808	94,008	105,624

¹ Excluding reexports. Effective Jan. 1, 1947, includes shipments under various special programs including ECA.
² Beginning January 1, 1933, includes paddy or rough rice in terms of milled.
³ Imports for consumption beginning 1933; general imports prior thereto.

Source: Department of Agriculture, Office of Foreign Agricultural Relations; compiled from official records of Bureau of Census. Published currently in *Foreign Agricultural Trade.*

No. 767.—COTTON AND COTTONSEED—ACREAGE, PRODUCTION, AND VALUE, BY
STATES: 1941 TO 1952

[Cotton production excludes linters. Values shown are for marketing season or crop year and should not be confused with calendar year income. Yields and prices for period are simple averages of figures for individual years. Tons are of 2,000 pounds. See also *Historical Statistics*, series E 217–224, for U. S. totals for acres harvested, production, and price]

YEARLY AVERAGE OR YEAR	COTTON					COTTONSEED			Total farm value
	Acres harvested	Bales (500 pounds gross)	Farm value	Yield per acre	Farm price per pound[1][9]	Quantity	Farm value	Farm price per ton[9]	
	Thou-sands	Thou-sands	1,000 dollars	Pounds	Cents	1,000 short tons	1,000 dollars	Dollars	1,000 dollars
United States:									
1941–1950	21,020	11,775	1,542,482	266	26.28	4,781	283,748	60.41	1,826,231
1951	26,687	15,144	2,867,668	272	37.88	6,286	435,891	69.30	3,303,559
1952 (prel.)	24,996	15,036	2,774,230	288	34.90	6,108	427,746	70.00	3,201,976
Alabama:									
1941–1950	1,570	899	117,984	277	26.70	347	19,627	57.35	137,611
1951	1,460	909	172,798	299	38.03	371	22,928	61.80	195,726
1952 (prel.)	1,500	890	166,430	285	37.40	361	23,517	67.00	189,947
Arizona:									
1941–1950	233	250	37,418	489	27.92	105	6,869	63.40	44,287
1951	545	803	155,835	705	38.87	345	23,770	68.90	179,606
1952 (prel.)	665	1,010	196,716	727	38.40	420	26,560	66.00	227,276
Arkansas:									
1941–1950	1,941	1,373	178,027	339	24.96	557	32,656	59.41	210,683
1951	2,025	1,249	237,643	296	38.06	594	35,580	67.90	273,223
1952 (prel.)	1,885	1,325	244,462	337	36.90	532	36,974	69.50	281,436
California:									
1941–1950	482	627	91,286	606	24.49	248	17,289	66.21	108,575
1951	1,320	1,765	346,343	640	38.25	704	50,618	71.90	396,961
1952 (prel.)	1,400	1,826	327,846	624	35.90	718	48,824	66.00	376,670
Florida:									
1941–1950	37	13	1,693	180	26.01	6	289	53.07	1,982
1951	62	33	5,764	260	34.67	14	840	60.70	6,604
1952 (prel.)	82	30	5,550	277	39.00	13	532	64.00	6,082
Georgia:									
1941–1950	1,409	686	89,497	236	26.99	278	16,038	59.00	105,535
1951	1,410	931	179,160	317	38.48	382	24,563	64.30	203,723
1952 (prel.)	1,395	725	137,025	249	37.80	296	19,832	67.00	156,857
Louisiana:									
1941–1950	862	524	68,471	290	26.53	213	12,039	57.34	80,510
1951	935	780	140,902	391	37.10	308	19,743	64.10	160,646
1952 (prel.)	890	750	142,875	405	38.10	300	20,250	67.50	163,125
Mississippi:									
1941–1950	2,372	1,552	220,126	333	27.18	675	40,428	60.83	260,554
1951	2,340	1,608	316,371	329	39.34	656	45,723	69.70	362,094
1952 (prel.)	2,375	1,885	354,380	380	37.60	751	54,072	72.00	408,452
Missouri:									
1941–1950	426	262	45,781	406	25.79	154	8,547	56.81	54,328
1951	490	309	55,373	302	35.80	136	8,514	62.60	63,887
1952 (prel.)	480	385	71,418	400	37.10	166	10,956	66.00	82,374
New Mexico:									
1941–1950	156	157	23,491	485	26.54	63	4,153	64.54	27,644
1951	315	273	56,939	415	43.34	116	8,965	77.20	67,904
1952 (prel.)	300	325	67,202	519	41.40	133	10,108	76.00	77,310
North Carolina:									
1941–1950	728	523	65,801	341	26.76	214	11,807	56.02	77,608
1951	690	542	106,019	376	38.75	228	15,778	69.20	120,797
1952 (prel.)	705	560	103,600	390	37.00	232	16,472	71.00	120,072
Oklahoma:									
1941–1950	1,277	456	51,382	166	24.50	180	10,476	61.04	61,858
1951	1,475	462	82,109	150	35.56	191	13,981	73.20	96,080
1952 (prel.)	1,150	390	43,550	108	33.80	107	7,597	71.00	51,147
South Carolina:									
1941–1950	1,071	651	86,115	293	25.81	255	15,148	57.71	101,263
1951	1,070	871	162,849	389	37.40	374	25,544	66.30	188,393
1952 (prel.)	1,090	680	122,760	292	37.20	272	19,040	70.00	141,800
Tennessee:									
1941–1950	707	549	70,942	373	26.21	213	12,501	59.67	83,443
1951	768	534	102,216	334	38.31	218	14,737	67.60	116,953
1952 (prel.)	800	625	115,988	374	37.10	249	17,056	68.50	133,994
Texas:									
1941–1950	7,706	3,020	390,147	153	25.44	1,241	75,090	61.74	465,237
1951	11,780	4,074	742,105	166	36.44	1,710	123,975	72.80	866,080
1952 (prel.)	10,300	3,750	666,003	175	33.80	1,555	112,738	72.50	778,741
Virginia:									
1941–1950	26	21	2,587	364	25.45	6	488	59.55	3,075
1951	19	14	2,695	347	38.09	6	412	68.60	3,107
1952 (prel.)	22	23	4,282	480	38.80	9	689	71.00	4,871
Other States:									
1941–1950	17	14	1,740	380	25.70	6	318	56.01	2,068
1951	16	8	1,536	245	37.13	3	220	64.30	1,776
1952 (prel.)	15	10	1,943	340	37.40	4	279	66.50	2,223

[1] Season average price for 1952, to Dec. 1 only. [9] Based on 1947–51 average ratio of lint to cottonseed. For cotton crop, and 1949–52 for cottonseed, season average prices include an allowance for unredeemed loans.

Source: Department of Agriculture, Bureau of Agricultural Economics; annual reports on Farm Production, Farm Disposition, and Value of Cotton and Cottonseed.

No. 768.—COTTON (EXCLUDING LINTERS)—PRODUCTION, CONSUMPTION, EXPORTS, IMPORTS, PRICES, AND CARRY-OVER: 1916 TO 1952

[All figures, except average price, in thousands of bales. Production figures relate to crop of preceding calendar year and are compiled from reports of individual ginners. Price per pound is average price received by growers. For data prior to 1916, see 1949 and earlier editions of the *Statistical Abstract*]

YEARLY AVERAGE OR YEAR ENDING JULY 31	PRODUCTION Running bales, counting round as half bales	PRODUCTION Equivalent 500-pound bales, gross weight	Average price per pound upland cotton (cents)	Consumption (running bales)	Exports of domestic cotton (running bales)	Imports (equivalent 500-pound bales)	Carry-over (running bales)
1916-20	11,382	11,481	24.0	6,388	5,524	361	3,432
1921-25	10,958	11,985	21.4	5,869	6,083	318	2,971
1926-30	15,101	15,268	17.4	6,735	8,251	365	3,337
1931-35	13,046	13,343	8.9	5,466	7,244	115	7,833
1936-40	12,783	13,148	9.9	6,938	5,306	171	9,008
1941-45	11,640	11,987	17.3	10,301	1,372	185	11,074
1946-50	11,875	12,102	29.4	9,038	3,929	252	5,014
1944	11,129	11,429	19.9	9,943	1,138	129	10,744
1945	11,839	12,230	20.7	9,568	2,007	190	11,164
1946	8,813	9,016	22.5	9,163	3,613	343	7,326
1947	8,517	8,639	32.6	10,025	3,544	270	2,530
1948	11,587	11,857	31.9	9,354	1,970	238	3,080
1949	14,580	14,868	30.4	7,795	4,747	163	5,297
1950	15,909	16,128	28.6	8,851	5,770	245	6,846
1951	9,908	10,012	40.1	10,654	4,117	188	2,278
1952	15,072	15,144	37.9	9,120	5,515	72	2,789

Source: Department of Commerce, Bureau of the Census (except price per pound from Department of Agriculture, Bureau of Agricultural Economics); annual report, *Cotton Production and Distribution*.

No. 769.—COTTONSEED AND COTTONSEED PRODUCTS—PRODUCTION AND EXPORTS: 1881 TO 1952

[Cottonseed production relates to preceding crop year: other data relate to 12 months ending July 31. Tons are 2,000 pounds. For value of cottonseed products, 1881-1945, see 1949 *Statistical Abstract*. See also *Historical Statistics*, series J 175, for data on cottonseed oil production]

YEARLY AVERAGE OR YEAR ENDING JULY 31 OR JUNE 30—	COTTONSEED Production	COTTONSEED Used in mills	COTTONSEED PRODUCTS Production Oil	Meal and cake	Hulls	Linters	COTTONSEED PRODUCTS Exports Oil	Meal and cake
	1,000 tons	1,000 tons	1,000 pounds	1,000 tons	1,000 tons	Bales [1]	1,000 pounds	1,000 tons
1881-1890	3,018	553	165,810	193	-----	-----	34,038	-----
1891-1900	4,280	1,625	483,015	570	[3]1,169	[3]114,544	191,157	[3]388
1901-1905	5,139	3,085	890,745	1,130	1,382	167,327	297,888	548
1906-1910	4,258	3,296	990,450	1,339	1,195	282,064	311,463	578
1911-1915	6,353	4,847	1,466,940	2,162	1,527	595,225	290,311	551
1916-1920	5,116	4,285	1,302,080	2,041	1,093	943,474	172,877	301
1921-1925	4,878	3,646	1,125,196	1,654	1,082	578,384	106,371	258
1926-1930	6,784	5,319	1,631,597	2,409	1,495	1,117,754	48,762	328
1931-1935	5,932	4,474	1,398,611	2,032	1,229	954,186	28,100	97
1936-1940	5,847	4,653	1,444,771	2,101	1,195	1,354,871	7,681	26
1941-1945	5,136	4,223	1,327,149	1,898	1,019	1,489,821	19,650	1
1946-1950	4,883	4,296	1,363,440	1,928	1,001	1,576,300	54,855	50
1944	4,680	3,955	1,235,829	1,834	927	1,412,340	8,061	1
1945	4,902	4,254	1,324,039	1,954	964	1,500,243	7,383	(4)
1946	3,663	3,202	1,017,546	1,434	783	1,191,553	5,878	(4)
1947	3,511	3,090	973,083	1,363	727	1,183,519	7,627	5
1948	4,683	4,082	1,275,603	1,898	923	1,523,820	32,588	9
1949	5,943	5,332	1,703,762	2,391	1,236	1,961,476	81,580	117
1950	6,614	5,712	1,847,205	2,555	1,338	2,021,123	146,600	121
1951	4,104	3,723	1,196,893	1,669	857	1,394,365	60,832	12
1952	6,301	5,475	1,750,783	2,847	1,234	2,054,032	99,368	44

[1] Of 500 pounds net.
[2] Figures for 1900.
[3] 6-year average, 1895-1900.
[4] Less than 500 tons.

Source: Department of Commerce, Bureau of the Census; annual report, *Cotton Production and Distribution*.

No. 770.—Cottonseed and Cottonseed Products—Production, by States: 1952

[Cottonseed production relates to preceding crop year; other data relate to 12 months ending July 31. Tons are 2,000 pounds. Bales are 500 pounds net]

STATE	COTTONSEED		COTTONSEED PRODUCTS			
	Production	Used in mills	Oil	Meal and cake	Hulls	Linters
	1,000 tons	*1,000 tons*	*1,000 pounds*	*1,000 tons*	*1,000 tons*	*Bales*
Total	6,301	5,476	1,789,783	2,847	1,284	2,664,632
Alabama	377	267	79,442	124	66	98,744
Arizona	348	286	86,307	112	66	94,073
Arkansas	636	303	130,907	173	91	147,281
California	702	603	220,081	260	144	279,081
Georgia	382	448	134,001	210	96	180,109
Louisiana	310	224	66,831	107	51	73,181
Mississippi	655	580	163,536	273	129	214,996
North Carolina	231	223	66,565	106	47	86,373
Oklahoma	188	171	30,453	63	37	64,697
South Carolina	373	339	74,804	111	46	105,218
Tennessee	217	365	119,962	161	86	131,321
Texas	1,718	1,806	486,429	723	344	818,004
All other States	275	132	43,217	67	31	54,826

Source: Department of Commerce, Bureau of the Census; annual reports, *Cotton Production* and *Cotton Production and Distribution.*

No. 771.—Sweetpotatoes—Acreage, Production, and Value, by States: 1941 to 1952

[Pounds per bushel, 55. Prices are season average prices received by farmers. See also *Historical Statistics,* series E 226-230, for U. S. totals for acreage harvested, production, and price]

STATE	ACREAGE HARVESTED			YIELD PER ACRE			PRODUCTION			PRICE FOR CROP OF—		FARM VALUE	
	1941-1950, average	1951	1952	1941-1950, average	1951	1952	1941-1950, average	1951	1952	1951	1952	1951	1952
	1,000 acres	*1,000 acres*	*1,000 acres*	*Bu.*	*Bu.*	*Bu.*	*1,000 bu.*	*1,000 bu.*	*1,000 bu.*	*Cts. per bu.*	*Cts. per bu.*	*1,000 dol.*	*1,000 dol.*
United States	635	314	326	93	92	87	57,768	28,796	28,232	305	332	87,867	93,897
New Jersey	16	14	14	142	165	150	2,266	2,310	2,100	336	345	7,762	7,245
Indiana	1	1	1	117	135	110	152	81	55	257	300	208	165
Illinois	3	1	1	92	110	90	240	132	99	282	310	372	307
Iowa	2	1	1	100	110	110	154	110	110	251	305	276	336
Missouri	6	3	2	100	110	80	506	275	176	275	320	756	563
Kansas	2	1	1	112	85	60	215	85	42	281	360	239	151
Delaware	1	1	1	126	150	125	150	105	75	227	285	240	214
Maryland	8	3	5	149	160	155	1,212	500	775	234	265	1,792	2,054
Virginia	24	17	17	116	130	130	2,765	2,210	2,210	241	260	5,326	5,746
North Carolina	65	37	39	106	94	100	6,850	3,478	3,900	314	340	10,921	13,260
South Carolina	54	26	26	96	85	80	5,115	2,380	2,080	296	355	7,092	7,384
Georgia	75	26	24	77	65	70	5,791	1,695	1,680	352	390	5,730	6,552
Florida	14	8	8	67	68	70	960	510	560	286	400	1,464	2,240
Kentucky	13	6	5	86	84	80	1,141	462	400	260	335	1,342	1,340
Tennessee	30	11	12	96	90	95	2,956	980	1,140	312	345	3,060	3,933
Alabama	59	21	17	82	65	60	4,832	1,365	1,020	282	340	3,849	3,468
Mississippi	53	22	19	91	60	57	4,830	1,320	1,083	348	415	4,594	4,494
Arkansas	18	7	7	82	74	60	1,453	518	402	296	390	1,533	1,568
Louisiana	102	73	88	92	100	90	9,453	7,300	7,920	284	285	20,732	22,572
Oklahoma	8	3	2	70	75	80	542	225	160	319	420	718	420
Texas	57	21	27	86	65	45	4,855	1,365	1,215	338	420	4,477	5,103
California	11	10	10	107	115	115	1,152	1,180	1,180	470	415	5,405	4,772

[1] Preliminary.

Source: Department of Agriculture, Bureau of Agricultural Economics; annual summaries, *Acreage, Yield, and Production of Principal Crops* and *Season Average Prices and Value of Production.*

No. 772.—POTATOES—ACREAGE, PRODUCTION AND VALUE, BY STATES: 1941 TO 1952

[Pounds per bushel, 60.   Prices are season average prices received by farmers.   See also *Historical Statistics*, series E 225–227, for U S. totals for acreage harvested, production, and price]

DIVISION AND STATE	ACREAGE HARVESTED			YIELD PER ACRE			PRODUCTION			PRICE FOR CROP OF—		FARM VALUE	
	1941–50, avg.	1951¹	1952¹	1941–50, avg.	1951¹	1952¹	1941–50, avg.	1951	1952¹	1951	1952¹	1951	1952¹
	1,000 acres	*1,000 acres*	*1,000 acres*	*Bu.*	*Bu.*	*Bu.*	*1,000 bu.*	*1,000 bu.*	*1,000 bu.*	*Dols. per bu.*	*Dols. per bu.*	*1,000 dol.*	*1,000 dol.*
U. S.	2,401	1,334	1,396	180	240	249	414,525	320,519	347,504	1.63	2.28	522,190	793,732
N. E.:													
Maine	180	100	145	348	445	360	61,882	44,500	52,200	1.78	2.15	79,210	112,230
N. H.	6	4	4	198	250	255	1,186	975	1,046	2.28	3.10	2,223	3,243
Vt.	9	4	4	163	180	180	1,405	738	774	2.19	3.15	1,616	2,438
Mass.	18	8	8	187	230	205	3,157	1,886	1,702	1.77	2.85	3,338	4,851
R. I.	6	4	5	223	265	245	1,293	1,060	1,152	1.85	2.90	1,961	3,341
Conn.	15	8	9	217	285	255	3,207	2,252	2,218	2.21	2.90	4,977	6,432
M. A.:													
N. Y.	166	102	107	200	274	287	33,182	27,900	30,725	1.48	2.45	41,292	75,276
N. J.	57	28	26	209	267	186	11,462	7,476	4,836	1.11	2.30	7,085	11,123
Pa.	128	69	64	168	235	225	19,990	16,215	14,400	1.95	2.75	31,619	39,600
E. N. C.:													
Ohio	55	25	24	156	230	200	7,656	5,750	4,800	1.74	3.05	10,005	14,640
Ind.	31	14	12	151	240	210	4,348	3,360	2,520	1.94	2.90	6,518	7,308
Ill.	20	8	7	91	110	80	1,721	825	520	1.80	3.05	1,485	1,586
Mich.	142	60	56	126	180	185	16,958	10,800	10,360	1.97	2.60	21,276	26,936
Wis.	118	53	56	122	185	215	12,820	9,805	12,040	1.67	2.40	16,374	28,896
W. N. C.:													
Minn.	154	70	66	121	170	180	17,209	11,900	12,240	1.77	2.35	21,063	28,764
Iowa	27	8	10	109	130	125	2,889	1,040	1,250	1.85	2.80	1,924	3,500
Mo.	28	14	12	111	112	90	3,022	1,568	1,080	1.65	2.40	2,587	2,592
N. Dak.	143	72	78	142	185	180	19,872	13,320	14,040	1.72	2.15	22,910	30,186
S. Dak.	27	11	11	94	150	115	2,467	1,650	1,265	1.75	2.40	2,888	3,036
Nebr.	62	31	31	176	190	245	10,518	5,890	7,595	1.52	1.75	8,953	13,291
Kans.	17	5	4	98	80	55	1,620	368	220	1.55	2.25	570	495
S. A.:													
Del.	3	5	5	103	188	176	330	940	862	1.18	2.70	1,109	2,327
Md.	15	8	6	120	150	122	1,762	1,230	781	1.22	2.70	1,501	2,109
Va.	63	37	34	139	186	138	8,352	6,882	4,692	1.27	3.00	8,740	14,076
W. Va.	27	15	14	102	105	85	2,694	1,575	1,190	2.00	3.10	3,150	3,689
N. C.	78	44	44	126	145	124	9,572	6,380	5,456	1.31	2.50	8,358	13,640
S. C.	22	13	12	107	149	154	2,295	1,937	1,848	1.52	2.98	2,944	5,507
Ga.	18	7	6	70	69	76	1,217	483	456	1.55	2.95	749	1,345
Fla.	29	25	31	155	258	246	4,398	6,321	7,626	1.84	2.44	11,631	18,607
E. S. C.:													
Ky.	36	20	19	90	98	82	3,265	1,960	1,558	1.47	2.65	2,881	4,129
Tenn.	36	19	17	86	81	80	3,005	1,539	1,360	1.46	2.85	2,247	3,876
Ala.	43	31	29	96	136	142	4,047	4,216	4,118	1.20	2.23	5,059	9,183
Miss.	22	9	8	69	58	56	1,531	522	448	1.73	3.20	903	1,434
W. S. C.:													
Ark.	35	14	12	83	79	65	2,820	1,106	780	1.65	3.05	1,825	2,379
La.	34	12	11	60	62	72	2,035	744	763	1.67	2.70	1,242	2,060
Okla.	20	7	5	71	81	80	1,359	526	400	1.79	2.95	942	1,180
Tex.	46	19	17	97	116	120	4,402	2,204	2,040	1.88	2.55	4,144	5,202
Mt.:													
Mont.	15	10	11	158	215	245	2,337	2,150	2,572	2.11	2.55	4,536	6,559
Idaho	159	131	138	247	280	310	39,312	36,680	42,780	1.37	1.75	50,252	74,865
Wyo.	12	7	7	180	185	240	2,035	1,202	1,680	1.84	2.15	2,212	3,612
Colo.	73	48	52	246	255	180	17,627	12,240	20,020	1.86	2.05	22,766	41,041
N. Mex.	3	1	1	101	120	100	277	144	80	1.59	2.25	229	180
Ariz.	5	4	4	262	365	370	1,292	1,387	1,517	1.98	2.50	2,219	3,792
Utah	15	11	12	196	205	255	2,938	2,214	3,162	1.98	2.00	4,384	6,324
Nev.	2	1	2	214	260	310	504	364	527	2.22	2.15	808	1,133
Pac.:													
Wash.	34	28	26	294	390	410	9,305	10,920	10,660	1.34	1.90	14,633	20,254
Oreg.	42	32	33	260	320	345	10,960	10,240	11,385	1.66	2.05	16,998	23,339
Calif.	102	80	102	357	439	409	36,388	35,135	41,760	1.59	2.45	55,854	102,126

¹ Preliminary.

Source: Department of Agriculture, Bureau of Agricultural Economics; annual summaries, *Acreage, Yield, and Production of Principal Crops* and *Season Average Prices and Value of Production.*

No. 773.—ALL HAY—ACREAGE, PRODUCTION, AND VALUE, BY STATES: 1941 TO 1952

[See also *Historical Statistics*, series E 211-216, for U. S. totals for acreage harvested, production, and price]

DIVISION AND STATE	ACREAGE HARVESTED			YIELD PER ACRE			PRODUCTION			PRICE FOR CROP OF [1]		FARM VALUE	
	1941-50, avg.	1951	1952[2]	1941-50, avg.	1951	1952[2]	1941-50, avg.	1951	1952[2]	1951	1952[2]	1951	1952[2]
	1,000 acres	1,000 acres	1,000 acres	Tons[3]	Tons[3]	Tons[3]	1,000 tons[3]	1,000 tons[3]	1,000 tons[3]	Dols. per ton	Dols. per ton	1,000 dol.	1,000 dol.
U. S.	74,536	74,442	74,664	1.36	1.45	1.40	101,072	107,901	104,424	22.09	25.20	2,451,028	2,636,059
N. E.:													
Maine	816	708	703	.97	1.12	1.17	790	796	825	28.10	26.00	22,368	21,450
N. H.	357	310	308	1.16	1.28	1.28	416	397	395	28.80	28.50	11,821	11,200
Vt.	982	917	912	1.37	1.46	1.44	1,351	1,341	1,310	27.80	26.50	37,280	34,715
Mass.	363	331	334	1.53	1.62	1.56	552	540	522	35.50	36.00	19,170	18,792
R. I.	23	29	31	1.42	1.69	1.68	47	49	52	34.80	34.50	1,705	1,946
Conn.	285	280	253	1.55	1.73	1.75	442	449	442	36.10	36.50	16,209	16,170
M. A.:													
N. Y.	3,804	3,397	3,250	1.51	1.72	1.66	5,748	5,678	5,390	20.30	21.50	115,283	115,885
N. J.	357	357	354	1.08	1.52	1.32	431	437	465	33.30	32.50	15,551	15,112
Pa.	2,390	2,314	2,269	1.45	1.53	1.49	3,470	3,544	3,378	25.10	27.50	88,954	92,895
E. N. C.:													
Ohio	2,511	2,578	2,601	1.44	1.52	1.47	3,630	3,916	3,677	24.40	26.50	95,550	97,440
Ind.	1,837	1,834	1,790	1.38	1.45	1.40	2,536	2,651	2,511	21.80	23.50	57,792	59,006
Ill.	2,712	2,799	2,723	1.46	1.69	1.63	3,965	4,736	4,443	20.90	23.00	98,982	102,189
Mich.	2,612	2,521	2,455	1.37	1.54	1.44	3,581	3,882	3,538	19.70	21.50	76,475	76,067
Wis.	4,061	4,064	4,056	1.67	2.20	2.10	6,786	8,986	8,508	16.70	19.00	149,231	161,652
W. N. C.:													
Minn.	4,267	3,770	3,821	1.47	1.84	1.53	6,284	6,921	6,986	15.30	16.50	105,199	115,269
Iowa	3,430	3,947	3,767	1.60	1.76	1.82	5,497	6,948	6,843	16.20	18.00	112,558	123,174
Mo.	3,670	3,715	3,425	1.20	1.29	1.08	4,396	4,790	3,702	21.80	26.50	104,422	98,103
N. Dak.	3,247	3,360	3,525	.96	.92	.96	3,114	3,077	3,382	15.90	17.80	48,924	57,435
S. Dak.	3,694	4,733	5,116	.84	.92	.78	3,079	4,346	4,007	16.50	18.00	71,709	72,126
Nebr.	4,216	5,215	5,369	1.06	1.18	1.12	4,481	6,157	6,009	17.50	25.00	107,748	150,225
Kans.	1,822	2,134	1,973	1.61	1.62	1.18	2,932	3,467	2,326	23.70	32.00	82,168	74,432
S. A.:													
Del.	74	69	70	1.37	1.45	1.46	100	100	102	25.70	27.50	2,570	2,805
Md.	444	450	473	1.36	1.52	1.46	605	683	689	27.50	29.50	18,782	20,326
Va.	1,330	1,380	1,460	1.14	1.18	1.21	1,552	1,641	1,760	34.60	26.00	56,779	63,360
W. Va.	808	818	818	1.22	1.28	1.21	989	1,048	986	28.50	30.50	29,866	30,134
N. C.	1,250	1,195	1,227	1.01	1.01	1.08	1,266	1,209	1,325	31.10	33.00	37,600	43,725
S. C.	555	455	492	.80	.82	.86	441	371	428	34.40	35.50	12,762	15,088
Ga.	1,357	991	883	.54	.63	.65	731	622	581	27.40	28.00	17,043	16,949
Fla.	116	80	78	.56	.71	.69	65	57	54	23.80	25.50	1,357	1,377
E. S. C.:													
Ky.	1,795	1,913	1,751	1.29	1.06	1.05	2,326	2,277	1,840	29.40	33.00	66,944	60,720
Tenn.	1,820	1,802	1,461	1.16	1.04	.88	2,114	1,666	1,290	32.40	34.50	53,978	44,805
Ala.	995	708	723	.75	.79	.79	739	563	572	30.80	31.00	17,340	17,732
Miss.	869	724	690	1.18	1.07	.94	1,024	774	650	29.30	31.50	22,678	20,475
W. S. C.:													
Ark.	1,311	1,137	1,009	1.12	1.14	.77	1,462	1,294	775	25.10	31.50	32,479	24,612
La.	317	296	343	1.22	1.15	1.18	387	344	404	26.50	30.50	9,804	12,322
Okla.	1,388	1,480	1,408	1.26	1.21	1.11	1,715	1,796	1,556	24.50	32.50	44,002	50,570
Tex.	1,583	1,448	1,517	.98	1.01	1.00	1,550	1,456	1,512	30.60	34.00	44,554	51,408
Mt.:													
Mont.	2,183	2,219	2,430	1.17	1.06	1.07	2,558	2,362	2,582	32.30	31.00	76,335	80,042
Idaho	1,119	1,066	1,097	2.12	2.14	2.41	2,372	2,281	2,643	27.60	24.50	62,906	64,754
Wyo.	1,102	1,117	1,139	1.12	1.12	1.17	1,235	1,255	1,327	28.60	32.00	35,362	42,464
Colo.	1,399	1,291	1,396	1.58	1.57	1.73	2,212	2,025	2,421	22.60	32.50	66,048	78,682
N. Mex.	208	200	207	2.09	2.09	2.20	435	418	455	39.30	40.00	16,427	18,200
Ariz.	275	251	251	2.34	2.53	2.70	642	634	678	34.40	33.50	21,310	22,713
Utah	566	508	548	2.03	2.01	2.39	1,154	1,022	1,310	30.30	26.00	30,997	34,060
Nev.	408	391	392	1.48	1.52	1.71	600	504	670	28.80	28.00	17,167	18,760
Pac.:													
Wash.	879	795	797	1.91	1.80	1.88	1,682	1,431	1,495	26.00	28.00	40,068	41,860
Oreg.	1,080	1,001	1,023	1.73	1.55	1.74	1,865	1,551	1,778	28.40	28.50	44,048	50,673
Calif.	1,938	1,744	1,862	2.96	3.11	3.19	5,728	5,425	5,932	28.80	31.50	161,685	186,856

[1] Price of hay sold baled.
[2] Preliminary.
[3] Tons of 2,000 pounds.

Source: Department of Agriculture, Bureau of Agricultural Economics; annual summaries, *Acreage, Yield, and Production of Principal Crops* and *Season Average Prices and Value of Production*.

No. 774.—Truck Crops, Commercial—Acreage, Production, and Value, By Kind, 1951 and 1952, and Leading States, 1952

[Production in equivalent tons of 2,000 pounds. Estimates relate to commercial production for fresh market and processing combined and include production in market-garden areas. Production for home use in farm and nonfarm gardens is not included. Value is for season or crop year and should not be confused with calendar year income]

CROP	ACREAGE [1]			PRODUCTION (EQUIVALENT TONS)			VALUE (1,000 DOLLARS)	
	1951	1952	1952, leading States	1951	1952	1952, leading States	1951	1952
Artichokes	7,400	8,100	California	12,600	17,000	California	2,816	2,975
Asparagus	130,600	130,830	California, New Jersey	167,900	151,700	California, New Jersey	40,280	34,962
Beans, lima	127,450	112,740	California, Delaware	120,000	113,600	California, Delaware	17,779	17,718
Beans, snap	305,510	276,600	Florida, New York	187,900	468,600	Florida, New York	74,415	76,990
Beets	23,820	22,000	Wisconsin, Texas	188,500	164,400	Wisconsin, Texas	5,152	4,020
Broccoli	33,650	41,000	California, Texas	90,700	102,200	California, Texas	15,112	17,669
Brussels sprouts	4,600	4,450	California, New York	24,300	17,400	California, New York	4,992	3,581
Cabbage	160,040	147,150	New York, Texas	1,285,400	1,243,700	New York, Texas	54,781	66,557
Cantaloupe	132,900	121,450	California, Arizona	489,900	477,900	California, Arizona	43,089	49,528
Carrots [4]	74,250	81,060	California, Texas	734,900	763,900	California, Texas	52,634	47,181
Cauliflower	28,900	28,430	California, New York	225,300	218,800	California, New York	16,804	17,025
Celery	37,080	37,320	California, Florida	709,300	721,300	California, Florida	63,470	87,973
Corn, sweet	648,800	709,920	Wisconsin, Minnesota	1,758,500	2,068,300	Wisconsin, Minnesota	66,509	78,152
Cucumbers	190,090	197,380	Michigan, Wisconsin	451,600	509,900	Michigan, Florida	34,011	42,676
Eggplant	4,500	5,400	Florida, New Jersey	27,600	30,100	Florida, New Jersey	2,379	2,673
Escarole	4,700	4,680	California, Texas	39,700	30,100	California, Texas	1,197	2,760
Garlic	300	2,050	California, Texas	7,100	6,700	California, Texas	144	1,986
Honeyball melons	143	250	California, Arizona	1,300	9,900	California, Arizona		105
Honeydew melons	10,100	9,500	California, Arizona	53,900	53,700	California, Arizona	6,259	7,036
Kale	2,800	2,700	Virginia	9,600	9,600	Virginia	904	1,013
Lettuce	204,600	212,450	California, Arizona	1,268,100	1,389,600	California, Arizona	122,456	124,986
Mint for oil [5]	55,700	58,500	Indiana, Oregon	1,005	1,156	Oregon, Indiana	12,571	13,845
Onions [4]	102,110	116,880	Texas, New York	984,200	965,100	New York, California	64,853	88,513
Peas, green	473,660	439,870	Wisconsin, Washington	543,200	453,500	Wisconsin, Washington	50,425	42,228
Peppers, green	37,430	36,650	Florida, New Jersey	112,200	113,500	Florida, New Jersey	18,755	22,935
Pimientos [7]	18,000	15,000	Georgia	15,300	12,300	Georgia	1,148	964
Potatoes, commercial early	204,900	216,750	California, Florida	1,670,800	1,675,600	California, Florida	76,297	138,277
Shallots	6,000	6,000	Louisiana	6,800	9,900	Louisiana	1,007	1,190
Spinach	84,470	74,760	Texas, California	255,500	213,400	Texas, California	18,457	17,080
Strawberries	143,830	130,560	Arkansas, Oregon	205,600	213,700	California, Washington	75,811	79,670
Tomatoes	651,850	605,750	California, Texas	5,181,500	4,314,200	California, New York	253,900	238,989
Watermelons	352,500	360,200	Texas, Florida	1,241,900	1,218,100	Florida, Texas	38,521	43,557

[1] Acreage of crops for harvest for fresh market, including any partially harvested or not harvested because of low prices or other economic factors, plus acreage harvested for processing.
[2] Processing production shelled basis plus fresh market production in the shell. Equivalent shelled basis: 1951, 107,600 tons; 1952, 102,000 tons.
[3] Includes some quantities not marketed and excluded in computing value.
[4] Includes quantities for dehydration.
[5] Peppermint and spearmint.
[6] Processing production shelled basis plus fresh market production in the shell. Equivalent shelled basis: 1951, 524,780 tons; 1952, 436,880 tons.
[7] Georgia, plus crop contracted in other States by Georgia processors.

Source: Department of Agriculture, Bureau of Agricultural Economics; annual report, Agricultural Statistics.

No. 775.—Fruits—Production and Price Received by Farmers: 1941 to 1952

[See also *Historical Statistics*, series E 231-243]

CROP	UNIT	PRODUCTION (1,000) [1]				PRICE PER UNIT [2]		
		1941-50, avg.	1950	1951	1952 [3]	1950	1951	1952 [3]
Apples [4]	Bu. (48 lbs.)	110,380	124,428	110,660	92,696	$1.50	$1.72	$2.44
Peaches	...do	65,195	50,627	65,627	62,746	2.05	2.02	2.05
Pears	Bu. [5]	30,306	29,312	30,028	30,744	2.14	2.48	1.87
Grapes	Ton	2,808	2,666	3,360	3,160	65.20	40.50	36.60
Cherries (12 States)	...do	191	230	260	216	167.00	135.00	155.00
Plums (3 States)	...do	84	84	168	61	172.00	142.00	155.00
Prunes (fresh basis) [6]	...do	575	416	558	434	99.30	66.80	87.80
Oranges and tangerines [7]	Box [8]	104,607	121,710	122,500	125,350	1.97	1.49	1.45
Grapefruit	...do [9]	51,222	45,550	40,500	33,440	1.09	.87	.94
Lemons	...do [10]	12,614	13,450	12,360	13,160	3.83	3.47	3.00

[1] Includes some quantities not harvested on account of economic conditions or scarcity of harvest labor or donated to charity.
[2] Season average prices, except citrus fruit prices, which are equivalent packing-house-door returns for all methods of sale. [3] Preliminary.
[4] Estimates refer to production of apples in commercial apple areas of each State and include fruit produced for sale to commercial processors, as well as that for sale for fresh consumption.
[5] California, 48 pounds; other States, 50 pounds.
[6] Fresh basis for California derived by multiplying dry basis estimate by 2½.
[7] Data for 5 States; 7 States prior to 1942. See also table 755, p. 654.
[8] Net content of box varies. In California and Arizona approximate average is 77 pounds; in Florida and other States, 90 pounds.
[9] In California and Arizona approximate average is 65 pounds net; in Florida and other States, 80 pounds net.
[10] About 79 pounds net.

Source: Department of Agriculture, Bureau of Agricultural Economics; annual summaries, *Acreage, Yield, and Production of Principal Crops* and *Season Average Prices and Value of Production*.

No. 776.—Apples, Peaches, Pears, and Grapes—Production, by States

[See also *Historical Statistics*, series E 232, 234, 236, and 238, for U. S. totals]

STATE	APPLES (1,000 BU.) [1][2]			PEACHES (1,000 BU.) [1]			PEARS (1,000 BU.) [1]			GRAPES (TONS) [1]		
	1941-1950, avg.	1951	1952 [3]	1941-1950, avg.	1951	1952 [3]	1941-1950, avg.	1951	1952 [3]	1941-1950, avg.	1951	1952 [3]
U. S.	110,380	110,660	92,696	65,195	65,627	62,746	30,306	30,028	30,744	2,807,770	3,359,500	3,159,900
Mass.	2,554	3,160	1,224	54	87	53	42	45	32			
Conn.	1,281	1,656	977	127	148	152	30	53	40			
N. Y.	14,591	17,291	11,395	1,247	1,312	1,311	679	486	396	55,540	60,700	56,800
N. J.	2,460	3,318	2,009	1,524	1,992	1,363				1,520	1,300	1,200
Pa.	6,084	7,626	4,914	2,051	2,162	2,290	277	200	186	16,940	17,460	17,300
Ohio	3,517	4,400	2,491	918	997	836	243	200	162	13,500	15,500	12,700
Ind.	1,403	1,806	1,069	507	72	472	136	100	81	1,800	800	1,100
Ill.	3,194	3,995	2,184	1,787	224	1,610	308	204	152	2,880	2,100	1,800
Mich.	6,982	9,085	5,508	2,851	605	3,397	721	986	1,096	33,250	10,000	36,300
Iowa	184	264	214							2,660	2,200	2,000
Mo.	1,208	1,440	799	613	304	673	194	132	120	4,490	4,400	3,500
Kans.	417	432	207	77	130	132	84	78	49	1,860	1,200	800
Del.	508	316	195	261	148	99						
Md.	1,357	1,127	1,116	499	476	415						
Va.	9,485	9,560	9,948	1,458	1,771	1,909	210	103	137	1,495	1,100	1,100
W. Va.	3,769	3,780	3,770	531	561	574	73	58	63	1,140	900	900
N. C.	1,090	1,259	2,053	1,867	1,805	1,646	202	154	172	4,070	3,300	2,700
S. C.				3,226	4,980	3,286	92	64	36	1,190	1,200	1,200
Ga.				4,114	3,975	2,496	314	241	221	1,980	1,900	1,900
Ky.	817	376	308	572	72	497	126	66	93			
Tenn.	592	399	380	707	80	459	168	58	113			
Ala.				1,036	266	585	241	99	99			
Miss.				702	255	432	275	128	162			
Ark.	882	510	270	2,027	1,044	1,530	153	94	56	9,480	10,800	8,800
La.				1,327	696	346	335	261	106			
Idaho	1,673	1,610	1,659	284	350	408	57	58	72			
Colo.	1,395	1,292	1,320	1,351	316	2,053	187	193	226			
Wash.	20,448	19,108	22,630	2,086	510	1,524	7,046	5,554	4,809	18,590	22,700	27,000
Oreg.	3,766	3,330	2,700	576	400	642	4,929	4,997	5,468	1,460	1,300	1,100
Calif.	7,990	7,522	5,820	30,608	35,678	30,127	12,466	15,001	16,084	2,827,100	3,225,000	2,995,600
Other	5,347	5,678	4,549	1,566	1,600	1,336	691	447	536	6,465	2,500	2,500

[1] See note 4, table 775. [2] See note 1, table 775. [3] Preliminary.
[4] U. S. average includes estimated production for certain States from 1941 to 1943. Estimates for those States discontinued beginning with 1944 crop.

Source: Department of Agriculture, Bureau of Agricultural Economics; annual summaries, *Acreage, Yield, and Production of Principal Crops* and *Season Average Prices and Value of Production*.

No. 777.—Sugar Beets—Acreage, Production, Prices Received by Farmers, and Value, 1901 to 1952, and by States, 1949 to 1952

[Prior to 1924 acreage and production include a small quantity produced in Canada for U. S. factories. U. S. totals include data for a few States not shown separately]

YEARLY AVERAGE OR YEAR AND STATE	Acres harvested (thousands)	Tons per acre	Production (1,000 tons)	Price per ton (dollars) [1]	Farm value (1,000 dollars)	YEAR AND STATE	Acres harvested (thousands)	Tons per acre	Production (1,000 tons)	Price per ton (dollars) [1]	Farm value (1,000 dollars)
United States:						Idaho:					
1901–1905...	228	9.22	[2] 2,079	4.89	10,166	1949........	60	17.8	1,067	10.20	10,883
1906–1910...	386	10.13	[2] 3,910	[2] 5.18	[2] 20,254	1950........	87	17.3	1,508	10.80	16,286
1911–1915...	541	10.66	[2] 5,738	5.63	32,318	1951........	66	18.6	1,227	11.40	13,968
1916–1920...	698	9.49	6,623	9.56	63,314	1952........	57	18.2	1,037	(4)	(4)
1921–1925...	693	10.06	6,972	7.46	52,040	Michigan:					
1926–1930...	701	11.01	7,718	7.32	56,480	1949........	77	9.6	743	11.60	8,619
1931–1935...	799	10.87	8,686	5.42	47,119	1950........	98	10.4	1,020	11.70	11,934
1936–1940...	857	12.20	10,452	5.13	53,569	1951........	53	11.4	605	12.40	7,502
1941–1945...	705	12.46	8,782	8.26	72,559	1952........	49	10.7	524	(4)	(4)
1946–1950...	797	14.09	11,244	11.15	125,395	Montana:					
1939........	918	11.7	10,781	4.76	51,342	1949........	59	11.8	697	10.50	7,318
1940........	912	13.4	12,194	5.11	62,287	1950........	62	12.0	744	11.50	8,556
1941........	755	13.7	10,342	6.43	66,522	1951........	45	11.9	537	12.00	6,444
1942........	954	12.2	11,685	6.84	79,905	1952........	37	14.0	518	(4)	(4) .
1943........	550	11.9	6,547	8.81	57,674	Nebraska:					
1944........	555	12.1	6,718	10.60	71,156	1949........	38	14.7	558	10.50	5,859
1945........	713	12.1	8,616	10.20	87,539	1950........	59	13.8	812	11.80	9,582
1946........	802	13.2	10,560	11.10	117,594	1951........	55	12.4	683	11.70	7,991
1947........	879	14.2	12,503	11.80	148,080	1952........	58	15.5	899	(4)	(4)
1948........	694	13.6	9,424	10.60	99,639	Ohio:					
1949........	687	14.8	10,196	10.80	110,369	1949........	24	10.5	252	11.40	2,873
1950........	925	14.6	13,535	11.20	151,293	1950........	22	12.6	277	11.50	3,186
1951........	691	15.2	10,485	11.70	122,507	1951........	13	9.8	127	12.50	1,588
1952........	667	15.3	10,217	11.90	121,582	1952........	12	11.0	132	(4)	(4)
California:						Utah:					
1949........	134	18.8	2,519	11.00	27,709	1949........	28	16.6	466	10.40	4,846
1950........	209	18.8	3,927	10.70	42,019	1950........	38	14.1	535	11.30	6,046
1951........	140	18.9	2,645	11.70	30,946	1951........	26	15.5	403	11.80	4,755
1952........	150	18.0	2,700	(4)	(4)	1952........	21	12.5	262	(4)	(4)
Colorado:						Wyoming:					
1949........	117	16.1	1,878	10.90	20,470	1949........	28	14.5	406	10.40	4,222
1950........	146	15.0	2,183	12.00	26,196	1950........	36	12.6	454	11.40	5,176
1951........	124	15.4	1,906	11.90	22,681	1951........	31	14.1	438	11.80	5,168
1952........	113	17.2	1,944	(4)	(4)	1952........	34	13.8	469	(4)	(4)

[1] Season average price.   [2] Beets used by factories 1901 to 1912.   [3] 4-year average.   [4] Not available.

No. 778.—Sugarcane Sirup—Production, 1941 to 1952, and by States, 1950 to 1952

[Excludes sorghum, sometimes confused with sugarcane. For molasses, a byproduct of sugar refineries not included in this table, see table 779]

STATE AND YEAR	Cane harvested for sirup	Sirup produced	STATE AND YEAR	Cane harvested for sirup	Sirup produced
	Acres	1,000 gallons		Acres	1,000 gallons
All States:			Florida:		
1941............	110,000	18,638	1950............	7,000	980
1942............	113,000	18,416	1951............	6,000	960
1943............	126,000	21,027	1952............	5,000	725
1944............	118,000	19,897	Alabama:		
1945............	131,000	26,251	1950............	10,000	1,150
1946............	114,000	23,335	1951............	6,000	480
1947............	103,000	18,545	1952............	5,000	450
1948............	67,000	11,245	Mississippi:		
1949............	58,000	9,745	1950............	8,000	1,040
1950............	49,000	9,230	1951............	4,000	360
1951............	33,000	6,040	1952............	4,000	360
1952............	30,000	6,100	Louisiana:		
Georgia:			1950............	12,000	3,960
1950............	12,000	2,100	1951............	9,000	2,880
1951............	8,000	1,360	1952............	9,000	3,375
1952............	7,000	1,190			

Source of tables 777 and 778: Department of Agriculture, Bureau of Agricultural Economics; annual summaries, *Acreage, Yield, and Production of Principal Crops* and *Season Average Prices and Value of Production.*

No. 779.—Sugarcane, Cane Sugar, and Molasses—Production in Continental
United States: 1924 to 1952

[Tons are of 2,000 pounds. Data include Louisiana for all years, and Florida beginning 1926]

YEAR	Total acreage harvested for sugar and seed	Average yield of cane per acre for sugar and seed [1]	Total production for sugar and seed	Season average price per ton received by farmers [2]	Farm value of cane used for sugar and seed	SUGAR PRODUCED			MOLASSES MADE	
						Raw value [3]	Equivalent refined [4]	Sugar per ton of cane, raw value [5]	Blackstrap [6]	Total [6]
	1,000 acres	Tons	1,000 tons	Dollars	1,000 dollars	1,000 tons	1,000 tons	Pounds	1,000 gallons	1,000 gallons
1924	251.0	7.6	1,900	5.58	10,602	90	84	147	3,336	9,580
1925	236.0	14.0	3,298	4.05	13,337	142	133	107	12,171	17,783
1926	161.0	6.8	1,088	4.92	5,353	48	45	111	2,745	6,614
1927	89.0	13.1	1,165	4.61	5,384	72	67	150	3,582	6,699
1928	146.5	14.4	2,115	3.85	8,153	136	127	145	5,817	12,660
1929	206.0	16.2	3,340	3.73	12,500	218	206	140	15,862	21,068
1930	208.5	15.5	3,153	3.31	10,430	215	201	148	14,294	19,039
1931	199.4	13.9	2,763	3.21	8,874	184	172	146	11,296	16,464
1932	241.9	14.9	3,599	2.98	10,741	265	248	160	13,472	15,934
1933	233.8	14.4	3,375	3.14	10,607	250	234	168	14,140	19,441
1934	262.6	15.1	3,955	2.33	9,211	262	245	148	16,602	22,698
1935	275.4	18.4	5,064	3.15	15,940	382	357	164	24,790	30,788
1936	264.2	22.2	5,867	3.67	21,526	438	410	162	33,495	38,793
1937	305.1	20.6	6,279	2.90	18,232	450	420	156	36,546	40,408
1938	315.9	22.7	7,174	2.70	19,400	584	546	173	42,117	45,514
1939	276.0	22.8	6,286	2.84	17,880	506	472	175	34,142	38,582
1940	271.9	15.9	4,313	2.96	12,355	332	311	172	23,171	34,970
1941	286.6	19.1	5,461	3.95	21,548	416	389	170	27,408	32,308
1942	315.7	18.5	5,837	4.39	25,630	458	428	170	29,184	36,867
1943	303.9	21.4	6,504	4.58	29,760	497	445	163	35,392	46,053
1944	294.3	20.9	6,144	4.95	30,393	437	409	153	36,178	43,100
1945	285.4	23.5	6,707	5.67	38,016	475	443	182	34,773	49,965
1946	310.9	19.2	5,962	6.61	39,431	425	397	154	27,947	41,536
1947	322.2	16.4	5,289	7.17	37,916	377	353	156	28,089	34,285
1948	334.6	20.2	6,768	5.77	39,040	477	446	152	43,350	47,376
1949	338.5	19.3	6,541	6.26	40,899	521	487	171	40,002	43,316
1950	322.5	20.6	6,644	7.80	54,153	564	527	174	45,095	49,434
1951	318.9	19.2	6,118	6.35	38,846	419	392	146	45,079	48,582
1952 (prel.)	331.0	21.5	7,132	6.83	48,721	557	521	166	(⁷)	49,500

[1] Growth of 9 months in Louisiana and 12 months in Florida. Sugar campaign usually ends by December or early January in Louisiana and in Florida by March following season of growth.
[2] Prices exclude Government payments under the Sugar Act. Price support payments for 1943–45 included.
[3] Raw value equals 96° raw sugar as defined in Sugar Act of 1948; prior to 1929, calculated by the Agricultural Adjustment Administration Method. (S. R. Series 1, No. 1.)
[4] Calculated on basis that 100 pounds of raw sugar required to produce 93.46 pounds of refined sugar.
[5] Converted to 80° Brix beginning with 1934. Data for previous years as reported.
[6] Sirup production excluded. See table 778.   [7] Not available.

Source: Department of Agriculture, Bureau of Agricultural Economics; annual report, *Agricultural Statistics.* Also published in *The World Sugar Situation.*

No. 780.—Sugarcane and Cane Sugar—Production in Hawaii: 1941 to 1952

[Tons are of 2,000 pounds]

YEAR BEGINNING JAN. 1—	Total acres in cane	CANE USED FOR SUGAR			SUGAR MADE (1,000 TONS)		Raw sugar 96° made per ton of cane (pounds)	Recovery of equivalent refined sugar from cane ground [4] (percent)
		Acres harvested	Production (1,000 tons)	Yield per acre (tons) [1]	Converted to 96° raw basis [2]	Equivalent refined [3]		
1941	238,111	130,768	8,840	65	947	885	221	10.34
1942	225,199	114,745	7,918	69	870	813	220	10.37
1943	220,928	113,754	8,185	72	896	836	216	10.11
1944	216,072	109,522	7,882	72	875	818	222	10.44
1945	211,231	103,173	7,371	71	821	768	223	10.41
1946	208,376	84,379	6,002	71	680	636	227	10.59
1947	211,624	113,020	7,942	70	872	815	220	10.26
1948	206,550	100,042	7,543	75	895	780	221	10.35
1949	213,354	108,794	8,046	74	966	862	238	11.10
1950	230,383	109,408	8,175	75	961	898	235	10.99
1951	221,212	109,404	8,477	77	996	931	235	10.98
1952	221,990	108,089	8,694	80	1,030	963	235	10.95

[1] Age of cane equals 18 to 24 months of growth.   [2] See note 3, table 779.
[3] One ton of raw sugar 96° test is assumed to be equivalent to 0.9346 ton of refined.
[4] Based on tonnage of cane used.

Source: Data collected by Department of Agriculture, Bureau of Agricultural Economics, through the Hawaiian Sugar Planters' Association. Published in annual report, *Agricultural Statistics,* and in *The World Sugar Situation.*

No. 781.—CANE SUGAR—PRODUCTION IN PUERTO RICO: 1941 TO 1952

YEAR [1]	ACREAGE IN CANE		SUGARCANE HARVESTED		SUGAR PRODUCED, RAW VALUE [2]		Blackstrap molasses produced
	Grown	Harvested	Total	Per acre	Total	Per ton of cane	
	1,000 acres	1,000 acres	1,000 tons	Tons	1,000 tons	Pounds	1,000 gallons
1941	337	236	7,	32.8	940	243	40, 277
1942	338	308	10,	32.5	1, 156	231	51, 458
1943	319	310	8,	27.9	1, 046	241	40, 098
1944	318	280	5,	20.0	729	260	28, 144
1945	335	289	7,	27.7	971	243	40, 531
1946	352	303	7,	24.9	916	243	38, 454
1947	365	325	9,	28.6	1, 096	236	50, 975
1948	369	336	9, 745	28.4	1, 118	234	55, 056
1949	376	353	10, 669	31.2	1, 288	234	59, 632
1950	382	367	10, 615	28.9	1, 299	245	49, 522
1951	391	366	10, 501	28.7	1, 238	236	60, 286
1952	⁸ 425	⁸ 388	12, 537	⁸ 32.3	1, 372	219	69, 755

[1] Grinding begins in January. About ⅓ of the crop is 18 months' growth and ⅔ is 12 months' growth.
[2] As defined in Sugar Act of 1948.
[3] Preliminary.

Source: Department of Agriculture, Bureau of Agricultural Economics; compiled from data of Sugar Branch, Production and Marketing Administration, and Association of Sugar Producers of Puerto Rico; annual report, *Agricultural Statistics*. Also published in *The World Sugar Situation*.

No. 782.—MAPLE SIRUP AND SUGAR—PRODUCTION, 1859 TO 1952, AND BY STATES, 1950, 1951, AND 1952

STATE AND YEAR	Trees tapped	Sugar made	Sirup made	Total product in terms of sugar [1]	STATE AND YEAR	Trees tapped	Sugar made	Sirup made	Total product in terms of sugar [1]
BUREAU OF THE CENSUS					DEPARTMENT OF AGRICULTURE—con.				
	Thou-sands	1,000 pounds	1,000 gallons	1,000 pounds	New Hampshire	Thou-sands	1,000 pounds	1,000 gallons	1,000 pounds
United States:					1950	281	22	64	534
1859		40, 120	1, 598	52, 901	1951	261	14	57	470
1869		28, 444	921	35, 812	1952	248	6	55	446
1879		36, 576	1, 796	50, 944	Vermont:				
1889		32, 953	2, 258	51, 020	1950	3, 465	103	875	7, 103
1899		11, 929	2, 057	28, 382	1951	3, 118	60	733	5, 924
1909	18, 900	14, 024	4, 106	46, 912	1952	2, 900	53	664	5, 365
1919	17, 457	9, 692	3, 508	37, 754	Massachusetts:				
1929	(²)	1, 341	2, 341	20, 070	1950	173	18	54	450
1939	9, 955	356	2, 456	20, 007	1951	166	16	53	440
1949	7, 691	147	1, 466	11, 876	1952	149	11	34	283
DEPARTMENT OF AGRICULTURE					New York:				
					1950	2, 107	46	505	4, 086
					1951	1, 960	43	466	3, 771
Total (10 States): [3] [4]					1952	1, 803	31	415	3, 351
1940	9, 970	394	2, 601	21, 202	Pennsylvania:				
1941	9, 850	324	2, 013	16, 428	1950	451	27	114	939
1942	10, 046	560	2, 987	24, 456	1951	422	22	98	806
1943	9, 444	463	2, 613	21, 367	1952	414	27	102	843
1944	8, 891	458	2, 630	21, 498	Ohio:				
1945	7, 657	202	1, 025	8, 402	1950	556	8	149	1, 200
1946	8, 257	310	1, 351	11, 118	1951	506	2	130	1, 042
1947	8, 834	303	2, 062	16, 799	1952	466	1	145	1, 161
1948	8, 404	281	1, 824	12, 422	Michigan:				
1949	8, 318	212	1, 611	13, 100	1950	432	5	93	749
1950	8, 146	257	2, 024	16, 449	1951	406	16	97	792
1951	7, 412	200	1, 763	14, 304	1952	402	6	92	742
1952	6, 958	158	1, 631	13, 206	Wisconsin:				
Maine: [5]					1950	378	15	103	839
1950	145	12	33	276	1951	284	12	79	644
1951	136	11	19	163	1952	284	10	65	530
1952	135	11	29	243	Minnesota:				
Maryland:					1950	130		20	160
1950	28	1	14	113	1951	125		19	152
1951	28	4	12	100	1952	128		16	128
1952	29	2	14	114					

[1] 1 gallon of sirup taken as equivalent to 8 pounds of sugar.   [2] Not called for on schedule.
[5] Excludes production on nonfarm lands in Somerset County, Maine.   [4] Beginning 1944, 11 States.

Source: Department of Agriculture, Bureau of Agricultural Economics, except Census figures; annual report, *Agricultural Statistics*. Data also published in *Crops and Markets* and in annual summary, *Acreage Yield, and Production of Principal Crops*.

No. 783.—SUGAR, BEET AND CANE—PRODUCTION, FOR CONTINENTAL UNITED STATES PUERTO RICO, HAWAII, PHILIPPINES, CUBA, AND WORLD: 1870 TO 1952

[In thousands of tons of 2,000 pounds. Prior to 1909, data refer to crop year beginning July 1; thereafter, crop year with beginning dates varying from Sept. to following June, except as noted for Hawaii]

YEARLY AVERAGE OR CROP YEAR (SEE HEADNOTE)	Continental U. S. and outlying areas [1]	CONTINENTAL U. S.			Puerto Rico [2]	Hawaii [3]	Philippine Islands [4]	Cuba	World total	PERCENT OF WORLD TOTAL IN—	
		Total (in terms of raw) [3]	Beet (reduced to raw) [3]	Cane (chiefly raw)						Continental U. S.	U. S. and outlying areas
1870–1874	291	73	(*)	73	95	[7] 13	110	------	(*)	(*)	(*)
1875–1879	347	96	(*)	96	78	20	132	------	(*)	(*)	(*)
1880–1884	476	135	1	130	57	64	196	------	(*)	(*)	(*)
1885–1889	542	155	1	152	73	119	196	------	(*)	(*)	(*)
1890–1894	730	304	14	271	63	145	205	------	(*)	(*)	(*)
1895–1899	312	325	46	279	56	256	174	10,944	3.0	7.5
1900–1904	1,141	542	194	348	115	359	94	12,321	4.1	8.6
1905–1909	1,603	808	447	362	255	459	141	14,786	5.1	10.7
1910–1914	2,806	980	697	291	363	604	243	19,706	5.0	11.6
1915–1919	2,838	1,069	845	224	463	600	447	19,675	5.7	13.7
1920–1924	2,938	1,233	1,017	215	476	643	531	22,394	5.5	13.1
1925–1929	3,567	1,169	1,065	128	687	804	830	30,419	4.0	13.2
1930–1934 [10]	4,662	1,632	1,396	235	896	1,042	1,111	1,847	30,820	4.5	14.8
1935–1939	4,008	1,901	1,518	474	974	980	1,068	3,192	28,630	6.7	17.0
1940–1944	3,931	1,879	1,451	428	961	981	[11] 1,065	3,685	26,402	7.1	15.3
1945–1949	4,350	1,925	1,513	455	1,134	961	353	3,761	27,436	7.2	15.3
1947	4,557	2,212	1,835	377	1,108	835	389	5,673	27,914	7.9	16.3
1948	4,815	1,847	1,370	477	1,277	966	730	5,761	31,628	5.8	15.3
1949	5,034	2,091	1,570	521	1,286	961	668	6,127	31,937	6.5	15.8
1950	5,742	2,576	2,012	564	1,228	995	935	6,349	36,186	7.1	15.9
1951	5,450	1,970	1,552	418	1,360	1,020	1,073	7,964	36,160	5.2	14.3
1952 (prel.)	5,609	2,067	1,530	557	1,190	1,075	1,345	5,680	36,699	5.7	15.3

[1] Excludes Cuba. Includes Puerto Rico, Hawaii, Phil. Isls., and beginning 1910, Virgin Islands not shown separately.
[2] Beet sugar not converted to raw prior to 1909. Refined reduced to raw basis by multiplying by 1.07.
[3] For 1900 to 1905, shipments to United States.
[4] Statistics for 1874 to 1880 represents exports. Normal grinding season begins Oct. 1. In 1923, production was from grindings of Oct. 1, 1923, to Dec. 31, 1924; beginning 1934, from grindings of the next calendar year.
[5] Exports 1871 to 1911; production 1912 and subsequently. Includes production of muscovado and panocha, low grades of sugar mostly for domestic consumption.
[6] Less than 500 tons. [7] One year only. [8] Not available.
[9] Louisiana and Texas 1909 to 1923; Louisiana only 1924 to 1927; Louisiana and Florida beginning 1928.
[10] Beginning 1930, includes centrifugal only. [11] Production for 1940; not available for 1941–44.

Sources: Department of Agriculture, Bureau of Agricultural Economics (from official sources and International Institute of Agriculture), annual report, Agricultural Statistics, and The World Sugar Situation.

No. 784.—SUGAR, CANE AND BEET: STOCKS, PRODUCTION, TRADE, AND SUPPLY AVAILABLE FOR CONSUMPTION IN CONTINENTAL UNITED STATES: 1940 TO 1952

CALENDAR YEAR	Production [1]	Visible stocks beginning of period [1] [2]	RECEIPTS FROM—		Commercial exports and shipments [3]	Dept. of Agri. net purchases for export [4]	DOMESTIC DISAPPEARANCE		
			Foreign sources [1]	Territories [1]			Military [6]	Civilian	Per capita consumption (refined) [6]
	1,000 tons	1,000 tons	1,000 tons	1,000 tons	1,000 tons	1,000 tons	1,000 tons	1,000 tons	Pounds
1940	2,104	2,613	3,006	1,855	193	------	------	7,029	94.2
1941	2,090	2,356	3,997	1,852	91	------	94	7,960	102.8
1942	2,151	2,149	1,928	1,607	55	184	424	5,035	85.7
1943	1,531	2,137	3,411	1,511	16	474	730	5,602	79.4
1944	1,512	1,706	3,926	1,848	24	317	1,014	6,172	86.3
1945	1,667	1,227	3,236	1,647	34	175	1,084	5,044	72.9
1946	1,900	1,416	3,087	1,804	256	139	119	5,541	75.9
1947	2,158	1,452	4,219	1,812	290	------	114	7,362	96.4
1948	1,917	1,939	3,220	1,734	115	------	76	7,219	96.4
1949	2,112	1,497	3,809	1,894	68	------	56	7,435	94.3
1950	2,400	1,759	3,859	2,051	100	------	64	8,104	96.7
1951	2,042	1,840	3,601	2,042	82	------	127	7,554	95.1
1952 (prel.)	2,094	1,762	3,876	2,004	29	------	184	7,859	95.9

[2] Data from Sugar Branch, Production and Marketing Administration.
[3] Includes raws for processing held by importers other than refiners.
[1] Includes sugar used in manufacture of other commodities. 1940–41, exports (Department of Commerce, Foreign Commerce and Navigation); 1942–48, quantities delivered for export (Sugar Branch, Production and Marketing Administration).
[4] Data based on allocation audits and records kept by armed forces.
[5] Adjusted for changes in invisible stocks (estimated) held by manufacturers, wholesalers, and retailers. Civilian per capita consumption, 1941–52.
[6] Includes exports for civilian feeding by military abroad.

Source: Department of Agriculture, Bureau of Agricultural Economics (except as noted); annual report, Agricultural Statistics. Also published in The World Sugar Situation.

No. 785.—Coffee, Tea, Cocoa and Chocolate—Imports: 1830 to 1952

[Coffee and tea imports represent imports from foreign countries and from Territories and possessions into continental United States. Reexports represent exports from continental United States to foreign countries and outlying Territories and possessions. Cocoa and chocolate figures represent general imports through 1932, imports for consumption, thereafter]

YEARLY AVERAGE OR YEAR	COFFEE				TEA			COCOA AND CHOCOLATE [1]	
	Imports	Reexports	Net imports per capita	Average import price	Net imports	Value	Net imports per capita	Imports	Value
	1,000 lbs.	*1,000 lbs.*	*Pounds*	*Cents per lb.*	*1,000 lbs.*	*$1,000*	*Pounds*	*1,000 lbs.*	*$1,000*
1830	51,488	3,125	2.99	8.2	6,873	1,532	0.54		
1840	94,996	18,608	5.04	9.0	16,883	4,067	.99		
1850	145,273	15,481	5.58	7.7	28,200	3,982	1.21		
1851–1860	203,190	14,710	6.78	9.0	21,028	5,361	.76		
1861–1870	173,290	8,229	4.66	10.8	32,394	8,969	.91		
1871–1880	331,925	7,911	7.19	14.7	59,536	18,550	1.32	[3] 5,132	[3] 706
1881–1890	513,039	24,725	8.52	10.8	76,534	15,071	1.34	13,504	1,891
1891–1895	585,270	8,792	8.61	[4] 16.8	89,675	13,689	1.34		
1896–1900	761,715	21,819	10.07	8.9	86,217	11,357	1.17	[3] 29,408	[3] 4,120
1901–1905	963,464	40,400	11.65	7.1	95,814	13,849	1.18	63,600	8,260
1906–1910	931,644	15,325	10.29	7.9	93,595	15,211	1.05	102,304	13,418
1911–1915	952,906	21,494	9.65	11.5	95,237	17,189	.99	161,473	19,002
1916–1920 [5]	1,227,523	67,347	11.20	13.5	106,988	22,528	1.03	346,623	45,480
1921–1925	1,343,579	35,265	11.73	15.4	92,230	24,658	.83	367,907	32,019
1926–1930	1,498,291	24,222	12.30	18.9	88,654	26,604	.74	429,338	47,044
1931–1935	1,626,316	19,520	12.81	8.7	86,892	15,359	.69	487,401	21,951
1936–1940	1,905,417	17,774	14.52	7.3	89,558	19,858	.69	622,802	33,563

			Excl. military [7]	Incl. military [8]			Excl. military [7]	Incl. military [8]		
1941–1945	2,300,918	12,309	15.02	16.63	11.5	81,121	25,527	0.58	0.59	568,728	39,022
1946–1950	2,673,293	43,673	18.12	18.08	27.6	89,396	39,424	.58	.60	626,754	143,015
1947	2,499,855	62,301	17.81	17.30	23.9	60,495	23,559	.58	.56	607,381	154,982
1948	2,770,589	38,157	18.42	18.41	25.1	88,969	43,531	.57	.57	557,293	196,864
1949	2,918,604	27,010	18.68	19.09	27.2	92,638	44,952	.59	.61	652,110	128,552
1950	2,441,910	16,784	16.30	16.48	44.6	113,376	53,099	.64	.75	711,751	176,147
1951	2,687,251	20,097	16.52	17.35	50.5	85,928	40,033	.65	.65	661,166	211,200
1952	2,685,832	22,429	16.74	16.79	51.3	92,820	38,812	.63	.63	626,519	193,269

[1] Includes prepared except confectionery.   [3] 3-year average.   [3] 9-year average
[4] Overvalued, due to depreciation of Brazilian paper milreis.   [4] Average for period 1891–1900.
[5] Average, July 1, 1915, to Dec. 31, 1920.
[7] Represents civilian consumption per capita, calculation of which excludes amounts allotted to military population, and takes into account changes in stock.
[8] Includes civilian population and military population in the U. S. and abroad.

Source: Department of Commerce, Bureau of the Census; annual report, *Foreign Commerce and Navigation of the U. S.*, records and data on shipments to and from Territories and possessions. Per capita figures from Department of Commerce, National Production Authority.

No. 786.—Silk and Silk Manufactures—Imports and Exports: 1871 to 1952

[Quantity in thousands of pounds; value, except average price per pound, in thousands of dollars]

YEARLY AVERAGE OR YEAR [1]	UNMANUFACTURED SILK, IMPORTS [2]			SILK MANUFACTURES, VALUE		YEARLY AVERAGE OR YEAR [1]	UNMANUFACTURED SILK, IMPORTS [2]			SILK MANUFACTURES, VALUE	
	Quantity	Value	Average price per pound	Imports [3]	Exports (excluding reexports) [4]		Quantity	Value	Average price per pound	Imports [3]	Exports (excluding reexports) [4]
1871–1880	[3] 1,340	[3] 6,390	$4.77	27,063	53	1946–1950	8,132	32,648	$4.01	20,708	2,947
1881–1890	5,328	16,775	3.15	34,162	83	1942	207	165	.80	1,775	1,200
1891–1900	9,259	26,843	2.90	29,776	268	1943	11	7	.64	1,069	303
1901–1905	15,798	45,968	2.91	32,215	425	1944	33	29	.88	1,419	203
1906–1910	20,281	67,414	3.32	33,725	835	1945	1,793	2,046	1.14	2,668	250
1911–1915	30,190	82,703	2.74	28,306	2,210	1946	15,587	102,587	6.58	7,408	2,330
1916–1920	45,641	235,332	5.16	47,121	16,735	1947	3,182	16,078	5.05	12,981	7,274
1921–1925	62,030	356,287	5.74	40,941	12,992	1948	7,361	15,900	2.16	24,393	1,428
1926–1930	86,458	374,715	4.33	36,383	17,293	1949	3,986	7,527	1.89	24,877	1,720
1931–1935	74,569	115,883	1.55	8,595	5,954	1950	10,543	21,151	2.01	33,881	1,985
1936–1940	58,326	109,947	1.89	8,254	6,938	1951	7,226	21,090	2.92	37,478	2,145
1941–1945	5,521	13,021	1.18	2,228	1,702	1952	12,586	37,383	2.97	34,832	2,603

[1] Fiscal years through 1915; calendar years thereafter.
[2] General imports through 1932; imports for consumption thereafter.   [3] Includes artificial silk prior to 1911.
[4] Include shipments under foreign aid programs such as UNRRA, Interim Aid, ECA, and MDAP (MSA); Civilian Supply shipments are included in 1948 and subsequent years only.   [5] Raw silk.

Source: Department of Commerce, Bureau of the Census; annual report, *Foreign Commerce and Navigation of the U. S.*, and records.

No. 787.—ANIMAL AND VEGETABLE FATS AND OILS—PRODUCTION, CONSUMPTION, AND STOCKS: 1951 AND 1952

[Data cover factory operations only, and therefore exclude considerable quantities of lard, tallow, and grease produced on farms and by local butcheries and small renderers, and quantities consumed and held in homes, hotels, restaurants, bakeries, and quantities consumed and held by painters, building contractors, garages, etc. Stocks include amounts held by and in transit to producers, factory consumers, and public storages, but exclude amounts held in private storages by retailers, wholesalers, and jobbers. Additional data on consumption and stocks of raw materials, such as cottonseed, copra, corn germs, flaxseed, soybeans, etc., and consumption data by process and end-use are contained in Facts for Industry Series M 17-1 and M 17-2]

[In thousands of pounds]

PRODUCT	1951			1952		
	Production	Consumption	Stocks, Dec. 31	Production	Consumption	Stocks, Dec. 31
VEGETABLE OILS						
Cottonseed, crude	1,415,012	1,296,592	186,292	1,710,162	1,646,430	178,154
Cottonseed, refined	1,196,575	1,105,537	292,861	1,522,945	1,277,271	344,575
Peanut, crude [1]	183,730	129,816	4,705	101,444	96,697	2,542
Peanut, refined	123,391	95,811	7,084	69,534	57,632	2,435
Corn, crude	232,126	246,065	10,508	231,567	237,136	14,215
Corn, refined	224,981	214,027	3,772	213,994	199,987	5,800
Soybean, crude	2,472,526	2,029,508	197,471	2,476,046	2,354,113	153,674
Soybean, refined	1,892,449	1,757,211	83,920	2,175,417	2,073,020	83,716
Sesame, crude	(⁷)	(⁷)	(⁷)	(⁷)	(⁷)	(⁷)
Sesame, refined	(⁷)	3,145	256	(⁷)	(⁷)	177
Olive, edible	1,943	2,415	17,701	4,429	(⁷)	4,464
Olive, inedible		787	283		196	85
Olive, sulphur foots	(⁷)	4,049	5,210	(⁷)	3,730	2,416
Palm, crude		40,307	⁵ 94,512		33,564	⁶ 16,686
Palm, refined	(⁷)	4,162	1,023	(⁷)	5,459	654
Coconut, crude	516,162	542,048	⁸ 92,073	454,562	531,219	⁹ 47,806
Coconut, refined	327,763	302,385	8,839	385,977	239,344	7,980
Palm kernel, crude		(⁷)	(⁷)		(⁷)	2,844
Palm kernel, refined	(⁷)	(⁷)	(⁷)	(⁷)	(⁷)	415
Babassu, crude	(⁷)	39,840	6,372	(⁷)	5,527	36
Babassu, refined	29,325	29,314	286	5,668	7,572	
Rapeseed, crude		3,274	395			(⁷)
Rapeseed, refined		3,485	1,926		5,372	2,293
Linseed, raw	756,838	652,379	646,147	545,318	554,096	634,069
Linseed, refined	292,306	296,003	42,031	252,132	267,274	36,566
Chinawood or tung	12,667	65,019	15,786	23,151	47,863	15,679
Perilla			(⁷)			(⁷)
Castor No. 1, crude	61,385	73,543	⁸ 13,486	55,053	57,236	⁸ 17,005
Castor No. 2, crude	17,864	30,333	⁸ 4,167	18,809	25,004	⁸ 4,068
Oiticica		10,294	7,349		10,215	3,977
Other vegetable oil, crude	42,789	31,670	11,356	20,120	34,599	13,922
Other vegetable oil, refined	22,604	22,385	3,347	19,851	19,068	3,426
ANIMAL FATS						
Lard, rendered [4]	2,531,000	⁸ 182,263	66,500	2,604,000	⁸ 188,883	154,245
Lard, refined [4]	1,669,000	94,454	37,679	1,542,000	193,244	86,749
Tallow, edible	69,224	45,086	4,742	122,475	64,465	5,609
Tallow, edible, refined	20,328	15,653	854	21,369	16,095	487
Tallow, inedible	1,901,081	1,155,567	231,102	1,442,602	1,117,612	245,739
Tallow, inedible, refined	275,078	255,520	13,488	261,354	265,342	15,022
Grease, other than wool	620,961	562,805	90,988	612,046	446,368	113,639
Wool grease	11,491	(⁷)	7,497	5,461	(⁷)	⁷ 811
Neat's-foot oil	1,929	3,976	1,092	1,777	4,180	787
FISH AND MARINE-MAMMAL OIL [9]						
Cod and cod-liver	1,466	15,153	7,377	1,524	14,465	5,576
Other liver oil	1,662	7,266	1,972	429	6,735	578
Menhaden	90,727	27,243	40,397	84,154	57,751	40,167
Sardine (pilchard) and herring	20,044	60,218	17,661	5,452	59,115	14,658
Other fish oil, except liver oil	13,130	8,360	3,352	12,551	9,739	9,475
Whale oil	93	(⁷)	496	(⁷)	(⁷)	926
Sperm oil		27,603	⁸ 24,897		⁸ 21,292	⁸ 12,522
Other marine-mammal oil	(⁷)	(⁷)	285	(⁷)	(⁷)	
Refined fish oil	22,741	22,403	1,399	(¹⁰)	19,005	1,360
FOOTS, RAW AND ACIDULATED SOAP STOCK						
Vegetable foots (100% basis)	236,463	163,673	49,534	261,656	192,104	44,996
Animal foots from refining (100% basis)	24,216	29,563	5,730	24,349	20,353	2,953
Fish and marine-mammal foots (100% basis)	4,639	6,321	1,609	(¹⁰)	2,466	1,155

See footnotes at end of table.

No. 787.—ANIMAL AND VEGETABLE FATS AND OILS—PRODUCTION, CONSUMPTION, AND STOCKS: 1951 AND 1952—Continued

[In thousands of pounds]

PRODUCT	1951			1952		
	Production	Consumption	Stocks, Dec. 31	Production	Consumption	Stocks. Dec. 31
SECONDARY PRODUCTS						
Winterised oil	497,718	285,561	26,826	569,077	324,098	31,351
Deodorised oil [11]	311,614	131,270	7,783	282,016	128,432	7,513
Stearin, vegetable oil, winter	99,228	82,873	10,793	116,446	103,761	14,819
Stearin, animal, edible	28,985	17,493	2,438	23,934	16,873	2,534
Stearin, animal, inedible	23,165	15,704	2,129	20,899	17,079	1,974
Oleo oil	46,339	4,809	3,097	45,522	6,216	3,215
Grease oil and lard oil	56,727	34,177	6,886	57,491	34,069	6,778
Tallow oil	10,711	8,440	2,594	11,568	9,319	2,885
Hydrogenated oils and fats, edible:						
Vegetable:						
Cottonseed	433,855	417,101	19,121	471,583	462,624	17,394
Soybean	660,159	621,131	16,853	886,361	838,434	30,831
Other [12]	103,613	77,012	3,371	70,425	50,233	2,629
Animal fats and oils [12]	12,666	4,739	1,637	56,883	16,583	1,935
Shortening	1,402,707	9,473	101,441	1,611,418	7,205	93,666
Margarine	1,040,718	(5)	19,004	1,285,975	(5)	25,437
Hydrogenated oils and fats, inedible:						
Vegetable	(16)	6,265	1,667	(16)	10,767	1,466
Animal	31,313	26,097	2,365	28,846	23,577	2,852
Fish	29,626	22,818	5,549	(16)	23,680	4,414
Chemically dehydrated castor oil	22,438	23,764	5,110	16,037	17,136	3,848
Fatty acid stock including spent and salvaged oils and fats, palm oil refuse, etc. (100% fatty acid basis)	4,267	18,448	3,921	3,309	13,105	3,129
Vegetable oil fatty acids from foots and other than from foots	151,307	141,989	23,233	166,956	160,642	27,351
Animal fat and oil fatty acids	207,562	206,103	15,616	155,324	153,767	12,914
Fish and marine mammal fatty acids	3,859	7,311	1,123	(16)	4,106	775
Fatty acids from fractionating or pressing:						
Stearic acid	68,134	58,051	13,807	55,978	57,835	8,819
Oleic acid	80,632	51,103	15,119	67,654	47,585	13,968
Other acids	(16)	18,091	6,083	53,602	11,905	5,186
Solid fatty acids produced by splitting hydrogenated fats and oils or by hydrogenation of fatty acids	47,890	19,626	5,381	48,065	22,558	5,558
Tall oil, crude	398,237	262,674	57,347	312,769	219,300	67,483
Tall oil, refined, including distilled and fractionated tall oil	134,580	85,021	19,179	102,860	78,322	17,530
Glycerin, crude (100% basis) [13]	211,348	229,391	14,960	187,902	212,321	11,751
Glycerin, high gravity and yellow distilled (100% basis)	77,282	83,124	15,284	81,291	76,872	11,370
Glycerin, chemically pure (100% basis) [13]	137,638	89,188	25,483	118,231	89,832	14,595

[1] Data for production and stocks held at crude oil mill locations collected by U. S. Department of Agriculture, October through December 1952.
[2] Included in "Other vegetable oils" to avoid disclosure of individual operations.
[3] Data are on a commercial stocks basis and do not include figures for stockpiles of strategic oils.
[4] Data on production collected by U. S. Department of Agriculture.
[5] Excludes quantities used in refining.
[6] Data not available.
[7] Held by wool scourers.
[8] Data from fish oil producers were collected by Fish and Wildlife Service, U. S. Department of the Interior.
[9] Included in "sperm oil."
[10] Not shown to avoid disclosure of individual operations.
[11] Winterized-deodorized oil, hydrogenated-deodorized oil and cooking and salad oil not included.
[12] Data prior to September 1951 for hydrogenated edible animal fats and oils included with other vegetable hydrogenated edible oils and fats.
[13] Includes data for synthetic glycerin.

Source: Department of Commerce, Bureau of the Census; annual report, *Animal and Vegetable Fats and Oils* (Facts for Industry, Series M17-1)

No. 788.—DOMESTIC ANIMALS ON FARMS—NUMBER, BY KIND, BY STATES: 1950 AND 1953

[All figures in thousands. See also *Historical Statistics*, series E 117-126 and 152 for U. S. totals]

DIVISION AND STATE	HORSES		MULES		ALL CATTLE		MILK COWS		SHEEP AND LAMBS		HOGS AND PIGS	
	1950 (Apr. 1)	1953 (Jan. 1)	1950 (Apr. 1)	1953 (Jan. 1)	1950 (Apr. 1)	1953 (Jan. 1)	1950 (Apr. 1)	1953 (Jan. 1) [1]	1950 (Apr. 1)	1953 (Jan. 1)	1950 (Apr. 1)	1953 (Jan. 1)
United States	5,402	3,870	2,302	1,788	76,762	94,694	21,299	23,996	31,357	31,611	55,712	54,623
New England	74	58	1		1,091	1,226	694	753	96	64	191	291
Maine	21	17	(2)		205	239	102	123	23	22	28	30
New Hampshire	9	7	(2)		110	120	67	70	7	9	12	12
Vermont	25	20	(2)		408	466	347	392	11	10	13	15
Massachusetts	10	8	(2)		190	189	113	126	10	11	96	107
Rhode Island	1	1	(2)		24	28	16	20	2	2	7	7
Connecticut	8	5	(2)		164	184	99	120	9	9	25	30
Middle Atlantic	345	179	15	12	3,876	4,493	3,196	2,523	435	430	999	1,013
New York	136	96	2	2	2,032	2,311	1,218	1,430	155	162	166	202
New Jersey	11	7	1	1	209	225	135	155	15	14	209	135
Pennsylvania	117	76	12	9	1,645	1,897	841	989	255	254	615	676
East North Central	775	562	43	29	12,151	14,627	5,308	6,068	3,844	3,372	14,283	16,051
Ohio	145	94	8	4	2,036	2,416	874	1,019	1,143	1,326	3,156	3,730
Indiana	113	71	14	9	1,781	1,997	656	671	408	330	4,580	4,406
Illinois	194	125	17	12	2,928	3,580	909	931	561	759	6,045	6,297
Michigan	103	65	2	2	1,696	2,002	794	963	366	442	900	794
Wisconsin	219	148	2	2	3,739	4,152	2,076	2,504	269	273	1,371	1,535
West North Central	1,552	988	96	85	22,100	25,600	5,393	5,415	4,813	5,343	28,200	23,705
Minnesota	257	156	3	2	3,110	3,750	1,364	1,454	665	971	3,385	3,307
Iowa	248	130	9	4	4,540	5,113	1,170	1,145	898	1,300	10,716	11,465
Missouri	326	206	63	54	3,261	3,950	923	1,014	1,160	943	3,912	3,736
North Dakota	161	113	1	1	1,668	1,742	367	422	396	513	343	362
South Dakota	171	115	2	1	2,513	3,052	345	350	889	1,084	1,245	1,008
Nebraska	210	135	7	4	3,629	4,965	460	450	314	810	3,360	2,397
Kansas	182	120	12	9	3,509	4,428	664	580	511	832	1,300	1,042
South Atlantic	444	353	737	607	5,449	6,989	1,767	2,119	996	761	5,106	5,401
Delaware	6	5	2	1	60	75	31	42	3	2	39	46
Maryland	40	23	8	7	431	539	204	255	50	45	349	275
District of Columbia	(2)		(2)		(2)		(2)		(2)		1	
Virginia	133	97	62	56	1,190	1,383	419	464	454	318	797	743
West Virginia	86	71	6	5	568	617	204	226	422	327	197	190
North Carolina	89	75	263	222	696	892	333	399	50	48	1,231	1,303
South Carolina	24	21	147	124	370	473	141	168	4	4	598	600
Georgia	39	37	215	186	1,003	1,358	308	387	10	13	1,837	1,813
Florida	27	24	34	24	1,101	1,662	131	156	4	3	450	531
East South Central	530	423	880	731	6,052	7,213	2,131	2,439	1,442	1,646	4,833	4,060
Kentucky	199	155	158	133	1,632	1,843	636	661	982	988	1,530	1,100
Tennessee	144	130	226	200	1,561	1,774	638	701	366	274	1,366	1,061
Alabama	68	55	220	179	1,269	1,708	355	444	25	21	1,061	1,143
Mississippi	118	93	275	219	1,569	1,888	502	504	67	83	875	756
West South Central	861	630	495	304	12,921	15,347	2,112	2,454	8,042	5,806	3,445	3,425
Arkansas	151	126	133	101	1,153	1,505	379	462	50	42	753	546
Louisiana	120	101	113	92	1,285	1,771	276	349	91	122	626	453
Oklahoma	203	135	30	22	2,656	3,218	534	556	151	131	774	406
Texas	387	286	129	89	7,825	8,853	923	1,085	7,750	5,511	1,292	1,119
Mountain	653	536	21	18	8,290	10,342	714	799	9,423	10,874	788	713
Montana	141	113	2	1	1,736	2,172	111	110	1,337	1,780	106	130
Idaho	88	66	3	3	949	1,237	186	222	1,500	1,113	161	143
Wyoming	83	66	1	1	1,028	1,201	46	50	1,829	2,261	50	59
Colorado	117	87	4	4	1,776	2,161	169	182	1,657	1,838	262	218
New Mexico	82	71	4	3	1,138	1,380	52	55	1,197	1,419	69	60
Arizona	64	61	6	4	656	974	42	52	473	430	26	26
Utah	53	44	1	1	562	733	93	111	1,101	1,528	72	55
Nevada	27	26	1	1	424	624	14	17	321	505	20	22
Pacific	349	298	11	10	4,734	5,780	1,171	1,365	3,338	3,615	828	782
Washington	62	46	2	2	878	1,032	254	375	368	338	123	116
Oregon	72	54	3	3	1,099	1,374	204	233	913	674	157	140
California	115	100	7	5	2,757	3,393	713	857	2,057	2,003	539	526

[1] Represents cows and heifers 2 years old and over kept for milk.
[2] Less than 500.

Source: 1950 data, Department of Commerce, Bureau of the Census; *U. S. Census of Agriculture: 1950*, Vol. II. 1953 data, Department of Agriculture, Bureau of Agricultural Economics, published in *Livestock on Farms Jan. 1,*

No. 789.—LIVESTOCK ON FARMS—VALUE BY STATES: 1945 AND 1950

[In thousands of dollars. 1950 covers horses, mules, cattle, hogs, sheep, goats (7 States), chickens, and turkeys; 1945 excludes turkeys]

DIVISION AND STATE	1945	1950	DIVISION AND STATE	1945	1950
United States	8,472,431	11,667,312	South Atlantic—Continued		
			Virginia	126,366	186,708
New England	176,541	184,394	West Virginia	52,366	80,663
Maine	27,755	30,393	North Carolina	144,248	146,287
New Hampshire	18,974	18,004	South Carolina	71,194	72,268
Vermont	51,637	58,493	Georgia	132,762	143,680
Massachusetts	39,292	40,028	Florida	67,956	101,673
Rhode Island	5,523	5,323			
Connecticut	33,360	32,153	East South Central	565,149	801,455
			Kentucky	160,584	257,415
Middle Atlantic	617,153	697,864	Tennessee	147,309	215,817
New York	319,417	349,391	Alabama	119,595	154,287
New Jersey	52,464	65,467	Mississippi	137,661	173,936
Pennsylvania	245,272	283,006			
			West South Central	1,042,842	1,600,372
East North Central	1,642,888	2,158,965	Arkansas	100,694	132,709
Ohio	262,203	352,495	Louisiana	110,874	147,861
Indiana	248,861	331,213	Oklahoma	206,952	300,242
Illinois	435,045	564,483	Texas	624,322	1,019,561
Michigan	206,056	262,834			
Wisconsin	490,724	647,941	Mountain	775,323	1,264,265
			Montana	174,633	253,354
West North Central	2,514,968	3,439,576	Idaho	97,254	150,086
Minnesota	422,294	535,226	Wyoming	99,886	178,885
Iowa	689,958	889,798	Colorado	152,086	261,143
Missouri	329,213	493,729	New Mexico	84,650	162,111
North Dakota	161,368	201,505	Arizona	55,677	90,105
South Dakota	238,962	364,750	Utah	69,320	103,817
Nebraska	357,216	495,180	Nevada	41,818	64,764
Kansas	315,957	459,386			
			Pacific	479,698	707,332
South Atlantic	657,869	813,089	Washington	82,279	118,065
Delaware	9,175	9,865	Oregon	95,592	141,040
Maryland	53,669	71,893	California	301,826	448,227
Dist. of Columbia	133	51			

Source: Department of Commerce, Bureau of Census; *U. S. Census of Agriculture: 1950*, Vol. II.

No. 790.—LIVESTOCK—NUMBER, VALUE PER HEAD, PRODUCTION, AND PRICES: 1910 TO 1953

[See also *Historical Statistics*, series E 117-134]

YEAR	NUMBER ON FARMS AND VALUE PER HEAD									
	All cattle		Hogs (incl. pigs)		Stock sheep		Horses [1]		Mules [1]	
	Number (1,000 head)	Value per head	Number (1,000 head)	Value per head	Number (1,000 head)	Value per head	Number (1,000 head)	Value per head	Number (1,000 head)	Value per head
CENSUS RETURNS [2]										
1910 (Apr. 15)........	53,997	$26.81	58,134	$10.02	39,644	$6.13	19,220	$107.23	4,101	$127.02
1920 (Jan. 1)........	66,640	54.80	59,346	16.66	35,094	11.20	19,767	90.15	5,432	145.45
1930 (Apr. 1)........	54,250	58.70	52,794	17.20	41,780	8.21	13,384	67.51	5,354	82.60
1940 (Apr. 1)........	60,675	42.52	34,087	8.36	40,129	5.90	10,087	75.92	3,845	112.46
1945 (Jan. 1)........	82,664	67.78	46,735	21.14	41,234	8.71	8,499	64.17	3,130	136.62
1950 (Apr. 1)........	76,762	119.02	55,722	19.70	31,387	17.60	5,402	49.50	2,202	95.38
ESTIMATES JAN. 1										
1940..............	66,309	40.60	61,165	7.73	46,266	6.35	10,444	77.30	4,084	116.00
1941..............	71,755	43.30	54,363	8.34	47,441	6.77	10,195	68.20	3,911	107.60
1942..............	76,025	55.00	60,607	15.60	49,346	8.66	9,873	64.70	3,782	107.00
1943..............	81,204	69.30	73,881	22.50	48,196	8.66	9,605	79.80	3,636	127.00
1944..............	85,334	68.40	83,741	17.50	44,370	8.08	9,192	78.60	3,421	143.00
1945..............	85,573	66.90	59,373	20.60	39,609	8.45	8,715	64.90	3,285	134.00
1946..............	82,235	76.20	61,306	24.00	35,525	9.57	8,081	57.50	3,027	133.00
1947..............	80,554	97.50	56,810	36.00	31,805	12.20	7,340	59.30	2,789	141.00
1948..............	77,171	117.00	54,590	42.90	29,486	15.00	6,704	55.70	2,575	133.00
1949..............	76,830	135.00	56,257	36.30	28,940	17.00	6,096	52.50	2,402	116.00
1950..............	77,963	124.00	58,852	27.20	26,182	17.80	5,548	46.00	2,253	99.10
1951..............	82,025	160.00	62,852	33.30	27,253	26.50	4,993	43.50	2,074	81.60
1952..............	87,844	179.00	62,582	30.00	26,080	28.00	4,330	45.80	1,913	72.40
1953 (prel.)......	93,696	128.00	54,632	25.90	27,857	15.80	3,870	47.20	1,766	65.30

YEAR	LIVE WEIGHT PRODUCTION AND ANNUAL AVERAGE PRICE RECEIVED BY FARMERS, PER 100 POUNDS						
	All cattle			Hogs		Sheep	
	Production [3] (1,000 lbs.)	Price, beef cattle	Price, veal calves	Production [3] (1,000 lbs.)	Price per 100 lbs.	Production [3] (1,000 lbs.)	Price, sheep	Price, lambs
1940..............	15,702,110	$7.56	$8.83	17,044,404	$5.39	2,100,928	$3.95	$8.10
1941..............	17,029,460	8.82	10.30	17,489,455	9.00	2,251,390	5.06	9.58
1942..............	18,567,996	10.70	12.30	21,105,123	13.00	2,313,319	5.80	11.70
1943..............	19,150,375	11.90	13.30	26,374,715	13.70	2,107,891	5.57	13.00
1944..............	19,708,296	10.80	12.40	30,582,573	13.10	1,988,399	6.01	12.50
1945..............	19,517,065	12.10	13.00	18,843,444	14.00	1,911,980	6.56	13.10
1946..............	18,998,709	14.50	15.20	18,744,289	17.30	1,761,938	7.48	15.60
1947..............	19,129,845	18.40	20.40	18,159,230	24.10	1,566,557	8.39	20.50
1948..............	18,401,950	22.20	24.40	15,222,066	23.10	1,368,456	9.60	22.80
1949..............	19,274,480	19.80	21.60	19,487,476	18.10	1,277,713	9.27	22.40
1950..............	20,487,888	23.30	26.30	20,000,834	18.00	1,330,696	11.80	25.10
1951 (prel.)......	21,692,410	28.70	32.00	21,349,211	20.00	1,349,355	16.00	31.00

[1] Jan. 1 estimates include colts.

[2] Census figures for 1910 are for animals over 3½ months old; 1920, 1945, and 1950, animals of all ages; 1930, animals 3 months and over except sheep (6 months and over); 1940, animals over 3 months, except hogs (over 4 months) and sheep (over 6 months).

[3] Includes adjustment for livestock shipped in and in inventory changes.

Source: Census returns—Department of Commerce, Bureau of the Census; *U. S. Census of Agriculture: 1950*, Vol. II. All other data—Department of Agriculture, Bureau of Agricultural Economics; annual report, *Agricultural Statistics*, and annual *U. S. Livestock Reports*.

No. 791.—Domestic Animals—Receipts and Shipments, by Kind, by Stockyards: 1948 to 1952

[In thousands. Total for all stockyards reporting covers about 65 stockyards]

ITEM AND YEAR	Total, all stockyards reporting	9 STOCKYARDS										All other stockyards reporting
		Total	Chicago	Denver	Fort Worth	Kansas City	Omaha	St. Joseph	St. Louis National Stock Yards	Sioux City	South St. Paul	
CATTLE												
Receipts:												
1948	18,673	10,048	1,694	849	786	1,543	1,521	573	991	1,132	959	8,625
1949	18,828	10,695	1,850	838	578	1,673	1,692	620	940	1,332	1,172	8,133
1950	17,917	10,100	1,780	872	540	1,438	1,638	566	863	1,292	1,111	7,817
1951	17,016	9,463	1,623	936	590	1,176	1,667	586	831	1,198	878	7,553
1952	18,942	10,634	1,853	979	692	1,550	1,824	617	970	1,221	928	8,308
Shipments:												
1948	9,245	4,740	685	535	391	846	776	163	290	746	307	4,505
1949	8,914	4,768	679	477	263	949	725	186	285	853	352	4,146
1950	8,357	4,304	630	478	245	764	674	176	217	796	323	4,053
1951	9,009	4,975	713	551	334	675	883	228	464	808	319	4,034
1952	9,784	5,328	834	514	332	952	928	221	472	796	279	4,456
CALVES												
Receipts:												
1948	6,277	2,056	188	112	329	222	107	99	435	73	490	4,221
1949	5,741	2,000	164	123	245	221	119	78	388	118	544	3,741
1950	5,225	1,850	115	107	276	213	107	58	379	105	491	3,375
1951	4,722	1,781	106	115	349	173	115	69	356	91	406	2,941
1952	4,786	1,969	112	117	266	311	161	80	368	144	410	2,817
Shipments:												
1948	2,601	756	22	75	185	85	35	28	127	54	145	1,845
1949	2,410	801	16	89	166	87	49	23	115	86	172	1,609
1950	2,389	838	12	84	211	112	39	24	95	87	174	1,551
1951	2,346	934	14	99	266	105	40	40	121	79	170	1,412
1952	2,266	939	17	92	170	190	60	39	135	114	122	1,327
SHEEP AND LAMBS												
Receipts:												
1948	19,814	10,604	888	2,394	1,587	1,380	1,301	943	741	581	788	9,210
1949	15,843	7,814	623	1,858	928	914	922	732	599	492	746	8,029
1950	15,435	7,996	654	1,880	1,055	1,042	899	673	676	494	624	7,439
1951	13,718	6,678	523	1,726	860	556	853	609	535	503	512	7,040
1952	15,772	8,087	887	1,872	899	746	1,160	616	670	518	719	7,685
Shipments:												
1948	10,236	4,572	236	1,546	587	619	573	188	194	266	365	5,664
1949	8,932	3,871	201	1,349	460	442	382	205	181	236	416	5,061
1950	8,859	4,133	230	1,367	582	573	359	208	233	260	320	4,726
1951	8,229	3,877	171	1,379	426	367	381	251	300	309	293	4,352
1952	9,037	4,223	200	1,408	392	496	518	222	357	270	360	4,814
HOGS												
Receipts:												
1948	30,611	16,000	3,342	897	749	738	2,331	1,373	2,681	1,812	2,076	14,611
1949	33,118	17,401	3,425	1,136	584	757	2,573	1,472	2,869	1,948	2,637	15,717
1950	35,325	18,479	3,670	1,092	687	758	2,734	1,610	3,109	2,044	2,775	16,846
1951	38,722	20,872	3,907	1,301	835	3,164	2,020	3,535	2,373	2,955	17,850	
1952	38,017	20,338	3,869	1,239	789	812	3,030	1,806	3,217	2,500	3,076	17,679
Shipments:												
1948	10,196	3,995	428	437	49	346	583	235	754	724	441	6,201
1949	10,885	4,283	434	546	72	364	566	248	824	724	505	6,602
1950	11,459	4,225	499	465	59	291	553	205	833	735	584	7,234
1951	12,773	5,422	501	609	67	306	681	374	1,429	535	620	7,351
1952	12,387	5,100	566	598	42	216	705	251	1,164	879	679	7,287
HORSES AND MULES												
Receipts:												
1948	252	62	(¹)	3	16	21	1	(¹)	16	4	1	190
1949	175	46	(¹)	2	13	19	(¹)	(¹)	9	1	1	129
1950	137	37	(¹)	2	9	16	(¹)	1	4	4	1	100
1951	124	21	(¹)	1	8	8	(¹)	(¹)	1	1		103
1952	84	9	(¹)	1	4	1	......	(¹)	1	2	(¹)	75

¹ Less than 500 head.

Source: Department of Agriculture, Production and Marketing Administration; annual report, *Agricultural Statistics*. Data are published currently in mimeographed form.

No. 792.—MEAT—SLAUGHTERING, PRODUCTION, AND PRICES: 1916 TO 1951

[Prices are simple averages of monthly prices at Chicago, except those for beef which are weighted average prices at Chicago. See also *Historical Statistics*, series E 136-151]

YEAR OR YEARLY AVERAGE	ANIMALS SLAUGHTERED (1,000 head)		Price (live weight) per cwt. (dollars)	Production, dressed weight (million pounds)	ANIMALS SLAUGHTERED (1,000 head)		Price (live weight) per cwt. (dollars)	Production, dressed weight (million pounds)
	Total [1]	Under Federal Inspection			Total [1]	Under Federal Inspection		
	BEEF [2]				VEAL			
1916-1920	15,025	9,536	12.91	6,897	7,633	3,380	14.35	764
1921-1925	13,974	8,979	9.13	6,617	9,289	4,556	9.78	910
1926-1930	13,800	8,982	11.82	6,309	8,123	4,739	12.07	830
1931-1935	13,964	8,799	7.44	6,618	8,585	5,175	7.08	959
1936-1940	15,110	10,001	9.97	7,051	9,580	5,668	9.91	1,080
1941-1945	18,766	12,686	14.41	8,977	11,240	6,344	14.36	1,351
1946-1950	19,739	13,349	24.29	8,371	12,056	6,396	31.40	1,407
1946	19,824	11,402	19.16	9,373	12,176	5,841	16.87	1,443
1947	22,404	15,524	26.83	10,452	13,738	7,963	24.68	1,405
1948	19,177	12,904	30.98	9,075	12,378	6,907	29.02	1,423
1949	18,765	13,222	25.80	9,439	11,898	6,449	27.04	1,364
1950	18,624	13,103	29.35	9,588	10,504	5,690	31.08	1,230
1951 (prel.)	17,100	11,879	35.72	8,945	8,912	4,985	37.19	1,051
	PORK				LAMB AND MUTTON [4]			
1916-1920	63,179	39,606	14.78	7,947	14,065	11,066	15.06	596
1921-1925	66,860	46,289	9.04	8,290	15,454	11,861	12.53	596
1926-1930	67,901	46,285	10.22	8,550	17,648	14,010	13.54	698
1931-1935	65,740	41,435	5.57	8,248	22,090	17,405	7.37	894
1936-1940	63,109	39,130	8.06	8,242	21,724	17,427	9.44	870
1941-1945	83,026	54,765	13.14	11,809	24,992	21,340	13.59	1,039
1946-1950	75,049	50,224	20.46	10,541	17,178	15,154	23.53	743
1946	76,115	44,394	18.40	11,180	22,788	19,664	18.40	968
1947	74,001	49,116	24.45	10,602	18,706	16,667	22.68	799
1948	70,859	47,615	23.14	10,055	17,871	15,843	26.04	747
1949	74,997	53,052	18.12	10,389	13,780	12,126	26.54	608
1950	79,563	56,964	18.20	10,714	13,344	11,739	27.54	597
1951 (prel.)	85,581	62,054	20.12	11,463	11,418	10,066	34.31	522

[1] Includes inspected, noninspected, retail, and farm slaughter.
[2] Prices are for beef steers, all grades, excluding western.
[3] Excludes animals slaughtered under government account.
[4] Includes slaughter under Emergency Government Relief Purchase Program in 1934-1935.
[5] Prices are for lambs only; (sheep represent smaller part of animals slaughtered).

Source: Department of Agriculture, Bureau of Agricultural Economics; annual report, *Agricultural Statistics* and records.

No. 793.—DOMESTIC ANIMALS—AVERAGE PRICES RECEIVED BY FARMERS AND AVERAGE CHICAGO MARKET PRICE, BY KIND: 1916 TO 1951

[Milk cows, dollars per head; others in dollars per 100 pounds, live weight. Prices are weighted calendar year averages, except those for milk cows at local markets, and calves, sheep, and lambs at Chicago, which are simple averages of monthly prices. See also *Historical Statistics*, series E 128, 129, 131, 132, 134, 139, 142, 147, and 151]

PERIOD	Milk cows at local market, per head	BEEF CATTLE [1]		CALVES, VEAL		SHEEP		LAMBS		HOGS	
		Local market	Chicago	Local market	Chicago	Local market	Chicago	Local market	Chicago	Local market	Chicago
1916-1920	79.80	8.77	12.91	11.00	14.35	8.81	10.26	11.90	15.06	12.54	14.78
1921-1925	56.30	5.91	9.13	7.96	9.78	6.34	7.02	10.15	12.53	8.34	9.04
1926-1930	79.56	8.21	11.82	10.61	13.07	6.76	6.57	11.01	13.54	9.65	10.22
1931-1935	40.18	4.74	7.44	5.72	7.08	2.87	2.81	5.67	7.37	5.08	5.57
1936-1940	57.16	6.81	9.97	8.09	9.91	3.94	4.04	7.97	9.44	7.68	8.06
1941-1945	96.68	10.86	14.41	12.36	14.36	6.48	6.44	11.96	13.59	12.36	13.14
1946-1950	169.90	19.66	26.20	21.82	25.92	9.39	9.85	21.28	23.53	20.16	20.46
1946	131.00	14.50	19.16	15.20	16.87	7.48	7.83	15.60	18.40	17.50	18.40
1947	182.00	18.40	26.83	20.40	24.68	8.50	8.46	20.80	22.68	24.10	24.45
1948	185.00	22.29	30.98	24.40	29.02	9.60	12.60	22.80	26.04	23.14	23.14
1949	182.00	19.80	25.80	22.60	27.54	9.27	10.07	22.40	26.54	18.10	18.12
1950	185.00	22.30	29.35	24.30	31.08	11.60	12.19	26.10	27.54	18.20	18.20
1951 (prel.)	346.00	28.70	35.72	32.00	37.19	14.00	16.98	31.00	34.31	20.00	20.12

[1] Chicago prices are for beef steers, all grades, excluding Western.

Source: Department of Agriculture, Bureau of Agricultural Economics and Production and Marketing Administration; annual report, *Agricultural Statistics*.

No. 794.—MEATS AND LARD—PRODUCTION, FOREIGN TRADE, AND CONSUMPTION BY KIND: 1943 TO 1951

[All quantities, except per capita, in millions of pounds of carcass weight equivalent. Edible byproducts are excluded. Production of pork excluding lard comprises weight of dressed hog carcass less head bones and less all carcass fat rendered into lard. Lard production represents rendered weight of lard. and lard exports represent rendered lard, including neutral lard. Federally inspected production omits production in Hawaii and Virgin Islands. Uninspected production is made up of farm and retail slaughter and all wholesale slaughter that is not Federally inspected. Commercial exports include commercial shipments to territories; they do not include USDA exports and shipments for Lend-Lease, UNRRA or other claimants, nor do they include shipments for military civilian feeding or voluntary relief feeding. Civilian consumption is calculated from production and foreign trade, with an allowance for changes in stocks, and with deduction of military takings, and of deliveries to USDA through 1947. See also *Historical Statistics*, series E 138, 142, 146, and 150 for total production of beef, veal, lamb and mutton, and pork]

	PRODUCTION			Exports of U. S. production	Imports for consumption	CIVILIAN CONSUMPTION	
ITEM AND YEAR	Total	Federally inspected	Uninspected			Total	Per capita (pounds)
All meats (excluding lard):							
1943	24,482	16,829	7,653	70	235	18,921	144.9
1944	25,178	17,921	7,257	98	190	19,827	152.2
1945	23,691	15,359	8,332	75	130	18,742	143.2
1946	22,934	13,795	9,139	117	20	21,344	152.1
1947	23,338	16,236	7,102	312	64	22,142	153.1
1948	21,300	14,721	6,579	138	350	21,110	143.4
1949	21,662	15,632	6,030	136	242	21,330	142.6
1950	22,079	16,040	6,039	135	368	21,680	142.4
1951	21,909	15,886	6,023	157	670	20,803	135.8
Beef:							
1943	8,571	5,966	2,605	26	225	6,860	52.5
1944	9,112	6,652	2,460	37	189	7,146	54.9
1945	10,276	7,236	3,040	34	127	7,665	58.6
1946	9,373	5,661	3,712	35	19	8,533	60.8
1947	10,432	7,535	2,897	176	64	9,916	68.6
1948	9,075	6,433	2,642	44	341	9,153	62.2
1949	9,439	6,998	2,441	27	228	9,420	63.0
1950	9,538	7,051	2,487	21	322	9,517	62.5
1951	8,843	6,431	2,412	18	147	8,462	55.2
Veal:							
1943	1,167	597	570	3	1	1,059	8.1
1944	1,738	926	812	4	1	1,594	12.2
1945	1,664	823	841	3	1	1,536	11.7
1946	1,443	642	801	3	1	1,382	9.8
1947	1,605	904	701	17	(¹)	1,545	10.7
1948	1,423	791	632	4	5	1,384	9.4
1949	1,334	746	588	2	7	1,311	8.8
1950	1,230	667	563	2	10	1,206	7.9
1951	1,061	583	478	2	14	1,005	6.6
Lamb and mutton:							
1943	1,104	958	146	3	1	830	6.4
1944	1,024	887	137	3	(¹)	857	6.6
1945	1,054	913	141	4	--------	943	7.2
1946	968	850	118	4	--------	923	6.6
1947	799	717	82	12	(¹)	762	5.2
1948	747	665	82	5	3	733	5.0
1949	603	536	67	3	4	606	4.0
1950	597	534	63	2	3	596	3.9
1951	522	465	57	1	10	518	3.4
Pork (excluding lard):							
1943	13,640	9,308	4,332	38	8	10,172	77.9
1944	13,304	9,456	3,848	54	(¹)	10,230	78.5
1945	10,697	6,387	4,310	34	2	8,598	65.7
1946	11,150	6,642	4,508	75	(¹)	10,506	74.9
1947	10,502	7,090	3,422	107	(¹)	9,919	68.6
1948	10,055	6,832	3,223	85	1	9,840	66.8
1949	10,286	7,352	2,934	104	3	9,993	66.8
1950	10,714	7,788	2,926	110	33	10,361	68.1
1951	11,483	8,407	3,076	136	499	10,818	70.6
Lard:							
1943	2,865	2,080	785	776	1	1,820	13.9
1944	3,054	2,367	687	894	(¹)	1,824	14.0
1945	2,066	1,311	755	559	(¹)	1,622	12.4
1946	2,136	1,344	792	470	(¹)	1,667	11.9
1947	2,402	1,722	680	387	(¹)	1,904	13.2
1948	2,321	1,680	641	322	(¹)	1,972	13.4
1949	2,534	1,923	611	663	(¹)	1,888	12.6
1950	2,631	2,009	622	522	(¹)	2,089	13.7
1951	2,864	2,225	639	742	(¹)	2,104	13.7

¹ Less than 500,000 pounds.

Source: Department of Agriculture, Bureau of Agricultural Economics; *The Livestock and Meat Situation* and *The National Food Situation*.

No. 795.—Dairying—Cows Kept for Milk and Production and Prices of
Dairy Products: 1930 to 1951

[See also *Historical Statistics*, series E 152-170]

ITEM	1930	1935	1940	1945	1949	1950	1951
Cows and heifers, 2 yrs. old and over, kept for milk, Jan. 1, number (1,000 head)	22,032	26,082	24,940	27,770	23,862	23,853	23,722
Value per head	$82.70	$30.17	$57.30	$99.40	$193.00	$177.00	$218.00
Milk produced on farms during year (million pounds)	100,158	101,205	109,412	119,828	116,103	116,602	114,841
Whole milk sold from farms during year (million pounds) [1]	41,344	42,694	53,261	74,895	77,824	78,140	78,447
Production of dairy products:							
Butter, total (1,000 lbs.) [2]	2,121,032	2,171,490	2,238,516	1,690,407	1,687,891	1,647,988	1,451,831
Factory	1,597,747	1,633,380	1,836,826	1,363,717	1,412,111	1,385,408	1,203,981
Farm	523,285	538,110	402,690	335,690	275,780	261,580	248,850
Cheese, factory (1,000 lbs.) [3]	499,698	620,731	765,490	1,114,772	1,199,442	1,191,487	1,160,996
Evaporated and condensed milk (unskimmed) (1,000 lbs.)	1,761,390	2,081,615	2,780,778	4,195,580	3,105,712	3,206,388	3,226,708
Ice cream (1,000 gallons) [4]	240,750	199,355	318,086	476,357	557,929	554,361	566,704
Milk equivalent of manufactured dairy products (million pounds) [5]	54,764	56,751	62,774	51,894	60,682	60,199	55,347
Wholesale prices:							
Wisconsin Cheese Exchange, twins (cents per lb.)	16.4	14.3	14.3	23.2	30.4	30.8	37.5
Butter, N. Y. (Grade A) (cents per lb.)	36.5	29.6	29.5	42.8	61.5	63.2	69.9
Prices received by farmers:							
Butter, per pound (cents)	36.3	26.7	26.6	45.3	58.0	56.8	60.8
Butterfat in cream, per pound (cents)	34.5	28.1	25.0	50.3	61.6	62.0	76.0
Whole milk:							
Wholesale, per 100 lbs.	$2.21	$1.74	$1.82	$3.19	$3.96	$3.89	$4.58
Retail, per quart (cents)	11.3	9.8	10.3	13.4	18.6	18.5	19.9

[1] Includes sales to plants and dealers, and retail deliveries by farmers direct to consumer.
[2] Includes whey butter.
[3] Excludes cottage, pot, bakers', and full skim American-type.
[4] Includes data for ice cream made by counter freezers and by other small retailers.
[5] Based on State data net. Includes whole milk equivalent of farm butter.

Source: Department of Agriculture, Bureau of Agricultural Economics; annual report, *Agricultural Statistics*.

No. 796.—Animals Butchered and Animals Sold Alive—Farms Reporting, Number, and Value, by Kind: 1949

ITEM	Cattle and calves, total	Cattle	Calves	Hogs and pigs	Sheep and lambs	Horses and mules
ANIMALS BUTCHERED						
Farms reporting	980,487	461,302	536,064	3,086,720	[1] 22,348	(²)
Number (thousands)	1,367	587	710	7,369	[1] 187	(²)
ANIMALS SOLD ALIVE						
Farms reporting	2,982,616	1,866,166	2,310,428	2,097,807	271,582	255,149
Number (thousands)	36,319	20,692	15,627	65,512	20,003	622
Value (thousands of dollars)	4,297,320	3,374,007	928,313	2,385,737	341,304	39,965

[1] Totals for Mountain and Pacific States and Texas.   ² Not available.

No. 797.—Specified Livestock Products—Quantity and Value, by Kind: 1944 and 1949

PRODUCT	FARMS REPORTING		Unit of quantity	QUANTITY (THOUSANDS)		VALUE (THOUSAND OF DOLLARS)	
	1944	1949		1944	1949	1944	1949
Any dairy products sold	2,472,709	2,006,831				2,531,406	3,079,133
Whole milk sold	1,162,218	1,096,650	Lb.	65,221,989	68,529,441	2,114,664	2,716,141
Cream sold (butterfat content)	1,176,457	862,128	Lb.	805,102	582,398	401,774	352,362
Butter, buttermilk, skim milk, and cheese sold	217,128	120,570	Lb.	35,042	(²)	[1] 14,950	10,428
Wool shorn	401,634	286,594	Lb.	278,979	178,753	115,282	86,533
Chicken eggs sold	(²)	2,420,718	Doz.	(²)	2,409,647	568,185	1,008,401
Chickens sold	(²)	1,712,435	No.	(²)	(²)	(²)	587,627
Turkeys raised	192,540	162,344	No.	27,202	36,484	156,680	(²)

[1] Butter sold.   ² Not available.

Source of tables 796 and 797: Department of Commerce, Bureau of Census; *U. S. Census of Agriculture: 1950*, Vol. V.

No. 798.—DAIRY PRODUCTS SOLD, BY STATES: 1944 AND 1949

DIVISION AND STATE	WHOLE MILK SOLD			CREAM SOLD (butterfat content)			OTHER MILK PRODUCTS SOLD, 1949	
	Farms reporting, 1949	Thousands of pounds		Farms reporting, 1949	Thousands of pounds		Farms reporting	Value ($1,000)
		1944	1949		1944	1949		
United States	1,096,650	65,221,989	68,529,441	862,128	805,102	582,398	129,570	18,428
New England	34,662	3,471,438	3,419,439	2,497	2,013	1,786	4,146	796
Maine	7,366	394,516	409,850	1,296	742	607	2,769	537
New Hampshire	4,186	282,425	283,639	361	155	181	516	100
Vermont	11,865	1,358,748	1,341,774	390	526	281	480	80
Massachusetts	5,774	719,232	677,488	268	519	463	234	44
Rhode Island	783	121,854	106,680	37	13	49	11	7
Connecticut	4,648	608,663	600,008	145	57	204	146	28
Middle Atlantic	122,731	12,224,347	12,726,222	14,035	7,817	7,719	9,268	1,530
New York	62,522	7,120,125	7,480,811	4,536	2,565	2,739	3,286	586
New Jersey	4,810	939,334	930,121	121	53	337	195	23
Pennsylvania	55,399	4,164,787	4,315,290	9,378	4,700	4,643	5,787	921
East North Central	414,742	25,174,741	25,550,179	130,808	125,610	84,608	5,054	718
Ohio	83,234	3,646,339	3,605,886	27,012	19,301	13,043	2,105	261
Indiana	65,853	2,367,314	2,354,709	27,477	21,287	14,821	731	108
Illinois	65,752	3,574,497	3,525,791	42,849	32,005	19,875	886	131
Michigan	62,997	3,373,765	3,432,349	28,429	38,312	26,571	1,209	212
Wisconsin	136,906	12,212,825	12,661,444	5,041	13,705	10,297	123	16
West North Central	177,044	6,885,614	8,088,461	454,094	501,690	390,294	2,725	216
Minnesota	56,843	3,138,502	3,844,359	80,963	147,114	111,510	364	21
Iowa	22,510	858,371	1,082,733	123,418	149,477	123,726	172	30
Missouri	58,638	1,634,221	1,816,061	56,801	31,061	25,193	1,898	102
North Dakota	2,632	75,724	98,906	41,244	46,657	33,124	84	6
South Dakota	3,506	113,677	138,048	37,842	33,398	26,605	98	21
Nebraska	10,118	327,919	327,436	60,353	48,618	38,094	142	22
Kansas	22,797	787,198	780,919	53,473	45,365	32,042	267	14
South Atlantic	76,374	3,141,825	3,781,061	45,060	13,250	12,959	47,549	3,573
Delaware	1,800	135,887	140,669	69	32	50	203	20
Maryland	8,821	844,629	970,262	2,050	909	927	1,347	174
Dist. of Columbia	2	3,345	1,086	1	6	6	--------	--------
Virginia	19,865	665,837	866,417	18,759	6,548	6,291	8,992	624
West Virginia	9,042	247,645	293,583	12,560	3,550	3,271	5,137	360
North Carolina	21,371	425,529	488,170	4,477	1,081	1,085	13,326	941
South Carolina	5,303	150,741	176,083	2,064	239	432	5,030	449
Georgia	8,675	313,798	376,566	4,644	811	717	12,864	910
Florida	1,695	354,415	468,254	436	75	181	650	95
East South Central	118,279	2,466,246	2,823,930	76,625	26,163	20,043	31,626	1,962
Kentucky	35,549	724,232	865,342	50,021	17,151	14,124	3,569	235
Tennessee	46,977	925,438	1,061,963	16,025	6,846	4,049	9,394	632
Alabama	13,131	309,216	337,661	5,589	714	954	13,518	792
Mississippi	22,622	507,359	558,944	4,990	1,452	916	5,145	302
West South Central	61,255	2,659,728	2,717,575	78,284	66,656	28,690	18,468	1,297
Arkansas	16,132	311,223	345,958	17,859	8,493	4,692	5,504	311
Louisiana	4,587	279,762	340,083	907	203	206	1,329	80
Oklahoma	18,301	621,129	649,123	35,477	37,632	17,530	1,229	122
Texas	22,235	1,447,614	1,382,410	24,041	20,328	6,263	10,406	783
Mountain	42,145	2,275,323	2,226,529	38,321	37,528	21,815	827	105
Montana	3,011	150,892	166,511	11,811	10,593	6,740	110	18
Idaho	18,391	887,081	770,986	6,295	7,305	3,665	73	26
Wyoming	1,471	92,466	84,962	3,851	3,271	1,977	37	2
Colorado	6,530	376,597	417,977	12,374	10,995	5,844	155	30
New Mexico	1,714	86,500	98,359	1,536	2,380	809	227	12
Arizona	1,523	183,529	210,180	256	317	196	108	9
Utah	8,996	460,510	433,410	1,782	1,874	914	98	6
Nevada	409	37,748	44,145	416	1,092	669	19	2
Pacific	49,478	6,872,828	7,166,026	22,404	24,877	14,484	907	233
Washington	17,403	1,311,428	1,179,960	9,856	9,456	5,341	327	73
Oregon	13,173	783,541	748,303	10,060	10,840	6,100	175	40
California	18,902	4,777,858	5,237,763	2,488	4,581	3,043	405	121

Source: Department of Commerce, Bureau of the Census; *U. S. Census of Agriculture: 1950*, Vol. II.

No. 799.—DAIRY PRODUCTS MANUFACTURED—QUANTITY, BY KIND: 1946 TO 1951

[See also *Historical Statistics*, series E 157, 158, and 162]

PRODUCT	1946	1947	1948	1949	1950	1951
	1,000 pounds	*1,000 pounds*	*1,000 pounds*	*1,000 pounds*	*1,000 pounds*	*1,000 pounds*
Creamery butter (incl. whey butter)	1,171,830	1,399,694	1,296,234	1,412,171	1,398,498	1,332,981
Renovated or process butter	1,441	1,219	1,080	1,419	1,504	903
American cheese:						
Whole milk	801,254	982,718	854,447	885,306	892,706	873,080
Part skim	2,696	4,906	3,987	769	3,319	886
Full skim	2,367	2,183	1,754	1,261	1,774	1,302
Swiss cheese (including block)	55,698	71,612	70,965	61,043	99,483	92,047
Brick and Munster cheese	17,478	36,533	29,505	30,376	30,148	31,190
Limburger cheese	9,648	7,753	7,356	7,180	6,008	6,691
Cream cheese and Neufchatel	72,003	64,508	56,816	56,406	45,753	72,089
All Italian varieties of cheese	72,288	38,100	43,579	54,863	61,704	57,376
All other varieties of cheese	65,275	34,821	35,608	31,510	30,371	25,712
Condensed milk (sweetened):						
Skimmed	818,878	542,056	328,652	215,296	210,728	211,376
Unskimmed	182,666	247,286	171,837	146,081	101,163	102,179
Unsweetened condensed milk (plain):						
Skimmed	487,219	408,194	494,024	857,648	893,182	485,624
Unskimmed	66,471	194,526	200,485	202,851	221,724	289,102
Evaporated milk, unskimmed (unsweetened)	3,060,643	3,206,027	3,362,608	2,755,780	2,662,478	2,864,989
Condensed skim milk (for animal feed)	23,408	18,642	22,633	13,573	13,671	8,134
Condensed or evaporated buttermilk (including concentrated product)	226,708	186,135	170,954	176,283	183,470	174,662
Dry buttermilk	36,627	45,437	41,830	49,250	48,537	45,346
Dry whole milk	183,405	164,888	170,087	182,541	194,986	131,017
Nonfat dry milk solids [1]	687,169	700,090	694,877	864,178	898,599	716,837
Dry cream	367	320	312	178	459	1,070
Dry whey	147,953	157,883	126,185	180,358	155,579	139,946
Dry casein (skim milk or buttermilk product)	18,319	35,531	14,372	13,846	18,531	21,092
Malted milk powder	45,029	37,354	31,361	25,369	30,710	33,391
	1,000 gallons	*1,000 gallons*	*1,000 gallons*	*1,000 gallons*	*1,000 gallons*	*1,000 gallons*
Ice cream of all kinds [2]	713,594	630,766	576,261	557,929	554,351	566,704
Sherbets (does not include water ices)	12,019	10,447	12,211	13,616	17,015	20,992
Ice milk	15,471	15,829	19,585	29,651	36,970	45,330
Other frozen dairy products [3]	5,636	5,542	4,966	6,754	8,330	9,168

[1] Includes dry skim milk for animal feed.
[2] Includes data for ice cream made by counter freezers and by other small retailers.
[3] Beginning 1949, change in question resulted in reporting of additional products.

Source: Department of Agriculture, Bureau of Agricultural Economics; annual report, *Production of Manufactured Dairy Products;* also published in annual report, *Agricultural Statistics.*

No. 800.—MARGARINE—PRODUCTION AND MATERIALS CONSUMED: 1945 TO 1952

[In thousands of pounds, except vitamin concentrate]

YEAR	PRODUCTION [1]			MATERIAL CONSUMED	1950	1951	1952
	Total	Colored	Uncolored				
1945	614,096	(2)	(2)	Total fats and oils	765,177	850,730	1,046,959
1946	572,520	(2)	(2)	Cottonseed oil, refined	74,416	75,944	75,256
1947	745,926	59,051	686,877	Soybean oil, refined	31,896	66,671	80,030
1948	906,642	96,397	811,645	Lard, rendered	3,722	(2)	2,791
1949	861,762	177,346	684,516	Stearin, vegetable oil, winter	10,766	(2)	10,298
1950	937,645	499,643	437,402	Stearin, animal, edible	3,876	3,285	3,763
				Oleo oil	4,137	2,213	2,618
1951	1,040,718	829,056	211,662	Hydrogenated cottonseed oil, edible	342,367	296,951	277,731
1952	1,255,975	1,135,249	120,726	Hydrogenated soybean oil, edible	279,377	402,659	570,726
				Hydrogenated other vegetable oils and fats, edible	(2)	(2)	76,186
				Other fats and oils	14,717	39,794	4,394
				Skim milk and skim milk powder (fluid equivalent basis)	(2)	175,365	212,629
				Vitamin concentrate (millions of U.S.P. units)	(2)	16,479,133	21,571,934
				Lecithin	[3] 1,460	1,918	2,616
				Soda (benzoate of)	[3] 566	771	906
				Mono- and di-glycerides	[3] 1,609	2,395	2,692

[1] Data through June 1950 from Bureau of Internal Revenue.   [2] Not available.
[3] Included in "other fats and oils" to avoid disclosure of figures for individual companies.

Source: Department of Commerce, Bureau of the Census; published in *Facts for Industry*, Series M17T.

No. 801.—POULTRY—NUMBER ON FARMS, VALUE, EGGS PRODUCED AND PRICES: 1930 TO 1951

[See also *Historical Statistics* series E 171-180]

YEAR	CHICKENS				EGGS		TURKEYS			
	Number, Jan. 1	Value per head, Jan. 1	Number produced	Price per pound [1]	Number produced	Price per dozen [1]	Number Jan. 1	Value per head, Jan. 1	Number produced	Price per pound [1]
	Thousands	*Dollars*	*Thousands*	*Cents*	*Millions*	*Cents*	*Thousands*	*Dollars*	*Thousands*	*Cents*
1930	466,491	0.928	714,380	18.4	39,067	23.7	5,969	3.00	17,052	20.0
1935	389,958	.544	597,769	15.3	33,609	23.4	5,499	2.18	20,487	20.1
1940	438,288	.605	555,563	13.0	39,695	18.0	8,569	2.14	33,572	15.2
1941	422,841	.654	664,115	15.6	41,878	23.5	7,193	2.26	32,497	19.9
1942	476,935	.833	751,843	18.7	45,597	30.0	7,485	3.06	32,359	27.5
1943	542,047	1.040	913,707	24.3	54,539	37.1	6,600	4.47	31,884	32.6
1944	582,197	1.180	724,871	23.7	58,530	32.5	7,429	5.33	35,170	34.0
1945	516,497	1.210	709,102	25.9	56,221	37.7	7,082	5.79	42,470	33.7
1946	523,227	1.270	646,490	27.6	55,962	37.6	7,862	5.75	39,746	36.3
1947	467,217	1.440	635,729	26.5	55,384	45.3	5,879	6.54	33,603	36.5
1948	449,644	1.440	536,107	30.1	54,899	47.2	3,959	6.97	31,346	46.8
1949	430,876	1.660	622,833	25.4	56,154	45.2	4,622	8.80	41,019	35.2
1950	455,549	1.360	550,595	22.3	58,734	36.3	5,124	6.34	43,533	32.8
1951	442,657	1.460	580,812	25.2	59,265	47.8	5,091	6.48	52,013	37.4

[1] Average annual price received by farmers.

Source: Department of Agriculture, Bureau of Agricultural Economics; annual report, *Agricultural Statistics*.

No. 802.—PROCESSING OF EGGS AND POULTRY: 1935 TO 1952

[In thousands of pounds]

YEAR	DRIED EGG PRODUCED			Liquid egg used for immediate consumption	Frozen egg produced	Poultry for sale certified for evisceration under U.S. Govt. inspection [1][2]	Canned poultry [1]
	Whole	Albumen	Yolk				
1935	61	133	2,806				
1936	126	267	1,093				
1937	74	541	1,776				
1938	179	1,510	4,313	10,400	116,100	8,264	
1939	184	2,305	7,550	12,089	177,144	20,202	
1940	392	1,916	5,179	12,646	189,578	26,181	
1941	31,241	4,391	9,648	18,765	237,182	31,335	
1942	226,127	2,253	7,269	21,429	[2]257,631	50,241	
1943	252,903	2,093	6,976	26,317	[2]412,615	94,517	89,763
1944	311,369	2,310	7,063	32,844	[2]511,791	79,349	131,801
1945	96,988	1,710	7,164	18,704	[2]397,579	113,175	146,587
1946	115,344	2,112	7,988	20,031	[2]392,218	155,576	125,197
1947	80,037	1,493	4,031	15,817	[2]371,096	121,487	87,552
1948	36,019	2,678	5,578	16,901	[2]345,192	149,673	146,993
1949	69,411	2,266	4,285	18,828	[2]318,327	212,853	128,231
1950	96,993	3,605	2,820	20,115	[2]354,148	337,909	152,049
1951	10,525	3,789	3,286	18,340	[2]339,537	525,798	170,774
1952	2,717	6,552	8,069	18,404	[2]320,352	700,300	193,790

[1] Dressed weight. [2] Source: Production and Marketing Administration.
[3] Includes amounts which were later dried: 115,782,000 pounds for 1942; 159,346,000 for 1943; 179,146,000 for 1944; 122,167,000 for 1945; 84,129,000 for 1946; 20,538,000 for 1947; 25,311,000 for 1948; 32,395,000 for 1949; 32,134,000 for 1950; 23,220,000 for 1951; 32,400 for 1952. Also included in dried figures for each year.

Source: Department of Agriculture, Bureau of Agricultural Economics, except as noted; annual report, *Agricultural Statistics*.

No. 803.—CHICKENS ON FARMS, 1945 AND 1950, EGGS AND CHICKENS SOLD, 1949, BY STATES

	CHICKENS [1]				CHICKEN EGGS SOLD, 1949		CHICKENS SOLD, 1949	
DIVISION AND STATE	Farms reporting (thousands)		Number on hand (thousands)		Farms reporting (thousands)	Number (thousands of dozens)	Farms reporting (thousands)	Number (thousands)
	1945 (Jan. 1)	1950	1945 (Jan. 1)	1950				
United States	4,906.9	4,215.6	422,111	342,464	2,429.7	2,469,647	1,712.4	526,185
New England	63.5	59.5	13,351	12,181	29.4	129,606	25.5	35,709
Maine	21.5	13.7	2,184	2,410	7.4	25,069	6.7	9,232
New Hampshire	9.9	6.6	2,267	1,986	4.3	22,576	3.5	4,519
Vermont	12.9	9.1	930	760	4.4	6,944	3.4	1,127
Massachusetts	22.0	11.4	4,779	4,001	7.2	40,944	6.6	11,037
Rhode Island	2.5	1.3	509	431	1.0	3,737	1.0	913
Connecticut	14.8	8.7	3,183	2,500	5.2	29,434	4.6	11,570
Middle Atlantic	287.3	260.4	42,065	38,117	127.7	352,941	106.4	55,218
New York	100.4	72.5	13,386	10,382	41.8	96,387	30.4	15,725
New Jersey	20.1	16.7	8,377	10,076	11.2	107,782	9.7	11,951
Pennsylvania	136.9	111.1	20,322	17,689	74.8	149,703	60.3	27,532
East North Central	795.0	666.6	82,071	63,692	491.6	486,486	379.1	72,699
Ohio	181.8	152.7	17,336	13,427	108.3	113,045	81.6	15,954
Indiana	150.6	128.7	16,103	12,512	97.1	102,978	83.4	25,902
Illinois	182.5	161.5	21,681	17,385	130.5	117,206	109.3	14,771
Michigan	133.5	104.7	11,338	8,456	64.0	59,282	47.2	8,693
Wisconsin	146.8	119.0	16,674	11,912	91.8	95,963	57.7	8,799
West North Central	995.5	798.4	125,741	96,738	647.9	797,460	520.1	75,532
Minnesota	157.7	136.3	26,672	22,964	123.4	222,925	94.8	16,306
Iowa	190.2	173.7	33,219	26,508	157.9	231,264	137.5	22,221
Missouri	212.7	192.6	21,455	16,836	136.0	103,458	105.9	15,367
North Dakota	58.2	45.9	5,235	3,340	34.2	16,093	21.7	1,762
South Dakota	60.5	54.0	8,513	7,204	47.4	51,347	38.1	5,281
Nebraska	101.4	89.0	14,685	10,569	77.9	84,061	61.1	7,850
Kansas	124.7	106.8	15,993	11,326	89.1	95,251	60.7	6,744
South Atlantic	881.9	791.5	42,462	33,928	297.5	137,210	265.3	297,468
Delaware	6.3	5.1	1,074	757	2.6	6,049	3.7	50,304
Maryland	34.0	28.2	3,793	2,950	16.6	18,828	13.4	30,672
District of Columbia	(²)	(²)	14	(²)	(²)	3	(²)	(²)
Virginia	180.5	128.4	8,955	6,785	66.1	33,912	43.2	24,604
West Virginia	79.1	66.6	3,541	2,962	32.6	12,621	21.9	11,365
North Carolina	244.6	237.2	10,792	9,002	53.9	27,572	61.7	17,300
South Carolina	128.6	115.9	4,646	3,551	28.5	7,093	15.9	3,411
Georgia	195.3	163.7	7,138	5,556	52.2	17,449	34.6	44,794
Florida	43.4	38.4	2,446	2,361	12.9	13,783	8.9	6,097
East South Central	838.5	779.1	35,468	27,819	355.0	74,496	234.0	31,774
Kentucky	203.9	185.8	10,256	8,175	107.4	25,709	73.9	4,326
Tennessee	208.3	200.1	10,404	8,041	112.8	24,243	76.2	4,014
Alabama	200.9	183.6	7,358	5,775	69.2	14,062	37.9	6,119
Mississippi	225.4	209.6	7,360	5,828	65.6	10,475	36.0	7,314
West South Central	779.1	644.8	52,514	33,435	314.4	134,568	172.4	61,656
Arkansas	173.3	182.3	7,349	5,464	59.5	13,793	42.0	29,960
Louisiana	116.9	107.0	4,946	3,736	34.1	5,866	14.0	1,166
Oklahoma	149.9	120.2	11,607	7,421	72.4	35,681	43.2	4,426
Texas	339.0	265.3	28,662	16,814	148.5	79,228	73.3	26,166
Mountain	165.3	135.7	13,447	10,084	68.5	62,290	40.5	8,463
Montana	29.7	25.1	2,029	1,401	14.1	6,196	7.9	809
Idaho	32.2	27.4	2,169	1,825	13.2	8,626	8.4	1,202
Wyoming	10.7	9.5	807	542	5.1	2,493	2.8	363
Colorado	40.1	34.8	3,444	2,570	20.2	14,485	11.9	2,411
New Mexico	22.3	16.4	1,198	831	5.8	3,106	3.4	551
Arizona	9.4	6.3	638	492	2.4	2,718	1.6	560
Utah	18.2	14.2	2,987	2,302	7.0	23,999	4.3	2,176
Nevada	2.7	2.2	285	170	.9	987	.5	122
Pacific	194.8	158.3	25,633	34,538	98.4	232,945	47.9	47,382
Washington	61.9	44.7	5,551	5,749	21.3	36,312	13.6	6,199
Oregon	48.6	40.1	2,501	2,542	18.7	24,237	11.6	3,534
California	84.1	73.5	16,772	17,988	58.4	172,397	22.3	37,369

[1] Chickens 4 months old and over. [2] 50 or less. [3] 500 or less.

Source: Department of Commerce, Bureau of the Census; U. S. Census of Agriculture: 1950, Vol. II.

No. 804.—POULTRY AND EGGS—FARM AND COMMERCIAL PRODUCTION, BY STATES: 1945-49 AVERAGE, AND 1952

[Eggs in millions; other figures in thousands]

DIVISION AND STATE	EGGS PRODUCED ON FARMS		CHICKENS RAISED ON FARMS		COMMERCIAL BROILERS PRODUCED		TURKEYS RAISED		CHICKS HATCHED BY COMMERCIAL HATCHERIES	
	1945-49 avg.	1952	1945-49 avg.	1952	1945-49 avg.	1952	1945-49 avg.	1952	1945-49 avg.	1952
United States	55,724	61,016	733,534	617,054	370,416	886,036	37,965	60,446	1,388,547	1,739,466
New England	2,469	2,997	27,287	33,123	24,912	66,891	939	1,834	97,256	133,969
Maine	419	663	5,474	6,980	4,826	23,048	60	464	8,709	22,008
New Hampshire	364	431	4,774	5,915	2,849	6,051	95	154	27,471	35,566
Vermont	168	171	1,794	1,877	436	550	143	138	1,562	1,666
Massachusetts	855	911	8,498	8,971	6,851	16,147	395	653	26,467	29,079
Rhode Island	92	108	910	1,067	549	1,136	39	55	2,572	1,334
Connecticut	542	713	5,837	8,303	9,399	19,950	206	370	30,475	44,316
Middle Atlantic	6,363	8,554	72,522	72,976	19,599	32,873	2,524	3,507	121,375	137,855
New York	2,094	2,368	21,431	19,681	6,069	8,194	710	943	25,685	29,935
New Jersey	1,397	2,503	14,519	16,444	6,185	6,644	317	384	31,739	41,000
Pennsylvania	2,872	3,683	36,572	36,851	7,346	18,035	1,496	2,180	63,951	66,920
East North Central	11,449	12,417	139,386	117,795	30,948	86,644	4,493	7,118	315,309	261,571
Ohio	2,562	2,795	30,213	24,852	4,228	11,102	1,158	1,878	62,420	59,800
Indiana	2,268	2,734	30,645	26,893	13,084	33,674	931	1,795	97,817	104,787
Illinois	2,769	3,148	35,838	27,271	8,160	27,393	887	999	103,379	71,717
Michigan	1,538	1,601	20,248	18,424	1,292	3,309	834	1,097	26,973	29,250
Wisconsin	2,312	2,139	22,442	20,355	4,184	11,166	682	1,349	24,720	24,221
West North Central	16,368	16,457	204,664	151,783	12,169	45,951	16,226	12,688	334,696	318,113
Minnesota	3,764	3,730	38,240	27,437	1,390	4,161	3,593	5,201	60,330	52,185
Iowa	4,345	4,602	54,205	41,669	3,471	8,590	2,615	3,415	87,928	75,000
Missouri	2,724	2,583	35,230	26,650	4,911	23,544	1,581	1,572	96,360	111,000
North Dakota	555	594	9,303	6,412	....	....	597	526	5,568	4,800
South Dakota	1,089	1,238	15,772	11,929	....	....	331	370	16,362	14,700
Nebraska	1,857	1,758	26,447	19,156	1,353	6,384	840	862	30,302	28,728
Kansas	2,034	1,862	26,458	18,530	1,044	3,272	668	742	37,848	31,700
South Atlantic	4,726	5,250	77,870	67,326	197,613	372,142	3,578	11,522	260,400	427,764
Delaware	139	138	2,210	1,571	61,163	65,191	106	360	40,154	49,342
Maryland	504	515	6,865	5,096	38,445	56,966	418	529	41,916	68,836
Virginia	1,149	1,149	13,300	10,749	27,431	50,642	1,368	5,762	41,916	68,836
West Virginia	489	478	5,500	4,351	9,771	19,075	486	1,800	6,373	10,050
North Carolina	1,121	1,298	21,016	18,981	18,032	43,366	404	1,018	38,437	59,909
South Carolina	390	462	9,477	8,520	4,204	14,301	471	1,252	7,696	12,850
Georgia	660	828	14,036	12,439	31,854	112,621	209	620	48,425	127,220
Florida	277	382	5,466	5,619	6,713	9,980	115	181	13,389	20,872
East South Central	3,572	3,648	67,067	55,175	14,259	66,674	650	1,062	43,297	101,353
Kentucky	1,237	1,244	20,550	16,502	1,220	3,677	238	412	11,764	12,800
Tennessee	1,063	1,023	18,251	15,006	2,273	8,762	153	211	12,337	18,450
Alabama	675	732	14,472	11,970	6,185	23,484	164	308	10,931	30,043
Mississippi	596	649	13,793	11,697	4,581	30,751	95	131	8,264	40,060
West South Central	5,279	5,134	80,662	57,611	40,679	148,462	3,702	5,065	101,190	176,657
Arkansas	677	705	13,286	10,470	22,788	72,627	158	550	14,984	59,244
Louisiana	369	385	9,071	8,005	1,490	8,113	56	122	5,326	8,175
Oklahoma	1,281	1,123	19,003	12,588	1,113	6,728	540	690	25,200	17,800
Texas	2,952	2,921	39,303	26,548	15,287	60,994	2,947	3,703	55,680	91,438
Mountain	1,646	1,675	23,132	18,948	1,475	5,714	3,155	3,360	16,903	21,555
Montana	231	254	3,697	3,562	....	....	137	140	1,921	2,667
Idaho	275	271	3,670	3,128	....	1,126	242	183	3,192	4,411
Wyoming	99	104	1,330	1,106	....	....	138	150	429	431
Colorado	415	393	6,418	5,043	820	2,129	784	723	6,385	9,020
New Mexico	126	115	1,826	1,266	....	....	65	68	1,085	810
Arizona	75	80	994	774	654	825	93	98	1,288	1,325
Utah	392	434	4,793	3,759	....	1,634	1,660	1,971	2,491	2,891
Nevada	33	24	405	310	....	....	36	27	111	....
Pacific	3,850	4,884	40,943	42,318	28,761	60,685	8,698	14,290	96,118	132,629
Washington	740	782	9,015	8,962	3,284	7,513	1,223	1,223	17,315	21,282
Oregon	485	552	5,670	5,310	2,131	5,093	2,031	2,134	8,760	14,865
California	2,625	3,550	26,258	28,046	23,346	48,079	5,444	10,933	72,043	96,482

Source: Department of Agriculture, Bureau of Agricultural Economics; annual report, *Agricultural Statistics.*

No. 805.—ANIMAL PRODUCTS AND FISH—COLD-STORAGE HOLDINGS, BY KIND, BY MONTHS: 1948 TO 1952

[In thousands of pounds, except shell eggs, thousands of 30-dozen cases and "all meats," millions of pounds. Quantities are net weights and are as of 1st of each month. Beef and pork figures cover frozen, cured, and in process of cure]

PRODUCT AND YEAR	Jan.	Feb.	Mar.	Apr.	May	June	July	Aug.	Sept.	Oct.	Nov.	Dec.
Creamery butter:												
1948	23, 672	13, 309	7, 323	3, 482	4, 449	18, 639	53, 072	53, 105	97, 624	93, 890	83, 412	60, 214
1949	33, 613	18, 727	8, 718	6, 315	15, 398	51, 056	102, 701	136, 795	143, 555	154, 455	142, 619	130, 452
1950	113, 993	103, 657	92, 886	93, 489	109, 030	136, 867	185, 167	230, 068	239, 908	234, 111	206, 228	180, 673
1951	106, 192	75, 320	52, 507	38, 378	32, 207	42, 590	72, 508	104, 405	116, 790	113, 601	94, 611	59, 340
1952	27, 061	13, 574	7, 879	6, 506	10, 532	30, 521	65, 616	99, 751	111, 400	111, 319	102, 177	53, 961
American cheese:												
1948	128, 186	107, 226	95, 570	80, 449	91, 907	196, 712	140, 038	168, 809	185, 324	182, 449	187, 535	140, 791
1949	126, 584	116, 779	111, 073	105, 608	109, 930	117, 021	140, 859	152, 548	153, 209	158, 329	185, 539	178, 794
1950	166, 670	169, 906	149, 004	141, 946	153, 135	186, 083	229, 785	256, 395	287, 977	292, 421	376, 920	283, 723
1951	187, 197	156, 117	137, 397	130, 955	144, 441	169, 553	204, 009	227, 190	253, 789	239, 500	239, 561	204, 663
1952	194, 784	167, 824	142, 945	133, 815	139, 705	164, 654	192, 920	211, 477	222, 933	231, 508	226, 317	210, 020
All varieties of cheese:												
1948	147, 693	134, 106	110, 125	103, 350	105, 263	123, 507	165, 201	197, 220	217, 819	212, 382	195, 470	164, 410
1949	146, 100	135, 110	128, 503	129, 569	125, 903	134, 765	162, 236	195, 617	210, 411	213, 483	209, 915	196, 125
1950	188, 659	176, 821	163, 922	156, 134	171, 553	208, 986	264, 346	280, 048	316, 661	336, 007	310, 240	261, 220
1951	212, 493	179, 577	160, 621	155, 096	169, 822	197, 412	234, 406	262, 540	280, 684	272, 003	269, 418	232, 968
1952	229, 136	193, 273	166, 040	155, 195	158, 949	185, 927	217, 604	230, 692	262, 853	262, 467	235, 885	242, 309
Shell eggs:												
1948	196	269	374	1, 168	3, 092	4, 908	5, 049	5, 525	4, 609	3, 200	1, 065	444
1949	139	152	144	530	954	1, 943	2, 290	1, 936	1, 476	810	501	230
1950	110	380	735	1, 296	2, 147	3, 413	3, 667	3, 163	2, 586	1, 486	802	61
1951	34	75	169	973	973	2, 053	2, 477	2, 270	1, 615	959	527	230
1952	141	238	942	1, 506	2, 184	3, 184	2, 387	2, 728	2, 169	1, 709	1, 080	308
Frozen eggs: [1]												
1948	138, 192	122, 438	120, 665	143, 268	195, 964	248, 574	264, 748	257, 367	233, 451	200, 988	189, 257	198, 208
1949	104, 932	71, 532	58, 621	77, 319	107, 058	141, 361	166, 582	168, 394	146, 866	121, 476	96, 392	72, 536
1950	53, 902	55, 052	72, 159	116, 546	155, 108	179, 732	185, 476	174, 761	155, 369	133, 002	104, 378	75, 582
1951	47, 210	31, 157	32, 712	62, 299	109, 253	162, 489	180, 980	190, 818	176, 373	151, 398	121, 382	85, 143
1952	67, 200	53, 055	60, 576	84, 295	111, 185	145, 863	166, 419	163, 389	144, 338	123, 681	96, 333	72, 462
Frozen poultry:												
1948	217, 468	203, 640	202, 374	206, 746	153, 494	117, 265	90, 597	91, 196	98, 234	108, 369	184, 617	171, 472
1949	140, 534	148, 418	131, 496	108, 732	89, 205	77, 833	74, 733	71, 261	83, 466	132, 280	211, 517	287, 508
1950	292, 513	285, 736	280, 523	212, 058	167, 000	126, 646	122, 238	103, 367	105, 179	146, 322	217, 969	286, 300
1951	301, 972	284, 623	242, 623	192, 912	147, 208	125, 359	112, 369	105, 692	121, 466	166, 242	209, 920	309, 943
1952	302, 151	306, 080	270, 397	232, 822	194, 965	158, 698	174, 049	157, 045	144, 508	182, 786	275, 191	294, 424
Beef:												
1948	175, 281	176, 110	165, 169	144, 254	112, 726	95, 755	82, 705	70, 559	66, 320	73, 299	87, 778	116, 687
1949	149, 329	130, 856	140, 125	127, 169	107, 506	84, 761	74, 237	66, 420	65, 063	61, 076	66, 721	91, 169
1950	120, 736	130, 430	112, 731	100, 298	90, 872	72, 402	60, 431	60, 508	72, 908	81, 156	94, 888	113, 235
1951	146, 925	160, 673	142, 040	131, 258	110, 740	100, 218	80, 986	87, 430	93, 636	94, 881	124, 856	182, 300
1952	217, 983	240, 296	253, 983	255, 582	240, 708	213, 316	180, 753	161, 342	195, 762	171, 708	195, 104	221, 219
Pork:												
1948	527, 150	659, 309	700, 114	661, 399	606, 827	540, 046	582, 496	506, 213	350, 794	234, 909	203, 169	210, 706
1949	489, 153	565, 215	611, 123	596, 429	545, 231	406, 108	419, 590	357, 043	283, 178	204, 678	209, 687	207, 206
1950	473, 741	582, 737	573, 108	543, 640	541, 965	492, 194	469, 361	394, 402	308, 522	240, 544	219, 758	236, 300
1951	499, 408	568, 007	641, 565	648, 384	654, 497	616, 231	572, 872	496, 171	401, 572	325, 969	276, 253	251, 870
1952	548, 604	704, 992	793, 870	822, 006	823, 741	727, 665	685, 033	542, 707	407, 568	290, 931	234, 694	319, 643
All meats:												
1948	857	996	1, 031	968	851	790	779	686	528	395	382	535
1949	763	889	903	861	791	673	612	547	451	362	370	403
1950	725	850	816	778	749	674	633	543	466	410	406	545
1951	770	957	918	906	892	839	778	701	605	522	499	686
1952	912	1, 096	1, 210	1, 242	1, 231	1, 095	1, 029	850	701	587	587	693
Frozen fish:												
1948	133, 844	112, 046	90, 491	76, 743	66, 266	85, 601	100, 537	127, 474	135, 928	140, 161	144, 049	156, 006
1949	150, 974	127, 635	104, 138	82, 722	74, 940	91, 453	114, 031	127, 216	146, 344	150, 608	156, 077	158, 719
1950	146, 813	125, 516	105, 818	87, 133	79, 027	97, 773	116, 897	137, 307	153, 625	158, 473	165, 105	165, 394
1951	157, 722	130, 880	106, 834	96, 367	88, 803	105, 944	127, 351	146, 891	161, 628	166, 100	171, 994	170, 134
1952	165, 792	146, 113	125, 704	113, 996	113, 544	123, 762	152, 396	170, 254	183, 826	190, 693	200, 944	210, 688
Lard and rendered pork fat:												
1948	113, 286	133, 513	137, 416	129, 025	138, 924	150, 660	181, 327	174, 304	139, 751	95, 587	66, 529	77, 021
1949	116, 397	160, 610	179, 628	156, 782	138, 216	125, 823	103, 890	96, 255	68, 819	43, 708	36, 230	39, 308
1950	73, 996	92, 949	81, 174	87, 306	108, 108	128, 467	136, 258	106, 613	75, 496	58, 241	52, 128	37, 262
1951	49, 857	80, 321	89, 433	78, 352	75, 171	68, 539	66, 754	46, 820	34, 702	28, 372	31, 344	37, 262
1952	53, 614	49, 284	52, 759	51, 127	88, 521	105, 749	132, 041	132, 589	124, 296	109, 157	78, 992	55, 926

[1] Frozen eggs may be converted to cases on basis of 37.5 pounds to a case.

Source: Frozen fish, Department of Interior, Fish and Wildlife Service; annual bulletins. Other figures, Department of Agriculture, Production and Marketing Administration; annual report, *Agricultural Statistics*; also published in monthly mimeographed reports.

No. 806.—WOOL—STOCKS, PRODUCTION, PRICE, IMPORTS, AND EXPORTS: 1921 TO 1952

ITEM	1921-1925, average	1926-1930, average	1931-1935, average	1936-1940, average	1941-1945, average	1946-1950, average
Sheep and lambs shorn (thousands)	32,160	39,753	45,891	45,069	45,366	29,404
Weight per fleece (pounds)	7.4	7.8	8.0	8.0	7.9	8.1
Shorn wool production (1,000 lbs.)	236,333	310,682	366,368	360,583	360,191	238,485
Price per pound (cents)[1]	32.0	30.0	16.8	25.7	40.3	49.0
Pulled wool production (1,000 lbs.)	44,720	53,600	64,780	64,680	68,340	46,500
Apparel wool (1,000 lbs.):						
Total production	283,053	364,282	431,148	425,263	428,531	284,985
Imports, less reexports[2]	183,293	[2]107,522	[2]37,404	122,572	[4]669,237	[4]589,483
Exports, domestic[3]	699	300	122	412	12,869	10,491
Total new supply[6]	465,647	471,504	468,430	547,423	[4]1,064,893	[4]863,978
Carpet wool, imports (1,000 lbs.)[5]	138,086	[3]134,601	[3]101,004	133,368	84,610	130,187

ITEM	1947	1948	1949	1950	1951	1952[7]
Stocks of apparel wool, Apr. 1 (1,000 lbs.)[1]	404,228	346,482	199,321	143,235	130,204	130,831
Sheep and lambs shorn (thousands)	30,953	28,649	26,382	26,387	27,357	28,172
Weight per fleece (pounds)	8.1	8.1	8.1	8.2	8.2	8.3
Shorn wool production (1,000 lbs.)	251,425	231,770	212,899	215,422	225,545	232,373
Price per pound (cents)[1]	42.0	49.2	49.4	62.1	97.0	53.3
Pulled wool production (1,000 lbs.)	56,600	46,600	35,600	32,400	25,900	33,600
Apparel wool (1,000 lbs.):						
Total production	308,025	278,370	248,499	247,822	251,445	265,973
Imports, less reexports[2]	528,171	596,466	347,964	550,801	469,188	439,020
Exports, domestic[3]	12,720	1,154	15,775	6,796	260	31
Total new supply[6]	823,476	873,682	580,088	791,827	720,373	704,962
Carpet wool, imports (1,000 lbs.)[5]	112,119	160,634	86,621	165,755	85,987	105,278

[1] Price received by farmers. Weighted season average 1946 to date, weighted calendar average earlier years. Season April-March.

[2] Imports for consumption beginning 1934, general imports prior thereto. Apparel wool for all years includes item "not finer than 40's" both free and dutiable. Carpet wool includes only Domskoi, Smyrna, East Indian, Chinese, and similar wool without merino or English blood.

[3] For the years 1930-35 the item "not finer than 40's" has been deducted from carpet wool totals reported by Department of Commerce and added to apparel wool, thus making entire series comparable.

[4] Includes 222,222,220 lbs. in 1942; 275,476,808 lbs. in 1943; 2,725,929 lbs. in 1944; 5,372,698 lbs. in 1945; and 14,840 lbs. in 1946, imported free of duty as an act of international courtesy. Wool so imported consisted almost entirely of wool stored in this country for the British Government, and later re-exported. This wool was not available to domestic mills.

[5] Includes hair of angora goat, alpaca, and other like animals. Includes a small amount of carpet wool beginning 1943.

[6] Production, minus exports, plus imports; stocks not taken into consideration.

[7] Preliminary.

[8] Scoured basis.

Source: Department of Agriculture, Bureau of Agricultural Economics; annual report, *Agricultural Statistics.* Exports and imports from Department of Commerce, Bureau of the Census; annual report, *Foreign Commerce and Navigation of the U. S.*

No. 807.—Wool—Production and Income, 1941 to 1952 and by Region, 1951 and 1952

YEAR AND REGION	Sheep shorn, number [1]	Weight per fleece	Production, shorn wool	Price per pound [2]	Cash receipts [3]
	1,000	*Lb.*	*1,000 lb.*	*Cents*	*$1,000*
1941-50, average	37,365	8.09	300,339	44.6	130,073
1941	47,729	8.12	387,820	32.5	127,704
1942	49,287	7.85	385,297	40.1	155,735
1943	47,802	7.91	378,342	41.6	157,367
1944	43,106	7.84	395,318	42.3	161,354
1945	38,763	7.96	307,978	41.9	128,870
1946	34,047	8.11	280,908	42.3	117,585
1947	30,153	8.12	251,436	42.0	105,644
1948	25,649	8.09	231,770	48.2	114,055
1949	26,362	8.07	212,899	48.4	105,362
1950	26,357	8.16	215,422	62.1	133,729
1951	27,257	8.24	225,845	97.0	218,952
North Atlantic	374	7.42	2,776	97.6	2,709
East North Central	2,231	8.05	18,694	94.8	17,687
West North Central	4,340	8.29	34,149	92.3	31,718
South Atlantic	659	5.42	3,468	99.3	3,438
South Central	7,863	7.07	55,363	99.0	55,035
Western	11,790	9.22	108,740	97.6	106,052
1952	26,172	8.26	252,373	4 53.3	135,073
North Atlantic	402	7.45	2,968	4 51.3	1,488
East North Central	2,385	8.12	21,004	4 49.6	10,427
West North Central	4,916	7.95	39,149	4 50.5	19,779
South Atlantic	673	5.30	3,689	4 52.4	1,932
South Central	7,160	7.48	53,537	4 57.0	30,522
Western	12,432	9.01	112,080	4 63.3	80,710

[1] Includes sheep shorn at commercial feeding yards.
[2] Beginning 1943, average price for marketing season April through March. Prior to 1943, average prices relate to calendar year.
[3] Computed using April-March average prices beginning 1943 and calendar year averages prior to 1943.
[4] Preliminary. Includes an allowance for wool under loan.

Source: Department of Agriculture, Bureau of Agricultural Economics; annual report, *Agricultural Statistics*

No. 808.—Wool Consumed in Manufactures: 1925 to 1952

[In millions of pounds. See also *Historical Statistics*, series J 176]

YEAR	SCOURED BASIS [1]			YEAR	SCOURED BASIS [1]		
	Total	Apparel class [2]	Carpet class		Total	Apparel class [2]	Carpet class
1925	349.9	251.7	98.2	1939	396.5	293.1	103.4
1926	342.7	254.7	88.0	1940	407.9	310.0	97.9
1927	334.1	238.7	95.4	1941	648.0	514.4	132.6
1928	352.2	252.4	100.2	1942	602.5	560.5	42.1
1929	368.1	253.2	114.9	1943	625.3	603.3	32.0
1930	362.9	300.7	62.5	1944	622.6	577.0	45.8
1931	311.0	237.7	73.3	1945	645.1	589.2	55.9
1932	230.1	188.5	41.6	1946	3 737.5	609.6	127.9
1933	317.1	245.5	71.6	1947	3 698.2	525.9	172.4
1934	229.6	167.6	62.1	1948	3 605.1	398.4	207.9
1935	417.5	319.0	98.5	1949	3 500.4	339.0	161.4
1936	406.1	299.8	106.3	1950	3 634.8	436.9	197.9
1937	388.5	274.2	106.6	1951	3 484.1	382.1	102.0
1938	284.5	219.6	64.9	1952	3 462.9	346.8	116.1

[1] Scoured wool, plus greasy wool reduced to a scoured basis, assuming average yields varying with class, origin, grade, and whether shorn or pulled.
[2] Wool regarded as more or less suitable for apparel purposes; formerly "Combing and clothing."
[3] Includes raw wool consumed on woolens and worsted systems only. Raw wool consumed on cotton and other systems and by felt and batting manufacture amounted to about 10 million pounds in 1946.

Source: Department of Commerce, Bureau of the Census; monthly data are published in *Facts for Industry*, Series M15H.

26. Forests and Forest Products

The Bureau of the Census, Department of Commerce, and the Forest Service, Department of Agriculture, are the principal Government agencies engaged in the collection and publication of statistics of forest land, forest industries, and forest products. The Forest Service, through its forest survey activities, makes an inventory of the forest resource and measures rates of forest growth and drain. A number of reports for surveyed areas have been published. A report based on a reappraisal of the Nation's forest situation made during 1945 and 1946 was published in 1948. Statistics from this report are shown in tables 809–812. Other publications of the Forest Service include data on stumpage and log prices, lumber consumption and distribution, lumber used in manufacture, and fire statistics. The *Statistical Supplement to the Annual Report of the Chief of the Forest Service* carries statistics of the administration of the national forests.

The Bureau of the Census, Department of Commerce, publishes information on forest industries and products in reports of the Census of Manufactures, in addition to current *Facts for Industry* reports. The Bureau of the Census also publishes statistics of foreign trade in forest products. Information on the domestic movement of forest products is reported by the Interstate Commerce Commission and the Association of American Railways.

The Bureau of Agricultural Economics of the Department of Agriculture publishes annual reports on the production of turpentine and rosin.

The Bureau of Labor Statistics of the Department of Labor publishes statistics of wholesale lumber prices monthly and annually.

A number of forest products trade associations and trade journals collect and publish statistics of forest products, production, markets, shipments, inventories, etc.

The completeness and reliability of published statistics of forests and forest products vary considerably. The data for forest land area and stand are, of course, much more reliable for areas which have been surveyed than for those areas which have not been covered. Forest fire statistics for federal lands are considered much better than for private lands, though too much reliance should not be placed in any estimates of fire damage or causes of fires.

In the field of forest products, data for lumber production and other manufactured products such as veneer and plywood, pulp and paper, cooperage, naval stores, etc., are much more complete than for the primary forest products such as poles and piling, fuelwood, and fence posts. The data for lumber production are subject to certain limitations because of incomplete coverage. Information for pulp and paper, and plywood, on the other hand, is believed to have practically complete coverage. Statistics relating to average value of lumber sawed may be subject to some special limitations due to under representation of small mills.

For a historical summation of raw materials production, imports, exports, and consumption, which includes figures for forest products, see table 1056.

Historical statistics.—See preface and historical appendix. Tabular headnotes (as "See also *Historical Statistics*, series F 69–73") provide cross-references, where applicable, to *Historical Statistics of the United States, 1789–1945*.

Note.—This section presents data for the most recent year or period available on May 20, 1953, when the material was organized and sent to the printer. In a few instances, more recent data were added after that date.

No. 809.—FOREST LAND AREA AND OWNERSHIP OF COMMERCIAL FOREST LAND, BY STATES

[In thousands of acres. Status beginning of 1945]

REGION AND STATE	Total forest land	All owner-ships	COMMERCIAL FOREST LAND [1]			State, county, and munic-ipal	Private		
			Federally owned or managed						
			Total	Na-tional	Other		Total	Farm	Indus-trial and other
Total	623,528	461,044	88,957	73,512	15,445	27,114	344,973	139,058	205,915
North	211,753	170,221	11,311	9,528	1,786	13,414	135,596	61,010	78,586
New England	31,992	30,551	891	822	69	666	28,294	6,477	21,817
Connecticut	1,907	1,900				155	1,745	711	1,034
Maine	16,788	16,668	74	47	27	50	16,541	2,172	14,368
Massachusetts	3,310	3,297	34	1	23	271	3,002	906	2,096
New Hampshire	4,800	4,722	621	613	8	79	4,022	1,086	2,936
Rhode Island	452	447				27	420	107	313
Vermont	3,835	3,820	172	161	11	84	3,564	1,494	2,070
Middle Atlantic	44,214	41,586	1,476	1,265	211	3,613	36,497	11,854	24,643
Delaware	442	442	2		2	7	433	228	205
Maryland	2,742	2,722	44	3	41	149	2,529	1,196	1,331
New Jersey	2,348	2,329	53		53	96	2,180	424	1,756
New York	13,800	11,114	75		75	732	10,307	3,651	6,656
Pennsylvania	15,228	15,127	470	442	28	2,514	12,143	3,369	8,774
West Virginia	9,954	9,852	832	820	12	115	8,905	2,984	5,921
Lake	53,700	50,345	5,455	4,455	1,040	14,995	29,445	12,330	16,115
Michigan	19,000	17,380	2,155	2,035	120	4,115	11,110	3,260	7,850
Minnesota	19,700	16,709	2,570	2,170	500	7,100	6,930	4,330	2,600
Wisconsin	17,000	16,265	1,670	1,250	420	3,590	11,005	4,340	4,665
Central	44,919	44,321	2,117	1,961	156	326	41,779	25,798	15,981
Illinois	3,396	3,319	192	175	17	10	3,117	3,092	26
Indiana	2,445	2,358	104	79	25	76	2,178	2,139	39
Iowa	2,248	2,226	16	5	11	19	2,191	2,186	5
Kentucky	11,857	11,604	534	427	107	35	11,125	5,421	5,704
Missouri	19,142	18,537	1,199	1,193	6	78	17,560	8,839	8,721
Ohio	4,831	4,779	72	72		108	4,599	3,112	1,487
Plains	35,526	3,326	332	30	302	4	2,990	2,960	30
Kansas	1,121	1,011					1,011	1,011	
Nebraska	1,112	987	39	15	24		948	948	
North Dakota	621	470	56		56	1	414	414	
Oklahoma (West) [2]	6,326								
South Dakota (East) [3]	662	618	215	15	200	3	400	400	
Texas (West) [2]	25,986	240	23		23		217	187	30
South	186,504	183,266	14,978	10,138	3,940	2,140	167,638	86,660	97,948
South Atlantic	43,843	42,923	3,485	2,775	710	536	38,902	23,377	15,526
North Carolina	18,400	17,997	1,312	960	352	242	16,443	10,072	6,371
South Carolina	10,611	10,549	720	549	171	187	9,642	6,084	3,908
Virginia	14,832	14,377	1,458	1,266	187	107	12,817	7,621	5,196
Southeast	91,542	89,396	5,908	3,802	2,107	1,216	82,345	33,134	49,131
Alabama	18,878	18,800	886	613	273	121	17,793	7,260	10,534
Florida	23,478	21,765	1,713	1,009	704	336	19,726	3,996	15,730
Georgia	21,432	21,107	1,202	646	556	72	19,833	10,362	9,471
Mississippi	15,899	15,868	1,307	979	328	410	14,151	6,323	7,828
Tennessee	12,165	11,850	801	555	246	287	10,762	5,194	5,568
West Gulf	51,119	50,953	4,684	3,561	1,123	406	45,861	12,549	33,312
Arkansas	20,036	19,928	2,645	2,214	431	104	17,179	6,142	11,037
Louisiana	16,196	16,196	747	536	211	265	15,187	2,969	12,186
Oklahoma (East) [2]	4,320	4,308	519	163	456	23	3,666	812	2,854
Texas (East) [2]	10,567	10,548	673	648	25	16	9,849	2,626	7,233
West	225,271	107,457	63,568	53,851	9,717	5,540	38,349	8,988	29,361
Pacific Northwest	63,855	46,284	23,012	17,341	5,671	3,435	19,757	3,334	16,423
Oregon	39,755	26,530	15,251	11,530	3,721	1,101	9,978	1,537	8,441
Washington	24,100	19,874	7,761	5,811	1,950	2,334	9,779	1,797	7,982
California	65,815	36,665	8,098	7,684	415	23	8,283	1,309	6,974
North Rocky Mountain	53,246	29,066	20,012	18,061	1,951	1,702	7,352	2,847	4,505
Idaho	19,813	10,149	6,436	5,838	598	925	2,788	841	1,947
Montana	24,238	14,758	10,122	9,118	1,004	699	3,937	1,614	2,322
South Dakota (West) [3]	1,317	1,147	920	918	2	4	223	144	79
Wyoming	8,878	3,012	2,534	2,187	347	74	404	248	156
South Rocky Mountain	72,455	15,783	12,445	10,745	1,690	360	2,967	1,498	1,469
Arizona	19,536	2,815	2,744	2,058	686	30	41	36	5
Colorado	19,902	7,574	5,928	5,387	536	152	1,790	630	1,140
Nevada	4,720	98	24	24			74	13	61
New Mexico	20,001	3,463	2,405	2,020	365	149	911	693	218
Utah	8,494	1,530	1,349	1,276	73	49	132	106	26

[1] Includes land capable of producing timber of commercial quantity and quality, and available now or prospectively, for commercial use.

[2] Western and central portions of Oklahoma and Texas included in the Plains region; eastern portions included in the West Gulf region.

[3] Eastern and central portions of South Dakota included in the Plains; southwestern portion (Black Hills) included in the North Rocky Mountain region.

Source: Department of Agriculture, Forest Service; A Reappraisal of the Forest Situation.

No. 810.—Saw Timber and Growth on Commercial Forest Land, by States

[In millions of board feet. Status beginning of 1945. Includes volume on land capable of producing timber of commercial quantity and quality and available now or prospectively for commercial use. Includes trees large enough for sawlogs regardless of actual use, in accordance with practice of region. Volumes on lumber-tally basis]

REGION AND STATE	VOLUME OF SAW TIMBER						SAW-TIMBER GROWTH		
	Total	Soft-wood	Hard-wood	On saw-timber areas		On other than saw-timber areas	Total	Soft-wood	Hard-wood
				On virgin areas	On second-growth areas				
Total	1,600,972	1,296,377	304,595	840,340	660,719	99,913	35,301	21,848	13,453
North	220,429	65,836	154,593	21,642	159,386	39,401	8,355	2,000	6,355
New England	53,197	33,263	24,934	726	48,605	8,866	1,799	910	889
Connecticut	1,642	258	1,384	....	1,111	531	107	14	93
Maine	36,787	24,279	12,508	525	31,912	4,350	760	491	269
Massachusetts	4,670	1,946	2,724	15	3,867	788	242	96	146
New Hampshire	7,620	3,424	4,186	88	5,739	1,783	389	174	215
Rhode Island	153	22	131	....	69	84	9	1	8
Vermont	7,335	3,334	4,001	98	5,907	1,330	292	134	158
Middle Atlantic	62,045	14,017	48,038	1,197	47,459	13,389	2,712	597	2,115
Delaware	1,183	519	664	25	1,029	129	62	27	35
Maryland	4,030	1,779	2,251	37	3,053	940	202	105	97
New Jersey	2,188	783	1,405	25	1,362	801	103	37	66
New York	25,279	6,926	18,353	329	21,088	3,862	785	191	594
Pennsylvania	20,582	3,087	17,495	162	13,406	7,014	1,111	193	918
West Virginia	8,783	923	7,860	619	7,521	643	449	44	405
Lake	50,710	15,670	35,040	17,390	23,280	10,040	1,408	346	1,067
Michigan	24,140	7,400	16,740	13,550	7,500	3,090	519	96	423
Minnesota	11,590	4,940	6,650	2,020	5,560	4,010	420	176	244
Wisconsin	14,980	3,330	11,650	1,820	10,220	2,940	464	74	390
Central	43,747	2,418	41,329	1,249	36,616	5,882	2,248	128	2,120
Illinois	3,717	22	3,695	71	3,092	554	208	1	207
Indiana	6,175	6	6,169	....	5,773	402	298	2	296
Iowa	5,344	43	5,301	....	4,842	502	295	2	293
Kentucky	12,392	1,611	10,781	797	10,356	1,239	638	83	555
Missouri	6,984	663	6,321	381	3,849	2,754	388	37	351
Ohio	9,135	73	9,062	....	8,704	431	421	3	418
Plains	5,730	468	5,262	1,084	3,426	1,224	193	19	174
Kansas	2,880	....	2,880	600	1,800	480	82	....	82
Nebraska	1,500	300	1,200	360	660	480	58	10	48
North Dakota	434	20	414	....	344	90	16	1	15
Oklahoma (West)[1]									
South Dakota (East)[2]	720	96	624	120	480	120	26	4	22
Texas (West)[1]	196	52	144	....	142	54	11	4	7
South	337,987	193,790	144,197	11,617	305,833	20,537	19,938	12,919	7,019
South Atlantic	97,141	59,326	37,815	....	90,205	6,936	6,106	4,016	2,090
North Carolina	42,241	27,962	14,279	....	40,109	2,132	2,589	1,835	754
South Carolina	29,580	19,362	10,218	....	28,452	1,128	1,733	1,234	499
Virginia	25,320	12,002	13,318	....	21,644	3,676	1,784	947	837
Southeast	135,887	76,992	58,895	4,674	121,473	9,740	8,224	5,284	2,940
Alabama	33,361	20,681	12,680	694	30,482	2,185	2,021	1,392	629
Florida	17,308	12,862	4,446	844	14,410	2,054	989	767	222
Georgia	40,543	28,941	11,602	2,005	36,121	2,417	2,501	1,995	506
Mississippi	30,483	11,592	18,861	1,131	27,206	2,116	1,866	904	962
Tennessee	14,222	2,916	11,306	....	13,254	968	847	226	621
West Gulf	104,959	57,472	47,487	6,943	94,155	3,861	5,608	3,619	1,989
Arkansas	37,528	22,315	15,213	2,080	33,940	1,508	1,929	1,186	743
Louisiana	36,895	13,930	22,965	2,492	33,184	1,219	1,893	970	923
Oklahoma (East)[1]	3,048	2,044	1,004	234	2,497	317	137	95	42
Texas (East)[1]	27,488	19,183	8,305	2,137	24,534	817	1,649	1,368	281
West	1,042,556	1,036,751	5,805	807,081	195,500	39,975	7,008	6,929	79
Pacific Northwest	630,894	626,941	3,953	513,149	111,706	6,039	4,224	4,152	72
Oregon	381,389	378,577	2,812	307,288	71,913	2,188	2,483	2,432	51
Washington	249,505	248,364	1,141	205,861	39,793	3,851	1,741	1,720	21
California	227,565	227,565	....	180,062	32,624	14,859	1,160	1,160	....
North Rocky Mountain	127,229	126,293	936	69,810	43,212	11,207	1,306	1,302	4
Idaho	60,796	60,764	32	27,078	28,076	5,642	826	826	(3)
Montana	52,515	52,112	403	32,020	12,531	7,964	418	414	4
South Dakota (West)[2]	2,866	2,866	....	....	1,249	1,333	284	22	(2)
Wyoming	11,052	10,551	501	9,463	1,272	317	40	40	(3)
South Rocky Mountain	56,868	55,952	916	44,040	7,958	4,870	318	315	3
Arizona	16,270	16,270	....	14,265	1,787	218	94	94	....
Colorado	27,658	26,742	916	18,727	4,860	4,071	145	142	3
Nevada	367	367	....	287	35	45	1	1	....
New Mexico	8,471	8,471	....	7,134	871	466	58	58	....
Utah	4,102	4,102	....	3,627	405	70	20	20	....

[1] Volume in western and central portions of Oklahoma and Texas included in the Plains region; that in eastern portions included in the West Gulf region.

[2] Volume in eastern and central portions of South Dakota included in the Plains; that in southwestern portion (Black Hills) included in North Rocky Mountain region.   [3] Less than 500,000 board feet.

Source: Department of Agriculture, Forest Service; *A Reappraisal of the Forest Situation.*

No. 811.—SAW TIMBER—VOLUME, BY SPECIES AND REGION

[In millions of board feet. Status beginning of 1945. For States represented in regions shown, see table 810]

KIND OF WOOD	Total North and South	New England	Middle Atlantic	Lake	Central	Plains	South Atlantic	South-east	West Gulf
Eastern softwoods, total	269,636	33,363	14,917	15,670	2,418	468	59,228	75,292	57,473
Southern yellow pine	188,327	143	4,035	3,600	1,727	51	54,964	70,927	56,491
Spruce and fir [1]	27,007	20,649	2,718	3,600			40		
White and Norway pine	15,383	7,320	3,060	3,990	161		817	335	
Hemlock	14,921	3,764	3,906	5,950	343		738	142	
Cypress	6,226				123	1	2,277	1,284	548
Other	7,753	1,373	218	2,430	61	[5] 416	512	2,304	433
Eastern hardwoods, total	[1] 296,730	34,934	[1] 65,636	36,546	[1] 41,329	5,262	[1] 37,815	[1] 95,896	47,487
Oak	101,381	2,355	19,012	5,090	20,270	703	12,815	21,017	20,110
Beech, birch, and maple	67,387	26,740	19,210	17,090	7,297		3,330	1,210	
Sweet gum	25,476				515	35	6,667	10,516	8,641
Tupelo and black gum	15,987				343	1	6,390	7,309	5,947
Cottonwood and aspen	15,582	1,385	1,154	6,380	2,472	2,414	116	907	534
Yellow poplar	12,347	56	1,710		2,160		4,512	3,900	
Other	56,080	488	6,942	6,490	8,147	2,107	5,125	14,696	12,355

KIND OF WOOD	Total West	PACIFIC NORTHWEST				California	North Rocky Mountain	South Rocky Mountain
		Total	Douglas-fir subregion	Pine subregion				
Western species, total	1,042,556	639,894	344,981	125,963	227,855	127,229	53,568
Douglas fir	430,028	331,237	330,833	30,704	[4] 85,623	26,718	3,470
Ponderosa pine	[5] 185,035	80,198	4,850	75,348	[7] 61,191	26,771	26,905
True firs	113,541	77,384	46,444	11,398	[7] 43,012	9,360	3,315
Western hemlock	97,207	96,555	94,460	1,336		1,352	
Sugar pine and western white pine	40,224	8,089	6,171	1,918	19,506	12,630	
Redwood	38,114				[8] 38,114		
Spruce	33,880	8,020	8,020			12,499	13,361
Larch	26,696	8,727	145	8,582		17,879	
Lodgepole pine	22,060	1,171	37	1,134		14,406	6,455
Other softwoods	42,066	35,800	30,386	5,414	7,130	4,678	456
Hardwoods	5,905	3,945	3,895	97		996	916

[1] Balsam fir.
[2] Ponderosa pine.
[3] Excludes dead chestnut of sawlog size still standing and usable.
[4] May include some white fir, Sitka spruce, western hemlock, Port Orford cedar and western red cedar commonly lumped with Douglas-fir in redwood cruising.
[5] Excludes 416 million board feet in Plains region.
[6] Includes Jeffrey pine.
[7] Includes western white pine, mountain hemlock, and lodgepole pine recorded in cruises of fir areas.
[8] Redwood exclusive of volume of 1,000 bigtrees on cruises in west-side Sierra subregion.

Source: Department of Agriculture, Forest Service; A Reappraisal of the Forest Situation.

No. 812.—ANNUAL DRAIN FROM COMMERCIAL FOREST LANDS BY CUTTING FOR COMMODITIES AND BY DESTRUCTIVE AGENCIES

[Includes drain in volume from land capable of producing timber of commercial quantity and quality and available now or prospectively for commercial use]

ITEM	ALL TIMBER DRAIN (MILLIONS OF CU. FT.)			SAW-TIMBER DRAIN (MILLIONS OF BD. FT.)		
	Total	Softwoods	Hardwoods	Total	Softwoods	Hardwoods
Aggregate	13,661	8,151	5,510	52,893	36,530	16,363
Timber cut for commodities (1944)	12,182	7,348	4,834	48,658	34,531	14,047
Lumber	8,711	4,778	1,933	34,391	26,130	8,261
Fuelwood	2,203	719	1,484	3,868	1,957	1,905
Pulpwood	1,308	1,163	143	4,787	4,500	287
Hewed ties	363	153	210	1,643	777	866
Fence posts	220	59	161	226	82	144
Mine timbers	392	165	227	1,971	942	1,029
Veneer logs	225	40	185	330	70	260
Cooperage	176	40	134	744	195	549
Shingles	72	72		334	334	
Other	516	159	357	1,409	604	805
Timber removed by destructive agencies (average 1934-45)	1,479	863	676	4,235	2,989	1,296
Fire	460	247	213	859	547	312
Insects, disease, wind, etc.	1,019	556	463	3,376	2,392	984

Source: Department of Agriculture, Forest Service; A Reappraisal of the Forest Situation.

No. 813.—NATIONAL FOREST AREAS AND PURCHASES: 1905 TO 1952

[National forest area data are cumulative totals as of June 30 and include Alaska and Puerto Rico. Forest reservation purchases are for fiscal year ending June 30, and include Puerto Rico. See also *Historical Statistics*, series F 69–73]

ITEM	1905	1910	1920	1930	1940	1945	1950	1952
NATIONAL FOREST AREAS [1]								
Gross area within established boundaries (1,000 acres)	85,693	192,931	180,300	183,976	228,174	228,703	229,341	229,165
Under Forest Service Administration (1,000 acres)	75,352	168,029	156,032	160,091	176,779	179,381	181,205	181,293
NATIONAL FOREST PURCHASES								
Gross area approved for purchase (acres)			101,428	538,048	553,077	5	61,078	10,181
Average price per acre (dollars)			4.44	2.73	3.98	194.00	8.71	10.42
Total price (1,000 dollars)			450	1,469	2,201	1	532	106

[1] See headnote, table 814.

Source: Department of Agriculture, Forest Service; annual reports on *National Forest Areas*, and annual reports of the National Forest Reservation Commission.

No. 814.—NATIONAL FOREST AND OTHER AREAS, BY STATES AND FOR ALASKA AND PUERTO RICO: JUNE 30, 1952

[Areas in acres; comprises national forests, purchase units, experimental areas, land utilization and other areas placed under Administration of Forest Service, but not given a national-forest status. See also *Historical Statistics*, series F 69–70, for gross area and area under Forest Service]

STATE OR OTHER AREA	Gross area	Not under Forest Service Administration	Under Forest Service Administration	STATE OR OTHER AREA	Gross area	Not under Forest Service Administration	Under Forest Service Administration
Total	229,164,852	47,871,523	181,293,329	Nebraska	207,209	1,181	206,028
				Nevada	5,378,726	320,993	5,057,733
Alabama	2,435,748	1,815,020	620,728	New Hampshire	802,714	125,540	677,174
Arizona	12,159,651	674,702	11,484,949	New Mexico	10,279,550	1,269,657	9,009,893
Arkansas	3,596,746	1,235,226	2,361,520	North Carolina	3,592,436	2,478,392	1,114,044
California	25,078,194	5,138,774	19,939,420	North Dakota	764,425	763,905	520
Colorado	15,232,996	1,504,097	13,728,899	Ohio	1,466,029	1,362,187	103,842
Florida	1,244,229	168,979	1,075,250	Oklahoma	344,269	163,552	180,717
Georgia	1,732,322	1,067,996	664,326	Oregon	17,378,050	2,561,151	14,816,899
Idaho	21,569,943	1,293,951	20,275,992	Pennsylvania	743,999	272,577	471,422
Illinois	812,654	591,759	220,895	South Carolina	1,423,339	836,378	586,961
Indiana	784,647	667,541	117,106	South Dakota	1,403,357	287,945	1,115,412
Iowa	218,671	213,922	4,749	Tennessee	1,532,124	940,849	591,275
Kentucky	1,411,699	954,521	457,178	Texas	1,716,965	1,058,886	658,079
Louisiana	1,274,977	714,292	560,685	Utah	9,009,452	1,128,236	7,881,216
Maine	878,283	829,155	49,128	Vermont	629,004	403,818	225,186
Maryland	4,318	3,208	1,110	Virginia	4,017,962	2,575,505	1,442,457
Massachusetts	1,651		1,651	Washington	10,746,707	1,063,484	9,683,223
Michigan	5,161,057	2,605,121	2,555,936	West Virginia	1,832,868	929,546	903,322
Minnesota	5,041,660	2,364,588	2,677,072	Wisconsin	2,023,858	562,142	1,461,716
Mississippi	2,777,325	1,728,649	1,048,676	Wyoming	9,016,134	449,031	8,567,103
Missouri	3,489,999	2,104,692	1,355,307	Alaska	20,777,547	34,785	20,742,762
Montana	19,015,176	2,452,521	16,562,655	Puerto Rico	186,182	153,069	33,113

Source: Department of Agriculture, Forest Service; annual report, *National Forest Areas*.

No. 815.—National Forest Land Purchases, by States and for Puerto Rico, to June 30, 1952

[Under Act of Mar. 1, 1911, as amended by Act of June 7, 1924, and other related acts]

STATE OR OTHER AREA	Gross area (acres)	TOTAL NET AREA APPROVED FOR PURCHASE			NET AREA PURCHASED		
		Acres	Average price per acre	Total price (1,000)	Acres	Average price per acre	Total price (1,000)
Total	62,575,951	18,883,186	$3.86	$72,761	18,500,012	$3.86	$72,856
Alabama	2,436,087	504,261	3.67	1,851	504,221	3.67	1,851
Arkansas	3,596,056	1,194,774	2.92	3,496	1,194,156	2.92	3,498
California	2,600,872	152,901	8.88	1,367	151,488	8.74	1,394
Florida	1,244,229	782,850	3.14	2,460	782,001	3.14	2,458
Georgia	1,727,885	600,328	4.93	2,989	599,836	4.93	2,965
Idaho	726,970	38,532	3.56	137	35,091	3.44	121
Illinois	801,944	196,637	6.41	1,290	196,271	4.49	1,256
Indiana	761,467	108,513	7.21	783	107,086	7.20	770
Iowa	218,671	4,749	9.11	43	4,749	9.11	43
Kentucky	1,411,686	457,071	4.05	1,852	456,837	4.05	1,851
Louisiana	1,274,977	551,596	3.00	1,656	551,476	3.00	1,654
Maine	375,253	49,531	6.60	327	49,117	6.63	325
Michigan	5,142,733	1,892,265	3.06	5,794	1,892,285	3.06	5,794
Minnesota	5,041,660	1,557,475	2.56	3,965	1,555,442	2.54	3,948
Mississippi	2,485,527	1,008,368	3.54	3,563	1,005,366	3.54	3,563
Missouri	3,459,999	1,324,408	2.32	3,067	1,323,996	2.32	3,066
Nevada	2,334,884	18,909	9.44	178	18,746	9.48	178
New Hampshire	802,714	674,794	7.76	5,235	671,755	7.77	5,219
New Mexico	92,514	20,715	1.92	40	20,715	1.92	40
North Carolina	2,605,153	1,035,699	5.18	5,369	1,034,470	5.18	5,355
North Dakota	764,425	480	10.00	5	480	10.00	5
Ohio	1,466,029	102,178	7.27	743	96,588	7.30	710
Oklahoma	344,369	178,277	1.79	319	178,177	1.79	319
Oregon	66,704	52,467	17.08	893	52,497	17.08	893
Pennsylvania	705,737	469,655	6.27	2,943	469,655	6.27	2,943
South Carolina	1,428,339	562,823	4.21	3,498	562,823	4.21	3,498
Tennessee	1,531,797	562,823	4.48	2,523	562,823	4.48	2,523
Texas	1,716,964	652,765	4.62	3,017	652,765	4.62	3,017
Utah	2,969,262	120,011	3.10	391	124,177	2.99	372
Vermont	629,004	223,191	9.22	2,056	221,312	9.21	2,039
Virginia	3,547,362	1,446,901	3.27	4,737	1,446,589	3.27	4,735
West Virginia	1,832,562	903,316	3.41	3,076	903,316	3.41	3,076
Wisconsin	2,023,838	1,366,853	2.17	2,971	1,366,823	2.17	2,970
Puerto Rico	186,155	14,111	13.96	197	14,066	13.96	196

Source: National Forest Reservation Commission, *Annual Report*.

No. 816.—Forest Tree Distribution Program, With Costs: 1926 to 1952

[In thousands. See also *Historical Statistics*, series F 84–87]

YEAR	Trees distributed (calendar year)	COSTS (YEAR ENDING JUNE 30)			YEAR	Trees distributed (calendar year)	COSTS (YEAR ENDING JUNE 30)		
		Total	Federal contribution [1]	State expenditure			Total	Federal contribution [1]	State expenditure
1926	22,610	$268	$45	$223	1944	37,980	$463	$119	$344
1930	25,896	403	81	322	1945	37,743	572	114	458
1936	25,150	206	55	151	1946	43,588	637	112	524
1938	15,360	344	70	295	1947	42,347	586	117	768
1939	64,212	368	97	301	1948	77,524	1,178	112	1,666
1940	87,468	524	140	384	1949	[2] 103,902	1,408	112	1,298
1941	97,460	526	113	413	1950	[2] 135,300	1,603	189	1,314
1942	74,219	527	115	412	1951	[2] 391,875	3,021	377	2,644
1943	46,350	448	115	332	1952	[2] 209,665	3,658	376	3,283

[1] Provided by Clarke-McNary law, Act of June 7, 1924, and the Norris-Doxey law, Act of May 18, 1937.
[2] Data for year ending June 30.

Source: Department of Agriculture, Forest Service.

No. 817.—National Forests—Grazing, Roads and Trails, Visitors, Timber Cut, Receipts, Payments to States, and Allotments to Forest Service: 1910 to 1952

[Data for years ending June 30. See also *Historical Statistics*, series F 74–83, 88–106]

ITEM AND UNIT OF MEASURE	1910	1920	1930	1940	1945	1950	1951	1952
Livestock grazing: [1]								
Cattle, horses, and hogs [2]....thousands..	1,498	[3] 96	1,358	1,177	1,206	1,092	1,088	1,096
Sheep and goats [2]...............do.....	7,649	[3] 557	6,714	4,949	3,889	3,006	3,013	3,000
Roads and trails:								
Road construction.................miles..			1,726	1,709	258	[4] 213	[4] 275	} [4] 545
Road betterment (reconstruction).do.....				1,945	138	[4] 240	[4] 230	
Trail construction...............do.....			6,176	2,221	77	828	300	116
Expenditures, total............$1,000..			10,356	23,511	8,407	[4] 15,036	[4] 13,968	[4] 19,868
Utilization of recreation								
resources [5]...............1,000 visits..			6,911	16,163	10,074	27,368	29,950	33,000
Improved public recreation areas..do...			5,253	13,053	5,072	12,941	17,988	19,600
Other public recreation resources..do....			1,658	3,110	5,002	14,427	11,962	13,400
Utilization of highways, roads,								
and water routes [5].........1,000 visits..			5,450	22,270	14,530	56,797	65,454	84,493
Forest products, total value.........$1,000..	1,082	1,887	4,930	5,168	13,291	31,140	48,227	59,759
Timber cut (commercial and cost sales,								
land exchanges):								
Volume...............million ft. b. m..	379	805	1,653	1,740	3,145	3,502	4,688	4,419
Value....................$1,000..	906	1,764	4,790	4,807	13,016	30,714	47,816	59,341
Timber cut (free use):								
Volume...............million ft. b. m..	105	88	116	326	154	121	106	98
Value.....................$1,000..	176	113	[6] 117	[7] 304	[7] 171	[7] 215	[7] 233	[7] 225
Misc. forest products, value.......do.....		10	23	58	104	211	178	193
Receipts, total.................do.....	2,041	4,793	6,752	5,859	16,048	33,595	56,147	69,720
Timber use.....................do.....	1,011	2,044	4,390	3,943	11,587	29,379	51,099	63,723
Grazing use....................do.....	970	2,486	1,943	1,463	2,159	3,385	4,165	5,023
Special land use, water power, etc..do....	60	263	419	453	2,302	831	883	974
Payments to States and								
territories, total [5]...........$1,000..	511	1,253	1,719	1,456	4,039	8,459	14,126	17,535
25-percent fund................do.....	510	1,180	1,678	1,433	4,003	8,343	13,974	17,358
Arizona and New Mexico								
school fund..................$1,000..	1	73	41	23	36	72	107	132
Payment to State of Minnesota...do.....						44	45	45
Allotments to Forest Service, total..do....		472	671	678	1,601	3,476	5,729	7,085
Roads and trails.................do....		472	671	573	1,601	3,338	5,590	6,945
Acquisition of lands.............do....				105		138	139	140

[1] Number permitted to graze under pay permit. Calendar year data beginning 1930.
[2] Excludes animals under 6 months of age.   [3] Figures cover 6 months period ending December.
[4] Excludes Forest Highway Construction.   [5] Calendar year data beginning 1930   [6] Calendar year.
[7] Includes free use not reducible to bd. ft.   Value as follows: 1940, $3,774; 1945, $8,291; 1950, $20,468; 1951, $20,081; 1952, $15,477.
[8] Payments made in following year.

No. 818.—Forest Tree Distribution Program, With Costs, by States, Year Ending June 30, 1952

STATE OR OTHER AREA	Trees distributed during year (thousands)	EXPENDITURES ($1,000)		STATE OR OTHER AREA	Trees distributed during year (thousands)	EXPENDITURES ($1,000)	
		Total	Federal contribution [1]			Total	Federal contribution [1]
Total.........	**299,665**	**3,658**	**376**	New Hampshire......	459	28	10
				New Jersey..........	1,398	44	10
Alabama............	16,141	213	10	New York...........	39,137	295	10
Arkansas............	19,343	74	10	North Carolina......	9,889	112	10
California..........	135	41	7	North Dakota.......	917	32	9
Colorado...........	423	17	2	Ohio...............	6,351	135	10
Connecticut........	873	35	7	Oklahoma..........	4,070	54	10
Delaware...........	177	9	2	Oregon............	4,468	40	10
Florida............	17,718	179	10	Pennsylvania.......	18,493	273	10
Georgia............	25,926	273	10	Rhode Island.......		6	2
Idaho..............	309	38	11	South Carolina......	15,516	81	10
Illinois............	4,063	109	10	South Dakota.......	1,689	57	4
Indiana............	5,946	172	10	Tennessee..........	2,245	59	10
Iowa..............	397	9	2	Texas.............	9,512	53	10
Kentucky..........	1,942	49	10	Utah..............	156	11	3
Louisiana..........	23,422	185	10	Vermont...........	1,333	37	10
Maine.............	611	20	7	Virginia...........	7,536	60	10
Maryland..........	2,546	43	10	Washington........	256	24	8
Massachusetts......	691	46	10	West Virginia.......	1,085	53	10
Michigan..........	4,701	72	10	Wisconsin..........	23,106	313	10
Mississippi.........	21,592	104	10	Wyoming...........	279	11	2
Missouri...........	1,474	51	10				
Montana...........	425	42	10	Hawaii............	140	36	10
Nebraska..........	1,563	40	....	Puerto Rico........	1,212	23	10

[1] Provided by Clarke-McNary law, Act of June 7, 1924, and Norris-Doxey law, Act of May 18, 1937.

Source of tables 817 and 818: Department of Agriculture, Forest Service.

No. 819.—LIVESTOCK UNDER PAY PERMIT ON NATIONAL FORESTS, AND RECEIPTS FROM GRAZING, BY STATES: 1951

[No livestock grazed or money received from Alaska or Puerto Rico. Receipts from grazing are for fiscal year ending June 30, other data are for calendar year]

STATE OR OTHER AREA	LIVESTOCK UNDER PAY PERMIT		Receipts from grazing (fiscal year)	STATE OR OTHER AREA	LIVESTOCK UNDER PAY PERMIT		Receipts from grazing (fiscal year) [3]
	Cattle and horses [1]	Sheep and goats [1]			Cattle and horses [1]	Sheep and goats [1]	
	Number	Number	$1,000		Number	Number	$1,000
Total	1,088,332	3,012,812	4,166	Nevada	53,828	128,546	180
				New Mexico	75,014	93,137	302
Alabama	20			North Carolina	71		(3)
Arizona	132,930	86,162	533	North Dakota	5		(3)
Arkansas	2,271		2	Ohio	147		(3)
California	104,401	121,599	328	Oklahoma	18		(3)
Colorado	152,035	606,599	630	Oregon	69,094	149,701	257
Florida	3,152		1	Pennsylvania	43		
Idaho	106,634	605,653	491	South Carolina	315		(3)
Illinois	207	8	(3)	South Dakota	23,652	15,183	50
Indiana	51		(3)	Tennessee	100		(3)
Iowa	199		(3)	Texas	2,226		2
Louisiana	1,287		(3)	Utah	104,463	481,091	435
Michigan	1,718	227	2	Vermont	92		(3)
Minnesota	514		(3)	Virginia	166	169	(3)
Mississippi	1,016		(3)	Washington	18,554	39,965	65
Missouri	3,029		8	West Virginia	1,117	1,427	4
Montana	113,185	255,521	418	Wisconsin	293		(3)
Nebraska	13,222		68	Wyoming	104,253	427,824	365

[1] Excludes animals under 6 months of age.　　[2] Includes grazing trespass.　　[3] Less than $500.

Source: Department of Agriculture, Forest Service.

No. 820.—PAYMENTS TO STATES, ALASKA, AND PUERTO RICO FROM RECEIPTS OF NATIONAL FORESTS: 1950 TO 1953

[In thousands of dollars. For years ending June 30. Payments are 25 percent of net receipts of preceding fiscal year from sales of timber, grazing fees, and miscellaneous uses of national forests (exclusive of school-fund payments to Arizona and New Mexico, and payments for acquisition of land), under Act of May 23, 1908]

STATE OR OTHER AREA	1950	1951	1952	1953	STATE OR OTHER AREA	1950	1951	1952	1953
Total	7,719	8,343	13,974	17,358	Nevada	35	42	46	58
					New Hampshire	23	24	39	33
Alabama	90	114	99	199	New Mexico	124	137	198	213
Arizona	244	291	434	533	North Carolina	85	64	84	125
Arkansas	375	499	538	565	North Dakota	(1)	(1)	(1)	(1)
California	1,133	973	2,345	3,292					
Colorado	218	225	283	302	Ohio	3	4	4	5
					Oklahoma	40	56	58	62
Florida	66	58	82	110	Oregon	2,045	2,230	4,292	4,960
Georgia	81	65	95	143	Pennsylvania	14	23	23	34
Idaho	418	496	821	887	South Carolina	100	150	151	240
Illinois	17	12	18	16					
Indiana	2	1	2	2	South Dakota	57	39	91	99
					Tennessee	40	51	51	78
Iowa	(1)	(1)	(1)	1	Texas	263	339	321	511
Kentucky	25	37	32	40	Utah	112	138	148	182
Louisiana	101	113	102	155	Vermont	26	24	40	35
Maine	6	2	3	2					
Michigan	65	82	128	158	Virginia	38	36	46	48
					Washington	1,106	1,224	2,321	2,806
Minnesota	68	69	111	138	West Virginia	29	21	34	42
Mississippi	197	265	309	432	Wisconsin	66	66	91	114
Missouri	25	26	36	38	Wyoming	109	119	142	165
Montana	251	207	330	500					
Nebraska	12	12	17	21	Alaska	5	6	5	8
					Puerto Rico	3	4	3	4

[1] Less than $500.

Source: Department of Agriculture, Forest Service; annual report, *Agricultural Statistics*.

No. 821.—Forest Fires—Number, and Area Burned Over on Federal, State, and Private Forest Lands: 1932 to 1951

[Area in thousands of acres. See also *Historical Statistics*, series F 145-150]

CALENDAR YEAR	FEDERAL LANDS, PROTECTED AREA [1]			STATE AND PRIVATE FORESTS [3]					
				On protected area			On unprotected area		
	Forest area [1]	Number of fires	Area burned over	Forest area [3]	Number of fires	Area burned over	Forest area [3]	Number of fires	Area burned over
1932	138,525	4,933	419	266,723	55,567	3,234	220,617	105,899	38,410
1933	176,698	4,517	380	266,259	48,770	3,343	218,664	87,435	40,167
1934	182,167	8,064	658	282,979	61,254	3,515	209,558	93,345	37,648
1935	180,443	7,962	228	288,751	54,502	2,311	204,379	77,743	27,798
1936	187,122	11,144	425	298,365	73,709	3,792	195,650	141,432	38,990
1937	182,872	9,468	90	301,911	54,292	1,254	182,763	121,449	20,637
1938	191,860	9,873	316	308,458	76,326	2,623	158,884	146,030	30,876
1939	157,691	12,356	522	278,919	85,677	3,266	148,812	114,638	26,680
1940	153,722	14,076	482	281,706	73,527	2,934	146,749	107,824	22,432
1941	153,559	10,002	437	282,074	80,994	3,138	143,743	108,706	22,830
1942	153,561	9,941	576	290,928	75,849	3,863	136,687	122,428	27,415
1943	183,052	9,892	702	299,331	78,815	3,860	131,275	121,619	27,772
1944	212,344	8,985	375	301,228	56,148	2,301	129,919	66,096	13,873
1945	213,210	8,539	445	302,942	48,176	2,456	126,959	68,013	14,780
1946	213,597	9,670	321	318,505	66,103	2,253	120,489	96,505	18,117
1947	215,361	8,928	318	327,968	71,442	2,814	111,026	120,429	20,093
1948	217,724	8,681	312	339,463	61,095	1,982	99,531	106,413	14,283
1949	214,805	9,592	317	357,168	78,649	2,320	81,826	105,533	12,760
1950	212,622	8,418	391	360,584	96,578	3,407	66,130	103,404	11,720
1951	212,502	8,638	471	363,414	97,230	3,056	63,280	58,222	7,253

[1] In continental U. S.; includes National Forests, Interior, Soil Conservation Service, TVA, Public Domain, etc.

[2] In continental U. S. and Hawaii. Data reported to Forest Service by its field offices, cooperating agencies, other Government bureaus, and similar sources. Statistics on unprotected areas based on State estimates only.

[3] Prior to 1939 forest area included total area needing protection. Beginning with 1939, this area included only forest area needing protection, which accounts for reduction in areas between 1938 and 1939.

Source: Department of Agriculture, Forest Service; annual report, *Forest Fire Statistics*, and records.

No. 822.—Forest Fires—Expenditures for Control on State and Private Forest Lands, 1920 to 1952 and by States, 1952

[In thousands of dollars. See also *Historical Statistics*, series F 151-154]

FISCAL YEAR AND STATE	Total expenditures	Federal	State and county	Private agencies	STATE	Total expenditures	Federal	State and county	Private agencies
1920	945	85	860		Florida	1,681	529	1,009	143
1930	5,500	1,252	4,248		Georgia	2,294	435	1,803	56
1940	9,188	1,988	7,200		Louisiana	1,137	277	853	7
					Maine	747	210	537	
1941	9,278	1,979	7,299		Michigan	1,695	404	1,291	
1942	11,168	2,703	6,272	2,193	Minnesota	1,134	252	882	
1943	13,743	4,624	6,714	2,405	Mississippi	996	244	752	
1944	13,960	5,870	6,351	1,739	Missouri	670	191	479	
1945	14,601	5,925	6,562	2,114	New York	1,064	228	836	
					North Carolina	1,013	267	724	22
1946	16,899	7,012	7,498	2,389	Oregon	3,372	661	1,149	1,562
1947	19,603	7,890	9,477	2,236	Pennsylvania	652	197	455	
1948	23,500	8,604	12,831	2,065	South Carolina	1,019	301	718	
1949	27,875	8,572	17,201	2,102	Tennessee	715	156	554	5
1950	28,934	8,551	18,121	2,262	Texas	634	158	331	145
1951	33,160	8,996	21,885	2,279	Virginia	668	197	468	3
1952	35,597	8,960	23,734	2,903	Washington	2,377	605	1,431	341
					Wisconsin	1,180	309	871	
Alabama	1,013	312	608	93	Other States [1]	4,114	1,245	2,421	445
Arkansas	839	254	507	78					
California	6,583	1,528	5,055						

[1] Includes Hawaii.

Source: Department of Agriculture, Forest Service; records.

No. 828.—LUMBER PRODUCTION, BY KIND OF WOOD, AND AVERAGE MILL VALUE: 1869 TO 1951

[Data not strictly comparable because of incomplete coverage of numerous small mills in the East prior to 1942 and exclusion of mills cutting less than 50 M ft. b. m. for all years prior to 1942 except 1899-1908, and 1919. Exclusion of under 50 M class of mills would affect totals less than 1 percent as reflected by 1942 survey. Data for 1943-46 and for 1949-51 are based on sample surveys and are subject to sampling errors; see source publications for evaluation of sampling reliability. See also *Historical Statistics*, series F 109-111 and F 120-122 for similar but not identical figures from Dept. of Agri. Forest Service]

YEAR	PRODUCTION (MILLION FT., BD. MEAS.)			AVERAGE MILL VALUE (DOLLARS PER 1,000 BD. FT.)		
	Total	Soft-wood	Hard-wood	Total	Soft-woods	Hard-woods
1869	12,756					
1879	18,091					
1889	23,842			11.41		
1899	1 35,078	26,146	8,634	11.13	10.27	12.53
1909	44,510	33,897	10,613	15.26	14.08	19.52
1919	34,552	27,407	7,145	30.21	28.39	37.32
1929	36,896	29,813	7,073	26.94	24.31	36.04
1935	19,539	16,248	3,291	20.43	19.08	27.09
1940	28,984	24,903	4,081	23.32	22.43	28.47
1943	34,289	26,917	7,371	36.96	35.57	41.57
1944	32,938	25,160	7,778	(2)	(2)	(2)
1945	28,123	21,140	6,983	(2)	(2)	(2)
1946	34,112	25,857	8,256	(2)	(2)	(2)
1947	35,404	27,937	7,467	55.00	55.00	55.00
1948	(2)	(2)	6,704	(2)	(2)	(2)
1949	32,176	26,472	5,704	(2)	(2)	(2)
1950	38,007	30,633	7,374	(2)	(2)	(2)
1951	37,204	29,493	7,711	(2)	(2)	(2)

KIND OF WOOD	PRODUCTION (MILLION FEET, BOARD MEASURE)								
	1899	1919	1929	1939	1945	1947	1949	1950	1951
Softwood, total	26,146	27,407	29,813	21,406	21,140	27,937	26,472	30,633	29,493
Balsam fir		68	38	20	(2)	27	(4)	(4)	(4)
Cedar	233	232	309	264	203	366	6 257	6 305	6 324
Cypress	496	656	532	422	228	240	239	(4)	(4)
Douglas fir	1,737	4,902	6,669	6,494	6,237	9,042	9,074	9,984	10,372
Hemlock	3,421	1,755	2,099	676	1,039	1,344	1,177	1,506	1,502
Larch	51	388	245	111	(2)	292	234	346	295
Lodgepole pine		16	31	55	65	100	96	(4)	(4)
Ponderosa pine	945	1,755	3,283	3,360	3,056	3,829	3,715	3,865	3,705
Redwood	360	410	486	345	444	529	744	875	860
Spruce	1,442	980	564	347	358	392	346	(4)	(4)
Sugar pine	54	134	349	309	228	343	380	425	400
White fir		223	307	98	499	673	759	1,114	1,285
White pine	7,742	1,724	1,248	1,158	1,269	1,370	1,119	1,292	1,314
Yellow pine	9,659	13,063	11,630	7,749	7,210	9,473	8,259	9,939	8,495
Other softwood	9				203	7	51	1,080	940
Hardwood, total	8,634	7,145	7,073	3,740	6,982	7,467	5,704	7,374	7,711
Alder		(4)	24	21	14	24	(2)	(4)	(4)
Ash	269	155	152	90	84	106	121	81	96
Basswood	305	184	133	96	100	126	103	(2)	100
Beech		359	187	120	352	330	256	325	332
Birch	133	375	374	141	152	175	153	137	152
Chestnut	207	546	268	74	(2)	33	(4)	(4)	(4)
Cottonwood	416	144	165	130	209	381	217	236	241
Elm	457	194	176	74	159	202	144	(2)	164
Hickory	97	170	57	38	159	156	102	125	(2)
Magnolia		2	42	20	(2)	(2)	(4)	(4)	(4)
Maple	632	857	824	445	522	490	408	546	584
Oak	4,438	2,708	2,574	1,432	2,859	3,193	2,515	3,347	3,590
Red gum	285	851	1,104	383	971	805	515	783	792
Sycamore	50	28	55	27	(2)	62	46	(2)	(2)
Tupelo		144	307	271	439	408	290	342	366
Walnut	39	39	72	27	(2)	34	23	(2)	(2)
Yellow poplar	1,115	329	436	276	578	636	646	638	742
Other hardwood	209	50	120	75	385	167	151	643	590

1 Includes 298,000,000 board feet of lumber not reported by kind of wood. 2 Not available.
2 Includes 165,305,000 board feet of softwood lumber and 7,805,000 board feet of hardwood lumber sawed by New England mills from timber salvaged from the hurricane of 1938.
4 Not available separately.
5 Incense and western red cedars only; data for Port Orford cedar and eastern cedar not available separately.
6 Less than 500,000 board feet.

Source: Department of Commerce, Bureau of the Census (in cooperation with Department of Agriculture, Forest Service, and Tennessee Valley Authority); reports of Census of Manufactures and annual report, *Lumber Production and Mill Stocks*, Facts for Industry, Series M13G.

No. 824.—LUMBER PRODUCTION, BY REGIONS AND STATES: 1889 TO 1951

[In millions of board feet. See headnote, table 823 for explanation of lack of comparability of statistics]

REGION AND STATE	1889	1899	1909	1919	1929	1939¹	1947	1949	1950	1951
United States	23,842	35,078	44,510	34,552	36,886	28,148	35,404	32,176	38,007	37,204
Northeastern States	4,726	5,709	5,197	2,584	1,232	1,140	2,324	1,900	2,103	2,367
Maine	597	785	1,112	596	258	215	459	(²)	(²)	(²)
New Hampshire	277	572	650	339	192	266	322	(²)	(²)	(²)
Vermont	384	376	352	218	120	126	204	236	(²)	(²)
Massachusetts	212	344	361	167	72	126	132	(²)	(²)	(²)
Connecticut	49	108	168	87	30	25	20	(²)	(²)	(²)
Rhode Island	8	19	25	11	7	12	2	(²)	(²)	(²)
New York	925	878	681	358	160	108	383	334	(²)	(²)
New Jersey	34	74	62	37	16	14	32	(²)	(²)	(²)
Pennsylvania	2,133	2,333	1,463	630	314	186	580	(²)	(²)	(²)
Maryland	82	184	268	113	55	51	154	(²)	(²)	(²)
Delaware	23	36	55	27	10	11	34	(²)	(²)	(²)
Central States	3,120	5,642	5,487	3,016	2,347	1,231	2,393	1,961	2,327	2,132
Ohio	565	990	543	280	176	111	265	(²)	(²)	(²)
Indiana	755	1,037	556	282	170	111	180	(²)	(²)	(²)
Illinois	222	388	170	65	38	27	100	(²)	(²)	(²)
Missouri	402	724	660	321	228	74	259	163	166	(²)
West Virginia	302	778	1,473	763	633	324	484	480	(²)	(²)
Kentucky	423	775	861	512	339	207	439	(²)	(²)	(²)
Tennessee	460	951	1,224	792	764	376	665	643	704	(²)
Southern States	3,718	8,464	14,796	12,704	12,484	7,549	9,397	7,358	9,383	8,429
Georgia	575	1,312	1,342	894	1,386	907	1,687	1,510	2,018	(²)
Florida	412	790	1,202	1,137	1,137	603	534	436	(²)	(²)
Alabama	589	1,101	1,691	1,799	2,059	1,412	1,795	1,297	2,139	(²)
Mississippi	454	1,206	2,573	2,390	2,669	1,201	1,397	872	1,242	(²)
Arkansas	538	1,624	2,111	1,772	1,348	1,110	1,285	(²)	(²)	(²)
Louisiana	304	1,115	3,552	3,164	2,232	1,036	1,269	919	950	(²)
Texas	843	1,232	2,099	1,380	1,452	1,137	1,347	1,122	1,336	(²)
Oklahoma	3	22	226	168	200	143	83	(²)	(²)	(²)
North Carolina Pine States	1,129	2,712	5,177	3,374	2,979	2,367	3,577	3,568	4,502	4,363
Virginia	416	959	2,102	1,098	708	679	1,166	1,033	1,557	(²)
North Carolina	515	1,287	2,178	1,654	1,202	1,042	1,540	1,730	1,994	(²)
South Carolina	199	466	898	622	1,068	646	871	804	951	(²)
Lake States	8,251	8,750	5,476	2,692	1,771	781	1,310	864	1,065	963
Michigan	4,300	3,018	1,800	876	571	333	580	(²)	(²)	(²)
Minnesota	1,084	2,342	1,562	700	357	111	244	(²)	(²)	(²)
Wisconsin	2,866	3,389	2,025	1,116	843	337	486	(²)	(²)	(²)
Pacific States	2,028	2,901	6,905	8,798	14,149	10,693	14,216	14,439	16,108	16,626
Washington	1,064	1,429	3,863	4,961	7,302	4,214	3,705	3,442	3,606	(²)
Oregon	446	735	1,899	2,577	4,784	4,765	7,102	7,185	8,239	(²)
California and Nevada	³ 518	738	³ 1,144	³ 1,259	2,063	1,685	3,409	3,812	4,263	(²)
Rocky Mountain States	249	556	1,292	1,299	1,843	1,336	2,062	1,990	2,419	2,237
Montana	90	256	309	287	389	271	500	459	480	(²)
Idaho	28	65	646	765	1,029	675	951	926	1,127	(²)
Arizona	5	36	63	74	175	119	220	(²)	(²)	(²)
New Mexico	26	31	92	87	148	106	127	10⁷	(²)	(²)
Colorado	80	134	142	65	72	84	145	135	(²)	(²)
Utah	14	18	13	12	5	15	39	(²)	(²)	(²)
Wyoming	6	17	29	9	26	65	81	(²)	(²)	(²)
All other	612	401	⁴ 179	⁴ 85	81	51	125	96	100	87
PERCENTAGE DISTRIBUTION										
United States	100.0	100.0	100.0	100.0	100.0	100.0	100.0	100.0	100.0	100.0
Northeastern States	19.8	16.3	11.7	7.5	3.3	4.5	6.6	5.9	5.5	6.3
Central States	13.1	16.1	12.3	8.7	6.4	4.9	6.8	6.1	6.1	5.8
Southern States	15.6	24.0	33.2	36.8	33.8	30.0	26.5	22.9	24.7	23.0
North Carolina Pine States	4.7	7.7	11.6	9.8	8.1	9.4	10.1	11.1	11.8	11.9
Lake States	34.6	24.9	12.3	7.8	4.8	3.1	3.7	2.7	2.8	2.6
Pacific States	8.5	8.3	15.5	25.5	38.4	42.5	40.1	44.9	42.4	44.1
Rocky Mountain States	1.0	1.6	2.9	3.8	5.0	5.3	5.8	6.2	6.4	6.1
All other	2.6	1.1	.4	.2	.2	.2	.4	.3	.3	.2

¹ Includes 165,305,000 board feet of softwood lumber and 7,605,000 board feet of hardwood lumber sawed by New England mills from timber salvaged from the hurricane of 1938.
² Not available separately.
³ California only; for 1909 and 1919 Nevada included with "All other." ⁴ Includes Nevada.

Source: Department of Commerce, Bureau of the Census (in cooperation with Department of Agriculture, Forest Service, and Tennessee Valley Authority); reports of Census of Manufactures and annual report, *Lumber Production and Mill Stocks, Facts for Industry*, Series M13G.

No. 825.—LUMBER AND SHINGLES—PRODUCTION, FOR ALASKA: 1899 TO 1950

YEAR	Number of mills reporting	LUMBER SAWED (M FEET, B. M.)					Shingles (squares) [1]
		Total	Spruce	Hemlock	Cedar	All other	
1899	10	6,571	6,088	15	[3]	[5] 500	
1904	6	7,974	7,883		[3]	[4] 41	1,156
1909	22	21,673	21,182	483			
1925	26	40,867	35,718	2,668	[3]	[5] 2,201	3,266
1927	19	30,348	21,850	6,205	[3]	[5] 333	2,943
1933	20	32,490	14,760	5,099	665	3	2,182
1939	24	26,885	16,162	6,071	1,895	57	2,471
1945	35	59,086	51,632	6,328	1,175		865
1946	43	57,506	47,487	6,719	1,296	13	2,632
1947	46	50,480	48,195	6,372	1,497	6	[5]
1948	55	62,181	43,976	12,432	1,008	765	[5]
1949	69	48,541	39,024	5,067	[5] 870		[5]
1950	79	61,936	54,582	6,100	[7] 1,264		[5]

[1] Reported in thousands for 1932 and prior years and converted on basis of 800 shingles to the square.
[2] Included in "All other." [3] Includes figures for cedar lumber.
[4] Data not published to avoid disclosing operations of indiv dual establishments.
[5] Not available. [6] Includes figures for birch. [7] Includes cottonwood and Douglas fir.

Source: Department of Commerce, Bureau of the Census (in cooperation with Department of Agriculture, Forest Service, and Tennessee Valley Authority); reports of Census of Manufactures and annual report, *Lumber, Lath, and Shingle Production, Facts for Industry, Series* M13C.

No. 826.—LATH AND SHINGLES—PRODUCTION: 1899 TO 1952

[Lath in thousands and shingles in squares. Shingles reported in thousands prior to 1932 and converted to squares on basis of 800 shingles to square. See headnote, table 825 for explanation of lack of comparability of statistics. Data for shingles reasonably comparable over a period of years, because of complete enumeration of Red Cedar Shingle Industry, this industry's production comprising over 90 percent of total shingle production]

YEAR	Lath	Shingles	YEAR	Lath	Shingles
1899	3,833,995	16,127,521	1943	180,512	[1] 3,735,961
1909	3,703,195	16,634,214	1944 [2]	132,859	[1] 3,587,502
1919	1,734,078	11,490,880	1945	113,268	[1] 3,136,613
1925	3,052,130	7,510,432	1946 [2]	134,602	[1] 3,463,612
1929	1,706,858	7,638,340	1947	197,078	[1] 3,953,485
1930	1,097,255	4,955,138	1948	[4]	[1] 3,421,863
1931	620,038	4,416,709	1949	[4]	[1] 3,088,058
1935	512,207	[1] 6,500,242	1950	[4]	[1] 3,738,929
1940	823,498	[1] 6,126,230	1951	[4]	[1] 2,973,274
1942	306,969	[1] 5,266,673	1952	[4]	[1] 2,870,822

[1] Includes data for shakes.
[2] Data incomplete since mills idle during war were not canvassed for 1944 production.
[3] Does not include Connecticut, Delaware, Illinois, Indiana, Iowa, Kansas, Kentucky, Maine, Maryland, Massachusetts, Michigan, Minnesota, Missouri, Nebraska, New Hampshire, New Jersey, New York, North Dakota, Ohio, Pennsylvania, Rhode Island, Vermont, West Virginia, and Wisconsin.
[4] Not available. [5] Red cedar shingles and shakes only; see headnote.

Source: Department of Commerce, Bureau of Census (in cooperation with Department of Agriculture, Forest Service, and Tennessee Valley Authority); reports of Census of Manufactures and annual report, *Red Cedar Shingles, Facts for Industry, Series* M13C.

No. 827.—COOPERAGE STOCK—PRODUCTION, BY KIND: 1909 TO 1947

[Staves and hoops in thousands; heading in thousand sets]

KIND	1909	1919	1927	1929	1931	1933	1935	1937	1939	1947 [1]
Staves:										
Tight	379,331	353,525	324,127	357,353	204,634	154,575	221,619	305,286	182,431	131,104
Slack	2,029,846	1,121,324	981,782	1,039,450	537,177	426,585	439,970	574,766	526,315	406,731
Heading:										
Tight	20,891	24,276	26,448	20,329	20,090	12,031	15,290	12,377	14,277	9,507
Slack	140,234	57,351	59,337	72,591	43,375	37,461	35,992	54,315	45,465	34,539
Hoops	378,703	140,772	134,506	133,054	94,311	61,161	51,818	68,152	32,209	10,457

[1] Excludes small amount produced in other than cooperage stock and cooperage industries.

Source: Department of Commerce, Bureau of the Census (in cooperation with Department of Agriculture, Forest Service); reports of Census of Manufactures.

No. 828.—PULPWOOD, WOOD PULP, PAPER AND PAPERBOARD: 1899 TO 1952

[Cords of 128 cu. ft.; short tons of 2,000 lbs. See also *Historical Statistics*, series F 132–133]

YEAR	Pulpwood consumption	Wood-pulp production	Paper and paperboard production	YEAR	Pulpwood consumption	Wood-pulp production	Paper and paperboard production
	Cords	*Short tons*	*Short tons*		*Cords*	*Short tons*	*Short tons*
1899	1,986,310	1,179,525	2,167,503	1941	16,580,000	10,375,422	[1] 17,933,607
1904	3,050,717	1,921,768	3,106,696	1945	16,911,861	10,167,200	17,370,965
1909	4,001,607	2,495,523	4,216,708	1946	17,817,560	10,606,527	19,277,667
1914	4,470,763	2,893,150	5,270,047	1947	19,714,229	11,945,864	21,114,000
1919	5,477,832	3,517,952	6,098,530	1948	21,189,458	12,872,292	21,897,301
1925	6,093,821	3,962,217	9,182,204	1949	19,945,440	12,207,279	20,315,436
1930	7,195,524	4,630,308	10,169,140	1950	23,627,217	14,848,951	24,375,468
1935	7,628,274	4,925,669	10,479,095	1951	26,521,795	16,524,408	26,048,143
1940	13,742,958	[1] 8,959,559	14,483,709	1952 [3]	26,462,219	16,466,810	24,413,212

[1] Beginning 1940, data on a new basis. i. e., figures include data for 6 mills not classified as pulp producers before 1940. For same reason, an additional mill was included in 1941 and 2 more added in 1943. 1940 figure on old basis, 8,851,740 tons.

[2] Beginning 1941, data on a new basis. i. e., figures include data for 25 mills not previously classified as producers of paper and paperboard. 1941 figure on old basis, 17,093,092 tons.

[3] Preliminary.

Source: Department of Commerce, Bureau of the Census. Published currently in *Facts for Industry*, Series M14A.

No. 829.—PULPWOOD CONSUMPTION AND VENEER AND PLYWOOD LOG CONSUMPTION AND PRODUCTION, BY KIND OF WOOD: 1943 TO 1952

YEAR	PULPWOOD CONSUMPTION			VENEER AND PLYWOOD				
				Log consumption		Production		
	Total	Softwood	Hardwood	Softwood [1]	Hardwood [2]	Softwood plywood [1]	Hardwood [2]	
							Veneer	Plywood
	Cords [3]	*Cords* [3]	*Cords* [3]	*M ft., log scale*	*M ft., log scale*	*M sq. ft., ⅜″ basis*	*M sq ft., surface meas.*	*M sq. ft., surface meas.*
1943	[4] 15,644,500	13,477,074	1,287,983	659,479	934,860	1,495,170	9,870,597	1,211,814
1944	[5] 16,757,400	13,931,075	1,550,117	646,946	885,960	1,484,889	9,270,351	1,166,243
1945	16,911,861	14,519,870	2,391,991	545,762		1,222,382		
1946	17,817,560	15,384,176	2,433,384	641,738		1,436,065		
1947	19,714,229	17,021,974	2,692,255	750,633		1,700,446		
1948	21,189,458	18,490,916	2,698,542	857,722		1,953,883		
1949	19,945,440	17,330,495	2,614,945	906,709		1,976,649		
1950	23,627,217	20,405,910	3,221,307	1,157,202		2,675,580		
1951	26,521,795	22,768,368	3,753,427	1,231,643	1,044,981	2,994,773	11,191,523	[6] 1,467,248
1952	26,462,219	22,662,381	3,799,838	1,303,605	([7])	3,153,909	([7])	([7])

[1] West coast softwood plywood industry, principally Douglas fir; includes some hardwood.

[2] Veneer and plywood industry other than west coast companies; includes some softwood.

[3] Cords of 128 cu. ft. (rough wood basis).

[4] Includes 641,838 cords of woods not classified by kind, and 237,605 cords of saw mill waste.

[5] Includes 988,873 cords of woods not classified by kind, and 287,335 cords of saw mill waste.

[6] Does not include 54,305 M square feet, ⅜″ basis, of hardwood plywood produced during period from April through December 31 in West Coast softwood plywood mills. Data not available on amount of hardwood plywood produced in these mills during period from January 1 through March 31.

[7] Not available.

Source: Department of Commerce, Bureau of the Census; *Facts for Industry*, Series 16–3, M13A, M13B and M14A, and records.

No. 830.—PAPER AND BOARD—PRODUCTION BY TYPE: 1949 TO 1952

[Tons of 2,000 pounds]

TYPE OF PAPER	1949	1950	1951	1952 [1]
All types	20,515,436	24,375,408	24,046,142	24,413,212
Paper, total	9,195,795	10,685,632	11,634,727	10,886,860
Newsprint	917,778	1,013,346	1,108,672	1,105,351
Groundwood printing and specialty paper, uncoated, total	674,542	705,229	780,114	903,512
Printing and converting paper, paper machine coated, total	887,371	1,680,962	1,112,990	1,006,251
Book paper, uncoated, total	1,413,165	1,579,755	1,610,450	1,493,628
Fine paper, total	1,012,491	1,197,809	1,366,438	1,285,279
Coarse paper, total	2,780,630	3,297,392	3,627,072	3,335,021
Special industrial	252,076	341,330	408,391	308,381
Sanitary	1,008,162	1,146,851	1,343,856	1,143,657
Tissue	186,687	216,965	226,174	208,181
Absorbent	86,113	119,113	127,591	117,790
Paperboard, total	8,994,777	10,925,731	11,630,048	10,778,452
Liners	3,131,627	3,572,051	4,213,228	3,904,756
Corrugating material	1,316,590	1,633,875	1,784,162	1,953,672
Container chip and filler board	242,589	204,651	320,391	303,044
Folding boxboard (for use in folding box plants only)	1,953,170	2,355,690	2,362,356	2,192,980
Set-up boxboard (for use in set-up box plants only)	617,349	708,782	733,475	687,070
Cardboard	78,722	98,748	85,208	68,407
All other paperboard	1,667,580	1,944,294	2,116,197	2,035,660
Wet machine board, total	129,761	104,621	148,381	137,385
Shoe board	42,522	49,128	45,690	(2)
Binder board	36,477	41,388	41,940	(2)
Other	50,462	73,900	60,451	(2)
Construction paper materials, total	1,990,188	2,046,444	2,654,997	2,606,755
Building paper (including flexible fibre insulation)	1,151,374	1,496,260	1,366,601	1,395,300
Building board	838,729	1,221,194	1,362,296	1,305,455

[1] Preliminary.
[2] Not available.

Source: Department of Commerce, Bureau of the Census; annual report, *Census of Pulp Mills and of Paper and Paperboard Mills*, Facts for Industry, Series M14A and M14D.

No. 831.—WOOD PRODUCTS TREATED WITH PRESERVATIVES: 1909 TO 1952

[In thousands of cubic feet. See also *Historical Statistics*, series F 125-131]

PRODUCT	1909	1919	1930	1935	1940	1945	1950	1951	1952 [1]
Total	75,946	146,061	332,319	179,439	265,473	279,450	289,788	302,471	316,925
Crossties	62,079	112,704	189,801	102,509	128,090	140,206	109,495	110,475	125,669
Poles [2]	660	6,061	75,268	34,708	74,129	74,391	109,470	104,066	93,109
Lumber [3]							27,064	32,945	35,995
Piles	4,422	9,169	17,027	5,575	15,660	20,525	12,282	17,325	16,577
Switch ties [4]			14,623	7,836	8,859	9,900	5,974	10,539	10,724
Fence posts [3]							5,382	8,641	11,197
Construction timbers	5,296	12,062	19,013	15,683	12,496	9,803	5,777	6,413	5,053
Wood blocks	2,904	4,714	5,013	1,484	2,790	3,294	2,684	4,537	6,545
Cross arms	42	75	1,299	351	675	1,469	1,812	3,103	1,896
Miscellaneous	464	676	10,264	6,207	22,994	19,863	2,955	5,040	4,800

[1] Preliminary, subject to revision.
[2] Includes both full-length pressure-treated poles and nonpressure (butt-treated) poles.
[3] Included in miscellaneous prior to 1950.
[4] Included in construction timbers prior to 1935.

Source: Department of Agriculture, Forest Service (in cooperation with American Wood-Preserver's Association); annual report, *Quantity of Wood Treated and Preservatives Used in the United States*.

No. 832.—WOOD PULP—PRODUCTION, BY STATES AND BY PROCESS: 1909 TO 1952

[Tons of 2,000 pounds]

STATE AND PROCESS	1909	1919	1929	1939	1947	1950	1951	1952[1]
Total	2,495,523	3,517,952	4,862,885	6,993,334	11,945,864	14,848,951	16,524,408	16,466,510
PROCESS								
Groundwood	1,179,266	1,518,829	1,637,653	1,444,875	2,049,814	2,215,883	2,473,796	2,379,740
Defibrated or exploded[2]					693,282	934,666	944,776	1,050,124
Special alpha and dissolving grades						478,849	616,202	706,033
Sulfite	}1,017,631	1,419,829	1,681,511	1,946,452	2,795,962	{2,369,587	2,525,325	2,366,735
Sulphate		120,378	918,084	2,962,657	5,356,710	7,501,429	8,571,779	8,568,704
Soda	298,626	411,693	520,729	441,565	491,580	522,221	446,260	425,415
Semi-chemical, off quality, screenings and misc.		47,223	104,908	197,785	558,516	826,316	946,279	961,059
STATE								
California	(2)	(2)	(2)		19,125	120,430	(2)	
Florida				449,162	783,258	1,207,538	1,326,157	
Georgia		(2)		(2)	(2)	1,091,708	1,209,445	
Illinois					(2)	78,928	74,880	
Louisiana		(2)	246,590	589,672	1,128,727	1,381,458	1,490,030	
Maine	620,705	916,764	981,433	941,273	1,237,075	1,182,759	1,349,568	
Michigan	64,369	106,194	178,015	200,325	232,678	239,762	272,837	
Minnesota	37,295	129,560	189,664	160,665	392,254	(2)	(2)	
Mississippi		(2)	(2)	(2)	476,264	778,977	778,259	
New Jersey					68,620	79,155	81,301	
New Hampshire	212,599	232,134	212,774	(2)	174,137	(2)	236,330	(4)
New York	679,534	811,958	662,988	460,652	645,955	578,997	711,216	
North Carolina	(2)	(2)	(2)	179,636	474,020	(2)	675,599	
Ohio	(2)	(2)	(2)	(2)	(2)	63,061	63,499	
Pennsylvania	135,525	215,686	213,083	193,958	288,757	308,359	315,551	
Oregon	(2)		85,945	(2)	288,047	436,078	526,874	625,457
Vermont			26,307	(2)	(2)	(2)	(2)	
Virginia	48,641	(2)	206,050	402,929	600,384	751,327	851,861	
Washington	(2)	83,575	523,948	1,126,114	1,501,229	1,870,662	2,066,202	
Wisconsin	324,509	506,549	733,617	655,816	922,732	975,634	1,060,293	
Other States	372,346	429,587	688,416	1,345,085	2,444,571	3,613,922	3,336,923	

[1] Preliminary.
[2] Recent developments; production for earlier years only a small proportion of total.
[3] Included in "Other States" to avoid disclosing data for individual establishments.
[4] Not available.

Source: Department of Commerce, Bureau of the Census; reports of Census of Manufactures; annual report, *Census of Pulp Mills and of Paper and Paperboard Mills*, Facts for Industry, Series M14A and M14D.

No. 833.—NEWSPRINT—PRODUCTION, STOCKS, CONSUMPTION, IMPORTS AND PRICE: 1935 TO 1952

[Monthly averages, in tons of 2,000 pounds, except as indicated]

COUNTRY AND ITEM	1935	1940	1945	1947	1948	1949	1950	1951	1952
CANADA, INCLUDING NEWFOUNDLAND[1]									
Production	256,916	314,162	299,325	401,680	415,236	431,361	439,882	459,690	473,921
Shipments from mills	254,145	316,985	296,076	406,107	413,920	430,361	442,553	458,626	472,204
Stocks at mills, end of month	245,293	261,342	139,763	161,182	137,511	159,770	146,397	138,042	146,094
UNITED STATES									
Consumption by publishers[2]	221,924	237,996	204,593	297,057	334,152	354,791	378,480	375,919	379,270
Production[1]	76,033	84,453	60,371	68,796	72,291	74,961	84,559	93,729	95,572
Shipments from mills[1]	76,436	84,411	60,455	69,373	72,237	74,805	84,773	93,785	95,226
Stocks, end of month:									
At mills[1]	17,735	16,869	7,135	11,251	7,663	11,892	8,543	8,452	8,926
At publishers[2]	224,535	297,813	252,956	257,265	320,756	398,068	332,299	386,874	506,699
In transit to publishers[2]	36,049	43,191	47,451	75,965	86,114	82,207	89,823	95,632	82,545
Imports[2]	198,610	230,212	222,400	329,839	366,273	386,630	405,338	413,569	419,679
Price, rolls, New York,[4] dollars per ton	40.00	50.00	60.25	88.62	97.69	100.00	100.92	111.00	-------
Wholesale price, standard newsprint, rolls, contract, delivered to principal ports,[4] dollars per ton				88.58	97.53	101.00	101.63	110.50	120.25

[1] Data from Newsprint Service Bureau and the Newsprint Association of Canada.
[2] Data from American Newspaper Publishers Association.
[3] Data from Bureau of the Census.   [4] Data from Bureau of Labor Statistics.

Source: Department of Commerce, Office of Business Economics; *Business Statistics Supplement to the Survey of Current Business* and records. Monthly data published currently in *Survey of Current Business*.

No. 834.—TURPENTINE AND ROSIN—PRODUCTION, 1899 TO 1952, AND BY STATES, 1948 TO 1952

[See also *Historical Statistics*, series F 127-142 where sources of figures for 1899-1952 are from *Gamble's International Naval Stores Year Book* and differ from census figures in this table]

YEAR [1]	TURPENTINE (BARRELS OF 50 GALLONS)			ROSIN (DRUMS 520 LBS. NET)		
	Total	From gum [2]	From wood [3]	Total	From gum [2]	From wood [3]
1899	754, 670	754, 670	(4)	1, 947, 946	1, 947, 946	(4)
1904	622, 585	613, 741	8, 844	1, 571, 739	1, 571, 739	(4)
1909	594, 266	579, 779	14, 137	1, 462, 206	1, 462, 206	(4)
1914	542, 979	530, 620	11, 511	1, 219, 326	1, 292, 514	22, 215
1919	384, 564	363, 877	30, 687	1, 015, 776	910, 926	104, 846
1929–30	718, 802	626, 417	92, 385	1, 963, 349	1, 580, 508	382, 841
1932–33	575, 131	501, 000	74, 131	1, 658, 664	1, 362, 720	296, 944
1933–34	594, 761	526, 000	68, 761	1, 897, 870	1, 490, 448	407, 422
1934–35	618, 008	516, 000	98, 008	1, 755, 268	1, 397, 200	358, 068
1935–36	602, 908	497, 000	105, 908	1, 821, 198	1, 360, 950	460, 248
1936–37	634, 520	482, 787	151, 733	1, 865, 869	1, 286, 347	579, 232
1937–38	700, 331	518, 454	181, 877	2, 049, 573	1, 388, 343	661, 230
1938–39	708, 218	534, 291	174, 927	2, 080, 912	1, 456, 344	625, 568
1939–40	604, 778	382, 781	221, 997	1, 825, 177	1, 064, 236	780, 941
1940–41	566, 341	343, 938	222, 403	1, 717, 492	938, 911	778, 581
1941–42	548, 796	285, 050	263, 746	1, 708, 474	791, 710	916, 764
1942–43	560, 351	321, 930	238, 421	1, 656, 808	868, 608	787, 105
1943–44	505, 432	286, 382	220, 060	1, 462, 831	783, 565	679, 206
1944–45	471, 342	245, 194	226, 049	1, 317, 912	692, 212	625, 700
1945–46	486, 131	344, 253	343, 879	1, 452, 086	664, 476	787, 680
1946–47	569, 985	270, 396	299, 699	1, 730, 248	762, 535	967, 713
1947–48	640, 903	294, 028	346, 875	1, 990, 831	826, 125	1, 163, 706
1948–49	659, 140	324, 330	334, 810	2, 076, 110	921, 220	1, 154, 890
1949–50	673, 300	323, 010	350, 290	2, 003, 610	994, 900	1, 008, 610
1950–51	708, 550	271, 880	436, 670	2, 137, 030	797, 620	1, 339, 410
1951–52	683, 960	246, 460	437, 500	2, 049, 390	716, 350	1, 333, 040

STATE	PRODUCTION FROM CRUDE GUM [1]							
	Turpentine (barrels of 50 gallons)				Rosin (drums 520 lbs. net) [6]			
	1948–49	1949–50	1950–51	1951–52	1948–49	1949–50	1950–51	1951–52
Alabama	21, 960	19, 600	16, 300	12, 390	61, 628	56, 263	47, 824	36, 688
Florida	59, 300	59, 030	47, 100	41, 450	167, 809	168, 849	137, 891	120, 347
Georgia	241, 370	242, 110	207, 270	189, 890	682, 241	691, 080	608, 157	552, 306
Louisiana / Mississippi / South Carolina	1, 800	2, 270	1, 210	1, 730	5, 502	6, 459	3, 185	5, 014

[1] Figures for turpentine and rosin from crude gum, beginning 1929–30, and from wood beginning 1933–34, relate to crop year ended Mar. 31. All other figures relate to calendar years.
[2] Figures compiled from data reported by establishments in turpentine and rosin industry.
[3] Figures compiled from data reported by establishments in Wood-Distillation Industry.
[4] Not reported.
[5] Includes, for 1909 and 1914, 366 barrels and 1,848 barrels respectively, of turpentine and, for 1914, 3,596 drums of rosin, reported by establishments engaged in manufacture of lumber and timber products.
[6] Estimated by J. E. Lockwood; complete data not available. Figures include estimates of rosin produced from reclaimed gum, as follows: 1932–33, 26,720 drums; 1933–34, 28,048; 1934–35, 27,300.
[7] Includes estimates by J. E. Lockwood for production of turpentine from steam-distilled wood.
[8] Includes data for rosin produced from reclaimed gum: For 1935–36, 42,350 drums; 1936–37, 34,155; 1937–38, 21,017; 1938–39, 31,983; 1939–40, 31,414; 1940–41, 20,181; 1941–42, 19,765; 1942–43, 11,397; 1943–44, 9,834; 1944–45, 3,056; 1945–46, 3,536; 1946–47, 5,449; 1947–48, 4,345; 1948–49, 4,230; 1949–50, 2,220; 1950–51, 560; 1951–52, amount insignificant.
[9] Prior to 1951–52, figures do not include data for rosin produced from reclaimed gum. See note 8.

Source: Department of Agriculture, Bureau of Agricultural Economics; *Annual Naval Stores Report*.

27. Fisheries

The Fish and Wildlife Service, Branch of Commercial Fisheries, in the Department of the Interior, conducts annual surveys for various statistical information on the fishery industries. These data are published in greater detail in publications of the Service and include data on the volume of the catch of individual species of fish and shellfish and their value, employment in the fisheries, quantity of gear operated, the number of fishing and transporting craft employed in the capture and transporting of fishery products, employment in wholesale and manufacturing establishments, and volume and value of the production of manufactured fishery products. In addition to the basic statistics on employment, yield, and the production of manufactured fishery products for individual States and various geographical sections, there are included in reports data on imports and exports of fishery commodities; landings by fishing craft at Boston, Gloucester, New Bedford, and on Cape Cod, Massachusetts; at Maine ports; and Seattle, Washington; shad fisheries of the Hudson and Potomac Rivers; alewife fishery in the Potomac; seed oyster fisheries; a review of the Pacific Coast halibut fishery; a statement on whaling operations by United States firms; data on the sponge fishery; and lists of firms producing various manufactured fishery products. These data are summarized in the *Statistical Abstract*. The more detailed information may be obtained from the Fish and Wildlife Service, Washington 25, D. C.

Historical statistics.—See preface and historical appendix. Tabular headnotes (as "See also *Historical Statistics*, series F 166–192") provide cross-references, where applicable, to *Historical Statistics of the United States, 1789–1945.*

Note—This section presents data for the most recent year or period available on May 20, 1953, when the material was organized and sent to the printer.

No. 835.—Fisheries—Summary of Total Catch and Value: 1930 to 1952

[Includes Alaska beginning with 1941, data partly estimated. See also *Historical Statistics*, series F 155]

YEAR	Quantity (1,000 pounds)	Value to fishermen (1,000 dollars)	YEAR	Quantity (1,000 pounds)	Value to fishermen (1,000 dollars)
1930	3,296,580	109,349	1945	4,575,500	269,900
1938	4,253,445	93,547	1946	4,455,600	310,000
1939	4,443,328	96,532	1947	4,344,000	307,600
1940	4,059,524	98,957	1948	4,575,000	367,000
1941	4,900,000	129,000	1949	4,796,000	339,000
1942	3,876,524	170,338	1950	4,884,909	343,876
1943	4,202,281	204,029	1951 (prel.)	4,400,000	335,000
1944	4,500,000	213,000	1952 (prel.)	4,300,000	325,000

No. 836.—Fisheries—Catch, by Sections: 1950

[See also *Historical Statistics*, series F 166–192, for data on quantity of catch]

SECTION	Fishermen	Fishing vessels	Fishing boats	CATCH	
				Quantity	Value to fishermen
	Number	Number	Number	1,000 pounds	1,000 dollars
New England States	23,434	868	13,439	1,006,590	60,576
Middle Atlantic States	15,476	577	5,991	491,685	28,843
Chesapeake Bay States	18,305	500	11,852	380,892	25,007
South Atlantic and Gulf States	37,296	3,778	17,028	831,522	69,302
Pacific Coast States	31,691	3,325	8,442	1,515,249	107,826
Great Lakes States	4,841	661	2,001	70,882	10,846
Mississippi River States	19,197		18,030	105,796	10,104
Alaska	11,233	1,787	4,031	482,293	31,372

Source of tables 835 and 836: Department of the Interior, Fish and Wildlife Service; annual bulletins.

No. 837.—Fisheries—Quantity and Value of Catch, by Sections and States: 1880 to 1950

[Values represent the value of fish to fishermen]

CALENDAR YEAR	NEW ENGLAND STATES					
	Total		Maine		New Hampshire	
	1,000 pounds	1,000 dollars	1,000 pounds	1,000 dollars	1,000 pounds	1,000 dollars
1880		12,503.0		2,742.6		170.6
1902	594,675	12,406.3	242,290	2,918.3	1,563	50.0
1908	536,029	15,139.0	173,843	3,347.0	677	58.0
1919	457,340	19,536.7	147,956	3,869.0	539	92.7
1930	791,361	27,463.5	145,534	4,539.4	1,069	98.1
1938	946,430	17,963.6	113,219	3,309.2	354	61.6
1940	636,044	20,493.7	85,088	2,604.4	788	105.2
1945	845,471	55,569.0	154,435	12,459.1	1,545	467.7
1948	908,380	67,987.9	305,504	70,077.0	530	282.2
1949	909,976	56,534.9	204,297	14,968.0	443	169.9
1950	1,006,580	60,676.5	386,266	14,689.7	645	228.9

	Massachusetts		Rhode Island		Connecticut	
		7,959.8		696.8		933.2
1880	220,646	6,462.4	21,614	1,155.7	37,832	1,799.4
1902	544,313	7,005.0	44,954	1,752.0	66,942	2,982.0
1908	348,951	10,839.7	48,251	2,206.6	23,653	1,700.6
1919	442,474	14,290.1	25,972	2,287.9	86,012	4,519.6
1930	566,417	12,147.9	24,534	1,347.9	14,916	1,227.0
1938	516,988	14,755.8	15,060	966.2	14,180	1,060.1
1940	635,978	20,643.3	20,526	2,376.0	18,094	1,852.0
1945	646,606	44,055.4	39,445	3,230.5	18,306	1,746.8
1948	647,613	38,201.5	34,428	3,230.9	24,196	2,157.6
1950	591,188	40,767.5	39,365	2,787.9	30,226	2,112.6

CALENDAR YEAR	MIDDLE ATLANTIC STATES									
	Total		New York		New Jersey		Pennsylvania		Delaware	
	1,000 pounds	1,000 dollars	1,000 pounds	1,000 dollars	1,000 pounds	1,000 dollars	1,000 pounds	1,000 dollars	1,000 pounds	1,000 dollars
1880	406,202	5,677.0	329,453	4,225.7	65,151	277.0	1,880	277.0	11,918	897.7
1901	357,866	9,104.7	228,092	5,294.3	117,931	4,755.5	6,080	251.5	5,995	801.1
1908	221,430	8,280.0	71,074	4,390.0	74,827	3,009.0	4,380	280.0	70,769	641.0
1921	333,962	11,557.6	210,377	4,906.9	95,937	5,083.4	595	44.6	25,023	642.4
1930	192,968	12,063.7	44,495	4,933.7	97,375	7,474.4	17	2.5	51,081	662.8
1938	279,438	6,415.7	84,939	3,135.4	107,502	2,844.3	31	5.7	86,965	630.4
1940	355,553	7,651.0	91,959	4,216.2	160,554	2,956.9	23	2.4	103,017	475.4
1945	494,192	25,224.2	117,548	10,082.7	207,647	11,062.5			168,996	2,109.0
1948	500,992	26,642.0	129,707	14,222.4	216,803	10,871.7			154,482	3,548.9
1949	520,977	27,117.1	145,505	14,364.5	205,988	9,744.5			168,474	3,007.8
1950	491,655	26,842.4	142,341	13,502.1	188,638	10,200.5			160,721	3,140.7

CALENDAR YEAR	CHESAPEAKE BAY STATES					
	Total		Maryland		Virginia	
	1,000 pounds	1,000 dollars	1,000 pounds	1,000 dollars	1,000 pounds	1,000 dollars
1880	254,587	8,346.2	95,713	5,221.7	158,875	3,134.4
1901	461,159	8,380.8	82,975	3,767.5	378,183	4,613.4
1908	426,311	8,022.0	113,796	3,306.0	312,515	4,716.0
1920	530,750	12,740.4	59,531	4,198.7	471,219	8,541.7
1930	316,393	11,472.0	71,099	3,984.7	245,294	7,487.3
1938	265,827	5,834.5	48,235	2,003.6	217,592	3,830.9
1940	320,736	7,456.4	51,085	2,598.6	269,651	4,857.9
1945	304,468	28,264.2	30,363.2	8,844.9	282,797	21,518.3
1948	364,336	27,604.2	54,213	8,220.9	310,123	19,384.2
1949	354,656	25,182.3	58,981	8,583.	275,675	16,598.5
1950	380,882	26,006.5	67,082	8,886.9	313,800	16,119.6

CALENDAR YEAR	SOUTH ATLANTIC STATES									
	Total		North Carolina		South Carolina		Georgia		Florida (east coast only)	
	1,000 pounds	1,000 dollars	1,000 pounds	1,000 dollars	1,000 pounds	1,000 dollars	1,000 pounds	1,000 dollars	1,000 pounds	1,000 dollars
1880	62,082	1,256.0	32,349	945.7	6,165	212.5	3,273	130.0	2,387	94.4
1902	109,446	2,530.6	67,196	1,782.7	8,174	362.0	12,103	249.1	19,364	477.9
1908	166,575	4,004.0	101,022	1,776.0	14,194	268.0	14,629	791.0	34,831	1,206.0
1918	322,514	5,345.6	216,989	1,976.7	3,747	207.7	27,134	416.0	61,311	1,744.2
1928	203,119	6,196.7	141,589	2,622.2	7,927	316.8	46,000	865.3	70,718	2,388.0
1934	361,060	5,634.1	166,469	1,572.2	8,406	228.3	27,141	329.5	64,896	1,387.1
1940	324,515	5,435.9	125,623	1,723.0	8,135	216.0	15,672	603.9	132,615	1,783.1
1950	404,880	14,453.5	181,653	5,168.0	8,563	484.4	28,525	1,236.4	176,024	7,394.1
1950	411,345	14,653.	165,483	4,558.	8,474	425.4	26,571	1,184.4	175,574	7,786.4

No. 887.—FISHERIES—QUANTITY AND VALUE OF CATCH, BY SECTIONS AND STATES: 1880 TO 1950—Continued

CALENDAR YEAR	GULF STATES					
	Total		Florida (west coast only)		Alabama	
	1,000 pounds	1,000 dollars	1,000 pounds	1,000 dollars	1,000 pounds	1,000 dollars
1880	23,561	1,227.5	8,376	564.8	3,542	119.3
1902	113,697	3,494.2	48,120	1,462.2	9,351	266.7
1908	118,274	4,860.0	37,566	2,120.0	10,665	387.0
1918	130,924	6,510.3	54,754	3,420.4	5,609	230.6
1930	141,963	6,794.9	53,525	3,001.4	7,113	315.5
1934	186,834	6,369.6	54,215	2,267.6	7,964	253.4
1940	250,018	10,580.8	54,676	3,451.6	11,344	561.9
1945	341,081	39,197.4	69,322	11,447.9	15,137	2,443.3
1948					12,556	2,157.3
1949	524,588	49,705.8	93,420	9,578.6	10,155	1,973.8
1950	570,641	50,357.9	62,013	9,954.6	10,988	2,122.4

CALENDAR YEAR	Mississippi		Louisiana		Texas	
	1,000 pounds	1,000 dollars	1,000 pounds	1,000 dollars	1,000 pounds	1,000 dollars
1880	788	22.5	6,996	392.6	3,859	128.3
1902	23,427	555.2	24,784	855.3	8,044	353.8
1908	17,302	459.0	42,302	1,448.0	10,439	446.0
1918	20,592	762.9	24,954	1,419.4	25,015	677.2
1930	15,796	740.1	49,886	1,960.4	15,693	777.5
1934	22,153	652.3	76,633	2,284.6	15,869	911.7
1940	38,002	623.1	126,627	4,951.5	19,369	992.7
1945	70,787	1,711.4	163,902	20,485.7	21,933	3,109.1
1948	80,450	2,588.6	209,106	24,382.0	55,580	6,145.0
1949	52,895	1,625.3	288,587	27,403.6	79,531	9,124.5
1950	84,139	3,371.2	316,250	23,644.5	97,251	11,265.2

CALENDAR YEAR	PACIFIC COAST STATES								Alaska	
	Total		Washington		Oregon		California			
	1,000 pounds	1,000 dollars	1,000 pounds	1,000 dollars	1,000 pounds	1,000 dollars	1,000 pounds	1,000 dollars	1,000 pounds	1,000 dollars
1888	87,043	4,010.0	20,468	811.0	26,048	734.0	40,527	2,465.0		
1899	206,911	6,278.6	119,340	2,871.4	22,752	855.7	64,819	2,551.5		
1908	193,056	6,839.0	111,356	3,513.0	28,221	1,356.0	53,479	1,970.0		
1915	304,796	9,306.0	170,594	5,321.0	34,693	1,479.0	99,509	2,506.0		
1925	627,025	24,580.5	139,457	9,476.4	40,008	3,442.4	447,560	11,661.7	616,136	9,860.7
1930	833,389	23,064.1	110,039	8,334.8	26,459	2,256.3	696,891	12,473.0	620,702	12,755.6
1935	1,676,236	23,088.8	124,086	6,328.7	85,392	2,076.8	1,466,758	14,683.3	648,710	9,093.2
1940	1,456,281	29,578.0	111,632	6,676.3	54,203	2,741.8	1,290,446	20,159.9	563,688	10,612.1
1945	1,428,278	62,694.3	196,136	18,154.6	72,774	7,507.3	1,159,369	37,032.4	596,052	22,288.1
1948	1,135,149	114,018.2	151,694	22,572.9	87,962	11,461.8	895,493	79,983.5	566,900	31,494.8
1949	1,364,518	100,373.1	174,161	20,802.9	61,096	7,065.5	1,129,261	72,504.7	472,889	39,299.0
1950	1,515,249	107,826.6	118,694	19,070.5	58,256	7,151.0	1,338,299	81,605.1	482,293	31,371.6

CALENDAR YEAR	GREAT LAKES [1]									
	Total [2]		Lake Superior		Lake Michigan		Lake Huron		Lake Erie	
	1,000 pounds	1,000 dollars	1,000 pounds	1,000 dollars	1,000 pounds	1,000 dollars	1,000 pounds	1,000 dollars	1,000 pounds	1,000 dollars
1885	99,842	2,691.9	8,826	291.5	23,518	878.8	11,457	276.4	51,457	1,109.1
1899	113,727	2,611.4	5,430	150.9	34,500	876.7	12,418	308.1	58,394	1,150.9
1908	106,631	3,768.0	10,198	342.0	40,019	1,554.0	12,932	486.0	41,922	1,280.0
1917	104,269	6,295.0	15,447	726.7	35,461	2,270.9	13,363	857.5	38,710	2,327.3
1927	81,327	6,794.9	15,302	918.1	23,681	2,354.8	15,711	1,444.4	23,796	1,831.3
1930	94,948	6,060.3	14,694	695.3	30,973	2,159.0	16,377	1,319.9	29,540	1,655.5
1935	90,323	5,944.9	17,874	940.6	25,089	1,942.6	13,676	1,224.1	30,357	1,643.6
1940	79,296	5,623.4	20,672	904.4	22,814	2,049.5	9,099	679.9	22,944	1,772.0
1945	78,643	13,800.1	18,726	2,574.0	22,090	5,570.9	7,475	1,129.0	28,631	4,256.9
1948	83,959	12,689.6	19,221	2,347.0	27,023	4,596.0	8,836	1,361.0	26,502	4,102.0
1949	85,693	11,458.4	17,730	2,190.1	25,573	3,822.7	5,580	594.9	34,249	4,618.1
1950	70,882	10,845.8	12,584	1,977.4	27,077	3,661.2	5,073	411.4	23,982	4,572.0

[1] Collected for most part by State fishery agencies and compiled by Fish and Wildlife Service since 1927.
[2] Includes, in addition to lakes shown, small amounts for Lake Ontario and also prior to 1927, Lake St. Clair and St. Clair and Detroit Rivers and beginning 1927, Lake-of-the-Woods, Namakan Lake, and Rainy Lake.

No. 837.—Fisheries—Quantity and Value of Catch, by Sections and States: 1880 to 1950—Continued

MISSISSIPPI RIVER AND TRIBUTARIES

CALENDAR YEAR	Total		TRIBUTARY [1]	1950	
	1,000 pounds	1,000 dollars		1,000 pounds	1,000 dollars
1894	44,845	1,384.6	Arkansas	1,660	247.2
1899 [2]	90,797	1,781.0	Atchafalaya	5,639	572.9
1908 [2]	93,374	1,841.2	Illinois [3]	5,761	344.3
1922 [2]	148,264	3,125.0	Missouri [3]	365	35.1
1922	105,734	4,508.5	Ohio River and minor tributaries	2,366	381.1
1931	82,382	2,887.3	Red Lake	663	141.9
1950	105,795	10,104.1	Red River [3]	11,255	1,342.2
			Tennessee [3]	34,606	1,376.5
			Inland lakes and streams	22,565	1,735.0
	Mississippi and minor tributaries				
1894	21,242	567.8			
1899	68,604	828.0			
1908	83,851	1,187.4			
1922	33,945	1,645.3			
1931	28,139	1,076.3			
1950	30,923	3,767.0			

[1] Excluding Atchafalaya River. [2] Tributary streams generally credited to streams into which they empty. Includes catch in Red Lake due to location and type of fishing. [3] Includes tributaries.

No. 838.—Fisheries—Catch of Principal Species: 1931 to 1951

[In thousands of pounds. Includes Alaska]

GROUP AND SPECIES	1931	1939	1945	1946	1947	1948	1949	1950	1951 [1]
FISH									
Cod	112,303	124,347	153,027	108,200	72,352	80,008	71,012	65,436	(2)
Haddock	195,419	176,824	164,988	155,035	146,871	158,375	194,971	182,550	155,000
Herring, sea	169,574	282,810	236,919	282,911	320,582	277,133	206,080	363,765	125,000
Mackerel	61,945	115,503	112,390	104,956	104,381	90,447	91,841	54,744	(2)
Menhaden	390,364	575,480	778,464	851,139	1,027,961	950,712	1,075,373	1,026,315	1,100,000
Pilchard or sardine	300,204	1,340,975	949,971	350,904	272,284	373,169	633,540	714,522	325,000
Salmon	601,095	536,973	498,892	476,257	496,048	403,750	484,206	326,645	400,000
Tuna and tuna-like	60,069	182,165	185,925	222,178	269,608	328,372	235,680	392,273	322,000
Ocean perch	237	76,306	131,534	176,152	146,587	238,096	236,987	207,793	260,000
SHELLFISH									
Crabs	82,701	109,414	121,050	(2)	(2)	(2)	(2)	159,278	(2)
Shrimp	90,622	130,260	191,345	(2)	(2)	(2)	(2)	191,674	210,000
Oysters	101,036	93,906	75,655	(2)	(2)	(2)	(2)	76,415	(2)
Whale products		5,159			520	1,178	790		(2)

[1] Preliminary. [2] Complete data not available.

No. 839.—Fisheries—Disposition of Domestic Catch: 1946 to 1952

[Round weight of catch in millions of pounds. Includes Alaska. A large portion of waste derived from canning, filleting, and dressing fish and shellfish is utilized in production of fish meal and oil in addition to whole fish used in manufacture of these products. About 600,000,000 pounds of waste were used in production of meal and oil each year shown. See also Historical Statistics, series F 155-159]

FORM MARKETED	1946	1947	1948	1949	1950	1951 [1]	1952 [1]
Total	4,486	4,344	4,575	4,796	4,884	4,498	4,396
Fresh and frozen	1,874	1,545	1,562	1,612	1,582	1,682	1,518
Canned	1,377	1,384	1,413	1,651	1,730	1,305	1,257
Cured	100	100	100	100	100	100	100
By-products, bait, etc	1,405	1,315	1,334	1,464	1,372	1,343	1,425

[1] Preliminary.

Source of tables 837-839: Department of the Interior, Fish and Wildlife Service; annual bulletins.

No. 840.—LANDINGS BY FISHING CRAFT AT PRINCIPAL ATLANTIC PORTS: 1945 TO 1951

[See also *Historical Statistics*, series F 193, 195]

PORT AND YEAR	Total, all species	Cod	Haddock	Hake	Pollock	Cusk	Whiting	Mackerel	Rosefish	Flounders	Miscellaneous
Quantity (thousands of pounds)											
Boston:											
1945	188,161	72,895	66,354	1,123	10,300	281	9,958	17,725	1,377	6,908	1,340
1946	158,596	35,722	71,473	2,263	13,077	411	6,776	14,139	5,219	8,047	1,468
1947	202,663	34,409	107,465	3,536	8,031	572	10,231	13,321	10,526	11,581	2,991
1948	199,980	34,710	105,308	3,462	17,064	1,077	11,428	3,473	11,383	9,153	2,302
1949	172,470	28,645	90,146	3,292	13,186	1,197	12,994	709	12,113	8,107	2,081
1950	172,033	24,360	107,379	2,998	9,886	1,265	4,887	1,051	7,740	10,028	2,439
1951	171,023	20,852	106,917	2,841	8,726	1,332	10,024	2,630	6,598	9,738	1,365
Gloucester:											
1945	213,498	25,797	21,786	11,544	15,792	773	16,830	11,890	102,038	4,830	2,218
1946	217,968	16,898	16,188	4,286	18,393	844	8,857	15,498	130,900	3,989	2,115
1947	163,713	8,276	12,692	2,524	5,569	487	9,126	24,011	95,357	2,115	3,556
1948	251,113	7,697	11,162	3,323	9,205	793	13,693	19,886	176,801	2,737	5,816
1949	250,910	6,976	8,516	2,768	6,147	777	19,442	6,876	169,281	7,643	22,484
1950	195,931	5,999	9,983	4,162	5,837	673	16,981	5,669	120,291	7,444	18,892
1951	259,670	4,970	5,842	4,402	5,591	841	36,917	3,785	177,694	4,534	15,094
New Bedford:											
1945	101,363	10,768	34,427	5,913	1,131	2	101	12,076	15	28,799	8,131
1946	90,324	11,568	33,020	323	1,394	2	8	2,252	195	31,364	10,198
1947	73,115	3,914	15,389	2,520	123	1	355	4,456	498	34,499	11,380
1948	77,572	6,330	11,410	4,345	380	3	60	1,683	350	40,958	12,053
1949	105,694	4,080	9,923	39,823	200	3	24	342	80	33,918	17,301
1950	116,911	5,110	11,514	97	207	6	85	258	474	29,412	69,748
1951	79,318	5,015	13,781	2,060	116	3	15	30	47	27,235	31,016
Provincetown and Cape Cod:											
1945	43,418	3,615	4,420	537	685	85	19,243	4,292	53	5,905	4,613
1946	40,970	3,765	5,568	477	1,249	56	14,520	4,868	764	5,512	4,201
1947	54,566	3,006	3,251	536	534	52	14,422	2,580	216	5,183	4,796
1948	44,455	2,767	2,340	362	457	72	16,766	8,897	517	4,313	7,964
1949	35,751	2,645	2,091	82	174	24	13,054	5,244	8	4,299	8,130
1950	37,760	3,034	2,555	359	384	39	11,618	2,379	7	5,912	11,473
1951	37,599	3,440	2,878	571	322	71	12,379	1,026	26	6,055	10,831
New York City:											
1945	16,596	1,006	7,788	232	142	......	227	91	......	3,517	3,503
1946	15,015	1,486	7,530	109	149	(1)	98	375	......	3,270	4,998
1947	10,778	740	4,111	109	58	......	31	210	......	2,388	3,133
1948	13,998	802	1,773	77	81	......	......	58	......	3,042	8,165
Value (thousands of dollars)											
Boston:											
1945	13,789.6	5,198.8	5,234.7	81.0	622.6	19.0	449.4	1,563.5	55.4	430.3	144.9
1946	13,725.3	2,785.4	7,392.9	156.6	564.2	25.3	504.5	1,108.6	237.7	667.5	482.5
1947	14,973.4	2,344.9	8,347.6	223.5	368.9	33.4	434.7	783.7	478.3	1,035.8	722.6
1948	16,182.5	2,680.7	9,765.8	246.6	794.1	62.5	501.8	256.8	497.6	907.3	469.3
1949	12,187	2,013	7,233	216	472	57	527	81	498	739	351
1950	13,557	1,787	9,180	191	451	62	199	107	326	924	330
1951	14,311	1,747	9,507	228	482	77	482	251	335	1,018	148
Gloucester:											
1945	11,183.9	1,813.3	1,744.5	401.8	832.8	46.5	742.5	925.2	3,956.8	311.5	409.0
1946	10,822.3	1,146.8	1,260.8	200.2	714.2	46.1	374.5	753.7	5,839.6	251.1	235.4
1947	7,636.0	433.9	881.0	93.4	205.3	17.7	371.8	1,121.3	4,199.7	114.4	197.5
1948	11,234.9	454.9	805.7	138.9	329.6	33.8	577.1	1,038.6	7,405.7	184.4	268.2
1949	10,456	391	547	113	155	24	718	362	7,304	447	395
1950	9,061	368	792	131	184	21	557	438	5,692	539	339
1951	12,694	330	463	175	244	32	1,320	295	8,829	386	620
New Bedford:											
1945	8,600.8	775.5	2,654.6	122.3	72.1	(1)	3.7	1,032.8	.6	2,302.0	1,637.2
1946	12,241.4	930.4	2,951.2	21.1	84.1	(1)	(1)	177.4	8.6	2,874.3	5,194.0
1947	10,417.3	279.7	1,155.3	37.0	4.7	(1)	7.2	198.7	14.5	3,347.5	5,372.8
1948	11,772.5	459.0	1,000.9	61.2	15.0	(1)	.9	127.9	14.3	4,605.3	5,488.0
1949	9,671	280	728	343	5	......	1	20	3	3,824	4,467
1950	11,343	369	991	4	8	......	1	40	17	3,724	6,189
1951	11,921	433	1,196	24	5	(1)	(1)	3	2	4,332	5,926
Provincetown and Cape Cod:											
1945	2,294.6	260.5	320.1	34.7	30.8	5.0	525.0	284.3	2.1	430.8	401.3
1946	2,399.7	310.6	462.0	24.9	56.0	2.3	337.4	360.1	32.5	418.1	395.8
1947	2,432.2	235.5	254.9	22.0	24.3	1.4	335.0	159.9	7.9	449.9	944.3
1948	3,332.9	230.3	213.4	15.9	19.4	2.3	396.3	933.4	17.6	479.4	1,024.9
1949	2,460	188	170	4	6	......	328	556	......	408	800
1950	2,560	230	232	8	14	1	289	194	......	677	915
1951	2,837	293	273	21	22	2	410	116	1	805	893

¹ Less than 500 pounds or $500.

Source: Department of Interior, Fish and Wildlife Service; annual bulletins.

No. 841.—Canned Fishery Products, Fish Meal, and Fish Oil—Production and Value: 1938 to 1951

[Includes Alaska]

YEAR	Canned		Scrap and meal		Oil (except vitamin)		Vitamin oil
	1,000 pounds	1,000 dollars	Tons	1,000 dollars	1,000 gallons	1,000 dollars	1,000 dollars
1938	645,156	89,446	205,216	7,418	30,445	9,876	2,476
1939	663,279	94,628	225,102	8,094	28,069	8,601	4,472
1940	675,661	94,182	193,244	7,534	15,250	5,632	5,088
1941	880,745	128,684	234,844	15,096	23,016	11,803	14,872
1942	656,907	144,997	171,080	11,626	19,549	12,515	10,272
1943	617,949	141,189	190,403	15,629	23,264	14,971	14,842
1944	655,680	152,914	212,000	15,200	27,324	17,771	13,237
1945	646,355	125,801	200,675	14,406	22,698	16,034	11,202
1946	669,375	227,629	199,621	20,439	19,135	21,228	13,619
1947	754,129	310,679	185,807	22,353	15,900	20,107	11,543
1948	782,208	326,181	198,544	22,087	16,343	18,476	15,508
1949	855,015	295,804	237,180	25,652	16,861	7,530	17,345
1950	967,115	331,335	236,713	29,226	21,432	14,042	3,431
1951	800,515	301,210	209,756	26,374	17,873	14,044	3,579

Source: Department of the Interior, Fish and Wildlife Service; annual bulletins.

No. 842.—Canned Fishery Products—Production and Value: 1936 to 1951

[Includes Alaska. See also *Historical Statistics*, series F 200-209, for total fishery products, salmon, sardines, and tuna and tuna-like fishes]

YEAR	Total	Salmon	SARDINES		Tuna and tuna-like fishes	Mackerel	Shrimp	Clam products	Oysters	Other
			Maine	Calif.						
	Quantity (thousands of pounds)									
1936	795,536	430,328	27,471	117,744	59,506	55,668	15,366	19,123	7,931	22,408
1937	712,532	342,642	34,109	126,560	69,522	37,837	21,323	19,577	10,634	30,123
1938	645,156	349,427	13,634	101,776	60,945	43,453	15,113	19,312	7,237	31,280
1939	663,279	287,621	44,872	130,564	79,666	40,023	20,651	24,515	9,080	36,958
1940	675,661	289,040	22,690	132,565	91,144	63,985	16,744	24,257	9,668	45,566
1941	880,745	375,918	64,245	225,322	61,663	43,075	13,273	25,271	9,199	63,879
1942	656,907	380,080	55,227	168,508	52,500	33,454	14,450	21,231	7,226	71,931
1943	617,949	273,802	50,854	150,961	56,563	42,176	9,907	12,197	4,842	16,647
1944	655,680	246,655	64,218	164,291	70,185	55,126	8,425	13,661	5,830	30,287
1945	646,355	235,506	55,322	160,469	85,978	31,174	3,226	21,502	5,164	37,925
1946	669,375	216,486	66,510	133,973	93,866	43,297	7,832	40,498	5,472	91,425
1947	754,129	270,787	61,182	74,367	117,469	78,973	7,085	36,136	5,747	102,383
1948	782,208	231,608	74,755	119,437	129,682	57,654	8,362	32,796	4,999	112,907
1949	855,015	265,196	62,413	169,570	141,701	47,247	9,971	31,112	6,341	121,464
1950	967,115	206,871	75,037	228,186	174,794	65,567	11,794	38,868	6,893	186,106
1951	800,515	222,367	34,688	128,924	157,336	47,183	13,068	39,187	6,529	151,272
	Value (thousands of dollars)									
1936	94,864	56,061	5,740	7,302	14,718	3,842	4,672	2,976	2,181	3,374
1937	104,175	52,934	4,998	8,592	16,995	2,674	7,131	3,013	2,933	3,904
1938	89,446	42,366	2,367	7,102	15,184	2,806	4,872	3,100	1,886	3,583
1939	94,628	41,781	7,075	9,554	20,080	2,889	5,398	3,798	2,379	3,974
1940	94,182	38,050	2,736	8,975	23,728	4,101	4,318	3,778	2,527	4,909
1941	128,684	67,417	12,591	18,092	19,398	3,504	4,883	3,711	2,997	4,091
1942	144,997	61,974	12,182	15,510	20,742	3,663	7,347	3,791	3,509	6,179
1943	141,189	62,525	11,166	14,352	31,430	5,271	4,361	2,802	2,822	5,111
1944	152,914	58,253	14,830	15,226	40,696	7,034	4,655	3,821	3,283	7,666
1945	125,801	52,852	13,077	15,349	47,407	4,647	1,919	7,391	3,030	9,906
1946	227,629	70,161	20,276	19,806	63,136	7,875	5,439	11,145	5,349	26,763
1947	310,679	130,636	28,311	16,536	90,609	15,029	8,192	9,642	4,260	18,474
1948	326,181	130,637	28,349	21,369	112,612	8,383	7,791	8,339	4,778	22,060
1949	295,804	146,431	22,062	21,538	97,716	6,849	11,503	8,770	6,636	15,639
1950	331,335	160,541	21,396	24,548	115,660	7,499	12,773	19,540	7,096	23,508
1951	301,210	108,625	14,685	19,363	98,046	6,259	12,187	11,774	5,961	23,380

Source: Department of the Interior, Fish and Wildlife Service; annual bulletins.

No. 848.—FRESH AND FROZEN PACKAGED FISH—PRODUCTION, BY PRINCIPAL SPECIES:
1935 TO 1951

YEAR	Total	Cod	Flounders	Haddock	Ocean perch	Whiting [1]	Other
			Quantity (thousands of pounds)				
1935	107,494	17,747	6,166	46,484	4,320		32,777
1936	113,356	17,896	5,850	41,187	15,521		32,902
1937	116,992	22,507	7,870	40,241	15,509		30,865
1938	129,976	21,189	8,115	41,453	19,152	7,603	32,464
1939	131,316	19,442	8,174	38,199	24,103	13,530	27,868
1940	129,420	14,805	11,245	37,140	23,014	13,256	29,960
1941	182,951	16,921	20,455	46,912	41,817	24,019	32,827
1942 [2]	173,362	13,010	24,869	41,882	37,680	24,583	31,338
1943 [2]	186,639	13,714	24,517	32,219	31,012	22,315	34,862
1944 [2]	172,294	22,083	18,073	38,403	34,531	18,510	40,694
1945 [2]	204,927	28,864	19,961	44,197	35,456	29,959	46,490
1946 [2]	196,572	18,132	21,900	42,441	49,507	22,129	34,463
1947	183,800	14,032	20,664	43,205	46,976	28,042	30,881
1948	180,297	13,879	23,466	42,219	67,696	5,122	36,915
1949	194,011	13,682	26,924	42,140	73,193	4,200	31,902
1950	191,524	12,990	28,321	51,192	63,128	2,537	33,346
1951	205,486	13,290	26,309	50,831	75,023	8,714	31,319
			Value (thousands of dollars)				
1935	11,202	1,751	973	4,427	440		3,611
1936	12,147	1,895	906	4,266	1,514		3,566
1937	12,861	2,262	1,287	4,162	1,495		3,655
1938	12,315	2,025	1,283	3,428	1,568	362	3,679
1939	13,030	1,927	1,123	3,754	2,394	668	3,164
1940	14,345	1,793	1,542	4,521	2,272	561	3,656
1941 [2]	23,930	2,451	3,171	6,848	4,808	1,484	5,168
1942 [2]	33,991	2,793	5,967	9,662	6,907	2,240	6,522
1943 [2]	37,589	3,516	7,299	9,091	6,952	2,194	8,537
1944 [2]	40,820	5,461	5,423	10,567	7,745	1,955	9,639
1945 [2]	48,371	7,452	6,086	12,349	7,673	3,098	11,713
1946 [2]	46,302	4,747	6,877	12,987	11,710	2,168	7,813
1947	44,272	3,458	7,027	12,094	10,912	2,662	8,119
1948	47,642	3,490	8,102	11,853	14,408	784	9,005
1949	48,339	3,232	9,096	11,845	15,335	686	8,145
1950	53,482	3,101	9,916	14,275	15,126	399	10,665
1951	59,487	3,436	10,817	14,546	18,733	1,338	10,617

[1] Data incomplete for years prior to 1938.
[2] Excludes California production. In 1941, yield of packaged fish in California totaled 5,384,000 pounds, valued at $1,032,000, of which 1,380,000 pounds were flounders, valued at $226,000.

Source: Department of the Interior, Fish and Wildlife Service; annual bulletins.

No. 844.—FROZEN FISHERY PRODUCTS—PRODUCTION: 1942 TO 1952

[In thousands of pounds. Includes Alaska. 1942 data for month ending on 15th, thereafter for calendar month. For cold storage holdings, see table 805. See also *Historical Statistics*, series F 199, for annual figures]

MONTH	1942	1943	1944	1945	1946	1947	1948	1949	1950	1951	1952
Total	247,165	246,063	266,537	286,001	280,065	246,625	291,988	285,822	287,190	325,504	313,173
January	8,740	6,740	9,021	4,925	6,228	4,394	6,384	7,435	7,302	10,651	12,897
February	6,559	6,792	8,813	4,191	6,231	3,439	7,927	6,914	9,318	10,292	10,195
March	7,018	9,180	11,262	6,890	11,077	8,225	14,365	11,873	13,207	12,721	11,800
April	10,376	9,958	17,375	12,962	12,504	11,711	15,227	16,484	14,249	20,199	19,455
May	22,569	22,220	32,640	27,630	34,375	25,188	38,088	37,775	33,846	43,289	34,172
June	25,459	36,025	34,849	39,392	38,203	30,039	40,920	38,910	39,310	44,809	49,306
July	34,035	34,438	40,573	42,856	43,269	33,280	40,351	34,469	35,727	42,220	44,093
August	35,634	34,766	32,602	45,623	37,940	39,809	34,598	40,046	37,289	42,217	34,242
September	28,564	26,913	28,004	33,257	27,372	27,730	29,112	33,095	30,527	30,393	31,849
October	26,281	18,806	23,733	27,472	29,983	29,625	27,113	24,308	29,493	30,666	32,311
November	22,701	24,948	18,104	26,212	20,306	16,848	22,379	21,336	22,230	23,604	20,689
December	19,126	15,297	9,561	14,591	12,575	16,337	15,524	13,177	14,692	14,443	12,154

Source: Department of the Interior, Fish and Wildlife Service; current and annual bulletins.

No. 845.—Fishery Products—Imports and Exports: 1939 to 1950

YEAR	IMPORTS			EXPORTS		
	Total	Edible products	Non-edible	Total	Edible products	Non-edible
	1,000 dollars	*1,000 pounds*	*1,000 dollars*	*1,000 dollars*	*1,000 dollars*	*1,000 pounds*	*1,000 dollars*	*1,000 dollars*
1939	45,908	346,240	32,404	13,595	14,207	124,974	13,581	627
1940	41,830	302,518	28,074	12,757	17,785	144,804	17,115	670
1941	40,981	305,875	28,040	12,941	22,008	215,990	21,479	529
1942	39,568	277,199	28,984	10,584	31,915	167,080	27,876	4,039
1943	57,183	234,476	43,689	23,494	45,584	239,290	43,244	5,290
1944	78,418	339,631	53,431	34,987	35,940	112,230	31,929	4,011
1945	101,264	404,788	76,434	24,520	38,510	135,979	30,856	7,655
1946	129,713	473,530	80,988	38,727	39,969	200,398	38,353	1,616
1947 [1]	108,972	407,636	83,275	26,697	52,536	207,486	49,281	3,556
1948 [1]	154,644	472,742	111,680	44,965	24,402	96,085	21,020	3,382
1949 [1]	151,610	670,517	113,768	27,857	34,574	146,660	29,212	5,662
1950 [1]	196,296	639,725	153,414	39,882	27,434	121,623	18,856	8,578

[1] Preliminary.

Source: Department of the Interior, Fish and Wildlife Service; compiled from data furnished by Department of Commerce, Bureau of the Census.

No. 846.—Fish Propagation by Fish and Wildlife Service—Output of Eggs, Fry, and Fingerlings, 1895 to 1951, and by Species, 1951

[All quantities in thousands]

YEAR ENDING JUNE 30—	Total	Eggs	Fry	Fingerlings or larger
1895	619,916	55,408	561,894	2,613
1900	1,164,537	88,692	1,070,737	4,906
1915	4,288,768	536,260	3,694,282	56,216
1920	4,770,388	630,749	3,872,218	267,388
1925	5,301,862	1,050,398	4,114,514	136,954
1930	7,570,482	2,553,481	4,766,831	250,170
1935	5,071,726	3,391,794	1,466,346	133,688
1940	7,407,347	5,826,069	1,466,157	83,031
1945 (Dec. 31)	4,454,558	2,176,357	2,203,672	74,529
1948	1,761,226	1,029,804	653,696	78,995
1949	835,571	141,309	586,349	107,912
1950 (Dec. 31)	287,200	55,853	121,730	109,617
1951 (Dec. 31)	332,465	66,917	134,389	121,149

GROUP	1951			GROUP	1951		
	Eggs	Fry	Fingerlings or larger		Eggs	Fry	Fingerlings or larger
Catfish (bullheads)			767	Northern pike	210	18,950	5
Channel catfish		60	93	Walleyed pike	1,145	2,400	32
Kokanee	525		668	Crappie (black)			97
Atlantic salmon		76	248	Crappie (white)			12
King salmon	24,207		50,401	Largemouth black bass		1,071	7,606
Chum salmon	5,259	14,056	491	Smallmouth black bass		414	174
Sockeye salmon			18	Rock bass			10
Silver salmon	2		660				
Red salmon	250	154	1,463	Warmouth bass			5
Steelhead trout		75	129	Bluegill sunfish			35,681
Rainbow trout	5,672		7,732	Buffalo fish			180
Cut-throat trout	15,544	100	6,731	Red-eared sunfish			2
Brown trout	2,480		1,810	Yellow perch			175
Lake trout			1,406	Flounder		91,407	
Brook trout	6,974	170	4,275	Lobster		224	
Dolly Varden			30	Pollock		2,635	
Grayling	546	507	24				

Source: Department of the Interior, Fish and Wildlife Service; annual bulletins and reports.

28. Mining and Mineral Products

This section summarizes the principal statistics relating to the mineral industries and mineral products. It includes not only crude minerals (such as coal, iron ore), but minerals which have gone through certain stages of preparation (such as refined copper, cement) and minerals such as magnesium whose extraction does not involve mining in the conventional sense. The latter two categories, while part of the mineral-raw-material sector of the economy, include the products of industries which are classified under the Standard Industrial Classification (Bureau of the Budget) as manufacturing.

The tables in this section are arranged in 4 groups which appear in the following sequence:

1. General summary statistics.
2. Fuels.
3. Nonmetals other than fuels.
4. Metals.

Most of the statistics are from the Bureau of Mines and the Bureau of the Census, with additional material from other Government agencies such as the Bureau of Labor Statistics, Bureau of the Mint, and the Interstate Commerce Commission and from non-Government sources such as the *Engineering and Mining Journal*, and *Metal Statistics*.

Mineral statistics, with principal emphasis on commodity detail, have been collected annually or at more frequent intervals by the United States Geological Survey or by the Bureau of Mines since 1880. The principal statistics have been published annually through 1931 in *Mineral Resources of the United States* and thereafter in the *Minerals Yearbook*. Data available from Bureau of Mines publications include quantities and values of minerals produced, sold or used by producers, or shipped; quantities of minerals stocked; crude materials treated and prepared minerals recovered; and consumption of mineral raw materials. The Bureau of Mines also collects and publishes separate data on man-hours, active days, length of shift, and accidents.

Censuses of mineral industries have been taken approximately every 10 years since 1840. The most recent Census taken, however, is for 1939. The statistics are collected and published in the Census volumes in such a manner as to relate the statistics on the production of the various minerals as nearly as possible to data on employment, principal expenses, fuels and power consumed, and other information available only for each establishment as a whole. Each establishment is classified according to its most valuable product. The data are also collected and compiled in a manner to permit integration with other Census statistics such as for manufactures and wholesale and retail trade. Commodity statistics on many of the manufactured mineral products are also collected by the Bureau of the Census at monthly, quarterly, or annual intervals.

To avoid misinterpretation, it should be noted that the Census of Mineral Industries statistics in table 855 relate to operations primarily engaged in extracting minerals and in such primary mineral-preparation activities (crushing, screening, washing,

---

Note.—This section presents data for the most recent year or period available on May 20, 1953, when the material was organized and sent to the printer.

flotation, etc.) as are needed to render the minerals marketable. Many of the statistics collected by the Bureau of Mines represent products of operations beyond the limits covered by the Census of Mineral Industries. Value totals based on Bureau of Mines publications, as shown in tables 847 to 849, are not wholly comparable with the Census value totals, as shown in table 855. Census values represent crude or prepared minerals f. o. b. the mine, well, or mineral-preparation plant. Bureau of Mines values for most nonferrous metals are based on the recovered value of contained metal rather than the value of the ores and concentrates as such and for certain nonmetals, such as cement, are based on the form in which the mineral is first generally marketed (even if a manufactured form) rather than on the imputed value of the mineral as first extracted.

In general, figures shown in the individual commodity tables include data for Territories and possessions, and may therefore not agree with summary table 849.

Data in other sections.—Data on mining and mineral products will also be found in other sections of this Abstract. For example, a historical summation of production and consumption of raw materials appears in section 32, Foreign Commerce (see table 1056); data on iron and steel, aluminum and magnesium, copper products, clay products, and others appear in section 30, Manufactures; financial data on mining corporations appear both in section 14, Federal Government Finances and Employment, and section 17, Business Enterprise; summary data for the Territories and possessions appear in section 33; for specific page references, consult the index.

Historical statistics.—See preface and historical appendix. Tabular headnotes (as "See also Historical Statistics, series G 1-5") provide cross-references, where applicable, to Historical Statistics of the United States, 1789-1945.

No. 847.—VALUE OF MINERAL PRODUCTION IN THE UNITED STATES: 1881 TO 1951

[All figures in millions of dollars. Principal differences between old basis and new basis are as follows: (1) Totals on the new basis represent continental U. S. only; on the old basis, production in Alaska, Hawaii, Philippine Islands (through 1945) and Puerto Rico was included, but no data were collected for other U. S. possessions now shown in table 1056; (2) U. S. totals on the new basis are a better representation than formerly of the production of primary minerals from domestic mines (or concentrating mills); on the old basis, totals include secondary products and mineral products made from foreign materials. However, value on new basis still includes some advanced products, like cement, lime, and natural gas liquids; also, mine value of nonferrous metals is based not on ore, but on value after refining of the recoverable metal content. Revised data for years prior to 1925 on new basis are not available. See also Historical Statistics, series G 1-5]

YEARLY AVERAGE OR YEAR	Total	NONMETALLIC			Metallic	YEAR	Total	NONMETALLIC			Metallic
		Total	Fuels [1]	Other				Total	Fuels [1]	Other	
1881-1885	426	232	171	61	194	1931	2,578	2,291	1,617	674	287
1886-1890	541	292	215	76	249	1932	2,000	1,872	1,457	415	128
1891-1895	592	347	248	99	245	1933	2,050	1,845	1,411	434	205
1896-1900	828	462	307	154	366	1934	2,744	2,467	1,944	523	277
1901-1905	1,392	814	546	267	578	1935	2,942	2,577	2,011	566	365
1906-1910	1,887	1,115	746	372	769	1936	3,606	3,090	2,401	689	516
1911-1915	2,220	1,400	967	433	821	1937	4,265	3,509	2,795	714	755
1916-1920	5,129	3,331	2,602	729	1,798	1938	3,518	3,058	2,433	625	460
1921-1925	5,151	3,997	2,943	1,054	1,154	1939	3,806	3,177	2,420	757	631
1926-1930	5,556	4,280	3,088	1,192	1,276	1940	4,411	3,446	2,659	787	752
NEW BASIS [2]						1941	5,107	4,217	3,224	993	890
1926-1930	4,675	4,015	2,865	1,150	661	1942	5,622	4,624	3,563	1,061	999
1931-1935	2,463	2,210	1,688	522	252	1943	5,931	4,944	4,023	921	987
1936-1940	3,879	3,256	2,543	714	623	1944	6,310	5,410	4,566	842	900
1941-1945	6,540	5,930	4,988	942	910	1945	6,231	5,457	4,563	894	774
1946-1950	10,276	9,179	7,671	1,500	1,097	1946	7,062	6,333	5,084	1,249	729
1925	4,812	4,097	2,905	1,192	715	1947	8,610	8,526	7,181	1,345	1,084
1926	5,311	4,590	3,366	1,224	721	1948	12,273	11,054	9,495	1,559	1,219
1927	4,695	4,076	2,869	1,207	622	1949	10,580	9,479	7,912	1,567	1,101
1928	4,484	3,829	2,650	1,207	685	1950	11,855	10,504	8,681	1,823	1,351
1929	4,905	4,106	2,934	1,172	802	1951 (prel.)	13,500	11,800	9,800	2,000	1,700
1930	3,980	3,473	2,495	978	507						

[1] Coal, natural gas, natural gas liquids, petroleum.
[2] See headnote.

Source: Department of the Interior, Bureau of Mines; Minerals Yearbook.

FIG. XLI.—VALUE OF MINERAL PRODUCTION: 1930 TO 1951

[This is a rate-of-change chart. The relation between plotting points represents percentage change or relative change in values rather than differences in amounts. The scale focuses attention on rate of increase and decrease. See table 847. 1951 data are preliminary]

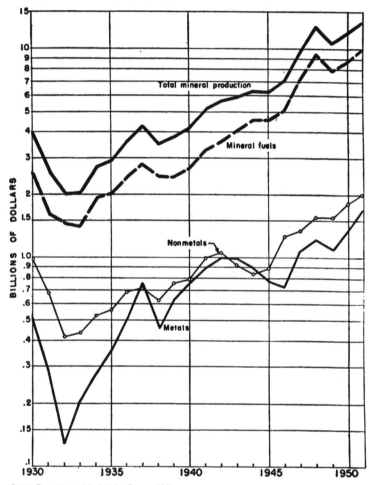

Source: Department of the Interior, Bureau of Mines.

No. 848.—Mineral Production—Value, by States and for Alaska: 1944 to 1950

[In thousands of dollars]

DIVISION AND STATE	1944	1945	1946	1947	1948	1949	1950
Continental United States...	6,316,000	6,281,000	7,082,000	9,610,000	12,273,000	10,536,000	11,855,000
New England	19,900	20,684	33,536	36,979	43,941	43,775	80,549
Maine	2,152	2,522	4,300	5,784	8,094	6,742	7,461
New Hampshire	1,164	802	1,451	1,264	1,331	1,364	1,711
Vermont	7,672	8,940	12,006	14,717	15,909	17,364	18,567
Massachusetts	5,363	5,450	9,745	10,876	12,583	12,449	16,014
Rhode Island	613	508	562	785	1,450	929	1,425
Connecticut	3,037	3,152	5,584	3,863	4,484	4,887	5,675
Middle Atlantic	1,673,755	1,632,177	1,311,698	1,469,583	1,874,971	1,213,047	1,390,132
New York	93,730	96,673	108,878	122,262	143,632	138,488	156,529
New Jersey	33,828	31,267	52,513	36,433	44,388	38,584	46,391
Pennsylvania	903,203	912,222	1,074,004	1,346,817	1,386,960	1,035,970	1,196,212
East North Central	741,532	740,542	849,231	1,004,811	1,207,797	1,079,137	1,390,908
Ohio	166,870	175,443	221,356	244,444	264,816	242,080	274,572
Indiana	60,760	66,602	107,479	123,862	161,960	141,025	166,532
Illinois	328,147	330,154	358,626	426,380	521,036	449,804	488,144
Michigan	132,938	123,806	153,162	166,634	202,865	201,280	229,862
Wisconsin	23,796	22,217	26,806	34,491	37,108	35,878	41,693
West North Central	451,356	440,744	505,410	654,528	813,844	789,696	911,497
Minnesota	170,486	167,130	155,744	218,374	257,248	257,540	331,567
Iowa	22,452	25,008	36,967	37,022	36,955	37,458	41,773
Missouri	72,890	74,347	86,857	105,926	105,291	111,206	113,191
North Dakota	4,334	4,806	5,118	6,256	8,478	8,818	9,614
South Dakota	5,472	7,138	18,394	22,890	24,327	26,723	32,716
Nebraska	5,080	4,962	7,277	6,704	8,385	10,102	14,022
Kansas	170,560	166,644	194,563	265,061	361,160	337,162	366,614
South Atlantic	717,654	690,591	793,104	1,112,489	1,296,977	974,683	1,146,348
Delaware	182	131	491	340	403	335	522
Maryland	15,264	15,329	21,991	23,291	25,002	20,461	22,725
District of Columbia	111	229	710	61	64	63	60
Virginia	96,962	61,965	90,822	130,296	143,332	116,408	137,806
West Virginia	547,551	537,212	586,925	857,670	1,012,402	718,119	829,634
North Carolina	22,301	14,766	20,628	16,396	18,281	19,753	26,343
South Carolina	4,192	5,043	8,130	7,899	8,885	9,026	11,394
Georgia	19,605	19,962	30,454	32,009	36,560	35,508	44,157
Florida	21,896	24,926	31,093	45,347	53,654	55,015	67,717
East South Central	441,620	439,753	496,460	731,961	900,793	697,178	811,670
Kentucky	250,735	280,919	272,558	426,101	504,090	372,229	450,956
Tennessee	62,461	57,104	66,201	79,941	96,890	77,333	89,604
Alabama	109,149	110,360	123,029	158,275	182,797	143,905	158,975
Mississippi	18,675	21,370	33,672	67,644	119,317	103,711	102,945
West South Central	1,618,316	1,665,690	1,912,728	2,795,687	4,065,416	3,605,393	4,013,294
Arkansas	64,098	58,262	65,998	90,527	122,090	109,523	115,642
Louisiana	217,522	222,173	273,882	404,779	604,198	631,913	695,607
Oklahoma	225,833	342,314	263,282	354,387	506,846	484,264	527,095
Texas	1,111,363	1,141,941	1,309,579	1,945,634	2,830,283	2,379,793	2,673,950
Mountain	668,761	636,391	632,606	944,931	1,151,358	1,048,334	1,211,605
Montana	51,730	66,537	61,833	87,735	103,841	98,070	103,389
Idaho	51,322	44,349	44,449	66,822	79,128	64,292	79,077
Wyoming	68,044	74,625	76,815	117,295	172,004	150,998	177,577
Colorado	79,147	77,237	77,630	102,448	125,861	139,858	154,997
New Mexico	112,186	104,239	111,968	157,648	230,080	198,825	210,294
Arizona	115,602	95,584	118,106	186,022	200,382	181,094	207,408
Utah	147,678	127,537	95,520	205,015	204,459	177,825	229,966
Nevada	37,852	31,193	35,484	40,928	42,503	37,372	48,499
Pacific	546,119	555,728	637,698	897,329	1,219,361	1,128,329	1,136,644
Washington	33,267	31,301	33,109	33,051	45,926	40,863	49,055
Oregon	9,687	9,443	12,107	15,965	32,923	21,845	21,542
California	503,165	514,984	592,372	843,413	1,140,419	1,078,612	1,065,047
Alaska	6,903	10,174	12,426	15,486	13,024	15,640	17,852

Source: Department of the Interior, Bureau of Mines; Minerals Yearbook.

No. 849.—MINERAL PRODUCTION IN CONTINENTAL UNITED STATES: 1947 to 1950

[Data represent production as measured by mine shipments or mine sales (including consumption by producers), except that fuels and the following additional minerals are strictly production: Gypsum, iodine, magnesite, pyrites, antimony, bauxite, and mercury. Excludes uranium ores and monazite. See headnote to table 847. See also *Historical Statistics*, series G 1–5, 13–18, and 43–130]

MINERAL	1947 Quantity	1947 Value ($1,000)	1948 Quantity	1948 Value ($1,000)	1949 Quantity	1949 Value ($1,000)	1950 Quantity	1950 Value ($1,000)
Total mineral production	....	9,616,000	....	12,273,000	....	10,889,000	....	11,855,000
Total mineral fuels	....	7,181,000	....	9,485,000	....	7,912,000	....	8,681,000
Coal:								
Bituminous [1] .... 1,000 short tons	627,389	2,614,561	596,024	2,953,465	534,342	2,196,226	512,529	2,489,229
Lignite .... do	2,874	6,519	3,066	7,012	3,092	7,336	3,370	8,112
Pennsylvania anthracite .... do	57,190	413,019	57,140	467,052	42,702	358,008	44,077	392,396
Natural gas .... 1,000,000 cubic feet	4,582,173	274,709	5,148,020	333,173	5,419,736	344,034	6,282,060	408,521
Natural-gas liquids:								
Natural gasoline and cycle products ... thousands of 42-gallon barrels	87,130	228,174	94,124	341,154	99,217	303,126	109,679	331,832
LP-gases .... do	45,043	64,820	52,597	117,823	57,899	96,054	72,282	97,773
Petroleum (crude) .... do	1,856,987	3,677,880	2,020,185	5,245,080	1,841,940	4,674,770	1,973,574	4,963,380
Total nonmetallic minerals (except fuels) [3]	....	1,345,000	....	1,559,000	....	1,567,000	....	1,823,000
Abrasive stone [3] .... short tons								
Grindstones and pulpstones	10,696	492	7,964	406	4,507	247	4,468	228
Millstones	(²)	23	(²)	18	(²)	9	(²)	11
Pebbles (grinding) .... short tons	5,990	123	4,098	102	2,374	64	923	11
Tube-mill liners (natural) .... do	1,496	40	1,297	42	1,166	47	1,533	63
Asbestos .... do	24,035	919	37,092	1,905	43,387	2,614	42,434	2,926
Asphalt and related bitumens (native) [3]:								
Bituminous limestone and sandstone ... do	1,004,740	3,756	1,094,004	3,635	1,150,931	4,265	1,184,676	3,522
Gilsonite .... do	67,165	1,746	52,122	1,391	51,462	1,394	66,186	1,774
Wurtzilite .... do	17							
Barite (crude) .... do	834,082	6,171	799,848	6,693	717,313	5,642	695,414	6,194
Boron minerals .... do	501,935	11,844	450,932	11,148	467,592	11,512	647,735	15,680
Bromine .... 1,000 pounds	78,178	14,837	76,048	14,825	88,726	16,298	98,502	18,706
Calcium-magnesium chloride short tons, 75-percent (Ca, Mg) Cl_2 basis	271,206	2,650	309,660	3,907	255,797	3,261	299,821	3,362
Carbon dioxide, natural (estimated) ... 1,000 cubic feet	581,000	412	645,000	397	489,000	376	472,334	369
Cement ... thousands of 376-pound barrels	188,516	356,639	205,259	446,465	207,142	475,074	228,788	537,652
Clays (including fuller's earth) ... 1,000 short tons	28,192	71,250	31,304	80,497	28,474	74,619	32,301	89,676
Emery .... short tons	5,736	67	5,305	69	4,909	61	5,919	76
Feldspar (crude) .... long tons	459,910	2,411	460,713	2,544	369,378	2,278	407,925	2,466
Fluorspar .... short tons	329,494	10,955	331,749	11,227	296,704	8,267	301,510	10,680
Garnet (abrasive) .... do	8,722	614	8,039	588	6,573	505	9,304	704
Gem stones (estimated)	(²)	540	(²)	450	(²)	450	(²)	450
Graphite .... short tons	5,207	221	9,871	451	5,213	475	5,605	435
Helium (shipments, calendar years) .... do	6,208,216	16,530	7,254,535	19,113	5,698,118	18,319	8,192,625	22,735
Gypsum (crude) .... do	52,322	501	50,915	610	51,501	689	80,889	1,026
Kyanite .... 1,000 cubic feet	(²)	(²)	14,552	527	12,115	403	(²)	(²)
Lime (open-market) .... short tons	6,759,949	63,363	7,245,211	74,677	6,302,651	68,908	7,462,109	52,947
Lithium minerals .... do	2,441	151	3,981	211	4,838	346	9,306	580

No. 849.—MINERAL PRODUCTION IN CONTINENTAL UNITED STATES: 1947 to 1950—Continued

MINERAL	1947		1948		1949		1950	
	Quantity	Value ($1,000)	Quantity	Value ($1,000)	Quantity	Value ($1,000)	Quantity	Value ($1,000)
Metals—Continued								
Mercury_____76-pound flasks__	20,117	1,488	14,888	1,088	9,880	781	4,889	386
Molybdenum (content of ore and concentrate)__1,000 pounds__	22,190	16,178	30,680	20,418	35,390	19,393	44,544	27,729
Platinum-group metals (crude)_____troy ounces__	384	(³)	(⁴)	(⁴)	(⁴)	(⁴)	(⁴)	(⁴)
Silver (recoverable content of ore, etc.)___1,000 troy ounces__	35,782	22,880	38,020	24,413	34,690	21,380	42,480	26,330
Tantalum concentrate_____pounds, gross weight__	3,350	(⁹)	800	(⁹)	17	37	15	31
Tin (content of ore and concentrate)_____long tons__			(⁴)	(⁹)				
Titanium concentrate:								
Ilmenite_____short tons, gross weight__	336,061	4,689	381,806	5,794	380,284	6,513	469,320	6,607
Rutile_____do__	5,157	584	9,907	647	10,559	480	(⁹)	(⁹)
Tungsten concentrate___short tons, 60-percent WO₃ basis__	3,061	4,256	4,088	5,355	2,765	4,377	4,807	8,157
Vanadium (content of ore and concentrate)____pounds__	2,117,969	1,288	(⁹)	(⁹)	(⁹)	(⁹)	(⁹)	(⁹)
Zinc (recoverable content of ore, etc.)___short tons__	657,565	183,112	650,905	167,974	563,321	145,913	657,300	178,067
Undistributed [¹¹]		3,676		10,496		6,671		10,257

¹ Includes small quantity of anthracite mined in States other than Pennsylvania.
² Excludes sharpening stones, included with "Nonmetallic minerals, undistributed."
³ Weight not recorded.
⁴ Excludes clays sold or used for cement as follows: 1947, 5,336,000 short tons, $2,967,000; 1948, 6,262,000 tons, $4,320,000; 1949, 6,676,000 tons, $4,573,000; 1950, 7,080,000 tons, $4,454,000.
⁵ Value included with "Nonmetallic minerals, undistributed."
⁶ Excludes production from Wyoming, value for which is included with "Nonmetallic minerals, undistributed."
⁷ Excludes abrasive stone, bituminous limestone, bituminous sandstone, and ground magnesium, all included elsewhere in table. Also excludes limestone for cement and lime.

⁸ Comprises andalusite (1947–49), aplite, brucite, diatomite (1949), gypsum salts from serpentine (1947) and gypsumite (1949–50), iodine, quartz crystal (1950), sharpening stones, sodium carbonate (Wyoming 1946–49), and minerals indicated by footnote 6.
⁹ Value included with "Metals, undistributed."
¹⁰ Less than 0.5 ton.
¹¹ Comprises magnesium chloride for magnesium metal, zirconium concentrate, and minerals indicated by footnote 9.

Source: Department of the Interior, Bureau of Mines: *Minerals Yearbook*.

No. 850.—Apparent Consumption of Principal Minerals and Percentage Distribution by Sources of Supply: 1950

[These data may not agree with similar data in subsequent tables due to use of somewhat different methods of calculation. For further detail, see Minerals Yearbook, 1950, p. 7]

Mineral and unit of measurement	Apparent consumption	Domestic production			Net imports [1]					Net decrease in stocks [4]
		Total	Primary	Secondary [2]	Total	Canada and Mexico	Other Western Hemisphere	Other "free world" [3]	U.S.S.R. bloc	
Antimony........short tons (Sb content)	38,517	55.5	5.6	49.9	43.5	18.7	17.0	9.4	0.4	
Bauxite, crude......thousand long tons (dried equivalent)	4,290	31.3	31.3	---	57.9	---	47.5	10.4	---	10.8
Boron minerals and compounds....thousand short tons (gross weight)	505	100.0	100.0		---					
Bromine and bromine in compounds...thousand pounds	97,729	100.0	100.0		---					
Cadmium.......thousand pounds (Cd content)	9,802	96.7	96.7		2.9	2.4	(*)	.5		10.4
Chromite......thousand short tons	1,453	(*)	(*)		89.6		7.4	77.3	4.9	10.4
Clays.......do	39,304	100.0	100.0		---					
Coal:										
Anthracite.......do	38,910	100.0	100.0		---					
Bituminous and lignite.......do	460,428	100.0	100.0		---					
Cobalt......thousand pounds (Co content)	11,913	7.8	6.8	1.0	78.4	4.6	12.8	78.4		13.8
Copper......thousand short tons (Cu content)	2,222	63.3	41.5	21.8	17.4	18.6		16.6		19.3
Fluorspar, finished......short tons	433,971	64.8	64.8		35.2	27.9				
Gypsum, crude......thousand short tons	11,360	72.1	72.1		27.9	27.9				
Iron ore......thousand short tons	103,435	94.5	94.5		8.8					4.4
Lead......thousand short tons (Pb content)	1,440	58.8	29.1	29.7	36.8	22.9	2.9	2.2		20.2
Magnesium......short tons (Mg content)	96,293	78.7	58.8	18.9	---		6.7	1.1		3.0
Manganese......thousand short tons (Mn content)	1,205	11.5	11.5		81.5	2.5	9.0	67.1	2.9	34.6
Molybdenum......thousand pounds (Mo content)	37,317	65.4	65.4		---					
Nickel......short tons (Ni content)	93,167	6.1	1.0	5.1	92.3	90.1				1.6
Petroleum, crude......million barrels	2,117	93.3	93.3		6.5		4.9	1.6		.3
Phosphate rock......thousand long tons (gross weight)	8,509	100.0	100.0		---					
Potash......thousand short tons (K₂O equivalent)	1,410	90.6	90.6		9.4			8.0	1.4	
Salt, common......thousand short tons	16,434	100.0	100.0		---					
Sulfur......thousand long tons (S content)	4,949	93.1	93.1		---					
Tin......long tons (Sn content)	129,883	18.2	(*)	18.2	81.8	1.1	11.0	69.4	1.8	6.9
Tungsten ore and concentrates [6]......short tons (gross weight)	20,850	19.7	19.7		80.3			28.4	37.0	
Zinc......thousand short tons (Zn content)	1,149	57.6	51.2	6.4	33.1	29.5	2.0	1.6	(*)	9.3

[1] Deduction for net export has been prorated among other sources of supply. Where there is an overall net import, but a net export to a particular country group, deduction for such net export is prorated among net imports from other country groups.
[2] From "old" scrap only, that is, from material previously in use.
[3] Other countries outside U.S.S.R. bloc.
[4] Deduction for net increase in stocks has been prorated among other sources of supply.
[5] Less than 0.05 percent.
[6] 60 percent W O₃ basis.

Source: Department of the Interior, Bureau of Mines; Minerals Yearbook.

No 851.—MINERAL PRODUCTION—INDEXES OF PHYSICAL VOLUME: 1925 TO 1952

[1935-39 average=100. See also *Historical Statistics*, series G 6-8]

Year	Total	Fuels	Metals	Year	Total	Fuels	Metals	Year	Total	Fuels	Metals
1925	92	87	121	1935	86	89	73	1945	137	143	101
1926	100	95	126	1936	99	99	102	1946	134	142	88
1927	100	97	116	1937	112	109	127	1947	149	155	118
1928	99	95	120	1938	97	99	86	1948	155	161	120
1929	107	103	134	1939	106	105	113	1949	135	139	107
1930	93	91	102	1940	117	114	134	1950	148	152	125
1931	80	82	68	1941	125	122	149	1951	164	169	134
1932	67	72	36	1942	129	125	148	1952	160	167	120
1933	76	80	51	1943	132	132	126				
1934	80	83	58	1944	140	145	113				

Source: Board of Governors of the Federal Reserve System. Totals and monthly data published in the *Federal Reserve Bulletin*.

No. 852.—IMPORTS AND EXPORTS OF PRINCIPAL MINERAL PRODUCTS: 1949 TO 1951

MINERAL		QUANTITY			VALUE ($1,000)		
	Unit	1949	1950	1951	1949	1950	1951
IMPORTS							
Fuels: Petroleum	1,000 barrels	154,719	173,920	177,356	340,658	369,208	374,869
Nonmetallic minerals:							
Asbestos	Short tons	509,365	705,454	761,873	33,940	47,293	56,521
Diamonds:							
Gem	1,000 carats	969	926	1,135	69,674	102,273	110,170
Industrial	do	6,380	11,198	12,287	17,643	37,001	46,799
Mica	Short tons	12,735	18,511	18,597	19,317	23,660	22,517
Ores and concentrates:							
Bauxite	Long tons	2,688,164	2,516,247	2,162,902	16,353	15,730	13,874
Chromite	Short tons	1,203,851	1,303,714	1,429,020	24,200	23,299	25,506
Copper	Short tons of metal	121,952	87,712	78,235	45,800	33,032	37,722
Iron ore	1,000 long tons	7,399	8,297	10,148	36,735	44,027	50,555
Lead	Short tons of metal	122,280	96,587	32,749	34,526	21,184	8,636
Manganese ore	1,000 short tons	1,453	2,014	2,075	26,798	41,882	45,598
Tin	Long tons of metal	38,311	25,960	29,621	78,176	47,163	82,462
Tungsten	Short tons of metal	3,344	8,024	3,188	6,390	15,309	17,604
Metals (incl. scrap):							
Aluminum	Short tons	125,327	255,692	161,834	36,082	67,533	59,263
Copper	do	438,337	481,068	379,031	169,313	184,394	193,442
Lead	do	287,755	460,035	184,636	84,805	110,644	66,992
Nickel	do	97,144	97,302	102,436	66,016	77,107	96,102
Platinum group	Troy ounces	190,051	391,126	576,260	10,333	21,123	34,111
Tin	Long tons	60,272	82,986	28,402	133,728	153,099	74,591
Zinc	Short tons	129,345	158,897	94,950	29,912	39,621	31,552
EXPORTS							
Fuels:							
Anthracite	1,000 short tons	4,943	3,892	5,956	64,786	62,502	89,024
Bituminous coal	do	27,842	25,468	56,722	232,393	206,545	495,992
Petroleum	1,000 barrels	33,068	34,824	28,603	98,425	102,717	81,767
Nonmetallic minerals:							
Cement	do	4,562	2,418	2,933	15,961	7,275	9,964
Phosphate rock	Long tons	1,257,962	1,832,048	1,726,834	11,405	14,874	14,735
Potash material	Short tons	126,757	117,138	124,212	7,111	5,534	7,594
Sulfur, native	1,000 long tons	1,431	1,441	1,288	30,490	30,951	31,761
Metals (incl. scrap):							
Aluminum	Short tons	37,179	21,283	13,415	21,455	11,029	8,107
Copper	do	196,130	192,339	166,274	95,377	86,712	96,837
Iron and steel, scrap [1]	1,000 short tons	294	208	220	6,897	5,255	6,457
Molybdenum [1]	Short tons	2,660	3,117	1,865	4,624	5,454	3,735
Nickel	do	4,471	3,645	4,622	5,268	4,064	6,050
Zinc	do	66,165	17,728	43,088	22,196	6,289	19,964

[1] Converted to short tons from content pounds.

Source: Department of Commerce, Bureau of Census; *Foreign Commerce and Navigation of the United States*, and current summary reports.

No. 853.—NUMBER OF MINING AND RELATED MANUFACTURING FIRMS: 1939 TO 1952

[In thousands]

SEPT. 30—	Mining firms	MINERAL MANUFACTURING FIRMS			
		Metal smelting and refining	Fabricated metal products	Products of petroleum and coal	Stone, clay, and glass products
1939	26.1	2.8	10.5	1.2	7.1
1940	27.7	4.0	10.8	1.2	7.2
1941	29.3	4.2	11.5	1.2	7.5
1942	25.2	4.3	11.7	1.2	7.5
1943	31.1	4.3	11.8	1.2	7.3
1944	31.0	4.5	12.4	1.2	7.2
1945	31.3	5.0	13.7	1.3	7.9
1946	22.9	6.0	16.3	1.4	12.6
1947	24.2	6.2	17.9	1.4	13.1
1948	25.8	6.2	18.0	1.4	12.0
1949	24.0	5.9	17.7	1.5	10.6
1950	24.4	5.8	18.0	1.4	10.1
1951	24.1	5.9	18.4	1.5	9.4
1952 (as of June 30)	24.2	4.0	18.7	1.6	8.9

Source: Department of Commerce, Office of Business Economics; *Survey of Current Business*.

No. 854.—AVERAGE PRICES OF SELECTED MINERAL PRODUCTS: 1896 TO 1952

[Prices per short ton for coal, per long ton for iron ore and sulfur]

YEARLY AVERAGE OR YEAR	Crude petroleum (at wells)	Bituminous coal (f.o.b. mines)	Iron ore (Lake Erie ports)	Copper, electrolytic (New York)	Lead (New York)	Tin (New York)	Zinc (St. Louis)	Aluminum, delivered	Sulfur, crude (f.o.b. works)
	Dollars per bbl.	Dollars per ton	Dollars per ton	Cents per lb.	Cents per lb.	Cents per lb.	Cents per lb.	Cents per lb.	Dollars per ton
1896–1900			2.91	12.61	3.64	19.54	4.56	8.15	
1901–1905			2.71	15.67	4.33	28.29	5.39	18.60	22.35
1906–1910			2.71	16.442	4.760	34.36	5.632	21.12	31.46
1901–1915			2.96	14.973	4.390	41.50	7.306	28.64	22.40
1916–1920	2.16		6.10	23.000	7.350	54.43	8.783	42.14	31.76
1921–1925	1.68	4.80	5.08	13.674	6.183	42.44	6.169	23.85	14.56
1926–1930	1.46	4.60	4.30	14.677	6.766	51.96	6.126	24.00	18.04
1931–1935	.86	5.48	4.50	7.066	3.643	37.64	3.000	22.60	18.00
1936–1940	1.13	4.30	4.71	10.990	5.136	46.34	5.446	20.12	13.00
1941–1945	1.16	4.90	4.45	11.775	6.350	52.01	8.695	15.87	10.00
1946–1950	2.21	7.6	5.99	19.451	13.897	8.32	11.705	10.18	17.45
1946	1.87	5.76	4.90	13.840	8.100	54.54	8.736	15.00	16.40
1947	1.90	5.87	5.55	20.956	14.673	77.96	10.500	15.00	16.20
1948	2.57	6.11	6.18	22.036	18.043	99.25	13.594	15.73	16.00
1949	2.57	6.05	7.20	19.202	15.304	99.34	12.144	17.00	18.00
1950	2.57	6.74	7.71	21.235	13.300	95.54	13.886	17.71	18.90
1951	2.57	9.90	8.30	24.200	17.800	127.95	18.000	19.00	21.00
1952	(1)	(1)	8.66	24.200	16.467	120.47	16.215	19.42	21.60

[1] Posted price. [2] Bituminous—Kansas, 1921, 33–1939, 1924–25, 1917–1918. [3] Run of mine, average weekly price. [4] Lake superior, Mesabi, non-bessemer. [5] Prices 1896 to 1939 for pure bessemer. (No 1 virgin, 98–99 percent; beginning 1941, for 96 percent+ virgin, etc.)

[6] Prices 1896 to 1899 are for Lake copper. [7] Data are for New York zinc. [8] Average, 1896–95, average for New York since 1901–05, Lake only. [9] Average for 4 years. [10] Average, 1896–95. [11] Not yet available.

Source: Compiled from *Engineering and Mining Journal*, *Metal Statistics*; *Petroleum Data Book*; *Wholesale Prices* (Bureau of Labor Statistics) and *Minerals Yearbook* (Bureau of Mines).

No. 855.—MINERAL INDUSTRIES—SUMMARY FOR THE UNITED STATES: 1919, 1929, AND 1939

]Statistics cover producing operations only. In general, those for 1939 cover only those operations (or concerns producing crude petroleum, natural gas, and natural gasoline, and rendering oil- and gas-field services) for which total value of all products, reported principal expenses, cost of buildings, machinery, and equipment during year, or cost of drilling and equipping wells during year amounted to $2,500 or more. For bituminous coal and lignite an output criterion of 1,000 tons of coal was substituted for value of all products. Statistics for common sand and gravel industry exclude data for operations that produce less than 15,000 tons of sand and gravel unless reported principal expenses or cost of buildings, machinery, and equipment during year amounted to $15,000 or more. Statistics for 1929 cover, in general, only those "enterprises" for which total value of all products or cost of development work amounted to $2,500 or more. Bituminous coal and lignite mines that produced less than 1,000 tons of coal and common sand and gravel operations that produced less than 25,000 tons of sand and gravel, were excluded. Statistics for 1919 exclude data for "enterprises" for which value of all products was less than $500 or cost of development work was less than $5,000. Noncommercial production of stone and sand and gravel obtained from mines or quarries operated by governmental agencies, public utilities, or by construction companies or contractors producing wholly for their own use or on contract for governmental agencies is excluded for all years. For summary data from 1939 Census of Mineral Industries by type of mineral industry, see 1949 Statistical Abstract, table 854]

ITEM	1939 (all industries)	COMPARATIVE STATISTICS FOR 1939 AND 1929		COMPARATIVE STATISTICS FOR 1939 AND 1919	
		1939 [1]	1929	1939 [2]	1919
Number of mines and quarries	13,395	12,736	11,602	10,888	13,844
Number of oil and gas wells producing December 31	347,645			347,645	257,673
Number of natural-gasoline plants	734			734	1,115
Value of all products [3] 1,000 dollars	3,221,927	1,721,771	2,392,831	3,089,904	3,122,550
Number of persons engaged, total	827,410	668,771	863,948	792,423	1,077,675
Wage earners (average for the year) [4]	736,150	616,614	806,418	705,872	981,560
Salaried employees [5]	77,019	44,124	52,623	73,238	74,197
Proprietors and firm members (not applicable to corporations) [6]	14,241	8,033	4,897	13,313	21,918
Performing manual labor	6,431	5,107	(7)	6,122	5,245
Principal expenses designated below, total 1,000 dollars	1,747,282	1,161,318	1,661,168	1,674,708	2,166,345
Wages [4] do	915,558	740,112	1,091,990	881,122	1,295,936
Salaries [5] do	189,355	103,807	137,639	180,372	149,329
Supplies and materials do	306,297	216,448	293,568	290,545	519,594
Fuel do	60,374	32,568	49,146	53,098	93,911
Purchased electric energy do	68,892	61,429	71,769	63,617	28,195
Contract work do	206,805	6,953	17,056	205,955	79,380
Cost of machinery and equipment installed during year [8] 1,000 dollars	261,475	60,334	84,508	253,688	(7)
Horsepower rating of power equipment, total [9]	13,045,784	8,754,546	7,514,843	12,112,357	[10] 6,723,786
Prime movers	7,149,168	3,332,089	2,743,025	6,653,204	5,111,531
Electric motors driven by purchased energy	5,896,616	5,422,457	4,771,818	5,459,153	[10] 1,612,255
Electric energy consumed, total 1,000 kilowatt-hours	8,371,670	7,396,870	7,462,790	(7)	(7)
Purchased do	6,301,497	5,627,091	5,382,178	(7)	(7)
Generated by reporting companies do	2,070,173	1,769,779	2,080,612	(7)	(7)

[1] Excludes statistics for common clay and shale, crude petroleum and natural gas, greensand, natural gasoline, peat, potash, and rock salt industries, for comparability with 1929.

[2] Excludes common clay and shale, common sand and gravel, glass-sand, foundry-sand, natural sodium compounds, peat, potash, and rock salt industries, and limestone mines and quarries operated in conjunction with cement and lime plants for comparability with 1919.

[3] Includes value of crude minerals produced, value added during year by preparation processes, receipts for services performed for other concerns, and value of electric energy generated and sold.

[4] Represents statistics for skilled and unskilled employees who perform manual labor, use tools, operate machines, handle materials, and care for property. Average numbers of wage earners were derived by adding numbers reported for each month and dividing sums by 12.

[5] Represents statistics for salaried employees at operations and at central and branch offices, including officers of corporations, managers, superintendents, and other supervisory personnel, responsible professional and technical employees, and clerical employees. Number of salaried employees represents number receiving pay on a representative or normal day or normal payroll period—for 1939, during normal payroll period ending nearest Oct. 14; for 1929, on Dec. 14 or on nearest representative day; for 1919, on Dec. 15 or on nearest representative day. Salaries represent total amount paid to salaried employees during calendar year.

[6] Represents statistics for proprietors and firm members at operations and at central and branch offices.

[7] Census statistics not available.

[8] For 1939 includes installation costs, which are excluded for 1929.

[9] Statistics for 1939 and 1929 refer to equipment in use or available for use at end of year.

[10] Includes equipment, with rating of 8,965 horsepower, operated by purchased power other than electric energy.

Source: Dept. of Commerce, Bureau of the Census; Census of Mineral Industries, 1939, Vol. I.

No. 856.—Employment and Injuries in Mineral Industries, by Industry Group: 1915 to 1951

[Excludes data on petroleum, natural gas, sand and gravel, clay, iron smelting and steel industries. For additional data for coal mines, see table 880. See also *Historical Statistics*, series G 131-118]

ITEM	1915	1930	1935	1940	1945	1949	1950	1951 (prel.)
Men working daily, total [1]	1,037,817	1,095,668	938,514	801,926	637,220	722,300	719,480	708,715
Coal mines	754,008	784,621	644,008	533,267	437,921	466,305	453,239	453,600
Metal mines [2]	152,118	136,563	105,233	130,120	71,665	53,741	80,289	52,400
Quarries	100,740	86,456	80,632	79,509	66,180	82,209	83,730	86,200
Coke plants	31,060	28,136	19,855	19,962	22,987	34,471	34,247	26,715
Metallurgical plants	49,891	50,232	40,737	49,088	46,467	47,853	46,277	45,800
Average active days, total	231	249	217	219	271	205	221	239
Coal mines	209	220	192	190	250	170	180	210
Metal mines [2]	280	296	270	342	290	256	275	261
Quarries	246	297	255	240	264	275	272	276
Coke plants	308	319	347	329	344	321	341	344
Metallurgical plants	333	332	327	295	329	294	314	310
Man-days worked, total (1,000 days)	246,947	272,526	192,536	175,665	172,672	148,304	159,442	165,008
Coal mines do	158,479	180,365	123,304	106,209	113,434	82,417	91,321	96,411
Metal mines [2] do	42,569	40,362	27,570	29,046	20,699	21,497	22,084	22,980
Quarries do	24,734	29,127	20,889	19,122	15,376	22,850	22,346	24,330
Coke plants do	9,424	8,976	6,851	6,774	7,915	7,880	8,293	8,534
Metallurgical plants do	16,611	19,676	13,321	14,484	15,368	14,051	14,639	16,444
Man-hours worked, total (1,000 hours)	(?)	(?)	(?)	1,365,128	1,427,533	1,170,581	1,399,637	1,327,350
Coal mines do	1,339,279	1,431,162	1,102,902	840,416	968,591	642,476	711,390	743,380
Metal mines [2] do	(?)	(?)	(?)	388,728	166,906	171,316	176,221	191,950
Quarries do	231,512	216,465	186,802	147,244	127,186	182,258	180,535	195,760
Coke plants do	(?)	86,070	55,960	53,694	64,375	62,446	66,361	70,180
Metallurgical plants do	(?)	(?)	(?)	162,116	131,461	112,096	116,430	124,090
Number of injuries:								
Fatal	3,076	2,965	2,492	1,716	1,270	760	845	974
Coal mines	2,290	2,272	2,053	1,386	1,068	585	645	785
Metal mines [2]	552	425	271	223	112	79	108	111
Quarries	148	178	105	72	53	66	54	85
Coke plants	38	49	28	15	18	7	14	10
Metallurgical plants	68	61	26	18	19	23	29	10
Nonfatal	(?)	(?)	126,740	80,856	72,411	51,578	55,299	54,538
Coal mines	(?)	(?)	98,981	57,776	57,117	35,405	37,264	37,640
Metal mines [2]	35,396	22,562	15,594	14,766	8,067	8,065	7,849	8,315
Quarries	9,071	11,217	7,447	5,188	4,121	4,826	4,762	5,010
Coke plants	3,862	3,145	1,022	844	826	713	780	768
Metallurgical plants	7,813	8,863	2,726	2,582	3,271	2,567	2,574	2,805
Permanent	(?)	(?)	3,664	2,912	1,707	1,540	(?)	(?)
Coal mines	(?)		2,728	2,151	1,100	845	(?)	(?)
Metal mines [2]	600	567	803	483	310	268	(?)	(?)
Quarries	538	237	265	172	89	171	(?)	(?)
Coke plants	(?)	79	32	22	34	47	(?)	(?)
Metallurgical plants		149	156	144	165	209	(?)	(?)
Injury rates per million man-hours:								
Fatal	(?)	(?)	(?)	1.34	.88	.65	.57	.73
Coal mines	1.99	1.57	1.97	1.65	1.11	.91	.90	1.06
Metal mines [2]	(?)	(?)	(?)	.97	.66	.46	.58	.58
Quarries	.64	.83	.86	.49	.43	.36	.28	.29
Coke plants	(?)	.57	.50	.28	.28	.11	.21	.14
Metallurgical plants	(?)	(?)	(?)	.16	.16	.21	.25	.06
Nonfatal	(?)	(?)	(?)	58.37	51.07	44.06	43.36	41.09
Coal mines	(?)	(?)	90.65	68.75	59.58	55.11	56.75	50.70
Metal mines [2]	(?)	(?)		64.00	48.62	47.08	44.54	43.32
Quarries	41.77	41.62	39.77	35.23	32.41	26.45	26.12	24.21
Coke plants	(?)	36.06	16.26	10.14	12.97	11.42	11.84	10.94
Metallurgical plants	(?)	(?)		22.63	26.92	22.90	22.11	22.60
Injury rates per thousand 300-day workers, for all mines except coal:								
Fatal	2.60	2.16	2.62	2.30	1.60	1.11	1.40	1.39
Nonfatal	241.86	243.21	167.76	132.51	116.96	113.61	106.57	104.02

[1] Average number of men at work each day, mine was active. Because absenteeism and labor turnover are taken into consideration, this number relates more than number of men available for work as measured by a count of names on payroll. [2] Includes nonmetal mines except coal and quarries. [?] Not available.

Source: Department of Interior, Bureau of Mines, *Minerals Yearbook* and records.

No. 857.—Coal—Production, Consumption, Imports, and Exports: 1910 to 1951

[Quantities in thousands of short tons except as indicated; values in thousands of dollars. Includes coal consumed at mines. See also *Historical Statistics*, series G 13–42]

ITEM	1910	1920	1930	1940	1945	1949	1950	1951
Total coal production:								
Quantity	501,596	658,265	536,911	512,257	632,551	480,570	560,388	576,335
Value, total	639,557	2,564,185	1,150,057	1,084,817	2,092,148	2,494,879	2,892,772	3,631,848
BITUMINOUS COAL [1]								
Production:								
Quantity	417,111	568,667	467,526	460,772	577,617	⁻437,868	516.311	533,665
Value, total	469,282	2,129,933	795,483	879,327	1,768,204	2,136,871	2,500,374	2,626,030
Average per ton	1.12	3.75	1.70	1.91	3.06	4.88	4.84	4.92
Exports:								
Quantity	12,078	38,517	15,877	16,466	27,956	27,842	25,468	56,726
Value	26,685	304,273	59,186	60,832	147,954	232,393	206,545	496,944
Imports:								
Quantity	2,225	1,245	250	372	467	315	347	292
Value	4,761	6,734	1,135	1,501	2,294	2,368	2,369	2,019
Consumption		508,595	454,990	430,910	559,567	445,536	454,302	466,904
Number of mines	5,818	8,921	5,891	6,324	7,033	8,559	9,429	8,009
Average number of men employed	555,533	639,547	493,202	439,075	383,100	[1]433,698	[1]415,582	[2]372,897
Calculated capacity [3] (millions of net tons):								
At 308 days per year	592	796	770	703	682	859	(4)	(4)
At 280 days per year	538	725	700	639	620	781	790	736
At 261 days per year	502	675	653	595	578	726	(4)	(4)
Average number of days worked	217	220	187	202	261	157	183	203
Average tons per man:								
Per day	3.46	4.00	5.06	5.19	5.78	6.43	6.77	7.04
Per year	751	881	948	1,049	1,508	1,010	1,239	1,429
Percent underground production:								
Cut by machines	41.7	60.7	81.0	88.4	90.8	91.4	92.6	94.9
Mechanically loaded			10.5	35.4	56.1	67.0	69.4	73.1
Percent total production:								
Mechanically cleaned	3.8	3.3	8.3	22.2	25.6	35.1	38.5	45.0
Mined by stripping		1.5	4.3	9.2	19.0	24.2	23.9	22.0
ANTHRACITE (PA.) [5]								
Production:								
Quantity	84,485	89,598	69,385	51,485	54,934	42,702	44,077	42,670
Value, total	160,275	434,252	354,574	205,490	323,944	358,008	392,398	405,818
Average per ton	1.90	4.85	5.11	3.99	5.90	8.38	8.90	9.51
Exports:								
Quantity	3,384	5,404	2,552	2,668	3,691	4,943	3,892	5,959
Value	14,785	45,538	24,509	21,210	36,435	64,786	62,502	89,112
Imports:								
Quantity	9	32	675	135	(4)		18	27
Value	42	258	4,376	976	1		255	394
Consumption (apparent)	81,110	85,786	67,628	49,000	51,600	37,700	39,900	37,000
Average number of men employed	169,497	145,074	150,804	91,313	72,842	75,377	72,624	68,995
Average number of days worked	229	271	208	186	269	195	211	208
Average tons per man:								
Per day	2.17	2.28	2.21	3.02	2.79	2.87	2.83	2.97
Per year	498	618	460	562	751	560	597	618
Quantity cut by machines	[7]70	938	1,410	1,816	1,210	558	612	496
Quantity mined by stripping		2,054	2,536	6,353	10,056	10,377	11,834	11,136
Quantity loaded mechanically underground			4,468	12,326	13,928	11,858	12,336	10,848
World total, bituminous coal, lignite and anthracite (1,000,000 metric tons)	1,166	1,319	1,414	1,799	1,356	1,654	1,805	1,915

[1] Data relate to mines having output of 1,000 tons a year or more, including lignite and small output of anthracite produced outside Pennsylvania. Includes Alaska.   [2] Average number of men working daily.
[3] Capacity of active mines with existing labor force, derived on basis of average output per day.
[4] Not available.
[5] Beginning 1945, production data include some bootleg coal purchased by anthracite industry for preparation and shipment to market. Data on employment, however, exclude such purchased coal as complete employment data on "bootleg" holes are not available.   [6] Less than 500 tons.   [7] For 1911.

Source: Department of Interior, Bureau of Mines; *Minerals Yearbook* and annual bulletins.

No. 858.—COAL—PRODUCTION, BY STATES: 1931 TO 1951

[In thousands of short tons. Includes coal consumed at mines. See also *Historical Statistics*, series G 13 and 16]

STATE	1931–1935, avg.	1936–1940, avg.	1941–1945, avg.	1946–1950, avg.	1947	1948	1949	1950	1951
Total quantity	405,106	465,860	636,667	585,972	687,814	656,653	480,570	560,399	576,335
Anthracite (Pa.)	53,674	51,101	59,105	52,323	57,190	57,140	42,702	44,077	42,670
Bituminous	351,434	417,758	578,842	543,640	630,624	599,518	437,868	516,311	536,065
Alabama	9,262	12,620	17,783	16,278	19,048	18,801	12,954	14,422	13,897
Arkansas	1,012	1,367	1,521	1,459	1,871	1,662	962	1,169	1,107
Colorado	6,711	6,435	7,830	5,360	6,338	5,631	4,636	4,259	4,103
Illinois	40,196	48,367	66,442	60,034	67,860	65,342	47,208	56,391	54,300
Indiana	14,286	17,232	25,216	21,500	26,449	23,849	16,580	19,967	19,451
Iowa	3,492	3,376	2,869	1,752	1,664	1,670	1,726	1,801	1,630
Kansas	2,270	2,949	2,654	2,386	2,745	2,538	2,631	2,126	1,961
Kentucky	38,130	44,970	64,020	74,791	84,341	82,084	62,583	75,495	74,972
Maryland	1,684	1,496	1,854	1,406	2,051	1,661	666	646	569
Michigan	492	510	196	26	14	13	12	11	7
Missouri	3,634	3,577	3,947	3,720	4,236	4,022	3,647	2,963	3,289
Montana	2,396	2,571	4,345	3,017	3,175	2,896	2,766	2,490	2,345
New Mexico	1,328	1,378	1,600	1,164	1,443	1,364	1,004	727	753
North Dakota [1]	1,780	2,161	2,447	2,901	2,760	2,961	2,967	3,251	3,334
Ohio	19,151	22,188	32,190	35,488	37,548	36,708	30,961	37,761	37,946
Oklahoma	1,368	1,446	2,623	3,046	3,421	3,462	2,622	2,679	2,223
Pennsylvania	86,592	101,586	138,576	130,441	147,079	134,542	89,215	105,870	108,164
Tennessee	4,063	5,197	7,184	5,920	6,326	6,683	4,172	6,070	5,401
Texas	738	816	200	48	61	87	49	16	...
Utah	2,846	3,373	6,012	6,613	7,429	6,813	6,160	6,670	6,136
Virginia	8,922	13,224	19,121	17,190	20,171	17,999	14,584	17,867	21,400
Washington	1,555	1,744	1,641	1,020	1,118	1,230	909	874	857
West Virginia	95,748	112,032	154,335	151,153	176,157	166,862	122,610	144,116	168,310
Wyoming	4,545	5,617	5,684	6,889	5,051	6,412	6,001	6,346	6,430
Other States and Alaska	301	368	374	476	363	448	502	499	557

[1] Lignite only.

Source: Department of the Interior, Bureau of Mines; *Minerals Yearbook*. Current data also published in annual report, *Bituminous Coal and Lignite*.

No. 859.—CONSUMPTION OF BITUMINOUS COAL AND LIGNITE, BY CONSUMER CLASS, WITH RETAIL DELIVERIES: 1940 TO 1951

[In thousands of short tons]

YEAR	Total of classes shown	Colliery fuel	Electric power utilities [1]	Bunker, foreign trade [2]	Rail-roads (class I) [3]	Coke		Steel and rolling mills	Coal-gas retorts	Cement mills [5]	Other industries [5]	Retail-dealer deliveries [6]
						Bee-hive ovens	By-product ovens					
1940	430,910	2,443	49,126	1,426	86,130	4,803	78,563	10,040	1,746	5,628	106,290	87,700
1941	492,115	2,480	59,388	1,943	97,384	10,529	82,609	10,902	1,649	6,522	120,720	97,460
1942	540,060	2,708	63,472	1,885	115,410	13,876	87,974	10,434	1,721	7,570	131,560	104,780
1943	595,797	2,702	74,096	1,847	130,263	12,441	90,019	11,288	1,605	8,551	141,211	123,764
1944	589,599	2,712	76,604	1,859	132,049	10,858	94,438	10,734	1,548	8,789	136,353	124,906
1945	549,867	2,442	71,808	1,795	125,120	8,135	87,214	10,084	(*)	4,215	127,164	121,965
1946	500,286	1,961	86,743	1,381	110,186	7,167	76,121	5,603	(*)	7,000	116,639	100,586
1947	548,891	(*)	94,099	1,690	109,296	10,475	94,325	10,045	(*)	7,938	126,946	96,163
1948	518,909	(*)	96,680	1,097	94,638	10,322	98,984	10,646	(*)	8,554	112,741	98,747
1949	448,536	(*)	90,610	874	65,122	5,364	85,663	7,451	(*)	7,959	93,967	95,299
1950	484,202	(*)	98,363	717	60,969	9,088	94,757	7,688	(*)	7,943	98,164	86,604
1951	488,904	(*)	101,308	880	54,005	11,418	102,030	7,973	(*)	8,826	106,684	76,591

[1] Federal Power Commission. Represents consumption by public-utility power plants in power generation, including a small quantity of coke amounting to approximately 100,000 tons annually.
[2] U. S. Bureau of Census.
[3] Association of American Railroads. Represents consumption by class I railways for all uses, including locomotive, powerhouse, shop, and station fuel. The I. C. C. reports that in 1951 consumption for all uses by class I line-haul railways, plus purchases for class II and class III railways, plus purchases by all switching terminal companies combined, was 55,196,153 tons of bituminous coal and lignite.
[4] Includes small amount of anthracite.
[5] Estimate based upon reports collected from a selected list of representative manufacturing plants and retailers.
[6] Included in "Other industrials."

Source: Department of the Interior, Bureau of Mines; *Minerals Yearbook*.

No. 860.—Coal—Employment, Fatalities and Injuries at Mines: 1911 to 1951

[See also table 856 and *Historical Statistics*, series G 144-158]

ITEM	1911	1920	1930	1940	1945	1949	1950	1951[1]
ALL COAL MINES								
Total coal production (1,000 tons)...	496,371	658,265	536,911	512,808	631,523	478,920	560,388	576,509
Tons per man-hour...................	.38	.45	.49	.61	.66	.75	.78	.78
Employment:								
Number of employees.............	728,348	784,621	644,006	533,267	437,921	485,306	483,239	453,600
Active days......................	220	230	192	199	259	170	189	210
Man-hours (1,000)................	1,302,108	1,451,162	1,102,902	840,416	958,591	642,476	711,390	742,360
Number of men killed.............	2,656	2,272	2,063	1,388	1,068	585	643	785
Per million tons coal mined.......	5.35	3.45	3.84	2.71	1.69	1.22	1.14	1.36
Per thousand men employed.....	3.65	2.90	3.20	2.60	2.44	1.21	1.33	1.73
Per thousand 300-day workers...	4.97	3.78	5.00	3.92	2.82	2.13	2.11	2.47
Number of men injured...........	[2]	[2]	99,981	57,776	57,117	35,405	37,264	37,640
Per million tons coal mined.......	[2]	[2]	186.22	112.67	90.44	73.93	66.50	65.29
BITUMINOUS COAL MINES								
Number of men killed.............	1,957	1,781	1,619	1,204	925	494	550	685
Per million tons coal mined.......	4.82	3.13	3.46	2.61	1.60	1.13	1.06	1.28
Per thousand men employed.....	3.53	2.78	3.28	2.73	2.53	1.21	1.35	1.78
Per thousand 300-day workers...	5.02	3.79	5.26	4.07	2.96	2.19	2.18	2.55
Number of men injured...........	[2]	[2]	71,217	43,994	46,194	27,548	28,390	30,525
Per million tons coal mined.......	[2]	[2]	152.33	95.37	80.12	63.22	54.80	57.06
ANTHRACITE MINES								
Number of men killed.............	699	491	444	184	143	91	93	100
Per million tons coal mined.......	7.73	5.48	6.40	3.57	2.60	2.11	2.09	2.41
Per thousand men employed.....	4.02	3.38	2.94	1.99	1.96	1.20	1.25	1.45
Per thousand 300-day workers...	4.90	3.74	4.22	3.16	2.19	1.83	1.77	2.07
Number of men injured...........	[2]	[2]	28,764	13,782	10,923	7,857	8,874	7,115
Per million tons coal mined.......	[2]	[2]	414.56	267.67	198.60	181.87	199.75	171.41

[1] Preliminary.   [2] Not available.

Source: Department of Interior, Bureau of Mines; *Minerals Yearbook*, annual bulletin, *Injury Experience in Coal Mining*, and records.

No. 861.—Consumption and Use of Fuels and Electric Energy in the Non-Energy-Producing Economy: 1929, 1939, and 1947

[In units of ten billion B. t. u.   Electric energy at central station fuel consumption rate.   Excludes exports]

USE	CONSUMPTION			PERCENT OF TOTAL		
	1929	1939	1947	1929	1939	1947
Total...........................	2,236,450	2,044,097	3,091,906	100.0	100.0	100.0
Manufacturing industries [1]....................	631,339	507,640	851,859	28.2	24.8	27.6
Food and kindred products................	55,460	54,943	71,101	2.5	2.7	2.3
Textile-mill products....................	36,735	30,688	38,582	1.6	1.5	1.2
Paper and allied products................	40,007	39,382	63,272	1.8	1.9	2.1
Chemicals and allied products............	50,927	51,482	102,266	2.3	2.5	3.3
Stone, clay, and glass products..........	84,300	59,430	88,960	3.8	2.9	2.9
Primary metals:						
Iron and steel..........................	231,503	168,221	287,150	10.3	8.2	9.3
Nonferrous............................	16,110	20,669	44,724	.7	1.0	1.5
Fabricated metal products................	21,318	12,396	19,838	1.0	.6	.6
Other manufacturing industries..........	94,979	69,834	128,672	4.2	3.4	4.2
Nonfuel mines and quarries................	23,530	16,462	21,841	1.1	.8	.7
Transportation [1]...........................	747,393	670,523	950,719	33.4	32.8	30.7
Pipeline and utility system use and loss.......	50,144	54,835	89,850	2.2	2.7	2.9
Railroads...............................	426,416	269,500	378,181	19.1	13.2	12.2
Bunkers (foreign trade only).............	67,672	53,118	77,359	3.0	2.6	2.5
Nonhighway:						
Aviation.............................	256	---------	11,275	---------	---------	.4
Other...............................	26,767	34,807	42,555	1.2	1.7	1.4
Highway...............................	176,138	257,979	350,546	7.9	12.6	11.3
Army, Navy, and Coast Guard...........	3,920	7,788	23,162	.2	.4	.7
Domestic and commercial..................	696,690	715,911	1,039,015	31.2	35.0	33.6
Nonfuel use............................	65,927	82,967	134,534	2.9	4.1	4.4
Miscellaneous..........................	67,651	42,806	70,776	3.0	2.1	2.3

[1] Includes certain small consumption not included in detail.

Source: Department of Interior, Bureau of Mines; *Production, Consumption, and Use of Fuels and Electric Energy in the United States in 1929, 1939, and 1947.*

No. 862.—Work Stoppages in Anthracite and Bituminous Coal-Mining Industries, by Major Issues Involved: 1940 to 1952

[Excludes work stoppages involving fewer than 6 workers or lasting less than 1 day. Figures are for stoppages beginning in years shown. For combined statistics covering work stoppages in all industries, see table 940]

COAL-MINING INDUSTRY AND YEAR	NUMBER OF WORK STOPPAGES [1]				NUMBER OF WORKERS INVOLVED [5]				NUMBER OF MAN-DAYS IDLE			
		Major issues				Major issues				Major issues		
	Total	Wages and hours	Union organization [3]	Miscellaneous	Total	Wages and hours	Union organization [3]	Miscellaneous	Total	Wages and hours	Union organization [3]	Miscellaneous
Anthracite:												
1940	26	1	3	21	17,255	62	3,208	14,085	106,399	496	30,470	74,433
1941	27	5	1	21	136,256	92,557	1,552	42,776	423,299	97,025	6,206	320,068
1942	31	10		21	36,153	19,142		17,011	226,921	148,440		77,461
1943	30	12		18	117,623	96,296		20,327	1,536,486	1,552,457		364,029
1944	61	18	1	42	46,624	14,278	6,726	19,616	336,922	209,054	63,590	74,378
1945	43	18		25	87,700	74,500		13,200	1,163,000	1,108,000		55,000
1946	34	6		28	109,000	81,700	20	27,600	649,000	545,000	260	104,000
1947	28	6		22	31,200	6,880		14,800	139,000	106,000		63,800
1948	39	11		20	54,300	5,710	20	48,300	274,000	33,000	100	241,800
1949	34	8		26	212,000	72,500		145,000	1,400,000	600,000		799,000
1950	41	13		28	22,200	11,200		10,900	80,100	27,700		52,400
1951	30	5		25	23,900	6,430		17,500	81,200	53,900		27,400
1952	41	6	1	34	22,300	890	110	31,300	104,000	13,600	120	90,100
Bituminous:												
1940	34	4	10	20	24,372	272	3,451	20,649	153,296	15,964	16,214	121,128
1941	75	19	13	43	592,352	283,529	63,180	146,343	6,747,985	5,586,678	710,230	446,088
1942	96	25	11	60	42,774	15,551	5,137	25,086	264,468	134,100	15,653	114,780
1943	400	177	17	206	487,474	423,801	3,127	60,546	7,510,397	7,247,829	23,141	239,427
1944	792	268	32	532	229,907	50,918	46,307	132,782	1,006,341	207,858	266,646	531,836
1945	586	144	49	399	581,500	203,100	238,500	139,400	5,007,000	984,000	3,308,000	713,000
1946	486	102	43	341	854,000	708,000	10,300	116,080	19,500,000	18,800,000	142,000	612,009
1947	415	72	22	319	460,000	20,400	247,000	122,000	2,190,000	184,000	1,560,000	456,000
1948	501	62	42	437	862,000	287,000	51,900	192,000	5,560,000	5,230,000	428,000	908,000
1949	421	50	27	344	1,120,000	345,000	8,000	780,000	15,708,000	12,400,000	39,800	4,220,069
1950	430	54	34	342	165,000	27,500	6,230	131,000	9,320,000	8,810,000	52,100	456,000
1951	549	75	56	418	213,000	26,400	13,400	171,000	887,000	81,200	80,700	725,000
1952	560	97	26	437	472,000	26,500	7,600	438,000	2,760,000	98,800	39,600	2,620,000

[1] Formerly designated "strikes and lockouts."
[3] Wages and hours were important issues also in some of these disputes. This is especially true in recent years.
[5] Includes some duplication (where same workers were involved in more than 1 stoppage). This is particularly significant in 1949, since over 60,000 anthracite miners and over 300,000 bituminous coal miners were involved in 3 separate stoppages during year.
[4] Totals include 6 stoppages, involving 500 workers and 2,000 man-days, in which issues were not reported.

Source: Department of Labor, Bureau of Labor Statistics; Bulletin No. 651, *Strikes in the United States, 1880–1936*; annual bulletins on work stoppages, and official records.

No. 863.—Coke—Production, Exports, and Imports: 1910 to 1951

[See also *Historical Statistics*, series G 43–56]

ITEM	1910	1920	1930	1940	1945	1949	1950	1951
Production, total 1,000 short tons	41,709	51,345	47,972	57,072	67,306	63,637	72,718	79,331
Oven coke do	7,139	30,834	45,196	54,014	62,094	60,222	66,391	71,987
Percent of total	17.1	60.1	94.2	94.6	92.3	94.6	92.0	90.7
Beehive coke 1,000 short tons	34,570	20,511	2,776	3,058	5,214	3,415	5,527	7,344
Value of coke at plant, total $1,000,000	106	581	878	442	699	1,111	1,279	1,474
Beehive coke do	75	163	10	14	38	44	77	103
Oven coke do	26	313	200	280	470	709	900	1,017
All coal-chemical materials do	6	106	168	168	191	368	302	355
Average value per ton at plant	$2.39	$0.27	$4.36	$4.50	$7.56	$13.24	$13.43	$14.11
Coal charged million short tons	63.1	76.2	59.8	81.4	95.7	91.4	104.0	113.7
Value, average per ton	$2.39	$4.44	$3.36	$2.56	$5.13	$3.34	$3.41	$3.66
Yield of coke from coal percent	66.1	67.4	68.7	70.1	70.4	69.6	69.9	69.8
Ovens in existence end of year number	104,440	86,179	26,726	27,884	26,689	25,795	22,680	25,777
Coke (slot type) do	4,078	16,881	12,821	12,734	14,510	15,104	14,983	15,319
Beehive do	100,362	74,398	23,907	15,150	12,179	13,052	17,708	20,458
Coke ovens under construction end of year do	1,200	396	878	492	335	582	706	1,446
Exports 1,000 short tons	985	820	1,004	804	1,479	548	366	1,027
Imports do	175	41	123	113	48	278	436	162

[1] Slot-type.

Source: Department of the Interior, Bureau of Mines; *Minerals Yearbook*.

No. 864.—COKE—OVEN AND BEEHIVE PRODUCTION, BY STATES: 1915 TO 1951

[In thousands of short tons.   Exclusive of screenings or breeze]

STATE	1915	1920	1925	1930	1935	1940	1945	1949	1950	1951
OVEN										
Total	14,073	36,534	39,912	45,196	34,224	54,014	62,094	60,222	66,891	71,987
Alabama	2,070	3,194	4,582	3,987	1,994	4,727	5,401	5,161	5,833	6,291
Colorado		517	490	379	207	544	639	730	805	995
Illinois	1,687	2,137	3,012	3,576	1,669	3,015	3,682	3,196	3,591	3,696
Indiana	2,768	4,554	5,142	4,984	3,768	6,413	7,814	7,533	8,256	8,843
Maryland	313	682	1,019	1,169	930	1,683	2,025	2,040	2,367	2,855
Massachusetts	504	488	535	863	1,006	1,130	1,180	891	855	1,109
Michigan	(¹)	1,303	1,751	2,604	2,482	2,872	2,806	2,484	2,731	2,920
Minnesota	128	675	518	641	430	524	826	782	834	972
New Jersey	269	726	904	919	917	1,016	1,284	1,345	1,481	1,539
New York	684	1,040	2,220	3,880	4,099	5,080	5,790	5,165	5,412	5,611
Ohio	666	5,615	7,105	6,163	5,101	7,896	9,406	8,911	10,314	11,151
Pennsylvania	3,092	7,780	9,853	12,530	8,078	14,862	15,255	14,769	16,333	17,250
West Virginia	141	447	1,056	1,479	1,604	1,900	2,462	3,183	3,389	3,830
All other States	1,749	1,706	1,725	2,051	1,989	2,350	3,586	4,032	4,690	4,935
BEEHIVE										
Total	27,506	26,511	11,355	2,776	917	3,058	5,214	3,415	5,527	7,344
Pennsylvania	22,531	15,908	9,574	2,011	564	2,580	4,584	2,899	5,193	6,396
Ohio	19	87	156							
West Virginia	1,250	1,381	490	422	155	233	288	177	302	432
Alabama	1,001	890	58							
Kentucky	285	273	(¹)			(¹)	74	48	(¹)	(¹)
Tennessee	284	163	128	25	3	5				2
Virginia	680	1,028	423	230	138	196	191	158	198	287
Colorado	671	273	155	79	49	62	73			1
Utah	(¹)	(¹)	146	7	6	7	4	133	85	102
All other States	887	509	196	12	2	1			49	124

¹ Included in figure for "All other States."

Source: Department of the Interior, Bureau of Mines; *Minerals Yearbook.*

No. 865.—NATURAL GAS—PRODUCTION, CONSUMPTION, AND VALUE: 1930 TO 1951

[See also *Historical Statistics*, series G 59–61 for production and value figures]

ITEM	1930	1935	1940	1945	1949	1950	1951
Total marketed production million cu. ft	1,943,421	1,916,595	2,660,222	3,918,686	¹ 5,419,736	¹ 6,282,060	¹ 7,457,359
Value (at wells) of gas produced..$1,000..	147,048	110,402	120,493	191,006	344,034	408,521	542,964
Average per M cu. ft cents..	7.6	5.8	4.5	4.9	6.3	6.5	7.3
Number of producing gas wells, Dec. 31..	55,020	53,790	53,880	60,660	63,346	64,900	65,100
Total consumption million cu.ft..	1,941,584	1,909,901	2,654,659	3,900,479	5,195,484	6,026,404	7,102,562
Domestic do....	295,700	313,498	443,646	607,400	992,544	1,198,369	1,474,725
Commercial do....	80,707	100,187	134,644	230,099	347,818	387,838	464,309
Industrial do....	1,565,237	1,496,216	2,076,369	3,062,980	3,855,122	4,440,197	5,163,528
Value (at point of consumption) of gas consumed, total..$1,000..	415,519	428,074	577,004	834,195	1,320,589	1,604,041	2,118,675
Domestic do....	200,615	233,940	315,515	415,122	665,536	826,393	1,120,819
Commercial do....	38,558	49,386	64,399	97,572	158,105	184,430	245,609
Industrial do....	176,346	144,748	197,090	321,501	496,948	593,218	752,247
Average per M cu. ft cents..	21.4	22.4	21.7	21.4	25.4	26.6	29.8
Domestic do....	67.8	74.6	71.1	68.3	67.1	69.0	76.0
Commercial do....	47.8	49.3	47.8	42.4	45.5	47.6	52.9
Industrial do....	11.3	9.7	9.5	10.5	12.9	13.4	14.6
Number of consumers:							
Domestic thousands..	5,035	7,391	9,245	10,959	14,690	16,906	21,444
Commercial do....	413	613	741	889	1,231	1,347	1,614
Industrial ³ do....	21	36	41	46	(²)	(²)	(²)

¹ Includes gas stored and lost in transmission.
² Excludes oil- and gas-field operators.
³ Not available.

Source: Department of the Interior, Bureau of Mines; *Minerals Yearbook.*

No. 866.—NATURAL GASOLINE—PRODUCTION AND VALUE: 1930 TO 1951

[Barrels of 42 gallons. See also *Historical Statistics*, series G 62–64]

ITEM	1930	1935	1940	1945	1949	1950	1951
Total produced..........1,000 barrels..	(¹)	(¹)	(¹)	112,004	157,086	181,961	204,754
Natural gasoline and natural-gasoline mixtures......1,000 barrels..	82,631	30,323	51,755	59,494	71,640	76,578	82,580
Liquefied petroleum gases......do....	(¹)	(¹)	(¹)	23,648	57,809	72,282	88,377
Other products............do....	....	....	8,945	18,863	27,877	32,906	34,497
Value at plants:							
Natural gasoline............$1,000..	128,160	70,940	³ 86,281	112,018	211,487	213,810	254,319
Liquefied petroleum gases......do....	(¹)	(¹)	(¹)	41,594	98,054	97,773	126,443
Other products............do....	....	....	(²)	32,552	91,648	108,023	115,599
Average value per gallon, all light products..........cents..	⁴ 5.8	⁴ 4.3	⁴ 2.9	4.0	6.1	5.5	5.9
Natural gas treated....million cu. ft..	2,088,778	1,898,009	2,471,400	3,653,870	4,666,142	5,341,804	6,208,070
Average yield, all light products gal. per M cu. ft..	(¹)	(¹)	(¹)	1.39	1.42	1.43	1.39

¹ Not available.
² Other products included with natural gasoline.
³ Does not cover liquefied petroleum gases.

Source: Department of the Interior, Bureau of Mines; *Minerals Yearbook*.

No. 867.—NATURAL GAS AND NATURAL GASOLINE—PRODUCTION, BY STATES

[Gas in millions of cubic feet; gasoline in thousands of barrels of 42 gallons. Production figures for gas (except as noted) refer only to that used by the ultimate consumer, in addition to which considerable quantities are used by producers, and large quantities are wasted or lost. Consumption figures by States differ greatly from production figures by reason of interstate transportation]

STATE	NATURAL GAS—MARKETED PRODUCTION					Natural gas reserves, 1950 ¹	NATURAL GASOLINE PRODUCED ²		
	1930	1935	1940	1945	1950		1949	1950	1951
Total........	1,943,421	1,916,595	2,660,322	3,918,696	⁵ 6,282,699	185,582,699	157,086	181,961	204,754
Arkansas..........	18,585	6,167	14,379	46,600	48,047	907,593	2,280	2,333	2,348
California.........	334,729	284,109	361,950	502,442	558,398	9,799,388	27,158	28,326	29,533
Illinois...........	2,890	1,448	8,359	16,653	12,285	229,893	3,219	3,107	⁴ 2,971
Kansas............	37,630	87,125	90,003	145,950	364,024	13,790,834	2,648	3,687	4,366
Kentucky.........	33,083	38,736	53,086	51,714	73,316	1,330,558	1,621	1,779	2,166
Louisiana.........	278,341	246,450	343,191	542,780	531,771	28,533,266	19,254	20,768	22,462
Michigan..........	2,075	4,203	12,648	21,874	11,280	195,074	86	79	(⁴)
Mississippi.......	179	3,643	6,365	4,467	114,153	2,519,206	1,271	1,312	1,202
Montana..........	10,050	16,570	28,281	31,820	39,186	797,361	230	261	277
New Mexico......	9,497	27,981	53,990	105,023	212,909	6,990,670	4,025	5,019	5,586
New York........	9,624	5,286	12,187	9,210	3,236	64,779	(⁴)	....	(⁶)
Ohio.............	63,304	46,802	40,639	46,967	43,163	656,562	123	103	107
Oklahoma........	345,116	274,313	267,824	357,580	482,360	11,634,287	12,485	14,733	17,543
Pennsylvania.....	85,708	94,464	98,725	82,188	91,137	627,171	245	246	⁶ 210
Texas............	517,580	642,305	1,082,538	1,711,401	3,126,402	102,404,077	77,631	93,650	106,531
West Virginia....	144,189	115,772	168,751	160,226	188,980	1,650,675	3,760	4,622	4,951
Wyoming.........	43,219	26,643	27,346	35,282	62,059	2,194,868	1,305	1,551	1,990
Other States......	6,233	5,475	9,238	13,408	17,281	⁷ 1,302,908	361	392	620

¹ Estimated recoverable proved reserves. Offshore reserves included for California, Louisiana, and Texas. Excludes gas lost due to natural-gas liquids recovery. Source: American Gas Association.
² Includes liquefied petroleum gases and other allied products.
³ Includes gas stored and lost in transmission.
⁴ Michigan included with Illinois.
⁵ Less than 500 barrels.
⁶ New York included with Pennsylvania.
⁷ Includes 1,116,873,000,000 cubic feet for Colorado.

Source: Department of the Interior, Bureau of Mines; *Minerals Yearbook*.

No. 868.—Crude Petroleum, Refined Products, and Natural Gasoline—Production and Stocks: 1910 to 1952

[Barrels of 42 gallons. See also *Historical Statistics*, series G 57–58]

ITEM	1910	1920	1930	1940	1945	1950	1951	1952 (prel.)
Crude petroleum:								
Domestic production...1,000 bbl..	209,557	442,929	898,011	1,353,214	1,713,655	1,973,574	2,247,711	2,291,997
Value...$1,000	127,900	1,360,745	1,070,200	1,385,440	2,094,250	4,963,380	5,690,410	(¹)
World production...1,000 bbl..	327,763	688,884	1,411,904	2,144,050	2,594,798	3,796,658	4,282,874	(¹)
U. S. proportion of world total percent..	64	64	64	63	66	52	52	(¹)
Imports²...1,000 bbl..	571	106,175	62,129	42,662	74,337	177,714	179,073	209,501
Exports²...do....	4,288	9,295	23,705	51,496	32,998	34,823	28,604	26,727
Stocks, end of period:								
Gasoline-bearing crude..do....	131,030	149,448	408,809	264,709	218,763 }	248.463	255,783	271,928
California heavy crude..do....	(¹)	(¹)	(²)	11,906	4,496			
Runs to stills...do....	(¹)	433,915	927,447	1,294,162	1,719,534	2,094,867	2,370,404	2,441,269
Total value at wells...$1,000	127,900	1,360,745	1,070,200	1,385,440	2,094,250	4,963,380	5,690,410	(¹)
Average price per barrel at wells..	$0.61	$3.07	$1.19	$1.02	$1.22	$2.51	$2.53	(¹)
Refined products:								
Imports²...1,000 bbl..	(¹)	2,647	43,489	41,089	39,282	132,547	129,121	140,716
Exports²...do....	(¹)	70,281	132,704	78,970	149,985	76,483	125,448	132,811
Stocks, end of period...do....	(¹)	³60,397	³254,311	260,958	235,998	326,892	⁴370,140	⁴394,019
Output of motor fuel...do....	(¹)	118,022	440,728	616,665	798,194	1,024,462	1,140,843	1,189,781
Yield of gasoline...percent..	(¹)	26.1	42.0	43.1	40.9	43.0	42.4	43.0
Completed refineries, end of year..	(¹)	415	435	556	393	357	350	(¹)
Daily crude-oil capacity of refineries...1,000 bbl..	(¹)	1,889	3,943	4,719	5,316	6,964	7,333	(¹)
Average dealer's net price (excl. tax) of gasoline in 50 U. S. cities⁵...cents per gal	(¹)	28.05	14.49	9.08	10.33	15.10	15.33	(¹)
Natural gasoline:								
Production...1,000 bbl..	(¹)	9,161	52,631	85,700	112,004	181,961	204,754	221,474
Stocks, end of period...do....	(¹)	(¹)	2,377	5,704	4,322	7,355	8,186	7,807

¹ Not available.
² Import and export figures from Bureau of Census, except for imports of crude petroleum for 1940 and later years which are as reported to Bureau of Mines. Exports include shipments to noncontiguous Territories and possessions.
³ Figure for California heavy crude included in refined products.
⁴ New basis.
⁵ American Petroleum Institute figures; prior to 1940, average tank-wagon prices.

Source: Department of the Interior, Bureau of Mines (except as noted); *Minerals Yearbook*.

No. 869.—Petroleum Pipe Lines—Summary: 1925 to 1951

[All figures, except miles of line operated, in thousands of dollars]

YEAR	Miles of line operated	Investment in pipe lines	Other investments	Pipe-line operating revenues	Pipe-line operating expenses	Pipe-line operating income	Net income
1925	70,009	511,088	93,896	164,645	80,232	70,966	88,495
1930	88,727	772,711	96,184	237,910	99,363	121,816	123,741
1935	92,037	763,009	119,071	197,368	89,364	79,586	78,249
1937	96,611	802,946	87,389	248,198	99,641	109,994	102,720
1938	96,775	807,657	70,666	228,211	98,756	95,128	92,734
1939	98,681	829,646	65,124	212,466	97,130	83,401	80,823
1940	100,156	841,977	64,095	225,760	101,919	82,558	79,857
1941	105,435	885,317	45,687	251,685	110,448	81,604	79,468
1942	106,485	918,848	44,525	245,061	123,507	58,332	56,845
1943	108,783	965,464	39,891	276,652	148,448	62,620	61,302
1944	111,615	1,000,741	62,767	310,194	172,368	67,840	65,715
1945	113,351	1,042,523	86,713	304,268	191,668	67,127	65,941
1946	116,544	1,106,454	69,991	293,723	183,869	56,485	56,094
1947	119,298	1,225,168	56,455	325,224	214,682	54,415	53,145
1948	124,092	1,381,402	52,168	377,034	252,971	58,806	56,679
1949	124,984	1,497,579	78,285	376,452	249,368	63,282	57,743
1950	128,589	1,655,973	100,798	441,627	254,701	89,047	81,303
1951	131,457	1,821,880	70,011	523,973	290,144	91,265	82,006

Source: Interstate Commerce Commission; annual report, *Statistics of Oil Pipe Line Companies*.

No. 870.—PETROLEUM, CRUDE—PRODUCTION, 1931 TO 1951, AND RESERVES, 1950 AND 1951, BY STATES

[In thousands of barrels of 42 gallons]

STATE	PRODUCTION							PROVED RESERVES	
	1931–1935 (average)	1936–1940 (average)	1941–45 (average)	1946–1950 (average)	1949	1950	1951	1950	1951
United States [1]	889,311	1,243,276	1,537,299	1,895,225	1,841,940	1,973,574	2,247,711	25,268,000	27,468,000
Arkansas	12,144	17,460	27,717	20,220	20,956	31,108	29,795	342,000	337,000
California	184,221	230,956	280,210	329,604	332,943	337,677	354,861	3,734,000	3,761,000
Colorado	1,289	1,539	2,509	15,463	22,587	33,308	27,823	330,000	336,000
Illinois	4,551	55,722	94,719	66,619	64,501	62,026	60,943	564,000	646,000
Indiana	800	1,870	5,888	8,098	9,606	10,699	11,100	57,000	51,000
Kansas	43,082	63,197	96,447	104,542	101,968	107,566	114,522	732,000	792,000
Kentucky	5,400	5,849	7,428	9,562	8,502	10,361	11,629	86,000	80,000
Louisiana	30,396	92,771	128,196	177,090	196,526	205,965	232,281	2,185,000	2,335,000
Michigan	9,094	15,169	18,926	16,501	15,617	15,595	13,927	79,000	64,000
Mississippi	(7)	4,567	19,673	36,237	37,986	38,296	37,039	266,000	266,000
Montana	3,152	5,261	6,117	8,595	9,119	9,109	6,955	111,000	105,000
New Mexico	15,520	35,730	37,260	44,144	47,045	47,347	53,719	592,000	812,000
New York	3,618	5,077	5,602	4,586	4,428	4,142	4,264	56,000	57,000
Ohio	4,504	3,460	3,502	3,586	3,358	3,388	3,140	27,000	20,000
Oklahoma	176,293	185,306	136,402	149,305	151,900	164,509	186,869	1,397,000	1,476,000
Pennsylvania	13,442	17,654	15,284	12,317	11,374	11,859	11,345	106,000	95,000
Texas	364,341	475,069	616,584	811,726	744,524	838,974	1,010,270	13,862,000	15,215,000
West Virginia	4,082	3,609	2,361	2,777	2,699	2,808	2,787	39,000	36,000
Wyoming	13,159	19,907	23,904	49,680	47,590	61,631	68,929	841,000	972,000

[1] Includes quantities for States not shown separately.
[2] Not shown separately.

Source: Department of the Interior, Bureau of Mines; Minerals Yearbook.

No. 871.—PETROLEUM—RUNS TO STILLS AND REFINERY PRODUCTS, BY CLASS: 1930 TO 1952

[In thousands of barrels of 42 gallons]

PRODUCT	1930	1935	1940	1945	1949	1950	1951	1952 (prel.)
Input, total	970,917	996,815	1,233,799	1,789,853	2,029,678	2,189,506	2,462,654	2,545,157
Crude petroleum, total	927,447	965,790	1,204,162	1,719,534	1,944,221	2,094,867	2,370,406	2,441,259
Domestic	866,615	943,659	1,252,364	1,645,862	1,759,766	1,916,084	2,185,677	2,235,198
Foreign	60,832	22,131	41,798	73,672	184,455	176,012	181,727	206,061
Natural gasoline	43,170	31,025	29,547	70,324	85,457	94,639	96,280	102,898
Output, total	970,917	996,815	1,233,799	1,789,853	2,029,678	2,189,506	2,462,654	2,545,157
Gasoline	432,241	457,842	597,375	774,460	939,051	998,093	1,105,880	1,155,916
Kerosene	48,208	55,813	73,882	81,024	168,182	118,512	136,742	182,300
Distillate fuel oil	81,551	100,235	183,304	249,224	340,825	398,912	475,891	521,264
Residual fuel oil	296,927	258,126	316,221	469,492	424,909	425,217	460,377	454,784
Lubricants	34,201	27,253	36,765	41,867	45,289	51,725	51,480	55,690
Wax (1 bbl. = 280 lb.)	1,906	1,608	1,533	2,921	3,208	4,482	4,514	4,331
Coke (5 bbl. = 1 s. ton)	6,306	7,390	7,633	10,115	16,959	17,294	18,977	18,122
Asphalt (5.5 bbl. = 1 s. ton)	15,194	17,133	29,405	39,196	49,007	55,240	65,302	70,312
Still gas (1 bbl. = 2,600 cu. ft.)	5,877	51,184	75,060	103,442	82,621	82,742	96,294	85,275
Road oil	1,436	6,030	7,771	2,665	7,491	5,925	6,100	6,998
Other finished products	2,277	1,698	3,302	19,080	27,705	33,800	40,244	44,226
Crude gasoline (net)		7,032	902	1,499	1,418	243	1,255	489
Other unfinished oils (net)	2,342	[3] 8,411	[3] 5,848	[3] 8,797	[3] 10,000	[3] 6,391	[3] 11,367	[3] 2,909
Shortage	37,003	11,493	3,313	6,954	888	[3] 718	[3] 2,642	[3] 2,662

[3] Negative quantity; represents net excess of unfinished oils rerun over unfinished oils produced.
[4] Negative quantity.

Source: Department of the Interior, Bureau of Mines; Minerals Yearbook.

No. 872.—Oil Wells, Number and Production, 1950 and 1951, and Number of Oil and Gas Wells Drilled, 1951 and 1952, by States

STATE	PRODUCING OIL WELLS				WELLS DRILLED [1]					
	Approximate number Dec. 31		Average production per well per day (barrels)		Oil		Gas		Dry	
	1950	1951	1950	1951	1951	1952	1951	1952	1951	1952
Total	465,870	474,990	11.8	13.1	23,453	23,466	3,030	3,255	16,653	17,618
Arkansas	3,700	3,800	22.2	21.8	235	217	10	7	184	202
California	28,080	29,630	34.2	33.7	1,735	1,790	40	43	580	590
Colorado	770	840	84.2	94.7	103	162	12	29	174	285
Illinois	27,500	27,420	6.2	6.0	918	825	10	18	1,484	1,299
Indiana	3,410	3,600	8.6	8.7	434	408	18	18	912	843
Kansas	31,000	32,460	9.7	9.9	2,177	2,194	376	316	1,886	2,013
Kentucky	15,650	16,900	1.8	2.0	594	406	155	227	629	661
Louisiana	11,860	12,490	50.4	52.3	1,318	1,286	176	206	843	886
Michigan	3,959	3,800	11.2	9.8	222	283	20	30	457	356
Mississippi	1,670	1,760	68.3	59.2	137	111	9	4	226	233
Montana	3,300	3,380	6.9	7.3	144	163	8	18	110	164
Nebraska [3]	221	346	30.2	20.5	77	100	15	16	167	193
New Mexico	6,020	6,350	22.7	23.4	350	525	254	319	189	209
New York	23,200	23,200	.5	.5	330	(²)	---	(²)	---	(²)
Ohio	18,580	17,650	.5	.5	334	(²)	226	(²)	344	(²)
Oklahoma	56,800	57,600	8.1	9.0	3,109	3,086	265	295	2,075	2,247
Pennsylvania	81,190	78,800	.4	.4	776	¹ 1,721	239	¹ 882	70	¹ 863
Texas	128,500	134,670	18.3	21.0	10,086	9,682	726	778	5,803	6,332
West Virginia	15,000	14,500	.5	.5	79	(²)	419	(²)	124	(²)
Wyoming	5,320	5,610	32.3	34.6	443	403	21	16	282	281
Other States	149	184	45.7	46.1	32	134	31	33	132	229

[1] Figures from Oil and Gas Journal.
[2] New York, Ohio, and West Virginia included in Pennsylvania.   [3] Missouri included with Nebraska.

No. 873.—Asphalt—Supply, Distribution, and Value: 1944 to 1951

ITEM	1944	1945	1946	1947	1948	1949	1950	1951
SUPPLY (1,000 TONS OF 2,000 LBS.)								
Total	8,483	8,609	9,832	10,947	11,551	11,360	13,064	14,911
Native asphalt and related bitumens:								
Produced	790	704	846	1,072	1,136	1,202	1,251	1,444
Imported (chiefly lake asphalt)	8	5	4	6	5	4	6	6
Petroleum asphalt (excluding road oil):								
Produced at refineries from domestic and foreign petroleum	6,996	7,127	8,166	8,961	9,440	8,910	10,589	12,056
Imported [1]	126	147	123	206	284	215	324	443
Stocks, Jan. 1	563	626	693	702	686	1,029	894	962
DISTRIBUTION (1,000 TONS OF 2,000 LBS.)								
Total	8,483	8,609	9,832	10,947	11,551	11,360	13,064	14,911
Native asphalt and related bitumens:								
Indicated domestic demand	752	657	819	1,048	1,127	1,189	1,233	1,419
Exports (unmanufactured)	37	47	27	24	14	17	18	25
Petroleum asphalt (excluding road oil):								
Indicated domestic demand (incl. lake asphalt)	6,949	6,999	7,888	8,533	9,111	9,028	10,707	12,080
Exports	119	213	396	556	270	234	144	183
Stocks, Dec. 31	626	693	702	686	1,029	894	962	1,204
VALUE (1,000 DOLLARS)								
Native asphalt and related bitumens:								
Sales	3,688	3,816	4,262	5,503	5,026	5,560	5,297	6,054
Imports (chiefly lake asphalt)	254	122	92	243	167	88	136	112
Exports (unmanufactured)	730	1,207	974	1,065	559	823	911	1,278
Petroleum asphalt (excluding road oil):								
Sales [2]	75,715	78,876	93,991	127,869	178,788	162,438	177,564	216,105
Imports [1]	726	842	771	1,692	2,419	2,615	3,481	5,294
Exports	2,606	5,172	9,708	14,208	8,985	7,402	4,520	6,391

[1] Includes cut-backs and road oil.   [2] Excludes export sales.

Source of tables 872 and 873: Department of Interior, Bureau of Mines; Minerals Yearbook, except as noted.

No. 874.—GYPSUM—SUPPLY, SALES, IMPORTS, AND EXPORTS: 1944 TO 1951

[Quantities in thousands of short tons; values in thousands of dollars. See also *Historical Statistics*, series G 67-68, for gypsum mined and total gypsum products sold]

ITEM	1944	1945	1946	1947	1948	1949	1950	1951
Active establishments [1]	77	75	80	93	95	88	87	85
Crude gypsum: [2]								
Mined	3,761	3,812	5,629	6,208	7,255	6,608	8,193	8,666
Imported	342	508	1,457	2,157	2,859	2,593	3,219	3,448
Apparent supply	4,104	4,320	7,087	8,365	10,114	9,201	11,412	12,114
Calcined gypsum produced: [2]								
Short tons	2,363	2,485	4,170	5,011	6,243	5,767	7,341	7,455
Value	13,841	14,474	29,273	38,726	46,145	45,455	60,480	65,761
Gypsum products sold, total value [3]	55,700	60,149	97,195	128,415	176,634	153,746	205,177	237,047
Uncalcined uses:								
Short tons	1,056	1,148	1,641	1,950	2,226	1,990	2,218	2,530
Value	2,954	3,433	5,106	7,012	7,927	7,127	7,812	9,413
Industrial uses:								
Short tons	200	158	207	207	219	212	266	269
Value	2,551	2,326	3,161	3,430	3,731	3,562	4,530	5,468
Building uses, value	50,196	54,390	88,928	117,973	165,176	148,057	193,735	222,166
Gypsum and gypsum products:								
Imported for consumption, value	395	549	1,833	2,522	3,115	2,851	3,584	3,685
Exported, value	490	1,503	1,065	1,600	1,317	1,936	1,045	1,584

[1] Each mine, plant, or combination mine and plant is counted as one establishment.
[2] Excludes byproduct gypsum.
[3] Made from domestic, imported, and byproduct crude gypsum.

Source: Department of the Interior, Bureau of Mines; *Minerals Yearbook.*

No. 875.—PORTLAND CEMENT—PRODUCTION, BY STATES: 1910 TO 1951

[In thousands of barrels of 376 pounds]

STATE	1910	1920	1930	1935	1940	1945	1950	1951
Production, total	76,550	100,023	161,197	76,742	[1]130,217	[1][2]102,805	[1]236,026	[1]246,022
Alabama	[3]1,481	1,182	4,521	2,498	5,122	5,542	10,372	10,773
California	[4]6,396	7,098	10,124	7,974	14,216	15,952	26,277	29,915
Illinois	4,489	5,539	7,935	3,368	4,975	4,367	7,924	8,484
Iowa	[4]2,010	4,849	7,088	3,520	4,606	3,194	7,418	8,365
Kansas	5,656	4,341	6,012	2,337	3,433	3,001	5,616	5,515
Michigan	3,688	4,891	11,511	4,579	8,603	5,839	12,967	14,804
Missouri	4,456	6,018	7,809	3,392	4,965	3,185	9,778	10,230
New York	3,296	5,885	10,373	4,285	5,437	[5]5,617	[5]14,196	[6]15,351
Ohio	1,528	1,780	8,632	3,576	5,664	4,604	10,607	11,574
Pennsylvania	26,676	28,209	37,844	15,502	26,853	15,564	38,646	41,961
Tennessee	(7)	(7)	3,875	2,703	3,808	2,882	6,685	7,222
Texas	[8]2,287	2,562	6,752	3,787	7,375	8,037	17,150	18,132
Other States	14,627	27,659	38,393	18,925	[1]31,156	[1][2]25,022	[1]55,392	[1]60,783

[1] Includes production of Puerto Rico.
[2] Includes production of Hawaii.
[3] Includes Georgia and Tennessee.
[4] Includes Washington.
[5] Includes Kentucky and West Virginia.
[6] Includes Maine.
[7] Included in figures for Alabama for 1910; "Other States," 1920.
[8] Includes Oklahoma

Source: Department of the Interior, Bureau of Mines; *Minerals Yearbook.*

No. 876.—Cement—Production: 1910 to 1951

[Figures include Puerto Rico beginning 1940 and Hawaii beginning 1945. See also *Historical Statistics*, series G 65–66]

ITEM	1910	1920	1930	1940	1945	1949	1950	1951
Production of finished cement, total 1,000 bbl..	77,785	100,790	162,989	132,751	104,289	212,912	230,272	249,472
Portland.................do....	76,550	100,023	161,197	130,216	102,805	209,727	226,026	246,023
Masonry, natural, and puzzolan (slag-lime)............1,000 bbl..	1,235	[1] 767	1,792	2,535	1,484	3,185	4,246	3,449
Active plants:								
Portland ....number..	111	117	163	152	145	150	150	155
Masonry, natural, and puzzolan (slag-lime)............number..	23	9	11	12	9	9	9	9
Shipments, total............1,000 bbl..	[2]	97,079	160,846	132,864	107,833	209,314	231,975	244,629
Portland.................do....	[2]	96,312	159,059	130,350	106,354	206,080	227,757	241,153
Value ....$1,000..	[2]	194,439	228,780	190,078	173,337	473,177	535,321	613,170
Per barrel............dollars..	[2]	2.02	1.44	1.46	1.63	2.30	2.35	2.55
Masonry, natural, and puzzolan (slag-lime)............1,000 bbl..	[2]	767	1,787	2,514	1,479	3,234	4,218	3,475
Value ....$1,000..	[2]	1,151	2,470	3,387	2,094	8,006	10,630	9,833
Per barrel............dollars..	[2]	1.50	1.38	1.35	1.42	2.48	2.52	2.83
Stocks at mills, Dec. 31 (finished portland cement)........1,000 bbl..	[2]	8,833	25,899	23,365	16,625	14,758	13,119	17,968
Imports....................do....	307	525	985	538	[1]	110	1,410	893
Exports....................do....	2,476	2,986	756	1,668	6,475	4,562	2,418	2,933
World production.............do....	[2]	[2]	416,880	474,927	290,233	671,934	771,024	863,077

[1] Shipments.   [2] Not available.   [3] Less than 500 bbls.

Source: Department of the Interior, Bureau of Mines; *Minerals Yearbook*.

No. 877.—Open-Market Lime—Production, by Type and Use, Exports and Imports: 1930 to 1951

[Includes only small quantities of captive tonnage. See also *Historical Statistics*, series G 69–70 for production and value data]

ITEM	1930	1935	1940	1945	1949	1950	1951
Active plants....................number..	375	301	314	189	180	168	155
Quantity sold by producers......1,000 short tons	3,388	2,987	4,887	5,921	6,318	7,478	8,256
Value................................$1,000..	25,616	21,749	33,956	45,918	69,319	83,248	96,935
Per ton................................	$7.56	$7.28	$6.95	$7.76	$10.97	$11.13	$11.74
By type:							
Quicklime................1,000 short tons..	2,058	1,981	3,501	4,566	4,624	5,593	6,336
Hydrated........................do....	1,330	1,006	1,386	1,355	1,694	1,885	1,920
By use:							
Agricultural........................do....	343	283	365	374	328	333	344
Building...........................do....	1,205	657	1,010	550	1,052	1,249	1,234
Chemical and industrial..............do....	1,488	1,592	2,644	3,810	3,619	4,137	4,711
Refractory (dead-burned dolomite)......do....	352	455	868	1,187	1,319	1,759	1,966
Imports for consumption.................do....	24	12	9	21	34	34	34
Value................................$1,000..	357	236	82	179	654	634	705
Exports......................1,000 short tons..	15	4	32	24	60	50	63
Value................................$1,000..	192	64	312	269	937	826	1,158

Source: Department of the Interior, Bureau of Mines; *Minerals Yearbook*.

No. 878.—SAND AND GRAVEL—QUANTITY SOLD OR USED BY PRODUCERS AND VALUE: 1930 TO 1950

[See also *Historical Statistics*, series G 71-72]

ITEM	1930	1935	1940	1945	1948	1949	1950
Sand and gravel, total....1,000 short tons..	197,052	132,924	226,366	195,534	319,266	318,104	370,465
Building...................................do....	46,606	32,182	65,096	61,568	115,082	113,523	132,673
Paving....................................do....	84,176	68,414	143,135	93,664	169,480	175,262	204,342
Other.....................................do....	66,271	32,326	27,114	40,397	34,804	30,018	33,340
Value.................................$1,000..	115,177	61,977	110,093	126,837	246,496	245,443	294,040
Average per ton.................dollars..	.58	.50	.46	.66	.79	.75	.80
Commercial sand............1,000 short tons..	81,754	27,776	63,930	65,077	109,796	105,008	124,923
Value.................................$1,000..	48,894	25,627	40,526	52,421	102,631	101,710	130,350
Average per ton.................dollars..	.60	.06	.63	.81	.94	.94	.96
Noncommercial (government-and-contractor) sand..........1,000 short tons..	1,905	2,656	14,744	6,649	3,965	9,096	13,916
Value.................................$1,000..	836	770	4,806	2,426	4,283	3,779	5,961
Average per ton.................dollars..	.46	.29	.33	.36	.46	.42	.46
Commercial gravel............1,000 short tons..	95,126	46,531	67,336	57,061	123,707	123,197	123,574
Value.................................$1,000..	58,475	26,147	37,745	57,992	107,668	109,625	130,974
Average per ton.................dollars..	.61	.56	.56	.67	.87	.89	.91
Noncommercial (government-and-contractor) gravel........1,000 short tons..	18,287	26,630	92,308	26,737	76,808	78,571	98,981
Value.................................$1,000..	6,930	9,984	27,612	15,999	36,915	32,829	47,755
Average per ton.................dollars..	.38	.27	.30	.44	.46	.63	.46

Source: Department of the Interior, Bureau of Mines; *Minerals Yearbook*.

No. 879.—STONE—SALES, BY KIND AND BY USE: 1930 TO 1950

[See also *Historical Statistics*, series G 75-76 for total]

VARIETY AND USE	QUANTITY SOLD, THOUSANDS OF SHORT TONS [1]							VALUE (1,000 DOLLARS)		
	1930	1935	1940	1945	1948	1949	1950	1948	1949	1950
Total...................	126,906	82,159	152,723	153,405	225,536	234,027	262,113	328,965	341,442	396,582
By kind:										
Granite................	10,048	6,014	10,890	7,740	13,086	16,944	22,553	38,908	42,567	52,221
Basalt and related rocks..	14,532	9,672	15,716	14,911	20,654	21,336	22,896	29,917	30,486	34,273
Sandstone.............	4,894	3,010	6,409	4,387	7,290	6,945	9,101	18,040	19,906	23,787
Marble................	477	132	240	171	276	240	267	10,421	12,293	10,932
Limestone.............	88,741	57,493	112,658	112,574	166,742	165,746	190,919	215,451	222,513	262,756
All other..............	8,604	6,838	7,740	13,623	16,887	14,786	16,378	16,239	13,677	16,612
By use:										
Building stone........	2,322	831	836	282	981	916	1,229	24,909	20,911	34,665
Monumental...........	291	180	196	251	307	368	344	20,541	18,735	17,525
Paving blocks.........	594	76	19	1	3	2	4	23	27	51
Curbing...............	262	69	72	13	63	59	78	1,332	1,689	2,490
Flagging..............	82	24	66	21	41	45	57	585	692	878
Rubble.	1,066	279	916	390	276	339	267	574	709	615
Riprap................	4,292	4,919	5,254	4,801	5,707	7,568	6,896	7,553	9,830	7,807
Crushed stone........	87,111	54,755	100,208	85,373	139,738	141,421	165,722	166,196	173,735	205,614
Furnace flux (limestone).	17,091	12,192	22,872	27,640	34,902	30,782	35,970	34,250	32,208	37,032
Refractory stone......	1,197	866	1,741	2,327	2,557	1,828	2,158	6,531	5,764	5,949
Agricultural (limestone).	2,542	2,140	8,734	17,396	20,942	21,483	19,349	32,035	33,251	30,392
Other uses...........	10,446	6,826	12,757	14,610	20,032	19,356	20,157	34,396	34,848	40,223

[1] Quantities of stones not sold by short ton are expressed in approximate equivalents in short tons; expressed in their selling units, quantities for 1950 are as follows: Building stone (cut stone, slabs, and mill blocks), 12,894,040 cubic feet; monumental stone, 2,942,630 cubic feet; paving blocks, 847,590 (number); curbing, 960,040 cubic feet; and flagging, 712,590 cubic feet.

Source: Department of the Interior, Bureau of Mines; *Minerals Yearbook*.

No. 880.—Salt—Production, by States and by Kind, Exports,
and Imports: 1880 to 1951

[In short tons (2,000 pounds). Production figures represent sales plus that used by producers; they include Puerto Rico. Imports are imports for consumption. See also *Historical Statistics*, series G 81–82 for production]

YEAR	Production	Exports	Imports	YEAR	Production	Exports	Imports
1880	834,548	1,642	509,703	1930	8,054,440	70,478	54,021
1890	1,342,779	2,464	257,323	1935	7,926,897	112,213	51,345
1900	2,921,708	7,511	199,909	1940	10,359,960	147,044	30,402
1905	3,635,257	34,238	161,189	1945	15,394,141	190,524	4,553
1910	4,242,792	49,013	137,103	1948	16,403,293	387,601	5,621
1915	5,352,409	80,474	122,326	1949	15,572,215	359,776	6,309
1920	6,840,029	139,272	137,654	1950	16,629,809	190,377	7,869
1925	7,397,500	155,079	85,788	1951	20,207,131	439,114	4,329

STATE OR KIND	1925	1930	1935	1940	1945	1949	1950	1951
Production, total	7,397,500	8,054,440	7,926,897	10,359,960	15,394,141	15,572,215	16,629,809	20,207,131
Michigan	2,172,600	2,558,290	2,128,171	2,863,035	4,285,493	4,064,106	4,446,667	5,137,639
New York	2,053,970	2,009,280	1,927,822	2,117,671	2,862,224	2,951,750	2,806,927	3,518,715
Ohio	1,173,590	1,311,440	1,487,315	2,080,133	2,764,926	2,195,778	2,515,205	3,112,472
Kansas	812,540	789,800	608,204	684,053	855,806	832,442	846,374	900,917
Louisiana	500,350	535,250	702,990	1,132,594	1,867,689	2,030,076	2,278,811	2,737,149
California	292,480	350,370	356,222	469,354	694,609	984,807	868,496	1,275,574
Texas	(1)	(1)	268,809	402,165	1,100,791	1,641,171	1,852,138	2,401,063
Utah	88,150	85,240	57,625	71,472	122,997	78,611	116,694	131,444
West Virginia	25,870	28,670	65,968	144,312	370,260	355,515	367,942	379,299
Other States	277,950	416,100	323,771	395,171	469,346	457,959	530,555	612,859
By kind:								
Manufactured (evaporated)	2,235,170	2,358,610	2,330,042	2,782,741	3,182,570	3,284,361	3,329,288	3,654,808
In brine	2,819,690	3,718,460	3,837,613	5,311,671	8,705,831	8,843,513	9,373,254	11,890,129
Rock salt	2,342,640	1,977,370	1,759,242	2,265,548	3,505,740	3,444,341	3,927,267	4,662,194
Total value [2] (dollars)	26,162,361	25,009,480	21,837,911	26,474,619	43,914,406	53,626,238	59,911,343	69,735,000

[1] Included in "Other States."
[2] F. o. b. mine or refinery; values exclude cost of cooperage or containers.

Source: Department of the Interior, Bureau of Mines; *Minerals Yearbook*.

No. 881.—Sulfur and Pyrites—Production, Exports, and Imports: 1930 to 1951

[See also *Historical Statistics*, series G 83–86]

ITEM	1930	1935	1940	1945	1949	1950	1951
SULFUR							
Production of crude sulfur ...1,000 long tons	2,559	1,633	2,732	3,753	4,745	5,192	5,278
Value ...$1,000	46,036	29,256	43,659	60,013	85,410	96,080	113,535
Price per long ton f. o. b. mines	$18	$18	$16	$16	$18	$18–22	$21–27
Shipments of crude sulfur ...1,000 long tons	1,990	1,635	2,559	3,833	4,789	5,505	4,988
For domestic consumption ...do	1,397	1,233	1,812	2,915	3,358	4,064	3,700
For export ...do	593	402	746	919	1,431	1,441	1,288
Imports (ore and other) ...do	(1)	2	28	(1)	(1)	(1)	2
Exports of treated sulfur ...do	12	11	20	24	30	38	24
PYRITES							
Production ...1,000 long tons	348	514	627	723	888	931	1,018
Sulfur content ...percent	35.7	39.5	41.8	41.0	42.6	42.2	42.5
Value ...$1,000	1,029	1,583	1,920	2,700	3,904	4,059	4,656
Imports ...1,000 long tons	355	397	407	187	121	209	221

[1] Less than 500 long tons.

Source: Department of the Interior, Bureau of Mines; *Minerals Yearbook*.

No. 882.—IRON ORE—SUMMARY: 1910 TO 1951

[In thousands of long tons, except as indicated. Nearly all exports are to Canada. Data exclude ore containing 5 percent or more of manganese. See also *Historical Statistics*, series G 93-95]

ITEM	1910	1920	1930	1940	1945	1949	1950	1951
Production, total	57,015	67,604	58,469	73,696	88,876	54,937	98,045	116,595
By districts:								
Lake Superior	46,420	57,945	49,383	61,471	74,821	68,494	79,627	93,947
Southeastern	6,895	6,768	5,838	[1]7,444	6,380	7,602	7,507	8,597
Northeastern	2,605	2,096	2,249	3,560	3,620	3,864	4,475	5,181
Western	1,095	795	989	[1]1,221	3,088	4,442	5,861	6,181
Undistributed (byproduct ore)	[2]	[2]	[2]	[2]	517	536	575	[5]608
By types of ore:								
Hematite	51,367	63,883	55,266	68,870	81,295	76,263	[4]87,156	[4]101,531
Brown ore	2,994	1,326	720	935	943	1,546	2,615	3,015
Magnetite	2,632	2,391	2,421	3,891	5,621	6,593	[4]7,699	[34]11,390
Carbonate	22	4	1	1	1	------	------	------
Byproduct material (pyrites cinder and sinter)	[2]	[2]	[2]	[2]	517	536	575	569
Number of mines	[2]191	403	208	230	199	221	247	289
Shipments	[2]	69,281	55,201	75,198	88,137	84,687	97,764	116,230
Value	[2]	285,006	145,619	189,087	243,761	381,516	487,990	634,729
Average value per ton at mine	[2]	$4.11	$2.64	$2.51	$2.77	$4.50	$4.99	$5.46
Stocks at mines, Dec. 31	9,422	11,379	10,383	3,614	4,432	5,334	5,726	5,599
Imports	2,591	1,273	2,775	2,479	1,198	7,402	8,222	10,145
Value	7,832	4,964	8,113	6,205	4,114	36,791	43,764	59,628
Exports	749	1,145	732	1,386	2,063	2,425	2,580	4,296
Value	2,474	6,199	2,734	4,625	6,688	14,654	15,737	30,622
World production (estimated) 1,000 metric tons	133,000	116,300	178,400	212,000	162,000	230,000	247,000	293,000

[1] Texas included with Southeastern district.
[2] Not available.
[3] Includes 39,000 tons iron ore (magnetite) from Puerto Rico.
[4] Small quantity of hematite included with magnetite.

Source: Department of the Interior, Bureau of Mines; *Minerals Yearbook* and records.

No. 883.—MANGANESE (INCLUDING FERROMANGANESE AND SPIEGELEISEN)—SUMMARY: 1910 TO 1951

[Gross weight in short tons]

ITEM	1910	1920	1930	1940	1945	1949	1950	1951
Manganese ore (35 percent or more Mn):								
Mine shipments	2,529	105,750	75,079	44,296	182,337	126,135	134,451	96,348
Metallurgical ore	[1]	[1]	59,725	30,416	174,295	110,928	122,944	85,496
Battery ore	[1]	[1]	13,168	10,383	8,042	14,963	11,507	9,752
Miscellaneous	[1]	[1]	2,186	4,137	------	224	------	------
General imports	271,430	671,736	655,536	1,449,634	1,461,945	1,544,584	1,834,925	1,766,773
Consumption	[1]	[1]	[1]	[1]	1,485,859	1,360,042	1,650,429	1,892,609
World production (estimate)	2,173,000	1,801,000	3,848,000	6,288,000	4,670,000	4,800,000	5,800,000	6,500,000
Ferromanganese:								
Domestic production	[2]253,362	309,785	307,810	514,682	619,760	577,345	719,680	791,260
Imports for consumption	127,935	66,364	[2]49,321	11,613	35,521	65,014	109,948	119,774
Exports	------	[3]3,868	[4]6,932	[4]14,600	836	6,627	580	633
Consumption	[1]	[1]	[1]	[1]	641,622	617,645	774,852	853,841
Spiegeleisen:								
Domestic production	[2]	116,113	97,506	114,119	139,039	78,167	42,375	77,017
Imports for consumption	28,429	5,862	[2]15,015	17,455	3,146	1,737	8,595	------
Exports	[4]	[4]	[4]	[4]	2,393	------	363	85
Consumption	[1]	[1]	[1]	[1]	148,087	75,841	76,280	80,556

[1] Not available.
[2] Production of spiegeleisen included with that of ferromanganese.
[3] Manganese content; gross weight not reported.
[4] Exports of spiegeleisen included with those of ferromanganese.

Source: Department of the Interior, Bureau of Mines; *Minerals Yearbook*.

No. 884.—Chromite—Production, Consumption, Imports, and Exports: 1930 to 1951

[Quantities in short tons; values in thousands of dollars. See also *Historical Statistics*, series G 106-107 for figures on shipments]

ITEM	1930	1935	1940	1945	1948	1949	1950	1951
Total supply	365,901	290,727	739,594	939,860	1,545,744	1,204,285	1,304,117	1,436,076
Domestic production (shipments)	90	577	2,982	13,973	3,619	433	404	7,056
Value	2	5	29	532	(¹)	12	(¹)	554
Imports for consumption	365,811	290,150	736,612	925,887	1,542,125	1,203,852	1,303,713	1,429,020
Value	3,513	3,604	8,755	17,530	33,010	24,200	23,299	25,506
Consumption by industry	(¹)	(¹)	562,915	806,120	875,033	672,773	980,369	1,212,480
Exports	(¹)	(¹)	(¹)	12,366	2,894	2,382	2,044	2,030

¹ Figure not available or Bureau of Mines not at liberty to publish.

Source: Department of the Interior, Bureau of Mines; *Minerals Yearbook*.

No. 885.—Nickel—Production, Price, Imports and Exports: 1930 to 1951

ITEM	1930	1935	1940	1945	1949	1950	1951
Production:							
Primary_____short tons	308	160	554	1,155	790	913	736
Secondary_____do	2,900	1,950	4,152	6,483	5,680	8,795	8,602
Imports (gross weight)¹_____do	30,143	37,848	92,468	122,528	97,144	97,333	102,325
Exports (gross weight)²_____do	1,420	2,193	11,994	3,876	4,471	3,645	4,622
Price per pound³_____cents	35	35	35	31½	40	40—50½	50½—56½
World production (approx.)_____short tons	59,700	85,300	154,000	160,000	161,000	160,000	177.000

¹ Excludes "All other manufactures of nickel"; weight not recorded; also excludes nickel bars, etc., scrap, and residues.
² Excludes "Manufactures"; weight not recorded.
³ Price quoted by International Nickel Co., Inc., for electrolytic nickel.

Source: Department of the Interior, Bureau of Mines; *Minerals Yearbook*.

No. 886.—Tungsten—Production, Imports, and Consumption: 1930 to 1951

[See also *Historical Statistics*, series G 108-109]

ITEM	1930	1935	1940	1945	1949	1950	1951
Production:							
Concentrates, 60 percent WO₃_____short tons	(¹)	(¹)	5,120	5,662	3,043	4,166	6,214
Tungsten content_____1,000 lb	(¹)	(¹)	4,873	5,389	2,896	3,965	5,914
Shipments from mines:							
Concentrates, 60 percent WO₃_____short tons	702	2,395	5,319	5,534	2,765	4,820	6,275
Tungsten content_____1,000 lb	668	2,279	5,062	5,267	2,632	4,588	5,973
Reported value f. o. b. mines_____$1,000	509	1,921	6,576	7,693	4,377	8,171	22,976
Average per pound of tungsten	$0.76	$0.84	$1.30	$1.46	$1.66	$1.78	$3.85
Imports (tungsten content):							
General_____1,000 lb	(¹)	(¹)	9,666	8,639	7,357	8,342	7,534
For consumption_____do	3,996	892	5,611	4,774	6,274	16,147	6,377
Consumption (tungsten content)_____do	4,642	2,372	9,955	14,146	4,958	6,597	11,410
Industry stocks, end of year (tungsten content) _____1,000 lb	(¹)	(¹)	2,897	4,341	5,056	5,338	4,272
World production_____metric tons²	16,652	22,458	43,592	22,802	33,000	39,000	50,100

¹ Not available.
² Metric tons of concentrates containing 60 percent WO₃.

Source: Department of the Interior, Bureau of Mines; *Minerals Yearbook*.

No. 887.—MOLYBDENUM CONCENTRATES—PRODUCTION, CONSUMPTION, AND STOCKS: 1920 TO 1951

[In thousands of pounds of contained molybdenum, except as indicated]

ITEM	1920	1930	1940	1945	1949	1950	1951
Production	(1)	3,723	34,313	30,802	22,530	28,480	38,855
Shipments from mines	35	3,759	25,329	33,683	28,280	44,544	37,955
Price per pound 2 dollars	1.23	3 0.73	0.75	0.75	0.90	0.91	1.00
Exports 4	(1)	(1)	6,585	2,863	5,320	6,235	3,729
Imports for consumption 5	(6)	145	--------	204	48	3	4
Consumption	(1)	(1)	(1)	32,696	19,960	26,029	33,591
Stocks (industry), Dec. 31 7	(1)	(1)	(1)	16,883	19,159	4,090	5,068
World production (estimate) metric tons	(1)	(1)	17,200	16,200	11,500	14,600	21,000

1 Not available.
2 Per pound of molybdenum contained. Source: Engineering and Mining Journal.
3 1930 price, July to December only.
4 Includes roasted concentrates.
5 Excludes imports for conversion and reexports as follows: 460,000 pounds in 1945, none in 1949–51.
6 Content not recorded for the 16,000 pounds of molybdenum ore imported.
7 At mines and at plants making molybdenum products.

Source: Department of the Interior, Bureau of Mines; Minerals Yearbook.

No. 888.—GOLD AND SILVER—PRODUCTION, BY STATES AND OTHER AREAS: 1930 TO 1951

Includes production of Alaska, Puerto Rico, and through 1945, Philippine Islands. See also Historical Statistics, series G 118–121, for data excluding Puerto Rico and Philippine Islands]

STATE OR OTHER AREA	GOLD (1,000 FINE OUNCES)					SILVER (1,000 FINE OUNCES)				
	1930	1940	1945	1950	1951	1930	1940	1945	1950	1951
Total	2,286	6,003	929	2,289	1,895	50,748	69,586	29,063	42,309	39,907
Alaska	407	757	60	276	208	392	173	9	50	30
Arizona	149	299	78	111	110	4,910	6,130	3,411	5,089	5,042
California	450	1,444	143	410	347	1,434	2,225	950	1,000	964
Colorado	218	369	102	124	108	4,852	9,378	2,407	3,343	2,970
Idaho	21	145	19	69	56	9,710	17,477	8,228	15,993	15,956
Illinois									7	3
Michigan						11	90	20	(1)	(1)
Missouri								21	233	173
Montana	47	273	42	57	32	8,597	12,152	5,494	7,178	6,414
Nevada	140	380	91	170	122	4,179	5,102	1,156	1,634	1,033
New Mexico	32	39	13	7	4	1,160	1,576	654	365	410
New York									33	25
Oregon	14	114	1	10	9	10	192	12	12	9
Pennsylvania				2	2				11	13
South Dakota	406	587	41	572	463	105	171	41	143	141
Tennessee				(1)	(1)				26	19
Texas	(1)	(1)	--------	(1)	(1)	469	1,295	21	4	1
Utah	209	382	271	392	362	14,451	11,686	6,244	6,799	6,292
Vermont				(1)	(1)				28	43
Virginia									(1)	--------
Washington	4	84	53	89	71	30	389	288	358	367
Wyoming				(1)	(1)				3	(1)
Philippine Islands	185	1,140	13	(2)	(2)	121	1,299	17	(2)	(2)
Other	3	20	2	--------	--------	317	251	90	--------	--------

1 Less than 500 ounces.
2 Excluded after 1945.

Source: Treasury Department, Bureau of the Mint; Annual Report of the Director.

No. 889.—GOLD AND SILVER—PRODUCTION, PRICE, IMPORTS, AND EXPORTS: 1910 TO 1951

[See also *Historical Statistics*, series G 118–121]

ITEM	1910	1920	1930	1940	1945	1949	1950	1951
Mine production:								
Gold..............1,000 fine ounces..	4,585	2,383	2,139	4,870	955	1,992	2,394	1,981
Silver......................do....	57,599	56,537	47,725	70,436	29,024	34,675	42,459	39,767
Value of production:								
Gold..................1,000 dollars..	94,778	49,261	44,211	170,448	33,410	69,712	83,798	69,322
Silver......................do....	31,102	61,625	18,374	50,088	20,639	31,383	38,425	35,991
Ore (dry and siliceous) produced: [1]								
Gold ore...........1,000 short tons..				16,550	1,364	3,376	3,584	2,606
Gold-silver ore................do....	9,646	8,590	7,767	948	277	412	433	368
Silver ore.....................do....				1,201	343	477	627	492
Net industrial consumption:								
Gold.................1,000 dollars..	34,10.	50,181	15,178	13,306	108,944	108,842	97,846	69,477
Silver............1,000 fine ounces..	23,187	19,280	26,874	44,499	126,300	88,000	110,000	105,000
Imports:								
Gold.................1,000 dollars..	66,549	417,068	396,054	4,749,467	93,718	771,390	162,749	81,259
Silver......................do....	48,401	88,060	42,761	58,434	27,278	73,536	110,035	108,469
Exports:								
Gold......................do....	47,425	322,091	115,987	4,995	199,968	84,936	534,036	630,382
Silver......................do....	71,962	113,616	54,157	3,674	90,937	23,281	6,202	8,590
Price, average per fine ounce: [2]								
Gold..	$20.67	$20.67	$20.67	$35.00	$35.00	$35.00	$35.00	$35.00
Silver..	$0.542	$1.019	$0.385	$0.711	$0.711	$0.905	$0.905	$0.905
World production:								
Gold..............1,000 fine ounces..	(3)	(3)	20,800	42,300	26,100	30,800	32,500	33,500
Silver......................do....	(3)	173,300	248,700	275,400	162,000	173,800	196,600	198,600

[1] Gold and silver are also produced from base-metal ores and placers. In 1951, dry and siliceous ores accounted for 39 percent of gold produced and 32 percent of silver.
[2] Treasury buying price, except for silver prices for 1910–30 which represent New York price.
[3] Not available.

Source: Department of the Interior, Bureau of Mines; *Minerals Yearbook*.

No. 890.—GOLD AND SILVER FOR USE IN MANUFACTURES AND THE ARTS: 1880 TO 1951

YEARLY AVERAGE OR YEAR	GOLD ($1,000) [1]			SILVER (1,000 FINE OUNCES)		
	Total amount of material issued	Amount of old material returned from use	Net material issued	Total amount of material issued	Amount of old material returned from use	Net material issued
1880..............................	10,105	1,294	8,811	2,794	204	2,300
1881–1885.......................	12,568	1,863	10,706	4,155	315	3,840
1886–1890.......................	16,041	4,029	12,012	5,662	676	4,986
1891–1895.......................	16,508	5,060	11,448	7,997	951	7,046
1896–1900.......................	16,965	4,067	12,899	10,214	1,200	9,014
1901–1905.......................	28,496	6,778	21,718	19,526	3,002	16,524
1906–1910.......................	38,149	7,708	30,441	24,553	3,669	20,884
1911–1915.......................	40,588	9,967	30,621	30,444	6,928	23,516
1916–1920.......................	61,864	22,033	39,831	31,214	9,126	22,089
1921–1925.......................	59,596	29,275	30,321	36,805	8,189	28,616
1926–1930.......................	55,197	30,450	24,747	38,461	10,325	28,137
1931–1935.......................	21,288	41,389	[2] 20,101	33,631	20,353	13,278
1936–1940.......................	36,543	32,393	4,150	52,481	21,249	31,232
1941–1945.......................	100,699	25,323	75,376	149,455	41,794	107,662
1942..............................	75,742	28,448	47,295	131,419	30,021	101,399
1943..............................	96,864	10,521	86,343	162,113	44,113	118,000
1944..............................	122,977	25,679	97,298	176,289	56,189	120,100
1945..............................	139,936	30,992	108,944	184,661	58,361	126,300
1946..............................	199,687	46,000	153,687	123,647	36,647	87,000
1947..............................	98,130	49,230	48,900	126,366	27,866	98,500
1948..............................	90,129	45,143	44,986	129,186	23,897	105,289
1949..............................	148,975	40,133	108,842	110,660	22,660	88,000
1950..............................	134,588	36,742	97,846	155,257	45,257	110,000
1951..............................	105,012	35,535	69,477	151,651	46,651	105,000

[1] Value prior to 1934 calculated on basis of $20.67+ per fine ounce; in 1934 and thereafter, $35.00 per fine ounce.
[2] Amount of old material returned from use exceeds total amount of material issued.

Source: Treasury Department, Bureau of the Mint; *Annual Report of the Director*.

No. 891.—COPPER—PRODUCTION, EXPORTS, IMPORTS, AND CONSUMPTION: 1910 TO 1951

[In short tons. Production figures cover United States and Alaska. See also *Historical Statistics*, series G 112-113]

ITEM	1910	1920	1930	1935	1940	1945	1950	1951
Primary production:								
Mine production	544,119	612,275	705,074	380,491	878,086	772,894	909,343	926,330
Smelter production from domestic ores	540,080	604,530	697,195	381,294	909,084	782,726	911,352	920,774
Value ($1,000)	137,180	222,467	181,271	63,296	205,453	¹184,759	379,122	450,495
Refinery production, total	711,019	763,083	1,078,530	588,805	1,313,556	1,108,899	1,236,834	1,206,988
From domestic ores	535,947	591,212	695,612	338,321	927,239	775,738	920,748	951,549
From foreign ores, matte, and blister	175,072	171,871	382,918	250,484	386,317	332,861	319,086	255,439
Secondary production, total	94,800	312,460	467,200	448,900	532,046	1,006,516	977,239	982,982
From new (purchased) scrap	30,000	143,500	125,000	87,200	196,186	509,421	492,028	474,188
From old scrap	64,800	168,960	342,200	361,700	333,890	497,095	485,211	458,124
Imports (unmanufactured) ²	172,218	242,835	408,577	257,182	491,342	853,196	690,289	489,376
Refined	(²)	54,372	43,105	18,071	68,337	831,367	317,353	284,547
Exports of metallic copper ⁴		³311,579	376,587	295,198	427,680	132,555	192,339	166,274
Refined (ingots, bars, rods, etc.)	⁵354,158	275,613	334,626	275,006	377,108	⁷48,862	⁷144,561	⁷123,305
Withdrawn on domestic account: ⁸								
New refined copper	366,203	526,919	632,508	441,371	1,008,785	1,415,000	1,447,000	1,303,000
New and old copper	460,700	839,500	1,099,500	860,000	1,541,000	⁹1,912,000	⁹1,932,000	⁹1,781,000
Stocks, producers, refined copper, Dec. 31	61,402	329,500	307,800	175,000	91,800	120,000	26,000	35,000
World smelter production, new copper	946,000	1,057,000	1,760,000	1,681,000	2,734,000	2,436,000	2,960,000	3,142,000

¹ Excludes bonus payments of Office of Metal Reserve.
² Data are for "general imports," i. e., include copper imported for immediate consumption plus material entering country under bond. Comprises copper in ingots, plates, and bars, ores and concentrates, regulus, blister and scrap.
³ Not separately recorded.
⁴ Total exports of copper, exclusive of ore, concentrate, composition metal, and unrefined copper. Exclusive also of "other manufactures of copper," for which quantity figures are not recorded.
⁵ Includes unrefined copper.
⁶ Includes small exports of unrefined black blister and converter copper (bars, pigs, etc.)
⁷ Excludes rods.
⁸ Apparent consumption; consumers' inventories not taken into account.
⁹ New copper and old scrap only.

Source: Department of the Interior, Bureau of Mines; *Minerals Yearbook*.

No. 892.—COPPER—MINE PRODUCTION, BY STATES: 1910 TO 1951

[In short tons of recoverable copper]

STATE	1910	1920	1930	1935	1940	1945	1950	1951
Total	544,119	612,275	705,074	380,491	878,086	772,894	909,343	926,330
Alaska	2,121	35,218	16,326	7,750	55	5	6	1
Arizona	148,746	270,126	286,095	130,015	361,169	267,203	405,201	415,870
California	34,350	6,313	13,643	977	6,436	6,473	921	921
Colorado	4,180	2,022	5,287	7,327	12,152	1,445	3,141	3,212
Idaho	3,519	1,269	1,556	1,048	3,349	1,548	2,107	2,160
Michigan	111,342	77,348	84,691	32,064	45,198	30,401	25,608	24,979
Missouri		756	88	34	685	3,399	2,982	2,422
Montana	142,404	85,530	96,094	77,479	126,391	98,505	54,475	57,405
Nevada	32,180	25,289	54,602	37,123	76,454	52,505	52,509	54,474
New Mexico	2,307	27,200	32,575	2,263	60,846	56,571	66,300	73,556
Tennessee	8,419	8,364	(¹)	(¹)	²12,722	²12,365	²14,497	²16,140
Utah	63,799	58,466	90,263	64,756	231,864	226,376	278,680	271,095
Washington	43	992	603	43	9,612	5,621	5,067	4,099
Other States	710	1,390	19,282	10,620	139	126	21	12

¹ Included under "Other States."   ³ Includes Pennsylvania and Vermont.
² Includes North Carolina and Pennsylvania.

Source: Department of the Interior, Bureau of Mines; *Minerals Yearbook*.

No. 893.—Copper—Exports and Imports: 1891 to 1952

[Exports are those classed as "domestic" in foreign trade statistics but include copper smelted or refined in United States from imported ore or unrefined metal. Values include all forms of copper; quantities represent all copper except the small item, "Other manufactures." Copper content of exports of ore for years 1891-1915 and of imports for years 1894-1903 was estimated]

[Quantities in short tons; values in thousands of dollars]

YEARLY AVERAGE OR YEAR	EXPORTS [1]		IMPORTS [2]		YEAR	EXPORTS [1]		IMPORTS [2]	
	Quantity	Value	Quantity	Value		Quantity	Value	Quantity	Value
1891-1895 [3]	65,586	14,392	5,477	896	1941	158,906	47,690	720,708	141,789
1896-1900 [3]	137,684	36,745	24,634	5,866	1942	217,082	82,348	782,361	165,307
1901-1905 [3]	190,451	54,942	83,237	22,611	1943	296,016	108,719	736,464	156,514
1906-1910 [3]	280,445	92,334	130,111	38,026	1944	237,821	102,697	764,228	165,479
1911-1915 [3]	416,840	123,655	176,635	46,129	1945	132,592	55,212	898,239	194,672
1916-1920 [4]	376,877	208,909	244,948	103,805	1946	97,513	38,587	355,008	86,384
1921-1925	438,337	129,761	298,975	77,811	1947	197,114	102,489	452,822	175,829
1926-1930	491,290	149,999	407,630	108,244	1948	209,494	113,563	489,567	213,042
1931-1935	246,658	39,920	211,116	29,662	1949	171,303	75,769	568,835	224,233
1936-1940	378,054	87,680	242,530	47,608	1950	174,274	73,262	605,831	242,810
1941-1945	208,423	79,333	780,000	164,752	1951	152,476	86,077	539,303	279,498
1946-1950	169,940	80,734	494,413	186,459	1952 (prel.)	195,968	134,035	637,777	411,651

[1] Export figures include shipments under foreign aid programs such as UNRRA, Interim Aid, ECA, and MDAP (MSA); Civilian Supply shipments are included in 1948 and subsequent years.
[2] Imports for consumption; general imports prior to 1933.
[3] Fiscal years ending June 30.　[4] Average for period July 1, 1915, to Dec. 31, 1920.

Source: Department of Commerce, Bureau of the Census; annual report, *Foreign Commerce and Navigation of the U. S.*, and records.

No. 894.—Lead—Production, Imports, Exports, and Prices: 1910 to 1951

[In short tons. See also *Historical Statistics*, series G 114-115]

ITEM	1910	1920	1930	1940	1945	1949	1950	1951
Smelter production of refined primary lead	470,272	529,657	643,033	533,179	443,585	477,338	508,314	417,693
From domestic ores and base bullion [1]	375,402	476,849	573,740	433,065	356,535	404,449	418,809	342,644
From foreign ores	18,065	8,414	34,348	83,563	86,932	71,413	86,241	71,984
From foreign base bullion	76,805	44,394	34,945	16,551	118	1,476	3,264	3,065
Recovery of secondary lead	55,422	124,650	255,800	260,346	363,039	412,183	482,275	518,110
Imports: [2]								
Lead in pigs, bars, and old	3,485	30,719	209	151,568	230,313	289,889	461,817	187,989
Lead in base bullion	57,742	48,052	38,630	19,624	8	2,373	3,488	2,281
Lead in ores and matte	47,376	14,744	39,377	111,300	70,005	107,279	76,520	67,651
Exports of refined pig lead [3]	[4]	[3] 20,093	[3] 48,307	[3] 23,755	1,408	969	2,735	1,281
Estimated consumption of primary and secondary lead	[4]	[4]	[3] 768,600	[3] 782,000	1,051,602	957,674	1,237,981	1,184,793
Prices (cents per pound):								
New York average	4.4	8.2	5.52	5.18	6.50	15.36	13.30	17.49
London average	2.8	6.15	3.92	[7]	4.99	16.95	13.29	20.25
Mine production of recoverable lead	382,692	496,814	558,313	457,392	390,831	409,908	430,827	388,164
World smelter production of lead	1,210,000	1,022,000	1,843,000	[4]	1,234,000	1,709,000	1,870,000	1,871,000

[1] Excludes lead content of antimonial lead.
[2] Includes lead imported for immediate consumption plus material entering country for storage under bond.
[3] Pigs, bars and anodes.　In addition, 17,363 tons of foreign refined lead were reexported in 1920, 25,324 tons in 1940, 377 tons in 1945, 86 tons in 1949, 53 tons in 1950, and none in 1951.
[4] Not available.
[5] Represents pigs, bars, and old.
[6] Source: American Bureau of Metal Statistics.
[7] Official maximum price fixed by British Ministry of Supply at £25 per long ton.　London Metal Exchange dealings suspended for duration of war.

Source: Department of the Interior, Bureau of Mines; *Minerals Yearbook*.

No. 895.—LEAD, RECOVERABLE—MINE PRODUCTION, BY STATES AND FOR ALASKA: 1920 TO 1951

[In short tons]

STATE	1920	1925	1930	1935	1940	1945	1949	1950	1951
Total	494,514	634,430	552,313	331,103	457,332	390,631	403,905	430,527	398,164
Western States and Alaska	242,121	304,387	312,422	193,439	244,974	194,132	242,800	257,803	231,337
Alaska	570	720	2,055	670	779	11	51	149	21
Arizona	5,500	11,935	4,346	7,752	13,206	22,957	35,303	26,382	17,274
Colorado	20,315	31,453	22,130	5,673	11,476	17,044	24,583	27,007	10,306
Idaho	112,385	125,631	134,059	79,020	104,534	68,447	79,300	100,025	74,722
Montana	14,946	18,765	10,663	15,589	23,036	9,599	17,398	19,617	8,882
Nevada	16,100	12,228	11,529	12,578	7,499	6,275	10,408	9,408	7,148
New Mexico	1,429	2,206	10,376	7,280	3,822	7,052	4,629	4,180	4,868
Utah	68,595	183,235	113,495	63,510	75,688	40,817	57,072	44,753	90,035
Washington	2,749	2,614	876	103	2,555	3,802	11,417	10,334	3,980
Other	3,412	2,394	1,983	1,126	2,019	7,228	10,606	13,977	10,614
Central States	245,789	317,375	237,583	132,662	207,597	191,520	162,621	165,173	153,915
Kansas	16,482	22,775	12,910	10,862	11,627	7,370	5,773	6,657	8,947
Missouri	161,812	211,566	190,632	97,493	172,032	176,876	127,332	134,625	128,702
Oklahoma	64,086	79,946	23,032	23,405	21,240	12,064	19,858	20,734	16,575
Other	4,630	3,088	1,939	892	2,368	4,911	4,669	3,336	4,691
Eastern States	[1] 1,995	2,677	8,367	4,982	4,531	5,189	4,687	4,651	3,622
New York					1,973	862	1,317	1,484	1,500
Tennessee	1,880	448	8,367	4,982	573	54	257	113	14
Virginia		2,229			2,285	4,263	3,213	3,204	1,508

[1] Includes small quantities produced in Massachusetts, Pennsylvania, and Georgia.

No. 896.—ZINC—PRODUCTION AND PRICES: 1910 TO 1951

[See also *Historical Statistics*, series G 116-117]

ITEM	1910	1920	1930	1940	1945	1949	1950	1951
Smelter production of primary slab zinc, total...........short tons	269,184	463,377	498,945	675,275	764,561	814,782	843,467	881,633
Value.......................$1,000	29,072	75,067	47,812	85,085	[1] 131,504	202,392	240,051	321,620
Source:								
From domestic ores.......short tons	252,479	450,045	489,361	589,968	467,084	591,454	588,291	621,826
From foreign ores................do	16,705	13,332	8,684	85,287	297,477	223,328	255,176	259,807
Method:								
Electrolytic.........percent of total		11	26	28	35	40	41	38
Distilled......................do	100	89	74	72	65	60	59	62
Production of redistilled secondary slab zinc.......................short tons	12,784	21,371	[2] 34,849	48,917	49,242	55,041	66,970	46,657
Average price common zinc at—								
St. Louis.............cents per pound	5.42	7.77	4.56	6.34	8.25	12.15	13.88	17.99
London [3]......................do	5.00	7.40	3.60	(4)	5.18	14.41	14.89	21.46
Mine production of recoverable zinc short tons	327,712	587,524	595,425	665,068	614,358	593,203	623,375	681,189
Arizona	2,742	729	815	15,456	40,226	70,658	60,480	52,999
Colorado	38,545	24,395	36,259	5,060	35,773	47,703	45,776	55,714
Idaho	2,802	13,966	37,649	70,601	83,463	76,555	87,890	78,121
Kansas	13,229	61,073	74,304	57,032	48,394	29,433	27,176	28,904
Missouri	128,589	24,509	10,811	12,703	22,175	5,911	8,189	11,416
Montana	15,819	92,189	26,421	52,587	17,403	54,195	67,678	85,551
Nevada	1,354	5,349	14,584	11,833	21,457	20,443	21,606	17,443
New Jersey	68,678	78,511	97,626	91,406	81,392	50,984	55,029	62,917
New Mexico	9,044	5,007	32,765	30,313	40,295	29,346	29,263	45,419
New York		5,654	22,471	35,686	24,978	37,973	38,321	40,051
Oklahoma	6,394	219,727	136,153	162,935	69,300	41,033	46,739	53,451
Tennessee	[5] 1,780	19,217	[5] 48,147	[5] 51,723	[5] 49,899	[5] 42,954	[5] 47,722	[5] 38,613
Utah	8,184	4,079	44,495	43,788	33,630	40,670	31,678	34,317
Washington		213	352	11,560	11,693	10,740	14,807	18,189
Wisconsin	25,927	27,288	12,558	5,770	15,561	5,295	5,722	15,754
Other States [6]	4,645	5,641	15	6,615	18,719	26,310	35,299	42,305
World smelter production 1,000 short tons	893	796	1,536	1,786	1,404	2,008	2,167	2,309

[1] Excludes bonus payments of Office of Metals Reserve.
[2] Includes small quantity of secondary electrolytic zinc.
[3] Average price for foreign zinc, based on average rates of exchange recorded by Federal Reserve Board.
[4] Not available. [5] Includes Virginia. [6] Includes Alaska.

Source of tables 895 and 896: Department of the Interior, Bureau of Mines; *Minerals Yearbook*.

No. 897.—TIN—PRODUCTION, PRICE, IMPORTS, AND EXPORTS: 1930 TO 1951

ITEM	1930	1935	1940	1945	1949	1950	1951
Production:							
Domestic mines..............long tons..	15	44. 5	49	....	68. 4	94. 1	88. 0
Domestic smelters [1]............do....	....	....	1, 391	40, 475	35, 834	33, 118	31, 852
Secondary sources..............do....	23, 303	24, 900	29, 700	31, 400	22, 230	31, 680	30, 745
Imports for consumption:							
Metal...........................do....	80, 734	64, 256	124, 810	8, 493	60, 224	82, 838	27, 784
Ore (tin content)..............do....	289	178	3, 000	33, 479	38, 311	25, 980	29, 618
Exports (domestic and foreign)......do....	2, 233	[3] 2, 292	[3] 2, 684	882	154	799	1, 513
Monthly price of Straits tin at New York, average [3] cents per pound..	31. 70	50. 39	49. 82	[4] 52. 00	99. 316	95. 557	126. 308
Apparent consumption [5]............long tons..	78, 801	61, 966	123, 537	48, 086	95, 904	115, 156	58, 123
World mine production..............do....	176, 000	[1] 135, 000	239, 600	87, 000	161, 500	168, 000	169, 100

[1] Includes tin content of ores used direct to make alloys.
[3] Foreign only, domestic not separately recorded.
[3] Source: American Metal Market.
[4] Ceiling price.
[5] May vary greatly from actual consumption.

Source: Department of the Interior, Bureau of Mines; *Minerals Yearbook.*

No. 898.—BAUXITE—PRODUCTION, IMPORTS, AND EXPORTS: 1910 TO 1951

[Quantities in thousands of long tons; values in thousands of dollars. See also *Historical Statistics*, series G 127–128 for figures on shipments]

ITEM	1910	1920	1930	1940	1945	1948	1949	1950	1951
Production:									
Crude ore....................	....	....	....	510	1, 145	1, 724	1, 352	1, 585	2, 193
Dried bauxite equivalent........	....	....	....	439	981	1, 457	1, 149	1, 335	1, 849
Value........................	....	....	....	1, 754	5, 591	8, 697	6, 778	7, 693	12, 478
Shipments: [1]									
Gross weight..................	....	....	....	....	....	1, 490	1, 279	1, 452	1, 622
Dried bauxite equivalent........	....	....	....	....	....	1, 374	1, 179	1, 337	1, 532
Value........................	....	....	....	....	....	9, 963	8, 545	9, 549	12, 358
Imports:									
Quantity [3]...................	16	43	410	630	740	2, 489	2, 688	2, 516	2, 830
Value........................	66	251	1, 996	4, 299	5, 273	15, 821	16, 353	15, 730	17, 863
Exports:									
Quantity [3]...................	(3)	22	105	82	126	54	35	45	90
Value........................	(3)	1, 844	3, 777	1, 543	2, 425	1, 202	513	1, 156	2, 217
World production..............	350	887	1, 603	4, 321	3, 376	8, 130	8, 160	8, 030	10, 480

[1] Shipments from mines and processing plants to consumers. Includes crude, dried, calcined, and activated bauxite.
[3] As shipped.
[3] Not separately classified.

Source: Department of the Interior, Bureau of Mines; *Minerals Yearbook.*

No. 899.—ALUMINUM—SUMMARY: 1915 TO 1951

[Quantities in short tons. See also *Historical Statistics*, series G 125-126 for earlier data on primary aluminum]

ITEM	1915	1920	1930	1940	1945	1949	1950	1951
PRODUCTION								
Total U. S.:								
Production............short tons..	53,752	84,521	153,119	286,642	793,447	784,224	962,288	1,129,489
Value.....................$1,000..	22,082	50,864	68,138	104,624	226,161	247,315	316.046	424,524
Primary aluminum:								
Production............short tons..	45,252	69,021	114,519	206,280	495,060	603,462	718,622	836,881
Value.....................$1,000..	16,280	41,375	50,961	75,292	140,864	190,303	235,977	318,015
Quoted price per pound [1]...cents..	34.13	30.61	23.8	18.7	15.0	17.0	17.7	19.0
Secondary aluminum:								
Production............short tons..	8,500	15,500	38,600	80,362	298,387	180,762	243,666	292,608
Value [2].....................$1,000..	5,802	9,489	17,177	29,332	85,297	57,012	80,069	106,509
World production [3].......short tons..	93,000	172,000	293,000	868,000	960,000	1,441,000	1,647,000	1,971,000
APPARENT CONSUMPTION								
Total U. S. consumption..short tons..	(4)	(4)	(4)	272,823	724,061	680,552	974,692	975,244
Primary aluminum [5].........do....	49,899	83,967	70,933	227,017	696,750	635,956	898,341	898,653
Secondary aluminum, recovered from old scrap..........short tons..	(6)	(6)	(6)	45,806	27,311	44,596	76,351	76,591
IMPORTS AND EXPORTS [6]								
Imports:								
Quantity.................short tons..	4,647	19,650	12,731	18,084	339,285	125,326	255,692	161,516
Value.....................$1,000..	1,766	12,184	4,690	4,737	98,285	36,082	67,533	59,256
Exports:								13,415
Quantity.................short tons..	(4)	4,704	8,665	27,841	6,703	37,179	21,284	
Value.....................$1,000..	(4)	3,068	3,916	17,919	3,116	21,455	11,029	8,107

[1] New York, No. 1 virgin 98-99 percent, 1915-20; 99-percent-plus virgin, 1930-51. Source: American Metal Market.
[2] Based upon average price of primary aluminum as reported to Bureau of Mines, or as quoted by the *Engineering and Mining Journal* and the American Metal Market.
[3] Estimated. Source, 1915-30: Imperial Institute.
[4] Not available.
[5] Data not available on fluctuations in consumers' stocks, 1915-40, and in producers' stocks, 1915 and 1920.
[6] Includes aluminum and aluminum alloy ingots, scrap, plates, sheets, bars, etc.

Source: Department of the Interior, Bureau of Mines; *Minerals Yearbook*.

No. 900.—MAGNESIUM—PRODUCTION, EXPORTS, IMPORTS AND APPARENT CONSUMPTION: 1920 TO 1951

[In short tons, except as noted]

ITEM	1920	1930	1940	1945	1949	1950	1951
Production, ingot equivalent.........................	(1)	587	6,261	32,792	11,598	15,726	40,881
Sales...	62	280	6,411	43,496	12,977	20,370	40,052
Price per pound (quoted).................cents..	160.0	48.0	27.0	20.5	20.5	21.6	24.3
Exports:							
Metal in primary form [2]......................	(1)	(1)	834	496	432	586	575
Powder, ribbons, etc...........................	(1)	(1)	(1)	860	276	322	186
Imports, metallic and scrap.....................	15	3	....	54	2,560	843	3,671
Apparent consumption [3].........................	(1)	280	5,577	43,000	12,545	19,784	39,571
World production................................	(1)	(1)	42,000	68,000	39,000	44,000	88,000

[1] Not available.
[2] Primary metal only. Alloy exports in addition: 25 tons in 1940, 22 tons in 1945, none in 1949-51.
[3] Not considering fluctuations in consumers' stocks and metal derived from scrap.

Source: Department of the Interior, Bureau of Mines; *Minerals Yearbook*.

29. Construction and Housing

Construction.—Monthly estimates of the value of work put in place are probably the most widely used of the current Federal statistics on construction. These estimates are prepared jointly by the Department of Commerce and the Bureau of Labor Statistics.

Estimates of privately financed nonresidential construction are primarily the responsibility of the Department of Commerce. Construction estimates for buildings such as stores, warehouses, and factories are based on F. W. Dodge Corporation reports of construction contracts awarded, supplemented by building permit data and information from secondary sources for States which the Dodge Corp. does not cover. Public utility construction estimates are derived from data reported by the Interstate Commerce Commission and other Federal regulatory agencies, and by private associations such as the American Gas Association and the American Transit Association.

Estimates of publicly financed construction of all types and housing construction activity are primarily the responsibilities of the Bureau of Labor Statistics. A considerable number of Federal agencies administer construction programs or award contracts for construction; some of them engage in construction themselves. In this field, construction activity data are derived by the Bureau of Labor Statistics from the reports of the respective Federal agencies; data on State and local governmental construction activity are derived from F. W. Dodge Corporation and Engineering News Record reports. Estimates of residential construction activity, including number of housing units started by type of structure and source of funds, and average construction costs, are based primarily upon reports of building permits granted which are received from nearly 6,000 permit-granting authorities. Field surveys on a sample basis are used to obtain data on housing activity in nonpermit areas. Statistics on housing starts in certain metropolitan areas are available from the Bureau of Labor Statistics for 1946 through the first quarter of 1951. The current program of the Bureau of Labor Statistics provides monthly estimates of the number of housing starts in the nation as a whole, but the series on the local area data have been discontinued.

The Bureau of the Census has taken a Census of Construction for 1929, 1935, and 1939. The last census covered all persons or establishments whose principal business in 1939 was utilizing construction materials and labor in construction work for others, or for themselves for speculative and investment purposes on projects located within the limits of continental United States. Because the census excluded force account work, its coverage was substantially less than current estimates of value of work put in place.

Housing.—The first Census of Housing was taken in 1940 as part of the Sixteenth Decennial Census, although some housing data were collected by the Bureau of the Census in earlier years in conjunction with Censuses of Population and Agriculture. Housing data, in less detail but roughly comparable to those obtained in the 1940 Census, were collected in sample surveys by the Bureau of the Census in October 1944, November 1945, and April 1947 as part of the Current Population Surveys; also, sample data on selected characteristics were collected in May 1948. The 1950 Census

Note.—This section presents data for the most recent year or period available on May 20, 1953, when the material was organized and sent to the printer.

of Housing was the second Census of Housing; this census was authorized by the Housing Act of 1949, which provided also that a Census of Housing be taken decennially thereafter.

Urban and rural, farm and nonfarm residence.—A new definition was adopted for use in the 1950 Census in response to requests from many users of Census data for a more realistic classification by urban and rural residence. For this definition and additional explanation, see page 2. In the 1950 Census, the enumerators in rural areas were specifically instructed to base the farm-nonfarm classification of a dwelling unit on the respondent's answer to the question, "Is this house on a farm?" Farm residence is therefore determined without regard to the occupation of the members of the household. The classification depends upon the respondent's conception of what is meant by the word "farm," and consequently there is considerable variability of response among families living in areas where farm operation is part-time or incidental to other activities.

In rural areas, dwelling units are classified into rural-farm units which comprise all dwelling units on farms, and rural-nonfarm units which are the remaining rural units. In the 1950 Census of Housing, as in 1940 and earlier, farm housing was defined to include all housing on farms. However, in the 1940 and previous censuses, there was no specific exclusion of dwelling units for which cash rent was paid for the house and yard only, nor of institutions, summer camps, and tourist courts; moreover, the enumerators were not specifically instructed to report farm-nonfarm residence according to the respondent's reply to the question concerning location on a farm.

Dwelling unit.—In general, a dwelling unit is a group of rooms or a single room occupied, or intended for occupancy, as separate living quarters by a family or other group of persons living together or by a person living alone. Living quarters of the following types are not included in the dwelling-unit inventory: Rooming houses with five lodgers or more, transient accommodations (tourist courts, hotels, etc., predominantly for transients), and barracks for workers (railroad, construction, etc.).

The count of dwelling units in the 1950 Census may be considered comparable with the count in the 1940 Census. The enumeration of vacant units in the 1950 Census of Housing is not entirely comparable with the procedure used in the 1940 Census. Counts of total vacant units in 1950 are considered more inclusive than in 1940. In 1940, vacant units were enumerated only if they were habitable; vacant units which were uninhabitable and beyond repair were omitted. In 1950, all vacant units, whether or not dilapidated, were included if they were intended for occupancy as living quarters.

Residential financing.—Statistics on residential financing were collected on a sample basis as part of the 1950 Census of Housing. The survey covered nonfarm residential mortgaged properties, both owner and rental. The data are expressed in terms of mortgaged properties, number of mortgages, and outstanding mortgage debt. Construction mortgages were excluded.

Data on home mortgages and foreclosures, based largely on reports from major holders, are provided by the Home Loan Bank Board. The Federal Housing Administration compiles, from its records, data on its real estate financial operations, such as volume of mortgages insured, type of lending institution, etc. The Veterans' Administration also compiles, from its records, data on amounts and types of loans. For explanation of the relationship between the data obtained in the 1950 Census of Housing and those compiled from other sources, see Department of Commerce, Bureau of the Census, 1950 Census of Housing, Volume IV, *Residential Financing.*

Historical statistics.—See preface and historical appendix. Tabular headnotes (as "See also *Historical Statistics,* series H 1-26") provide cross-references, where applicable, to *Historical Statistics of the United States, 1789-1945.*

FIG. **XLII.**—NEW CONSTRUCTION ACTIVITY: 1930 TO 1952

[See table 901]

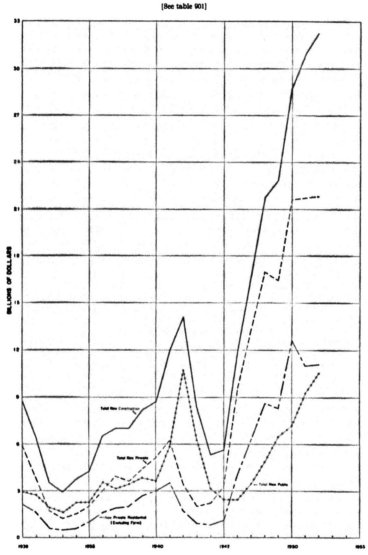

Source: Department of Commerce, Bureau of the Census. Data are from National Production Authority.

No. 901.—CONSTRUCTION IN THE UNITED STATES—ESTIMATED EXPENDITURES FOR PRIVATE AND PUBLIC CONSTRUCTION: 1915 TO 1952

[In millions of dollars. Represents value of work put-in-place during year; consequently differs from building permit and construction contract data which measure value of work started. In addition, coverage generally broader than permit and contract data. Includes value and cost of installation of equipment which is integral part of structure, but not that of machinery, shipbuilding, or land costs. See also Historical Statistics, series H 1-26]

TYPE OF CONSTRUCTION	1915	1920	1925	1930	1935	1940	1941	1942	1943
Total	4,800	9,500	14,752	12,391	7,136	12,069	16,136	16,186	12,890
New construction, total	3,202	6,749	11,439	8,741	4,292	8,062	11,907	14,028	8,691
Adjusted values, 1939 prices	5,600	8,069	10,874	8,661	4,549	8,928	10,480	10,608	4,191
Adjusted values, 1947-49 prices	11,630	10,876	22,569	17,558	9,188	16,873	21,881	22,814	15,811
Private, total	2,543	5,397	9,301	5,883	1,990	6,064	6,305	5,413	1,079
Residential (excl. farm)	1,220	2,015	5,615	2,075	1,010	2,985	3,129	1,714	635
Nonresidential building [1]	478	1,964	2,060	2,008	472	1,025	1,482	685	232
Industrial	197	1,099	513	532	188	442	901	348	144
Warehouses, office and loft bldgs	(²)	258	357	596	78	91	153	62	14
Stores, restaurants and garages	(²)	367	583	297	136	257	286	98	19
Other nonresidential bldgs	(²)	240	607	578	103	234	272	134	44
Farm construction	229	866	811	193	136	340	316	360	264
Operators' dwellings	109	385	141	107	61	145	182	138	131
Service buildings	120	200	170	95	65	96	192	138	163
Public utility	349	771	1,302	1,827	363	771	872	736	470
Railroad	241	184	368	521	116	167	187	197	211
Telephone and telegraph	43	124	210	333	52	122	179	155	61
Other public utility	265	462	699	672	195	482	508	434	298
All other private	67	81	113	85	28	32	32	19	7
Public, total [3]	719	1,362	2,138	2,858	2,223	2,928	4,751	10,660	6,322
Residential					9	300	630	546	739
Nonresidential building	217	263	573	666	226	615	1,646	3,965	2,010
Industrial	(¹)	(¹)	(¹)	(¹)	2	164	1,290	3,477	1,570
Educational	(²)	190	400	364	148	186	188	128	63
Hospital and institutional	(²)	33	61	118	38	54	42	35	44
Other nonresidential	(²)	60	112	178	138	241	186	83	33
Military and naval	17	161	8	29	37	325	1,520	5,016	2,800
Highway	302	666	1,082	1,316	845	1,302	1,086	724	446
Sewer and water	106	152	272	343	175	228	262	169	107
Misc. public service enterprises	40	39	120	167	71	131	141	88	40
Conservation and development	36	55	73	137	700	526	500	257	285
All other public	1	5	4	16	68	120	96	90	134
Maintenance and repair	1,626	2,811	3,343	3,660	2,964	3,378	4,169	4,100	4,190

TYPE OF CONSTRUCTION	1944	1945	1946	1947	1948	1949	1950	1951	1952
Total	8,636	10,524	17,562	22,945	28,793	31,005	37,527	40,252	(⁴)
New construction, total	5,299	5,633	12,000	16,680	21,678	22,750	26,740	30,803	32,290
Adjusted values, 1939 prices	3,918	4,061	7,430						
Adjusted values, 1947-49 prices	8,175	8,439	15,244	17,795	20,759	22,750	26,650	30,650	30,780
Private, total	2,186	3,225	9,638	13,256	16,853	16,364	21,610	21,684	21,785
Residential (excl. farm)	815	1,100	4,015	6,310	8,580	8,257	12,600	10,973	11,101
Nonresidential building	351	1,020	3,341	3,142	3,621	3,226	3,777	5,152	4,950
Industrial	208	642	1,689	1,702	1,397	972	1,062	2,117	2,298
Warehouses, office and loft bldgs	17	86	331	227	328	321	402	544	479
Stores, restaurants and garages	39	147	801	679	901	708	886	627	616
Other nonresidential bldg	87	178	530	564	971	1,220	1,427	1,864	1,567
Farm construction	263	267	856	1,397	1,544	1,488	1,701	1,800	1,700
Operators' dwellings	108	100	409	683	738	695	837	850	800
Service buildings	175	167	447	714	806	798	954	950	900
Public utility	725	827	1,374	2,338	3,043	3,333	3,320	2,995	2,950
Railroad	247	264	288	318	379	382	315	399	405
Telephone and telegraph	52	117	308	510	713	833	440	652	480
Other public utility	395	446	811	1,510	1,951	2,425	2,875	2,809	2,685
All other private	12	21	89	69	65	75	113	64	84
Public, total [3]	3,073	2,398	2,362	3,428	4,825	6,405	7,130	9,209	10,544
Residential	211	80	374	300	138	359	345	398	967
Nonresidential building	1,361	987	354	599	1,301	2,085	2,402	3,471	4,061
Industrial	1,290	755	118	96	199	177	234	925	1,609
Educational	41	50	101	257	615	994	1,149	1,331	1,615
Hospital and institutional	58	55	85	85	223	477	476	495	549
Other nonresidential	22	38	49	132	264	430	500	484	240
Military and naval	537	680	188	204	145	127	177	387	1,940
Highway	383	398	895	1,432	1,774	2,181	2,341	2,400	1,760
Sewer and water	79	97	104	385	625	679	671	709	690
Misc. public service enterprises	49	69	99	164	135	202	159	212	190
Conservation and development	163	150	240	390	551	683	583	840	680
All other public	14	11	18	70	57	95	65	77	84
Maintenance and repair	4,476	4,391	3,962	3,565	5,114	6,153	6,352	6,535	(⁴)

[1] Public industrial and commercial building not separable from private construction, 1915-25; amount believed negligible. [2] Not available separately. [3] Includes work-relief construction, 1933-1943. [4] Not available.

Source: Department of Commerce, National Production Authority. Current estimates are published monthly in *Construction and Building Materials Industry Report* and in *Survey of Current Business*.

No. 902.—BUILDING CONSTRUCTION IN ALL URBAN AREAS—VALUE, BY CLASS OF
CONSTRUCTION AND BY SOURCE OF FUNDS: 1951 AND 1952

[In thousands of dollars. Compiled from estimates of construction costs made by prospective builders when
applying for permits to build and value of contracts awarded by Federal Government. Covers entire urban
area of United States which includes all incorporated places of 2,500 or more in 1940 and, by special rule, a small
number of unincorporated civil divisions]

CLASS OF CONSTRUCTION	TOTAL		NON-FEDERAL		FEDERAL [1]	
	1951	1952	1951	1952	1951	1952
All building construction	8,918,168	8,926,672	7,902,588	8,132,109	1,015,580	794,563
New buildings	7,821,156	7,796,138	6,873,854	7,046,918	947,302	749,220
Residential buildings [1]	5,005,487	5,189,102	4,418,012	4,668,727	587,478	490,375
1-family dwellings	3,846,616	4,067,189	3,817,697	4,060,435	28,919	16,754
2-family dwellings [2]	171,941	213,790	171,343	213,790	498	
Multifamily dwellings [3]	949,156	826,411	391,097	382,780	558,058	443,631
Nonhousekeeping buildings	37,875	51,713	37,875	51,713		
Nonresidential buildings	2,815,699	2,657,037	2,455,642	2,348,191	359,827	288,845
Amusement buildings	32,564	33,899	32,564	33,826		74
Churches	161,328	179,906	161,328	179,906		
Factories and workshops	513,007	351,520	470,624	338,620	42,383	12,900
Public garages	44,114	37,861	44,114	37,861		
Private garages	113,801	123,504	113,801	123,504		
Service stations	34,953	46,256	34,953	46,256		
Institutions	441,963	337,661	186,790	198,554	255,173	139,107
Office buildings	197,406	166,029	197,406	166,029		
Public buildings	109,306	132,537	67,469	61,914	41,740	90,623
Public works and utilities	115,708	135,525	109,530	129,846	5,875	5,679
Schools and libraries	523,217	583,574	508,563	543,112	14,653	40,462
Sheds, stables and barns	11,324	10,726	11,324	10,726		
Stores and warehouses	430,875	400,302	430,875	400,302		
All other	66,101	75,738	66,101	75,738		
Additions, alterations and repairs	[1] 1,097,011	1,130,534	1,028,734	1,085,251	68,277	45,283

[1] Housing financed solely by State and local governments is included under "Federal" to segregate public from
private housing.
[2] Includes 1- and 2-family dwellings with stores.   [3] Includes multifamily dwellings with stores.

Source: Department of Labor, Bureau of Labor Statistics; annual and current data are published in the monthly
pamphlet, Construction, in monthly releases, and in Monthly Labor Review.

No. 903.—NEW PERMANENT DWELLING UNITS STARTED IN NONFARM AREAS,
BY TYPE: 1920 TO 1952

[Figures are estimates covering construction of all new permanent family dwelling units in nonfarm area of United
States, based upon building-permit reports, and from 1946, on building-permit information, supplemented by
data from field surveys in non-permit-issuing places. This area consists of all urban and rural nonfarm places.
Urban designation is applied to all incorporated places with a population of 2,500 or more in 1940, and, by special
rule, to a small number of unincorporated civil divisions. Rural nonfarm construction includes all construction
for nonagricultural use in unincorporated areas and incorporated places of less than 2,500 population. See also
Historical Statistics, series H 40-45; data for 1941-1945 in historical volume include temporary units]

YEAR	Total nonfarm	NUMBER OF DWELLING UNITS STARTED							ESTIMATED CONSTRUCTION COST (MILLIONS OF DOLLARS)[4]		
		Area [1]		Type of dwelling			Ownership		Total	Privately financed	Publicly financed
		Urban	Rural nonfarm	1-family	2-family [2]	Multi-family [3]	Private	Public			
1920	247,000	196,000	51,000	202,000	24,000	21,000	247,000		1,068	1,068	
1925	937,000	752,000	185,000	572,000	157,000	208,000	937,000		4,475	4,475	
1930	330,000	236,000	94,000	227,000	29,000	74,000	330,000		1,494	1,494	
1935	221,000	117,000	104,000	183,000	8,000	30,000	215,705	5,295	757	733	25
1940	603,000	397,000	206,000	486,000	37,000	80,000	530,000	73,000	2,299	2,072	227
1944	141,800	96,200	45,600	117,700	10,600	13,500	138,692	3,108	496	453	13
1945	209,300	133,900	75,400	184,600	8,800	15,900	208,159	1,241	966	959	6
1946	670,500	403,700	266,800	590,000	24,300	56,200	662,473	8,027	3,770	3,714	56
1947	849,000	479,800	369,200	740,200	33,900	74,900	845,560	3,440	5,643	5,617	25
1948	931,600	524,900	406,700	766,600	46,900	118,100	913,500	18,100	7,203	7,029	174
1949	1,025,100	588,800	436,300	794,300	36,500	194,300	988,800	36,300	7,703	7,374	329
1950	1,396,000	827,800	568,200	1,154,100	44,800	197,100	1,352,200	43,800	11,789	11,418	370
1951	1,091,300	595,300	496,000	900,100	40,400	150,800	1,020,100	71,200	9,801	9,186	615
1952	1,127,000	609,600	517,400	942,500	45,900	138,600	1,068,500	58,500	10,209	9,706	503

[1] Urban and rural nonfarm classification for 1920 and 1925 are based on 1930 Census; for 1930-52, on 1940 Census.
[2] Includes 1- and 2-family dwellings with stores.   [3] Includes multifamily dwellings with stores.
[4] Private construction costs based on permit valuation, adjusted for understatement of costs shown on permit
applications. Public construction costs based on contract values or estimated construction costs for individual
projects.

Source: 1920 and 1925, National Bureau of Economic Research; later years, Department of Labor, Bureau of
Labor Statistics. Published in monthly releases and in the monthly pamphlet, Construction.

No. 904.—FEDERAL CONTRACT AWARDS FOR NEW CONSTRUCTION (VALUE), BY TYPE OF PROJECT: 1935 TO 1952

[In thousands of dollars. Includes force-account construction started, which is work done directly by Federal agency (not through contractor), using separate work force to perform nonmaintenance work on agency's own property. For Federal-aid programs, includes funds to be contributed by owners as well as Federal Government. Major additions and alterations considered new construction. Secret projects sometimes excluded]

TYPE OF PROJECT	1935	1940	1945	1948	1949	1950	1951	1952 [1]
Total new construction	1,478,073	2,316,467	1,092,181	1,906,666	2,174,399	2,995,214	4,291,999	4,628,996
Airfields [2]	(2)	137,112	41,219	55,577	49,317	55,183	278,630	110,144
Building	442,782	1,537,910	806,917	543,118	880,101	1,369,617	2,176,280	2,380,784
Residential	7,833	244,671	60,535	47,198	46,980	15,445	5,966	11,031
Nonresidential	434,949	1,293,239	746,382	496,920	833,201	1,354,172	2,170,314	2,339,753
Conservation and development	438,725	197,589	72,150	404,571	455,457	321,456	306,841	280,669
Reclamation	158,027	69,028	30,765	147,732	142,703	81,766	96,928	92,812
River, harbor, and flood control	280,698	128,561	41,385	347,139	312,754	239,690	209,913	187,857
Highways	361,037	364,048	100,969	757,460	690,469	536,015	550,946	997,767
All other [4]	215,529	78,806	70,926	45,440	98,850	219,941	496,242	691,344

[1] Preliminary.
[2] Excludes hangars and other buildings, which are included under nonresidential building.
[3] Included in "All other."
[4] Covers electrification projects, water-supply and sewage-disposal systems, railroad construction, etc.

Source: Department of Labor, Bureau of Labor Statistics; Handbook of Labor Statistics, 1950 edition. Current data published in Monthly Labor Review.

No. 905.—FEDERAL EXPENDITURES FOR PUBLIC WORKS: 1952 AND 1953

[In millions of dollars. For years ending June 30. Includes direct Federal works and grants and loans to State and local governments for public works]

FUNCTION AND TYPE OF FACILITY	1952 actual	1953 estimate	FUNCTION AND TYPE OF FACILITY	1952 actual	1953 estimate
Civil public works, total	3,116	3,419	Natural resources	2,082	2,187
Veterans' services and benefits	128	107	Water resources and related development: irrigation, flood control, navigation, and power	980	989
Hospitals and other facilities	123	103	Roads, buildings, and utilities on Indian lands	11	17
Memorials and cemeteries	5	4	Forest roads and structures	12	14
International security and foreign relations: Radio facilities and buildings	16	28	Mineral and other research facilities	3	4
			Fish and wildlife facilities	1	2
Social security, welfare and health	80	84	Parkways, roads, buildings, and utilities in national parks	14	16
Grants for public hospital construction	61	59	Atomic energy facilities	1,071	1,145
Other hospitals and facilities	18	20			
Construction of Federal prisons	1	3	Transportation and communication	806	765
Defense community facilities for health		2	Water navigation aids and facilities	45	72
			Federal-aid highways	614	602
Housing and community development			Forest and other highways	21	25
Loans for low-rent housing (net)	176	149	Alaska Railroad and roads	27	32
Public works in Alaska and Virgin Islands	150	36	Federal-aid airports	23	22
	6	14	Other airways and airports	23	19
Defense housing and community facilities	7	93	General government: Government buildings	27	37
Other community facilities	6	4			
Education and general research	35	141	Military public works and defense construction, total	1,831	1,730
Research facilities	1	3			
Grants for school construction	35	130	Army, Navy, and Air Force construction	1,751	1,625
Agriculture and agricultural research			Stockpile storage facilities	23	30
Grain storage facilities	1	6	Synthetic rubber and other defense-related facilities	57	75
Water facilities and other	1	3			

Source: Bureau of the Budget; Budget of the U.S. Government, 1953, Special Analysis F.

No. 906.—CONSTRUCTION CONTRACTS AWARDED IN 37 STATES—VALUE OF CONSTRUCTION AND FLOOR SPACE OF BUILDINGS, BY CLASS OF CONSTRUCTION: 1925 TO 1952

[Public works and public utilities cover some projects not measurable in terms of floor space, such as highways, pipe lines, subways, etc. Statistics for the 37 States were not compiled for years prior to 1925, but available figures covering a varying number of States for earlier years have been published in the 1932 and previous issues of the *Statistical Abstract*. Figures for individual States and districts in table 907 represent value of construction contracts awarded in States and districts where work was actually done. See also *Historical Statistics*, series H 51-57]

[Values in millions of dollars; floor space in thousands of square feet]

YEAR	Total	Residential	Commercial[1]	Manufacturing buildings[2]	Public works	Public utilities[1][2]	Educational	Hospital and institutional	Public buildings	Religious	Social and recreational	Miscellaneous nonresidential
VALUE OF CONSTRUCTION												
1925	6,006.4	2,747.7	872.4	326.6	653.9	403.0	418.7	111.1	54.5	153.1	253.0	12.4
1929	5,750.8	1,915.7	929.2	545.9	940.1	469.6	369.6	152.2	120.8	106.1	146.6	54.9
1930	4,523.1	1,101.3	616.3	256.6	969.6	629.8	366.2	163.1	139.8	92.8	116.6	70.9
1933	1,255.7	249.3	99.4	127.5	504.5	84.5	38.9	37.3	50.9	17.7	27.2	18.7
1934[4]	1,543.1	248.6	150.6	116.1	631.6	111.5	112.3	37.3	55.7	18.3	46.2	14.7
1935	1,844.5	478.8	164.5	108.9	589.1	95.7	168.3	47.1	97.8	23.7	54.9	16.0
1936	2,675.3	801.6	249.1	196.0	721.8	192.1	219.0	74.1	102.2	28.3	74.9	14.2
1937	2,913.1	905.3	297.0	313.7	588.7	262.9	223.2	81.8	104.9	36.9	83.8	14.8
1938	3,196.9	985.8	215.8	121.1	850.2	288.8	334.1	115.6	114.1	35.8	108.0	27.7
1939	3,550.5	1,334.3	246.9	174.8	961.7	289.0	201.4	82.9	110.0	38.4	82.2	28.9
1940	4,004.0	1,596.9	318.3	442.4	831.3	281.1	147.2	94.1	80.2	45.7	62.6	104.2
1941	6,007.5	1,953.8	471.2	1,181.5	1,109.3	628.7	140.9	88.5	89.4	52.5	78.1	213.6
1942	8,255.1	1,817.7	302.2	2,227.5	1,302.5	1,238.1	147.9	184.9	101.6	23.5	101.3	807.7
1943	3,274.0	867.8	120.7	766.2	470.6	511.4	62.4	110.7	24.7	7.1	58.2	274.2
1944	1,994.0	348.4	80.8	472.7	429.6	316.6	69.2	59.2	11.9	11.6	32.7	161.3
1945	3,299.3	563.5	346.4	1,027.0	482.6	402.8	100.2	112.6	15.9	34.8	60.3	153.2
1946	7,489.7	3,142.1	773.2	1,317.3	1,194.7	436.6	221.4	130.9	25.1	67.6	92.5	88.3
1947	7,759.9	3,153.8	785.5	941.4	1,344.0	546.4	391.9	192.0	73.1	117.5	122.1	92.2
1948	9,429.6	3,608.0	975.0	839.8	1,627.1	528.0	724.6	404.9	83.5	245.2	232.4	161.0
1949	10,359.2	4,239.4	885.0	558.6	1,778.6	697.4	824.4	554.8	118.9	275.5	222.1	204.7
1950	14,501.1	6,741.0	1,208.5	1,142.3	1,930.0	648.4	1,179.8	655.2	124.3	336.3	261.3	273.9
1951[4]	15,751.1	6,205.4	915.3	2,883.3	1,824.0	899.2	1,334.6	580.8	158.2	299.3	136.4	514.6
1952[4]	16,774.9	6,667.5	979.2	2,558.1	2,267.6	1,144.8	1,471.6	443.7	233.2	317.5	153.4	538.3
FLOOR SPACE OF BUILDINGS												
1925	936,226	559,499	160,066	66,901	3,040	11,358	60,543	14,037	8,294	18,870	32,261	1,357
1929	791,099	387,670	161,264	105,524	450	5,353	58,639	19,496	12,626	12,818	21,457	5,802
1930	510,382	230,040	96,586	48,019	826	7,611	56,955	19,121	17,023	10,864	16,089	7,248
1933	147,063	72,783	22,551	18,985	170	1,491	5,598		9,474	2,633	5,606	2,239
1934	152,394	64,255	28,261	17,566	292	1,804	16,775	4,222	9,425	2,650	6,532	612
1935	251,558	135,416	35,391	20,638	915	1,077	26,046	6,176	13,522	3,534	7,909	934
1936	409,676	222,514	57,178	40,291	1,035	3,360	41,985	10,369	14,282	4,312	12,852	1,495
1937	446,084	235,515	62,283	60,816	1,301	5,197	36,489	11,141	12,464	5,730	13,544	1,334
1938	429,028	240,568	41,789	25,246	1,038	1,679	57,022	17,235	15,564	5,303	17,591	5,893
1939	513,380	332,656	48,798	44,268	603	1,319	34,418	11,593	15,121	6,213	12,371	6,020
1940	690,459	420,531	66,588	94,772	330	1,536	24,761	14,401	11,869	7,108	11,909	36,653
1941	956,719	502,676	105,851	187,923	11,647	2,104	24,499	15,394	14,453	8,567	14,761	68,844
1942	1,314,220	449,454	74,079	446,055	13,400	3,837	30,586	34,083	19,806	3,477	23,326	216,117
1943	448,244	200,547	22,171	105,822	1,851	1,090	11,969	19,947	4,754	1,001	12,862	66,130
1944	234,549	73,955	12,490	84,356	1,290	3,748	9,797	7,637	1,999	1,420	5,896	32,769
1945	412,423	111,244	63,197	158,207	1,348	13,701	12,453	11,331	1,858	4,569	8,097	26,423
1946	959,610	516,256	118,563	235,238	919	10,537	25,883	15,245	2,211	8,404	11,292	15,060
1947	831,965	478,713	100,043	142,990	648	3,943	41,042	19,915	6,320	12,282	14,235	11,838
1948	850,651	464,256	100,602	109,693	243	1,046	72,345	35,487	6,184	21,162	21,972	17,664
1949	869,366	520,477	86,446	61,143	14	5,216	79,046	42,076	7,726	24,598	20,992	21,638
1950	1,313,879	828,140	122,430	114,800	(3)	2,407	110,554	44,526	9,456	29,371	24,219	27,922
1951	1,158,347	684,512	77,214	148,231	(6)	3,719	109,490	37,881	10,800	25,133	11,255	50,115
1952	1,166,947	723,793	82,072	114,823	(6)	2,235	106,717	26,177	14,698	22,295	11,723	62,421

[1] Data for airports now included with "Public utilities"; prior to 1930, included with "Commercial."
[2] Data for pipe lines now included with "Public utilities"; prior to 1929, included with "Manufacturing buildings."
[3] Excludes data for 23 Civil Works Program projects, valued at $29,551,900, not available by class of construction.
[4] Includes data for Atomic Energy Commission projects ($980,000,000 in 1951 and $923,000,000 in 1952) for which floor space data are excluded because of security restrictions.
[5] Not shown separately; negligible amount with respect to total. [6] Data no longer reported.

Source: The F. W. Dodge Corporation, New York, N. Y.; Statistical and Research Division, historical record. Figures published currently in *Statistical Research Service*.

No. 907.—CONSTRUCTION CONTRACTS AWARDED IN 37 STATES—VALUE, BY DISTRICTS AND STATES: 1945 TO 1952

[Value in thousands of dollars. See headnote, table 906]

DISTRICT AND STATE	1945	1946	1947	1948	1949	1950	1951	1952
Total (37 states)	2,296,366	7,490,722	7,750,565	9,429,618	10,359,250	14,591,055	15,761,131	16,774,936
New England	164,637	863,411	528,097	665,599	642,230	969,993	1,015,919	1,616,130
Connecticut	55,313	172,129	167,034	183,495	192,274	290,850	303,698	327,848
Maine	6,816	38,347	24,729	25,974	20,705	30,599	65,871	64,239
Massachusetts	82,995	292,511	264,290	304,173	330,944	465,577	530,110	490,064
New Hampshire	4,704	17,367	25,131	27,845	25,492	33,879	30,964	34,125
Rhode Island	12,121	29,741	29,866	45,963	46,379	90,192	77,721	81,573
Vermont	2,778	13,316	17,075	17,998	13,436	20,896	18,066	16,591
Metrop. N. Y. and No. N. J.	247,454	897,442	945,550	1,111,098	1,440,153	1,667,363	1,065,277	1,919,997
Northern New Jersey	101,818	307,755	299,750	346,460	332,476	607,868	533,746	536,530
Metropolitan New York[1]	145,636	589,687	645,800	765,148	1,107,677	1,299,460	1,131,631	1,382,217
Upstate New York[2]	79,290	369,767	363,333	363,298	439,957	597,194	521,459	579,140
Middle Atlantic	488,360	965,407	963,233	1,227,366	1,358,631	1,852,456	1,567,124	1,962,376
Delaware	12,913	17,915	25,231	57,326	51,933	52,418	72,427	86,345
District of Columbia	41,510	61,633	78,946	71,980	138,777	96,514	66,861	73,687
Maryland	101,725	297,933	270,402	226,085	371,813	536,364	460,787	416,612
Southern New Jersey	30,745	71,995	54,809	66,213	78,531	130,878	162,712	158,980
Eastern Pennsylvania	157,784	316,083	342,441	507,304	472,122	634,747	645,342	735,092
Virginia	112,631	192,895	191,302	190,558	266,256	392,687	460,045	435,279
Southeast	482,917	1,026,527	936,611	1,115,929	1,232,290	1,793,169	2,431,666	2,389,321
Alabama	50,870	141,245	118,905	126,234	176,354	236,588	233,428	212,695
Florida	106,027	287,847	344,726	392,092	361,988	531,938	508,435	654,991
Georgia	66,759	195,737	149,219	181,531	215,067	304,170	315,082	391,108
North Carolina	80,564	180,286	161,038	188,987	192,673	297,820	304,000	335,347
South Carolina	21,948	119,020	78,651	86,861	101,387	134,250	762,486	160,630
Eastern Tennessee	157,749	101,202	89,007	137,115	184,045	292,494	226,640	784,495
Pittsburgh	91,797	245,649	275,969	216,409	391,463	642,444	489,399	451,729
Western Pennsylvania	60,953	161,377	209,821	286,878	319,132	512,988	386,421	340,780
West Virginia	30,844	84,072	66,148	102,228	71,926	95,856	102,948	110,979
Cleveland (North and East Ohio)	184,637	431,458	362,979	462,597	496,343	709,342	718,541	775,654
Cincinnati	136,110	226,539	343,670	352,397	315,483	400,606	667,654	1,051,541
Kentucky	45,565	100,582	115,807	119,747	186,016	191,187	506,155	761,760
Southwest Ohio	64,545	134,988	127,963	135,640	184,446	365,519	362,369	290,591
Southern Michigan	172,979	390,315	412,591	478,776	642,199	638,369	625,399	777,429
Chicago	596,695	963,097	886,126	1,194,463	1,125,769	1,663,673	1,662,911	1,672,228
Northern Illinois	201,114	426,158	408,970	467,828	504,151	755,536	749,282	767,286
Indiana	184,712	253,537	195,283	344,090	256,055	389,188	464,319	422,342
Iowa	48,792	118,846	95,186	156,703	150,225	193,960	186,045	182,371
Northern Michigan	2,680	12,254	9,226	19,345	17,779	17,267	14,861	18,135
Southeast Wisconsin	72,397	151,912	177,517	216,409	231,560	300,595	296,518	200,798
St. Louis	214,981	336,689	342,973	396,361	413,815	683,563	660,469	596,663
Arkansas	76,568	99,103	108,388	105,623	101,010	126,076	107,394	146,344
Southern Illinois	46,043	65,867	154,580	143,808	130,993	174,299	231,990	276,708
Eastern Missouri	63,314	106,385	131,466	167,734	191,695	279,144	256,112	202,171
Western Tennessee	29,056	61,904	69,643	81,419	80,376	104,194	108,982	132,469
New Orleans	70,413	119,327	231,364	271,329	315,597	414,673	396,365	386,151
Louisiana	46,312	74,638	151,823	190,217	227,495	311,198	281,231	177,640
Mississippi	24,101	44,680	79,533	72,722	85,392	103,475	114,167	120,511
Minneapolis	83,386	243,448	341,388	299,249	292,573	457,686	462,513	463,166
Minnesota	55,635	170,743	180,340	182,238	207,009	301,443	307,131	295,731
North Dakota	6,708	22,747	37,487	45,685	84,745	62,790	40,078	70,169
South Dakota	7,626	26,581	30,206	30,329	70,256	62,002	100,817	61,661
Northwest Wisconsin	12,971	21,772	29,154	31,809	20,563	31,431	35,286	32,227
Kansas City	163,797	292,363	346,128	443,467	478,273	641,589	723,275	667,499
Kansas	49,511	92,986	118,475	122,978	152,534	913,574	233,794	266,208
Western Missouri	30,080	59,315	52,917	61,051	96,656	99,321	115,204	178,095
Nebraska	38,217	50,036	64,369	69,879	73,507	106,071	111,990	136,760
Oklahoma	44,949	89,994	103,308	130,979	162,588	302,963	242,287	273,620
Texas	264,604	535,569	634,155	716,164	676,466	1,071,582	1,231,515	1,394,159
Totals for States in more than one district:								
Illinois	247,157	491,755	562,550	709,033	644,064	930,827	981,243	1,044,344
Michigan	176,659	402,672	421,819	466,315	659,908	627,635	858,143	790,444
Missouri	93,394	164,700	185,583	242,785	278,382	366,465	371,317	441,108
New Jersey	132,363	379,751	354,550	411,673	408,007	747,771	675,488	660,770
New York	225,126	850,454	821,953	1,146,428	1,386,614	1,786,654	1,665,081	1,972,987
Ohio	348,572	560,576	511,842	602,327	858,709	976,181	1,080,910	1,071,675
Pennsylvania	218,787	477,410	443,262	763,889	791,364	1,137,735	1,031,768	1,076,685
Tennessee	186,815	162,809	146,710	218,494	264,221	396,578	330,622	916,904
Wisconsin	84,768	172,684	200,671	243,516	283,413	332,326	321,680	341,928

[1] Includes Bronx borough, Nassau, Orange, Putnam, Rockland, Suffolk, and Westchester Counties.
[2] All counties north of Orange, Putnam, and Rockland.

Source: The F. W. Dodge Corp., New York, N. Y.; figures published currently in Statistical Research Service.

No. 908.—Construction Contracts Awarded—Indexes of Value: 1920 to 1952

[1947–49=100. Indexes are derived from monthly figures of construction contracts awarded reported by F. W. Dodge Corporation. Reports covered 37 States beginning with May 1924 and a varying number for earlier years. In order to obtain comparable figures from 1919 to date, total value of construction contracts awarded in 37 States was estimated for January 1919 through April 1924. Seasonal adjustments computed separately for "residential" and "all other" types of construction and the two series combined. Indexes based on a 3-month moving average, centered at middle month. More detailed description of indexes obtainable from the Division of Research and Statistics, Board of Governors of the Federal Reserve System]

YEAR	Total	Residential	All other	YEAR	Total	Residential	All other	YEAR AND MONTH	Total	Residential	All other
1920	34	18	45	1937	32	25	36	**1952**			
1922	43	41	43	1938	35	27	40				
1923	45	49	42	1939	39	37	40	January	161	142	173
1924	51	57	46	1940	44	43	44	February	156	163	152
1925	66	75	59	1941	66	54	74	March	164	174	157
1926	69	73	67	1942	89	49	116	April	171	189	158
1927	69	71	68	1943	37	24	45	May	168	186	156
1928	73	76	70	1944	22	10	30	June	172	193	158
1929	63	52	70	1945	36	16	50	July	177	196	165
1930	49	30	62	1946	82	87	79	August	207	193	217
1931	34	22	41	1947	84	86	83	September	207	191	218
1932	15	8	20	1948	102	98	105	October	210	185	227
1933	14	7	18	1949	113	116	111	November	196	178	207
1934	17	7	24	1950	159	185	142	December	205	183	219
1935	20	13	25	1951	171	170	172				
1936	30	22	35	1952 [1]	183	183	183				

[1] Preliminary.

Source: Board of Governors of the Federal Reserve System; published currently in *Federal Reserve Bulletin*.

No. 909.—Engineering Construction Contracts Awarded and Backlog of Proposed Construction—Volume, by Type: 1932 to 1952

[In millions of dollars. Covers continental U. S. construction projects of following minimum costs: For 1932–35, waterworks, excavation, drainage, and irrigation, $10,500; other public works, $17,500; industrial buildings, $28,000; other buildings, $105,000. For 1936–45, minimums used were $15,000, $25,000, $40,000, and $150,000. For 1946–47, these minimums were raised to $22,500, $40,000, $55,000, and $205,000, respectively, to account for rise in construction costs. For 1948–50, minimums used were: $28,000, $50,000, $58,000, and $250,000. For 1951–52, minimums used were: $34,000, $60,000, $82,000, and $300,000]

YEAR	Total	PUBLIC WORKS						PRIVATE BUILDINGS		Unclassified
		Waterworks	Sewerage	Bridges [1]	Earthwork, irr., drain.	Streets, roads	Buildings	Industrial	Commercial	
CONTRACTS AWARDED										
1932	1,219	35	25	84	101	380	241	93	166	95
1933	1,068	67	22	98	137	288	121	152	106	77
1934	1,361	92	61	99	266	345	204	105	81	106
1935	1,590	81	100	98	259	325	298	172	109	148
1936	2,387	92	121	188	182	483	436	309	275	300
1937	2,437	104	95	133	110	415	333	477	460	309
1938	2,792	131	136	135	268	638	503	152	550	279
1939	3,003	163	160	151	233	644	593	283	388	390
1940	3,987	70	91	120	234	678	1,196	594	400	603
1941	5,869	77	89	112	245	583	2,786	496	486	996
1942	9,306 [2]	151	118	50	251	531	5,678	200	292	2,034
1943	3,062 [3]	46	41	26	47	227	1,419	167	231	858
1944	1,730	33	32	17	64	196	658	174	140	416
1945	2,289	61	35	53	57	227	463	635	387	371
1946	5,176	109	114	129	328	769	414	1,113	1,846	354
1947	5,659	139	175	196	327	794	615	862	1,898	652
1948	7,219	209	228	303	519	996	1,161	1,096	1,888	820
1949	8,157	207	277	357	524	897	1,736	950	2,406	803
1950	13,342 [4]	215	287	369	417	1,268	3,754 [4]	1,683	4,092	1,256
1951	13,605	209	335	316	505	1,167	2,701	4,124	2,632	1,617
1952	15,689	231	304	413	496	1,397	4,899	2,722	3,845	1,382
BACKLOG OF PROPOSED PROJECTS										
1950	52,113	1,387	2,182	1,692	7,282	4,598	12,050	5,753	6,963	10,206
1951	62,147	1,432	2,372	2,030	7,444	5,129	13,569	9,400	7,993	12,777
1952	68,728	1,533	2,762	2,266	7,983	5,614	14,737	10,593	9,439	13,801

[1] Includes private; amount of contracts awarded in 1952, $17,989,000.   [3] $1,300 million canceled by W. P. B.
[2] Add $1,357 million for Atomic Bomb plants.   [4] Includes $990 million Atomic Energy contract for Savannah River project.

Source: Engineering News-Record, New York, N. Y.

No. 910.—ENGINEERING CONSTRUCTION CONTRACTS AWARDED—VOLUME, BY TYPE, BY STATES: 1952

[In thousands of dollars. Covers continental U. S. construction projects of following minimum costs: Waterworks, excavation, and irrigation, $54,000; other public works, $80,000; industrial buildings, $93,000; other buildings, $300,000]

STATE	Total	PUBLIC WORKS CONTRACTS						PRIVATE CONTRACT BUILDINGS		Unclassified
		Waterworks	Sewerage	Bridges[1]	Earthwork, irr., drain.	Streets, roads	Buildings	Industrial	Commercial	
United States	15,689,344	231,668	304,372	418,300	426,900	1,396,532	4,686,847	2,722,369	3,845,400	1,361,402
Alabama	177,843	2,443	2,376	5,976	236	12,137	78,580	21,661	36,142	16,325
Arizona	77,825	1,502		909	5,410	10,884	3,286	16,636	26,128	9,490
Arkansas	184,127	2,374	1,556	62	14,674	16,312	26,963	96,010	12,875	6,672
California	961,617	26,585	27,058	31,453	60,812	73,268	207,120	153,167	170,080	190,220
Colorado	124,980	3,512	2,090	1,051	5,794	14,609	22,840	22,419	20,621	11,445
Connecticut	149,845	262	5,321	2,426	185	6,054	48,972	22,601	30,929	13,215
Delaware	95,366	267	7,472	172	154	2,422	11,148	8,713	52,726	11,806
Dist. of Columbia	83,076	840	2,468	2,472		2,099	20,148	320	51,769	2,362
Florida	385,101	3,461	6,618	4,142	21,229	30,696	26,605	50,389	154,608	76,963
Georgia	319,895	6,206	3,415	20,166	2,936	30,212	76,746	63,160	76,216	40,647
Idaho	109,690	362	344	726	45,900	10,902	37,720	98	2,990	11,127
Illinois	692,610	10,748	18,855	20,746	7,503	97,072	91,096	205,359	187,251	32,081
Indiana	220,744	3,280	7,746	5,034	1,101	20,386	68,508	34,991	72,686	4,183
Iowa	177,844	544	1,826	9,834	3,884	38,811	15,768	77,279	28,916	4,945
Kansas	224,552	576	4,308	13,010		25,807	36,636	40,767	35,947	52,635
Kentucky	716,841	3,082	7,826	3,454	10,052	32,518	541,863	51,001	57,944	9,082
Louisiana	365,654	11,925	3,669	14,043	17,092	24,478	47,296	146,779	96,577	24,735
Maine	39,965		632	8,477	79	11,131	2,623	2,623	2,169	20,295
Maryland	282,128	8,492	7,806	7,016	1,620	27,708	76,262	46,945	26,926	12,811
Massachusetts	326,194	4,200	14,609	19,303	3,589	42,925	93,373	53,380	87,190	18,295
Michigan	594,510	12,780	12,096	11,903	864	52,910	92,919	115,302	211,460	13,830
Minnesota	130,480	1,201	3,290	5,322	2,452	39,140	22,318	12,772	30,844	4,620
Mississippi	122,666	1,305	5,432	3,381	8,053	13,554	29,940	36,082	12,268	11,023
Missouri	326,206	1,322	5,772	10,488	9,126	26,966	42,182	50,296	124,290	45,601
Montana	91,084	780	519	965	14,497	10,772	4,734	47,086	800	10,331
Nebraska	121,330	371	2,749	1,159	5,563	13,496	41,411	27,166	8,266	21,145
Nevada	27,233	224	780	117	273	6,227	6,089		4,250	7,273
New Hampshire	18,210	236	267	139	30	6,977	2,209	262	1,290	6,660
New Jersey	327,551	4,510	8,079	16,946	3,302	22,373	80,314	34,784	148,277	16,184
New Mexico	73,902	348	368	836	2,472	14,072	19,287	9,978	9,604	16,760
New York	1,186,377	4,112	11,704	64,209	4,825	129,443	224,905	34,319	653,630	46,099
North Carolina	248,064	5,400	4,788	5,995	3,172	37,787	40,086	21,847	72,064	57,855
North Dakota	44,172	947	691	2,710	20,153	11,667	2,489	1,282	1,270	5,999
Ohio	1,891,782	12,493	10,531	17,342	3,214	37,354	1,292,446	214,365	260,991	53,226
Oklahoma	218,200	3,965	4,654	11,768	3,192	40,080	37,178	42,735	27,322	47,306
Oregon	125,102	5,789	3,775	6,545	34,638	33,711	16,622	4,072	4,399	12,102
Pennsylvania	689,391	3,869	15,394	17,534	2,133	76,927	107,789	145,186	306,694	14,345
Rhode Island	46,045	1,540	1,731	778	6	6,859	21,369	2,533	5,309	6,366
South Carolina	180,700	2,122	2,082	4,779	1,609	16,049	37,688	16,729	82,088	27,022
South Dakota	69,779	727	472	3,450	31,637	11,722	2,080	690	2,179	15,616
Tennessee	304,102	1,919	4,321	3,510	21,869	27,913	601,650	46,378	64,511	30,362
Texas	1,587,142	58,802	44,735	20,167	30,307	94,686	178,446	557,927	366,688	207,220
Utah	62,603	480	897	741	2,622	16,786	16,941	11,505	6,802	18,377
Vermont	11,318	306	60	1,227	13	2,956	4,767	660	559	671
Virginia	373,090	4,432	3,611	3,316	4,630	23,036	73,767	60,198	147,306	44,673
Washington	470,947	3,832	6,321	17,292	17,106	24,426	209,174	86,808	30,444	41,540
West Virginia	37,715	227	554	2,441	526	6,949	10,510	3,875	3,429	1,920
Wisconsin	167,980	1,386	9,764	9,582	1,797	44,578	24,467	42,307	18,772	2,049
Wyoming	43,035	50		896	1,987	6,191	2,431	100	3,398	22,590

[1] Includes bridges under private contracts amounting to $17,996,000.

Source: Engineering News-Record, New York, N. Y.

No. 911.—Building Construction in Cities of 50,000 or More Inhabitants—
Value of All Construction and Number of New Dwelling Units: 1948
to 1952

[Valuation figures are derived from estimates of construction costs made by prospective builders when applying for permits to build and value of contracts awarded by Federal Government. No land costs are included. For type of building covered see table 902. Cities shown had a population of 50,000 and over in 1950]

CITY	VALUE OF ALL CONSTRUCTION ($1,000)					NUMBER OF NEW DWELLING UNITS				
	1948	1949	1950	1951	1952 [1]	1948	1949	1950	1951	1952 [1]
Akron, Ohio	24,754	19,110	33,343	28,382	40,634	1,154	1,111	2,041	1,377	1,468
Alameda, Calif	2,353	2,038	2,488	7,092	6,829	151	103	103	143	91
Albany, N.Y	19,743	9,148	11,063	7,547	9,896	201	187	949	347	608
Albuquerque, N. Mex	(?)	23,881	30,703	19,427	28,219	(?)	3,137	4,092	1,721	3,207
Alexandria, Va	13,409	13,836	6,516	7,845	10,165	495	1,413	595	536	712
Alhambra, Calif	12,314	8,008	7,772	5,783	5,787	1,283	637	671	515	322
Allentown, Pa	6,979	6,192	11,267	8,858	9,282	429	226	486	468	629
Altoona, Pa	2,807	1,442	3,044	3,386	3,347	100	75	117	212	99
Amarillo, Tex	10,094	16,939	26,082	21,252	24,248	1,444	1,986	2,350	2,477	2,903
Arlington Co., Va	21,280	27,173	29,904	40,395	28,468	1,909	2,468	2,052	1,646	1,285
Asheville, N.C	2,929	4,352	4,602	7,699	3,554	194	664	447	430	190
Atlanta, Ga	31,832	30,415	48,569	35,678	41,188	1,071	2,144	3,773	2,352	2,851
Atlantic City, N.J	2,077	1,777	8,015	3,538	(?)	28	38	981	146	(?)
Augusta, Ga	4,152	3,304	4,688	5,773	6,270	340	233	243	559	278
Aurora, Ill	2,469	3,098	5,957	5,636	4,740	169	294	406	246	191
Austin, Tex	27,295	31,090	28,913	28,913	27,898	2,609	1,840	2,837	1,808	1,643
Baltimore, Md	57,562	55,921	91,430	83,241	55,710	5,923	5,039	7,918	5,789	3,917
Baton Rouge, La	(?)	(?)	18,695	10,960	10,584	(?)	(?)	1,807	897	707
Bay City, Mich	2,930	4,171	3,999	3,583	2,958	170	196	289	226	173
Bayonne, N.J	4,206	1,908	2,770	4,018	4,009	20	115	278	357	343
Beaumont, Tex	9,434	9,336	9,279	7,033	8,525	1,286	1,116	823	810	1,019
Berkeley, Calif	10,388	8,499	14,888	9,022	5,176	367	385	433	298	305
Berwyn, Ill	2,320	2,808	4,480	3,122	4,004	132	103	233	168	221
Bethlehem, Pa	5,315	3,369	13,894	7,800	7,276	304	240	1,066	463	767
Binghamton, N.Y	4,872	4,839	3,767	2,795	6,446	204	325	246	133	253
Birmingham, Ala	18,143	37,865	38,236	24,719	21,603	1,803	4,193	4,019	2,010	1,699
Boston, Mass	54,987	43,175	68,078	63,303	46,681	1,642	1,598	2,353	3,686	1,390
Bridgeport, Conn	7,243	4,014	16,710	5,483	16,584	352	222	1,301	303	1,587
Brockton, Mass	2,285	3,664	3,933	21,467	3,993	157	304	170	247	244
Buffalo, N.Y	15,049	15,934	20,810	22,091	21,749	630	873	1,355	872	1,087
Burbank, Calif	15,976	10,376	12,953	25,978	14,724	1,459	1,035	1,152	1,807	1,131
Cambridge, Mass	8,996	14,580	6,424	9,829	5,353	91	810	55	221	186
Camden, N.J	8,274	5,901	8,527	4,876	8,936	336	470	805	118	551
Canton, Ohio	4,938	5,861	7,886	6,623	8,775	345	351	517	499	332
Cedar Rapids, Iowa	5,273	7,019	12,062	8,313	6,610	427	353	859	664	555
Charleston, S.C	4,536	3,637	3,736	5,342	2,590	178	402	135	306	125
Charleston, W.Va	9,861	9,683	13,242	4,672	13,532	378	347	702	357	780
Charlotte, N.C	17,582	23,351	32,049	20,586	20,578	1,198	3,338	3,136	1,276	1,489
Chattanooga, Tenn	7,810	9,027	12,336	10,148	10,403	349	442	982	782	314
Chester, Pa	2,613	1,234	5,545	5,444	1,045	74	9	418	481	22
Chicago, Ill	173,300	163,177	270,079	218,773	192,560	6,285	8,091	16,196	9,535	10,718
Cicero, Ill	3,354	3,619	5,894	5,261	(?)	126	54	139	173	(?)
Cincinnati, Ohio	40,899	37,004	61,471	68,236	47,223	1,307	1,090	2,349	3,793	1,331
Cleveland, Ohio	40,766	40,753	66,492	65,977	57,256	1,032	2,195	2,913	1,683	2,567
Cleveland Heights, Ohio	3,512	5,202	6,565	6,704	5,962	138	220	352	330	258
Clifton, N.J	8,554	8,455	10,958	8,897	10,277	893	1,427	1,802	468	716
Columbia, S.C	6,842	8,571	9,163	11,834	10,404	436	561	664	915	896
Columbus, Ga	3,856	5,133	11,207	8,830	6,567	199	493	1,040	639	267
Columbus, Ohio	30,653	34,074	48,733	32,486	38,261	1,991	2,619	4,549	1,811	1,712
Corpus Christi, Tex	15,757	16,113	29,919	17,352	21,691	1,075	1,855	2,661	1,270	1,783
Covington, Ky	1,242	2,090	634	748	(?)	30	17	22	36	(?)
Cranston, R.I	3,782	4,401	6,071	6,830	5,584	414	476	645	531	501
Dallas, Tex	76,061	69,079	132,949	96,978	102,408	6,981	6,309	12,197	7,315	6,972
Davenport, Iowa	5,761	5,540	10,542	9,739	10,644	310	251	547	436	472
Dayton, Ohio	12,039	13,918	21,825	24,843	19,872	759	1,009	1,743	1,141	730
Dearborn, Mich	20,562	30,582	44,098	36,067	57,700	1,354	1,873	2,486	1,292	898
Decatur, Ill	3,027	3,750	6,535	5,796	3,122	220	320	389	236	169
Denver, Colo	48,372	43,713	66,275	68,177	66,884	3,079	3,947	6,911	4,861	5,990
Des Moines, Iowa	12,471	26,582	24,877	15,973	19,432	938	1,468	1,842	921	753
Detroit, Mich	141,388	188,382	209,274	163,900	136,789	7,235	13,336	13,565	7,029	5,443
Duluth, Minn	5,937	6,649	7,562	6,414	6,166	412	325	651	530	298
Durham, N.C	8,698	8,604	17,090	9,137	9,291	554	493	617	267	812
East Chicago, Ind	1,832	1,728	2,966	5,797	3,413	38	34	132	47	203
East Orange, N.J	3,891	10,806	3,724	2,104	2,258	322	1,644	515	95	36
East St. Louis, Ill	2,568	4,080	3,437	5,179	7,322	255	212	264	438	576

For footnotes, see p. 768.

CITY	VALUE OF ALL CONSTRUCTION ($1,000)					NUMBER OF NEW DWELLING UNITS				
	1948	1949	1950	1951	1952	1948	1949	1950	1951	1952
eth, N. J.	2,944	4,101	5,897	4,634	3,509	82	544	768	272	194
o, Tex.	13,171	16,204	24,897	14,590	15,417	878	1,264	2,879	1,394	1,514
Pa.	13,422	7,557	15,306	16,812	11,312	596	634	1,226	1,629	498
ton, Ill.	10,264	11,087	14,150	8,946	7,827	282	285	580	329	282
ville, Ind.	4,874	5,108	5,636	3,834	5,954	399	419	717	476	527
iver, Mass.	2,260	4,196	3,961	8,908	1,776	130	430	290	447	98
Mich.	12,171	14,924	26,367	21,672	24,580	658	978	2,045	1,036	1,388
ayne, Ind.	8,829	10,062	13,726	17,357	11,027	600	779	1,234	782	560
orth, Tex.	29,517	29,963	49,161	42,690	47,409	3,228	4,131	7,131	4,466	6,458
, Calif.	12,938	12,993	18,698	17,962	13,304	709	1,231	1,757	1,513	846
an, Ala.	4,898	3,524	7,492	4,875	4,185	891	373	977	622	362
ton, Tex.	8,683	7,969	7,373	10,606	3,621	404	300	322	688	228
Ind.	11,458	13,941	17,131	12,884	19,454	1,066	1,836	1,508	963	1,443
le, Calif.	14,693	8,560	13,200	10,022	11,353	1,369	868	1,170	700	1,593
Rapids, Mich.	16,130	12,879	18,208	12,288	6,917	782	686	1,510	725	570
Bay, Wis.	10,980	5,446	18,000	6,659	6,014	371	306	825	420	354
boro, N. C.	10,315	10,956	21,150	13,923	8,940	838	1,116	1,089	1,688	844
ville, S. C.	7,187	10,635	12,077	9,829	9,515	555	1,429	846	1,030	984
ton, Ohio	8,156	3,505	5,114	5,399	4,846	228	356	475	411	316
ond, Ind.	7,784	7,555	12,654	18,809	11,101	571	713	1,129	916	588
burg, Pa.	6,354	7,791	8,423	9,384	5,678	354	478	392	742	108
rd, Conn.	12,943	12,250	20,150	14,382	8,822	670	647	882	843	484
nd Park, Mich.	2,679	2,063	4,669	1,668	1,520	7	4	4	4	
an, N. J.	2,088	1,060	6,360	6,860	6,597		2	696	(4)	(4)
re, Mass.	2,007	1,492	8,556	3,845	2,696	88	74	321	115	180
n, Tex.	96,952	82,613	185,979	127,225	114,652	7,517	5,822	11,909	7,997	7,546
agton, W. Va.	7,928	8,378	7,778	9,980	7,230	494	406	625	499	214
apolis, Ind.	32,495	40,654	36,403	63,677	36,049	1,826	3,033	3,556	1,350	1,698
ton, N. J.	2,816	11,022	2,614	1,227	3,180	77	1,994	174	96	179
n, Mich.	2,073	1,339	4,164	1,706	2,888	74	64	152	113	76
n, Miss.	13,377	16,558	14,939	12,341	13,779	854	1,993	1,557	691	868
aville, Fla.	16,111	22,480	21,701	17,890	16,873	1,172	1,987	2,082	1,354	898
City, N. J.	7,683	7,150	9,633	8,252	12,312	10	459	695	209	727
own, Pa.	1,485	2,441	6,158	4,751	1,883	80	65	282	361	54
Ill.	4,753	4,074	4,607	4,582	7,412	250	180	278	344	400
azoo, Mich.	2,079	4,934	3,962	2,533	2,215	146	108	130	86	44
City, Kans.	5,693	6,846	7,046	6,612	12,327	266	356	854	451	375
City, Mo.	25,562	36,864	44,606	33,596	42,542	2,008	2,363	2,957	1,283	2,606
ha, Wis.	5,471	4,532	5,270	5,325	8,611	496	317	566	478	427
ille, Tenn.	11,560	7,347	19,964	7,982	11,228	445	433	1,790	440	570
ood, Ohio	1,390	2,022	7,827	3,272	4,302	30	53	283	46	36
ter, Pa.	4,194	6,078	3,353	2,692	5,372	212	104	192	100	70
g, Mich.	6,286	7,125	13,314	14,680	12,523	320	406	757	496	577
, Tex.	1,308	730	1,108	794	2,127	281	250	267	196	379
ce, Mass.	3,321	3,118	2,723	5,456	2,325	183	305	88	485	37
ton, Ky.	9,745	3,247	9,433	8,560	5,089	81	62	69	508	108
Ohio	1,887	3,249	3,289	2,648	2,529	84	88	208	164	112
n, Nebr.	8,510	7,064	12,010	13,061	12,360	510	622	1,223	1,502	1,414
Rock, Ark.	20,534	9,244	21,090	21,930	8,888	666	663	1,539	632	482
beach, Calif.	32,264	33,762	28,579	37,737	42,907	3,299	2,542	1,810	1,483	2,642
Ohio	3,091	3,406	5,408	4,846	4,554	272	226	585	366	366
geles, Calif.	373,978	392,301	407,393	274,734	371,272	30,226	26,101	30,796	18,687	26,070
ille, Ky.	16,270	22,349	23,179	32,539	16,691	1,280	1,378	2,310	2,174	1,228
, Mass.	1,141	4,305	2,008	5,617	1,401	130	391	136	367	82
ck, Tex.	14,817	16,758	26,529	19,835	20,300	1,289	1,810	2,135	1,142	1,268
Mass.	6,229	4,943	7,564	9,042	4,792	188	344	584	450	278
, Ga.	2,973	2,809	4,174	2,520	2,720	149	190	341	293	223
n, Wis.	7,309	16,772	15,252	8,796	9,996	543	696	1,168	541	698
, Mass.	1,658	2,280	2,236	1,080	4,799	81	196	165	60	469
ster, N. H.	10,694	5,186	8,941	6,557	5,542	731	469	449	555	417
sport, Pa.	1,960	2,191	3,645	1,803	2,201	71	93	156	316	264
d, Mass.	2,343	2,726	2,986	2,701	1,649	99	157	270	148	118
his, Tenn.	33,223	34,926	44,289	37,158	46,690	3,443	4,218	6,682	4,697	5,189
Fla.	54,888	43,627	47,037	38,946	37,425	5,711	4,900	4,664	4,911	5,023
kee, Wis.	53,996	58,154	87,850	76,091	65,740	2,859	3,437	6,822	3,887	5,677
apolis, Minn.	37,282	39,920	46,888	46,842	38,728	1,658	2,477	2,900	1,679	1,946
Ala.	10,025	12,606	13,952	7,296	11,091	1,091	862	1,743	808	979
mpery, Ala.	4,029	8,614	13,200	9,748	11,462	786	2,190	2,388	1,688	982
Vernon, N. Y.	4,031	11,227	7,681	5,303	5,528	196	1,104	693	167	208
, Ind.	3,751	3,457	3,639	4,033	2,150	270	276	307	277	120

No. 911.—BUILDING CONSTRUCTION IN CITIES OF 50,000 OR MORE INHABITANTS—
VALUE OF ALL CONSTRUCTION AND NUMBER OF NEW DWELLING UNITS: 1948
TO 1952—Continued

CITY	VALUE OF ALL CONSTRUCTION ($1,000)					NUMBER OF NEW DWELLING UNITS				
	1948	1949	1950	1951	1952 [1]	1948	1949	1950	1951	1952 [1]
Nashville, Tenn	9,785	18,774	16,391	42,793	18,267	321	688	1,024	2,017	1,514
Newark, N. J	25,914	9,641	23,499	34,783	34,376	397	849	293	2,700	2,809
New Bedford, Mass	2,125	3,948	4,217	6,948	2,002	151	336	387	534	168
New Britain, Conn	2,434	3,408	4,658	9,788	10,373	189	277	645	518	596
New Haven, Conn	11,111	7,559	14,051	13,821	8,601	577	247	1,093	469	164
New Orleans, La	28,288	56,036	77,547	77,677	82,734	3,446	4,248	5,091	4,793	3,510
New Rochelle, N. Y	8,312	3,312	8,534	6,247	9,773	549	195	879	444	596
Newton, Mass	9,834	8,040	12,436	14,121	8,560	820	356	735	482	465
New York, N. Y.:[18]										
Bronx	47,753	92,147	45,730	71,175	84,243	4,751	9,513	3,689	6,599	5,237
Brooklyn	46,667	117,080	71,811	45,776	78,251	3,397	11,535	6,566	2,507	5,434
Manhattan	80,513	177,374	117,080	120,034	63,067	3,304	6,619	4,389	2,818	1,934
Queens	129,348	133,353	194,562	120,417	118,662	13,303	15,104	24,336	12,680	8,919
Richmond	10,990	11,388	4,574	2,632	11,477	1,054	1,097	428	183	971
Niagara Falls, N. Y	7,521	8,320	10,255	8,602	10,292	610	492	913	627	563
Norfolk, Va	16,035	12,234	20,012	29,640	21,807	1,936	1,509	2,182	2,153	2,920
Oakland, Calif	37,408	30,596	31,227	31,946	27,564	1,354	1,339	1,491	1,301	1,241
Oak Park, Ill	3,815	1,574	2,257	3,850	4,169	30	52	93	151	110
Ogden, Utah	3,460	4,145	8,842	7,566	4,952	364	385	802	445	409
Oklahoma City, Okla	12,430	16,688	50,646	28,310	23,647	985	1,025	4,120	2,401	2,131
Omaha, Nebr	22,043	13,971	26,014	15,296	21,111	777	1,307	2,533	1,068	1,467
Orlando, Fla	10,233	9,222	12,155	12,862	11,970	1,129	1,025	1,383	899	1,029
Pasadena, Calif	16,809	16,646	20,590	22,627	14,355	1,012	1,100	1,497	1,451	750
Passaic, N. J	2,085	3,607	5,659	2,361	[19] 5,564	78	490	103	173	[19] 426
Paterson, N. J	4,488	4,258	7,340	10,010	5,831	132	194	472	726	279
Pawtucket, R. I	4,998	4,126	5,566	7,275	3,358	508	456	547	687	296
Peoria, Ill	8,451	6,103	11,122	12,733	5,542	367	255	597	670	190
Philadelphia, Pa	93,597	86,126	157,332	111,725	118,322	5,061	6,555	12,464	7,362	7,094
Phoenix, Ariz	16,571	12,071	15,400	21,424	14,604	1,416	467	1,169	1,306	838
Pittsburgh, Pa	26,464	43,034	105,335	48,332	29,501	938	1,842	3,320	2,813	1,150
Pittsfield, Mass	6,402	4,018	5,332	6,893	7,826	430	195	299	333	266
Pontiac, Mich	4,238	8,336	9,387	18,123	4,838	203	592	584	712	187
Port Arthur, Tex	4,296	4,697	5,135	7,394	4,291	238	353	490	605	239
Portland, Maine	4,490	3,346	5,478	3,717	3,543	155	137	233	163	137
Portland, Oreg	52,258	47,656	63,325	37,787	49,546	3,067	2,976	3,824	1,721	1,880
Portsmouth, Va	2,483	2,013	4,124	13,222	4,392	275	188	419	734	312
Providence, R. I	11,853	10,222	17,778	19,071	8,225	454	267	775	1,275	322
Pueblo, Colo	3,633	4,171	7,008	8,230	13,109	496	504	919	723	1,208
Quincy, Mass	4,458	7,361	3,957	6,869	3,215	278	651	311	403	237
Racine, Wis	5,175	4,346	9,532	8,554	8,435	204	261	604	521	502
Raleigh, N. C	9,070	8,962	16,594	12,753	17,779	674	1,003	683	486	741
Reading, Pa	2,004	3,253	4,766	4,285	8,501	40	377	79	80	600
Richmond, Calif	8,943	8,848	[19] 5,759	8,744	7,532	657	492	[19] 555	483	441
Richmond, Va	21,466	18,074	32,949	31,333	21,488	943	890	1,336	1,723	677
Roanoke, Va	7,221	14,075	17,487	14,427	8,327	391	968	1,216	1,241	521
Rochester, N. Y	16,091	19,313	16,406	21,153	16,974	459	1,083	1,040	1,058	668
Rockford, Ill	6,553	4,909	11,686	9,621	11,162	456	370	891	843	804
Sacramento, Calif	17,432	18,814	30,524	14,177	12,908	1,473	1,267	3,048	1,151	954
Saginaw, Mich	7,747	4,240	6,108	5,549	7,167	348	352	575	433	375
St. Joseph, Mo	1,291	1,220	1,727	1,486	1,780	147	122	212	172	176
St. Louis, Mo	28,242	30,413	74,659	39,758	58,381	1,337	1,559	4,145	1,633	2,799
St. Paul, Minn	23,846	21,602	47,424	36,345	34,283	998	1,295	3,216	1,797	1,275
St. Petersburg, Fla	20,523	21,675	30,869	23,954	28,927	2,088	2,496	3,306	2,867	3,219
Salt Lake City, Utah	14,960	16,086	33,740	15,595	16,667	1,350	1,513	2,207	943	727
San Angelo, Tex	6,012	4,230	10,678	9,050	5,590	525	517	1,333	605	467
San Antonio, Tex	35,822	36,941	57,040	53,547	47,964	4,675	5,293	5,989	6,159	4,945
San Bernardino, Calif	11,554	[19] 13,359	17,420	14,927	14,577	977	[19] 1,171	1,810	1,434	1,067
San Diego, Calif	42,882	37,052	60,770	74,419	97,197	4,107	3,224	5,951	6,072	9,730
San Francisco, Calif	62,990	68,281	85,104	56,417	51,005	3,951	3,664	3,785	1,692	1,708
San Jose, Calif	19,486	15,231	20,937	22,155	12,227	1,629	1,221	2,034	1,005	955
Santa Monica, Calif	12,672	10,664	10,276	11,481	9,448	1,356	930	869	718	902
Savannah, Ga	5,458	4,753	7,867	6,047	6,032	750	743	1,095	755	904
Schenectady, N. Y	3,734	8,637	4,149	5,822	4,699	184	912	229	223	203
Scranton, Pa	2,812	3,137	5,761	2,709	2,937	41	42	324	68	225
Seattle, Wash	61,005	53,673	57,742	54,136	63,481	2,860	3,115	3,415	2,249	2,548
Shreveport, La	17,062	27,487	25,851	15,186	20,381	1,296	1,775	3,261	1,439	982
Sioux City, Iowa	7,251	6,196	10,814	6,449	4,910	357	349	763	505	443

For footnotes, see p. 763.

No. 911.—BUILDING CONSTRUCTION IN CITIES OF 50,000 OR MORE INHABITANTS—
VALUE OF ALL CONSTRUCTION AND NUMBER OF NEW DWELLING UNITS: 1948 TO
1952—Continued

CITY	VALUE OF ALL CONSTRUCTION ($1,000)					NUMBER OF NEW DWELLING UNITS				
	1948	1949	1950	1951	1952 [1]	1948	1949	1950	1951	1952 [1]
Sioux Falls, S. Dak	6,530	5,909	9,511	5,226	6,621	543	421	848	287	283
Somerville, Mass	1,191	3,088	3,313	909	592	3	174	349	6	5
South Bend, Ind	12,978	12,143	21,247	17,985	16,715	963	1,078	2,012	1,087	1,094
South Gate, Calif	10,705	4,944	4,361	4,584	5,205	1,252	577	491	282	430
Spokane, Wash	26,392	15,254	33,473	21,908	21,773	1,536	1,742	2,436	1,420	1,361
Springfield, Ill	5,241	3,876	6,754	4,850	4,644	380	367	399	217	380
Springfield, Mass	9,905	9,294	13,346	21,587	10,251	389	696	1,192	587	654
Springfield, Mo	4,988	4,684	20,388	6,781	7,551	367	446	763	531	360
Springfield, Ohio	3,200	4,661	6,252	3,964	7,964	241	292	540	245	475
Stamford, Conn	7,089	5,211	18,285	15,139	11,113	502	508	1,469	970	384
Stockton, Calif	10,013	4,627	9,397	11,543	7,704	682	486	942	689	440
Syracuse, N.Y	11,684	26,037	16,940	18,166	10,259	1,110	681	1,416	680	492
Tacoma, Wash	14,494	13,371	23,331	18,159	13,132	963	1,105	1,750	1,108	852
Tampa, Fla	8,721	9,361	15,658	12,973	13,987	886	827	1,548	1,102	1,450
Terre Haute, Ind	3,121	1,382	2,293	3,968	3,011	136	111	147	177	130
Toledo, Ohio	20,396	18,292	22,645	19,494	17,622	868	894	1,660	1,145	1,612
Topeka, Kans	4,632	5,068	9,940	8,623	6,980	508	514	823	461	406
Trenton, N.J	4,190	3,286	4,050	11,580	4,696	157	140	67	595	142
Troy, N.Y	3,363	5,217	2,619	4,802	9,353	37	390	218	217	447
Tulsa, Okla	14,405	15,490	19,173	12,742	12,758	1,034	1,371	1,430	745	761
Union City, N.J	870	1,287	414	1,200	1,772	------	27	------	95	167
Upper Darby Township, Pa.[4]	19,692	7,610	11,267	6,114	6,392	3,653	857	611	221	221
Utica, N.Y	2,691	6,927	2,323	5,574	2,299	340	296	212	345	285
Waco, Tex	10,087	12,944	19,310	14,898	12,341	930	1,070	1,577	1,261	1,180
Washington, D.C	80,096	114,734	59,194	60,345	54,297	3,797	5,254	4,857	4,494	4,761
Waterbury, Conn	6,050	3,757	9,529	7,436	12,065	477	396	742	549	690
Waterloo, Iowa	4,644	6,746	9,186	7,882	6,372	253	350	695	418	315
Wheeling, W. Va	3,668	3,294	4,423	3,029	3,383	100	68	130	85	63
Wichita, Kans	22,457	22,540	26,204	30,436	23,065	2,387	2,653	3,828	2,984	2,623
Wichita Falls, Tex	4,511	5,416	8,624	7,285	16,510	456	539	865	530	1,623
Wilkes-Barre, Pa	13,681	2,157	3,715	1,779	3,632	23	13	47	19	22
Wilmington, Del	5,633	10,619	8,620	8,968	12,816	136	100	276	280	581
Winston-Salem, N.C	15,074	8,080	14,087	14,075	11,341	311	680	1,189	1,087	698
Woonsocket, R.I	1,256	1,408	2,357	5,292	1,199	130	102	122	434	72
Worcester, Mass	9,992	6,978	16,314	26,763	12,145	748	485	1,383	1,031	447
Yonkers, N.Y	9,855	19,195	15,847	8,422	17,808	975	2,586	1,430	694	1,390
York, Pa	3,851	3,608	2,728	3,311	4,471	66	22	77	59	252
Youngstown, Ohio	5,279	6,676	11,372	11,135	15,158	343	514	1,088	570	655

[1] Preliminary.
[2] Not available.
[3] Excludes data for Nov.
[4] Classified as urban under special rule by Bureau of the Census, 1940, but omitted from list of urban places in 1950.
[5] Excludes data for Sept.
[6] Excludes data for July.
[7] Excludes data for June.
[8] Represents applications filed.
[9] Excludes data for Sept. and Oct.
[10] Excludes data for Oct.
[11] Excludes data for July and Aug.
[12] Excludes data for Feb.
[13] Excludes data for May.
[14] Excludes data for July and Oct.
[15] Excludes data for April, May, and Oct.; no new dwelling units.
[16] Excludes data for June and Nov.; no new dwelling units.
[17] Excludes data for April.
[18] Represents work actually started, based on inspection records.
[19] Excludes data for July and Nov.
[20] Excludes data for Feb. and Oct.

Source: Department of Labor, Bureau of Labor Statistics.

No. 912.—CONSTRUCTION AND BUILDING COST INDEXES: 1917 TO 1952

[1913=100 except Aberthaw for which base year is 1914. See also *Historical Statistics*, series H 64, 65, and 73, for AAC, ENR (const.), and Turner indexes]

YEAR	AAC (new) [1]	AGC [2]	ENR Const. [3]	ENR Bldg. [3]	Boeckh, U. S. [4]	Aber-thaw [5]	Fuller [6]	Turner [7]	M & S [8]	S. H. & G. [9]
1917....	143	152	181	167	142	126	156	147	127	--------
1918....	177	175	189	159	156	147	160	166	148	--------
1919....	229	198	196	159	172	172	168	196	185	--------
1920....	283	247	251	207	214	234	209	252	233	--------
1921....	216	200	202	166	175	179	188	183	178	--------
1922....	200	184	174	155	162	170	175	175	172	--------
1923....	224	201	214	186	181	202	190	196	182	190
1924....	222	204	215	186	181	198	194	194	183	193
1925....	217	199	207	183	179	195	193	195	185	187
1926....	217	197	208	185	181	197	202	195	185	185
1927....	217	200	206	186	179	193	197	190	182	183
1928....	217	199	207	188	179	191	196	190	184	188
1929....	217	203	207	191	184	190	201	185	179	190
1930....	200	200	203	185	181	186	199	165	165	181
1931....	178	196	181	168	168	176	180	145	156	148
1932....	155	171	157	141	144	168	157	136	130	128
1933....	150	163	170	148	148	170	155	141	143	137
1934....	161	178	198	167	161	176	171	160	156	157
1935....	162	176	196	166	159	177	167	162	164	161
1936....	170	179	206	172	164	184	168	166	166	173
1937....	196	188	235	196	183	199	187	193	180	200
1938....	199	189	236	197	189	191	192	188	178	200
1939....	200	188	236	197	191	190	195	182	183	199
1940....	204	189	242	203	195	193	196	194	190	204
1941....	217	198	258	211	204	208	206	217	202	217
1942....	241	209	276	222	214	223	229	245	218	226
1943....	252	216	290	229	223	225	238	257	227	245
1944....	261	223	299	235	237	227	240	244	234	264
1945....	271	231	308	239	252	236	241	257	248	285
1946....	322	257	346	262	275	279	290	318	288	319
1947....	430	296	413	313	323	304	354	380	338	371
1948....	490	332	461	345	365	321	380	422	368	403
1949....	490	342	477	352	369	312	382	414	365	395
1950....	500	357	509	375	386	321	377	427	390	426
1951....	532	377	542	401	415	370	405	478	430	476
1952....	553	388	569	416	430	381	416	493	436	499

[1] American Appraisal Co. Average for 30 cities of 4 types of buildings: Wood frame, brick-wood frame, brick-steel frame, reinforced concrete. Mechanicals not included. Based on actual appraisal costs. Available for individual cities.

[2] Associated General Contractors of America. Wages and materials for 12 cities combined in 40-60 ratio. Wages, prevailing rates for hod carriers and common labor. Materials, weighted: Sand, gravel and crushed stone, 1; cement, 1; lumber, 1; hollow tile, ½; structural and reinforcing steel, ½.

[3] Engineering News Record construction cost index has 4 components: (1) Structural steel shapes, base price; (2) cement, which is 20-cities average but prior to July, 1948, was Chicago only; (3) lumber, which until 1935 was 12 x 12 long leaf yellow pine wholesale at New York, and since 1935 is 2 x 4 S*S pine and fir in carload lots. ENR 20-cities average: (4) common labor, ENR 20-cities average of wage rates in force, ENR Building Cost index provides a more representative measure of building cost movement, the skilled labor trend having been substituted for the common labor trend in the ENR Construction Cost index, and the ENR Building Cost index computed.

[4] E. H. Boeckh & Assoc., Inc. Individual series for 10 types of buildings for 20 areas. Weights based on studies of actual building costs—vary with different type of structures. Material prices are those paid by contractors to material dealers. Prevailing skilled and common wage rates from contractors. Base: United States average, 1926-29=100. Series given here is commercial and factory buildings, U. S. average converted to 1913=100 base.

[5] Aberthaw. Until Mar. 31, 1946, New England, 7-story and basement (62' 4" x 202' 4"), reinforced concrete building built in 1914, repriced quarterly as a construction bid to duplicate original building; labor costs based on current experience with similar construction. Since Mar. 31, 1946, New England, composite of 36 major cost items in 3 multi-story and 2 one-story industrial buildings, including all mechanical trades, repriced using actual and estimated labor and material costs.

[6] George A. Fuller Company. Composite of 36 major cost elements, in 3 commercial type buildings, including mechanicals, elevators, wiring, heating and ventilating, repriced.

[7] Turner Construction Co. Eastern Cities. Own building cost experience applied to these factors: Labor rates, material prices, productivity of labor, efficiency of plant and management, competitive conditions.

[8] Marshall and Stevens. Averages for 4 types of building: Fireproof protected steel, fireproof reinforced concrete, masonry, and frame. Designed to reflect normal costs in line with recognized or published prices of building materials, equipment, and labor. Base: U. S. average, 1926=100, converted to 1913=100 base.

[9] Smith, Hinchman, and Grylls, Inc. Actual in-place costs, using building material costs, freight rates, skilled and unskilled labor rates and labor efficiency and premiums, bidding competition, contractor profit margins and overhead. Figured with the contractor overhead as taxes, duration of projects, material expediting and labor procurement. This index is reported monthly on a 1926=100 base, converted to 1913=100 base.

Source: Engineering News-Record, New York, N. Y.

No. 913.—NUMBER OF PUBLIC HOUSING UNITS COMPLETED FOR OCCUPANCY:
1935 to 1952

[Covers programs administered by Housing and Home Finance Agency or Public Housing Administration]

		LOW-RENT				
YEAR	All public housing	Total	U. S. Housing Act	All other [1]	War and defense housing	Veterans' reuse housing
Total	1,265,654	279,367	239,644	39,363	729,586	265,652
1935	3,932	3,932	----------	3,932		
1936	1,213	1,213	----------	1,213		
1937	7,849	7,849	----------	7,840		
1938	17,319	17,319	----------	17,319		
1939	3,858	3,858	3,858			
1940	31,940	31,940	31,940			
1941	119,634	59,848	59,848		59,786	
1942	156,366	27,537	27,537		120,739	
1943	374,729	27,325	27,325		347,404	
1944	153,158	2,831	2,831		150,327	
1945	45,026	2,949	2,949		40,171	1,906
1946	134,726	1,804	1,804		4,061	128,871
1947	107,097	466	466			106,631
1948	30,054	1,336	1,336		1,550	27,168
1949	1,242	547	547			695
1950	1,582	1,201	1,201			381
1951	10,595	10,346	10,346			
1952	62,553	57,956	57,956		5,877	

[1] Includes PWA, subsistence homestead and Greenbelt town projects.
[2] Includes 80 PWA units completed in 1934.
[3] Includes 60,489 units completed as war housing of which all but 2,898 units have been returned to low-rent use.
[4] 2,469 permanent family dwelling units have since been conveyed to local authorities for low-rent use under Public Law 475.
[5] Units completed for emergency flood projects in Portland-Vancouver area.
[6] Defense housing.

Source: Housing and Home Finance Agency, Public Housing Administration.

No. 914.—NUMBER OF DWELLING UNITS OWNED OR SUPERVISED BY THE PUBLIC HOUSING ADMINISTRATION, BY PROGRAM, AS OF DEC. 31, 1952

[Excludes units which have been sold to mutual housing associations, limited dividend corporations (PWA) and homesteads associations on which FHA holds mortgages for collection]

	TOTAL		Federally owned	Locally owned
PROGRAM	Number	Net change since Dec. 31, 1951		
Total	731,699	+4,289	320,133	410,966
Active	718,547	+8,651	307,581	410,966
Veterans' reuse housing	24,909	−6,519	1,573	23,136 [1]
Defense housing	10,456	+10,456	10,456	
Public war housing (Lanham constructed)	246,116	−26,780	246,116	
Low-rent housing	436,792	+31,960	48,963	387,830
Under management	271,261	+60,000	48,963	222,313
Under construction	87,596	−3,026		87,588
Not under construction	77,934	−25,015		77,934
Public Law 171	226,206	+29,915		226,206
Public Law 412	117,430	−10	10,840	106,590
Public Law 671	49,695	−309	7,139	43,556
PWA	21,625	−18	21,625	
Farm labor camps	9,350	−1	9,350	
Public Law 475	2,469	+2,469		2,469
Subsistence homesteads and Greenbelt towns	373	−1,196	373	
Inactive—Public war housing (Lanham constructed)	12,552	−4,362	12,552	

[1] This veterans' housing is so classified even though title or income rights may not be formally transferred.
[2] Excludes 1,438 rural farm units not yet built but which are parts of active rural projects.

Source: Housing and Home Finance Agency, Public Housing Administration; Annual Report.

No. 915.—Number of Active Projects and Dwelling Units, Owned or Supervised by the Public Housing Administration, by State or Other Area, as of Dec. 31, 1952

[See headnote, table 914]

STATE OR OTHER AREA	TOTAL PROGRAM [1]		LOW-RENT HOUSING [2]		WAR HOUSING [3]		DEFENSE HOUSING		VETERANS' RE-USE HOUSING	
	Projects	Units	Projects	Units	Projects	Units	Projects	Units	Projects	Units
Total	2,339	716,547	2,125	436,738	879	246,116	64	10,466	165	24,809
Alabama	157	21,622	128	14,151	23	6,460	2	226	4	685
Arizona	50	6,461	18	2,752	27	3,406	3	200	2	122
Arkansas	30	3,020	26	2,528	2	274			2	218
California	397	115,729	165	36,450	187	71,001	9	1,353	36	6,925
Colorado	17	4,114	16	3,784					1	330
Connecticut	88	21,301	35	10,116	48	10,525	2	300	3	360
Delaware	9	2,377	4	760	5	1,617				
Dist. of Columbia	31	7,481	14	4,506	16	1,989			1	886
Florida	102	18,057	80	14,843	18	2,965	2	160	2	99
Georgia	294	27,793	272	22,507	17	4,629	2	258	3	399
Idaho	12	1,197	4	430	4	258	3	401	1	28
Illinois	131	31,178	113	28,719	13	1,901			5	558
Indiana	50	9,060	28	5,297	14	2,826	1	190	7	747
Iowa	9	1,769			4	871			5	898
Kansas	14	6,591			10	5,865	4	726		
Kentucky	53	9,656	49	9,285	2	249	1	110	1	32
Louisiana	70	14,286	62	13,185	2	255	4	748	2	98
Maine	17	2,556	2	86	14	2,195	1	275		
Maryland	50	19,144	28	8,763	29	9,971	3	113		
Massachusetts	66	19,525	49	16,621	11	2,535			6	369
Michigan	86	30,315	26	13,475	56	16,568	1	120	3	152
Minnesota	12	2,639	10	2,506					2	133
Mississippi	59	5,406	49	3,219	6	1,621			3	565
Missouri	15	9,510	9	7,685	1	60	2	809	3	956
Montana	9	747	8	697	1	50				
Nebraska	12	3,001	6	1,778	6	1,223				
Nevada	12	1,627	1	100	10	1,427	1	100		
New Hampshire	6	1,511	4	626	2	885				
New Jersey	112	25,340	90	22,022	11	2,875			10	438
New Mexico	7	455	2	148	4	287			1	20
New York	90	53,519	60	45,407	16	4,239			14	3,873
North Carolina	72	11,504	59	9,097	9	1,953	3	526	1	18
North Dakota	2	63							2	63
Ohio	108	33,266	44	17,547	55	14,124			8	1,557
Oklahoma	7	912	2	434	1	184			4	294
Oregon	34	3,409	12	1,066	19	2,207			3	136
Pennsylvania	174	45,071	104	25,599	69	19,445			1	27
Rhode Island	19	5,199	13	4,008	2	800	2	300	2	91
South Carolina	97	7,924	87	5,458	10	2,466				
South Dakota										
Tennessee	88	15,950	82	15,384	5	561				
Texas	243	36,026	210	27,975	24	6,906	3	353	6	792
Utah	13	2,979			13	2,979				
Vermont	3	323			3	323				
Virginia	77	29,582	35	9,554	29	17,666	9	1,766	4	596
Washington	91	19,860	24	4,486	57	14,498	4	420	6	456
West Virginia	17	2,202	13	2,076					4	126
Wisconsin	17	3,431	8	1,949	4	828	2	612	2	27
Wyoming	7	796			7	795				
Alaska	16	680	4	325	12	355				
Hawaii	12	4,132	6	1,409	1	999			5	1,724
Puerto Rico	63	17,454	63	17,454						
Virgin Islands	3	476	3	476						

[1] Includes 6 projects and 373 units in the subsistence homestead Greenbelt towns programs not shown separately by program.

[2] Includes Public Law 412, Public Law 671, PWA, Public Law 171, Public Law 475 and farm labor camps programs.

[3] Includes homes conversion program, 126 units in California.

Source: Housing and Home Finance Agency, Public Housing Administration; *Annual Report*.

No. 916.—Occupied Dwelling Units—Tenure, and Population Per Dwelling Unit, by Color of Occupants, and by Nonfarm and Farm Residence: 1890 to 1950

[Minus sign (—) denotes decrease. See also *Historical Statistics*, series H 89-112]

COLOR OF OCCUPANTS, RESIDENCE, AND CENSUS YEAR	OCCUPIED DWELLING UNITS (OR FAMILIES)[1]						PERCENT INCREASE OVER PRECEDING CENSUS		Population per occupied dwelling unit (or family)[2]
	Total	Reporting tenure	Owner-occupied		Renter-occupied		Total occupied dwelling units (or families)[1]	Total population	
			Number	Percent	Number	Percent			
1890	12,690,152	12,690,152	6,066,417	47.8	6,623,735	52.2			5.0
1900	15,963,965	15,428,967	7,205,212	46.7	8,223,775	53.3	25.8	20.7	4.8
1910	20,255,555	19,781,606	9,063,711	45.9	10,697,895	54.1	25.9	21.0	4.5
1920	24,351,676	23,810,558	10,866,960	45.6	12,943,598	54.4	20.2	14.9	4.3
1930	29,904,663	29,221,891	14,002,074	47.8	15,319,817	52.2	22.8	16.1	4.1
1940	34,854,532	34,854,532	15,195,763	43.6	19,658,769	56.4	16.6	7.2	3.8
1950	42,826,281	42,826,281	23,559,966	55.0	19,266,315	45.0	22.9	14.5	3.5
COLOR OF OCCUPANTS									
White									
1890	11,255,169	11,255,169	5,793,660	51.5	5,461,509	48.5			4.9
1900	14,063,791	13,659,106	6,788,069	49.7	6,871,037	50.3	25.0	21.2	4.8
1910	(³)	(³)	(³)	(³)	(³)	(³)		22.3	(³)
1920	21,825,654	21,379,163	10,286,267	48.1	11,092,896	51.9	(³)	16.0	4.3
1930	26,982,904	26,492,256	13,288,429	50.2	13,203,827	49.8	23.6	16.3	4.1
1940	31,561,126	31,561,126	14,418,092	45.7	17,143,034	54.3	17.0	7.2	3.7
1950	39,043,595	39,043,595	22,240,970	57.0	16,802,625	43.0	23.7	14.1	3.5
Nonwhite									
1890	1,434,983	1,434,983	272,757	19.0	1,162,226	81.0			5.5
1900	1,900,174	1,769,881	417,143	23.6	1,352,738	76.4	32.4	17.1	4.8
1910	(³)	(³)	(³)	(³)	(³)	(³)		11.5	(³)
1920	2,526,022	2,431,395	580,693	23.9	1,850,702	76.1	(³)	6.5	4.3
1930	2,921,669	2,829,635	713,645	25.2	2,115,990	74.8	15.7	14.7	4.3
1940	3,293,406	3,293,406	777,671	23.6	2,515,735	76.4	12.7	7.7	4.1
1950	3,782,686	3,782,686	1,318,996	34.9	2,463,690	65.1	14.9	17.1	4.2
RESIDENCE									
Nonfarm									
1890	7,922,973	7,922,973	2,923,671	36.9	4,999,302	63.1			(³)
1900	10,274,127	9,779,979	3,566,809	36.5	6,213,170	63.5	29.7	(³)	(³)
1910	14,131,945	13,672,044	5,245,380	38.4	8,426,664	61.6	37.5	(³)	4.2
1920	17,600,472	17,229,394	7,041,283	40.9	10,188,111	59.1	24.5	(³)	4.0
1930	23,300,026	22,917,072	10,549,972	46.0	12,367,100	54.0	32.4	25.0	4.0
1940	27,747,973	27,747,973	11,413,036	41.1	16,334,937	58.9	19.1	9.5	3.7
1950	37,105,259	37,105,259	19,801,646	53.4	17,303,613	46.6	33.7	26.8	3.4
Farm[4]									
1890	4,767,179	4,767,179	3,142,746	65.9	1,624,432	34.1			(³)
1900	5,689,838	5,649,008	3,638,403	64.4	2,010,605	35.6	19.4	(³)	(³)
1910	6,123,610	6,109,562	3,826,331	62.8	2,271,231	37.2	7.6	(³)	4.7
1920	6,751,204	6,581,164	3,825,677	58.1	2,755,487	41.9	10.2	(³)	4.6
1930	6,604,637	6,404,819	3,452,102	53.9	2,952,717	46.1	-2.2	-4.6	4.3
1940	7,106,559	7,106,559	3,782,727	53.2	3,223,832	46.8	7.6	.2	4.3
1950	5,721,022	5,721,022	3,758,320	65.7	1,982,702	34.3	-19.5	-22.7	4.0

[1] "Occupied dwelling units" for 1940 and 1950 is not exactly same as "Families" for earlier years, but differences are so small as to be negligible. Count of families for 1900 and 1930 represents private families only; that for 1890, 1910, and 1920, includes small number of quasi-family groups which were counted as families in those years.

[2] Since population in private families was not tabulated separately for all years, population per occupied dwelling unit (or family) is based on total population (including population in quasi-households). See table 10, p. 14.

[3] Not available.

[4] For 1890 to 1920, "Farm" contains a small proportion of urban-farm families in addition to the rural-farm families. For changes in definition of "Farm," see "Farm and Nonfarm Residence," p. 3.

Source: Department of Commerce, Bureau of the Census, *U. S. Census of Housing: 1950*, Vol. I, Part 1.

No. 917.—DWELLING UNITS—OCCUPANCY, TENURE, AND RACE OF OCCUPANTS: 1940 AND 1950

[In thousands of dwelling units]

OCCUPANCY, TENURE, AND RACE OF OCCUPANTS	1950								1940, TOTAL	
	Number				Percent distribution				Number	Percent
	Total	Urban	Rural nonfarm	Rural farm	Total	Urban	Rural nonfarm	Rural farm		
All dwelling units................	45,983	29,569	10,056	6,358	100.0	100.0	100.0	100.0	37,325	100.0
Urban-farm dwelling units........	96	96	......	......	.2	.3	......	......	88	.2
Occupied dwelling units................	42,826	28,492	8,613	5,721	93.1	96.4	85.6	90.0	34,855	93.4
Owner occupied......................	23,560	14,377	5,425	3,758	51.2	48.6	53.9	59.1	15,196	40.7
White..............................	22,241	13,567	5,135	3,539	48.4	45.9	51.1	55.7	14,418	38.6
Negro............................	1,252	787	265	199	2.7	2.7	2.6	3.1	720	1.9
Other races.....................	67	22	25	20	.1	.1	.2	.3	58	.2
Renter occupied....................	19,266	14,116	3,188	1,963	41.9	47.7	31.7	30.9	19,659	52.7
White............................	16,803	12,434	2,846	1,522	36.5	42.1	28.3	23.9	17,143	45.9
Negro...........................	2,381	1,630	324	428	5.2	5.5	3.2	6.7	2,437	6.5
Other races.....................	82	51	18	13	.2	.2	.2	.2	79	.2
Nonresident dwelling units............	127	56	28	44	.3	.2	.3	.7	106	.3
Vacant dwelling units [1].............	3,030	1,021	1,416	593	6.6	3.5	14.1	9.3	2,365	6.3
Nonseasonal not dilapidated, for rent or sale........................	732	493	146	93	1.6	1.7	1.5	1.5	(²)	(²)
For rent [³]......................	517	354	106	57	1.1	1.2	1.1	.9	(²)	(²)
For sale only...................	215	138	40	36	.5	.5	.4	.6	(²)	(²)
Nonseasonal not dilapidated, not for rent or sale [⁴]...................	743	276	297	170	1.6	.9	3.0	2.7	(²)	(²)
Nonseasonal dilapidated.................	505	103	183	219	1.1	.3	1.8	3.4	(²)	(²)
Seasonal.............................	1,050	150	790	111	2.3	.5	7.9	1.7	678	1.8

[1] 1940 and 1950 data not strictly comparable. See text, p. 751.
[2] Not available.
[3] Includes those offered for rent or for sale.
[4] Includes units already rented or sold but not yet occupied, and units held off market for other reasons.

Source: Department of Commerce, Bureau of the Census; *U. S. Census of Housing: 1950*, Vol. I, Part 1, and Sixteenth Census Reports, *Housing*, Vol. II, Part 1.

No. 918.—DWELLING UNITS FOR GEOGRAPHIC DIVISIONS: 1950

REGION AND DIVISION	TOTAL		URBAN		RURAL NONFARM		RURAL FARM	
	Number	Percent	Number	Percent	Number	Percent	Number	Percent
United States................	45,983,398	100.0	29,569,073	100.0	10,056,382	100.0	6,357,943	100.0
Northeast:								
New England....................	2,879,409	6.3	2,080,539	7.0	676,930	6.7	121,940	1.9
Middle Atlantic................	9,171,773	19.9	7,271,291	24.6	1,498,371	14.9	402,111	6.3
North Central:								
East North Central.............	9,334,211	20.3	6,399,303	21.6	1,869,849	18.6	1,065,059	16.8
West North Central.............	4,411,435	9.6	2,274,630	7.7	1,050,053	10.4	1,086,752	17.1
South:								
South Atlantic..................	5,996,267	13.0	3,116,394	10.5	1,758,337	17.5	1,121,536	17.6
East South Central.............	3,195,164	6.9	1,330,434	4.5	851,620	8.5	1,013,110	15.9
West South Central.............	4,462,354	9.7	2,516,479	8.5	1,008,094	10.0	937,781	14.7
West:								
Mountain........................	1,608,421	3.5	884,417	3.0	468,824	4.7	255,180	4.0
Pacific.........................	4,924,364	10.7	3,695,586	12.5	874,304	8.7	354,474	5.6

Source: Department of Commerce, Bureau of the Census; *U. S. Census of Housing: 1950*, Vol. I, Part 1.

No, 919.—DWELLING UNITS—SELECTED HOUSING CHARACTERISTICS, BY STATES: 1950

DIVISION AND STATE	TOTAL DWELLING UNITS				ALL DWELLING UNITS, 1950			
						Percent of dwelling units—		
	1950	1940	Percent increase, 1940 to 1950	Median number of rooms	In one-dwelling-unit detached structures [1]	In structures built in 1940 or later [2]	With hot running water, private toilet and bath, not dilapidated	Vacant non-seasonal not dilapidated, for rent or sale
United States...	45,983,398	37,325,470	23.2	4.6	64.0	22.7	63.1	1.6
New England...	2,879,469	2,436,229	18.1	5.1	47.4	11.6	72.9	1.2
Maine...	311,441	280,630	10.5	5.3	67.9	12.0	52.4	1.4
New Hampshire...	190,563	158,044	20.6	5.2	61.6	11.5	64.8	1.6
Vermont...	121,911	106,362	14.6	5.5	66.1	9.0	65.3	1.6
Massachusetts...	1,400,185	1,221,222	14.7	5.3	40.6	9.5	79.2	1.0
Rhode Island...	244,147	203,400	20.0	4.9	40.3	11.9	68.2	1.4
Connecticut...	611,102	486,543	25.1	5.0	47.2	17.3	81.9	1.1
Middle Atlantic...	9,171,773	7,874,463	16.5	4.9	39.1	11.9	79.3	1.1
New York...	4,632,806	4,032,460	14.9	4.5	22.7	11.1	83.6	1.2
New Jersey...	1,501,473	1,223,487	22.7	5.0	46.7	15.2	83.5	1.2
Pennsylvania...	3,036,494	2,618,056	16.0	5.5	45.0	11.6	71.6	.9
E. N. Central...	9,354,211	7,661,568	21.5	5.0	64.9	16.2	66.1	1.0
Ohio...	2,402,565	1,977,608	21.5	5.2	66.1	14.5	69.5	.9
Indiana...	1,232,314	1,005,962	22.5	4.8	75.9	17.2	58.6	1.1
Illinois...	2,671,647	2,280,821	17.1	4.7	52.3	12.3	67.0	.9
Michigan...	1,971,842	1,519,378	29.8	5.1	71.9	22.6	70.4	1.2
Wisconsin...	1,056,843	897,719	17.6	5.2	66.1	14.1	66.5	1.0
W. N. Central...	4,411,435	3,915,963	12.7	4.8	75.4	14.9	59.9	1.1
Minnesota...	916,434	773,042	18.6	4.9	73.0	16.4	52.7	1.0
Iowa...	811,912	726,654	11.7	5.3	80.4	11.2	51.4	.8
Missouri...	1,268,354	1,140,493	11.2	4.3	67.8	14.1	45.5	1.1
North Dakota...	175,769	162,881	7.9	4.8	82.6	14.2	33.6	1.1
South Dakota...	194,573	179,744	8.3	5.0	82.8	14.2	38.0	1.0
Nebraska...	417,245	387,368	7.7	5.0	80.3	11.5	56.5	1.1
Kansas...	625,148	545,721	14.6	4.8	80.1	16.8	57.8	1.0
South Atlantic...	5,996,357	4,547,316	31.9	4.5	70.7	27.4	48.5	2.1
Delaware...	97,013	75,867	28.4	5.6	53.8	21.9	60.6	1.4
Maryland...	689,116	500,156	37.8	5.1	46.1	26.1	71.3	1.9
Dist. of Columbia...	229,788	186,128	24.1	4.1	13.2	22.3	87.0	1.2
Virginia...	901,483	659,787	36.6	4.7	71.5	29.0	49.7	1.7
West Virginia...	544,075	459,725	18.3	4.6	79.4	19.1	44.6	1.2
North Carolina...	1,055,367	820,688	28.9	4.5	83.3	28.0	34.5	1.4
South Carolina...	557,672	458,809	21.5	4.3	82.1	25.3	34.3	1.8
Georgia...	966,672	796,715	21.3	4.2	74.3	24.6	38.6	1.6
Florida...	952,131	560,451	61.3	4.2	73.2	39.2	60.1	5.1
E. S. Central...	3,196,164	2,736,526	16.8	4.2	80.1	24.6	32.7	1.4
Kentucky...	820,141	728,205	12.5	4.3	78.7	18.7	35.5	1.1
Tennessee...	921,537	742,030	24.2	4.2	75.6	26.7	36.0	1.5
Alabama...	843,557	706,043	19.2	4.1	79.3	27.3	31.6	1.6
Mississippi...	609,329	557,346	9.3	4.0	85.2	25.8	25.2	1.5
W. S. Central...	4,463,354	3,562,215	24.3	4.1	80.6	31.0	47.6	2.3
Arkansas...	575,163	520,613	10.5	4.0	84.5	26.9	28.7	1.6
Louisiana...	777,672	619,283	25.6	4.1	73.1	30.0	40.5	1.7
Oklahoma...	715,691	647,465	10.5	4.2	83.6	24.0	51.7	2.2
Texas...	2,393,828	1,804,854	32.6	4.1	79.6	34.4	53.2	2.5
Mountain...	1,666,431	1,238,888	29.9	4.6	75.9	36.0	63.3	2.7
Montana...	194,256	177,443	9.5	4.0	78.0	19.1	56.5	1.7
Idaho...	188,328	152,535	23.2	4.1	82.1	27.5	61.6	1.4
Wyoming...	92,066	76,568	19.8	3.9	78.3	26.7	60.5	1.0
Colorado...	436,226	354,360	23.0	4.2	71.9	22.7	61.1	1.9
New Mexico...	198,706	145,042	37.1	3.7	76.3	38.7	51.0	2.9
Arizona...	240,750	147,079	63.7	3.7	73.3	46.0	62.5	4.1
Utah...	200,554	147,291	34.2	4.2	76.5	29.1	79.2	2.2
Nevada...	56,515	34,770	62.7	3.8	75.6	55.6	73.7	3.6
Pacific...	4,934,344	3,368,628	46.3	4.3	71.3	38.5	83.5	2.7
Washington...	809,701	590,430	37.1	4.3	77.6	29.7	78.5	2.7
Oregon...	534,003	366,811	41.7	4.4	78.5	36.6	74.0	2.7
California...	3,590,680	2,540,375	46.4	4.3	68.6	34.9	86.0	2.7

[1] Includes occupied trailers.
[2] Based on 20-percent sample.

No. 919.—Dwelling Units—Selected Housing Characteristics, by States: 1950—Continued

DIVISION AND STATE	Total number	Popula-tion in dwelling units	Me-dian num-ber of per-sons	With 1.01 or more per-sons per room	Occu-pied by non-white	Own-er occu-pied	With cen-tral heat-ing [2]	With me-chan-ical refri-gera-tor [1]	Per-cent mort-gaged [2]	Median value of one-dwell-ing-unit struc-tures [4] (dol-lars)	Median contract monthly rent (dollars)	Median gross monthly rent (dollars)
				Percent of dwelling units								
U. S.	42,826,281	145,636,888	3.1	15.7	8.8	55.0	50.4	80.2	44.6	7,354	35.50	42.47
New England	2,613,421	8,880,812	3.1	9.9	1.4	58.9	65.9	86.2	56.6	8,943	38.45	45.06
Maine	254,443	881,015	3.1	12.1	.2	62.8	48.1	71.1	31.8	4,856	27.95	41.35
N. H.	155,203	509,828	3.0	8.9	.2	58.1	57.0	82.1	45.0	6,190	26.67	40.52
Vermont	103,496	363,298	3.1	9.0	.1	61.3	51.4	77.5	41.1	6,277	27.54	41.22
Mass.	1,305,194	4,455,319	3.1	9.8	1.5	47.9	71.4	87.2	62.6	9,144	31.61	46.80
R. I.	225,447	750,558	3.1	9.7	1.6	45.3	58.5	86.0	54.0	9,767	25.62	40.17
Conn.	569,638	1,922,794	3.1	9.7	2.2	51.1	68.9	93.6	61.1	11,862	31.85	45.18
Mid. Atlantic	8,614,655	28,987,149	3.1	11.4	4.8	47.7	79.4	90.1	48.9	8,627	38.42	44.37
New York	4,325,139	14,152,766	3.0	12.4	5.4	37.9	82.2	90.2	56.7	10,152	41.02	45.30
New Jersey	1,373,637	4,658,598	3.1	10.2	5.3	53.1	79.7	92.6	51.3	10,408	39.12	48.74
Pa.	2,915,879	10,175,785	3.2	10.7	5.5	59.7	75.0	88.7	40.7	6,992	31.28	39.76
E. N. Central	8,823,056	29,306,167	3.1	11.9	5.0	60.0	65.6	86.2	42.9	7,720	33.33	43.46
Ohio	2,313,990	7,692,196	3.0	10.9	5.4	61.1	66.5	87.5	45.2	8,304	34.28	41.56
Indiana	1,168,916	3,816,485	2.9	13.8	3.9	65.5	54.0	82.6	46.6	6,226	34.26	41.97
Illinois	2,582,600	8,341,171	3.0	12.6	6.6	50.1	68.7	87.8	39.9	8,646	41.91	47.19
Michigan	1,790,702	6,136,272	3.1	10.9	5.4	67.5	68.2	87.0	43.6	7,496	40.29	47.36
Wisconsin	967,448	3,320,043	3.1	11.2	.9	63.5	64.4	81.9	37.8	7,937	37.85	45.99
W. N. Central	4,148,910	13,581,307	2.9	13.8	3.1	61.3	78.9	78.9	36.2	6,391	33.76	39.83
Minnesota	845,265	2,876,145	3.1	13.0	.8	66.4	60.1	79.5	41.1	7,805	35.72	43.27
Iowa	780,167	2,538,841	2.9	10.3	.7	63.4	57.3	82.3	32.3	6,320	34.80	42.53
Missouri	1,197,597	3,813,053	2.8	16.8	6.8	57.7	47.2	76.0	41.1	6,399	30.38	36.44
N. Dak.	162,105	600,012	3.4	20.5	1.2	66.2	51.9	68.1	22.8	5,396	36.14	42.80
S. Dak.	182,978	631,235	3.1	15.4	2.5	62.2	41.4	73.6	25.0	5,410	33.54	42.30
Nebraska	394,148	1,279,013	2.9	12.6	1.5	60.6	51.5	82.1	32.0	5,918	36.71	42.50
Kansas	586,650	1,843,008	2.8	11.6	3.6	63.9	41.8	82.1	33.7	5,462	35.43	37.55
S. Atlantic	5,539,658	20,344,644	3.3	21.4	20.9	52.1	27.2	69.5	42.6	6,391	28.92	35.91
Delaware	90,390	307,314	3.1	9.6	12.1	58.9	65.2	83.2	51.0	9,079	35.80	46.03
Maryland	641,222	2,245,275	3.2	12.3	13.6	56.3	70.3	81.9	49.0	8,033	39.68	46.16
D. C.	224,142	715,861	2.7	14.1	27.9	32.3	90.8	92.0	60.1	14,498	53.72	57.09
Virginia	845,250	3,141,756	3.3	19.1	19.4	55.1	34.9	72.6	43.5	6,581	31.71	39.16
W. Va.	518,281	1,963,114	3.4	22.6	5.3	55.0	25.1	74.2	32.5	5,478	21.63	28.43
N. C.	994,356	3,931,516	3.5	25.1	22.7	53.3	14.8	64.1	36.4	4,901	20.83	29.58
S. C.	514,638	2,061,697	3.5	28.9	34.5	45.1	8.0	58.6	40.2	5,112	17.39	26.03
Georgia	889,269	3,335,172	3.3	27.2	28.0	46.5	14.2	58.5	40.2	5,235	19.97	27.42
Florida	821,501	2,642,939	2.8	18.0	18.8	57.6	6.5	71.4	42.1	6,512	38.46	39.35
E. S. Central	2,991,832	11,192,665	3.3	27.9	22.0	53.6	16.6	60.4	34.9	4,933	21.63	38.11
Kentucky	778,754	2,865,393	3.2	25.1	7.3	58.7	24.8	65.9	38.5	5,283	24.66	30.77
Tennessee	871,474	3,200,784	3.3	25.3	15.5	56.5	20.3	65.6	37.2	5,268	24.13	30.73
Alabama	786,839	2,999,317	3.4	30.5	29.3	49.4	11.2	58.7	34.6	4,473	17.51	24.52
Mississippi	554,765	2,128,171	3.3	32.1	42.3	47.8	7.0	46.6	29.4	4,150	18.81	24.62
W. S. Central	4,101,717	14,102,683	3.0	23.7	15.9	55.8	22.5	69.5	37.3	5,446	31.57	33.60
Arkansas	524,391	1,874,484	3.1	26.7	21.2	54.5	10.1	55.1	29.1	4,087	22.60	27.91
Louisiana	724,945	2,616,079	3.2	26.2	30.8	50.3	16.7	62.5	37.1	5,141	22.21	26.74
Oklahoma	663,203	2,166,511	2.9	20.0	7.8	60.0	20.9	72.4	40.0	5,228	32.78	34.20
Texas	2,189,178	7,445,609	3.0	23.3	12.1	56.7	11.1	74.3	37.9	5,805	33.96	37.13
Mountain	1,445,433	4,877,377	3.0	22.8	3.4	59.4	38.8	77.1	38.8	6,582	34.65	40.29
Montana	175,470	566,284	2.9	19.0	2.1	60.3	40.0	77.0	27.2	5,797	35.35	40.83
Idaho	169,110	572,854	3.1	22.2	1.0	65.5	31.8	82.5	34.7	5,852	35.91	43.85
Wyoming	84,185	274,991	3.0	22.2	1.6	54.0	37.9	77.5	36.9	6,811	38.41	41.22
Colorado	391,235	1,257,727	2.9	18.0	1.8	58.1	52.2	77.6	41.7	7,151	36.31	39.25
N. Mex.	176,993	659,051	3.3	34.0	5.6	58.8	23.9	63.5	36.2	5,697	39.19	40.93
Arizona	210,374	721,992	3.0	27.6	9.7	56.4	19.0	72.2	42.8	5,936	35.50	36.83
Utah	187,825	673,447	3.3	23.4	1.4	65.3	54.8	88.3	42.7	7,409	36.05	39.93
Nevada	50,241	151,031	2.6	16.3	5.2	48.7	25.4	80.3	39.6	8,859	42.33	47.34
Pacific	4,548,199	13,757,084	2.7	12.2	4.1	57.2	43.2	84.0	49.9	8,872	39.56	42.62
Wash.	735,746	2,243,893	2.7	11.3	2.0	65.0	43.5	81.6	43.0	7,169	36.57	43.46
Oregon	479,047	1,467,556	2.8	12.7	1.2	65.3	36.6	80.6	40.3	6,846	38.01	44.19
California	3,333,406	10,045,635	2.7	12.3	5.0	54.3	44.1	85.1	53.0	9,564	40.48	42.30

[1] Based on 20-percent sample.
[2] Restricted to units in 1- to 4-dwelling-unit structures without business.
[4] Restricted to 1-dwelling-unit properties without business.

Source: Department of Commerce, Bureau of the Census; U. S. Census of Housing: 1950, Vol. 1, Part 1, and Sixteenth Census Reports, Housing, Vol. II, Part 1.

929.—Dwelling Units—Selected Characteristics for Standard Metropolitan Areas: 1950

[Detailed explanation of standard metropolitan area concept, and data for geographic components of each area, see source and *County and City Data Book, 1952*, a supplement to the *Statistical Abstract*]

STANDARD METROPOLITAN AREA	TOTAL DWELLING UNITS		ALL DWELLING UNITS, 1950		OCCUPIED DWELLING UNITS, 1950				
			Percent in structures built in 1940 or later [1]	Percent with hot running water, private toilet and bath, not dilapidated				Nonfarm	
	1940	1950			Total number	Percent owner-occupied	Percent occupied by non-white	Median value [2]	Median gross monthly rent [3]
(Ohio) area	92,994	122,545	19.0	79.3	119,444	69.4	5.0	8,511	42.94
...ny-Schenectady-Troy (N.Y.) area	142,085	160,114	10.6	79.4	158,713	52.9	1.4		44.20
...querque (N. Mex.) area	19,039	43,443	54.2	68.4	40,340	62.0	2.3		
...town-Bethlehem-Easton (Pa.) area	106,671	127,183	11.1	72.4	122,287	61.6		7,472	
...na (Pa.) area	37,227	40,941	6.5	70.1	39,158	64.0			
...lic (Tex.) area	17,790	32,280	46.9	76.3	30,805	58.8	4.0	7,110	
...ville (N. C.) area	29,323	34,616	20.2	53.5	32,649	50.6	11.4		
...na (Ga.) area	146,027	192,552	20.1	61.9	186,250	59.6	21.0		
...tic City (N. J.) area	41,232	44,604	9.4	56.4	40,155	54.7	14.2	7,467	
...ta (Ga.) area	35,340	44,006	22.9	42.6	42,450	41.5	56.2	4,984	
...n (Tex.) area	35,320	42,606	28.4	67.5	42,505	53.4	12.8	7,094	
...more (Md.) area	300,346	362,263	22.5	76.7	350,235	55.0	14.2	7,080	
...n Rouge (La.) area	22,940	34,087	47.1	62.5	42,162	50.3	21.0	7,165	37.65
... City (Mich.) area	20,514	26,417	29.6	67.7	24,808	75.7	.4	6,178	41.11
...ont-Port Arthur (Tex.) area	40,584	52,586	31.3	66.6	55,776	58.2	22.3	6,736	
...ton (N. Y.) area	44,942	55,354	13.9	84.2	52,640	58.4		8,159	
...ngham (Ala.) area	122,744	158,377	14.6	49.2	146,545	50.7	34.1	4,830	
...n (Miss.) area		667,412	6.9	87.5	648,166	44.5	2.2	10,830	51.81
...port (Conn.) area	(4)	77,919	20.0	84.6	74,954	62.1	2.6	12,163	44.32
...ton (Miss.) area		28,996	5.6	83.2	27,825	58.0	.6	7,806	42.15
...lo (N. Y.) area	294,692	317,423	13.9	84.5	306,000	58.2	3.4	9,692	45.66
...n (Ohio) area	43,471	58,152	19.1	78.1	50,906	53.9	3.3	7,690	41.46
...Rapids (Iowa) area	37,156	23,789	14.0	64.3	31,221	64.9	.7	6,329	42.15
...ston (S.C.) area	34,340	47,157	19.3	64.4	45,287	41.5	44.4	6,627	
...ston (W. Va.) area	65,694	67,464	38.2	38.2	64,844	47.6	6.4	6,440	31.45
...otte (N. C.) area	37,175	54,132	23.3	62.2	52,608	44.8	23.4	8,194	
...anooga (Tenn.) area	65,600	71,380	34.3	52.1	68,710	53.7	17.0	5,372	
...go (Ill.) area	1,254,322	1,652,387	11.6	78.3	1,607,490	41.8	9.1	11,477	
...mati (Ohio) area	340,929	392,967	12.0	72.1	378,401	48.1	10.3	10,170	
...land (Ohio) area	364,534	438,902	14.2	86.7	427,768	53.4	8.5	12,135	
...mbia (S. C.) area	35,399	35,189	36.1	57.1	34,306	45.2	30.0	7,690	
...mbus (Ga.) area	35,990	61,750	39.3	39.6	41,664	37.9	32.4	6,640	
...mbus (Ohio) area	106,737	140,214	29.3	78.0	146,654	53.7	8.9	9,550	
...s Christi (Tex.) area	27,041	53,077	47.9	61.5	49,648	47.9	6.2	7,681	
...s (Tex.) area	130,164	197,308	41.5	73.9	187,172	57.2	12.4	7,696	45.70
...port (Iowa)-Rock Island-Moline (Ill.) area	67,257	76,326	16.5	68.5	66,302	60.5	1.2	9,185	
...n (Ohio) area	64,632	152,337	27.5	68.6	132,822	58.6	7.1	9,341	
...ur (Ill.) area	24,949	31,484	16.2	68.1	30,680	64.4	3.9	7,690	
...er (Colo.) area	128,351	151,410	27.2	74.4	172,504	55.5	3.0	9,165	41.13
...Moines (Iowa) area	65,444	72,609	17.5	66.2	70,138	66.7	3.6	7,360	
...t (Mich.) area	645,940	645,027	26.9	82.9	628,822	61.6	9.3	9,946	46.44
...que (Iowa) area	14,288	19,611	16.2	45.6	18,574	60.2	.1	8,390	
...th (Minn.)-Superior (Wis.) area	76,147	84,901	11.6	46.6	73,620	64.7	.4	6,116	34.23
...am (N. C.) area		36,917	29.2	41.9		41.1	30.4	8,119	34.14
...o (Tex.) area		35,764	40.9	46.6		44.1	3.3	6,661	
...a (Pa.) area		34,812	14.0	77.6		61.1	1.1	7,690	
...ville (Ind.) area		54,573	24.4	66.9	47,897	54.7	4.2	7,670	
...River (Mass.) area	(4)	42,632		46.9	36,714	54.7		6,115	
...(Mich.) area		42,652	9.4	86.6		78.6	1.6		
...Wayne (Ind.) area	47,315	56,444	18.5	76.5	54,616	68.2	1.6	9,185	
...Worth (Tex.) area	87,190	114,512	41.1	62.2		56.7	14.4		
...o (Calif.) area		63,642	34.5						
...den (Ala.) area		20,206	27.4						
...eston (Tex.) area		34,642							
...d Rapids (Mich.) area		87,191							
...n Bay (Wis.) area									
...sboro-High Point (N. C.) area	37,490	58,547	24.9	45.4		55.5	17.5	5,958	34.50

No. 920.—Dwelling Units—Selected Characteristics for Standard Metropolitan Areas: 950—Continued

STANDARD METROPOLITAN AREA	TOTAL DWELLING UNITS		ALL DWELLING UNITS, 1950		OCCUPIED DWELLING UNITS, 1950			Nonfarm	
	1940	1950	Percent in structures built in 1940 or later [1]	Percent with hot running water, private toilet and bath, not dilapidated	Total number	Percent owner-occupied	Percent occupied by nonwhite	Median value [2]	Median gross monthly rent [3]
Greenville (S. C.) area	35,093	47,857	28.9	48.6	45,345	48.1	17.0	6,311	28.60
Hamilton-Middletown (Ohio) area	33,366	42,173	19.0	61.3	41,124	63.7	4.6	8,205	40.24
Hampton-Newport News-Warwick (Va.) area	20,262	40,360	(4)	(4)	(4)	(4)	(4)	(4)	(4)
Harrisburg (Pa.) area	69,510	87,356	15.1	70.8	83,970	57.9	4.5	7,497	42.77
Hartford (Conn.) area	(4)	103,456	20.9	88.4	101,071	44.5	3.2	13,277	49.67
Houston (Tex.) area	154,628	257,154	42.7	73.2	240,392	55.5	17.5	7,403	45.20
Huntington (W. Va.)-Ashland (Ky.) area	56,934	70,165	19.0	59.1	67,321	60.5	2.9	6,102	31.66
Indianapolis (Ind.) area	136,877	171,642	18.9	69.0	167,571	58.5	10.5	7,544	44.03
Jackson (Mich.) area	27,764	33,254	14.3	63.2	30,814	73.6	2.4	6,157	45.55
Jackson (Miss.) area	27,404	40,111	39.3	53.0	37,809	46.8	40.8	7,876	34.41
Jacksonville (Fla.) area	57,816	91,027	35.0	62.0	85,277	55.8	23.4	6,905	39.05
Johnstown (Pa.) area	70,447	78,749	10.6	54.2	76,209	58.5	1.0	5,205	30.99
Kalamazoo (Mich.) area	29,768	38,853	20.5	69.8	36,664	70.5	1.6	7,315	46.45
Kansas City (Mo.) area	218,880	263,708	15.7	70.3	256,223	58.3	10.4	7,006	38.51
Kenosha (Wis.) area	19,387	25,413	20.0	72.7	21,988	62.6	.3	8,866	48.34
Knoxville (Tenn.) area	61,832	94,610	35.3	53.8	88,809	56.3	7.8	5,067	36.42
Lancaster (Pa.) area	56,950	67,376	11.4	67.0	65,128	59.4	1.1	7,821	38.26
Lansing (Mich.) area	38,491	50,953	23.0	71.1	49,613	66.3	1.6	7,042	46.87
Laredo (Tex.) area	11,044	14,117	28.7	32.3	12,823	56.4	.3	2,178	18.39
Lawrence (Mass.) area	(4)	37,955	6.1	74.7	36,959	39.3	.3	9,210	42.06
Lexington (Ky.) area	21,963	27,905	18.1	65.9	27,124	49.0	16.7	8,698	36.74
Lima (Ohio) area	20,650	26,662	17.3	68.6	25,969	60.0	3.7	6,895	44.03
Lincoln (Nebr.) area	30,844	37,116	14.6	74.5	35,991	57.3	.9	7,134	42.12
Little Rock-North Little Rock (Ark.) area	43,567	59,228	29.1	60.0	56,569	54.7	22.4	6,425	36.97
Lorain-Elyria (Ohio) area	31,666	43,044	22.6	77.0	41,326	68.3	3.8	9,154	44.55
Los Angeles (Calif.) area	1,010,550	1,521,849	33.9	91.0	1,440,451	54.1	5.0	9,899	44.61
Louisville (Ky.) area	130,827	170,858	21.2	64.5	166,112	55.6	11.5	7,212	36.62
Lowell (Mass.) area	(4)	38,489	7.5	69.2	36,178	49.1	.2	6,460	39.19
Lubbock (Tex.) area	14,888	31,475	52.9	63.9	28,230	50.5	5.9	7,370	48.19
Macon (Ga.) area	26,822	38,859	30.7	48.3	37,196	41.6	33.7	4,924	27.52
Madison (Wis.) area	37,514	48,022	18.8	64.9	46,082	58.1	.5	10,919	54.50
Manchester (N. H.) area	(4)	27,192	9.9	73.2	26,000	42.3	.3	7,866	37.88
Memphis (Tenn.) area	99,413	137,985	29.5	55.4	133,683	48.0	34.8	7,725	33.00
Miami (Fla.) area	90,472	180,658	48.2	82.6	154,462	53.9	9.7	9,473	56.46
Milwaukee (Wis.) area	216,530	253,384	14.3	81.5	249,036	49.8	1.9	11,922	56.18
Minneapolis-St. Paul (Minn.) area	276,575	337,792	16.9	75.2	327,791	60.3	1.3	9,963	44.68
Mobile (Ala.) area	37,134	67,044	41.2	50.2	62,138	53.4	32.2	4,511	32.53
Montgomery (Ala.) area	30,462	40,459	28.5	51.8	37,740	39.7	39.9	7,151	30.23
Muncie (Ind.) area	22,181	28,330	20.7	63.6	27,308	63.6	4.8	6,102	40.25
Nashville (Tenn.) area	69,639	91,575	24.9	56.0	88,741	52.9	19.3	6,808	31.51
New Bedford (Mass.) area	(4)	43,241	6.0	46.1	41,127	41.0	2.1	7,189	36.03
New Britain-Bristol (Conn.) area	(4)	43,436	20.3	83.3	42,505	49.0	.8	10,615	42.96
New Haven (Conn.) area	(4)	77,482	12.3	83.7	75,108	46.6	3.7	11,914	44.45
New Orleans (La.) area	152,284	207,086	23.8	60.0	197,311	38.3	27.7	8,956	28.30
New York-Northeastern New Jersey area	3,421,913	3,953,876	12.2	87.8	3,774,306	31.7	6.8	11,144	49.27
Norfolk-Portsmouth (Va.) area	69,417	119,623	38.6	67.7	113,532	42.7	26.7	6,659	40.09
Ogden (Utah) area	15,914	24,696	33.1	85.4	23,574	59.1	2.3	7,417	37.89
Oklahoma City (Okla.) area	76,025	108,083	34.2	76.5	101,924	58.5	7.8	7,536	39.94
Omaha (Nebr.) area	94,514	107,762	12.2	73.1	105,407	63.4	4.3	7,137	46.69
Orlando (Fla.) area	23,298	40,212	41.0	65.2	35,833	61.4	16.2	7,540	38.50
Peoria (Ill.) area	61,113	76,675	21.7	64.4	74,119	63.9	2.1	7,784	43.80
Philadelphia (Pa.) area	875,513	1,052,537	13.4	83.0	1,017,729	61.9	12.1	7,593	44.50
Phoenix (Ariz.) area	64,358	108,047	52.6	70.0	96,435	57.0	5.8	6,615	37.19
Pittsburgh (Pa.) area	537,809	628,470	14.5	67.9	614,557	54.8	5.4	7,740	40.10
Pittsfield (Mass.) area	(4)	19,627	10.0	88.3	18,997	53.1	1.0	9,688	48.63
Portland (Maine) area	(4)	37,801	12.2	81.3	34,994	46.0	.3	8,341	45.27
Portland (Oreg.) area	174,190	243,840	30.3	83.1	229,046	65.6	1.7	7,472	44.14
Providence (R. I.) area	(4)	221,800	10.6	62.3	211,471	45.3	1.3	9,714	39.53
Pueblo (Colo.) area	19,331	25,551	20.5	60.3	24,357	63.7	2.0	6,228	35.51

See footnotes at end of table.

920.—DWELLING UNITS—SELECTED CHARACTERISTICS FOR STANDARD METROPOLITAN AREAS: 1950—Continued

ARD METROPOLITAN AREA	TOTAL DWELLING UNITS		ALL DWELLING UNITS, 1950		OCCUPIED DWELLING UNITS, 1950				
		Percent in structures built in 1940 or later [1]	Percent with hot running water, private toilet and bath, not dilapidated	Total number	Percent owner-occupied	Percent occupied by non-white	Nonfarm	
							Median value [2]	Median gross monthly rent [3]
(Wis.) area	27,633	112	16.5	70.9	31,402	64.2	1.3	9,306	44.49
h (N. C.) area	25,248	539	27.3	50.1	33,249	46.4	25.0	7,360	34.57
ng (Pa.) area	60,503	843	8.9	72.5	73,230	64.3	.9	7,014	38.57
ond (Va.) area	71,094	539	20.3	47.8	90,987	54.7	23.1	8,000	40.15
ke (Va.) area	28,905	990	22.3	67.7	36,660	63.2	11.6	7,180	41.23
ster (N. Y.) area	127,776	923	10.9	88.5	143,685	60.9	1.3	9,739	46.76
rd (Ill.) area	35,453	875	23.3	65.9	43,645	00.7	1.9	9,345	45.77
nento (Calif.) area	51,715	253	42.7	84.0	82,728	63.4	4.7	8,110	43.10
w (Mich.) area	35,802	491	17.3	62.4	42,931	72.2	4.6	8,400	43.36
sph (Mo.) area	28,673	624	5.7	57.6	28,610	53.6	3.0	4,497	33.13
uis (Mo.) area	608	213	14.9	65.9	494,235	51.4	11.5	8,919	38.12
ake City (Utah) area	071	490	26.6	87.8	78,377	61.9	1.2	8,865	44.35
ngelo (Tex.) area	283	175	41.7	65.0	16,073	60.7	5.0	4,954	42.02
ntonio (Tex.) area	252	853	32.7	60.9	130,959	57.5	6.7	4,694	34.57
ernardino (Calif.) area	175	428	42.5	81.2	85,631	62.5	2.5	7,116	38.84
iego (Calif.) area	245	440	44.5	83.8	160,010	52.7	3.4	8,446	41.59
rancisco-Oakland (Calif.)									
	518	668	29.9	90.5	706,207	49.1	7.5	11,333	41.82
us (Calif.) area	406	670	34.4	80.4	85,421	64.8	2.5	10,644	44.45
nah (Ga.) area	281	928	23.9	53.4	43,074	37.6	37.3	6,192	28.85
on (Pa.) area	450	000	1.5	73.5	71,769	52.6	.3	5,719	37.50
(Wash.) area	151	306	31.0	86.9	236,278	63.2	3.5	8,768	44.65
eport (La.) area	566	677	20.1	53.3	50,358	50.1	34.3	7,376	38.02
City (Iowa) area	630	945	8.6	61.2	31,253	60.7	1.0	7,008	43.32
Falls (S. Dak.) area	923	627	23.7	60.9	20,600	69.2	.3	8,059	43.76
Bend (Ind.) area	842	732	24.6	74.4	50,230	73.0	3.5	7,364	47.60
ne (Wash.) area	376	505	25.4	83.5	68,949	66.4	1.0	7,215	44.01
field (Ill.) area	943	848	15.9	68.3	40,659	61.8	3.3	8,961	43.97
field (Mo.) area	012	562	21.6	54.1	33,007	55.1	1.9	6,514	33.72
field (Ohio) area	540	507	16.1	69.0	32,733	57.3	7.9	7,985	41.43
field-Holyoke (Mass.)									
		294	12.5	85.0	113,531	47.4	1.5	9,114	44.64
ord-Norwalk (Conn.)									
		909	18.4	89.2	55,329	56.0	3.1	14,308	55.82
on (Calif.) area	210	430	32.7	78.9	58,004	60.1	7.0	7,314	35.35
se (N. Y.) area	649	206	11.4	78.0	90,803	54.8	1.3	9,861	44.70
a (Wash.) area	372	258	27.4	83.1	78,850	60.5	1.9	9,960	41.31
a-St. Petersburg (Fla.)									
	775	612	36.4	65.0	131,683	61.7	11.7	6,725	36.85
Haute (Ind.) area	135	988	10.0	49.8	33,510	65.4	4.0	4,554	34.04
o (Ohio) area	903	111	15.3	83.1	116,599	65.4	4.9	8,000	44.39
a (Kans.) area	009	917	16.6	67.7	32,774	65.4	7.0	6,488	44.61
a (N. J.) area	502	784	14.2	84.6	59,383	63.6	6.5	7,810	48.17
(Okla.) area	857	251	29.7	73.2	78,003	60.2	8.4	7,817	54.95
Rome (N. Y.) area	343	149	8.1	72.8	79,081	57.4	.7	7,690	42.39
(Tex.) area	114	168	30.1	65.3	37,650	56.8	16.0	6,877	32.47
ngton (D. C.) area	997	885	35.2	87.1	405,111	42.6	18.2	14,062	60.55
bury (Conn.) area		210	15.5	81.0	42,879	49.0	2.1	11,085	42.76
loo (Iowa) area	653	938	22.3	61.8	29,189	65.0	1.8	7,886	44.64
ing (W. Va.)-Steuben									
(Ohio) area	218	644	9.9	61.0	100,362	58.6	3.0	6,376	31.92
ta (Kans.) area	503	829	30.3	77.8	69,426	57.5	4.1	7,781	39.48
ta Falls (Tex.) area	577	374	21.8	62.9	20,173	53.5	6.5	5,566	41.43
-Barre—Hazleton (Pa.)									
	105,633	931	4.1	72.4	106,663	53.7	.2	6,440	30.05
ngton (Del.) area	60,025	453	22.8	77.7	75,075	57.6	10.4	9,675	47.92
n-Salem (N. C.) area	32,205	41,338	21.6	47.4	39,094	54.8	27.7	6,435	38.38
ter (Mass.) area	(*)	70,586	9.5	79.3	74,442	46.1	.9	9,383	44.46
Pa.) area	50,104	61,054	13.5	62.1	58,912	64.4	1.3	7,189	38.11
stown (Ohio) area	121,012	149,623	16.8	71.9	145,863	68.5	5.3	7,627	41.71

No. 921.—Dwelling Units—Type of Structure, Number of Rooms, Number of Persons, and Persons Per Room: 1940 and 1950

[In thousands of dwelling units. Percent not shown where less than 0.1]

	1950								1940, TOTAL	
	Number				Percent distribution					
SUBJECT	Total	Urban	Rural non-farm	Rural farm	Total	Urban	Rural non-farm	Rural farm	Number	Per-cent
TYPE OF STRUCTURE										
Total dwelling units........	45,963	29,569	10,056	6,358	100.0	100.0	100.0	100.0	37,325	100.0
1 to 4 dwelling unit..........	40,591	24,470	9,788	6,332	88.3	82.8	97.3	99.6	33,397	89.5
1 dwelling unit, detached [1].....	29,116	14,471	8,567	6,078	63.3	48.9	85.2	95.6	23,898	64.0
1 dwelling unit, attached.......	1,210	1,056	110	44	2.6	3.6	1.1	.7	(²)	(²)
1 and 2 dwelling unit, semi-detached.....................	1,589	1,312	237	40	3.5	4.4	2.4	.6	(²)	(²)
2 dwelling unit, other..........	5,302	4,518	634	149	11.5	15.3	6.3	2.3	(²)	(²)
3 and 4 dwelling unit [1]........	3,374	3,113	240	21	7.3	10.5	2.4	.3	2,259	6.1
5 to 9 dwelling unit............	2,138	2,028	102	8	4.6	6.9	1.0	.1	1,492	4.0
10 to 19 dwelling unit..........	1,085	1,051	29	4	2.4	3.6	.3	.1	854	2.3
20 dwelling unit or more........	1,855	1,846	8	1	4.0	6.2	.1	......	1,582	4.2
Trailers.....................	315	174	128	12	.7	.6	1.3	.2	(²)	(²)
NUMBER OF ROOMS										
Total dwelling units......	45,963	29,569	10,056	6,358	......	......	......	......	37,325	......
Number reporting................	44,898	29,044	9,687	6,167	100.0	100.0	100.0	100.0	36,832	100.0
1 room.....................	1,296	836	349	110	2.9	2.9	3.6	1.8	1,307	3.5
2 rooms....................	3,384	2,233	828	323	7.5	7.7	8.5	5.2	3,215	8.7
3 rooms....................	6,670	4,582	1,408	680	14.9	15.8	14.5	11.0	5,332	14.5
4 rooms....................	9,814	6,195	2,326	1,293	21.9	21.3	24.0	21.0	6,892	18.7
5 rooms....................	9,522	6,486	1,904	1,131	21.2	22.3	19.7	18.3	7,302	19.8
6 rooms....................	7,565	5,044	1,450	1,070	16.8	17.4	15.0	17.4	6,322	17.2
7 rooms....................	3,320	1,965	704	651	7.4	6.8	7.3	10.6	2,869	7.8
8 rooms....................	1,835	953	398	483	4.1	3.3	4.1	7.8	1,886	5.1
9 rooms....................	1,493	749	319	425	3.3	2.6	3.3	6.9	1,707	4.6
Not reported...................	1,086	525	369	191					493	
Median number of rooms........	4.6	4.6	4.5	5.1	......	......	......	......	4.7	......
NUMBER OF PERSONS										
Occupied dwelling units...	42,826	28,492	8,613	5,721	100.0	100.0	100.0	100.0	34,855	100.0
1 person...................	3,993	2,839	867	288	9.3	10.0	10.1	5.0	2,677	7.7
2 persons..................	12,023	8,340	2,347	1,336	28.1	29.3	27.2	23.4	8,630	24.4
3 persons..................	9,763	6,727	1,870	1,165	22.8	23.6	21.7	20.4	7,796	22.4
4 persons..................	7,878	5,287	1,557	1,034	18.4	18.6	18.1	18.1	6,325	18.1
5 persons..................	4,466	2,813	921	733	10.4	9.9	10.7	12.8	4,013	11.5
6 persons..................	2,258	1,302	491	465	5.3	4.6	5.7	8.1	2,360	6.8
7 persons..................	1,160	613	261	285	2.7	2.2	3.0	5.0	1,341	3.8
8 persons..................	594	282	139	174	1.4	1.0	1.6	3.0	768	2.2
9 persons..................	324	141	77	106	.8	.5	.9	1.9	436	1.3
10 persons or more..........	367	148	84	135	.9	.5	1.0	2.4	509	1.5
Median number of persons......	3.1	3.0	3.1	3.6	......	......	......	......	3.3	......
PERSONS PER ROOM										
Occupied dwelling units...	42,826	28,492	8,613	5,721	......	......	......	......	34,855	......
Number reporting................	42,154	28,096	8,451	5,606	100.0	100.0	100.0	100.0	34,447	100.0
0.75 or less..................	25,357	17,245	4,895	3,216	60.2	61.4	57.9	57.4	18,910	54.9
0.76 to 1.00.................	10,170	7,119	1,912	1,140	24.1	25.3	22.6	20.3	8,573	24.9
1.01 to 1.50.................	4,020	2,426	916	678	9.5	8.6	10.8	12.1	3,879	11.3
1.51 or more.................	2,606	1,308	728	572	6.2	4.7	8.6	10.2	3,086	9.0
Not reported...................	672	395	162	115					408	

[1] 1950 statistics include units with business; 1940 statistics exclude units with business and include "other dwelling places."
[2] 1940 classification not strictly comparable with 1950. See source publication.
[3] Included with "1 dwelling unit, detached."

Source: Department of Commerce, Bureau of the Census; *U. S. Census of Housing: 1950*, Vol. I, Part 1, and Sixteenth Census Reports, *Housing*, Vol. II, Part 1.

No. 922.—DWELLING UNITS—YEAR BUILT: 1950

[In thousands of dwelling units. Asterisk (*) denotes statistics based on 20-percent sample]

YEAR BUILT	NUMBER				PERCENT DISTRIBUTION			
	Total	Urban	Rural non-farm	Rural farm	Total	Urban	Rural non-farm	Rural farm
All dwelling units	45,983	29,860	10,085	6,368				
Number reporting year built*	44,290	28,547	9,585	6,145	100.0	100.0	100.0	100.0
1945 or later	5,946	3,366	1,954	626	13.4	11.8	20.5	10.2
1940 to 1944	3,228	2,154	757	317	7.3	7.5	7.9	5.2
1930 to 1939	5,868	3,303	1,678	918	13.3	11.6	17.5	14.9
1920 to 1929	8,904	6,464	1,439	1,000	20.1	22.6	15.0	16.3
1919 or earlier	20,364	13,350	3,719	3,286	45.8	46.4	39.0	53.4

Source: Department of Commerce, Bureau of the Census; U. S. Census of Housing: 1950, Vol. I, Part 1.

No. 923.—DWELLING UNITS—WATER SUPPLY, CONDITION AND PLUMBING FACILITIES, AND KITCHEN SINK: 1950

[In thousands of dwelling units. Asterisk (*) denotes statistics based on 20-percent sample]

SUBJECT	NUMBER				PERCENT DISTRIBUTION			
	Total	Urban	Rural non-farm	Rural farm	Total	Urban	Rural non-farm	Rural farm
All dwelling units	45,983	29,560	10,056	6,368				
WATER SUPPLY								
Number reporting	45,299	29,240	9,709	6,249	100.0	100.0	100.0	100.0
Hot and cold piped running water inside structure	31,759	25,063	4,922	1,784	70.1	85.7	50.2	28.5
Only cold piped running water inside structure	5,746	3,119	1,740	887	12.7	10.7	17.8	14.2
Piped running water outside structure	1,064	560	335	169	2.3	1.9	3.4	2.7
No piped running water	6,720	500	2,802	3,409	14.8	1.7	28.6	54.6
Not reported	696	320	257	109				
CONDITION AND PLUMBING FACILITIES								
Number reporting	44,502	28,763	9,606	6,135	100.0	100.0	100.0	100.0
Not dilapidated:								
With private toilet and bath, and hot running water [1]	28,102	22,371	4,301	1,431	63.1	77.8	44.9	23.3
With private toilet and bath, and only cold water [1]	1,435	935	373	128	3.2	3.2	3.9	2.1
With running water, lacking private toilet or bath	5,491	3,034	1,537	921	13.2	10.6	16.0	15.0
No running water [2]	5,123	569	2,104	2,460	11.5	2.0	21.9	40.1
Dilapidated: [3]								
With private toilet and bath, and hot running water	627	510	86	30	1.4	1.8	.9	.5
Lacking hot water, private toilet or bath	3,713	1,344	1,204	1,164	8.3	4.7	12.5	19.0
Condition or plumbing facilities not reported	1,481	806	452	223				
Occupied dwelling units	42,836	28,492	8,612	5,721				
KITCHEN SINK [4]								
Number reporting	42,186	28,006	8,459	5,620	100.0	100.0	100.0	100.0
With kitchen sink	35,911	26,509	6,113	3,057	85.1	94.7	72.6	54.5
No kitchen sink	6,275	1,497	2,345	2,543	14.9	5.3	28.5	45.2

[1] Units with both flush toilet and bathtub (or shower) inside structure.
[2] Includes units with only piped running water outside structure.
[3] Below generally accepted minimum standard for housing because of either deterioration or inadequate construction; and should be torn down or extensively repaired or rebuilt.

Source: Department of Commerce, Bureau of the Census; U. S. Census of Housing: 1950, Vol. I, Part 1.

No. 924.—DWELLING UNITS—SELECTED CHARACTERISTICS OF OCCUPIED UNITS: 1940 AND 1950

[In thousands of dwelling units. Asterisk (*) denotes 1950 statistics based on 20-percent sample; all 1940 statistics based on complete enumeration]

SUBJECT	1950								1940, TOTAL	
	Number				Percent distribution				Number	Percent
	Total	Urban	Rural non-farm	Rural farm	Total	Urban	Rural non-farm	Rural farm		
Occupied dwelling units	42,826	28,492	8,613	5,721	.....	.....	.....	.....	34,855	.....
REFRIGERATION EQUIPMENT*										
Number reporting	42,060	27,996	8,442	5,622	100.0	100.0	100.0	100.0	34,205	100.0
Mechanical	33,720	24,092	6,102	3,526	80.2	86.1	72.3	62.7	15,093	44.1
Ice	4,445	2,798	985	663	10.6	10.0	11.7	11.8	9,253	27.1
Other or none	3,894	1,106	1,355	1,433	9.3	4.0	16.1	25.5	9,859	28.8
RADIO*										
Number reporting	42,234	28,109	8,472	5,653	100.0	100.0	100.0	100.0	33,891	100.0
With radio	40,411	27,321	7,891	5,199	95.7	97.2	93.1	92.0	28,048	82.8
No radio	1,823	789	581	454	4.3	2.8	6.9	8.0	5,842	17.2
TELEVISION*										
Number reporting	42,030	27,971	8,434	5,625	100.0	100.0	100.0	100.0	(1)	(1)
With television	5,030	4,381	495	154	12.0	15.7	5.9	2.7	(1)	(1)
No television	36,999	23,589	7,939	5,471	88.0	84.3	94.1	97.3	(1)	(1)
HEATING EQUIPMENT*										
Number reporting heating equipment	42,056	28,045	8,423	5,588	100.0	100.0	100.0	100.0	34,149	100.0
Central heating	21,191	17,558	2,620	1,013	50.4	62.6	31.1	18.1	14,347	42.0
Piped steam or hot water	9,890	8,922	786	183	23.5	31.8	9.3	3.3	7,428	21.8
Warm air furnace	11,301	8,637	1,834	830	26.9	30.8	21.8	14.9	6,919	20.3
Noncentral heating or not heated	20,865	10,487	5,808	4,575	49.6	37.4	68.9	81.9	19,802	58.0
Noncentral heating	20,295	10,065	5,720	4,510	48.3	35.9	67.9	80.7	(1)	(1)
Other means with flue	15,122	6,690	4,591	3,841	36.0	23.9	54.5	68.7	(1)	(1)
Other means without flue	5,173	3,375	1,129	669	12.3	12.0	13.4	12.0	(1)	(1)
Not heated	570	422	83	65	1.4	1.5	1.0	1.2	(1)	
HEATING FUEL*										
Number reporting heating equipment	42,056	28,045	8,423	5,588	100.0	100.0	100.0	100.0	34,149	100.0
Central heating	21,191	17,558	2,620	1,013	50.4	62.6	31.1	18.1	14,347	42.0
Coal	9,637	7,714	1,323	599	22.9	27.5	15.7	10.7	10,903	31.9
Wood	261	87	55	120	.6	.3	.7	2.1	373	1.1
Gas	5,897	5,400	404	93	14.0	19.3	4.8	1.7	1,110	3.2
Utility gas	5,727	5,337	346	44	13.6	19.0	4.1	.8	(1)	(1)
Bottled gas	170	63	58	50	.4	.2	.7	.9	(1)	(1)
Liquid and other fuel	5,236	4,214	825	197	12.5	15.0	9.8	3.5	1,766	5.2
Liquid fuel	4,832	3,912	751	168	11.5	14.0	8.9	3.0	(1)	(1)
Other fuel	405	301	74	29	1.0	1.1	.9	.5	(1)	(1)
Not reported	160	144	12	4	.4	.5	.1	.1	195	.6
Noncentral heating	20,295	10,065	5,720	4,510	48.3	35.9	67.9	80.7	19,540	57.2
Coal	4,847	2,093	1,644	1,110	11.5	7.5	19.5	19.9	7,622	22.3
Wood	3,910	531	1,262	2,117	9.3	1.9	15.0	37.9	7,362	21.6
Gas	6,200	4,630	1,111	460	14.7	16.5	13.2	8.2	2,728	8.0
Utility gas	5,395	4,462	781	152	12.8	15.9	9.3	2.7	(1)	(1)
Bottled gas	805	167	329	308	1.9	.6	3.9	5.5	(1)	(1)
Liquid and other fuel	5,270	2,770	1,687	812	12.5	9.9	20.0	14.5	1,757	5.1
Liquid fuel	4,629	2,451	1,480	697	11.0	8.7	17.6	12.5	(1)	(1)
Electricity	276	135	91	50	.7	.5	1.1	.9	(1)	(1)
Other fuel	365	184	115	65	.9	.7	1.4	1.2	(1)	(1)
Not reported	68	41	16	11	.2	.1	.2	.2	70	.2
Not heated	570	422	83	65	1.4	1.5	1.0	1.2	2 263	.8
COOKING FUEL*										
Number reporting	42,100	28,014	8,449	5,637	100.0	100.0	100.0	100.0	34,342	100.0
Coal	3,295	1,614	990	691	7.8	5.8	11.7	12.3	3,962	11.5
Wood	4,150	667	1,303	2,180	9.9	2.4	15.4	38.7	8,102	23.6
Gas									16,776	48.8
Utility gas	21,710	19,897	1,560	253	51.6	71.0	18.5	4.5	(1)	(1)
Bottled gas	3,360	809	1,524	1,026	8.0	2.9	18.0	18.2	(1)	(1)
Electricity	6,295	3,447	1,949	900	15.0	12.3	23.1	16.0	1,838	5.4
Liquid and other fuel	3,168	1,492	1,096	581	7.5	5.3	13.0	10.3	3,523	10.3
Liquid fuel	2,834	1,354	982	499	6.7	4.8	11.6	8.9	(1)	(1)
Other fuel	334	138	114	82	.8	.5	1.4	1.5	(1)	(1)
None	122	88	27	6	.3	.3	.3	.1	143	.4

1 Not available.
2 Units without central heating equipment and reporting "None" for fuel were considered "Not heated."

Source: Department of Commerce, Bureau of the Census; U. S. Census of Housing: 1950, Vol. I, Part 1, and Sixteenth Census Reports, Housing, Vol. II, Part 1.

No. 925.—DWELLING UNITS—ELECTRIC LIGHTING, TOILET, AND BATHING FACILITIES: 1940 AND 1950

[In thousands of dwelling units. Asterisk (*) denotes 1950 statistics based on 20-percent sample; all 1940 statistics based on complete enumeration]

SUBJECT	1950								1940, TOTAL	
	Number				Percent distribution				Number	Percent
	Total	Urban	Rural non-farm	Rural farm	Total	Urban	Rural non-farm	Rural farm		
All dwelling units..............	45,983	29,569	10,056	6,358	......	......	......	....	37,325	......
ELECTRIC LIGHTING										
Number reporting................	45,046	29,092	9,752	6,202	100.0	100.0	100.0	100.0	36,747	100.0
With electric lights...............	42,359	28,734	8,808	4,818	94.0	98.8	90.3	77.7	28,915	78.7
No electric lights..................	2,687	358	944	1,384	6.0	1.2	9.7	22.3	7,831	21.3
TOILET FACILITIES										
Number reporting................	45,261	29,204	9,803	6,254	100.0	100.0	100.0	100.0	36,776	100.0
Flush toilet inside structure, exclusive use.........................	32,335	25,363	5,240	1,732	71.4	86.8	53.5	27.7	21,967	59.7
Flush toilet inside structure, shared.	1,839	1,655	160	24	4.1	5.7	1.6	.4	1,827	5.0
Other toilet facilities (including privy).............................	10,157	1,994	4,063	4,100	22.4	6.8	41.4	65.6	11,957	32.5
No toilet...........................	930	192	340	398	2.1	.7	3.5	6.4	1,015	2.8
Not reported......................	722	365	254	104	......	......	......	......	556	......
BATHING FACILITIES										
Number reporting................	44,776	28,929	9,660	6,187	100.0	100.0	100.0	100.0	36,640	100.0
Installed bathtub or shower, exclusive use........................	31,022	24,165	5,013	1,845	69.3	83.6	51.8	29.8	20,606	56.2
Installed bathtub or shower, shared.	1,734	1,560	151	23	3.9	5.4	1.6	.4	1,723	4.7
No bathtub or shower..............	12,020	3,195	4,505	4,320	26.8	11.0	46.6	69.8	14,321	39.1
Not reported......................	1,207	649	387	171	......	......	......	......	676	......

Source: Department of Commerce, Bureau of the Census; *U. S. Census of Housing: 1950*, Vol. I, Part 1, and Sixteenth Census Reports, *Housing*, Vol. II, Part 1.

No. 926.—DWELLING UNITS—VALUE OF NONFARM OWNER-OCCUPIED UNITS: 1950

[In thousands of dwelling units. Value represents amount which owner-occupant estimates property (including structure and its land) would sell for under ordinary conditions and not at forced sale]

VALUE	NUMBER			PERCENT DISTRIBUTION		
	Urban and rural nonfarm	Urban	Rural non-farm	Urban and rural nonfarm	Urban	Rural non-farm
Owner-occupied dwelling units [1].......	15,878	11,160	4,718	......	......	......
Number reporting...................	14,974	10,865	4,109	100.0	100.0	100.0
Less than $2,000...................	1,165	446	720	7.8	4.1	17.5
$2,000 to $2,999...................	857	397	460	5.7	3.7	11.2
$3,000 to $3,999...................	1,094	597	497	7.3	5.5	12.1
$4,000 to $4,999...................	1,104	696	407	7.4	6.4	9.9
$5,000 to $5,999...................	1,290	878	415	8.6	8.0	10.1
$6,000 to $7,499...................	2,114	1,612	501	14.1	14.8	12.2
$7,500 to $9,999...................	2,618	2,178	439	17.5	20.0	10.7
$10,000 to $14,999.................	2,995	2,577	418	20.0	23.7	10.2
$15,000 to $19,999.................	1,008	873	135	6.7	8.0	3.3
$20,000 or more...................	731	615	116	4.9	5.7	2.8
Not reported......................	905	295	610			
Median value......................	$7,354	$8,380	$4,878	......	......	......

[1] Restricted to 1-dwelling-unit structures without business and with one dwelling unit in property.

Source: Department of Commerce, Bureau of the Census; *U. S. Census of Housing: 1950*, Vol. I, Part 1.

No. 927.—Dwelling Units—Mortgage Status of Nonfarm Owner-Occupied Units: 1890 to 1950

For 1940 and 1950, mortgage statistics are for owner-occupied dwelling units in 1- to 4-dwelling unit structures without business. An owner-occupied dwelling unit was reported as mortgaged if property on which it was located had an indebtedness in form of a mortgage or deed of trust, or if occupants had contract to purchase property. For 1920 and earlier, mortgage data are for owner-occupied units in all types of structures. Although types of units for which mortgage data were reported are not the same for all censuses, differences are not large enough to invalidate comparisons]

CENSUS YEAR	Total owner-occupied dwelling units	Reporting mortgage status	MORTGAGED		Not mort-gaged
			Number	Percent	
1890	2,923,671	2,923,671	809,933	27.7	2,113,738
1900	3,568,809	3,394,967	1,086,605	32.0	2,308,362
1910	5,245,380	5,109,916	1,701,062	33.3	3,408,854
1920	7,041,283	6,867,546	2,735,668	39.8	4,131,878
1930	10,549,972	(1)	(1)	(1)	(1)
1940	11,413,086	10,611,259	4,804,778	45.3	5,806,481
1950	19,801,646	17,795,844	7,825,116	44.0	9,970,728
Urban	14,376,594	13,296,133	6,429,743	48.4	6,866,390
Rural nonfarm	5,425,052	4,499,711	1,395,373	31.0	3,104,338

[1] Not available.

Source: Department of Commerce, Bureau of the Census; U. S. Census of Housing: 1950, Vol. I, Part 1.

No. 928.—Dwelling Units—Contract and Gross Monthly Rent of Nonfarm Renter-Occupied Units: 1940 and 1950

[In thousands of dwelling units. Contract monthly rent is rent contracted for, regardless of whether it includes furniture, heating fuel, electricity, cooking fuel, water, or other services sometimes supplied. Gross monthly rent is contract monthly rent plus reported average monthly cost of utilities (water, electricity, gas) and fuels such as wood, coal, and oil; if furniture was included in contract rent, reported estimated rent of dwelling unit without furniture was used in computation rather than contract rent]

MONTHLY RENT	1950						1940, URBAN AND RURAL NONFARM	
	Number			Percent distribution				
	Urban and rural nonfarm	Urban	Rural nonfarm	Urban and rural nonfarm	Urban	Rural nonfarm	Number	Percent
CONTRACT MONTHLY RENT								
Total dwelling units	17,304	14,116	3,188	....	....	....	16,335	....
Number reporting	15,503	13,252	2,251	100.0	100.0	100.0	16,178	100.0
Less than $10	638	298	340	4.1	2.3	15.1	2,822	17.4
$10 to $14	990	623	367	6.4	4.7	16.3	2,280	14.1
$15 to $19	1,175	869	306	7.6	6.6	13.6	2,217	13.7
$20 to $24	1,436	1,177	259	9.3	8.9	11.5	2,013	12.4
$25 to $29	1,611	1,372	239	10.4	10.4	10.6	1,840	11.4
$30 to $39	3,178	2,854	324	20.5	21.5	14.4	2,526	15.6
$40 to $49	2,577	2,402	175	16.6	18.1	7.8	1,300	8.0
$50 to $59	1,603	1,500	103	10.3	11.3	4.6	570	3.5
$60 to $74	1,221	1,141	79	7.9	8.6	3.5	327	2.0
$75 to $99	710	674	36	4.6	5.1	1.6	164	1.0
$100 or more	363	341	22	2.3	2.6	1.0	118	.7
Rent free	1,257	555	702				(1)	(1)
Not reported	543	308	235				157	
Median rent	$35.50	$37.54	$21 67	....	....	....	$21.41	....
GROSS MONTHLY RENT								
Total dwelling units	17,304	14,116	3,188	.....	.....	.....	16,335	.....
Number reporting	15,190	13,007	2,182	100.0	100.0	100.0	15,144	100.0
Less than $10	227	98	130	1.5	.8	5.9	1,404	9.3
$10 to $14	444	258	186	2.9	2.0	8.5	1,614	10.7
$15 to $19	702	464	238	4.6	3.6	10.9	1,735	11.5
$20 to $24	979	725	254	6.4	5.6	11.6	1,838	12.1
$25 to $29	1,197	956	241	7.9	7.4	11.0	1,768	11.7
$30 to $39	3,123	2,696	427	20.6	20.8	19.6	3,029	20.0
$40 to $49	3,105	2,805	300	20.4	21.6	13.8	1,967	13.0
$50 to $59	2,302	2,122	179	15.2	16.3	8.2	925	6.1
$60 to $74	1,740	1,601	139	11.5	12.3	6.4	513	3.4
$75 to $99	941	881	59	6.2	6.8	2.7	228	1.5
$100 or more	429	400	28	2.8	3.1	1.3	123	.8
Rent free or not reported	2,114	1,108	1,006				[1] 1,191	
Median rent	$42.47	$44.16	$30 44	....	....	....	$27.28	....

[1] In 1940, rent-free units were distributed according to estimated rents.

Source: Department of Commerce, Bureau of the Census; U. S. Census of Housing: 1950, Vol. I, Part 1, and Sixteenth Census Reports, Housing, Vol. II, Part 1.

No. 929.—Mortgaged Residential Nonfarm Properties, by Government Insurance Status of First Mortgage: 1950

[In thousands of properties. Based on a sample; excludes structures completed after April 1950. A mortgaged property consists of all structures and land given as security for a mortgage loan]

TENURE AND NUMBER OF DWELLING UNITS ON PROPERTY	TOTAL MORT- GAGED PROP- ERTIES		PROPERTIES WITH—					
			FHA insured first mortgage		VA guaranteed first mortgage		Conventional first mortgage	
	Num- ber	Per- cent	Num- ber	Per- cent	Num- ber	Per- cent	Num- ber	Per- cent
Total	9,443	100	1,329	100	1,364	100	6,850	100
Owner-occupied properties	8,288	88	1,228	92	1,196	96	5,862	86
1 dwelling unit	7,052	75	1,179	89	1,032	82	4,840	71
2 to 4 dwelling units	1,236	13	50	4	163	13	1,023	15
Rental properties	1,155	12	100	8	67	5	987	14
1 dwelling unit	560	6	75	6	49	4	436	6
2 to 4 dwelling units	324	3	20	1	15	1	290	4
5 to 49 dwelling units	260	3	5		3		253	4
50 dwelling units or more	11		1				10	

Source: Department of Commerce, Bureau of the Census; *U. S. Census of Housing: 1950*, Vol. IV.

No. 930.—Mortgaged Residential Nonfarm Properties—Outstanding Debt, by Holder of Mortgage: 1950

[In millions of dollars. Based on a sample; excludes structures completed after April 1950. A mortgaged property consists of all structures and land given as security for a mortgage loan]

SUBJECT	Total out- stand- ing debt	OUTSTANDING DEBT BY HOLDER OF MORTGAGE							
		Com- mercial bank or trust com- pany	Mu- tual sav- ings bank	Sav- ings and loan asso- ciation	Life insur- ance com- pany	Mort- gage com- pany	Fed- eral Na- tional Mort- gage Asso- ciation	Indi- vidual	Other
Total	44,486	8,368	5,847	10,089	8,985	699	1,685	7,817	1,728
GOVERNMENT INSURANCE STATUS OF MORTGAGE									
First mortgages	42,942	8,187	5,794	9,976	8,790	666	1,038	6,985	1,606
FHA insured	8,583	2,318	1,021	667	3,842	239	194		253
VA guaranteed	7,501	2,149	905	2,194	1,176	117	844	5	110
Conventional	26,909	3,720	3,869	7,115	3,771	209		6,980	1,245
Junior mortgages	1,544	182	73	92	190	25	17	523	116
VA guaranteed	425	102	43	40	181	19	17	1	12
Conventional	1,118	80	30	53	15	16		522	104
TENURE AND NUMBER OF DWELL- ING UNITS ON PROPERTY									
Owner-occupied properties	33,755	6,995	5,262	8,878	6,140	449	983	5,957	1,079
1 dwelling unit	25,566	6,194	3,542	7,096	5,795	411	947	4,664	920
2 to 4 dwelling units	8,188	801	730	1,783	345	38	36	1,304	160
Rental properties	10,732	1,373	2,805	1,190	2,845	151	72	1,550	644
1 dwelling unit	1,858	382	129	630	303	20	53	422	82
2 to 4 dwelling units	1,474	270	169	382	171	17	12	365	89
5 to 49 dwelling units	4,222	500	1,206	349	532	65	2	894	274
50 dwelling units or more	3,178	222	1,091	29	1,442	49	4	113	229

Source: Department of Commerce, Bureau of the Census; *U. S. Census of Housing: 1950*, Vol. IV.

No. 931.—Occupied Farm Dwelling Units—Percent Distribution by Condition and Plumbing Facilities, and by Year Built: 1950

[Data based on sample; see source for explanation of sampling variability]

SUBJECT	Total occu-pied dwelling units	OWNER Total [1]	OWNER 1 to 4 rooms	OWNER 5 rooms or more	RENTER AND RENT-FREE Total [1]	RENTER AND RENT-FREE 1 to 4 rooms	RENTER AND RENT-FREE 5 rooms or more	Non-white occu-pied units
Number of occupied farm dwelling units.............(thousands).....	5,660	3,702	1,021	2,606	1,958	1,002	911	664
CONDITION AND PLUMBING FACILITIES [2]								
Total reporting.....................	100	100	100	100	100	100	100	100
Not dilapidated.....................	83	88	76	92	73	61	85	54
All facilities.....................	24	29	12	36	14	6	22	2
Some facilities.....................	18	20	15	22	14	10	19	4
No facilities.....................	41	39	50	34	44	45	44	48
Dilapidated.....................	17	12	24	8	27	39	15	46
All or some facilities.....................	2	2	2	2	2	3	2	2
No facilities.....................	15	10	22	6	25	36	13	45
KITCHEN SINK [3]								
Total reporting condition and plumbing.....................	100	100	100	100	100	100	100	100
With running water.....................	44	51	29	60	31	19	43	7
No running water.....................	56	49	71	40	69	81	57	93
With kitchen sink.....................	14	14	12	15	13	7	19	3
No kitchen sink or not reporting sink..	42	35	59	25	57	74	37	90
YEAR BUILT								
Total reporting.....................	100	100	100	100	100	100	100	100
1945 or later.....................	10	12	19	9	7	11	4	11
1940 to 1944.....................	5	6	9	5	4	5	2	6
1930 to 1939.....................	15	14	19	12	15	21	9	21
1920 to 1929.....................	16	15	16	14	19	23	14	24
1919 or earlier.....................	54	53	37	60	54	40	70	38

[1] Includes dwelling units for which number of rooms was not reported.
[2] Units with all plumbing facilities have all of following facilities inside structure: Private flush toilet, private bath, and hot and cold running water. Units with no facilities have no private flush toilet, no private bath, and no running water inside structure.
[3] Tabulation restricted to units with no running water inside structure.
Source: Department of Commerce, Bureau of the Census, U. S. Census of Housing: 1950, Vol. III.

No. 932.—Occupied Farm Dwelling Units—Year Built, Electric Lighting, and Heating Equipment by Condition and Plumbing Facilities: 1950

[Data based on sample; see source for explanation of sampling variability]

CONDITION AND PLUMBING FACILITIES [1]	ALL OCCUPIED UNITS Num-ber (1,000)	Percent with— Elec-tric lights	Heating equipment Central	Heating equipment Non-central, with flue	Built in 1940 or later Num-ber (1,000)	Built in 1940 or later Percent of total	NONWHITE-OCCUPIED UNITS Num-ber (1,000)	Percent with— Elec-tric lights	Heating equipment Central	Heating equipment Non-central, with flue
Total [2].............	5,660	80	18	69	853	15	664	44	1	85
Not dilapidated..........	4,541	87	21	66	750	17	345	54	2	83
All facilities	1,319	99	49	39	237	18	12	99	23	51
Some facilities..........	983	95	20	66	138	14	23	80	4	76
No facilities..........	2,239	75	5	82	376	17	310	50	1	85
Dilapidated..............	961	53	3	83	87	9	298	32	1	85
All or some facilities....	122	86	13	70	10	8	10	51	5	79
No facilities..........	839	48	1	85	77	9	288	31	1	86

[1] See footnote 2, table 931.
[2] Includes dwelling units for which condition or plumbing facilities were not reported.
Source: Department of Commerce, Bureau of the Census; U. S. Census of Housing: 1950, Vol. III.

30. Manufactures

Census of Manufactures.—The basic source of comprehensive data on manufacturing production is the Census of Manufactures conducted by the Bureau of the Census. The first Census of Manufactures covered the year 1809 and a census was taken at 10-year intervals in connection with the Decennial Census of Population up to and including 1899, with the exception of 1829. It was conducted at 5-year intervals from 1904 through 1919, and every other year from 1921 through 1939, but was suspended during the war period. The 1947 Census of Manufactures was the first to be taken since 1939. Present legislation provides for a Census of Manufactures to cover the year 1953 and every fifth year thereafter.

The 1947 Census of Manufactures covered all establishments primarily engaged in manufacturing, as defined in the 1945 revision of the Standard Industrial Classification sponsored by the Bureau of the Budget. This Census, as well as the Annual Survey of Manufactures, which is described below, covers operating manufacturing establishments only, omitting separate administrative offices and auxiliary units of operating establishments. Operating establishments, however, account for approximately 98 percent of total manufacturing employment. To the extent possible, this Census was conducted on an establishment basis. As a rule, the term "establishment" signifies a single plant or factory and is not necessarily identical with the business unit or company which may consist of one or more establishments. A company operating establishments at more than one location is required to submit a report for each location; also, companies engaged in distinctly different lines of activity at one location are required to submit separate reports if separate payroll and inventory records are kept for each activity. Census figures differ, therefore, from those prepared on a company basis. They also differ to some extent from other tabulations based on establishment reports, where the definition of an establishment as to location and line of activity is not so rigidly applied.

In the 1947 Census, reports were required from all establishments employing one or more persons at any time during the census year. In other recent censuses, establishments having less than $5,000 value of products were designated as outside the scope of the census. The change in the minimum size limit in 1947 as compared with 1939 has not appreciably affected the comparability of the figures for these two years, except for data on number of establishments for a few industries.

Each of the establishments covered in the census was classified in one of 458 manufacturing industries in accordance with the industry definitions embodied in the Standard Industrial Classification system. Under this system of classification, an industry is generally defined as a group of establishments producing a single product or a more or less closely related group of products. This product or group of products is in turn said to be "primary" to that industry. Accordingly, an establishment is classified in a particular industry if its production of the primary products of that industry exceeds in value its production of any other group of products. In a few instances, however, the industry classification of an establishment is determined not only by the products it makes but also by the processes employed in making those products.

While some establishments produce only the primary products of the industry in which they are classified, it rarely happens that all the establishments in an industry specialize to this extent. The statistics on employment, payrolls, value added, inventories, and expenditures, therefore, reflect not only the primary activities of the

Note.—This section presents data for the most recent year or period available on May 20, 1951, when the material was organized and sent to the printer. In a few instances, more recent data were added after that date.

establishments in that industry but also their activities of a secondary nature. For this reason the industry statistics usually cannot be directly related to statistics on the total shipments of commodities.

Comparative figures shown for 1939 are generally slightly lower than those published in the 1939 reports. The 1939 figures have been revised to exclude retail bakeries, machine-shop repairs, and some other types of establishments also omitted from the 1947 Census. Cost of materials and value of products for 1947 were not compiled for summary tables because of the duplication which arises in the combination of individual industries representing successive stages in the production of finished manufactures.

The Bureau of the Census is prohibited by law from publishing any statistics that disclose information reported by individual companies. Figures are, therefore, not shown for an industry or a geographic unit which is represented by only one or two companies, or by more companies when one or two companies produce a very large proportion of the combined output of all the companies. This restriction has no effect upon statistics by industry for the entire United States, or statistics for all industries within States and standard metropolitan areas. There are many instances, however, where this restriction makes it necessary to withhold figures for counties and cities, and for industries within States and areas.

Annual Survey of Manufactures.—This survey, which was conducted for the first time in 1949 and was repeated in 1950 and 1951, carries forward, for the intercensal years, the key measures of manufacturing activity covered in detail by the quinquennial Census of Manufactures. It is designed to yield estimates of general statistics (employment, payrolls, value added by manufacture, inventories, and capital expenditures) for industry groups, important individual industries, geographic divisions, States, and important cross-tabulations of major industry groups by division and by State.

The annual survey is based on a sample of approximately 45,000 out of a total of almost 250,000 manufacturing establishments. Included are all large plants and a representative sample of the much more numerous small plants. The large plants in the survey account for approximately two-thirds of total manufacturing employment in the United States.

The annual survey estimates vary from the totals that would have been obtained from a comparable complete canvass of all manufacturing establishments. The relative magnitude of this sampling variation, expressed in percentage form, is given in the table column captioned "Standard error." The standard error should be interpreted to mean that the sample estimates will differ from complete canvass totals by *less than:* (a) the percentage shown in approximately 2 cases out of 3; (b) twice the percentage shown in approximately 19 cases out of 20; and (c) three times the percentage shown in almost every case. It should be noted that standard errors are shown only for selected items. The standard errors of other measures are shown in the source report cited.

In making any study of the historical trend of the 1947, 1949, 1950 and 1951 figures, it is important to take account of the effect of the sampling variation on the apparent increase or decrease shown between years. In addition to sampling errors, individual figures may be subject to biases arising from undetected response or procedural errors which are not reflected in the "standard errors." In general, figures are withheld from publication in the original source volumes if (a) the standard error of the estimate exceeds 15 percent, or (b) survey estimates are inconsistent with other census series and related data. It must be noted that any estimate which can be derived by subtraction of one published figure from another may have a standard error considerably in excess of 15 percent.

The basic statistical measures of manufacturing activity, such as employment, payrolls, value added, etc., were defined in essentially the same way for the annual surveys as for the quinquennial census. Consequently, historical series shown in the following tables may be considered to be comparable except as specifically noted. It should be pointed out that for 1949, 1950, and 1951, average employment was calculated from the figures reported for the pay periods ending nearest the fifteenth of March, May, August, and November, whereas for 1947 such averages were based on twelve monthly employment figures.

Current and other statistics.—Monthly, quarterly, and annual commodity surveys are also conducted by the Bureau of the Census. These data are published currently in the *Facts for Industry* series. This series also includes releases of information collected by or for the War Production Board and successor agencies during the war and reconversion periods by the Census Bureau or other Federal agencies.

Reports on current activities of industries, or current movements of individual commodities, are also compiled by trade associations and trade journals, commercial agencies, and by such governmental bureaus as Labor Statistics, Agricultural Economics, Foreign and Domestic Commerce, Fish and Wildlife Service, Tariff Commission, and Internal Revenue, in addition to the Census Bureau previously mentioned.

Abbreviated balance sheet and income account data on all United States manufacturing corporations are compiled and published annually by the Bureau of Internal Revenue from corporation income and profits tax returns and holding company returns.

Data on financial operations and intercorporate relations of manufacturing corporations are collected from time to time by the Securities and Exchange Commission, the Tariff Commission, the Federal Trade Commission, and special investigating agencies. Financial statistics for certain manufacturing industries in the form of balance sheets, profit and loss statements, analyses of sales and expenses, lists of subsidiaries, types and amounts of security issues, and selected data on the salaries paid to officers and directors, are summarized and published for the leading corporations that are registered with the Securities and Exchange Commission. The Tariff Commission publishes commodity surveys which cover economic and competitive aspects of production, distribution, and international trade in selected important industries. Each survey deals with several products which are related because of the raw materials consumed, or competitive uses. The Federal Trade Commission has made several comprehensive studies of individual industries.

Material in other sections.—In addition to the statistics presented in this section, statistics on the output and activities of manufacturers will be found in various other sections of the *Statistical Abstract*. For example, a historical summation of production and consumption of raw materials appears in section 32, Foreign Commerce (see table 1056); data on wages and hours appear in section 8, Labor Force, Employment, and Earnings; statistics on manufacturing corporations compiled from corporation income tax returns appear in section 14, Federal Government Finances and Employment, and in section 17, Business Enterprise; and statistics on lumber production in section 26, Forests and Forest Products. For page references to the commodity or industry, consult the index. For references to the important sources of statistics on manufacturing and related activities, see the listings under the appropriate subjects in the "Bibliography of Sources of Statistical Data," page 969.

Geographic coverage.—Statistics in this section relate to continental United States except as noted.

Historical statistics.—See preface and historical appendix. Tabular headnotes (as "See also *Historical Statistics*, series J 1–12") provide cross-references, where applicable, to *Historical Statistics of the United States, 1789–1945.*

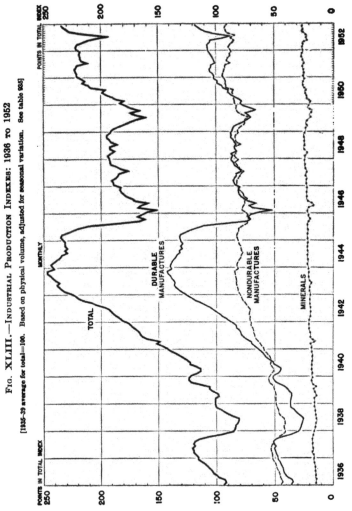

FIG. XLIII.—INDUSTRIAL PRODUCTION INDEXES: 1936 TO 1952

[1935-39 average for total=100. Based on physical volume, adjusted for seasonal variation. See table 935]

Source: Board of Governors of the Federal Reserve System.

No. 983.—MANUFACTURES—SUMMARY: 1849 TO 1951

[Figures for 1849 to 1919 include establishments whose products were valued at $500 or more; for 1921 to 1939, establishments whose products were valued at $5,000 or more; for 1947, figures cover all establishments employing 1 or more persons at any time during year. See also 1948 *Abstract* and *Historical Statistics*, series J 1-13, for unrevised data for 1939 and earlier years]

CENSUS YEAR	Number of establishments	Number of proprietors and firm members	ALL EMPLOYEES [1]		PRODUCTION WORKERS		Value added [3] ($1,000)
			Number (average for year) [2]	Salaries and wages ($1,000)	Number (average for year)	Wages ($1,000)	
Factories and hand and neighborhood industries:							
1849	123,025				957,059	236,755	463,983
1859	140,433		(4)	(4)	1,311,346	378,879	854,257
1869	252,148				2,053,996	620,467	1,395,119
1879	253,852	(4)			2,732,595	947,954	1,972,756
1889	355,504		4,895,494	2,283,063	4,129,355	1,930,554	4,165,596
1899	509,490		5,478,361	2,895,366	4,997,922	2,326,547	4,674,596
Factories, excluding hand and neighborhood industries:							
1899	204,750	(4)	4,830,019	2,235,654	4,501,919	1,892,574	4,646,981
1904	213,444	226,118	5,674,967	2,960,927	5,181,690	2,440,581	6,019,171
1909	264,810	272,421	7,012,066	4,108,470	6,261,736	3,426,213	8,162,073
1914	268,496	268,560	7,814,196	4,815,977	6,932,287	3,782,222	9,385,662
1919	270,231	240,955	9,636,801	12,495,992	8,464,916	9,664,009	23,841,624
1921	192,008	172,291	7,457,344	9,570,199	6,675,674	7,451,390	17,253,712
1923	192,004	147,968	9,474,688	12,906,460	8,194,170	10,145,634	24,569,587
1925	183,877	132,971	9,142,417	12,927,767	7,871,850	9,976,949	25,667,994
1927	187,629	132,151	9,072,063	13,132,135	7,848,570	10,098,948	26,736,264
1929	206,663	132,686	9,659,742	14,284,282	8,369,705	10,884,919	30,591,435
1931	171,450	(4)	(4)	(4)	6,182,144	6,688,841	18,550,683
1933	139,325	72,267	6,557,925	6,327,800	5,787,611	4,940,146	14,007,949
1935	167,916	81,521	6,853,590	8,944,754	7,308,794	7,311,339	18,552,963
1937	166,794	90,385	9,795,452	13,299,749	8,569,231	10,112,883	25,174,092
1939	173,802	128,555	8,537,380	12,705,102	7,808,205	8,997,516	24,487,304
1947	240,881	128,948	14,294,304	39,696,537	11,916,188	30,249,345	74,430,131
1949 [9]	(4)	(4)	12,980,060	42,752,063	11,016,301	30,358,971	72,896,137
1950 [9]	347,307	(4)	14,769,981	47,882,804	11,778,908	34,600,685	89,749,765
1951 [9]	262,000	(4)	15,612,619	55,992,091	12,808,914	40,684,582	103,035,814

[1] Beginning 1899 includes data for employees of manufacturing establishments engaged in distribution and construction work. Extent to which data for such employees were included in figures for earlier years is not known.
[2] Data for 1949-50 based on pay periods ending nearest 15th of Mar., May, Aug., and Nov. For 1947, figures represent average of 12 monthly figures; for earlier years, sum of average number of production workers for year and number of nonproduction workers reported for 1 pay-roll period (usually in October).
[3] Value of products less cost of materials, supplies, fuel, electricity, and contract work. For 1849-1933, cost of contract work was not subtracted from value of products in calculating value added by manufacture.
[4] Not available. [5] Reduced to gold basis. [6] Excludes data for salaried officers of corporations.
[7] Revised on basis of retabulation of returns to exclude data for establishments classified as nonmanufacturing in 1947. Value added by manufacture on a basis comparable with 1937 and previous years, was $34.7 billion.
[8] Number of proprietors and firm members not revised. Figures for "All employees" revised on basis of estimates rather than by retabulation of 1939 reports. (See footnote 7.)
[9] Estimates based on sample survey: see text, p. 783. For standard errors of estimates, see subsequent tables.
[10] Figures include data for plants idle throughout year, administrative offices, and units auxiliary to manufacturing.

Source: Department of Commerce, Bureau of the Census; 1947 Census of Manufactures reports and *Annual Survey of Manufactures: 1949, 1950* and *1951.*

No. 984.—POPULATION, WAGE EARNERS, AND PRODUCTION—INDEXES: 1899 TO 1947

[1899=100. See also *Historical Statistics*, series J 13 for indexes of production]

CENSUS YEAR	Population	Wage earners	Production (quantity) [1]	Production per wage earner	CENSUS YEAR	Population	Wage earners	Production (quantity) [1]	Production per wage earner
1899	100	100	100	100	1927	156	175	217	179
1904	110	119	134	108	1929	160	186	264	142
1909	125	139	166	114	1931	166	143	198	
1914	131	147	186	127	1933	169	131	199	
1919	140	167	206	126	1935	170	146	246	
1921	146	147	189	132	1937	173	164	308	
1923	150	168	258	154	1939	176	157	287	
1925	154	175			1947	193	(2)	449	(2)

[1] Index of physical output for 1899-1939 from National Bureau of Economic Research. [2] Not available.

Source: Department of Commerce, Bureau of the Census; *1939 Census of Manufactures*, Vol. I, and records.

No. 935.—Industrial Production—Indexes, by Groups: 1933 to 1952

[1935–39 average=100. Monthly data adjusted for seasonal variation. See also *Historical Statistics*, series J 30–48 and G 6–8]

YEAR AND MONTH	Total	MANUFACTURES										
		Total	Durable manufactures								Nondurable manufactures	
			Total	Iron and steel	Machinery	Transportation equipment	Nonferrous metal and products	Lumber and products	Stone, clay, and glass products		Total	Textiles and products	Leather and products
1933	69	68	54	54	50	48	60	63	54		79	88	88
1934	75	74	65	61	69	69	62	64	64		81	76	91
1935	87	87	83	81	83	93	80	85	77		90	93	99
1936	103	104	106	114	105	110	104	105	103		100	104	103
1937	113	113	122	123	126	123	122	113	114		106	106	102
1938	89	87	78	68	82	72	80	90	92		96	86	93
1939	109	109	109	114	104	103	113	106	114		109	112	105
1940	125	126	139	147	136	145	139	116	124		115	114	98
1941	162	168	201	186	221	245	191	134	162		142	152	123
1942	199	212	279	340	464	214	134	168			158	157	122
1943	239	258	360	208	443	735	267	129	173		176	153	114
1944	235	252	353	206	439	719	259	125	164		171	148	113
1945	203	214	274	183	343	457	204	109	163		166	146	117
1946	170	177	192	150	240	232	157	131	192		165	162	122
1947	187	194	220	195	276	230	187	143	206		172	163	116
1948	192	198	225	206	277	235	193	145	206		177	170	111
1949	176	183	202	188	234	235	160	130	188		168	147	106
1950	200	209	237	229	270	261	206	160	209		187	182	111
1951	220	229	273	259	336	307	207	157	231		194	174	101
December	218	228	282	263	358	320	207	154	219		185	152	88
1952	219	230	280	243	356	338	222	154	220		189	161	106
March	221	231	285	263	359	327	218	158	222		188	152	106
June	204	214	247	140	352	339	210	146	222		186	154	103
September	228	237	290	270	354	353	225	155	222		194	177	112
December	235	247	313	286	385	393	246	165	222		194	169	107

YEAR AND MONTH	MANUFACTURES—continued								MINERALS		
	Nondurable manufactures—Continued										
	Manufactured food products	Alcoholic beverages	Tobacco products	Paper and products	Printing and publishing	Petroleum and coal products	Chemical products	Rubber products	Total	Fuels	Metals
1933	83	....	80	76	75	74	76	77	76	80	51
1934	88	74	87	75	80	79	83	86	80	83	58
1935	89	89	90	86	89	85	89	93	86	89	73
1936	98	109	99	98	99	97	99	107	99	99	102
1937	103	108	103	107	109	108	112	104	112	109	127
1938	101	96	102	95	96	100	96	83	97	99	86
1939	108	98	106	114	106	110	112	113	106	105	113
1940	113	101	109	123	112	120	130	123	117	114	134
1941	127	117	120	150	127	135	176	163	125	122	148
1942	134	118	131	142	115	147	278	172	129	125	148
1943	145	117	133	139	111	185	384	228	132	132	126
1944	152	144	125	139	101	247	324	234	140	145	113
1945	150	178	136	139	108	236	284	215	137	143	101
1946	149	191	156	145	127	173	236	225	134	142	88
1947	157	190	160	158	144	193	251	226	149	155	116
1948	159	182	164	164	154	218	254	206	155	161	120
1949	163	172	165	156	155	209	241	183	135	139	107
1950	164	188	168	187	170	229	264	223	148	152	123
1951	165	186	175	201	175	267	299	243	164	169	134
December	160	176	147	184	174	281	298	250	163	170	122
1952	164	160	180	189	171	270	301	248	160	167	120
March	166	170	174	192	177	278	294	242	164	170	125
June	166	152	189	181	176	251	298	246	147	161	65
September	168	155	187	192	165	282	302	252	175	180	149
December	163	166	172	196	168	291	309	273	168	176	117

Source: Board of Governors of the Federal Reserve System. Figures published monthly in *Federal Reserve Bulletin*.

No. 936.—MANUFACTURES—SELECTED STATISTICS, BY SIZE OF ESTABLISHMENT, FOR MAJOR INDUSTRY GROUPS: 1951

[Value added figures in thousands of dollars. Figures are based on sample and subject to sampling variation (see standard error columns). Figures for value added by manufacture derived by subtracting from total value of products the cost of materials, supplies, containers, fuel, purchased electric energy and contract work]

MAJOR INDUSTRY GROUP AND ITEM	All estab-lishments	ESTABLISHMENTS WITH AVERAGE EMPLOYMENT OF—					Standard error (percent)	
		1-249 em-ployees	250-499 em-ployees	500-999 em-ployees	1,000-2,499 em-ployees	2,500 em-ployees and more		
	A	B	C	D	E	F	B	C
All industries, total:								
Number of establishments								
All employees								
Value added by manufacture								
Food and kindred products:								
Number of establishments								
All employees								
Value added by manufacture								
Tobacco manufactures:								
Number of establishments								
All employees								
Value added by manufacture								
Textile mill products:								
Number of establishments								
All employees								
Value added by manufacture								
Apparel and related products:								
Number of establishments								
All employees								
Value added by manufacture								
Lumber and products (except furniture):								
Number of establishments								
All employees								
Value added by manufacture								
Furniture and fixtures:								
Number of establishments								
All employees								
Value added by manufacture								
Paper and allied products:								
Number of establishments								
All employees								
Value added by manufacture								
Printing and publishing industries:								
Number of establishments								
All employees								
Value added by manufacture								
Chemicals and allied products:								
Number of establishments								
All employees								
Value added by manufacture								
Petroleum and coal products:								
Number of establishments								
All employees								
Value added by manufacture								
Rubber products:								
Number of establishments								
All employees								
Value added by manufacture								
Leather and leather products:								
Number of establishments								
All employees								
Value added by manufacture								
Stone, clay, and glass products:								
Number of establishments								
All employees								
Value added by manufacture								
Primary metal industries:								
Number of establishments								
All employees								
Value added by manufacture								
Fabricated metal products:								
Number of establishments								
All employees								
Value added by manufacture								

See footnotes at end of table.

No. 996.—MANUFACTURES—SELECTED STATISTICS, BY SIZE OF ESTABLISHMENT, FOR MAJOR INDUSTRY GROUPS: 1951—Continued

[Value added figures in thousands of dollars]

MAJOR INDUSTRY GROUP AND ITEM	All establishments	ESTABLISHMENTS WITH AVERAGE EMPLOYMENT OF—					Standard error (percent) [1]	
		1-249 employees	250-499 employees	500-999 employees	1,000-2,499 employees	2,500 employees and more		
	A	B	C	D	E	F	B	C
Machinery (except electrical):								
Number of establishments ...	14,734	17,527	564	280	223	5	5	5
All employees	1,488,167	446,466	280,726	284,432	337,342	65,326	4	5
Value added by manufacture	11,254,654	3,196,223	1,653,980	1,664,488	2,342,480	2,752,489	4	4
Electrical machinery:								
Number of establishments ...	4,284	3,451	247	206	114	6	5	5
All employees	826,561	190,477	95,168	146,900	172,982	315,989	6	4
Value added by manufacture	5,732,225	921,468	571,114	1,061,670	1,114,488	2,131,544	7	3
Transportation equipment:								
Number of establishments ...	3,368	2,402	146	134	144	127	15	7
All employees	1,668,570	192,237	40,563	94,386	208,664	908,330	9	7
Value added by manufacture	9,780,628	501,659	302,791	568,377	2,042,961	6,162,880	9	6
Instruments and related products:								
Number of establishments ...	2,496	2,514	74	54	30	14	9	10
All employees	283,091	40,426	26,263	38,090	40,527	75,165	8	10
Value added by manufacture	1,608,236	264,219	120,963	245,465	315,831	466,525	9	10
Miscellaneous manufactures:								
Number of establishments ...	15,057	14,720	199	83	45	10	7	9
All employees	539,105	291,021	66,602	56,579	49,291	36,522	7	7
Value added by manufacture	2,842,250	1,446,082	358,524	341,630	366,867	289,237	6	5
Administrative and auxiliary: [10]								
Number of establishments ...	2,107	1,822	142	73	51	9		
All employees..............	282,940	97,312	48,672	59,442	73,067	33,487		

[1] See text, p 782, for explanation of standard error. Standard errors for column A are approximately the same as corresponding standard errors for column B for "Number of establishments"; and are 5 percent or less for "All employees" and "Value added." Standard errors for column D are: From 5 to 8 percent for apparel and related products, lumber and products, petroleum and coal products, and leather and leather products; and from 1 to 4 percent for textile mill products, fabricated metal products, transportation equipment, and instruments and related products. Other estimates in columns D, E, and F, unless otherwise indicated, are based on reports from all establishments known to be in appropriate size classification.

[2] Standard error 1 percent.

[3] Standard error 3 percent for "Number of establishments," 2 percent for "All employees," and 2 percent for "Value added."

[4] Withheld because estimate did not meet publication standards. See text, p 782.

[5] Data for any size class which cannot be shown without disclosing information for individual companies have been combined with figures for adjacent size class.

[6] Standard error 3 percent for "Number of establishments," 4 percent for "All employees," and 4 percent for "Value added."

[7] Data for logging industry and for sawmills producing less than 200,000 board feet of lumber included in these estimates.

[8] Standard error 2 percent

[9] Standard error 5 percent for "Number of establishments," 6 percent for "All employees," and 30 percent for "Value added."

[10] Based on number of employees reported as of mid-March under Old-Age and Survivors Insurance Program.

Source: Department of Commerce, Bureau of the Census; Annual Survey of Manufactures: 1951.

No. 945.—Manufactures—Selected Statistics for Geographic Divisions, by Major Industry Groups: 1947 and 1951

[Money figures in thousands of dollars. Division totals include estimates for component industry groups not shown separately. See table 942 for United States figures. 1951 figures based on sample and subject to sampling variation]

MAJOR INDUSTRY GROUP	NEW ENGLAND						
	1947		1951				
			All employees [1]		Number of production workers (average)	Value added by manu- facture [1]	Stand- ard error (per- cent) [1]
	All em- ployees (average)	Value added by manu- facture [1]	Number (average)	Salaries and wages			
All industries, total	1,474,634	6,813,606	1,494,739	5,800,962	1,226,395	5,465,600	2
Food and kindred products	66,625	364,608	66,142	305,702	50,060	364,012	6
Textile mill products	263,017	1,345,169	249,236	530,644	227,063	1,322,563	4
Apparel and related products	74,322	278,963	72,584	162,651	63,060	262,622	8
Lumber and products (exc. furniture) [4]	23,734	115,905	22,520	68,394	23,471	744,456	15
Furniture and fixtures	18,159	74,619	22,383	74,546	21,167	105,603	15
Paper and allied products	66,345	367,012	70,611	251,751	65,169	310,068	2
Printing and publishing industries	54,169	281,170	51,697	180,726	26,650	322,114	15
Chemicals and allied products	36,573	214,958	38,617	115,122	26,707	266,169	3
Rubber products	44,963	222,783	46,800	182,606	38,766	262,762	2
Leather and leather products	109,032	453,690	104,121	305,220	98,325	448,135	15
Stone, clay, and glass products	21,519	106,475	22,439	84,264	18,759	162,421	6
Primary metal industries	61,696	283,199	64,520	307,307	55,073	265,421	18
Fabricated metal products	106,696	305,176	106,696	306,642	85,963	662,421	3
Machinery (except electrical)	202,098	923,120	200,301	508,545	161,122	1,205,206	2
Electrical machinery	96,606	451,306	113,781	350,160	89,310	726,646	4
Transportation equipment	51,600	306,974	64,365	278,906	50,060	365,600	4
Instruments and related products	34,419	165,632	33,077	116,997	28,770	197,236	6
Miscellaneous manufactures [5]	106,452	463,700	106,098	340,670	90,169	561,813	4
Administrative and auxiliary			15,386	80,268			

MAJOR INDUSTRY GROUP	MIDDLE ATLANTIC						
	1947		1951				
			All employees [1]		Number of pro- duction workers (average)	Value added by manu- facture [1]	Stand- ard error (per- cent) [1]
	All em- ployees (average)	Value added by manu- facture [1]	Number (average)	Salaries and wages			
All industries, total	4,253,736	20,796,696	4,165,609	16,363,446	3,373,735	26,466,411	1
Food and kindred products	295,851	1,912,172	294,173	962,513	206,612	2,321,762	3
Tobacco manufactures	36,957	102,095	32,316	49,562	20,363	115,662	3
Textile mill products	293,690	1,375,639	278,606	861,696	241,327	1,322,167	4
Apparel and related products	802,741	2,665,194	873,160	1,696,669	508,160	2,571,193	4
Lumber and products (exc. furniture) [4]	37,380	142,694	43,232	120,628	36,642	152,170	15
Furniture and fixtures	64,297	265,219	67,046	237,074	55,946	669,369	6
Paper and allied products	121,600	752,611	125,609	453,171	104,929	666,696	3
Printing and publishing industries	341,350	1,576,611	347,360	1,066,649	162,752	1,544,166	6
Chemicals and allied products	196,341	1,665,360	204,843	841,371	130,697	2,227,662	3
Petroleum and coal products	53,602	515,666	54,600	943,460	43,422	656,666	5
Rubber products	40,797	210,466	37,323	143,504	30,620	276,666	3
Leather and leather products	110,666	466,162	102,666	276,342	100,660	456,666	4
Stone, clay, and glass products	140,770	662,361	132,667	526,621	120,662	1,027,662	4
Primary metal industries	378,597	1,664,345	400,167	1,660,261	315,666	1,666,666	3
Fabricated metal products	304,145	1,306,394	304,661	1,609,946	235,666	1,466,666	3
Machinery (except electrical)	398,666	1,676,796	387,666	1,466,626	296,666	2,666,666	3
Electrical machinery	266,666	1,362,167	312,661	1,161,666	236,666	2,666,666	3
Transportation equipment	262,666	666,666	247,666	666,666	176,666	1,666,666	3
Instruments and related products	132,666	666,666	155,666	666,666	666,666	666,666	3
Miscellaneous manufactures [5]	176,666	666,616	667,666	666,666	176,646	1,696,726	3
Administrative and auxiliary			103,666	666,662			7

See footnotes at end of table.

No. 945.—MANUFACTURES—SELECTED STATISTICS FOR GEOGRAPHIC DIVISIONS, BY MAJOR INDUSTRY GROUPS: 1947 AND 1951—Continued

[Money figures in thousands of dollars]

MAJOR INDUSTRY GROUP	EAST NORTH CENTRAL						
	1947		1951				
			All employees [1]		Number of production workers (average)	Value added by manufacture [1]	Standard error (percent) [1]
	All employees (average)	Value added by manufacture [1]	Number (average)	Salaries and wages			
All industries, total	4,314,892	23,473,563	4,684,191	15,637,941	3,795,677	33,543,646	1
Food and kindred products	353,615	2,382,765	362,195	1,305,344	265,818	2,899,579	3
Textile mill products	45,330	206,617	42,485	137,526	37,522	200,400	5
Apparel and related products	126,395	505,872	128,366	339,170	111,221	553,668	7
Lumber and products (exc. furniture)[4]	63,329	280,060	77,965	237,587	68,951	396,594	7
Furniture and fixtures	112,539	510,622	114,067	404,365	97,430	671,974	4
Paper and allied products	122,989	776,060	131,966	517,130	109,939	1,094,690	3
Printing and publishing industries	195,263	1,169,861	211,895	881,569	134,132	1,485,978	2
Chemicals and allied products	143,733	1,356,796	155,225	641,842	106,254	1,896,725	2
Petroleum and coal products	49,055	431,152	52,431	235,279	42,064	667,722	4
Rubber products	125,502	588,746	113,513	457,687	90,838	742,771	2
Leather and leather products	75,158	318,894	63,659	187,927	56,643	269,555	4
Stone, clay, and glass products	131,596	688,262	149,896	541,546	130,402	1,011,050	4
Primary metal industries	478,422	2,416,939	508,967	2,185,274	443,215	4,047,492	1
Fabricated metal products	406,058	2,159,830	437,550	1,750,047	361,684	3,169,988	2
Machinery (except electrical)	762,315	4,013,422	787,270	3,430,187	619,594	5,692,777	2
Electrical machinery	325,509	1,634,719	343,378	1,263,467	275,432	2,351,246	2
Transportation equipment	631,049	3,283,208	728,382	3,033,765	616,494	5,326,614	1
Miscellaneous manufactures [1]	111,601	499,884	120,237	420,205	96,724	712,617	5
Administrative and auxiliary			99,027	432,500			

MAJOR INDUSTRY GROUP	WEST NORTH CENTRAL						
	1947		1951				
			All employees [1]		Number of production workers (average)	Value added by manufacture [1]	Standard error (percent) [1]
	All employees (average)	Value added by manufacture [1]	Number (average)	Salaries and wages			
All industries, total	785,064	4,119,409	897,931	3,090,495	691,971	5,688,029	2
Food and kindred products	206,986	1,204,953	213,117	703,521	154,975	1,462,087	4
Textile mill products	8,374	28,279	7,394	22,241	6,167	44,789	15
Apparel and related products	54,451	187,519	56,163	131,650	50,139	207,881	10
Lumber and products (exc. furniture)[4]	20,613	77,023	28,485	78,178	25,686	126,759	15
Furniture and fixtures	14,873	58,025	11,979	38,668	10,027	56,587	20
Paper and allied products	21,061	124,804	23,539	82,090	19,573	165,471	6
Printing and publishing industries	60,520	335,192	71,067	251,219	47,082	453,838	6
Chemicals and allied products	32,586	328,481	33,996	130,321	23,595	387,723	4
Petroleum and coal products	8,947	79,401	9,370	40,558	6,361	68,706	15
Rubber products	5,785	31,032	6,503	22,637	5,553	42,822	1
Leather and leather products	45,395	128,775	41,986	97,086	38,129	160,718	3
Stone, clay, and glass products	28,049	148,796	35,427	127,624	30,305	251,049	7
Primary metal industries	26,002	115,014	27,920	108,622	24,012	181,984	6
Fabricated metal products	44,909	232,093	51,518	194,706	40,310	337,436	5
Machinery (except electrical)	86,729	422,902	96,690	368,482	77,385	660,041	4
Electrical machinery	41,351	191,232	31,772	113,554	25,265	189,475	4
Transportation equipment	45,576	261,527	86,990	353,294	71,231	595,475	1
Miscellaneous manufactures [1]	25,819	135,818	30,690	108,297	23,455	209,063	5
Administrative and auxiliary			16,374	57,940			

See footnotes at end of table.

No. 945.—Manufactures—Selected Statistics for Geographic Divisions, by Major Industry Groups: 1947 and 1951—Continued

[Money figures in thousands of dollars]

MAJOR INDUSTRY GROUP	SOUTH ATLANTIC						
	1947		1951				
	All employees (average)	Value added by manufacture [1]	All employees		Number of production workers (average)	Value added by manufacture [1]	Standard error (percent) [2]
			Number (average)	Salaries and wages			
All industries, total	1,822,495	6,942,054	1,999,392	4,722,485	1,451,139	9,216,678	1
Food and kindred products	141,948	696,422	144,466	377,982	103,729	838,108	4
Textile mill products	484,285	2,021,525	505,755	1,314,176	477,680	2,144,672	1
Apparel and related products	95,515	237,514	112,695	264,163	106,947	455,591	7
Lumber and products (exc. furniture) [4]	135,388	288,376	176,380	306,532	162,385	387,775	15
Furniture and fixtures	55,709	306,806	55,061	168,430	52,205	344,009	6
Paper and allied products	46,045	312,432	52,013	161,942	45,066	346,649	2
Printing and publishing industries	40,335	365,272	51,467	180,277	31,088	392,711	7
Chemicals and allied products	105,719	778,062	116,978	417,625	85,950	1,305,250	6
Petroleum and coal products	5,894	47,900	5,808	21,970	4,581	40,671	3
Leather and leather products	17,413	68,143	18,480	40,941	15,098	64,392	5
Stone, clay, and glass products	60,791	261,549	71,419	208,985	43,174	288,179	14
Primary metal industries	64,782	322,372	69,004	270,021	60,489	397,684	1
Fabricated metal products	45,211	207,287	50,982	171,308	36,090	204,260	5
Machinery (except electrical)	31,305	134,846	35,611	138,770	26,590	192,611	5
Electrical machinery	20,964	94,829	26,276	161,083	21,794	182,066	4
Transportation equipment	63,631	296,812	76,774	276,356	63,383	433,292	3
Instruments and related products	3,049	9,585	3,633	12,086	2,739	17,190	15
Miscellaneous manufactures [6]	16,512	50,481	18,189	44,919	14,112	72,083	7
Administrative and auxiliary			22,623	80,694			

MAJOR INDUSTRY GROUP	EAST SOUTH CENTRAL						
	1947		1951				
	All employees (average)	Value added by manufacture [1]	All employees [5]		Number of production workers (average)	Value added by manufacture [1]	Standard error (percent) [2]
			Number (average)	Salaries and wages			
All industries, total	632,765	2,875,436	682,525	1,895,277	595,549	4,911,636	2
Food and kindred products	65,070	510,352	67,528	193,194	44,692	685,801	4
Textile mill products	90,987	366,078	94,512	256,898	88,723	401,380	3
Apparel and related products	53,845	133,696	65,016	126,436	61,587	189,046	6
Lumber and products (exc. furniture) [4]	96,761	277,203	105,345	175,108	98,516	315,678	14
Furniture and fixtures	18,358	89,940	19,616	51,117	17,315	84,088	15
Paper and allied products	16,987	116,864	21,851	72,714	18,494	175,624	5
Printing and publishing industries	20,854	102,062	28,669	77,910	16,122	121,028	6
Chemicals and allied products	46,950	291,960	51,709	182,987	32,622	467,680	6
Petroleum and coal products	4,782	89,104	5,102	18,540	4,166	104,560	
Leather and leather products	14,311	60,696	17,374	27,133	11,382	65,785	6
Stone, clay, and glass products	20,587	88,460	22,102	67,350	19,582	128,564	5
Primary metal industries	62,474	267,068	61,911	217,373	54,507	428,010	5
Fabricated metal products	32,911	144,419	33,334	107,442	28,077	162,560	5
Machinery (except electrical)	22,692	94,814	28,564	108,443	22,348	208,282	4
Electrical machinery	4,732	27,663	12,396	46,407	11,505	80,660	6
Transportation equipment	21,305	104,804	15,006	40,118	13,126	88,066	6
Instruments and related products	1,015	13,819	3,210	11,380	2,460	88,086	
Miscellaneous manufactures [6]	4,386	16,211	7,891	17,434	7,204	34,486	20
Administrative and auxiliary			6,549	29,686			

See footnotes at end of table.

No. 945.—MANUFACTURES—SELECTED STATISTICS FOR GEOGRAPHIC DIVISIONS, BY MAJOR INDUSTRY GROUPS: 1947 AND 1951—Continued

[Money figures in thousands of dollars]

MAJOR INDUSTRY GROUP	WEST SOUTH CENTRAL						
	1947		1951				
	All employees (average)	Value added by manufacture [1]	All employees [2]		Number of production workers (average)	Value added by manufacture [1]	Standard error (percent) [3]
			Number (average)	Salaries and wages			
All industries, total	559,241	3,027,769	653,719	2,095,470	539,007	4,399,571	3
Food and kindred products	110,744	593,694	109,199	289,311	77,767	667,269	5
Textile mill products	12,259	43,525	12,465	29,128	11,994	52,467	6
Apparel and related products	31,533	96,203	45,721	97,052	41,999	159,531	20
Lumber and products (exc. furniture) [4]	90,348	269,573	78,407	155,605	73,225	255,364	15
Furniture and fixtures	11,587	43,420	17,466	44,834	15,677	84,647	15
Paper and allied products	22,371	156,090	30,040	105,693	26,475	293,534	15
Printing and publishing industries	29,037	154,406	33,567	112,625	23,279	201,734	9
Chemicals and allied products	42,138	389,299	54,441	211,585	40,752	909,137	4
Petroleum and coal products	59,035	578,617	60,184	273,960	47,416	830,200	2
Leather and leather products	3,093	9,343	3,875	7,532	3,534	16,092	2
Stone, clay, and glass products	20,366	107,883	31,126	94,151	26,133	216,673	15
Primary metal industries	18,778	96,122	24,963	92,325	22,158	191,679	4
Fabricated metal products	21,171	105,190	19,647	72,220	15,735	146,077	9
Machinery (except electrical)	31,826	175,449	39,346	162,500	29,233	323,417	7
Electrical machinery	2,300	14,109	3,618	10,618	3,159	34,261	4
Transportation equipment	31,750	132,722	59,281	226,661	50,323	339,905	4
Instruments and related products	2,484	7,999	3,473	11,425	3,101	18,630	15
Miscellaneous manufactures [4]	5,378	21,382	5,944	13,875	5,344	27,543	15
Administrative and auxiliary			17,863	71,784			

MAJOR INDUSTRY GROUP	MOUNTAIN						
	1947		1951				
	All employees (average)	Value added by manufacture [1]	All employees [2]		Number of production workers (average)	Value added by manufacture [1]	Standard error (percent) [3]
			Number (average)	Salaries and wages			
All industries, total	141,638	839,202	167,171	588,886	133,435	1,257,762	4
Food and kindred products	40,583	245,359	38,294	117,275	28,934	249,806	6
Lumber and products (exc. furniture) [4]	21,177	101,926	29,654	98,486	27,741	167,059	20
Paper and allied products	782	4,758	1,549	6,956	1,364	16,479	15
Chemicals and allied products	4,758	39,796	11,184	47,698	8,375	105,481	4
Petroleum and coal products	5,470	52,093	6,280	27,930	4,501	79,649	15
Leather and leather products	1,319	4,811	2,287	7,275	1,965	12,223	1
Stone, clay, and glass products	6,345	31,891	5,788	20,721	4,996	49,671	15
Primary metal industries	23,094	175,735	26,842	103,150	23,509	318,740	1
Fabricated metal products	4,361	22,460	6,269	24,958	4,199	45,459	20
Machinery (except electrical)	6,163	29,966	6,822	23,301	5,317	38,841	15
Transportation equipment	1,026	4,811	1,778	6,197	1,396	7,747	20
Instruments and related products	399	1,902	507	1,440	404	2,797	4
Administrative and auxiliary [5]			2,435	11,008			

See footnotes at end of table.

No. 945.—MANUFACTURES—SELECTED STATISTICS FOR GEOGRAPHIC DIVISIONS, BY MAJOR INDUSTRY GROUPS: 1947 AND 1951—Continued

[Money figures in thousands of dollars]

MAJOR INDUSTRY GROUP	PACIFIC						
	1947		1951				
			All employees [3]		Number of production workers (average)	Value added by manufacture [1]	Standard error (percent) [3]
	All employees (average)	Value added by manufacture [1]	Number (average)	Salaries and wages			
All industries, total............	913,787	5,544,634	1,179,411	4,696,190	929,344	8,422,245	2
Food and kindred products..........	164,415	1,108,506	185,450	658,236	142,347	1,339,803	5
Textile mill products.................	9,097	48,557	7,068	24,729	5,697	39,296	15
Apparel and related products........	47,805	205,770	63,302	180,948	55,763	202,265	9
Lumber and products(exc. furniture)[4].	133,043	860,202	189,896	739,904	175,039	1,374,382	10
Furniture and fixtures................	25,183	120,467	22,483	81,824	19,136	135,847	15
Paper and allied products.............	29,555	253,033	37,599	151,189	31,993	421,174	4
Printing and publishing industries...	53,080	328,055	62,324	267,663	35,009	414,179	8
Chemicals and allied products........	30,591	307,515	45,216	195,649	31,228	533,029	10
Petroleum and coal products.........	22,008	217,571	20,174	92,750	13,877	369,910	5
Stone, clay, and glass products.......	31,652	177,623	37,035	133,502	31,095	273,740	6
Primary metal industries..............	42,502	256,115	55,886	243,126	50,114	524,611	4
Fabricated metal products............	62,689	335,727	65,215	262,199	54,536	505,526	5
Machinery (except electrical).........	61,606	329,482	70,689	296,438	53,485	520,314	6
Electrical machinery..................	19,329	116,236	27,047	99,760	20,844	194,113	5
Transportation equipment............	137,114	643,778	219,666	931,871	161,336	1,240,801	2
Instruments and related products....	7,111	31,836	9,006	36,452	6,776	57,982	15
Administrative and auxiliary [5]........	....	....	19,082	78,788	....	....	....

[1] Value of products less cost of materials, supplies, fuel, electric energy, and contract work.
[2] Includes data for plants idle throughout year, administrative offices and units auxiliary to manufacturing.
[3] See text, p. 782, for explanation of standard error. Refers to column "All employees—Number"; standard errors of estimates for other columns usually of same magnitude.
[4] Data for logging industry and for sawmills producing less than 200,000 board feet of lumber included in estimates for 1951, but excluded from figures for 1947.
[5] Includes privately owned and/or operated establishments classified in "Ordnance and accessories." Government owned and operated establishments excluded from annual survey.

Source: Department of Commerce, Bureau of the Census; advance reports of *1951 Annual Survey of Manufactures.*

No. 946.—MANUFACTURES—GENERAL STATISTICS, BY STATES: 1950 AND 1951

[Money figures in thousands of dollars. For comparable 1947 and 1939 data, see table 947. Figures are based on sample and subject to sampling variation]

DIVISION AND STATE	1950		1951					STANDARD ERROR (per cent)[3]	
	All employees (average for the year)[1]	Value added by manufacture[2]	All employees[1]		Production workers		Value added by manufacture[2]	1950	1951
			Number (average for the year)	Salaries and wages, total	Number (average for the year)	Wages, total			
United States	14,769,931	89,749,765	15,612,619	55,992,091	12,506,914	40,654,832	102.085.814	1	1
New England	1,433,359	7,417,675	1,490,750	5,099,902	1,226,365	3,816,755	8,469,850	2	2
Maine	108,309	454,278	106,930	306,848	95,753	255,732	520,998	15	4
New Hampshire	80,832	353,710	85,400	244,896	75,466	197,658	407,474	5	6
Vermont	40,636	205,938	42,343	141,867	36,450	113,242	264,622	6	15
Massachusetts	696,777	3,665,666	710,857	2,435,581	572,340	1,764,671	4,024,945	2	3
Rhode Island	135,473	614,636	136,936	436,053	114,475	332,191	666,552	4	3
Connecticut	371,332	2,123,447	408,284	1,534,687	332,501	1,153,261	2,584,459	2	2
Middle Atlantic	4,006,194	23,503,166	4,165,028	15,263,445	3,273,735	10,732,197	26,666,411	1	1
New York	1,829,479	10,511,860	1,883,085	7,003,629	1,427,398	4,649,236	11,933,729	2	2
New Jersey	730,650	4,967,312	772,032	2,933,683	610,018	2,095,668	5,310,912	2	2
Pennsylvania	1,446,065	8,123,994	1,509,911	5,326,133	1,236,319	3,987,293	9,421,770	2	1
East North Central	4,427,093	29,518,015	4,684,191	18,637,941	3,705,677	13,569,131	33,543,646	1	1
Ohio	1,192,224	7,972,073	1,299,492	5,209,001	1,028,445	3,802,661	9,396,104	1	1
Indiana	563,730	3,832,892	596,925	2,280,368	487,909	1,735,432	4,278,221	1	2
Illinois	1,187,296	7,933,449	1,243,681	4,817,311	956,588	3,347,116	8,835,548	2	1
Michigan	1,054,441	7,392,255	1,084,622	4,572,223	868,748	3,397,426	7,858,442	1	1
Wisconsin	429,402	2,687,346	459,471	1,759,038	363,987	1,286,496	3,175,331	2	3
West North Central	828,111	5,154,364	897,931	3,090,495	691,971	2,180,216	5,688,029	2	2
Minnesota	186,123	1,200,204	202,160	730,027	151,568	499,307	1,301,396	3	3
Iowa	147,429	925,762	156,969	546,036	118,440	392,223	1,018,667	3	5
Missouri	340,239	2,045,318	358,594	1,176,075	279,791	815,322	2,177,950	2	2
North Dakota[4] }	17,906	99,001	16,855	51,423	12,472	34,440	103,958	20	8
South Dakota[4] }									
Nebraska	48,025	270,579	50,692	166,976	40,433	124,996	336,725	5	6
Kansas	88,389	613,500	112,641	419,958	89,267	313,928	749,333	3	4
South Atlantic	1,627,284	8,471,115	1,690,593	4,722,485	1,451,120	3,647,683	9,316,475	2	1
Delaware	45,269	287,592	47,447	157,893	35,578	105,733	326,715	5	8
Maryland	222,439	1,455,095	249,999	849,622	200,199	609,380	1,603,006	2	3
Dist. of Columbia	17,282	113,746	17,339	66,714	9,944	33,254	126,803	15	15
Virginia	225,133	1,326,495	232,228	644,517	197,146	494,011	1,447,535	3	2
West Virginia	129,242	882,401	139,431	470,926	114,761	355,654	1,036,456	4	2
North Carolina	408,295	1,862,825	412,488	1,029,530	370,698	844,282	1,948,452	2	3
South Carolina	195,954	857,716	201,227	524,299	184,684	447,697	926,277	2	4
Georgia	292,273	1,235,957	285,334	696,609	253,182	556,350	1,332,659	5	2
Florida	91,397	449,288	105,100	282,375	84,928	201,322	568,572	6	5
East South Central	649,792	3,452,683	683,825	1,885,277	585,640	1,460,885	3,911,625	2	2
Kentucky	138,444	957,640	147,426	463,836	122,963	349,158	1,093,896	3	3
Tennessee	226,372	1,174,446	240,986	665,164	203,826	503,702	1,294,384	3	3
Alabama	211,162	1,039,831	215,568	585,913	188,999	473,499	1,192,019	3	2
Mississippi	73,814	280,766	79,845	170,364	69,832	134,526	331,326	6	3
West South Central	603,787	3,849,399	653,719	2,095,470	520,007	1,497,745	4,809,571	2	3
Arkansas	72,926	320,723	76,194	182,227	66,757	143,700	378,979	7	6
Louisiana	126,035	915,976	136,138	418,677	112,083	304,155	1,073,822	4	5
Oklahoma	63,494	344,037	69,504	230,251	51,244	150,809	433,706	4	4
Texas	341,332	2,268,663	371,883	1,264,315	289,923	899,081	2,923,064	3	4
Mountain	157,142	1,042,063	167,171	588,886	133,435	439,031	1,257,762	4	4
Montana	17,040	107,837	17,497	62,948	14,226	48,828	149,776	5	1
Idaho	15,832	117,673	19,330	76,897	18,784	66,464	147,853	15	10
Wyoming	7,099	37,739	5,891	21,809	4,938	16,429	37,245	7	15
Colorado	56,508	340,795	58,195	195,694	44,340	139,252	393,899	4	8
New Mexico	13,527	102,897	14,736	50,479	11,041	35,726	121,633	20	9
Arizona	14,721	127,946	17,441	60,959	14,018	47,683	156,762	7	6
Utah	29,377	177,504	30,993	109,065	24,263	77,886	223,221	15	8
Nevada	3,038		3,088	11,035	1,825	6,763	27,373	40	20
Pacific	1,037,169	7,041,285	1,179,411	4,608,190	920,344	3,311,189	8,423,245	2	2
Washington	162,661	1,113,362	193,695	760,370	159,585	590,253	1,343,983	4	3
Oregon	119,419	806,947	132,447	498,685	114,710	411,621	945,875	4	3
California	755,089	5,120,976	853,269	3,349,135	646,049	2,309,315	6,133,387	2	2

[1] Includes data for plants idle throughout year, administrative offices and units auxiliary to manufacturing.
[2] Value of products less cost of materials, supplies, fuel, electric energy, and contract work.
[3] See text, p. 782, for explanation of standard error. Refers to columns "All employees—Number (average for the year)"; standard errors of estimates for other columns usually of same magnitude.
[4] Data for North Dakota and South Dakota combined because of high standard errors associated with each State.

Source: Department of Commerce, Bureau of the Census; advance report of *1951 Annual Survey of Manufactures.*

No. 947.—MANUFACTURES—GENERAL STATISTICS, BY STATES: 1947 AND 1939

[Money figures in thousands of dollars. See text, p. 781]

DIVISION AND STATE	Number of establishments	All employees [1]		Production workers		Value added by manufacture [2]	Number of production workers (average for year)	Value added by manufacture [2]
		Number (average for year)	Salaries and wages, total	Number (average for year)	Wages, total			
							1939 [3]	
United States....	240,881	14,294,304	39,695,527	11,916,136	30,342,343	74,425,835	7,808,205	24,487,304
New England........	30,274	1,274,684	3,941,811	1,343,228	3,864,112	6,813,800	947,412	2,414,388
Maine.............	1,635	100,181	288,994	90,375	198,204	432,123	74,069	180,388
New Hampshire......	1,124	74,782	177,670	68,463	146,324	306,832	55,494	104,422
Vermont...........	580	34,872	85,021	30,390	64,409	140,025	20,495	49,741
Massachusetts......	10,586	718,443	1,933,141	601,668	1,464,047	2,370,094	458,372	1,151,493
Rhode Island.......	2,214	140,550	374,582	128,130	297,680	458,420	108,569	257,688
Connecticut........	3,047	300,586	1,148,794	331,827	851,548	1,906,840	383,970	650,228
Middle Atlantic........	75,383	3,853,738	11,412,746	3,245,673	8,613,489	39,796,626	2,384,380	7,393,709
New York..........	47,849	1,778,976	4,279,680	1,494,705	3,816,374	9,686,380	940,888	3,313,640
New Jersey.........	10,785	728,229	2,214,150	601,748	1,644,397	4,177,080	621,803	1,512,260
Pennsylvania.......	16,789	1,639,534	5,918,903	1,319,436	3,053,879	6,966,958	833,571	3,476,803
East North Central....	86,578	4,317,362	13,697,891	3,545,172	9,195,490	26,473,383	2,359,020	7,744,488
Ohio.............	12,306	1,194,603	3,590,075	988,446	2,727,661	6,388,005	586,089	2,116,434
Indiana...........	5,408	646,846	1,967,848	487,582	1,394,445	3,077,608	275,812	984,746
Illinois...........	18,988	1,184,820	3,683,083	964,415	2,627,312	6,660,137	800,385	2,187,240
Michigan..........	9,892	973,673	3,060,656	821,721	2,436,027	8,156,336	320,166	1,794,016
Wisconsin.........	6,979	418,448	1,184,347	342,006	908,119	2,380,674	198,648	661,970
West North Central....	17,462	782,064	2,042,729	638,940	1,511,383	4,111,089	376,189	1,349,167
Minnesota.........	4,567	179,986	501,346	146,153	353,568	1,022,586	78,362	353,300
Iowa............	2,965	140,425	372,339	112,660	275,454	671,300	64,772	289,360
Missouri..........	5,726	227,515	527,184	203,711	467,464	1,363,148	175,388	681,804
North Dakota......	262	5,318	12,341	4,220	8,948	29,461	2,000	13,809
South Dakota......	404	10,388	25,706	8,380	19,289	51,328	4,521	19,619
Nebraska.........	1,344	47,031	119,028	37,328	87,422	300,658	18,448	69,139
Kansas...........	1,940	74,634	204,301	59,348	151,399	661,061	30,885	112,301
South Atlantic.........	24,081	1,539,496	3,376,875	1,344,444	2,790,342	6,942,654	977,886	2,234,970
Delaware..........	682	34,465	99,183	26,014	70,607	182,088	19,568	74,028
Maryland.........	2,524	238,582	612,034	185,464	449,343	1,126,407	140,569	460,189
Dist. of Columbia...	428	17,815	88,972	10,007	27,491	89,067	7,579	42,367
Virginia..........	3,644	216,637	453,904	190,035	384,441	1,081,629	132,689	376,290
West Virginia......	1,602	127,353	337,809	106,994	285,499	668,909	74,411	213,394
North Carolina.....	5,322	331,480	746,895	350,207	641,086	1,646,672	200,344	444,161
South Carolina.....	2,187	185,601	376,364	175,734	330,464	794,312	128,409	168,204
Georgia..........	4,784	249,936	484,946	228,807	309,830	1,015,900	155,070	320,082
Florida..........	2,828	78,066	145,818	66,026	125,240	349,978	51,149	115,885
East South Central....	10,967	633,765	1,366,231	529,191	1,092,380	2,375,436	365,696	823,191
Kentucky.........	2,344	139,304	304,668	110,602	240,803	740,772	62,491	196,485
Tennessee........	3,346	221,454	473,211	192,367	369,820	967,539	131,394	348,378
Alabama.........	3,335	205,136	444,647	185,648	376,923	367,366	114,866	205,577
Mississippi.......	1,942	70,671	137,706	60,877	114,580	300,194	45,688	72,661
West South Central....	18,181	589,341	1,333,884	468,338	965,389	3,627,700	262,689	829,270
Arkansas.........	1,924	65,321	124,167	57,254	101,360	300,144	33,672	74,444
Louisiana........	2,389	132,464	309,371	111,553	229,673	934,674	76,668	348,497
Oklahoma........	1,740	53,405	143,806	44,302	105,277	341,667	27,468	149,769
Texas...........	7,128	337,053	755,411	242,014	565,480	1,727,444	125,113	481,808
Mountain............	5,040	161,636	373,990	116,199	232,491	688,368	67,691	299,301
Montana.........	682	16,092	61,481	12,806	34,380	68,266	8,568	37,388
Idaho...........	664	16,907	43,748	14,602	37,504	100,484	9,884	39,738
Wyoming........	256	5,607	16,696	4,385	12,391	34,987	2,389	15,399
Colorado........	1,602	54,071	144,307	44,153	105,734	296,774	24,369	93,589
New Mexico......	432	7,800	18,222	6,349	14,173	55,488	3,381	14,668
Arizona.........	545	14,188	35,209	11,167	29,080	105,300	5,589	23,448
Utah...........	772	24,516	62,804	19,973	48,063	128,368	11,386	61,243
Nevada.........	126	2,667	8,049	2,064	6,416	37,777	1,098	11,341
Pacific.............	24,133	913,737	2,639,370	746,915	2,129,080	5,544,094	411,089	1,665,197
Washington......	3,410	144,324	434,090	129,488	354,896	874,099	62,989	397,714
Oregon.........	3,075	105,391	317,897	92,144	265,557	875,037	56,389	178,789
California......	17,648	663,573	2,094,383	530,388	1,532,365	3,904,958	291,389	1,292,545

[1] Includes all full-time and part-time production and related workers, force-account construction workers, clerical and routine office workers, administrative, supervisory, sales, technical, and all other personnel on payroll of manufacturing establishments. Excludes employees of central administrative offices operated by companies having 3 or more manufacturing establishments. Wages and salaries represent gross earnings of employees before deductions, dismissal pay, nonproduction bonuses, vacation and sick leave pay, and compensation in kind, and prior to such deductions as employees' social security contributions, withholding taxes, group insurance, union dues, and savings bonds.

[2] Value of products less cost of materials, supplies, fuel, electricity, and contract work.

[3] Figures will not add to totals because of rounding.

Source: Department of Commerce, Bureau of the Census; 1947 Census of Manufactures report.

No. 948.—MANUFACTURES—EXPENDITURES FOR NEW PLANT AND EQUIPMENT, BY INDUSTRY GROUPS: 1947, 1950, AND 1951[1]

[Dollar figures in thousands. 1950 and 1951 figures based on sample and subject to sampling variation. See text, p. 781. 1947 and 1950 figures exclude expenditures: (1) for plant under construction but not in operation; (2) for plants idle throughout year; (3) for nonmanufacturing establishments of manufacturing companies; (4) for plants and equipment leased to manufacturers by owners; and (5) for used plant and equipment acquired from others. 1951 figures include, for the first time, expenditures for plants under construction but not in operation]

INDUSTRY GROUP	1947[1]			1950			1951			STANDARD ERROR (percent)[2]	
	Total expenditures for new plant and equipment	New structures and additions to plant	New machinery and equipment	Total expenditures for new plant and equipment	New structures and additions to plant	New machinery and equipment	Total expenditures for new plant and equipment	New structures and additions to plant	New machinery and equipment	1950	1951
All industries, total	6,003,873	2,122,143	3,881,730	5,110,252	1,411,330	3,698,922	7,781,731	2,893,220	5,188,511	1	1
Food and kindred products	820,847	276,803	544,044	649,445	216,421	433,024	722,872	254,449	468,423	5	5
Tobacco manufactures	35,645	12,919	22,726	17,664	6,633	10,831	17,992	7,388	10,604	5	2
Textile mill products	367,510	104,706	262,804	420,183	74,449	345,734	413,536	98,264	315,252	4	4
Apparel and related products	83,945	22,114	61,831	62,558	14,279	48,279	69,363	18,555	50,926	8	4
Lumber and products (exc. furniture)	171,574	56,048	115,526	[3] 191,817	80,887	140,930	240,076	69,535	170,538	10	7
Furniture and fixtures	77,441	26,247	51,194	[3] 68,087	(4)	(4)	53,444	18,629	34,815	9	8
Paper and allied products	406,779	117,231	289,548	290,083	62,906	226,177	433,104	100,957	334,147	3	3
Printing and publishing industries	225,368	82,143	144,225	244,396	54,322	190,074	244,290	78,097	166,303	10	15
Chemicals and allied products	810,732	279,739	530,993	602,998	149,183	453,815	1,087,690	297,170	790,501	2	4
Petroleum and coal products	399,754	317,440	82,314	331,541	201,360	130,181	449,532	229,858	219,674	3	5
Rubber products	109,783	30,893	78,890	79,958	16,944	63,014	116,769	23,263	93,506	4	3
Leather and leather products	31,301	8,064	23,237	25,791	4,638	21,153	29,385	6,323	17,062	15	8
Stone, clay, and glass products	285,066	104,378	180,688	222,652	138,698	106,014	343,453	100,753	242,730	5	3
Primary metal industries	692,177	212,687	379,490	548,253	93,061	409,555	1,233,749	478,909	856,940	2	3
Fabricated metal products	304,822	92,119	212,703	[3] 317,027	93,061	223,936	359,924	112,170	247,754	3	3
Machinery (except electrical)	517,569	167,396	350,193	337,212	96,877	259,340	653,098	228,956	423,331	3	4
Electrical machinery	244,606	64,874	179,732	194,458	50,733	143,407	320,314	119,325	200,980	3	3
Transportation equipment	354,974	99,511	255,460	343,426	79,738	256,690	653,783	283,771	400,991	2	1
Instruments and related products	55,000	15,313	40,687	64,446	16,418	48,028	85,004	30,918	54,086	8	8
Miscellaneous manufactures	106,960	31,515	75,445	98,275	19,895	78,880	146,426	67,169	79,257	6	6

[1] Smaller establishments submitting "short" form reports were not requested to include data on capital expenditures. Resulting understatement is negligible (see Ch. VI of Vol. I, "General Summary," Census of Manufactures, 1947).

[2] See text, p. 782, for explanation of standard error. Refers to total expenditures columns. Standard errors for new machinery columns approximately same as those for total expenditures; for new structures columns, vary, usually between 1 and 3 times the standard errors shown for total expenditure, up to a maximum of 18 percent for published totals; corresponding understatement of "All industries" total is less than 0.5 percent.

[3] Not fully represented in sample; capital expenditures understated by approximately 1 to 10 percent;

[4] Withheld because estimate did not meet publication standards. See text, p. 782.

Source: Department of Commerce, Bureau of the Census; Annual Survey of Manufactures: 1950 and 1951.

No. 949.—Manufactures—Expenditures for New Plant and Equipment,
BY States: 1947 AND 1951

[In thousands of dollars. See headnote, table 948]

DIVISION AND STATE	1947			1951			Standard error (percent)
	Total expenditures	New structures and additions to plant	New machinery and equipment	Total expenditures	New structures and additions to plant	New machinery and equipment	
United States	6,063,873	2,182,143	3,881,730	7,781,731	2,593,220	5,188,511	1
New England	413,580	114,151	368,429	462,306	121,440	330,958	4
Maine	35,055	12,708	22,347	42,636	12,565	30,062	8
New Hampshire	34,010	6,904	15,016	35,449	5,609	19,849	15
Vermont	9,608	3,061	6,647	(?)	(?)	(?)	4
Massachusetts	198,985	52,425	146,556	172,920	41,311	131,609	4
Rhode Island	34,609	9,117	26,492	43,206	(?)	(?)	20
Connecticut	116,225	32,845	83,366	180,576	43,147	107,429	6
Middle Atlantic	1,385,206	444,579	898,636	1,743,687	596,390	1,147,587	2
New York	497,443	152,173	345,270	542,114	154,949	387,769	3
New Jersey	303,287	93,130	210,857	263,290	118,595	244,568	3
Pennsylvania	533,806	201,376	332,439	837,874	321,756	615,590	4
East North Central	1,908,332	607,536	1,301,796	2,455,906	868,136	1,617,765	2
Ohio	498,254	179,298	318,961	606,782	271,492	336,270	2
Indiana	302,104	146,724	155,389	357,564	127,206	328,345	3
Illinois	476,431	166,046	310,385	509,046	181,096	327,978	4
Michigan	427,746	119,354	308,492	665,457	165,792	366,695	3
Wisconsin	162,787	55,189	107,568	195,057	70,498	134,560	7
West North Central	248,462	123,342	217,129	370,812	147,134	223,672	4
Minnesota	82,500	29,438	53,342	66,486	22,640	43,940	5
Iowa	64,686	23,041	41,645	98,651	32,166	66,462	20
Missouri	122,166	50,531	81,635	114,905	43,236	71,667	3
North Dakota	2,286	956	1,301	(?)	(?)	(?)	—
South Dakota	3,371	1,252	2,119	4,861	(?)	(?)	20
Nebraska	16,402	6,472	11,930	16,563	6,225	10,628	20
Kansas	36,767	11,739	26,048	74,364	(?)	(?)	20
South Atlantic	677,651	234,397	463,444	871,216	243,511	637,365	2
Delaware	21,137	5,504	15,543	38,074	19,261	19,639	3
Maryland	123,509	49,106	74,403	100,329	28,765	71,564	4
District of Columbia	4,602	976	3,526	6,983	2,305	4,778	9
Virginia	113,353	33,902	78,481	4 127,982	4 36,922	4 91,080	3
West Virginia	82,322	27,354	54,968	113,356	30,104	83,252	4
North Carolina	137,582	42,812	94,771	166,786	46,932	118,854	3
South Carolina	61,743	20,189	41,554	4 130,806	4 27,573	4 102,982	2
Georgia	84,320	28,147	56,173	115,460	41,044	74,416	10
Florida	50,052	16,117	33,935	76,936	15,699	60,287	7
East South Central	255,662	80,991	175,971	339,742	167,576	232,166	2
Kentucky	77,135	27,197	49,948	87,428	22,150	65,273	2
Tennessee	83,792	34,384	54,436	113,694	23,432	80,192	4
Alabama	73,362	22,752	49,610	97,132	32,794	64,398	3
Mississippi	22,713	6,658	16,087	41,565	9,200	32,365	6
West South Central	487,920	205,644	282,276	717,571	237,389	459,329	4
Arkansas	20,332	11,109	15,423	46,163	15,322	34,940	9
Louisiana	97,210	32,597	64,613	159,206	58,682	100,238	4
Oklahoma	25,504	12,352	12,353	36,147	12,206	34,685	7
Texas	304,944	146,235	153,718	605,036	172,019	385,077	5
Mountain	95,023	33,396	61,727	123,777	51,379	72,909	7
Montana	7,446	1,708	5,736	(?)	(?)	(?)	—
Idaho	11,447	3,903	7,544	14,731	2,395	12,346	10
Wyoming	10,236	3,756	7,479	13,328	3,230	8,790	9
Colorado	22,169	8,406	22,783	31,481	11,699	19,692	15
New Mexico	5,431	1,810	3,621	5,060	(?)	(?)	20
Arizona	6,238	2,131	4,197	9,463	(?)	(?)	20
Utah	16,988	4,171	12,817	33,057	11,794	18,392	7
Nevada	2,900	1,411	1,546	1,774	(?)	(?)	20
Pacific	553,678	225,277	332,391	766,123	299,082	466,670	7
Washington	81,476	29,707	52,769	100,629	26,671	72,967	4
Oregon	61,699	23,635	38,234	111,540	35,618	78,248	20
California	410,533	172,236	237,398	554,730	236,793	316,010	9

1 Smaller establishments submitting "short" form reports were not requested to include data on capital expenditures. Resulting understatement is negligible (see Ch. VI of Vol. 1, "General Summary," Census of Manufactures, 1947).
2 See text, p. 793, for explanation of standard error. Refers to total expenditures column. Standard errors for new machinery column approximately same as those for total expenditures; for new structures column, vary, usually between 1 and 3 times the standard errors shown for total expenditures, up to a maximum of 15 percent for published total. 3 Withheld because estimates did not meet publication standards. 4 Excludes data for establishments under construction; withheld to avoid disclosure of data for individual companies.

Source: Department of Commerce, Bureau of the Census; 1947 Census of Manufactures reports, and advance report of 1951 Annual Survey of Manufactures.

No. 948.—MANUFACTURES—EXPENDITURES FOR NEW PLANT AND EQUIPMENT, BY INDUSTRY GROUPS: 1947, 1950, AND 1951

[Dollar figures in thousands. 1950 and 1951 figures based on sample and subject to sampling variation. See text, p. 781. 1947 and 1950 figures exclude expenditures: (1) for plant under construction but not in operation; (2) for plants idle throughout year; (3) for nonmanufacturing establishments of manufacturing companies; (4) for plants and equipment leased to manufacturers by owners; and (5) for used plant and equipment acquired from others. 1951 figures include, for the first time, expenditures for plants under construction but not in operation]

INDUSTRY GROUP	1947 [1]			1950			1951			STANDARD ERROR (percent) [2]	
	Total expenditures for new plant and equipment	New structures and additions to plant	New machinery and equipment	Total expenditures for new plant and equipment	New structures and additions to plant	New machinery and equipment	Total expenditures for new plant and equipment	New structures and additions to plant	New machinery and equipment	1950	1951
All industries, total	6,003,873	2,122,143	3,881,730	5,110,262	1,411,330	3,698,932	7,761,731	2,568,220	5,188,511	1	1
Food and kindred products	820,847	276,803	544,044	649,445	216,421	433,024	722,872	254,449	468,423	5	5
Tobacco manufactures	35,645	12,919	22,726	17,654		10,464	11,992	7,388	10,604	5	2
Textile mill products	367,810	104,706	263,304	420,183	74,449	345,274	413,386	98,384	315,302	4	4
Apparel and related products	83,945	22,114	61,831	62,558	14,879	46,279	66,883	19,155	50,696	5	4
Lumber and products (exc. furniture)	171,574	56,048	115,526	[5] 191,817	50,857	140,930	240,076	69,838	170,238	10	7
Furniture and fixtures	77,441	26,247	51,194	[5] 58,087	(4)	228,177	65,444	18,629	36,815	9	8
Paper and allied products	406,779	117,231	289,548	299,083	62,906	190,074	435,104	100,987	334,147	3	3
Printing and publishing industries	225,368	82,143	144,225	244,396	54,322	453,815	244,290	78,087	166,203	10	15
Chemicals and allied products	810,732	270,739	530,993	602,094	149,183	130,181	1,067,680	397,179	790,501	2	4
Petroleum and coal products	399,734	317,440	82,314	331,541	201,360		449,583	229,838	219,674	3	5
Rubber products	109,763	30,893	78,890	76,958	16,944	63,014	116,769	23,283	93,506	4	3
Leather and leather products	31,301	8,064	23,237	25,701	(4)	(4)	32,888	6,323	17,062	15	8
Stone, clay, and glass products	285,066	104,378	180,668	222,652	64,638	108,014	343,468	100,718	242,780	5	3
Primary metal industries	692,177	212,687	379,490	546,253	133,668	409,555	1,335,749	475,008	865,940	2	2
Fabricated metal products	304,822	92,119	212,703	[5] 317,027	93,091	223,936	386,924	113,170	247,764	3	3
Machinery (except electrical)	517,559	167,396	350,193	237,212	86,872	250,340	652,026	228,695	423,331	3	4
Electrical machinery	244,606	64,874	170,732	195,458	50,051	145,407	320,314	119,326	200,989	3	3
Transportation equipment	354,974	99,514	255,460	343,426	78,738	264,690	663,783	283,771	409,991	3	1
Instruments and related products	55,050	16,313	40,687	64,446	18,418	45,028	85,004	30,918	64,086	3	3
Miscellaneous manufactures	105,960	31,515	76,445	98,275	19,395	78,880	146,420	67,100	79,257	6	6

[1] Smaller establishments submitting "short" form reports were not requested to include data on capital expenditures. Resulting understatement is negligible (see Ch. VI of Vol. I, "General Summary," Census of Manufactures, 1947).
[2] See text, p. 782, for explanation of standard error. Refers to total expenditures columns. Standard errors for new machinery columns approximately same as those for total expenditures; for new structure columns, vary, usually between 1 and 3 times the standard errors shown for total expenditure, up to a maximum of 18 percent for published totals.
[3] Not fully represented in sample; capital expenditures understated by approximately 1 to 10 percent; corresponding understatement of "All industries" total is less than 0.5 percent.
[4] Withheld because estimate did not meet publication standards.

Source: Department of Commerce, Bureau of the Census; Annual Survey of Manufactures: 1950 and 1951.

No. 949.—MANUFACTURES—EXPENDITURES FOR NEW PLANT AND EQUIPMENT, BY STATES: 1947 AND 1951

[In thousands of dollars. See headnote, table 948]

DIVISION AND STATE	1947 [1]			1951			Standard error (percent) [2]
	Total expenditures	New structures and additions to plant	New machinery and equipment	Total expenditures	New structures and additions to plant	New machinery and equipment	
United States	6,003,873	3,122,143	2,881,730	7,731,731	2,543,220	5,186,511	1
New England	413,630	115,151	303,429	452,396	121,446	330,105	4
Maine	35,055	12,708	22,347	42,638	12,585	30,053	8
New Hampshire	34,010	5,994	18,019	23,449	5,609	18,849	13
Vermont	9,696	3,051	6,647	(?)	(?)	(?)	
Massachusetts	198,066	52,486	146,580	172,920	41,311	131,609	4
Rhode Island	34,609	5,117	29,492	43,206	(?)	(?)	20
Connecticut	116,228	32,855	83,368	160,576	43,147	117,430	6
Middle Atlantic	1,385,285	444,679	903,630	1,743,687	305,300	1,437,387	2
New York	497,443	152,173	345,270	542,114	154,949	387,165	3
New Jersey	303,937	93,130	210,867	363,390	118,536	244,805	3
Pennsylvania	583,306	201,376	332,430	837,874	331,765	516,909	4
East North Central	1,869,332	667,536	1,301,796	2,455,896	839,126	1,617,790	2
Ohio	496,254	179,293	318,961	606,732	271,462	335,270	2
Indiana	302,104	145,724	156,380	357,554	137,206	220,348	4
Illinois	476,431	166,066	310,365	509,046	151,068	357,978	4
Michigan	427,746	119,254	308,492	566,487	156,792	360,695	3
Wisconsin	162,737	55,199	107,588	196,067	70,488	134,500	7
West North Central	348,482	122,322	227,159	376,812	147,124	239,679	6
Minnesota	82,890	29,438	53,362	95,486	32,640	62,945	5
Iowa	64,686	22,041	41,645	96,651	32,168	64,482	20
Missouri	133,166	50,531	81,635	114,905	43,398	71,627	3
North Dakota	2,250	859	1,391	(?)	(?)	(?)	
South Dakota	3,371	1,262	2,119	4,861	(?)	(?)	20
Nebraska	15,402	6,472	11,930	16,553	(?)	10,638	20
Kansas	36,757	11,790	26,048	74,304	(?)	(?)	20
South Atlantic	677,651	234,397	453,444	871,316	243,511	627,805	2
Delaware	21,137	5,594	15,543	33,074	13,261	19,698	3
Maryland	123,599	49,106	74,492	100,239	28,766	71,364	4
District of Columbia	4,502	976	3,526	6,983	2,206	4,778	9
Virginia	112,365	33,902	78,481	[4] 127,952	[4] 36,922	[4] 91,030	2
West Virginia	82,332	27,364	54,968	113,356	30,104	83,252	4
North Carolina	137,583	42,812	94,771	160,786	44,682	116,564	3
South Carolina	61,748	20,193	41,554	[4] 130,806	[4] 27,573	[4] 102,682	2
Georgia	84,320	30,147	54,173	115,460	41,044	74,416	10
Florida	50,062	16,117	33,935	78,926	18,639	60,287	7
East South Central	258,662	80,961	175,971	309,742	107,576	242,166	2
Kentucky	77,136	27,197	49,988	87,432	32,130	55,273	2
Tennessee	53,792	34,366	58,426	112,024	33,432	80,192	4
Alabama	72,302	22,752	49,610	97,132	32,794	64,339	3
Mississippi	22,713	6,636	16,087	41,563	9,200	32,368	6
West South Central	467,920	205,644	262,276	717,671	237,255	480,335	4
Arkansas	20,362	11,569	18,660	40,153	15,338	24,920	6
Louisiana	97,210	32,597	64,613	136,206	36,652	100,532	9
Oklahoma	25,504	12,242	13,262	38,147	12,390	24,689	7
Texas	304,944	149,226	155,718	503,036	172,919	330,027	5
Mountain	95,662	33,236	61,727	122,777	61,178	72,500	7
Montana	7,446	1,708	5,738	(?)	(?)	(?)	
Idaho	11,447	3,903	7,544	16,731	3,385	13,346	20
Wyoming	10,228	5,765	1,479	13,828	3,530	8,795	6
Colorado	32,190	9,606	23,763	37,481	11,680	18,089	15
New Mexico	5,431	1,810	3,621	5,009	(?)	(?)	20
Arizona	8,339	2,131	6,197	8,463	(?)	(?)	3
Utah	16,988	4,171	12,817	26,057	11,794	(?)	7
Nevada	2,960	1,411	1,548	1,774	(?)	(?)	20
Pacific	552,673	235,377	352,301	705,132	259,603	485,670	7
Washington	61,478	32,707	52,769	100,599	36,571	72,400	4
Oregon	61,669	32,435	35,234	111,500	30,033	52,407	20
California	410,533	172,235	237,298	493,734	192,739	300,303	6

No. 950.—VALUE OF MANUFACTURERS' INVENTORIES, BY MAJOR INDUSTRY GROUPS: 1947 AND 1951

[In thousands of dollars. 1947 data exclude all small establishments reporting on "short" forms. 1951 figures based on sample and subject to sampling variation. See text, p. 781]

| MAJOR INDUSTRY GROUP | 1947 | | | | | |
| | Inventories at beginning of year | | | Inventories at end of year | | |
	Total	Finished products [1]	Materials, supplies, and work in process [3]	Total	Finished products [1]	Materials, supplies, and work in process [1]
All industries, total	22,432,422	6,159,703	16,272,719	26,129,137	7,908,637	18,220,500
Food and kindred products	3,489,199	1,522,149	1,967,050	4,078,750	1,943,108	2,135,642
Tobacco manufactures	1,033,759	391,569	642,190	1,117,664	466,754	651,910
Textile mill products	1,609,619	339,750	1,269,869	1,788,166	385,472	1,402,694
Apparel and related products	1,087,339	365,489	721,850	1,257,372	449,094	808,278
Lumber and products, exc. furniture	497,580	200,015	297,565	653,637	275,277	378,360
Furniture and fixtures	342,280	61,108	281,172	401,311	83,053	318,258
Paper and allied products	536,913	91,644	445,269	714,223	125,316	588,907
Printing and publishing industries	(2)	(2)	(2)	(2)	(2)	(2)
Chemicals and allied products	1,743,370	505,525	1,237,845	2,062,730	650,037	1,412,693
Petroleum and coal products	730,588	400,293	330,295	888,583	453,606	434,977
Rubber products	373,058	98,427	274,631	413,785	152,967	260,818
Leather and leather products	447,705	102,289	345,416	508,276	120,257	388,619
Stone, clay, and glass products	391,146	137,933	253,213	494,666	184,543	310,123
Primary metal industries	1,719,943	368,501	1,351,442	1,968,469	441,282	1,527,187
Fabricated metal products	1,254,132	233,753	1,020,379	1,500,320	315,639	1,184,681
Machinery (except electrical)	2,833,852	677,792	2,156,060	3,354,237	890,262	2,463,975
Electrical machinery	1,342,423	188,439	1,153,994	1,489,516	291,340	1,198,176
Transportation equipment	2,048,774	242,172	1,806,602	2,377,482	296,994	2,090,488
Instruments and related products	382,008	83,172	298,926	429,047	103,757	325,290
Miscellaneous manufactures	568,634	149,683	418,951	630,903	180,879	450,024

| MAJOR INDUSTRY GROUP | 1951 | | | | | | |
| | Inventories at beginning of year | | | Inventories at end of year | | | Standard error (percent) [4] |
	Total	Finished products	Materials, supplies and work in process	Total	Finished products	Materials, supplies and work in process	
All industries, total	30,473,462	9,555,807	20,917,655	38,073,024	12,111,804	25,961,220	1
Food and kindred products	4,351,199	2,312,885	2,038,314	4,866,796	2,647,538	2,219,258	3
Tobacco manufactures	1,335,481	505,862	829,619	1,423,104	525,644	897,460	1
Textile mill products	2,413,840	624,515	1,789,325	2,772,403	941,258	1,831,145	2
Apparel and related products	1,677,321	602,220	1,075,101	1,631,142	623,709	1,007,433	4
Lumber and products (except furniture)	839,141	374,571	464,570	1,012,222	453,805	558,417	3
Furniture and fixtures	515,686	121,771	393,915	583,042	148,316	434,726	5
Paper and allied products	786,527	176,929	609,598	1,014,020	227,474	786,546	2
Printing and publishing industries	(2)	(2)	(2)	(2)	(2)	(2)	------
Chemicals and allied products	2,290,987	713,177	1,577,810	2,932,396	1,048,241	1,884,155	2
Petroleum and coal products	1,229,155	606,557	622,598	1,371,056	705,012	666,044	2
Rubber products	406,266	143,580	262,686	591,288	224,759	366,529	2
Leather and leather products	585,911	158,550	427,361	596,935	183,369	413,566	4
Stone, clay, and glass products	635,329	248,132	387,197	805,706	331,474	474,232	3
Primary metal industries	2,476,452	556,055	1,920,397	2,822,582	619,871	2,202,711	1
Fabricated metal products	1,877,853	429,574	1,448,279	2,455,851	597,426	1,858,425	2
Machinery (except electrical)	3,623,453	1,011,026	2,612,427	5,181,316	1,443,961	3,737,355	1
Electrical machinery	1,592,811	325,196	1,267,615	2,326,717	494,378	1,832,339	2
Transportation equipment	2,522,236	293,380	2,228,856	3,809,915	403,062	3,406,853	1
Instruments and related products	516,002	117,970	398,032	749,841	155,056	594,785	2
Miscellaneous manufactures [5]	797,812	233,857	563,955	1,126,692	337,451	789,241	6

[1] Includes value of goods produced by contract work on materials owned by manufacturers reporting.
[2] Includes value of fuel and all other inventories.   [3] Data not collected.
[4] See text, p. 782, for explanation of standard error. Refers to total inventories columns. Standard errors for other columns are the same or one percent higher.   [5] Includes "Ordnance and accessories."

Source: Department of Commerce, Bureau of the Census; advance report of 1951 Annual Survey of Manufactures.

PRODUCT	1941-42	1942-43	1943-44	1944-45	1945-46	1946-47	1947-48	1948-49	1949-50	1950-51	1951-52	1952-53
Fruits, total [1]	61.3	59.1	46.6	54.4	52.1	52.9	64.2	65.1	69.6	74.2	81.5	72.6
Apples	4.0	3.9	2.9	3.0	1.1	4.0	2.1	1.6	3.9	4.9	3.1	2.4
Applesauce	3.3	3.6	2.2	3.1	1.9	6.2	4.5	3.4	3.9	5.3	5.5	5.5
Apricots	4.3	3.3	1.3	7.8	4.4	10.7	3.3	4.8	2.4	3.7	4.6	4.0
Berries	1.9	1.4	1.0	.5	.4	.6	1.0	1.8	2.0	1.3	1.7	1.4
Cherries, red pitted	1.7	2.6	.6	2.6	1.1	2.4	1.5	2.7	2.6	3.8	3.4	2.9
Cherries, other	.9	1.1	.9	.6	1.3	1.8	.6	.8	1.7	.7	.9	1.3
Cranberries	1.7	.8	1.1	.6	1.8	3.3	2.3	1.3	1.8	2.5	2.7	2.3
Figs	.5	.8	1.0	.9	.7	1.3	.6	.6	.3	.6	.7	.6
Grapefruit	3.3	.8	.6	.6	2.1	4.0	3.3	3.1	2.4	3.3	2.4	(?)
Mixed fruits	3.7	6.2	3.8	6.6	8.5	6.0	10.3	11.0	7.6	8.2	10.0	6.3
Peaches	14.4	16.2	11.6	13.6	14.8	20.0	19.6	17.4	19.1	14.6	22.3	15.3
Pears	6.6	6.2	4.7	4.5	4.7	5.2	5.7	4.0	6.9	6.4	6.6	6.5
Pineapple [2]	9.2	9.9	10.3	9.1	7.9	8.4	9.4	10.3	10.8	11.3	12.3	14.6
Plums and prunes	2.5	1.7	2.4	1.8	2.5	4.2	2.3	.9	1.8	1.9	2.4	1.9
Olives, ripe	1.2	.8	1.1	1.0	.9	1.6	1.0	.9	1.4	1.8	2.3	1.8
Juices, total [4]	68.1	75.1	80.7	96.7	110.6	118.0	97.3	94.3	87.6	96.4	98.5	85.3
Apple	1.6	1.7	1.4	2.7	1.1	4.4	1.4	1.1	3.7	2.4	3.0	2.1
Apricot, peach, pear	(?)	.8	.3	.9	.3	1.5	1.8	1.0	1.5	(?)	(?)	(?)
Grape	3.3	2.9	1.6	2.0	2.5	2.4	2.4	3.4	3.5	2.8	(?)	(?)
Grapefruit	12.9	34.0	35.6	22.0	26.4	17.6	17.5	14.2	13.2	13.8	8.3	(?)
Lemon	.2	.2	(?)	.6	.6	.4	.5	.4	.6	.4	.7	.4
Orange	4.5	2.9	4.3	16.8	22.6	70.7	37.3	19.3	19.6	32.6	38.0	(?)
Orange-grapefruit	3.3	2.7	6.0	9.0	14.0	11.0	13.4	10.8	7.4	9.4	6.4	(?)
Pineapple [2]	9.5	10.4	9.4	8.9	6.9	6.6	6.9	11.5	12.0	13.7	13.2	(?)
Prune	.4	1.5	1.9	.2	4.9	4.0	3.9	4.0	3.4	4.5	4.0	(?)
Other fruit	1.4		.2	.3	1.3	3.5	(?)	.1	1.1	1.7	.7	(?)
Tomato	23.4	26.1	22.5	29.4	23.4	20.2	19.5	27.8	23.5	24.3	24.2	35.3
Other vegetable	4.0	2.8	2.6	3.1	4.0	6.3	(?)	(?)	(?)	2.0	2.5	2.3
Seasonal vegetables, total [3]	146.3	168.6	146.4	132.9	125.5	146.2	173.1	117.1	135.3	134.3	149.3	129.5
Asparagus	3.8	4.5	4.2	4.2	4.5	4.6	3.2	3.6	4.4	4.5	4.8	4.4
Beans, green and wax	15.8	25.2	23.3	18.6	17.5	18.3	13.1	15.2	20.6	21.0	19.4	16.3
Beans, lima	4.0	2.0	2.0	1.7	1.6	1.7	2.2	2.8	4.4	3.2	3.0	2.3
Beets	9.0	7.3	7.2	8.7	9.5	7.0	3.4	4.4	7.3	8.2	7.6	8.7
Carrots	2.9	3.0	3.1	3.1	3.6	3.7	1.0	3.1	1.6	1.9	3.3	3.3
Corn	28.9	32.6	29.3	25.4	27.7	31.0	26.1	31.5	29.8	18.2	34.6	22.3
Greens, leafy	.9	1.4	1.2	1.0	3.0	1.5	.9	1.7	2.5	2.4	1.6	1.7
Mixed vegetables	(?)	(?)	(?)	(?)	(?)	(?)	(?)	(?)	1.1	1.7	1.4	1.3
Peas, field	(?)	(?)	(?)	(?)	(?)	(?)	(?)	(?)	(?)	(?)	(?)	(?)
Peas, green	31.9	36.9	36.4	21.7	30.7	40.9	33.1	33.4	33.6	39.1	38.9	38.5
Pimientos	.3	.2	.2	.1	.8	.8	.6	.8	.6	1.3	.4	.3
Pumpkin and squash	3.5	3.3	2.1	2.9	1.0	4.6	3.4	1.8	1.1	2.2	4.4	3.4
Spinach	8.5	8.4	7.7	9.0	8.4	8.9	3.0	4.7	3.6	7.5	6.1	4.1
Tomatoes	34.6	41.6	29.7	26.1	16.9	28.0	27.7	34.4	21.5	24.1	32.3	22.0
Other vegetable packs [3]	(?)	(?)	(?)	(?)	(?)	(?)	(?)	(?)	(?)	2.0	2.5	2.3
Nonseasonal vegetables, total [4]	39.4	46.3	40.2	53.2	35.5	91.0	35.5	57.0	38.9	34.1	12.3	6.3
Beans, all dry varieties	34.5	10.5	15.1	25.5	34.7	35.0	37.1	(?)	(?)	(?)	(?)	(?)
Hominy	2.5	.6	.4	(?)	(?)	(?)	4.3	4.5	4.8	(?)	(?)	.7
Mushrooms	.9		.4	.4	.5	.5	.9	.7	.9	(?)	(?)	(?)
Sauerkraut	8.2	3.5	3.7	3.2	5.5	8.3	4.2	4.5	7.8	8.7	7.2	(?)
Spaghetti and macaroni	6.5	1.4	.1	1.7	1.1	4.1	4.3	4.2	.7	4.3	3.3	(?)
Sweet potatoes	2.0	.9	1.3	1.7	3.1	4.2	1.7	1.3	3.1	4.3	2.3	4.0
Soups	34.5	27.7	23.0	29.7	39.1	43.0	43.5	42.0	41.0	(?)	(?)	(?)
White potatoes	(?)	1.3	4.3	1.6	(?)	(?)	.9	1.6	1.5	1.6	1.3	2.6
Tomato products [4]	21.6	23.4	29.6	32.5	33.8	45.6	36.7	36.4	33.9	39.0	42.0	37.2
Catsup and chili sauce	10.6	11.0	8.9	12.0	10.1	12.0	10.9	13.2	8.7	11.7	19.6	16.5
Paste and sauce	5.0	5.9	9.1	10.0	11.5	14.2	12.9	8.5	2.0	10.7	19.4	17.0
Pulp and puree	6.0	6.5	10.6	11.5	12.2	18.5	3.9	3.7	4.1	4.0	7.7	4.7
Canned baby foods, total [7]	38.3	44.3	54.6	77.5	104.1	132.3	90.0	133.7	132.1	130.3	119.6	134.1
Desserts		2.2	3.0	7.8	9.8	10.6	7.3	10.1	8.6	9.3	9.9	12.1
Fruits	(?)	13.5	15.7	24.4	36.0	44.0	34.8	41.6	46.0	44.9	44.4	49.4
Meat compounds		9.6	12.9	16.1	21.0	36.0	34.7	38.0	30.1	44.4	43.2	41.2
Vegetables		18.6	23.2	27.3	34.4	27.8	23.3	37.6	37.6	31.3	36.4	38.4

No. 952.—DENATURED ALCOHOL:[1] 1910 TO 1952

YEAR ENDING JUNE 30—	Alcohol produced at industrial alcohol plants [2]	Denaturing plants operated	Ethyl alcohol used for denaturation [3]	DENATURED ALCOHOL PRODUCED [4]		
				Total	Completely denatured	Specially denatured
	Proof gallons		Proof gallons	Wine gallons	Wine gallons	Wine gallons
1910		12	10,603,571	6,079,027	3,076,888	3,002,108
1915		23	26,411,719	13,985,469	5,386,647	8,598,822
1920	16,983,551	32	45,640,949	28,536,350	13,538,403	15,997,947
1925	166,165,518	91	152,254,089	81,805,273	46,983,970	34,894,308
1930	193,822,717	68	185,000,927	108,776,975	59,063,510	47,713,468
1935	180,645,920	39	166,253,606	97,051,074	26,746,879	59,304,385
1940	243,727,756	40	225,160,792	126,761,530	15,352,033	111,408,797
1945	[5] 663,431,544	65	971,445,910	527,085,537	33,057,533	494,008,004
1947	248,798,639	49	338,029,989	183,744,086	36,395,715	147,348,371
1948	532,282,148	43	338,651,745	184,281,826	34,887,789	149,394,657
1949	351,015,364	47	322,925,930	174,494,703	10,221,482	164,273,221
1950	312,535,129	46	322,836,727	174,673,641	4,414,088	170,259,583
1951	444,935,011	48	455,909,873	245,437,178	1,438,584	243,998,614
1952	467,389,720	55	489,788,861	262,493,485	988,027	261,500,458

[1] Includes data for Hawaii for all years and data for Puerto Rico beginning with Aug. 1, 1928.
[2] Separate accounts for alcohol produced at industrial alcohol plants required commencing May 1, 1920.
[3] Through 1940, represents *withdrawals* of all products for denaturation, that is, domestic ethyl alcohol, spirits produced by registered distilleries (redesignated upon receipt at denaturing plants as alcohol), and rum. Beginning 1944, represents all products (except rum) *used* for denaturation, that is, domestic ethyl alcohol, imported ethyl alcohol, and spirits. Rum is included for 1935 and 1940 because denatured rum is included with specially denatured alcohol for those years.
[4] Prior to 1944 includes denatured rum.
[5] Represents gross production. Net production (gross production minus products used in redistillation) for 1945, 650,089,874.

Source: Treasury Department, Bureau of Internal Revenue: *Annual Report of the Commissioner.*

No. 953.—ALCOHOLIC BEVERAGES—PRODUCTION, TAX-PAID WITHDRAWALS, AND STOCKS: YEARS ENDING JUNE 30, 1946 TO 1952

[Includes data for Alaska and Hawaii. See also *Historical Statistics*, series J 172 for production of fermented malt liquor]

CLASS	Unit	1946	1947	1948	1949	1950	1951	1952
Fermented malt liquor:								
Production	Thous. of bbl.[1]	84,978	87,857	91,291	89,736	88,807	88,976	89,601
Tax-paid withdrawals	do	81,287	82,629	86,993	85,809	83,512	83,246	84,294
Stocks on hand June 30	do	8,035	9,565	9,888	9,879	10,982	11,344	10,982
Distilled spirits, total:								
Production [3]	Thous. of tax gal.[2]	[4] 275,148	315,158	244,127	266,542	208,235	401,453	221,866
Tax-paid withdrawals [3]	do	178,131	173,505	147,160	141,767	144,124	174,625	141,791
Stocks on hand June 30 [3]	do	420,262	525,828	594,733	677,344	708,562	901,106	937,156
Whiskey:								
Production	do	147,465	167,995	129,597	149,595	118,760	205,702	103,544
Tax-paid withdrawals	do	63,227	58,823	53,603	52,675	60,499	76,442	64,908
Stocks on hand June 30	do	374,072	464,825	522,261	602,926	643,280	751,233	767,558
Rectified spirits and wines, production, total	Thous. of proof gal.	150,879	148,560	125,733	118,955	107,861	122,373	93,928
Whiskey, production	do	124,727	130,701	114,917	107,782	94,908	108,152	83,146
Still wines: [6]								
Production [7]	Thous. of wine gal.[8]	379,936	515,335	314,328	425,925	297,857	425,821	594,006
Tax-paid withdrawals	do	107,965	102,212	110,114	119,107	133,055	123,253	121,809
Stocks on hand June 30 [9]	do	102,014	160,211	147,708	162,586	127,000	133,978	170,606
Sparkling wines: [10]								
Production	Thous. of half pints [11]	40,569	48,548	20,422	22,836	21,225	25,014	24,314
Tax-paid withdrawals	do	35,721	30,985	20,414	21,665	20,934	23,789	22,500
Stocks on hand June 30	do	24,498	39,491	36,465	34,859	32,387	30,994	30,294

[1] Barrels of 31 wine gallons.
[2] A tax gallon for spirits of 100 proof or over is equivalent to the proof gallon. For spirits of less than 100 proof the tax gallon is equivalent to the wine gallon.
[3] Excludes ethyl alcohol.
[4] Excludes high-proof spirits and unfinished spirits produced at registered distilleries for industrial purposes.
[5] Includes ethyl alcohol.
[6] Excludes vermouth and other aperitif wines.
[7] Production represents total amount removed from fermenters, including distilling material (substandard wines produced with excessive water or residue materials). In 1952, 354,886,942 gallons of distilling materials were produced.
[8] Standard United States gallon.
[9] Excludes distilling materials.
[10] Includes champagne, other sparkling wines, and artificially carbonated wines.
[11] Tax is payable on each ½ pint or fraction thereof in each bottle or container.

Source: Treasury Department, Bureau of Internal Revenue; *Annual Report of the Commissioner.*

No. 954.—ETHYL ALCOHOL AND OTHER DISTILLED SPIRITS, EXCEPT BRANDY AND SPIRITS (FRUIT)—MATERIALS USED IN PRODUCTION, BY KINDS: 1901 TO 1952

YEARLY AVERAGE OR YEAR ENDING JUNE 30—	Molasses (thousand gallons)	GRAIN (THOUSANDS OF POUNDS) [1]				ETHYL SULPHATE	PINE-APPLE JUICE	OTHER MATERIALS [3]	
		Corn	Malt	Rye	Other [2]	Thousand gallons		Thousand gallons	Thousand pounds
1901-1905	14,059	1,094,027	197,602	208,038	2,349				
1906-1910	20,680	1,114,277	202,720	280,112	1,893				
1911-1915	71,738	1,183,706	209,194	278,874	5,029				
1916-1920	109,627	958,003	125,430	65,130	5,298			46,457	
1921-1925	144,652	256,134	55,562	5,219	654			42,340	95,357
1926-1930	299,279	472,682	29,613	2,722	1,008	1,274		63,546	55,021
1931-1935	167,254	490,276	101,183	245,457	5,362	10,696	5,671	5,902	35,405
1936-1940	185,214	1,398,797	257,247	455,205	3,179	31,520	3,449	12,059	1,196
1941-1945	340,247	1,652,322	552,455	345,848	2,096,179	77,809	2,945	15,085	46,745
1946-1950	182,504	1,769,024	381,054	345,640	604,308	116,613	3,212	215,945	660,389
1946	117,520	1,370,401	537,373	452,522	1,963,382	108,208	2,274	152,506	645,520
1947	73,382	2,451,731	455,336	287,166	148,396	108,457	2,590	222,581	982,782
1948	178,502	1,852,653	344,069	368,099	617,550	109,945	4,909	246,189	274,429
1949	161,790	1,716,278	328,347	375,986	233,767	131,819	2,966	349,203	1,326,397
1950	131,327	1,593,057	240,216	272,298	53,902	172,237	3,211	205,520	72,530
1951	131,206	2,790,404	554,952	428,736	1,001,429	149,398	4,404	292,063	75,299
1952	160,801	1,624,372	294,647	235,281	855,898	168,020	7,498	315,744	72,125

[1] Conversion factor used was 56 pounds per bushel when reported in bushels.
[2] Wheat, barley, rice, sorghum grain, etc., also mixtures of corn, malt, and rye.
[3] Dismalt, sulphite liquors, manioca meal, maguey juice, maple sirup, cider, corn sirup, potatoes, crude alcohols, mixtures, cellulose pulp and chemical mixtures, ethylene gas, etc.
[4] Average for 4 years.
[5] Average for 3 years.
[6] 1930 figure.

Source: Treasury Department: 1901 to 1933, Bureau of Industrial Alcohol; *Statistics Concerning Intoxicating Liquors.* 1934 and subsequent years, Bureau of Internal Revenue; annual and special reports.

No. 955.—DISTILLED SPIRITS, MALT LIQUORS, AND WINES—APPARENT AVERAGE ANNUAL PER CAPITA CONSUMPTION: 1850 TO 1952

[In gallons, except distilled spirits which is shown in tax gallons]

FISCAL YEAR	DISTILLED SPIRITS			MALT LIQUORS			WINES		
	Total	Domestic	Imported	Total	Domestic	Imported	Total	Domestic	Imported
1850	2.24	2.02	0.22	1.58	1.57	0.01	0.27	0.01	0.26
1860	2.86	2.67	.19	3.22	3.18	.04	.34	.06	.28
1870	2.07	1.89	.18	5.31	5.25	.06	.32	.08	.24
1871-80 [5]	1.39	1.35	.04	6.98	6.90	.08	.47	.31	.16
1881-90 [5]	1.34	1.31	.03	11.37	11.34	.03	.45	.29	.16
1891-00 [5]	1.37	1.35	.02	15.20	15.13	.07	.30	.23	.07
1898-1900 [5]	1.13	1.10	.03	15.48	15.44	.04	.36	.31	.05
1901-05 [5]	1.39	1.36	.03	17.20	17.20	.05	.47	.40	.07
1906-10 [5]	1.43	1.39	.04	19.81	19.73	.08	.62	.52	.10
1915	1.36	1.28	.08	18.40	18.37	.03	.33	.27	.06
1920	.22	.22	(7)	2.61	2.61	(7)	.13	.13	(7)
1925 [6]	.09	.09	(7)				.08	.08	(7)
1930 [6]	.08	.08	(7)				.30	.30	(7)
1935	.70	.67	.03	10.46	10.44	.04	.30	.30	.06
1940	1.02	.93	.09	12.56	12.57	.03	.87	.86	.08
1945	1.23	1.06	.17	18.96	18.70	.07	.78	.70	.08
1946	1.39	1.27	.12	18.56	18.47	.09	.87	.82	.05
1947	1.28	1.17	.11	18.58	18.52	.06	.77	.74	.03
1948	1.06	.97	.09	18.58	18.56	.06	.79	.77	.07
1949	1.08	.98	.10	18.06	18.08	.08	.84	.84	.09
1950	1.08	.93	.10	17.30	17.34	.06	.84	.84	.09
1951	1.20	1.06	.14	16.97	16.97	.06	.96	.93	.03
1952	1.00	.87	.13	16.94	16.93	.08	.93	.93	.06

[5] Average for the period. [7] Less than .005.
[8] Excludes quantities withdrawn for certain manufacturing, compounding, medicinal, and sacramental uses.

Source: Department of Commerce, National Production Authority; published in *World Trade in Commodities.*

No. 956.—Tobacco Products—Production, by Kind: 1901 to 1951

[Compiled from monthly returns of manufacturers. Data relate to products manufactured in continental United States, excluding those manufactured in customs bonded manufacturing warehouses, class 6. There were 173,325,273 large cigars manufactured in these warehouses in 1951. Large cigars are those weighing more than 3 pounds per thousand. See also *Historical Statistics*, series J 174 for data on cigarettes]

CALENDAR YEAR OR YEARLY AVERAGE	TOBACCO AND SNUFF (THOUSANDS OF POUNDS)						CIGARS (THOUSANDS)		CIGARETTES (THOUSANDS)	
	Total	Plug	Twist	Fine cut	Smoking [1]	Snuff	Large	Small	Large	Small
1901–1905....	346,841	175,981	11,903	138,402	20,556	6,513,095	716,720	7,143	3,227,698
1906–1910....	413,054	167,460	13,524	12,525	192,700	26,845	6,883,272	1,059,501	16,113	6,192,571
1911–1915....	437,346	158,529	15,017	10,795	221,865	31,140	7,087,530	1,053,654	15,696	14,882,414
1916–1920....	455,584	150,869	14,346	9,758	237,808	34,805	7,364,937	810,327	26,026	41,565,670
1921–1925....	409,457	115,445	10,105	6,972	239,151	37,785	6,691,913	557,300	16,704	65,903,981
1926–1930....	389,244	99,470	8,374	5,821	235,421	40,159	6,360,650	414,044	10,479	109,361,216
1931–1935....	349,785	64,662	5,404	3,660	239,072	36,987	4,648,368	245,412	20,417	121,702,676
1936–1940....	344,331	54,402	6,029	4,703	241,561	37,636	5,184,661	164,652	2,956	174,117,549
1941–1945....	327,473	56,967	6,223	4,535	217,829	41,919	5,457,472	125,370	23,938	285,475,535
1946–1950....	242,865	45,321	5,522	3,250	148,725	40,047	5,520,509	82,664	846	376,602,999
1938.........	345,369	54,495	5,659	4,572	243,470	37,173	5,014,758	152,990	2,638	171,686,368
1939.........	343,307	51,263	5,733	4,701	243,640	37,970	5,197,627	156,940	4,369	180,066,594
1940.........	344,423	48,759	5,605	4,176	248,011	37,872	5,235,271	134,758	2,349	189,371,286
1941.........	342,427	50,230	5,614	5,069	241,897	39,616	5,610,176	146,711	1,790	217,934,925
1942.........	330,413	54,300	6,024	5,084	224,002	41,003	5,840,805	133,150	2,503	257,520,963
1943.........	327,089	58,945	6,257	4,460	214,249	43,179	5,363,027	125,480	6,111	296,173,333
1944.........	306,935	61,655	6,496	4,692	192,728	41,962	5,198,679	123,340	26,870	323,563,886
1945.........	330,502	59,704	6,723	3,970	216,271	43,834	5,274,675	98,167	82,416	332,184,670
1946.........	253,231	51,810	5,773	3,756	152,531	39,361	5,617,700	92,262	1,656	350,032,003
1947.........	242,283	47,306	5,152	3,793	146,869	39,163	5,487,656	79,890	537	369,662,709
1948.........	244,681	45,346	5,632	3,207	149,687	40,809	5,645,104	89,134	641	396,825,746
1949.........	238,942	41,903	5,586	2,757	147,788	40,908	5,452,994	83,440	707	384,961,686
1950.........	235,189	40,242	5,467	2,738	146,751	39,992	5,399,089	68,877	696	391,955,743
1951 [2]......	227,151	39,918	4,551	2,817	140,412	39,453	5,594,291	69,216	815	418,801,801

[1] Includes scrap chewing tobacco.
[2] Number of factories on Jan. 1, 1952: Tobacco and snuff (excluding 169 "quasi" manufacturers), 270; cigars, 1,478; cigarettes, 46.

Source. Treasury Department, Bureau of Internal Revenue; *Annual Report of the Commissioner.*

No. 957.—Tobacco, Leaf—Amounts Consumed in the Manufacture of Cigars, Cigarettes, Chewing and Smoking Tobacco, and Snuff: 1896 to 1951

[All figures in thousands of pounds. Figures represent the equivalent in unstemmed leaf tobacco of stemmed leaf or scraps, cuttings, and clippings. In the following table the tobacco used in the manufacture of cigars and cigarettes was converted on the basis of 3 pounds of stemmed leaf or scraps, etc., to 4 pounds of unstemmed beginning 1915 (conversion prior to 1915 was at the ratio of 3 to 5) and of tobacco and snuff beginning 1903. For 1896 to 1902, tobacco used in manufactured tobacco and snuff was shown only under two heads, namely, "leaf" and "scraps." It is probable that stemmed leaf was included with unstemmed tobacco under the head of "leaf" without the one kind being converted to the equivalent in the other. The conversion ratio of 3 to 4 was applied only to "scraps" for these years. Data exclude tobacco used in bonded manufacturing warehouses. See also *Historical Statistics*, series J 171, for annual total consumption]

CALENDAR YEAR OR YEARLY AVERAGE	Total	Cigars	Cigarettes	Tobacco and snuff	CALENDAR YEAR	Total	Cigars	Cigarettes	Tobacco and snuff
1896–1900....	359,053	87,851	16,235	254,967	1938........	865,302	118,751	483,840	262,710
1901–1905....	451,461	124,411	12,444	314,606	1939........	885,299	122,681	509,133	253,485
1906–1910....	524,193	139,206	22,079	362,908	1940........	922,716	126,835	535,218	260,663
1911–1915....	578,283	151,890	52,207	374,186					
1916–1920....	650,460	155,312	130,320	364,828	1941........	1,009,085	136,066	626,842	246,178
					1942........	1,131,065	140,679	754,550	235,837
1921–1925....	672,077	151,421	198,069	322,588	1943........	1,228,703	131,896	860,459	236,349
1926–1930....	762,540	149,240	312,533	300,767	1944........	1,254,541	129,882	920,418	204,241
1931–1935....	740,934	112,296	345,985	282,652	1945........	1,291,176	128,390	944,286	218,499
1936–1940....	878,722	124,700	492,296	261,726					
1941–1945....	1,182,914	133,383	821,311	228,221	1946........	1,306,667	137,539	1,000,938	168,190
1946–1950....	1,367,515	133,056	1,071,586	162,873	1947........	1,355,117	135,338	1,055,594	164,185
					1948........	1,400,091	139,823	1,099,176	161,092
1935........	775,932	113,742	399,458	262,731	1949........	1,382,348	125,173	1,096,154	161,020
1936........	847,367	126,578	453,327	267,462	1950........	1,393,355	127,409	1,106,067	159,878
1937........	872,924	128,653	479,961	264,309	1951........	1,464,663	129,819	1,184,633	150,211

Source: Treasury Department, Bureau of Internal Revenue; *Annual Report of the Commissioner.*

No. 958.—Cotton Manufactures—Production by Kind: 1939 to 1952

[In thousands of linear yards]

PRODUCT	1939	1947	1949	1950	1951	1952 (prel.)
Cotton woven goods over 12 inches in width, except tire fabrics, total [1]	8,227,349	9,515,769	8,406,351	10,012,656	10,135,969	9,606,582
Cotton duck	173,979	206,415	216,816	248,990	362,777	365,935
Narrow sheeting and allied coarse and medium yarn fabrics	1,585,084	2,308,084	1,764,985	2,026,071	2,118,627	1,752,451
Print-cloth yarn fabrics	2,999,356	3,228,025	3,156,320	3,663,440	3,709,439	3,626,215
Napped fabrics [2]	451,412	502,393	335,737	308,614	408,682	314,544
Colored yarn cotton goods and related fabrics	688,639	751,749	688,162	860,318	779,053	813,174
Fine cotton-goods (all combed or part-combed cotton fabrics, including fabrics having rayon or other synthetic fiber or silk decorations and fine carded goods)	1,036,206	1,312,583	[3] 1,009,985	[3] 1,216,361	[3] 1,283,133	[3] 1,117,855
Towels, toweling, washcloths, and terry-woven fabrics other than towels	482,641	408,606	346,786	483,692	481,607	437,968
Wide cotton fabrics	557,475	670,591	590,558	711,620	717,636	665,977
Specialties and all other fabrics	317,487	367,034	334,069	432,681	385,085	434,366

[1] All data for fabrics in the gray except 1939 blanket and blanketing data which are for finished fabrics.
[2] 1949 and 1950 data exclude 10,172,000 yards and 14,263,000 yards, respectively, of blankets and blanketings, less than 25 percent wool, produced on woolen and worsted looms. 1951 and 1952 data include all chiefly cotton blankets including those produced on woolen and worsted looms.
[3] Includes fabrics containing 51 percent or more cotton by weight, balance rayon and/or acetate.

Source: Department of Commerce, Bureau of the Census; 1939 and 1947 Census of Manufactures reports, and *Facts for Industry*, Series M15A.

No. 959.—Tire Cord and Fabric—Production by Kind: 1939 to 1952

[In thousands of pounds]

PRODUCT	1939	1947	1949	1950	1951	1952 (prel.)
Tire cord and fabrics, total	260,473	546,301	435,401	532,083	565,913	537,994
Cotton	260,473	330,688	155,928	225,040	290,160	126,016
Tire cord fabrics woven (except chafer)	145,949	285,076	96,597	126,806	168,920	74,894
Chafer fabrics and all other tire fabrics	17,420	65,609	41,644	60,656	65,124	[4] 44,900
Tire cord not woven	97,084	(1)	17,662	25,580	55,116	[1] 15,222
Rayon and nylon	(2)	214,576	279,476	288,983	314,753	[4] 403,806
Tire cord fabrics and all other tire fabrics	(2)	186,938	234,872	346,901	275,805	[4] 318,084
Tire cord not woven	(2)	30,638	44,608	50,082	35,948	[4] 85,572
Nylon						8,082

[1] 4th quarter data for tire cord not woven included with chafer fabrics.
[2] Included with tire cord fabrics woven.
[3] Not available.
[4] Rayon only.

Source: Department of Commerce, Bureau of the Census; 1939 and 1947 Census of Manufactures reports, and *Facts for Industry*, Series M15A.

No. 960.—COTTON-SYSTEM SPINDLES, COTTON CONSUMPTION, AND STOCKS: 1840 TO 1952

[Statistics for 1915 to 1949 relate to 12 months ending July 31 and those for prior years to 12 months ending Aug. 31. For 1946–52, spindles in place include all cotton-system spindles in place regardless of fiber spun. Prior to 1946, "in place" figure represents all spindles in place used exclusively for spinning cotton. Consumption and stocks are expressed in running bales, counting round as half bales, except that all figures, 1840 to 1870, inclusive, and foreign cotton for all years are in equivalent 500-pound bales. See also *Historical Statistics*, series J 179–189 for data on active cotton-system spindles in the U. S. and total cotton consumed including linters]

YEAR	COTTON-SYSTEM SPINDLES (THOUSANDS)					Active cotton spindle hours (millions)	COTTON CONSUMED, EXCLUDING LINTERS (THOUSANDS OF BALES) [1]			
	Total in place	Active [1]					United States	Cotton-growing States	New England	Other States
		United States	Cotton-growing States	New England	Other States					
1840	(2)	2,265	181	1,597	506	(2)	207	71	129	7
1850	(2)	3,998	265	2,959	775	(2)	576	78	431	67
1860	(2)	5,236	324	3,859	1,053	(2)	845	94	367	104
1870	(2)	7,122	326	5,498	1,306	(2)	797	69	551	177
1880	(2)	10,653	4 561	4 8,622	4 1,460	(2)	4 1,570	4 190	4 1,129	4 232
1890	(2)	14,384	1,570	10,934	1,880	(2)	2,518	529	1,502	477
1900	(2)	19,472	4,368	13,171	1,933	(2)	3,573	1,528	1,908	148
1910	28,929	28,267	10,494	15,735	2,038	(2)	4,632	2,294	1,995	284
1920	35,834	35,481	15,231	18,287	1,963	(2)	6,420	3,853	2,397	48
1925	37,929	35,032	17,292	15,975	1,765	91,055	6,163	4,230	1,639	335
1930	34,025	31,245	18,586	11,351	1,308	87,515	6,106	4,749	1,143	214
1935	30,093	26,701	18,212	7,763	726	72,526	5,361	4,306	818	237
1940	24,750	23,586	17,641	5,279	666	97,006	7,784	6,647	918	229
1944	23,293	23,019	17,652	4,784	582	118,263	9,943	8,739	950	254
1945	23,128	22,675	17,610	4,511	554	111,896	9,566	8,455	891	222
1946	23,862	22,777	17,700	4,536	551	105,366	9,162	8,074	854	235
1947	23,824	22,519	17,502	4,541	476	114,727	10,025	8,776	968	281
1948	23,796	22,675	17,807	4,429	438	119,017	9,354	8,254	887	213
1949	23,501	20,134	16,491	3,276	367	98,217	7,795	6,986	644	165
1950	22,995	21,790	17,673	3,739	378	109,243	8,851	8,030	664	157
1951	23,195	22,140	18,129	3,637	374	126,852	10,654	9,642	840	172
1952	23,205	21,298	18,119	2,927	252	106,932	9,120	8,443	559	118

YEARLY AVERAGE OR YEAR	CONSUMPTION (THOUSANDS OF BALES)							STOCKS IN CONSUMING ESTABLISHMENTS AT END OF YEAR (THOUSANDS OF BALES)			
	Cotton, excluding linters						Linters	Cotton, excluding linters [1]			Linters
	Total	Domestic				Foreign		Total	Domestic	Foreign	
		Total	Upland	Sea Island	American-Egyptian						
1906–1910	4 4,829	4 4,680	4 4,616	4 64		149	7 163	8 731	8 673	58	7 39
1911–1915	5,257	5,051	4 4,976	75	(8)	206	293	822	738	84	86
1916–1920	6,388	6,105	8 6,034	71	(8)	282	734	1,452	1,352	100	179
1921–1925	5,869	5,577	5,531	9	37	292	599	1,003	911	92	139
1926–1930	6,735	6,434	6,419	1	15	301	815	1,150	1,050	100	188
1931–1935	5,466	5,325	5,311	1	14	140	720	1,116	1,061	55	261
1936–1940	6,938	6,799	6,780	2	18	139	864	7,133	7,060	74	273
1941–1945	10,301	10,151	10,105	3	42	149	1,399	10,354	10,233	121	391
1946–1950	9,038	8,829	8,820	1	8	209	1,243	4,678	4,570	108	218
1945	9,568	9,448	9,404	1	44	120	1,481	10,339	10,215	124	247
1946	9,163	8,966	8,946	1	19	197	1,055	6,746	6,593	153	255
1947	10,025	9,765	9,755	1	9	260	984	2,310	2,178	132	201
1948	9,354	9,109	9,101	2	5	246	1,156	2,806	2,717	89	190
1949	7,795	7,634	7,629	1	4	161	1,406	5,031	4,962	69	237
1950	8,851	8,669	8,666	1	2	182	1,616	6,496	6,399	97	208
1951	10,654	10,487	10,452	1	34	167	1,396	1,371	1,313	58	171
1952	9,120	9,036	9,011	1	24	84	1,306	1,035	999	36	241

[1] For 1945 and earlier years data represent sum of greatest number of cotton spindles reported by each mill as active at any time during year, regardless of length of time operated. Beginning with 1946, active figure includes all cotton-system spindles active last day of year, regardless of type of fiber spun. On August 2, 1952, there were 19,033,000 spindles active on cotton, 1,159,000 on synthetics, 217,000 on other fibers and blends, and 1,907,000 idle.
[1] Includes linters for 1840 to 1908. Figures for all years include foreign and domestic cotton.
[2] Not available. [4] Cotton mills only.
[3] Includes stocks held in public storage and at compresses beginning 1938.
[4] Includes linters for 1906 to 1908. [7] Average, 1909 and 1910.
[8] "Upland" includes "American-Egyptian" beginning 1912 (first year produced).

Source: Department of Commerce, Bureau of Census; annual report *Cotton Production and Distribution*.

No. 961.—COTTON-SYSTEM SPINDLE ACTIVITY, 1950, 1951, 1952, AND COTTON CONSUMPTION, 1948 TO 1952, BY REGION AND STATE

[Years ending July 31. Consumption includes domestic and foreign cotton and is in running bales counting round as half bales, except foreign cotton which is in equivalent 500-pound bales]

REGION AND STATE	COTTON SPINDLES IN PLACE (THOUSANDS)[1]			ACTIVE COTTON SPINDLE HOURS (MILLIONS)			COTTON CONSUMED, EXCLUDING LINTERS (THOUSANDS OF BALES)				
	1950	1951	1952	1950	1951	1952	1948	1949	1950	1951	1952
United States	22,995	23,195	23,205	109,243	126,852	106,932	9,354	7,795	8,851	10,654	9,130
Cotton-growing States	18,244	18,545	18,857	92,746	107,474	95,044	8,254	6,986	8,030	9,642	8,443
New England	4,332	4,241	4,024	15,274	18,043	11,051	887	644	664	840	559
Other States	419	409	324	1,223	1,335	837	213	165	157	172	118
Alabama	1,693	1,732	1,722	9,127	10,836	9,309	1,106	945	1,088	1,312	1,122
Connecticut	490	467	453	1,319	1,814	1,209	61	48	56	72	51
Georgia	3,194	3,225	3,272	16,317	19,288	16,492	1,927	1,600	1,879	2,370	1,992
Maine	631	625	610	2,829	3,253	2,327	170	147	170	207	166
Massachusetts	2,263	2,193	2,041	7,579	8,980	5,057	476	340	310	392	244
New York	218	6,069	125	666	688	345	96	71	61	66	38
North Carolina	5,975	691	6,127	27,651	32,614	28,344	2,524	2,098	2,433	2,870	2,483
Rhode Island	696	210	688	2,374	2,556	1,537	89	53	69	84	50
South Carolina	5,679	5,839	6,033	31,613	35,332	32,843	1,962	1,740	1,963	2,276	2,155
Tennessee	554	527	530	2,780	3,118	2,639	215	179	200	235	197
Texas	209	213	226	963	1,164	1,050	155	144	153	175	149
Virginia	650	649	648	3,086	3,563	2,922	211	154	186	223	189
All other States	741	755	730	2,939	3,646	2,858	362	276	293	362	284

[1] Includes all cotton-system spindles in place regardless of fiber spun.

Source: Department of Commerce, Bureau of Census; annual report, *Cotton Production and Distribution*.

No. 962.—COTTON AND SYNTHETIC WOVEN GOODS, BLEACHED, DYED OR PRINTED: 1946 TO 1951

[In thousands of linear yards. Data cover bleaching, dyeing, and printing of cotton and synthetic woven textiles. Fabrics are classified by chief fiber content]

PRODUCT	1946	1947	1948	1949	1950	1951 (prel.)
Bleached, dyed or printed goods	8,648,290	8,915,147	8,848,437	8,230,712	9,328,681	8,677,496
Cotton	6,922,822	6,944,456	6,779,692	6,239,821	7,063,046	6,676,499
Synthetic and silk[1]	1,725,468	1,970,691	2,060,745	2,050,891	2,265,635	2,000,907
Bleached and white finished goods	3,578,225	3,814,867	3,529,268	3,980,233	3,466,795	3,463,327
Cotton	3,379,892	3,616,001	3,316,637	2,812,950	3,296,423	3,294,382
Synthetic and silk[1]	198,333	198,866	212,631	167,283	170,372	168,955
Plain dyed and finished goods	3,037,150	3,175,230	3,340,402	3,505,218	3,950,245	3,427,490
Cotton	1,871,852	1,757,386	1,819,096	1,942,054	2,166,113	2,040,664
Synthetic and silk[1]	1,165,298	1,418,934	1,521,306	1,563,184	1,784,132	1,386,826
Printed and finished goods[1]	2,032,915	1,923,940	1,970,787	1,965,261	1,911,641	1,646,679
Cotton	1,671,078	1,571,069	1,643,959	1,634,837	1,600,510	1,401,453
Synthetic and silk[1]	361,837	352,891	326,808	330,424	311,131	245,126

[1] Includes fabrics made of rayon, acetate, nylon, silk, glass, acrylic fibers, etc.
[2] Includes roller, screen, flock and block printed fabrics.

Source: Department of Commerce, Bureau of Census; 1947 Census of Manufactures reports and *Facts for Industry*, Series M15G.

No. 963.—Synthetic Broad Woven Fabrics—Production, by Type: 1947 to 1952

[Data cover production of synthetic broad woven fabrics, classified by chief fiber content. Prior to 1951, fabrics containing 25 percent or more wool by weight were classified as woolen fabrics and are not included in this table]

[In thousands of linear yards]

PRODUCT	1947	1949	1950	1951	1952 (prel.)
Rayon and acetate broad woven fabrics, total [1]	1,976,835	1,957,105	2,406,205	2,063,836	1,812,689
100 percent filament rayon and/or acetate fabrics, total	1,236,805	1,296,678	1,601,282	1,296,967	968,622
Flat fabrics, total	652,252	756,141	860,375	768,280	684,900
Bright viscose taffetas	50,828	49,214	53,561	56,579	47,144
Pigment viscose taffetas	103,706	125,871	151,189	116,526	62,563
Acetate taffetas	76,516	163,998	201,561	183,889	234,196
Cross-dyed taffetas	13,281	7,245	9,868	18,457	26,945
Jersey weaves	5,559	(2)		(2)	(2)
Sharkskins	15,530	10,341	4,058	3,972	1,972
Twills and serges	109,325	158,758	200,296	177,619	153,847
Viscose satins	26,331	27,647	23,992	19,132	13,785
Acetate satins	142,254	159,018	165,506	137,280	101,400
All other flat fabrics	48,922	54,049	50,344	54,826	53,955
Twisted yarn fabrics, total	584,553	540,534	740,907	528,687	283,513
Crepe satins	28,258	19,906	28,692	17,905	9,838
Flat, faille and canton crepes	111,964	151,555	193,701	115,925	44,407
French crepes	119,856	136,370	168,275	123,264	49,906
Plied yarn fabrics, plain weave	118,303	72,840	125,012	81,301	46,730
Plied yarn fabrics, fancy weave	46,422	7,879	10,183	5,597	6,616
Marquisettes	57,959	78,816	87,922	90,964	55,636
Ninons and voiles	39,082	22,755	37,069	30,505	31,512
Other sheers (georgettes, triple sheers, etc.)	49,896	43,720	79,663	51,793	17,339
All other twisted yarn fabrics	12,723	6,693	9,790	11,413	21,530
100 percent spun rayon and/or acetate fabrics, total	332,451	340,603	434,085	407,601	401,629
Twills (including serges, gabardines, etc.)	86,429	166,678	251,848	248,456	189,602
Ribbed and corded fabrics (poplins, bedford cord, etc.)	(3)	3,894	5,534	3,746	6,021
Challis	59,974	72,318	49,816	29,261	80,19?
Linen type flakes	25,672	14,140	37,663	35,627	86,331
Plied yarn fabrics	55,860	26,981	35,952	40,655	31,411
All other 100 percent spun rayon and/or acetate fabrics	104,516	56,592	53,272	49,856	37,484
Combination filament and spun rayon and/or acetate fabrics, total	178,982	184,533	202,450	190,238	226,642
Poplins and failles	67,350	62,351	74,180	63,315	66,108
Shantungs	23,750	15,176	22,533	19,282	35,38?
Fujis	66,440	26,503	18,890	14,485	10,398
All other filament and spun rayon and/or acetate	21,442	80,503	86,847	93,156	114,79?
Pile, upholstery, drapery, tapestry, and tie fabrics, total [4]	57,060	29,860	37,763	36,496	45,433
Velvets, plushes and other pile fabrics	14,587	9,300	12,784	13,168	15,738
Upholstery, drapery, and tapestry fabrics	21,273	7,151	11,957	13,737	18,734
Yarn-dyed tie fabrics	13,282	6,544	4,212	4,054	6,703
Non-yarn-dyed tie fabrics	7,918	6,865	8,810	5,537	4,258
All other rayon mixtures, total	171,537	105,434	130,625	152,534	169,963
Rayon and/or acetate and wool	33,038	23,158	7,931	21,835	15,803
Filament rayon and/or acetate and cotton	55,279	49,323	50,037	42,250	31,165
Spun rayon and/or acetate and cotton	48,360	19,028	41,888	40,138	42,307
Rayon and/or acetate and other fibers	34,860	13,925	30,769	48,311	80,988
Silk, nylon, glass, and other fabrics, total [4]	61,673	145,264	201,312	292,036	477,444
100 percent nylon fabrics	21,881	92,997	110,233	167,561	266,254
100 percent silk fabrics	9,986	15,380	28,213	25,147	31,430
Other woven fabrics, not classified above [4]	29,806	36,887	62,866	99,328	119,760

[1] Includes estimated production for a few mills not reporting, estimates distributed by fabric classification.
[2] Included with "All other flat fabrics" to avoid disclosing data for individual establishments.
[3] Included with "All other 100 percent spun rayon and/or acetate fabrics" to avoid disclosing data for individual establishments.
[4] Fabrics containing 51 percent or more rayon and/or acetate by weight, without separation as to type of yarn used; includes filament, spun and mixtures of rayon and/or acetate and other fibers.
[5] Includes fabrics made of glass, acrylic, and other synthetic fibers and mixtures not chiefly cotton, wool, rayon, or acetate.

Source: Department of Commerce, Bureau of the Census; 1947 Census of Manufactures reports, and Facts for Industry, Series M15C.

No. 964.—WOOL MANUFACTURING EQUIPMENT, BY TYPE: 1899 TO 1947

[Represents equipment in possession of wool manufacturing establishments, regardless of condition. 1943 data based on reports of machinery "in place," and include estimates of number in possession but not in place. Data for 1899, 1914, and 1929 exclude mills whose product was valued at less than $500 in 1899 and 1914, and less than $5,000 in 1929; 1943 and 1947 include all mills, regardless of size]

TYPE	1899	1914	1929	1943	1947
Rag pickers [1]	(2)	1,769	1,466	1,346	----------
Garnetts [1]	(2)	412	467	377	----------
Cards (sets), except shoddy cards	(2)	(2)	8,831	7,172	----------
Woolen	7,765	6,819	6,610	6,347	----------
Worsted [1]	(2)	(2)	2,221	825	----------
Combs	1,451	2,425	2,661	2,612	2,335
Spinning spindles, total	3,220,792	4,307,865	4,558,803	3,643,603	3,632,673
Woolen [1]	2,228,283	2,079,635	2,343,297	1,961,643	1,116,947
Worsted	904,500	2,227,730	2,347,401	1,681,960	2,515,590
Twisting spindles, total [1]	442,572	676,783	917,148	742,000	----------
Woolen	98,252	91,792	96,779	142,000	----------
Worsted	344,420	784,661	821,368	644,760	----------
Looms, except carpet and rug [3]	62,304	76,738	69,564	43,318	35,445
Carpet and rug looms	9,795	8,821	10,387	5,607	5,685

[1] Data for 1899, 1914, and 1929 include estimates to provide for those machines in knitting mills. 1929 data also include estimates on number of woolen spinning spindles and worsted cards in knitting mills.
[2] Data not available.
[3] 1943 and other years not strictly comparable. Census of Manufactures for 1899, 1914, 1929, and 1947 called for a report on looms from those mills whose principal products were wool and hair goods while 1943 inquiry covered all mills consuming weaving yarns spun on woolen or worsted spinning spindles. Includes pile fabric looms conforming with these definitions.

Source: Department of Commerce, Bureau of the Census; 1947 Census of Manufactures reports, and *Facts for Industry*, Series M15H.

No. 965.—WOOL MANUFACTURING EQUIPMENT IN PLACE, 1943 TO 1952, AND BY REGION AND STATE, 1949

[Machinery in place is that which is set up in operating position]

YEAR, REGION, AND STATE	Worsted combs	Woolen spinning spindles	Worsted spinning spindles	Woolen and worsted looms	WOOL CARPET AND RUG LOOMS Broad	Narrow
1943	2,662	1,682,560	1,967,863	43,313	2,429	5,463
1947	2,666	1,561,198	1,920,642	36,872	2,336	2,384
1948	2,679	1,535,127	1,860,306	35,145	2,360	3,300
1949	2,739	1,436,660	1,896,744	37,400	2,307	4,501
1950	2,806	1,306,170	1,814,430	36,337	2,356	4,644
1951	2,990	1,252,400	1,831,304	34,517	2,049	3,310
1952	2,721	1,134,390	1,662,132	34,501	2,334	3,266
1949						
United States	2,739	1,436,660	1,896,744	37,400	2,307	4,501
New England	1,915	749,919	1,266,740	21,695		853
Connecticut	(1)	126,673	(1)	2,663		
Maine	(1)	123,332	84,600	3,417		
Massachusetts	1,185	270,789	615,606	5,508		
New Hampshire	(1)	112,045	55,630	3,616		
Rhode Island	601	65,586	473,876	5,047		
Vermont	(1)	61,204	(1)	550		
Middle Atlantic	671	329,530	414,100	4,680		2,669
New Jersey	403	39,907	149,622	2,304		469
New York	74	173,545	67,560	1,640		2,099
Pennsylvania	194	111,787	192,963	736		101
Southern [2]	(1)	168,785	95,480	4,408		88
North Central [3]	80	132,904	84,780	2,180		(1)
Western [4]	(1)	28,708	13,896	598		----------

[1] Not shown separately to avoid disclosing information for individual establishments.
[2] Ala., Del., Ga., Ky., N. C., S. C., Tenn., Texas, Va., W. Va., Md., and Okla.
[3] Ill., Ind., Iowa, Mich., Minn., Mo., Ohio, S. Dak., and Wis.
[4] Calif., Oreg., Utah, Wash., and Wyo.

Source: Department of Commerce, Bureau of the Census; *Facts for Industry*, Series M15H.

No. 966.—KNIT GOODS: CLOTH, UNDERWEAR, AND OUTERWEAR—PRODUCTION BY TYPE: 1947 TO 1951

PRODUCT	Unit	1947	1949	1950	1951
Knit cloth for sale, total[1]	Million pounds	152.6	147.8	162.8	148.7
Warp knit fabrics	do	41.5	42.9	47.2	43.8
Circular knit fabrics	do	111.1	104.9	115.6	104.9
Knit underwear and nightwear:					
Made from warp knit fabrics, all fibers	Thousand dozens	7,708	15,496	16,617	17,822
Made from circular knit fabrics:					
Rayon, silk, and synthetics	do	10,932	13,326	12,371	11,197
Cotton and wool	do	40,557	37,076	43,271	41,744
Knit outerwear:					
Sweaters, jackets, and jerseys	do	6,677	7,573	8,733	7,722
Bathing suits and trunks	do	500	355	326	291
Knit headwear and neckwear	do	1,556	1,375	1,599	1,578

[1] Figures for 1949, 1950 and 1951 represent shipments.

Source: Department of Commerce, Bureau of the Census; 1947 Census of Manufactures reports and *Facts for Industry*, Series M15K, M67C, and M67G.

No. 967.—WOMEN'S, MISSES', AND JUNIORS' OUTERWEAR: 1939 TO 1951

TYPE OF GARMENT	Unit	GARMENTS CUT					
		1939	1947	1948	1949	1950	1951
Blouses	1,000 dozens	2,886	7,496	7,851	9,329	10,764	12,049
Unit price dresses	1,000 units	194,383	127,791	134,951	147,023	139,607	138,559
Dozen price dresses	do		75,456	92,088	105,936	9,097	8,506
Suits	do	4,297	14,352	14,963	15,643	18,048	18,179
Skirts	1,000 dozens	1,084	2,020	2,907	3,691	4,784	4,567
Untrimmed coats	1,000 units	17,428	18,956	22,936	22,022	22,598	21,992
Fur-trimmed coats	do		1,924	2,638	1,927	2,105	1,907

Source: Department of Commerce, Bureau of Census; 1947 Census of Manufactures reports and *Facts for Industry*, Series M67H.

No. 968.—MEN'S AND BOYS' CLOTHING—SELECTED GARMENTS CUT: 1937 TO 1952

[Leaders indicate comparable data not available]

TYPE OF GARMENT AND UNIT OF MEASURE	1937	1939	1947	1949	1950	1951	1952[1]
Suits thousands	23,743	27,354	28,882	22,437	27,145	22,140	
Men's and youths' do	20,733	24,737	26,428	19,497	23,695	19,559	19,398
Boys' do	3,010	2,617	2,454	2,940	3,450	2,581	
Separate trousers do			60,905	58,603	65,819	59,644	
Separate coats do			5,286	7,300	8,855	8,361	
Men's and youths' do			4,760	5,767	7,039	6,328	
Boys' do			526	1,533	1,816	2,033	
Dress and sport shirts, men's and youths' thousand dozens	[2]12,027	13,362	17,042	16,462	18,100	16,614	18,283
Overalls do	4,114	3,973	6,807	8,190	9,824	8,619	
Men's and youths' do			4,241	4,755	6,100	5,214	5,419
Boys' do			2,566	3,435	3,724	3,405	
Work shirts (includes flannel) do	6,062	6,850	5,815	5,774	5,796	5,669	
Men's and youths' do			4,959	5,429	5,471	5,315	5,165
Boys' do			856	345	325	354	

[1] Preliminary.
[2] Includes polo, tennis, and basque shirts of knitted fabrics.

Source: Department of Commerce, Bureau of the Census, monthly data published in *Facts for Industry*, Series M67B.

No. 969.—HOSIERY—PRODUCTION, BY TYPE: 1946 TO 1952

[Thousands of dozens of pairs]

TYPE	1946	1947	1948	1949	1950	1951	1952
Total, all types	157,359	149,545	147,687	144,512	160,406	155,730	163,204
Women's full-fashioned, total	40,338	38,875	44,706	45,238	51,855	51,195	51,366
Silk	1,600	1,603	603	313	330	190	120
Nylon	26,307	33,484	42,657	44,642	51,039	40,749	76
Rayon	11,401	3,919	1,290	187	111	49	127
Cotton	347	300	142	124	199	141	19
All other yarns	100	64	54	35	17	14	19
Seamless, total (including men's full-fashioned)	117,000	110,660	102,382	99,284	105,801	105,935	111,438
Silk	5,489	11,346	8,417	7,085	7,440	5,088	4,673
Women's seamless, total		3		35			
Nylon	2,999	3,843	3,706	3,600	4,398	4,388	5,413
Rayon	3,519	3,084	1,689	1,476	1,161		
Cotton	2,449	3,312	2,276	2,361	1,419		1,281
Wool	105	105	90	77			
Ribbed hose	687	895	860	246	238	362	284
Men's full-fashioned	171	139	76	79	35		
Men's seamless half-hose, total	26,734	24,642	16,131	14,430	14,033	16,977	16,376
Silk	66	19	21				
Nylon	365	430	364	404	909		
Rayon	8,399	8,654	6,146	4,578	5,403	3,685	6,866
Cotton	13,182	12,156	7,955	7,557	7,271	7,014	8,049
Wool	4,687	3,401	1,722	2,006	1,932	2,397	2,137
Synthetics, other							
Men's slack socks, total	21,885	21,911	26,690	26,997	28,693	30,126	30,688
Silk	40	40	33	4	35		
Nylon	140	648	220	3,390	2,000	3,645	6,885
Rayon	6,491	5,163	9,444	6,766	7,802	6,330	5,671
Cotton	12,007	11,667	14,600	16,467	20,391	16,695	15,184
Wool	3,206	1,414	1,026	1,010	1,305	1,100	1,164
Synthetics, other							207
Cotton bundle goods	5,216	5,627	6,077	4,577	6,011	5,288	4,729
Woolen bundle goods	2,104	1,590	1,747	1,642	1,000		
Athletic socks	2,305	1,670	7,006	8,108	8,200		
Crew socks	3,828	3,230	2,785	6,961	8,000		
Slipper socks					440		
Children's and infants'	8,180	8,231	8,462	8,367	9,580	9,399	10,979
Anklets, total	37,138	30,196	30,368	36,360	36,197	35,163	34,437
Misses' and women's	26,012	14,660	13,440	14,000	14,360	14,880	14,427
Men's and boys'	3,015	3,473	3,382	3,348	4,130	4,300	5,046
Children's	(1)	5,500	6,760	6,000	5,130	4,880	4,980
Infants'	9,111	6,056	7,229				

[1] Included with infants' anklets.

Source: National Association of Hosiery Manufacturers, New York, N. Y.; published annually in Hosiery Statistics.

No. 970.—SHOES AND SLIPPERS (EXCEPT RUBBER FOOTWEAR)—PRODUCTION BY CLASS: 1939 TO 1952

[Thousands of pairs]

CLASS	1939	1947	1949	1950	1951	1952
Total	455,329	454,954	478,390	512,644	445,000	454,904
Dress and work shoes	361,578	398,904	387,600	404,362	346,000	344,340
Men's dress, including moccasin type dress shoes	78,687	84,967	86,000	85,000	81,000	77,000
Men's work, including moccasins	26,135	31,765	19,000	21,000	19,000	18,000
Youths' and boys'	17,316	19,226	18,000	19,000	16,000	16,000
Women's, including sandal type dress shoes	193,777	182,816	163,278	181,000	141,000	145,000
Misses', including sandal type dress shoes	46,601	27,096	25,340	34,000	23,000	24,437
Children's		28,362	22,366	24,000	18,000	18,000
Infants'	34,083	16,800	15,000	15,000	11,000	13,000
Babies'		14,502	13,642	15,000	13,000	13,000
Slippers for housewear	48,682	47,000	44,726	48,000	47,000	52,000
Athletic shoes	4,144	4,333	3,166	5,044	3,166	3,000
Play shoes	19,574	31,000	77,000	63,000	74,000	52,000
Footwear, not specified by kind		2,193	2,004	4,350	5,000	6,143

Source: Department of Commerce, Bureau of the Census; 1939 and 1947 Census of Manufactures reports, and Facts for Industry, Series M15A.

No. 971.—CHEMICALS—PRODUCTION, BY KIND, 1939 TO 1952

[Data for chemicals shown are restricted to a selected group comprised for the most part of inorganic chemicals and related products which are sufficiently important economically to justify publication. Data for production by Government-owned arsenals, ordnance works, and certain plants operated for Government by private industry are excluded, except that data for chemicals manufactured by Tennessee Valley Authority are included]

CHEMICAL AND BASIS	Unit	1939	1947	1950	1951	1952[1]
Ammonia, synthetic anhydrous	Short tons	310,822	1,114,000	1,565,569	1,767,043	2,053,796
Ammonium nitrate, original solution (100%NH4NO3)	do	(2)	1,086,869	1,213,911	1,346,443	1,466,570
Ammonium sulfate, synthetic (technical)[3]	do	(2)	195,848	1,137,721	622,084	811,022
Calcium arsenate (100%Ca3(AsO4)2)	do	[4] 20,674	23,452	22,674	20,450	3,586
Calcium carbide (commercial)	do	(2)	607,113	671,492	775,284	703,360
Calcium phosphate:						
Monobasic (100%CaH4(PO4)2)	do	37,038	36,898	39,472	(5)	35,363
Dibasic (100%CaHPO4)	do	(2)	41,323	53,046	52,033	62,336
Carbon, activated[6]	do	16,168	35,548	37,921	41,656	32,449
Carbon dioxide:						
Liquid and gas	do	(2)	117,600	200,380	[7] 161,784	[7] 163,398
Solid (dry ice)	do	178,447	360,200	439,526	482,462	535,731
Chlorine, gas[3]	do	514,401	1,443,219	2,084,161	2,517,913	2,506,536
Chrome green (C. P.)	do	5,014	6,991	7,688	7,766	6,509
Chrome yellow and orange (C. P.)	do	[9] 19,466	23,235	27,098	31,046	24,681
Hydrochloric acid (100%HCl)	do	123,831	442,558	618,784	693,541	678,373
Hydrofluoric acid, anhydrous and technical (100%H2F2)	do	7,421	27,933	35,174	43,660	41,085
Hydrogen	Mil. cu. ft	(2)	21,185	45,163	[10] 26,442	[10] 26,532
Lead arsenate (acid and basic)	Short tons	29,784	15,503	19,717	12,708	7,144
Methanol (natural) (100%CH3OH)	M gallons	4,005	2,598	2,082	2,017	2,237
Molybdate chrome orange (C. P.)	Short tons	(2)	2,238	3,905	4,021	3,503
Nitric acid (100%HNO3)	do	167,740	1,189,411	1,335,718	1,512,609	1,630,673
Oxygen	Mil. cu. ft	(2)	14,429	17,848	22,282	22,962
Phosphoric acid:						
Total (50%H3PO4)	Short tons	(2)	1,012,971	1,640,599	1,845,727	2,048,532
From phosphorus (50%H3PO4)	do	(2)	529,848	814,668	911,364	976,263
From phosphate rock (50%H3PO4)	do	(2)	483,123	825,931	934,363	1,072,269
Silver nitrate (100%AgNO3)	M ounces	(2)	38,336	55,549	60,452	59,498
Soda ash (commercial sodium carbonate):						
Ammonia soda process—						
Total wet and dry (98-100%Na2CO3)[11]	Short tons	2,826,000	4,524,668	3,991,199	5,093,927	4,442,459
Finished light (98-100%Na2CO3)[12]	do		2,206,590	2,049,506	2,575,677	2,316,509
Finished dense (98-100%Na2CO3)	do		1,629,406	1,410,110	1,802,022	1,591,170
Natural (Na2CO3 equivalent)[13]	do	121,858	276,428	338,379	363,951	312,643
Sodium bicarbonate (refined) (100%NaHCO3)	do	[14] 150,913	180,596	146,906	172,640	138,101
Sodium bichromate and chromate	do	58,164	90,285	89,829	127,634	89,283
Sodium hydroxide (caustic soda):[15]						
Electrolytic process—						
Liquid (100%NaOH)	do	512,492	1,353,429	2,005,420	2,437,997	2,499,915
Solid (100%NaOH)	do		247,054	316,816	445,917	347,381
Lime—soda process—						
Liquid (100%NaOH)	do	532,914	749,721	505,300	668,310	510,996
Solid (100%NaOH)	do		246,303	121,562	204,706	134,769
Sodium phosphate:						
Monobasic (100%NaH2PO4)	do	(2)	14,690	15,703	18,478	19,366
Dibasic (100%Na2HPO4)	do	32,382	78,806	158,756	182,649	175,764
Tribasic (100%Na3PO4)	do	116,731	88,568	66,801	67,607	51,26
Meta (100%NaPO3)	do	(2)	30,460	39,412	52,398	48,902
Tetra (100%Na4P2O7)	do	48,691	56,641	85,657	86,384	84,498
Sodium silicate (soluble silicate glass, liquid and solid) (anhydrous)	do	(2)	492,837	486,203	547,387	517,842
Sodium sulfate:						
Anhydrous (refined) (100%Na2SO4)	do	(2)	134,969	184,254	233,666	202,813
Glauber's salt (100%Na2SO4,10H2O)[15]	do	(2)	202,285	185,626	219,942	176,838
Salt cake (crude) (commercial)[15]	do	(2)	693,517	561,395	707,388	661,945

For footnotes, see next page.

No. 971.—CHEMICALS—PRODUCTION, BY KIND, 1939 TO 1952—Continued

CHEMICAL AND BASIS	Unit	1939	1947	1950	1951	1952
Sulfuric acid:						
Gross (100% H₂SO₄)	Short tons	4,795,003	10,780,166	13,029,268	13,372,300	13,824,628
Chamber process (100% H₂SO₄)	do	2,120,963	3,274,753	2,956,007	2,885,672	2,712,713
Contact process (gross) (100% H₂SO₄)	do	2,674,040	7,505,413	10,073,352	10,486,628	16,663,606
Contact process (new) (100% H₂SO₄)	do		6,828,640	9,180,784	9,562,100	6,665,267
Fortified spent acid (100% H₂SO₄)	do		676,773	886,568	903,546	957,339
Zinc yellow (zinc chromate) (C. P.)	do		3,476	4,565	5,142	7,304

^{1} Preliminary. ^{2} No comparable data.
^{3} Excludes byproduct coke-oven production. Data for 1950-1952 include synthetic ammonium sulfate produced in coke plants, as well as quantities produced for the account of Department of the Army.
^{4} Proportion of estimate, 5 percent. ^{5} Not shown separately to avoid disclosure of individual operations.
^{6} Includes data for deodorizing, decolorizing, and water purification grades. Data for gas-mask solvent recovery grades excluded.
^{7} Excludes quantities produced and consumed in the same plants manufacturing soda ash.
^{8} Total production including quantities liquefied for use, storage or shipment.
^{9} Includes data for molybdate chrome orange.
^{10} Excludes quantities produced and consumed in manufacture of methanol and ammonia but includes an unspecified amount of hydrogen produced for sale or interplant transfer to plants consuming this gas in production of ammonia.
^{11} Includes quantities diverted to manufacture of caustic soda and sodium bicarbonate and quantities processed to finished light and finished dense soda ash.
^{12} Excludes quantities converted to finished dense soda ash.
^{13} Collected in cooperation with Bureau of Mines.
^{14} Proportion of estimate, 3 percent or less.
^{15} Liquid production figures represent total production for each process, including quantities later evaporated to solid caustic and reported as such.
^{16} Includes sulfuric acid of oleum grades.

Source: Department of Commerce, Bureau of the Census 1939 and 1947 Census of Manufactures reports; 1950-52 compiled from manufacturers' reports and published in Facts for Industry, Series M19A. Monthly data published currently.

No. 972.—SYNTHETIC ORGANIC CHEMICALS—PRODUCTION AND SALES, BY GROUP: 1950 AND 1951

GROUP	1950			1951		
	Production	Sales	Sales value	Production	Sales	Sales value
ORGANIC CHEMICALS, CYCLIC	1,000 lbs.	1,000 lbs.	$1,000	1,000 lbs.	1,000 lbs.	$1,000
Intermediates	4,596,659	1,466,661	339,899	4,527,925	1,601,990	437,879
Finished products	3,472,585	2,102,877	1,274,694	4,715,024	3,957,761	1,780,312
Dyes	195,713	195,282	100,780	187,032	159,992	176,870
Color index	142,403	138,443	101,064	136,618	113,320	
Prototype	38,464	38,840	47,108	32,354	26,218	
Uncoded	34,966	32,860	42,409	94,670	30,247	
Lakes and toners	47,417	38,970	38,279	47,272	40,109	
Medicinals	41,434	37,611	128,644	61,315	48,787	
Flavor and perfume materials			38,417	75,934	14,812	
Plastics and resin materials	1,238,583	1,077,865	445,782	1,421,762	1,152,642	
Rubber processing chemicals	95,789	74,791	43,909	176,009	87,642	
Elastomers (synthetic rubbers)	802,877	870,840	176,664	1,003,856	1,406,196	
Pesticides and other organic agricultural chemicals	245,848	218,810	60,256	406,986	318,801	
Miscellaneous	762,144	616,760	140,685	867,826	726,930	
ORGANIC CHEMICALS, ACYCLIC						
Intermediates and finished products	15,456,626	7,512,879	1,261,074	18,253,406	8,905,704	1,788,607
Medicinals	7,900	6,387	27,189	12,228	9,779	26,922
Flavor and perfume materials	9,662	8,680	14,557	10,652	10,496	17,366
Plastics and resin materials	664,662	616,819	212,154	1,019,670	871,676	
Rubber processing chemicals	16,349	15,866	10,409	22,439	16,099	
Elastomers (synthetic rubbers)	363,949	356,385	195,790	442,279		
Pesticides and other organic agricultural chemicals	36,790	31,729	8,457	57,032	46,616	14,512
Miscellaneous	14,156,164	6,272,457	777,381	16,688,875	7,623,589	1,122,525

^{1} Excludes quantity and value of interplant transfers.

Source: U. S. Tariff Commission annual report, "Synthetic Organic Chemicals, United States Production and Sales."

No. 973.—Industrial Explosives Manufactured and Sold in the United States: 1929 to 1951

[In thousands of pounds. Excludes exports]

YEAR	Total	Permissible explosives [1]	High explosives other than permissible	BLACK BLASTING POWDER Granular	BLACK BLASTING POWDER Pellet	USE	Total	Permissible explosives [1]	High explosives other than permissible	Black blasting powder
1929	509,708	62,669	326,993	86,818	33,227	**1950**	[2]719,841	109,420	575,962	20,655
1930	445,090	53,826	291,391	63,139	36,735					
1931	337,565	41,578	216,157	46,300	33,530	Coal mining	[2]296,633	108,351	156,839	17,702
1932	238,887	32,225	137,908	35,793	27,961	Metal mining	127,750	53	127,749	[3]51
1933	255,987	33,927	157,849	33,887	30,323	Quarrying and nonmetallic				
1934	314,768	39,208	206,625	37,193	31,742	mineral mining	[2]141,249	895	138,857	1,435
1935	308,381	39,170	200,324	34,223	34,665	Railway and other construction work	129,856	74	138,886	896
1936	391,605	47,859	262,047	40,420	41,278	All other purposes	14,353	46	13,631	676
1937	404,744	49,579	288,924	29,837	36,404					
1938	332,130	41,859	238,576	23,552	28,143	**1951**	[2]753,821	108,258	611,236	13,985
1939	386,438	49,960	278,250	28,322	29,915	Coal mining	[2]291,787	107,182	152,500	11,836
1940	423,369	56,436	305,180	29,084	30,670	Metal mining	147,213	131	147,073	9
						Quarrying and nonmetallic				
1941	481,927	70,612	351,857	27,882	31,576	mineral mining	[2]152,353	815	150,230	1,235
1942	499,255	84,022	359,699	24,167	31,367	Railway and other construction work	150,511	106	149,851	554
1943	477,651	92,656	338,573	19,814	26,608	All other purposes	11,956	24	11,582	351
1944	464,111	102,538	318,613	16,282	26,677					
1945	457,311	97,407	322,956	12,303	24,644					
1946	536,315	100,258	399,233	13,539	23,285					
1947	[2]651,391	122,349	476,017	9,837	26,627					
1948	[2]725,227	126,282	550,086	8,236	25,004					
1949	[2]631,230	91,630	505,601	5,853	14,224					
1950	[2]719,841	109,420	575,962	5,441	15,214					
1951	[2]753,821	108,258	611,236	3,752	10,233					

[1] Represents type of high explosives approved by Bureau of Mines as suitable for safe use in coal mines provided specifications of use are followed.
[2] Includes 16,562,000 liquid oxygen explosive in 1947, 15,620,000 in 1948, 13,922,000 in 1949, 13,804,000 in 1950, and 20,341,000 in 1951.
[3] Includes 13,742,000 liquid oxygen explosive in 1950, and 20,268,000 in 1951.
[4] Includes 62,000 liquid oxygen explosive in 1950 and 72,000 in 1951.
[5] Sold by manufacturer but later returned unused.

Source: Department of the Interior, Bureau of Mines; *Production of Explosives in the United States.*

No. 974.—Asphalt and Tar Roofing and Siding Products—Shipments: 1933 to 1952

PRODUCT AND UNIT OF MEASURE	1933	1938	1943	1947	1948	1949	1950	1951	1952
Asphalt roofing, total 1,000 squares	24,737	34,610	51,349	71,461	59,939	52,357	65,024	59,117	57,935
Smooth-surfaced do	13,838	15,027	19,236	22,482	16,344	13,038	14,377	13,577	12,458
Mineral-surfaced do	5,685	8,799	16,688	16,357	13,569	12,510	14,116	13,961	13,764
Strip shingles do	4,223	9,054	13,014	28,569	26,216	23,573	32,109	27,401	27,806
Individual shingles do	991	1,730	2,411	4,053	3,810	3,236	4,422	4,178	3,969
Asphalt sidings, total do	(1)	[2]590	2,338	4,316	3,280	2,499	2,009	2,078	1,858
Roll form do	(1)	(1)	2,140	3,903	2,866	2,090	1,659	1,754	1,540
Shingle form do	(1)	(1)	198	413	414	409	350	324	317
Mineral-surfaced insulating board base siding 1,000 squares	(1)	(1)	1,012	3,686	2,560	2,188	2,402	2,411	2,718
Asphalt board products 1,000 sq. ft.	(1)	(1)	(1)	86,086	31,932	32,184	48,376	56,200	45,933
Saturated felts, total tons of 2,000 lb.	(1)	(1)	(1)	457,870	538,042	500,688	650,389	662,961	640,214
Asphalt do	(1)	(1)	(1)	354,291	448,751	421,510	550,017	538,005	531,112
Tar do	(1)	(1)	(1)	103,579	89,291	79,178	100,372	124,956	109,102
Saturated and coated sheathings, total tons of 2,000 lb.	(1)	(1)	(1)	37,619	14,619	10,284	12,025	13,571	9,587
Asphalt do	(1)	(1)	(1)	(3)	(3)	(3)	(3)	(3)	(3)
Tar do	(1)	(1)	(1)	(3)	(3)	(3)	(3)	(3)	(3)

[1] Not available. [2] Represents brick and all other types of siding.
[3] Not shown separately, to avoid disclosing operations of individual companies.

Source: Department of Commerce, Bureau of the Census; 1947 Census of Manufactures reports, and *Facts for Industry,* Series M26D.

No. 975.—Rubber (Natural, Reclaimed, and Synthetic)—New Supply, Distribution, and Stocks: 1945 to 1952

[In tons of 2,240 pounds. Natural rubber refers to dry weights of all types, including liquid latex, guayule, etc. Synthetic includes GR–S, Neoprene, Butyl, and Butadiene-Acrylonitrile; reclaimed includes both natural and synthetic rubber reclaims]

ITEM	1945	1946	1947	1948	1949	1950	1951	1952
New supply, total	1,399,761	1,444,074	1,489,562	1,506,225	1,295,552	1,620,112	1,954,869	1,899,436
Domestic production	1,064,218	1,035,650	800,097	755,204	617,719	789,190	1,211,092	1,071,962
Natural	536	12						
Reclaimed	243,309	295,612	291,395	266,861	224,029	313,006	365,933	272,396
Synthetic	820,373	740,026	508,702	488,343	393,690	476,184	845,159	798,566
Imports	145,543	408,424	689,465	751,021	677,883	830,922	743,777	827,452
Natural	135,136	400,675	688,354	735,340	660,566	804,142	732,925	806,997
Reclaimed	(1)	40	18	10	25	1,059	757	1,595
Synthetic	10,407	7,709	1,093	15,671	17,242	25,721	10,085	19,891
Distribution, total	1,143,979	1,406,202	1,440,764	1,353,492	1,234,585	1,590,334	1,586,993	1,577,736
Domestic consumption	1,040,045	1,314,706	1,410,722	1,330,517	1,211,582	1,562,290	1,560,419	1,541,415
Natural	105,429	277,597	562,661	627,332	574,522	720,268	454,015	453,846
Reclaimed	241,036	275,410	288,395	261,113	222,679	303,733	347,507	280,532
Synthetic	693,580	761,699	559,666	442,072	414,381	538,289	758,897	807,037
Exports	103,934	91,496	30,042	22,975	23,103	28,034	26,574	36,305
Natural	6,743	4,338	4,101	6,673	6,253	5,640	2,603	3,024
Reclaimed	13,413	14,461	14,556	11,428	6,483	11,741	14,722	11,180
Synthetic	83,778	72,697	11,385	4,874		7,653	9,249	22,101
Stocks, end of year [2]	350,234	387,926	227,347	288,394	232,396	177,681	261,963	344,911
Natural	118,715	237,467	129,038	141,541	106,619	99,215	76,369	95,260
Reclaimed	28,155	33,666	35,943	32,630	28,263	35,708	45,082	30,664
Synthetic [3]	203,454	116,793	62,366	115,123	98,054	52,758	139,962	118,987

[1] Less than 0.5 long tons.
[2] Differences between "new supply" and "distribution" not precisely comparable with "stocks" due to year-end and inventory adjustments.   [3] Includes stocks shipped for export which had not yet cleared port.
Source: Department of Commerce, National Production Authority. Monthly data published in Survey of Current Business.

No. 976.—Leather—Production, by Principal Types of Raw Stock: 1937 to 1952

[Cattle hide in thousands of hides, other figures in thousands of skins]

YEAR	Cattle hide	Calf and kip	Goat and kid	Sheep and lamb [1]	YEAR	Cattle hide	Calf and kip	Goat and kid	Sheep and lamb [1]
1937	22,380	12,027	46,554	34,232	1945	27,576	11,636	24,026	51,847
1938	19,047	12,991	31,905	28,941	1946	27,033	10,882	24,137	47,971
1939	22,095	14,027	40,419	39,384	1947	25,612	12,471	37,256	36,555
1940	21,013	11,387	37,697	27,920	1948	26,071	10,484	37,991	53,532
1941	28,099	13,098	45,355	51,865	1949	23,388	10,173	34,752	28,736
1942	30,822	12,264	41,122	53,634	1950	24,385	10,669	37,162	31,307
1943	25,656	11,112	37,351	59,315	1951	22,706	7,962	31,091	24,504
1944	26,114	10,930	34,666	53,959	1952	22,689	9,971	30,482	27,936

[1] Prior to 1940, includes skivers and excludes fleshers; beginning 1940, includes fleshers and excludes skivers.
Source: Tanners' Council of America. Monthly figures published in Survey of Current Business.

No. 977.—Pressed and Blown Glassware—Quantity and Value of Shipments, by Class: 1950 and 1951

[Includes only products manufactured from glass produced in reporting establishment]

CLASS	Unit of measure	1950		1951	
		Quantity	Value ($1,000)	Quantity	Value ($1,000)
Shipments, total value			324,696		324,929
Tumblers, goblets, and other stemware	Thous. of doz	74,815	51,999	75,244	54,133
Cooking ware [1]	Thous. pieces	54,608	10,977	69,444	12,539
Ornamental, decorative, novelty glassware, and smokers' accessories, total			12,020		12,853
Lighting glassware, total			133,268		166,162
Electric-light bulb blanks, electronic-tube blanks (including radio, X-ray, radar, and special tubes), and fluorescent tubes			109,051		82,617
Bowls, all types			3,316		3,367
Enclosing globes, all types			3,570		3,379
Shades, reflectors, and torcheres			5,887		5,416
Railroad, marine, and traffic lighting glassware			888		1,339
Lamp chimneys	Thous. of doz	1,317	1,300	1,265	1,334
Lantern globes (oil and electric)	do	426	889	424	967
All other lighting glassware			8,367		9,443
All other pressed and blown glassware (except glass containers).[2]			116,432		137,571

[1] Heat-resistant, heat-treated, and annealed.
[2] Includes tubing (except fluorescent and neon), technical, scientific, and industrial glassware.

Source: Department of Commerce, Bureau of the Census; published in *Facts for Industry*, Series M77E.

No. 978.—Glass Containers—Direct Exports and Domestic Production and Shipments, by Kind: 1950, 1951, and 1952

[In thousand gross]

ITEM	1950		1951		1952	
	Production	Shipments	Production	Shipments	Production	Shipments
Total	106,380	107,897	117,692	114,738	115,631	114,115
Direct exports		2,643		3,062		2,677
Domestic production and shipments:						
Narrow-neck, total	66,398	65,322	78,052	73,066	73,363	70,379
Food		11,061		11,528		11,917
Medicinal and health supplies	39,526	14,685	41,688	13,726	40,512	13,009
Chemical, household, and industrial		7,320		7,788		7,791
Toiletries and cosmetics		5,977		6,241		6,584
Beverage, returnable	6,678	6,291	7,086	6,308	8,672	7,916
Beverage, nonreturnable	146	168	177	180	520	446
Beer, returnable	3,237	3,155	5,175	4,524	2,836	2,256
Beer, nonreturnable	3,213	3,211	10,251	9,816	8,170	8,196
Liquor	9,805	9,709	10,302	9,644	8,771	8,518
Wine	3,793	3,745	3,371	3,219	3,882	3,677
Wide-mouth, total	39,982	39,932	39,641	38,610	42,268	41,098
Food		[1] 28,309		[1] 26,841		28,914
Medicinal and health supplies	[1] 34,758	3,449	[1] 34,467	3,849	37,066	3,975
Chemical, household, and industrial		1,418		1,310		1,542
Toiletries and cosmetics		1,595		1,603		1,615
Dairy products	3,731	3,695	3,639	3,517	3,250	3,157
Fruit jars	(1)	(1)	(1)	(1)	(1)	(1)
Jelly glasses	(1)	(1)	(1)	(1)	(1)	(1)
Packers' tumblers	1,493	1,466	1,534	1,489	1,952	1,895

[1] Data for fruit jars and jelly glasses combined with wide-mouth food containers to avoid disclosing operations of individual companies.

Source: Department of Commerce, Bureau of the Census; published in *Facts for Industry*, Series M77C.

No. 979.—REFRACTORIES—SHIPMENTS: 1950 AND 1951

PRODUCT	Unit of measure	1950		1951	
		Quantity	Value f. o. b. plant	Quantity	Value f. o. b. plant
Clay refractories, total.............................			$1,000 128, 684		$1,000 171, 864
Fire-clay brick, standard and special shapes, except super-duty.	M 9" equiv	555, 103	57, 489	710, 299	78, 648
Superduty fire-clay brick, standard and special shapes..........	......do....	64, 046	10, 106	92, 783	14, 148
Insulating fire-brick, standard and special shapes...............	......do....	45, 204	7, 685	56, 606	11, 670
High-alumina brick, standard and special shapes (50% Al₂O₃ and over, except fused alumina and mullite).	......do....	17, 670	4, 787	22, 414	6, 690
Ladle brick...	......do....	198, 230	12, 078	205, 848	14, 688
Glass-house pots, tank blocks, upper structure, and floaters....	Short ton	21, 294	3, 177	23, 708	3, 818
Hot-top refractories...................................	M 9" equiv	43, 040	4, 459	54, 944	5, 817
Sleeves, nozzles, runner brick, and tuyeres...................	......do....	52, 108	6, 586	68, 591	9, 090
High-temperature bonding mortars.....................	Short ton	65, 817	5, 494	82, 746	6, 577
Plastic refractories....................................	......do....	97, 455	4, 511	90, 277	5, 600
Cast and castables (hydraulic setting)...................	......do....	87, 200	4, 590	95, 780	5, 680
Ground crude fire clay and high-alumina material..........	......do....	261, 162	3, 611	444, 670	5, 697
Other clay refractories................................			2, 040		
Nonclay refractories, total............................			111, 977		208, 758
Silica brick and shapes................................	M 9" equiv	308, 353	28, 223	374, 357	34, 688
Magnesite and magnesite-chrome brick and shapes..........	......do....	27, 779	14, 418	35, 133	27, 688
Chrome and chrome-magnesite brick and shapes............	......do....	44, 499	16, 672	53, 948	22, 495
Graphite and other carbon crucibles and retorts...........	Short ton	10, 229	5, 506	13, 345	7, 680
Other graphite and carbon refractories..................	......do....	1, 206	508	1, 527	677
High temperature bonding mortars......................	......do....	31, 173	4, 346	46, 787	6, 644
Plastic refractories...................................	......do....	69, 658	7, 175	133, 392	15, 682
Dead-burned magnesia and magnesite...................	......do....	286, 690	12, 908	372, 009	116, 650
Other nonclay brick and shapes........................			17, 594		23, 493
Other nonclay refractory materials sold in lump or ground form.			5, 905		4, 346

¹ Excluded from total to avoid duplication.

Source: Department of Commerce, Bureau of the Census; published in *Facts for Industry*, Series M27C.

No. 980.—STRUCTURAL CLAY PRODUCTS—PRODUCTION AND SHIPMENTS, BY KIND: 1948 TO 1951

PRODUCT AND UNIT OF MEASURE	1948	1949	1950	1951
Unglazed brick, common and face:				
Production.....................1,000 standard bricks..	5, 342, 479	5, 534, 305	6, 253, 260	6, 695, 308
Shipments: Quantity...........................do....	5, 706, 526	5, 361, 622	6, 464, 252	6, 356, 895
Value..........................1,000 dollars..	134, 665	129, 179	164, 479	170, 769
Hollow facing tile, glazed and unglazed:				
Production.....................1,000 brick equivalent..	394, 292	370, 405	454, 699	454, 699
Shipments: Quantity.........................do....	391, 841	357, 461	452, 697	452, 727
Value..........................1,000 dollars..	16, 099	16, 717	22, 698	25, 692
Unglazed structural tile:				
Production......................short tons..	1, 365, 968	1, 357, 687	1, 394, 380	1, 355, 680
Shipments: Quantity.........................do....	1, 390, 904	1, 380, 445	1, 396, 972	1, 166, 879
Value..........................1,000 dollars..	13, 384	14, 080	14, 698	14, 689
Vitrified clay sewer pipe:				
Production......................short tons..	1, 495, 247	1, 463, 013	1, 549, 637	1, 686, 580
Shipments: Quantity.........................do....	1, 623, 512	1, 349, 859	1, 867, 654	1, 640, 271
Value..........................1,000 dollars..	46, 721	44, 641	59, 692	56, 698
Floor and wall tile and accessories ¹:				
Production......................1,000 square feet..	104, 094	98, 146	134, 798	146, 873
Shipments: Quantity.........................do....	102, 391	98, 115	127, 699	141, 199
Value..........................1,000 dollars..	46, 646	43, 695	61, 679	70, 277
Drain tile:				
Production......................short tons..	710, 399	720, 769	667, 685	689, 797
Shipments: Quantity.........................do....	734, 251	668, 039	667, 648	657, 646
Value..........................1,000 dollars..	10, 696	11, 694	14, 296	14, 491

¹ Glazed and unglazed floor and wall tile, and accessories, including quarry tile.

Source: Department of Commerce, Bureau of the Census. *Facts for Industry, Series M27B.*

No. 981.—Pig Iron and Ferro-Alloys—Production, by Disposition, Kind, and Fuel and Materials Used: 1900 to 1951

[In thousands of short tons (2,000 lbs.)]

ITEM	1900	1910	1920	1925	1930	1935	1940	1945	1950	1951
Total pig iron and ferro-alloys	15,444	30,580	41,357	41,105	35,562	23,237	47,399	54,919	66,400	72,449
By disposition:										
For sale	(1)	(1)	12,011	10,070	7,933	4,505	6,837	8,351	8,957	9,745
For maker's use	(1)	(1)	29,346	31,034	27,630	19,432	40,561	46,569	57,443	62,704
By kind:										
Basic	1,201	10,175	18,746	22,027	20,601	15,253	33,988	39,867	49,880	54,213
Bessemer and low-phosphorus	8,936	12,595	13,510	10,550	8,193	4,747	7,835	8,570	8,426	9,361
Foundry (incl. ferro-silicon)	3,781	5,892	6,673	6,059	4,436	2,137	2,791	3,067	3,646	3,970
Malleable	194	944	1,468	1,740	1,760	1,350	1,832	2,350	3,181	3,363
Forge	888	632	355	270	57	6	4			
Ferromanganese, spiegeleisen, and all other	442	342	604	458	517	444	949	1,066	1,267	1,542
By fuel:										
Coke and charcoal [3]	13,566	29,853	41,018	41,105	35,564	23,938	47,396	54,919	66,400	72,449
Anthracite	1,878	727	339							
Materials used: [3]										
Iron ore, briquettes, etc	27,027	57,948	74,424	73,304	60,101	39,405	79,672	91,276	112,156	121,194
Cinder, scale, scrap, etc	1,792	3,136	5,585	5,619	7,052	4,768	7,480	9,749	10,731	10,950
Coke [4]	(1)	(1)	42,046	39,296	31,168	20,272	40,451	48,965	59,549	64,983
Limestone	8,313	16,271	19,964	16,973	12,431	8,425	16,678	20,863	27,708	30,335
Total number furnaces Dec. 31 [5]	406	473	452	395	300	258	231	241	250	251
Furnaces in blast Dec. 31 [5]	232	206	216	238	97	124	206	201	234	242

[1] Not available.   [3] Includes ferro-alloys made in electric furnaces   Charcoal pig iron last produced in 1945.
[3] Materials consumed in manufacture of pig iron only, beginning 1930.
[4] Coke and bituminous coal 1900 to 1925.   [5] Or as of Jan. 1 of following year.
Source: American Iron and Steel Institute, annual report.

No. 982.—Pig Iron and Ferro-Alloys—Production by States: 1944 to 1951

[In thousands of short tons (2,000 pounds)]

STATE	1944	1945	1946	1947	1948	1949	1950	1951
Grand total	62,866	54,919	46,200	60,117	61,912	54,917	66,400	72,449
Pig iron, total	61,007	53,223	44,779	58,329	60,055	53,413	64,587	70,274
Massachusetts, New York	3,947	3,295	2,780	3,869	3,875	3,541	4,302	4,699
Pennsylvania	18,510	16,171	13,251	17,563	17,742	15,037	18,240	20,221
Maryland, West Virginia	[1] 4,781	3,519	2,949	3,662	4,240	4,383	5,203	5,339
Kentucky, Tennessee, Texas	(1)	808	656	818	1,228	1,089	1,460	1,596
Alabama	3,949	3,582	3,149	3,929	4,013	3,663	4,347	4,371
Ohio	13,371	11,259	9,534	12,317	12,471	10,640	12,510	13,710
Indiana	[2] 8,474	5,982	4,829	6,401	6,493	5,991	7,018	7,756
Illinois	5,686	5,045	4,357	5,600	5,513	4,913	6,024	6,566
Michigan, Minnesota	(2)	1,921	1,893	1,924	2,101	2,002	2,830	2,904
Colorado, Utah, California	[2] 2,289	1,642	1,381	2,245	2,379	2,154	2,653	3,112
Ferro-alloy, total	1,859	1,696	1,421	1,788	1,856	1,504	1,813	2,174
New York, New Jersey	478	449	386	431	451	316	392	391
Pennsylvania	637	573	437	553	616	467	554	658
Virginia, West Virginia, South Carolina	[3] 380	171	141	278	302	266	287	306
Tennessee	(3)	66	64	84	88	47	60	77
Alabama	(3)	85	60	53	28	37	59	47
Ohio	[4] 363	204	200	212	210	166	198	242
Other States		148	133	177	161	206	264	454

[1] Production for Kentucky, Tennessee, and Texas included with Maryland and West Virginia.
[2] Production for Michigan included with Indiana, production for Minnesota included with Colorado, Utah, and California.
[3] Production for Tennessee and Alabama included with Virginia, West Virginia, and South Carolina.
[4] Includes production for Indiana, Illinois, Iowa, Colorado, and Washington.

Source: American Iron and Steel Institute, annual report.

No. 983.—Pig Iron and Ferro-Alloys and Steel Ingots and Castings— Production, Exports, and Imports: 1871 to 1951

[In short tons (2,000 pounds). Prior to 1921 exports and imports are for years ending June 30 following year specified; calendar years thereafter. Imports are imports for consumption beginning with 1933. All production figures are for calendar years. For figures for earlier years, see Abstract for 1951]

YEARLY AVERAGE OR YEAR	PIG IRON AND FERRO-ALLOYS			Steel ingots and castings, production [1]	YEAR	PIG IRON AND FERRO-ALLOYS			Steel ingots and castings, production [1]
	Production	Exports of domestic	Imports			Production	Exports of domestic	Imports	
1871–1875..	2,318,088	5,901	154,109	429,575 [2]	1933......	25,937,423	19,940	211,901	
1876–1880..	2,870,295	3,118	305,798		1934......	34,722,083	20,430	294,437	
1881–1885..	4,817,226	5,948	254,328	1,685,940	1937......	41,852,540	516,160	150,035	
1886–1890..	7,058,520	15,608	277,588	2,067,898	1938......				
1891–1895..	9,102,970	23,741	61,261	5,354,058	1939......	34,677,067		152,477	
1896–1900..	12,370,049	251,190	26,036	9,452,781	1940......	47,503,328	344,017	48,035	
1901–1905..	20,429,435	50,921	257,427	17,215,063	1941......		480,720	20,944	
1906–1910..	25,907,650	82,022	308,040	24,532,707	1942......	60,769,947	191,181	37,306	
1911–1915..	30,320,405	225,252	145,451	31,721,304	1943......	63,886,165		24,160	
1916–1920..	41,421,650	462,552	115,715	44,622,586	1944......			74,306	
1921–1925..	34,132,119	41,444	492,735	41,122,917	1945......	54,912,029	182,819		
1926–1930..	42,215,084	55,316	285,030	44,152,988	1946......	45,199,329	134,294	55,106	
1931–1935..	17,468,486	14,522	177,494	27,538,544	1947......	60,117,319	32,670	251,472	
1936–1940..	36,174,308	476,409	144,094	52,384,086	1948......	61,911,509	113,971	210,452	
1941–1945..	52,683,017	260,039	26,376	65,410,089	1949......	54,915,776	115,971	174,573	
1946–1950..	57,909,160	167,094	248,490	60,290,306	1950......		92,411	644,320	
1951......	18,675,202	16,091	178,273	29,121,924	1951......	72,443,542	35,366	1,228,170	

[1] Beginning 1904, includes only steel castings produced in foundries producing steel ingots.
[2] 1875 only.

Source: Production, American Iron and Steel Institute, annual report. Exports and imports, Department of Commerce, Bureau of Census; annual report. Foreign Commerce and Navigation of the U. S., and reports.

No. 984.—Rolled and Miscellaneous Steel Products—Production, by Kind: 1925 to 1951

[In short tons (2,000 pounds). See also Historical Statistics, series J 170]

KIND	1925	1930	1935	1940	1945	1950 [4]	1951
Hot-rolled products, total......	37,300,205	32,654,305	26,648,205	45,600,200	60,012,000	75,104,004	81,921,320
Plates......	4,323,895	4,102,262	1,609,407	3,325,403	7,246,082	7,308,130	
Sheets......	4,395,462	3,992,944	4,795,404	11,705,404	13,067,437	22,622,918	25,152,388
Black plate......	2,102,261	2,130,144	2,307,452	532,524	941	632,664	
Strip......	1,905,471	2,174,855	2,935,200	2,677,744	3,542,995	3,903,657	3,971,125
Strip and sheets for cold reduced black plate and tin plate......	[1]	[1]	[1]	3,109,607	4,095,524	5,600,547	6,923,420
Hoops......	220,544	96,426	106,404	97,074		97,391	
Cotton ties and baling bands......	300,205	81,737	27,485	44,918	34,216	49,211	
Bars—merchant......		4,632,810	4,142,944		9,045,282	9,286,500	10,926,400
Bars—concrete......	917,487	908,169	624,342	1,562,082	2,322,082	2,345,487	
Structural shapes......	4,094,082	3,962,970	1,968,700	4,236,700	4,487,104	5,442,104	
Steel piling......	64,130	115,275	60,082	322,289	169,080	262,779	
Rails......	3,118,400	2,095,061	793,972	1,678,509	2,417,550	1,848,580	1,...
Long splice bars and tie plate bars......	922,341	679,187	200,471	313,022	328,022	328,078	
Skelp......	3,012,540	3,005,882	1,814,236	2,705,000	2,804,082	4,164,404	4,...
Blanks, tube rounds or pierced billets for seamless tubes......	[1]	1,297,082	1,087,776	4,325,082	3,204,482	4,451,082	4,447,...
Wire rods......	3,302,615	2,652,082	2,723,482	4,328,082	4,252,187	4,210,677	
Rolled forging billets......	361,170	343,482		1,477,082	382,082	1,214,482	
Blooms, billets, etc. for export......	[1]	60,622	44,720		176,000	11,242	
Rolled steel car wheels......	[1]		98,714	101,160			
All other......	1,704,189	765,306	227,485	114,482	776,082	101,282	
Miscellaneous products [3]							
Tin plate and terneplate......	1,896,610	1,896,610	1,800,082	2,705,804	2,897,082	4,082,080	
Galvanized sheets......	1,308,560	1,176,482	1,151,745	1,896,082	1,076,582	2,275,700	
Galvanized formed products......	88,130		87,482	522,082	822,717	117,482	
Wire (plain)......	779,687	44,082	2,177,082	2,671,082	3,444,082		
Wire nails......	88,085	84,821	44,082	56,082	84,082		
Cut nails and spikes......	[1]		14,082	9,577	13,100		
Pipes and tubes (black)......	1,973,082	4,572,082	6,082,082				
Forgings made by rolling mills [4]	494,414	488,670	392,330	622,082	1,602,942	457,482	

[1] Not available.
[2] Included in all other.
[3] These are mostly further elaborations of products listed above.
[4] Includes forged axles, beginning 1950.

Source: American Iron and Steel Institute, annual report.

No. 985.—Steel—Production of Ingots and Steel for Castings: 1890 to 1951

[In short tons (2,000 pounds). See also *Historical Statistics*, series J 165–169]

YEAR	Total [1]	OPEN HEARTH			Bessemer	Electric	Crucible
		Total	Basic	Acid			
1890	4,790,320	574,820	(²)	(²)	4,131,536	(³)	79,714
1900	11,410,928	3,805,911	2,850,502	955,409	7,486,942	(³)	112,469
1910	29,236,309	18,485,050	17,127,408	1,357,642	10,542,305	56,398	136,979
1915	36,009,161	26,520,594	24,985,772	1,534,822	9,281,679	77,741	127,428
1920	47,188,886	36,592,522	35,140,810	1,451,712	9,949,057	566,370	80,987
1925	50,840,747	42,598,627	41,537,823	1,060,804	7,530,837	689,373	21,919
1930	45,583,421	39,255,073	38,380,514	874,559	5,639,714	686,111	2,523
1935	38,183,705	34,401,280	34,004,585	396,695	3,175,235	606,471	719
1940	66,982,686	61,573,063	60,882,840	690,243	3,708,573	1,700,006	1,034
1941	82,839,259	74,389,619	73,312,851	1,076,768	5,578,071	2,869,256	2,313
1942	86,031,931	76,501,987	75,183,065	1,318,892	5,553,424	3,974,540	2,080
1943	88,836,512	78,621,804	77,207,870	1,413,934	5,625,492	4,589,070	146
1944	89,641,600	80,363,953	79,168,294	1,195,659	5,039,923	4,237,699	25
1945	79,701,648	71,939,602	71,069,876	869,726	4,305,318	3,456,704	24
1946	66,602,724	60,711,963	60,112,300	599,663	3,327,737	2,563,024	(³)
1947	84,894,071	76,873,793	76,209,268	664,525	4,232,543	3,787,735	(³)
1948	88,640,470	79,340,157	78,714,852	625,305	4,243,172	5,057,141	(³)
1949	77,978,176	70,248,803	69,742,110	596,693	3,946,656	3,782,717	(³)
1950	96,836,075	86,262,509	85,661,651	600,858	4,534,558	6,039,008	(³)
1951	105,199,848	93,166,518	92,387,447	779,071	4,890,946	7,142,384	(³)

[1] Includes all other grades not shown separately, as follows: 1890, 4,248 tons; 1900, 5,445; 1910, 3,577; 1915, 1,719. Beginning 1935, figures include only that part of steel for castings which was made in foundries producing steel ingots.
[2] Not available.
[3] Included with electric steel.

Source: American Iron and Steel Institute, annual report.

No. 986.—Blast Furnaces and Steel Mills—Summary: 1889 to 1947

[Data for years prior to 1937 include figures for steel castings, thereafter such data are excluded]

YEAR	Number of establishments	Production and related workers (average number)	Wages ($1,000)	Value added by manufacture ($1,000) [1]
1889	719	171,181	89,273	151,415
1899	668	222,490	120,820	281,884
1909	654	278,505	187,807	399,013
1919	695	416,748	711,407	1,321,885
1923	658	424,913	696,761	1,289,918
1925	595	399,914	660,297	1,281,957
1927	602	389,270	645,534	1,219,534
1929	591	419,534	730,974	1,622,832
1931	526	278,206	357,645	623,193
1933	466	288,945	270,367	481,528
1935	468	374,808	458,584	893,681
1937	352	461,118	755,427	1,503,959
1939	334	388,441	598,037	1,234,631
1947	301	470,785	1,431,536	2,603,757
Blast furnaces:				
1937 [2]	87	23,075	38,001	127,644
1939 [2]	81	19,537	28,312	87,083
1947	86	32,697	93,598	328,060
Steel works and rolling mills:				
1937	265	438,043	717,425	1,376,314
1939	253	368,904	569,724	1,147,548
1947	215	438,088	1,337,938	2,275,697

[1] Value of products less cost of materials, supplies, fuel, electricity, and contract work. For 1889–1933, cost of contract work was not deducted.
[2] Includes data for 5 establishments in 1937 and 2 in 1939 engaged in production of sintered ore and flue dust and operated independently of blast furnaces.

Source: Department of Commerce, Bureau of the Census; 1947 Census of Manufactures reports.

No. 994.—SELECTED METAL PRODUCTS—FACTORY SHIPMENTS: 1950 AND 1951

[Leaders indicate no data available]

PRODUCT AND UNIT OF MEASURE	1950		1951	
	Quantity	Value ($1,000)	Quantity	Value ($1,000)
Containers and closures:				
Steel shipping barrels and drums............number	24,773,806		41,250,228	
Steel packages, kegs, and pails............do..	66,187,830		70,725,970	
Metal cans............short tons of steel consumed..	3,808,344		3,804,803	
Food............do..	2,550,949		2,555,401	
Non-food............do..	1,342,435		1,348,400	
Crowns............gross..	342,576,467		342,044,044	
Closures (except crowns)............1,000..				
Commercial............do..	14,236,465		13,705,500	
Home canning............gross..				
Heating and cooking equipment:				
Domestic cooking stoves and ranges............number	4,990,776	471,060	3,968,277	
Electric............do..	1,632,382	169,193	1,360,000	
Gas, including bungalow............do..	2,944,326	245,490	2,297,400	
Liquid fuel............do..	160,776	7,377	133,000	
Coal and wood............do..	151,140	7,611	123,000	
Combination............do..	100,065	14,397		
Domestic heating stoves............do..	4,382,400	68,000	4,185,000	
Gas............do..	2,023,275	34,057	1,805,000	
Liquid fuel............do..	1,330,400	44,015	1,350,000	
Coal and wood............do..	668,515	8,970	1,057,000	
Water heaters............do..	3,722,600	177,000	3,017,517	164,000
Electric............do..	800,854	51,000	671,000	
Non-electric............do..	2,914,134	126,000	2,345,700	133,000
Direct-fired............do..	2,642,354	116,000	2,137,100	133,000
Indirect............do..	271,560	10,100	208,000	10,000
Range boilers............do..	404,575	7,500	421,000	8,000
Cast iron boilers............1,000 pounds..	297,911	54,676	210,305	47,000
Cast iron radiators and convectors				
............1,000 sq. ft. heating surf..	46,175	36,436	43,000	36,000
Oil burners............number..	913,000		701,000	
Residential............do..	879,000		666,000	
Non-residential............do..	34,447		34,000	
Mechanical stokers............do..	34,067			
Warm air furnaces............do..	1,069,734	258,000	871,000	195,000
Forced air............do..	689,000	176,000	677,000	
Gravity air............do..	380,081	90,000	300,000	
Construction machinery:				
Power cranes and shovels............do..	8,108	108,006	7,000	135,000
Dozers............do..	21,044	26,540	20,000	51,000
Track-laying tractors............do..	43,500	223,043	46,000	262,000
Plumbing fixtures:				
Bathtubs, cast iron and steel............do..	2,308,310		1,817,500	
Lavatories............do..	3,808,474		3,300,500	
Vitreous china............do..	1,412,126		1,400,000	
Cast iron and steel............do..	2,006,848		1,900,000	
Kitchen sinks............do..	2,900,708		2,410,000	
Vitreous china............do..	7,797		7,000	
Cast iron............do..	1,414,519		1,200,000	
Steel............do..	1,477,442		1,100,000	
Transportation equipment:				
Truck trailers............do..	68,900	238,000	64,000	346,316
Complete trailers............do..	63,419			
Trailer chassis only............do..	2,347			
Complete aircraft (civilian)............do..	3,520	100,007	2,477	85,844
Aircraft engines (civilian)............do..	4,314	20,008	4,300	20,000
Domestic water systems............do..	722,547	60,204	617,000	65,000

[1] Includes a small quantity of other metals and glazed earthenware.

Source: Department of Commerce, Bureau of Census; Facts for Industry series. Data for power cranes and shovels from Power Crane and Shovel Association. Data on electric stoves and electric water heaters from National Electric Manufacturers' Association.

No. 995.—MACHINERY—VALUE OF PRINCIPAL CLASSES MANUFACTURED: 1929 TO 1947

[In thousands of dollars. Figures represent total value of production (or shipments) of specified commodities reported by all establishments producing these commodities. Data for selected groups of commodities only are shown. For 1929 and 1947, value represents value of shipments; for other years, value of production]

CLASS	1929	1933	1935	1937	1939	1947
Agricultural machinery (except tractors) [1]	278, 271	(²)	139, 098	226, 274	182, 688	758, 228
Automatic merchandising machines (except refrigerated)	8, 821	5, 472	5, 989	8, 978	6, 154	14, 538
Bakery machinery and equipment	21, 730	7, 332	11, 869	18, 120	17, 583	38, 441
Blowers and fans	26, 243	6, 955	15, 830	26, 282	[³] 24, 561	[³] 129, 913
Bottlers' machinery (except dairy)	11, 082	9, 157	8, 364	21, 135	11, 969	34, 442
Cash registers, adding, calculating, and card tabulating machines, and typewriters	151, 583	46, 577	[⁴] 83, 217	118, 552	104, 675	[³] 441. 972
Cement-making machinery and equipment	4, 387	545	1, 646	2, 065	3, 035	8, 111
Clay-working machinery (brick, pottery, etc.)	4, 402	591	1, 071	2, 727	2, 069	6, 983
Commercial laundry, dry-cleaning, and pressing machinery	[³] 36, 110	[³] 7, 993	[³] 14, 241	21, 969	20, 727	93, 078
Concrete products machinery and equipment	4, 132	224	1, 809	4, 053	1, 739	17, 974
Conveyors and conveying systems	48, 537	11, 413	22, 045	38, 911	29, 773	142, 573
Cotton-ginning machinery	11, 760	2, 165	4, 892	11, 300	5, 115	20, 433
Elevators, escalators, and dumb-waiters	44, 044	8, 322	9, 110	21, 235	16, 244	82, 845
Engines (steam and internal-combustion) and turbines:						
Steam engines	(²)	(²)	(²)	1, 738	1, 155	2, 183
Steam turbines	(²)	(²)	(²)	16, 214	15, 439	18, 722
Hydraulic turbines	(²)	(²)	(²)	(²)	5, 885	10, 740
Internal-combustion engines	(²)	(²)	(²)	91, 843	90, 817	423, 040
Flour-mill and grain-mill machinery	8, 286	2, 354	5, 167	6, 916	6, 087	25, 437
Foundry machinery [⁶]	10, 639	1, 957	5, 585	9, 156	6, 904	34, 431
Glass-making machinery	3, 688	1, 895	3, 543	4, 729	4, 459	21, 609
Locomotives	82, 909	2, 748	21, 735	65, 163	42, 667	302, 251
Machine tools	147, 316	16, 457	64, 515	162, 046	166, 649	322, 356
Motor vehicles:						
Passenger cars, complete	(²)	(²)	(²)	(²)	1, 799, 503	4, 080, 311
Trucks, truck tractors, truck chassis, motor coaches, and fire department vehicles	(²)	(²)	(²)	(²)	462, 517	1, 864, 669
Oil-field machinery and tools	(²)	(²)	(²)	121, 881	84, 153	262, 939
Petroleum refinery machinery and equipment	30, 210	4, 807	7, 931	14, 816	16, 360	22, 473
Printing trades machinery and equipment	(²)	(²)	(²)	74, 013	52, 583	191, 282
Pulp and paper industries machinery	(²)	(²)	(²)	41, 341	31, 227	134, 713
Pumps, pumping equipment, and air compressors:						
Reciprocating pumps	(²)	(²)	(²)	8, 159	5, 479	13, 919
Centrifugal pumps	(²)	(²)	(²)	19, 539	18, 630	74, 904
Rotary pumps	(²)	(²)	(²)	7, 663	8, 450	27, 734
Turbine pumps	(²)	(²)	(²)	(²)	(²)	31, 015
Air compressors	(²)	(²)	(²)	28, 325	21, 233	101, 686
Rolling mill machinery and equipment	13, 552	3, 347	4, 883	52, 139	34, 605	96, 074
Rubber-working machinery	13, 552	3, 347	4, 883	12, 271	13, 685	46, 445
Scales and balances	25, 385	6, 805	12, 191	17, 169	13, 544	49, 272
Sewing machines (domestic and industrial)	37, 378	10, 274	18, 250	24, 593	20, 304	63, 643
Shoemaking and repairing machinery	12, 317	8, 130	10, 245	10, 903	10, 603	23, 708
Stokers, mechanical	14, 054	5, 629	11, 537	22, 176	20, 275	18, 392
Sugar plant machinery	5, 046	794	1, 260	4, 344	2, 935	16, 949
Textile machinery and parts	115, 525	57, 892	64, 899	[³] 100, 696	85, 601	379, 988
Tobacco manufacturing machinery and equipment	5, 018	1, 106	1, 693	3, 679	3, 337	20, 146
Tractors (all types)	214, 721	(²)	137, 990	258, 855	203, 865	744, 272
Vacuum cleaners (household type)	35, 108	14, 411	24, 191	36, 029	44, 160	[³] 133, 107
Washing machines and other domestic laundry equipment	79, 011	42, 422	59, 513	73, 291	[⁷] 66, 282	[⁷] 433, 955

[1] From annual survey, Farm Machines and Equipment, series M35A.
[2] No comparable data.
[3] Not strictly comparable with figures for earlier years.
[4] Includes postal meters.
[5] Excludes dry-cleaning machinery.
[6] Excludes patterns and molds (of wood, metal, etc.).
[7] Includes parts and attachments.

Source: Department of Commerce, Bureau of the Census; Census of Manufactures reports.

No. 996.—ELECTRICAL MACHINERY—VALUE OF SELECTED PRODUCTS: 1933 TO 1947

[In thousands of dollars. Figures represent total value of production (or shipments) of specified commodities reported by all establishments producing these commodities. Data for selected groups of commodities only are shown. For 1947, value represents value of shipments; for other years, value of production]

PRODUCT	1933	1935	1937	1939	1947
Batteries, storage and primary (dry and wet):					
Storage batteries	52,129	66,904	78,260	81,122	220,298
Dry batteries (cells)	12,929	15,307	20,680	28,900	72,073
Wet primary batteries and parts and supplies for dry batteries and wet primary batteries	3,386	4,510	3,947	4,196	5,092
Carbon and graphite products:					
Brushes (carbon, graphite, metal-graphite and metal-impregnated)	2,282	4,150	6,511	6,664	16,243
Other carbon and graphite products (including electrodes)	6,715	8,329	13,921	13,931	82,341
Electric hearing aids	(²)	(²)	(²)	3,671	16,888
Electrical appliances					
Fans (direct motor-driven)			94,784	93,349	666,237
Water heaters (for permanent installation)	(²)	(²)	15,855		
Mixers, whippers and juicers			5,605		
Commercial cooking apparatus			7,272		
Other electrical appliances			2,765	3,394	
			63,447	61,730	469,162
Electrical measuring instruments:					
Electrical integrating instruments	(²)	(²)	32,636	19,383	36,946
Other electrical measuring instruments			14,390	17,912	94,497
Electric lamps:					
Incandescent-filament	45,949	62,705	74,304	73,129	
Other		2,072	3,858	6,184	
Electro-therapeutic apparatus	(²)	(²)		4,990	7,091
Engine electrical equipment:					
Battery charging generators (not including automotive starter-motors)	(²)	(²)	23,320	14,940	52,422
Ignition apparatus for internal-combustion engines	23,489	40,826	55,381	66,727	140,110
Fuse and fuse equipment under 2,300 volts (except power distribution cut-outs)	4,826	5,013	7,117	6,679	
Industrial electrical control equipment (except railway and motor-vehicle controllers)	15,166	35,230	47,388		
Insulated wire and cable	64,697	122,236	205,343		
Magnet wire	10,141	16,809	20,850		
Armored cable or conductor	4,434	8,946	5,977		
Weatherproof and slow burning		13,344	22,080		
Other	51,685	84,136	153,940	145,136	
Radios, radio tubes and phonographs:					
Household radio receivers, television sets, radio phonographs, phonographs, and record players					
Home radio receivers, socket powered					
Radio-phonograph combinations (except television sets)	(²)	(²)	(²)		
Phonographs and record players					
Television sets					
Automobile radios (broadcast receivers only)					
Other					
Electronic type components for communications and industrial electronic controls	(²)	(²)	(²)	75,349	
Radio receiving type tubes (except ballast tubes, voltage regulators and indicators)	(²)	(²)	(²)		
Transmitting and industrial type tubes except X-ray					
Phonograph records					
Switchboard apparatus (circuit breakers, panelboards, switchboards and switches):					
Panelboards and distribution boards		7,908	16,663	16,451	
Knife, power and other switches		6,888	13,649	15,447	
Circuit breakers		6,610	23,462	17,190	
Power switchboards	(²)	9,008	21,231	18,121	
Power switching equipment, power connectors, distribution cut outs and fuse links for 2,300 volts and over A. C. service		5,864	14,730	11,733	
Telephone and telegraph apparatus (not incl. wireless)	21,180	42,364	114,862		
Transformers (except for measuring instruments)	15,094	26,681	58,613		
Wiring devices and supplies	38,945		102,690		
X-ray equipment and X-ray tubes	(²)	(²)	(²)		

¹ Includes parts and supplies.
² Not strictly comparable with data for earlier years.
³ Not available.
⁴ Includes X-ray tubes for later years data are included in nonradio electronic tubes and X-ray tubes in "X-ray and therapeutic apparatus and electronic tubes" industry.
⁵ Includes television sets and facsimile sets.
⁶ Includes radio transformers.

Source: Department of Commerce, Bureau of the Census; Census of Manufactures reports.

No. 997.—SALES OF HOME APPLIANCES, 1940 TO 1952, AVERAGE RETAIL PRICE, 1952, AND HOMES OWNING AND WITHOUT APPLIANCES, JANUARY 1953

[In thousands of units, except light bulbs and tubes in millions. Compiled from sales reports and estimates of associations and manufacturers, and from Census Bureau surveys of manufactures. Sales figures represent manufacturers' shipments. Unless otherwise specified, figures are for electric appliances only. Estimates for homes owning appliances and homes without appliances are based on the accumulation of yearly sales totals with certain allowances for replacement, trade-ins, junking, and other factors]

| | | | | | | | 1952 | | Jan. 1953 | |
PRODUCT	1940	1946	1948	1949	1950	1951	Sales	Average retail price	Homes owning [1]	Homes without [1]
Air conditioners, room	11	30	77	96	195	238	341	$360.00	560	41,747
Bed coverings, electric		200	675	440	800	776	830	42.50	3,638	38,679
Blenders			215	175	225	290	425	41.50	1,475	40,832
Broilers		800	280	260	295	312	435	30.30	2,513	39,494
Cleaners, vacuum:										
Floor type	1,341	2,290	3,361	2,890	3,529	2,729	2,855	91.52	25,145	17,162
Hand type	359	80	290	191	230	176	153	30.85		
Clocks	3,600	6,500	9,995	5,280	8,100	7,500	6,700	7.25	34,249	8,058
Coffee makers	1,873	5,000	2,700	2,450	2,975	2,825	3,000	20.06	21,570	20,737
Dehumidifiers				25	45	75	90	143.00		
Dishwasher, motor-driven			225	160	230	260	210	300.00	1,253	41,054
Driers, clothes, electric and gas			92	106	319	492	610	257.54	1,524	40,783
Evaporated air coolers							175	86.50		
Fans:										
Attic			85	77	95	90	95	150.00		
Desk and bracket	1,682	1,239	3,470	2,776	2,450	2,225	1,570	20.95		
Hassock or floor					180	185	257	48.50		
Ventilating, wall and ceiling	107	203	240	255	495	445	525	32.54		
Window ventilating						320	480	54.95		
Floor polishers					240	275	287	60.95		
Food waste units			175	155	320	352	275	130.00	1,379	40,927
Freezers, home		210	690	485	890	1,050	1,140	370.00	4,885	37,422
Fryers, deep fat					500	725	1,250	29.95		
Heaters, electric, total	528	2,000	1,300	835	1,115	930	1,202	25.96	9,672	32,634
Heating pads	932	2,900	1,600	1,350	1,725	1,450	1,500	6.95	12,938	29,369
Hotplates	415	2,000	1,225	820	1,160	940	905	9.50	8,965	33,342
Ironing machines	176	175	477	307	409	284	208	209.00	3,910	36,397
Irons	5,171	9,600	7,360	6,310	7,475	7,585	6,135	15.52	37,890	4,417
Kitchen cabinets, steel (wall, base, accessory)		1,348	3,236	2,132	2,969	2,672	2,970	51.85		
Lamp bulbs and tubes	1,115	1,305	1,837	1,757	2,007	2,012	1,838	.26		
Incandescent	568	726	845	814	934	950	900	.24		
Other types	548	578	992	942	1,073	1,062	938	.28		
Lawn mowers, power	42	139	397	529	1,080	1,241	1,155	95.24		
Mixers, food:										
Standard	460	1,500	1,550	1,375	1,700	1,475	1,375	44.00	12,565	29,741
Portable			20	150	145	125	355	18.95		
Oil space heaters	390	1,006	1,235	742	886	764	755	93.00	7,260	38,204
Radio:										
Home radios	11,860	14,031	10,466	6,620	8,175	6,751	3,602	34.25	43,720	1,744
Other radios [3]			2,643	1,351	1,675	2,110	2,998	35.62		
Ranges	450	577	1,600	1,056	1,830	1,400	1,060	255.00	10,200	32,107
Refrigerators	2,700	2,100	4,766	4,450	6,200	4,075	3,570	285.00	37,750	4,557
Roasters	260	150	675	350	400	442	460	39.95	3,762	38,545
Shavers	900	2,115	1,650	1,725	2,150	2,200	2,550	24.95	13,508	28,799
Television		7	975	3,000	7,464	5,385	6,000	282.00	19,751	22,555
Toasters	2,307	3,500	4,850	4,200	4,525	3,725	2,992	21.12	30,000	12,307
Waffle irons and sandwich grills	1,545	3,600	3,670	1,960	2,535	1,875	1,570	20.49	13,323	28,984
Washing machines [4]	1,553	2,124	4,616	3,200	4,406	3,488	3,218	214.16	32,217	10,090
Water heaters, storage	125	488	1,040	695	990	845	720	132.00	5,821	36,483
Water systems	259	626	650	600	723	625	680	162.00		

[1] All figures except radio and oil space heaters, based on 42,307,000 domestic and farm electric customers. Radio and oil space heaters based on 45,464,000 total homes.
[2] Convector and radiant.
[3] Portable and clock radios.
[4] Includes gas engine washers except as noted.
[5] Represents electric washers only.

Source: *Electrical Merchandising*, January 1953; published by McGraw-Hill Publishing Co., Inc., New York, N. Y.

No. 998.—Exports of Electric Home Appliances—Number: 1940 to 1952

[Export figures include shipments under foreign aid programs such as UNRRA, Interim Aid, ECA, and MDAP (MSA); Civilian Supply shipments are included in 1946 and subsequent years]

PRODUCT	1940	1945	1946	1947	1948	1949	1950	1951	1952 (prel.)
Vacuum cleaners	9,994	1,470	14,194	74,221	51,511	27,941	19,986	18,089	26,272
Clocks	36,086	27,306	140,134	410,673	192,531	259,840	315,272	241,544	174,815
Irons	182,587	53,762	296,484	563,947	354,984	243,747	241,471	206,765	155,475
Radios and televisions	556,398	28,547	622,377	1,520,518	710,400	532,679	622,988	632,896	452,146
Refrigerators [1]	102,082	7,134	102,708	273,712	271,354	166,129	199,527	377,094	395,602
Razors	36,758	1,913	55,435	125,553	22,413	22,180	25,410	54,619	[2]
Washing machines	29,667	1,100	30,304	118,821	70,504	66,587	52,582	62,440	60,485
Ranges	7,302	1,156	4,668	15,506	13,409	6,406	5,841	13,620	15,353

[1] Beginning 1949 includes home freezers. [2] Not separately reported.

Source: Department of Commerce, Bureau of the Census; annual report, *Foreign Commerce and Navigation of the U. S.*, and records.

No. 999.—Farm Machines and Equipment—Shipments, by Class: 1945 to 1951

[In thousands of dollars. Excludes data for tractors for nonfarm use. Data prior to 1947 represent sales, which do not differ significantly from shipments]

CLASS	1945	1946	1947	1948	1949	1950	1951
Total	790,177	966,478	1,394,686	1,795,745	1,813,866	1,793,427	2,204,337
Farm machines and equipment (complete units)	680,504	622,674	975,982	1,394,345	1,424,988	1,427,824	1,796,982
Attachments and parts	209,673	327,804	318,666	399,401	388,946	364,608	445,835
COMPLETE UNITS, ATTACHMENTS, AND PARTS							
Plows and listers	40,168	50,694	82,529	100,605	90,974	100,329	112,108
Harrows, rollers, pulverizers, and stalk cutters	22,598	36,694	57,433	80,964	76,980	77,716	93,692
Planting, seeding, and fertilizing machinery	43,294	53,598	75,977	108,504	114,878	113,069	132,760
Cultivators and weeders	32,527	53,947	50,363	80,069	70,169	57,333	61,641
Sprayers and dusters	14,715	36,280	39,556	44,469	32,159	36,779	42,539
Harvesting machinery	90,301	112,728	191,579	247,620	269,546	295,168	345,084
Haying machinery	49,456	50,835	94,845	158,395	151,781	154,970	200,546
Machines for preparing crops for market or for use	35,520	36,046	42,013	52,216	55,383	50,558	58,409
Farm poultry equipment	24,508	22,925	20,602	20,379	25,844	20,127	24,611
Farm dairy machines and equipment	46,782	41,533	31,415	38,443	30,067	25,969	32,310
Barn equipment	7,087	9,854	11,808	13,207	19,680	11,860	19,719
Barnyard equipment	6,087	8,544	8,508	10,915	12,466	17,777	21,641
Farm elevators and blowers	6,144	10,595	14,399	26,311	32,735	34,671	38,278
Farm wagons, trucks, and other farm transportation equipment	15,564	26,470	36,014	26,918	24,538	30,108	33,596
Tractors for farm use	282,586	264,638	506,380	743,682	813,313	706,059	683,535

No. 1000.—Farm Machines and Equipment—Shipments: 1929 to 1951

[In thousands of dollars. Includes data for tractors for nonfarm use; for figures excluding these data, see table 999. Survey suspended 1932-34. Data prior to 1947 represent sales not significantly different from shipments]

YEAR	Total	Farm machines and equipment	Attachments and parts	YEAR	Total	Farm machines and equipment	Attachments and parts
1929	492,993	411,681	81,311	1942	669,588	614,688	248,888
1930	417,926	340,376	77,689	1943	668,588	446,388	248,388
1931	208,875	157,744	50,388	1944	668,388	446,388	248,388
1933	237,089	201,388	35,622	1945	663,815		
1934	375,128	301,688	73,445	1946	668,988	668,988	248,988
1937	484,180	405,897	78,588	1947	1,500,588	1,188,388	248,388
1938	404,047	316,688	87,188	1948	1,888,888	1,488,888	448,888
1939	384,849	299,388	85,383	1949	1,888,888	1,488,888	448,888
1940	482,418	381,388	101,452	1950	1,888,888	1,427,773	448,888
1941	628,608	506,170	122,455	1951			

Source of tables 999 and 1000: Dept. of Commerce, Bureau of the Census; *Facts for Industry*, Series M38A.

No. 1001.—Tractors, Attachments, and Parts (Farm and Nonfarm)—Shipments, by Kind: 1945 to 1951

[Value in thousands of dollars. Data prior to 1947 represents sales, which do not differ significantly from shipments]

Year and type of product	Total value	Complete units				Attachments and parts (value)	
		Farm		Nonfarm		Farm	Nonfarm
		Number	Value	Number	Value		
Total:							
1945	559,378	263,164	177,578	52,486	206,917	85,421	98,462
1946	449,561	364,725	221,840	32,119	77,282	94,583	53,746
1947	744,272	890,963	392,212	47,488	124,604	144,148	52,308
1948	970,792	697,633	547,704	41,053	141,653	194,847	86,321
1949	1,064,476	¹686,416	¹628,514	¹34,226	¹164,367	186,704	54,591
1950	1,096,049	¹663,344	¹620,583	¹35,000	¹179,448	170,686	107,962
1951	1,417,030	¹734,168	¹771,596	¹43,299	¹271,123	213,929	146,382
Wheel type:							
1945	250,069	224,985	153,170	18,707	15,726	74,695	8,473
1946	279,470	243,271	180,363	12,067	11,909	80,360	6,526
1947	475,086	413,783	331,653	14,882	17,682	117,586	8,165
1948	658,879	510,847	468,083	18,845	29,215	148,975	12,606
1949	723,129	¹534,946	¹543,005	¹10,422	¹29,425	141,920	5,779
1950	705,152	¹490,539	¹535,374	¹9,378	¹38,921	121,642	9,215
1951	930,064	¹545,663	¹680,423	¹14,310	¹77,578	141,081	30,982
Tracklaying type:							
1945	303,269	11,149	20,974	32,849	191,033	8,400	82,502
1946	142,150	8,898	18,118	17,367	64,817	10,569	48,645
1947	225,256	11,630	28,332	25,904	105,996	16,281	74,845
1948	268,930	17,365	49,569	22,208	112,438	32,941	72,962
1949	311,113	20,043	64,481	23,805	134,942	35,578	78,111
1950	360,437	18,978	62,960	25,622	160,527	38,233	94,717
1951	449,478	20,153	66,415	28,989	193,545	60,118	129,460
Garden type:							
1945	6,040	27,030	3,434	932	158	2,326	12
1946	27,941	112,556	23,359	2,685	566	3,755	26
1947	43,930	165,550	32,227	6,702	924	10,281	456
1948	42,983	169,421	30,052	(²)	(²)	12,931	(²)
1949	30,234	131,427	21,028	(²)	(²)	9,206	(²)
1950	32,460	153,827	22,249	(²)	(²)	10,211	(²)
1951	37,488	168,352	24,758	(²)	(²)	12,730	(²)

¹ Data for small number of nonfarm tractors included with "Farm."
² Included with "Farm."

Source: Department of Commerce, Bureau of the Census; published in *Facts for Industry*, Series M35A.

No. 1002.—Machine Tools—Shipments, by Major Types: 1949, 1950, and 1951

[Includes light type machine tools, particularly in drilling machines, lathes, grinding and polishing machines, and milling machines. Excludes machine tools specifically designed for home workshops, model makers, garages, and service shops]

Major type	1949		1950		1951	
	Number	Value ($1,000)	Number	Value ($1,000)	Number	Value ($1,000)
Total		241,370		315,743		629,722
Boring machines	1,212	29,430	1,363	29,402	2,518	75,065
Broaching machines	290	3,411	374	4,883	681	11,973
Drilling machines	6,305	25,271	9,917	33,129	19,257	70,916
Gear cutting and finishing machines	1,095	14,231	1,402	19,819	2,452	38,336
Grinding and polishing machines (except gear tooth grinding, honing, lapping, and buffing)	64,257	45,660	79,274	60,859	109,782	121,115
Lathes	18,631	62,289	30,251	89,716	43,107	170,529
Milling machines	4,397	31,400	6,975	36,452	11,287	70,257
Planers	99	3,699	84	3,035	111	5,966
Shapers (except gear shapers)	666	2,831	794	3,397	1,096	6,095
All other machine tools		23,148		35,051		59,465

Source: Department of Commerce, Bureau of the Census; published in *Facts for Industry*, Series M34A.

No. 1003.—MOTION-PICTURE PRODUCTION—SUMMARY: 1921 TO 1947

[Money figures in thousands of dollars]

YEAR, TYPE OF WORK, AND DIVISION	Number of establishments	ALL EMPLOYEES		Total expenses other than salaries and wages	Total cost of work done during the year
		Number (average for the year)	Salaries and wages, total		
UNITED STATES					
1921	127	10,659	$37,693	(1)	$77,397
1923	97	9,904	36,495	(1)	86,418
1925	132	11,518	49,017	$44,619	93,636
1927	142	16,013	74,936	59,407	134,343
1929	142	19,602	85,028	99,074	184,102
1931	140	² 14,839	² 70,637	(1)	154,436
1933	92	19,037	71,344	47,999	119,343
1935	129	27,592	104,430	57,435	161,865
1937	98	32,398	139,551	58,190	197,741
1939	178	35,345	142,543	73,157	215,700
1947	277	34,799	293,046	167,097	460,143
TYPE OF WORK, 1947					
Theatrical-film producers	100	27,549	261,276	121,806	383,082
Nontheatrical-film producers	127	2,445	8,746	9,613	18,359
Laboratories and other service organizations	50	4,805	23,024	35,678	58,702
DIVISION, 1947					
New England	4	17	50	112	162
Middle Atlantic	79	3,701	15,549	29,643	45,192
East North Central	28	1,219	4,216	3,435	7,651
West North Central	10	181	495	1,042	1,537
South Atlantic	4	43	197	433	630
South Central	7	88	204	146	350
West	145	29,550	272,335	132,286	404,621
Los Angeles Metropolitan Area	130	29,393	271,974	131,206	403,180
Other West	15	157	361	1,080	1,441

¹ Not available.
² Represents production-department employees only; not comparable other years.

Source Department of Commerce, Bureau of the Census; 1947 Census of Manufactures reports.

No. 1004.—SHIPMENTS OF AIR-CONDITIONING EQUIPMENT AND COMPONENTS AND ACCESSORIES FOR AIR-CONDITIONING AND COMMERCIAL-REFRIGERATION EQUIPMENT: 1940 TO 1951

[Value figures in thousands of dollars; represent manufacturer's billing prices for units actually billed and shipped. Data for earlier years are less complete, and thus not strictly comparable]

PRODUCT	1940		1945		1950		1951	
	Number	Value	Number	Value	Number	Value	Number	Value
Condensing units	211,021	18,808	354,401	36,902	885,913	75,833	840,176	75,672
Ammonia refrigerants	985	964	1,785	2,503	245	352	240	404
Refrigerants except ammonia	210,036	17,844	352,616	34,399	885,668	75,481	839,936	75,268
Air-cooled	187,468	12,313	327,031	23,378	835,239	69,035	796,303	58,604
Water-cooled	22,568	5,531	25,585	11,021	50,429	16,446	43,633	16,664
Compressors and compressor units	84,880	7,084	107,340	9,578	954,368	46,977	1,051,937	56,699
Centrifugal-refrigeration systems	112	2,494	185	2,994	382	12,249	441	15,369
Heat-exchanger equipment		17,110		22,422		61,337		55,677
Evaporative condensers	2,413	1,769	2,885	2,829	7,818	5,569	6,216	5,652
Unit coolers	63,417	7,076	91,083	10,186	133,300	28,588	121,981	27,296
Other heat-exchanger equipment		8,265		9,407		27,880		29,139
Self-contained air-conditioning units	¹ 5,880	¹ 4,467	14,973	11,230	257,263	86,913	382,488	93,573
Ice-making machines	1,045	628	2,895	4,044	14,914	8,907	12,998	8,504

¹ Other than room-type.

Source: Department of Commerce, Bureau of the Census; published in *Facts for Industry*, Series M33A.

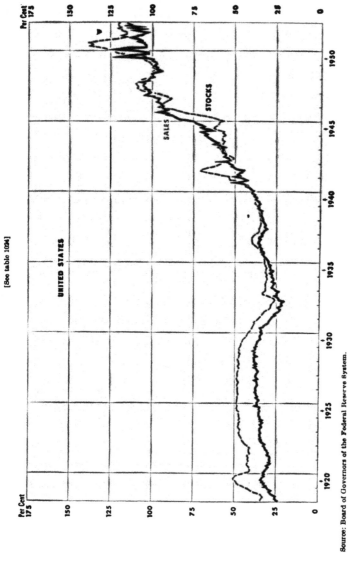

Fig. XLIV.—Indexes of Department Store Sales and Stocks: 1919 to 1952

[See table 1024]

Source: Board of Governors of the Federal Reserve System.

OF OPERATION AND KIND OF BUSINESS: 1929, 1939, AND 1948

PAYROLL, ENTIRE YEAR ($1,000)		ACTIVE PROPRIETORS [1] (number)		PAID EMPLOYEES, WORK-WEEK ENDED NEAREST NOV. 15 (number)		STOCKS ON HAND, END OF YEAR, AT COST ($1,000)		
1939	1948	1939	Nov. 1948	1939	1948	1939	1948	
2,589,876	7,990,713	132,466	182,490	1,665,347	2,382,789	3,847,552	10,167,965	1
1,406,353	5,064,281	71,924	106,522	948,601	1,307,990	2,620,862	7,206,634	2
224,304	549,042	11,846	13,780	153,704	182,847	632,585	860,204	3
132,383	462,581	10,206	13,660	94,212	155,923	47,466	144,624	4
73,677	224,362	4,507	6,422	48,211	62,637	121,471	276,746	5
60,006	186,477	1,885	2,637	40,226	54,042	114,560	306,617	6
26,946	75,458	2,237	2,768	18,785	34,143	49,627	116,746	7
126,554	346,731	6,390	9,304	69,086	79,451	273,752	673,545	8
33,372	118,362	1,445	2,712	18,817	22,187	70,538	168,340	9
56,490	179,640	1,686	2,601	31,912	49,047	74,366	194,622	10
37,871	90,960	1,560	2,094	27,712	34,548	204,679	466,622	11
100,927	424,694	5,236	10,130	87,380	126,229	141,134	602,569	12
71,599	321,918	1,555	2,577	38,862	60,448	63,485	314,471	13
102,030	361,604	1,643	3,126	62,718	102,740	309,770	623,516	14
63,029	302,907	1,466	3,072	27,437	87,064	60,308	277,077	15
157,192	673,944	6,533	13,480	88,779	189,617	236,155	944,111	16
32,620	137,398	479	537	17,226	33,368	63,741	192,446	17
46,040	167,546	5,966	7,410	44,428	59,817	87,201	105,079	18
144,232	438,968	7,522	11,477	68,801	138,532	277,038	665,911	19
983,950	1,501,413	260	537	267,514	411,725	682,297	1,748,779	20
104,219	212,363	31	16	56,154	65,360	98,974	291,984	21
11,321	60,977	3	12	6,564	17,682	11,313	22,662	22
15,532	32,105	5	16	6,487	8,378	10,810	33,862	23
81,432	126,270	13	12	22,870	31,726	68,581	147,692	24
8,637	7,896	6	8	4,059	2,660	11,760	26,346	25
31,197	64,877	76	48	13,917	11,453	63,348	121,596	26
8,634	26,097	4	51	3,961	7,348	11,724	30,473	27
12,183	18,166	1	13	6,173	4,115	14,961	35,062	28
(²)	91,007	(²)	31	(²)	20,602	(²)	228,697	29
20,274	170,411	4	19	12,608	44,962	29,366	123,678	30
21,207	30,468	9	23	11,944	13,778	23,804	54,723	31
18,350	56,088	12	54	9,821	15,788	23,404	65,317	32
114,378	390,734	80	189	57,785	90,976	145,442	944,309	33
19,402	50,800	2	12	10,026	13,228	82,412	167,942	34
(²)	151,098	(²)	68	(²)	43,367	(²)	212,847	35
131,949	420,341	126	354	47,374	89,890			36
156,366	345,847	23,061	32,963	98,956	112,466	236,366	708,266	37
162,602	330,146	18,605	21,530	92,822	101,630	88,794	68,550	38
19,123	44,528	2,423	2,608	(²)	10,982	12,686	9,022	39
17,850	28,660	1,113	862	(²)	7,440	8,749	3,640	40
471	727	70	75	262	171	861	647	41
4,082	7,381	366	346	1,772	1,626	1,819	1,437	42
207	84	32	20	78	20	134	21	43
29,340	69,214	3,791	3,690	11,357	12,117	6,447	8,142	44
3,208	9,337	713	789	1,307	2,221	682	512	45
2,684	3,604	382	340	1,132	876	777	333	46
36,568	38,367	2,376	3,705	(²)	34,692	37,307	16,142	47
1,556	6,107	737		662	1,626	646	447	48
3,342	18,970	811	1,397	2,021	3,226	980	1,673	49
3,126	14,969	722	1,126	1,872	2,603	985	1,566	50
4,926	7,168		644	2,287	1,901	709	7,663	51
19,372	34,669	3,631	2,941	9,354	6,535	6,520	1,660	52
3,990	6,577	832	698	1,744	1,343	3,135	1,668	53
1,152	3,267	88	20	336	357	1,386	628	54
21,264	42,697	1,646	2,384	(²)	9,357	6,487	6,866	55
106,066	306,066	16,063	16,714	49,130	180,066	313,119	63,663	56
4,449	14,347	681	601	11,407	13,364	1,368	3,868	57
2,841	12,680	167	125	(²)	12,366	1,386	863	58
17,804	51,380	7,897	7,808	(²)	8,877	1,263	271	59
49,717	144,088	1,677	1,668	(²)	64,686	13,868	366,608	60
34,700	161,173	6,776	4,114	(²)	48,371	161,862	366,708	61
1,281	6,080	444	346	(²)	2,735	2,777	9,080	62
382	389	31	20	286	177	436	486	63

Source: Department of Commerce, Bureau of Census; U. S. Census of Business: 1948, Vol. V.

No. 1007.—WHOLESALE ESTABLISHMENTS—

DIVISION AND STATE	ESTABLISHMENTS (number)			SALES, ENTIRE YEAR ($1,000)			ACTIVE PROPRIETORS [1] (number)	
	1929	1939	1948	1929	1939	1948	1939	Nov. 1948
United States	[2] 168,262	199,726	243,366	[2] 66,739,607	54,888,480	185,688,801	133,466	163,499
New England	9,721	10,064	13,122	3,368,607	3,149,541	9,341,451	5,461	6,683
Maine	986	1,032	927	175,853	166,548	490,529	608	424
New Hampshire	325	363	518	60,500	64,263	188,996	196	260
Vermont	308	383	392	57,393	57,112	166,216	209	206
Massachusetts	6,015	5,932	7,798	2,935,089	2,214,403	6,396,231	3,182	3,791
Rhode Island	734	761	1,136	275,357	238,989	722,552	458	679
Connecticut	1,353	1,593	2,361	484,415	408,926	1,374,925	808	1,242
Middle Atlantic	37,913	45,179	64,046	22,606,345	18,807,570	57,747,882	30,122	44,525
New York	25,110	30,255	43,786	17,072,380	14,452,737	43,140,120	19,541	29,358
New Jersey	2,334	3,523	5,695	935,521	1,082,078	3,596,934	1,928	3,794
Pennsylvania	10,469	11,401	14,565	4,596,944	3,322,755	11,010,826	8,653	11,373
East North Central	31,973	40,504	47,412	13,401,820	11,164,583	40,345,543	26,815	31,131
Ohio	8,005	9,545	11,099	2,910,629	2,606,812	9,468,871	6,017	6,652
Indiana	3,726	4,821	5,325	588,816	842,092	3,227,141	3,356	3,596
Illinois	11,534	14,468	17,454	6,560,084	4,977,030	18,136,506	9,552	11,963
Michigan	5,222	6,891	8,434	2,018,328	1,918,154	6,683,754	4,874	5,878
Wisconsin	3,486	4,779	5,100	923,963	820,495	2,829,271	3,016	3,032
West North Central	29,591	33,039	31,514	8,442,430	5,768,120	21,968,833	21,835	20,631
Minnesota	5,243	6,433	6,075	1,667,535	1,448,297	5,026,505	4,075	3,632
Iowa	4,936	5,790	5,980	1,040,840	787,208	3,361,733	4,306	4,418
Missouri	6,621	7,606	7,846	3,296,777	2,238,054	7,420,888	5,196	5,341
North Dakota	2,618	2,682	2,261	261,131	170,252	939,420	1,300	1,021
South Dakota	1,972	2,020	1,829	236,095	133,139	791,606	1,100	1,014
Nebraska	2,856	3,378	3,183	1,053,441	564,601	2,354,449	2,338	2,072
Kansas	4,315	5,128	4,640	886,611	427,569	2,094,230	3,518	3,133
South Atlantic	15,556	17,341	22,430	4,473,555	4,537,886	16,287,633	11,722	14,060
Delaware	286	316	370	118,067	157,474	483,721	189	217
Maryland	2,192	2,461	3,076	711,372	665,138	2,057,749	1,904	2,130
District of Columbia	478	735	1,114	216,791	338,233	1,242,601	437	585
Virginia	2,331	2,426	3,000	621,139	626,477	2,033,470	1,489	1,856
West Virginia	1,127	1,423	1,737	341,433	254,119	1,076,754	754	849
North Carolina	2,403	2,842	3,962	695,118	826,694	3,129,656	2,068	2,617
South Carolina	1,539	1,447	1,609	333,528	297,078	1,008,042	1,101	1,056
Georgia	3,159	3,009	3,844	992,009	797,580	3,264,294	2,086	2,516
Florida	2,041	2,682	3,718	444,078	522,093	1,991,316	1,694	2,234
East South Central	7,711	8,154	10,318	2,495,203	1,957,572	7,897,253	6,278	7,686
Kentucky	2,024	2,168	2,456	500,389	463,769	1,784,338	1,672	1,854
Tennessee	2,238	2,634	3,529	1,043,463	835,369	3,477,171	1,910	2,469
Alabama	1,737	1,934	2,597	566,403	413,607	1,677,829	1,565	2,027
Mississippi	1,712	1,418	1,736	384,948	244,827	957,915	1,131	1,336
West South Central	17,480	18,380	20,441	4,726,740	3,425,977	13,005,080	13,257	14,490
Arkansas	2,045	1,782	2,147	366,510	248,643	851,613	1,466	1,647
Louisiana	1,711	2,360	3,068	828,056	698,804	2,227,055	1,419	2,007
Oklahoma	4,155	3,985	3,668	766,817	458,709	1,729,240	2,767	2,540
Texas	9,569	10,253	11,558	2,765,357	2,019,821	8,197,169	7,605	8,296
Mountain	5,743	7,259	8,615	1,167,413	1,080,863	4,270,113	4,598	5,644
Montana	1,243	1,333	1,396	158,227	130,334	587,330	506	657
Idaho	673	988	1,147	97,157	105,496	415,822	605	734
Wyoming	283	397	463	34,661	37,031	153,477	312	339
Colorado	2,056	2,274	2,650	536,353	431,118	1,628,603	1,572	1,826
New Mexico	315	542	718	53,143	66,387	259,969	414	566
Arizona	356	605	864	97,024	96,426	420,481	390	605
Utah	721	945	1,123	177,130	190,840	724,933	601	726
Nevada	96	175	254	13,718	23,231	79,498	108	191
Pacific	13,664	19,806	25,167	5,456,553	4,995,368	17,805,013	13,378	18,720
Washington	2,572	3,565	4,147	955,070	762,974	2,643,174	1,817	2,734
Oregon	1,437	1,916	2,561	465,196	437,954	1,891,251	1,019	1,649
California	9,655	14,325	18,459	4,036,287	3,794,440	13,270,588	10,542	14,337

[1] Proprietors of unincorporated businesses.
[2] To avoid disclosures, where scope changes involved only one or two establishments, adjustments were not made at the State and geographic division levels. Hence, figures will not add to United States totals.

SUMMARY, BY STATES: 1929, 1939, AND 1948

PAID EMPLOYEES, WORKWEEK ENDED NEAREST NOV. 15 (number)		PAYROLL, ENTIRE YEAR ($1,000)			STOCKS ON HAND, END OF YEAR, AT COST ($1,000)			DIVISION AND STATE
1929	1948	1929	1939	1948	1929	1939	1948	
1,005,347	2,382,789	2,941,008	2,590,878	7,908,713	5,042,041	3,947,882	10,107,000	U.S. total
95,342	136,330	302,387	104,498	621,890	318,535	226,639	941,286	N. E.
7,454	6,616	11,302	10,126	27,126	22,972	19,122	42,019	Maine
2,570	4,087	3,057	3,785	11,291	6,261	5,184	14,408	N. H.
2,364	3,141	2,899	3,484	9,206	5,433	5,140	15,411	Vt.
58,355	51,564	143,528	118,061	350,915	214,210	182,768	390,000	Mass.
7,624	11,105	14,634	17,453	25,210	22,806	20,972	60,600	R. I.
16,005	58,558	27,287	24,070	88,141	46,984	33,428	117,718	Conn.
434,989	616,213	945,513	554,708	2,385,318	1,662,286	1,172,280	2,988,888	M. A.
297,728	347,770	677,860	635,440	1,651,426	1,226,942	884,306	2,022,888	N. Y.
36,089	86,512	54,648	63,044	204,040	67,615	74,123	333,738	N. J.
100,233	183,661	213,274	167,224	469,852	283,709	208,207	342,888	Pa.
316,385	474,780	673,388	539,786	1,697,848	982,170	642,468	1,895,614	E. N. C.
76,798	120,822	180,208	136,011	431,175	191,342	146,305	635,219	Ohio
28,761	45,056	42,531	42,387	144,878	60,212	57,912	185,167	Ind.
124,884	182,512	336,877	225,544	648,089	410,090	204,302	628,740	Ill.
53,305	84,705	98,411	55,318	304,771	113,976	105,680	235,741	Mich.
28,068	41,513	50,094	43,238	167,388	106,061	72,318	180,721	Wis.
164,504	238,400	321,140	245,665	719,894	615,894	445,391	1,099,917	W. N. C.
28,308	52,366	62,438	39,660	166,428	151,304	120,109	278,157	Minn.
24,281	34,028	40,841	31,860	90,434	68,566	47,866	137,728	Iowa
64,056	87,916	147,963	104,126	261,276	226,139	146,663	365,682	Mo.
6,325	4,916	9,686	7,195	24,788	34,418	52,864	74,613	N. Dak.
4,067	6,088	5,614	6,568	21,306	16,850	12,179	40,894	S. Dak.
15,419	22,178	26,047	20,378	54,896	58,442	25,402	98,007	Nebr.
15,149	22,966	28,612	15,151	61,490	57,986	41,666	110,049	Kans.
197,806	304,516	196,900	219,519	738,175	252,387	300,362	988,274	S. A.
2,982	5,153	5,778	6,018	17,784	10,516	4,466	39,877	Del.
25,178	33,689	32,760	23,300	98,048	48,906	41,460	172,888	Md.
10,087	17,105	13,103	17,616	63,327	12,886	17,960	80,614	D. C.
53,008	89,625	29,875	25,610	229,122	77,714	72,091	152,993	Va.
11,620	17,746	18,286	17,143	54,346	26,268	28,777	76,913	W. Va.
43,841	63,641	35,670	32,397	107,716	48,288	35,184	192,609	N. C.
5,874	13,840	10,585	9,979	37,337	17,694	16,368	171,899	S. C.
24,849	44,004	34,184	24,009	133,380	61,388	52,864	144,824	Ga.
37,089	40,588	25,371	34,357	126,370	32,239	40,864	144,824	Fla.
62,343	168,104	94,190	81,396	296,380	234,492	194,687	468,047	E. S. C.
17,303	56,680	29,672	28,672	34,471	90,196	67,544	104,088	Ky.
23,343	40,726	34,248	30,897	114,988	67,510	64,196	213,088	Tenn.
14,494	26,988	22,451	15,737	73,798	43,731	34,812	162,088	Ala.
7,224	13,607	10,520	6,123	32,110	34,066	24,222	66,015	Miss.
117,137	182,006	105,463	147,808	546,060	265,384	310,605	884,189	W. S. C.
8,045	14,705	11,040	6,604	25,908	28,349	32,088	90,451	Ark.
24,012	26,187	28,900	21,787	108,918	55,715	66,070	166,088	La.
16,011	28,188	30,426	21,168	72,717	60,904	35,742	109,897	Okla.
69,069	116,930	95,209	85,214	336,106	267,423	196,600	848,277	Tex.
39,362	79,346	54,777	53,977	398,880	104,720	82,889	304,798	Mt.
4,262	7,470	6,099	6,106	21,779	19,029	14,688	48,770	Mont.
5,819	8,969	4,479	5,202	19,842	10,912	9,440	17,088	Idaho
1,204	2,225	1,885	1,671	4,144	4,215	3,888	17,088	Wyo.
14,211	28,483	28,520	19,930	75,036	37,436	27,861	97,088	Colo.
2,822	4,368	3,313	3,492	13,452	4,744	7,782	28,088	N. Mex.
3,594	8,077	3,407	3,614	34,022	9,377	7,728	28,088	Ariz.
6,008	12,130	9,847	6,666	37,308	17,861	14,604	28,088	Utah
707	1,338	677	1,394	4,614	1,334	2,105	7,888	Nev.
130,889	307,100	289,130	286,432	872,851	546,368	398,888	1,397,847	Pac.
28,780	45,088	60,537	44,116	146,811	78,390	35,600	198,088	Wash.
15,696	28,814	24,088	34,421	94,419	46,680	35,341	143,188	Oreg.
136,088	212,151	215,844	251,991	722,122	429,563	305,476	987,637	Calif.

No. 1008.—Wholesale Administrative Offices and Auxiliary U[illegible]
Summary, by Type of Operation and Kind of Business: 1948

Type of operation and kind of business	Establishments	Sales, entire year	Payroll, entire year	Paid employees and payroll, workweek ended nearest Nov. 15: Employees	Paid employees and payroll, workweek ended nearest Nov. 15: Payroll
	Number	*$1,000*	*$1,000*	*Number*	*Dollars*
United States, total	1,339	1,791,497	319,893	80,644	6,272,228
Merchant wholesalers, total	275	49,174	44,842	11,623	838,245
Groceries, confectionery, meats	22	6,383	3,232	654	47,643
Farm products (edible)[1]	21	4,736	4,349	1,137	85,780
Beer, wines, distilled spirits	7	4	1,531	475	28,972
Drugs, chemicals, allied products	20	947	1,997	360	37,096
Tobacco and products (exc. leaf)	3		1,271	315	26,192
Dry goods, apparel	28	1,323	5,703	1,493	112,817
Furniture, home furnishings	7	22,033	232	36	3,443
Paper and its products	8	181	2,879	1,284	56,676
Farm products (raw materials)[1]	35	1,108	4,175	1,074	71,906
Automotive	10	1,589	1,737	471	34,926
Electrical goods	9	739	2,949	709	58,617
Hardware, plumbing, heating	5		691	135	13,052
Lumber, construction materials	24	1,417	3,012	754	57,540
Machinery, equipment, supplies	31	2,238	3,078	733	53,617
Metals, metal work (exc. scrap)	9	[illegible]	449	90	10,436
Waste materials	3	1,314	90	29	1,543
Other merchant wholesalers	33	4,157	7,497	1,984	137,499
Manufacturers' sales branches (with stocks), total	353	73,634	51,891	12,738	983,999
Groceries, confectionery, meats	17	20,312	[illegible]	[illegible]	106,213
Farm products (edible)	[illegible]	6,[illegible]	[illegible]	349	[illegible]
Drugs, chemicals, allied products	[illegible]	[illegible]	[illegible]	153	[illegible]
Tobacco and products (exc. leaf)	[illegible]		[illegible]	[illegible]	[illegible]
Dry goods, apparel	[illegible]		[illegible]	[illegible]	[illegible]
Furniture, home furnishings	[illegible]				
Paper and its products	[illegible]				
Automotive equipment, tires and tubes	[illegible]	[illegible]	[illegible]	[illegible]	[illegible]
Electrical goods	[illegible]	[illegible]	[illegible]	[illegible]	[illegible]
Lumber, construction materials	[illegible]		[illegible]	[illegible]	[illegible]
Machinery, equipment, supplies	[illegible]	[illegible]	[illegible]	[illegible]	[illegible]
Metals, metal work (exc. scrap)	[illegible]				
Other manufacturers' sales branches	[illegible]	[illegible]	[illegible]	[illegible]	[illegible]
Manufacturers' sales offices (without stocks), total	[illegible]	[illegible]	[illegible]	4,568	[illegible]
Groceries, confectionery, meats			[illegible]	[illegible]	[illegible]
Farm products (edible)	[illegible]	[illegible]	[illegible]	[illegible]	[illegible]
Beer, wines, distilled spirits	[illegible]		[illegible]	[illegible]	[illegible]
Drugs, chemicals, allied products	[illegible]	[illegible]	[illegible]	[illegible]	[illegible]
Dry goods, apparel	[illegible]	[illegible]	[illegible]	[illegible]	[illegible]
Furniture, home furnishings	[illegible]	[illegible]	[illegible]	[illegible]	[illegible]
Paper and its products					
Automotive equipment, tires and tubes	[illegible]	[illegible]	[illegible]	[illegible]	[illegible]
Electrical goods	[illegible]	[illegible]	[illegible]	[illegible]	[illegible]
Lumber, construction materials					
Machinery, equipment, supplies	[illegible]	[illegible]	[illegible]	[illegible]	[illegible]
Metals, metal work (exc. scrap)					
Other manufacturers' sales offices	[illegible]	[illegible]	[illegible]	[illegible]	[illegible]
Petroleum bulk stations	[illegible]	[illegible]	[illegible]	[illegible]	[illegible]
Agents, brokers, total	[illegible]	[illegible]	[illegible]	[illegible]	[illegible]
Farm products (edible)	[illegible]	[illegible]	[illegible]	[illegible]	[illegible]
Dry goods, apparel					
Farm products (raw materials)	[illegible]	[illegible]	[illegible]	[illegible]	[illegible]
[illegible]					
Other agents, brokers					
Assemblers (mainly farm products), total	[illegible]	[illegible]	[illegible]	[illegible]	[illegible]
[illegible]			[illegible]	[illegible]	[illegible]
[illegible]	[illegible]	[illegible]	[illegible]	[illegible]	[illegible]
Farm products (raw materials)	[illegible]	[illegible]	[illegible]	[illegible]	[illegible]
Farm supplies	[illegible]	[illegible]	[illegible]	[illegible]	[illegible]

[1] [illegible]

Source: Department of Commerce, Bureau of the Census; [illegible]

No. 1008.—WHOLESALE ADMINISTRATIVE OFFICES AND AUXILIARY UNITS— SUMMARY, BY TYPE OF OPERATION AND KIND OF BUSINESS   948

TYPE OF OPERATION AND KIND OF BUSINESS	Establishments	Sales, entire year	Payroll, entire year	PAID EMPLOYEES AND PAYROLL, WORKWEEK ENDED NEAREST NOV. 15		Stocks on hand, end of year, at cost
				Employees	Payroll	
	Number	$1,000	$1,000	Number	Dollars	$1,000
United States, total	1,339	1,791,497	319,893	80,644	6,272,228	162,425
Merchant wholesalers, total	275	49,174	44,842	11,623	838,245	69,800
Groceries, confectionery, meats	23	6,383	3,232	654	47,643	443
Farm products (edible)	21	4,726	4,349	1,137	85,780	269
Beer, wines, distilled spirits	7	4	1,531	475	28,972	4,879
Drugs, chemicals, allied products	20	947	1,987	360	37,096	393
Tobacco and products (exc. leaf)	3		1,271	315	26,192	2,733
Dry goods, apparel	28	1,323	5,703	1,493	112,817	6,230
Furniture, home furnishings	7	22,033	232	36	3,443	
Paper and its products	8	181	2,879	1,284	56,676	1,025
Farm products (raw materials)	35	1,108	4,175	1,074	71,906	5,531
Automotive	10	1,589	1,727	471	34,926	581
Electrical goods	9	729	2,949	709	58,817	531
Hardware, plumbing, heating	5		691	135	13,052	
Lumber, construction materials	24	1,417	3,012	754	57,540	2,292
Machinery, equipment, supplies	31	2,238	3,078	733	53,617	41,236
Metals, metal work (exc. scrap)	9	1,045	449	80	10,426	331
Waste materials	3	1,314	80	29	1,843	145
Other merchant wholesalers	33	4,137	7,497	1,884	137,499	3,181
Manufacturers' sales branches (with stocks), total	283	75,654	51,501	12,788	993,809	60,263
Groceries, confectionery, meats	17	20,312	5,250	1,207	109,213	1,708
Farm products (edible)	5	6,195	1,542	349	28,805	41
Drugs, chemicals, allied products	6	1,331	593	155	10,851	5,122
Tobacco and products (exc. leaf)	22		663	222	13,009	1,178
Dry goods, apparel	8		667	232	15,343	1,664
Furniture, home furnishings	1	(¹)	(¹)	(¹)	(¹)	(¹)
Paper and its products	1	(¹)	(¹)	(¹)	(¹)	(¹)
Automotive equipment, tires and tubes	34	31,757	6,110	2,158	119,107	23,955
Electrical goods	14	11,780	10,477	2,616	198,541	7,156
Lumber, construction materials	7		265	76	4,879	
Machinery, equipment, supplies	138	1,632	19,172	4,373	361,265	18,891
Metals, metal work (exc. scrap)	1	(¹)	(¹)	(¹)	(¹)	(¹)
Other manufacturers' sales branches	29	1,947	5,808	1,174	114,768	460
Manufacturers' sales offices (without stocks), total	116	44,147	17,238	4,568	343,691	13,275
Groceries, confectionery, meats	7		421	127	9,347	967
Farm products (edible)	10	3,858	3,022	866	57,395	42
Beer, wines, distilled spirits	24		1,475	363	29,397	
Drugs, chemicals, allied products	19	1,502	888	288	17,128	257
Dry goods, apparel	8	2,526	563	117	9,612	248
Furniture, home furnishings	6	3,789	1,821	496	36,235	1,468
Paper and its products	1	(¹)	(¹)	(¹)	(¹)	(¹)
Automotive equipment, tires and tubes	9	24,251	1,981	586	35,746	5,558
Electrical goods	6	1,808	1,463	474	37,081	3,290
Lumber, construction materials	4	(¹)	(¹)	(¹)	(¹)	(¹)
Machinery, equipment, supplies	9	560	1,639	344	35,292	591
Metals, metal work (exc. scrap)	1	(¹)	(¹)	(¹)	(¹)	(¹)
Other manufacturers' sales offices	12	5,853	2,962	721	58,378	798
Petroleum bulk stations	607	1,586,628	193,214	48,377	3,854,890	15,646
Agents, brokers, total	16	9,116	6,592	1,608	126,603	2,714
Farm products (edible)	6	6,608	3,503	889	70,942	
Dry goods, apparel	5	(¹)	(¹)	(¹)	(¹)	(¹)
Farm products (raw materials)	3	1,275	97	31	1,769	13
Electrical goods	1	(¹)	(¹)	(¹)	(¹)	(¹)
Other agents, brokers	1	(¹)	(¹)	(¹)	(¹)	(¹)
Assemblers (mainly farm products), total	42	26,778	6,506	1,680	114,990	727
Dairy, poultry products	3		465	145	9,093	
Fruits, vegetables (fresh)	4	7,438	676	150	11,419	3
Farm products (raw materials)	29	15,522	3,248	639	48,589	536
Farm supplies	6	3,818	2,117	746	45,889	188

¹ Withheld to avoid disclosure of individual operations.

Source: Department of Commerce, Bureau of the Census; U. S. Census of Business: 1948, Vol. V.

No. 1009.—WHOLESALE TRADE—SUMMARY, BY TYPE OF OPERATION AND NUMBER OF EMPLOYEES: 1948

TYPE OF OPERATION, EMPLOYEE-SIZE GROUP [1]	Establishments	Sales, entire year	Payroll, entire year	Active proprietors, [2] November	PAID EMPLOYEES AND PAYROLL, WORK-WEEK ENDED NEAREST NOV. 15	
					Employees	Payroll
	Number	$1,000	$1,000	Number	Number	Dollars
United States, total	244,705		5,216,696	163,460	2,462,433	
Administrative, auxiliary units	1,339	1,791,497	319,893		90,644	6,272,228
Wholesale establishments	243,366	186,688,801	7,990,713	163,460	2,382,789	
No paid employees	36,682	4,680,719	25,071	62,007		
1–2 paid employees	64,150	13,262,057	264,792	48,172		
3–5 paid employees	64,608	22,955,456	551,520	34,646		
6–9 paid employees	32,304	21,762,944	797,082	17,648		
10–19 paid employees	29,309	31,482,641	1,364,616	12,245		
20–49 paid employees	19,468	40,482,979	1,822,518	4,608		
50 or more paid employees	7,896	69,132,406	2,912,507	1,504		
Merchant wholesalers, total	146,768	79,835,768	5,188,228	164,828	1,536,613	
Administrative, auxiliary units	275	48,174	44,542		11,632	
Wholesale establishments	146,849	79,769,889	5,064,381	164,828	1,607,660	
No paid employees	15,201	1,942,127	9,634	26,006		
1–2 paid employees	33,606	4,040,080	131,666	25,007		
3–5 paid employees	32,602	8,164,620	392,881	34,602		
6–9 paid employees	23,431	9,871,804	531,366	14,146		
10–19 paid employees	20,608	14,748,680	946,606	10,064		
20–49 paid employees	12,239	19,430,471	1,364,670	4,630		
50 or more paid employees	4,760	23,882,810	1,606,686	765		
Manufacturers' sales branches, offices, total	34,147	52,888,379	1,990,288	781	816,971	
Administrative, auxiliary units	360	119,501	62,730		17,280	
Wholesale establishments	33,702	52,738,877	1,921,664	781	801,614	
No paid employees	267	34,182	1,578	122		
1–2 paid employees	4,438	1,324,142	32,280	301	6,744	
3–5 paid employees	4,737	3,480,521	94,163	167	13,463	
6–9 paid employees	3,740	4,446,866	116,973	151	27,341	
10–19 paid employees	4,673	9,395,000	261,626	67	64,397	
20–49 paid employees	3,862	12,097,367	447,380	27	117,513	
50 or more paid employees	3,941	25,666,308	976,171	34	267,896	
Petroleum bulk stations, terminals, total	36,682	13,282,278	520,051	36,063	169,848	
Administrative, auxiliary units	697	1,688,689	132,214		40,897	
Wholesale establishments	29,441	10,618,680	345,847	36,063	132,466	
No paid employees	5,116	696,382	1,610	6,469		
1–2 paid employees	10,792	1,698,680	36,660	9,018	13,366	
3–5 paid employees	6,176	1,906,218	60,504	4,427	23,040	
6–9 paid employees	2,194	1,346,380	44,736	1,716	15,466	
10–19 paid employees	1,207	1,680,761	35,440	424	17,186	
20–49 paid employees	669	1,909,181	66,402	242	26,799	
50 or more paid employees	282	1,978,696	76,266	64	31,396	
Agents, brokers, total	34,277	34,603,308	382,740	21,620	169,308	
Administrative, auxiliary units	16	9,116	6,892		1,003	
Wholesale establishments	34,361	34,638,662	350,148	21,620	161,660	
No paid employees	7,900	2,198,245	4,648	6,006		
1–2 paid employees	8,399	3,627,384	36,846	7,362	13,668	
3–5 paid employees	4,948	4,766,601	72,861	4,307	13,888	
6–9 paid employees	1,949	4,388,917	62,945	1,576	10,647	
10–19 paid employees	1,461	5,766,330	62,466	1,104	76,647	
20–49 paid employees	774	6,264,660	61,404	861	31,168	
50 or more paid employees	188	4,197,670	52,278	96	17,606	
Assemblers (mainly farm products), total	19,320	16,904,671	325,180	16,114	169,748	
Administrative, auxiliary units	48	36,778	6,606		1,668	
Wholesale establishments	19,308	10,997,848	308,608	16,114	126,408	
No paid employees	2,026	620,768	7,196	2,012		
1–2 paid employees	7,066	2,513,678	26,351	3,080	16,348	
3–5 paid employees	4,542	2,679,487	71,369	2,666	17,121	
6–9 paid employees	1,991	1,637,680	54,070	867	94,166	
10–19 paid employees	1,227	1,152,696	37,085	687	97,688	
20–49 paid employees	816	1,621,366	90,610	260	97,663	
50 or more paid employees	608	1,362,208	113,066	269	72,368	

[1] Based on total number of paid employees as of Nov. 15, 1948.
[2] Proprietors of unincorporated businesses.

Source: Department of Commerce, Bureau of the Census; U. S. Census of Business: 1948, Vol. IV.

No. 1010.—WHOLESALE TRADE—SUMMARY FOR SELECTED STANDARD METROPOLITAN AREAS: 1948

[Metropolitan areas with 1950 population of 1,000,000 inhabitants or more (as defined by the Bureau of the Budget) listed in order of population]

METROPOLITAN AREA	Estab-lish-ments	Sales, entire year	Payroll, entire year	Active propri-etors,[1] No-vember	PAID EMPLOYEES AND PAYROLL, WORK-WEEK ENDED NEAREST NOV. 15	
					Employ-ees	Payroll
	Number	*$1,000*	*$1,000*	*Number*	*Number*	*Dollars*
Entire United States	244,705	190,480,298	8,310,606	163,490	2,463,433	159,496,195
Administrative, auxiliary units	1,339	1,791,497	319,893	....	80,644	6,272,228
Wholesale establishments	343,366	188,688,801	7,990,713	163,490	2,382,789	153,223,967
Metropolitan areas with population of 1,000,000 or more inhabitants	100,107	163,855,536	4,400,110	68,506	1,132,514	83,269,306
Administrative, auxiliary units	583	1,233,463	181,651	....	43,114	3,543,018
Wholesale establishments	99,524	102,622,073	4,218,459	68,506	1,089,400	79,726,258
New York-Northeastern New Jersey area	41,202	42,209,821	1,661,790	28,207	390,340	30,796,906
Administrative, auxiliary units	149	438,876	62,256	....	13,625	1,197,535
Wholesale establishments	41,053	41,770,945	1,599,534	28,207	376,715	29,599,368
Chicago (Ill.) area	11,879	15,266,089	622,232	7,981	156,899	11,881,039
Administrative, auxiliary units	72	185,981	24,951	....	6,080	506,588
Wholesale establishments	11,807	15,080,108	597,281	7,981	150,819	11,374,451
Los Angeles (Calif.) area	8,415	6,060,357	343,092	6,554	95,981	6,763,246
Administrative, auxiliary units	40	125,508	16,042	....	4,075	332,388
Wholesale establishments	8,375	5,934,849	327,050	6,554	91,906	6,430,858
Philadelphia (Pa.) area	6,539	(²)	258,169	5,412	74,717	4,582,808
Administrative, auxiliary units	36	(²)	9,597	....	2,293	184,080
Wholesale establishments	6,503	5,736,681	248,572	5,412	72,424	4,698,728
Detroit (Mich.) area	4,136	(²)	207,934	2,829	52,635	4,079,172
Administrative, auxiliary units	36	(²)	10,559	....	2,618	209,688
Wholesale establishments	4,100	4,866,105	197,375	2,829	50,017	3,869,484
Boston (Mass.) area	5,532	5,474,986	240,042	2,651	63,667	4,343,391
Administrative, auxiliary units	45	134,582	13,448	....	3,126	261,953
Wholesale establishments	5,457	5,340,404	226,594	2,651	60,541	4,081,438
San Francisco-Oakland (Calif.) area	5,086	(²)	250,245	3,913	65,464	4,517,570
Administrative, auxiliary units	34	(²)	9,007	....	2,162	176,841
Wholesale establishments	5,052	5,006,634	241,235	3,913	63,302	4,640,729
Pittsburgh (Pa.) area	2,945	(²)	131,764	2,604	37,676	2,580,877
Administrative, auxiliary units	22	(²)	3,403	....	850	70,595
Wholesale establishments	2,923	3,107,418	128,361	2,604	36,826	2,510,282
St. Louis (Mo.) area	3,525	(²)	(²)	(²)	(²)	(²)
Administrative, auxiliary units	29	(²)	(²)	(²)	(²)	(²)
Wholesale establishments	3,496	3,990,234	162,761	2,050	48,325	3,120,283
Washington (D. C.) area	1,295	1,336,616	69,053	671	19,186	1,322,072
Administrative, auxiliary units	19		1,601	....	418	34,010
Wholesale establishments	1,276	1,336,616	67,452	671	18,768	1,288,062
Cleveland (Ohio) area	3,035	3,539,302	154,229	1,706	39,684	2,959,324
Administrative, auxiliary units	21	43,388	5,950	....	1,453	110,929
Wholesale establishments	3,014	3,495,914	148,279	1,706	38,231	2,848,395
Baltimore (Md.) area	2,285	1,800,574	89,863	1,586	27,589	1,710,293
Administrative, auxiliary units	22	25,966	5,896	....	1,489	101,983
Wholesale establishments	2,263	1,774,608	83,967	1,586	26,100	1,608,310
Minneapolis-St. Paul (Minn.) area	2,476	(²)	(²)	(²)	(²)	(²)
Administrative, auxiliary units	46	(²)	(²)	(²)	(²)	(²)
Wholesale establishments	2,430	3,652,701	122,964	1,306	36,098	2,377,357
Buffalo (N. Y.) area	1,757	(²)	69,701	1,038	20,093	1,331,023
Administrative, auxiliary units	12	(²)	2,670	....	765	52,480
Wholesale establishments	1,745	1,528,856	67,031	1,038	19,328	1,278,543

[1] Active proprietors of unincorporated businesses.
[2] Withheld to avoid disclosure of individual operations.

Source: Department of Commerce, Bureau of the Census; *U. S. Census of Business: 1948*, Vol. V.

No. 1011.—RETAIL TRADE—SALES, BY KIND-OF-BUSINESS GROUPS; AND TOTAL INVENTORIES: 1929 TO 1952

[Millions of dollars]

KIND-OF-BUSINESS GROUP	1929	1935	1939	1945	1946	1949	1950	1951	NEW SERIES [1]	
									1951	1952
SALES										
All retail stores [3]	[2] 48, 459	32, 791	42, 042	78, 034	130, 521	136, 721	143, 689	152, 975	153, 223	164, 685
Durable goods stores [2]	15, 610	8, 321	11, 312	16, 026	41, 876	43, 882	52, 935	53, 179	54, 479	55, 270
Automotive group	7, 031	4, 237	5, 549	5, 855	20, 104	22, 940	26, 289	27, 316	28, 156	28, 337
Motor vehicle, other automotive dealers	6, 432	3, 863	5, 025	5, 000	18, 744	21, 669	26, 702	26, 634	26, 282	26, 393
Tire, battery, accessory dealers	599	374	524	855	1, 360	1, 271	1, 587	1, 982	1, 874	1, 944
Furniture and appliance group	2, 755	1, 290	1, 733	2, 740	6, 914	6, 790	8, 249	8, 073	8, 604	8, 926
Furniture and home furnishings	1, 813	852	1, 200	2, 101	4, 371	4, 155	4, 847	4, 943	5, 095	5, 255
Household appliances and radio	942	438	533	639	2, 543	2, 635	3, 402	3, 130	3, 509	3, 671
Jewelry	536	235	362	997	1, 225	1, 136	1, 174	1, 256	1, 351	1, 452
Lumber, building and hardware group	3, 327	1, 572	2, 390	3, 739	8, 766	8, 287	10, 092	10, 648	10, 208	10, 200
Lumber and building materials	2, 621	1, 105	1, 761	2, 502	6, 272	5, 895	7, 458	7, 798	7, 470	7, 572
Hardware	706	467	629	1, 237	2, 494	2, 342	2, 634	2, 850	2, 738	2, 698
Nondurable goods stores [2]	32, 849	24, 470	30, 730	62, 008	88, 645	86, 839	90, 754	99, 895	103, 744	108, 815
Apparel group	4, 241	2, 656	3, 259	7, 689	9, 803	9, 332	9, 333	10, 043	10, 209	10, 633
Men's and boys' wear	1, 358	727	840	1, 769	2, 309	2, 183	2, 175	2, 320	2, 461	2, 497
Women's apparel and accessory	1, 480	1, 026	1, 323	3, 338	3, 961	3, 698	3, 606	3, 923	4, 049	4, 353
Family and other apparel	596	392	479	1, 442	2, 066	1, 997	2, 041	2, 163	2, 015	2, 210
Shoes	807	511	617	1, 140	1, 467	1, 454	1, 511	1, 637	1, 684	1, 693
Drug and proprietary stores	1, 690	1, 233	1, 563	3, 155	4, 013	4, 037	4, 166	4, 500	4, 547	4, 717
Eating and drinking places	2, 132	2, 395	3, 529	9, 575	10, 683	10, 470	10, 626	11, 626	12, 207	12, 068
Food group [2]	10, 980	8, 358	10, 156	19, 233	30, 986	30, 965	32, 768	36, 940	37, 626	39, 771
Grocery	7, 353	6, 352	7, 722	14, 593	24, 770	24, 800	26, 412	29, 316	30, 346	32, 238
Gasoline service stations [4]	1, 787	1, 968	2, 822	3, 284	6, 483	6, 957	7, 553	8, 390	9, 151	9, 976
General merchandise group	9, 015	5, 730	6, 475	11, 802	17, 135	16, 307	17, 235	18, 170	18, 202	18, 694
Department, excluding mail order	3, 903	2, 833	3, 408	6, 484	9, 344	8, 862	9, 403	9, 846	10, 095	10, 277
Mail order (catalog sales)	447	386	464	608	1, 301	1, 156	1, 238	1, 284	1, 309	1, 339
Variety	904	873	1, 080	1, 845	2, 507	2, 506	2, 587	2, 807	2, 859	2, 996
Other general merchandise	3, 761	1, 638	1, 523	2, 865	3, 983	3, 783	4, 010	4, 233	3, 939	4, 082
Other nondurable goods stores: [2]										
Liquor		328	586	2, 288	2, 580	2, 474	2, 550	2, 834	2, 975	3, 165
INVENTORIES										
All retail stores, inventories, end of year	[5]	[5]	5, 285	7, 442	15, 190	14, 570	17, 781	18, 719	19, 530	19, 544

[1] New series for 1951 and 1952 not comparable to prior years due to change in methodology used to compute retail store sales and inventory estimates; see *Survey of Current Business*, September 1952.
[2] Sales of other durable goods stores, other food stores, and other nondurable goods stores not shown separately but included in totals.
[3] Includes sales of certain milk dealers in the amount of $130,000,000, not included in tables 1012 and 1020. Data for these concerns were received too late for inclusion in summary tables for 1929.
[4] Much of increase in sales from 1929 to 1939 results from change in classification. Garages primarily selling gasoline and oil were classified separately as garages in 1929 Census of Retail Trade and included in filling station category in 1939 Census of Retail Trade.
[5] Not available.

Source: Department of Commerce, Office of Business Economics and Bureau of the Census; published currently in *Survey of Current Business*.

No. 1012.—Retail Stores—Summary, by

	KIND OF BUSINESS	NUMBER OF STORES			SALES, ENTIRE YEAR ($1,000)		
		1929	1939	1948	1929	1939	1948
1	United States, total	1,474,365	1,776,355	1,769,540	48,329,652	42,041,790	130,520,548
2	Food group	481,891	568,549	564,439	10,837,421	10,164,987	30,965,674
3	Grocery stores, without fresh meat	191,876	200,303	154,277	3,449,129	2,225,435	4,026,835
4	Grocery stores, with fresh meat	115,549	187,034	222,662	3,903,662	5,496,318	20,743,288
5	Meat markets	43,788	35,630	24,242	1,253,260	700,243	1,641,697
6	Fish (sea food) markets	6,077	6,730	5,223	53,608	50,554	133,572
7	Fruit stores, vegetable markets	22,904	27,666	15,763	308,379	222,239	308,968
8	Candy, nut, confectionery stores	63,265	48,015	32,876	571,548	296,800	649,347
9	Dairy products stores	4,488	7,382	6,743	165,965	142,728	358,965
10	Milk dealers	3,990	9,452	4,984	560,996	597,283	1,527,907
11	Bakery products stores [1]	12,013	16,985	20,152	201,093	168,027	725,021
12	Bakeries, without baking on premises	(²)	(²)	4,466	(²)	(²)	162,649
13	Bakeries, with baking on premises	(²)	(²)	15,686	(²)	(²)	562,372
14	Egg, poultry dealers	3,258	6,532	5,582	70,858	63,350	256,664
15	Delicatessen stores	11,166	9,909	8,212	194,820	132,365	306,777
16	Other food stores	3,517	4,911	2,723	74,012	71,125	194,243
17	Eating and drinking places	134,293	365,386	346,556	2,124,890	3,520,052	10,683,324
18	Restaurants, cafeterias, caterers [1]	96,950	99,068	131,190	1,802,913	1,764,554	5,303,004
19	Restaurants, cafeterias	96,950	99,068	130,192	1,802,913	1,764,854	5,236,920
20	Caterers	(¹)	(¹)	998	(¹)	(¹)	66,174
21	Lunch counters, refreshment stands	37,343	70,724	62,933	321,977	370,166	1,165,129
22	Drinking places		135,594	152,433		1,385,032	4,215,101
23	General stores	104,089	39,688	21,557	2,570,744	810,342	1,159,361
24	General merchandise group	54,636	50,267	52,644	6,444,101	5,665,007	15,975,257
25	Department stores	4,221	4,074	2,580	4,350,098	3,974,998	10,644,747
26	Dry goods, general merchandise stores	38,305	29,247	29,754	1,189,856	713,208	2,823,869
27	Variety stores	12,110	16,946	20,210	904,147	976,801	2,506,741
28	Apparel group	114,296	106,959	115,246	4,240,893	3,258,772	9,803,218
29	Men's, boys' clothing stores	17,435	15,577	14,775	936,947	664,511	1,609,902
30	Men's, boys' furnishings stores	10,762	5,924	8,955	255,776	106,801	556,051
31	Family clothing stores	10,551	10,053	12,533	552,353	429,454	1,791,317
32	Women's ready-to-wear stores	18,253	25,820	30,677	1,087,601	1,009,494	3,305,162
33	Millinery stores	12,433	10,799	5,725	161,807	118,586	108,556
34	Hosiery stores	1,943	2,293	1,658	54,830	35,307	71,911
35	Corset, lingerie stores	2,390	2,338	2,512	49,556	27,938	89,179
36	Apparel accessory, specialty stores	925	1,863	3,086	19,588	37,312	167,221
37	Men's shoe stores	1,402	2,472	2,246	61,507	78,770	199,331
38	Women's shoe stores	1,666	2,735	2,985	130,681	154,138	372,579
39	Family shoe stores	21,191	15,250	13,707	614,641	384,156	873,354
40	Children's, juveniles' shoe stores	(¹)	(¹)	613	(¹)	(¹)	22,043
41	Custom tailors	11,284	5,674	4,963	165,048	66,282	142,861
42	Furriers, fur shops	2,280	2,214	2,350	106,862	94,133	219,290
43	Children's infants' wear stores	1,309	} 3,917	6,730	29,965	} 49,884	231,644
44	Other apparel stores	472		1,231	13,731		42,817
45	Furniture, furnishings, appliance group	58,941	52,827	85,555	2,754,721	1,733,257	6,914,179
46	Furniture stores	25,854	19,902	29,031	1,578,632	973,157	3,427,168
47	Floor covering stores	1,503	1,986	4,568	73,428	58,618	358,953
48	Drapery, curtain, upholstery stores	973	930	3,178	18,735	15,843	141,403
49	China, glassware, metalware stores	1,066	778	1,626	35,128	21,821	116,916
50	Antique stores	2,099	3,324	4,963	60,373	17,743	53,062
51	Other home furnishing stores	2,080	4,994	5,288	37,592	112,702	273,318
52	Household appliance stores	9,329	18,002	29,700	389,061	484,698	2,159,302
53	Radio stores	16,087	2,911	7,231	561,772	48,675	384,057

See footnotes at end of table.

Kind of Business: 1929, 1939, and 1948

PAYROLL, ENTIRE YEAR ($1,000)			NUMBER OF ACTIVE PROPRIE-TORS OF UNINCORPORATED BUSINESSES			NUMBER OF PAID EMPLOYEES, WORK-WEEK ENDED NEAREST NOV. 15				
						Total		Full workweek	
1929	1939	1948	1939	1939	Nov. 1948	1939	1948	1939	1948	
5,044,139	4,536,496	12,967,697	1,494,704	1,633,673	1,763,045	4,621,396	6,912,061	3,976,196	5,686,396	1
767,387	769,762	1,943,987	495,321	636,926	649,721	614,746	1,065,987	614,386	782,386	3
163,430	118,988	149,338	171,691	172,189	187,086	131,543	59,043	62,186	60,136	4
254,364	364,140	1,112,687	113,296	172,700	224,406	421,691	597,313	307,333	633,736	5
84,396	80,594	89,645	46,248	36,568	76,232	46,590	49,309	39,524	31,690	6
7,800	4,395	5,800	6,671	4,995	5,673	3,816	3,345	3,671	4,061	7
20,583	15,986	24,249	25,706	28,382	17,380	20,283	14,862	14,806	10,687	8
45,734	20,144	54,696	67,696	45,777	31,276	31,368	48,746	23,546	24,607	9
12,683	17,982	38,136	3,579	4,111	4,406	18,160	20,570	14,543	14,607	10
101,027	140,078	262,071	4,069	9,387	4,690	81,106	89,161	78,663	78,290	10
31,081	21,736	140,716	11,732	14,294	39,905	28,983	82,608	21,409	68,397	11
(3)	(3)	22,469	(3)	(3)	4,676	(3)	94,699	(3)	90,415	12
		116,280			14,080		931		931	13
3,320	3,514	11,480	3,612	4,646	6,416	3,466	7,466	3,443	4,486	15
10,996	6,913	14,198	12,194	6,466	4,426	4,643	6,466	3,476	4,466	16
11,109	14,462	36,026	2,062	4,060	2,660	14,513	14,772	11,317	12,296	16
344,973	464,468	1,646,497	146,469	365,279	372,044	636,969	1,382,096	764,469	1,466,469	17
346,700	364,453	1,146,696	109,627	101,276	146,696	544,913	515,924	473,469	469,469	17
(1)	(1)	1,163,984			945		12,139	(1)		17
47,375	42,446	172,069	30,111	96,736	94,451	96,990	130,816	47,473	148,469	18
	150,696	906,417		136,217	164,377	222,181	368,522	174,697	266,397	19
115,211	47,379	66,737	121,296	38,666	21,962	62,623	41,444	38,364	28,191	20
818,980	368,466	2,304,386	47,631	34,693	34,993	368,694	1,361,387	674,496	1,634,496	22
620,980	611,706	1,680,702	1,441	580	381	637,199	843,479	662,766	764,444	23
102,878	68,979	231,672	30,087	34,990	34,736	98,346	175,469	146,469	146,469	27
96,982	171,804	341,926	7,943	9,862	14,853	229,449	232,670	115,303	197,469	27

No. 1012.—RETAIL STORES—SUMMARY, BY KIND

KIND OF BUSINESS	NUMBER OF STORES			SALES, ENTIRE YEAR ($1,000)		
	1929	1939	1948	1929	1939	1948
1 Automotive group				7,031,177	5,545,485	29,104,654
2 Motor vehicle (new and used) dealers				6,295,590	4,510,245	16,562,781
3 Motor vehicle (used) dealers	2,007		16,512	140,982	190,790	2,442,377
4 Tire, battery, accessory dealers	22,318	15,625	22,655	599,235	525,085	1,320,595
5 Motorcycle dealers	735	513	1,224	8,035	8,619	50,856
6 Aircraft dealers	110	61	304	3,504	2,358	30,136
7 Boat dealers	219	454	1,087	10,741	9,990	66,288
8 Other automotive dealers	(²)	(²)	2,196	(²)	(²)	200,063
9 Gasoline service stations	121,513	245,658	199,253	1,787,423	2,822,455	6,483,301
10 Lumber, building, hardware group	98,596	78,313	98,988	3,345,634	2,734,914	11,131,470
11 Lumber yards	28,237	20,652	20,802	1,081,264	(1,196,817)	4,396,380
12 Building materials dealers		4,448	5,307		281,642	840,700
13 Paint, glass, wallpaper stores	4,570	5,480	9,043	196,372	152,673	490,098
14 Heating and plumbing equipment dealers	12,709	4,262	7,606	384,277	102,404	555,679
15 Electrical supply stores	4,558	1,888	3,092	110,131	27,069	128,907
16 Hardware stores	26,580	26,147	24,674	705,089	626,276	2,423,669
17 Farm equipment dealers	12,943	16,499	17,615	518,507	344,432	2,305,172
18 Drug and proprietary stores	58,258	57,258	58,796	1,690,399	1,562,502	4,612,231
19 Drug stores, with fountain	34,844	39,432	32,480	1,140,260	1,305,341	2,797,235
20 Proprietary stores, with fountain			6,225			940,196
21 Drug stores, other	23,414	15,451	15,538	541,190	257,351	861,286
			2,546			95,583
22 Liquor stores		19,126	23,632		886,351	2,576,507
23 Second-hand stores	15,465	28,962	16,808	148,068	128,067	394,654
24 Furniture stores	5,643	7,875	6,491	37,749	31,463	74,317
25 Tire, battery, accessory dealers	2,820	6,403	2,365	26,843	30,868	64,962
26 Clothing, shoe stores	2,606	3,558	3,731	12,042	9,766	38,067
27 Book stores	175	588	374	2,372	4,050	5,693
28 Pawn shops	1,509	1,273	1,374	35,537	22,868	53,718
29 Other second-hand stores	2,312	4,165	2,634	34,525	29,907	67,907
31 Other retail stores	174,782	172,375	164,073	4,854,191	3,496,437	10,383,218
32 Fuel dealers, except fuel oil	15,444	38,320	14,953	920,829	887,617	1,607,658
33 Ice dealers	3,674		3,192	83,540		84,630
34 Fuel oil dealers	(²)	2,843	4,325	(²)	136,925	732,119
35 Hay, grain, feed stores	21,304	16,772	18,213	990,743	622,977	2,790,333
36 Other farm, garden supply stores	5,749	4,915	3,345	128,422	155,312	356,526
37 Jewelry stores	19,586	14,589	21,209	536,381	361,505	1,224,878
38 Book stores	2,509	2,845	2,905	117,051	73,842	267,682
39 Stationery stores [4]	4,047	5,036	4,083	155,113	118,184	251,442
40 Sporting goods stores	1,990	2,505	6,859	65,465	56,914	309,632
41 Bicycle stores	1,134	941	1,738	12,210	6,837	35,229
42 Florists	9,326	16,055	14,749	176,201	148,741	377,260
43 Cigar stores and stands	33,348	18,504	14,536	410,063	207,781	535,255
44 News dealers, newsstands	10,285	7,407	6,801	149,866	73,427	216,866
45 Gift, novelty, souvenir stores	5,186	7,429	12,516	61,502	53,568	195,664
46 Music stores	2,232	2,930	6,120	54,742	65,127	237,358
47 Luggage, leather goods stores	1,367	769	1,188	40,312	79,345	68,828
48 Optical goods stores	3,001	5,995	1,897	50,000	60,567	73,921
49 Camera, photographic supply stores	710	1,112	3,080	29,810	32,343	202,099
50 Office, store machine and equipment dealers	3,486	3,600	2,347	262,199	140,216	109,507
51 All other retail stores	29,727	19,739	19,867	601,872	277,119	576,371

[1] Data for "Caterers" for 1929 and 1939 included with "Bakery products stores."
[2] Not available.
[3] Not separately classified in 1929 and 1939.
[4] Includes data for two 1939 classifications "Stationery stores" and "Office, store, school supply dealers."

OF BUSINESS: 1929, 1939, AND 1948—Continued

PAYROLL, ENTIRE YEAR ($1,000)			NUMBER OF ACTIVE PROPRIETORS OF UNINCORPORATED BUSINESSES			NUMBER OF PAID EMPLOYEES, WORK-WEEK ENDED NEAREST NOV. 15				
						Total		Full workweek	
1929	1939	1948	1929	1939	Nov. 1948	1939	1948	1939	1948	
628,317	507,947	1,846,376	64,948	51,238	77,647	400,166	633,553	386,240	604,624	1
537,205	420,588	1,584,430	40,425	29,069	37,290	324,688	519,378	316,323	503,014	2
11,805	14,177	90,401	3,036	6,806	17,782	13,744	32,059	12,215	29,155	3
76,104	70,665	165,647	20,961	14,424	18,018	59,800	72,366	55,962	63,774	4
988	1,023	4,548	292	504	1,235		2,082		1,808	5
1,344	375	4,726	26	22	117	1,934	1,634	1,740	1,517	6
871	1,119	6,125	208	411	956		2,211		1,911	7
(²)	(²)	10,498	(²)	(²)	2,249	(²)	3,823	(²)	2,345	8
159,212	198,934	488,350	100,746	231,475	196,532	246,600	285,954	204,978	226,058	9
468,362	312,160	1,182,354	85,579	65,755	91,213	257,641	475,413	222,620	428,850	10
222,855	143,269	459,947	17,056	10,615	11,603	112,888	170,254	96,363	155,450	11
	34,002	111,629		3,387	4,642	26,069	41,133	21,896	27,335	12
33,268	19,495	56,054	8,570	6,781	8,853	15,465	23,611	13,613	21,044	13
80,323	18,924	115,984	12,959	3,644	7,741	16,258	44,094	13,450	39,443	14
23,539	4,938	18,170	4,895	1,708	3,301	4,043	7,940	3,401	6,902	15
73,272	63,679	244,093	27,692	28,709	36,017	57,998	113,165	52,008	96,311	16
35,105	27,853	176,497	14,407	10,911	18,966	24,920	75,216	22,281	70,156	17
195,742	172,733	468,485	87,415	49,673	51,525	192,296	262,891	158,240	211,988	18
136,915	137,994	343,709	33,034	33,257	30,552	158,674	214,191	131,073	160,276	19
		23,331			6,244		19,244		13,536	20
58,827	34,739	94,930	24,381	16,416	12,675	33,622	45,043	27,167	34,916	21
		6,515			2,354		4,413		3,360	22
....	30,782	116,303	....	13,670	29,637	27,065	52,404	23,901	43,980	23
20,163	20,758	39,557	16,699	24,014	17,265	24,122	30,652	19,448	17,366	24
3,959	3,061	5,551	6,042	7,882	6,720	4,285	3,843	3,238	2,942	25
4,685	6,888	8,804	3,145	6,814	2,593	8,616	4,349	7,326	3,752	26
1,109	922	4,240	2,697	3,430	3,489	1,836	3,391	1,265	2,717	27
320	488	617	172	578	383	449	300	373		28
4,331	4,357	8,736	1,599	1,252	1,453	3,080	3,237	2,802	2,890	29
5,759	5,042	11,609	2,444	4,068	2,627	5,866	5,532	4,444	4,740	30
565,161	407,699	1,037,262	171,906	154,525	154,959	362,444	469,266	300,327	401,859	31
101,158	109,910	176,130	14,787	12,674		102,037	73,682	79,460	64,063	32
20,189		19,203	2,042	34,784	2,796		9,128		7,589	33
(²)	13,873	69,068	(²)	2,426	3,893	9,847	25,040	8,620	22,389	34
45,745	33,949	129,412	22,523	13,953	15,363	36,368	60,611	30,605	54,300	35
15,294	13,447	27,077	5,818	4,074	3,001	13,104	12,381	10,289	10,902	36
69,560	53,965	178,306	19,982	13,077	20,424	37,609	68,808	34,245	62,054	37
18,283	13,932	47,504	2,451	2,156	2,359	13,038	23,836	11,050	20,880	38
28,817	19,003	46,659	3,671	4,441	3,802	15,257	20,088	13,601	17,603	39
7,066	6,653	28,766	1,917	2,393	7,173	5,348	12,693	4,756	10,765	40
1,332	630	2,733	1,203	937	1,813	796	1,586	632	1,320	41
30,760	22,641	53,497	10,015	16,074	15,840	22,561	30,519	18,898	25,292	42
34,235	14,085	32,689	33,982	16,748	14,098	14,449	16,560	11,739	13,806	43
14,890	6,335	17,632	8,608	6,038	5,914	11,725	15,886	6,624	9,178	44
6,653	5,548	17,005	5,445	7,227	13,109	6,438	13,829	4,836	9,340	45
8,915	11,049	45,380	1,943	2,534	5,864	8,566	19,249	7,682	16,941	46
4,556	2,601	8,406	1,255	606	1,176	2,012	3,721	1,809	3,264	47
10,132	11,919	18,886	2,697	5,412	1,431	7,844	6,287	7,054	5,957	48
4,251	4,086	22,231	653	982	2,875	3,300	9,594	3,069	8,453	49
58,086	29,049	17,085	1,730	2,850	2,382	20,398	7,652	19,396	6,854	50
87,239	34,934	79,873	30,294	18,113	18,961	31,747	38,526	26,024	32,410	51

No. 1013.—RETAIL TRADE—WAREHOUSES AND ADMINISTRATIVE OFFICES, SUMMARY, BY KIND OF BUSINESS: 1948

[Warehouses and administrative offices operated primarily in connection with retail stores]

KIND OF BUSINESS	WAREHOUSES				ADMINISTRATIVE OFFICES AND AUXILIARY UNITS			
	Total	Payroll, entire year	Paid employees, workweek ended nearest Nov. 15		Total	Payroll, entire year	Paid employees, workweek ended nearest Nov. 15	
			Total	Full workweek			Total	Full workweek
	Number	*$1,000*	*Number*	*Number*	*Number*	*$1,000*	*Number*	*Number*
United States	1,308	496,651	132,072	128,197	697	135,651	32,183	31,513
Food group	389	205,642	57,445	54,418	94	25,512	6,985	5,568
Grocery, grocery-meat stores	337	202,621	56,774	53,785	44	16,306	3,517	3,443
Candy, nut, confectionery stores	10	465	101	94	16	1,785	437	437
Dairy products stores, milk dealers	7	512	307	295	14	6,065	1,366	1,646
Bakery products stores					9	1,467	308	300
All other food stores	16	1,944	363	363	11	514	180	170
Eating and drinking places	40	6,666	1,851	1,699	81	14,908	3,425	3,230
General stores	4	987	319	298	5	338	73	73
General merchandise group	117	125,223	35,580	33,658	80	31,962	6,119	6,082
Department stores	43	57,343	24,452	22,800	22	8,099	1,484	1,467
Dry goods, general merchandise stores	28	23,400	5,290	5,436	20	2,236	332	336
Variety stores	46	25,431	5,527	5,351	38	21,657	4,303	4,270
Apparel group	270	68,751	18,352	17,116	191	17,452	4,463	4,245
Men's, boys' clothing, furnishings stores	29	5,909	1,347	1,199	21	1,957	436	410
Family clothing stores	30	4,655	1,177	1,090	24	3,743	1,055	977
Women's ready-to-wear stores	84	27,132	8,130	7,472	48	3,680	1,217	1,151
Military stores	17	1,830	462	453	49	3,015	685	657
Other apparel accessory, specialty stores	24	3,235	847	821	10	565	150	142
Shoe stores	81	25,680	7,038	6,006	33	4,386	886	874
All other apparel stores	5	310	73	73	6	154	34	34
Furniture, furnishings, appliance group	49	9,668	2,918	2,761	46	9,024	2,205	2,146
Furniture stores	23	5,616	1,612	1,472	10	3,145	806	785
Other home furnishing stores	13	1,748	601	584	24	2,549	451	450
Household appliance stores	10	1,556	428	428	12	3,330	948	911
Radio stores	3	748	277	277				
Automotive group	26	4,625	1,181	1,130	6	3,615	1,148	1,144
Tire, battery, accessory dealers [1]	26	4,625	1,181	1,130	6	3,615	1,148	1,144
All other automotive dealers								
Gasoline service stations	11	828	227	223	37	5,228	1,210	1,194
Lumber, building, hardware group	23	2,552	681	673	82	12,622	2,358	2,326
Lumber yards, building materials dealers	9	867	237	235	69	11,455	2,042	2,013
Plumbing, paint, electrical stores	8	719	174	174	7	843	239	237
Hardware stores and farm equipment dealers	6	966	270	264	6	324	77	76
Drug and proprietary stores	97	29,517	8,904	8,281	10	4,388	1,120	1,117
Liquor stores	31	3,844	1,547	1,455	7	3,202	1,366	1,356
Other retail stores	43	10,766	3,507	3,490	58	8,778	2,539	2,513
Fuel, fuel oil dealers	1	(²)	(²)	(²)	10	(²)	(²)	(²)
Ice dealers					4	427	137	136
Feed, farm, garden supply stores	5	671	202	194	10	3,313	1,042	1,022
Jewelry stores	7	1,153	250	245	16	2,216	545	541
Book, stationery stores	4	2,188	915	915	3	250	86	66
Florists	2	(²)	(²)	(²)	1	(²)	(²)	(²)
Cigar stores and stands	6	(²)	(²)	(²)	1	(²)	(²)	(²)
News dealers, newsstands	14	2,927	857	853	3	517	224	224
Music stores	1	(²)	(²)	(²)	4	(²)	(²)	(²)
Optical goods stores					3	163	25	25
All other retail stores	3	1,039	482	482	3	127	35	33

[1] Includes data for 2 "All other automotive dealers" administrative offices.
[2] Withheld to avoid disclosure of individual operations.

Source: Department of Commerce, Bureau of the Census; *U. S. Census of Business: 1948*, Vol. III.

No. 1014.—SALES OF RETAIL STORES, BY MONTHS: 1951 AND 1952

[Millions of dollars. Figures are seasonally adjusted. Data not comparable to that published for earlier years due to change in methodology; see *Survey of Current Business*, September 1952. See also table 1011]

MONTH	ALL RETAIL STORES		DURABLE GOODS STORES [1]		NONDURABLE GOODS STORES[1]	
	1951	1952	1951	1952	1951	1952
Year	158,223	164,085	54,479	55,270	103,744	108,815
January	14,027	13,170	5,260	4,364	8,767	8,806
February	13,859	13,421	5,179	4,608	8,680	8,813
March	13,162	13,033	4,680	4,312	8,482	8,721
April	12,885	13,363	4,441	4,494	8,444	8,869
May	12,979	13,850	4,472	4,927	8,507	8,923
June	12,913	14,014	4,399	4,883	8,514	9,131
July	12,796	13,667	4,223	4,494	8,573	9,173
August	13,074	13,359	4,387	4,199	8,687	9,160
September	12,992	13,570	4,398	4,505	8,594	9,045
October	13,230	14,202	4,437	4,844	8,793	9,358
November	13,239	14,026	4,352	4,769	8,887	9,257
December	13,067	14,410	4,251	4,871	8,816	9,539

[1] Durable goods include automotive group; furniture and appliance group; jewelry stores; lumber, building, hardware group; and other durable goods stores. Nondurable goods stores include all other kinds of business.

Source. Department of Commerce, Office of Business Economics and Bureau of the Census; published currently in *Survey of Current Business*.

No. 1015.—RETAIL STORES—NUMBER AND SALES, BY SIZE OF STORE: 1929, 1939, AND 1948

ANNUAL SALES GROUP AND YEAR		STORES		SALES	
		Number	Percent	Amount ($1,000)	Percent
$300,000 or more:	1929	15,029	1.0	12,323,766	25.5
	1939	12,630	.7	9,555,631	22.4
	1948	67,615	3.8	54,674,754	41.9
$100,000 to $299,999:	1929	62,009	4.2	9,786,669	20.2
	1939	50,097	2.8	7,955,285	18.9
	1948	194,829	11.0	31,871,978	24.4
$50,000 to $99,999:	1929	127,148	8.6	8,631,797	17.9
	1939	93,318	5.3	6,304,769	15.3
	1948	295,555	16.9	20,854,524	16.0
$30,000 to $49,999:	1929	173,269	11.7	6,617,160	13.7
	1939	133,231	7.5	5,077,007	12.1
	1948	296,599	16.8	11,491,605	8.8
$10,000 to $29,999:	1929	468,885	31.8	8,349,491	17.3
	1939	522,117	29.5	8,938,632	21.3
	1948	519,258	29.3	9,826,110	7.5
Less than $10,000:	1929	630,025	42.7	2,620,760	5.4
	1939	958,972	54.2	3,820,532	9.1
	1948	392,284	22.3	1,901,677	1.4

No. 1016.—FIRMS WITH FOUR OR MORE RETAIL STORES: 1939 AND 1948

ITEM	1939	1948	ITEM	1939	1948
Firms (number)	6,969	6,159	Payroll, entire year (thousand dollars)	1,439,117	4,260,838
Warehouses (number)	1,176	1,080	Stores (thousand dollars)	1,215,540	3,632,656
Administrative offices and other auxiliary units (number)	(¹)	697	Warehouses (thousand dollars)	105,236	480,081
Retail stores (number)	132,763	107,409	Administrative offices and other auxiliary units (thousand dollars)	118,341	138,081
Sales, entire year, by stores (thousand dollars)	10,104,713	30,425,024	Paid employees, workweek ended nearest Nov. 15, total	1,339,496	2,013,258
Billings by warehouses to own stores (thousand dollars)	2,726,428	8,945,663	Stores	1,228,161	1,848,004
Sales by warehouses to others (thousand dollars)	64,295	145,208	Warehouses	60,774	138,072
Merchandise inventories, at warehouses, end of year, at cost (thousand dollars)	167,122	592,936	Administrative offices, and other auxiliary units	(¹)	22,182

[1] Comparable data not available.

Source of tables 1015 and 1016: Department of Commerce, Bureau of Census; *U. S. Census of Business: 1948*, Vol. I.

No. 1017.—Retail Stores—Number and Sales, by Type of Operation and Kind of Business: 1948

	TOTAL		TYPE OF OPERATION					
KIND OF BUSINESS			Consumer cooperatives		Retail stores of farm co-operatives		Mail order houses	
	Stores	Sales, entire year	Stores	Sales, entire year	Stores	Sales, entire year	Establishments	Sales, entire year
	Number	$1,000	Number	$1,000	Number	$1,000	Number	$1,000
United States, total	1,769,540	130,520,548	728	108,529	3,670	958,312	880	1,485,352
Food group	504,439	30,965,674	402	48,629	384	91,234	54	5,602
Eating and drinking places	346,556	10,683,324	41	6,122	42	1,740		
General merchandise group, general stores	74,101	17,134,718	46	10,278	148	26,723	60	1,300,867
Apparel group	115,246	9,805,218	9	1,483			108	47,287
Furniture, furnishings, appliance group	85,585	6,914,179	18	729	14	1,295	80	11,138
Automotive group	86,162	20,104,054	12	6,243	16	1,481	10	2,236
Gasoline service stations	188,253	6,483,301	97	11,501	723	96,440		
Lumber, building, hardware group	98,938	11,151,470	18	5,690	243	38,724	18	6,034
Drug and proprietary stores	55,796	4,013,231	11	921			23	925
Other retail stores	214,464	13,267,379	74	16,933	2,100	700,675	859	111,273

	TYPE OF OPERATION—continued					
KIND OF BUSINESS	Direct selling (house to house) organizations		Merchandise vending machine operators		Other types	
	Establishments	Sales, entire year	Establishments	Sales, entire year	Stores	Sales, entire year
	Number	$1,000	Number	$1,000	Number	$1,000
United States, total	3,451	634,763	881	199,703	1,759,930	127,133,889
Food group	414	112,806	322	56,484	502,862	30,650,919
Eating and drinking places			103	8,279	346,370	10,667,183
General merchandise group, general stores	313	33,290			73,534	15,763,560
Apparel group	264	33,186			114,867	9,721,262
Furniture, furnishings, appliance group	1,355	304,852			84,148	6,596,165
Automotive group					86,124	20,094,094
Gasoline service stations					187,433	6,375,360
Lumber, building, hardware group					98,659	11,101,032
Drug and proprietary stores	9	58			55,753	4,011,327
Other retail stores	1,096	150,571	455	134,940	210,180	12,152,987

Source: Dept. of Commerce, Bureau of the Census; *U. S. Census of Business: 1948*, Vol. II, and records.

No. 1018.—Retail Stores—Number, Sales, Payroll and Personnel, by Number of Employees: 1948

	STORES		SALES, ENTIRE YEAR		PAYROLL, ENTIRE YEAR		UNINCORPORATED BUSINESSES				PAID EMPLOYEES WORKWEEK ENDED NEAREST NOV. 15	
NUMBER OF EMPLOYEES PER STORE [1]							Active proprietors, November		Unpaid family workers, November			
	Number	Percent	Amount ($1,000)	Percent	Amount ($1,000)	Percent	Number	Percent	Number	Percent	Number	Percent
Total, all stores	1,769,540	100.0	130,520,548	100.0	13,567,997	100.0	1,742,046	100.0	930,546	100.0	6,918,061	100.0
No paid employees	669,317	37.8	11,111,704	8.5	75,891	.6	736,341	42.3	512,697	55.1		
1 paid employee	289,170	16.3	9,020,653	6.9	413,686	3.0	303,959	17.4	148,917	16.0	289,170	4.2
2 paid employees	217,597	12.3	9,810,800	7.5	683,980	5.0	219,111	12.6	94,310	10.1	435,194	6.3
3 paid employees	149,109	8.4	8,926,538	6.8	749,728	5.5	142,566	8.2	57,052	6.1	447,327	6.5
4 or 5 paid employees	170,213	9.6	13,720,554	10.5	1,326,290	9.8	154,750	8.9	58,097	6.3	754,408	10.9
6 or 7 paid employees	92,956	5.3	10,305,105	7.9	1,104,393	8.1	78,930	4.5	27,993	3.0	597,317	8.6
8 or 9 paid employees	46,163	2.6	6,856,456	5.3	772,703	5.7	34,034	2.0	11,129	1.2	389,282	5.6
10 to 19 paid employees	84,456	4.8	19,008,835	14.6	2,303,131	17.0	54,817	3.1	16,226	1.8	1,117,606	16.2
20 to 49 paid employees	38,880	2.2	18,798,875	14.4	2,479,947	18.3	15,649	.9	3,725	.4	1,130,366	16.3
50 to 99 paid employees	8,005	.5	7,847,605	6.0	1,177,676	8.7	1,556	.1	334	(²)	536,272	7.8
100 or more paid employees	3,674	.2	15,083,423	11.6	2,480,572	18.3	333	(²)	66	(²)	1,221,119	17.6

[1] Based on number of paid employees for workweek ended nearest Nov. 15, 1948.
² Less than 0.05 percent.

Source: Department of Commerce, Bureau of the Census; *U. S. Census of Business: 1948*, Vol. I.

No. 1019.—Retail Trade—Single and Multiunits by Kind-of-Business Groups: 1948

KIND OF BUSINESS AND SINGLE AND MULTIUNITS	Stores	Sales, entire year	Payroll, entire year	PAID EMPLOYEES, WORKWEEK ENDED NEAREST NOV. 15	
				Total	Full work-week
	Number	$1,000	$1,000	Number	Number
United States, total	1,769,540	130,520,548	12,557,597	6,915,661	5,663,266
Single units	1,606,884	91,089,227	8,946,407	4,857,202	
2 or 3 store multiunits	57,547	6,904,751	1,191,084		
4 or more store multiunits	105,188	20,736,570	2,320,558	1,780,120	
Food group	504,430	20,985,974	1,543,987	1,006,067	
Single units	462,058	19,028,648		601,700	
2 or 3 store multiunits	9,500	1,264,208	118,000		42,781
4 or more store multiunits	32,874	10,462,788	622,475	351,029	264,007
Eating and drinking places	348,556	10,683,394	1,540,507	1,387,130	
Single units	332,619	9,516,258		1,151,048	
2 or 3 store multiunits	6,804	431,696	110,608		
4 or more store multiunits	6,123	741,840	202,784	119,306	97,281
General stores	21,837	1,289,981	65,785	41,468	
Single units	20,877	861,215	42,307	38,737	
2 or 3 store multiunits		49,039	4,531	2,130	
4 or more store multiunits		179,088	13,587	9,551	6,776
General merchandise group	83,544	15,922,567	3,334,208	1,351,307	
Single units	26,615	5,719,388	812,536	446,946	
2 or 3 store multiunits	3,298	1,208,349	240,099	121,123	
4 or more store multiunits	12,727	5,780,761	1,345,682	770,208	
Department stores	2,880	10,664,747	1,461,702	845,479	
Single units		3,472,478	648,616	336,775	
2 or 3 store multiunits	179	1,248,168	215,229	110,288	
4 or more store multiunits	1,665	5,882,101	791,857	504,146	611,176
Apparel group	115,300	9,102,218	1,175,820	888,700	
Single units	91,306	5,684,122	677,434	339,776	
2 or 3 store multiunits	9,135	1,120,467	160,488	75,927	
4 or more store multiunits	14,815	2,782,860	342,704		
Furniture, furnishings, appliance group	86,866	6,914,179	986,625	376,311	
Single units	74,490	5,148,919	680,306	345,461	
2 or 3 store multiunits	5,863	748,840	115,757	91,388	
4 or more store multiunits	6,607	1,037,401	221,048	92,844	
Automotive group	94,166	20,194,664	1,468,370		
Single units	78,384	17,622,604	1,283,602		
2 or 3 store multiunits	5,072	1,448,404	167,284	44,280	
4 or more store multiunits	4,668	760,381	87,008	32,328	
Gasoline service stations	188,253	6,462,301	482,190	305,964	
Single units	178,617	5,992,889		248,072	
2 or 3 store multiunits	5,091	322,091		10,888	
4 or more store multiunits	4,446	470,874	65,087	28,988	
Lumber, building, hardware group	98,288	11,191,070	1,185,344	678,413	
Single units	86,122	9,882,600	973,318	552,221	
2 or 3 store multiunits	4,906	1,006,566	116,012	58,289	
4 or more store multiunits	7,361	1,852,804	196,013	71,888	
Drug and proprietary stores	56,798	4,611,331	591,761	392,891	
Single units	49,774	3,805,271	391,761	304,469	
2 or 3 store multiunits	2,387	344,387	42,488	18,278	
4 or more store multiunits	4,715			70,132	
Drug stores	44,664	3,672,465	584,730	398,864	
Single units	42,056	2,513,714	394,730	176,104	
2 or 3 store multiunits	4,506	227,751	48,013	17,000	
4 or more store multiunits				87,000	
Proprietary stores		501,907			
Single units		15,492			
2 or 3 store multiunits	313	15,598	3,874	2,364	
Liquor stores	32,422	2,185,807	128,248	88,444	
Single units		1,051,344		37,542	
2 or 3 store multiunits				5,417	
4 or more store multiunits				11,488	
Second-handstores	14,168			10,888	
Single units		971,088			
2 or 3 store multiunits		15,888			
4 or more store multiunits		17,088			
Other retail stores	184,073	10,282,218			
Single units					
2 or 3 store multiunits					
4 or more store multiunits		1,888,888			

Source: Department of Commerce, Bureau of the Census; U. S. Census of Business: 1948, Vol. I.

No. 1020.—Retail Stores—Summary,

DIVISION AND STATE	NUMBER OF STORES			SALES, ENTIRE YEAR ($1,000)			ACTIVE PROPRIETORS[1] (number)	
	1929	1939	1948	1929	1939	1948	1939	Nov. 1948
United States.....	1,476,365	1,770,355	1,769,540	48,329,652	42,041,790	130,520,548	1,613,673	1,742,046
New England........	104,618	121,888	115,219	3,732,087	3,318,214	8,557,443	101,716	99,626
Maine.............	10,453	13,455	11,843	300,010	281,386	755,651	11,821	10,752
New Hampshire....	6,181	7,435	7,541	180,248	183,100	470,742	6,600	6,938
Vermont...........	4,831	5,423	5,075	148,281	123,369	337,804	4,942	4,567
Massachusetts....	52,661	59,217	53,902	2,031,839	1,737,680	4,302,147	47,538	42,608
Rhode Island......	9,155	10,485	10,371	313,978	275,447	716,064	9,100	9,687
Connecticut.......	21,337	25,873	26,487	757,731	717,262	1,975,035	21,715	25,044
Middle Atlantic....	372,026	412,819	395,268	12,527,976	10,291,937	28,175,162	376,063	389,727
New York........	183,615	209,425	196,282	6,968,931	5,578,159	14,626,526	191,259	190,977
New Jersey......	57,780	68,851	69,090	1,811,257	1,580,401	4,479,205	59,277	67,487
Pennsylvania.....	130,631	134,543	129,896	3,747,788	3,133,377	9,069,431	125,532	131,263
East North Central..	394,986	364,508	350,319	11,113,186	9,251,114	28,901,766	332,029	351,815
Ohio.............	80,155	93,041	86,971	2,829,354	2,441,293	7,373,173	82,712	83,610
Indiana..........	39,402	47,317	44,754	1,200,458	1,066,383	3,532,337	44,003	45,309
Illinois..........	93,432	109,132	103,405	3,658,560	2,857,646	8,805,257	100,099	105,863
Michigan.........	53,952	67,414	68,689	2,202,405	1,820,798	5,950,278	61,129	71,579
Wisconsin........	38,045	47,604	46,500	1,222,409	1,064,994	3,240,721	44,086	45,954
West North Central..	161,393	197,909	179,246	5,178,845	4,128,883	13,268,296	185,927	179,339
Minnesota........	29,206	40,448	35,241	1,036,012	1,017,195	2,906,062	38,932	34,965
Iowa.............	30,933	39,034	33,725	966,006	822,905	2,556,224	37,111	34,412
Missouri.........	44,586	52,196	50,616	1,422,449	1,102,503	3,568,337	49,328	50,014
North Dakota.....	7,511	8,549	8,201	230,602	156,137	608,182	7,818	8,279
South Dakota.....	8,330	9,817	8,993	249,935	169,396	622,192	8,954	8,616
Nebraska.........	16,852	19,330	16,873	553,611	397,196	1,317,813	18,004	17,135
Kansas...........	24,045	27,545	25,597	730,228	473,551	1,689,396	25,750	25,918
South Atlantic........	162,295	199,371	222,848	4,138,337	4,368,947	14,772,800	174,561	211,034
Delaware.........	3,527	4,544	4,433	101,861	110,052	382,305	4,001	4,155
Maryland.........	20,371	25,566	25,037	610,967	619,273	1,914,689	23,774	25,240
District of Columbia.	5,815	6,893	7,094	332,393	402,768	1,111,643	5,498	6,437
Virginia..........	25,036	29,610	32,124	591,763	628,172	2,227,407	25,389	30,073
West Virginia.....	16,501	18,928	21,265	441,072	403,989	1,287,983	16,202	19,527
North Carolina....	27,660	33,826	40,880	642,550	633,240	2,248,360	29,890	38,994
South Carolina....	14,452	18,520	20,970	296,674	332,224	1,148,170	15,759	19,190
Georgia..........	27,640	32,870	35,655	627,171	624,765	2,111,539	28,797	33,362
Florida...........	21,293	28,614	35,390	493,886	614,464	2,340,395	25,251	34,056
East South Central..	86,315	101,065	112,879	2,137,499	1,845,037	6,417,719	93,025	111,053
Kentucky.........	25,927	30,919	29,890	577,929	520,135	1,682,087	28,970	29,986
Tennessee........	22,368	28,196	32,692	632,612	606,489	2,088,439	25,980	32,390
Alabama..........	20,456	23,916	28,756	518,972	435,973	1,638,859	21,715	27,976
Mississippi.......	16,564	18,032	21,541	407,986	282,440	1,008,334	16,860	20,701
West South Central.	128,542	159,768	169,520	3,654,572	3,101,358	10,923,488	148,785	165,469
Arkansas.........	17,107	20,328	22,243	406,206	298,301	1,083,262	19,071	22,517
Louisiana.........	22,559	25,469	29,679	469,755	486,250	1,681,334	22,845	28,312
Oklahoma........	25,984	28,722	26,924	781,121	513,091	1,640,015	27,221	27,046
Texas............	62,832	85,249	90,674	1,997,490	1,803,716	6,518,877	79,648	87,594
Mountain...........	42,022	57,459	59,861	1,515,313	1,427,541	4,665,554	53,112	60,561
Montana..........	6,521	8,481	8,108	238,293	222,008	602,623	7,367	8,304
Idaho............	4,624	6,804	7,323	165,352	175,873	581,844	6,223	7,128
Wyoming.........	2,837	4,113	3,869	101,457	100,233	300,109	3,863	4,037
Colorado.........	13,139	16,785	15,426	457,413	409,103	1,257,095	15,770	16,010
New Mexico......	3,941	6,617	7,842	116,533	125,765	477,553	6,139	7,934
Arizona..........	4,766	6,242	8,043	193,818	162,003	657,587	5,726	7,984
Utah.............	4,964	6,372	6,840	193,286	170,728	570,767	5,520	6,682
Nevada...........	1,230	2,045	2,410	48,861	61,828	200,016	2,004	2,482
Pacific..............	115,168	155,568	164,380	4,331,837	4,298,759	14,838,410	148,450	173,422
Washington.......	20,836	26,682	25,731	745,891	668,790	2,221,306	24,798	25,819
Oregon...........	13,544	16,458	17,538	443,303	442,160	1,597,300	15,757	19,678
California........	80,788	112,428	121,111	3,142,643	3,187,809	11,019,804	107,895	127,925

[1] Of unincorporated businesses.

BY STATES: 1929, 1939, AND 1948

UNPAID FAMILY WORKERS [1] (number)		PAID EMPLOYEES, WORKWEEK ENDED NEAREST NOV. 15				PAYROLL, ENTIRE YEAR ($1,000)			DIVISION AND STATE
		Total (number)		Full workweek (number)					
1939	Nov. 1948	1939	1948	1939	1948	1929	1939	1948	
923, 878	930, 546	4, 521, 806	4, 915, 061	3, 870, 195	5, 608, 206	5, 044, 123	4, 529, 490	11, 547, 997	U. S.
46, 389	46, 696	372, 789	474, 286	296, 923	375, 381	411, 532	377, 987	521, 488	N. E.
5, 567	5, 546	26, 093	28, 025	22, 945	30, 696	26, 895	26, 079	66, 500	Maine
5, 007	5, 514	18, 198	24, 178	14, 881	19, 136	18, 214	17, 322	43, 576	N. H.
2, 259	2, 092	12, 174	16, 046	9, 554	13, 070	12, 210	10, 707	25, 516	Vt.
20, 632	19, 890	210, 116	268, 087	164, 540	298, 902	326, 204	312, 006	406, 509	Mass.
4, 318	4, 777	31, 174	39, 448	24, 322	31, 283	35, 223	30, 978	72, 308	R. I.
10, 806	10, 537	73, 044	98, 562	60, 401	78, 382	85, 003	79, 906	210, 578	Conn.
224, 795	196, 084	1, 112, 888	1, 675, 414	917, 902	1, 306, 371	1, 362, 975	1, 170, 490	3, 004, 500	M. A.
106, 507	85, 998	567, 180	752, 941	495, 744	694, 585	773, 533	660, 098	1, 644, 297	N. Y.
37, 306	35, 323	186, 377	208, 786	128, 421	199, 380	187, 835	171, 619	433, 177	N. J.
80, 922	74, 763	306, 329	513, 715	293, 836	412, 427	408, 007	336, 712	945, 603	Pa.
192, 399	181, 251	1, 065, 879	1, 540, 997	864, 347	1, 291, 486	1, 217, 630	1, 026, 315	3, 065, 083	E. N. C.
49, 129	64, 541	282, 968	406, 646	234, 862	321, 980	310, 045	271, 073	857, 155	Ohio
23, 643	21, 784	120, 757	182, 488	101, 960	151, 153	125, 182	110, 998	340, 758	Ind.
54, 963	54, 046	353, 496	474, 488	298, 897	448, 987	438, 583	380, 072	930, 079	Ill.
36, 708	34, 470	208, 645	290, 880	168, 887	290, 842	227, 340	204, 030	440, 599	Mich.
27, 866	27, 540	111, 088	170, 896	89, 734	123, 534	116, 580	103, 580	325, 579	Wis.
90, 675	91, 444	479, 424	694, 377	378, 166	547, 878	663, 899	601, 399	1, 349, 599	W. N. C.
20, 372	17, 573	109, 539	154, 414	86, 485	119, 011	101, 245	104, 304	291, 612	Minn.
16, 960	16, 206	92, 127	138, 064	70, 383	98, 781	92, 602	72, 514	224, 834	Iowa
25, 318	27, 013	139, 651	200, 311	112, 065	148, 901	149, 362	119, 337	369, 683	Mo.
4, 307	3, 998	16, 026	27, 390	12, 675	21, 718	17, 487	12, 960	62, 591	N. Dak.
4, 570	5, 095	17, 708	30, 430	13, 849	23, 782	18, 562	13, 582	69, 490	S. Dak.
10, 656	5, 112	45, 516	84, 706	35, 623	51, 418	68, 168	36, 221	112, 489	Nebr.
14, 195	12, 421	58, 266	87, 198	44, 946	70, 377	64, 871	42, 510	151, 873	Kans.
104, 971	125, 676	551, 496	809, 680	443, 383	694, 341	607, 304	447, 047	1, 672, 777	S. A.
2, 440	2, 274	11, 459	16, 572	9, 367	14, 102	8, 551	11, 188	39, 599	Del.
14, 069	12, 208	75, 458	102, 791	61, 227	91, 306	62, 764	66, 079	204, 575	Md.
2, 838	2, 651	30, 838	50, 943	23, 365	56, 246	62, 808	55, 007	142, 475	D. C.
14, 687	16, 842	79, 147	134, 313	64, 443	103, 890	63, 600	63, 867	214, 088	Va.
10, 894	13, 610	44, 943	69, 205	36, 075	57, 414	45, 699	35, 262	115, 477	W. Va.
16, 464	34, 608	88, 147	131, 846	65, 691	108, 361	62, 128	50, 062	212, 489	N. C.
9, 203	12, 149	43, 997	64, 623	33, 113	48, 460	32, 316	28, 060	202, 199	S. C.
17, 124	22, 010	83, 346	122, 618	67, 239	102, 308	68, 702	58, 874	302, 198	Ga.
16, 532	20, 364	77, 312	131, 486	64, 668	116, 184	50, 727	64, 344	341, 582	Fla.
61, 448	74, 093	224, 191	252, 341	179, 946	290, 436	127, 322	162, 675	596, 562	E. S. C.
20, 982	19, 409	57, 636	94, 986	46, 047	70, 503	38, 144	45, 098	147, 989	Ky.
15, 941	20, 212	76, 787	118, 800	61, 766	95, 981	39, 144	55, 936	200, 302	Tenn.
14, 436	19, 484	54, 774	91, 842	44, 651	75, 196	49, 721	37, 623	128, 509	Ala.
10, 189	14, 988	34, 884	54, 311	27, 582	45, 364	35, 721	22, 738	119, 502	Miss.
92, 331	107, 989	387, 347	509, 897	319, 512	561, 290	335, 629	282, 418	1, 611, 606	W. S. C.
12, 208	14, 379	35, 800	54, 491	29, 016	45, 618	27, 396	23, 176	95, 578	Ark.
15, 537	19, 973	66, 882	87, 080	54, 228	84, 680	37, 809	40, 000	196, 897	La.
18, 079	16, 683	62, 774	90, 302	50, 302	73, 204	71, 581	46, 083	151, 832	Okla.
46, 097	56, 132	222, 130	348, 333	155, 371	364, 090	166, 614	171, 080	631, 780	Tex.
28, 740	32, 361	151, 600	294, 373	121, 968	192, 635	189, 590	146, 305	409, 590	Mt.
3, 542	3, 387	20, 714	34, 480	16, 530	22, 362	22, 599	21, 066	63, 497	Mont.
3, 763	3, 051	17, 499	26, 599	14, 387	22, 687	16, 399	14, 198	54, 497	Idaho
1, 608	2, 154	9, 019	16, 590	7, 307	11, 690	8, 340	6, 390	123, 790	Wyo.
6, 340	7, 892	46, 016	67, 615	36, 714	42, 979	42, 100	63, 588	128, 790	Colo.
4, 294	5, 700	13, 613	24, 390	11, 341	19, 779	11, 860	11, 880	33, 199	N. Mex.
3, 764	3, 431	17, 594	31, 671	14, 144	27, 790	22, 890	17, 119	62, 399	Ariz.
3, 130	3, 570	20, 397	34, 673	14, 673	34, 087	24, 590	18, 743	34, 199	Utah
1, 021	1, 127	6, 027	9, 190	4, 704	7, 726	21, 500	7, 204	28, 621	Nev.
73, 880	74, 382	454, 975	711, 244	349, 196	594, 659	457, 615	503, 736	1, 729, 539	Pac.
12, 199	12, 510	68, 771	106, 696	54, 614	89, 698	54, 900	73, 000	262, 529	Wash.
8, 192	8, 571	42, 898	72, 541	34, 625	66, 157	44, 384	44, 104	182, 599	Oreg.
52, 638	53, 871	341, 296	584, 319	272, 198	446, 140	358, 195	387, 138	1, 283, 539	Calif.

No. 1021.—Retail Stores—Number and Sales, for Specified Metropolitan Areas: 1948

[Listed in order of 1948 sales volume]

METROPOLITAN AREA	THE METROPOLITAN AREA					CENTRAL CITIES [1]			
	Sales, entire year		Stores (number)	Population rank, 1950 [2]	Per capita sales [3] (dollars)	Stores (number)	Sales, entire year ($1,000)	Population, 1950, percent of area total	Per capita sales [3] (dollars)
	Rank	Amount ($1,000)							
United States, total..		130,520,548	1,769,540		857	1,769,540	130,520,548		857
Total, 147 areas..........		86,898,778	932,124		967	595,942	57,747,493	58.2	1,210
Percent of United States total..........		62.0	52.7			33.7	44.2		
New York-Northeastern New Jersey area.........	1	12,652,074	171,105	1	966	115,473	8,839,001	66.8	1,032
Chicago (Ill.) area.........	2	5,969,723	62,030	2	1,094	43,540	4,348,901	65.9	1,206
Los Angeles (Calif.) area....	3	4,721,241	49,133	3	1,088	23,183	2,370,761	45.1	1,211
Philadelphia (Pa.) area....	4	3,345,506	45,506	4	914	28,243	2,115,759	56.4	1,026
Detroit (Mich.) area.......	5	3,014,275	28,189	5	1,014	18,242	2,084,748	61.8	1,134
San Francisco-Oakland (Calif.) area............	6	2,366,588	25,069	7	1,069	15,542	1,581,566	51.5	1,386
Boston (Mass.) area........	7	2,261,260	24,417	6	960	9,926	1,086,720	33.6	1,374
Pittsburgh (Pa.) area.......	8	1,985,201	23,341	8	900	7,536	882,806	30.5	1,310
St. Louis (Mo.) area.......	9	1,567,167	19,843	9	936	11,706	987,731	50.9	1,158
Cleveland (Ohio) area.....	10	1,523,834	15,630	11	1,048	11,823	1,178,241	62.3	1,301
Washington (D. C.) area....	11	1,485,845	10,171	10	1,019	7,094	1,111,643	54.7	1,394
Minneapolis-St. Paul (Minn.) area...........	12	1,263,527	10,227	13	1,141	8,316	1,133,172	74.7	1,371
Baltimore (Md.) area......	13	1,227,103	15,342	12	929	12,586	1,052,945	71.2	1,120
Buffalo (N. Y.) area......	14	1,027,228	14,252	14	946	8,328	664,284	53.2	1,150
Kansas City (Mo.) area....	15	990,626	8,982	17	1,226	5,301	782,963	56.1	1,661
Milwaukee (Wis.) area.....	16	926,279	9,792	16	1,072	7,791	794,283	73.2	1,255
Cincinnati (Ohio) area.....	17	879,847	10,114	15	980	6,372	619,086	55.7	1,237
Houston (Tex.) area.......	18	818,603	8,018	18	1,021	5,874	697,060	74.1	1,173
Portland (Oreg.) area.....	19	772,318	7,382	21	1,101	4,642	574,822	52.9	1,549
Seattle (Wash.) area.......	20	783,744	7,862	20	1,038	5,754	613,665	63.7	1,327
Dallas (Tex.) area.........	21	704,804	5,986	24	1,154	4,713	621,858	70.9	1,436
Atlanta (Ga.) area........	22	675,307	5,792	23	1,017	3,552	528,446	49.3	1,616
Providence (R. I.) area....	23	671,380	9,390	19	916	3,842	328,351	33.8	1,326
Indianapolis (Ind.) area...	24	627,565	5,294	28	1,143	4,650	586,192	77.3	1,380
Denver (Colo.) area........	25	594,701	5,422	26	1,061	4,234	510,219	73.7	1,236
Miami (Fla.) area.........	26	581,134	6,799	34	1,189	3,725	388,283	50.5	1,572
Albany-Schenectady-Troy (N. Y.) area.............	27	562,302	6,763	31	1,097	4,625	409,045	58.2	1,373
New Orleans (La.) area.....	28	553,211	7,750	22	812	6,678	506,924	83.3	894
Louisville (Ky.) area......	29	517,109	5,727	25	900	4,082	411,095	63.9	1,119
San Diego (Calif.) area....	30	507,440	5,711	29	947	3,666	367,780	60.0	1,144
Columbus (Ohio) area.....	31	506,564	4,700	32	1,009	3,973	460,363	74.7	1,228
Rochester (N. Y.) area....	32	491,277	5,472	35	1,013	4,286	411,367	66.3	1,242
Memphis (Tenn.) area.....	33	485,432	4,153	36	1,011	3,554	461,826	82.1	1,172
Youngstown (Ohio) area...	34	468,623	5,383	30	890	1,812	214,134	31.8	1,277
Dayton (Ohio) area........	35	446,616	3,962	37	986	2,550	342,636	53.6	1,409
Toledo (Ohio) area........	36	442,946	4,170	43	1,128	3,393	393,567	76.8	1,306
Birmingham (Ala.) area...	37	441,752	5,157	27	797	3,083	342,491	53.9	1,147
Akron (Ohio) area........	38	403,116	3,884	40	988	2,764	323,486	67.0	1,184
Fort Worth (Tex.) area....	39	402,391	3,873	46	1,120	3,142	370,077	77.1	1,336
Allentown-Bethlehem-Easton (Pa.) area.......	40	401,807	5,972	38	924	2,368	205,494	39.6	1,193
Hartford (Conn.) area.....	41	396,377	3,924	47	1,113	2,468	267,621	49.7	1,511
San Antonio (Tex.) area...	42	392,717	5,038	33	792	4,642	377,840	82.0	929
Springfield-Holyoke (Mass.) area.............	43	389,191	4,780	41	957	2,773	260,317	53.4	1,199
Omaha (Nebr.) area.......	44	383,009	3,530	45	1,057	2,451	308,452	68.3	1,247
Tampa-St. Petersburg (Fla.) area.............	45	364,475	5,193	42	897	3,195	274,081	54.1	1,247
Syracuse (N. Y.) area......	46	353,617	3,787	49	1,037	2,621	290,191	64.6	1,319
Norfolk-Portsmouth (Va.) area....................	47	347,270	4,216	39	848	3,147	299,391	63.5	1,152
Richmond (Va.) area......	48	339,794	3,153	52	1,040	2,606	319,524	70.3	1,390
Oklahoma City (Okla.)area..	49	317,913	3,539	53	986	2,760	290,068	75.2	1,196
Phoenix (Ariz.) area.......	50	311,336	3,472	51	946	1,593	209,171	32.0	1,984

See footnotes at end of table.

No. 1021.—Retail Stores—Number and Sales, for Specified Metropolitan Areas 1948—Continued

METROPOLITAN AREA	THE METROPOLITAN AREA				CENTRAL CITIES [1]			
	Sales, entire year	Stores (number)	Population rank, 1950 [2]	Per capita sales [3] (dollars)	Stores (number)	Sales, entire year ($1,000)	Population, 1950, percent of area total	Per capita sales [3] (dollars)
	Rank	Amount ($1,000)							
Wilkes-Barre-Hazleton (Pa.) area	51	305,435	6,350	44	781	2,025	148,861	26.7	1,228
Sacramento (Calif.) area	52	297,303	2,921	65	1,079	1,987	236,730	49.2	1,744
Grand Rapids (Mich.) area	53	296,140	3,051	60	1,032	2,126	240,356	61.2	1,366
Fresno (Calif.) area	54	285,519	3,218	66	1,041	1,562	185,945	33.0	2,062
San Jose (Calif.) area	55	279,967	2,840	59	969	1,254	147,734	32.9	1,584
Nashville (Tenn.) area	56	278,063	3,032	54	868	2,235	238,412	54.1	1,375
Wilmington (Del.) area	57	276,534	3,382	70	1,036	1,962	189,444	41.1	1,724
Jacksonville (Fla.) area	58	272,034	3,153	56	899	2,492	247,762	67.2	1,218
Wheeling (W. Va.)-Steubenville (Ohio) area	59	268,024	4,193	48	759	1,446	139,101	26.7	1,478
Canton (Ohio) area	60	268,010	3,054	62	950	1,525	150,489	41.2	1,294
Des Moines (Iowa) area	61	267,871	2,337	84	1,191	1,999	250,325	78.7	1,415
Salt Lake City (Utah) area	62	267,573	2,433	67	976	1,697	218,642	66.3	1,203
Bridgeport (Conn.) area	63	266,455	3,318	72	1,031	2,498	214,461	61.7	1,348
Harrisburg (Pa.) area	64	265,132	3,650	57	911	1,531	140,795	30.6	1,580
Worcester (Mass.) area	65	265,030	3,058	66	967	2,316	228,376	73.7	1,131
New Haven (Conn.) area	66	262,070	3,833	71	1,000	2,847	205,995	62.3	1,261
Charleston (W. Va.) area	67	259,302	3,258	55	812	1,105	141,982	22.8	1,960
Utica-Rome (N. Y.) area	68	256,150	4,078	61	910	2,092	160,017	50.4	1,130
Tulsa (Okla.) area	69	254,405	2,677	77	1,023	2,123	230,985	72.6	1,279
Knoxville (Tenn.) area	70	250,505	3,012	80	746	1,680	174,752	37.0	1,407
Davenport (Iowa)-Rock Island-Moline (Ill.) area	71	246,739	2,632	81	1,059	1,939	207,515	66.5	1,301
Flint (Mich.) area	72	246,724	2,794	69	914	1,822	196,510	60.3	1,207
San Bernardino (Calif.) area	73	246,338	3,581	63	879	964	96,907	22.4	1,575
Trenton (N. J.) area	74	242,259	3,194	82	1,056	2,253	169,276	55.7	1,324
Peoria (Ill.) area	75	242,123	2,613	76	969	1,368	165,191	44.6	1,461
Duluth (Minn.)-Superior (Wis.) area	76	238,859	3,281	75	949	1,761	186,378	55.3	1,124
Reading (Pa.) area	77	230,547	3,741	74	904	1,975	139,995	42.8	1,264
Wichita (Kans.) area	78	225,074	2,414	85	1,022	1,961	201,582	75.5	1,212
Spokane (Wash.) area	79	223,147	2,173	86	1,014	1,738	196,014	72.9	1,234
Tacoma (Wash.) area	80	218,285	2,612	64	791	1,709	171,114	51.8	1,197
South Bend (Ind.) area	81	217,908	2,164	88	1,064	1,481	169,129	56.5	1,462
Stamford-Norwalk (Conn.) area	82	217,066	2,574	93	1,117	1,594	133,456	63.3	1,065
Lancaster (Pa.) area	83	215,371	2,872	80	920	1,042	90,805	27.2	1,493
Erie (Pa.) area	84	215,241	2,527	87	966	1,607	162,569	59.6	1,249
Johnstown (Pa.) area	85	210,329	3,080	58	724	836	90,846	21.6	1,448
Scranton (Pa.) area	86	205,268	3,811	73	801	1,796	136,904	48.7	1,097
Stockton (Calif.) area	87	202,242	2,260	90	1,009	1,210	131,448	35.7	1,834
Chattanooga (Tenn.) area	88	197,849	2,717	79	806	1,829	166,989	53.1	1,281
Beaumont-Port Arthur (Tex.) area	89	193,671	2,447	94	998	2,030	177,353	77.9	1,175
Fort Wayne (Ind.) area	90	193,390	1,774	96	1,057	1,400	171,638	72.6	1,292
Lansing (Mich.) area	91	184,141	1,582	100	1,068	978	142,734	53.2	1,557
Charlotte (N. C.) area	92	183,964	1,642	92	938	1,275	169,702	67.9	1,274
Binghamton (N. Y.) area	93	181,878	2,017	97	985	1,061	115,546	43.9	1,434
Greensboro-High Point (N. C.) area	94	177,448	1,810	96	933	1,274	162,429	59.8	1,429
Huntington (W. Va.)-Ashland (Ky.) area	95	174,853	2,628	78	712	1,464	130,229	47.8	1,109
Little Rock (Ark.) area	96	174,746	2,311	95	906	1,923	167,392	74.4	1,166
Atlantic City (N. J.) area	97	173,260	2,986	127	1,304	1,909	121,682	46.4	1,974
Madison (Wis.) area	98	172,963	1,860	102	1,026	1,035	122,620	56.7	1,263
York (Pa.) area	99	172,775	7,689	89	853	1,263	81,094	29.5	1,356
Shreveport (La.) area	100	170,289	1,743	99	975	1,320	155,531	71.8	1,240
Mobile (Ala.) area	101	169,797	2,227	83	742	1,390	137,859	55.6	1,064
Rockford (Ill.) area	102	163,760	1,673	112	1,078	1,271	137,663	60.9	1,488
El Paso (Tex.) area	103	159,834	1,941	91	808	1,474	141,984	65.7	1,092
Evansville (Ind.) area	104	149,941	1,636	108	947	1,434	139,279	69.4	1,208
Springfield (Ill.) area	105	143,875	1,565	130	1,101	1,092	124,100	61.9	1,535

See footnotes at end of table.

No. 1021.—RETAIL STORES—NUMBER AND SALES, FOR SPECIFIED METROPOLITAN AREAS: 1948—Continued

METROPOLITAN AREA	THE METROPOLITAN AREA					CENTRAL CITIES [1]			
	Sales, entire year		Stores (number)	Population rank, 1950 [2]	Per capita sales [2] (dollars)	Stores (number)	Sales, entire year ($1,000)	Population, 1950, percent of area total	Per capita sales [3] (dollars)
	Rank	Amount ($1,000)							
Corpus Christi (Tex.) area.	106	141,350	1,819	104	859	1,364	123,226	65.6	1,140
Waterbury (Conn.) area...	107	141,237	2,021	110	914	1,523	111,132	67.5	1,066
Austin (Tex.) area.........	108	138,692	1,539	106	865	1,343	134,085	82.3	1,016
Baton Rouge (La.) area...	109	134,751	1,587	109	861	1,171	116,738	79.2	942
Portland (Maine) area.....	110	134,179	1,356	136	1,127	1,015	113,945	64.6	1,481
Hamilton-Middletown (Ohio) area..............	111	132,802	1,542	114	905	1,176	114,683	62.2	1,255
Saginaw (Mich.) area......	112	132,435	1,522	111	866	1,035	107,045	60.4	1,159
Roanoke (Va.) area........	113	130,719	1,251	129	984	972	117,634	68.6	1,291
New Britain-Bristol (Conn.) area..............	114	127,720	1,862	116	873	1,423	103,030	74.9	941
Sioux City (Iowa) area.....	115	125,931	1,293	146	1,211	1,028	113,912	80.8	1,356
Lincoln (Nebr.) area.......	116	124,734	1,091	137	1,055	912	117,984	82.4	1,211
Kalamazoo (Mich.) area...	117	122,824	1,249	133	975	810	99,806	45.5	1,741
Savannah (Ga.) area.......	118	120,765	2,030	113	800	1,657	109,693	79.3	916
Columbia (S. C.) area.....	119	120,446	1,471	119	849	1,110	111,000	60.6	1,291
New Bedford (Mass.) area.	120	120,216	1,884	123	875	1,627	107,657	79.4	987
Cedar Rapids (Iowa) area.	121	118,353	1,097	147	1,141	768	100,311	69.6	1,390
Fall River (Mass.) area....	122	117,211	1,813	124	856	1,518	105,148	81.6	941
Muskegon (Mich.) area.....	123	116,628	1,382	(4)	966	755	75,075	39.8	1,563
Galveston (Tex.) area......	124	116,620	1,524	139	1,039	993	82,697	58.7	1,255
Lawrence (Mass.) area.....	125	115,662	1,769	134	921	1,367	93,316	64.1	1,160
Brockton (Mass.) area....	126	115,163	1,530	131	891	824	71,171	48.6	1,132
Racine (Wis.) area........	127	114,884	1,450	141	1,053	965	87,328	64.8	1,234
Waco (Tex.) area..........	128	114,536	1,659	132	891	1,139	97,634	65.6	1,158
Charleston (S. C.) area...	129	113,208	1,834	107	708	1,107	88,153	42.7	1,292
Altoona (Pa.) area.........	130	113,101	1,628	121	814	928	78,430	55.3	1,021
Jackson (Miss.) area.......	131	112,765	1,273	120	797	848	100,585	69.0	1,030
Montgomery (Ala.) area...	132	109,527	1,261	122	796	1,006	103,401	76.4	984
Augusta (Ga.) area........	133	106,896	1,760	105	659	1,040	83,111	44.1	1,162
Columbus (Ga.) area......	134	106,607	1,644	101	627	1,133	92,338	46.8	1,161
Springfield (Ohio) area....	135	105,634	1,168	140	952	940	93,817	70.3	1,202
Decatur (Ill.) area.........	136	105,627	1,064	150	1,053	797	92,412	67.6	1,363
Terre Haute (Ind.) area...	137	104,944	1,376	143	1,000	1,052	94,666	61.0	1,478
Lowell (Mass.) area........	138	104,640	1,464	128	788	1,201	92,920	72.7	963
Raleigh (N. C.) area.......	139	104,098	1,382	125	766	740	82,157	47.9	1,262
Springfield (Mo.) area.....	140	99,815	1,381	145	959	1,006	85,587	63.7	1,291
Topeka (Kans.) area.......	141	99,627	1,196	144	954	993	92,014	74.5	1,182
Macon (Ga.) area.........	142	97,239	1,313	126	723	911	83,441	52.1	1,190
Winston-Salem (N. C.) area.....................	143	97,003	1,319	118	669	953	86,978	59.8	1,002
Asheville (N. C.) area.....	144	91,799	1,261	135	749	813	79,435	42.6	1,522
Durham (N. C.) area......	145	90,125	995	148	896	797	85,366	69.9	1,214
St. Joseph (Mo.) area......	146	89,798	1,186	156	959	984	81,508	80.7	1,079
Manchester (N. H.) area...	147	89,497	1,052	159	1,015	998	86,977	93.6	1,053

[1] Central cities are those named in title of metropolitan area, with exception of New York-Northeastern New Jersey which includes New York, Newark, and Jersey City.
[2] Based on advance 1950 population estimates.
[3] Per capita sales is ratio of 1948 sales to advance 1950 population estimates.
[4] Not included in ranking of metropolitan areas by 1950 Census of Population.

Source: Department of Commerce, Bureau of Census; U. S. Census of Business: 1948, Vol. III.

No. 1022.—RETAIL SALES OF CHAIN STORES AND MAIL-ORDER HOUSES, BY KIND OF BUSINESS: 1929 TO 1952

[Millions of dollars]

KIND OF BUSINESS	1929	1935	1939	1945	1948	1950	1951	NEW SERIES [1]	
								1951	1952
Total sales	10,412	5,040	9,870	17,230	29,727	31,222	34,000	29,536	30,130
Durable goods stores	1,583	813	1,024	1,027	3,497	3,843	3,525	2,521	2,605
Automotive group	745	356	372	391	741	989	984		
Motor vehicle, other automotive dealers	594	198	130	96	257	409	390		
Tire, battery, accessory dealers	152	157	204	285	454	541	575	363	
Furniture and appliance group	392	163	230	329	1,027	1,214	1,141	879	917
Furniture, home furnishings stores	235	97	151	277	553	646	666	357	
Household appliance, radio stores	157	66	80	112	468	534	438	66	70
Jewelry stores	35	23	33	108	154	136	135		
Lumber, building, hardware group [2]	500	274	372	739	1,806	1,851	1,692	1,306	1,355
Lumber, building materials dealers	422	256	336	695	1,107	1,142	1,147	796	
Nondurable goods stores	8,729	7,227	8,846	16,653	24,380	27,340	30,178	26,615	27,140
Apparel group	1,197	758	899	2,090	2,728	2,398	2,705	3,009	3,065
Men's and boys' wear stores	371	241	175	252	286	320	342	315	
Women's apparel, accessory stores	415	256	304	695	1,117	1,049	1,127	700	
Family and other apparel stores	146	78	60	339	648	613	469	526	
Shoe stores	365	270	346	621	695	695	745	729	797
Drug and proprietary stores	312	317	400	704	800	852	905	722	
Eating and drinking places	385	246	304	483	743	736	770		
Food group [2]	3,476	2,916	3,340	5,614	10,480	11,344	12,906	11,585	13,324
Grocery stores	2,963	2,468	2,896	4,705	9,316	10,140	11,060	10,712	11,566
Gasoline service stations	696	435	532	395	271	470	446	478	174
General merchandise group	2,272	2,134	2,334	3,603	5,375	5,760	6,149	2,520	6,002
Department stores, excluding mail order	1,016	666	1,720	2,085	5,375	5,760	6,149	2,520	2,002
Mail order (catalog sales)	447	386	404	603	1,201	1,384	1,284	1,280	1,364
Variety stores	818	802	982	1,840	2,077	2,142	2,229	2,322	2,322
Other general merchandise stores		39	51	128	179	179	191	1,302	1,225
Other retail stores	566	441	535	1,463	2,037	2,013	2,348	1,603	2,144

[1] Based on sales of organizations operating 11 or more retail stores in same kind of business; data for prior years represented sales of organizations with 4 or more retail stores. See *Survey of Current Business*, Sept. 1953.
[2] Not available. [3] Group total includes other related business not separately shown.

Source: Department of Commerce, Office of Business Economics and Bureau of the Census; published currently in *Survey of Current Business*.

No. 1023.—SALES OF FIRMS WITH 11 OR MORE RETAIL STORES, BY SELECTED KIND OF BUSINESS, AND BY MONTHS: 1951 AND 1952

[Millions of dollars. Figures are seasonally adjusted]

MONTH	TOTAL [1]		APPAREL STORES		DRUG AND PROPRIETARY STORES		EATING AND DRINKING PLACES		FOOD STORES		GENERAL MERCHANDISE STORES AND MAIL ORDER	
	1951	1952	1951	1952	1951	1952	1951	1952	1951	1952	1951	1952
Annual sales	29,536	30,130	2,609	2,065	722	797	800	632	11,785	12,594	5,575	6,798
January	2,409	2,420	175	170	60	61	44	50	967	1,010	516	567
February	2,371	2,421	166	164	61	63	48	46	955	958	734	738
March	2,315	2,356	161	157	61	60	47	47	973	1,013	557	555
April	2,317	2,446	140	176	59	60	47	51	975	1,013	557	774
May	2,395	2,476	162	164	62	62	50	51	975	1,015	557	746
June	2,340	2,469	162	159	60	62	50	50	955	1,040	557	798
July	2,390	2,529	169	177	60	60	50	44	967	1,068	667	739
August	2,420	2,502	172	174	60	60	50	50	1,005	1,068	734	737
September	2,351	2,516	165	165	61	60	47	50	955	1,050	557	719
October	2,430	2,502	167	164	60	61	47	50	1,005	1,050	557	748
November	2,432	2,502	170	170	61	60	50	50	1,005	1,050	734	759
December	2,430	2,502	169	177	60	60	50	48	1,005	1,050	734	817

[1] Includes businesses not shown separately.

Source: Department of Commerce, Office of Business Economics and Bureau of the Census; published currently in *Survey of Current Business*.

245354°—53——56

No. 1024.—DEPARTMENT STORE SALES AND STOCKS—INDEXES, BY FEDERAL RESERVE DISTRICT: 1919 TO 1952

[1947-49 average=100. Based on retail value figures. Monthly data adjusted for seasonal variation]

YEAR OR MONTH	United States	FEDERAL RESERVE DISTRICT											
		Boston	New York	Philadelphia	Cleveland	Richmond	Atlanta	Chicago	St. Louis	Minneapolis	Kansas City	Dallas	San Francisco
SALES													
1919	27	37	34	40	27	21	20	---	---	37	---	21	18
1920	32	42	41	47	34	23	24	---	---	42	---	26	22
1925	36	48	47	50	35	26	22	35	36	41	38	23	26
1930	35	47	51	44	34	26	22	33	33	35	34	22	28
1935	29	35	36	34	28	25	19	30	25	30	27	19	24
1940	37	42	43	41	38	34	29	40	35	36	34	27	33
1942	50	56	52	53	51	51	39	52	48	44	46	37	49
1943	55	60	55	58	56	58	50	57	54	51	57	50	59
1944	62	66	61	62	61	65	61	62	61	57	64	58	65
1945	70	72	70	68	68	72	70	68	70	66	72	66	72
1946	90	92	91	87	88	92	90	89	90	88	90	85	91
1947	98	99	99	98	97	97	96	98	97	98	98	94	99
1948	104	102	103	104	105	103	103	104	104	104	103	105	104
1949	98	99	98	100	98	100	101	97	98	90	99	102	98
1950	105	103	101	105	105	105	109	104	104	105	108	113	105
1951	109	105	105	109	111	113	115	108	105	104	111	117	109
1952	110	104	99	109	110	116	124	106	106	104	113	124	114
January	109	102	99	110	116	116	119	105	111	97	115	122	106
February	106	100	100	110	108	112	112	104	100	113	106	115	108
March	105	104	98	109	106	114	114	103	99	94	105	115	102
April	103	99	96	102	104	108	116	100	98	98	104	114	105
May	108	101	96	107	103	116	127	104	102	104	112	128	118
June	111	103	96	107	112	122	138	105	111	100	114	132	114
July	105	106	95	106	105	106	120	97	99	104	114	123	110
August	114	109	102	115	113	127	131	111	110	115	119	127	116
September	106	101	95	105	105	112	121	103	104	98	108	119	114
October	115	109	105	114	116	120	126	113	114	110	113	128	118
November	113	105	98	109	113	115	128	108	106	107	117	129	125
December	115	106	101	111	117	121	130	116	113	110	119	130	119
STOCKS													
1919	37	53	44	---	37	---	29	---	---	48	---	34	27
1920	48	62	60	---	51	---	38	---	---	59	---	46	35
1925	48	64	58	76	50	35	33	43	55	56	59	40	36
1930	44	56	58	58	45	32	30	44	46	41	52	29	36
1935	31	43	40	40	31	26	22	30	33	32	32	23	26
1940	38	47	44	42	39	33	29	38	39	39	36	29	34
1942	63	75	78	70	68	58	47	64	63	59	55	42	57
1943	55	65	62	60	54	54	44	55	54	52	53	42	53
1944	58	68	65	62	57	59	51	55	56	58	55	48	54
1945	59	71	69	64	59	62	53	55	58	57	56	52	56
1946	77	85	85	81	78	80	75	73	77	74	74	69	73
1947	93	95	98	93	93	94	90	89	93	91	89	89	93
1948	107	105	105	107	107	105	108	111	106	110	108	110	107
1949	100	100	97	99	100	101	102	100	100	100	100	101	100
1950	109	110	104	108	106	114	120	110	112	104	113	112	110
1951	129	124	124	127	128	133	140	128	131	117	132	132	131
1952	118	110	110	113	111	132	130	115	122	107	124	126	125
January	118	115	113	116	116	126	133	114	106	106	122	124	121
February	115	112	106	113	110	125	129	113	112	102	122	122	123
March	115	109	108	113	110	127	126	113	111	103	120	124	119
April	116	111	111	112	111	126	125	114	114	104	121	122	123
May	118	109	112	114	109	131	126	114	124	106	124	124	128
June	118	110	113	113	107	139	125	113	125	105	122	123	128
July	120	110	116	114	113	140	129	118	120	108	128	130	125
August	118	109	111	112	109	136	129	115	129	109	127	127	123
September	120	109	110	113	112	132	130	118	132	113	129	131	126
October	120	109	110	114	111	130	133	118	130	113	124	129	134
November	120	111	111	113	113	132	136	118	130	111	124	130	127
December	119	110	111	114	112	132	142	114	128	107	123	130	126

Source: Board of Governors of the Federal Reserve System; *Federal Reserve Bulletin.*

No. 1025.—Estimated Membership and Business of Consumers' Cooperatives, by Type of Association: 1950

TYPE OF ASSOCIATION	Total number of associations	Number of members (1,000)	Amount of business ($1,000)	TYPE OF ASSOCIATION	Total number of associations	Number of members (1,000)	Amount of business ($1,000)
LOCAL ASSOCIATIONS				**LOCAL ASSOCIATIONS—con.**			
Retail distributive	3,215	2,642	1,263,300	Electric light and power [6]	905	[7] 3,250	219,000
Stores and buying clubs	1,800	1,575	825,000	Telephone (mutual and co-op.)	22,000	620	10,000
Petroleum associations	1,340	1,085	420,000	Credit unions [9]	10,950	4,600	305,000
Other [1]	85	48	18,500	Insurance associations [10]	2,600	11,780	210,000
Service	779	364	41,351				
Rooms and/or meals	175	19	7,875				
Housing	175	26	10,730			**Member-ships in unions**	
Medical and/or hospital care:				**FEDERATIONS [12]**			
On contract	25	85	800	Wholesale:			
Own facilities	66	177	12,460	Interregional	2	77	10,160
Burial: [3]				Regional	30	4,702	430,320
Complete funeral	28	28	200	District	12	1,220	7,000
Caskets only	3	1	8	Service	12	1,120	2,400
Burial on contract	8	8	77	Productive	11	400	82,000
Cold storage [4]	165	85	6,349	Electric light and power [6]	15	160	11,000
Other [5]	135	18	2,380				

[1] Such as consumers' dairies, creameries, bakeries, fuel yards, lumber yards, etc. [2] Gross income.
[3] Local associations only; excludes associations of fraternal type (included with service associations) and funeral departments of store associations. [4] Excludes cold-storage departments of other types of associations.
[5] Such as water supply, cleaning and dyeing, recreation, printing and publishing, nursery schools, etc.
[6] Data furnished by Rural Electrification Administration. [7] Number of patrons.
[8] Actual figures, not estimates. Includes, for first time, data on credit unions in Puerto Rico.
[9] Number of policyholders. [10] Premium income. [11] Includes an allowance for nonreporting associations.
[12] Includes wholesale distributive, retail distributive, and service business.

Source: Department of Labor, Bureau of Labor Statistics; published in *Monthly Labor Review*.

No. 1026.—Department Store Merchandising Data: 1939 to 1952

[These figures are not estimates for all department stores in the United States. Figures for sales, stocks, and outstanding orders are based on actual reports from 226 stores. Receipts of goods are derived from reported figures on sales and stocks. New orders are derived from receipts and reported figures on outstanding orders]

PERIOD	REPORTED DATA (millions of dollars) [1]			DERIVED DATA (millions of dollars) [1]		RATIOS				
	Sales (total for month)	Stocks (end of month)	Outstanding orders (end of month)	Receipts (total for month)	New orders (total for month)	Stocks to sales	Outstanding orders to sales	Outstanding orders to stocks	Stocks plus outstanding orders to sales	Receipts to sales
Monthly average:										
1939	130	388	[2]	141	[2]	2.8	[2]	[2]	[2]	1.0
1940	147	370	115	145	134	2.7	0.8	0.3	2.6	1.0
1941	169	450	205	179	194	2.8	1.3	.5	4.0	1.1
1942	194	643	280	197	208	3.5	1.8	.4	5.1	1.1
1943	221	548	288	220	269	2.6	2.7	1.0	5.3	1.0
1944	246	574	295	244	298	2.4	2.5	1.0	5.0	1.0
1945	278	604	775	277	271	2.3	3.0	1.3	5.3	1.0
1946	348	707	804	372	384	2.3	3.0	1.3	5.3	1.1
1947	362	827	671	366	383	2.4	1.7	.7	4.2	1.0
1948	361	858	460	355	355	2.4	1.4	.4	3.8	1.0
1949	353	808	401	357	348	2.3	1.1	.4	3.4	1.0
1950	378	1,013	461	371	380	2.5	1.3	.4	3.8	1.0
1951	391	1,059	462	383	382	2.8	1.3	.4	4.0	1.0
1952	385	1,063	438	385	372	2.9	1.2	.4	4.1	1.0

[1] Not adjusted for seasonal variation. [2] Not available.

Source: Board of Governors of the Federal Reserve System. *Federal Reserve Bulletin*.

No. 1027.—SELECTED SERVICES—SUMMARY, BY KIND OF BUSINESS: 1939 AND 1948

[Covers establishments primarily engaged in providing personal, business and repair services, amusement or entertainment, and accommodations in hotels and tourist courts. 1939 figures adjusted to secure comparability with 1948]

KIND OF BUSINESS	ESTABLISHMENTS		RECEIPTS, ENTIRE YEAR		PAYROLL, ENTIRE YEAR		PAID EMPLOYEES AND PAYROLL, WORKWEEK ENDED NEAREST NOV. 15			UNINCORPORATED BUSINESSES			
							Employees		Payroll, 1948	Active proprietors		Unpaid family workers, Nov. 1948	
	1939	1948	1939	1948	1939	1948	1939	1948		1939	Nov. 1948	1939	Nov. 1948
	Number	Number	$1,000	$1,000	$1,000	$1,000	Number	Number	Dollars	Number	Number	Number	Number
SELECTED SERVICES													
Personal, business, and repair services	570,057	559,559	2,973,593	8,578,162	911,248	2,971,214	924,271	1,342,496	56,828,496	579,633	571,610	123,467	
Amusements [1]	44,917	91,903	908,079	2,349,601	225,481	596,012	91,903	64,509	2,357,296	124,596	68,970	3,783	
Hotels	50,347	74,497	863,155	2,172,756	243,228	660,804	330,216	398,293	11,451,185	33,971	75,111	17,488	
Tourist courts and camps	27,987	29,650	36,722	195,605	4,226	22,804	6,938	16,973	621,809	13,365	27,715	18,916	
	13,521	25,919										24,397	
PERSONAL, BUSINESS, AND REPAIR SERVICES													
Personal services, total	389,726	351,985	1,521,584	4,440,189	571,610	1,862,832	653,072	861,024	31,357,304	398,721	360,548	77,117	
Barber, beauty shops	205,268	169,081	481,271	844,968	137,374	275,862	184,742	157,164	5,688,684	214,896	174,099	19,949	
Barber shops	117,998	91,903	230,983	404,441	85,557	196,012	70,783	64,509	2,357,296	124,596	68,970	3,783	
Beauty shops	83,071	74,497	231,670	417,570	74,496	143,274	104,501	87,290	2,907,787	85,419	75,111	6,245	
Barber and beauty shops combined	4,199	2,591	18,618	22,987	7,321	9,666	9,458	6,365	193,691	4,821	2,973	861	
Cleaning, dyeing plants	12,616	25,534	193,316	844,357	83,682	390,434	87,421	210,026	7,972,704	12,704	36,145	12,759	
Cleaning, dyeing plants (ex. rug cleaning)	11,604	24,017	182,698	807,673	80,014	385,155	83,970	203,867	7,688,985	11,845	35,601	12,128	
Rug cleaning, repairing plants	1,012	1,517	10,618	36,684	3,948	14,279	3,451	6,159	283,719	949	1,547	631	
Funeral service, crematories	18,196	18,675	261,617	572,335	40,676	90,010	33,122	40,726	1,780,831	18,239	18,792	10,183	
Laundries, laundry services	22,736	19,182	527,733	1,257,867	259,052	620,550	266,528	339,728	11,699,671	13,018	18,674	10,966	
Power laundries (exc. power laundries of linen supply and diaper services)	17,491	6,781	481,970	913,036	241,647	501,646	254,618	272,496	9,604,700	8,520	8,560	1,705	
Linen supply service	(²)	1,176	(²)	238,203	(²)	91,101	(²)	39,877	1,731,983	(²)	675	106	
Diaper service	(²)	384	(²)	25,687	(²)	10,061	(²)	4,685	194,973	(²)	333	106	
Laundries (exc. power)	15,245	10,859	45,783	80,861	7,515	17,781	12,010	12,671	365,436	17,498	12,097	4,019	
Photographic studios (inc. commercial photography)	10,957	14,712	64,185	212,025	15,660	57,670	16,045	27,609	1,206,853	10,417	14,410	5,313	
Photographic studios (exc. commercial photography)	(²)	11,549	(²)	147,118	(²)	35,993	(²)	19,756	779,297	(²)	11,227	4,384	
Commercial photography	(²)	3,163	(²)	64,907	(²)	21,877	(²)	7,853	427,556	(²)	3,183	929	
Pressing, alteration, garment repair shops	54,696	47,888	151,254	395,661	23,772	67,704	35,024	41,893	1,459,966	54,664	49,783	19,054	
Fur repair and storage shops	52,516	45,554	140,578	320,148	21,478	59,197	31,665	37,488	1,344,842	52,898	47,401	18,254	
Shoe-repair shops, shoeshine parlors, hat cleaning	2,180	2,334	12,676	45,513	2,294	8,507	3,369	4,405	214,854	2,106	2,382	760	
	59,371	44,151	119,321	218,800	15,497	36,409	23,447	22,900	736,367	59,125	44,263	7,988	
Shoe-repair shops	50,115	39,763	106,737	202,176	13,340	32,711	18,929	19,191	659,836	49,646	39,701	7,008	
Shoeshine parlors	7,908	2,902	8,210	6,668	1,133	1,166	2,961	1,690	24,605	8,064	3,020	435	

No. 1027.—SELECTED SERVICES—SUMMARY, BY KIND OF BUSINESS: 1939 AND 1948—Continued

KIND OF BUSINESS	ESTABLISHMENTS		RECEIPTS, ENTIRE YEAR		PAYROLL, ENTIRE YEAR		PAID EMPLOYEES AND PAYROLL, WORKWEEK ENDED NEAREST NOV. 15			UNINCORPORATED BUSINESSES		
							Employees		Payroll, 1948 [2]	Active proprietors		Unpaid family workers, Nov. 1948
	1939	1948	1939 [1]	1948	1939	1948 [2]	1939	1948 [2]		1939	Nov. 1948	
	Number	Number	$1,000	$1,000	$1,000	$1,000	Number	Number	Dollars	Number	Number	Number
PERSONAL, BUSINESS, AND REPAIR SERVICES—con.												
Automobile repair services and garages—Con.												
Automobile storage, parking	11,065	8,553	102,070	190,347	25,320	55,990	25,320	25,618	1,122,452	8,126	5,628	1,134
Storage garages	4,821	2,606	70,315	114,796	18,193	35,729	16,608	14,294	702,803	3,844	3,918	319
Parking lots	6,274	5,927	31,755	74,868	4,961	20,261	8,812	11,324	419,649	4,282	3,910	816
Automobile services (exc. repair)	(5)	1,125		14,809		6,119	1,057	3,880	144,557	987	1,061	191
Automobile laundries	960	792	2,941	10,375	889	4,046	1,057	3,880	116,252	(5)	763	111
Automobile services, n. e. c.	(5)	333		4,434	(5)	1,404	618		28,305		326	90
Miscellaneous repair services, total	75,262	86,023	224,266	947,351	42,660	232,668	43,294	94,914	4,727,446	76,947	84,275	19,184
Blacksmith shops	10,797	8,249	22,567	44,411	2,627	7,466	3,149	3,550	144,552	17,266	8,963	1,236
Electrical repair shops	15,644	19,440	47,835	214,796	2,638	46,631	7,961	21,100	1,025,197	16,143	20,131	5,443
Radio repair shops	10,732	12,558	21,687	100,679	2,094	30,701	2,842	10,262	500,643	11,000	12,933	3,211
Refrigerator-service and repair shops	1,297	2,581	9,222	45,507	2,538	9,598	1,884	4,919	184,390	1,410	2,738	189
Other electrical repair shops	3,615	4,351	16,926	68,610	3,466	16,692	3,235	4,919	194,144	3,733	4,463	386
Upholstery, furniture repair shops	12,685	10,297	35,005	129,375	4,915	30,167	7,740	13,666	665,514	12,261	11,346	3,180
Watch, clock, jewelry repair shops	20,631	12,250	29,902	86,401	2,946	13,464	2,977	6,314	288,376	12,690	13,033	2,534
Miscellaneous repair shops	976	29,287	88,906	475,268	22,384	134,380	30,489	60,104	2,688,370	2,748	30,962	6,466
Armature rewinding shops	1,601	2,023	12,873	60,472	3,783	17,749	4,163	6,468	338,920	1,623	2,224	450
Bicycle repair shops	1,601	1,283	3,433	7,390	307	649	484	446	11,049	1,021	1,300	331
Leather goods repair shops	2,168	560	3,809	3,617	249	694	346	240	14,100	2,178	676	199
Locksmith, gunsmith shops	2,252	1,518	5,261	11,529	722	1,815	734	863	33,634	2,346	1,683	364
Musical instrument repair shops	982	789	1,946	5,534	251	1,186	233	598	24,579	1,012	629	173
Repair shops, n. e. c.	12,670	23,114	61,482	386,826	17,042	112,335	15,894	41,460	2,333,203	12,655	24,420	5,029
Lawn mower sharpening and repair shops [10]												
Saw, knife, and tool sharpening and repair shops	(5)	774	(5)	2,385	(5)	200	119	968	3,383	(5)	805	145
Sewing machine repair shops	1,451	1,304	3,875	9,801	882	2,462	706	968	49,445	1,501	1,332	220
Stove repair shops	355	488	1,058	3,961	136	395	126	196	8,136	361	681	162
Taxidermists	365	207	977	2,692	173	573	242	243	11,947	380	225	89
Typewriter repair shops	363	211	853	1,670	197	453	201	191	7,420	364	220	71
Welding shops	618	638	2,322	7,618	423	1,661	446	770	33,068	643	138	(5)
Other repair shops, n. e. c.	(5)	3,636	(5)	7,614	(5)	1,661		3,444	178,997		2,333	696
	(5) 9,518	15,966	(5) 62,397	322,043	(5) 16,231	97,838	(5) 14,190	38,560	1,941,527	(5) 9,407	14,765	3,665

[1] Include Federal, State, and local amusement, sales, and excise taxes collected directly from customer and paid directly to taxing agency.

[2] Includes paid executives of corporations but not proprietors of unincorporated businesses.

[3] Includes motion picture theaters.

[4] Not available.

[5] Percent; laundries include industrial laundries, linen supply and diaper service.

[6] Includes self-service laundries and electrolysis establishments.

[7] Includes miscellaneous advertising service, news syndicates, miscellaneous service to dwellings, etc., and telephone-answering service.

[8] Includes glass-replacement and repair shops and automobile services, n. e. c.

[9] Included in custom industries with custom welders in 1939.

[10] Includes lawn-mower-sharpening and repair shops.

Source: Department of Commerce, Bureau of the Census; U. S. Census o J Business: 1948, Vol. VII.

No. 1028.—Personal, Business, and Repair Services—Summary, by States: 1948

[For kinds of personal, business, and repair services covered, see table 1027]

DIVISION AND STATE	Establishments	Receipts, entire year	Payroll, entire year	UNINCORPORATED BUSINESSES		PAID EMPLOYEES, WORKWEEK ENDED NEAREST NOV. 15 [1]		PAYROLL, WORKWEEK ENDED NEAREST NOV. 15 [1]	
				Active proprietors, November	Unpaid family workers, November	Total	Full workweek	Total	Full workweek
	Number	$1,000	$1,000	Number	Number	Number	Number	Dollars	Dollars
United States	589,559	8,578,162	2,871,214	574,616	120,407	1,342,496	1,196,415	51,628,496	54,264,092
New England	38,789	597,272	188,281	28,210	6,247	73,190	69,324	3,971,632	
Maine	3,129	30,016	8,340	2,077	549	3,673	4,121	115,326	
New Hampshire	2,167	22,155	5,880	2,210	410	3,300	1,843		
Vermont	1,420	11,724	2,833	1,428	229	1,698	1,484	34,819	
Massachusetts	19,886	280,002	97,352	19,392	3,574	45,294	39,675	1,762,033	
Rhode Island	3,771	45,107	18,966	3,740	672	8,556	8,086	266,137	
Connecticut	8,330	117,069	36,584	8,370	1,312	17,359	15,114	715,161	
Middle Atlantic	141,635	2,195,360	838,066	144,817	27,621	346,064	311,121	16,499,694	
New York	77,310	1,341,959	570,360	78,210	19,720	217,725	196,419	11,278,103	
New Jersey	21,249	313,030	90,540	22,595	5,215	45,669	40,974	1,985,224	
Pennsylvania	42,379	540,371	162,136	43,912	8,750	82,670	78,731	3,232,207	
East North Central	110,129	1,848,908	638,455	112,836	23,128	278,281	242,187	12,673,262	
Ohio	28,060	437,447	143,680	29,310	6,016	67,452	59,149	2,867,582	
Indiana	13,640	184,266	57,387	14,192	2,740	29,207	25,730	1,147,394	
Illinois	35,218	709,562	259,050	36,155	7,775	101,513	89,955	5,070,273	
Michigan	21,370	367,266	130,292	22,230	4,552	55,572	45,313	2,589,401	
Wisconsin	10,935	153,262	41,432	10,963	2,207	22,335	16,037	597,406	
West North Central	53,682	652,463	189,845	55,865	10,532	98,282	85,905	3,738,712	
Minnesota	10,104	134,571	46,767	10,503	1,706	19,521	16,827	824,667	
Iowa	9,881	108,409	29,083	10,327	1,863	14,766	13,606		
Missouri	16,243	235,513	74,672	16,055	3,154	37,463	33,074	1,498,980	
North Dakota	1,958	21,016	4,982	2,130	460	2,312	1,966		
South Dakota	2,667	19,831	4,743	2,786	419	2,730	2,328		
Nebraska	3,987	63,634	16,143	3,859	1,017	9,040	7,862		
Kansas	8,611	63,716	22,042	8,514	1,963	12,446	11,018	444,910	
South Atlantic	58,652	879,008	305,536	58,832	12,741	178,347	160,838	8,996,154	
Delaware	1,192	15,409	4,794	1,190	257	2,521	2,307	96,677	
Maryland	7,910	121,055	40,056	7,867	1,919	20,559	18,335	791,004	
District of Columbia	3,480	88,430	34,353	3,014	719	16,267	14,570		
Virginia	7,944	120,811	41,706	7,914	1,497	25,015	22,620		
West Virginia	4,476	59,306	19,541	4,443	637	10,836	9,880	401,287	
North Carolina	9,677	122,426	43,646	9,873	2,121	30,081	27,640	933,500	
South Carolina	4,674	58,062	19,458	4,538	1,080	15,922	12,884	392,840	
Georgia	9,121	130,969	85,597	9,148	1,994	28,450	35,412	907,940	
Florida	10,354	155,306	52,379	10,335	2,704	28,440	36,340	1,043,825	
East South Central	26,349	351,764	116,122	27,208	6,562	74,854	65,465	2,148,022	
Kentucky	6,600	98,229	28,560	7,221	1,484	16,834	15,081		
Tennessee	7,900	123,477	43,655	8,134	1,962	20,189	18,087	916,169	
Alabama	6,082	82,798	31,037	7,095	1,780	20,963	18,940	918,830	
Mississippi	4,001	47,258	12,472	4,717	1,314	10,195	9,050	308,841	
West South Central	50,923	634,099	196,932	52,307	14,688	115,695	105,396	4,036,649	
Arkansas	3,882	40,865	14,965	5,480	1,310	10,734	9,564		
Louisiana	6,682	90,866	35,302	6,488	1,865	18,470	17,002		
Oklahoma	8,201	101,379	24,368	8,880	2,609	16,851	14,990		
Texas	28,981	392,804	124,247	30,624	9,000	70,520	63,839	2,527,417	
Mountain	17,946	233,328	78,032	17,998	4,148	36,178	31,965	1,491,833	
Montana	1,961	21,833	6,231	2,172	369	3,229	2,845		
Idaho	1,890	22,090	6,121	2,010	431	3,164	2,815		
Wyoming	923	13,364	3,690	999	264	1,800	1,600	79,734	
Colorado	5,117	72,763	22,879	5,098	1,265	10,491	454,013		
New Mexico	1,847	24,661	7,318	2,010	637	4,147	148,062		
Arizona	3,030	34,813	10,850	2,845	735	6,425	4,676	215,970	
Utah	2,332	31,111	9,300	2,334	729	4,710	3,968	185,131	
Nevada	946	11,122	3,672	681	100	1,505	1,472	74,481	
Pacific	62,328	1,072,837	353,047	65,596	14,227	123,497	123,526	7,013,699	
Washington	8,787	134,550	46,127	9,172	1,611	17,603	15,363	666,037	
Oregon	5,468	96,723	29,972	6,259	1,265	12,195	11,318	465,176	
California	47,073	841,564	276,948	49,765	11,351	93,699	96,845	5,882,486	

[1] Includes paid executives of corporations but not proprietors of unincorporated businesses.

Source: Department of Commerce, Bureau of the Census; U. S. Census of Business: 1948, Vol. VII.

No. 1029.—PERSONAL SERVICES—SUMMARY, BY STATES: 1948

DIVISION AND STATE	Establishments	Receipts, entire year	Payroll, entire year	UNINCORPORATED BUSINESSES		PAID EMPLOYEES, WORKWEEK ENDED NEAREST NOV. 15		PAYROLL, WORKWEEK ENDED NEAREST NOV. 15	
				Active proprietors, November	Unpaid family workers, November	Total	Full workweek	Total	Full workweek
	Number	$1,000	$1,000	Number	Number	Number	Number	Dollars	Dollars
United States	351,985	4,440,189	1,582,532	360,568	77,317	851,024	765,494	31,357,304	29,929,790
New England	26,171	288,013	99,158	25,839	4,095	53,307	47,070	1,910,442	1,808,129
Maine	1,925	16,838	5,494	1,580	207	3,208	2,533	102,306	96,554
New Hampshire	1,393	12,763	3,982	1,417	245	2,381	2,073	76,261	71,880
Vermont	817	6,643	1,978	800	104	1,240	1,092	37,753	35,575
Massachusetts	13,858	157,295	55,303	13,588	2,118	30,187	26,710	1,074,178	1,017,902
Rhode Island	2,623	26,916	9,081	2,599	478	4,609	4,120	171,115	162,879
Connecticut	5,555	67,558	23,230	5,555	853	11,682	10,242	448,829	423,339
Middle Atlantic	95,607	1,145,053	383,365	98,011	19,447	190,734	170,809	7,625,679	7,266,312
New York	51,485	662,940	228,060	52,827	9,822	107,324	96,328	4,542,103	4,332,508
New Jersey	15,283	184,983	63,039	15,460	3,653	30,982	27,523	1,244,169	1,180,044
Pennsylvania	28,839	297,130	92,266	29,724	5,972	52,428	46,958	1,839,407	1,753,760
East North Central	71,015	982,265	345,575	73,096	15,237	170,382	151,411	6,830,527	6,505,632
Ohio	18,605	242,442	84,006	18,807	3,932	43,318	38,669	1,651,237	1,578,874
Indiana	8,452	110,461	38,159	8,881	1,653	20,794	18,587	766,233	731,140
Illinois	23,624	354,661	127,440	24,425	5,412	58,896	52,642	2,515,046	2,400,615
Michigan	13,777	191,790	68,219	14,341	2,990	32,699	28,779	1,358,457	1,284,437
Wisconsin	6,557	82,911	27,751	6,552	1,250	14,675	12,734	539,552	510,567
West North Central	30,847	334,300	111,014	31,856	6,679	63,314	56,393	2,217,207	2,106,869
Minnesota	5,790	68,703	23,926	5,903	955	12,187	10,859	484,996	461,680
Iowa	5,673	57,460	17,189	5,950	1,032	9,552	8,412	341,975	325,752
Missouri	9,809	115,809	41,353	10,030	1,965	23,862	21,405	811,645	770,270
North Dakota	1,080	9,478	2,479	1,129	192	1,695	1,457	54,973	51,286
South Dakota	1,138	10,837	3,275	1,140	280	1,932	1,670	64,364	60,048
Nebraska	2,925	30,119	9,407	3,060	545	5,648	5,018	187,357	178,410
Kansas	4,432	41,804	13,385	4,644	1,110	8,438	7,572	271,897	259,444
South Atlantic	37,101	519,944	205,080	36,837	8,055	130,006	119,067	4,049,935	3,896,172
Delaware	799	9,990	2,960	788	191	1,722	1,592	57,848	56,208
Maryland	5,269	67,250	25,328	5,295	913	14,194	12,883	491,611	470,558
District of Columbia	2,489	52,243	22,468	2,442	526	11,061	10,087	434,076	416,689
Virginia	5,054	75,563	30,022	4,958	887	19,245	17,399	591,177	566,541
West Virginia	3,008	37,390	13,593	2,954	604	8,073	7,366	270,607	259,105
North Carolina	6,051	54,136	34,197	6,120	1,323	24,075	22,219	694,013	670,068
South Carolina	2,844	37,040	14,425	2,779	715	11,025	10,070	286,212	274,876
Georgia	5,500	72,584	29,221	5,458	1,318	20,805	19,100	588,952	567,730
Florida	6,087	84,748	32,864	6,043	1,578	19,806	18,351	635,439	614,057
East South Central	16,289	212,857	81,624	16,783	4,168	56,875	52,209	1,619,721	1,562,508
Kentucky	4,243	57,191	20,241	4,556	917	12,592	11,424	400,266	384,056
Tennessee	4,869	74,020	29,145	5,029	1,206	19,517	18,218	577,722	562,497
Alabama	4,244	51,699	20,906	4,211	1,118	15,637	14,372	417,272	401,712
Mississippi	2,933	29,947	11,332	2,987	927	9,129	8,195	224,461	214,243
West South Central	29,820	331,485	123,172	30,627	9,383	80,734	73,728	2,484,680	2,386,286
Arkansas	3,182	33,121	11,010	3,256	854	7,913	7,338	222,961	216,004
Louisiana	4,159	46,551	17,950	4,190	1,113	12,492	11,608	358,425	345,430
Oklahoma	5,390	50,703	17,674	5,703	1,700	11,236	10,235	356,781	343,045
Texas	17,089	203,110	76,538	17,478	5,716	49,093	44,547	1,546,513	1,481,807
Mountain	9,689	125,406	45,408	10,183	2,569	25,026	22,531	896,282	855,206
Montana	1,134	12,891	4,204	1,234	173	2,354	2,072	83,338	78,631
Idaho	974	11,943	4,096	1,028	235	2,223	2,004	79,695	76,210
Wyoming	560	7,184	2,442	611	154	1,410	1,270	49,710	47,542
Colorado	2,947	37,385	13,833	3,086	763	7,689	6,944	268,959	256,898
New Mexico	1,104	13,356	4,931	1,154	375	4,609	2,842	98,378	95,264
Arizona	1,301	19,664	7,659	1,339	425	4,002	3,612	151,624	144,974
Utah	1,289	16,758	5,774	1,328	320	3,128	2,693	114,418	106,728
Nevada	380	6,225	2,469	403	104	1,150	1,094	50,160	48,959
Pacific	35,446	500,866	188,136	37,426	8,284	80,646	72,276	3,722,831	3,542,684
Washington	4,964	67,021	25,864	5,140	1,033	10,891	9,656	497,586	470,938
Oregon	3,178	44,811	16,347	3,432	621	7,441	6,738	330,912	316,156
California	27,304	389,034	145,925	28,854	6,630	62,314	55,882	2,894,333	2,755,590

Source: Department of Commerce, Bureau of Census; U. S. Census of Business: 1948, Vol. VII.

No. 1030.—BUSINESS SERVICES—SUMMARY, BY STATES: 1948

[Corresponds with Standard Industrial Classification "Miscellaneous Business Services," except that Census data do not include the classification "Accounting, Auditing, and Bookkeeping Services"]

DIVISION AND STATE	Establishments	Receipts entire year	Payroll entire year	UNINCORPORATED BUSINESSES		PAID EMPLOYEES WORKWEEK ENDED NEAREST NOV. 15		PAYROLL, WORKWEEK ENDED NEAREST NOV. 15	
				Active proprietors, November	Unpaid family workers, November	Total	Full workweek	Total	Full workweek
	Number	$1,000	$1,000	Number	Number	Number	Number	Dollars	Dollars
United States	32,007	1,629,513	701,326	27,918	5,366	242,382	209,091	12,872,326	12,935,000
New England	2,084	69,772	25,989	1,737	310	16,839	8,646	492,448	
Maine	94	1,453	437	77	18	201	207	9,379	
New Hampshire	61	1,257	347	74	20	165	138	6,925	
Vermont	19	342	90	45	11	40	39	1,380	
Massachusetts	1,134	45,529	17,558	910	156	8,908	5,744	324,602	
Rhode Island	205	6,906	2,237	164	20	944	768	42,051	
Connecticut	623	14,253	5,283	694	73	2,202	1,735	102,986	
Middle Atlantic	9,597	562,366	310,830	5,227	1,137	99,985	86,480	5,530,352	
New York	6,752	544,080	202,641	5,647	673	77,772	69,700	4,984,137	
New Jersey	996	35,008	13,170	907	189	8,182	4,630	202,320	
Pennsylvania	1,849	54,027	35,319	1,673	275	14,029	12,151	694,591	
East North Central	6,552	291,163	175,363	5,392	1,109	58,725	49,761	3,404,978	
Ohio	1,062	77,114	32,707	1,443	280	11,656	9,646	625,711	
Indiana	661	19,026	6,890	608	127	2,932	2,404	131,490	
Illinois	2,472	187,612	89,064	2,080	303	26,852	23,245	1,723,000	
Michigan	1,117	81,020	37,764	1,025	215	13,490	11,309	741,491	
Wisconsin	660	25,291	8,949	206	112	3,785	3,033	181,222	
West North Central	2,459	90,742	25,748	2,325	434	14,148	11,148	662,183	
Minnesota	500	31,366	8,280	492	96	2,460	2,537	162,118	
Iowa	420	11,982	3,787	397	81	1,010	1,540	74,441	
Missouri	885	41,201	10,547	782	124	6,207	4,978	218,059	
North Dakota	50	795	277	54	3	139	117	5,051	
South Dakota	70	1,073	229	69	20	204	146	4,978	
Nebraska	200	8,053	2,028	178	51	1,429	1,290	55,811	
Kansas	255	6,270	1,800	253	67	931	734	28,020	
South Atlantic	2,752	93,704	35,958	2,125	325	14,589	12,293	699,959	
Delaware	71	2,635	771	42	11	444	440	172,924	
Maryland	417	24,272	6,771	282	41	2,144	2,180	132,500	
District of Columbia	295	16,471	5,512	261	41	2,562	1,370	114,721	
Virginia	316	9,471	2,512	301	43	1,362	944	71,520	
West Virginia	180	5,896	1,962	143	64	737	644	30,906	
North Carolina	274	7,018	2,400	208	47	1,097	916	47,444	
South Carolina	112	2,916	1,028	84	17	505	440	19,711	
Georgia	427	15,072	7,041	349	60	2,780	2,372	137,511	
Florida	682	17,354	4,905	616	175	2,629	2,208	110,743	
East South Central	965	33,430	12,949	733	169	6,239	4,688	229,116	
Kentucky	222	7,060	2,636	207	35	1,071	962	30,060	
Tennessee	351	14,400	4,701	233	47	2,345	2,109	104,147	
Alabama	213	7,413	2,882	173	47	1,390	1,231	56,913	
Mississippi	119	2,964	938	80	40	437	386	17,976	
West South Central	1,908	65,945	22,374	1,732	482	10,085	8,742	449,786	
Arkansas	129	3,442	909	100	37	492	477	18,420	
Louisiana	261	11,065	4,757	211	43	2,261	1,019	66,222	
Oklahoma	274	8,089	2,763	235	76	1,271	1,057	52,388	
Texas	1,244	42,349	13,945	1,146	326	6,064	6,329	291,328	
Mountain	541	23,218	7,474	579	226	3,771	2,890	162,918	
Montana	75	1,573	592	83	70	184	160	11,697	
Idaho	90	2,950	695	71	39	317	247	13,309	
Wyoming	27	670	257	30	9	94	84	4,399	
Colorado	168	8,526	3,683	322	62	1,751	1,176	63,389	
New Mexico	102	1,790	609	90	28	214	234	10,377	
Arizona	136	3,670	986	130	40	467	394	21,266	
Utah	121	3,897	1,281	107	20	592	454	25,821	
Nevada	22	1,016		37	3	100	90	6,065	
Pacific	4,129	200,767	78,634	4,476	971	25,746	24,292	1,459,634	
Washington	663	17,669	7,960	476	90	2,670	2,341	148,300	
Oregon	327	13,508	3,359	290	80	1,000	1,787	105,504	
California	3,044	169,290	65,315	3,711	816	23,076	20,204	1,205,834	

Source: Department of Commerce, Bureau of the Census, U.S. Census of Business 1948, Vol. VII.

No. 1031.—Personal, Business, and Repair Services—Employment by Size of Establishment, Based on Number Employed: 1948

[For kinds of personal, business and repair services covered, see table 1027]

NUMBER OF EMPLOYEES PER ESTABLISHMENT	ESTABLISHMENTS		Receipts, entire year ($1,000)	Payroll, entire year [1] ($1,000)	Paid employees [2]
	Number	Percent of total			
Total	599, 599	100. 0	5, 575, 162	2, 871, 214	1, 342, 496
No paid employees	295, 305	52. 9	1, 131, 579	16, 865	
1 paid employee	104, 717	18. 7	880, 533	167, 007	104, 717
2 paid employees	56, 549	10. 1	762, 076	197, 000	113, 098
3 paid employees	30, 758	5. 5	584, 525	170, 865	92, 274
4 or 5 paid employees	25, 800	5. 1	787, 017	256, 199	127, 190
6 or 7 paid employees	13, 547	2. 4	522, 347	184, 161	57, 134
8 or 9 paid employees	6, 656	1. 2	333, 462	125, 806	56, 003
10 to 19 paid employees	12, 331	2. 2	900, 032	376, 064	164, 394
20 to 49 paid employees	7, 244	1. 3	1, 024, 109	488, 137	219, 653
50 to 99 paid employees	2, 293	. 4	645, 375	342, 045	157, 482
100 or more paid employees	1, 150	. 2	1, 006, 781	547, 062	230, 991

[1] Includes paid executives of corporations but not proprietors of unincorporated businesses.
[2] Workweek ended nearest Nov. 15.

Source: Department of Commerce, Bureau of the Census; U. S. Census of Business: 1948, Vol. VI.

No. 1032.—Amusements—Summary, by Kind of Business: 1948

[Covers establishments primarily engaged in providing amusement or entertainment. Excludes establishments operated by educational institutions, religious bodies, fraternal groups, government agencies and nonprofit organizations]

KIND OF BUSINESS	Establishments	Receipts (exc. taxes), entire year	Taxes [1]	Payroll, entire year [2]	UNINCORPORATED BUSINESSES		PAID EMPLOYEES AND PAYROLL, WORKWEEK ENDED NEAREST NOV. 15 [3]	
					Active proprietors, Nov.	Unpaid family workers, Nov.	Employees	Payroll
	Number	$1,000	$1,000	$1,000	Number	Number	Number	Dollars
United States	58, 347	2, 349, 601	323, 396	616, 634	37, 874	17, 458	341, 931	11, 551, 16
Motion picture theaters	15, 631	1, 352, 580	261, 402	302, 511	8, 486	6, 004	187, 031	6, 732, 12
Bands, orchestras, and entertainers	2, 026	25, 509	(F)	17, 066	1, 742	122	10, 335	367, 14
Bowling alleys, billiard and pool parlors	14, 166	202, 773	1, 364	64, 315	13, 790	3, 445	76, 543	1, 555, 90
Billiard and pool parlors	9, 661	65, 464	442	12, 413	9, 586	2, 007	9, 706	255, 30
Bowling alleys	4, 505	137, 274	922	51, 902	4, 172	1, 441	66, 773	1, 296, 52
Dance halls, studios and schools	1, 074	32, 996	4, 207	9, 579	1, 018	565	5, 397	194, 17
Race track operation, total	198	177, 032	10, 573	35, 538	55	33	7, 615	503, 90
Sports promoters and commercial operators	6, 518	149, 964	23, 369	57, 553	5, 969	4, 420	17, 196	943, 95
Baseball and football clubs, athletic fields, sports promoters	589	110, 655	39, 142	42, 903	164	35	8, 985	775, 45
Baseball clubs inc promoters	357	65, 092	12, 127	28, 394	34	10	3, 094	396, 57
Football clubs inc promoters	21	11, 239	1, 761	5, 464	5		1, 047	375, 68
Stadiums, athletic fields, promoters of boxing, wrestling, and other athletic events	211	35, 354	6, 290	5, 945	125	25	4, 777	235, 74
Bathing beaches	261	3, 849	229	1, 014	234	27	207	4, 77
Golf courses	325	5, 304	64	2, 501	252	157	907	26, 57
Riding academies	709	5, 19	17	1, 145	449	460	605	22, 55
Skating rinks	1, 424	19, 775	2, 144	5, 283	1, 459	1, 257	4, 753	115, 57
Swimming pools	499	6, 672	668	1, 538	351	371	444	12, 47
Commercial sports operators, n. e. c.	2, 711	15, 531	105	2, 949	2, 790	1, 983	1, 294	49, 99
Theaters and theatrical producers exc motion picture	1, 425	133, 902	(F)	56, 903	1, 294	143	13, 285	1, 116, 35
Miscellaneous amusement and recreation services	6, 338	251, 555	11, 777	66, 369	5, 675	2, 423	22, 829	1, 574, 93
Amusement devices	1, 654	22, 653	1, 447	4, 703	1, 663	704	1, 094	36, 77
Amusement parks	368	38, 690	3, 388	12, 287	270	221	2, 706	161, 37
Shooting galleries	151	1, 581	5	539	164	56	139	5, 35
Coin-operated amusement device services	2, 447	97, 460	1, 731	20, 232	2, 598	555	7, 965	385, 07
Misc. amusement and recreation services n. e. c.	1, 708	91, 902	5, 206	28, 658	1, 587	887	10, 115	660, 37

[1] Consists of Federal, State and local amusement, sales and excise taxes collected directly from customer and paid directly to taxing agency.
[2] Includes paid executives of corporations but not proprietors of unincorporated businesses.
[3] Withheld to avoid disclosure of individual operations.
[4] Includes legalized gambling operations. Net revenues of pari-mutuel betting at race tracks included in "Race track operation."

Source: Department of Commerce, Bureau of the Census: U. S. Census of Business: 1948, Vol. VII.

No. 1033.—Power Laundries, Cleaning and Dyeing Establishments, and Rug Cleaning Establishments—Summary: 1919 to 1948

[All money figures in thousands of dollars. Statistics for 1948 cover establishments reporting receipts of $500 or more; statistics for 1939 cover establishments reporting receipts of $100 or more; for preceding specified census years statistics cover establishments reporting receipts of $5,000 or more. The Business Censuses of 1948 and 1939 classified establishments shown in this table as service establishments. (See also table 1027.) Statistics for 1935 and earlier years were compiled in connection with the Census of Manufactures. Rug cleaning was treated, in general, as an activity of the power laundry industry for 1929 and earlier years]

YEAR	Number of establishments	Proprietors and firm members	Salaried employees	Wage earners (average for year)[1]	Salaries[1]	Wages[1]	Cost of supplies, fuel and purchased electric energy	Cost of contract work	Receipts for work done
Power laundries:									
1919	4,881	(²)	(²)	130,400	(²)	91,026	52,342	1,599	195,974
1925	4,650	2,651	15,412	166,200	21,613	162,400	55,407	1,197	322,326
1929	5,770	5,250	21,964	222,187	40,522	229,861	50,285	(²)	541,152
1935	6,316	4,344	19,920	235,354	34,806	164,791	62,796	2,155	409,422
1939	6,773	5,174	(³)	249,009	(³)	222,600	(²)	(²)	463,879
1948	6,763	5,669	(⁴)	272,495	(⁵)	501,646	(²)	(²)	913,006
Cleaning and dyeing establishments:									
1919	1,769	(²)	(²)	16,402	(²)	17,596	11,511	461	53,153
1925	3,406	2,258	3,769	30,350	10,550	37,260	16,198	514	102,994
1929	4,595	4,613	9,744	50,140	20,290	75,951	26,607	(²)	201,300
1935	4,610	4,350	9,284	57,386	13,423	49,792	21,306	1,150	130,687
1939	11,604	11,946	(³)	82,610	(³)	60,014	(²)	(²)	152,666
1948	24,617	26,601	(⁴)	203,897	(⁵)	356,156	(²)	(²)	657,673
Rug cleaning establishments:									
1935	606	366	670	3,344	1,136	3,300	1,311	93	9,501
1939	1,612	949	(³)	4,659	(³)	3,998	(²)	(²)	10,618
1948	1,517	1,847	(⁴)	6,155	(⁵)	14,279	(²)	(²)	35,654

[1] Includes data for paid executives of corporations but not for proprietors of unincorporated businesses.
[2] No comparable data.   [3] Included in figure for cost of supplies, fuel, and purchased electric energy.
[4] Data for "Salaried employees" included in "Wage earners (average for year)." 1948 data covered all paid employees who were on the payroll during the November 15 workweek.
[5] Data for "Salaries" included in "Wages."

Source: Department of Commerce, Bureau of the Census: Biennial Census of Manufactures reports for 1935 and earlier years; 1939 Census of Business, Vol. III; and U. S. Census of Business: 1948, Vol. VII.

No. 1034.—Hotels—Summary, 1929 to 1948, and by Size, 1948

[Covers commercial establishments known to the public as hotels and primarily engaged in providing lodging, or lodging and meals, to the general public. For 1935, 1939, and 1948 hotels having less than 5 guest rooms or receipts of less than $500 for a full year's operations were excluded]

YEAR	Number of hotels	Number of guest rooms	Receipts (thousands of dollars)	Paid employees[1]	Total payroll (thousands of dollars)[1]
All hotels:					
1939	27,987	1,444,390	863,156	395,029	370,128
1948	29,085	1,546,623	3,172,756	384,203	666,004
Year-round hotels with 25 or more guest rooms:					
1929	11,975	1,006,694	972,595	307,902	359,127
1933	10,990	959,565	392,074	190,153	119,420
1935	11,372	994,681	545,317	294,491	148,460
1939	14,084	1,143,704	788,664	308,661	254,577
1948	14,847	1,192,723	1,864,656	370,422	591,586

SIZE	Less than 25 rooms	25 to 49 rooms	50 to 99 rooms	100 to 299 rooms	300 rooms or more
Number of hotels	12,207	8,679	4,599	2,849	531
Receipts (1,000 dollars)	187,371	222,460	341,128	681,580	739,600
Active proprietors of unincorporated businesses	13,513	9,401	4,909	1,949	135
Paid employees[1]	31,600	54,361	80,603	134,408	148,481

[1] Includes data for paid executives of corporations but not for proprietors of unincorporated businesses. For 1929, 1933, and 1935, average based on number of employees for April, July, October, and December; for 1939, average for year; for 1948, number for workweek ending nearest Nov. 15.
[2] Figures for California not included.

Source: Department of Commerce, Bureau of the Census: 1939 Census of Business, Vol. III, and U. S. Census of Business: 1948, Vol. VI.

No. 1035.—HOTELS—SUMMARY BY STATES: 1948

[See headnote, table 1034]

DIVISION AND STATES	Hotels	Guest rooms	Active proprietors,[1] November	Payroll, entire year[2]	RECEIPTS, ENTIRE YEAR				PAID EMPLOYEES AND PAYROLL, WORKWEEK ENDED NEAREST NOV. 15	
					Total	Room rentals and sales of meals[3]	Sales of alcoholic drinks[3]	Other sources	Employees	Payroll
	Number	*Number*	*Number*	*$1,000*	*$1,000*	*$1,000*	*$1,000*	*$1,000*	*Number*	*$1,000*
United States	29,650	1,549,823	26,411	660,004	2,172,756	1,762,905	248,441	161,410	398,293	12,449
Year-round hotels	24,448	1,343,081	21,116	614,538	1,981,626	1,592,164	237,393	152,069	389,025	12,127
Seasonal hotels	5,202	206,742	5,295	45,466	191,130	170,741	11,048	9,341	9,268	322
New England	2,192	94,233	1,810	42,572	143,273	111,034	24,981	7,258	22,765	690
Maine	462	17,699	411	4,796	17,975	13,944	3,059	972	2,517	65
New Hampshire	460	15,446	459	3,962	15,096	13,266	1,158	672	1,377	35
Vermont	221	6,670	173	2,304	8,318	6,623	1,267	428	1,308	35
Massachusetts	665	35,302	454	22,004	70,503	53,433	13,469	3,601	12,457	393
Rhode Island	96	4,522	76	2,660	8,481	6,167	2,029	285	1,352	46
Connecticut	288	14,294	237	6,846	22,900	17,601	3,999	1,300	3,694	116
Middle Atlantic	5,058	342,628	4,615	194,325	610,165	488,771	87,745	33,649	99,949	3,443
New York	2,664	220,637	2,324	134,701	409,571	330,831	55,470	23,270	64,373	2,390
New Jersey	1,170	60,322	1,112	34,322	83,655	69,614	10,538	3,503	11,842	390
Pennsylvania	1,224	61,669	1,179	35,302	116,939	88,396	21,737	6,876	22,834	663
East North Central	4,545	286,264	3,949	131,221	418,125	327,413	56,735	33,977	79,349	2,535
Ohio	766	52,889	553	29,902	92,320	72,235	13,499	6,586	19,337	891
Indiana	522	26,796	439	10,539	35,605	26,790	4,289	2,527	7,678	268
Illinois	1,259	117,254	1,003	57,548	171,403	138,538	17,467	15,398	31,664	1,125
Michigan	1,136	58,929	1,129	20,627	73,946	54,839	12,587	6,520	13,237	412
Wisconsin	862	30,366	825	12,305	44,850	33,011	8,893	2,946	7,433	219
W. North Central	3,303	145,270	3,115	49,716	170,446	142,678	14,960	12,808	36,172	1,068
Minnesota	818	33,479	832	12,090	40,690	32,889	4,838	2,963	7,469	226
Iowa	442	21,082	308	6,991	23,782	21,053	1,010	1,719	5,678	138
Missouri	818	45,621	703	18,434	59,321	48,421	6,404	4,496	12,812	380
North Dakota	219	7,648	226	1,857	8,368	6,387	1,122	859	1,544	38
South Dakota	194	6,535	168	1,439	5,841	5,093	270	478	1,156	31
Nebraska	347	14,348	328	4,985	17,834	15,395	1,210	1,229	4,038	96
Kansas	465	16,557	480	3,920	14,610	13,440	106	1,064	3,475	51
South Atlantic	3,697	187,590	3,094	75,285	268,231	231,321	17,099	19,811	52,721	1,451
Delaware	71	1,981	72	1,380	4,638	2,784	972	882	753	25
Maryland	262	11,159	231	5,668	19,358	14,775	3,042	1,541	4,026	162
Dist. of Columbia	100	16,699	63	13,465	40,931	32,287	5,027	3,617	7,884	268
Virginia	447	19,839	353	9,619	32,091	28,575	777	2,739	7,178	173
West Virginia	255	11,453	197	4,622	14,630	13,275	234	1,121	3,847	104
North Carolina	405	18,805	319	5,837	21,987	20,612	266	1,109	4,937	110
South Carolina	196	7,877	155	2,629	9,676	9,053	182	441	2,351	47
Georgia	346	17,878	270	6,570	25,109	21,182	1,485	2,442	6,252	129
Florida	1,615	81,899	1,434	25,495	99,811	88,778	5,114	5,919	15,463	490
East South Central	1,035	47,838	863	18,579	67,471	58,512	2,864	6,095	17,348	369
Kentucky	308	13,311	281	5,480	19,186	16,097	1,525	1,564	4,421	105
Tennessee	323	16,427	263	6,683	23,623	20,919	285	2,419	6,422	131
Alabama	214	9,386	173	3,606	13,285	11,484	737	1,064	3,519	71
Mississippi	190	8,714	146	3,110	11,377	10,012	317	1,048	2,986	62
W. South Central	2,705	110,826	2,231	37,456	132,472	111,953	4,481	16,038	31,250	759
Arkansas	319	12,094	309	3,632	13,329	11,549	195	1,585	3,427	71
Louisiana	287	12,452	221	6,478	22,953	17,813	2,908	2,232	5,494	122
Oklahoma	607	23,308	530	5,412	17,751	16,002	122	1,627	4,442	109
Texas	1,492	62,972	1,171	21,934	78,439	66,589	1,256	10,594	17,887	444
Mountain	2,322	85,233	2,252	30,841	105,604	78,564	12,684	14,356	17,147	612
Montana	308	13,673	430	3,266	12,498	9,426	2,257	815	2,118	69
Idaho	220	7,460	203	3,279	9,309	7,209	821	1,279	1,727	66
Wyoming	208	7,928	202	2,158	8,039	6,183	1,367	489	932	31
Colorado	652	25,525	669	6,690	24,316	20,238	2,452	1,626	4,341	155
New Mexico	237	7,216	226	2,058	7,882	6,372	922	588	1,569	45
Arizona	266	9,479	213	4,392	14,606	11,968	1,638	1,000	2,485	89
Utah	188	7,561	173	2,599	8,470	7,375	221	874	1,682	46
Nevada	153	6,391	136	6,399	20,484	9,793	3,006	7,685	2,293	15
Pacific	4,793	249,941	4,482	79,709	256,969	212,659	26,892	17,418	42,552	1,571
Washington	781	42,243	712	10,618	32,207	29,134	888	2,185	6,048	211
Oregon	468	23,389	502	6,212	19,881	17,893	476	1,512	3,664	133
California	3,544	184,309	3,268	62,879	204,581	165,632	25,528	13,721	32,840	1,262

[1] Active proprietors of unincorporated businesses.
[2] Includes paid executives of corporations but not proprietors of unincorporated businesses.
[3] 8,998 hotels with total receipts of $1,634,401,000 reported rentals and sales of meals separately as follows: rentals, $720,113,000; meals, $554,992,000.

Source: Department of Commerce, Bureau of the Census; *U. S. Census of Business: 1948,* Vol. VI.

36.—ADVERTISING—ESTIMATED EXPENDITURES, BY MEDIUM: 1948 TO 1952

[Amounts in millions]

IUM	1948 Amount	1948 Per-cent of total	1949 Amount	1949 Per-cent of total	1950 Amount	1950 Per-cent of total	1951 Amount	1951 Per-cent of total	1952[1] Amount	1952[1] Per-cent of total
	$4,864	100.0	$5,292	100.0	$5,710	100.0	$6,427	100.0	$7,220	100.0
	2,776	57.1	2,965	57.2	3,257	57.0	3,736	57.5	4,121	57.1
	2,088	42.9	2,237	42.8	2,453	43.0	2,760	42.5	3,099	42.9
	1,750	36.0	1,916	36.6	2,076	36.3	2,258	34.7	2,459	34.1
	394	8.1	476	8.9	533	9.3	549	8.4	552	7.7
	1,356	27.9	1,440	27.7	1,542	27.0	1,709	26.3	1,907	26.4
	617	12.7	628	12.2	668	11.7	712	10.9	723	10.1
	387	8.0	363	7.5	394	6.9	406	6.2	402	5.6
	230	4.7	245	4.7	273	4.8	306	4.7	321	4.5
	513	10.5	493	9.5	515	9.0	574	8.9	614	8.5
	258	5.3	245	4.7	261	4.6	297	4.6	323	4.5
	133	2.7	129	2.5	129	2.3	144	2.2	149	2.0
	87	1.8	84	1.6	88	1.5	95	1.5	101	1.4
rs	35	.7	35	.7	37	.6	38	.6	41	.6
l	20	.4	21	.4	21	.4	26	.4	30	.4
pers.	689	14.2	756	14.5	803	14.1	924	14.2	1,011	14.0
	251	5.2	248	4.8	251	4.4	292	4.5	336	4.6
	132	2.7	131	2.5	143	2.5	149	2.4	162	2.2
	89	1.8	88	1.7	96	1.7	101	1.6	109	1.5
	43	.9	43	.8	46	.8	49	.8	53	.7
			68	1.2	201	3.5	388	6.0	580	8.0
			49	1.0	146	2.5	297	4.6	442	6.1
			19	.2	55	1.0	92	1.4	138	1.9
us.	892	18.3	942	18.3	1,033	18.1	1,174	18.0	1,306	18.1
	453	9.3	473	9.3	518	9.1	594	9.1	655	9.1
	438	9.0	470	9.0	515	9.0	580	8.9	651	9.0

nary.

Compiled by McCann-Erickson, Inc., for Printers' Ink Publications, New York, N. Y. Published Ink.

37.—ADVERTISING—INDEXES OF NATIONAL ADVERTISING EXPENDITURES, BY MEDIA TYPE: 1935 TO 1952

[for all indexes is the average monthly expenditure for those media which give national coverage]

TYPE	1935	1940	1945	1947	1948	1949	1950	1951	1952
PRINTERS' INK									
se: 1935-1939=100)									
dex	83	118	198	268	290	299	337	405	453
gazines	81	119	217	315	327	314	330	361	390
	73	147	263	396	415	396	421	479	527
's.	96	90	183	247	248	236	238	265	274
l.	79	109	189	273	277	267	282	285	303
	64	123	211	304	367	363	384	396	422
	69	144	289	296	309	292	284	271	251
ers.	95	102	132	210	246	284	318	312	315
	76	112	168	264	299	296	322	338	367
papers.	82	122	326	374	394	389	392	458	526
TIDE									
se: 1947-49=100)									
dex							113.1	126.4	137.8
ers.							126.7	128.1	130.3
s.							102.3	111.9	122.9
radio							95.3	90.4	84.8
television[1]								100.0	141.1
							114.3	118.0	128.8
							106.5	107.9	114.0
papers.							100.3	125.5	146.8

riod: 1951=100.

Printers' Ink Publications, New York, N. Y.; Tide Publishing Co., New York, N. Y.

No. 1088.—Advertising—Expenditures for National Advertising in Newspapers, by Type of Product: 1950, 1951, and 1952

[In thousands of dollars. Data are compiled on basis of actual space measurements of bulk of "national" advertising carried by weekday and Sunday newspapers]

TYPE OF PRODUCT	1950 [1]	1951 [2]	1952 [3]	TYPE OF PRODUCT	1950 [1]	1951 [2]	1952 [3]
Total	499,019	513,484	536,066	Industrial	8,480	9,809	11,681
				Hotels and resorts	9,946	10,588	11,639
Groceries	123,354	127,481	120,825	Public utilities	8,341	10,126	11,236
Automotive	98,094	97,038	97,874	Wearing apparel	6,240	5,840	6,789
Alcoholic beverages	45,473	51,046	51,525	Agriculture	6,819	6,969	9,888
Toilet requisites	34,904	35,606	43,049	Insurance	4,152	4,970	5,780
Transportation	21,587	22,716	24,163	Confections	3,105	2,866	3,670
Tobacco	19,935	15,938	16,918	Sporting goods	1,997	1,846	2,467
Household equipment				Jewelry and silverware	1,190	1,424	1,179
and supplies	20,001	24,572	20,646	Educational	1,339	1,404	1,422
Medical	24,588	24,748	23,646	Amusements	1,272	1,788	1,668
Publications	17,470	17,124	17,853	Professional and service	730	717	768
Radio and television	22,760	22,549	18,782	Miscellaneous	17,242	16,321	22,850

[1] Totals are projections to 100 percent; newspapers actually measured account for 89.2 percent of total weekday circulation and 95.6 percent of total Sunday circulation.

[2] Totals are projections to 100 percent; newspapers actually measured account for 88.9 percent of total weekday circulation and 92.3 percent of total Sunday circulation.

[3] Totals are projections to 100 percent; newspapers actually measured account for 88.0 percent of total weekday circulation and 93.8 percent of total Sunday circulation.

Source: Compiled by Media Records, Inc., for Bureau of Advertising of American Newspaper Publishers Association; published in *Advertising Age*.

No. 1039.—Advertising—Newspaper Advertising Linage for 52 Cities: 1928 to 1952

[In thousands of lines. Data represent newspaper linage in all newspapers, daily and Sunday, in the following 52 cities: Akron, Albany, Albuquerque, Atlanta, Baltimore, Birmingham, Boston, Buffalo, Chicago, Cincinnati, Cleveland, Columbus, Dallas, Dayton, Denver, Detroit, El Paso, Fort Worth, Hartford, Houston, Indianapolis, Jacksonville, Knoxville, Los Angeles, Memphis, Milwaukee, Minneapolis, Nashville, New Orleans, Oakland, Oklahoma City, Omaha, Pittsburgh, Portland, Reading, Richmond, Rochester, Salt Lake City, San Antonio, San Diego, San Francisco, Seattle, South Bend, Spokane, St. Louis, Syracuse, Tacoma, Toledo, Tulsa, Washington, Worcester, and Youngstown. List of cities is unchanged throughout the period covered by the data. General advertising is the advertising of specific products on general sale, as distinguished from the advertising of retail stores, and automotive or financial advertising]

YEAR	Total	Classified	DISPLAY				
			Total	Automotive	Financial	General	Retail
Monthly average:							
1928	150,207	28,820	121,387	11,860	5,500	24,148	79,57
1929	158,101	28,787	129,314	12,539	6,181	28,240	82,354
1930	137,854	24,913	112,941	8,932	4,938	25,254	73,817
1931	122,072	22,106	99,966	6,718	3,415	21,818	68,015
1932	97,064	18,363	78,701	5,316	1,973	16,819	54,592
1933	88,793	16,439	72,354	5,220	1,682	15,670	49,782
1934	98,240	17,110	81,130	6,109	1,594	17,615	55,812
1935	103,912	19,081	84,831	6,077	1,776	18,081	58,897
1936	115,010	22,123	92,887	6,069	2,085	20,959	63,773
1937	117,472	23,618	93,854	5,650	1,873	20,566	65,737
1938	102,097	21,251	80,846	3,938	1,598	15,996	59,317
1939	103,629	21,060	82,569	4,390	1,692	15,988	60,499
1940	105,719	21,901	83,818	5,167	1,619	15,719	61,312
1941	109,436	22,714	86,722	4,704	1,707	16,171	64,140
1942	103,473	21,443	82,030	2,235	1,469	16,388	61,938
1943	116,368	27,920	88,448	2,696	1,480	20,619	63,653
1944	113,437	25,741	87,696	2,623	1,530	20,910	62,633
1945	115,969	26,680	89,289	2,888	1,841	20,504	64,056
1946	144,143	35,305	108,838	3,509	2,198	22,190	80,941
1947	167,378	39,467	127,911	5,723	2,035	26,217	93,936
1948	188,621	43,537	145,083	6,895	2,149	28,220	107,819
1949	191,831	40,335	151,495	8,790	2,112	29,565	111,028
1950	203,346	42,553	160,793	10,049	2,356	32,464	115,924
1951	206,539	48,501	158,037	9,166	2,514	30,555	115,802
1952	208,783	51,459	157,323	8,952	2,690	29,094	116,587

Source: Compiled by Media Records, Inc. and published currently in Department of Commerce, Office of Business Economics, *Survey of Current Business*.

No. 1040.—ADVERTISING—COST OF MAGAZINE ADVERTISING: 1948 TO 1952

[In thousands of dollars. Data represent advertising revenue of national general magazines, farm magazines, and magazine sections of newspapers. Space cost is based on one-time rate; special rates are used where applicable. Retail advertising and direct-mail advertising are not distributed according to type of product, but are included in "All other." Figures for certain publications not shown separately by product classes, are also accounted for in "All other." Figures from year to year may not be strictly comparable, as publications are added or deleted]

TYPE OF PRODUCT	1948	1949	1950	1951	1952
Cost, total	458,677	440,795	458,451	513,851	552,699
Apparel, footwear and accessories	47,629	41,718	39,038	44,517	44,549
Automotive, automotive accessories and equipment	38,189	40,906	41,969	41,379	47,337
Beer, wine and liquor	27,120	26,847	26,581	31,278	30,156
Building materials, equipment and fixtures	19,106	17,817	20,064	24,851	26,276
Drugs and remedies	11,341	11,591	12,774	14,354	16,217
Food and food products	49,543	50,950	53,591	57,628	61,334
Household equipment and supplies	34,243	27,913	34,326	34,774	35,674
Household furnishings	24,945	23,475	24,820	28,433	26,837
Industrial materials	21,602	20,904	24,490	33,348	40,500
Smoking materials	12,021	14,309	12,997	13,663	14,406
Toiletries and toilet goods	39,007	37,402	37,541	40,061	41,039
Transportation, hotels and resorts, industrial and agricultural development	14,267	14,663	15,627	18,014	21,086
All other	119,664	112,390	114,633	131,551	145,268

Source: Publishers' Information Bureau, Inc., New York, N. Y.

No. 1041.—ADVERTISING—GROSS TIME COST FOR RADIO AND TELEVISION ADVERTISING: 1949 TO 1952

[In thousands of dollars. Gross time charges computed at the one-time rate, before application of size and frequency discounts. Net time charges, after application of such discounts, are currently approximately 40 percent less for radio and 25 percent less for television. No allowance included for talent, production, and wire charges]

TYPE OF PRODUCT	RADIO				TELEVISION			
	1949	1950	1951	1952	1949	1950 [1]	1951	1952
Cost of facilities, total	187,800	183,519	174,719	163,453	12,294	40,779	127,990	180,795
Apparel, footwear and accessories	1,292	1,506	601	420	285	901	3,141	2,985
Automotive, automotive accessories and equipment	6,719	5,009	4,298	4,376	1,546	5,325	11,061	15,466
Beer, wine and liquor	1,345	2,775	3,178	2,203	326	1,704	5,756	5,650
Confectionery and soft drinks	6,253	6,148	6,264	5,297	188	1,839	3,411	5,042
Drugs and remedies	21,055	24,483	22,132	21,030	943	392	2,800	6,103
Food and food products	45,312	44,861	42,486	36,834	1,296	6,602	25,840	33,807
Gasoline, lubricants and other fuel	5,641	5,809	5,722	5,180	720	1,516	2,925	3,613
Household equipment and supplies	6,118	3,086	3,160	6,651	457	2,653	8,528	11,460
Household furnishings	904	601	1,005	1,435	820	2,090	3,556	2,328
Insurance	3,738	2,853	3,284	3,336		79	391	605
Radios, TV sets, phonographs, musical instruments and accessories	749	1,232	2,747	2,877	2,392	3,421	4,661	5,662
Smoking materials	23,667	22,489	20,610	15,960	2,397	6,250	17,993	26,430
Soaps, cleansers and polishes	19,335	20,700	17,949	18,326	107	863	11,038	21,004
Toiletries and toilet goods	29,370	25,783	25,787	23,215	1,026	4,183	16,455	24,804
All other	16,302	16,532	15,501	16,313	491	2,961	10,444	13,817

[1] Excluding Du Mont.

Source: Publishers' Information Bureau, Inc., New York, N. Y.

32. Foreign Commerce

Including International Accounts and Aid

Balance of payments.—The statistics shown for international balance of payments and the international investment position are compiled in the Balance of Payments Division, Office of Business Economics of the Department of Commerce.

The international accounts of the United States comprise the international balance of payments (tables 1042, 1044, 1045 and 1046) and the international investment position (table 1043). The balance of payments shows for given time periods, e. g., one year, the transfers of assets and the form of compensation for these transfers between this country and the rest of the world; the international investment position indicates for specific dates the value of United States investments abroad and of foreign investments in the United States. The two types of accounts, however, are not strictly comparable; the transfers of assets between countries as shown in the balance of payments is only one of the factors affecting the value of foreign investments. Other factors not shown in the balance of payments are changes in security values and revaluation of assets, and reinvested earnings and losses. For a detailed discussion and analysis of these accounts, see the Department of Commerce publications, *International Transactions of the United States During the War, 1940–45, Economic Series No. 65,* 1948, *The Balance of International Payments of the United States, 1946–48,* 1949, and *Balance of Payments of the United States, 1949–51,* a supplement to the *Survey of Current Business,* published in 1952. For current data and revisions, see the monthly *Survey of Current Business.*

Foreign assistance.—Statistics on United States Government grants to and credits utilized by foreign countries and reverse grants and credit repayments received by the Government from abroad are prepared by the Clearing Office for Foreign Transactions, Office of Business Economics. These data are obtained from Federal agencies which report such transactions to the Clearing Office. For detailed information on the statistics provided in tables 1047 and 1048, and on other foreign activities of the Government, see the Department of Commerce publication, *Foreign Aid by the United States Government, 1940–51,* a supplement to the *Survey of Current Business,* published in 1952. For current data and revisions, see the regular quarterly reports of the Clearing Office.

Foreign aid is defined to comprise two categories—grants and credits. Grants are largely outright gifts for which no payment is expected, or which at most involve an obligation on the part of the receiver to extend aid to the United States or other countries to achieve a common objective. Credits are loans or other agreements which give rise to specific obligations to repay or return, over a period of years, usually with interest. In some instances assistance has been given with the understanding that a decision as to repayment will be made at a later date; such assistance is included in grants. At such time as an agreement is reached for repayment over a period of years, a credit is established. Because such credits cannot, as a rule, be deducted from specific grants recorded in previous periods, they are included in both grants (at the earlier period) and credits (at the time of the agreement), and the amounts of such *credit-agreement offsets to grants* must therefore be deducted from the total of grants and credits in arriving at gross foreign aid. All known returns to the United States Government stemming from grants and credits are also taken into account in net foreign aid. Gross foreign aid less the returns is net foreign aid, which is shown as net grants and net credits. The Government's capital investments in the International Bank ($635 million) and International Monetary Fund ($2,750 million) are not in-

Note.—This section presents data for the most recent year or period available on May 20, 1953, when the material was organized and sent to the printer.

cluded in gross foreign aid although they constitute an additional measure taken by this Government to promote foreign economic recovery. Payments to these international financial institutions do not result in immediate equivalent aid to foreign countries. Use of available dollar funds is largely determined by the managements of the two institutions, subject to certain restraints which can be exercised by the United States Government.

The major activities of the Mutual Security Agency (changed to Foreign Operations Administration on August 1, 1953) are summarized in tables 1049–1054, prepared by the Division of Statistics and Reports of that agency. Data are presented on the European Program and the separate program for the Far East.

In these tables, colonies and overseas territories of European countries are reported with mother countries; the Saar is shown with France. Commodity groups shown are based on the Mutual Security Agency commodity classification. In determining the various reporting groups, an attempt has been made to align the coverage of the summary groups shown in these tables as closely as possible with that of reports on United States exports originating in the Bureau of the Census.

These and other data are published in more detail in the several monthly publications of the Division of Statistics and Reports of the Mutual Security Agency.

Foreign trade.—Statistics on foreign trade are compiled by the Bureau of the Census of the Department of Commerce. Annual statistics through 1946 are published in the annual report, *Foreign Commerce and Navigation of the United States*. Preliminary statistics for later years are from current corrected data. Monthly data are published in the *Summary of Foreign Commerce of the United States* (monthly and quarterly through April 1951, quarterly thereafter) and other monthly reports of the foreign trade series. For a complete list of these reports see *Catalog of United States Foreign Trade Statistical Publications* issued by the Bureau of the Census.

Statistics covering shipments made after World War II under the Department of the Army Civilian Supply Program are included in the export statistics for 1948 but not for earlier years. In addition, export data include United States exports under the Lend-Lease, United Nations Relief and Rehabilitation Administration, Economic Cooperation Administration, Mutual Defense Assistance, and other foreign aid programs. Shipments to United States armed forces for their own use are not included in export statistics for any period.

Certain commodity classifications in the export statistics were grouped for security reasons into special categories beginning with May 1949 and data for the individual commodities withheld from publication. The special category list of commodities was amended in July 1949, July 1950, and January 1951 to include additional commodities. With the adoption of new security regulations, effective July 1950, the publication of the country of destination and Customs District detail for the special category commodities and groups were discontinued. Data for special commodities are included, however, in all total export statistics issued by the Bureau of the Census.

Except as noted (as, for example, in table 1076) the values stated are in United States dollars without reference to changes in the gold content of the dollar. (The statutory price of gold—$20.67 per ounce—in effect prior to Jan. 31, 1934, was changed on that date by Executive Order to $35 per ounce. Between Mar. 10, 1933, and Jan. 31, 1934, the foreign exchange value of the dollar was permitted to depreciate as a result of the restrictions placed on gold shipments to foreign countries.) The geographic area covered by these statistics, except as noted, is the United States Customs area, which includes Alaska, Hawaii, and Puerto Rico; and from Jan. 1, 1935, through Dec. 31, 1939, the Virgin Islands (see headnote, table 1060). Other explanations of the trade tables are given in the introduction to the annual report, *Foreign Commerce and Navigation of the United States*.

Historical statistics.—See preface and historical appendix. Tabular headnotes (as "See also *Historical Statistics*, series M 14–41") provide cross references, where applicable, to *Historical Statistics of the United States, 1789–1945*.

Fig. XLV.—Foreign Trade by Economic Classes: 1916 to 1952

See table 1066]

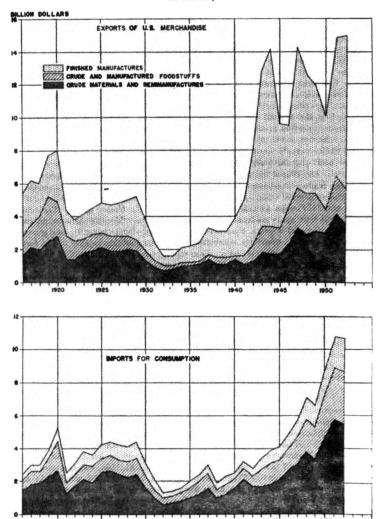

Source: Department of Commerce, Bureau of the Census.

No. 1042.—BALANCE OF INTERNATIONAL PAYMENTS: 1946 TO 1952

[In millions of dollars. 1952 data preliminary. See also *Historical Statistics*, series M 14–41 for data as presented in 1950 *Abstract*, table 988]

ITEM	1946	1947	1948	1949	1950	1951	1952
Exports of goods and services, total	14,741	19,796	16,967	15,974	14,425	20,218	20,701
Merchandise, adjusted	11,672	15,977	13,346	12,337	10,658	15,485	15,859
Transportation	1,420	1,788	1,299	1,176	926	1,487	1,373
Travel	252	342	308	363	377	420	512
Miscellaneous services: Private	459	472	522	540	551	623	623
Government	128	71	117	153	160	211	423
Income on investments: Private	789	1,080	1,273	1,307	1,634	1,800	1,711
Government	21	66	102	98	109	192	200
Imports of goods and services, total	7,637	8,318	10,368	9,603	12,128	15,054	15,728
Merchandise, adjusted	5,242	6,129	7,822	7,066	9,315	11,668	11,519
Transportation	509	761	630	676	796	933	1,051
Travel	457	548	600	678	727	722	823
Miscellaneous services: Private	137	181	201	224	250	249	253
Government	386	450	731	606	601	1,084	1,661
Income on investments: Private	201	233	267	328	406	351	357
Government	15	16	17	25	31	47	64
Balance on goods and services	+7,704	+11,678	+6,699	+6,371	+2,297	+5,164	+4,973
Unilateral transfers (net), total	−2,893	−2,563	−4,835	−5,843	−4,601	−4,913	−5,043
Private	−679	−665	−678	−522	−481	−412	−415
Government grants and other transfers [1]	−2,214	−1,918	−4,157	−5,321	−4,120	−4,501	−4,628
Balance on goods and services and unilateral transfers (net foreign investment)	+4,811	+8,896	+1,844	+528	−2,304	+251	−70
United States capital (net), total	−3,381	−7,956	−1,780	−1,256	−1,481	−1,229	−1,350
Private, long-term	−59	−810	−748	−796	−1,166	−963	−831
Private, short-term	−310	−189	−116	+187	−149	−103	−65
Government, long term	−3,262	−6,849	−973	−474	−127	−140	−409
Government, short-term	+250	−108	+87	−173	−37	−23	−45
Foreign capital (net), total	−986	+243	+379	+107	+1,896	+495	+1,560
Long-term	−347	−96	−170	+144	+974	−543	+419
Short-term	−639	+339	+549	−37	+912	+1,036	+1,141
Gold purchases (−), or sales (+)	−623	−2,162	−1,530	−164	+1,743	−53	−378
Transfers of funds between foreign areas [receipts from other areas (−), payments to other areas (+)] and errors and omissions	+179	+980	+1,037	+785	+156	+536	+238

[1] Unilateral transfers include Government aid contributions as shown in table 1047 plus various other transfers such as payments of pensions, claims, etc.

Source: Department of Commerce, Office of Business Economics; *Balance of Payments of the United States, 1949–51*, and the *Survey of Current Business*, March 1953.

No. 1043.—INTERNATIONAL INVESTMENT POSITION OF THE UNITED STATES: 1939 TO 1951

[In millions of dollars. Estimates for end of year; subject to considerable error due to nature of basic data. Direct investments at book value; other types at market or stated values. For 1945–51, value of securities of former enemy countries, or countries where no realistic market can be determined, has been eliminated. For 1950–51, direct investments abroad revised in accordance with latest data; revisions not yet carried back to earlier years. See also *Historical Statistics*, series M 1–13]

ITEM	1939	1940	1945	1946	1947	1948	1949	1950	1951
U. S. investments abroad, total	12,480	12,275	16,818	20,618	25,927	31,172	32,482	32,926	36,665
Private	12,445	12,195	14,683	18,033	16,876	18,335	18,960	19,250	22,172
Long-term	11,385	11,310	13,608	14,199	16,343	16,886	17,542	17,609	19,407
Direct	7,280	7,340	8,309	8,854	9,965	11,206	12,418	11,782	13,121
Portfolio	4,105	3,970	5,299	5,344	6,378	5,380	5,124	5,827	6,286
Short-term	1,060	885	1,028	1,237	1,533	1,649	1,427	1,641	1,765
U. S. Government	35	80	2,136	4,053	12,051	12,937	13,514	13,676	13,894
Long-term	35	80	1,644	4,900	11,756	12,722	13,202	13,364	13,536
Short-term			491	177	296	209	312	312	348
Foreign investments in U. S., total	12,520	12,535	17,594	16,452	16,448	17,087	17,568	20,108	23,146
Private obligations	12,195	12,225	13,294	12,806	13,702	13,084	14,733	14,972	15,723
Long-term	8,095	8,100	8,031	7,615	7,400	7,297	7,792	8,457	9,092
Direct	2,900	2,875	2,514	2,548	2,650	2,843	3,066	3,293	2,499
Portfolio	5,795	5,225	5,517	5,067	4,750	4,454	4,726	5,164	5,593
Short-term	3,800	4,125	5,263	5,281	6,302	5,787	6,941	6,516	6,631
U. S. Government obligations	325	310	4,300	3,556	2,944	4,003	3,835	5,135	5,443
Long-term	150	150	487	205	421	434	405	1,426	738
Short-term	175	160	3,813	3,361	2,523	3,569	3,340	3,769	4,705
Net debtor (−) or creditor (+) position	−340	−1,260	−776	+4,166	+12,281	+14,085	+14,915	+12,726	+13,890
Net private	−50	−1,030	+1,389	+2,639	+4,174	+5,151	+5,226	+4,277	+5,449
Net U. S. Government	−290	−230	−2,165	+1,527	+8,107	+8,934	+9,679	+8,451	+8,441
Net long-term, private and U. S. Government	+2,575	+3,140	+6,784	+11,194	+19,277	+21,563	+22,457	+21,090	+23,113
Net short-term, private and U. S. Government	−2,915	−4,400	−7,560	−7,028	−6,996	−7,498	−7,542	−8,332	−9,233

Source: Department of Commerce, Office of Business Economics; *International Transactions of the United States During the War, 1940–45* (as revised in release of June 29, 1950), *The Balance of International Payments of the United States, 1946–48*, and *Balance of Payments of the United States, 1949–51*.

No. 1044.—INTERNATIONAL INVESTMENTS—INCOME RECEIPTS AND PAYMENTS, BY AREA: 1947 TO 1952

[In millions of dollars. Figures represent investment income receipts and payments abstracted from the general pattern of the United States balance of payments. "Direct" investments represent private enterprises in one country controlled by investors in another country or in the management of which foreign investors have an important voice. "Other private" investments represent long-term miscellaneous holdings such as government or corporate bonds, interests in trusts and estates, or bank loans]

AREA AND TYPE OF INVESTMENT	1947		1948		1949		1950		1951		1952	
	Receipts	Payments	Receipts	Payments	Receipts	Payments	Receipts	Payments	Receipts	Payments	Receipts	Payments
Total, all areas	1,146	249	1,375	284	1,405	353	1,743	437	1,982	398	1,911	421
Direct	924	84	1,111	109	1,148	159	1,469	196	1,632	134	1,538	153
Other private	156	149	162	158	159	169	165	210	166	217	173	204
U. S. Government	66	16	102	17	98	25	109	31	192	47	200	64
Canada	302	32	319	54	387	66	406	76	401	78	372	102
Direct	203	11	223	25	295	39	305	39	292	35	261	59
Other private	99	19	94	25	92	20	101	27	109	28	111	27
U. S. Government	(1)	2	2	4	(1)	7	(1)	10	(1)	15	(1)	16
Latin American republics	477	11	556	12	455	11	696	14	704	17	672	16
Direct	451	1	525	1	425	(1)	664		731	(1)	636	(1)
Other private	17	9	19	10	18	9	18	12	17	13	17	12
U. S. Government	9	1	12	1	12	2	14	2	16	4	19	4
OEEC countries [2]	153	183	195	196	262	252	216	322	307	277	312	270
Direct	80	71	93	82	97	118	108	155	123	98	122	92
Other private	30	110	32	111	32	130	30	160	26	165	27	154
U. S. Government	43	2	70	2	73	4	78	7	156	14	163	24
OEEC dependencies [3]	32	3	75	2	78	2	90	3	102	2	103	7
Direct	32		73		77		90		102		103	
Other private		2		2		2		2		2		4
U. S. Government	(1)	1	2	(1)	1	(1)		1	(1)			3
Other foreign countries	182	20	230	20	283	2	335	22	418	24	452	28
Direct	158	1	197	1	254	2	302	2	384	1	416	2
Other private	10	9	17	10	17	8	16	9	16	9	18	7
U. S. Government	14	10	16	9	12	12	17	11	18	14	18	17

[1] Less than $500,000.
[2] Countries formerly under ERP (Marshall Plan) and now participating in Organization of European Economic Cooperation
[3] Includes British West Indies, Malaya and Hong Kong, Netherlands East Indies, Netherlands West Indies and Surinam, and other dependencies of OEEC countries.
Source: Department of Commerce, Office of Business Economics; Survey of Current Business, August 1952, and records.

No. 1045.—INTERNATIONAL INVESTMENTS—DIRECT-INVESTMENT INCOME RECEIPTS BY AREA AND INDUSTRY: 1948 TO 1951

[In millions of dollars. See headnote, table 1044]

AREA	Year	Total	Manufacturing	Distribution	Agriculture	Mining and smelting	Petroleum	Public utilities	Miscellaneous
All areas, total	1948	1,111	248	84	89	129	472	31	58
	1949	1,148	301	93	80	88	487	39	60
	1950	1,469	328	97	98	112	705	45	84
	1951	1,632	344	126	138	146	741	44	93
Canada	1948	223	123	16	(1)	34	8	12	30
	1949	295	179	29	2	29	11	18	27
	1950	305	181	27	2	33	12	11	39
	1951	292	169	20	2	35	18	16	37
Latin American republics	1948	525	50	33	80	84	243	19	16
	1949	425	35	24	68	44	217	21	16
	1950	664	54	36	90	64	362	33	25
	1951	731	84	56	119	87	335	23	27
OEEC countries [2]	1948	93	51	18		1	18		5
	1949	97	60	19		(1)	8		10
	1950	108	68	21		1	7	(1)	11
	1951	123	65	31		(1)	15	(1)	12
OEEC dependencies [3]	1948	73	1	5	1	7	58	(1)	1
	1949	77	2	7	1	12	54	(1)	1
	1950	90	2	3	5	9	68	(1)	3
	1951	102	2	4	3	14	75	(1)	4
Other foreign countries	1948	197	23	12	8	3	145	(1)	6
	1949	254	25	14	9	3	197	(1)	6
	1950	302	23	10	1	5	256	(1)	6
	1951	384	24	15	14	10	303	5	13

[1] Less than $500,000. [2] See footnote 2, table 1044. [3] See footnote 3, table 1044.
Source: Department of Commerce, Office of Business Economics; Survey of Current Business, August 1952.

No. 1046.—INTERNATIONAL INVESTMENTS—VALUE OF UNITED STATES DIRECT INVESTMENTS IN FOREIGN COUNTRIES BY AREA AND INDUSTRY GROUPS: 1929 TO 1950

[In millions of dollars. Areas and industry groups for 1950 based on new census of American direct investments abroad conducted by OBE]

YEAR AND INDUSTRY	Total all areas	Canada	Latin American republics	Western Europe	Western European dependencies	Other countries
1929	[1] 7,527.7	2,010.3	3,461.9	1,263.8	169.0	534.0
1936	[1] 6,690.5	1,951.6	2,803.1	1,165.3	170.1	481.0
1943	[1] 7,861.6	2,377.6	2,721.2	1,785.5	231.8	485.5
1950 [2]	11,788.0	3,579.2	4,735.2	1,720.2	435.2	1,316.1
Agriculture, total	589.0	20.5	519.6	.8	9.4	38.7
Fruit	154.6		147.7	.1	.8	5.9
Sugar	356.7		346.4		1.5	8.9
Rubber	26.3		1.2		5.8	21.3
All other agriculture	49.5	20.5	24.4	.6	1.3	2.7
Mining and smelting, total	1,128.5	334.3	628.4	20.9	88.4	56.5
Iron	88.3	20.6	63.7	(²)		4.0
Gold, silver, and platinum	74.4	24.9	21.7	2.2	.1	25.4
Other metals	871.7	276.0	486.0	5.6	77.1	27.0
Nonmetallic minerals	94.2	12.7	57.1	13.1	11.2	.1
Petroleum	3,390.3	418.3	1,407.8	424.1	296.0	844.1
Manufacturing, total	3,831.4	1,896.6	779.8	932.5	8.9	213.6
Food	483.2	226.5	158.2	64.4	.9	33.2
Paper and allied products	377.8	367.5	4.5	5.0		.8
Chemicals and allied products	512.2	198.3	206.0	74.3	.1	34.5
Rubber products	181.6	59.0	60.3	30.7	2.8	28.8
Primary and fabricated metals	385.2	248.7	21.7	111.2	.8	2.9
Machinery (other than electrical)	420.4	203.8	13.0	178.0	.1	26.5
Electrical machinery, equipment, and supplies	386.5	140.5	78.9	152.8	1.2	13.0
Motor vehicles and their equipment	485.2	160.0	83.0	191.5	.3	50.5
All other manufacturing	599.2	292.3	155.3	127.5	2.7	21.3
Transportation, communication, and public utilities, total	1,424.9	284.4	1,041.5	27.3	18.1	53.6
Railroads	286.6	91.3	186.4			9.0
Water transportation [4]	182.6	11.7	145.7	10.2	13.4	1.6
All other transportation	62.5	16.2	31.7	8.8	1.9	3.8
Communication	155.2	11.2	131.5	6.1	2.4	4.0
Electric light, power, and gas	737.9	154.1	546.2	2.2	.4	35.1
Trade, total	762.2	239.8	242.5	185.5	13.1	81.4
Wholesale trade	541.6	178.9	191.3	101.5	5.1	64.8
Retail trade	220.6	60.9	51.1	84.0	8.0	16.6
Finance and insurance, total	424.7	313.2	71.1	37.3	.2	2.9
Banking and other finance	169.7	105.9	37.8	21.3	.4	4.3
Holding companies	56.2	12.5	28.6	12.8		2.4
Insurance	198.8	194.9	4.8	3.1	−.1	−3.7
Miscellaneous, total	237.1	72.0	44.5	92.0	1.2	27.4
Real estate	37.7	9.5	7.5	17.0	.5	3.3
Motion pictures	111.7	22.9	16.9	55.9	.4	15.7
All other	87.6	39.6	20.1	19.1	.4	8.5

[1] Includes Eastern Europe and China. 1936 also includes $26.2 million shown as "International."
[2] Excludes Eastern Europe and China; valuations for properties not generally available for end of 1950.
[3] Less than $50,000.
[4] Excluding tankers owned by petroleum companies.

Source: Department of Commerce, Office of Business Economics; *Foreign Investment Supplement to Survey of Current Business.*

No. 1048.—U. S. Government Foreign Aid by Country, Postwar to 1952

[In millions of dollars. See headnote, table 1047]

COUNTRY	Total postwar period [1]	July-Dec. 1945	1946	1947	1948	1949	1950	1951	1952
Gross foreign aid (grants and credits)	41,034	2,140	5,649	6,206	5,707	6,045	4,613	5,074	5,575
Less: Returns	3,422	162	204	543	522	483	481	452	574
Equals: Net foreign aid	37,612	1,978	5,465	5,665	5,185	5,563	4,132	4,622	5,004
Net grants	27,760	1,153	2,457	1,836	4,092	5,108	4,003	4,506	4,605
Net credits	9,852	825	3,008	3,828	1,093	455	129	116	399
MILITARY AID									
Gross foreign aid	6,672	615	110	43	326	216	528	1,495	2,739
Less: Returns	86						4	16	66
Equals: Net foreign aid: Net grants	5,986	615	110	43	326	216	524	1,479	2,673
Western Europe (including Greece and Turkey):									
Gross foreign aid	4,271			43	255	172	451	1,098	2,252
Less: Returns	84						4	15	64
Equals: Net foreign aid: Net grants	4,187			43	255	172	446	1,083	2,188
Asia and Pacific:									
Gross foreign aid	1,590	615	110		72	44	63	296	391
Less: Returns	2							1	1
Equals: Net foreign aid: Net grants	1,588	615	110		72	44	63	295	390
American republics:									
Gross foreign aid (net grants)	123							64	59
Unspecified areas:									
Gross foreign aid (net grants)	88						15	37	36
ECONOMIC AID									
Gross foreign aid	34,362	1,525	5,539	6,165	5,381	5,829	4,085	3,579	2,840
Less: Returns	3,336	162	204	543	522	483	477	436	509
Equals: Net foreign aid	31,626	1,363	5,355	5,622	4,859	5,346	3,608	3,143	2,331
Net grants	21,774	538	2,347	1,794	3,766	4,892	3,479	3,627	1,932
Net credits	9,852	825	3,008	3,828	1,093	455	129	116	399
Western Europe and dependent areas:									
Gross foreign aid	25,857	976	3,585	4,740	4,150	4,666	3,135	2,611	1,994
Less: Returns	2,129	134	136	253	191	338	323	348	417
Equals: Net foreign aid	23,729	842	3,450	4,488	3,959	4,329	2,811	2,263	1,578
Net grants	15,440	253	1,036	783	2,842	3,941	2,764	2,385	1,436
Net credits	8,289	589	2,422	3,705	1,117	388	47	−122	142
Austria:									
Gross foreign aid	1,013	18	73	151	195	206	113	161	95
Less: Returns	58			(²)	1	18	13	14	13
Equals: Net foreign aid	956	18	73	150	196	190	100	147	82
Net grants	944	18	72	146	181	185	103	151	88
Net credits	12		1	4	14	5	−2	−4	−5
Belgium-Luxembourg:									
Gross foreign aid	806	36	155	(²)	89	253	191	55	28
Less: Returns	66		2	2	8	12	15	12	14
Equals: Net foreign aid	740	36	153	−2	80	240	176	43	13
Net grants	568	36	25	(²)	56	202	190	52	8
Net credits	172		128	−2	24	38	−14	−9	6
British Commonwealth: United Kingdom:									
Gross foreign aid	7,441	167	862	2,850	1,017	1,107	710	236	492
Less: Returns	875	133	112	188	81	98	82	106	75
Equals: Net foreign aid	6,567	34	750	2,662	937	1,009	629	129	418
Net grants	2,151	−524	125	−143	443	976	657	215	403
Net credits	4,415	558	625	2,805	494	33	−28	−86	15
Denmark:									
Gross foreign aid	291	8	7	1	40	108	55	62	10
Less: Returns	15				(²)	6	3	4	2
Equals: Net foreign aid	276	8	7	1	40	102	52	58	8
Net grants	224		(²)		17	89	52	59	7
Net credits	52	8	7	1	23	14	(⁴)	−1	1
Finland:									
Gross foreign aid	128	(²)	53	32	26	12	5		
Less: Returns	37			13	3	7	8	3	3
Equals: Net foreign aid	91	(²)	53	19	24	5	−3	−3	−3
Net grants	2	(²)	1	1					
Net credits	89		51	18	24	5	−3	−3	−3
France:									
Gross foreign aid	5,070	151	1,163	607	808	856	514	476	495
Less: Returns	386	1	5	19	25	90	50	55	141
Equals: Net foreign aid	4,684	149	1,158	588	783	766	464	421	354
Net grants	2,581	149	−132	17	619	738	481	439	269
Net credits	2,103		1,290	571	164	28	−17	−18	85
Germany:									
Gross foreign aid	3,891	6	288	446	1,161	965	484	386	155
Less: Returns	173			3	38	28	23	29	51
Equals: Net foreign aid	3,718	6	288	442	1,123	937	461	357	103
Net grants	3,479	6	267	419	955	933	466	362	71
Net credits	239		21	24	168	4	−5	−5	32

See footnotes at end of table.

No. 1048.—U. S. Government Foreign Aid by Country, Postwar to 1952—Con.

[In millions of dollars]

COUNTRY	Total postwar period	July-Dec. 1945	1946	1947	1948	1949	1950	1951	1952
Greece:									
Gross foreign aid	1,299	121	166	159	148	126	121	166	139
Less: Returns	72			3	4	18	14	16	14
Equals: Net foreign aid	1,127	121	166	156	164	145	107	180	124
Net grants	1,046	121	132	98	154	112	108	182	129
Net credits	92		36	58	20	—4	—2	—2	—5
Iceland:									
Gross foreign aid	28			2	5	5	9	6
Less: Returns	1				(²)	(²)	(²)	(²)
Equals: Net foreign aid	26			2	5	5	9	5
Net grants	21			(²)	5	4	7	4
Net credits	5			2	(²)	(²)	2	1
Ireland:									
Gross foreign aid	147		(²)		6	55	25	(²)
Less: Returns	1					(²)	1	(²)
Equals: Net foreign aid	146		(²)		6	55	24	(²)
Net grants	17		(²)		3	(²)	14	(²)
Net credits	128				64	55	10	
Italy:									
Gross foreign aid	2,647	126	514	317	422	457	280	300	230
Less: Returns	166		1	11	22	29	38	41	35
Equals: Net foreign aid	2,480	126	513	305	400	427	254	260	175
Net grants	2,153	126	370	246	314	375	249	284	179
Net credits	327		143	60	86	62	5	—25	—4
Netherlands:									
Gross foreign aid	1,243	63	135	99	124	300	275	150	88
Less: Returns	184	(²)	1	11	3	24	52	48	44
Equals: Net foreign aid	1,059	63	133	88	120	266	222	102	44
Net grants	759	30	26	—46	73	203	253	142	65
Net credits	300	34	107	134	47	82	—31	—40	—21
Norway:									
Gross foreign aid	328	(²)	8	24	64	73	76	40	32
Less: Returns	46			(²)	3	10	16	9	8
Equals: Net foreign aid	282	(²)	8	24	61	64	61	41	23
Net grants	182	(²)	1	(²)	11	37	69	45	18
Net credits	100		8	23	50	27	—8	—5	²
Portugal:									
Gross foreign aid	47						19	20	8
Less: Returns	1			(²)	(²)		1	(²)	(²)
Equals: Net foreign aid	46			(²)	(²)		18	20	8
Net grants	10							1	2
Net credits	35			(²)	(²)		10	19	6
Spain:									
Gross foreign aid (net credits)	41							17	24
Sweden:									
Gross foreign aid	112	1			3	40	45	27	—3
Less: Returns	3				1	2	(²)	(²)
Equals: Net foreign aid	109	1			3	39	43	27	—4
Net grants	87	1			1	38	24	27	—3
Net credits	21				2	1	19	(²)	(²)
Trieste:									
Gross foreign aid	46			11	10	9	8	8	
Less: Returns	2				(²)	0	(²)	1	(²)
Equals: Net foreign aid: Net grants	44			11	10	9	8	7	(²)
Turkey:									
Gross foreign aid	239			3	10	13	39	47	59	68
Less: Returns	38			4	1	2	4	8	7	9
Equals: Net foreign aid	202			—1	9	10	34	39	52	59
Net grants	100			—4			7	7	38	53
Net credits	101			3	9	10	28	32	14	6
Yugoslavia:									
Gross foreign aid	525	115	150	34			36	108	83
Less: Returns	5						(²)	2	3
Equals: Net foreign aid	520	115	150	34			36	106	80
Net grants	466	115	150	34	—1			91	77
Net credits	54				1		36	15	3
Unspecified Western Europe [6]									
Gross foreign aid (net grants)	605	156	5		8	30	85	258	63
Other Europe:									
Gross foreign aid	1,160	274	679	186	19	1			
Less: Returns	72		2	1	16	25	9	—15	4
Equals: Net foreign aid	1,088	274	677	186	3	—24	—9	—15	4
Net grants	775	52	605	155	—8	—8	—9	—13	
Net credits	313	223	72	30	11	—16	—1	—1	—4
Czechoslovakia:									
Gross foreign aid	213	54	120	39	(²)				
Less: Returns	26			(²)	—7	17	(²)	(²)	(²)
Equals: Net foreign aid	188	54	120	39	—7	—17	(²)	(²)	(²)
Net grants	183	54	98	31	(²)				
Net credits	5		22	8	—7	—17	(²)	(²)	(²)

See footnotes at end of table.

No. 1048.—U. S. Government Foreign Aid by Country, Postwar to 1952—Con.

[In millions of dollars]

COUNTRY	Total postwar period [1]	July-Dec. 1945	1946	1947	1948	1949	1950	1951	1952
Poland:									
Gross foreign aid	443	75	251	96	19	1			
Less: Returns	6			(?)	1	(?)	(?)	1	3
Equals: Net foreign aid	437	75	251	96	19	1	(?)	-1	-3
Net grants	365	75	216	74					
Net credits	72		35	21	19	1	(?)	-1	-3
U. S. S. R.:									
Gross foreign aid	465	133	287	45					
Less: Returns	39		2			8	9	13	
Equals: Net foreign aid	426	133	285	45	-8	-8	-9	-13	
Net grants	204	-89	285	45	-8	-8	-9	-13	
Net credits	223	223							
Unspecified other Europe: [7]									
Gross foreign aid	39	11	21	6					
Less: Returns	2			(?)	1	(?)	(?)	(?)	(?)
Equals: Net foreign aid	36	11	21	6	-1	(?)	(?)	(?)	(?)
Net grants	23	11	6	5					
Net credits	14		15	1	-1	(?)	(?)	(?)	(?)
Near East and Africa:									
Gross foreign aid	448	2	30	12	6	48	69	94	187
Less: Returns	152	3	2	111	16	4	2	3	12
Equals: Net foreign aid	296	-1	28	-99	-10	44	67	91	176
Net grants	104	-7	1	-91		15	20	44	122
Net credits	192	6	28	-8	-10	29	47	47	53
Egypt:									
Gross foreign aid	19	(?)	9	1	2	5	(?)	(?)	(?)
Less: Returns	11			1	9	1			1
Equals: Net foreign aid	7	(?)	9	(?)	-5	4	(?)	(?)	(?)
Net grants	1	(?)	(?)	1					
Net credits	7		9	-1	-5	4	(?)		-1
Iran:									
Gross foreign aid	42	1	4	(?)	(?)	17	2	4	14
Less: Returns	15		1	4	2	2	(?)	(?)	4
Equals: Net foreign aid	27		3	-3	-2	15	2	4	10
Net grants	3	-8				(?)	(?)	2	10
Net credits	24	9	3	-3	-2	15	2	2	
Israel:									
Gross foreign aid	218					7	41	57	113
Less: Returns	4								4
Equals: Net foreign aid	214					7	41	57	109
Net grants	98							16	81
Net credits	117					7	41	41	27
Liberia:									
Gross foreign aid	24	1	4	3	2	4	4	3	4
Less: Returns	1							(?)	1
Equals: Net foreign aid	23	1	4	3	2	4	4	3	3
Net grants	2					(?)	(?)	1	1
Net credits	21	1	4	3	2	4	3	2	2
Saudi Arabia:									
Gross foreign aid	21	1	10	5	(?)		1	3	1
Less: Returns	7				3	1	1	1	1
Equals: Net foreign aid	14	1	10	5	-3	-1	(?)	2	(?)
Net grants	2	1	1			(?)	(?)		
Net credits	12		9	5	-3	-1	(?)	2	-1
Union of South Africa:									
Gross foreign aid	28			1					26
Less: Returns	94			92	(?)		1	(?)	(?)
Equals: Net foreign aid	-66			-91	(?)		-1	(?)	26
Net grants	-92			-92					
Net credits	26			1	(?)		-1	(?)	26
Unspecified Near East and Africa: [8]									
Gross foreign aid	97		3	1	(?)	15	21	27	30
Less: Returns	21	-3	(?)	14	1	(?)	(?)	2	1
Equals: Net foreign aid	76	-3	3	-13	-1	15	21	25	29
Net grants	91		(?)	(?)		15	20	26	29
Net credits	-15	-3	3	-13	-1	(?)	1	-1	-1
Asia and Pacific:									
Gross foreign aid	5,600	187	866	988	869	898	657	647	487
Less: Returns	534	16	50	148	120	72	84	21	22
Equals: Net foreign aid	5,067	171	817	840	749	826	573	625	465
Net grants	4,427	181	406	792	799	826	579	526	318
Net credits	640	-10	411	48	-50	(?)	-6	99	147
Afghanistan:									
Gross foreign aid (net foreign aid)	17					(?)	(?)	11	6
Net grants	(?)					(?)	(?)	(?)	(?)
Net credits	17							11	6
Australia—New Zealand:									
Gross foreign aid	27	12	13	1	1				
Less: Returns	24		20			1	1	(?)	1
Equals: Net foreign aid	3	12	-7	1	1	-1	-1	(?)	-1
Net grants	-6	12	-18	(?)					
Net credits	9		11	(?)	1	-1	-1	(?)	-1

See footnotes at end of table.

No. 1048.—U. S. Government Foreign Aid by Country, Postwar to 1952—Con.

[In millions of dollars]

COUNTRY	Total postwar period [1]	July-Dec. 1945	1946	1947	1948	1949	1950	1951	1952
Burma:									
Gross foreign aid	17			5	([2])	([2])	([2])	6	5
Less: Returns	2				([2])		1	1	1
Equals: Net foreign aid	15			5	([4])	([2])	−1	5	5
Net grants	11				([2])	([2])	([2])	6	5
Net credits	3			5	([4])	([2])	−1	([4])	([4])
China—Taiwan (Formosa):									
Gross foreign aid	1,070	129	342	207	155	66	23	71	79
Less: Returns	125	14	10	18	35	34	6	6	2
Equals: Net foreign aid	946	115	332	189	119	32	17	65	76
Net grants	837	124	172	173	135	62	22	70	77
Net credits	109	−10	159	16	−15	−30	−5	−5	−1
India—Pakistan:									
Gross foreign aid	258	2	40		3	([2])	1	110	102
Less: Returns	33	2	20		6	([2])		2	
Equals: Net foreign aid	225	([4])	20	−3	−2	([4])	1	108	102
Net grants	−11	([4])	−19	−3	−6	([2])	1	4	12
Net credits	236		39		3	([4])		104	90
Indochina:									
Gross foreign aid	37						1	14	22
Less: Returns	1							([2])	1
Equals: Net foreign aid: Net grants	36						1	14	22
Indonesia:									
Gross foreign aid	206	4	64		20	43	39	3	35
Less: Returns	9				([2])	2	2	3	2
Equals: Net foreign aid	198	4	64		20	41	36	1	33
Net grants	91	4	([2])		14	30	35	3	4
Net credits	107		64		6	10	1	−3	29
Japan and Ryukyu Islands:									
Gross foreign aid	2,414	9	329	532	413	500	283	285	62
Less: Returns	293			116	76	25	69	3	4
Equals: Net foreign aid	2,121	9	329	415	337	475	214	282	58
Net grants	2,074	9	209	457	394	453	246	285	22
Net credits	48		121	−41	−56	22	−32	−3	36
Korea:									
Gross foreign aid	717	1	31	83	142	85	109	119	148
Less: Returns	13					7	5	([2])	
Equals: Net foreign aid	704	1	31	83	142	78	104	118	148
Net grants	683	1	24	74	132	78	108	118	148
Net credits	21		7	8	10		−4		
Philippines:									
Gross foreign aid	807	29	42	161	133	203	202	17	21
Less: Returns	30			11	2	([2])	([2])	4	11
Equals: Net foreign aid	778	29	42	150	131	203	201	13	9
Net grants	692	29	36	91	130	203	166	17	20
Net credits	86		6	59	1	([4])	35	−4	−11
Thailand:									
Gross foreign aid	17		5	([2])	1	([2])	([2])	6	5
Less: Returns	4				([2])	([2])	([2])	1	2
Equals: Net foreign aid	13		5	([4])	1	([4])	([4])	5	3
Net grants	9					([2])	([2])	5	5
Net credits	4		5	([2])	1	([4])	([4])	([4])	−1
Unspecified Asia and Pacific:[9]									
Gross foreign aid (net grants)	11	3	2					4	3
American republics:									
Gross foreign aid	818	32	115	130	78	107	94	142	120
Less: Returns	305	9	25	31	40	44	57	47	52
Equals: Net foreign aid	514	24	91	99	38	63	37	95	68
Net grants	165	8	15	46	16	29	17	14	19
Net credits	349	16	75	53	22	34	19	81	49
Canada:									
Gross foreign aid	150				140	1	2	1	6
Less: Returns	143	([2])	([2])	([4])	140	([2])	1	([2])	1
Equals: Net foreign aid: Net credits	7	([4])	([4])	([4])	([4])	([2])	1	1	5
International and unspecified:									
Gross foreign aid	928	53	283	108	119	108	128	84	44
Less: Returns	2							1	1
Equals: Net foreign aid	926	53	283	108	119	108	128	83	43
Net grants	863	53	283	108	117	89	106	71	37
Net credits	63				3	20	22	12	6

[1] July 1, 1945 through Dec. 31, 1952. All lend-lease and credit-agreement offsets to grants are from V-J Day (Sept. 2, 1945).
[2] Less than $500,000.
[3] Net (+) of less than $500,000.
[4] Net (−) of less than $500,000.
[5] Negative entry results from refunds of cash aid.
[6] Includes Switzerland.
[7] Includes Albania and Hungary.
[8] Includes Bahrein, Eritrea—Ethiopia, Iraq, Jordan, Lebanon, Libya, and Syria.
[9] Includes Ceylon, Nepal, and Trust Territory of the Pacific Islands.

Source: Department of Commerce, Office of Business Economics; quarterly report, *Foreign Aid by the United States Government*.

No. **1049.**—MSA European Program—Authorizations and Paid Shipments, by Commodity Group and Area of Source: April 3, 1948, to Dec. 31, 1952

[In millions of dollars]

COMMODITY GROUP	Total	AREA OF SOURCE				
		United States	Canada	Latin America	Participating (OEEC) countries	Other countries
Procurement authorizations, total	13,813.4	(¹)	(¹)	(¹)	(¹)	(¹)
Commodity total	²12,081.9	8,439.9	1,465.8	918.7	554.3	723.0
Food and agricultural commodities	5,700.6	4,560.4	602.4	423.9	50.3	63.6
Industrial commodities	6,401.1	3,879.5	863.5	494.8	504.0	659.4
Technical services	61.4	60.3				1.1
Ship disbursements	9.4	(¹)	(¹)	(¹)	(¹)	(¹)
Assistance via European Payments Union	312.7	(¹)	(¹)	(¹)	(¹)	(¹)
European Payments Union—capital fund	361.4	(¹)	(¹)	(¹)	(¹)	(¹)
General freight account	33.5	(¹)	(¹)	(¹)	(¹)	(¹)
Ocean freight	932.1	(¹)	(¹)	(¹)	(¹)	(¹)
Paid shipments, total ³	12,986.5	(¹)	(¹)	(¹)	(¹)	(¹)
Commodity total	⁴11,357.5	7,785.2	1,437.0	887.3	548.5	719.9
Food and agricultural commodities	5,503.2	4,366.3	603.0	420.9	49.7	63.2
Industrial commodities	5,874.7	3,418.9	834.0	466.4	498.7	656.7
Technical services	49.0	47.9				1.1
Ship disbursements	9.1	(¹)	(¹)	(¹)	(¹)	(¹)
Assistance via European Payments Union	300.4	(¹)	(¹)	(¹)	(¹)	(¹)
European Payments Union—capital fund	361.4	(¹)	(¹)	(¹)	(¹)	(¹)
Ocean freight	903.1	(¹)	(¹)	(¹)	(¹)	(¹)
COMMODITY DETAIL ON SHIPMENTS						
Food, feed, and fertilizer	3,430.6	2,323.9	662.9	397.9	48.8	47.0
Bread grains	1,769.3	1,278.7	490.7			
Coarse grains	451.2	438.8	7.5			4.9
Fats and oils	359.1	291.4	10.1	9.4	19.3	28.8
Sugar and related products	312.9	21.5		284.0	1.0	6.4
Meat	132.7	24.1	67.5	39.2	1.8	.2
Dairy products	118.1	107.7	10.0	.1	.3	
Feeds and fodder	58.6	36.8	2.8	13.6	1.9	3.4
Fertilizer	49.3	16.6	3.4	16.2	10.5	2.6
Fruits and nuts, except peanuts	36.9	31.3	.3		5.2	
Rice	31.1	28.1		3.0		
Coffee	29.1			29.0		
Vegetables and preparations	20.2	10.9	.1	.3	8.4	.4
Eggs	18.4	18.4				
Fish, and products, except fish oil and meal	15.8	6.3	9.3		.2	
Miscellaneous grain preparations	7.0	6.5	.5			
Seeds, other than oilseeds	6.9	6.0	.8		.1	
Miscellaneous edible agricultural products	4.1	.8		3.0		.3
Fuel	1,833.7	643.3	.1	170.4	421.6	596.1
Petroleum and products	1,414.2	332.4	.1	170.4	325.3	586.0
Coal and related fuels	419.5	310.8			96.6	12.1
Raw materials and semifinished products	3,844.8	2,620.3	771.8	316.7	68.4	73.9
Cotton	1,517.7	1,517.4		.3		
Nonferrous metals and products	838.8	172.6	482.3	142.7	35.5	5.7
Iron and steel mill materials and products, including ferro-alloys	397.5	334.4	39.5	.7	21.8	1.1
Chemicals and related products	288.9	268.1	9.9	6.0	4.7	.1
Metallic ores and concentrates	151.1	13.2	46.2	88.7		3.0
Fabricated basic textiles	124.6	69.9	2.5	1.6	4.0	46.6
Lumber and lumber manufactures	123.8	57.3	62.2	2.5	.6	1.3
Pulp and paper	122.7	30.1	92.3		.2	
Nonmetallic minerals	116.3	83.1	32.9	.2	.1	
Hides, skins, and leather	83.4	25.4	4.1	53.7		.4
Fibers, except unmanufactured cotton and wool	36.9	6.8	.1	13.9	.3	15.7
Naval stores	27.3	27.1				.1
Wool, unmanufactured	14.0	13.9		.1		
Miscellaneous fiber products	1.8	.9			.9	
Machinery and vehicles	1,666.8	1,646.7	41.1		7.6	.1
Machinery and equipment	1,318.5	1,278.9	33.1		6.4	.1
Motor vehicles, engines, and parts	222.8	230.9	1.5		.4	
Aircraft, engines, and parts	95.7	95.6				
Other transportation equipment	51.8	45.3	6.4		.1	
Miscellaneous and unclassified	⁴569.7	567.0	21.0		2.5	.8
Tobacco	465.9	460.7		4.7	.6	
Miscellaneous industrial commodities	103.3	79.8	21.0	.1	1.9	.5
Misc. inedible animal and vegetable products	20.8	16.5		3.9		.3

¹ Not available.
² Includes refunds totaling $19.8 million for unclassified commodities not shown separately.
³ MSA expenditures supplemented by movement reports from U. S. Government agencies; total paid shipments are less than actual movements because of time required for receipt and processing of documents requesting payment.
⁴ Includes refunds totaling $20.3 million for unclassified commodities not shown separately, and for which source is not ascertainable.

Source: Mutual Security Agency; *Monthly Report to the Public Advisory Board,*

No. 1050.—MSA European Program—Authorizations and Paid Shipments, by Commodity Group and Country of Destination: April 3, 1948, to Dec. 31, 1952

[In millions of dollars]

COMMODITY GROUP	Total	Aus-tria	Bel-gium-Lux-em-bourg	Den-mark	France	Ger-many (Fed. Rep.)	Greece	Ice-land	Ire-land	Italy	Neth-er-lands	Nor-way	Por-tugal	Swe-den	Tri-este	Tur-key	United King-dom	Yugo-sla-via
Procurement authorizations, total	18,812.4	700.1	845.4	271.9	2,798.1	1,369.4	699.0	28.7	146.3	1,681.0	1,077.0	383.6	88.3	197.1	82.0	283.4	3,491.0	195.0
Commodity total	12,081.9	576.9	528.5	284.1	2,420.7	1,274.2	505.6	22.0	144.4	1,344.6	1,043.7	348.4	47.8	107.1	57.5	146.0	3,381.4	146.3
Food and agricultural commodities	6,700.6	415.6	171.1	120.6	729.6	979.6	335.9	6.4	105.2	660.6	482.3	110.3	18.5	.6	11.3	118.3	1,472.6	88.2
Industrial commodities	6,401.1	162.0	367.9	144.1	1,695.1	290.5	171.7	18.7	36.3	712.8	428.3	110.0	18.8	106.6	11.3	133.3	1,709.6	60.1
Unclassified commodity adjust-ments	116.8	−.8	−.4	−.6	−3.0	−1.9	−1.0	−.1	...	−8.1	−7.9	−.8	−.3	−.9	...	...	−7.9	...
Technical services	61.4	...	...	...	14.9	2.0	6.7	−.7	...	11.4	2.5	1.4	...	...	2.4	12.7	3.0	...
Ship disbursements	9.4	...	1.4	...	2.0	.2	.9	...	...	...	...	...	...	...	...	...	...	...
Assistance via European Pay-ments Union	212.7	46.0	...	...	...	...	123.4	6.9	...	...	...	...	...	...	...	47.8	64.0	...
European Payments Union — cap-ital fund	261.4	...	...	...	260.6	...	...	...	...	...	...	...	...	...	...	...	...	...
General freight account	33.6	...	26.6	...	...	113.0	52.4	...	...	...	...	...	...	...	...	...	87.7	...
Ocean freight	162.1	80.2	...	11.6	...	...	...	...	1.8	...	...	...	44.9	...	...	...	...	4.7
Paid shipments, total	12,596.9	647.7	816.1	296.5	2,611.0	1,289.5	656.6	27.8	146.3	1,543.2	1,046.5	358.5	...	197.1	...	194.1	3,069.1	195.6
Commodity total	11,387.0	544.0	...	367.6	2,344.5	1,256.6	473.7	15.8	144.6	2,105.0	1,004.4	...	42.0	197.1	...	120.0	3,089.1	113.6
Food and agricultural commod-ities	4,196.7	588.4	171.1	117.7	704.3	973.6	...	...	...	...	...	...	18.5	...	...	...	...	...
Industrial commodities	6,876.7	185.5	343.5	146.5	1,642.4	341.6	...	...	...	...	...	...	...	103.6	...	...	...	...
Technical services	40.0	...	...	...	11.7	1.8	...	...	...	...	...	...	...	...	...	...	1.0	...
Ship disbursements	9.1	...	1.4	...	2.0	.3	...	...	...	...	...	...	...	...	...	...	...	...
Assistance via European Pay-ments Union	360.4	46.0	...	...	...	...	100.2	6.9	...	...	...	...	...	...	...	47.8	64.0	...
European Payments Union — cap-ital fund	881.1	92.7	6.5	11.7	361.6	119.7	42.6	6.1	9.1	2.0	6.0	...	...	...	...	6.1	...	...

Meat
Dairy products
Other
Fuel
Petroleum and products
Coal and related fuels
Raw materials and semifinished products
Cotton
Nonferrous metals and products
Iron and steel mill materials and products, including ferro-alloys
Chemicals and related products
Metallic ores and concentrate
Fabricated basic textiles
Lumber and lumber manufactures
Pulp and paper
Nonmetallic minerals
Hides, skins, and leather
Fibers, except unmanufactured
Naval stores
Wool, unmanufactured
Miscellaneous fiber products
Machinery and vehicles
Machinery and equipment
Motor vehicles, engines, and parts
Aircraft engines, and parts
Other transportation equipment
Miscellaneous manufactured
Tobacco
Misc. industrial commodities
Misc. inedible animal and vegetable products
Unclassified commodity refund

1 Includes $101.4 million authorized and expended for Indonesia in 1948 and 1949 when this country was a Netherlands dependency.

2 Not available.

3 MSA expenditures supplemented by movement reports from U. S. Government agencies; total paid shipments are less than actual movements because of time required for receipt and processing of documents requesting payment.

4 Includes refunds totaling $20.3 million for unclassified commodities not shown separately.

Source: Mutual Security Agency; Monthly Report to the Public Advisory Board.

No. 1050.—MSA EUROPEAN PROGRAM—AUTHORIZATIONS AND PAID SHIPMENTS, BY COMMODITY GROUP AND COUNTRY OF DESTINATION: APRIL 3, 1948, TO DEC. 31, 1952

[In millions of dollars]

COMMODITY GROUP	Total	Austria	Belgium-Luxembourg	Denmark	France	Germany (Fed. Rep.)	Greece	Iceland	Ireland	Italy	Netherlands[1]	Norway	Portugal	Sweden	Trieste	Turkey	United Kingdom	Yugoslavia
Procurement authorizations, total	13,812.4	702.1	655.4	275.0	2,736.1	1,389.4	699.0	29.7	146.2	1,611.0	1,677.0	363.5	88.3	197.1	32.8	232.4	3,431.0	185.0
Commodity total	12,081.9	578.9	528.5	264.1	2,420.7	1,274.2	506.6	22.0	144.4	1,344.6	1,042.7	345.4	47.8	107.1	27.8	149.0	3,231.4	146.3
Food and agricultural commodities	5,700.6	415.6	171.1	120.6	739.5	978.6	335.9	6.4	105.2	940.0	480.4	110.2	18.8	1.5	11.3	11.5	1,473.6	95.2
Industrial commodities	6,401.1	162.0	357.9	144.1	1,685.1	296.5	171.7	15.7	39.2	713.8	563.2	138.6	29.2	105.6	16.2	138.2	1,759.6	51.1
Unclassified commodity adjustments	-19.8	-.8	-.4	-.6	-3.9	-1.9	-1.0	-.7		-8.1	-1.0	-.8	-.3	-.3			-7.0	
Technical services	61.4				14.0	2.0	8.9			11.4	1.9	1.1				12.7	7.0	
Ship disbursements	9.4		1.4		2.0	.2		6.9			2.5	.4					2.0	
Assistance via European Payments Union	312.7	45.0					121.4									47.8	91.9	
European Payments Union—capital fund	361.4						22.4	.1										
General freight account	33.5	80.2	25.5	11.8	300.5	113.0	52.4		1.8	164.9	30.0	3.6	2.4		6.1	12.3	67.7	8.7
Ocean freight	962.1																	
Paid shipments, total[3]	12,960.5	667.7	540.9	269.3	2,611.0	1,369.5	635.6	27.3	146.2	1,343.2	1,643.5	344.9	44.9	197.1	31.7	194.1	3,318.2	118.9
Commodity total[4]	11,357.5	546.0	514.1	257.6	2,345.5	1,256.8	473.7	19.8	144.4	1,106.5	1,009.4	339.8	43.0	107.1	26.6	130.0	3,098.5	112.6
Food and agricultural commodities	5,603.2	390.4	171.1	117.7	706.3	973.6	222.7	6.4	105.2	906.8	497.3	110.1	18.7	1.5	11.3	15.0	1,403.0	48.2
Industrial commodities	5,874.7	150.4	343.5	140.5	1,643.4	285.0	152.4	13.5	39.2	696.9	522.5	130.2	23.6	105.6	15.4	114.1	1,694.4	63.5
Technical services	49.0		1.4		11.7	1.8	7.4	.5		8.7	1.6	1.1				8.3	8.0	
Ship disbursements	9.1				2.0	.2	.6	6.9			2.5	.4					2.0	
Assistance via European Payments Union	300.4	45.0					109.2									47.8	91.9	
European Payments Union—capital fund	361.4							6.9										
Ocean freight	903.1	76.7	26.3	11.7	361.8	110.7	44.8	.1	1.8	144.0	30.0	2.8	1.9		6.1	8.3	76.8	7.3

COMMODITY DETAIL ON SHIPMENTS [1]

Feed, feed and fertilizer	3,420.6	333.7	147.0	295.6	596.2	311.4	6.3	69.1	225.9	332.4	90.0	19.7		10.9	12.9	881.1	19.9
Bread grains	1,769.3	168.4	54.0	122.8	232.8	175.1	1.7	20.2	196.0	155.8	50.3	19.7		7.0	12.8	545.1	1.3
Coarse grains	451.2	63.5	4.6	56.9	162.6	4.8		46.5	2.8	58.0	19.0					6.4	1.4
Fats and oils	359.1	59.6	24.0	65.8	93.4	5.7	.8	.6	17.3	49.7	10.6		2.5			9.3	4.7
Sugar and related products	312.9	16.2	14.2	12.6	53.3	48.9	.3	.2		29.7	2.8					134.4	
Meat	132.7	4.4	10.7	1.1	18.5	17.6				4.4						76.5	
Dairy products	118.1	.4	13.4	11.8		20.9				1.3		1.2				69.0	
Other	277.2	21.2	24.6	24.7	35.5	38.3	3.5	1.5	9.7	33.6	7.2	8.4	13.3	2.9	41.4	27.5
Fuel	1,633.7	41.6	61.1	469.0	64.2	37.7	1.7	13.3	252.5	89.1	42.9	8.4	12.7	2.9	385.4	11.1
Petroleum and products	414.2	3.9	59.1	78.2	60.2	27.0			156.5	68.5	41.3				11.1	
Coal and related fuels	419.5	37.7	2.1	433.4		27.6			95.8	20.7			12.6		388.4	16.3
Raw materials and semifinished products	3,844.8	100.8	96.9	738.3	447.3	56.0	2.8	14.2	8.5	386	64.3	2.1	1.7	21.1	1,283.4	79.6
Cotton	1,517.7	46.2	6.6	371.5	263.2	9.0	.3		733.	120.0	1.9		.2	1.6	268.7	30.9
Nonferrous metals and products	838.8	9.2	.7	150.3	48.2	2.7			43.5	54.4	6.5			1.2	503.3	2.4
Iron and steel mill materials and products, including ferro-alloys	397.5	7.2	14.8	47.9	3.5	12.6	.8	2.1	21.0	75.9	30.9	1.9	.3	8.1	137.7	13.0
Chemicals and related products	288.9	14.3	27.5	84.4	30.0	14.4	.1	.4	16.4	23.0	2.7	.1	.3	5.9	66.1	7.8
Metallic ores and concentrates	151.1	2.8	19.7	19.8	20.3		.7		7.3	8.9	1.9		.4		67.6	
Fabricated basic textiles	134.6	.8	3.6	9.7	6.4	1.3		1.9	5.3	65.7	11.1		2.3	4.2	9.2	3.8
Lumber and lumber manufactures																
Pulp and paper	123.8	1.0	6.5	6.3	7.1	6.1	.1	3.6	1.4	7.0	1.1		.6	1.6	81.4	1.0
Nonmetallic minerals	122.7	3.6	10.7	1.0	16.4	1.5	.7	4.2	3.9	6.1	1.0	.1			76.6	.4
Hides, skins, and leather	83.4		2.5	28.4	5.9	2.2	.1	.7	6.3	11.7	1.2		5.1	.3	52.7	3.2
Fibers, except unmanufactured cotton and wool				.3	40.7	6.3									2.8	
Naval stores	36.9	.6	.9		8.7	2.4		.1	2.4	8.7	2.2	.1			6.5	
Wool, unmanufactured	27.3	.1	.3	12.7	10.4					4.5	3		.1		8.7	
Miscellaneous fiber products	14.0	6.2			7.6					.7						
Machinery and vehicles	1.8		.2	.2		1.3										1.2
Machinery and equipment	1,658.8	57.1	194.0	492.8	28.2	64.2	8.8	19.8	233.4	170.7	39.4	13.0	.7	83.8	224.9	9.9
Motor vehicles, engines, and parts	1,318.6	55.3	76.5	380.0	32.4	51.4	7.6	6.8	228.2	92.6	27.8	9.1	.6	70.1	230.5	2.2
Aircraft engines, and parts	222.8	1.3	104.7	19.5	5.2	.7		3.9		45.3	1.1	.5		13.0	3.3	1.5
Other transportation equipment	95.7	.7	4.2	54.2			.6		4.6	30.2	1.0					
Miscellaneous and unclassified	31.8			.8	.7		.1			2.7		3.3		.7	1.1	1.6
Tobacco	460.7	12.7	34.1	45.9	84.8	12.6	.6	27.0	9.5	34.6	17.9	-.2	.1	7.3	243.7	
Commercial commodities	103.3	10.2	15.8	33.3	62.9		.2	35.7	12.6	22.4	15.7	.3	.1	8.3	230.5	1.6
Misc. inedible animal and vegetable products	20.8	-.6	.6	2.6	4.5	2.4		1.2		9.0	1.7	.3			10.6	
Unclassified commodity refund	-20.3	-.8	-.4	-4.2	-1.7	-1.4	-.1	.1	-8.2	-1.0	-.5	-.4	-.1	2.0	-.8	.1

[1] Includes $101.4 million authorized and expended for Indonesia in 1948 and 1949 when this country was a Netherlands dependency.

[2] Not available.

[3] MSA expenditures supplemented by movement reports from U. S. Government agencies; total paid shipments are less than actual movements because of time required for receipt and processing of documents requesting payment.

[4] Includes refunds totaling $20.3 million for unclassified commodities not shown separately.

Source: Mutual Security Agency; Monthly Report to the Public Advisory Board.

No. 1051.—MSA Far East Program—Authorizations and Paid Shipments, by Commodity Group and Area of Source: June 5, 1950, to Dec. 31, 1952

[In thousands of dollars]

COMMODITY GROUP	Total	AREA OF SOURCE					
		United States	Canada	Latin America	European participating (OEEC) countries	Other countries	World-wide source[1]
Authorizations, total	413,342	[2]	[2]	[2]	[2]	[2]	[2]
Commodity total	378,985	275,103	723	1,277	18,237	43,800	39,896
Food and agricultural commodities	151,304	119,704		1,277	14,753	9,218	6,352
Industrial commodities	227,639	155,360	723		3,479	34,553	33,525
Unclassified commodities	92	39			4	30	19
Unclassified commodity reductions	−51	[2]	[2]	[2]	[2]	[2]	[2]
Technical services	5,215	5,210			5		
Technical assistance	8,665	8,665					
Ocean freight	20,477	[2]	[2]	[2]	[2]	[2]	[2]
Paid shipments, total[3]	234,255	[2]	[2]	[2]	[2]	[2]	[2]
Commodity total	209,877	136,283	1,558	2,000	32,136	37,947	13
Food and agricultural commodities	107,991	76,504	1,420	1,268	22,934	5,864	
Industrial commodities	101,932	59,779	137	732	9,201	32,083	
Unclassified commodities	13						13
Unclassified commodity refunds	−59	[2]	[2]	[2]	[2]	[2]	[2]
Technical services	3,840	3,840					
Technical assistance	4,804	4,604					
Ocean freight	15,934	[2]	[2]	[2]	[2]	[2]	[2]
COMMODITY DETAIL ON SHIPMENTS							
Food, feed, and fertilizer	74,833	43,402	1,420	1,268	22,934	5,809	
Fertilizer	44,018	14,653	922		22,934	5,509	
Fats and oils	15,905	15,905					
Bread grains	10,876	10,876					
Sugar, raw or refined	1,536			1,268		267	
Feeds and fodder	1,145	1,145					
Dairy products, milk	566	566					
Fish and products, except fish oil and meal	498			498			
Meat	129	98				32	
Fruits and nuts, except peanuts	128	128					
Vegetables and preparations	23	23					
Seeds, other than oilseeds	9	9					
Fuel	17,521	9,315			80	8,125	
Petroleum and products	17,423	9,298				8,125	
Coal and related fuels	97	17			80		
Raw materials and semifinished products	79,120	55,564	114	732	7,144	15,566	
Cotton	30,664	30,664					
Fabricated basic textiles	16,910	6,530			4,758	5,622	
Chemicals and related products	11,797	10,194		95	1,131	377	
Iron and steel mill materials and products, including ferro-alloys	10,356	3,466			348	6,543	
Nonferrous metals and products	2,848	184	91		535	2,039	
Pulp and paper	2,323	2,083	23		96	120	
Lumber and lumber manufactures	1,377	1,248				128	
Hides, skins, and leather	1,325	443		637		246	
Nonmetallic minerals	1,161	514			222	425	
Miscellaneous fiber products	306	235			5	67	
Metallic ores and concentrates	51				51		
Naval stores	2	2					
Machinery and vehicles	28,657	20,149	22		925	7,561	
Machinery and equipment	20,179	13,486	22		697	5,974	
Motor vehicles, engines, and parts	6,100	5,645			229	226	
Aircraft, engines, and parts	246	246					
Other transportation equipment	2,132	772				1,360	
Miscellaneous and unclassified	9,746	7,853	2		1,051	887	13
Scientific and professional instruments	2,979	2,402			506	71	
Tobacco	2,436	2,436					
Rubber and rubber products	707	671	2		1	32	
Miscellaneous industrial commodities	3,614	2,343			544	727	
Misc. inedible animal and vegetable prod.	55					55	
Unclassified commodities	13						13
Unclassified commodity refunds	−59	[2]	[2]	[2]	[2]	[2]	[2]

[1] Procurement authorizations issued with "worldwide source," except for exclusion of recipient country itself and Communist-dominated areas. These authorizations identified as "worldwide source" until closed, at which time actual source countries will be determined.

[2] Not available.

[3] MSA expenditures supplemented by movement reports from U. S. Government agencies; total paid shipments less than actual movements because of time required for receipt and processing of documents requesting payment.

Source: Mutual Security Agency; *Monthly Report to the Public Advisory Board.*

No. 1052.—MSA Far East Program—Authorizations and Paid Shipments, by Commodity Group and Country of Destinations: June 5, 1950, to Dec. 31, 1952

[In thousands of dollars]

COMMODITY GROUP	Total	China (Formosa)	Indochina, Associated States	Philippines	Thailand	General account [1]	Burma [2]	Indonesian Republic [2]
				COUNTRY OF DESTINATION				
Authorizations, total	413,342	246,726	78,575	55,949	17,831	915	10,246	6,099
Commodity total	378,985	221,653	72,746	55,297	15,034		9,040	5,184
Food and agricultural commodities	151,304	122,898	13,914	11,582	278		1,587	1,045
Industrial commodities	227,639	98,775	58,785	43,746	14,740		7,454	4,139
Unclassified commodities	92	28	49		15			
Unclassified commodity reductions	−51	−18	−2	−31				
Technical services	5,215	2,676	189	194	247	404	858	648
Technical assistance	8,665	1,310	776	3,382	2,330	383	308	175
Ocean freight	20,477	15,056	4,864	76	220	128	40	93
Paid shipments, total [3]	234,255	150,903	35,634	21,038	9,399	1,026	10,246	6,099
Commodity total	209,877	136,170	32,177	19,095	7,611		9,040	5,184
Food and agricultural commodities	107,991	87,723	10,277	7,266	93		1,587	1,045
Industrial commodities	101,932	48,465	21,887	12,471	7,518		7,454	4,139
Unclassified commodities	13		13					
Unclassified commodity refunds	−59	−18		−41				
Technical services	3,840	1,403	182	116	247	386	858	648
Technical assistance	4,604	606	500	1,217	1,284	512	308	175
Ocean freight	15,934	12,734	2,774	9	167	128	40	93
COMMODITY DETAIL ON SHIPMENTS								
Food, feed, and fertilizer	74,833	63,983	2,789	6,899	93		24	1,045
Fertilizer	44,018	35,045	1,044	6,771	93		21	1,045
Fats and oils	15,905	15,905						
Bread grains	10,876	10,876						
Sugar, raw or refined	1,536		1,536					
Feeds and fodder	1,145	1,053		92				
Dairy products, milk	566	454	111					
Fish and fish products, except fish oil and meal	498	498						
Meat	129		96	32				
Fruits and nuts, except peanuts	128	128						
Vegetables and preparations	23	23						
Seeds, other than oilseeds	9			5			3	
Fuel	17,521	12,073	5,336	94	17			
Petroleum and products	17,423	12,073	5,336	14				
Coal and related fuels	97			80	17			
Raw materials and semifinished products	79,120	50,893	12,769	5,620	1,750		6,219	1,869
Cotton	30,664	22,737	6,054	311			1,563	
Fabricated basic textiles	16,910	12,531	1,706	689	9		1,972	
Chemicals and related products	11,797	2,975	4,149	1,843	1,233		718	880
Iron and steel mill materials and products, including ferro-alloys	10,356	6,697	408	480	505		1,500	766
Nonferrous metals and products	2,848	2,452	112	60	1			223
Pulp and paper	2,323	357	178	1,662	1		125	
Lumber and lumber manufactures	1,377	1,377						
Hides, skins, and leather	1,325	882		443				
Nonmetallic minerals	1,161	634	139	46			342	
Miscellaneous fiber products	306	199	22	85				
Metallic ores and concentrates	51	51						
Naval stores	2	2						
Machinery and vehicles	28,687	7,343	7,792	5,450	4,933		1,653	1,466
Machinery and equipment	20,179	6,143	3,537	4,420	3,027		1,312	540
Motor vehicles, engines and parts	6,100	815	3,471	1,030	443		341	
Aircraft, engines, and parts	246		246					
Other transportation equipment	2,132	384	238		864			646
Miscellaneous and unclassified	9,746	1,878	3,491	1,631	818		1,144	784
Scientific and professional instruments	2,979	177	1,027	548	553		414	260
Tobacco	2,436	1,001	1,435					
Rubber and rubber products	707	420	162	119	6			
Miscellaneous industrial commodities	3,614	297	854	949	249		730	535
Misc. inedible animal and veg. prods	55			55				
Unclassified commodities	13		13					
Unclassified commodity refunds	−59	−18		−41				

[1] For services provided by U.S. Public Health Service and Emergency Procurement Service, not assignable by country.

[2] Transferred to Technical Cooperation Administration, July 1, 1952.

[3] MSA expenditures supplemented by movement reports from U.S. Government agencies; total paid shipments less than actual movements because of time required for receipt and processing of documents requesting payment.

Source: Mutual Security Agency; *Monthly Report to the Public Advisory Board.*

No. 1053.—MSA European Program—Allotments for Defense Support and Economic Assistance, by Country and Fiscal Year: April 3, 1948, to Dec. 31, 1952

[In millions of dollars]

COUNTRY	Total April 3, 1948, through Dec. 31, 1952	FISCAL YEAR			
		1948–49 (15 months)	1949–50	1950–51	1951–52	1952–53 through Dec. 31, 1952
Total	13,998.9	5,952.0	3,523.0	2,465.9	1,486.2	549.8
Austria	711.8	280.0	166.5	114.3	116.0	35.0
Belgium-Luxembourg	555.5	261.4	210.9	74.3	8.9	
Denmark	275.9	126.2	86.1	45.1	14.0	4.5
France	2,806.3	1,313.4	698.3	433.1	261.5	100.0
Germany (Federal Republic)	1,412.8	613.5	284.7	399.1	91.7	23.8
Greece	693.9	191.7	156.3	167.1	178.8	
Iceland	29.8	8.3	7.0	8.4	5.5	.6
Ireland	146.2	86.3	44.9	15.0		
Italy	1,515.0	668.0	403.7	244.0	159.3	40.8
Netherlands, excl. Indonesia	977.3	507.0	268.3	101.9	100.0	
Indonesia [1]	101.4	64.1	37.3			
Norway	253.5	101.1	89.5	46.1	16.8	
Portugal	50.5		38.8	11.7		
Sweden	107.1	45.4	51.9	21.2	[2] –11.4	
Trieste	32.6	17.9	12.5	2.1		
Turkey	242.5	49.0	58.5	45.0	70.0	20.0
United Kingdom	3,442.8	1,619.7	907.9	298.4	350.0	266.9
Yugoslavia	159.3			29.0	80.3	50.0
General Freight Account	33.5				33.5	
European Payments Union—Capital Fund	361.4			350.0	11.4	

[1] Allotments received by Indonesia in 1948 and 1949 when this country was Netherlands dependency.
[2] Reduction in aid to Sweden—a portion of Sweden's fiscal 1951 allotment. A like amount was allotted to European Payments Union in fiscal year 1952 to offset the reductions in Sweden's grant to this institution.

Source: Mutual Security Agency; *Monthly Report to the Public Advisory Board.*

No. 1054.—MSA Far East Program—Allotments for Technical and Economic Assistance, by Country and Fiscal Year: June 5, 1950, to Dec. 31, 1952

[In thousands of dollars]

COUNTRY	Total June 5, 1950, through Dec. 31, 1952	FISCAL YEAR			
		1949–50 (1 month)	1950–51	1951–52	1952–53 through Dec. 31, 1952
Total	[1] 439,829	750	162,697	167,010	[1] 133,400
Programs administered by MSA	423,484	750	144,324	145,010	133,400
China (Formosa)	245,761		98,034	81,480	66,247
Indochina, Associated States	92,432	750	21,728	24,561	45,393
Philippines	64,915		15,000	32,000	17,915
Thailand	19,270		8,876	6,994	3,400
General Account [2]	1,106		246	415	445
Far East Inventory [3]			440	–440	
Programs transferred to TCA, July 1, 1952	[1] 16,345		18,373	22,000	(1)
Burma	[1] 10,246		10,400	14,000	(1)
Indonesian Republic	[1] 6,099		7,973	8,000	(1)

[1] Adjusted to exclude funds transferred to Technical Cooperation Administration, as of July 1, 1952, for assistance to Burma and Indonesian Republic.
[2] For services provided by United States Public Health Service and Emergency Procurement Service, not assignable to a specific country.
[3] For commodities distributed among Far East countries after deliveries; such commodities were held in a pool and assigned to particular countries as required.

Source: Mutual Security Agency; *Monthly Report to the Public Advisory Board.*

No. 1055.—FOREIGN TRADE OF THE UNITED STATES—SUMMARY: 1936 TO 1952

[In thousands of dollars. For calendar years]

ITEM	1936–1940, average	1941–1945, average	1946–1950, average	1949	1950	1951	1952
Merchandise:							
Exports (incl. reexports)....	3,219,581	10,051,075	11,829,455	12,051,108	10,275,043	15,032,379	15,163,982
U. S. merchandise.... . ..	3,166,518	9,922,152	11,672,622	11,936,125	10,142,423	14,879,499	15,025,655
Reexports of foreign merchandise	53,063	128,923	156,834	114,984	132,620	152,880	138,327
General imports..	2,482,030	3,514,080	6,659,363	6,622,390	8,852,161	10,967,300	10,713,518
Entered for immediate consumption......	2,092,793	3,054,652	5,895,465	5,942,177	7,814,743	9,599,925	9,765,339
Entered for warehouse....	389,237	459,428	763,898	680,213	1,037,419	1,367,376	948,179
Excess of exports..............	737,552	6,536,995	5,170,092	5,428,718	1,422,882	4,065,079	4,450,444
Imports for consumption	2,440,042	3,475,593	6,583,595	6,591,640	8,743,082	10,817,341	10,744,634
.Entered for immediate consumption..............	2,092,793	3,054,652	5,895,465	5,942,177	7,814,743	9,599,925	9,765,339
Withdrawn from warehouse	347,249	420,941	688,130	649,463	928,339	1,217,416	979,285
Free.	1,475,825	2,293,945	3,842,818	3,883,186	4,766,778	5,993,442	6,256,990
Dutiable	964,217	1,181,648	2,740,777	2,708,454	3,976,304	4,823,900	4,487,634
Percent free................	60.48	66.00	58.37	58.91	54.52	55.41	58.23
Duties calculated............	365,151	379,704	(1)	(1)	(1)	(1)	(1)
Ratio of duties (percent):							
To total imports for consumption................	14.97	10.92	(1)	(1)	(1)	(1)	(1)
To dutiable imports........	37.87	32.13	(1)	(1)	(1)	(1)	(1)
Gold:							
Exports......................	16,989	238,443	270,890	84,936	534,036	630,382	55,921
Imports	2,615,845	321,514	1,105,573	771,390	162,749	81,259	740,254
Excess of: Imports...........	2,598,856	83,070	834,683	686,455			684,333
Exports............					371,287	549,123	
Silver:							
Exports......................	9,879	51,243	21,797	23,281	6,202	8,590	4,921
Imports......................	129,793	33,342	76,035	73,536	110,035	103,469	67,296
Excess of: Imports...........	119,914		54,237	50,255	103,833	94,878	62,375
Exports............		17,901					

1 Not available.

Source· Department of Commerce, Bureau of Census; annual report, *Foreign Commerce and Navigation of the United States*, and records.

No. 1056.—RAW MATERIALS PRODUCTION, IMPORTS, EXPORTS, AND APPARENT CONSUMPTION, VALUE IN CONSTANT DOLLARS: 1900 TO 1952

[Millions of 1935–39 dollars]

YEAR	All raw materials [1]	AGRICULTURAL MATERIALS			Fishery and wildlife products	Forest products	MINERALS			
		Total	Foods	Non-foods			Total [1]	Metallic ores [1]	Mineral fuels	Other minerals
PRODUCTION										
1900	8,620	6,289	4,829	1,430	107	1,238	996	180	699	108
1910	10,481	7,131	5,529	1,602	113	1,347	1,890	327	1,356	207
1920	12,133	8,278	6,416	1,862	102	1,161	2,592	399	1,941	252
1930	13,070	8,825	7,270	1,555	145	994	3,106	387	2,308	411
1940	14,793	9,920	8,082	1,838	149	957	3,767	507	2,763	497
1950	18,689	12,190	10,050	2,140	157	1,100	5,242	572	3,788	882
1951	19,721	12,633	10,468	2,165	152	1,115	5,821	647	4,192	982
1952	20,284	13,200	10,630	2,570	145	1,139	5,800	628	4,144	1,028
IMPORTS										
1900	490	314	189	125	44	17	115	91	4	20
1910	749	463	253	210	68	33	185	144	5	36
1920	1,350	792	428	364	66	51	351	200	120	31
1930	1,405	900	510	390	93	79	333	175	118	40
1940	1,647	985	493	472	115	68	499	370	93	36
1950	2,274	1,089	584	505	122	140	923	514	334	75
1951	2,129	1,020	575	445	116	137	856	436	337	83
1952	2,279	1,015	570	445	115	127	1,022	561	381	80
EXPORTS										
1900	1,284	1,074	510	564	27	43	140	89	47	4
1910	951	650	186	464	39	49	213	130	77	6
1920	1,470	1,074	635	439	33	35	328	137	176	15
1930	1,316	848	359	489	32	58	378	152	206	20
1940	893	455	173	282	30	34	374	170	181	23
1950	1,382	1,020	541	479	22	28	312	92	178	42
1951	1,773	1,276	816	460	27	31	439	107	290	42
1952	1,538	1,066	689	377	23	24	425	117	269	39
APPARENT CONSUMPTION [2]										
1900	7,826	5,499	4,508	991	124	1,232	971	191	656	124
1910	10,279	6,944	5,596	1,348	142	1,331	1,862	341	1,284	237
1920	11,923	7,996	6,209	1,787	135	1,177	2,615	462	1,885	268
1930	13,159	8,877	7,421	1,456	206	1,015	3,061	410	2,220	431
1940	15,547	10,430	8,402	2,028	234	991	3,892	707	2,675	510
1950	19,581	12,259	10,093	2,166	257	1,212	5,853	994	3,944	915
1951	20,077	12,377	10,227	2,150	241	1,221	6,238	976	4,239	1,023
1952	21,025	13,149	10,511	2,638	237	1,242	6,397	1,072	4,256	1,069

[1] Excludes gold.
[2] Represents "production" plus "imports," minus "exports."

Source: The President's Materials Policy Commission, *Resources for Freedom*, Vol. II (June 1952), as revised by the Bureau of the Census and the Office of Business Economics.

No. 1057.—EXPORTS AND IMPORTS OF MERCHANDISE, GOLD, AND SILVER: 1791 TO 1952

[In thousands of dollars. For basis of dollar values, see general note, p. 880. Figures are for fiscal years ending Sept. 30, 1791 to 1842, and June 30, 1843 to 1915; calendar years thereafter. For total exports and imports of merchandise by individual years prior to 1942, see table 1058. Merchandise figures include gold and silver prior to 1821. See also *Historical Statistics*, series M 42-55]

YEARLY AVERAGE OR YEAR	TOTAL MERCHANDISE, GOLD, AND SILVER			GOLD			SILVER		
	Exports	Imports	Excess of exports (+) or imports (−)	Exports	Imports	Excess of exports (+) or imports (−)	Exports	Imports	Excess of exports (+) or imports (−)
1821-1830....	76,575	79,863	−3,288	(¹)	(¹)	(¹)	¹7,154	¹6,914	¹+229
1831-1840....	109,234	130,268	−21,034	2,154	3,394	−1,240	3,530	7,358	−3,828
1841-1850 ². .	129,288	130,029	−741	3,222	5,463	−2,241	3,445	3,443	+2
1851-1860....	298,389	292,226	+6,163	46,372	3,762	+42,610	3,130	3,988	−858
1861-1870 . . .	320,313	350,712	−30,399	53,633	13,956	+39,678	12,354	4,890	+7,464
1871-1880 . . .	650,325	565,793	+84,532	33,732	19,144	+14,588	27,293	11,428	+15,865
1881-1890 . . .	816,503	740,511	+75,992	24,457	33,248	−8,791	26,911	15,077	+11,834
1891-1900 . . .	1,137,586	845,452	+292,134	64,265	57,040	+7,225	48,451	25,085	+23,367
1901-1910 . . .	1,740,599	1,271,244	+469,355	69,540	76,218	−6,678	54,809	36,526	+18,284
1911-1915 . . .	2,515,144	1,837,027	+678,117	83,173	85,969	−2,796	61,432	38,739	+22,693
1915-1920 ². .	6,897,886	3,804,593	+3,093,293	235,245	382,022	−146,775	143,447	64,217	+79,231
1921-1925...	4,558,940	3,866,937	+692,003	83,729	347,425	−264,696	79,174	60,409	+8,765
1926-1930...	5,077,974	4,348,594	+729,076	222,094	255,528	−33,434	78,888	60,868	+18,488
1931-1935...	2,383,679	2,645,517	−261,838	330,539	819,256	−478,717	18,946	113,159	−94,213
1936-1940...	3,246,449	5,227,957	−1,981,218	16,989	2,615,845	−2,598,856	9,879	129,793	−119,914
1941-1945....	10,340,761	3,868,936	+6,471,825	258,443	321,514	−63,070	51,243	33,342	+17,901
1946-1950....	12,122,143	7,840,971	+4,281,172	270,800	1,105,573	−834,683	21,797	76,035	−54,237
1945	10,096,534	4,290,134	+5,816,396	190,985	93,718	+106,250	90,937	27,278	+63,659
1946	9,996,243	5,532,593	+4,463,650	221,468	532,962	−311,494	36,455	57,578	−21,123
1947	14,673,636	7,904,062	+6,769,574	215,341	2,076,888	−1,866,348	30,649	68,140	−37,492
1948	12,966,229	9,175,937	+3,790,292	300,771	1,981,175	−1,680,404	12,400	70,865	−58,484
1949	12,159,325	7,467,316	+4,692,009	84,996	771,390	−686,455	23,281	73,538	−50,255
1950	10,815,281	9,134,945	+1,680,336	535,036	163,749	+371,287	6,302	110,035	−103,533
1951	15,671,351	11,152,027	+4,519,324	680,287	81,259	+549,122	8,900	103,460	−94,878
1952	15,224,824	11,520,169	+3,704,655	55,921	740,254	−684,333	4,921	67,296	−62,375

YEARLY AVERAGE OR YEAR	MERCHANDISE					
	Total exports and imports	Exports			General imports	Excess of exports (+) or imports (−)
		Total	U.S. merchandise	Reexports		
1791-1800	105,959	46,774	27,740	19,034	59,185	−12,411
1801-1810	167,298	74,532	38,178	36,354	92,766	−18,234
1811-1820	139,801	58,989	46,270	12,719	80,812	−21,823
1821-1830	142,370	69,421	53,221	16,200	72,949	−3,528
1831-1840	223,070	103,550	88,168	15,382	119,520	−15,970
1841-1850 ²	243,743	122,620	114,894	7,727	121,123	+1,498
1851-1860	533,362	248,887	232,283	16,604	284,475	−35,588
1861-1870	586,194	254,327	238,947	15,380	331,867	−77,541
1871-1880	1,124,523	589,301	574,889	14,412	535,222	+54,080
1881-1890	1,467,322	765,136	750,146	14,990	692,187	+72,949
1891-1900	1,788,198	1,024,670	1,006,183	18,667	763,328	+261,342
1901-1910	2,774,750	1,616,250	1,589,000	27,250	1,158,500	+457,780
1911-1915	4,062,858	2,370,539	2,331,648	38,891	1,712,319	+658,220
1915-1920 ²	9,879,545	6,521,190	6,416,519	104,677	3,358,354	+3,162,836
1921-1925	7,847,129	4,397,027	4,310,221	86,806	3,450,103	+946,924
1926-1930	8,810,782	4,777,314	4,687,788	89,526	4,033,469	+743,845
1931-1935	3,738,296	2,025,195	1,999,964	26,231	1,713,102	+312,088
1936-1940	5,701,611	3,219,581	3,166,518	63,063	2,482,030	+737,522
1941-1945	12,565,155	10,051,075	9,924,155	126,922	2,514,080	+6,536,995
1946-1950	18,488,818	11,829,455	11,672,622	156,834	6,659,363	+5,170,092
1945	13,964,763	9,805,625	9,584,684	220,941	4,159,138	+5,646,487
1946	14,680,374	9,738,321	9,500,184	238,137	4,942,054	+4,796,267
1947	20,186,080	14,429,747	14,252,285	177,462	5,756,333	+8,673,414
1948	19,776,935	12,653,058	12,532,068	120,965	7,123,877	+5,529,181
1949	18,673,498	12,051,108	11,936,125	114,984	6,622,390	+5,428,718
1950	19,127,205	10,275,043	10,142,423	132,620	8,852,161	+1,422,882
1951	25,999,680	15,032,379	14,879,499	152,880	10,967,300	+4,065,079
1952	25,876,601	15,163,982	15,025,655	138,327	10,712,619	+4,451,363

¹ Silver figures include gold, 1821-30: not available separately prior to 1825.
² Period Oct. 1, 1840, to June 30, 1850. ³ Period July 1, 1915, to Dec. 31, 1920.
⁴ Represents later data than that shown in table 1055.

Source: Department of Commerce, Bureau of Census; annual report, *Foreign Commerce and Navigation of the United States*, and records.

No. 1058.—Exports and Imports of Merchandise, With Trade Balances:
1790 to 1952

[In thousands of dollars. For basis of dollar values, see general note, p. 880. Fiscal years ending Sept. 30, 1790 to 1842, June 30 through 1915; calendar years thereafter. See also *Historical Statistics*, series M 51–55]

YEAR	Exports[1]	Imports[1]	Excess of exports (+) or imports (−)	YEAR	Exports	Imports	Excess of exports (+) or imports (−)	YEAR	Exports	Imports	Excess of exports (+) or imports (−)
1790...	20, 205	23, 000	−2, 795	1845..	106, 040	113, 184	−7, 144	1900...	1, 394, 483	849, 941	+544, 542
1791...	19, 012	29, 200	−10, 188	1846..	109, 583	117, 914	−8, 331				
1792...	20, 753	31, 500	−10, 747	1847..	156, 742	122, 424	+34, 318	1901...	1, 487, 765	823, 172	+664, 592
1793...	26, 110	31, 100	−4, 990	1848..	138, 191	148, 639	−10, 448	1902...	1, 381, 719	903, 321	+478, 398
1794...	33, 044	34, 600	−1, 556	1849..	140, 351	141, 206	−855	1903...	1, 420, 142	1, 025, 719	+394, 423
1795...	47, 990	69, 756	−21, 766	1850..	144, 376	173, 510	−29, 134	1904...	1, 460, 827	991, 087	+469, 740
1796...	58, 575	81, 436	−22, 861					1905...	1, 518, 562	1, 117, 513	+401, 049
1797...	51, 295	75, 379	−24, 084	1851	188, 915	210, 771	−21, 856	1906...	1, 743, 865	1, 226, 562	+517, 303
1798...	61, 327	68, 552	−7, 225	1852	166, 984	207, 440	−40, 456	1907...	1, 880, 851	1, 434, 421	+446, 430
1799...	78, 665	79, 069	−403	1853	203, 489	263, 777	−60, 288	1908...	1, 860, 773	1, 194, 342	+666, 431
1800...	70, 972	91, 253	−20, 281	1854	237, 044	297, 804	−60, 760	1909...	1, 663, 011	1, 311, 920	+351, 091
				1855	218, 916	257, 809	−38, 899	1910...	1, 744, 985	1, 556, 947	+188, 038
1801...	93, 021	111, 364	−18, 343	1856	281, 219	310, 432	−29, 213				
1802...	71, 957	76, 333	−4, 376	1857	293, 824	348, 428	−54, 604	1911...	2, 049, 320	1, 527, 226	+522, 094
1803...	55, 800	64, 667	−8, 867	1858	272, 011	263, 339	+8, 672	1912...	2, 204, 322	1, 653, 265	+551, 057
1804...	77, 699	85, 000	−7, 301	1859	292, 902	331, 333	−38, 431	1913...	2, 465, 884	1, 813, 008	+652, 876
1805...	95, 566	120, 600	−25, 034	1860	333, 576	353, 616	−20, 040	1914...	2, 364, 579	1, 893, 926	+470, 653
1806...	101, 537	129, 410	−27, 873					1915...	2, 768, 589	1, 674, 170	+1, 094, 419
1807...	108, 343	138, 500	−30, 157	1861	219, 554	289, 311	−69, 757	1915			
1808...	22, 431	56, 990	−34, 559	1862	190, 671	189, 357	+1, 314	(6 mos.)	1, 852, 863	912, 787	+940, 076
1809...	52, 203	59, 400	−7, 197	1863	203, 964	243, 336	−39, 372	1916...	5, 482, 641	2, 391, 635	+3, 091, 006
1810...	66, 758	85, 400	−18, 642	1864	158, 838	316, 447	−157, 609	1917...	6, 233, 513	2, 952, 468	+3, 281, 045
				1865	166, 029	238, 746	−72, 717	1918...	6, 149, 088	3, 031, 213	+3, 117, 875
1811...	61, 317	53, 400	+7, 917	1866	348, 860	434, 812	−85, 952	1919...	7, 920, 426	3, 904, 365	+4, 016, 061
1812...	38, 527	77, 030	−38, 503	1867	294, 506	395, 761	−101, 255	1920...	8, 228, 016	5, 278, 481	+2, 949, 535
1813...	27, 856	22, 005	+5, 851	1868	281, 953	357, 436	−75, 483				
1814...	6, 927	12, 965	−6, 038	1869	286, 118	417, 506	−131, 388	1921...	4, 485, 031	2, 509, 148	+1, 975, 883
1815...	52, 558	113, 041	−60, 482	1870	392, 772	435, 958	−43, 186	1922...	3, 831, 777	3, 112, 747	+719, 030
1816...	81, 920	147, 103	−65, 183					1923...	4, 167, 493	3, 792, 066	+375, 427
1817...	87, 672	99, 250	−11, 578	1871	442, 820	520, 224	−77, 404	1924...	4, 590, 984	3, 609, 963	+981, 021
1818...	93, 281	121, 750	−28, 469	1872	444, 178	626, 595	−182, 417	1925...	4, 909, 848	4, 226, 589	+683, 258
1819...	70, 143	87, 125	−16, 982	1873	522, 480	642, 136	−119, 656	1926...	4, 808, 660	4, 430, 888	+377, 772
1820...	69, 692	74, 450	−4, 758	1874	586, 283	567, 406	+18, 877	1927...	4, 865, 375	4, 184, 742	+680, 633
				1875	513, 443	533, 005	−19, 562	1928...	5, 128, 356	4, 091, 444	+1, 036, 912
1821...	54, 496	54, 521	−25	1876	540, 385	460, 741	+79, 644	1929...	5, 240, 995	4, 399, 361	+841, 534
1822...	61, 350	79, 872	−18, 522	1877	602, 475	451, 323	+151, 152	1930...	3, 843, 181	3, 060, 908	+782, 273
1823...	68, 326	72, 481	−4, 155	1878	694, 866	437, 052	+257, 814				
1824...	68, 972	72, 169	−3, 197	1879	710, 439	445, 778	+264, 661	1931...	2, 424, 289	2, 090, 635	+333, 654
1825...	90, 738	90, 189	+549	1880	835, 639	667, 955	+167, 684	1932...	1, 611, 016	1, 322, 774	+288, 242
1826...	72, 891	78, 094	−5, 203					1933...	1, 674, 994	1, 449, 559	+225, 435
1827...	74, 310	71, 333	+2, 977	1881	902, 377	642, 665	+259, 712	1934...	2, 132, 800	1, 655, 055	+477, 745
1828...	64, 021	81, 020	−16, 999	1882	750, 542	724, 640	+25, 902	1935...	2, 282, 874	2, 047, 485	+235, 389
1829...	67, 435	67, 089	+346	1883	823, 839	723, 181	+100, 658	1936...	2, 455, 978	2, 422, 592	+33, 386
1830...	71, 671	62, 721	+8, 950	1884	740, 514	667, 698	+72, 816	1937...	3, 349, 167	3, 083, 668	+265, 499
				1885	742, 190	577, 527	+164, 663	1938...	3, 094, 440	1, 960, 428	+1, 134, 012
1831...	72, 296	95, 885	−23, 589	1886	679, 525	635, 436	+44, 089	1939...	3, 177, 176	2, 318, 081	+859, 095
1832...	81, 521	95, 122	−13, 601	1887	716, 183	692, 320	+23, 863	1940...	4, 021, 146	2, 625, 379	+1, 395, 767
1833...	87, 529	101, 048	−13, 519	1888	695, 955	723, 957	−28, 002				
1834...	102, 260	108, 610	−6, 350	1889	742, 401	745, 132	−2, 731	1941...	5, 147, 154	3, 345, 005	+1, 802, 149
1835...	115, 216	136, 764	−21, 548	1890	857, 829	789, 310	+68, 519	1942...	8, 078, 988	2, 755, 893	+5, 323, 095
1836...	124, 339	176, 579	−52, 240					1943...	12, 964, 906	3, 381, 498	+9, 583, 408
1837...	111, 443	130, 473	−19, 030	1891	884, 481	844, 916	+39, 565	1944...	14, 258, 702	3, 928, 866	+10, 329, 837
1838...	104, 979	95, 970	+9, 009	1892	1, 030, 278	827, 402	+202, 876	1945...	9, 805, 625	4, 159, 138	+5, 646, 487
1839...	112, 252	156, 497	−44, 245	1893	847, 665	866, 401	−18, 736	1946...	9, 738, 321	4, 942, 054	+4, 796, 267
1840...	123, 669	98, 259	+25, 410	1894	892, 141	654, 995	+237, 146	1947...	14, 429, 747	5, 756, 333	+8, 673, 413
				1895	807, 538	731, 970	+75, 568	1948...	12, 653, 058	7, 123, 877	+5, 529, 181
1841...	111, 817	122, 958	−11, 141	1896	882, 607	779, 725	+102, 882	1949...	12, 051, 108	6, 622, 390	+5, 428, 718
1842...	99, 878	96, 075	+3, 803	1897	1, 050, 994	764, 730	+286, 264	1950...	10, 275, 043	8, 852, 161	+1, 422, 882
1843[3]..	82, 826	42, 433	+40, 393	1898	1, 231, 482	616, 050	+615, 432	1951...	15, 032, 379	10, 967, 300	+4, 065, 079
1844...	105, 746	102, 605	+3, 141	1899	1, 227, 023	697, 148	+529, 875	1952[3]..	15, 163, 982	10, 712, 619	+4, 451, 363

[1] Includes gold and silver prior to 1821. [2] Period beginning Oct. 1, 1842, and ending June 30, 1843.
[3] Represents later data than that shown in table 1055.

Source: Department of Commerce, Bureau of Census; annual report, *Foreign Commerce and Navigation of the United States*, and records.

No. 1059.—Exports and Imports of Merchandise, Per Capita: 1791 to 1952

[Export figures for 1791 to 1820 are based on total exports including reexports (the latter were then relatively large) and for 1821 to date, on exports of United States merchandise only. Import figures for 1791 to 1820 are based on general imports; for 1821 to 1870, total imports less reexports; and for 1871 to date, imports for consumption. (See tables 1057 and 1077)]

YEARLY AVERAGE	Exports	Imports	YEARLY AVERAGE OR YEAR	Exports	Imports	YEAR	Exports	Imports	YEAR	Exports	Imports
	Dollars	Dollars		Dollars	Dollars		Dollars	Dollars		Dollars	Dollars
1791–1800..	10.08	12.75	1926–1930..	26.80	23.02	1928......	36.11	32.95	1938......	28.14	14.75
1801–1810..	11.82	14.71	1931–1935..	15.55	13.23	1924......	39.12	31.10	1939......	32.44	17.08
1811–1820..	6.96	9.53	1936–1940..	25.96	18.48	1925......	41.30	35.90	1940¹.....	29.25	15.90
1821–1830..	4.71	5.03	1941–1945..	71.14	24.92	1926......	39.81	37.34	1941¹.....	36.96	22.71
1831–1840..	5.58	6.01	1946–1950¹.	78.13	44.07	1927......	39.08	34.67	1942¹.....	56.19	20.23
1841–1850..	5.67	5.80	1913......	34.97	18.17	1928......	41.31	33.06	1943¹.....	91.98	24.28
1851–1860..	8.46	9.78	1914......	23.61	19.23	1929......	41.77	34.14	1944¹.....	100.11	27.48
1861–1870..	6.73	8.94	1915......	27.13	16.46	1930......	30.34	24.90	1945¹.....	67.06	28.67
1871–1880..	12.86	11.67	1916......	63.01	22.06	1931......	15.96	16.67	1946¹.....	65.92	33.46
1881–1890..	13.31	12.12	1917......	58.48	28.14	1932......	12.42	10.44	1947¹.....	97.01	38.67
1891–1900..	14.41	10.51	1918......	57.51	28.06	1933......	12.90	11.22	1948¹.....	88.80	47.48
1901–1910..	18.54	13.29	1919......	72.09	35.90	1934......	16.34	12.73	1949¹.....	78.51	43.36
1911–1915..	23.96	17.46	1920......	74.70	47.16	1935......	17.33	15.75	1950¹.....	65.64	56.58
1916–1920¹.	61.20	31.37	1921......	39.96	23.27	1936......	18.57	18.61	1951¹.....	94.66	65.81
1921–1925..	38.06	30.23	1922......	33.75	27.55	1937......	25.16	22.96	1952¹.....	94.01	67.23

¹ Based on estimated population including armed forces overseas.   ² Period July 1, 1918, to Dec. 31, 1920.

Source: Department of Commerce, Bureau of Census; annual report, *Foreign Commerce and Navigation of the United States*, and records.

No. 1060.—Merchandise Trade of Continental United States With Foreign Countries and Outlying Territories and Possessions: 1903 to 1950

IMPORTANT NOTE.—This table differs as to its geographic basis from all other foreign trade tables in this section and in other publications: (1) In the case of other tables the data represent the trade of the United States customs area with all foreign countries, including the Philippine Islands and prior to 1935, the Virgin Islands. The U. S. customs area comprises continental U. S., Alaska, Hawaii, Puerto Rico, and during 1935 through 1939, the Virgin Islands. Trade between continental U. S. and the territories mentioned as part of the customs area are therefore excluded from these data. (2) The present table takes continental United States as the basis. In the totals, trade between it and all United States Territories and possessions is included, while the trade between that part of the customs area outside of continental United States and foreign countries is excluded. Practically all other nations calculate their foreign trade in the manner followed in the present table; that is, totaling the trade of the home country with foreign countries and with all outlying areas. Prior to 1901 Alaska was our only outlying area. Therefore, our foreign trade statistics for 1900 and earlier years very nearly represent the trade of continental United States with foreign countries. Data are for years ending June 30 through 1918; thereafter, for years ending Dec. 31. For purposes of continuity of the data in this table, trade with the Republic of the Philippines has been treated as trade with a Territory through calendar year 1946, even though Philippine independence was established in July 1946.

[In thousands of dollars]

YEARLY AVERAGE OR YEAR	EXPORTS¹			IMPORTS		
	Total	To foreign countries	To U. S. Territories and possessions	Total	From foreign countries	From U. S. Territories and possessions
1903–1905............	1,496,616	1,466,122	30,494	1,090,764	1,026,341	64,423
1906–1910............	1,838,286	1,761,625	97,651	1,419,329	1,294,564	94,754
1911–1915............	2,441,254	2,337,591	103,664	1,811,324	1,691,207	120,027
1915–1920³...........	6,642,453	6,462,130	203,303	3,666,065	3,374,499	221,568
1921–1925............	4,552,455	4,335,343	217,114	3,851,375	3,630,488	221,082
1926–1930............	4,961,904	4,699,505	262,442	4,273,903	3,993,079	272,828
1931–1935............	2,172,705	1,976,604	196,152	1,953,073	1,839,804	173,686
1936–1940............	3,445,009	3,135,300	305,060	2,725,964	2,551,000	174,000
1941–1945............	10,560,012		417,000	3,772,364		172,000
1941...............	4,442,728		637,000			
1942...............						
1943...............						
1944...............						
1945...............						
1946...............						
1947...............						
1948...............						
1949...............						
1950...............						

¹ Including reexports of foreign merchandise.   ² Period July 1, 1918, to Dec. 31, 1920.
³ Excludes certain aircraft originating in continental U. S. cleared for foreign country through Alaska, valued as follows: 1943, $210,414,000; 1944, $279,000,000; 1945, $166,070,000.
⁴ Excludes Alaska and Hawaii; data no longer available.

Source: Department of Commerce, Bureau of Census; annual report, *Foreign Commerce and Navigation of the United States*, and records.

No. 1061.—Exports (Including Reexports) and General Imports of Merchandise, by Months: 1947 to 1952

[In millions of dollars]

MONTH	1947		1948		1949		1950		1951		1952	
	Ex-ports	Im-ports	Ex-ports	Im-ports	Ex-ports	Im-ports	Ex-ports	Im-ports	Ex-ports	Im-ports	Ex-ports	Im-ports [1]
January___	1,113.7	533.0	1,091.6	546.6	1,105.1	589.7	740.9	623.4	974.0	1,024.7	1,254.0	922.4
February__	1,146.0	437.8	1,084.6	589.0	1,043.4	566.6	764.3	600.2	1,075.9	910.0	1,344.1	882.7
March____	1,326.4	444.5	1,138.6	674.6	1,189.2	632.6	860.2	664.9	1,295.2	1,101.9	1,446.8	963.9
April_____	1,294.3	515.1	1,121.3	531.6	1,172.9	534.5	803.5	585.0	1,369.4	1,033.6	1,352.0	932.2
May_____	1,413.5	475.0	1,102.5	553.5	1,095.0	540.6	829.5	659.1	1,354.4	1,017.8	1,472.9	834.4
June_____	1,234.9	464.1	1,014.0	624.8	1,107.7	526.0	876.9	686.7	1,296.6	930.2	1,166.8	860.8
July_____	1,154.7	451.8	1,019.2	563.6	900.4	456.5	778.6	708.9	1,186.2	894.5	1,026.9	839.2
August____	1,145.0	405.8	.9	605.5	884.8	490.7	761.6	820.4	1,270.3	880.8	1,086.5	817.2
September_	1,111.7	475.2	.6	560.2	910.0	530.4	911.0	856.9	1,231.7	721.3	1,225.3	876.5
October___	1,234.7	493.1	1	600.2	855.7	557.0	906.3	922.6	1,152.4	833.6	1,213.4	917.9
November_	1,141.2	455.6	991 2	554.3	841.9	592.9	977.0	855.1	1,388.0	818.6	1,185.9	804.3
December__	1,113.6	605.4	1,822.5	720.0	945.0	604.8	1,065.2	867.0	1,438.4	800.3	1,389.5	1,051.1

[1] Represents later data than that shown in table 1055.

No. 1062.—Exports and Imports of Gold, by Months: 1947 to 1952

[In thousands of dollars]

MONTH	1947		1948		1949		1950		1951		1952 (prel.)	
	Ex-ports	Im-ports	Ex-ports	Im-ports	Ex-ports	Im-ports	Ex-ports	Im-ports	Ex-ports	Im-ports	Ex-ports	Im-ports
January___	102,593	85,774	6,590	241,568	6,399	72,612	7,223	46,201	107,834	2,240	13,223	76,864
February__	49,215	69,577	2,560	161,948	4,499	25,978	4,119	4,350	110,136	2,257	17,805	168,129
March____	17,691	171,325	27,385	127,328	5,108	24,879	4,338	2,706	125,704	2,242	1,473	158,600
April_____	17,458	61,508	28,178	292,334	12,020	25,615	2,130	55,419	112,842	2,245	1,313	97,932
May_____	3,028	132,762	61,887	213,214	1,612	11,142	1,553	14,628	43,357	2,308	2,824	30,060
June_____	2,685	202,917	44,782	222,523	5,483	12,399	2,246	12,274	41,422	3,840	3,445	40,051
July_____	3,639	222,839	2,486	269,178	6,890	137,986	4,069	2,556	28,374	12,165	1,580	26,047
August____	5,118	116,776	47,353	86,431	11,563	268,936	46,368	4,146	19,183	15,533	2,861	5,947
September_	2,085	111,685	25,993	79,283	15,857	114,002	108,446	11,998	3,462	14,341	1,244	34,590
October___	5,619	456,450	8,337	129,908	2,397	58,527	95,967	2,519	26,326	7,896	2,988	86,465
November_	1,600	267,301	21,097	75,321	2,998	10,629	161,750	3,117	9,366	7,302	1,580	1,872
December_	2,509	180,674	24,123	112,141	10,110	8,697	95,825	2,833	2,375	8,800	5,587	13,697

No. 1063.—Exports and Imports of Silver, by Months: 1947 to 1952

[In thousands of dollars]

MONTH	1947		1948		1949		1950		1951		1952 (prel.)	
	Ex-ports	Im-ports	Ex-ports	Im-ports	Ex-ports	Im-ports	Ex-ports	Im-ports	Ex-ports	Im-ports	Ex-ports	Im-ports
January___	2,945	13,295	1,636	7,222	581	2,116	47	8,065	3,623	10,999	157	6,125
February__	12,700	4,589	220	6,196	261	3,278	30	4,355	282	8,101	513	6,177
March____	3,523	5,332	229	5,331	214	6,444	110	6,317	1,932	17,486	142	8,126
April_____	1,865	7,220	5,763	5,560	4,783	2,825	62	3,412	332	10,016	587	4,678
May_____	1,387	4,488	2,564	9,146	514	12,190	70	8,253	273	7,015	1,535	4,680
June_____	1,685	4,408	42	5,747	1,818	10,237	1,219	6,126	182	16,828	215	5,038
July_____	1,636	3,410	278	4,352	11,910	6,824	375	10,408	665	4,686	236	5,733
August____	630	4,659	13	4,781	2,090	6,056	425	8,904	194	6,616	216	4,877
September_	374	4,440	52	5,758	160	5,628	334	17,371	678	4,807	382	4,499
October___	2,509	6,087	61	6,910	86	7,508	335	12,350	250	6,975	411	7,778
November_	1,042	6,917	123	4,973	184	6,370	947	13,870	88	6,284	258	5,009
December_	352	3,296	1,419	4,908	680	4,060	2,246	10,602	89	3,656	270	4,578

Source of tables 1061-1063: Department of Commerce, Bureau of Census; annual report, *Foreign Commerce and Navigation of the United States*, and records.

No. 1064.—Gold Under Earmark for Foreign Account in the United States: 1945 to 1952

[All figures in thousands of dollars at rate of $35 a fine ounce. Gold under earmark is gold held by Federal Reserve banks in custody for foreign central banks and governments. Minus sign (−) denotes decrease. See also *Historical Statistics*, series N 170-171]

MONTH	AMOUNT UNDER EARMARK AT END OF MONTH [1]							
	1945	1946	1947	1948	1949	1950	1951	1952
January	3, 995, 330	4, 306, 254	3, 632, 326	3, 633, 286	3, 780, 349	4, 366, 800	5, 874, 260	4, 870, 715
February	4, 032, 722	4, 312, 128	4, 316, 800	3, 705, 452	3, 802, 549	4, 416, 911	6, 058, 617	4, 718, 496
March	4, 079, 646	4, 292, 296	4, 113, 260	3, 768, 827	3, 819, 274	4, 512, 348	6, 160, 856	4, 821, 588
April	4, 132, 836	4, 277, 305	3, 841, 270	3, 880, 374	3, 837, 015	4, 571, 518	6, 087, 942	4, 896, 045
May	4, 199, 693	4, 249, 945	3, 828, 213	3, 883, 215	3, 799, 240	4, 601, 391	6, 080, 889	4, 869, 861
June	4, 103, 667	4, 234, 834	3, 709, 254	3, 801, 544	3, 677, 608	4, 619, 018	6, 034, 619	4, 850, 595
July	4, 204, 014	4, 226, 838	3, 682, 509	3, 989, 955	3, 697, 844	4, 708, 987	6, 043, 409	4, 881, 989
August	4, 267, 004	4, 166, 716	3, 640, 192	3, 930, 480	3, 906, 094	5, 140, 385	5, 906, 433	4, 914, 609
September	4, 286, 013	4, 154, 410	3, 487, 080	3, 832, 342	4, 060, 893	5, 206, 284	5, 729, 779	4, 928, 385
October	4, 251, 366	4, 038, 721	3, 491, 049	3, 531, 373	4, 150, 000	5, 352, 474	5, 486, 308	5, 020, 815
November	4, 289, 567	3, 911, 236	3, 573, 835	3, 731, 714	4, 213, 989	5, 287, 786	5, 298, 028	5, 049, 819
December	4, 293, 825	3, 828, 406	3, 618, 427	3, 777, 659	4, 273, 338	5, 636, 730	5, 008, 167	5, 313, 008
Increase during year of gold under earmark	356, 655	−465, 419	−209, 979	159, 232	495, 679	1, 352, 382	−617, 553	304, 841

[1] On certain occasions during this period, figures include gold earmarked in the names of domestic banks as security for foreign loans; beginning August 1945 they include gold held for the account of international institutions.

Source: Board of Governors of the Federal Reserve System; *Banking and Monetary Statistics* through 1941 *Federal Reserve Bulletin* thereafter.

No. 1065.—Exports and Imports of Merchandise, by Economic Classes— Percent Distribution: 1820 to 1952

[Percentages based on figures shown in table 1066]

YEAR OR YEARLY AVERAGE	PERCENT OF TOTAL EXPORTS OF UNITED STATES MERCHANDISE					PERCENT OF TOTAL IMPORTS [2]				
	Crude materials	Crude foodstuffs	Manufactured foodstuffs [1]	Semimanufactures	Finished manufactures	Crude materials	Crude foodstuffs	Manufactured foodstuffs [1]	Semimanufactures	Finished manufactures
1820	60.62	4.79	19.51	9.42	5.66	[3] 4.66	[3] 11.15	[3] 19.85	[3] 7.48	[3] 56.86
1830	62.65	4.65	16.32	7.04	9.34	7.65	11.77	15.39	8.22	56.97
1840	67.83	4.09	14.27	4.34	9.47	12.36	15.54	15.46	11.58	45.09
1850	62.36	5.59	14.84	4.49	12.72	7.24	10.38	12.37	15.08	54.92
1851-1860	61.67	6.51	15.39	4.01	12.32	9.63	11.70	15.43	12.50	50.74
1861-1870	38.80	15.59	24.09	5.19	16.34	12.53	13.64	18.98	13.77	40.98
1871-1880	38.59	19.70	21.99	4.61	15.10	17.34	15.98	20.72	13.05	33.01
1881-1890	35.96	17.99	25.26	5.15	15.65	21.36	15.35	17.77	14.78	30.74
1891-1900	29.89	18.06	25.62	7.98	18.45	26.45	16.92	16.96	13.87	25.80
1901-1910	30.96	10.55	20.14	12.77	25.57	34.07	11.80	12.04	17.32	24.77
1911-1915	30.74	8.83	14.32	15.41	30.70	34.91	12.80	12.56	17.37	22.36
1915-1920 [4]	18.22	9.16	17.66	15.39	39.58	40.13	12.15	16.21	17.10	14.40
1921-1925	27.54	9.74	13.93	12.45	36.33	37.40	11.09	12.99	17.56	20.86
1926-1930	24.40	6.40	9.72	14.14	45.35	36.80	12.56	9.88	18.89	21.88
1931-1935	30.23	3.85	8.83	14.51	42.57	29.91	15.61	13.73	16.72	23.03
1936-1940	19.08	3.77	5.53	19.30	52.36	33.08	13.10	14.16	20.94	18.72
1941-1945	5.78	1.67	11.64	9.39	71.54	33.01	16.86	11.51	21.15	17.97
1946-1950	13.96	8.33	9.95	11.10	56.66	30.26	18.79	10.72	22.34	17.89
1943	5.15	.84	12.06	8.48	73.45	30.60	17.23	12.42	19.98	19.76
1944	3.91	.94	11.52	7.74	75.87	27.73	21.64	13.40	18.17	19.05
1945	9.08	4.51	13.00	8.13	65.26	28.87	16.92	11.26	22.65	20.30
1946	14.90	6.82	16.02	9.42	52.83	35.84	16.88	10.44	19.29	17.55
1947	11.08	6.96	10.41	12.17	60.39	31.17	17.90	11.57	21.97	17.34
1948	11.88	10.10	10.48	10.94	56.60	30.27	17.93	10.31	23.03	18.46
1949	14.91	11.24	7.42	11.36	55.07	28.12	20.23	11.24	21.51	18.90
1950	18.60	7.49	5.94	11.05	56.92	28.20	20.01	10.28	24.31	17.20
1951	16.61	9.42	5.65	11.19	57.13	31.10	19.20	9.44	22.73	17.53
1952	13.19	9.10	4.84	10.80	62.07	27.32	19.25	10.06	23.89	19.48

[1] Includes beverages.
[2] "General imports" through 1932, "imports for consumption" thereafter.
[3] Data are for 1821.
[4] Period July 1, 1915, to Dec. 31, 1920.

Source: Department of Commerce, Bureau of Census; annual report, *Foreign Commerce and Navigation of the United States*, and records.

No. 1068.—EXPORTS OF UNITED STATES MERCHANDISE, BY COMMODITY GROUPS: 1936 TO 1952

[In thousands of dollars. See general note, p. 830]

COMMODITY	1936-1940, average	1941-1945, average	1946-1950, average	1949	1950	1951	1952
Total exports of domestic merchandise	3,166,518	9,922,152	11,672,622	11,936,125	10,142,423	14,879,499	15,025,653
Group 00.—Animals and animal products, edible, total	67,355	896,205	517,628	380,884	235,596	384,727	263,591
Animals, edible	492	1,965	4,886	3,511	3,818	5,753	7,490
Meat products	26,409	379,553	124,405	51,454	43,107	60,032	51,506
Animal oils and fats, edible [1]	17,141	106,747	83,693	92,906	63,759	134,817	91,486
Dairy products	7,879	181,987	201,294	174,157	96,646	120,852	72,318
Fish	14,097	31,086	31,568	29,195	18,856	27,073	15,511
Other edible animal products	1,337	198,865	71,783	29,661	19,319	36,200	25,262
Group 0.—Animals and animal products, inedible, total	46,396	67,244	154,796	187,671	138,973	180,809	155,842
Hides and skins, raw, except furs	4,509	1,124	15,726	21,035	11,610	12,745	19,495
Leather	14,418	20,497	25,270	28,286	20,003	19,063	17,344
Leather manufactures	8,372	27,270	37,635	28,345	18,962	21,809	23,361
Furs and manufactures	14,763	10,976	35,605	25,902	24,459	32,375	29,832
Animal oils and greases, inedible	1,346	3,489	27,794	45,745	55,485	86,229	58,370
Other inedible animals and animal products	2,991	3,888	12,769	8,355	8,455	8,588	7,541
Group 1.—Vegetable food products and beverages, total	226,272	417,609	1,609,889	1,839,596	1,118,677	1,850,037	1,831,397
Grains and preparations	104,622	174,020	1,205,384	1,457,382	833,512	1,483,875	1,481,776
Fodders and feeds	9,736	4,124	19,443	33,427	17,051	33,870	13,277
Vegetables and preparations	15,304	83,002	113,863	87,753	59,973	83,796	106,212
Fruits and nuts	76,111	87,718	180,914	139,762	99,850	108,159	125,031
Vegetable oils and fats, edible [1]	3,342	14,038	30,515	60,516	31,014	64,371	28,984
Cocoa and coffee	2,749	1,686	8,982	8,844	6,189	6,510	8,239
Spices	243	675	1,206	581	672	962	809
Sugar and related products	10,444	31,272	38,534	18,714	38,251	36,538	31,275
Beverages	3,720	21,075	31,737	32,619	32,166	31,964	36,373
Group 2.—Vegetable products, inedible, except fibers and wood, total	194,282	355,081	642,039	625,702	601,423	812,756	648,536
Rubber and manufactures	33,293	118,585	146,782	114,432	91,192	143,273	159,788
Naval stores, gums, and resins	16,117	13,778	36,006	32,044	42,442	48,031	23,309
Drugs, herbs, leaves, and roots, crude	1,798	1,662	3,509	2,729	2,341	3,265	2,782
Oilseeds	3,998	5,604	39,284	80,721	65,196	97,088	82,609
Vegetable oils	4,693	30,618	46,345	54,414	70,632	102,199	52,263
Vegetable dyeing and tanning extracts	1,800	1,406	1,461	774	635	933	1,292
Seeds except oilseeds	2,463	13,034	14,983	12,014	6,962	7,988	5,527
Nursery and greenhouse stock	433	447	1,138	925	1,035	1,135	1,904
Tobacco and manufactures	123,099	183,557	328,092	308,556	298,594	382,246	304,423
Miscellaneous vegetable products	6,590	16,390	24,437	19,093	22,393	26,602	12,693
Group 3.—Textiles, total	386,213	523,510	1,509,613	1,547,332	1,550,842	1,968,005	1,536,099
Cotton, unmanufactured	282,940	151,727	674,203	874,216	1,024,397	1,146,372	873,320
Cotton semimanufactures	13,199	14,586	49,192	41,401	36,605	87,863	57,773
Cotton manufactures	47,710	170,752	422,063	324,939	226,879	390,384	312,307
Jute and manufactures	1,988	3,909	7,634	5,473	6,191	13,445	6,394
Flax, hemp, and ramie, and manufactures	527	1,219	5,786	4,940	1,867	2,329	3,598
Other vegetable fibers and manufactures	1,162	2,683	1,363	1,646	1,509	1,761	1,233
Wool, mohair, and Angora rabbit hair, unmanufactured	149	5,500	6,408	11,726	6,118	409	79
Wool semimanufactures	2,009	5,748	14,332	13,422	10,920	18,371	9,518
Wool manufactures	2,810	72,775	47,230	18,004	13,144	18,898	9,367
Hair and manufactures	2,156	1,646	4,618	5,196	4,740	4,666	2,721
Silk manufactures	6,838	1,702	2,947	1,720	1,985	2,145	2,603
Rayon and other synthetic textiles	12,397	49,238	212,251	204,761	176,699	226,436	205,803
Miscellaneous textile products	12,327	42,026	61,947	39,889	39,787	54,926	51,283
Group 4.—Wood and paper, total	118,374	161,836	247,432	214,469	189,561	379,964	318,771
Wood, unmanufactured	4,898	2,423	6,502	7,359	5,362	11,066	12,599
Wood semimanufactures—sawmill products	43,162	29,752	68,684	59,956	48,484	96,417	76,670
Wood manufactures	16,211	36,039	39,189	31,078	24,761	36,575	32,482
Cork manufactures	935	1,871	3,514	4,107	3,791	4,663	3,370
Paper base stocks	17,668	19,582	18,638	18,349	16,890	52,179	39,143
Paper and manufactures	35,500	72,168	110,865	93,620	90,272	179,064	154,507

[1] Beginning 1949, margarine included with "Vegetable oils and fats, edible"; with "Animal oils and fats, edible" in prior years.

No. 1068.—Exports of United States Merchandise, by Commodity Groups: 1936 to 1952—Continued

[In thousands of dollars]

COMMODITY	1936–1940, average	1941–1945, average	1946–1950, average	1949	1950	1951	1952
Group 5.—Nonmetallic minerals, total	466,369	848,002	1,175,713	1,081,861	965,057	1,535,845	1,545,187
Coal and related fuels	66,745	164,497	405,244	307,940	277,823	605,119	509,845
Petroleum and products	345,619	572,545	559,105	561,850	499,474	783,007	799,909
Stone, cement, and lime	2,526	8,724	18,235	18,566	9,102	12,401	14,031
Glass and glass products	10,310	27,265	58,442	51,547	47,673	64,479	55,415
Clays and clay products	9,449	19,550	42,153	47,968	41,564	59,601	56,952
Other nonmetallic minerals, including precious	31,718	55,122	92,534	93,990	89,420	114,238	109,034
Group 6.—Metals and manufactures, except machinery and vehicles, total	476,637	884,491	1,626,284	1,123,526	792,106	1,036,852	1,234,414
Iron ore	3,232	7,259	11,924	14,654	15,717	30,997	37,421
Iron and steel semimanufactures	196,955	324,347	315,314	352,286	239,469	320,334	309,872
Steel-mill products—manufactures	72,617	218,736	309,773	379,642	232,994	290,834	221,287
Iron and steel, advanced manufactures	50,304	116,442	193,337	183,672	149,793	196,179	[1] 310,834
Ferro-alloys, ores, and metals, n. e. s	13,392	6,719	5,455	5,040	3,001	5,575	7,796
Nonferrous metals, except precious	137,421	209,114	185,742	182,909	146,825	186,565	242,222
Precious metals and plated ware, except jewelry, and gold and silver in ore, bullion, and coin	2,717	1,873	4,739	5,323	4,308	6,368	4,982
Group 7.—Machinery and vehicles, total	912,154	4,274,262	3,427,633	3,539,965	3,232,774	4,680,159	5,121,829
Electrical machinery and apparatus	105,605	257,992	454,905	482,344	438,832	633,347	748,408
Industrial machinery [2]	281,807	675,193	1,173,214	1,322,216	1,105,566	1,364,005	1,549,994
Office appliances	29,370	17,086	82,730	84,017	90,473	119,578	89,131
Printing machinery	9,816	4,465	35,027	44,839	39,768	35,823	28,327
Agricultural machinery and implements [4]	68,027	118,232	98,557	128,405	108,533	140,790	140,751
Automobiles and other vehicles [3][4]	417,439	3,201,294	1,583,201	1,478,135	1,449,603	2,386,655	2,565,217
Group 8.—Chemicals and related products, total	153,099	399,936	711,677	773,671	721,848	977,075	802,023
Coal-tar products	16,297	32,604	84,666	84,384	53,892	77,071	49,753
Medicinal and pharmaceutical preparations	20,208	75,709	184,681	198,205	210,666	281,380	221,169
Chemical specialties	29,182	66,669	[5] 155,427	[5] 184,366	[5] 180,020	[5] 271,936	[5] 261,155
Industrial chemicals	32,888	97,405	119,212	117,248	96,110	172,391	129,262
Pigments, paints, and varnishes	20,638	25,276	74,386	76,359	79,348	103,174	78,645
Fertilizers and fertilizer materials	17,676	17,489	60,740	91,637	76,392	50,682	43,371
Explosives, fuses, etc	7,203	60,063	[7] 7,616	(6)	(6)	(6)	[8] 123
Soap and toilet preparations	9,007	18,729	27,993	19,472	16,410	19,861	18,547
Group 9.—Miscellaneous, total	119,365	1,091,359	649,915	651,454	595,657	976,268	1,576,394
Photographic and projection goods	19,617	22,361	55,420	53,744	[5] 52,391	[5] 60,082	[5] 56,711
Scientific and professional instruments, apparatus, and supplies	12,648	107,760	67,815	60,762	54,201	[5] 63,869	[5] 55,773
Musical instruments	2,582	2,988	15,001	13,545	15,848	22,260	19,596
Miscellaneous office supplies	5,056	11,413	37,833	23,178	22,698	26,414	21,212
Toys, athletic and sporting goods	4,906	3,707	16,790	13,734	12,238	15,667	17,460
Firearms and ammunition	17,800	751,909	[10] 18,580	[10][4] 4,240	[10] 2,636	[10] 4,263	[10] 4,762
Books, maps, pictures, and other printed matter	21,794	32,712	63,893	57,966	51,628	67,512	71,670
Clocks and watches	2,828	3,962	10,437	12,092	9,064	9,166	10,090
Art works—painting and statuary	1,025	1,002	1,938	1,218	1,051	1,188	1,396
Jewelry	2,775	5,621	21,820	25,062	13,130	13,391	14,293
Miscellaneous, n. e. s	27,020	148,504	[11] 340,688	[11] 385,912	[11] 260,777	[11] 686,457	[11] 1,303,431

[1] Includes some nonferrous articles.
[2] Beginning 1950, certain commodities excluded under security regulations from "Industrial machinery" and included with "Automobiles and other vehicles."
[3] Beginning 1946, tractors, parts and accessories included with "Automobiles and other vehicles"; with "Agricultural machinery and implements" in prior years.
[4] Includes explosives, fuses, and blasting caps January 1949 to June 1950.
[5] Under security regulations, certain commodities included with "Miscellaneous, n. e. s."
[6] 3-year average, 1946–1948.
[7] For security reasons, beginning July 1950, data included with "Miscellaneous, n. e. s." See also note 5.
[8] Black powder only.
[10] Includes only sporting rifles, shotguns, fireworks and pyrotechnics in 1949, and only sporting rifles and shotguns in 1950–1952.
[11] Includes certain chemical specialties; explosives, fuses, etc.; photographer's goods, scientific and professional supplies; firearms, and ammunition excluded under security regulations from commodity groups in which they belong. See notes 6, 9, and 10.

Source: Department of Commerce, Bureau of Census; annual report, *Foreign Commerce and Navigation of the United States*, and records.

No. 1069.—IMPORTS OF MERCHANDISE, BY COMMODITY GROUPS: 1936 TO 1952

[In thousands of dollars. Represents imports for consumption. See general note, p. 880]

COMMODITY	1936-1940 average	1941-1945 average	1946-1950 average	1949	1950	1951	1952
Total imports of merchandise.....	2,440,042	3,475,523	6,583,596	6,591,640	8,743,082	10,817,341	10,744,624
Group 00.—Animals and animal products, edible, total.................	90,761	103,985	243,767	269,413	376,396	429,779	398,367
Animals, edible....................	15,535	21,225	49,073	60,390	71,989	52,945	14,404
Meat products...................	28,064	26,823	62,901	71,790	113,028	187,485	156,842
Animal oils and fats, edible.......	661	793	83	110	91	76	534
Dairy products..................	13,013	4,757	14,641	17,586	24,301	25,194	36,300
Fish..........................	30,819	46,030	110,639	112,402	157,046	157,171	181,258
Other edible animal products.....	2,670	2,358	6,432	7,136	9,942	6,908	7,239
Group 0.—Animals and animal products, inedible, total.................	169,882	236,821	360,826	277,516	365,864	406,366	222,157
Hides and skins, raw (except furs).	50,591	67,789	92,458	72,533	115,681	132,770	60,080
Leather.......................	8,748	14,355	22,674	13,556	25,646	24,647	16,149
Leather manufactures...........	7,644	9,361	15,890	9,067	15,585	20,687	20,940
Furs and manufactures..........	69,781	107,797	149,405	108,836	109,372	114,275	78,656
Animal oils, fats, and greases, inedible.....................	6,512	9,820	8,783	7,307	8,598	14,085	10,207
Other animals and animal products, inedible.................	26,606	27,699	71,614	66,217	87,982	101,901	106,116
Group 1.—Vegetable food products and beverages, total.................	574,365	864,797	1,699,290	1,304,237	2,271,583	2,654,764	2,748,695
Grains and preparations...........	44,342	112,296	42,787	75,311	78,443	131,428	165,791
Fodders and feeds................	11,315	16,397	23,092	24,062	33,389	42,103	74,175
Vegetables and preparations......	19,413	29,678	52,762	52,439	46,512	52,894	55,367
Fruits and nuts..................	59,902	63,291	151,263	146,812	168,847	168,961	163,327
Vegetable oils and fats, edible.....	17,503	8,427	13,841	8,966	24,034	14,431	14,649
Cocoa, coffee, and tea............	191,568	331,852	916,112	960,753	1,322,140	1,613,792	1,608,461
Spices........................	12,501	15,689	40,406	37,881	69,497	58,362	58,069
Sugar and related products........	152,536	211,915	366,095	396,409	408,242	444,406	477,314
Beverages......................	65,282	75,262	92,921	92,585	120,477	128,386	131,402
Group 2.—Vegetable products, inedible, except fibers and wood, total...	393,850	369,791	734,045	604,239	886,499	1,279,225	1,041,641
Rubber and manufactures........	211,308	165,642	323,780	251,312	478,303	829,894	642,653
Gums, resins, and balsams, n.e.s.	12,758	25,118	36,707	28,578	31,049	35,733	29,380
Drugs, herbs, leaves, roots, etc....	10,398	17,050	29,123	25,981	28,140	31,031	35,414
Oilseeds......................	40,066	40,564	108,707	95,178	105,660	104,112	56,090
Vegetable oils.................	60,773	45,662	95,646	72,501	102,565	116,207	98,925
Dyeing and tanning materials, n.e.s.	6,790	11,852	20,214	16,581	20,706	32,099	47,846
Seeds, except oilseeds...........	5,512	3,932	14,858	19,735	21,172	20,636	21,127
Nursery and greenhouse stock.....	3,255	1,602	9,323	9,162	9,851	10,155	13,222
Tobacco and manufactures........	37,706	54,223	83,441	75,535	78,873	88,107	83,468
Miscellaneous vegetable products.	5,263	4,146	10,249	9,677	10,180	11,250	13,516
Group 3.—Textiles, total.............	382,072	461,117	801,068	685,764	1,054,590	1,495,121	1,111,110
Cotton, unmanufactured..........	11,425	20,208	41,202	22,415	43,302	42,364	41,245
Cotton semimanufactures........	3,404	2,740	9,315	6,675	16,371	11,993	7,683
Cotton manufactures............	38,735	16,202	42,502	43,171	64,533	68,547	59,287
Jute and manufactures..........	47,056	63,255	133,919	142,072	127,920	159,838	142,137
Flax, hemp, and ramie, and manufactures......................	27,450	12,556	34,252	33,700	44,292	45,044	31,876
Other vegetable fiber and manufactures......................	25,993	41,764	73,248	73,616	87,924	154,100	141,407
Wool, including mohair, etc., unmanufactured.................	61,291	247,905	291,210	222,223	427,802	713,533	382,036
Wool semimanufactures..........	6,405	6,496	20,728	25,162	38,346	58,878	74,896
Wool manufactures.............	19,601	16,067	48,375	46,803	75,508	92,662	89,739
Hair and manufactures, n.e.s.....	4,117	8,200	10,348	8,508	11,762	15,646	7,033
Silk, unmanufactured...........	109,947	13,021	32,649	7,527	21,151	21,090	37,353
Silk manufactures..............	8,250	2,228	20,708	24,877	33,881	37,478	34,832
Manufactures of rayon or other synthetic textiles.................	7,815	2,186	22,795	9,206	38,441	52,149	37,570
Miscellaneous textile products....	10,584	8,287	19,816	19,809	23,357	21,799	23,993

No. 1069.—Imports of Merchandise, by Commodity Groups: 1936 to 1952—
Continued

[In thousands of dollars]

COMMODITY	1936–1940, average	1941–1945, average	1946–1950, average	1949	1950	1951	1952
Group 4.—Wood and paper, total......	261,779	327,821	845,849	841,894	1,114,086	1,304,370	1,280,706
Wood, unmanufactured...........	7,903	11,182	23,388	19,382	27,306	29,484	28,258
Wood semimanufactures—sawmill products.........................	19,328	80,290	142,082	113,176	265,195	229,200	221,515
Wood manufactures.............	11,371	11,569	37,696	33,515	61,055	66,648	68,442
Cork and manufactures...........	5,872	9,023	14,376	10,295	13,948	20,803	17,163
Paper base stocks................	93,396	101,123	252,303	212,889	273,809	414,059	325,354
Paper and manufactures.........	123,911	144,645	396,004	452,638	472,774	544,176	599,974
Group 5.—Nonmetallic minerals, total.	137,276	246,662	632,068	694,101	904,841	977,978	1,060,796
Coal and related fuels............	4,844	4,297	4,833	6,468	8,063	4,470	6,961
Petroleum and products.........	47,654	93,981	379,027	477,788	591,905	601,261	691,046
Stone, cement, lime, and gypsum.	3,564	9,547	8,454	7,174	11,169	13,684	12,180
Glass and glass products.........	6,102	1,084	7,564	7,365	14,357	21,684	17,381
Clays and clay products.........	9,515	6,175	19,434	23,782	29,304	40,962	45,317
Other nonmetallic minerals......	21,466	46,834	67,020	69,749	94,636	119,394	111,267
Precious stones and imitations...	44,034	84,133	146,736	101,775	155,509	175,753	176,626
Group 6.—Metals and manufactures, except machinery and vehicles, total.	242,551	519,481	841,041	963,445	1,183,371	1,435,403	1,922,620
Iron ore and concentrates........	5,697	3,088	28,107	36,735	44,027	59,555	83,156
Iron and steel semimanufactures.	4,840	1,764	35,878	48,344	94,289	217,354	89,856
Steel-mill products—manufactures.	10,807	5,811	15,395	17,988	37,169	125,338	122,989
Iron and steel, advanced manufactures......................	2,882	3,178	5,686	5,774	8,647	21,266	24,755
Ferro-alloys....................	25,513	64,793	80,126	76,590	111,869	132,905	199,575
Nonferrous metals, except precious.	183,770	427,085	613,381	759,745	854,819	829,801	1,361,632
Precious metals, jewelry, and plated ware, except gold and silver in ore, bullion, and coin...	9,042	13,762	22,468	18,288	32,552	49,184	40,037
Group 7.—Machinery and vehicles, total.......................	17,532	82,125	111,537	135,113	157,486	243,334	353,602
Electrical machinery and apparatus.	2,075	14,438	5,189	4,291	9,443	18,039	27,136
Industrial, office and printing machinery......................	9,074	9,999	22,408	26,742	36,871	71,340	125,767
Agricultural machinery and implements......................	4,519	6,051	58,734	82,993	77,372	96,626	98,222
Automobiles and other vehicles, except agricultural.............	1,864	52,638	25,206	21,087	33,800	57,329	102,476
Group 8.—Chemicals and related products, total.................	79,662	130,741	118,762	106,819	179,362	300,697	242,969
Coal-tar chemicals..............	15,501	9,719	14,977	13,200	25,754	53,791	46,442
Medicinal and pharmaceutical preparations.................	4,847	7,920	7,191	5,925	7,811	11,823	6,124
Industrial chemicals............	19,036	28,835	33,264	18,288	52,757	120,036	63,925
Pigments, paints, and varnishes..	1,605	780	1,992	1,425	3,603	5,328	3,569
Fertilizers and materials........	35,280	31,688	54,489	62,685	74,803	102,100	114,568
Explosives.....................	621	49,401	1,866	1,740	1,216	1,682	4,747
Soap and toilet preparations.....	2,801	2,398	4,904	3,557	4,439	5,847	4,604
Group 9.—Miscellaneous, total.......	96,412	131,861	214,414	209,698	257,983	289,296	318,717
Photographic goods.............	6,601	1,433	6,327	7,059	10,092	17,023	21,295
Scientific and professional instruments, apparatus, and supplies, n. e. s.	2,047	1,523	3,337	4,709	6,869	9,811	11,735
Musical instruments............	2,795	1,211	9,392	9,726	12,866	13,817	14,971
Toys, athletic and sporting goods.	2,964	800	4,858	5,884	6,010	8,646	11,609
Firearms......................	294	13,080	1,427	1,807	2,193	4,103	6,474
Books and other printed matter...	8,388	6,394	13,162	13,680	13,956	20,004	18,920
Clocks, watches, etc.............	10,175	36,682	57,387	50,766	57,320	67,381	72,555
Art works.....................	19,224	3,678	19,615	19,725	26,257	21,634	24,119
Miscellaneous articles, n. e. s.....	36,824	66,090	98,909	96,280	120,418	126,876	129,030

Source: Department of Commerce, Bureau of Census; annual report, *Foreign Commerce and Navigation of the United States*, and records.

No. 1070.—Exports of United States Merchandise—Value of Selected Articles: 1821 to 1952

[In thousands of dollars. For basis of dollar values, except export figures for 1870–78, see general note, p. 890. Export figures for those years are mixed gold and currency values. Figures are for fiscal years ending Sept. 30 through 1840, and June 30, 1850 through 1915; calendar years thereafter. In some cases blanks represent entire absence of trade; in other cases the item is not available separately]

YEAR OR YEARLY AVERAGE	Meat products	Animal fats and oils [1]	Leather	Rye	Wheat and wheat flour	Oil cake and oil-cake meal	Fruits and nuts [3]	Rubber and manufactures [3]	Naval stores, gums, and resins	Tobacco, unmanufactured
1821					4,476				315	5,649
1830					6,132		24		356	5,586
1840					11,779		55		666	9,884
1850					7,742		25		1,372	9,951
1860	8,080	6,200	698		19,525	1,609	206	241	3,886	15,907
1870	11,630	9,909	111	217	68,341	3,419	543	186	3,277	21,100
1871–1880	50,299	20,635	5,521	1,452	108,067	4,732	1,485	237	4,852	24,028
1881–1890	64,539	36,330	8,271	1,263	131,966	6,847	3,309	709	6,187	21,246
1891–1900	91,521	52,251	15,317	3,323	147,694	10,433	6,235	1,865	8,735	24,083
1901–1910	102,256	79,130	27,627	1,150	124,399	21,471	15,555	6,218	16,668	31,530
1911–1915	81,315	83,806	44,656	3,613	172,788	25,570	31,865	13,362	21,882	46,064
1915–1920 [4]	401,251	166,868	110,215	52,009	512,963	21,978	61,501	46,430	20,417	139,509
1921–1925	139,833	144,085	44,287	39,475	321,864	24,695	82,869	30,003	22,379	164,596
1926–1930	77,988	116,071	47,481	14,767	230,647	24,392	122,234	67,366	30,353	144,549
1931–1935	28,724	36,987	17,120	139	39,237	7,613	84,798	22,961	14,722	103,742
1936–1940	26,409	18,183	14,418	1,392	55,708	8,188	76,111	33,293	15,117	109,798
1941–1945	379,553	109,189	20,497	1,580	104,941	908	87,718	118,585	12,778	137,730
1946–1950	124,405	108,565	25,270	7,393	872,128	11,124	160,914	146,782	36,008	257,888
1945	289,540	102,532	19,547	7,639	329,852	739	128,442	154,962	12,964	238,802
1946	341,413	95,327	24,228	6,840	609,696	177	171,459	181,367	27,288	351,274
1947	129,300	111,445	33,373	5,454	868,078	14,992	199,096	214,516	47,763	270,687
1948	56,753	88,978	20,462	2,934	1,392,663	7,044	194,404	132,402	30,494	214,528
1949	51,454	134,966	28,286	15,841	1,001,608	24,541	139,762	114,482	32,044	251,945
1950	43,107	112,107	20,003	5,896	488,597	8,867	99,830	91,192	42,442	251,060
1951	60,032	214,341	19,063	11,604	996,802	22,443	105,159	148,273	40,030	325,528
1952 (prel.)	51,506	147,319	17,244	9,608	941,873	2,826	125,031	159,788	25,309	245,499

YEAR OR YEARLY AVERAGE	Cotton, unmanufactured	Cotton manufactures [5]	Saw-mill products	Other wood manufactures	Coal and coke	Petroleum and products	Iron and steel-mill products	Copper and manufactures	Machinery, all classes	Automobiles including engines and parts
1821	20,157		1,513					27		
1830	29,675	1,318	1,650	426				37		
1840	63,870	3,550	2,072	921				87		
1850	71,985	4,734	2,545	2,279	167			105		
1860	191,807	10,935	3,714	6,318	741			1,864		
1870	227,028	3,787	4,921	7,625	1,306	32,669	539	1,042	5,783	
1871–1880	194,577	6,622	7,341	8,470	2,506	40,361	1,150	1,687	8,365	
1881–1890	221,689	12,558	12,549	9,134	4,912	49,452	1,622	5,530	13,607	
1891–1900	225,819	16,924	18,856	11,509	12,095	59,055	11,840	25,589	36,093	
1901–1910	386,513	33,237	43,397	18,448	32,491	93,032	43,528	78,638	95,971	[6] 6,292
1911–1915	537,044	52,525	62,458	23,608	58,648	137,466	96,313	123,555	158,897	35,805
1915–1920 [4]	768,361	214,697	63,213	33,973	151,569	349,316	491,191	208,909	354,216	157,775
1921–1925	804,985	133,052	88,233	27,690	131,112	406,267	166,776	129,761	320,048	177,164
1926–1930	765,674	124,079	104,580	32,848	121,800	525,265	170,666	149,999	488,042	406,164
1931–1935	366,539	45,423	38,573	12,622	51,678	232,081	62,931	39,920	212,499	146,503
1936–1940	282,940	60,909	43,162	16,211	66,745	345,619	269,571	87,680	494,612	456,273
1941–1945	151,727	185,337	29,752	36,039	164,497	572,845	543,083	79,333	1,072,968	456,273
1946–1950	674,203	471,256	68,684	39,189	405,244	559,105	625,086	85,745	2,065,354	820,815
1945	278,678	235,924	34,402	54,637	196,258	753,084	457,446	55,312	1,190,961	587,868
1946	538,155	375,242	50,364	36,323	315,735	435,759	447,120	38,587	1,369,145	548,548
1947	423,241	852,492	120,589	68,266	632,448	641,395	824,465	102,489	2,351,731	1,149,433
1948	511,005	498,720	64,027	35,518	492,275	667,456	649,456	113,568	2,259,052	380,367
1949	874,216	366,340	[7] 59,956	[7] 31,078	307,940	561,850	731,928	97,111	[2]2,334,073	[7] 752,592
1950	1,024,397	263,484	[7] 48,484	[7] 24,761	277,823	499,474	472,463	88,437	[2]2,012,770	[7] 723,143
1951	1,146,372	478,247	[7] 96,417	[7] 36,575	605,119	783,007	611,167	100,993	[2]2,588,800	[9]1,190,512
1952 (prel.)	873,520	399,980	[7] 76,670	[7] 32,482	509,845	799,909	[10]621,159	155,516	[2]2,824,250	[3] 988,353

[1] Includes margarine of vegetable origin through 1948. Excludes inedible fish oils. Excludes "lard compounds" beginning 1921; now classified as "vegetable cooking fats." [3] Includes fruit and nut preparations.
[3] Natural and synthetic rubber. [4] Average for period July 1, 1915, to Dec. 31, 1920.
[5] Includes semimanufactures. [6] Average for 1906–10.
[7] Box, crate and package shooks (except fruit and vegetable) included with "Other wood manufactures" beginning 1949; classified as "Sawmill products" in prior years.
[8] Exclusive of truck-laying tractors of 95 and over drawbar horsepower beginning July 1949.
[9] Exclusive of machinery and vehicles manufactured to military specifications beginning July 1949.
[10] Includes a small amount of nonferrous metal articles.

Source: Department of Commerce, Bureau of the Census; annual report, *Foreign Commerce and Navigation of the United States*, and records.

No. 1071.—Imports—Value of Selected Commodities: 1821 to 1952

[In thousands of dollars. For basis of dollar values, see general note, p. 880. Figures represent "general imports" through 1932, "imports for consumption" thereafter. Figures cover fiscal years ending Sept. 30 through 1840, and June 30, 1850 through 1915; calendar years thereafter. In some cases blanks represent entire absence of trade; in other cases the item is not available separately]

YEAR OR YEARLY AVERAGE	Hides and skins	Furs, and manufactures [1]	Fruits and nuts	Vegetable oils and fats, expressed or extracted	Coffee	Sugar [2]	Rubber, crude	Tobacco, unmanufactured	Cotton manufactures [3]	Burlaps
1821	893	224	181		4,490	3,554			7,391	
1830	2,410	306	520	15	4,227	4,631			7,865	
1840	2,756	423	1,405	263	8,546	5,581			6,504	
1850	4,799	1,014	1,191	922	11,235	7,556		272	20,781	
1860	16,525	1,838	4,804	1,619	21,894	31,079	1,427	1,366	53,216	
1870	14,402	2,236	7,417	2,153	24,236	56,924	3,460	2,534	23,380	
1871-1880	17,443	4,192	11,237	1,164	48,574	75,216	3,695	4,363	36,691	
1881-1890	24,776	7,224	18,732	1,796	55,381	85,760	13,262	6,682	30,299	2,276
1891-1900	32,143	9,406	19,492	3,371	83,026	97,371	21,135	12,083	31,588	6,626
1901-1910	69,363	18,236	28,363	10,676	71,473	84,863	47,755	20,824	57,845	18,549
1911-1915	102,967	19,341	43,033	26,554	108,970	118,240	82,735	31,576	63,049	30,749
1915-1920 [4]	201,517	47,620	61,755	84,462	165,265	203,906	192,149	51,012	65,816	62,591
1921-1925	93,057	80,552	75,499	59,552	208,792	295,389	192,922	64,831	86,568	60,406
1926-1930	118,003	114,785	84,868	81,940	281,707	207,318	294,428	57,018	63,627	72,250
1931-1935	39,795	43,125	48,407	45,912	141,173	115,110	74,573	27,118	34,472	25,141
1936-1940	50,591	69,781	59,902	72,766	137,736	138,521	206,312	34,294	42,139	35,667
1941-1945	67,789	107,798	63,291	48,840	205,688	171,975	148,694	50,496	18,942	50,074
1946-1950	92,456	149,405	151,263	94,812	731,709	334,782	311,446	80,763	51,816	102,062
1945	49,954	144,148	109,815	48,714	345,952	201,554	96,930	75,443	37,869	65,313
1946	77,471	228,378	143,281	73,531	472,380	196,963	232,800	85,904	44,503	76,183
1947	85,539	125,889	136,053	117,379	601,318	410,516	316,740	90,694	31,029	109,019
1948	107,765	164,548	161,324	103,636	697,679	313,059	309,137	77,590	82,800	131,313
1949	72,533	108,836	146,812	70,014	795,145	372,167	240,312	73,239	49,846	103,237
1950	118,681	109,372	168,847	109,496	1,002,022	381,187	448,241	76,387	80,904	90,558
1951	132,770	114,275	168,961	107,569	1,361,837	387,182	808,330	85,441	80,540	112,128
1952	60,089	78,656	163,827	95,500	1,375,867	414,790	619,101	80,699	66,970	113,716

YEAR OR YEARLY AVERAGE	Wool and mohair	Wool manufactures (including rags, noils, waste)	Silk, raw	Sawmill products	Wood pulp	Paper and manufactures	Petroleum and products	Copper, including ore and manufactures	Tin, including ore	Fertilizers and materials [5]
1821		7,289				58		233	149	
1830	97	5,901	119			170		807	108	
1840	846	10,503	234			70		1,688	229	
1850	1,680	19,621	386			432		2,418	674	92
1860	4,543	42,149	1,236			497		1,830	1,158	526
1870	6,743	34,491	3,018			1,100		656	2,043	2,192
1871-1880	12,538	32,152	6,390	5,618		1,591		1,094	3,032	2,517
1881-1890	15,531	42,889	15,963	8,074		2,082		498	6,028	4,700
1891-1900	25,171	38,914	26,160	7,887	1,478	3,016		3,591	9,146	6,642
1901-1910	32,410	18,957	55,509	14,699	5,378	4,124		30,319	25,897	20,969
1911-1915	42,664	22,777	80,079	18,276	16,254	12,932	8,868	46,129	41,493	39,631
1915-1920 [4]	170,173	26,562	213,940	36,521	42,814	47,214	31,174	105,805	73,739	67,142
1921-1925	102,369	64,592	348,123	30,653	67,002	105,230	91,857	77,811	59,225	57,140
1926-1930	78,790	69,295	368,232	44,503	85,044	151,219	132,794	108,243	89,058	67,997
1931-1935	18,731	17,114	115,054	10,540	50,544	95,523	50,990	29,662	43,837	28,659
1936-1940	61,291	26,406	108,723	19,328	77,094	123,911	47,654	47,608	85,303	35,250
1941-1945	247,608	22,852	12,508	50,280	84,130	144,645	92,981	164,807	77,610	31,687
1946-1950	291,210	66,180	142,082	217,455	396,004	376,027	186,450	149,165	54,480	
1945	241,300	24,535	1,116	57,240	115,764	157,542	151,969	194,672	54,009	41,327
1946	289,400	41,112	101,246	79,374	135,782	159,373	86,384	89,179	35,230	
1947	308,942	36,608	15,709	101,587	256,439	263,169	250,400	175,829	85,932	43,449
1948	307,463	78,067	6,496	152,078	272,409	437,779	415,689	203,042	176,153	56,180
1949	222,223	71,964	7,272	115,176	162,432	482,638	477,788	224,232	212,304	62,085
1950	427,602	113,853	20,566	265,195	240,211	472,774	591,906	242,810	202,255	74,803
1951	712,433	151,440	19,485	229,200	352,411	544,176	601,780	279,507	158,885	102,100
1952	382,648	164,426	33,625	221,515	271,303	596,974	691,046	411,651	298,319	114,558

[1] Includes fur hats beginning 1921; formerly classified as miscellaneous textile products.
[2] Includes sirups and maple sugar prior to Oct. 4, 1913. [3] Includes semimanufactures.
[4] Average for period July 1, 1915, to Dec. 31, 1920.
[5] Saltpeter transferred to fertilizers from chemicals beginning 1921.

Source: Department of Commerce, Bureau of Census; annual report, *Foreign Commerce and Navigation of the United States*, and records.

No. 1072.—EXPORTS (INCLUDING REEXPORTS) AND GENERAL IMPORTS OF MERCHANDISE, BY CONTINENTS: 1821 TO 1952

[In thousands of dollars. For basis of dollar values, see general note, p. 880. Figures cover fiscal years to and including 1915; calendar years thereafter, except as noted. Philippine Islands included with Asia for all years; Turkey in Europe is with Asia from 1926 through 1951 and with Europe thereafter; U. S. S. R. in Asia is with Europe beginning 1924; and Hawaiian Islands with Oceania prior to 1901. See also *Historical Statistics*, series M 87-102]

YEARLY AVERAGE OR YEAR	EXPORTS							
	Total	North America		South America	Europe	Asia	Australia and Oceania	Africa
		Northern	Southern					
1821	54,496	2,392	11,965	2,208	35,575	1,977	71	309
1830	71,671	2,802	14,723	4,586	47,393	1,906	27	234
1840	123,669	6,090	17,241	5,714	92,039	1,560	330	696
1850	144,376	9,519	14,284	7,730	108,638	3,028	190	987
1860	333,576	22,883	20,273	15,706	249,425	8,100	4,962	3,227
1870	392,772	21,703	31,100	15,188	313,315	5,773	3,873	1,830
1871-1880	589,301	32,874	36,246	21,161	482,235	8,133	5,703	2,980
1881-1890	765,136	40,697	43,945	30,129	613,783	18,958	13,928	3,728
1891-1900	1,024,870	64,636	63,050	34,473	798,320	32,068	20,132	11,272
1901-1910	1,616,250	182,606	126,238	64,194	1,131,789	87,091	31,048	23,222
1911-1915	2,370,539	337,091	182,315	122,243	1,517,404	133,348	51,506	26,632
1915-1920 ¹	6,521,190	780,221	503,439	360,744	4,123,523	562,476	109,121	81,668
1921-1925	4,397,027	627,382	444,577	297,115	2,318,244	496,553	141,426	69,729
1926-1930	4,777,314	829,858	403,175	447,880	2,236,801	573,085	177,239	109,986
1931-1935	2,025,196	300,372	162,435	141,074	960,158	349,911	45,868	62,377
1936-1940	3,219,581	521,798	291,178	317,400	1,332,706	535,283	89,150	132,086
1941-1945	10,061,075	1,297,384	574,985	500,039	5,673,543	799,063	363,562	842,499
1946-1950 ²	11,829,455	1,895,406	1,399,158	1,664,671	4,120,070	1,826,927	183,572	613,214
1944	14,258,702	1,460,921	625,938	540,277	9,363,897	995,782	410,484	861,404
1945	9,805,625	1,194,814	794,279	645,226	5,514,814	849,252	353,569	523,671
1946	9,738,321	1,462,917	1,072,097	1,148,500	4,122,358	1,326,870	116,671	488,819
1947	14,429,747	2,114,505	1,714,979	2,353,642	5,187,322	1,917,504	320,324	821,471
1948	12,653,058	1,944,706	1,450,572	1,911,582	4,279,188	2,129,566	152,772	784,672
1949	12,051,108	1,959,180	1,339,502	1,561,882	4,118,159	2,255,766	194,864	621,755
1950 ²	10,275,043	1,995,732	1,418,642	1,347,660	2,893,324	1,504,931	133,229	349,334
1951 ²	15,032,379	2,588,417	1,703,877	2,070,809	4,044,487	2,243,589	244,142	580,967
1952 ³ (prel.)	15,163,982	2,785,404	1,700,496	1,831,664	3,341,681	2,113,112	224,253	568,423

YEARLY AVERAGE OR YEAR	GENERAL IMPORTS							
	Total	North America		South America	Europe	Asia	Australia and Oceania	Africa
		Northern	Southern					
1821	54,521	402	11,816	1,570	35,000	5,324	34	375
1830	62,721	398	10,793	4,919	40,117	6,241	18	234
1840	98,259	1,228	15,421	8,606	61,721	10,686	152	445
1850	173,509	5,180	16,116	16,038	123,115	12,434	9	615
1860	353,616	23,730	44,180	34,929	216,661	29,239	1,170	3,706
1870	435,958	36,265	74,435	42,964	240,187	37,773	1,612	2,722
1871-1880	535,222	30,720	91,365	65,771	284,294	55,715	4,287	3,051
1881-1890	692,187	41,113	97,564	79,184	384,644	72,173	13,764	3,746
1891-1900	763,328	36,801	102,025	107,255	393,733	96,584	19,519	7,412
1901-1910	1,158,500	66,137	154,913	139,437	594,067	177,289	12,818	13,840
1911-1915	1,712,319	131,455	248,943	219,923	798,115	270,797	19,020	24,065
1915-1920 ¹	3,358,354	425,337	588,103	591,295	682,298	910,340	70,134	90,848
1921-1925	3,450,103	396,668	514,233	421,336	1,049,565	942,808	53,994	71,499
1926-1930	4,033,469	479,737	460,457	545,788	1,207,213	1,195,930	53,137	91,207
1931-1935	1,713,102	236,164	177,257	244,160	516,313	490,909	16,209	32,088
1936-1940	2,482,030	368,521	246,139	337,703	627,085	784,989	36,372	81,220
1941-1945	3,514,080	963,196	588,916	801,021	287,826	478,314	187,281	217,526
1946-1950	6,659,363	1,429,229	955,066	1,479,231	1,011,596	1,245,432	167,102	371,706
1944	3,928,866	1,275,898	757,844	931,271	289,295	321,940	130,305	222,312
1945	4,159,138	1,145,388	782,934	976,101	409,480	407,315	170,935	297,015
1946	4,942,054	910,529	733,222	1,118,138	804,326	886,946	182,574	306,317
1947	5,756,333	1,126,124	1,015,661	1,254,222	820,036	1,055,195	155,761	327,538
1948	7,123,877	1,593,546	946,114	1,559,644	1,121,123	1,346,073	163,673	393,703
1949	6,622,390	1,552,351	941,348	1,501,273	925,082	1,239,488	125,364	337,516
1950 ²	8,852,161	1,961,593	1,138,987	1,962,879	1,387,445	1,699,457	208,140	493,661
1951	10,967,301	2,277,692	1,220,873	2,327,098	2,042,944	2,059,072	450,546	589,076
1952 ³	10,712,619	2,388,317	1,350,426	2,283,093	2,027,858	1,813,385	242,984	606,556

¹ Period July 1, 1915, to Dec. 31, 1920.
² Total includes $632,171,000 for 1950, $1,556,192,000 for 1951 and $2,598,948,000 for 1952 not shown by continents for security reasons.   ³ Represents later data than that shown in table 1055.

Source: Department of Commerce, Bureau of Census; annual report, *Foreign Commerce and Navigation of the United States*, and records.

No. 1073.—Exports and General Imports, by Continents—Percent
Distribution: 1821 to 1952

[Percentages based on figures shown in table 1072, except that calculations were made from unrounded figures.
See headnote to that table]

YEARLY AVERAGE OR YEAR	PERCENT OF TOTAL EXPORTS							PERCENT OF TOTAL IMPORTS						
	North America		South America	Europe	Asia	Australia and Oceania	Africa	North America		South America	Europe	Asia	Australia and Oceania	Africa
	Northern	Southern						Northern	Southern					
1821...............	4.4	22.0	4.1	65.3	3.6	0.1	0.6	0.7	21.7	2.9	64.2	9.8	0.1	0.7
1830...............	3.9	20.5	6.4	66.1	2.7	(¹)	.3	.6	17.2	7.8	64.0	10.0	(¹)	.4
1840...............	4.9	13.9	4.6	74.4	1.3	.3	.6	1.2	15.7	8.8	62.8	10.9	.2	.5
1850...............	6.6	9.9	8.4	75.2	2.1	.1	.7	3.0	9.3	3.2	71.0	7.2	(¹)	.4
1860...............	6.9	8.5	4.7	74.8	2.4	1.5	1.0	6.7	12.5	8.9	61.3	8.3	.3	1.0
1870...............	5.5	7.9	3.9	79.8	1.5	1.0	.5	8.3	17.1	2.9	55.1	8.7	.4	.6
1871–1880.........	5.6	6.2	3.6	81.8	1.4	1.0	.5	5.7	17.1	12.3	53.1	10.4	.8	.6
1881–1890.........	5.3	5.7	3.9	80.2	2.5	1.8	.5	5.9	14.1	11.4	55.6	10.4	2.0	.5
1891–1900.........	6.8	6.2	3.4	77.9	3.2	2.0	1.1	4.8	13.4	14.1	51.6	12.7	2.6	1.0
1901–1910.........	9.4	7.8	4.0	70.0	5.4	1.9	1.4	5.7	13.4	12.0	51.3	15.3	1.1	1.2
1911–1915.........	14.2	7.7	5.2	64.0	5.6	2.2	1.1	7.7	14.8	12.8	46.6	15.8	1.1	1.4
1915–1920 ².......	12.0	7.7	5.5	63.2	8.6	1.7	1.3	12.7	17.5	17.6	20.3	27.1	2.1	2.7
1921–1925.........	14.2	10.1	6.8	52.7	11.3	3.2	1.6	11.5	14.9	12.2	30.4	27.3	1.6	2.1
1926–1930.........	17.4	8.4	9.4	46.8	12.0	3.7	2.3	11.9	11.4	12.5	29.9	29.7	1.3	2.3
1931–1935.........	14.8	8.0	7.0	47.4	17.3	2.4	3.1	12.8	10.3	14.3	30.1	26.7	.9	1.9
1936–1940.........	16.2	9.0	9.9	41.4	16.6	2.7	4.2	14.8	9.9	13.6	25.3	31.6	1.5	3.3
1941–1945.........	12.9	5.7	5.0	36.4	8.0	3.6	4.4	27.1	16.8	22.8	8.2	13.6	4.3	6.2
1946–1950 ².......	16.0	11.8	14.1	34.8	13.4	1.6	5.2	21.5	14.3	22.2	13.2	18.7	2.5	5.6
1941	19.7	9.9	10.2	35.9	12.1	2.6	9.6	17.1	12.3	20.2	8.4	32.5	4.8	4.8
1942.............	16.8	5.9	4.7	49.6	8.5	4.4	10.1	26.6	12.8	26.5	8.0	12.3	8.4	7.4
1943.............	11.3	4.2	3.2	58.9	6.5	4.4	11.4	30.8	19.0	22.9	7.1	6.9	7.3	6.0
1944.............	10.2	4.4	3.8	65.7	7.0	2.6	6.0	32.5	19.3	25.7	7.4	8.2	3.3	5.7
1945.............	12.2	7.4	6.6	56.2	8.7	2.6	5.3	27.5	18.1	22.5	9.3	9.3	4.1	7.1
1946.............	16.0	11.0	11.8	42.3	12.6	1.9	4.9	18.6	14.8	22.6	16.3	17.9	3.7	6.2
1947.............	14.7	11.9	16.3	35.9	12.8	2.2	5.7	19.6	17.6	21.8	14.2	18.3	2.7	5.7
1948.............	15.4	11.5	15.1	32.8	16.8	1.2	6.2	22.4	13.3	21.9	15.7	18.9	2.3	5.5
1949 ²...........	16.3	11.1	13.0	34.2	18.7	1.6	5.2	26.4	14.2	22.7	14.0	18.7	1.9	5.1
1950 ²...........	19.4	13.8	13.1	28.2	14.6	1.3	3.4	22.2	12.9	22.2	15.7	19.2	2.4	5.6
1951 ²..........	17.2	11.3	13.8	28.9	14.9	1.6	5.9	20.5	11.1	21.2	18.6	18.8	4.1	5.4
1952 ² (prel.).....	18.4	11.2	12.1	29.0	13.9	1.5	5.7	22.3	12.6	21.3	18.9	16.9	2.3	5.7

¹ Less than ⅒ of 1 percent.
² Period July 1, 1915, to Dec. 31, 1920.
³ Percentages for individual continents are understated since basic continent data excludes, for security reasons, exports of Special Category commodities representing 6.2 percent of total exports in 1950, 10.4 percent in 1951 and 17.1 percent in 1952.

Source: Department of Commerce, Bureau of Census; annual report, *Foreign Commerce and Navigation of the United States*, and records.

No. 1074.—EXPORTS (INCLUDING REEXPORTS) AND GENERAL IMPORTS OF MERCHANDISE, BY COUNTRY OF DESTINATION AND ORIGIN: 1941 TO 1952

[In thousands of dollars. See also *Historical Statistics*, series M 87-102, for group totals, historically]

AREA AND COUNTRY	1941-45, average Exports	1941-45, average Imports	1946-50, average Exports	1946-50, average Imports	1947 Exports	1947 Imports	1948 Exports	1948 Imports	1949 Exports	1949 Imports	1950 Exports	1950 Imports	1951 Exports	1951 Imports	1952 Exports	1952 Imports
Grand total	10,051,075	3,514,080	11,829,455	6,659,363	14,429,747	5,756,333	12,653,058	7,123,877	12,051,109	6,622,390	10,275,043	8,852,181	15,032,379	10,967,390	15,163,982	10,712,619
North America	1,872,369	1,542,113	3,294,566	2,384,296	3,829,484	2,143,784	3,395,277	2,539,661	3,298,662	2,493,695	3,414,374	3,160,579	4,292,294	3,498,585	4,485,900	3,735,744
Northern Area	1,297,334	953,196	1,895,408	1,429,229	2,114,505	1,128,124	1,944,706	1,593,546	1,969,180	1,852,331	1,995,732	1,961,593	2,588,417	2,277,592	2,785,494	2,388,817
Greenland	1,149	2,568		336	621	1,565	158	210	137		43	1,036	212	2,337	402	3,034
Canada (inc. Newfoundland and Labrador)	1,296,060	950,621	1,894,919	1,428,211	2,113,671	1,126,528	1,944,435	1,593,320	1,968,912	1,851,037	1,995,498	1,960,467	2,588,177	2,275,312	2,784,904	2,385,189
Miquelon and St. Pierre	178	8	182	27	213	31	113	16	132	1	192	90	28	43	98	94
Southern Area	574,985	588,917	1,399,158	955,047	1,714,979	1,015,661	1,450,572	946,114	1,339,802	941,348	1,418,642	1,198,987	1,703,877	1,220,873	1,700,496	1,350,435
Mexico	212,916	170,032	527,250	255,843	629,896	396,680	521,505	246,297	498,105	486,105	511,864	315,884	713,010	325,050	691,427	410,572
Central America	194,399	57,349	270,174	134,805	368,146	125,332	281,058	134,222	284,946	243,631	280,547	152,642	354,733	217,134	281,228	420,396
Guatemala	11,199	17,363	39,436	43,299	41,377	44,042	44,817	44,171	44,859	43,292	43,047	63,716	47,277	64,443	40,381	64,236
British Honduras	2,211	2,690	3,126	2,409	4,505	3,237	2,984	2,646	2,100	2,198	3,175	1,037	2,530	1,143	2,995	4,708
El Salvador	8,635	13,023	25,164	33,013	28,433	27,168	28,764	31,136	33,506	40,214	32,092	51,037	42,021	63,712	38,994	61,083
Honduras	7,161	7,016	26,787	33,917	20,901	11,877	20,901	11,277	33,590	15,217	21,436	20,182	33,968	23,680	42,326	22,464
Nicaragua	11,880	4,774	16,828	10,657	17,403	8,953	20,577	11,698	15,705	6,697	18,333	19,459	31,302	20,700	25,223	22,848
Costa Rica	8,358	8,358	27,976	29,243	20,933	35,033	25,622	22,935	26,994	22,965	26,584	24,613	31,611	27,881	33,092	32,806
Panama, Republic of	30,934	2,705	108,049	8,474	172,162	6,719	91,913	5,949	115,740	11,199	110,964	9,714	46,633	12,275	75,416	14,854
Panama, Canal Zone	26,308	1,418	31,806	2,803	39,365	2,612	39,112	4,487	29,123	2,482	22,997	2,361	29,191	2,150	24,774	1,908
Bermuda and Caribbean	257,679	361,536	592,735	563,419	716,941	643,640	648,007	560,666	577,362	554,195	628,100	640,576	736,134	677,721	702,600	719,453
Bermuda	6,370	501	10,110	509	12,463	652	9,690	997	11,961	680	8,458	356	10,997	1,066	11,005	877
Bahamas	118,545	11,910	8,307	1,058	9,505	1,362	9,850	1,645	8,225	881	7,207	658	10,363	1,733	13,597	1,614
Cuba	151,213	271,704	408,218	401,696	491,843	560,624	440,996	374,240	380,292	387,540	456,173	406,401	539,809	417,782	515,724	438,135
Jamaica	7,542	3,651	13,492	945	23,961	1,539	12,948	1,833	10,394	2,064	8,282	2,307	10,606	2,877	19,784	5,018
Haiti	7,448	10,004	21,340	19,908	23,214	20,144	20,304	20,604	23,536	10,782	25,142	23,060	28,232	32,679	32,835	29,531
Dominican Republic	12,753	12,197	41,043	29,574	49,324	30,228	46,966	35,212	38,311	24,379	41,151	37,652	48,506	49,061	54,201	55,767
Leeward Isls. and Windward Isls	1,585	2,196	2,784	2,597	4,549	3,529	3,291	2,480	3,042	1,876	1,160	2,262	1,924	1,788	1,981	2,018
Barbados	1,279	240	2,426	326	4,429	481	2,506	141	2,628	194	1,057	403	1,600	396	2,049	288
Trinidad and Tobago	18,324	3,032	12,800	5,024	19,373	3,079	14,275	6,398	13,432	5,405	8,004	9,004	8,920	10,317	10,674	7,733
Netherlands Antilles	29,325	54,153	65,599	101,693	66,935	72,935	81,512	120,048	75,939	111,407	69,063	157,827	68,033	150,831	88,363	178,038
French West Indies	6,373	2,191	6,617	189	9,415	126	5,809	51	7,361	200	2,527	193	1,124	575	2,110	427

Row labels (left column):

- South America
- Northern Area
  - Colombia
  - Venezuela
  - British Guiana
  - Surinam
  - French Guiana
- Western Area
  - Ecuador
  - Peru
  - Bolivia
  - Chile
- Eastern Area
  - Brazil
  - Paraguay
  - Uruguay
  - Argentina
  - Falkland Islands
- Europe
- Northwestern and Central Area
  - Iceland
  - Sweden
  - Norway
  - Denmark
  - Faroe Islands
  - United Kingdom
  - Ireland (Eire)
  - Netherlands
  - Belgium and Luxembourg
  - France
  - West Germany
  - East Germany
  - Austria
  - Czecho-Slovakia
  - Hungary
  - Switzerland

[1] Total includes $682,171,000 in 1960, $1,558,192,000 in 1931, and $2,568,948,000 in 1962 not shown by continents for security reasons.

[2] Country designations established January 1962; data for prior years represent combined trade with East and West Germany.

[3] Average for 1942–46; not separately reported prior to 1942.

Less than $500.

No. 1075.—Exports (Including Reexports) and Imports of Merchandise, 1949, 1950, and 1951, and Duties Collected, 1951, by Customs Districts

[In thousands of dollars]

CUSTOMS DISTRICT	EXPORTS, DOMESTIC AND FOREIGN			IMPORTS FOR CONSUMPTION			Duties collected, 1951 [2]
	1949	1950 [1]	1951 [1]	1949	1950	1951	
Total	[3]12,051,108	[3]10,275,043	[3]15,022,379	6,591,640	8,743,662	10,817,342	604,733
Maine and New Hampshire	27,487	23,203	34,410	60,851	73,327	104,037	3,227
Vermont	96,109	86,116	129,017	124,163	160,353	201,837	4,385
Massachusetts	(4)	(4)	77,592	358,574	586,066	880,400	75,934
Rhode Island	(4)	(4)	796	23,429	31,696	45,379	4,571
Connecticut	(4)	(4)	44	9,776	20,853	23,211	2,364
St. Lawrence	189,687	179,048	254,133	165,437	202,846	339,843	7,367
Rochester	20,514	23,934	22,658	7,417	7,187	9,240	1,133
Buffalo	390,296	385,647	522,675	231,065	293,822	400,179	11,805
New York	(4)	(4)	4,290,801	2,442,279	3,380,369	3,988,568	230,274
Philadelphia	(4)	(4)	400,405	474,405	667,219	778,442	46,570
Pittsburgh	894	97	205	14,054	25,916	30,759	3,134
Maryland	(4)	(4)	482,373	239,976	287,844	373,860	16,130
Virginia	(4)	(4)	637,163	94,097	104,829	140,059	9,462
North Carolina	(4)	(4)	17,149	35,574	41,043	56,050	11,466
South Carolina	(4)	(4)	110,344	16,667	39,605	42,771	2,798
Georgia	(4)	(4)	53,928	45,744	46,946	53,890	3,718
Florida	(4)	(4)	285,625	55,662	110,353	136,252	8,392
Mobile	(4)	(4)	65,258	29,835	49,175	46,545	1,998
New Orleans	(4)	(4)	1,117,169	417,125	509,640	695,386	21,645
Sabine	(4)	(4)	117,142	31,305	3,024	3,716	15
Galveston	(4)	(4)	1,213,535	201,068	209,913	336,708	12,256
Laredo	304,245	301,474	455,745	61,123	72,817	47,136	4,764
El Paso	32,427	32,516	47,847	22,843	24,978	29,333	2,674
San Diego	36,196	40,717	60,662	11,307	12,992	16,905	975
Arizona	22,966	21,935	40,515	28,989	24,360	32,050	3,696
Los Angeles	(4)	(4)	349,626	151,417	214,494	281,379	12,284
San Francisco	(4)	(4)	375,625	211,447	269,792	333,559	11,576
Oregon	(4)	(4)	238,034	16,764	25,853	33,140	2,049
Washington	150,306	116,592	247,462	140,973	184,798	217,930	6,352
Alaska	2,600	2,524	2,825	1,397	904	1,161	73
Hawaii	3,462	2,224	3,505	16,007	13,587	19,158	1,554
Montana and Idaho	35,081	28,589	47,492	14,765	28,140	26,455	614
Dakota	140,838	131,121	172,298	123,330	158,970	154,249	3,483
Minnesota	3,822	3,364	5,821	17,744	21,458	14,696	1,525
Duluth and Superior	55,785	70,703	72,874	69,752	94,396	126,795	1,872
Wisconsin	12,138	15,293	6,563	28,961	34,529	42,547	1,598
Michigan	688,836	727,231	973,741	395,131	479,377	562,134	17,224
Chicago	42,874	51,431	53,663	82,217	97,481	124,969	13,147
Indiana	100	60	50	4,349	4,812	5,438	1,053
Ohio	106,905	145,200	141,555	36,628	55,853	65,049	7,206
Kentucky	(5)	9	(5)	2,314	2,615	3,913	459
Tennessee	22	7	2	1,387	1,423	18,251	2,073
St. Louis	724	1	8	17,156	24,409	32,204	3,595
Colorado	34	9	1	2,373	3,297	3,308	197
Puerto Rico	8,571	29,047	13,898	24,708	30,541	38,399	4,077
Virgin Islands [6]	806	769	609	1,791	1,679	2,554	[7]77
Vessels under own power or afloat	171,012	117,510	28,499	22	30	59	
Shipments valued under $100 [8]	122,515	113,980	122,692				
Parcel Post	(4)	(4)	49,926				
Shipments on vessels operated by U. S. Army or Navy	1,003,788	190,756	132,838				

[1] Customs district data exclude certain commodity shipments under security regulations.
[2] As reported to Treasury Department by collectors of customs, subject in certain cases to subsequent refund as well as drawback. These figures are somewhat higher than duties as calculated on basis of imports for consumption (see table 1077).
[3] Includes $8,380,874,000 in 1949, $7,434,703,000 in 1950 and $1,556,192,000 in 1951, not shown by districts.
[4] Data not individually reported.
[5] Less than $500.
[6] Excluded from totals; not part of U. S. customs area, assessed under tariff law of Virgin Islands.
[7] Duties less cost of collection are turned into the Island's treasury; excluded from totals.
[8] Export shipments individually valued under $100.

Source: Department of Commerce, Bureau of the Census; annual report, *Foreign Commerce and Navigation of the United States*, and records.

No. 1076.—Exports (Including Reexports) and Imports of Merchandise,
by Principal Customs Districts: 1860 to 1952

[In thousands of dollars. For basis of dollar values, except export figures for 1870-78, see general note, p. 880.
Export figures for those years represent mixed gold and currency values. Figures cover fiscal years to and
including 1915; thereafter, calendar years. Import data are "general imports" through 1933; "imports for
consumption" thereafter. Areas of districts were rearranged July 1, 1913. Prior to that date some of the districts were more restricted. However, in most cases this change only slightly affects the comparability of the
figures. Prior to 1914 the statistics given in the table for Buffalo include the (former) districts of Buffalo Creek
and Niagara; those for Michigan include the (former) districts of Superior, Huron, and Detroit; and those for
Massachusetts and Maryland were the former districts of Boston and Baltimore, respectively]

YEAR OR YEARLY AVERAGE	MASSACHUSETTS		NEW YORK		PHILADELPHIA		MARYLAND		GEORGIA	
	Exports	Imports	Exports	Imports	Exports	Imports	Exports	Imports	Exports	Imports
1860	12,745	36,294	80,048	231,310	4,327	14,612	8,940	9,781	18,352	782
1870	14,129	47,484	196,615	281,049	14,298	14,488	14,811	13,819	28,747	1,659
1871-1880	30,440	52,450	290,762	237,431	35,308	23,586	24,919	28,392	25,670	645
1881-1890	64,126	66,480	348,771	463,476	34,604	35,479	31,322	13,335	22,405	603
1891-1900	97,381	68,708	397,396	486,204	45,964	50,451	51,683	12,663	26,117	603
1901-1910	96,432	96,670	575,272	697,726	81,315	64,135	90,218	30,383	86,232	1,643
1911-1915	76,794	141,012	913,312	975,410	74,326	86,381	107,096	30,196	84,982	4,882
1916-1920	217,236	273,049	2,912,639	1,708,482	415,361	144,049	350,388	45,329	138,775	16,745
1921-1925	53,559	297,227	1,611,536	1,676,764	117,533	182,857	113,608	77,606	71,380	18,714
1926-1930	40,686	297,466	1,499,191	1,957,940	208,066	205,662	94,543	100,108	73,680	17,614
1931-1935	16,304	96,790	675,065	868,790	55,628	100,712	53,832	45,312	34,837	9,333
1936-1940	23,743	157,488	1,294,347	1,210,233	90,947	145,182	98,031	79,580	22,052	12,323
1941-1945	80,056	196,328	4,396,688	1,278,003	838,370	172,136	361,782	96,332	143,978	37,030
1946-1950	74,392	407,488	6,022,498	3,650,768	397,820	463,607	636,657	335,328	78,739	41,084
1943	105,861	172,284	5,016,108	1,146,981	1,280,890	146,086	819,386	83,618	140,236	35,341
1944	55,608	162,451	5,605,423	1,275,209	1,400,861	206,132	1,073,726	101,396	166,688	37,146
1945	65,132	296,274	4,019,920	1,477,340	806,908	236,491	694,006	117,906	162,691	42,436
1946	60,052	397,540	4,016,104	2,281,777	403,448	406,589	344,461	147,587	94,624	39,730
1947	63,729	342,367	5,056,022	2,981,684	580,187	390,070	265,408	288,579	83,236	43,630
1948	(4)	482,736		2,676,212		467,397		241,997		45,375
1949	(4)	348,574		2,443,379		474,466		388,968		46,704
1950		566,066		3,380,369		667,219		287,844		46,946
1951	77,982	580,400	4,200,801	3,955,556	401,496	775,442	452,373	372,800	55,928	53,850
1952	68,437	577,215	3,784,126	4,184,006	284,739	673,175	452,604	363,026	26,200	56,673

YEAR OR YEARLY AVERAGE	NEW ORLEANS		GALVESTON		BUFFALO		CHICAGO		MICHIGAN	
	Exports	Imports	Exports	Imports	Exports	Imports	Exports	Imports	Exports	Imports
1860	109,165	20,690	5,772	585	3,040	4,920	1,145	90	1,627	986
1870	107,487	14,377	14,376	509	365	5,275	2,612	736	2,114	1,730
1871-1880	94,785	13,245	16,491	1,354	648	6,002	4,088	653	3,115	3,048
1881-1890	85,612	11,130	19,655	1,328	445	6,118	4,361	7,489	14,617	3,486
1891-1900	92,790	16,268	65,956	1,051	9,878	9,846	8,580	14,366	21,274	6,483
1901-1910	139,173	27,650	150,302	3,386	90,122	30,814	4,804	21,439	50,561	30,963
1911-1915	179,066	78,696	243,254	7,611	82,713	34,321	30,341	33,060	102,360	20,067
1916-1920	488,307	149,070	345,964	15,560	204,696	40,117	204,275	41,088
1921-1925	391,842	167,731	523,306	30,060	94,639	77,447	27,451	44,094	211,725	74,000
1926-1930	388,633	201,460	542,304	31,809	70,062	75,769	16,608	48,674	266,845	83,423
1931-1935	141,711	98,747	285,702	15,521	70,062	45,601	18,501	40,311	113,045	49,718
1936-1940	197,604	171,468	300,614	27,060	134,001	75,762	18,503	60,317	282,077	83,537
1941-1945	304,441	240,661	283,304	22,081	304,960	125,349	18,508	42,717	648,607	83,348
1946-1950	704,028	367,188	781,337	155,361	204,380	324,639				
1943	365,206	246,900	189,806	40,586	304,870	304,301	5,608	34,031	628,345	87,887
1944	355,790	268,606	281,609	49,703				39,314		
1945	394,800	286,664	417,846	62,206						
1946	666,845	308,022	728,367	92,080						
1947	913,307	332,077	1,232,686	111,491						
1948	(4)		(4)		173,384					
1949	(4)		(4)		192,306					
1950										
1951	1,013,309		1,212,386							
1952	948,090		1,176,006							

[1] Period July 1, 1913, to Dec. 31, 1913.
[2] For security reasons Customs district of exportation for certain commodities not reported in export statistics.
[3] Average for 1946 and 1947.
[4] Customs district data not available.

No. 1076.—Exports (Including Reexports) and Imports of Merchandise, by Principal Customs Districts: 1860 to 1952—Continued

[In thousands of dollars]

YEAR OR YEARLY AVERAGE	SAN FRANCISCO		WASHINGTON		YEAR OR YEARLY AVERAGE	SAN FRANCISCO		WASHINGTON	
	Exports	Imports	Exports	Imports		Exports	Imports	Exports	Imports
1860	4,868	7,367			1941–1945	326,645	83,972	214,186	78,802
1870	13,992	15,963	428	35	1946–1950 [1]	[2]347,288	188,514	162,685	127,890
1871–1880	23,597	27,629	493	32	1942	303,600	98,074	90,626	56,361
1881–1890	37,388	41,726	2,178	263	1943	677,022	88,038	386,206	71,329
1891–1900	34,486	42,000	9,788	3,734	1944	304,255	64,476	310,879	115,072
1901–1910	35,255	43,707	34,638	16,658	1945	213,143	56,052	222,427	92,657
					1946	297,117	102,651	136,291	65,738
1911–1915	60,154	63,760	57,711	50,200	1947	397,459	174,575	224,651	101,122
1915–1920 [2]	186,317	197,613	222,702	206,862	1948	(4)	184,104	185,583	146,712
1921–1925	158,275	155,500	110,361	214,213	1949	(4)	211,447	180,308	140,673
1926–1930	182,236	195,331	136,896	212,134	1950 [3]	(4)	269,793	116,592	184,788
1931–1935	96,950	65,233	48,974	35,216	1951 [3]	378,625	333,589	247,462	217,930
1936–1940	120,922	74,986	77,816	36,543	1952 [3]	400,582	320,215	290,404	217,639

[1] Period July 1, 1915, to Dec. 31, 1920.
[2] For security reasons Customs district of exportation for certain commodities not reported in export statistics.
[3] Average for 1946 and 1947. [4] Customs district data not available.

Source: Department of Commerce, Bureau of Census; annual report, *Foreign Commerce and Navigation of the United States*, and records.

No. 1077.—Imports Entered for Consumption and Duties Thereon: 1821 to 1952

[For basis of dollar values, see general note, p. 880. From 1821 to 1866, inclusive, figures of import values represent total imports less reexports, and for 1867 and later years imports entered for consumption. "Ratio of duties to total" is based upon values of imports shown in table. Figures cover fiscal years ending Sept. 30, 1821 to 1842, and June 30, 1843 to 1915; calendar years thereafter. See also *Historical Statistics*, series M 66–74]

YEARLY AVERAGE OR YEAR	VALUES				Duties calculated[1]	RATIO OF DUTIES TO TOTAL		Amount duties per capita
	Total	Free	Dutiable	Percent free		Free and dutiable	Dutiable	
	1,000 dollars	1,000 dollars	1,000 dollars		1,000 dollars	Percent	Percent	Dollars
1821–1830	56,749	3,325	53,424	5.86	26,282	46.31	49.20	2.32
1831–1840	104,139	39,680	64,459	38.10	24,509	23.53	38.02	1.63
1841–1850	110,561	20,347	90,214	18.40	26,738	24.18	29.64	1.32
1851–1860	267,871	40,685	227,186	15.19	54,511	20.35	23.99	1.99
1861–1870	315,637	35,676	279,961	11.30	120,042	38.03	42.88	3.32
1871–1880	522,653	133,480	389,173	25.54	163,201	31.23	41.94	3.55
1881–1890	682,681	220,986	461,695	32.37	205,580	30.11	44.53	3.59
1891–1900	749,584	371,837	377,747	49.61	177,580	23.69	47.01	2.53
1901–1910	1,142,514	522,123	620,391	45.70	280,955	24.59	45.29	3.37
1911–1915	1,698,028	966,141	731,887	56.89	283,408	16.69	38.72	2.91
1915–1920 [2]	3,289,748	2,262,412	1,027,336	68.77	227,035	6.90	22.10	2.17
1921–1925	3,422,748	2,088,932	1,333,816	61.03	478,911	13.99	35.90	4.22
1926–1930	4,020,350	2,645,610	1,374,740	65.81	550,743	13.70	40.06	4.52
1931–1935	1,704,294	1,075,585	628,709	63.11	314,477	18.45	50.02	2.46
1936–1940	2,440,042	1,475,825	964,217	60.48	365,151	14.96	37.87	2.76
1941–1945	3,475,593	2,293,945	1,181,648	66.00	379,704	10.92	32.13	[3]2.72
1946–1950	6,583,595	3,842,818	2,740,777	58.37	439,453	6.67	16.03	[3]2.94
1943	3,390,101	2,192,852	1,197,249	64.68	392,540	11.57	32.79	[3]2.51
1944	3,887,490	2,717,986	1,169,504	69.92	367,296	9.45	31.41	[3]2.60
1945	4,098,101	2,749,345	1,348,756	67.09	380,827	9.29	28.24	[3]2.66
1946	4,824,902	2,934,955	1,889,946	60.83	477,854	9.90	25.28	[3]3.32
1947	5,666,321	3,454,647	2,211,674	60.97	427,679	7.55	19.34	[3]2.91
1948	7,092,032	4,174,523	2,917,509	58.86	404,778	5.71	13.87	[3]2.71
1949	6,591,640	3,883,186	2,708,454	58.91	364,618	5.53	13.46	[3]2.40
1950	8,743,082	4,766,778	3,976,304	54.52	522,337	5.97	13.14	[3]3.36
1951	10,817,341	5,993,442	4,828,900	55.41	591,261	5.47	12.26	[3]3.75
1952	10,744,624	6,256,990	4,487,634	58.23	569,557	5.30	12.69	[3]3.55

[1] Beginning 1947, data from Bureau of Customs and represent unrevised figures based on reports at time of entry.
[2] Period July 1, 1915, to Dec. 31, 1920.
[3] Based on estimated population including armed forces overseas.

Source: Department of Commerce, Bureau of Census; annual report, *Foreign Commerce and Navigation of the United States*, and records, except as noted.

No. 1078.—IMPORTED DUTIABLE MERCHANDISE ENTERED FOR CONSUMPTION—
VALUES, CALCULATED DUTIES, AND AVERAGE RATE OF DUTY, BY TARIFF SCHED-
ULES: 1934 TO 1951

[All figures except percentages in thousands of dollars. For basis of dollar values, see general note, p. 880.
Includes articles on which countervailing and antidumping duties are assessed. Free list commodities taxable
under revenue acts excluded from various schedules. Percents represent average ad valorem rate or ratio of
duties to values of dutiable merchandise]

YEAR	Values	Duties	Per-cent	Values	Duties	Per-cent	Values	Duties	Per-cent
	Schedule 1.—Chemicals, oils, and paints			Schedule 2.—Earths, earthenware, and glassware			Schedule 3.—Metals and manufactures		
1934	45,438	17,375	38.24	19,195	10,675	55.61	57,802	20,284	35.09
1935	66,105	28,205	42.67	22,853	11,636	50.92	68,013	23,305	34.27
1936	69,317	25,349	36.57	28,104	13,620	48.46	94,778	29,496	31.12
1937	83,316	29,265	35.13	36,954	18,067	48.89	114,020	37,135	32.57
1938	51,958	19,417	37.37	24,693	11,049	44.75	68,172	21,493	31.53
1939	56,586	19,634	34.70	25,369	10,794	42.55	89,728	25,749	28.70
1940	41,204	12,356	29.99	22,336	8,806	39.45	102,303	31,161	30.46
1941	48,695	13,291	27.29	25,857	7,742	29.94	126,095	43,435	34.45
1942	47,209	10,621	22.50	19,031	4,786	25.15	102,300	28,040	27.41
1943	61,480	7,634	18.40	18,399	4,071	22.13	120,054	31,434	26.18
1944	54,123	8,037	14.85	10,764	3,103	28.83	117,660	28,919	24.58
1945	71,809	10,051	13.99	14,760	3,884	26.31	150,019	38,496	25.66
1946	90,586	13,622	15.10	30,941	9,546	30.85	197,984	50,628	25.57
1947	119,262	16,578	13.90	44,308	13,643	30.79	246,376	51,079	20.73
1948	114,896	14,252	12.40	60,710	15,321	25.24	348,465	53,421	15.33
1949	77,975	10,635	13.64	59,496	16,220	27.26	337,977	48,513	14.35
1950	149,773	23,133	15.45	82,737	21,935	26.51	658,793	85,475	12.97
1951	200,441	25,749	12.85	120,317	31,663	26.32	927,602	108,145	11.66
	Schedule 4.—Wood and manufactures			Schedule 5.—Sugar, molasses, and manufactures			Schedule 6.—Tobacco and manufactures		
1934	9,904	2,270	22.92	64,948	43,706	67.30	25,235	22,486	89.11
1935	12,687	2,923	23.09	94,963	39,985	42.11	25,974	21,958	84.54
1936	16,975	2,782	16.39	113,425	40,578	35.78	29,931	25,231	84.30
1937	19,861	3,188	16.05	126,645	45,371	35.83	31,776	24,213	76.20
1938	13,503	2,156	15.97	95,496	45,506	47.66	35,803	24,408	68.17
1939	17,002	2,096	12.33	90,543	46,213	51.05	35,999	23,927	66.47
1940	17,461	1,723	9.87	87,780	42,826	48.79	36,665	22,173	60.44
1941	36,089	2,536	7.04	145,375	63,586	43.74	38,026	23,017	60.53
1942	46,185	2,413	5.22	134,811	36,066	26.75	37,779	22,505	59.87
1943	27,852	1,642	5.90	194,349	55,730	28.68	43,209	23,044	53.33
1944	37,299	2,297	6.16	101,071	29,096	28.79	65,930	24,882	37.74
1945	44,563	2,867	6.43	35,418	10,430	29.45	82,278	28,253	34.34
1946	54,940	4,191	7.67	42,594	10,167	23.91	89,337	24,916	27.89
1947	42,112	3,073	7.30	496,404	87,280	18.42	92,367	25,737	27.80
1948	127,501	4,624	3.63	336,010	34,665	10.29	79,943	23,784	29.75
1949	97,541	4,364	4.68	345,663	37,206	10.76	73,278	22,832	31.35
1950	227,168	5,414	3.50	359,948	37,635	10.46	78,654	19,534	24.54
1951	211,560	9,366	4.66	368,691	34,967	9.48	87,831	20,484	23.33
	Schedule 7.—Agricultural products and provisions			Schedule 8.—Spirits, wines, and other beverages			Schedule 9.—Cotton manufactures		
1934	138,787	53,269	38.23	50,292	42,471	84.60	23,892	10,514	45.26
1935	219,133	87,550	39.96	42,384	39,326	92.79	27,136	10,852	39.99
1936	247,183	90,589	36.64	77,109	43,954	56.96	35,087	14,008	39.92
1937	310,186	106,775	34.43	74,973	46,093	61.48	44,052	17,155	38.94
1938	147,857	51,088	34.53	59,460	34,498	58.02	24,288	9,490	38.86
1939	173,508	56,419	32.46	59,076	34,206	57.90	27,284	9,841	36.07
1940	147,228	46,083	31.30	53,900	32,753	60.87	20,106	7,050	35.06
1941	173,113	56,518	32.82	49,635	30,186	60.82	15,003	5,002	33.34
1942	178,729	41,368	23.15	56,695	28,811	50.82	8,270	2,548	30.81
1943	245,557	40,526	16.30	83,094	61,563	74.09	8,946	2,707	30.26
1944	265,284	37,584	14.11	115,304	85,671	74.30	6,709	1,900	28.32
1945	314,005	42,542	13.55	67,923	45,340	66.75	26,392	4,533	17.18
1946	354,680	43,405	12.24	95,150	50,520	53.10	23,451	5,453	23.26
1947	311,800	36,347	11.66	67,305	31,718	47.13	15,986	4,921	30.78
1948	529,066	56,729	10.72	86,434	23,834	27.57	26,079	6,224	23.87
1949	480,055	51,914	10.62	89,594	24,145	26.95	22,510	5,376	23.88
1950	623,196	66,673	10.70	116,485	29,284	25.14	40,999	9,742	23.76
1951	785,114	71,369	9.09	125,405	31,496	25.08	47,661	10,873	22.83

No. 1078.—IMPORTED DUTIABLE MERCHANDISE ENTERED FOR CONSUMPTION—VALUES, CALCULATED DUTIES, AND AVERAGE RATE OF DUTY, BY TARIFF SCHEDULES: 1934 TO 1951—Continued

[All figures except percentages in thousands of dollars]

YEAR	Values	Duties	Per cent	Values	Duties	Per cent	Values	Duties	Per cent	Values	Duties	Per cent
	Schedule 10.—Flax, hemp, jute, and manufactures			Schedule 11.—Wool and manufactures			Schedule 12.—Silk manufactures			Schedule 13.—Rayon and other synthetic textiles, manufactures		
1934	53,547	13,271	24.78	21,648	17,187	79.39	4,624	2,586	55.93	1,098	794	72.45
1935	62,430	15,063	24.16	28,857	23,510	81.47	6,039	3,557	58.90	1,730	831	48.08
1936	68,147	16,819	24.68	59,298	44,687	75.36	6,833	3,810	55.76	5,209	2,197	42.18
1937	77,456	19,029	24.50	82,560	51,617	62.52	8,736	4,756	54.44	7,499	3,240	43.21
1938	49,402	12,092	24.48	27,418	18,531	67.50	6,184	3,327	53.79	6,041	2,274	37.64
1939	54,765	10,829	19.77	49,271	33,624	68.24	5,286	2,776	52.52	10,210	3,080	30.26
1940	68,033	10,255	15.07	77,829	51,601	66.30	4,074	2,148	52.72	3,898	1,280	32.33
1941	69,846	9,526	13.64	185,672	123,118	66.31	2,829	1,457	51.50	2,550	753	29.53
1942	52,309	6,639	12.69	178,771	112,972	63.19	855	411	48.07	202	81	40.10
1943	40,635	4,857	11.95	218,316	134,369	61.54	438	209	47.72	219	113	51.69
1944	10,047	2,252	22.41	179,016	114,379	63.89	596	307	51.34	362	198	54.70
1945	17,863	3,982	22.29	228,513	144,039	62.76	1,928	927	48.08	2,529	1,252	48.51
1946	106,202	15,394	14.50	276,042	167,759	60.77	5,159	2,459	47.66	15,819	5,341	33.76
1947	149,880	13,878	9.26	199,090	95,072	47.75	10,930	5,272	48.23	15,686	4,621	29.47
1948	173,155	10,000	5.77	291,730	81,410	27.91	20,398	6,258	30.68	26,136	6,744	21.97
1949	141,656	7,035	4.97	239,329	58,040	24.25	21,483	5,670	26.40	7,233	1,706	23.59
1950	144,843	9,279	6.41	394,178	94,294	23.91	29,272	8,953	30.59	35,209	7,877	22.37
1951	184,027	11,098	6.03	721,552	103,170	14.30	31,687	9,672	30.52	49,146	9,296	18.92

YEAR	Values	Duties	Per cent	Values	Duties	Per cent	Values	Duties	Per cent
	Schedule 14.—Pulp, paper, and books			Schedule 15.—Sundries			Free-list commodities taxable under Revenue Act of 1932 and subsequent acts,[1] dutiable under section 466, Tariff Act of 1930, etc.		
1934	9,482	2,346	24.74	85,185	31,647	37.15	33,862	9,987	29.49
1935	11,118	2,697	24.26	111,030	36,172	32.58	32,011	10,008	31.26
1936	13,201	3,029	22.95	136,546	41,545	30.43	37,049	10,396	25.06
1937	15,113	3,394	21.99	169,064	49,246	29.13	41,153	12,033	29.24
1938	11,970	2,531	21.14	110,444	33,959	30.75	33,285	9,636	28.95
1939	11,461	2,152	18.78	133,270	35,245	26.45	38,394	11,753	30.61
1940	7,550	1,278	16.93	114,987	29,558	25.71	86,582	17,235	19.91
1941	13,641	2,791	20.46	132,757	25,438	19.16	126,091	29,901	23.71
1942	9,534	1,643	17.23	96,819	13,411	13.85	40,185	6,183	15.39
1943	7,432	1,029	13.85	115,815	17,457	15.07	38,506	5,163	13.41
1944	7,711	1,038	13.46	118,006	21,069	17.85	73,677	7,502	10.18
1945	8,773	1,260	14.36	170,234	33,008	19.39	112,430	11,347	10.09
1946	15,692	1,980	12.62	354,144	60,854	18.20	156,996	16,626	10.59
1947	23,304	3,186	13.67	207,728	39,468	19.00	231,207	15,794	6.83
1948	29,803	3,442	11.54	267,551	45,419	16.98	389,100	18,750	4.82
1949	21,443	2,199	10.26	225,844	43,374	19.21	457,636	24,499	5.35
1950	27,144	2,691	9.91	338,043	61,370	18.15	650,803	35,947	5.52
1951	39,231	3,673	9.36	336,008	58,832	17.51	615,319	50,956	8.28

[1] Taxes collected on dutiable commodities under revenue acts and Sugar Act of 1937 are included in appropriate schedules.

Source: Treasury Department, Bureau of Customs; *Annual Report of the Secretary.*

No.,1079.—IMPORTS OF MERCHANDISE, FREE AND DUTIABLE, AND PERCENT FREE, BY ECONOMIC CLASSES: 1821 TO 1952

[In thousands of dollars. For basis of dollar values, see general note, p. 880. Figures cover fiscal years ending Sept. 30, 1821 to 1840, and June 30, 1850 to 1918; calendar years thereafter, except as noted. Data are "general imports" through 1933; "imports for consumption" beginning 1934. Percentage free in general imports is normally slightly lower than in imports for consumption because relatively more of dutiable general imports are reported as reexported than of free general imports. Moreover, in the period 1922-1933, there is an understatement of free goods in general imports because, for 1922 to 1933, carpet wool used for making carpets and, for 1922 to 1928, wheat imported for milling in bond for exports were reported as dutiable when entered, although no duty was ultimately paid on these products. For adjusted figures see table 492 of 1935 issue of Statistical Abstract. See also Historical Statistics, series M 74-86]

YEAR OR YEARLY AVERAGE	TOTAL			CRUDE MATERIALS			CRUDE FOODSTUFFS AND FOOD ANIMALS		
	Free	Dutiable	Percent free	Free	Dutiable	Percent free	Free	Dutiable	Percent free
1821	2,018	52,504	3.7	1,476	1,096	58.1	----	8,082	----
1830	4,590	55,131	7.3	2,348	1,480	60.5	----	7,382	----
1840	49,314	49,946	49.3	8,780	2,380	80.6	13,514	60	69.6
1850	18,082	155,628	10.4	602	11,964	4.8	18,508	2,908	87.7
1851-1860	44,790	239,746	15.7	6,456	20,936	23.6	30,148	3,131	90.6
1861-1870	38,388	286,470	11.6	10,285	31,805	24.6	19,904	34,389	34.1
1871-1880	129,985	405,537	34.3	44,492	27,775	39.1	16,916	28,675	70.1
1881-1890	223,623	488,550	32.3	96,173	49,680	66.4	52,276	23,089	73.4
1891-1900	372,344	391,084	48.8	140,491	41,229	70.9	105,884	22,089	83.5
1901-1910	520,831	637,870	45.0	205,690	98,960	74.9	109,577	77,089	80.2
1911-1915	941,439	780,880	54.1	491,946	105,752	82.3	181,170	37,304	82.7
1915-1920 [1]	3,258,688	1,050,747	67.3	1,196,808	152,074	88.7	349,938	58,135	85.7
1921-1925	2,950,302	1,339,900	68.7	1,004,561	253,794	80.3	302,242	80,297	75.0
1926-1930	2,597,197	1,436,271	64.4	1,228,971	254,152	82.8	407,540	68,075	85.4
1931-1935	1,087,146	648,430	62.4	380,689	111,703	77.4	220,717	44,582	82.2
1936-1940	1,476,825	964,217	60.5	627,299	176,948	77.7	288,255	81,247	74.0
1941-1945	2,285,944	1,181,646	66.0	777,319	369,539	67.6	434,586	134,135	76.4
1946-1950	3,542,818	2,740,777	56.4	1,363,002	729,397	65.4	1,082,802	205,168	83.4
1945	2,740,345	1,348,756	67.1	745,819	437,326	63.0	501,485	191,781	72.3
1946	2,934,055	1,899,946	60.6	1,166,749	562,325	67.6	652,307	162,086	80.1
1947	3,454,457	2,211,874	61.0	1,151,334	284,526	66.9	878,525	128,150	89.4
1948	4,174,623	2,917,860	58.9	1,385,692	788,815	60.3	1,096,122	282,668	81.7
1949	3,982,186	2,798,454	58.9	1,126,880	728,951	60.8	1,068,320	256,340	80.5
1950	4,792,778	2,976,804	54.5	1,481,571	965,918	62.1	1,492,335	207,221	83.2
1951	5,908,648	4,828,900	54.4	2,057,598	1,227,016	61.5	1,772,033	208,285	85.4
1952	5,288,980	4,487,634	56.2	1,875,876	1,089,178	62.9	1,772,800	208,830	85.7

YEAR OR YEARLY AVERAGE	MANUFACTURED FOODSTUFFS [2]			SEMIMANUFACTURES			FINISHED MANUFACTURES		
	Free	Dutiable	Percent free	Free	Dutiable	Percent free	Free	Dutiable	Percent free
1821	----	10,821	----	488	3,591	12.0	55	30,944	0.2
1830	----	9,654	----	1,312	8,942	18.5	31	35,703	.1
1840	1,021	14,108	6.7	4,948	6,804	42.7	17,337	32,488	35.1
1850	----	31,486	----	765	39,380	2.9	811	94,491	1.0
1851-1860	2,486	44,477	5.5	3,439	32,140	9.6	2,284	143,087	1.6
1861-1870	2,239	30,738	5.2	7,351	38,327	16.1	6,540	129,442	4.8
1871-1880	1,808	108,106	1.6	7,986	62,186	11.0	6,084	170,867	3.4
1881-1890	11,488	111,877	9.3	17,188	85,163	16.8	13,088	199,230	6.4
1891-1900	36,514	73,911	42.9	30,090	75,880	28.4	19,427	177,512	9.9
1901-1910	4,344	138,086	3.1	81,071	119,628	40.4	30,180	208,686	20.6
1911-1915	36,685	150,817	11.9	167,982	128,612	56.6	94,622	266,121	34.6
1915-1920 [1]	73,142	471,407	13.4	434,343	150,177	73.9	215,704	267,602	44.6
1921-1925	86,488	381,480	13.6	411,602	197,495	67.6	353,068	466,617	39.2
1926-1930	72,706	326,608	58.5	545,349	218,589	71.2	343,735	559,450	36.0
1931-1935	72,488	164,388	30.6	242,078	101,498	69.1	175,348	215,286	44.1
1936-1940	72,488	272,088	21.2	337,519	172,494	66.1	349,100	257,757	40.8
1941-1945	129,910	270,189	32.4	514,875	215,772	70.2	413,789	181,713	69.5
1946-1950	170,484	506,548	12.6	632,812	642,776	46.9	613,488	561,453	38.5
1945	265,324	266,280	44.9	665,576	288,398	71.8	581,541	261,709	40.8
1946	288,390	392,462	42.6	406,536	443,996	68.6	409,729	399,204	43.2
1947	29,157	616,871	4.9	605,129	419,773	66.6	710,316	445,236	46.5
1948	60,366	432,629	11.1	686,342	502,088	65.1	742,808	467,529	46.5
1949	62,868	442,420	13.3	682,185	492,398	64.8	748,588	464,262	46.3
1950	112,464	785,530	12.5	667,156	1,188,717	42.1	746,862	498,506	43.9
1951	128,734	864,321	13.4	1,176,489	1,264,322	48.1	866,693	1,036,762	44.4
1952	132,333	628,387	14.1	1,466,804	1,657,767	46.6	855,806	1,468,612	42.7

[1] Period July 1, 1916, to Dec. 31, 1920.   [2] Includes beverages.

Source: Department of Commerce, Bureau of Census; annual report, Foreign Commerce and Navigation of the United States, and records.

No. 1080.—Duties on Imports for Consumption, and Ratio to Dutiable Imports, by Principal Countries: 1948 to 1952

[Duties in thousands of dollars. Represents unrevised data based on reports at date of entry]

COUNTRY	DUTIES CALCULATED					RATIO OF DUTIES TO VALUE OF DUTIABLE IMPORTS FOR CONSUMPTION (PERCENT)				
	1948	1949	1950	1951	1952	1948	1949	1950	1951	1952
Grand total	404,776	364,518	522,337	591,261	569,587	12.91	13.46	12.17	12.19	12.70
Northern North America	45,673	45,893	61,734	61,180	56,888	7.60	8.09	7.25	6.24	6.22
Canada[1]	45,473	45,893	61,721	61,141	56,873	7.60	8.09	7.25	6.24	6.22
Other			13	9	15			9.35	4.50	6.17
Southern North America	55,402	59,072	69,509	73,944	71,369	10.36	10.93	10.07	10.77	10.66
Mexico	10,799	9,577	16,869	19,117	20,305	10.66	10.96	10.03	11.56	12.23
Central American countries	508	393	404	387	550	6.90	9.69	7.87	6.22	8.12
Guatemala	69	46	97	225	199	12.04	15.92	10.52	12.10	10.66
El Salvador	188	62	38	29	54	15.42	10.46	7.09	5.53	6.94
Other	251	285	269	134	207	4.51	8.94	7.32	3.47	6.13
Bermuda and Caribbean	44,095	49,002	52,236	54,440	50,514	10.34	10.92	10.10	10.57	9.44
Cuba	38,873	41,794	42,623	40,290	39,362	10.89	11.35	11.05	10.46	10.01
Dominican Republic	1,269	1,705	1,031	1,631	762	12.23	18.40	10.70	10.10	5.15
Netherlands Antilles	2,705	4,581	7,449	11,321	9,186	5.02	7.04	6.65	11.05	7.96
Other	1,248	922	1,133	1,198	1,202	23.86	16.60	11.50	10.60	9.90
South America	61,994	46,152	74,732	75,987	66,864	12.19	9.86	10.79	10.19	16.23
Argentina	22,670	11,170	21,494	19,656	18,038	21.02	30.01	18.02	13.51	16.76
Bolivia	235	82	981	269	166	35.13	35.04	16.33	11.53	16.13
Brazil	5,198	3,756	3,778	4,239	3,294	10.10	9.70	8.92	7.18	7.92
Chile	2,118	1,217	5,433	4,096	2,006	27.71	22.53	10.37	9.88	19.53
Colombia	955	1,253	1,704	3,112	2,452	4.19	4.40	4.50	7.49	5.17
Peru	2,502	2,560	5,052	3,885	2,663	15.90	15.97	14.66	10.45	10.17
Uruguay	16,687	12,003	20,898	17,565	15,929	28.04	23.71	22.04	14.52	22.90
Venezuela	9,980	11,099	13,467	21,158	19,681	4.46	4.44	4.73	7.57	6.10
Other	1,656	1,912	1,966	1,985	2,635	8.61	8.97	9.27	8.09	8.65
Europe[1]	146,387	128,396	193,852	215,338	243,969	21.32	21.35	19.39	17.16	17.53
Belgium and Luxembourg	8,994	7,419	12,632	17,782	15,187	12.80	11.60	11.83	10.69	10.54
Finland	543	329	915	1,194	634	18.02	18.80	17.66	12.86	14.28
France	12,578	11,261	20,507	31,671	23,182	24.34	24.89	20.51	16.10	17.67
Germany	5,057	6,021	14,290	30,036	29,077	26.62	25.23	18.12	15.85	17.25
Italy	15,746	13,811	19,724	23,672	24,473	24.06	26.18	23.17	21.27	20.12
Netherlands	3,438	2,992	5,321	5,957	7,273	11.12	10.60	9.93	8.91	9.33
Norway	3,320	1,885	3,182	2,897	2,875	15.00	10.58	11.19	9.60	4.75
Spain	5,832	3,706	7,434	7,120	9,093	18.75	16.46	18.46	15.92	17.30
Sweden	2,004	1,535	2,190	4,165	4,783	18.94	18.60	14.23	13.86	14.62
Switzerland	29,944	27,518	32,564	35,824	36,662	31.62	31.83	31.44	30.16	29.96
Turkey[2]					9,709					22.97
United Kingdom	42,323	36,819	55,510	63,668	64,121	20.27	21.25	20.72	19.49	19.35
Other	16,608	15,100	19,623	21,349	16,900	21.08	19.50	17.11	15.32	12.92
Asia[1]	56,267	58,309	80,684	81,193	75,715	14.75	15.11	16.50	15.86	14.47
British Malaya	179	88	118	819	321	17.18	13.77	11.76	8.77	8.82
Ceylon	275	65	65	105	75	9.08	7.25	8.00	7.95	7.96
China	10,039	10,106	13,262	2,896	1,006	16.86	17.45	16.20	10.72	10.29
India	10,026	6,184	7,398	9,755	8,799	5.85	4.33	5.48	5.67	5.17
Indonesia	808	571	893	1,052	1,448	23.93	17.48	17.41	17.27	12.22
Japan	11,536	17,685	35,307	40,217	44,607	30.85	30.42	27.94	27.81	26.24
Pakistan	49	21	70	136	42	6.19	6.36	10.00	6.02	9.33
Republic of Philippines	109	97	106	72	45	23.04	45.75	47.53	17.56	34.35
Siam (Thailand)	319	240	385	468	652	10.10	13.28	21.13	18.59	13.31
Turkey[2]	15,585	15,187	12,298	11,445		35.59	41.69	29.53	26.32	
Other	7,342	8,065	10,782	14,228	18,720	12.79	9.65	11.42	13.83	12.26
Australia and Oceania	26,523	18,017	29,164	38,867	41,186	23.72	20.90	20.78	11.20	38.22
Australia	23,274	15,548	23,846	32,775	25,886	22.49	19.91	20.07	10.84	18.75
New Zealand	3,231	2,453	5,287	6,079	15,248	40.27	30.80	24.93	13.64	23.80
Other	18	16	31	13	52	5.63	11.27	9.54	6.95	7.35
Africa	12,532	9,779	12,662	14,782	13,566	14.85	16.09	12.21	10.32	12.46
Belgian Congo	72	63	90	105	97	20.57	15.07	9.70	5.94	6.12
Egypt	1,963	632	2,246	1,914	1,422	6.57	7.39	7.38	6.50	3.64
Gold Coast	571	699	940	896	687	13.19	13.52	10.89	8.92	7.65
Nigeria	34	13	74	44	23	18.48	11.40	7.28	6.62	9.79
Union of South Africa	6,290	5,514	5,955	8,684	8,240	17.56	15.49	13.36	10.34	15.97
Other	3,602	2,858	3,357	3,139	3,097	26.03	11.35	18.53	18.17	14.58

[1] Includes Newfoundland and Labrador.
[2] Turkey included in Europe as of January 1, 1952.

Source: Treasury Department, Bureau of Customs.

33. Territories, Possessions, and Other Areas Under the Jurisdiction of the United States

Statistics in this section are presented for the two territories, Alaska and Hawaii; the four principal possessions, Puerto Rico (a commonwealth), Virgin Islands, Guam, and American Samoa; and the Canal Zone. The circumstances under which the Territories, possessions, and other areas were acquired by or came under the jurisdiction of the United States are as follows:

Alaska.—Alaska was acquired by purchase from Russia in 1867 and was organized as a Territory in 1912.

Hawaii.—Hawaii, by voluntary action of its people, ceded its sovereignty to the United States in 1898 and was organized as a Territory on June 14, 1900.

Puerto Rico.—The island of Puerto Rico was formally surrendered by Spain to the United States in October 1898, and was ceded to the United States, together with a few adjacent islands, by the Treaty of Paris, signed December 10, 1898, and ratified in the following year. Puerto Rico acquired the status of a commonwealth on July 25, 1952.

Virgin Islands of the United States.—The Virgin Islands, formerly known as the Danish West Indies, were acquired by the United States by purchase from Denmark in 1917, the formal transfer of possession having taken place on March 31 of that year.

Guam.—The island of Guam was ceded by Spain to the United States under the terms of the Treaty of Paris, signed December 10, 1898, and ratified in the following year.

American Samoa.—American Samoa was acquired by the United States in accordance with a convention between the United States, Great Britain, and Germany, signed December 2, 1899, ratified February 16, 1900, and proclaimed by the President of the United States on the latter date.

Canal Zone.—The use, occupation, and control of the Canal Zone were granted to the United States under the terms of a treaty with the Republic of Panama, signed November 18, 1903, and ratified in the following year.

Trust Territory of the Pacific Islands.—The United States became the administering authority over the Trust Territory of the Pacific Islands (which comprises the Caroline, Marshall, and Marianas Islands except Guam) under an agreement approved by the Security Council of the United Nations on April 2, 1947, and by the United States Government on July 18, 1947.

For a brief summary of the territorial development of the United States, see tables 1 and 3, in section 1.

Sources.—Many of the statistics were obtained from the results of the 1950 Censuses of Agriculture, Population, and Housing conducted by the Bureau of the Census. Other agencies which furnished material for this section are the National Office of Vital Statistics of the Department of Health, Education, and Welfare, the Bureau of Mines of the Department of Interior, and the Department of the Navy.

Material in other sections.—In addition to the statistics presented in this section there are a number of tables on Territories and possessions appearing in other sections of this volume. Thus, statistics on the Alaska Railroad are presented in section 21, Transportation, Air and Land; statistics on cane sugar production in Hawaii and Puerto Rico are given in section 25, Agriculture—Production and Related Subjects; lumber and shingle production for Alaska are given in section 26, Forests and Forest Products; and data on the Panama Canal are presented in section 22, Waterways, Water Traffic, and Shipping. In addition, other data are included as integral parts of several State tables in various sections of the volume.

Note.—This section presents data for the most recent year or period available on May 20, 1953, when the material was organized and sent to the printer. In a few instances, more recent data were added after that date.

Population, Housing, and Agriculture.—Due to the difference in the population and housing characteristics and the variation in agriculture products between the Territories and possessions, the collection and presentation of data from the 1950 Censuses varies slightly between areas. The tables in this section attempt to take into account these differences and give, as nearly as possible, comparable data between the areas. For definition and explanation of terms see section 1, Area and Population; section 29, Construction and Housing; section 24, Agriculture—General Statistics; and section 25, Agriculture—Production and Related Subjects. However, for detailed treatment of the Territories and possessions, see the original sources.

Commerce.—The statistics on commerce are published by the Bureau of the Census in the *Summary of Foreign Commerce of the United States.* In section 32, Foreign Commerce, the Virgin Islands is treated as a foreign country prior to 1935. On the other hand, Alaska, Hawaii, and Puerto Rico, and for 1935–39, the Virgin Islands, are treated as integral parts of the United States. Neither trade of American Samoa and Guam with foreign countries nor shipments between them and the United States are included in the general tables on foreign trade. See also table 1060, p. 901.

The tables on commerce in this section present the total foreign trade of each of the U. S. Territories and possessions and show separately the trade with United States (unless otherwise indicated) and with foreign countries. The trade with foreign countries represents exports and imports through the respective territorial Customs Districts and does not necessarily represent exports of commodities originating within the designated territory nor imports for direct consumption within the territory. For basis of dollar values, see general note, p. 881.

No. 1081.—Population and Characteristics—Summary for Alaska, Hawaii, Puerto Rico, Virgin Islands, Guam, American Samoa, and Canal Zone: 1930 to 1950

ITEM	Alaska	Hawaii [1]	Puerto Rico	Virgin Islands	Guam	American Samoa	Canal Zone
AREA AND POPULATION							
Land area (sq. mi.), 1950	571,065	6,407	3,423	132	203	76	362
Population:							
1930	[3] 59,278	368,336	1,543,913	22,012	18,509	10,055	39,467
1940	[3] 72,524	423,330	1,869,255	24,889	22,290	12,908	51,827
1950	128,643	499,794	2,210,703	26,665	59,498	18,937	52,822
Per square mile	[3] 28	78	646	202	293	249	146
Percent increase, 1940 to 1950	77.4	18.1	18.3	7.1	166.9	46.7	1.9
Urban [4]	34,262	344,869	894,813	15,581			
Rural [4]	94,381	154,925	1,315,890	11,084			
Male	79,472	273,895	1,110,946	13,075	40,485	9,818	30,729
Female	49,171	225,899	1,099,757	13,590	19,013	9,119	22,093
Married couples	23,317	88,510	254,779	2,644	6,455	2,556	10,281
Households, number	31,047	112,095	429,429	7,742	7,373	2,687	11,507
Population in households	100,779	463,230	2,177,898	25,854	36,816	18,033	42,536
Population per household	3.25	4.13	5.07	3.34	4.99	6.71	3.70
Quasi households, population	27,864	36,564	32,805	811	22,682	904	10,286
MARITAL STATUS, 1950							
Persons 14 years old and over	96,008	351,389	1,301,130	16,789	44,133	10,596	38,595
Male	62,775	197,874	[5] 649,414	[8] 8,118	32,572	5,428	23,433
Single	27,289	81,921	264,854	3,536	17,952	2,373	10,426
Married	30,380	103,470	274,597	3,309	12,932	2,872	12,097
Widowed or divorced	5,106	12,483	27,531	416	1,688	183	908
Female	33,233	153,515	[5] 651,716	[8] 8,671	11,561	5,168	15,162
Single	5,570	43,447	193,897	3,373	3,644	1,608	3,301
Married	24,441	94,521	282,078	3,318	6,826	2,951	10,898
Widowed or divorced	3,222	15,547	83,750	1,105	1,091	609	963
LABOR FORCE, 1950							
Total labor force	67,311	207,971	597,467	9,021	(²)		24,900
Civilian labor force	46,989	155,115	591,909	8,809	(²)		15,255
Male	34,801	134,531	453,483	5,954	(²)		11,322
Employed	31,240	120,986	428,934	5,648	[7] 15,584	[7] 3,574	10,504
Unemployed	3,561	13,545	24,549	306	(²)		406
Female	12,168	20,584	138,426	2,855	(²)		3,953
Employed	11,149	46,602	131,337	2,621	[7] 3,087	[7] 1,976	3,564
Unemployed	1,019	3,982	7,089	234	(²)		389
Employed persons by industry group	42,389	167,588	560,271	8,269	[7] 18,671	[7] 5,550	14,458
Agriculture, forestry, and fisheries	5,626	31,789	215,978	1,661	1,189	(²)	(²)
Mining	1,328	166	1,481		36	(²)	(²)
Construction	5,635	11,662	27,019	939	6,269	(²)	(²)
Manufacturing	3,957	21,292	92,864	464	401	(²)	(²)
Transportation, communication, and other public utilities	5,413	13,179	31,078	613	2,750	(²)	(²)
Wholesale and retail trade	5,430	31,650	68,249	1,088	1,837	(²)	(²)
Finance, insurance, and real estate	540	3,951	3,501	97	85	(²)	(²)
Business and repair services	708	4,129	6,545	119	342	(²)	(²)
Personal services	1,720	10,883	43,232	1,436	998	(²)	(²)
Entertainment and recreation services	351	2,712	4,472	54	68	(²)	(²)
Professional and related services	3,062	16,722	34,012	767	943	(²)	(²)
Public administration	7,193	18,436	24,642	803	3,556	(²)	(²)
Industry not reported	1,426	1,019	7,498	228	175	(²)	(²)
INCOME IN 1949 OF PERSONS 14 YEARS OLD AND OVER, 1950 [5]							
Persons 14 years old and over	96,008	[8] 153,690	1,301,130	16,789	44,133	10,596	38,595
Number reporting income	[9] 86,059	148,835	[10] 1,279,981	[11] 16,078	(²)	(²)	(²)
Under $300	8,334	16,730	277,186	3,573	(²)	(²)	(²)
$300 to $499			108,295	1,670	(²)	(²)	(²)
$500 to $699	8,387	7,815	59,887	1,176	(²)	(²)	(²)
$700 to $999			58,212	1,061	(²)	(²)	(²)
$1,000 to $1,499	16,705	14,470	66,894	971	(²)	(²)	(²)
$1,500 to $1,999		12,680	27,708	458	(²)	(²)	(²)
$2,000 to $2,499	8,577	31,220	13,533	257	(²)	(²)	(²)
$2,500 to $2,999			6,221	151	(²)	(²)	(²)
$3,000 to $3,999	8,409	23,600	9,179	194	(²)	(²)	(²)
$4,000 to $4,999	6,517	13,215	3,991	98	(²)	(²)	(²)
$5,000 to $6,999	7,539	15,025	7,570	202	(²)	(²)	(²)
$7,000 and over	2,312	14,080			(²)	(²)	(²)
Income not reported	9,939	4,855	21,149	711	(²)	(²)	(²)
Median income (dollars)	[12] 2,072	2,726	[13] 378	460	(²)	(²)	(²)

See footnotes at end of table.

245354°—53——60

No. 1081.—POPULATION AND CHARACTERISTICS—SUMMARY FOR ALASKA, HAWAII, PUERTO RICO, VIRGIN ISLANDS, GUAM, AMERICAN SAMOA, AND CANAL ZONE: 1930 TO 1950—Continued

ITEM	Alaska	Hawaii [1]	Puerto Rico	Virgin Islands	Guam	American Samoa	Canal Zone
SCHOOL ENROLLMENT							
Persons enrolled in school, 5 to 29 years old..	18,517	109,970	416,206	7,034	([6])	([6])	([7])
5 and 6 years	1,260	8,170	10,435	959	238	380	733
7 to 13 years..	11,122	59,185	279,019	4,288	5,779	3,065	5,094
14 to 17 years	4,531	29,500	84,685	1,485	2,567	1,388	1,998
18 and 19 years	759	7,050	18,051	201	4	448	217
20 to 24 years	598	4,310	13,373	61	9	376	280
25 to 29 years	247	1,755	10,643	40	([6])	([6])	([7])
YEARS OF SCHOOL COMPLETED BY PERSONS 25 YEARS OLD AND OVER							
Total persons, 25 years old and over	66,576	247,480	842,266	12,296	24,853	6,383	26,898
Years of school completed:							
None: Male	2,293	16,480	120,340	378	966	504	351
Female	1,989	9,725	160,345	353	850	874	186
1 to 4 years:							
Male	2,681	20,940	140,332	1,296	3,102	613	1,113
Female	1,632	11,945	125,439	1,416	2,378	831	823
5 to 8 years:							
Male	11,023	38,595	106,502	2,832	4,387	1,684	5,297
Female	4,637	33,210	88,558	3,465	1,502	1,207	3,955
High school: [13]							
Male	16,999	47,845	42,082	806	6,248	185	5,197
Female	10,687	37,665	27,757	788	1,893	65	4,154
College or more: [13]							
Male	7,526	14,270	15,405	348	2,172	101	2,349
Female	5,541	13,515	13,198	248	1,084	48	2,052
Median school years completed	11.3	8.7	3.7	6.2	8.4	5.3	9.9

[1] Data for married couples, income of families and unrelated individuals, school enrollment and years of school completed based on 20-percent sample.
[2] Censuses taken in 1929 and 1939.
[3] Per 100 square miles.
[4] Urban population is that living in cities, towns, or villages of 2,500 or more. The remainder is classified as rural.
[5] Includes consensually married.
[6] Not available.
[7] Worked as civilians in 1949.
[8] For Hawaii, income is for families and unrelated individuals.
[9] Includes 17,989 persons with no income.
[10] Includes 641,508 persons with no income.
[11] Includes 6,257 persons with no income.
[12] Median computed on basis of those persons reporting income greater than zero, excludes those reporting no income.
[13] Represents persons completing 1 or more years.

Source: Department of Commerce, Bureau of the Census; *U. S. Census of Population: 1950*, Vol. II, Parts 51-54 (as corrected).

No. 1082.—ESTIMATED POPULATION OF ALASKA, HAWAII, PUERTO RICO, AND VIRGIN ISLANDS: JULY 1, 1940 TO 1952

[Total population estimates include estimates of armed forces stationed in area]

YEAR	ALASKA		HAWAII		PUERTO RICO		VIRGIN ISLANDS	
	Total	Civilian	Total	Civilian	Total	Civilian	Total	Civilian
1940	74,000	73,000	428,000	398,000	1,878,000	1,875,000	25,000	24,900
1941	83,000	74,000	459,000	411,000	1,927,000	1,904,000	25,800	25,400
1942	137,000	77,000	556,000	420,000	1,973,000	1,939,000	26,100	24,800
1943	226,000	74,000	629,000	429,000	2,013,000	1,975,000	26,400	24,900
1944	180,000	76,000	844,000	437,000	2,038,000	2,010,000	27,100	26,200
1945	138,000	78,000	815,000	460,000	2,071,000	2,040,000	26,700	26,300
1946	103,000	85,000	533,000	467,000	2,096,000	2,082,000	27,100	27,000
1947	117,000	91,000	528,000	489,000	2,140,000	2,131,000	27,200	27,100
1948	125,000	98,000	517,000	484,000	2,172,000	2,163,000	26,900	26,900
1949	134,000	104,000	510,000	479,000	2,193,000	2,184,000	26,700	26,700
1950	138,000	112,000	491,000	470,000	2,207,000	2,202,000	26,800	25,600
1951	159,000	121,000	514,000	470,000	2,233,000	2,214,000	24,800	24,800
1952	182,000	132,000	522,000	467,000	2,240,000	2,214,000	24,000	23,800

Source: Department of Commerce, Bureau of the Census; *Current Population Reports*, Series P-25, Nos. 25, and 76.

No. 1083.—POPULATION, BY AGE AND SEX, OF ALASKA, HAWAII, PUERTO RICO, GUAM, AND VIRGIN ISLANDS: 1930 TO 1950

AGE	ALASKA		1950			HAWAII		1950		
	1929	1939	Total	Male	Female	1930	1940	Total	Male	Female
Total, all ages	59,278	72,524	128,643	79,472	49,171	368,336	423,330	499,794	273,895	225,899
Under 9 years	12,434	14,410	26,223	13,358	12,865	95,299	83,516	115,785	59,443	56,342
10 to 19 years	9,830	11,707	18,673	11,602	7,071	71,532	95,832	84,260	43,869	40,391
20 to 29 years	8,430	13,046	31,178	21,342	9,836	79,438	93,406	100,040	53,506	46,534
30 to 39 years	8,221	11,032	23,005	14,049	8,956	49,725	62,275	80,417	45,787	34,630
40 to 49 years	8,496	8,086	14,122	8,708	5,414	34,393	39,598	53,889	33,268	20,621
50 to 59 years	6,548	7,303	7,965	5,195	2,770	23,383	26,244	32,831	18,149	14,682
60 to 69 years	3,744	4,601	4,861	3,378	1,483	10,683	16,055	20,581	12,470	8,111
70 years and over	1,436	2,068	2,616	1,840	776	3,780	6,249	11,991	7,403	4,588
Median age	28.7	27.8	25.8	26.1	25.3	22.0	23.2	24.9	26.2	23.6

AGE	PUERTO RICO		1950			GUAM			VIRGIN ISLANDS		
	1930	1940	Total	Male	Female	1930	1940	1950	1930	1940	1950
Total, all ages	1,543,913	1,869,255	2,210,703	1,110,946	1,099,757	18,509	22,290	59,498	22,012	24,889	26,665
Under 9 years	450,490	532,092	684,549	346,382	338,167	5,618	7,007	12,021	4,743	5,608	7,551
10 to 19 years	385,487	433,246	490,958	247,590	243,368	4,084	5,055	11,246	4,174	4,753	5,102
20 to 29 years	249,116	354,334	350,922	167,424	183,498	3,326	3,589	18,653	2,902	4,214	3,526
30 to 34 years	94,709	102,596	131,737	66,583	65,154	1,188	1,455	5,452	1,239	1,509	1,697
35 to 44 years	164,904	187,110	224,346	114,907	109,439	1,794	2,149	6,805	2,731	2,510	2,746
45 to 54 years	103,163	125,993	146,982	76,460	70,522	1,181	1,411	3,230	2,721	2,446	2,202
55 to 64 years	56,418	69,831	95,631	50,634	44,997	850	936	1,293	1,783	2,056	1,830
65 to 74 years	25,828	41,905	54,587	27,334	27,253	366	501	550	1,213	1,213	1,378
75 years and over	13,576	21,201	30,991	13,632	17,359	102	174	248	535	561	633
Median age	18.3	19.2	18.4	18.2	18.6	18.8	17.9	22.8		24.6	22.0

1 Includes age not reported.
Source: Department of Commerce, Bureau of Census, U. S. Census of Population: 1950, Vol. II, Parts 51-54.

No. 1084.—POPULATION BY RACE, NATIVITY, AND SEX, WITH MALES PER 100 FEMALES, FOR ALASKA, HAWAII, AND PUERTO RICO: 1930 TO 1950

NATIVITY AND RACE	1930		1940		1950		MALES PER 100 FEMALES		
	Male	Female	Male	Female	Male	Female	1930	1940	1950
ALASKA 1									
Total	35,764	23,514	43,003	29,521	79,472	49,171	152.1	145.7	161.6
White	19,904	8,736	25,595	13,575	60,390	32,418	227.8	188.5	186.3
Native	11,515	6,945	18,651	11,733	55,846	30,486	165.8	159.0	183.2
Foreign born	8,389	1,791	6,944	1,842	4,544	1,932	468.4	377.0	235.2
Aboriginal stock	15,359	14,624	16,790	15,668	17,548	16,315	105.0	107.2	107.6
Aleut	(2)	(2)	2,988	2,631	2,110	1,782	(2)	112.8	118.4
Eskimo			8,034	7,542	8,200	7,662		106.5	106.7
Indian			5,788	5,495	7,238	6,851		105.3	105.6
Other races	501	154	618	278	1,534	438	325.3	222.3	350.2
HAWAII									
Total	222,640	145,696	245,135	178,195	273,895	225,899	152.5	137.6	121.2
Native	180,627	119,172	214,645	156,072	221,553	201,621	151.6	137.5	109.9
Foreign born	42,013	26,524	30,490	22,123	52,342	24,278	158.4	137.8	215.6
Hawaiian	25,353	25,507	32,063	32,247	42,785	43,306	99.4	99.4	98.8
Caucasian	48,705	31,667	64,473	39,318	65,409	49,384	153.8	164.0	132.4
Chinese	16,561	10,618	16,131	12,643	17,044	15,332	156.0	127.6	111.2
Filipino	52,566	10,486	40,791	11,778	43,587	17,514	501.3	346.3	248.7
Japanese	75,008	64,623	82,820	75,085	93,250	91,361	116.1	110.3	102.1
Other races	4,446	2,795	8,857	7,124	11,830	9,002	159.1	124.3	131.6
PUERTO RICO									
Total	771,761	772,152	938,280	930,975	1,110,946	1,099,757	99.9	100.8	101.0
Native	767,683	770,213	935,088	929,128	1,106,176	1,096,074	99.7	100.6	100.9
Foreign born	4,078	1,939	3,192	1,847	4,770	3,683	210.3	172.8	129.5
White	574,369	572,380	718,398	712,346	883,603	878,809	100.4	100.8	100.5
Negro	197,392	199,802	219,882	218,629	226,293	220,655	98.8	100.6	102.6
Other races					1,051	293			356.7

1 Censuses taken in 1929 and 1939.   2 Not available.
Source: Department of Commerce, Bureau of the Census; U. S. Census of Population: 1950, Vol. II, Parts 51-53.

No. 1085.—Births and Deaths in Alaska, 1945 to 1950, and in Hawaii, Puerto Rico, and the Virgin Islands, 1940 to 1950

TERRITORY OR POSSESSION AND YEAR	BIRTHS		DEATHS		DEATHS UNDER 1 YEAR	
	Number	Rate per 1,000 population [1]	Number	Rate per 1,000 population [2]	Number	Rate per 1,000 live births
Alaska: 1945	1,829	23.4	1,213	8.8	138	75.5
1946	2,271	26.7	1,227	11.9	161	70.9
1947	2,701	23.1	1,165	10.0	173	63.7
1948	3,079	24.6	1,197	9.6	146	47.1
1949	3,527	24.3	1,182	8.6	168	47.6
1950	3,725	20.0	1,263	9.7	198	51.8
Hawaii: 1940	9,414	22.2	3,069	7.3	421	44.7
1945	12,305	26.8	3,396	4.2	336	27.3
1946	12,808	27.4	3,229	6.1	385	30.1
1947	14,592	27.6	3,219	6.1	452	31.0
1948	14,463	28.0	3,104	6.0	414	28.6
1949	14,150	27.7	3,020	5.9	358	25.3
1950	14,054	28.1	2,919	5.8	337	24.0
Puerto Rico: 1940			34,468	18.4	8,221	
1945	86,680	42.5	28,837	13.9	8,064	93.0
1946	88,421	42.5	27,517	13.1	7,397	83.7
1947	91,305	42.7	25,407	11.9	6,527	71.5
1948	87,809	40.4	26,209	12.1	6,876	78.3
1949	85,625	39.0	23,389	10.7	5,797	67.7
1950	86,038	38.9	21,895	9.9	5,803	67.4
Virgin Islands: 1940	755	30.4	553	22.2	103	136.3
1945	964	37.4	401	15.0	122	134.0
1946	917	34.0	408	15.1	84	91.6
1947	876	32.2	394	14.5	78	89.0
1948	826	30.7	340	12.6	73	88.4
1949	886	33.2	362	13.6	80	90.3
1950	894	33.5	374	14.0	51	57.0

[1] 1945 and 1946 based on civilian population in area; other years based on total population present in area.
[2] Based on total population present in area.

Source: Department of Health, Education and Welfare, Public Health Service, National Office of Vital Statistics; basic figures published in annual report, *Vital Statistics of the United States.*

No. 1086.—Housing Characteristics—Summary for Alaska, Hawaii, Puerto Rico, and Virgin Islands: 1950

SUBJECT	Alaska	Hawaii	Puerto Rico	Virgin Islands
ALL DWELLING UNITS				
Number of dwelling units	33,072	120,606	453,572	8,370
Median number of rooms per unit	(1)	(1)	3.2	1.9
Percent of dwelling units:				
In one-dwelling-unit detached structures	77.1	71.9	83.0	64.5
In structures built in 1940 or later	48.0	30.6	50.6	14.9
With running water, private toilet and bath, not dilapidated	48.6	58.6	[3] 15.1	(1)
With flush toilet inside structure, exclusive use	54.8	78.1	16.7	13.1
With installed bathtub or shower, exclusive use	52.8	80.6	25.6	12.6
Vacant, available [3]	2.8	2.4	1.0	2.5
Using wood as exterior material	89.8	93.1	78.3	70.2
With electric lights	77.9	96.7	49.1	52.6
OCCUPIED DWELLING UNITS				
Number of occupied dwelling units	30,329	112,290	431,300	7,765
Owner occupied	16,537	37,025	282,172	2,177
Renter occupied	13,792	75,265	149,128	5,588
Median number of persons per unit	2.8	3.8	4.7	2.5
Percent of occupied dwelling units:				
In one-dwelling-unit detached structures	76.1	71.8	82.9	64.0
With 1.51 or more persons per room	22.8	11.8	43.7	35.8
Median value (owner-occupied units) [4]	3,477	12,283	667	1,317
Median contract monthly rent (renter-occupied units) [5]	59.24	32.34	10.01	4.88

[1] Not available. [2] With running water from municipal water system.
[3] Represents not dilapidated, for rent or sale.
[4] Represents nonfarm units, except in Hawaii where farm is also included; restricted to 1-dwelling-unit structures, including land.
[5] Represents nonfarm units, except in Hawaii where farm is also included.

Source: Department of Commerce, Bureau of the Census; *U. S. Census of Housing: 1950*, Vol. I, Parts 51-54.

No. 1087.—FARMS AND FARM PROPERTY—SUMMARY FOR ALASKA, HAWAII, PUERTO RICO, VIRGIN ISLANDS, GUAM, AND AMERICAN SAMOA

[Figures are as of Apr. 1, except 1939 figures for Alaska, as of Oct. 1]

ITEM	ALASKA		HAWAII		PUERTO RICO		
	1939	1950	1940	1950	1930	1940	1950
Number of farms, total	633	525	4,995	5,750	52,965	56,519	53,515
Operated by owners	471	495	1,345	2,335	43,101	42,990	50,184
Full owners	397	445	956	1,638	40,480	40,622	47,821
Part owners	74	50	389	697	2,621	2,368	2,363
Operated by managers	27	10	123	109	3,374	1,303	421
Operated by tenants	125	20	3,527	3,306	6,490	11,226	2,910
Land in farms, total [1]	1,775,752	421,799	2,485,648	2,432,049	1,979,474	1,885,874	1,844,886
Operated by owners	51,566	62,510	490,396	493,212	1,166,976	1,072,144	1,378,636
Full owners	43,522	53,105	41,966	85,460	1,040,161	931,931	1,174,157
Part owners	8,044	9,405	448,430	407,752	126,815	140,213	204,469
Operated by managers	526,619	157,152	1,882,113	1,897,242	676,760	573,699	340,194
Operated by tenants	1,197,567	202,137	113,139	41,615	135,738	240,031	126,066
Number of farms, by size:[1]							
Under 10 acres or cuerdas	75	58	2,870	3,558	26,520	29,370	27,965
10 to 19 acres or cuerdas	24	19	952	979	11,067	11,288	10,526
20 to 49 acres or cuerdas	86	58	739	690	8,535	8,575	8,667
50 to 99 acres or cuerdas	117	81	163	193	3,351	3,200	3,166
100 to 174 acres or cuerdas	190	231	60	105	1,570	1,504	1,440
175 to 259 acres or cuerdas	26	32	40	41	674	646	627
260 to 499 acres or cuerdas	45	32	36	} 184	561	504	} 1,072
500 acres or cuerdas and over	60	14	135		367	342	
Land in farms, by size of farm:[1]							
Under 10 acres or cuerdas	307	248	11,344	13,184	131,432	145,438	143,008
10 to 19 acres or cuerdas	306	242	12,892	13,033	147,503	151,510	144,449
20 to 49 acres or cuerdas	3,288	2,185	23,030	20,533	264,712	258,563	262,720
50 to 99 acres or cuerdas	8,403	6,047	11,228	13,061	226,464	215,540	216,148
100 to 174 acres or cuerdas	26,295	34,000	7,579	13,663	201,902	191,675	186,530
175 to 259 acres or cuerdas	5,459	6,721	8,475	8,688	143,884	135,569	133,055
260 to 499 acres or cuerdas	15,041	10,455	12,955	} 2,349,887	196,061	206,789	} 757,967
500 acres or cuerdas and over	1,714,653	361,904	2,398,145		667,490	550,786	
Value of farm property ($1,000):							
Land and buildings	3,841	6,544	112,788	195,277	182,112	173,863	(2)
Buildings	2,140	(2)	17,829	(2)	16,948	16,556	(2)
Implements and machinery	377	(2)	13,805	(2)	4,617	8,445	(2)

ITEM	VIRGIN ISLANDS		GUAM	
	1940	1950	1940	1950
Number of farms, total	828	755	2,529	2,362
Operated by owners	540	573	1,209	901
Full owners	498	540	(2)	(2)
Part owners	42	33	(2)	(2)
Operated by managers	58	36		
Operated by tenants	230	146		
Operated by lessees, renters, and borrowers (squatters)			1,320	1,361
Land in farms, total [1]	55,219	63,753	26,264	18,625
Operated by owners	24,107	41,623	15,094	5,405
Full owners	22,623	37,039	(2)	(2)
Part owners	1,484	4,504	(2)	(2)
Operated by managers	24,782	17,813		
Operated by tenants	6,330	4,307		
Operated by lessees, renters, and borrowers (squatters)			11,170	4,620
Number of farms, by size:				
Under 10 acres or hectares	504	364	(2)	2,072
10 to 19 acres or hectares	145	140	(2)	119
20 to 49 acres or hectares	53	94	(2)	55
50 to 499 acres or hectares	96	126	(2)	} 16
500 acres or hectares and over	30	31	(2)	
Land in farms, by size of farm:[1]				
Under 10 acres or hectares	2,784	1,723	(2)	3,675
10 to 19 acres or hectares	1,816	1,844	(2)	1,535
20 to 49 acres or hectares	1,526	2,858	(2)	1,509
50 to 499 acres or hectares	20,092	24,096	(2)	} 3,216
500 acres or hectares and over	29,021	33,232	(2)	
Value of farm property ($1,000):				
Land and buildings	2,399	6,493	(2)	(2)
Buildings	771	(2)	(2)	(2)
Implements and machinery	113	(2)	(2)	(2)

ITEM	AMERICAN SAMOA	
	1940	1950
Number of farms	1,038	1,490
Farms operated by owners	709	952
Land in farms (acres)	(2)	14,690

[1] For Alaska, Hawaii, and Virgin Islands, figures are for acres; for Puerto Rico, cuerdas; and for Guam, hectares. A cuerda is equivalent to 0.9712 acre and a hectare to 2.471 acres. [2] Data not available.

Source: Department of Commerce, Bureau of the Census; U. S. Census of Agriculture: 1950, Vol. I, Part 34.

No. 1088.—Domestic and Other Animals on Farms, by Kind—Summary for Alaska, American Samoa, Guam, Hawaii, Puerto Rico, and Virgin Islands

[Figures are as of Apr. 1, except 1939 figures for Alaska as of Oct. 1]

CLASS	NUMBER					
	Alaska		American Samoa		Guam	
	1939	1950	1940	1950	1940	1950
Horses	} 496	} 207	121	170	128	5
Mules						
Asses and burros						
Carabaos						1,580	671
Cattle	3,749	2,236	272	223	5,945	2,847
Milk cows	1,217	¹ 1,324	26	75	980	661
Sheep	17,076	6,046	34	15		(²)
Goats	280	(²)		(²)		762
Swine	959	1,201	8,641	9,080	1,383	
Chickens	18,374	20,278	22,906	28,011	14,089	7,035
Fur-bearing animals	34,433	³ 1,378			208,465	132,781
Reindeer	312,854	(²)				

	Hawaii		Puerto Rico		Virgin Islands	
	1940	1950	1940	1950	1940	1950
Horses	⁴ 10,044	7,564	33,688	36,390	⁴ 954	1,077
Mules	} ⁴ 4,491	1,918	{ 4,652	} 5,419	{ ⁴ 623	265
Asses and burros			1,547		⁴ 544	399
Carabaos	52					
Cattle	⁴ 139,078	155,739	299,734	289,389	⁴ 8,796	11,355
Milk cows	10,952	9,449	89,217	⁴ 81,056	2,480	5,331
Sheep	⁶ 26,207	13,513	3,488	3,121	⁴ 819	2,786
Goats	⁷ 765	379	42,861	39,311	⁷ 2,134	3,576
Swine	⁷ 31,684	65,435	97,306	91,069	⁷ 1,124	978
Chickens	272,590	472,183	⁷ 981,358	⁸ 799,353	⁷ 8,046	10,074

¹ Cows including heifers that have calved.
² Not available.
³ Females over 3 months old.
⁴ Excluding data for animals under 3 months old.
⁵ Cows milked.
⁶ Excluding data for sheep and lambs under 6 months old.
⁷ Excluding data for animals or chickens under 4 months old.
⁸ Chicken hens only.

Source: Department of Commerce, Bureau of the Census; *U. S Census of Agriculture: 1950*, Vol. I, Part 34.

No. 1089.—Principal Crops, Land Harvested and Production—Summary for Alaska, Hawaii, Virgin Islands, Puerto Rico, Guam, and American Samoa

[Leaders indicate no data available]

AREA AND CROP	LAND HARVESTED (ACRES)		PRODUCTION		
			Unit	Quantity	
	1939	1949		1939	1949
ALASKA					
Barley	654	55	Bushel	13,219	661
Oats	527	333	do	13,661	11,616
Potatoes	388	1,030	do	41,887	184,862
Wheat	527	204	do	9,479	5,263
HAWAII	1940	1949		1940	1949
Coffee	4,136	3,403	Pound	8,546,783	4,648,155
Corn	1,862	752	Hundredweight	16,320	9,639
Pineapples	48,598	51,018	Ton	614,484	654,915
Potatoes, white	487	106	Hundredweight	19,916	4,956
Rice	509	170	do	19,018	6,585
Sugarcane	135,945	108,298	Ton	8,535,023	7,886,338
Sweetpotatoes and yams	180	279	Hundredweight	9,271	12,177
Taro	622	591	do	115,800	104,897
VIRGIN ISLANDS	1939	1949		1939	1949
Sugarcane	4,097	4,142	Ton	42,641	49,091
Sweetpotatoes and yams	131	137	Pound	180,100	154,116

No. 1089.—PRINCIPAL CROPS, LAND HARVESTED AND PRODUCTION—SUMMARY FOR
ALASKA, HAWAII, VIRGIN ISLANDS, PUERTO RICO, GUAM, AND AMERICAN SAMOA—Con.

AREA AND CROP	LAND HARVESTED OR NUMBER OF TREES OR PLANTS		PRODUCTION		
			Unit	Quantity	
	1939	1940		1939	1940
PUERTO RICO	*Cuerdas*	*Cuerdas*			
Coffee	181,106	176,386	Pound	32,652,044	25,661,626
Corn	50,350	39,497	do	36,811,000	23,122,102
Cotton	3,381	2,736	do	1,637 to 7	1,175,677
Dry beans	48,363	19,962	do	19,248,800	5,808,972
Pigeon peas	34,301	20,436	do	15,722,200	6,698,152
Rice	13,753	5,342	do	7,915,100	2,480,090
Sugarcane	229,780	344,067	Ton	7,237,717	10,699,147
Sweetpotatoes	49,565	23,818	Pound	103,160,600	32,485,183
Tobacco	26,584	26,834	do	19,895,377	22,254,360
Taniers (Yautias)	22,080	14,663	do	42,707,200	34,105,774
Bananas	47,114	44,341	Bunch	16,014,474	12,032,378
Coconuts	12,961	12,581	Number	21,776,289	25,496,475
Grapefruit	4,869	2,701	do	24,879,531	14,140,951
Oranges	9,879	16,532	do	116,273,562	178,994,691
Pineapples	1,912	3,553	Tons	11,971	33,452
Plantains	16,775	15,125	Number	6,166,226	168,401,070
	1939	1949		1939	1949
GUAM	*Hectares*	*Hectares*			
Arrowroot	78	(¹)	Pound	126,640	3,461
Cassava	74	4	do	472,657	15,710
Corn	881	270	do	2,033,528	571,413
Sweetpotatoes	128	22	do	756,415	107,044
Taro	293	77	do	(²)	280,742
Yams	80	15	do	840,015	87,252
	Number of trees or plants	*Number of trees or plants*			
Alligator pears (avocados)	10,220	1,870	Number	989,861	67,054
Bananas	535,240	142,222	Bunch	301,264	65,265
Breadfruit	36,615	12,405	Number	2,855,708	371,589
Coconuts	885,424	241,816	do	20,849,546	3,172,106
Coffee	90,254	7,968	Pound	42,686	2,465
Kapok	9,629	418	Number	18,263	1,131
Lemons	11,270	1,330	do	868,684	54,027
Mangoes	4,602	1,788	do	1,933,761	428,072
Oranges	5,477	800	do	365,073	25,008
Papayas	7,719	2,211	do	78,153	10,504
Pineapples	134,263	35,603	do	87,026	10,726
Tangerines	3,961	1,996	do	647,719	74,713

AREA AND CROP	FARMS REPORTING		LAND HARVESTED OR NUMBER OF TREES OR PLANTS	
	1939	1949	1939	1949
AMERICAN SAMOA	*Number*	*Number*	*Acres*	*Acres*
Arrowroot	690	101		20
Sugarcane for thatching	(²)	537	(²)	118
Taro	1,027	1,630		1,576
Tobacco	197	40		13
Yams	542	224		40
			Number of trees or plants	*Number of trees or plants*
Alligator pears (avocados)	348	215	1,275	934
Bananas	1,027	(²)	³ 450,000	(²)
Breadfruits	1,026	1,427	⁴ 46,000	637,405
Coconuts		(²)	⁴ 245,000	(²)
Limes	559	422	2,383	2,304
Mangoes	631	445	3,203	2,182
Oranges	671	605	4,699	5,173

¹ Reported in small fractions. ² Data not available. ³ Estimated in part.
⁴ Based on estimates supplied by Governor of Samoa.

Source: Department of Commerce, Bureau of the Census; *U. S. Census of Agriculture: 1940*, Vol. I, Part 34.

No. 1090.—Mineral Production in Territories, Possessions, Etc., of the United States: 1947 to 1950

MINERAL	1947 Quantity	1947 Value ($1,000)	1948 Quantity	1948 Value ($1,000)	1949 Quantity	1949 Value ($1,000)	1950 Quantity	1950 Value ($1,000)
Territories, total		20,193		15,196		16,537		19,637
Alaska, total		18,488		13,094		16,549		17,833
Antimony ore and concentrate ... short tons, gross weight	40	16	68	29	74	31		
Coal ... 1,000 short tons	361	2,635	408	2,789	434	3,309	412	3,033
Copper (recoverable content of ores, etc.) ... short tons	12	6	16	7	4	2	6	3
Gold (recoverable content of ores, etc.) ... troy ounces	279,988	9,900	248,385	8,694	229,416	8,030	269,272	10,126
Lead (recoverable content of ores, etc.) ... short tons	264	76	329	118	61	16	140	40
Mercury (content of ore) ... 76-pound flasks	127	11	100	8	100	8		
Platinum-group metals (crude) ... troy ounces	13,512	(3)	(3)	(3)	(3)	(3)	(3)	(3)
Sand and gravel ... 1,000 short tons	(3)	(3)	67	61	36	33	3,050	2,877
Silver (recoverable content of ores, etc.) ... 1,000 troy ounces	66	90	41	54	51		53	48
Stone ... 1,000 short tons	(3)	2	6		51	116	13	170
Tin (content of ore and concentrate) ... long tons	1						70	
Tungsten concentrate ... short tons, 60-percent WO3 basis	13						6	
Zinc (recoverable content of ores, etc.) ... short tons	25	6	23	6	2	(3)		2
Undistributed: Clay (1948), gem stones (1947), pumice (1948), and minerals as indicated by footnote 1								
Hawaii, total		5,987		1,288		4,006		2,046
Lime (open market) ... short tons	9,130	1,705	8,767	2,171	8,404	948	8,141	1,776
Stone ... 1,000 short tons	796	1,228	838	237	654	727	648	1,533
Undistributed (nonmetallic)	6	1,471		1,917		711		
				17		43		
Possessions, total		8,171		10,798		12,841		12,886
Guam: Stone ... 1,000 short tons	1,142	2,265	1,537	3,073	2,606	5,299	1,528	5,035
Puerto Rico, total		5,674		7,051		7,336		9,307
Cement ... 1,000 (376-lb.) barrels	1,004	5,339	2,440	6,947	2,171	6,100	3,147	8,260
Lime (open market) ... short tons					7,347	144	8,105	181
Salt (common) ... 1,000 short tons	13	101	16	112	13	77	14	137
Sand and gravel ... do.	(3)		(3)	(3)	(3)		101	104
Stone ... do.	104	196	1,169	312	820	827	1,260	1,576
Undistributed: Other nonmetallic minerals and minerals indicated by footnote 1								
Virgin Islands: Stone (crushed) ... 1,000 short tons	(3)	239	9	290	10	139	8	(3)
		12		14		116		4
Other areas:								
Canal Zone, total		220		330		222		98
Sand and gravel ... 1,000 short tons	45	68	58	62	29	58	23	10
Stone (crushed) ... do	102	182	170	268	100	164	53	58
Trust Territories of the Pacific Islands (Angaur Island): Phosphate rock exports ... 1,000 long tons	106	425	76	380	155	747	135	677

1 Included with "Undistributed." 2 Less than $500. 3 Estimate. 4 Excludes certain stone included with "Undistributed." 5 St. Croix Island only. Data for St. Thomas Island not available. 6 Not available. 10 Conjectural.

1 Quantities are estimated short-ton equivalents of cubic yards reported.
2 Distribution of quantities by years estimated for 1947-49 from reported totals and a partial breakdown.
3 Data are for years ending June 30.

Source: Department of the Interior, Bureau of Mines; Minerals Yearbook.

No. 1091.—Puerto Rico—Manufactures by Industry Groups and Industries: 1949 and 1939

[Figures for 1949 include data for all establishments. Figures for 1939 include data only for establishments with products valued at $2,000 or more. Certain industries not shown separately to avoid disclosing operations of individual companies]

INDUSTRY GROUP AND INDUSTRY	1949							1939 [1]		
	Number of establishments	Number of proprietors and partners	All employees		Production workers		Value added by manufacture [2] ($1,000)	Number of establishments	Number of production workers (average for year)	Value added by manufacture ($1,000)
			Number (average for year)	Salaries and wages, total ($1,000)	Number (average for year)	Wages, total ($1,000)				
All industries, total [3]	1,998	1,821	55,137	49,395	47,735	35,736	93,421	(4)	(4)	(4)
All industries (excl. coffee roasting and grinding and tobacco stemming and redrying), total [3]	1,987	1,768	49,052	46,816	42,012	33,174	87,043	796	23,484	35,219
Food and kindred products	536	473	23,243	25,516	19,615	18,251	52,432	(4)	(4)	(4)
Food and kindred products, exc. coffee roasting and grinding	507	450	23,102	25,398	19,526	18,203	51,821	379	12,996	22,997
Dairy products	31	29	311	391	166	133	651	9	36	40
Natural cheese	4	5	37	32	31	23	47	3	9	12
Ice cream and ices	27	24	274	360	135	110	604	6	27	27
Canning, preserving, and freezing	23	14	1,159	650	872	464	906	7	307	105
Canning and preserving, except fish	19	12	1,132	630	851	454	894	7	307	105
Pickles and sauces	4	2	27	19	21	9	53			
Bakery products	277	286	2,750	2,441	2,275	1,946	3,928	219	1,470	1,215
Bread and other bakery products	265	278	2,235	1,995	1,839	1,656	3,144	212	1,143	1,022
Biscuits, crackers, and pretzels	12	8	515	446	436	291	784	7	327	193
Sugar	41	22	14,241	17,246	12,900	13,254	35,704	44	9,658	18,666
Raw cane sugar	36	22	13,562	16,496	12,280	12,680	32,228	40	7,765	16,497
Cane sugar refining	5		679	750	620	574	[5] 3,476	4	1,893	2,170
Chocolate and cocoa products	4	4	141	116	98	43	329	1	(4)	(4)
Beverages	73	42	3,174	3,533	2,287	1,836	6,527	53	1,008	2,344
Bottled soft drinks	33	18	863	927	428	397	1,973	10	(4)	(4)
Malt liquors	4		799	1,050	637	652	2,419	2	(4)	(4)
Wines and brandy	5	12	85	57	52	26	262	4	42	20
Distilled liquors, except brandy	31	12	1,427	1,499	1,170	779	[5] 3,852	37	657	1,696
Misc. food preparations [6]	66	78	1,085	889	675	441	1,659	(4)	(4)	(4)
Misc. food preparations, exc. coffee roasting and grinding [6]	49	55	944	771	586	393	1,048	36	467	580
Manufactured ice	29	37	515	445	241	170	640	25	265	382
Macaroni and spaghetti	10	10	193	185	171	156	300	8	154	(4)
Food preparations, n. e. c.	25	27	361	245	249	105	703	(4)	(4)	(4)
Food preparations, n. e. c., etc. coffee roasting and grinding	6	4	220	128	160	56	92	1	(4)	(4)
Tobacco manufactures	626	609	7,116	3,403	6,732	2,956	6,743	(4)	(4)	(4)
Tobacco manufactures, exc. tobacco stemming and redrying	584	579	1,172	531	1,096	443	977	47	446	339
Cigars	577	574	1,097	496	1,034	409	935	41	(4)	(4)
Chewing and smoking tobacco	7	5	75	35	74	34	42	5	30	11
Tobacco stemming and redrying	42	30	5,944	2,873	5,634	2,513	5,767	(4)	(4)	(4)
Textile mill products	10	2	1,450	596	1,273	475	607	3	101	(4)
Apparel and related products	262	244	10,805	6,464	9,361	4,983	9,251	135	6,307	7,265
Men's and boys' suits and coats	111	17	684	549	642	450	861	5	688	709
Men's and boys' furnishings	68	73	2,216	1,381	2,006	965	1,993	36	1,604	799
Men's dress shirts and nightwear	17	13	741	541	657	333	781	9	505	305
Separate trousers	35	41	1,058	603	978	468	920	12	382	260
Men's and boys' clothing, n. e. c.	6	10	260	129	234	91	132	1	(4)	(4)
Women's and misses' outerwear	33	29	1,149	562	1,066	451	701	15	269	582
Blouses and waists	18	13	757	387	700	313	497	7	(4)	(4)
Women's and children's undergarments	31	22	1,401	831	1,300	688	1,076	25	(4)	(4)

See footnotes at end of table.

No. 1091.—Puerto Rico—Manufactures by Industry Groups and Industries: 1949 and 1939—Continued

INDUSTRY GROUP AND INDUSTRY	1949							1939 [1]		
	Number of establishments	Number of proprietors and partners	All employees		Production workers		Value added by manufacture [2] ($1,000)	Number of establishments	Number of production workers (average for year)	Value added by manufacture ($1,000)
			Number (average for year)	Salaries and wages, total ($1,000)	Number (average for year)	Wages, total ($1,000)				
Apparel and related products— Continued										
Children's outerwear	27	22	946	552	894	483	711	11	(4)	(4)
Miscellaneous apparel and accessories [7]	74	68	3,828	2,284	2,989	1,650	3,485	32	1,292	1,878
Handkerchiefs	45	44	2,453	1,517	2,118	1,200	2,030	31	(4)	(4)
Housefurnishings, n. e. c	8	6	395	147	306	123	177	8	173	402
Canvas products	6	5	51	48	37	32	80	1	(4)	(4)
Lumber and products (except furniture)	51	53	327	302	313	245	611	13	119	134
Millwork plants	43	47	300	289	266	232	589	11	(4)	(4)
Furniture and fixtures	186	193	1,888	1,519	1,727	1,229	2,338	62	630	825
Household furniture	177	180	1,837	1,468	1,681	1,194	2,205	49	823	512
Wood house furniture, except upholstery	152	161	1,443	1,071	1,343	926	1,467	39	610	317
Mattresses and bedsprings	13	9	266	276	222	177	511	9	(4)	(4)
Paper and allied products	5	1	294	352	256	263	825	1	(4)	(4)
Printing and publishing industries	77	63	1,459	2,216	975	1,266	3,670	59	653	1,067
Chemicals and allied products	49	21	1,268	1,510	1,011	884	4,394	39	400	981
Pharmaceutical preparations	20	6	209	231	149	96	542	13	(4)	(4)
Fertilizers (mixing only)	7	5	504	659	428	402	2,731	7	197	634
Compressed and liquefied gases	6	1	239	354	153	187	716	2	(4)	(4)
Insecticides and fungicides	3	3	7	3	7	3	12	--	--	--
Leather and leather products	22	12	911	611	859	446	925	15	79	64
Handbags and small leather goods	7	1	389	246	367	172	380	--	--	--
Stone, clay, and glass products	87	82	2,562	3,097	2,224	2,162	6,353	23	254	248
Products of purchased glass	3	2	21	21	17	15	38	--	--	--
Structural clay products	18	12	715	724	654	548	1,034	12	155	156
Concrete products	42	50	317	268	281	193	498	--	--	--
Cut-stone and stone products	7	6	46	71	44	66	183	3	9	4
Fabricated metal products	33	32	310	338	290	292	710	10	49	63
Structural metal products	24	22	194	255	187	221	538	6	29	29
Structural and ornamental products	15	17	123	153	122	151	251	3	(4)	(4)
Machinery (except electrical)	13	9	617	949	517	670	1,352	7	477	690
Farm machinery (except tractors)	6	4	86	133	74	85	217	3	30	(4)
Miscellaneous manufactures [9]	44	26	2,389	1,591	2,230	1,275	2,451	12	574	619
Jewelry and silverware	7	2	382	320	345	234	406	1	(4)	(4)
Costume jewelry and notions	16	6	1,595	951	1,497	788	1,393	2	(4)	(4)
Artificial flowers	5	1	629	375	600	344	380	--	--	--
Buttons	5	2	572	470	509	347	863	2	(4)	(4)
Morticians' goods	8	8	13	10	13	10	20	6	8	10
Signs and advertising displays	4	6	19	20	17	17	33	1	(4)	(4)

[1] Retabulated to provide industry statistics comparable with those for 1949.

[2] Computed by subtracting costs of materials and supplies, fuels, electric energy, and contract work from value of products.

[3] Includes data for industry groups not shown separately (to avoid disclosing operations of individual companies) as follows: Rubber, primary metal industries, electrical machinery, and transportation equipment, 1 establishment each; and for instruments and related products, 2 establishments.

[4] Comparable statistics for 1939 not available. Figures for 1949 include statistics for activities of (1) coffee roasting and grinding and (2) tobacco stemming and redrying, which were classified as manufacturing in 1949 but considered nonmanufacturing in 1939.

[5] This figure may include an undetermined amount of excise taxes.

[6] Also includes shortening, cooking oils, and flavorings.

[7] Also includes fabric and combination dress and work gloves.

[9] Also includes sporting and athletic goods, hand stamps and stencils, needles, pins, and fasteners, plastic products, brooms and brushes, matches, and hair work.

[4] Withheld to avoid disclosing figures for individual companies.

Source: Department of Commerce, Bureau of the Census; *Puerto Rico Census of Manufactures, 1949.*

No. 1092.—ALASKA AND HAWAII—SUMMARY OF MANUFACTURES: 1899 TO 1939

[Figures for 1939 do not include data for plants reporting products valued at less than $2,000; those for earlier years cover all plants having products valued at $500 or more. This increase in minimum value-of-products limit resulted in some reduction in "Number of establishments" reported as compared with what it would have been had minimum of $500 been retained, but did not seriously impair comparability of figures for 1939 with those for earlier years]

INDUSTRY	Census year	Number of establishments	Wage earners (average for the year)	Wages	Cost of materials, etc., fuel, electric energy	Value of products	Value added by manufacture [1]
Alaska, all industries	1899	48	2,260	$1,374,680	$1,762,583	$4,194,421	$2,431,838
	1909	152	3,009	1,948,026	5,119,613	11,340,105	6,220,492
	1919	147	6,575	8,530,452	19,482,485	41,495,243	22,012,758
	1939[2]	230	4,816	6,883,988	20,916,757	38,815,436	17,898,679
Hawaii, all industries	1899[3]	222	3,655	1,473,000	12,251,000	23,354,000	11,103,000
	1909[3]	500	5,904	2,108,903	25,817,734	47,403,880	21,586,146
	1919[3]	496	9,969	6,635,763	81,178,956	133,096,412	51,917,456
	1939	474	17,002	11,458,311	75,651,675	134,005,264	58,353,589

[1] Value of products less cost of materials, etc., fuel, and purchased electric energy.
[2] Figures for 1939 cover the 12-month period ended Sept. 30, 1939.
[3] Includes data for coffee roasting and spice grinding which are no longer treated as manufacturing activities.
Source: Department of Commerce, Bureau of the Census; 1939 Census of Manufactures reports.

No. 1093.—IMPORTS AND EXPORTS OF ALASKA: 1882 TO 1952

[In 1947 Alaska shipped domestic silver valued at $2,067 to the United States]

YEARLY AVERAGE OR YEAR ENDING—	MERCHANDISE IMPORTS			MERCHANDISE EXPORTS			Shipments domestic gold to United States
	Total	From United States [1]	From other countries [2]	Total	To United States	To other countries	
June 30:	Dollars	Dollars	Dollars	Dollars	Dollars	Dollars	Dollars
1882–1885		680,250	9,198			24,955	
1886–1890		1,455,600	23,697			8,748	
1891–1895		2,422,600	42,530			15,524	
1896–1900		9,843,000	185,182			135,069	
1901–1905	[3] 11,238,265	[3] 11,159,017	721,110	[3] 11,820,379	[3] 10,398,365	1,882,464	[3] 7,703,283
1906–1910	18,051,314	17,255,687	804,627	12,960,141	11,589,320	1,370,821	15,773,847
1911–1915	20,726,443	20,034,397	692,046	23,095,710	21,945,625	1,150,087	14,934,009
Dec. 31:							
1916–1920[4]	37,099,688	35,707,204	1,392,484	68,445,011	66,590,595	1,854,417	11,880,362
1921–1925	28,955,839	28,216,438	739,401	52,009,911	80,730,865	1,279,046	8,787,818
1926–1930	33,661,490	32,754,859	906,631	61,476,709	60,960,208	516,501	6,449,570
1931–1935	25,252,071	24,951,064	301,008	37,964,038	37,703,765	260,273	11,974,339
1936–1940	43,572,951	43,380,029	192,922	52,804,870	52,323,674	481,196	19,380,455
1941–1945	75,893,346	74,255,643	1,637,602	199,556,432	66,938,416	130,618,015	6,744,079
1946–1950	[5] 96,443,910	[5] 95,907,254	1,245,715	[5] 97,720,815	[5] 95,239,395	[7] 2,099,132	[5] 5,128,957
1940	48,180,293	48,039,460	149,833	40,585,267	40,173,952	411,315	20,925,957
1941	82,206,608	82,029,238	177,367	68,471,531	67,699,708	771,823	17,848,450
1942	91,524,276	89,497,621	2,026,655	59,018,262	58,199,935	818,327	12,104,445
1943	76,007,574	73,558,796	2,448,776	267,899,094	73,164,753	214,734,341	1,980,296
1944	62,638,819	62,042,363	596,456	343,470,611	72,359,111	271,111,500	1,009,125
1945	67,088,955	64,150,197	2,938,758	238,922,661	73,268,575	165,654,086	778,081
1946	75,576,054	75,005,229	570,825	69,892,767	68,837,904	1,054,863	4,363,386
1947	117,311,766	116,809,279	502,487	125,548,863	123,640,885	1,907,978	5,884,527
1948	(6)	(6)	2,779,449	(6)	(6)	2,408,928	(6)
1949	(6)	(6)	1,397,255	(6)	(6)	2,599,870	(6)
1950	(6)	(6)	993,561	(6)	(6)	[7] 2,524,020	(6)
1951	(6)	(6)	1,160,922	(6)	(6)	[7] 2,594,861	(6)
1952	(6)	(6)	906,665	(6)	(6)	[7] 3,041,956	(6)

[1] Unofficial estimates of value of merchandise shipped from Pacific coast ports to Alaska from 1882 to 1901; from 1903 to date, official figures of shipments to Alaska.
[2] General imports through 1933; imports for consumption thereafter.
[3] 5-year average.   [4] 4-year average.   [5] 2-year average.   [6] Period July 1, 1915 to Dec. 31, 1920.
[7] For security reasons Customs district of exportation for certain commodities are not reported in export statistics.
[8] Not available; legal requirement for filing of export declarations for shipments between U. S. and Alaska and Hawaii was removed in April 1948.

Source: See general note, p. 927.

No. **1094.**—IMPORTS AND EXPORTS OF PUERTO RICO: 1901 TO 1952

YEARLY AVERAGE OR YEAR ENDING—	MERCHANDISE IMPORTS			MERCHANDISE EXPORTS		
	Total	From United States	From other countries [1]	Total	To United States	To other countries
June 30:	Dollars	Dollars	Dollars	Dollars	Dollars	Dollars
1901–1905	13, 255, 464	11, 055, 607	2, 200, 857	14, 226, 464	10, 485, 414	3, 743, 050
1906–1910	26, 819, 987	23, 660, 948	3, 158, 988	29, 850, 006	25, 118, 813	4, 731, 195
1911–1915	37, 790, 207	33, 959, 225	3, 830, 982	46, 237, 403	38, 982, 507	7, 254, 896
Dec. 31:						
1915–1920 [2]	51, 192, 853	47, 846, 373	3, 346, 480	67, 831, 644	60, 818, 903	7, 012, 741
1921–1925	78, 901, 764	70, 355, 330	8, 546, 434	82, 878, 547	76, 481, 329	6, 397, 218
1926–1930	92, 500, 964	80, 640, 700	11, 860, 264	98, 613, 291	92, 468, 856	6, 144, 435
1931–1935	65, 055, 632	58, 128, 726	6, 926, 906	83, 942, 503	81, 464, 920	2, 477, 583
1936–1940	96, 916, 409	89, 512, 394	7, 404, 015	94, 701, 265	92, 837, 006	1, 864, 259
1941–1945	136, 612, 529	120, 136, 052	16, 476, 477	119, 403, 190	114, 301, 879	5, 101, 312
1946–1950	345, 256, 034	320, 169, 438	25, 088, 596	[3] 206, 295, 625	195, 007, 759	[3] 11, 287, 866
1940	110, 629, 960	103, 972, 709	6, 657, 251	85, 041, 449	83, 733, 274	1, 308, 173
1941	153, 259, 895	143, 691, 759	9, 568, 136	101, 580, 919	99, 651, 309	1, 929, 618
1942	102, 378, 764	90, 380, 869	11, 997, 895	105, 477, 270	104, 214, 641	1, 262, 629
1943	109, 066, 388	87, 419, 797	21, 646, 591	115, 946, 349	99, 221, 148	16, 725, 201
1944	136, 445, 478	120, 499, 206	15, 946, 272	125, 604, 083	123, 747, 071	1, 857, 012
1945	181, 912, 120	158, 688, 630	23, 223, 490	148, 407, 331	144, 675, 234	3, 732, 107
1946	298, 697, 281	274, 430, 616	24, 266, 665	168, 190, 917	163, 941, 239	4, 249, 678
1947	341, 842, 882	320, 118, 678	21, 724, 204	199, 363, 482	191, 136, 679	8, 366, 803
1948	360, 403, 762	336, 201, 027	24, 202, 735	194, 533, 110	188, 208, 149	6, 334, 961
1949	333, 674, 462	308, 966, 549	24, 707, 913	222, 455, 322	213, 884, 768	8, 570, 554
1950	390, 945, 172	361, 130, 319	29, 814, 853	[3] 246, 915, 294	217, 867, 960	[3] 29, 047, 334
1951	442, 900, 808	404, 502, 271	38, 398, 537	[3] 264, 527, 351	250, 629, 829	[3] 13, 897, 522
1952	468, 729, 223	431, 187, 309	37, 541, 914	[3] 291, 816, 589	271, 512, 753	[3] 20, 303, 836

[1] General imports through 1933; imports for consumption thereafter.   [2] Period July 1, 1915, to Dec. 31, 1920.
[3] For security reasons Customs district of exportation for certain commodities are not reported in export statistics.

No. **1095.**—IMPORTS AND EXPORTS OF HAWAII: 1901 TO 1951

YEARLY AVERAGE OR YEAR ENDING—	MERCHANDISE IMPORTS			MERCHANDISE EXPORTS		
	Total	From United States	From other countries [1]	Total	To United States	To other countries
June 30:	Dollars	Dollars	Dollars	Dollars	Dollars	Dollars
1901–1905	[2] 14, 778, 085	[2] 11, 459, 879	3, 165, 296	28, 093, 757	28, 029, 059	64, 698
1906–1910	20, 120, 188	15, 970, 287	4, 149, 852	37, 097, 102	36, 842, 145	254, 936
1911–1915	31, 532, 670	25, 600, 469	5, 932, 201	48, 983, 610	48, 352, 547	631, 063
Dec. 31:						
1915–1920 [3]	39, 271, 498	33, 236, 198	6, 035, 299	76, 008, 709	73, 691, 927	2, 316, 751
1921–1925	74, 514, 123	65, 429, 082	9, 085, 041	92, 977, 893	91, 487, 972	1, 489, 922
1926–1930	89, 454, 566	79, 666, 569	9, 787, 997	108, 096, 755	105, 937, 984	2, 158, 771
1931–1935	73, 500, 296	67, 592, 513	5, 907, 783	95, 000, 597	93, 944, 684	1, 055, 913
1936–1940	112, 155, 544	104, 106, 212	8, 049, 332	115, 133, 303	113, 516, 846	1, 616, 457
1941–1945	197, 510, 876	187, 516, 126	9, 994, 750	101, 427, 047	99, 041, 911	2, 385, 136
1946–1950	[4] 292, 967, 186	[4] 283, 742, 195	12, 153, 998	[4] 188, 237, 691	[4] 180, 845, 275	[4] 5, 435, 234
1940	135, 446, 957	127, 439, 539	8, 007, 418	103, 067, 965	102, 145, 130	922, 835
1941	192, 855, 457	186, 662, 139	6, 193, 318	133, 653, 066	122, 640, 189	11, 012, 877
1942	143, 377, 345	141, 701, 552	1, 675, 793	96, 903, 345	96, 650, 450	253, 095
1943	185, 766, 176	182, 594, 027	3, 172, 149	103, 391, 067	103, 370, 901	20, 186
1944	198, 509, 464	185, 793, 636	12, 715, 828	85, 140, 644	85, 087, 249	53, 395
1945	267, 045, 937	240, 829, 274	26, 216, 663	88, 046, 893	87, 460, 764	586, 129
1946	236, 306, 962	227, 072, 997	9, 233, 965	140, 042, 662	133, 337, 539	6, 705, 123
1947	349, 627, 410	340, 411, 393	9, 216, 017	236, 432, 720	228, 353, 010	8, 079, 710
1948	[6]	[6]	12, 725, 649	[6]	[6]	6, 704, 891
1949	[6]	[6]	16, 007, 450	[6]	[6]	3, 462, 131
1950	[6]	[6]	13, 586, 910	[6]	[6]	[5] 2, 224, 317
1951	[6]	[6]	19, 158, 467	[6]	[6]	[5] 3, 504, 790
1952	[6]	[6]	20, 076, 009	[6]	[6]	[5] 4, 124, 809

[1] See note 1, table 1094.   [2] Average for 1903 to 1905.
[3] Period July 1, 1915, to Dec. 31, 1920.   [4] 2-year average.
[5] For security reasons Customs district of exportation for certain commodities are not reported in export statistics.
[6] Not available; legal requirement for filing of export declarations for shipments between U. S. and Alaska and Hawaii was removed in April 1948.

Source of tables 1094 and 1095: See general note, p. 927.

No. 1096—Shipments of Principal Products to the United States From Alaska, Hawaii, and Puerto Rico

[Totals include items not shown separately. Legal requirements for filing of export declarations for shipments between U. S. and Alaska and Hawaii was removed in April 1948; 1947 data latest available. For gold shipments from Alaska, see table 1093]

TERRITORY AND PRODUCT	QUANTITY			VALUE (THOUSANDS OF DOLLARS)			
	1945	1946	1947	1944	1945	1946	1947
ALASKA							
Total, all merchandise				72,359	73,269	68,838	123,641
Articles produced in U. S. returned				4,165	3,815	4,933	6,825
Foreign merchandise				1			1
Total, Alaskan products				68,194	69,454	63,904	117,115
Fish _____ 1,000 pounds	274,075	199,678	269,744	58,950	57,767	52,082	100,712
Halibut, fresh and frozen _____ do	24,081	19,848	25,036	3,578	4,406	4,058	6,370
Salmon, fresh and frozen _____ do	16,812	13,206	15,108	2,156	3,177	2,727	3,841
Canned salmon _____ do	214,095	149,857	216,716	50,489	45,852	40,032	86,528
Cured or preserved fish _____ do	9,129	9,459	7,624	1,009	2,226	2,826	2,430
Shellfish _____ do	2,127	2,539	1,338	866	1,016	1,751	908
Other fish products:							
Meal _____ tons	9,463	12,791	15,018	702	852	1,374	2,229
Oil _____ 1,000 gallons	2,930	3,799	4,409	1,602	1,831	1,972	3,664
Furs and fur skins _____ number	315,279	315,238	382,731	3,997	5,791	5,818	7,022
Beaver _____ do	9,968	18,929	20,395	301	306	946	834
Blue fox _____ do	1,731	1,523	2,275	28	45	26	60
Red fox _____ do	7,809	4,754	3,303	171	99	58	32
Seal skins _____ do	77,003	64,887	61,472	1,764	3,849	2,007	3,559
Marten _____ do	482	2,670	15,071	309	36	214	586
Mink _____ do	42,691	64,837	55,584	747	874	1,945	1,291
Muskrat _____ do	152,346	137,656	195,818	307	287	310	334
Platinum _____ troy ounces	23,529	19,809	11,534	1,335	937	1,187	658
HAWAII							
Total, all merchandise				85,087	87,461	133,338	228,353
Articles produced in U. S. returned				2,466	2,994	19,039	47,021
Foreign merchandise				(7)		12	1
Total, Hawaiian products				82,619	84,467	114,286	181,330
Cattle hides _____ 1,000 pounds	1,468	1,370	1,644	230	207	204	334
Fruits				18,750	14,388	40,752	49,561
Pineapples (canned) _____ 1,000 pounds	143,762	378,515	381,222	18,728	14,360	40,538	48,793
Vegetables, fresh, canned, etc. _____ do	(7)	68	79		(7)	11	17
Coffee _____ do	2	7,147	5,080		1	882	1,531
Sugar, unrefined _____ do	1,487,321	1,196,495	1,596,013	52,278	50,011	45,458	92,397
Sugar, refined _____ do		58	16,773			8	1,418
Molasses _____ 1,000 gallons	36,942	32,226	37,461	2,788	2,703	2,600	4,800
Pineapple juice _____ 1,000 pounds	149,068	277,095	302,387	7,297	12,566	21,487	25,619
Fiber insulating board _____ do	30,395	30,689	44,832	509	805	764	1,607
PUERTO RICO	1950	1951	1952	1949	1950	1951	1952
Total, all merchandise				213,885	217,868	250,639	271,513
Articles produced in U. S. returned				4,012	4,310	6,273	5,645
Foreign merchandise				18	26	160	115
Total, Puerto Rican products				209,855	213,532	244,197	265,753
Fruits				5,235	3,564	2,428	2,238
Pineapples, canned, etc. _____ 1,000 pounds	17,350	9,299	6,913	3,320	2,253	1,255	1,042
Coconuts _____ thousands	14,105	20,169	21,194	892	809	800	681
Coconut, prepared _____ 1,000 pounds	1,862	1,856	711	172	374	351	143
Sugar, unrefined _____ do	1,572,595	1,761,383	1,711,177	118,454	91,175	111,409	105,452
Sugar, refined _____ do	310,785	219,111	253,949	17,256	21,563	16,325	18,783
Candy and confectionery _____ do	3,068	3,263	1,958	222	536	683	454
Molasses _____ 1,000 gallons	31,224	49,951	52,252	1,725	1,825	10,977	7,659
Fruit juice _____ do	309	465	344	407	202	355	191
Rum _____ 1,000 proof gallons	1,332	1,596	1,467	3,011	3,962	4,353	4,871
Leaf tobacco _____ 1,000 pounds	9,958	13,666	15,200	9,222	9,099	10,168	15,500
Stems, scraps, etc	9,259	3,009	6,511	2,484	3,024	1,383	2,876
Cigars and cheroots _____ thousands	364	354	1,351	191	33	25	64
Cotton manufactures				22,336	30,559	33,643	
Wearing apparel, except gloves				4,926	5,289	5,838	8,506
Gloves _____ dozen pairs	1,154,566	891,479	934,542	8,868	12,722	9,278	10,288
Handkerchiefs _____ 1,000 dozen	4,825	4,617	5,154	8,135	9,833	9,965	10,811
Linen handkerchiefs _____ do	995	810	596	2,679	3,801	3,204	2,413
Rugs, woven and hooked _____ number	23,665	296,424	324,821	1,200	2,756	3,632	4,259
Silk manufactures				5,368	9,246	1,990	1,825
Rayon manufactures				5,480	6,444	6,230	
Blouses, dresses, housecoats _____ dozen	106,956	106,397	(4)	2,058	2,655	3,256	(4)
Underwear _____ 1,000 dozen	53	45	(4)	2,265	1,259	1,199	(4)
Other wearing apparel				749	1,262	1,775	(4)
Diamonds				1,188	1,234	1,317	1,315
Leather gloves _____ dozen pairs	29,255	39,678	85,002	321	502	917	1,849
Alcohols _____ 1,000 gallons	38	1,573	1,645	52	13	200	156
Buttons, pearl or shell _____ 1,000 gross	1,126	969	869	729	1,193	1,281	1,235

[1] Of 2,240 pounds.   [2] Less than 500 pounds or $500.   [3] Reported in 1,000 pounds beginning 1951.
[4] Reported in square yards beginning 1951.   [5] Not separately reported.

Source: See general note, p. 927.

No. 1097.—Imports and Exports of the Virgin Islands: 1911 to 1952

[For 1911 to 1917 figures for trade with United States cover years ending June 30, for total trade years ending Mar. 31; thereafter, all figures cover calendar years]

YEARLY AVERAGE OR YEAR	MERCHANDISE IMPORTS			MERCHANDISE EXPORTS		
	Total	From United States[1]	From other countries	Total	To United States	To other countries
	Dollars	*Dollars*	*Dollars*	*Dollars*	*Dollars*	*Dollars*
1911–1915	1,617,225	844,729	....	416,930	210,597	....
1916–1920	(²)	1,945,396	(²)	(²)	1,718,822	(²)
1921–1925	³ 2,254,547	1,894,229	³ 365,579	³ 673,710	650,718	³ 104,349
1926–1930	(²)	2,020,197	(²)	(²)	969,170	(²)
1931–1935	⁴ 2,503,027	1,293,347	⁴ 836,612	⁴ 553,842	479,024	⁴ 64,716
1936–1940	3,743,219	2,611,010	1,132,210	1,369,532	1,241,445	128,087
1941–1945	5,230,224	4,257,447	962,777	3,845,923	3,647,908	128,815
1946–1950	9,602,012	7,787,153	1,814,859	2,927,295	2,238,174	688,121
1933	(²)	1,075,512	(²)	(²)	516,846	(²)
1934	(²)	1,544,424	(²)	(²)	575,082	(²)
1935	2,503,027	1,666,415	836,612	553,842	489,126	64,716
1936	3,599,617	2,208,570	1,391,047	793,551	725,746	68,905
1937	4,148,593	2,976,146	1,172,447	1,319,895	1,253,429	65,495
1938	3,346,563	2,358,548	988,015	1,541,472	1,220,806	320,986
1939	3,456,895	2,487,905	969,090	1,664,933	1,569,532	105,410
1940	4,164,428	3,023,979	1,140,449	1,527,709	1,448,020	79,689
1941	6,307,730	5,190,548	1,117,182	2,564,856	2,419,597	145,259
1942	4,862,986	3,768,497	1,094,489	1,846,367	1,588,414	257,953
1943	4,847,655	4,025,839	821,816	3,622,139	3,456,235	165,904
1944	4,750,640	3,726,484	1,024,156	6,839,921	6,657,669	182,232
1945	5,332,106	4,575,955	756,290	4,356,431	4,117,624	238,807
1946	8,640,560	6,722,914	1,917,496	4,136,205	3,690,130	446,075
1947	8,690,546	7,003,157	1,687,499	2,300,915	1,448,536	852,379
1948	9,465,562	7,655,939	1,799,623	1,796,308	1,236,434	559,874
1949	9,967,225	8,176,045	1,791,180	2,543,879	1,737,524	806,355
1950	11,046,262	9,367,711	1,678,571	3,857,166	3,088,945	768,202
1951	11,686,154	9,131,904	2,554,250	2,715,901	2,105,744	608,157
1952	13,870,399	11,162,888	2,707,511	3,385,419	2,477,655	907,764

[1] For change in statistical reporting, 1935 to 1939, see general note, p. 928.   [2] Not available.
[3] Average for 1921 to 1924.   [4] For year 1935.

Source: Total trade, 1911 to 1915, from Danish Yearbook; 1916, from "The Virgin Islands of the United States of America," by Luther K. Zabriski. For source of other figures, see general note, p. 927.

No. 1098.—Imports and Exports of Guam: 1915 to 1952

YEARLY AVERAGE OR YEAR	MERCHANDISE IMPORTS			MERCHANDISE EXPORTS		
	Total	From United States	From other countries	Total	To United States	To other countries
	Dollars	*Dollars*	*Dollars*	*Dollars*	*Dollars*	*Dollars*
1915–1920 (July 1, 1915, to Dec. 31, 1920)	342,651	211,744	130,908	77,894	41,741	36,153
1921–1925	594,583	378,094	216,489	72,681	57,302	15,379
1926–1930	608,026	295,398	312,628	212,352	98,335	114,017
1931–1935	498,513	228,509	270,004	69,921	21,386	48,535
1936–1940	786,273	403,928	382,345	139,697	97,694	42,003
1941–1945	(1)	² 483,870	(1)	(1)	(1)	(1)
1946–1950	(1)	8,487,026	(1)	3,236,530	2,813,056	423,474
1937	857,904	345,543	512,361	228,229	164,879	63,330
1938	698,433	357,838	340,595	118,122	79,065	39,057
1939	735,906	402,963	332,943	112,104	88,468	23,636
1940	859,624	545,430	314,194	103,094	83,785	19,309
1941	1,060,980	788,325	272,655	50,175	29,303	20,872
1944	(1)	656,777	(1)	(1)	(1)	(1)
1945	(1)	6,508	(1)	(1)	(1)	(1)
1946	(1)	1,096,858	(1)	3,433,354	2,710,833	722,521
1947	(1)	9,368,182	(1)	3,639,977	2,312,410	1,327,567
1948	(1)	9,530,325	(1)	5,980,079	5,968,686	11,393
1949	(1)	11,296,882	(1)	2,358,142	2,708,534	49,608
1950	13,702,182	11,142,910	2,559,272	771,098	764,818	6,290
1951	16,870,079	15,181,661	1,688,418	4,881,399	3,961,798	919,601
1952 (prel.)	19,832,213	17,419,149	2,413,064	4,095,564	982,326	3,113,228

[1] Not available.   [2] Three-year average; no shipments reported for 1942 and 1943.

Source: Returns of the Navy Department and (beginning July 1950) the Department of Interior to the Department of Commerce. See general note, p. 927.

No. 1099.—IMPORTS AND EXPORTS OF AMERICAN SAMOA: 1915 TO 1952

	MERCHANDISE IMPORTS			MERCHANDISE EXPORTS		
YEARLY AVERAGE OR YEAR	Total	From United States	From other countries	Total	To United States	To other countries
	Dollars	*Dollars*	*Dollars*	*Dollars*	*Dollars*	*Dollars*
1915–1920 (July 1, 1915 to Dec. 31, 1920).......	179,041	115,278	63,763	140,757	140,757	....
1921–1925...	201,005	101,038	99,967	122,288	88,087	34,201
1926–1930..	226,856	142,774	84,084	(¹)	121,026	(¹)
1931–1935..	198,517	121,035	76,882	(¹)	43,702	(¹)
1936–1940..	336,365	220,070	116,295	(¹)	87,939	(¹)
1941–1945..	878,378	642,094	236,282	(¹)	³ 46,923	(¹)
1946–1950..	945,007	608,910	336,097	282,573	282,573	....
1938...	355,731	221,787	133,944	(¹)	110,657	(¹)
1939...	277,318	164,758	112,560	(¹)	84,853	(¹)
1940...	332,718	230,007	102,711	(¹)	72,598	(¹)
1941...	714,589	506,510	208,079	(¹)	103,129	(¹)
1942...	866,498	710,559	155,937	(¹)	5,664	(¹)
1943...	1,081,442	1,017,252	64,190	(¹)	(¹)	(¹)
1944...	1,009,574	635,266	374,308	(¹)	(¹)	(¹)
1945...	689,782	340,883	348,899	31,975	31,975	....
1946...	678,344	379,637	298,707	190,925	190,925	....
1947...	892,027	540,695	351,332	261,297	261,297	....
1948...	1,043,171	662,553	380,618	259,648	259,648	....
1949...	1,194,287	863,054	371,233	304,238	304,238	....
1950...	917,208	596,613	314,595	306,758	306,758	....
1951...	963,190	562,286	400,904	282,863	282,863	....
1952 (prel.)...	1,055,772	628,800	436,972	315,865	315,865	....

¹ Not available. ³ Average for 1941, 1942 and 1945.

Source: Returns of the Navy Department to the Department of Commerce. See general note, p. 927.

34. Comparative International Statistics

The statistics of the various individual nations may be found primarily in the official publications or compendia, generally in the form of Yearbooks, issued by most of the nations at various intervals in their own national languages, expressed in their customary national units of measurement. For handier reference, especially for international comparisons, the Statistical Office of the United Nations compiles and issues a number of international summary publications, generally in English and French. Among these, the annual *Statistical Yearbook*, the annual *Demographic Yearbook*, and the *Monthly Bulletin of Statistics* may be most helpful for both general and special users. The Statistical Office of the United Nations also publishes a *Yearbook of International Trade Statistics* and the *National Income Statistics of Various Countries*. For international agricultural statistics, the outstanding source is the *Yearbook of Food and Agricultural Statistics* which is published by the Food and Agricultural Organization of the United Nations. These publications usually present data covering an extensive period of time, frequently up to 20 years.

The information shown in this section was obtained almost entirely from the *Statistical Yearbook, 1952*, a United Nations publication, prepared by the Statistical Office of the United Nations. To facilitate comparison in terms of familiar units, items shown in metric units in the source have been converted to U. S. equivalents by means of the conversion factors given in the *Statistical Yearbook* (see table of conversion factors, p. 945).

Countries and items shown.—Problems of space and availability (or nonavailability) of data are restrictive factors in this presentation of statistics for the various nations.

In particular, the space problem makes it necessary to limit the number of countries for which statistics are shown on a somewhat arbitrary basis. The list of countries included comprises all those who are members of the United Nations or are members of the larger agencies affiliated with the U. N. (see table 1108). In a few instances, such member countries were omitted because of an almost complete lack of data. Data for the Union of Soviet Socialist Republics have been included for those few items for which they were available. For the most part, however, official data for the U. S. S. R. have not been released since the prewar period.

Statistics are shown for a standardized list of countries. No attempt was made to vary the list according to the relative standing or significance of each country with respect to each specific subject item shown. In consequence, there may be instances, with respect to certain subject items shown, in which one or more of the countries omitted from the list are more important, statistically, than some of the countries included. However, cases of this kind are not believed to be numerous.

A high degree of selection also was necessary with respect to subject items included. The items shown here are believed to be among those more significant in reflecting the general industrial structure and the social level of a country.

Certain subject materials of basic import, such as those on national income, are omitted because of the inability to convert the available statistics, stated in terms of the national currencies, to meaningful consistency in United States measures. Finally, items for which figures are available for a large number of countries were favored over items for which information is scanty in order to broaden the scope of comparison as much as possible.

Note.—This section presents data for the most recent year or period available on May 20, 1953, when the material was organized and sent to the printer.

Quality and comparability of the data.—The quality and the comparability of the data presented here are affected by a number of factors which should be kept in mind:

(1) The data shown are for the latest year available for each country; the latest year, however, may vary from item to item for a particular country and within items for different countries. All such variations have been noted (see table headnotes) and should be taken into account. In most instances, the data shown are for calendar years. In a number of instances, however, the 12-month totals shown do not correspond with the calendar year. Problems of space unfortunately made it impracticable to present the data for a series of years.

(2) The bases, methods of estimating, methods of data collection, extent of coverage, precision of definition, scope of territory, and margins of error may vary from item to item within a particular country and within items for different countries. Footnotes and headnotes to the tables give some measure of the qualifications and differences attached to the figures. Again, the compelling limits of space made necessary some condensation and editing of the more detailed notes appearing in the source. The user is, therefore, cautioned to proceed with care in analysis and comparison, since, at best, many of the measures shown are merely rough indicators of magnitude.

(3) Figures shown in this section for the United States may not always agree with figures shown in the preceding sections. Such differences may be attributable to the use of differing original sources, a difference in the definition of geographic limits (continental United States only, or including certain territories and possessions), or to possible adjustments made in the United States figures by the United Nations in order to improve their comparability with figures from other countries.

Because of the many difficult problems inherent in bringing together summary statistics in this fashion, those readers who are interested in detailed comparisons should consult the publications of the United Nations mentioned above.

CONVERSION FACTORS

Metric units	U. S. equivalents
1 km	0.621370 mile
1 sq. km	0.386101 sq. mile
1 metric ton (1,000 kg.)	1.102311 short tons
1 passenger-km	0.621370 passenger-mile
1 ton-km	0.684943 short ton-mile

No. 1102.—MANUFACTURING, IMPORTS, EXPORTS, GOLD HOLDINGS, AND EXCHANGE RATES

[See text, p. 944, for general comments concerning quality of the data. Years for which data are shown may vary from column to column and from country to country. Figures which are set for the year shown in the "year" column are prefixed by a letter to indicate the year represented as follows: a represents 1950; b, 1949; c, 1948; d, 1947; e, 1946; f, 1945; g, 1944; h, 1943; i, 1942; j, 1941]

COUNTRY	Year	MANUFACTURING [1]		Imports [4]	Exports [4]	Gold holdings [5]	EXCHANGE RATES	
		Establishments [2]	Persons employed, total [3]				Unit	Average [6]
		Number	Thousands	Million dollars	Million dollars	Million dollars		
United States	1949		[7] 13, 567	[1][1] 6, 696	[1] 12, 074	24, 563	Dollar	
	1950	247, 300	[7] 14, 369	[1][1] 8, 962	[1] 10, 261	22, 820	do	
	1951			[1][1] 11, 071	[1] 15, 038	22, 873	do	
Afghanistan	1949			52	47			
Argentina	1951	e 84, 895	e 1, 171	d 1, 343	d 1, 613	266	Peso	20. 00-4. 95
Australia	1951	[10] 42, 693	921	[1] 1, 661	2, 199	112	Pound	224. 0
Austria	1951			657	451	5	Schilling	4. 685-3. 827
Belgium	1951			[11] 2, 528	[11] 2, 647	685	Franc	2. 000
Bolivia	1951	e 1, 144	e 16	b 78	151	23	Boliviano	1. 660-1. 009
Brazil	1951	e [11] 11, 180	e [13] 540	2, 011	1, 757	317	Cruzeiro	5. 405
Bulgaria	1950			d 74	d 86	j 35	Lev	.3460
Burma	1951	d [10] 473	[13] [14] 47	143	206			
Canada	1951	a 35, 942	a 1, 183	[1] [15] 3, 877	[15] 3, 766	842	Dollar	95. 00
Ceylon	1951			328	400			
Chile	1951	b [16] 4, 649	b [16] 176	329	372	45	Peso	5. 163-1. 667
China	1948			[17] 140	[17] 104	d 97	Yuan	5. 000-0. 833
Colombia	1951	f [16] 7, 853	f [16] 135	416	460	[19] 122	Peso	51. 28-52. 54
Costa Rica	1951			56	41	2	Colon	17. 64-12. 66
Cuba	1951			[1] 640	766	311	Peso	[20]
Czechoslovakia	1951	d 18, 193	d 1, 098	a [21] 516	a [21] 538	f 35	Koruna	2. 000
Denmark	1951	a [22] 7, 710	a [22] 302	1, 012	899	31	Krone	14. 45
Dominican Republic	1951	a 3, 412	a 48	[1] 48	108	12	Peso	[20]
Ecuador	1951			[1] 56	57	22	Sucre	6. 601-5. 620
Egypt	1951	e 133, 619	e 577	[23] 666	[23] 583	174	Pound	287. 2
El Salvador	1951			64	85	26	Colon	40 00
Ethiopia	1951			38	45			
Finland	1951	a 5, 479	a 290	676	813	26	Markka	.435
France	1951			[24] 4, 551	[24] 4, 175	547	Franc	.2857
Germany, Western	1951	[23] 48, 309	[23] 5, 332	3, 493	3, 465		D. mark	23. 81
Greece	1951		b 210	398	102	4	Drachma	.0067
Guatemala	1951	e [25] 757	e [25] 22	81	76	27	Quetzal	[20]
Haiti	1951			45	50			
Honduras	1951			[1] 39	[1] 27	0. 11	Lempira	[20]
Hungary	1950	d 4, 342	d 350	e 167	e 166	b 41	Forint	8. 519
Iceland	1951			57	45	1	Krona	6. 14
India	1951	b [15] 6, 753	b [15] 1, 692	[20] 1, 811	[20] 1, 504	247	Rupee	21. 00
Indonesia	1951			805	1, 259	280	Gulden	26. 30-5. 26
Iran	1951			223	350	138	Rial	3. 101-2. 116
Iraq	1951			143	[20] 82		Dinar	[20]
Ireland, Republic of	1951	a [15] 3, 331	a [15] 134	573	229	18	Pound	280. 0
Israel	1951			343	47		do	280. 0
Italy	1951	a 156, 223	a 3, 861	2, 119	1, 629	333	Lira	.1600
Japan	1951			2, 044	1, 355		Yen	.2778
Korea, South	1949	d [23] 3, 246	d [23] 201	139	14			
Lebanon	1951			136	41	26	Pound	45. 63-26. 91
Liberia	1950			8	27			
Luxembourg	1951		a 28	(11)	(11)		Franc	2. 000
Mexico	1951	g [23] 50, 894	g 559	[1] 760	573	207	Peso	11. 56
Netherlands	1951	a 116, 000	a 1, 013	2, 550	1, 948	316	Gulden	26. 32
New Zealand	1951	[24] 8, 178	[24] 142	579	693	32	Pound	280. 0
Nicaragua	1951			[1] 30	37	3	Cordoba	20. 00-14. 15
Norway	1951	a [15] 5, 964	a [15] [16] 250	[27] 878	[27] 620	50	Krone	14. 00
Pakistan	1951			[29] 518	[28] 529	27	Rupee	30. 22
Panama	1951			[1] [15] 66	[29] 12		Balboa	[20]
Paraguay	1951			[1] 33	31	0. 20	Guarani	16. 67-3. 69
Peru	1951	d [23] 2, 742	d [23] 125	261	255	46	Sol	6. 631-6. 588
Philippines	1951			[1] 480	410	7	Peso	[27]
Poland	1950	d [40] 28, 996	d [40] 1, 443	c 516	c 533	b 46	Zloty	1. 000-0. 250
Portugal	1951	a 16, 674	a 166	330	263	264	Escudo	3. 475
Romania	1950	d [41] 3, 834	d [41] 338			d 216	Leu	.6667
Spain	1951			384	462	51	Peseta	9. 132-2. 513
Sweden	1951	a [16] 16, 062	a [30] 777	1, 777	1, 779	152	Krona	19. 33
Switzerland	1951			1, 365	1, 082	1, 451	Franc	23. 07

See footnotes at end of table.

No. 1102.—Manufacturing, Imports, Exports, Gold Holdings, and Exchange
Rates—Continued

[See text, p. 944, for general comments concerning quality of the data. Years for which data are shown may vary from column to column and from country to country. Figures which are *not* for the year shown in the "year" column are prefixed by a letter to indicate the year represented as follows: a represents 1950; b, 1949; c, 1948; d, 1947; e, 1946; f, 1945; g, 1944; h, 1943; i, 1942; j, 1941]

COUNTRY	Year	MANUFACTURING		Imports	Exports	Gold holdings	EXCHANGE RATES	
		Establishments	Persons employed, total				Unit	Average
		Number	Thousands	Million dollars	Million dollars	Million dollars		
Syria	1951			134	127		Pound	a 45.69–26.15
Thailand	1951			d 112	d 98	119	Baht	8.000–4.646
Turkey	1951	a 98,826	h 264	462	314	151	Pound	35.71
Union of South Africa	1951	b 12,429	b 560	e 1,216	961	190	do	280.0
United Kingdom	1951	c 54,847	c 6,587	10,979	7,896	e 2,335	do	280.0
Uruguay	1951		f 77	316	236	221	Peso	65.63–60.52
Venezuela	1951			e 642	1,448	378	Bolivar	33.36–30.03
Yugoslavia	1951	c 1,042	c 338	342	184		Dinar	3.000
World total	1951			55 51,700	55 76,600			

1 Manufacturing relates to production (including repair work) in factories, and excludes mining, building and construction, and public utilities (gas, electricity and water supply).

2 In general, single plants or factories.

3 Includes wage earners and salaried employees and represents average number engaged on production (excluding sales and distribution staff). Salaried employees include working proprietors and directing, managing, clerical, and technical staff.

4 Figures expressed in United States dollars of gold content fixed on Jan. 31, 1934, and refer to merchandise, including silver, in all forms, excluding gold and issued paper currency. Imports are generally valued c. i. f.; exports, i. e. b. Postal and governmental trade are generally included; war reparations and restitutions are generally excluded. Figures for United States are for "general trade." For other countries, figures shown are not distinguished here as to "general trade" or "special trade." Roughly half the countries fall into each category; see source publication for distinction as to categories. Comparability between countries is undoubtedly affected by this distinction.

5 Refers to gross holdings of gold of central banks, treasuries, exchange stabilization funds, and other official institutions as of end of period indicated. Gold used in payment of subscriptions to International Monetary Fund or International Bank for Reconstruction and Development are not included. Gold holdings reported at 35 dollars per fine troy ounce. U. S. data refer to holdings of treasury, and gold in active portion of stabilization fund.

6 In U. S. cents per unit of foreign exchange. Represents domestic par values or basic official rates for single rate countries, and range of significant rates for countries employing multiple rates. For fluctuating or nearest rates, data represent annual averages. For administratively determined or nonfluctuating rates, data represent, for any given period during which a change occurred, the rate in effect for major portion of that period. The exchange rates shown are not necessarily those used to convert trade figures to U. S. dollars.

7 Includes distribution and construction employees on payrolls of manufacturing establishments.

8 Imports valued f. o. b.

9 United States customs area including Alaska, Hawaii, Puerto Rico.

10 Establishments employing 4 or more persons or using mechanical power.

11 Belgium and Luxembourg combined.

12 Establishments in 22 State capitals having annual sales of not less than 100,000 cruzeiros.

13 Factories employing 20 or more wage earners.

14 Wage earners. 15 Includes Newfoundland.

16 Establishments having a capital of 100,000 pesos or more or production exceeding 200,000 pesos.

17 January to October.

18 Establishments employing 6 or more wage earners and with products valued at 5,000 pesos or more.

19 Gold and net foreign exchange.

20 Currency maintained at par with U. S. dollar.

21 January to September.

22 Establishments employing 6 or more wage earners. Excludes dairies and bacon factories but includes their preserving and canning plants. Persons employed exclude home workers and working proprietors but include canteen and sales staff.

23 Excludes trade with Anglo-Egyptian Sudan.

24 Includes flour.

25 Establishments employing 10 or more persons. Includes flour.

26 Establishments employing 5 or more persons.

27 Currency maintained at 2 units per United States dollar.

28 Reporting establishments employing 20 or more wage earners and using power. Persons employed includes distribution staff of salaried workers.

29 Excludes land trade.

30 Excludes pipe-line exports of crude petroleum.

31 Establishments employing 3 or more wage earners.

32 Includes public utilities.

33 Includes mining.

34 Establishments employing 2 or more persons or using mechanical power.

35 Establishments whose wage earners were employed a total of 12,000 hours or more during the year.

36 Excludes working proprietors.

37 Includes Svalbard.

38 Excludes Panama Canal Zone and national exports to the zone.

39 Registered establishments.

40 Establishments employing 5 or more wage earners. Includes mining.

41 Establishments employing more than 10 wage earners or having an installed capacity of more than 20 hp.

42 Quotations for Syria and Lebanon.

43 Excludes establishments in villages with 500 or less population.

44 Establishments employing 3 or more persons, using any form of mechanical power or using boilers for producing steam.

45 Excludes Northern Ireland. Establishments employing 10 or more persons.

46 Includes sales and distribution staff.

47 Includes United States and Canadian dollar holdings of the Exchange Equalization Account.

48 Excludes electrical products, precision instruments, and miscellaneous industries.

49 Establishments employing 20 or more wage earners or having an installed capacity of 20 hp. or more.

55 World totals exclude trade of Bulgaria, China, Hungary, Romania, U. S. S. R. and Eastern Germany.

Source: Statistical Office of the United Nations Statistical Yearbook, 1952.

No. 1103.—FARM CROPS, MEAT, AND NET FOOD SUPPLY

[Crop production data pertain to harvests of the year indicated (or to harvests continuing into the first half of the following year for Southern Hemisphere and southerly regions of Northern Hemisphere). Meat production data pertain to calendar year. See text, p. 944, for general comments concerning quality of the data. Years for which data are shown may vary from column to column and from country to country. Figures which are not for the year shown in the "year" column are prefixed by a letter to indicate the year represented, as follows: a represents 1950; b, 1949; c, 1948; d, 1947]

COUNTRY	PRODUCTION OF FARM CROPS AND MEAT (thousands of short tons)								NET FOOD SUPPLY PER PERSON [1]	
	Year	Wheat	Rye	Rice	Corn	Potatoes	Sugar [1]	Meat [2]	Year	Calories per day
United States.......	1949	34, 237	525	2, 037	94, 623	12, 347	2, 189	10. 651	1948–49	3, 140
	1950	30, 583	595	1, 935	85, 618	12, 897	2, 488	10, 832	1949–50	3, 170
	1951	29, 625	600	2, 190	82, 359	9, 771	1, 942	11, 040	1950–51	3, 210
Argentina...........	1951	2, 260	96	211	2, 194	1, 378	718	a 1, 305	1948–49	3, 190
Australia...........	1951	4, 785		56	112	473	a 1, 106	a 1, 125	1950–51	3, 290
Austria.............	1951	377	368		152	2, 380	186	4 216	1950–51	2, 740
Belgium............	1951	567	225			2, 222	293	a 335	1950–51	5 2, 990
Brazil..............	1951	467		3, 053	6, 945	796	2, 183	a 6 71, 351	1948–49	2, 340
Bulgaria...........	1951						68			
Burma.............	1951			6, 063					1947–48	1, 980
Canada............	1951	16, 580	494		430	1, 451	133	958	1950–51	3, 290
Ceylon.............	1951			347					1950–51	2, 060
Chile...............	1951	1, 089		88		521		a 184	1948–49	2, 330
China..............	1951	9 23, 652		9 953, 242	6 6, 963	b 9 1, 918	10 441			
Colombia...........	1951	140		351	820	a 397	a 203	a 369	1948–49	2, 290
Costa Rica.........	1951			36						
Cuba..............	1951			127	306		7, 964		1948–49	2, 730
Czechoslovakia......	1950	1, 698	1, 257		259	6, 267	882	b 320	1948–49	2, 660
Denmark...........	1951	301	298			2, 152	396	a 4 11 579	1950–51	3, 130
Dominican Republic.	1951			77	108		648			
Ecuador...........	1951			116		a 52				
Egypt.............	1951	1, 333		683	1, 566	192	220		1949–50	2, 300
El Salvador........	1951			29						
Ethiopia...........	1951	99			165					
Finland............	1951	276	228			1, 633			1950–51	3, 210
France.............	1951	7, 844	540		761	14, 815	1, 360	a 2, 095	1950–51	2, 790
Germany, Western.	1951	3, 251	3, 344			26, 569	12 2, 023	a 1, 543	1950–51	2, 810
Greece.............	1951	1, 025	53		243	455			1950–51	2, 570
Guatemala.........	1949				417					
Haiti..............	1951						64			
Honduras..........	1950			11	418					
Hungary...........	1951	a 2, 249	a 871		c 3, 155	b 2, 116	281			
Iceland............	1950							9	1948–49	3, 230
India..............	1951	7, 381		34, 542	2, 223	a 1, 824	13 1, 841		1950–51	1, 570
Indonesia..........	1951			7, 244	1, 764		471			
Iran...............	1951	1, 984		397			76			
Iraq...............	1951	717		198						
Ireland, Rep. of.....	1951	278				3, 097	104	a 161	1950–51	3, 500
Israel.............	1951	15							1949–50	2, 680
Italy..............	1951	7, 610	134	804	3, 031	3, 106	827	a 563	1950–51	2, 400
Japan.............	1951	1, 642		12, 458		2, 832	61	a 7 150	1950–51	2, 100
Korea, South.......	1951			2, 320		a 209				
Luxembourg........	1951					139		a 18		(1)
Mexico............	1951	408		165	3, 748	143	762			
Netherlands........	1951	296	505			4, 184	383	a 353	1950–51	3, 090
New Zealand.......	1951	120				94		a 623	1950–51	3, 430
Norway............	1951					1, 119		a 112	1950–51	3, 180
Pakistan...........	1951	4, 427		13, 007	443				1948–49	2, 020
Panama............	1951			94						
Paraguay..........	1950				110					
Peru..............	1951	173		237		1, 461	551			
Philippines.........	1951			3, 121	840		14 1, 080	a 149		

See footnotes at end of table.

No. 1103.—FARM CROPS, MEAT, AND NET FOOD SUPPLY—Continued

[See text, p. 944, for general comments concerning quality of the data. Years for which data are shown may vary from column to column and from country to country. Figures which are *not* for the year shown in the "year" column are prefixed by a letter to indicate the year represented, as follows: a represents 1950; b, 1949; c, 1948; d, 1947]

COUNTRY	PRODUCTION OF FARM CROPS AND MEAT (thousands of short tons)								NET FOOD SUPPLY PER PERSON [3]	
	Year	Wheat	Rye	Rice	Corn	Potatoes	Sugar [1]	Meat [2]	Year	Calories per day
Poland	1951	2,513	a 7,167			a 40,604	1,213		1948–49	2,620
Portugal	1951	666	219	141	466	1,333		a 83		
Romania	1951				d 5,819		143			
Spain	1951	4,702	562	314	700	4,409	355	a 476		
Sweden	1951	526	193			1,936	333	a 321	1950–51	3,240
Switzerland	1951	258				1,067		195	1950–51	3,250
Syria	1951	545								
Thailand	1951			7,992						
Turkey	1951	6,173	661	118	935	745	228	a 97	1950–51	2,510
Union of South Africa	1951	761			1,893	265	592	a 15 464	1950–51	2,640
United Kingdom	1951	2,594	53			9,278	743	a 1,246	1950–51	3,100
Uruguay	1951	521		51	306			a 438	1949–50	2,920
Venezuela	1951			a 35	a 398		60		1949–50	2,210
Yugoslavia	1951	2,510	305		4,446	1,787	246			
World total [10]	1951	157,190	21,385	166,669	145,505	168,213	35,605			

[1] Beet and cane. Figures expressed generally in terms of raw sugar. Most of series relate to a crop year beginning September of year shown.
[2] In terms of carcass weight; refers to beef and veal (including buffalo meat), pork (including bacon and ham), mutton, lamb (including goat meat). Excludes lard, tallow, and edible offals. Figures relate to commercial and farm slaughter.
[3] Represents net supply of foodstuffs, other than alcoholic beverages, available at retail level for human consumption within the country.
[4] Includes offals.
[5] Belgium and Luxembourg combined.
[6] Includes fat.
[7] Commercial slaughter only.
[8] 22 provinces.
[9] Includes Manchuria.
[10] Excludes Formosa and Manchuria.
[11] Includes allowance for export of live animals.
[12] Includes Eastern and Western Germany.
[13] Includes Pakistan.
[14] Centrifugal sugar only.
[15] Excludes meat from animals slaughtered in villages.
[16] Excludes U. S. S. R.

Source: Statistical Office of the United Nations; *Statistical Yearbook, 1952.*

No. 1104.—ELECTRIC ENERGY, COAL, PETROLEUM, IRON ORE, STEEL, AND CEMENT

[See text, p. 944, for general comments concerning quality of the data. Years for which data are shown may vary from column to column and from country to country. Figures which are *not* for the year shown in the "year" column are prefixed by a letter to indicate the year represented, as follows: a represents 1950; b, 1949; c, 1948; d, 1947; e, 1946; f, 1945; g, 1944; h, 1943; i, 1942; j, 1941]

COUNTRY	Year	ENERGY			PRODUCTION (thousand short tons)				
		Installed capacity of electric energy [1]	Production of electric energy [1]	Consumption of commercial sources of energy expressed in terms of coal [2]	Coal [3]	Crude petroleum [4]	Iron ore [5] (Iron content)	Steel [6]	Cement [7]
		Thousand kw	*Million kwh*	*Thousand short tons*					
United States.......	1949	76,570	345,066	1,137,640	477,478	278,136	[8] 47,717	77,977	39,616
	1950	82,851	388,674	1,256,409	557,019	296,013	[8] 54,351	96,836	42,686
	1951	90,128	435,649	1,364,617	573,185	338,928	[8] 65,462	105,134	46,403
Argentina............	1951	e 1,444	[9] 4,718	16,946	44	3,902			1,722
Australia............	1951	[9] 2,478	10,503	29,826	19,721		1,634	1,574	1,382
Austria.............	1951	2,070	7,375	13,900	216	2,535	829	1,133	1,626
Belgium.............	1951	3,170	9,496	[10] 41,201	32,702		31	5,590	4,845
Bolivia.............	1951		a 175	440		75			b 46
Brazil.............	1951	a 1,883	[11] 2,988	13,970	2,138	99	a 1,489	913	1,541
Bulgaria............	1950		d [9] 480	2,390	c	360			f 270
Burma.............	1951			443		107	j 15		
Canada.............	1951	a [9] 9,960	[9] 57,400	[11] 107,428	16,342	6,819	[11][12] 2,605	3,567	2,982
Ceylon.............	1951	42	[14] 108	567					
Chile.............	1951		[9] 1,682	5,962	[12] 2,437	107	2,162	196	769
China.............	1950			443	c [16] 15,212	[17] 3	e [16] 13	[16] 18	d [16] 836
Colombia............	1951		[16] 743	3,578	[36] 590	5,961			714
Costa Rica..........	1951			209					
Cuba.............	1951	[9] 168	[9] 836	3,131		20	a 1		421
Czechoslovakia.....	1951		a 9,100	a 41,061	19,731	105	582	[21] 3,651	b 1,916
Denmark...........	1951	1,076	2,410	9,879				181	1,086
Dominican Republic	1951		[9] 96	239					a 79
Ecuador...........	1951		a 118	442		392			87
Egypt.............	1951			5,362		2,571			1,246
El Salvador.........	1951			205					
Ethiopia............	1951			53					
Finland............	1951	1,284	4,423	5,788				147	914
France.............	1951	15,900	[9] 36,024	[22] 109,042	[23] 58,388	324	12,621	[22] 10,838	[22] 9,211
Germany, Western..	1951	[9] 7,822	51,355	157,432	131,092	1,507	3,829	14,888	13,460
Greece............	1951	[9] 223	[9] 790	2,241			29		457
Guatemala..........	1951		[9] 79	467					63
Haiti.............	1951			79					
Honduras...........	1951			258					
Hungary............	1951		e [9] 1,162	a 10,032	1,653	551	110	1,323	220
Iceland............	1951	[9] 44	[9] 210	379					
India.............	1951	2,409	5,852	41,089	38,424	e 332	2,616	1,680	3,579
Indonesia..........	1951	k	[9] 364	4,760	956	8,207			c 42
Iran.............	1951			331		[22] 18,567			
Iraq.............	1951		a [14] 38	1,054		9,205			
Ireland, Republic of.	1951	[9] 266	[9] 1,009	4,019	195				477
Israel.............	1951	139	[9][25] 558	1,371					484
Italy.............	1951	8,788	29,223	41,495	1,286	20	288	3,376	[26] 6,149
Japan.............	1951	[27] 10,808	[27] 47,729	81,014	47,743	370	522	7,167	7,219
Korea, South........	1951		314		123		f [28] 371	1	8
Lebanon............	1951		a 114	[29] 854					334
Liberia............	1950		13	31					
Luxembourg........	1951	146	810	(10)			1,861	3,392	146
Mexico.............	1951	a 1,235	4,896	19,192	1,217	12,102	345	499	1,780
Netherlands	1951	c 2,275	7,816	23,253	13,695	787		611	774
New Zealand........	1951	[9] 725	[9] 3,450	5,025	758		3		166
Nicaragua..........	1951			132					c 13
Norway............	1951	3,156	17,663	16,656	518		[30] 276	96	794
Pakistan............	1951		222	3,943	[16] 567	168			559
Panama............	1951	[31] 20	[31] 88	294					

See footnotes at end of table.

No. 1104.—ELECTRIC ENERGY, COAL, PETROLEUM, IRON ORE, STEEL, AND CEMENT—Continued

[See text, p. 944, for general comments concerning quality of the data. Years for which data are shown may vary from column to column and from country to country. Figures which are not for the year shown in the "year" column are prefixed by a letter to indicate the year represented, as follows: a represents 1950; b, 1949; c, 1948; d, 1947; e, 1946; f, 1945; g, 1944; h, 1943; i, 1942; j, 1941]

COUNTRY	Year	ENERGY		Consumption of commercial sources of energy expressed in terms of coal [3]	PRODUCTION (thousand short tons)				
		Installed capacity of electric energy [1]	Production of electric energy [1]		Coal [4]	Crude petroleum [4]	Iron ore [5] (iron content)	Steel [6]	Cement [7]
		Thousand kw	Million kwh	Thousand short tons					
Paraguay	1951		b 26	44					262
Peru	1951		b 287	1,781	220	2,368			346
Philippines	1951	c 167	b 497	2,302	168		526		343
Poland	1951		11,100	57,540	90,331	216	c 736	b 3,075	2,952
Portugal	1951	555	1,043	2,607	460				706
Romania	1951		a 2,100	8,090	381	7,360	237	712	302
Spain	1951	2,362	b 6,367	16,807	12,492		1,361	896	3,461
Sweden	1951	5,065	19,582	27,456	308		10,362	b 1,658	3,249
Switzerland	1951		12,347	13,153			80		1,485
Syria	1951		b 57	(20)					42
Thailand	1951	a 22	b 80	491					261
Turkey	1951	424	894	6,402	5,214	31	156	140	437
Union of South Africa	1951	a 2,405	11,660	b 30,436	26,337		844	1,110	2,184
United Kingdom	1951	b c 16,595	b c 61,537	269,084	a 946,653	81	4,922	17,515	11,449
Uruguay	1951		d c 396	1,896				c	366
U.S.S.R.	1951		c 104,600		c 313,065	c 46,625		c 34,802	e
Venezuela	1951		b 618	4,760	c 31	96,125	506		685
Yugoslavia	1951	a c 775	c 2,540	7,203	1,096	172	306	475	1,278
World total	1951	c 953,000	b c 2,746,187	c 1,395,707	c 606,271	c 121,916	c 195,211	c 140,604

[1] Includes utilities (publicly and privately owned plants supplying energy to consumers), plus industrial, transport and other plants generating electricity primarily for their own use. Capacity represents nominal power of all generators available for simultaneous operation in hydroelectric and thermoelectric plants.

[2] Figures are provisional and refer to gross inland consumption of mineral fuels and water power. Computed mainly from data on production, trade and processing of major sources of energy, with allowance for, as far as possible, changes in stocks, and fuels loaded in bunkers of vessels and aircraft in international trade. Production data employed cover coal and lignite; petroleum, shale oil, natural gasoline and, when available, motor alcohol; natural gas; and hydroelectric power. Trade data include foregoing and derivatives: briquettes, coke (including petroleum coke), motor spirit (petrol, gasoline), kerosene, fuel oils, and, when available, benzol; manufactured and bottled gas; and electric power. In calculating consumption, duplication has been eliminated in all cases. Fuel wood and other vegetal fuels and peat omitted for want of adequate data although believed to provide a major share of energy supply in all but a few countries. Minimum amount of energy obtained from each source estimated, for most countries, as equivalent to about 0.25 ton of coal per capita per annum.

[3] Anthracite and bituminous coal (including semibituminous). Excludes lignite and brown coal.

[4] Excludes natural gasoline and shale oil. In many cases figures represent conversions from original data expressed in units of capacity.

[5] Including manganiferous iron ores but excluding pyrites. Data are sometimes only rough estimates obtained by applying a fixed percentage to figures for production of crude ore.

[6] Total production of crude steel, both ingots and steel for castings, whether obtained from pig iron or scrap. Excludes wrought (puddled) iron.

[7] Covers, as far as possible, both natural and artificial (portland, etc.) cements.

[8] Excludes manganiferous iron ore.

[9] Public utility plants only.

[10] Luxembourg combined with Belgium.

[11] Consumption in cities of Rio de Janeiro and São Paulo.

[12] Includes Newfoundland.

[13] Shipments.

[14] Plants under Government control only.

[15] Includes lignite.

[16] Excludes Formosa and Manchuria.

[17] Formosa only.

[18] Excludes Manchuria.

[19] Production by 3 principal enterprises.

[20] Partial production only; coal transported by rail.

[21] Includes wrought (puddled) iron.

[22] Excludes Saar.

[23] Production of the Anglo-Iranian Oil Co.

[24] Consumption in Baghdad.

[25] Sales.

[26] About 90 percent of total production.

[27] Excludes private plants of less than 500 kw.

[28] All of Korea, North and South.

[29] Syria combined with Lebanon.

[30] Includes ferro-titanium.

[31] Cities of Panama and Colon.

[32] Consumption in cities of Lima and Callao.

[33] Manila only.

[34] Crude ore.

[35] Ingots and finished castings for February-December.

[36] Ingots and finished castings.

[37] Includes Basutoland, Bechuanaland, Swaziland and South West Africa.

[38] Great Britain only; includes production of railway and transport stations.

[39] Great Britain only. Excludes coal produced at quarries but includes open-cast coal.

[40] Estimated by Economic Commission for Europe.

[41] U.S.S.R. (excludes Sakhalin) estimated by Economic Commission for Europe. Includes lignite.

[42] Production in States of Guerrero and Yucatan.

[43] Plants with installed capacity of 100 kw. or more.

[44] Excludes U.S.S.R. and China.

[45] Excludes U.S.S.R., China, and Korea.

[46] Excludes U.S.S.R.

[47] Excludes China, Manchuria, and U.S.S.R.

Source: Statistical Office of the United Nations, Statistical Yearbook, 1952.

No. 1105.—TRANSPORTATION—SHIPPING, RAILWAY TRAFFIC, CIVIL AVIATION, AND MOTOR VEHICLES

[See text, p. 944, for general comments concerning quality of the data. Years for which data are shown may vary from column to column and from country to country. Figures which are *not* for the year shown in the "year" column are prefixed by a letter to indicate the year represented, as follows: a represents 1950; b, 1949; c, 1948; d, 1947; e, 1946]

COUNTRY	Year	SHIPPING				RAILWAY TRAFFIC [4]		Civil aviation: Miles flown [5]	Motor vehicles in use [6]
		Merchant shipping fleets [1]	Vessels entered [2]	Freight loaded [3]	Freight unloaded [3]	Passenger miles	Short ton miles		
		Thousand gross tons	*Thousand net tons*	*Thousand short tons*	*Thousand short tons*	*Millions*	*Millions*	*Thousands*	*Thousands*
United States	1949	[7] 27,814	[8] 59,360	[9] 71,865	[9] 77,871	35,133	529,111	459,022	44,129
	1950	[7] 27,513	[8] 66,792	[9] 62,685	[9] 96,704	31,790	591,550	471,617	48,549
	1951	[7] 27,331	[8] 70,280	[9] 115,586	[9] 100,545	34,618	646,607	520,574	51,291
Argentina	1951	979	[10] 9,246	6,273	13,008	8,690	11,685	9,196	348
Australia	1951	554	8,200	7,021	13,153	[11] 7,030	[12] 51,531	1,534
Austria	1951					[12] 2,904	[13] 5,021		100
Belgium	1951	493	21,958	16,101	18,791	4,507	4,540	[14] 9,391	452
Bolivia	1951					b 86	b 186	1,678	[15] 12
Brazil	1951	688		[16] 5,348	[16] 12,119	6,462	[17][16] 5,609	51,958	[a] 298
Bulgaria	1947					1,568	846		
Burma	1951		1,688	a 1,142	a 618	206	[19] 137		20
Canada	1951	[20] 1,647		[21] 27,280	[21] 38,269	[22] 3,085	[22] 64,071	32,719	[22] 2,557
Ceylon	1951		7,857	790	2,351			1,444	56
Chile	1951	168		5,841	2,576	1,128	[23] 1,622	[24] 3,041	79
China	1951	633				e 9,443	[23] 3,514	[25] 14,396	[d] 35
Colombia	1951		[16] 6,861	4,815	1,221	a 491	[17] 421	[26] 21,748	[a] 64
Costa Rica	1951		[16] 1,472	[27] 375	[27] 292	31	31		8
Cuba	1951	b 36	[28] 6,392	8,135	4,893	347	795	5,046	123
Czechoslovakia	1949					11,587	[19] 8,904	3,098	168
Denmark	1951	1,344	[29] 9,519	2,603	13,215	a 2,051	a 887	4,664	185
Dominican Republic	1951			864	360				a 8
Ecuador	1951			525	190	83	[19] 82		12
Egypt	1951	92		b [31] 2,332	b [31] 3,963	a 1,538	a 1,026	2,849	85
El Salvador	1951		[19][39] 1,569	[37] 109	[37] 477				a 9
Finland	1951	552	3,597	8,297	6,103	a 1,401	3,216	1,668	71
France	1951	3,367	42,033	[33] 24,916	45,125	[13] 17,460	[13] 31,096	[33] 30,013	[34] 605
Germany, Western	1951	1,031	22,860	11,164	22,567	[33] 18,624	[13] 37,714		1,501
Greece	1951	1,277	[16] 4,528	500	3,880	[34] 478	[19] [35] 151		31
Guatemala	1948								9
Haiti	1950								4
Honduras	1951	508							
Hungary	1949					3,262	c [19] 2,245	c [37] 626	[d] 48
Iceland	1951								11
India	1951	452	9,360			a 40,052	a [13] 30,249	19,493	[39] 283
Indonesia	1951			[39][39] 9,868	[39] 2,798			5,704	[19] 60
Iran	1951							744	
Iraq	1951		b [40] 980			b 322	b [17] 451	593	[a] 19
Ireland, Rep. of	1951		7,498				[19] [41] 353	3,288	132
Israel	1951		[19] 2,191	[43] 230	[43] 1,754		[19] 71	741	27
Italy	1951	[43] 2,917	a [44] 19,968	[43] 5,882	[43] 30,321	[13] 12,915	[13] [17] 7,671		[47] 169
Japan	1951	[46] 2,182	[10] 14,449	[46] 4,087	[46] 23,281	[11] 47,875	[11] 25,261		16
Korea, South	1949		[19] 369			1,678	753		16
Lebanon	1951		[10][31][46] 2,921	[49] 248	[49] 1,004	3	31		17
Liberia	1950		b [10][31][41] 356	56	76				1
Luxembourg	1951					144	[17] 401		16
Mexico	1951	168	a 1,597	4,273	1,166	2,082	[19] 6,523	a 26,053	[a] 267
Netherlands	1951	3,235	28,045	[50] 15,190	[50] 37,751	3,909	[17] 2,230	23,218	[39] 368
New Zealand	1951	232	2,316	1,365	4,361		1,197	7,199	344
Nicaragua	1951					c 60	c 13	994	[c] 2
Norway	1951	5,816	5,425			[51] 982	[17] 963	5,550	129
Pakistan	1951		4,454			6,118	3,407		25
Panama	1951	3,609							[b] 12
Paraguay	1948								3
Peru	1951	91		a 1,985	a 711	a 150	[19] 276	a 6,166	[a] 59
Philippines	1951			3,443	2,907	258	95	7,159	[19] 95
Poland	1951	237	a [16] 7,250	a [53][54] 13,727	a [53] 3,544	a 16,375	a 21,918	b 1,492	[c] 53
Portugal	1951	492	[16] 6,372	[50] 920	[50] 1,516	897	401	1,184	96
Romania	1947	33				[53] 3,378	2,642		
Spain	1951	1,216	7,361	6,462	5,082	[51] 4,526	4,799	5,215	[55] 179
Sweden	1951	2,113	21,884	[55] 16,723	[55] 21,774	4,044	6,863	[55] 7,332	410

See footnotes at end of table.

No. 1105.—TRANSPORTATION—SHIPPING, RAILWAY TRAFFIC, CIVIL AVIATION, AND MOTOR VEHICLES—Continued

[See text, p. 944, for general comments concerning quality of the data. Years for which data are shown may vary from column to column and from country to country. Figures which are not for the year shown in the "year" column are prefixed by a letter to indicate the year represented, as follows: a represents 1950; b, 1949; c, 1948; d, 1947; e, 1946]

COUNTRY	Year	SHIPPING				RAILWAY TRAFFIC		Civil aviation: Miles flown	Motor vehicles in use
		Merchant shipping fleets	Vessels entered	Freight loaded	Freight unloaded	Passenger-miles	Short ton miles		
		Thousand gross tons	Thousand net tons	Thousand short tons	Thousand short tons	Millions	Millions	Thousands	Thousands
Switzerland	1951		a 1,349			a 3,904	a 10 1,527	6,458	20 212
Thailand	1951					1,123	367	1,381	15
Turkey	1951	424	a 10 21 4,290			21 1,402	17 21 1,982		27
Union of South Africa	1951	10 527	2,004	3,599	7,154		17 23 12,783	6,482	625
United Kingdom	1951	e 12,550	62,579			25 30,799	52 54 55,680	11 53,992	22 3,458
Uruguay	1949					c 221	53 367		76
Venezuela	1951	167	b 6,654	92,992	2,148			16,534	136
Yugoslavia	1951	229		2,000	1,480	4,709	53 5,982		25
World total	1951	87,345		705,479			1,446,000		

1 Figures relate to merchant fleets on June 30. They are given in gross registered tons (100 cubic feet or 2.83 cubic meters) and represent total volume of all permanently enclosed spaces of vessels to which figures refer. Only vessels of 100 gross tons and over are included. Excludes vessels without mechanical means of propulsion, but includes sailing vessels with auxiliary power. Excludes the following classes of ships, not entered in Lloyd's Register: Ships trading on Caspian Sea; wooden or composite ships trading on Great Lakes of North America.

2 In general, represents sum of net registered tonnage of seagoing foreign and domestic merchant vessels (power and sailing) entered with cargo to a foreign port and refer to only 1 entrance for each foreign voyage including foreign commerce on inland waterways, such as Great Lakes. Excludes, if possible, "in ballast," i. e. entering without unloading goods.

3 Represents weight of all goods (including its packing) in external trade loaded to and unloaded from seagoing vessels of all flags at ports of country in question. Excludes mail, bullion, specie, passengers' baggage, bunkers, ships' stores, ballast, floating appliances when delivered as goods without being loaded on other ships, government stores when carried in government vessels or without revenue in merchant vessels, and transshipment (goods transshipped from an importing vessel to an exporting vessel). Includes goods unloaded into or landed from bonded warehouses.

4 Relates to domestic and international traffic on all railway lines within each country shown except railways entirely within an urban unit and plantation, industrial, mining, funicular and cable railways. Passenger miles include all passengers except military, government and railway personnel when carried without revenue; ton miles relate to freight net ton miles and include all goods whether carried by fast or ordinary trains except service traffic, mail, baggage and nonrevenue government stores.

5 Covers both domestic and international scheduled services operated by companies registered in each country. Includes supplementary services occasioned by overflow traffic on regularly scheduled trips and preparatory flights for new scheduled services.

6 For years in which a census or registration took place, census or registration figure is shown; for other years officially estimated number of vehicles in use is shown. Includes passenger cars and commercial vehicles. Excludes trams, trolley-buses, special and government service vehicles, motorcycles, trailers, farm and road tractors.

7 Includes Great Lakes. 8 Includes Alaska, Hawaii, Puerto Rico, Virgin Islands.

9 Excludes international traffic in Great Lakes. Based on special Treasury and Department of Defense imports and exports and commodities classified as "special category."

10 Including vessels in ballast.
11 Government railways.

12 Joint United Kingdom-Australia service of QEA includes some duplication. 13 State railways.
14 Operations of Sabena in Belgian Congo included.
15 Government vehicles included.
16 Excluding goods to and from bonded warehouse.
17 Excluding livestock.
18 Including nonrevenue traffic.
19 Including service traffic.
20 Including vessels trading on Great Lakes (701,947 gross tons).
21 Great Lakes traffic included.
22 Including Newfoundland.
23 Gross. 24 Lines Aeres Nacional only.
25 Nonscheduled operations of Civil Air Transport included.
26 Nonrevenue traffic and nonscheduled flights included.
27 Total imports and exports. 28 All entrances counted.
29 International ferry traffic excluded. 30 Danish share of Scandinavian Airways System included.
31 Including coastwise traffic.
32 Including bunkers and ships' stores.
33 Traffic of Air France only.
34 Commercial vehicles only.
35 Excluding occupation traffic.
36 Excluding "Franco-Hellenique" lines.
37 Domestic traffic of Hungarian line and foreign lines on Budapestvecsei; foreign traffic of annexined foreign lines.
38 Special service vehicles included.
39 Federal area only. 40 Principal port only.
41 2 principal railways, including some lines in North Ireland. 42 Excluding petroleum.
43 Including Trieste. 44 Excluding Trieste.
45 Excludes wooden or composite ships with auxiliary power under 300 tons.
46 Goods carried by steel vessels. Excluding military goods. 47 Small size vehicles excluded.
48 All entrances counted.
49 Port of Beirut only.
50 Including floating appliances when delivered as goods without being loaded on ships.
51 Excluding suburban traffic. 52 Taxis included.
53 Excluding live animals. 54 Including bunkers.
55 Including Canary Islands and Spanish Morocco.
56 Swedish portion of SAS included.
57 Includes nonmilitary government vehicles.
58 Foreign vessels only. 59 Main line railways.
60 Including British Colonies (except Hong Kong) and British dependencies (70 percent of gross tonnage).
61 Including South-West Africa and Vryburg-Bulawayo line of Rhodesia railways.
62 Including tonnage on bare boat charter from U. S. A. and Canada.
63 Excluding Northern Ireland.
64 Includes service trains carried on revenue-earning trains.

Source: Statistical Office of the United Nations; Statistical Yearbook, 1955.

No. 1106.—COMMUNICATIONS—TELEPHONES, TELEGRAMS, MAIL, NEWSPAPERS, AND RADIO

[See text, p. 944, for general comments concerning quality of the data. Years for which data are shown may vary from column to column and from country to country. Figures which are *not* for the year shown in the "year" column are prefixed by a letter to indicate the year represented, as follows: ∞ represents 1951; a, 1950; b, 1949; c, 1948; d, 1947; e, 1946; f, 1945; g, 1944; h, 1943; i, 1942]

COUNTRY	Year	Telephones in use [1]	Telegrams sent, domestic [2]	Letters sent, domestic [3]	NEWSPAPERS			RADIO (WIRELESS)	
					Dailies [4]	Circulation		Transmitting stations [5]	Receiving sets [6]
						Total	Copies per 1,000 population		
		Number	*Thousands*	*Thousands*	*Number*	*Thousands*		*Number*	*Thousands*
United States	1949	40,665,000	f 174,343					g 4,085	
	1950	43,004,000	f 175,077					g 4,510	
	1951				f 1,773	54,000	356		10 105,000
Afghanistan	1950				4	14	1		10 5
Albania	1948								48
Argentina	1951	a 796,391	b 22,604	1,493,000	b 180	b 3,460	b 207		10 11 1,500
Australia	1952	a 1,109,984	a 35,486	∞ 1,376,000	54	3,600	455	e 153	∞ 2,257
Austria	1952	a 412,989		∞ 826,049	34	1,486	214	e 42	a 1,027
Belgium	1952	a 687,012	a 4,890	∞ 1,819,000	49	2,850	313	e 13	a 1,627
Bolivia	1949				9	56	14		10 180
Brazil	1950			c 1,794,000	b 220	b 1,500	b 30	d 178	731
Bulgaria	1950	59,000	d 5,575	d 527,724	9	717	100		e 270
Burma	1952				32	153	8		b 11
Canada	1951	a 2,911,900	a 11 18,113	a 11 2,707,000	95	a 3,889	287	d 161	2,221
Ceylon	1952	a 16,860		228,343	7	300	39	a 2	10 51
Chile	1949			118,828	39	450	79		10 556
China	1948		d 18,424	d 1,028,000		4,500	10		10 900
Colombia	1950				37	605	53		10 500
Costa Rica	1952				5	78	97		10 22
Cuba	1949				c 33	c 448	c 87		11 573
Czechoslovakia	1951	385,000	a 5,368	a 800,766	a 20	a 2,400	a 193	d 15	2,545
Denmark	1952	721,821	a 11 1,914	b 336,415	131	1,650	386	a 6	∞ 1,229
Dominican Republic	1952				5	54	25	d 26	a 11 35
Ecuador	1950				c 25	c 85	c 26		10 50
Egypt	1952	a 115,500	d 2,796	∞ 155,583	50	515	25		a 234
El Salvador	1950				9	68	32		10 21
Ethiopia	1950								11 5
Finland	1952	a 328,394	a 722	∞ 142,348	64	1,100	274	a 15	757
France	1952	a 2,405,802	a 18 16,516	b 14 2,827,000	135	9,800	231	a 15 81	e 7,297
Germany, Western	1951	a 2,393,013	a 21,501	a 4,149,000					120	10,040
Greece	1952	a 82,101	a 4,915	∞ 126,794	68	550	72		e 229
Guatemala	1951				a 6	a 50	a 18		31
Haiti	1952	a 3,059			6	10	3	a 11	4
Honduras	1952				5	30	20		11 25
Hungary	1951	116,000	d 3,264	d 380,000	b 20	b 834	b 90	d 5	701
Iceland	1952			a 6,288	5	65	455		a 35
India	1952	a 168,397	a 22,605		578	3,000	8	a 25	e 650
Indonesia	1952	a 43,000	a 1,790	b 80,649	95	570	7	a 15	a 193
Iran	1950		4,825	∞ 32,799	20	100	5		194
Iraq	1952			h 8,030	54	108	21		b 30
Ireland, Republic of	1952	83,730	a 1,682	∞ 208,157	12	700	237	a 4	∞ 277
Israel	1952	a 29,761	a 509	44,161	17	300	198	a 6	a 159
Italy	1952	a 1,244,152	a 28,544		107	5,000	106	a 68	∞ 11 3,709
Japan	1952	a 1,664,490	a 85,788	d 2,540,000	186	30,218	358	a 81	∞ 9,230
Korea	1950								134
Lebanon	1952		a 51	a 5,691	40	100	80		e 40
Liberia	1950								11 2
Luxembourg	1952	a 23,412	a 128	∞ 31,545	5	135	452	a 3	∞ 63
Mexico	1952	a 285,600	c 30,350	∞ 419,819	162	1,300	49	b 212	b 10 750
Netherlands	1952	a 781,678	a 3,509	∞ 1,416,000	108	2,581	255	a 9	∞ 2,106
New Zealand	1952	a 369,986	a 7,159	b 290,645	43	713	366	a 30	e 475
Nicaragua	1952				11	56	51		10 20
Norway	1952	a 451,727	a 6,060	∞ 248,878	96	1,317	403	a 22	∞ 824

See footnotes at end of table.

No. 1106.—COMMUNICATIONS—TELEPHONES, TELEGRAMS, MAIL, NEWSPAPERS, AND RADIO—Continued

[See text, p. 944, for general comments concerning quality of the data. Years for which data are shown may vary from column to column and from country to country. Figures which are *not* for the year shown in the "year" column are prefixed by a letter to indicate the year represented, as follows: æ represents 1951; a 1950, b, 1949; c, 1948; d, 1947; e, 1946; f, 1945; g, 1944; h, 1943; i, 1942]

COUNTRY	Year	Telephones in use [1]	Telegrams sent, domestic [2]	Letters sent, domestic [3]	NEWSPAPERS			RADIO (WIRELESS)	
					Dailies [4]	Circulation		Transmitting stations [5]	Receiving sets [6]
						Total	Copies per 1,000 population		
		Number	*Thousands*	*Thousands*	*Number*	*Thousands*		*Number*	*Thousands*
Pakistan	1951	a 19,364	a 2,847	a 279,025	c 35	e 150	c 2	e 4	80
Panama	1952				11	100	122		10 55
Paraguay	1950	5,273			b 3	b 17	b 13		
Peru	1952	a 46,733	a 5,850		60	380	41	b 49	10 600
Philippines	1950	19,675			20	500	26		b 79
Poland	1951	230,000	e 385	737,121	b 115	b 3,000	b 123		1,628
Portugal	1952	152,973	a 2,424	æ 220,682	20	530	62	a 26	e 310
Romania	1950		f 7,137	æ 200,189					270
Spain	1952	651,516	a 19,202	æ 1,075,000	104	5,540	196		e 805
Sweden	1952	a 1,615,200	a 5,008	a 859,646	160	3,490	490	a 32	a 2,305
Switzerland	1952	896,398	æ 795	a 922,900	147	1,442	304	a 8	a 1,082
Syria	1950	14,301	110		33	66	21		45
Thailand	1952				30	75	4		10 100
Turkey	1952	65,150	b 6,249	b 109,419	116	692	33	a 3	a 368
Union of South Africa	1952	456,851	a 11,411	b 567,140	17 19	17 730	17 59	a 10	æ 583
United Kingdom	1952	a 5,376,053	a 41,614	b 8,045,000	18 121	31,000	612	a 42	19 12,807
Uruguay	1950	89,871			c 31	e 400	e 172	58	e 19 800
Venezuela	1949			38,513	29	300	65		e 10 150
Yugoslavia	1952	a 110,170	æ 5,581	æ 345,176	16	690	42		æ 854

[1] Figures relate to number of public and private telephones (including extension instruments) connected to a central exchange.
[2] Figures cover, in general, all types of telegrams including cablegrams and radiograms, but exclude messages in transit.
[3] Letters mailed for distribution within national territories. Figures cover letters (airmail, ordinary mail and registered), postcards, printed matter, business papers, small merchandise samples, small packets, and phonopost packets. Includes mail carried without charge, but excludes ordinary packages, and letters and packages with a declared value.
[4] Publications devoted mainly to recording current events and appearing 6 or 7 times a week.
[5] Figures relate only to stations broadcasting to the public; excludes service stations (e. g., aeronautical and naval stations). Each station counted for as many units as it possesses different transmitting frequencies (wave lengths).
[6] Figures shown for most countries relate to number of licenses issued for receiving sets, figures which are estimates of number of sets actually in use are footnoted. In general, figures should be used with considerable caution as number of licenses falls, in varying degree from country to country, to represent full number in use. On the other hand, figures given for estimated number in use may in some cases be overstatements. Data apply to all types of sets for radio broadcasts to the public, including loud-speakers connected to a "radio redistribution system" but excluding television sets.
[7] Includes messages to Canada, Mexico, St. Pierre, and Miquelon.
[8] Includes Alaska, Guam, Hawaii, and Puerto Rico.
[9] English language dailies only.
[10] Estimates of number of sets actually in use.
[11] All telegrams sent and received by land are counted as domestic. Letters sent include foreign.
[12] Including Faeroe Islands and Greenland.
[13] Including Algeria, Guadeloupe, Martinique, French Guianas, and Reunion.
[14] Excluding Saar.
[15] Includes Algeria.
[16] Excluding free licenses. A single license may cover several sets.
[17] Comprising English language dailies and dailies in Afrikaans.
[18] Includes newspapers published in Channel Islands and Isle of Man.
[19] Includes 1,597,900 combined sound-television licenses.

Source: Statistical Office of the United Nations; *Statistical Yearbook, 1953*.

COMPARATIVE INTERNATIONAL STATISTICS

No. 1107.—Education and Health

[Education: Figures usually refer to both official (public) and independent (private) schools, to school year beginning in year stated, and generally exclude adult education, evening classes, apprenticeship courses and correspondence schools; intercountry comparisons are subject to caution owing to variations in definitions employed and in scope of data; usually excludes (unless otherwise stated) nursery schools, kindergarten and other preschool education. Health: Data do not allow of a close comparison between countries which present a similar standard, whether high or low, in respect of strength and character of their medical facilities. However, they may be used to judge approximate difference in standard between advanced and underdeveloped countries. Data for hospital beds usually refer to both private and public hospitals, nursing homes, infirmaries and dispensaries, but are not always quite complete. See text, p. 944, for general comments concerning quality of the data. Years for which data are shown may vary from column to column and from country to country. Figures which are not for the year shown in the "year" column are prefixed by a letter to indicate the year represented, as follows: a represents 1950; b, 1949; c, 1948; d, 1947; e, 1946; f, 1945]

COUNTRY	Year	PRIMARY SCHOOLS		SECONDARY SCHOOLS		HEALTH		
		Schools	Students enrolled	Schools	Students enrolled	Physicians	Dentists	Hospital beds
United States	1950	c 156,831	c 20,828,958	d 28,354	d 7,929,484	201,277	87,000	1,436,090
Albania	1949	1,817	1 162,000	668	(1)			
Argentina	1950	b 14,722	b 2,119,940	388	68,633	c 18,301	c 6,643	c 66,386
Australia	1950	c 8,700	c 1,017,000	1,290	236,000	7,400		c 70,682
Austria	1951	5,147	844,986	169	61,539	b 10,760	b 2,147	b 57,213
Belgium	1950	b 8,733	b 768,283	727	129,146	8,132	1,214	28,950
Bolivia	1950	2,199	183,506	104	18,029	e 633	e 215	f 5,180
Brazil	1950	b 54,900	b 4,132,604	e 1,365	e 282,179	b 19,044	b 11,632	162,515
Bulgaria	1947	8,631	907,846	295	167,660			
Burma	1950	3,108	358,111	176	26,735			
Canada	1950	c 1 31,665	c 1,838,767	(1)	c 477,992	14,596	c 4,355	c 132,630
Ceylon	1951	a 5,645	a 1,105,052	a 601	a 244,293	1,318		17,668
Chile	1951	b 5,684	b 752,254	a 323	a 80,937	3,251	1,592	33,738
China	1950	1 210,918	1 16,180,000	1 3,690	1 1,090,000	e 4 13,447	e 4 371	e 4 13,357
Colombia	1949	c 12,559	6 761,915	e 4 397	c 4 42,293	c 3,223		e 22,310
Costa Rica	1951	a 1,046	112,500		6,000	257	81	4,161
Cuba	1950	7 7,598	7 546,984			c 3,100		c 17,112
Czechoslovakia	1947	17,768	1,571,337	5 342	5 119,469	9,959		90,764
Denmark	1951	a 3,640	a 427,856	423	93,555	b 4,334	b 1,202	b 44,712
Dominican Republic	1950	2,656	379,469	54	7,433	b 636	b 225	b 5,757
Ecuador	1949	3,216	309,376	c 71	c 15,769	e 808	e 220	
Egypt	1949	8,361	1,340,606	335	96,625	4,000	600	22,000
El Salvador	1951	1,867	142,927			380	96	b 3,553
Ethiopia	1950					98	10	3,200
Finland	1950		490,882	b 336	b 92,986	1,999	1,303	29,953
France	1951	a 80,952	a 5,232,000	a 2,577	a 794,070	9 36,636	10,915	10 612,800
Germany, Western	1951	11 29,224	11 5,920,898	a 2,106	a 828,631			a 510,987
Greece	1951					7,300	2,490	21,109
Guatemala	1951	a 3,397	a 164,815			492	116	12 6,783
Haiti	1951	638	121,844	30	5,882	a 298	a 74	d 1,513
Honduras	1950	1,930	97,209	d 12 26	d 1,274			e 1,512
Hungary	1950	b 6,205	b 1,143,608	405	91,956	e 9,809		e 38,079
Iceland	1950	214	16,218			b 161	b 17	b 1,177
India	1950	b 220,000	b 17,394,000	19,705	4,675,441	b 55,321	b 1,950	13 112,781
Indonesia	1951	26,670	5,318,014	811	178,339	e 14 1,101		e 14 30,867
Iran	1950	15 9,900	15 762,908	333	51,039			
Iraq	1950	b 1,194	b 196,334	121	22,706	c 811	c 72	c 5,103
Ireland, Republic of	1951	b 16 4,886	b 16 463,703	b 416	b 47,065	e 2,674	e 536	42,114
Israel	1951	a 841	a 153,617	a 117	a 13,025	a 2,801		8,379
Italy	1950	c 38,766	c 4,878,149	2,854	503,943			
Japan	1950	21,081	11,190,794	17 15,266	17 7,266,032	69,000	26,000	275,804
Korea, South	1948	3,536	2,354,977					
Lebanon	1951	b 7,171	b 198,987		d 30,000	1,038	385	5,389
Liberia	1950	265	24,353		1,047			
Luxembourg	1951	b 18 1,014	b 18 28,216	a 7	a 2,843	240	117	5,177
Mexico	1949	24,493	2,880,527	440	72,733	d 10,605	d 1,498	d 27,816
Netherlands	1950	8,058	1,371,511	19 1,426	19 227,447	b 8,000	b 1,500	b 49,388
New Zealand	1951		303,674	a 19 270	a 19 59,046	2,463	806	20 16,782
Nicaragua	1950	1,341	90,544			293	84	2,437
Norway	1949		d 298,222	c 155	c 33,266	3,227	1,688	29,253
Pakistan	1951	40,295	3,212,312		21 1,164,342	c 2,190		

See footnotes at end of table.

No. 1107.—EDUCATION AND HEALTH—Continued

[See text, p. 944, for general comments concerning quality of the data. Years for which data are shown may vary from column to column and from country to country. Figures which are not for the year shown in the "year" column are prefixed by a letter to indicate the year represented, as follows: a represents 1950; b, 1949; c, 1948; d, 1947; e, 1946; f, 1945]

COUNTRY	Year	PRIMARY SCHOOLS		SECONDARY SCHOOLS		HEALTH		
		Schools	Students enrolled	Schools	Students enrolled	Physicians	Dentists	Hospital beds
Panama	1950	950	110,059	b 17	b 8,122	d 195	d 72	d 3,071
Paraguay	1950	1,477	195,607	....	d 6,545	507	211	13 2,076
Peru	1951	a 10,454	a 926,367	1,896	37,762	f 1,358	f 372	f 16,204
Philippines	1948	19,116	3,811,981	1,328	549,659			
Poland	1948	22,530	3,375,061	486	219,500	d 7,869	d 1,672	d 106,354
Portugal	1950	b 11,700	b 609,329	b 333	b 46,490	5,493	469	c 33,049
Spain	1949	e 7 56,747	7 2,063,646	7 119	7 214,847			102,594
Sweden	1951		b 611,869	390	143,179	a 4,890	a 3,470	a 79,390
Switzerland	1950		c 434,496	c 237	c 91,899	6,507	1,861	b 71,763
Syria	1951	a 1,794	a 261,857	a 135	a 34,874	670	269	2,399
Thailand	1950	18,539	2,523,839	b 1,242	b 105,146			
Turkey	1951	a 17,029	a 1,625,499	534	102,022	6,570	953	a 18,837
Union of South Africa 22	1950	d 8,347	d 1,267,273		d 100,730	5,703	957	43,700
United Kingdom 22	1950	15 24,135	16 4,041,382	c 5,373	e 1,875,997		b 10,000	b 504,209
Uruguay	1950		b 223,049					13,931
Venezuela	1950	c 5,755	485,668	b 115	b 23,336	2,165	472	17,983
Yugoslavia	1950	13,836	1,552,360	1,696	485,876	5,138	23 525	53,700

1 Secondary schools included with primary schools.
2 Excludes Formosa and 10 provinces.
3 Excludes Formosa and Southwest Region.
4 Government hospitals personnel only.
5 In 428 public hospitals.
6 Data refer to reporting institutions only.
7 Public schools only.
8 Includes normal schools.
9 Civil personnel.
10 Includes 114,900 beds in homes for the aged.
11 Excludes Hamburg and Bremen.
12 In general hospitals only.
13 Includes technical schools.
14 Area under authority of Interim Federal Government before Dec. 18, 1948.
15 Includes preschool.
16 Includes infant departments.
17 Includes vocational schools.
18 Public schools only, excluding higher primary.
19 Includes advanced primary and normal schools.
20 Excludes beds in mental hospitals.
21 Excludes vocational schools.
22 England and Wales only.
23 Personnel of health institutions only.

Source: Statistical Office of the United Nations; Statistical Yearbook, 1952.

No. 1108.—United Nations and Certain Specialized Agencies—Member Contributions: 1953

COUNTRY	UNITED NATIONS (UN) Percent	Amount	FOOD AND AGRICULTURE ORGANIZATION (FAO) Percent	Amount	INTERNATIONAL CIVIL AVIATION ORGANIZATION (ICAO) Units	Percent	Amount	INTERNATIONAL LABOR ORGANIZATION (ILO) Percent	Amount	U. N. EDUCATIONAL, SCIENTIFIC AND CULTURAL ORGANIZATION (UNESCO) Percent	Amount	WORLD HEALTH ORGANIZATION (WHO) Units	Percent	Amount
1953 budget		$48,327,700		$5,250,000			$3,259,384		$5,550,585		$9,017,849			$9,832,764
Total member assessments	100.00	$44,290,000	100.00	$5,180,000	1,500	100.00	$2,817,187	100.00	$6,469,665	100.00	$8,638,551	12,915	100.00	$9,590,290
Afghanistan	.08	35,360	.16	8,288	4	.27	7,512	.12	7,763	.09	7,685	6	.08	4,201
Albania								.12	7,763			5		3,501
Argentina	1.45	640,900	1.83	94,704	36	2.40	67,612	2.18	141,059	1.85	132,348	222	1.72	155,533
Australia	1.75	773,500	2.00	103,600	52	3.47	97,662	2.35	152,004	1.88	160,525	236	1.77	168,732
Austria			.38	19,664	2	.13	3,756	.35	22,663	.17	13,504	17	.13	11,905
Belgium	1.37	605,540	1.78	92,204	32	2.13	60,100	1.72	111,265	1.47	125,517	163	1.06	111,605
Bolivia	.06	26,530	.06	3,108	2	.13	3,756	.12	7,763	.06	5,123	10	.06	7,002
Brazil	1.45	640,900	1.52	78,736	39	2.60	73,246	2.22	143,614	1.55	132,348	222	1.72	155,533
Bulgaria								.28	18,113			98	.13	11,905
Burma	.13	57,460	.16	8,288	5	.34	9,391	.19	12,291	.14	11,964	6	.08	4,201
Canada	3.30	1,458,600	4.76	246,568	74	4.93	138,980	3.98	257,470	3.54	302,265	384	2.90	269,854
Ceylon			.13	6,734	5	.34	9,391	.15	9,704	.14	11,964	6	.04	3,501
Chile	.33	145,860	.31	16,058	9	.60	16,903	.50	32,345			54	.42	37,807
China	5.62	2,484,040			16	1.07	30,040	3.04	196,660	6.03	514,875	730	5.61	504,102
Colombia	.35	154,040	.40	20,720				.45	29,111	.38	32,447			
Costa Rica	.04	17,680	.05	2,590				.12	7,763	.04	3,415	6	.04	3,501
Cuba	.34	150,280	.46	23,528	14	.93	26,296	.38	24,083	.35	30,739	35	.27	24,605
Czechoslovakia	1.05	464,100	1.08	55,944	20	1.34	37,688	1.16	75,041	1.13	96,488	108	.84	75,613
Denmark	.78	344,760	.05	2,590	20	1.34	37,688	.97	63,780	.84	71,724	96	.90	60,813
Dominican Republic	.05	22,100	.05	2,590	2	.13	3,756	.12	7,763	.06	6,123	6	.06	4,201
Ecuador	.04	17,680	.05	2,590	15	1.00	28,172	.12	7,763	.04	3,415	6	.06	4,201
Egypt	.50	221,000	.55	28,490	3	.20	5,634	.85	55,634	.54	46,108	96	.74	66,813
El Salvador	.05	22,100	.15	7,770	6	.40	11,269	.12	7,763	.06	5,123	6	.06	4,201
Ethiopia	.10	44,200	.43	22,274	6	.40	11,269	.30	19,407	.13	11,269	10	.08	7,002
Finland												17	.13	11,905
France	5.75	2,541,500	6.70	347,060	86	5.73	161,513	7.49	484,535	6.17	526,529	720	5.61	504,102
Germany, Fed. Republic	4.73		4.73	245,014				4.87	315,044	4.52	385,943	387	3.03	270,968
Greece	.19	83,980	.27	13,986	9	.60	16,903	.22	14,232	.20	17,077	20	.16	14,002
Guatemala	.06	26,520	.08	4,144	3	.20	5,634	.12	7,763	.04	4,123	6	.08	4,201
Haiti	.04	17,680	.05	2,590	2	.13	3,756	.12	7,763	.04	3,415	6	.04	3,501
Honduras	.04	17,680	.05	2,590				.12	7,763	.04	3,415	6	.04	3,501
Hungary	.04	17,680	.18		3	.20	4,634	.63	34,286	.51	43,547	34	.19	16,003
Ireland	.27		.52	26,940	52	.47	97,662	.13	7,763	.70	59,327	50	.04	3,476
India	3.45	1,524,900				3.20		4.13	267,172	3.70	316,327	390	3.04	272,055
Indonesia	.60	265,200	.52			.63	17,023	.43	27,617	.64	54,547	40	.31	28,006

1 Unofficial percentages, calculated from official scale of assessments.

2 Includes contributions for the following countries not shown separately: Byelorussian S. S. R., Cambodia, Hashemite Kingdom of Jordan, Libya, Monaco, Morocco, Nepal, Saudi Arabia, Southern Rhodesia, Tunisia, Ukrainian S. S. R., Viet Nam, Yemen.

3 Regular 1953 budget less $4,228,200 estimated miscellaneous income, plus $2,780,680 adjustment in 1952 budget and miscellaneous income, less $670,380 savings in 1953 and 1951 accounts.

4 Regular 1953 budget less an estimated miscellaneous income of $70,000.

5 Regular 1953 budget less $442,217 casual revenue.

6 Regular 1953 budget less supplementary receipts of $81,800. Gross assessments against which credits in respect of 1949, 1950 and 1951 balances ($479,346), and of working capital fund ($245,717) are to be deducted for certain members.

7 Regular 1953 budget less $479,298 estimated miscellaneous income. Gross assessments against which credits in respect of working capital fund ($86,700) are to be deducted for certain members.

8 Regular 1953 budget less transfer of assets from "officer" of $23,164, miscellaneous income of $277,180 and $452,240 in adjustments.

9 Inactive members. This scale of assessments included inactive members, even though these States have announced that they no longer consider themselves as members.

10 Gross assessment. Due to credit of $356,000 as result of adjustment of advances to working capital fund on basis of 1953 scale of assessments, U. S. net assessment is $15,167,040.

11 Gross assessment. Due to credit of $132,552 in respect of 1951 balance, and a credit of $63,420 in respect of working capital fund, U. S. net assessment is $1,421,299.

Source: Department of State, Bureau of United Nations Affairs.

No. 1109.—Net Geographical Product by Industrial Origin (Percent Distribution)

[Net geographical product relates to the product of all industry within a nation's boundaries; it is given in this table at factor cost, and therefore equals the sum of factor incomes (wages, rent, profits, interest) paid by industry. Exceptions are listed in the footnotes. Estimates are not fully uniform from country to country in items of income covered and industrial classifications used. Some of the major differences are indicated in footnotes below. In general, "Agriculture" includes also forestry, hunting and fishing; "Manufacturing and construction" includes mining; "Trade" covers wholesale and retail distribution; "Transport and communications" includes public utilities; "Government" includes administration, defense and public services but not public enterprises, which are classified under relevant industry; category "All others" comprises finance, insurance, ownership of dwellings and personal and other nongovernment services. See text, p. 944, for general comments concerning quality of the data]

COUNTRY	Year	PERCENT BY INDUSTRIAL ORIGIN					
		Agriculture	Manufacturing and construction	Trade	Transport and communication	Government	All others
United States	1949	7.8	36.3	19.0	8.5	[1]10.1	[2]18.4
	1950	7.3	38.5	17.9	8.5	9.8	17.9
	1951	7.2	39.4	17.3	8.3	10.9	16.9
Canada	1950	14.2	38.7	15.0	9.5	7.9	[2]14.6
Chile [3]	1950	16.5	31.0	16.0	6.2	7.4	22.9
Colombia	1950	42.0	20.2	9.3	6.6	6.5	15.4
Denmark [4]	1951	21.0	36.4	14.8	10.1	7.1	10.6
Finland	1951	27.2	[5]41.4	[6]12.0	[6]6.6	8.3	[6]4.5
Germany (Western)	1951	12.6	[5]56.1	9.1	[5]7.4	7.7	7.7
Greece [7]	1949	38.4	25.2	11.3	6.1	9.8	9.2
Guatemala [8]	1949	45.5	21.4	8.5	14.3	7.1	3.2
Honduras	1951	59.2	14.0	[5]13.4	5.4	2.7	[5]5.4
India	1948	47.5	17.2	18.9		5.3	11.1
Ireland	1950	30.6	25.3	20.6		7.4	[10]16.2
Israel [9]	1950	9.5	[5]36.2	14.8	[8][11]6.2	14.8	15.5
Italy	1951	28.0	37.2	[8]12.7	7.6	9.5	[8]5.0
Japan	1951	21.3	34.6	18.5	7.1	3.7	14.9
Netherlands	1950	[12]12.8	41.1	13.3	[12]10.9	8.3	[12][13]13.6
Nicaragua [14]	1950	40.5	25.2	[13]10.5	4.7	6.1	[11]13.0
Norway [9]	1951	15.2	41.8	12.4	15.8	3.0	11.9
Paraguay [9]	1950	44.3	21.2	13.3	2.7	9.4	[16]9.0
Peru [9]	1951	37.0	[17]25.3	16.2	[17]5.4	8.4	7.8
Phillippines [9]	1951	40.3	16.0	13.5	3.7	5.4	21.1
Turkey	1951	57.8	12.8	9.5	4.6	9.4	5.9
Union of South Africa	1950	17.5	35.3	14.5	8.6	[16]9.1	15.0
United Kingdom [18]	1951	5.2	50.0	12.7	10.3	9.6	12.2

[1] Includes public enterprises.
[2] Includes cash rents paid by business.
[3] Includes net income from abroad.
[4] Gross geographical product at factor cost.
[5] Public utilities included under "Manufacturing and construction."
[6] Banking and insurance included under "Trade."
[7] Income from ocean shipping excluded.
[8] Gross geographical product at market prices.
[9] Finance, insurance and real estate included under "Trade."
[10] Includes personal and business rent and government payments to teachers.
[11] Excludes postal services.
[12] Beginning 1946, all farm rent included under "All others."
[13] Hotels and restaurants included under "Transport and communication."
[14] Gross national income.
[15] Finance included under "Trade."
[16] Includes public enterprises other than transport, etc.
[17] Construction included under "Transport and communication."
[18] Gross geographical product at factor cost before deduction of adjustment for stock appreciation.

Source: Statistical Office of the United Nations; basic data from the *Monthly Bulletin of Statistics, February 1953.*

APPENDIX I

HISTORICAL APPENDIX: INDEX OF HISTORICAL STATISTICS SERIES AND STATISTICAL ABSTRACT TABLES IN WHICH THOSE SERIES APPEAR

[Comprises statistical time series (identified by number) shown in the historical supplement entitled *Historical Statistics of the United States, 1789–1945*. Historical series are listed only: (1) where comparable data are available for a year or years later than 1945; (2) where data are included in a table in this *Abstract*. For a more complete listing of series for which data are available for the years 1946 to 1951, see Appendix I of the 1949, 1950, 1951, and 1952 editions of the *Statistical Abstract*]

Historical Statistics series	1953 Abstract table number	Historical Statistics series	1953 Abstract table number	Historical Statistics series	1953 Abstract table number	Historical Statistics series	1953 Abstract table number
A 101–107	305	C 37	41	E 244–255	489	G 131–143	956
A 110–116	305	C 39	69	E 258	488	G 144–158	960
A 117–133	307	C 40–41	77	E 261–266	488	G 162	568
A 134–144	308	C 42	69	F 4–7	191	G 165	568
B 1–3	3	C 45–51	67	F 8	200	G 170	568
B 6–9	3	C 52	68	F 9	192	G 171–190	590
B 13	3	C 56–61	73	F 11–16	192	G 194–199	567
B 14–15	20	C 65–76	68	F 26	710	G 200–224	590
B 16–17	19	C 77–78	54	F 28–41	710	G 225–233	594
B 18	15	C 79–84	95	F 52	697	H 1–23	901
B 19–20	28	C 92–107	84	F 56	692	H 25–26	903
B 21	15	C 122–127	97	F 69–73	813	H 51–57	906
B 23	15	C 128–155	96	F 74–83	817	H 64–65	913
B 25	1	D 11–19	206	F 84–87	816	H 73	913
B 26–30	2	D 20	208	F 88–91	817	H 89	916
B 40–47	24	D 23	208	F 94–108	817	H 90	10
B 48	10	D 26–31	206	F 123–131	831	H 91–97	916
B 54	10	D 32–35	208	F 132–134	828	H 99–105	916
B 60	10	D 37–40	208	F 137–142	834	H 106	21
B 66	10	D 42–45	206	F 145–150	821	H 107–112	916
B 72–94	21	D 117–119	231	F 151–154	822	H 114	451
B 96–109	21	D 145–147	232	F 155–159	839	H 120–126	457
B 145	17	D 176	214	F 160	838	H 128–132	451
B 146	16	D 214–217	229	F 166	836	H 133–135	454
B 149–163	16, 17	D 218–223	239	F 173	836	J 1	988
B 167	21	D 224–229	240	F 175	836	J 4–5	988
B 170	19	D 230–238	241	F 178	836	J 7	983
B 171	47	E 1–16	709	F 180–181	836	J 10	983
B 173	50	E 19	711	F 186	836	J 30–48	983
B 174	47	E 20–24	717	F 189–190	836	J 165–169	963
B 183	38	E 31	711	F 193	840	J 170	985
B 185	38	E 32–35	718	F 195	840	J 171	985
B 187	38	E 37	716	F 199	844	J 172	987
B 189–192	38	E 43–47	716	F 201–207	842	J 174	987
B 193–194	27	E 49–52	716	F 209	842	J 175	763
B 195	33	E 54–59	716	G 6–8	851	J 176	806
B 237	24	E 61–64	214	G 13–24	857	J 179–180	969
B 238–239	26	E 72–75	745	G 27–42	857	K 28–30	628
B 244–247	32	E 76–87	729	G 43–56	863	K 31–33	620
B 250	32	E 88–93	726	G 57–58	868	K 34–39	623
B 251–253	24	E 98–102	726	G 59–61	865	K 40	622
B 258	23	E 104	726	G 62–64	866	K 41–47	623
B 265–267	24	E 105–110	733	G 65–66	876	K 48–49	636
B 272	23	E 117–134	790	G 67–68	874	K 50	623
B 279–282	30	E 136–151	792	G 69–70	877	K 51	637
B 285–286	30	E 152–158	796	G 71–72	878	K 52	643
B 290	30	E 160–162	795	G 73–74	849	K 54–59	647
B 293	30	E 164–170	795	G 75–76	879	K 60–62	620
B 297–300	30	E 171–180	801	G 77–80	849	K 63–65	623
B 304–307	105	E 181–183	755	G 81–82	880	K 66–67	623
B 310–312	105	E 186–188	755	G 83–86	881	K 68–70	631
B 314–326	105	E 190–195	757	G 87–92	849	K 71–72	623
B 328	105	E 196–198	755	G 93–95	882	K 75–76	621
B 331	107	E 200–202	755	G 104–105	849	K 77	633
B 333–335	107	E 204–206	755	G 106–107	884	K 78	623
B 337–339	114	E 208–211	755	G 108–109	886	K 79	632
B 340–341	115	E 213	755	G 110–111	849	K 80–83	623
B 350–352	102	E 215	755	G 112–113	891	K 84–93	643
C 1	7	E 217–219	755	G 114	894	K 94–98	653
C 6–9	66	E 222	755	G 116–117	896	K 100–102	654
C 24	54	E 225–230	755	G 118–121	889	K 105	655
C 25–26	56	E 232–240	775	G 125–126	899	K 107	655
C 28–35	60	E 242	775	G 127–128	898	K 113–116	656

HISTORICAL APPENDIX: INDEX OF HISTORICAL STATISTICS SERIES AND STATISTICAL ABSTRACT TABLES IN WHICH THOSE SERIES APPEAR—Continued

Historical Statistics series	1953 Abstract table number	Historical Statistics series	1953 Abstract table number	Historical Statistics series	1953 Abstract table number	Historical Statistics series	1953 Abstract table number
K 119-123	680	M 42-55	1057	N 183-184	452	P 144	288
K 124-126	685	M 56-67	1066	N 185-187	500	P 146-147	390
K 132	664	M 68-70	1077	N 197-200	505	P 152-153	386
K 134-139	664	M 75-86	1079	N 204-205	505	P 155-157	386
K 141-144	664	M 87-102	1072	N 213-214	503	P 160	386
K 146-151	661	N 43-48	453	N 221-227	514	P 162	386
K 152-157	682	N 60-67	465	N 228-232	508	P 164	386
K 170-171	678	N 68-69	487	P 29	352	P 165-167	351
K 178-180	608	N 73-75	457	P 30	354	P 171-174	589
K 181	606	N 76-79	448	P 31	352	P 176-179	588
K 184-188	608	N 87	449	P 32-37	364	P 180	557
K 189-191b	612	N 109-113	460	P 40-49	363	P 181	556
K 193-204	609	N 114-116	459	P 50-56	362	P 185-187	555
K 205-219	613	N 118-119	459	P 59	353	P 189A	419
K 221-224	613	N 120-122	460	P 62	407	P 188B-201B	433
K 225-232	615	N 131-134	463	P 63	405	P 189C	419
K 233-235	616	N 135	473	P 65-66	407	P 202B-208B	433
K 246-251	650	N 140-141	473	P 80-93	366	P 224B-234B	432
K 253-256	689	N 146	473	P 96	366	P 224C	432
K 257	657	N 148-151	446	P 98	366	P 227C	433
K 259-260	657	N 153-156	447	P 99-103	367	P 230C	433
K 264	657	N 158-160	447	P 109	374	P 232C	433
K 265	659	N 162	447	P 110-115	375	P 234D	433
L 41-47	339	N 164-165	447	P 117-121	375	P 227D	433
M 1-10	1043	N 166	450	P 125	375	P 232D	433
M 13	1043	N 168-171	450	P 127-129	375	P 235-239	433
M 15-18	1042	N 172-178	445	P 132-136	392	P 242-245	433
M 24-27	1042	N 179	451	P 137-138	395	P 246	419
M 33-41	1042	N 181-182	451	P 139-143	393	P 247-249	433

APPENDIX II

Weights, measures, and foreign exchange

UNITED STATES UNITS WITH METRIC EQUIVALENTS

1 inch = 2.540 centimeters.
1 foot = 0.3048 meter.
1 yard = 0.9144 meter.
1 mile = 1.609 kilometers.
1 square yard = 0.8361 square meter.
1 acre = 0.4047 hectare.
1 square mile = 2.590 square kilometers.
1 cubic inch = 16.39 cubic centimeters.
1 cubic foot = 0.02832 cubic meter.
1 cubic yard = 0.7646 cubic meter.

1 liquid quart = 0.9463 liter.
1 gallon = 231 cubic inches = 3.785 liters.
1 bushel (measured) = 2,150.4 cubic inches = 35.24 liters.
1 avoirdupois ounce = 28.35 grams.
1 troy ounce = 31.10 grams.
1 pound = 0.4536 kilogram.
1 long ton = 2,240 pounds = 1.0160 metric tons of 1,000 kilograms.
1 short ton = 2,000 pounds = 0.9072 metric ton.

UNITED STATES GALLON AND BUSHEL WITH BRITISH EQUIVALENTS

1 United States gallon = 231 cubic inches = 0.8331 imperial gallon.

1 United States bushel = 2,150.4 cubic inches = 0.9694 imperial bushel.

OFFICIAL WEIGHTS OF THE BARREL OF NONLIQUID PRODUCTS

	Pounds	Kilograms
Wheat flour, barley flour, rye flour, and corn meal (net) [1]	196	88.90
Rosin, tar, and pitch (gross)	500	226.80
Fish, pickled (net)	200	90.72
Lime (net)	200	90.72
Cement (4 bags counted as 1 barrel) (net) [1]	376	170.55

[1] Except as noted in the tables.

OFFICIAL WEIGHTS OF THE UNITED STATES BUSHEL

	Pounds	Kilograms
Wheat, beans, peas, potatoes (Irish or white)	60	27.22
Rye, corn (maize), linseed (flaxseed), maslin (mixed grain)	56	25.40
Barley, buckwheat	48	21.77
Onions	57	25.86
Rough rice	45	20.41
Malt	34	15.42
Oats	32	14.51
Peanuts, green, in shell	22	9.98
Castor beans	50	22.68

APPROXIMATE WEIGHT OF PETROLEUM AND PRODUCTS

In the United States petroleum and its products are measured by bulk, not weight. Whether handled in containers or without them the quantities are customarily reduced to the equivalent of barrels of 42 United States gallons (barrel thus equals 158.984 liters). In many foreign countries these commodities are measured by weight. The specific gravity of the different grades of crude petroleum and of the finished products varies materially. On the basis of approximate averages the Department of Commerce in converting foreign weight statistics to gallons or barrels of 42 gallons uses the factors shown in the following table:

	WEIGHT OF UNITED STATES GALLON		WEIGHT OF BARREL OF 42 GALLONS	
	Pounds	Kilograms	Pounds	Kilograms
Crude petroleum	7.3	3.311	306.6	139.07
Lubricating oils	7.0	3.175	294.0	133.36
Illuminating oils (kerosene)	6.6	2.994	277.2	125.74
Gasoline and related products (motor spirit, benzine, etc.)	6.1	2.767	256.2	116.21
Fuel and gas oils	7.7	3.493	323.4	146.69

967

APPENDIX II

FOREIGN EXCHANGE RATES

[Averages of certified noon buying rates in New York for cable transfers. In cents per unit of foreign currency]

COUNTRY	MONETARY UNIT	1941	1946	1947	1948	1949	1950	1951	1952
Argentina:									
Basic	Peso	29.773	29.773	29.773	[1] 29.744	[1] 29.774	26.571	20.000	20.000
Preferential	do						[1] 13.333	13.333	13.333
Free	do						[1] 8.2888	7.067	7.163
Australia:									
Official	Pound	322.80	} 321.34	321.00	321.22	293.80	223.15	223.07	222.63
Free	do	321.27							
Belgium	Franc		2.2829	2.2817	2.2816	2.2009	1.9906	1.9859	1.9876
Foreign "Bank Notes" account	do					[1] 2.1407	[1] 1.9722	[1] 1.9622	
Brazil:									
Official	Cruzeiro [1]	6.0575	[1] 6.0602	}5.4403	5.4406	5.4406	5.4406	5.4406	5.4406
Free	do	5.0705							
British Malaya [1]	Dollar					[1] 42.973	32.788	32.849	32.603
Canada:									
Official	do	90.909	95.198	100.00	100.00	97.491	[1] 90.909		
Free	do	87.345	93.288	91.999	91.691	92.881	91.474	94.989	102.149
Ceylon	Rupee					[1] 27.839	20.850	20.849	20.903
Chile:									
Official	Peso	[1] 5.1664							
Export	do	[1] 4.0000							
China	Yuan Shanghai	[1] 5.3133							
Colombia	Peso	57.004	57.020	57.001	[1] 57.006				
Czechoslovakia	Koruna		[1] 2.0060	2.0060	2.0060	2.0060	2.0060	[1] 2.0060	
Denmark	Krone		[1] 20.876	20.864	20.857	19.117	14.494	14.491	[4] 14.482
Finland	Markka	[1] 2.0101					[1] .4354	.4354
France (Metropolitan):									
Official	Franc		} .8409	.8407	{ [1] .4929	[1] .4671			
Free	do				{ [1] .3240	.3017	.2858	.2856	.2856
Germany	D. Mark	[1] 39.970					[1] 23.838	23.838	[1] 23.838
Hong Kong	Dollar	[1] 24.592							
India [1]	Rupee	30.137	30.155	30.164	30.169	27.706	20.870	20.869	20.922
Ireland	Pound							[1] 280.38	279.66
Italy	Lira	[1] 5.0703	[1] .4434						
Mexico	Peso	20.538	20.581	20.577	[1] 18.860	12.620	11.570	11.564	11.588
Netherlands	Guilder		37.813	37.760	37.668	34.528	26.252	26.264	26.315
New Zealand	Pound	322.54	322.63	322.29	350.48	365.07	277.28	277.19	276.49
Norway	Krone		[1] 20.176	20.160	20.159	18.481	14.015	14.015	14.015
Philippine Republic	Peso					[1] 49.723	49.621	49.639	49.673
Portugal	Escudo	[4] 4.0023	[4] 4.0501	4.0273	4.0183	3.8800	3.4704	3.4739	3.4853
South Africa	Pound	398.00	400.50	400.74	400.75	366.62	278.38	278.33	278.20
Spain	Peseta	[1] 9.1300	[1] 9.1324	9.1324	[1] 9.1324				
Sweden	Krona	[1] 23.829	[1] 25.859	27.824	27.824	25.480	19.332	19.327	19.326
Switzerland	Franc	[1] 23.210	[1] 23.363	23.363	23.363	23.314	23.136	23.060	23.148
United Kingdom:									
Official	Pound	403.50	} 403.28	402.86	403.13	368.72	280.07	279.96	279.26
Free	do	403.18							
Uruguay [7]	Peso	65.830	65.830	65.830	[1] 65.830	[1] 65.830	65.833	65.833	65.833
	do	43.380	56.280	56.239	[1] 56.182	[1] 56.180	56.180	56.180	56.180
	do					[1] 42.553	42.553	42.553	42.553

[1] Average of daily rates for part of year during which quotations were certified (see previous *Abstracts* for exact periods)
[2] Prior to Nov. 1, 1942, official designation for Brazilian cruzeiro was milreis.
[3] As of Aug. 27, 1951, quotations on Straits Settlements dollar discontinued and quotations on Malayan dollar substituted. The two rates had been identical for a considerable period.
[4] Based on quotations through Aug. 14, 1952.
[5] Based on quotations through May 8, 1952.
[6] Excludes Pakistan, beginning April 1948.
[7] Beginning October 1948, application depends upon type of merchandise.

Source: Board of Governors of the Federal Reserve System; annual and monthly figures published in *Federal Reserve Bulletin*.

BIBLIOGRAPHY OF SOURCES OF STATISTICAL DATA

This bibliography contains under the various subject headings references to the important primary sources of statistical information for the United States. Secondary sources have been referred to if the information contained therein is presented in a particularly convenient form or if primary sources are not readily available. Non-recurrent studies presenting compilations or estimates for several years or new types of data not available in regular series are included.

Much valuable information will also be found in State reports and in reports for particular commodities, industries, or similar segments of our economic and social structure. However, because of the large number of such references, they are not included here.

Section references on the right-hand side of each page indicate where data from the report cited appear in the *Statistical Abstract*. Where current reports and a summary volume are both cited in the bibliography the section reference will often appear opposite the summary volume only. Reference to the sections indicated will enable the user to ascertain the type of information presented in the original source. However, it should not be assumed that all of the subjects from that source are summarized in the *Abstract*.

The location of the publisher of the report is given except for Federal governmental agencies located in Washington. Major inquiries, such as the Census of Population, are referred to by name rather than by specific volume references under the various topic headings. The final reports of the Seventeenth Census, which include those on the Censuses of Agriculture, Population, and Housing, are listed at the end of the bibliography together with the final reports of the 1948 Census of Business and the 1947 Census of Manufactures.

Abstract
Sec. No.

Accidents—*see* Vital Statistics.

Advertising—*see* Service Establishments.

Agriculture—*see also* Irrigation; *and* Population:

National Fertilizer Association, Inc., Washington, D. C.:

The Fertilizer Review. Quarterly------------------------------- 24

U. S. Bureau of Agricultural Economics:

The Agricultural Finance Review. Annual----------------------- 16, 24

The Balance Sheet of Agriculture. Annual---------------------- 24

Cash Receipts from Farming, by States and Commodities, 1924–44. Later and revised data published in "The Farm Income Situation" reports. (*See* Situation Reports.)

Crop and livestock reports. (Farm production and disposition of principal crops, meat animals, milk, chickens, eggs, turkeys, etc.) Monthly, quarterly, annual-- 25

Crops and Markets. Annual----------------------------------- 24, 25

Farm Labor. (Farm wage rates, farm employment, and related data.) Monthly and special releases. -------------------------------- 8

Farm Mortgage Credit Facilities in the United States. 1942.

Farm Population Estimates. Annual. ------------------------- ▲

The Farm Real Estate Situation. Annual. Quarterly release, "Current Developments in the Farm Real Estate Market"------------------- 24

Farmer Bankruptcies, 1898–1935. 1936. Subsequent annual data included in The Agricultural Finance Review.

Child Welfare—Continued

Abstract
Sec. No.

U. S. Department of Health, Education, and Welfare:

Annual Report_____ 10

U. S. Social Security Administration:

Children's Bureau Statistical Series: (1) Maternal and Infant Mortality in 1944, by George Wolff, M. D., 1947. (2) Deaths of Premature Infants in the United States, by Ethel C. Dunham, M. D., 1947. (3) Children Served by Public Welfare Agencies and Institutions, Dec. 31, 1945, published in 1947. (4) Further Progress in Reducing Maternal and Infant Mortality, by George Wolff and Eleanor P. Hunt, 1949. (5) Mortality from Premature Birth and Associated Causes of Death, 1948, published in 1950. (6) Changes in Infant, Childhood, and Maternal Mortality Over the Decade 1939–48, published in 1950. (7) Personnel in Public Child Welfare Programs, 1950, published in 1950. (8) Juvenile Court Statistics, 1946–49, published in 1951. (9) Charts on Infant, Childhood and Maternal Mortality, 1949, published in 1951.

Social Security Bulletin. Monthly. Beginning 1950, annual statistical supplement in September issue_____ 10

Social Security Yearbook. (Last issue 1948.)

Civil Aeronautics—*see* Transportation.

Civil Service—*see* Federal Government; *and* State and Local Government.

Climate:

U. S. Department of Agriculture:

Yearbook of Agriculture, 1941: Climate and Man.

U. S. Department of Agriculture and U. S. Department of Commerce:

Fluctuations in Crops and Weather, 1866–1948.

U. S. Weather Bureau:

Climatological Data. Issued monthly and annually for each State.

Climatological Data. National Summary. Issued monthly and annually.

Daily and Hourly Precipitation. Monthly. (Hydrologic bulletins issued for eight regions of the United States until about June 1948, then published in monthly Climatological Data until September 1951 after which the publication of hourly values was discontinued.)

Daily River Stages at River Gage Stations on the Principal Rivers of the United States. Issued annually.

Daily Weather Bulletin. (For local areas.)

Local Climatological Data. Issued monthly and annually for local areas.

Meteorological Yearbook. (Through 1949. Period from 1943 to 1949 in one volume.)

Monthly Weather Review.

Weekly Weather and Crop Bulletin, National Summary.

Commodity Prices:

Commodity Research Bureau, Inc., New York, N. Y.:

Commodity Handbook. Annual.

Fairchild Publications, New York, N. Y.:

Retail Price Index. Monthly. (Published regularly in Wall Street Journal.)

Guaranty Trust Company of New York, New York, N. Y.:

The Guaranty Survey. Monthly. (Wholesale price index.)

Journal of Commerce Corporation, New York, N. Y.:

Journal of Commerce. Daily except Sunday holidays.

National Bureau of Economic Research, New York, N. Y.:

The Structure of Postwar Prices (Occasional Paper No. 27), by Frederick C. Mills. 1948.

Construction, Housing, and Real Estate—Continued

Abstract Sec. No.

National Bureau of Economic Research, New York, N. Y.:
Urban Mortgage Lending by Life Insurance Companies, by R. J. Saulnier. 1950.
U. S. Board of Governors of the Federal Reserve System:
Federal Reserve Bulletin. Monthly------------------ 8, 11, 14, 16, 17, 28–32
U. S. Bureau of Agricultural Economics:
The Farm Real Estate Situation. Annual. Quarterly release, "Current Developments in the Farm Real Estate Market"-------------------- 24
U. S. Bureau of the Census:
Census of Agriculture. Quinquennial. (Tenure and equipment data.)_ 23–25, 33
Census of Business. (Construction Industry.) Decennial. Special report for 1935--- 31
Census of Housing. Decennial----------------------------------- 29, 33
Census of Population. Decennial. (Tenure and family data.)_ 1, 4, 8, 11, 13, 33
Current Population Reports. Housing.
Housing Vacancy and Occupancy Surveys. Reports on housing of World War II veterans and dwelling unit vacancy and occupancy in selected areas.
U. S. Bureau of the Census and U. S. Bureau of Agricultural Economics:
Farm Mortgage Debt (U. S. Census of Agriculture: 1950, Vol. V, pt. 8)__ 24
U. S. Bureau of Labor Statistics:
Building Construction in Principal Cities of the United States, 1921–48. Based on building permits issued. Pamphlet. June 1949. 25 pp.
Construction Activity in the United States. Monthly press release issued jointly with the U. S. Department of Commerce.
Construction. Annual Review. 1942–45, 1946–47, 1948, 1950, and 1951.
Construction. Monthly report on selected phases--------------------- 29
Consumer Price Index. (Rent indexes.) Monthly release.
Employment and Payrolls. Monthly------------------------------- 8
Handbook of Labor Statistics, 1950 Edition and 1951 Supplement____ 8, 12, 29
Hours and Earnings. Monthly Industry Report.
Housing Series. Monthly press release.
Housing Volume and Construction Cost of One-Family Houses, 1946–50. 15 Metropolitan Areas. May 1951 Supplement to Construction.
Monthly Labor Review--------------------------- 8, 9, 11, 12, 14, 16, 29, 31
New Construction—Expenditures, 1915–51; Labor Requirements, 1939–51. Bulletin. 1953.
Union Wages and Hours in the Building Trades. Annual bulletins. Quarterly releases list scales in selected trades in key cities.
Urban Building Authorized. Monthly press release.
Wholesale Prices. Monthly release, "Prices and Price Relatives for Individual Commodities." Annual bulletin--------------------- 12, 28
U. S. Federal Housing Administration:
Annual Report.
Insured Mortgage Portfolio. Quarterly.
U. S. Home Loan Bank Board:
Annual Report-- 16
Mortgage Investment of Life Insurance Companies. Annual.
Statistical Summary. Annual.
U. S. Housing and Home Finance Agency:
Annual Report-- 29
The Housing Situation. 1950.
Housing Statistics Monthly.
Housing Statistics Handbook. 1948.

Construction, Housing, and Real Estate—Continued

Abstract
Sec. No.

U. S. Interstate Commerce Commission:
Railroad Construction Indices. Annual.

U. S. National Production Authority:
Construction and Building Materials Industry Report. Monthly. Statistical Supplement, May 1951_____ 29

U. S. Office of Business Economics:
Survey of Current Business. Monthly statistics and special articles_____ 11,
14, 16, 17, 24, 26, 28–32

U. S. War Production Board:
Facts for Industry. (Various series on construction compiled in cooperation with Bureau of Labor Statistics and Bureau of Census.)

Consumer Incomes and Expenditures—see also National Income:

National Bureau of Economic Research, New York, N. Y.:
Shares of Upper Income Groups in Income and Savings, by Simon Kuznets. 1952.
Studies in Income and Wealth. Vol. 13—Ten Papers on Size Distribution of Income, 1951, and Vol. 15—Eight Papers on Income Size Distribution, 1952.

National Industrial Conference Board, New York, N. Y.:
Conference Board Business Record. Monthly.
The Economic Almanac. Annual_____ 12

U. S. Board of Governors of the Federal Reserve System:
A National Survey of Liquid Assets (1945), Parts 1–3. Reported in Federal Reserve Bulletin, June, July, and August 1946. Estimates of Liquid Assets are published yearly in July issue of Federal Reserve Bulletin.
Survey of Consumer Finances. Annual. Published in Federal Reserve Bulletin, June, July, August, and sometimes additional issues_____ 11, 16

U. S. Bureau of the Census:
Census of Agriculture. Quinquennial_____ 23–25, 33
Current Population Reports: Periodic releases on Consumer Income. The latest, "Family Income in the United States, 1951" and "Income of Persons in the United States, 1951."_____ 11
Family and Individual Money Income in the United States, 1945 and 1944.

U. S. Bureau of Human Nutrition and Home Economics:
Rural Family Spending and Saving in Wartime (1941–42). 1943.

U. S. Bureau of Internal Revenue:
Statistics of Income. Parts 1 and 2. Annual_____ 14, 17

U. S. Bureau of Labor Statistics:
Family Income, Expenditures, and Savings in 10 Cities   Bulletin No 1065.
Family Spending and Saving in Wartime, 1941 and First Quarter of 1942.
Monthly Labor Review_____ 8, 9, 11, 12, 14, 16, 29, 31
Survey of Consumer Expenditures in 1950. Preliminary report in Monthly Labor Review for August, 1952.
Survey of Prices Paid by Consumers, 1944

U. S. Council of Economic Advisers:
Economic Report of the President. Annual_____ 11, 17

U. S. Department of Agriculture:
Agricultural Statistics. Annual_____ 2, 16, 24–26

U. S. Office of Business Economics:
Survey of Current Business. Monthly statistics and special articles_____ 11,
14, 16, 17, 24, 26, 28–32

Education—Continued

Abstract
Sec. No.

U. S. Library of Congress:
Annual Report. (Copyrights)_____ 18
U. S. Office of Education:
Biennial Survey of Education_____ 4
Digest of Annual Reports of State Boards for Vocational Education_____ 4
Directory of Secondary Schools (showing accredited status, enrollment, staff, and other data for publicly and privately controlled schools). 1949, 1952.
Earned Degrees Conferred by Higher Educational Institutions. Annual__ 4
Education in Rural and City School Systems: Some Statistical Indices for 1947–48. Circular No. 329. Nov. 1951.
Expenditure per Pupil in City Schools. Annual.
Fall Enrollment in Higher Educational Institutions. Annual_____ 2
Federal Funds for Education. Annual.
Public Library Statistics. Bulletin No. 12, 1947_____ 4
Statistics of State School Systems. Annual, 1940 through 1949_____ 4

Elections:

Congressional Quarterly News Features, Washington, D. C.:
Congressional Quarterly Almanac_____ 13
The Council of State Governments:
The Book of the States. Biennial_____ 13
George Gallup and the American Institute of Public Opinion:
The Political Almanac, 1952.
U. S. Bureau of the Census:
Elections. (1947 and previous years, series of reports including calendar of elections and State and city proposals voted upon. Special reports, The Soldier Vote in 1942 and Army and Navy Voting in 1944.)_____ 13
Vote Cast in Presidential and Congressional Elections, 1928–44_____ 13
U. S. Congress, Clerk of the House:
Statistics of Presidential and Congressional Elections. Biennial_____ 13
Electrical Industries—*see* Communications; *and* Power.
Emigration—*see* Immigration.
Employment—*see* Labor.
Exports—*see* Foreign Commerce.
Family Characteristics—*see* Population.
Farms and Farm Characteristics—*see* Agriculture.
Federal Employees—*see* Federal Government; *and* Labor.

Federal Government—*see also* Elections; *and* State and Local Government:

Moody's Investors Service, New York, N. Y.:
Moody's Government and Municipals. (American and Foreign government securities.) Annual.
National Bureau of Economic Research, New York, N. Y.:
Federal Grants and the Business Cycle, by James A. Maxwell. 1952.
Trend of Government Activity in the United States Since 1900, by Solomon Fabricant. 1952.
U. S. Board of Governors of the Federal Reserve System:
Banking and Monetary Statistics. 1943____ _____ _ _ _____ 14, 16, 32
Federal Reserve Bulletin. Monthly_____ _ 8, 11, 14, 16, 17, 28–32
Federal Reserve Charts on Bank Credit, Money Rates, and Business. Monthly.
U. S. Bureau of the Budget:
The Budget of the United States Government. Annual_____ 9, 14, 15, 29

Institutions—Continued
Abstract Sec. No.

U. S. Public Health Service:
Patients in Mental Institutions. Annual.. 2
U. S. Public Health Service, National Office of Vital Statistics:
Vital Statistics—Special Reports. (Hospitals and Other Institutional
Facilities and Services.).. 1, 2
U. S. Veterans' Administration:
Annual Report. (Data on veterans' facilities.).......................... 9

Insurance—*see also* Money:

Alfred M. Best Company, New York, N. Y.:
Best's Insurance Reports. Annual. (Separate volumes on life, casualty,
and surety companies.)
Institute of Life Insurance, New York, N. Y.:
Life Insurance Fact Book. Annual.
National Board of Fire Underwriters, New York, N. Y.:
Report of the Committee on Statistics and Origin of Fires. Annual...... 16
The Spectator, Philadelphia, Pa.:
Life Insurance in Action. Annual statistical issue.
Property Insurance Review. Annual statistical issue.
Spectator Insurance Yearbook. Annual. (Three volumes: Life Insur-
ance; Fire and Marine Insurance; and Casualty, Surety, and Miscella-
neous Insurance.)... 16
Survey Research Center, Ann Arbor, Mich.:
Life Insurance Ownership Among American Families, 1952.
U. S. Bureau of Employment Security:
Reports on unemployment insurance.. 10
U. S. Bureau of Old-Age and Survivors Insurance:
Handbook of Old-Age and Survivors Insurance Statistics, 1949. 1952.
U. S. Office of Business Economics:
Survey of Current Business. Monthly statistics. Admitted assets and
premium collections from Life Insurance Association of America; pay-
ments to policyholders and beneficiaries from Institute of Life Insurance;
insurance written from Life Insurance Management Association........ 11,
14, 16, 17, 24, 26, 28–32
U. S. Veterans' Administration:
Annual Report.. 9

International Accounts and Aid:

Guaranty Trust Company of New York, New York, N. Y.:
The Guaranty Survey. Monthly.
International Bank for Reconstruction and Development:
Annual Report.
International Monetary Fund:
Annual Report.
Balance of Payments Yearbook. 1949.
National Association of Manufacturers, New York, N. Y.:
Capital Export Potentialities After 1952. 1949.
U. S. Board of Governors of the Federal Reserve System:
Federal Reserve Bulletin. Monthly..................... 8, 11, 14, 16, 17, 28–32
U. S. Export-Import Bank:
Semiannual Report to Congress.
U. S. Foreign Operations Administration:
Monthly Report for the Public Advisory Board........................ 32

Military Services and Veterans' Affairs: Abstract Sec. No.
  U. S. Bureau of the Budget:
    The Budget of the United States Government. Annual_____ 9, 14, 15, 29
  U. S. Bureau of the Census:
    Elections. (Special reports, The Soldier Vote in 1942 and Army and
      Navy Voting in 1944.)_____ 13
  U. S. Bureau of Labor Statistics:
    Monthly Labor Review_____ 8, 9, 11, 12, 14, 16, 29, 31
  U. S. Department of the Army:
    The Army Almanac, 1950_____ 7
  U. S. Department of Defense:
    Annual Report of Office of Secretary of Defense_____ 9
  U. S. Selective Service System, National Headquarters:
    Various reports on registrants and rejections_____ 9
  U. S. Veterans' Administration:
    Annual Report_____ 9

Minerals—see also Manufactures:
  American Bureau of Metal Statistics, New York, N. Y.:
    Year Book.
  American Gas Association, New York, N. Y.:
    Gas Facts. Annual_____ 19
    Monthly and quarterly reports of utility gas sales.
  American Iron and Steel Institute, New York, N. Y.:
    Annual Statistical Report_____ 30
  American Metal Market, New York, N. Y.:
    Metal Statistics. Annual_____ 28
  American Petroleum Institute, New York, N. Y.:
    Petroleum Facts and Figures. Annual.
  Bituminous Coal Institute, Washington, D. C.:
    Bituminous Coal. Annual.
  Commodity Research Bureau, Inc., New York, N. Y.:
    Commodity Handbook. Annual.
  McGraw-Hill Publishing Company, New York, N. Y.:
    Engineering and Mining Journal. Monthly_____ 28
  National Bureau of Economic Research, New York, N. Y.:
    The Mining Industries, 1899–1939: A study of Output, Employment, and
      Productivity by Harold Barger and Sam H. Schurr. 1944.
  Petroleum Engineer Publishing Co., Dallas, Tex.:
    Petroleum Data Book. (Latest edition 1948.)_____ 28
  Petroleum Publishing Company, Tulsa, Okla.:
    The Oil and Gas Journal. Weekly.
  U. S. Bureau of the Census:
    Census of Manufactures. Quinquennial. (Biennial 1921–39. Latest
      census covers 1947.)_____ 18, 26, 30, 33
    Census of Mineral Industries. (Latest census, 1939.)_____ 25
    Facts for Industry. Monthly, quarterly, and annual series issued by
      Bureau of the Census. Many of these are compiled in cooperation with
      other U. S. Government agencies. Statistics cover production, sales,
      stock, shipments, inventories, and in a few instances consumption of
      commodities and products of manufacture_____ 24–26, 30
    Foreign Commerce and Navigation of the United States. Annual_____ 12,
                                                           22, 25, 28, 30, 32
    Monthly and Quarterly Summary of Foreign Commerce of the United
      States_____ 32, 33

Minerals—Continued

U. S. Bureau of Mines:

Injury Experience in Coal Mining. Annual. (Similar reports are also issued for accidents in metallurgical plants, coke ovens, metal mines, nonmetallic mineral mines, quarries, and the petroleum industry.)_____ 28

Mineral Industry Surveys. Weekly, monthly, quarterly, or annual reports on production, stocks, consumption, shipments, and similar data relating to minerals. Examples of these reports are: Weekly Coal Report, Weekly Crude Oil Stock Report, Quarterly Gypsum Report, Monthly Coke Report, Monthly Iron Ore Report, Monthly and Annual Petroleum Statement, etc._____ 28

Minerals Yearbook. Annual_____ 19, 28, 33

U. S. Bureau of the Mint:

Annual Report_____ 16, 28

U. S. Federal Power Commission:

Statistics of Natural Gas Companies. Annual_____ 19

U. S. Interstate Commerce Commission:

Statistics of Oil Pipe Line Companies. Annual; also quarterly report on large companies.

U. S. Office of Business Economics:

Survey of Current Business. Monthly and supplements thereto_____ 11, 14, 16, 17, 24, 26, 28–32

U. S. President's Materials Policy Commission:

Resources for Freedom_____ 32

U. S. Securities and Exchange Commission:

Plant and Equipment Expenditures of U. S. Business. Quarterly_____ 17

Statistical Bulletin. Monthly_____ 16, 17

U. S. Treasury Department:

Treasury Bulletin. Monthly. (Gold and silver statistics.)_____ 14

Money, Banking, and Investments:

American Bankers' Association, New York, N. Y.:

Condition and Operation of State Banks. Annual.

The Brookings Institution, Washington, D. C.:

Share Ownership in the United States. 1952_____ 16

William B. Dana Company, New York, N. Y.:

Commercial and Financial Chronicle. Semiweekly_____ 16

Commercial and Financial Chronicle's Bank and Quotation Record. Monthly.

Dow-Jones and Company, New York, N. Y.:

Wall Street Journal. Daily except Sunday and holidays.

Dun and Bradstreet, Inc., New York, N. Y.:

Dun's Statistical Review. Monthly_____ 17

Moody's Investors Service, New York, N. Y.:

Moody's Manual of Investments. Annual. (Volumes on Industrials; Banks, Insurance, Real Estate, and Investment Trusts; Government and Municipals; Railroads; and Public Utilities.)_____ 16

National Bureau of Economic Research, New York, N. Y.:

Basic Yields of Bonds, 1926–47: Their Measurement and Pattern (Technical Paper No. 6), by David Durand and Willis J. Winn. 1947.

Corporate Income Retention, 1915–43, by Sergei P. Dobrovolsky. 1952.

Money, Banking, and Investments—Continued   Abstract Sec. No.

National Bureau of Economic Research, New York, N. Y.—Continued

The Nature and Tax Treatment of Capital Gains and Losses, by Lawrence H. Seltzer. 1951.

A Study of Money Flows in the United States, by Morris A. Copeland. 1952

The Volume of Corporate Bond Financing since 1900, by W. Braddock Hickman. 1953.

New York Stock Exchange, New York, N. Y.:

Year Book. Annual--- 16

Standard and Poor's Corporation, New York, N. Y.:

Corporation Records, 6 basic volumes; News Supplements, daily; and Dividend Record, daily with monthly and annual cumulative sections.. 16

Statistical Section (basic business, industry, and financial statistics with monthly supplement).

U. S. Board of Governors of the Federal Reserve System:

Annual Report-- 16

Banking and Monetary Statistics. 1943 ------------------------ 14, 16, 32

Federal Reserve Bulletin. Monthly. (Also monthly and annual releases on bank debits, weekly releases on condition of banks, monthly releases on consumer credit, and weekly and monthly releases on foreign exchange rates.) ------------------------------------- 8, 11, 14, 16, 17, 28–32

Federal Reserve Charts on Bank Credit, Money Rates, and Business. Monthly.

Member Bank Call Report. (Each official call.)

U. S. Bureau of Agricultural Economics:

The Agricultural Finance Review. Annual-------------------------- 16, 24

The Balance Sheet of Agriculture. Annual----------------------------- 24

Farm Mortgage Credit Facilities in the United States. 1942.

Farm Mortgage Interest Charges and Interest Rates, 1940·48.

Farm Mortgage Loans and Their Distribution by Lender Groups, 1940–48.

Farmer Bankruptcies, 1898–1935. 1936. Subsequent annual data included in The Agricultural Finance Review.

U. S. Bureau of the Census:

Census of Housing. Decennial. (Mortgage data.)-------------------- 29, 33

Foreign Commerce and Navigation of the United States. Annual. (Gold and silver exports and imports.)---------------------- 12, 22, 25, 28, 30, 32

Monthly and Quarterly Summary of Foreign Commerce of the United States. (Gold and silver exports and imports.)-------------------- 32, 33

U. S. Bureau of the Census and U. S. Bureau of Agricultural Economics:

Farm Mortgage Debt (U. S. Census of Agriculture: 1950, Vol. V, pt. 8)__ 24

U. S. Bureau of Federal Credit Unions:

Annual Report of Operations.

U. S. Bureau of Labor Statistics:

Monthly Labor Review. (Credit Unions)------------ 8, 9, 11, 12, 14, 16, 29, 31

U. S. Bureau of the Mint:

Annual Report-- 16, 28

U. S. Comptroller of the Currency:

Abstract of Reports of Condition of National Banks. Quarterly-------- 16

Annual Report--- 16

U. S. Council of Economic Advisers:

Economic Indicators. Monthly--------------------------------------- 8, 16

Economic Report of the President. Annual-------------------------- 11, 17

National Park System—*see* Public Lands.
Naturalization—*see* Immigration.
Navy—*see* Military Services.
Occupations—*see* Labor; Population; *and* Social Security.

Population and Population Characteristics—*see also* Vital Statistics:

Princeton University School of Public Affairs and Population Association of
America, Inc., Princeton, N. J.:
Population Index. Quarterly.
U. S. Bureau of Agricultural Economics:
Farm Population Estimates. Annual------------------------------------- ₁
U. S. Bureau of the Census:
Census of Agriculture. Quinquennial-------------------------- 23–25, 33
Census of Housing. Decennial-------------------------------- 29, 33
Census of Population. Decennial---------------------- 1, 4, 8, 11, 13, 33
Current Population Reports: Population Characteristics, Population
Estimates, Farm Population (issued jointly with Bureau of Agricultural
Economics), Special Censuses, Negro Statistics-------------------- ₁
Forecasts of the Population of the United States, 1945–75.
U. S. Bureau of the Census and U. S. Bureau of Agricultural Economics:
Farm Population Estimates.
U. S. National Resources Planning Board:
Estimates of Future Population of the United States, 1940–2000. 1943.
U. S. Public Health Service, National Office of Vital Statistics:
United States Life Tables and Actuarial Tables, 1939–41. Decennial---- 2
Vital Statistics—Special Reports. (Series include Natality and Mortality;
Hospitals and Other Institutional Facilities and Services; Marriage and
Divorce; Life Tables; and other selected subjects.)------------------ 1, 2
Postal Service—*see* Communications.

Power—*see also* Communications; Manufactures; Minerals; *and* Transportation:

American Gas Association, New York, N. Y.:
Gas Facts. Annual--- 19
Monthly and quarterly reports of utility gas sales.
Edison Electric Institute, New York, N. Y.:
The Electric Light and Power Industry. Monthly and annual---------- 19
Weekly Electric Power Output.
National Bureau of Economic Research, New York, N. Y.:
Output and Productivity in the Electric and Gas Utilities, 1899–1942, by
Jacob Martin Gould. 1946.
U. S. Bureau of the Census:
Census of Electrical Industries, 1937. (Central Electric Light and Power
Stations; Street Railways and Trolley-Bus and Motorbus Operations;
Telephones and Telegraphs. Survey discontinued.)-------------- 18, 19, 21
U. S. Bureau of Mines:
Minerals Yearbook. Annual----------------------------------- 19, 28, 33
U. S. Federal Power Commission:
Annual Report.
Consumption of Fuel for Production of Electric Energy. Annual and
monthly--- 19
Electric Utility Depreciation Practices. Annual--------------------- 19
Electric Utility System Loads and Capacity. Monthly.
National Electric Rate Book. Summaries of Rate Schedules. Revised
annually.
Production of Electric Energy and Capacity of Generating Plants.
Annual-- 19

Service Establishments—*see also* Wholesale and Retail Trade:

Advertising Publications, Inc., Chicago, Ill.:

Advertising Age. Weekly------------------------------------

Horwath and Horwath, New York, N. Y.:

Horwath Hotel Accountant. Monthly.

Media Records, Inc., New York, N. Y.:

Media Records. Monthly.

Printers' Ink Publishing Company, New York, N. Y.:

Printers' Ink. Weekly-------------------------------------

Publishers' Information Bureau, Inc., New York, N. Y.:

National Advertising Records. Semimonthly.

U. S. Bureau of the Census:

Census of Business (Service Establishments). Decennial, 1930 and quinquennial, 1948 (latest census). (Special census in 1933 and 193

Shipping—*see* Transportation.

Social Security—*see also* Labor:

U. S. Bureau of Employees' Compensation:

Annual Report---

U. S. Bureau of Employment Security:

Reports on unemployment insurance-----------------------

U. S. Bureau of Labor Statistics:

Handbook of Labor Statistics, 1950 Edition and 1951 Supplement-----

Monthly Labor Review--------------------------- 8, 9, 11, 12, 1

U. S. Bureau of Old-Age and Survivors Insurance:

Handbook of Old-Age and Survivors Insurance Statistics, 1949. 1952.

U. S. Civil Service Commission:

Retirement Report. Annual-----------------------------------

U. S. Department of Health, Education, and Welfare:

Annual Report--

U. S. President's Commission on the Health Needs of the Nation:

Building America's Health. Five volumes, especially Volumes 2, 3, an

U. S. Railroad Retirement Board, Chicago, Ill.:

Annual Report--

Compensation and Service of Railroad Employees. Annual.

The Monthly Review-------------------------------------

U. S. Social Security Administration:

Social Security Bulletin. Monthly. Beginning 1950, annual statis supplement in September issue---------------------------

Social Security Yearbook. (Last issue 1948.)

U. S. Veterans' Administration:

Annual Report--

Soil Conservation—*see* Irrigation.

State and Local Government—*see also* Elections; *and* Federal Government

The Council of State Governments:

The Book of the States. Biennial------------------------------

International City Managers' Association, Chicago, Ill.:

Municipal Year Book. Annual.

Moody's Investors Service, New York, N. Y.:

Moody's Government and Municipals. Annual.

U. S. Bureau of the Budget:

The Budget of the United States Government. Annual-----------

State and Local Government—Continued

Abstract
Sec. No.

U. S. Bureau of the Census:

Census of Governments, 1942. Decennial. (1932 title, Financial Statistics of State and Local Governments; 1922 and earlier censuses, Wealth, Public Debt, and Taxation.) Includes reports, Governmental Finances in the United States, Governmental Units in the United States, Finances of Cities Having Populations Less than 25,000, Finances of School Districts, and Finances of Townships and New England Towns. *See also* Revised Summary of State and Local Government Finances in 1942.

City Finances. (Annual series relating to cities having populations over 25,000: Summary report, Summary of City Government Finances; detailed data, Compendium of City Government Finances; advance report for cities with populations over 250,000, Large City Finances.) __ 15

County Finances. (1946 and previous years; basic items of county government finances.)

Elections. (1947 and previous years, series of reports including calendar of elections and State and city proposals voted upon.)_____ 13

Government Employment. (Quarterly reports showing monthly national aggregates of employees and payrolls, and annual reports, State Employment, City Employment, and State Distribution of Public Employment.)_____ 15

Governmental Finances in the United States. (Annual series on revenue and debt of Federal, State, and local governments, as shown in reports, Governmental Revenue and Governmental Debt.)_____ 15

Governments in the United States in 1952._____ 15

Historical Review of State and Local Government Finances (1890–1946). Special Study No. 25.

Retirement Coverage of State and Local Government Employees. (1952) Special Study No. 30.

State Aid to Local Governments. Special Study No. 28.

State Finances. (Annual series providing individual State data and totals: Summary of State Government Finances, detailed Compendium of State Government Finances, Revenue and Expenditure of Selected States, and State Tax Collections.)_____ 15

U. S. Bureau of Internal Revenue:

Annual Report_____ 14, 30

Comparative Statement of Internal Revenue Collections. Monthly.

Statistics of Income. Parts 1 and 2. Annual_____ 14, 17

U. S. Bureau of Public Roads:

The Financing of Highways by Counties and Local Rural Governments, 1931–41. 1949.

U. S. Treasury Department:

Annual Report_____ 14, 16, 32

Federal, State, and Local Government Fiscal Relations. (S. Doc. No. 69, 78th Cong. 1st sess. Report of the Committee on Intergovernmental Fiscal Relations.)

Stocks and Bonds—*see* Money.

Stores—*See* Service Establishments; *and* Wholesale and Retail Trade.

Tax Collections—*see* Government.

Telephone and Telegraph Systems—*see* Communications.

Territories, Possessions, and Other Areas—*see also* Foreign Commerce:

Economic Development Administration, Puerto Rico:

Current Business Statistics, Puerto Rico. (Retail Trade, October, 1952.)
Statistical Yearbook, Puerto Rico, 1950–51. 1952.

Unemployment Insurance—*see* Insurance; *and* Social Security.
Utilities, Public—*see* Communications; Power; *and* Transportation.
Veterans—*see* Military Services.
Virgin Islands of the United States—*see* Territories.

Vital Statistics, Health, and Medical Care:

American Medical Association, Council on Medical Education and Hospitals, Chicago, Ill.:
Hospital Service in the United States. Annual _
Metropolitan Life Insurance Company, New York, N. Y.:
Health Progress, 1936 to 1945, by Louis I. Dublin. (Supplement to Twenty-five Years of Health Progress). 1948.
Statistical Bulletin. Monthly.
National Safety Council, Chicago, Ill.:
Accident Facts. Annual.
U. S. Bureau of Agricultural Economics:
National Food Situation. Quarterly _
U. S. Bureau of Labor Statistics:
Monthly Labor Review. (Accident data.) _ _ _ _ _ _ _ _ _ _ _ 8, 9, 11, 12, 14, 16,
U. S. Bureau of Mines:
Injury Experience in Coal Mining. Annual. (Similar reports are also issued for accidents in metallurgical plants, coke ovens, metal mines, nonmetallic mineral mines, quarries, and the petroleum industry.) _ _ _ _ _
Coal Mine Fatalities. Monthly.
U. S. Department of the Army:
Annual Report, Surgeon General.
U. S. Department of Health, Education, and Welfare:
Annual Report _
U. S. Department of the Navy:
Annual Report, Surgeon General, U. S. N.
U. S. Interstate Commerce Commission:
Accident Bulletin—Steam Railways. Annual; also monthly summary _ _ _
Accidents, Steam Railways. Monthly.
U. S. President's Commission on the Health Needs of the Nation:
Building America's Health. Five volumes, especially Volumes 2, 3, and 4.
U. S. Public Health Service:
Annual Report of the Surgeon General of the United States Public Health Service.
Journal of Venereal Disease Information. Monthly.
National Institute of Health Bulletins. (Series of reports largely on laboratory research but include some statistical studies. Nos. 1–182.)
Patients in Mental Institutions. Annual _
Public Health Bulletins. (Series of reports on research studies in public health, including many statistical studies. Nos. 1–285.)
Public Health Reports. Monthly.
Supplements to the Public Health Reports, including some statistical material.
U. S. Public Health Service, National Office of Vital Statistics:
Monthly Vital Statistics Report _
Morbidity and Mortality Weekly Report.
Motor-Vehicle Accident Fatalities. Annual 1941–49 _ _ _ _ _ _ _ _ _ _ _ _ _ _ _ _
United States Life Tables and Actuarial Tables, 1939–41. Decennial _ _ _ _
Vital Statistics Rates in the United States, 1900–40 _ _ _ _ _ _ _ _ _ _ _ _ _ _ _ _
Vital Statistics—Special Reports. (Series include Natality and Mortality; Marriage and Divorce; Life Tables; and other selected subjects.) _ _ _ _ _ _

Wholesale and Retail Trade—Continued Abstract
Sec. No.

U. S. Council of Economic Advisers:

Economic Report of the President. Annual 11, 17

U. S. Office of Business Economics:

Industry Reports. Monthly, bimonthly, and quarterly series. Statistics on production, manufacturing, distribution, and consumption of specific commodities.

Survey of Current Business. Monthly statistics and special articles. Biennial Supplement 11, 14, 16, 17, 24, 26, 28–32

U. S. Securities and Exchange Commission:

Survey of American Listed Corporations. (Individual industry reports and statistical studies covering periods from 1936–47.)

Wholesale Prices—*see* Commodity Prices.

Workmen's Compensation—*see* Social Security.

Work Relief—*see* Social Security.

Work Stoppages—*see* Labor.

PUBLICATIONS OF MAJOR CENSUSES

[Each part of a volume in this list is a separate book or pamphlet. Preliminary bulletins, which were issued in advance of final reports, are not included in the list. A detailed catalog of Census publications is available upon request]

17th DECENNIAL CENSUS

Agriculture:

Vol. I: Counties and State Economic Areas. Detailed statistics by counties and economic areas. Economic areas within each State comprise groups of counties having similar agricultural, demographic, and other characteristics. A series of 34 separately published parts.

Vol. II: General Report. Summary data and analyses by subjects for States, for geographic divisions, and for the United States. Subject matter chapters also issued as separate bulletins.

Vol. III: Irrigation of Agricultural Lands. State reports with statistics for counties and drainage basins, and a summary for the United States. State reports also issued as separate bulletins.

Vol. IV: Drainage of Agricultural Lands. Data for States, for counties, and for the United States; all in one part.

Vol. V: Special Reports (10 parts).

Part 1. Horticultural Specialties.

Part 2. Multiple-Unit Operations.

Part 3. Ranking Agricultural Counties.

Part 4. Land Utilization—A Graphic Summary.

Part 5. Farm Tenure—A Graphic Summary.

Part 6. 1950 Census of Agriculture—A Graphic Summary.

Part 7. Irrigation of Agricultural Lands—A Graphic Summary.

Part 8. Farm Mortgage Debt.

Part 9. Economic Class and Type of Farm—A Graphic Summary.

Part 10. Farms and Farm Characteristics, by Subregions.

Housing:

Vol. I: General Characteristics. A separate bulletin is also issued for the United States, each State and the District of Columbia, Alaska, Hawaii, Puerto Rico, and the Virgin Islands of the United States. Characteristics by States, counties, standard metropolitan areas, urban places, and other constituent areas.

Vol. II: Nonfarm Housing Characteristics. Chapters also issued as separate bulletins for the United States and the 9 geographic divisions, and for each of the 152 standard metropolitan areas of 100,000 or more inhabitants including the 106 cities of 100,000 inhabitants or more in the United States.

Vol. III: Farm Housing Characteristics. Analytical data for the rural-farm segment of the dwelling-unit inventory; for the United States and each of the 119 economic subregions. Subregions usually are combinations of two or more counties having relatively homogeneous agricultural conditions.

Vol. IV: Residential Financing. Financial characteristics of nonfarm mortgaged residential properties, for the United States, the 4 geographic regions, and for the 25 largest standard metropolitan areas as measured by 1940 population figures (2 parts).

Part 1. United States.

Part 2. Large standard metropolitan areas and comparable data for the United States.

Vol. V: Block Statistics. Separate reports for each of the 209 cities in the United States which had a population of 50,000 or more inhabitants in 1940, or in a subsequent special census prior to 1950. (These bulletins *not* bound in a single publication.)

Population:

Vol. I: Number of Inhabitants. General characteristics of the population by States, counties, standard metropolitan areas, urban places, and other constituent areas. State chapters also issued as separate bulletins.

Vol. II: Characteristics of the Population. A series of separately published parts, one for each State and the District of Columbia, a summary for the United States, and another part for the Territories and possessions. Each part comprises the following chapters: (A) Number of Inhabitants, (B) General Characteristics, and (C) Detailed Characteristics. Each of these chapters also issued separately as State bulletins.

Vol. III: Census Tract Statistics. Selected population and housing data by census tracts. 64 separate bulletins for tracted cities. (These bulletins *not* bound in a single publication.)

Vol. IV: Special Reports. Comprises Series P-E Bulletins including: Employment and Personal Characteristics; Institutional Population; Marital Status; Nonwhite Population by Race; Persons of Spanish Surname; Puerto Ricans in Continental U. S.; State of Birth; Characteristics by Size of Place; Education.

Subject and area volumes: Subject volumes include a United States Summary chapter, a separate chapter for each subject, a miscellaneous chapter, and a chapter on Territories (Alaska and Hawaii). Area volumes contain statistics for standard metropolitan areas, cities, and counties as well as for the United States, geographic divisions, and States.

Retail Trade:

Vol. I: General Statistics, Part 1.
Vol. II: General Statistics, Part 2, and Merchandise Line Sales Statistics.
Vol. III: Area Statistics.

Wholesale Trade:

Vol. IV: General Statistics and Commodity Line Sales Statistics.
Vol. V: Area Statistics.

Service Trade:

Vol. VI: General Statistics.
Vol. VII: Area Statistics.

Trade bulletins (data for continental United States only):

The Grocery Trade.
Department Stores.
Variety Stores.
The Electrical Goods Trade.
The Automotive Trade.
The Drug Trade.
The Jewelry Trade.
The Apparel Trade.
The Furniture Trade.
The Lumber Trade.
The Hardware, Plumbing and Heating Equipment Trade.
Marketing by Producers of Basic Iron and Steel Products.
The Motion Picture Trade.
The Optical Goods Trade.

Census monograph: The Manufacturers' Agent as a Marketing Institution.

Vol. I: General Summary. Detailed comparative statistics for industries and for geographic areas.
Vol. II: Reports for Industries. Also issued as 82 separate bulletins for approximately 460 industries.
Vol. III: Reports for States. Also issued as separate bulletins for each State and the District of Columbia.
Product Supplement. Data on shipments and/or production for more than 6,000 manufactured products.
Indexes of Production. Measures of the physical volume of 1947 production as compared with 1939 production for total manufacturing, for 20 major industry groups, and for approximately 200 individual industries.
Classes of Products, by State. Value of shipments by State for 890 classes of products.

INDEX

1038 INDEX